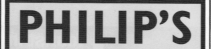

5-STAR NAVIGATOR® Britain

www.philips-maps.co.uk

First published in 1994 by Philip's,
a division of Octopus Publishing Group Ltd
www.octopusbooks.co.uk
Endeavour House, 189 Shaftesbury Avenue,
London WC2H 8JY
An Hachette UK Company
www.hachette.co.uk

Third edition 2014
First impression 2014

ISBN 978 1 84907 315 8

Cartography by Philip's

Data for the speed cameras provided by **PocketGPSWorld.com Ltd**.

Data for the caravan sites provided by The Camping and Caravanning Club.

Information for the selection of Wildlife Trust nature reserves provided by The Wildlife Trusts.

Information for National Parks, Areas of Outstanding Natural Beauty, National Trails and Country Parks in Wales supplied by the Countryside Council for Wales.

Information for National Parks, Areas of Outstanding Natural Beauty, National Trails and Country Parks in England supplied by Natural England. Data for Regional Parks, Long Distance Footpaths and Country Parks in Scotland provided by Scottish Natural Heritage.

Information for Forest Parks supplied by the Forestry Commission

Information for the RSPB reserves provided by the RSPB

Gaelic name forms used in the Western Isles provided by Comhairle nan Eilean.

Data for the National Nature Reserves in England provided by Natural England. Data for the National Nature Reserves in Wales provided by Countryside Council for Wales. Darparwyd data'n ymwneud â Gwarchodfeydd Natur Cenedlaethol Cymru gan Gyngor Cefn Gwlad Cymru.

Information on the location of National Nature Reserves in Scotland was provided by Scottish Natural Heritage.

Data for National Scenic Areas in Scotland provided by the Scottish Executive Office. Crown copyright material is reproduced with the permission of the Controller of HMSO and the Queen's Printer for Scotland. Licence number C02W0003960.

Printed in China

Contents

II Key to map symbols

III The Death of the Full English?

VI Restricted motorway junctions

VIII Route planning maps

XIV Distances and journey times

1 Road maps of Britain

315 Urban approach maps

- 315 Bristol *approaches*
- 316 Birmingham *approaches*
- 318 Cardiff *approaches*
- 319 Edinburgh *approaches*
- 320 Glasgow *approaches*
- 321 Leeds *approaches*
- 322 London *approaches*
- 326 Liverpool *approaches*
- 327 Manchester *approaches*
- 328 Newcastle *approaches*
- 329 Nottingham *approaches*
- 330 Sheffield *approaches*

331 Town plans

- 331 Aberdeen, Aberystwyth, Ashford, Ayr, Bangor
- 332 Barrow-in-Furness, Bath, Berwick-upon-Tweed, Birmingham, Blackpool
- 333 Bournemouth, Bradford, Brighton, Bristol, Bury St Edmunds
- 334 Cambridge, Canterbury, Cardiff, Carlisle, Chelmsford, Cheltenham
- 335 Chester, Chichester, Colchester, Coventry, Derby, Dorchester
- 336 Dumfries, Dundee, Durham, Edinburgh, Exeter
- 337 Fort William, Glasgow, Gloucester, Grimsby, Hanley
- 338 Harrogate, Holyhead, Hull, Inverness, Ipswich, Kendal
- 339 King's Lynn, Leeds, Lancaster, Leicester, Lewes
- 340 London
- 342 Lincoln, Liverpool, Llandudno, Llanelli, Luton
- 343 Macclesfield, Manchester, Maidstone, Merthyr Tydfil, Middlesbrough
- 344 Milton Keynes, Newcastle, Newport, Newquay, Newtown, Northampton
- 345 Norwich, Nottingham, Oban, Oxford, Perth, Peterborough
- 346 Plymouth, Poole, Portsmouth, Preston, Reading, St Andrews
- 347 Salisbury, Scarborough, Shrewsbury, Sheffield, Southampton
- 348 Southend-on-Sea, Stirling, Stoke, Stratford-upon-Avon, Sunderland, Swansea
- 349 Swindon, Taunton, Telford, Torquay, Truro, Wick
- 350 Winchester, Windsor, Wolverhampton, Worcester, Wrexham, York

351 Index to town plans

367 Index to road maps of Britain

Inside back cover: County and unitary authority boundaries

Road map symbols

Motorway

Motorway junctions – full access, restricted access

Toll motorway

Motorway service area

Motorway under construction

Primary route – dual, single carriageway, services – under construction, narrow

Primary destination

Numbered junctions – full, restricted access

A road – dual, single carriageway – under construction, narrow

B road – dual, single carriageway – under construction, narrow

Minor road – dual, single carriageway

Drive or track

Urban side roads

Roundabout, multi-level junction

Distance in miles

Tunnel

Toll, steep gradient – points downhill

Speed camera – single, multiple

National trail – England and Wales

Long distance footpath – Scotland

Railway with station, level crossing, tunnel

Preserved railway with level crossing, station, tunnel

Tramway

National boundary

County or unitary authority boundary

Car ferry, catamaran

Passenger ferry, catamaran

Ferry destination, journey time – hours: minutes

Hovercraft

Internal ferry – car, passenger

Principal airport, other airport or airfield

Area of outstanding natural beauty, National Forest – England and Wales, Forest park, National park, National scenic area – Scotland, Regional park

Woodland

Beach – sand, shingle

Navigable river or canal

Lock, flight of locks, canal bridge number

Caravan or camping sites – CCC* Club Site, Camping in the Forest Site – CCC Certificated Site, Listed Site

*Categories defined by the Camping and Caravanning Club of Great Britain

Viewpoint, park and ride, spot height – in metres

Linear antiquity

Adjoining page number

Ordnance Survey National Grid reference – see inside back cover

Road map scale 1: 112 903 or 1.78 miles to 1 inch

0   1   2   3 miles

0   1   2   3   4   5 km

Road map scale (Isle of Man and parts of Scotland)

1: 225 806 or 3.56 miles to 1 inch

0   1   2   3   4   5   6 miles

0   1   2   3   4   5   6   7   8   9   10 km

Tourist information

BYLAND ABBEY	Abbey or priory
WOODHENGE	Ancient monument
SEALIFE CENTRE	Aquarium or dolphinarium
CITY MUSEUM AND ART GALLERY	Art collection or museum
TATE ST IVES	Art gallery
1644	Battle site and date
ABBOTSBURY SWANNERY	Bird sanctuary or aviary
BAMBURGH CASTLE	Castle
YORK MINSTER	Cathedral
SANDHAM MEMORIAL CHAPEL	Church of interest
SEVEN SISTERS	Country park – England and Wales
LOCHORE MEADOWS	– Scotland
ROYAL BATH & WEST SHOWGROUND	County show ground
MONK PARK FARM	Farm park
HILLIER GARDENS AND ARBORETUM	Garden, arboretum
ST ANDREWS	Golf course – 18-hole
TYNTESFIELD	Historic house
SS GREAT BRITAIN	Historic ship
HATFIELD HOUSE	House and garden
CUMBERLAND PENCIL MUSEUM	Museum
MUSEUM OF DARTMOOR LIFE	– Local
NAT MARITIME MUSEUM	– Maritime or military

	Marina
SILVERSTONE	Motor racing circuit
	Nature reserves
HOLTON HEATH	– National nature reserve
BOYTON MARSHES	– RSPB reserve
DRAYCOTT SLEIGHTS	– Wildlife Trust reserve
	Picnic area
WEST SOMERSET RAILWAY	Preserved railway
THIRSK	Racecourse
LEAHILL TURRET	Roman antiquity
THRIGBY HALL	Safari park
FREEPORT BRAINTREE	Shopping village
MILLENNIUM STADIUM	Sports venue
ALTON TOWERS	Theme park
	Tourist information centres – open all year – open seasonally
NATIONAL RAILWAY MUSEUM	Transport collection
LEVANT MINE	World heritage site
HELMSLEY	Youth hostel
MARWELL	Zoo
SUTTON BANK VISITOR CENTRE	Other place
GLENFIDDICH DISTILLERY	of interest

Approach map symbols

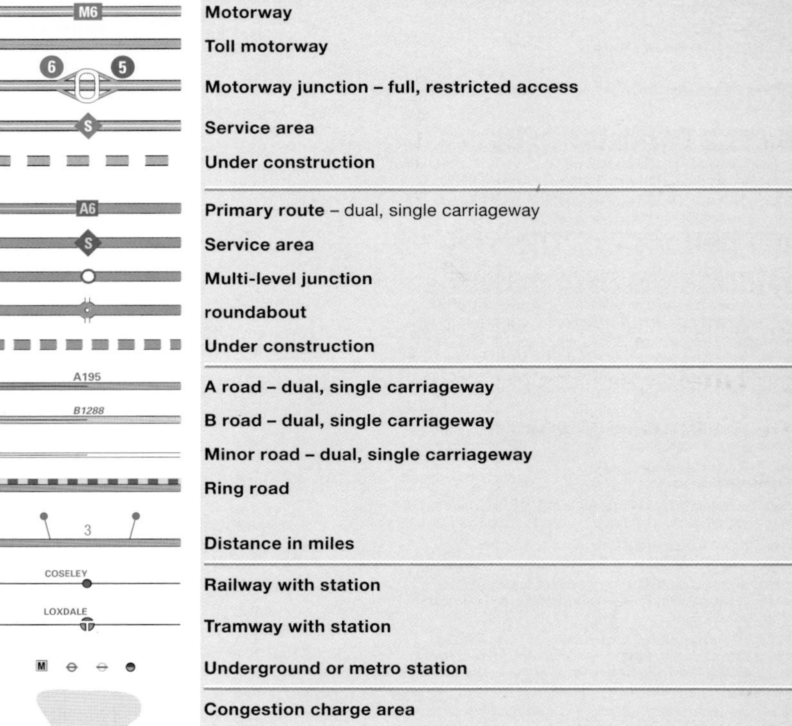

Motorway

Toll motorway

Motorway junction – full, restricted access

Service area

Under construction

Primary route – dual, single carriageway

Service area

Multi-level junction

roundabout

Under construction

A road – dual, single carriageway

B road – dual, single carriageway

Minor road – dual, single carriageway

Ring road

Distance in miles

Railway with station

Tramway with station

Underground or metro station

Congestion charge area

Speed Cameras

Fixed camera locations are shown using the 40 symbol. In congested areas the 40 symbol is used to show that there are two or more cameras on the road indicated.

Due to the restrictions of scale the camera locations are only approximate and cannot indicate the operating direction of the camera. Mobile camera sites, and cameras located on roads not included on the mapping are not shown. Where two or more cameras are shown on the same road, drivers are warned that this may indicate that a SPEC system is in operation. These cameras use the time taken to drive between the two camera positions to calculate the speed of the vehicle. At the time of going to press, some local authorities were considering decommissioning their speed cameras.

The Death of the Full English?

A Motorway pile up you'll want to avoid

by Stephen Mesquita,
Philip's On The Road Correspondent

Now come on. Be honest. When you're away from home and on the road early, haven't you been tempted by a Full English? Live it up. Put the new diet on hold. Build up your strength for the day ahead. Won't have to eat again till dinner. (A full list of excuses may be available on our web site).

shutterstock

One Full English can be a struggle. But, on a hot and sunny day last August, your intrepid Philip's On The Road Correspondent, ably assisted by his right-hand man Stuart the Sales Supremo, consumed eight of them. Our location: a typical stretch of Middle England – otherwise known as Milton Keynes. Our guide: The Philip's atlas, dotted with Post-it notes for each location (we won't mention the sat-nav). Our mission: to see if the hungry early-morning motorist is adequately catered for.

I'm sad to report that, in my view, The Full English for the motorist in a hurry has become an endangered species. Here are a few of the threats to one of our great traditions:

- **Low-quality ingredients** – most of the sausages and bacon served up seem to be from the 'we've got something cheaper out the back' counter.

- **Sausages have more than one side** – the striped sausage reigns supreme, burnt on two sides.

- **Baked Beans** – OK for the Full American but they alter the taste of the Full English. They should be offered as an option only.

- **Triangles of frozen Hash Browns** – these have no place in the Full English and should not be allowed through Passport Control.

- **Bring back the Fried Bread, please** – it may be horribly unhealthy but it's the forbidden pleasure of the Full English, the apple in the Garden of Eden. Where is it now?

- **Tinned tomatoes** – some people may prefer them but we don't. We like a lightly cooked ripe tomato, not one that's been refrigerated for six months and then burnt.

- **Cold, lukewarm or barely warm?** These seem to be the thermal options. None of the breakfasts were piping hot and many were stone cold.

- **Value for money** – not a concept understood by Motorway Service Areas.

So here is what we thought of what we tasted – a bite-by-bite account of the whole gory episode:

1 Moto Toddington Services
Eat and Drink Company ⏲ 6.20am

Price: £8.49

The Highlights

- **Eggs cooked to order and cover provided** (but still not hot)
- **Fried bread** (hurrah – the only one)
- **A decent amount for your money** (but needs to be for £8.49)
- **Sausages like rubber**
- **Bacon unappetising**
  - **Hash browns superfluous and tasted of frozen goo**
    - **Black pudding** – a terrible mistake
    Verdict: 5 out of 10

    Comment: a reasonable attempt let down by less than adequate ingredients.

▼ 6.20am Moto Toddington, Stuart decides

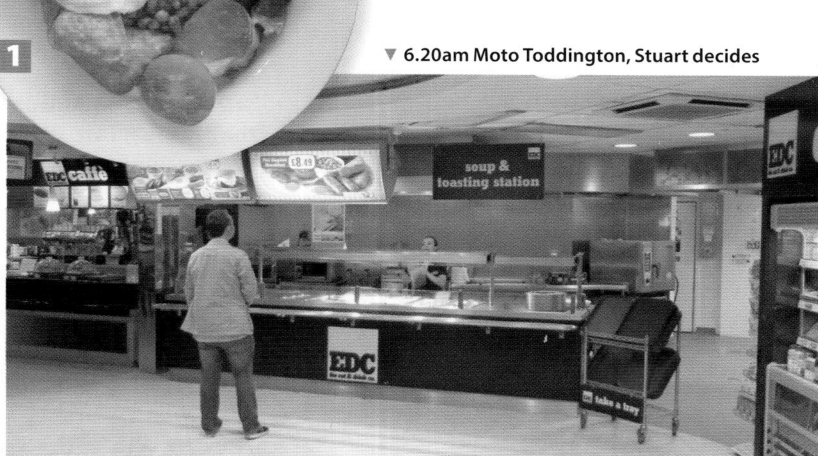

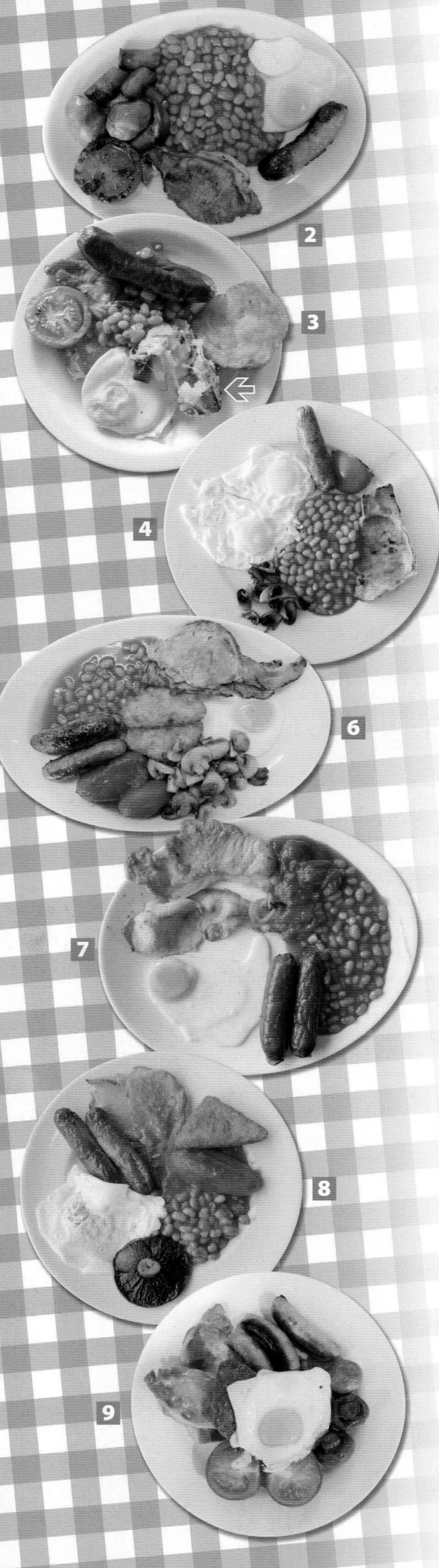

2 Premier Inn ⏱ 7.30am

Price: £8.25

The Highlights
- **Egg** – rubbery and covered in grease (with an extra greasy bit thrown in)
- **Tomato** – unripe
- **Sausage** –not a disaster but rather sweet
- **Bacon** – mainly salt
- **Mushrooms** – a bit chewy
- **Swamped** by baked beans
- **Intrusive drivel** from local radio station

Comment: Lovely location, pity about the breakfast. We liked the windmill.

Verdict: 4 out of 10

3 Toby Carvery, Travel Lodge ⏱ 8.05am

Price: £3.99

The Highlights
- **Egg** –beyond repair
- **Sausage** – seemed to be a veteran of many campaigns
- **Bacon** – tasted like 99% salt
- **Hash brown** – completely tasteless pancake
- **Tomato** – unripe
- **2 orange juices** cost nearly as much as the breakfast

Comment: The unseemly mess highlighted by the arrow is a triumph of innovation over taste. Overall, this breakfast was not what you want to be faced with first thing in the morning.

Verdict: 2 out of 10

4 Comfort Inn Milton Keynes Hotel ⏱ 8.45am

Price: £7.50 but didn't accept credit cards or have change so accepted £6.70 (all the change we had)

The Highlights
- **An unspeakable experience**
- **Mushrooms** – like cardboard filings, late 20th Century
- **Eggs** – greasy and unappetising
- **Sausage** – tasted as if it had made only passing contact with meat.
- **Tomato** – a quarter, slightly burnt

Comment: The website says this hotel is an unrivalled experience. That's true.

Verdict: 1 out of 10

5 McDonald's

Price: Big Breakfast £3.39 including OJ/ Sausage and Egg McMuffin £3.29 including OJ

The Highlights:
- **The Full American** – not really an English breakfast as we know it
- **You can't fault the price**
- **Couldn't look more unappetising**
- **Hash brown slab mainly fat**
- **A confession:** the sausage burger's quite nice
- **Stick to the scrambled egg in the Big Breakfast** – the flying saucer in the Egg McMuffin is dire
- **Here's what the others don't tell you:** the Big Breakfast is 550 calories

Verdict: 4 out of 10

Comment: It doesn't pretend to be an English breakfast but you know what you're getting.

6 Super Sausage A5 Towcester ⏱ 9.50am

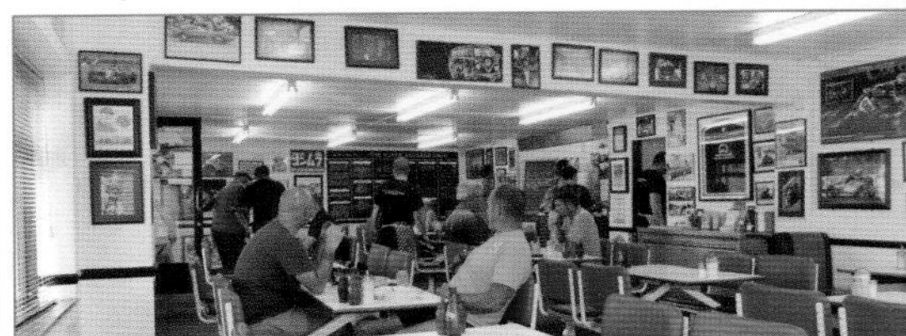

The Price: £6.20

The Highlights
- **Tasty sausages** (bravo!)
- **Good value for money**
- **Egg** – nicely cooked and not too greasy
- **Bacon** –tasted of bacon
- **A bit let down by some of the extras** (hash browns were tasteless, except slightly burnt)
- **Excellent service**

Comment: not a classic Full English but by some way the best we tasted. Great for families as well as motorists.

Verdict: 7 out of 10

7 Jack's Hill Café A5/A43 ⏱ 10.20am

The Price: £4.50

The Highlights
- **Excellent value for money**
- **Reasonably tasty**
- **Ingredients** – you get what you pay for

Comment: you expect truck stops to be cheap and filling and this fits the bill. You won't (and we didn't) get a gourmet experience.

Verdict: 6 out of 10

8 Road Chef Watford Gap Services Fresh Food Cafe ⏱ 11.00am

The Price:

The Highlights
- **Arrived in 1 minute**
- **All lukewarm**
- **Egg** – cooked both sides (not asked for)
- **Bacon** – like salty mdf
- **Hash Brown** – a fried mush
- **A real mushroom (hurrah)** but rubbery and watery
- **Comment:** As Julius Caesar said, 'We Came, We Saw, We Left'.

Verdict: 3 out of 10

9 Welcome Break Newport Pagnell Services ⏱ 11.55

The Price: £7.99

The Highlights
- **Mushrooms** –a bit wizened
- **Bacon** – tough, cold and horrible, with watery white residue
- **3 sausages** with the designer 'zebra' look
- **Hash brown** – like a fishcake without the fish
- **Tomatoes** – lukewarm
- **Egg specially cooked (hurrah!)** – two cooked, only one put on plate. Where did it go?

Comment: sausages would win a 'Find the Meat' competition

Verdict: 3 out of 10

10 Home – the £2 Challenge

The Price: £1.98

I've been impolite about almost all the breakfasts we tasted – so it seems only fair that I have a go myself.

And to make things harder, I set myself a stiff challenge. To create a Full English with the best ingredients I could find for no more than £2.

Why £2? Because then I could sell it for a four times mark up for £7.99. That's a reasonable price for good breakfast. And – I'm sure you'll agree, beleaguered consumers and travellers, a more than generous profit margin for me as the supplier. I'm sure that most of the breakfasts we ate on the road were making substantially more profit – great for them but not so good for us.

Part 1: The shopping

Off to the market in my local town of Halesworth in Suffolk and the tension is mounting. Armed with a calculator, I was asking the big question: could I buy the ingredients for my Under £2 Full English and bring it in under budget?

First stop – the local farm for absolutely fresh, speckled eggs, laid in the last 24 hours. Then to the Wednesday market stall for the tomatoes and mushrooms. Next the Farmhouse Bakery for a small granary loaf and – last stop – Allen's The Butcher for the meat (best Suffolk pork, of course).

That was the easy bit. Now the fun really started, as I retired to Frapa's for a cup of their excellent coffee and agonised over the costings with a calculator. The ingredients were great: fresh, wholesome and local. But could I bring it in on budget?

The shopping list – in the best traditions of male shopping, created on a spreadsheet – reveals all.

Ingredients	Price per portion	Notes
Eggs (2)	£0.33	Six farm-laid eggs £1.00
Bacon (1)	£0.30	Best Suffolk Pork Smoked Bacon £10.99 per kilo £1.21 for 4 rashers
Sausages (2)	£0.84	Best Suffolk Pork Sausages £6.99 per kilo £1.68 for 4
Tomato (1)	£0.145	Ripe English vine tomatoes £0.60 per lb
Mushrooms (4)	£0.28	Fresh mushrooms £1.20 per lb
Bread (1)	£0.085	Granary loaf £0.95 for 11 slices
Total	**£1.98**	

The spreadsheet

The total cost: £1.98. Just 2p to spare! I'd done it! Now I had to cook it.

Part 2: The Preparation
◄ The picture says it all

Part 3: The Cooking

I took the view that a Full English shouldn't pretend to be 100% healthy – but my personal preference was for something not too cholesterol-soaked. So the sausages, bacon and tomatoes were cooked in the oven, the bread was toasted not fried and the eggs fried in almost no olive oil. Here are the results:

Part 4: The Eating

It may sound immodest to say this – but this was the most pleasurable 10 minutes of the whole exercise. Actually, it isn't immodest because the pleasure had almost nothing to do with my cooking and almost everything to do with the ingredients. They were yummy. Where do I start?

- **The eggs were as good as they looked**
- **The sausages tasted of meat and were not too salty.**
- **The bacon was lean and beautifully flavoured**
- **The tomatoes were ripe and succulent**
- **The mushrooms were juicy and nicely flavoured**
- **Even the toast had a pleasant aroma**

This Full English actually tasted quite healthy (all right – the bacon and sausage were a bit of an indulgence) and didn't require 3 litres of water to recover from it. All for £1.98.

▲ Allen's Butchers Halesworth

▼ Halesworth Market

Enter the 'Death of the Full English Breakfast' competition

and you could win a copy of the Royal Geographical Society Atlas of the World (worth £100).
Create the Full English Breakfast from Hell using the numbered pictures in this article.

THE ROYAL GEOGRAPHICAL SOCIETY
ATLAS OF THE WORLD

shutterstock

Here's how you enter:

Look at the pictures and read the text of this article. Choose the picture which you think has the worst ingredient from the list on the right. So, for example, if you think that Picture 1 has the worst eggs (check the text and look at the pictures), choose that one.

E-mail your list to deadenglishbreakfast@octopusbooks.co.uk
or tweet it to @deadenglishbrekkie

The competition closes 15th March 2015. The first 25 winners drawn out of a hat will receive a copy of the Royal Geographical Society Atlas of the World, the magnificent flagship atlas of the Philip's range, with a retail price of £100.

Here's the list:

Eggs	Picture ☐
Bacon	Picture ☐
Sausage	Picture ☐
Mushrooms	Picture ☐
Tomatoes	Picture ☐
Black Pudding	Picture ☐

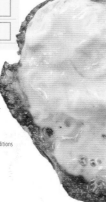

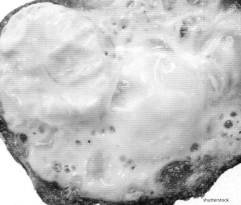

shutterstock

Restricted motorway junctions

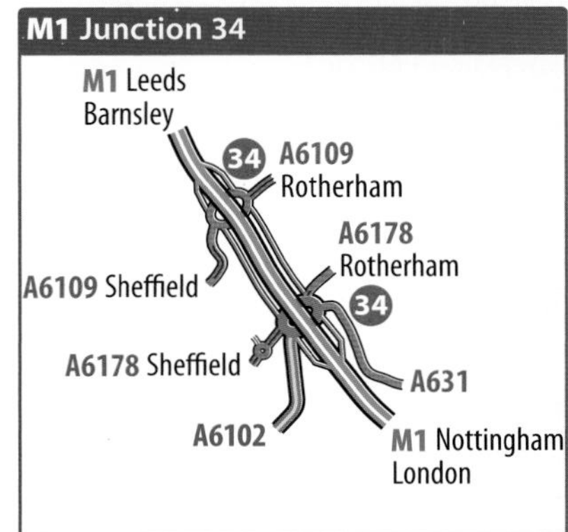

M1 Junction 34

M1 Leeds
Barnsley
34 — A6109 Rotherham
A6178 Rotherham
A6109 Sheffield
34
A6178 Sheffield — A631
A6102
M1 Nottingham London

M1 Junctions 6, 6A
M25 Junctions 21, 21A

M1 The North Luton
A405 Hatfield St Albans
6A
21A
21
M25 (M40, M4) Heathrow
M25 (M11, M20) Dartford
6
A405 North Watford
M1 Watford Central London

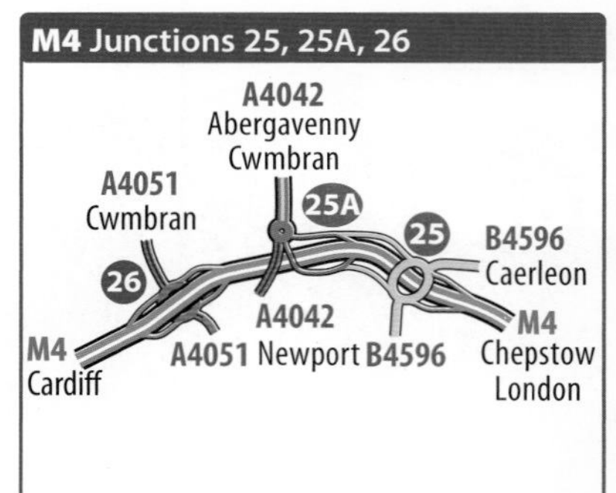

M4 Junctions 25, 25A, 26

A4042 Abergavenny Cwmbran
A4051 Cwmbran
25A
25 — B4596 Caerleon
26
A4042
A4051 Newport B4596
M4 Cardiff
M4 Chepstow London

M8 Junctions 8, 9 · M73 Junctions 1, 2 · M74 Junctions 2A, 3, 3A, 4

9
M8 Glasgow
M73 Stirling
8
A89 Coatbridge
2
A8 Edinburgh
A74 B765 B7058
M74 A74
M73
M74 Glasgow
1/4
B7001
2A 3 M74
3A
A763
B758 A721
M74 Carlisle
B7071

M5 Junction 11A

A417 Gloucester
M5 Cheltenham (A40)
11A
M5 Bristol B4641
A417 Cirencester

M1	Northbound	Southbound
2	No exit	No access
4	No exit	No access
6A	No exit. Access from M25 only	No access. Exit to M25 only
7	No exit. Access from A414 only	No access. Exit to A414 only
17	No access. Exit to M45 only	No exit. Access from M45 only
19	No exit to A14	No access from A14
21A	No access	No exit
23A		Exit to A42 only
24A	No exit	No access
35A	No access	No exit
43	No access. Exit to M621 only	No exit. Access from M621 only
48	No exit to A1(M) southbound	

M3	Eastbound	Westbound
8	No exit	No access
10	No access	No exit
13	No access to M27 eastbound	
14	No exit	No access

M4	Eastbound	Westbound
1	Exit to A4 eastbound only	Access from A4 westbound only
2	Access from A4 eastbound only	Access to A4 westbound only
21	No exit	No access
23	No access	No exit
25	No exit	No access
25A	No exit	No access
29	No exit	No access
38		No access
39	No exit or access	No exit
41	No access	No access
41A	No exit	No access
42	Access from A483 only	Exit to A483 only

M5	Northbound	Southbound
10	No exit	No access
11A	No access from A417 eastbound	No exit to A417 westbound

M6	Northbound	Southbound
3A	No access. Exit to M42 northbound only	No exit. Access from M6 eastbound only
4A	No exit. Access from M42 southbound only	No access. Exit to M42 only
5	No access	No exit
10A	No access. Exit to M54 only	No exit. Access from M54 only
11A	No exit. Access from M6 Toll only	No access. Exit to M6 Toll only
20	No exit to M56 eastbound	No access from M56 westbound
24	No exit	No access
25	No access	No exit
30	No exit. Access from M61 northbound only	No access. Exit to M61 southbound only
31A	No access	No exit
45	No access	No exit

M6 Toll	Northbound	Southbound
T1		No exit
T2	No exit, no access	No access
T5	No exit	No access
T7	No access	No exit
T8	No access	No exit

M8	Eastbound	Westbound
8	No exit to M73 northbound	No access from M73 southbound
9	No access	No exit
13	No exit southbound	Access from M73 southbound only
14	No access	No exit
16	No exit	No access
17	No exit	No access
18		No exit
19	No exit to A814 eastbound	No access from A814 westbound
20	No exit	No access
21	No access from M74	No exit
22	No exit. Access from M77 only	No access. Exit to M77 only
23	No exit	No access
25	Exit to A739 northbound only. Access from A739 southbound only	Access from A739 southbound only
25A	No exit	No access
28	No exit	No access
28A	No exit	No access

M9	Eastbound	Westbound
1A	No exit	No access
2	No access	No exit
3	No exit	No access
6	No access	No exit
8	No exit	No access

M11	Northbound	Southbound
4	No exit	No access
5	No access	No exit
9	No access	No exit
13	No access	No exit
14	No exit to A428 westbound	No exit. Access from A14 westbound only

M20	Eastbound	Westbound
2	No access	No exit
3	No exit	No access. Access from M26 eastbound only
11A	No access	No exit

M23	Northbound	Southbound
7	No exit to A23 southbound	No access from A23 northbound
10A	No exit	No access

M25	Clockwise	Anticlockwise
5	No exit to M26 eastbound	No access from M26 westbound
19	No access	No exit
21	No exit to M1 southbound. Access from M1 southbound only	No exit to M1 southbound. Access from M1 southbound only
31	No exit	No access

M27	Eastbound	Westbound
10	No exit	No access
12	No access	No exit

M40	Eastbound	Westbound
3	No exit	No access
7	No exit	No access
8	No exit	No access
13	No exit	No access
14	No access	No exit
16	No access	No exit

M42	Northbound	Southbound
1	No exit	No access
7	No access Exit to M6 northbound only	No exit Access from M6 northbound only
7A	No access. Exit to M6 southbound only	No exit
8	No exit. Access from M6 southbound only	Exit to M6 northbound only. Access from M6 southbound only

M45	Eastbound	Westbound
M1 J17	Access to M1 southbound only	No access from M1 southbound
With A45	No access	No exit

M48	Eastbound	Westbound
M4 J21	No exit to M4 westbound	No access from M4 eastbound
M4 J23	No access from M4 westbound	No exit to M4 eastbound

M49	Southbound	Northbound
18A	No exit to M5 northbound	No access from M5 southbound

M53	Northbound	Southbound
11	Exit to M56 eastbound only. Access from M56 westbound only	Exit to M56 eastbnd only. Access from M56 westbound only

M56	Eastbound	Westbound
2	No exit	No access
3	No access	No exit
4	No exit	No access
7		No access
8	No exit or access	No exit
9	No access from M6 northbound	No access to M6 southbound
15	No exit to M53	No access from M53 northbound

M57	Northbound	Southbound
3	No exit	No access
5	No exit	No access

M58	Eastbound	Westbound
1	No exit	No access

M60	Clockwise	Anticlockwise
2		
3	No exit to A34 northbound	No exit to A34 northbound
4	No access from M56	No exit to M56
5	No exit to A5103 southbound	No exit to A5103 northbound
14	No exit	No access
16	No exit	No access
20	No access	No exit
22		No access
25	No access	
26		No exit or access
27	No exit	No access

M61	Northbound	Southbound
2	No access from A580 eastbound	No exit to A580 westbound
3	No access from A580 eastbound. No access from A666 southbound	No exit to A580 westbound
M6 J30	No exit to M6 southbound	No access from M6 northbound

M62	Eastbound	Westbound
23	No access	No exit

M65	Eastbound	Westbound
9	No exit	No access
11	No access	No access

M66	Northbound	Southbound
1	No access	No exit

M67	Eastbound	Westbound
1A	No access	No exit
2	No exit	No access

M69	Northbound	Southbound
2	No exit	No access

M73	Northbound	Southbound
2	No access from M8 or A89 eastbound. No exit to A89	No exit to M8 or A89 westbound. No access from A89

M74	Northbound	Southbound
3	No access	No exit
3A	No exit	No access
7	No exit	No access
9	No exit or access	No access
10		No access
11	No exit	No access
12	No access	No exit

M77	Northbound	Southbound
4	No access	No access
6	No exit	No access
7	No exit or access	
8	No access	No access

M80	Northbound	Southbound
4A	No access	No exit
6A	No exit	
8	Exit to M876 northbound only. No access	Access from M876 southbound only. No exit

M90	Northbound	Southbound
2A	No access	No exit
7	No exit	No access
8	No access	No exit
10	No access from A912	No exit to A912

M180	Eastbound	Westbound
1	No access	No exit

M621	Eastbound	Westbound
2A	No exit	No access
4	No exit	
5	No access	No access
6	No access	No exit

M876	Northbound	Southbound
2	No access	No exit

A1(M)	Northbound	Southbound
2	No access	No exit
3		No access
5	No exit	No access
14	No exit	No access
40	No access	No access
43	No access. Access from M1 only	No access. Exit to M1 only
57	No access	No exit
65	No access	No exit

A3(M)	Northbound	Southbound
1	No exit	No access
4	No access	No exit

A38(M) with Victoria Rd, (Park Circus) Birmingham

Northbound	No exit
Southbound	No access

A48(M)	Northbound	Southbound
M4 Junc 29	Exit to M4 eastbound only	Access from M4 westbound only
29A	Access from A48 eastbound only	Exit to A48 westbound only

A57(M)	Eastbound	Westbound
With A5103	No access	No exit
With A34	No access	No exit

A58(M)		Southbound
With Park Lane and Westgate, Leeds		No access

A64(M)	Eastbound	Westbound
With A58 Clay Pit Lane, Leeds	No access	No exit
With Regent Street, Leeds	No access	No access

A74(M)	Northbound	Southbound
18	No access	No access
22		No exit

A194(M)	Northbound	Southbound
A1(M) J65 Gateshead Western Bypass	Access from A1(M) northbound only	Exit to A1(M) southbound only

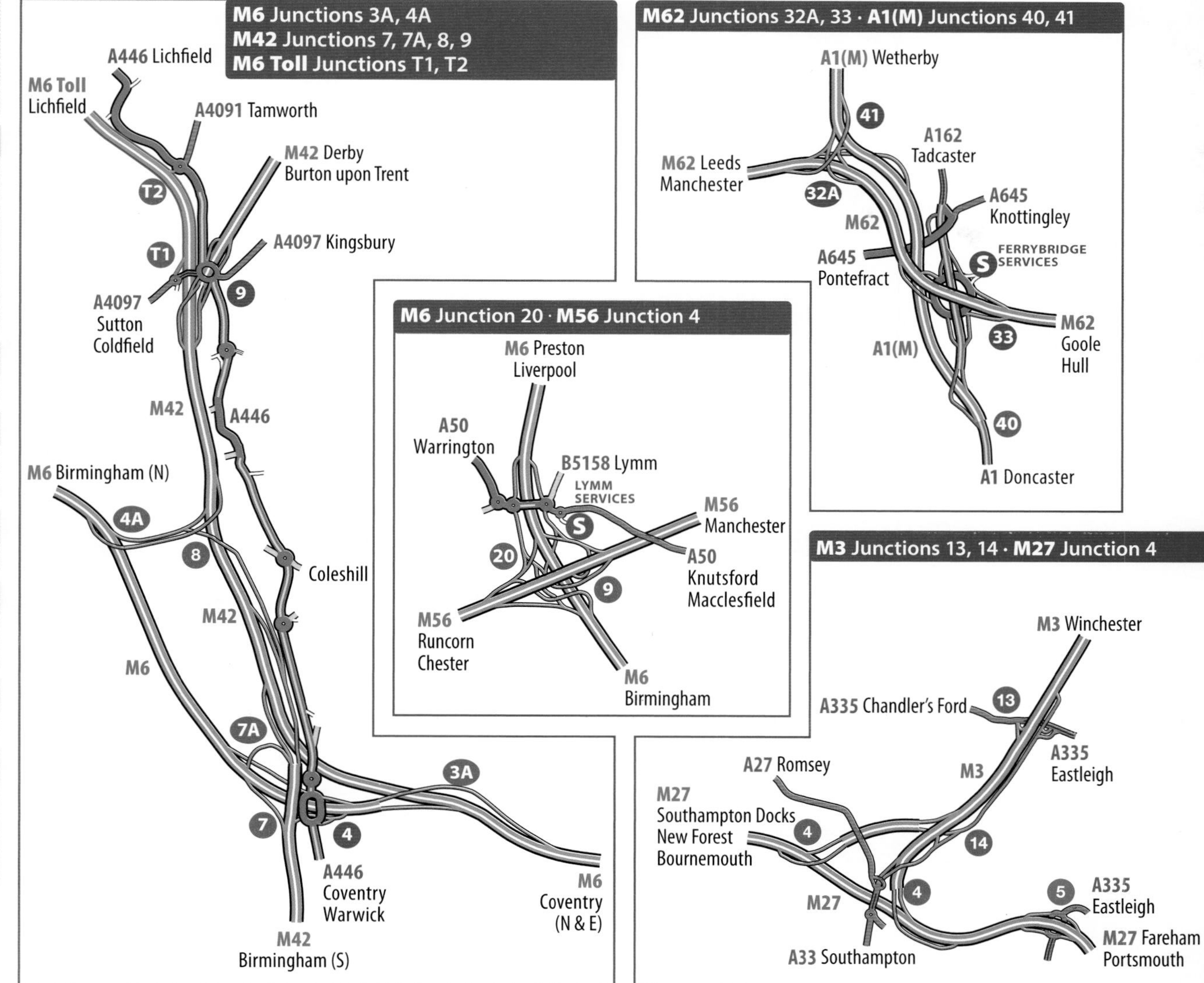

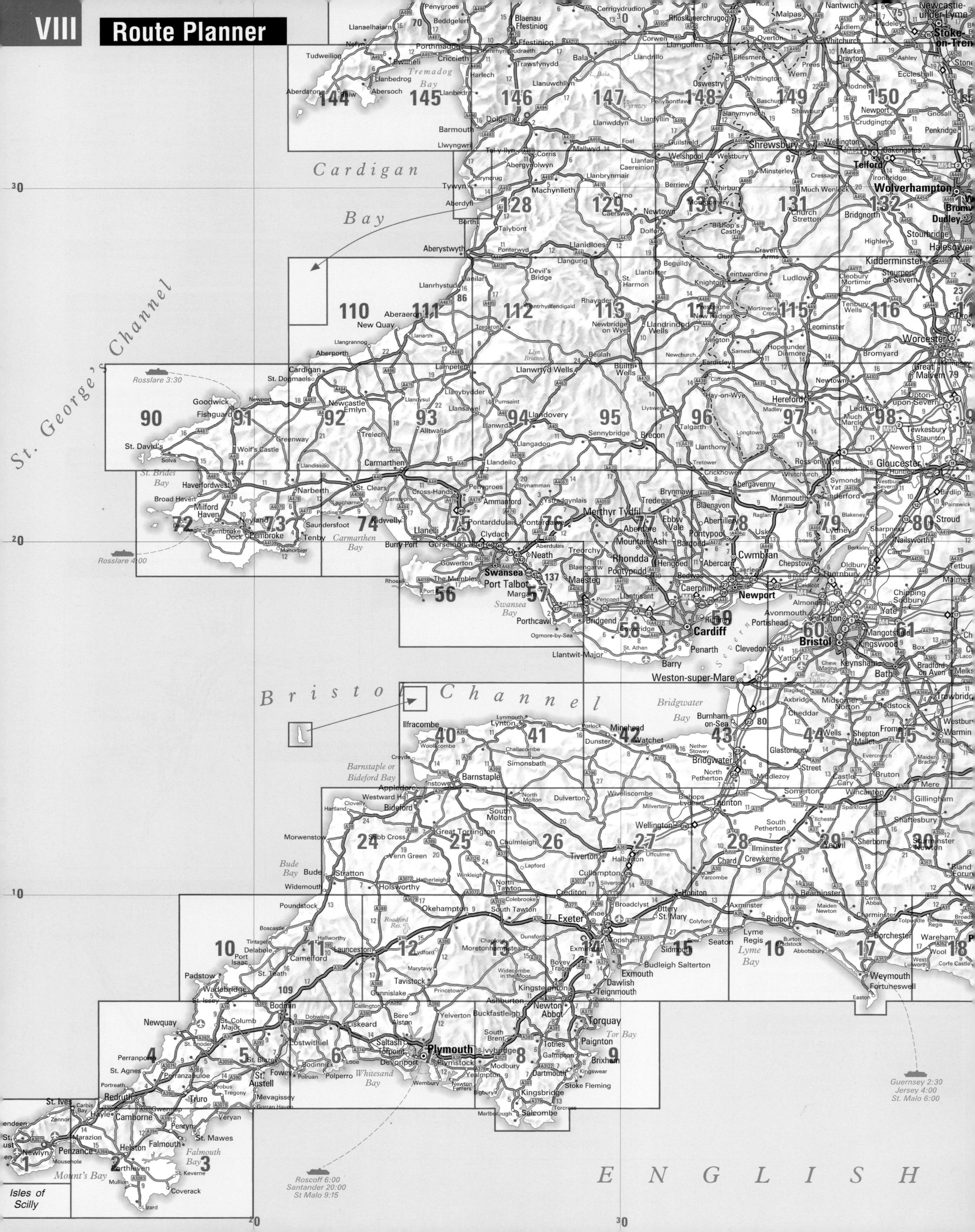
Cardigan Bay
St. George's Channel
Bristol Channel
ENGLISH
Tremadog Bay
Carmarthen Bay
Swansea Bay
Bridgwater Bay
Barnstaple or Bideford Bay
Bude Bay
Lyme Bay
Tor Bay
Whitesand Bay
Falmouth Bay
Mount's Bay
Isles of Scilly
Rosslare 3:30
Rosslare 4:00
Roscoff 6:00
Santander 20:00
St Malo 9:15
Guernsey 2:30
Jersey 4:00
St. Malo 6:00
Pwllheli
Criccieth
Porthmadog
Blaenau Ffestiniog
Bala
Llangollen
Oswestry
Whitchurch
Dolgellau
Barmouth
Shrewsbury
Welshpool
Telford
Wolverhampton
Dudley
Tywyn
Aberdyfi
Machynlleth
Newtown
Aberystwyth
Llanidloes
Kidderminster
Aberaeron
New Quay
Rhayader
Llandrindod Wells
Leominster
Worcester
Cardigan
Lampeter
Builth Wells
Hereford
Fishguard
Newcastle Emlyn
Llandovery
Brecon
Ledbury
St. David's
Carmarthen
Llandeilo
Abergavenny
Gloucester
Haverfordwest
Narberth
Monmouth
Milford Haven
Pembroke
Tenby
Llanelli
Merthyr Tydfil
Stroud
Swansea
Neath
Port Talbot
Rhondda
Pontypridd
Cwmbran
Chepstow
Newport
Bridgend
Cardiff
Bristol
Bath
Barry
Weston-super-Mare
Ilfracombe
Lynton
Minehead
Barnstaple
Bridgwater
Glastonbury
Wells
Frome
Bideford
Taunton
Yeovil
Tiverton
Bude
Exeter
Honiton
Okehampton
Launceston
Tavistock
Exmouth
Newton Abbot
Torquay
Paignton
Bodmin
Newquay
Plymouth
St. Austell
Truro
Falmouth
Redruth
Camborne
Penzance
Helston
Dorchester
Weymouth
Dartmouth
Salcombe

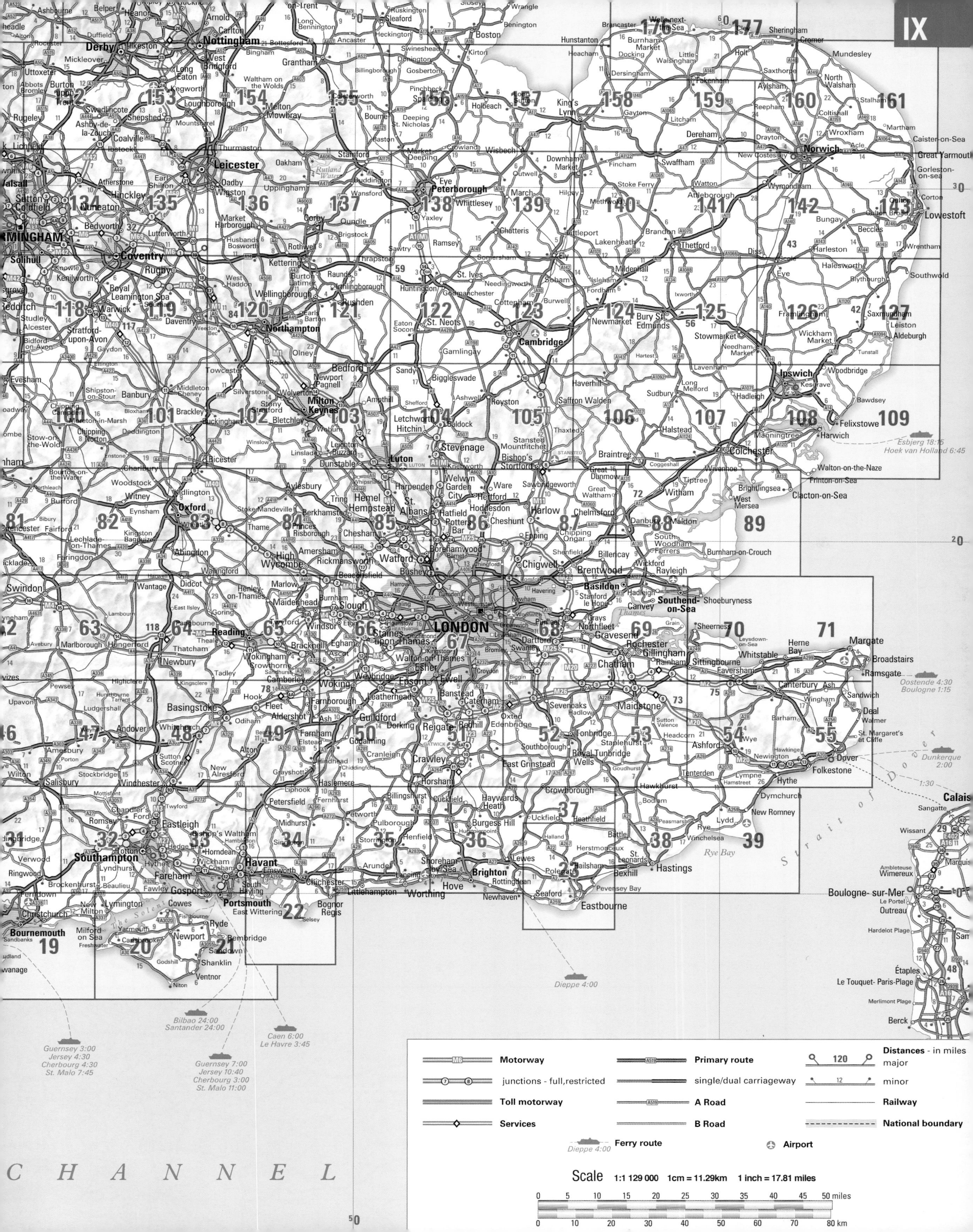

Motorway
junctions - full,restricted
Toll motorway
Services
Primary route
single/dual carriageway
A Road
B Road
Distances - in miles
major
minor
Railway
National boundary
Ferry route
Dieppe 4:00
Airport
Scale 1:1 129 000 1cm = 11.29km 1 inch = 17.81 miles
0 5 10 15 20 25 30 35 40 45 50 miles
0 10 20 30 40 50 60 70 80 km
CHANNEL
Strait of Dover
Esbjerg 18:15
Hoek van Holland 6:45
Oostende 4:30
Boulogne 1:15
Dunkerque 2:00
1:30
Dieppe 4:00
Caen 6:00
Le Havre 3:45
Bilbao 24:00
Santander 24:00
Guernsey 3:00
Jersey 4:30
Cherbourg 4:30
St. Malo 7:45
Guernsey 7:00
Jersey 10:40
Cherbourg 3:00
St. Malo 11:00
LONDON
Nottingham
Derby
Leicester
Coventry
Northampton
Peterborough
Cambridge
Norwich
Ipswich
Colchester
Oxford
Reading
Southampton
Portsmouth
Brighton
Luton
Milton Keynes
Bedford
Chelmsford
Southend-on-Sea
Canterbury
Dover
Folkestone
Hastings
Eastbourne
Bournemouth
Great Yarmouth
Lowestoft
King's Lynn
Felixstowe
Harwich
Margate
Calais
Boulogne-sur-Mer

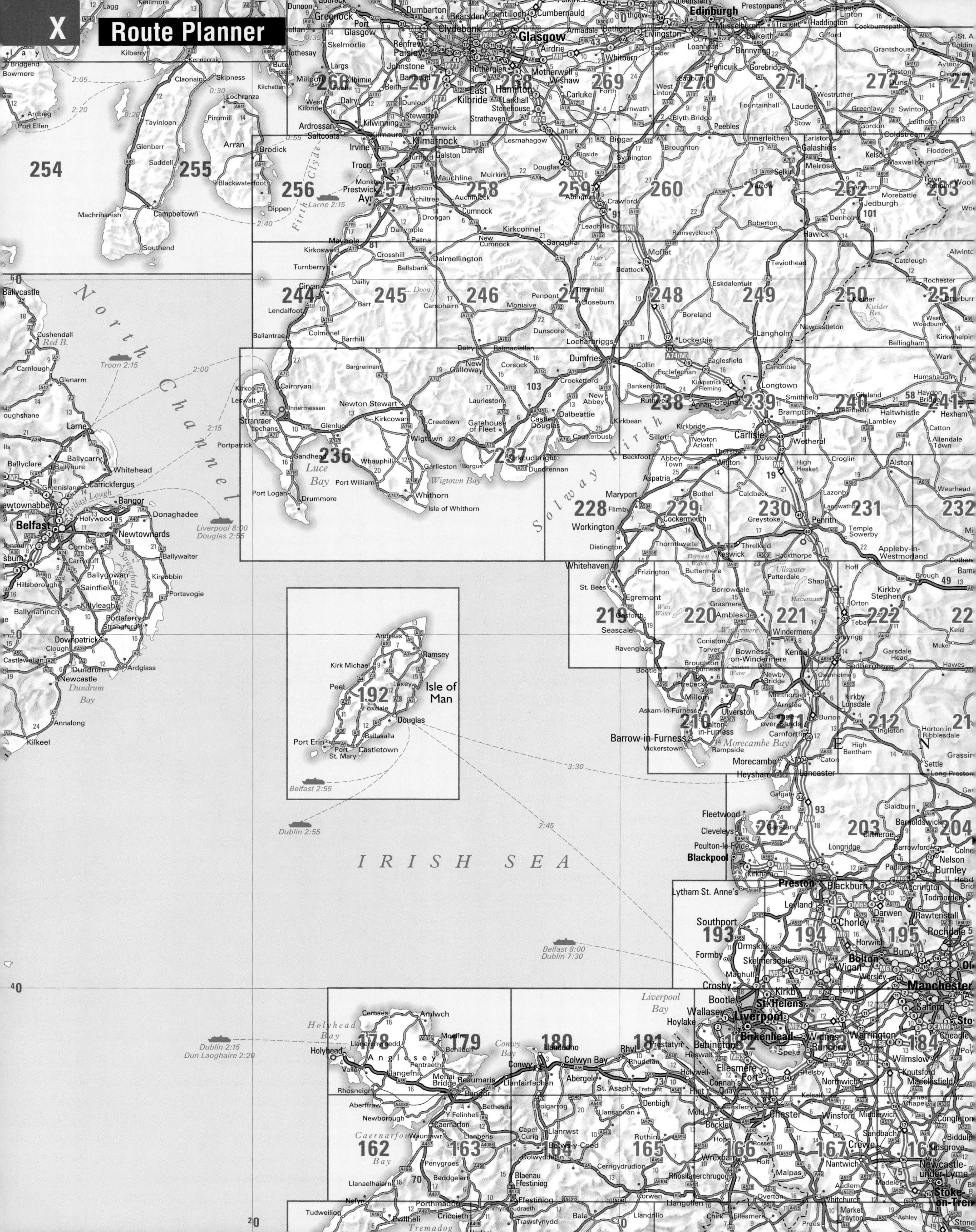

Edinburgh
Glasgow
Greenock
Dumbarton
Paisley
Motherwell
Hamilton
East Kilbride
Kilmarnock
Ayr
Prestwick
Troon
Irvine
Arran
Campbeltown
Girvan
Stranraer
Newton Stewart
Dumfries
Lockerbie
Moffat
Hawick
Jedburgh
Carlisle
Gretna
Annan
Solway Firth
Workington
Whitehaven
Keswick
Penrith
Kendal
Windermere
Barrow-in-Furness
Morecambe Bay
Lancaster
Fleetwood
Blackpool
Preston
Blackburn
Southport
Bolton
Wigan
Manchester
Liverpool
Birkenhead
Chester
Wrexham
Crewe
Stoke-on-Trent
Holyhead
Anglesey
Bangor
Caernarfon
Conwy
Rhyl
Belfast
Larne
Bangor
Newtownards
Carrickfergus
Downpatrick
Newcastle
Dundrum Bay
Kilkeel
North Channel
Isle of Man
Douglas
Ramsey
Peel
Castletown
Port Erin
IRISH SEA
Liverpool Bay
Caernarfon Bay
Tremadog
Troon 2:15
Larne 2:15
Liverpool 8:00
Douglas 2:55
Belfast 2:55
Dublin 2:55
Belfast 8:00
Dublin 7:30
Dublin 2:15
Dun Laoghaire 2:20
254
255
256
257
258
259
260
261
262
263
244
245
246
247
248
249
250
251
236
237
238
239
240
241
228
229
230
231
232
219
220
221
222
210
211
212
192
202
203
204
193
194
195
178
179
180
181
182
183
184
162
163
164
165
166
167
168

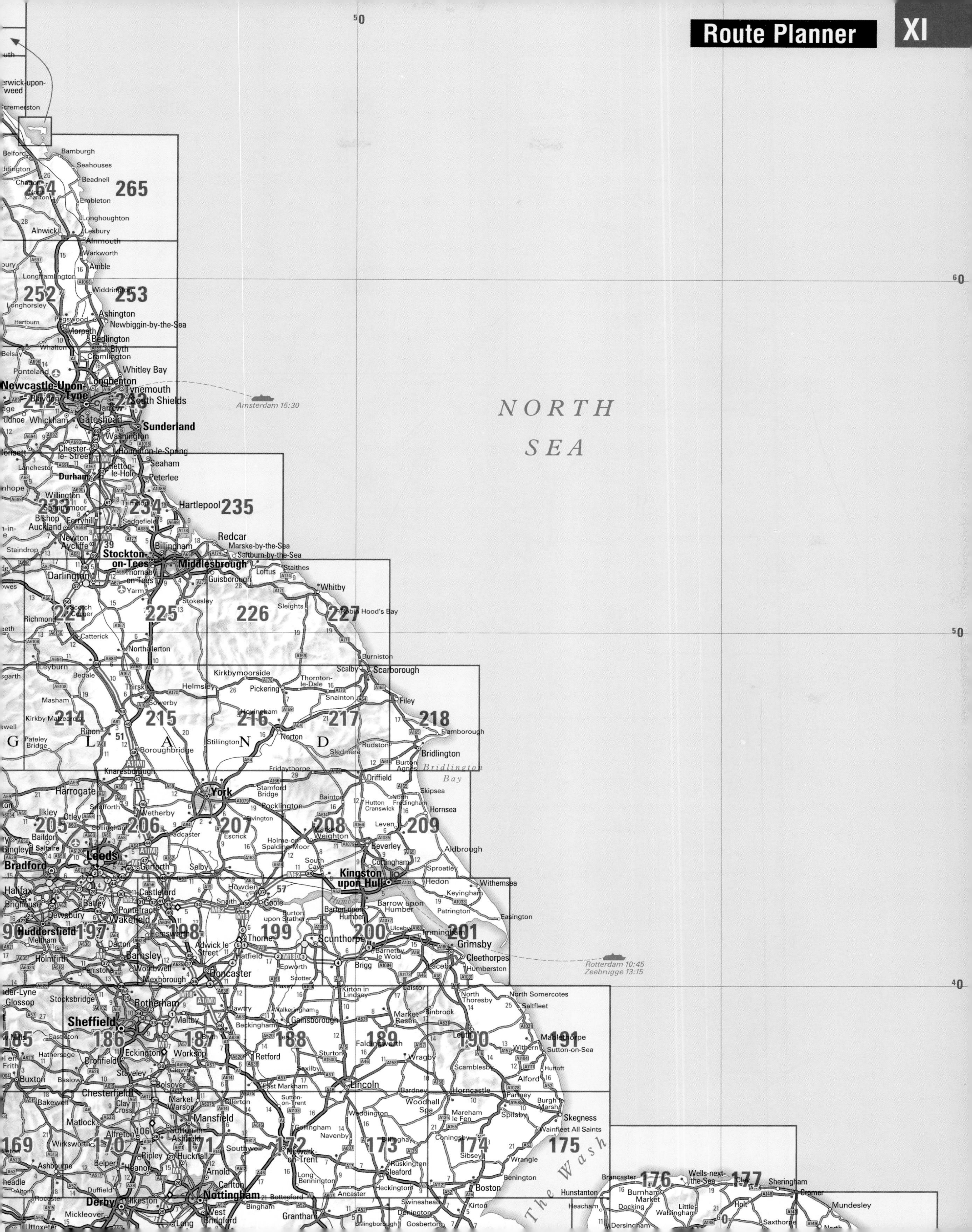
NORTH
SEA
Amsterdam 15:30
Rotterdam 10:45
Zeebrugge 13:15
Bamburgh
Seahouses
Beadnell
Embleton
Longhoughton
Alnwick
Lesbury
Alnmouth
Warkworth
Amble
Widdrington
Ashington
Newbiggin-by-the-Sea
Morpeth
Bedlington
Blyth
Cramlington
Whitley Bay
Ponteland
Longbenton
Newcastle-Upon-Tyne
Tynemouth
South Shields
Jarrow
Gateshead
Whickham
Sunderland
Washington
Chester-le-Street
Houghton-le-Spring
Seaham
Durham
Hetton-le-Hole
Peterlee
Hartlepool
Bishop Auckland
Newton Aycliffe
Sedgefield
Redcar
Marske-by-the-Sea
Saltburn-by-the-Sea
Billingham
Stockton-on-Tees
Middlesbrough
Darlington
Guisborough
Loftus
Staithes
Whitby
Yarm
Stokesley
Sleights
Robin Hood's Bay
Richmond
Catterick
Northallerton
Burniston
Scalby
Scarborough
Kirkbymoorside
Helmsley
Pickering
Thornton-le-Dale
Snainton
Filey
Leyburn
Bedale
Thirsk
Masham
Ripon
Norton
Flamborough
Bridlington
Bridlington Bay
Pateley Bridge
Boroughbridge
Stillington
Knaresborough
Driffield
Harrogate
York
Stamford Bridge
Pocklington
Skipsea
Hornsea
Ilkley
Otley
Wetherby
Tadcaster
Market Weighton
Beverley
Aldbrough
Leeds
Bradford
Garforth
Selby
Cottingham
Kingston upon Hull
Hedon
Withernsea
Halifax
Castleford
Howden
Goole
Barton-upon-Humber
Patrington
Easington
Dewsbury
Wakefield
Huddersfield
Hemsworth
Thorne
Scunthorpe
Immingham
Grimsby
Cleethorpes
Barnsley
Doncaster
Brigg
Rotherham
Sheffield
Gainsborough
Market Rasen
Louth
North Somercotes
Saltfleet
Mablethorpe
Sutton-on-Sea
Worksop
Retford
Lincoln
Alford
Chesterfield
Mansfield
Horncastle
Woodhall Spa
Spilsby
Skegness
Wainfleet All Saints
Matlock
Newark-on-Trent
Sleaford
Boston
The Wash
Hunstanton
Brancaster
Wells-next-the-Sea
Sheringham
Cromer
Mundesley
Derby
Nottingham
Grantham
ENGLAND

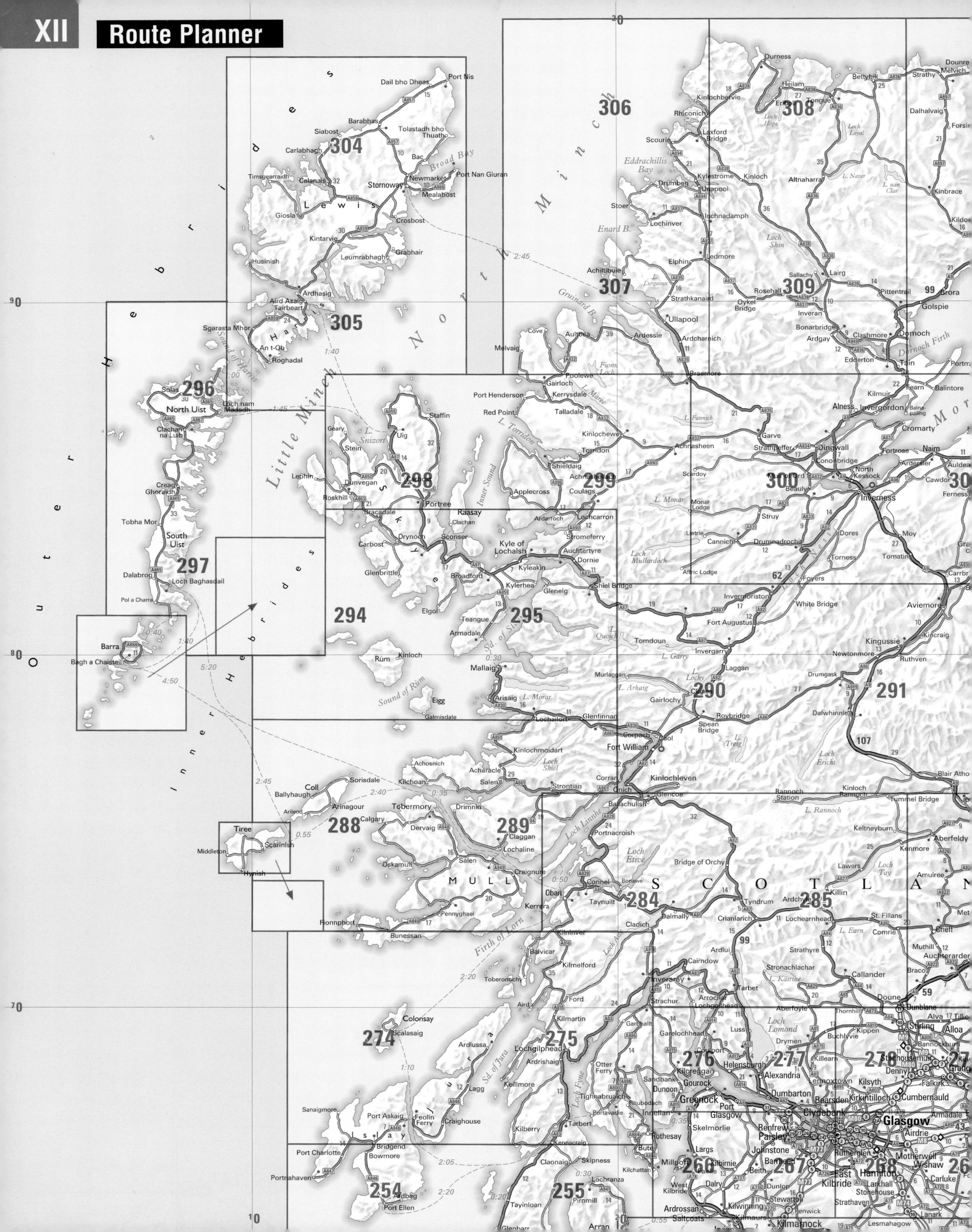
Outer Hebrides
Inner Hebrides
North Minch
Little Minch
Lewis
Harris
North Uist
South Uist
Barra
Skye
Raasay
Rùm
Eigg
Coll
Tiree
Mull
Colonsay
Jura
Islay
SCOTLAND
Stornoway
Ullapool
Inverness
Fort William
Oban
Glasgow
Greenock
Paisley
Kilmarnock
Stirling
Durness
Thurso
Portree
Mallaig
Tobermory
Inveraray
Campbeltown
304
305
306
307
308
309
296
297
298
299
300
294
295
290
291
288
289
284
285
274
275
276
277
278
254
255
266
267
268

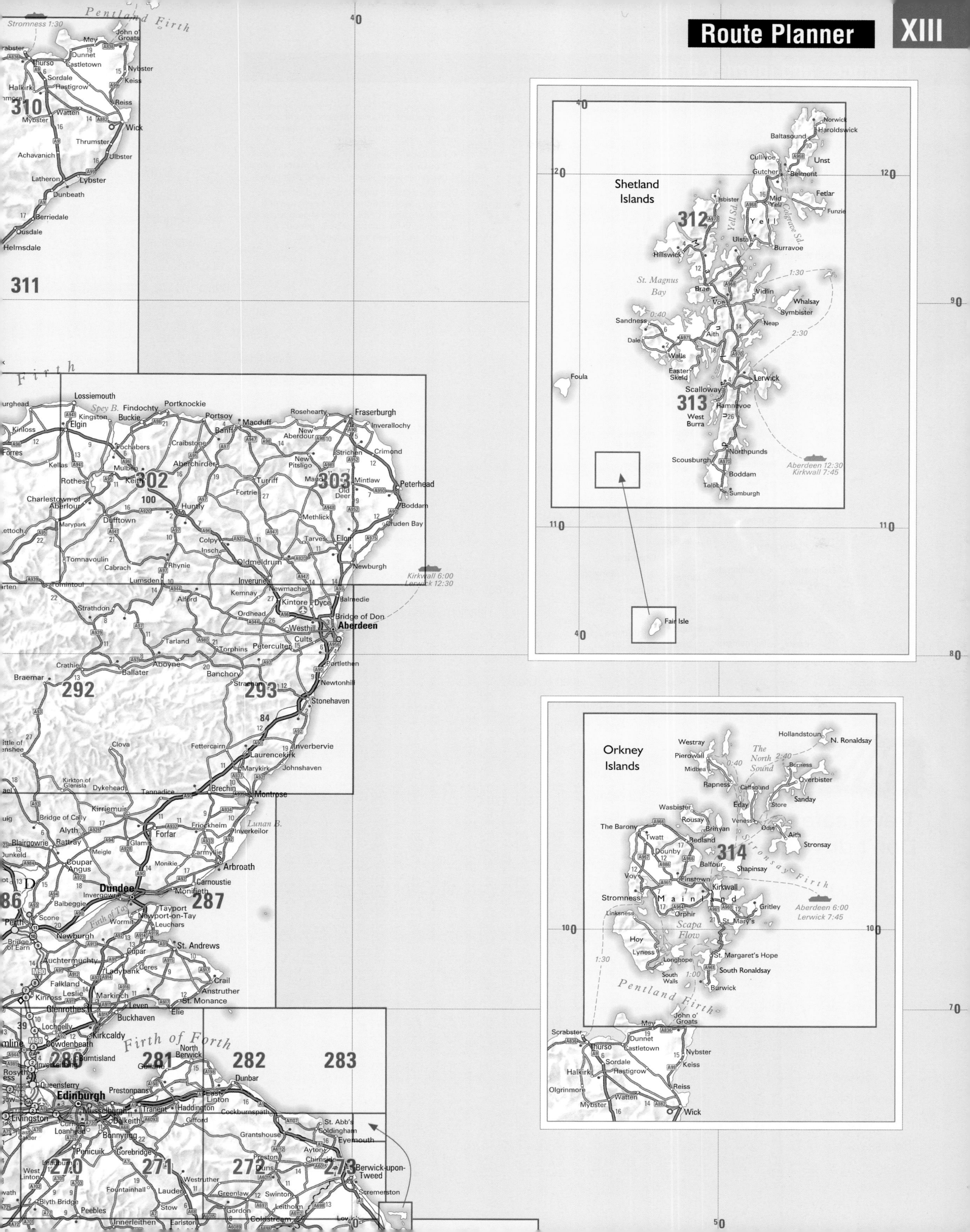

Pentland Firth

Stromness 1:30

Dunnet
Mey
John of Groats
Castletown
Nybster
15
Thurso
Sordale
Keiss
Hastigrow
Reiss
Halkirk
Watten
14
Wick
Mybster
16
Thrumster
Achavanich
Ulbster
Latheron
Lybster
Dunbeath
Berriedale
Ousdale
Helmsdale

310

311

Firth

Lossiemouth
Findochty
Portknockie
Spey B.
Portsoy
Rosehearty
Fraserburgh
Kingston
Buckie
Macduff
Inverallochy
Elgin
Banff
New Aberdour
Kinloss
Portsoy
Crimond
Forres
Craibstone
New Pitsligo
Strichen
Kellas
Fochabers
Aberchirder
Rothes
Mulben
Turriff
Maud
Mintlaw
Keith
Fortrie
Old Deer
Peterhead
302 **100** Huntly
Charlestown of Aberlour
Dufftown
Colpy
Methlick
Boddam
Maryculter
303
Tomnavoulin
Rhynie
Insch
Tarves
Elon
Gruden Bay
Cabrach
Oldmeldrum
Newburgh
Lumsden
Inverurie
Strathdon
Alford
Kemnay
Newmachar
Kintore
Dyce
Balmedie
Ordhead
Bridge of Don
Tarland
Westhill
Aberdeen
Torphins
Peterculter
Cults
Crathie
Aboyne
Banchory
Portlethen
Braemar
Ballater
Strachan
Newtonhill
292
293
Stonehaven
Clova
Fettercairn
84
Inverbervie
Kirkton of Glenisla
Laurencekirk
Johnshaven
Dykehead
Tannadice
Marykirk
Brechin
Montrose
Kirriemuir
Friockheim
Inverkeilor
Bridge of Cally
Glamis
Blairgowrie
Forfar
Lunan B.
Rattray
Meigle
Carmylie
Coupar Angus
Monikie
Arbroath
Dundee
Carnoustie
86
Invergowrie
Monifieth
287
Scone
Tayport
Perth
Newport-on-Tay
Wormit
Newburgh
Leuchars
Bridge of Earn
Cupar
St. Andrews
Auchtermuchty
Ladybank
Ceres
Falkland
Crail
Kinross
Leslie
Markinch
Anstruther
Glenrothes
Leven
St. Monance
39
Lochgelly
Buckhaven
Elie
Dunfermline
Kirkcaldy
Cowdenbeath
Burntisland
North Berwick
Firth of Forth
280 **281** **282** **283**
Inverkeithing
Gullane
Dunbar
Queensferry
Prestonpans
East Linton
Edinburgh
Tranent
Haddington
Cockburnspath
Musselburgh
St. Abb's
Livingston
Dalkeith
Gifford
Coldingham
Curne
Loanhead
Grantshouse
Eyemouth
Bonnyrigg
Gorebridge
Ayton
Chirnside
Penicuik
Preston
Berwick-upon-Tweed
West Linton
Westruther
Duns
270 **271** **27** **27**
Blyth Bridge
Fountainhall
Lauder
Greenlaw
Swinton
Scremerston
Peebles
Stow
Gordon
Leitholm
Coldstream
Innerleithen
Earlston

Kirkwall 6:00
Lerwick 12:30

Shetland Islands

Norwick
Haroldswick
Baltasound
Cullivoe
Unst
Gutcher
Belmont
Isbister
Mid Yell
Fetlar
312
Yell
Funzie
Hillswick
Ulsta
Burravoe
St. Magnus Bay
Brae
Vidlin
Whalsay
Voe
Symbister
Sandness
Dale
Aith
Neap
Walls
Easter Skeld
Lerwick
Foula
Scalloway
313
West Burra
Hamnavoe
Scousburgh
Northpunds
Boddam
Aberdeen 12:30
Kirkwall 7:45
Toab
Sumburgh

Fair Isle

Orkney Islands

Westray
Hollandstoun
N. Ronaldsay
Pierowall
The North Sound
Midbea
Burness
Rapness
Calfsound
Overbister
Wasbister
Eday
Sanday
Rousay
Store
The Barony
Brinyan
Veness
Odin
Twatt
Redland
Aith
Dounby
Balfour
Stronsay
314
Voy
Finstown
Shapinsay
Stromness
Mainland
Kirkwall
Linksness
Orphir
Gritley
Aberdeen 6:00
Lerwick 7:45
Hoy
Scapa Flow
St. Mary's
Lyness
Longhope
St. Margaret's Hope
South Walls
South Ronaldsay
Burwick
Pentland Firth

Scrabster
Dunnet
May
John o' Groats
Thurso
Castletown
Nybster
Sordale
Keiss
Halkirk
Hastigrow
Reiss
Olgrinmore
Watten
Mybster
Wick

Distances and journey times

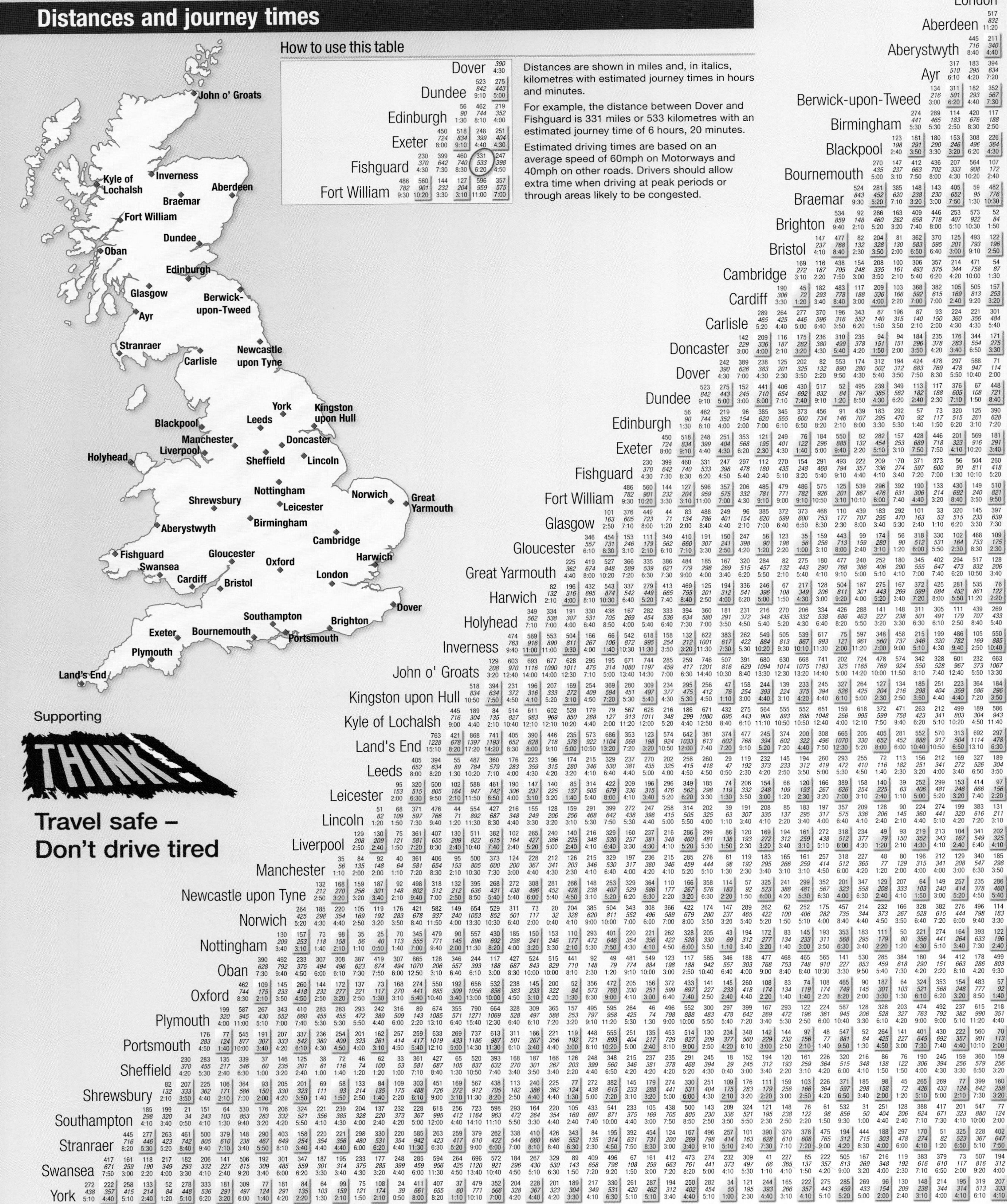

How to use this table

	Dover					
Dover	390 4:30					
Dundee	523 *842* 9:10	275 *443* 5:00				
Edinburgh	56 *90* 1:30	462 *744* 8:10	219 *352* 4:00			
Exeter	450 *724* 8:00	518 *834* 9:10	248 *399* 4:40	251 *404* 4:30		
Fishguard	230 *370* 4:30	399 *642* 7:30	460 *740* 8:30	331 *533* 6:20	247 *398* 4:50	
Fort William	486 *782* 9:30	560 *901* 10:20	144 *232* 3:30	127 *204* 3:10	596 *959* 11:00	357 *575* 7:00

Distances are shown in miles and, in italics, kilometres with estimated journey times in hours and minutes.

For example, the distance between Dover and Fishguard is 331 miles or 533 kilometres with an estimated journey time of 6 hours, 20 minutes.

Estimated driving times are based on an average speed of 60mph on Motorways and 40mph on other roads. Drivers should allow extra time when driving at peak periods or through areas likely to be congested.

	Swansea	Stranraer	Southampton	Shrewsbury	Sheffield	Portsmouth	Plymouth	Oxford	Oban	Nottingham	Norwich	Newcastle upon Tyne	Manchester	Liverpool	Lincoln	Leicester	Leeds	Land's End	Kyle of Lochalsh	Kingston upon Hull	John o' Groats	Inverness	Holyhead	Harwich	Great Yarmouth	Gloucester	Glasgow	Fort William	Fishguard	Exeter	Edinburgh	Dundee	Dover	Doncaster	Carlisle	Cardiff	Cambridge	Bristol	Brighton	Braemar	Bournemouth	Blackpool	Birmingham	Berwick-upon-Tweed	Ayr	Aberystwyth	Aberdeen	London
Aberdeen																																																517 *832* 11:20
Aberystwyth																																															445 *716* 8:40	211 *340* 4:40
Ayr																																														317 *510* 6:10	183 *295* 4:20	394 *634* 7:20
Berwick-upon-Tweed																																													134 *216* 3:00	311 *501* 6:20	182 *293* 4:40	352 *567* 7:30
Birmingham																																												274 *441* 5:30	289 *465* 5:30	114 *183* 2:50	420 *676* 8:30	117 *188* 2:50
Blackpool																																											123 *198* 2:40	181 *291* 3:50	180 *290* 3:30	153 *246* 3:20	308 *496* 6:20	226 *364* 4:30
Bournemouth																																										270 *435* 5:00	147 *237* 3:10	412 *663* 7:50	436 *702* 8:00	207 *333* 4:30	564 *908* 10:20	107 *172* 2:40
Braemar																																									524 *843* 9:30	281 *452* 5:20	385 *620* 7:10	148 *238* 3:20	143 *230* 3:00	405 *652* 7:50	59 *95* 1:30	482 *776* 10:30
Brighton																																								534 *859* 9:40	92 *148* 2:10	286 *460* 5:20	163 *262* 3:20	409 *658* 7:40	446 *718* 8:00	253 *407* 5:10	573 *922* 10:30	52 *84* 1:50
Bristol																																							147 *237* 4:10	477 *768* 8:40	82 *132* 2:30	204 *328* 3:50	81 *130* 2:00	362 *583* 6:50	370 *595* 6:40	125 *201* 3:00	493 *793* 9:10	122 *196* 2:50
Cambridge																																						169 *272* 3:10	116 *187* 2:20	438 *705* 7:50	154 *248* 3:00	208 *335* 3:50	100 *161* 2:10	306 *493* 5:40	357 *575* 6:20	214 *344* 4:20	471 *758* 10:00	54 *87* 1:30
Cardiff																																					190 *306* 3:30	45 *72* 1:20	182 *293* 3:40	483 *778* 8:40	117 *188* 3:00	209 *336* 4:00	103 *166* 2:20	368 *592* 7:00	382 *615* 7:00	105 *169* 2:40	505 *813* 9:20	157 *253* 3:20
Carlisle																																				289 *465* 5:20	264 *425* 4:40	277 *446* 5:00	370 *596* 6:40	196 *316* 3:50	343 *552* 6:20	87 *140* 1:50	196 *315* 3:50	87 *140* 2:10	93 *150* 2:00	224 *360* 4:30	221 *356* 4:30	301 *484* 5:40
Doncaster																																			142 *229* 3:00	209 *336* 4:00	116 *187* 2:10	175 *282* 3:20	236 *380* 4:30	310 *499* 5:40	235 *378* 4:20	94 *151* 1:50	94 *151* 2:00	184 *296* 3:50	235 *378* 4:20	176 *283* 3:40	344 *554* 6:50	171 *275* 3:30
Dover																																		242 *390* 4:30	389 *626* 7:00	238 *383* 4:30	125 *201* 2:30	202 *325* 3:50	82 *132* 2:20	553 *890* 9:50	174 *280* 4:30	312 *502* 5:40	194 *312* 3:50	424 *683* 7:50	478 *769* 8:30	297 *478* 5:50	588 *947* 10:40	71 *114* 2:00
Dundee																																	523 *842* 9:10	275 *443* 5:00	152 *245* 3:00	441 *710* 8:00	406 *654* 7:10	430 *692* 7:40	517 *832* 9:10	52 *84* 1:20	495 *797* 8:50	239 *385* 4:30	349 *562* 6:20	113 *182* 2:40	117 *188* 2:30	376 *605* 7:10	67 *108* 1:50	448 *721* 8:40
Edinburgh																																56 *90* 1:30	462 *744* 8:10	219 *352* 4:00	96 *154* 2:00	385 *620* 7:00	345 *555* 6:10	373 *600* 6:50	456 *734* 8:20	91 *146* 2:10	439 *707* 8:00	183 *295* 3:30	292 *470* 5:30	57 *92* 1:40	73 *117* 1:50	320 *515* 6:20	125 *201* 3:10	390 *628* 7:20
Exeter																															450 *724* 8:00	518 *834* 9:10	248 *399* 4:40	251 *404* 4:30	353 *568* 6:20	121 *195* 2:30	249 *401* 4:30	76 *122* 1:40	184 *296* 5:00	550 *885* 9:40	82 *132* 2:20	282 *454* 5:10	157 *253* 3:10	428 *689* 7:50	446 *718* 7:50	201 *323* 4:10	569 *916* 10:20	181 *291* 3:40
Fishguard																														230 *370* 4:30	399 *642* 7:30	460 *740* 8:30	331 *533* 6:20	247 *398* 4:50	297 *478* 5:40	112 *180* 2:40	270 *435* 5:10	154 *248* 3:20	291 *468* 5:40	493 *794* 9:10	222 *357* 4:40	209 *336* 4:10	170 *274* 3:40	371 *597* 7:20	373 *600* 7:00	56 *90* 1:30	504 *811* 10:10	260 *418* 5:20
Fort William																													486 *782* 9:30	560 *901* 10:20	144 *232* 3:30	127 *204* 3:10	596 *959* 11:00	357 *575* 7:00	206 *332* 4:30	485 *781* 9:10	479 *771* 9:00	486 *782* 9:10	575 *926* 10:50	125 *201* 3:10	539 *867* 10:10	296 *476* 6:00	392 *631* 7:40	190 *306* 4:40	133 *214* 3:20	430 *692* 8:40	149 *240* 3:50	510 *821* 9:50
Glasgow																												101 *163* 2:50	376 *605* 7:10	449 *723* 8:00	44 *71* 1:20	83 *134* 2:00	488 *786* 8:40	249 *401* 4:40	96 *154* 2:10	385 *620* 7:00	372 *599* 6:40	373 *600* 6:50	468 *753* 8:30	110 *177* 2:30	439 *707* 8:00	183 *295* 3:40	292 *470* 5:30	101 *163* 2:40	33 *53* 1:10	320 *515* 6:20	145 *233* 3:30	397 *639* 7:30
Gloucester																											346 *557* 6:10	454 *731* 8:30	153 *246* 3:10	111 *179* 2:10	349 *562* 6:10	410 *660* 7:10	191 *307* 3:30	150 *241* 2:50	247 *398* 4:20	56 *90* 1:20	123 *198* 2:20	35 *56* 1:00	159 *256* 3:10	443 *713* 8:00	99 *159* 2:40	174 *280* 3:10	56 *90* 1:20	318 *512* 6:00	330 *531* 5:50	102 *164* 2:30	468 *753* 8:30	109 *175* 2:30
Great Yarmouth																										225 *362* 4:40	419 *674* 8:00	527 *848* 10:20	366 *589* 7:20	335 *539* 6:30	386 *621* 7:30	484 *779* 9:00	185 *298* 4:00	167 *269* 3:40	320 *515* 6:20	284 *457* 5:50	82 *132* 2:10	275 *443* 5:40	180 *290* 4:10	477 *768* 9:10	240 *386* 5:00	252 *406* 5:10	180 *290* 4:10	345 *555* 7:00	402 *647* 7:40	294 *473* 6:20	517 *832* 10:50	128 *206* 3:40
Harwich																									82 *132* 2:10	196 *316* 4:00	432 *695* 8:10	543 *874* 10:30	337 *542* 6:40	279 *449* 5:20	413 *665* 7:40	469 *755* 8:40	125 *201* 2:50	194 *312* 4:00	336 *541* 6:20	246 *396* 5:00	67 *108* 1:50	217 *349* 4:30	128 *206* 3:00	504 *811* 9:20	187 *301* 4:00	275 *443* 5:20	167 *269* 3:40	372 *599* 7:20	425 *684* 8:00	281 *452* 5:50	535 *861* 11:20	76 *122* 2:20
Holyhead																								349 *562* 7:10	334 *538* 7:00	191 *307* 4:00	330 *531* 6:40	438 *705* 8:50	167 *269* 4:00	282 *454* 5:40	333 *536* 6:40	394 *634* 7:30	360 *580* 7:00	181 *291* 3:50	231 *372* 4:50	216 *348* 5:40	270 *435* 5:20	206 *332* 4:30	334 *538* 6:40	426 *686* 8:20	288 *463* 5:50	141 *227* 3:20	148 *238* 3:30	311 *501* 6:30	305 *491* 6:10	111 *179* 2:50	439 *707* 8:40	269 *433* 5:40
Inverness																							474 *763* 9:40	569 *916* 11:00	553 *890* 11:00	504 *811* 9:30	166 *267* 4:00	66 *106* 1:40	542 *872* 10:30	618 *995* 11:30	158 *254* 3:50	132 *212* 3:20	622 *1001* 11:30	383 *617* 7:30	262 *422* 5:30	549 *884* 10:20	505 *813* 9:30	539 *867* 10:10	617 *993* 11:30	75 *121* 2:00	597 *961* 11:20	348 *560* 7:00	458 *737* 9:00	215 *346* 5:10	199 *320* 4:30	486 *782* 9:40	105 *169* 2:50	550 *885* 10:40
John o' Groats																						129 *208* 3:20	603 *970* 12:40	693 *1116* 14:00	677 *1090* 14:00	628 *1011* 12:30	295 *475* 7:10	195 *314* 5:00	671 *1080* 13:40	744 *1197* 14:30	285 *459* 7:00	259 *417* 6:30	746 *1201* 14:40	507 *816* 10:30	391 *629* 8:40	680 *1094* 13:30	630 *1014* 12:30	668 *1075* 13:20	741 *1193* 14:40	202 *325* 5:00	724 *1165* 14:20	478 *769* 10:00	574 *924* 11:50	342 *550* 8:10	328 *528* 7:40	601 *967* 12:40	232 *373* 5:50	663 *1067* 13:30
Kingston upon Hull																					518 *834* 10:50	394 *634* 7:50	231 *372* 4:50	196 *316* 4:10	207 *333* 5:20	169 *272* 3:10	254 *409* 4:50	369 *594* 7:20	280 *451* 5:30	309 *497* 5:40	234 *377* 4:30	295 *475* 5:30	256 *412* 4:50	47 *76* 1:10	158 *254* 3:00	244 *393* 4:40	139 *224* 3:10	233 *375* 4:20	245 *394* 4:40	327 *526* 6:10	264 *425* 5:00	127 *204* 2:30	134 *216* 2:50	185 *298* 3:50	251 *404* 4:40	223 *359* 4:40	364 *586* 7:20	184 *296* 3:50
Kyle of Lochalsh																				445 *716* 9:00	189 *304* 4:40	84 *135* 2:10	514 *827* 10:40	611 *983* 12:10	602 *969* 12:10	528 *850* 10:20	179 *288* 4:40	79 *127* 2:00	567 *913* 11:20	628 *1011* 12:00	216 *348* 5:20	186 *299* 4:40	671 *1080* 12:50	432 *695* 8:40	275 *443* 6:10	564 *908* 11:10	555 *893* 10:50	552 *888* 10:50	651 *1048* 12:40	159 *256* 4:00	618 *995* 12:10	372 *599* 7:50	471 *758* 9:40	263 *423* 6:20	212 *341* 5:10	499 *803* 10:20	189 *304* 4:50	586 *943* 11:40
Land's End																			763 *1228* 15:10	421 *678* 8:20	868 *1397* 17:20	741 *1193* 14:20	405 *652* 8:30	390 *628* 8:00	446 *718* 9:10	235 *378* 5:00	573 *922* 10:50	686 *1104* 13:20	353 *568* 7:20	123 *198* 3:20	574 *924* 10:50	642 *1033* 12:00	381 *613* 7:40	374 *602* 7:20	477 *768* 9:10	245 *394* 5:20	374 *602* 7:20	200 *322* 4:40	308 *496* 7:50	665 *1070* 12:30	205 *330* 5:20	405 *652* 8:00	281 *452* 6:00	552 *888* 10:40	570 *917* 10:50	313 *504* 6:50	692 *1114* 13:10	297 *478* 6:30
Leeds																		405 *652* 8:00	394 *634* 8:20	55 *89* 1:30	487 *784* 10:20	360 *579* 7:10	176 *283* 4:00	223 *359* 4:30	196 *315* 4:20	174 *280* 3:20	215 *346* 4:10	329 *530* 6:40	237 *381* 4:40	270 *435* 5:00	202 *325* 4:00	258 *415* 4:50	260 *418* 4:50	29 *47* 0:50	119 *192* 2:30	232 *373* 4:20	145 *233* 2:50	194 *312* 3:50	260 *419* 5:00	293 *472* 5:30	255 *410* 4:50	72 *116* 1:40	113 *182* 2:30	156 *251* 3:20	212 *341* 4:00	169 *272* 3:40	327 *526* 6:50	189 *304* 3:50
Leicester																	95 *153* 2:00	320 *515* 6:30	500 *805* 9:50	102 *164* 2:10	588 *947* 11:50	461 *742* 8:50	190 *306* 4:00	147 *237* 3:10	140 *225* 3:20	85 *137* 1:40	314 *505* 5:40	422 *679* 8:00	209 *336* 4:10	196 *315* 3:40	296 *476* 5:20	349 *562* 6:20	185 *298* 3:30	74 *119* 1:30	206 *332* 3:50	154 *248* 3:00	68 *109* 1:20	120 *193* 2:30	166 *267* 3:20	389 *626* 7:00	158 *254* 3:10	140 *225* 2:40	39 *63* 1:10	252 *406* 5:00	299 *481* 5:20	153 *246* 3:20	414 *666* 7:40	97 *156* 2:20
Lincoln																51 *82* 1:20	68 *109* 1:50	371 *597* 7:30	476 *766* 9:40	44 *71* 1:20	554 *892* 11:30	427 *687* 8:30	216 *348* 4:40	155 *249* 3:30	128 *206* 3:20	159 *256* 3:10	291 *468* 5:30	399 *642* 7:50	272 *438* 5:30	247 *398* 4:40	258 *415* 5:00	314 *505* 5:50	202 *325* 4:00	39 *63* 1:10	191 *307* 3:40	208 *335* 4:10	85 *137* 2:20	183 *295* 3:40	197 *317* 4:00	357 *575* 6:40	209 *336* 4:10	128 *206* 2:40	90 *145* 2:10	224 *360* 4:40	274 *441* 5:10	199 *320* 4:20	383 *616* 7:20	131 *211* 3:10
Liverpool															129 *208* 2:50	130 *209* 2:40	75 *121* 1:50	361 *581* 7:20	407 *655* 8:30	130 *209* 2:40	511 *822* 10:40	382 *615* 7:40	102 *164* 2:40	265 *427* 5:20	240 *386* 5:00	140 *225* 2:40	216 *348* 4:10	329 *530* 6:40	160 *257* 3:30	237 *381* 4:30	216 *348* 4:10	286 *460* 5:20	299 *481* 5:30	86 *138* 1:50	120 *193* 2:30	169 *272* 3:20	194 *312* 3:40	161 *259* 3:10	272 *438* 5:10	318 *512* 6:00	234 *377* 4:30	49 *79* 1:20	93 *150* 2:10	219 *352* 4:30	213 *343* 4:10	104 *167* 2:40	341 *549* 6:40	202 *325* 4:10
Manchester														35 *56* 1:10	84 *135* 2:00	92 *148* 2:00	40 *64* 1:10	361 *581* 7:20	406 *654* 8:30	95 *153* 2:10	500 *805* 10:30	373 *600* 7:30	124 *200* 3:00	228 *367* 4:40	212 *341* 4:30	126 *203* 2:30	215 *346* 4:10	329 *530* 6:40	197 *317* 4:00	236 *380* 4:20	215 *346* 4:10	285 *459* 5:20	276 *444* 5:10	61 *98* 1:30	119 *192* 2:30	183 *295* 3:40	165 *266* 3:10	161 *259* 3:10	257 *414* 4:50	318 *512* 6:00	227 *365* 4:20	48 *77* 1:20	80 *129* 2:00	196 *315* 4:00	212 *341* 4:00	129 *208* 3:00	340 *547* 6:30	185 *298* 3:50
Newcastle upon Tyne													132 *212* 2:50	168 *270* 3:20	159 *256* 3:20	187 *301* 3:40	92 *148* 2:10	498 *802* 9:40	318 *512* 7:00	132 *212* 2:50	395 *636* 8:50	268 *431* 5:40	272 *438* 5:40	308 *496* 6:00	281 *452* 5:40	266 *428* 4:50	148 *238* 3:10	253 *407* 5:20	329 *529* 6:20	364 *586* 6:30	110 *177* 2:20	166 *267* 3:20	358 *576* 6:30	114 *183* 2:20	57 *92* 1:50	325 *523* 6:00	241 *388* 4:20	299 *481* 5:30	352 *567* 6:30	201 *323* 4:00	347 *558* 6:30	129 *208* 2:40	207 *333* 4:10	64 *103* 1:50	149 *240* 3:00	257 *414* 5:20	235 *378* 4:50	286 *460* 5:40
Norwich												264 *425* 5:20	185 *298* 4:30	220 *354* 4:40	105 *169* 2:50	119 *192* 3:20	176 *283* 3:50	421 *678* 8:40	582 *937* 11:50	149 *240* 4:00	654 *1053* 13:30	529 *852* 10:30	311 *501* 6:40	73 *117* 2:00	20 *32* 0:40	204 *328* 4:10	385 *620* 9:00	504 *811* 10:00	343 *552* 7:00	308 *496* 6:00	366 *589* 7:00	422 *679* 8:00	174 *280* 3:50	147 *237* 3:20	289 *465* 5:40	262 *422* 5:20	62 *100* 1:50	252 *406* 5:10	175 *282* 4:00	457 *735* 8:40	214 *344* 4:40	232 *373* 4:50	166 *267* 3:50	328 *528* 6:40	382 *615* 7:20	276 *444* 6:00	496 *798* 9:40	114 *183* 3:30
Nottingham											130 *209* 3:40	157 *253* 3:10	73 *118* 1:40	98 *158* 2:10	35 *56* 1:10	25 *40* 0:50	70 *113* 1:40	345 *555* 7:00	479 *771* 9:40	90 *145* 2:00	557 *896* 11:30	430 *692* 8:20	185 *298* 4:00	150 *241* 3:20	153 *246* 3:30	110 *177* 2:10	293 *472* 5:30	401 *646* 7:50	220 *354* 4:30	221 *356* 4:10	262 *422* 4:50	328 *528* 6:00	205 *330* 3:50	43 *69* 1:10	194 *312* 3:40	172 *277* 3:20	83 *134* 1:40	145 *233* 3:00	193 *311* 3:50	353 *568* 6:30	183 *295* 3:40	111 *179* 2:20	50 *80* 1:20	221 *356* 4:30	274 *441* 5:10	164 *264* 3:40	393 *633* 7:30	122 *196* 2:40
Oban										390 *628* 7:30	492 *792* 9:40	233 *375* 4:50	307 *494* 6:00	308 *496* 6:10	387 *623* 7:30	419 *674* 7:50	307 *494* 6:00	665 *1070* 12:50	128 *206* 3:10	346 *557* 6:40	244 *393* 6:10	117 *188* 3:00	427 *687* 8:30	524 *843* 10:00	515 *829* 10:00	441 *710* 8:10	92 *148* 2:30	49 *79* 1:20	481 *774* 9:10	549 *884* 10:00	123 *198* 3:00	117 *188* 2:50	585 *942* 10:40	346 *557* 6:40	188 *303* 4:00	477 *768* 9:00	468 *753* 8:40	465 *748* 8:40	565 *910* 10:30	141 *227* 3:30	530 *853* 9:50	285 *459* 5:40	384 *618* 7:30	180 *290* 4:20	94 *151* 2:20	412 *663* 8:10	178 *286* 4:20	499 *803* 9:30
Oxford									462 *744* 8:30	109 *175* 2:10	145 *233* 3:50	260 *418* 4:50	144 *232* 2:50	172 *277* 3:20	137 *221* 2:50	73 *117* 1:30	168 *270* 3:10	274 *441* 5:40	550 *885* 10:40	192 *309* 3:40	656 *1056* 13:00	532 *856* 10:00	238 *383* 4:50	145 *233* 3:10	200 *322* 4:20	52 *84* 1:30	356 *573* 6:30	472 *760* 9:00	205 *330* 4:10	156 *251* 3:00	372 *599* 6:40	433 *697* 7:40	141 *227* 2:50	145 *233* 2:40	260 *418* 4:40	108 *174* 2:20	83 *134* 1:40	74 *119* 1:40	108 *174* 2:20	465 *749* 8:20	90 *145* 2:00	187 *301* 3:30	64 *103* 1:30	324 *521* 6:10	353 *568* 6:20	154 *248* 3:20	483 *777* 8:50	57 *92* 1:40
Plymouth								199 *320* 4:00	587 *945* 11:00	267 *430* 5:10	343 *552* 7:00	410 *660* 7:40	283 *455* 5:30	283 *455* 5:30	293 *472* 5:50	242 *389* 4:40	316 *509* 6:00	89 *143* 2:20	674 *1085* 13:10	355 *571* 6:40	790 *1271* 15:40	664 *1069* 12:30	328 *528* 6:40	309 *497* 6:10	365 *588* 7:20	157 *253* 3:20	495 *797* 9:10	595 *958* 11:20	264 *425* 5:30	46 *74* 1:30	496 *798* 9:00	552 *888* 10:00	300 *483* 5:50	297 *478* 5:40	399 *642* 7:20	167 *269* 3:40	293 *472* 5:30	122 *196* 2:50	224 *361* 6:00	587 *945* 10:40	128 *206* 3:30	328 *528* 6:10	203 *327* 4:20	474 *763* 9:00	492 *792* 9:00	237 *382* 5:10	615 *990* 11:20	218 *351* 4:40
Portsmouth							176 *283* 4:50	77 *124* 1:40	545 *877* 10:00	191 *307* 3:40	207 *333* 4:20	337 *542* 6:10	236 *380* 4:30	254 *409* 4:50	201 *323* 4:00	162 *261* 3:10	257 *414* 4:50	259 *417* 5:40	633 *1019* 12:10	269 *433* 5:00	737 *1186* 14:30	613 *987* 11:30	311 *501* 6:10	166 *267* 3:40	221 *356* 4:40	119 *192* 3:00	448 *721* 8:10	555 *893* 10:20	251 *404* 5:00	135 *217* 2:40	453 *729* 8:10	514 *827* 9:00	130 *209* 2:50	234 *377* 4:20	348 *560* 6:10	142 *229* 3:00	144 *232* 2:50	97 *156* 2:10	48 *77* 1:40	547 *881* 9:50	52 *84* 1:30	264 *425* 4:50	141 *227* 3:00	401 *645* 7:30	430 *692* 7:40	222 *357* 4:40	560 *901* 10:10	70 *113* 2:00
Sheffield						230 *370* 4:20	283 *455* 5:30	135 *217* 2:40	339 *546* 6:30	37 *60* 1:00	146 *235* 3:20	125 *201* 2:40	38 *61* 1:00	72 *116* 1:40	46 *74* 1:20	62 *100* 1:20	33 *53* 1:00	361 *581* 7:10	427 *687* 8:40	65 *105* 1:30	520 *837* 10:50	393 *632* 7:40	168 *270* 3:40	187 *301* 3:50	166 *267* 3:40	126 *203* 2:20	248 *399* 4:40	348 *560* 6:50	215 *346* 4:20	237 *381* 4:20	235 *378* 4:20	291 *468* 5:20	245 *394* 4:30	18 *29* 0:40	152 *245* 3:00	194 *312* 3:40	120 *193* 2:20	161 *259* 3:10	226 *364* 4:20	320 *515* 6:00	216 *348* 4:10	86 *138* 1:50	76 *122* 1:50	190 *306* 4:00	245 *394* 4:30	159 *256* 3:30	360 *579* 6:50	159 *256* 3:20
Shrewsbury					82 *132* 2:10	207 *333* 3:50	225 *362* 4:40	106 *171* 2:10	364 *586* 7:00	93 *150* 2:00	205 *330* 4:20	201 *323* 3:50	69 *111* 1:40	58 *93* 1:50	133 *214* 2:50	84 *135* 1:40	109 *175* 2:20	303 *488* 6:10	451 *726* 9:00	169 *272* 3:10	567 *912* 11:30	438 *705* 8:20	113 *182* 2:50	240 *386* 4:40	225 *362* 4:40	77 *124* 1:30	272 *438* 5:00	382 *615* 7:20	145 *233* 3:10	179 *288* 3:20	274 *441* 5:00	330 *531* 6:00	251 *404* 4:30	109 *175* 2:10	176 *283* 3:20	111 *179* 2:20	159 *256* 3:00	103 *166* 2:50	226 *364* 4:20	371 *597* 6:50	185 *298* 3:40	98 *158* 2:00	45 *72* 1:20	265 *426* 5:10	269 *433* 5:00	77 *124* 2:10	399 *642* 7:30	160 *258* 3:20
Southampton				185 *298* 4:10	199 *320* 3:40	21 *34* 0:50	151 *243* 4:10	64 *103* 1:30	530 *853* 9:40	176 *283* 3:20	206 *332* 4:20	324 *521* 5:50	221 *356* 4:10	239 *385* 4:30	204 *328* 4:00	137 *220* 2:40	232 *373* 4:20	228 *367* 5:00	618 *995* 12:00	256 *412* 4:40	723 *1164* 14:10	598 *963* 11:10	293 *472* 5:50	164 *264* 3:30	220 *354* 4:40	105 *169* 2:40	433 *697* 7:40	541 *871* 10:00	233 *375* 4:40	105 *169* 3:00	438 *705* 7:50	500 *805* 8:50	143 *230* 2:50	209 *336* 3:50	324 *521* 5:50	121 *195* 2:30	148 *238* 2:50	76 *122* 2:20	61 *98* 1:50	532 *856* 9:30	31 *50* 1:00	251 *404* 4:40	128 *206* 2:40	388 *624* 7:10	417 *671* 7:30	201 *323* 4:10	547 *880* 10:00	77 *124* 2:00
Stranraer			445 *716* 8:20	277 *446* 5:30	263 *423* 5:20	461 *742* 8:40	500 *805* 9:40	379 *610* 7:10	148 *238* 3:40	290 *467* 5:50	403 *649* 8:10	158 *254* 3:40	220 *354* 4:40	221 *356* 4:40	298 *480* 6:00	330 *531* 6:20	220 *354* 4:40	585 *942* 11:30	263 *423* 6:30	259 *417* 5:20	379 *610* 9:00	262 *422* 6:00	338 *544* 7:00	410 *660* 8:10	426 *686* 8:40	343 *552* 6:30	84 *135* 2:30	195 *314* 4:50	392 *631* 7:50	454 *731* 8:30	124 *200* 3:00	167 *269* 3:40	496 *798* 9:10	257 *414* 5:10	101 *163* 2:40	390 *628* 7:30	379 *610* 7:10	378 *608* 7:20	475 *765* 9:00	194 *312* 4:20	444 *715* 8:30	188 *303* 4:00	297 *478* 6:00	170 *274* 4:10	51 *82* 1:20	325 *523* 6:50	228 *367* 5:10	402 *647* 7:50
Swansea		417 *671* 7:50	161 *259* 3:00	118 *190* 2:20	217 *349* 4:00	182 *293* 3:30	206 *332* 4:10	141 *227* 2:40	506 *815* 9:20	192 *309* 3:40	301 *485* 6:00	347 *559* 6:20	187 *301* 3:30	195 *314* 3:40	233 *375* 4:30	177 *285* 3:20	248 *399* 4:40	285 *459* 6:00	594 *956* 11:30	264 *425* 4:50	696 *1120* 13:40	572 *921* 10:40	184 *296* 4:50	267 *430* 5:10	329 *530* 6:30	89 *143* 1:50	409 *658* 7:20	496 *798* 9:20	67 *108* 1:50	161 *259* 3:00	412 *663* 7:20	473 *761* 8:20	274 *441* 5:00	232 *373* 4:10	309 *497* 5:30	41 *66* 1:10	227 *365* 4:10	85 *137* 1:50	222 *357* 4:20	505 *813* 9:00	167 *269* 3:20	216 *348* 4:00	119 *192* 2:30	383 *616* 7:10	379 *610* 6:50	73 *117* 2:00	507 *816* 9:20	194 *312* 4:00
York	272 *438* 5:10	222 *357* 4:40	258 *415* 5:10	133 *214* 2:40	52 *84* 1:20	278 *448* 5:10	333 *536* 6:20	181 *291* 3:20	309 *497* 6:00	77 *124* 1:40	181 *291* 4:20	84 *135* 2:20	64 *103* 1:30	99 *159* 2:10	75 *121* 1:50	108 *174* 2:10	24 *39* 0:50	411 *661* 8:00	407 *655* 8:20	37 *60* 1:10	479 *771* 10:10	352 *566* 7:00	204 *328* 4:20	228 *367* 4:40	201 *323* 4:20	189 *304* 3:30	217 *349* 4:10	330 *531* 6:30	261 *420* 5:10	287 *462* 5:10	194 *312* 3:40	250 *402* 4:40	282 *454* 5:10	34 *55* 1:00	121 *195* 2:30	244 *393* 4:40	165 *266* 3:10	222 *357* 4:10	275 *443* 5:10	285 *459* 5:20	269 *433* 5:00	96 *154* 2:00	130 *209* 2:40	148 *238* 3:10	214 *344* 4:00	195 *314* 4:10	319 *513* 6:10	207 *333* 4:10

Supporting

THINK!

Travel safe – Don't drive tired

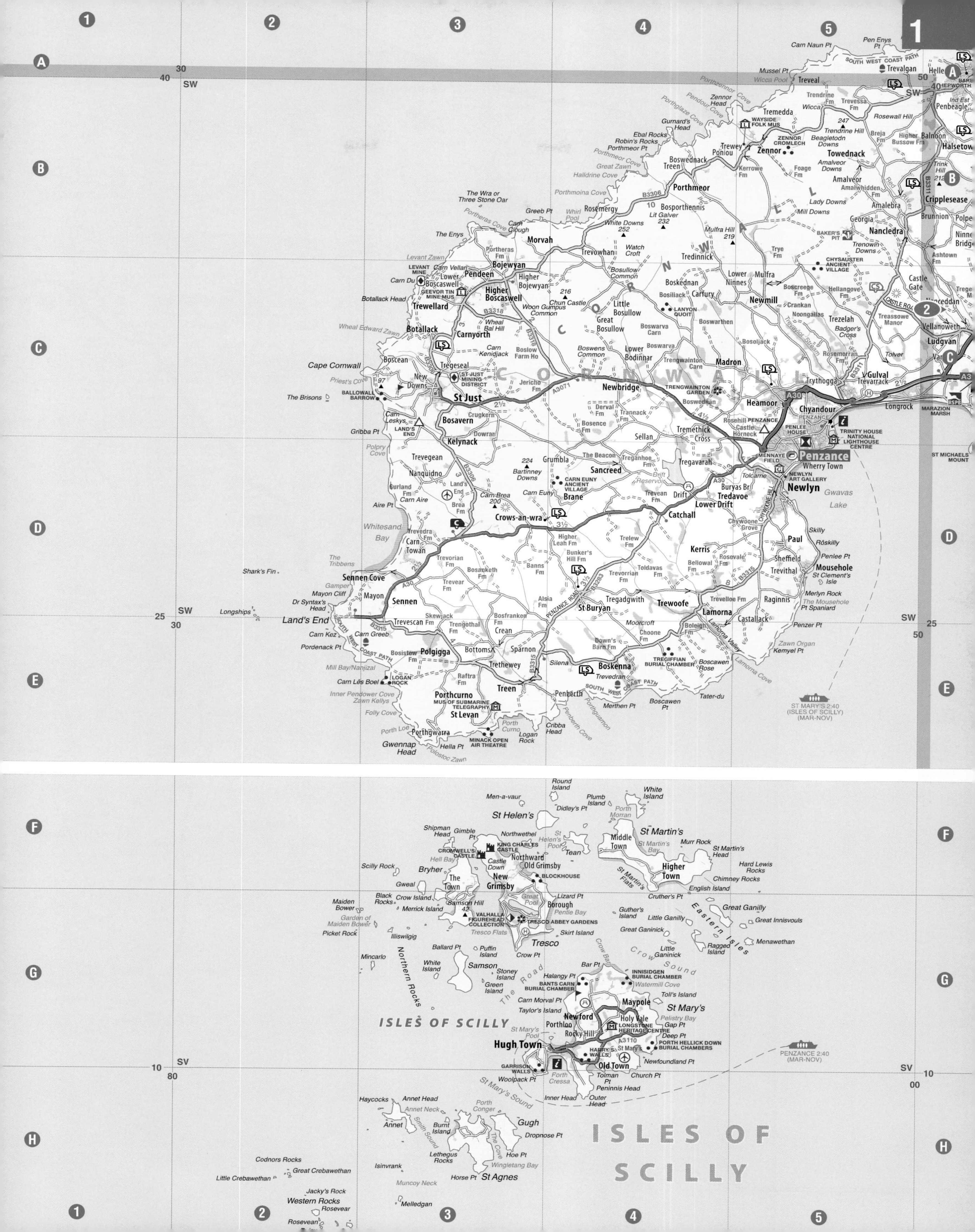

Carn Naun Pt
Pen Enys Pt
SOUTH WEST COAST PATH
Trevalgan
Mussel Pt
Wicca Pool
Treveal
Zennor Head
Tremedda
Wicca
Trendrine Fm
Trevessa Fm
Rosewall Hill
Penbeagle
WAYSIDE FOLK MUS
Gurnard's Head
Ebal Rocks
Robin's Rocks
Porthmeor Pt
Trewey
Poniou
Zennor
ZENNOR CROMLECH
247
Trendrine Hill
Beagletodn Downs
Towednack
Breja
Higher Bussow Fm
Balnoon
Halsetown
Great Zawn
Halldrine Cove
Bosweddnack
Treen
Kerrowe Fm
Foage Fm
Amalveor Downs
Amalveor
Porthmoina Cove
Porthmeor
Amalwhidden
Cripplesease
The Wra or Three Stone Oar
Greeb Pt
Rosemergy
Bosporthennis
Lit Galver 232
Lady Downs
Mill Downs
Amalebra
Brunnion
Porthers Cove
Carn Clough
White Downs 252
Mulfra Hill 219
Georgia
Nancledra
The Enys
Morvah
Watch Croft
BAKER'S PIT
Trye Fm
Tredinnick
Trenowin Downs
Levant Zawn
Portheras Fm
Trevowhan
CHYSAUSTER ANCIENT VILLAGE
Castle Gate
LEVANT MINE
Carn Vellan
Bojewyan
Bosullow Common
Lower Ninnes
Mulfra
Carn Du
Lower Boscaswell
Pendeen
Higher Bojewyan
Boskednan
Boscreege Fm
Hellangove Fm
GEEVOR TIN MINE MUS
Higher Boscaswell
216
Bosiliack
Carfury
Botallack Head
Trewellard
Chun Castle
Little Bosullow
LANYON QUOIT
Newmill
Crankan
Noongallas
Trezelah
Treassowe Manor
Woon Gumpus Common
Wheal Edward Zawn
Botallack
Carnyorth
Wheal Bal Hill
Great Bosullow
Boswarva Carn
Boswarthen
Badger's Cross
Vellanoweth
Ludgvan
Carn Kenidjack
Boslow Farm Ho
Boswens Common
Lower Bodinnar
Boswarva
Bosoljack
Tolver
Rosemorran Fm
Cape Cornwall
Boscean
Tregeseal
ST JUST MINING DISTRICT
Trengwainton Carn
Madron
Gulval
Trevarrack
Priest's Cove
97
New Downs
Jericho Fm
CORNWALL
Newbridge
TRENGWAINTON GARDEN
Trythogga
The Brisons
BALLOWALL BARROW
St Just
Heamoor
Chyandour
Longrock
MARAZION MARSH
Boswednan
Carn Leskys
LAND'S END
Crugkern
Bosavern
Derval Fm
Trannack Fm
Rosehill
PENZANCE
Castle Horneck
TRINITY HOUSE NATIONAL LIGHTHOUSE CENTRE
PENLEE HOUSE
Gribba Pt
Kelynack
Dowran
Bosence Fm
Sellan
Tremethick Cross
Polpry Cove
Trevegean
224
Grumbla
The Beacon
Treganhoe Fm
Tregavarah
MENNAYE FIELD
Penzance
Wherry Town
ST MICHAELS MOUNT
Nanquidno
Bartinney Downs
CARN EUNY ANCIENT VILLAGE
Sancreed
Drift Reservoir
Tolcarne
NEWLYN ART GALLERY
Gurland Fm
Carn Aire
Land's End
Carn Brea 200
Carn Euny
Brane
Trevean Fm
Drift
Buryas Br
Tredavoe
Newlyn
Gwavas Lake
Aire Pt
Brea Fm
Lower Drift
Crows-an-wra
Catchall
Whitesand Bay
Trevedra Fm
Carn Towan
Higher Leah Fm
Trelew Fm
Chywoone Grove
Skilly
Paul
Roskilly
The Tribbens
Trevorian Fm
Bunker's Hill Fm
Kerris
Rosevale
Sheffield
Penlee Pt
Shark's Fin
Sennen Cove
Bosanketh Fm
Banns Fm
Trevorrian Fm
Toldavas Fm
Bellowal Fm
Trevithal
Mousehole
St Clement's Isle
Gamper
Mayon Cliff
Mayon
Trevear Fm
Merlyn Rock
Dr Syntax's Head
Sennen
Alsia Fm
Tregadgwith
Trewoofe
Trevelloe Fm
Raginnis
The Mousehole
Pt Spaniard
Longships
Land's End
Skewjack
St Buryan
Lamorna
Castallack
Trevescan Fm
Bosfranken Fm
Moorcroft
Carn Kez
Carn Greeb
Trengothal Fm
Crean
Choone Fm
Boleigh Fm
Penzer Pt
Pordenack Pt
Zawn Organ
Kemyel Pt
Bosistow Fm
Polgigga
Bottoms
Sparnon
Down's Barn Fm
TREGIFFIAN BURIAL CHAMBER
Boscawen Rose
Lamorna Valley
Lamorna Cove
Mill Bay/Nanjizal
Trethewey
Silena
Boskenna
Carn Lès Boel
LOGAN ROCK
Raftra Fm
Trevedran
Inner Penolver Cove
Zawn Kellys
Porthcurno
Treen
Penberth
Tater-du
ST MARY'S 2:40 (ISLES OF SCILLY) (MAR-NOV)
MUS OF SUBMARINE TELEGRAPHY
Merthen Pt
Boscawen Pt
Folly Cove
St Levan
Porth Curno
Cribba Head
Porthguarnon
Porth Loe
Porthgwarra
Logan Rock
Penberth Cove
MINACK OPEN AIR THEATRE
Gwennap Head
Hella Pt
Folostoc Zawn
SW
25
30
40
50
Round Island
White Island
Men-a-vaur
Plumb Island
Didley's Pt
St Helen's
Porth Morran
St Martin's
Shipman Head
Gimble Pt
Northwethel
St Helen's Pool
Middle Town
Murr Rock
KING CHARLES CASTLE
CROMWELL'S CASTLE
Tean
St Martin's Bay
St Martin's Head
Hell Bay
Castle Down
Northward
Scilly Rock
Bryher
Old Grimsby
Higher Town
Hard Lewis Rocks
The Town
New Grimsby
BLOCKHOUSE
St Martin's Flats
Chimney Rocks
Gweal
English Island
Black Rocks
Crow Island
Lizard Pt
Cruther's Pt
Maiden Bower
Samson Hill 42
Great Pool
Borough
Great Ganilly
Merrick Island
Pentle Bay
Guther's Island
Little Ganilly
Great Innisvouls
Garden of Maiden Bower
VALHALLA FIGUREHEAD COLLECTION
TRESCO ABBEY GARDENS
Eastern Isles
Picket Rock
Tresco Flats
Skirt Island
Great Ganinick
Menawethan
Illiswilgig
Tresco
Ragged Island
Ballard Pt
Puffin Island
Little Ganinick
Mincarlo
Crow Pt
Crow Bar
Crow Sound
Northern Rocks
White Island
Samson
Bar Pt
Stoney Island
Halangy Pt
INNISIDGEN BURIAL CHAMBER
Green Island
BANTS CARN BURIAL CHAMBER
Watermill Cove
The Road
Toll's Island
Carn Morval Pt
Maypole
St Mary's
Taylor's Island
Newford
Holy Vale
Pelistry Bay
ISLES OF SCILLY
St Mary's Pool
Porthloo
LONGSTONE HERITAGE CENTRE
Gap Pt
Rocky Hill
Deep Pt
A3110
PORTH HELLICK DOWN BURIAL CHAMBERS
Hugh Town
HARRY'S WALLS
St Mary's
PENZANCE 2:40 (MAR-NOV)
GARRISON WALLS
Old Town
Newfoundland Pt
Woolpack Pt
Porth Cressa
Tolman Pt
Church Pt
St Mary's Sound
Peninnis Head
Haycocks
Annet Head
Inner Head
Outer Head
Annet Neck
Porth Conger
Annet
Smith Sound
Burnt Island
Gugh
The Cove
Dropnose Pt
ISLES OF SCILLY
Lethegus Rocks
Hoe Pt
Codnors Rocks
Isinvrank
Wingletang Bay
Little Crebawethan
Great Crebawethan
Horse Pt
St Agnes
Muncoy Neck
Jacky's Rock
Western Rocks
Rosevear
Melledgan
Rosevean
SV
10
80
00

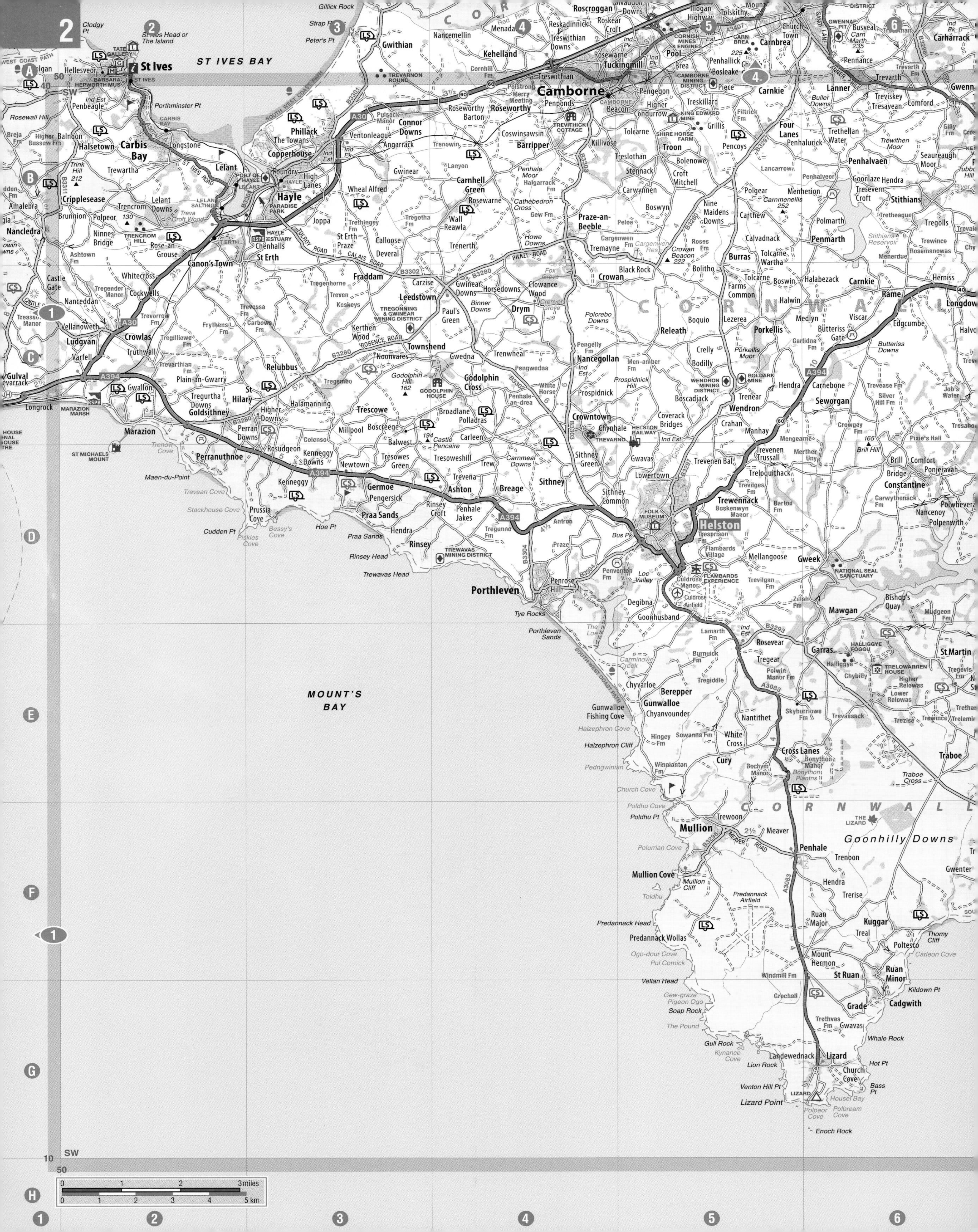

2
ST IVES BAY
St Ives
Carbis Bay
Halsetown
Lelant
Hayle
Copperhouse
Phillack
Connor Downs
Camborne
Tuckingmill
Pool
Carn Brea
Carnbrea
Illogan Highway
Roscroggan
Kehelland
Gwithian
Nancemellin
Reskadinnick
Treswithian
Roseworthy
Barripper
Praze-an-Beeble
Crowan
Troon
Four Lanes
Lanner
Carharrack
Stithians
Penhalvaen
Carnkie
Leedstown
Fraddam
St Erth
Canon's Town
Crowlas
Ludgvan
Nancledra
Cripplesease
Gulval
Longrock
Marazion
Marazion Marsh
St Michaels Mount
Perranuthnoe
Goldsithney
St Hilary
Relubbus
Townshend
Godolphin Cross
Trescowe
Germoe
Praa Sands
Rinsey
Ashton
Breage
Sithney
Porthleven
Crowntown
Nancegollan
Releath
Porkellis
Wendron
Helston
Trewennack
Constantine
Gweek
Mawgan
Garras
St Martin
Gunwalloe
Cury
Cross Lanes
Traboe
Mullion
Mullion Cove
Penhale
Goonhilly Downs
Kuggar
Ruan Minor
Cadgwith
Grade
St Ruan
Lizard
Lizard Point
Landewednack
Church Cove
Predannack Wollas
Predannack Head
Mount's Bay
CORNWALL
Culdrose Airfield
Loe Valley
Flambards Experience
Trevarno
Helston Railway
Goonhusband
Degibna
Chyvarloe
Berepper
Halzephron Cliff
Poldhu Pt
Polurrian Cove
Vellan Head
Soap Rock
Gull Rock
Kynance Cove
Lion Rock
Venton Hill Pt
Enoch Rock
Hot Pt
Bass Pt
Kildown Pt
Thorny Cliff
Cudden Pt
Hoe Pt
Rinsey Head
Trewavas Head
Tye Rocks
Porthleven Sands
Maen-du-Point
Prussia Cove
Stackhouse Cove
Trevean Cove
A30
A394
A3083
B3293
B3297
B3303
B3302
B3280
B3304
B3296
B3301
B3311
B3074
SW
0 1 2 3 miles
0 1 2 3 4 5 km
A B C D E F G H
1 2 3 4 5 6

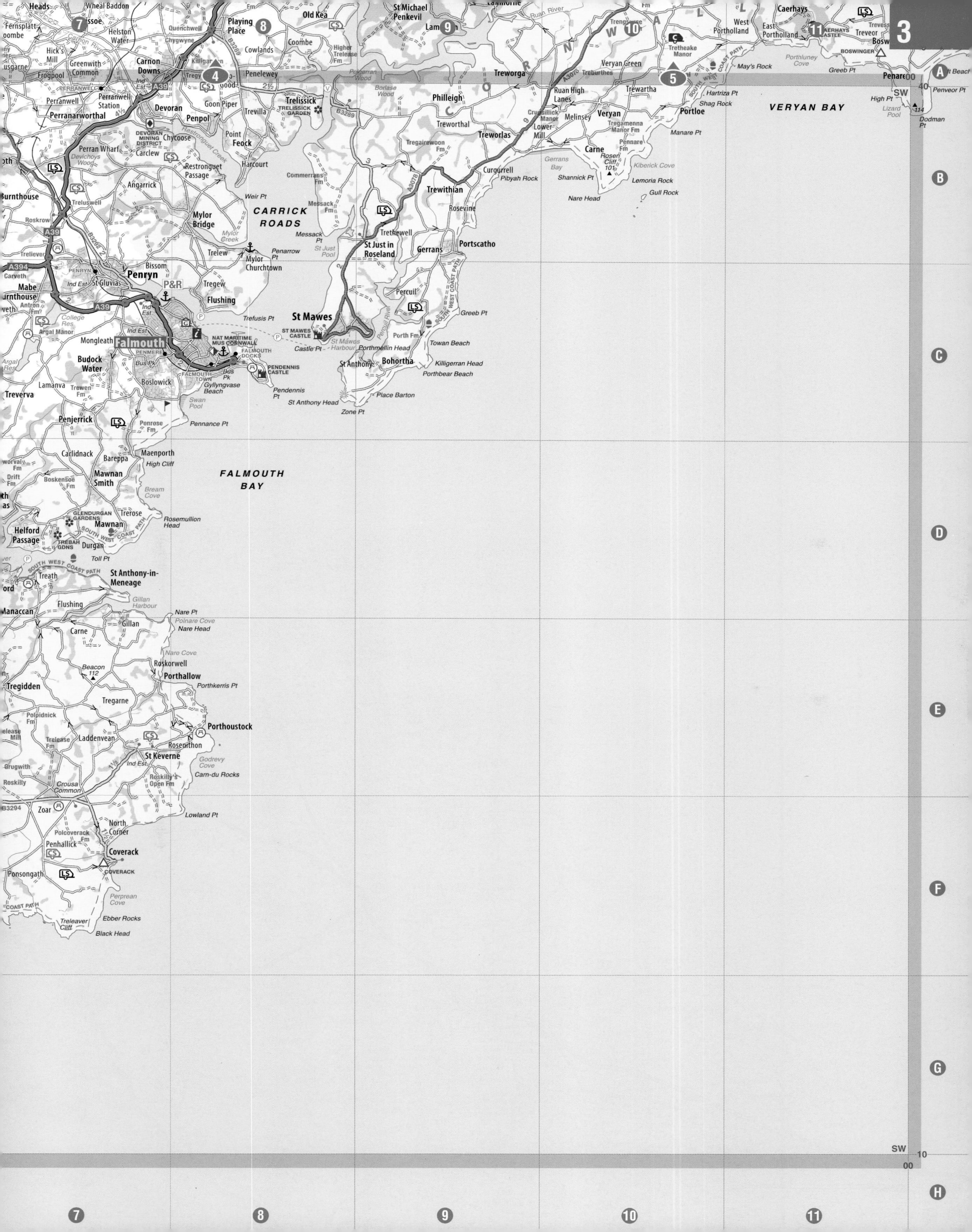
3
Playing Place
Old Kea
St Michael Penkevil
Caerhays
West Portholland
East Portholland
Treveor
Carnon Downs
Greenwith Common
Frogpool
Penelewey
Treworga
Veryan Green
Tretheake Manor
May's Rock
Greeb Pt
Perranwell
Perranwell Station
Devoran
Perranarworthal
Penpol
Goon Piper
Trevilla
Trelissick
TRELISSICK GARDEN
Phillegh
Ruan High Lanes
Trewartha
Portloe
VERYAN BAY
Dodman Pt
Melinsey
Veryan
Treworthal
Treworlas
Lower Mill
Carne
Point
Feock
Chycoose
Carclew
Perran Wharf
DEVORAN MINING DISTRICT
Restronguet Passage
Harcourt
Gerrans Bay
Pibyah Rock
Shannick Pt
Nare Head
Lemoria Rock
Gull Rock
Curgurrell
Trewithian
Rosevine
Angarrick
Burnthouse
CARRICK ROADS
Mylor Bridge
Weir Pt
Trethewell
St Just in Roseland
Gerrans
Portscatho
Trelew
Mylor Churchtown
Penarrow Pt
Penryn
Bissom
Mabe
Tregew
Flushing
St Gluvias
Trefusis Pt
St Mawes
Percuil
Greeb Pt
Falmouth
Mongleath
NAT MARITIME MUS CORNWALL
FALMOUTH DOCKS
PENDENNIS CASTLE
ST MAWES CASTLE
Castle Pt
Porthmellin Head
Porth Fm
Towan Beach
Budock Water
St Anthony
Bohortha
Killigerran Head
Porthbear Beach
Boslowick
Gyllyngvase Beach
Pendennis Pt
St Anthony Head
Place Barton
Zone Pt
Treverva
Lamanva
Penjerrick
Pennance Pt
Carlidnack
Bareppa
Maenporth
High Cliff
FALMOUTH BAY
Mawnan Smith
Trerose
Mawnan
GLENDURGAN GARDENS
Rosemullion Head
Helford Passage
TREBAH GDNS
Durgan
Toll Pt
SOUTH WEST COAST PATH
Treath
St Anthony-in-Meneage
Gillan Harbour
Flushing
Manaccan
Nare Pt
Nare Head
Carne
Gillan
Roskorwell
Porthallow
Porthkerris Pt
Tregidden
Tregarne
Porthoustock
Laddenvean
Rosenithon
St Keverne
Carn-du Rocks
Crousa Common
Zoar
Lowland Pt
North Corner
Penhallick
Coverack
Ponsongath
Ebber Rocks
Black Head
7
8
9
10
11
A
B
C
D
E
F
G
H

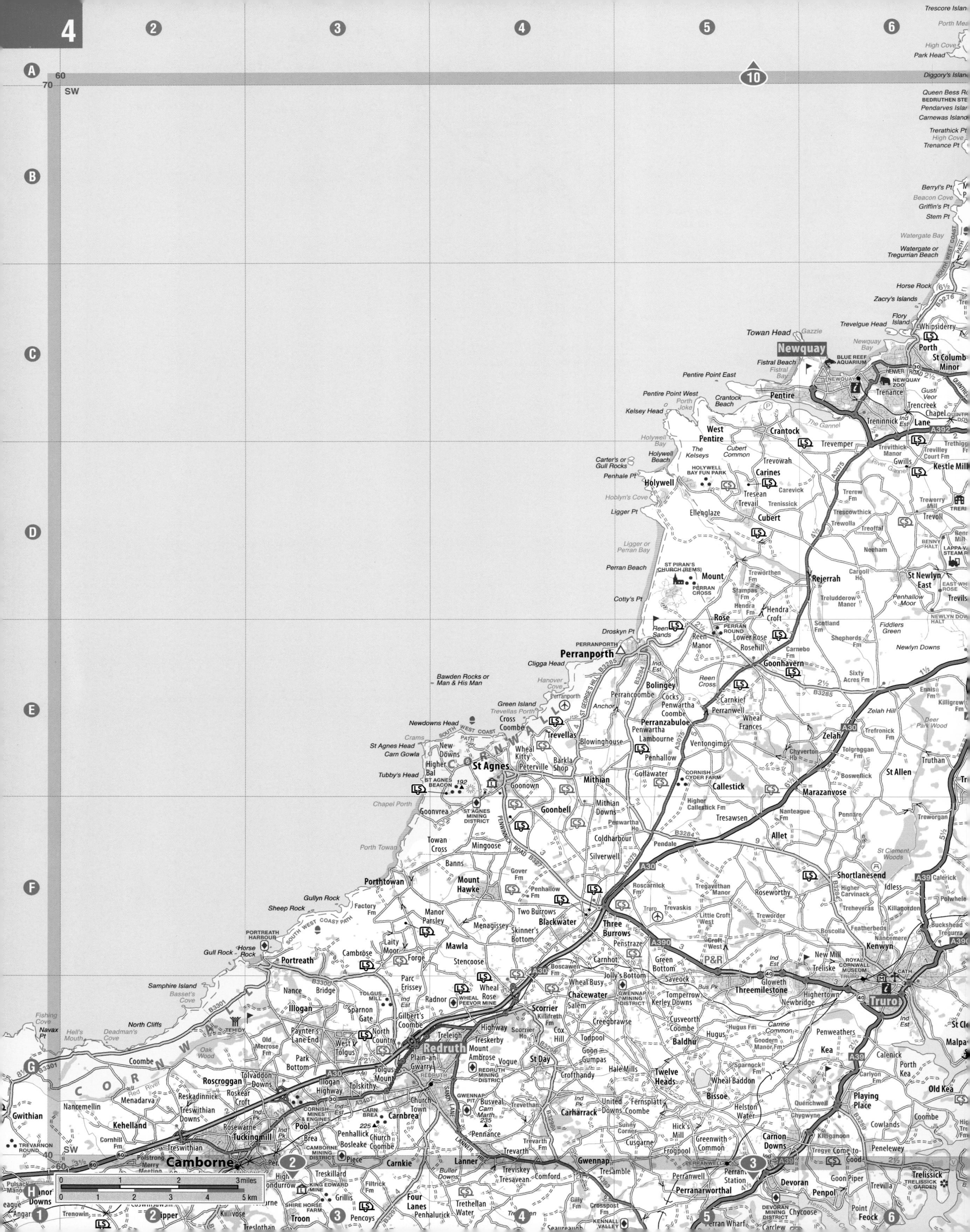

4
2
3
4
5
6
A
B
C
D
E
F
G
H
SW
10
Trescore Islands
Porth Mear
High Cove
Park Head
Diggory's Island
Queen Bess Rock
Bedruthen Steps
Pendarves Island
Carnewas Island
Trerathick Pt
High Cove
Trenance Pt
Berryl's Pt
Beacon Cove
Griffin's Pt
Stem Pt
Watergate Bay
Watergate or Tregurrian Beach
Horse Rock
Zacry's Islands
Flory Island
Trevelgue Head
Whipsiderry
Porth
St Columb Minor
Towan Head
Gazzle
Newquay
Newquay Bay
Blue Reef Aquarium
Fistral Beach
Fistral Bay
Newquay Zoo
Trenance
Pentire Point East
Pentire Point West
Porth Joke
Crantock Beach
Pentire
Kelsey Head
Gusti Veor
Trencreek
Chapel
Treninnick
Lane
The Gannel
Holywell Bay
West Pentire
Crantock
Trevemper
Holywell Beach
The Kelseys
Cubert Common
Trevowah
Carter's or Gull Rocks
Penhale Pt
Carines
Holywell
Holywell Bay Fun Park
Tresean
Carevick
Hoblyn's Cove
Trevail
Trenissick
Ligger Pt
Ellenglaze
Cubert
Trevithick Manor
Gwills
Trevilley Court Fm
Kestle Mill
Trerew Fm
Trescowthick
Trewolla
Treoffal
Trewerry Mill
Trevoll
Neeham
Ligger or Perran Bay
Perran Beach
St Piran's Church (rems)
Mount
Perran Cross
Treworthen
Rejerrah
Cargoll Ho
St Newlyn East
Stampas Fm
Hendra Fm
Hendra Croft
Treluddérow Manor
Penhallow Moor
Cotty's Pt
Rose
Perran Round
Reen Sands
Lower Rose
Rosehill
Scotland Fm
Shepherds Fm
Fiddlers Green
Droskyn Pt
Reen Manor
Carnebo Fm
Perranporth
Newlyn Downs
Cligga Head
Goonhavern
Bawden Rocks or Man & His Man
Hanover Cove
Bolingey
Reen Cross
Sixty Acres Fm
Perrancoombe
Anchor
Cocks
Penwartha Coombe
Carnkief
Perranwell
Green Island
Trevellas Porth
Cross Coombe
Perranzabuloe
Wheal Frances
Newdowns Head
Crams
Trevellas
Penwartha
Lambourne
Zelah
Zelah Hill
Trefronick Fm
St Agnes Head
Carn Gowla
New Downs
Wheal Kitty
Blowinghouse
Ventongimps
Chyverton Ho
Tolgroggan Fm
Truthan
Tubby's Head
Higher Bal
St Agnes
Barkla Shop
Peterville
Penhallow
Boswellick
St Allen
St Agnes Beacon
Goonown
Mithian
Gollawater
Cornish Cyder Farm
Callestick
Marazanvose
Chapel Porth
Goonvrea
St Agnes Mining District
Goonbell
Mithian Downs
Higher Callestick Fm
Tresawsen
Nanteague Fm
Pennare
Treworgan
Towan Cross
Penwartha Ho
Coldharbour
Allet
Porth Towan
Mingoose
Pendale
Silverwell
Banns
St Clement Woods
Porthtowan
Mount Hawke
Gover Fm
Penhallow Fm
Shortlanesend
Gullyn Rock
Sheep Rock
Factory Fm
Manor Parsley
Two Burrows
Blackwater
Roscarnick Fm
Tregavethan Manor
Roseworthy
Higher Carvinack
Idless
Calerick
Truro
Trevaskis
Little Croft West
Treworder
Treheveras
Killagorden
Polwhele
Menagissey
Skinner's Bottom
Three Burrows
Boscolla
Featherbeds
Buckshead
Tregurra
Portreath Harbour
Laity Moor
Mawla
Penstraze
Croft West
Nancemere
Kenwyn
Gull Rock
Horse Rock
Cambrose
Forge
Stencoose
Carnhot
P&R
New Mill
Treliske
Royal Cornwall Museum
Portreath
Parc Erissey
Boscawen Fm
Jolly's Bottom
Green Bottom
Saveock
Samphire Island
Basset's Cove
Nance
Bridge
Tolgus Mill
Wheal Rose
Wheal Busy
Chacewater
Gwennap Mining District
Tomperrow
Threemilestone
Gloweth
Highertown
Illogan
Sparnon Gate
Radnor
Wheal Peevor Mine
Scorrier
Killifreth Fm
Salem
Kerley Downs
Newbridge
Truro
Fishing Cove
Navax Pt
Hell's Mouth
Deadman's Cove
North Cliffs
Tehidy
Paynter's Lane End
Gilbert's Coombe
North Country
Highway
Scorrier Ho
Cox Hill
Creegbrawse
Cusveorth Coombe
Carrine Common
Penweathers
St Clement
Old Merrose Fm
West Tolgus
Redruth
Treleigh
Treskerby
Mount Ambrose
Todpool
Baldhu
Hugus Fm
Hugus
Goodern Manor Fm
Kea
Malpas
Oak Wood
Coombe
Park Bottom
Plain-an-Gwarry
Vogue
St Day
Goon Gumpas
Calenick
Porth Kea
Roscroggan
Tolvaddon Downs
Illogan Highway
Tolgus Mount
Redruth Mining District
Crofthandy
Hale Mills
Twelve Heads
Sparnock Fm
Wheal Baddon
Carlyon Fm
Old Kea
Menadarva
Reskadinnick
Roskear Croft
Tolskithy
Church Town
Gwennap Pit
Busveal
Carn Marth
Trevethan
Carharrack
United Downs
Fernsplatt Coombe
Bissoe
Quenchwell
Playing Place
Gwithian
Nancemellin
Treswithian Downs
Cornish Mines & Engines
Carn Brea
Carnbrea
Helston Water
Chygwyne
Coombe
Kehelland
Rosewarne
Tuckingmill
Pool
Pennance
Sunny Corner
Hick's Mill
Carnon Downs
Cowlands
Trevarnon Round
Cornhill Fm
Treswithian
Brea
Penhallick
Bosleake
Church Coombe
Trevarth Fm
Cusgarne
Greenwith Common
Killiganoon
Camborne
Polstrong
Camborne Mining District
Piece
Carnkie
Lanner
Trevarth
Gwennap
Frogpool
Tregye
Come-to-Good
Penelewey
Merry Meeting
Treskillard
Buller Downs
Treviskey
Comford
Tresamble
Perranwell
Perranwell Station
Devoran
Goon Piper
Trelissick
Trelissick Garden
Pulsack Manor
Manor Downs
High
Condurrow
King Edward Mine
Filtrick Fm
Tresavean
Gilly Fm
Perranarworthal
Penpol
Trevilla
Grillis
Shire Horse Farm
Four Lanes
Trethellan Water
Crosspost Fm
Kennall Vale
Devoran Mining District
Chycoose
Point
Feock
Angarrack
Trenowin
Killivose
Troon
Pencoys
Penhalurick
Perran Wharf
Carclew
Restronguet
Treslothan
Seaureaugh
South West Coast Path
Cornwall
0 1 2 3 miles
0 1 2 3 4 5 km

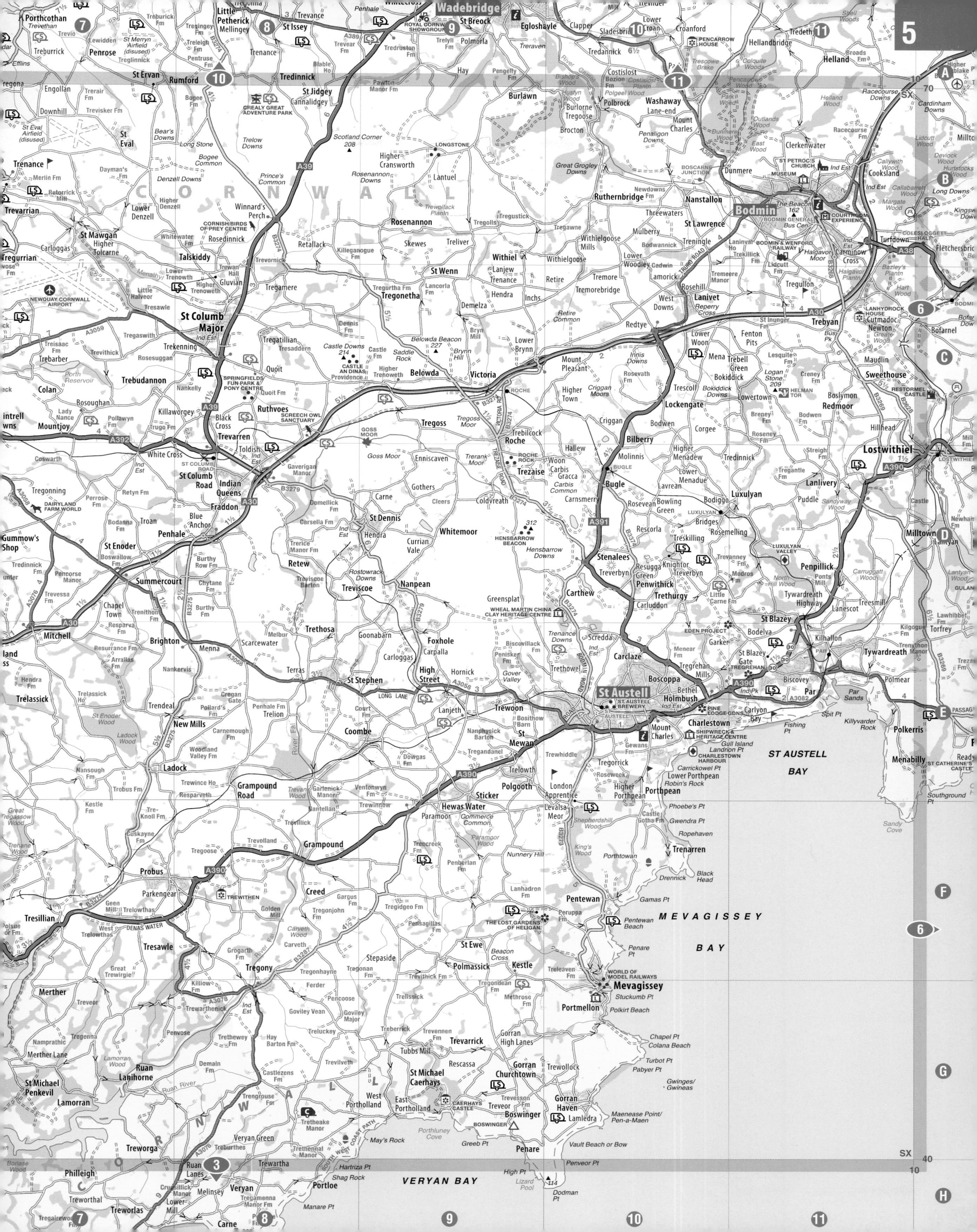

5
Wadebridge
Porthcothan
Trevethan
Little Petherick
Mellingey
St Issey
Trevance
Penhale
ROYAL CORNWALL SHOWGROUND
St Breock
Egloshayle
Clapper
Sladesbridge
Lower Croan
Croanford
Tredethy
Pencarrow House
Hellandbridge
Helland
Treburrick
Penrose
St Mawgan
Trenance
Tredinnick
Polmorla
Trevio
Lewidden
St Merryn Airfield (disused)
Treleigh Fm
Treglinnick
Trevear Fm
Tredruston Fm
Trelyll Fm
Treraven
Tredannick
Costislost
Bozion Fm
Polgeel Wood
Trescowe Brake
Colquite Woods
Broads Fm
St Ervan
Rumford
Engollan
Trerair Fm
Trevisker Fm
Bogee Fm
CREALY GREAT ADVENTURE PARK
St Jidgey
Cannalidgey
Pawton Manor Fm
Burlawn
Pengelly Fm
Hay
Hustyn Wood
Burlorne Tregoose
Polbrock
Washaway
Lane-end
Mount Charles
Penaligon Downs
Brocton
Dunmere Wood
Helland Wood
Racecourse Downs
Cardinham Downs
Downhill
St Eval Airfield (disused)
St Eval
Bear's Downs
Long Stone
Trelow Downs
Bogee Common
Scotland Corner 208
LONGSTONE
Higher Cransworth
Lantuel
Rosenannon Downs
Great Grogley Downs
Outlands Wood
Clerkenwater
Racecourse Fm
Lidcutt Wood
Milltown
Trenance
Merlin Fm
Dayman's Fm
Denzell Downs
Prince's Common
CORNWALL
Winnard's Perch
CORNISH BIRDS OF PREY CENTRE
Rosedinnick
Higher Denzell
Lower Denzell
Trevarrian
Tregurrian
Carloggas
Higher Tolcarne
Whitewater Fm
Talskiddy
Rosenannon
Trewollack Plantn
Tregolls
Tregustick
Tregawne
Withielgoose Mills
Rutherbridge
Newdowns Fm
Threewaters
Mulberry
Nanstallon
St Lawrence
Treningle
Bodwannick
Dunmere
BOSCARNE JUNCTION
ST PETROC'S CHURCH
MUSEUM
Bodmin
The Beacon 162
BODMIN GENERAL Bus Cen
COURTROOM EXPERIENCE
Cooksland
Callybith Wood
Long Downs
Margate Wood
Devlock Wood
Hurtstocks Wood
Trewan Hall
Gluvian
Lower Trenowth
Higher Trenowth
Little Halveor
NEWQUAY CORNWALL AIRPORT
Trevornick
Retallack
Killaganogue Fm
Skewes
Treliver
St Wenn
Withiel
Lanjew
Trenance
Withielgoose
Retire
Tremore
Lower Woodley
Cadwin
Lamorick
Laninval Ho
Trekillick Fm
BODMIN & WENFORD RAILWAY
Lidcutt Fm
Halgavor Moor
Carminow Cross
Turfdown
COLESLOGGETT HALT
Fletchersbridge
Bazley's Plantn
Tregamere
Tregurtha Fm
Tregonetha
Lancorla Fm
Demelza
Hendra
Inchs
Tremorebridge
Rosehill
Lanivet
Tremeere Manor
Tregullon
Hart Wood
Tresawle
St Columb Major
Ind Est
A3059
Tregaswith
Trekenning
Tregatillian
Tresaddern
Dennis Fm
Castle Downs 214
Castle Fm
Saddle Rock
Belowda Beacon 227
Bryn Mill
Brynn Hill
Retire Common
Redtye
West Downs
Reperry Cross
St Ingunger
Trebyan
LANHYDROCK HOUSE
Cutmadoc
Newton
Bofarnel
Treisaac Fm
Trebarber
Trevithick
Rosesuggan
Quoit
CASTLE AN DINAS
Providence
Higher Trenowth
Belowda
Victoria
Lower Bryn
Mount Pleasant
Innis Downs
Rosevath Fm
Trebell Green
Bokiddick
Fenton Pits
Lesquite Fm
Logan Stone 209
HELMAN TOR
Maudlin
Sweethouse
RESTORMEL CASTLE
Colan
Porth Reservoir
Trebudannon
Nankelly
SPRINGFIELDS FUN PARK & PONY CENTRE
Quoit Fm
Ruthvoes
SCREECH OWL SANCTUARY
ROCHE
Higher Town
Criggan Moors
Trescoll
Bokiddick Downs
Lowertown
Boslymon
Redmoor
Bosoughan
Lady Nance
Mountjoy
Pollawyn Fm
Killaworgey
Trugo Fm
Black Cross
Trevarren
GOSS MOOR
Tregoss
Tregoss Moor
Trebilcock
Roche
Criggan
Lockengate
Bodwen
Corgee
Bodwen Fm
Roseney Fm
Hillhead
Lostwithiel
A392
White Cross
Toldish
Coswarth
ST COLUMB ROAD
St Columb Road
Indian Queens
Gaverigan Manor
Goss Moor
Enniscaven
Trerank Moor
ROCHE ROCK
Hallew
Woon
Carbis
Gracca
Carbis Common
Trezaise
Bilberry
Molinnis
BUGLE
Higher Menadew
Lower Menadue
Tredinnick
Tregantle Fm
Streigh Fm
Lanlivery
Sandyway Wood
Tregonning
DAIRYLAND FARM WORLD
Perrose Fm
Retyn Fm
Fraddon
Bodanna Fm
Troan
Blue Anchor
Penhale
B3279
Domellick Fm
Carsella Fm
Carne
Gothers
Cleers
Coldvreath
Carnsmerry
Bugle
Lavrean
Rosevean
Bowling Green
Bodiggo
LUXULYAN
Luxulyan
Puddle
Castle
Gummow's Shop
St Enoder
Boswallow Fm
St Dennis
Hendra
Trerice Manor Fm
Currian Vale
Whitemoor
312
HENSBARROW BEACON
Hensbarrow Downs
Stenalees
Treverbyn
Rescorla
Bridges
Rosemelling
Treskilling
Milltown
Lantyan
Tredinnick Fm
Pencorse Manor
Summercourt
Burthy Row Fm
Chytane Fm
Retew
Rostowrack Downs
Treviscoe Barton
Treviscoe
Nanpean
Resugga Green
Penwithick
Knightor
Trevarney Fm
LUXULYAN VALLEY
Penpillick
Carruggatt Wood
Trevessa Fm
Chapel Town
Trenithon Fm
Burthy Fm
Greensplat
WHEAL MARTIN CHINA CLAY HERITAGE CENTRE
Carthew
Carluddon
Trethurgy
Little Carne Fm
North Hill Wood
Tywardreath Highway
Treesmill
Lanescot
Lawhibbet Fm
A30
Mitchell
Resparva Fm
Brighton
Melbur
Trethosa
Goonabarn
Foxhole
Carpalla
EDEN PROJECT
Garker
Bodelva
St Blazey
Kilhallon
Torfrey
Resurrance Fm
Arrallas Fm
Menna
Scarcewater
Carloggas
Trenance Downs
Screddha
Carclaze
Menear Fm
St Blazey Gate
TREGREHAN
Tywardreath
Trenython Manor
Nankervis
Terras
High Street
Hornick
Gover Valley
Trethowel
Boscoppa
Tregrehan Mills
Biscovey
Polmear
Trelassick
St Stephen
LONG LANE
A3058
St Austell
ST AUSTELL BREWERY
Bethel
Holmbush
PINE LODGE GDNS
Par
Par Sands
Carlyon Bay
Trendeal
Gregan Gate
Pollard's Fm
Penhale Fm
Trelion
Court Fm
Lanjeth
Trewoon
Bosithow Barn
Charlestown
Spit Pt
Killyvarder Rock
Polkerris
St Enoder Wood
New Mills
Carnemough Fm
Coombe
Nanphysick Barton
St Mewan
Gewans Fm
Mount Charles
SHIPWRECK & HERITAGE CENTRE
CHARLESTOWN HARBOUR
Fishing Pt
Gull Island
Landrion Pt
ST AUSTELL BAY
Menabilly
ST CATHERINE'S CASTLE
Ladock Wood
Woodland Valley Fm
Dowgas Fm
Tregandaei
Trewhiddle
Tregorrick
Roseweek
Carrickowel Pt
Lower Porthpean
Robin's Rock
Nansough Fm
Ladock
Trewince Ho
Grampound Road
Resparveth
Trewoon Wood
Garlenick Manor
Ventonwyn Fm
Trelowth
Polgooth
London Apprentice
Higher Porthpean
Porthpean
Southground Pt
Sandy Cove
Kestle Fm
Trobus Fm
Great Tregassow Wood
Tre-Knoll Fm
Nantellan
Trewinnow
Trevillick
A390
Sticker
Hewas Water
Paramoor
Commerce Common
Levalsa Meor
Shepherdshill Wood
Phoebe's Pt
Castle Gotha Fm
Gwendra Pt
Ropehaven
Trehane Wood
Cuskayne Fm
Trevolland
Grampound
Tregoose
Trencreek Fm
Paramoor Wood
Nunnery Hill
King's Wood
Porthtowan
Trenarren
Probus
Parkengear
TREWITHEN
Creed
Gargus Fm
Penberian Fm
Lanhadron Fm
Drennick
Black Head
Pentewan
Gamas Pt
Tresillian
Green Mill
Trelowthas
West Trelowthas
DENAS WATER
Golden Mill
Tregonjohn Fm
Tregidgeo Fm
Pensagillas Fm
THE LOST GARDENS OF HELIGAN
Peruppa Fm
Pentewan Beach
MEVAGISSEY
Tresawle
Carveth Wood
Carveth
Grogarth Fm
Stepaside
St Ewe
Beacon Cross
Kestle
Penare Pt
BAY
Great Trewirgie
Tregony
Tregonhayne
Tregonan Fm
Trevithick Fm
Polmassick
Treleaven Fm
WORLD OF MODEL RAILWAYS
Mevagissey
Stuckumb Pt
Merther
Treveor
Killiow Fm
Ferder
Pencoose
Tregondean Fm
Trelissick
Methrose Fm
Portmellon
Polkirt Beach
Trewarthenick
Ind Est
Goviley Vean
Goviley Major
Namprathic
Tregenna
Penvose
Trethewey Fm
Treluckey
Treberrick
Trevennen Fm
Trevarrick
Gorran High Lanes
Chapel Pt
Colana Beach
Merther Lane
Lamorran Wood
Ruan Lanihorne
Demain Fm
Hay Barton Fm
Trevilveth
Tubbs Mill
Rescassa
Gorran Churchtown
Trewollock
Turbot Pt
Pabyer Pt
St Michael Penkevil
Ruan River
Castlezens Fm
St Michael Caerhays
Gwinges/ Gwineas
Lamorran
Trengrouse Fm
West Portholland
East Portholland
CAERHAYS CASTLE
Trevesson Fm
Treveor
Boswinger
Gorran Haven
Lamledra
Maenease Point/ Pen-a-Maen
Tretheake Manor
BOSWINGER
Porthluney Cove
Veryan Green
Treburthes
May's Rock
Greeb Pt
Penare
Vault Beach or Bow
Treworga
Trethennal Manor
SOUTH WEST COAST PATH
Penveor Pt
Borlase Wood
Ruan Lanes
Trewartha
Hartriza Pt
High Pt
Lizard Pool
114
SX
40
Philleigh
Crugsillick Manor
Lower Mill
Melinsey
Veryan
Tregamenna Manor
Carne
Shag Rock
Portloe
VERYAN BAY
Dodman Pt
Manare Pt
Treworthal
Treworlas
Tregairewoon
7
8
9
10
11
A
B
C
D
E
F
G
H
6

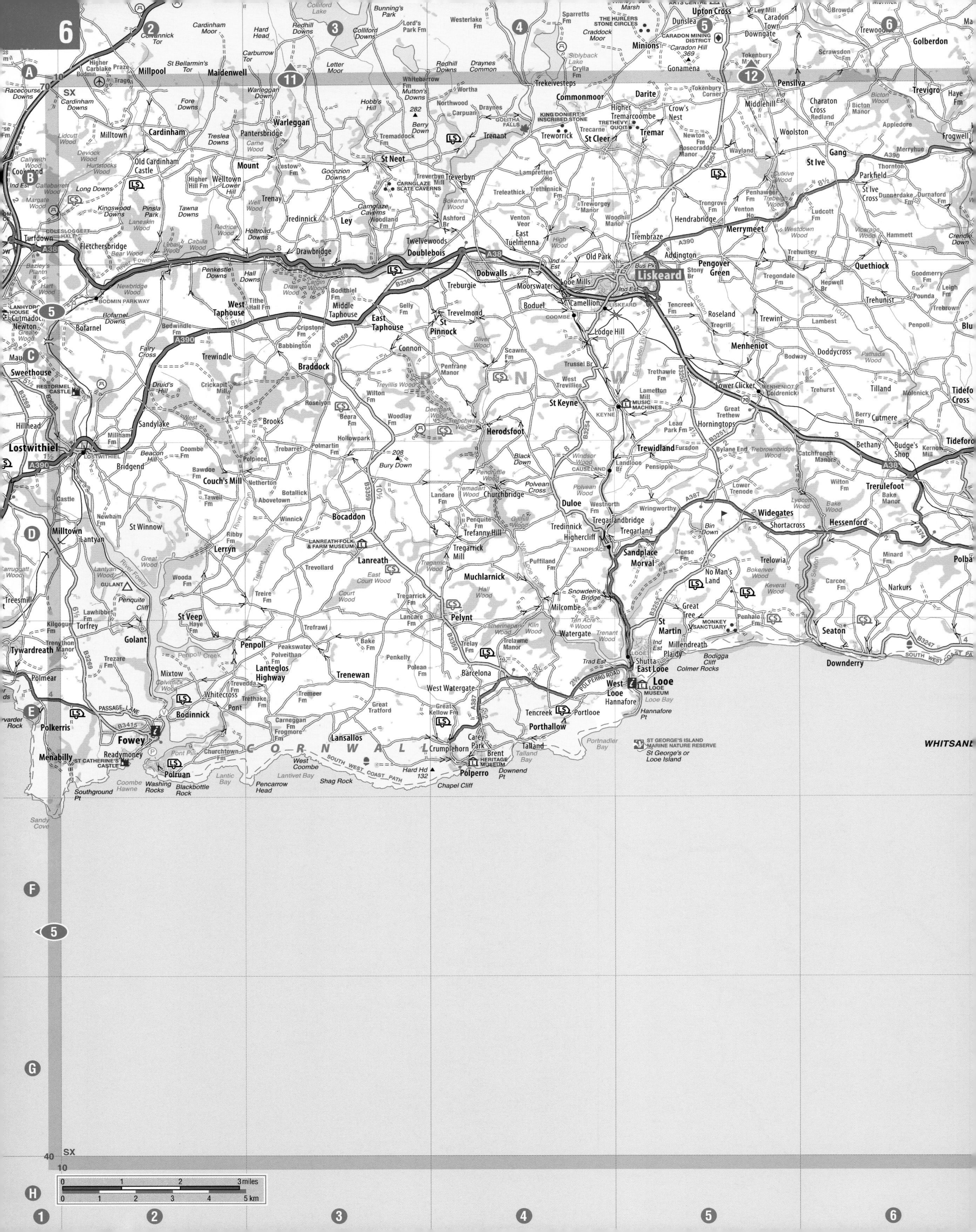

Cardinham Moor
Hard Head
Redhill Downs
Colliford Downs
Bunning's Park
Lord's Park Fm
Westerlake Fm
Sparretts Fm
THE HURLERS STONE CIRCLES
Craddock Moor
Minions
Upton Cross
Dunslea
CARADON MINING DISTRICT
Caradon Hill 369
Gonamena
Caradon Town
Downgate
Tokenbury Manor
Trewoodloe
Golberdon
Higher Carblake
Praze
Millpool
St Bellarmin's Tor
Maidenwell
Carburrow Tor
Letter Moor
Whitebarrow
Redhill Downs
Draynes Common
Siblyback Lake
Crylla Fm
Trekeivesteps
Commonmoor
Darite
Tokenbury Corner
Pensilva
Middlehill
Charaton Cross
Bicton Manor
Trevigro
Haye Fm
Racecourse Downs
SX
Cardinham Downs
Fore Downs
Warleggan Down
Hobb's Hill
Mutton's Downs
Wortha
Northwood
Carpuan
Draynes
GOLITHA FALLS
KING DONIERT'S INSCRIBED STONE
Higher Tremarcoombe
Crow's Nest
TRETHEVY QUOIT
Tremar
Redland Fm
Appledore
Milltown
Cardinham
Treslea Downs
Pantersbridge
Warleggan
282
Berry Down
Tremaddock
Trenant
Treworrick
Trecarne
St Cleer
Newton Fm
Rosecraddoc Manor
Wayland
Woolston
Frogwell
Lidcutt Wood
Deviock Wood
Hurtstocks Wood
Old Cardinham Castle
Carne Wood
Mount
Lestow Fm
St Neot
Goonzion Downs
Treverbyn Mill
Treverbyn
CARNGLAZE SLATE CAVERNS
Lampretten Ho
Gang
St Ive
Merryhue
A390
Thornton
Parkfield
Callywith Wood
Cooksland
Ind Est
Callabarrett Wood
Long Downs
Higher Hill Fm
Welltown
Lower Hill
Trethinnick Fm
Treleathick
St Ive Cross
Dunnerdake
Durnaford Fm
Penhawger Fm
Trebeigh Wood
Cutkive Wood
Margate Wood
Kingswood Downs
Pinsla Park
Tawna Downs
Trenay
Carnglaze Caverns
Woodland Fm
Bokenna Wood
Ashford Fm
Treworgey Manor
Trengrove Fm
Venton Ho
Ludcott Fm
Well Wood
Laneskin Wood
Tredinnick
Ley
Venton Veor
Woodhill Manor
Hendrabridge
Merrymeet
Turfdown
COLESLOGGETT HALT
Redrice Wood
Holtroad Downs
Twelvewoods
East Tuelmenna
High Wood
Trembraze
Westdown Wood
Vicarage Wood
Hammett
Crendle Down
Fletchersbridge
Bear Wood
Lebail Wood
Cabilla Wood
Drawbridge
Doublebois
A38
Old Park
Addington
Trehunsey Br
Quethiock
Bazley's Plantn
River Fowey
Penkestle Downs
Hall Downs
Dobwalls
Moorswater
Ind Est
Looe Mills
Bus Pk
Liskeard
Stony Br
Pengover Green
Tregondale Fm
Goodmerry Fm
Hart Wood
Newbridge Wood
BODMIN PARKWAY
Draw Wood
Largin Wood
Bodithiel Fm
B3360
Treburgie
Camellion
Ind Est
Hepwell Br
Leigh Fm
Pounda
Trehunist
Trebrown
LANHYDROCK HOUSE
Cutmadoc
West Taphouse
Tithe Hall Fm
Middle Taphouse
Gelly Fm
Boduel
COOMBE
LISKEARD
Tencreek Fm
Roseland
River Tiddy
Newton
Bofarnel Downs
Bofarnel
Great Wood
Bedwindle Fm
A390
Cripstone Fm
East Taphouse
Trevelmond
St Pinnock
Lodge Hill
Tregrill
Trewint
Lambest
Penpoll
Babbington
Connon
Scawns Fm
Menheniot
Doddycross
Pathada Wood
Fairy Cross
Trewindle
Braddock
Cliver Wood
Trussel Br
Bodway
Sweethouse
RESTORMEL CASTLE
Druid's Hill
Crickapit Mill
Trevillis Wood
Penfrane Manor
CORNWALL
West Trevillies
Trethawle Fm
Lower Clicker
MENHENIOT
Coldrenick
Trehurst
Tilland
Molenick
Tideford Cross
Roselyon
Wilton Fm
Lametton Mill
MUSIC MACHINES
St Keyne
Great Trethew
Berry Fm
Cutmere
Hillhead
Sandylake
West Drive
Brooks
Beara Fm
Woodlay Fm
Deerpark Wood
Trebchway Wood
Herodsfoot
B3254
Lean Park Fm
Horningtops
Lostwithiel
Millham
LOSTWITHIEL
Beacon Hill
Coombe Fm
Trebarret
Polmartin Fm
Hollowpark
208
Bury Down
Windsor Wood
Trewidland
Fursdon
Bylane End
Trebrownbridge Wood
Catchfrench Manor
Bethany
Budge's Shop
Kernow Mill
Tideford
Bridgend
Polpiece
Black Down
CAUSELAND
Landlooe Br
Pensipple
Bawdoe Fm
Couch's Mill
Netherton
Pendruffle Wood
Polvean Cross
Lower Trenode
Wilton Fm
Trerulefoot
Bake Manor
Castle
Tawell Fm
Abovetown
Botallick
Landare Fm
Tremadart Wood
Churchbridge
Polvean Wood
Duloe
Westnorth Fm
Wringworthy
A387
Lydcott Wood
Bake Wood
Newham Fm
St Winnow
Winnick
Bocaddon
Penquite Fm
Trefanny Hill
Gillhill Wood
Tredinnick
Highercliff
Tregartandbridge
Tregarland
Widegates
Shortacross
Bin Down
Hessenford
Milltown
Lantyan
Ribby Fm
Lerryn
LANREATH FOLK & FARM MUSEUM
Tregarrick Mill
SANDPLACE
Sandplace
Morval
Cleese Fm
Minard Fm
Polbathic
Great Wood
Lanreath
Trevollard
Tregarrick Wood
Puffiland Fm
No Man's Land
Trelowia
Bokenver Wood
Keveral Wood
Carcoe Fm
Narkurs
Lantyan Wood
River Fowey
Wooda Fm
East Court Wood
Muchlarnick
Hall Wood
Snowden's Bridge
GULANT
Penquite Cliff
Treire Fm
Court Wood
Tregarrick Fm
Milcombe
B3253
Great Tree
Treesmill
Lawhibbet Fm
Torfrey
St Veep
Haye Fm
Lancare Fm
Pelynt
Ten Acre Wood
Kiln Wood
MONKEY SANCTUARY
Penhale Fm
Seaton
Kilgogue Fm
Trenython Manor
Golant
Penpoll
Trefrawl
Bake Fm
Catherinepark Wood
Watergate
Trenant Wood
St Martin
Ind Est
Millendreath
Tywardreath
Penpoll Creek
Peakswater
Polveithan Fm
Trelay Fm
Trelawne Manor
LOOE
Plaidy
Bodigga Cliff
Colmer Rocks
Downderry
B3247
SOUTH WEST COAST PATH
Trezare Fm
Lanteglos Highway
Penkelly
Polean Fm
Barcelona
Trad Est
Shutta
East Looe
Polmear
Mixtow
Colvithick Wood
Trevedda Fm
Trenewan
West Watergate
POLPERRO ROAD
West Looe
Looe
Hannafore
LOOE MUSEUM
Looe Bay
Hannafore Pt
E
PASSAGE LANE
Whitecross
Bodinnick
Pont
Trethake Fm
Tremeer Fm
Great Tratford
Great Kellow Fm
A387
Tencreek
Portlooe
Porthallow
Gribbin Head
Polkerris
B3415
Fowey
Carneggan Fm
Frogmore Fm
Lansallos
Crumplehorn
Carey Park
Brent
Talland
Portnadler Bay
ST GEORGE'S ISLAND MARINE NATURE RESERVE
St George's or Looe Island
WHITSAND
Menabilly
Readymoney
ST CATHERINE'S CASTLE
Pont Pill
Churchtown Fm
Polruan
West Coombe
Lantivet Bay
SOUTH WEST COAST PATH
Hard Hd 132
HERITAGE MUSEUM
Polperro
Talland Bay
Downend Pt
Chapel Cliff
Southground Pt
Coombe Hawne
Washing Rocks
Blackbottle Rock
Lantic Bay
Pencarrow Head
Shag Rock
Sandy Cove
SX
0 1 2 3 miles
0 1 2 3 4 5 km

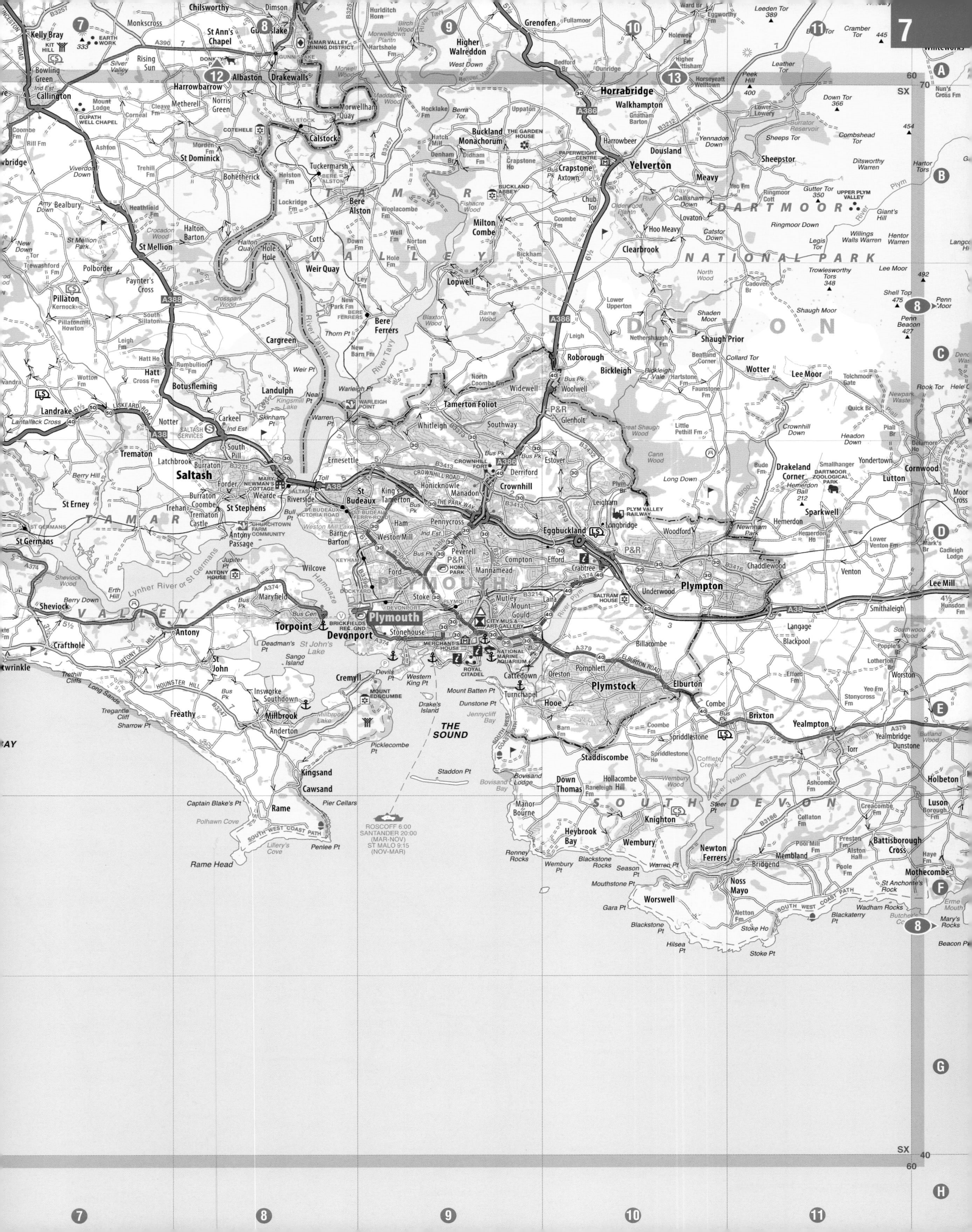
Chilsworthy
Dimson
Hurlditch Horn
Grenofen
Fullamoor
Ward Br
Eggworthy Fm
Leeden Tor 389
Kelly Bray
Kit Hill
333
Earth Work
Monkscross
St Ann's Chapel
Gunnislake
Tamar Valley Mining District
Morwelldown Plantn
Hartshole Fm
Higher Walreddon
West Down
Holewell Fm
Higher Pittisham
Cramber Tor
445
Whiteworks
Leather Tor
Bowling Green
Silver Valley
Rising Sun
Albaston
Drakewalls
Bedford Br
Dunridge
Horseyeatt
Welltown
Peek Hill 400
Harrowbarrow
Horrabridge
Walkhampton
Nun's Cross Fm
Callington
Mount Lodge
Cleave Fm
Metherell
Norris Green
Morwellham Quay
Maddacleave Wood
Hocklake Fm
Berra Tor
Uppaton
Gnatham Barton
Lower Lowery
Down Tor 366
Dupath Well Chapel
Corneal
Calstock
Cotehele
Buckland Monachorum
The Garden House
Burrator Reservoir
Combshead Tor
454
Coombe Fm
Rill Fm
Ashton
Morden Fm
St Dominick
Tuckermarsh
Hatch Mill
Denham Br
Didham Fm
Crapstone Ho
Harrowbeer
Yennadon Down
Sheeps Tor
Dousland
Paperweight Centre
Crapstone
Axtown
Yelverton
Sheepstor
Ditsworthy Warren
Harford Tors
Viverdon Down
Trehill Fm
Bohetherick
Helston Fm
Bere Alston
Buckland Abbey
Meavy
Neo Fm
Ringmoor Cott
Gutter Tor 350
Upper Plym Valley
Giant's Hill
Amy Down
Bealbury
Heathfield Fm
Lockridge Fm
Tamar
Bere Alston
Woolacombe Fm
Fishacre Wood
Chub Tor
Callisham Down
Dartmoor
Lovaton
Ringmoor Down
Crocadon Wood
Halton Barton
Milton Combe
Coombe Fm
Oldenwood Plantn
Hoo Meavy
Catstor Down
Willings Walls Warren
Hentor Warren
St Mellion Park
New Down
St Mellion
Halton Quay
Hole's Hole
Cotts
Well Fm
Down Fm
Norton Fm
Valley
Legis Tor
Trewashford Fm
Polborder
Weir Quay
Hole Fm
Bickham
Clearbrook
National Park
Lee Moor
Paynter's Cross
Ley Fm
Lopwell
North Wood
Trowlesworthy Tors 348
492
Pillaton
Kernock
A388
Crosspark Wood
New Park Fm
Bere Ferrers
Blaxton Wood
Bame Wood
Lower Upperton
Cadover Br
Shell Top 475
Penn Moor
Pillatonmill
Howton
South Sillaton
Thorn Pt
Bere Ferrers
A386
Shaden Moor
Shaugh Moor
Penn Beacon 427
Leigh Fm
Cargreen
River Tamar
New Barn Fm
River Tavy
Leigh
Devon
Nethershaugh Fm
Shaugh Prior
Hatt Ho
Rumbleford Fm
Roborough
Bickleigh
Beatland Corner
Collard Tor
Hatt
Cross Fm
Weir Pt
Bickleigh Vale
Hartstone Fm
Wotter
Lee Moor
Tolchmoor Gate
Wotton Fm
Botusfleming
Landulph
Kingsmill Lake
North Coombe Fm
Widewell
Woolwell
Faunstone Fm
Rook Tor
Neal Pt
Warleigh Pt
Warleigh Point
Tamerton Foliot
Newpark Waste
Quick Br
Landrake
Liskeard Road
Carkeel
Skinham Pt
P&R
Glenholt
Lantallack Cross
Notter
Saltash Services
Ind Est
Warren Pt
Whitleigh
Southway
Great Shaugh Wood
Little Pethill Fm
Crownhill Down
Headon Down
Plall Br
Delamore Ho
A38
Trematon
South Pill
Ernesettle
B3373
Estover
B3432
Cann Wood
Yondertown
Latchbrook
Burraton
Bus Pk
Crownhill Fort
A386
Derriford
Bude Fm
Drakeland Corner
Smallhanger
Dartmoor Zoological Park
Cornwood
Berry Hill
Saltash
B3271
Mary Newman's Cottage
Toll
A38
Crownhill Road
B3413
Long Down
Lutton
Forder
Saltash
Riverside
St Budeaux
King's Tamerton
Honicknowle
Manadon
Crownhill
Plym Br
Hemerdon Ball 212
Moor Cross
Burraton Coombe
Wearde
The Parkway
Leigham
Plym Valley Railway
Sparkwell
St Erney
Trehan
St Stephens
Bull Pt
Ham
Pennycross
B3413
Longbridge
Woodford
Hemerdon
Tamar
Trematon Castle
Churchtown Farm Community
St Budeaux Victoria Road
St Budeaux Ferry Road
Weston Mill Lake
Weston Mill
Ind Est
Eggbuckland
Newnham Park
Hemerdon Ho
St Germans
Antony Passage
Barne Barton
Peverell
P&R
Home Park
Compton
Efford
P&R
Lower Venton Fm
Mark's Br
Cadleigh Lodge
Jupiter Pt
Keyham
Ford
Mannamead
Crabtree
Chaddlewood
Venton
A374
Sheviock Wood
Antony House
Wilcove
Hamoaze
Plymouth
Lee Mill
Erth Hill
Lynher River or St Germans
Maryfield
Dockyard
Stoke
Mutley
Laira
Saltram House
Underwood
Plympton
Berry Down
Sheviock
Valley
Bus Cen
Devonport
Plymouth
Mount Gould
River Plym
A38
Smithaleigh
Hunsdon Fm
Torpoint
Brickfields Rec Gnd
Devonport
Stonehouse
City Mus & Art Gallery
Langage
Antony
Crafthole
Deadman's Pt
St John's Lake
A374
Merchant's House
National Marine Aquarium
Billacombe
Blackpool
Southwood Wood
Popple's Br
Sango Island
St John
Royal Citadel
A379
Elburton Road
Lotherton Br
Portwrinkle
Trethill Cliffs
Long Sands
Hounster Hill
Cremyll
Devils Pt
Western King Pt
Cattedown
Oreston
Pomphlett
Plymstock
Elburton
Efford Fm
Worston
Inswork
Southdown
Mount Edgcumbe
Mount Batten Pt
Drake's Island
Dunstone Pt
Turnchapel
Hooe
Combe
Yeo Fm
Stonycross Fm
Tregantle Cliff
Sharrow Pt
Freathy
B3247
Millbrook
Millbrook Lake
Jennycliff Bay
The Sound
Brixton
Yealmpton
A379
Yealmbridge
Dunstone
Bulland Wood
Whitsand Bay
Anderton
Barn Fm
Coombe Fm
Spriddlestone
Picklecombe Pt
South West Coast Path
Staddiscombe
Spriddlestone Ho
Coffleet Creek
Torr
Kingsand
Staddon Pt
Bovisand Lodge
Bovisand Bay
Down Thomas
Hollacombe Hill
Raneleigh Fm
Wembury Wood
River Yealm
Ashcombe Fm
Holbeton
Cawsand
Captain Blake's Pt
Pier Cellars
Rame
Manor Bourne
South Devon
Steer Pt
Creacombe Fm
Luson
Borough Fm
Polhawn Cove
Roscoff 6:00
Santander 20:00 (Mar-Nov)
St Malo 9:15 (Nov-Mar)
Knighton
Collaton Fm
B3186
Heybrook Bay
Wembury
Newton Ferrers
Pool Mill Fm
Preston Fm
Alston Hall
Battisborough Cross
Lillery's Cove
Penlee Pt
Rame Head
Renney Rocks
Wembury Pt
Blackstone Rocks
Season Pt
Warren Pt
Membland
Bridgend
Poole Fm
Haye Fm
Mothecombe
Mouthstone Pt
Noss Mayo
St Anchorite's Rock
Erme Mouth
Worswell
Gara Pt
Netton Fm
South West Coast Path
Blackaterry Pt
Wadham Rocks
Butcher's Cove
Mary's Rocks
Blackstone Pt
Stoke Ho
Hilsea Pt
Stoke Pt
Beacon Pt
SX
60
70
40
A
B
C
D
E
F
G
H
7
8
9
10
11
12
13

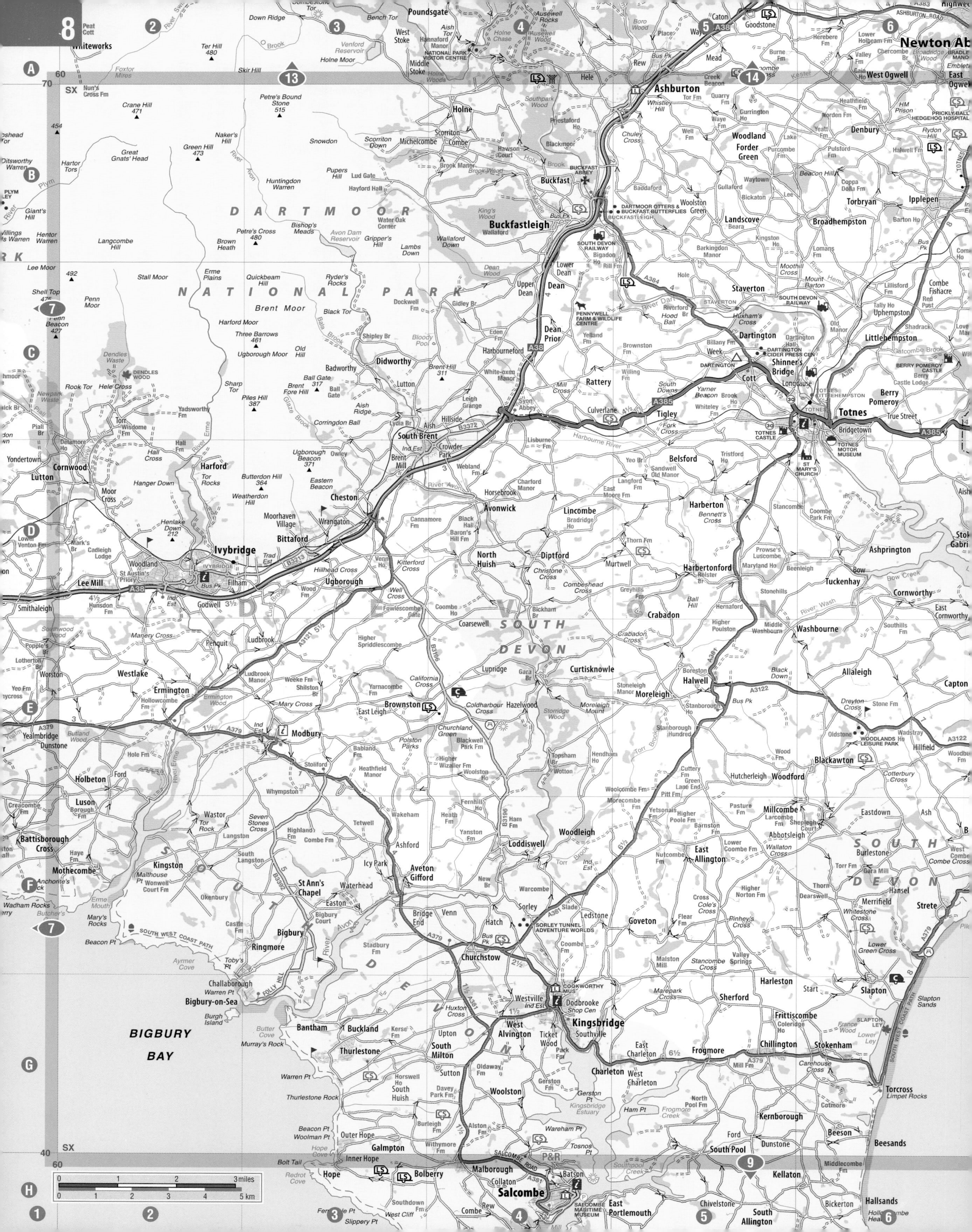

DARTMOOR
NATIONAL PARK
DEVON
SOUTH DEVON
BIGBURY BAY
Newton Abbot
Ashburton
Buckfast
Buckfastleigh
Totnes
Dartington
Staverton
Ipplepen
Denbury
Woodland
Landscove
Broadhempston
Torbryan
Littlehempston
Berry Pomeroy
Bridgetown
South Brent
Ivybridge
Cornwood
Lutton
Harford
Bittaford
Ugborough
Modbury
Ermington
Westlake
Yealmbridge
Holbeton
Kingston
Mothecombe
Battisborough Cross
Bigbury
Bigbury-on-Sea
Ringmore
Aveton Gifford
Loddiswell
Woodleigh
Kingsbridge
Churchstow
West Alvington
Thurlestone
South Milton
Bantham
Buckland
Hope
Galmpton
Bolberry
Malborough
Salcombe
East Portlemouth
Chivelstone
South Allington
Kellaton
Hallsands
Beesands
Torcross
Stokenham
Chillington
Frogmore
Charleton
Sherford
Slapton
Strete
Harleston
Goveton
East Allington
Halwell
Moreleigh
Curtisknowle
Diptford
North Huish
Avonwick
Harberton
Harbertonford
Ashprington
Tuckenhay
Cornworthy
Washbourne
Allaleigh
Capton
Blackawton
Woodford
Millcombe
Brownston
Rattery
Dean Prior
Tigley
Belsford
Crabadon
Lee Mill
Smithaleigh
Holne
Poundsgate
Whiteworks
0 1 2 3 miles
0 1 2 3 4 5 km

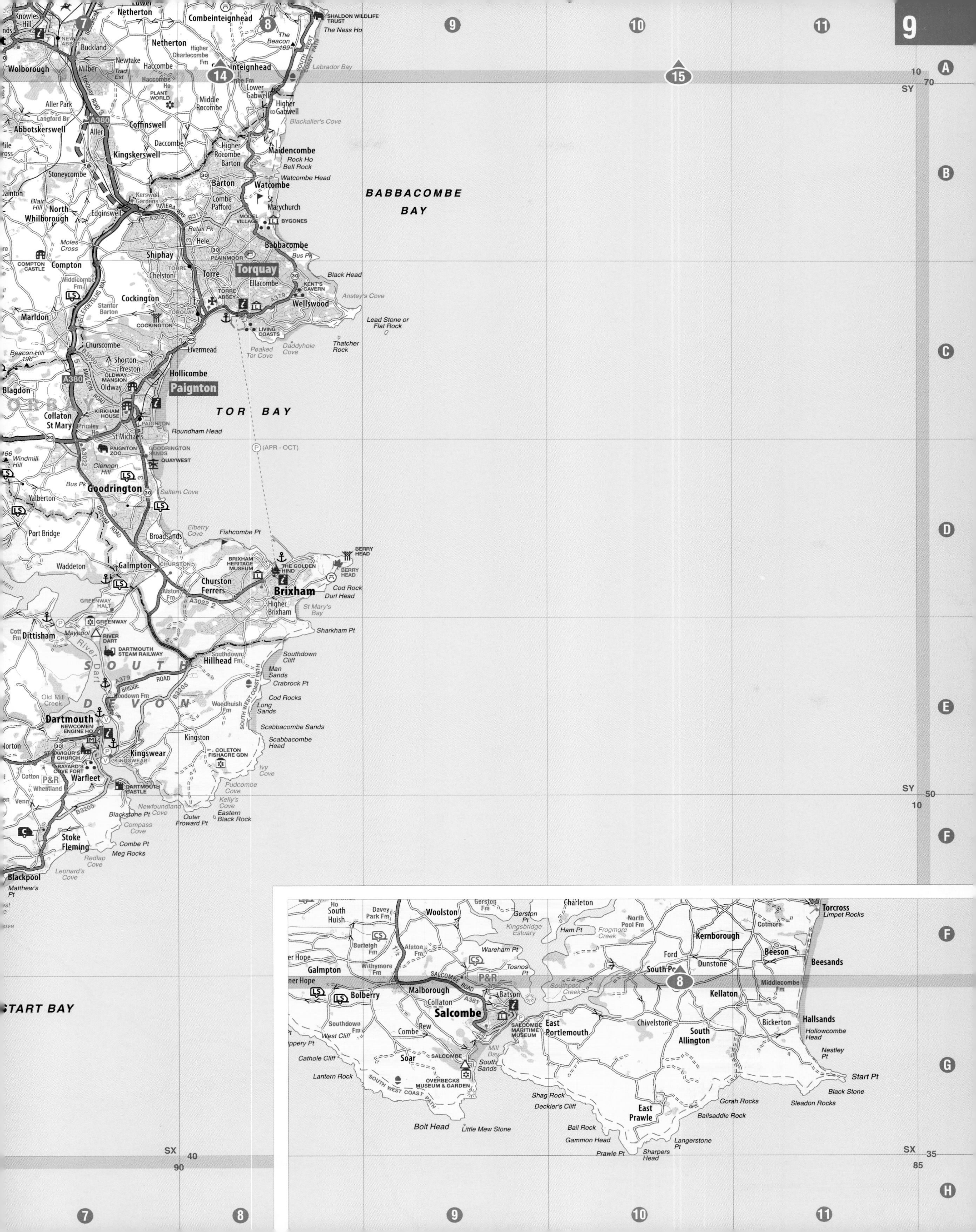

BABBACOMBE BAY
TOR BAY
START BAY
Torquay
Paignton
Brixham
Dartmouth
Salcombe
Babbacombe
Goodrington
Kingswear
Combeinteignhead
Netherton
Wolborough
Aller Park
Abbotskerswell
Coffinswell
Kingskerswell
Maidencombe
Watcombe
Barton
Shiphay
Torre
Chelston
Cockington
Ellacombe
Wellswood
Marldon
Churscombe
Livermead
Hollicombe
Preston
Oldway
Collaton St Mary
St Michaels
Churston Ferrers
Galmpton
Hillhead
Dittisham
Kingston
Warfleet
Stoke Fleming
Blackpool
Berry Head
Hope's Nose
Black Head
Thatcher Rock
Lead Stone or Flat Rock
Roundham Head
Sharkham Pt
Scabbacombe Sands
Woolston
South Huish
Malborough
Bolberry
East Portlemouth
Chivelstone
South Allington
Kernborough
Beeson
Beesands
Torcross
Kellaton
Bickerton
Hallsands
Start Pt
East Prawle
Bolt Head
Soar
Galmpton
Charleton
South Pool
SOUTH WEST COAST PATH
SX
SY

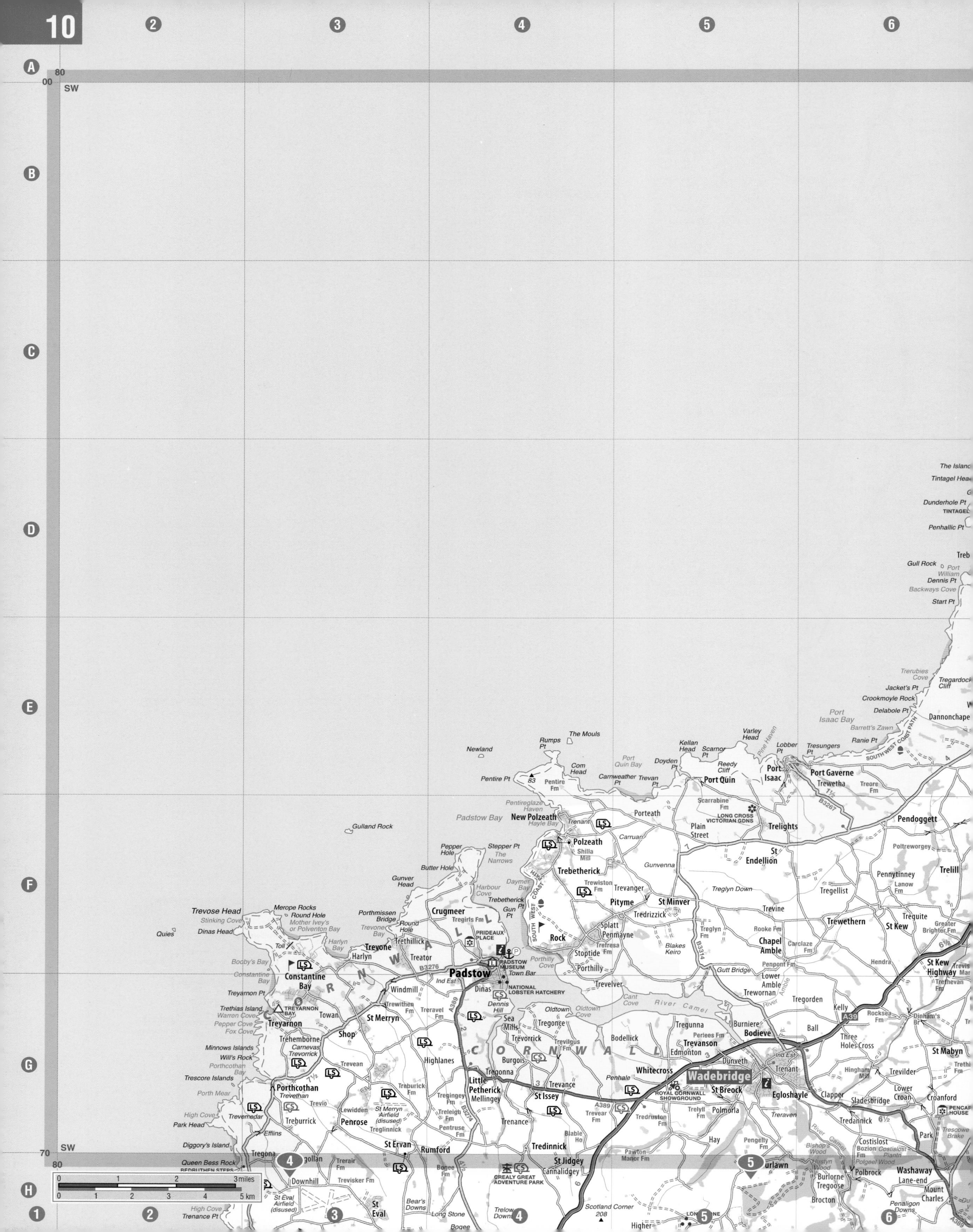

SW

The Island
Tintagel Head
Dunderhole Pt
TINTAGEL
Penhallic Pt
Treb
Gull Rock
Port
William
Dennis Pt
Backways Cove
Start Pt

Trerubies
Cove
Tregardock
Cliff
Jacket's Pt
Crookmoyle Rock
Delabole Pt
Dannonchape
Port
Isaac Bay
Barrett's Zawn
SOUTH WEST COAST PATH

Rumps
Pt
The Mouls
Kellan
Head
Scarnor
Pt
Varley
Head
Pine Haven
Lobber
Pt
Ranie Pt
Newland
Com
Head
Port
Quin Bay
Doyden
Pt
Reedy
Cliff
Port Quin
Tresungers
Pt
Port
Isaac
Port Gaverne
Pentire Pt
83
Pentire
Fm
Carnweather
Pt
Trevan
Pt
Trewetha
Treore
Fm
B3267
Pendoggett
Padstow Bay
New Polzeath
Hayle Bay
Trenant
Porteath
Scarrabine
Fm
LONG CROSS
VICTORIAN GDNS
Plain
Street
Trelights
Poltreworgey
Gulland Rock
Polzeath
Shilla
Mill
Carruan
Gunvenna
St
Endellion
Pennytinney
Lanow
Fm
Trelill
Pepper
Hole
Stepper Pt
The
Narrows
Trebetherick
Trewiston
Fm
Trevanger
Tregellist
Trevine
Trewethern
Trequite
Butter Hole
Daymer
Bay
Pityme
St Minver
Tregryn Down
Chapel
Amble
St Kew
Gunver
Head
Trebetherick
Pt
Tredrizzick
Rooke Fm
Carclaze
Fm
Greater
Brighter Fm
Trevose Head
Merope Rocks
Round Hole
Porthmissen
Bridge
Round
Hole
Gun Pt
Rock
Splatt
Penmayne
Tregigo
Fm
B3314
Hendra
St Kew
Highway
Stinking Cove
Mother Ivey's
or Polventon Bay
Trevone
Bay
Tregirts Fm
PRIDEAUX
PLACE
Tresfrata
Fm
Penpont Fm
Trefrevva
Mar
Quies
Dinas Head
Trevone
Trethillick
Stoptide
Porthilly
Lower
Amble
Trewornan
Booby's Bay
Toll
Harlyn
Bay
Harlyn
Treator
B3276
PADSTOW
MUSEUM
Town Bar
Porthilly
Cove
Porthilly
Tregorden
Constantine
Bay
Constantine
Bay
Padstow
Ind Est
Dinas
Trevelver
Rocksea
Fm
Dinham's
A39
Treyarnon Pt
Windmill
NATIONAL
LOBSTER HATCHERY
Cant
Cove
River Camel
Tregunna
Burniere
Fm
Kelly
Trethias Island
Warren Cove
TREYARNON
BAY
Trewithen
Fm
Treravel
Fm
Dennis
Hill
Oldtown
Oldtown
Cove
Perlees Fm
Trevanson
Bodieve
Ball
Pepper Cove
Fox Cove
Treyarnon
Towan
St Merryn
Sea
Mills
Tregonce
Bodellick
Edmonton
Three
Holes Cross
St Mabyn
Minnows Islands
Will's Rock
Trehemborne
Carnevas
Trevorrick
Shop
Trevorrick
Fm
Trevilgus
Fm
Burgois
CORNWALL
Dunveth
Ind Est
Trenant
Trevilder
Porthcothan
Bay
Trescore Islands
Trevean
Highlanes
Whitecross
Penhale
Wadebridge
ROYAL CORNWALL
SHOWGROUND
St Breock
Egloshayle
Clapper
Sladesbridge
Hingham
Mill
Lower
Croan
Porth Mear
Porthcothan
Trevethan
Little
Petherick
Mellingey
Trevance
St Issey
A389
Trelyll
Fm
Polmorla
Traven
River
Croanford
PENCAR
ROUS
High Cove
Park Head
Trevemedar
Trevio
Lewidden
Treginegy
Fm
Treleigh
Fm
Penruse
Fm
Trenance
A389
Trevear
Fm
Tredruston
Fm
Hay
Pengelly
Fm
Tredannick
6½
Trescowe
Brake
Effins
Treburrick
Penrose
Treglinnick
Blable
Ho
Pawton
Manor Fm
Bishop's
Wood
Costislost
Costislost
Polgoof
Wood
Park
Diggory's Island
Tregona
gollan
Trerair
Fm
St Ervan
Rumford
St Jidgey
Cannalidgey
Higher
Hustyn
Washaway
Lane-end
Queen Bess Rock
REDRUTHEN STEPS
Downhill
Trevisker Fm
Bogee
Tredinnick
urlawn
Polbrock
Burlorne
Tregoose
Mount
Charles
St Eval
Airfield
(disused)
Bear's
Downs
Long Stone
GREALY GREAT
ADVENTURE PARK
Trelow
Downs
Scotland Corner
208
LONG
NE
Brocton
Penaligon
Downs

SW

High Cove
Trenance Pt
St
Eval
Bogee

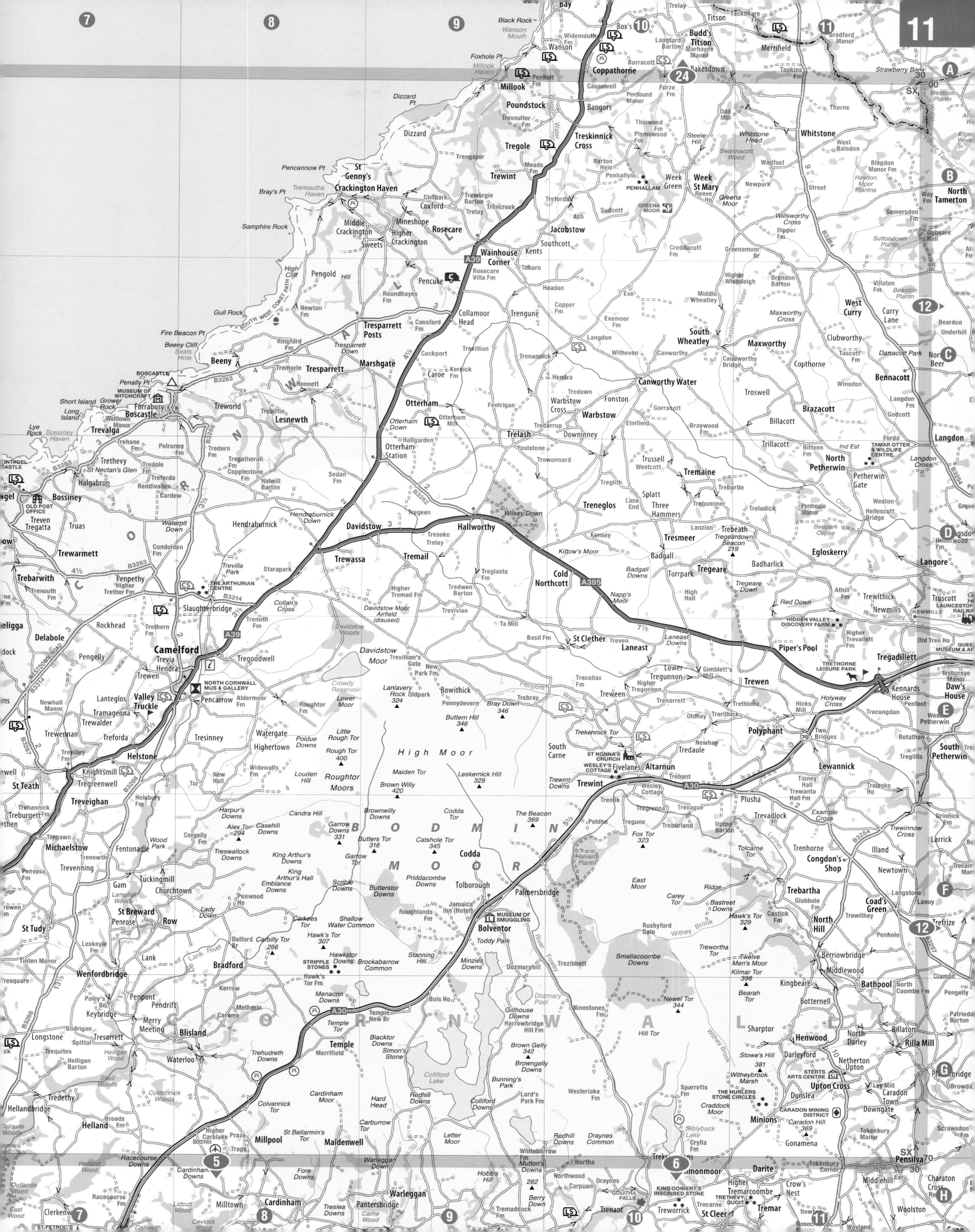

11
Black Rock
Wanson Mouth
Wanson
Bay
Box's
Budd's Titson
Titson
Merrifield
Bradford Manor
Foxhole Pt
Millook Haven
Millook
Penhalt
Coppathorne
Burracott
Bakesdown
Strawberry Bank
Causewell
Poundstock
Bangors
Penfound Manor
Dizzard Pt
Dizzard
Tregole
Treskinnick Cross
Whitstone
Thorne
Pencannow Pt
St Genny's
Crackington Haven
Bray's Pt
Tremoutha Haven
Trewint
Week Green
Week St Mary
North Tamerton
Samphire Rock
Middle Crackington
Higher Crackington
Sweets
Mineshope
Rosecare
Coxford
Jacobstow
Southcott
Wainhouse Corner
Kents
High Cliff
Pengold
Pencuke
Gull Rock
Collamoor Head
Trengune
West Curry
Curry Lane
Fire Beacon Pt
Beeny Cliff
Seals Hole
Beeny
Trespareett Posts
Tresparrett
Marshgate
South Wheatley
Maxworthy
Canworthy Water
Bennacott
Boscastle
Penally Pt
Museum of Witchcraft
Forrabury
Short Island
Grower Rock
Long Island
Lye Rock
Bossiney Haven
Trevalga
Treworld
Lesnewth
Otterham
Otterham Station
Warbstow
Warbstow Cross
Trelash
Brazacott
Langdon
Tintagel Castle
Trethevy
St Nectan's Glen
Halgabron
Bossiney
Old Post Office
Treven
Tregatta
Truas
Trewarmett
Trebarwith
Delabole
Pengelly
Davidstow
Hallworthy
Trewassa
Tremail
Treneglos
Three Hammers
Tresmeer
Tremaine
North Petherwin
Tamar Otter & Wildlife Centre
Egloskerry
Langore
The Arthurian Centre
Slaughterbridge
Rockhead
Cold Northcott
Tregeare
Camelford
Trevia
Hendra
Trewen
Lanteglos
Valley Truckle
North Cornwall Mus & Gallery
Pencarrow
Davidstow Moor
St Clether
Laneast
Piper's Pool
Tregadillett
Launceston
Trewen
Polyphant
Kennards House
Daw's House
South Petherwin
Tramagenna
Trewalder
Treforda
Trewennan
Helstone
Knightsmill
Tregreenwell
St Teath
Treveighan
Michaelstow
Fentonadle
High Moor
Roughtor Moors
Rough Tor 400
Brown Willy 420
Altarnun
Fivelanes
St Nonna's Church
Wesley's Cottage
Trewint
Lewannick
South Carne
Bodmin Moor
Codda
Tolborough
Palmersbridge
Bolventor
Museum of Smuggling
Jamaica Inn (Hotel)
Dozmary Pool
Trevenning
St Tudy
St Breward
Row
Churchtown
Tuckingmill
Penrose
Gam
Trebartha
Congdon's Shop
Coad's Green
North Hill
Wenfordbridge
Bradford
Blisland
Merry Meeting
Keybridge
Longstone
Tresarrett
Temple
Waterloo
Henwood
Rilla Mill
Upton Cross
Minions
Caradon Hill 369
Stripple Stones
Tredethy
Hellandbridge
Helland
Millpool
Maidenwell
Cardinham
Warleggan
Pantersbridge
Colliford Lake
Siblyback Lake
Golitha Falls
King Doniert's Inscribed Stone
Trethevy Quoit
Darite
Tremar
St Cleer
Treworrick
Trenant
Pensilva
Woolston
Clerkenwater
Milltown
A39
A30
A395
B3263
B3266
B3314
B3254
B3257

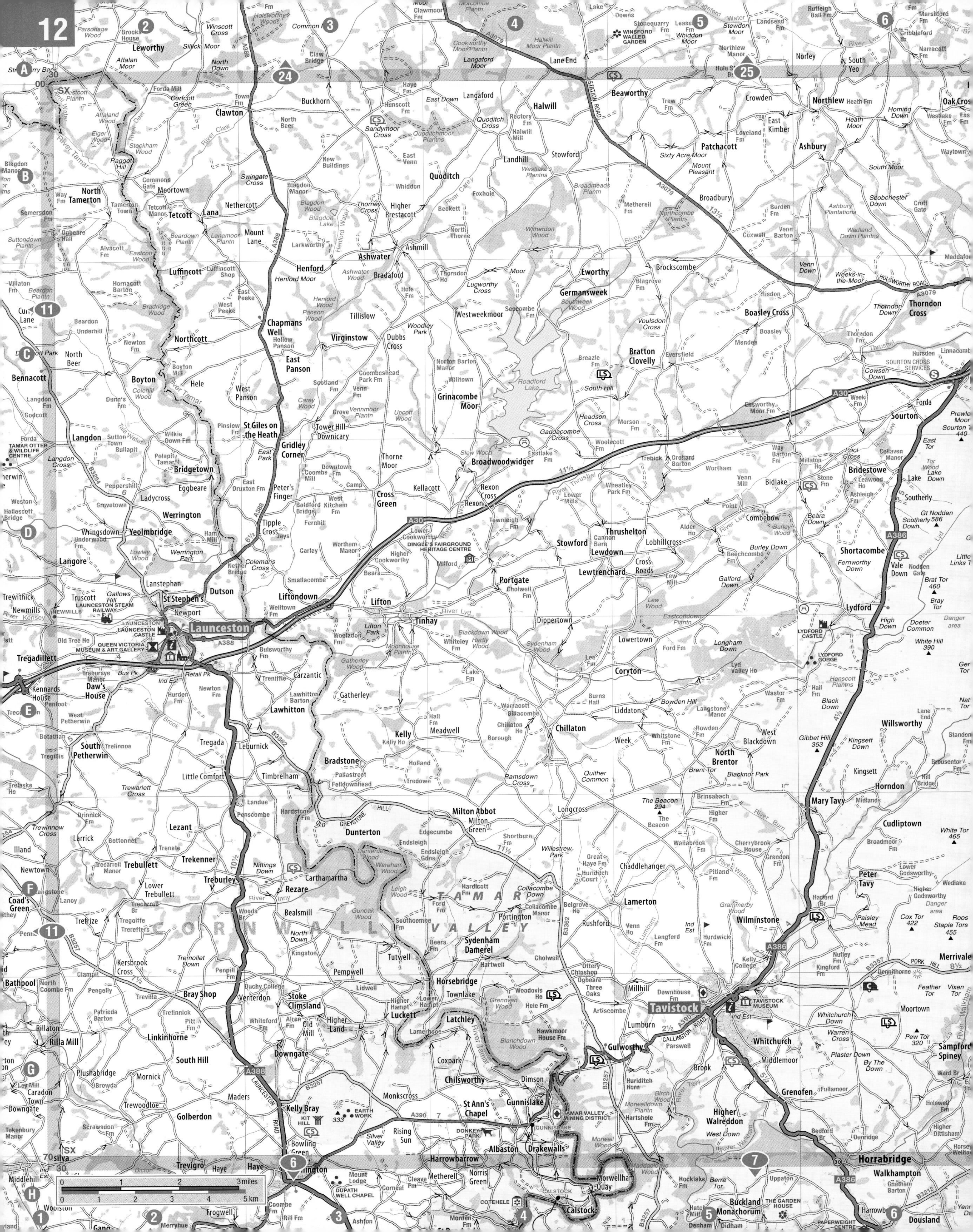
24
25
Leworthy
Clawton
Halwill
Beaworthy
Northlew
Ashbury
Patchacott
Quoditch
North Tamerton
Tetcott
Lana
Henford
Ashwater
Luffincott
Eworthy
Germansweek
Chapmans Well
Virginstow
Northcott
East Panson
Boyton
Bratton Clovelly
Boasley Cross
Thorndon Cross
Bennacott
Grinacombe Moor
Roadford Lake
St Giles on the Heath
Langdon
Gridley Corner
Broadwoodwidger
Sourton
Bridgetown
Bridestowe
Werrington
Cross Green
Yeolmbridge
Thrushelton
Stowford
Lewdown
Lewtrenchard
Shortacombe
Langore
Dutson
Liftondown
Portgate
Lifton
Tinhay
Lydford
St Stephen's
Launceston
Tregadillett
Daw's House
Coryton
Lawhitton
Kelly
Chillaton
Willsworthy
South Petherwin
North Brentor
Bradstone
Mary Tavy
Milton Abbot
Dunterton
Lezant
Trebullett
Trekenner
Treburley
Rezare
Peter Tavy
Lamerton
Wilminstone
T A M A R   V A L L E Y
C O R N W A L L
Sydenham Damerel
Horsebridge
Bray Shop
Stoke Climsland
Luckett
Latchley
Tavistock
Rilla Mill
Linkinhorne
South Hill
Downgate
Gulworthy
Whitchurch
Grenofen
Higher Walreddon
Kelly Bray
St Ann's Chapel
Gunnislake
Golberdon
Harrowbarrow
Albaston
Drakewalls
Horrabridge
Walkhampton
Trevigro
Haye
Callington
Metherell
Morwellham Quay
Buckland Monachorum
Calstock
Dousland
A30
A386
A388
A3079
A390
B3257
B3362
0 1 2 3 miles
0 1 2 3 4 5 km

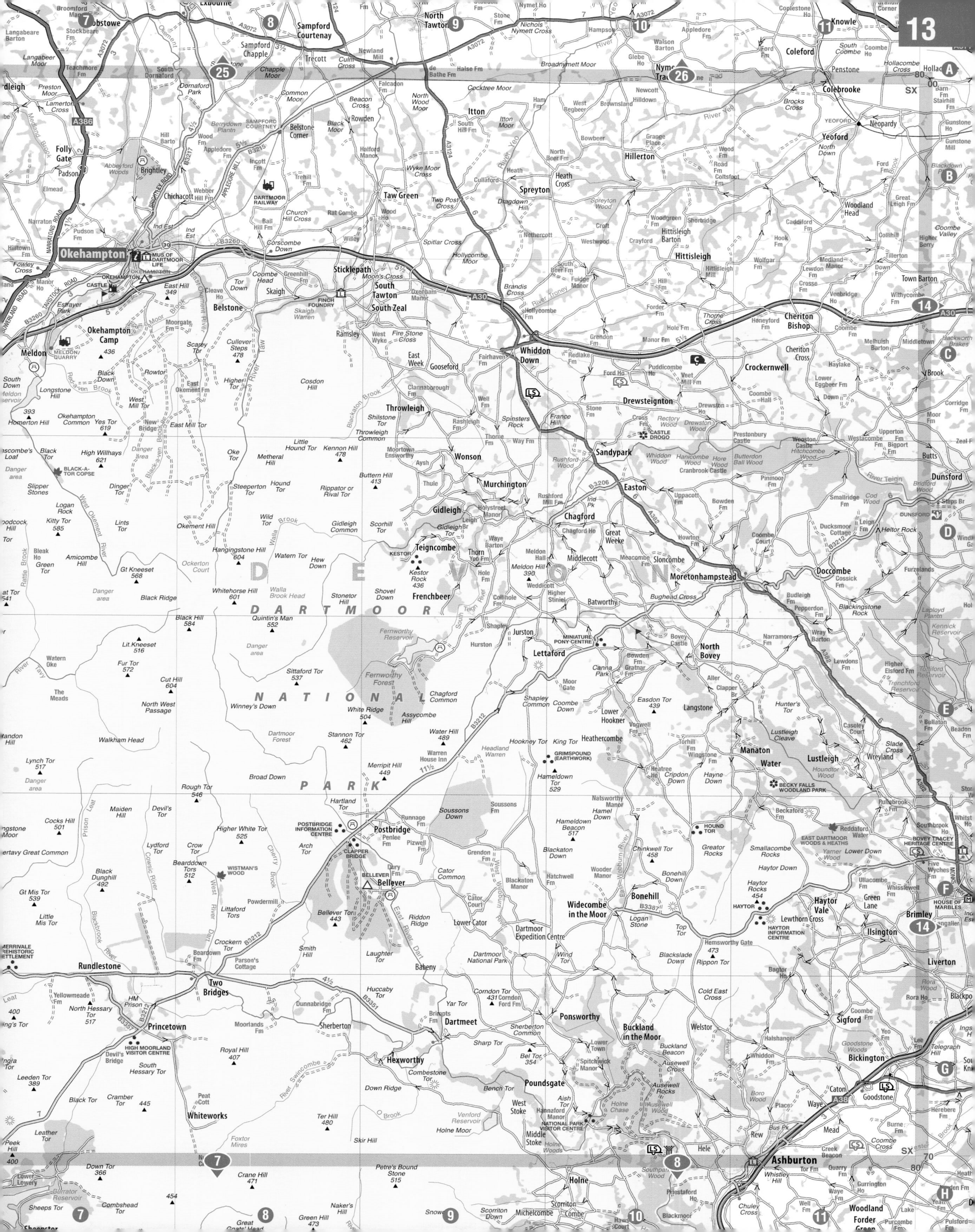

Okehampton
Sampford Courtenay
North Tawton
Sampford Chapple
Knowle
Coleford
Colebrooke
Yeoford
Neopardy
Itton
Belstone Corner
Hillerton
Spreyton
Taw Green
Folly Gate
Brightley
Chichacott
DARTMOOR RAILWAY
Hittisleigh
Sticklepath
South Tawton
South Zeal
Belstone
Okehampton Camp
Meldon
Whiddon Down
Cheriton Bishop
Crockernwell
Drewsteignton
Throwleigh
Wonson
Murchington
Gidleigh
Sandypark
CASTLE DROGO
Easton
Chagford
Teigncombe
Frenchbeer
Moretonhampstead
Doccombe
Dunsford
D E V O N
DARTMOOR
NATIONAL
PARK
Cosdon Hill
Yes Tor 619
High Willhays 621
Kennon Hill 478
Hangingstone Hill 604
Kestor Rock 436
Meldon Hill 390
Whitehorse Hill 601
Quintin's Man 552
Black Hill 584
Fernworthy Reservoir
Fernworthy Forest
Sittaford Tor 537
Cut Hill 604
Lit. Kneeset 516
Fur Tor 572
North Bovey
Lettaford
Jurston
Langstone
Manaton
Water
Lustleigh
Wreyland
BECKY FALLS WOODLAND PARK
Easdon Tor 439
Hameldown Tor 529
GRIMSPOUND (EARTHWORK)
Warren House Inn
Postbridge
CLAPPER BRIDGE
Bellever
Bellever Tor 443
Widecombe in the Moor
Bonehill
Haytor Vale
HAYTOR INFORMATION CENTRE
Ilsington
Brimley
Liverton
Sigford
Bickington
Buckland in the Moor
Ponsworthy
Poundsgate
Dartmeet
Hexworthy
Two Bridges
Rundlestone
Princetown
HIGH MOORLAND VISITOR CENTRE
Whiteworks
Dartmoor Expedition Centre
Holne
Ashburton
Goodstone
Woodland
Sheepstor
Burrator Reservoir
A30
A386
A3072
A3124
A382
B3212
B3357
B3351
B3387
B3260
B3206
A38
SX
80
70

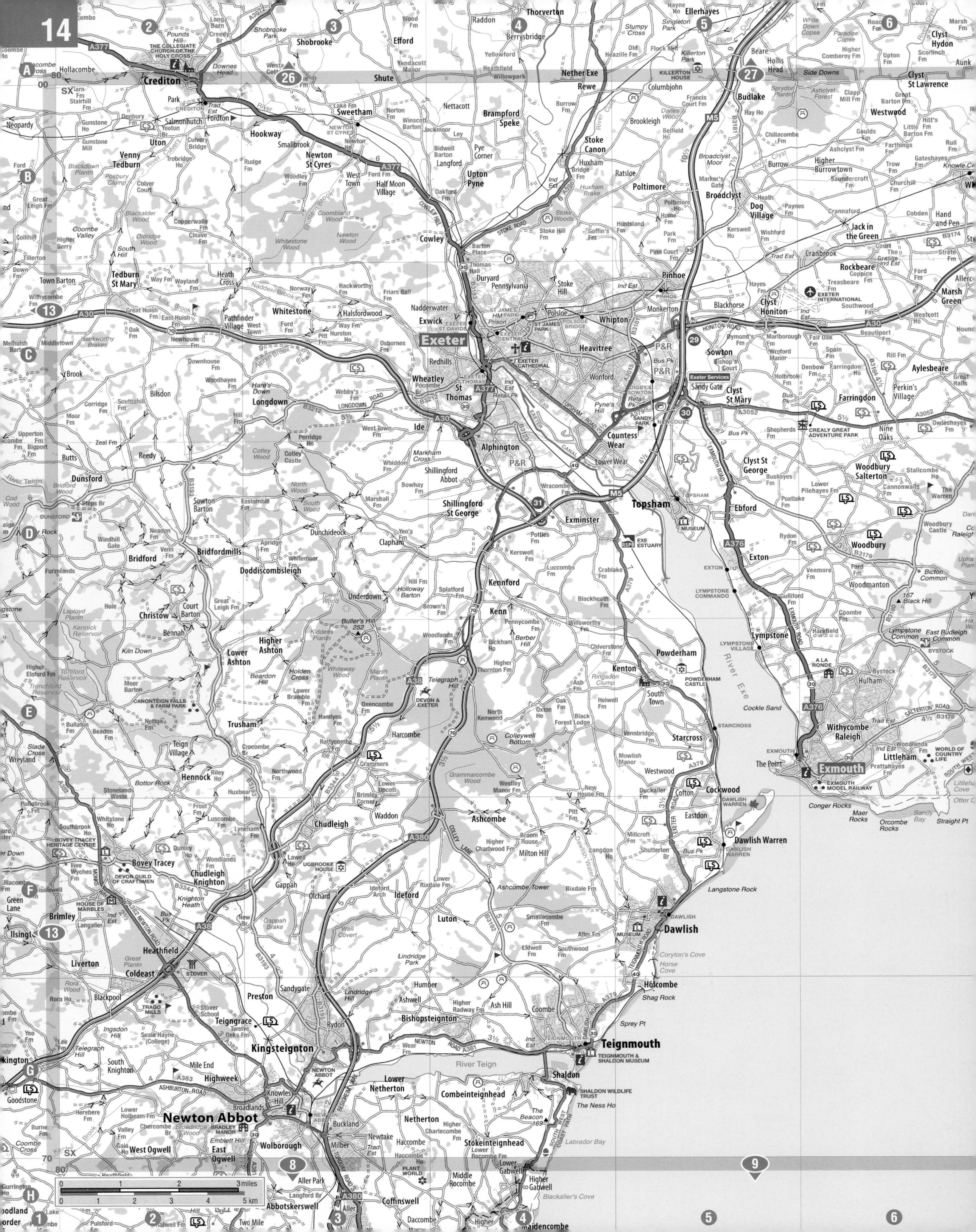
Crediton
Exeter
Exmouth
Topsham
Dawlish
Teignmouth
Newton Abbot
Kingsteignton
Bovey Tracey
Chudleigh
Exminster
Dawlish Warren
River Exe
River Teign
Heavitree
Countess Wear
Lympstone
Starcross
Shaldon
Heathfield

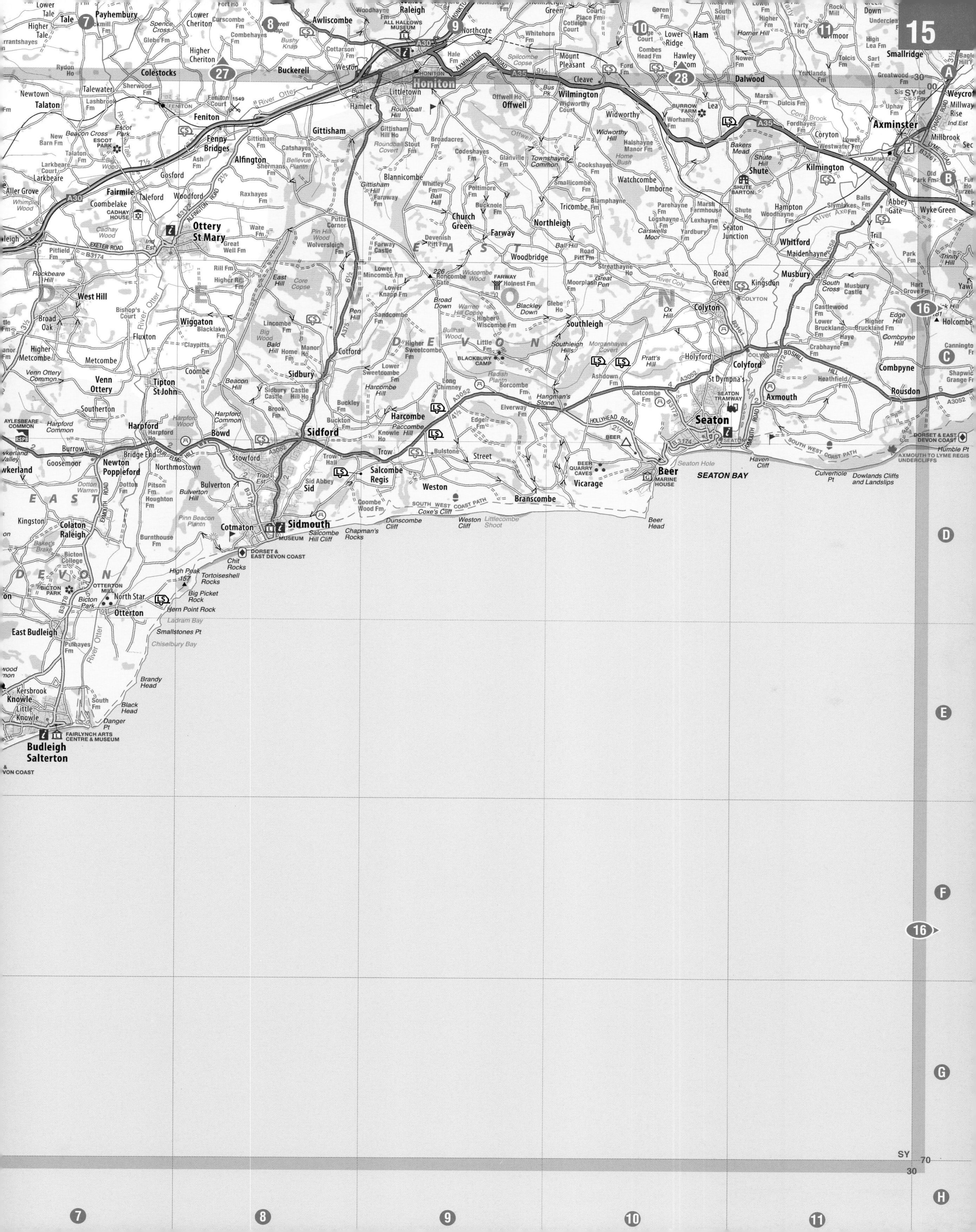

15
Lower Tale
Tale
Payhembury
Higher Tale
Lower Cheriton
Curscombe Fm
Awliscombe
Raleigh
ALL HALLOWS MUSEUM
Northcote
Whitehorn Fm
Cotleigh Court
Court Place Fm
Gøren Fm
Lower Ridge
Ham
South Mill
Horner Hill
Yarty Ho
Yarmoor
Smallridge
Down
Spence Cross
Glebe Fm
Combehayes Fm
Bushy Knap
Cottarson Fm
Weston
Higher Cheriton
Rydon Ho
Colestocks
Buckerell
Honiton
Hale Fm
Spilcombe Copse
Mount Pleasant
Cleave
Ford Fm
Combes Head Fm
Hawley Bottom
Dalwood
Nower Fm
Tolcis Fm
High Lea Fm
Sart Fm
Greatwood Fm
Yeatlands Fm
Newtown
Talewater
Talaton
Sherwood Fm
Lashbrook Fm
Feniton Court
1549
FENITON
River Otter
Feniton
Littletown
Hamlet
Roundball Hill
Offwell Ho
Offwell
Bus Pk
Wilmington
Widworthy Court
Widworthy
BURROW FARM
Lea
Worhams Fm
Marsh Fm
Dulcis Fm
Uphay Fm
Fordhayes Fm
Corry Brook
Coryton
Westwater Fm
Axminster
Weycroft
Millway Rise
Ind Est
Millbrook
New Barn Fm
Beacon Cross
ESCOT PARK
Escot Park
Talaton Fm
Larkbeare Court
Larkbeare
Fenny Bridges
Gittisham Fm
Catshayes Fm
Bellevue Plantn
Gittisham
Gittisham Hill Ho
Roundball Covert
Stout Fm
Broadacres Fm
Codeshayes Fm
Glanville Fm
Townshayne Common
Offwell Brook
Widworthy Hill
Halshayne Manor Fm
Home Bush
Bakers Mead
Shute Hill
Shute
Kilmington
AXMINSTER
Old Park Fm
Allen Grove
Whimple Wood
Ash Fm
Gosford
Alfington
Shermans Fm
Blannicombe
Fairmile
Coombelake
CADHAY HOUSE
Taleford
Woodford
ALFINGTON ROAD
Raxhayes Fm
Gittisham Hill
Faraway Fm
Whitley Fm
Ball Hill
Poltimore Fm
Bucknole Fm
Smallicombe Fm
Cookshayes Fm
Watchcombe
Umborne
Umborne Brook
SHUTE BARTON
Hampton
Slymlakes Fm
Balls Fm
Abbey Gate
Wyke Green
Cadhay Wood
Ottery St Mary
Ware Fm
Great Well Fm
Putts Corner
Pin Hill Wood
Wolverstleigh Fm
Church Green
Farway
Northleigh
Tricombe Fm
Blamphayne Fm
Parehayne Fm
Logshayne Fm
Marsh Farmhouse
Lexhayne Fm
Carswells Moor
Yardbury Fm
Seaton Junction
Shute Ho
Woodhayne Fm
River Axe
Whitford
Trill
Maidenhayne
Park Fm
Trinity Hill
Pitfield Fm
EXETER ROAD
Ind Est
Rill Fm
Higher Rill Fm
Farway Castle
Devenish Pitt Fm
EAST
Ball Hill
Road Pitt Fm
Woodbridge
Streathayne Ho
Rockbeare Hill
West Hill
East Hill
Core Copse
Lower Mincombe Fm
226
Roncombe Gate
Widcombe Wood
FARWAY
Holnest Fm
Moorplash Fm
Great Pen
River Coly
Road Green
Kingsdon
Musbury
South Cross
Musbury Castle
Hart Grove Fm
DEVON
Bishop's Court
Lower Knapp Fm
Broad Down
Warren Hill Copse
Blackley Down
Glebe Ho
Ox Hill
Colyton
COLYTON
Castlewood Fm
Edge Hill
Holcombe
Broad Oak
Fluxton
Wiggaton
Blacklake Fm
Lincombe Fm
Sandcombe Fm
Pen Hill
Higher Wiscombe Fm
Southleigh
Lower Bruckland Fm
Higher Bruckland Fm
Combpyne Hill
Higher Metcombe
Metcombe
Claypitts Fm
Big Wood
Bald Hill
Home Fm
Manor Ho
Cotford
Higher Sweetcombe Fm
Bullhall Wood
Little Fm
BLACKBURY CAMP
Southleigh Hills
Morganhayes Covert
Pratt's Hill
Holyford
Colyford
BOSHILL
Crabhayne Fm
Haye Fm
Cannington Fm
Venn Ottery Common
Venn Ottery
Tipton St John
Coombe
Beacon Hill
Sidbury
Lower Sweetcombe Fm
Harcombe Hill
Long Chimney
Radish Plantn
Borcombe Fm
Ashdown Fm
St Dympna's
Combpyne
Heathfield Fm
Shapwick Grange Fm
Rousdon
Southerton
Sidbury Castle
Castle Hill Ho
Brook Fm
Buckley Fm
Buckton Fm
Harcombe
Paccombe Hill
Knowle Ho
A3052
Elverway Fm
Hangman's Stone
Gatcombe Fm
SEATON TRAMWAY
Axmouth
AYLESBEARE COMMON
RSPB
Harpford Common
Harpford
Harpford Ho
Harpford Wood
Harpford Common
Bowd
Sidford
Edgell Fm
HOLLYHEAD ROAD
BEER
Seaton
SEATON
AXMOUTH ROAD
SOUTH WEST COAST PATH
DORSET & EAST DEVON COAST
Humble Pt
AXMOUTH TO LYME REGIS UNDERCLIFFS
Burrow
Woodbury Valley
Goosemoor
Newton Poppleford
Bridge End
FOUR ELMS HILL
Northmostown
Stowford
Trow Hall
Trow
Bulstone
Street
BEER QUARRY CAVES
Vicarage
Beer
MARINE HOUSE
Seaton Hole
SEATON BAY
Haven Cliff
Culverhole Pt
Dowlands Cliffs and Landslips
Woodbury
Dotton Warren
Dotton Fm
Pitson Fm
Houghton Fm
Bulverton
Bulverton Hill
Trad Est
Salcombe Regis
Sid Abbey
Sid
Weston
Branscombe
Coombe Wood Fm
Coxe's Cliff
Weston Cliff
Littlecombe Shoot
Beer Head
Kingston
Colaton Raleigh
EXMOUTH ROAD
Pinn Beacon Plantn
Cotmaton
Sidmouth
MUSEUM
Salcombe Hill Cliff
Chapman's Rocks
Dunscombe Cliff
Burnthouse Fm
Baker's Brake
Bicton College
DORSET & EAST DEVON COAST
Chit Rocks
High Peak
157
Tortoiseshell Rocks
BICTON PARK
OTTERTON MILL
Bicton Park
North Star
Otterton
Big Picket Rock
Hern Point Rock
Ladram Bay
Smallstones Pt
Chiselbury Bay
East Budleigh
Pulhayes Fm
River Otter
Brandy Head
Black Head
Danger Pt
South Fm
Kersbrook
Knowle
Little Knowle
FAIRLYNCH ARTS CENTRE & MUSEUM
Budleigh Salterton
EAST DEVON COAST
A30
A35
A375
B3174
B3177
B3176
B3172
B3161
B3261
B3178
A3052
CHARD ROAD
LYME ROAD
AXMINSTER ROAD
SY
00
30
70
A
B
C
D
E
F
G
H
7
8
9
10
11
16
27
28

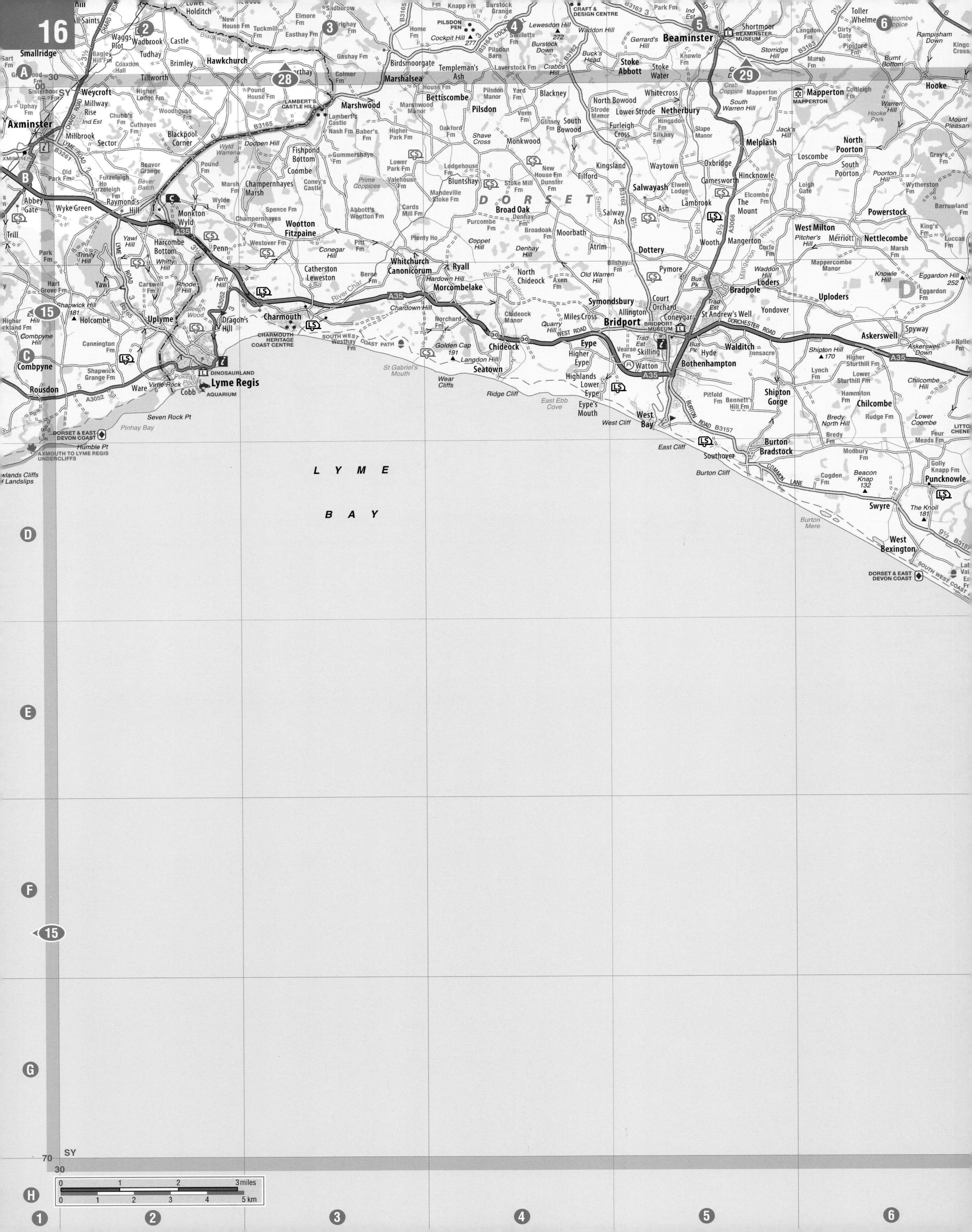

16
Smallridge
Axminster
Weycroft
Millway Rise
Chubb's Fm
Cuthayes Fm
Ind Est
Millbrook
Sector
Wadbrook
Waggs Plot
Tudhay
Castle
Brimley
Tillworth
Hawkchurch
Higher Lodge Fm
Woodhouse Fm
Blackpool Corner
Pound House Fm
Lambert's Castle Hill
Marshwood
Lambert's Castle
Nash Fm
Baber's Fm
Gummershaye Fm
Fishpond Bottom
Coombe
Champernhayes Marsh
Coney's Castle
Prime Coppices
Abbott's Wootton Fm
Wootton Fitzpaine
Spence Fm
Westover Fm
Conegar Hill
Pitt Fm
Catherston Leweston
Berne Fm
Charmouth
Charmouth Heritage Coast Centre
Dinosaurland
Lyme Regis
Aquarium
Cobb
Ware
Virtle Rock
Seven Rock Pt
Pinhay Bay
Rousdon
Combpyne
Cannington Fm
Shapwick Grange Fm
Holcombe
Uplyme
Dragon's Hill
Sleech Wood
Fern Hill
Rhode Hill
Carswell Fm
Whitty Hill
Harcombe Bottom
Harcombe Hill
Yawl Hill
Yawl
Trinity Hill
Hart Grove Fm
Shapwick Hill
Park Fm
Trill
Abbey Gate
Wyke Green
Raymond's Hill
Monkton Wyld
Penn
Furzeleigh Ho
Beavor Grange
Beaver Batch
Old Park Fm
Pound Fm
Marsh Fm
Wylde Fm
Dodpen Hill
Wyld Warren
Tuckmill Fm
Easthay Fm
Elmore Fm
Sadborow
Frighay Fm
Gashay Fm
Colmer Fm
New House Fm
Lower Holditch
Blackwater River
Birdsmoorgate
Marshalsea
Home Fm
Templeman's Ash
House Fm
Bettiscombe
Marshwood Manor
Higher Park Fm
Oakford Fm
Lower Park Fm
Valehouse Fm
Lodgehouse Fm
Bluntshay
Mandeville Stoke Fm
Cards Mill Fm
Plenty Ho
Whitchurch Canonicorum
Ryall
Hardown Hill
Morcombelake
Chardown Hill
Norchard Fm
Golden Cap
191
Langdon Hill
Seatown
St Gabriel's Mouth
Wear Cliffs
Chideock
Chideock Manor
North Chideock
Ridge Cliff
Pilsdon Pen
Cockpit Hill
277
Knapp Fm
Burstock Grange
Swilletts Fm
Pilsdon Barn
Pilsdon Manor
Pilsdon
Laverstock Fm
Yard Fm
Venn Fm
Shave Cross
Monkwood
Stoke Mill Fm
Purcombe Fm
Coppet Hill
Broad Oak
Denhay Fm
Broadoak Fm
Denhay Hill
New House Fm
Dunster Fm
D O R S E T
Moorbath
Atrim
Axen Fm
Old Warren Hill
Symondsbury
Miles Cross
Quarry Hill
West Road
Eype
Higher Eype
Highlands
Lower Eype
Eype's Mouth
East Ebb Cove
West Cliff
Lewesdon Hill
272
Burstock Down
Crabbs Hill
Blackney
Glitney Fm
South Bowood
Craft & Design Centre
Waddon Hill
Buck's Head
Stoke Abbott
Stoke Water
Gerrard's Hill
North Bowood
Strode Manor
Lower Strode
Furleigh Cross
Kingsland
Filford
Salway Ash
Bilshay Fm
Dottery
Pymore
Court Orchard
Allington
Bridport
Bridport Museum
Coneygar
Trad Est
Skilling
Vearse Fm
Watton
West Bay
East Cliff
Burton Cliff
Southover
Beaminster
Beaminster Museum
Shortmoor
Knowle Fm
Storridge Hill
Whitecross
Netherbury
Hingsdon Fm
Silkhay Fm
Slape Manor
Waytown
Oxbridge
Camesworth
Salwayash
Elwell Lodge
Lambrook
Ash
Wooth
River Brit
Melplash
Hincknowle
The Mount
Elcombe Fm
Mangerton
Corfe Fm
Waddon Hill
Loders
Bradpole
St Andrew's Well
Bus Pk
Hyde
Bothenhampton
Walditch
Innsacre
Dorchester Road
Burton Road
Pitfold Fm
Bennett's Hill Fm
Shipton Gorge
Burton Bradstock
Common Lane
Cogden Fm
Beacon Knap
132
Swyre
Burton Mere
West Bexington
The Knoll
181
Puncknowle
Golly Knapp Fm
Modbury Fm
Bredy Fm
Bredy North Hill
Rudge Fm
Chilcombe
Hammiton Fm
Lower Sturthill Fm
Higher Sturthill Fm
Shipton Hill
170
Lynch Fm
Askerswell
Askerswell Down
Spyway
Yondover
Uploders
Knowle Hill
Eggardon Hill
252
Eggardon Fm
Mappercombe Manor
West Milton
Pitcher's Hill
Merriott
Nettlecombe
Marsh Fm
Powerstock
King's Fm
Luccas Fm
Barrowland Fm
Wytherston Fm
Poorton Hill
South Poorton
North Poorton
Loscombe
Loigh Gate
Mapperton
Crab Coppice
South Warren Hill
Coltleigh Fm
Warren Hill
Hooke Park
Hooke
Jack's Hill
Langdon Fm
Dirty Gate
Pipsford Fm
Marsh Fm
Burnt Bottom
Toller Whelme
Rampisham Down
Mount Pleasant
Gray's Fm
Lower Coombe
Four Meads Fm
Dorset & East Devon Coast
Humble Pt
Axmouth to Lyme Regis Undercliffs
South West Coast Path
Westhay Fm
L Y M E
B A Y
A35
A3052
B3165
B3161
B3162
B3163
B3164
B3157
A3066
28
29
15
SY
30
70
0 1 2 3 miles
0 1 2 3 4 5 km
A
B
C
D
E
F
G
H
1
2
3
4
5
6

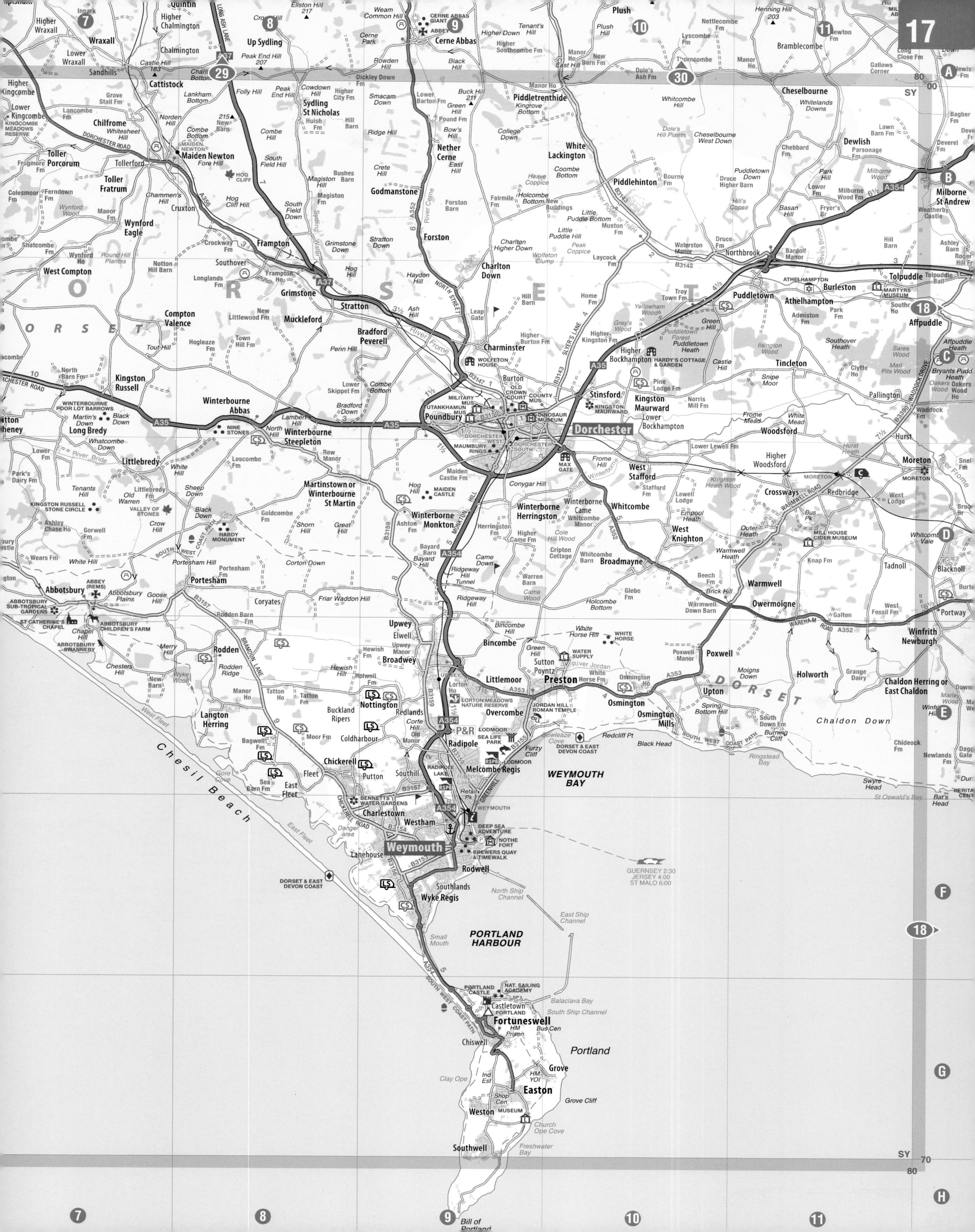
Higher Wraxall
Wraxall
Lower Wraxall
Sandhills
Higher Chalmington
Chalmington
Cattistock
Up Sydling
Cerne Abbas
Plush
Piddletrenthide
Cheselbourne
Bramblecombe
Higher Kingcombe
Lower Kingcombe
Chilfrome
Sydling St Nicholas
Nether Cerne
White Lackington
Dewlish
Toller Porcorum
Tollerford
Maiden Newton
Toller Fratrum
Godmanstone
Piddlehinton
Milborne St Andrew
Cruxton
Wynford Eagle
Forston
Frampton
Charlton Down
Northbrook
West Compton
Southover
Grimstone
Stratton
Puddletown
Athelhampton
Burleston
Tolpuddle
Affpuddle
Compton Valence
Muckleford
Bradford Peverell
Charminster
Higher Bockhampton
Tincleton
Kingston Russell
Burton
Stinsford
Kingston Maurward
Pallington
Winterbourne Abbas
Poundbury
Dorchester
Lower Bockhampton
Woodsford
Long Bredy
Winterbourne Steepleton
Littlebredy
Martinstown or Winterbourne St Martin
West Stafford
Higher Woodsford
Moreton
Crossways
Redbridge
Winterborne Monkton
Winterborne Herringston
Winterborne Came
Whitcombe
West Knighton
Portesham
Broadmayne
Abbotsbury
Coryates
Warmwell
Owermoigne
Upwey
Elwell
Bincombe
Broadwey
Rodden
Littlemoor
Sutton Poyntz
Preston
Poxwell
Winfrith Newburgh
Langton Herring
Nottington
Overcombe
Osmington
Upton
Osmington Mills
Holworth
Chaldon Herring or East Chaldon
Chickerell
Radipole
Melcombe Regis
Fleet
East Fleet
Charlestown
Westham
Weymouth
Rodwell
Wyke Regis
WEYMOUTH BAY
PORTLAND HARBOUR
Chesil Beach
Fortuneswell
Castletown
Chiswell
Portland
Grove
Easton
Weston
Southwell
Bill of Portland

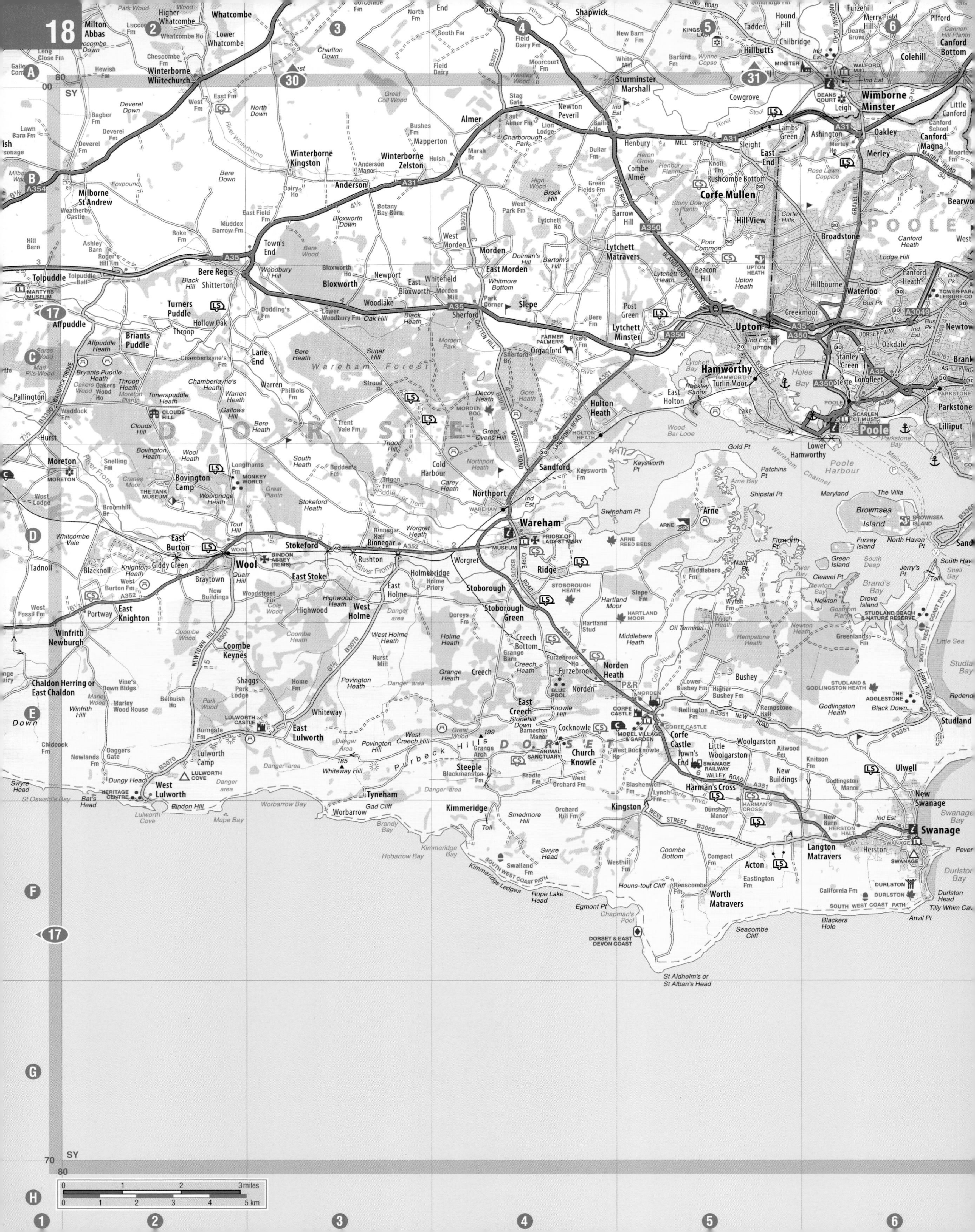

18
Milton Abbas
Higher Whatcombe
Whatcombe
Lower Whatcombe
Charlton Down
North Fm
South Fm
Shapwick
Field Dairy Fm
New Barn Fm
Kingston Lacy
Tadden
Hound Hill
Merry Field Hill
Furzehill
Pilford
Canford Bottom
Chilbridge
Hillbutts
Colehill
Winterborne Whitechurch
Sturminster Marshall
Wimborne Minster
30
31
Great Coll Wood
Stag Gate
Newton Peveril
Cowgrove
Little Canford
Deverel Down
North Down
Almer
East Almer Fm
Charborough Park
Lion Lodge
Henbury
Sleight
Lambs Green
Ashington
Oakley
Canford Magna
Mapperton
Winterborne Kingston
Winterborne Zelston
Huish
Marsh Br
Dullar Fm
Combe Almer
East End
Merley
Milborne St Andrew
Anderson
Anderson Manor
Corfe Mullen
Rushcombe Bottom
Weatherby Castle
Bere Down
Bloxworth Down
Botany Bay Barn
West Park Fm
Barrow Hill
Hill View
Broadstone
POOLE
Bearwood
Muddox Barrow Fm
Roke Fm
Town's End
West Morden
Morden
Lytchett Matravers
Poor Common
Canford Heath
Bere Regis
Shitterton
Tolpuddle
Tolpuddle Ball
Martyrs Museum
Bloxworth
Newport
East Bloxworth
Whitefield
Morden Mill
East Morden
Whitmore Bottom
Beacon Hill
Upton Heath
Hillbourne
Waterloo
Turners Puddle
Hollow Oak
Throop
Affpuddle
Briants Puddle
Woodlake
Sherford
Slepe
Park Corner
Post Green
Bere Fm
Lytchett Minster
Upton
Creekmoor
Oakdale
Newtown
Lane End
Bere Heath
Wareham Forest
Sugar Hill
Morden Park
Farmer Palmer's
Organford
Pike's Fm
Hamworthy
Turlin Moor
Holes Bay
Stanley Green
Sterte
Longfleet
Branksome
Pallington
Warren
Phillols Fm
Stroud Br
Decoy Heath
Morden Bog
Gore Heath
Holton Heath
East Holton
Rockley Sands
Lake
Poole
Parkstone
Lilliput
Clouds Hill
Hurst
D O R S E T
Bere Heath
Trent Vale Fm
Great Ovens Hill
Wood Bar Looe
Lower Hamworthy
Gold Pt
Moreton
Bovington Camp
Monkey World
The Tank Museum
South Heath
Cold Harbour
Northport Heath
Sandford
Keysworth Fm
Keysworth Pt
Patchins Pt
Poole Harbour
Main Channel
Woolbridge Heath
Great Plantn
Stokeford Heath
Carey Heath
Northport
Wareham
Maryland
The Villa
Brownsea Island
Swineham Pt
Arne
Arne Reed Beds
Priory of Lady St Mary
Whitcombe Vale
East Burton
Wool
Stokeford
Binnegar
Rushton
Worgret
Ridge
Fitzworth Pt
Furzey Island
North Haven Pt
Sandbanks
South Haven Pt
Tadnoll
Blacknoll
Knighton Heath
Giddy Green
Braytown
Bindon Abbey
River Frome
Holmebridge
East Stoke
Stoborough
Middlebere Fm
Green Island
South Deep
Cleavel Pt
Jerry's Pt
West Fossil Fm
Portway
East Knighton
Woodstreet Fm
Highwood
West Holme
East Holme
Stoborough Green
Stoborough Heath
Hartland Moor
Slepe Fm
Newton
Brand's Bay
Drove Island
Studland Beach & Nature Reserve
Winfrith Newburgh
Coombe Keynes
West Holme Heath
Holme Heath
Creech Bottom
Hartland Stud
Oil Terminal
Middlebere Heath
Rempstone Heath
Newton Heath
Greenlands Fm
Little Sea
South West Coast Path
Chaldon Herring or East Chaldon
Vine's Down Bldgs
Marley Wood House
Shaggs
Park Lodge
Home Fm
Povington Heath
Grange Heath
Creech
Furzebrook
Norden Heath
Norden
Blue Pool
P&R
Bushey
Higher Bushey Fm
Lower Bushey Fm
Studland & Godlingston Heath
The Agglestone
Studland Bay
Winfrith Hill
Lulworth Castle
East Lulworth
Whiteway
East Creech
Knowle Hill
Corfe Castle
Rollington Fm
Rempstone Hall
Godlingston Heath
Black Down
Studland
Redend Pt
Burngate Fm
Lulworth Camp
Povington Hill
West Creech Hill
Great Wood
Grange Arch
Barneston Manor
Cocknowle
Church Knowle
Model Village & Garden
Town's End
Little Woolgarston
Woolgarston
Ailwood
Knitson Fm
Chideock Fm
Newlands Fm
Daggers Gate
Dungy Head
Lulworth Cove
Heritage Centre
West Lulworth
Bindon Hill
Purbeck Hills
Steeple
Blackmanston Fm
Animal Sanctuary
West Bucknowle Ho
Swanage Railway
Harman's Cross
New Buildings
Ulwell
Swyre Head
St Oswald's Bay
Bat's Head
Mupe Bay
Worbarrow Bay
Worbarrow
Tyneham
Gad Cliff
Kimmeridge
Smedmore Hill
Orchard Hill Fm
Kingston
Lynch Fm
Dunshay Manor
Godlingston Manor
New Swanage
Swanage Bay
Brandy Bay
Kimmeridge Bay
Hobarrow Bay
Kimmeridge Ledges
Swalland Fm
Swyre Head
Rope Lake Head
Westhill Fm
Coombe Bottom
Compact Fm
Acton
Langton Matravers
Herston
Swanage
Peveril Pt
Durlston Bay
Durlston Head
Tilly Whim Caves
Anvil Pt
Houns-tout Cliff
Renscombe Fm
Eastington Fm
Worth Matravers
California Fm
Blackers Hole
Egmont Pt
Chapman's Pool
Dorset & East Devon Coast
Seacombe Cliff
St Aldhelm's or St Alban's Head
A31
A35
A350
A351
A352
A354
B3075
B3070
B3071
B3069
B3351
0 1 2 3 miles
0 1 2 3 4 5 km
A B C D E F G H
1 2 3 4 5 6
SY
00
70
80
17

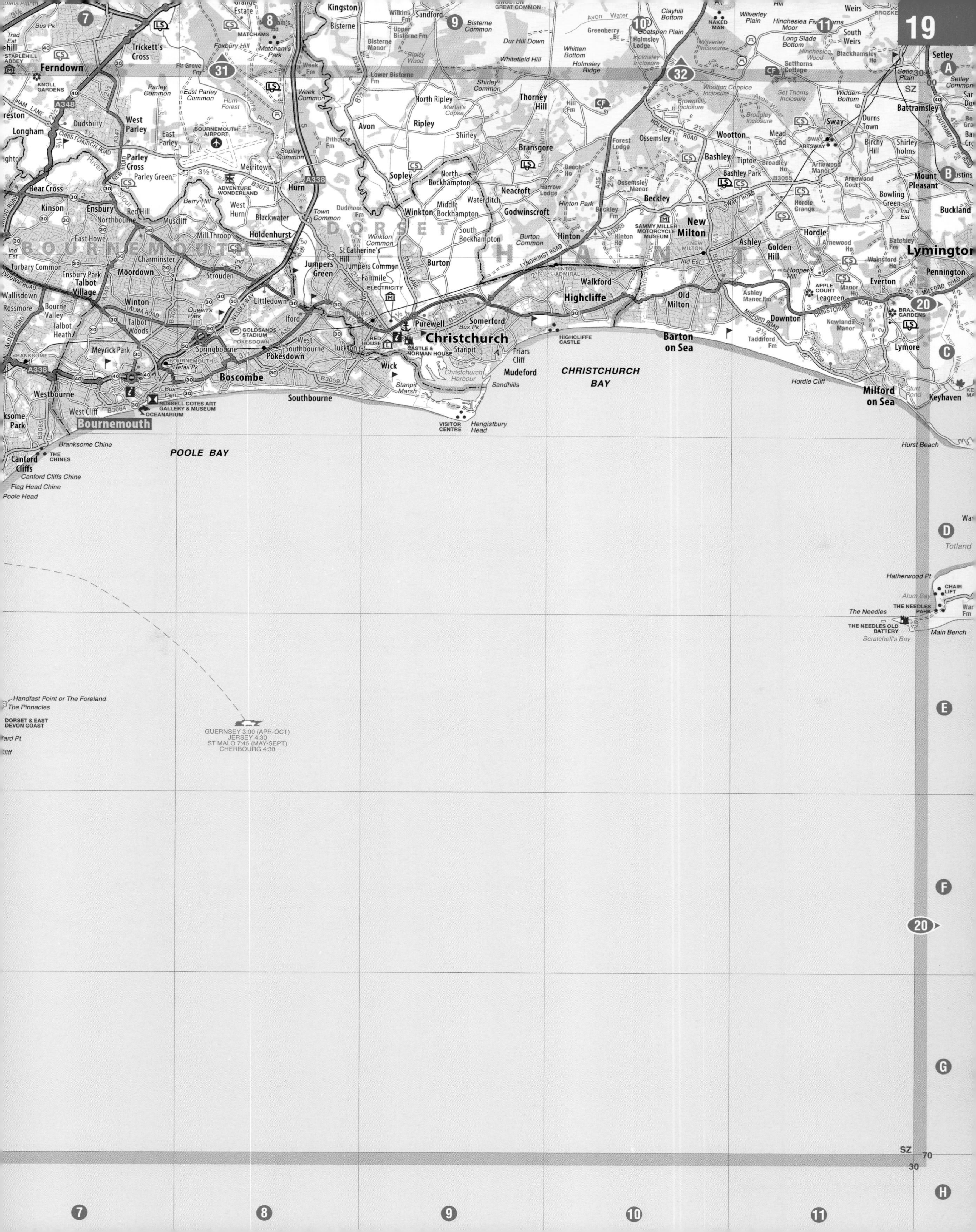

Ferndown
Trickett's Cross
West Parley
Parley Cross
Bournemouth Airport
Hurn
Kinson
Ensbury
Northbourne
Moordown
Winton
Charminster
Holdenhurst
Jumpers Green
Talbot Village
Boscombe
Southbourne
Pokesdown
Westbourne
Bournemouth
Russell Cotes Art Gallery & Museum
Oceanarium
Canford Cliffs
Poole Bay
Christchurch
Christchurch Harbour
Mudeford
Hengistbury Head
Highcliffe
Highcliffe Castle
Christchurch Bay
Barton on Sea
New Milton
Sammy Miller Motorcycle Museum
Milford on Sea
Keyhaven
Lymington
Pennington
Everton
Sway
Bransgore
Sopley
Burton
Winkton
Ripley
Avon
Kingston
Bisterne
Hordle
Ashley
Bashley
Wootton
Dorset
Hants
Bournemouth
The Needles
The Needles Old Battery
Alum Bay
Totland
Hurst Beach
Handfast Point or The Foreland
The Pinnacles
Dorset & East Devon Coast
GUERNSEY 3:00 (APR-OCT)
JERSEY 4:30
ST MALO 7:45 (MAY-SEPT)
CHERBOURG 4:30
7
8
9
10
11
20

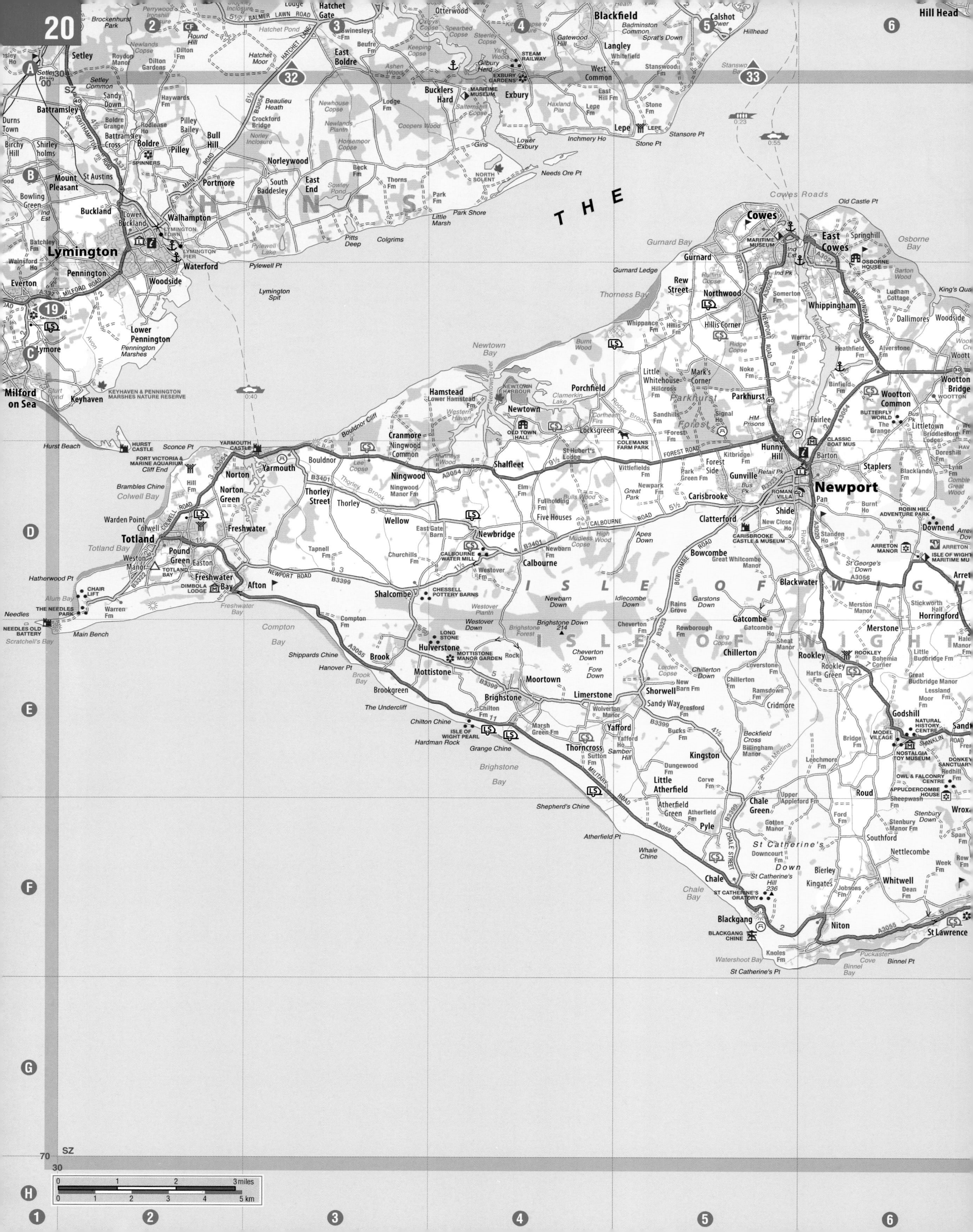

Setley
Battramsley
Boldre
Pilley
Bull Hill
Portmore
Norleywood
South Baddesley
East End
East Boldre
Hatchet Gate
Beaulieu Heath
Bucklers Hard
Exbury
Blackfield
Langley
Calshot
Hill Head
West Common
Lepe
Needs Ore Pt
Buckland
Lower Buckland
Walhampton
Lymington
Pennington
Woodside
Waterford
Everton
Lower Pennington
Pennington Marshes
Lymore
Milford on Sea
Keyhaven
KEYHAVEN & PENNINGTON MARSHES NATURE RESERVE
Hurst Beach
HURST CASTLE
Pylewell Pt
Lymington Spit
THE
Cowes Roads
Old Castle Pt
Cowes
East Cowes
Osborne Bay
Gurnard Bay
Gurnard
Rew Street
Northwood
Thorness Bay
Whippingham
Newtown Bay
Hamstead
Newtown
Porchfield
Parkhurst
Parkhurst Forest
Wootton Common
Wootton Bridge
Bouldnor
Cranmore
Ningwood Common
Shalfleet
Norton
Yarmouth
Norton Green
Colwell Bay
Warden Point
Colwell
Totland
Totland Bay
Freshwater
Freshwater Bay
Pound Green
Afton
Thorley Street
Thorley
Wellow
Ningwood
Newbridge
Calbourne
Five Houses
Hunny Hill
Newport
Carisbrooke
Gunville
Shide
Clatterford
Staplers
Downend
Shalcombe
Bowcombe
Blackwater
ISLE OF WIGHT
Compton Bay
Brook
Hulverstone
Mottistone
Brookgreen
Brighstone
Moortown
Limerstone
Shorwell
Gatcombe
Chillerton
Rookley
Merstone
Horringford
Godshill
Yafford
Thorncross
Kingston
Brighstone Bay
Little Atherfield
Chale Green
Roud
Pyle
Chale
Chale Bay
St Catherine's Down
Whitwell
Niton
St Lawrence
Blackgang
St Catherine's Pt
Needles
The Needles
Scratchell's Bay
Alum Bay
Hatherwood Pt
Shippards Chine
The Undercliff
Atherfield Pt
Shepherd's Chine
Whale Chine
Hanover Pt
0 1 2 3 miles
0 1 2 3 4 5 km

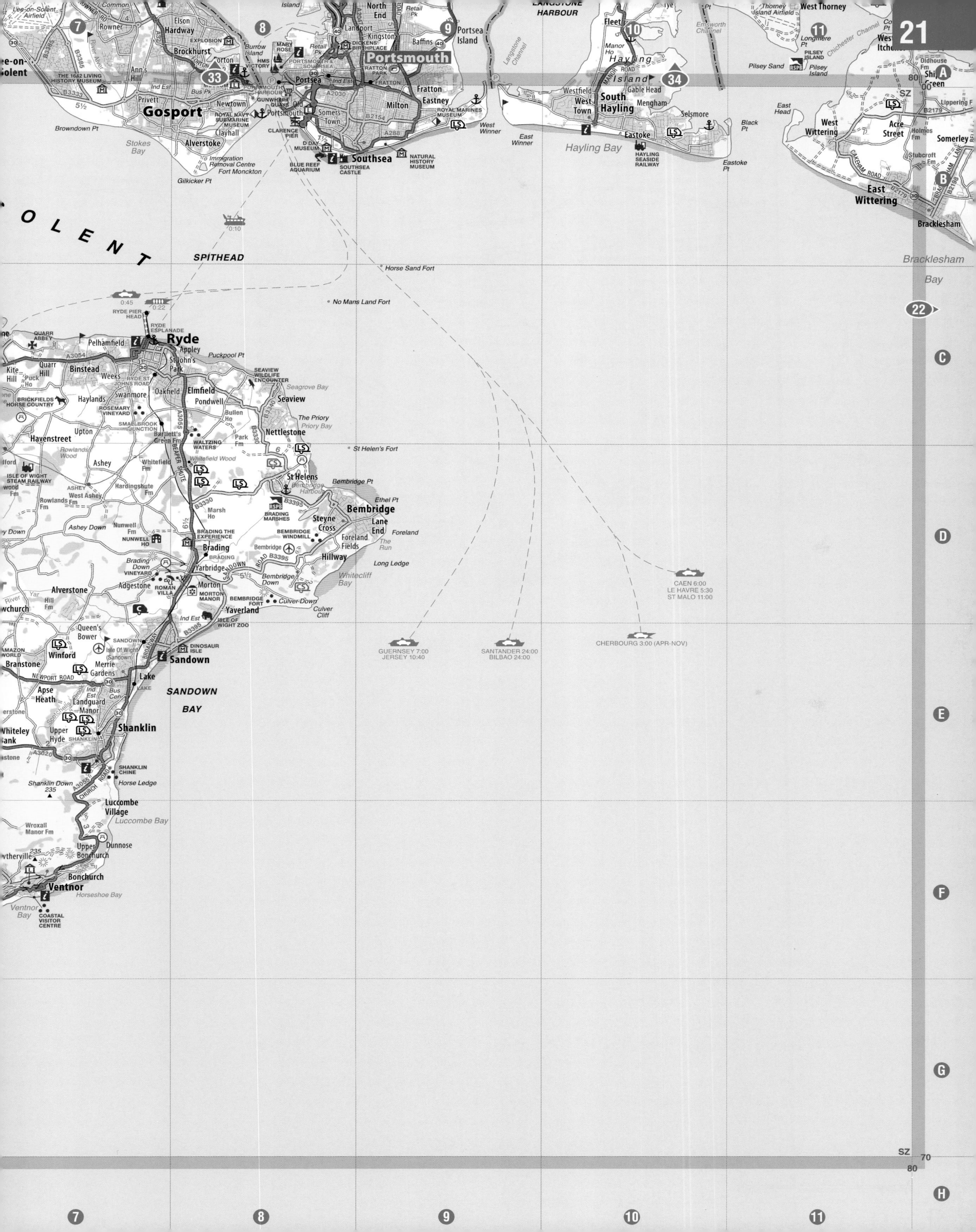
Portsmouth
Gosport
Southsea
Ryde
Sandown
Shanklin
Ventnor
Bembridge
Brading
South Hayling
West Wittering
East Wittering
Bracklesham
SPITHEAD
SANDOWN BAY
Hayling Bay
Bracklesham Bay
CAEN 6:00
LE HAVRE 5:30
ST MALO 11:00
GUERNSEY 7:00
JERSEY 10:40
SANTANDER 24:00
BILBAO 24:00
CHERBOURG 3:00 (APR-NOV)

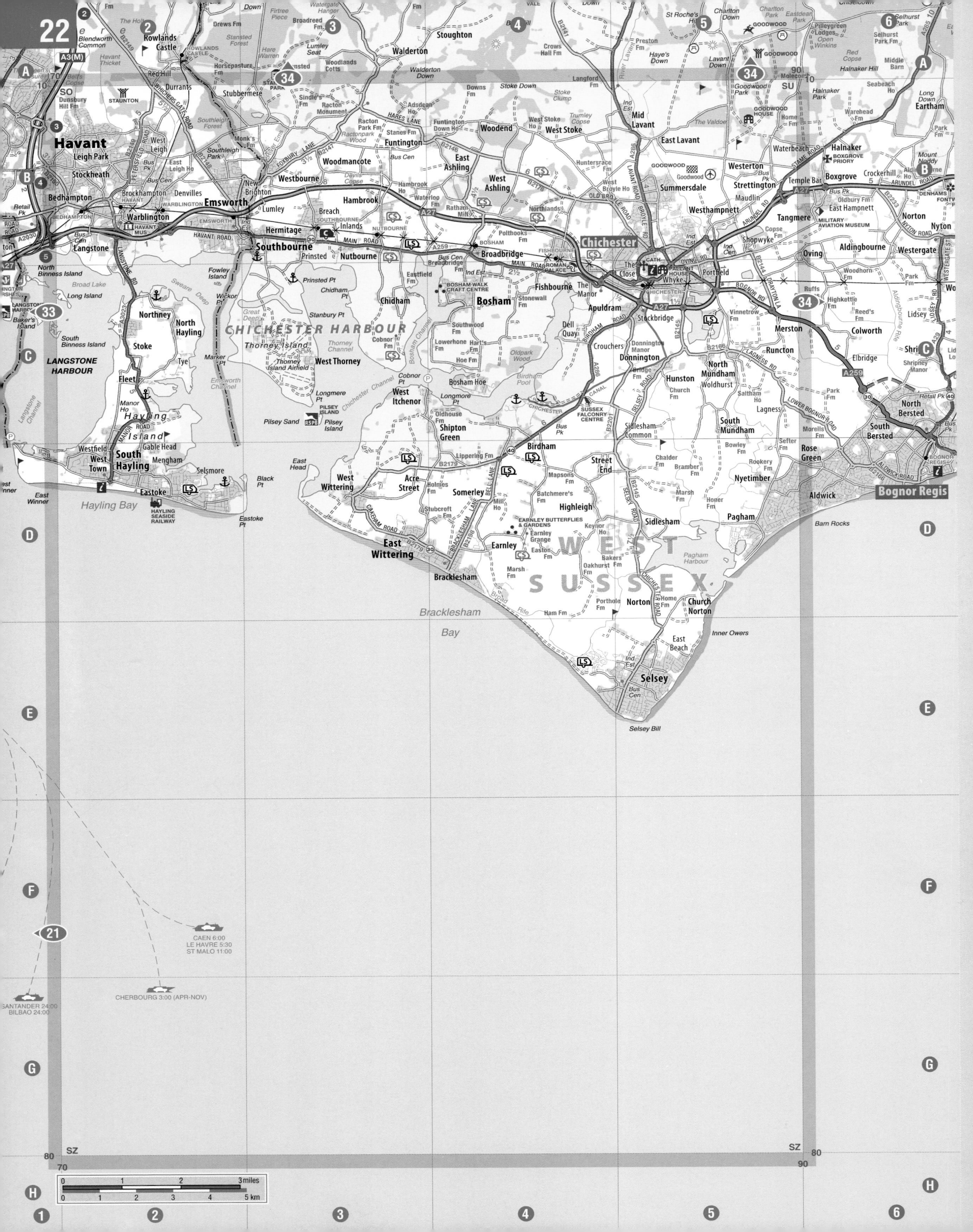
Havant
Leigh Park
Stockheath
Bedhampton
Rowlands Castle
Red Hill
Durrants
Stubbermere
Walderton
Stoughton
Woodmancote
Westbourne
Emsworth
Warblington
Denvilles
Brockhampton
Langstone
Southbourne
Hermitage
Lumley
Hambrook
Nutbourne
Chidham
Bosham
Broadbridge
Funtington
East Ashling
West Ashling
Woodend
West Stoke
Mid Lavant
East Lavant
Summersdale
Westhampnett
Chichester
Fishbourne
Apuldram
Donnington
Hunston
North Mundham
Tangmere
Boxgrove
Halnaker
Westerton
Strettington
Oving
Aldingbourne
Westergate
Norton
Nyton
Merston
Colworth
Runcton
Lidsey
Elbridge
North Bersted
South Bersted
Bognor Regis
Aldwick
Rose Green
Pagham
Nyetimber
South Mundham
Sidlesham
Highleigh
Street End
Birdham
Somerley
Earnley
East Wittering
West Wittering
Bracklesham
Acre Street
West Itchenor
Shipton Green
Bosham Hoe
Selsey
Selsey Bill
Church Norton
East Beach
Norton
Pagham Harbour
Bracklesham Bay
Hayling Bay
Hayling Island
North Hayling
South Hayling
West Town
Eastoke
Mengham
Stoke
Northney
Fleet
LANGSTONE HARBOUR
CHICHESTER HARBOUR
Thorney Island
West Thorney
Pilsey Sand
Pilsey Island
WEST SUSSEX
A27
A259
A3(M)
34
33
21
CAEN 6:00
LE HAVRE 5:30
ST MALO 11:00
CHERBOURG 3:00 (APR-NOV)
SANTANDER 24:00
BILBAO 24:00
SZ
SU
0 1 2 3 miles
0 1 2 3 4 5 km

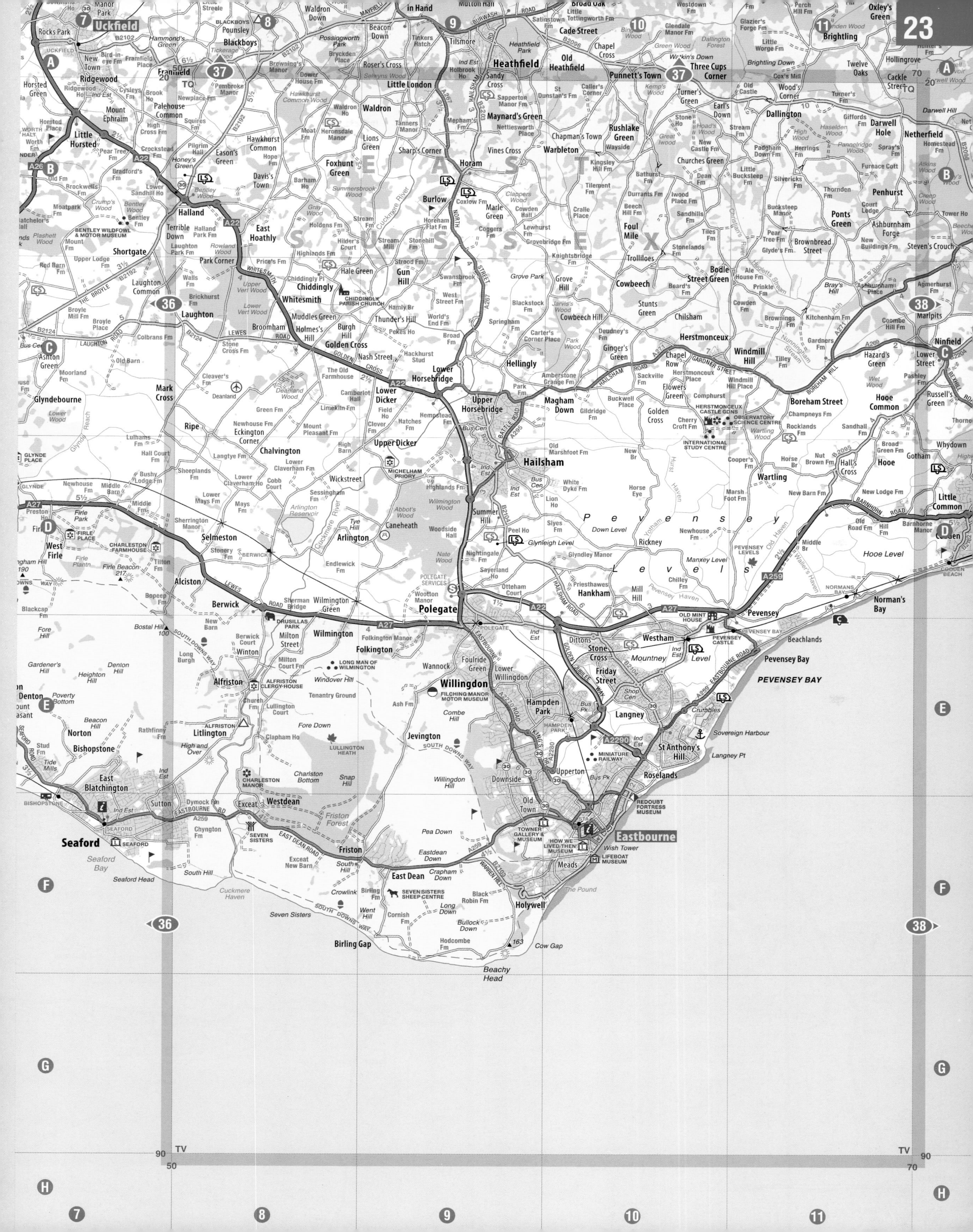
Uckfield
Rocks Park
Ridgewood
Framfield
Blackboys
Pounsley
Waldron Down
Beacon Down
Tilsmore
Heathfield
Old Heathfield
Cade Street
Punnett's Town
Three Cups Corner
Brightling
Oxley's Green
Twelve Oaks
Hollingrove
Cackle Street
Little London
Waldron
Horsted Green
Little Horsted
Mount Ephraim
Palehouse Common
Hawkhurst Common
Foxhunt Green
Sharp's Corner
Horam
Vines Cross
Maynard's Green
Warbleton
Rushlake Green
Dallington
Darwell Hole
Netherfield
Halland
East Hoathly
Terrible Down
Shortgate
Burlow
Marle Green
Foul Mile
Trolliloes
Penhurst
Ponts Green
Ashburnham Forge
Brownbread Street
Steven's Crouch
Park Corner
Laughton Common
Laughton
Chiddingly
Whitesmith
Gun Hill
Hale Green
Cowbeech
Bodle Street Green
Muddles Green
Holmes's Hill
Burgh Hill
Golden Cross
Thunder's Hill
Stunts Green
Chilsham
Herstmonceux
Windmill Hill
Hellingly
Lower Horsebridge
Ninfield
Lower Street
Glyndebourne
Mark Cross
Ripe
Lower Dicker
Upper Horsebridge
Magham Down
Flowers Green
Boreham Street
Hooe Common
Eckington Corner
Chalvington
Upper Dicker
Hailsham
Golden Cross
Wartling
Hooe
Little Common
Selmeston
Arlington
Caneheath
Summer Hill
Pevensey Levels
Rickney
Cooden
Alciston
Berwick
Wilmington Green
Polegate
Hankham
Mill Hill
Pevensey
Norman's Bay
Wilmington
Milton Street
Folkington
Westham
Stone Cross
Friday Street
Pevensey Bay
Willingdon
Alfriston
Denton
Norton
Bishopstone
Litlington
Jevington
Hampden Park
Langney
St Anthony's Hill
Roselands
East Blatchington
Seaford
Sutton
Exceat
Westdean
Friston
East Dean
Eastbourne
Upperton
Old Town
Meads
Holywell
Birling Gap
Beachy Head
Seven Sisters
EAST SUSSEX
PEVENSEY BAY
A22
A27
A259
A267
A271
A2290
TV
TQ

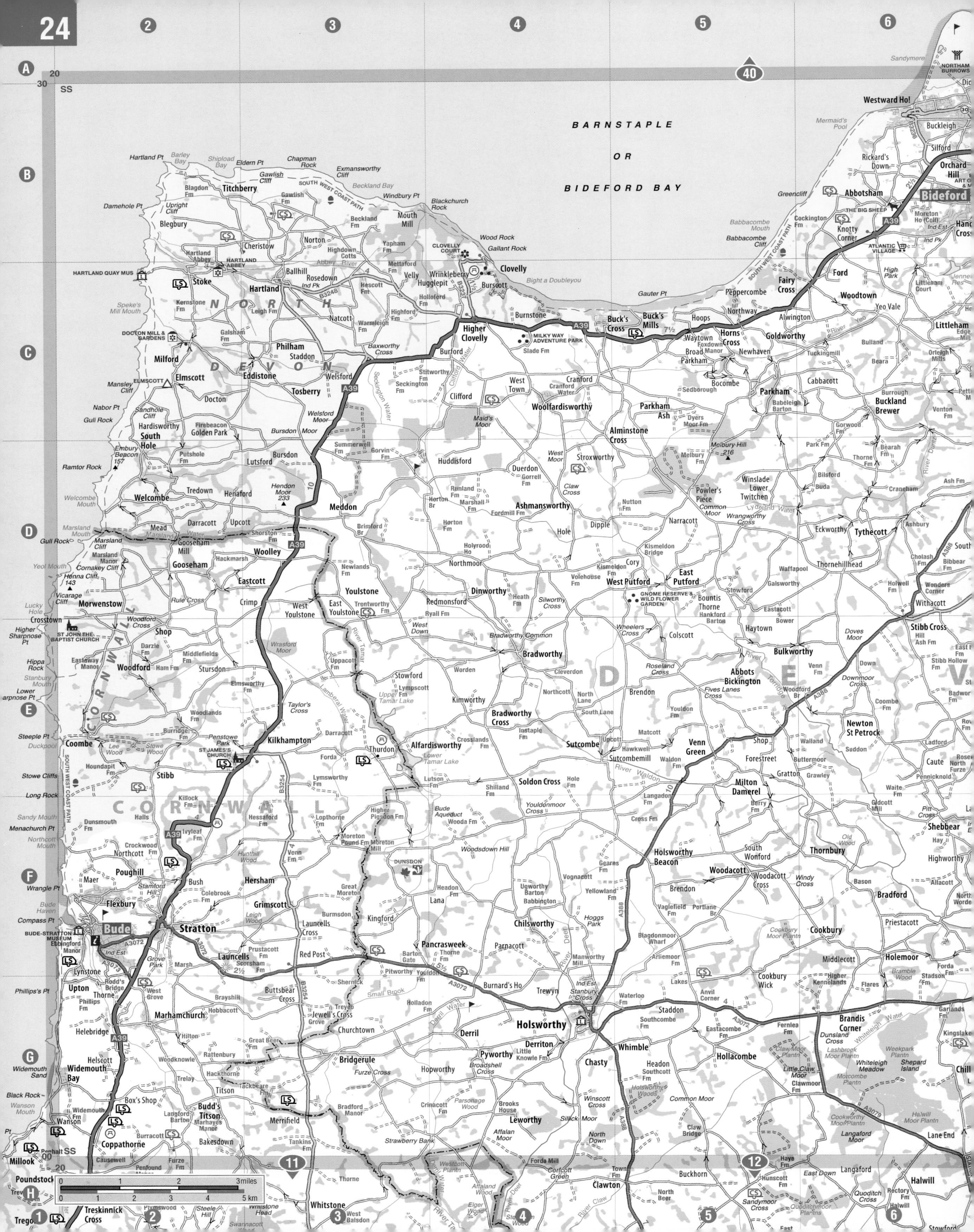
BARNSTAPLE
OR
BIDEFORD BAY
40
11
12
Westward Ho!
Northam Burrows
Sandymere
Mermaid's Pool
Buckleigh
Silford
Rickard's Down
Orchard Hill
Bideford
Abbotsham
The Big Sheep
Greencliff
Cockington Fm
Knotty Corner
Babbacombe Mouth
Babbacombe Cliff
Atlantic Village
Ford
Fairy Cross
Woodtown
Peppercombe
Northway
Alwington
Yeo Vale
Littleham
Hoops
Horns Cross
Goldworthy
Waytown
Broad Parkham
Newhaven
Bulland
Buck's Cross
Buck's Mills
Gauter Pt
Bocombe
Parkham
Cabbacott
Sedborough
Buckland Brewer
Parkham Ash
Alminstone Cross
Melbury Hill 216
Hartland Pt
Barley Bay
Shipload Bay
Eldern Pt
Chapman Rock
Gawlish Cliff
Exmansworthy Cliff
Beckland Bay
Windbury Pt
Blackchurch Rock
Titchberry
Blagdon Fm
Damehole Pt
Upright Cliff
Blegbury
Beckland Fm
Mouth Mill
Cheristow
Norton
Yapham Fm
Clovelly Court
Wood Rock
Gallant Rock
Clovelly
Hartland Abbey
Hartland Quay Mus
Stoke
Hartland
Ballhill
Rosedown
Velly
Wrinkleberry
Hugglepit
Bursdon
Burscott
Bight a Doubleyou
Speke's Mill Mouth
NORTH
DEVON
Leigh Fm
Natcott
Docton Mill & Gardens
Higher Clovelly
Burnstone
Milky Way Adventure Park
Slade Fm
Milford
Philham
Baxworthy Cross
Burford
Elmscott
Eddistone
Welsford
West Town
Cranford
Tosberry
Clifford
Woolfardisworthy
Docton
Nabor Pt
Guli Rock
Hardisworthy
South Hole
Firebeacon Golden Park
Welsford Moor
Maid's Moor
Bursdon Moor
Embury Beacon 157
Ramtor Rock
Lutsford
Bursdon
Summerwell Fm
Gorvin Fm
Huddisford
Duerdon
Stroxworthy
Welcombe Mouth
Welcombe
Tredown
Henaford
Hendon Moor 233
Meddon
Ashmansworthy
Powler's Piece
Winslade
Lower Twitchen
Marsland Mouth
Mead
Darracott
Upcott
Brimford Br
Horton Fm
Hole
Dipple
Narracott
Eckworthy
Tythecott
Gull Rock
Marsland Cliff
Gooseham Mill
Woolley
Gooseham
Eastcott
Northmoor
Holyrood Ho
Cory
Kismeldon Bridge
Thornehillhead
Waffapool
Yeol Mouth
Cornakey Cliff
Henna Cliff 143
Youlstone
Dinworthy
West Putford
East Putford
Morwenstow
Crimp
West Youlstone
East Youlstone
Redmonsford
Gnome Reserve & Wild Flower Garden
Withacott
Crosstown
St John the Baptist Church
Shop
Woodford Cross
Higher Sharpnose Pt
Bradworthy Common
Bradworthy
Colscott
Haytown
Stibb Cross
Hippa Rock
Woodford
Sturdon
Stowford
Worden
Bulkworthy
Abbots Bickington
Doves Moor
Lower Sharpnose Pt
Kimworthy
Brendon
Northcott
Fives Lanes Cross
Taylor's Cross
Upper Tamar Lake
CORNWALL
Steeple Pt
Duckpool
Coombe
Kilkhampton
Thurdon
Alfardisworthy
Bradworthy Cross
Sutcombe
Sutcombemill
Venn Green
Newton St Petrock
Stowe Cliffs
Long Rock
Stibb
Lower Tamar Lake
Soldon Cross
Forestreet
Milton Damerel
Gratton
Shebbear
Sandy Mouth
Menachurch Pt
Northcott Mouth
Halls
Dunsmouth Fm
Hessaford Fm
Higher Pigsdon Fm
Bude Aqueduct
Youldonmoor Cross
Northcott
Poughill
Maer
Hersham
Bush
Woodsdown Hill
Holsworthy Beacon
South Wonford
Thornbury
Highworthy
Wrangle Pt
Flexbury
Bude Haven
Compass Pt
Bude
Stratton
Bude-Stratton Museum
Grimscott
Launcells Cross
Kingford
Lana
Chilsworthy
Woodacott
Brendon
Bradford
Cookbury
Priestacott
Launcells
Red Post
Pancrasweek
Parnacott
Holemoor
Middlecott
Lynstone
Upton
Marsh
Buttsbear Cross
Pitworthy
Burnard's Ho
Trewyn
Cookbury Wick
Phillips's Pt
Thorne
Marhamchurch
Jewell's Cross
Churchtown
Derril
Holsworthy
Staddon
Brandis Corner
Helebridge
Helscott
Widemouth Sand
Widemouth Bay
Bridgerule
Pyworthy
Derriton
Chasty
Whimble
Hollacombe
Shepard Island
Black Rock
Wanson Mouth
Box's Shop
Budd's Titson
Titson
Merrifield
Hopworthy
Leworthy
Common Moor
Wanson
Coppathorne
Bakesdown
Strawberry Bank
Lane End
Millook
Penhalt
Forda Mill
Clawton
Buckhorn
Langaford
Halwill
Poundstock
Whitstone
Tregole
Treskinnick Cross
Sandymoor Cross
Quoditch Cross
SS
20
30
1
2
3
4
5
6
A
B
C
D
E
F
G
H
0 1 2 3 miles
0 1 2 3 4 5 km

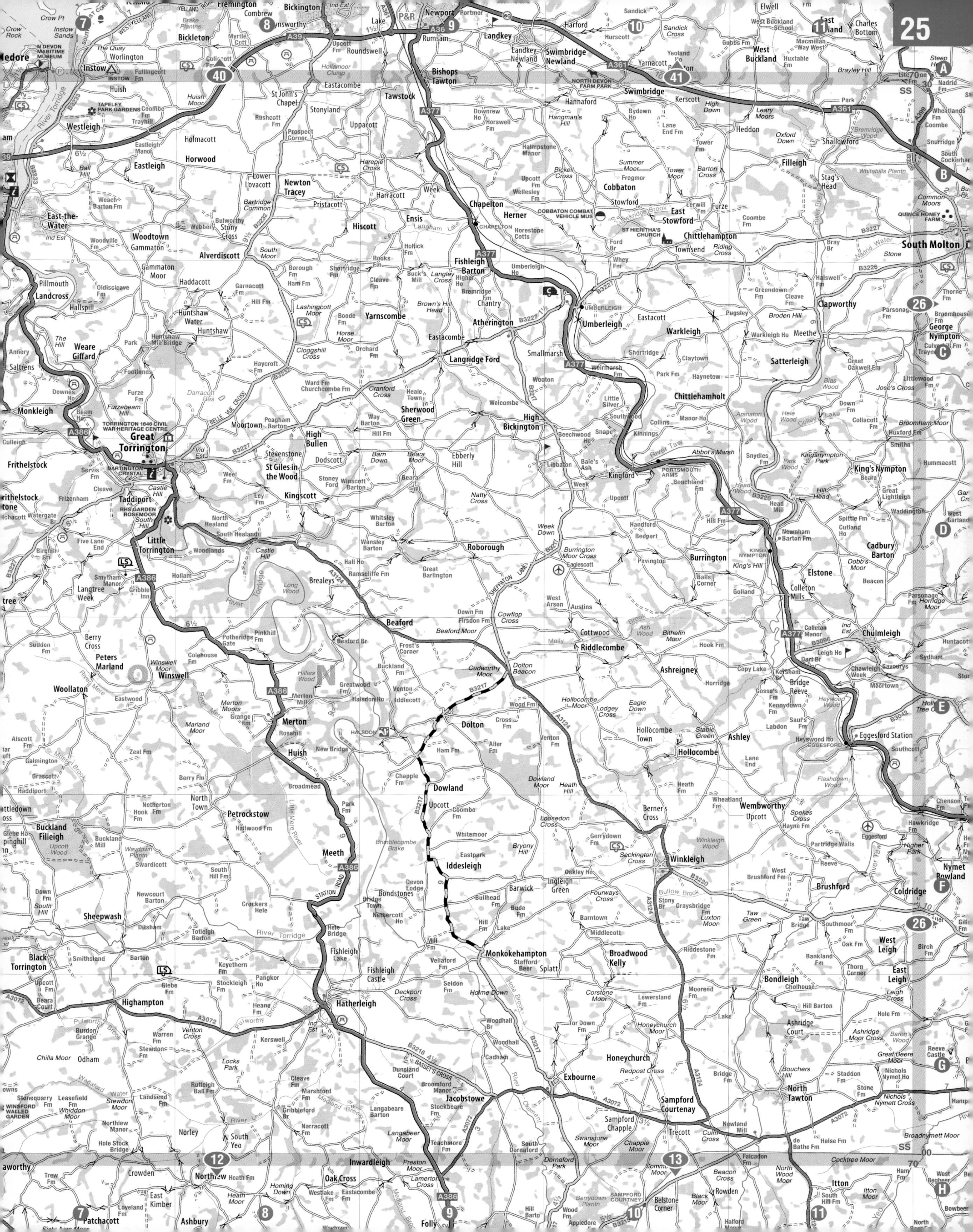

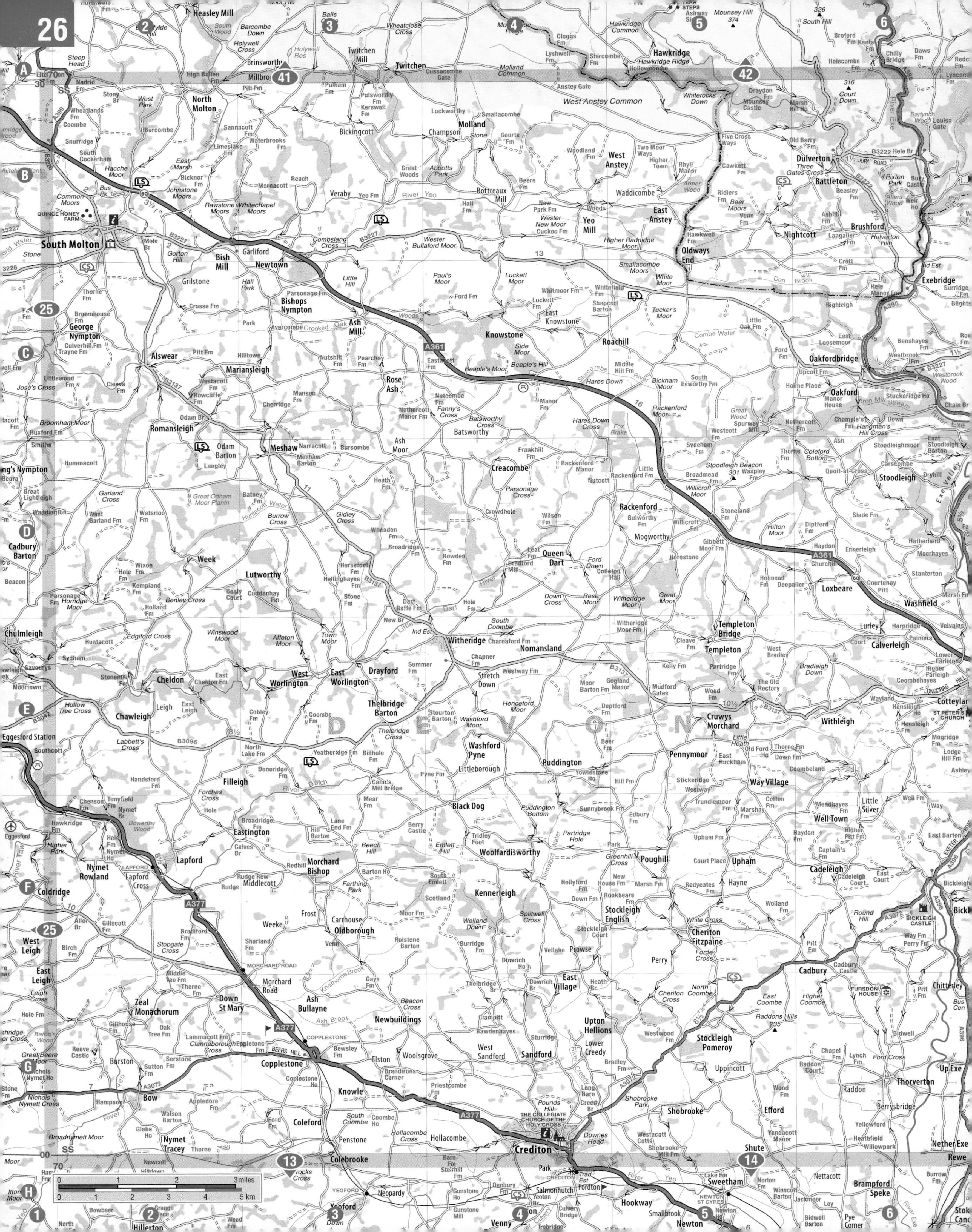

Heasley Mill
Barcombe Down
Holywell Cross
Brinsworthy
Twitchen Mill
Twitchen
Wheatclose Cross
Hawkridge Common
Hawkridge
Hawkridge Ridge
Mounsey Hill 374
South Hill
Steep Head
High Bullen Fm
Millbrook
Molland Common
Anstey Gate
West Anstey Common
Whiterocks Down
Mounsey Castle
Court Down
North Molton
West Park
Wheatlands Fm
Coombe
Snurridge
South Cockerham
Hacche Moor
Burcombe
Sannacott Fm
Limeslake Fm
Waterbrooks Fm
East Marsh
Bicknor Fm
Johnstone Moors
Mornacott
Reach
Bickingcott
Champson
Molland
Smallacombe
Stone
Great Woods
Abbotts Park
Veraby
Yeo Fm
River Yeo
Bottreaux Mill
Hall Fm
Beere Fm
Woodland Fm
West Anstey
Two Moor Ways
Higher Town
Rhyll Manor
Armer Wood
Five Cross Ways
Cawkett Fm
Old Berry Fm
Dulverton
Three Gates Cross
Battleton
Pixton Park
Bury Castle
Weir Ho
Hele Br
Common Moors
Quince Honey Farm
Bus Pk
South Molton
Rawstone Moors
Whitechapel Moors
New Park Fm
Wester New Moor
Cuckoo Fm
Yeo Mill
Waddicombe
East Anstey
Ridlers Fm
Beer Moors
Venn Fm
Nightcott
Langaller Fm
Brushford
Hulverton Hill
Mole Br
Gorton Hill
Bish Mill
Garliford
Newtown
Combsland Cross
Wester Bullaford Moor
Higher Radnidge Moor
Hawkwell Fm
Oldways End
Smallacombe Moors
White Moor
Den Brook
Exebridge
Grilstone
Hall Park
Parsonage Fm
Little Hill
Paul's Moor
Luckett Moor
Whitmoor Fm
Whitefield Fm
Shapcott Barton
Tucker's Moor
Thorne Fm
Bishops Nympton
Ford Fm
Luckett Fm
East Knowstone
Little Oak Fm
Highleigh
Broomhouse Fm
George Nympton
Culverhill Fm
Trayne Fm
Crosse Fm
Park
Avercombe
Crooked Oak
Ash Mill
Woods
Knowstone
Side Moor
Beaple's Hill
Roachill
Combe Water
East Loosemoor
Oakfordbridge
Westbrook Fm
Alswear
Pitt Fm
Hilltown
Mariansleigh
Nutshill Fm
Pearchay Fm
Rose Ash
Eastacott Fm
Beaple's Moor
Hares Down
Middle Hill Fm
Bickham Moor
South Esworthy Fm
Upcott Fm
Holme Place
Oakford
Manor House
Stuckeridge Ho
Iron Mill Stream
Littlewood Fm
Jose's Cross
Cleave Fm
Westacott Fm
Rowcliffe Fm
Munson Fm
Nutcombe
Fanny's Cross
Nethercott Manor Fm
Manor Fm
Rackenford Moor
Great Wood
Spurway Mill
Westcott Fm
Nethercott Fm
Chample's Fm
Hangman's Hill Cross
Broomham Moor
Huxford Fm
Odam Br
Cherridge
Romansleigh
Odam Barton
Langley
Meshaw
Narracott
Meshaw Barton
Burcombe
Ash Moor
Batsworthy Cross
Batsworthy
Hares Down Cross
Fox Brake
Sydeham Fm
Stoodleigh Beacon 301
Waspley Fm
Thorne Fm
Coleford Bottom
Stoodleighmoor
East Stoodleigh Barton
Carscombe
Quoit-at-Cross
Stoodleigh
Exe Valley
Hummacott
King's Nympton
Great Lightleigh
Garland Cross
Great Odham Moor Plantn
Frankhill Fm
Creacombe
Rackenford Manor
Little Rackenford Fm
Nutcott
Parsonage Cross
Broadmead Fm
Willicroft Moor
Heath Fm
Waddington
West Garland Fm
Waterloo Fm
Batney Fm
Huntacott Water
Burrow Cross
Gidley Cross
Crowdhole
Rackenford
Bulworthy Fm
Willicroft Fm
Stoneland Fm
Rifton Moor
Diptford Fm
Slade Fm
Cadbury Barton
Wheadon Fm
Broadridge Fm
Wilson Fm
Mogworthy
Gibbett Moor Fm
Haydon
Hatherland
Week
Rowden Fm
Queen Dart
Leat Fm
Bradford Mill
Ford Down
Colleton Hall
Horestone
Ennerleigh
Moorhayes
Churchill
Beacon
Wixon Fm
Hole Fm
Kempland Fm
Lutworthy
Horseford Fm
Hellinghayes Fm
Stanterton
Parsonage Fm
Horridge Moor
Benley Cross
Bealy Court
Cuddenhay Fm
Stone Fm
Down Cross
Rose Moor
Witheridge Moor
Great Moor
Holmead Fm
Deepaller
Loxbeare
Courtenay Pitt
Washfield
Holland Fm
Dart Raffe Fm
Hole Fm
Marsh Fm
Chulmleigh
Winswood Moor
Affeton Moor
Town Moor
New Br
Little Dart
Ind Est
South Coombe
Witheridge
Charnaford Fm
Witheridge Moor Fm
Templeton Bridge
Lurley
Harpridge
Velvains
Edgiford Cross
Huntacott
Cleave Fm
Templeton
Calverleigh
Sydham
Nomansland
Chapner Fm
Summer Fm
West Bradley
Kelly Fm
Partridge Fm
Bradleigh Down
Lower Farleigh
Higher Farleigh
Savoury's
Stonemill
Cheldon
Cheldon Fm
East Leigh
West Worlington
East Worlington
Drayford
Stretch Down
Westway Fm
Moor Barton Fm
Gogland Manor
Mudford Gates
The Old Rectory
Coombehayes
Moortown
Hollow Tree Cross
Chawleigh
Leigh
Cobley Fm
Coombe Fm
Thelbridge Barton
Stourton Barton
Washford Moor
Henceford Moor
Deptford Fm
Wood Fm
Cruwys Morchard
Wayland
Hensleigh Ho
Cotteylands
St Peter's Church
Withleigh
D E V O N
Eggesford Station
Southcott
Labbett's Cross
Thelbridge Cross
Washford Pyne
Beer Fm
Little Heath
Old Ford Ho
Thorne Fm
Down Fm
Mogridge Fm
Lodge Hill Fm
Ashley
North Lake Fm
Yeatheridge Fm
Billhole Fm
Littleborough
Puddington
Pennymoor
East Ruckham
Coombeland
Handsford Fm
Tonyfield Fm
Deneridge Fm
Cann's Mill Bridge
Pyne Fm
Yowlestone Ho
Hill Fm
Stickeridge Fm
Westway
Way Village
Filleigh
River Dalch
Forches Cross
Chenson Fm
Nymet Br
Hole
Mear Fm
Black Dog
Puddington Bottom
Sunnybrook Fm
Trundlemoor Fm
Marshay Fm
Cotten Fm
Meadhayes Fm
Little Silver
Well Fm
Way
Hawkridge Fm
Eggesford
Bowerthy Wood
Broadridge Fm
Eastington
Lane End Fm
Berry Castle
Edbury Fm
Well Town
Higher Park
Hele Fm
Nymet Br
Calves Br
Hill Barton
Beech Hill
Emlett Hill
Tridley Foot
Woolfardisworthy
Partridge Hole
Park
Upham Fm
Haydon Fm
Higher Pitt Fm
East Barton
Nymet Rowland
Lapford
Lapford Cross
Morchard Bishop
Redhill
Barton Ho
Greenhill Cross
Poughill
Court Place
Upham
Captain's Fm
Cadeleigh
Cadeleigh Court
East Court
Coldridge
Rudge
Rudge Rew
Middlecott
Farthing Park
South Emlett
Kennerleigh
Hollyford Fm
New House Fm
Marsh Fm
Redyeates Fm
Hayne
Bickleigh
Aller Br
Gillscott Fm
Frost
Scotland
Down Fm
Rookbeare Fm
Stockleigh English
Wolland Fm
Round Hill
Bickleigh Castle
West Leigh
Weeke
Carrhouse
Oldborough
Moor Fm
Welland Down
Splitwell Cross
Stockleigh Court
White Cross
Cheriton Fitzpaine
Way Fm
Perry Fm
Birch Fm
Stopgate Cross
Bradiford Fm
Sharland Fm
Venn
Rolstone Barton
Burridge Fm
Vellake
Prowse
Forde Cross
Pitt Fm
East Leigh
Middle Yeo Fm
Morchard Road
Dowrich Ho
Perry
Cadbury
Cadbury Castle
Leigh Cross
Thorne Fm
Gays Fm
Knathorne Brook
Thelbridge Ho
Dowrich Br
East Village
Heath Br
Cheriton Cross
North Coombe
Fursdon House
Pitt Fm
Chitterley
Hole Fm
Zeal Monachorum
Oak Tree Fm
Down St Mary
Ash Bullayne
Beacon Cross
Clampitt
Higher Coombe
East Coombe
Raddons Hills 235
Ash Brook
Newbuildings
Bawdenhayes
Sturridge
Upton Hellions
Westwood Fm
Bidwell
Gillhouse Fm
Lammacott Fm
Clannaborough Cross
Eppletons Fm
Copplestone
Reeve Castle
Burston
Sutton Fm
Serstone Fm
Beers Hill
Copplestone
Bewsley Fm
Elston
Woolsgrove
West Sandford
Sandford
Lower Creedy
Stockleigh Pomeroy
Chapel Fm
Lynch Fm
Ford Cross
Up Exe
Great Beere Moor
Nichols Nymet Ho
Coplestone Ho
Brandirons Corner
Bradley Fm
Uppincott
Raddon Court
Thorverton
Bow
Hampson
Appledore Fm
Knowle
Priestcombe
Shobrooke Park
Long Barn
Creedy Br
Shobrooke
Wood Fm
Raddon
Berrysbridge
Nichols Nymett Cross
Walson Barton
Glebe Ho
Ford Fm
Coleford
South Coombe
Coombe Ho
Pounds Hill
The Collegiate Church of the Holy Cross
Downes Head
Westacott Cotts
Efford
Yellowford
Heathfield
Willowpark
Yendacott Manor
Broadnymett Moor
Nymet Tracey
Thorne
Penstone
Hollacombe Cross
Hollacombe
Crediton
Shobrooke Mill Fm
Shute
Nether Exe
Moor
Newcott
Colebrooke
Crocks Cross
Barn Fm
Stairhill Fm
Park
Trad Est
Fordton
River Yeo
Lake Fm
Sweetham
Nettacott
Rewe
Burrow Fm
Itton Moor
Yeoford
Neopardy
Gunstone Ho
Denbury Fm
Salmonhutch
Yeoton
Hookway
Smallbrook
Norton Fm
Winscott Barton
Newton St Cyres
Jackmoor
Ley
Brampford Speke
Bowbeer
Grange
Hillerton
Gunstone Mill
Culvery Bridge
Wood Fm
Yeoford
Down
Venny
Newton
Bidwell Barton
Pye Corner
Troubridge
3miles
5 km

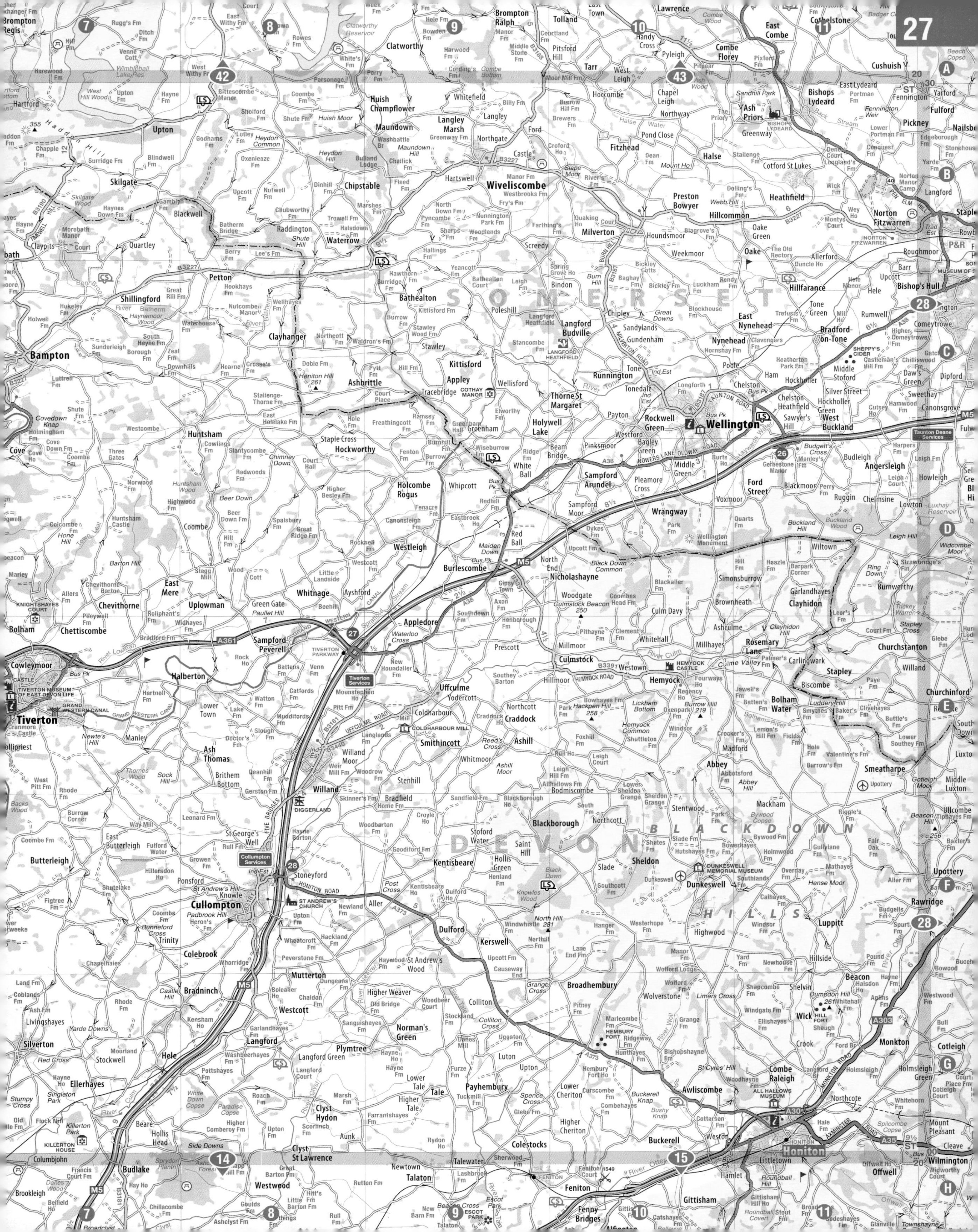

Brompton Regis
Clatworthy
Brompton Ralph
Tolland
Lawrence
East Combe
Cothelstone
Combe Florey
Cushuish
Huish Champflower
Bishops Lydeard
Yarford
Fulford
Hartford
Upton
Langley Marsh
Maundown
Northgate
Fitzhead
Halse
Pickney
Skilgate
Chipstable
Wiveliscombe
Preston Bowyer
Heathfield
Blackwell
Raddington
Waterrow
Milverton
Hillcommon
Norton Fitzwarren
Oake
Petton
Shillingford
Bathealton
S O M E R S E T
Hillfarance
Bishop's Hull
Clayhanger
Langford Budville
Chipley
East Nynehead
Nynehead
Bradford-on-Tone
Bampton
Kittisford
Appley
Runnington
Ashbrittle
Thorne St Margaret
Huntsham
Holywell Lake
Rockwell Green
Wellington
West Buckland
Hockworthy
Sampford Arundel
Angersleigh
Holcombe Rogus
Whipcott
Ford Street
Wrangway
Westleigh
Burlescombe
Nicholashayne
Chevithorne
Uplowman
Whitnage
East Mere
Appledore
Culm Davy
Clayhidon
Bolham
Chettiscombe
Sampford Peverell
Rosemary Lane
Churchstanton
Cowleymoor
Halberton
Culmstock
Hemyock
Stapley
Tiverton
Uffculme
Craddock
Bolham Water
Churchinford
Ash Thomas
Smithincott
Ashill
Abbey
Willand
Smeatharpe
Blackborough
B L A C K D O W N
Butterleigh
D E V O N
Sheldon
Upottery
Kentisbeare
Dunkeswell
Cullompton
Dulford
Kerswell
H I L L S
Luppitt
Rawridge
Colebrook
Mutterton
Broadhembury
Bradninch
Westcott
Norman's Green
Beacon
Wick
Monkton
Silverton
Langford
Plymtree
Hele
Combe Raleigh
Cotleigh
Ellerhayes
Payhembury
Awliscombe
Clyst Hydon
Honiton
Clyst St Lawrence
Colestocks
Buckerell
Budlake
Talaton
Feniton
Wilmington
Offwell
Westwood
Gittisham
Fenny Bridges
M5
A38
A361
A373
A30
A35
A303

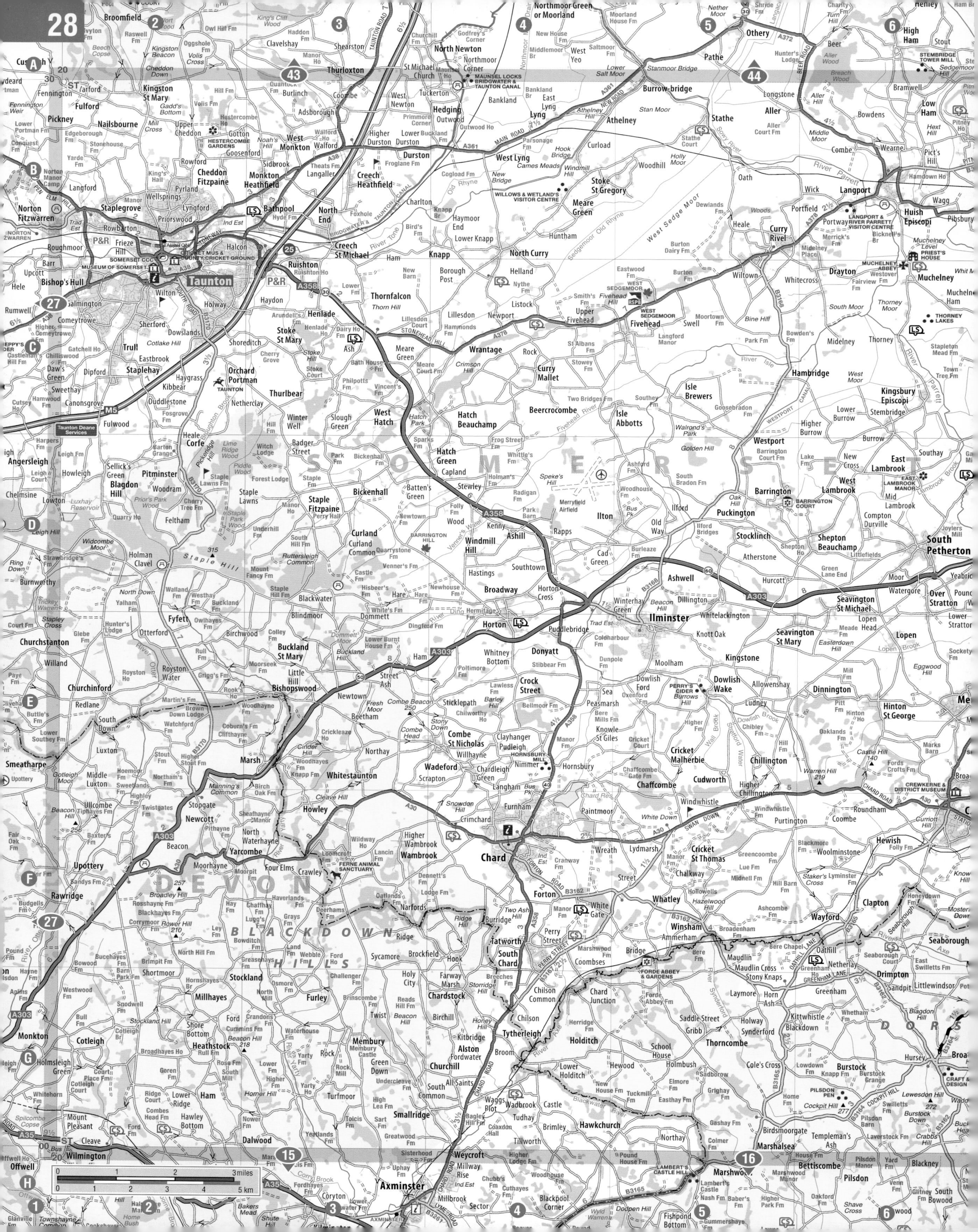

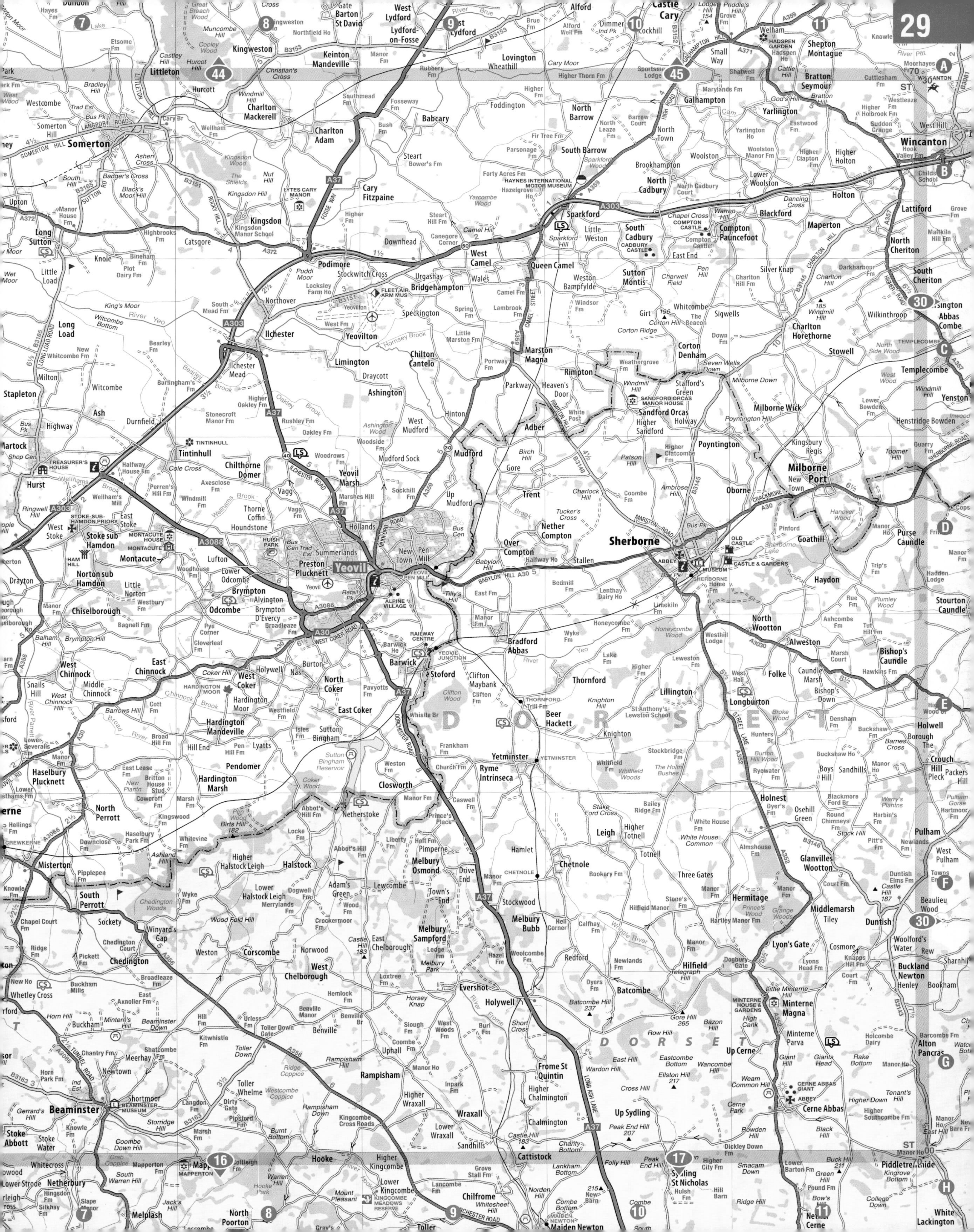
Somerton
Langport
Littleton
Kingweston
Charlton Mackerell
Charlton Adam
Keinton Mandeville
Lydford-on-Fosse
West Lydford
Lovington
Babcary
North Barrow
South Barrow
Castle Cary
Galhampton
Yarlington
Wincanton
Bratton Seymour
Shepton Montague
North Cadbury
South Cadbury
Sparkford
Queen Camel
West Camel
Compton Pauncefoot
Blackford
Maperton
North Cheriton
South Cheriton
Kingsdon
Long Sutton
Podimore
Bridgehampton
Ilchester
Yeovilton
Limington
Chilton Cantelo
Marston Magna
Rimpton
Corton Denham
Charlton Horethorne
Stowell
Templecombe
Sandford Orcas
Milborne Wick
Milborne Port
Mudford
Yeovil
Preston Plucknett
Tintinhull
Montacute
Stoke sub Hamdon
Norton sub Hamdon
Chiselborough
Odcombe
Brympton
West Coker
East Coker
North Coker
Barwick
Stoford
Bradford Abbas
Nether Compton
Over Compton
Sherborne
Goathill
Haydon
North Wootton
Thornford
Beer Hackett
Yetminster
Ryme Intrinseca
Longburton
Lillington
Folke
Alweston
Bishop's Caundle
Hardington Mandeville
Hardington Marsh
Pendomer
Closworth
Haselbury Plucknett
North Perrott
South Perrott
Misterton
Crewkerne
Halstock
Melbury Osmond
Melbury Sampford
Leigh
Chetnole
Holnest
Glanvilles Wootton
Hermitage
Middlemarsh
Pulham
Corscombe
Chedington
West Chelborough
Evershot
Holywell
Batcombe
Hilfield
Minterne Magna
Beaminster
Rampisham
Wraxall
Frome St Quintin
Cattistock
Up Cerne
Up Sydling
Sydling St Nicholas
Cerne Abbas
Alton Pancras
Piddletrenthide
Chilfrome
Maiden Newton
Hooke
Netherbury
Melplash
North Poorton
Toller
Buckland Newton
Duntish
DORSET
A303
A37
A30
A3088
A359
A356
A352
A371

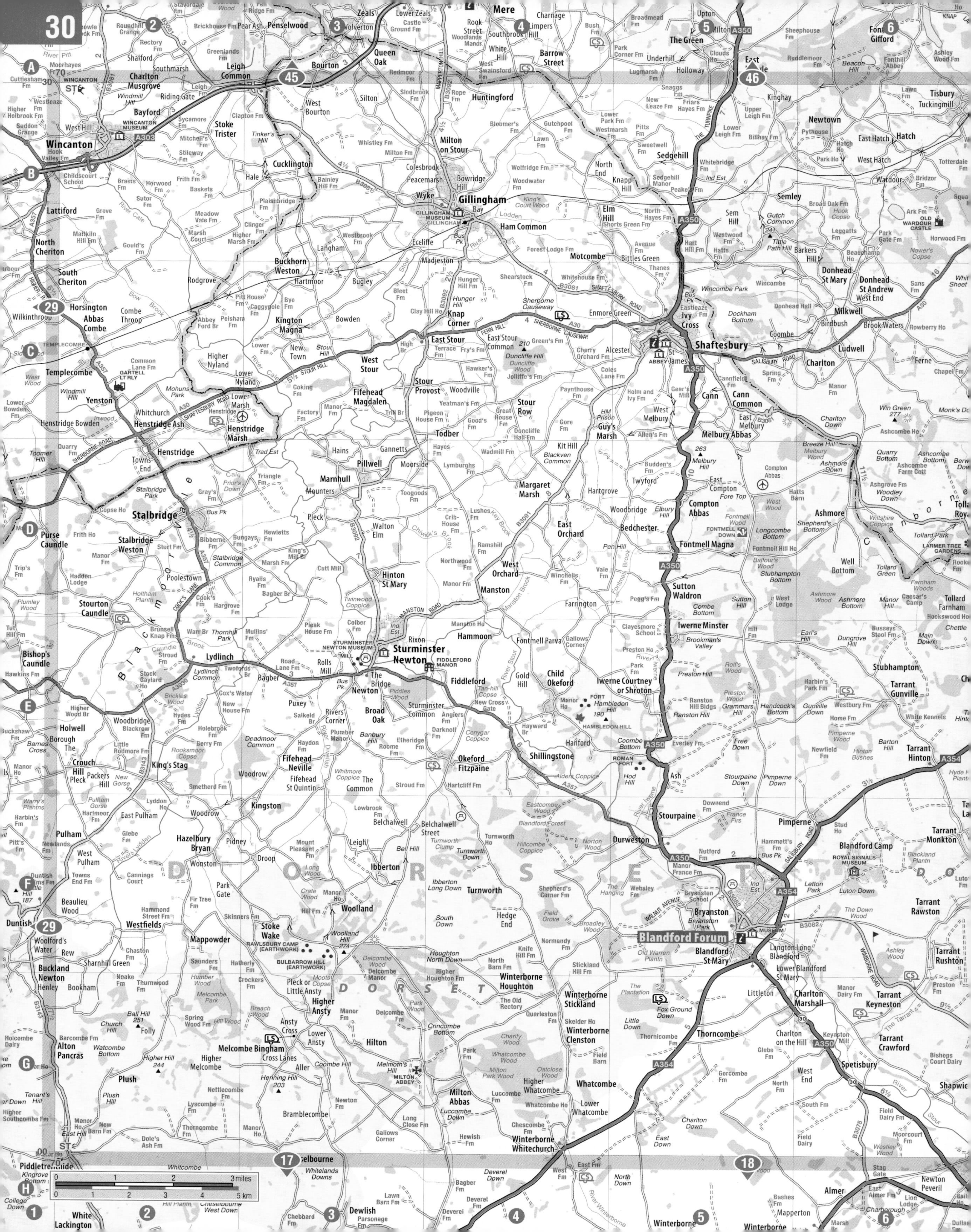

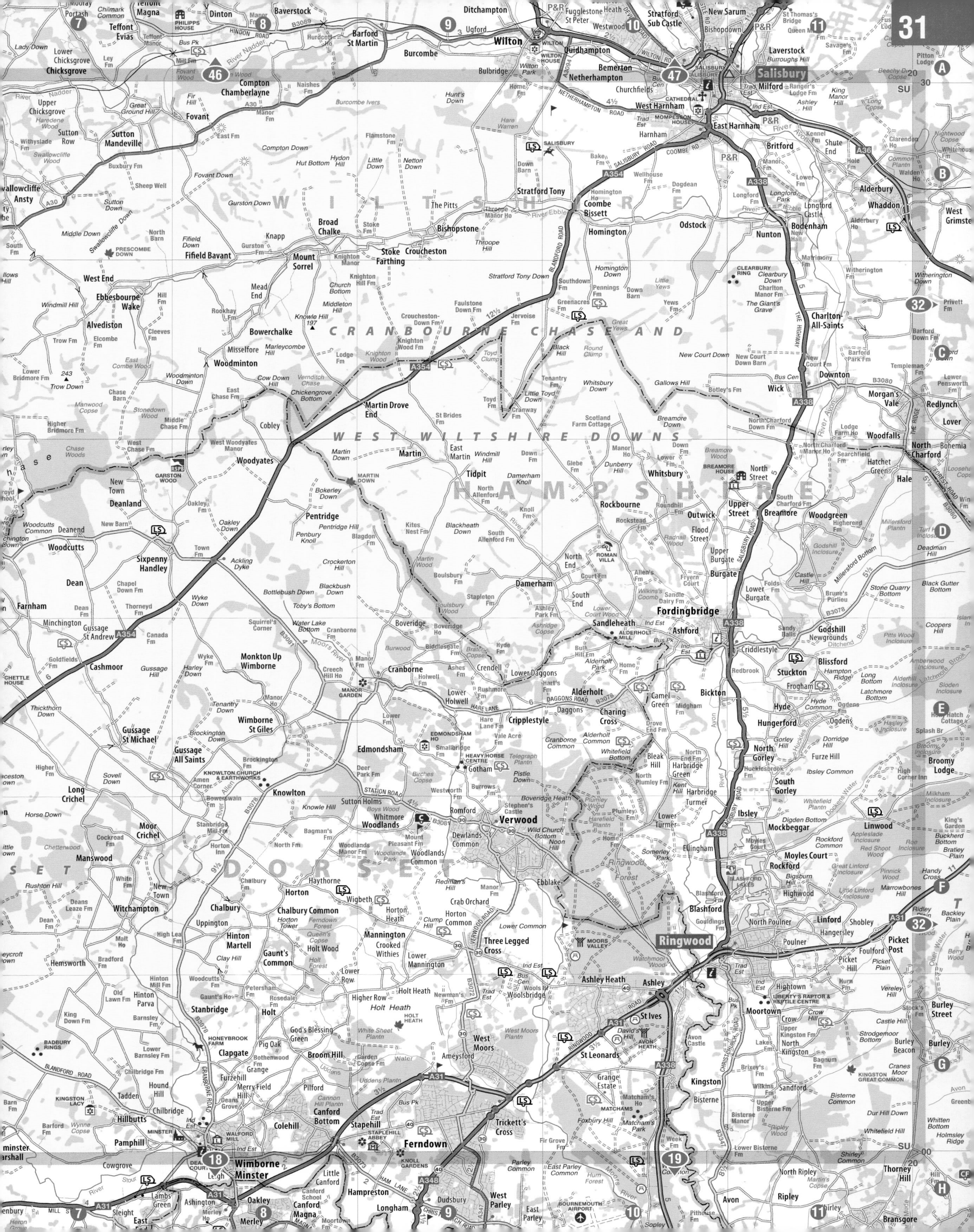
Teffont Evias
Dinton
Baverstock
Barford St Martin
Ditchampton
Wilton
Fugglestone St Peter
Stratford Sub Castle
New Sarum
Bishopdown
Laverstock
Chicksgrove
Compton Chamberlayne
Burcombe
Quidhampton
Bemerton
Netherhampton
Salisbury
Milford
West Harnham
East Harnham
Harnham
Fovant
Sutton Mandeville
Britford
Alderbury
Whaddon
West Grimstead
Ansty
Stratford Tony
Coombe Bissett
Homington
Odstock
Nunton
Bodenham
Broad Chalke
Bishopstone
Stoke Farthing
Croucheston
Mount Sorrel
Fifield Bavant
West End
Ebbesbourne Wake
Alvediston
Bowerchalke
Woodminton
Charlton-All-Saints
Downton
Wick
Morgan's Vale
Redlynch
Lover
Woodfalls
North Charford
Hale
W I L T S H I R E
C R A N B O U R N E   C H A S E   A N D
W E S T   W I L T S H I R E   D O W N S
H A M P S H I R E
D O R S E T
Martin Drove End
Martin
East Martin
Tidpit
Cobley
Woodyates
New Town
Deanland
Pentridge
Rockbourne
Whitsbury
Outwick
Upper Street
Breamore
Woodgreen
Woodcutts
Sixpenny Handley
Dean
Farnham
Gussage St Andrew
Cashmoor
Damerham
South End
North End
Burgate
Lower Burgate
Fordingbridge
Sandleheath
Ashford
Godshill
Boveridge
Cranborne
Monkton Up Wimborne
Wimborne St Giles
Gussage St Michael
Gussage All Saints
Alderholt
Cripplestyle
Daggons
Charing Cross
Camel Green
Bickton
Stuckton
Blissford
Hyde
Hungerford
North Gorley
South Gorley
Broomy Lodge
Edmondsham
Gotham
Knowlton
Long Crichel
Moor Crichel
Manswood
Witchampton
Verwood
Romford
Dewlands Common
Woodlands
Bleak Hill
Harbridge
Ibsley
Mockbeggar
Linwood
Moyles Court
Rockford
Ellingham
Blashford
Highwood
Horton
Chalbury
Chalbury Common
Hinton Martell
Gaunt's Common
Holt Wood
Mannington
Three Legged Cross
Ringwood
North Poulner
Poulner
Linford
Hangersley
Picket Post
Ashley Heath
Ashley
St Ives
St Leonards
West Moors
Holt
Stanbridge
Clapgate
Broom Hill
Pilford
Canford Bottom
Colehill
Stapehill
Ferndown
Trickett's Cross
Moortown
Crow
Kingston
Bisterne
Sandford
Burley
Burley Street
Hillbutts
Pamphill
Wimborne Minster
Little Canford
Hampreston
Longham
West Parley
East Parley
Avon
Ripley
Thorney Hill
Bransgore
Sopley
Canford Magna
Oakley
Merley
Ashington
Sleight
Lambs' Green
A30
A354
A338
A31
A348
A36
B3078
B3081
B3072
B3089
B3080

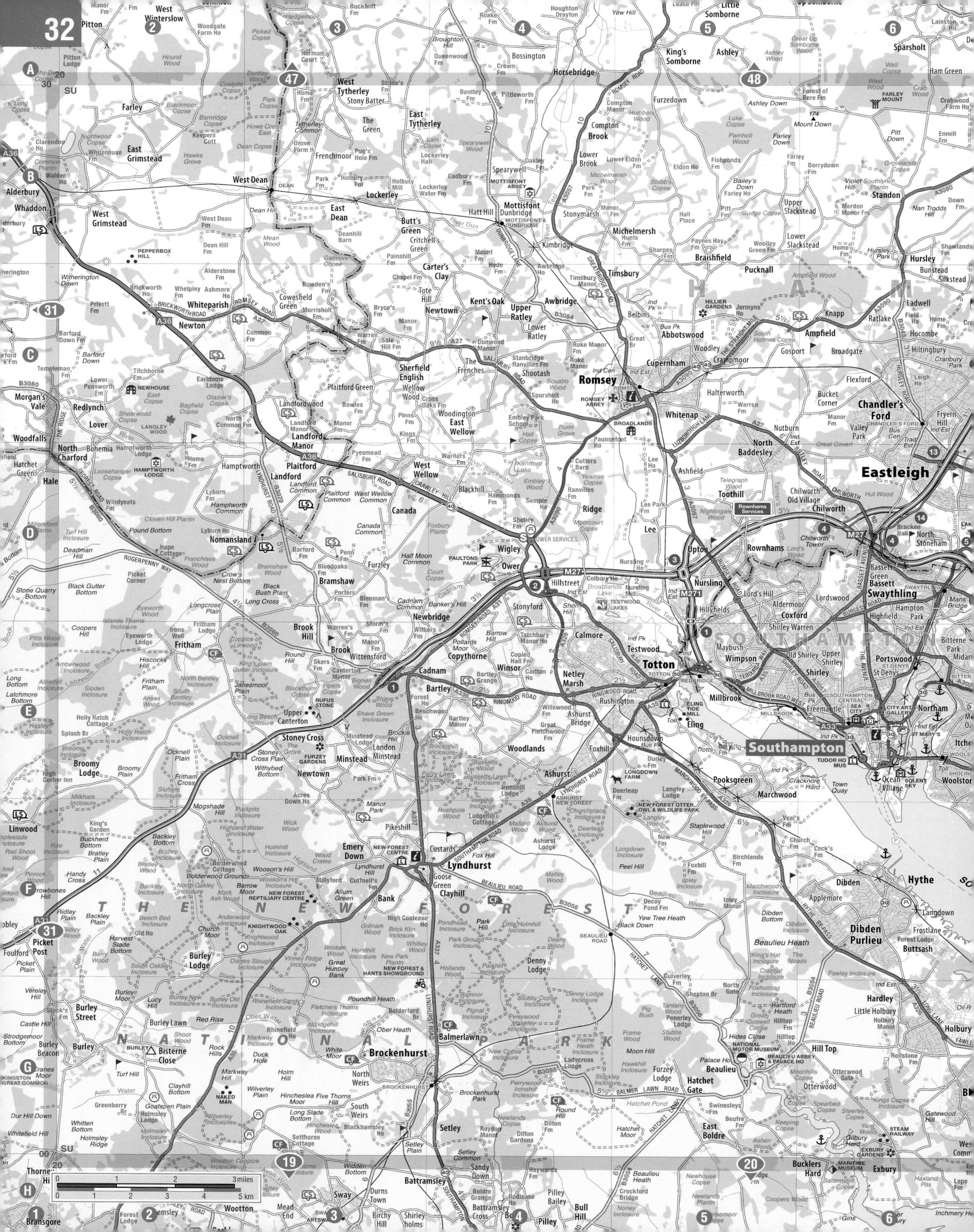

Pitton
West Winterslow
Farley
East Grimstead
West Grimstead
West Dean
Alderbury
Whaddon
Whiteparish
Newton
Redlynch
Lover
Woodfalls
Morgan's Vale
North Charford
Hale
Hamptworth
Landford
Plaitford
Nomansland
Bramshaw
Canada
Furzley
West Tytherley
East Tytherley
Lockerley
East Dean
Butt's Green
Carter's Clay
Newtown
Sherfield English
East Wellow
West Wellow
Mottisfont
Horsebridge
Kimbridge
King's Somborne
Ashley
Little Somborne
Sparsholt
Compton
Brook
Michelmersh
Timsbury
Awbridge
Upper Ratley
Kent's Oak
Romsey
Braishfield
Ampfield
Hursley
Standon
Chandler's Ford
Eastleigh
North Baddesley
Chilworth
Nursling
Rownhams
Bassett
Swaythling
Upton
Totton
Calmore
Testwood
Netley Marsh
Cadnam
Bartley
Copythorne
Ower
Wigley
Brook
Minstead
Stoney Cross
Lyndhurst
Emery Down
Bank
Ashurst
Woodlands
Marchwood
Eling
Redbridge
Millbrook
Shirley
Portswood
Northam
Southampton
Hythe
Dibden
Dibden Purlieu
Fawley
Holbury
Hardley
Beaulieu
Hatchet Gate
East Boldre
Bucklers Hard
Exbury
Brockenhurst
Balmerlawn
Setley
Battramsley
Sway
Burley
Burley Street
Bisterne Close
Picket Post
Linwood
Fritham
Rockford
Boldre
Pilley
Bull Hill
Bransgore
Wootton
THE NEW FOREST NATIONAL PARK
SOUTHAMPTON
HAMPSHIRE
M27
M271
A36
A31
A35
A337
A326
A33
A3090
A27
B3079
B3078
B3056
B3054
B3055
0 1 2 3 miles
0 1 2 3 4 5 km

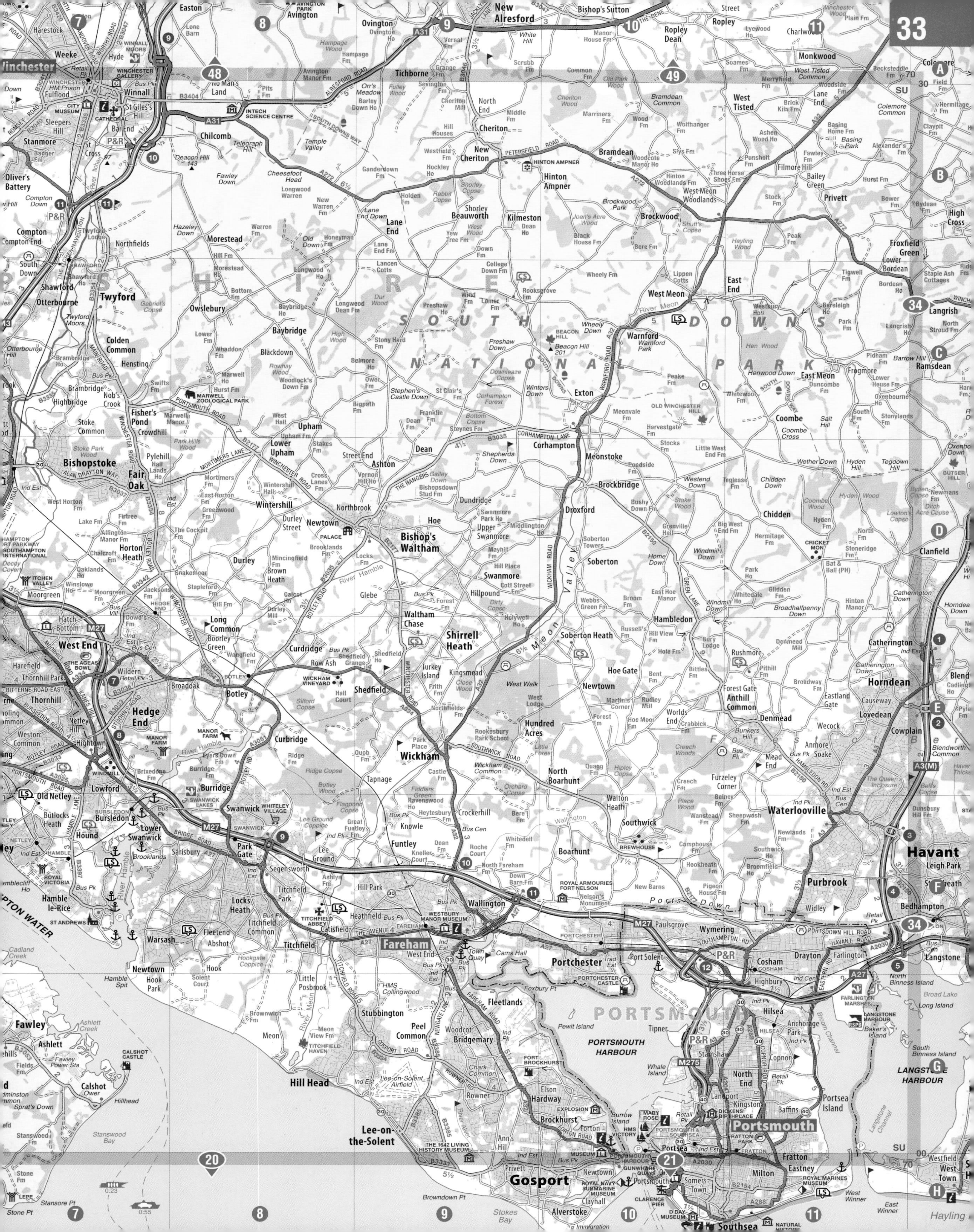

Winchester
Weeke
Harestock
Fulflood
Winnall
St Giles's Hill
Bar End
Stanmore
Chilcomb
Oliver's Battery
Compton
Compton End
South Down
Shawford
Otterbourne
Twyford
Colden Common
Hensting
Owslebury
Morestead
Baybridge
Brambridge
Highbridge
Nob's Crook
Fisher's Pond
Crowdhill
Stoke Common
Bishopstoke
Fair Oak
Pylehill
Horton Heath
Durley
Upham
Lower Upham
Ashton
Dean
Corhampton
Meonstoke
Exton
Droxford
Soberton
Soberton Heath
Hambledon
Brockbridge
Northbrook
Newtown
Bishop's Waltham
Hoe
Upper Swanmore
Swanmore
Hillpound
Waltham Chase
Shirrell Heath
Curdridge
Botley
Broadoak
Hedge End
West End
Moorgreen
Harefield
Thornhill Park
Thornhill
Netley
Hightown
Weston Common
Lowford
Old Netley
Bursledon
Butlocks Heath
Hound
Lower Swanwick
Swanwick
Burridge
Curbridge
Park Gate
Sarisbury
Segensworth
Locks Heath
Titchfield Common
Warsash
Hamble-le-Rice
Titchfield
Titchfield Park
Fareham
Wickham
Knowle
Funtley
Shedfield
Wallington
North Fareham
Portchester
Fleetlands
Peel Common
Bridgemary
Stubbington
Hill Head
Lee-on-the-Solent
Rowner
Hardway
Brockhurst
Gosport
Alverstoke
Clayhall
Cosham
Drayton
Farlington
Hilsea
North End
Portsmouth
Southsea
Fratton
Milton
Eastney
Portsea Island
Portsmouth Harbour
Purbrook
Waterlooville
Havant
Bedhampton
Langstone
Horndean
Cowplain
Lovedean
Denmead
Southwick
Boarhunt
North Boarhunt
Hundred Acres
Clanfield
Chidden
East Meon
Langrish
Ramsdean
Frogmore
Warnford
West Meon
East End
Privett
Froxfield Green
High Cross
Coombe
Bramdean
Brockwood
Hinton Ampner
Kilmeston
Beauworth
Cheriton
New Cheriton
North End
Lane End
Tichborne
New Alresford
Ovington
Avington
Easton
Bishop's Sutton
Ropley
Ropley Dean
West Tisted
Monkwood
Colemore
Fawley
Ashlett
Calshot
SOUTH DOWNS NATIONAL PARK
PORTSMOUTH
LANGSTONE HARBOUR
Hayling

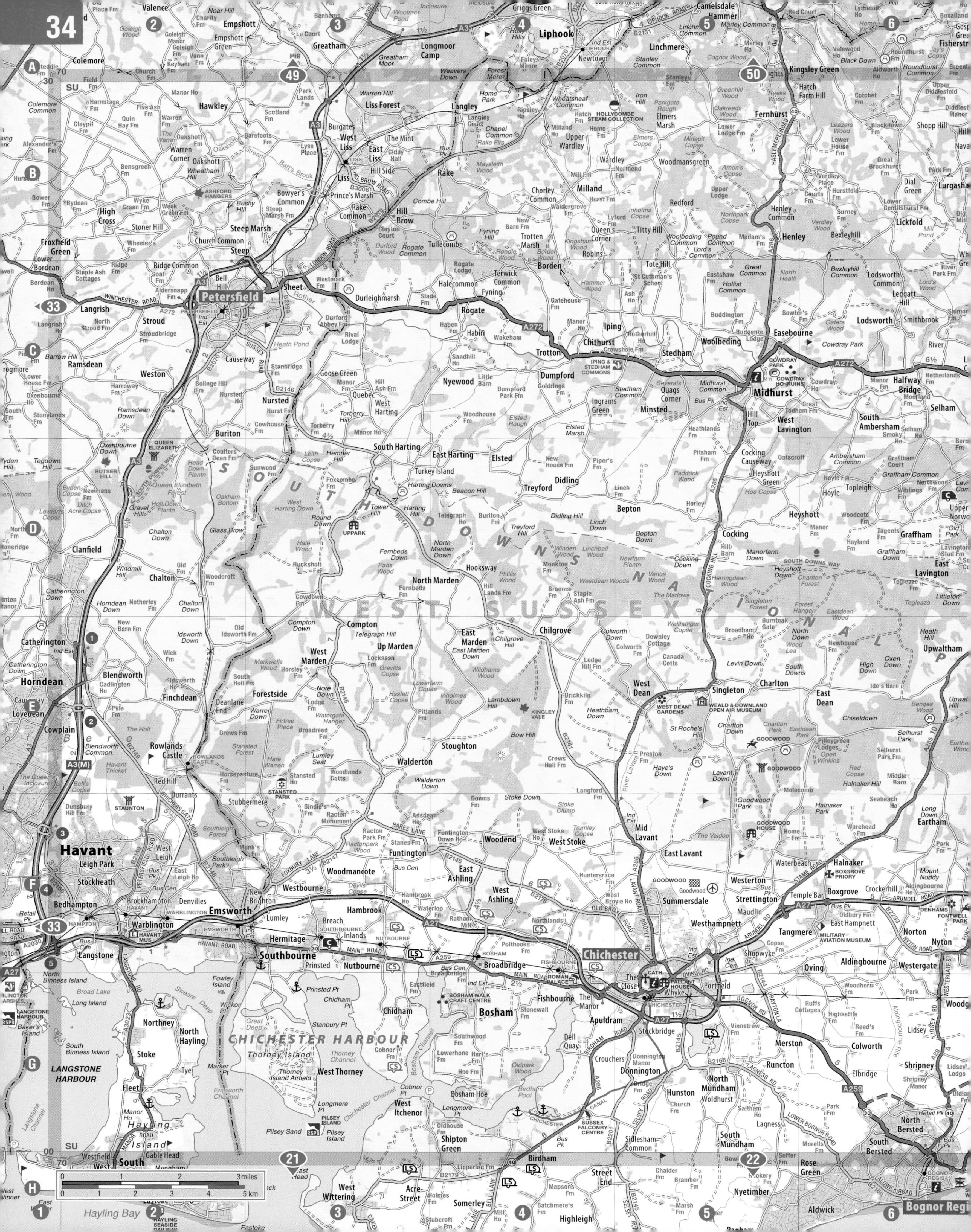
Valence
Empshott
Greatham
Longmoor Camp
Liphook
Camelsdale
Hammer
Linchmere
Colemore
Kingsley Green
Hawkley
Liss Forest
Langley
HOLLYCOMBE STEAM COLLECTION
Fernhurst
West Liss
East Liss
Liss
Hill Side
Rake
Milland
Wardley
Woodmansgreen
ASHFORD HANGERS
Prince's Marsh
Hill Brow
Redford
Henley
Lickfold
Lurgashall
High Cross
Steep Marsh
Church Common
Steep
Froxfield Green
Tullecombe
Borden
Titty Hill
Bexleyhill
Petersfield
Sheet
Durleighmarsh
Rogate
Langrish
Stroud
Iping
Chithurst
Woolbeding
Easebourne
Lodsworth
Ramsdean
Causeway
Trotton
Stedham
Dumpford
Midhurst
Halfway Bridge
Selham
Weston
Nyewood
Minsted
Nursted
West Harting
Buriton
South Harting
East Harting
Elsted
West Lavington
South Ambersham
QUEEN ELIZABETH
Turkey Island
Treyford
Didling
Bepton
Heyshott
Cocking
Graffham
UPPARK
Clanfield
Chalton
North Marden
Hookway
WEST SUSSEX
SOUTH DOWNS NATIONAL PARK
Lavington
Catherington
Compton
Up Marden
East Marden
Chilgrove
Upwaltham
Horndean
Blendworth
West Marden
Charlton
Finchdean
Forestside
West Dean
Singleton
East Dean
WEALD & DOWNLAND OPEN AIR MUSEUM
WEST DEAN GARDENS
Lovedean
Cowplain
KINGLEY VALE
Rowlands Castle
Stoughton
GOODWOOD
Walderton
A3(M)
STANSTED PARK
STAUNTON
Stubbermere
Mid Lavant
GOODWOOD HOUSE
Havant
Leigh Park
Woodend
West Stoke
Funtington
East Lavant
Halnaker
Stockheath
Woodmancote
East Ashling
BOXGROVE PRIORY
Westbourne
West Ashling
Westerton
Boxgrove
Bedhampton
Warblington
Emsworth
Hambrook
Summersdale
Strettington
Crockerhill
Westhampnett
Tangmere
Norton
Nyton
HAVANT MUS
Hermitage
Lumley
Southbourne
Nutbourne
Broadbridge
Chichester
MILITARY AVIATION MUSEUM
Langstone
Prinsted
Fishbourne
CATH
PALLANT HOUSE
Portfield
Oving
Aldingbourne
Westergate
Whyke
Apuldram
Stockbridge
BOSHAM WALK CRAFT CENTRE
Bosham
Chidham
North Binness Island
Long Island
Northney
North Hayling
CHICHESTER HARBOUR
Thorney Island
West Thorney
Merston
Colworth
Runcton
Shripney
LANGSTONE HARBOUR
Stoke
Donnington
Hunston
North Mundham
Woldhurst
Fleet
Bosham Hoe
West Itchenor
SUSSEX FALCONRY CENTRE
Hayling Island
Shipton Green
South Mundham
North Bersted
South Bersted
Birdham
Sidlesham Common
Rose Green
West Wittering
Acre Street
Somerley
Street End
Highleigh
Nyetimber
Aldwick
Bognor Regis
Hayling Bay
0 1 2 3 miles
0 1 2 3 4 5 km

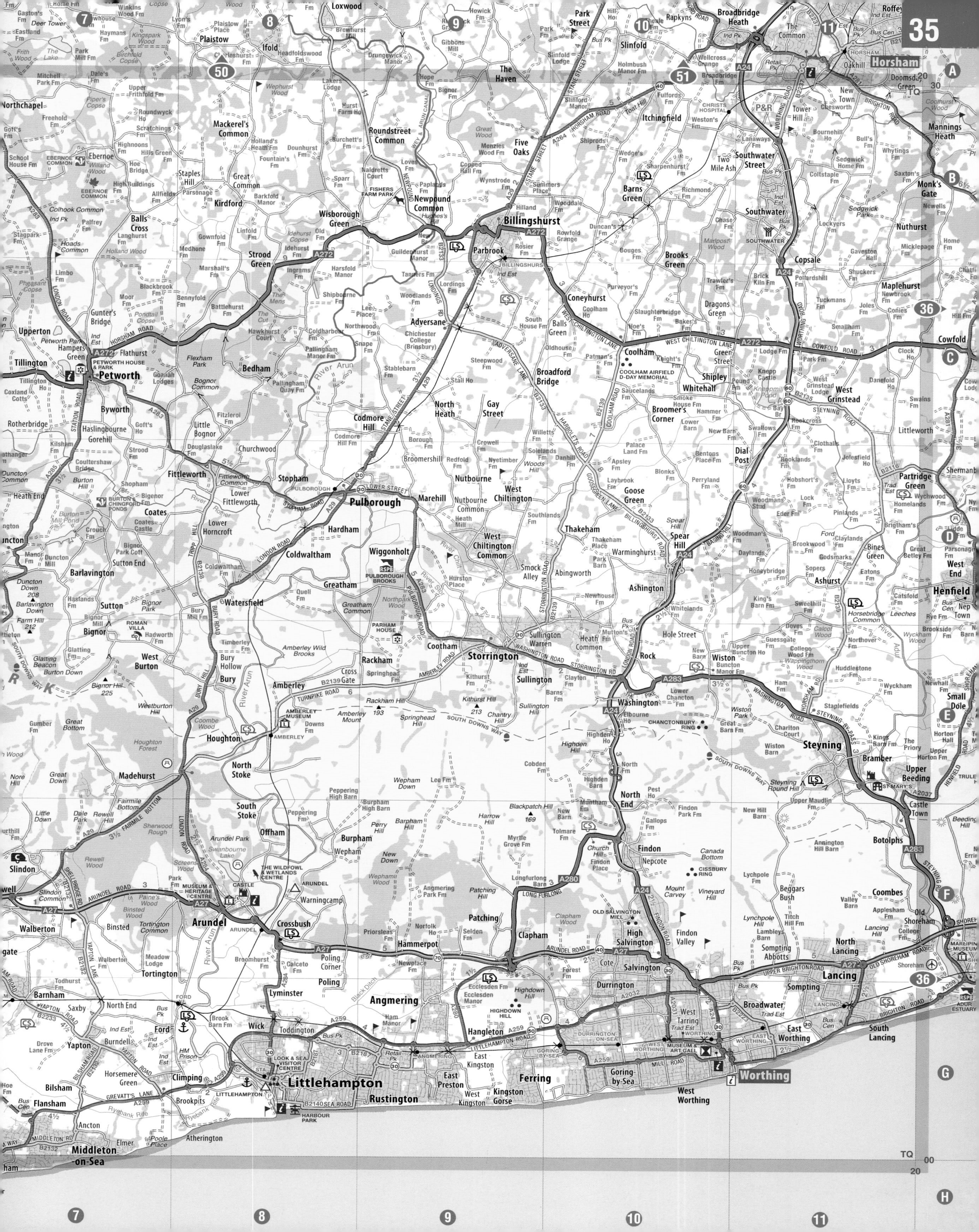
Horsham
Worthing
Petworth
Billingshurst
Pulborough
Storrington
Steyning
Arundel
Littlehampton
Rustington
Angmering
Lancing
Henfield
Ferring
Goring-by-Sea
Middleton-on-Sea
Findon
Washington
Ashington
Cowfold
West Grinstead
Southwater
Slinfold
Loxwood
Plaistow
Kirdford
Wisborough Green
Coolham
Shipley
Amberley
Bramber
Upper Beeding
Shoreham
Sompting
Durrington
Salvington
Clapham
Patching
Yapton
Ford
Climping
Fittleworth
Sutton
Bignor
Slindon
Walberton
Barnham

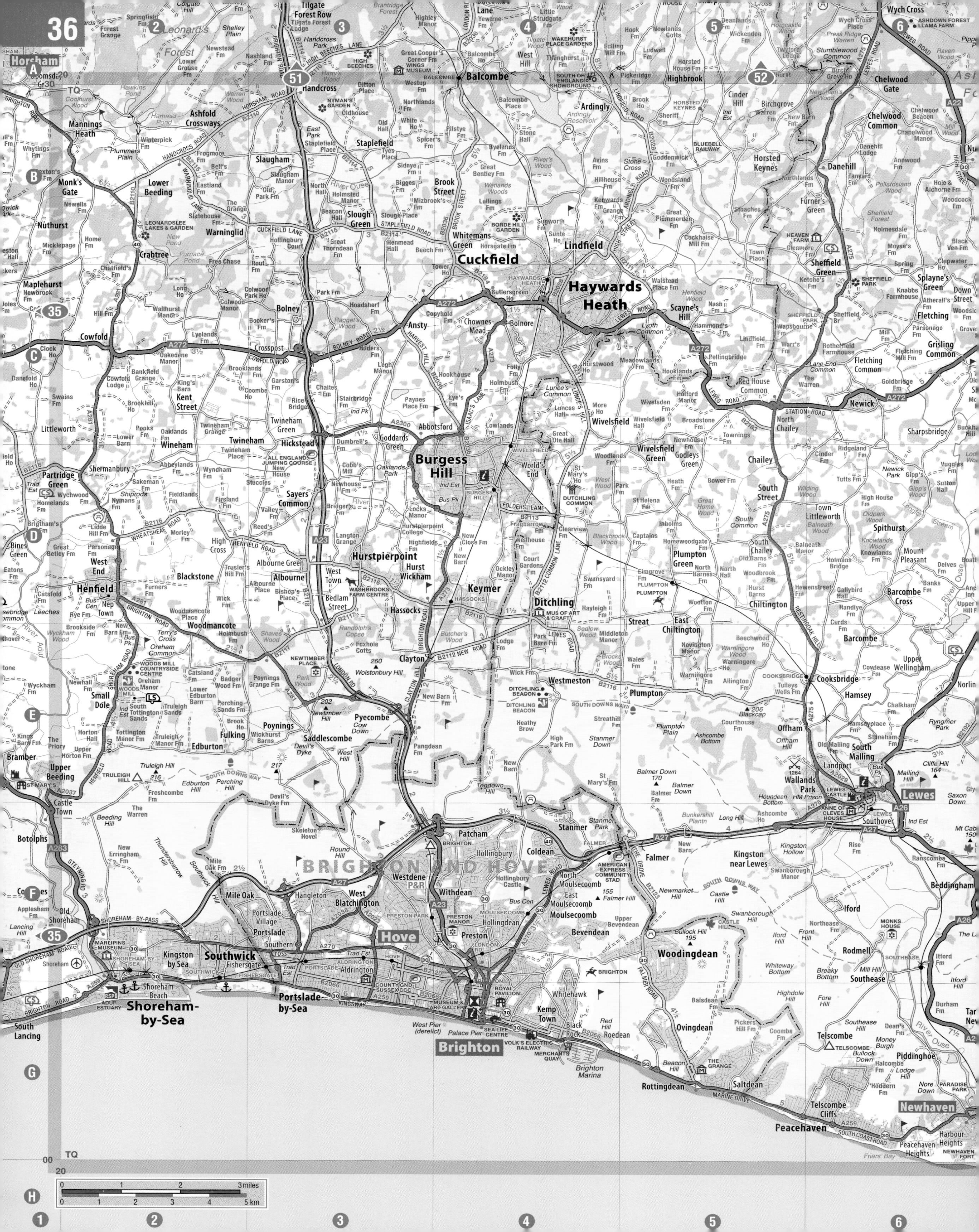

Horsham
Handcross
Balcombe
Ardingly
Highbrook
Chelwood Gate
Mannings Heath
Ashfold Crossways
Slaugham
Staplefield
Lower Beeding
Monk's Gate
Nuthurst
Warninglid
Crabtree
Cuckfield
Lindfield
Haywards Heath
Horsted Keynes
Danehill
Sheffield Green
Maplehurst
Bolney
Ansty
Cowfold
Crosspost
Scayne's Hill
Fletching
Newick
North Chailey
Kent Street
Wivelsfield
Littleworth
Twineham
Hickstead
Abbotsford
Burgess Hill
Wineham
Partridge Green
Shermanbury
Sayers Common
Wivelsfield Green
Chailey
South Street
Spithurst
Henfield
West End
Blackstone
Albourne
Hurstpierpoint
Hurst Wickham
Keymer
Ditchling
Plumpton Green
Hassocks
Chiltington
East Chiltington
Barcombe Cross
Barcombe
Woodmancote
Clayton
Westmeston
Plumpton
Cooksbridge
Hamsey
Small Dole
Poynings
Pyecombe
Saddlescombe
Fulking
Edburton
Offham
South Malling
Bramber
Upper Beeding
Wallands Park
Lewes
Castle Town
Botolphs
Patcham
Coldean
Stanmer
Falmer
Kingston near Lewes
Southover
BRIGHTON AND HOVE
Westdene
Withdean
Hollingbury
Mile Oak
Hangleton
West Blatchington
Portslade
Moulsecoomb
Bevendean
Woodingdean
Iford
Beddingham
Rodmell
Southease
Hove
Preston
Kingston by Sea
Southwick
Shoreham-by-Sea
Portslade-by-Sea
Brighton
Kemp Town
Whitehawk
Roedean
Ovingdean
Rottingdean
Saltdean
Telscombe
Telscombe Cliffs
Peacehaven
Piddinghoe
Newhaven
Peacehaven Heights
Brighton Marina
Lancing
South Lancing
Old Shoreham
miles
km

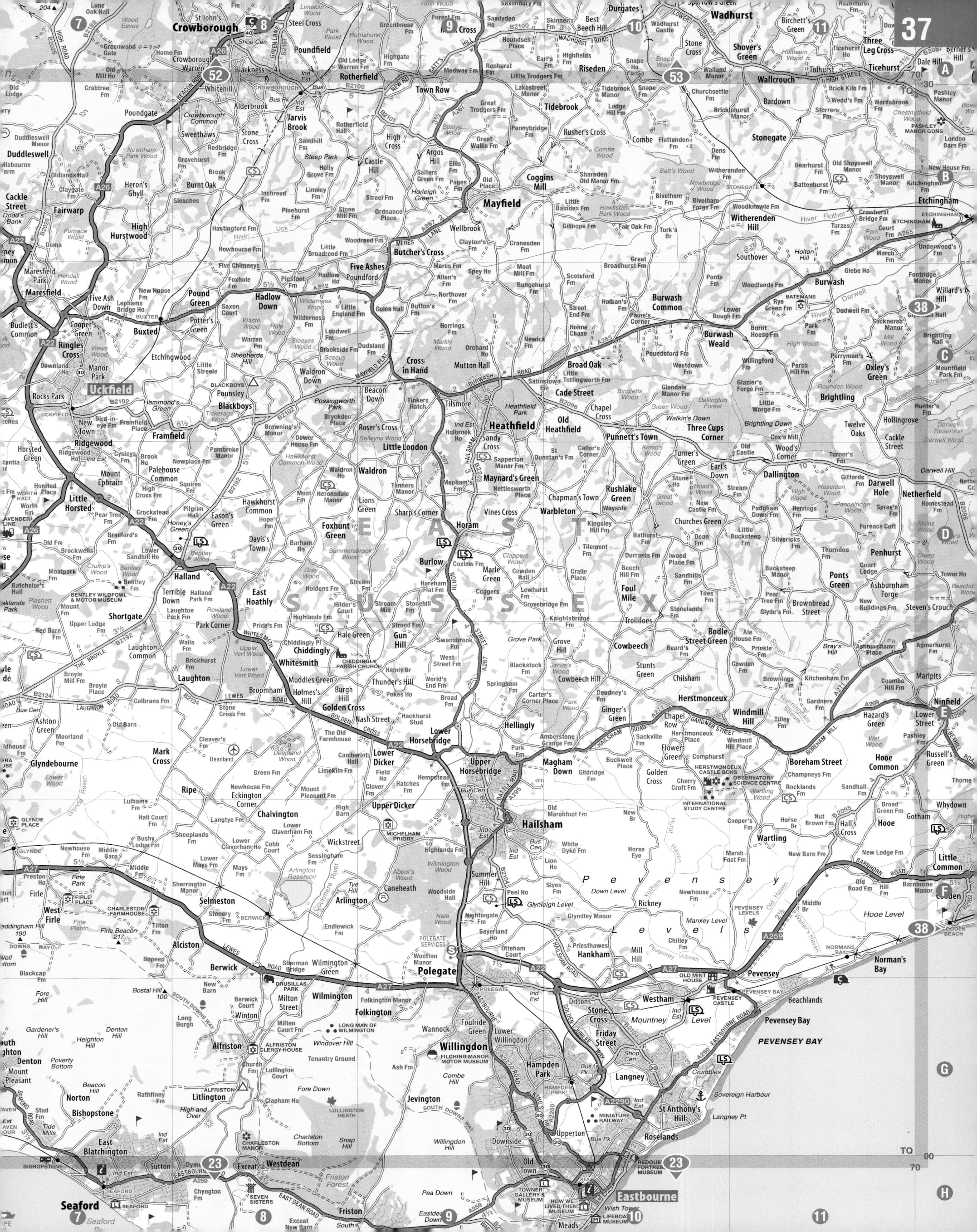
Crowborough
St John's
Steel Cross
Poundfield
Rotherfield
Town Row
Mark Cross
Durgates
Wadhurst
Best Beech Hill
Birchett's Green
Three Leg Cross
Shover's Green
Stone Cross
Riseden
Wallcrouch
Ticehurst
Dale Hill
Tidebrook
Bardown
Stonegate
Jarvis Brook
Poundgate
Alderbrook
Whitehill
Crowborough Warren
Blackness
Stone Cross
Sweethaws
Duddleswell
High Cross
Argos Hill
Castle Hill
Rushers Cross
Combe
Coggins Mill
Mayfield
Etchingham
Witherenden Hill
Burnt Oak
Heron's Ghyll
Cackle Street
Fairwarp
High Hurstwood
Maresfield
Butcher's Cross
Five Ashes
Hadlow Down
Pound Green
Five Ash Down
Buxted
Burwash Common
Burwash
Burwash Weald
Southover
Ringles Cross
Uckfield
Etchingwood
Cross in Hand
Mutton Hall
Broad Oak
Cade Street
Oxley's Green
Brightling
Blackboys
Framfield
Ridgewood
Heathfield
Old Heathfield
Punnett's Town
Three Cups Corner
Little London
Waldron
Maynard's Green
Dallington
Darwell Hole
Netherfield
Little Horsted
Horam
Warbleton
Rushlake Green
Foxhunt Green
Halland
East Hoathly
Burlow
Foul Mile
Penhurst
Ponts Green
Shortgate
Chiddingly
Whitesmith
Gun Hill
Laughton
Golden Cross
Cowbeech
Bodle Street Green
Herstmonceux
Windmill Hill
Ninfield
Hellingly
Lower Horsebridge
Upper Horsebridge
Magham Down
Boreham Street
Hooe Common
Glyndebourne
Mark Cross
Ripe
Chalvington
Upper Dicker
Lower Dicker
Hailsham
Wartling
Hooe
Selmeston
Arlington
Alciston
Berwick
Polegate
Pevensey Levels
Pevensey
Norman's Bay
Wilmington
Westham
Pevensey Bay
Willingdon
Hampden Park
Langney
Alfriston
Litlington
Jevington
St Anthony's Hill
Denton
Norton
Bishopstone
East Blatchington
Westdean
Friston
Seaford
Eastbourne
Old Town
PEVENSEY BAY
EAST SUSSEX

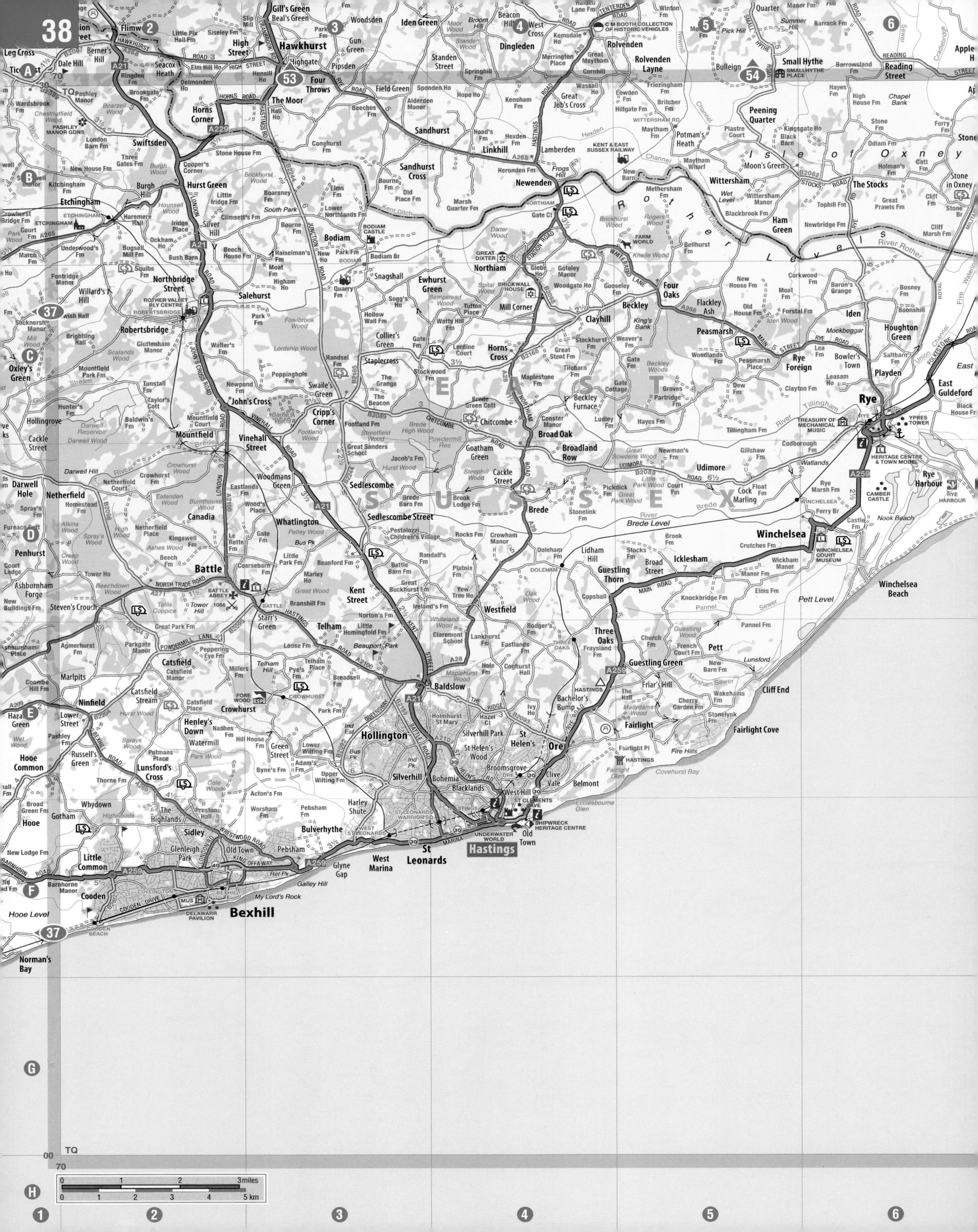
Hawkhurst
Gill's Green
Beal's Green
Iden Green
Four Throws
The Moor
Highgate
Pipsden
Woodsden
Standen Street
Dingleden
West Cross
Rolvenden
Rolvenden Layne
C M BOOTH COLLECTION OF HISTORIC VEHICLES
Bulleign
Small Hythe
SMALLHYTHE PLACE
Reading Street
Peening Quarter
Isle of Oxney
Wittersham
Stone in Oxney
The Stocks
Ham Green
Moon's Green
Potman's Heath
KENT & EAST SUSSEX RAILWAY
Newenden
Lamberden
Linkhill
Sandhurst
Sandhurst Cross
Great Job's Cross
Horns Corner
Swiftsden
Hurst Green
Etchingham
Burgh Hill
Silver Hill
Bodiam
BODIAM CASTLE
Northiam
GREAT DIXTER
BRICKWALL HOUSE
Mill Corner
Ewhurst Green
Snagshall
Salehurst
Northbridge Street
ROTHER VALLEY RLY CENTRE
Robertsbridge
Four Oaks
Beckley
Clayhill
Flackley Ash
Peasmarsh
Iden
Houghton Green
Playden
Rye Foreign
Rye
East Guldeford
TREASURY OF MECHANICAL MUSIC
YPRES TOWER
HERITAGE CENTRE & TOWN MODEL
Rye Harbour
CAMBER CASTLE
River Rother
Rother Levels
Horns Cross
Staplecross
Cripp's Corner
John's Cross
Swaile's Green
Chitcombe
Broad Oak
Broadland Row
Beckley Furnace
Udimore
Cock Marling
Winchelsea
WINCHELSEA COURT MUSEUM
Winchelsea Beach
Icklesham
Guestling Thorn
Brede
Brede Level
Cackle Street
Goatham Green
Sedlescombe
Sedlescombe Street
Whatlington
Vinehall Street
Mountfield
Netherfield
Darwell Hole
Canadia
Battle
BATTLE ABBEY
Kent Street
Telham
Starr's Green
Westfield
Three Oaks
Guestling Green
Pett
Pett Level
Cliff End
Fairlight
Fairlight Cove
Ore
St Helen's
Baldslow
Hollington
Silverhill
Bohemia
West Hill
Old Town
Hastings
SHIPWRECK HERITAGE CENTRE
UNDERWATER WORLD
St Leonards
West Marina
Bulverhythe
Glyne Gap
Crowhurst
Catsfield
Ninfield
Henley's Down
Lunsford's Cross
Hooe
Hooe Common
Sidley
Little Common
Cooden
Bexhill
DELAWARR PAVILION
Hooe Level
Norman's Bay
Penhurst
Ashburnham Forge
EAST SUSSEX
0 1 2 3 miles
0 1 2 3 4 5 km

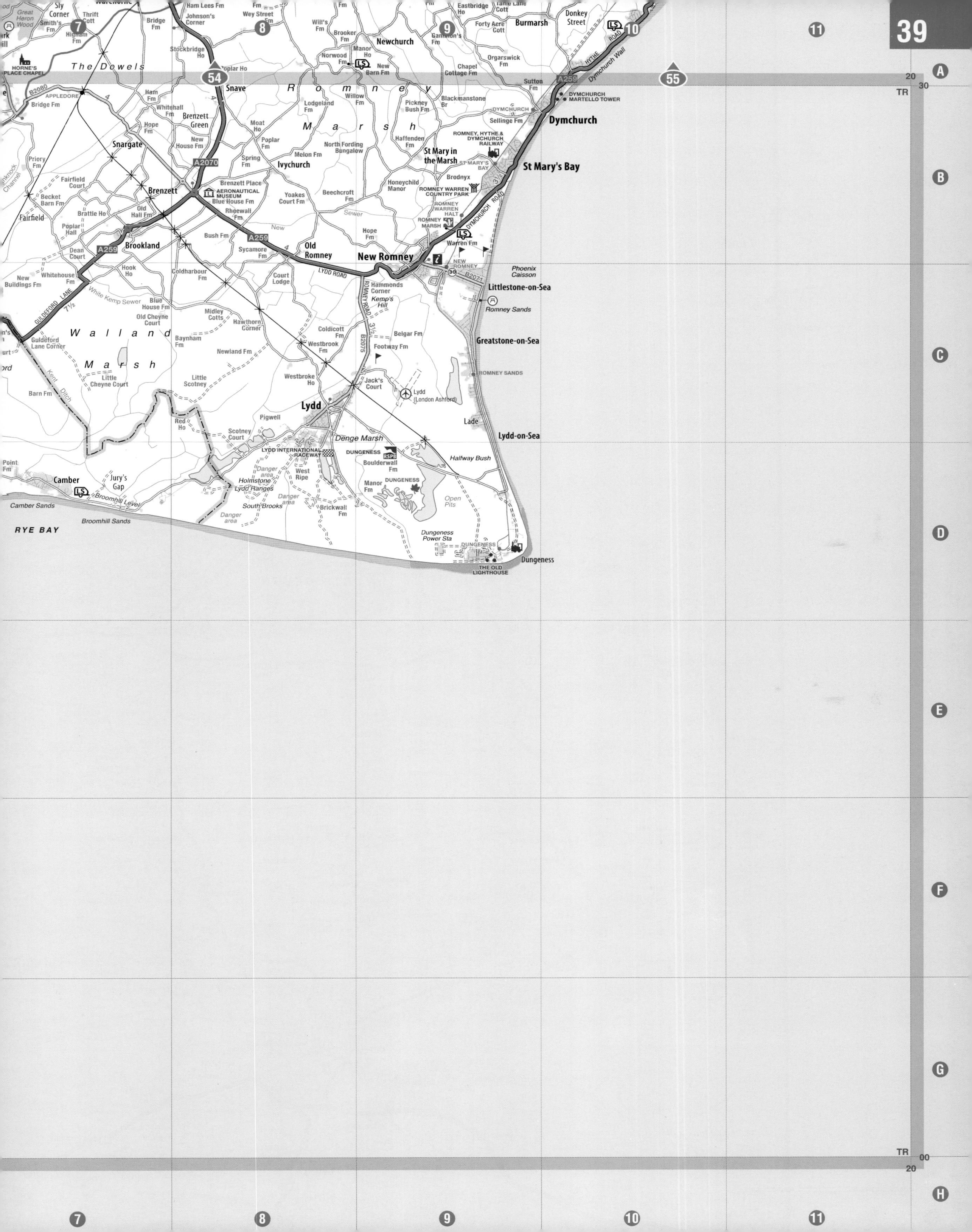

The Dowels
Great Heron Wood
HORNE'S PLACE CHAPEL
Smith's
Higham Fm
Thrift Cott
Sly Corner
Warehorne
Ham Lees Fm
Johnson's Corner
Bridge Fm
Stockbridge Ho
Wey Street Fm
Will's Fm
Brooker Fm
Norwood Fm
Manor Ho
New Barn Fm
Newchurch
Gammon's
Chapel Cottage Fm
Orgarswick Fm
Sutton Fm
Eastbridge Ho
Forty Acre Cott
Fame Lane Cott
Burmarsh
Donkey Street
7 **8** **9** **10** **11**

APPLEDORE
B2080
Bridge Fm
Whitehall Fm
Ham Fm
Snave
54
Romney
Marsh
Willow Fm
Lodgeland Fm
Pickney Bush Fm
Blackmanstone Br
DYMCHURCH
Sellinge Fm
A259
Dymchurch Wall
55
HYTHE
DYMCHURCH
MARTELLO TOWER
Dymchurch
20 30
TR **A**

Brenzett Green
Snargate
Priory Fm
Hope Fm
A2070
Brenzett
AERONAUTICAL MUSEUM
Blue House Fm
Brenzett Place
Ivychurch
Melon Fm
North Fording Bungalow
Haffenden
Beechcroft Fm
Honeychild Manor
Brodnyx
St Mary in the Marsh
ST MARY'S BAY
ROMNEY, HYTHE & DYMCHURCH RAILWAY
St Mary's Bay
B

Becket Barn Fm
Fairfield Court
Fairfield
Brattle Ho
Old Hall Fm
Poplar Hall
Dean Court
A259
Brookland
Hook Ho
Bush Fm
Coldharbour Fm
Rheewall Fm
Yoakes Court Fm
Sycamore Fm
Hope Fm
New
Old Romney
LYDD ROAD
New Romney
B2021
NEW ROMNEY
30
Warren Fm
ROMNEY WARREN COUNTRY PARK
ROMNEY WARREN HALT
ROMNEY MARSH
DYMCHURCH ROAD

New Buildings Fm
Whitehouse Fm
Guldeford Lane Corner
GUILDEFORD LANE
7½
White Kemp Sewer
Blue House Fm
Old Cheyne Court
Midley Cotts
Hawthorn Corner
Coldicott Fm
Westbrook
B2075
Footway Fm
ROMNEY ROAD
3½
Belgar Fm
Hammonds Corner
Kemp's Hill
Phoenix Caisson
Littlestone-on-Sea
Romney Sands
Greatstone-on-Sea
ROMNEY SANDS
C

Walland
Marsh
Barn Fm
Little Cheyne Court
Baynham Fm
Newland Fm
Little Scotney
Westbroke Ho
Court Lodge
Jack's Court
Lydd (London Ashford)
Lydd
Lade
Lydd-on-Sea

Point
Camber
Jury's Gap
Red Ho
Scotney Court
Pigwell
Lydd
Denge Marsh
LYDD INTERNATIONAL RACEWAY
Danger area
Holmstone
Lydd Ranges
West Ripe
Boulderwall Fm
DUNGENESS
RSPB
Manor Fm
DUNGENESS
Halfway Bush
Open Pits
D

Camber Sands
Broomhill Level
South Brooks
Danger area
Brickwall Fm
Danger area
Dungeness Power Sta
DUNGENESS
Dungeness
THE OLD LIGHTHOUSE

RYE BAY
Broomhill Sands

E

F

G

TR
00
20
H

7 **8** **9** **10** **11**

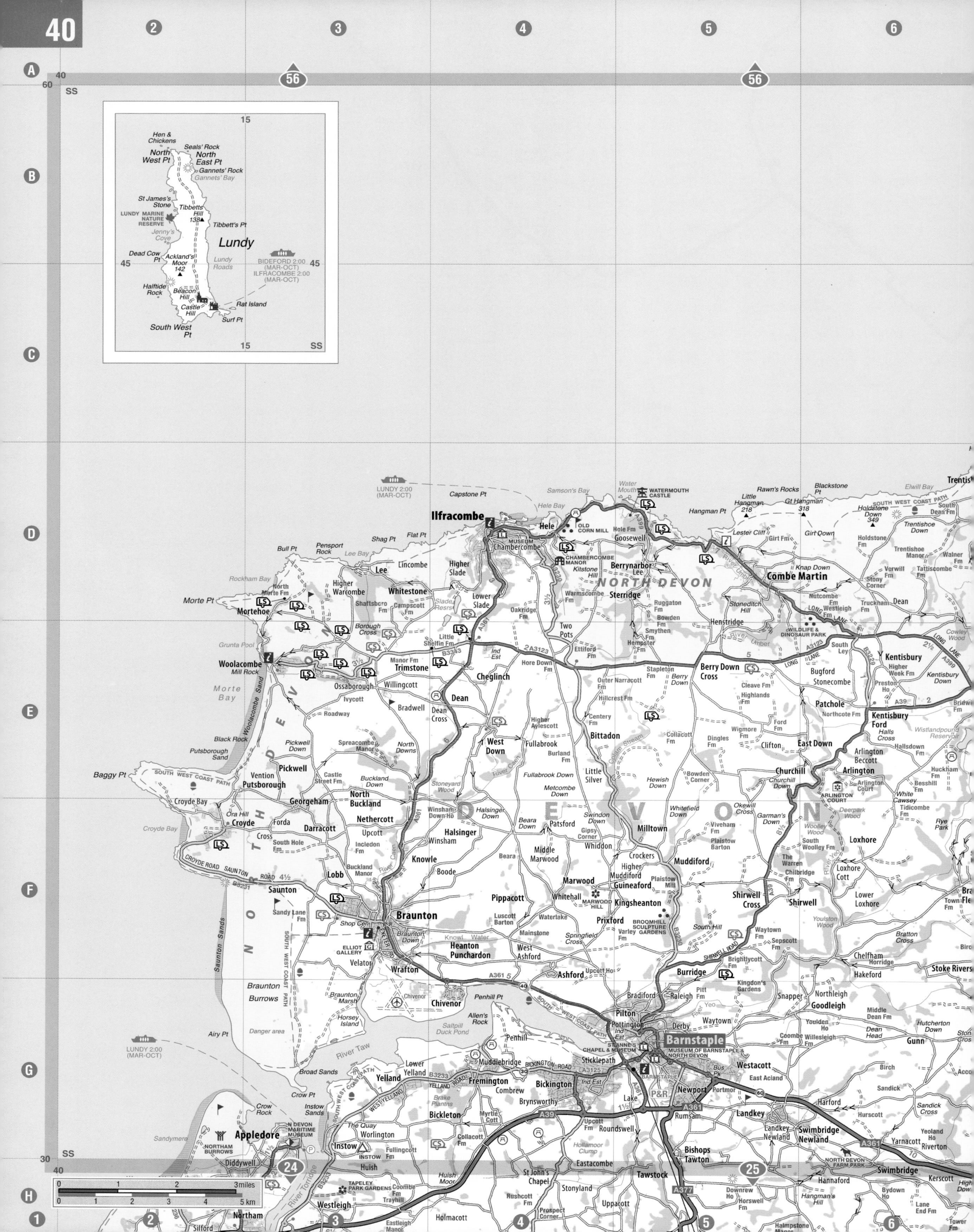

Lundy (inset map)

Hen & Chickens
North West Pt
Seals' Rock
North East Pt
Gannets' Rock
Gannets' Bay
St James's Stone
LUNDY MARINE NATURE RESERVE
Tibbetts Hill 138▲
Tibbett's Pt
Jenny's Cove
Lundy
Dead Cow Pt
Ackland's Moor 142▲
Lundy Roads
Halftide Rock
Beacon Hill
Castle Hill
Rat Island
South West Pt
Surf Pt
BIDEFORD 2:00 (MAR–OCT)
ILFRACOMBE 2:00 (MAR–OCT)

15   45   SS

LUNDY 2:00 (MAR–OCT)
Capstone Pt
Samson's Bay
Water Mouth
WATERMOUTH CASTLE
Rawn's Rocks
Blackstone Pt
Elwill Bay
Trentis
Hele Bay
Little Hangman 218
Gt Hangman 318
Holdstone Down 349
SOUTH WEST COAST PATH
South

Ilfracombe
MUSEUM
Chambercombe
OLD CORN MILL
Hole Fm
Goosewell
Hangman Pt
Trentishoe Down
Trentishoe Manor
Walner Fm
Holdstone Fm

Shag Pt
Flat Pt
Pensport Rock
Lee Bay
Higher Slade
CHAMBERCOMBE MANOR
Kitstone Hill
Berrynarbor Lee
Lester Cliff
Girt Fm
Girt Down
Verwill Fm
Stony Corner
Tattiscombe
Dean

Bull Pt
Rockham Bay
North Morte Fm
Lee
Lincombe
Whitestone
Lower Slade
Slade Resrs
Warmscombe Fm
Sterridge
N O R T H   D E V O N
Combe Martin
Knap Down
Nutcombe Fm
LONG Fm
Westleigh Fm
Truckham Fm
Cowley Wood

Morte Pt
North Morte Fm
Higher Warcombe
Shaftsboro Fm
Campscott Fm
Slade
Oakridge Fm
Two Pots
Ruggaton Fm
Bowden Fm
Smythen Fm
Hempster Fm
Stapleton Fm
Henstridge
Berry Down Cross
Berry Down
Cleave Fm
Bugford
Stonecombe
Preston Ho
Kentisbury
Higher Week Fm
Kentisbury Down

Mortehoe
Borough Cross
Little Sheflin Fm
Ind Est
2A3123
Hore Down
Ettiford Fm
Highlands
Ford Fm
Wigmore Fm
Dingles Fm
Clifton
Patchole
Northcote Fm
Kentisbury Ford
Halls Cross
Hallsdown
Bridw

Grunta Pool
Trimstone
Manor Fm
Cheglinch
Higher Aylescott
Centery Fm
Bittadon
Collacott Fm
Little Silver
Bowden Corner
Hewish Down
East Down
Churchill Down
Arlington Beccott
Huckham Fm
Besshill Fm

Woolacombe
Mill Rock
Ossaborough
Willingcott
Ivycott
Dean
Dean Cross
West Down
Fullabrook
Burland Fm
Fullabrook Down
Metcombe Down
Whitefield Down
Swindon Down
Gipsy Corner
Milltown
Viveham Fm
Plaistow Fm
Churchill
Woolley Wood
ARLINGTON COURT
White Cawsey
Deerpark Wood
Arlington
Tidicombe Fm
Rye Fm

Morte Bay
Roadway
Bradwell
Spreacombe Manor
North Downs
Stoneyard Wood
Beara Down
Whiddon
Middle Marwood
Higher Muddiford
Bowden Corner
South Woolley Fm
The Warren
Chilbridge Fm
Loxhore
Loxhore Cott

Black Rock
Pickwell Down
Castle Street Fm
Buckland Fm
Winsham Down
Halsinger Down
Patsford
Crockers
Muddiford
Garman's Down
Woolley Fm
Lower Loxhore

Baggy Pt
Putsborough Sand
SOUTH WEST COAST PATH
Pickwell
Vention
Putsborough
North Buckland
Halsinger
Winsham
Beara
Marwood
MARWOOD HILL
Guineaford
Plaistow Mill
Shirwell Cross
Shirwell
Bra Town Fle
Youlston Wood

Croyde Bay
Ora Hill
Georgeham
Nethercott
Upcott
Incledon Fm
Knowle
Boode
Kingsheanton
Prixford
BROOMHILL SCULPTURE GARDENS
Varley Fm
South Hill
Waytown Fm
Sepscott Fm
Bratton Cross
Chelfham
Horridge
Stoke Rivers

Croyde
Forda
Darracott
South Hole Fm
Buckland Manor
Pippacott
Luscott Barton
Whitehall
Kingsheanton
Waterlake
Mainstone
Springfield Cross

CROYDE ROAD
SAUNTON ROAD 4½
Lobb
Braunton
Shop Cen
ELLIOT GALLERY
Braunton Down
West Ashford
Ashford
Upcott Ho
Burridge
Brightlycott
Kingdon's Gardens
Hakeford
Goodleigh
Middle Dean Fm
Dean Head
Hutcherton Down
Ston Cro

Saunton Sands
Saunton
Sandy Lane
Heanton Punchardon
Knowl Water
Wrafton
Velator
A361
Mainstone
Bradiford
Raleigh
Pilton
Pottington Ind Est
Snapper
Youlden Ho
Coombe Witsleigh
Gunn

Braunton Burrows
Braunton Marsh
Chivenor
Penhill Pt
Allen's Rock
Penhill
Barnstaple
STANNES CHAPEL & MUSEUM
Derby
Waytown
Westacott
East Acland
Birch
Sandick

Airy Pt
LUNDY 2:00 (MAR–OCT)
Danger area
Horsey Island
Saltpill Duck Pond
MUSEUM OF BARNSTAPLE & NORTH DEVON
Pilton
Bus Pk
P&R
Newport
Portmor
Harford
Hurscott
Sandick Cross

River Taw
Broad Sands
Yelland
Crow Pt
Broad Sands
Lower Yelland
Muddlebridge
BICKINGTON ROAD
Fremington
Combrew
Bickington
Ind Est
Sticklepath
Lake
Landkey
Landkey Newland
Swimbridge Newland
Yeoland Fm
Riverton

Crow Rock
N DEVON MARITIME MUSEUM
Appledore
NORTHAM BURROWS
Instow Sands
WEST YELLAND
Brynsworthy
A39
Upcott Fm
Roundswell
Hollamoor Clump
Bishops Tawton
NORTH DEVON FARM PARK
Hannaford
Kerscott

Sandymere
Diddywell
Instow
INSTOW
The Quay
Worlington
Bickleton
Myrtle Cott
Collacott Fm
Tawstock
Downrew Ho
Horswell
Hangman's Hill
Bydown Ho
Lane End Fm

Westleigh
Northam
Silford
Holmacott
TAPELEY PARK GARDENS
Coombe Fm
Trayhill
Fullingcott Fm
Huish
Westcott
St John's Chapel
Stonyland
Eastacombe
Huish Moor
Rushcott
Prospect Corner
Uppacott
Eastleigh Manor
Hampsteon Manor

River Torridge

SS 30 40

24   25
56   56

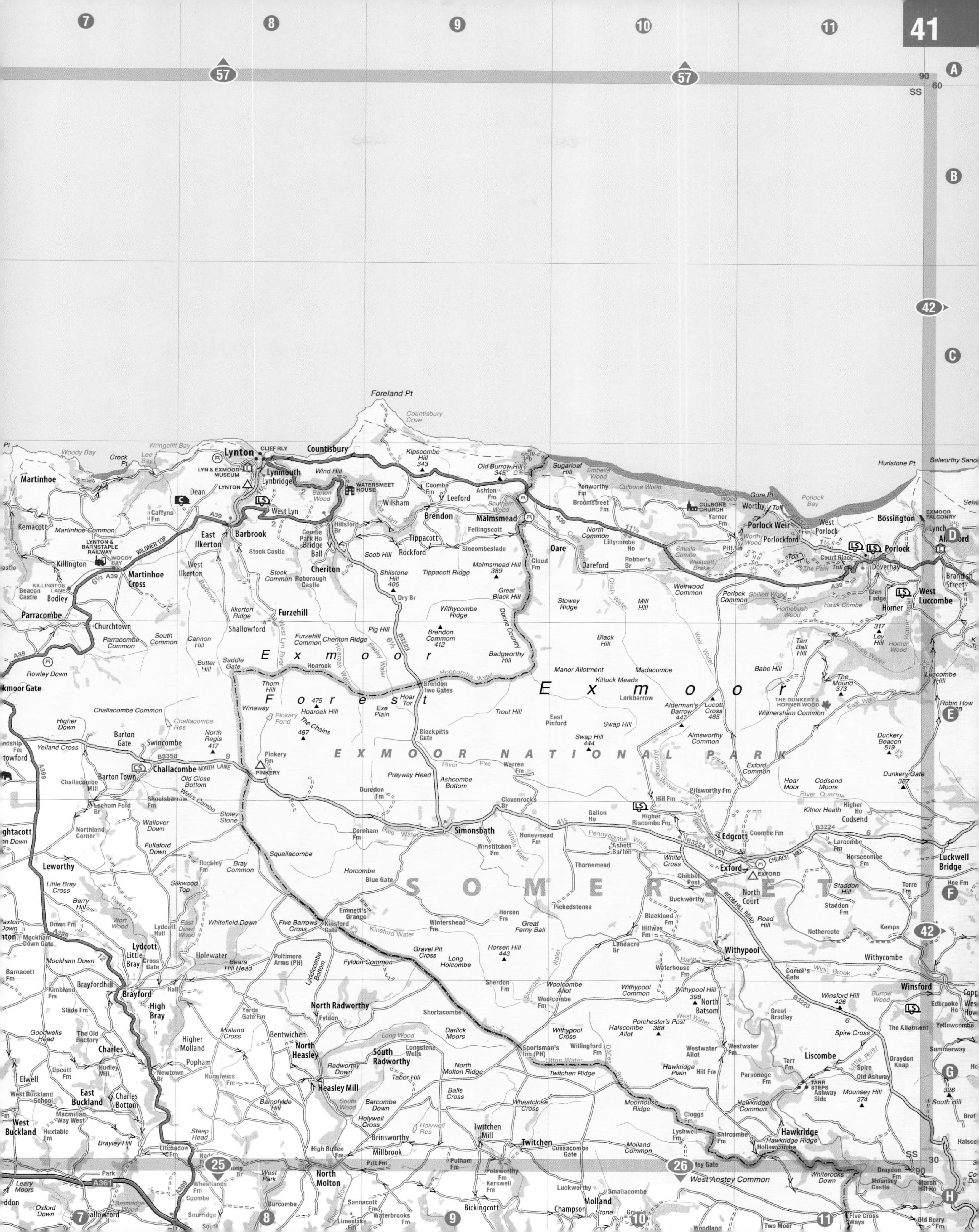
Foreland Pt
Lynton
Lynmouth
Countisbury
Martinhoe
Barbrook
Brendon
Malmsmead
Oare
Porlock
Porlock Weir
Exford
Simonsbath
Withypool
Challacombe
Parracombe
Brayford
North Molton
Twitchen
Hawkridge
Winsford
Exmoor Forest
EXMOOR NATIONAL PARK
SOMERSET

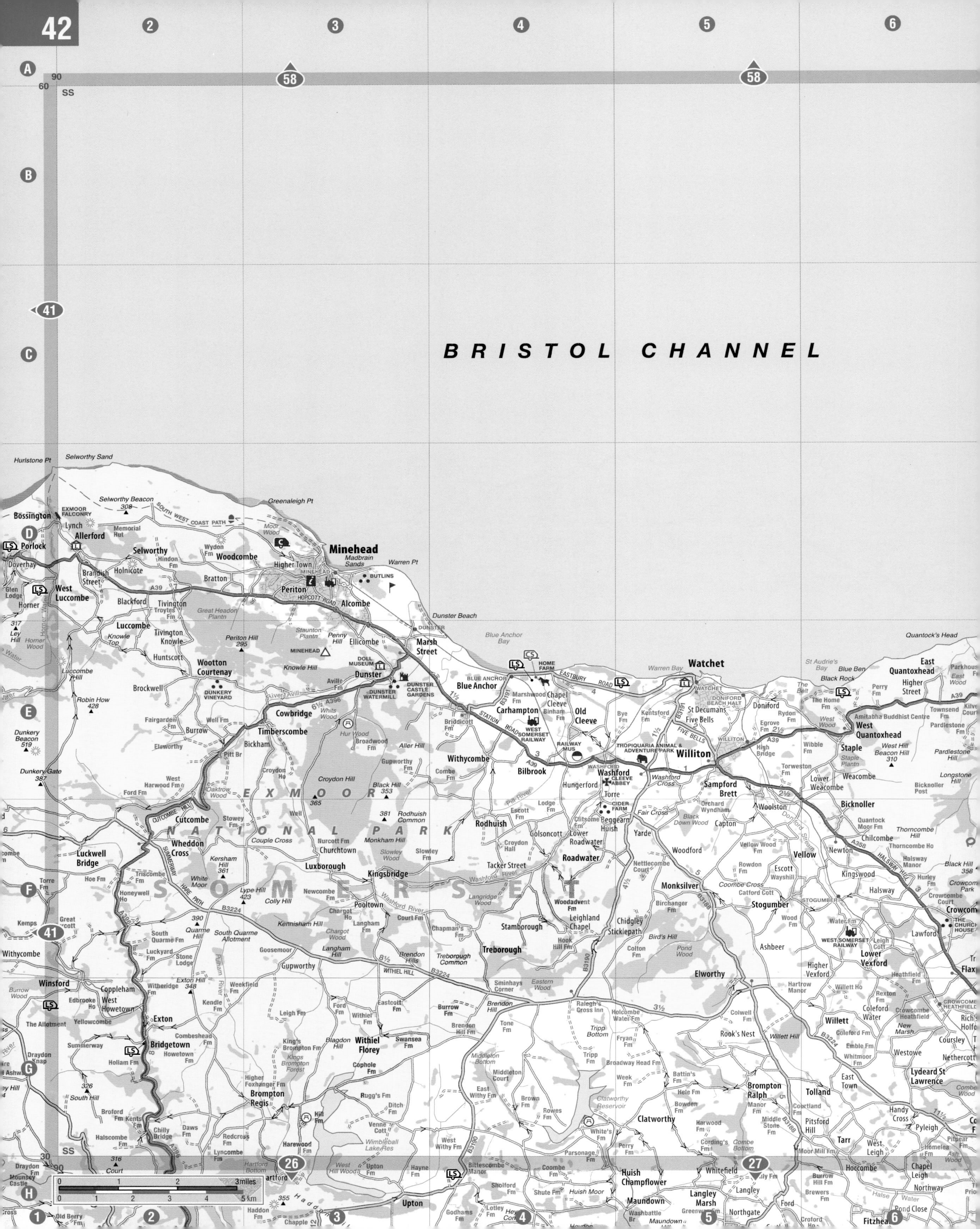

BRISTOL CHANNEL
E X M O O R
N A T I O N A L P A R K
S O M E R S E T
Hurlstone Pt
Selworthy Sand
Selworthy Beacon
308
Greenaleigh Pt
SOUTH WEST COAST PATH
Bossington
EXMOOR FALCONRY
Lynch
Allerford
Porlock
Memorial Hut
Selworthy
Wydon Fm
Woodcombe
Moor Wood
Minehead
Madbrain Sands
Warren Pt
Higher Town
BUTLINS
Doverhay
Brandish Street
Holnicote
Hindon Fm
Bratton
Periton
Alcombe
HOPCOTT ROAD
Glen Lodge
West Luccombe
Horner
Blackford
Tivington
Troytes Fm
Great Headon Plantn
Dunster Beach
317
Ley Hill
Horner Wood
Luccombe
Knowle Top
Tivington Knowle
Periton Hill
295
Staunton Plantn
Penny Hill
Ellicombe
Marsh Street
Blue Anchor Bay
MINEHEAD
Huntscott
Wootton Courtenay
Knowle Hill
DOLL MUSEUM
Dunster
Aville Fm
DUNSTER CASTLE GARDENS
DUNSTER WATERMILL
HOME FARM
Blue Anchor
BLUE ANCHOR
EASTBURY ROAD
Watchet
Warren Bay
WATCHET
DONIFORD BEACH HALT
Quantock's Head
St Audrie's Bay
Blue Ben
Black Rock
East Quantoxhead
Parkhouse
Higher Street
Perry Fm
The Belt
The Home Fm
West Wood
Luccombe Hill
Robin How
428
Brockwell
DUNKERY VINEYARD
River Avill
Cowbridge
Whits Wood
Hur Wood
Broadwood Fm
Marshwood Fm
Chapel Cleeve
Binham Fm
Carhampton
Old Cleeve
Bye Fm
Kentsford Fm
St Decumans
Five Bells
FIVE BELLS
Doniford
Rydon Fm
Egrove Fm
Amitabha Buddhist Centre
Townsend Fm
Pardlestone Fm
West Quantoxhead
Dunkery Beacon
519
Fairgarden Fm
Burrow
Well Fm
Timberscombe
Elsworthy
Bickham
Pitt Br
Aller Hill
Briddicott Fm
STATION ROAD
WEST SOMERSET RAILWAY
RAILWAY MUS
TROPIQUARIA ANIMAL & ADVENTURE PARK
Williton
WILLITON
High Bridge
Wibble Fm
Staple
West Hill Beacon Hill
310
Pardlestone Hill
Dunkery Gate
387
West Harwood Fm
Ford Fm
Croydon Ho
Gupworthy Fm
Croydon Hill
Black Hill
353
Withycombe
Combe Fm
Bilbrook
WASHFORD
Washford
CLEEVE ABBEY
Hungerford
Washford Cross
Sampford Brett
Torweston Fm
Lower Weacombe
Weacombe
Bicknoller Post
Longstone Hill
Oaktrow Wood
365
381
Rodhuish Common
Pill River
Lodge Fm
Escott Fm
Torre
CIDER FARM
Orchard Wyndham
Woolston
Bicknoller
Quantock Moor Fm
CUTCOMBE HILL
Cutcombe
Stowey Fm
Well
Rodhuish
Clitsome Fm
Beggearn Huish
Fair Cross
Black Down Wood
Capton
Chilcombe
Thorncombe Hill
Thorncombe Ho
Wheddon Cross
Couple Cross
Nurcott Fm
Churchtown
Monkham Hill
Slowley Wood
Slowley Fm
Croydon Hall
Golsoncott
Lower Roadwater
Yarde
Woodford
Yellow Wood Fm
Newton
Vellow
Halsway Manor
Black Hill
358
Luckwell Bridge
Kersham Hill
361
White Moor
Luxborough
Kingsbridge
Tacker Street
Roadwater
Washford River
Nettlecombe Court
Rowdon Fm
Escott Wayshill
Kingswood
Hurley Fm
Crowcombe Park
Torre Fm
Hoe Fm
Triscombe Fm
Honeywell Ho
Lype Hill
423
Colly Hill
Newcombe Fm
Pooltown
Langridge Wood
Woodadvent Fm
Monksilver
Coombe Cross
Catford Cott
Stogumber
STOGUMBER
Halsway
Crowcombe Court
Crowcombe
THE CHURCH HOUSE
Great Cott
Kemps
Withycombe
South Quarme Fm
Quarme Hill
390
South Quarme Allotment
B3224
Chargot Ho
Kennisham Hill
Langham Fm
Court Fm
Chapman's Fm
Stamborough
Leighland Chapel
Chidgley
Sticklepath
Birchanger Fm
Wood Fm
Water Fm
Lawford
Bird's Hill
WEST SOMERSET RAILWAY
Leigh Cott
Luckyard Fm
Stone Lodge
Goosemoor
Langham Hill
Chargot Wood
Brendon Hills
Treborough Common
Treborough
Hook Hill Fm
Colton Fm
Pond Wood
Ashbeer
Lower Vexford
Winsford
Coppleham
West Howetown
Burrow Wood
Edbrooke Ho
Witheridge Fm
Exton Hill
348
Weekfield Fm
Kendle Fm
Gupworthy
WITHIEL HILL
Smithays Corner
Eastern Wood
Elworthy
Higher Vexford
Heathfield Fm
Flax
The Allotment
Yellowcombe
Exton
Leigh Fm
Ford Fm
Withiel Fm
Eastcott Fm
Burrow Fm
Brendon Hill
Raleigh's Cross Inn
Holcombe Water Fm
Colwell Fm
Hartrow Manor
Willett Ho
Rexton Fm
Coleford Water
CROWCOMBE HEATHFIELD
Crowcombe Heathfield
Willett
Combeshead Fm
Summerway
Bridgetown
Howetown Fm
King's Brompton Fm
Blagdon Hill
Withiel Florey
Swansea Fm
Brendon Hill Fm
Tone Fm
Tripp Bottom
Rook's Nest
Willett Hill
Coleford Fm
New Marsh
Emble Fm
Whitmoor Fm
Westowe
Coursley
Draydon Knap
Holfam Fm
Kings Brompton Forest
Cophole Fm
Middleton Bottom
Fryan Fm
Tripp Fm
Broadway Head Fm
Nethercott
Lydeard St Lawrence
326
South Hill
Higher Foxhanger Fm
Brompton Regis
Rugg's Fm
Middleton Court
East Withy Fm
Week Fm
Battin's Fm
Hele Fm
Brompton Ralph
Manor Fm
East Town
Tolland
Broford Fm
Kents
Chilly Bridge
Ditch Fm
Hill Fm
Brown Fm
Rowes Fm
Clatworthy Reservoir
Bowden Fm
Middle Stone Fm
Courtland
Pitsford Hill
Handy Cross
Pyleigh
Halscombe Fm
Daws Fm
Redcross Fm
Venne Cott
Wimbleball Lake Res
Harewood
West Withy Fm
White's Fm
Clatworthy
Harwood Fm
Cording's Fm
Combe Bottom
Tarr
West Leigh
Pitpear Fm
SS
Lyncombe Fm
316
Court
Hartford Bottom
Draydon Fm
Mounsey Castle
West Hill Wood
Upton Fm
Hayne Fm
Bittescombe Manor
Coombe Fm
Parsonage Fm
Perry Fm
Huish Champflower
Whitefield
Moor Mill Fm
Hoccombe
Chapel Leigh
Northway
Sholford Fm
Shute Fm
Huish Moor
Langley Marsh
Langley
Burrow Hill Fm
Brewers Fm
Halse Water
355
Haddon Hill
Upton
Godhams Fm
Lotley Fm
Maundown
Washbattle Br
Greenway Fm
Northgate
Ford
Pond Close
Fitzhead
Old Berry Fm
Chapple
Maundown Hill
Croford Ho
0 1 2 3 miles
0 1 2 3 4 5 km
A39
A396
A358
B3191
B3190
B3188
B3224
B3227
HALSWAY HILL
1½
2½
3½
4½
6½
8½
11½

58
58
41
41
26
27

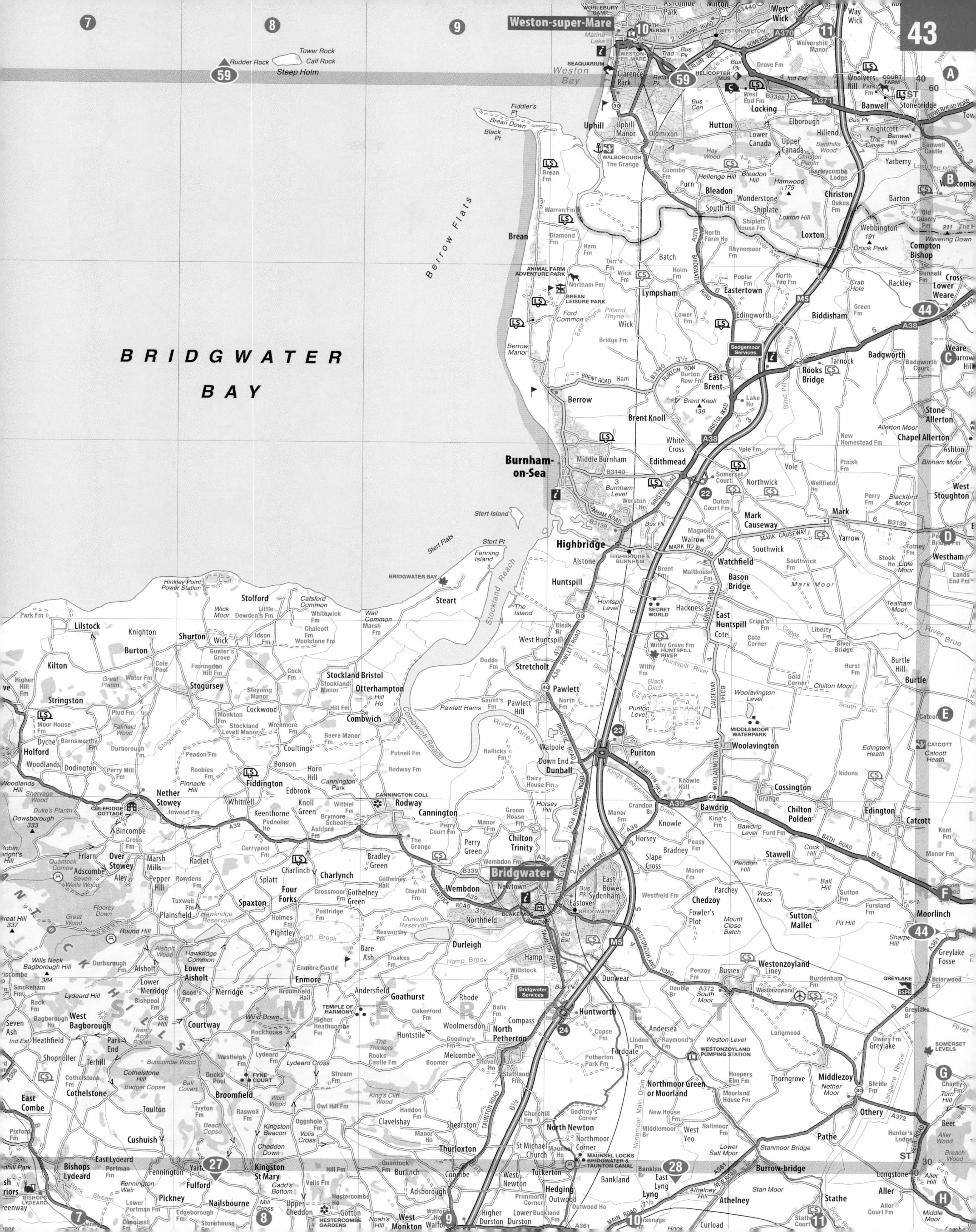

43
BRIDGWATER BAY
Weston-super-Mare
Weston Bay
Steep Holm
Tower Rock
Calf Rock
Rudder Rock
59
Berrow Flats
Stert Flats
Stert Island
Stert Pt
Fenning Island
Brean Down
Fiddler's Pt
Black Pt
Uphill
Uphill Manor
Oldmixon
Hutton
Locking
Banwell
Bleadon
Christon
Loxton
Webbington
Compton Bishop
Brean
Lympsham
Eastertown
Biddisham
Edingworth
Badgworth
Rooks Bridge
East Brent
Berrow
Brent Knoll
Burnham-on-Sea
Middle Burnham
Edithmead
Highbridge
Alstone
Watchfield
Mark
Mark Causeway
Southwick
Yarrow
Westham
Huntspill
East Huntspill
Bason Bridge
Hackness
Steart
Stolford
Hinkley Point Power Station
Lilstock
Kilton
Burton
Shurton
Stogursey
Stringston
Holford
Dodington
Nether Stowey
Over Stowey
Fiddington
Stockland Bristol
Otterhampton
Combwich
Cannington
Rodway
Stretcholt
Pawlett
West Huntspill
Puriton
Woolavington
Cossington
Bawdrip
Chilton Polden
Edington
Catcott
Dunball
Chilton Trinity
Bridgwater
Wembdon
Charlynch
Spaxton
Four Forks
Durleigh
Enmore
Goathurst
Aisholt
Lower Aisholt
Courtway
West Bagborough
Cothelstone
Broomfield
North Petherton
Huntworth
Chedzoy
Westonzoyland
Middlezoy
Othery
Sutton Mallet
Stawell
Moorlinch
Greylake
Burrow-bridge
Athelney
Stathe
Lyng
North Newton
Thurloxton
Kingston St Mary
Bishops Lydeard
Fulford
Pickney
Nailsbourne
Hedging
Durston
West Monkton
QUANTOCK HILLS
SOMERSET
River Parrett
River Brue
River Axe
Sedgemoor Services
Bridgwater Services
M5
A38
A39
A372
A361
44
22
23
24
27
28

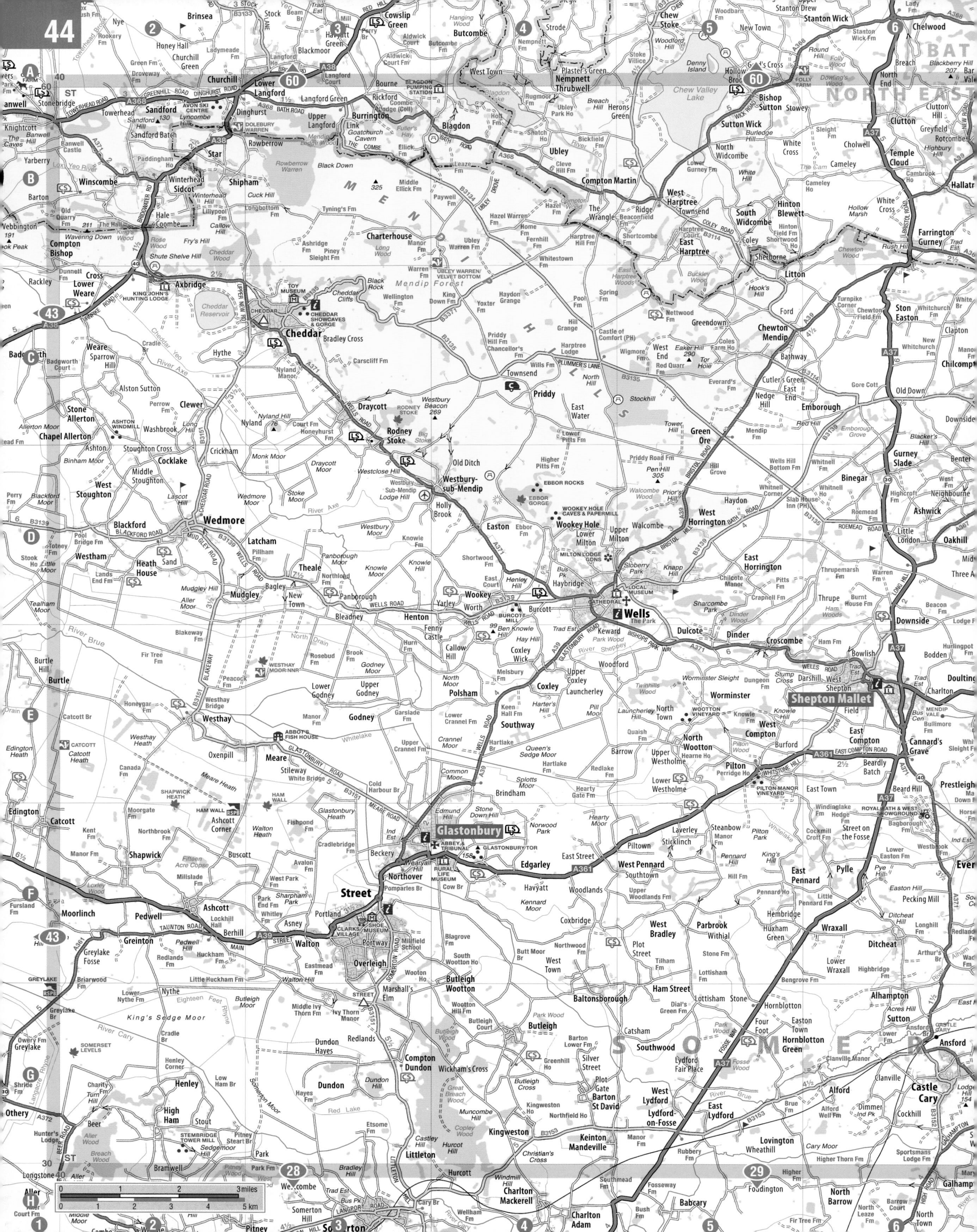
Brinsea
Churchill
Lower Langford
Sandford
Winscombe
Axbridge
Cheddar
Cheddar Reservoir
Draycott
Rodney Stoke
Westbury-sub-Mendip
Wedmore
Blackford
Mudgley
Theale
Wookey
Wookey Hole
Wells
Priddy
Charterhouse
Blagdon
Burrington
Ubley
Compton Martin
West Harptree
East Harptree
Chew Valley Lake
Bishop Sutton
Chew Stoke
Butcombe
Litton
Chewton Mendip
Emborough
Binegar
Gurney Slade
Ston Easton
Chelwood
Clutton
Temple Cloud
Farrington Gurney
Hinton Blewett
Shipham
Compton Bishop
Chapel Allerton
Westhay
Meare
Godney
Glastonbury
Street
Walton
Ashcott
Shapwick
Catcott
Edington
Moorlinch
Pedwell
Greinton
Butleigh
Baltonsborough
West Pennard
Pilton
Croscombe
Dinder
Dulcote
Shepton Mallet
Evercreech
Ditcheat
Alhampton
Castle Cary
Ansford
Alford
Lydford-on-Fosse
Keinton Mandeville
Kingweston
Charlton Mackerell
Charlton Adam
Babcary
Somerton
Compton Dundon
Dundon
Littleton
Henley
High Ham
Othery
Polsham
Coxley
Southway
North Wootton
Worminster
Doulting
Oakhill
Ashwick
Wraxall
Pylle
East Pennard
Parbrook
West Bradley
Southwood
Lovington
North Barrow
SOMERSET
MENDIP HILLS
BATH AND NORTH EAST SOMERSET
3 miles
5 km

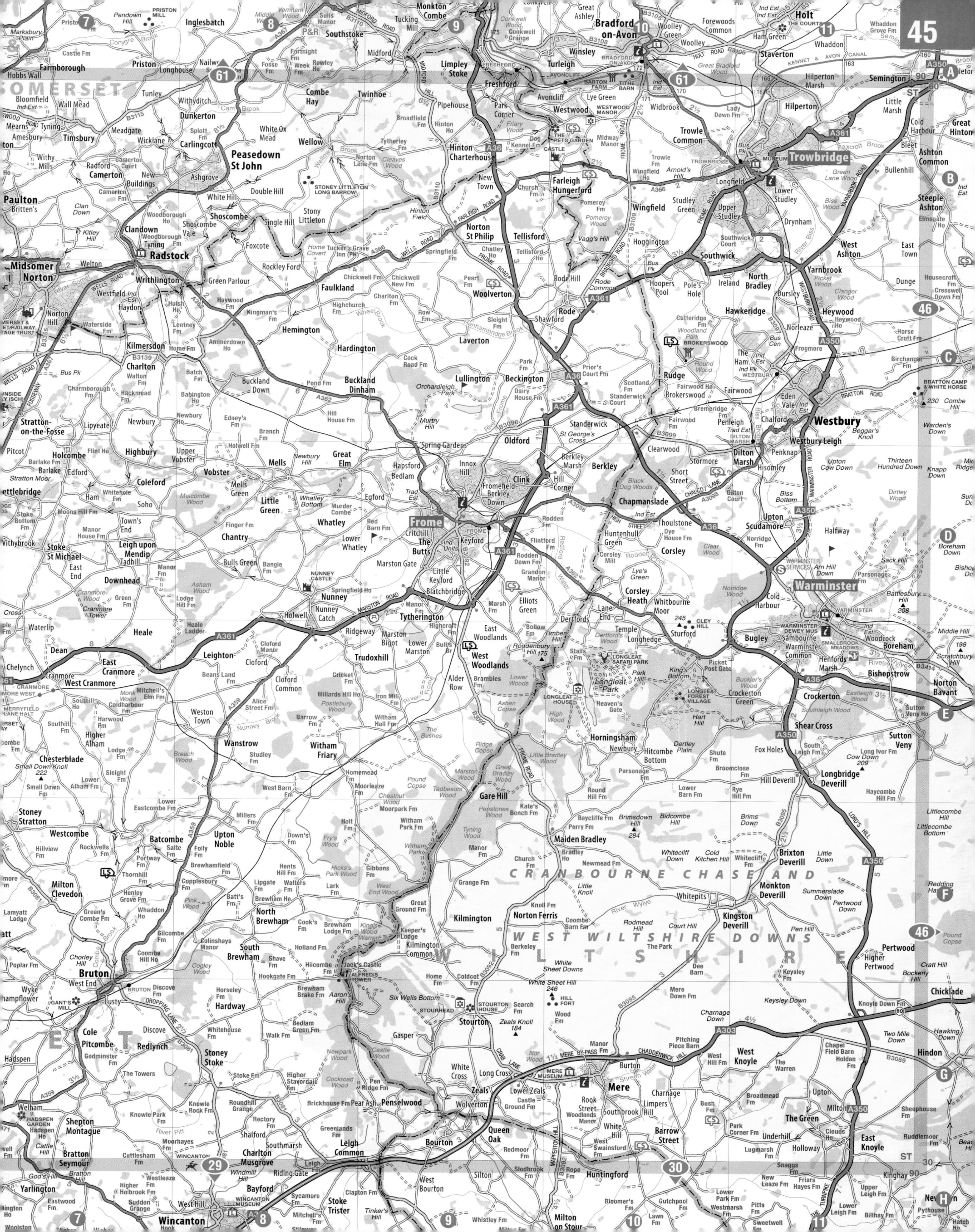
SOMERSET
WILTSHIRE
CRANBOURNE CHASE AND
WEST WILTSHIRE DOWNS
Bradford on Avon
Trowbridge
Westbury
Warminster
Frome
Radstock
Midsomer Norton
Peasedown St John
Bruton
Mere
Wincanton
Holt
Staverton
Semington
Hilperton
Freshford
Limpley Stoke
Monkton Combe
Southstoke
Midford
Wellow
Dunkerton
Camerton
Timsbury
Paulton
Farmborough
Priston
Inglesbatch
Combe Hay
Twinhoe
Hinton Charterhouse
Norton St Philip
Farleigh Hungerford
Westwood
Avoncliff
Turleigh
Winsley
Wingfield
Southwick
North Bradley
Heywood
Dilton Marsh
Rode
Beckington
Woolverton
Laverton
Lullington
Tellisford
Rudge
Standerwick
Berkley
Chapmanslade
Corsley
Corsley Heath
Upton Scudamore
Westbury Leigh
Hemington
Hardington
Faulkland
Kilmersdon
Charlton
Writhlington
Buckland Dinham
Mells
Great Elm
Vobster
Coleford
Holcombe
Highbury
Stratton-on-the-Fosse
Leigh upon Mendip
Stoke St Michael
Downhead
Chantry
Whatley
Nunney
Tytherington
Marston Bigot
Trudoxhill
Witham Friary
Wanstrow
West Woodlands
Horningsham
Longleat Park
Longleat House
Bugley
Boreham
Bishopstrow
Norton Bavant
Crockerton
Shear Cross
Sutton Veny
Longbridge Deverill
Hill Deverill
Brixton Deverill
Monkton Deverill
Kingston Deverill
Maiden Bradley
Kilmington
Norton Ferris
Gare Hill
Stourton
Stourhead
Zeals
Penselwood
Bourton
Queen Oak
Silton
Huntingford
West Knoyle
Hindon
East Knoyle
Chicklade
Pertwood
Batcombe
Upton Noble
North Brewham
South Brewham
Hardway
Redlynch
Pitcombe
Cole
Stoney Stoke
Charlton Musgrove
Shepton Montague
Bratton Seymour
Yarlington
Bayford
Stoke Trister
Leigh Common
East Cranmore
West Cranmore
Leighton
Heale
Dean
Chesterblade
Stoney Stratton
Westcombe
Milton Clevedon
Alfred's Tower
White Sheet Hill
A36
A361
A350
A362
A366
A303
A359
A367
A3098
B3092
B3109
B3099
B3095
B3089
61
46
30
29
7
8
9
10
11

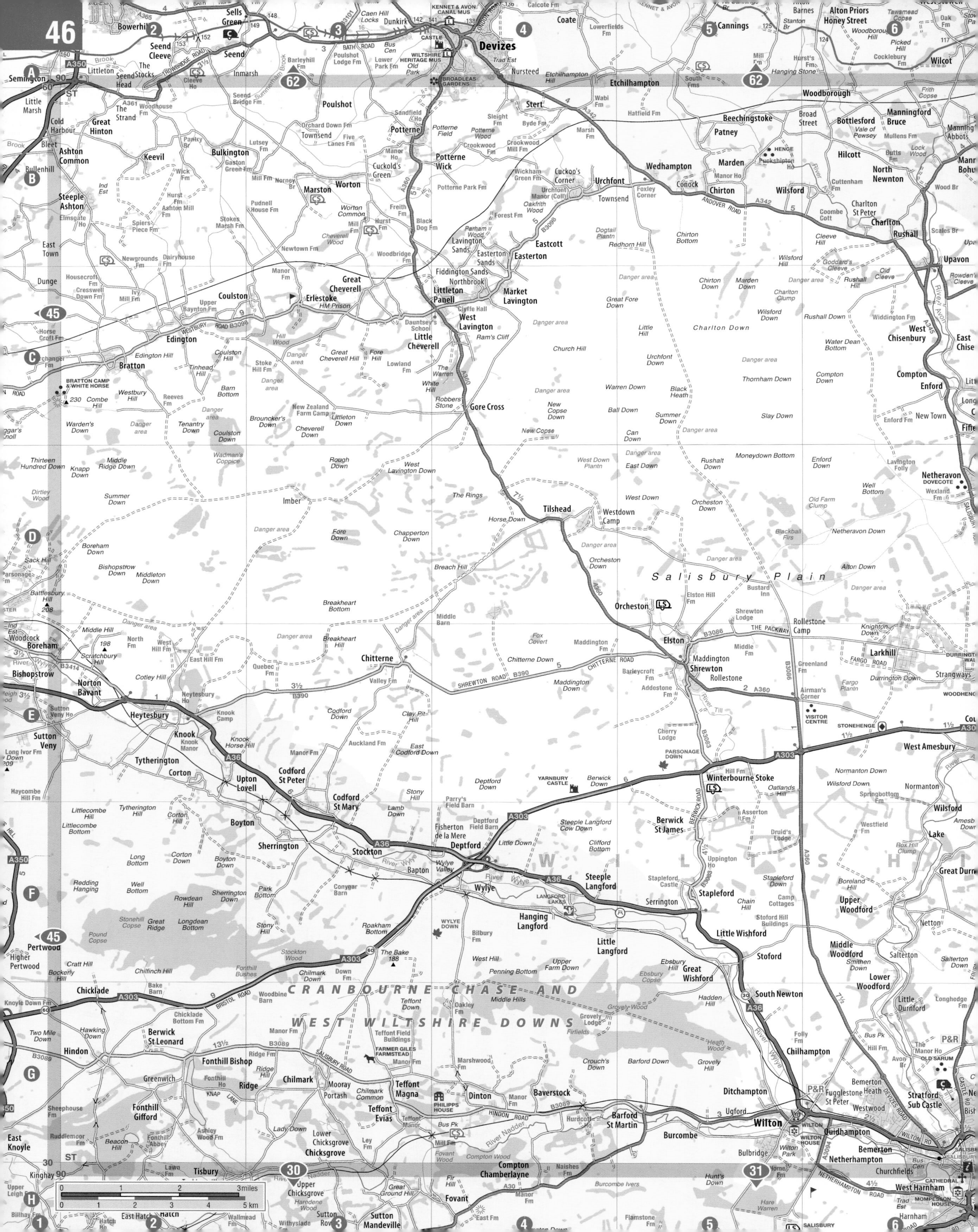

46
Bowerhill
Sells Green
Seend Cleeve
Seend
Semington
Littleton
Seend Head
The Stocks
Inmarsh
Caen Hill Locks
Dunkirk
Kennet & Avon Canal Mus
Devizes
Castle
Wiltshire Heritage Mus
Old Park
Broadleas Gardens
Nursteed
Trad Est
Calcote Fm
Coate
Lowerfields Fm
Etchilhampton Hill
Etchilhampton
Cannings
Alton Priors
Honey Street
Woodborough Hill
Stanton Br
Barnes
Tawsmead Copse
Oak Fm
Picked Hill
Cocklebury Fm
Wilcot
Hurst's Fm
Hanging Stone
Mill Fm
South Fms
Woodborough
Frith Copse
Little Marsh
Cold Harbour
Great Hinton
The Strand
Woodhouse Fm
Poulshot
Seend Bridge Fm
Barleyhill Fm
Poulshot Lodge Fm
Lower Park Fm
Bus Cen
Sandfield Ho
Potterne
Potterne Field
Potterne Wood
Sleight Fm
Stert
Byde Fm
Wabi Fm
Hatfield Fm
Beechingstoke
Broad Street
Bottlesford
Manningford Bruce
Vale of Pewsey
Mullens Fm
Manningford Abbots
Orchard Down Fm
Townsend
Five Lanes Fm
Bleet
Ashton Common
Keevil
Bulkington
Gaston Green Fm
Pantry Br
Lutsey Fm
Manor Ho
Cuckold's Green
Potterne Wick
Crookwood Fm
Crookwood Mill Fm
Marsh Fm
Wedhampton
Patney
Marden
Henge
Puckshipton Ho
Hilcott
Butts Fm
Lock Wood
North Newnton
Bullenhill
Ind Est
Wick Fm
Hurst Fm
Ashton Mill Fm
Norney Br
Mill Fm
Marston
Worton
Potterne Park Fm
Wickham Green Fm
Cuckoo's Corner
Urchfont Manor (Coll)
Urchfont
Townsend
Foxley Corner
Conock
Manor Ho
Chirton
Wilsford
Cuttenham Fm
Wood Br
Steeple Ashton
Elmsgate Ho
Spiers Piece Fm
Stokes Marsh Fm
Pudnell House Fm
Worton Common
Freith Fm
Hurst Fm
Black Dog Fm
Oakfrith Wood
Forest Fm
Andover Road
Coombe Cott
Charlton St Peter
Charlton
Rushall
Scales Br
East Town
Newgrounds Fm
Dairyhouse Fm
Newtown Fm
Cheverell Wood
Woodbridge Fm
Parham Wood
Lavington Sands
Easterton Sands
Easterton
Eastcott
Dogtail Plantn
Redhorn Hill
Chirton Bottom
Cleeve Hill
Wilsford Hill
Goddard's Cleeve
Old Cleeve
Upavon
Rowden's Cleeve
Dunge
Housecroft Fm
Cresswell Down Fm
Ivy Mill Fm
Manor Fm
Coulston
Upper Baynton Fm
Great Cheverell
Erlestoke
HM Prison
Fiddington Sands
Northbrook
Littleton Panell
Market Lavington
Clyffe Hall
West Lavington
Danger area
Great Fore Down
Chirton Down
Marden Down
Charlton Clump
Rushall Hill
Wilsford Down
Rushall Down
Widdington Fm
West Chisenbury
East Chisenbury
Horse Croft Fm
Edington
Westbury Road
Hill Wood
Dauntsey's School
Little Cheverell
Ram's Cliff
Little Hill
Charlton Down
Water Dean Bottom
Edington Hill
Bratton
Coulston Hill
Tinhead Hill
Stoke Hill Fm
Great Cheverell Hill
Fore Hill
Lowland Fm
Church Hill
Urchfont Down
Thornham Down
Compton Down
Compton
Enford
Bratton Camp & White Horse
Combe Hill
Westbury Hill
Reeves Fm
Barn Bottom
The Warren
White Hill
Robbers Stone
Gore Cross
Warren Down
Black Heath
Ball Down
Summer Down
Slay Down
New Town
Enford Fm
Warden's Down
Tenantry Down
Coulston Down
Brouncker's Down
New Zealand Farm Camp
Littleton Down
Cheverell Down
New Copse Down
New Copse
Can Down
Thirteen Hundred Down
Knapp Down
Middle Ridge Down
Wadman's Coppice
Rough Down
West Lavington Down
West Down Plantn
East Down
Rushalt Down
Moneydown Bottom
Enford Down
Lavington Folly
Netheravon
Dovecote
Well Bottom
Wexland Fm
Dirtley Wood
Summer Down
Imber
The Rings
West Down
Orcheston Down
Old Farm Clump
Tilshead
Westdown Camp
Horse Down
Fore Down
Chapperton Down
Blackball Firs
Netheravon Down
Boreham Down
Bishopstrow Down
Middleton Down
Breach Hill
Orcheston Down
Salisbury Plain
Alton Down
Bustard Inn
Sack Hill
Battlesbury Hill
Breakheart Bottom
Middle Barn
Orcheston
Elston Hill Fm
Shrewton Lodge
Rollestone Camp
The Packway
Knighton Down
Larkhill
Durrington Walls
Woodcock
Boreham
Middle Hill
North Fm
West Hill Fm
Scratchbury Hill
Breakheart Hill
Fox Covert
Maddington Fm
Elston
Maddington
Shrewton
Middle Fm
Greenland Fm
Fargo Road
Durrington Down
Strangways
Fargo Plantn
Bishopstrow
Norton Bavant
Cotley Hill
East Hill Fm
Quebec Fm
Chitterne
Chitterne Down
Chitterne Road
Shrewton Road
Barleycroft Fm
Rollestone
Valley Fm
Maddington Down
Addestone Fm
Airman's Corner
Woodhenge
Heytesbury
Sutton Veny Ho
Sutton Veny
Codford Down
Clay Pit Hill
Visitor Centre
Stonehenge
Knook Camp
Knook
Knook Manor
Knook Horse Hill
Auckland Fm
East Codford Down
Cherry Lodge
Parsonage Down
West Amesbury
Long Ivor Fm
Tytherington
Corton
Manor Fm
Codford St Peter
Deptford Down
Yarnbury Castle
Berwick Down
Hill Fm
Winterbourne Stoke
Normanton Down
Wilsford Down
Normanton
Haycombe Hill Fm
Upton Lovell
Codford St Mary
Stony Hill
Parry's Field Barn
Oatlands Hill
Springbottom Fm
Wilsford
Littlecombe Hill
Tytherington Hill
Corton Hill
Littlecombe Bottom
Boyton
Lamb Down
Deptford Field Barn
Fisherton de la Mere
Steeple Langford Cow Down
Berwick Road
Berwick St James
Asserton Fm
Druid's Lodge
Westfield Fm
Amesbury Down
Sherrington
Stockton
Deptford
Little Down
Clifford Bottom
Lake
Long Bottom
Corton Down
Boyton Down
River Wylye
Bapton
Wylye Valley
Uppington Fm
Fox Hill Clump
Wiltshire
Steeple Langford
Stapleford Castle
Stapleford Down
Great Durnford
Redding Hanging
Well Bottom
Rowdean Hill
Sherrington Down
Park Bottom
Conygar Barn
Wylye
Langford Lakes
Serrington
Stapleford
Chain Hill
Camp Cottages
Boreland Hill
Upper Woodford
Stonehill Copse
Great Ridge
Longdean Bottom
Stony Hill
Roakham Bottom
Wylye Down
Bilbury Fm
Hanging Langford
Stoford Hill Buildings
Little Wishford
Netton
Pound Copse
Pertwood
Higher Pertwood
Craitt Hill
Bockerly Hill
Chiltinch Hill
Stockton Wood
The Bake
Chilmark Down
West Hill
Penning Bottom
Upper Farm Down
Little Langford
Ebsbury Hill
Ebsbury Copse
Great Wishford
Stoford
Middle Woodford
Salterton
Smithen Down
Lower Woodford
Salterton Down
Fonthill Bushes
Down Fm
Chicklade
Bake Barn
Woodbine Barn
Cranbourne Chase and West Wiltshire Downs
Teffont Down
Oakley Fm
Middle Hills
Grovely Wood
Grovely Lodge
Hadden Hill
South Newton
Little Durnford
Longhedge Fm
Knoyle Down Fm
Chicklade Bottom Fm
Bristol Road
Two Mile Down
Hawking Down
Berwick St Leonard
Manor Fm
Teffont Field Buildings
Firfields
Heath Wood
Folly Fm
Chilhampton
Bus Pk
Hill Fm
P&R
Hindon
Ridge Fm
Salisbury Road
Farmer Giles Farmstead
Manor Fm
Marshwood Fm
Crouch's Down
Barford Down
Grovely Hill
Avon Br
The Manor Ho
Old Sarum
Fonthill Bishop
Greenwich
Fonthill Ho
Ridge Hill
Ridge
Knap Lane
Chilmark
Mooray
Portash
Teffont Magna
Chilmark Common
Philipps House
Dinton
Manor Fm
Baverstock
Ditchampton
Bemerton Heath
Fugglestone St Peter
Westwood
Devizes Road
Stratford sub Castle
Castle Road
Bishopdown
Fonthill Gifford
Sheephouse Fm
Teffont Evias
Teffont Manor
Hindon Road
Hurdcott Ho
Barford St Martin
Ugford
Wilton
Quidhampton
Wilton Rd
East Knoyle
Ruddlemoor Fm
Beacon Hill
Fonthill Abbey
Ashley Wood Fm
Lady Down
Lower Chicksgrove
Chicksgrove
Ley Fm
Bus Pk
Mill Fm
River Nadder
Compton Wood
Burcombe
Wilton House
Bulbridge
Wilton Park
Bemerton
Netherhampton
Salisbury
Kinghay
Lawn Fm
Tisbury
Upper Chicksgrove
Harebedene Wood
Great Ground Hill
Fir Hill
Fovant
Compton Chamberlayne
Naishes Fm
Burcombe Ivers
Hunt's Down
Home Fm
Netherhampton Road
Churchfields
Cathedral
West Harnham
Trad Est
Mompesson House
Upper Leigh
Billhay Fm
East Hatch
Hatch
Wallmead Fm
Withyslade
Sutton Row
Sutton Mandeville
East Fm
Manor Fm
Flamstone Fm
Hare Warren
Harnham
0 1 2 3 miles
0 1 2 3 4 5 km

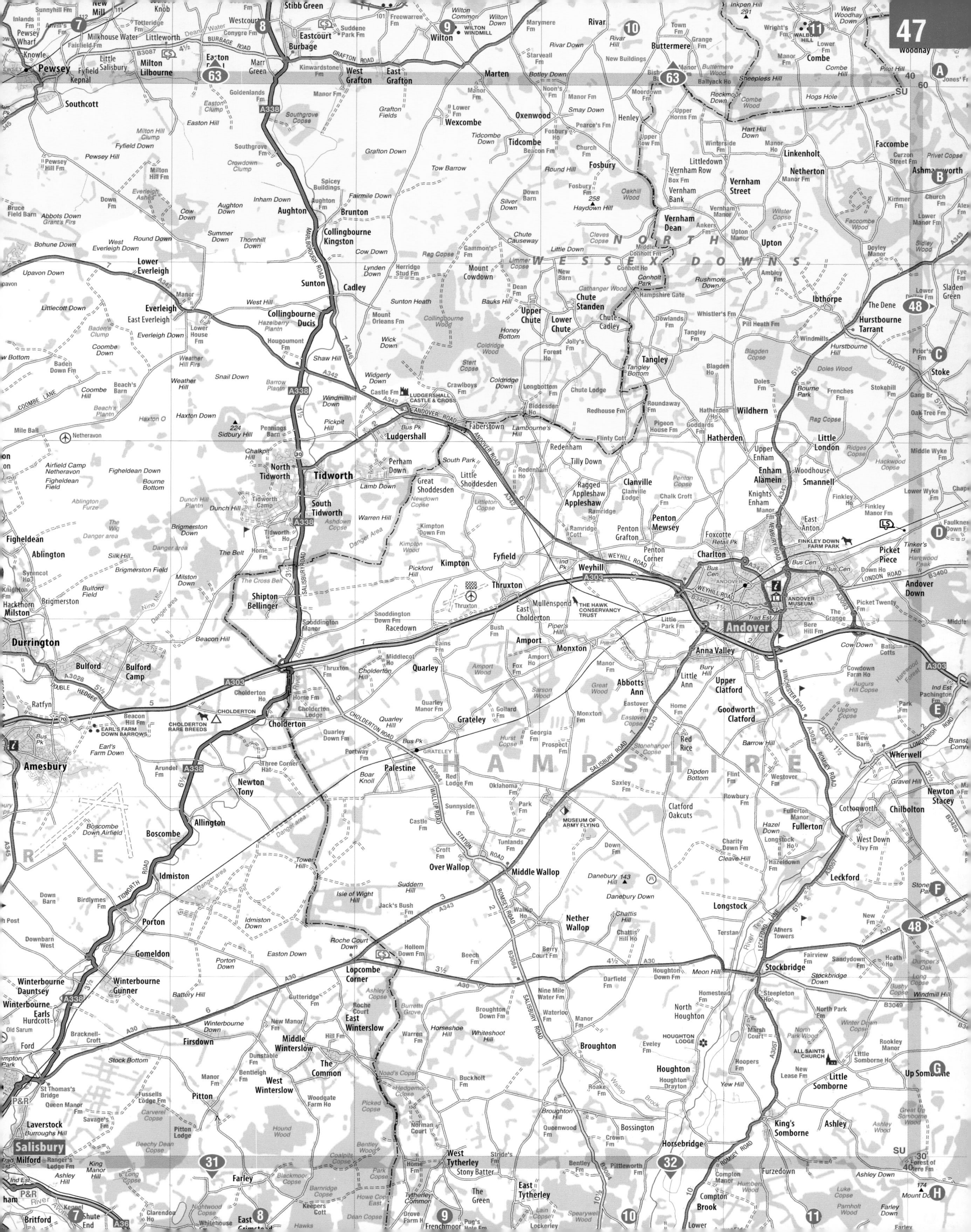
Pewsey
Knowle
Pewsey Wharf
Milkhouse Water
Littleworth
Milton Lilbourne
Little Salisbury
Fyfield
Kepnal
Southcott
Easton
Marr Green
Stibb Green
Eastcourt
Burbage
Sudden Park Fm
Freewarren Fm
Wilton
Wilton Windmill
Wilton Common
Wilton Down
Marten
Rivar
Rivar Hill
Buttermere
Combe
Woodhay
West Grafton
East Grafton
Goldenlands Fm
Kinwardstone Fm
Easton Hill
Manor Fm
Grafton Fields
Southgrove Copse
Grafton Down
Wexcombe
Tidcombe
Oxenwood
Fosbury
Henley
Linkenholt
Faccombe
Netherton
Ashmansworth
Littledown
Vernham Row
Vernham Street
Vernham Dean
Upton
NORTH WESSEX DOWNS
Pewsey Hill
Aughton
Brunton
Collingbourne Kingston
Cadley
Sunton
Lower Everleigh
Everleigh
East Everleigh
Collingbourne Ducis
Upavon Down
Mount Cowdown
Chute Standen
Upper Chute
Lower Chute
Chute Cadley
Tangley
Ibthorpe
Hurstbourne Tarrant
The Dene
Stoke
Ludgershall
Ludgershall Castle & Cross
Faberstown
Redenham
Wildhern
Hatherden
Little London
Netheravon
Sidbury Hill
Haxton Down
North Tidworth
Tidworth
South Tidworth
Perham Down
Great Shoddesden
Little Shoddesden
Clanville
Appleshaw
Ragged Appleshaw
Upper Enham
Enham Alamein
Knights Enham
Smannell
Penton Mewsey
Penton Grafton
Penton Corner
Charlton
Fighelden
Ablington
Kimpton
Fyfield
Weyhill
Thruxton
Mullenspond
The Hawk Conservancy Trust
East Cholderton
Andover
Andover Museum
Picket Piece
Andover Down
Anna Valley
Finkley Down Farm Park
Milston
Durrington
Bulford
Bulford Camp
Shipton Bellinger
Racedown
Amport
Monxton
Quarley
Abbotts Ann
Little Ann
Upper Clatford
Goodworth Clatford
Cholderton
Cholderton Rare Breeds
Earl's Farm Down Barrows
Ratfyn
Amesbury
Grateley
Palestine
HAMPSHIRE
Red Rice
Wherwell
Newton Stacey
Chilbolton
Cottonworth
Newton Tony
Allington
Boscombe
Boscombe Down Airfield
Idmiston
Porton
Gomeldon
Over Wallop
Middle Wallop
Museum of Army Flying
Nether Wallop
Danebury Hill
Clatford Oakcuts
Fullerton
Leckford
Longstock
Stockbridge
Winterbourne Dauntsey
Winterbourne Gunner
Winterbourne Earls
Hurdcott
Old Sarum
Ford
Lopcombe Corner
East Winterslow
Middle Winterslow
The Common
West Winterslow
Firsdown
Broughton
Houghton
Houghton Lodge
North Houghton
Little Somborne
All Saints Church
Up Somborne
King's Somborne
Ashley
Laverstock
Salisbury
Milford
Pitton
Bossington
Horsebridge
West Tytherley
Stony Batter
East Tytherley
The Green
Farley
Britford
Compton Brook
Furzedown
A338
A342
A343
A303
A30
A3057
A36
A345
B3087
B3400
B3048
B3084
B3420
B3049
63
48
31
32
7
8
9
10
11

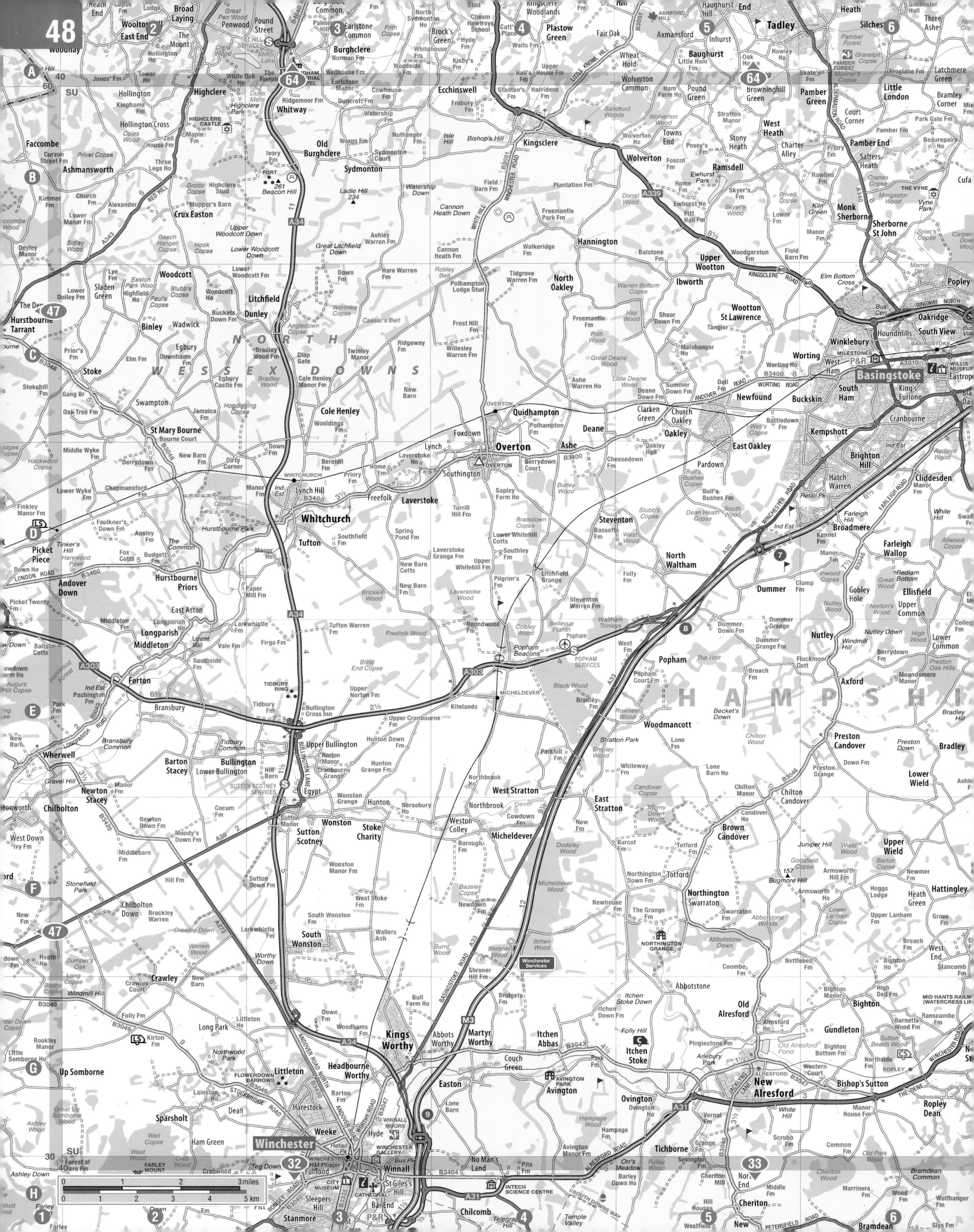
A
B
C
D
E
F
G
H
1
2
3
4
5
6
Woolton Hill
East End
Broad Laying
Pound Street
Burghclere
Earlstone Common
Plastow Green
Axmansford
Baughurst
Tadley
Silchester
Highclere
Whitway
Ecchinswell
Kingsclere
Wolverton
Ramsdell
Pamber Green
Little London
Faccombe
Ashmansworth
Old Burghclere
Sydmonton
Beacon Hill
Crux Easton
Hannington
Monk Sherborne
Sherborne St John
Woodcott
Litchfield
Dunley
North Oakley
Ibworth
Upper Wootton
Wootton St Lawrence
Hurstbourne Tarrant
Binley
Stoke
NORTH WESSEX DOWNS
Cole Henley
Quidhampton
Overton
Deane
Ashe
Oakley
East Oakley
Newfound
Worting
Winklebury
Basingstoke
Buckskin
South Ham
Kempshott
Brighton Hill
Cliddesden
Oakridge
South View
St Mary Bourne
Whitchurch
Freefolk
Laverstoke
Tufton
Steventon
North Waltham
Dummer
Farleigh Wallop
Ellisfield
Picket Piece
Hurstbourne Priors
Andover Down
Longparish
Middleton
Popham
Nutley
Axford
Forton
Bransbury
Woodmancott
Preston Candover
Bradley
Wherwell
Barton Stacey
Bullington
Upper Bullington
West Stratton
East Stratton
Chilton Candover
Lower Wield
Newton Stacey
Chilbolton
Sutton Scotney
Wonston
Hunton
Stoke Charity
Micheldever
Brown Candover
Upper Wield
Northington
Hattingley
South Wonston
Crawley
Abbotstone
Old Alresford
Bighton
Gundleton
Kings Worthy
Martyr Worthy
Itchen Abbas
Itchen Stoke
Littleton
Headbourne Worthy
Up Somborne
Avington
New Alresford
Bishop's Sutton
Ropley Dean
Easton
Ovington
Tichborne
Sparsholt
Weeke
Winchester
Winnall
Chilcomb
Cheriton
Bramdean
HAMPSHI
A34
A303
A30
A33
M3
A31
A339
B3400
B3047
B3046
B3049
B3048
0 1 2 3 miles
0 1 2 3 4 5 km

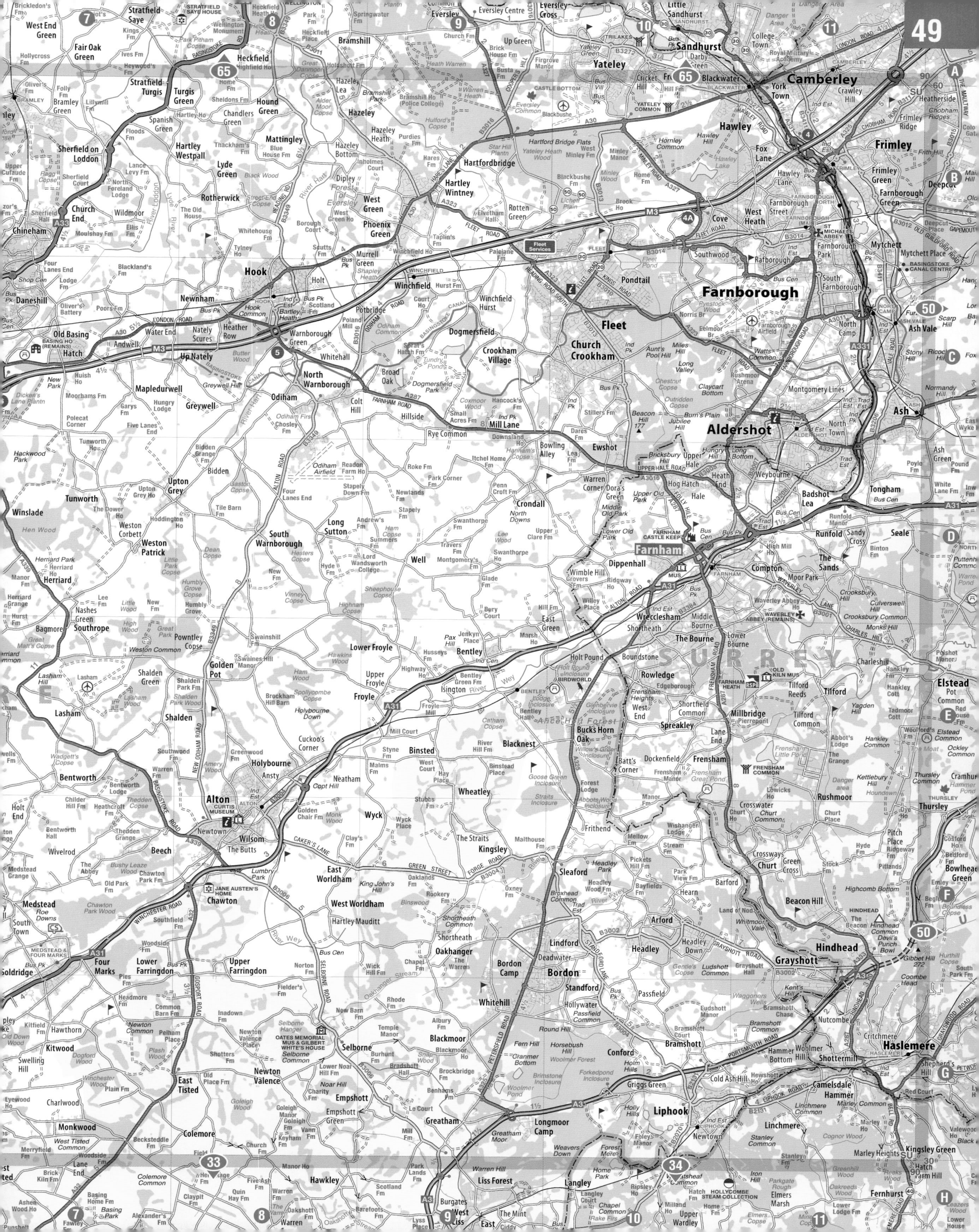

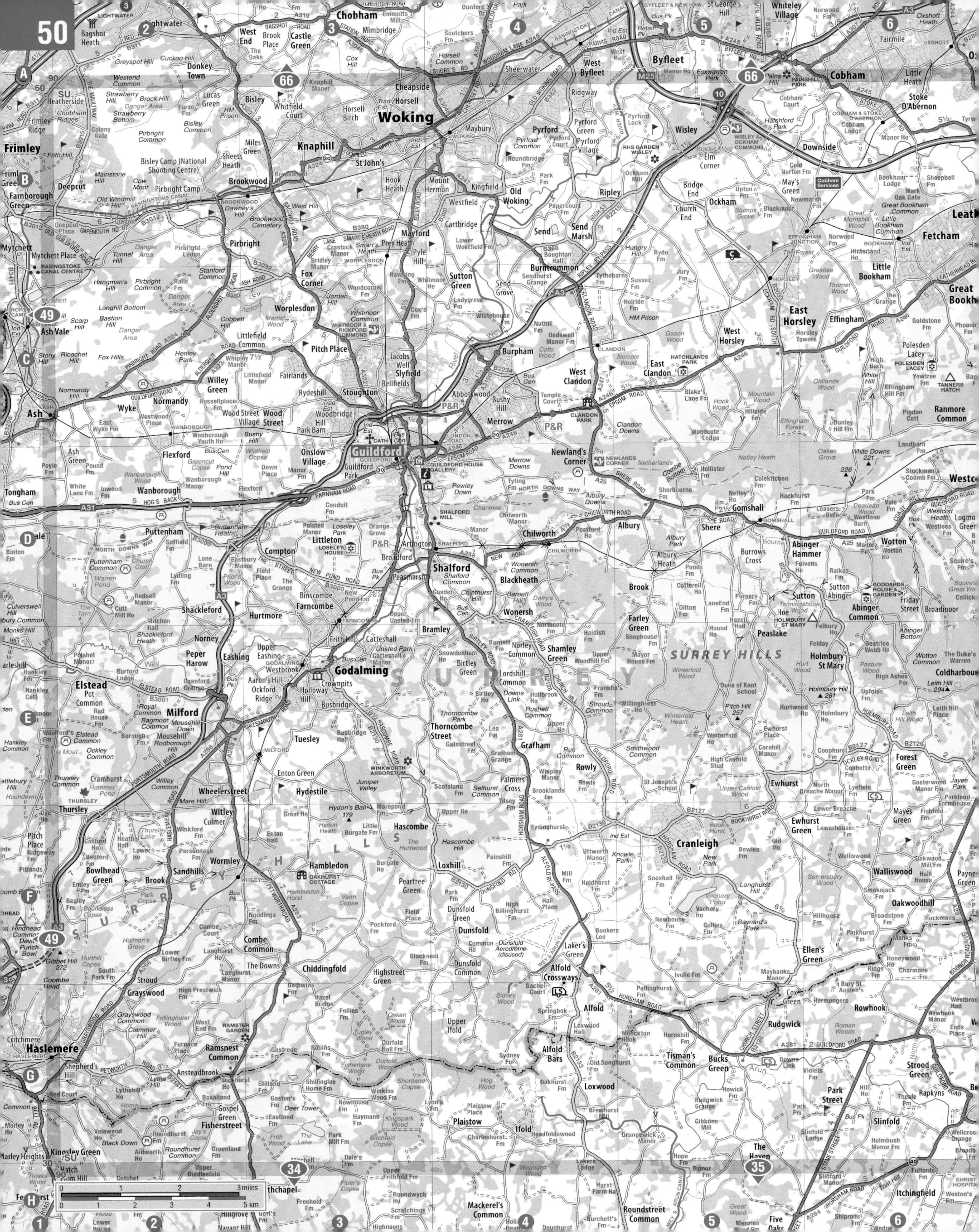
Lightwater
Bagshot Heath
Chobham
West End
Brook Place
Castle Green
Mimbridge
Byfleet
West Byfleet
Whiteley Village
Cobham
Fairmile
Little Heath
Stoke D'Abernon
Frimley
Frimley Ridge
Heatherside
Donkey Town
Lucas Green
Bisley
Whitfield Court
Horsell
Cheapside
Woking
Sheerwater
Maybury
Pyrford
Pyrford Green
Pyrford Village
Ridgway
Wisley
Downside
Knaphill
St John's
Bisley Camp (National Shooting Centre)
Pirbright Camp
Deepcut
Farnborough Green
Brookwood
Mount Hermon
Kingfield
Old Woking
Ripley
Ockham
Bridge End
Church End
Elm Corner
Mytchett
Mytchett Place
Pirbright
Mayford
Westfield
Send
Send Marsh
Burntcommon
Fetcham
Little Bookham
Great Bookham
Worplesdon
Fox Corner
Sutton Green
Send Grove
East Horsley
West Horsley
Effingham
Ash Vale
Pitch Place
Jacobs Well
Slyfield
Burpham
West Clandon
East Clandon
Polesden Lacey
Willey Green
Normandy
Wyke
Ash
Stoughton
Rydeshill
Wood Street Village
Merrow
Ranmore Common
Guildford
Onslow Village
Flexford
Ash Green
Guildford Park
Newland's Corner
Tongham
Wanborough
Puttenham
Compton
Littleton
Artington
Chilworth
Albury
Shere
Gomshall
Abinger Hammer
Wotton
Shalford
Blackheath
Farncombe
Binscombe
Peasmarsh
Brook
Farley Green
Peaslake
Sutton Abinger
Abinger Common
Shackleford
Hurtmore
Bramley
Wonersh
Peper Harow
Eashing
Godalming
Norney
Shamley Green
SURREY HILLS
SURREY
Holmbury St Mary
Coldharbour
Elstead
Milford
Tuesley
Thorncombe Street
Grafham
Rowly
Ewhurst
Forest Green
Thursley
Wheelerstreet
Hydestile
Hascombe
Cranleigh
Witley
Ewhurst Green
Wormley
Hambledon
Sandhills
Brook
Bowlhead Green
Loxhill
Peartree Green
Walliswood
Oakwoodhill
Dunsfold
Combe Common
Chiddingfold
Ellen's Green
Alfold Crossways
Grayswood
Alfold
Rudgwick
Rowhook
Haslemere
Ramsnest Common
Alfold Bars
Tisman's Common
Bucks Green
Strood Green
Loxwood
Park Street
Shepherd's Hill
Gospel Green
Fisherstreet
Plaistow
Ifold
Slinfold
Kingsley Green
The Haven
Itchingfield
Mackerel's Common
Roundstreet Common
Five Oaks
3 miles
5 km

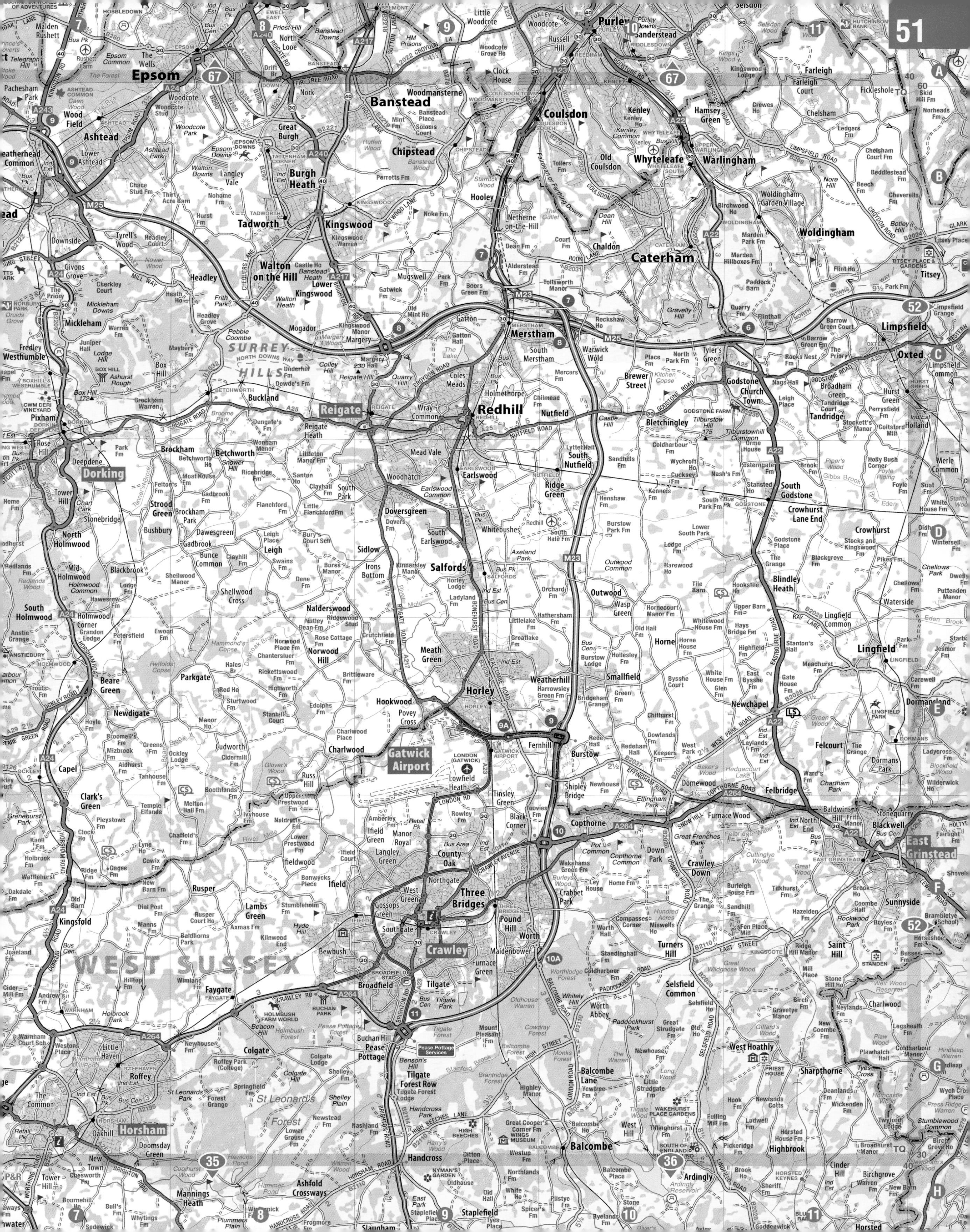
Epsom
Banstead
Purley
Sanderstead
Coulsdon
Ashtead
Chipstead
Burgh Heath
Whyteleafe
Warlingham
Tadworth
Kingswood
Hooley
Caterham
Woldingham
Walton on the Hill
Headley
Lower Kingswood
Titsey
Mickleham
Merstham
Limpsfield
Oxted
SURREY HILLS
Buckland
Reigate
Redhill
Nutfield
Bletchingley
Godstone
Tandridge
Pixham
Dorking
Brockham
Betchworth
Earlswood
South Nutfield
South Godstone
Salfords
Sidlow
Leigh
Outwood
Horne
Lingfield
Beare Green
Parkgate
Horley
Smallfield
Newchapel
Newdigate
Charlwood
Gatwick Airport
Felbridge
Capel
Copthorne
East Grinstead
Crawley Down
Ifield
Three Bridges
Crawley
Sunnyside
Kingsfold
WEST SUSSEX
Faygate
Turners Hill
Saint Hill
Colgate
Pease Pottage
West Hoathly
Sharpthorne
Roffey
Horsham
Balcombe
Handcross
Ardingly
Staplefield
Mannings Heath
Highbrook
Forest Row
Dormansland
Felcourt
Blindley Heath
Crowhurst
Burstow
Worth
Pound Hill
Broadfield
Tilgate
Little Haven
Rusper
Lambs Green

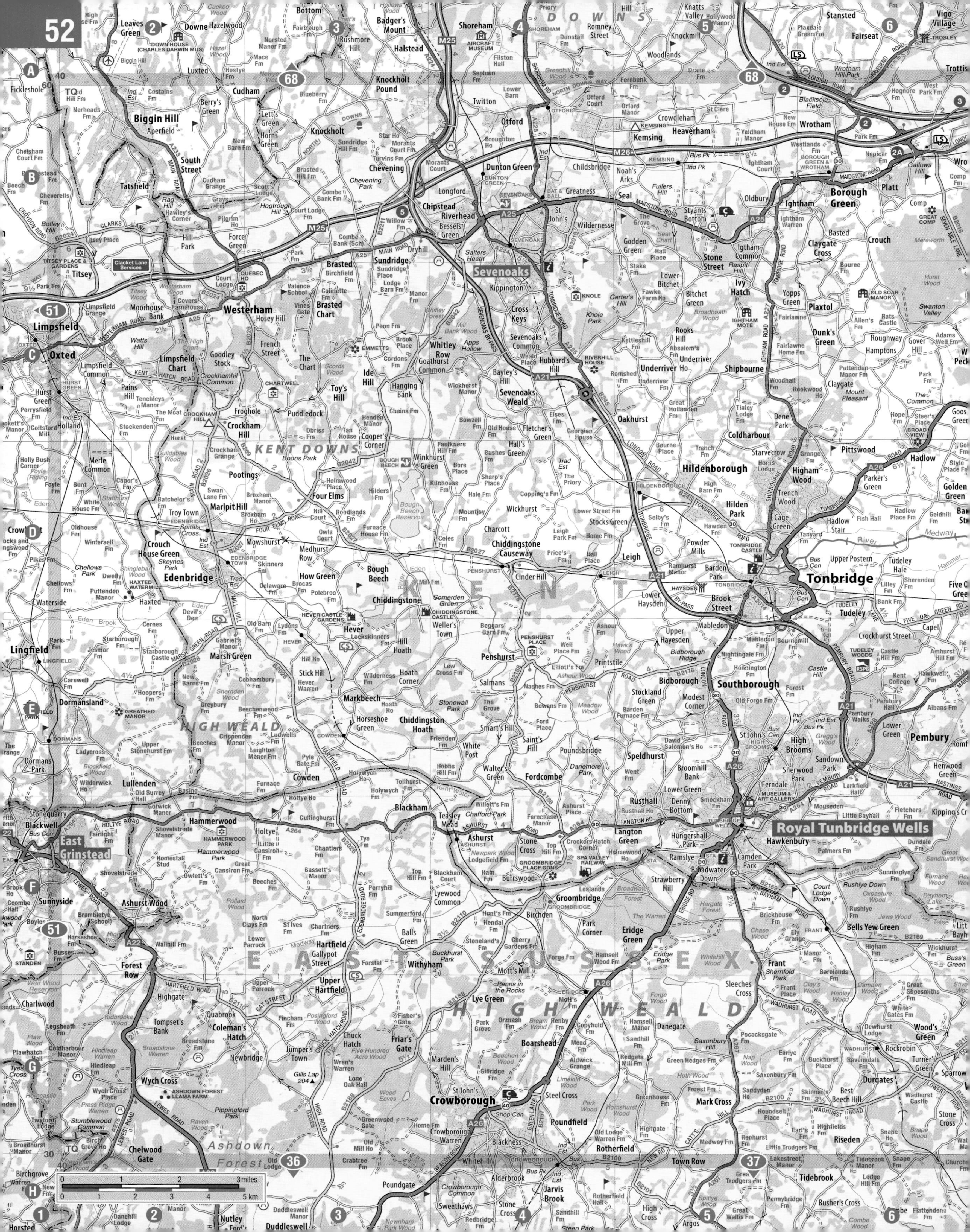

Biggin Hill
Westerham
Limpsfield
Oxted
Edenbridge
Lingfield
East Grinstead
Sevenoaks
Otford
Kemsing
Wrotham
Borough Green
Tonbridge
Hildenborough
Southborough
Royal Tunbridge Wells
Pembury
Crowborough
Hartfield
Forest Row
Penshurst
Chiddingstone
Hever
Kent Downs
KENT
HIGH WEALD
EAST SUSSEX
Ashdown Forest
M25
M26
A21
A25
A26
A22
68
51
36
37
0 1 2 3 miles
0 1 2 3 4 5 km

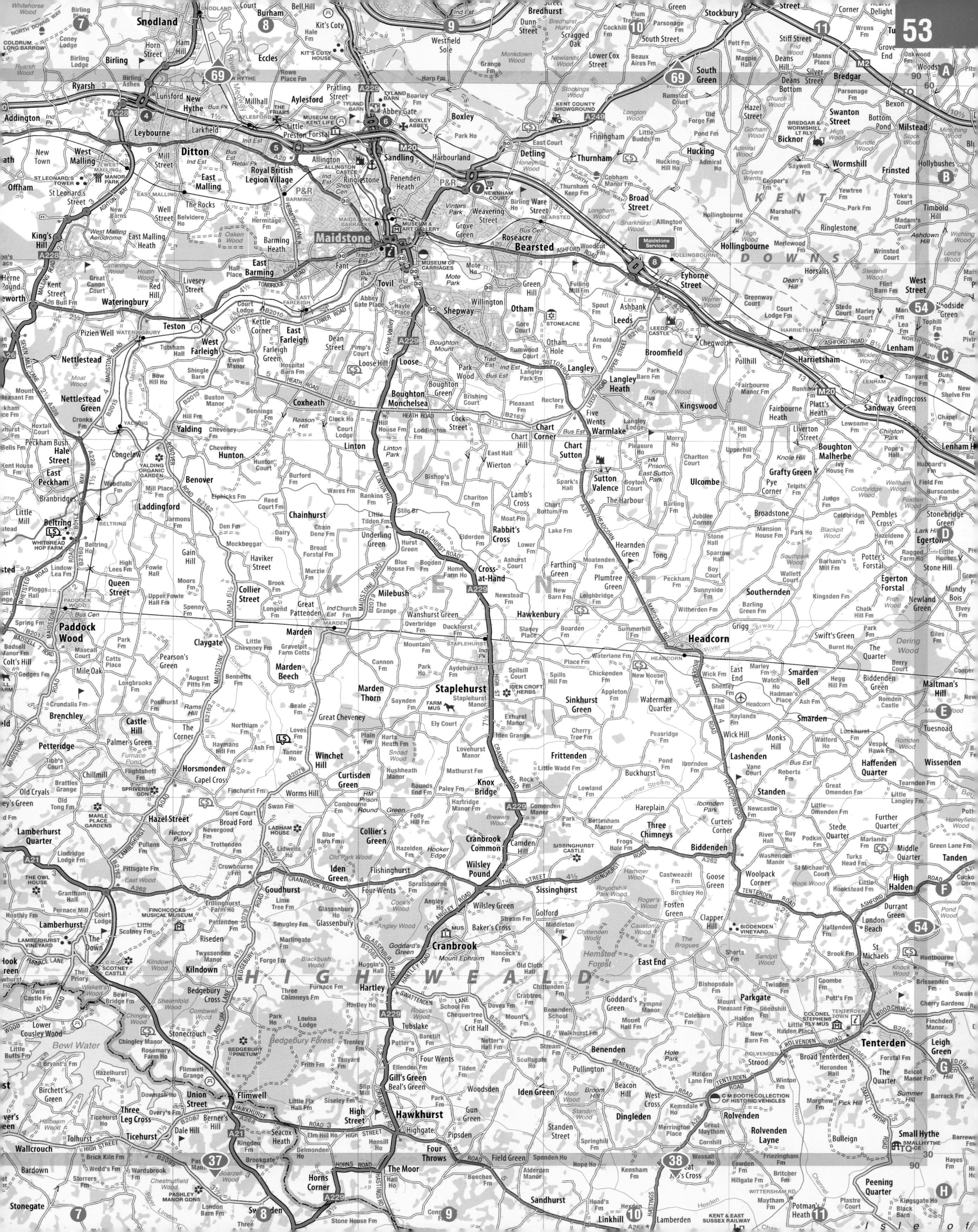
Snodland
Burham
Eccles
Aylesford
Boxley
Bredhurst
Stockbury
Bredgar
Ryarsh
Birling
Leybourne
Larkfield
Ditton
Addington
West Malling
East Malling
Royal British Legion Village
Allington
Sandling
Penenden Heath
Detling
Thurnham
Hucking
Bicknor
Milstead
Frinsted
Wormshill
Maidstone
Bearsted
Hollingbourne
Eyhorne Street
Harrietsham
Lenham
Kings Hill
Wateringbury
Teston
East Barming
Barming Heath
Tovil
Shepway
Otham
Leeds
Langley
Langley Heath
Kingswood
Broomfield
East Farleigh
West Farleigh
Loose
Coxheath
Boughton Monchelsea
Yalding
Nettlestead
Nettlestead Green
Hunton
Linton
Chart Sutton
Sutton Valence
Ulcombe
Boughton Malherbe
Grafty Green
Charing
Egerton
Egerton Forstal
Laddingford
Beltring
Chainhurst
Collier Street
Marden
Staplehurst
Headcorn
Paddock Wood
Claygate
Marden Beech
Marden Thorn
Sinkhurst Green
Frittenden
Smarden
Biddenden
Brenchley
Castle Hill
Horsmonden
Petteridge
Lamberhurst Quarter
Lamberhurst
Goudhurst
Kilndown
Hartley
Cranbrook
Sissinghurst
Three Chimneys
High Halden
Tenterden
St Michaels
Rolvenden
Rolvenden Layne
Benenden
Iden Green
Hawkhurst
Flimwell
Ticehurst
Union Street
Sandhurst
Small Hythe
Wissenden
Bethersden
Bewl Water
Bedgebury Forest
Bedgebury Pinetum
Scotney Castle
Sissinghurst Castle
Leeds Castle
Stoneacre
Maidstone Services
C M Booth Collection of Historic Vehicles
Colonel Stephens Rly Mus
Biddenden Vineyard
Iden Croft Herbs
Whitbread Hop Farm
Yalding Organic Garden
Marle Place Gardens
Finchcocks Musical Museum
Lamberhurst Vineyard
Pashley Manor Gdns
Kent & East Sussex Railway
K E N T
K E N T
D O W N S
H I G H W E A L D
M20
M2
A20
A21
A26
A228
A229
A249
A262
A274
A268
B2010
B2079
B2160
B2162
B2163
Tunbridge Wells
A
B
C
D
E
F
G
H
69
37
38
54
7
8
9
10
11

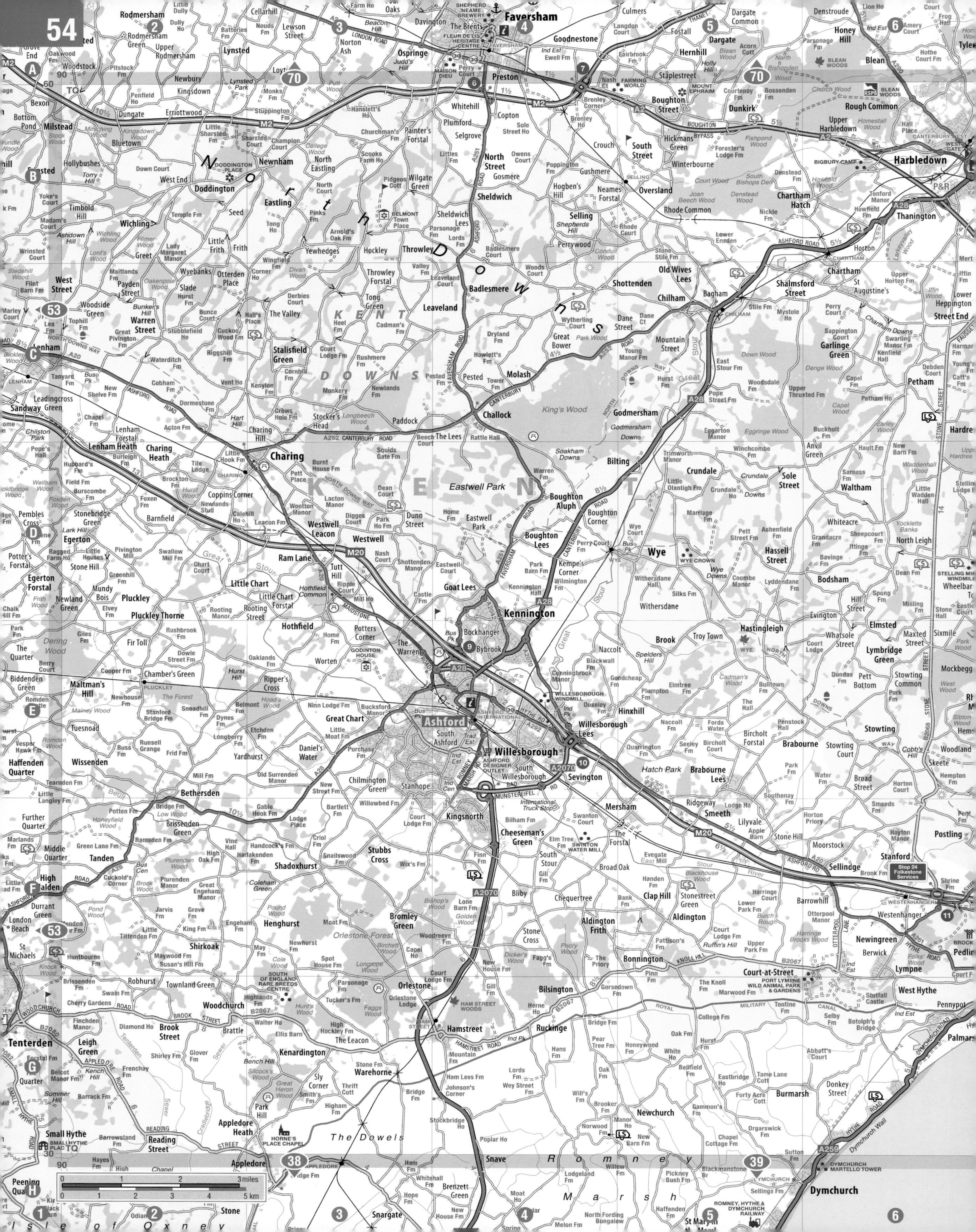
Rodmersham
Rodmersham Green
Upper Rodmersham
Lynsted
Lewson Street
Norton Ash
Ospringe
Davington
The Brents
Faversham
Goodnestone
Culmers
Dargate Common
Dargate
Hernhill
Denstroude
Honey Hill
Blean
Preston
Boughton Street
Dunkirk
Rough Common
Upper Harbledown
Harbledown
Milstead
Bexon
Bottom Pond
Bluetown
Hollybushes
Newnham
Doddington
North Eastling
Eastling
Whitehill
Plumford
Selgrove
Copton
North Street
Gosmere
Sheldwich
Sheldwich Lees
Painter's Forstal
Wilgate Green
South Street
Gushmere
Oversland
Hogben's Hill
Neames Forstal
Selling
Perrywood
Winterbourne
Chartham Hatch
Thanington
Timbold Hill
Wichling
Seed
Little Frith
Frith
Yewhedges
Hockley
Throwley
Throwley Forstal
Leaveland
Badlesmere
Old Wives Lees
Shottenden
Chilham
Bagham
Chartham
Shalmsford Street
St Augustine's
Lower Hepington
Street End
West Street
Woodside Green
Warren Street
Slade
Otterden Place
Payden Street
The Valley
Tong Green
Stalisfield Green
Molash
Challock
Pested
Dane Street
Mountain Street
Great Bower
Godmersham
Garlinge Green
Petham
Lenham
Sandway
Leadingcross Green
Lenham Heath
Charing Heath
Charing
Paddock
Stocker's Head
The Lees
King's Wood
Bilting
Crundale
Sole Street
Waltham
Hardres
Pembles Cross
Egerton
Stonebridge Green
Barnfield
Coppins Corner
Westwell Leacon
Westwell
Dunn Street
Eastwell Park
Boughton Aluph
Boughton Corner
Boughton Lees
Wye
Hassell Street
Bodsham
North Leigh
Potter's Forstal
Egerton Forstal
Stone Hill
Pluckley
Pluckley Thorne
Little Chart
Little Chart Forstal
Ram Lane
Tutt Hill
Hothfield
Potters Corner
Goat Lees
Kennington
Withersdane
Hastingleigh
Elmsted
Sixmile
Brook
Troy Town
Evington
Hill Street
Whatsole Street
Lymbridge Green
Mockbegg
Biddenden Green
Maltman's Hill
Chamber's Green
Ripper's Cross
Worten
The Warren
Bockhanger
Bybrook
Naccolt
Hinxhill
Stowting Common
Pett Bottom
Ashford
South Ashford
Willesborough
Willesborough Lees
Great Chart
Daniel's Water
Yardhurst
Tuesnoad
Haffenden Quarter
Wissenden
Bethersden
Chilmington Green
Stanhope
South Willesborough
Sevington
Brabourne
Brabourne Lees
Stowting
Stowting Court
Woodland
Kingsnorth
Mersham
Smeeth
Ridgeway
Lilyvale
Stone Hill
Moorstock
Sellindge
Postling
Stanford
Further Quarter
Brissenden Green
Middle Quarter
Tanden
Shadoxhurst
Stubbs Cross
Cheeseman's Green
South Stour
Broad Oak
The Forstal
High Halden
Bliby
Chequertree
Clap Hill
Aldington
Barrowhill
Westenhanger
Newingreen
Berwick
Lympne
Pedlinge
Durrant Green
London Beach
Henghurst
Bromley Green
Stone Cross
Aldington Frith
Bonnington
Court-at-Street
West Hythe
St Michaels
Shirkoak
Robhurst
Townland Green
Woodchurch
Orlestone
Bilsington
Hamstreet
Ruckinge
Brattle
Brook Street
Tenterden
Leigh Green
Kenardington
Warehorne
Sly Corner
Newchurch
Burmarsh
Donkey Street
Palmarsh
Small Hythe
Reading Street
Appledore Heath
Appledore
The Dowels
Snave
Romney Marsh
Brenzett Green
Dymchurch
Snargate
Stone
Isle of Oxney
Kent
North Downs

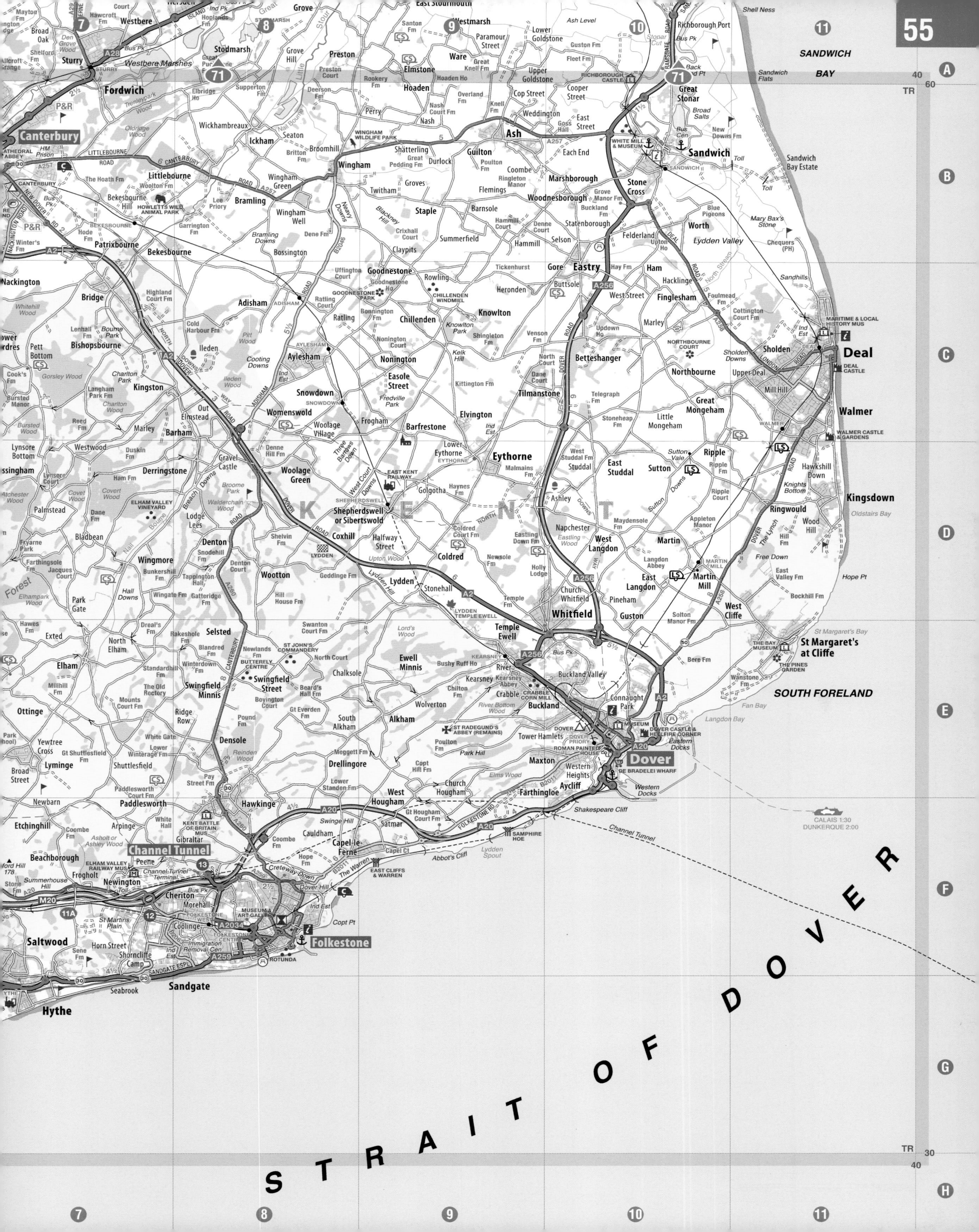

SANDWICH BAY
Shell Ness
Richborough Port
Sandwich Flats
Sandwich
Sandwich Bay Estate
Great Stonar
Broad Salts
New Downs Fm
Stone Cross
Worth
Lydden Valley
Mary Bax's Stone
Chequers (PH)
Sandhills
Deal
DEAL CASTLE
MARITIME & LOCAL HISTORY MUS
Sholden
Upper Deal
Mill Hill
Walmer
WALMER CASTLE & GARDENS
Hawkshill Down
Knights Bottom
Kingsdown
Oldstairs Bay
Ringwould
Wood Hill
Free Down
Hope Pt
East Valley Fm
Bockhill Fm
St Margaret's Bay
THE BAY MUSEUM
St Margaret's at Cliffe
THE PINES GARDEN
SOUTH FORELAND
Fan Bay
Langdon Bay
CALAIS 1:30
DUNKERQUE 2:00
Channel Tunnel
STRAIT OF DOVER
Canterbury
Sturry
Fordwich
Westbere
Westbere Marshes
Stodmarsh
Grove
Preston
Elmstone
Hoaden
Westmarsh
Ware
Lower Goldstone
Upper Goldstone
RICHBOROUGH CASTLE
Cop Street
Weddington
Ash
Guilton
Wickhambreaux
Ickham
Seaton
Wingham
WINGHAM WILDLIFE PARK
Shatterling
Durlock
Littlebourne
Bramling
HOWLETTS WILD ANIMAL PARK
Bekesbourne
Patrixbourne
Nackington
Bridge
Bishopsbourne
Kingston
Barham
Adisham
Aylesham
Nonington
Goodnestone
GOODNESTONE PARK
CHILLENDEN WINDMILL
Chillenden
Knowlton
Staple
Barnsole
Marshborough
Woodnesborough
Eastry
Betteshanger
Northbourne
NORTHBOURNE COURT
Great Mongeham
Little Mongeham
Ripple
Sutton
East Studdal
Tilmanstone
Eythorne
Elvington
Barfrestone
Snowdown
Womenswold
Woolage Green
Shepherdswell or Sibertswold
EAST KENT RAILWAY
K E N T
Coxhill
Coldred
West Langdon
East Langdon
Martin
Martin Mill
West Cliffe
Guston
Pineham
Whitfield
Temple Ewell
Lydden
Denton
Wootton
Selsted
Wingmore
Elham
Ottinge
Lyminge
Densole
Swingfield Minnis
Swingfield Street
ST JOHN'S COMMANDERY
Ewell Minnis
Alkham
River
Kearsney
Crabble
CRABBLE CORN MILL
Buckland
Buckland Valley
Connaught Park
Dover
DOVER CASTLE & HELLFIRE CORNER
Eastern Docks
Western Docks
DE BRADELEI WHARF
ROMAN PAINTED HOUSE
Tower Hamlets
Maxton
Western Heights
Aycliff
Farthingloe
Shakespeare Cliff
West Hougham
Church Hougham
Drellingore
Capel-le-Ferne
EAST CLIFFS & WARREN
SAMPHIRE HOE
Abbot's Cliff
Hawkinge
KENT BATTLE OF BRITAIN MUS
Paddlesworth
Etchinghill
Channel Tunnel
Peene
Newington
Frogholt
Beachborough
ELHAM VALLEY RAILWAY MUS
Cheriton
Morehall
Cooling
Folkestone
MUSEUM & ART GALLERY
ROTUNDA
Sandgate
Seabrook
Saltwood
Hythe
Horn Street
Shorncliffe Camp
ST RADEGUND'S ABBEY (REMAINS)
TR

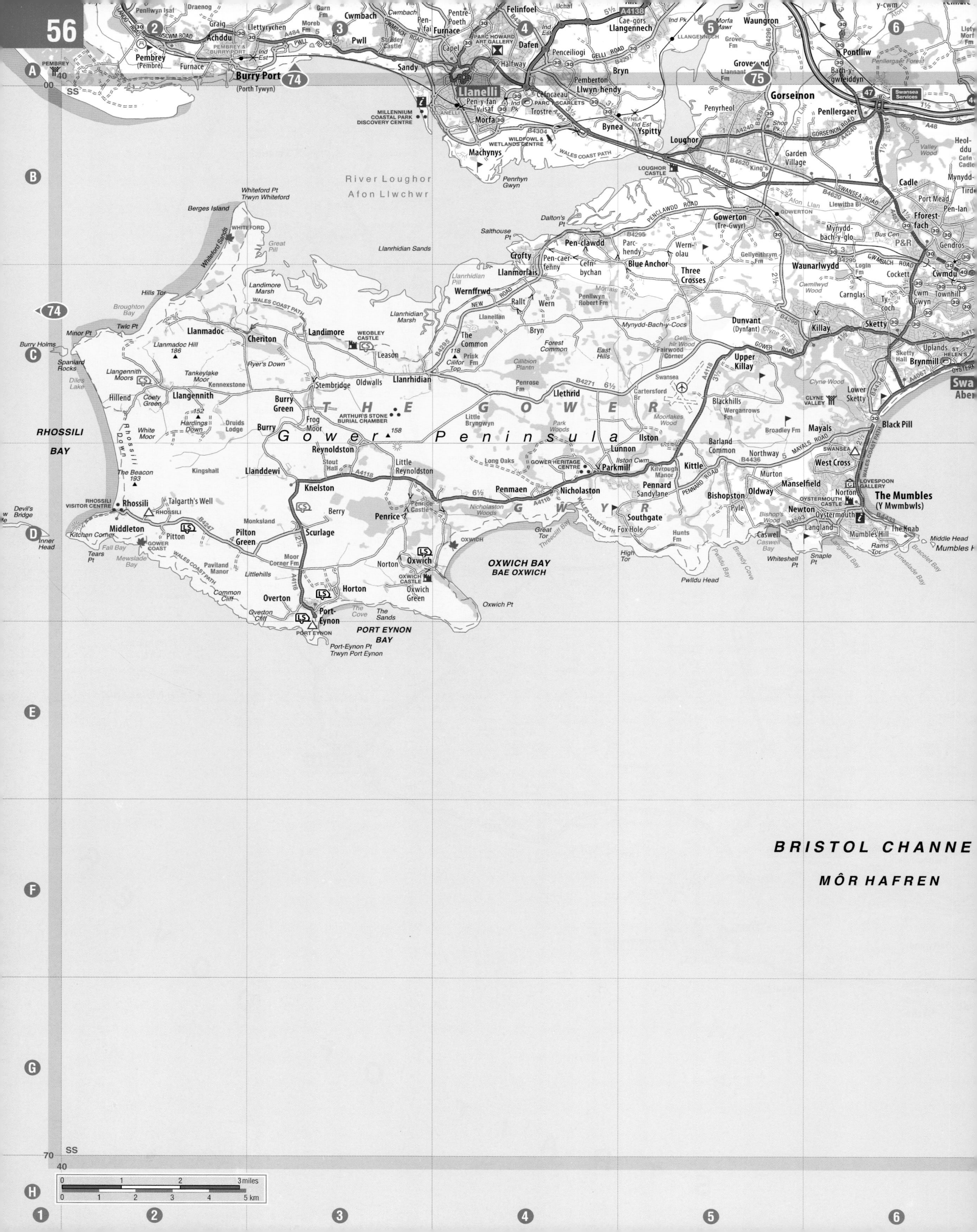
Pembrey
(Pembre)
Burry Port
(Porth Tywyn)
Achddu
Cwmbach
Pwll
Furnace
Sandy
Felinfoel
Dafen
Llanelli
Llangennech
Waungron
Pontlliw
Gorseinon
Penllergaer
Loughor
Bynea
Yspitty
Machynys
Morfa
River Loughor
Afon Llwchwr
Llanrhidian Sands
Whiteford Pt
Trwyn Whiteford
Berges Island
Whiteford Sands
Gowerton
(Tre-Gwyr)
Pen-clawdd
Crofty
Llanmorlais
Blue Anchor
Three Crosses
Waunarlwydd
Cwmdu
Cockett
Killay
Sketty
Dunvant
(Dynfant)
Upper Killay
Brynmill
Swansea
Black Pill
Mayals
West Cross
The Mumbles
(Y Mwmbwls)
Oystermouth
Mumbles Hill
Mumbles Head
Langland
Caswell
Newton
Norton
Manselfield
Bishopston
Kittle
Murton
Oldway
Pennard
Southgate
Parkmill
Ilston
Lunnon
Nicholaston
Penmaen
Llethrid
THE GOWER
Gower Peninsula
GŴYR
Llanrhidian
Oldwalls
Landimore
Cheriton
Llanmadoc
Llangennith
Burry Green
Burry
Reynoldston
Llanddewi
Knelston
Scurlage
Pilton Green
Rhossili
Middleton
RHOSSILI BAY
Rhossili Down
Burry Holms
Port-Eynon
Horton
Overton
Oxwich
Penrice
OXWICH BAY
BAE OXWICH
PORT EYNON BAY
Port-Eynon Pt
Trwyn Port Eynon
Worms Head
BRISTOL CHANNEL
MÔR HAFREN
0 1 2 3 miles
0 1 2 3 4 5 km

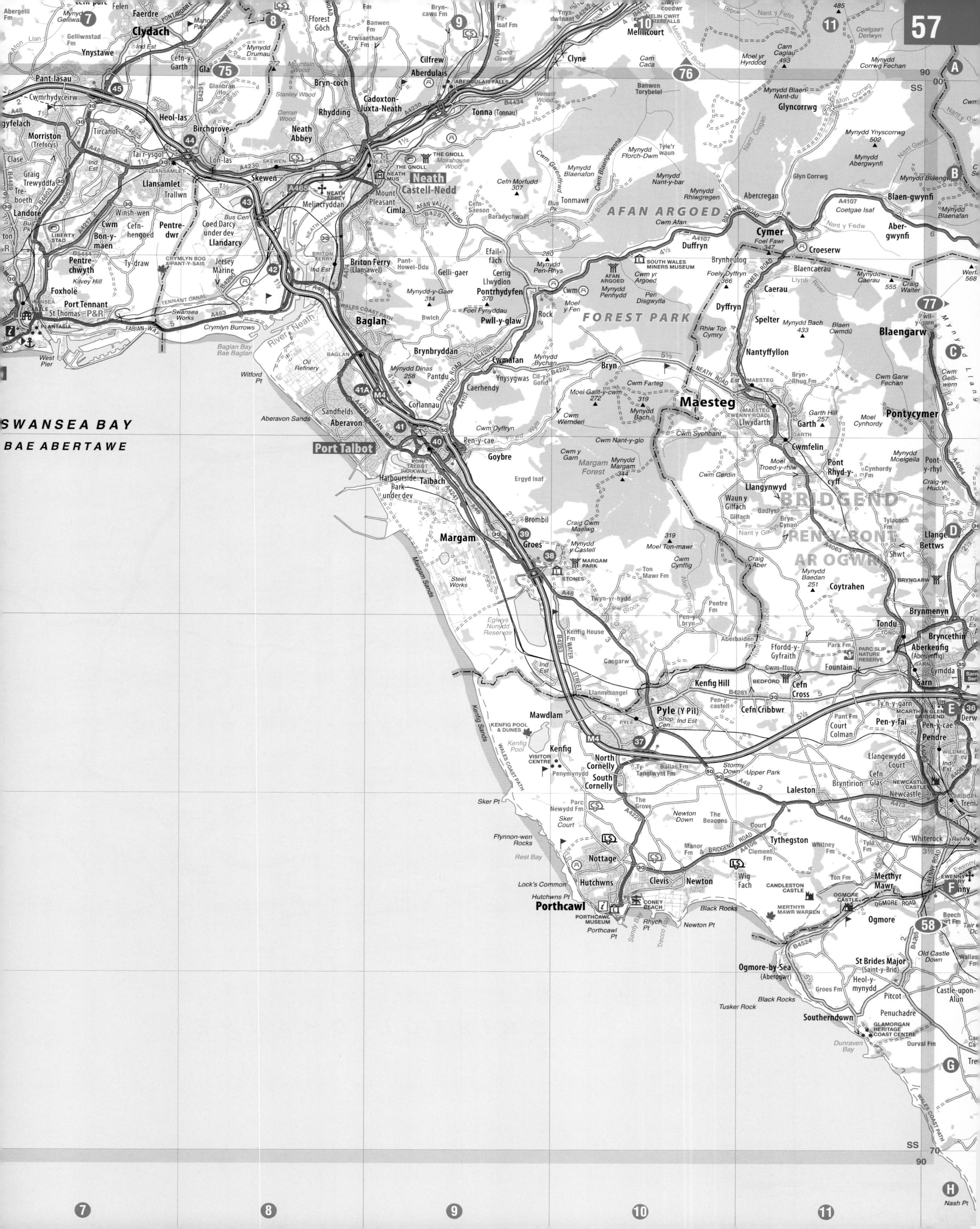

SWANSEA BAY
BAE ABERTAWE
Clydach
Morriston
Neath
Castell-Nedd
Port Talbot
Baglan
Aberavon
Margam
AFAN ARGOED
FOREST PARK
Maesteg
Cymer
BRIDGEND
PEN-Y-BONT AR OGWR
Pyle (Y Pîl)
Kenfig Hill
Porthcawl
Nottage
Ogmore-by-Sea
Laleston
Pontycymer
Blaengarw
Margam Sands
Kenfig Sands
Skewen
Llansamlet
Briton Ferry
Cwmafan
Tonna
Glyncorrwg

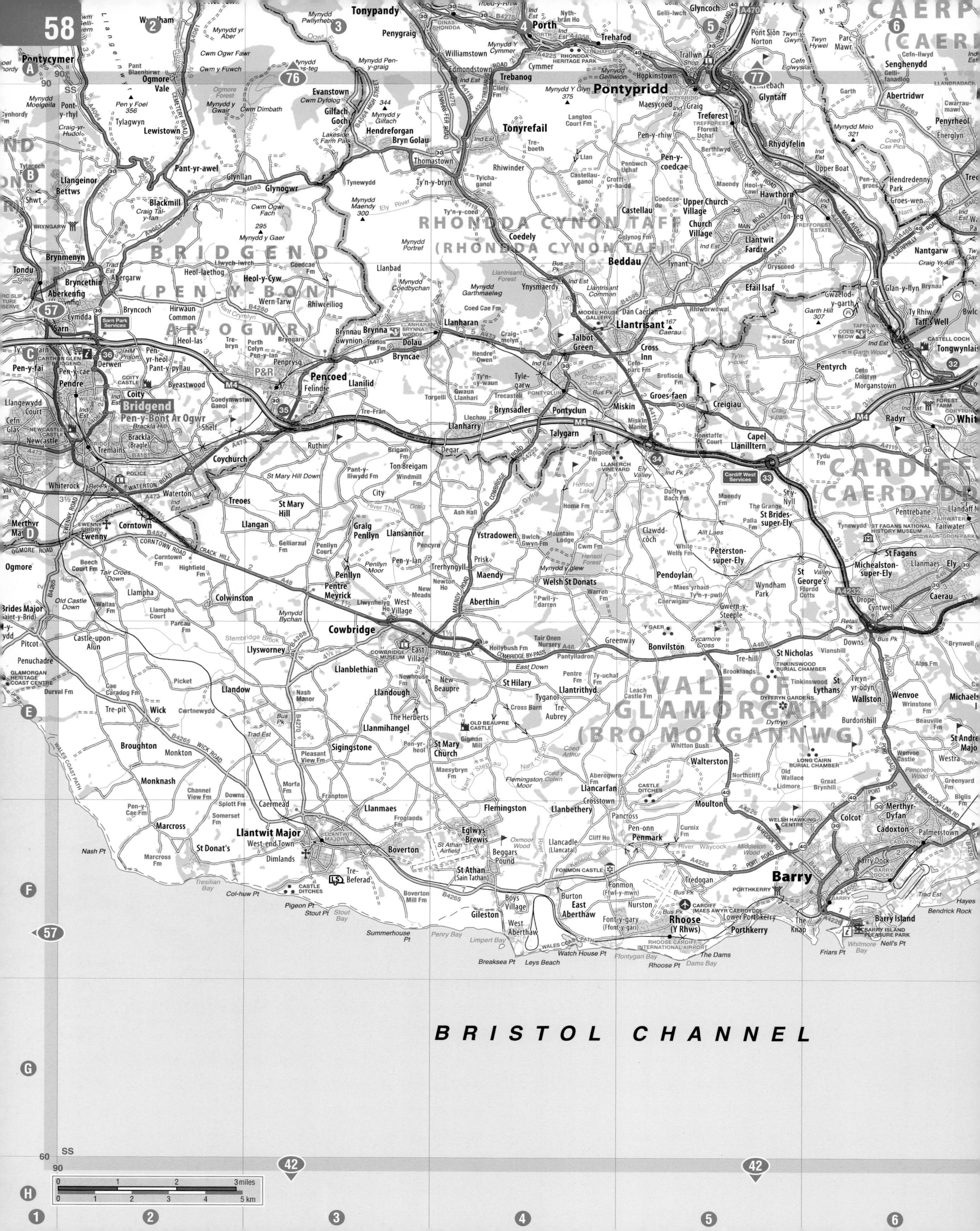
Tonypandy
Porth
Glyncoch
CAERP
Pontycymer
Penygraig
Trehafod
Williamstown
Edmondstown
Trebanog
Cymmer
Pontypridd
Hopkinstown
Trallwn
Pont Siôn Norton
Senghenydd
Ogmore Vale
Evanstown
Gilfach Goch
Hendreforgan
Tonyrefail
Maesycoed
Treforest
Glyntaff
Abertridwr
Lewistown
Tylagwyn
Bryn Golau
Thomastown
Rhydyfelin
Pen-y-rhiw
Pen-y-coedcae
Upper Boat
Llangeinor
Bettws
Pant-yr-awel
Glynllan
Glynogwr
Ty'n-y-bryn
Rhiwinder
Castellau
Upper Church Village
Church Village
Hawthorn
Hendredenny Park
Groes-wen
Blackmill
RHONDDA CYNON TAFF
(RHONDDA CYNON TAF)
Coedely
Llantwit Fardre
Nantgarw
BRIDGEND
(PEN-Y-BONT AR OGWR)
Brynmenyn
Tondu
Bryncethin
Abergarw
Heol-laethog
Heol-y-Cyw
Llanbad
Beddau
Tynant
Efail Isaf
Aberkenfig
Wern Tarw
Rhiwceiliog
Ynysmaerdy
Dan Caerlan
Llantrisant
Glan-y-llyn
Taff's Well
Tongwynlais
Cymdda
Sarn
Bryncoch
Hirwaun Common
Heol-las
Brynna
Brynnau Gwynion
Dolau
Bryncae
Llanharan
Talbot Green
Cross Inn
Pentyrch
Morganstown
Derwen
Pen-y-fai
Pen-y-cae
Pendre
Coity
Bridgend
Pen-y-Bont Ar Ogwr
Pen-yr-heol
Pant-y-pyllau
Byeastwood
Pencoed
Felindre
Llanilid
Tyle-garw
Pontyclun
Miskin
Groes-faen
Creigiau
Radyr
Whitchurch
Llangewydd Court
Newcastle
Brackla
Tremains
Coychurch
Shelf
Ruthin
Llanharry
Brynsadler
Talygarn
Capel Llanilltern
Degar
Ton Breigam
Whiterock
Waterton
Treoes
St Mary Hill
City
Ash Hall
Home Fm
Duffryn Bach Fm
Sty-Nyll
CARDIFF
(CAERDYDD)
Merthyr Mawr
Corntown
Ewenny
Llangan
Graig Penllyn
Llansannor
Ystradowen
Bwlch Gwyn Fm
Mountain Lodge
Clawdd-côch
Peterston-super-Ely
St Brides-super-Ely
Pentrebane
St Fagans
Michaelston-super-Ely
Ely
Caerau
Ogmore
Pen-y-lan
Prisk
Trerhyngyll
Maendy
Welsh St Donats
Pendoylan
Wyndham Park
St George's
Drope
Cyntwell
Colwinston
Penllyn
Pentre Meyrick
West Village
Aberthin
Gwern-y-Steeple
St Brides Major
Llampha
Castle-upon-Alun
Pitcot
Penuchadre
Cowbridge
Llysworney
East Village
Bonvilston
St Nicholas
Downs
Llanblethian
St Hilary
Pentre Fm
Tre-hill
Tinkinswood
St Lythans
Twyn-yr-odyn
Wallston
Wenvoe
Michaelston
Llandow
Llandough
New Beaupre
Tyganol
Llantrithyd
Tre-Aubrey
VALE OF GLAMORGAN
(BRO MORGANNWG)
Burdonshill
Tre-pit
Wick
Llanmihangel
Broughton
Monkton
Sigingstone
St Mary Church
Whitton Bush
Walterston
Monknash
Llancarfan
Moulton
Marcross
Llantwit Major
Llanmaes
Flemington
Llanbethery
Colcot
Merthyr-Dyfan
Cadoxton
Palmerstown
St Donat's
Dimlands
Boverton
Eglwys-Brewis
Beggars Pound
Llancadle
Penmark
Barry
Barry Dock
St Athan
Tre-Beferad
Fonmon
Tredogan
Nash Pt
Gileston
West Aberthaw
East Aberthaw
Nurston
Rhoose
(Y Rhws)
Porthkerry
The Knap
Barry Island
Breaksea Pt
Leys Beach
Rhoose Pt
Friars Pt
Nell's Pt
BRISTOL CHANNEL
0 1 2 3 miles
0 1 2 3 4 5 km

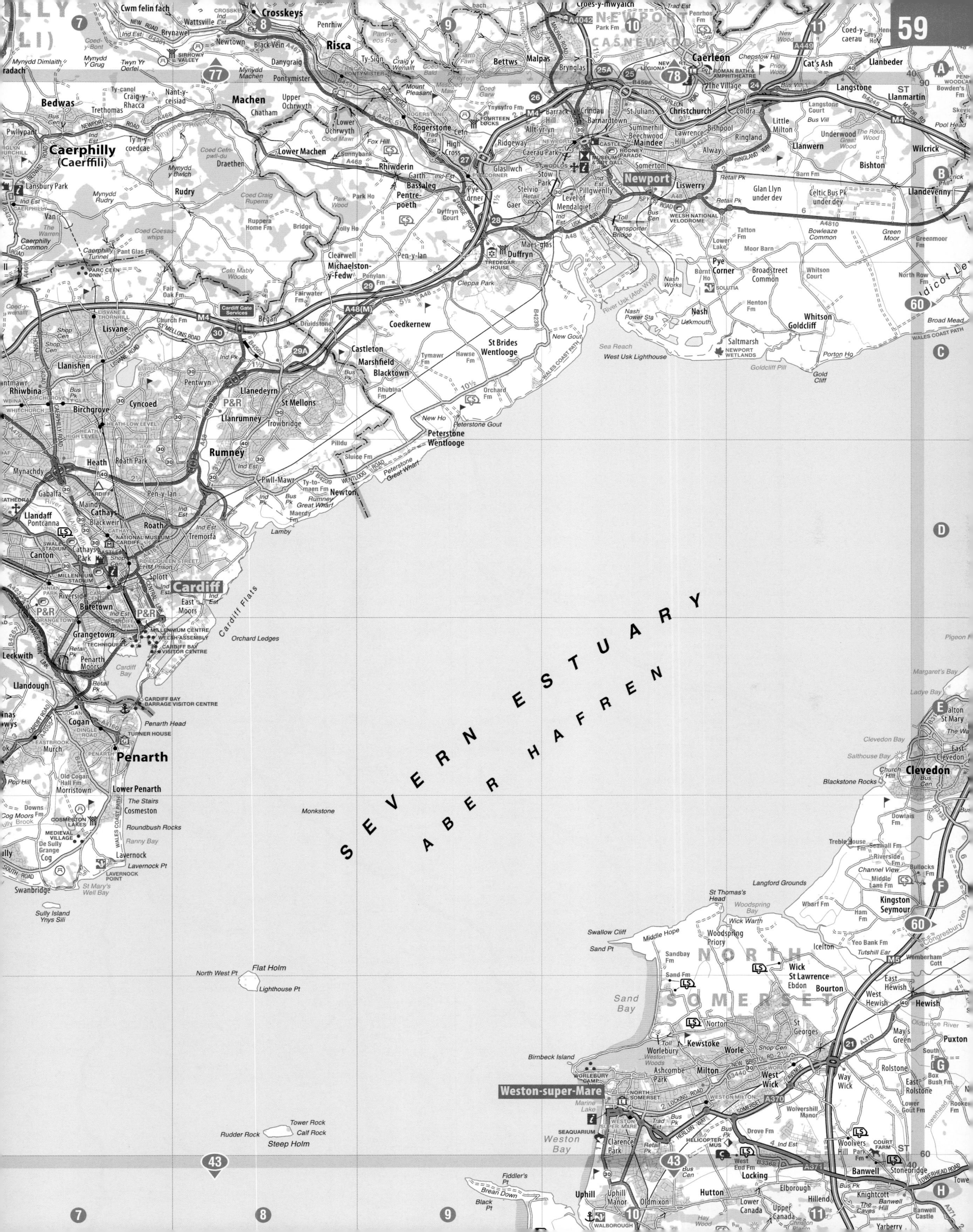
SEVERN ESTUARY
ABER HAFREN
NEWPORT
CASNEWYDD
NORTH SOMERSET
Caerphilly
(Caerffili)
Cardiff
Newport
Weston-super-Mare
Penarth
Clevedon
Crosskeys
Cwm felin fach
Risca
Machen
Bedwas
Caerleon
Bettws
Malpas
Rogerstone
Bassaleg
Duffryn
Lisvane
Llanishen
Rhiwbina
Cyncoed
Llanedeyrn
St Mellons
Llanrumney
Rumney
Heath
Roath
Llandaff
Canton
Cathays
Riverside
Butetown
Grangetown
Leckwith
Llandough
Cogan
Lower Penarth
Cosmeston
Lavernock
Swanbridge
Sully Island
Ynys Sili
Flat Holm
Steep Holm
Monkstone
Orchard Ledges
Cardiff Flats
Castleton
Marshfield
Coedkernew
St Brides
Wentlooge
Peterstone
Wentlooge
Nash
Goldcliff
Whitson
Saltmarsh
Liswerry
Christchurch
Langstone
Llanmartin
Llandevenny
Bishton
Wilcrick
Kingston
Seymour
Wick
St Lawrence
Worle
Kewstoke
Milton
Uphill
Hutton
Locking
Banwell
Puxton
Hewish
Sand Bay
Weston
Bay
M4
M5
A48(M)
60
77
78
43
7
8
9
10
11
A
B
C
D
E
F
G
H

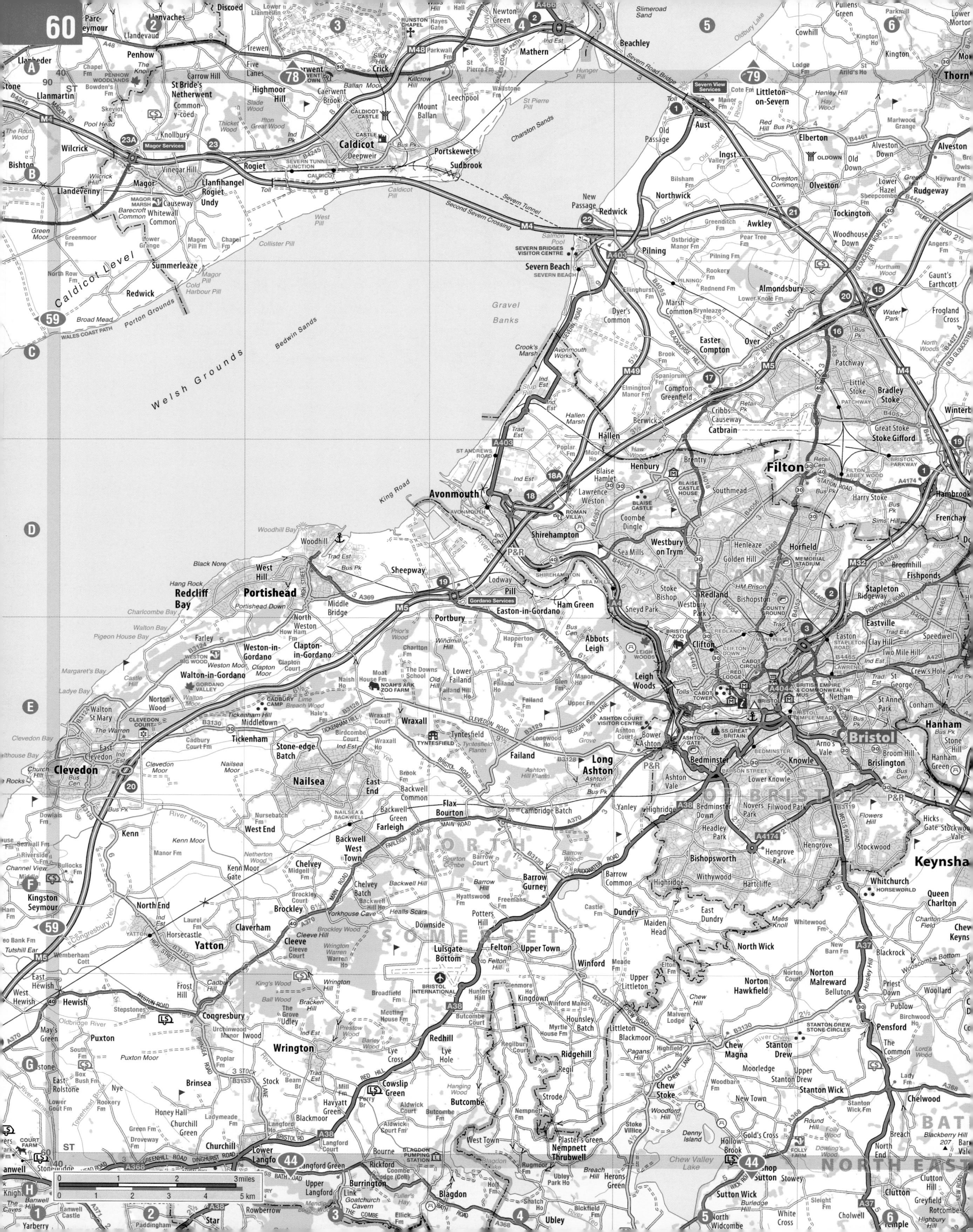

Caldicot
Magor
Rogiet
Portskewett
Sudbrook
Severn Beach
Pilning
Aust
Olveston
Almondsbury
Thornbury
Avonmouth
Shirehampton
Portishead
Redcliff Bay
Pill
Portbury
Easton-in-Gordano
Clevedon
Nailsea
Wraxall
Long Ashton
Flax Bourton
Backwell
Filton
Bristol
Keynsham
Yatton
Congresbury
Wrington
Winford
Chew Magna
Chew Stoke
Blagdon
Pensford
Whitchurch
Kingston Seymour
Caldicot Level
Welsh Grounds
Gravel Banks
Severn Bridge
Second Severn Crossing
Bristol International
Chew Valley Lake
SOMERSET
NORTH
CITY AND COUNTY OF BRISTOL
BATH
NORTH EAST
M4
M5
M48
M49
M32
A38
A370
A4
A403
A368
A37
Magor Services
Severn View Services
Gordano Services
0 1 2 3 miles
0 1 2 3 4 5 km

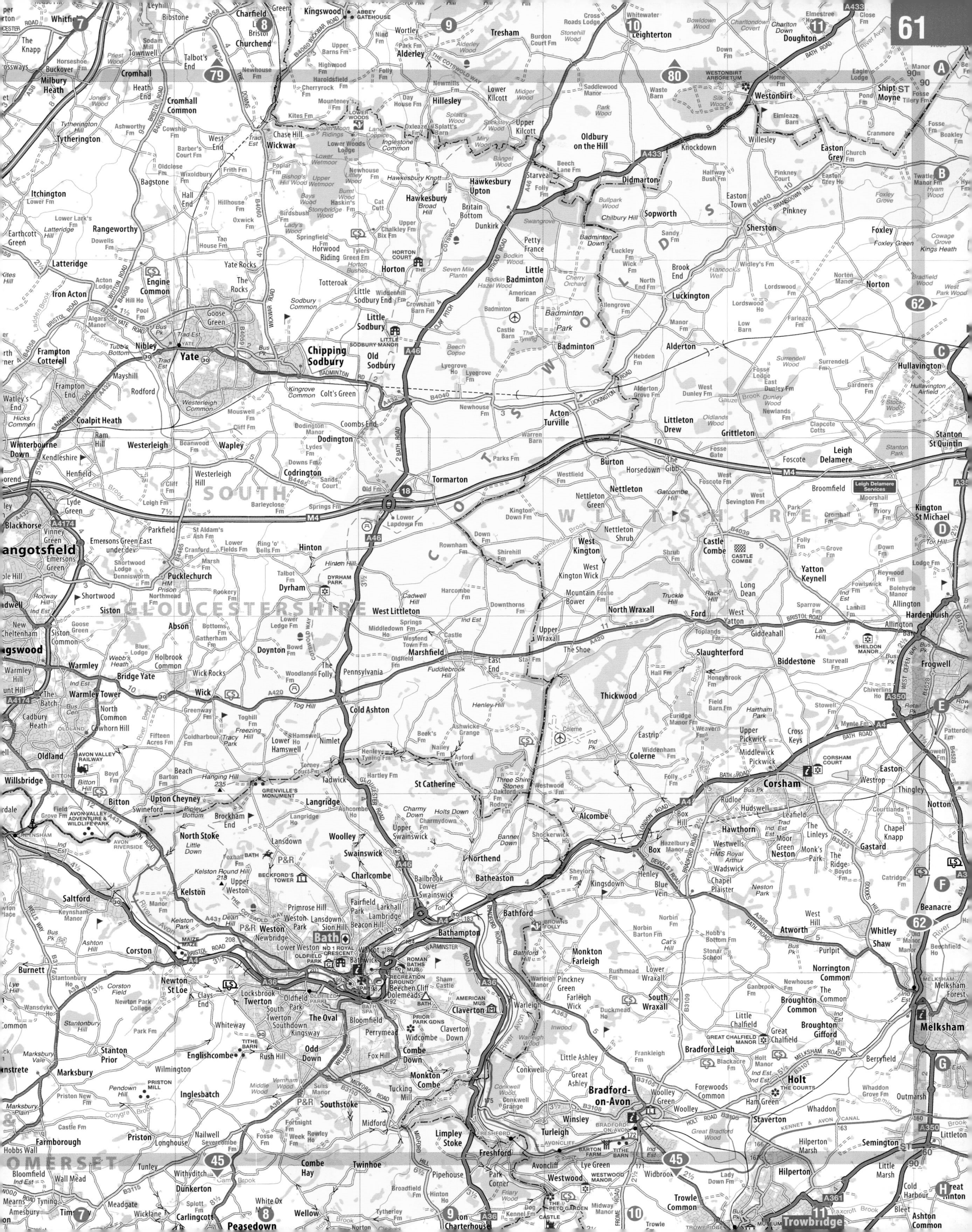

Whitfield
Charfield
Bristol
Churchend
Kingswood
ABBEY GATEHOUSE
Wortley
Alderley
Tresham
Leighterton
Doughton
Cromhall
Cromhall Common
Milbury Heath
Tytherington
Wickwar
Hillesley
Lower Kilcott
Upper Kilcott
Westonbirt
WESTONBIRT ARBORETUM
Shipton Moyne
Oldbury on the Hill
Didmarton
Easton Grey
Itchington
Rangeworthy
Latteridge
Iron Acton
Engine Common
Yate Rocks
The Rocks
Hawkesbury
Hawkesbury Upton
Horton
HORTON COURT
Little Badminton
Petty France
Sopworth
Sherston
Luckington
Foxley
Norton
Nibley
Yate
Chipping Sodbury
Old Sodbury
Little Sodbury
Badminton
Alderton
Hullavington
Frampton Cotterell
Coalpit Heath
Westerleigh
Wapley
Dodington
Codrington
Tormarton
Acton Turville
Littleton Drew
Grittleton
Stanton St Quintin
Winterbourne Down
Burton
Nettleton
Leigh Delamere
Leigh Delamere Services
Kington St Michael
SOUTH
GLOUCESTERSHIRE
COTSWOLDS
WILTSHIRE
Mangotsfield
Pucklechurch
Hinton
Dyrham
DYRHAM PARK
West Kington
Castle Combe
Yatton Keynell
Siston
Abson
West Littleton
North Wraxall
Ford
Kingswood
Warmley
Bridge Yate
Doynton
Marshfield
Upper Wraxall
The Shoe
Slaughterford
Biddestone
Frogwell
Chippenham
Wick
Cold Ashton
Thickwood
Oldland
Willsbridge
AVON VALLEY RAILWAY
Bitton
Upton Cheyney
Langridge
St Catherine
Colerne
Corsham
CORSHAM COURT
Keynsham
North Stoke
Woolley
Swainswick
Charlcombe
Northend
Batheaston
Alcombe
Box
Hawthorn
Gastard
Saltford
Kelston
Weston
Bath
Bathampton
Bathford
Monkton Farleigh
Atworth
Whitley
Corston
Newton St Loe
Twerton
Odd Down
Combe Down
Claverton
South Wraxall
Broughton Gifford
Melksham
Stanton Prior
Englishcombe
Marksbury
Inglesbatch
Southstoke
Monkton Combe
Bradford Leigh
Holt
THE COURTS
Bradford-on-Avon
Winsley
Turleigh
Staverton
Farmborough
Priston
Midford
Limpley Stoke
Freshford
Westwood
Semington
Hilperton
SOMERSET
Dunkerton
Combe Hay
Twinhoe
Wellow
Peasedown
Carlingcott
Trowle Common
Trowbridge
M4
A46
A4
A36
A420
A433
A350
A432

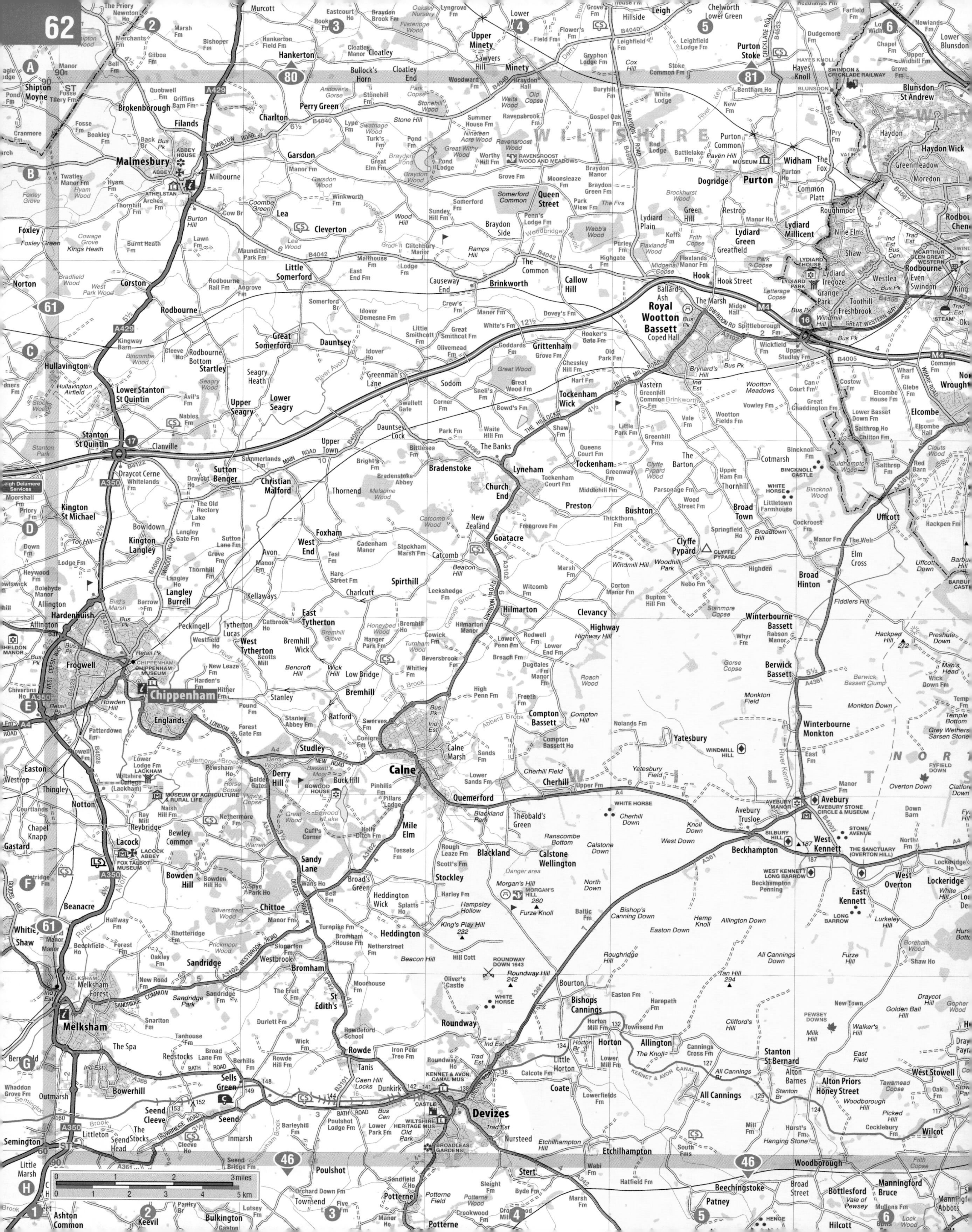

The Priory
Newnton Ho
Murcott
Eastcourt Ho
Braydon Brook Fm
Oaksey Nursery
Lyngrove Fm
Lower Moor
Leigh
Hillside
Chelworth Lower Green
Farfield Fm
Newlands Fm
Lower Blunsdon
Marsh Fm
Bishoper Fm
Hankerton Field Fm
Rookery Fm
Flisteridge Wood
Upper Minety
Sawyers Hill
Flower's Fm
Field Fm
Leighfield Ho
Leighfield Lodge Fm
Purton Stoke
Dudgemore Fm
Chapel Fm
Upper Widhill Fm
Merchants Fm
Gilboa Fm
Bell Fm
Manor Fm
Hankerton
Cloatley Manor
Cloatley
Gryphon Lodge Fm
Cox Hill
Stoke Common Fm
Hayes Knoll
Swindon & Cricklade Railway
Grove Fm
Shipton Moyne
Tillery Fm
Fosse
Bullock's Horn
Cloatley End
Minety
Braydon Hall
Woodward Fm
Buryhill Fm
White Lodge
Bentham Ho
Blunsdon
Blunsdon St Andrew
Quobwell Fm
Griffins Barn Fm
Brokenborough
Andover's Gorse
Stonehill Fm
Park Copse
Stonehill Wood
Old Copse
Walts Wood
Perry Green
Charlton
Filands
Fosse Fm
Boakley Fm
Cranmore Fm
Back Br
Lype Fm
Swatnage Wood
Turk's Fm
Stone Hill
Summer House Fm
Nineteen Acre Wood
Ravensbrook Fm
Gospel Oak Fm
New Fm
Pry Fm
Haydon
Haydon Wick
Malmesbury
Abbey House
Abbey
Athelstan
Garsdon
Great Elm Fm
Pond Fm
Great Withy Wood
Pond Lodge
Braydon Pond
Braydon Wood
Ravensroost Wood
Worthy Hill Fm
Ravensroost Wood and Meadows
Grove Fm
WILTSHIRE
Red Lodge
Battlelake Fm
Purton Common
Paven Hill
Museum
Widham
The Fox
Greenmeadow
Moredon
Twatley Manor Fm
Hyam Fm
Hyam Wood
Foxley Grove
Milbourne
Manor Fm
Garsdon Wood
Moonsleaze Fm
Braydon Manor
Braydon Green Fm
Somerford Common
Queen Street
Park View Fm
The Firs
Brockhurst Wood
Dogridge
Purton
Purton Ho
Common Platt
Thornhill Fm
Arches Fm
Coombe Green
Cow Br
Lea
Winkworth Fm
Woodbridge
Wood Hill
Sundey Hill Fm
Somerford Fm
Penn's Lodge Fm
Lydiard Plain
Green Hill
Restrop
Manor Ho
Roughmoor
Lydiard Millicent
Nine Elms
Rodbourne Cheney
Foxley
Foxley Green
Burton Hill
Cowage Grove
Kings Heath
Lawn Fm
Burnt Heath Fm
Clevercon
Cleverton
Lea Wood
Braydon Side
Webb's Wood
Koffs Fm
Flaxlands Wood
Frith Copse
Lydiard Green
Greatfield
Shaw
Ind Est
Trad Est
Clitchbury Manor
Ramps Hill
Purley Fm
Highgate Fm
Park Copse
McArthur Glen Great Western
Maunditts Park Fm
Malthouse Fm
B4042
The Common
Lydiard House
Lydiard Tregoze
Westlea
Rodbourne
Even Swindon
Norton
Bradfield Wood
West Park Wood
Corston
Little Somerford
East End Fm
Lodge Fm
Causeway End
Brinkworth
Callow Hill
Flaxlands Manor Fm
Midgehall Copse
Hook
Hook Street
Lydiard Park
Grange Park
Toothill
Rodbourne Rail Fm
Angrove Fm
Somerford Br
Idover Demesne Fm
Crew's Fm
Manor Fm
Dovey's Fm
Ballard's Ash
Royal Wootton Bassett
Coped Hall
The Marsh
Midge Hall
Letterage Copse
Windmill Hill
Freshbrook
Great Western Way
Steam
Rodbourne
Little Smithcot Fm
Great Smithcot Fm
White's Fm
Spittleborough Fm
Great Somerford
Dauntsey
Goddards Fm
Grittenham
Hooker's Gate Fm
Wickfield Fm
Upper Studley Fm
Kingway Barn
Cleeve Ho
Rodbourne Bottom
Binscombe Wood
Idover Ho
Olivemead Fm
Grove Fm
Chessley Hill Fm
Old Park Fm
Brynard's Hill
Common Fm
Hullavington
Startley
Seagry Heath
River Avon
Greenman's Lane
Great Wood
Hart Fm
Costow Fm
Wharf Fm
Wroughton
Hullavington Airfield
Lower Stanton St Quintin
Seagry Wood
Lower Seagry
Sodom
Snell's Fm
Great Wood Fm
Tockenham Wick
Vastern
Greenhill Common Fm
Brinkworth Brook
Ind Est
Can Court Fm
Elcombe House Fm
Glebe Fm
Stock Wood
Avil's Fm
Upper Seagry
Swallett Gate
Corner Fm
Bowd's Fm
Wootton Meadows
Vowley Fm
Great Chaddington Fm
Lower Basset Down Fm
Elcombe
Nables Fm
Dauntsey Lock
Waite Hill Fm
The Hillocks
Shaw Fm
Little Park Fm
Vale Fm
Wootton Fields Fm
Salthrop Ho
Chilton Fm
Elcombe Hall
Stanton St Quintin
Stanton Park
Clanville
Upper Town
Park Fm
Bittlesea Fm
The Banks
Greenhill Fms
Binknoll Fm
Cotmarsh
Clouts Wood
Red Barn Fm
Salthrop Fm
Leigh Delamere Services
Draycot Cerne
Whitelands Fm
Summerlands Fm
Main Road
Sutton Benger
Christian Malford
Bright's Fm
Bradenstoke Abbey
Bradenstoke
Lyneham
Queens Court Fm
Tockenham
Greenway Fm
Clyffe Pypard Wood
The Barton
Upper Ham Fm
Thornhill
Binknoll Castle
Quidhampton Wood
Draycot Ho
Moorshall Fm
Kington St Michael
Priory Fm
The Old Rectory
Lake Fm
Thornend
Melsome Wood
Church End
Tockenham Court Fm
Middlehill Fm
Parsonage Fm
White Horse
Littletown Farmhouse
Binknoll Wood
Bowldown Fm
Langley Gate Fm
Preston
Bushton
Wood Street Fm
Broad Town
Uffcott
Hackpen Fm
Kington Langley
Tor Hill
Foxham
Catcomb Wood
New Zealand
Freegrove Fm
Thickthorn Fm
Springfield Ho
Broadtown Hill
Cockroost Fm
Down Fm
Sutton Lane Fm
West End
Cadenham Manor
Stockham Marsh Fm
Goatacre
Clyffe Pypard
Manor Fm
The Weir
Heywood Fm
Lodge Fm
Grove Fm
Avon
Teal Fm
Catcomb
Windmill Hill
Woodhill Park
Elm Cross
Uffcott Down
Bolehyde Manor
Swindon Road
Thornhill Fm
Manor Fm
Hare Street Fm
Beacon Hill
Marsh Fm
Highden
Broad Hinton
Langley Fm
Spirthill
Leekshedge Fm
Witcomb Fm
Corton Manor Fm
Nebo Fm
Barbury Castle
Allington
Langley Burrell
Kellaways
Charlcutt
Bupton Hill Fm
Fiddlers Hill
Hardenhuish
Bird's Marsh
Barrow Fm
Cowage Brook
Hilmarton
Clevancy
Stanmore Copse
Winterbourne Bassett
Rabson Manor
Allington Bar
Bus Pk
Peckingell
Tytherton Lucas
Catbrook Ho
East Tytherton
Honeybed Wood
Bremhill Fm
Hilmarton Manor
Highway
Highway Hill
Whyr Fm
Hackpen Hill
Preshute Down
Sheldon Manor
Westfield Ho
River Marden
West Tytherton
Bremhill Grove
Bremhill Wick
Hanger Park Fm
Turnham Wood
Cowick Fm
Lower Penn Fm
Rodwell Fm
Lower End Fm
Retail Pk
Chippenham Museum
Frogwell
New Leaze Fm
Scotts Mill
Bencroft Hill
Wick Hill
Low Bridge
Whitley Fm
Beversbrook Fm
Breach Fm
Dugdales Fm
Manor Fm
Roach Wood
Gorse Copse
Berwick Bassett
Berwick Bassett Clump
Man's Head
Wick Down Fm
Chiverlins Ho
Harden's Fm
Hither Fm
Stanley
Bremhill
Fisher's Brook
High Penn Fm
Freeth Fm
Monkton Field
Monkton Down
Temple Fm
Temple Bottom
Rowden Hill
Chippenham
Englands
Pound Fm
Stanley Abbey Fm
Ratford
Swerves Fm
Abberd Brook
Compton Bassett
Compton Hill
Nolands Fm
Yatesbury
Winterbourne Monkton
Grey Wethers Sarsen Stone
Patterdown Fm
London Road
Forest Gate Fm
Conigre Fm
Calne Marsh
Compton Bassett Ho
Windmill Hill
River Kennet
East Fm
Fyfield Down
Easton
Westrop
Showell Fm
Studley
Lower Lodge Fm
Cocklemore Brook
Derry Wood
New Road
Bassett's Moor
Sands Fm
Calne
Cherhill Field
Yatesbury Field
Overton Down
Thingley
Lackham
Wiltshire College (Lackham)
Pewsham Ho
Golden Gates
Derry Hill
Buck Hill
Bowood House
Pinhills Fm
Lower Sands Fm
Cherhill
Upper Fm
Manor Fm
Avebury
Avebury Manor
Avebury Stone Circle & Museum
Clatford Down
Notton
Museum of Agriculture & Rural Life
Piggy Copse
Pillars Lodge
Quemerford
White Horse
Cherhill Down
Avebury Trusloe
Down Barn
Courtlands
Naish Hill Fm
Ray Mill
Reybridge
Nethermore Fm
Great Wood
Bowood Lake
Holly Ditch Fm
Blackland Park
Theobald's Green
Knoll Down
West Down
Silbury Hill
Stone Avenue
Chapel Knapp
Bewley Common
Lacock
Lacock Abbey
Fox Talbot Museum
The Warren
Cuff's Corner
Mile Elm
Tossels Fm
Rough Leaze Fm
Ranscombe Bottom
Calstone Down
Beckhampton
West Kennett
North Fm
The Sanctuary (Overton Hill)
Lockeridge Ho
Gastard
Sandy Lane
Scott's Fm
Blackland
Calstone Wellington
Danger area
West Kennett Long Barrow
Beckhampton Penning
West Overton
Lockeridge
Bowden Hill
Bowden Hill Ho
Spye Park Ho
West Park
Broad's Green
Stockley
Morgan's Hill
North Down
East Kennett
Partridge Fm
Bell Fm
Heddington Wick
Splatts Ho
Harley Fm
Hampsley Hollow
Furze Knoll
Baltic Fm
Bishop's Canning Down
Hemp Knoll
Allington Down
Long Barrow
Lurkeley Hill
Beanacre
Chittoe
Silverstreet Wood
Manor Fm
Turnpike Fm
Heddington
King's Play Hill
Easton Down
Whitley
Shaw
Halfway Fm
Rhotteridge Fm
Bromham House Fm
Netherstreet Fm
Hill Cott
Roughridge Hill
All Cannings Down
Boreham Wood
Beechfield Ho
Forest Fm
Prickmoor Wood
Sloperton Fm
Westbrook
Beacon Hill
Furze Hill
Shaw Ho
Oakley Fm
Sandridge
Bromham
Roundway Down 1643
Roundway Hill
Tan Hill
Melksham Forest
New Road Fm
Westbrook Road
Moorhouse Fm
Oliver's Castle
Bourton
Harepath Fm
Easton Fm
New Town
Draycot Hill
Sandridge Common
Sandridge Park
Sandridge Fm
The Fruit Fm
St Edith's
White Horse
Bishops Cannings
Pewsey Downs
Golden Ball Hill
Melksham
Snarlton Fm
Durlett Fm
Rowdeford School
Roundway
Horton Mill Fm
Townsend Fm
Clifford's Hill
Milk Hill
Walker's Hill
Tanhouse Fm
The Spa
Wick Fm
Rowde Hill Fm
Rowde
Iron Pear Tree Fm
Roundway Ho
Ind Est
Horton
Little Horton
Allington
The Knoll
Cannings Cross Fm
Stanton St Bernard
East Field
Redstocks
Broad Lane Fm
Bath Road
Berhills Fm
Tanis
Trad Est
Lower Mill Fm
Kennet & Avon Canal
Berryfield
Ind Est
Bowerhill
Sells Green
Caen Hill Locks
Dunkirk
Kennet & Avon Canal Mus
Calcote Fm
Coate
All Cannings Br
All Cannings
Alton Barnes
Alton Priors
Honey Street
West Stowell
Tawsmead Copse
Whaddon Grove Fm
Outmarsh
Seend Cleeve
Seend
Barleyhill Fm
Poulshot Lodge Fm
Bus Cen
Lower Park Fm
Castle
Wiltshire Heritage Mus
Devizes
Trad Est
Lowerfields Fm
Stanton Br
Woodborough Hill
Picked Hill
Cocklebury Fm
Wilcot
Semington
Littleton
The Stocks
Seend Head
Cleeve Ho
Inmarsh
Old Park
Broadleas Gardens
Nursteed
Etchilhampton Hill
Etchilhampton
Mill Fm
South Fms
Hanging Stone
Hurst's Fm
Little Marsh
Seend Bridge Fm
Sunnamble Brook
Poulshot
Stert
Wabi Fm
Woodborough
Frith Copse
Orchard Down Fm
Sandfield Ho
Potterne Field
Sleight Fm
Byde Fm
Hatfield Fm
Beechingstoke
Broad Street
Bottlesford
Vale of Pewsey
Manningford Bruce
Mullens Fm
Ashton Common
Keevil
Pantry Br
Bulkington
Lutsey Fm
Townsend
Potterne
Potterne Wood
Crookwood Fm
Marsh Fm
Patney
Henge
Hilcott
Lock Wood
Manningford Abbots
miles
km

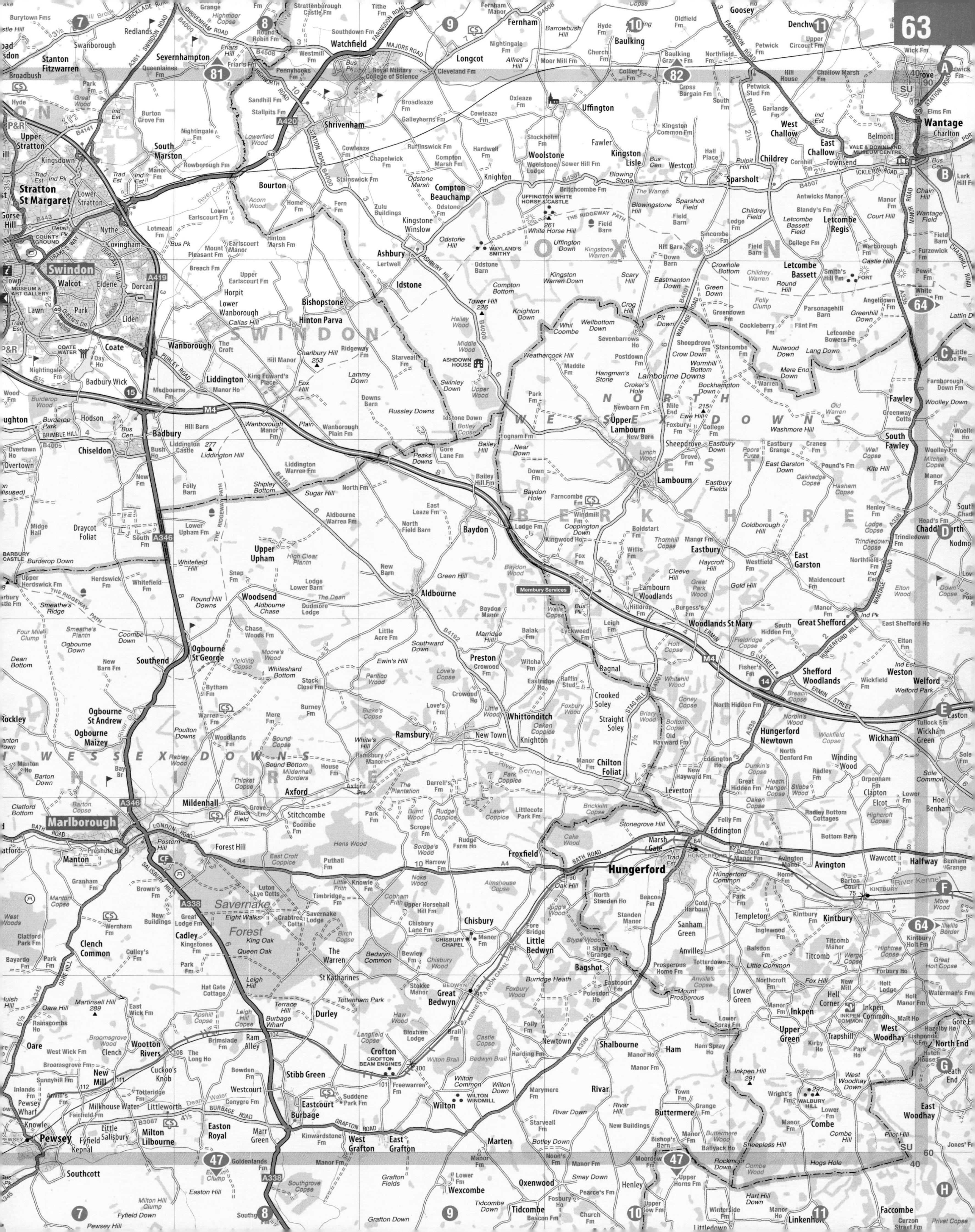
Swindon
Stratton St Margaret
Upper Stratton
Stanton Fitzwarren
Swanborough
Redlands
Severnhampton
Watchfield
Longcot
Fernham
Baulking
Goosey
Denchworth
Wantage
Charlton
Grove
Shrivenham
Bourton
South Marston
Uffington
Woolstone
Kingston Lisle
Compton Beauchamp
Knighton
Fawler
Childrey
West Challow
East Challow
Sparsholt
Letcombe Regis
Letcombe Bassett
Ashbury
Idstone
Bishopstone
Hinton Parva
Uffington White Horse & Castle
White Horse Hill
Wayland's Smithy
Ashdown House
Lambourne Downs
Upper Lambourn
Lambourn
Eastbury
East Garston
Great Shefford
Shefford Woodlands
Weston
Welford
Wickham
Fawley
South Fawley
Chaddleworth
Baydon
Aldbourne
Membury Services
Woodlands St Mary
Lambourn Woodlands
Ramsbury
Whittonditch
Knighton
Chilton Foliat
Leverton
Eddington
Hungerford
Hungerford Newtown
Kintbury
Avington
Halfway
Inkpen
Upper Green
West Woodhay
East Woodhay
Combe
Walbury Hill
Faccombe
Linkenholt
Buttermere
Ham
Shalbourne
Rivar
Bagshot
Little Bedwyn
Great Bedwyn
Chisbury
Froxfield
Crofton
Crofton Beam Engines
Wilton
Wilton Windmill
Marten
Oxenwood
Tidcombe
Wexcombe
East Grafton
West Grafton
Burbage
Eastcourt
Easton Royal
Milton Lilbourne
Pewsey
Southcott
New Mill
Wootton Rivers
Durley
Savernake Forest
Cadley
Marlborough
Mildenhall
Axford
Manton
Clench Common
Oare
Ogbourne St George
Ogbourne St Andrew
Ogbourne Maizey
Rockley
Southend
Upper Upham
Woodsend
Draycot Foliat
Chiseldon
Badbury
Liddington
Wanborough
Coate
Walcot
Eldene
Covingham
Nythe
Dorcan
Liden
Lawn
Park
Hodson
Burderop Park
Hungerford Common
Templeton
Sanham Green
Anvilles
Titcomb
Hell Corner
Inkpen Common
Trapshill
Kirby
North End
Heath End
Henley
Lower Green
Mount Prosperous
Newtown
Oxon
North Wessex Downs
West Berkshire
Swindon
Wessex Downs
River Kennet
The Ridgeway Path
M4
A4
A338
A346
A419
B4000
B4192
B4507
81
82
47
64
7
8
9
10
11

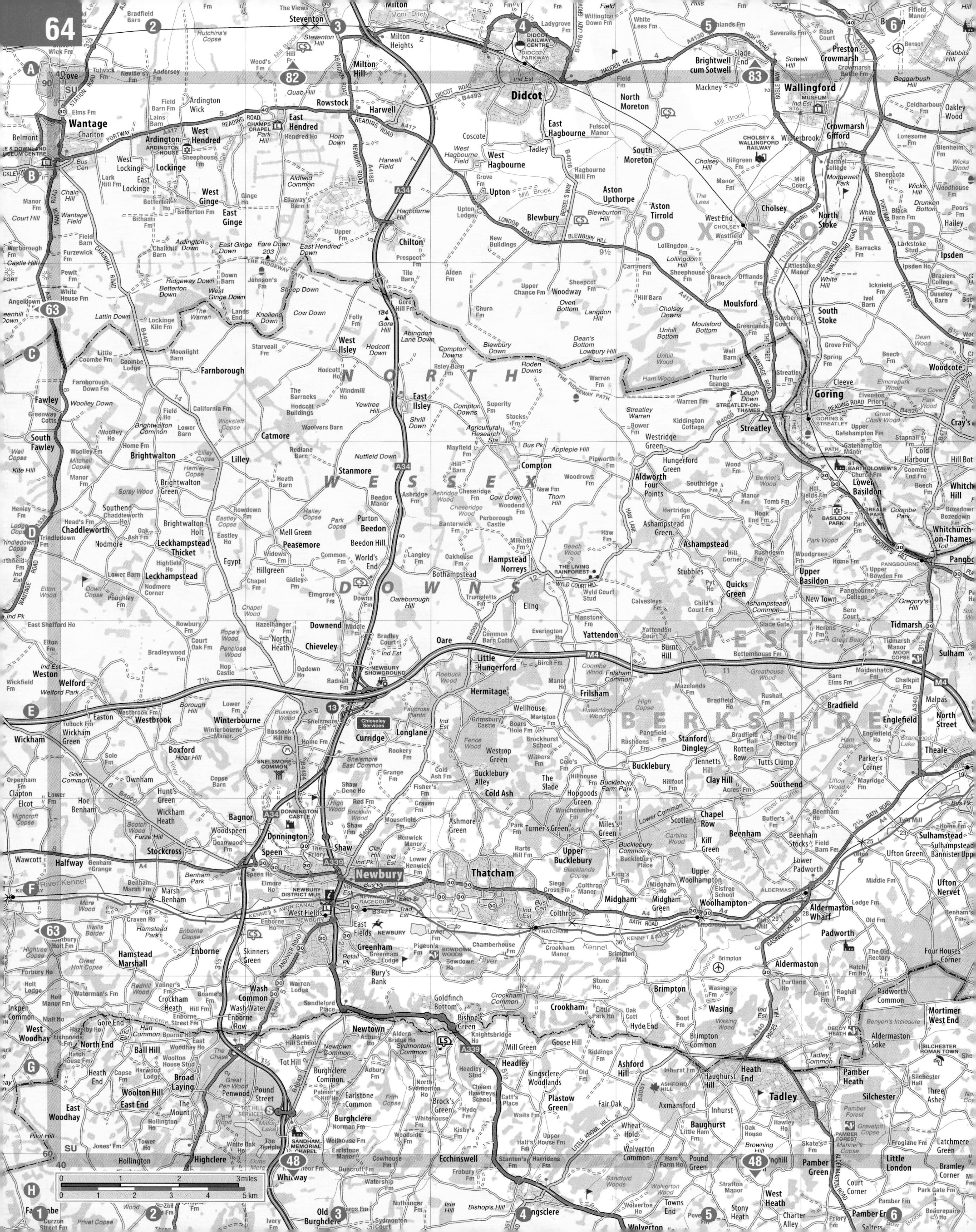

Steventon
Milton
Milton Heights
Milton Hill
Didcot
Ladygrove
Willington Down Fm
Brightwell cum Sotwell
Slade End
Mackney
Wallingford
Preston Crowmarsh
Crowmarsh Gifford
Benson
Grove
Wantage
Charlton
Belmont
Ardington
Ardington Wick
West Hendred
East Hendred
Rowstock
Harwell
West Lockinge
Lockinge
East Lockinge
West Ginge
East Ginge
Chilton
East Hagbourne
West Hagbourne
Coscote
Tadley
Upton
Blewbury
Aston Upthorpe
Aston Tirrold
North Moreton
South Moreton
Cholsey
Winterbrook
North Stoke
South Stoke
Moulsford
Ipsden
Woodcote
Goring
Streatley
Cleeve
Farnborough
Fawley
South Fawley
West Ilsley
East Ilsley
Compton
Catmore
Lilley
Brightwalton
Brightwalton Green
Stanmore
Aldworth
Ashampstead
Ashampstead Green
Upper Basildon
Lower Basildon
Whitchurch-on-Thames
Pangbourne
Tidmarsh
Sulham
Chaddleworth
Leckhampstead
Leckhampstead Thicket
Peasemore
Beedon
Beedon Hill
World's End
Hampstead Norreys
Eling
Yattendon
Quicks Green
Chieveley
North Heath
Downend
Oare
Little Hungerford
Hermitage
Frilsham
Bradfield
Englefield
Theale
North Street
Weston
Welford
Wickham
Westbrook
Winterbourne
Boxford
Curridge
Longlane
Bucklebury
Stanford Dingley
Southend
Clay Hill
Cold Ash
Bagnor
Donnington
Shaw
Speen
Stockcross
Halfway
Wawcott
Newbury
Thatcham
Upper Bucklebury
Midgham
Woolhampton
Aldermaston Wharf
Padworth
Ufton Nervet
Sulhamstead
Beenham
Greenham
Enborne
Hamstead Marshall
Wash Common
Aldermaston
Brimpton
Wasing
Crookham
Headley
Newtown
Ball Hill
North End
West Woodhay
East Woodhay
Woolton Hill
East End
Burghclere
Highclere
Whitway
Ecchinswell
Kingsclere
Plastow Green
Ashford Hill
Axmansford
Baughurst
Heath End
Tadley
Pamber Heath
Silchester
Little London
Pamber Green
West Heath
Charter Alley
Wolverton
Old Burghclere
NORTH WESSEX DOWNS
OXFORD
WEST BERKSHIRE
M4
A34
A4
A339
A417
A329
A340
Newbury
Wallingford
0 1 2 3 miles
0 1 2 3 4 5 km

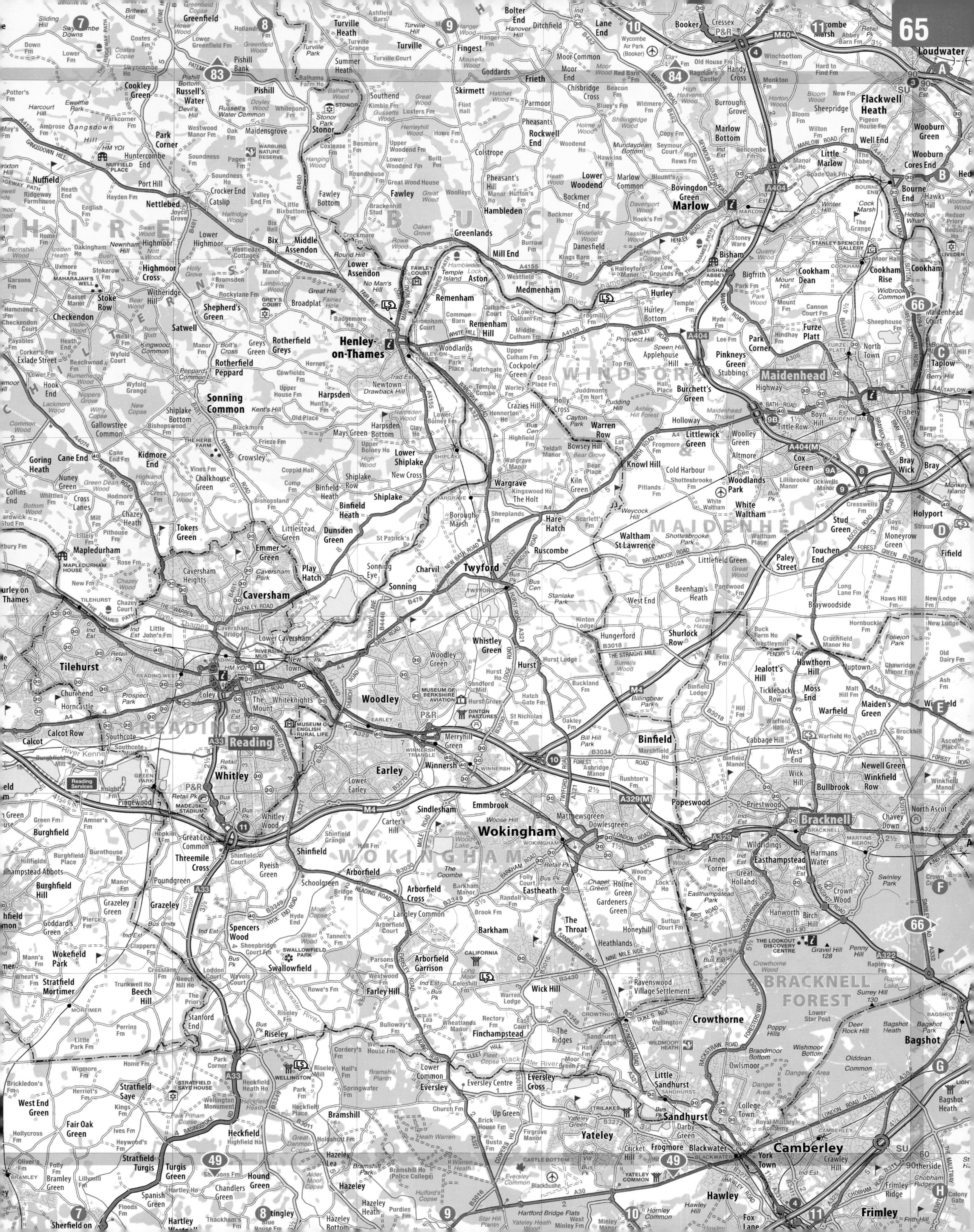
Greenfield
Turville Heath
Turville
Fingest
Bolter End
Lane End
Booker
Cressex
Loudwater
Pishill Bank
Pishill
Southend
Skirmett
Frieth
Moor Common
Moor End
Handy Cross
Flackwell Heath
Cookley Green
Russell's Water
Stonor
Parmoor
Chisbridge Cross
Burroughs Grove
Wooburn Green
Park Corner
Maidensgrove
Pheasants
Rockwell End
Marlow Bottom
Little Marlow
Wooburn Cores End
Nuffield
Huntercombe End
Colstrope
Lower Woodend
Marlow Common
Bovingdon Green
Bourne End
Port Hill
Nettlebed
Crocker End
Catslip
Fawley Bottom
Fawley
Pheasant's Hill
Hambleden
Bockmer End
Marlow
Greenlands
Mill End
Danesfield
Bisham
Cookham Dean
Cookham Rise
Cookham
Bix
Middle Assendon
Lower Assendon
Highmoor
Highmoor Cross
Aston
Medmenham
Hurley
Temple
Bigfrith
Stoke Row
Checkendon
Shepherd's Green
Satwell
Broadplat
Remenham
Remenham Hill
Hurley Bottom
Furze Platt
Henley-on-Thames
Rotherfield Greys
Rotherfield Peppard
Greys Green
Woodlands
Cockpole Green
WINDSOR
Applehouse Hill
Pinkneys Green
Park Corner
Maidenhead
Taplow
Exlade Street
Harpsden
Sonning Common
Kent's Hill
Burchett's Green
Holly Cross
Crazies Hill
Warren Row
Littlewick Green
Woolley Green
Knowl Hill
Cox Green
Bray Wick
Bray
Gallowstree Common
Goring Heath
Cane End
Kidmore End
Shiplake
Lower Shiplake
Wargrave
Kiln Green
Woodlands Park
White Waltham
Chalkhouse Green
Binfield Heath
Hare Hatch
MAIDENHEAD
Holyport
Stud Green
Tokers Green
Mapledurham
Dunsden Green
Emmer Green
Caversham
Play Hatch
Sonning Eye
Sonning
Charvil
Twyford
Ruscombe
Waltham St Lawrence
Paley Street
Touchen End
Fifield
Purley on Thames
Tilehurst
Woodley
Whistley Green
Hurst
West End
Beenham's Heath
Shurlock Row
Hungerford
Braywoodside
Hawthorn Hill
Jealott's Hill
Moss End
Warfield
Maiden's Green
Calcot
Calcot Row
Reading
READING
Whitley
Earley
Lower Earley
Winnersh
Binfield
Newell Green
Winkfield Row
Bullbrook
Sindlesham
Emmbrook
Popeswood
Priestwood
Bracknell
North Ascot
Wokingham
Burghfield
Shinfield
Threemile Cross
Arborfield
WOKINGHAM
Easthampstead
Harmans Water
Burghfield Hill
Grazeley
Ryeish Green
Arborfield Cross
Eastheath
The Throat
Crown Wood
Spencers Wood
Barkham
Swallowfield
Arborfield Garrison
Honeyhill
Heathlands
Hanworth
Birch Hill
Wokefield Park
Stratfield Mortimer
Beech Hill
Farley Hill
Wick Hill
BRACKNELL FOREST
Riseley
Finchampstead
Crowthorne
Bagshot
Eversley
Eversley Cross
Little Sandhurst
Sandhurst
Stratfield Saye
West End Green
Fair Oak Green
Heckfield
Bramshill
Up Green
Yateley
College Town
Bagshot Heath
Stratfield Turgis
Turgis Green
Bramley Green
Hound Green
Hazeley
Cricket Hill
Frogmore
Blackwater
Camberley
York Town
Hawley
Frimley
Sherfield on

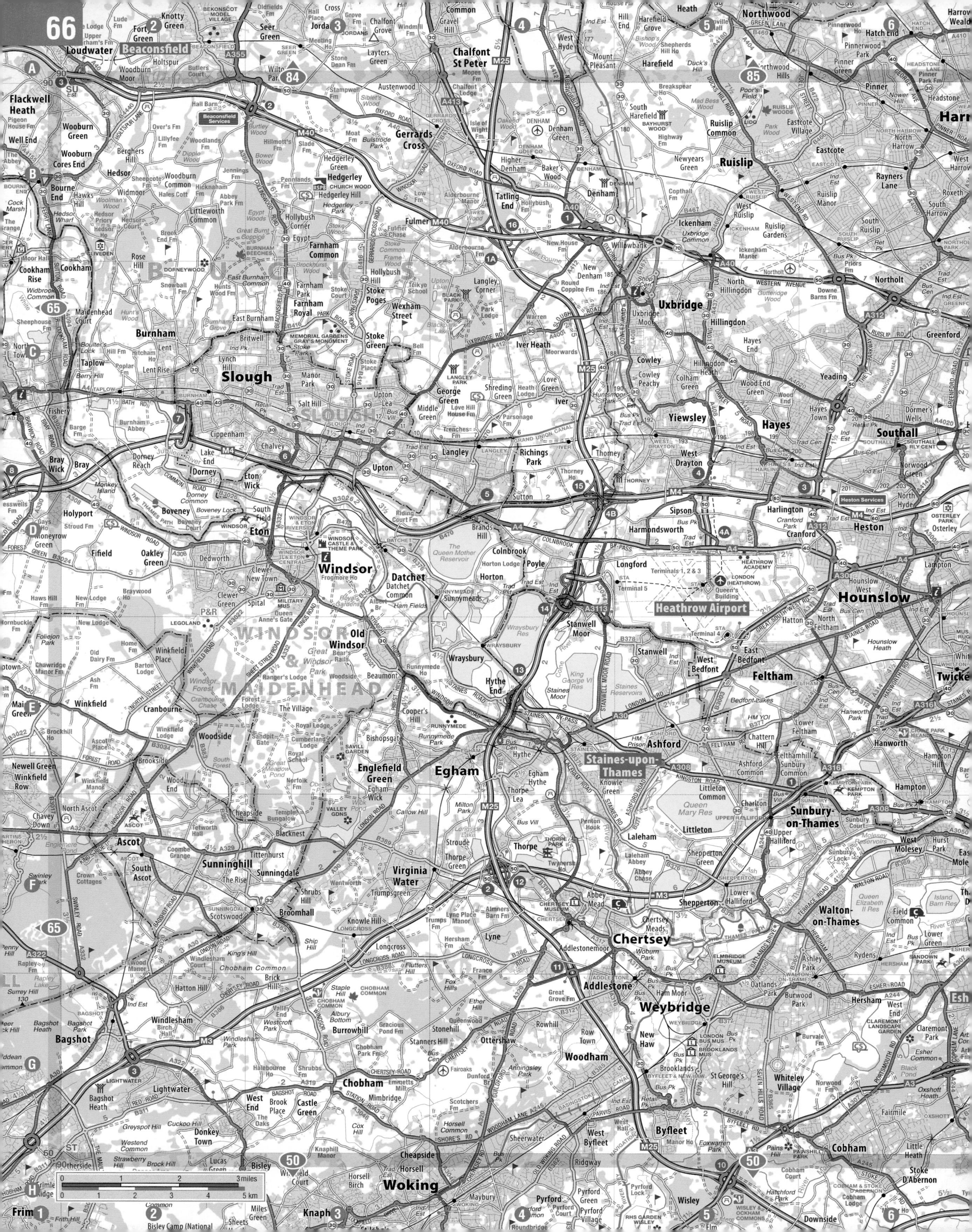
Beaconsfield
Loudwater
Flackwell Heath
Gerrards Cross
Chalfont St Peter
Northwood
Harefield
Ruislip
Denham
Uxbridge
Hillingdon
Northolt
Burnham
Slough
Farnham Royal
Stoke Poges
Iver
Yiewsley
Hayes
Southall
West Drayton
Windsor
Eton
Datchet
Colnbrook
Heathrow Airport
Hounslow
Heston
Feltham
Egham
Staines-upon-Thames
Ashford
Sunbury-on-Thames
Ascot
Sunninghill
Virginia Water
Chertsey
Addlestone
Weybridge
Walton-on-Thames
Bagshot
Chobham
Woking
Byfleet
Cobham
Windsor & Maidenhead
Bucks

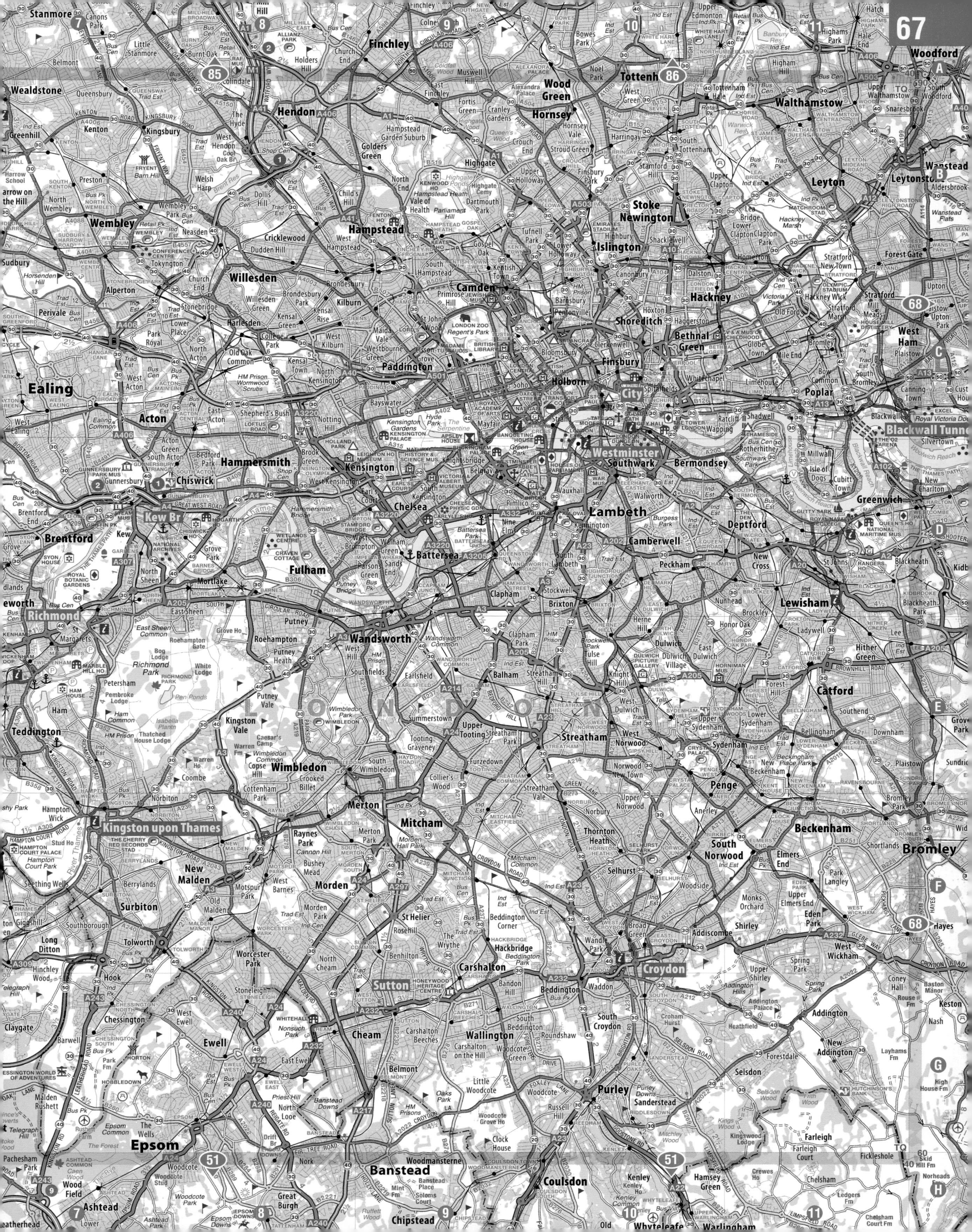
Stanmore
Canons Park
Little Stanmore
Belmont
Burnt Oak
Colindale
Mill Hill
Finchley
Church End
Colney Hatch
Holders Hill
East Finchley
Muswell Hill
Wood Green
Bowes Park
Noel Park
Tottenham
Edmonton
Highams Park
Hale End
Woodford
South Woodford
Walthamstow
Snaresbrook
Wealdstone
Queensbury
Kingsbury
Hendon
West Hendon
Hampstead Garden Suburb
Golders Green
Fortis Green
Cranley Gardens
Hornsey
Crouch End
Stroud Green
Harringay
South Tottenham
Tottenham Hale
Kenton
Greenhill
Preston
Harrow on the Hill
North Wembley
Wembley
Neasden
Welsh Harp
Dollis Hill
Cricklewood
Dudden Hill
Child's Hill
West Hampstead
Hampstead
Highgate
Upper Holloway
Finsbury Park
Stamford Hill
Upper Clapton
Leyton
Leytonstone
Stoke Newington
Islington
Highbury
Lower Holloway
Tufnell Park
Dartmouth Park
Gospel Oak
Kentish Town
South Hampstead
Camden
Clapton Park
Lower Clapton
Lea Bridge
Hackney Marsh
Hackney
Homerton
Dalston
Canonbury
Stratford
Forest Gate
Stratford New Town
Hackney Wick
Upton
Sudbury
Alperton
Tokyngton
Willesden
Church End
Harlesden
Stonebridge
Kensal Green
Kensal Rise
Brondesbury
Kilburn
Primrose Hill
St John's Wood
Maida Vale
West Kilburn
Barnsbury
Pentonville
Hoxton
Haggerston
Shoreditch
Bethnal Green
Old Ford
Globe Town
Mile End
Bow Common
West Ham
Plaistow
Perivale
Park Royal
North Acton
Old Oak Common
College Park
Kensal Town
North Kensington
Westbourne Green
Lisson Grove
Paddington
Bloomsbury
Clerkenwell
Finsbury
Holborn
City
Spitalfields
Whitechapel
Limehouse
Poplar
Canning Town
Ealing
West Ealing
Ealing Common
Acton
East Acton
Shepherd's Bush
Bayswater
Notting Hill
Hyde Park
Mayfair
Soho
Strand
Westminster
Southwark
Bermondsey
Shadwell
Ratcliff
Wapping
Rotherhithe
Millwall
Isle of Dogs
Cubitt Town
Blackwall
Silvertown
Blackwall Tunnel
Acton Green
South Acton
Bedford Park
Hammersmith
Kensington
West Kensington
Earl's Court
Knightsbridge
Belgravia
Chelsea
Pimlico
Vauxhall
Lambeth
Kennington
Walworth
Camberwell
Deptford
Greenwich
New Charlton
Gunnersbury
Chiswick
Kew Br
Kew
Brentford
Fulham
Walham Green
Parsons Green
Sands End
Battersea
Nine Elms
South Lambeth
Stockwell
Brixton
Peckham
New Cross
St John's
Blackheath
Isleworth
Richmond
St Margarets
Mortlake
East Sheen
Putney
Roehampton
Wandsworth
Clapham
Herne Hill
Nunhead
Brockley
Lewisham
Ladywell
Honor Oak
Dulwich
Dulwich Village
East Dulwich
Catford
Hither Green
Lee
Richmond Park
Petersham
Ham
Teddington
Kingston Vale
Putney Vale
Putney Heath
West Hill
Southfields
Earlsfield
Balham
Streatham Hill
Tulse Hill
West Dulwich
Sydenham
Upper Sydenham
Lower Sydenham
Forest Hill
Southend
Downham
Bellingham
LONDON
Summerstown
Upper Tooting
Tooting Graveney
Streatham
Streatham Park
West Norwood
Norwood New Town
Wimbledon
South Wimbledon
Coombe
Crooked Billet
Collier's Wood
Furzedown
Streatham Vale
Upper Norwood
Penge
Anerley
New Beckenham
Beckenham
Plaistow
Bromley
Shortlands
Norbiton
Cottenham Park
Merton
Mitcham
Norbury
Thornton Heath
South Norwood
Elmers End
Hampton Wick
Kingston upon Thames
New Malden
Raynes Park
Morden
Hampton Court Palace
Seething Wells
Berrylands
Surbiton
Old Malden
Motspur Park
West Barnes
St Helier
Rosehill
Beddington Corner
Hackbridge
Selhurst
Woodside
Monks Orchard
Upper Elmers End
Eden Park
Park Langley
Long Ditton
Southborough
Tolworth
Worcester Park
North Cheam
Benhilton
The Wrythe
Carshalton
Broad Green
Wandle Park
Croydon
Addiscombe
Shirley
Upper Shirley
Spring Park
West Wickham
Hayes
Hinchley Wood
Hook
Chessington
Stoneleigh
Sutton
Cheam
Bandon Hill
Beddington
Waddon
Wallington
South Beddington
Roundshaw
South Croydon
Addington
New Addington
Coney Hall
Keston
Claygate
West Ewell
Ewell
East Ewell
Carshalton Beeches
Carshalton on the Hill
Woodcote Green
Selsdon
Forestdale
Malden Rushett
Belmont
Little Woodcote
Purley
Sanderstead
Epsom
The Wells
North Looe
Banstead
Woodmansterne
Coulsdon
Kenley
Hamsey Green
Farleigh
Fickleshole
Chelsham
Ashtead
Woodcote
Great Burgh
Chipstead
Whyteleafe
Warlingham
Wood Field

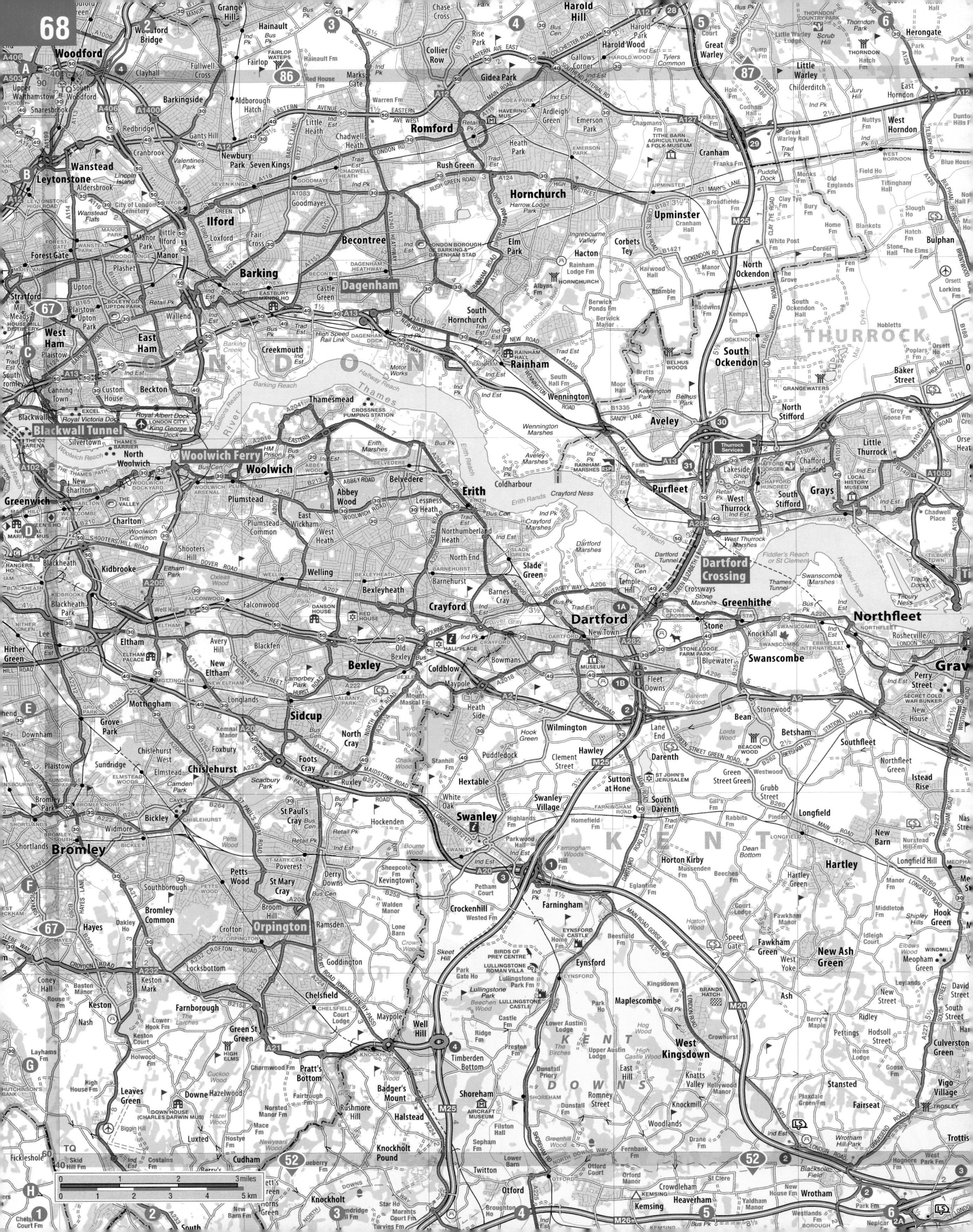
Woodford
Leytonstone
Wanstead
Stratford
West Ham
East Ham
Beckton
Ilford
Barking
Becontree
Dagenham
Romford
Gidea Park
Hornchurch
Upminster
Rainham
South Hornchurch
Harold Hill
Harold Wood
Great Warley
Little Warley
Cranham
North Ockendon
South Ockendon
Aveley
Purfleet
Grays
Little Thurrock
THURROCK
North Stifford
South Stifford
West Thurrock
Lakeside
LONDON
Blackwall Tunnel
Woolwich Ferry
Woolwich
Greenwich
Charlton
Thamesmead
Plumstead
Abbey Wood
Belvedere
Erith
Welling
Bexleyheath
Crayford
Dartford
Dartford Crossing
Greenhithe
Stone
Swanscombe
Northfleet
Eltham
Blackheath
Kidbrooke
Lee
Bexley
Sidcup
Chislehurst
Foots Cray
Swanley
Bromley
Orpington
Petts Wood
St Mary Cray
St Paul's Cray
Hayes
Keston
Farnborough
Chelsfield
Green Street Green
Knockholt
Halstead
Badgers Mount
Shoreham
Otford
Kemsing
Eynsford
Farningham
Horton Kirby
South Darenth
Darenth
Wilmington
Hextable
Hawley
Sutton at Home
Longfield
Hartley
New Ash Green
West Kingsdown
Heaverham
Wrotham
KENT
KENT DOWNS
River Thames
M25
M20
M26
A2
A13
A12
A20
0 1 2 3 miles
0 1 2 3 4 5 km

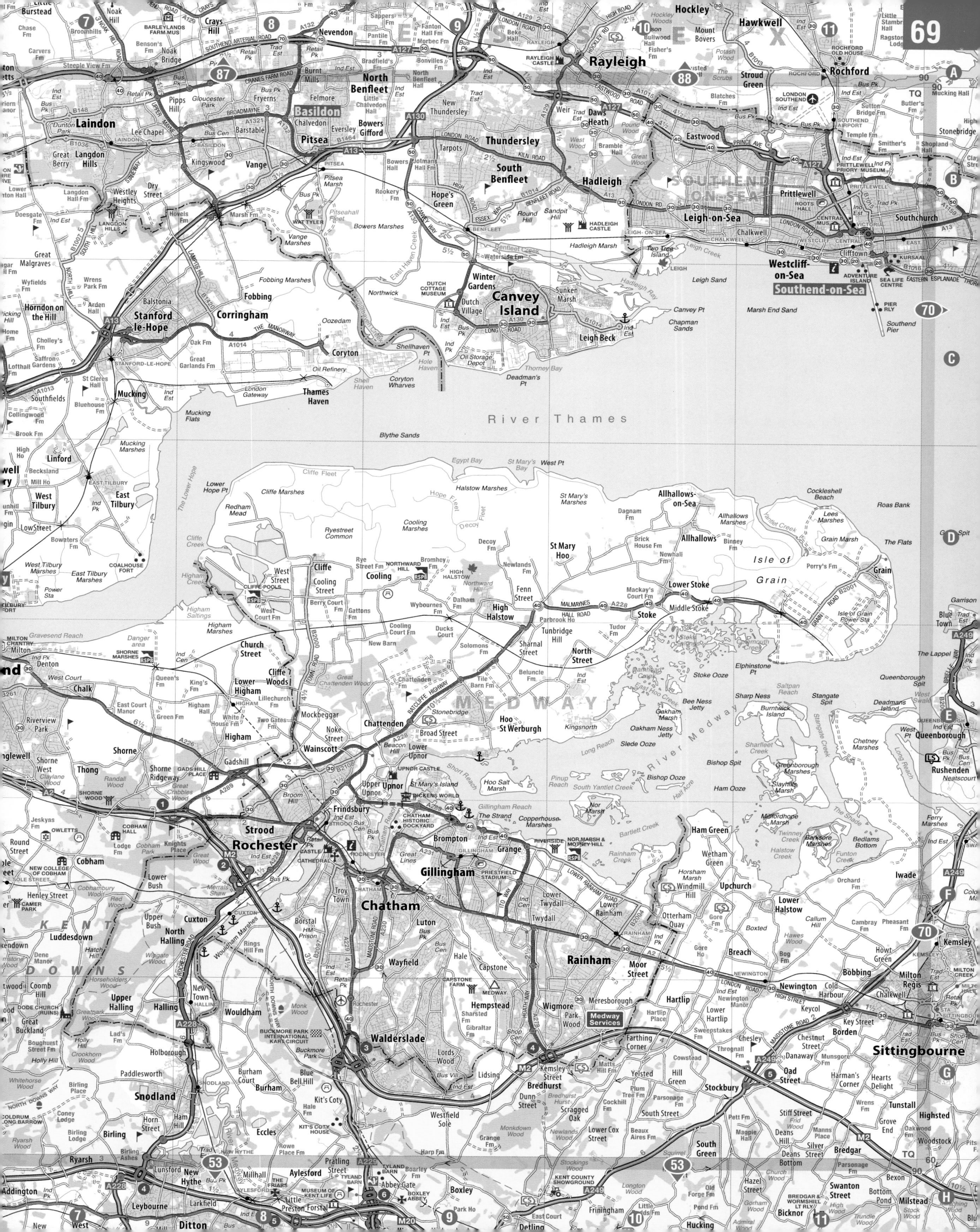

69
ESSEX
Burstead
Noak Hill
Crays Hill
Nevendon
Hockley
Hawkwell
Rochford
Basildon
Laindon
Langdon Hills
Lee Chapel
Pipps Hill
Noak Bridge
North Benfleet
Bowers Gifford
Pitsea
Vange
Kingswood
Chalvedon
Barstable
Felmore
Fryerns
Great Berry
Dry Street
Westley Heights
Rayleigh
Eastwood
Daws Heath
Thundersley
New Thundersley
South Benfleet
Hadleigh
Tarpots
Hope's Green
Leigh-on-Sea
Southend-on-Sea
Prittlewell
Southchurch
Westcliff-on-Sea
Chalkwell
Clifftown
London Southend Airport
Stroud Green
Canvey Island
Winter Gardens
Leigh Beck
Stanford-le-Hope
Corringham
Fobbing
Coryton
Thames Haven
Mucking
Horndon on the Hill
Linford
East Tilbury
West Tilbury
River Thames
Blythe Sands
Allhallows-on-Sea
Allhallows
St Mary Hoo
Isle of Grain
Grain
Lower Stoke
Stoke
Middle Stoke
High Halstow
Fenn Street
Cliffe
Cooling
Cliffe Woods
Church Street
Lower Higham
Higham
Shorne
Chalk
Riverview Park
Denton
Milton
Chattenden
Hoo St Werburgh
Kingsnorth
Wainscott
Upper Upnor
Upnor
Frindsbury
Strood
Rochester
Chatham
Gillingham
Brompton
Grange
Rainham
Lower Rainham
Twydall
Lower Twydall
Luton
Wayfield
Walderslade
Hempstead
Capstone
Wigmore
Medway Services
Lordswood
Borstal
Cuxton
North Halling
Halling
Upper Halling
Luddesdown
Cobham
Thong
Gadshill
Shorne Ridgeway
Upper Bush
Lower Bush
Wouldham
Burham
Snodland
Birling
Holborough
Paddlesworth
Bluebell Hill
Kit's Coty
Eccles
Aylesford
Larkfield
Leybourne
Ditton
New Hythe
Boxley
Detling
Bredhurst
Kemsley Street
Lidsing
Westfield Sole
Upchurch
Otterham Quay
Lower Halstow
Iwade
Newington
Hartlip
Stockbury
Oad Street
Borden
Sittingbourne
Milton Regis
Kemsley
Bobbing
Key Street
Chalkwell
Tunstall
Highsted
Bredgar
Swanton Street
Milstead
Queenborough
Rushenden
River Medway
MEDWAY
KENT
DOWNS
M2
M20
A2
A13
A127
A130
A228
A229
A249
87
88
53
70

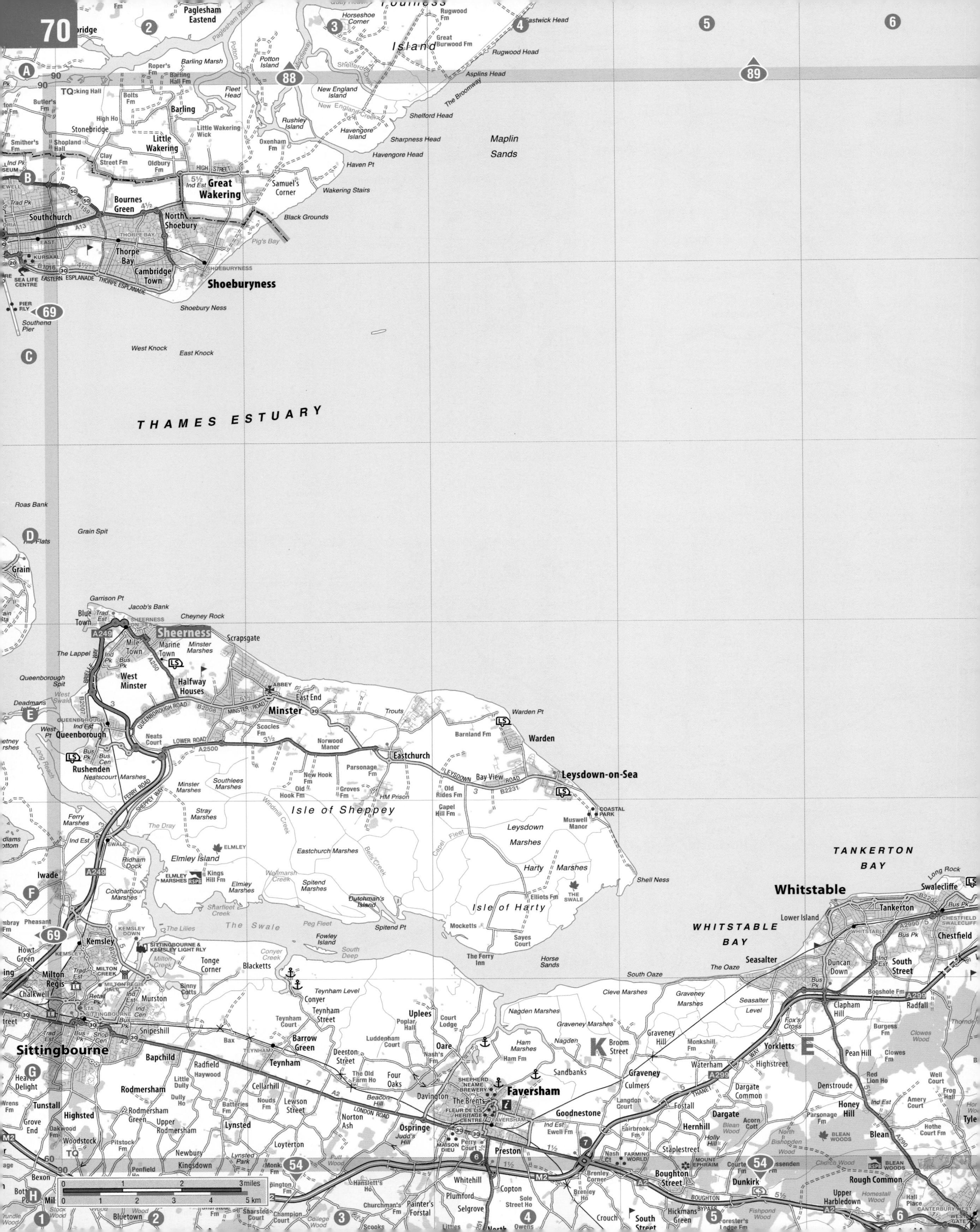

THAMES ESTUARY

Isle of Sheppey

Isle of Harty

TANKERTON BAY

WHITSTABLE BAY

Sheerness

Minster

Eastchurch

Warden

Leysdown-on-Sea

Whitstable

Tankerton

Chestfield

Seasalter

Queenborough

Rushenden

Iwade

Kemsley

Sittingbourne

Milton Regis

Chalkwell

Murston

Teynham

Barrow Green

Conyer

Faversham

Ospringe

Preston

Goodnestone

Graveney

Yorkletts

Dargate

Dunkirk

Hernhill

Boughton Street

Shoeburyness

Great Wakering

Little Wakering

Barling

Southchurch

Thorpe Bay

Cambridge Town

North Shoebury

Bournes Green

Maplin Sands

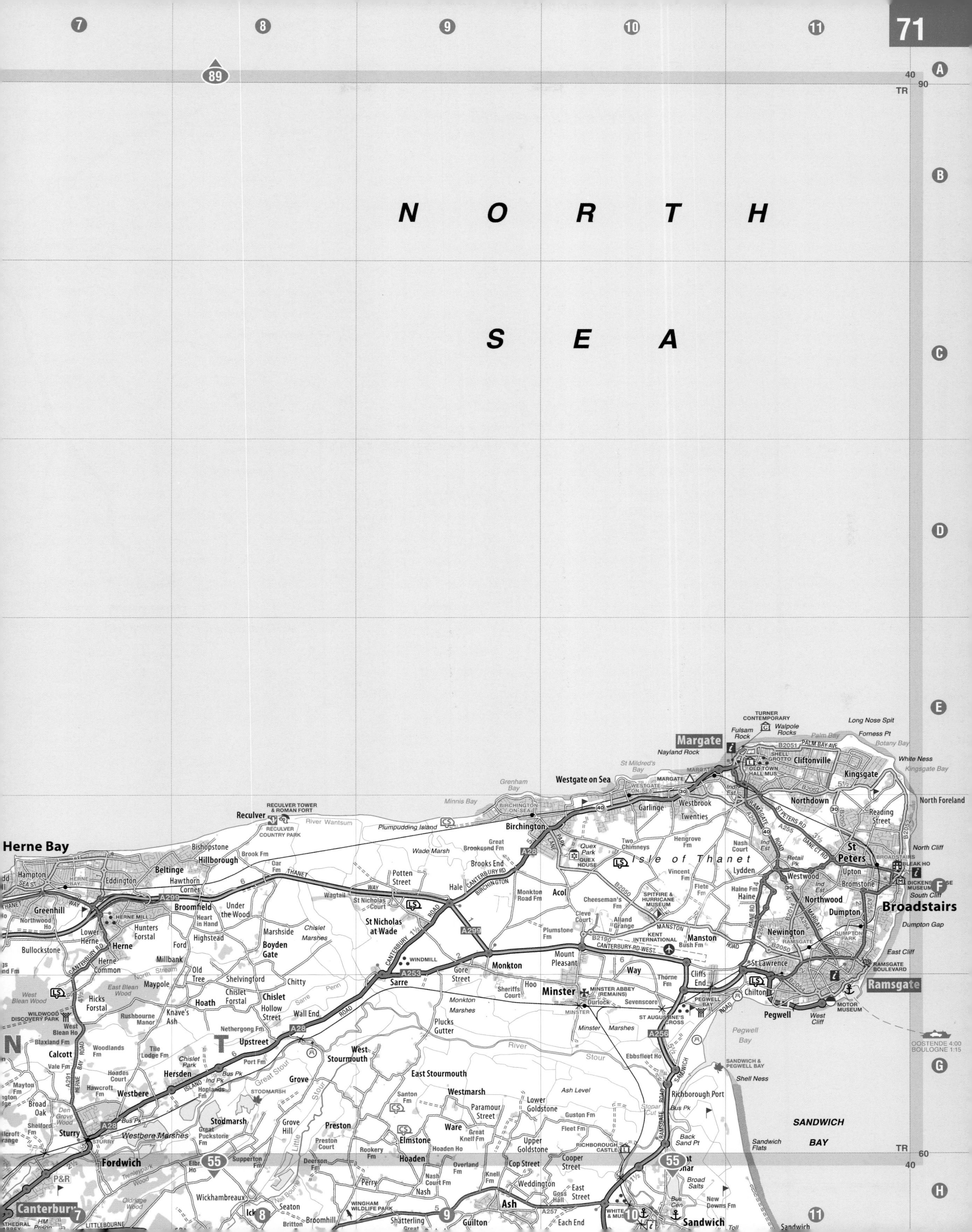

N O R T H

S E A

Margate
Westgate on Sea
Birchington
Cliftonville
Kingsgate
Northdown
Reading Street
North Foreland
Garlinge
Westbrook
Twenties
White Ness
St Peters
Broadstairs
Herne Bay
Reculver
Isle of Thanet
Minster
Ramsgate
Pegwell
Sandwich
Canterbury
Fordwich
Sturry

SANDWICH
BAY

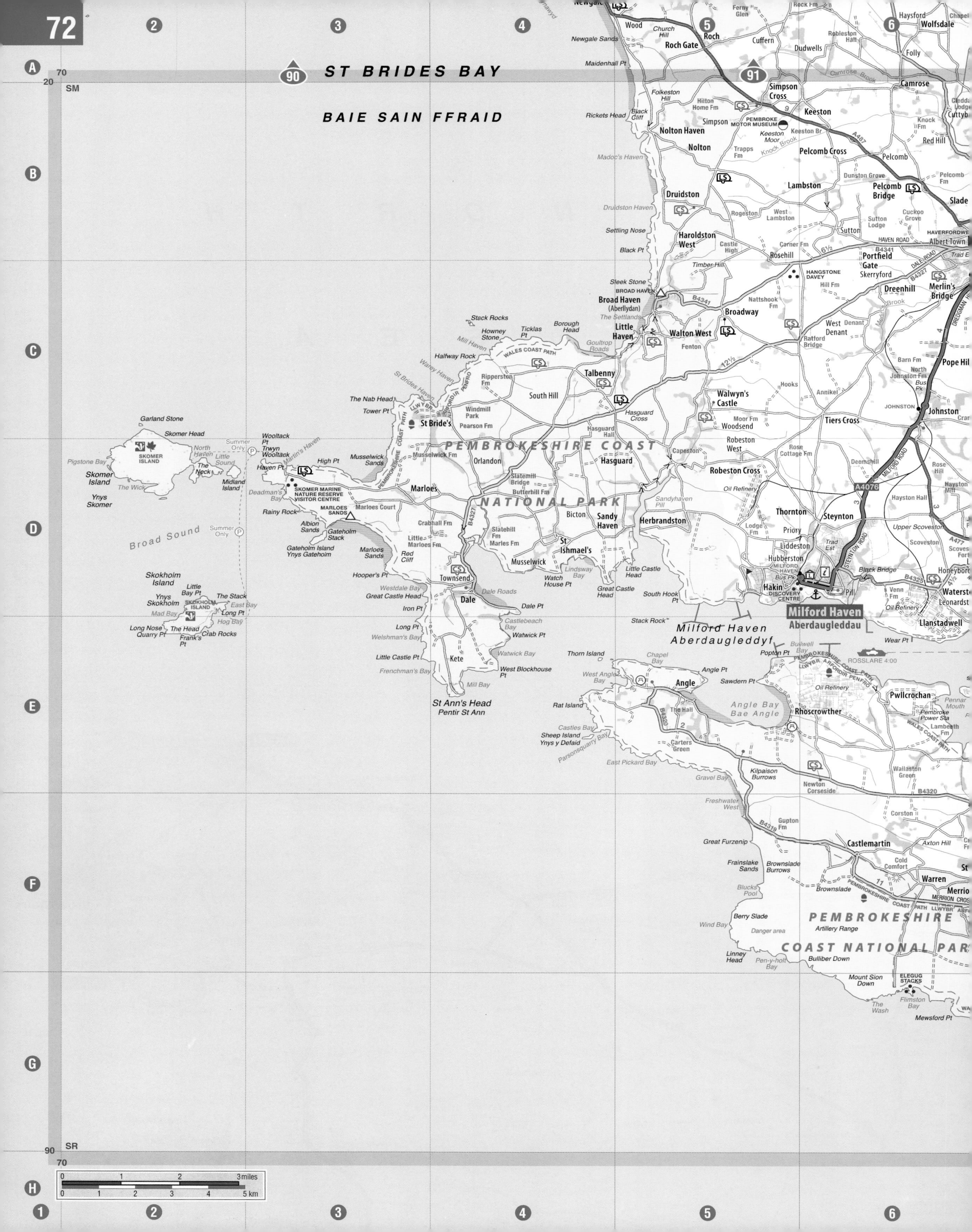
ST BRIDES BAY
BAIE SAIN FFRAID
90
91
SM
SR
Skomer Island
Skokholm Island
Broad Sound
Garland Stone
Skomer Head
Pigstone Bay
The Neck
North Haven
Little Sound
Midland Island
The Wick
Ynys Skomer
SKOMER ISLAND
Summer Only
Wooltack Pt
Trwyn Wooltack
Martin's Haven
Haven Pt
Deadman's Bay
SKOMER MARINE NATURE RESERVE VISITOR CENTRE
MARLOES SANDS
Rainy Rock
Albion Sands
Gateholm Stack
Gateholm Island
Ynys Gateholm
Marloes Sands
Little Bay Pt
The Stack
East Bay
Ynys Skokholm
SKOKHOLM ISLAND
Mad Bay
Long Pt
Hog Bay
Long Nose
Quarry Pt
The Head
Crab Rocks
Frank's Pt
High Pt
Musselwick Sands
Marloes
Marloes Court
Crabhall Fm
Little Marloes Fm
Red Cliff
Hooper's Pt
Westdale Bay
Great Castle Head
Iron Pt
Long Pt
Welshman's Bay
Little Castle Pt
Frenchman's Bay
Kete
Mill Bay
St Ann's Head
Pentir St Ann
West Blockhouse Pt
Watwick Bay
Watwick Pt
Castlebeach Bay
Dale Pt
Dale
Dale Roads
Townsend
The Nab Head
Tower Pt
St Bride's
St Brides Haven
Musselwick Fm
Orlandon
Windmill Park
Pearson Fm
Ripperston Fm
South Hill
Halfway Rock
Mill Haven
Warey Haven
Stack Rocks
Howney Stone
Ticklas Pt
Borough Head
WALES COAST PATH
Goultrop Roads
Talbenny
PEMBROKESHIRE COAST
NATIONAL PARK
Slatemill Bridge
Butterhill Fm
Slatehill Fm
Marles Fm
Musselwick
Bicton
St Ishmael's
Sandy Haven
Lindsway Bay
Watch House Pt
Great Castle Head
Little Castle Head
Hasguard
Hasguard Hall
Hasguard Cross
Capeston
Herbrandston
Sandyhaven Pill
South Hook Pt
Stack Rock
Milford Haven
Aberdaugleddyf
Thorn Island
Chapel Bay
Angle Pt
West Angle Bay
Angle
Rat Island
The Hall
Castles Bay
Sheep Island
Ynys y Defaid
Parsonsquarry Bay
Carters Green
East Pickard Bay
Angle Bay
Bae Angle
Sawdern Pt
Popton Pt
Bullwell Bay
Oil Refinery
Rhoscrowther
Pwllcrochan
Pennar Mouth
Pembroke Power Sta
Lambeeth Fm
Wallaston Green
Kilpaison Burrows
Gravel Bay
Newton Corseside
B4320
Freshwater West
B4319
Gupton Fm
Corston
Great Furzenip
Castlemartin
Axton Hill
Frainslake Sands
Brownslade Burrows
Cold Comfort
Warren
Brownslade
Blucks Pool
Berry Slade
Danger area
Wind Bay
PEMBROKESHIRE
Artillery Range
COAST NATIONAL PARK
Bulliber Down
Linney Head
Pen-y-holt Bay
Mount Sion Down
ELEGUG STACKS
Flimston Bay
The Wash
Mewsford Pt
Newgale Sands
Wood
Church Hill
Roch
Roch Gate
Ferny Glen
Cuffern
Dudwells
Robleston Hall
Hayesford
Wolfsdale
Folly
Maidenhall Pt
Camrose Brook
Camrose
Folkeston Hill
Simpson Cross
Hilton Home Fm
Keeston
Black Cliff
Rickets Head
Simpson
PEMBROKE MOTOR MUSEUM
Keeston Moor
Keeston Br
Nolton Haven
Nolton
Trapps Fm
Knock Brook
Pelcomb Cross
A487
Pelcomb
Red Hill
Knock Fm
Madoc's Haven
Dunston Grove
Lambston
Pelcomb Bridge
Pelcomb Fm
Slade
Druidston
Druidston Haven
Rogeston
West Lambston
Sutton Lodge
Cuckoo Grove
Settling Nose
Haroldston West
Castle High
Sutton
HAVEN ROAD
HAVERFORDWEST
Albert Town
Black Pt
Corner Fm
Rosehill
B4341
Portfield Gate
Timber Hill
HANGSTONE DAVEY
Skerryford
Hill Fm
DALE ROAD
B4327
Dreenhill
Merlin's Bridge
Sleek Stone
BROAD HAVEN
Broad Haven
(Aberllydan)
The Settlands
Nattshook Fm
Broadway
Little Haven
Walton West
Fenton
West Denant
Denant
Ratford Bridge
Merlin's Brook
Barn Fm
North Johnston Fm
Pope Hill
Walwyn's Castle
Hooks
Anniket
Moor Fm
Woodsend
JOHNSTON
Johnston
Tiers Cross
Robeston West
Rose Cottage Fm
Deemshill
MILFORD ROAD
Rose Hill
Robeston Cross
Oil Refinery
A4076
Hayston Hall
Hayston Mill
Thornton
Steynton
Lodge Fm
Priory
Upper Scoveston
Liddeston
Trad Est
STEYNTON ROAD
Scoveston
A477
Hubberston
MILFORD HAVEN
Black Bridge
Honeyborough
Hakin
DISCOVERY CENTRE
Bus Pk
Pill
Venn Fm
B4325
Waterston
Leonardston
Oil Refinery
Milford Haven
Aberdaugleddau
Llanstadwell
Wear Pt
ROSSLARE 4:00
PEMBROKESHIRE COAST PATH
LLWYBR ARFORDIR PENFRO
MERRION CROSS
Merrion
0 1 2 3 miles
0 1 2 3 4 5 km

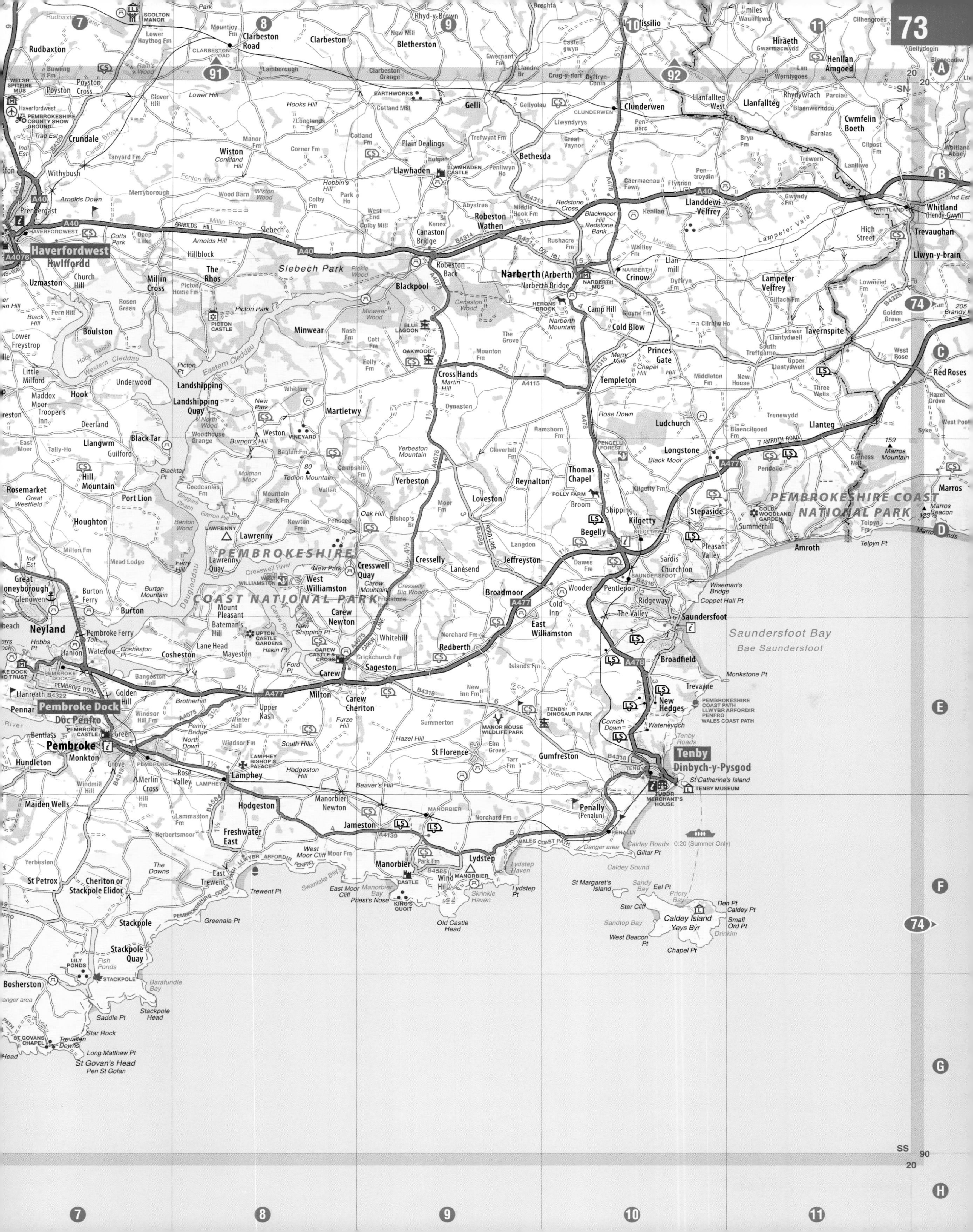
Rudbaxton
Scolton Manor
Clarbeston Road
Clarbeston
Bletherston
Rhyd-y-Brown
Llandissilio
miles
Hiraeth
Henllan Amgoed
Cilhengroes
Gellydogin
91
92
Poyston Cross
Lamborough
Clarbeston Grange
Crug-y-deri
Dyffryn-Conin
Welsh Spitfire Mus
Haverfordwest
Pembrokeshire County Show Ground
Earthworks
Gelli
Clunderwen
Llanfallteg West
Llanfallteg
Rhydywrach
Cwmfelin Boeth
Crundale
Wiston
Plain Dealings
Bethesda
Withybush
Llawhaden
Llawhaden Castle
Caermaenau Fawr
Llanddewi Velfrey
Whitland (Hendy-Gwyn)
Prendergast
Arnolds Down
Merryborough
Robeston Wathen
Redstone Cross
Trevaughan
Haverfordwest Hwlffordd
Slebech
Slebech Park
Canaston Bridge
Robeston Back
Narberth (Arberth)
Narberth Bridge
Narberth Mus
Crinow
Lampeter Velfrey
Llwyn-y-brain
Uzmaston
Millin Cross
The Rhos
Blackpool
Picton Castle
Picton Park
Minwear
Blue Lagoon
Oakwood
Camp Hill
Cold Blow
Princes Gate
Tavernspite
Boulston
Western Cleddau
Eastern Cleddau
Hook Reach
Landshipping
Landshipping Quay
Cross Hands
Templeton
Red Roses
Little Milford
Hook
Underwood
Martletwy
Ludchurch
Llanteg
Deerland
Llangwm
Black Tar
Weston
Vineyard
Yerbeston
Longstone
Amroth Road
Marros
Rosemarket
Hill Mountain
Port Lion
Reynalton
Thomas Chapel
Folly Farm
Loveston
Kilgetty
Stepaside
Pembrokeshire Coast National Park
Colby Woodland Garden
Summerhill
Houghton
Lawrenny
Begelly
Pleasant Valley
Amroth
Cresselly
Jeffreyston
Cresswell Quay
West Williamston
Sardis
Churchton
Great Honeyborough
Burton Ferry
Burton
Broadmoor
Wooden
Pentlepoir
Ridgeway
Saundersfoot
Saundersfoot Bay
Bae Saundersfoot
Neyland
Pembroke Ferry
Carew Newton
Upton Castle Gardens
East Williamston
The Valley
Broadfield
Cosheston
Carew
Sageston
Redberth
Milton
Carew Cheriton
Pembroke Dock
Doc Penfro
Pembroke
Monkton
New Hedges
Trevayne
Manor House Wildlife Park
Tenby Dinosaur Park
St Florence
Gumfreston
Tenby
Dinbych-y-Pysgod
St Catherine's Island
Tenby Museum
Tudor Merchant's House
Hundleton
Lamphey
Lamphey Bishop's Palace
Maiden Wells
Hodgeston
Freshwater East
Manorbier Newton
Jameston
Penally (Penalun)
Manorbier
Manorbier Castle
Lydstep
Caldey Roads
Giltar Pt
Caldey Sound
St Margaret's Island
Caldey Island
Ynys Byr
0:20 (Summer Only)
St Petrox
Cheriton or Stackpole Elidor
Stackpole
Stackpole Quay
Bosherston
Lily Ponds
Stackpole Head
St Govan's Head
Pen St Gofan
St Govans Chapel
Old Castle Head
Wales Coast Path
74
SN
SS
A
B
C
D
E
F
G
H
7
8
9
10
11

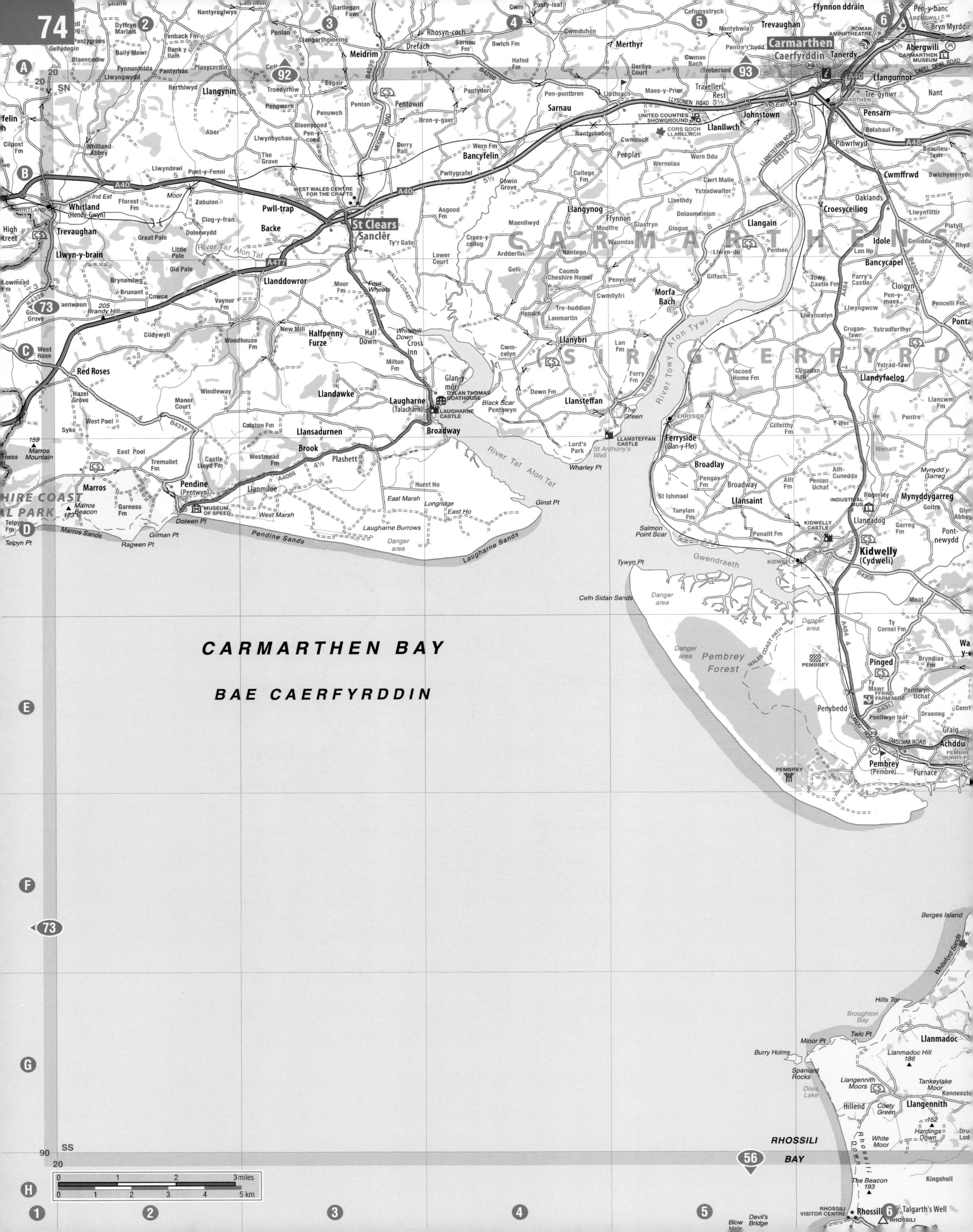
CARMARTHEN BAY
BAE CAERFYRDDIN
Carmarthen
Caerfyrddin
St Clears
Sanclêr
Laugharne
(Talacharn)
Kidwelly
(Cydweli)
Pembrey
(Pembre)
Pembrey Forest
Pendine Sands
Laugharne Sands
Cefn Sidan Sands
RHOSSILI
BAY
Whitland
(Hendy-Gwyn)
Llansteffan
Ferryside
(Glan-y-Fferi)
Llanmadoc
Llangennith
Rhossili

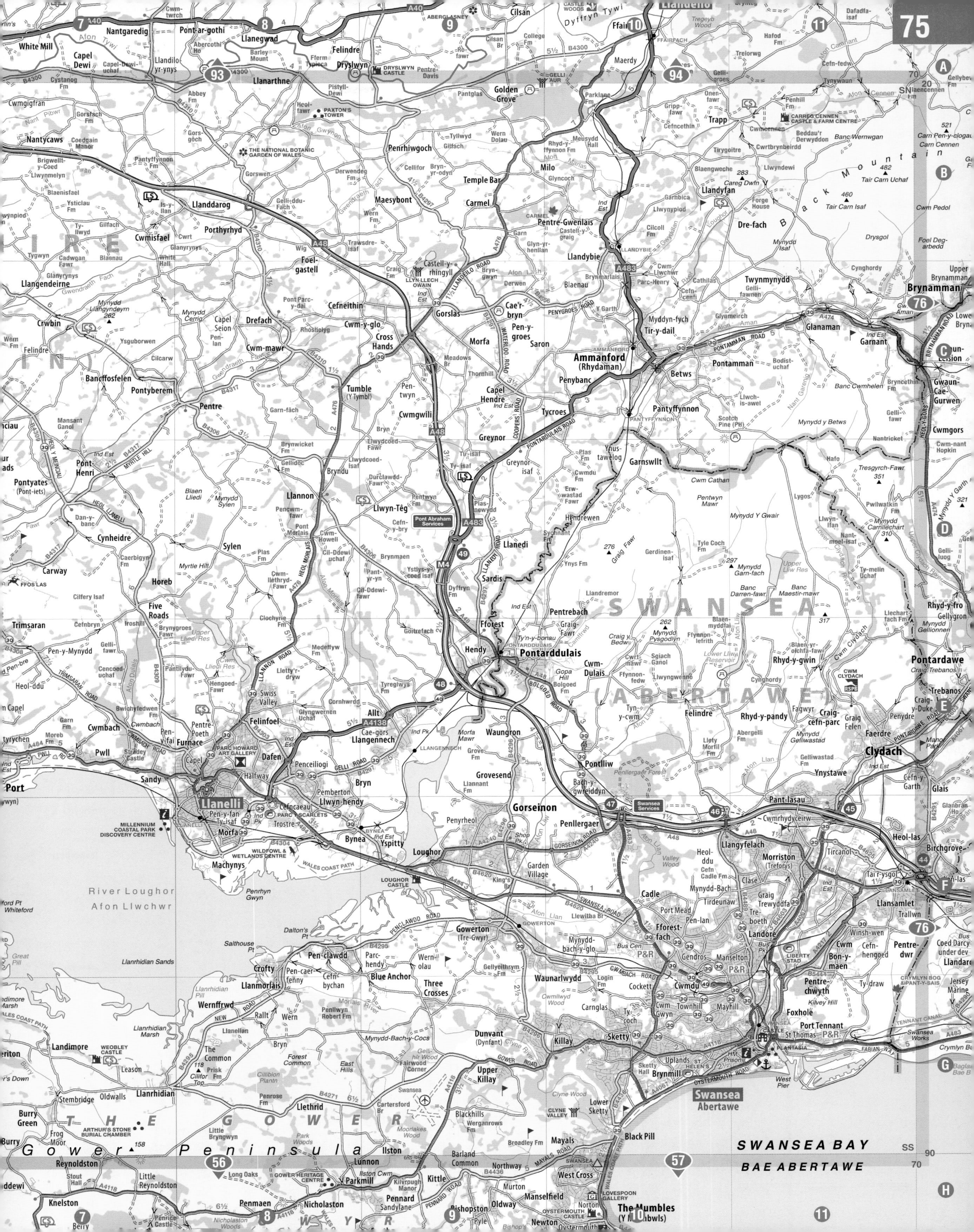
Llandeilo
Nantgaredig
Pont-ar-gothi
Llanegwad
Felindre
Dryslwyn
Llanarthne
Golden Grove
Ffairfach
Trapp
Penrhiwgoch
Llanddarog
Porthyrhyd
Maesybont
Temple Bar
Carmel
Milo
Llandyfan
Pentre-Gwenlais
Llandybie
Foel-gastell
Llangendeirne
Cefneithin
Gorslas
Cwm-y-glo
Cross Hands
Drefach
Morfa
Saron
Ammanford (Rhydaman)
Tir-y-dail
Glanaman
Garnant
Brynamman
Betws
Pontamman
Tumble (Y Tymbl)
Pontyberem
Pentre
Cwmgwili
Capel Hendre
Penybanc
Tycroes
Pantyffynnon
Greynor
Pontyates (Pont-iets)
Pont-Henri
Llannon
Llwyn-Têg
Garnswllt
Llanedi
Sylen
Horeb
Five Roads
Sardis
Fforest
Pentrebach
Hendy
Pontarddulais
Cwm-Dulais
Rhyd-y-gwin
Pontardawe
Trimsaran
SWANSEA (ABERTAWE)
Felinfoel
Allt
Llangennech
Waungron
Felindre
Rhyd-y-pandy
Clydach
Pwll
Furnace
Dafen
Llanelli
Bryn
Pontlliw
Gorseinon
Penllergaer
Llangyfelach
Morriston (Treforys)
Llwyn-hendy
Bynea
Yspitty
Loughor
Machynys
River Loughor
Afon Llwchwr
Gowerton (Tre-Gwyr)
Fforest-fach
Landore
Pen-clawdd
Blue Anchor
Three Crosses
Waunarlwydd
Cwmdu
Llanmorlais
Dunvant (Dynfant)
Killay
Sketty
Swansea Abertawe
Upper Killay
Brynmill
Landimore
Llanrhidian
Black Pill
Mayals
SWANSEA BAY
BAE ABERTAWE
Gower Peninsula
THE GOWER
Reynoldston
Ilston
Parkmill
Kittle
West Cross
Knelston
Penmaen
Nicholaston
Bishopston
Oldway
Newton
The Mumbles (Y Mwmbwls)
Black Mountain

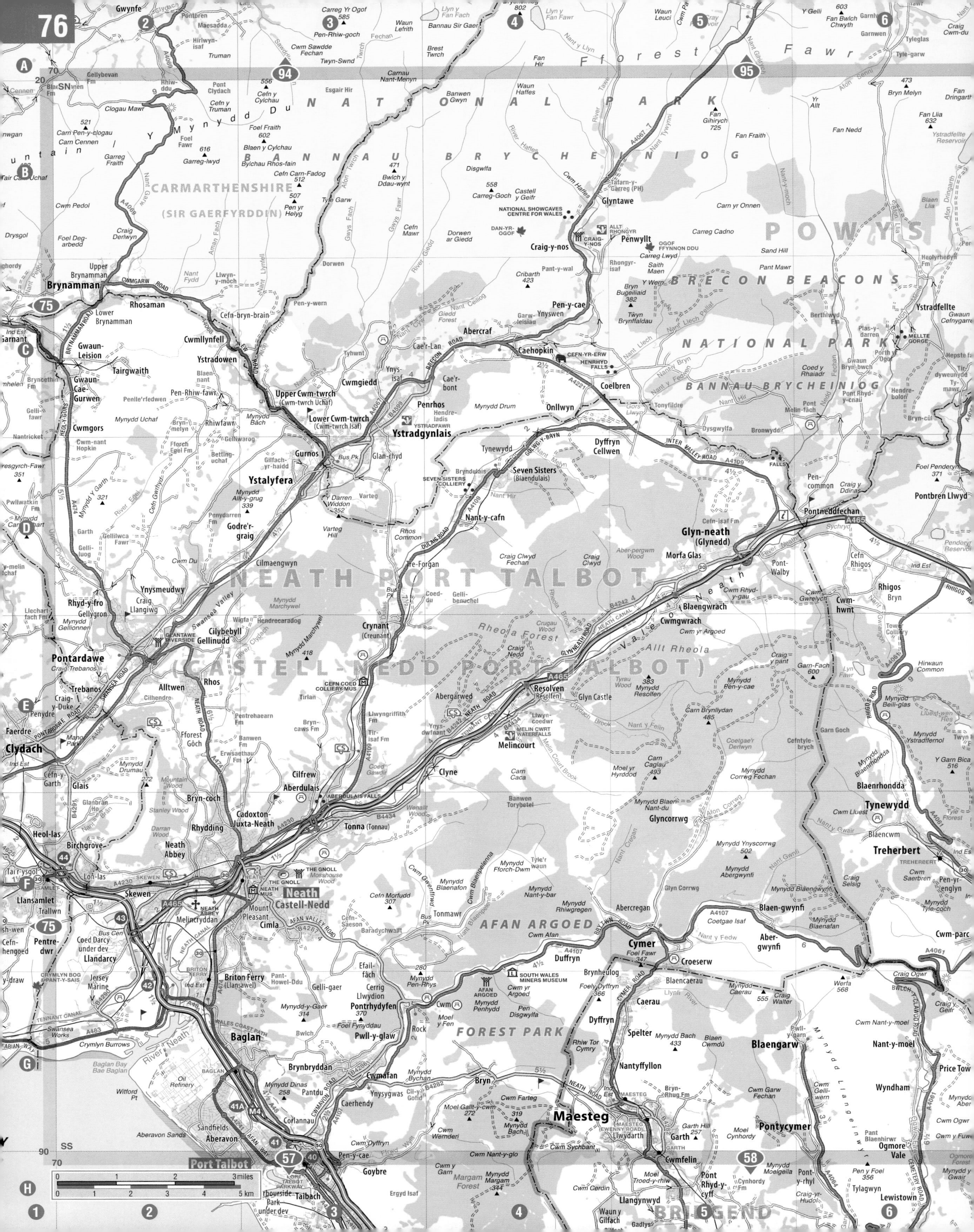

94
95
75
57
58
NATIONAL PARK
BANNAU BRYCHEINIOG
BRECON BEACONS
NATIONAL PARK
BANNAU BRYCHEINIOG
POWYS
CARMARTHENSHIRE
(SIR GAERFYRDDIN)
NEATH PORT TALBOT
(CASTELL-NEDD PORT TALBOT)
Fforest Fawr
Mynydd Du
AFAN ARGOED
FOREST PARK
BRIDGEND
Gwynfe
Carreg Yr Ogof
Pen-Rhiw-goch
Cwm Sawdde Fechan
Twyn-Swnd
Waun Lefrith
Bannau Sir Gaer
Brest Twrch
Carnau Nant-Menyn
Waun Leuci
Y Gelli
Fan Bwlch Chwyth
Garnwen
Craig Cwm-du
Tyleglas
Tyle-garw
Maesadda
Hirlwyn-isaf
Truman
Gellybevan Fm
Rhiw-ddu
Pont Clydach
Cefn y Truman
Esgair Hir
Cefn y Cylchau
Clogau Mawr
Carn Pen-y-clogau
Carn Cennen
Foel Fraith
Blaen y Cylchau
Bylchau Rhos-fain
Cefn Carn-Fadog
Pen yr Helyg
Garreg Fraith
Garreg-lwyd
Foel Fawr
Bwlch y Ddau-wynt
Waun Haffes
Banwen Gwyn
Fan Hir
Fan Gihirych
Fan Fraith
Bryn Melyn
Fan Dringarth
Fan Llia
Fan Nedd
Yr Allt
Ystradfellte Reservoir
Disgwlfa
Carreg-Goch
Castell y Geifr
Tatarn-y-Garreg (PH)
Glyntawe
Carn yr Onnen
NATIONAL SHOWCASES CENTRE FOR WALES
DAN-YR-OGOF
ALLT RHONGYR
Craig-y-nos
Penwyllt
OGOF FFYNNON DDU
Carreg Cadno
Carreg Lwyd
Saith Maen
Sand Hill
Pant Mawr
Heolyrhedyn Fm
Tyle Garw
Cefn Mawr
Dorwen ar Giedd
Dorwen
Cribarth
Pant-y-wal
Rhongyr-isaf
Bryn Bugeiliaid
Y Wern
Twyn Bryntfaldau
Cwm Pedol
Drysgol
Foel Deg-arbedd
Craig Derlwyn
Upper Brynamman
Brynamman
Lower Brynamman
CWMGARW ROAD
Nant Fydd
Llwyn-y-moch
Rhosaman
Cefn-bryn-brain
Pen-y-wern
Giedd Forest
Garw-leisiau
Ynyswen
Pen-y-cae
Abercraf
Caehopkin
CEFN-YR-ERW
HENRHYD FALLS
Coelbren
Ystradfellte
Berthlwyd Fm
Plas-y-darren
MELLTE GORGE
Porth yr Ogof
Gwaun Cefnygarreg
Hepste fa
Coed y Rhaiadr
Gwaun Bryn-bwch
Pont Rhyd-y-cnau
Hendre-bolon
Pont Melin-fach
Bryn-cûl
Garnant
Gwaun-Leision
Cwmllynfell
Ystradowen
Tairgwaith
Gwaun-Cae-Gurwen
Tyhwnt
Cae'r-Lan
BRECON ROAD
Ynys-isaf
Cwmgiedd
Cae'r-bont
Penrhos
Hendre-ladis
Mynydd Drum
Onllwyn
Tonyfildre
Dysgwylfa
Bronwydd
Pen-Rhiw-fawr
Penlle'rfedwen
Mynydd Uchaf
Upper Cwm-twrch
(Cwm-twrch Uchaf)
Lower Cwm-twrch
(Cwm-twrch Isaf)
YSTRADFAWR
Ystradgynlais
Rhiwfawr
Mynydd Bach
Bryn-melyn
Cwmgors
Cwm-nant Hopkin
Fforch Egel Fm
Gelliwarog
Betting-uchaf
Gilfach-yr-haidd
Gurnos
Bus Pk
Glan-rhyd
Tynewydd
COLWG-Y-BRYN
Dyffryn Cellwen
INTER VALLEY ROAD
FALLS
Pen-common
Craig y Ddinas
Pontneddfechan
Foel Penderyn
Pontbren Llwyd
Ystalyfera
Mynydd Allt-y-grug
Bryndulais
SEVEN SISTERS COLLIERY
Seven Sisters
(Blaendulais)
Nant Hir
Darren Widdon
Varteg
Mynydd Y Garth
Cefn Gwrhyd
Penydarren Fm
Godre'r-graig
Nant-y-cafn
Varteg Hill
Rhos Common
DULAIS ROAD
Cefn-isaf Fm
Glyn-neath
(Glynedd)
Morfa Glas
Pont-Walby
Cefn Rhigos
Ind Est
Garth
Gellilwca Fawr
Gelli-luog
Cwm Du
Tre-Forgan
Craig Clwyd Fechan
Craig Clwyd
Aber-pergwm Wood
Cilmaengwyn
Ynysmeudwy
Craig Llangiwg
Rhyd-y-fro
Gellygron
Mynydd Gellionnen
Swansea Valley
Mynydd Marchywel
Wigfa
Hendrecaradog
Cilybebyll
Gellinudd
GLANTAWE RIVERSIDE
Bus Pk
Coed-du
Gelli-benuchel
Cwm Rhyd-y-gau
Blaengwrach
Cwmgwrach
Cwm yr Argoed
Rhigos
Bryn
Cwm-hwnt
Tower Colliery
Pontardawe
Craig Trebanos
Trebanos
Mynydd Marchywel
Crynant
(Creunant)
Crugau Wood
Rheola Forest
Craig Nedd
Allt Rheola
Vale of Neath
Craig y pant
Garn-Fach
Hirwaun Common
Craig-y-Duke
Penydre
Faerdre
Clydach
Alltwen
Cilhendre
Rhos
CEFN COED COLLIERY MUS
Tirlan
Abergarwed
Resolven
(Resolfen)
Glyn Castle
Tyrau Wood
Mynydd Resolfen
Mynydd Pen-y-cae
Mynydd Beili-glas
Pentreheaarn Fm
Fforest Goch
Banwen Fm
Erwsaethau Fm
Bryn-caws Fm
Llwyngriffith Fm
Tir-isaf Fm
Ynys-dwfnant
Llwyn-coedwr
MELIN CWRT WATERFALLS
Melincourt
Carn Brynllydan
Coetgae'r Derlwyn
Cefntyle-brych
Garn Goch
Mynydd Ystradfernol
Twyn
Y Garn Bica
Cefn-y-Garth
Glais
Mynydd Drumau
Mountain Wood
Coed Gawdir
Cilfrew
Aberdulais
ABERDULAIS FALLS
Clyne
Carn Caca
Moel yr Hyrddod
Carn Caglau
Mynydd Corrwg Fechan
Mynydd Blaenrhondda
Blaenrhondda
Glanbran Ho
Stanley Wood
Bryn-coch
Cadoxton-Juxta-Neath
Rhydding
Darran Wood
Tonna (Tonnau)
Wenallt Wood
Banwen Torybetel
Mynydd Blaen Nant-du
Glyncorrwg
Tynewydd
Cwm Lluest
Blaencwm
Heol-las
Birchgrove
Neath Abbey
Treherbert
TREHERBERT
Mynydd Ynyscorrwg
Mynydd Abergwynfi
Tai'r-ysgol
Lon-las
SKEWEN
Skewen
Llansamlet
Trallwn
Pentre-dwr
Coed Darcy under dev
Llandarcy
Bus Cen
NEATH ABBEY
Melincryddan
Mount Pleasant
Cimla
THE GNOLL
Mosshouse Wood
NEATH MUS
Neath
Castell-Nedd
Cefn Morfudd
Cwm Gwenffrwd
Mynydd Blaenafon
Mynydd Ffforch-Dwm
Tyle'r waun
Mynydd Nant-y-bar
Mynydd Rhiwgwreg
Glyn Corrwg
Mynydd Blaengwynfi
Craig Selsig
Cwm Saerbren
Pen-yr-englyn
Mynydd Tyle-coch
Cefn-Saeson
Baradychwalt
AFAN VALLEY ROAD
Tonmawr
Abercregan
Blaen-gwynfi
Coetgae Isaf
Mynydd Blaenafan
Cwm-parc
Cwm Afan
Cymer
Foel Fawr
Croeserw
Aber-gwynfi
Briton Ferry
(Llansawel)
Pant-Howel-Ddu
Efail-fâch
Cerrig Llwydion
Gelli-gaer
Mynydd Pen-Rhys
SOUTH WALES MINERS MUSEUM
Cwm yr Argoed
Duffryn
Brynheulog
Foel y Dyffryn
Blaencaerau
Mynydd Caerau
Craig Walter
Werfa
Craig Ogwr
BWLCH
Craig-y-Geifr
CRYMLYN BOG
PANT-Y-SAIS
Jersey Marine
Ind Est
Pontrhydyfen
Foel Fynyddau
Pwll-y-glaw
Mynydd-y-Gaer
Bwlch
AFAN ARGOED
Mynydd Penhydd
Pen Disgwylfa
Cwm
Moel y Fen
Rock
Caerau
Dyffryn
Spelter
Mynydd Bach
Blaen Cwmdu
Pwll-y-garn
Cwm Nant-y-moel
Nant-y-moel
Rhiw Tor Cymry
TENNANT CANAL
Swansea Works
Crymlyn Burrows
Baglan
WALES COAST PATH
River Neath
Baglan Bay
Bae Baglan
Oil Refinery
Witford Pt
Brynbryddan
Mynydd Dinas
Pantdu
Cwmafan
Mynydd Bychan
Ynysygwas
Cil-y-Gofid
Bryn
Nantyffyllon
Blaengarw
Cwm Farteg
Moel Gallt-y-cwm
Mynydd Bach
Bryn-Rhug Fm
Cwm Garw Fechan
Price Town
Wyndham
Cwm Gelli-wern
Mynydd Llangeinwyr
Mynydd Aber
Cwm Ogwr
Cwm y Fuwch
Sandfields
Aberavon
Aberavon Sands
Corlannau
Caerhendy
Cwm Wernderi
Maesteg
Garth Hill
Moel Cynhordy
Pontycymer
Pant Blaenhirwr
Ogmore Vale
Cwm Dyffryn
Cwm Sychbant
Llwydarth
EWENNY ROAD
Garth
GARTH
Cwmfelin
Pen-y-cae
Cwm Nant-y-glo
Port Talbot
PORT TALBOT PARKWAY
Goybre
Cwm y Garn
Margam Forest
Mynydd Margam
Moel Troed-y-rhiw
Cwm Cerdin
Pont Rhyd-y-cyff
Cynhordy Fm
Mynydd Moelgeila
Pont-y-rhyl
Pen y Foel
Tylagwyn
Lewistown
Craig-yr-Hudol
Mynydd Gwaith y Gwyr
CEMETERY ROAD
Ergyd Isaf
Taibach
Llangynwyd
Waun y Gilfach
Gadlys
rbourside Park under dev
Ind Est
0 1 2 3 miles
0 1 2 3 4 5 km
SN
SS
1 2 3 4 5 6
A B C D E F G H

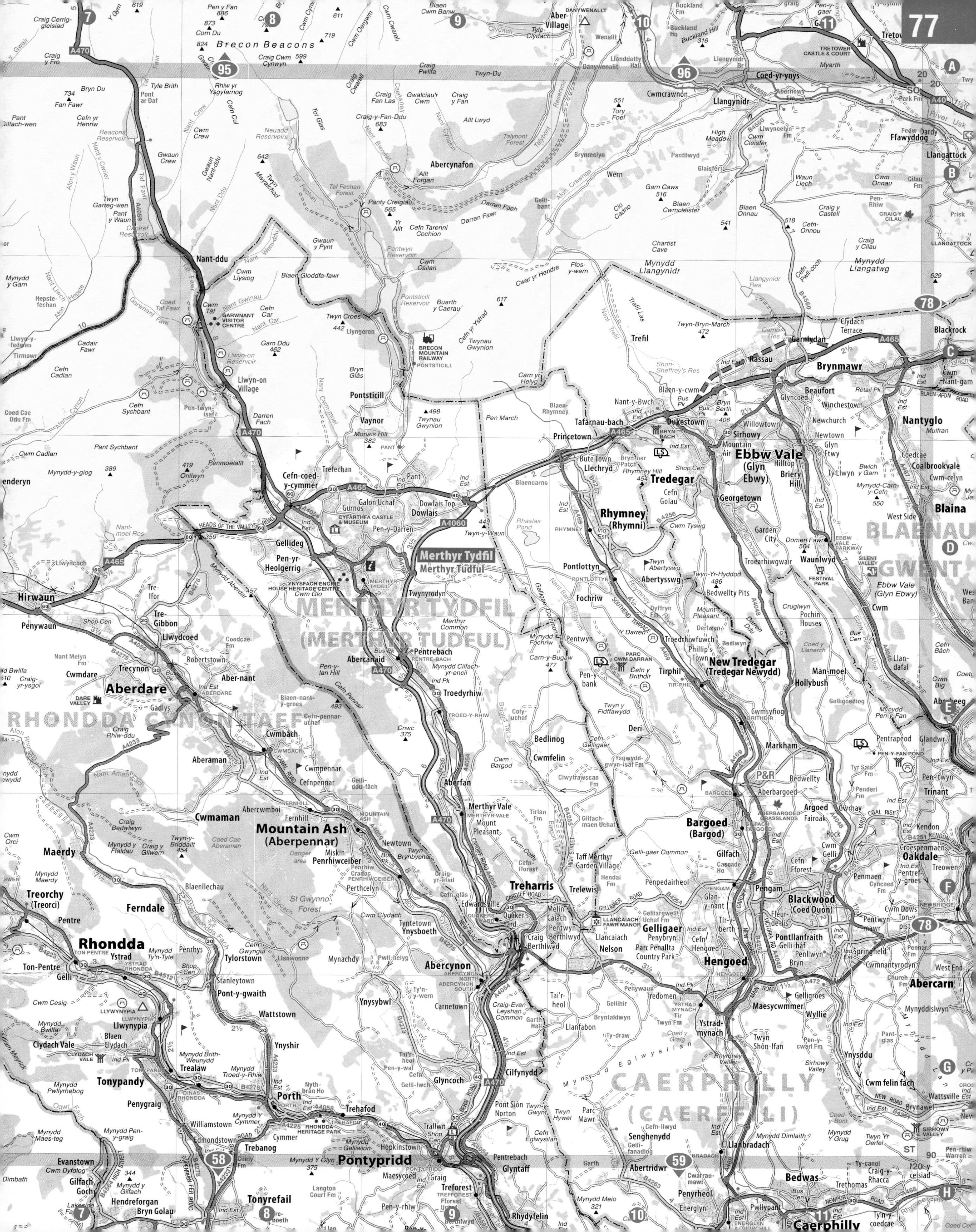
Brecon Beacons
MERTHYR TYDFIL
(MERTHYR TUDFUL)
RHONDDA CYNON TAFF
CAERPHILLY
(CAERFFILI)
BLAENAU GWENT
Merthyr Tydfil
Merthyr Tudful
Aberdare
Mountain Ash
(Aberpennar)
Rhondda
Pontypridd
Ebbw Vale
(Glyn Ebwy)
Tredegar
Rhymney
(Rhymni)
New Tredegar
(Tredegar Newydd)
Bargoed
(Bargod)
Blackwood
(Coed Duon)
Hengoed
Gelligaer
Treharris
Abercynon
Porth
Tonypandy
Treorchy
(Treorci)
Ferndale
Maerdy
Hirwaun
Brynmawr
Nantyglo
Blaina
Abercarn
Oakdale
Caerphilly
Tonyrefail
Llangattock
Crickhowell

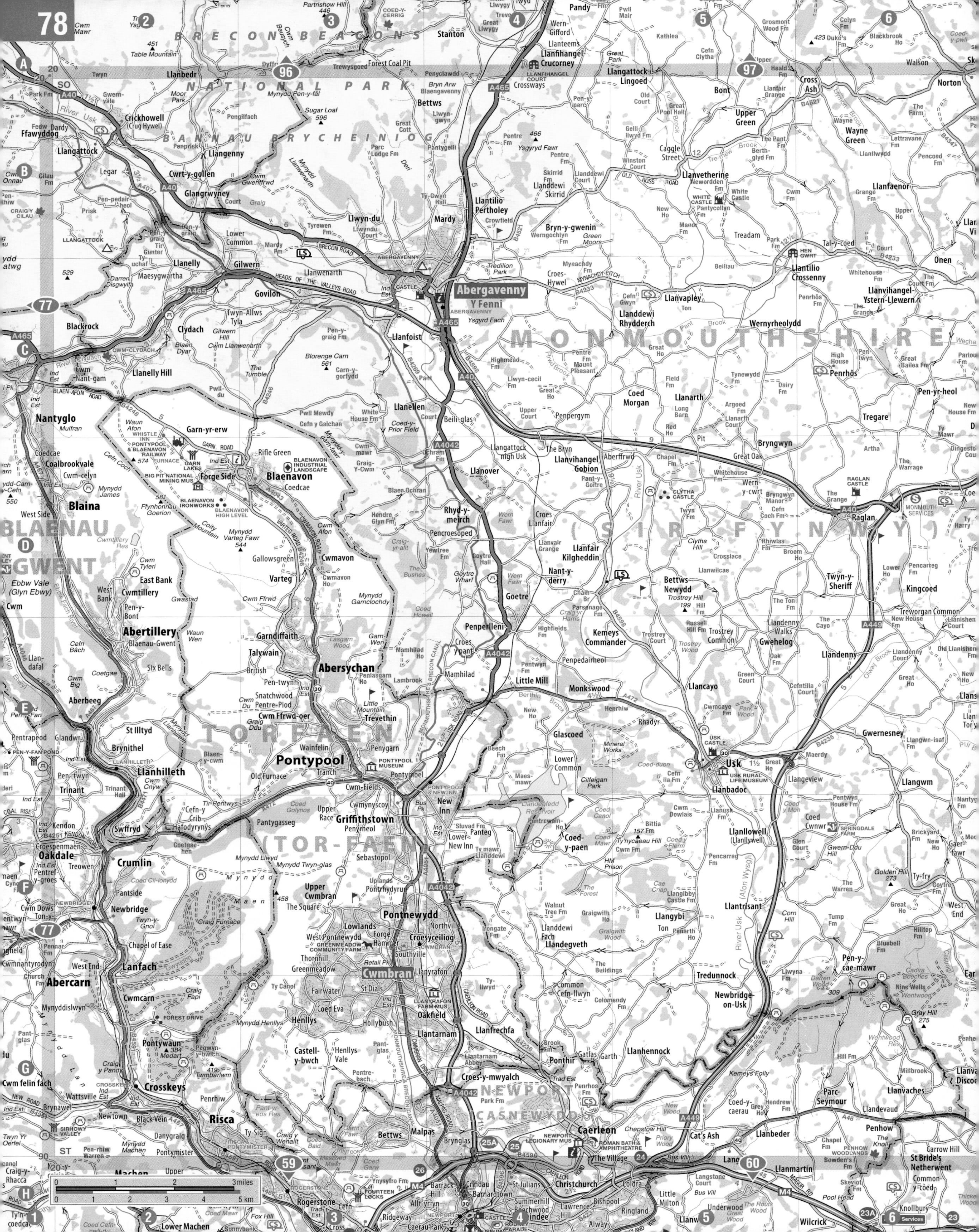
BRECON BEACONS
NATIONAL PARK
BANNAU BRYCHEINIOG
MONMOUTHSHIRE
(SIR FYNWY)
BLAENAU GWENT
TORFAEN
(TOR-FAEN)
NEWPORT
CASNEWYDD
Abergavenny
Y Fenni
Pontypool
Cwmbran
Caerleon
Usk
Raglan
Crickhowell
(Crug Hywel)
Blaenavon
Blaina
Nantyglo
Abertillery
Ebbw Vale
(Glyn Ebwy)
Abersychan
Griffithstown
Pontnewydd
Crosskeys
Risca
Abercarn
Newbridge
Crumlin
Oakdale
Llanhilleth
Brynithel
Gilwern
Govilon
Llanfoist
Llanellen
Llanover
Goetre
Penperlleni
Little Mill
Monkswood
Glascoed
Llanbadoc
Llangybi
Llantrisant
Tredunnock
Newbridge-on-Usk
Llanhennock
Ponthir
Christchurch
Llanmartin
Penhow
Llanvaches
Parc-Seymour
Llanbeder
Cat's Ash
Llangattock
Llangenny
Llanbedr
Llanelly
Llanelly Hill
Clydach
Blackrock
Mardy
Llantilio Pertholey
Llanvapley
Llantilio Crossenny
Llanvetherine
Llanarth
Coed Morgan
Bryngwyn
Tregare
Kingcoed
Llandenny
Gwehelog
Llancayo
Llangwm
Llanllowell
Gwernesney
Wernyrheoldydd
Llandewi Rhydderch
Llanvihangel Gobion
Llanfair Kilgheddin
Kemeys Commander
Bettws Newydd
Twyn-y-Sheriff
Pen-yr-heol
Llanfaenor
Cross Ash
Norton
Onen
Bont
Upper Green
Wayne Green
Llangattock Lingoed
Llanfihangel-Crucorney
Pandy
Stanton
Bettws
Forest Coal Pit
Coed-y-paen
Llandegveth
Llanfrechfa
Croes-y-mwyalch
Malpas
Bettws
Rogerstone
Henllys
Oakfield
Llantarnam
New Inn
Sebastopol
Upper Cwmbran
Varteg
Talywain
Garndiffaith
Cwmavon
Trevethin
Rhyd-y-meirch
Pontywaun
Wattsville
Lanfach
Cwmcarn
Machen
Lower Machen
A40
A465
A4042
A472
A449
A48
M4
B4598
B4233
B4246
B4248
B4591
B4251
B4235
B4236
B4596
HEADS OF THE VALLEYS ROAD
596
Sugar Loaf
Blorenge Carn
561
Mynydd Varteg Fawr
544
Ysgyryd Fawr
466
Table Mountain
451
Partrishow Hill
446
Wentwood
0
1
2
3 miles
0
1
2
3
4
5 km

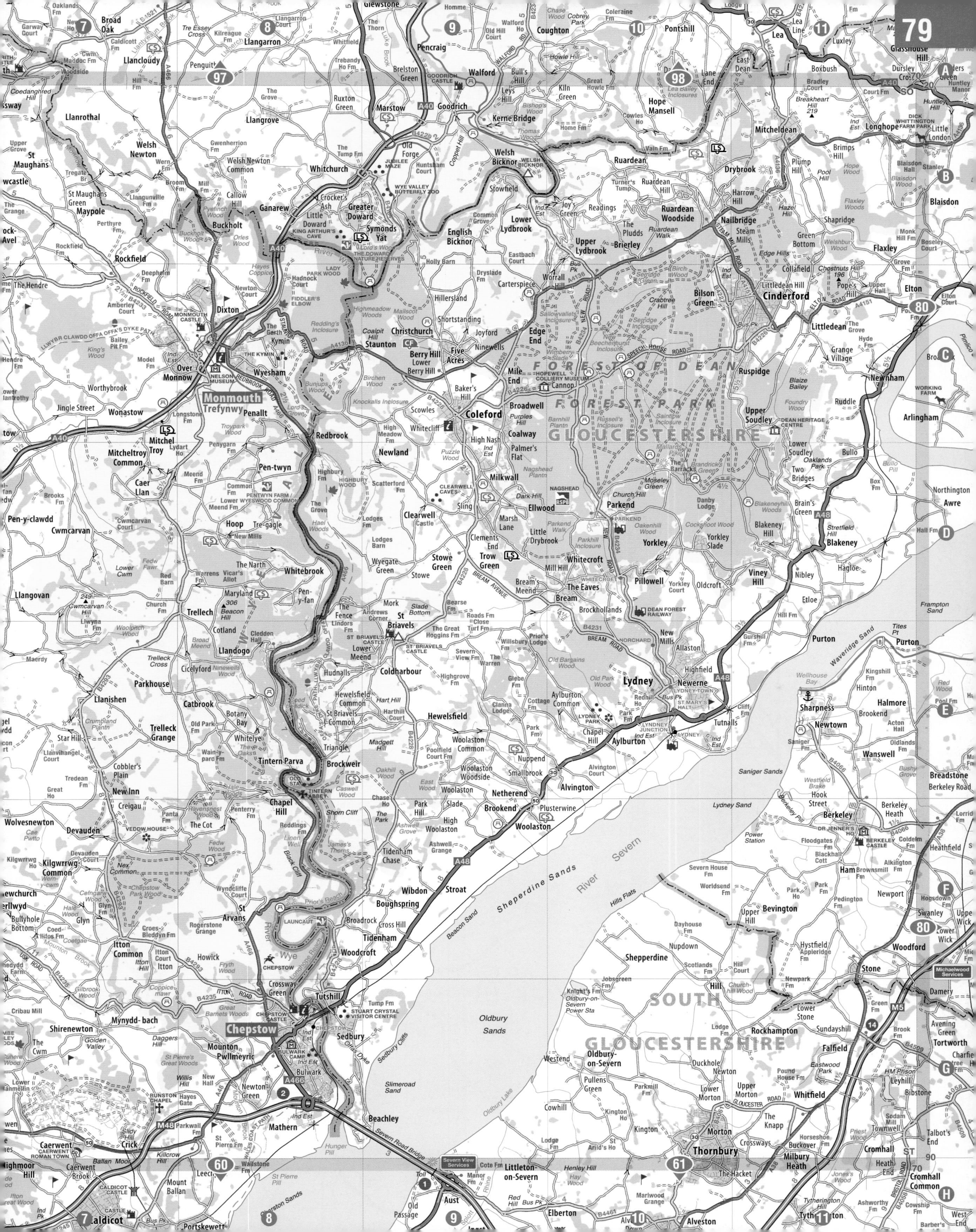

79
Broad Oak
Llangarron
Llancloudy
Glewstone
Pencraig
Walford
Coughton
Pontshill
Lea
Glasshouse Hill
Goodrich
Marstow
Kerne Bridge
Hope Mansell
Mitcheldean
Longhope
Llanrothal
Llangrove
Welsh Newton
St Maughans
Whitchurch
Welsh Bicknor
Ruardean
Drybrook
Blaisdon
Ganarew
Symonds Yat
Lower Lydbrook
Upper Lydbrook
Ruardean Woodside
Nailbridge
Buckholt
Rockfield
English Bicknor
Brierley
Flaxley
Dixton
Cinderford
Elton
Monmouth
Trefynwy
Over Monnow
Wyesham
Christchurch
Staunton
Berry Hill
Five Acres
Edge End
Mile End
Littledean
Ruspidge
Newnham
FOREST OF DEAN
FOREST PARK
GLOUCESTERSHIRE
Coleford
Broadwell
Coalway
Cannop
Upper Soudley
Arlingham
Penallt
Redbrook
Newland
Mitchel Troy
Mitcheltroy Common
Pen-twyn
Milkwall
Ellwood
Parkend
Awre
Clearwell
Sling
Hoop
Cwmcarvan
Pen-y-clawdd
Yorkley
Blakeney
Trow Green
Whitecroft
Whitebrook
Pillowell
Viney Hill
Llangovan
Trellech
St Briavels
Bream
Llandogo
Coldharbour
Purton
Parkhouse
Lydney
Newerne
Llanishen
Catbrook
Hewelsfield
Aylburton
Sharpness
Trelleck Grange
Tintern Parva
Brockweir
Newtown
Wanswell
New Inn
Chapel Hill
Netherend
Alvington
Brookend
Woolaston
Berkeley
Devauden
Kilgwrrwg Common
Stroat
Wibdon
River Severn
Sheperdine Sands
Bevington
St Arvans
Tidenham
Itton Common
Woodcroft
Shepperdine
Woodford
Stone
Tutshill
Chepstow
Sedbury
SOUTH GLOUCESTERSHIRE
Shirenewton
Mynydd-bach
Mounton
Pwllmeyric
Oldbury Sands
Oldbury-on-Severn
Rockhampton
Falfield
Tortworth
Newton Green
Beachley
Mathern
Crick
Whitfield
Morton
Thornbury
Caerwent
Littleton-on-Severn
Aust
Elberton
Alveston
Cromhall
Caldicot
Portskewett

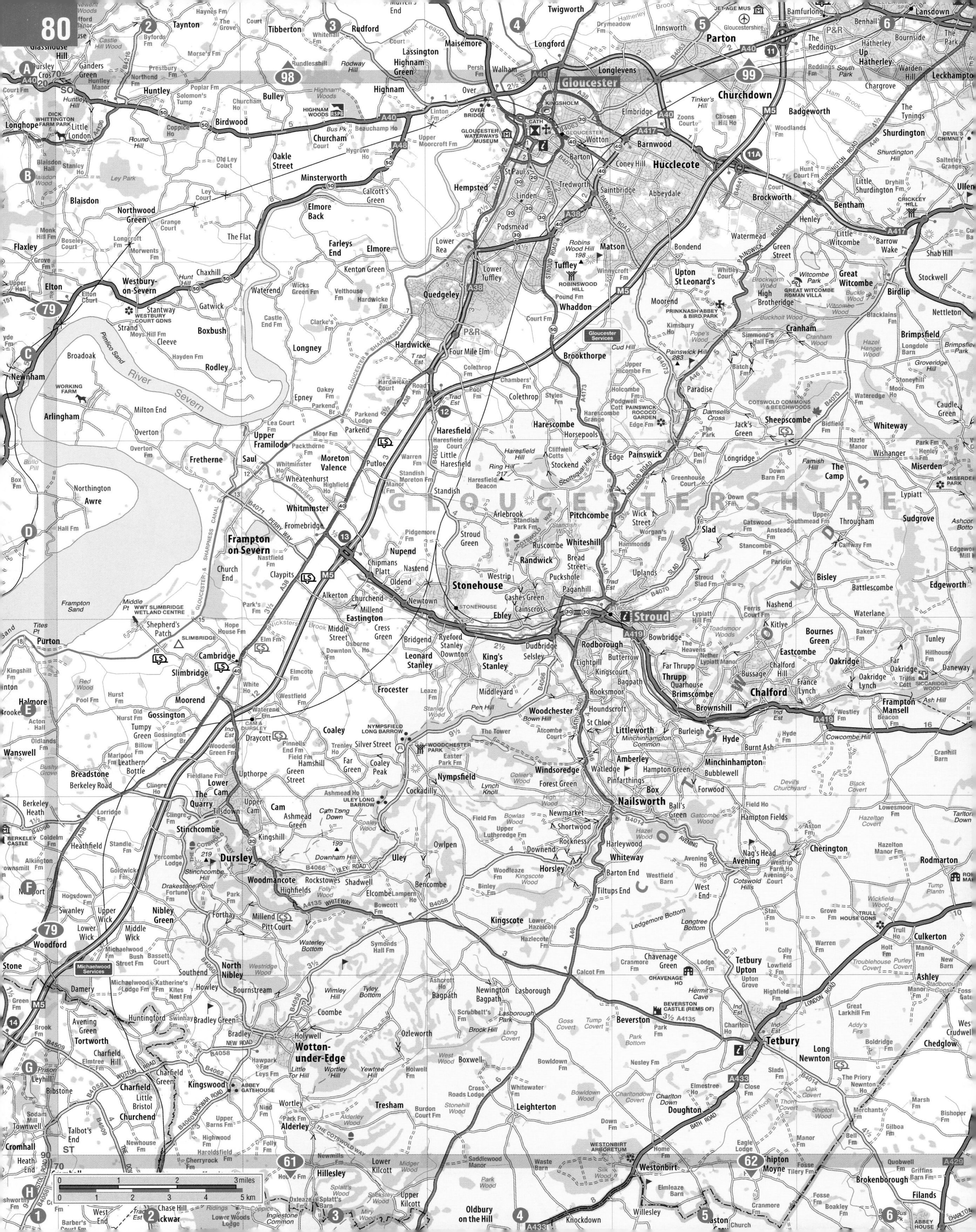
GLOUCESTERSHIRE
COTSWOLDS
River Severn
Gloucester
Stroud
98
99
79
61
62
Taynton
Tibberton
Rudford
Twigworth
Innsworth
Parton
Bamfurlong
Lansdown
Benhall
Maisemore
Longford
Lassington
Highnam Green
Highnam
Longlevens
Churchdown
Up Hatherley
Leckhampton
Huntley
Bulley
Over
Kingsholm
Elmbridge
Badgeworth
Longhope
Birdwood
Churcham
Barnwood
Hucclecote
Shurdington
Little London
Oakle Street
Minsterworth
Hempsted
Coney Hill
Brockworth
Bentham
Blaisdon
Northwood Green
Elmore Back
Tredworth
Saintbridge
Abbeydale
Linden
Podsmead
Matson
Tuffley
Flaxley
The Flat
Farleys End
Elmore
Lower Rea
Lower Tuffley
Upton St Leonard's
Great Witcombe
Birdlip
Elton
Westbury-on-Severn
Chaxhill
Quedgeley
Whaddon
Moorend
Stantway
Gatwick
Boxbush
Strand
Cleeve
Longney
Hardwicke
Four Mile Elm
Brookthorpe
Cranham
Brimpsfield
Newnham
Broadoak
Rodley
Epney
Colethrop
Paradise
Sheepscombe
Arlingham
Milton End
Overton
Parkend
Haresfield
Harescombe
Horsepools
Whiteway
Upper Framilode
Fretherne
Saul
Moreton Valence
Putloe
Little Haresfield
Edge
Painswick
Longridge
Miserden
Awre
Whitminster
Standish
Stockend
The Camp
Lypiatt
Sudgrove
Frampton on Severn
Fromebridge
Nupend
Arlebrook
Pitchcombe
Wick Street
Slad
Througham
Church End
Claypits
Chipmans Platt
Nastend
Stroud Green
Whiteshill
Ruscombe
Randwick
Bisley
Edgeworth
Oldend
Stonehouse
Westrip
Puckshole
Paganhill
Uplands
Battlescombe
Alkerton
Churchend
Eastington
Millend
Newtown
Ebley
Cashes Green
Cainscross
Nashend
Waterlane
Purton
Hope
Middle Street
Cress Green
Bridgend
Ryeford
Stanley Downton
King's Stanley
Dudbridge
Selsley
Rodborough
Bowbridge
Kitlye
Bournes Green
Tunley
Slimbridge
Cambridge
Leonard Stanley
Lightpill
Butterrow
Far Thrupp
Thrupp
Brimscombe
Chalford
Eastcombe
Oakridge
Daneway
Halmore
Frocester
Middleyard
Rooksmoor
Bussage
France Lynch
Frampton Mansell
Moorend
Gossington
Woodchester
Houndscroft
St Chloe
Brownshill
Wanswell
Coaley
Draycott
Silver Street
Littleworth
Burleigh
Hyde
Burnt Ash
Breadstone
Berkeley Road
Far Green
Coaley Peak
Hamshill
Nympsfield
Windsoredge
Forest Green
Amberley
Minchinhampton
Bubblewell
Upthorpe
Lower Cam
The Quarry
Cam
Cockadilly
Watledge
Pinfarthings
Box
Forwood
Berkeley Heath
Ashmead Green
Nailsworth
Ball's Green
Hampton Fields
Stinchcombe
Tilsdown
Kingshill
Owlpen
Newmarket
Shortwood
Rockness
Harleywood
Heathfield
Dursley
Uley
Downend
Whiteway
Avening
Cherington
Rodmarton
Woodmancote
Rockstowes
Shadwell
Elcombe
Bencombe
Horsley
Barton End
Tiltups End
West End
Swanley
Upper Wick
Nibley Green
Forthay
Millend
Pitt Court
Kingscote
Woodford
Lower Wick
Middle Wick
North Nibley
Tetbury Upton
Culkerton
Stone
Southend
Howley
Bournstream
Chavenage Green
Ashley
Damery
Bagpath
Newington Bagpath
Lasborough
Coombe
Avening Green
Tortworth
Bradley Green
Bradley
Holywell
Ozleworth
Beverston
Tetbury
Chedglow
Charfield Hill
Charfield
Charfield Green
Wotton-under-Edge
Boxwell
Long Newnton
Leyhill
Bibstone
Little Bristol
Kingswood
Churchend
Wortley
Tresham
Leighterton
Doughton
Townwell
Talbot's End
Alderley
Cromhall
Heath End
Hillesley
Lower Kilcott
Westonbirt
Shipton Moyne
Brokenborough
Upper Kilcott
Oldbury on the Hill
Willesley
Knockdown
Filands
Michaelwood Services
Gloucester Services
Slimbridge WWT Wetland Centre
Westonbirt Arboretum
Chavenage Ho
Beverston Castle (Rems of)
0 1 2 3 miles
0 1 2 3 4 5 km

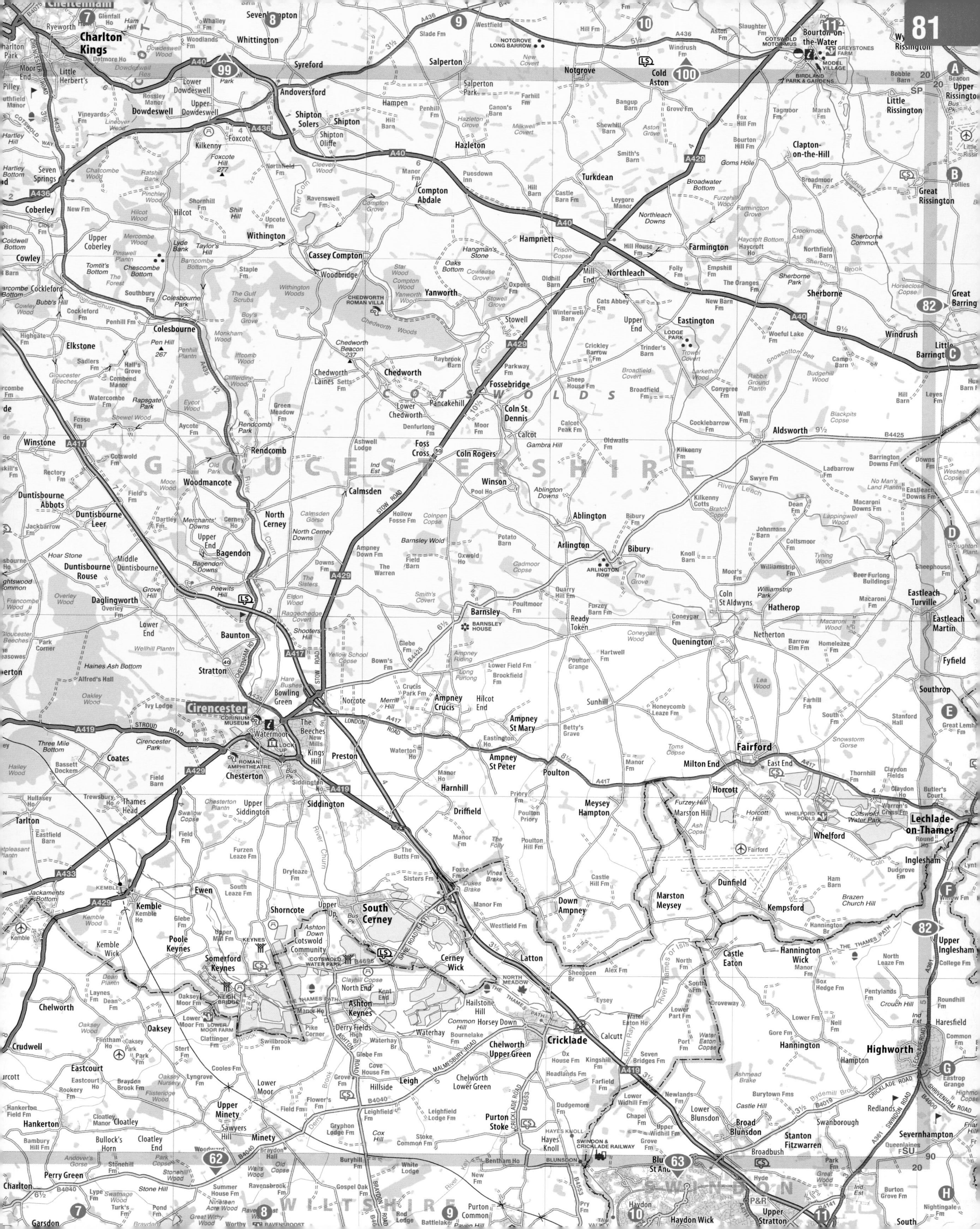

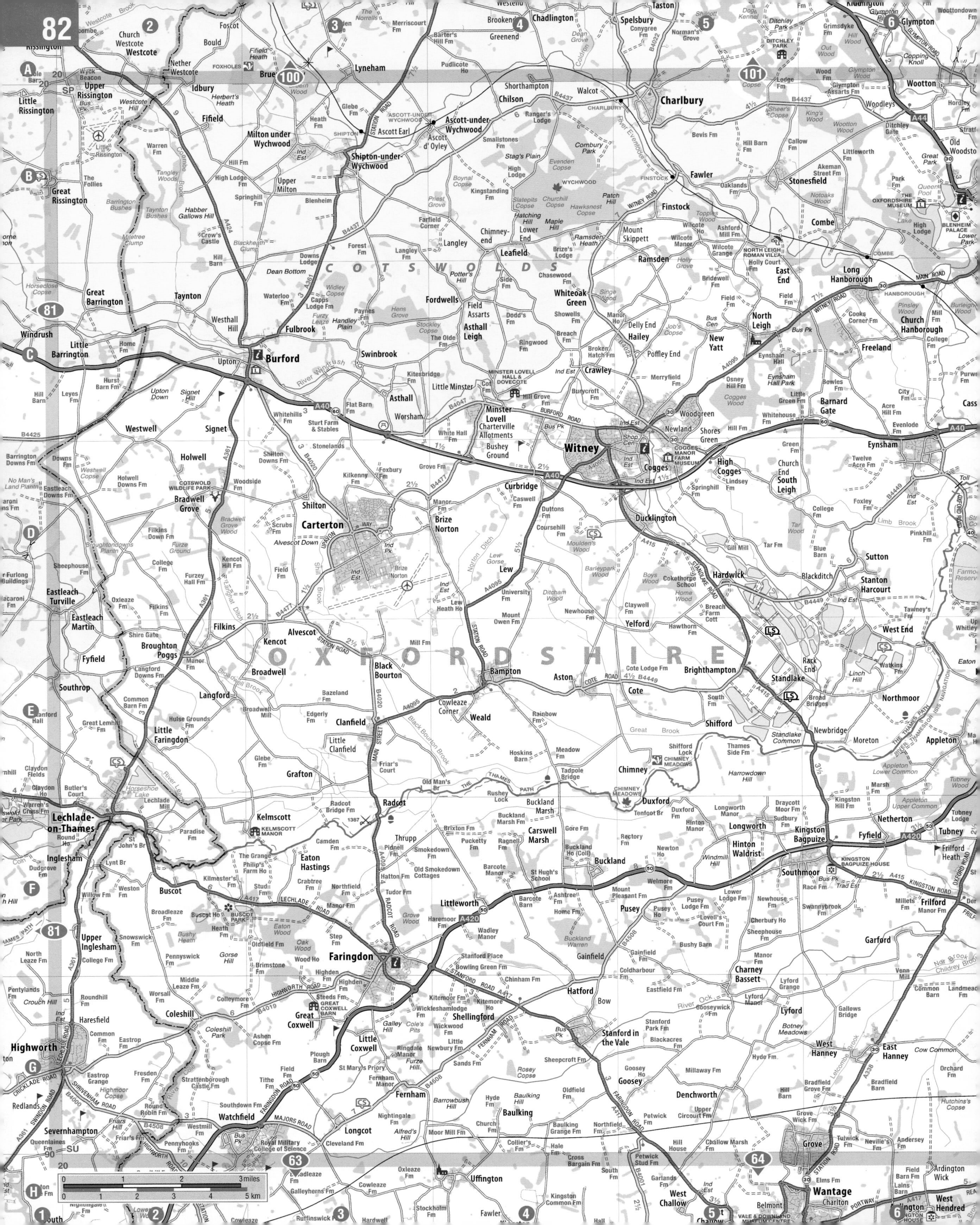
Rissington
Church Westcote
Westcote
Foscot
Bould
Nether Westcote
Fifield Heath
Bruern
100
Lyneham
Merriscourt Fm
Barter's Hill Fm
Pudlicote Ho
Brookend
Chadlington
Greenend
Taston
Spelsbury
Conygree Fm
Dean Grove
Norman's Grove
Ditchley Park
Grimsdyke Fm
Glympton
Wootton
Upper Rissington
Little Rissington
Idbury
Herbert's Heath
Westcote Hill
Fifield
Milton under Wychwood
Ascott Earl
Ascott-under-Wychwood
Ascott d'Oyley
Shorthampton
Chilson
Walcot
Charlbury
101
Shipton-under-Wychwood
Great Rissington
Upper Milton
Smallstones Fm
Stag's Plain
Cornbury Park
Wychwood
Fawler
Finstock
Stonesfield
Oxfordshire Museum
Blenheim Palace
Great Barrington
Taynton
Westhall Hill
Fulbrook
Burford
Swinbrook
Asthall Leigh
Fordwells
Field Assarts
Leafield
Langley
Chimney-end
Ramsden
Whiteoak Green
Hailey
Crawley
Delly End
Poffley End
New Yatt
North Leigh
East End
Long Hanborough
Church Hanborough
Freeland
Windrush
Little Barrington
Upton
Asthall
Worsham
Little Minster
Minster Lovell
Charterville Allotments
Bushey Ground
Witney
Cogges
Woodgreen
Newland
Shores Green
High Cogges
Eynsham
Barnard Gate
South Leigh
Church End
Westwell
Signet
Holwell
Shilton
Carterton
Brize Norton
Curbridge
Ducklington
Bradwell Grove
Lew
Hardwick
Sutton
Stanton Harcourt
Eastleach Turville
Eastleach Martin
Filkins
Broughton Poggs
Alvescot
Kencot
Black Bourton
Bampton
Aston
Cote
Yelford
Brighthampton
Standlake
West End
Fyfield
Southrop
Langford
Broadwell
Clanfield
Cowleaze Corner
Weald
Shifford
Northmoor
Little Faringdon
Little Clanfield
Grafton
Radcot
Chimney
Duxford
Newbridge
Moreton
Appleton
Lechlade-on-Thames
Kelmscott
Buckland Marsh
Carswell Marsh
Longworth
Hinton Waldrist
Kingston Bagpuize
Netherton
Fyfield
Tubney
Inglesham
Eaton Hastings
Buscot
Buckland
Southmoor
Frilford
Littleworth
Pusey
Upper Inglesham
Faringdon
Gainfield
Charney Bassett
Garford
Coleshill
Great Coxwell
Shellingford
Hatford
Lyford
Highworth
Little Coxwell
Stanford in the Vale
West Hanney
East Hanney
Goosey
Denchworth
Watchfield
Fernham
Baulking
Longcot
Severnhampton
Grove
Uffington
West Challow
Wantage
West Hendred
OXFORDSHIRE
COTSWOLDS
A40
A361
A415
A420
A4095
A417
A338
A44
B4437
B4020
B4477
B4449
B4047
B4022
B4019
B4508
B4000
B4425
81
63
64
0 1 2 3 miles
0 1 2 3 4 5 km

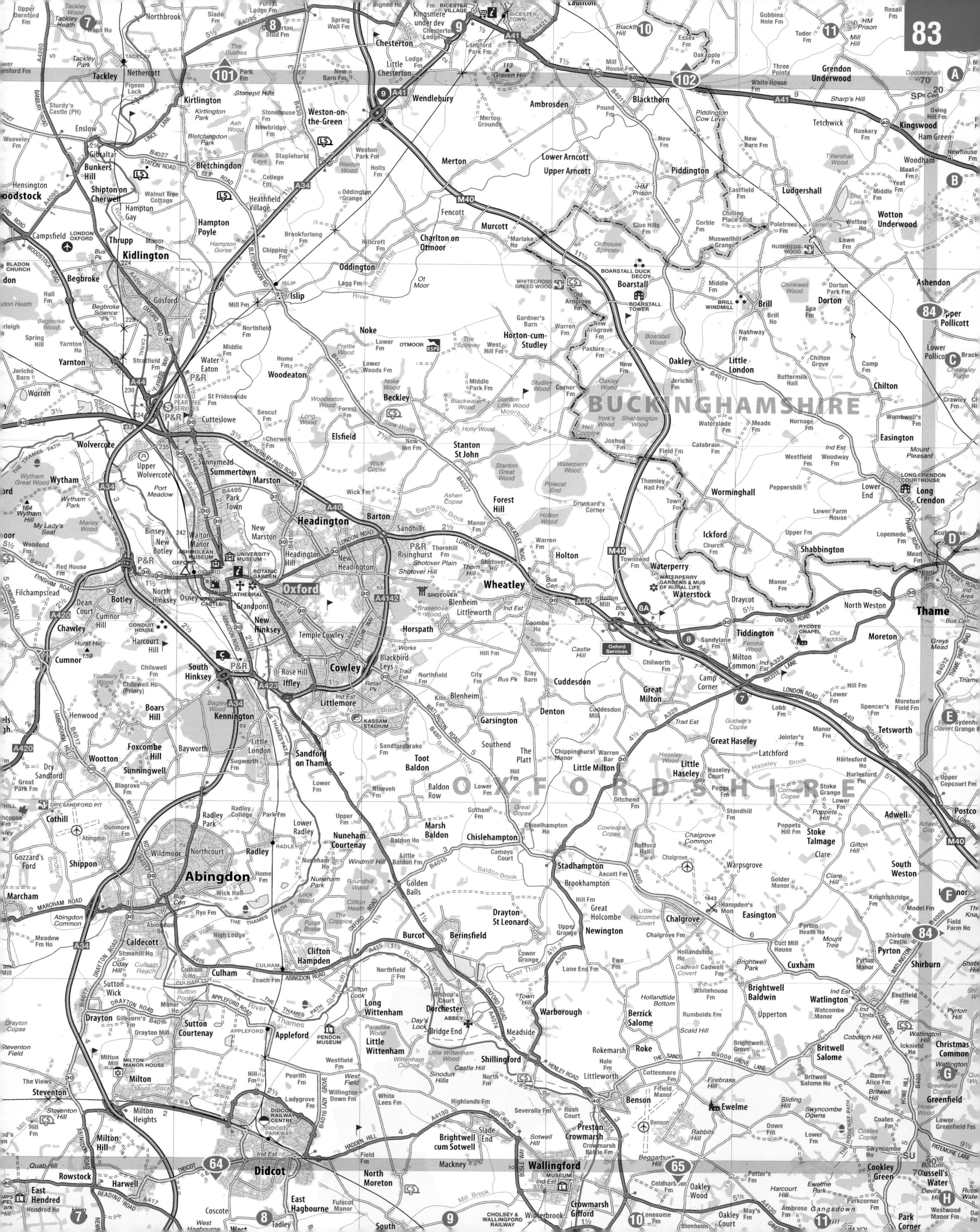

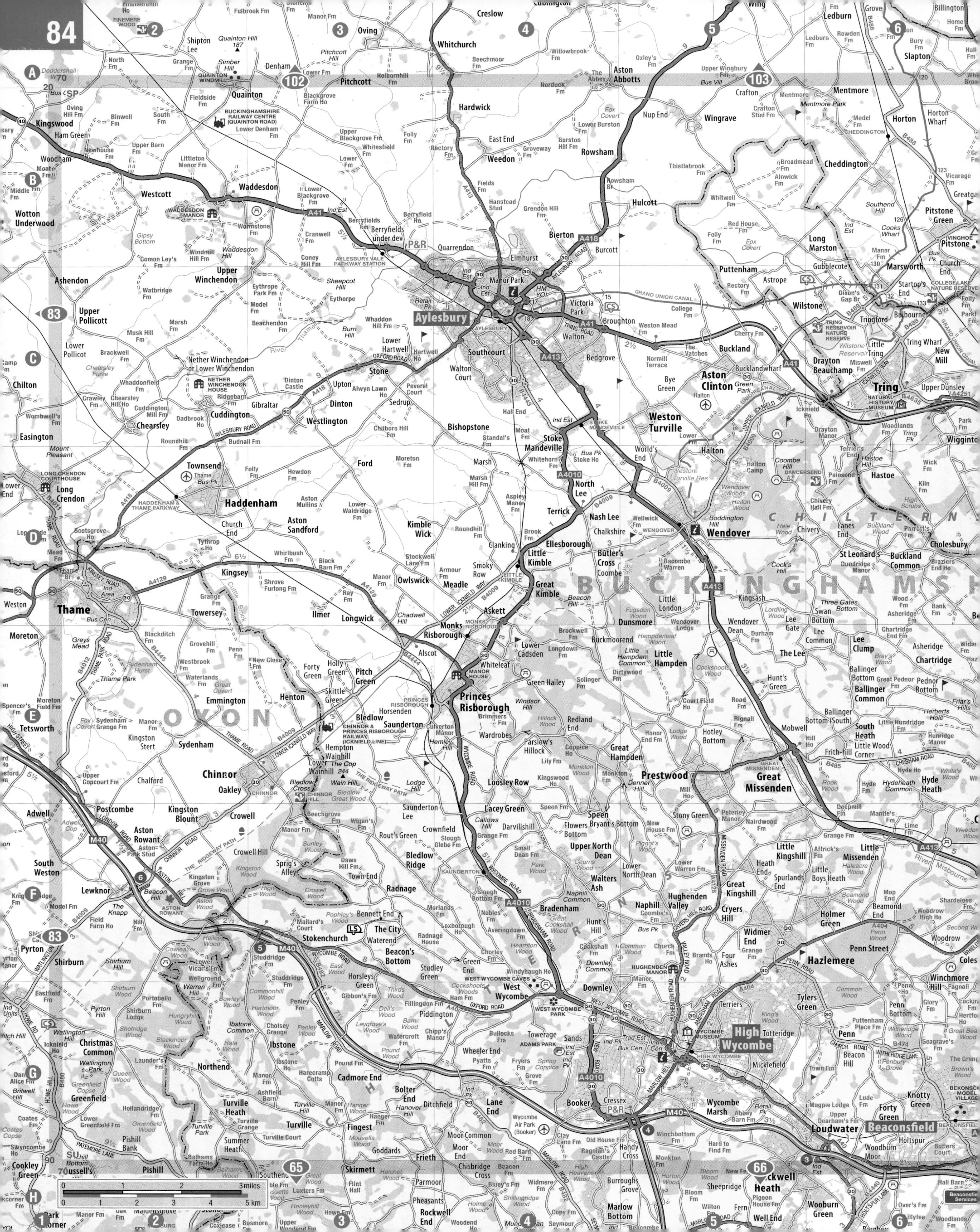

Creslow
Oving
Whitchurch
Quainton
Denham
Pitchcott
Aston Abbotts
Wing
Ledburn
Slapton
Mentmore
Crafton
Wingrave
Horton
Kingswood
Hardwick
Weedon
Rowsham
Cheddington
Waddesdon
Westcott
Wotton Underwood
Hulcott
Pitstone Green
Pitstone
Bierton
Long Marston
Quarrendon
Elmhurst
Burcott
Puttenham
Marsworth
Ashendon
Upper Winchendon
Manor Park
Aylesbury
Victoria Park
Broughton
Wilstone
Tringford
Bulbourne
Upper Pollicott
Lower Pollicott
Southcourt
Walton
Bedgrove
Buckland
Aston Clinton
Drayton Beauchamp
Tring
New Mill
Chilton
Stone
Upton
Dinton
Cuddington
Gibraltar
Chearsley
Westlington
Sedrup
Bishopstone
Weston Turville
Stoke Mandeville
Halton
Easington
Townsend
Haddenham
Long Crendon
Ford
Marsh
North Lee
Terrick
Nash Lee
Wendover
Aston Sandford
Kimble Wick
Ellesborough
Butler's Cross
Little Kimble
Chalkshire
Cholesbury
Kingsey
Owlswick
Meadle
Great Kimble
Thame
Towersey
Ilmer
Longwick
Askett
Monks Risborough
Dunsmore
Little London
Kingsash
Wendover Dean
Buckland Common
St Leonard's
Moreton
Alscot
Whiteleaf
Little Hampden
The Lee
Lee Clump
Chartridge
Forty Green
Pitch Green
Henton
Emmington
Princes Risborough
Ballinger Common
Tetsworth
Bledlow
Saunderton
Sydenham
Kingston Stert
Great Hampden
Hotley Bottom
South Heath
Chinnor
Oakley
Chalford
Prestwood
Great Missenden
Hyde Heath
Loosley Row
Lacey Green
Speen
Adwell
Postcombe
Kingston Blount
Crowell
Aston Rowant
Bledlow Ridge
Upper North Dean
Little Kingshill
Little Missenden
South Weston
Lewknor
Radnage
Walters Ash
Great Kingshill
Naphill
Hughenden Valley
Cryers Hill
Holmer Green
Bradenham
Stokenchurch
The City
Beacon's Bottom
Widmer End
Hazlemere
Penn Street
Pyrton
Shirburn
Studley Green
West Wycombe
Downley
Four Ashes
Tylers Green
Winchmore Hill
Piddington
Christmas Common
Ibstone
Northend
Wheeler End
Sands
High Wycombe
Totteridge
Penn
Cadmore End
Bolter End
Lane End
Booker
Cressex
Wycombe Marsh
Loudwater
Beaconsfield
Knotty Green
Greenfield
Turville Heath
Turville
Fingest
Ditchfield
Moor Common
Frieth
Handy Cross
Holtspur
Pishill
Skirmett
Cookley Green
Parmoor
Chisbridge Cross
Burroughs Grove
Marlow Bottom
Wooburn Green
Flackwell Heath
Rockwell End
0 1 2 3 miles
0 1 2 3 4 5 km

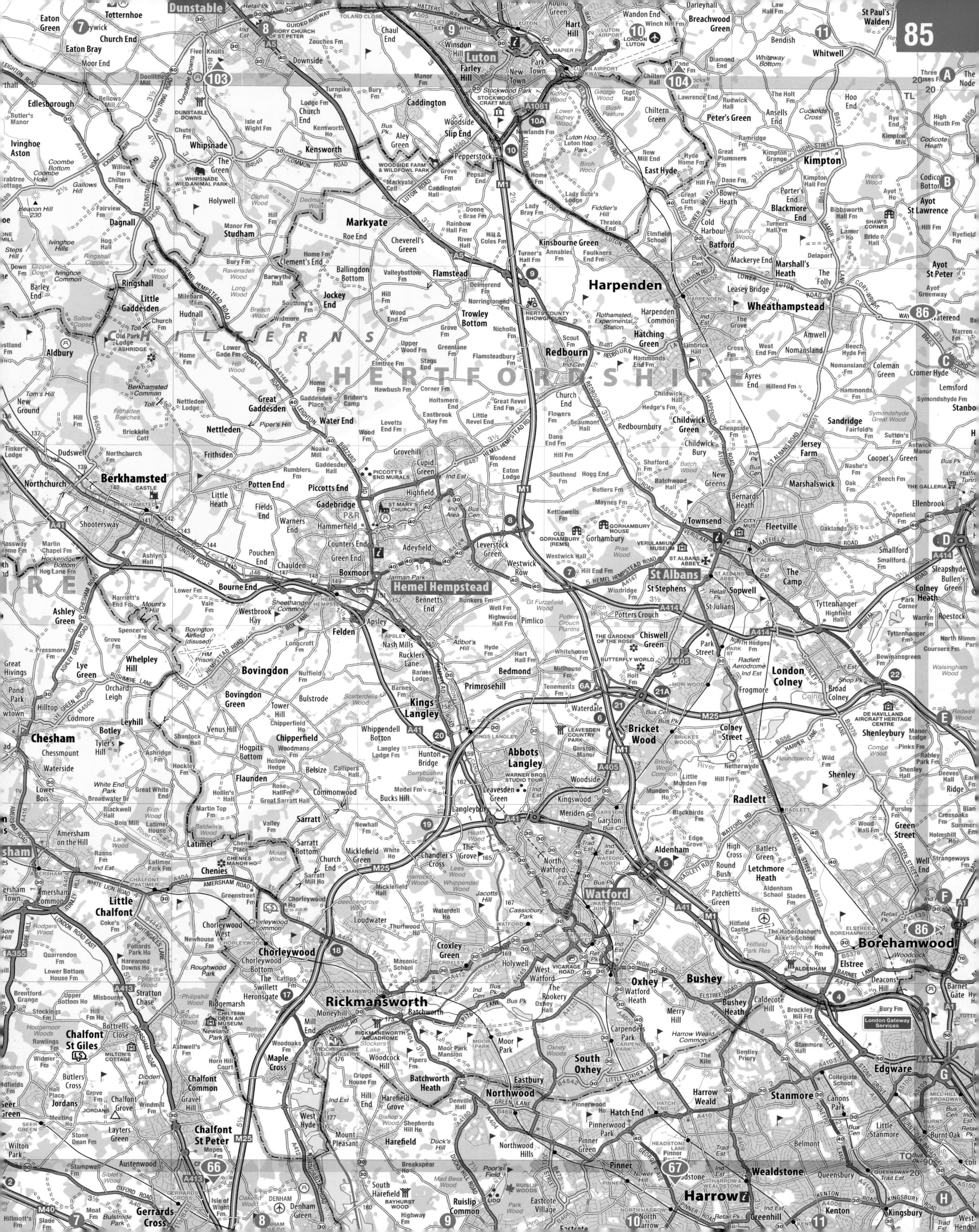
Dunstable
Totternhoe
Eaton Green
Church End
Eaton Bray
Moor End
Edlesborough
Ivinghoe Aston
Whipsnade
Kensworth
Caddington
Slip End
Luton
Farley Hill
Park Town
New Town
Luton Airport
Hart Hill
Wandon End
Breachwood Green
St Paul's Walden
Whitwell
Bendish
Kimpton
Peter's Green
East Hyde
Chiltern Green
Pepperstock
Markyate
Flamstead
Dagnall
Studham
Holywell
Ringshall
Little Gaddesden
Hudnall
Jockey End
Trowley Bottom
Harpenden
Batford
Wheathampstead
Kinsbourne Green
Redbourn
Hatching Green
Harpenden Common
Aldbury
CHILTERNS
HERTFORDSHIRE
Great Gaddesden
Water End
Nettleden
Frithsden
Berkhamsted
Northchurch
Dudswell
Potten End
Piccotts End
Gadebridge
Highfield
Adeyfield
Leverstock Green
Hemel Hempstead
Boxmoor
Bourne End
Felden
Apsley
Nash Mills
Bovingdon
Kings Langley
Abbots Langley
Bedmond
Chiswell Green
St Albans
St Stephens
Sopwell
Fleetville
Marshalswick
Sandridge
Jersey Farm
Smallford
Colney Heath
London Colney
Park Street
Bricket Wood
Shenleybury
Shenley
Radlett
Chesham
Ashley Green
Lye Green
Whelpley Hill
Botley
Chipperfield
Sarratt
Chenies
Latimer
Flaunden
Little Chalfont
Amersham
Chorleywood
Croxley Green
Rickmansworth
Watford
Garston
Aldenham
Letchmore Heath
Elstree
Borehamwood
Bushey
Bushey Heath
Oxhey
South Oxhey
Carpenders Park
Northwood
Eastbury
Moor Park
Harefield
Maple Cross
Chalfont St Giles
Chalfont St Peter
Chalfont Common
Jordans
Gerrards Cross
Denham
Ruislip Common
Eastcote Village
Pinner
Hatch End
Harrow Weald
Harrow
Wealdstone
Stanmore
Edgware
Canons Park
Kenton
Kingsbury
Queensbury
M1
M25
M40
A41
A5
A414
86
104
103
66
67

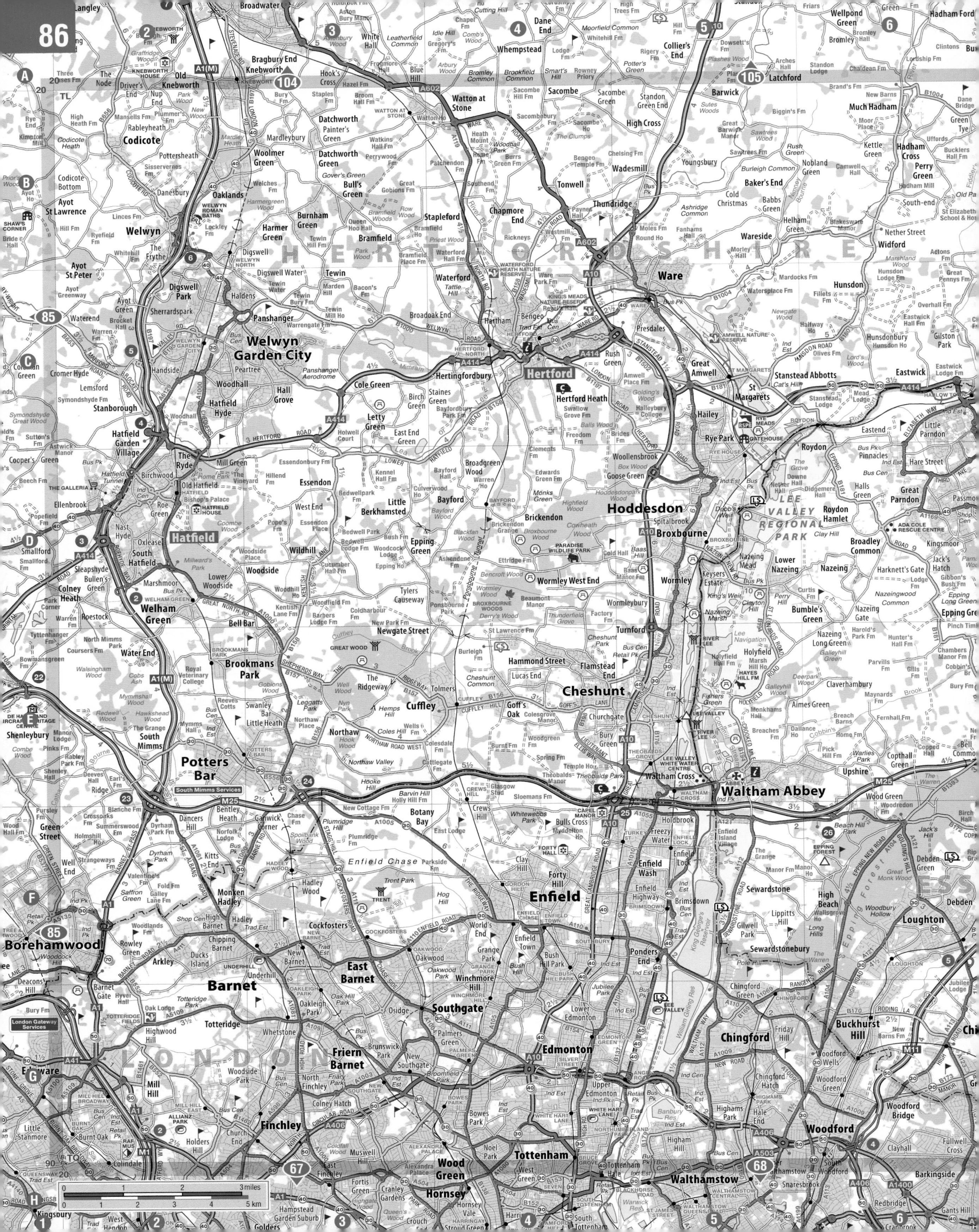
HERTFORDSHIRE
LONDON
Welwyn Garden City
Hertford
Ware
Hoddesdon
Broxbourne
Cheshunt
Waltham Abbey
Enfield
Hatfield
Potters Bar
Borehamwood
Barnet
East Barnet
Southgate
Edmonton
Tottenham
Wood Green
Hornsey
Finchley
Friern Barnet
Chingford
Walthamstow
Woodford
Loughton
Buckhurst Hill
Edgware
Mill Hill
Welwyn
Codicote
Knebworth
Watton at Stone
Stanstead Abbotts
Cuffley
Brookmans Park
Welham Green
South Mimms
Lee Valley Regional Park
Epping Forest
Enfield Chase
South Mimms Services
London Gateway Services
0 1 2 3 miles
0 1 2 3 4 5 km

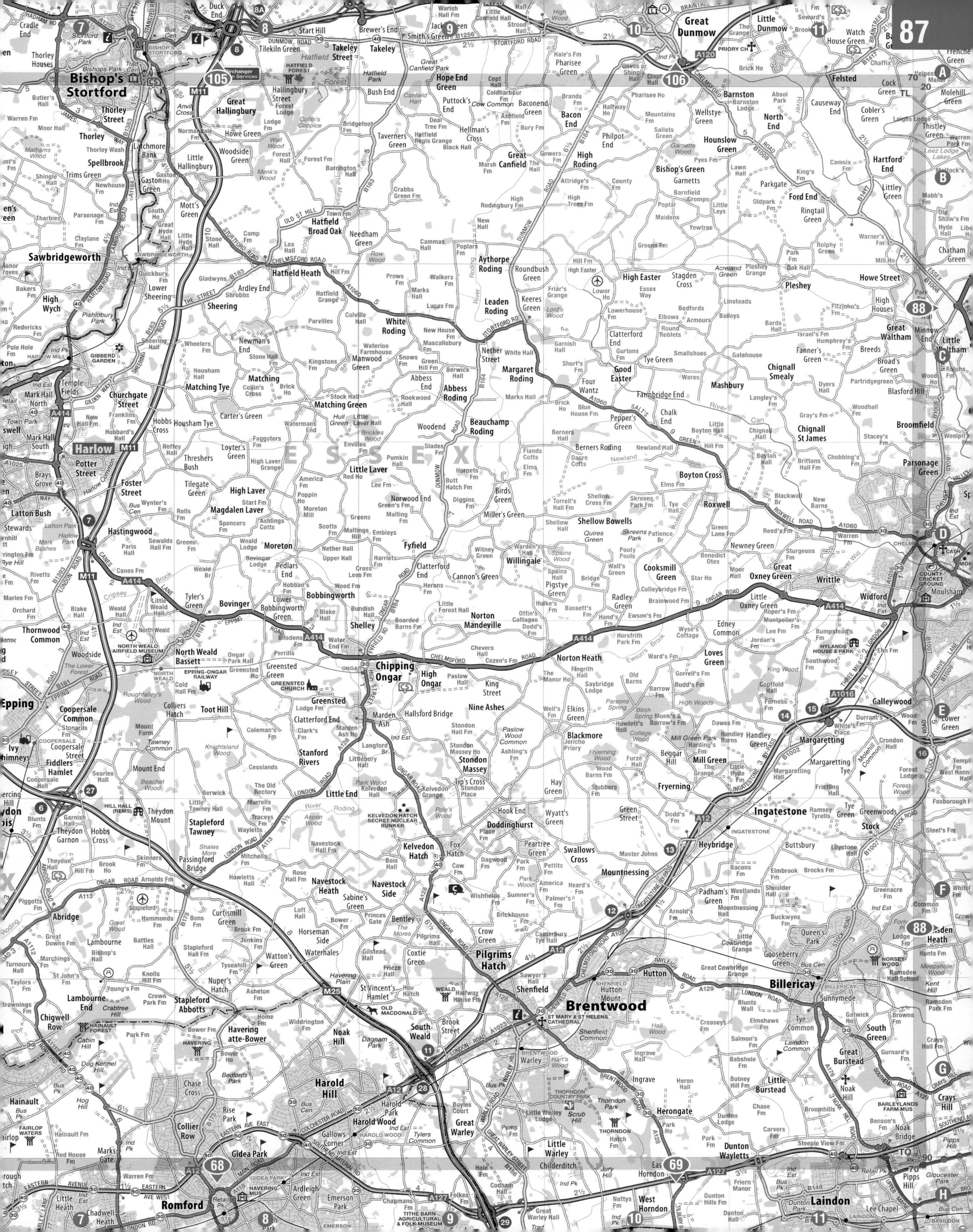
Bishop's Stortford
Great Dunmow
Takeley
Hatfield Forest
Great Hallingbury
Little Hallingbury
Sawbridgeworth
Hatfield Heath
Hatfield Broad Oak
Great Canfield
High Roding
Aythorpe Roding
Leaden Roding
White Roding
High Easter
Pleshey
Barnston
Felsted
Great Waltham
Little Waltham
Harlow
Potter Street
Sheering
Matching Green
Matching Tye
Abbess Roding
Margaret Roding
Good Easter
Mashbury
Chignall Smealy
Chignall St James
Broomfield
Beauchamp Roding
Berners Roding
ESSEX
Little Laver
High Laver
Magdalen Laver
Moreton
Fyfield
Willingale
Roxwell
Writtle
Chelmsford
Widford
Bovinger
Bobbingworth
Shelley
Norton Mandeville
North Weald Bassett
Chipping Ongar
High Ongar
Norton Heath
Epping
Coopersale Common
Toot Hill
Greensted
Stanford Rivers
Blackmore
Mill Green
Fryerning
Ingatestone
Margaretting
Galleywood
Stock
Theydon Mount
Stapleford Tawney
Kelvedon Hatch
Doddinghurst
Navestock Heath
Navestock Side
Mountnessing
Heybridge
Abridge
Lambourne
Chigwell Row
Lambourne End
Stapleford Abbotts
Havering atte-Bower
Noak Hill
South Weald
Pilgrims Hatch
Shenfield
Brentwood
Hutton
Billericay
Great Burstead
Little Burstead
Harold Hill
Harold Wood
Gidea Park
Romford
Hainault
Collier Row
Great Warley
Little Warley
Herongate
Ingrave
Dunton Wayletts
West Horndon
Laindon
Crays Hill
M11
M25
A12
A414
A127
A1060
105
106
68
69
88

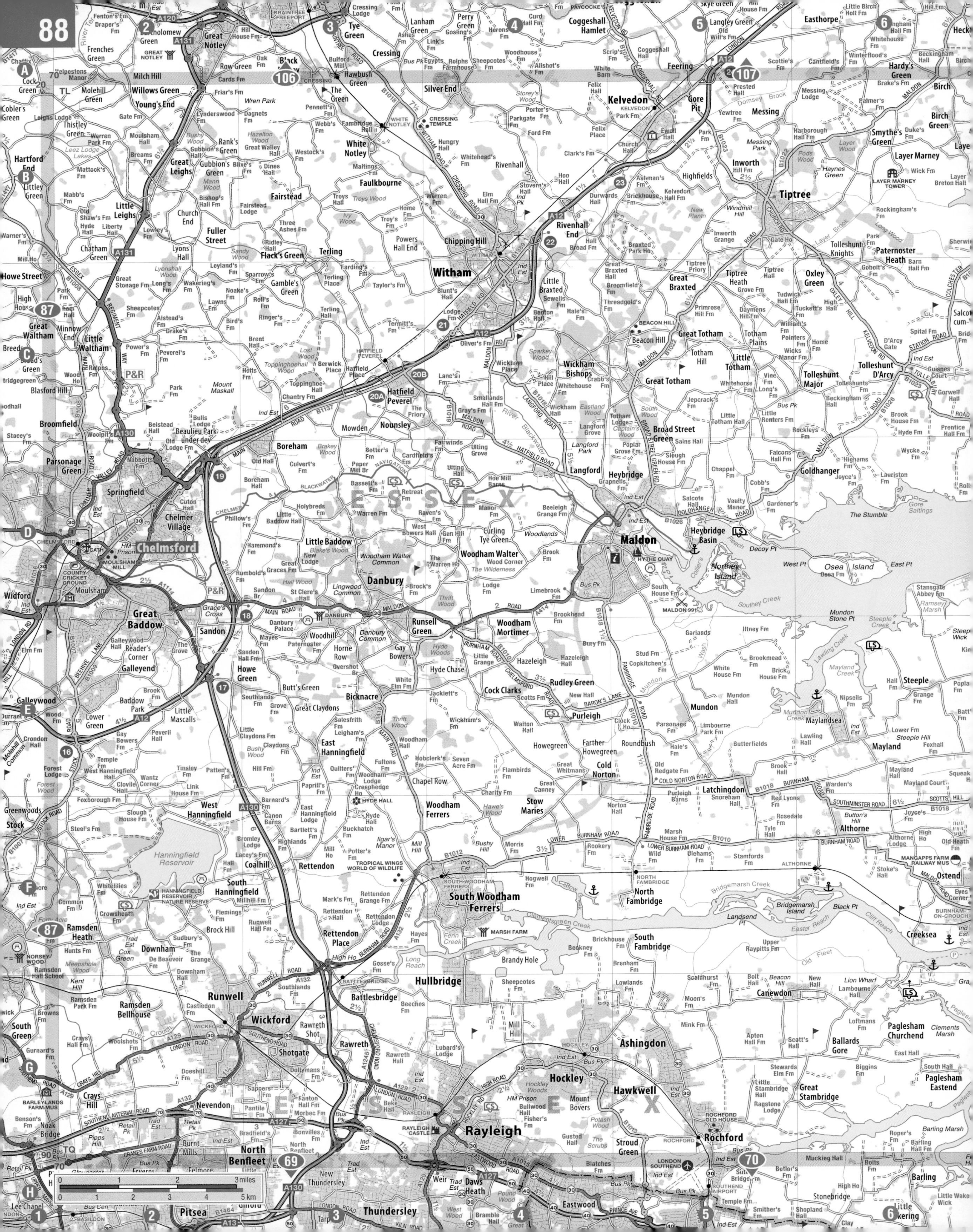

106
107
87
69
70
Great Notley
Black Notley
Tye Green
Cressing
Silver End
Coggeshall Hamlet
Feering
Kelvedon
Gore Pit
Messing
Easthorpe
Birch
Birch Green
Layer Marney
Tiptree
Inworth
Willows Green
Young's End
Great Leighs
Little Leighs
White Notley
Faulkbourne
Fairstead
Rivenhall
Rivenhall End
Chipping Hill
Witham
Terling
Flack's Green
Fuller Street
Church End
Great Braxted
Little Braxted
Tiptree Heath
Tolleshunt Knights
Paternoster Heath
Oxley Green
Great Totham
Little Totham
Tolleshunt Major
Tolleshunt D'Arcy
Goldhanger
Wickham Bishops
Hatfield Peverel
Nounsley
Boreham
Heybridge
Heybridge Basin
Langford
Maldon
Northey Island
Osea Island
Hartford End
Howe Street
Great Waltham
Little Waltham
Broomfield
Springfield
Chelmer Village
Chelmsford
Moulsham
Widford
Great Baddow
Sandon
Danbury
Little Baddow
Woodham Walter
Runsell Green
Woodham Mortimer
Hazeleigh
Purleigh
Rudley Green
Cock Clarks
Mundon
Maylandsea
Mayland
Steeple
Galleywood
Howe Green
Bicknacre
East Hanningfield
West Hanningfield
Hanningfield Reservoir
South Hanningfield
Stock
Woodham Ferrers
Stow Maries
Cold Norton
Latchingdon
Althorne
North Fambridge
South Woodham Ferrers
Rettendon
Rettendon Place
Ramsden Heath
Downham
Runwell
Wickford
Shotgate
Battlesbridge
Hullbridge
South Fambridge
Canewdon
Ashingdon
Hockley
Hawkwell
Rayleigh
Rochford
Ballards Gore
Paglesham Churchend
Paglesham Eastend
Great Stambridge
Crays Hill
Nevendon
North Benfleet
Thundersley
Pitsea
Daws Heath
Eastwood
Barling
Creeksea
Ostend
ESSEX

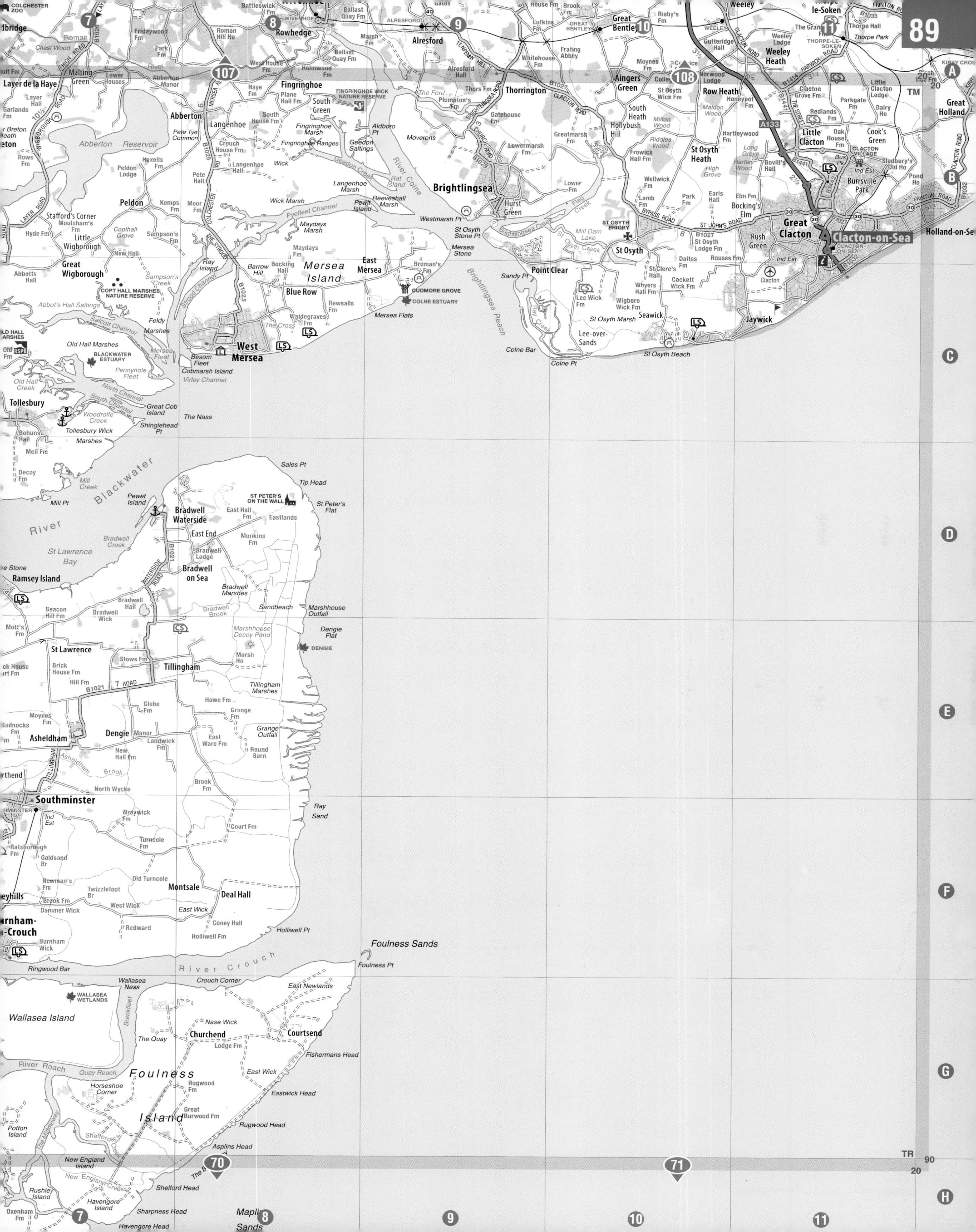
COLCHESTER ZOO
Rowhedge
Wivenhoe
Alresford
Great Bentley
Weeley
Thorpe-le-Soken
Weeley Heath
Layer de la Haye
Malting Green
Abberton
Fingringhoe
FINGRINGHOE WICK NATURE RESERVE
South Green
Langenhoe
Abberton Reservoir
Thorrington
Aingers Green
Row Heath
Little Clacton
Great Holland
Cook's Green
Burrsville Park
Peldon
Brightlingsea
Hurst Green
St Osyth Heath
Great Clacton
Clacton-on-Sea
Holland-on-Sea
Stafford's Corner
Little Wigborough
Great Wigborough
Mersea Island
East Mersea
ST OSYTH PRIORY
St Osyth
Point Clear
Blue Row
CUDMORE GROVE
COLNE ESTUARY
Mersea Flats
Brightlingsea Reach
COPT HALL MARSHES NATURE RESERVE
West Mersea
Old Hall Marshes
BLACKWATER ESTUARY
Seawick
Jaywick
Lee-over-Sands
St Osyth Beach
Colne Bar
Colne Pt
Tollesbury
Tollesbury Wick Marshes
The Nass
River Blackwater
St Lawrence Bay
Ramsey Island
Bradwell Waterside
ST PETER'S ON THE WALL
Bradwell on Sea
Dengie Flat
DENGIE
St Lawrence
Tillingham
Tillingham Marshes
Asheldham
Dengie
Southminster
Ray Sand
Montsale
Deal Hall
Foulness Sands
Foulness Pt
River Crouch
Burnham-on-Crouch
WALLASEA WETLANDS
Wallasea Island
Churchend
Courtsend
Foulness Island
River Roach
Potton Island
New England Island
Havengore Island
Rushley Island
Maplin Sands
TM
TR
A B C D E F G H
7 8 9 10 11

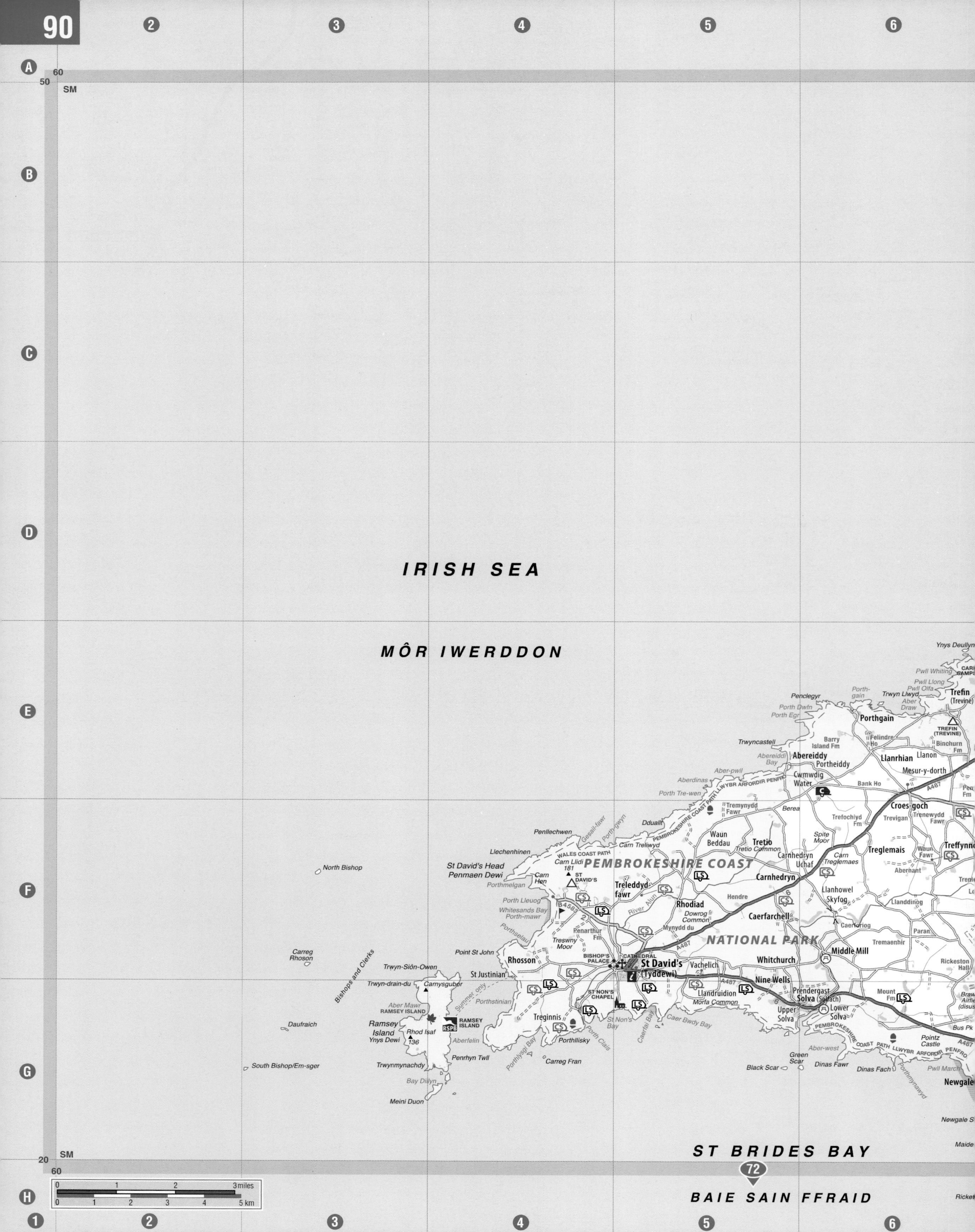

IRISH SEA

MÔR IWERDDON

PEMBROKESHIRE COAST

NATIONAL PARK

St David's
(Tyddewi)

RAMSEY
ISLAND

Ramsey
Island
Ynys Dewi

ST BRIDES BAY

BAIE SAIN FFRAID

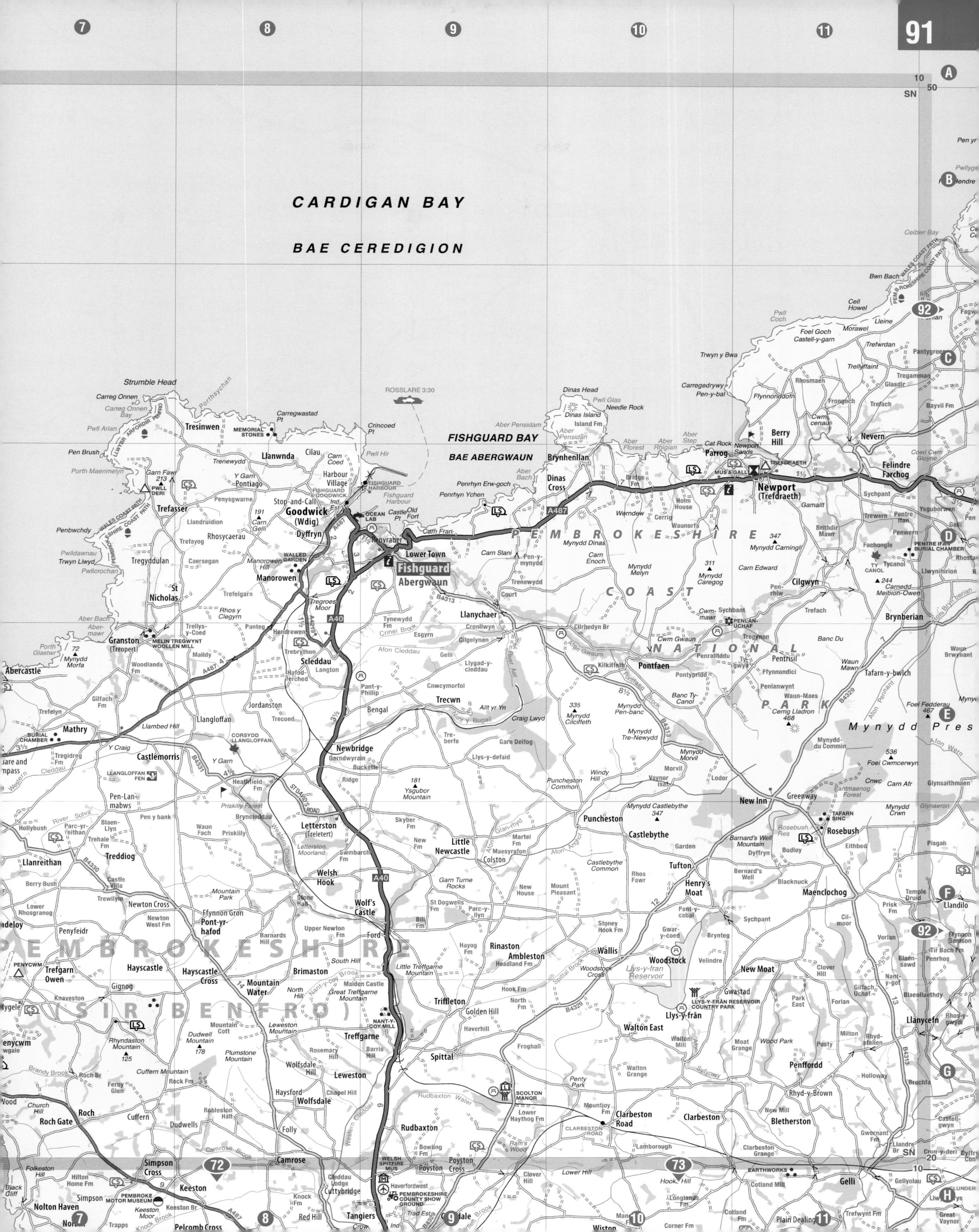

CARDIGAN BAY
BAE CEREDIGION
FISHGUARD BAY
BAE ABERGWAUN
ROSSLARE 3:30
Strumble Head
Carreg Onnen
Carreg Onnen Bay
Pwll Arian
Pen Brush
Porth Maenmelyn
Tresinwen
Memorial Stones
Carregwastad Pt
Llanwnda
Cilau
Crincoed Pt
Pwll Hir
Carn Coed
Harbour Village
Fishguard Harbour
Trenewydd
Y Garn
Pontiago
Garn Fawr
Pwll Deri
Trefasser
Penysgwarne
Stop-and-Call
Goodwick (Wdig)
Dyffryn
Ocean Lab
Castle Pt
Old Fort
Carn Fran
Penyraber
Lower Town
Fishguard
Abergwaun
Penbwchdy
Pwlldawnau
Trwyn Llwyd
Pwllcrochan
Llandruidion
Trefayog
Rhosycaerau
Tregyddulan
Caersegan
Manorowen Hill
Walled Garden
Manorowen
St Nicholas
Trefelgarn
Rhos y Clegyrn
Aber Bach
Aber-mawr
Granston (Treopert)
Melin Tregwynt Woollen Mill
Trellys-y-Coed
Panteg
Hendrewen
Tregroes Moor
Trebrython
Scleddau
Langton
Hafod-Perched
Maildy
72 Mynydd Morfa
Porth Glastwr
Abercastle
Woodlands Fm
Gilfach Fm
Trefelyn
Burial Chamber
Mathry
Llambed Hill
Llangloffan
Jordanston
Trecoed
Corsydd Llangloffan
Y Craig
Tregidreg Fm
Castlemorris
Y Garn
Llangloffan Fen
Heathfield Fm
Priskilly Forest
Pen-Lan-mabws
Pen y bank
Bryncleddau
Priskilly
Waun Fach
Hollybush
Parc-yr-eithan
Blaen-Llyn
Trehale Fm
Treddiog
Llanreithan
Castle Villa
Berry Bush
Lower Rhosgranog
Trewilym
Newton Cross
Mountain Park
Ffynnon Gron
Newton West Fm
Pont-yr-hafod
Penyfeidr
Barnards Hill
Trefgarn Owen
Hayscastle
Hayscastle Cross
Gignog
Knaveston
Mountain Water
North Hill
Mountain Cott
Dudwell Mountain
Rhyndaston Mountain
Plumstone Mountain
Cuffern Mountain
Rock Fm
Roch Br
Ferny Glen
Church Hill
Roch Gate
Roch
Cuffern
Dudwells
Robleston Hall
Simpson Cross
Folkeston Hill
Hilton Home Fm
Simpson
Keeston
Pembroke Motor Museum
Keeston Moor
Keeston Br
Nolton Haven
Pelcomb Cross
Trapps
Camrose
Camrose Brook
PEMBROKESHIRE
(SIR BENFRO)
Penycwm
Letterston (Treletert)
Letterston Moorland
Swmbarch Fm
Welsh Hook
Stone Hall
Wolf's Castle
Upper Newton Fm
Ford
South Hill
Brimaston
Maiden Castle
Great Treffgarne Mountain
Nant-y-Coy Mill
Leweston Mountain
Treffgarne
Rosemary Hill
Barris Hill
Wolfsdale Hill
Leweston
Haysford
Wolfsdale
Chapel Hill
Folly
Cleddau Lodge
Cuttybridge
Knock Fm
Red Hill
Tangiers
Haverfordwest
Pembrokeshire County Show Ground
Welsh Spitfire Mus
Poyston
Poyston Cross
Trad Est
Crow
Ind
Newbridge
Garndwyrain
Buckett
Ridge
St David's Road
Pant-y-Phillip
Bengal
Trecwn
Cnwcymorfol
Gelli
Cilgelynen
Llygad-y-cleddau
Esgyrn
Tynewydd Fm
Crinei Brook
Afon Cleddau
Allt yr Yn
Nant y Bugail
Craig Lwyd
Tre-berfe
Garn Deilog
Llys-y-defaid
181 Ysgubor Mountain
Skyber Fm
New Fm
Little Newcastle
Maesyrafon
Colston
Martel Fm
Garn Turne Rocks
St Dogwells Fm
Parc-y-llyn
Bill Fm
Hayog Fm
Rinaston
Ambleston
Headland Fm
Little Treffgarne Mountain
Hook Fm
North Fm
Triffleton
Golden Hill
Haverhill
Spittal
Froghall
Scolton Manor
Lower Haythog Fm
Rudbaxton
Rudbaxton Water
Bowling Fm
Ram's Wood
Llanychaer
Cronllwyn
Court
Trenewydd
Pen-y-mynydd
Carn Slani
Cilrhedyn Br
Afon Gwaun
Kilkiffeth
Pontfaen
Pontypridd
Penrallt Ddu
River Aer
335 Mynydd Cilciffeth
Mynydd Pen-banc
Mynydd Tre-Newydd
Puncheston Common
Windy Hill
Mynydd Morvil
Morvil
Vaynor Isaf
Lodor
Puncheston
Mynydd Castlebythe 347
Castlebythe
Castlebythe Common
Rhos Fawr
New House
Mount Pleasant
Stoney Hook Fm
Wallis
Woodstock
Woodstock Cross
Spittal Brook
Llys-y-fran Reservoir
Llys-y-fran Reservoir Country Park
Llys-y-frân
Walton East
Walton Mill
Walton Grange
Penty Park
Mountjoy Fm
Clarbeston Road
Clarbeston
Lamborough
Lower Hill
Hook
Longlands Fm
Cotland Fm
Corner Fm
Wiston
Dinas Head
Pwll Glas
Needle Rock
Dinas Island
Island Fm
Aber Pensidan
Aber Pensidam
Brynhenllan
Dinas Cross
Aber Bach
Penrhyn Erw-goch
Penrhyn Ychen
Aber Fforest
Aber Rhigian
Aber Step
Bridge Fm
Werndew
Cerrig
Holm House
Waunorfa
Cat Rock
Parrog
Newport Sands
Mus & Gall
Trefdraeth
Newport (Trefdraeth)
Gamallt
PEMBROKESHIRE COAST NATIONAL PARK
Mynydd Dinas
Carn Enoch
Mynydd Melyn
311 Mynydd Caregog
347 Mynydd Carningli
Carn Edward
Pen-rhiw
Cwm-mawr
Sychbant
Penlan-Uchaf
Cwm Gwaun
Tregynon
Penralltddu
Pentrisil
Ffynnondici
Penlanwynt
Banc Ty-Canol
Waun-Maes
Cerrig Lladron 468
Afon Cwmau
Trwyn y Bwa
Carregedrywy
Pen-y-bal
Berry Hill
Nevern
Ffynnonddofn
Rhosmaen
Frongoch
Trefach
Cwm-cenau
Pwll Coch
Foel Goch
Castell-y-garn
Morawel
Trefwrdan
Trellyffaint
Tregamman
Glasdir
Cell Howel
Lleine
Bwn Bach
Ceibwr Bay
Pantygroes
Bayvil Fm
Coed Cwm Gloyne
Felindre Farchog
Sychpant
Pentre Ifan
Trewern
Penwern
Brithdir Mawr
Fachongle
Pentre Ifan Burial Chamber
Ty Canol
Tycanol
Llwynihirion
244 Carnedd Meibion-Owen
Cilgwyn
Trefach
Brynberian
Banc Du
Waun Mawn
Tafarn-y-bwlch
Foel Feddau 467
Mynydd Preseli
Mynydd-du Commin
536 Foel Cwmcerwyn
Cnwc
Carn Afr
Pantmaenog Forest
Glynsaithmaen
Mynydd Crwn
New Inn
Greenway
Tafarn Sinc
Rosebush
Rosebush Res
Budloy
Bernard's Well Mountain
Dyffryn
Garden
Tufton
Bernard's Well
Henry's Moat
Blacknuck
Maenclochog
Pant-y-cabal
Sychpant
Gwar-y-coed
Brynteg
Velindre
New Moat
Gwastad
Clover Hill
Forlan
Park East
Moat Grange
Wood Park
Posty
Penffordd
Holloway
Rhyd-y-Brown
New Mill
Bletherston
Clarbeston Grange
Earthworks
Gelli
Cotland Mill
Plain Dealing
Trefwynt Fm
Eithbed
Pisgah
Temple Druid
Llandilo
Prisk Fm
Cil-moor
Vorlan
Blaen-sawd
Nant-y-gof
Gilfach Uchaf
Blaenllaethdy
Llanycefn
Rhos-y-gwydl
Milton
Rhyd-afallen
Brechfa
Gwernant Fm
Llandre Br
Gellyolau
Llwyn
Ffynnon Samson
Tir Bach Fm
Penrhos
Castell-gwyn
Wales Coast Path
Llwybr Arfordir Penfro
Pembrokeshire Coast Path
Llwybr Arfordir Cymru
A40
A487
A4219
B4313
B4329
B4330
B4331
Western Cleddau
Afon Anghof
Glan-rhyd
Brandy Brook
Nant-y-coy Brook
Sylvwny
Cleddau
SN

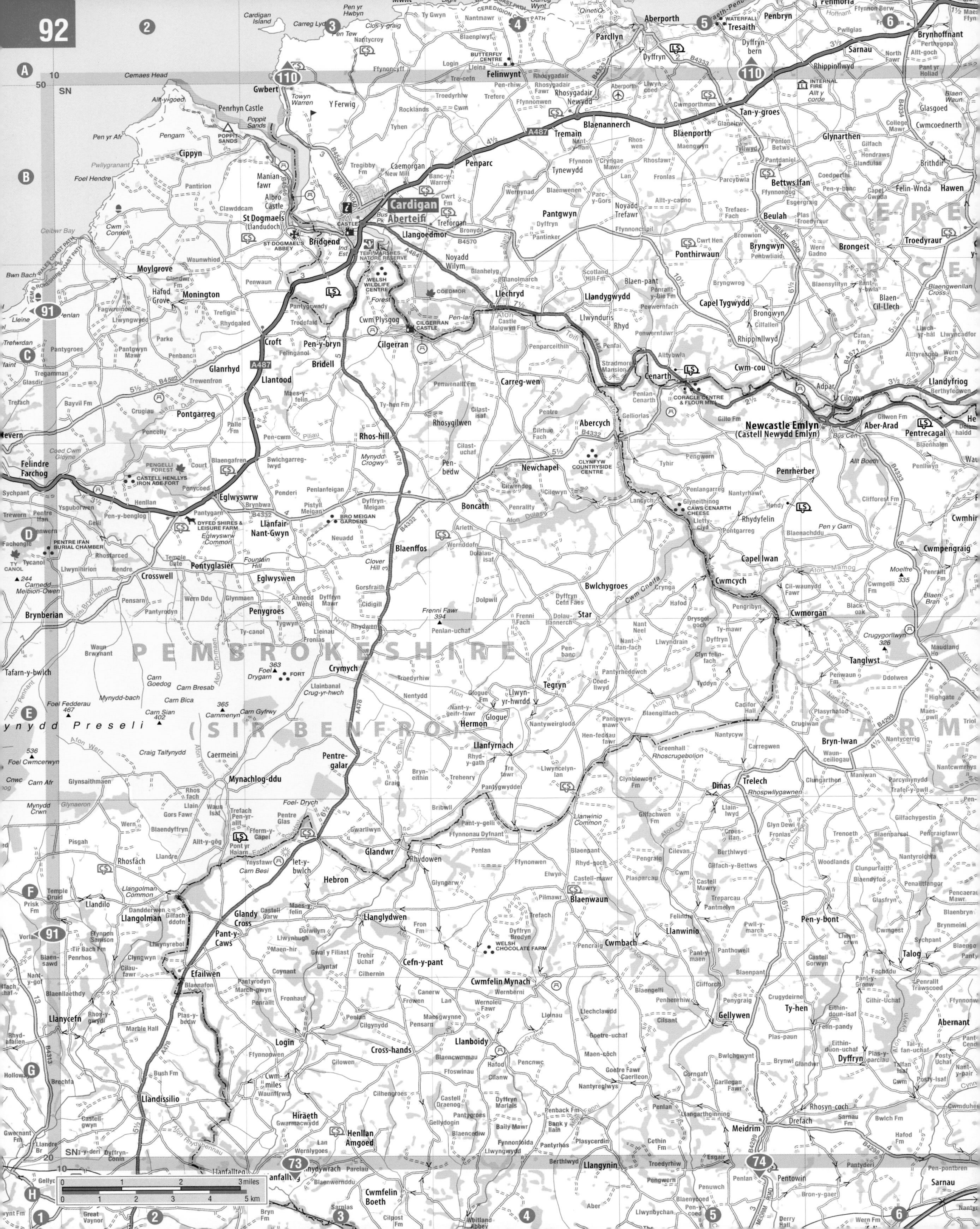
Cardigan Island
Cemaes Head
Gwbert
Aberporth
Tresaith
Penbryn
Brynhoffnant
Parcllyn
Felinwynt
Tan-y-groes
Blaenannerch
Tremain
Blaenporth
Glynarthen
Penparc
Cardigan
Aberteifi
St Dogmaels
(Llandudoch)
Bridgend
Llangoedmor
Pantgwyn
Beulah
Bettws Ifan
Brongest
Troedyraur
Hawen
Ponthirwaun
Bryngwyn
Moylgrove
Monington
Hafod Grove
Llechryd
Llandygwydd
Capel Tygwydd
Cilgerran
Croft
Pen-y-bryn
Bridell
Glanrhyd
Llantood
Cenarth
Cwm-cou
Adpar
Llandyfriog
Carreg-wen
Pontgarreg
Rhos-hill
Abercych
Newcastle Emlyn
(Castell Newydd Emlyn)
Aber-Arad
Pentrecagal
Felindre Farchog
Newchapel
Penrherber
Eglwyswrw
Boncath
Llanfair-Nant-Gwyn
Blaenffos
Capel Iwan
Crosswell
Pontyglasier
Eglwyswen
Bwlchygroes
Cwmcych
Cwmpengraig
Brynberian
Penygroes
Star
Cwmorgan
PEMBROKESHIRE
(SIR BENFRO)
Crymych
Tegryn
Tanglwst
Mynydd Preseli
Hermon
Llanfyrnach
Bryn-Iwan
Pentre-galar
Mynachlog-ddu
Dinas
Trelech
Glandwr
Rhydowen
Hebron
Blaenwaun
Llanglydwen
Glandy Cross
Llangolman
Pant-y-Caws
Llanwinio
Pen-y-bont
Cefn-y-pant
Cwmbach
Talog
Efailwen
Cwmfelin Mynach
Llanycefn
Gellywen
Ty-hen
Abernant
Login
Llanboidy
Cross-hands
Dyffryn
Llandissilio
Hiraeth
Henllan Amgoed
Meidrim
Llangynin
Cwmfelin Boeth
Sarnau
CARM
CERE
A487
A478
A484
B4332
B4333
B4313
B4299
B4298
Frenni Fawr 394
Foel Drygarn 363
Foel Cwmcerwyn 536
Foel Feddarau 467
Carn Sian 402
0 1 2 3 miles
0 1 2 3 4 5 km

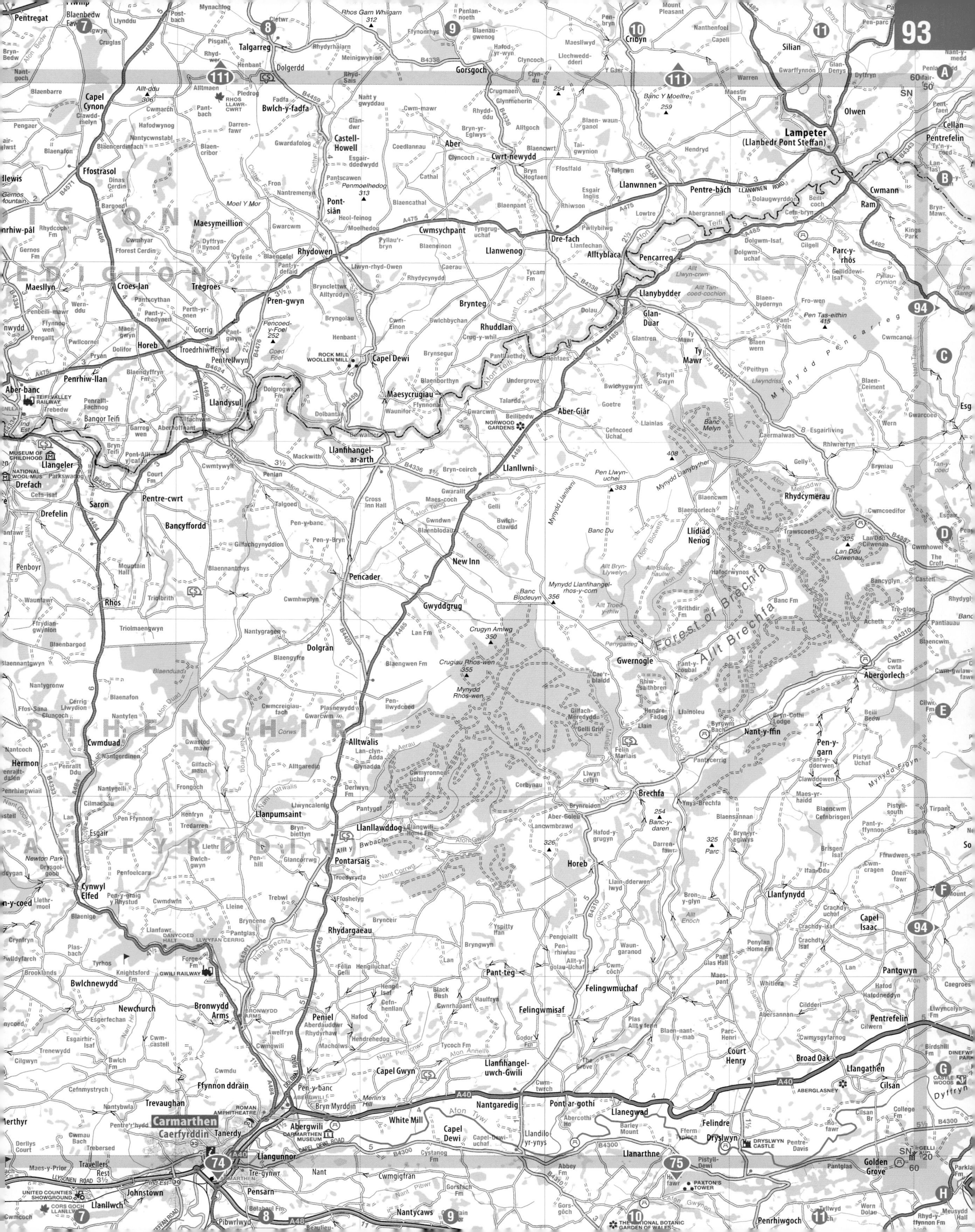
93
Pentregat
Blaenbedw Fawr
Talgarreg
Dolgerdd
Gorsgoch
Cribyn
Silian
Capel Cynon
Bwlch-y-fadfa
Castell-Howell
Aber
Cwrt-newydd
Lampeter
(Llanbedr Pont Steffan)
Olwen
Cellan
Pentrefelin
Ffostrasol
Llanwnnen
Pentre-bach
Cwmann
Ram
Pont-siân
Maesymeillion
Cwmsychpant
Dre-fach
Llanwenog
Alltyblaca
Pencarreg
Parc-y-rhôs
Rhydowen
Croes-lan
Tregroes
Pren-gwyn
Llanybydder
Glan-Duar
Brynteg
Rhuddlan
Maesllyn
Horeb
Troedrhiwffenyd
Pentrellwyn
Capel Dewi
Rock Mill Woollen Mill
Ty Mawr
Aber-banc
Penrhiw-llan
Teifi Valley Railway
Llandysul
Maesycrugiau
Aber-Giâr
Norwood Gardens
Llanllwni
Llanfihangel-ar-arth
Museum of Childhood
National Wool Mus
Llangeler
Drefach
Saron
Pentre-cwrt
Bancyffordd
Drefelin
Rhydcymerau
Llidiad Nenog
Penboyr
New Inn
Pencader
Rhos
Gwyddgrug
Forest of Brechfa
Allt Brechfa
Dolgran
Gwernogle
Abergorlech
Cwmduad
Hermon
Alltwalis
Nant-y-ffin
Brechfa
Llanpumsaint
Llanllawddog
Pontarsais
Horeb
Cynwyl Elfed
Llanfynydd
Capel Isaac
Rhydargaeau
Bwlchnewydd
Gwili Railway
Pant-teg
Pantgwyn
Newchurch
Bronwydd Arms
Peniel
Felingwmuchaf
Felingwmisaf
Pentrefelin
Capel Gwyn
Llanfihangel-uwch-Gwili
Court Henry
Broad Oak
Llangathen
Cilsan
Ffynnon ddrain
Trevaughan
Carmarthen
Caerfyrddin
Abergwili
Carmarthen Museum
White Mill
Nantgaredig
Pont-ar-gothi
Llanegwad
Aberglasney
Capel Dewi
Felindre
Dryslwyn
Dryslwyn Castle
Tanerdy
Llangunnor
Llanarthne
Golden Grove
Johnstown
Llanllwch
United Counties Showground
Pensarn
Nantycaws
Paxton's Tower
The National Botanic Garden of Wales
Penrhiwgoch
Mynydd Pencarreg
Mynydd Llanybyther
Mynydd Llanfihangel-rhos-y-corn
A40
A48
A475
A485
A482
A484
A486
B4459
B4336
B4310
B4300
B4337
B4338
111
74
75
94

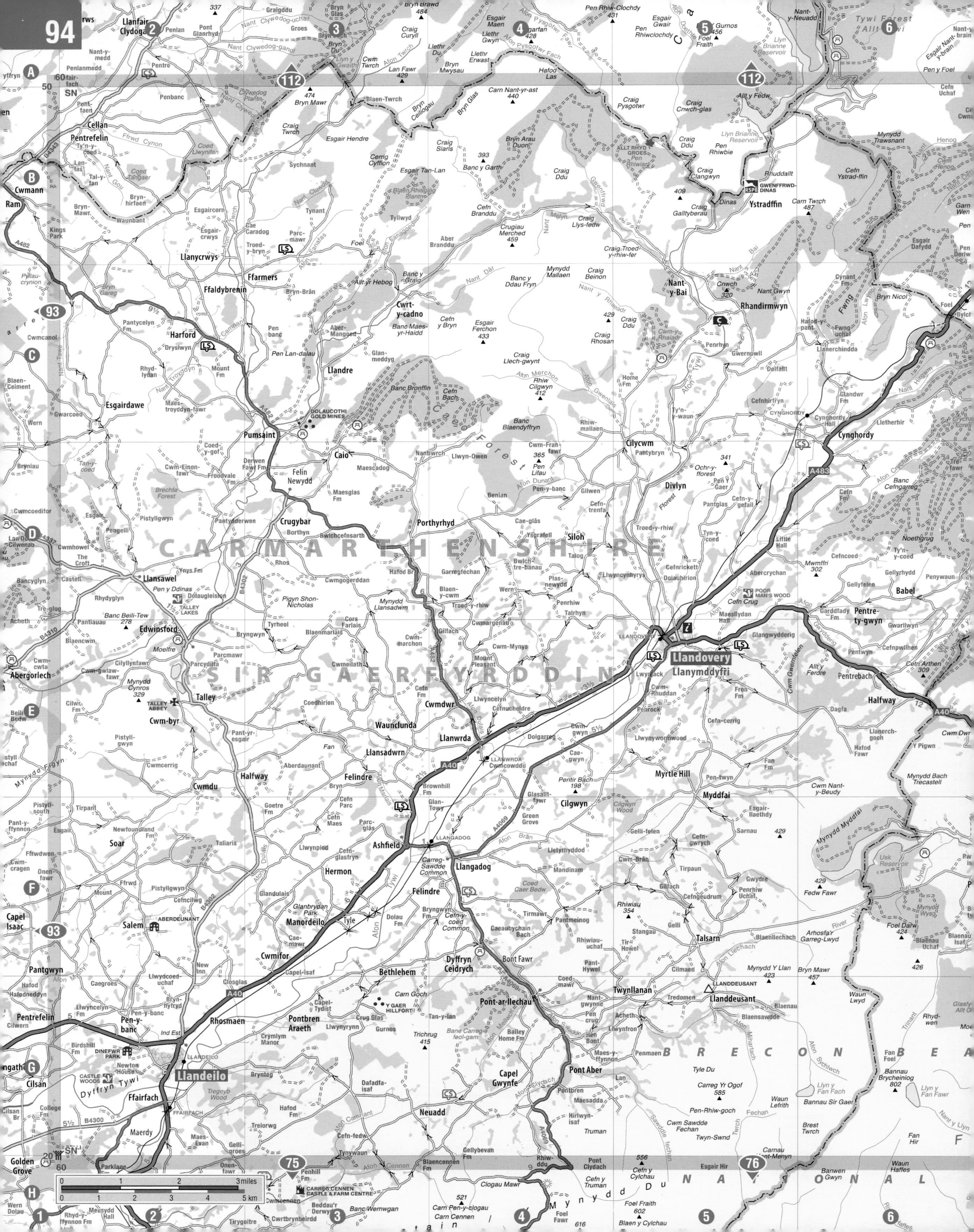
CARMARTHENSHIRE
SIR GAERFYRDDIN
BRECON BEACONS NATIONAL
Llandovery
Llanymddyfri
Llandeilo
Llangadog
Pumsaint
Cwmann
Harford
Llanycrwys
Ffarmers
Ffaldybrenin
Caio
Crugybar
Porthyrhyd
Siloh
Cilycwm
Rhandirmwyn
Cynghordy
Llansawel
Edwinsford
Talley
Cwm-byr
Cwmdu
Halfway
Llanwrda
Llansadwrn
Wauncluda
Cwmdwr
Myddfai
Myrtle Hill
Cilgwyn
Talsarn
Twynllanan
Llanddeusant
Pont-ar-llechau
Capel Gwynfe
Pont Aber
Bethlehem
Manordeilo
Cwmifor
Rhosmaen
Ffairfach
Salem
Soar
Ashfield
Hermon
Felindre
Pontbren Araeth
Dyffryn Ceidrych
Neuadd
Babel
Pentre-ty-gwyn
Halfway
Ystradffin
Nant-y-Bai
Divlyn
A40
A482
A483
A4069
B4302
B4343
B4337
B4310
B4300
93
75
76
112
DOLAUCOTHI GOLD MINES
TALLEY ABBEY
TALLEY LAKES
DINEFWR PARK
CASTLE WOODS
Y GAER HILLFORT
CARREG CENNEN CASTLE & FARM CENTRE
GWENFFRWD-DINAS
POOR MAN'S WOOD
Usk Reservoir
Llyn Brianne Reservoir
Mynydd Du
Bannau Brycheiniog 802
Fan Foel
Llyn y Fan Fach
Llyn y Fan Fawr
Carreg Yr Ogof 585
Tywi Forest
0 1 2 3 miles
0 1 2 3 4 5 km

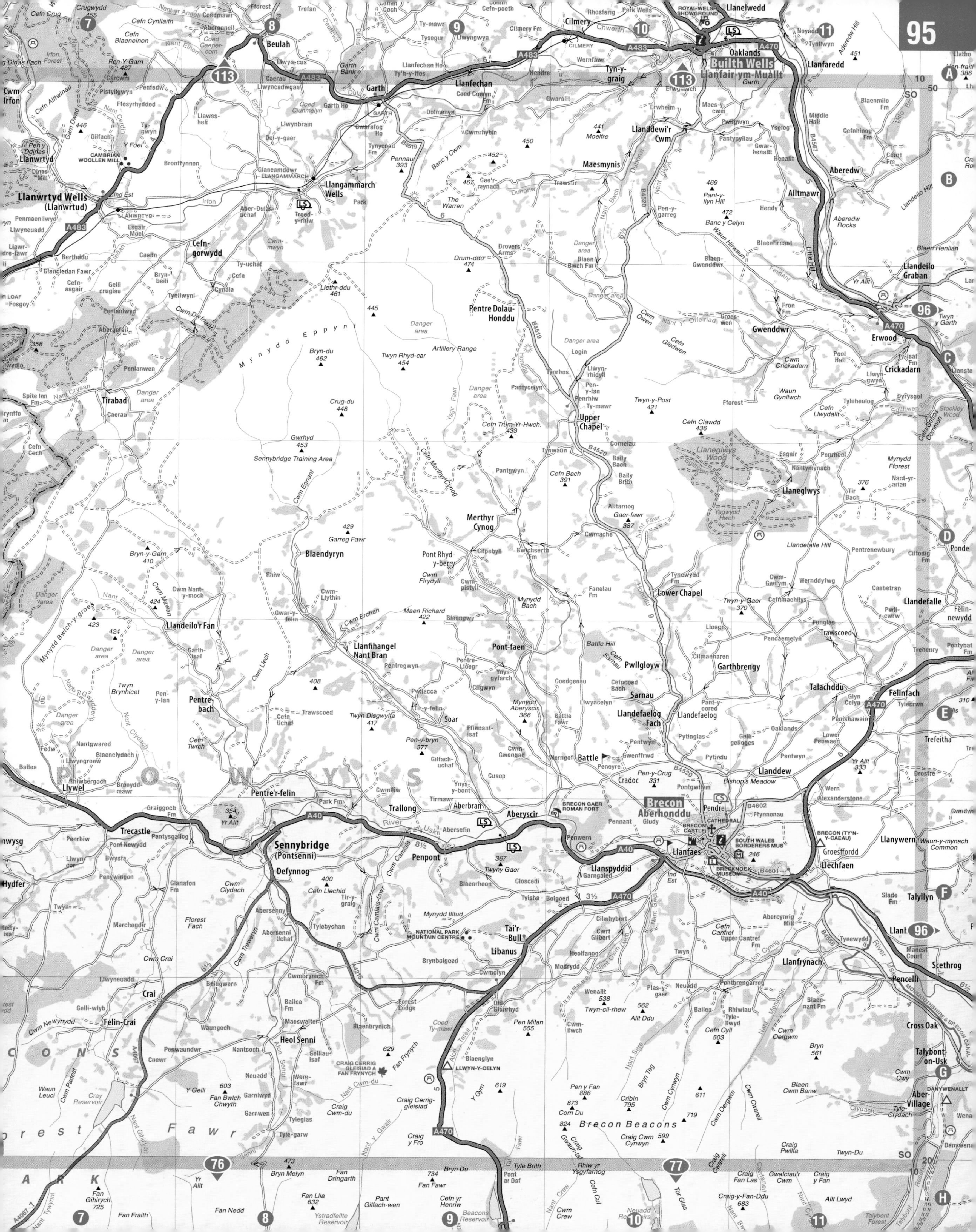

Llanelwedd
ROYAL WELSH SHOWGROUND
Builth Wells
Llanfair-ym-Muallt
Oaklands
Cilmery
Beulah
Garth
Llanfechan
Llanwrtyd Wells
(Llanwrtyd)
Llangammarch Wells
Cefn-gorwydd
CAMBRIAN WOOLLEN MILL
Tyn-y-graig
Llanddewi'r Cwm
Maesmynis
Llanfaredd
Aberedw
Alltmawr
Llandeilo Graban
Erwood
Gwenddwr
Crickadarn
Mynydd Eppynt
Pentre Dolau-Honddu
Upper Chapel
Tirabad
Sennybridge Training Area
Merthyr Cynog
Blaendyryn
Llaneglwys
Lower Chapel
Llandefalle
Llandeilo'r Fan
Llanfihangel Nant Bran
Pont-faen
Pwllgloyw
Garthbrengy
Sarnau
Llandefaelog Fach
Talachddu
Felinfach
Pentre-bach
Battle
Llanddew
Llywel
Pentre'r-felin
Trecastle
Sennybridge
(Pontsenni)
Defynnog
Trallong
Aberyscir
Penpont
Brecon
Aberhonddu
BRECON GAER ROMAN FORT
CATHEDRAL
BRECON CASTLE
SOUTH WALES BORDERERS MUS
BRECKNOCK MUSEUM
Llanfaes
Llanspyddid
Groesffordd
Llechfaen
Llanywern
Talyllyn
Libanus
Tai'r-Bull
NATIONAL PARK MOUNTAIN CENTRE
Llanfrynach
Pencelli
Scethrog
Cross Oak
Talybont-on-Usk
Aber-Village
Crai
Felin-Crai
Heol Senni
CRAIG CERRIG GLEISIAD A FAN FRYNYCH
LLWYN-Y-CELYN
Brecon Beacons
Pen y Fan 886
Corn Du 873
Cribin 795
Fforest Fawr
Fan Gihirych 725
Fan Llia 632
Fan Fawr 734
POWYS
A483
A470
A40
A4215
A4067
B4519
B4520
B4602
B4601
B4558
B4567
7
8
9
10
11
76
77
96
113
A
B
C
D
E
F
G
H
SO

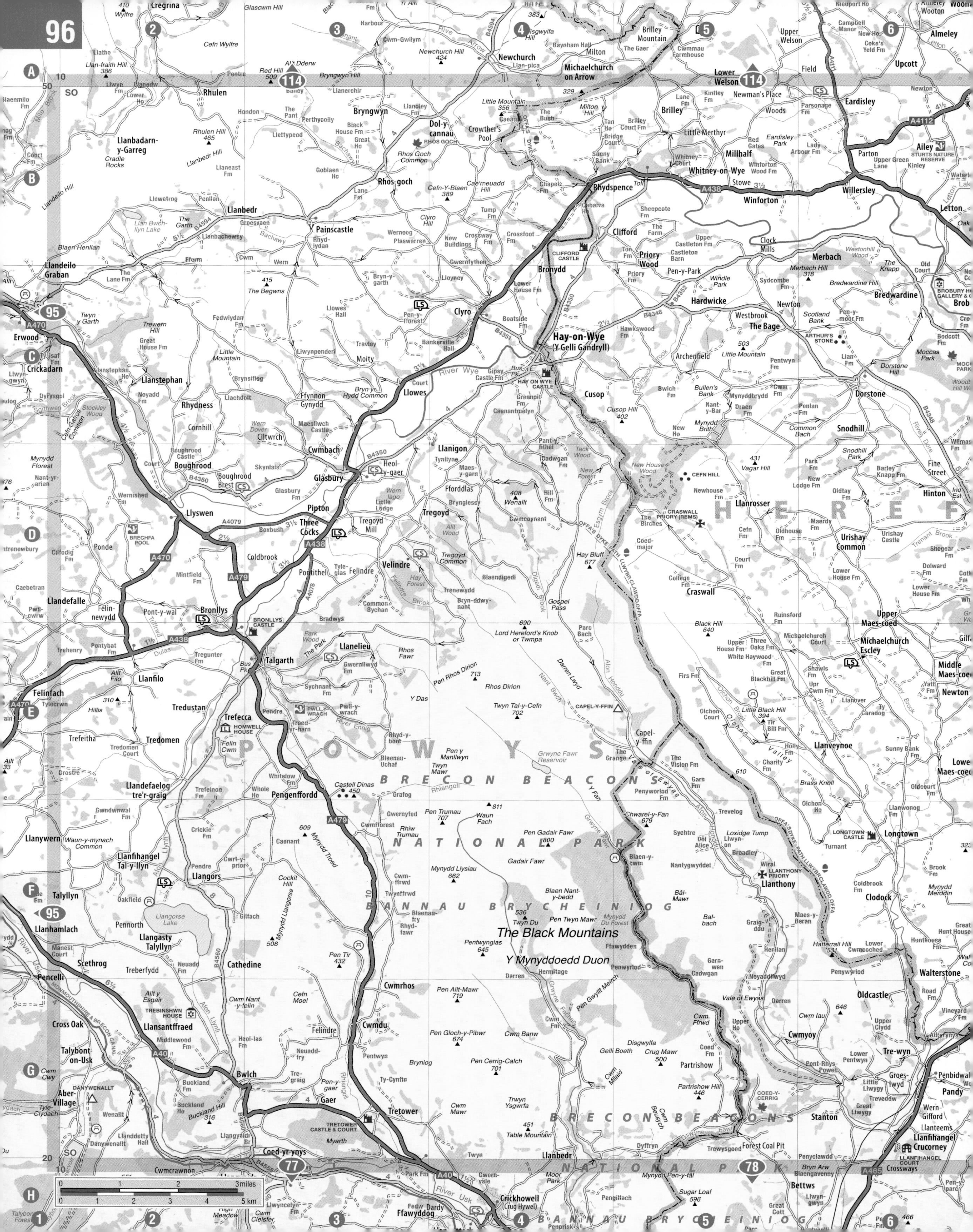
Cregrina
Glascwm Hill
Harbour
Newchurch
Brilley Mountain
Upper Welson
Almeley
Wootton
Rhulen
Red Hill 509
Aly Dderw
114
Michaelchurch on Arrow
Lower Welson
Field
Upcott
Llanbadarn-y-Garreg
Bryngwyn
Dol-y-cannau
Crowther's Pool
Brilley
Kintley Fm
Newman's Place
Eardisley
Woods
A4112
Little Mountain 356
Rhulen Hill 465
Cradle Rocks
Rhos Goch Common
Little Merthyr
Millhalf
Whitney-on-Wye
Ailey
Parton
Rhos-goch
Bhydspence
Winforton
Willersley
Letton
Llanbedr
Painscastle
Clyro Hill
Clifford
Clock Mills
Merbach
Llandeilo Graban
The Begwns
Priory Wood
Pen-y-Park
Hardwicke
Bredwardine
CLIFFORD CASTLE
Bronydd
Merbach Hill 318
Bredwardine Hill
95
A470
Erwood
Clyro
Hay-on-Wye
(Y Gelli Gandryll)
Westbrook
The Bage
Newton
ARTHUR'S STONE
Crickadarn
Llanstephan
Moity
Llowes
River Wye
Archenfield
Little Mountain 503
Dorstone
Moccas Park
HAY ON WYE CASTLE
Cusop
Cusop Hill 402
Rhydness
Ffynnon Gynydd
Cornhill
Ciltwrch
Maesllwch Castle
Cwmbach
Llanigon
Snodhill
Boughrood
Boughrood Brest
Glasbury
Heol-y-gaer
Vagar Hill 431
CEFN HILL
Fine Street
Hinton
Mynydd Fforest
Nant-yr-arian
Pipton
Three Cocks
Llyswen
Tregoyd
Wenallt 408
Llanrosser
HEREF
CRASWALL PRIORY (REMS)
Urishay Common
BRECHFA POOL
A4079
A479
A438
Ponde
Coldbrook
Felindre
Velindre
Tregoyd Common
Hay Bluff 677
Craswall
Upper Maes-coed
Llandefalle
Bronllys
BRONLLYS CASTLE
Pont-y-wal
Gospel Pass
Lord Hereford's Knob or Twmpa 690
Black Hill 640
Michaelchurch Escley
Talgarth
Llanelieu
Rhos Fawr
Pen Rhos Dirion 713
Rhos Dirion
Darren Lwyd
Middle Maes-coed
Felinfach
Llanfilo
Y Das
Twyn Tal-y-Cefn 702
CAPEL-Y-FFIN
Newton
Tredustan
Trefecca
HOMWELL HOUSE
Pwll-y-wrach
Capel-y-ffin
Little Black Hill 394
Tredomen
P O W Y S
Grwyne Fawr Reservoir
Llanveynoe
Llandefaelog-tre'r-graig
Pen y Manllwyn
Twyn Mawr
B R E C O N   B E A C O N S
Castell Dinas 450
Pengenffordd
Vale of Ewyas
Trevelog
Penyworlod Fm
Chwarel-y-Fan 679
Waun Fach 811
Pen Trumau 707
A479
Pen Gadair Fawr 800
N A T I O N A L   P A R K
Llanywern
Mynydd Troed 609
Gadair Fawr
Longtown
LONGTOWN CASTLE
Llanfihangel Tal-y-llyn
Llangors
Mynydd Llysiau 662
LLANTHONY PRIORY
Llanthony
Talyllyn
B A N N A U   B R Y C H E I N I O G
Blaen Nant-y-bedd
Clodock
Llanhamlach
Langorse Lake
Pennorth
Llangasty Talyllyn
Mynydd Llangorse 508
Twyn Du 536
Pen Twyn Mawr
The Black Mountains
Y Mynyddoedd Duon
Pentwynglas 645
Hatterrall Hill 531
Scethrog
Pencelli
Cathedine
Pen Tir 432
Walterstone
Cwmrhos
Darren
Pen Allt-Mawr 719
Pen Gwyllt Meirch
Oldcastle
Cross Oak
Llansantffraed
Cwmdu
Pen Gloch-y-Pibwr 674
Cwm Banw
Cwmyoy
Talybont-on-Usk
Bwlch
Pen Cerrig-Calch 701
Crug Mawr 500
Partrishow
Tre-wyn
Aber-Village
Gaer
Tretower
TRETOWER CASTLE & COURT
Partrishow Hill 446
Stanton
Pandy
Table Mountain 451
Llanbedr
Forest Coal Pit
Llanfihangel Crucorney
Coed-yr-ynys
77
78
A40
Crickhowell
(Crug Hywel)
Sugar Loaf 596
Bettws
Ffawyddog
Mynydd Pen-y-fal
Cwmcrawnon
0 1 2 3 miles
0 1 2 3 4 5 km

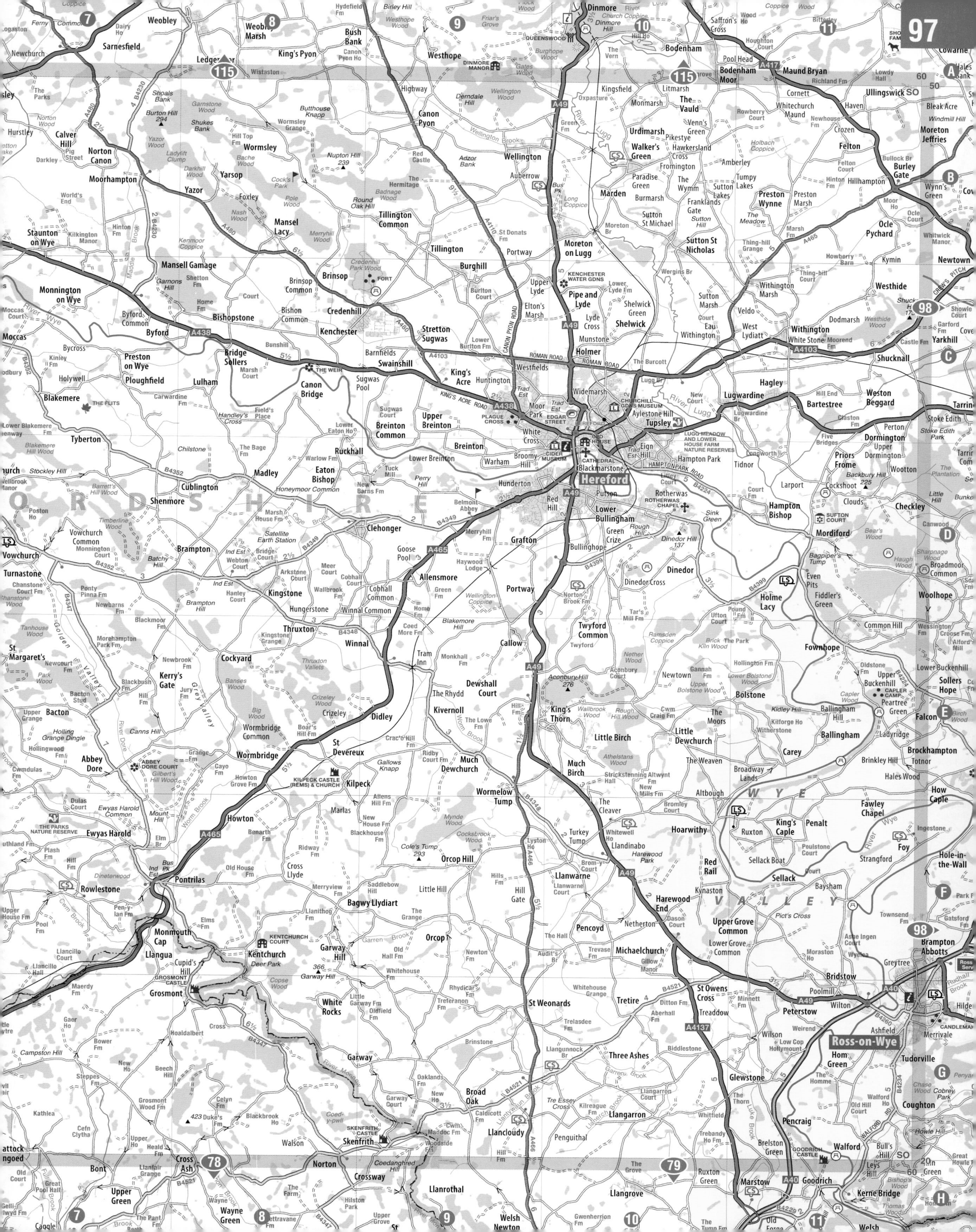
Weobley
Sarnesfield
Weobley Marsh
King's Pyon
Bush Bank
Westhope
Dinmore
Bodenham
Maund Bryan
Bodenham Moor
Ledgemoor
Canon Pyon
Dinmore Manor
Queenswood
Litmarsh
Kingsfield
The Vauld
Monmarsh
Urdimarsh
Walker's Green
Marden
Ullingswick
Felton
Moreton Jeffries
Burley Gate
Calver Hill
Norton Canon
Moorhampton
Yazor
Yarsop
Wormsley
Mansel Lacy
Tillington Common
Tillington
Wellington
Auberrow
Preston Wynne
Sutton St Michael
Sutton St Nicholas
Ocle Pychard
Staunton on Wye
Mansell Gamage
Brinsop
Brinsop Common
Burghill
Moreton on Lugg
Pipe and Lyde
Shelwick
Westhide
Withington Marsh
Withington
Monnington on Wye
Bishopstone
Credenhill
Kenchester
Stretton Sugwas
Byford
Bridge Sollers
Swainshill
King's Acre
Holmer
Shucknall
Yarkhill
Moccas
Preston on Wye
Ploughfield
Lulham
Canon Bridge
Blakemere
Tyberton
Upper Breinton
Breinton Common
Breinton
Ruckhall
Eaton Bishop
Madley
Hereford
Tupsley
Lugwardine
Hagley
Bartestree
Weston Beggard
Dormington
Priors Frome
Hampton Bishop
Mordiford
Checkley
Cublington
Shenmore
Clehonger
Lower Bullingham
Grafton
Dinedor
Holme Lacy
Fownhope
Woolhope
Vowchurch
Turnastone
Brampton
Kingstone
Allensmore
Portway
Twyford Common
Thruxton
Winnal
Callow
Cockyard
Kerry's Gate
St Margaret's
Dewshall Court
Kivernoll
King's Thorn
Little Birch
Little Dewchurch
Bolstone
Ballingham
Carey
Sollers Hope
Falcon
Brockhampton
Bacton
Abbey Dore
Wormbridge
St Devereux
Didley
Kilpeck
Much Dewchurch
Much Birch
Wormelow Tump
Ewyas Harold
Howton
Orcop Hill
Llanwarne
Hoarwithy
King's Caple
Fawley Chapel
How Caple
Foy
Hole-in-the-Wall
Pontrilas
Rowlestone
Bagwy Llydiart
Harewood End
Red Rail
Sellack
Monmouth Cap
Llangua
Kentchurch
Garway Hill
Orcop
Pencoyd
Michaelchurch
Upper Grove Common
Brampton Abbotts
Grosmont
White Rocks
St Weonards
Tretire
St Owens Cross
Peterstow
Bridstow
Wilton
Ross-on-Wye
Garway
Broad Oak
Three Ashes
Glewstone
Tudorville
Llancloudy
Llangarron
Pencraig
Coughton
Skenfrith
Cross Ash
Walford
Bont
Norton
Crossway
Llanrothal
Llangrove
Marstow
Goodrich
Kerne Bridge
Upper Green
Wayne Green
Welsh Newton
WYE VALLEY
A49
A438
A465
A466
A4103
A480
A417
A40
A4137
B4349
B4352
B4399
B4224
B4521
B4347
B4348
B4230
B4229
B4234
115
78
79
98
7
8
9
10
11

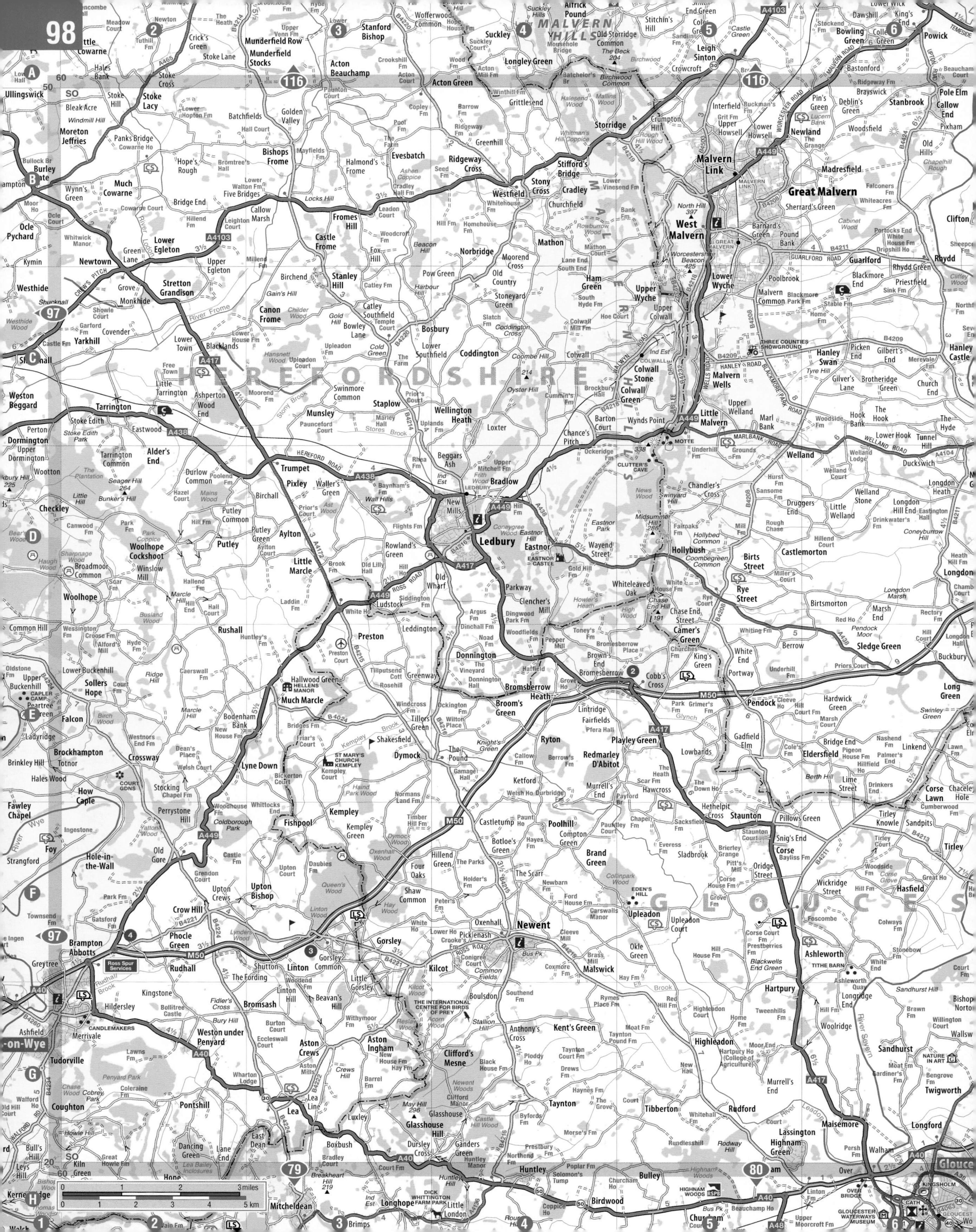
HEREFORDSHIRE
MALVERN HILLS
GLOUCES
116
97
79
80
Ullingswick
Stoke Lacy
Moreton Jeffries
Burley Gate
Much Cowarne
Ocle Pychard
Lower Egleton
Newtown
Westhide
Stretton Grandison
Yarkhill
Weston Beggard
Tarrington
Dormington
Checkley
Woolhope
Woolhope Cockshoot
Munderfield Row
Munderfield Stocks
Acton Beauchamp
Stanford Bishop
Acton Green
Bishops Frome
Evesbatch
Fromes Hill
Castle Frome
Canon Frome
Stanley Hill
Bosbury
Coddington
Munsley
Staplow
Wellington Heath
Trumpet
Pixley
Aylton
Putley
Little Marcle
Ledbury
Eastnor
Preston
Much Marcle
Rushall
Sollers Hope
Falcon
Brockhampton
Crossway
Lyne Down
Dymock
Kempley
Fishpool
Upton Bishop
Crow Hill
Phocle Green
Brampton Abbotts
Rudhall
Linton
Gorsley
Kilcot
Newent
Malswick
Bromsash
Weston under Penyard
Aston Crews
Aston Ingham
Clifford's Mesne
Tudorville
Coughton
Pontshill
Lea
Glasshouse Hill
Huntley
Tibberton
Rudford
Maisemore
Longford
Mitcheldean
Longhope
Birdwood
Suckley
Longley Green
Storridge
Ridgeway Cross
Stifford's Bridge
Cradley
Mathon
Colwall
Colwall Stone
Colwall Green
Little Malvern
Welland
Malvern Link
West Malvern
Great Malvern
Lower Wyche
Upper Wyche
Malvern Wells
Hanley Swan
Hanley Castle
Guarlford
Rhydd
Madresfield
Newland
Callow End
Powick
Hollybush
Castlemorton
Birts Street
Rye Street
Longdon
Berrow
Sledge Green
Pendock
Redmarley D'Abitot
Playley Green
Bromsberrow Heath
Donnington
Ryton
Poolhill
Brand Green
Upleadon
Staunton
Corse
Eldersfield
Tirley
Hasfield
Ashleworth
Hartpury
Sandhurst
Twigworth
Highleadon
Kent's Green
Taynton
M50
A40
A417
A449
A438
A4103
Ross-on-Wye
Gloucester

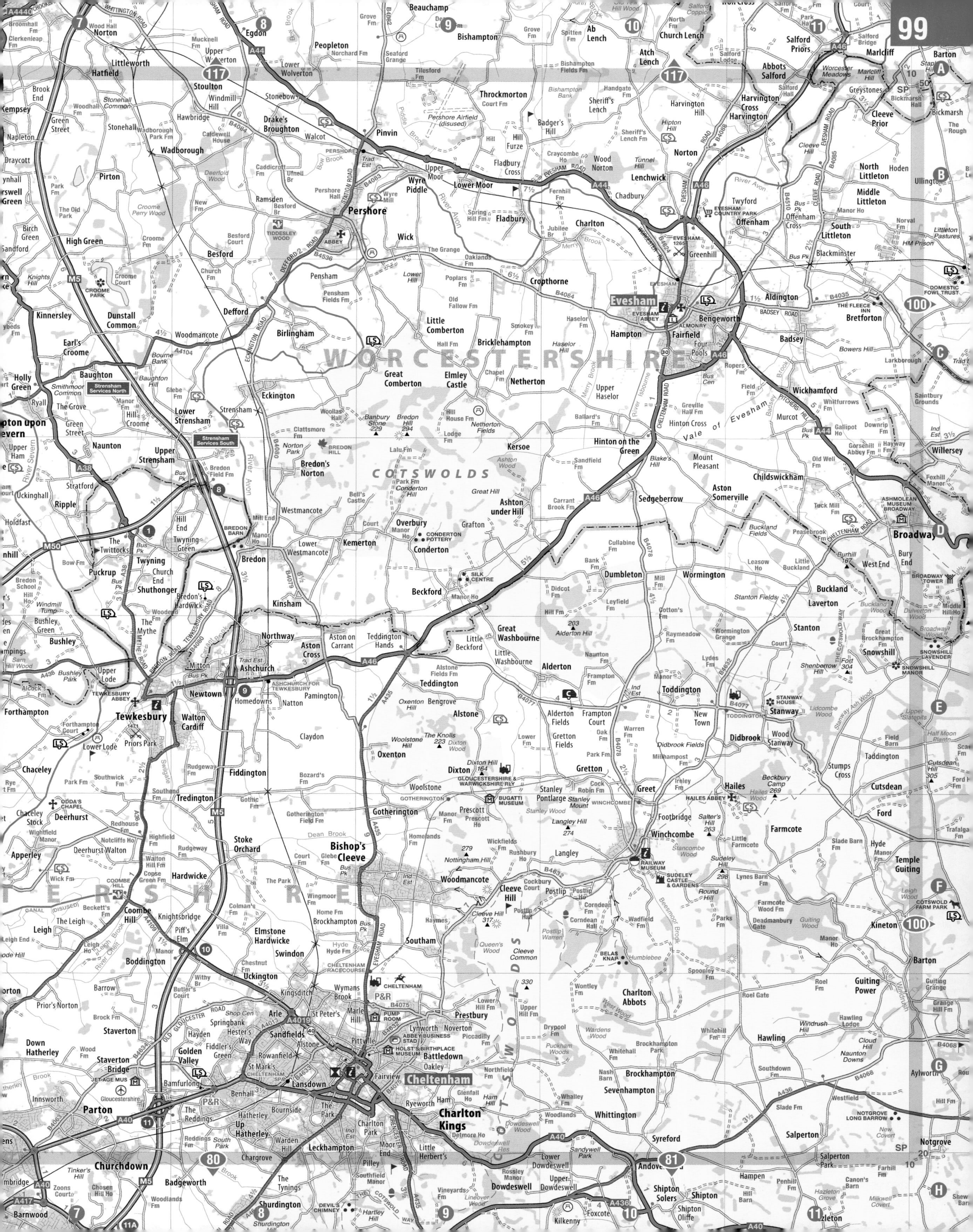
WORCESTERSHIRE
COTSWOLDS
Vale of Evesham
Evesham
Pershore
Tewkesbury
Cheltenham
Broadway
Winchcombe
Bishop's Cleeve
Charlton Kings
Churchdown
Norton
Egdon
Beauchamp
Bishampton
Ab Lench
Atch Lench
Church Lench
Salford Priors
Abbots Salford
Marlcliff
Barton
Littleworth
Hatfield
Stoulton
Peopleton
Throckmorton
Harvington
Cleeve Prior
Bickmarsh
Kempsey
Wadborough
Drake's Broughton
Pinvin
Hill Furze
Badger's Hill
Norton
Lenchwick
North Littleton
Middle Littleton
South Littleton
Pirton
Wyre Piddle
Lower Moor
Fladbury
Chadbury
Offenham
Charlton
High Green
Besford
Wick
Cropthorne
Greenhill
Aldington
Bretforton
Kinnersley
Dunstall Common
Defford
Birlingham
Little Comberton
Bricklehampton
Hampton
Bengeworth
Fairfield
Badsey
Earl's Croome
Great Comberton
Elmley Castle
Netherton
Holly Green
Baughton
Eckington
Upper Haselor
Wickhamford
Ryall
Lower Strensham
Strensham
Murcot
Upton upon Severn
Naunton
Upper Strensham
Bredon's Norton
Kersoe
Hinton on the Green
Willersey
Ripple
Mount Pleasant
Childswickham
Uckinghall
Westmancote
Ashton under Hill
Sedgeberrow
Aston Somerville
Overbury
Grafton
Twyning
Puckrup
Bredon
Kemerton
Conderton
Dumbleton
Wormington
Buckland
Laverton
Shuthonger
Beckford
Kinsham
Northway
Stanton
Bushley
Aston Cross
Great Washbourne
Snowshill
Ashchurch
Alderton
Teddington
Toddington
Newtown
Stanway
Forthampton
Walton Cardiff
Alstone
Didbrook
Oxenton
Taddington
Chaceley
Fiddington
Dixton
Gretton
Greet
Hailes
Cutsdean
Tredington
Gotherington
Deerhurst
Ford
Stoke Orchard
Farmcote
Apperley
Woodmancote
Langley
Hardwicke
Temple Guiting
Cleeve Hill
Coombe Hill
Leigh
Elmstone Hardwicke
Southam
Kineton
Swindon
Boddington
Uckington
Charlton Abbots
Barton
Guiting Power
Staverton
Arle
Prestbury
Golden Valley
Hawling
Down Hatherley
Staverton Bridge
Battledown
Brockhampton
Sevenhampton
Parton
Up Hatherley
Leckhampton
Whittington
Salperton
Syreford
Notgrove
Badgeworth
Dowdeswell
Shipton Solers
Shipton
Shurdington
Barnwood
Kilkenny
Foxcote

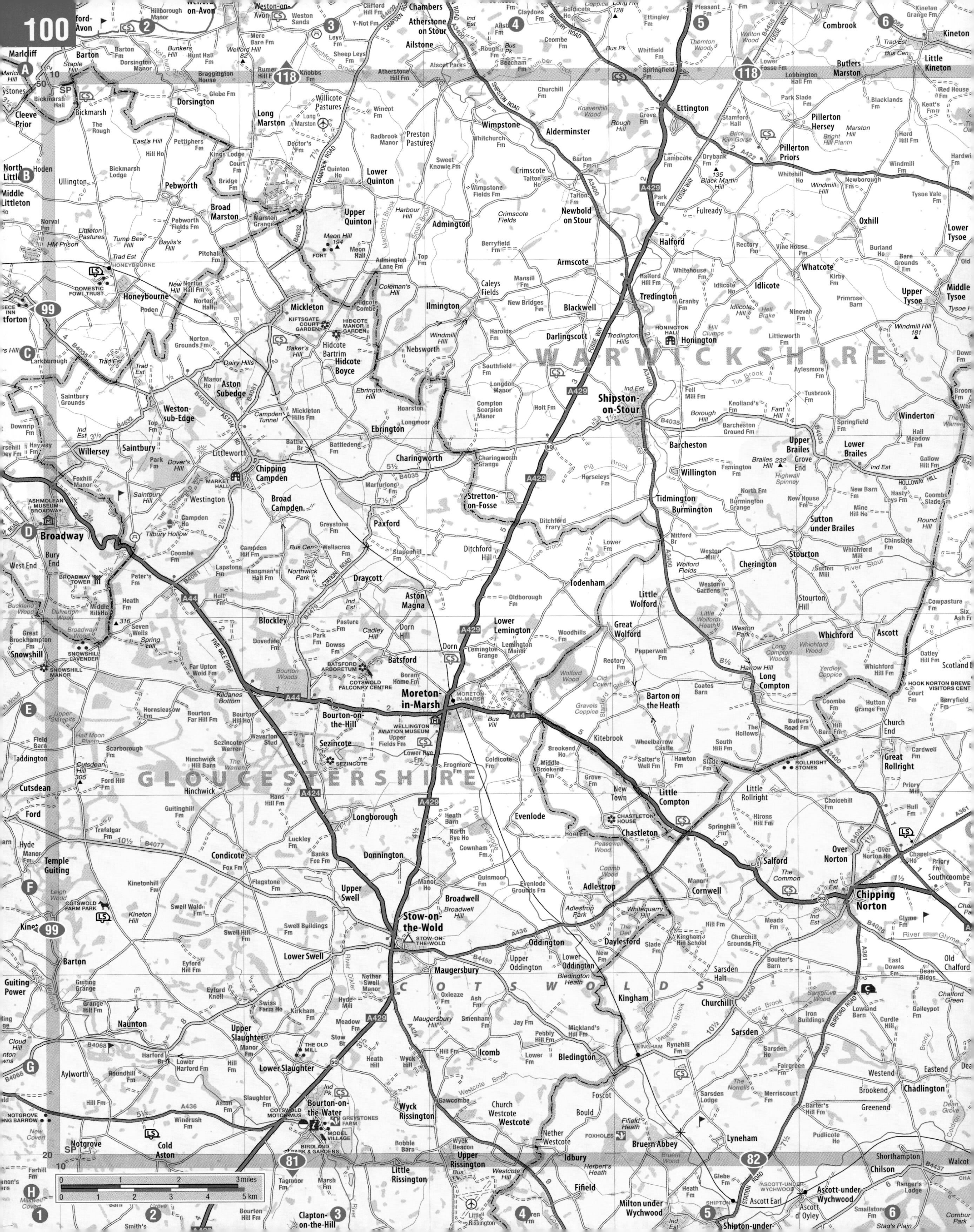

Marlcliff
Barton
Bickmarsh
Cleeve Prior
Dorsington
Long Marston
Welford Hill
Weston-on-Avon
Atherstone on Stour
Ailstone
Alscot Park
Whitfield Fm
Ettington
Combrook
Kineton
Butlers Marston
Little Kineton
Pillerton Hersey
Pillerton Priors
Wimpstone
Alderminster
Preston Pastures
North Littleton
Middle Littleton
Ullington
Pebworth
Broad Marston
Lower Quinton
Upper Quinton
Admington
Crimscote
Newbold on Stour
Fulready
Oxhill
Lower Tysoe
Honeybourne
Mickleton
Kiftsgate Court Garden
Hidcote Manor Garden
Hidcote Bartrim
Hidcote Boyce
Ilmington
Nebsworth
Caleys Fields
Armscote
Blackwell
Darlingscott
Halford
Tredington
Idlicote
Whatcote
Upper Tysoe
Middle Tysoe
Honington
Honington Hall
WARWICKSHIRE
Larkborough
Aston Subedge
Weston-sub-Edge
Saintbury
Willersey
Ebrington
Charingworth
Shipston-on-Stour
Barcheston
Upper Brailes
Lower Brailes
Winderton
Chipping Campden
Broad Campden
Westington
Stretton-on-Fosse
Willington
Tidmington
Burmington
Sutton under Brailes
Broadway
Broadway Tower
Paxford
Draycott
Ditchford Hill
Todenham
Cherington
Stourton
Blockley
Aston Magna
Lower Lemington
Little Wolford
Great Wolford
Whichford
Ascott
Long Compton
Snowshill
Snowshill Manor
Batsford
Batsford Arboretum
Moreton-in-Marsh
Barton on the Heath
Bourton-on-the-Hill
Sezincote
Wellington Aviation Museum
Kitebrook
Little Rollright
Great Rollright
Rollright Stones
Taddington
Cutsdean
GLOUCESTERSHIRE
Hinchwick
Longborough
Evenlode
Little Compton
Chastleton
Chastleton House
Ford
Temple Guiting
Condicote
Donnington
Adlestrop
Salford
Over Norton
Chipping Norton
Cornwell
Upper Swell
Broadwell
Stow-on-the-Wold
Oddington
Daylesford
Cotswold Farm Park
Barton
Lower Swell
Maugersbury
Upper Oddington
Lower Oddington
Sarsden Halt
Kingham
Churchill
Sarsden
COTSWOLDS
Guiting Power
Naunton
Upper Slaughter
Lower Slaughter
Icomb
Bledington
Aylworth
Wyck Rissington
Church Westcote
Westcote
Bourton-on-the-Water
Cotswold Motor Museum
Model Village
Birdland Park & Gardens
Notgrove
Cold Aston
Nether Westcote
Foscot
Bould
Bruern Abbey
Lyneham
Chadlington
Idbury
Little Rissington
Upper Rissington
Fifield
Milton under Wychwood
Ascott-under-Wychwood
Ascott Earl
Ascott d'Oyley
Chilson
Shorthampton
Shipton-under-
Clapton-on-the-Hill
A429
A44
A424
A436
A3400
A361
B4035
B4632
118
99
81
82
0 1 2 3 miles
0 1 2 3 4 5 km

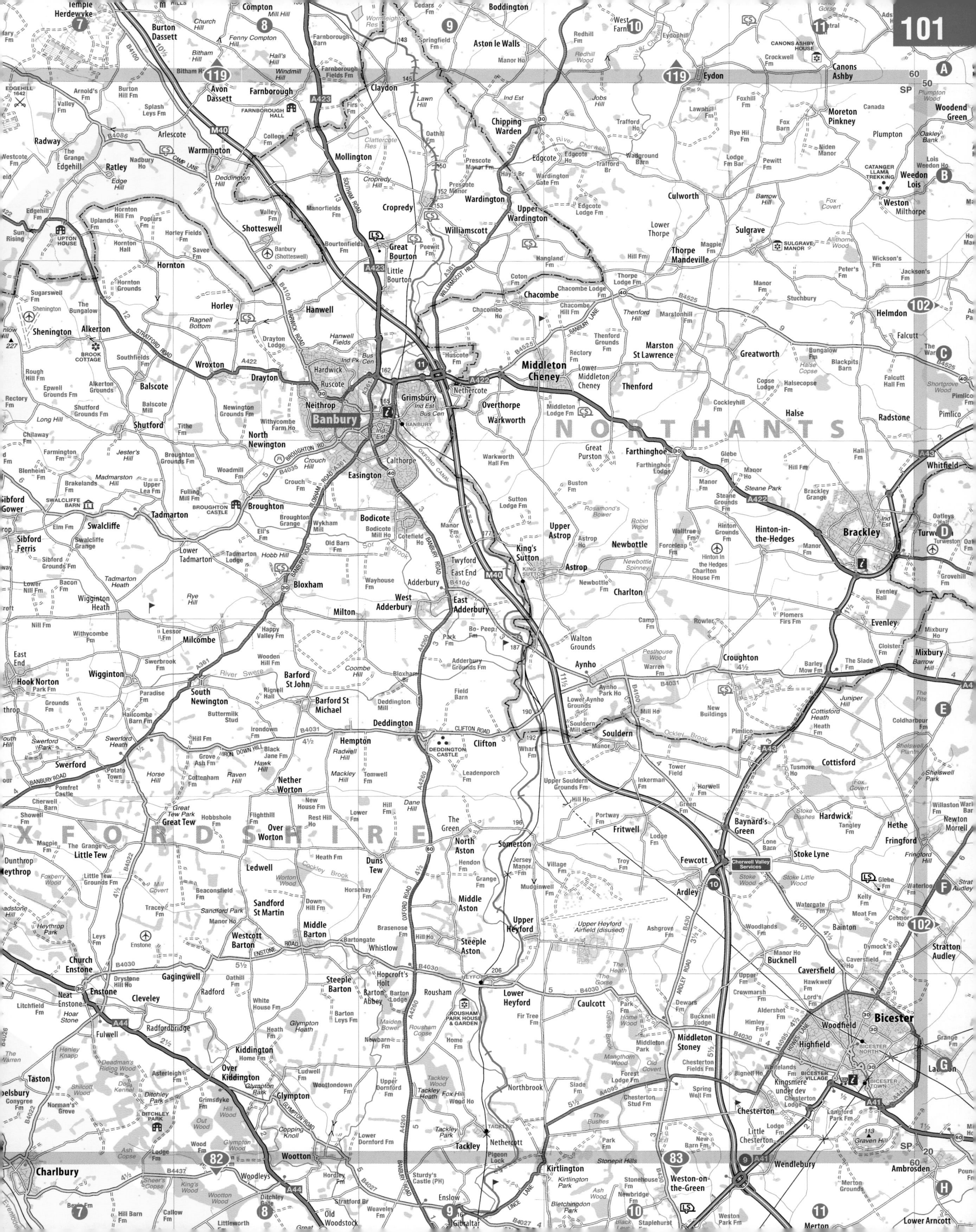

NORTHANTS
OXFORDSHIRE
Banbury
Bicester
Brackley
Middleton Cheney
Chacombe
Thenford
Marston St Lawrence
Greatworth
Helmdon
Falcutt
Sulgrave
Culworth
Thorpe Mandeville
Moreton Pinkney
Canons Ashby
Eydon
Plumpton
Woodend Green
Weedon Lois
Weston
Milthorpe
Chipping Warden
Edgcote
Aston le Walls
Boddington
Claydon
Farnborough
Avon Dassett
Burton Dassett
Temple Herdewyke
Compton
Warmington
Arlescote
Radway
Edgehill
Ratley
Mollington
Cropredy
Wardington
Upper Wardington
Williamscott
Great Bourton
Little Bourton
Shotteswell
Hornton
Horley
Hanwell
Shenington
Alkerton
Wroxton
Drayton
Balscote
Shutford
North Newington
Neithrop
Grimsbury
Nethercote
Overthorpe
Warkworth
Easington
Calthorpe
Broughton
Tadmarton
Swalcliffe
Sibford Ferris
Sibford Gower
Bodicote
Bloxham
Milton
Adderbury
West Adderbury
East Adderbury
Twyford
King's Sutton
Astrop
Upper Astrop
Newbottle
Charlton
Farthinghoe
Halse
Radstone
Whitfield
Hinton-in-the-Hedges
Evenley
Mixbury
Croughton
Aynho
Souldern
Cottisford
Hardwick
Hethe
Fringford
Stoke Lyne
Baynard's Green
Fritwell
Fewcott
Ardley
Somerton
North Aston
Middle Aston
Steeple Aston
Upper Heyford
Lower Heyford
Caulcott
Middleton Stoney
Bucknell
Caversfield
Stratton Audley
Bainton
Chesterton
Little Chesterton
Wendlebury
Ambrosden
Lower Arncott
Merton
Weston-on-the-Green
Kirtlington
Tackley
Rousham
Steeple Barton
Middle Barton
Westcott Barton
Sandford St Martin
Ledwell
Over Worton
Nether Worton
Duns Tew
Deddington
Clifton
Hempton
Barford St John
Barford St Michael
Milcombe
Wigginton
South Newington
Hook Norton
Swerford
Great Tew
Little Tew
Church Enstone
Enstone
Neat Enstone
Cleveley
Gagingwell
Radford
Kiddington
Over Kiddington
Glympton
Wootton
Woodleys
Charlbury
Fulwell
Taston
Old Woodstock
Enslow
Gibraltar
Whistlow
Woodfield
Highfield
Kingsmere
Cherwell Valley Services
M40
A422
A423
A361
A4260
A43
A41
A44
B4100
B4525
B4031
B4030
B4035
B4022
B4027
OXFORD CANAL
River Cherwell
River Swere

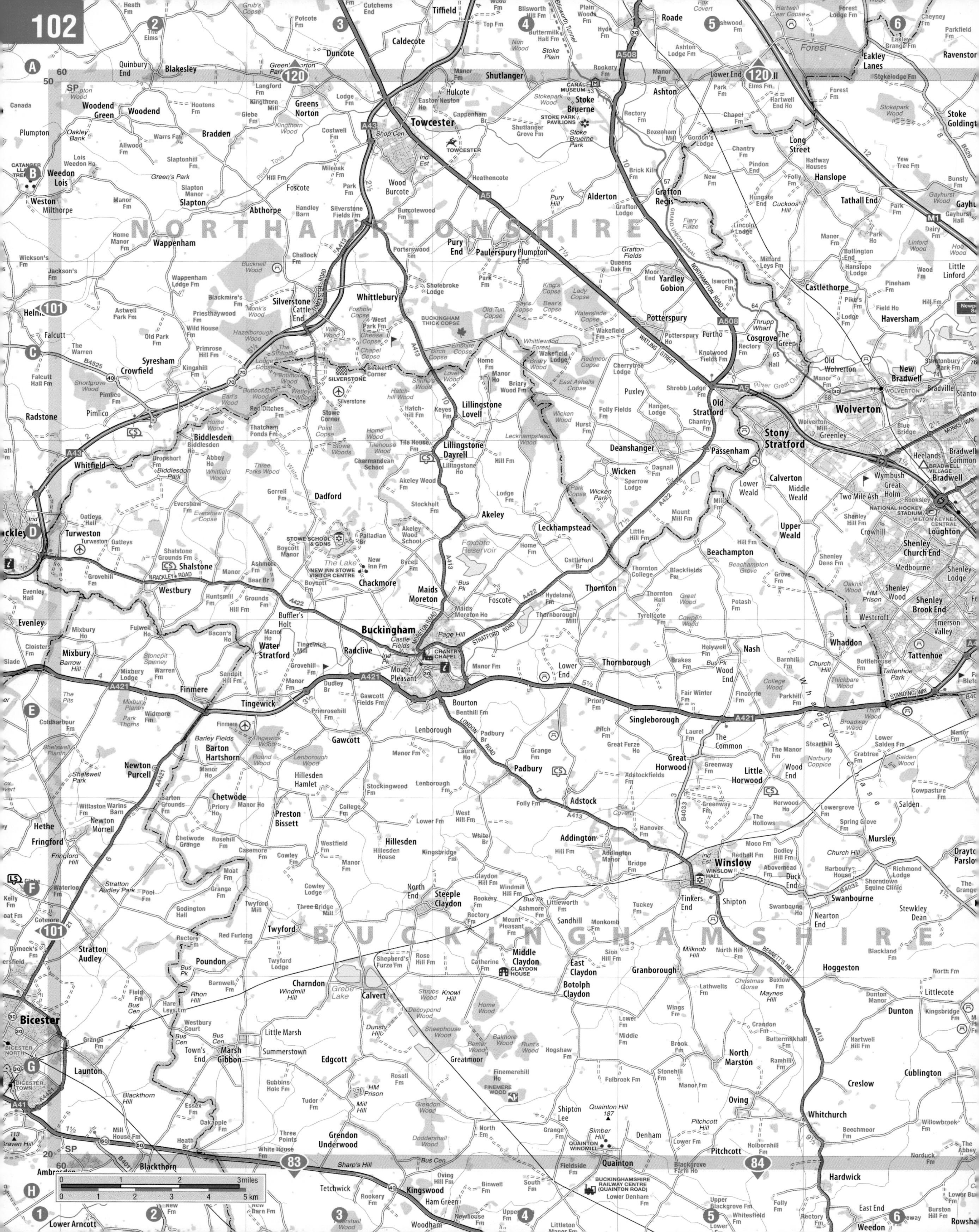
NORTHAMPTONSHIRE
BUCKINGHAMSHIRE
Blakesley
Quinbury End
Duncote
Caldecote
Tiffield
Roade
Ashton
Shutlanger
Stoke Bruerne
Towcester
Woodend Green
Woodend
Greens Norton
Bradden
Plumpton
Weedon Lois
Weston
Slapton
Abthorpe
Foscote
Wood Burcote
Heathencote
Alderton
Grafton Regis
Long Street
Hanslope
Tathall End
Wappenham
Pury End
Paulerspury
Plumpton End
Yardley Gobion
Castlethorpe
Silverstone
Cattle End
Whittlebury
Potterspury
Furtho
Cosgrove
Haversham
Helmdon
Falcutt
Syresham
Crowfield
Radstone
Pimlico
Biddlesden
Lillingstone Lovell
Old Stratford
Wolverton
New Bradwell
Stony Stratford
Lillingstone Dayrell
Deanshanger
Passenham
Wicken
Whitfield
Dadford
Akeley
Leckhampstead
Calverton
Upper Weald
Turweston
Shalstone
Westbury
Chackmore
Maids Moreton
Foscote
Thornton
Beachampton
Loughton
Evenley
Mixbury
Buckingham
Water Stratford
Radclive
Nash
Whaddon
Tattenhoe
Finmere
Tingewick
Bourton
Thornborough
Singleborough
Gawcott
Lenborough
Padbury
Great Horwood
Little Horwood
Newton Purcell
Barton Hartshorn
Chetwode
Preston Bissett
Hillesden Hamlet
Adstock
Newton Morrell
Hethe
Fringford
Hillesden
Addington
Winslow
Mursley
Steeple Claydon
Shipton
Swanbourne
Stratton Audley
Twyford
Middle Claydon
East Claydon
Granborough
Hoggeston
Poundon
Charndon
Calvert
Botolph Claydon
Dunton
Bicester
Launton
Marsh Gibbon
Little Marsh
Summerstown
Edgcott
Greatmoor
North Marston
Creslow
Cublington
Oving
Whitchurch
Grendon Underwood
Pitchcott
Quainton
Blackthorn
Kingswood
Hardwick
A5
A43
A413
A422
A421
A508
A4421
A41
M1
3 miles
5 km

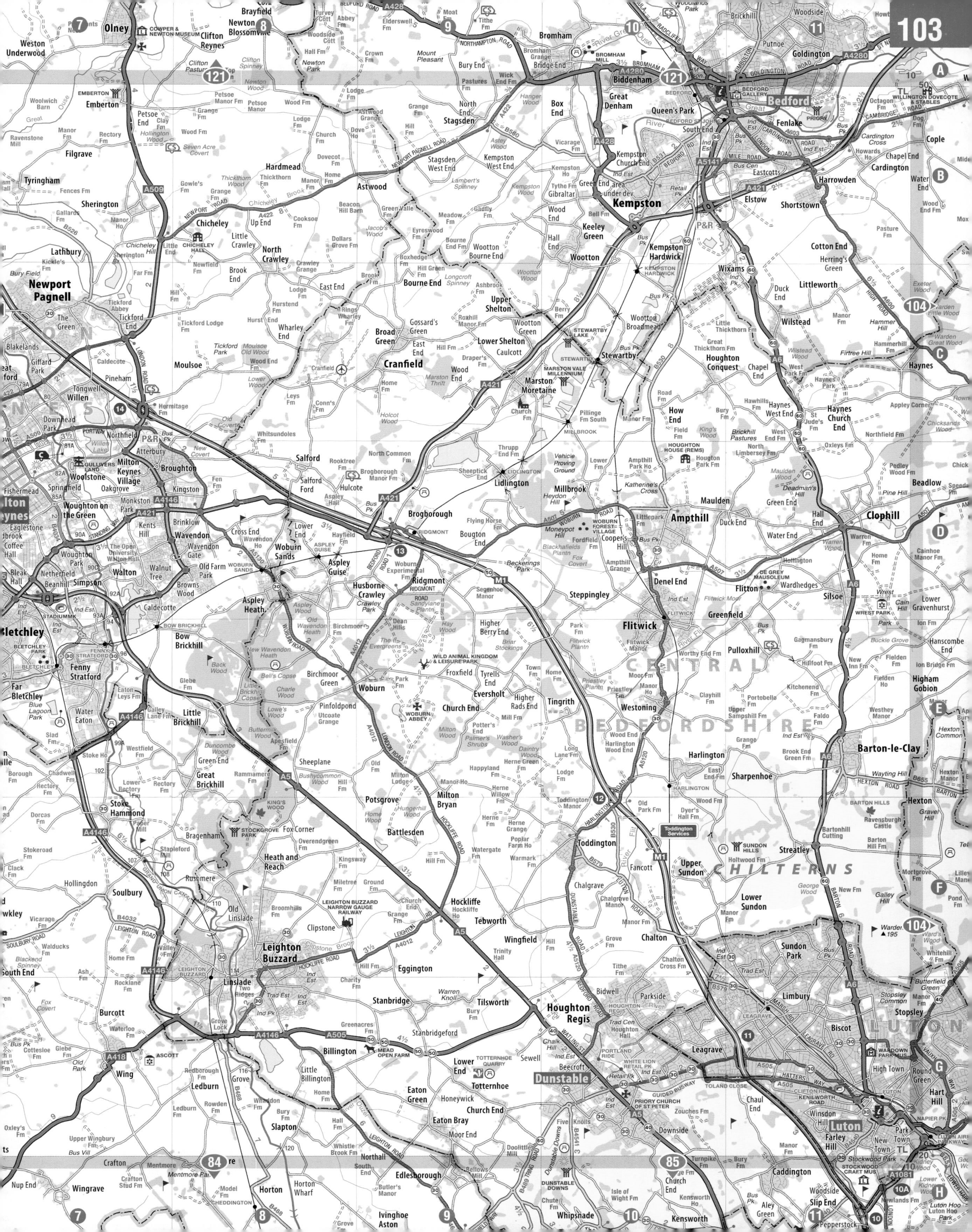
103
Olney
Cowper & Newton Museum
Weston Underwood
Clifton Reynes
Newton Blossomville
Brayfield
Turvey
Bromham
Bromham Mill
Biddenham
Bedford
Bedford Gallery
Putnoe
Goldington
Woodside
Brickhill
Emberton
Petsoe End
Filgrave
Tyringham
Sherington
Chicheley
Chicheley Hall
Hardmead
Astwood
Stagsden
Stagsden West End
Kempston West End
Kempston Church End
Kempston
Great Denham
Queen's Park
Fenlake
Cardington
Cople
Harrowden
Elstow
Shortstown
Lathbury
Newport Pagnell
Tickford End
North Crawley
Little Crawley
Bourne End
Wootton
Keeley Green
Kempston Hardwick
Wixams
Cotton End
Upper Shelton
Lower Shelton
Broad Green
Cranfield
Stewartby
Marston Moretaine
Marston Vale Millennium
Houghton Conquest
Wilstead
Haynes
Haynes Church End
Moulsoe
Tongwell
Willen
Milton Keynes
Milton Keynes Village
Broughton
Woolstone
Salford
Hulcote
Lidlington
Millbrook
Ampthill
Maulden
Clophill
Brogborough
Ridgmont
Woburn Sands
Aspley Guise
Aspley Heath
Husborne Crawley
Wavendon
Walton
Simpson
Bletchley
Fenny Stratford
Far Bletchley
Water Eaton
Bow Brickhill
Little Brickhill
Great Brickhill
Woburn
Woburn Abbey
Wild Animal Kingdom & Leisure Park
Eversholt
Steppingley
Flitwick
Flitton
Wrest Park
Silsoe
Greenfield
Pulloxhill
Westoning
Tingrith
Harlington
Sharpenhoe
Barton-le-Clay
Hexton
Higham Gobion
Potsgrove
Milton Bryan
Battlesden
Toddington
Toddington Services
Streatley
Upper Sundon
Lower Sundon
Chalton
CHILTERNS
CENTRAL BEDFORDSHIRE
Stoke Hammond
Soulbury
Heath and Reach
Hockliffe
Tebworth
Wingfield
Leighton Buzzard
Linslade
Eggington
Stanbridge
Tilsworth
Houghton Regis
Dunstable
Sundon Park
Limbury
Leagrave
Luton
Biscot
Stopsley
High Town
Round Green
Hart Hill
Farley Hill
Caddington
Wing
Burcott
Billington
Little Billington
Ledburn
Slapton
Eaton Bray
Totternhoe
Edlesborough
Northall
Whipsnade
Kensworth
Wingrave
Horton
Ivinghoe Aston
Slip End
Pepperstock
M1
A5
A6
A421
A428
A509
A4146
A505
A507
A4012
A5120

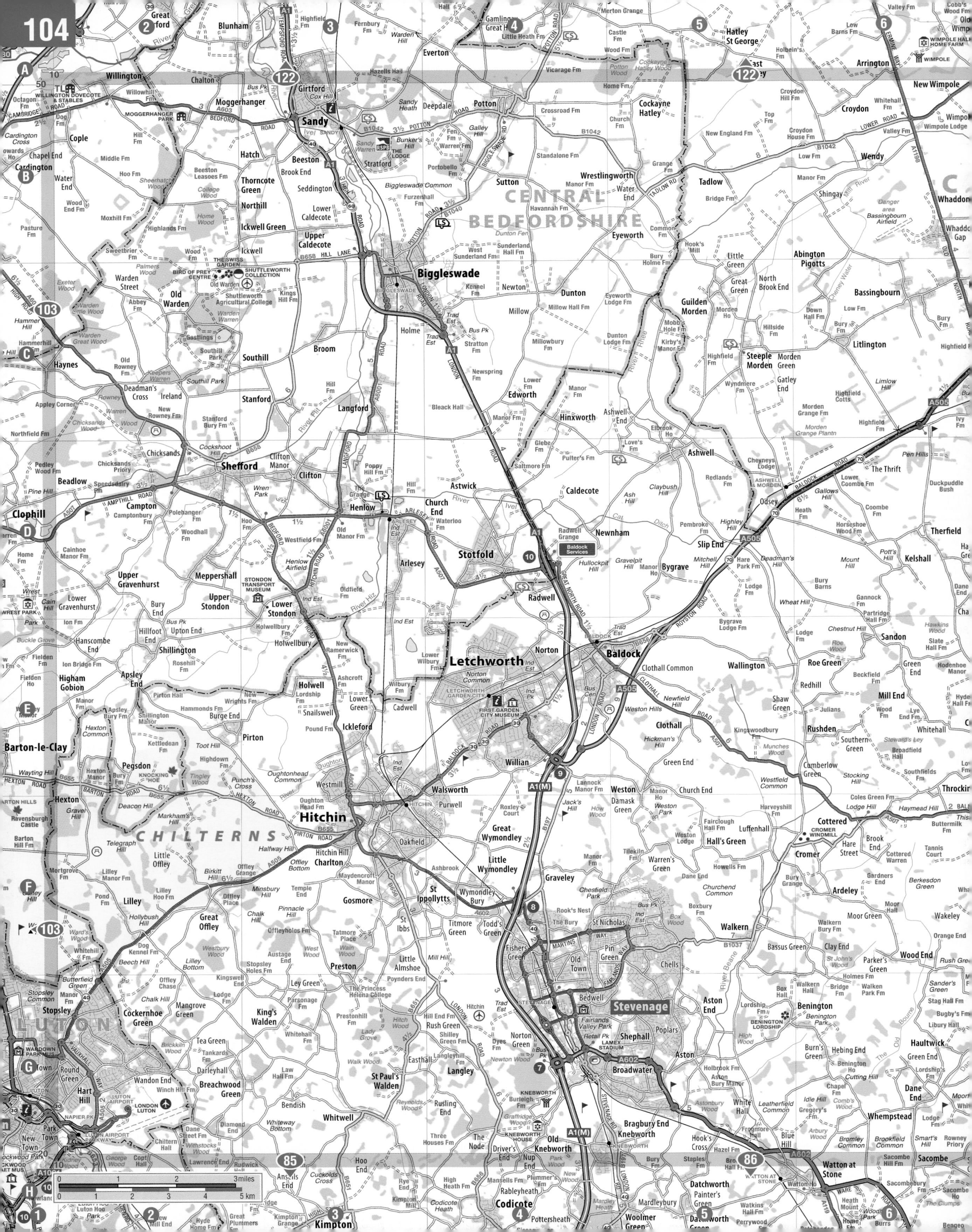
CENTRAL
BEDFORDSHIRE
CHILTERNS
LUTON
Blunham
Great Barford
Willington
Willington Dovecote & Stables
Moggerhanger
Moggerhanger Park
Chalton
Sandy
Girtford
Beeston
Everton
Potton
Deepdale
Sandy Heath
Gamlingay
Little Heath Fm
Hatley St George
East Hatley
Cockayne Hatley
Arrington
New Wimpole
Wimpole Hall Home Farm
Croydon
Wendy
Tadlow
Shingay
Whaddon
Abington Pigotts
Bassingbourn
Litlington
Steeple Morden
Guilden Morden
Wrestlingworth
Sutton
Stratford
Biggleswade Common
Biggleswade
Upper Caldecote
Lower Caldecote
Ickwell Green
Northill
Thorncote Green
Hatch
Seddington
Cople
Cardington
Old Warden
The Shuttleworth Collection
Shuttleworth Agricultural College
Southill
Broom
Holme
Dunton
Eyeworth
Newton
Millow
Edworth
Hinxworth
Ashwell
Ashwell End
Haynes
Ireland
Stanford
Langford
Chicksands
Shefford
Clifton
Campton
Clophill
Henlow
Arlesey
Church End
Astwick
Stotfold
Caldecote
Newnham
Radwell
Baldock Services
Bygrave
Slip End
Odsey
Therfield
Kelshall
Sandon
Upper Gravenhurst
Lower Gravenhurst
Meppershall
Upper Stondon
Lower Stondon
Stondon Transport Museum
Shillington
Apsley End
Higham Gobion
Holwell
Letchworth
Letchworth Garden City
First Garden City Museum
Norton
Baldock
Clothall Common
Clothall
Wallington
Roe Green
Rushden
Cumberlow Green
Barton-le-Clay
Hexton
Pegsdon
Pirton
Ickleford
Hitchin
Walsworth
Willian
Weston
Great Wymondley
Little Wymondley
Graveley
Cottered
Cromer
Ardeley
Walkern
Lilley
Great Offley
Little Offley
Charlton
Gosmore
St Ippollytts
St Ibbs
Preston
Stevenage
Old Town
Bedwell
Shephall
Broadwater
Aston
Aston End
Benington
Stopsley
Luton
London Luton Airport
Cockernhoe Green
King's Walden
St Paul's Walden
Langley
Knebworth
Knebworth House
Old Knebworth
Whitwell
Kimpton
Codicote
Datchworth
Watton at Stone
Whempstead
Sacombe
A1
A1(M)
A505
A507
A600
A602
A6001
B1042
B197
B655
B656
B658
103
104
122
85
86
0 1 2 3 miles
0 1 2 3 4 5 km

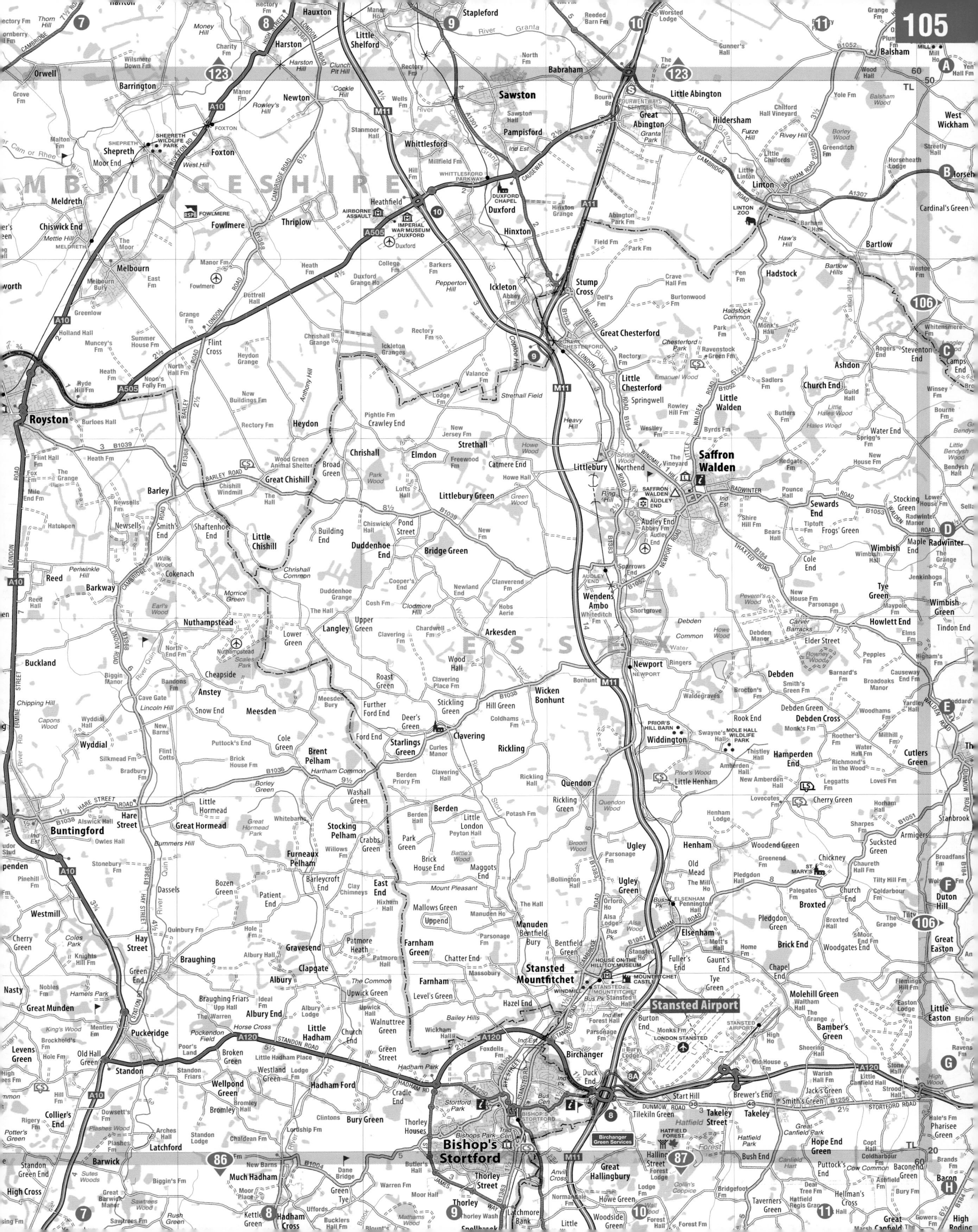
CAMBRIDGESHIRE
ESSEX
Orwell
Barrington
Harston
Hauxton
Little Shelford
Stapleford
Babraham
Balsham
Newton
Sawston
Pampisford
Little Abington
Great Abington
Hildersham
West Wickham
Shepreth
Foxton
Whittlesford
Linton
Meldreth
Fowlmere
Thriplow
Heathfield
Duxford
Hinxton
Bartlow
Chiswick End
Melbourn
Ickleton
Stump Cross
Hadstock
Great Chesterford
Ashdon
Little Chesterford
Springwell
Little Walden
Royston
Heydon
Crawley End
Strethall
Chrishall
Elmdon
Littlebury
Saffron Walden
Barley
Great Chishill
Littlebury Green
Audley End
Little Chishill
Duddenhoe End
Bridge Green
Wimbish
Radwinter
Reed
Barkway
Nuthampstead
Langley
Arkesden
Wendens Ambo
Newport
Buckland
Anstey
Meesden
Wicken Bonhunt
Debden
Clavering
Rickling
Widdington
Wyddial
Brent Pelham
Starlings Green
Quendon
Buntingford
Great Hormead
Stocking Pelham
Berden
Furneaux Pelham
Ugley
Henham
Chickney
Broxted
Manuden
Elsenham
Braughing
Farnham
Stansted Mountfitchet
Stansted Airport
Westmill
Puckeridge
Albury
Little Hadham
Birchanger
Standon
Bishop's Stortford
Takeley
Much Hadham
Great Hallingbury
Thorley
Barwick
High Cross
Great Easton
Little Easton
M11
A10
A505
A120

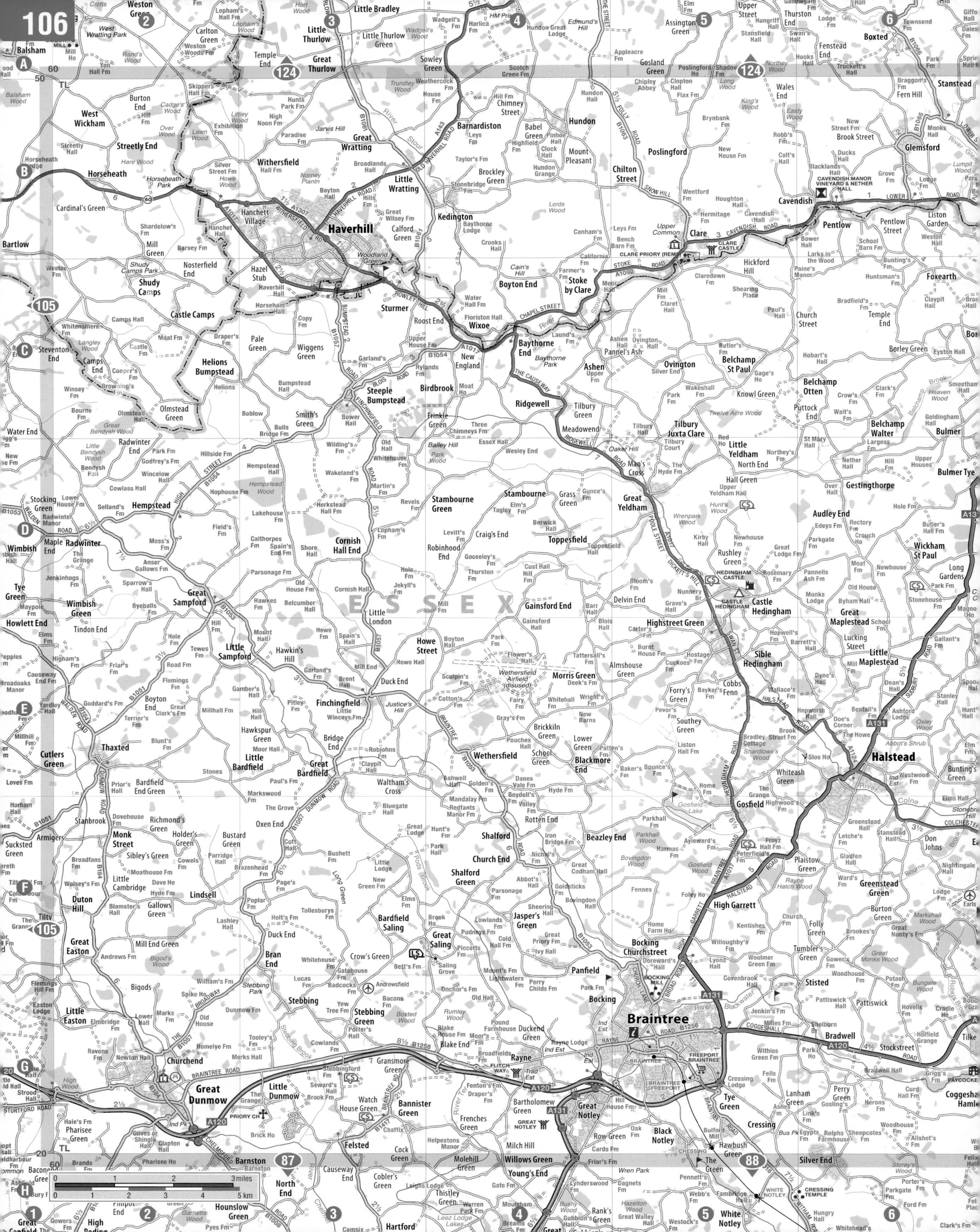
Balsham
Weston Green
Carlton Green
Little Thurlow
Great Thurlow
Little Bradley
Little Thurlow Green
Haverhill
Withersfield
Great Wratting
Little Wratting
Barnardiston
Kedington
Hundon
Poslingford
Chilton Street
Stansfield
Clare
Cavendish
Pentlow
Glemsford
Boxted
Stanstead
Foxearth
Liston
Cavendish Manor Vineyard & Nether Hall
Clare Priory (Rems)
Clare Castle
Upper Common
Stoke by Clare
Boyton End
Sturmer
Wixoe
Roost End
Baythorne End
Birdbrook
Ridgewell
Steeple Bumpstead
Helions Bumpstead
Castle Camps
Shudy Camps
Horseheath
West Wickham
Streetly End
Bartlow
Hempstead
Radwinter
Great Sampford
Little Sampford
Wimbish Green
Thaxted
Cutlers Green
Great Easton
Little Easton
Great Dunmow
Little Dunmow
Stebbing
Lindsell
Bardfield Saling
Great Saling
Great Bardfield
Finchingfield
Wethersfield
Shalford
Stambourne
Toppesfield
Great Yeldham
Little Yeldham
Tilbury Juxta Clare
Ovington
Belchamp St Paul
Belchamp Otten
Belchamp Walter
Gestingthorpe
Bulmer
Castle Hedingham
Sible Hedingham
Halstead
Gosfield
High Garrett
Braintree
Bocking
Bocking Churchstreet
Rayne
Great Notley
Black Notley
Cressing
Bradwell
Stisted
Coggeshall
Silver End
Felsted
Barnston
Great Maplestead
Little Maplestead
Wickham St Paul
ESSEX
A120
A131
A1017
A1307
B1054
B1057
B1053
B1256
124
105
87
88
0 1 2 3 miles
0 1 2 3 4 5 km

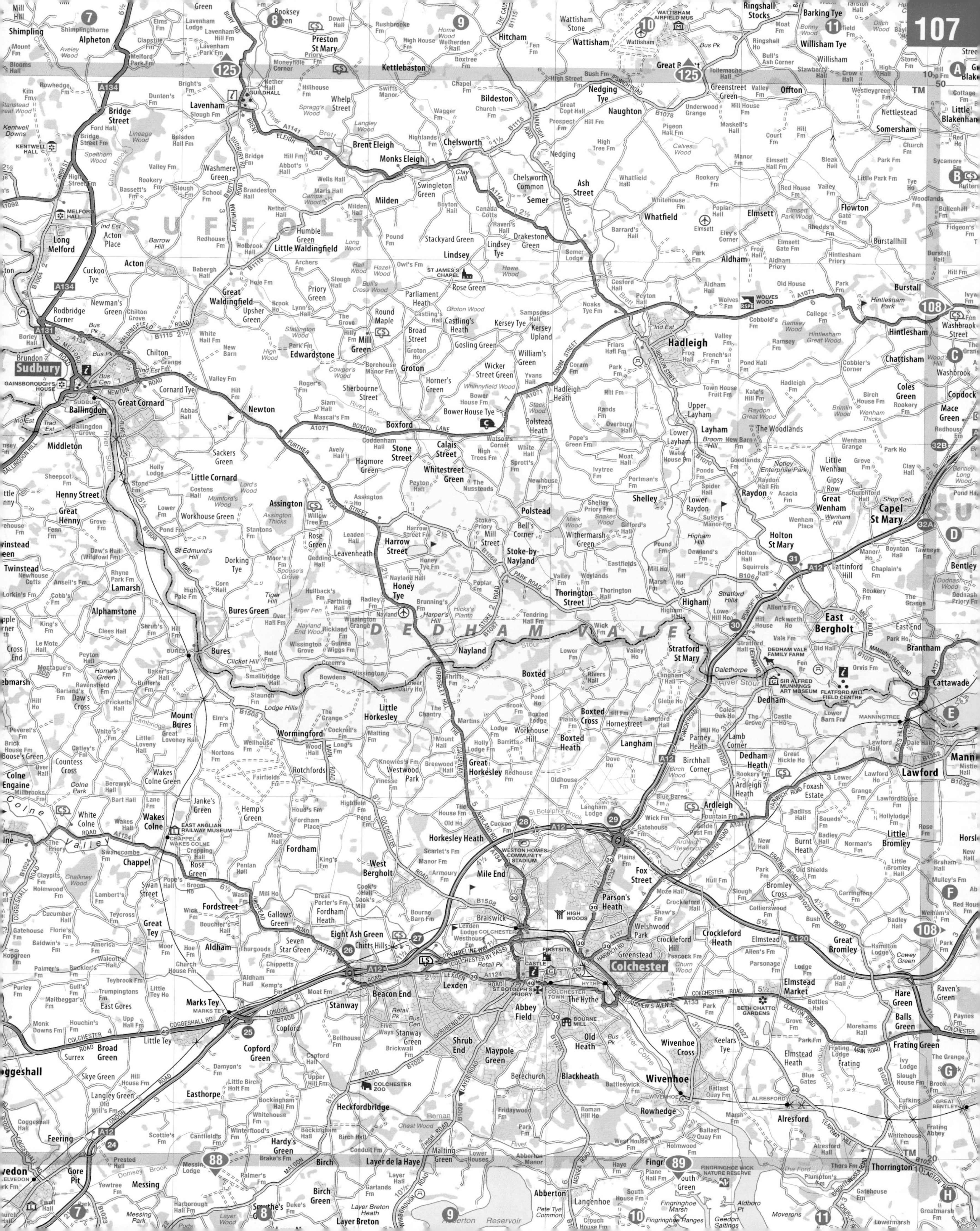
SUFFOLK
DEDHAM VALE
Shimpling
Alpheton
Preston St Mary
Kettlebaston
Hitcham
Wattisham Stone
Wattisham
WATTISHAM AIRFIELD MUS
Ringshall Stocks
Barking Tye
Willisham Tye
Willisham
Offton
Nedging Tye
Naughton
Bildeston
Lavenham
GUILDHALL
Bridge Street
Brent Eleigh
Monks Eleigh
Chelsworth
Nedging
Long Melford
MELFORD HALL
KENTWELL HALL
Acton
Milden
Swingleton Green
Chelsworth Common
Semer
Ash Street
Whatfield
Elmsett
Flowton
Somersham
Little Blakenham
Nettlestead
Burstall
Burstallhill
Little Waldingfield
Great Waldingfield
Lindsey
Lindsey Tye
Stackyard Green
Drakestone Green
ST JAMES'S CHAPEL
Aldham
Hintlesham
Chattisham
Washbrook
Copdock
Hadleigh
Kersey
Kersey Tye
Kersey Upland
Rose Green
Castling's Heath
Gosling Green
Groton
Edwardstone
Mill Green
Round Maple
Sudbury
GAINSBOROUGH'S HOUSE
Chilton
Ballingdon
Great Cornard
Cornard Tye
Newton
Boxford
Bower House Tye
Polstead Heath
Layham
Upper Layham
Lower Layham
Raydon
Great Wenham
Little Wenham
Capel St Mary
Holton St Mary
Middleton
Little Cornard
Sackers Green
Henny Street
Great Henny
Assington
Stone Street
Calais Street
Whitestreet Green
Polstead
Shelley
Lower Raydon
Harrow Street
Leavenheath
Stoke-by-Nayland
Withermarsh Green
Thorington Street
Higham
Twinstead
Lamarsh
Alphamstone
Bures Green
Honey Tye
Nayland
Bures
Boxted
Stratford St Mary
East Bergholt
Brantham
Cattawade
DEDHAM VALE FAMILY FARM
SIR ALFRED MUNNINGS ART MUSEUM
FLATFORD MILL FIELD CENTRE
Dedham
Mount Bures
Wormingford
Little Horkesley
Boxted Cross
Hornestreet
Langham
Boxted Heath
Great Horkesley
Dedham Heath
Lawford
Manningtree
Colne Engaine
White Colne
Wakes Colne
EAST ANGLIAN RAILWAY MUSEUM
Chappel
Fordham
Horkesley Heath
West Bergholt
Mile End
WESTON HOMES COMMUNITY STADIUM
Ardleigh
Little Bromley
Fox Street
Parson's Heath
Crockleford Heath
Great Bromley
Fordstreet
Great Tey
Aldham
Eight Ash Green
Braiswick
HIGH WOODS
Colchester
Greenstead
Elmstead
Elmstead Market
Marks Tey
Stanway
Lexden
Beacon End
Abbey Field
The Hythe
BETH CHATTO GARDENS
Hare Green
Balls Green
Frating Green
Frating
Little Tey
Copford
Copford Green
Shrub End
Maypole Green
Old Heath
Wivenhoe Cross
Wivenhoe
Coggeshall
Easthorpe
Heckfordbridge
COLCHESTER ZOO
Blackheath
Rowhedge
Alresford
Feering
Kelvedon
Messing
Birch
Layer de la Haye
Abberton
Fingringhoe
FINGRINGHOE WICK NATURE RESERVE
Thorrington
Layer Breton
Abberton Reservoir
Langenhoe
Great Bentley

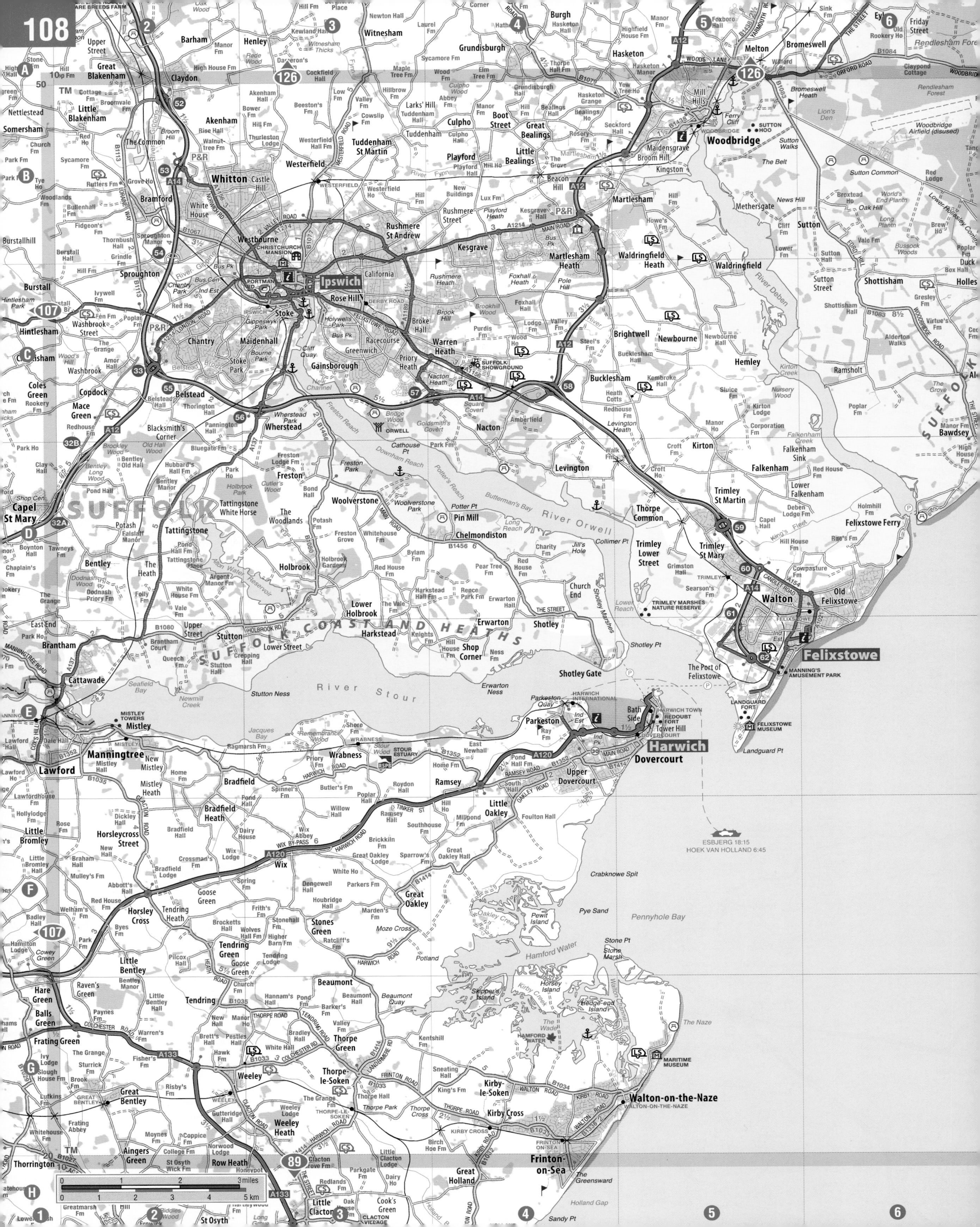
Barham
Henley
Witnesham
Grundisburgh
Burgh
Hasketon
Melton
Bromeswell
Friday Street
Great Blakenham
Claydon
Little Blakenham
Nettlestead
Somersham
Akenham
Westerfield
Tuddenham St Martin
Playford
Culpho
Boot Street
Great Bealings
Little Bealings
Woodbridge
Sutton Hoo
Woodbridge Airfield (disused)
Whitton
Bramford
Castle Hill
White House
Westbourne
Rushmere St Andrew
Kesgrave
Martlesham
Martlesham Heath
Waldringfield Heath
Waldringfield
Sutton
Sutton Street
Shottisham
Sproughton
Burstall
Ipswich
California
Rose Hill
Stoke
Chantry
Maidenhall
Gainsborough
Greenwich
Priory Heath
Warren Heath
Hintlesham
Washbrook
Copdock
Belstead
Brightwell
Newbourne
Bucklesham
Hemley
Ramsholt
Mace Green
Blacksmith's Corner
Wherstead
Nacton
Levington
Kirton
Falkenham
Bawdsey
SUFFOLK
Freston
Woolverstone
Pin Mill
Chelmondiston
River Orwell
Thorpe Common
Trimley St Martin
Trimley St Mary
Trimley Lower Street
Felixstowe Ferry
Capel St Mary
Tattingstone
Bentley
Holbrook
Shotley
Church End
Erwarton
Walton
Old Felixstowe
Felixstowe
Lower Holbrook
Harkstead
Brantham
Stutton
SUFFOLK COAST AND HEATHS
Shop Corner
Shotley Gate
The Port of Felixstowe
Cattawade
River Stour
Stutton Ness
Mistley
Manningtree
Lawford
Wrabness
Parkeston
Harwich
Dovercourt
Upper Dovercourt
Landguard Pt
Bradfield
Ramsey
Little Oakley
Mistley Heath
Bradfield Heath
Little Bromley
Horsleycross Street
Wix
ESBJERG 18:15
HOEK VAN HOLLAND 6:45
Great Oakley
Horsley Cross
Tendring Heath
Stones Green
Pennyhole Bay
Hamford Water
Tendring Green
Little Bentley
Beaumont
Hare Green
Balls Green
Tendring
Frating Green
Thorpe Green
Weeley
Thorpe-le-Soken
Kirby-le-Soken
Walton-on-the-Naze
Great Bentley
Weeley Heath
Kirby Cross
Frinton-on-Sea
Aingers Green
Row Heath
Thorrington
Great Holland
Little Clacton
St Osyth
The Naze
Holland Gap
0 1 2 3 miles
0 1 2 3 4 5 km

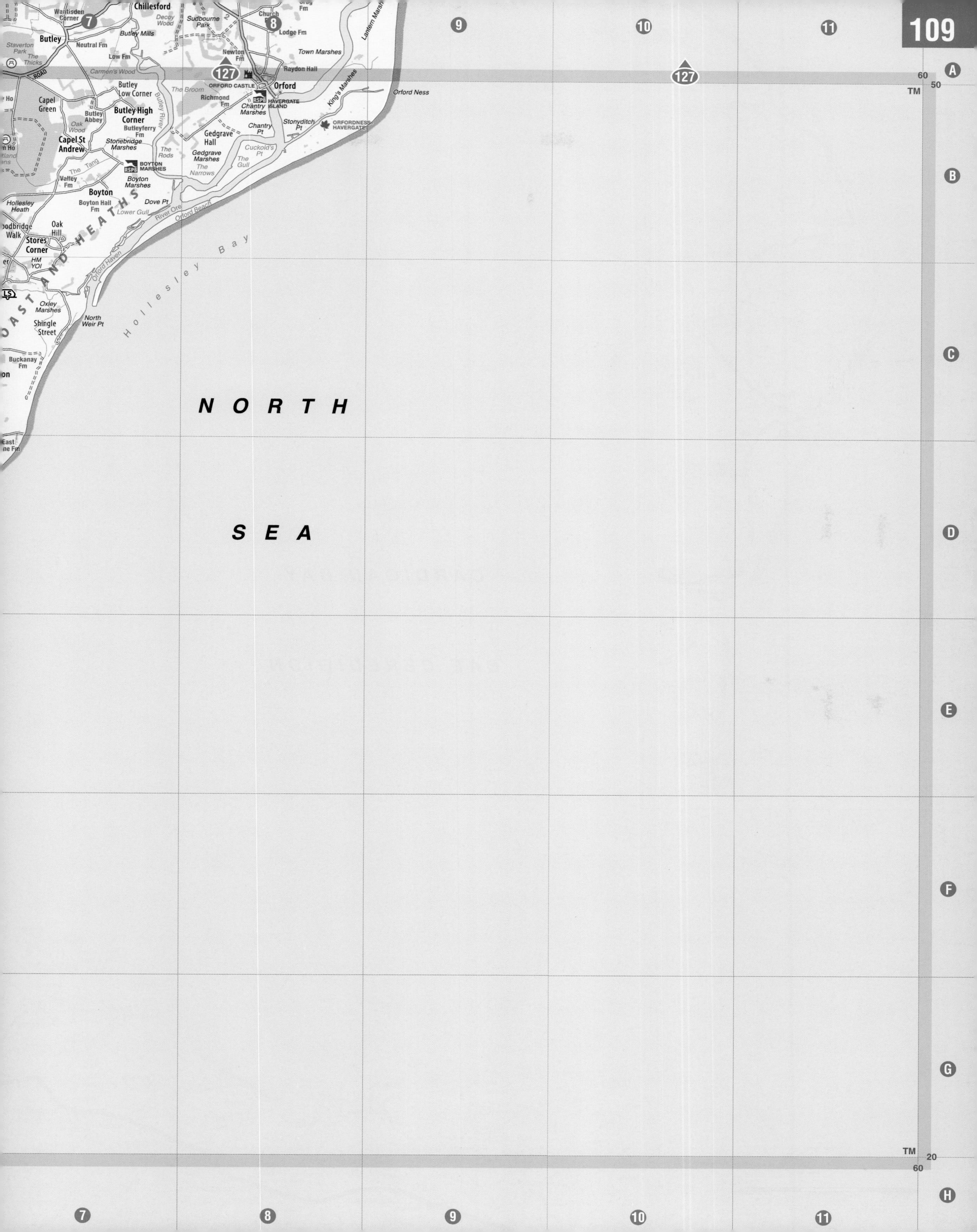
Chillesford
Wantisden Corner
Decoy Wood
Sudbourne Park
Church
Lodge Fm
Butley
Neutral Fm
Butley Mills
Staverton Park
The Thicks
Low Fm
Newton Fm
Town Marshes
Raydon Hall
Lantern Marsh
Carmen's Wood
127
ORFORD CASTLE
Orford
The Broom
Butley Low Corner
Capel Green
Richmond Fm
HAVERGATE ISLAND
Chantry Marshes
King's Marshes
Orford Ness
Butley High Corner
Butley Abbey
Butley River
Butleyferry Fm
Oak Wood
Capel St Andrew
Stonebridge Marshes
Gedgrave Hall
Chantry Pt
Stonydicth Pt
ORFORDNESS HAVERGATE
Cuckold's Pt
The Rods
Gedgrave Marshes
The Narrows
The Gull
The Tang
BOYTON MARSHES
Valley Fm
Boyton Marshes
Boyton
Boyton Hall Fm
Dove Pt
Hollesley Heath
Lower Gull
River Ore
Orford Beach
Oak Hill
Stores Corner
HM YOI
Orford Haven
Hollesley Bay
Oxley Marshes
Shingle Street
North Weir Pt
Buckanay Fm
NORTH
SEA
TM
50
60
20
A
B
C
D
E
F
G
H
7
8
9
10
11

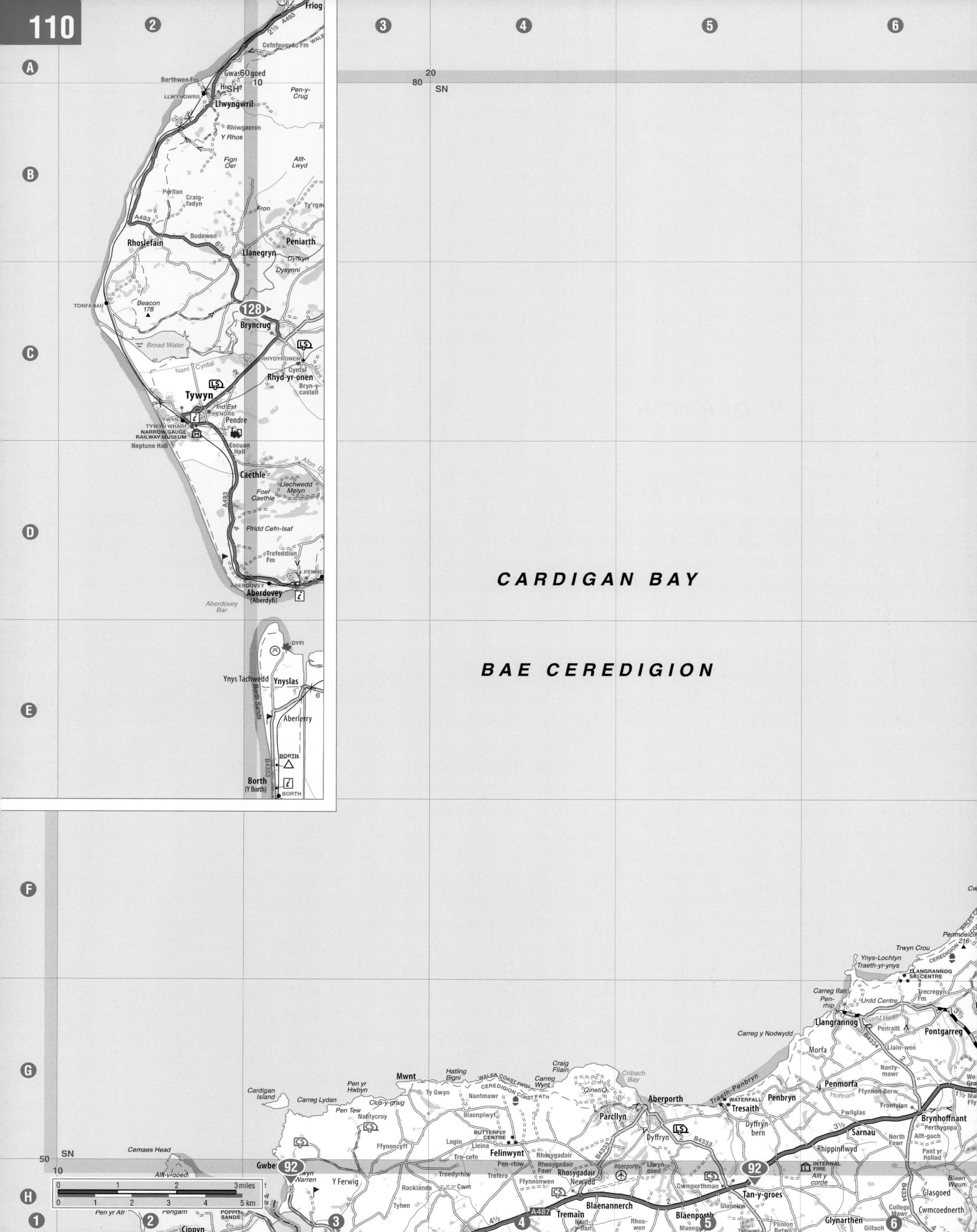
CARDIGAN BAY
BAE CEREDIGION
Friog
Llwyngwril
Rhoslefain
Llanegryn
Peniarth
Bryncrug
Tywyn
Rhyd-yr-onen
Pendre
Caethle
Aberdovey
(Aberdyfi)
Ynyslas
Ynys Tachwedd
Borth Sands
Aberleri
Borth
(Y Borth)
Mwnt
Aberporth
Parcllyn
Tresaith
Penbryn
Llangrannog
Pontgarreg
Penmorfa
Brynhoffnant
Sarnau
Felinwynt
Rhosygadair Newydd
Blaenannerch
Tremain
Tan-y-groes
Blaenporth
Glynarthen
Gwbert
Y Ferwig
Cardigan Island
Cemaes Head
Carreg y Nodwydd
Ynys-Lochtyn
Traeth-yr-ynys
Trwyn Crou
Aberdovey Bar
Broad Water
Beacon 178
128
92
A493
A487
B4333
B4334
B4353
SN
SH

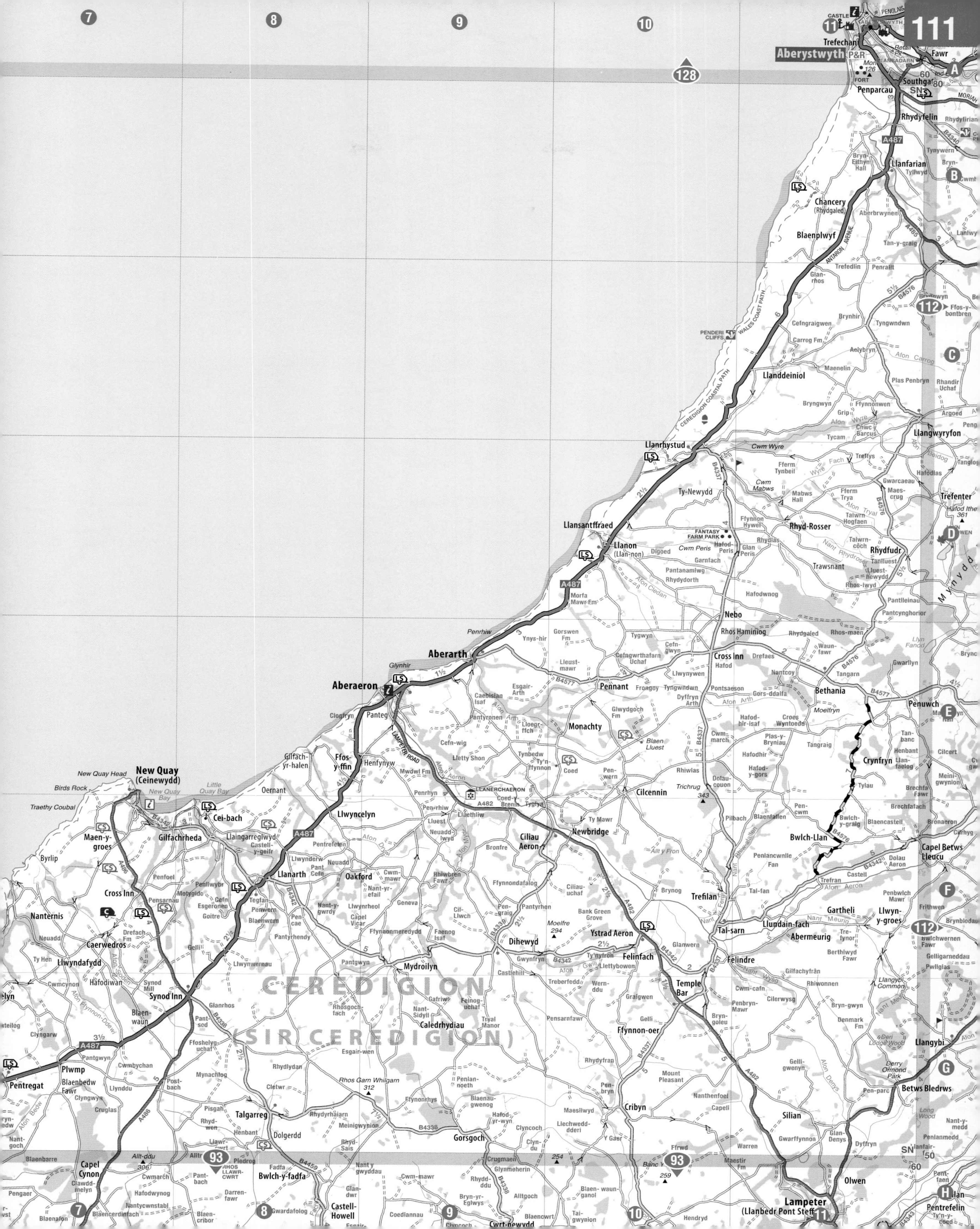
Aberystwyth
Trefechan
Penparcau
Rhydyfelin
Llanfarian
Chancery (Rhydgaled)
Blaenplwyf
Penderi Cliffs
Wales Coast Path
Ceredigion Coastal Path
Llanddeiniol
Llanrhystud
Cwm Wyre
Ty-Newydd
Llansantffraed
Llanon (Llan-non)
Fantasy Farm Park
Rhyd-Rosser
Rhydfudr
Trawsnant
Llangwyryfon
Trefenter
Nebo
Rhos Haminiog
Penrhiw
Aberarth
Aberaeron
Cross Inn
Pennant
Bethania
Penuwch
Monachty
Crynfryn
Cilcennin
Llanerchaeron
New Quay (Ceinewydd)
New Quay Head
Birds Rock
Traethy Coubal
Little Quay Bay
Cei-bach
Oernant
Ffos-y-ffin
Henfynyw
Llwyncelyn
Gilfachrheda
Maen-y-groes
Byrlip
Cross Inn
Nanternis
Llanarth
Oakford
Ciliau Aeron
Newbridge
Bwlch-Llan
Capel Betws Lleucu
Trefilan
Tal-sarn
Llundain-fach
Abermeurig
Gartheli
Llwyn-y-groes
Caerwedros
Llwyndafydd
Synod Inn
Dihewyd
Mydroilyn
Ystrad Aeron
Felinfach
Temple Bar
Felindre
CEREDIGION
(SIR CEREDIGION)
Caledrhydiau
Ffynnon-oer
Llangybi
Betws Bledrws
Plwmp
Pentregat
Talgarreg
Gorsgoch
Cribyn
Silian
Capel Cynon
Bwlch-y-fadfa
Castell-Howell
Lampeter (Llanbedr Pont Steffan)
Olwen
A487
A482
A485
A486
B4337
B4342
B4576
B4577
B4338
B4459
128
112
93

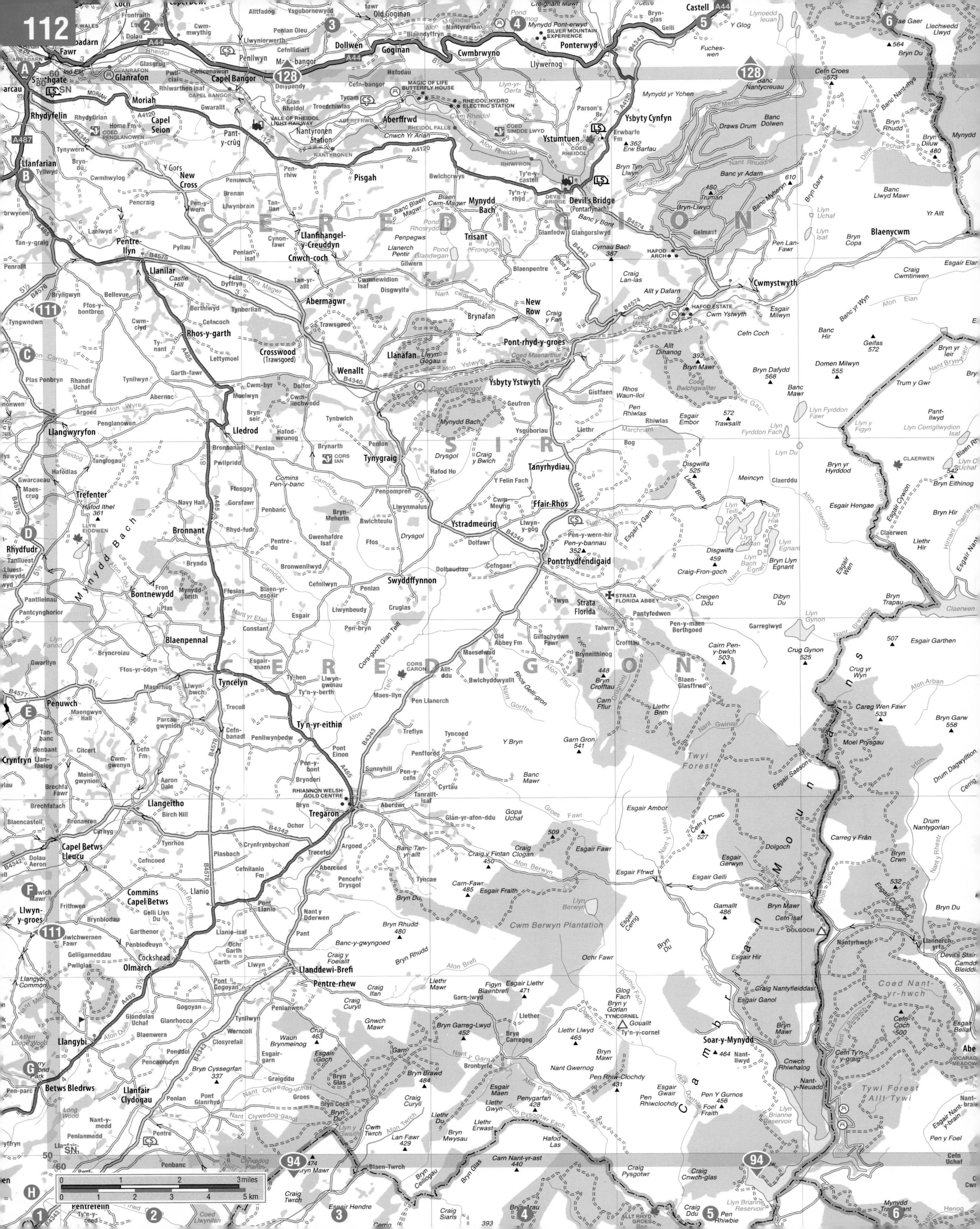

Castell
A44
Llynoedd Ieuan
Y Glog
Lechwedd Llwyd
Bryn Du
Old Goginan
Ysguborneydd
Alltfadog
Penlan Oleu
Cwm-mwythig
Llwyniorwerth
Cefnllidiart
Dollwen
Goginan
Cwmbrwyno
Blaendyffryn
Nantyrarian
Mynydd Pont-erwyd
SILVER MOUNTAIN EXPERIENCE
Ponterwyd
Fuches-wen
Llywernog
Bryn-glas
Gelli
Glasgrug
Penllwyn
Pwll-clai
Pwllcenawon
Capel Bangor
Glanrafon
Southgate
Fawr
Moriah
Rhydyfelin
Capel Seion
Home Fm
COED PENGLANOWEN
Tynywern
Llanfarian
Tyllwyd
Rhiwarthen Isaf
Gwarallt
Pant-y-crûg
Nantyronen Station
VALE OF RHEIDOL LIGHT RAILWAY
Aberffrwd
Troedrhiwlas
Glan Rheidol
Tycam
Cefn-bangor
Dolypandy
Hafodau
MAGIC OF LIFE BUTTERFLY HOUSE
RHEIDOL HYDRO ELECTRIC STATION
Cwm Rheidol Res
RHEIDOL FALLS
Cwnch Yr Arian
NANTYRONEN
COED SIMDDE LWYD
Ystumtuen
COED RHEIDOL
Afon Rheidol
RHIWFRON
Ty'n-y-castell
Parson's Br
Ysbyty Cynfyn
Erwbarfe Fm
Erw Barfau
Mynydd yr Ychen
Banc Nantycreuau
Cefn Croes
Draws Drum
Banc Dolwen
Bryn Rhudd
Bryn Diluw
Banc Nant-rhys
Bryn Tyn-Llwyn
Banc yr Adarn
Truman
Bryn-Llwyd
Banc Myherin
Bryn Garw
Banc Llwyd Mawr
Yr Allt
Llyn Uchaf
Llyn Isaf
Bryn Copa
Blaenycwm
Gelmast
Pen Lan-Fawr
HAFOD ARCH
Cwmystwyth
Craig Cwmtinwen
Esgair Elan
Y Gors
New Cross
Penuwch
Brenan
Llwynbrain
Pen-y-wern
Tan-llan
Pen-rhiw
Pisgah
Bwlchcrwys
Ty'n-y-rhyd
Devil's Bridge (Pontarfynach)
Banc y Bont
Glanfedw
Glangorslwyd
Cyrnau Bach
Mynydd Bach
Blaen Cwm-Magwr
Banc Blaen Magwr
Penpegws
Llanerch Pentir
Trisant
Llyn Frongoch
Pond Glandwgan
Rhosrydd
Gilwern
Blaenpentre
Rhos y Gell
Craig Lan-las
Allt y Dafarn
HAFOD ESTATE
Cwm Ystwyth
Llanfihangel-y-Creuddyn
Cnwch-coch
Cynon-fawr
Penlan-isaf
Pencraig
Lanlwyd
Pentre-llyn
Llanilar
Castle Hill
Felin Dyffryn
Pyllau
Tan-y-graig
Penrallt
Tan-yr-allt
Abermagwr
Cwmnewidion Isaf
Disgwylfa
Nant cwm-newydion
Brynafan
New Row
Craig y Fan
Bryngwyn
Ffos-y-bontbren
Bellevue
Cwm-clyd
Berthlwyd
Cefncoch
Tynberllan
Trawsgoed
Rhos-y-garth
Tyngwndwn
Ty-nant
Crosswood (Trawsgoed)
Llanafan
Llwyn Gogau
Pont-rhyd-y-groes
Coed Maenarthur
Afon Ystwyth
Allt Dihanog
Bryn Mawr
Coed Bwlchgwallter
Cefn Coch
Banc Hir
Geifas
Banc yr Wyn
Afon Elan
Cefn Milwyn
Esgair Milwyn
Lettymoel
Garth-fawr
Plas Penbryn
Rhandir Uchaf
Tynllwyn
Abernac
Cwm-byr
Moelwyn
Dolfor
Wenallt
Cwm-llechwedd
Coed Craigyrogof
Ysbyty Ystwyth
Gistfaen
Rhos Waun-lloi
Bryn Dafydd
Domen Milwyn
Banc Mawr
Trum y Gwr
Pant-llwyd
Llyn Cerrigllwydion Isaf
Argoed
Afon Wyre
Penglanowen
Llangwyryfon
Bryn-seir
Lledrod
Hafod-weunog
Tynbwlch
Mynydd Bach
Geufron
Ysguboriau
Pen Rhiwlas
Rhiwlas
Esgair Embor
Trawsallt
Llyn Fyrddon Fawr
Llyn Fyrddon Fach
Marchnant
Bog
Llethr
Beidog
Tanglogau
Hafodlas
Bronbanadl
Pwllpridd
Penlan
Brynarth
CORS IAN
Tynygraig
Drysgol
Craig y Bwlch
Hafod Ho
Tanyrhydiau
Disgwilfa
Llethr Brith
Meincyn
Claerddu
Bryn yr Hyrddod
CLAERWEN
Bryn Eithinog
Gwarcaeau
Maes-crug
Trefenter
Hafod Ithel
LLYN EIDDWEN
Flosgoy
Gorsfawr
Navy Hall
Comins Pen-y-banc
Camddwr Fach
Penpompren
Bryn-Meherin
Bwlchteulu
Llwynmalus
Y Felin Fach
Cwm-Meurig
Ffair-Rhos
Ystradmeurig
Esgair Hengae
Llyn Teifi
Bryn Hir
Esgair Cywion
Mynydd Bach
Bronnant
Rhyd-fudr
Gwenhafdre Isaf
Ffos
Drysgol
Lllwyn-y-gog
Dolfawr
Pen-y-wern-hir
Pen-y-bannau
Esgair y Gam
Llyn y Gorlan
Llyn Bach
Llyn Egnant
Bryn Llyn Egnant
Claerwen
Llethr Hir
Esgair Wen
Rhydfudr
Tanllwyst
Lluest-newydd
Bryncla
Pentre-du
Bronwenllwyd
Dolbeudiau
Cefngaer
Pontrhydfendigaid
Craig-Fron-goch
Afon Du
Bontnewydd
Fron
Mynydd-brith
Ffoslas
Blaen-yr-esgair
Cefnllwyn
Penlan
Swyddffynnon
Pantllleinau
Pantcynghorior
Plas
Nant yr Efail
Esgair
Llwynbeudy
Cruglas
STRATA FLORIDA ABBEY
Strata Florida
Twyn
Creigen Ddu
Dibyn Du
Bryn Trapau
Pantyfedwen
Constant
Pen-bryn
Cors-goch Glan Teifi
Old Abbey Fm
Gilfachydwn Fawr
Talwrn
Pen-y-maen Berthgoed
Garreglwyd
Llyn Gynon
Esgair Garthen
Blaenpennal
Bryncroiau
Esgair-maen
Crofftau
Bryneithinog
Cairn Pen-y-bwlch
Crug Gynon
Crug yr Wyn
Llyn Fanod
Gwarllyn
Ffos-yr-odyn
Tyncelyn
Llwyn-bwch
Ty-hen
Llwyn-gwinau
Ty'n-y-berth
CORS CARON
Maeselwad
Allt-ddu
Bwlchyddwyallt
Rhos Gelli-gron
Crofftau
Blaen-Glasffrwd
Afon Arban
Penuwch
Maesrhug
Maes-llyn
Pen Llanerch
Carn Fflur
Llethr Brith
Careg Wen Fawr
Bryn Garw
Maengwyn Hall
Parcau-gwynion
Trecoll
Ty'n-yr-eithin
Nant Gorffen
Nant Gwinau
Moel Prysgau
Tan-banc
Henbant
Cilcert
Cefn-banadl
Penllwynbedw
Treflyn
Tyncoed
Y Bryn
Garn Gron
Twyi Forest
Esgair Saeson
Drum Dagwyllton
Crynfryn
Llan-faelog
Cefn Fm
Cwm-gwenyn
Pont Einon
Penffordd
Pen-y-bont
Sunnyhill
Pen-y-cefn
Meini-gwynion
Aeron Dale
Brynderi
Banc Mawr
Brechfa Fawr
RHIANNON WELSH GOLD CENTRE
Tanrallt-isaf
Cyrtau
Brechfatach
Llangeitho
Birch Hill
Bryn
Tregaron
Aberdwr
Gopa Uchaf
Esgair Ambor
Blaencastell
Bronaeron
Ochor
Glan-yr-afon-ddu
Groes Fawr
Cefn y Cnwc
Drum Nantygorlan
Cilrhyg
Crynfrynbychan
Argoed
509
Carreg y Frân
Capel Betws Lleucu
Tynrhos
Plasbach
Trecefel
Banc Tan-yr-allt
Craig y Fintan
Craig Clogan
Esgair Fawr
Nant y Maen
Dolgoch
Bryn Crwn
Dolau Aeron
Cefncoed
Cefnllanio Fm
Abercoed
Afon Berwyn
Esgair Ffrwd
Esgair Gelli
Esgair Gerwyn
Commins Capel Betws
Pencefn Drysgol
Tyncae
Carn-Fawr
Esgair Fraith
Llyn Berwyn
Frithwen
Gelli Llyn Du
Llanio
Pont Llanio
Bryn Du
Gamallt
Bryn Mawr
Cefn Isaf
Llwyn-y-groes
Brynblodau
Nant y Dderwen
Bryn Rhudd
Cwm Berwyn Plantation
Esgair Cerrig
Bryn Du
DOLGOCH
Nantyrhwch
Bwlchwernen Fawr
Garthenor
Llanio-isaf
Pant
Banc-y-gwyngoed
Lannerch-yrfa
Devil's Stair
Gelligameddau
Penblodeuyn
Ochr Garth
Craig y Foelallt
Bryn Rhudd
Ochr Fawr
Esgair Hir
Pwllglas
Cockshead
Olmarch
Garth
Llwyn
Llanddewi-Brefi
Afon Brefi
Llangybi Common
Pont Gogoyan
Pentre-rhew
Craig Ifan
Llethr Mawr
Figyn Blaenbrefi
Esgair Llethr
Doethie Fach
Craig Nantyfleiddast
Esgair Ganol
Coed Nant-yr-hwch
Gogoyan
Garn-lwyd
Glog Fach
Bryn y Gorlan
TYNCORNEL
Goualt
Ty'n-y-cornel
Glandulas Uchaf
Glanrhocca
Craig Curyll
Penlanwen
Gnwch Mawr
Llether
Blaenwern
Tynllwyn
Werncoli
Crug
Waun Brynmeinog
Bryn Garreg-Lwyd
Llethr Llwyd
Soar-y-Mynydd
Nant-llwyd
Cefn Coch
Llangybi
Closyrefail
Esgair Goch
Garn
Bryn Carregog
Bryn Mawr
Cwnch Rhiwhalog
Cefn Ty'n-y-graig
Pencaerodyn
Penddol
Esgair-garn
Bryn Glas
Bronbyrfe
Nant y Garn
Nant Gwernog
Bryn Mawr
Pen Rhiw-Clochdy
VICARAGE MEADOW
Bryn Cyssegrfan
Graigddu
Bryn Brawd
Esgair Maen
Esgair Gwair
Nant-y-Neuadd
Tywi Forest Allt Tywi
Betws Bledrws
Llanfair Clydogau
Groes
Nant Clywedog-uchaf
Pont Glanrhyd
Penlan
Bryn Coch
Bryn Du
Craig Curyll
Penygarfan
Llethr Gwinau
Pen Rhiwclochdy
Pen Y Gurnos
Foel Fraith
Afon Pysgotwr Fawr
Afon Pysgotwr Fach
Nant Clywedog-ganol
Long Wood
Nant-y-medd
Penlanmedd
Pentre
Llyn y Gwaith
Cwm Twrch
Afon Twrch
Lan Fawr
Llethr Du
Bryn Mwysau
Llethr Erwast
Hafod Las
Llyn Brianne Reservoir
Esgair Nant-y-brain
Pen y Foel
Cefn Uchaf
Penbanc
Clywedog Bach
Blaen-Twrch
Carn Nant-yr-ast
Craig Pysgotwr
Craig Cwnch-glas
Bryn Glas
Bryn Celliogau
Craig Twrch
Esgair Hendre
Craig Siarls
ALLT RHYD Y GROES
Craig Ddu
Pen Rhiwbie
Llyn Brianne Reservoir
Mynydd Trawsnant
Henog
Pentrefelin
Ty'n-y-coed
Coed Llwynllan
C E R E D I G I O N
S I R
C E R E D I G I O N
C a m b r i a n   M o u n t a i n s
A44
A487
A485
A4120
B4340
B4575
B4576
B4577
B4578
B4342
B4343
B4574
A
B
C
D
E
F
G
H
1
2
3
4
5
6
111
128
94
0 1 2 3 miles
0 1 2 3 4 5 km

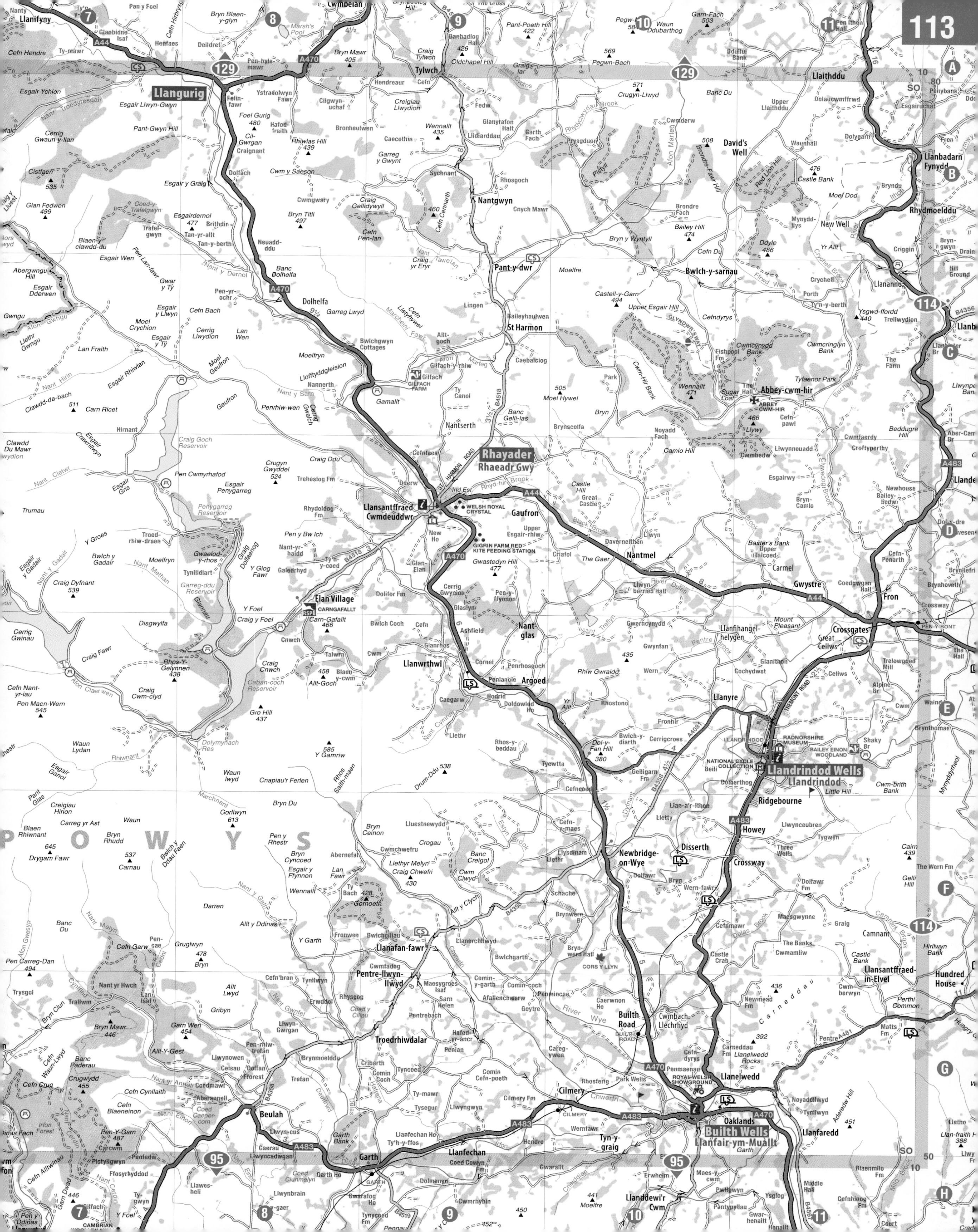
Llanifyny
Llangurig
Cwmbelan
Tylwch
Llaithddu
Pant-y-dwr
St Harmon
David's Well
Llanbadarn Fynydd
Rhydmoelddu
New Well
Bwlch-y-sarnau
Llananno
Abbey-cwm-hir
Nantgwyn
Dolhelfa
Gamallt
Nantserth
Rhayader
Rhaeadr Gwy
Llansantffraed Cwmdeuddwr
Gaufron
Elan Village
Nantmel
Gwystre
Fron
Crossgates
Nant-glas
Llanwrthwl
Argoed
Llanyre
Llandrindod Wells
Llandrindod
Ridgebourne
Howey
Disserth
Crossway
Newbridge-on-Wye
Llanafan-fawr
Pentre-llwyn-llwyd
Troedrhiwdalar
Builth Road
Cwmbach Llechrhyd
Llanelwedd
Beulah
Cilmery
Builth Wells
Llanfair-ym-Muallt
Garth
Llanfechan
Tyn-y-graig
Llanfaredd
Llansantffraed-in-Elvel
Hundred House
Llanddewi'r Cwm
P O W Y S
Craig Goch Reservoir
Penygarreg Reservoir
Garreg-ddu Reservoir
Caban-coch Reservoir
Dolymynach Res
River Wye
Gigrin Farm Red Kite Feeding Station
Welsh Royal Crystal
Radnorshire Museum
National Cycle Collection
Royal Welsh Showground
Cors y Llyn
Gilfach Farm
Carngafallt
A44
A470
A483
A4081
B4518
B4358
B4356
129
114
95
7
8
9
10
11
A
B
C
D
E
F
G
H
SO

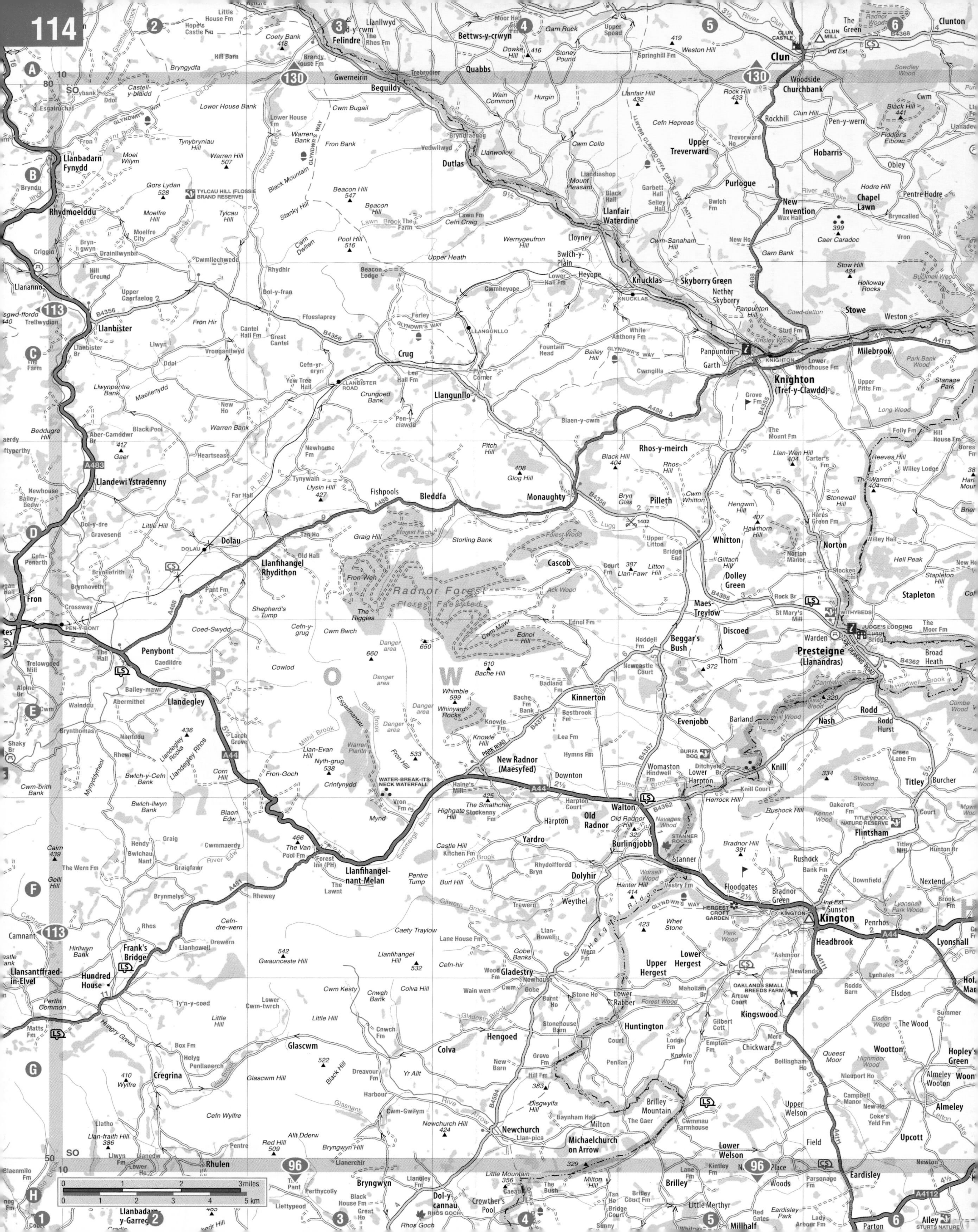
Clun
Knighton (Tref-y-Clawdd)
Presteigne (Llanandras)
Kington
New Radnor (Maesyfed)
Radnor Forest
Fforest Faesyfed
POWYS
Llanbister
Llandewi Ystradenny
Penybont
Llandegley
Bleddfa
Knucklas
Newchurch
Gladestry
Huntington
Eardisley
Glyndŵr's Way
Offa's Dyke Path
0 1 2 3 miles
0 1 2 3 4 5 km

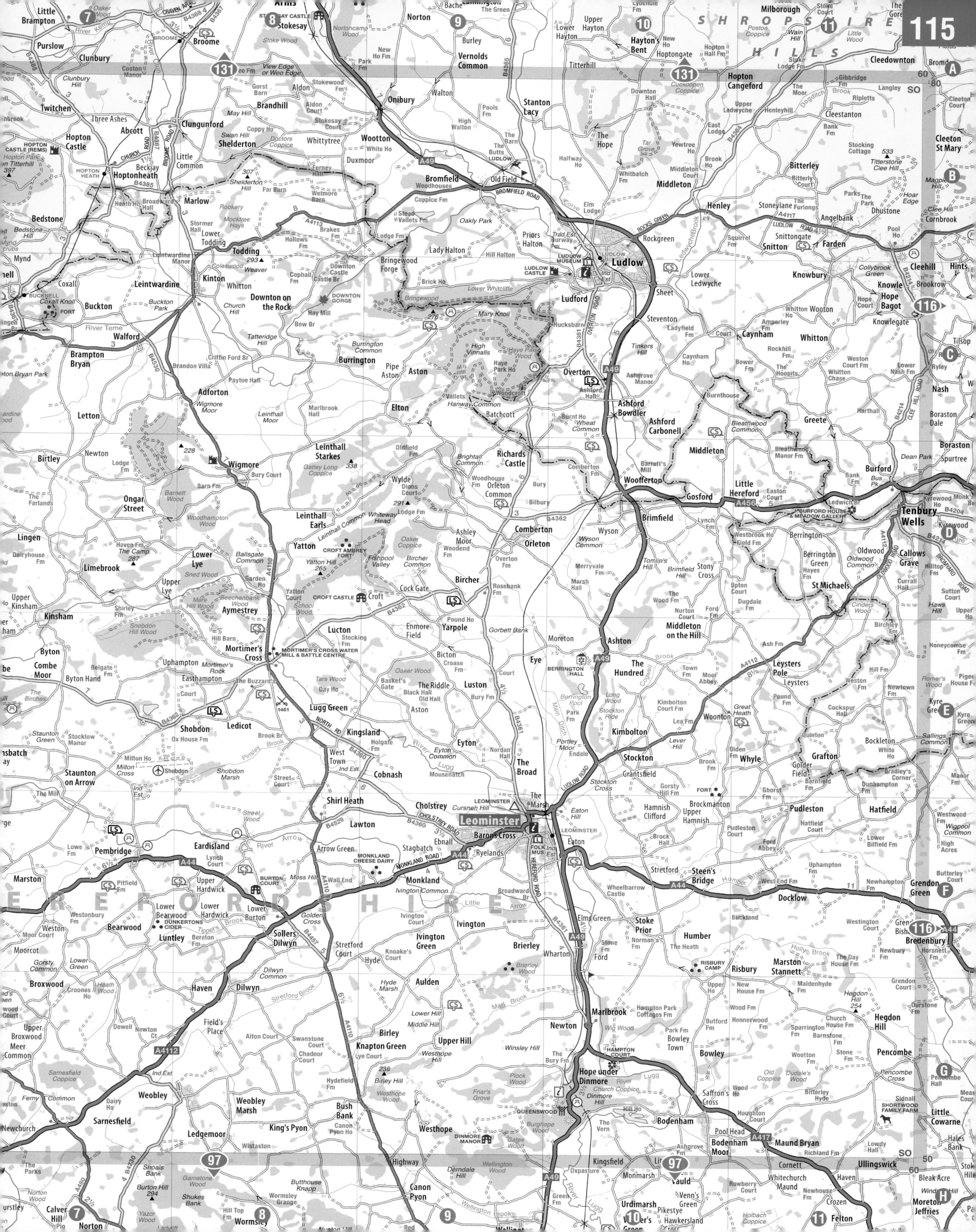
SHROPSHIRE HILLS
HEREFORDSHIRE
Little Brampton
Purslow
Clunbury
Twitchen
Abcott
Hopton Castle
Hoptonheath
Clungunford
Shelderton
Little Common
Broome
Stokesay
Stokesay Castle
Norton
Onibury
Wootton
Whittytree
Duxmoor
Bromfield
Vernolds Common
Walton
Stanton Lacy
Old Field
Upper Hayton
Lower Hayton
Hayton's Bent
Hoptongate
Titterhill
Hopton Cangeford
Milborough
Cleedownton
Cleestanton
Cleeton St Mary
The Hope
Middleton
Bitterley
Henley
Stoneylane
Angelbank
Dhustone
Cornbrook
Rockgreen
Snitton
Farden
Ludlow
Ludford
Sheet
Lower Ledwyche
Knowbury
Cleehill
Hints
Knowle
Hope Bagot
Caynham
Whitton
Steventon
Knowlegate
Nash
Bedstone
Marlow
Lower Todding
Todding
Leintwardine
Kinton
Whitton
Downton on the Rock
Bringewood Forge
Lady Halton
Priors Halton
Coxall
Buckton
Walford
Brampton Bryan
Burrington
Pipe Aston
Aston
Overton
Adforton
Letton
Elton
Ashford Bowdler
Ashford Carbonell
Greete
Boraston
Middleton
Burford
Tenbury Wells
Birtley
Wigmore
Leinthall Starkes
Richards Castle
Woofferton
Little Hereford
Gosford
Brimfield
Ongar Street
Leinthall Earls
Lingen
Yatton
Comberton
Orleton
Wyson
Berrington
Oldwood
Callows Grave
Lower Lye
Limebrook
Upper Lye
Kinsham
Aymestrey
Bircher
Croft Castle
Cock Gate
St Michaels
Lucton
Yarpole
Moreton
Ashton
Middleton on the Hill
Mortimer's Cross
Byton
Combe Moor
Byton Hand
Uphampton
Eye
The Hundred
Leysters Pole
Leysters
Shobdon
Ledicot
Lugg Green
Kingsland
Luston
Eyton
Kimbolton
Woonton
Staunton on Arrow
West Town
Cobnash
The Broad
Stockton
Whyle
Grafton
Shirl Heath
Cholstrey
Lawton
Leominster
Barons Cross
The Marsh
Eaton
Hamnish Clifford
Brockmanton
Pudleston
Hatfield
Pembridge
Eardisland
Arrow Green
Stagbatch
Monkland
Ebnall
Stretford
Steen's Bridge
Docklow
Grendon Green
Marston
Lower Bearwood
Bearwood
Luntley
Lower Hardwick
Lower Burton
Sollers Dilwyn
Stretford Court
Ivington
Ivington Green
Brierley
Wharton
Stoke Prior
Humber
Risbury
Marston Stannett
Bredenbury
Broxwood
Haven
Dilwyn
Aulden
Marlbrook
Hegdon Hill
Field's Place
Birley
Knapton Green
Upper Hill
Newton
Bowley
Pencombe
Weobley
Weobley Marsh
Sarnesfield
Ledgemoor
King's Pyon
Bush Bank
Westhope
Hope under Dinmore
Bodenham
Bodenham Moor
Maund Bryan
Little Cowarne
Canon Pyon
Kingsfield
Vauld
Ullingswick
Urdimarsh
Felton
Moreton Jeffries
A49
A44
A4110
A4112
A4113
A456
A4117
A417
B4361
B4362
B4385
B4529
B4360
B4214
B4457
B4230

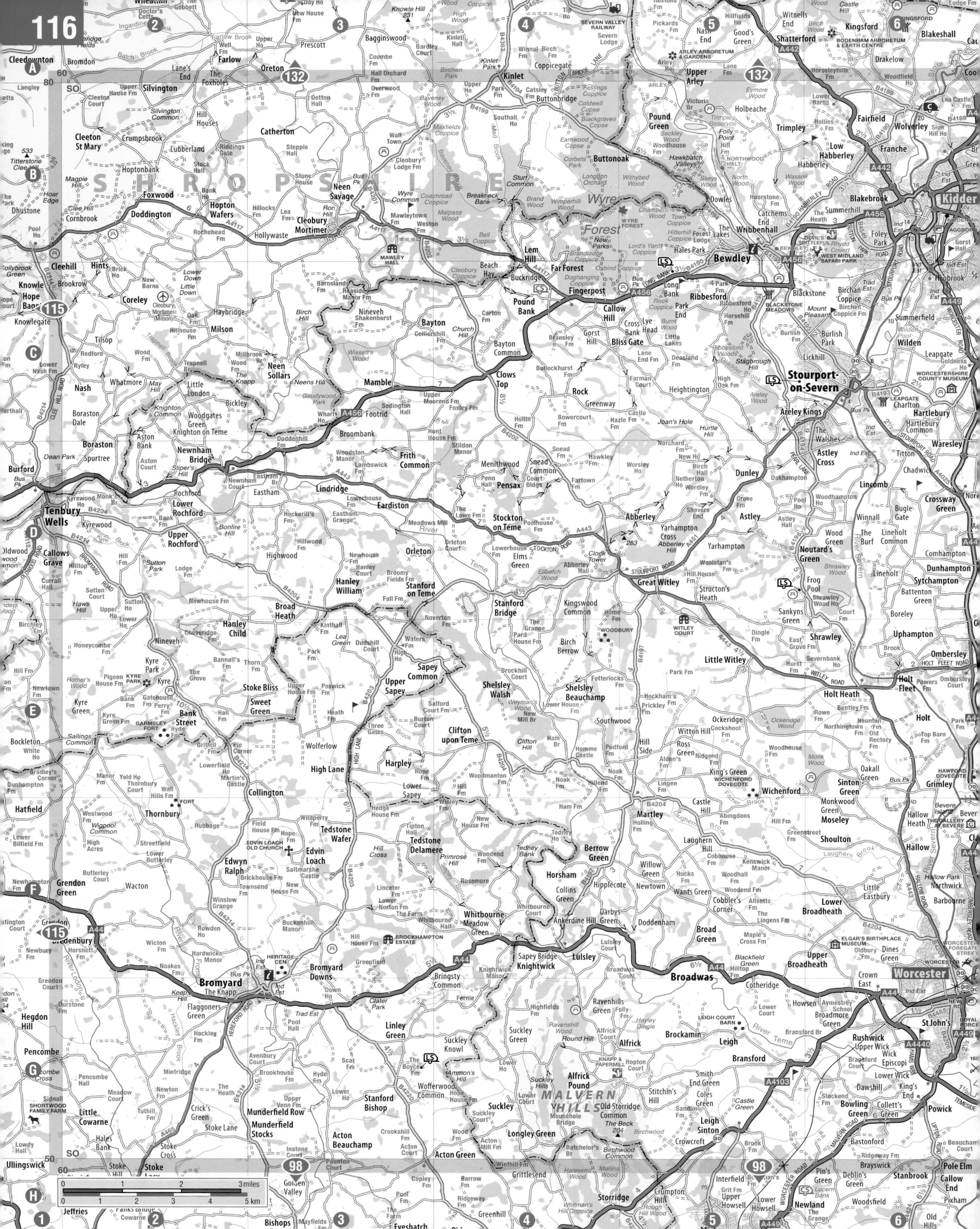
SHROPSHIRE
Cleobury Mortimer
Kinlet
Bewdley
Kidderminster
Stourport-on-Severn
Tenbury Wells
Wyre Forest
Far Forest
Callow Hill
Bliss Gate
Clows Top
Mamble
Bayton
Neen Savage
Neen Sollars
Milson
Coreley
Cleehill
Hopton Wafers
Doddington
Foxwood
Farlow
Oreton
Silvington
Catherton
Buttonoak
Upper Arley
Shatterford
Kingsford
Wolverley
Hartlebury
Areley Kings
Astley
Astley Cross
Dunley
Abberley
Great Witley
Stockton on Teme
Pensax
Lindridge
Eardiston
Newnham Bridge
Boraston
Burford
Orleton
Stanford on Teme
Stanford Bridge
Hanley William
Hanley Child
Kyre Green
Upper Sapey
Sapey Common
Shelsley Walsh
Shelsley Beauchamp
Clifton upon Teme
Little Witley
Holt Heath
Holt Fleet
Ombersley
Shrawley
Wichenford
Martley
Hallow
Grimley
Worcester
Broadwas
Lulsley
Knightwick
Bromyard
Bromyard Downs
Tedstone Wafer
Tedstone Delamere
Edvin Loach
Edwyn Ralph
Thornbury
Collington
Whitbourne
Alfrick
Leigh
Bransford
Suckley
Longley Green
Acton Green
Acton Beauchamp
Stanford Bishop
Munderfield Row
Little Cowarne
Pencombe
Grendon Green
Malvern Hills
Powick
Bowling Green
St John's
Rushwick
Lower Broadheath
Upper Broadheath
Bishops Frome
Storridge
Grittlesend
Newland
Callow End
Stanbrook
Kingsford
ARLEY ARBORETUM & GARDENS
BODENHAM ARBORETUM & EARTH CENTRE
SEVERN VALLEY RAILWAY
WEST MIDLAND SAFARI PARK
WORCESTERSHIRE COUNTY MUSEUM
WITLEY COURT
BROCKHAMPTON ESTATE
ELGAR'S BIRTHPLACE MUSEUM
LEIGH COURT BARN
SHORTWOOD FAMILY FARM
132
115
98
0 1 2 3 miles
0 1 2 3 4 5 km

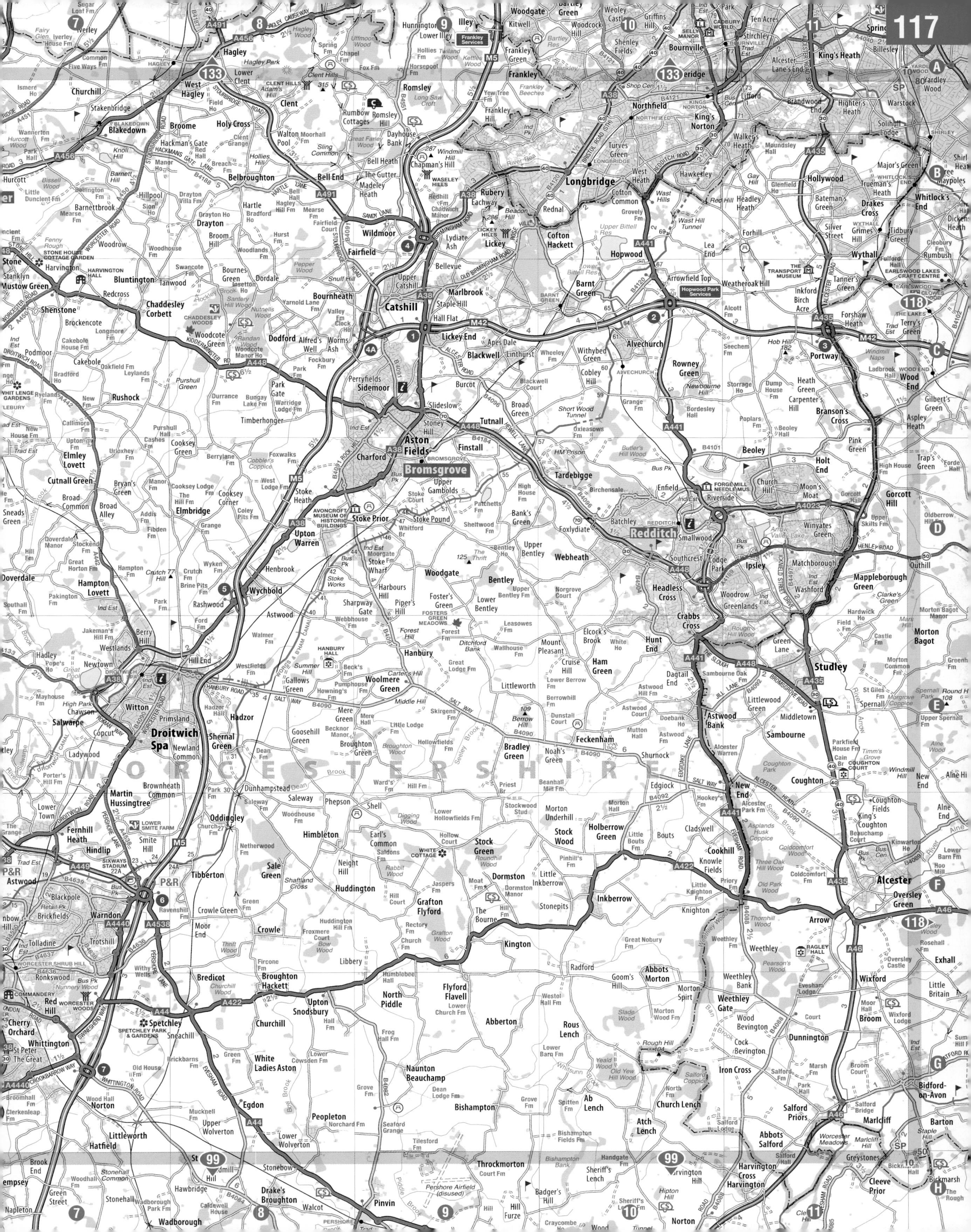
WORCESTERSHIRE
Bromsgrove
Redditch
Droitwich Spa
Alcester
Studley
Longbridge
Northfield
Bournville
Kings Norton
Hagley
West Hagley
Blakedown
Belbroughton
Catshill
Sidemoor
Aston Fields
Charford
Alvechurch
Hopwood
Barnt Green
Cofton Hackett
Rubery
Lickey
Blackwell
Tardebigge
Wychbold
Hanbury
Feckenham
Inkberrow
Upton Snodsbury
Spetchley
Whittington
Warndon
Hartlebury
Chaddesley Corbett
Rushock
Elmbridge
Hampton Lovett
Hindlip
Tibberton
Oddingley
Crowle
Huddington
Grafton Flyford
Kington
Flyford Flavell
North Piddle
Abberton
Bishampton
Throckmorton
Pinvin
Abbots Morton
Weethley Gate
Dunnington
Salford Priors
Abbots Salford
Bidford-on-Avon
Harvington
Coughton
Sambourne
Mappleborough Green
Matchborough
Winyates Green
Hollywood
Wythall
Portway
Wood End
Beoley
Holt End
Headless Cross
Crabbs Cross
Astwood Bank
Webheath
Bentley
Stoke Prior
Upton Warren
Romsley
Clent
Frankley
Illey
Hunnington
M5
M42
A38
A441
A435
A448
A422
A44
A46
133
118
99

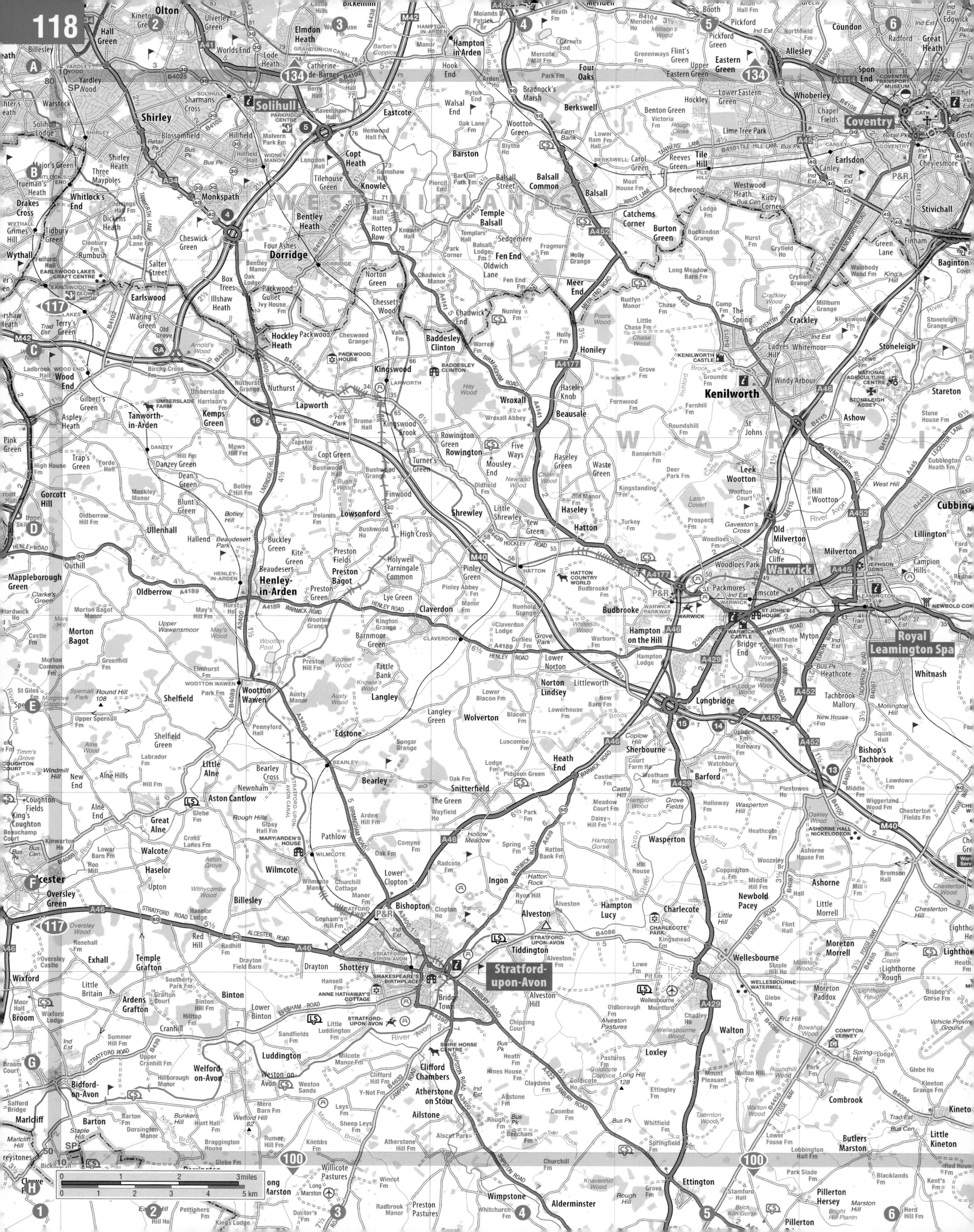
Olton
Hall Green
Elmdon Heath
Catherine-de-Barnes
Hampton in Arden
Solihull
Shirley
Blossomfield
Monkspath
Knowle
Copt Heath
Eastcote
Barston
Berkswell
Balsall Common
Balsall
Temple Balsall
Burton Green
Allesley
Coventry
Coventry Transport Museum
Whoberley
Chapel Fields
Earlsdon
Canley
Cheylesmore
Stivichall
Finham
Baginton
Westwood Heath
Tile Hill
Lime Tree Park
Eastern Green
Pickford Green
Four Oaks
Bentley Heath
Dorridge
Four Ashes
Cheswick Green
Tidbury Green
Wythall
Earlswood
Earlswood Lakes Craft Centre
Hockley Heath
Packwood
Packwood House
Baddesley Clinton
Kingswood
Lapworth
Chadwick End
Fen End
Meer End
Honiley
Kenilworth
Kenilworth Castle
Crackley
Stoneleigh
Stoneleigh Abbey
National Agriculture Centre
Ashow
Leek Wootton
Hill Wootton
Old Milverton
Milverton
Warwick
Warwick Castle
Royal Leamington Spa
Lillington
Cubbington
Whitnash
Tachbrook Mallory
Bishop's Tachbrook
Heathcote
Myton
Emscote
Packmores
Budbrooke
Hampton on the Hill
Hatton
Hatton Country World
Haseley
Haseley Knob
Beausale
Wroxall
Rowington
Shrewley
Claverdon
Lowsonford
Preston Bagot
Henley-in-Arden
Beaudesert
Tanworth-in-Arden
Umberslade Farm
Ullenhall
Oldberrow
Mappleborough Green
Morton Bagot
Wootton Wawen
Shelfield
Langley
Edstone
Norton Lindsey
Wolverton
Longbridge
Barford
Sherbourne
Snitterfield
Bearley
Aston Cantlow
Great Alne
Little Alne
Mary Arden's House
Wilmcote
Pathlow
Alcester
Oversley Green
Exhall
Temple Grafton
Ardens Grafton
Binton
Wixford
Broom
Bidford-on-Avon
Marlcliff
Barton
Welford-on-Avon
Luddington
Weston-on-Avon
Clifford Chambers
Atherstone on Stour
Ailstone
Stratford-upon-Avon
Shakespeare's Birthplace
Anne Hathaway's Cottage
Shottery
Drayton
Bishopton
Tiddington
Alveston
Charlecote
Charlecote Park
Hampton Lucy
Wasperton
Wellesbourne
Wellesbourne Watermill
Walton
Loxley
Ettington
Alderminster
Wimpstone
Newbold Pacey
Ashorne
Ashorne Hall Nickelodeon
Moreton Morrell
Moreton Paddox
Lighthorne
Compton Verney
Combrook
Butlers Marston
Kineton
Pillerton Hersey
Long Marston
Preston Pastures
Willicote Pastures
Shire Horse Centre
WEST MIDLANDS
WARWICK
M40
M42
A46
A452
A429
A3400
A4189
A4177
0 1 2 3 miles
0 1 2 3 4 5 km

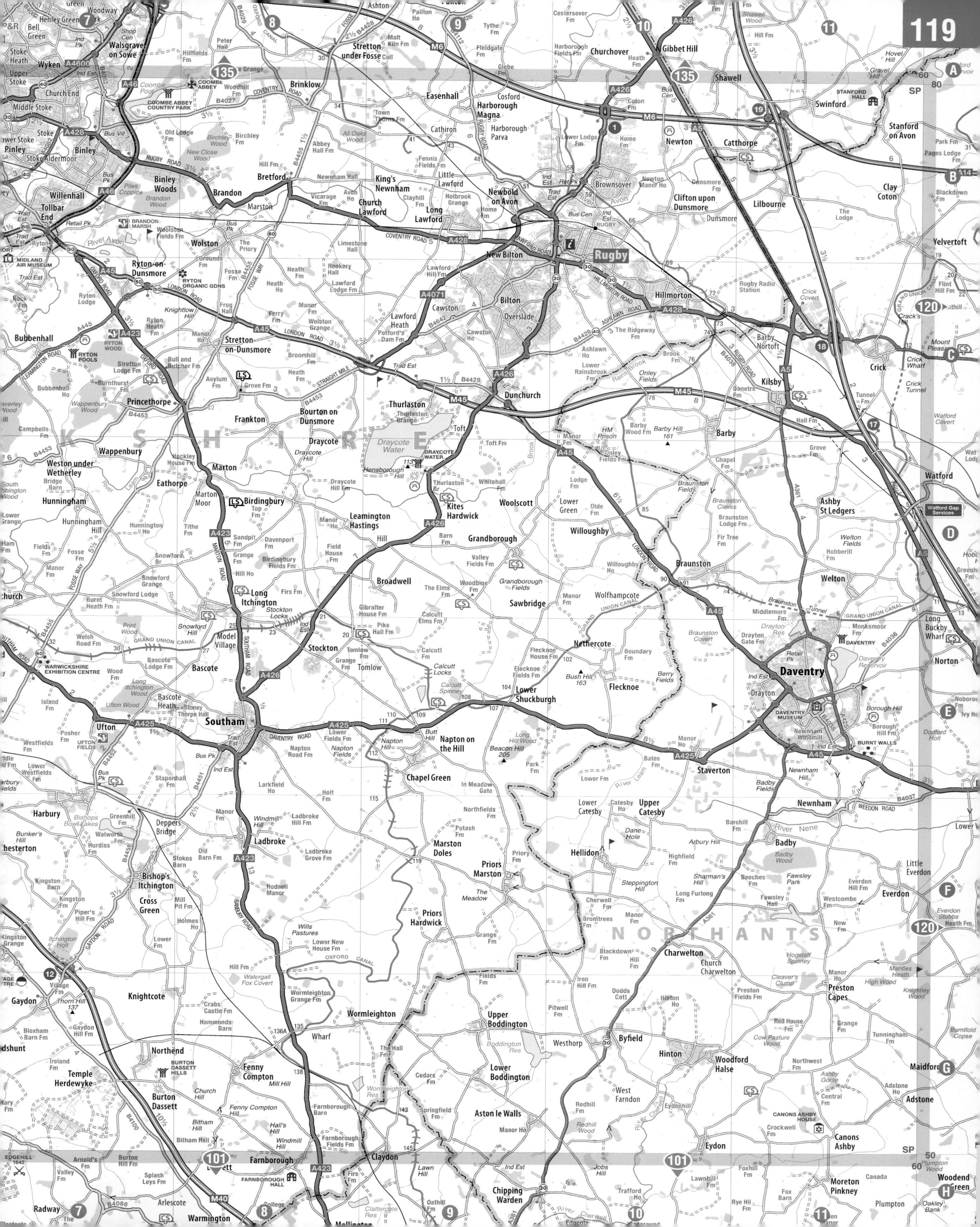

Henley Green
Woodway
Bell Green
Walsgrave on Sowe
Ashton
Pailton Ho
Cestersover Fm
Wyken
Stoke Heath
Upper Stoke
Peter Hall
Stretton under Fosse
Tythe Fm
Harborough Fields Fm
Churchover
Gibbet Hill
Heath Fm
Shawell
Coombe Abbey
COOMBE ABBEY COUNTRY PARK
Woodhill Fm
Brinklow
Easenhall
Cosford
Harborough Magna
Coton Fm
Swinford
STANFORD HALL
Church End
Middle Stoke
Stoke
Pinley
Binley
Stoke Aldermoor
Old Lodge Fm
Birchley Wood
Birchley Fm
Abbey Hall Fm
All Oaks Wood
Cathiron
Harborough Parva
Lower Lodge Fm
Home Fm
Newton
Catthorpe
Stanford on Avon
Park Fm
Pages Lodge Fm
New Close Wood
Hill Fm
Fennis Fields Fm
Little Lawford
Binley Woods
Willenhall
Tollbar End
Brandon
Bretford
Newnham Hall
King's Newnham
Newbold on Avon
Brownsover
Newton Manor Ho
Clifton upon Dunsmore
Dunsmore Fm
Lilbourne
Clay Coton
Blackdown Fm
Brandon Wood
Piles Coppice
Marston
Vicarage Fm
Avon Ho
Church Lawford
Clayhill Fm
Long Lawford
Holbrook Grange
Home Fm
Dunsmore
The Lodge
BRANDON MARSH
Woolston Fields Fm
Wolston
The Priory
River Avon
Limestone Hall
COVENTRY ROAD
New Bilton
Rugby
Yelvertoft
MIDLAND AIR MUSEUM
Ryton-on-Dunsmore
Grounds Fm
Fosse Fm
Heath Fm
Rookery Hall
Lawford Hill Fm
Hillmorton
Rugby Radio Station
Crick Covert
Flint Hill Fm
RYTON ORGANIC GDNS
Heath Ho
Lawford Lodge Fm
Bilton
Overslade
Cawston
Lawford Heath
Ryton Lodge
Rock Fm
Knightlow Hill
Frog Hall
Ferry Fm
Manor Fm
Wolston Grange
Potford's Dam Fm
Cawston Ho
The Ridgeway Fm
Ashlawn Ho
Barby Nortoft
Crick's Hill
Bubbenhall
Ryton Heath Fm
Manor Ho
Stretton-on-Dunsmore
Broomhill Fm
Lower Rainsbrook Fm
Brook Fm
Rains Brook
Mount Pleasant
Crick Wharf
RYTON WOOD
RYTON POOLS
Stretton Lodge Fm
Bull and Butcher Fm
Heath Fm
Trad Est
Dunchurch
Onley Fields
Kilsby
Danetre Fm
Crick
Crick Tunnel
Bubbenhall Ho
Burnthurst Fm
Asylum Fm
Grove Fm
Tunnel Fm
Princethorpe
Wappenbury Wood
Frankton
Bourton on Dunsmore
Thurlaston
Thurlaston Grange
Toft
Barby Wood Fm
Barby Hill 161
HM Prison
Manor Fm
Barby
Hall Fm
Watford Covert
Campbells Fm
Draycote
Draycote Water
Toft Fm
Onley Fields Fm
Grove Fm
Wappenbury
Hockley House Fm
Draycote Hill
DRAYCOTE WATER
Chapel Fm
Weston under Wetherley
Marton
Hensborough Hill
Whitehall Fm
Watford
Bridge Barn
Eathorpe
Draycote Hill Fm
Thurlaston Br
Braunston Fields
Braunston Claves
Ashby St Ledgers
Watford Gap Services
Hunningham
Marton Moor
Birdingbury
Top Fm
Kites Hardwick
Woolscott
Lower Green
Olde Fm
Lodge Fm
Braunston Lodge Fm
Hunningham Hill
Hunnington Ho
Tithe Fm
Manor Ho
Leamington Hastings
Hill
Grandborough
Willoughby
Fir Tree Fm
Welton Fields
Hobberill Fm
Fields Fm
Fosse Fm
Sandpit Fm
Davenport Fm
Barn Fm
Manor Fm
Snowford Br
Grange Fm
Birdingbury Fields Fm
Field House Fm
Valley Fields Fm
Willoughby Ho
Braunston
Welton
Hill Ho
Snowford Grange
Broadwell
Grandborough Fields
Woodbine Fm
The Elms Fm
Sawbridge
Manor Fm
Wolfhampcote
Long Itchington
Firs Fm
Snowford Lodge
Burnt Heath Fm
Stockton Locks
Gibralter House Fm
Calcutt Elms Fm
Middlemore Fm
Braunston Tunnel
GRAND UNION CANAL
Long Buckby Wharf
Print Wood
Snowford Hill
Model Village
Pike Hall Fm
Braunston Covert
Drayton Res
Monksmoor Fm
Welsh Road Fm
Stockton
Tomlow Fm
Calcutt Fm
Nethercote
Boundary Fm
Drayton Gate Fm
DAVENTRY
Daventry Reservoir
WARWICKSHIRE EXHIBITION CENTRE
Bascote Lodge Fm
Bascote
Grange Fm
Tomlow
Calcutt Locks
Flecknoe House Fm
Flecknoe Fields Fm
Bush Hill 163
Berry Fields
Retail Pk
Daventry
Norton
Wood Fm
Long Itchington Wood
Calcutt Spinney
Lower Shuckburgh
Flecknoe
Ind Est
Drayton
Island Fm
Ulton Wood
Bascote Heath
Stoney Thorpe Hall
Borough Hill
DAVENTRY MUSEUM
Newnham Windmill
Ufton
Southam
Butt Hill
Napton on the Hill
Long Hill Wood
Borough Hill Fm
Dodford Holt
Posher Fm
UFTON FIELDS
Westfields Fm
DAVENTRY ROAD
Lower Fields Fm
Napton Hill
Napton Fields
Napton Road Fm
Beacon Hill 205
Park Fm
Manor Ho
Bates Fm
Staverton
BURNT WALLS
Lower Westfields Fm
Bus Pk
Ind Est
Stapenhall Fm
Larkfield Ho
Chapel Green
In Meadow Gate
Lower Fm
Newnham Hill
Badby Fields
Holt Fm
Newnham
WEEDON ROAD
Harbury
Greenhill Fm
Deppers Bridge
Manor Fm
Windmill Hill
Ladbroke Hill Fm
Northfields Fm
Lower Catesby
Catesby Ho
Upper Catesby
Dane Hole
Barehill Fm
River Nene
Lower
Bishops Bowl Lakes
Walworth Fm
Ladbroke
Potash Fm
Marston Doles
Arbury Hill
Badby
Bunker's Hill
Chesterton
Hurdiss Fm
Old Barn Fm
Ladbroke Grove Fm
Priors Marston
Priory Fm
Hellidon
Highfield Fm
Badby Wood
Stokes Barn
Sharman's Hill
Beeches Fm
Fawsley Park
Little Everdon
Kingston Barn
Bishop's Itchington
Hodnell Manor
The Meadow
Steppington Hill
Long Furlong Fm
Fawsley Hall
Everdon Hill Fm
Everdon
Kingston Fm
Cross Green
Mill Pit Fm
Priors Hardwick
Cherwell Fm
Westcombe Fm
Piper's Hill Fm
Holmes Ho
Wills Pastures
Bromtrees Fm
Manor Fm
Everdon Stubbs
Heath Fm
Itchington Holt
Lower Fm
Lower New House Fm
Grange Fm
NORTHANTS
New Fm
Kingston Grange
Blackdown Fm
Hill Fm
Charwelton
Church Charwelton
Hogstaff Spinney
OXFORD CANAL
Hill Fm
Watergall Fox Covert
Fields Fm
Iron Hill Fm
Mantles Heath
Wormleighton Grange Fm
Manor Fm
Preston Capes
Gaydon
Thorn Hill 137
Knightcote
Crabs Castle Fm
Dodds Cott
Hinton Ho
Preston Fields Fm
High Wood
Cleaver's Clump
Knightley Wood
Wormleighton
Upper Boddington
Pitwell Fm
Hammonds Barn
Red House Fm
Grange Fm
Bloxham Barn Fm
Gaydon Hill Fm
Wharf
Boddington Res
Westhorp
Byfield
Cow Pasture Wood
Tunningham Fm
Burntfold Copse
Northend
The Hall Fm
Hinton
Woodford Halse
Northwest Fm
Ireland Fm
BURTON DASSETT HILLS
Fenny Compton
Mill Hill
Lower Boddington
Maidford
Temple Herdewyke
Cedars Fm
Ashby Gorse
Adstone Ho
Church Hill
Wormleighton Res
West Farndon
Central Fm
Adstone
Burton Dassett
Fenny Compton Hill
Farnborough Barn
Springfield Fm
Aston le Walls
Redhill Fm
Eydonhill
CANONS ASHBY HOUSE
Bitham Hill
Hall's Hill
Windmill Hill
Manor Ho
Redhill Wood
Crockwell Fm
Canons Ashby
Bitham Hall
Farnborough Fields Fm
Eydon
EDGEHILL 1642
Arnold's Fm
Burton Hill Fm
Avon Dassett
Farnborough
Claydon
Lawn Hill
Ind Est
Jobs Hill
Foxhill Fm
Lawnhill Fm
Pimpton Wood
Woodend Green
Valley Fm
FARNBOROUGH HALL
Firs Fm
Chipping Warden
Trafford Ho
Moreton Pinkney
Canada
Splash Leys Fm
Arlescote
Fox Barn
Radway
Warmington
Clattercote Res
Oathill Fm
Rye Hill Fm
Plumpton
Oakley Bank
Mollington
Edgcote

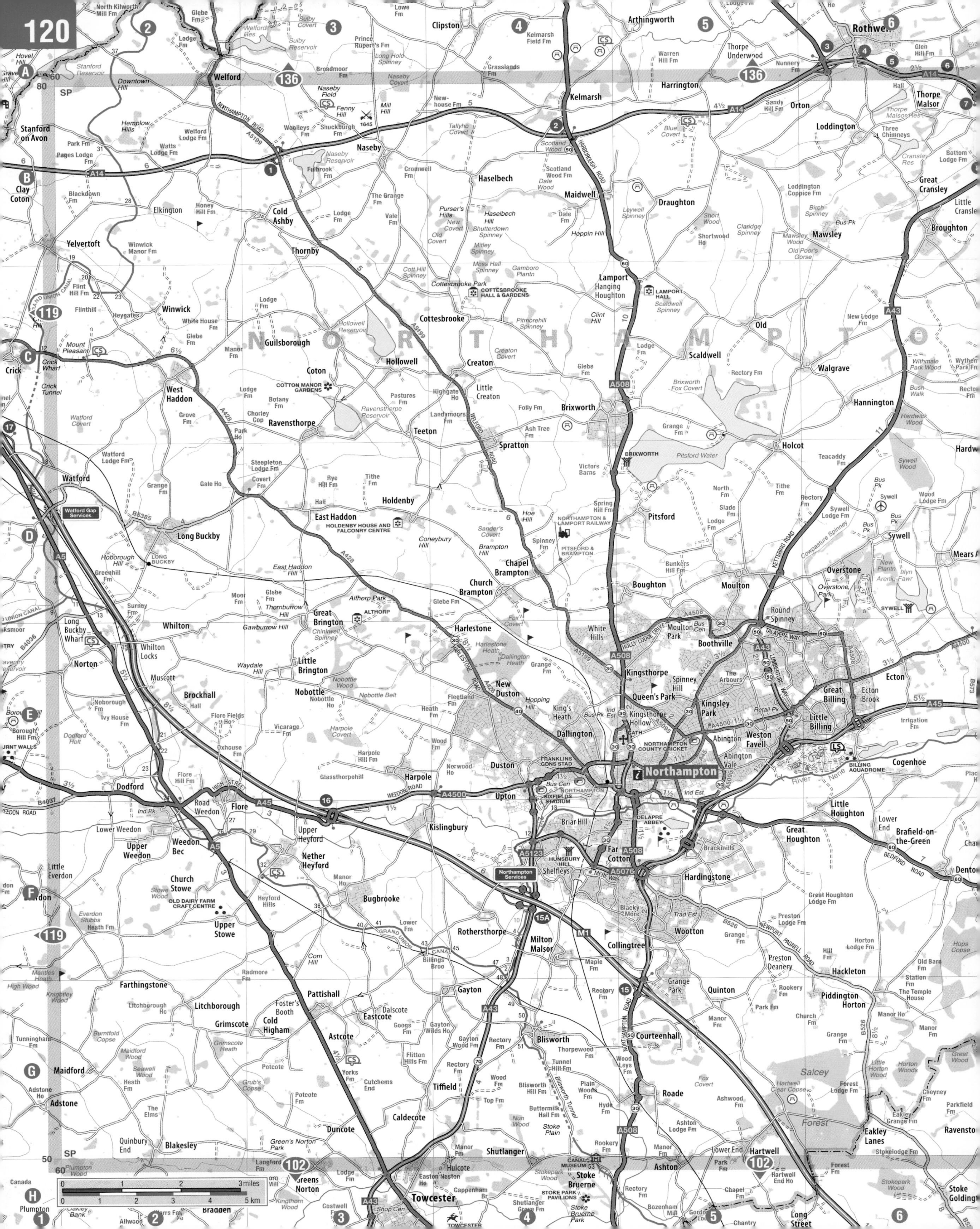

North Kilworth Mill Fm
Glebe Fm
Sulby Covert
Lowe Fm
Clipston
Arthingworth
Rothwell
Hovel Hill
Lodge Fm
Welford Res
Sulby Reservoir
Prince Rupert's Fm
Long Hold Spinney
Kelmarsh Field Fm
Thorpe Underwood
Glen Hill Fm
Stanford Reservoir
Welford
136
Broadmoor Fm
Naseby Covert
Grasslands Fm
Warren Hill Fm
Nunnery Fm
Downtown Hill
SP
Naseby Field
Fenny Hill
Mill Hill
1645
New-house Fm
Kelmarsh
Harrington
Sandy Hill Fm
Orton
Hall
Thorpe Malsor
Stanford on Avon
Hemplow Hills
Welford Lodge Fm
Woolleys Fm
Shuckburgh Fm
Naseby
Tallyho Covert
Scotland Wood
Blue Covert
Loddington
Thorpe Malsor Res
Three Chimneys
Park Fm
Pages Lodge Fm
Watts Lodge Fm
Naseby Reservoir
Harborough Road
Cransley Res
Bottom Lodge Fm
Clay Coton
Fullbrook Fm
Cromwell Fm
Haselbech
Scotland Wood Fm
Dale Wood
Maidwell
Great Cransley
Blackdown Fm
The Grange Fm
Draughton
Loddington Coppice Fm
Little Cransley
Elkington
Honey Hill Fm
Cold Ashby
Lodge Fm
Vale Fm
Purser's Hills
Haselbech Hill
Shutterdown Spinney
Dale Fm
Hoppin Hill
Leywell Spinney
Short Wood
Claridge Spinney
Birch Spinney
Bus Pk
Mawsley
Broughton
New Covert
Old Covert
Mitley Spinney
Shortwood Ho
Mawsley Wood
Old Poor's Gorse
Yelvertoft
Winwick Manor Fm
Thornby
Moss Hall Spinney
Gamboro Plantn
Cott Hill Spinney
Lamport
Hanging Houghton
Flint Hill Fm
Cottesbrooke Park
COTTESBROOKE HALL & GARDENS
LAMPORT HALL
Scaldwell Spinney
Grand Union Canal
Flinthill
Heygates
Lodge Fm
Winwick
Hollowell Reservoir
Cottesbrooke
Pitmorehill Spinney
Clint Hill
New Lodge Fm
Old
A43
119
White House Fm
Glebe Fm
Guilsborough
NORTHAMPTON
Mount Pleasant
Manor Fm
Creaton Covert
Lodge Fm
Glebe Fm
Scaldwell
Withmale Park Wood
Wythen Park Fm
Crick
Crick Wharf
Crick Tunnel
West Haddon
Coton
Hollowell
Creaton
Walgrave
Rectory Fm
COTTON MANOR GARDENS
Lodge Fm
Botany Fm
Pastures Fm
Highgate Ho
Little Creaton
Brixworth Fox Covert
Bush Walk
Hannington
Watford Covert
Grove Fm
Chorley Cop
Ravensthorpe
Park Ho
Ravensthorpe Reservoir
Landymoors Fm
Teeton
Folly Fm
Brixworth
Ash Tree Fm
Hardwick Wood
Grange Fm
Holcot
Spratton
Pitsford Water
Hardwick
Watford Lodge Fm
Steepleton Lodge Fm
BRIXWORTH
Teacaddy Fm
Sywell Wood
Watford
Grange Fm
Gale Ho
Covert Fm
Rye Hill Fm
Tithe Fm
Victors Barns
North Fm
Tithe Fm
Bus Pk
Watford Gap Services
Hall
Holdenby
East Haddon
Hoe Hill
Spring Hill Fm
Slade Fm
Rectory Fm
Sywell
Wood Lodge Fm
Sywell Lodge Fm
B5385
HOLDENBY HOUSE AND FALCONRY CENTRE
NORTHAMPTON & LAMPORT RAILWAY
Pitsford
Lodge Fm
Long Buckby
Sander's Covert
Coneybury Hill
Spinney Fm
Kettering Road
Bus Pk
Sywell
Brampton Hill
PITSFORD & BRAMPTON
Cowpasture Spinney
Mears Ashby
Hoborough Hill
LONG BUCKBY
Chapel Brampton
Bunkers Hill Fm
Overstone
Greenhill Fm
East Haddon Hill
Church Brampton
Boughton
Moulton
New Plantn
Blyn Arenig-Fawr
Overstone Park
Moor Fm
Glebe Fm
Thornburrow Hill
Althorp Park
Glebe Fm
SYWELL
Surney Fm
Great Brington
ALTHORP
Fox Covert
A4508
Round Spinney
Long Buckby Wharf
Whilton
Gawburrow Hill
Chinkwell Spinney
Harlestone
White Hills
Moulton Park
Bus Cen
Talavera Way
Whilton Locks
Harlestone Heath
Dallington Heath
Holly Lodge Drive
Boothville
A4500
Norton
Waydale Hill
Little Brington
Grange Fm
A5199
A508
Kingsthorpe
The Arbours
Ecton
Muscott
Nobottle Wood
Spinney Hill
Lumbertubs Way
Brockhall
Nobottle
Nobottle Belt
New Duston
Hopping Hill
Queen's Park
Great Billing
Ecton Brook
Noborough Fm
Nobottle Ho
Fleetland Fm
King's Heath
Kingsley Park
Hall
Heath Fm
Bus Pk
Ind Est
Kingsthorpe Hollow
Retail Pk
Little Billing
A45
Ivy House Fm
Flore Fields Ho
A5095
A4500
Irrigation Fm
Borough Hill
Dodford Holt
Vicarage Fm
Harpole Covert
Dallington
Abington
Weston Favell
Borough Hill Fm
Oxhouse Fm
Wood Fm
NORTHAMPTON COUNTY CRICKET
BURNT WALLS
Harpole Hill Fm
Norwood Ho
Duston
FRANKLINS GDNS STAD
Abington Vale
Cogenhoe
BILLING AQUADROME
Flore Hill Fm
Glassthorpehill
Harpole
Northampton
River Nene
Dodford
High Street
Weedon Road
A4500
Upton
Bus Cen
NORTHAMPTON
SIXFIELDS STADIUM
Ind Est
Road Weedon
Flore
A45
Kislingbury
Briar Hill
DELAPRE ABBEY
Little Houghton
Lower End
Ind Pk
Brafield-on-the-Green
Lower Weedon
Upper Heyford
Great Houghton
Upper Weedon
Weedon Bec
A5
Nether Heyford
A5123
HUNSBURY HILL
Far Cotton
Brackmills
Bedford Road
Denton
Little Everdon
Church Stowe
Shelfleys
Mere Way
A5076
Hardingstone
Northampton Services
Everdon
Stowe Wood
OLD DAIRY FARM CRAFT CENTRE
Heyford Hills
Manor Ho
Bugbrooke
Great Houghton Lodge Fm
Everdon Stubbs
Heath Fm
Upper Stowe
Blacky More
Trad Est
Preston Lodge Fm
119
Lower Fm
Grand Union
Rothersthorpe
15A
B526
Wootton
Grange Fm
Newport Pagnell Road
Horton Lodge Fm
Hops Copse
Corn Hill
Canal
Billings Broo
Milton Malsor
M1
Collingtree
Preston Deanery
Hill Fm
Old Barn Fm
Mantles Heath
Radmore Fm
Maple Fm
Hackleton
Station Fm
High Wood
Knightley Wood
Farthingstone
Grange Park
Rookery Fm
The Temple House
Gayton
Rectory Fm
Quinton
Piddington
Horton
Litchborough Ho
Litchborough
Foster's Booth
Pattishall
Dalscote
A43
Park Fm
Manor Ho
Cold Higham
Eastcote
Grimscote
Goggs Fm
Gayton Wilds Ho
Church Fm
Tunningham Fm
Blisworth
Manor Fm
Courteenhall
Burntfold Copse
Grimscote Heath
Gayton Wood Fm
Rectory Fm
Thorpewood Fm
Maidford Wood
Astcote
Grange Fm
Northampton Road
Great Wood
Seawell Wood
Potcote
Flitton Hills Fm
Tunnel Hill Fm
Wood Leys Fm
Little Horton Wood
Horton Woods
Maidford
Rectory Fm
Salcey
Heath Fm
Grub's Copse
Yorks Fm
Cutchems End
Wood Fm
Blisworth Hill Fm
Plain Woods Fm
Fox Covert
Hartwell Clear Copse
Forest Lodge Fm
Cheyney Fm
Adstone Ho
Adstone
Potcote Fm
Tiffield
Top Fm
Blisworth Tunnel
Roade
Ashwood Fm
The Elms
Buttermilk Hall Fm
Nun Wood
Hyde Fm
Parkfield Fm
Eakley Grange Fm
Caldecote
Stoke Plain
Ashton Lodge Fm
Ravenstone
Forest
Quinbury End
Blakesley
Duncote
Eakley Lanes
Green's Norton Park
Shutlanger
Rookery Fm
Manor Fm
SP
Manor Fm
CANAL MUSEUM
Lower End
Hartwell
Stokelodge Fm
Plumpton Wood
102
Langford Fm
Greens Norton
Lodge Fm
Hulcote
Easton Neston Ho
Stoke Bruerne
Stokepark Wood
Ashton
Park Fm
Hartwell End Ho
Forest Fm
102
Stokepark Wood
Canada
Plumpton
Cappenham Br
STOKE PARK PAVILIONS
Rectory Fm
Chapel Fm
Stoke Goldington
Oakley Bank
Allwood
Farrs Fm
Bradden
Kingthorn Wood
Costwell
A43
Towcester
Shop Cen
Shutlanger Grange Fm
Stoke Bruerne Park
Bozenham Mill
Gordon Lodge
Chantry
Long Street
TOWCESTER
0 1 2 3 miles
0 1 2 3 4 5 km

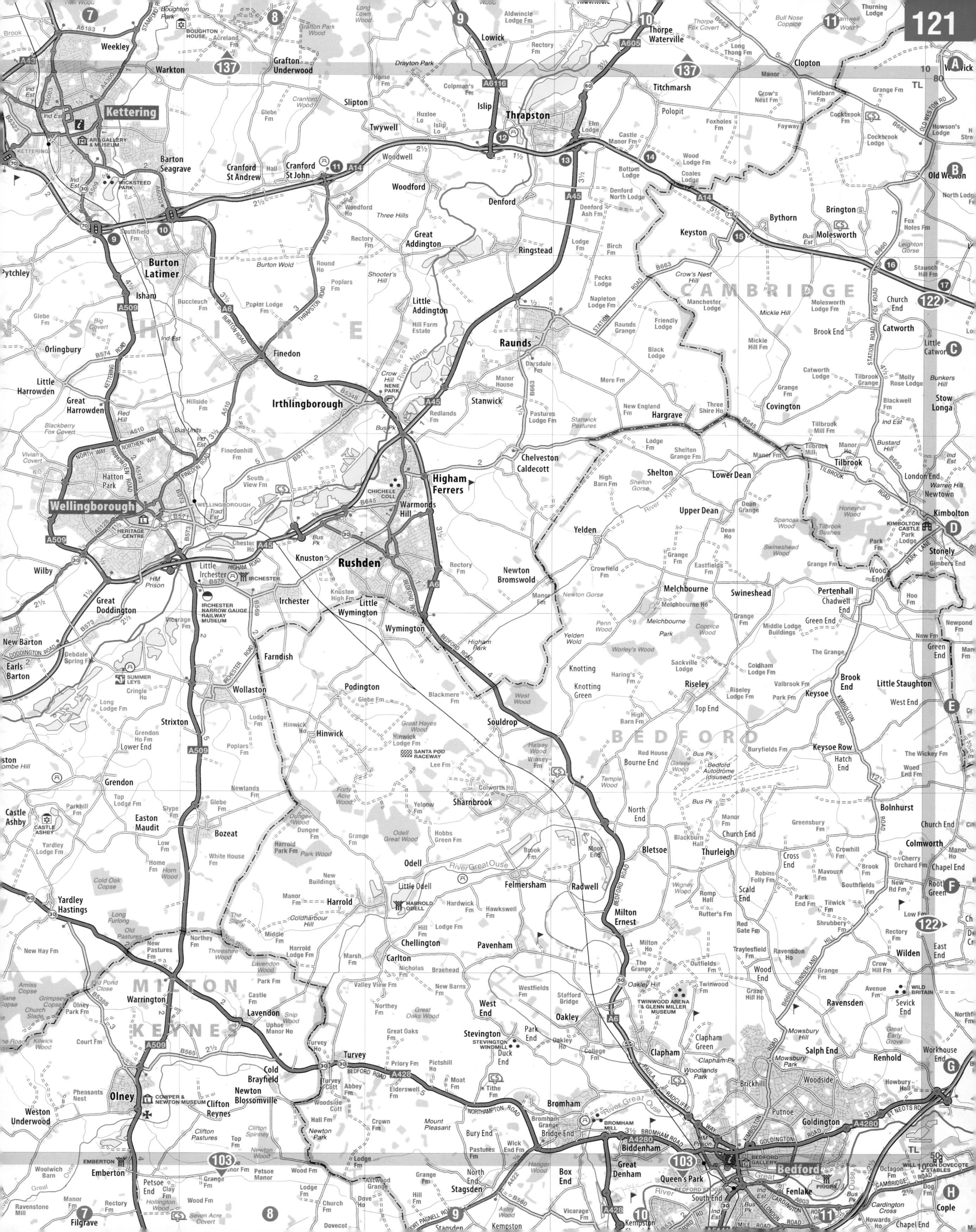
Weekley
Boughton Park
Boughton House
Acreland Fm
Grafton Park Wood
Long Low Wood
Lowick
Aldwincle Lodge Fm
Thorpe Waterville
Thorpe Fox Covert
Bull Nose Coppice
Thurning Lodge
Warkton
Grafton Underwood
Drayton Park
Rectory Fm
Long Thong Fm
Clopton
Manor
Titchmarsh
Kettering
Glebe Fm
Cranford Wood
Slipton
Home Fm
Colpman's Fm
Islip
Crow's Nest Fm
Fieldbarn Fm
Grange Fm
Polopit
Art Gallery & Museum
Huxloe Lo
Twywell
Islip Lo
Thrapston
Elm Lodge
Castle Manor Fm
Foxholes Fm
Fayway
Cockbrook Fm
Cockbrook Lodge
Howson's Lodge
Barton Seagrave
Cranford St Andrew
Cranford St John
Woodwell
Wood Lodge Fm
Coales Lodge
Bottom Lodge
Old Weston
Wicksteed Park
Woodford
Denford
Denford North Lodge
Denford Ash Fm
Woodford Ho
Three Hills
Bythorn
Brington
Keyston
Molesworth
Fox Holes Fm
North Lodge
Southfield Fm
Burton Latimer
Burton Wold
Round Ho
Rectory Fm
Great Addington
Ringstead
Lodge Fm
Birch Fm
Leighton Gorse
Staunch Hill Fm
Pytchley
Isham
Poplars Fm
Shooter's Hill
Pecks Lodge
Crow's Nest Hill
Buccleuch Fm
Poplar Lodge Fm
Little Addington
Napleton Lodge Fm
Cambridge
Manchester Lodge
Mickle Hill
Molesworth Lodge Fm
Church End
Glebe Fm
Big Covert
Hill Farm Estate
Raunds
Raunds Grange
Friendly Lodge
Mickle Hill Fm
Brook End
Catworth
Orlingbury
Finedon
Darsdale Fm
Black Lodge
Little Catworth
Little Harrowden
Crow Hill
Nene Park
Manor House
Mere Fm
Catworth Lodge
Grange Fm
Tilbrook Grange
Molly Rose Lodge
Bunkers Hill
Great Harrowden
Irthlingborough
Hillside Fm
Stanwick
New England Fm
Hargrave
Three Shire Ho
Covington
Blackwell Fm
Stow Longa
Red Hill
Redlands Fm
Pastures Lodge Fm
Stanwick Pastures
Tillbrook Mill Fm
Ind Est
Blackberry Fox Covert
Bus Units
Lodge Fm
Shelton Grange Fm
Bustard Hill
Vivian's Covert
Finedonhill Fm
Chelveston
Caldecott
Manor Fm
Tilbrook Mill
Manor Ho
Tilbrook
Hatton Park
High Barn Fm
Shelton
Lower Dean
London End
South View Fm
Chichele Coll
Higham Ferrers
Shelton Gorse
Warren Hill
Newtown
Wellingborough
Warmonds Hill
Upper Dean
Dean Grange
Honeyhill Wood
Kimbolton
Trad Est
Heritage Centre
Spanoak Wood
Tilbrook Bushes
Kimbolton Castle
Park Lodge
Yelden
Dean Ho
Chester Ho
Bus Pk
Swineshead Wood
Park Fm
Stonely
Wilby
Knuston
Rushden
Rectory Fm
Newton Bromswold
Grange Fm
Eastfields Fm
Crowfield Fm
Grange Fm
Gimbers End
Wood End
Little Irchester
HM Prison
Irchester
Melchbourne
Swineshead
Pertenhall
Chadwell End
Hoo Fm
Great Doddington
Irchester Narrow Gauge Railway Museum
Knuston High Fm
Little Wymington
Manor Fm
Newton Gorse
Melchbourne Ho
Newpond Hill
Vicarage Fm
Wymington
Penn Wood
Melchbourne Park
Grange Fm
Coppice Wood
Middle Lodge Buildings
Green End
New Fm
New Barton
Debdale Spring Fm
Farndish
Higham Park
Yelden Wold
Worley's Wood
The Grange
Green End
Earls Barton
Knotting
Haring's Fm
Sackville Lodge
Coldham Lodge Fm
Summer Leys
Podington
Knotting Green
Riseley
Valbrook Fm
Brook End
Little Staughton
Cringle Ho
Wollaston
Glebe Fm
Blackmere Fm
Riseley Lodge Fm
Park Fm
Keysoe
West End
Long Lodge Fm
West Wood
High Barn Fm
Top End
Strixton
Lodge Fm
Hinwick Ho
Hinwick
Great Hayes Wood
Souldrop
Grendon Ho Fm
Lower End
Hinwick Lodge Fm
Santa Pod Raceway
Bedford
Halsey Wood
Red House
Bourne End
Buryfields Fm
Keysoe Row
The Wickey Fm
Poplars Fm
Lee Fm
Wilsey Fm
Gaisey Wood
Bedford Autodrome (disused)
Hatch End
Wood End Fm
Grendon
Temple Wood
Top Lodge Fm
Newlands Fm
Forty Acre Wood
Colworth Ho
Bus Pk
Bolnhurst
Castle Ashby
Parkhill Fm
Slype Fm
Glebe Fm
Yelnow Fm
Sharnbrook
North End
Manor Fm
Greensbury Fm
Church End
Easton Maudit
Dungee Wood
Dungee Fm
Hobbs Green Fm
Blackburn Hall
Church End
Colmworth
Yardley Lodge Fm
Low Fm
Bozeat
Grange Fm
Odell Great Wood
Moor End
Bletsoe
Thurleigh
Crowhill Fm
Cherry Orchard Fm
Chapel End
Harrold Park Fm
Park Wood
Brook Fm
Cross End
Home Fm
White House Fm
Horn Wood
Odell
Mavourn Fm
Brook Fm
Cold Oak Copse
New Buildings
Little Odell
Felmersham
Radwell
Robins Folly Fm
Scald End
Southfields Fm
New Rd Fm
Root Green
Yardley Hastings
Manor Fm
Harrold
Harrold Odell
Hardwick Fm
Hawkswell Fm
Wigney Wood
Romp Hall
Park End Fm
Tilwick Fm
Goldharbour Hill
Rutter's Fm
Low Fm
Long Furlong
The Slipe
Hill Fm
Lodge Fm
Milton Ernest
Shrubbery Fm
Old Pastures
Northey Fm
Middle Fm
Chellington
Pavenham
Milton Ho
Red Gate Fm
Rectory Fm
New Pastures Fm
Harrold Lodge Fm
Traylesfield Fm
Ravensden Ho
Wilden
East End
New Hay Fm
Threeshire Wood
Marsh Fm
Carlton
Nicholas Fm
Braehead
The Grange
Outfields Fm
Crow Hill Fm
Lavendon Wood
Wood End
Grange Fm
Milton Keynes
Park Fm
Old Pond Close
Valley View Fm
New Barns Fm
Westfields Fm
Oakley Hill
Twinwood Fm
Avenue Fm
Wild Britain
Arniss Copse
Grimpsey Copse
Castle Fm
Northey Fm
Stafford Bridge
Twinwood Arena & Glenn Miller Museum
Graze Hill Ho
Sevick End
Warrington
West End
Great Oaks Wood
Oakley
Ravensden
Olney Park Fm
Lavendon
Snip Wood
Church Slade
Uphoe Manor Ho
Great Oaks Fm
Stevington
Stevington Windmill
Park End
Mowsbury Hill
Great Early Grove
Kilwick Wood
Court Fm
Keynes
Turvey Ho
Oakley Ho
Clapham Green
Salph End
Workhouse End
Duck End
College Fm
Clapham
Mowsbury Park
Renhold
Cold Brayfield
Turvey
Priory Fm
Pictshill Ho
Clapham Pk
Woodlands Park
Pheasants Nest
Turvey Cott
Abbey Fm
Elderswell Fm
Moat Fm
Tithe Fm
Brickhill
Woodside
Howbury Hall
Olney
Cowper & Newton Museum
Clifton Reynes
Newton Blossomville
Woodside Cott
Bromham
Putnoe
Weston Underwood
Hall Fm
Crown Fm
Mount Pleasant
Bromham Grange
Bromham Mill
Goldington
Clifton Pastures
Clifton Spinney
Newton Park
Bury End
Bridge End
Biddenham
Top Fm
Pastures Fm
Wick End Fm
Hanger Wood
Box End
Great Denham
HM Prison
Bedford Gallery
Bedford
Octagon Fm
Willington Dovecote & Stables
Emberton
Newton Wood
Lodge Fm
Woolwich Barn
Petsoe Manor
Wood Fm
Grange Fm
North End
Queen's Park
Priory
Cambridge Fm
Petsoe End
Clay Fm
Astwood Grange
Stagsden
Fenlake
Manor Fm
Hollington Wood
Wood Fm
Lodge Fm
Hill Fm
Vicarage Fm
South End
Bus Pk
Dog Fm
Ravenstone Mill
Rectory Fm
Seven Acre Covert
Church Fm
Dove Ho
Astey Wood
Kempston
Cardington Cross
Copie
Filgrave
Dovecot
Stagsden
Kempston
Howards
Chapel End
Seven Acre Covert

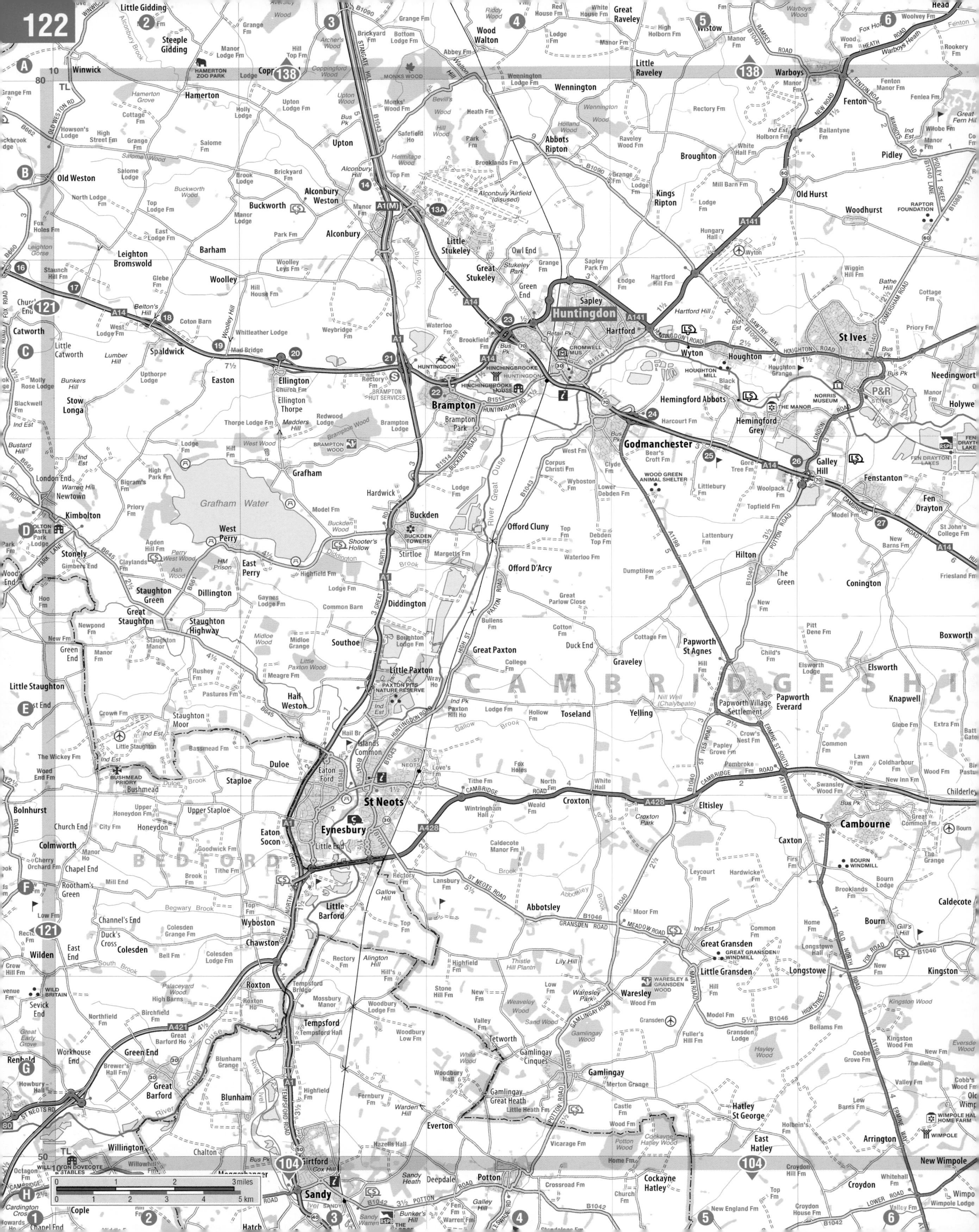

122
Little Gidding
Steeple Gidding
Hamerton Zoo Park
Copple
138
Wood Walton
Great Raveley
Little Raveley
Wistow
Warboys
Winwick
Hamerton
Monks Wood
Wennington
Upton
Abbots Ripton
Broughton
Fenton
Old Weston
Alconbury Weston
Buckworth
Alconbury
Barham
Little Stukeley
Great Stukeley
Kings Ripton
Old Hurst
Woodhurst
Pidley
Raptor Foundation
Leighton Bromswold
Woolley
Owl End
Sapley
Huntingdon
Hartford
Wyton
Houghton
St Ives
Catworth
Little Catworth
Spaldwick
Easton
Ellington
Ellington Thorpe
Brampton
Hinchingbrooke House
Brampton Park
Godmanchester
Hemingford Abbots
Hemingford Grey
Needingworth
Holywell
Stow Longa
Grafham
Grafham Water
Kimbolton
Kimbolton Castle
West Perry
Buckden
Buckden Towers
Offord Cluny
Offord D'Arcy
Hilton
Fenstanton
Fen Drayton
Conington
Stonely
Staughton Green
Dillington
East Perry
Diddington
Great Staughton
Staughton Highway
Southoe
Great Paxton
Papworth St Agnes
Boxworth
Graveley
Little Paxton
Paxton Pits Nature Reserve
Elsworth
Little Staughton
Hail Weston
Toseland
Yelling
Papworth Village Settlement
Papworth Everard
Knapwell
CAMBRIDGESHIRE
Staughton Moor
Duloe
Staploe
Eaton Ford
St Neots
Croxton
Eltisley
Cambourne
Bushmead
Bushmead Priory
Upper Staploe
Eaton Socon
Eynesbury
Bolnhurst
Colmworth
Honeydon
Chapel End
Rootham's Green
Abbotsley
Caxton
Caldecote
Bourn
Bourn Windmill
BEDFORD
Little Barford
Wyboston
Chawston
Colesden
Channel's End
Wilden
Great Gransden
Little Gransden
Longstowe
Kingston
Roxton
Tempsford
Waresley
Gransden
Tetworth
Wild Britain
Sevick End
Great Barford
Blunham
Gamlingay
Gamlingay Cinques
Gamlingay Great Heath
Hatley St George
East Hatley
Arrington
Wimpole Hall Home Farm
Everton
Willington
Sandy
Girtford
Potton
Deepdale
Cockayne Hatley
Croydon
New Wimpole
104
A14
A1
A1(M)
A141
A428
A1198
A421
B1040
B1043
B1046
0 1 2 3 miles
0 1 2 3 4 5 km

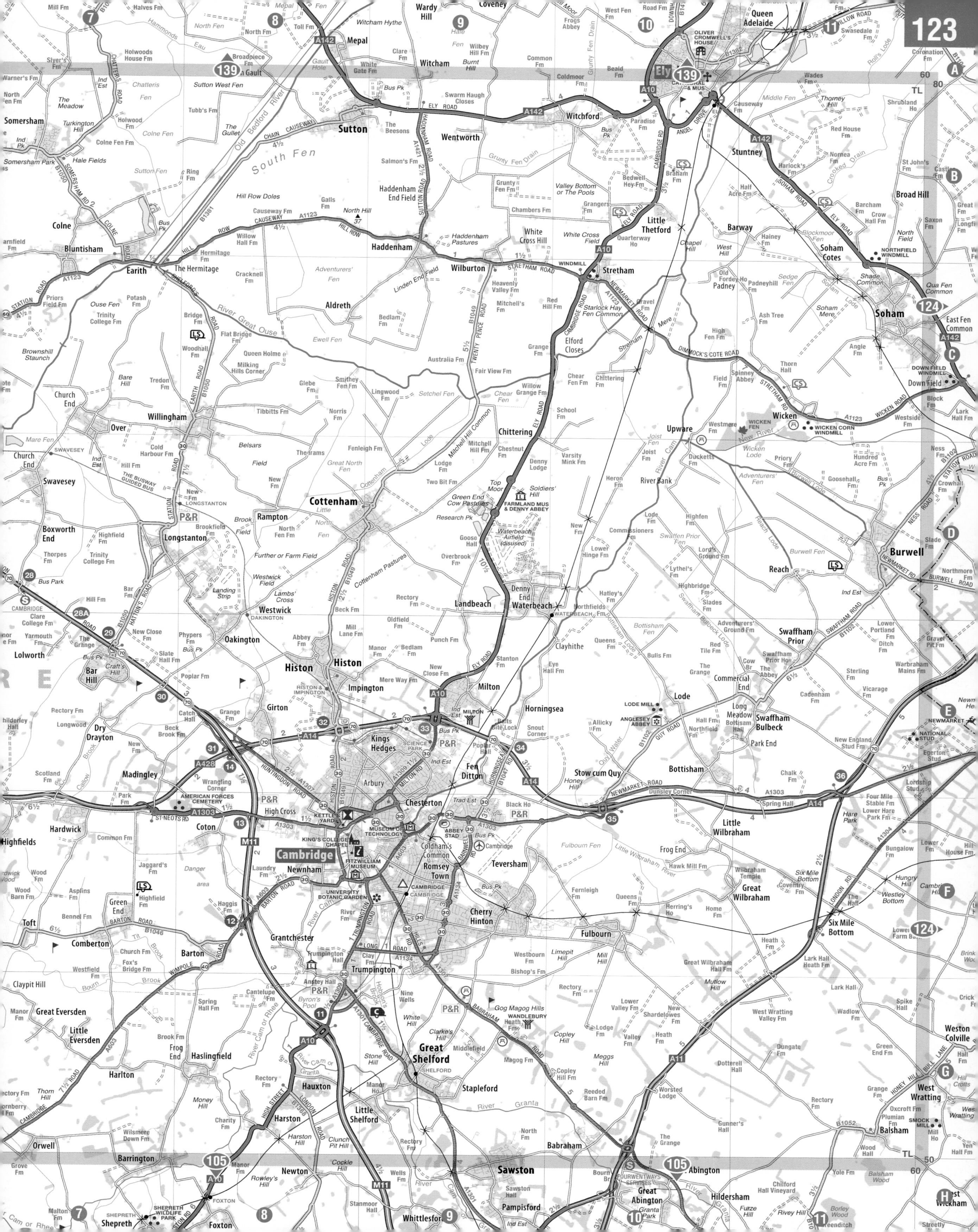
Ely
Queen Adelaide
Oliver Cromwell's House
Mepal
Wardy Hill
Coveney
Witcham
Witcham Hythe
Sutton
Haddenham
Wentworth
Witchford
Stuntney
Somersham
Colne
Bluntisham
Earith
The Hermitage
Aldreth
Wilburton
Stretham
Little Thetford
Barway
Soham
Soham Cotes
Broad Hill
East Fen Common
Wicken
Wicken Corn Windmill
Upware
Chittering
Willingham
Over
Swavesey
Cottenham
Rampton
Longstanton
Boxworth End
Westwick
Oakington
Landbeach
Denny End
Waterbeach
Farmland Mus & Denny Abbey
Burwell
Reach
Swaffham Prior
Commercial End
Lode
Anglesey Abbey
Swaffham Bulbeck
Bottisham
Clayhithe
Horningsea
Milton
Histon
Impington
Girton
Kings Hedges
Chesterton
Fen Ditton
Stow cum Quy
Little Wilbraham
Great Wilbraham
Dry Drayton
Madingley
Bar Hill
Lolworth
Hardwick
Highfields
Coton
Cambridge
Newnham
Kettle's Yard
King's College Chapel
Fitzwilliam Museum
Museum of Technology
University Botanic Garden
Romsey Town
Coldham's Common
Teversham
Cherry Hinton
Fulbourn
Grantchester
Trumpington
Comberton
Toft
Barton
Great Eversden
Little Eversden
Haslingfield
Harlton
Hauxton
Great Shelford
Little Shelford
Stapleford
Harston
Newton
Barrington
Orwell
Foxton
Shepreth
Sawston
Babraham
Pampisford
Whittlesford
Great Abington
Hildersham
Balsham
West Wratting
Weston Colville
Six Mile Bottom
Newmarket
Wandlebury
Gog Magog Hills
American Forces Cemetery
River Great Ouse
Old Bedford River
South Fen
River Cam
A10
A14
A142
A1123
A1303
A1307
A11
M11
139
124
105

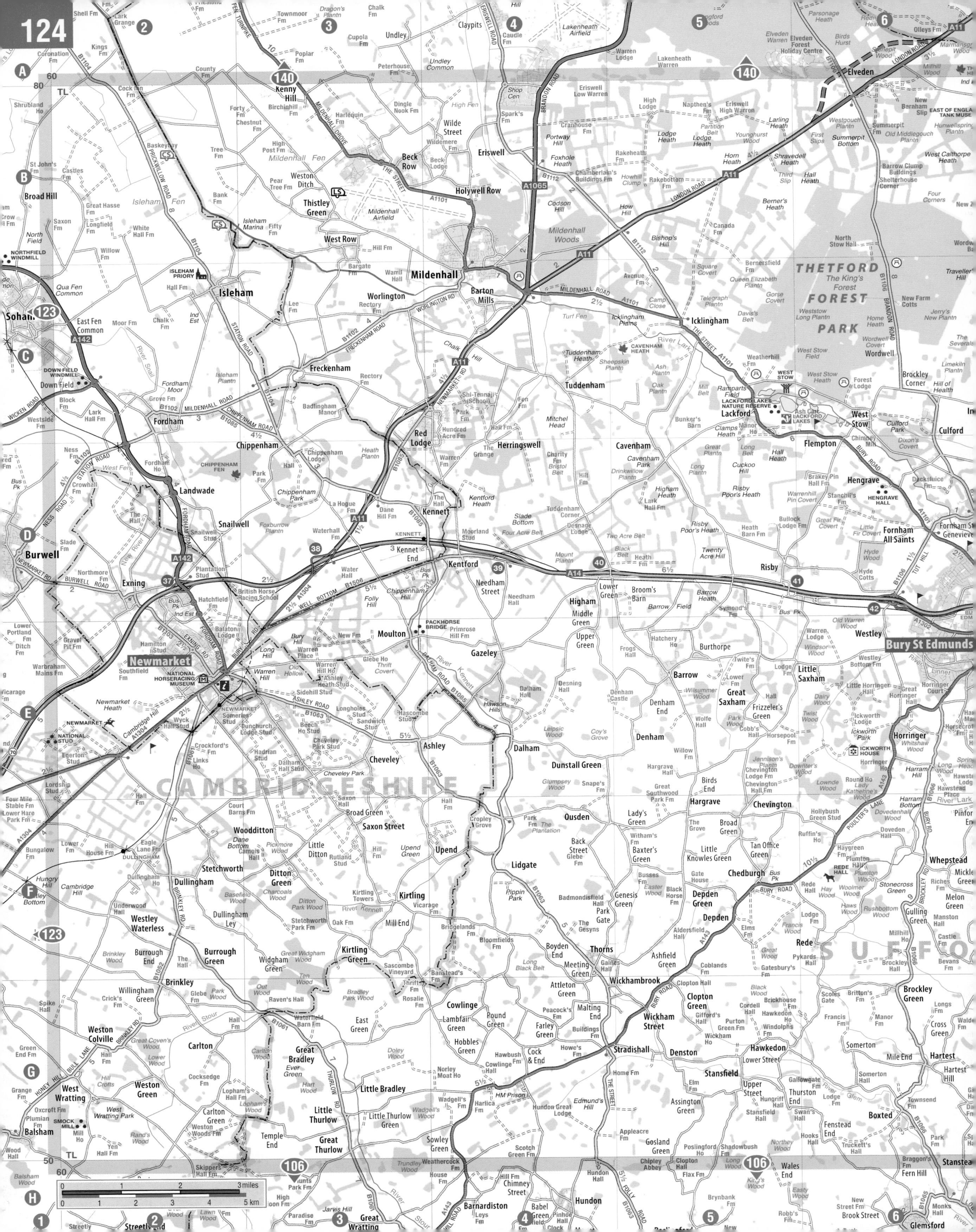

Shell Fm
Lark Grange
Townmoor Fm
Dragon's Plantn
Chalk Fm
Cupola Fm
Undley
Claypits
Caudle Fm
Lakenheath Airfield
Parsonage Heath
Olleys Fm
Kings Fm
Coronation Fm
Poplar Fm
Peterhouse Fm
Undley Common
Warren Lodge
Lakenheath Warren
Elveden Warren
Elveden Forest Holiday Centre
Birds Hirst
Elveden
County Fm
Kenny Hill
Birchinhill Fm
Cock Inn Fm
Harlequin Fm
Dingle Nook Fm
High Fen
Wilde Street
Shop Cen
Spark's Fm
Eriswell
Eriswell Low Warren
High Lodge
Napthen's Fm
Eriswell High Warren
Larling Heath
Shrubland Ho
Forty Fm
Chestnut Fm
Baskeybay Fm
High Post Fm
Mildenhall Fen
Wildemere Fm
Beck Row
Beck Lodge
Portway Hill
Cranhouse Fm
Lodge Heath
Partition Belt
Youngs Wood
First Slips
Summerpit Bottom
Summerpit Fm
Old Middlegouch Plantn
New Barnham Slip
EAST OF ENGLAND TANK MUSEUM
West Calthorpe Heath
St John's Fm
Castles Fm
Tree Fm
Pear Tree Fm
Weston Ditch
Thistley Green
Bank Fm
Holywell Row
Foxhole Heath
Chamberlain's Buildings Fm
Rakeheath Fm
Horn Heath
Shravedell Heath
Barrow Clump Buildings
Shelterhouse Corner
Broad Hill
Isleham Fen
Great Hasse Fm
Longfield Fm
Saxon Fm
White Hall Fm
Isleham Marina
Fifty Fm
Mildenhall Airfield
Codson Hill
Howhill Clump
Rakebottom Fm
Third Slip
Hall Heath
Berner's Heath
Four Corners
North Field
Willow Fm
NORTHFIELD WINDMILL
West Row
Hill Fm
Bargate Fm
Mildenhall Woods
How Hill
Bishop's Hill
Canada Fm
North Stow Hall
ISLEHAM PRIORY
Hall Fm
Wamil Hall
Mildenhall
Avenue Fm
Square Covert
Bernersfield Fm
Queen Elizabeth Plantn
THETFORD
The King's Forest
FOREST
PARK
Traveller's Hill
Qua Fen Common
Isleham
Worlington
Barton Mills
Rectory Fm
Lee Fm
Telegraph Plantn
Camp Close
Gorse Covert
Davis's Belt
New Farm Cotts
Jerry's New Plantn
Soham
East Fen Common
Chalk Fm
Ind Est
Moor Fm
Turf Fen
Icklingham Plains
Icklingham
Westslow Long Plantn
Home Heath
Wordwell Covert
Wordwell
The Severals
Chalk Hill
River Lark
Tuddenham Heath
Sheepskin Plantn
CAVENHAM HEATH
Ash Plantn
Weatherhill Fm
West Stow Field
West Stow Heath
WEST STOW
Forest Lodge
Brockley Corner
Limekiln Plantn
Hill of Health
DOWN FIELD WINDMILL
Down Field
Freckenham
Rectory Fm
Isleham Plantn
Fordham Moor
Grove Fm
Tuddenham
Oak Plantn
Mill Belt
Ramparts Field
LACKFORD LAKES NATURE RESERVE
Lackford
Ash Cast
LACKFORD LAKES
Block Fm
Lark Hall Fm
Badlingham Manor
Shi-Tennoji (School)
Fen Fm
Mitchel Head
Bunker's Barn
Clamps Heath
Manor Ho
West Stow
Culford Park
Culford
Westside Fm
Fordham
Chippenham
Red Lodge
Hundred Acre Fm
Park Fm
Hall Fm
Herringswell
The Grange
Charity Fm
Bristol Belt
Cavenham
Cavenham Park
Great Plantn
Long Belt
Hall Heath
Flempton
Chimney Mill
Dixon's Covert
Ness Fm
Fordham Ho
West Fen
CHIPPENHAM FEN
Chippenham Lodge
Heath Plantn
Warren Fm
Drinkwillow Plantn
Long Plantn
Cuckoo Hill
Brakey Pin Hall Fm
Hengrave
Decksluice Fm
Crowhall Fm
Landwade
Park Fm
Chippenham Park
Hall
Higham Heath
Lark Hall Fm
Risby Poor's Heath
Warrenhill Pin Covert
Stanchil's Fm
HENGRAVE HALL
The Hall
La Hogue Fm
Dane Hill Fm
The Hall
Kennett
Kentford Heath
Slade Bottom
Four Acre Belt
Tuddenham Corner
Desnage Lodge
Risby Poor's Heath
Heath Barn Fm
Bullock Lodge Fm
Great Fir Covert
Little Fir Covert
Fornham All Saints
Fornham St Genevieve
Snailwell
Snailwell Stud
Foxburrow Plantn
Waterhall Fm
Moorland Stud
Two Acre Belt
Burwell
Slade Fm
KENNETT
Kennet End
Kentford
Mount Plantn
Black Belt
Heath Fm
Twenty Acre Hill
Risby
Hyde Wood
Hyde Cotts
Tut Hill
Northmore Fm
Exning
Plantation Stud
Water Hall
Bus Pk
Needham Street
Needham Hall
Lower Green
Broom's Barn
Barrow Heath
Barrow
Field
Symond's Fm
Old Warren Wood
Westley
Burwell Road
British Horse Racing School
Hatchfield Stud
Ind Est
Folly Hill
Chippenham Hill
Well Bottom
Higham
Middle Green
Lower Portland Fm
Gravel Pit Fm
Ditch Fm
Balaton Lodge
Hamilton Stud
Bury Hill
New Fm
Moulton
PACKHORSE BRIDGE
Primrose Hill Fm
Upper Green
Gazeley
Hatchery Ho
Frogs Hall
Burthorpe
Warren Lodge
Windsor Wood
Westley Bottom Fm
Bury St Edmunds
Warbraham Mains Fm
Newmarket
Southfield Fm
NATIONAL HORSERACING MUSEUM
Long Hill
Warren Place
Warren Hill
Old Hollow
Warren Hill Ho
Ashley Heath Stud
Glebe Ho
Thrift Covert
River Kennett
Dalham Hall
Desning Hall
Barrow
Twite's Fm
Lower Fm
Great Saxham
Lodge Fm
Little Saxham
Little Horringer Hall
Great Horringer Hall
Horringer Court
Linnet
Vicarage Fm
Newmarket Heath
NEWMARKET
Sidehill Stud
Ashley Road
Longholes Stud
Sandwich Stud
Hascombe Stud
Hawson Hills
Denham Castle
Summer Wood
Denham End
Wolfe Hall
Hall
Frizzeler's Green
Dairy Wood
Ickworth Lodge
Ickworth Park
Horringer
Whitehaw Wood
NATIONAL STUD
Egerton Stud
Cambridge Hill
Wyck Hall Stud
NEWMARKET Somerries Stud
Dunchurch Lodge Stud
Beech Ho Stud
Cheveley Park Stud
Ashley
Leipsic Wood
Coy's Grove
Park Wood
Cobb's Hall
Twist Wood
Horsepool Fm
Denham
ICKWORTH HOUSE
Crockford's Fm
Hadrian Stud
Links Ho
Dalham Hall Stud
Cheveley
Dalham
Willow Fm
Jennison's Plantn
Chevington Lodge Fm
Horringer Ho
Harram Hill
Long Wood
Lordship Stud
Cheveley Park
Dunstall Green
Hargrave Hall
Downter's Wood
Lownde Wood
Round Ho
Lady Katherine's Wood
Hawstead Place
CAMBRIDGESHIRE
Glumpsey Wood
Snape's Fm
Birds End
Chevington Hall Fm
Great Southwood Park Fm
Four Mile Stable Fm
Lower Hare Park Fm
Hall Fm
Court Barns Fm
Saxon Hall
Broad Green
Hall Fm
Cropley Grove
Hargrave
Chevington
Hollybush Green Stud
Harram Bottom
Dovedenhall Wood
River Lark
Pinford End
Woodditton
Saxon Street
Park Fm
The Plantation
Ousden
Lady's Green
Broad Green
The Grove
Doveden Hall
Dane Bottom
Camois Hall
Pickmore Wood
Little Ditton
Hill Fm
Upend Green
Upend
Back Street
Glebe Fm
Witham's Fm
Baxter's Green
Little Knowles Green
Tan Office Green
Ruffin's Ho
Haygreen Fm
Plumton Hall
Bungalow Fm
Lower Fm
Hill House Fm
Eagle Lane Fm
DULLINGHAM
Rutland Stud
Lidgate
Whepstead
Mickle Green
Hungry Hill
Stetchworth
Ditton Green
Busses Fm
Caster Wood
Gate House
Chedburgh
Bus Pk
REDE HALL
Plumton Wood
Stonecross Green
Cambridge Hill
Dullingham Ho
Dullingham
Charcoals Wood
Kirtling Towers
Kirtling
Pippin Park
Badmondisfield Hall
Genesis Green
Black Horse Fm
Depden Green
Rede Hall
Woolmer Wood
Hay Wood
Riches Fm
Melon Green
Underwood Hall
Basefield Wood
Ditton Park Wood
Vicarage Fm
Park Gate
Depden
Lodge Fm
Haws Wood
Rushbottom Wood
Gulling Green
Manston Hall
Westley Waterless
Dullingham Ley
Stetchworth Park Fm
Oak Fm
Mill End
Bridgelands Fm
The Gesyns
Aldersfield Hall
Francis Wood
Rede
Millhill Ho
Castle Fm
Brinkley Wood
Burrough End
The Hall
Burrough Green
Widgham Green
Great Widgham Wood
Kirtling Green
Sascombe Vineyard
Bloomfields Fm
Boyden End
Thorns
Ashfield Green
Elms Fm
Great Wood
Pykards Hall
Brockley Hall
Bevans Fm
SUFFO
Gaines Hall
Coblands Fm
Gatesbury's Fm
Ten Wood
Banstead's Fm
Long Black Belt
Meeting Green
Willingham Green
Brinkley
Glebe Fm
Park Wood
Out Wood
Raven's Hall
Thrift Fm
Rosalie Fm
Bradley Park Wood
Attleton Green
Wickhambrook
Clopton Hall
Clopton Green
Black Wood
Brickhouse Fm
Scales Gate
Britton's Fm
Brockley Green
Spike Hall
Crick's Fm
Cowlinge
Lambfair Green
Pound Green
Peacock's Fm
Malting End
Cordell Hall
Gifford's Hall
Hawkedon Hall
Manor Fm
Longs Fm
Waterfield Barn Fm
East Green
Farley Green
Buildings Fm
Wickham Street
Purton Green Fm
Windolphs Fm
Francis Fm
Cross Green
Weston Colville
Hall Fm
Carlton
River Stour
Great Coven's Wood
Hobbles Green
Howe's Fm
Wickham Ho
Somerton
Hall Fm
Great Bradley
Doley Wood
Hawbush Fm
Cock & End
Stradishall
Denston
Hawkedon
Lower Street
Mile End
Hartest
Green End Fm
Carlton Wood
Lower Wood
Ever Green
Cowlinge Hall
Norley Moat Ho
Home Fm
Hartest Hill
Somerton Hall
Grange Fm
Hill Crofts
Cocksedge Fm
Hart Wood
Little Bradley
HM Prison
Edmund's Hill
Stansfield
Gallowgate Fm
Lodge Fm
River Glem
Townsend Fm
West Wratting
Weston Green
Lopham's Hall
Lopham Wood
Wadgell's Fm
Harlica Fm
Hundon Great Lodge
Assington Green
Elm Fm
Upper Street
Thurston End
Hungriff Hall
Oxcroft Fm
Plumian Fm
SMOCK MILL
West Wratting Park
Carlton Green
Weston Woods Fm
Little Thurlow
Little Thurlow Green
Wadgell's Wood
Stansfield Hall
Swan's Hall
Boxted
Balsham
Mill Ho
Rand's Wood
Temple End
Great Thurlow
Sowley Green
Scotch Green Fm
Applecare Fm
Gosland Green
Fenstead End
Hooks Hall
Northey Wood
Park Fm
Wood Hall
Yen Hall Fm
Skippers Hall Fm
Trundley Wood
Weathercock Fm
Hundon Hall
Chipley Abbey
Poslingford Ho
Clopton Hall
Shadowbush Fm
Long Wood
Wales End
Truckett's Hall
Bragon's Fm
Fern Hill
Stanstead
Balsham Wood
Hunts Park Fm
House Fm
Hill Fm
Chimney Street
Flax Fm
Kirk's Wood
Easty Wood
High Moon Fm
Paradise Fm
Jarvis Hill
Great Wratting
Barnardiston
Leys Fm
Babel Green
Pinhoe Hall
Hundon
Brynbank Fm
New Street Fm
Brook Street
Monks Hall
Glemsford
Robb's Fm
Streetly End
Lawn Wood
Clock
Folly Road
Brandon Road
Bury Road
Newmarket Rd
Station Road
Fordham Road
Mildenhall Road
Chippenham Road
Worlington Rd
Freckenham Road
London Road
Wicken Road
Ness Road
Well Bottom
Honey Hill
Bull Lane
Brinkley Rd
Thurlow Rd
The Street
Prickwillow Road
Mildenhall Drove
Fen Turnpike
Cheveley Park
A11
A14
A142
A1065
A1101
A1304
A1302
A143
A1088
B1104
B1102
B1085
B1063
B1061
B1506
B1112
B1103
B1106
B1066
B1065
B1052
B1057
1
2
3
4
5
6
A
B
C
D
E
F
G
H
TL
60
80
50
70
37
38
39
40
41
42
123
140
106
0
1
2
3 miles
0
1
2
3
4
5 km

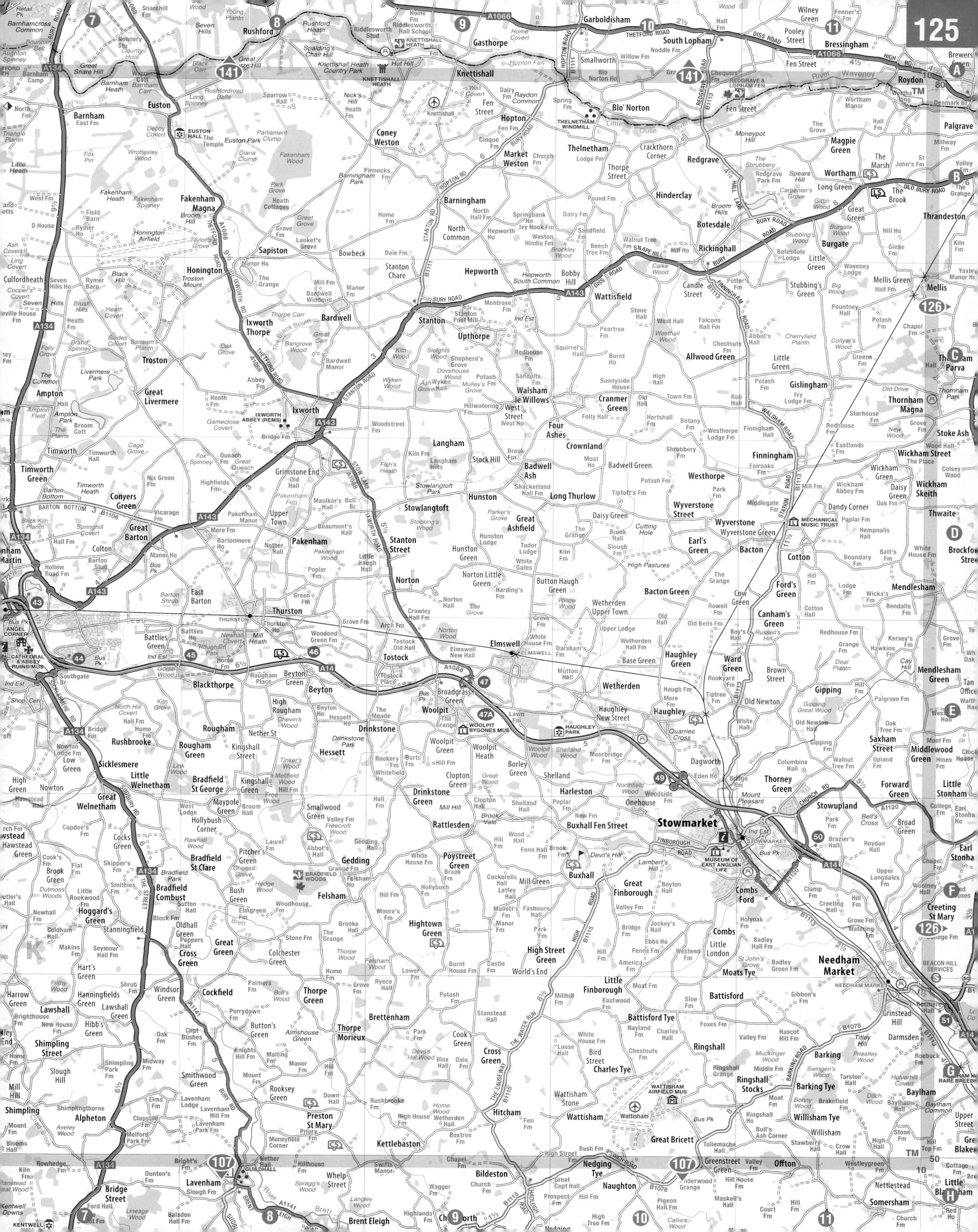
Barnhamcross Common
Rushford
Garboldisham
South Lopham
Bressingham
Gasthorpe
Knettishall
Roydon
Euston
Barnham
Coney Weston
Hopton
Market Weston
Blo' Norton
Thelnetham
Redgrave
Palgrave
Wortham
Fakenham Magna
Barningham
Hinderclay
Botesdale
Rickinghall
Sapiston
Honington
Bardwell
Stanton
Hepworth
Wattisfield
Mellis
Ixworth Thorpe
Troston
Upthorpe
Walsham le Willows
Allwood Green
Gislingham
Ampton
Great Livermere
Ixworth
Thornham Magna
Langham
Four Ashes
Crownland
Finningham
Timworth Green
Conyers Green
Badwell Ash
Westhorpe
Stowlangtoft
Hunston
Long Thurlow
Wickham Street
Wickham Skeith
Great Barton
Pakenham
Stanton Street
Great Ashfield
Wyverstone Street
Wyverstone
Earl's Green
Bacton
Cotton
Thurston
Norton
Mendlesham
Elmswell
Haughley Green
Beyton
Tostock
Woolpit
Wetherden
Haughley
Drinkstone
Rougham
Rushbrooke
Sicklesmere
Little Welnetham
Great Welnetham
Hessett
Stowupland
Harleston
Stowmarket
Rattlesden
Buxhall Fen Street
Gedding
Bradfield St Clare
Felsham
Buxhall
Great Finborough
Combs Ford
Combs
Needham Market
Bradfield Combust
Hightown Green
High Street Green
Cockfield
Lawshall
Thorpe Green
Thorpe Morieux
Brettenham
Battisford
Cross Green
Ringshall
Barking
Hitcham
Wattisham
Great Bricett
Willisham Tye
Preston St Mary
Kettlebaston
Lavenham
Bildeston
Nedging Tye
Naughton
Offton
Somersham
Brent Eleigh
Chelsworth
Bridge Street
Alpheton
Shimpling

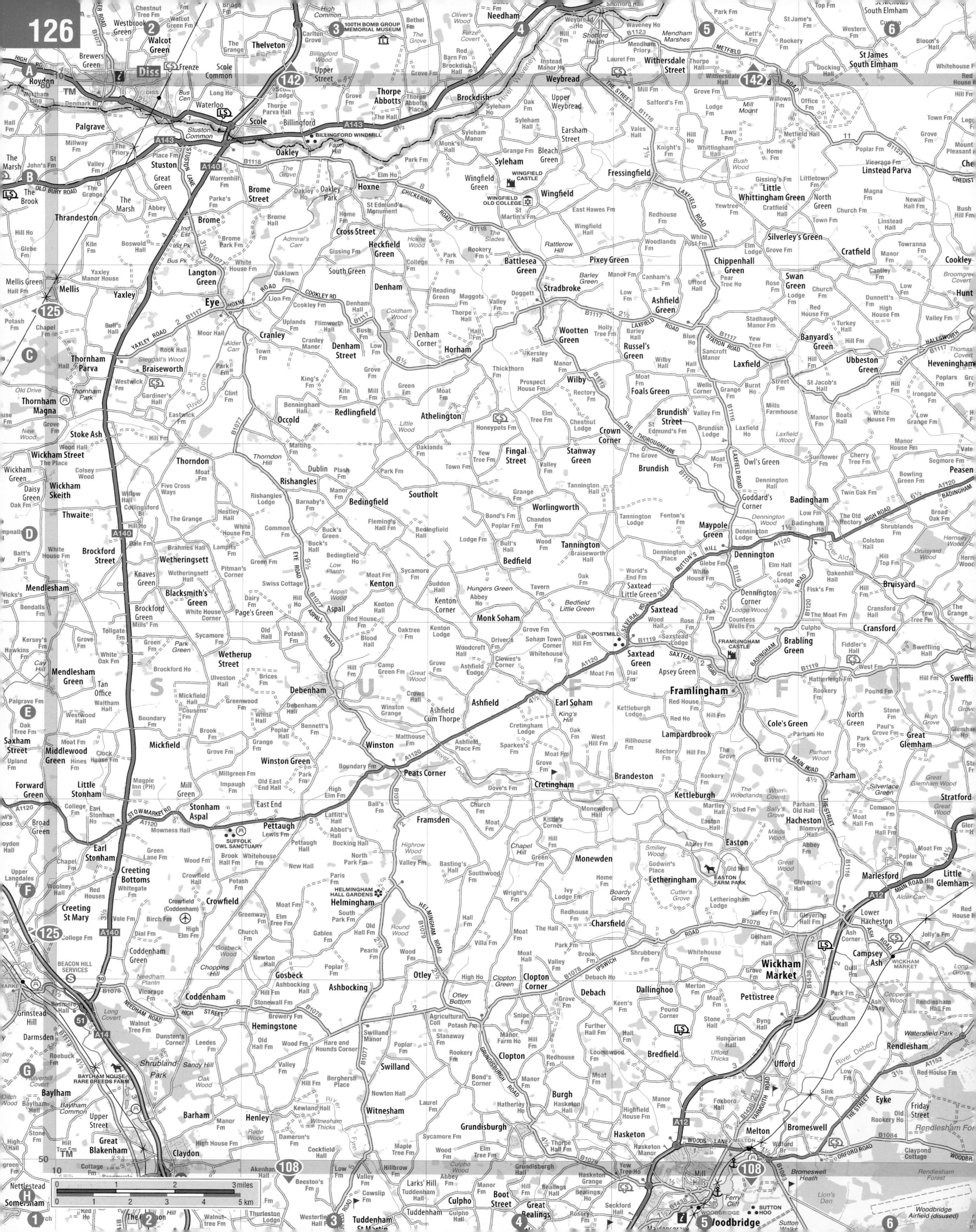

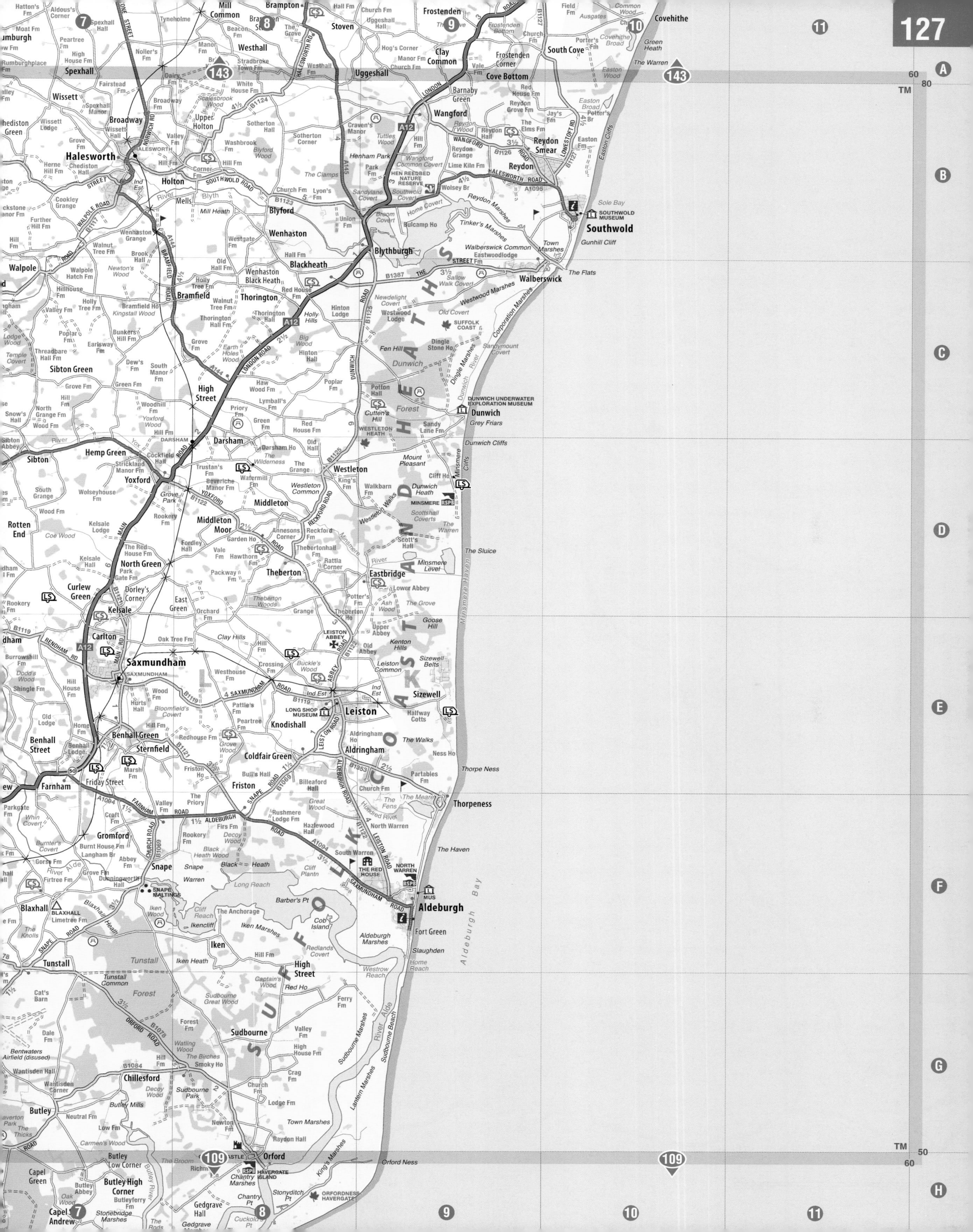

Halesworth
Southwold
Walberswick
Blythburgh
Wangford
Reydon
Covehithe
Dunwich
Westleton
Yoxford
Saxmundham
Leiston
Sizewell
Thorpeness
Aldeburgh
Snape
Orford
Orford Ness
Tunstall
Sudbourne
Chillesford
Butley
Farnham
Kelsale
Theberton
Middleton
Darsham
Wenhaston
Thorington
Bramfield
Holton
Spexhall
Uggeshall
Frostenden
South Cove
Sibton
Knodishall
Aldringham
Friston
Iken
SUFFOLK COAST AND HEATHS
SOUTHWOLD MUSEUM
DUNWICH UNDERWATER EXPLORATION MUSEUM
LEISTON ABBEY
LONG SHOP MUSEUM
SNAPE MALTINGS
Aldeburgh Bay

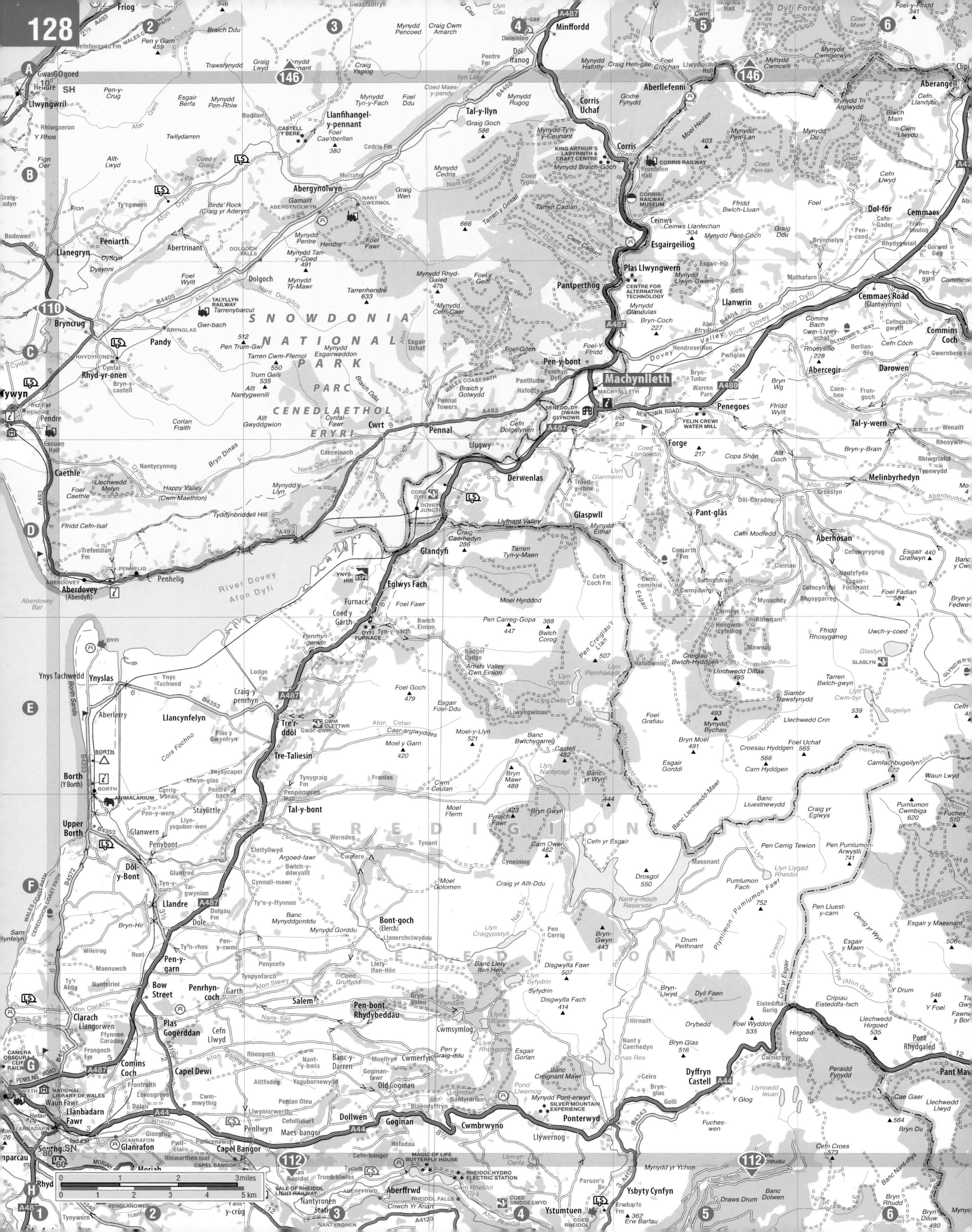

Minffordd
Corris Uchaf
Aberllefenni
Aberangell
Corris
Tal-y-llyn
Llanfihangel-y-pennant
Abergynolwyn
Llwyngwril
Peniarth
Llanegryn
Abertrinant
Dolgoch
Bryncrug
Pandy
Rhyd-yr-onen
Tywyn
Pendre
Esgairgeiliog
Plas Llwyngwern
Pantperthog
Llanwrin
Cemmaes
Cemmaes Road
Dol-fôr
Commins Coch
Darowen
Abercegir
Penegoes
Machynlleth
Pen-y-bont
Pennal
Cwrt
Tal-y-wern
Forge
Derwenlas
Llugwy
Caethle
Glaspwll
Pant-glâs
Melinbyrhedyn
Aberhosan
Glandyfi
Eglwys Fach
Aberdovey (Aberdyfi)
Penhelig
River Dovey
Afon Dyfi
Furnace
Ynyslas
Llancynfelyn
Tre'r-ddôl
Tre-Taliesin
Borth (Y Borth)
Upper Borth
Tal-y-bont
Dôl-y-Bont
Llandre
Bont-goch (Elerch)
Penrhyn-coch
Bow Street
Pen-y-garn
Clarach
Salem
Pen-bont Rhydybeddau
Plas Gogerddan
Capel Dewi
Comins Coch
Llanbadarn Fawr
Waun Fawr
Glanrafon
Capel Bangor
Goginan
Dollwen
Cwmbrwyno
Ponterwyd
Dyffryn Castell
Aberffrwd
Ystumtuen
Ysbyty Cynfyn
Rhydgaled
Pant Mawr
S N O W D O N I A
N A T I O N A L
P A R K
P A R C
C E N E D L A E T H O L
E R Y R I
C E R E D I G I O N
(S I R   C E R E D I G I O N)
Nant-y-moch Reservoir
Pumlumon Fawr
0 1 2 3 miles
0 1 2 3 4 5 km

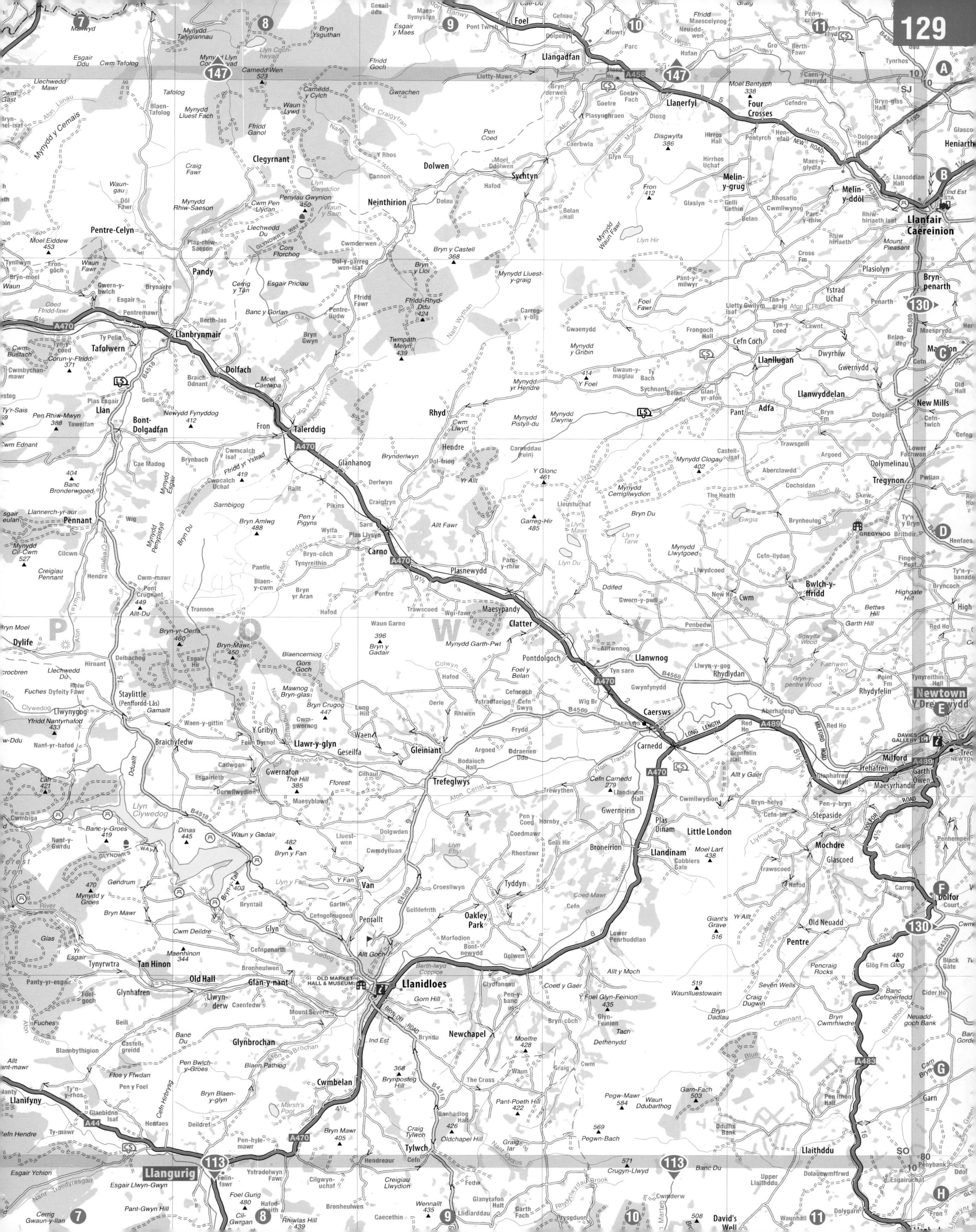

Mallwyd
Mynydd Talyglannau
Bryn Ysguthan
Esgair y Maes
Foel
Pont Twrch
Llangadfan
Dolpebyll
Blowty
Parc
Ffridd Maescelynog
Neuadd-wen
Hafan
Tynrhos
Esgair Ddu
Cwm Tafolog
Carnedd Wen 523
Ffridd Goch
Letty-Mawr
Stone Ho.
A458
Goetre Fach
Goetre
Llanerfyl
Moel Bentyrch 338
Four Crosses
Cefndre
SJ
A495
Heniarth
Llechwedd Mawr
Tafolog
Blaen-Tafolog
Carnedd y Cylch
Waun Lwyd
Gwrachen
Nant Craigyfran
Mynydd y Cemais
Mynydd Lluest Fach
Ffridd Ganol
Plasynghraen
Diosg
Pentyrch
Henefail
NEW ROAD
Dolgead Hall
Pen Coed
Caerbwla
Disgwylfa 386
Hirros Hall
Hirrhos Uchaf
Melin-y-grug
Maes-y-glydfa
Clegyrnant
Y Rhos
Dolwen
Moel Ddolwen
Sychtyn
Glyn
Craig Fawr
Waun-gau
Dôl Fawr
Cannon
Hafod
Fron 412
Llanoddian Hall
Ind Est
Mynydd Rhiw-Saeson
Cwm Pen Llydan
Penylau Gwynion 450
Neinthirion
Dolau
Belan Hall
Glaslyn
Gelli Gethin
Belan
Rhosaflo
Cwmllwynog
Melin-y-ddôl
Rhiw-hiriaeth Isaf
Llanfair Caereinion
Pentre-Celyn
Moel Eiddew 453
Llechwedd Du
Plas-rhiw-Saeson
Cors Fforchog
GLYNDŴR'S WAY
Cwmderwen
Mynydd Waun Fawr
Llyn Hir
Rhiw hiriaeth
Mount Pleasant
Cross Fm
Bryn y Castell 368
Waun Fawr
Frongôch
Bryn-moel
Waun
Pandy
Cerrig y Tân
Esgair Priciau
Dol-y-garreg wen-isaf
Bryn y Lloi
Mynydd Lluest-y-graig
Pant-y-milwyr
Plasiolyn
Bryn-penarth
Ystrad Uchaf
Gwern-y-bwlch
Brynaere
Esgair
Coed Ffridd-fawr
Pentremawr
Berth-las
Banc y Gorlan
Ffridd Fawr
Pentre-llwdw
Ffridd-Rhyd-Ddu 424
Foel Fawr
Lletty Gwilym Isaf
Tan-y-graig
Penarth
130
A470
Ty Pella
Llanbrynmair
Tafolwern
Tyn-y-coed
Cwm-Bustach
Corun-y-Ffridd 371
Bryn Gwyn
Twmpath Melyn 439
Carreg-y-big
Gwaenydd
Frongoch Hall
Cefn Coch
Tyn-y-coed
Lawnt
B4389
Maesprydd
Cwmbychan-mawr
Dolfach
Braich-Odnant
Moel Caetwpa
Mynydd y Gribin
Llanllugan
Dwyrhiw
Gwernydd
B4518
Gelli
Plas Esgair
Llan
Bont-Dolgadfan
Newydd Fynyddog 412
Afon Iaen
Mynydd yr Hendre
414 Y Foel
Gwaun-y-maglau
Ty Bach
Sychnant
Belan-ddu
Glan-yr-afon
Llanwyddelan
Old Hall
New Mills
Ty'r-Sais
Pen Rhiw-Mwyn 388
Tawelfan
Fron
Talerddig
Rhyd
Cwm Llwyd
Mynydd Pistyll-du
Mynydd Dwyriw
Pant
Adfa
Bryn Fm
Dolgair
Cefn-twlch
Cwm Ednant
Cae Madog
Brynbach
Cwmcalch isaf
Ffridd yr Ystrad
Glanhanog
Hendre
Brynderlwyn
Dol-friog
Carneddau (ruin)
Castell-isaf
Mynydd Clogau 402
Trawsgelli
Argoed
Lower Fachwen
Dolymelinau
404 Banc Bronderwgoed
Mynydd Esgair
Cwmcalch Uchaf
419
Rallt
Derlwyn
Yr Allt
Y Glonc 461
Mynydd Cerriglwydion
Aberclawdd
Cochsidan
Tregynon
Pwllan
Llannerch-yr-aur
Pennant
Wig
Sarnbigog
Pikins
Craigfryn
Lleustuchaf
The Heath
Bechan Brook
Skew Br
Bryn Du
Mynydd Penypistyll
Bryn Amlwg 488
Pen y Pigyns
Sarn
Plas Llysyn
Allt Fawr
Garreg-Hir 485
Llyn Mawr
Bryn Du
Llyn y Tarw
Gwgia
Brynheulog
Ty'n y Bryn
GREGYNOG
Brithdir
Henfaes
Mynydd Cil-Cwm 527
Cilcwn
Wylfa
Bryn-côch
Carno
Tynyreithin
Parc-y-rhiw
Llyn Du
Mynydd Llwytgoed
Cefn-llydan
Finger Post
Creigiau Pennant
Hendre
Cwm-mawr
Pantle
Blaen-y-cwm
Plasnewydd
Ddifed
Llwydcoed
Bwlch-y-ffridd
Ty'n-y-banadl
Bryncoch
Pont Crugnant 449
Allt-Du
Trannon
Bryn yr Aran
Pentre
Trawscoed
Wgi-fawr
Maesypandy
Gwern-y-pwll
New Ho
Cwm
Highgate Hill
Bettws Hall
Hafod
Waun Garno
396 Bryn y Gadair
Clatter
Mynydd Garth-Pwt
Penbedw
Garth Hill
Red Ho
POWYS
Dylife
Bryn-yr-Oerfa 460
Bryn-Mawr 450
Esgair Hir
Blaencerniog
Gors Goch
Alltwnnog
Llanwnog
Pontdolgoch
Sgwylfa Wood
Dolbachog
Llechwedd Du
Hirnant
Foel y Belan
Tyn sarn
Llwyn-y-gog
Rhydlydan
B4568
Fachwen Pool
Bryn-y-pentre Wood
Point Fm
Tynyreithin Hall
Fuches Dyfeity Fawr
Staylittle (Penffordd-Lâs)
Gamallt
Mawnog Bryn-glas
Bryn Crugog 447
Long Hill
Oerle
Rhiwen
Ystradfaelog
Cefn Gwyn
Cefncoch
Wig Br
B4569
Gwynfynydd
Caersws
Aberhafesp
Red Ho
Rhydyfelin
Newtown Y Drenewydd
Llwynygog
Yfridd Nantyrhafod 433
Waen-y-gittin
Y Gribyn
Cwm-gwernog
Waen
Llawr-y-glyn
Gleiniant
Frydd
Carnedd
LONG LENGTH
A489
MILFORD ROAD
DAVIES GALLERY
Nant-yr-hafod
Braichyfedw
Felin Dyrnol
Geseilfa
Argoed
Bodaioch Hall
Ddraenen Ddu
Cefn
Bronfelin Hall
Allt y Gaer
Milford
Trehafren
Garth Owen
Maesyrhandir
Lan 421
Cadwgan
Esgairieth
Gwernafon
The Hill 385
Fforest
Cilhaul
Trefeglwys
Cefn Carnedd 279
Llandinam Hall
Trewythen
Cwmllwydion
Glanhafren Hall
Derwlwydion
Maesyblawd
Afon Cerist
Llyn Clywedog
Cwmbiga
Banc-y-Groes 419
Dinas 445
B4518
Waun y Gadair
Lluest-wen
Dolgwden
Pen y Coed
Hornby
Coedmawr
Plas Dinam
Gwerneirin
Little London
Bryn-helyg
Cefn-bir
Pen-y-bryn
Stepaside
DOLFOR ROAD
Penhempen
Nant-y-Gwrdu
GLYNDŴR'S WAY
482 Bryn y Fan
Cwmdyliuan
Llyn Ebyr
Rhosfawr
Gelli Hir
Broneirion
Llandinam
Moel Lart 438
Cobblers Gate
Mochdre
Glascoed
Graig
Gendrum
470 Mynydd y Groes
Bryn-y-tail 403
Llyn y Fan
Y Fan
Van
Croesllwyn
Tyddyn
Coed Mawr
Trawscoed
Hafod
Carreg
Dolfor Court
Bryn Mawr
Bryntail
Garth
Cefngoleugoed
Penrallt
Gellilefrith
Oakley Park
Cefn
Yr Allt
Giant's Grave 516
Old Neuadd
Pentre
Gias
Cwm Deildre
Glyn
Morfodion
Bont-newydd
Lower Penrhuddlan
130
Cwm
Yr Esgair
Tynyrwtra
Tan Hinon
Maenhinon 344
Cefnpenarth
Allt Goch
Dolwen
Allt y Moch
Pencraig Rocks
480 Glôg Fm Glog
Black Gate
B4355
Panty-yr-esgair
Old Hall
Bronheulwen
Glan-y-nant
OLD MARKET HALL & MUSEUM
Llanidloes
Berth-lwyd Coppice
Clydfannau
Coed y Gaer
519 Waunlluestowain
Seven Wells
Banc Cefnperfedd
Cider Ho
Glynhafren
Foel-goch
Llwyn-derw
Caenfedw
Mount Severn
Gorn Hill
Pen-y-banc
Y Foel Glyn-Feinion 435
Craig Dugwin
Bryn Dadlau
Camnant
Bryn Cwmrhiwdre
Neuadd-goch Bank
Fuches
Beili
BRYN-DU ROAD
Bryndu
Newchapel
Bryn-côch
Glyn-Feinion
Tach
Banc Du
Castell-greidd
Glynbrochan
Ind Est
Moelfre 428
Dethenydd
Allt ant-mawr
Blaenbythigion
Pen Bwlch-y-Groes
Blaen Pathog
368 Brynposteg Hill
Waun
Graig
Cwm
Blue Lins Brook
A483
Flos y Ffwdan
Ty'n-y-rhos
Pen y Foel
Cwmbelan
The Cross
Garn
Bryn Blaen-y-glyn
Marsh's Pool
Pant-Poeth Hill 422
Pegw-Mawr 584
Waun Ddubarthog
Garn-Fach 503
Pen Ithon Hall
Llanifyny
Glanbidno Isaf
Cefn Hirbrysg
Henfaes
Deildref
Pen-hyle-mawr
Bryn Mawr 405
Craig Tylwch
426 Banhadlog Hall
Oldchapel Hill
Graig-lar
569 Pegwn-Bach
Ddulfu Bank
Llaithddu
SO
Penybank
Efn Hendre
Ty-mawr
A44
A470
Tylwch
Nant Gwenth
Llangurig
113
Felin-fawr
Ystradolwyn Fawr
Cilgwyn-uchaf
Hendreaur
Cefn
571 Crugyn-Llwyd
Banc Du
Upper Llaithddu
Dolaucwmffrwd
Esgairuchaf
Esgair Ychion
Esgair Llwyn-Gwyn
Foel Gurig 480
Creigiau Llwydion
Fedw
Glanyrafon Halt
Cwmderw
Pant-Gwyn Hill
Cerrig Gwaun-y-llan
Cil-Gwrgan
Hafod-with
Rhiwlas Hill 439
Bronheulwen
Caecethin
Wennallt 435
Llidiarddau
Garth Fach
Rhysgduon
508
David's Well
Waunhall
Dolygarn
Fron

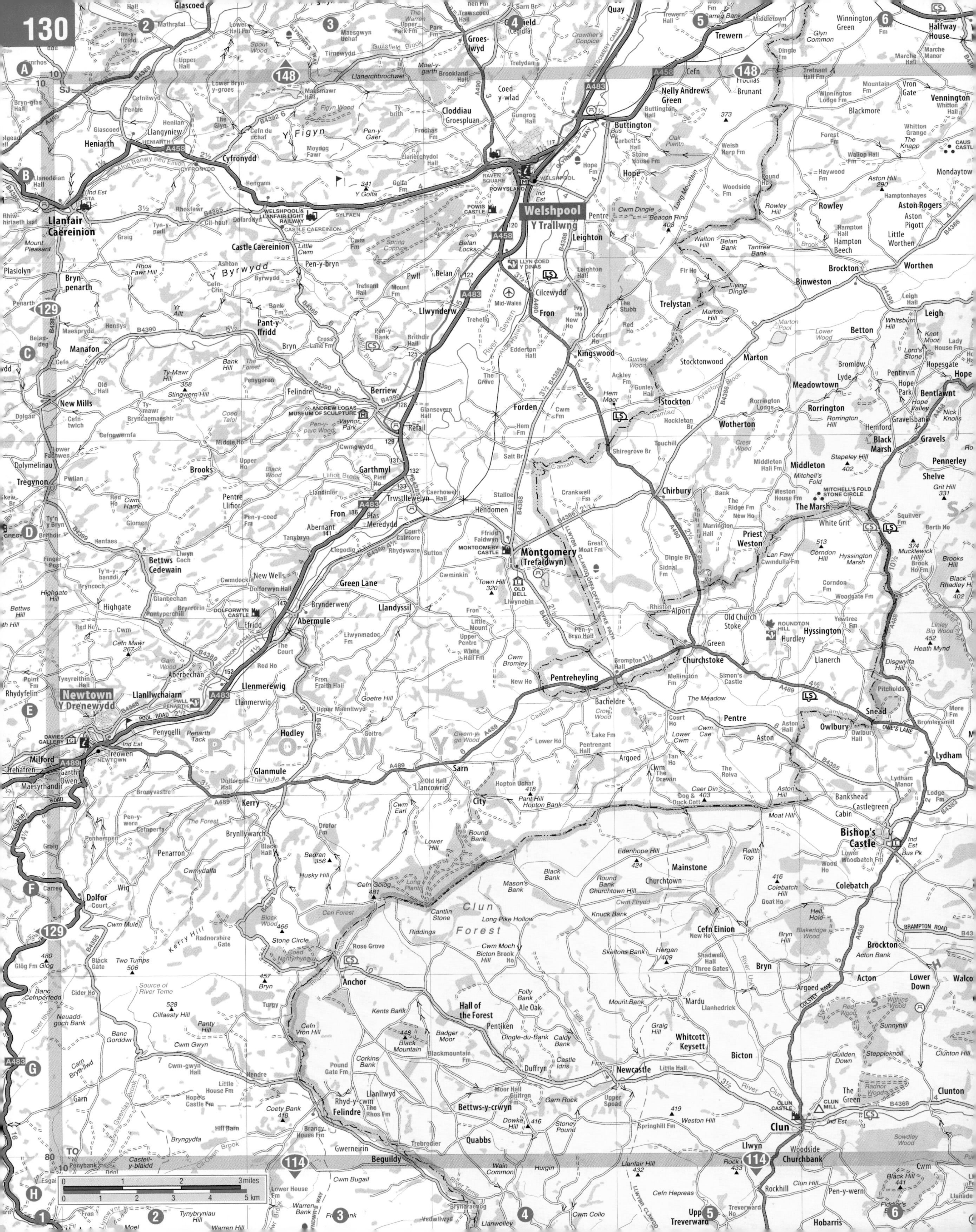

Welshpool
Y Trallwng
Newtown
Y Drenewydd
Montgomery
(Trefaldwyn)
Llanfair Caereinion
Bishop's Castle
Clun
Churchstoke
Chirbury
Guilsfield
Groes-lwyd
Cloddiau
Buttington
Nelly Andrews Green
Trewern
Halfway House
Winnington Green
Vennington
Heniarth
Cyfronydd
Castle Caereinion
Leighton
Hope
Rowley
Aston Rogers
Brockton
Worthen
Binweston
Trelystan
Leigh
Betton
Marton
Kingswood
Forden
Berriew
Manafon
New Mills
Stockton
Wotherton
Rorrington
Meadowtown
Bentlawnt
Gravels
Black Marsh
Middleton
Pennerley
Shelve
The Marsh
Priest Weston
Tregynon
Brooks
Garthmyl
Fron
Llwynderw
Cilcewydd
Bettws Cedewain
Abermule
Llandyssil
Green Lane
Hyssington
Pentreheyling
Pentre
Aston
Owlbury
Snead
Lydham
Llanllwchaiarn
Llanmerewig
Hodley
Glanmule
Sarn
Kerry
City
Milford
Dolfor
Mainstone
Churchtown
Colebatch
Cefn Einion
Brockton
Acton
Bryn
Lower Down
Anchor
Hall of the Forest
Whitcott Keysett
Bicton
Newcastle
Clunton
Felindre
Bettws-y-crwyn
Quabbs
Beguildy
Llwyn
Churchbank
Clun Forest
Kerry Hill
POWYS

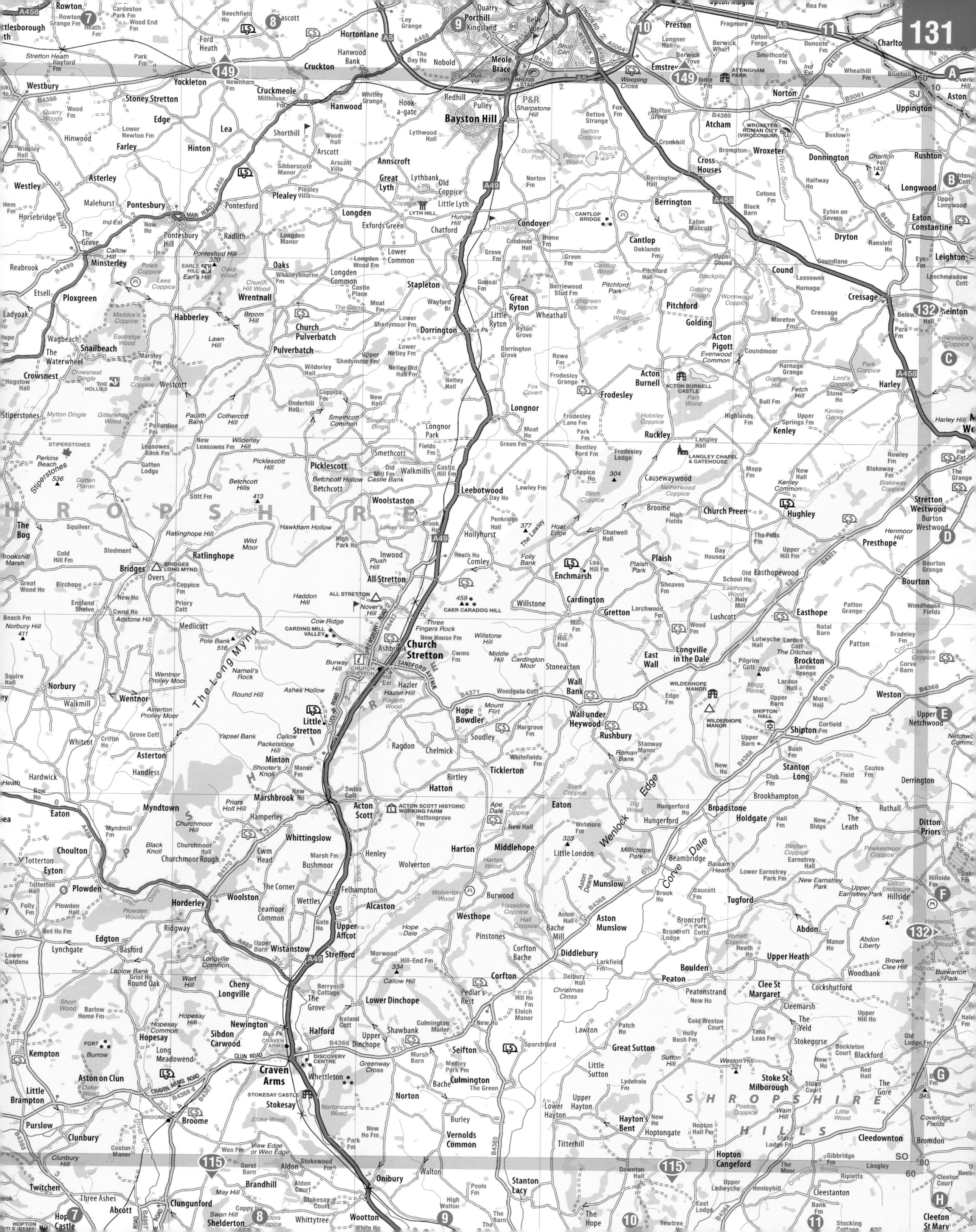
Rowton
Cardeston
Alberbury Park Fm
Wood End Fm
Beechfield Ho
Cascott
Quarry
Porthill
Kingsland
Belle Vue
Preston
Upton Magna
Rea Fm
Frogmore
Charlton
Hortonlane
Ley Grange
Ford Heath
Hanwood Bank
Meole Brace
Shop Cen
Longner Hall
Berwick Wharf
Upton Forge
Duncote Fm
Cruckton
The Day Ho
Nobold
Emstrey
Berwick Grove
Smethcote Ho
Stretton Heath
Hayford Fm
Park Fm
Yockleton
Weeping Cross
Home Fm
Attingham Park
Ind Est
Wheathill Fm
Bluebell
Westbury
Newnham Fm
Cruckmeole
Millhouse Fm
Redhill
Greenhous Stad
P&R
Norton
Aston
Stoney Stretton
Whitley Grange
Hanwood
Hook-a-gate
Pulley
Sharpstone Hill
Fox Fm
Betton Strange
Chilton Grove
Uppington
Quarry Woods
Wood Fm
Edge
Bayston Hill
Atcham
Wroxeter Roman City (Viroconium)
Bell Brook
Hinwood
Lower Newton Fm
Lea
Shorthill
Wood Hall
Lythwood Hall
Betton Coppice
Cronkhill
Beslow
Farley
Hinton
Arscott
Bomere Pool
Bomere Wood
Betton Pool
Cross Houses
Brompton
Wroxeter
Donnington
Charlton Hill
Rushton
Asterley
Sibberscote Manor
Arscott Villa
Annscroft
Great Lyth
Lythbank
Old Coppice
Norton Fm
Berrington Hall
Halfway Ho
Westley
Plealey Villa
Plealey
Spring Coppice
Little Lyth
Lyth Hill
Longwood
Upper Longwood
Malehurst
Pontesbury
Pontesford
Longden
Exfords Green
Chatford
Hunger Hill
Condover
Cantlop Bridge
Berrington
Black Barn
Cotons Fm
Eaton Mascott
Eyton on Severn
Eaton Constantine
Hem Fm
Horsebridge
Ind Est
New Ho
Radlith
Longden Manor
Cound Brook
Home Fm
Cantlop
Oaklands Fm
Dryton
Ransiett Ho
Leighton
The Grove
Pontesbury Hill
Pontesford Hill
Lower Common
Condover Hall
Grove Fm
Green Fm
Cantlop Wood
Pitchford Hall
Upper Cound
Cound
Soundlane
Eye Fm
Reabrook
Callow Hill
Minsterley
Earl's Hill
Oaks
Longden Wood Fm
Longden Common
Whaileybourne Fm
Leechmeadow Cott
Poles Coppice
Oaks Wood
Church Hill Wood
Castle Place
Stapleton
Gonsal Fm
Berriewood Stud Fm
Pitchford Park
Blackpits
Golding Rough
Wormwood Coppice
Leasowes
Harnage
Etsell
Ploxgreen
Lees Coppice
Wrentnall
Moat Fm
Wayford Br
Great Ryton
Lightgreen Coppice
Cressage
Ladyoak
Maddox's Coppice
Habberley
Broom Hill
The Gorse
Lower Shadymoor Fm
Little Ryton
Wheathall
Big Wood
Pitchford
Golding
Acton Pigott
Cressage Ho
Kenton
Belswardine Hall
Church Pulverbatch
Dorrington
Bus Pk
Ryton Grove
Row Brook
Moreton Fm
Wagbeach
Eastridge Wood
Pulverbatch
Lower Netley Fm
Upper Shadymoor Fm
Dorrington Grove
Evenwood Common
Coundmoor
Park Fm
Bannister's Coppice
Snailbeach
The Waterwheel
Lawn Hill
Marsley Fm
Wilderley Hall
Netley Old Hall Fm
Rowe Fm
Acton Burnell
Harnage Grange
Park Coppice
Crowsnest
Crowsnest Dingle
The Hollies
Brook Coppice
Westcott
Coppice Fm
New Hall
Netley Hall
Fox Covert
Frodesley Grange
Frodesley
Acton Burnell Castle
Park Wood
Grange Hill
Lord's Coppice
Harley
Hogstow Hall
Underhill Hall
Smethcott Common
Smethcott Dingle
Longnor Park
Longnor
Bull Fm
Fetch Hill
Stone Ho
Stiperstones
Mytton Dingle
Gittinshay Wood
Paulith Bank
Cothercott Hill
Moat Ho
Frodesley Lane Fm
Hobsley Coppice
Highlands Fm
Springs Fm
Upper Kenley Gorse
Harley Hill
Pollardine Fm
Park Fm
Ruckley
Kenley
Stiperstones
Perkins Beach
Leasowes Bank Fm
New Leasowes Fm
Wilderley Hill
Smethcott
Fields Fm
Green Fm
Bentley Ford Fm
Frodesley Lodge
Langley Hall
Langley Chapel & Gatehouse
Rowley Fm
Blakeway Fm
Gatten Lodge
Picklescott Hill
Picklescott
Old Mill Fm
Walkmills
Castle Hill Fm
Coppice Ho
Mapp Fm
New Hall
The Grange
Gatten Plantn
Betchcott Hills
Betchcott Hollow
Castle Bank
Betchcott
Leebotwood
Lawley Fm
Causewaywood
Netherwood Coppice
Kenley Common
Blakeway Coppice
Stitt Fm
Woolstaston
Day Ho
Birch Coppice
Broome
Church Preen
Hughley
Stretton Westwood
Burton Westwood
The Bog
Squilver
Damford Brook
Hawkham Hollow
Lower Wood
Brook Ho
Penkridge Hall
The Lawley
Hoar Edge
High Fields
Chatwell Hall
The Falls Fm
Henmoor Hill
Presthope
Ratlinghope Hill
Wild Moor
High Park Ho
Hollyhurst
Brookshill Marsh
Stedment
Cold Hill Fm
Ratlinghope
Inwood
Plush Hill
Heath Ho
Comley
Folly Bank
Enchmarsh
Lea Hill Fm
Plaish
Plaish Park
Day Houses
Upper Hill Fm
Bourton Grange
Bridges
Bridges Long Mynd
Overs
All Stretton
Sheaves Fm
School Ho
Easthopewood
Bourton
Great Wood Ho
Birchope
Coppice Fm
Haddon Hill
Caer Caradog Hill
Cardington
Eastope Wood
Hays Mill
England Shelve
New Ho
Priory Cott
Nover's Hill
Willstone
Gretton
Larchwood Fm
Lushcott
Patton Grange
Woodhouse Fields
Beach Fm
Adstone Hill
Cwnd Ho
Medlicott
Cow Ridge
Carding Mill Valley
Three Fingers Rock
Mill Fm
Easthope
Norbury Hill
New House Fm
Willstone Hill
Hill End
Wood Fm
Natal Barn
Lutwyche Hall
Larden Cott
Bradeley Fm
Pole Bank
Boiling Well
Church Stretton
Cwms Fm
Middle Hill
Cardington Moor
East Wall
Longville in the Dale
Pilgrim Cott
The Ditches
Patton
Cawleys Coppice
Ashbrook
Stoneacton
Brockton
Larden Grange
Corve Barn
Squire Hill
Wentnor Prolley Moor
Narnell's Rock
Burway Hill
Sandford Avenue
Mogg Forest
Larden Hall
Norbury
Hazler
Hazler Hill
Ragleth Wood
Wall Bank
Woodgate Cott
Wilderhope Manor
Weston
Walkmill
Wentnor
The Long Mynd
Round Hill
Ashes Hollow
Edge Fm
Upper Barn
More Hall
Asterton Prolley Moor
Little Stretton
Hope Bowdler
Mount Flirt
Wall under Heywood
Shipton Hall
Upper Netchwood
Netchwood Common
Grove Cott
Callow Hill
Hargrove Fm
Rushbury
Corfield Fm
Whitcot
Crifton Ho
Asterton
Yapsel Bank
Packetstone Hill
Ragdon
Chelmick
Soudley
Stanway Manor
Upper Barn
Shipton
Bush Fm
Minton
Whitefields Fm
Roman Bank
Stanton Long
Trow Brook
Coates Fm
Hardwick
Handless
Shooter's Knoll
Manor Fm
Birtley
Ticklerton
New Ho
Club Fm
Field Ho
Derrington
Heath
Bow Ho
Marshbrook
Hatton
Brookhampton
Eaton
Myndtown
Priors Holt Hill
Hamperley
Swiss Cott
Acton Scott
Acton Scott Historic Working Farm
Hattongrove Fm
Ape Dale
Eaton Coppice
Stars Coppice
Big Wood
Hungerford Ho
Broadstone
Holdgate
Ruthall
Myndmill Fm
Churchmoor Hill
New Hall
Wetmore Fm
Wenlock Edge
Hungerford
Hall Fm
New Bldgs
The Leath
Ditton Priors
Choulton
Black Knoll
Churchmoor Hall
Churchmoor Rough
Whittingslow
Harton
Middlehope
Little London
Millichope Park
Birchen Coppice
Earnstrey Hall
Powkesmoor Coppice
Totterton
Eyton
Cwm Head
Marsh Fm
Bushmoor
Henley
Wolverton
Harton Wood
Aston Deans
Munslow
Beambridge
Balaam's Heath
Lower Earnstrey Park Fm
New Earnstrey Park
Upper Earnstrey Park
Ditton Enclosure
Hillside
Totterton Hall
Plowden
The Corner
Felhampton
Alcaston
Wolverton Wood
Burwood
Corve Dale
Brook Ho
Baucott Fm
Tugford
Folly Fm
Plowden Hall
Plowden Woods
Horderley
Woolston
Leamoor Common
Wettles
Westhope
Hazeldine Coppice
Aston Hall
Aston Munslow
Broncroft Park Cotts
Broncroft Lodge
Abdon
Red Ho Fm
Edgton
Ridgway
Gate Ho
Upper Affcot
Hope Dale
Pinstones
Bache Mill
Wynett Coppice
Heath Fm
Manor Ho
Abdon Liberty
Lower Gardens
Lynchgate
Basford
Longville Common
Upper Barn
Wistanstow
Strefford
Morwood
Hill-End Fm
Corfton Bache
Diddlebury
Larkfield Fm
Upper Heath
Brown Clee Hill
Burwarton Park
Laplow Bank
Grist Ho
Round Oak
Wart Hill
Cheny Longville
Berrymill Cottage
Callow Hill
Corfton
Delbury Hall
Boulden
Woodbank
Short Wood
Barlow Home Fm
The Grove
Lower Dinchope
Pedlar's Rest
Christmas Cross
Peaton
Peatonstrand
New Ho
Clee St Margaret
Cockshutford
Hopesay Hill
Newington
Ireland Cott
Halford
Culmington Manor
New Ho
Hill Ho Fm
Elsich Manor
Cleemarsh
The Yeld
Upper Hill Ho
Fort Burrow
Hopesay Common
Hopesay
Sibdon Carwood
Bus Pk
Craven Arms
Upper Dinchope
Shawbank
Marsh Barn
Seifton
Sparchford
Lawton
Patch Ho
Cold Weston Court
Holly Bush Fm
Tana Leas Fm
Stokegorse
Bockleton Court
Blackford
Old Lodge Fm
Kempton
Long Meadowend
Clun Road
Discovery Centre
Greenway Cross
Medley Park Fm
Great Sutton
Sutton Hill
Weston Hill
New Ho
Red Hill
Aston on Clun
Oaker Wood
Craven Arms Road
Whettleton
Culmington
The Green
Bache
Little Sutton
Lydehole Fm
Stoke St Milborough
Stoke Court
The Gore
Little Brampton
River Kemp
Stokesay Castle
Stokesay
Norton
Upper Hayton
Lower Hayton
Hayton's Bent
New Ho
Hoptongate
Hopton Hall Fm
Poston Coppice
Wain Hill
Little Wood
Coverige Fields
Broome
Nortoncamp Wood
Stoke Wood
Burley
Shropshire Hills
Purslow
River Clun
Clunbury
Coston Manor
New Ho Fm
Vernolds Common
Titterhill
Stoke Lodge Fm
Cleedownton
Bromdon
Clunbury Hill
Weo Fm
View Edge or Weo Edge
Park Fm
Hopton Cangeford
Gibbridge Fm
Gorst Barn
Aldon
Stokewood Fm
Downton Hall
The Moor
Langley
Twitchen
Brandhill
Aldon Court
Onibury
Walton
Stanton Lacy
Upper Ledwyche
Henleyhill
Ripletts
Cleeton Court
Three Ashes
May Hill
Pools Fm
Cleestanton
Abcott
Clungunford
Swan Hill
Coppy Ho
Stokesay Court
High Walton
The Hope
East Lodge
Bank Fm
Hopton Castle
Shelderton
Whittytree
Wootton
White Ho
The Barn
Yewtree
Stocking Fm
Cleeton St Mary
Shropshire
River Severn
River Onny
Byne Brook
Pye Brook
Eaton Brook
Hughley Brook
Rea Brook
Corve Brook
Lakehouse Brook
Dogditch Brook
A458
A5
A488
A49
A489
A4169
B4386
B4380
B4394
B5061
B4499
B4370
B4371
B4368
B4378
B4365
B4364
B4368
B4367
B4385
B4386
London Rd
Wenlock Rd
Shrewsbury Road
Ludlow Road
SJ
SO
149
132
115
1
2
3
4
5
6
7
8
9
10
11
A
B
C
D
E
F
G
H

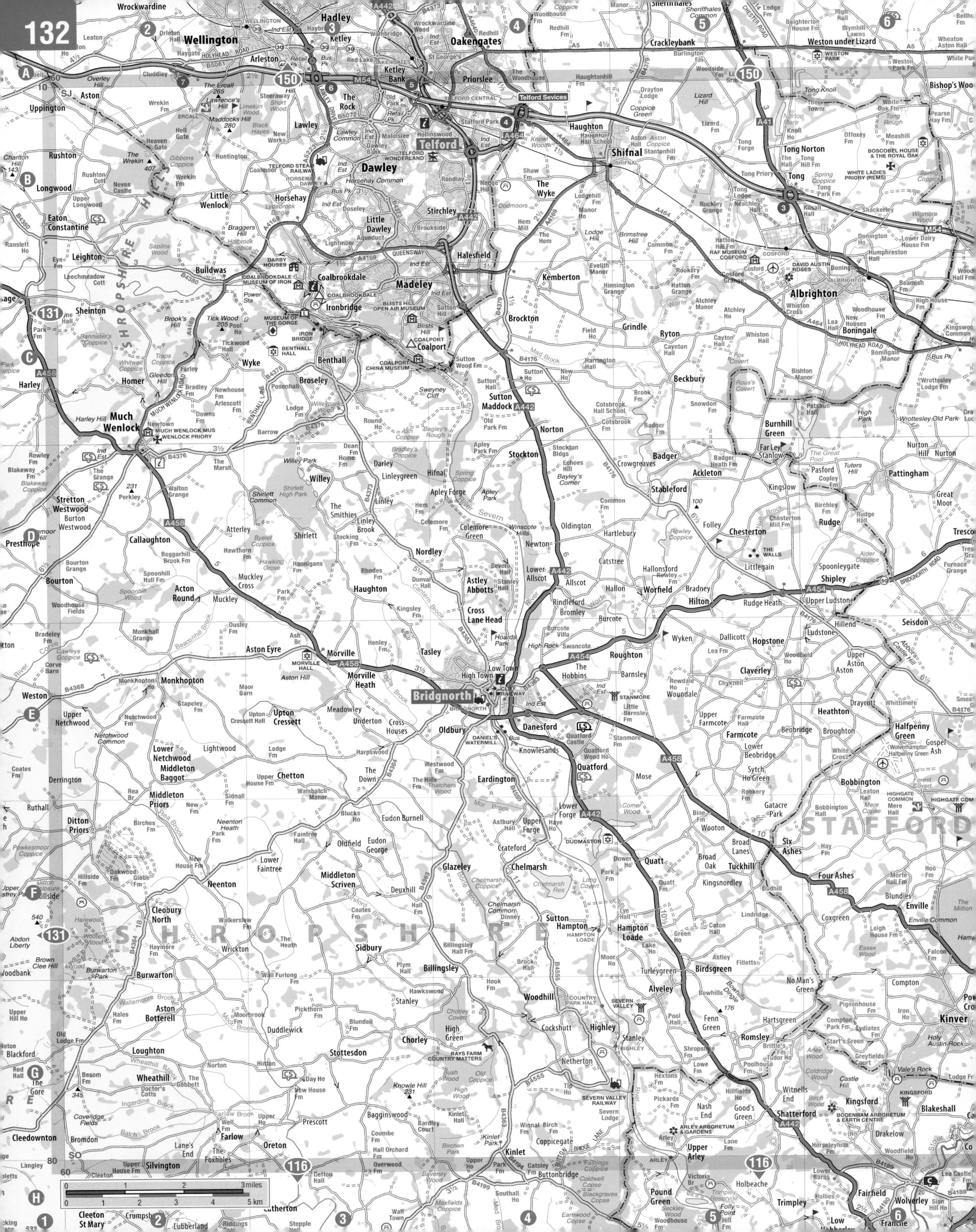

Wrockwardine
Wellington
Hadley
Ketley
Oakengates
Crackleybank
Weston under Lizard
Arleston
St George's
Priorslee
Ketley Bank
Telford Sevices
Haughton
Bishop's Wood
Overley Hill
Aston
Uppington
Cluddley
The Ercall
Lawrence's Hill
Maddocks Hill
Wrekin Fm
Steeraway
Short Wood
The Rock
Lawley
Telford
Dawley
Shifnal
Tong Norton
Tong
Tong Knoll
Lizard Hill
The Wrekin
Heaven Gate
Rushton
Longwood
Little Wenlock
Horsehay
Stirchley
Little Dawley
The Wyke
Shaw Fm
Eaton Constantine
Leighton
Buildwas
Coalbrookdale
Madeley
Halesfield
Kemberton
Ironbridge
Brockton
Grindle
Ryton
Albrighton
Boningale
Sheinton
Coalport
Benthall
Broseley
Wyke
Homer
Harley
Much Wenlock
Sutton Maddock
Norton
Beckbury
Burnhill Green
Badger
Ackleton
Stableford
Pattingham
Barrow
Willey
Darley
Linleygreen
Hifnal
Apley Forge
Stockton
Crowgreaves
Kingslow
Chesterton
Rudge
Stretton Westwood
Burton Westwood
Callaughton
Shirlett
Atterley
Nordley
Oldington
Hartlebury
Folley
Littlegain
Presthope
Bourton
Acton Round
Muckley Cross
Muckley
Haughton
Astley Abbotts
Allscot
Worfield
Hallon
Catstree
Hallonsford
Hilton
Shipley
Cross Lane Head
Rindleford
Bromley
Burcote
Wyken
Upper Ludstone
Seisdon
Aston Eyre
Morville
Tasley
Roughton
Hopstone
Claverley
Weston
Monkhopton
Morville Heath
Bridgnorth
Low Town
High Town
The Hobbins
Barnsley
Woundale
Upton Cressett
Meadowley
Underton
Oldbury
Danesford
Quatford
Heathton
Halfpenny Green
Upper Netchwood
Lower Netchwood
Middleton Baggot
Chetton
Eardington
Mose
Farmcote
Broughton
Bobbington
Derrington
Middleton Priors
Ditton Priors
Ruthall
Eudon Burnell
Lower Forge
Upper Forge
Oldfield
Eudon George
Grateford
Quatt
Six Ashes
Tuckhill
STAFFORD
Lower Faintree
Chelmarsh
Middleton Scriven
Glazeley
Deuxhill
Four Ashes
Neenton
Cleobury North
Sutton
Hampton
Hampton Loade
Enville
SHROPSHIRE
Sidbury
Billingsley
Birdsgreen
Burwarton
Alveley
Compton
Stanley
Aston Botterell
Woodhill
Highley
Kinver
Duddlewick
Chorley
High Green
Romsley
Loughton
Stottesdon
Blackford
Wheathill
Netherton
The Gobbett
Kingsford
Blakeshall
Shatterford
Prescott
Bagginswood
Cleedownton
Bromdon
Farlow
Oreton
Kinlet
Upper Arley
Silvington
Buttonbridge
Holbeache
Fairfield
Wolverley
Pound Green
Trimpley
Cleeton St Mary
Crumpsbrook
Catherton
Lubberland
A442
A458
A454
A464
A5
M54
A41
B4176
B4363
B4364
B4555
B4194
B4373
B4376
B4378
B4380
B4368
B4379
B4169
A4169
B4190
B4189
150
131
116
3 miles
5 km

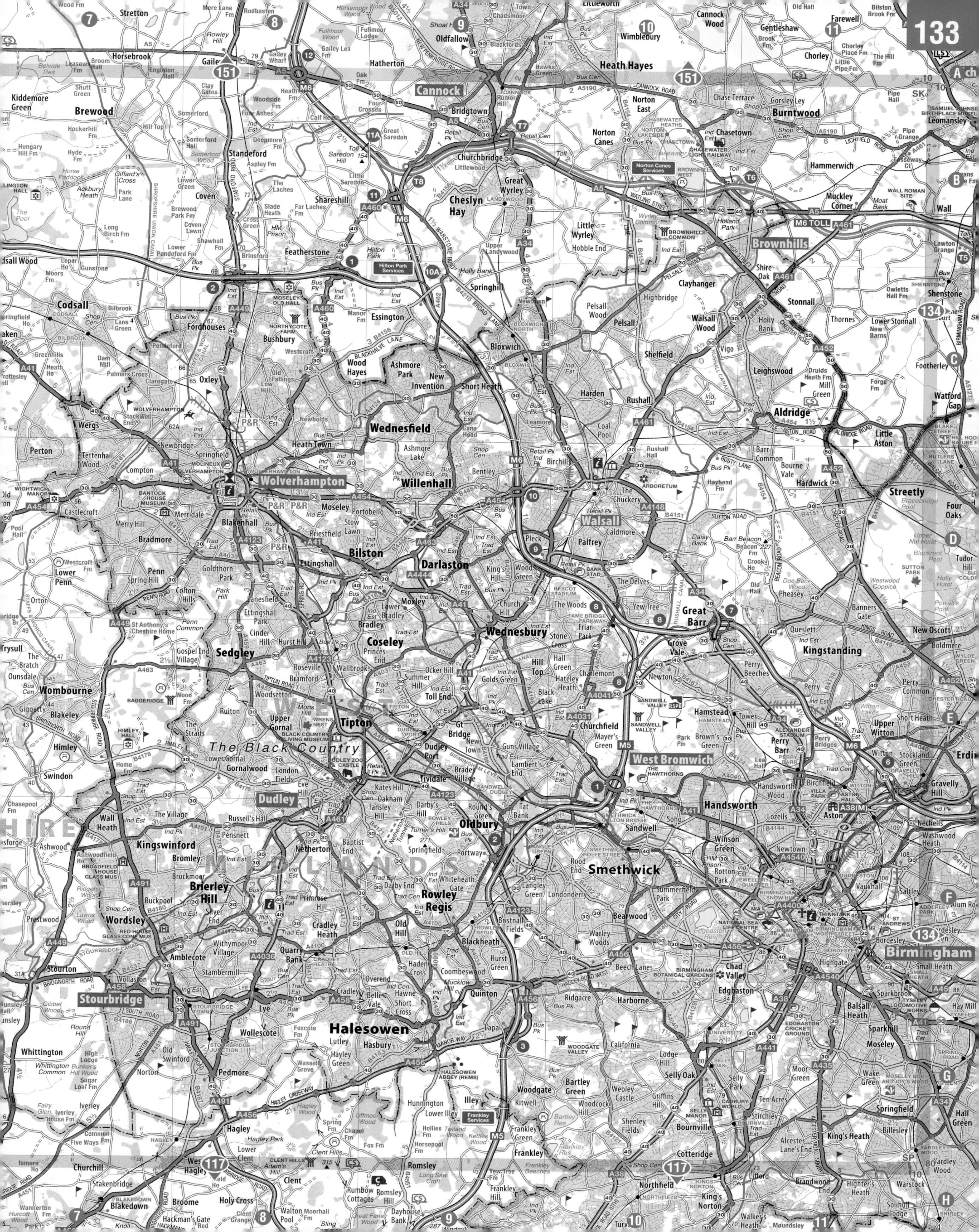

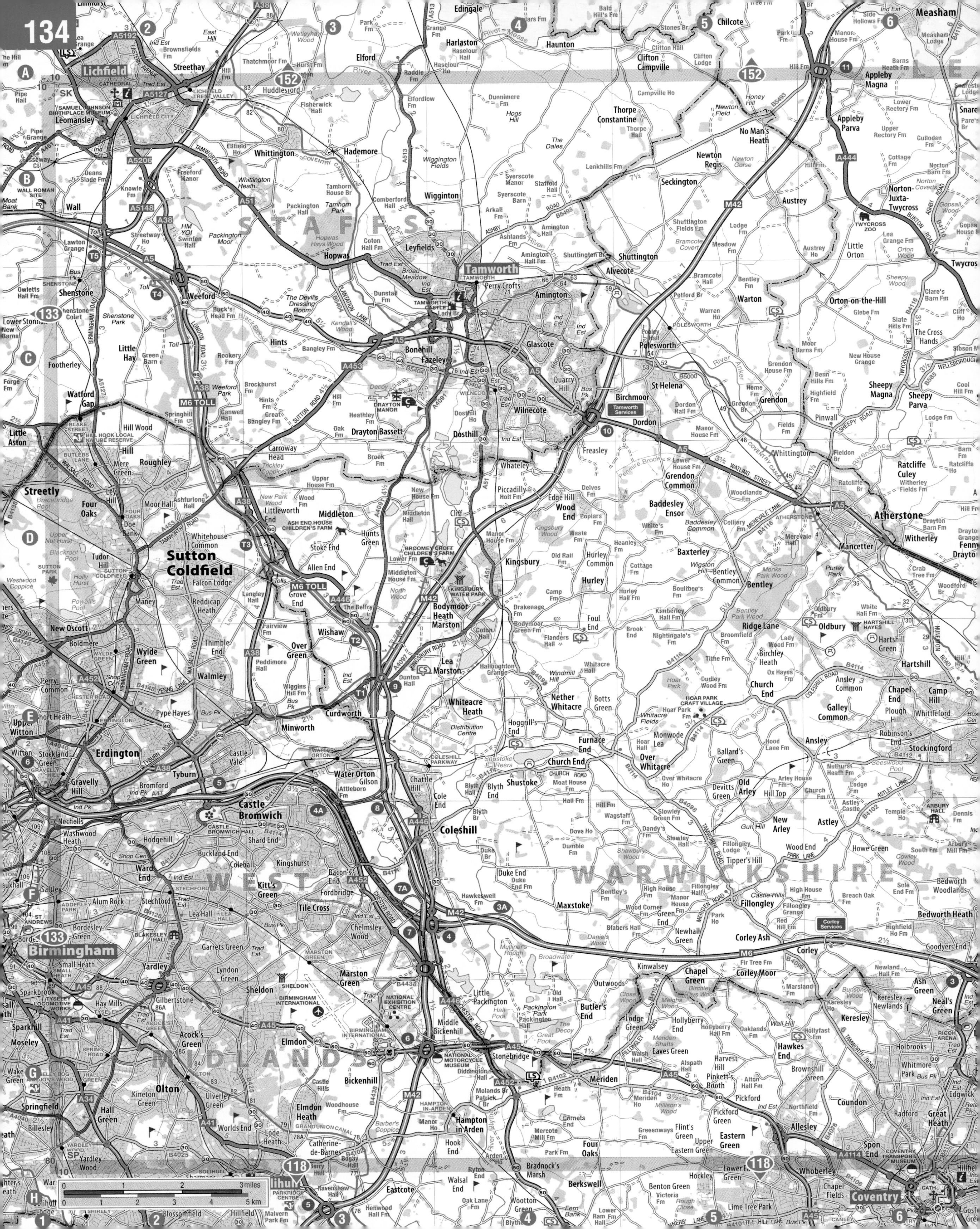
Lichfield
Streethay
Elford
Harlaston
Edingale
Haunton
Clifton Campville
Chilcote
Measham
Appleby Magna
Appleby Parva
Leomansley
Whittington
Hademore
Wigginton
Thorpe Constantine
No Man's Heath
Newton Regis
Seckington
Austrey
Norton-Juxta-Twycross
Wall
STAFFS
Hopwas
Leyfields
Tamworth
Shuttington
Alvecote
Amington
Warton
Orton-on-the-Hill
Shenstone
Weeford
Hints
Bonehill
Fazeley
Glascote
Polesworth
St Helena
Grendon
Sheepy Magna
Sheepy Parva
Little Hay
Watford Gap
Wilnecote
Birchmoor
Dordon
Drayton Bassett
Dosthill
Little Aston
Hill Wood
Roughley
Streetly
Four Oaks
Middleton
Edge Hill
Wood End
Baddesley Ensor
Grendon Common
Atherstone
Mancetter
Witherley
Sutton Coldfield
Kingsbury
Hurley
Baxterley
Bentley
Oldbury
New Oscott
Wylde Green
Walmley
Bodymoor Heath
Marston
Wishaw
Over Green
Lea Marston
Ridge Lane
Hartshill
Erdington
Curdworth
Minworth
Whitacre Heath
Nether Whitacre
Church End
Ansley
Stockingford
Castle Vale
Water Orton
Shustoke
Furnace End
Over Whitacre
Old Arley
New Arley
Astley
Castle Bromwich
Coleshill
WEST
WARWICKSHIRE
Maxstoke
Fillongley
Corley Ash
Corley
Birmingham
Yardley
Marston Green
Sheldon
Little Packington
Chapel Green
Corley Moor
Keresley
Elmdon
Bickenhill
Meriden
MIDLANDS
Olton
Hampton in Arden
Allesley
Coundon
Eastcote
Berkswell
Coventry
M6 TOLL
M42
M6
A5
A38
A45
A446
A452

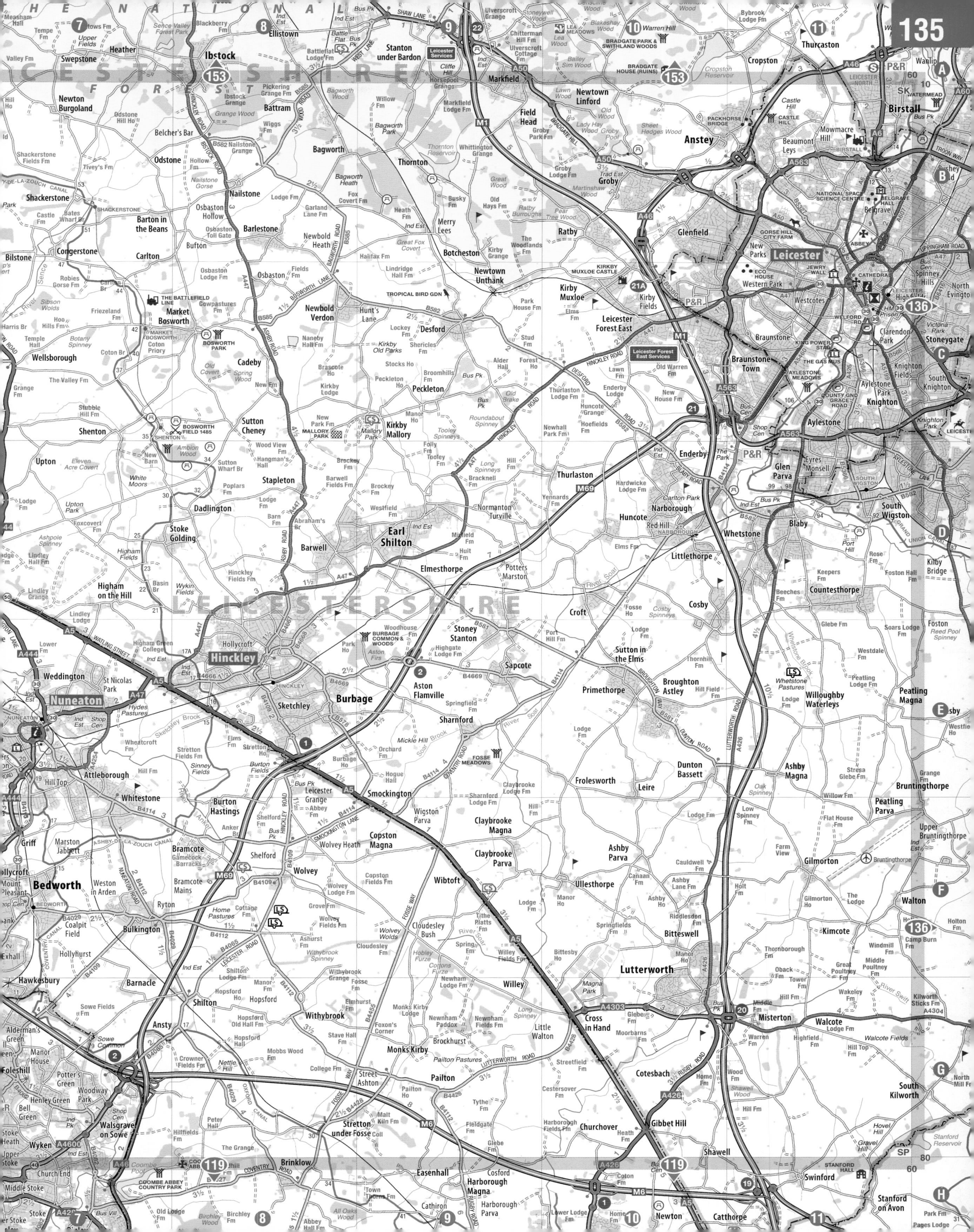

LEICESTERSHIRE
Ibstock
Ellistown
Stanton under Bardon
Markfield
Newtown Linford
Thurcaston
Cropston
Birstall
Anstey
Field Head
Groby
Ratby
Glenfield
Leicester
Kirby Muxloe
Leicester Forest East
Braunstone Town
Aylestone
Knighton
Stoneygate
Glen Parva
South Wigston
Blaby
Enderby
Narborough
Whetstone
Thurlaston
Huncote
Cosby
Countesthorpe
Kilby Bridge
Croft
Sapcote
Stoney Stanton
Sutton in the Elms
Broughton Astley
Primethorpe
Dunton Bassett
Frolesworth
Leire
Ashby Magna
Willoughby Waterleys
Peatling Magna
Peatling Parva
Bruntingthorpe
Gilmorton
Kimcote
Walton
Lutterworth
Bitteswell
Ullesthorpe
Ashby Parva
Claybrooke Magna
Claybrooke Parva
Misterton
Walcote
South Kilworth
Cotesbach
Gibbet Hill
Shawell
Swinford
Catthorpe
Stanford on Avon
Churchover
Harborough Magna
Pailton
Monks Kirby
Brinklow
Easenhall
Stretton under Fosse
Withybrook
Wibtoft
Willey
Cross in Hand
Little Walton
Hinckley
Burbage
Sketchley
Aston Flamville
Sharnford
Smockington
Wolvey
Copston Magna
Earl Shilton
Barwell
Elmesthorpe
Kirkby Mallory
Peckleton
Desford
Newbold Verdon
Bagworth
Thornton
Battram
Nailstone
Barlestone
Osbaston
Market Bosworth
Cadeby
Carlton
Congerstone
Shackerstone
Barton in the Beans
Odstone
Newton Burgoland
Swepstone
Heather
Sutton Cheney
Shenton
Stapleton
Dadlington
Stoke Golding
Higham on the Hill
Upton
Wellsborough
Nuneaton
Attleborough
Whitestone
Burton Hastings
Bramcote
Bulkington
Bedworth
Weddington
Shilton
Ansty
Barnacle
Hawkesbury
Walsgrave on Sowe
Wyken
Botcheston
Newtown Unthank
Merry Lees
M1
M69
M6
A5
A47
A46
A426
A447

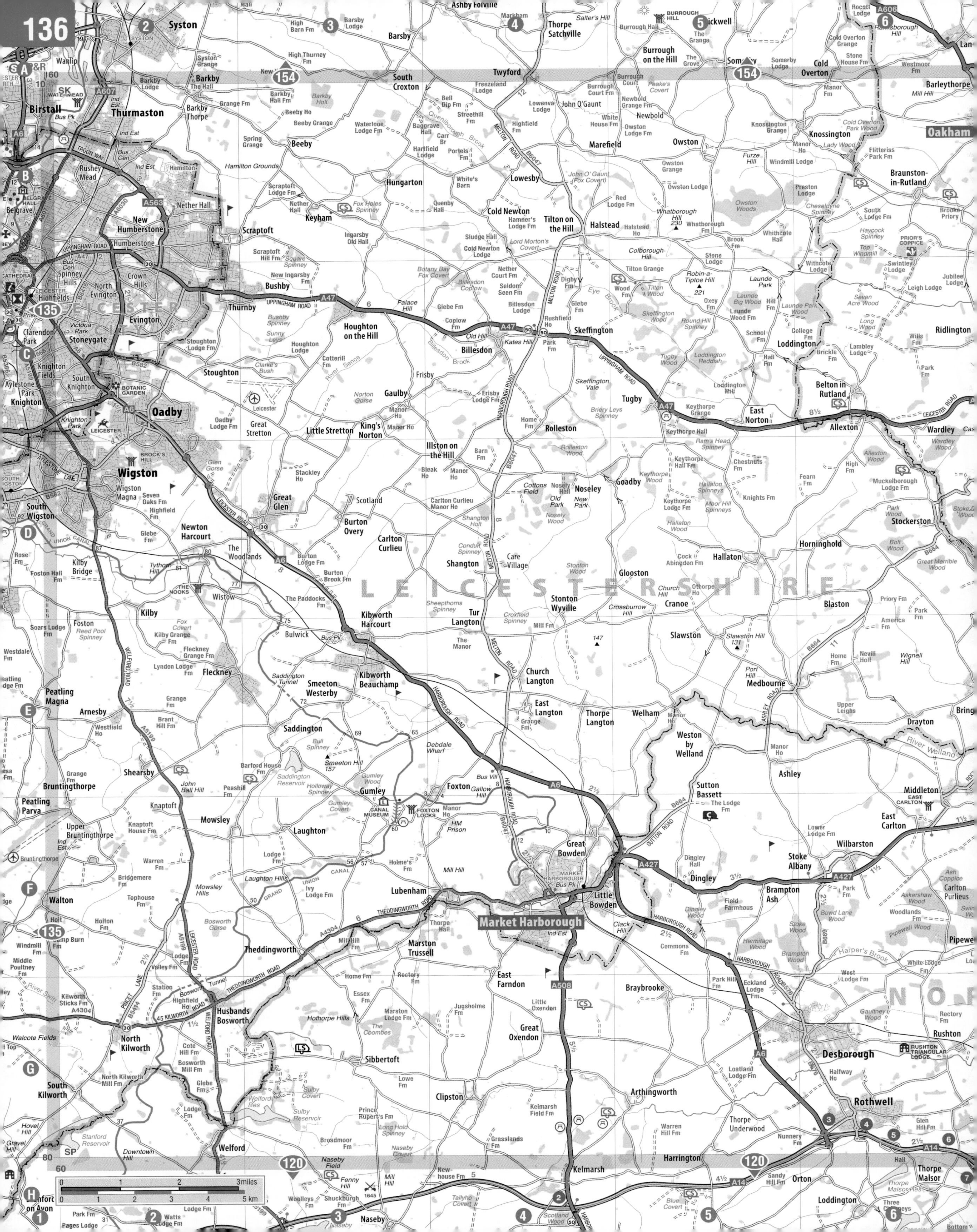
LEICESTERSHIRE
Leicester
Oadby
Wigston
Market Harborough
Desborough
Rothwell
Oakham
Syston
Birstall
Thurmaston
Barsby
Twyford
Hungarton
Billesdon
Skeffington
Tugby
Allexton
Kibworth Harcourt
Kibworth Beauchamp
Fleckney
Saddington
Gumley
Foxton
Lubenham
Husbands Bosworth
North Kilworth
South Kilworth
Welford
Theddingworth
Sibbertoft
Clipston
Kelmarsh
Naseby
Harrington
Arthingworth
Braybrooke
Great Bowden
Little Bowden
Medbourne
Hallaton
Church Langton
Great Glen
Houghton on the Hill
Scraptoft
Thurnby
Rolleston
Noseley
Goadby
Blaston
Drayton
Ashley
Wilbarston
Stoke Albany
Dingley
Brampton Ash
East Farndon
Great Oxendon
Marston Trussell
Thorpe Malsor
Orton
Loddington
Rushton
154
135
120

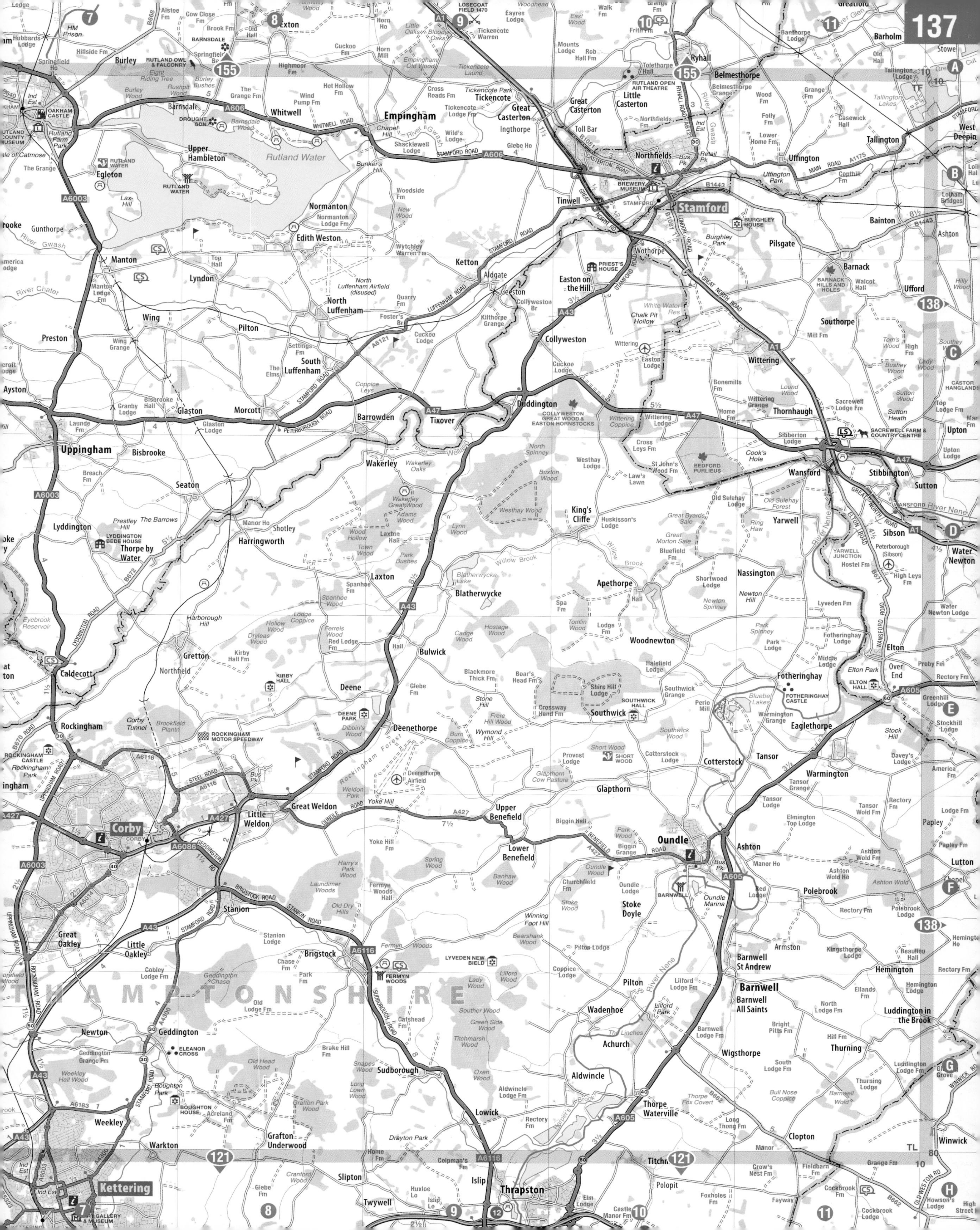
Burley
Exton
Empingham
Tickencote
Great Casterton
Little Casterton
Ryhall
Belmesthorpe
Barholm
Stowe
Oakham
Barnsdale
Whitwell
Rutland Water
Upper Hambleton
Egleton
Normanton
Edith Weston
Tinwell
Northfields
Stamford
Uffington
Tallington
West Deeping
Burghley House
Pilsgate
Bainton
Ashton
Manton
Lyndon
Ketton
Aldgate
Geeston
Wothorpe
Easton on the Hill
Barnack
Ufford
North Luffenham
Wing
Pilton
Preston
South Luffenham
Collyweston
Southorpe
Wittering
Ayston
Glaston
Morcott
Barrowden
Tixover
Duddington
Thornhaugh
Uppingham
Bisbrooke
Wakerley
Wansford
Stibbington
Upton
Sutton
Seaton
King's Cliffe
Yarwell
Sibson
Lyddington
Harringworth
Thorpe by Water
Laxton
Nassington
Water Newton
Apethorpe
Blatherwycke
Woodnewton
Elton
Caldecott
Gretton
Bulwick
Deene
Fotheringhay
Southwick
Rockingham
Deenethorpe
Eaglethorpe
Tansor
Cotterstock
Corby
Great Weldon
Little Weldon
Upper Benefield
Glapthorn
Warmington
Lower Benefield
Oundle
Ashton
Papley
Lutton
Stanion
Stoke Doyle
Polebrook
Great Oakley
Little Oakley
Brigstock
Barnwell St Andrew
Armston
Hemington
NORTHAMPTONSHIRE
Pilton
Barnwell
Barnwell All Saints
Newton
Geddington
Wadenhoe
Luddington in the Brook
Achurch
Thurning
Wigsthorpe
Sudborough
Aldwincle
Weekley
Lowick
Thorpe Waterville
Clopton
Winwick
Warkton
Grafton Underwood
Slipton
Islip
Thrapston
Titchmarsh
Twywell
Kettering
Polopit

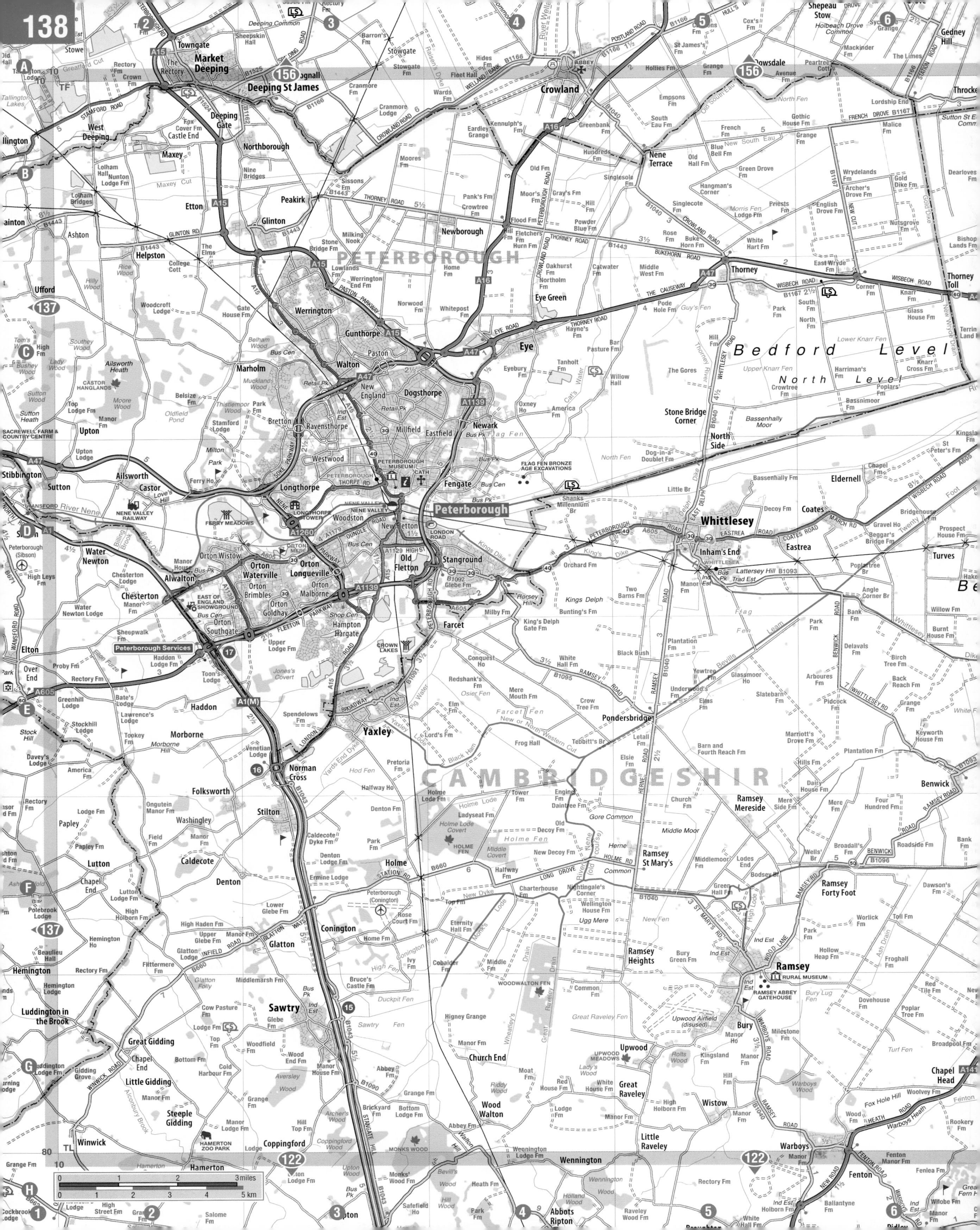

Market Deeping
Deeping St James
Crowland
Peterborough
PETERBOROUGH
Werrington
Gunthorpe
Paston
Walton
Dogsthorpe
Eye
Eye Green
Newborough
Thorney
Thorney Toll
Bedford Level
North Level
Whittlesey
Eastrea
Coates
Turves
Stanground
Old Fletton
Woodston
Longthorpe
Orton Longueville
Orton Waterville
Orton Wistow
Alwalton
Chesterton
Castor
Ailsworth
Sutton
Stibbington
Elton
Yaxley
Farcet
Norman Cross
Folksworth
Stilton
Holme
Conington
Glatton
Sawtry
Caldecote
Denton
Morborne
Haddon
Washingley
Lutton
Papley
Hemington
Luddington in the Brook
Great Gidding
Little Gidding
Steeple Gidding
Winwick
Hamerton
Coppingford
Wood Walton
Upwood
Great Raveley
Little Raveley
Wistow
Bury
Ramsey
Ramsey St Mary's
Ramsey Heights
Ramsey Mereside
Ramsey Forty Foot
Pondersbridge
Benwick
Warboys
Fenton
Wennington
Abbots Ripton
Chapel Head
CAMBRIDGESHIRE
Peterborough Services
Glinton
Peakirk
Etton
Helpston
Maxey
Northborough
Deeping Gate
West Deeping
Ufford
Ashton
Upton
Marholm
Bretton
Ravensthorpe
Westwood
Newark
Eastfield
Millfield
Fengate
Nene Terrace
Stone Bridge Corner
North Side
Inham's End
Eldernell
Gedney Hill
Shepeau Stow
Dowsdale
Towngate

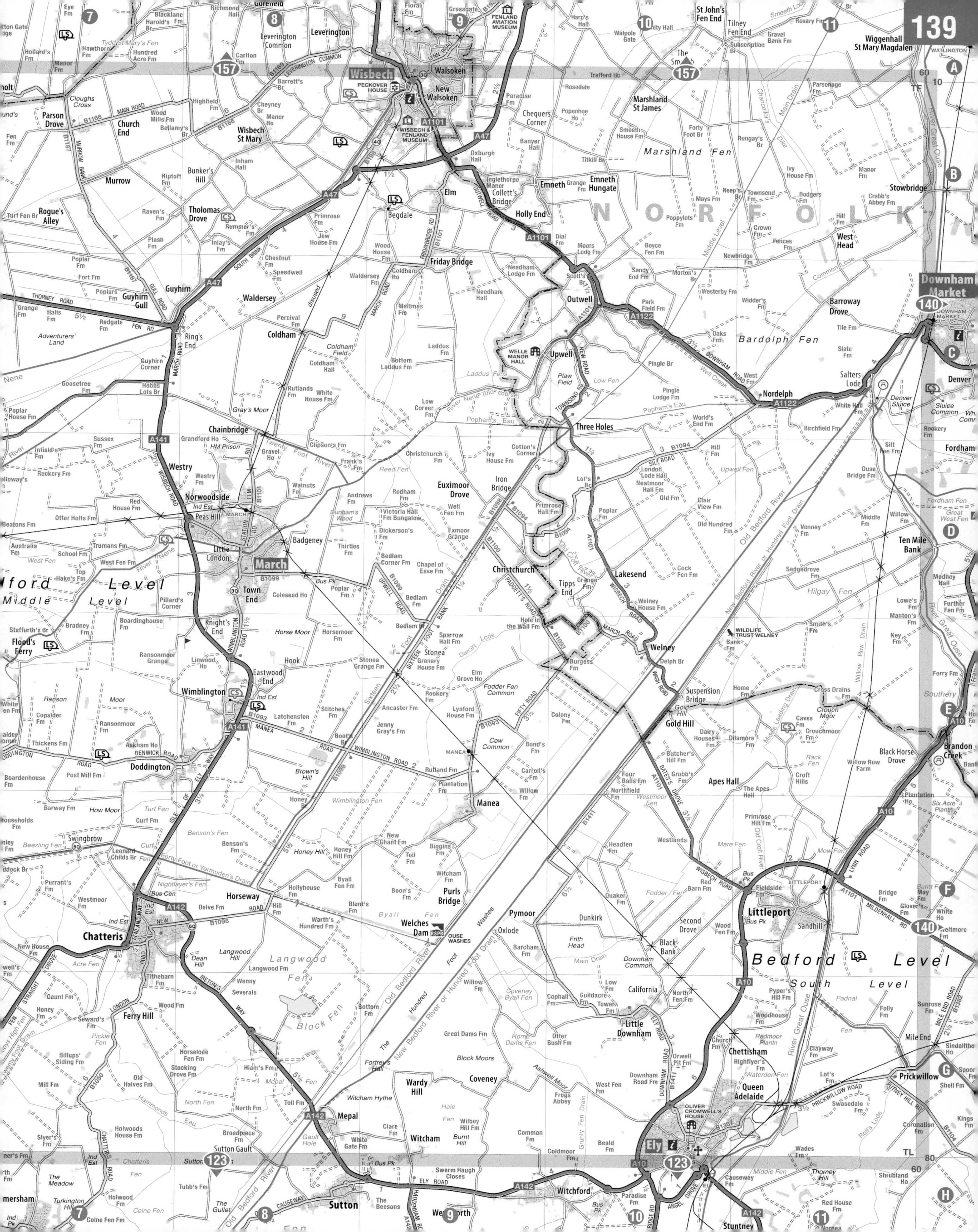
Wisbech
Walsoken
New Walsoken
Peckover House
Wisbech & Fenland Museum
Fenland Aviation Museum
Leverington
Leverington Common
Gorefield
Parson Drove
Church End
Wisbech St Mary
Murrow
Rogue's Alley
Tholomas Drove
Guyhirn
Guyhirn Gull
Waldersey
Coldham
Ring's End
Elm
Begdale
Friday Bridge
Emneth
Emneth Hungate
Holly End
Outwell
Upwell
Welle Manor Hall
Marshland St James
Marshland Fen
St John's Fen End
Tilney Fen End
Wiggenhall St Mary Magdalen
Stowbridge
NORFOLK
West Head
Downham Market
Barroway Drove
Bardolph Fen
Nordelph
Salters Lode
Denver
Denver Sluice
Three Holes
Chainbridge
Westry
Norwoodside
Peas Hill
March
Little London
Town End
Badgeney
Euximoor Drove
Iron Bridge
Christchurch
Tipps End
Lakesend
Welney
Wildlife Trust Welney
Ten Mile Bank
Hilgay Fen
Fordham
Bedford Level
Middle Level
Flood's Ferry
Knight's End
Wimblington
Eastwood End
Hook
Stonea
Doddington
Manea
Horseway
Chatteris
Swingbrow
Welches Dam
Ouse Washes
Pymoor
Oxlode
Gold Hill
Suspension Bridge
Apes Hall
Littleport
Sandhill
Brandon Creek
Black Horse Drove
Dunkirk
Black Bank
Downham Common
California
Little Downham
Ferry Hill
Langwood Fen
Block Fen
Wardy Hill
Coveney
Mepal
Witcham
Chettisham
Queen Adelaide
Prickwillow
Mile End
Oliver Cromwell's House
Ely
Sutton
Witchford
Wentworth
Stuntney
Sutton Gault
Old Bedford River
New Bedford River or Hundred Foot Drain
Sixteen Foot Drain
Forty Foot or Vermuden's Drain
River Great Ouse
A47
A141
A142
A1101
A1122
A10
B1098
B1093
B1099
B1100
B1094
B1411
B1382
157
140
123

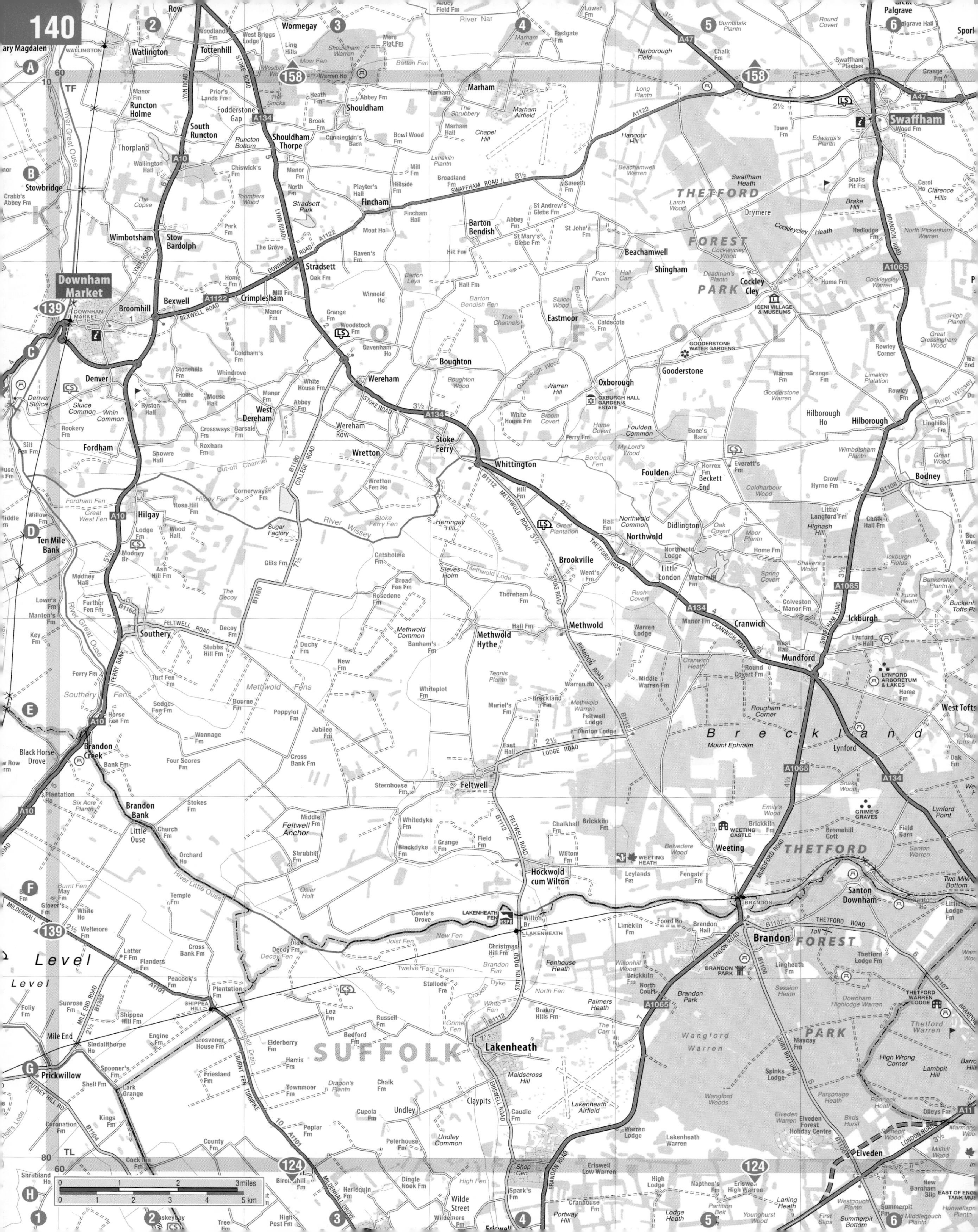
Row
Wormegay
Woodlands Fm
West Briggs Lodge
Ling Hills
Shouldham Warren
Mere Plot Fm
Mow Fen
Warren Ho
Button Fen
River Nar
Marham Fen
Eastgate Fm
Lower Fm
Narborough Field
Burntstalk Plantn
Round Covert
Great Palgrave
Palgrave Hall
Sporle
Watlington
Tottenhill
Runcton Holme
Manor Fm
Prior's Lands Fm
Fodderstone Gap
Heath Fm
Abbey Fm
Shouldham
Marham
Marham Ho
The Shrubbery
Marham Airfield
Long Plantn
Chalk Fm
Swaffham Plashes
Grange Fm
Swaffham
Wood Fm
South Runcton
Runcton Bottom
Shouldham Thorpe
Brook Fm
Cunnington's Barn
Bowl Wood
Marham Hall
Chapel Hill
Hangour Hill
Town Fm
Edwards's Plantn
Thorpland
Wallington Hall
Chiswick's Fm
Manor Fm
North Fm
Stradsett Park
Playter's Hall
Mill Fm
Hillside Fm
Limekiln Plantn
Broadland Fm
Smeeth Fm
Beachamwell Warren
Swaffham Heath
Snails Pit Fm
Carol Ho
Clarence Hills
Stowbridge
Crabb's Abbey Fm
The Copse
Toombers Wood
Fincham
Fincham Hall
SWAFFHAM ROAD
St Andrew's Glebe Fm
Larch Wood
THETFORD
Drymere
Brake Hill
North Pickenham Warren
Wimbotsham
Stow Bardolph
Park Fm
The Grove
Moat Ho
Barton Bendish
Abbey Fm
St Mary's Glebe Fm
St John's Fm
Cockleycley Heath
Redlodge Fm
FOREST
Cockleycley Wood
Beachamwell
Downham Market
Home Fm
Stradsett
Raven's Fm
Hill Fm
Oak Fm
Barton Leys
Hall Fm
Fox Plantn
Hall Carr
Shingham
Deadman's Plantn
PARK
Cockley Cley
Home Fm
Cockleycley Warren
Broomhill
Bexwell
Crimplesham
Mill Fm
Winnold Ho
Barton Bendish Fen
Sluice Wood
Eastmoor
Caldecote Fm
ICENI VILLAGE & MUSEUMS
High Plantn
Manor Fm
Grange Fm
Woodstock Fm
The Channels
NORFOLK
GOODERSTONE WATER GARDENS
Great Cressingham Wood
Rowley Corner
Coldham's Fm
Stonehills Fm
Whindrove Fm
Gavenham Ho
Boughton
Oxborough Wood
Gooderstone
Warren Fm
Grange Fm
Limekiln Plantation
Denver
Denver Sluice
Home Fm
Mouse Hall
White House Fm
Wereham
Boughton Wood
Warren Hill
Oxborough
OXBURGH HALL GARDEN & ESTATE
Gooderstone Warren
Rowley Fm
Sluice Common
Whin Common
Ryston Hall
Manor Fm
West Dereham
Abbey Fm
White House Fm
Broom Covert
Hilborough Ho
Hilborough
Linghills Fm
Rookery Fm
Crossways Fm
Barsale Fm
Wereham Row
Stoke Ferry
Home Covert
Foulden Common
Bone's Barn
Fordham
Silt Fen Fm
Roxham Fm
Snowre Hall
Wretton
My Lord's Wood
Ferry Fm
Everett's Fm
Wimbotsham Plantn
Great Wood
Whittington
Borough Fen
Cut-off Channel
Foulden
Horrex Fm
Beckett End
Bodney
Fordham Fen
Great West Fen
Cornerways Fm
Wretton Fen Ho
Hill Fm
Coldharbour Wood
Crow Hyrne Fm
Willow Fm
Rose Hill Fm
Hilgay Fen
Herringay Hill
Stoke Ferry Fen
Great Plantation
Hall Fm
Northwold Common
Didlington
Oak Covert
Little Langford Fm
Highash Hill
Chalk-Hall Fm
Hilgay
Lodge Fm
Wood Hall
Sugar Factory
River Wissey
Northwold
Moor Plantn
Ten Mile Bank
Modney Br
Ash Hill Fm
Gills Fm
Catsholme Fm
Sleves Holm
Methwold Lode
Brookville
Northwold Lodge
Little London
Home Fm
Shakers Wood
Ickburgh Fields
Watermill Fm
Went's Fm
Spring Covert
Bunkershill Plantn
Buckenham Tofts Park
Modney Hall
Further Fen Fm
The Decoy
Broad Fen Fm
Rosedene Fm
Thornham Fm
Rush Covert
Furze Heath
Lowe's Fm
Manton's Fm
Southery
FELTWELL ROAD
Decoy Fm
Methwold Common
Banham's Fm
Methwold Hythe
Hall Fm
Methwold
Warren Lodge
Manor Fm
Cranwich
Colveston Manor Fm
Ickburgh
Key Fm
Stubbs Hill Fm
Duchy Fm
Lynford Hall
West Hall
Mundford
Ferry Fm
Turf Fen Fm
New Fm
Tennis Plantn
Cranwich Heath
Round Covert Fm
LYNFORD ARBORETUM & LAKES
Southery Fens
Methwold Fens
Whiteplot Fm
Warren Ho
Middle Warren Fm
Home Fm
Sedge Fen Fm
Bourne Fm
Poppylot Fm
Muriel's Fm
Breckland Fm
Methwold Warren
Fieltwell Lodge
Rougham Corner
West Tofts
Horse Fen Fm
Jubilee Fm
Denton Lodge
Breckland
Wannage Fm
East Hall
LODGE ROAD
Mount Ephraim
Lynford
Black Horse Drove
Brandon Creek
Bank Fm
Four Scores Fm
Cross Bank Fm
Feltwell
Sternhouse Fm
Snake Wood
Oak Fm
Plantation Ho
Six Acre Plantn
Brandon Bank
Stokes Fm
Middle Fm
Feltwell Anchor
Whitedyke Fm
Chalkhall Fm
Bricklin Fm
Emily's Wood
Brickkiln Fm
GRIME'S GRAVES
Lynford Point
Little Ouse
Church Fm
Orchard Ho
Shrubhill Fm
Blackdyke Fm
Grange Fm
Field Fm
WEETING CASTLE
Bromehill Cott
Field Barn
Belvedere Wood
Wilton Fm
Weeting
THETFORD
Santon Warren
Temple Fm
Osier Holt
Hockwold cum Wilton
WEETING HEATH
Leylands Fm
Fengate Fm
Two Mile Bottom
River Little Ouse
Santon Downham
Burnt Fen
May Fm
Glover's Fm
White Ho
Weltmore Fm
Cowle's Drove
LAKENHEATH FEN
Wilton Br
Limekiln Fm
Foord Ho
Brandon Hall
BRANDON
Brandon
FOREST
THETFORD ROAD
Level
Letter F Fm
Flanders Fm
Old Decoy Fm
Decoy Fen
Joist Fen
New Fen
Christmas Hill Fm
Twelve Foot Drain
Fenhouse Heath
Wiltonhill Wood
Brickkiln Fm
BRANDON PARK
Thetford Lodge Fm
Lingheath Fm
Level
Peacock's Fm
Cross Bank Fm
Plantation Fm
SHIPPEA HILL
Brandon Fen
Dyke
Stallode Fm
North Fen
North Court
Brandon Park
Session Heath
Downham Highlodge Warren
THETFORD WARREN LODGE
Folly Fm
Sunrose Fm
Shippea Hill Fm
Lea Fm
Russell Fm
Grime Fen
White Fen
Brakey Hills Fm
Palmers Heath
Thetford Warren
Mile End
Sindallthorpe Ho
Engine Fm
Grosvenor House Fm
Elderberry Fm
Bedford Fm
SUFFOLK
Lakenheath
The Carr
Wangford Warren
PARK
Mayday Fm
High Wrong Corner
Prickwillow
Spooner's Fm
Shell Fm
Lark Grange
Friesland Fm
Harris Fm
Townmoor Fm
Dragon's Plantn
Chalk Fm
Maidscross Hill
Spinks Lodge
Lambpit Hill
Claypits
Lakenheath Airfield
Parsonage Heath
Redneck Heath
Wangford Woods
Kings Fm
Coronation Fm
Cupola Fm
Undley
Caudle Fm
Elveden Warren
Elveden Forest Holiday Centre
Birds Hurst
Olleys Fm
Poplar Fm
Undley Common
Warren Lodge
Lakenheath Warren
County Fm
Peterhouse Fm
Mildenhall Wood
Elveden
Cock Inn Fm
Shop Cen
Eriswell Low Warren
Shrubland Ho
Birch Hill
Dingle Nook Fm
High Fen
High Lodge
Napthen's Fm
Eriswell High Warren
Larling Heath
New Barnham Slip
EAST OF ENGLAND TANK MUSEUM
Harlequin Fm
Wilde Street
Spark's Fm
Portway Hill
Cranhouse Fm
Partition Belt
Lodge Heath
Youngsharst Wood
Westgouch Plantn
Summerpit Fm
Middlegouch Plantn
Hunwellspring Plantn
High Post Fm
Wildemere
Tree
Summerpit Bottom
First Slips
0 1 2 3 miles
0 1 2 3 4 5 km

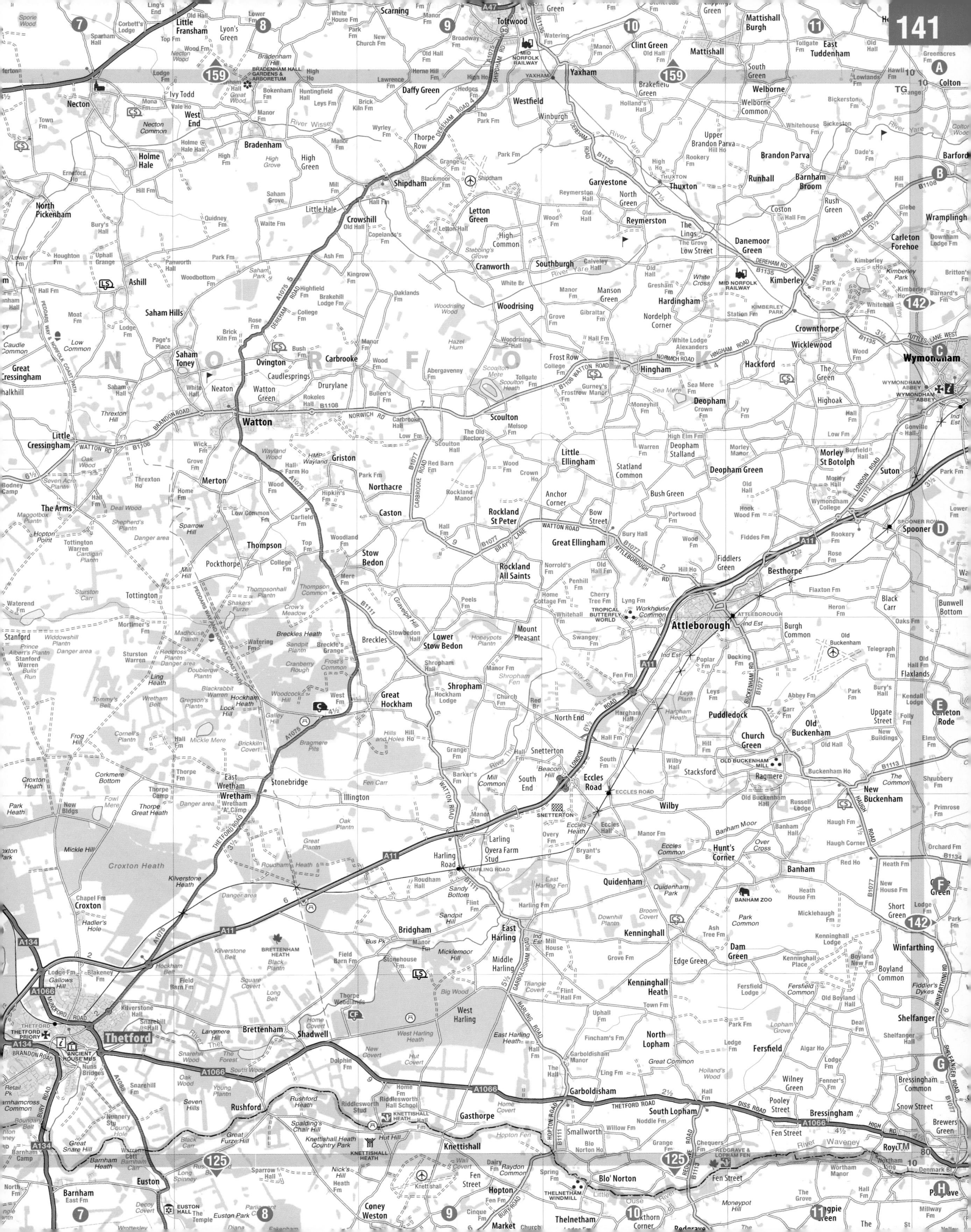
NORFOLK
Little Fransham
Lyon's Green
Scarning
Toftwood
Mattishall Burgh
Mattishall
Clint Green
East Tuddenham
Colton
Necton
Ivy Todd
West End
Bradenham
Daffy Green
Westfield
Yaxham
Welborne
Thorpe Row
Holme Hale
High Green
Shipdham
Garvestone
Thuxton
Runhall
Brandon Parva
Barnham Broom
Barford
North Pickenham
Little Hale
Crowshill
Letton Green
Reymerston
Danemoor Green
Carleton Forehoe
Wramplingham
Ashill
Cranworth
Southburgh
Kimberley
Woodrising
Hardingham
Saham Hills
Saham Toney
Ovington
Carbrooke
Great Cressingham
Hingham
Hackford
Crownthorpe
Wicklewood
Wymondham
Watton
Scoulton
Deopham
Little Cressingham
Griston
Little Ellingham
Morley St Botolph
Suton
Merton
Northacre
Deopham Green
The Arms
Caston
Rockland St Peter
Great Ellingham
Spooner Row
Thompson
Stow Bedon
Rockland All Saints
Besthorpe
Tottington
Attleborough
Stanford
Breckles
Lower Stow Bedon
Mount Pleasant
Shropham
Great Hockham
Puddledock
Old Buckenham
Carleton Rode
Church Green
Snetterton
Eccles Road
Stacksford
Stonebridge
Wretham
Illington
Wilby
New Buckenham
Harling Road
Quidenham
Banham
Croxton
Bridgham
East Harling
Kenninghall
Winfarthing
Thetford
Brettenham
Shadwell
West Harling
North Lopham
Fersfield
Shelfanger
Rushford
Garboldisham
South Lopham
Bressingham
Gasthorpe
Knettishall
Blo' Norton
Barnham
Euston
Coney Weston
Thelnetham
Market
A11
A1075
A1066
A134
A47
B1108
B1077
B1111
B1135
159
142
125
TG
TM

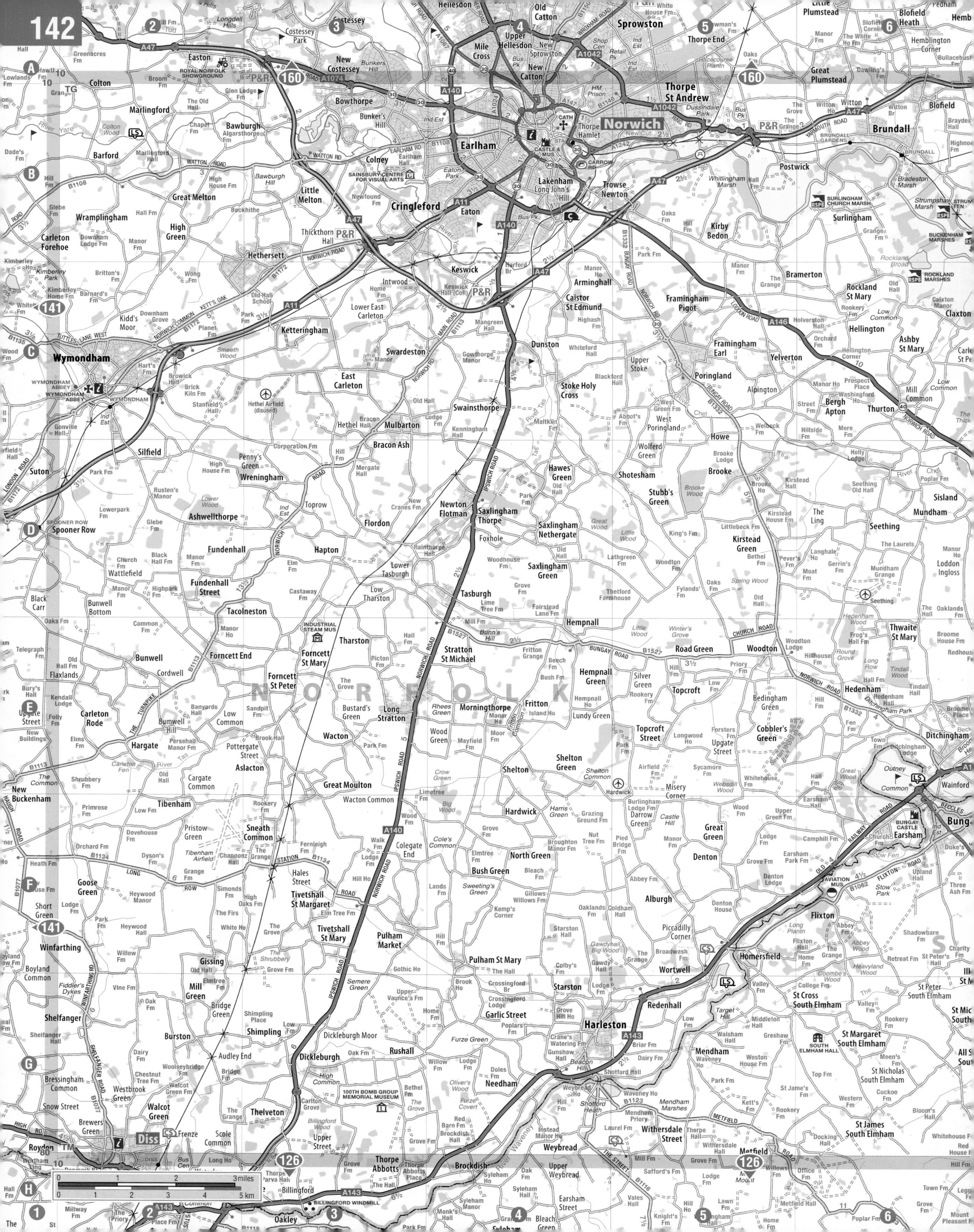
Norwich
Wymondham
Diss
Harleston
Earlham
Cringleford
Hethersett
Long Stratton
Brundall
NORFOLK

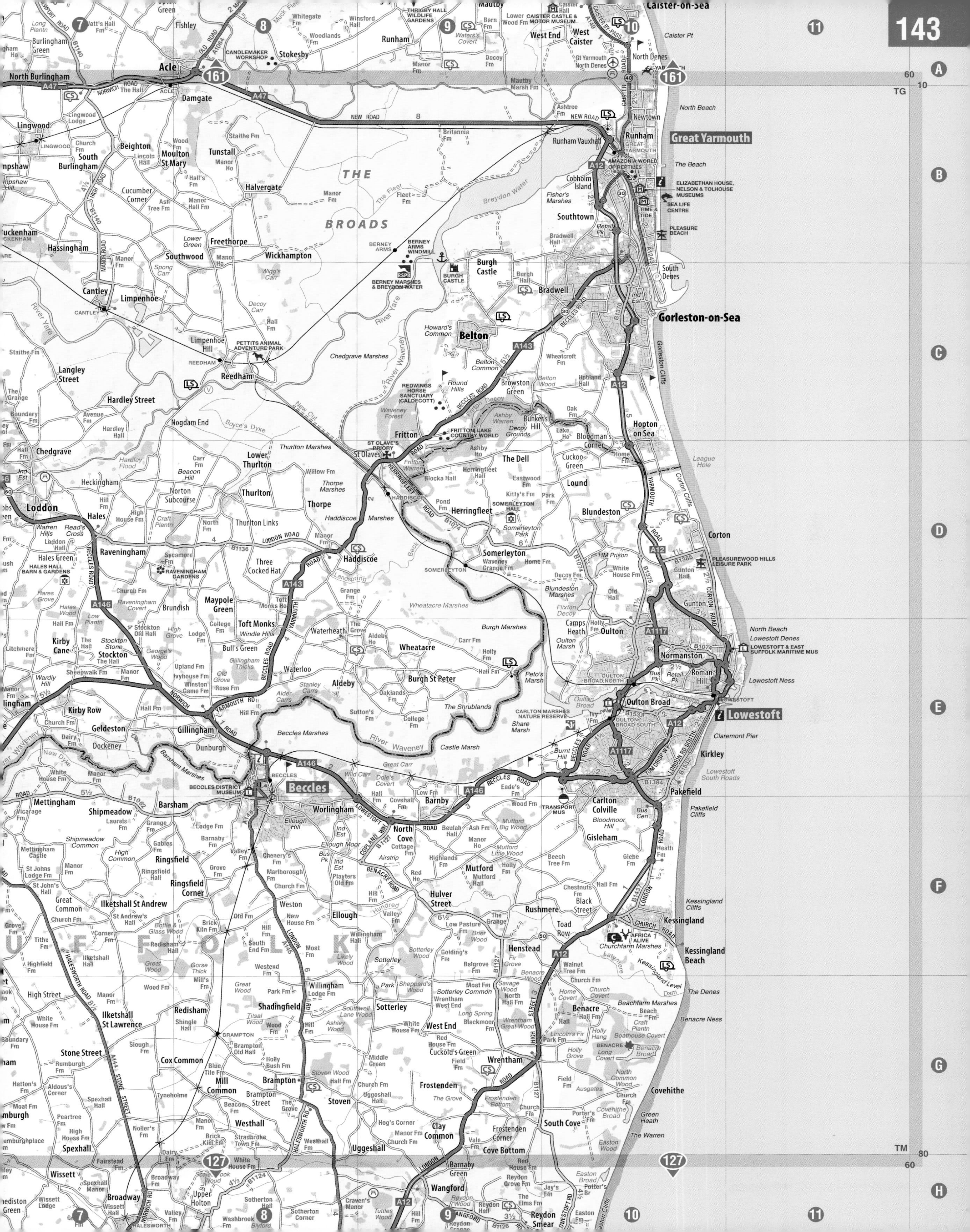
143
Caister-on-Sea
Caister Pt
West Caister
West End
Runham
Stokesby
Fishley
Acle
North Burlingham
Burlingham Green
Damgate
Lingwood
Beighton
Moulton St Mary
Tunstall
South Burlingham
Halvergate
THE
BROADS
Breydon Water
North Denes
North Beach
Newtown
Runham
Great Yarmouth
The Beach
ELIZABETHAN HOUSE, NELSON & TOLHOUSE MUSEUMS
SEA LIFE CENTRE
PLEASURE BEACH
Cobholm Island
Southtown
South Denes
Freethorpe
Wickhampton
Southwood
Hassingham
Cantley
Limpenhoe
BERNEY ARMS WINDMILL
BERNEY MARSHES & BREYDON WATER
Burgh Castle
Bradwell
Gorleston-on-Sea
Gorleston Cliffs
Belton
Belton Common
Limpenhoe Hill
PETTITS ANIMAL ADVENTURE PARK
Reedham
Chedgrave Marshes
Langley Street
Hardley Street
Nogdam End
REDWINGS HORSE SANCTUARY (CALDECOTT)
Round Hills
Browston Green
Hopton on Sea
Fritton
FRITTON LAKE COUNTRY WORLD
Bunker's Hill
Bloodman's Corner
Chedgrave
Loddon
Hales
Heckingham
Lower Thurlton
Thurlton
Norton Subcourse
Thorpe
St Olaves
Herringfleet
The Dell
Lound
Blundeston
Corton
Haddiscoe
Somerleyton
SOMERLEYTON HALL
Raveningham
RAVENINGHAM GARDENS
Three Cocked Hat
PLEASUREWOOD HILLS LEISURE PARK
Gunton
Maypole Green
Toft Monks
Wheatacre
Burgh Marshes
Oulton
North Beach
Lowestoft Denes
LOWESTOFT & EAST SUFFOLK MARITIME MUS
Normanston
Kirby Cane
Stockton
Waterloo
Aldeby
Burgh St Peter
Lowestoft Ness
Kirby Row
Geldeston
Gillingham
Dockeney
Dunburgh
Oulton Broad
Lowestoft
CARLTON MARSHES NATURE RESERVE
River Waveney
Beccles Marshes
Castle Marsh
Claremont Pier
Kirkley
BECCLES DISTRICT MUSEUM
Beccles
Barsham
Mettingham
Shipmeadow
Worlingham
North Cove
Barnby
TRANSPORT MUS
Carlton Colville
Pakefield
Gisleham
Ringsfield
Ringsfield Corner
Mutford
Ilketshall St Andrew
Weston
Ellough
Hulver Street
Rushmere
Kessingland
Kessingland Beach
AFRICA ALIVE
Henstead
Sotterley
Shadingfield
Redisham
Ilketshall St Lawrence
High Street
Benacre
Benacre Ness
West End
Wrentham
Stone Street
Cox Common
Mill Common
Brampton
Frostenden
Stoven
Westhall
Clay Common
South Cove
Covehithe
Spexhall
Uggeshall
Cove Bottom
Wissett
Broadway
Upper Holton
Wangford
Reydon Smear
SUFFOLK
161
127

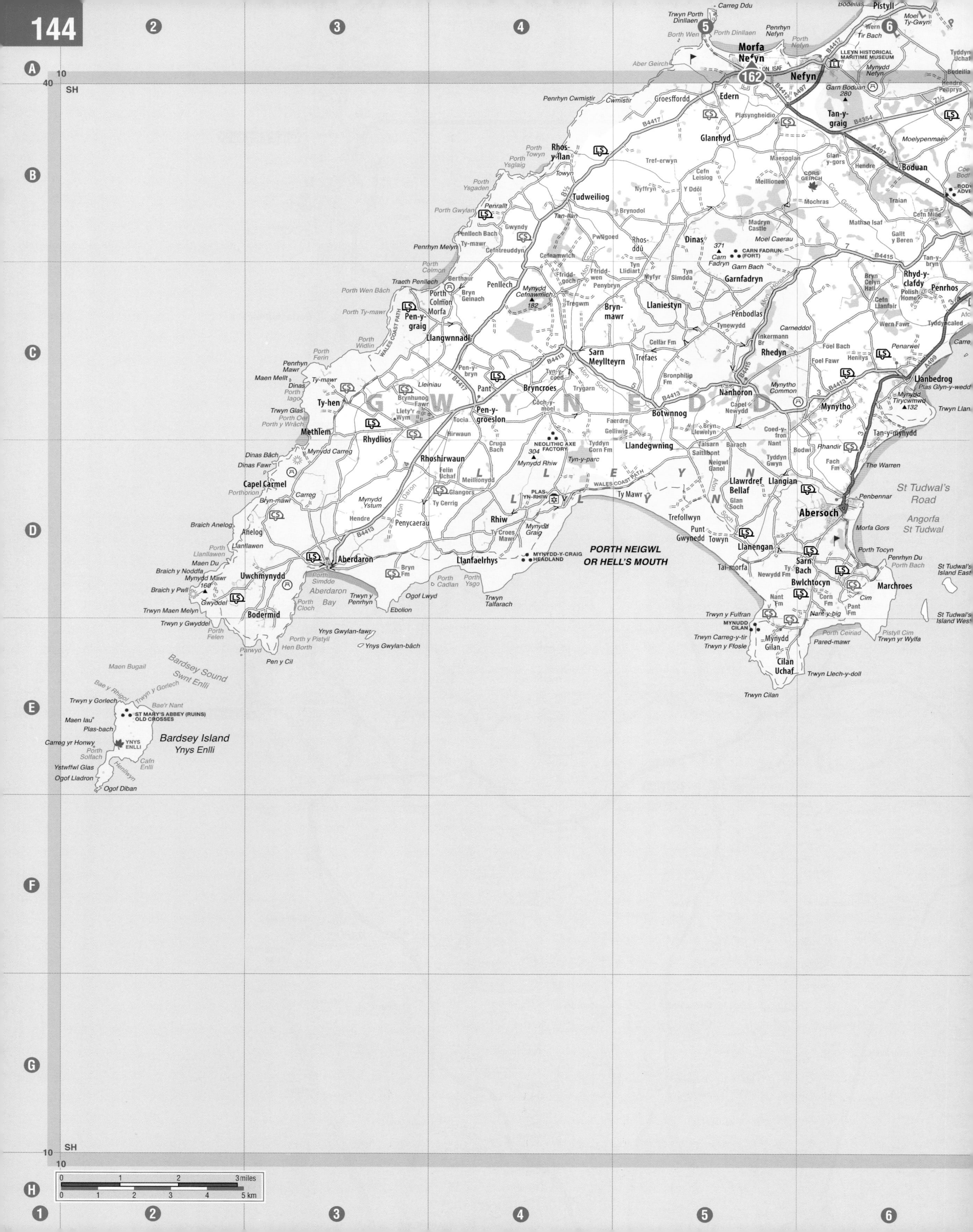

Bardsey Island
Ynys Enlli

Bardsey Sound
Swnt Enlli

GWYNEDD

LLEYN

PORTH NEIGWL
OR HELL'S MOUTH

St Tudwal's
Road

Angorfa
St Tudwal

Morfa
Nefyn

Nefyn

Nefyn

Abersoch

Aberdaron

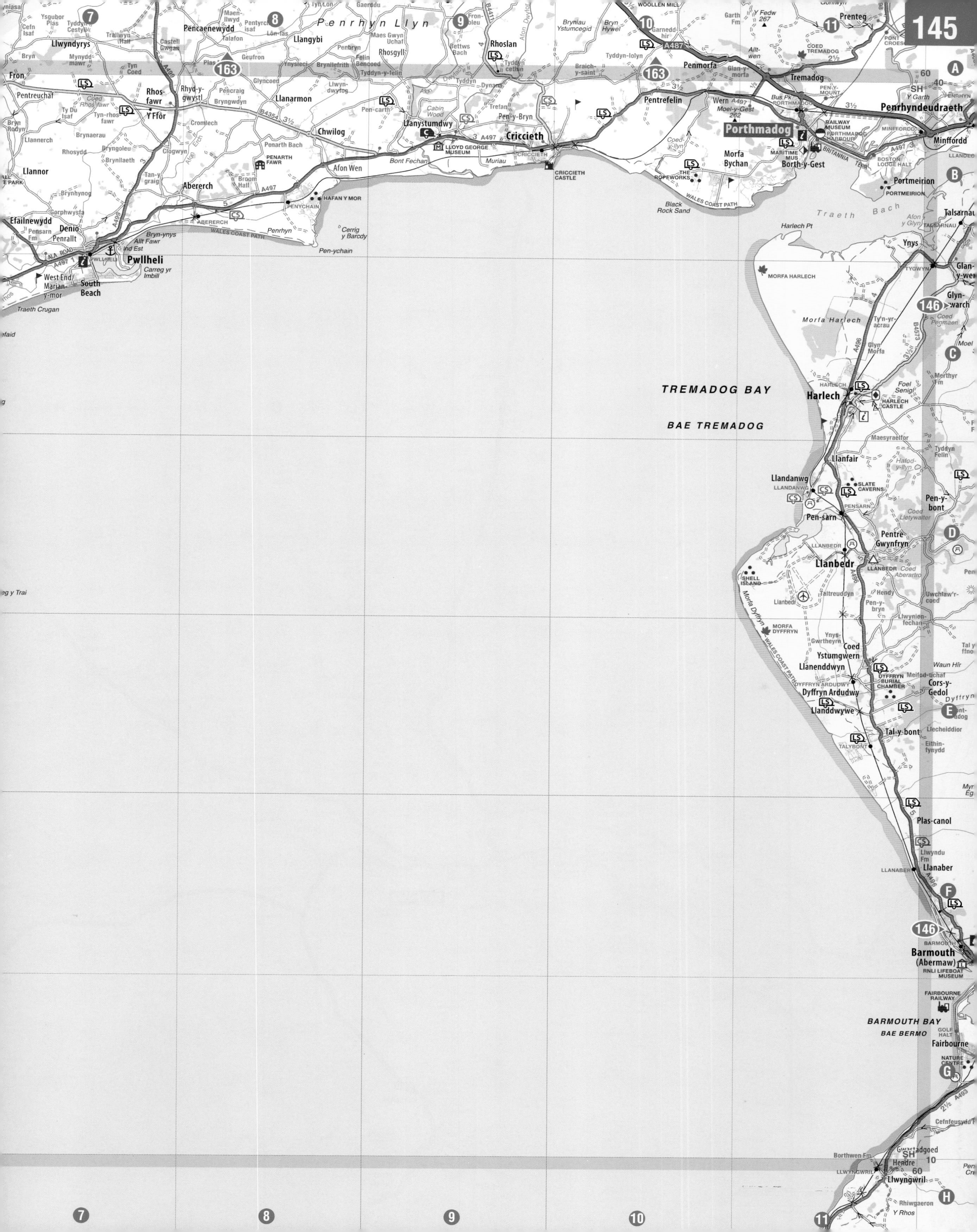

Penrhyn Llyn
Pencaenewydd
Llangybi
Llwyndyrys
Rhoslan
Penmorfa
Tremadog
Prenteg
Penrhyndeudraeth
Minffordd
Porthmadog
Borth-y-Gest
Morfa Bychan
Pentrefelin
Criccieth
CRICCIETH CASTLE
Llanystumdwy
LLOYD GEORGE MUSEUM
Pen-y-Bryn
Chwilog
Llanarmon
Rhos-fawr
Y Ffôr
Rhyd-y-gwystl
Fron
Pentreuchaf
Llannor
Abererch
Afon Wen
Penarth Bach
PENARTH FAWR
HAFAN Y MOR
Efailnewydd
Denio
Penrallt
Pwllheli
West End/ Marian-y-mor
South Beach
Traeth Crugan
WALES COAST PATH
Black Rock Sand
THE ROPEWORKS
Portmeirion
PORTMEIRION
Talsarnau
Traeth Bach
Harlech Pt
MORFA HARLECH
Morfa Harlech
Ynys
Glan-y-wern
Glyn-y-warch
TREMADOG BAY
BAE TREMADOG
Harlech
HARLECH CASTLE
Llanfair
Llandanwg
SLATE CAVERNS
Pen-sarn
Pentre Gwynfryn
Llanbedr
SHELL ISLAND
Morfa Dyffryn
MORFA DYFFRYN
Coed Ystumgwern
Llanenddwyn
Dyffryn Ardudwy
DYFFRYN BURIAL CHAMBER
Llanddwywe
Cors-y-Gedol
Tal-y-bont
Plas-canol
Llanaber
Barmouth (Abermaw)
RNLI LIFEBOAT MUSEUM
FAIRBOURNE RAILWAY
BARMOUTH BAY
BAE BERMO
Fairbourne
Cefnfeusydd
Gwastadgoed
Hendre
Llwyngwril
Rhiwgaeron
A497
A499
A487
A496
B4354
B4573
163
146
7
8
9
10
11
A
B
C
D
E
F
G
H

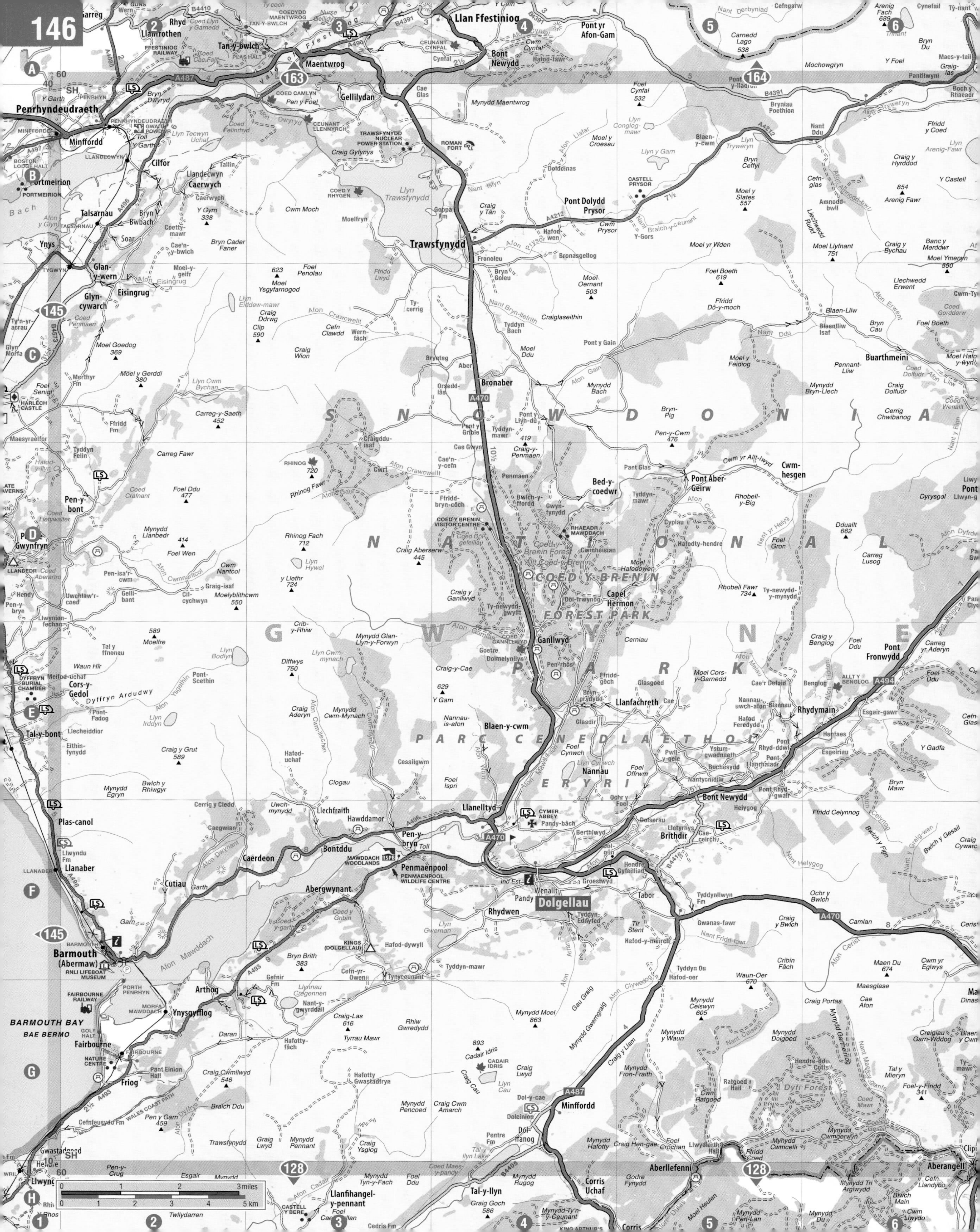

Llan Ffestiniog
Pont yr Afon-Gam
Carnedd Lago 538
Rhyd
Llanfrothen
Tan-y-bwlch
Maentwrog
Bont Newydd
163
164
Penrhyndeudraeth
Minffordd
Gellilydan
Cilfor
Portmeirion
Talsarnau
Llandecwyn
Caerwych
Trawsfynydd
Llyn Trawsfynydd
Pont Dolydd Prysor
Castell Prysor
Ynys
Glan-y-wern
Eisingrug
Glyn-cywarch
145
Moel Goedog 369
Harlech Castle
Bronaber
S N O W D O N I A
N A T I O N A L
G W Y N E D D
P A R K
PARC CENEDLAETHOL
ERYRI
Coed y Brenin Forest Park
Rhinog Fawr
Rhinog Fach 712
Y Llethr 724
Diffwys 750
Capel Hermon
Ganllwyd
Bed-y-coedwr
Pont Aber-Geirw
Cwm-hesgen
Buarthmeini
Arenig Fawr 854
Moel Llyfnant 751
Llanfachreth
Rhydymain
Pont Fronwydd
Cors-y-Gedol
Tal-y-bont
Plas-canol
Llanaber
Barmouth (Abermaw)
Barmouth Bay
Bae Bermo
Fairbourne
Friog
Arthog
Ynysgyffiog
Bontddu
Caerdeon
Cutiau
Abergwynant
Penmaenpool
Llanelltyd
Cymer Abbey
Pen-y-bryn
Dolgellau
Brithdir
Bont Newydd
Rhydwen
Cadair Idris 893
Minffordd
Dol-y-cae
Dolffanog
Tal-y-llyn
Corris Uchaf
Aberllefenni
Aberangell
Llanfihangel-y-pennant
Dyfi Forest
128
A470
A487
A493
A494
A496
B4416
B4391
B4405
0 1 2 3 miles
0 1 2 3 4 5 km

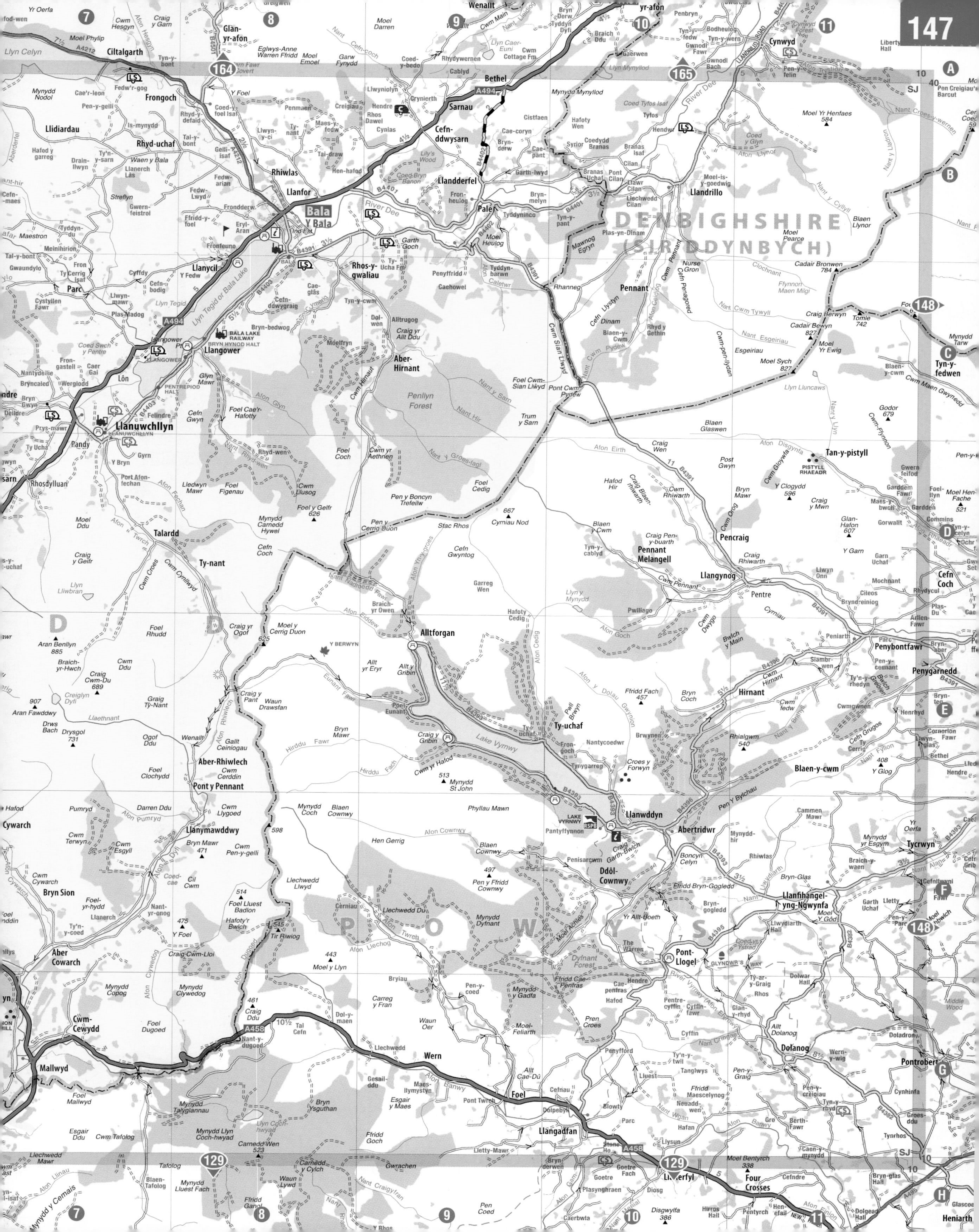

Yr Oerfa
Cwm Hesgyn
Craig y Garn
Glan-yr-afon
Wenallt
yr-afon
Penbryn
Cynwyd
Liberty Hall
Moel Phylip
Llyn Celyn
Ciltalgarth
Tyn-y-bont
Eglwys-Anne Warren Ffridd
Moel Emoel
Garw Fynydd
Moel Darren
Coed-y-bedo
Rhydywernen
Cablyd
Bethel
Llyn Caer-Euni
Cwm Cottage Fm
Braich Ddu
Gaerwen
Bryn Derw
Tyddyn Dyfi
Tyn-y-fedw
Gwnodl Fawr
Gwnodl Bach
Bodheulog
Tyn-y-wern
Pen-y-felin
Llyn Mynyllod
Mynydd Mynyllod
Y Foel
Mynydd Nodol
Cae'r-leon
Frongoch
Fedw'r-gog
Coed-y-foel Isaf
Rhyd-y-defaid
Penmaen
Creigiau
Llwyniolyn
Hendre
Crynierth
Sarnau
Pen Creigiau'r Barcut
Pen-y-gelli
Is-mynydd
Rhos Dawel
Cynlas
Cefn-ddwysarn
Cistfaen
Coed Tyfos Isaf
Tyfos
Hafoty Wen
Moel Yr Henfaes 584
Llidiardau
Rhyd-uchaf
Tal-y-bont
Llwyn-y-ci
Ty-nant
Maes-y-fedw
Cae-coryn
Bryn-derw
Syrior
Coedydd Branas
Branas isaf
Hendwr
Coed y Glyn
Afon Llynor
Hafod y garreg
Ty'n-y-sarn
Waen y Bala
Drain-llwyn
Llanerch Las
Gelli-isaf
Tai-draw
Lily's Wood
Cae-pant
Cilan
Rhiwlas
Hen-hafod
Garth-lwyd
Branas Uchaf
Pont Cilan
Llawr Cilan
Moel-is-y-goedwig
Llandrillo
Coed Bryn Banon
Llandderfel
Streflyn
Fedw-Lwyd
Fedw-arian
Llanfor
Fron-heulog
Bryn-melyn
Llechwedd Cilan
Gwern-feistrol
Fronddderw
Bala
Y Bala
River Dee
Pale
Tyddyninco
Tyn-y-pant
DENBIGHSHIRE
(SIR DDYNBYCH)
Blaen Llynor
Maestron
Ffridd-y-foel
Eryl-Aran
Ind Est
Moel Heulog
Mawnog Egryn
Plas-yn-Dinam
Moel Pearce
Tyddyn-du
Meinihirion
Fronfeuno
Garth Goch
Tal-y-bont
Gwaunydyle
Fron
Ty Cerrig Isaf
Cyffdy
Cefn-bodig
Llanycil
Y Fedw
Ty-Ucha Fm
Rhos-y-gwaliau
Penyffridd
Tyddyn-barwn
Afon Caletwr
Caehowel
Cae-glâs
Rhanneg
Nurse Gron
Clochnant
Cadair Bronwen 784
Ffynnon Maen Milgi
Parc
Llwyn-mawr
Llyn Tegid
Cefn-ddwygraig
Tyn-y-cwm
Pennant
Cefn Penagored
Cystyllen Fawr
Plas-Madog
Llyn Tegid or Bala Lake
Dol-wen
Alltrugog
Cefn Llystyn
Dinam
Nant Cwm Tywyll
Craig Berwyn
Tomle 742
Bryn-bedwog
BALA LAKE RAILWAY
Craig yr Allt Ddu
Blaen-y-Cwm
Rhyd y Gethin
Nant Esgeiriau
Cadair Berwyn 827
Mynydd Tarw
Coed Swch y Pentre
Llangower
BRYN HYNOD HALT
Moelfryn
Cwm Hirnant
Nant Cwm Pydew
Esgeiriau
Moel Yr Ewig
Frongastell
Caer Gai
Llangower
Aber-Hirnant
Cwm Sian Llwyd
Cwm-pen-llydan
Moel Sych 827
Blaen-y-cwm
Tyn-y-fedwen
Cwm Maen Gwynedd
Nantydeilie
Wergloedd
Bryncaled
Lôn
Glyn Mawr
PENTREPIOD HALT
Penllyn Forest
Nant y Sarn
Foel Cwm-Sian Llwyd
Pont Cwm Pydew
Llyn Lluncaws
Bryn Gwyn
Afon Glyn
Felindre
Cefn Gwyn
Foel Cae'r-Hafotty
Nant Hir
Trum y Sarn
Godor 679
Cwm-Ffynnon
Prys-mawr
Llanuwchllyn
LLANUWCHLLYN
Nant y Llyn
Blaen Glaswen
Pandy
Ty Ucha
Gyrn
Nant Rhyd-wen
Rhyd-wen
Foel Goch
Cwm yr Aethnen
Nant y Groes-fagl
Afon Eirth
Craig Wen
Afon Disgynfa
Tan-y-pistyll
PISTYLL RHAEADR
Y Bryn
Port Afon-fechan
Ledwyn Mawr
Foel Figenau
Cwm Llusog
Foel Cedig
Hafod Hir
Craig Blaen-rhiwarth
Post Gwyn
Cwm Glogwyn
Gwern feifod
Rhosdylluan
Afon Fechan
Pen y Boncyn Trefeilw
Cwm Rhiwarth
Bryn Mawr
Y Clogydd 596
Garddem Fawr
Foel-llyn
Moel Hen-Fache 521
Moel Ddu
Foel y Gelfr 626
Mynydd Carnedd Hywel
Cwm Croes
Pen y Cerrig Buon
667 Cyrniau Nod
Stac Rhos
Cwm Orog
Craig y Mwn
Maes-y-bwcll
Gorwallt
Glan-Hafon 607
Commins
Talardd
Ty-nant
Cefn Coch
Cefn Gwyntog
Blaen y Cwm
Tyn-y-cablyd
Craig Pen-y-buarth
Pennant Melangell
Pencraig
Y Garn
Craig y Geifr
Cwm Cynllwyd
Garreg Wen
Nant Nadroedd Fawr
Afon Ybyn-y-groes
Llyn y Mynydd
Craig Rhiwarth
Llangynog
Garn Uchaf
Llwyn Onn
Cefn Coch
Mochnant
Cileos
Rhydycul
Llyn Llwibran
Braich-yr Owen
Cwm Pennant
Pentre
Bryndreiniog
Plas-Du
Afon Eiddew
Pwlliago
Cyrniau
Arllen-Fawr
Moel y Cerrig Duon
625
Hafoty Cedig
Afon Goch
Cwm Dwygo
Penybontfawr
Aran Benllyn 885
Foel Rhudd
Craig yr Ogof
Alltforgan
Bwlch y Main
Peniarth
Parc
Braich-yr-Hwch
Cwm Ddu
Y BERWYN
Allt yr Eryr
Allt y Gribin
Afon Cedig
Afon y Dolau Gwynion
Siambr-wen
Pen-y-ceunant
Ty'n-y-rhedyn
Bwlch Gredyn
Penygarnedd
Craig Cwm-Du 689
Craiglyn Dyfi
Eunant Fawr
Craig y Pant
Waun Drawsfan
Ffridd Fach 457
Bryn Coch
Hirnant
Cwm fedw
Cwmgwnen
Henrhyd
907 Aran Fawddwy
Graig Tŷ-Nant
Pont Eunant
Pwll Bryn
Llaethnant
Drws Bach
Drysgol 731
Ogof Ddu
Wenallt
Afon Rhiwlech
Gallt Ceiniogau
Bryn Mawr
Craig y Gribin
Ty-uchaf
Ty-uchaf
Fron-goch
Nantycoedwr
Brwynen
Rhialgwm 540
Cefn Grugos
Corporlen Fawr
Aber-Rhiwlech
Cwm Cerddin
Hirddu Fawr
Lake Vyrnwy
Hirddu Fach
Tynygarreg
Croes y Forwyn
Blaen-y-cwm
408 Y Glog
Bethel
Hendre
Foel Clochydd
Pont y Pennant
Cwm yr Hafod
513 Mynydd St John
Hafod
Cywarch
Pumryd
Darren Ddu
Afon Pumryd
Cwm Llygoed
Mynydd Coch
Blaen Cownwy
Phyllau Mawn
LAKE VYRNWY
RSPB
Pantyffynnon
Llanwddyn
Abertridwr
Pen Y Bylchau
Cammen Mawr
Yr Oerfa
Llanymawddwy
598
Afon Cownwy
Hen Gerrig
Mynydd-hir
Mynydd yr Esgym
Tycrwyn
Cwm Terwyn
Cwm Esgyll
Bryn Mawr 471
Cwm Pen-y-gelli
Blaen Cownwy
Penisarcwm
Craig Garth-Bwlch
Boncyn Celyn
Rhiwlas
Braich-y-waen
Afon Cywarch
Cwm Cywarch
Coed-cae
Cil Cwm
497 Pen y Ffridd Cownwy
Llechwedd Llwyd
Ddôl-Cownwy
Ffridd Bryn-Gogledd
Bryn-Glas
Llanfihangel-yng-Ngwynfa
Cefnllwyni Fawr
Bryn Sion
Foel-yr-hydd
Llanerch
514 Foel Lluest Badlon
Hafoty'r Bwlch
Cerniau
Llechwedd Du
Mynydd Dyfnant
Moel Achles
Yr Allt-Boeth
Bryn-gogledd
Garth Uchaf
Lletty
Pen-y-Parc
Moel Y Gôd
Moel Bwlch
Nant-yr-onog
Ty'n-y-coed
475 Y Foel
545 Tir Riwiog
POWYS
Afon Twrch
The Warren
Pont-Llogel
GLYNDWR'S WAY
Llwydiarth Hall
Coed-y-Ystrad
Aber Cowarch
Craig-Cwm-Lloi
Afon Clywedog
Afon Dugoed
443 Moel y Llyn
Afon Llechog
Dylnant Forest
Ffridd Cae-Penfras
Hendre
Cae-penfras
Ty-ar-y-Graig
Rhos
Dolwar Hall
Mynydd Copog
Mynydd Clywedog
Bryniau
Carreg y Fran
Pen-y-coed
Mynydd y Gadfa
Hafod
Pentre-cyffin
Cyffin-fawr
River Vyrnwy (Afon Efyrnwy)
Glan-rhyd
Middle Wood
Cwm-Cewydd
Foel Dugoed
461 Craig Ddu
Tal Cefn
Dol-y-maen
Waun Oer
Moel-Feliarth
Pren Croes
Allt Dolanog
Cyffin
Doladron
Nant-y-dugoed
Llechwedd
Wern
Penyfford
Nant Cringae
Dolanog
Wern-y-wig
Mallwyd
Ty'n-y-twil
Tanglwys
Pen-y-Graig
Pontrobert
Foel Mallwyd
Gesail-ddu
Maes-llymystyn
Afon Banwy
Allt Cae-Dû
Lluest
Ffridd Maescelynog
Neuadd-wen
Pen-y-creigiau
Tyn-y-rhyd
Cynhinfa
Esgair y Maes
Bryn Ysguthan
Pont Twrch
Foel
Cefnau
Blowty
Dolpebyll
Nant Wgan
Groes-ddu
Mynydd Talyglannau
Llyn Coch-hwyad
Parc
Hafan
Gro
Berth-Fawr
Tynrhos
Esgair Ddu
Cwm Tafolog
Mynydd Llyn Coch-hwyad
Carnedd Wen 523
Ffridd Goch
Llangadfan
Llysun
Caen-y-mynydd
Llechwedd Mawr
Letty-Mawr
Bryn-derwen
Goetre Fach
Moel Bentyrch 338
Tafolog
Camedd y Cylch
Gwrachen
Goetre
Llanerfyl
Four Crosses
Cefndre
Bryn-glas Hall
Glascoed
Afon Llinau
Blaen-Tafolog
Mynydd Lluest Fach
Waun Lywd
Nant Craigyfran
Plasynghraen
Diosg
Mynydd y Cemais
Ffridd Ganol
Pen Coed
Caerbwla
Disgwylfa 386
Hirros Hall
Pentyrch
Hen-efail
Dolgead Hall
Heniarth

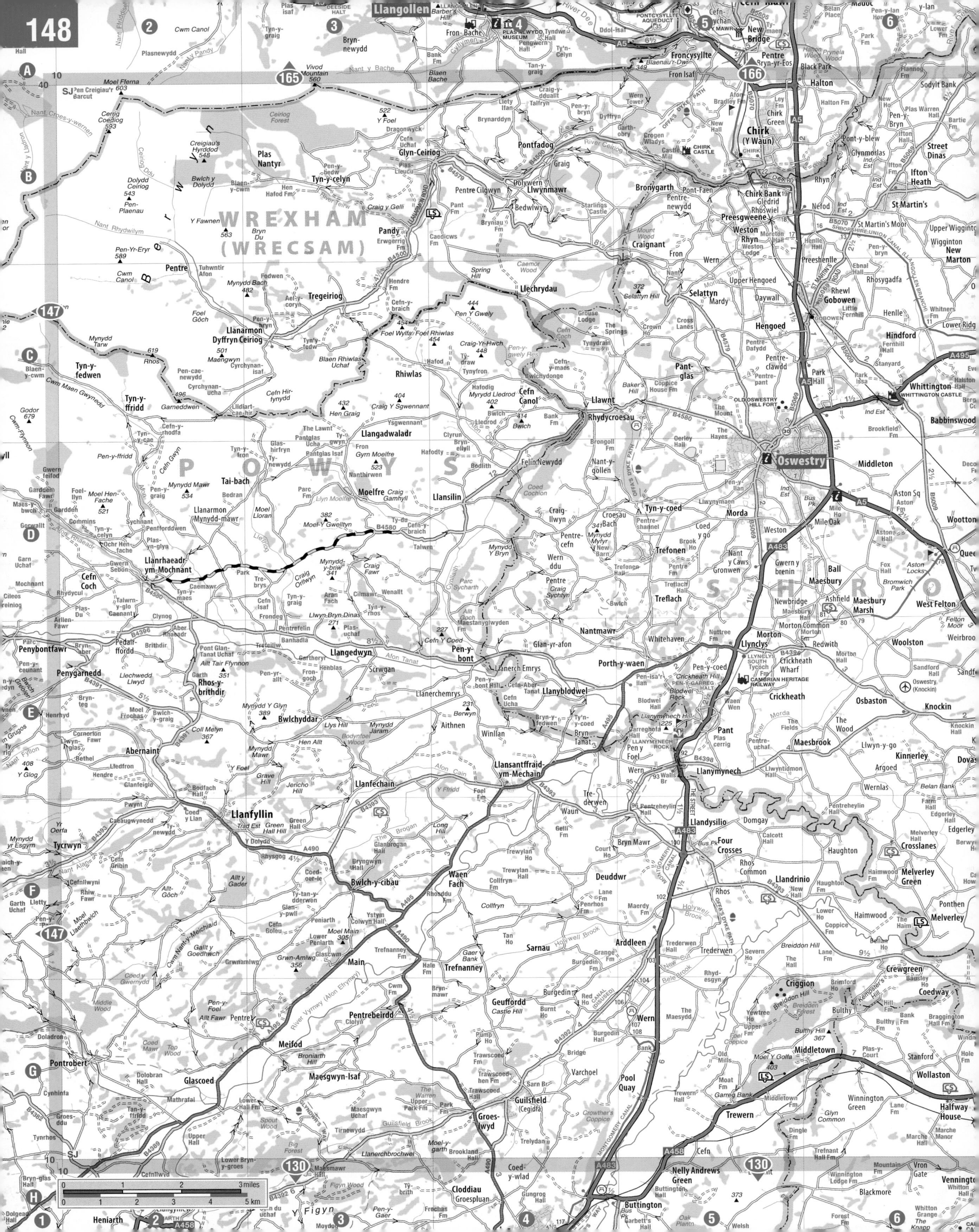
Llangollen
Froncysyllte
Chirk
(Y Waun)
Chirk Castle
Glyn-Ceiriog
Pontfadog
Llwynmawr
Bronygarth
Preesgweene
Weston Rhyn
St Martin's
Ifton Heath
Halton
Black Park
WREXHAM
(WRECSAM)
Berwyn
Tyn-y-celyn
Pandy
Tregeiriog
Llanarmon Dyffryn Ceiriog
Llechrydau
Selattyn
Craignant
Hengoed
Gobowen
Hindford
Whittington
Whittington Castle
Babbinswood
Rhiwlas
Cefn Canol
Llawnt
Rhydycroesau
Pant-glas
Old Oswestry Hill Fort
Oswestry
Middleton
Llangadwaladr
Tyn-y-fedwen
Tyn-y-ffridd
POWYS
SHROPSHIRE
Tai-bach
Moelfre
Llansilin
Felin Newydd
Tyn-y-coed
Morda
Trefonen
Llanrhaeadr-ym-Mochnant
Llanarmon Mynydd-mawr
Cefn Coch
Maesbury
Maesbury Marsh
West Felton
Treflach
Nantmawr
Llangedwyn
Pen-y-bont
Porth-y-waen
Llynclys
Morton
Penybontfawr
Penygarnedd
Rhos-y-brithdir
Llanyblodwel
Crickheath
Osbaston
Knockin
Bwlchyddar
Abernaint
Pant
Llanymynech
Maesbrook
Kinnerley
Llansantffraid-ym-Mechain
Llanfechain
Llanfyllin
Llandysilio
Four Crosses
Tycrwyn
Bwlch-y-cibau
Waen Fach
Deuddwr
Llandrinio
Crosslanes
Melverley Green
Melverley
Arddleen
Sarnau
Main
Trefnanney
Geuffordd
Pentrebeirdd
Wern
Criggion
Crewgreen
Coedway
Pontrobert
Meifod
Glascoed
Maesgwyn-Isaf
Guilsfield
(Cegidfa)
Groes-lwyd
Pool Quay
Middletown
Trewern
Wollaston
Halfway House
Cloddiau
Nelly Andrews Green
Buttington
Vennington
Heniarth
Y Figyn
147
165
166
130
0 1 2 3 miles
0 1 2 3 4 5 km

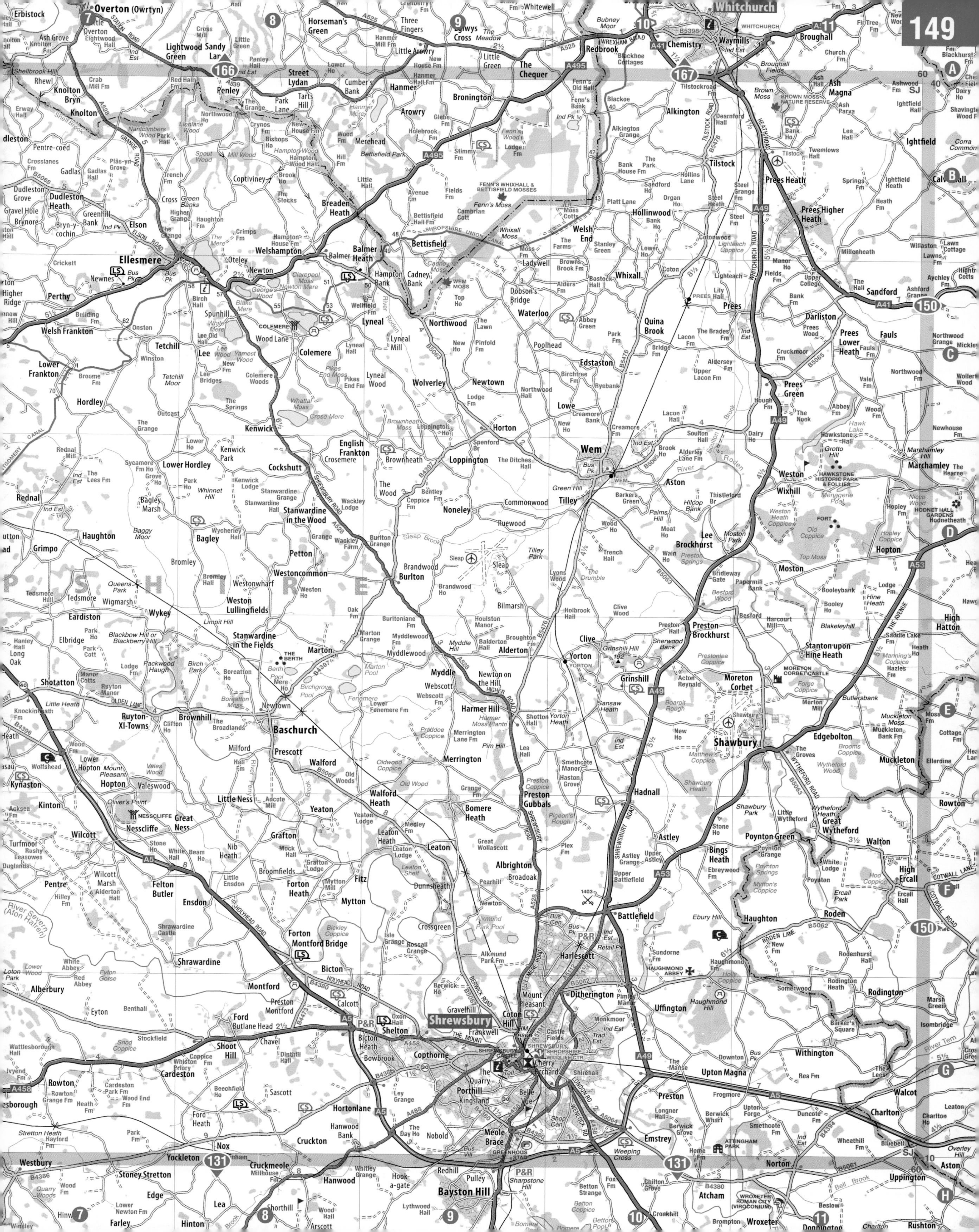
Overton (Owrtyn)
Whitchurch
Erbistock
Horseman's Green
Three Fingers
Eglwys Cross
Whitewell
Redbrook
Chemistry
Waymills
Broughall
Lightwood Green
Sandy Lane
Penley
Street Lydan
Hanmer
Bronington
The Chequer
Little Green
Tilstock
Alkington
Ash Magna
Ightfield
Knolton
Knolton Bryn
Dudleston Heath
Elson
Ellesmere
Welshampton
Bettisfield
Balmer Heath
Hampton Bank
Cadney Bank
Fenn's Moss
Whixall
Welsh End
Hollinwood
Prees Heath
Prees Higher Heath
Prees
Sandford
Darliston
Fauls
Prees Lower Heath
Perthy
Welsh Frankton
Tetchill
Lee
Colemere
Lyneal
Northwood
Waterloo
Quina Brook
Edstaston
Wolverley
Newtown
Lowe
Lower Frankton
Hordley
Kenwick
Horton
Wem
Aston
English Frankton
Loppington
Cockshutt
Lower Hordley
Noneley
Tilley
Weston
Wixhill
Marchamley
Hawkstone Historic Park & Follies
Lee Brockhurst
Haughton
Grimpo
Bagley
Petton
Burlton
Sleap
Hopton
Moston
Tedsmore
Eardiston
Weston Lullingfields
Wykey
Preston Brockhurst
High Hatton
Stanton upon Hine Heath
Stanwardine in the Fields
Marton
Myddlewood
Alderton
Clive
Yorton
Grinshill
Moreton Corbet
Shotatton
Ruyton-XI-Towns
Baschurch
Myddle
Harmer Hill
Shawbury
Edgebolton
Muckleton
Walford
Merrington
Kynaston
Hopton
Kinton
Nesscliffe
Great Ness
Wilcott
Little Ness
Walford Heath
Yeaton
Bomere Heath
Preston Gubbals
Hadnall
Rowton
Grafton
Leaton
Albrighton
Astley
Poynton Green
Great Wytheford
Walton
Pentre
Felton Butler
Ensdon
Fitz
Mytton
Forton Heath
Battlefield
High Ercall
Haughton
Roden
Shrawardine
Montford Bridge
Bicton
Harlescott
Alberbury
Montford
Mount Pleasant
Ditherington
Uffington
Rodington
Shrewsbury
Shelton
Coton Hill
Frankwell
Upton Magna
Withington
Rowton
Cardeston
Shoot Hill
Copthorne
Porthill
Kingsland
Belle Vue
Hortonlane
Meole Brace
Emstrey
Preston
Walcot
Charlton
Cructon
Nox
Yockleton
Westbury
Stoney Stretton
Edge
Cruckmeole
Hanwood
Bayston Hill
Atcham
Norton
Uppington
Aston
Lea
Hinton
Farley
Wroxeter
Rushton
A41
A49
A5
A495
A528
A53
A458
B5476
B5063
B4397

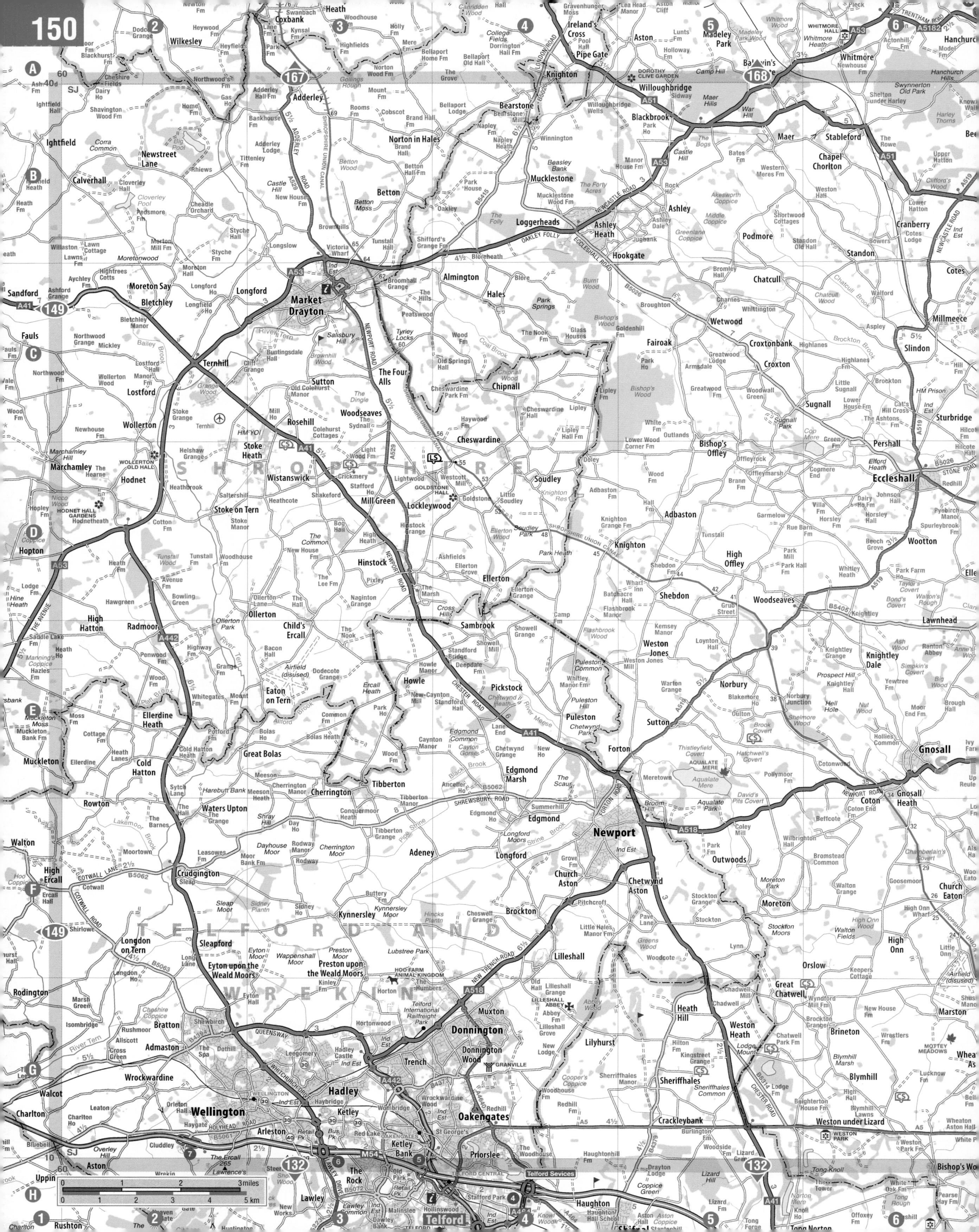

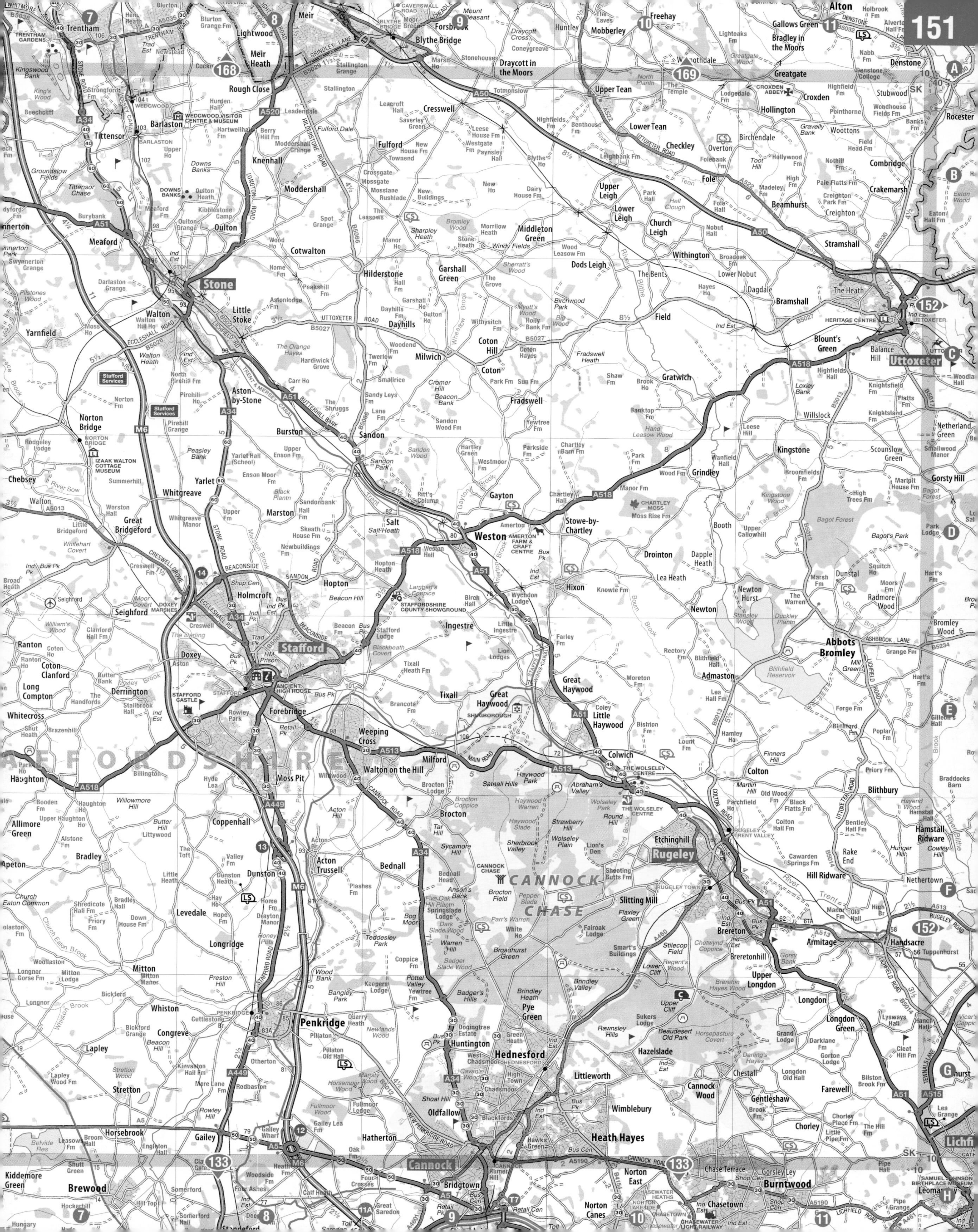
Trentham
Trentham Gardens
Meir
Lightwood
Meir Heath
Blurton
Blythe Bridge
Forsbrook
Mount Pleasant
Draycott Cross
Coneygreave
Draycott in the Moors
Huntley
The Eaves
Mobberley
Freehay
Alton
Gallows Green
Bradley in the Moors
Denstone
Rough Close
Stallington
Stallington Grange
Totmonslow
Upper Tean
Greatgate
Croxden Abbey
Croxden
Hollington
Stubwood
Rocester
Barlaston
Wedgwood Visitor Centre & Museum
Tittensor
Cresswell
Fulford
Lower Tean
Checkley
Birchendale
Overton
Woottons
Combridge
Knenhall
Moddershall
Hilderstone
Upper Leigh
Lower Leigh
Church Leigh
Fole
Crakemarsh
Beamhurst
Creighton
Meaford
Oulton
Cotwalton
Middleton Green
Withington
Dods Leigh
Stramshall
Stone
Garshall Green
The Bents
Lower Nobut
Dagdale
Bramshall
The Heath
Little Stoke
Walton
Yarnfield
Dayhills
Milwich
Coton Hill
Field
Blount's Green
Uttoxeter
Heritage Centre
Balance Hill
Stafford Services
Norton Bridge
Aston-by-Stone
Coton
Fradswell
Gratwich
Izaak Walton Cottage Museum
Burston
Sandon
Chebsey
Yarlet
Whitgreave
Marston
Gayton
Grindley
Kingstone
Gorsty Hill
Great Bridgeford
Salt
Weston
Stowe-by-Chartley
Chartley Moss
Amerton Farm & Craft Centre
Drointon
Dapple Heath
Bagot Forest
Hopton
Holmcroft
Staffordshire County Showground
Hixon
Lea Heath
Newton
Newton Hurst
Dunstal
Seighford
Ingestre
Abbots Bromley
Ranton
Coton Clanford
Doxey
Stafford
Derrington
Long Compton
Whitecross
Stafford Castle
Ancient High House
Forebridge
Tixall
Great Haywood
Shugborough
Little Haywood
Admaston
Blithfield Reservoir
Weeping Cross
Milford
Walton on the Hill
Colwich
The Wolseley Centre
Colton
Blithbury
Haughton
Moss Pit
Brocton
Allimore Green
Coppenhall
Acton Trussell
Bednall
Etchinghill
Rugeley
Hamstall Ridware
Bradley
Dunston
Cannock Chase
Slitting Mill
Hill Ridware
Nethertown
Levedale
Brereton
Armitage
Handsacre
Longridge
Upper Longdon
Mitton
Longdon
Longdon Green
Whiston
Penkridge
Pye Green
Congreve
Lapley
Huntington
Hednesford
Hazelslade
Stretton
Littleworth
Cannock Wood
Farewell
Gentleshaw
Oldfallow
Wimblebury
Chorley
Horsebrook
Gailey
Hatherton
Heath Hayes
Cannock
Kiddemore Green
Brewood
Bridgtown
Norton East
Chase Terrace
Burntwood
Norton Canes
Chasetown
Chasewater Light Railway
STAFFORDSHIRE

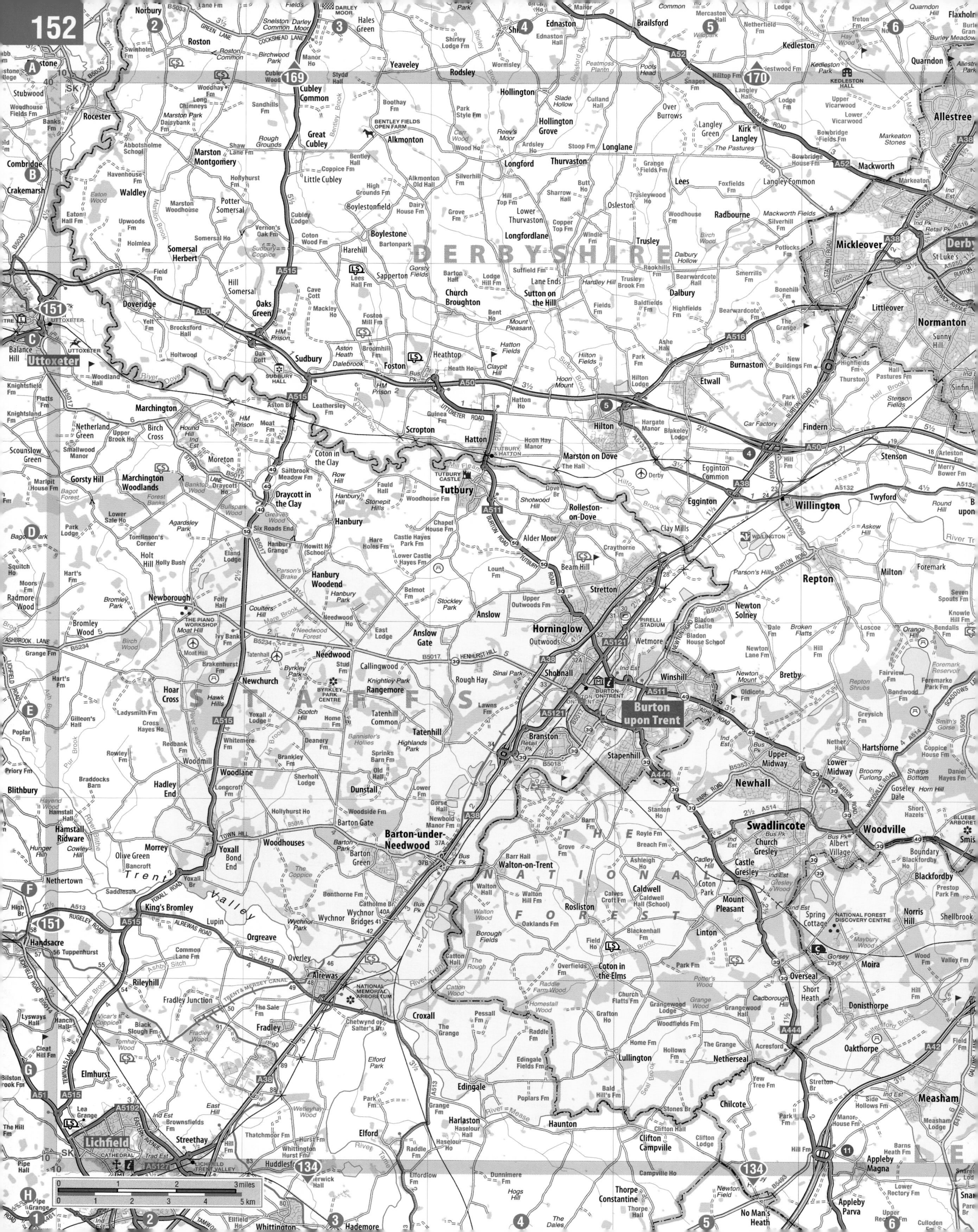
Norbury
Roston
Snelston Common
Darley Moor
Hales Green
Ednaston
Brailsford
Mercaston
Kedleston
Quarndon
Flaxholme
Stubwood
Rocester
Cubley Common
Yeaveley
Rodsley
Hollington
Hollington Grove
Over Burrows
Kirk Langley
Allestree
Great Cubley
Alkmonton
Longlane
Mackworth
Combridge
Crakemarsh
Marston Montgomery
Waldley
Little Cubley
Longford
Thurvaston
Lees
Radbourne
Langley Common
Potter Somersal
Boylestonfield
Lower Thurvaston
Osleston
Mickleover
Derby
Boylestone
Longfordlane
Trusley
Somersal Herbert
Harehill
DERBYSHIRE
Sapperton
Church Broughton
Sutton on the Hill
Dalbury
Hill Somersal
Doveridge
Oaks Green
Littleover
Normanton
Uttoxeter
Sudbury
Foston
Heathtop
Burnaston
Etwall
Marchington
Scropton
Hatton
Hilton
Findern
Stenson
Tutbury
Marston on Dove
Egginton
Willington
Twyford
Gorsty Hill
Marchington Woodlands
Draycott in the Clay
Hanbury
Rolleston-on-Dove
Clay Mills
Alder Moor
Repton
Milton
Foremark
Stretton
Newborough
Hanbury Woodend
Anslow
Newton Solney
Horninglow
Anslow Gate
Outwoods
Wetmore
Needwood
Bromley Wood
Winshill
Shobnall
Burton upon Trent
Hoar Cross
Newchurch
Rangemore
Rough Hay
Bretby
Tatenhill
Branston
Stapenhill
Hartshorne
Newhall
Blithbury
Hadley End
Woodlane
Dunstall
Midway
Hamstall Ridware
Morrey
Yoxall
Woodhouses
Barton-under-Needwood
Swadlincote
Woodville
Walton-on-Trent
Castle Gresley
Blackfordby
Handsacre
King's Bromley
Lupin
Orgreave
Wychnor
Rosliston
Caldwell
Linton
Norris Hill
Mount Pleasant
NATIONAL FOREST DISCOVERY CENTRE
Rileyhill
Fradley Junction
Alrewas
Coton in the Elms
Overseal
Moira
Donisthorpe
NATIONAL MEMORIAL ARBORETUM
Fradley
Croxall
Lullington
Netherseal
Oakthorpe
Elmhurst
Edingale
Chilcote
Measham
Lichfield
Streethay
Elford
Harlaston
Haunton
Clifton Campville
Appleby Magna
Huddlesford
Thorpe Constantine
No Man's Heath
Appleby Parva
Whittington
Hademore
STAFFS
THE NATIONAL FOREST
Trent Valley
A50
A38
A515
A511
A52
A444
A513
A51
A5121
A516
169
170
151
134
0 1 2 3 miles
0 1 2 3 4 5 km

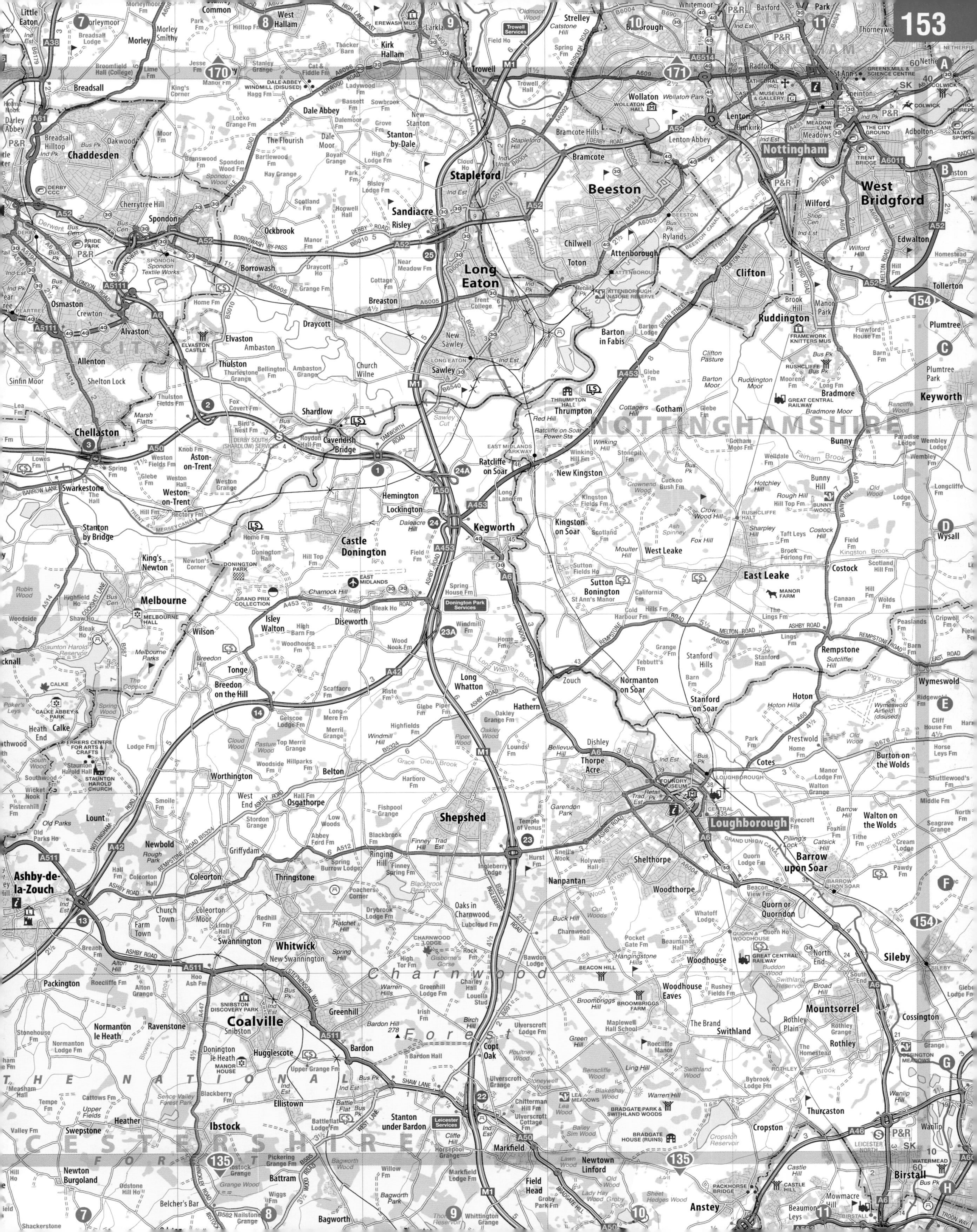
153
Nottingham
West Bridgford
Beeston
Stapleford
Long Eaton
Sandiacre
Risley
Spondon
Chaddesden
Derby City
Alvaston
Chellaston
Elvaston
Thulston
Shardlow
Cavendish Bridge
Aston-on-Trent
Weston-on-Trent
Swarkestone
Stanton by Bridge
King's Newton
Melbourne
Castle Donington
Hemington
Lockington
Kegworth
Sawley
Draycott
Breaston
Borrowash
Ockbrook
Dale Abbey
Stanton-by-Dale
Trowell
Bramcote
Chilwell
Toton
Attenborough
Clifton
Ruddington
Barton in Fabis
Thrumpton
Gotham
Ratcliffe on Soar
Kingston on Soar
West Leake
East Leake
Sutton Bonington
Normanton on Soar
Zouch
Hathern
Long Whatton
Diseworth
Isley Walton
Tonge
Breedon on the Hill
Wilson
Calke
Worthington
Belton
Osgathorpe
Shepshed
Loughborough
Thorpe Acre
Dishley
Shelthorpe
Nanpantan
Woodthorpe
Quorn or Quorndon
Barrow upon Soar
Sileby
Mountsorrel
Rothley
Cossington
Thurcaston
Cropston
Anstey
Birstall
Wanlip
Woodhouse
Woodhouse Eaves
Swithland
Newtown Linford
Markfield
Field Head
Stanton under Bardon
Bardon
Coalville
Hugglescote
Ibstock
Whitwick
Thringstone
Swannington
Coleorton
Ashby-de-la-Zouch
Packington
Normanton le Heath
Ravenstone
Heather
Swepstone
Newton Burgoland
Battram
Bagworth
Ellistown
Lount
Newbold
Griffydam
Keyworth
Plumtree
Tollerton
Edwalton
Bunny
Bradmore
Costock
Wysall
Rempstone
Wymeswold
Hoton
Prestwold
Burton on the Wolds
Cotes
Stanford on Soar
Walton on the Wolds
Nottinghamshire
Charnwood Forest
Leicestershire
The National Forest
East Midlands Airport
Donington Park Services
Trowell Services
Leicester Services
M1
A52
A6
A453
A42
A50
A511
A512
A60
A46
170
171
154
135

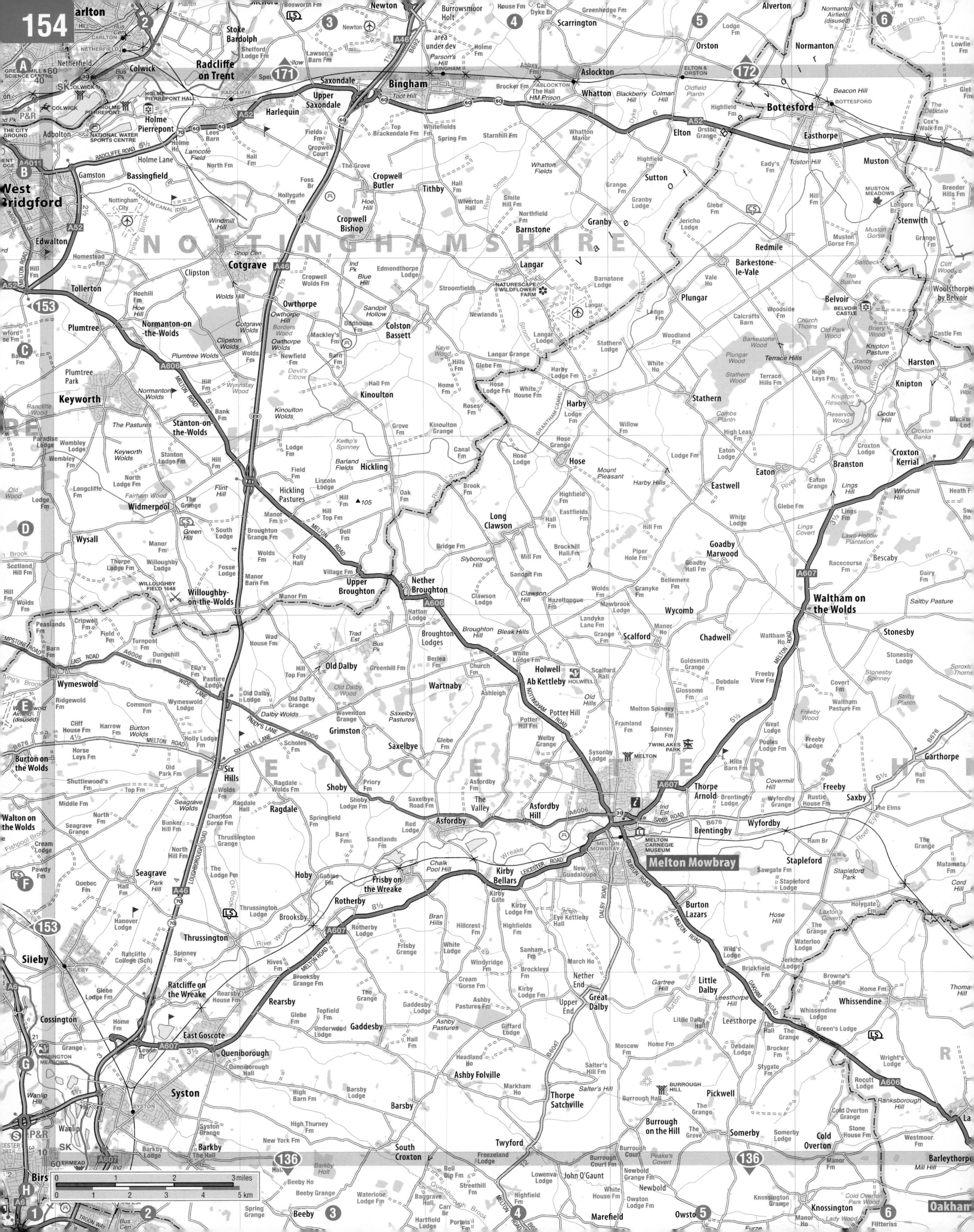

NOTTINGHAMSHIRE
LEICESTERSHIRE
Vale of Belvoir
Carlton
Netherfield
Colwick
Stoke Bardolph
Radcliffe on Trent
Newton
Burrowsmoor Holt
Scarrington
Alverton
Normanton
Orston
Aslockton
Whatton
Bingham
Saxondale
Upper Saxondale
Harlequin
Holme Pierrepont
Adbolton
West Bridgford
Gamston
Bassingfield
Holme Lane
Cropwell Butler
Tithby
Cropwell Bishop
Elton
Bottesford
Easthorpe
Muston
Sutton
Granby
Barnstone
Langar
Redmile
Barkestone-le-Vale
Plungar
Stenwith
Belvoir
Woolsthorpe by Belvoir
Harston
Knipton
Edwalton
Tollerton
Cotgrave
Clipston
Owthorpe
Colston Bassett
Plumtree
Normanton-on-the-Wolds
Plumtree Park
Keyworth
Stanton-on-the-Wolds
Kinoulton
Harby
Stathern
Hose
Hickling
Hickling Pastures
Eastwell
Eaton
Branston
Croxton Kerrial
Widmerpool
Wysall
Long Clawson
Goadby Marwood
Nether Broughton
Upper Broughton
Willoughby-on-the-Wolds
Waltham on the Wolds
Wycomb
Scalford
Chadwell
Stonesby
Wymeswold
Old Dalby
Broughton Lodges
Holwell
Ab Kettleby
Wartnaby
Grimston
Saxelbye
Burton on the Wolds
Six Hills
Shoby
Ragdale
Asfordby
Asfordby Hill
Thorpe Arnold
Brentingby
Wyfordby
Freeby
Saxby
Garthorpe
Walton on the Wolds
Seagrave
Hoby
Frisby on the Wreake
Rotherby
Kirby Bellars
Melton Mowbray
Stapleford
Burton Lazars
Brooksby
Thrussington
Sileby
Ratcliffe on the Wreake
Rearsby
Cossington
Gaddesby
Great Dalby
Little Dalby
Leesthorpe
Whissendine
East Goscote
Queniborough
Ashby Folville
Syston
Thorpe Satchville
Pickwell
Barsby
Barkby
Burrough on the Hill
Somerby
Cold Overton
South Croxton
Twyford
Barleythorpe
John O'Gaunt
Beeby
Marefield
Owston
Knossington
Oakham
A46
A52
A606
A607
A6006
B676
171
172
153
136
0 1 2 3 miles
0 1 2 3 4 5 km

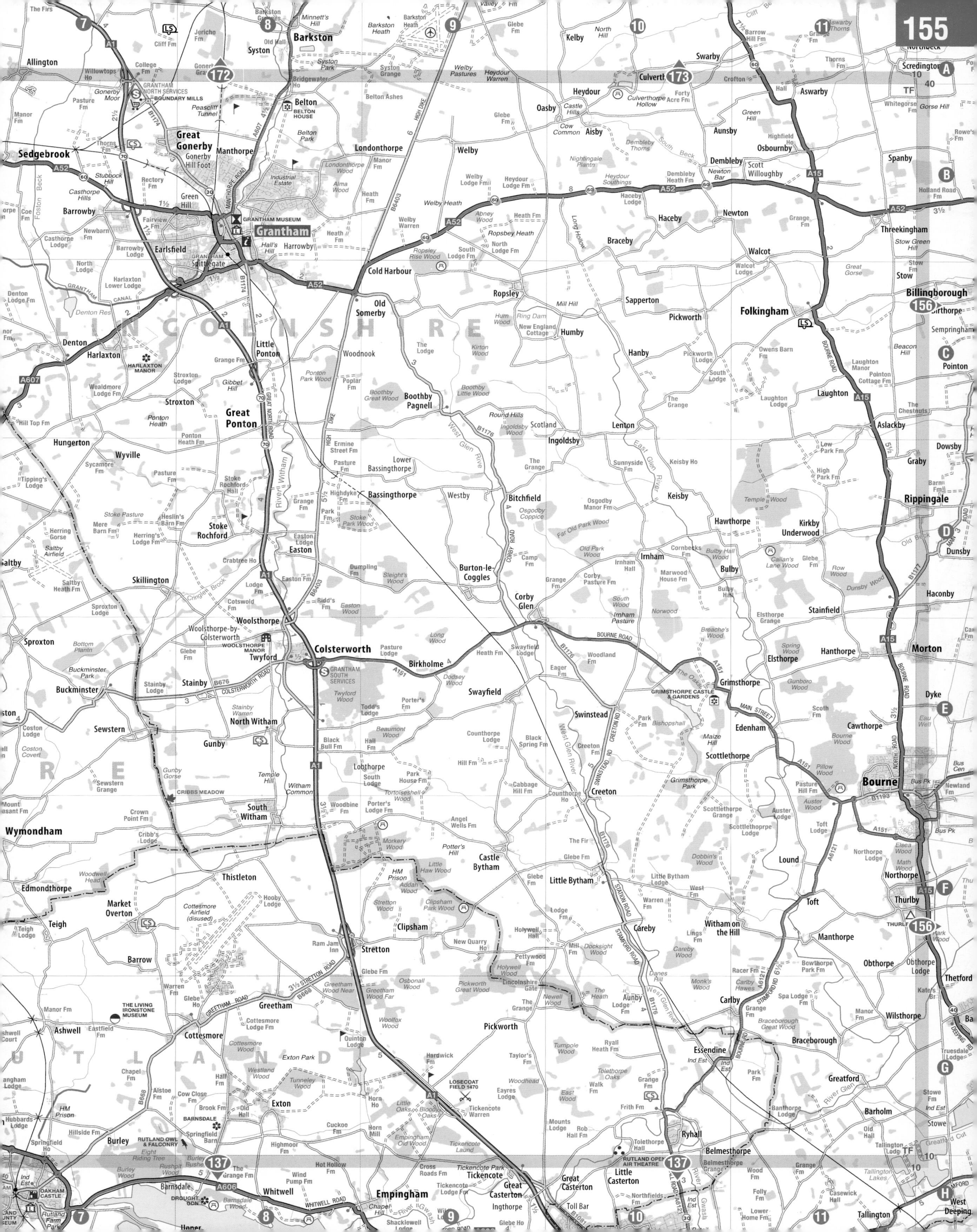

155
LINCOLNSHIRE
RUTLAND
Grantham
Barkston
Syston
Belton
BELTON HOUSE
Great Gonerby
Gonerby Hill Foot
Manthorpe
Londonthorpe
Sedgebrook
Allington
Barrowby
Earlsfield
Spittlegate
GRANTHAM MUSEUM
GRANTHAM NORTH SERVICES
BOUNDARY MILLS
Harrowby
Cold Harbour
Old Somerby
Welby
Oasby
Aisby
Heydour
Kelby
Culverthorpe
Swarby
Aswarby
Aunsby
Dembleby
Scott Willoughby
Osbournby
Newton
Haceby
Braceby
Walcot
Spanby
Threekingham
Stow
Billingborough
Sempringham
Pointon
Folkingham
Sapperton
Pickworth
Ropsley
Humby
Hanby
Laughton
Aslackby
Dowsby
Graby
Rippingale
Kirkby Underwood
Dunsby
Haconby
Stainfield
Morton
Hanthorpe
Dyke
Cawthorpe
Bourne
Denton
Harlaxton
HARLAXTON MANOR
Little Ponton
Great Ponton
Stroxton
Woodnook
Boothby Pagnell
Scotland
Ingoldsby
Lenton
Keisby
Hawthorpe
Irnham
Bulby
Hungerton
Wyville
Bassingthorpe
Lower Bassingthorpe
Westby
Bitchfield
Burton-le-Coggles
Corby Glen
Stoke Rochford
Easton
Saltby
Skillington
Sproxton
Woolsthorpe
Woolsthorpe-by-Colsterworth
WOOLSTHORPE MANOR
Colsterworth
Twyford
Birkholme
Stainby
Buckminster
GRANTHAM SOUTH SERVICES
Swayfield
Swinstead
GRIMSTHORPE CASTLE & GARDENS
Grimsthorpe
Edenham
Elsthorpe
Scottlethorpe
Sewstern
North Witham
Gunby
South Witham
Lobthorpe
Creeton
Wymondham
CRIBBS MEADOW
Castle Bytham
Little Bytham
Thistleton
Edmondthorpe
Market Overton
Teigh
Clipsham
Stretton
Careby
Witham on the Hill
Toft
Lound
Northorpe
Thurlby
Manthorpe
Obthorpe
Thetford
Barrow
Greetham
THE LIVING IRONSTONE MUSEUM
Ashwell
Cottesmore
Pickworth
Aunby
Carlby
Wilsthorpe
Braceborough
Essendine
Exton
Greatford
Barlholm
Stowe
Burley
BARNSDALE
RUTLAND OWL & FALCONRY
Whitwell
Empingham
Tickencote
Great Casterton
Ingthorpe
Little Casterton
RUTLAND OPEN AIR THEATRE
Ryhall
Belmesthorpe
Tallington
West Deeping
OAKHAM CASTLE
LOSECOAT FIELD 1470
Toll Bar
A1
A52
A15
A151
A606
A607
B1176
B676
B6403
HIGH DIKE
GREAT NORTH ROAD
BOURNE ROAD
STAMFORD ROAD
172
173
156
137

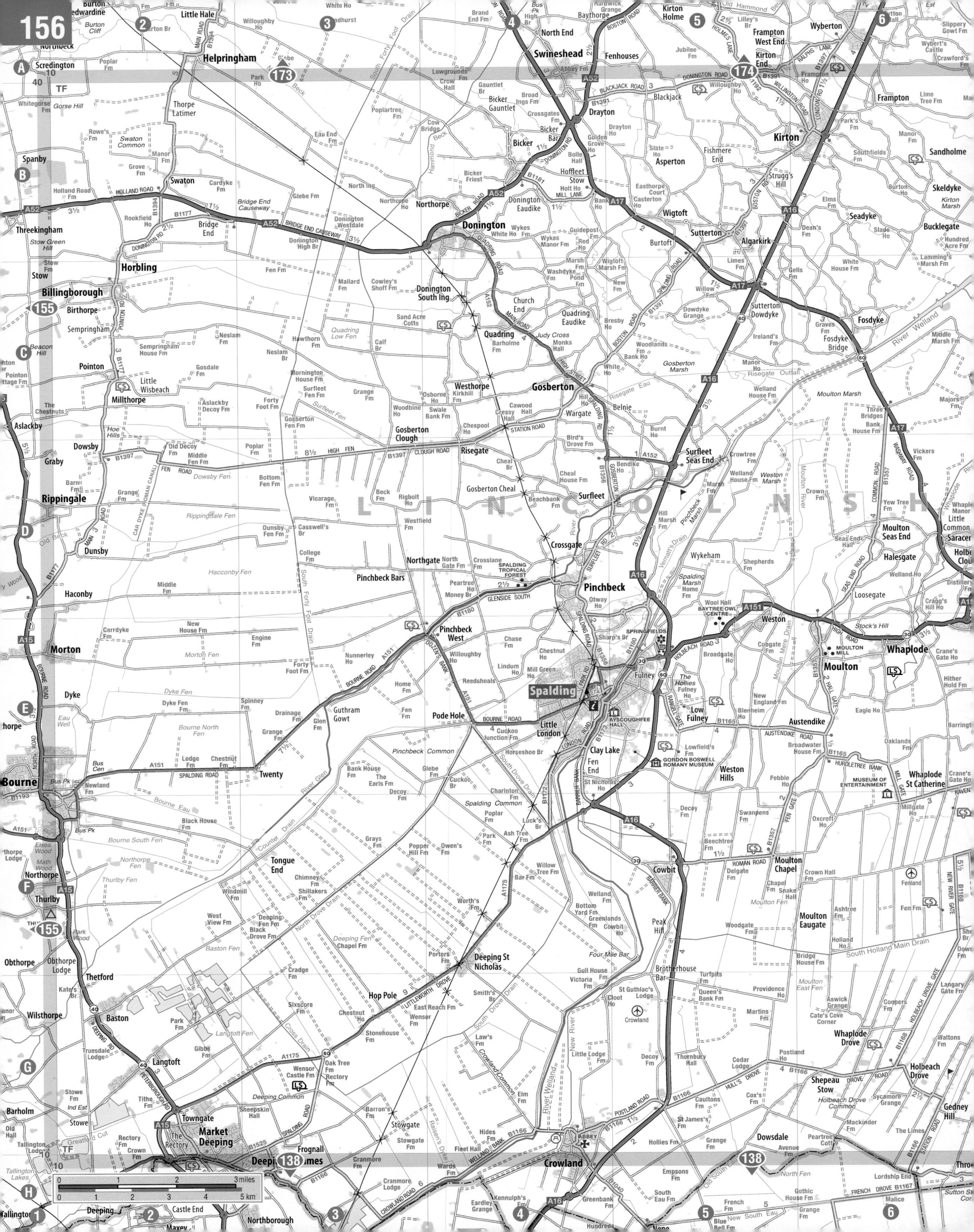
Burton
Pedwardine
Burton Cliff
Little Hale
Willoughby Ho
White Ho
Brand End Fm
Bus Pk
High Br
Hardwick Grange
Baythorpe
Kirton Holme
Old Hammond Beck
Lilley's Br
Frampton West End
Wyberton
Slippery Gowt Fm
Northbeck
Helpringham
Glebe
Park Ho
North End
Swineshead
Fenhouses
Jubilee Fm
Kirton End
Wybert's Castle
Crawford's Fm
Screditon
Poplar Fm
TF
Lowgrounds Fm
Crow Hall
Abbey Fm
Blackjack
Donington Road
Frampton Ho
Frampton
Lime Tree Fm
Whitegorse Fm
Gorse Hill
Thorpe Latimer
Poplartree Fm
Gauntlet Br
Bicker Gauntlet
Broad Ings Fm
Crossgates Fm
Drayton
Drayton Ho
Willoughby Ho
Park's Fm
Rowe's Fm
Swaton Common
Eau End Fm
Cow Bridge
Hammond Beck
Bicker
Bicker Bar
Golden Grove Ho
Bolle Hall
Slate Ho
Asperton
Fishmere End
Kirton
Manor Fm
Sandholme
Spanby
Manor Fm
Grove Fm
Southfields Fm
Holland Road Fm
Holland Road
Swaton
Cardyke Fm
Glebe Fm
North Ing
Bicker Friest
Hoffleet Stow
Holt Ho
Mill Lane
Easthorpe Court
Casterton Ho
Strugg's Hill
Burton Ho
Skeldyke
Kirton Marsh
Bridge End Causeway
Northorpe Ho
Northorpe
Donington Eaudike
Bank Ho
Elms Fm
Rookfield Ho
Bridge End
Donington Westdale
Donington
White Ho
Wykes Fm
Wigtoft
Seadyke
Threekingham
Stow Green Hill
Donington Rd
Donington High Br
Wykes Manor Fm
Guidepost Fm
Red Ho
Sutterton
Algarkirk
Burtoft
Dean's Fm
Slade Ho
Bucklegate
Hundred Acre Fm
Stow Fm
Stow
Horbling
Fen Fm
Marsh Ho
Wigtoft Marsh Fm
Washdyke Fm
Pond Fm
New Fm
Limes Fm
Gells Fm
White House Fm
Lamming's Marsh Fm
Billingborough
Birthorpe
Sempringham
Mallard Fm
Cowley's Shoff Fm
Donington South Ing
Church End
Quadring Eaudike
Bresby Ho
Willow Fm
Dowdyke Grange
Sutterton Dowdyke
Fosdyke
Sand Acre Cotts
Quadring Low Fen
Quadring
Barholme Fm
Judy Cross
Monks Hall
Woodlands Fm
Bank Ho
Graves Fm
Fosdyke Bridge
River Welland
Middle Marsh Fm
Beacon Hill
Sempringham House Fm
Neslam Fm
Neslam Br
Hawthorn Fm
Calf Br
Ireland's Fm
Gosberton Marsh
Pointon
Pointon Cottage Fm
Gosdale Fm
Mornington House Fm
Manor Ho
Risegate Outfall
Little Wisbeach
Millthorpe
Surfleet Fen Fm
Grange Fm
Westhorpe
Kirkhill Fm
Osborne Ho
Gosberton
White Ho
Welland House Fm
Moulton Marsh
The Chestnuts
Aslackby Decoy Fm
Forty Foot Fm
Surfleet Fen
Woodbine Ho
Swale Bank Fm
Cawood Hall
Cressy Hall
Hill Ho
Wargate
Belnie
Risegate Eau
Three Bridges
Bank House Fm
Majors Fm
Aslackby
Hoe Hills
Gosberton Fen Fm
Gosberton Clough
Chespool Ho
Station Road
Burnt Ho
Bird's Drove Fm
Dowsby
Old Decoy Fm
Poplar Fm
High Fen
Clough Road
Risegate
Surfleet Seas End
Crowtree Fm
Vickers Fm
Graby
Middle Fen Fm
Fen Road
Dowsby Fen
Bottom Fen Fm
Cheal Br
Bendike Ho
Welland House Fm
Weston Marsh
Moulton River
Barn Fm
Grange Fm
Car Dyke (Roman Canal)
Beck Fm
Rigbolt Ho
Gosberton Cheal
Cheal House Fm
Surfleet
Beachbank Fm
Marsh Fm
Crown Fm
Yew Tree Fm
Rippingale
Rippingdale Fen
Vicarage Fm
Westfield Fm
River Glen
Hill Marsh Fm
Pinchbeck Marsh
Moulton Seas End
Whaple Manor
Little Common
Saracen's Head
Old Beck
Dunsby Fen Fm
Casswell's Br
L I N C O L N S H I R E
Crossgate
Vernatt's Drain
Seas End Hall
Dunsby
College Fm
Northgate
North Gate Fm
Crosslane Ho
Spalding Tropical Forest
Wykeham
Shepherds Fm
Halesgate
Holbeach Clough
Hacconby Fen
Pinchbeck Bars
Peartree Ho
Money Br
Pinchbeck
Spalding Marsh Home Fm
Welland Ho
Distillery Fm
Haconby
Middle Fm
Glenside South
Otway Ho
Loosegate
Cragg's Hill Ho
Wool Hall
Baytree Owl Centre
Weston
Stock's Hill
Carrdyke Fm
New House Fm
Engine Fm
Pinchbeck West
Chase Fm
Sharp's Br
Springfields
Holbeach Road
Cobgate Fm
Moulton Mill
Whaplode
Crane's Gate Ho
Morton
Morton Fen
Nunnerley Ho
Willoughby Ho
Chestnut Ho
Broadgate Ho
Moulton
Forty Foot Fm
Bourne Road
Lindum Ho
Mill Green Ho
Fulney
Moulton Mere Drain
Hither Hold Fm
Home Fm
Reedshoals
The Hollies
Fulney Ho
Dyke
Dyke Fen
Spinney Fm
Dyke Fen Fm
Spalding
Park Road
Ayscoughfee Hall
Low Fulney
New England Fm
Eagle Ho
Guthram Gowt
Drainage Fm
Fen Fm
Pode Hole
Little London
Blenheim Ho
Austendike
Eau Well
Bourne North Fen
Glen Fm
Cuckoo Junction Fm
Austendike Road
Barrington Gate
Grange Fm
Clay Lake
Lowfield's Fm
Broadwater House Fm
Oaklands Fm
Pinchbeck Common
Horseshoe Br
Gordon Boswell Romany Museum
Hurdletree Bank
Bourne
Bus Pk
Bus Cen
Lodge Fm
Chestnut Fm
Spalding Road
Twenty
Fen End
Weston Hills
Museum of Entertainment
Mill Gate
Whaplode St Catherine
Crane's Gate Ho
Newland Fm
Bank House Fm
The Earls Fm
Glebe Fm
Decoy Fm
Cuckoo Br
Charinton Ho
St Nicholas Ho
Pebble Ho
Ravens Gate
Bourne Eau
Spalding Common
Poplar Fm
Millgate Ho
Black House Fm
River Glen
Park Fm
Luck's Br
Swanpens Fm
Oxcroft Fm
Decoy Fm
Fen Gate
Haconby
Elsea Wood
Bourne South Fen
Counter Drain
Grays Fm
Pepper Hill Fm
Owen's Fm
Ash Tree Fm
Beechtree Fm
Thorpe Lodge
Math Wood
Northorpe Fen
Northorpe
Tongue End
Bar Fm
Willow Tree Fm
Cowbit
Roman Road
Moulton Chapel
Crown Hall Fm
Delgate Fm
Chapel Fm
Snake Hall
Fenland
Thurlby Fen
Thurlby
Chimney Fm
Shillakers Fm
Barrier Bank
Windmill Fm
Worth's Fm
Welland Fm
Bottom Yard Fm
Greenlands Fm
Cowbit Ho
Moulton Fen
Ashtree Fm
Fen Fm
Park Wood
West View Fm
Deeping Fen Fm
Black Drove Fm
North Drove Drain
Peak Hill
Woodgate Fm
Moulton Eaugate
Holland Ho
South Holland Main Drain
Obthorpe
Obthorpe Lodge
Baston Fen
Deeping Fen
Chapel Fm
Porters Fm
Deeping St Nicholas
Four Mile Bar
Bridge House Fm
Thetford
Cradge Fm
Gull House Fm
Victoria Fm
Brotherhouse Bar
Turfpits Fm
Moulton East Fen
Langary Gate Fm
Kate's Br
Hop Pole
Littleworth Drove
Smith's Br
St Guthlac's Lodge
Cloot Ho
Queen's Bank Fm
Providence Ho
Coopers Fm
Wilsthorpe
Park Fm
Sixscore Fm
Chestnut Ho
East Reach Fm
Wensor Fm
Crowland
Martins Fm
Aswick Grange
Cate's Cove Corner
Baston
Langtoft Fen
Cross Drain
Stonehouse Fm
Law's Fm
South Drove Drain
New River
Whaplode Drove
Waltons Fm
Truesdale Lodge
Gibbs Fm
A1175
Wensor Castle Fm
Oak Tree Fm
Rectory Fm
Crowland Common
Little Lodge Fm
Decoy Ho
Thornbury Hall
Cedar Lodge
Postland Ho
Holbeach Drove
Langtoft
River Welland
Elm Fm
Shepeau Stow
Holbeach Drove Common
Sycamore Grange
Gedney Hill
Deeping Common
Postland Road
Hull's Drove
Cox's Fm
Caultons Fm
Stowe Fm
Ind Est
Tithe Fm
Sheepskin Hall
Barron's Fm
Stowgate
St James's Fm
Mackinder Fm
The Limes
Station Road
Stowe
Towngate
Market Deeping
Spalding Road
Stowgate Fm
Hides Fm
Abbey
Hollies Fm
Grange Fm
Dowsdale
Peartree Cotts
Barholm
Old Hall
Greatford Cut
Rectory Fm
Crown Fm
The Rectory
Frognall
Fleet Hall
Welland Bank
Avenue Fm
Tallington Lodge
Tallington Lakes
Deeping St James
Cranmore Fm
Wards Fm
Crowland
Empsons Fm
North Fen
Lordship End
Cranmore Lodge
Crowland Road
Raisen's Dyke
Kennulph's Fm
Eardley Grange
Greenbank Fm
South Eau Fm
Old South Eau
Gothic House Fm
French Drove
Sutton St Edmund
Malice
Tallington
Deeping
Castle End
Maxey
Northborough
Hundreds
French Fm
Blue Bell Fm
New South Eau
Grange Fm
0 1 2 3 miles
0 1 2 3 4 5 km
A52
A17
A16
A15
A151
A152
A1175
B1394
B1177
B1397
B1181
B1391
B1357
B1356
B1180
B1172
B1173
B1165
B1166
B1168
B1193
B1525
B1040
B1167
155
173
174
138
A B C D E F G H
1 2 3 4 5 6

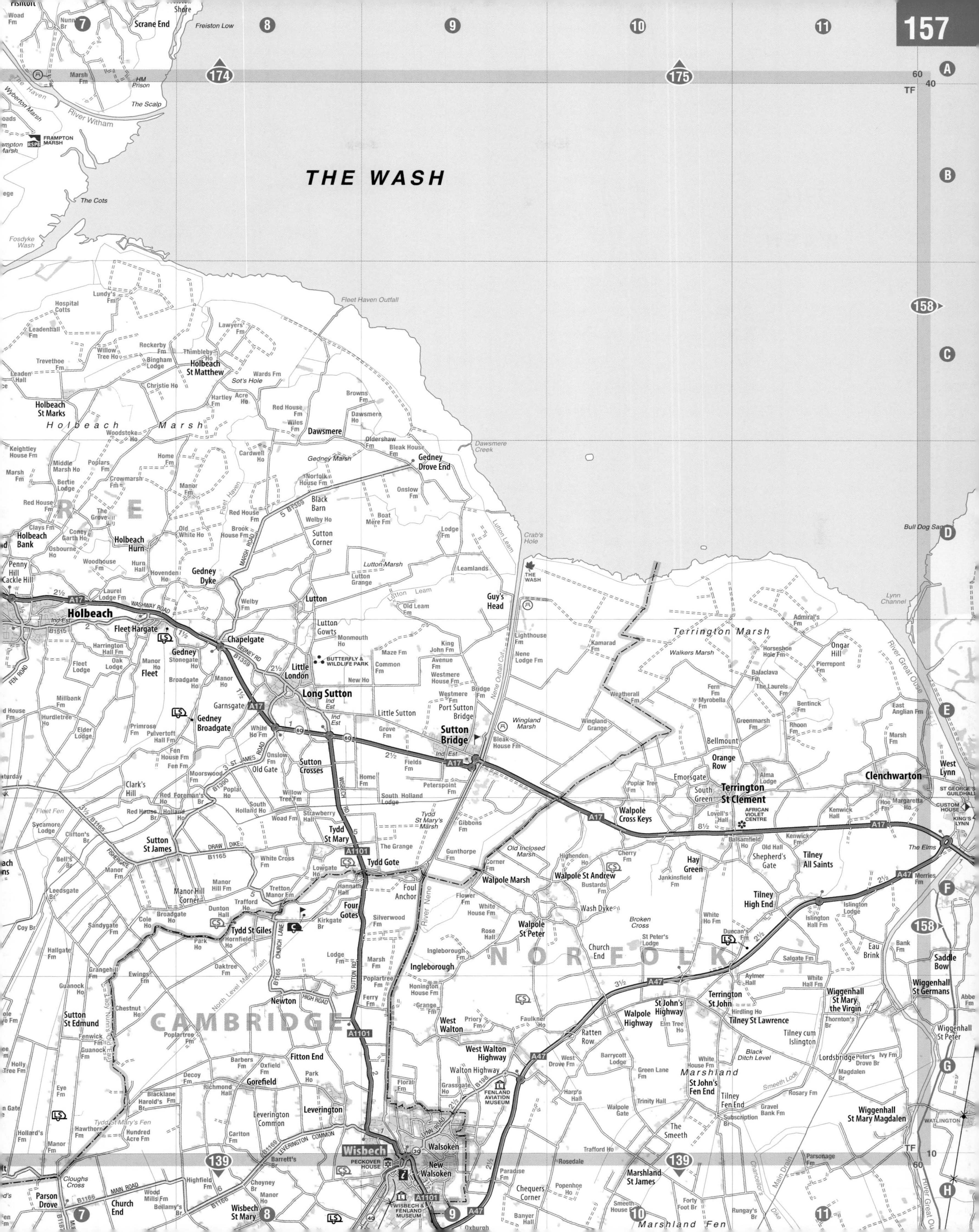
THE WASH
Scrane End
Freiston Low
HM Prison
The Scalp
River Witham
FRAMPTON MARSH
The Cots
Fosdyke Wash
Fleet Haven Outfall
Holbeach St Matthew
Holbeach St Marks
Holbeach Marsh
Dawsmere
Gedney Drove End
Gedney Marsh
Black Barn
Sutton Corner
Lutton Marsh
Holbeach Bank
Holbeach Hurn
Gedney Dyke
Lutton
Guy's Head
Holbeach
Fleet Hargate
Chapelgate
Gedney
Fleet
Little London
Long Sutton
BUTTERFLY & WILDLIFE PARK
Little Sutton
Sutton Bridge
Port Sutton Bridge
Gedney Broadgate
Garnsgate
Old Gate
Sutton Crosses
Terrington Marsh
Walkers Marsh
Ongar Hill
Bellmount
Orange Row
Terrington St Clement
Clenchwarton
West Lynn
KING'S LYNN
Walpole Cross Keys
AFRICAN VIOLET CENTRE
Tilney All Saints
Hay Green
Shepherd's Gate
Walpole St Andrew
Walpole Marsh
Tydd St Mary
Tydd Gote
Sutton St James
Four Gotes
Foul Anchor
Tydd St Giles
Walpole St Peter
Church End
NORFOLK
Tilney High End
Ingleborough
Terrington St John
St John's Highway
Walpole Highway
Tilney St Lawrence
Wiggenhall St Mary the Virgin
Wiggenhall St Germans
Saddle Bow
Tilney cum Islington
Newton
CAMBRIDGE
Sutton St Edmund
West Walton
West Walton Highway
Walton Highway
FENLAND AVIATION MUSEUM
Ratten Row
Fitton End
Gorefield
Leverington
Leverington Common
Marshland St John's Fen End
Tilney Fen End
Wiggenhall St Peter
Wiggenhall St Mary Magdalen
The Smeeth
Wisbech
PECKOVER HOUSE
Walsoken
New Walsoken
Marshland St James
Chequers Corner
WISBECH & FENLAND MUSEUM
Cloughs Cross
Parson Drove
Church End
Wisbech St Mary
Marshland Fen
River Great Ouse
River Nene
A17
A47
A1101
B1359
B1165
B1166
174
175
158
139
7
8
9
10
11
A
B
C
D
E
F
G
H
TF

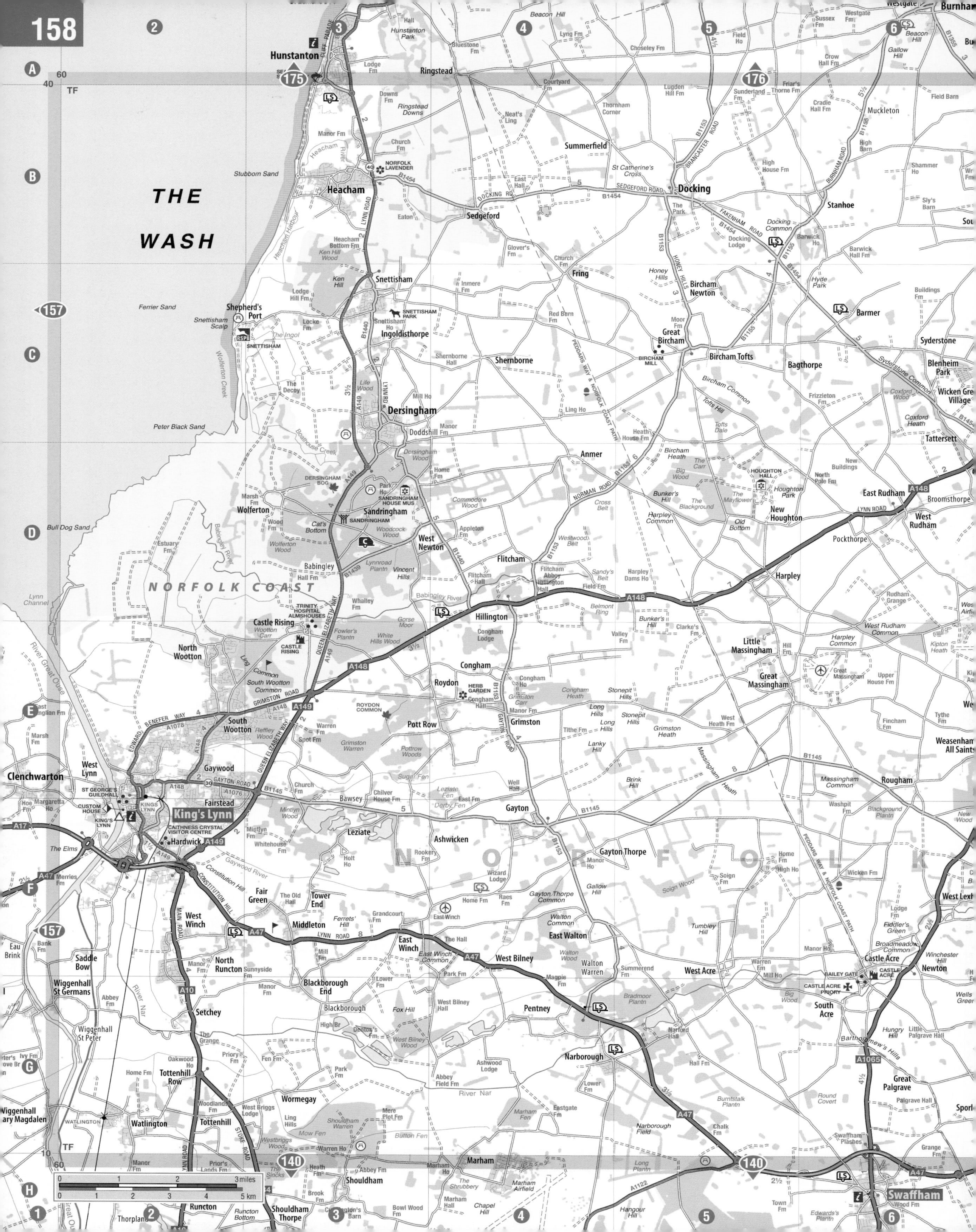
THE WASH
NORFOLK COAST
NORFOLK
Hunstanton
Heacham
Snettisham
Ingoldisthorpe
Dersingham
Sandringham
Wolferton
West Newton
Babingley
Castle Rising
North Wootton
South Wootton
Gaywood
King's Lynn
West Lynn
Clenchwarton
Hardwick
Fairstead
Ringstead
Sedgeford
Docking
Fring
Summerfield
Stanhoe
Bircham Newton
Great Bircham
Bircham Tofts
Barmer
Syderstone
Bagthorpe
Shernborne
Anmer
Houghton Hall
New Houghton
East Rudham
West Rudham
Tattersett
Flitcham
Hillington
Harpley
Congham
Roydon
Grimston
Pott Row
Little Massingham
Great Massingham
Rougham
Gayton
Gayton Thorpe
Bawsey
Leziate
Ashwicken
East Winch
West Winch
Middleton
Tower End
Fair Green
North Runcton
Setchey
Blackborough End
West Bilney
East Walton
Walton Warren
Pentney
Narborough
West Acre
Castle Acre
South Acre
Newton
Great Palgrave
Swaffham
Marham
Shouldham
Shouldham Thorpe
Wormegay
Tottenhill
Tottenhill Row
Watlington
Saddle Bow
Wiggenhall St Germans
Wiggenhall St Peter
Runcton
Peter Black Sand
Stubborn Sand
Ferrier Sand
Bull Dog Sand
Shepherd's Port
Pockthorpe
Weasenham All Saints
West Lexham
Burnham
Mileage
Scale: 0 1 2 3 miles; 0 1 2 3 4 5 km
TF
175
176
157
140

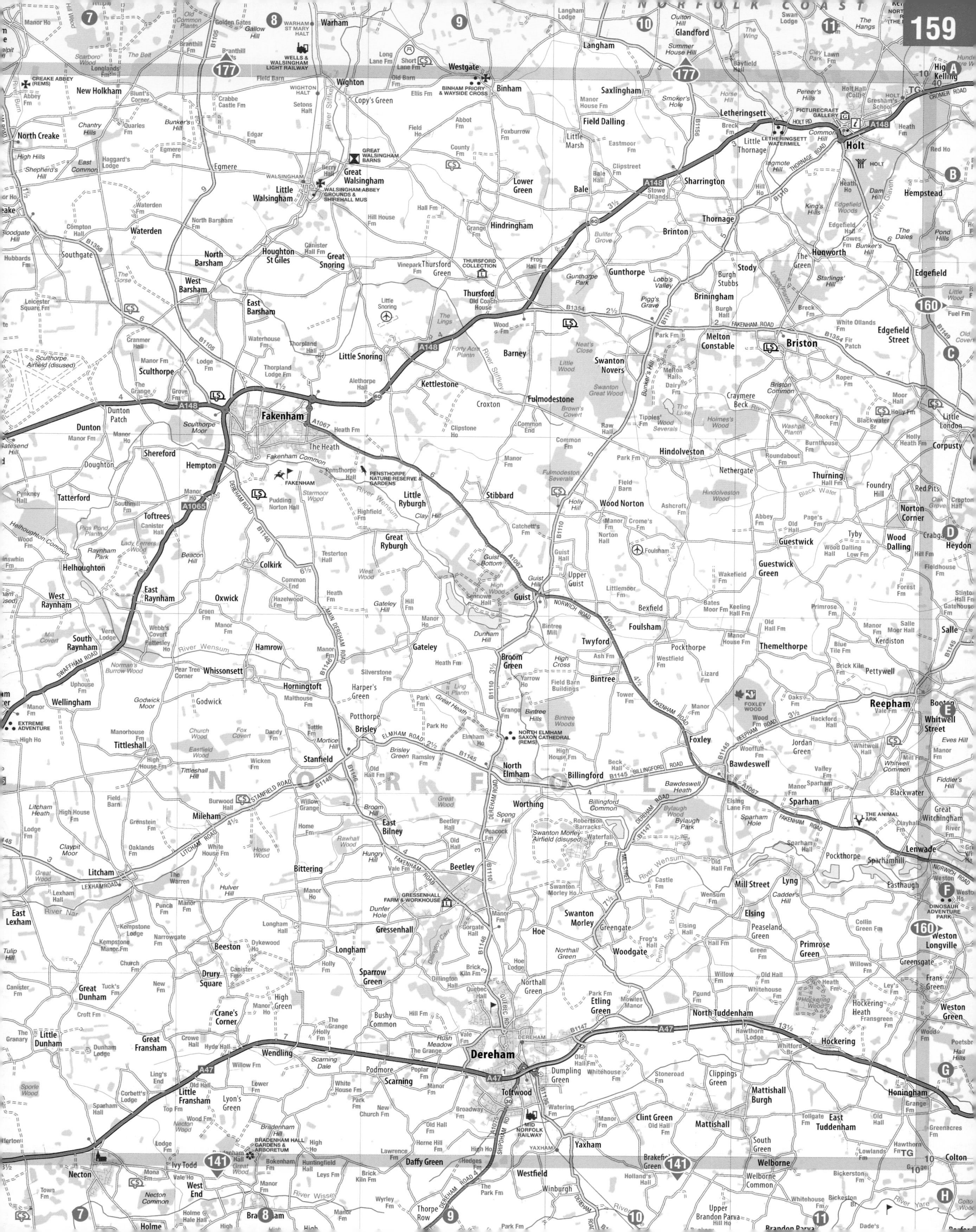

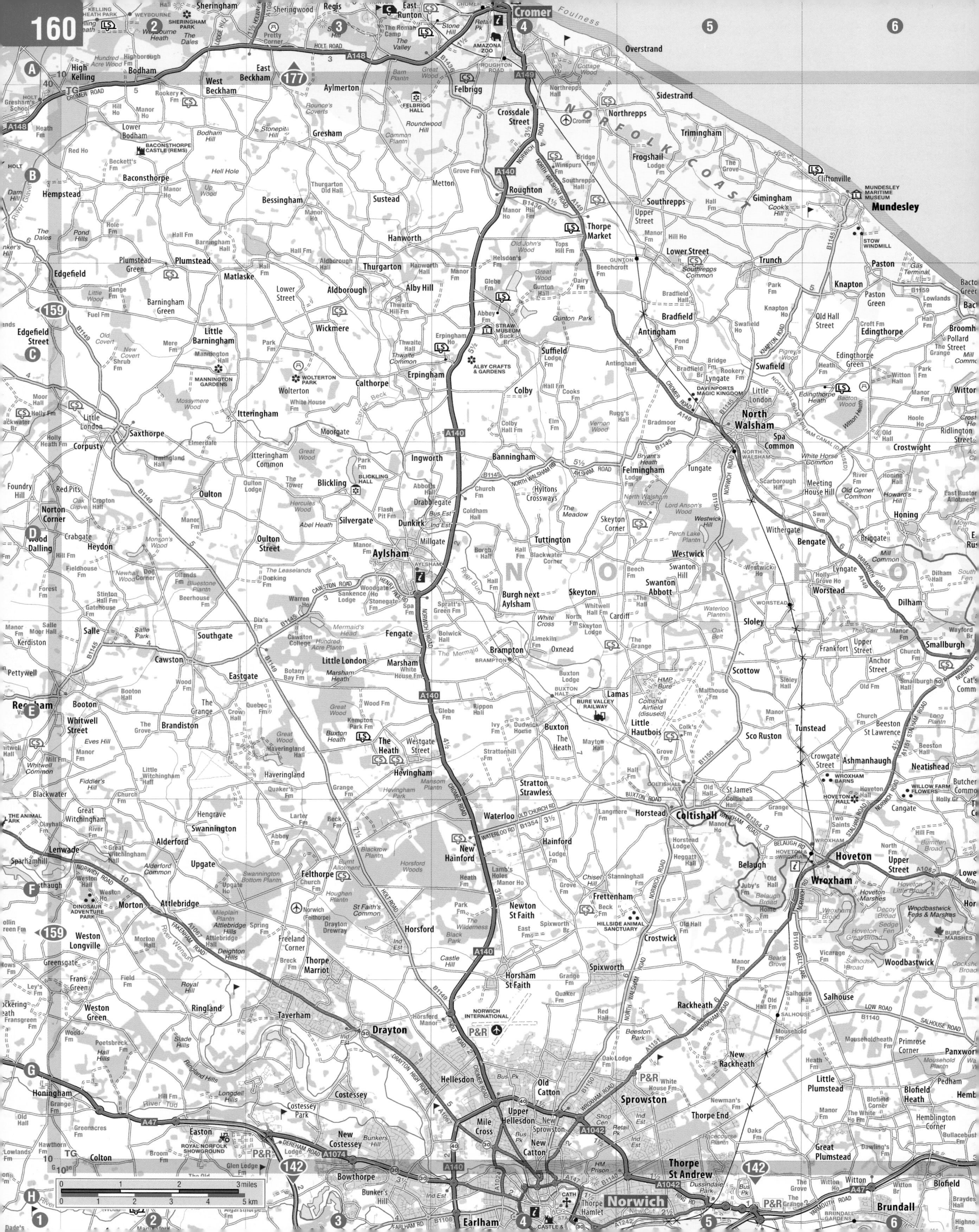

Sheringham
Weybourne
Sheringwood
Regis
East Runton
Cromer
Foulness
Overstrand
Sidestrand
Northrepps
Trimingham
Mundesley
High Kelling
Bodham
West Beckham
East Beckham
Aylmerton
Felbrigg
Crossdale Street
Gresham
Baconsthorpe
Hempstead
Bessingham
Sustead
Metton
Roughton
Southrepps
Gimingham
Thorpe Market
Lower Street
Trunch
Paston
Knapton
Edgefield
Plumstead
Matlaske
Thurgarton
Alby Hill
Aldborough
Hanworth
Antingham
Bradfield
Swafield
Edingthorpe
Wickmere
Little Barningham
Barningham Green
Edgefield Street
Calthorpe
Erpingham
Suffield
Colby
North Walsham
Wolterton
Saxthorpe
Corpusty
Itteringham
Ingworth
Banningham
Felmingham
Tungate
Crostwight
Blickling
Oulton
Silvergate
Dunkirk
Aylsham
Tuttington
Westwick
Honing
Bengate
Norton Corner
Wood Dalling
Heydon
Oulton Street
Burgh next Aylsham
Skeyton
Swanton Abbott
Worstead
Dilham
Salle
Southgate
Cawston
Eastgate
Little London
Marsham
Fengate
Brampton
Oxnead
Sloley
Smallburgh
Scottow
Booton
Brandiston
Whitwell Street
The Heath
Hevingham
Buxton
Lamas
Little Hautbois
Tunstead
Sco Ruston
Ashmanhaugh
Neatishead
Swannington
Alderford
Great Witchingham
Lenwade
Waterloo
Stratton Strawless
Horstead
Coltishall
Hainford
New Hainford
Belaugh
Hoveton
Wroxham
Upgate
Felthorpe
Attlebridge
Morton
Frettenham
Newton St Faith
Crostwick
Horsford
Weston Longville
Thorpe Marriott
Horsham St Faith
Spixworth
Woodbastwick
Ringland
Taverham
Drayton
Rackheath
Salhouse
Weston Green
New Rackheath
Hellesdon
Old Catton
Sprowston
Honingham
Costessey
Upper Hellesdon
Mile Cross
Thorpe End
Easton
New Costessey
New Catton
Little Plumstead
Great Plumstead
Blofield Heath
Colton
Bowthorpe
Thorpe St Andrew
Norwich
Thorpe Hamlet
Earlham
Brundall
Blofield
NORFOLK COAST
NORFOLK
A148
A149
A140
A1067
A1042
A47
A1074
B1145
B1149
B1150
B1354
177
159
142
TG
0 1 2 3 miles
0 1 2 3 4 5 km

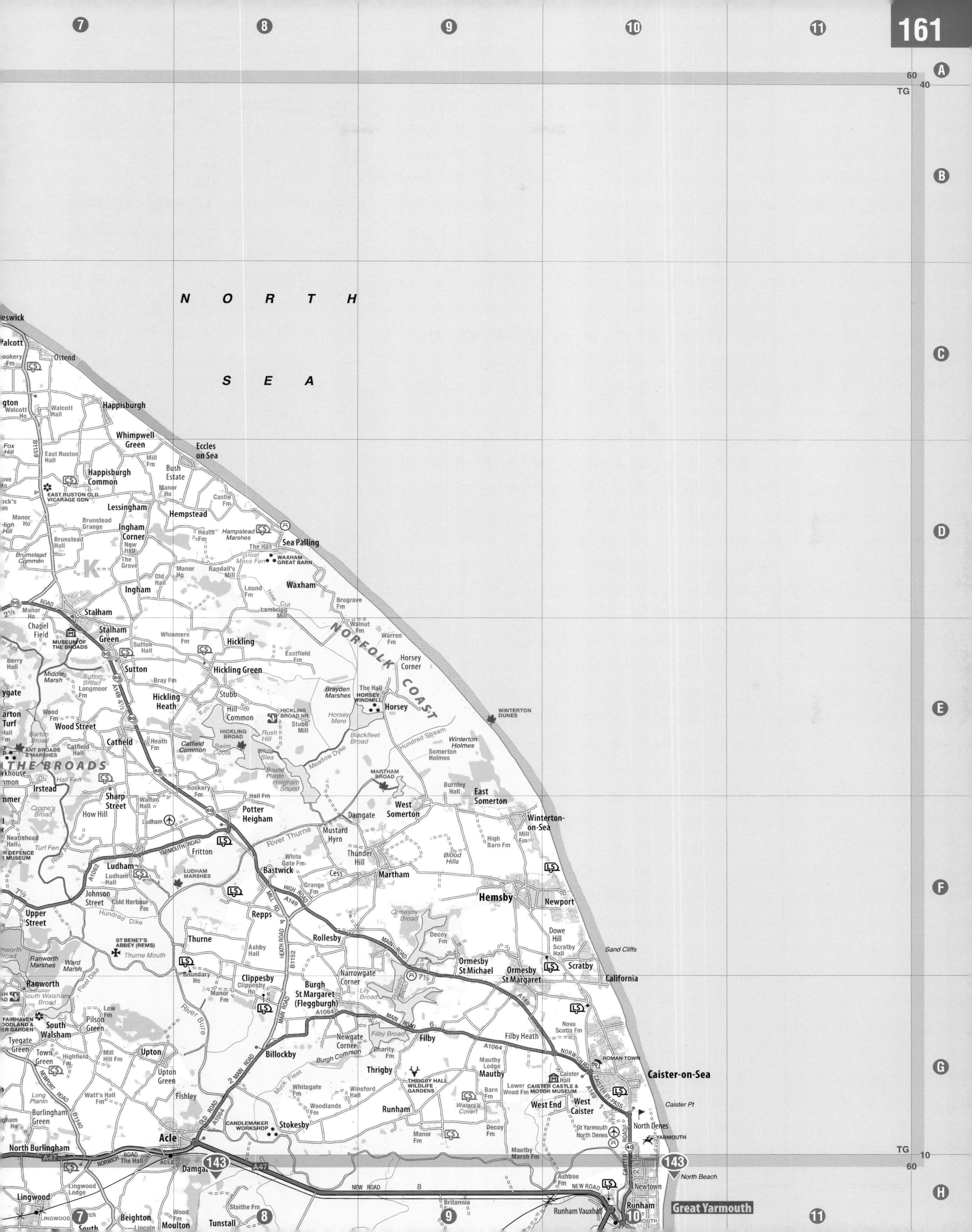

NORTH

SEA

NORFOLK COAST

THE BROADS

Great Yarmouth

Top/left grid and margin labels:

7 8 9 10 11

A B C D E F G H

60 40 TG

TG 10 60

143 143

Place names (north to south, west to east):

eswick
Walcott
Rookery Fm
Ostend
Happisburgh
Fox Hill
East Ruston Hall
Walcott Ho
Whimpwell Green
Eccles on Sea
Happisburgh Common
EAST RUSTON OLD VICARAGE GDN
Mill Ho
Castle Fm
Bush Estate
Manor Ho
Lessingham
Hempstead
Manor High Ho
Brunstead Grange
Ingham Corner
Hampstead Marshes
Sea Palling
Brunstead Hall
New Hall
Heath
The Hall
WAXHAM GREAT BARN
Great Moss Fen
Brumstead Common
The Grove
Old Hall
Randall's Mill
Waxham
K
Stalham
Ingham
Manor Ho
Lound Fm
Brograve Fm
Chapel Field
Manor Ho
Whimere Fm
Lambrigg Mill
Walnut Fm
Stalham Green
Sutton Hall
Hickling
Eastfield Fm
Warren Fm
Horsey Corner
Berry Hall
Sutton
Hickling Green
HICKLING BROAD NR
The Hall
HORSEY WINDMILL
Middle Marsh
Sutton Broad Longmoor
Bray Fm
Brayden Marshes
Horsey
ygate
Stubb
Hickling Heath
Hill Common
Stubb Mill
Wood Fm
Winterton Dunes
arton Turf
Wood Street
HICKLING BROAD
Horsey Mere
Winterton Holmes
ANT BROADS & MARSHES
Catfield
Heath Fm
Rush Hill
Blackfleet Broad
Somerton Holmes
Barton Broad
Catfield Common
Mill Slea
Hundred Stream
Crome's Broad
Catfield Hall
Swim Coots
Meadow Dyke
Winterton Holmes
THE BROADS
Hall Fen
Sound Plantn Heigham Sound
MARTHAM BROAD
Burnley Hall
East Somerton
rkhouse
Irstead
Rookery Fm
Hall Fm
Damgate
West Somerton
Winterton-on-Sea
Sharp Street
Walton Hall
mmer
How Hill
Ludham
Potter Heigham
Mustard Hyrn
High Barn Fm
Mill Fm
Neatishead Hall
Ludham
River Thurne
White Gate Fm
Thunder Hill
Blood Hills
DEFENCE MUSEUM
Turf Fen
Fritton
Cess
Martham
Ludham Hall
Grange Fm
Johnson Street
LUDHAM MARSHES
Bastwick
Hemsby
Cold Harbour
Repps
Newport
Upper Street
Hundred Dike
Thurne
Ashby Hall
Ormesby Broad
Dowe Hill
Scratby Hall
ST BENET'S ABBEY (REMS)
Thurne Mouth
Rollesby
Decoy Fm
Sand Cliffs
nworth
Ranworth Marshes
Ward Marsh
Boundary Ho
Clippesby
Narrowgate Corner
Ormesby St Michael
Ormesby St Margaret
Scratby
Ranworth
South Walsham Broad
Manor Fm
Clippesby Ho
Lily Broad
Rollesby Broad
California
FAIRHAVEN WOODLAND & WATER GARDEN
Low Fm
Pilson Green
Burgh St Margaret (Fleggburgh)
A1064
Nova Scotia Fm
South Walsham
Tyegate Green
Upton
Newgate Corner
Filby Broad
Filby
Filby Heath
ROMAN TOWN
Town Green
Highfield
Mill Hill Fm
Upton Green
Billockby
Burgh Common
Charity Fm
A1064
Caister-on-Sea
Long Plantn
Watt's Hall Fm
Fishley
Thrigby
Mautby Lodge Fm
Mautby
CAISTER CASTLE & MOTOR MUSEUM
Burlingham Green
Whitegate Fm
Winsford Hall
THRIGBY HALL WILDLIFE GARDENS
Barn Fm
Lower Wood Fm
Caister Hall
West End
West Caister
Caister Pt
North Burlingham
Woodlands
Runham
Water's Covert
Mautby
Gt Yarmouth North Denes
North Denes
Acle
CANDLEMAKER WORKSHOP
Stokesby
Decoy Fm
Manor Fm
GT YARMOUTH
Lingwood
ACLE
Damgate
Mautby Marsh Fm
North Beach
Lingwood Lodge
Staithe Fm
NEW ROAD
Ashtree Fm
NEW ROAD
Newtown
Beighton
Moulton
Tunstall
Britannia
Runham Vauxhall
Runham
GREAT YARMOUTH

Road numbers: A47, A149, A1064, A1062, B1152, B1159, B1140, B1140

Distances: 2½, 7½, 2½, 7½, 8

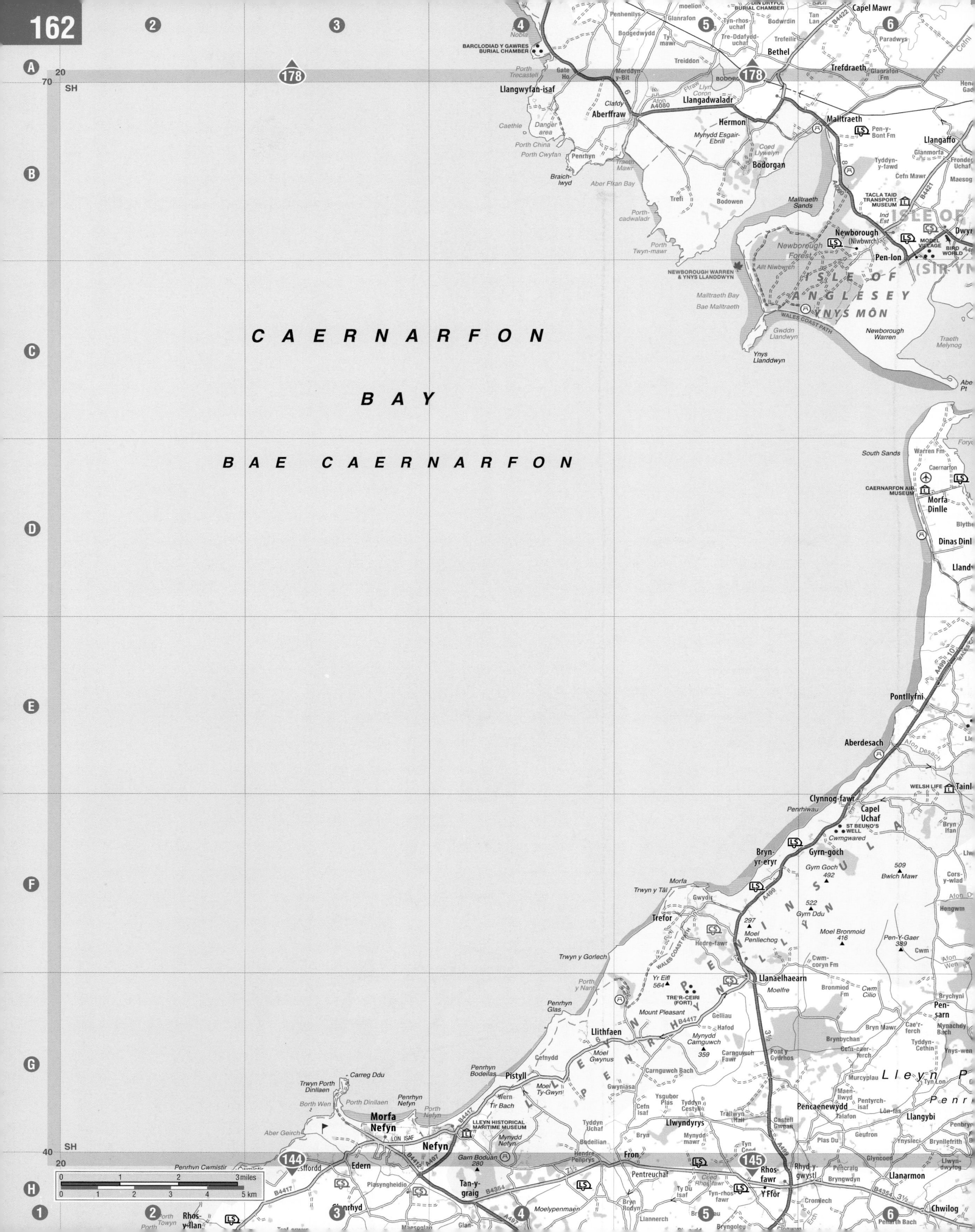

❷ ❸ ❹ ❺ ❻

A

B

C

D

E

F

G

H

❶ ❷ ❸ ❹ ❺ ❻

20
70
SH

Penhenllys
Bodgedwydd
moelion
Glanfaron
Tyn-rhos-uchaf
Bodwrdin
Tan Lan
B4422
Capel Mawr

DIN DRYFOL
BURIAL CHAMBER
Tre-feilir
Trefeilir
Trefeilir
Paradwys

BARCLODIAD Y GAWRES
BURIAL CHAMBER
178
Bethel
Trefdraeth
Glanrafon
/Fm

178
178
Trefdraeth
Hen
Gae

Llangwyfan-isaf
Merddyn
y-Bit
Ffrwd
Llyn
Coron
A4080
Bodorg

Clafdy
Llangadwaladr
Malltraeth
Pen-y-Bont Fm
B4421

Aberffraw
A4080
Hermon
Llangaffo

Caethle
Danger
area
Mynydd Esgair-Ebrill
Glanmorfa
Cefn Mawr

Porth China
Penrhyn
Coed
Llywelyn
Tyddyn-y-fawd
Maesog

Porth Owyfan
Traeth
Mawr
Bodorgan
TACLA TAID
TRANSPORT
MUSEUM
ISLE OF

Braich-
lwyd
Trefi
Newborough
(Niwbwrch)
MODEL
VILLAGE
Dwyr

Aber Ffraw Bay
Bodowen
Newborough
Forest
Pen-lon
BIRD
WORLD

Porth-
cadwaladr
Malltraeth
Sands
Allt Niwbwren
ISLE OF
(SIR YN

NEWBOROUGH WARREN
& YNYS LLANDDWYN
ANGLESEY
YNYS MÔN

Malltraeth Bay
Bae Malltraeth
Newborough
Warren

C A E R N A R F O N
WALES COAST PATH
Gwddn
Llandwyn
Traeth
Melynog

Ynys
Llanddwyn
Abe
Pt

B A Y

South Sands
Warren Fm
Foryd

B A E   C A E R N A R F O N
CAERNARFON AIR
MUSEUM
Caernarfon
Morfa
Dinlle

D

Blythe

Dinas Dinl

Lland

E
Pontllyfni

Aberdesach
Afon Desach

Clynnog-fawr
WELSH LIFE
Tainl

Penrhiwau
Capel
Uchaf
ST BEUNO'S
WELL
Bryn
Ifan

Cwmgwared

Bryn-
yr-eryr
Gyrn-goch
Cers-
y-wlad

F
Morfa
Gyrn Goch
492
509
Bwlch Mawr
Hengwm

Trwyn y Tâl
Gwydir
522
Gyrn Ddu
Afon O

Trefor
297
Moel
Penllechog
Moel Bronmoid
416
Pen-Y-Gaer
389
Cwm

Twyn y Gorlech
Hedre-fawr
Cwm-
coryn Fm
Afon
Wen

G
Yr Eifl
564
TRE'R-CEIRI
(FORT)
Llanaelhaearn
Moelfre
Bronmiod
Fm
Cwm
Cilio
Brychyni
Pen-
sarn

Penrhyn
Glas
Mount Pleasant
B4417
Gelliau
Bryn Mawr
Cae'r-
ferch
Mynachdy
Bach

Llithfaen
Moel
Gwynus
Hafod
Carnguwch
Fawr
Brynbychan
Cefn-caer-
ferch
Ynys-wen

Cefnydd
Mynydd
Camguwch
359
Carnguwch Bach
Pont y
Gydrhos
Tyddyn-
Cethin
Lleyn P

Penrhyn
Bodeilas
Pistyll
Gwyniasa
Cefn Isaf
Castell
Gwgan
Penr

Carreg Ddu
Moel
Ty-Gwyrf
Ysgubor
Plas
Tyddyn
Cestyll
Trallwyn
Pencaenewydd
Llangybi

Trwyn Porth
Dinllaen
Wern
Tir Bach
Penrhyn
Nefyn
Tyddyn
Uchaf
Bryn
Talafon
Lôn-las

Borth Wen
Porth Dinllaen
Porth
Nefyn
LLEYN HISTORICAL
MARITIME MUSEUM
Bodeilan
Mynydd-
mawr
Plas Tu

Morfa
Nefyn
LÔN ISAF
Ynysau
Nefyn
Llwyndyrys
Ynysleci
Brynllefrith

Aber Geirch
Nefyn
B4412
Garn Boduan
280
Hendre
Penprys
Fron
Tyn
Coed
Rhyd y
gwystl
Glyncoed
Llwyn-
dwyrfa

40
20
SH
144
145
Rhos-
fawr
B4354

Penrhyn Cwmistir
/sffordd
Edern
B4417
Tan-y-
graig
B4354
Pentreuchaf
Ty Du
Isaf
Tyn-rhos
fawr
Y Ffôr
Pencraig
Bryngwdyn
Llanarmon

0 1 2 3miles
0 1 2 3 4 5 km

❷
orth
Towyn
Rhos-
y-llan
❸
nrhyd
Plasyngheidio
❹
Moelypenmaen
A497
Moelfre
Bryn
Rodyn
❺
Tyn-rhos
fawr
❻
Penrhin Bach
Chwilog
Cromlech

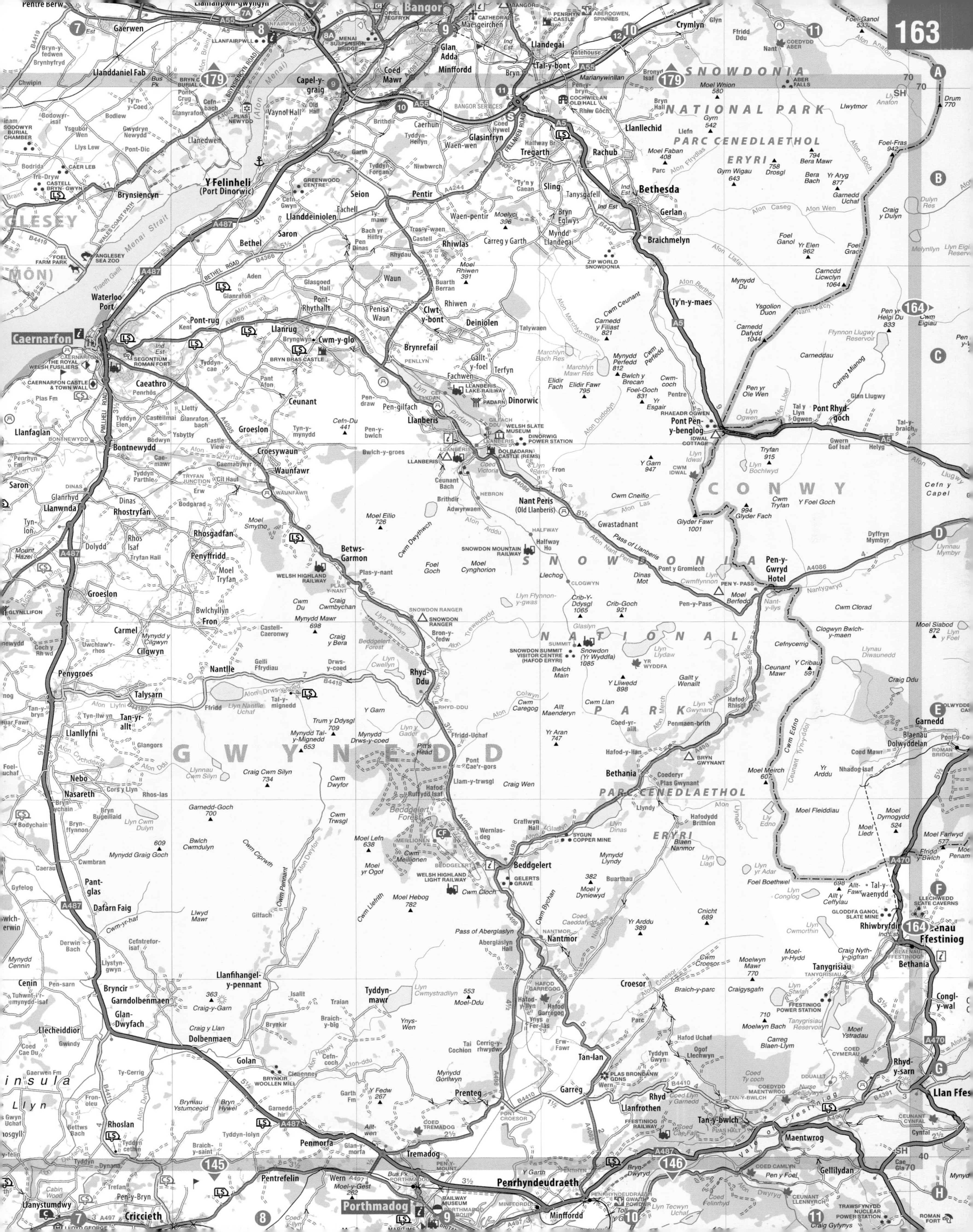
Bangor
Gaerwen
Llanfairpwll
Llanddaniel Fab
Capel-y-graig
Coed Mawr
Glan Adda
Minffordd
Maesgeirchen
Llandegai
Tal-y-bont
Crymlyn
SNOWDONIA
NATIONAL PARK
PARC CENEDLAETHOL
ERYRI
Moel Whion 580
Aber Falls
Drum 770
Foel-Ganol 533
Foel-Fras 942
Vaynol Hall
Bangor Services
Glasinfryn
Llanllechid
Tregarth
Rachub
Bethesda
Gerlan
Braichmelyn
Y Felinheli (Port Dinorwic)
Brynsiencyn
Menai Strait
Seion
Pentir
Sling
Llanddeiniolen
Saron
Bethel
Rhiwlas
Waen-pentir
Moel Rhiwen 391
Zip World Snowdonia
Yr Elen 962
Foel Grach
Carnedd Llewelyn 1064
Waterloo Port
Caernarfon
Caernarfon Castle & Town Wall
Segontium Roman Fort
Pont-rug
Llanrug
Cwm-y-glo
Bryn Bras Castle
Clwt-y-bont
Deiniolen
Brynrefail
Ty'n-y-maes
Carnedd y Filiast 821
Carnedd Dafydd 1044
Carneddau
Caeathro
Ceunant
Llanberis
Llyn Padarn
Dinorwic
Llanberis Lake Railway
Welsh Slate Museum
Dinorwig Power Station
Dolbadarn Castle
Elidir Fawr 795
Y Garn 947
Pont Pen-y-benglog
Pont Rhyd-goch
Tryfan 915
Llanfaglan
Bontnewydd
Groeslon
Croesywaun
Waunfawr
Saron
Llanwnda
Rhostryfan
Rhosgadfan
Nant Peris (Old Llanberis)
Gwastadnant
Glyder Fawr 1001
Glyder Fach 994
CONWY
Pass of Llanberis
Snowdon Mountain Railway
Betws-Garmon
Welsh Highland Railway
Penyffridd
Groeslon
Pen-y-Pass
Pen-y-Gwryd Hotel
Carmel
Cilgwyn
Nantlle
Penygroes
Talysarn
Llyn Cwellyn
Snowdon Ranger
Crib-y-Ddysgl 1065
Crib-Goch 921
Snowdon (Yr Wyddfa) 1085
Snowdon Summit Visitor Centre (Hafod Eryri)
Y Lliwedd 898
Rhyd-Ddu
Moel Siabod 872
Llanllyfni
GWYNEDD
Nebo
Nasareth
Trum y Ddysgl 709
Mynydd Tal-y-Mignedd 653
Craig Cwm Silyn 734
Garnedd-Goch 700
Pitt's Head
Beddgelert Forest
Yr Aran 747
Bethania
Dolwyddelan
Garnedd
Moel Meirch 607
Moel Hebog 782
Beddgelert
Sygun Copper Mine
Gelerts Grave
Welsh Highland Light Railway
Pant-glas
Dafarn Faig
Pass of Aberglaslyn
Nantmor
Cnicht 689
Moelwyn Mawr 770
Blaenau Ffestiniog
Tanygrisiau
Llechwedd Slate Caverns
Bryncir
Garndolbenmaen
Glan-Dwyfach
Llanfihangel-y-pennant
Dolbenmaen
Golan
Tyddyn-mawr
Croesor
Tan-lan
Plas Brondanw Gdns
Garreg
Rhyd
Llanfrothen
Tan-y-bwlch
Ffestiniog Railway
Maentwrog
Rhyd-y-sarn
Llan Ffestiniog
Rhoslan
Penmorfa
Prenteg
Tremadog
Coed Tremadog
Pentrefelin
Criccieth
Llanystumdwy
Porthmadog
Penrhyndeudraeth
Minffordd
Gellilydan
Trawsfynydd Nuclear Power Station
Vale of Ffestiniog
A55
A5
A487
A4086
A4085
A498
A4244
A470
A496
A497
B4366
B4418
B4410
179
164
145
146

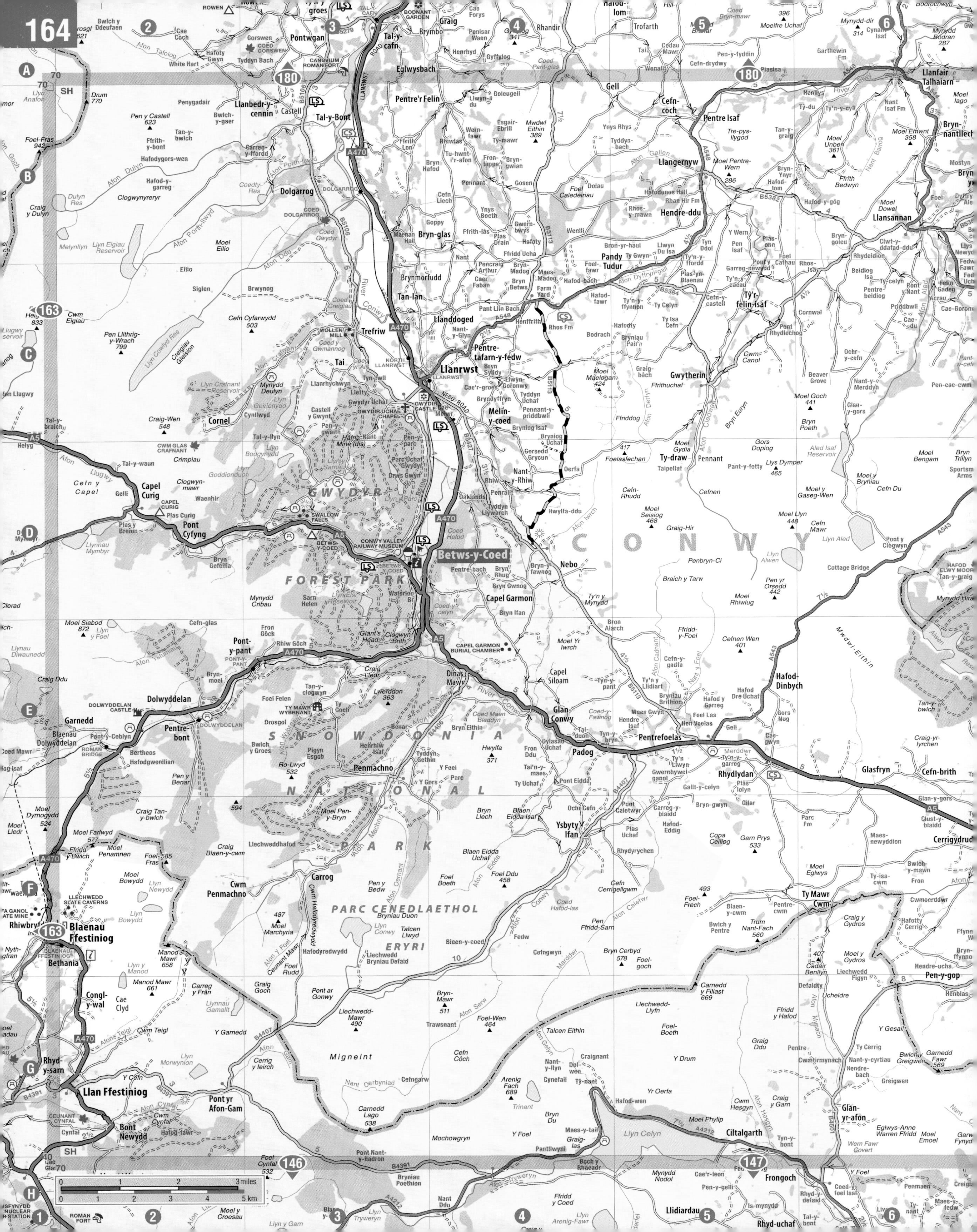

Bwlch y Ddeufaen
Pontwgan
Tal-y-cafn
Bodnant Garden
Graig
Brymbo
Eglwysbach
Rhandir
Trofarth
Moelfre Uchaf
Llanfair Talhaiarn
Llanbedr-y-cennin
Castell
Tal-y-Bont
Pentre'r Felin
Gell
Cefn-coch
Pentre Isaf
Foel-Fras 942
Drum 770
Pen y Castell 623
Dolgarrog
Llangernyw
Bryn-nantllech
Moel Eilio
Melynllyn
Llyn Eigiau Reservoir
Eilio
Siglen
Brwynog
Bryn-glas
Pandy Tudur
Hendre-ddu
Llansannan
Moel Unben 361
Moel Emwnt 358
Brynmorfudd
Tan-lan
Llanddoged
Pentre-tafarn-y-fedw
Rhos Fm
Tŷ'r-felin-isaf
Cefn Cyfarwydd 503
Pen Llithrig-y-Wrach 799
Trefriw
Tai
Llanrwst
Gwytherin
Moel Maelogan 424
Cornel
Craig-Wen 548
Melin-y-coed
Moel Goch 441
Gwydyr Castle
Gwydyr
Capel Curig
Pont Cyfyng
Swallow Falls
Plas y Brenin
Ty-draw
Pennant
Foelasfechan
Oerfa
Nant-y-Rhiw
Gors Dopiog
Moel Bengam
Moel Seisiog 468
Graig-Hir
Moel Llyn 448
Cefn Mawr
Llyn Aled
Forest Park
Betws-y-Coed
Conwy Valley Railway Museum
Nebo
Conwy
Capel Garmon
Bryn Ifan
Penbryn-Ci
Braich y Tarw
Moel Rhiwlug
Pen yr Orsedd 442
Mynydd Cribau
Moel Siabod 872
Pont-y-pant
Capel Garmon Burial Chamber
Moel Yr Iwrch
Cefnen Wen 401
Hafod-Dinbych
Dolwyddelan
Dolwyddelan Castle
Pentre-bont
Dinas Mawr
Capel Siloam
Glan-Conwy
Padog
Pentrefoelas
Garnedd
Lwerddon 363
Snowdonia National Park
Penmachno
Hwylfa 371
Ro-Lwyd 532
Glasfryn
Cefn-brith
Rhydlydan
Moel Dyrnogydd 524
Moel Farlwyd 577
Craig Tan-y-bwlch
Ysbyty Ifan
Foel-fras 585
Craig Blaen-y-cwm
Llechwedd Slate Caverns
Carrog
Cwm Penmachno
Foel Ddu 458
Blaenau Ffestiniog
Bethania
Parc Cenedlaethol Eryri
Garn Prys 533
Cerrigydrudion
Ty Mawr Cwm
Manod Mawr 658
Manod Mawr 661
Congl-y-wal
Carreg y Frân
Pont ar Gonwy
Bryn-Mawr 511
Foel-Wen 464
Carnedd y Filiast 669
Pen-y-gop
Llechwedd-Mawr 490
Migneint
Talcen Eithin
Rhyd-y-sarn
Llan Ffestiniog
Pont yr Afon-Gam
Arenig Fach 689
Carnedd Lago 538
Moel Phylip
Llyn Celyn
Ciltalgarth
Glan-yr-afon
Bont Newydd
Cwm Teigl
Mochowgryn
Foel Cynfal 532
Frongoch
Llidiardau
Rhyd-uchaf
0 1 2 3 miles
0 1 2 3 4 5 km

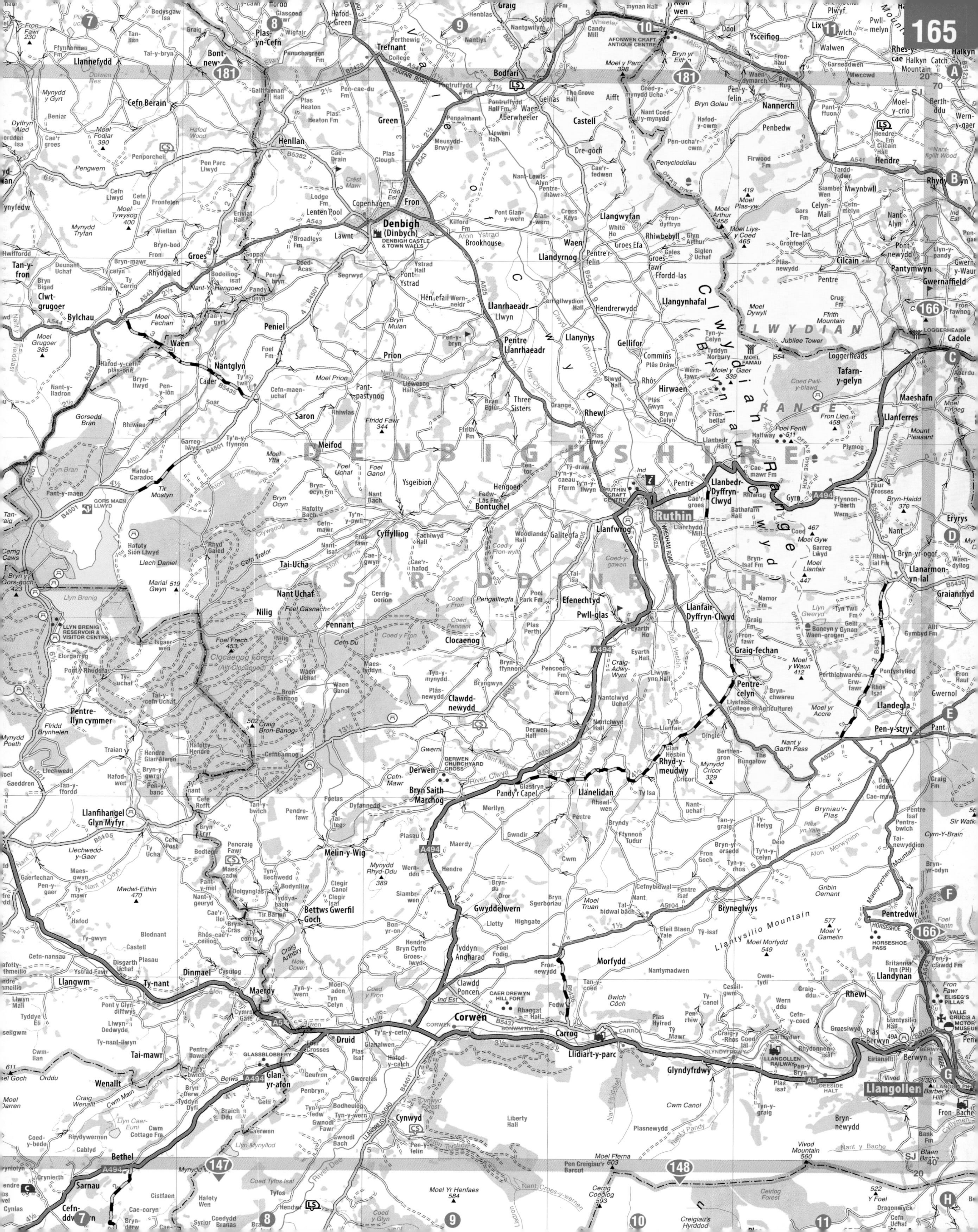

7
8
9
10
11
181
166
147
148
A
B
C
D
E
F
G
H
DENBIGHSHIRE
(SIR DDINBYCH)
CLWYDIAN RANGE
(Bryniau Clwyd)
Vale of Clwyd
Denbigh
(Dbych)
DENBIGH CASTLE & TOWN WALLS
Ruthin
RUTHIN CRAFT CENTRE
Corwen
Llangollen
Bodfari
Trefnant
Henllan
Cefn Berain
Llannefydd
Plas-yn-Cefn
Bont-newydd
Green
Copenhagen
Fron
Lenten Pool
Lawnt
Brookhouse
Groes
Rhydgaled
Bylchau
Clwt-grugoer
Tan-y-fron
Waen
Nantglyn
Peniel
Prion
Saron
Meifod
Bryn Mulan
Llanrhaeadr
Pentre Llanrhaeadr
Llanynys
Gellifor
Hirwaen
Rhewl
Llandyrnog
Llangwyfan
Waen
Aifft
Caerwys
Castell
Dre-gôch
Nannerch
Ysceifiog
Walwen
Cilcain
Pantymwyn
Gwernaffield
Loggerheads
Cadole
Tafarn-y-gelyn
Maeshafn
Llanferres
Rhydymwyn
Hendre
Halkyn
Moel Famau
Moel Fenlli
Jubilee Tower
Llanbedr-Dyffryn-Clwyd
Pentre
Gyrn
Eryrys
Llanarmon-yn-Ial
Graianrhyd
Llanfwrog
Cyffylliog
Bontuchel
Ysgeibion
Clocaenog
Clocaenog Forest
Efenechtyd
Pwll-glas
Llanfair-Dyffryn-Clwyd
Graig-fechan
Pentre-celyn
Llandegla
Pen-y-stryt
Nilig
Pennant
Nant Uchaf
Tai-Ucha
Llyn Brenig
LLYN BRENIG RESERVOIR & VISITOR CENTRE
Pentre-llyn cymmer
Clawdd-newydd
Derwen
DERWEN CHURCHYARD CROSS
Bryn Saith Marchog
Llanelidan
Rhyd-y-meudwy
Llanfihangel Glyn Myfyr
Melin-y-Wig
Bettws Gwerfil Goch
Gwyddelwern
Bryneglwys
Llantysilio Mountain
Horseshoe Pass
Pentredwr
Llandynan
Rhewl
Valle Crucis Abbey
Eliseg's Pillar
Berwyn
Glyndyfrdwy
Carrog
Llidiart-y-parc
Morfydd
Tyddyn Angharad
Caer Drewyn Hill Fort
Druid
Maerdy
Ty-nant
Dinmael
Llangwm
Glan-yr-afon
Glassblobbery
Tai-mawr
Wenallt
Cynwyd
Bethel
Sarnau
Cefn-ddwysarn
Llangollen Railway
A5
A494
A525
A543
A541
A542
A5104
B5105
B5429
B4501
B5437

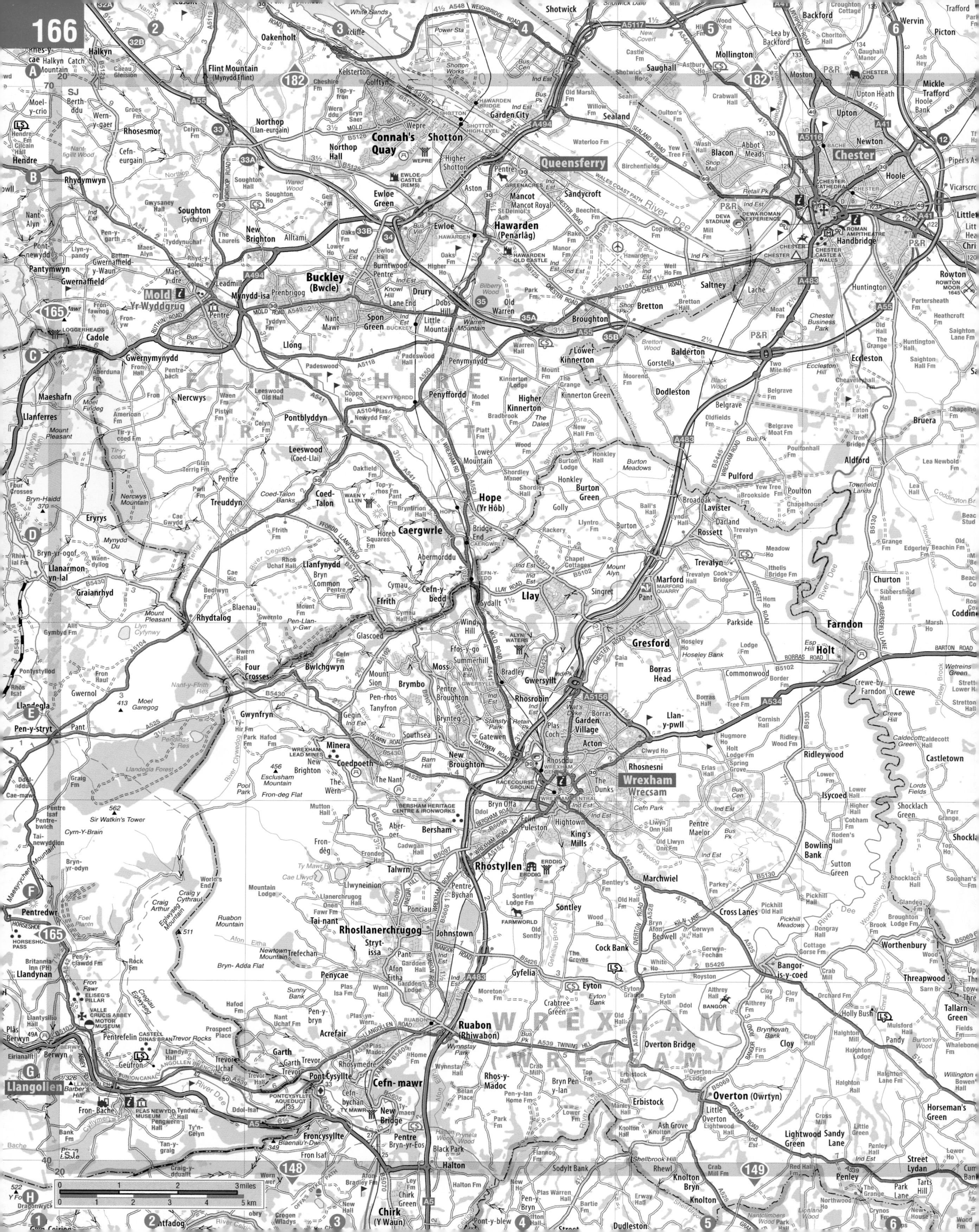
Halkyn
Flint Mountain (Mynydd Fflint)
Oakenholt
Shotwick
Backford
Wervin
Picton
Trafford
Mollington
Saughall
Lea by Backford
Kelsterton
Golftyn
Connah's Quay
Shotton
Garden City
Sealand
Queensferry
Northop (Llan-eurgain)
Northop Hall
Rhosesmor
Hendre
Rhydymwyn
Soughton (Sychdyn)
Ewloe
Ewloe Green
Aston
Mancot
Sandycroft
Hawarden (Penarlâg)
Buckley (Bwcle)
New Brighton
Alltami
Mold
Yr Wyddgrug
Mynydd-isa
Prenbrigog
Leadmill
Gwernaffield
Pantymwyn
Cadole
Gwernymynydd
Nant Mawr
Spon Green
Llong
Drury
Little Mountain
Broughton
Old Warren
Bretton
Saltney
Lache
Blacon
Upton
Newton
Chester
Hoole
Handbridge
Huntington
Mickle Trafford
Rowton
Eccleston
Balderton
Gorstella
Lower Kinnerton
Dodleston
Higher Kinnerton
Kinnerton Green
Penymynydd
Penyffordd
Padeswood
Pontblyddyn
Leeswood (Coed-Llai)
Nercwys
Maeshafn
Llanferres
FLINTSHIRE
(SIR Y FFLINT)
Hope (Yr Hôb)
Caergwrle
Abermorddu
Coed-Talon
Treuddyn
Eryrys
Llanfynydd
Cefn-y-bedd
Ffrith
Llay
Lower Mountain
Burton Green
Burton
Golly
Belgrave
Bruera
Aldford
Pulford
Poulton
Lavister
Rossett
Trevalyn
Marford
Pant
Singret
Churton
Farndon
Holt
Gresford
Borras Head
Llanarmon-yn-Ial
Graianrhyd
Rhydtalog
Four Crosses
Bwlchgwyn
Glascoed
Brymbo
Moss
Summerhill
Gwersyllt
Bradley
Rhosrobin
Llan-y-pwll
Crewe-by-Farndon
Crewe
Pen-y-stryt
Llandegla
Gwynfryn
Minera
Coedpoeth
New Broughton
Acton
Garden Village
Rhosnesni
Wrexham
Wrecsam
Ridleywood
Castletown
Isycoed
Bersham
Hightown
King's Mills
Rhostyllen
Marchwiel
Bowling Bank
Shocklach Green
Talwrn
Ponciau
Johnstown
Rhosllanerchrugog
Tai-nant
Stryt-issa
Sontley
Cock Bank
Cross Lanes
Bangor-is-y-coed
Worthenbury
Threapwood
Penycae
Gyfelia
Eyton
Ruabon (Rhiwabon)
Acrefair
Garth
Trevor
Cefn-mawr
Pont Cysyllte
WREXHAM
(WRECSAM)
Overton Bridge
Cloy
Pandy
Llangollen
Berwyn
Fron-Bache
Froncysyllte
Newbridge
Erbistock
Overton (Owrtyn)
Horseman's Green
Lightwood Green
Sandy Lane
Halton
Chirk (Y Waun)
Penley
Street Lydan
Rhewl
Knolton
Bryn
Dudleston
182
165
148
149

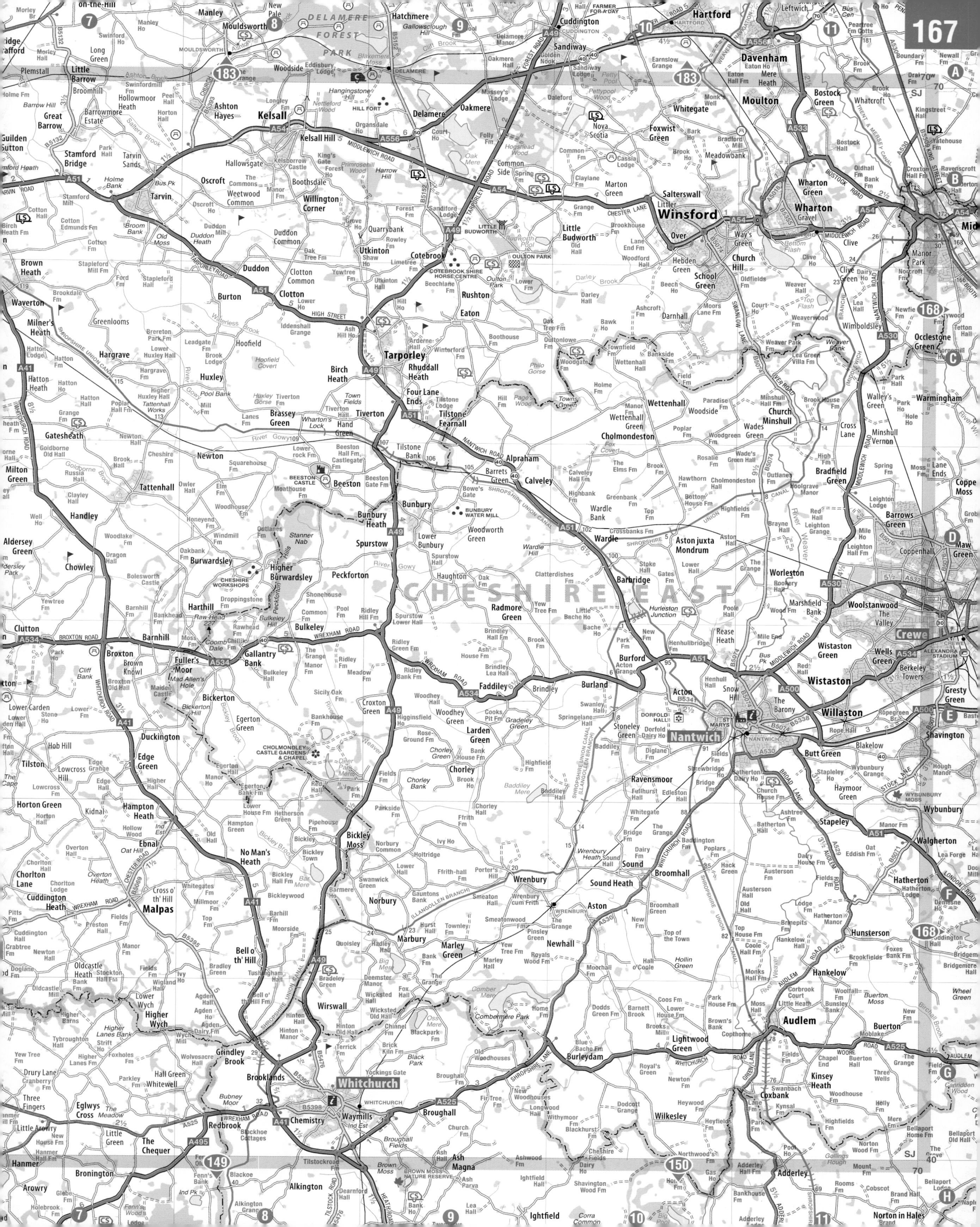
DELAMERE FOREST PARK
CHESHIRE EAST
Hartford
Davenham
Moulton
Winsford
Kelsall
Tarporley
Cuddington
Sandiway
Mouldsworth
Manley
Hatchmere
Delamere
Oakmere
Whitegate
Wharton
Over
Little Budworth
Cotebrook
Eaton
Rushton
Tarvin
Oscroft
Duddon
Clotton
Utkinton
Willington Corner
Kelsall Hill
Ashton Hayes
Great Barrow
Little Barrow
Stamford Bridge
Tarvin Sands
Waverton
Milner's Heath
Hargrave
Huxley
Burton
Birch Heath
Tiverton
Four Lane Ends
Rhuddall Heath
Tilstone Fearnall
Alpraham
Calveley
Wettenhall
Church Minshull
Cholmondeston
Beeston
Bunbury
Bunbury Heath
Spurstow
Peckforton
Higher Burwardsley
Burwardsley
Harthill
Bulkeley
Tattenhall
Newton
Gatesheath
Handley
Chowley
Aldersey Green
Clutton
Barnhill
Broxton
Fuller's Moor
Gallantry Bank
Bickerton
Faddiley
Brindley
Burland
Wardle
Barbridge
Radmore Green
Aston juxta Mondrum
Worleston
Wistaston
Willaston
Crewe
Nantwich
Acton
Burford
Stoneley Green
Ravensmoor
Sound
Broomhall
Aston
Wrenbury
Newhall
Marbury
Norbury
Chorley
Larden Green
Egerton Green
Duckington
Edge Green
Tilston
Hampton Heath
Malpas
No Man's Heath
Bickley Moss
Bell o' th' Hill
Wirswall
Grindley Brook
Brooklands
Whitchurch
Chemistry
Redbrook
Broughall
Burleydam
Lightwood Green
Audlem
Buerton
Coxbank
Kinsey Heath
Wilkesley
Adderley
Ash Magna
Alkington
Bronington
Hanmer
Higher Wych
Hankelow
Hunsterson
Hatherton
Walgherton
Stapeley
Wybunbury
Shavington
Butt Green
Blakelow
Wistaston Green
Wells Green
Woolstanwood
Coppenhall
Warmingham
Wimboldsley
Occlestone Green
Bradfield Green
Leighton
Barrows Green
Clive
Church Hill
School Green
Darnhall
Salterswall
Marton Green
Foxwist Green
Nova Scotia
A49
A51
A54
A41
A534
A530
A525
A500
A556
A533
A495
183
168
149
150

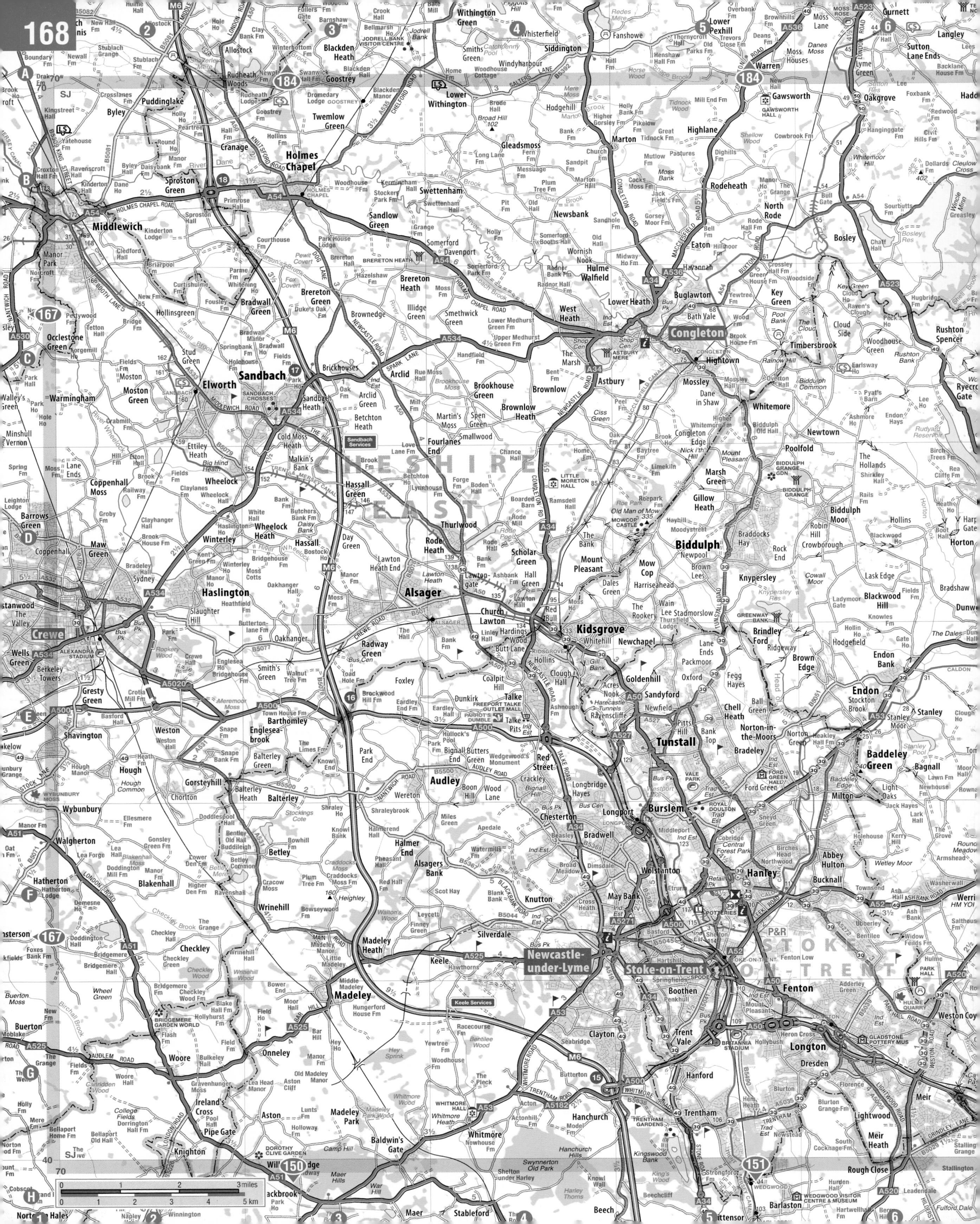
CHESHIRE EAST
STOKE-ON-TRENT
Middlewich
Holmes Chapel
Goostrey
Sandbach
Elworth
Congleton
Biddulph
Alsager
Kidsgrove
Crewe
Haslington
Tunstall
Burslem
Hanley
Stoke-on-Trent
Newcastle-under-Lyme
Fenton
Longton
Madeley
Audley
Keele
Trentham
Bucknall
Baddeley Green
Endon
Betley
Woore
Knighton
Whitmore
Meir
Barlaston
Astbury
Mow Cop
Talke
Kidsgrove
Swettenham
Marton
Gawsworth
Bosley
Rushton Spencer
Sandbach Services
Keele Services
Shavington
Wybunbury
Hough
Weston
Barthomley
Chesterton
Bradwell
Wolstanton
Silverdale
Knutton
Clayton
Hanford
Blurton
Lightwood
Meir Heath
Rough Close
Abbey Hulton
Milton
Norton-in-the-Moors
Brown Edge
Knypersley
Timbersbrook
Buglawton
Eaton
Rodeheath
North Rode
Warren
Sutton Lane Ends
Langley
Gurnett
Oakgrove
Byley
Cranage
Brereton Green
Brereton Heath
Arclid
Wheelock
Winterley
Coppenhall
Warmingham
Moston
Hassall Green
Rode Heath
Church Lawton
Scholar Green
Radway Green
Onneley
Madeley Heath
Blakenhall
Checkley
Hatherton
Walgherton
Pipe Gate
Ireland's Cross
Aston
Baldwin's Gate
Stableford
Maer
Beech
Hanchurch
Trent Vale
Boothen
Penkhull
Dresden
Heron Cross
3 miles
5 km

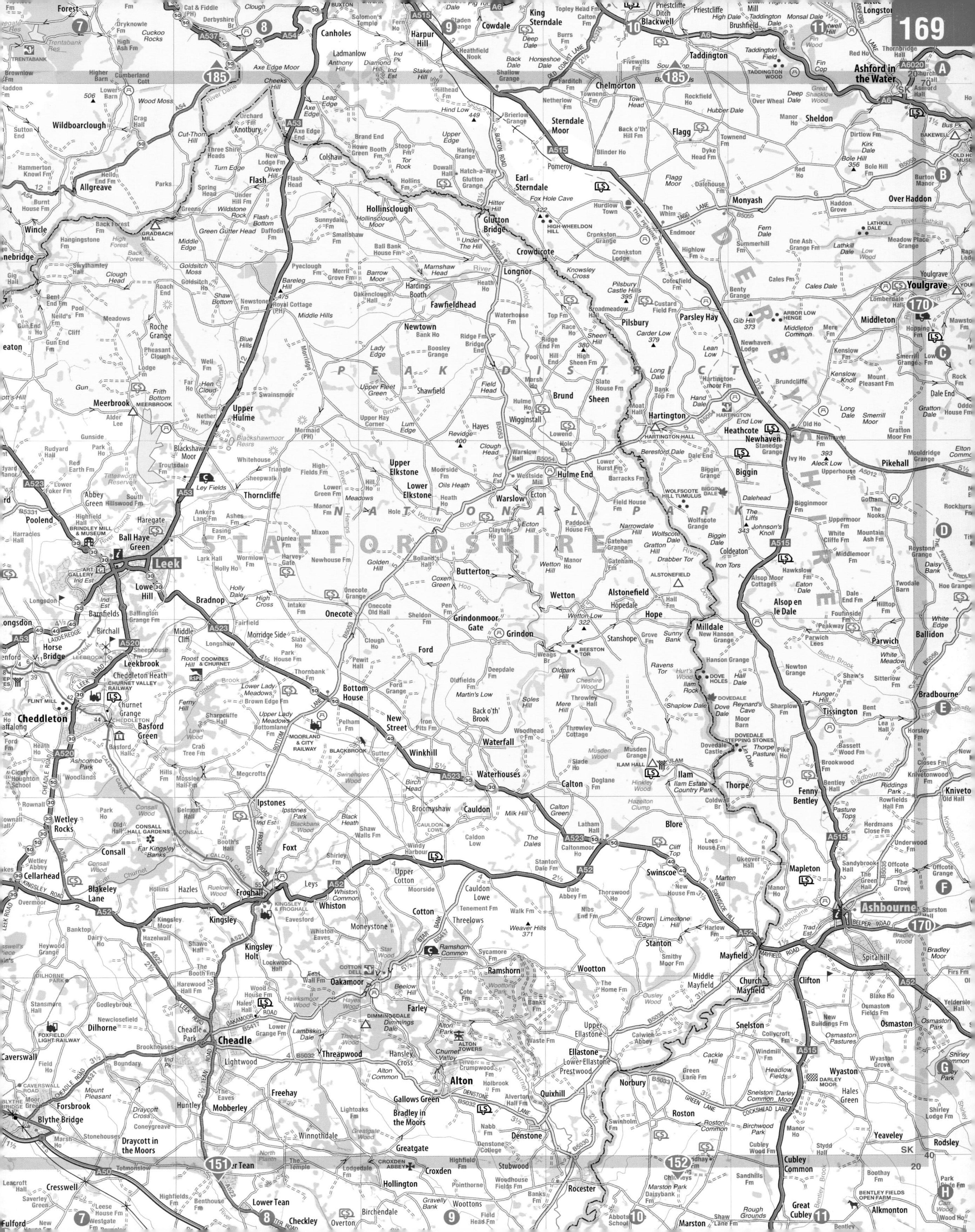
Forest
Cat & Fiddle (PH)
Derbyshire Br
Canholes
Harpur Hill
Cowdale
King Sterndale
Blackwell
Priestcliffe
Taddington
Longstone
Thornbridge Hall
Ashford in the Water
TRENTABANK
Axe Edge Moor
185
Cumberland Cott
Cheeks Hill
Ladmanlow
Staker Hill
Chelmorton
Flagg
Sheldon
Wildboarclough
Knotbury
Axe Edge End
Brand End
Upper Edge
Sterndale Moor
Dowall Hall
Pomeroy
Bakewell
Allgreave
Flash
Hollinsclough
Earl Sterndale
Monyash
Over Haddon
Wincle
GRADBACH MILL
Glutton Bridge
Fox Hole Cave
HIGH WHEELDON HILL
Crowdicote
Longnor
LATHKILL DALE
Youlgrave
170
Fawfieldhead
Pilsbury
Parsley Hay
ARBOR LOW HENGE
Middleton
Newtown
Meerbrook
MEERBROOK
Upper Hulme
P E A K D I S T R I C T
Brund
Sheen
Hartington
HARTINGTON HALL
Heathcote
Newhaven
Pikehall
Blackshaw Moor
Upper Elkstone
Lower Elkstone
Hulme End
Biggin
Ley Fields
Thorncliffe
Warslow
Ecton
WOLFSCOTE HILL TUMULUS
BIGGIN DALE
D E R B Y S H I R E
Poolend
BRINDLEY MILL & MUSEUM
Haregate
Ball Haye Green
N A T I O N A L P A R K
S T A F F O R D S H I R E
Leek
ART GALLERY
Lowe Hill
Butterton
Alstonefield
ALSTONEFIELD
Alsop en le Dale
Bradnop
Onecote
Grindonmoor Gate
Grindon
Wetton
Hope
Milldale
Parwich
Ballidon
Longsdon
Horse Bridge
Birchall
Leekbrook
Cheddleton Heath
CHURNET VALLEY RAILWAY
Ford
BEESTON TOR
DOVE HOLES
Bradbourne
Cheddleton
Basford Green
Bottom House
New Street
DOVEDALE
Tissington
MOORLAND & CITY RAILWAY
Winkhill
Waterfall
DOVEDALE STEPPING STONES
Thorpe Pasture
Waterhouses
Calton
ILAM HALL
Ilam
Ilam Estate Country Park
Thorpe
Fenny Bentley
Kniveton
Wetley Rocks
Ipstones
Cauldon
CONSALL HALL GARDENS
Consall
Foxt
Blore
Mapleton
Cellarhead
Blakeley Lane
Froghall
KINGSLEY & FROGHALL
Whiston
Upper Cotton
Cauldon Lowe
Swinscoe
Ashbourne
Kingsley
Cotton
Threelows
Stanton
Weaver Hills 371
Kingsley Holt
Ramshorn Common
Ramshorn
Wootton
Mayfield
Spitalhill
Oakamoor
Farley
Church Mayfield
Clifton
Dilhorne
FOXFIELD LIGHT RAILWAY
DIMMINGSDALE
Cheadle
Threapwood
ALTON TOWERS
Upper Ellastone
Ellastone
Snelston
Osmaston
Caverswall
Lightwood
Alton
Prestwood
Norbury
Wyaston
DARLEY MOOR
Forsbrook
Blythe Bridge
Mobberley
Huntley
Freehay
Gallows Green
Bradley in the Moors
Quixhill
Roston
Yeaveley
Rodsley
Draycott in the Moors
Greatgate
Denstone
Stubwood
Cubley Common
151
152
CROXDEN ABBEY
Croxden
Hollington
Rocester
Cresswell
Lower Tean
Checkley
Overton
Woottons
Great Cubley
Alkmonton
BENTLEY FIELDS OPEN FARM
Fulford
Marston
Abbots School

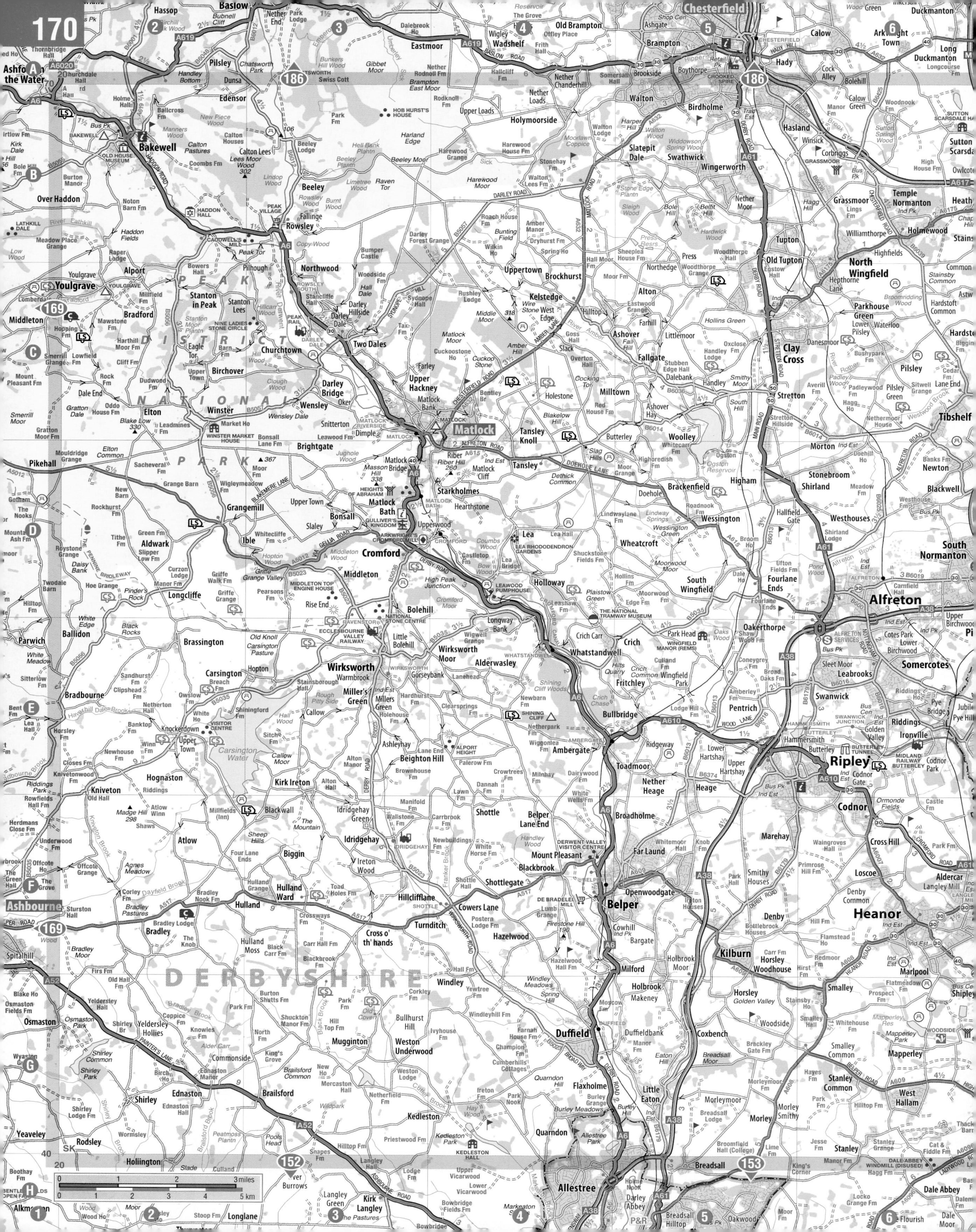
Chesterfield
Matlock
Alfreton
Ripley
Belper
Heanor
Ashbourne
Bakewell
Wirksworth
Cromford
Duffield
Allestree
DERBYSHIRE
PEAK
DISTRICT
NATIONAL
PARK
Baslow
Hassop
Pilsley
Edensor
Beeley
Rowsley
Youlgrave
Middleton
Bradford
Stanton in Peak
Birchover
Winster
Elton
Darley Dale
Two Dales
Darley Bridge
Tansley
Matlock Bath
Bonsall
Grangemill
Aldwark
Brassington
Carsington
Carsington Water
Hognaston
Kniveton
Kirk Ireton
Idridgehay
Shottle
Hulland Ward
Hulland
Turnditch
Windley
Mugginton
Weston Underwood
Kedleston
Quarndon
Brailsford
Ednaston
Shirley
Osmaston
Yeaveley
Rodsley
Holymoorside
Walton
Brampton
Old Brampton
Ashover
Kelstedge
Brockhurst
Uppertown
Milltown
Woolley
Higham
Shirland
Stonebroom
Clay Cross
Stretton
Tupton
North Wingfield
Wingerworth
Holmewood
Tibshelf
Pilsley
Blackwell
South Normanton
Westhouses
South Wingfield
Crich
Whatstandwell
Holloway
Lea
Ambergate
Heage
Nether Heage
Pentrich
Swanwick
Somercotes
Leabrooks
Riddings
Ironville
Codnor
Marehay
Denby
Kilburn
Horsley
Smalley
Holbrook
Milford
Little Eaton
Morley
Stanley
Breadsall
Oakwood
Darley Abbey
Dale Abbey
West Hallam
Mapperley
Shipley
Marlpool
Loscoe
Aldercar
Fritchley
Bullbridge
Whatstandwell
Alderwasley
Middleton
Longcliffe
Ballidon
Bradbourne
Atlow
Biggin
Blackwall
Hazelwood
Mount Pleasant
Openwoodgate
Far Laund
Broadholme
Toadmoor
Coxbench
Calow
Hasland
Duckmanton
Temple Normanton
Grassmoor
Heath
Pikehall
Over Haddon
Alport
Churchtown
Wensley
Dimple
Starkholmes
Upper Hackney
Riber
Brightgate
Slaley
Ible
Upperwood
Bolehill
Heights of Abraham
Gulliver's Kingdom
Arkwright's Cromford Mill
National Stone Centre
Ecclesbourne Valley Railway
The National Tramway Museum
Haddon Hall
Chatsworth Park
Kedleston Hall
Derwent Valley Visitor Centre
186
169
152
153
A6
A38
A61
A52
A517
A610
A615
A619
A632
A609
A608
B5023
B5035
B5057
0 1 2 3 miles
0 1 2 3 4 5 km

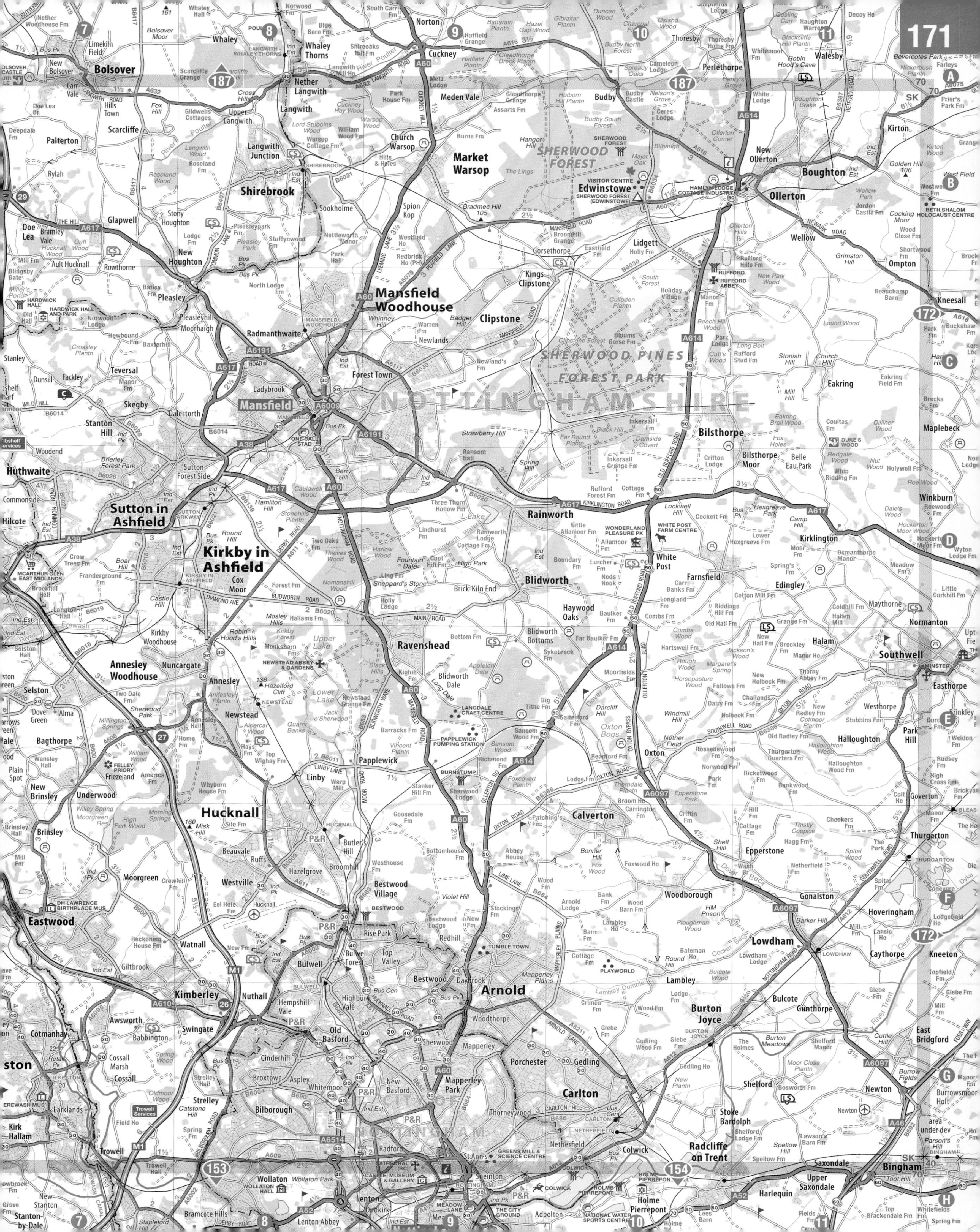

Bolsover
New Bolsover
Whaley
Whaley Thorns
Norton
Cuckney
Nether Langwith
Langwith
Upper Langwith
Scarcliffe
Palterton
Langwith Junction
Shirebrook
Church Warsop
Market Warsop
Meden Vale
Budby
Thoresby
Perlethorpe
Walesby
Kirton
SHERWOOD FOREST
Edwinstowe
New Ollerton
Boughton
Ollerton
Wellow
Ompton
Glapwell
Stony Houghton
New Houghton
Rowthorne
Pleasley
Mansfield Woodhouse
Clipstone
Kings Clipstone
Gorsethorpe
Lidgett
Kneesall
Radmanthwaite
Newlands
Forest Town
SHERWOOD PINES FOREST PARK
NOTTINGHAMSHIRE
Eakring
Maplebeck
Teversal
Skegby
Ladybrook
Mansfield
Stanton Hill
Dalestorth
Bilsthorpe
Bilsthorpe Moor
Huthwaite
Sutton in Ashfield
Sutton Forest Side
Rainworth
Kirklington
Winkburn
Hilcote
Kirkby in Ashfield
White Post
Farnsfield
Edingley
Blidworth
Haywood Oaks
Normanton
Halam
Southwell
Easthorpe
Ravenshead
Annesley Woodhouse
Nuncargate
Annesley
Newstead
Selston
Bagthorpe
Papplewick
Linby
Oxton
Halloughton
Underwood
Hucknall
Calverton
Goverton
Thurgarton
Brinsley
Moorgreen
Westville
Bestwood Village
Epperstone
Gonalston
Hoveringham
Eastwood
Watnall
Woodborough
Lowdham
Caythorpe
Kneeton
Kimberley
Nuthall
Bulwell
Arnold
Lambley
Bulcote
Gunthorpe
Awsworth
Swingate
Cotmanhay
Cinderhill
Old Basford
Woodthorpe
Mapperley
Burton Joyce
East Bridgford
Porchester
Gedling
Carlton
Shelford
Newton
Strelley
Bilborough
Mapperley Park
Stoke Bardolph
Netherfield
Colwick
Radcliffe on Trent
Bingham
Trowell
Wollaton
Lenton
Sneinton
Holme Pierrepont
Upper Saxondale
Saxondale
Harlequin
NOTTINGHAM

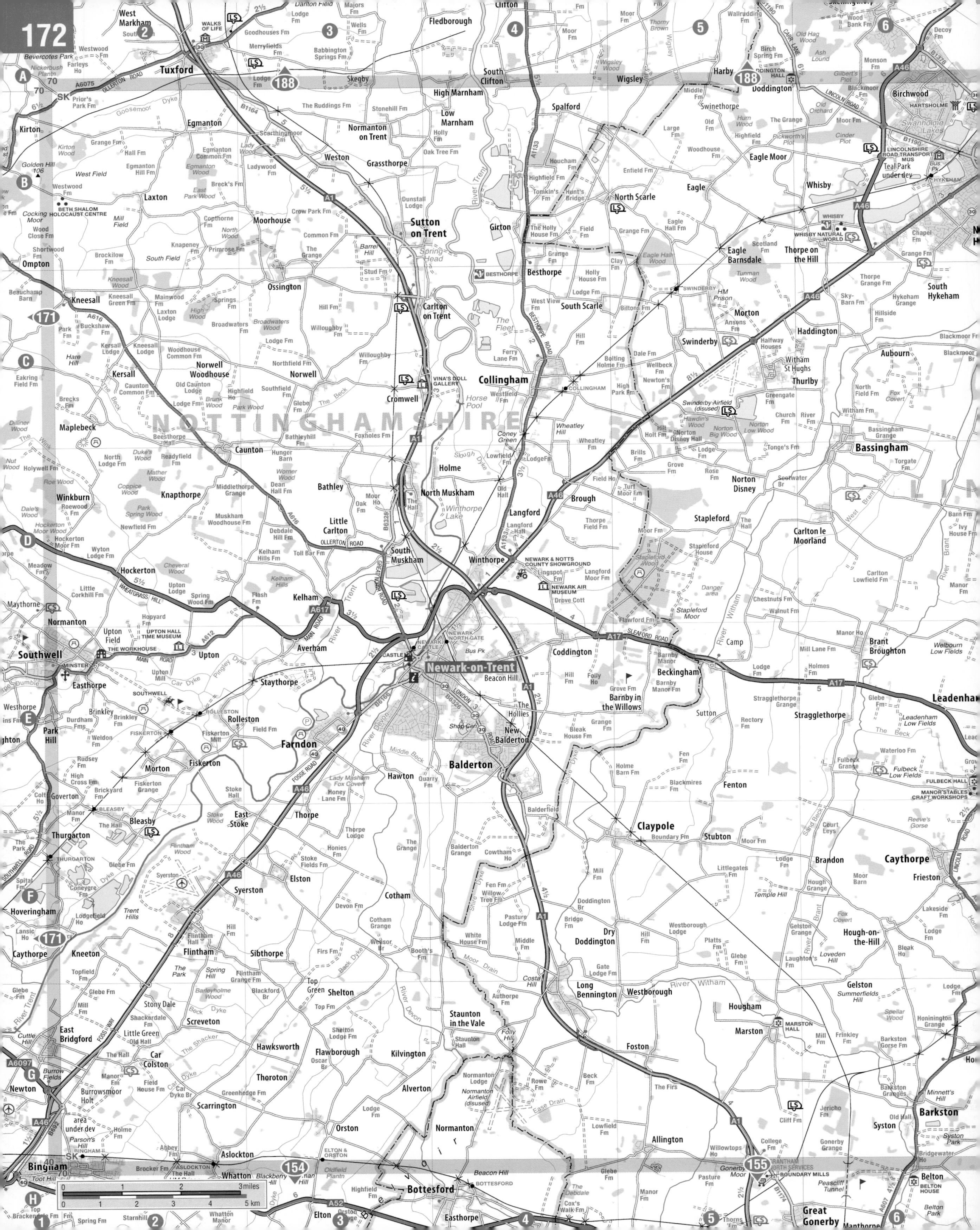
West Markham
Tuxford
Fledborough
Clifton
Wigsley
Harby
Doddington
Birchwood
Kirton
Egmanton
High Marnham
Low Marnham
Normanton on Trent
Spalford
Eagle Moor
Laxton
Weston
Grassthorpe
North Scarle
Eagle
Whisby
Ompton
Moorhouse
Sutton on Trent
Girton
Eagle Barnsdale
Thorpe on the Hill
Ossington
Besthorpe
Kneesall
Carlton on Trent
South Scarle
Morton
South Hykeham
Swinderby
Haddington
Kersall
Norwell Woodhouse
Norwell
Cromwell
Collingham
Witham St Hughs
Thurlby
Aubourn
NOTTINGHAMSHIRE
Maplebeck
Caunton
Holme
Bassingham
Winkburn
Knapthorpe
Bathley
North Muskham
Brough
Norton Disney
Langford
Stapleford
Little Carlton
Carlton le Moorland
Hockerton
South Muskham
Winthorpe
Kelham
Maythorne
Normanton
Upton
Averham
Coddington
Camp
Brant Broughton
Southwell
Newark-on-Trent
Beacon Hill
Beckingham
Easthorpe
Staythorpe
Barnby in the Willows
Leadenham
Rolleston
The Hollies
New Balderton
Sutton
Stragglethorpe
Park Hill
Farndon
Fiskerton
Balderton
Hawton
Fenton
Morton
Goverton
Thorpe
Claypole
Bleasby
East Stoke
Stubton
Thurgarton
Brandon
Caythorpe
Frieston
Elston
Syerston
Cotham
Hoveringham
Dry Doddington
Hough-on-the-Hill
Caythorpe
Kneeton
Flintham
Sibthorpe
Long Bennington
Westborough
Shelton
Gelston
Hougham
Screveton
Staunton in the Vale
Marston
East Bridgford
Hawksworth
Flawborough
Kilvington
Foston
Car Colston
Thoroton
Newton
Alverton
Scarrington
Barkston
Orston
Normanton
Syston
Aslockton
Allington
Bingham
Whatton
Bottesford
Belton
Great Gonerby
Elton
Easthorpe
0 1 2 3 miles
0 1 2 3 4 5 km

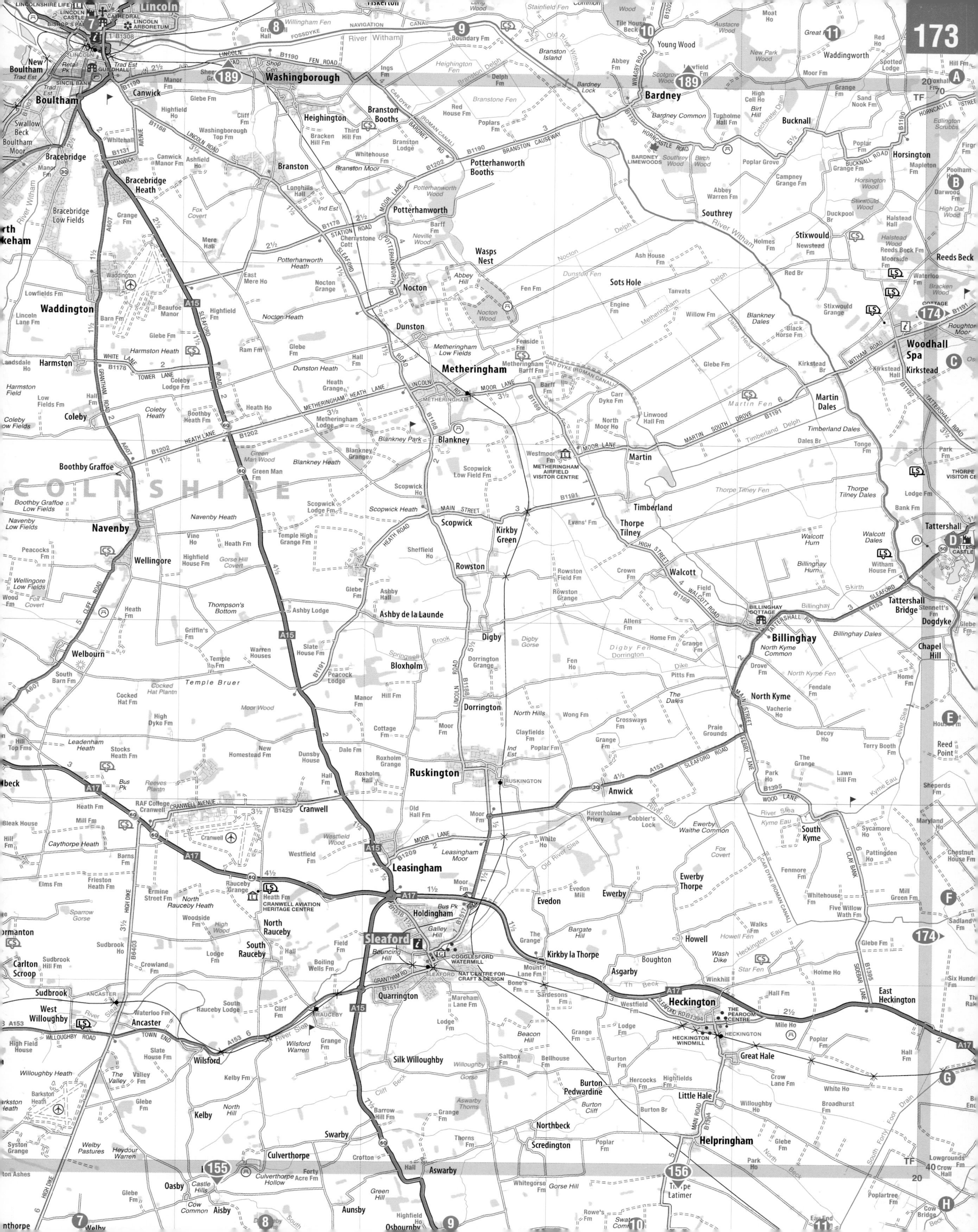
Lincoln
Lincoln Castle
Cathedral
Lincoln Arboretum
Lincolnshire Life
New Boultham
Boultham
Swallow Beck
Boultham Moor
Bracebridge
Bracebridge Heath
Bracebridge Low Fields
Canwick
Washingborough
Heighington
Branston
Branston Booths
Potterhanworth
Potterhanworth Booths
Nocton
Dunston
Metheringham
Blankney
Scopwick
Kirkby Green
Rowston
Digby
Ashby de la Launde
Bloxholm
Dorrington
Ruskington
Anwick
Cranwell
Leasingham
Sleaford
Holdingham
Quarrington
North Rauceby
South Rauceby
Wilsford
Ancaster
Sudbrook
West Willoughby
Kelby
Silk Willoughby
Swarby
Culverthorpe
Aswarby
Aisby
Oasby
Osbournby
Aunsby
Evedon
Ewerby
Ewerby Thorpe
Kirkby la Thorpe
Asgarby
Howell
Heckington
East Heckington
Great Hale
Little Hale
Helpringham
Burton Pedwardine
Scredington
Northbeck
Threkingham
Waddington
Harmston
Coleby
Boothby Graffoe
Navenby
Wellingore
Welbourn
Bardney
Bucknall
Horsington
Southrey
Stixwould
Woodhall Spa
Kirkstead
Martin
Martin Dales
Timberland
Thorpe Tilney
Walcott
Billinghay
North Kyme
South Kyme
Tattershall
Tattershall Bridge
Dogdyke
Chapel Hill
Wasps Nest
Sots Hole
Young Wood
Waddingworth
Reeds Beck
Tupholme
LINCOLNSHIRE
A15
A17
A153
A607
B1188
B1189
B1190
B1191
B1202
Metheringham Airfield Visitor Centre
Cranwell Aviation Heritage Centre
Cogglesford Watermill
Nat Centre for Craft & Design
Heckington Windmill
The Pearoom Centre
189
155
156
174
TF

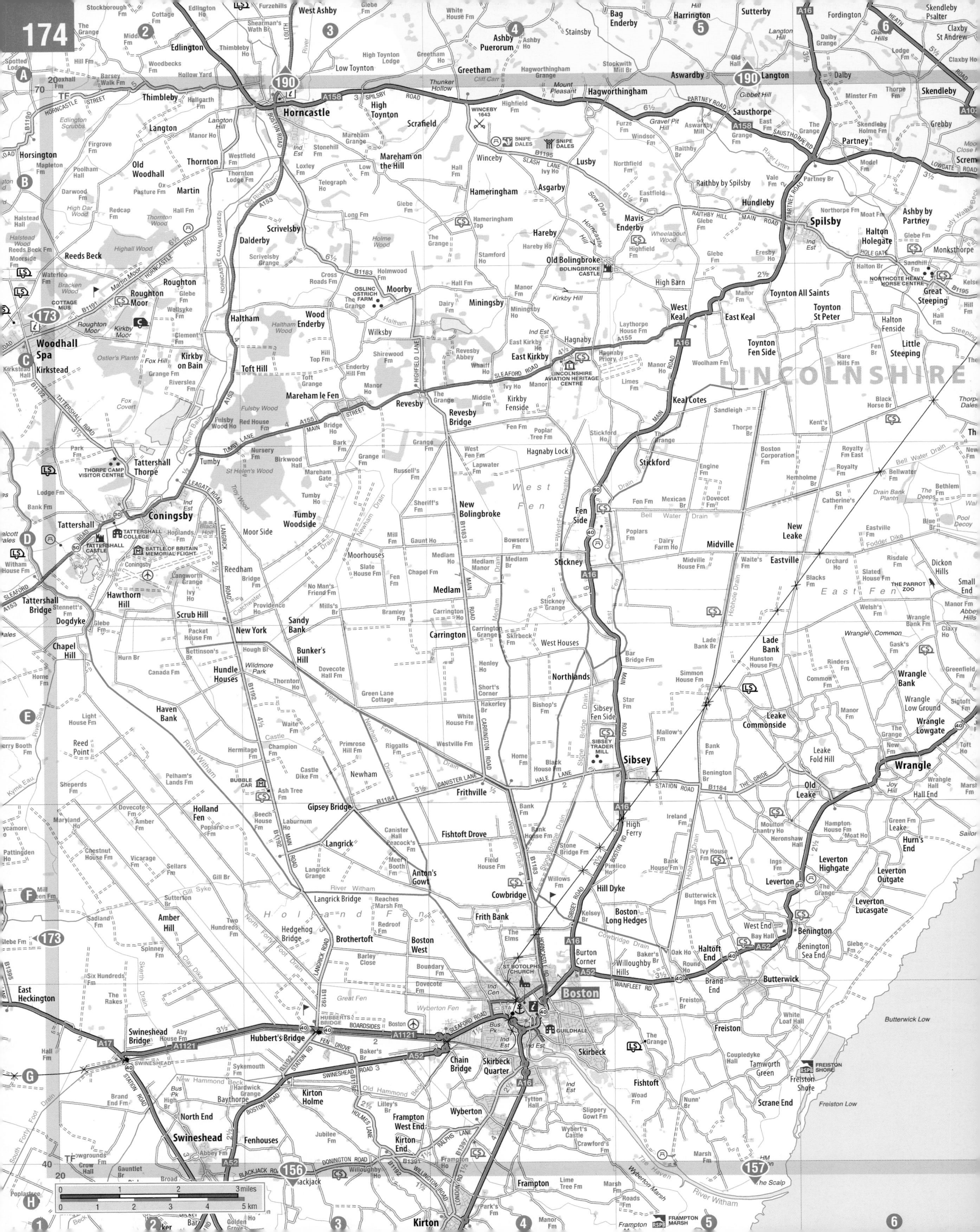
Stockborough Fm
Edlington
West Ashby
Ashby Puerorum
Stainsby
Bag Enderby
Harrington
Sutterby
Fordington
Skendleby Psalter
Claxby St Andrew
Horncastle
High Toynton
Scrafield
Greetham
Hagworthingham
Aswardby
Langton
Dalby
Skendleby
Thimbleby
Langton
Mareham on the Hill
Winceby
Lusby
Sausthorpe
Partney
Grebby
Horsington
Old Woodhall
Thornton
Martin
Hameringham
Asgarby
Raithby by Spilsby
Hundleby
Spilsby
Ashby by Partney
Halton Holegate
Monksthorpe
Scrivelsby
Dalderby
Hareby
Mavis Enderby
Old Bolingbroke
Bolingbroke Castle
Reeds Beck
Roughton
Roughton Moor
Moorby
Miningsby
High Barn
West Keal
East Keal
Toynton All Saints
Toynton St Peter
Great Steeping
Woodhall Spa
Kirkstead
Haltham
Wood Enderby
Wilksby
Hagnaby
East Kirkby
Little Steeping
Toynton Fen Side
Kirkby on Bain
Toft Hill
Mareham le Fen
Revesby
Revesby Bridge
Kirkby Fenside
Keal Cotes
LINCOLNSHIRE
Lincolnshire Aviation Heritage Centre
Tumby
Tattershall Thorpe
Thorpe Camp Visitor Centre
Hagnaby Lock
Stickford
Coningsby
Tattershall
Tattershall Castle
Tattershall College
Battle of Britain Memorial Flight
Tumby Woodside
Moor Side
New Bolingbroke
West Fen
Fen Side
Midville
New Leake
Eastville
Reedham
Moorhouses
Medlam
Stickney
Dickon Hills
Small End
East Fen
The Parrot Zoo
Tattershall Bridge
Dogdyke
Hawthorn Hill
Scrub Hill
New York
Sandy Bank
Carrington
West Houses
Chapel Hill
Bunker's Hill
Lade Bank
Wrangle Common
Hundle Houses
Northlands
Wrangle Bank
Haven Bank
Sibsey Fen Side
Leake Commonside
Wrangle Lowgate
Sibsey Trader Mill
Sibsey
Wrangle
Reed Point
Newham
Frithville
Old Leake
Holland Fen
Gipsey Bridge
Fishtoft Drove
High Ferry
Langrick
Anton's Gowt
Hill Dyke
Leverton Highgate
Leverton
Leverton Outgate
Leverton Lucasgate
Amber Hill
Langrick Bridge
Cowbridge
Frith Bank
Boston Long Hedges
Hedgehog Bridge
Brothertoft
Boston West
Benington
Benington Sea End
Haltoft End
Burton Corner
Willoughby Hills
Brand End
Butterwick
East Heckington
St Botolph's Church
Boston
Guildhall
Freiston
Butterwick Low
Swineshead Bridge
Hubbert's Bridge
Chain Bridge
Skirbeck Quarter
Skirbeck
Fishtoft
Tamworth Green
Freiston Shore
Freiston Low
Scrane End
Kirton Holme
Wyberton
Bicker Fen
North End
Swineshead
Fenhouses
Frampton West End
Kirton End
Frampton
Frampton Marsh
Wyberton Marsh
The Haven
River Witham
The Scalp
Kirton
Blackjack
156
157
173
190

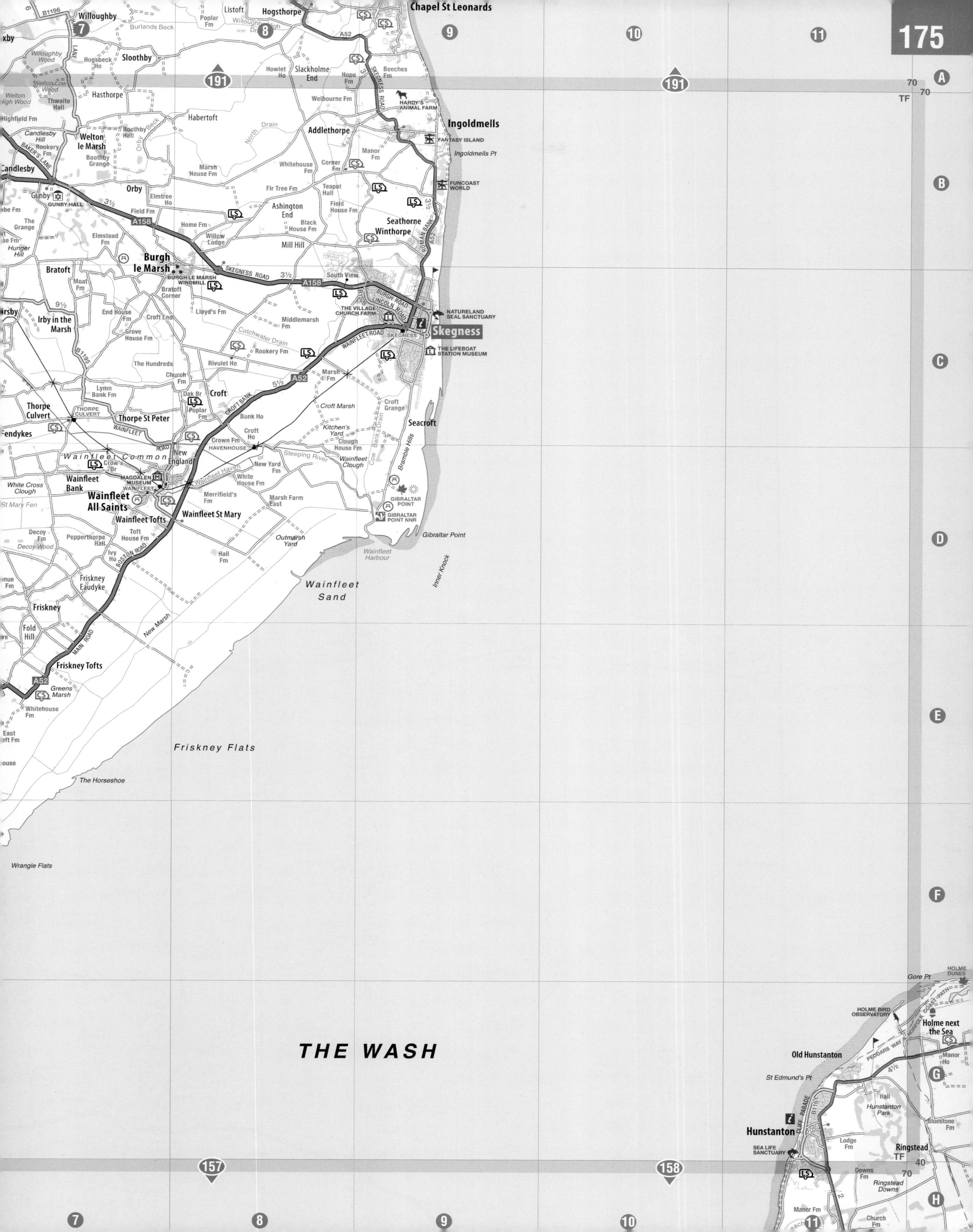
Willoughby
Hogsthorpe
Chapel St Leonards
Sloothby
Slackholme End
Hasthorpe
Welbourne Fm
Hardy's Animal Farm
Habertoft
Ingoldmells
Fantasy Island
Ingoldmells Pt
Addlethorpe
Welton le Marsh
Candlesby
Gunby Hall
Orby
Funcoast World
Ashington End
Seathorne
Winthorpe
Burgh le Marsh
Burgh-le-Marsh Windmill
Bratoft
Mill Hill
South View
Irby in the Marsh
The Village Church Farm
Natureland Seal Sanctuary
Skegness
The Lifeboat Station Museum
Croft
Thorpe Culvert
Thorpe St Peter
Seacroft
Croft Marsh
Wainfleet Common
New England
Wainfleet Bank
Magdalen Museum
Wainfleet All Saints
Wainfleet Tofts
Wainfleet St Mary
Gibraltar Point
Gibraltar Point NNR
Wainfleet Harbour
Inner Knock
Wainfleet Sand
Friskney
Friskney Eaudyke
Friskney Tofts
Friskney Flats
The Horseshoe
Wrangle Flats
THE WASH
Gore Pt
Holme Dunes
Holme Bird Observatory
Holme next the Sea
Old Hunstanton
St Edmund's Pt
Hunstanton
Hunstanton Park
Sea Life Sanctuary
Ringstead
Ringstead Downs
A52
A158
B1196
B1195
B1161

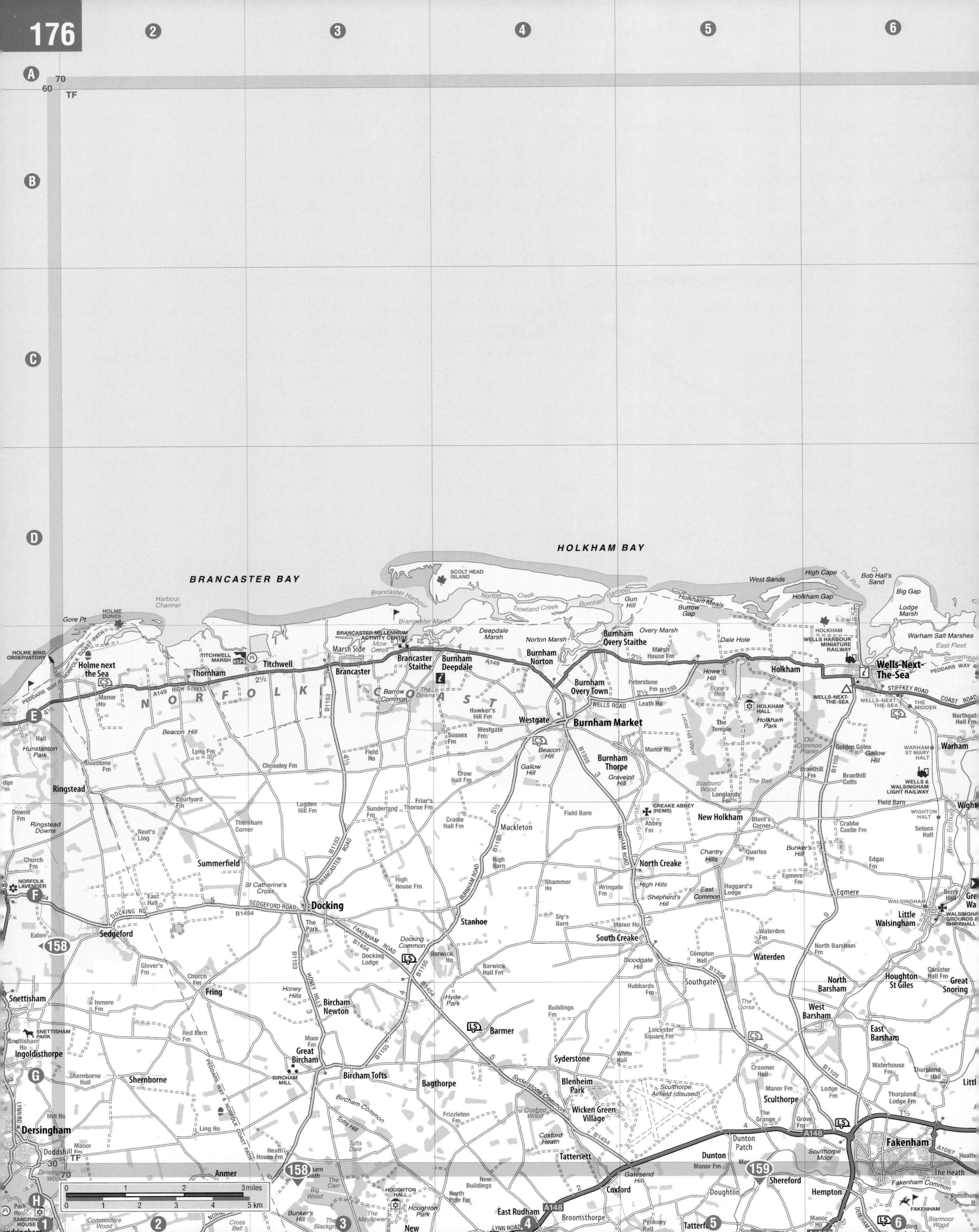
HOLKHAM BAY
BRANCASTER BAY
SCOLT HEAD ISLAND
Harbour Channel
Gore Pt
HOLME DUNES
HOLME BIRD OBSERVATORY
Holme next the Sea
Thornham
TITCHWELL MARSH
Titchwell
Brancaster
BRANCASTER MILLENNIUM ACTIVITY CENTRE
Marsh Side
Brancaster Staithe
Burnham Deepdale
Deepdale Marsh
Norton Marsh
Burnham Norton
Burnham Overy Staithe
Overy Marsh
Burnham Overy Town
Burnham Market
Westgate
Holkham
HOLKHAM HALL
Holkham Park
Wells-Next-The-Sea
WELLS HARBOUR MINIATURE RAILWAY
Holkham Meals
Holkham Gap
West Sands
High Cape
Bob Hall's Sand
Big Gap
Lodge Marsh
Warham Salt Marshes
East Fleet
STIFFKEY ROAD
THE MIDDEN
Warham
WARHAM ST MARY HALT
WELLS & WALSINGHAM LIGHT RAILWAY
Wighton
N O R F O L K C O A S T
PEDDARS WAY
NORFOLK COAST PATH
Hunstanton Park
Ringstead
Ringstead Downs
Downs Fm
Church Fm
NORFOLK LAVENDER
Sedgeford
Eaton
Snettisham
SNETTISHAM PARK
Ingoldisthorpe
Shernborne
Dersingham
Doddshill
Fring
Summerfield
Docking
Stanhoe
Bircham Newton
Great Bircham
BIRCHAM MILL
Bircham Tofts
Bagthorpe
Barmer
Muckleton
North Creake
South Creake
CREAKE ABBEY (REMS)
New Holkham
Egmere
Little Walsingham
Waterden
Southgate
Syderstone
Blenheim Park
Wicken Green Village
Sculthorpe Airfield (disused)
Sculthorpe
Tattersett
Dunton
Fakenham
North Barsham
West Barsham
East Barsham
Houghton St Giles
Great Snoring
Anmer
HOUGHTON HALL
Houghton Park
New Buildings
North Pole Fm
East Rudham
Broomsthorpe
Coxford
Shereford
Hempton
Doughton
Fakenham Common
The Heath
SANDRINGHAM HOUSE
A149
A148
A1067
B1153
B1155
B1355
B1454
B1105
0 1 2 3 miles
0 1 2 3 4 5 km
158
159

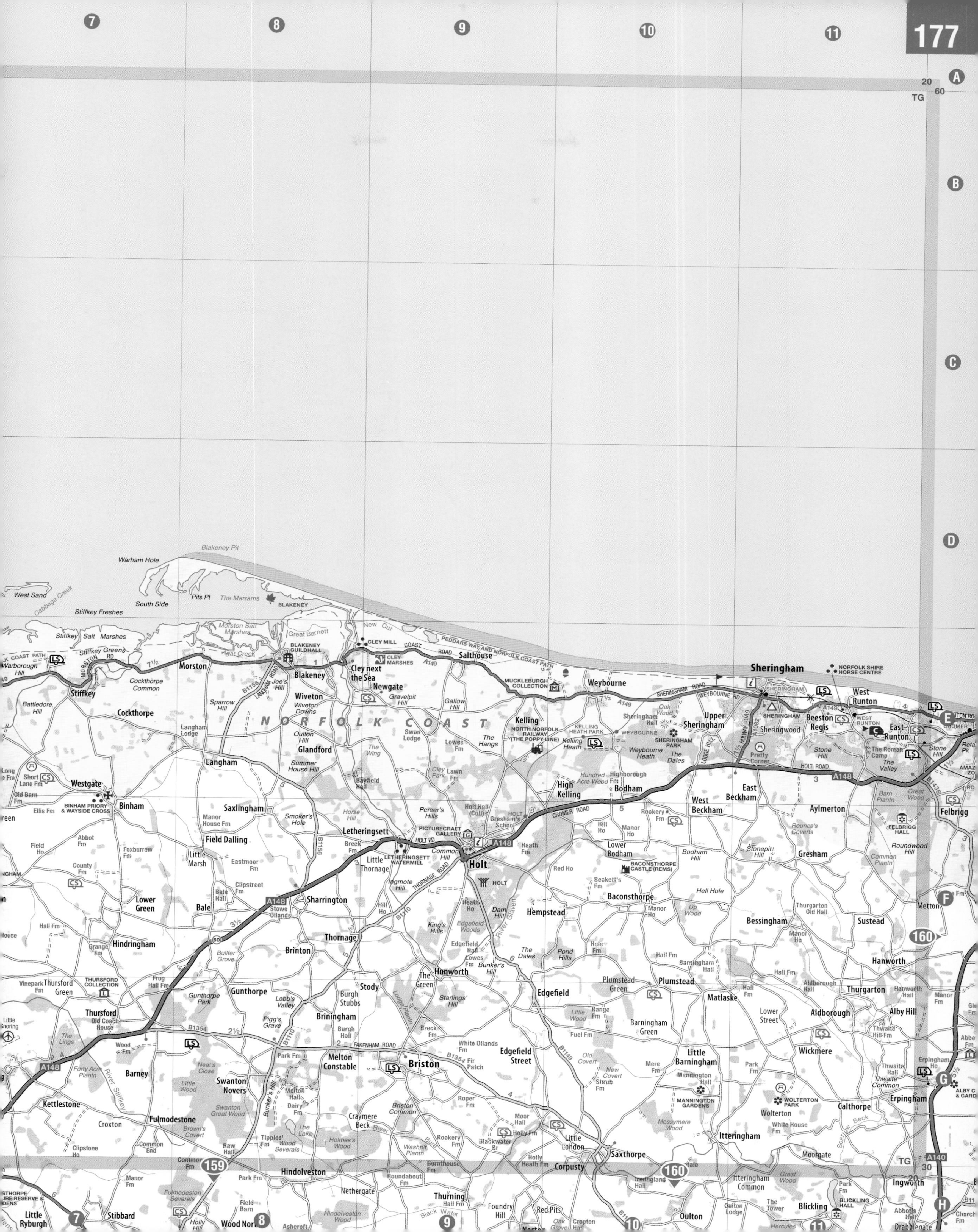

7
8
9
10
11
A
B
C
D
E
F
G
H
TG
Blakeney Pit
Warham Hole
West Sand
South Side
Pits Pt
The Marrams
BLAKENEY
Stiffkey Freshes
Stiffkey Salt Marshes
Morston
Blakeney
Cley next the Sea
Newgate
Salthouse
Stiffkey
Cockthorpe
Wiveton
Glandford
NORFOLK COAST
Weybourne
Kelling
Sheringham
Upper Sheringham
Beeston Regis
West Runton
East Runton
Langham
Westgate
Binham
Saxlingham
Field Dalling
Letheringsett
Holt
High Kelling
Bodham
West Beckham
East Beckham
Aylmerton
Felbrigg
Gresham
Lower Bodham
Baconsthorpe
Hempstead
Bessingham
Sustead
Metton
Hanworth
Thurgarton
Aldborough
Alby Hill
Sharrington
Little Thornage
Thornage
Brinton
Bale
Lower Green
Hindringham
Thursford
Thursford Green
Gunthorpe
Stody
Briningham
Hunworth
Edgefield
Plumstead
Matlaske
Wickmere
Barney
Swanton Novers
Melton Constable
Briston
Edgefield Street
Little Barningham
Erpingham
Kettlestone
Croxton
Fulmodestone
Hindolveston
Little London
Saxthorpe
Corpusty
Itteringham
Calthorpe
Wolterton
Ingworth
Blickling
Oulton
Thurning
Stibbard
Little Ryburgh
Nethergate
A148
A149
B1156
B1110
B1354
B1149
A140
159
160

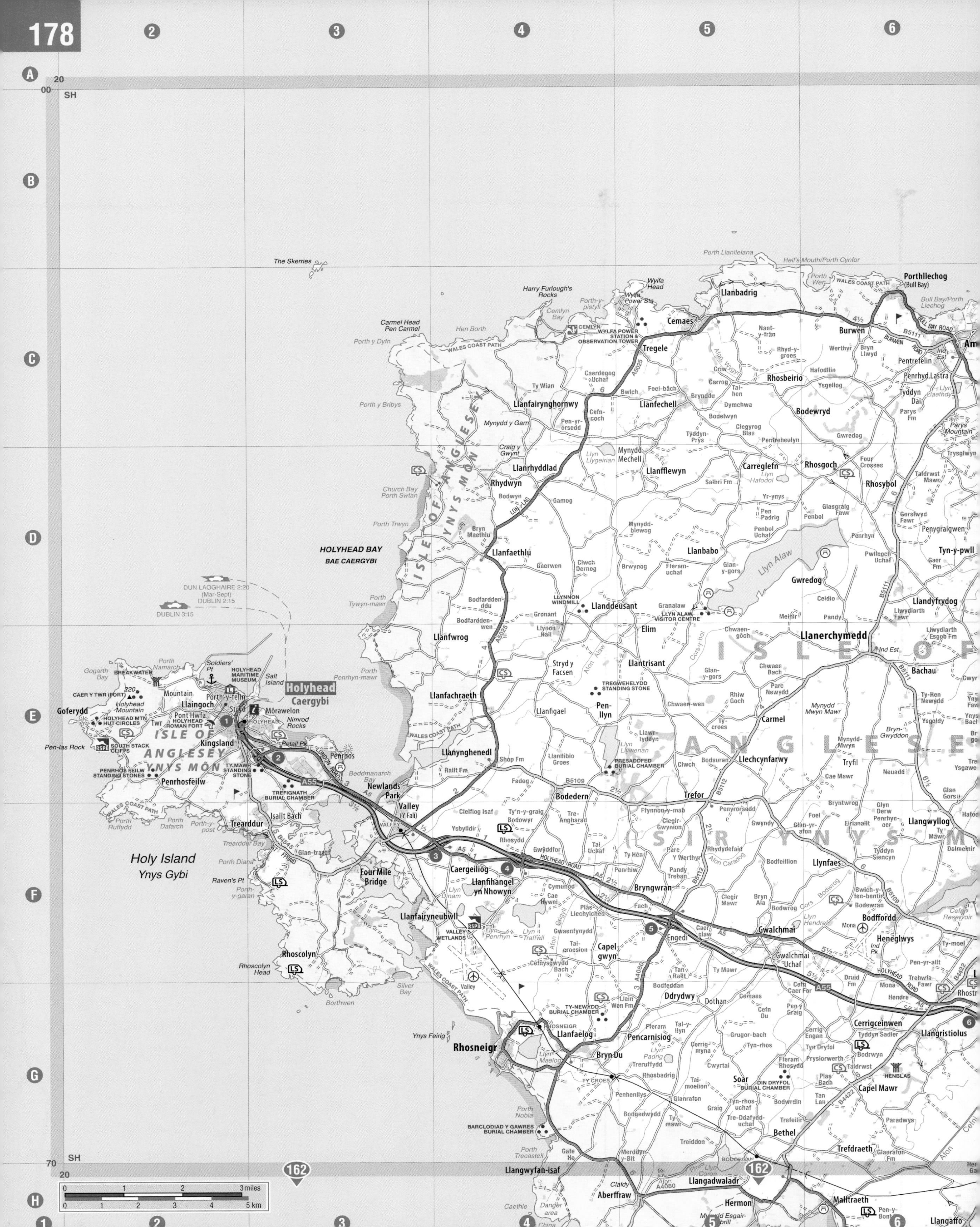

The Skerries
Harry Furlough's Rocks
Wylfa Head
Porth Llanlleiana
Hell's Mouth/Porth Cynfor
Porthllechog (Bull Bay)
Llanbadrig
Cemaes
Burwen
WYLFA POWER STATION & OBSERVATION TOWER
Carmel Head
Pen Carmel
Tregele
Llanfairynghornwy
Llanfechell
Rhosbeirio
Bodewryd
Llanrhyddlad
Mynydd Mechell
Llanfflewyn
Carreglefn
Rhosgoch
Rhosybol
Rhydwyn
Church Bay
Porth Swtan
ISLE OF ANGLESEY
YNYS MÔN
HOLYHEAD BAY
BAE CAERGYBI
Llanfaethlu
Llanbabo
Llyn Alaw
Gwredog
Llandyfrydog
DUN LAOGHAIRE 2:20 (Mar-Sept)
DUBLIN 2:15
DUBLIN 3:15
Llanddeusant
Elim
Llanerchymedd
Llanfwrog
Llantrisant
Bachau
Holyhead
Caergybi
Soldiers' Pt
Salt Island
Mountain
Llaingoch
Porth-y-felin
Môrawelon
Goferydd
Kingsland
Pen-las Rock
SOUTH STACK CLIFFS
Penrhosfeilw
Llanfachraeth
Pen-llyn
Carmel
Llanynghenedl
Penrhos
Llechcynfarwy
Newlands Park
Valley (Y Fali)
Bodedern
Trefor
Trearddur
Isallt Bach
Holy Island
Ynys Gybi
Caergeiliog
Llanfihangel yn Nhowyn
Four Mile Bridge
Bryngwran
Llynfaes
Llanfairyneubwll
VALLEY WETLANDS
Gwalchmai
Bodffordd
Heneglwys
Rhoscolyn
Rhoscolyn Head
Capel-gwyn
Engedi
Ddrydwy
Cerrigceinwen
Llangristiolus
Rhosneigr
Llanfaelog
Pencarnisiog
Bryn Du
Soar
Capel Mawr
BARCLODIAD Y GAWRES BURIAL CHAMBER
Bethel
Trefdraeth
Llangwyfan-isaf
Aberffraw
Llangadwaladr
Hermon
Malltraeth
Llangaffo
0 1 2 3 miles
0 1 2 3 4 5 km

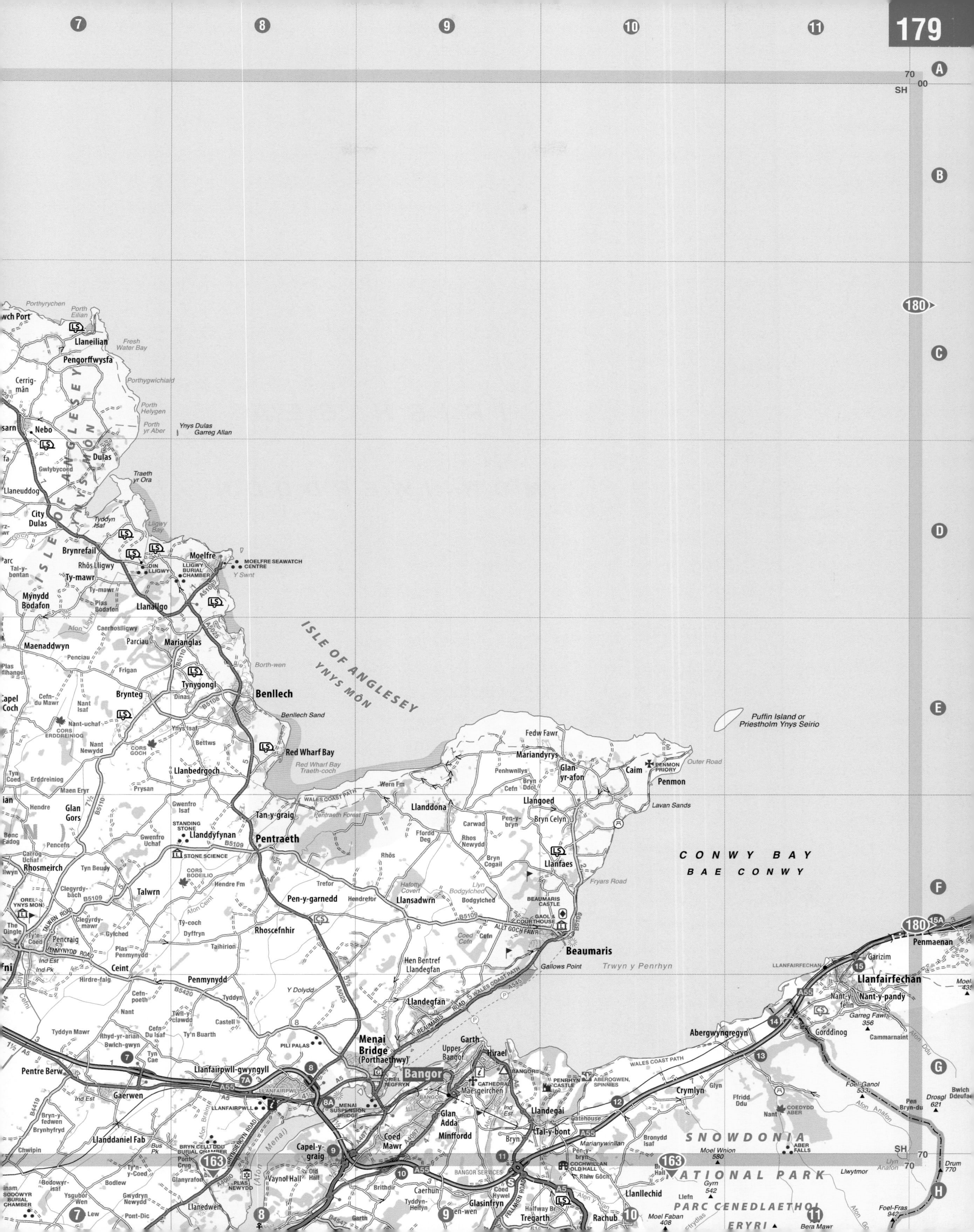

7
8
9
10
11
A
B
C
D
E
F
G
H
180
SH
ISLE OF ANGLESEY
YNYS MÔN
CONWY BAY
BAE CONWY
Puffin Island or Priestholm Ynys Seirio
Llaneilian
Pengorffwysfa
Nebo
Dulas
City Dulas
Brynrefail
Moelfre
MOELFRE SEAWATCH CENTRE
Llanallgo
Marianglas
Maenaddwyn
Tynygongl
Benllech
Benllech Sand
Red Wharf Bay
Brynteg
Llanbedrgoch
Pentraeth
Llanddyfnan
STONE SCIENCE
Rhosmeirch
Talwrn
Pen-y-garnedd
Rhoscefnhir
Llanddona
Llansadwrn
Fedw Fawr
Mariandyrys
Glan-yr-afon
Caim
PENMON PRIORY
Penmon
Llangoed
Lavan Sands
Llanfaes
BEAUMARIS CASTLE
GAOL & COURTHOUSE
Beaumaris
Gallows Point
Trwyn y Penrhyn
Fryars Road
Outer Road
Hen Bentref Llandegfan
Llandegfan
Ceint
Penmynydd
Pentre Berw
Gaerwen
Llanfairpwll-gwyngyll
LLANFAIRPWLL
PILI PALAS
Menai Bridge (Porthaethwy)
MENAI SUSPENSION BRIDGE
Bangor
Garth
Upper Bangor
Hirael
Maesgeirchen
Glan Adda
Minffordd
Coed Mawr
Capel-y-graig
Llanddaniel Fab
Vaynol Hall
Llanedwen
Llandegai
Tal-y-bont
PENRHYN CASTLE
ABEROGWEN, SPINNIES
Crymlyn
Abergwyngregyn
Llanfairfechan
Nant-y-pandy
Penmaenan
Gorddinog
Glasinfryn
Tregarth
Rachub
Llanllechid
SNOWDONIA
NATIONAL PARK
PARC CENEDLAETHOL ERYRI
Moel Wnion 580
Moel Faban 408
Gyrn 542
Drosgl 621
Foel-Ganol 533
Foel-Fras 942
Drum 770
ABER FALLS
A55
A5
A5025
B5109

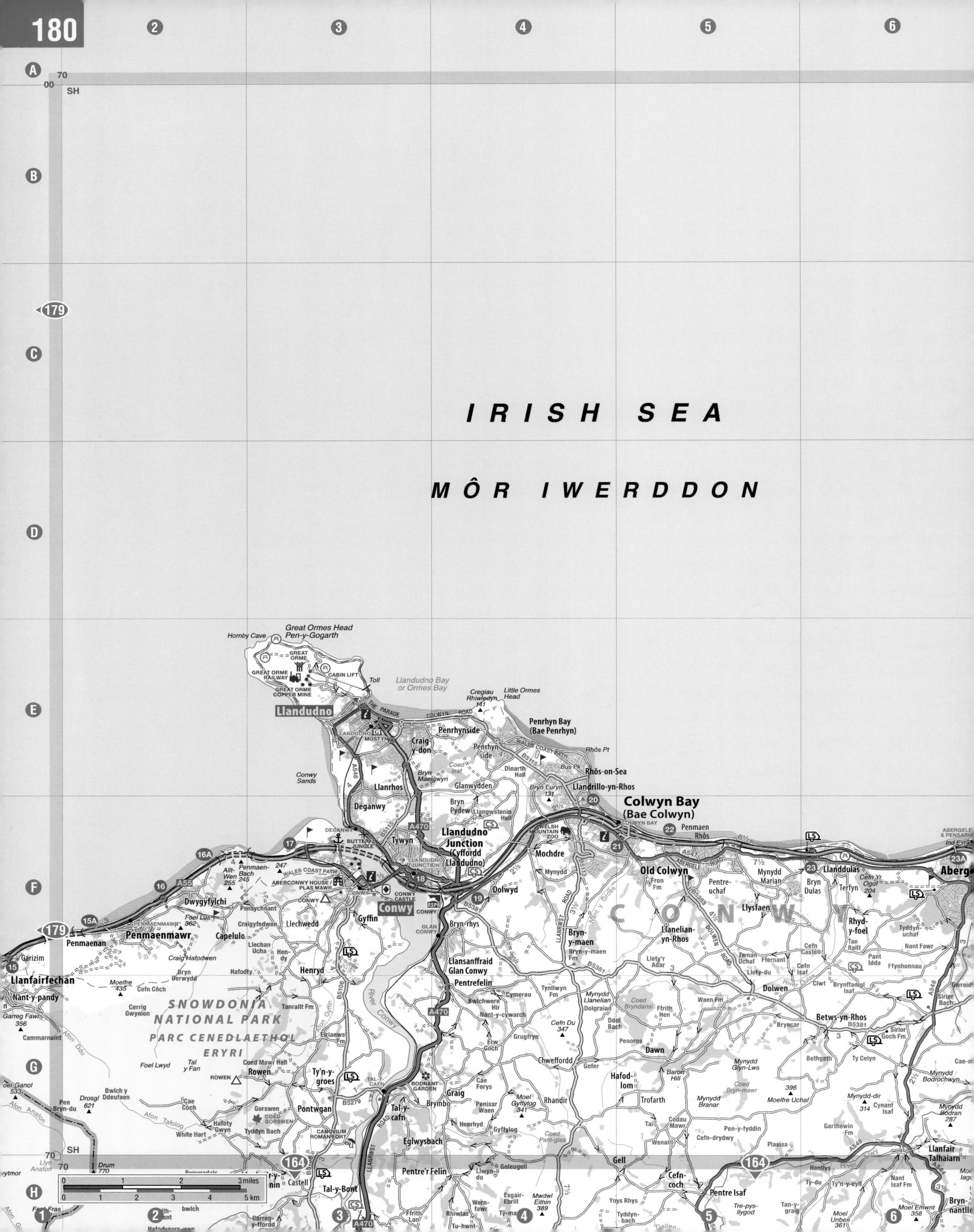

IRISH SEA
MÔR IWERDDON
Great Ormes Head
Pen-y-Gogarth
Llandudno Bay
or Ormes Bay
Little Ormes Head
Llandudno
Penrhyn Bay
(Bae Penrhyn)
Penrhynside
Craig-y-don
Rhôs-on-Sea
Llandrillo-yn-Rhos
Colwyn Bay
(Bae Colwyn)
Conwy Sands
Llanrhos
Deganwy
Tywyn
Llandudno Junction
(Cyffordd Llandudno)
Mochdre
Old Colwyn
Llanddulas
Penmaenmawr
Dwygyfylchi
Conwy
Gyffin
Llanfairfechan
SNOWDONIA NATIONAL PARK
PARC CENEDLAETHOL ERYRI
Henryd
Rowen
Llansanffraid Glan Conwy
Pentrefelin
Dolwyd
Bryn-y-maen
Llanelian-yn-Rhos
Betws-yn-Rhos
Dolwen
Llysfaen
Rhyd-y-foel
CONWY
Tal-y-cafn
Eglwysbach
Pentre'r Felin
Tal-y-Bont
Pentre Isaf
Llanfair Talhaiarn

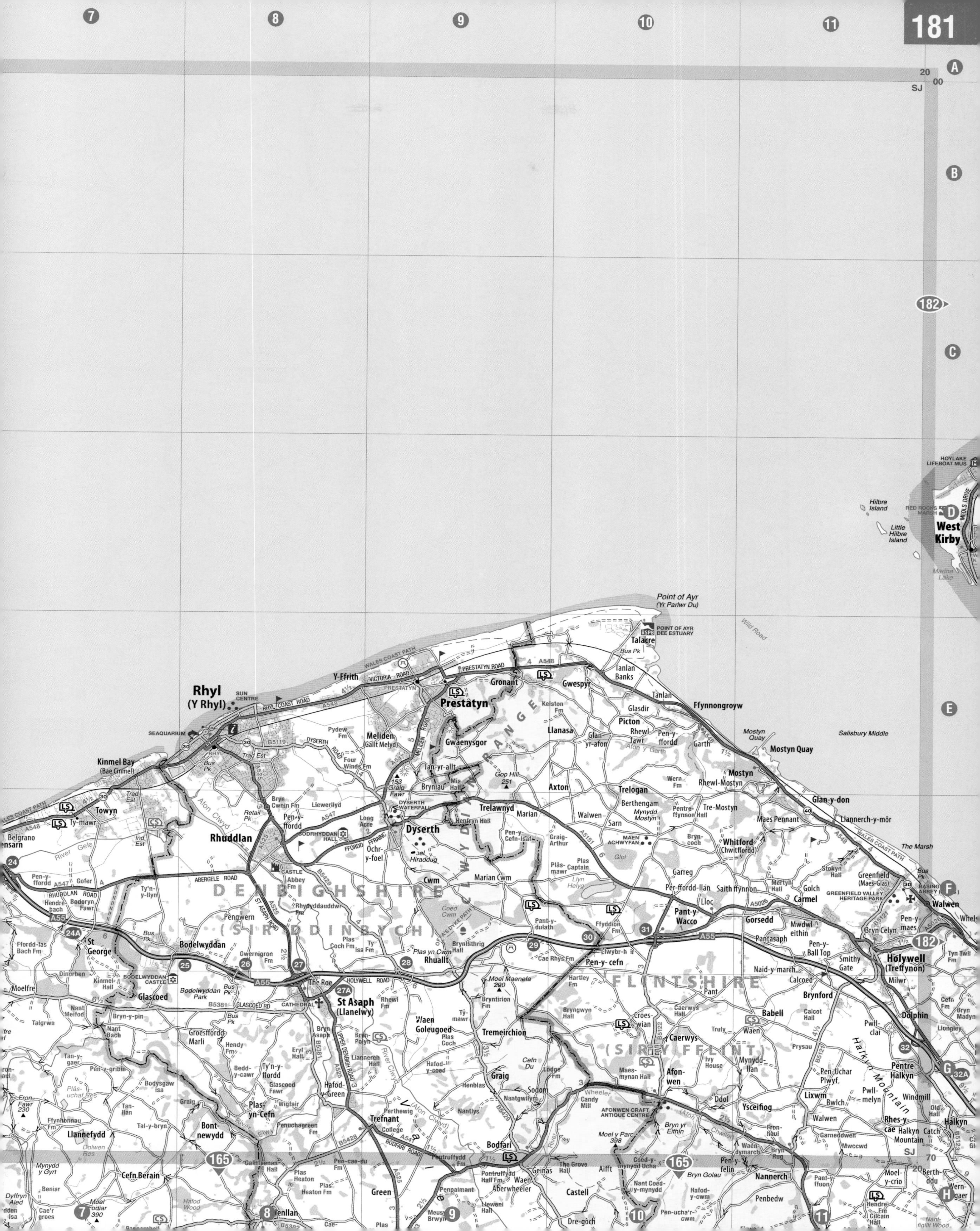

7
8
9
10
11
A
B
C
D
E
F
G
H
SJ
182
Hoylake Lifeboat Mus
Hilbre Island
Little Hilbre Island
Red Rocks Marsh
Meols Drive
West Kirby
Marine Lake
Point of Ayr
(Yr Parlwr Du)
Point of Ayr Dee Estuary
Wild Road
Talacre
Bus Pk
Tanlan Banks
Tanlan
Ffynnongroyw
Salisbury Middle
Mostyn Quay
Mostyn
Rhewl-Mostyn
Glan-y-don
Llannerch-y-môr
The Marsh
Wales Coast Path
Greenfield
(Maes-Glas)
Greenfield Valley Heritage Park
Basingwerk Abbey
Walwen
Holywell
(Treffynnon)
Milwr
Dolphin
Pwll-clai
Halkyn Mountain
Pentre Halkyn
Halkyn
Rhyl
(Y Rhyl)
Sun Centre
Seaquarium
Kinmel Bay
(Bae Cinmel)
Towyn
Ty-mawr
Belgrano
Rhuddlan
Prestatyn
Y-Ffrith
Gronant
Gwespyr
Meliden
(Gallt Melyd)
Gwaenysgor
Llanasa
Picton
Glasdir
Dyserth
Trelawnyd
Gop Hill 251
Axton
Trelogan
Berthengam
Maen Achwyfan
Whitford
(Chwitffordd)
Carmel
Lloc
Pant-y-Wacco
Gorsedd
Denbighshire
(Sir Ddinbych)
Clwydian Range
Flintshire
(Sir y Fflint)
St George
Bodelwyddan
Bodelwyddan Castle
Glascoed
St Asaph
(Llanelwy)
The Roe
Cathedral
Rhuallt
Waen Goleugoed
Tremeirchion
Moel Maenefa 290
Pen-y-cefn
Caerwys
Babell
Brynford
Afon-wen
Afonwen Craft Antique Centre
Ysceifiog
Lixwm
Rhes-y-cae
Halkyn Mountain
Graig
Sodom
Bodfari
Trefnant
Bont-newydd
Llannefydd
Cefn Berain
Moel Fodiar 390
Moelfre
Nannerch
Caerwys
Moel y Parc 398
Castell
Green
Henllan
Aberwheeler
A55
A548
A547
A525
A5151
A5026
A541
B5119
B5381
B5429
B5122
B5428
B5382
24
24A
25
26
27
27A
28
29
30
31
32
32A
165

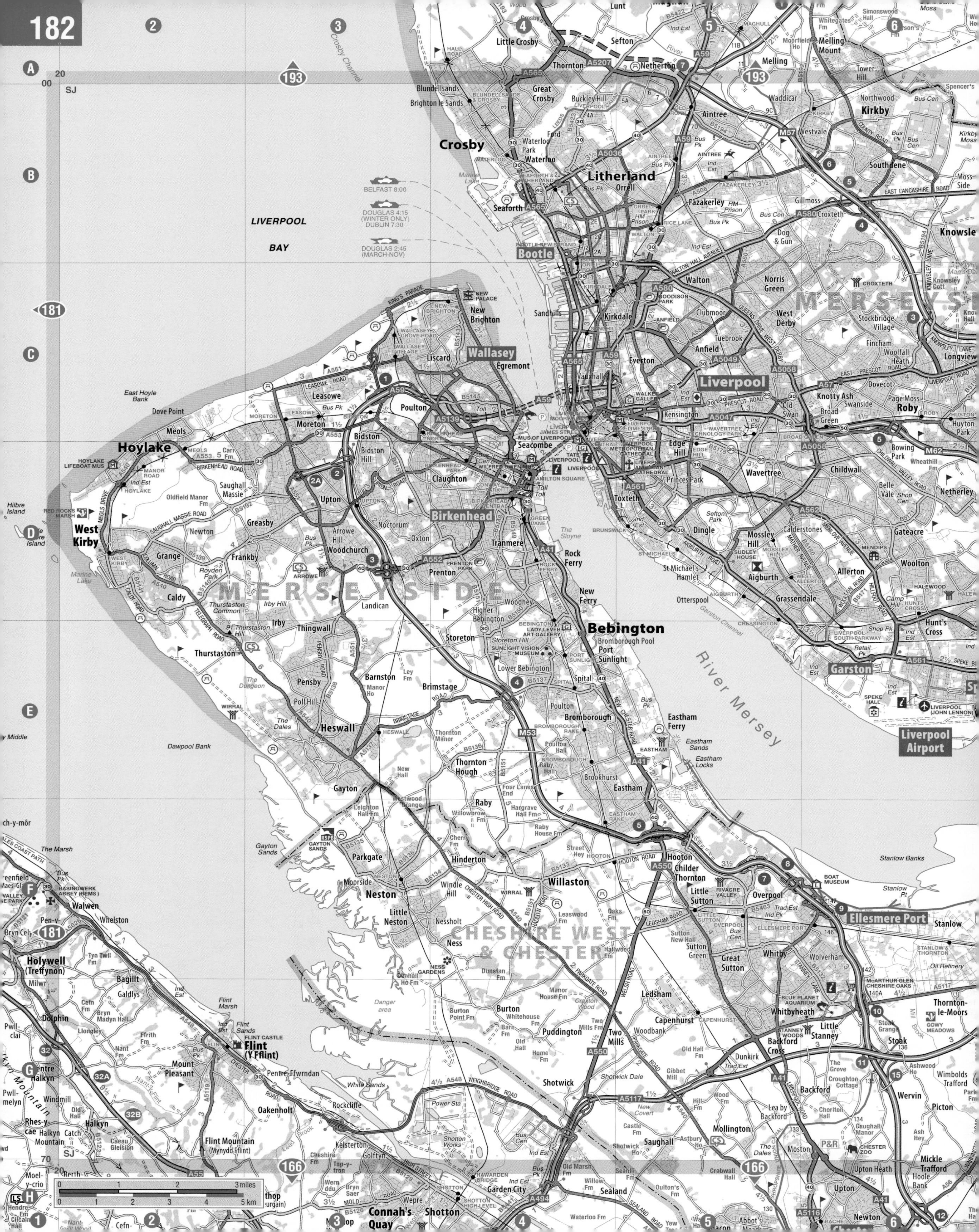
193
181
166
LIVERPOOL
BAY
BELFAST 8:00
DOUGLAS 4:15 (WINTER ONLY) DUBLIN 7:30
DOUGLAS 2:45 (MARCH-NOV)
Crosby Channel
Crosby
Little Crosby
Great Crosby
Blundellsands
Brighton le Sands
Waterloo
Seaforth
Bootle
Litherland
Orrell
Thornton
Sefton
Netherton
Aintree
Melling
Kirkby
Fazakerley
Walton
Kirkdale
Everton
Anfield
Norris Green
West Derby
Knowsle
Liverpool
Kensington
Edge Hill
Wavertree
Toxteth
Dingle
Aigburth
Allerton
Grassendale
Woolton
Gateacre
Childwall
Roby
Huyton
Netherley
Hunt's Cross
Garston
Liverpool Airport
MERSEYSIDE
New Brighton
Wallasey
Egremont
Liscard
Leasowe
Moreton
Poulton
Bidston
Seacombe
Birkenhead
Claughton
Tranmere
Rock Ferry
New Ferry
Bebington
Port Sunlight
Bromborough
Eastham
Hoylake
Meols
West Kirby
Hilbre Island
Greasby
Upton
Woodchurch
Prenton
Frankby
Caldy
Irby
Thurstaston
Pensby
Heswall
Barnston
Thornton Hough
Gayton
Parkgate
Neston
Little Neston
Willaston
Hooton
Little Sutton
Overpool
Ellesmere Port
Stanlow
Great Sutton
Whitby
Ledsham
Capenhurst
Backford
Mollington
Saughall
Upton
Hoole
CHESHIRE WEST & CHESTER
River Mersey
Dee Estuary
Holywell (Treffynon)
Flint (Y Fflint)
Bagillt
Connah's Quay
Shotton
Garden City
Sealand
Shotwick
Puddington
Burton
Ness
Dawpool Bank
Gayton Sands
Halkyn

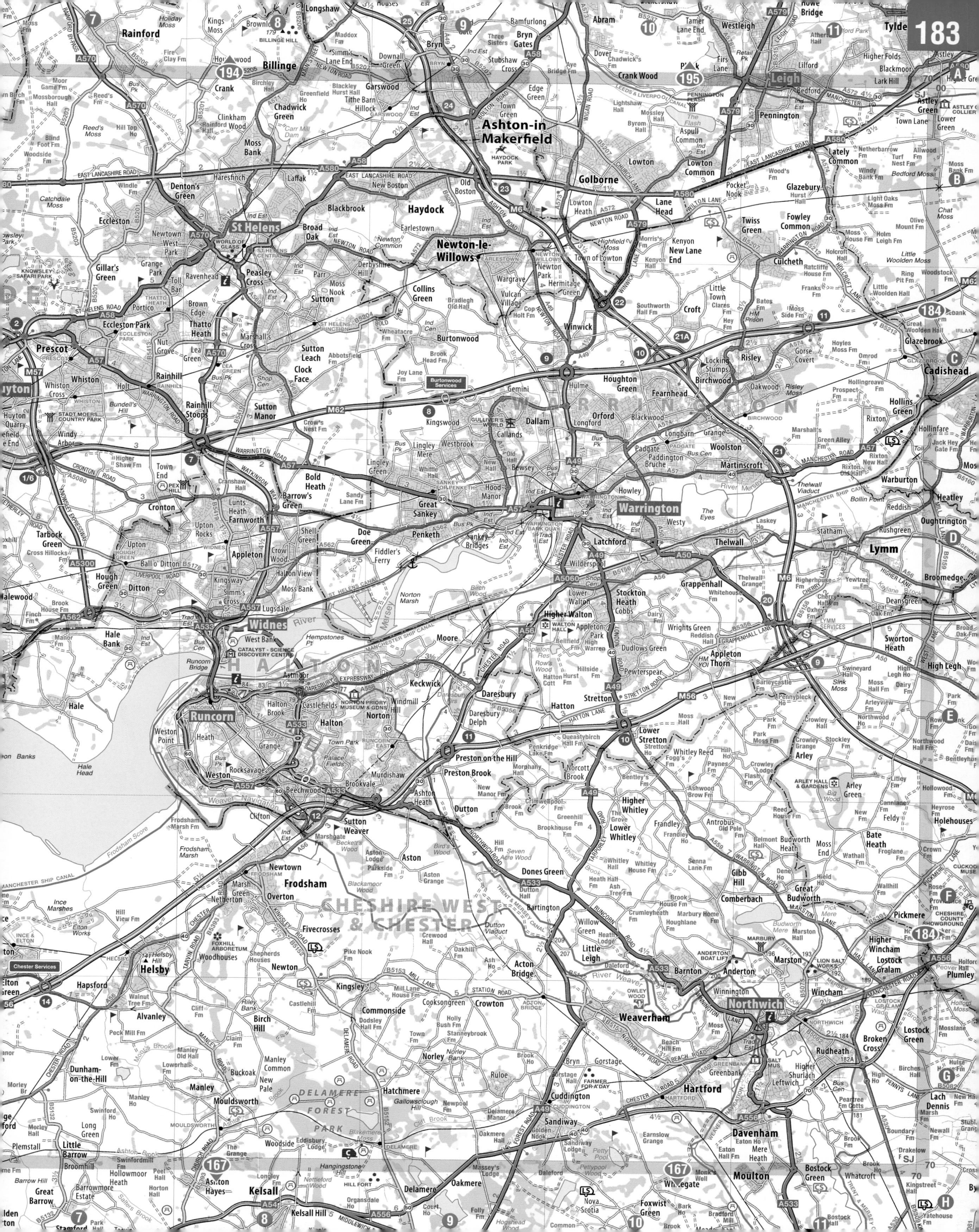
Rainford
Billinge
Bryn
Abram
Westleigh
Tyldesley
Leigh
Ashton-in Makerfield
Golborne
Lowton
Haydock
St Helens
Eccleston
Newton-le-Willows
Prescot
Whiston
Rainhill
Culcheth
Glazebury
Croft
Risley
Birchwood
Cadishead
Winwick
Burtonwood
Warrington
Orford
Woolston
Great Sankey
Penketh
Lymm
Thelwall
Grappenhall
Latchford
Widnes
Halton
Runcorn
Hale
Daresbury
Stretton
Arley
Frodsham
Helsby
Cheshire West & Chester
Kingsley
Weaverham
Barnton
Northwich
Hartford
Davenham
Moulton
Cuddington
Sandiway
Delamere Forest Park
Kelsall
Ashton Hayes
Manley
Mouldsworth
Alvanley
Dunham-on-the-Hill
Great Barrow
Plumley
Lostock Gralam
Rudheath
Marston
Comberbach
Great Budworth
Pickmere
Higher Whitley
Lower Whitley
Preston on the Hill
Dutton
Acton Bridge
Crowton
Norley
Sutton Weaver
Aston
Hapsford
Kingswood
Dallam
Bewsey
Howley
Appleton
Ditton
Cronton
Tarbock Green
Hough Green
Halewood

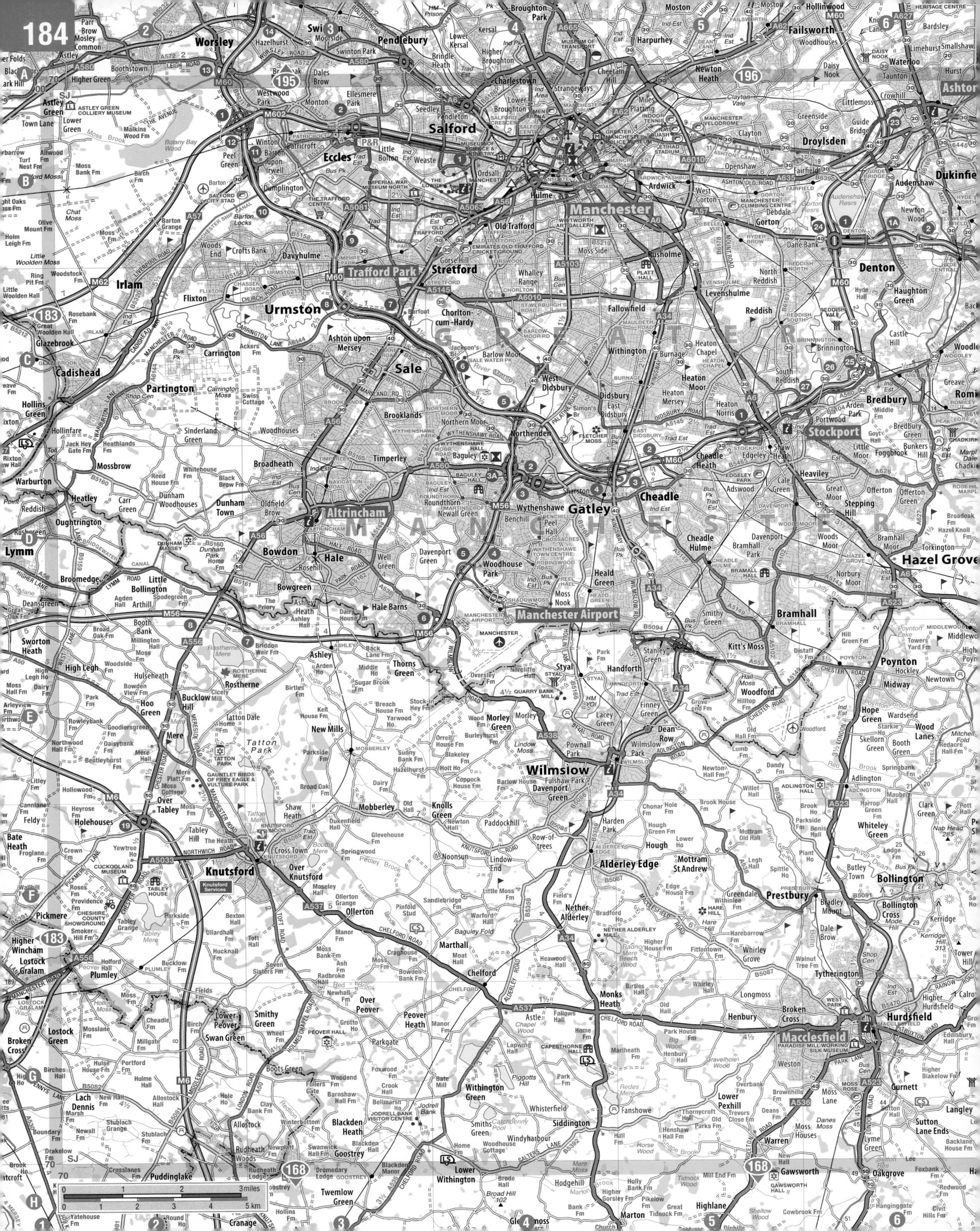
Worsley
Pendlebury
Broughton Park
Moston
Failsworth
Hollinwood
Salford
Eccles
Manchester
Droylsden
Ashton
Dukinfield
Audenshaw
Denton
Trafford Park
Stretford
Irlam
Urmston
Flixton
Davyhulme
Cadishead
Glazebrook
Partington
Carrington
Sale
Ashton upon Mersey
Chorlton-cum-Hardy
Fallowfield
Levenshulme
Reddish
Withington
Didsbury
West Didsbury
Heaton Moor
Stockport
Bredbury
Brooklands
Northenden
Timperley
Altrincham
Cheadle
Gatley
Wythenshawe
Cheadle Hulme
Bramhall
Hazel Grove
Lymm
Heatley
Bowdon
Hale
Hale Barns
Manchester Airport
Dunham Town
Ashley
Styal
Handforth
Poynton
Woodford
Wilmslow
Mobberley
Knutsford
Mere
Rostherne
Tatton Park
Alderley Edge
Prestbury
Bollington
Macclesfield
Hurdsfield
Chelford
Monks Heath
Henbury
Ollerton
Plumley
Lower Peover
Goostrey
Jodrell Bank Visitor Centre
Siddington
Lower Withington
Gawsworth
Warren
Sutton Lane Ends
Langley
Oakgrove
Pickmere
Lostock Gralam
Higher Wincham
GREATER MANCHESTER
195
196
183
168
0 1 2 3 miles
0 1 2 3 4 5 km

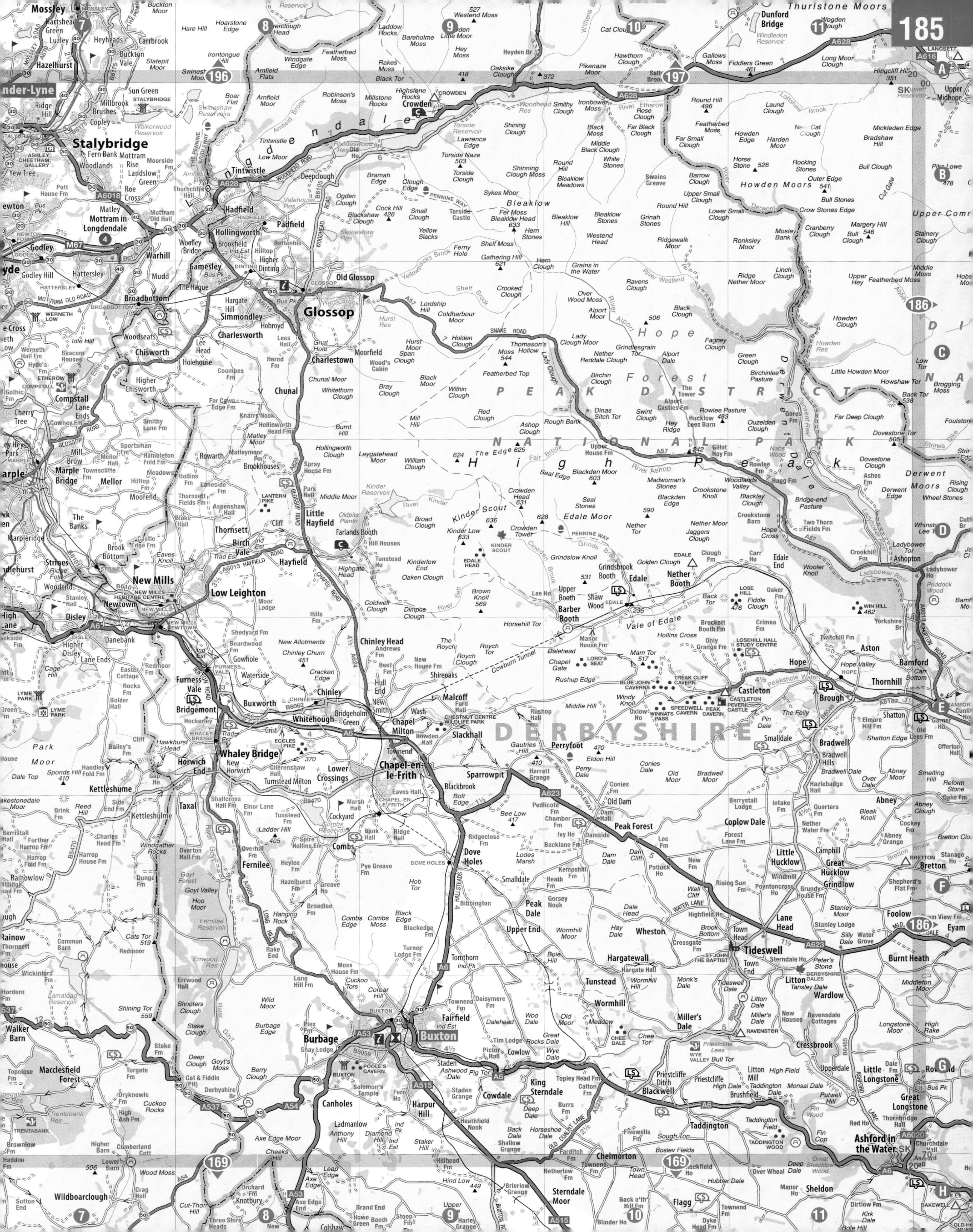

Mossley
Stalybridge
Hazelhurst
Mottram in Longdendale
Godley
Hattersley
Broadbottom
Hollingworth
Hadfield
Padfield
Tintwistle
Crowden
Longdendale
Glossop
Old Glossop
Simmondley
Charlesworth
Chisworth
Compstall
Marple Bridge
Mellor
Charlestown
Chunal
Little Hayfield
Hayfield
Birch Vale
Thornsett
New Mills
Low Leighton
Newtown
Disley
Furness Vale
Bridgemont
Buxworth
Chinley
Whitehough
Chinley Head
Chapel Milton
Malcoff
Slackhall
Whaley Bridge
Horwich End
Chapel-en-le-Frith
Sparrowpit
Kettleshulme
Taxal
Combs
Dove Holes
Peak Dale
Peak Forest
Fernilee
Burbage
Buxton
Fairfield
Harpur Hill
Cowdale
King Sterndale
Chelmorton
Flagg
Sterndale Moor
Taddington
Blackwell
Tideswell
Wheston
Hargatewall
Tunstead
Wormhill
Miller's Dale
Litton
Wardlow
Cressbrook
Little Longstone
Great Longstone
Ashford in the Water
Sheldon
Bradwell
Castleton
Hope
Brough
Aston
Bamford
Thornhill
Edale
Barber Booth
Nether Booth
Upper Booth
Ashopton
Little Hucklow
Great Hucklow
Grindlow
Foolow
Bretton
Eyam
Abney
Wildboarclough
Macclesfield Forest
Walker Barn
Kinder Scout
Bleaklow
Howden Moors
Edale Moor
Vale of Edale
Hope Forest
High Peak
PEAK DISTRICT NATIONAL PARK
DERBYSHIRE
Thurlstone Moors
Dunford Bridge
Langsett
Derwent Moors
Snake Road
Pennine Way
Cowburn Tunnel
A628
A57
A6
A623
A624
A626
A53
A54
A537
A515
A5004
A6187
A6013
A6020
A6024
B6101
M67
196
197
186
169

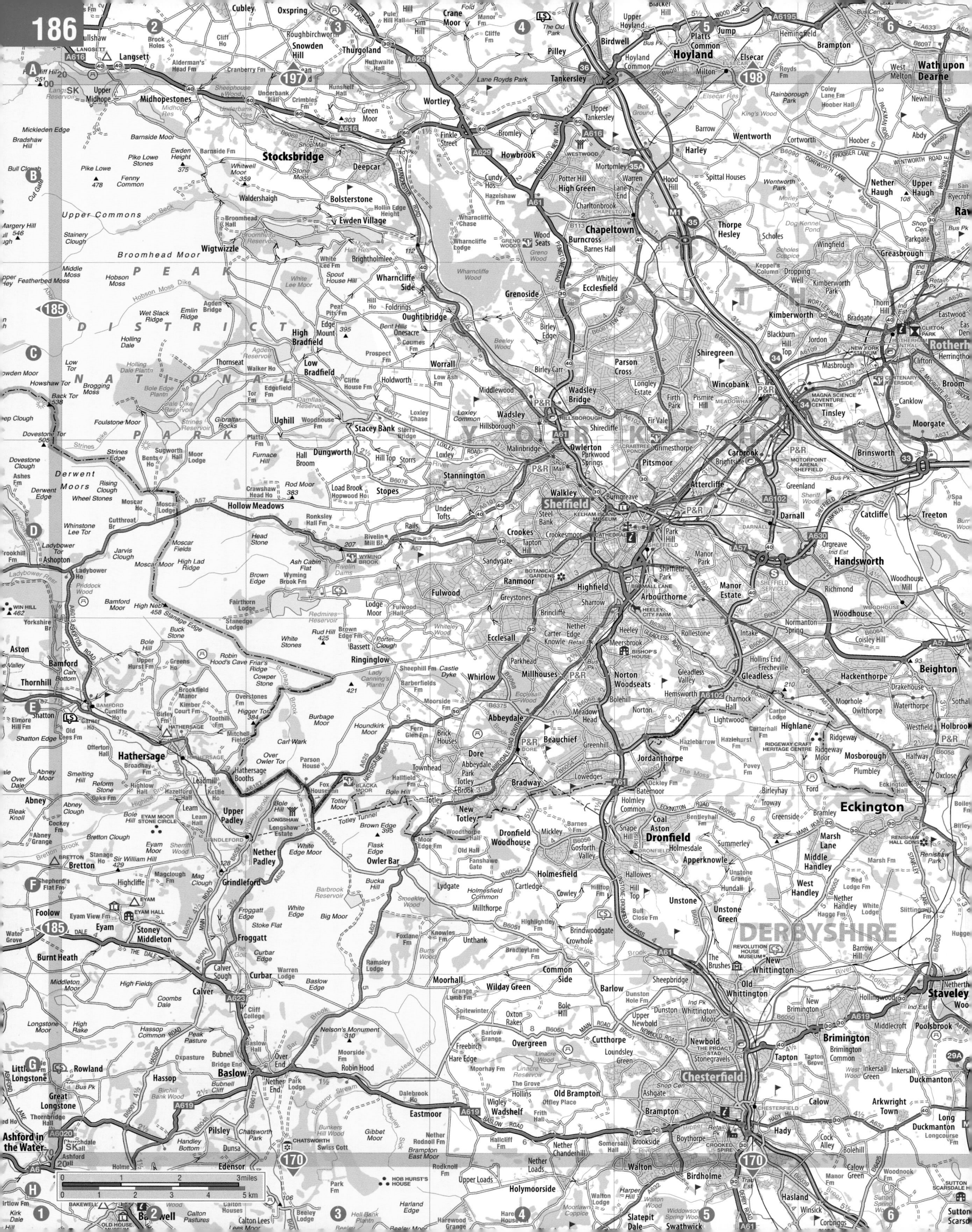

Cubley
Oxspring
Roughbirchworth
Snowden Hill
Thurgoland
Crane Moor
Pilley
Upper Hoyland
Birdwell
Hoyland
Platts Common
Jump
Elsecar
Hemingfield
Brampton
Wath upon Dearne
West Melton
Langsett
Midhopestones
Upper Midhope
Brock Holes
Cliff Ho
Alderman's Head Fm
Cranberry Fm
197
198
Tankersley
Chapeltown
Wortley
Upper Tankersley
Finkle Street
Bromley
Howbrook
Westwood
Mortomley
Warren
Harley
Wentworth
Cortworth
Hoober
Abdy
Newhill
Rainborough Park
Stocksbridge
Deepcar
Bolsterstone
Ewden Village
Upper Commons
Broomhead Moor
Wigtwizzle
Pike Lowe
Fenny Common
Bull Clough
Cut Gate
Margery Hill
Mickleden Edge
Bradshaw Hill
Barnside Moor
Ewden Height
Whitwell Moor
Waldershaigh
Cundy Hos
Hazelshaw Fm
Potter Hill
High Green
Charltonbrook
Burncross
Barnes Hall
Hood Hill
Spittal Houses
Thorpe Hesley
Scholes
Wentworth Park
Nether Haugh
Upper Haugh
Greasbrough
Parkgate
Wingfield
Kimberworth
Kimberworth Park
Dropping Well
Keppel's Column
Bradgate
Thorn Hill
Eastwood
Rotherham
Clifton
Herringthorpe
Broom
Canklow
Moorgate
Brinsworth
Tinsley
Jordon
Masbrough
Blackburn
PEAK DISTRICT NATIONAL PARK
Brightholmlee
Wharncliffe Side
Wharncliffe Chase
Grenoside
Ecclesfield
Whitley
Birley Edge
Oughtibridge
Worrall
Middlewood
Wadsley
Hillsborough
Wadsley Bridge
Parson Cross
Longley Estate
Shiregreen
Wincobank
Firth Park
Pismire Hill
Fir Vale
Shirecliffe
Birley Carr
High Bradfield
Low Bradfield
Holdworth
Dungworth
Storrs
Stacey Bank
Loxley
Stannington
Ughill
Hollow Meadows
Thornseat
Emlin Ridge
Wet Slack Ridge
Agden Bridge
Holling Dale
Low Tor
Howshaw Tor
Back Tor
Foulstone Moor
Dovestone Tor
Derwent Moors
Featherbed Moss
Hobson Moss
Middle Moss
Stainery Clough
185
YORKSHIRE
SOUTH
Malinbridge
Owlerton
Parkwood Springs
Pitsmoor
Grimesthorpe
Brightside
Carbrook
Attercliffe
Darnall
Catcliffe
Treeton
Handsworth
Orgreave
Woodhouse
Richmond
Sheffield
Walkley
Burngreave
Crookes
Crookesmoor
Tapton Hill
Steel Bank
Park Hill
Manor Park
Manor Estate
Heeley
Sandygate
Ranmoor
Fulwood
Greystones
Highfield
Sharrow
Arbourthorne
Brincliffe
Nether Edge
Carter Knowle
Ecclesall
Meersbrook
Rollestone
Intake
Normanton Spring
Coisley Hill
Gleadless
Gleadless Valley
Hackenthorpe
Beighton
Drakehouse
Waterthorpe
Westfield
Holbrook
Halfway
Owlthorpe
Moorhole
Hollins End
Frecheville
Rivelin Mill Br
Under Tofts
Rails
Stopes
Load Brook
Lodge Moor
Bassett
Ringinglow
Whirlow
Parkhead
Millhouses
Norton Woodseats
Bolehill
Norton
Hemsworth
Charnock Hall
Lightwood
Highlane
Ridgeway
Mosborough
Plumbley
Oxclose
Eckington
Abbeydale
Beauchief
Greenhill
Meadow Head
Jordanthorpe
Dore
Totley
Totley Brook
Bradway
Lowedges
Batemoor
Holmley Common
Coal Aston
Dronfield
Dronfield Woodhouse
Mickley
Gosforth Valley
Apperknowle
Summerley
Marsh Lane
Middle Handley
West Handley
Unstone
Unstone Green
Hallowes
Holmesfield
Cowley
Cartledge
Lydgate
Millthorpe
Unthank
DERBYSHIRE
Ashopton
Ladybower
Win Hill
Yorkshire Br
Aston
Bamford
Thornhill
Shatton
Hathersage
Hathersage Booths
Stanage Edge
High Neb
Burbage Moor
Higger Tor
Carl Wark
Owler Tor
Fox House
Upper Padley
Nether Padley
Grindleford
Longshaw Estate
Owler Bar
Big Moor
Froggatt
Curbar
Calver
Stoney Middleton
Eyam
Foolow
Bretton
Abney
Highcliffe
Grindleford
Burnt Heath
Hassop
Baslow
Rowland
Little Longstone
Great Longstone
Ashford in the Water
Pilsley
Edensor
Chatsworth
Over End
Nether End
Robin Hood
Eastmoor
Moorhall
Wilday Green
Common Side
Barlow
Overgreen
Cutthorpe
Old Whittington
New Whittington
Sheepbridge
Newbold
Chesterfield
Brimington
Staveley
Tapton
Duckmanton
Calow
Arkwright Town
Long Duckmanton
Hady
Old Brampton
Wadshelf
Brampton
Ashgate
Brookside
Boythorpe
Walton
Birdholme
Holymoorside
Nether Loads
Hasland
Swathwick
Slatepit Dale
170
Bakewell
0 1 2 3 miles
0 1 2 3 4 5 km

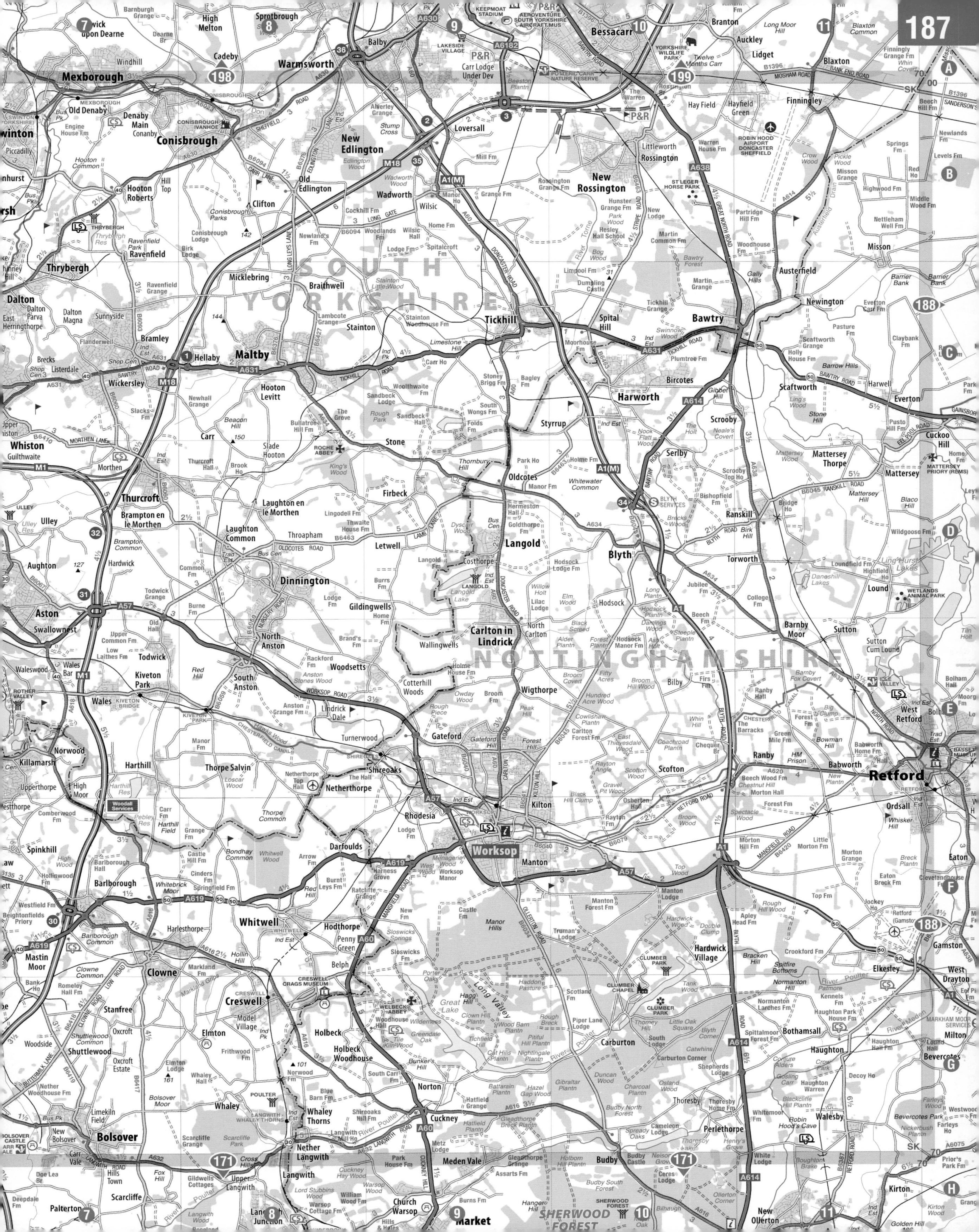
Mexborough
Conisbrough
Warmsworth
Sprotbrough
Cadeby
High Melton
Balby
Bessacarr
Branton
Auckley
Lidget
Blaxton
Finningley
Loversall
New Edlington
Old Edlington
Wadworth
Wilsic
Littleworth
Rossington
New Rossington
Hooton Roberts
Clifton
Thrybergh
Ravenfield
Micklebring
Braithwell
Stainton
Tickhill
Spital Hill
Bawtry
Austerfield
Misson
Newington
SOUTH YORKSHIRE
Dalton
Bramley
Wickersley
Hellaby
Maltby
Hooton Levitt
Harworth
Bircotes
Scrooby
Scaftworth
Everton
Whiston
Carr
Stone
Styrrup
Serlby
Mattersey Thorpe
Mattersey
Thurcroft
Brampton en le Morthen
Laughton en le Morthen
Laughton Common
Firbeck
Oldcotes
Ulley
Letwell
Langold
Blyth
Ranskill
Torworth
Aughton
Dinnington
Aston
Swallownest
Gildingwells
North Anston
Carlton in Lindrick
Barnby Moor
Sutton
Todwick
Kiveton Park
South Anston
Woodsetts
NOTTINGHAMSHIRE
Wales
Wigthorpe
Bilby
West Retford
Norwood
Killamarsh
Harthill
Thorpe Salvin
Gateford
Shireoaks
Netherthorpe
Ranby
Scofton
Babworth
Retford
Kilton
Rhodesia
Ordsall
Worksop
Manton
Darfoulds
Spinkhill
Barlborough
Whitwell
Hodthorpe
Clowne
Creswell
Hardwick Village
Elkesley
Gamston
West Drayton
Mastin Moor
Belph
Stanfree
Elmton
Holbeck
Carburton
Bothamsall
Haughton
Milton
Shuttlewood
Norton
Thoresby
Perlethorpe
Walesby
Whaley
Whaley Thorns
Cuckney
Bolsover
Nether Langwith
Langwith
Meden Vale
Budby
Scarcliffe
Palterton
Church Warsop
Market Warsop
New Ollerton
Kirton
SHERWOOD FOREST

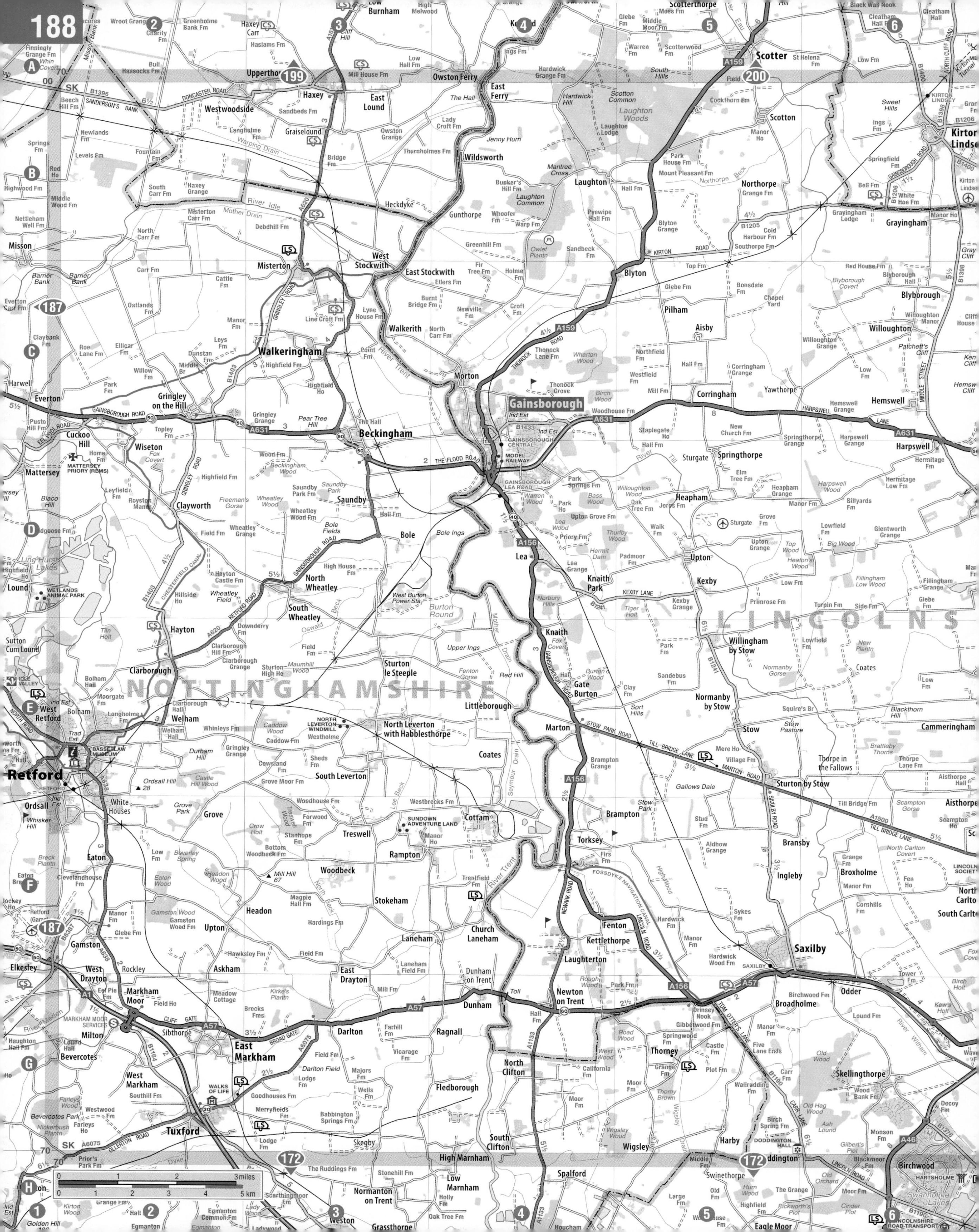
199
200
187
172
NOTTINGHAMSHIRE
LINCOLNS
Finningly Grange Fm
Wroot Grange
Charity Fm
Greenholme Bank Fm
Haxey Carr
Haslams Fm
Low Burnham
High Melwood
Cliff Hill
Scotterthorpe
Moss Fm
Glebe Fm
Middle Moor Fm
Warren Fm
Scotterwood Fm
Black Wall Nook
Cleatham Hall Fm
Cleatham Hall
Bull Hassocks Fm
Upperthorpe
Mill House Fm
Low Hall Fm
Owston Ferry
East Ferry
Ings Fm
Hardwick Grange Fm
South Hills
Scotter
St Helena Fm
Low Fm
Kirton Lindsey
Haxey
East Lound
The Hall
Scotton Common
Laughton Woods
Laughton Lodge
Cookthorn Fm
Scotton
Sweet Hills
Ings Fm
Westwoodside
Sandbeds Fm
Beech Hill Fm
Sanderson's Bank
Doncaster Road
Lady Croft Fm
Hardwick Hill
Newlands Fm
Langholme Fm
Graiselound
Owston Grange
Jenny Hurn
Manor Ho
Springs Fm
Levels Fm
Fountain Fm
Warping Drain
Thurnholmes Fm
Wildsworth
Park House Fm
Mount Pleasant Fm
Springfield Fm
Bridge Fm
Mantree Cross
Northorpe Beck
Red Ho
Highwood Fm
South Carr Fm
Haxey Grange
River Idle
Bunker's Hill Fm
Laughton Common
Laughton
Hall Fm
Northorpe
Northorpe Grange Fm
Bell Fm
White Hoe Fm
Middle Wood Fm
Heckdyke
Mother Drain
Misterton Carr Fm
Gunthorpe
Whoofer Fm
Warp Fm
Pyewipe Hall Fm
Blyton Grange
Cold Harbour Fm
Grayingham Lodge
Grayingham
Manor Ho
Nettleham Well Fm
Debdhill Fm
North Carr Fm
Greenhill Fm
Owlet Plantn
Sandbeck Fm
Kirton Road
Southorpe Fm
Misson
Misterton
West Stockwith
East Stockwith
Ellers Fm
Fir Tree Fm
Holme Fm
Blyton
Top Fm
Red House Fm
Blyborough Covert
Blyborough Hall
Gray Cliff
Carr Fm
Barrier Bank
Cattle Fm
Glebe Fm
Bonsdale Fm
Chapel Yard
Blyborough
Everton Carr Fm
Oatlands Fm
Lyne House Fm
Line Croft Fm
Burnt Bridge Fm
Newville Fm
Croft Fm
Pilham
Willoughton Manor
Willoughton
Cliff House
Manor Fm
Gringley Road
Walkerith
North Carr Fm
Aisby
Willoughton Grange
Patchett's Cliff
Claybank Fm
Roe Lane Fm
Ellicar Fm
Leys Fm
Dunstan Fm
Walkeringham
Highfield Fm
Point Fm
River Trent
Thonock Road
Thonock Lane Fm
Wharton Wood
Northfield Fm
Hall Fm
Corringham Grange
Low Fm
Ken Cliff
Middle Br
Willow Fm
Park Fm
Highfield Ho
Morton
Westfield Fm
Mill Fm
Thonock Grove
Birch Wood
Corringham
Yawthorpe
Hemswell Grange
Hemswell
Hemswell Cliff
Harwell
Everton
Gringley on the Hill
Gringley Grange
Pear Tree Hill
The Hall
Gainsborough
Ind Est
Woodhouse Fm
Harpswell Lane
Middle Street
Gainsborough Road
Pusto Hill Fm
Cuckoo Hill
Topley Fm
Beckingham
Staplegate Ho
New Church Fm
Springthorpe Grange
Harpswell Grange
Harpswell
Hermitage Fm
Wiseton
Fox Covert
Home Fm
Mattersey Priory (Rems)
Mattersey
Wood Fm
Beckingham Wood
The Flood Road
Gainsborough Central
Model Railway
Hall Fm
River Till
Sturgate
Springthorpe
Elm Tree Fm
Hermitage Low Fm
Highfield Fm
Leyfield Fm
Saundby Park Fm
Saundby Park
Gainsborough Lea Road
Park Springs Fm
Willoughton Wood
Heapham
Heapham Grange
Harpswell Wood
Billyards Fm
Blaco Hill
Royston Manor
Clayworth
Freeman's Gorse
Wheatley Wood
Saundby
Warren Wood
Bass Wood
Oak Tree Fm
Jorus Fm
Manor Fm
Wheatley Wood Fm
Hall Fm
Park Ho
Upton Grove Fm
Sturgate
Grove Fm
Lowfield Fm
Glentworth Grange
Bridgoose Fm
Field Fm
Wheatley Grange
Bole Fields
Bole
Bole Ings
Lea Wood
Priory Fm
Walk Fm
Thurlby Wood
Big Wood
Ling Hurst Lakes
Chesterfield Canal
Gainsborough Road
Lea
Hermit Dam
Padmoor Fm
Upton
Upton Grange
Top Wood
Heaton's Wood
Highfield Fm
High House Fm
Hayton Castle Fm
North Wheatley
Lea Grange
Knaith Park
Kexby Lane
Kexby
Fillingham Low Wood
Fillingham Grange
Lound
Wetlands Animal Park
Hillside Ho
Wheatley Field
West Burton Power Sta
Burton Round
Norbury Hills
Kexby Grange
Tiger Holt
Low Fm
Primrose Fm
Turpin Fm
Side Fm
Glebe Fm
Retford Road
South Wheatley
Oswald Beck
Mother Drain
Willingham by Stow
Lowfield Fm
New Plantn
Sutton Cum Lound
Tiln Holt
Hayton
Downderry Fm
Field Fm
Upper Ings
Knaith
Fox Covert
Park Fm
Clarborough Hill Fm
Clarborough Grange
Sturton High Ho
Maumhill Wood
Sturton le Steeple
Fenton Gorse
Red Hill
Burton Wood
Sandebus Fm
Normanby Gorse
Coates
Low Fm
Idle Valley
Clarborough
Bolham Hall
Moorgate Fm
Gate Burton
Clay Fm
Normanby by Stow
Squire's Br
Blackthorn Hill
West Retford
Bolham
Longholme Fm
Clarborough Hall
Welham
Littleborough
Sort Hills
Stow
Stow Pasture
Cammeringham
North Road
Trad Est
Bassetlaw Museum
Whinleys Fm
Welham Hall
Caddow Wood
Caddow Fm
North Leverton Windmill
North Leverton with Habblesthorpe
Westholme
Marton
Stow Park Road
Till Bridge Lane
Mere Ho
Brattleby Thorns
Gringley Grange
Durham Hill
Cawsland Fm
Sheds Fm
Coates
Brampton Grange
Village Fm
Marton Road
Thorpe in the Fallows
Thorpe Lane Fm
Retford
Ordsall Hill
Castle Hill Wood
Grove Moor Fm
South Leverton
Seymour Drain
Gallows Dale
Sturton by Stow
Aisthorpe Hall
Ordsall
White Houses
Grove Park
Grove
Woodhouse Fm
Westbrecks Fm
Lee Beck
Cottam
Brampton
Stow Park
Saxilby Road
Till Bridge Fm
Scampton Gorse
Aisthorpe
Whisker Hill
Treswell Wood
Forwood Fm
Crow Holt
Sundown Adventure Land
Stud Fm
Scampton Ho
Treswell
Stanhope Fm
Manor Ho
Torksey
Aldhow Grange
Bransby
North Carlton Covert
Eaton
Low Fm
Beverley Spring
Bottom Woodbeck Fm
Rampton
Flrs Fm
Fossdyke Navigation Canal
Grange Fm
Broxholme
Lincolnshire Society
Breck Plantn
Eaton Wood
Headon Wood
Mill Hill
Woodbeck
Trentfield Fm
Ingleby
Fen Ho
North Carlton
Eaton Brecks
Clevelandhouse Fm
Magpie Hall Fm
North Beck
Stokeham
Newark Road
Lincoln Road
Hardwick Fm
Manor Fm
Cornhills Fm
South Carlton
Headon
Hardings Fm
Sykes Fm
Manor Fm
Gamston Wood
Gamston Wood Fm
Upton
Church Laneham
Fenton
Kettlethorpe
Glebe Fm
Laneham
Hardwick Wood Fm
Saxilby
Gamston
Hawksley Fm
Field Fm
Laughterton
Elkesley
West Drayton
Rockley
Askham
East Drayton
Laneham Field Fm
Dunham on Trent
Rough Wood
Park Fm
Tower Fm
Birch Holt
Markham Moor
Meadow Cottage
Kirke's Plantn
Mill Fm
Toll
Newton on Trent
Birchwood Fm
Broadholme
Odder
Field Ho
Brecks Fms
Dunham
Hall Fm
Drinsey Nook
Gibbetwood Fm
Tom Otter's Lane
Lound Fm
Kew's Holt
Markham Moor Services
Milton
Sibthorpe
Cliff Gate
Broad Gate
Darlton
Farhill Fm
Ragnall
Road Wood
Springwood Fm
Manor Fm
Five Lane Ends
River Witham
Haughton Hall Fm
Lound Hall
Bevercotes
East Markham
Field Fm
Vicarage Fm
West Wood
Castle Fm
Thorney
Old Wood
River Meden
Darlton Field
Majors Fm
North Clifton
California Fm
Grange Fm
Plot Fm
Carr Fm
Skellingthorpe
West Markham
Southill Fm
Walks of Life
Lodge Fm
Wells Fm
Fledborough
Moor Fm
Wallrudding Fm
Old Hag Wood
Wood Bank Fm
Farleys Wood
Westwood Fm
Goodhouses Fm
Merryfields Fm
Babbington Springs Fm
Moor Fm
Thorny Brown
Birch Spring Fm
Ash Lound
Decoy Fm
Bevercotes Park
Farleys Fm
Nickerbush Plantn
Tuxford
Ollerton Road
Lodge Fm
Skegby
South Clifton
Wigsley Wood
Wigsley
Harby
Doddington Hall
Gilbert's Plot
Monson Fm
Carr Lane
Prior's Park Fm
Dyke
The Ruddings Fm
High Marnham
Middle Fm
Doddington
Blackmoor Fm
Birchwood
Hartsholme
Swanholme Lakes
Stonehill Fm
Low Marnham
Spalford
Swinethorpe
Old Orchard
Lincoln Road
Scarthingmoor Fm
Normanton on Trent
Holly Fm
Oak Tree Fm
Large Fm
Old Fm
Hurn Wood
The Grange
Moor Fm
Highfield Fm
Pickworth's Plot
Cinder Plot
Lincolnshire Road Transport
Kirton Wood
Grange Fm
Hall
Egmanton Common Fm
Ladywood
Weston
Grassthorpe
Houcham
Eagle Moor
Golden Hill
Egmanton
0 1 2 3 miles
0 1 2 3 4 5 km

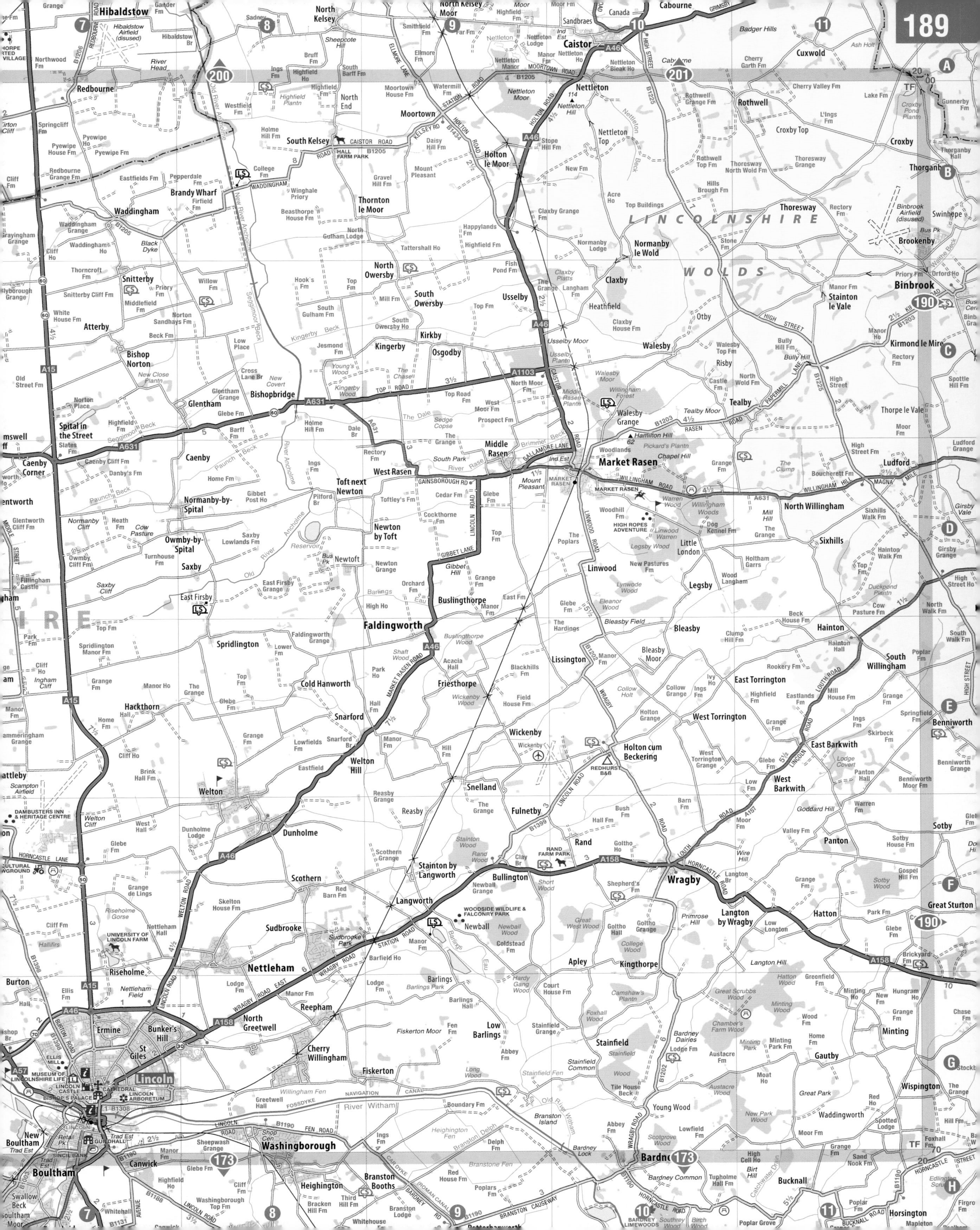

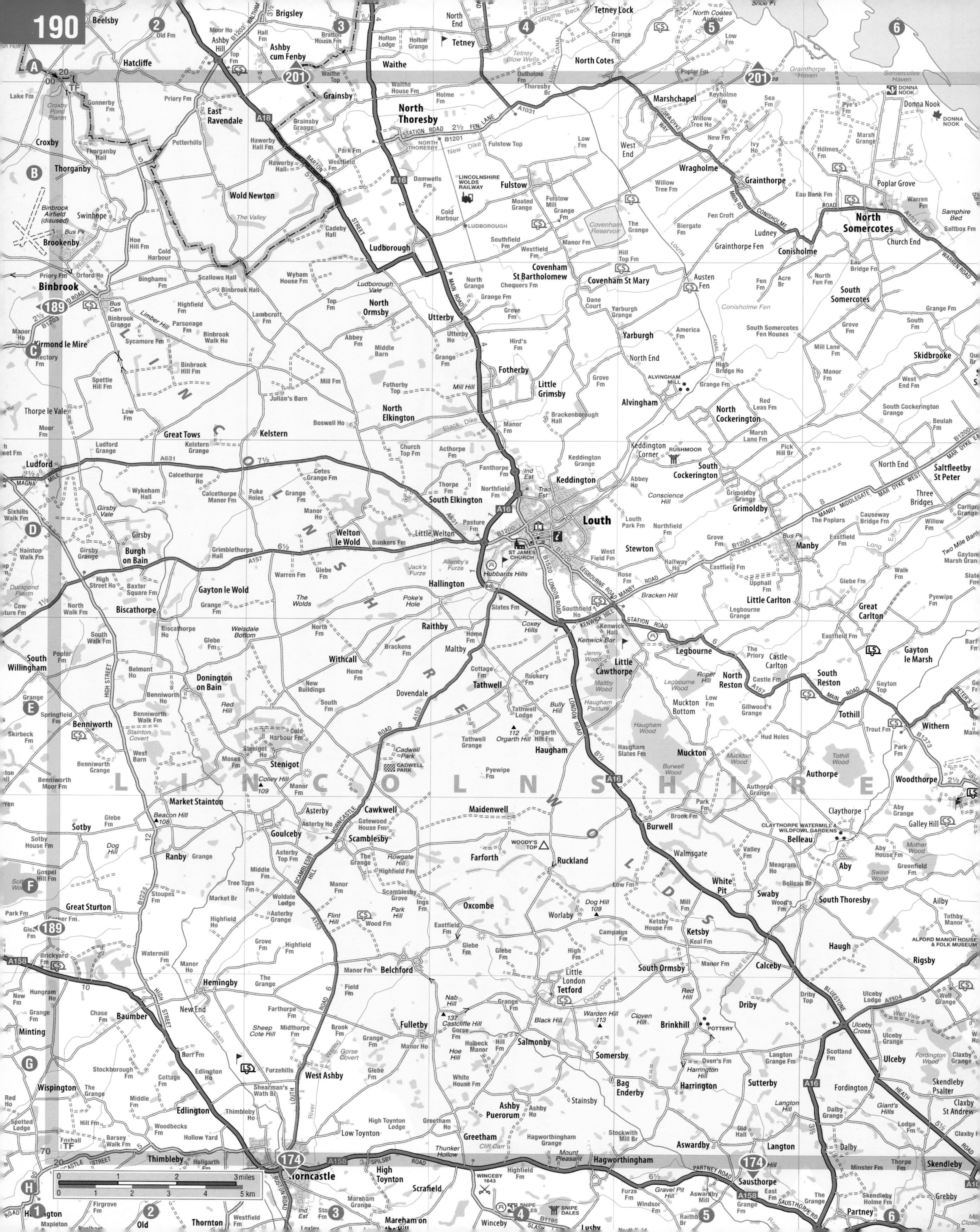

Beelsby
Brigsley
Tetney Lock
North Coates
Hatcliffe
Ashby cum Fenby
Waithe
North End
Tetney
North Cotes
Grainsby
North Thoresby
Marshchapel
East Ravendale
Croxby
Thorganby
Wold Newton
Fulstow
Wragholme
Grainthorpe
North Somercotes
Poplar Grove
Donna Nook
Swinhope
Brookenby
Ludborough
Covenham St Bartholomew
Covenham St Mary
Conisholme
Ludney
Church End
Binbrook
North Ormsby
Utterby
Yarburgh
South Somercotes
Kirmond le Mire
Fotherby
Little Grimsby
North End
Skidbrooke
Alvingham
Thorpe le Vale
North Elkington
North Cockerington
Great Tows
Kelstern
Ludford
Keddington
South Cockerington
Saltfleetby St Peter
South Elkington
Louth
Grimoldby
Manby
Welton le Wold
Little Welton
Stewton
Burgh on Bain
Girsby
Hallington
Gayton le Wold
Little Carlton
Great Carlton
Biscathorpe
Raithby
Legbourne
Gayton le Marsh
Maltby
Withcall
Little Cawthorpe
South Willingham
Castle Carlton
North Reston
South Reston
Donington on Bain
Tathwell
Dovendale
Tothill
Withern
Benniworth
Haugham
Muckton
Stenigot
Authorpe
Woodthorpe
L I N C O L N S H I R E
Market Stainton
Cawkwell
Maidenwell
Claythorpe
Sotby
Asterby
Goulceby
Scamblesby
Burwell
Belleau
Ranby
Farforth
Ruckland
Aby
Oxcombe
White Pit
Swaby
South Thoresby
Great Sturton
Worlaby
Ketsby
Belchford
South Ormsby
Calceby
Rigsby
Hemingby
Tetford
Baumber
Fulletby
Brinkhill
Driby
Minting
Salmonby
Somersby
Ulceby
West Ashby
Harrington
Sutterby
Wispington
Edlington
Bag Enderby
Ashby Puerorum
Fordington
Skendleby Psalter
Greetham
Aswardby
Langton
Thimbleby
Horncastle
High Toynton
Scrafield
Hagworthingham
Sausthorpe
Skendleby
Partney
Winceby
Lusby
Thornton
Old
Mareham on the Hill
A16
A18
A631
A157
A153
A158
A1031
A1104
B1200
B1201
B1203
B1225
B1373
189
201
174
miles
km

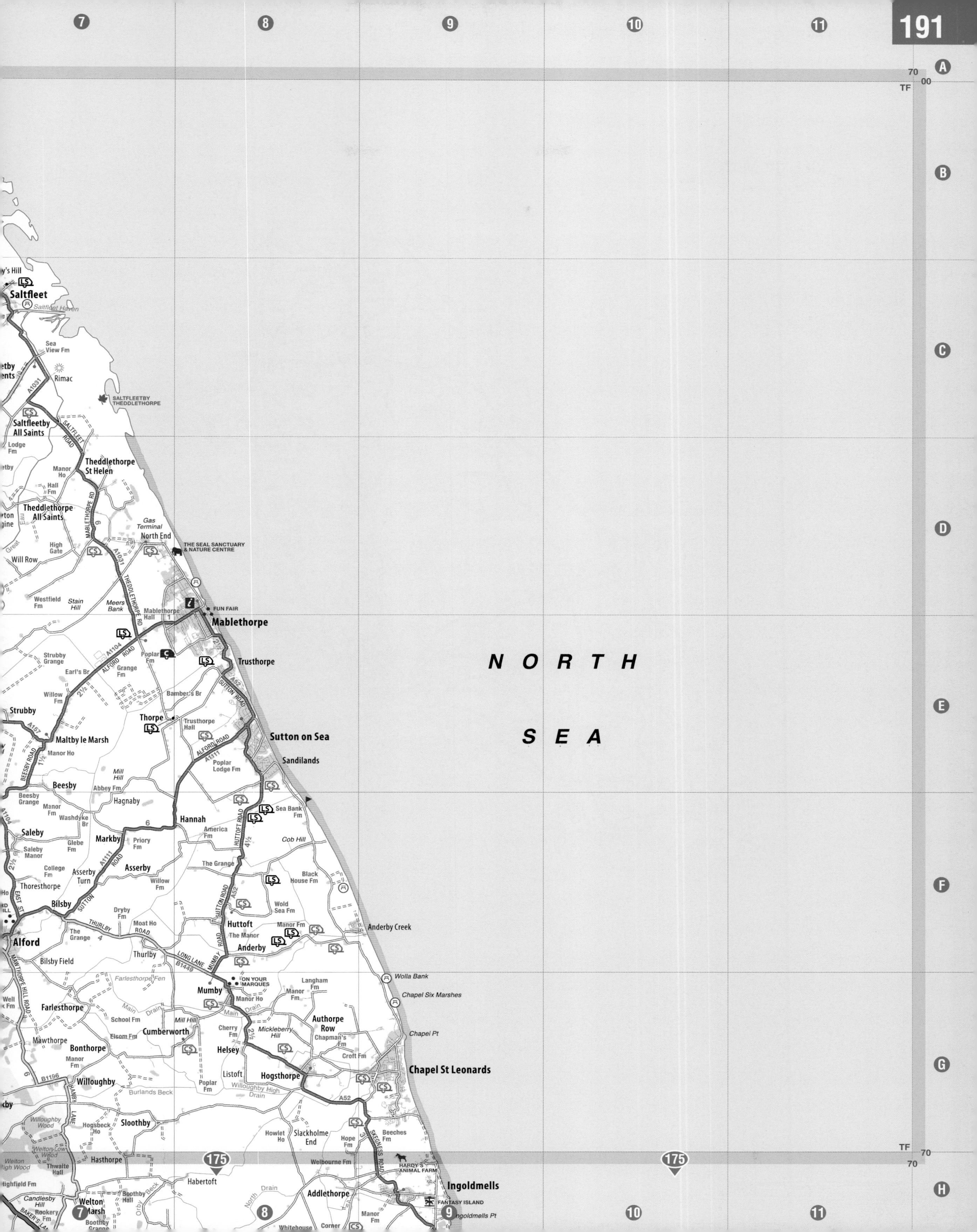

⑦ ⑧ ⑨ ⑩ ⑪

A
70
00
TF

B

C

Saltfleet
Saltfleet Haven
Sea View Fm
etby ents
Rimac

SALTFLEETBY THEDDLETHORPE

Saltfleetby All Saints
Lodge Fm
etby

Theddlethorpe St Helen
Manor Ho
Hall Fm

Theddlethorpe All Saints
ton gine
High Gate
Will Row
Great

Gas Terminal
North End
THE SEAL SANCTUARY & NATURE CENTRE

D

Westfield Fm
Stain Hill
Meers Bank

Mablethorpe Hall
FUN FAIR
Mablethorpe

NORTH

Strubby Grange
Earl's Br
Grange Fm
Poplar Fm
Trusthorpe

Willow Fm
Bamber's Br

Strubby
Thorpe
Trusthorpe Hall
Sutton on Sea

SEA

E

Maltby le Marsh
Manor Ho
Sandilands

Mill Hill
Poplar Lodge Fm

Beesby
Abbey Fm
Beesby Grange
Manor Fm
Washdyke Br
Hagnaby

Sea Bank Fm
Hannah
America Fm

Saleby
Markby
Priory Fm
Glebe Fm
Saleby Manor
Cob Hill

College Fm
Asserby
The Grange

Asserby Turn
Thoresthorpe
Willow Fm
Black House Fm

Ho LL
Bilsby

F

Dryby Fm
Moat Ho
Wold Sea Fm

Alford
The Grange
Huttoft
Manor Fm
Anderby Creek

Bilsby Field
Thurlby
The Manor
Anderby

Farlesthorpe Fen
Wolla Bank

Mumby
ON YOUR MARQUES
Manor Ho
Langham Fm
Manor Fm
Chapel Six Marshes

Farlesthorpe
School Fm
Mill Hill
Authorpe Row
Chapel Pt

Mawthorpe
Elsom Fm
Cumberworth
Cherry Fm
Mickleberry Hill
Chapman's Fm

Bonthorpe
Manor Fm
Helsey
Croft Fm

G

Willoughby
Listoft
Poplar Fm
Hogsthorpe
Chapel St Leonards

Burlands Beck
Willoughby High Drain
A52

kby
Hogsbeck Ho
Sloothby
Willoughby Wood

TF
70
70

Welton Low Wood
Thwaite Hall
Hasthorpe
175
Howlet Ho
Slackholme End
Hope Fm
Beeches Fm
HARDY'S ANIMAL FARM
Welbourne Fm
175
Ingoldmells

ighfield Fm
Candlesby Hill
Rookery
Welton Marsh
Boothby Hall
Habertoft
Addlethorpe
FANTASY ISLAND

⑦ ⑧ ⑨ ⑩ ⑪

H

Manor Fm
Ingoldmells Pt
Whitehouse Corner

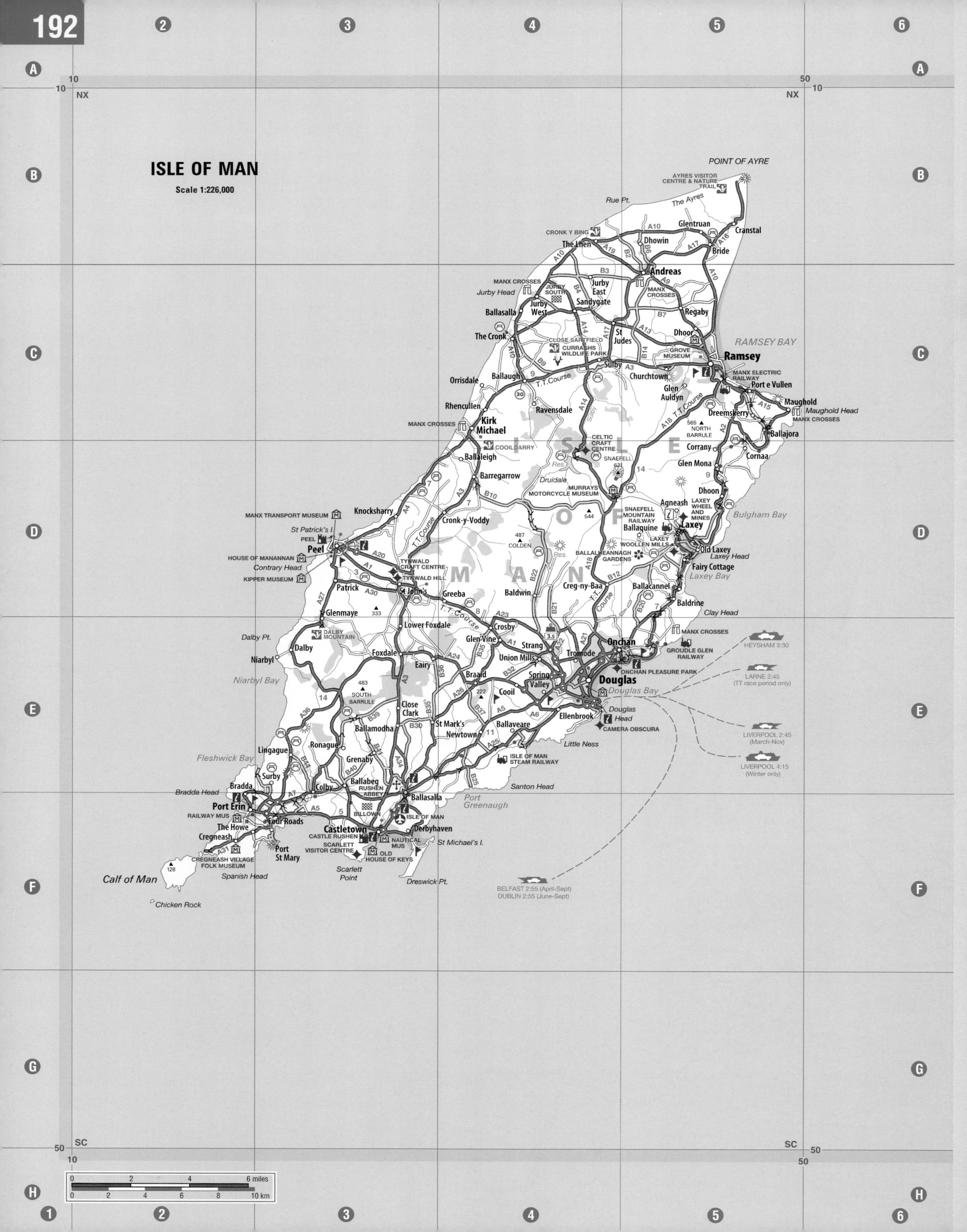

ISLE OF MAN

Scale 1:226,000

POINT OF AYRE

AYRES VISITOR
CENTRE & NATURE
TRAIL

Rue Pt.

The Ayres

CRONK Y BING

Glentruan
Cranstal
The Lhen
Dhowin
A17
Bride
A19
A10

B3
Andreas
A9

MANX CROSSES
Jurby
East
A10

Jurby Head
JURBY
SOUTH
Sandygate
MANX
CROSSES

Ballasalla
Jurby
West
Regaby
B7

The Cronk
CLOSE SARTFIELD
St
Jude's
A13
Dhoor

CURRAGHS
WILDLIFE PARK
GROVE
MUSEUM

RAMSEY BAY

Orrisdale
Ballaugh
9
Subby
A3
Ramsey

T.T.Course
Churchtown
MANX ELECTRIC
RAILWAY

Rhencullen
30
Glen
Auldyn
Port e Vullen

A14
Maughold

Kirk
Michael
A18 T.T. Course
Maughold Head
MANX CROSSES

MANX CROSSES
565
NORTH
BARRULE
Ballajora

Ballaleigh
COOILDARRY
Dreemskerry
A15

CELTIC
CRAFT
CENTRE
A2

Barregarrow
B10
Snaefell
621
Corrany
Cornaa

Druidale
MURRAYS
MOTORCYCLE MUSEUM
Glen Mona
9

MANX TRANSPORT MUSEUM
Knocksharry
A4
14

St Patrick's I.
Cronk-y-Voddy
544
Dhoon

PEEL
Agneash
LAXEY WHEEL
AND MINES

HOUSE OF MANANNAN
487
COLDEN
SNAEFELL
MOUNTAIN
RAILWAY
Bulgham Bay

Peel
A20
Laxey

Contrary Head
TYNWALD
CRAFT
CENTRE
Ballaquine
LAXEY
WOOLLEN MILLS

KIPPER MUSEUM
B22
BALLAHEANNAGH
GARDENS
Old Laxey
Laxey Head

Patrick
A30
TYNWALD HILL
St John's
Creg-ny-Baa
Fairy Cottage
Laxey Bay

Glenmaye
333
Greeba
B12
Ballacannel

Dalby Pt.
Lower Foxdale
Baldwin
B20
Baldrine

DALBY
MOUNTAIN
Crosby
Clay Head

Dalby
Glen Vine
A1
3.5
Onchan
MANX CROSSES

Niarbyl
Foxdale
Strang
Tromode
GROUDLE GLEN
RAILWAY
HEYSHAM 3:30

Niarbyl Bay
483
SOUTH
BARRULE
Eairy
Braaid
Spring
Valley
ONCHAN PLEASURE PARK
LARNE 2:45
(TT race period only)

14
222
Cooil
Douglas

Lingague
Close
Clark
St Mark's
Newtown
11
Ballaveare
A6
Ellenbrook
Douglas Bay
LIVERPOOL 2:45
(March-Nov)

Ronague
Ballamodha
B30
*Douglas
Head*
CAMERA OBSCURA

Surby
Grenaby
ISLE OF MAN STEAM RAILWAY
Little Ness
LIVERPOOL 4:15
(Winter only)

Bradda
Colby
Ballabeg
RUSHEN ABBEY
Ballasalla
*Port
Greenaugh*

Bradda Head
Port Erin
A5
5
BILLOWN
ISLE OF MAN
Santon Head

RAILWAY MUS
Four Roads
Derbyhaven

The Howe
Castletown
St Michael's I.

Cregneash
CASTLE RUSHEN
NAUTICAL
MUS

Fleshwick Bay
Port
St Mary
SCARLETT
VISITOR
CENTRE
OLD
HOUSE OF KEYS
Dreswick Pt.

CREGNEASH VILLAGE
FOLK MUSEUM
128
*Scarlett
Point*

Calf of Man
Spanish Head
BELFAST 2:55 (April-Sept)
DUBLIN 2:55 (June-Sept)

Chicken Rock

0   2   4   6 miles
0 2 4 6 8 10 km

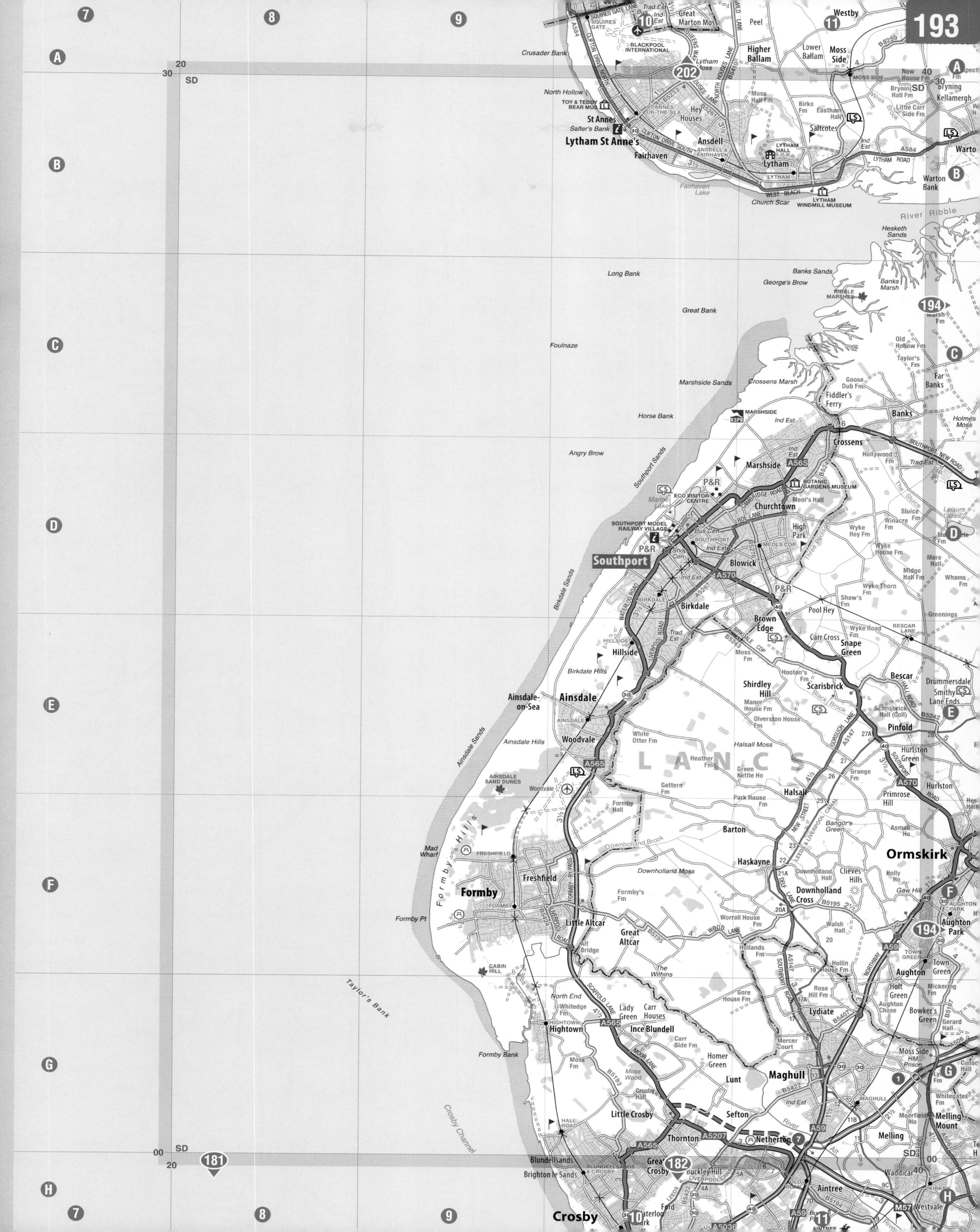
Westby
Great Marton Moss
Peel
Higher Ballam
Lower Ballam
Moss Side
Blackpool International
Crusader Bank
North Hollow
Toy & Teddy Bear Mus
St Annes
Salter's Bank
Lytham St Anne's
Fairhaven
Ansdell
Hey Houses
Moss Hall Fm
Birks Fm
Eastham Hall
Saltcotes
Lytham Hall
Lytham
Lytham Windmill Museum
Fairhaven Lake
Church Scar
Brynin Hall Fm
Little Carr Side Fm
Kellamergh
Warton Bank
River Ribble
Hesketh Sands
Long Bank
Banks Sands
George's Brow
Banks Marsh
Ribble Marshes
Great Bank
Foulnaze
Marshside Sands
Crossens Marsh
Old Hollow Fm
Taylor's Fm
Goose Dub Fm
Fiddler's Ferry
Far Banks
Banks
Horse Bank
Marshside
Holmes Moss
Angry Brow
Southport Sands
Crossens
Hollywood Fm
Botanic Gardens Museum
Meol's Hall
Eco Visitor Centre
Marine Lake
Churchtown
Southport Model Railway Village
High Park
Wyke Hey Fm
Winacre Fm
Sluice Fm
Leisure Lakes
Southport
Blowick
Wyke House Fm
Mere Hall
Midge Hall Fm
Whams Fm
Birkdale Sands
Birkdale
Wyke Thorn Fm
Shaw's Fm
Pool Hey
Greenings
Brown Edge
Carr Cross
Wyke Road Fm
Snape Green
Hillside
Moss Fm
Birkdale Hills
Hooton's Fm
Shirdley Hill
Scarisbrick
Bescar
Drummersdale
Smithy Lane Ends
Manor House Fm
Olverston House Fm
Scarisbrick Hall (Coll)
Ainsdale-on-Sea
Ainsdale
Pinfold
Ainsdale Sands
Woodvale
White Otter Fm
Halsall Moss
Hurlston Green
Ainsdale Hills
Heather Fm
LANCS
Green Kettle Ho
Grange Fm
Hurlston
Ainsdale Sand Dunes
Gettern Fm
Halsall
Primrose Hill
Formby Hall
Park House Fm
Bangor's Green
Asmall Ho
Barton
Mad Wharf
Formby Hills
Downholland Brook
Ormskirk
Freshfield
Haskayne
Downholland Moss
Downholland Hall
Clieves Hills
Holly Ho
Gaw Hill
Formby
Formby's Fm
Downholland Cross
Formby Pt
Little Altcar
Worrall House Fm
Aughton Park
Great Altcar
Walsh Hall
Alt Bridge
Hollands Fm
Town Green
Cabin Hill
The Withins
Hollin House Fm
Aughton
Taylor's Bank
North End
Gore House Fm
Rose Hill Fm
Holt Green
Mickering Fm
Whitedge Fm
Lady Green
Carr Houses
Aughton Chase
Bowker's Green
Hightown
Ince Blundell
Lydiate
Carr Side Fm
Mercer Court
Moss Side
HM Prison
Formby Bank
Moss Fm
Homer Green
Lunt
Maghull
Moss Wood
Crosby Hall
Ind Est
Whitegates Fm
Crosby Channel
Little Crosby
Sefton
Moorfield Ho
Melling Mount
Melling
Thornton
Netherton
Blundellsands
Great Crosby
Buckley Hill
Waddicar
Brighton le Sands
Aintree
Westvale
Crosby
Waterloo Park
Ford
A584
A565
A570
A5147
A59
A5207
M57
B5195
B5422
B5407
B5242
202
181
182
194
SD

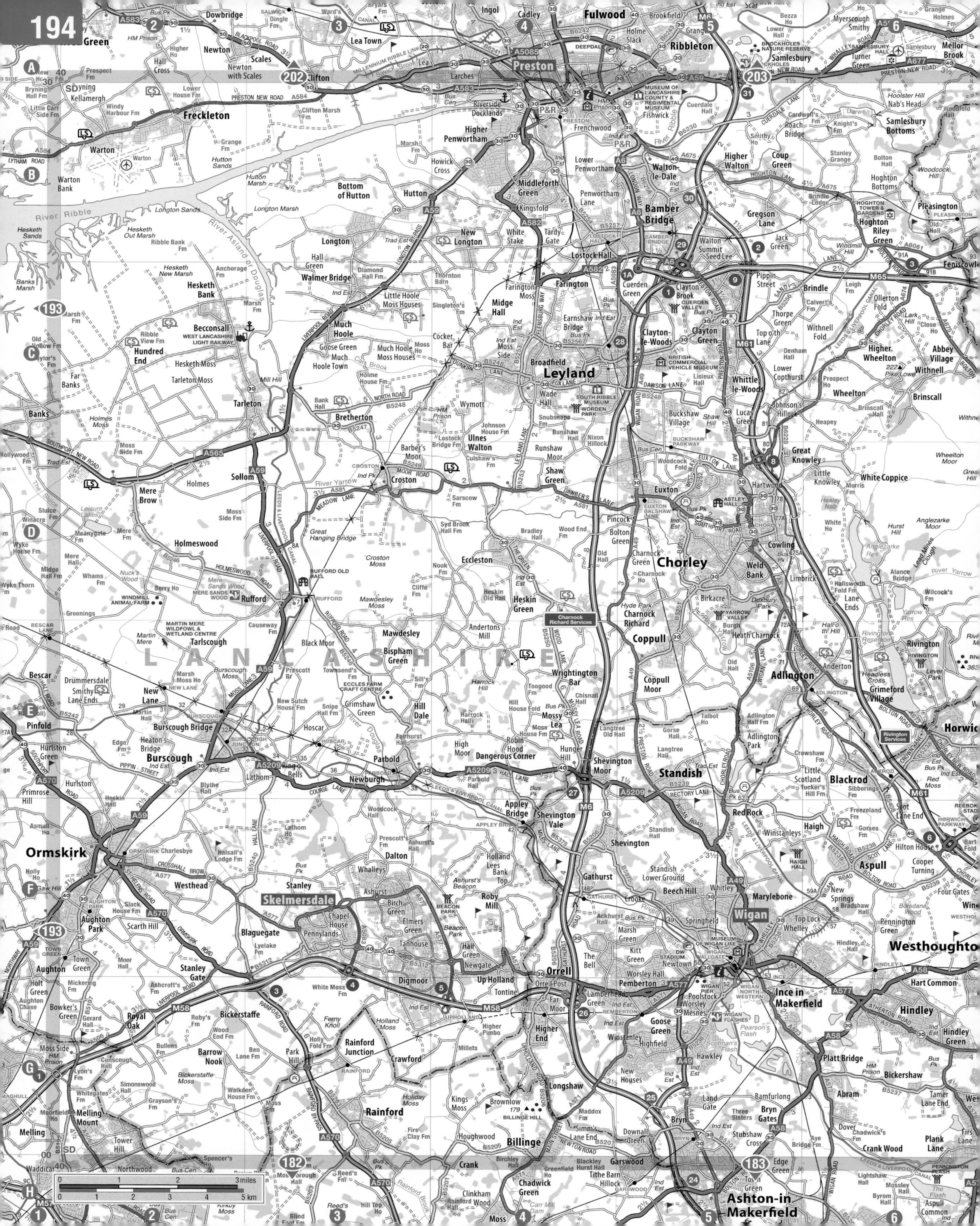
194
Preston
Fulwood
Ribbleton
Ingol
Cadley
Lea Town
Clifton
Newton with Scales
Scales
Freckleton
Warton
Lytham Road
Samlesbury
Mellor Brook
Higher Penwortham
Lower Penwortham
Riverside Docklands
Frenchwood
Fishwick
Walton-le-Dale
Bamber Bridge
Higher Walton
Coup Green
Hoghton
Pleasington
River Ribble
Longton Sands
Longton Marsh
Bottom of Hutton
Hutton
Middleforth Green
Kingsfold
Longton
New Longton
Lostock Hall
Farington
Walmer Bridge
Hesketh Bank
Much Hoole
Midge Hall
Leyland
Broadfield
Clayton-le-Woods
Clayton Green
Whittle-le-Woods
Wheelton
Brinscall
Becconsall
Tarleton
Hundred End
Banks
Bretherton
Croston
Ulnes Walton
Euxton
Chorley
Buckshaw Village
Great Knowley
White Coppice
Holmeswood
Sollom
Mere Brow
Rufford
Eccleston
Heskin Green
Mawdesley
Charnock Richard
Coppull
Adlington
Rivington
Horwich
Tarlscough
Bescar
New Lane
Burscough Bridge
Burscough
Parbold
Newburgh
Lathom
Shevington Moor
Standish
Blackrod
LANCASHIRE
Ormskirk
Westhead
Dalton
Appley Bridge
Shevington Vale
Shevington
Gathurst
Aspull
Skelmersdale
Aughton Park
Aughton
Up Holland
Orrell
Pemberton
Wigan
Ince in Makerfield
Hindley
Westhoughton
Bickerstaffe
Rainford Junction
Rainford
Billinge
Garswood
Ashton-in-Makerfield
Abram
Platt Bridge
Melling Mount
Melling
Crank
Chadwick Green
Bryn
Goose Green
Higher End
Marylebone
Haigh
M6
M61
M65
M58
A59
A6
A49
A5209
A570
A577
202
203
193
182
183
0 1 2 3 miles
0 1 2 3 4 5 km

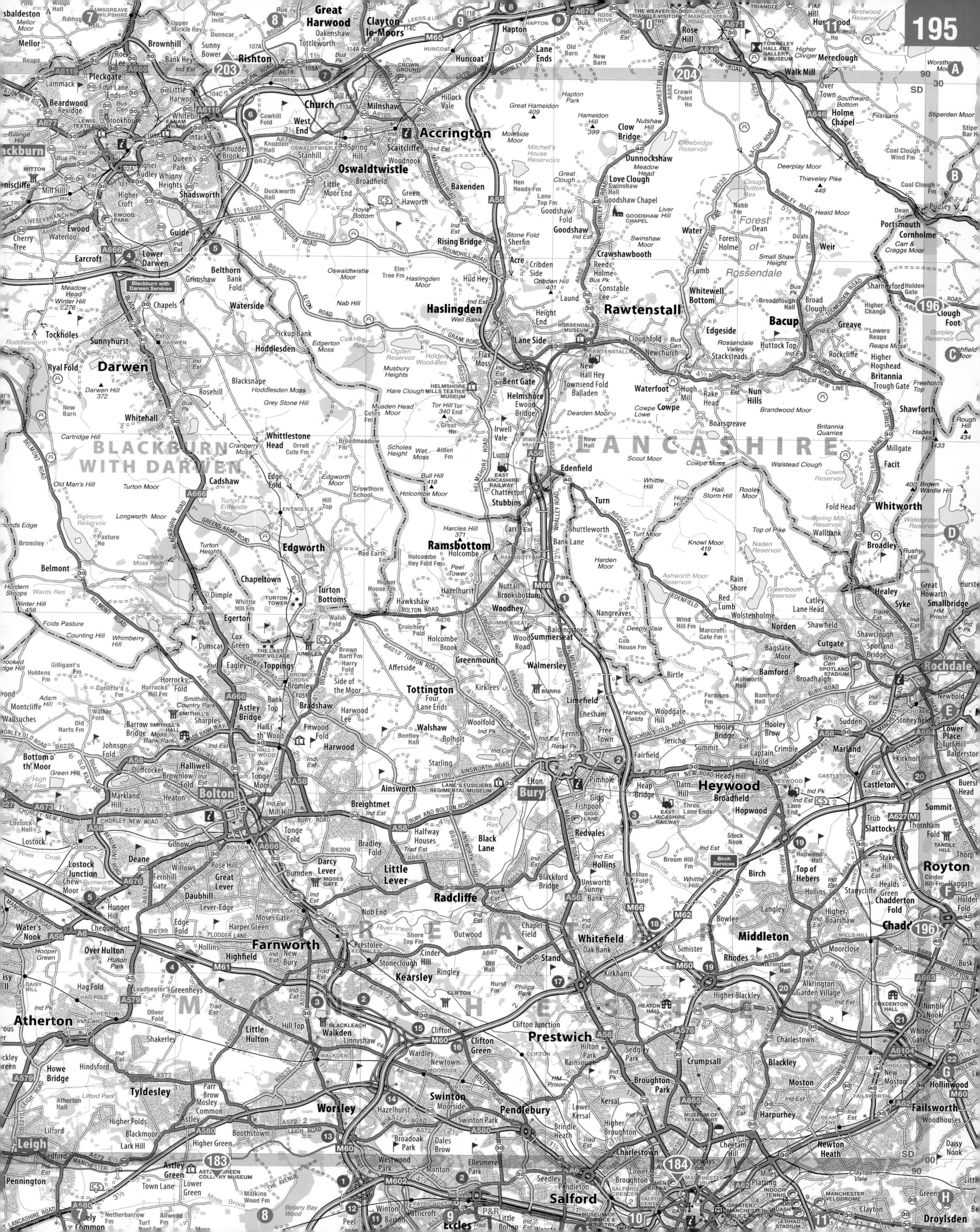
Great Harwood
Clayton-le-Moors
Rishton
Accrington
Oswaldtwistle
Church
Blackburn
Darwen
BLACKBURN WITH DARWEN
Haslingden
Rawtenstall
Bacup
LANCASHIRE
Ramsbottom
Edgworth
Edenfield
Whitworth
Rochdale
Bury
Bolton
Heywood
Middleton
Royton
Radcliffe
Farnworth
Little Lever
Prestwich
Whitefield
Atherton
Tyldesley
Walkden
Worsley
Swinton
Pendlebury
Salford
Leigh
Eccles
Failsworth
Droylsden
GREATER MANCHESTER

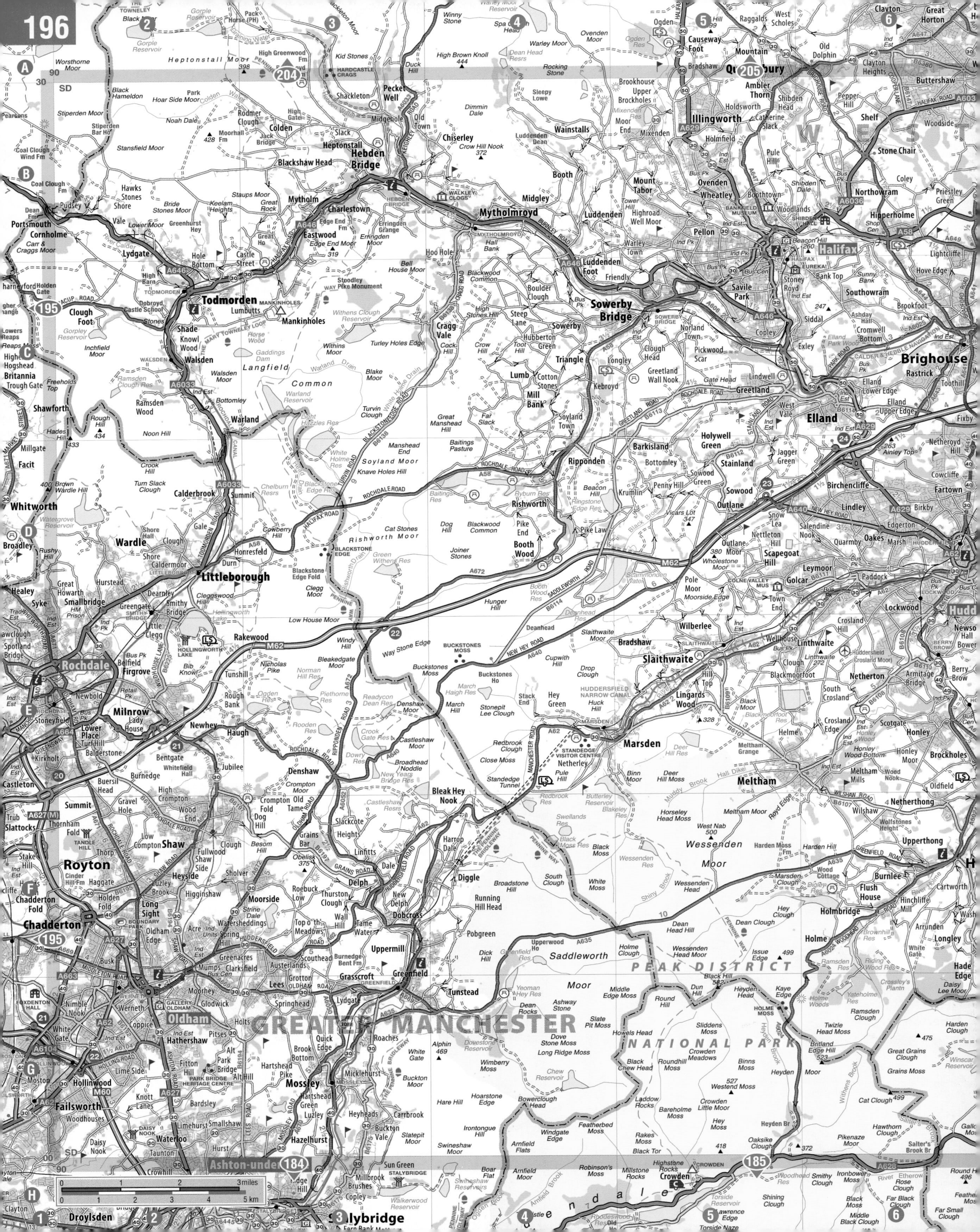

Heptonstall Moor
Hebden Bridge
Heptonstall
Colden
Blackshaw Head
Pecket Well
Old Town
Chiserley
Wainstalls
Illingworth
Queensbury
Mountain
Causeway Foot
Ogden
Clayton
Great Horton
West Scholes
Raggalds
Shelf
Stone Chair
Northowram
Hipperholme
Halifax
Lightcliffe
Hove Edge
Brighouse
Rastrick
Elland
Southowram
Siddal
Copley
Sowerby Bridge
Savile Park
Pellon
Ovenden
Wheatley
Mount Tabor
Luddenden
Luddenden Foot
Midgley
Mytholmroyd
Mytholm
Charlestown
Eastwood
Todmorden
Lumbutts
Mankinholes
Cornholme
Portsmouth
Lydgate
Walsden
Cragg Vale
Sowerby
Triangle
Ripponden
Rishworth
Booth Wood
Barkisland
Stainland
Greetland
Holywell Green
Outlane
Lindley
Birchencliffe
Fartown
Golcar
Leymoor
Scapegoat Hill
Slaithwaite
Linthwaite
Lockwood
Netherton
Marsden
Meltham
Honley
Brockholes
Netherthong
Upperthong
Holmbridge
Holme
Hade Edge
Wessenden Moor
Littleborough
Wardle
Calderbrook
Summit
Whitworth
Shawforth
Facit
Healey
Rochdale
Smallbridge
Milnrow
Newhey
Rakewood
Firgrove
Belfield
Denshaw
Delph
Dobcross
Diggle
Uppermill
Greenfield
Grasscroft
Lees
Springhead
Mossley
Stalybridge
Ashton-under-Lyne
Droylsden
Failsworth
Hollinwood
Oldham
Chadderton
Royton
Shaw
Moorside
Hathershaw
Waterloo
Hazelhurst
Saddleworth Moor
Crowden
GREATER MANCHESTER
PEAK DISTRICT
NATIONAL PARK
WEST
Longdendale
204
205
195
184
185
M62
A62
A58
A646
A629
A640
A672
A635
A627
A6033
0 1 2 3 miles
0 1 2 3 4 5 km

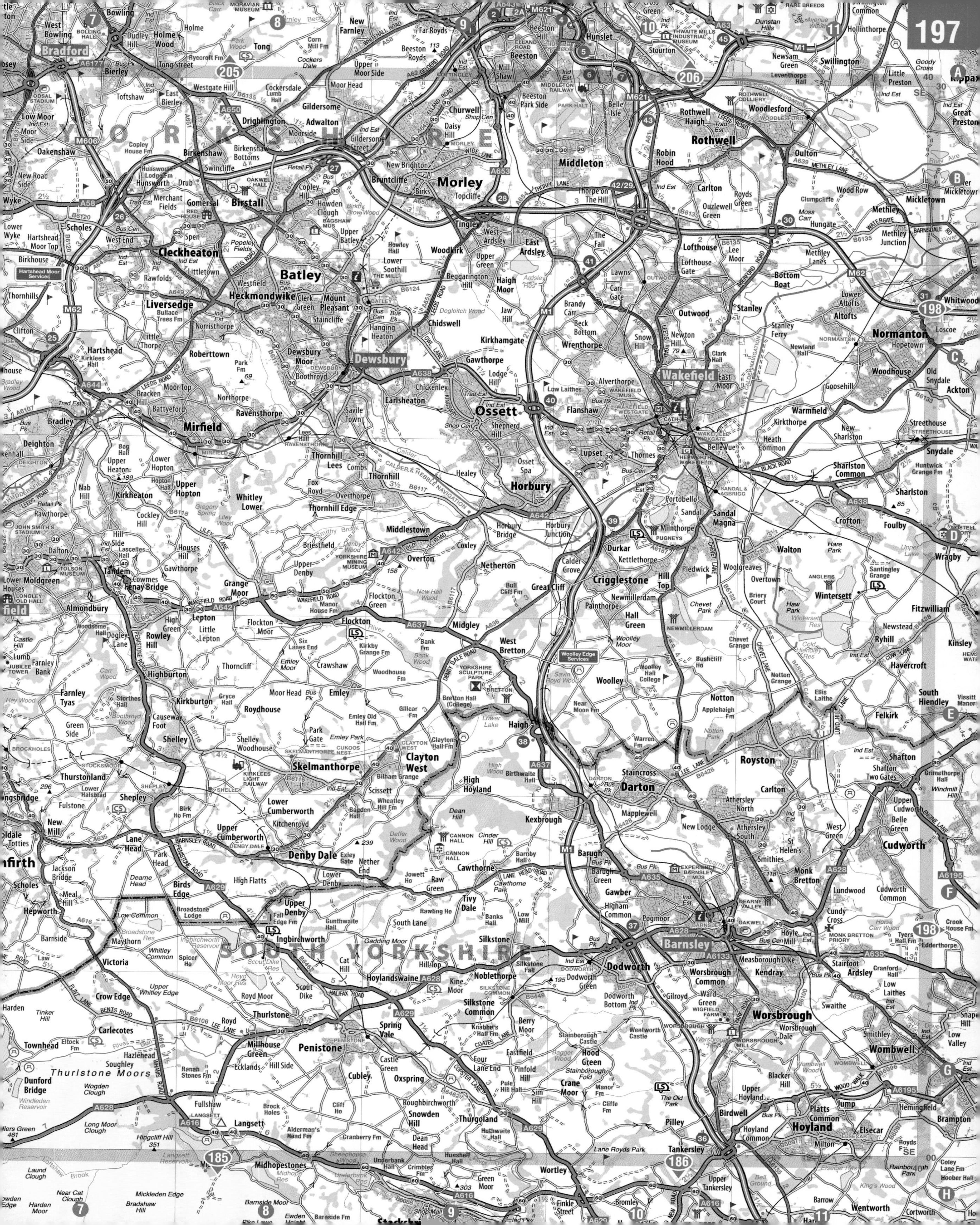
Bradford
Dewsbury
Wakefield
Barnsley
Batley
Morley
Ossett
Horbury
Mirfield
Cleckheaton
Heckmondwike
Liversedge
Birstall
Rothwell
Middleton
Normanton
Cudworth
Worsbrough
Wombwell
Hoyland
Penistone
Denby Dale
Skelmanthorpe
Clayton West
Darton
Royston
Crigglestone
Dodworth
Y O R K S H I R E
SOUTH YORKSHIRE
Thurlstone Moors
205
206
198
185
186

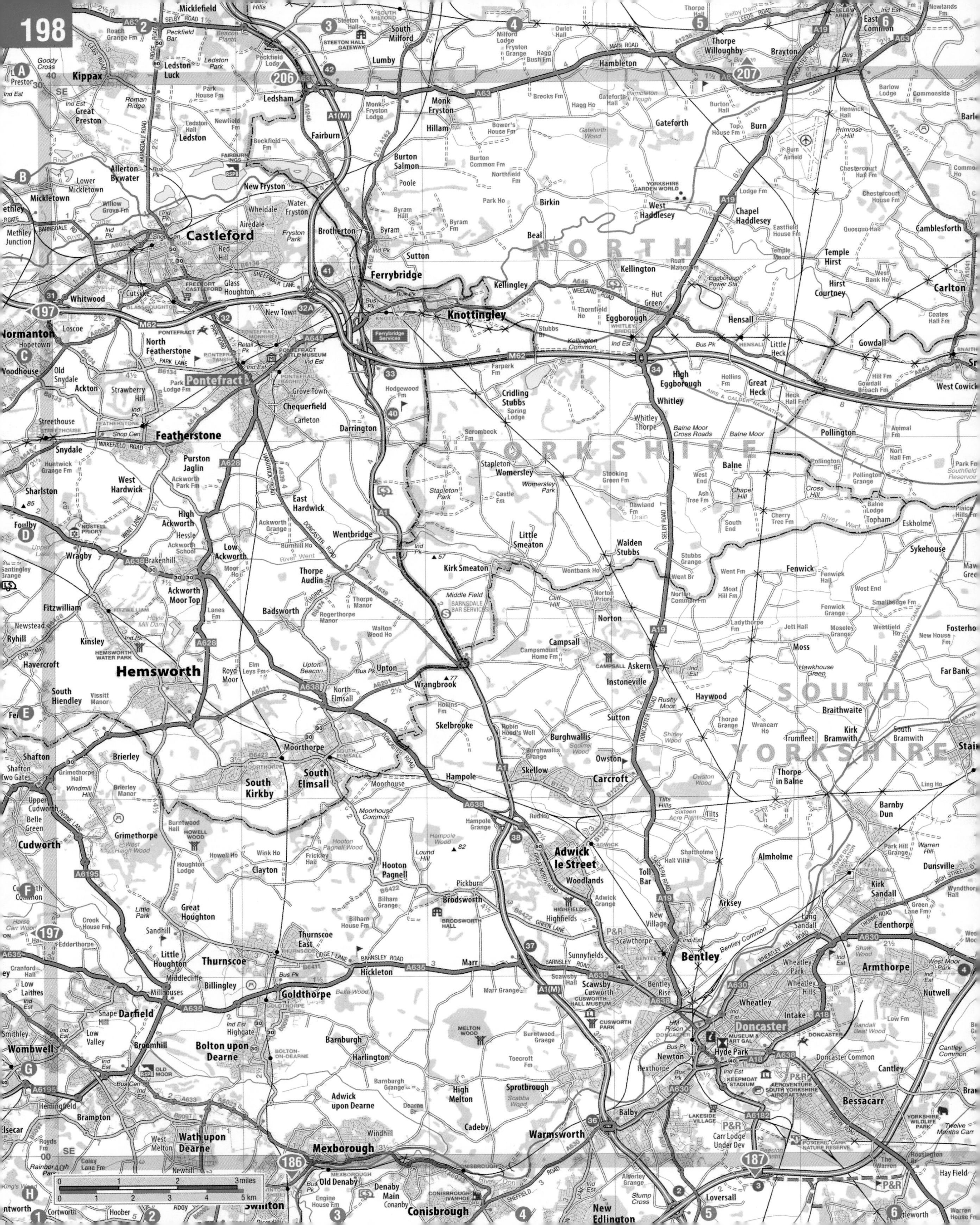
Micklefield
Kippax
Ledston Luck
Ledston
Great Preston
Ledsham
Fairburn
Lumby
South Milford
Monk Fryston
Hillam
Burton Salmon
Hambleton
Thorpe Willoughby
Brayton
Gateforth
Burn
Allerton Bywater
Mickletown
Lower Mickletown
New Fryston
Water Fryston
Brotherton
Byram
Birkin
West Haddlesey
Chapel Haddlesey
Camblesforth
Castleford
Red Hill
Glass Houghton
Sutton
Ferrybridge
Beal
Kellingley
Kellington
Temple Hirst
Hirst Courtney
Carlton
NORTH
Whitwood
Normanton
Knottingley
Eggborough
Hensall
Gowdall
Little Heck
Great Heck
High Eggborough
Whitley
West Cowick
North Featherstone
Pontefract
Ackton
Strawberry Hill
Chequerfield
Carleton
Darrington
Cridling Stubbs
Whitley Thorpe
Pollington
Featherstone
Snydale
Purston Jaglin
West Hardwick
Sharlston
High Ackworth
Stapleton
Womersley
Balne
YORKSHIRE
East Hardwick
Wentbridge
Little Smeaton
Walden Stubbs
Topham
Eskholme
Sykehouse
Wragby
Low Ackworth
Thorpe Audlin
Kirk Smeaton
Fenwick
Ackworth Moor Top
Fitzwilliam
Badsworth
Norton
Ryhill
Kinsley
Campsall
Moss
Fosterhouses
Havercroft
Hemsworth
Upton
Askern
Instoneville
Far Bank
Wrangbrook
Haywood
South Hiendley
North Elmsall
Skelbrooke
Sutton
Braithwaite
SOUTH
Kirk Bramwith
Shafton
Brierley
Moorthorpe
Burghwallis
Owston
Trumfleet
South Bramwith
South Kirkby
South Elmsall
Hampole
Skellow
Carcroft
Thorpe in Balne
Upper Cudworth
Barnby Dun
Cudworth
Grimethorpe
Clayton
Hooton Pagnell
Adwick le Street
Woodlands
Toll Bar
Almholme
Dunsville
Kirk Sandall
Great Houghton
Brodsworth
Highfields
Arksey
Edenthorpe
Thurnscoe East
Thurnscoe
Little Houghton
Hickleton
Marr
Bentley
Armthorpe
Billingley
Goldthorpe
Scawsby
Cusworth
Wheatley
Intake
Nutwell
Darfield
Bolton upon Dearne
Barnburgh
Harlington
Doncaster
Hyde Park
Newton
Cantley
Wombwell
Broomhill
Sprotbrough
High Melton
Adwick upon Dearne
Bessacarr
Brampton
Wath upon Dearne
West Melton
Cadeby
Warmsworth
Balby
Mexborough
Old Denaby
Denaby Main
Conisbrough
Swinton
New Edlington
Loversall
Hay Field
0 1 2 3 miles
0 1 2 3 4 5 km

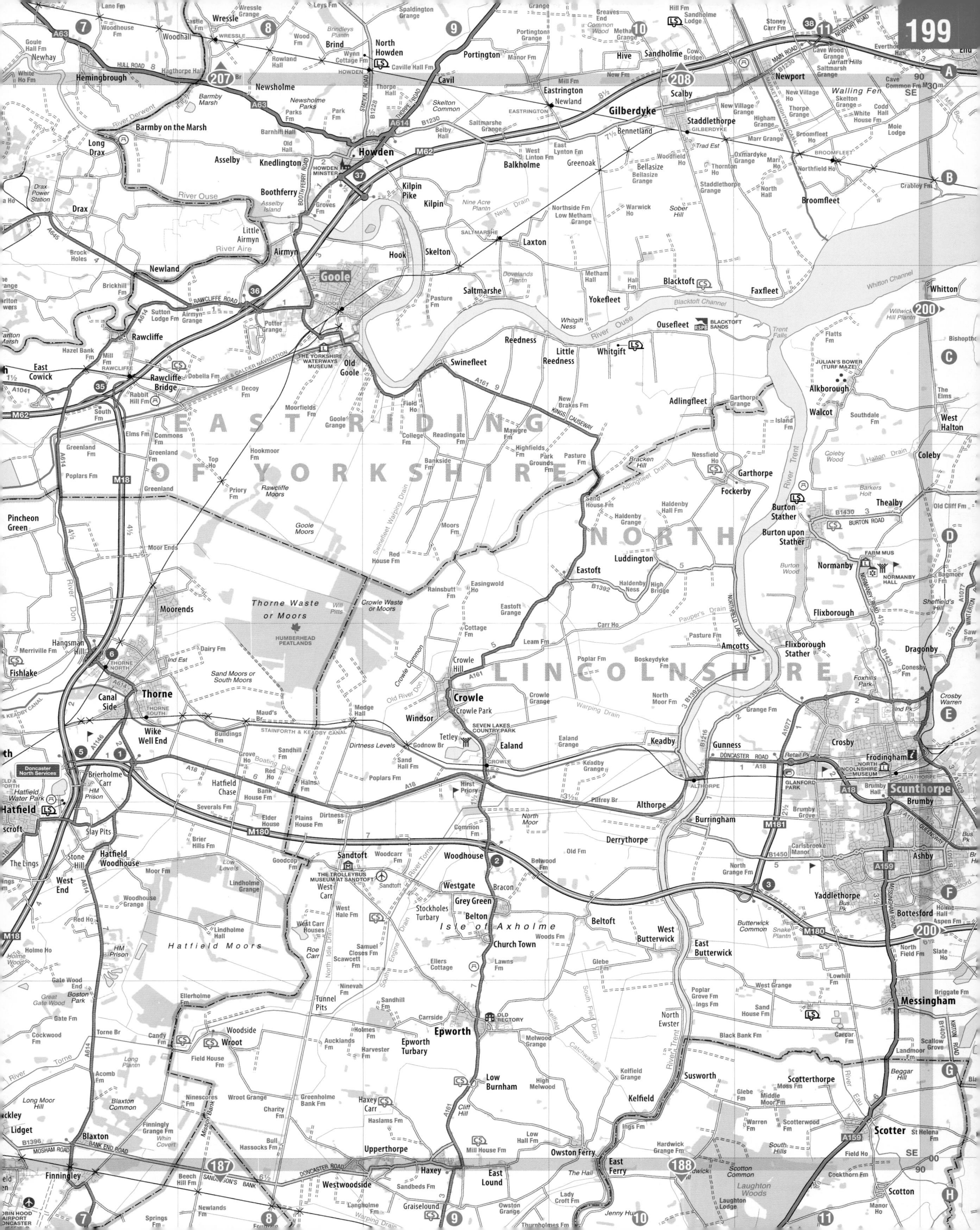

EAST RIDING OF YORKSHIRE
NORTH LINCOLNSHIRE
Goole
Howden
Gilberdyke
Scunthorpe
Thorne
Crowle
Epworth
Hatfield
Isle of Axholme
Thorne Waste or Moors
Hatfield Moors
River Ouse
River Trent
River Aire
Whitton Channel
Blacktoft Channel
Drax
Rawcliffe
Swinefleet
Reedness
Ousefleet
Whitgift
Adlingfleet
Garthorpe
Fockerby
Luddington
Eastoft
Amcotts
Keadby
Gunness
Althorpe
Burringham
Crosby
Frodingham
Brumby
Ashby
Bottesford
Yaddlethorpe
Messingham
Scotter
Scotton
Burton upon Stather
Normanby
Flixborough
Alkborough
Walcot
West Halton
Whitton
Coleby
Thealby
Dragonby
Belton
Westgate
Woodhouse
Sandtoft
Haxey
Westwoodside
Owston Ferry
East Ferry
Kelfield
Susworth
Scotterthorpe
Finningley
Blaxton
Wroot
Moorends
Stainforth & Keadby Canal
Aire & Calder Navigation
M62
M18
M180
M181
A63
A614
A161
A18
A159
A1077
B1392

207
208
200
187
188

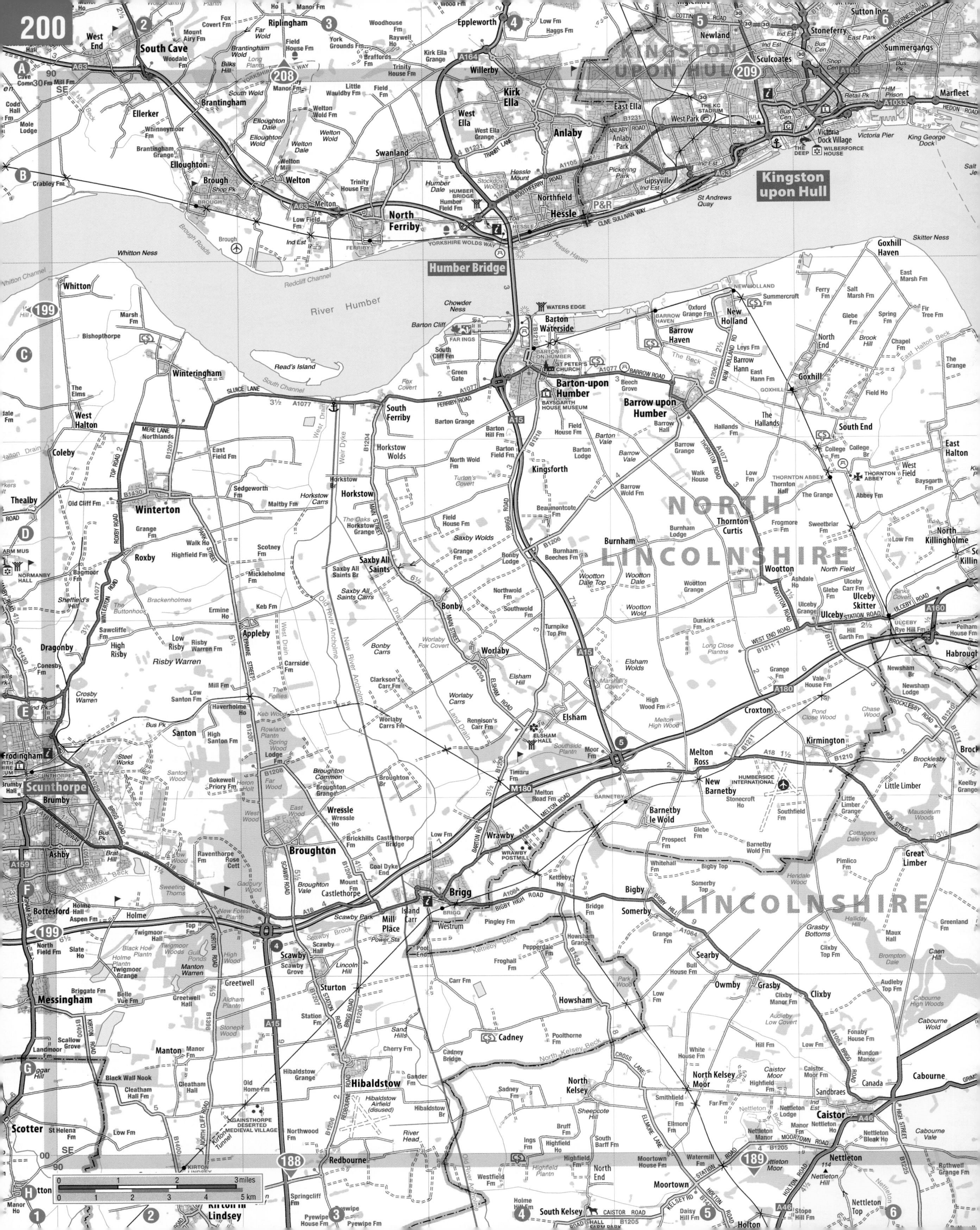
West End
South Cave
Riplingham
Eppleworth
Newland
Kingston upon Hull
Sculcoates
Stoneferry
Sutton Ings
East Park
Summergangs
Marfleet
Ellerker
Brantingham
Willerby
Kirk Ella
West Ella
Anlaby
East Ella
West Park
Anlaby Park
Swanland
Elloughton
Brough
Welton
Melton
North Ferriby
Hessle
Northfield
Gipsyville
Victoria Dock Village
Victoria Pier
King George Dock
The Deep
Wilberforce House
Humber Bridge
River Humber
Whitton Ness
Redcliff Channel
Whitton
Read's Island
Winteringham
West Halton
Coleby
Thealby
Winterton
Roxby
Barton Waterside
Barton-upon Humber
Baysgarth House Museum
Barrow Haven
Barrow upon Humber
New Holland
Goxhill Haven
Goxhill
South End
East Halton
South Ferriby
Horkstow
Horkstow Wolds
Kingsforth
Thornton Curtis
Thornton Abbey
North Killingholme
North Lincolnshire
Wootton
Ulceby
Ulceby Skitter
Saxby All Saints
Bonby
Appleby
Dragonby
Risby Warren
Worlaby
Elsham
Elsham Hall
Croxton
Santon
Frodingham
Scunthorpe
Brumby
Ashby
Bottesford
Kirmington
Melton Ross
New Barnetby
Barnetby le Wold
Humberside International
Little Limber
Great Limber
Wressle
Broughton
Wrawby
Wrawby Postmill
Brigg
Castlethorpe
Holme
Scawby
Sturton
Messingham
Manton
Hibaldstow
Scotter
Redbourne
Kirton in Lindsey
Howsham
Cadney
Bigby
Somerby
Searby
Owmby
Grasby
Clixby
North Kelsey
North Kelsey Moor
Caistor
Cabourne
Nettleton
Moortown
South Kelsey
Holton
Lincolnshire
0 1 2 3 miles
0 1 2 3 4 5 km

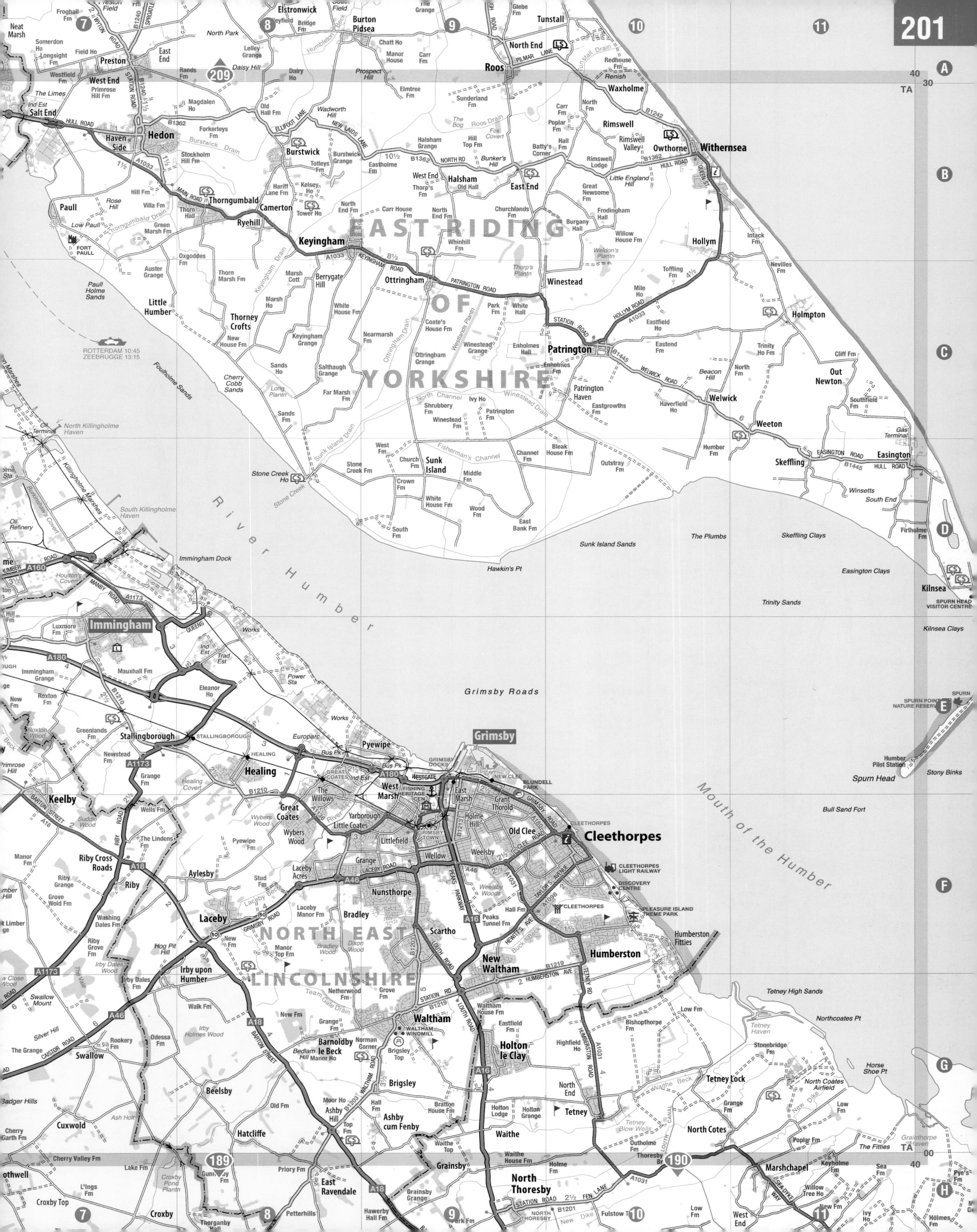
Neat Marsh
Froghall Fm
Somerdon Ho
Longsight Fm
Field Ho
Preston
East End
Westfield Fm
West End
Primrose Hill Fm
The Limes
Ind Est
Salt End
HULL ROAD
Haven Side
Hedon
Elstronwick
Burton Pidsea
Bridge Fm
North Park
Lelley Grange
Daisy Hill
Rands Fm
Dairy Ho
Magdalen Ho
Chatt Ho
Manor House
Carr Fm
Prospect Hill
Elmtree Fm
Glebe Fm
Tunstall
North End
Roos
PILMAR LANE
Redhouse Fm
Renish
Waxholme
Old Hall Fm
Forkerleys Fm
Burstwick Drain
Stockholm Hill Fm
Burstwick
Wadworth Hill
ELLIFOOT LANE
NEW LAIDS LANE
Sunderland Fm
The Bog
Roos Drain
Fox Covert
Carr Fm
Poplar Fm
North Fm
Rimswell
Rimswell Valley
Owthorne
Withernsea
Burstwick Grange
Totleys Fm
Halsham Grange
Hill Top Fm
Bunker's Hill
Batty's Corner
Hall Fm
Rimswell Lodge
B1362
NORTH RD
HULL ROAD
QUEEN ST
Little England Hill
Eastholme Fm
West End
Thorp's Fm
Halsham
Old Hall
East End
Great Newsome Fm
Paull
Rose Hill
Hill Fm
Villa Fm
MAIN ROAD
Thorngumbald
Camerton
Hariff Lane Fm
Kelsey Ho
Tower Ho
North End Fm
Carr House Fm
North End Fm
Churchlands Fm
Burgany Hall
Frodingham Hall
Thorn Hall
Low Paull
Thorngumbald Drain
Green Marsh Fm
Ryehill
FORT PAULL
Keyingham
EAST RIDING
OF
YORKSHIRE
Whinhill Fm
Willow House Fm
Weldon's Plantn
Hollym
Intack Fm
Oxgoddes Fm
Auster Grange
Thorn Marsh Fm
Marsh Cott
Berrygate Hill
KEYINGHAM ROAD
Ottringham
PATRINGTON ROAD
Thorp's Plantn
Winestead
Toffling Fm
Nevilles Fm
Paull Holme Sands
Little Humber
Marsh Ho
Thorney Crofts
White House Fm
Coate's House Fm
Park Fm
White Hall
Mile Ho
HOLLYM ROAD
Eastfield Ho
Holmpton
STATION ROAD
New House Fm
Keyingham Grange
Nearmarsh Fm
Ottringham Drain
Westlands Plantn
Winestead Grange
Enholmes Hall
Patrington
Eastend Fm
Trinity Ho Fm
Cliff Fm
ROTTERDAM 10:45
ZEEBRUGGE 13:15
Foulholme Sands
Sands Ho
Salthaugh Grange
Ottringham Grange
Enholmes Fm
WELWICK ROAD
Beacon Hill
North Fm
Out Newton
Cherry Cobb Sands
Long Plantn
Far Marsh Fm
North Channel
Ivy Ho
Winestead Drain
Patrington Haven
Eastgrowths Fm
Haverfield Ho
Welwick
Southfield Fm
Sands Fm
Shrubbery Fm
Winestead Fm
Patrington Fm
Weeton
Gas Terminal
North Killingholme Haven
Oil Terminal
West Fm
Sunk Island Drain
Fisherman's Channel
Church Fm
Sunk Island
Channel Fm
Bleak House Fm
Outstray Fm
Humber Fm
Skeffling
EASINGTON ROAD
Easington
HULL ROAD
Stone Creek Ho
Stone Creek Fm
Crown Fm
Middle Fm
Winsetts
South End
Killingholme Marshes
Stone Creek
White House Fm
Wood Fm
South Killingholme Haven
River Humber
Oil Refinery
South Fm
East Bank Fm
Sunk Island Sands
The Plumbs
Skeffling Clays
Firtholme Fm
Immingham Dock
Hawkin's Pt
Easington Clays
Kilnsea
Houlton's Covert
MANBY ROAD
Trinity Sands
SPURN HEAD VISITOR CENTRE
Luxmore Fm
Immingham
QUEENS RD
Works
Kilnsea Clays
Ind Est
Trad Est
Mauxhall Fm
Immingham Grange
Eleanor Ho
Power Sta
Grimsby Roads
New Fm
Roxton Fm
Works
SPURN POINT NATURE RESERVE
SPURN
Roxton Wood
Greenlands Fm
Stallingborough
STALLINGBOROUGH
Europarc
Pyewipe
Grimsby
Newstead Fm
HEALING
Bus Pk
GRIMSBY DOCKS
Humber Pilot Station
Primrose Hill
Grange Fm
Healing
Healing Covert
GREAT COATES
Ind Est
WESTGATE
NEW CLEE
Spurn Head
Stony Binks
Keelby
BARTON STREET
B1210
The Willows
West Marsh
FISHING HERITAGE CEN
East Marsh
Grant Thorold
BLUNDELL PARK
Mouth of the Humber
Suddle Wood
Wells Fm
Great Coates
Wybers Wood
Yarborough
Little Coates
Holme Hill
Old Clee
GRIMSBY TOWN
CLEETHORPES
Bull Sand Fort
The Lindens Fm
Pyewipe Fm
Wybers Wood
Littlefield
Cleethorpes
Manor Fm
Riby Cross Roads
Wellow
Weelsby
CLEE ROAD
Riby Grange
Aylesby
Grange
LACEBY ROAD
Laceby Acres
PEAKS PARKWAY
CLEETHORPES LIGHT RAILWAY
Riby
Stud Fm
Nunsthorpe
Weelsby Woods
TAYLOR'S AVENUE
DISCOVERY CENTRE
Grove Wold Fm
Lacey Beck
Laceby Manor Fm
Bradley
CLEETHORPES
PLEASURE ISLAND THEME PARK
Washing Dales Fm
Laceby
GRIMSBY ROAD
Hall Fm
Peaks Tunnel Fm
Scartho
HEWITT'S AVE
Humberston Fitties
NORTH EAST
Riby Grove Fm
New Fm
Dixon Wood
Bradley Wood
LOUTH ROAD
Buck Beck
Hog Pit Hill
Manor Top Fm
New Waltham
Humberston
Irby Dales Wood
Irby upon Humber
LINCOLNSHIRE
HUMBERSTON AVE
Irby Dales Fm
Netherwood Fm
Grove Fm
TETNEY RD
Swallow Mount
Team Gate Drain
STATION RD
Tetney High Sands
Walk Fm
Waltham House Fm
Low Fm
Irby Holmes Wood
New Fm
Grange Fm
Waltham
WALTHAM WINDMILL
Eastfield Fm
Bishopthorpe Fm
Northcoates Pt
Silver Hill
Odessa Fm
Barnoldby le Beck
Norman Corner
Tetney Haven
The Grange
Rookery Fm
BARTON STREET
Bedlam Hill
Manor Ho
Brigsley Top
Holton le Clay
Highfield Ho
HUMBERSTON ROAD
Stonebridge Fm
CAISTOR ROAD
Swallow
Horse Shoe Pt
Brigsley
North End
Waithe Beck
Tetney Lock
North Coates Airfield
Badger Hills
Beelsby
Old Fm
Moor Ho
Ashby Hill
Hall Fm
Bratton House Fm
Holton Lodge
Holton Grange
Tetney
Grange Fm
New Dike
Low Fm
Ash Holt
Ashby cum Fenby
Tetney Blow Wells
Cherry Garth Fm
Cuxwold
Hatcliffe
Top Fm
Waithe
North Cotes
Poplar Fm
Outholme Fm
Waithe Top
Thoresby Br
Grainthorpe Haven
The Fitties
Cherry Valley Fm
Lake Fm
Waithe House Fm
Holme Fm
Keyholme Fm
Sea Fm
Pye's Fm
Gunby Fm
Priory Fm
Grainsby
North Thoresby
Marshchapel
othwell
L'Ings Fm
Croxby Pond Plantn
East Ravendale
Grainsby Grange
STATION ROAD
FEN LANE
SEA DYKE WAY
Willow Tree Ho
Crosby Top
Croxby
Petterhills
Hawerby Hall Fm
NORTH THORESBY
Fulstow
Low Fm
West End
New Fm
Ivy Ho
Holmes Fm
Thorganby Hall
TA
30
40
00

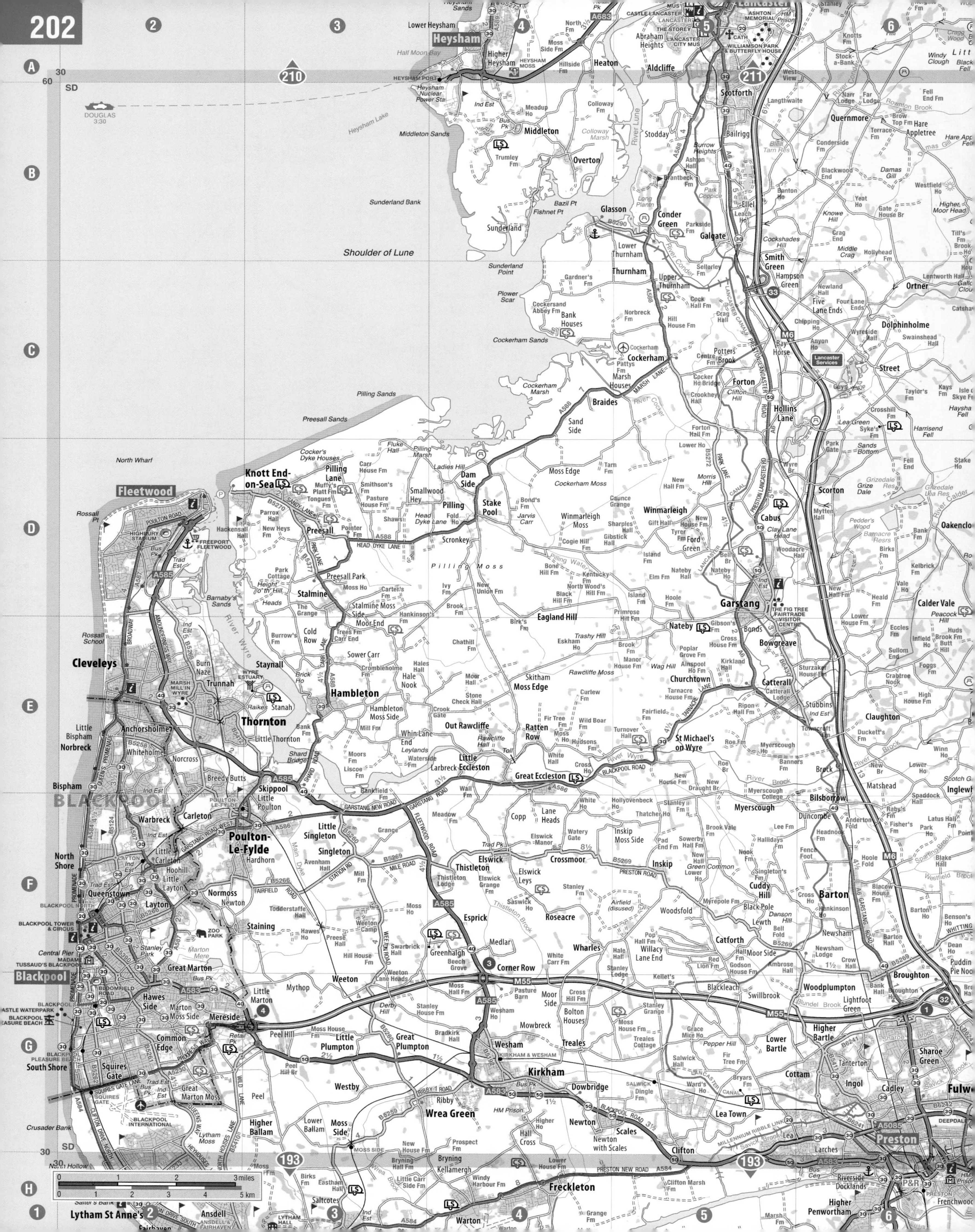
202
Heysham
Lower Heysham
Higher Heysham
Heysham Nuclear Power Sta
Half Moon Bay
Heysham Lake
Middleton Sands
Middleton
Overton
Heaton
Aldcliffe
Abraham Heights
Lancaster
Castle Lancaster
Ashton Memorial
Williamson Park & Butterfly House
Scotforth
Bailrigg
Stodday
Quernmore
Hare Appletree
Douglas 3:30
Sunderland Bank
Sunderland
Sunderland Point
Shoulder of Lune
Bazil Pt
Fishnet Pt
Glasson
Conder Green
Galgate
Ellel
Lower Thurnham
Thurnham
Upper Thurnham
Smith Green
Hampson Green
Ortner
Plower Scar
Cockersand Abbey Fm
Bank Houses
Cockerham Sands
Cockerham
Cockerham Marsh
Marsh Houses
Pattys Fm
Potters Brook
Forton
Hollins Lane
Bay Horse
Lancaster Services
Dolphinholme
Street
Pilling Sands
Preesall Sands
Braides
Sand Side
North Wharf
Fleetwood
Knott End-on-Sea
Pilling Lane
Cocker's Dyke Houses
Pilling Marsh
Dam Side
Pilling
Stake Pool
Moss Edge
Cockerham Moss
Winmarleigh
Winmarleigh Moss
Scorton
Cabus
Rossall Pt
Hackensall Hall
Preesall
Head Dyke Lane
Scronkey
Pilling Moss
Preesall Park
Stalmine
Stalmine Moss Side
Moor End
Cold Row
Eagland Hill
Nateby
Garstang
Bonds
Bowgreave
Calder Vale
Cleveleys
Rossall School
River Wyre
Staynall
Burn Naze
Trunnah
Thornton
Stanah
Hambleton
Churchtown
Catterall
Skitham
Moss Edge
Out Rawcliffe
Ratten Row
St Michael's on Wyre
Claughton
Little Bispham
Anchorsholme
Norbreck
Whiteholme
Little Thornton
Norcross
Shard Bridge
Little Eccleston
Larbreck
Great Eccleston
Bispham
Breedy Butts
Skippool
Little Poulton
Carleton
Blackpool
Warbreck
Poulton-Le-Fylde
Hardhorn
Little Singleton
Singleton
Copp
Lane Heads
Crossmoor
Inskip
Myerscough
Bilsborrow
Barton
North Shore
Little Carleton
Hoohill
Little Layton
Queenstown
Layton
Normoss
Newton
Staining
Thistleton
Elswick
Elswick Leys
Esprick
Roseacre
Woodsfold
Cuddy Hill
Lewth
Catforth
Newsham
Blackpool Tower & Circus
Central Pier
Zoo Park
Stanley Park
Great Marton
Medlar
Greenhalgh
Corner Row
Wharles
Moor Side
Broughton
Woodplumpton
Hawes Side
Marton Moss Side
Little Marton
Mythop
Weeton
Mereside
Moor Side
Swillbrook
Lightfoot Green
Peel Hill
Little Plumpton
Great Plumpton
Wesham
Mowbreck
Treales
Higher Bartle
Lower Bartle
Common Edge
South Shore
Squires Gate
Great Marton Moss
Westby
Kirkham
Dowbridge
Cottam
Ingol
Sharoe Green
Tanterton
Cadley
Fulwood
Blackpool International
Peel
Ribby
Wrea Green
Newton
Scales
Lea Town
Lea
Preston
Crusader Bank
Lytham Moss
Higher Ballam
Lower Ballam
Moss Side
Hall Cross
Newton with Scales
Clifton
Larches
Bryning
Kellamergh
Freckleton
Riverside Docklands
Higher Penwortham
Frenchwood
Lytham St Anne's
Ansdell
Saltcotes
Warton
Fairhaven
M55
M6
0 1 2 3 miles
0 1 2 3 4 5 km

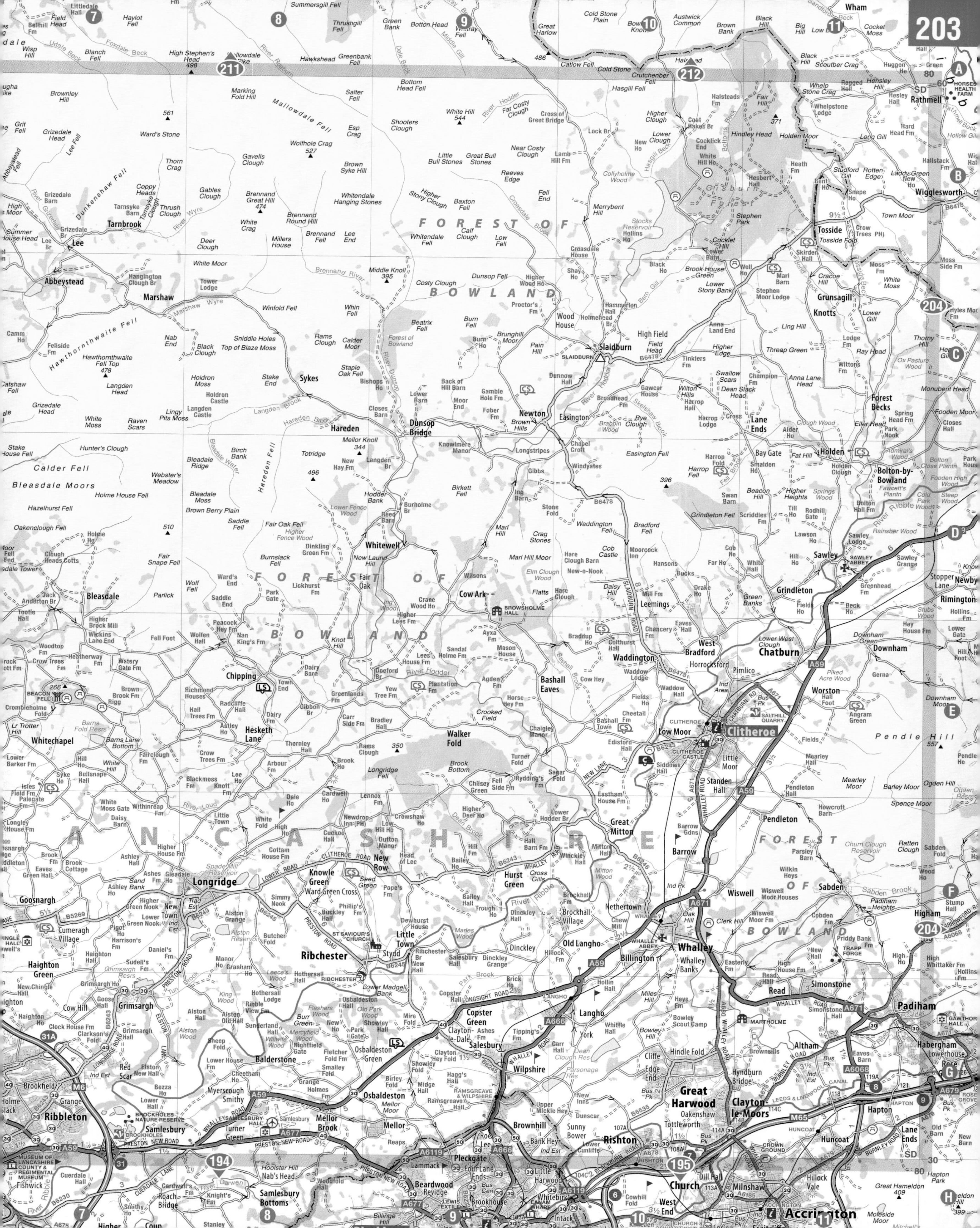

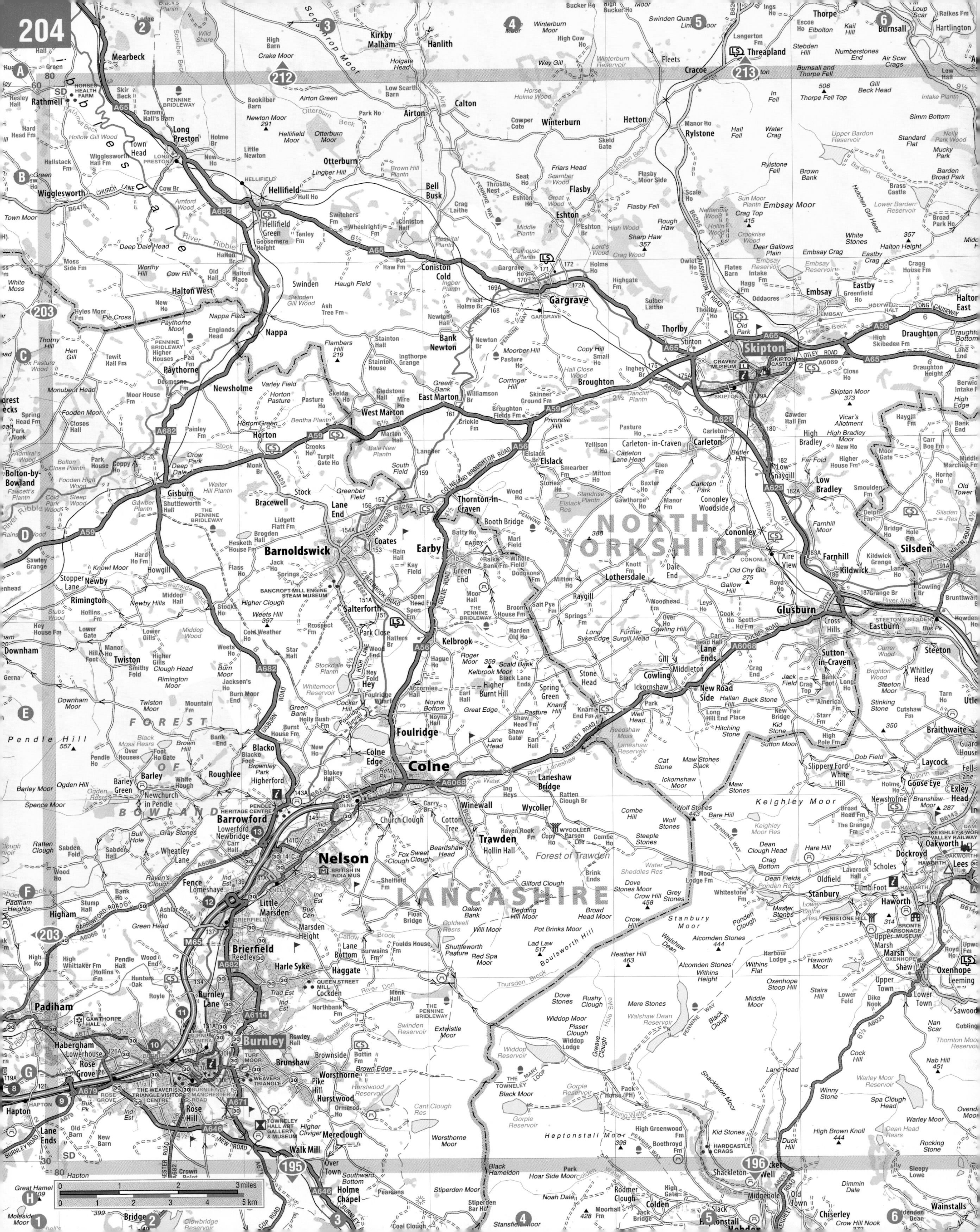
Mearbeck
Kirkby Malham
Hanlith
Threapland
Burnsall
Hartlington
Rathmell
Long Preston
Airton
Calton
Winterburn
Hetton
Rylstone
Cracoe
Wigglesworth
Hellifield
Otterburn
Bell Busk
Flasby
Eshton
Embsay Moor
Halton West
Coniston Cold
Gargrave
Embsay
Nappa
Thorlby
Stirton
Skipton
Draughton
Paythorne
Bank Newton
Newsholme
East Marton
West Marton
Broughton
Horton
Carleton
Elslack
Bolton-by-Bowland
Gisburn
Bracewell
Lane End
Thornton-in-Craven
Snaygill
Low Bradley
Coates
Barnoldswick
Earby
NORTH YORKSHIRE
Cononley
Farnhill
Kildwick
Silsden
Lothersdale
Glusburn
Eastburn
Steeton
Rimington
Salterforth
Kelbrook
Downham
Twiston
Sutton-in-Craven
Cowling
Middleton
FOREST OF BOWLAND
Pendle Hill 557
Foulridge
Colne
Laycock
Barley
Roughlee
Blacko
Laneshaw Bridge
Barrowford
Winewall
Wycoller
Trawden
Keighley Moor
Oakworth
Nelson
Forest of Trawden
LANCASHIRE
Stanbury
Haworth
Fence
Little Marsden
Higham
Brierfield
Harle Syke
Haggate
Oxenhope
Padiham
Burnley
Brunshaw
Worsthorne
Hapton
Hurstwood
Mereclough
Walk Mill
Heptonstall Moor
Wainstalls
A65
A59
A682
A56
A6068
A629
A6069
M65
A646
A671
A6114
A679
203
212
213
195
196
3 miles
5 km

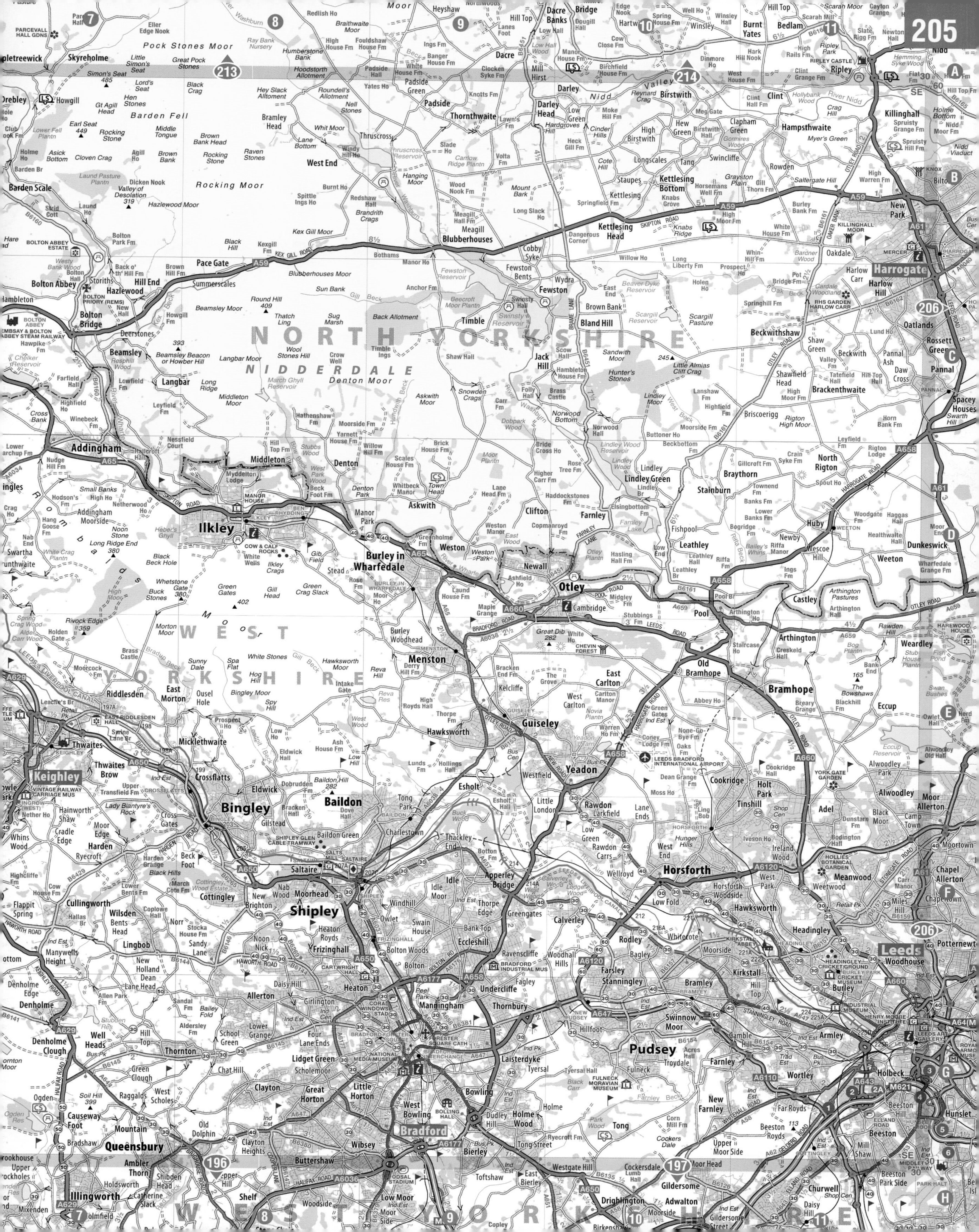

NORTH YORKSHIRE
NIDDERDALE
WEST YORKSHIRE
Harrogate
Leeds
Bradford
Keighley
Ilkley
Otley
Burley in Wharfedale
Bingley
Baildon
Shipley
Guiseley
Yeadon
Horsforth
Pudsey
Queensbury
Illingworth
Skyreholme
Pock Stones Moor
Barden Fell
Rocking Moor
Thruscross
Padside
Darley
Dacre Banks
Dacre
Birstwith
Hampsthwaite
Killinghall
Ripley
Clint
Kettlesing
Blubberhouses
Pace Gate
Bolton Abbey
Bolton Bridge
Hazlewood
Timble
Fewston
Bland Hill
Beckwithshaw
Pannal
Oatlands
Harlow Hill
Langbar
Denton Moor
Addingham
Middleton
Denton
Askwith
Menston
Burley Woodhead
Clifton
Farnley
Leathley
Stainburn
Huby
Weeton
Dunkeswick
Castley
Pool
Arthington
Bramhope
Riddlesden
East Morton
Micklethwaite
Crossflatts
Eldwick
Hawksworth
Esholt
Rawdon
Cookridge
Adel
Alwoodley
Moor Allerton
Saltaire
Cottingley
Idle
Calverley
Rodley
Farsley
Stanningley
Bramley
Kirkstall
Headingley
Burley
Armley
Wortley
Holbeck
Beeston
Hunslet
Heaton
Manningham
Allerton
Thornton
Clayton
Wibsey
Buttershaw
Low Moor
Bowling
Tong
Farnley
Gildersome
Drighlington
LEEDS BRADFORD INTERNATIONAL AIRPORT

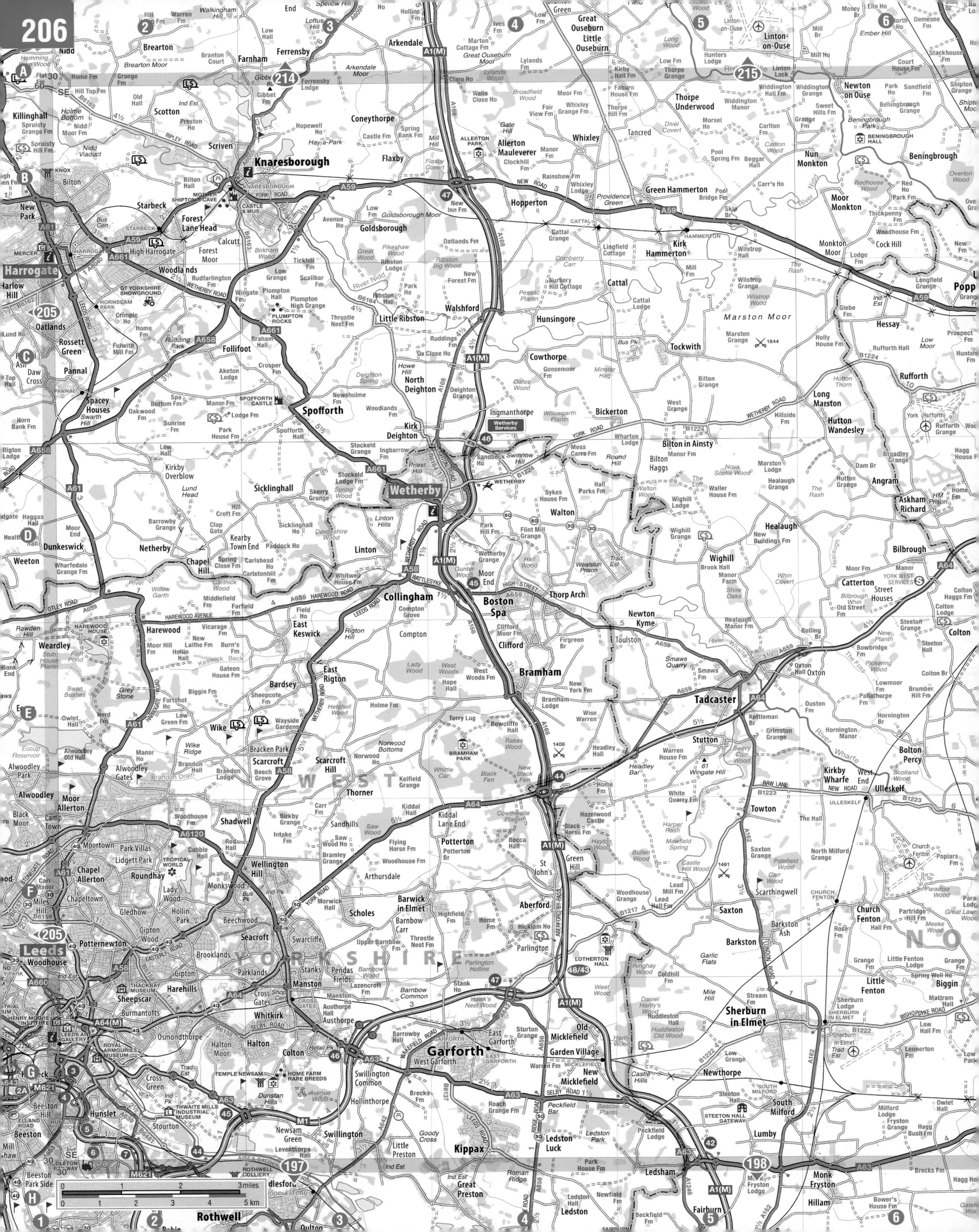
Brearton
Farnham
Ferrensby
Arkendale
Great Ouseburn
Little Ouseburn
Linton-on-Ouse
Newton on Ouse
Killinghall
Scotton
Scriven
Knaresborough
Coneythorpe
Flaxby
Allerton Mauleverer
Whixley
Tancred
Thorpe Underwood
Nun Monkton
Beningbrough
Bilton
New Park
Starbeck
Forest Lane Head
Calcutt
High Harrogate
Harrogate
Hopperton
Green Hammerton
Moor Monkton
Goldsborough
Kirk Hammerton
Woodlands
Harlow Hill
Oatlands
Rossett Green
Pannal
Follifoot
Little Ribston
Walshford
Hunsingore
Cattal
Marston Moor
Hessay
Tockwith
Cowthorpe
Spacey Houses
Spofforth
North Deighton
Kirk Deighton
Ingmanthorpe
Bickerton
Long Marston
Rufforth
Hutton Wandesley
Bilton in Ainsty
Bilton Haggs
Wetherby
Sicklinghall
Kirkby Overblow
Angram
Askham Richard
Dunkeswick
Weeton
Netherby
Linton
Walton
Healaugh
Bilbrough
Wighill
Collingham
Boston Spa
Thorp Arch
Catterton
Newton Kyme
Harewood
East Keswick
Clifford
Compton
Weardley
Bramham
Tadcaster
Colton
Oxton
East Rigton
Bardsey
Wike
Scarcroft
Scarcroft Hill
Thorner
Stutton
Kirkby Wharfe
Bolton Percy
Ulleskelf
Towton
Alwoodley
Alwoodley Gates
Moor Allerton
Shadwell
Sandhills
Kiddal Lane End
Potterton
Moortown
Park Villas
Lidgett Park
Roundhay
Chapel Allerton
Wellington Hill
Monkswood
Barwick in Elmet
Scholes
Aberford
Saxton
Church Fenton
Barkston
Barkston Ash
Chapeltown
Gledhow
Gipton Wood
Potternewton
Seacroft
Swarcliffe
Parlington
Leeds
Woodhouse
Brooklands
Parklands
YORKSHIRE
WEST
Sheepscar
Harehills
Stanks
Pendas Fields
Manston
Little Fenton
Biggin
Burmantofts
Whitkirk
Austhorpe
Cross Gates
Sherburn in Elmet
Osmondthorpe
Halton
Colton
Garforth
Old Micklefield
Garden Village
New Micklefield
Newthorpe
South Milford
Swillington Common
Hunslet
Beeston
Stourton
Swillington
Kippax
Ledston Luck
Lumby
Ledsham
Great Preston
Rothwell
Ledston
Fairburn
Monk Fryston
Hillam
A1(M)
A59
A61
A64
A659
A168
0 1 2 3 miles
0 1 2 3 4 5 km

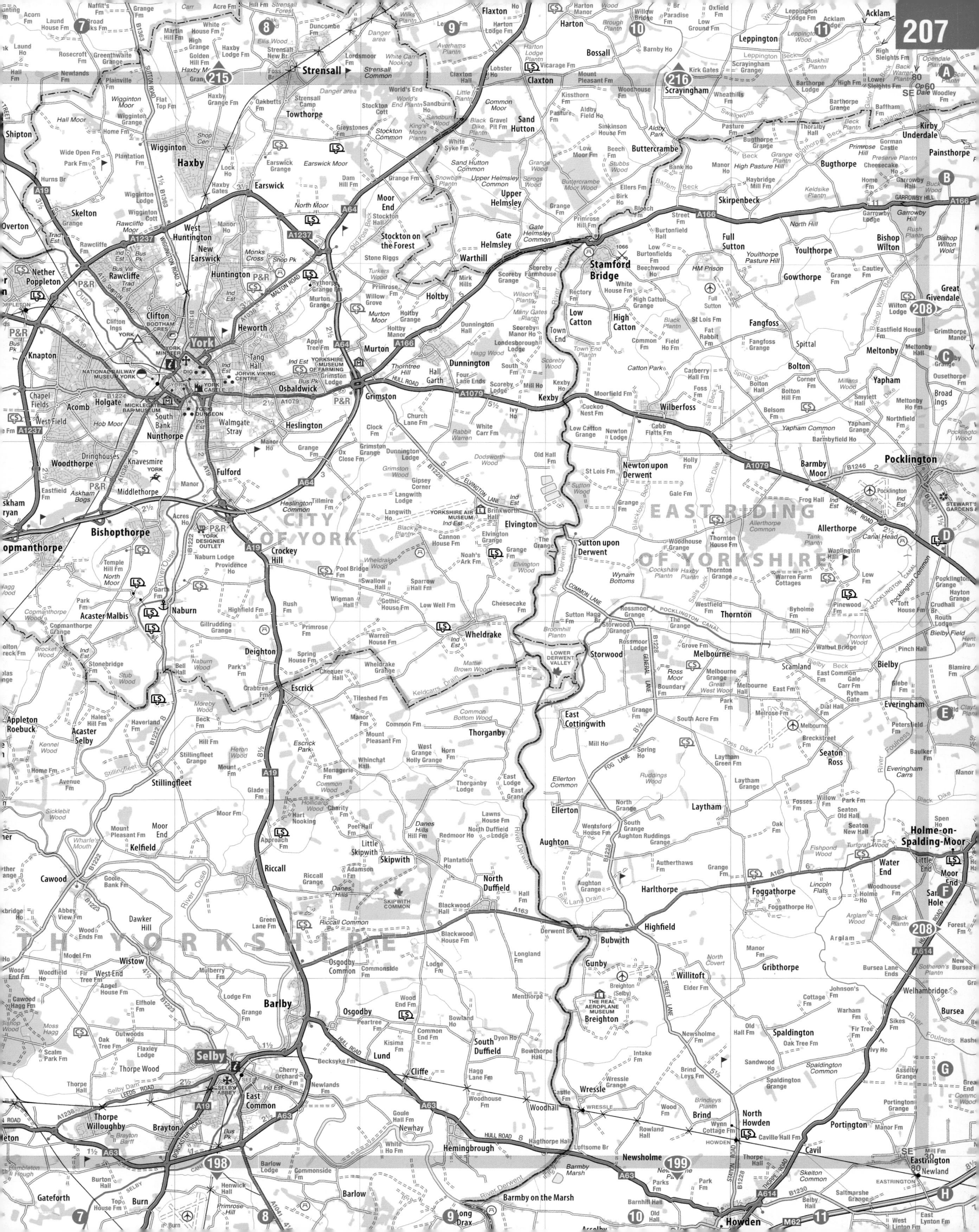
Strensall
Haxby
Wigginton
Earswick
Huntington
York
Heworth
Osbaldwick
Heslington
Fulford
Bishopthorpe
Acomb
Holgate
Clifton
Rawcliffe
Skelton
Knapton
Dunnington
Murton
Stockton on the Forest
Stamford Bridge
Claxton
Flaxton
Harton
Bossall
Leppington
Acklam
Scrayingham
Buttercrambe
Sand Hutton
Upper Helmsley
Gate Helmsley
Warthill
Holtby
Kexby
Wilberfoss
Full Sutton
Skirpenbeck
Bugthorpe
Kirby Underdale
Bishop Wilton
Youlthorpe
Great Givendale
Fangfoss
Yapham
Meltonby
Bolton
Pocklington
Barmby Moor
Allerthorpe
Newton upon Derwent
Elvington
Sutton upon Derwent
Thornton
Melbourne
Storwood
Wheldrake
Escrick
Deighton
Naburn
Acaster Malbis
Stillingfleet
Kelfield
Riccall
Skipwith
North Duffield
Thorganby
East Cottingwith
Ellerton
Aughton
Laytham
Seaton Ross
Everingham
Holme-on-Spalding-Moor
Harlthorpe
Foggathorpe
Bubwith
Highfield
Gunby
Willitoft
Breighton
Spaldington
Wressle
Brind
Newsholme
Howden
Barlby
Osgodby
Cliffe
Hemingbrough
South Duffield
Selby
Brayton
Thorpe Willoughby
Wistow
Cawood
Barlow
Barmby on the Marsh
Long Drax
Gateforth
Burn
Portington
Cavil
Eastrington
CITY OF YORK
EAST RIDING OF YORKSHIRE
NORTH YORKSHIRE
A64
A166
A1079
A19
A163
A63
A614
M62
A1237
B1228

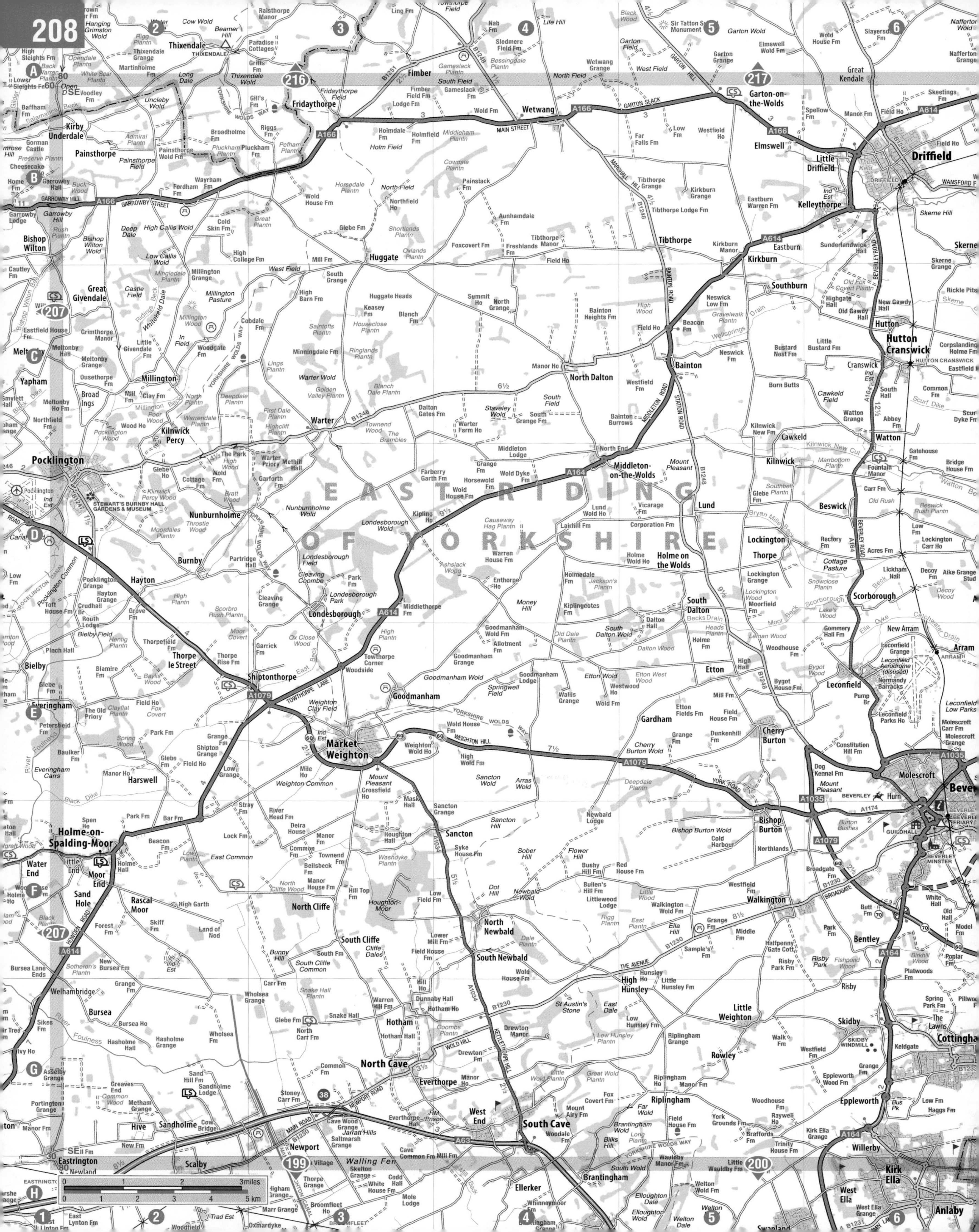
EAST RIDING OF YORKSHIRE
Thixendale
Cow Wold
Beamer Hill
Raisthorpe Manor
Hanging Grimston Wold
Rigg Plantn
Paradise Cottages
Martinholme Fm
Thixendale Grange
Grits Fm
High Sleights Fm
Lower Sleights Fm
Opendale Plantn
White Scar Plantn
Long Dale
Thixendale Wold
Ling Fm
Nab Fm
Life Hill
Sledmere Field Fm
Bessingdale Plantn
Gameslack Plantn
South Field
Gameslack Fm
Fimber
Fimber Field Fm
Lodge Fm
Fridaythorpe Field
Fridaythorpe
Woodley Fm
Uncleby Wold
Baffham Fm
Salamanca Beck
Kirby Underdale
Gorman Castle
Preserve Plantn
Painsthorpe
Painsthorpe Field
Painsthorpe Wold Fm
Admiral Plantn
Broadholme Fm
Pluckham Plantn
Pluckham Fm
Riggs Fm
Gill's Fm
Pelham Plantn
Holmdale Fm
Holmfield Fm
Holm Field
Middleham Plantn
Wold Fm
Wetwang
MAIN STREET
North Field
Wetwang Grange
West Field
Garton Field
Garton Grange
Garton Wold
GARTON HILL
GARTON SLACK
Sir Tatton Sykes Monument
Black Wood
Wold House Fm
Elmswell Wold Fm
Slayersdale Fm
Nafferton Wold
Nafferton Grange
Great Kendale
Garton-on-the-Wolds
Skeetings Fm
Spellow Fm
Manor Fm
Field Ho
Far Falls Fm
Low Fm
Westfield Ho
Elmswell
Little Driffield
Driffield
WANSFORD RD
Cheesecake Fm
Home Fm
Garrowby Hall
Buck Wood
GARROWBY HILL
Garrowby Lodge
Garrowby Hill
Fordham Fm
Wayrham Fm
GARROWBY STREET
Horsedale Plantn
Wold House Fm
North Field
Northfield Ho
Cowdale Plantn
Painslack Fm
MARSHALL HILL
Tibthorpe Grange
Kirkburn Grange
Eastburn Warren Fm
Tibthorpe Lodge Fm
Kelleythorpe
Ind Est
Skerne Hill
Bishop Wilton
Bishop Wilton Wold
Rush Plantn
Deep Dale
High Callis Wold
Cold Skin Fm
Great Plantn
Glebe Fm
Shortlands Plantn
Aunhamdale Fm
Oxlands Plantn
Foxcovert Fm
Freshlands Fm
Tibthorpe Manor
Field Ho
Tibthorpe
Kirkburn Manor
Eastburn
Kirkburn
Sunderlandwick Hall
Skerne
Skerne Grange
Cautley Fm
Low Callis Wold
Mingledale Plantn
Millington Grange
High College Fm
West Field
Mill Fm
Huggate
South Grange
Southburn
Rickle Pits
Great Givendale
Castle Field
Whiteleaf Dale
Millington Pasture
High Barn Fm
Huggate Heads
Summit Ho
North Grange
High Wood
Bainton Heights Fm
Neswick Low Fm
Gravelwalk Plantn
Old Fox Covert Plantn
Highgate Hall
New Gawdy Hall
Old Gawdy Hall
Eastfield House Fm
Grimthorpe Manor
Millington Wood
Cobdale Fm
Keasey Fm
Houseclose Plantn
Blanch Fm
Saintofts Plantn
Field Ho
Beacon Fm
Wellsprings
Hutton
Hutton Cranswick
Corpslanding Holme Fm
Meltonby Hall
Meltonby Grange
Little Givendale Fm
In Field
Woodgate Fm
Lings Plantn
Minningdale Fm
Ringlands Plantn
Manor Ho
North Dalton
Bainton
Bustard Nest Fm
Little Bustard Fm
Neswick Fm
Cranswick
Eastfield Ho
Yapham
Ousethorpe Fm
Millington
Warter Wold
Golden Valley Plantn
Blanch Dale Plantn
Westfield Fm
Burn Butts
Cawkeld Field
Common Fm
Broad Ings
Mill Fm
Clay Fm
Meltonby Ho Fm
Deepdale Plantn
6½
South Field
Staveley Wold
South Grange Fm
Dalton Gates Fm
Warter Farm Ho
Bainton Burrows
MIDDLETON ROAD
STATION ROAD
Watton Grange
Abbey Fm
Scurf Dike
Northfield Fm
Wood Ho
Pocklington Wood
Poor Wood
Kilnwick Percy
Warrendale Plantn
First Dale Plantn
Highcliff Plantn
Warter
B1246
Townend Wood
The Brambles
Middleton Lodge
North End
Middleton-on-the-Wolds
Mount Pleasant
Kilnwick New Fm
Cawkeld
Kilnwick New Cut
Watton
Gatehouse Fm
Bridge House Fm
Pocklington
The Park
High Wood
Wold Fm
Warter Priory
Methill Hall
Glebe Ho
Cottage Fm
Garforth Fm
Farberry Garth Fm
Grange Fm
Horsewold Fm
Wold Dyke Fm
Wold House Fm
Kilnwick
Marrbottom Plantn
Fountain Manor
Pocklington Ind Est
STEWART'S BURNBY HALL GARDENS & MUSEUM
Kilnwick Percy Wood
Bratt Wood
Nunburnholme Wold
Nunburnholme
Throstle Wood
Moordales Plantn
Kipling Ho
9½
Causeway Hag Plantn
Lund Wold Ho
Vicarage Fm
Lund
Southburn Plantn
Glebe Fm
Bryan Mills
Carr Fm
Old Rush
Beswick
Beswick Rush Plantn
Watton Beck
Pocklington Canal
Burnby
Partridge Hall
Londesborough Wold
Lairhill Fm
Corporation Fm
Lockington
Low Fm
Rectory Fm
Lockington Carr Ho
Thorpe
Acres Fm
Holme Wold Ho
Holme on the Wolds
Cottage Pasture
Lickham Hall
Decoy Fm
Aike Grange Stud
Pocklington Grange
Pocklington Common
Hayton
Hayton Grange
Crudhall Fm
Toft House Fm
Routh Lodge
Bielby Field
Hentig Plantn
Grove Fm
High Plantn
Scorbro Rush Plantn
Cleaving Grange
Cleaving Coombe
Londesborough Field
Park Fm
Londesborough Park
Londesborough
Warren House Fm
Ashslack Wood
Enthorpe Ho
Holmedale Fm
Jackson's Plantn
South Dalton
Becks Drain
Lockington Grange
Lockington Wood
Moorfield Fm
Snowclose Plantn
Scorborough
Decoy Wood
Lake's Wood
Middlethorpe Fm
Money Hill
Kiplingcotes Fm
Dalton Hall
Moor Beck
Ella Dyke
Catchwater Drain
Pinch Hall
Thorpefield Fm
Moor Covert
Garrick Fm
Ox Close Wood
High Plantn
Goodmanham Wold Fm
Allotment Fm
Old Dale Plantn
South Dalton Wold
Heads Plantn
Dalton Wood
Holme Fm
Leman Wood
Gommery Hall Fm
New Arram
Arram
Woodhouse Fm
Leconfield Grange
Leconfield Aerodrome (disused)
Normandy Barracks
Bielby
Blamire Fm
Thorpe le Street
Thorpe Rise Fm
Baylis Wood
Towthorpe Corner
Woodside
Goodmanham Grange
Goodmanham Wold
Goodmanham Lodge
Springwell Field
Etton Wold
Westwood Ho
Etton West Wood
Etton
High Hall
Bygot Wood
Bygot House Fm
Leconfield
Pump Br
Leconfield Low Parks
Glebe Fm
Everingham
The Old Priory
Clayflat Plantn
Field Ho
Fox Covert
Shiptonthorpe
TOWTHORPE LANE
Weighton Clay Field
Goodmanham
Wallis Grange
Wold Fm
Gardham
Etton Fields Fm
Mill Fm
Field House Fm
Leconfield Parks Ho
Molescroft Carr Fm
Molescroft Grange
Petersfield Fm
Park Fm
Spring Wood
Grange Fm
Shipton Grange
Glebe Fm
Field Ho
Ind Est
Market Weighton
Weighton Wold Ho
Wold House Fm
WEIGHTON HILL
YORKSHIRE WOLDS WAY
7½
Grange Fm
Dunkenhill Fm
Cherry Burton
Cherry Burton Wold
Constitution Hill Fm
Molescroft
Baulker Fm
Everingham Carrs
River Foulness
Manor Ho
Harswell
Low Grange
Mile Ho
Weighton Common
High Wold Fm
Sancton Wold
Arras Wold
Deepdale Plantn
YORK ROAD
Dog Kennel Fm
Mount Pleasant
BEVERLEY
Hurn
Mount Pleasant Crossfield Ho
Mask Hall
Black Dike
Park Fm
Bar Fm
Stray Fm
River Head Fm
Deira House
Sancton Grange
Sancton
Sancton Hill
Newbald Lodge
Bishop Burton
Bishop Burton Wold
Cold Harbour
Burton Bushes
GUILDHALL
BEVERLEY MINSTER
BEVERLEY FRIARY
Spen Ho
Holme-on-Spalding-Moor
Lock Fm
Manor Fm
Houghton Hall
Syke House Fm
Sober Hill
Flower Hill
Northlands
Beacon Fm
Low Plantn
East Common
Common Fm
Townend Fm
Washdyke Plantn
Bushy Hill Fm
Red House Fm
Water End
Little End
Moor End
Holme Hall
Beilsbeck Fm
Manor House Fm
North Cliffe Wood
Hill Top Fm
Low Field Fm
Dot Hill
Newbald Wold
Bullen's Hill Fm
Littlewood Lodge
Little Wood
Walkington Wold Fm
Westfield Fm
Walkington
Broadgate Fm
BROADGATE
Sand Hole
Rascal Moor
High Garth
North Cliffe
Houghton Moor
North Newbald
Rigg Plantn
East Plantn
Ella Hill
Grange Fm
8½
Middle Fm
Butt Fm
White Hall
Old Hall
Model Fm
Black Plantn
Forest Fm
Skiff Fm
Land of Nod
South Cliffe
Cliffe Dales
Lower Mill Fm
Dale Plantn
B1230
Halfpenny Gate Cott
Sample's Fm
Park Fm
Bentley
Birkhill Wood
Poplar Fm
HOWDEN ROAD
New Bursea Fm
Sotheron's Plantn
Ind Est
Bunny Hill
South Fm
South Cliffe Common
Field House Fm
South Newbald
Wold House Fm
THE AVENUE
Risby Park Fm
Risby Park
Fishpond Wood
Platwoods Fm
Bursea Lane Ends
Grange Fm
Carr Fm
Snake Hall Plantn
Hill Ho
Hunsley Ho
High Hunsley
Little Hunsley Fm
Risby
Welhambridge
Wholsea Grange
Warren Hill Fm
Dunnaby Hall
Hotham Ho
St Austin's Stone
East Dale
Little Weighton
Spring Park Fm
Pillwoods
Bursea
Bursea Ho
Glebe Fm
North Carr Fm
Snake Hall
Hotham
Hotham Hall
Coombs Plantn
Drewton Manor
Low Hunsley Fm
Low Hunsley Plantn
Skidby
The Lawns
Cottingham
Sikes Fm
River Foulness
Hasholme Hall
Hasholme Grange
Wholsea Fm
WOLD HILL
Drewton Fm
KETTLETHORPE HILL
Riplingham Grange
Rowley
Walk Fm
SKIDBY WINDMILL
Keldgate
Westfield Fm
Ivy Ho
Asselby Grange
Common Fm
North Cave
3½
Everthorpe
Manor Ho
Little Wold Plantn
Great Wold Plantn
Riplingham Ho
Manor Fm
Grange Fm
Epplewort Wood Fm
Sand Hill Fm
Sandholme Lodge
Greaves End Common Wood
Metham Grange
Portington Grange
Stoney Carr Fm
NEWPORT ROAD
Everthorpe Fm
HM Prison
West End
South Cave
Woodale Fm
Fox Covert Fm
Mount Airy Fm
Far Wold
Riplingham
Woodhouse Fm
Raywell Ho
Eppleworth
Bus Pk
Low Fm
Haggs Fm
Manor Fm
Hive
Sandholme
Cow Bridge
MAIN ROAD
Cave Wold Grange
Jarratt Hills
Saltmarsh Grange
Riplingham Wold
Long Plantn
Field House Fm
York Grounds Fm
Braffords Fm
Kirk Ella Grange
Willerby
New Fm
Newport
Cave Common Fm
Mill Fm
Bilks Hill
YORKSHIRE WOLDS WAY
Trinity House Fm
Eastrington
Scalby
Walling Fen
South Wold
Wauldby Manor Fm
Little Wauldby Fm
Kirk Ella
Newland
EASTRINGTON
Thorpe Grange
Skelton Grange
White House Fm
Codd Hall
Higham Grange
Broomfleet Ho
Mole Lodge
Ellerker
Brantingham
Welton Wold Fm
Elloughton Dale
Elloughton Wold
Welton Dale
West Ella
West Ella Grange
Anlaby
Marr Grange
Trad Est
Woodfield
Oxmardyke
BROOMFLEET
Whinneymoor Fm
Swanland
East Lynton Fm
0 1 2 3 miles
0 1 2 3 4 5 km

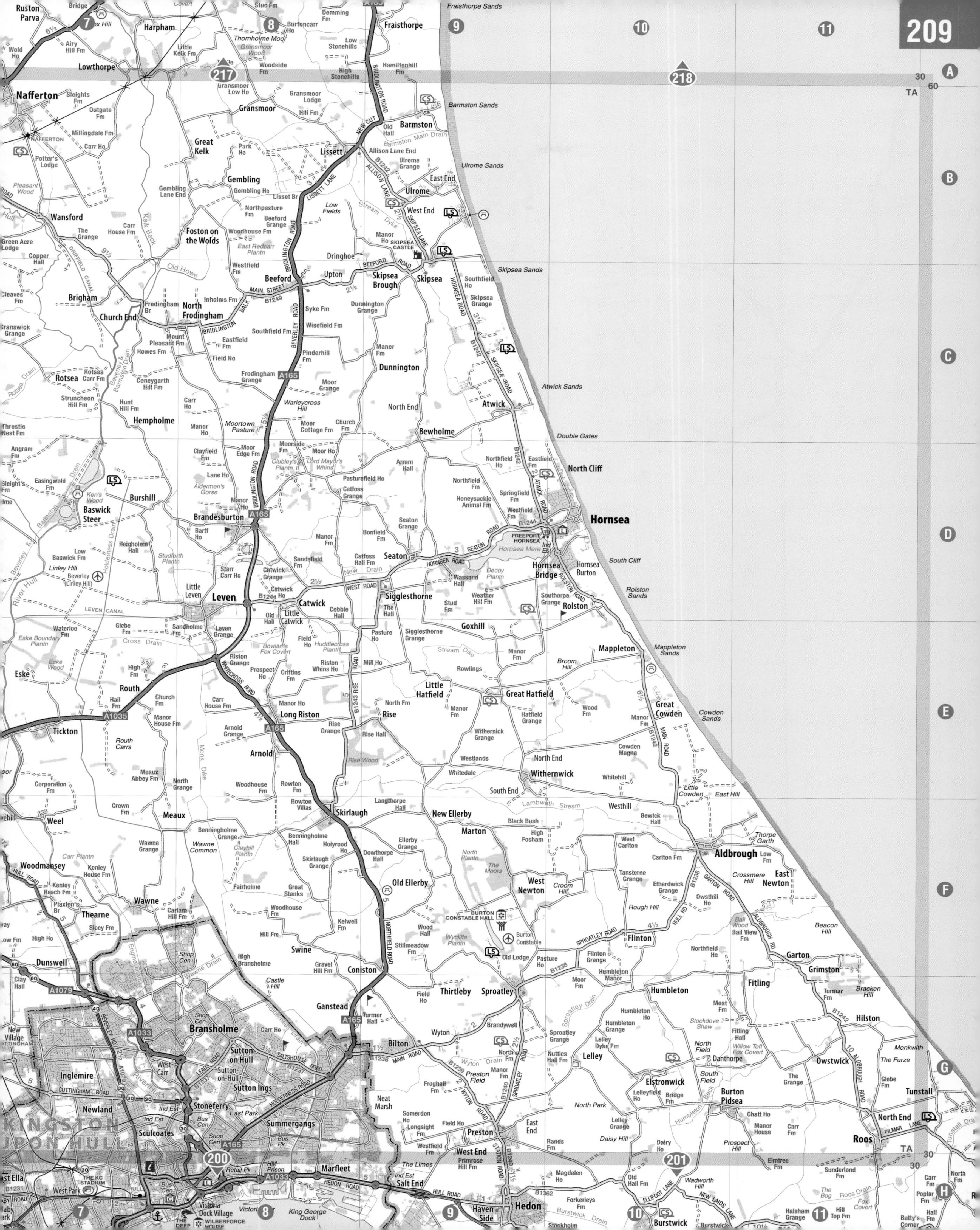
Ruston Parva
Harpham
Burtoncarr Ho
Demming Fm
Fraisthorpe
Fraisthorpe Sands
Wold Ho
Airy Hill Fm
Thornholme Moor
Little Kelk Fm
Low Stonehills
Lowthorpe
Woodside Fm
High Stonehills
Hamiltonhill Fm
217
218
Nafferton
Sleights Fm
Gransmoor Low Ho
Gransmoor Lodge
Outgate Fm
Gransmoor
Hill Fm
Barmston Sands
Barmston
Old Hall
Millingdale Fm
Carr Ho
Great Kelk
Park Ho
Lissett
Allison Lane End
Ulrome Grange
Potter's Lodge
Barmston Main Drain
Ulrome Sands
Gembling
Gembling Ho
East End
Ulrome
Pleasant Wood
Gembling Lane End
Lisset Br
Northpasture Fm
Low Fields
West End
Wansford
The Grange
Carr House Fm
Foston on the Wolds
Beeford Grange
Woodhouse Fm
East Redcarr Plantn
Manor Ho
Skipsea Castle
Green Acre Lodge
Copper Hall
Westfield Fm
Dringhoe
Old Howe
Beeford
Upton
Skipsea Brough
Skipsea
Skipsea Sands
Southfield Ho
Skipsea Grange
Cleaves Fm
Brigham
Frodingham Br
North Frodingham
Inholms Fm
Syke Fm
Dunnington Grange
Church End
Southfield Fm
Wisefield Fm
Mount Pleasant Fm
Eastfield Fm
Howes Fm
Field Ho
Pinderhill Fm
Manor Fm
Dunnington
Rotsea
Rotsea Carr Fm
Frodingham Grange
Coneygarth Hill Fm
Moor Grange
Atwick Sands
Struncheon Hill Fm
Hunt Hill Fm
Carr Ho
Warleycross Hill
North End
Atwick
Hempholme
Throstle Nest Fm
Manor Ho
Moortown Pasture
Moor Cottage Fm
Church Fm
Bewholme
Double Gates
Angram Fm
Clayfield Fm
Moor Edge Fm
Moorside Fm
Moor Ho
Clubley's Plantn
Lord Mayor's Whins
Arram Hall
Northfield Ho
Eastfield Fm
North Cliff
Easingwold Fm
Lane Ho
Pasturefield Ho
Aldermen's Gorse
Catfoss Grange
Northfield Fm
Honeysuckle Animal Fm
Springfield Fm
Ken's Wood
Burshill
Manor Ho
Westfield Fm
Hornsea
Baswick Steer
Brandesburton
Seaton Grange
Freeport Hornsea
Barff Ho
Bonfield Fm
Manor Fm
Heigholme Hall
Hornsea Mere
Low Baswick Fm
Studforth Plantn
Sandsfield Fm
Catfoss Hall Fm
Seaton
Hornsea Bridge
Hornsea Burton
South Cliff
Linley Hill
Beverley (Linley Hill)
Starr Carr Ho
Catwick Grange
Wassand Hall
Decoy Plantn
Rolston Sands
Little Leven
Catwick Ho
Sigglesthorne
Weather Hill Fm
Southorpe Grange
Rolston
Leven
Catwick
Stud Fm
Leven Canal
Old Hall
Little Catwick
Cobble Hall
The Hall
Goxhill
Waterloo Fm
Glebe Fm
Sandholme Fm
Leven Grange
Eske Boundary Plantn
Field Ho
Pasture Ho
Sigglesthorne Grange
Mappleton
Mappleton Sands
Cross Drain
Bowlams Fox Covert
Huddlecross Plantn
Stream Dike
Manor Fm
Broom Hill
Eske Wood
Riston Grange
Mill Ho
Rowlings
Eske
High Fm
Prospect Ho
Riston Whins Ho
Criftins Fm
Routh
Little Hatfield
Great Hatfield
Great Cowden
Hall Fm
Church Fm
Carr House Fm
Manor Ho
North Fm
Manor Fm
Wood Fm
Manor Fm
Cowden Sands
Tickton
Long Riston
Rise
Hatfield Grange
Manor House Fm
Arnold Grange
Rise Grange
Witherwick Grange
Routh Carrs
Rise Hall
Cowden Magna
Arnold
Westlands
North End
Rise Wood
Whitedale
Withernwick
Whitehill
Meaux Abbey Fm
North Grange
South End
Little Cowden
East Hill
Corporation Fm
Woodhouse Fm
Rowton Fm
Rowton Villas
Langthorpe Hall
Crown Fm
Meaux
Skirlaugh
New Ellerby
Lambwath Stream
Westhill
Weel
Benningholme Grange
Marton
Black Bush
Bewick Hall
Benningholme Hall
High Fosham
Thorpe Garth
Wawne Grange
Wawne Common
Claybill Plantn
Holyrood Ho
Ellerby Grange
West Carlton
Aldbrough
Low Fm
Carr Plantn
Dowthorpe Hall
North Plantn
Carlton Fm
Woodmansey
Kenley House Fm
Skirlaugh Grange
The Moors
Tansterne Grange
Crossmere Hill
East Newton
Kenley Reach Fm
Fairholme
Great Stanks
Old Ellerby
West Newton
Croom Hill
Etherdwick Grange
Owsthill Ho
Plaxton's Br
Wawne
Woodhouse Fm
Rough Hill
Thearne
Carlam Hill Fm
Burton Constable Hall
Kelwell Fm
Wood Hall
Bail Wood
Bail View Fm
Beacon Hill
Sicey Fm
Hill Fm
Stillmeadow Fm
Wycliffe Plantn
Burton Constable
Flinton
High Ho
Shop Cen
High Bransholme
Swine
Northfield Ho
Garton
Dunswell
Wawne Drain
Gravel Hill Fm
Coniston
Old Lodge
Pasture Ho
Flinton Grange
Grimston
Clay Hall
Castle Hill
Humbleton Manor
Fitling
Field Ho
Thirtleby
Sproatley
Moor Fm
Humbleton
Turmar Fm
Bracken Hill
Ganstead
Turmer Hall
Moat Fm
Bransholme
Carr Ho
Brandywell
Humbleton Ho
Humbleton Grange
Stockdove Shaw
Hilston
New Village
Sutton on Hull
Wyton
Sproatley Grange
Lelley Dyke Fm
Fitling Hall
Willow Toft Fox Covert
Monkwith
Saltshouse Road
Bilton
North Fm
Nuttles Hall Fm
Lelley
North Field
Danthorpe
Owstwick
The Furze
Inglemire
West Carr
Sutton-on-Hull
Wyton Drain
Manor Fm
Preston Field
Elstronwick
South Field
The Grange
Glebe Fm
Sutton Ings
Foxghall Fm
Lelleyfield Ho
Bridge Fm
Burton Pidsea
Tunstall
Newland
Stoneferry
Ind Est
East Park
Neat Marsh
North Park
Chatt Ho
North End
Kingston upon Hull
Sculcoates
Summergangs
Bus Cen
Shop Cen
Bus Pk
Somerdon Ho
Longsight Fm
Field Ho
Preston
East End
Lelley Grange
Manor House
Carr Fm
Daisy Hill
Rands Fm
Dairy Ho
Prospect Hill
Roos
Westfield Fm
West End
Primrose Hill Fm
The Limes
200
201
Elmtree Fm
HM Prison
Retail Pk
Marfleet
Ind Est
Salt End
Magdalen Ho
Old Hall Fm
Wadworth Hill
Sunderland Fm
Carr Fm
North Fm
East Ella
The KC Stadium
West Park
Victoria Dock Village
Victoria
King George Dock
Haven Side
Hedon
Forkerleys Fm
Burstwick Drain
The Bog
Roos Drain
Fox Covert
Poplar Fm
Hall Fm
Batty's Corner
Stockholm
Burstwick
Halsham Grange
Hill Top Fm
The Deep
Wilberforce House
Bridlington Road
Beverley Road
Hornsea Road
Seaton Road
Skipsea Road
Atwick Road
Rolston Road
Main Road
Garton Road
Aldbrough Road
Spratley Road
Northfield Road
Whitecross Road
Holderness Road
Hedon Road
Hull Road
Station Road
Pilmar Lane
Elliffoot Lane
New Laids Lane
A165
A1035
A1079
A1033
B1242
B1244
B1249
B1243
B1238
B1239
B1240
B1362
TA

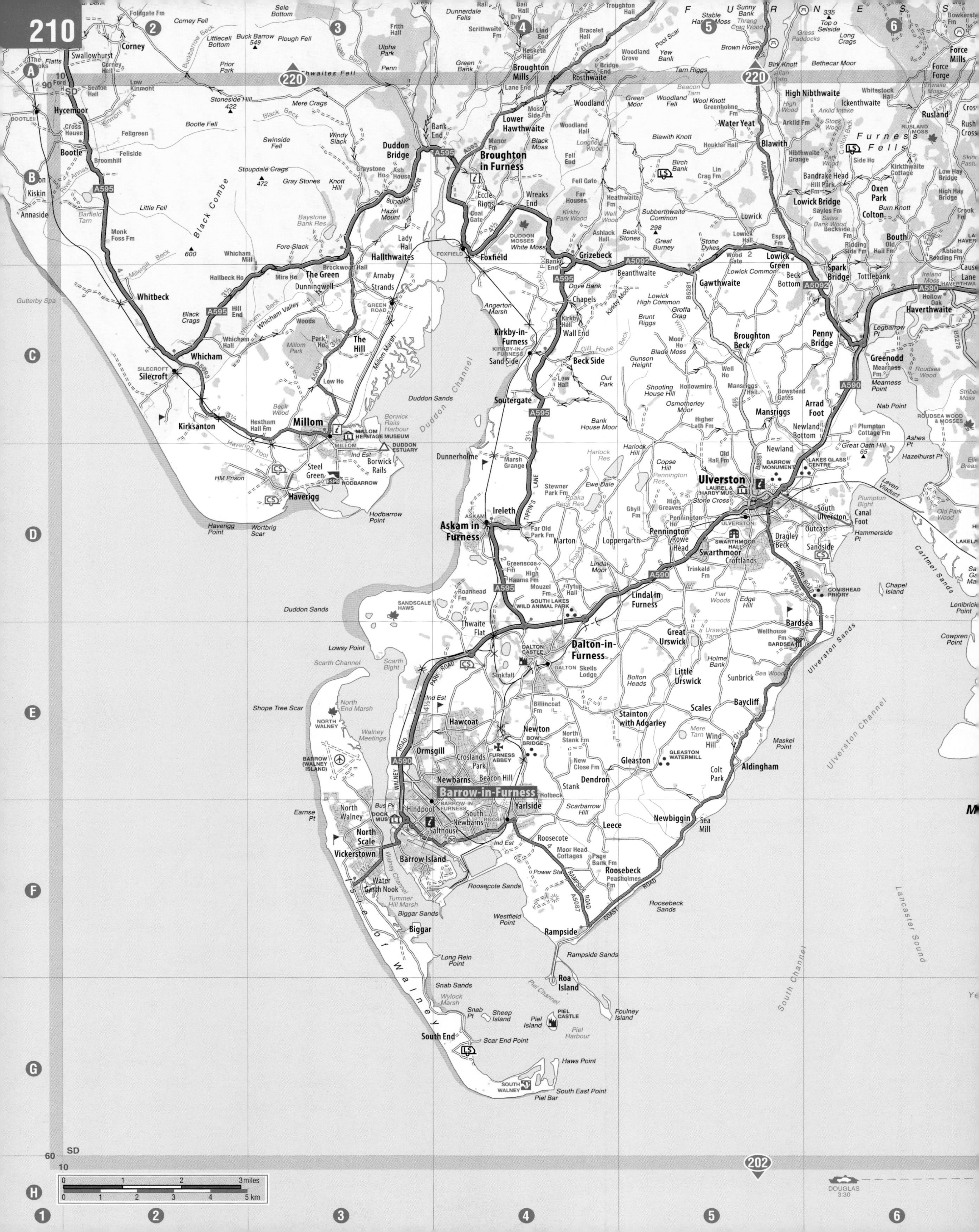

Corney
Bootle
Whitbeck
Whicham
Silecroft
Kirksanton
Millom
Haverigg
Black Combe
The Green
Hallthwaites
The Hill
Duddon Bridge
Broughton in Furness
Foxfield
Grizebeck
Kirkby-in-Furness
Askam in Furness
Ireleth
Dalton-in-Furness
Lindal in Furness
Ulverston
Swarthmoor
Pennington
Great Urswick
Little Urswick
Bardsea
Baycliff
Aldingham
Gleaston
Newbiggin
Barrow-in-Furness
Vickerstown
North Scale
Barrow Island
Biggar
Rampside
Roa Island
Piel Island
South End
Isle of Walney
Duddon Sands
Ulverston Sands
Lancaster Sound
Greenodd
Haverthwaite
Lowick Bridge
Penny Bridge
Spark Bridge
Rusland
Furness Fells
A595
A590
A5092
A5093
220
202
DOUGLAS 3:30

0 1 2 3 miles
0 1 2 3 4 5 km

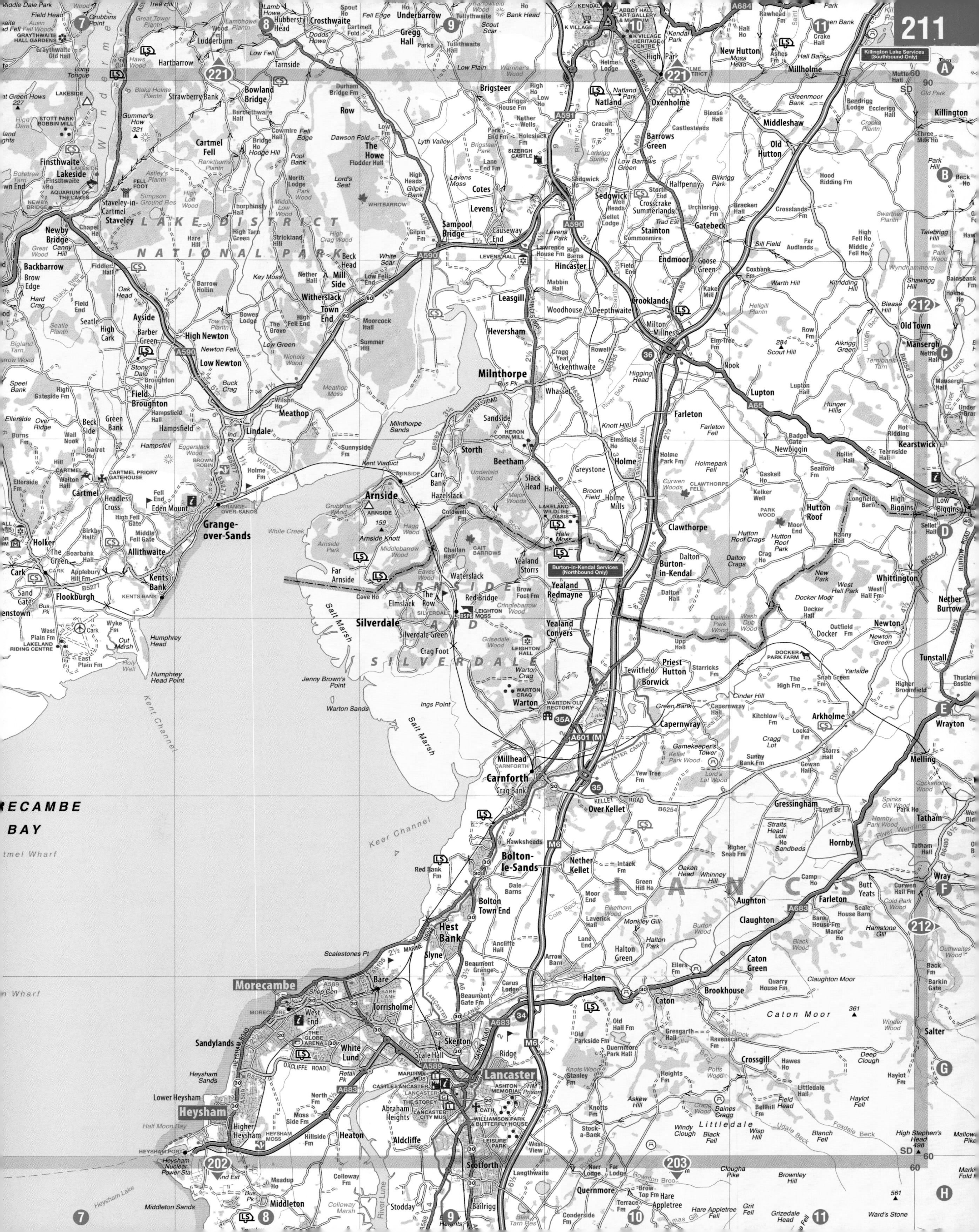
LAKE DISTRICT
NATIONAL PARK
ARNSIDE AND SILVERDALE
MORECAMBE BAY
Kent Channel
Keer Channel
Salt Marsh
Kendal
Abbot Hall Art Gallery & Museum
K Village Heritage Centre
Killington Lake Services (Southbound Only)
Burton-in-Kendal Services (Northbound Only)
Crosthwaite
Underbarrow
Gregg Hall
Ludderburn
Hartbarrow
Tarnside
Bowland Bridge
Strawberry Bank
Brigsteer
Natland
Oxenholme
New Hutton
Millholme
Killington
Middleshaw
Old Hutton
Halfpenny
Barrows Green
Sedgwick
Crosscrake
Summerlands
Stainton
Gatebeck
Endmoor
Cartmel Fell
Row
The Howe
Lyth Valley
Sizergh Castle
Levens
Cotes
Sampool Bridge
Levens Hall
Hincaster
Leasgill
Heversham
Woodhouse
Deepthwaite
Crooklands
Milton
Milnthorpe
Ackenthwaite
Whasset
Lupton
Old Town
Mansergh
Farleton
Kearstwick
Finsthwaite
Lakeside
Staveley-in-Cartmel
Newby Bridge
Backbarrow
Witherslack
Town End
High Newton
Low Newton
Ayside
Field Broughton
Meathop
Lindale
Hampsfield
Cartmel
Grange-over-Sands
Eden Mount
Allithwaite
Holker
Cark
Flookburgh
Kents Bank
Arnside
Storth
Beetham
Hale
Holme
Greystone
Clawthorpe
Hutton Roof
Low Biggins
High Biggins
Burton-in-Kendal
Dalton
Yealand Redmayne
Yealand Conyers
Silverdale
Warton
Priest Hutton
Borwick
Capernwray
Arkholme
Whittington
Nether Burrow
Newton
Docker
Tunstall
Wrayton
Melling
Millhead
Carnforth
Over Kellet
Gressingham
Hornby
Tatham
Wray
Bolton-le-Sands
Nether Kellet
Aughton
Farleton
Claughton
Hest Bank
Slyne
Halton
Caton Green
Caton
Brookhouse
Caton Moor
Morecambe
Bare
Torrisholme
West End
Sandylands
White Lund
Skerton
Lancaster
Heysham
Higher Heysham
Heaton
Aldcliffe
Scotforth
Quernmore
Littledale
Crossgill
Salter
Middleton
Bailrigg
Stodday
Ward's Stone
M6
A6
A65
A590
A591
A683
A589
A601(M)
221
212
202
203
A
B
C
D
E
F
G
H
7
8
9
10
11

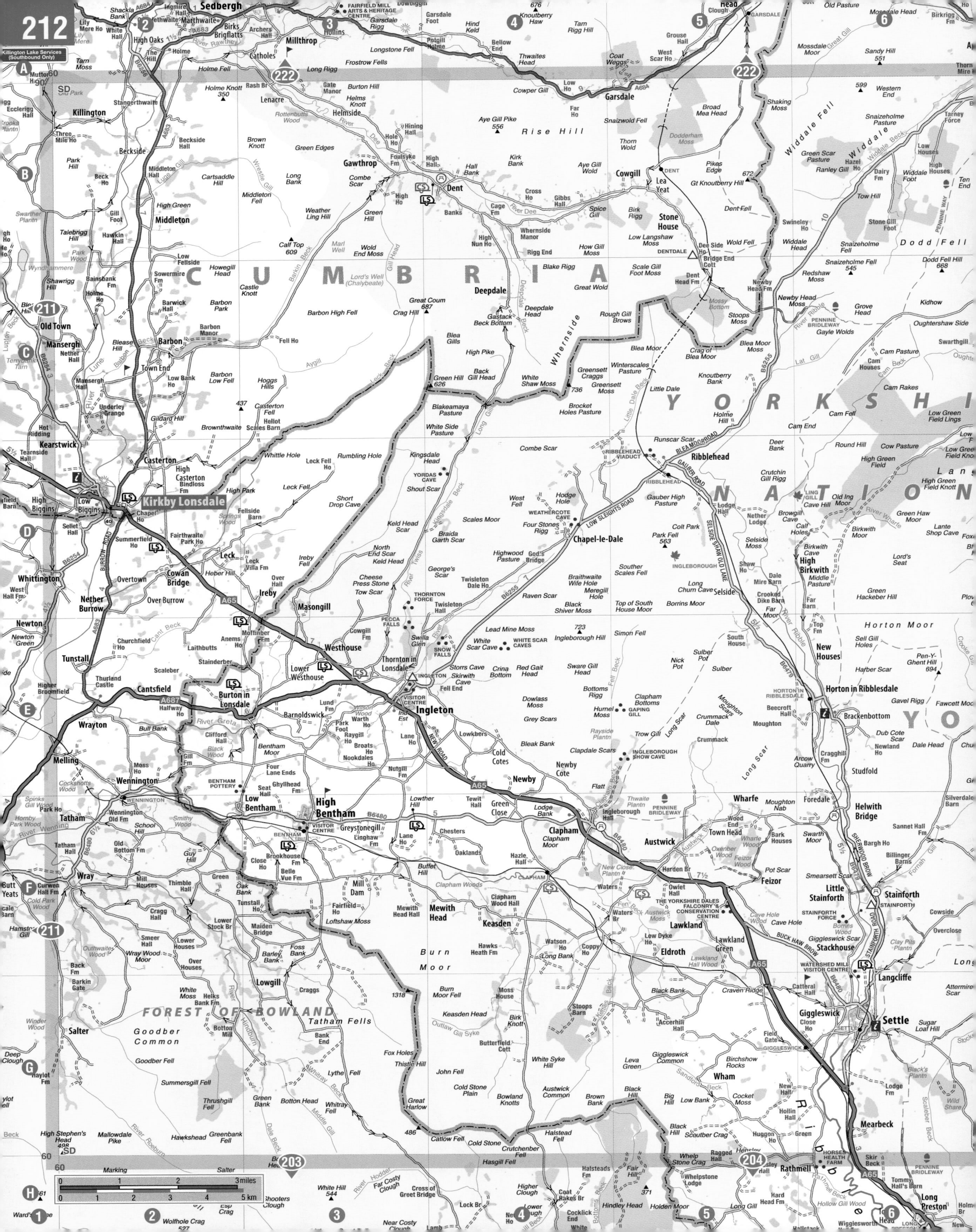
Killington Lake Services (Southbound Only)
Sedbergh
Millthrop
Garsdale
Garsdale Head
Killington
Gawthrop
Dent
Cowgill
Lea Yeat
Stone House
Middleton
C U M B R I A
Y O R K S H I R E
N A T I O N
Deepdale
Rise Hill
Whernside
Dodd Fell
Old Town
Mansergh
Barbon
Casterton
Kearstwick
Kirkby Lonsdale
Ribblehead
Ribblehead Viaduct
Chapel-le-Dale
Ingleborough
High Birkwith
Selside
Leck
Cowan Bridge
Ireby
Masongill
Whittington
Nether Burrow
Newton
Tunstall
Westhouse
Thornton in Lonsdale
Ingleton
Burton in Lonsdale
Cantsfield
Wrayton
Melling
Wennington
Low Bentham
High Bentham
Clapham
Austwick
Newby
Horton in Ribblesdale
Brackenbottom
Helwith Bridge
Studfold
Wray
Tatham
Feizor
Little Stainforth
Stainforth
Lawkland
Eldroth
Keasden
Mewith Head
Stackhouse
Langcliffe
Giggleswick
Settle
Lowgill
Salter
FOREST OF BOWLAND
Tatham Fells
Burn Moor
Goodber Common
Wham
Rathmell
Long Preston
Mearbeck
Austwick Common
A65
A683
A684
A687
B6255
B6480
B6479
222
211
203
204
0 1 2 3 miles
0 1 2 3 4 5 km

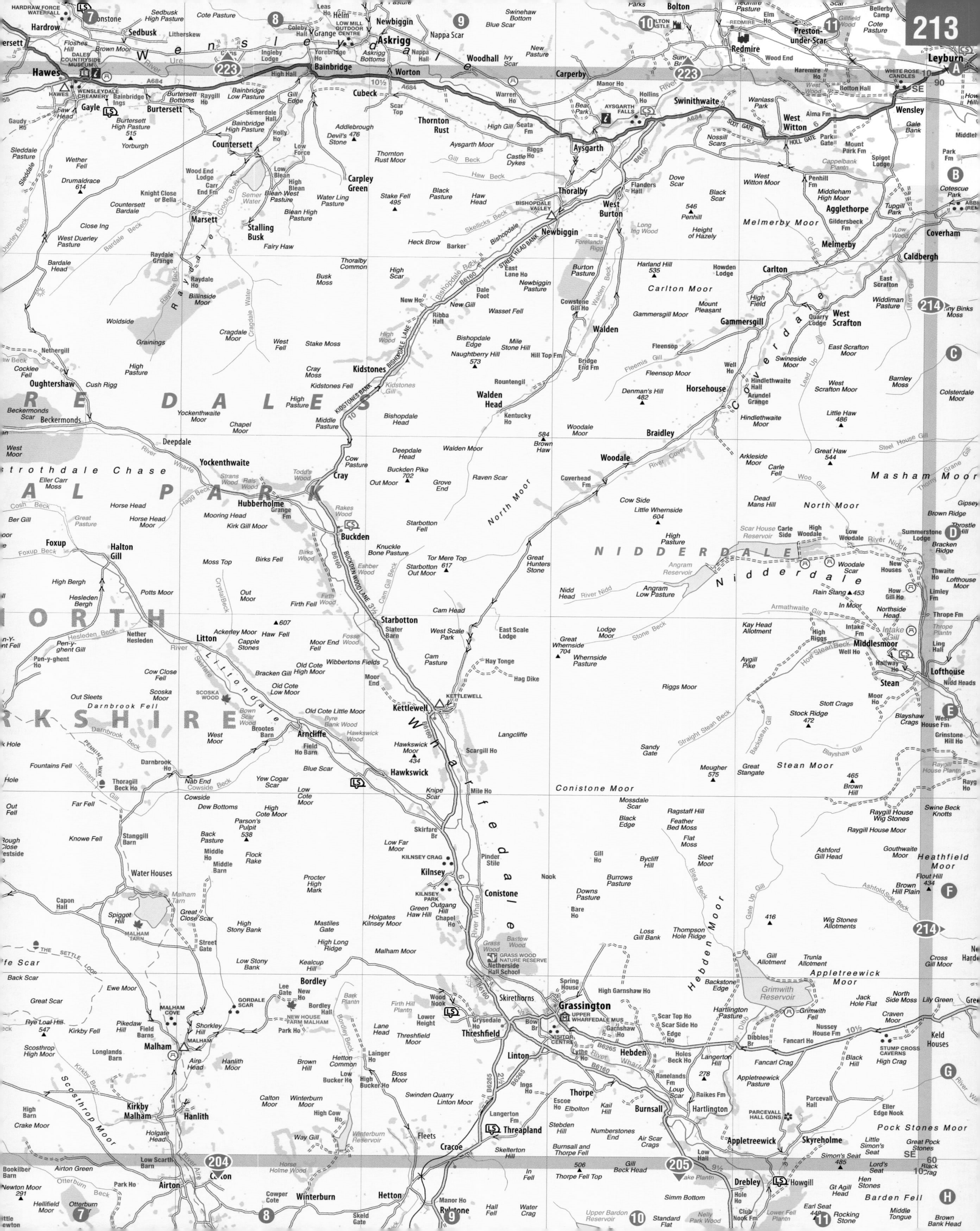

HARDRAW FORCE WATERFALL
Hardrow
Sedbusk
Sedbusk High Pasture
Cote Pasture
Litherskew
Leas Ho
Helm
LOW MILL OUTDOOR CENTRE
Newbiggin
Nappa Scar
Swinehaw Bottom
Blue Scar
Bolton
Redmire
Preston-under-Scar
Bellerby Camp
Cote Pasture
Elm Ho
Askrigg
Askrigg Bottoms
Nappa Hall
Woodhall
Ivy Scar
New Pasture
Wood End
Leyburn
W e n s l e y d a l e
Hawes
Gayle
Burtersett
Burtersett Bottoms
Burtersett High Pasture
Raygill Ho
Bainbridge
Bainbridge Ings
Bainbridge Low Pasture
Bainbridge High Pasture
WENSLEYDALE CREAMERY
DALES COUNTRYSIDE MUSEUM
Brown Moor
Ingleby Lodge
Yorebridge Ho
High Hall
Worton
Cubeck
Scar Top
Carperby
Manor Ho
Hollins Ho
Swinithwaite
Harmire Ho
WHITE ROSE CANDLES
Bolton Hall
Wanlass Park
West Witton
Wensley
Alma Fm
Gale Bank
Gaudy Ho
Semerdale Hall
Holly Ho
Countersett
Yorburgh
Addlebrough 476
Devil's Stone
Thornton Rust
Thornton Rust Moor
High Gill
Seata Fm
Riggs Ho
Castle Dykes
Aysgarth Moor
Bear Park
AYSGARTH FALLS
Aysgarth
Nossill Scars
Park Gate
Mount Park Fm
Spigot Lodge
Cappelbank Plantn
Sleddale Pasture
Wether Fell
Drumaldrace 614
Low Force
Low Blean
Wood End Lodge
Carr End Fm
Semer Water
High Blean
Blean West Pasture
Carpley Green
Water Ling Pasture
Stake Fell 495
Black Pasture
Haw Head
Haw Beck
Thoralby
Flanders Hall
Dove Scar
Black Scar
Penhill Fm
Middleham High Moor
Agglethorpe
Tupgill Park
Cotescue Park
Knight Close or Bella
Countersett Bardale
Marsett
Stalling Busk
Blean High Pasture
Fairy Haw
BISHOPDALE VALLEY
West Burton
Newbiggin
546 Penhill
Height of Hazely
Long Ing Wood
Melmerby Moor
Gildersbeck Fm
Melmerby
Coverham
Caldbergh
Close Ing
West Duerley Pasture
Bardale Beck
Raydale Grange
Raydale Ho
Billinside Moor
Bardale Head
Heck Brow
Barker
Thoralby Common
Busk Moss
High Scar
East Lane Ho
Newbiggin Pasture
Burton Pasture
Harland Hill 535
Howden Lodge
Carlton
East Scrafton
Carlton Moor
Dale Foot
Wasset Fell
New Ho
New Gill
Ribba Hall
Cowstone Gill Ho
Mount Pleasant
Gammersgill Moor
High Field
Widdiman Pasture
Any Binks Moss
West Scrafton
Quarry Lodge
Gammersgill
Woldside
Grainings
Cragdale Moor
Bishopdale Edge
Mile Stone Hill
Walden
Fleensop
East Scrafton Moor
Swineside Moor
Hill Top Fm
Bridge End Fm
Fleensop Moor
Well Ho
Nethergill
Cocklee Fell
West Fell
Stake Moss
High Pasture
Cray Moss
Naughtberry Hill 573
Kidstones
Kidstones Fell
Kidstones Bank
Rountengil
Walden Head
Denman's Hill 482
Horsehouse
Hindlethwaite Hall
Arundel Grange
West Scrafton Moor
Barnley Moss
Colsterdale Moor
Oughtershaw
Cush Rigg
Beckermonds Scar
Beckermonds
Yockenthwaite Moor
Chapel Moor
Middle Pasture
Bishopdale Head
Kentucky Ho
584 Brown Haw
Woodale Moor
Braidley
Hindlethwaite Moor
Little Haw 486
Y O R K S H I R E   D A L E S   N A T I O N A L   P A R K
West Moor
Deepdale
Yockenthwaite
Strans Wood
Rais Wood
Todd's Wood
Cow Pasture
Cray
Deepdale Head
Walden Moor
Buckden Pike 702
Out Moor
Grove End
Raven Scar
Woodale
Coverhead Fm
River Cover
Arkleside Moor
Carle Fell
Great Haw 544
Masham Moor
Langstrothdale Chase
Eller Carr Moss
Horse Head
Horse Head Moor
Hagg Beck
Hubberholme
Grange Fm
Cosh Beck
Ber Gill
Great Pasture
Mooring Head
Kirk Gill Moor
Rakes Wood
Buckden
Starbotton Fell
North Moor
Cow Side
Little Whernside 604
Dead Mans Hill
North Moor
Gipsey
Brown Ridge
Throstle Hill
Foxup
Halton Gill
Scar House Reservoir
Carle Side
High Woodale
Low Woodale
Summerstone Lodge
Bracken Ridge
N I D D E R D A L E
High Pasture
Knuckle Bone Pasture
Tor Mere Top 617
Starbotton Out Moor
Great Hunters Stone
Angram Reservoir
Woodale Scar
New Houses
Moss Top
Birks Fell
Birks Wood
Eshber Wood
Thwaite Ho
Lofthouse Moor
Limley Fm
High Bergh
Hesleden Bergh
Potts Moor
Out Moor
Crystal Beck
Firth Fell
Firth Wood
Nidd Head
River Nidd
Angram Low Pasture
N i d d e r d a l e
Rain Stang 453
How Gill Ho
In Moor
Northside Head
Cam Head
Armathwaite Gill
Thrope Fm
N O R T H   Y O R K S H I R E
607
Starbotton
Slater Barn
Ackerley Moor
Haw Fell
Nether Hesleden
Pen-y-ghent Gill
Pen-y-ghent Ho
Pen-y-ghent Fell
Litton
Capple Stones
Moor End Fell
Fosse Wood
West Scale Park
East Scale Lodge
Lodge Moor
Great Whernside 704
Whernside Pasture
Stone Beck
Kay Head Allotment
High Riggs
Intake Fm
Middlesmoor
Ling Hall
Well Ho
Halfway Ho
Lofthouse
Nidd Heads
Aygill Pike
Cam Pasture
Hay Tonge
Hag Dike
Wibbertons Fields
Old Cote High Moor
Bracken Gill
Old Cote Low Moor
Moor End
Littondale
Cow Close Fell
Scoska Moor
SCOSKA WOOD
Riggs Moor
Stean
Stott Crags
Moor Ho
Stock Ridge 472
Blayshaw Crags
West House Fm
Out Sleets
Darnbrook Fell
Bown Scar Wood
Old Cote Little Moor
Byre Bank Wood
KETTLEWELL
Kettlewell
Langcliffe
Grinstone Hill Ho
Arncliffe
Brootes Barn
West Moor
Hawkswick Wood
Field Ho Barn
Hawkswick Moor 434
Scargill Ho
Straight Stean Beck
Sandy Gate
Blayshaw Gill
Fountains Fell
Darnbrook Ho
PENNINE WAY
Tennant Gill
Thoragill Beck Ho
Blue Scar
Hawkswick
Meugher 575
Great Stangate
Stean Moor
465 Brown Hill
Nab End
Cowside Beck
Yew Cogar Scar
Knipe Scar
Mile Ho
Conistone Moor
Mossdale Scar
Raygill House Plantn
Swine Beck Knotts
Far Fell
Cowside
Dew Bottoms
High Cote Moor
Low Cote Moor
Black Edge
Ragstaff Hill
Feather Bed Moss
Raygill House Wig Stones
Raygill House Moor
Parson's Pulpit 538
Back Pasture
Middle Ho
Middle Barn
Flock Rake
Stanggill Barn
Knowe Fell
Skirfare Br
Low Far Moor
KILNSEY CRAG
Kilnsey
Pinder Stile
Gill Ho
Bycliff Hill
Sleet Moor
Flat Moss
Ashford Gill Head
Gouthwaite Moor
Heathfield Moor
Water Houses
Procter High Mark
Nook
Burrows Pasture
Downs Pasture
Flout Hill 434
Brown Hill Plain
Ashfold Side Beck
Malham Tarn
Capon Hall
Spiggot Hill
Great Close Scar
MALHAM TARN
KILNSEY PARK
Outgang Hill
Green Haw Hill
Chapel Ho
Conistone
Bare Ho
Gate Up Gill
416
Holgates Kilnsey Moor
Mastiles Gate
High Stony Bank
Loss Gill Bank
Thompson Hole Ridge
Wig Stones Allotments
Street Gate
High Long Ridge
Malham Moor
Bastow Wood
GRASS WOOD NATURE RESERVE
Netherside Hall School
Hebden Moor
Gill Allotment
Trunla Allotment
Appletreewick Moor
Cross Gill Moor
THE SETTLE LOOP
Low Stony Bank
Kealcup Hill
Back Scar
Ewe Moor
Bordley
Lee Gate
New Ho
Bordley Hall
Bark Plantn
Firth Hill Plantn
Wood Nook
Skirethorns
Spring House
Grassington
High Garnshaw Ho
Backstone Edge
Grimwith Reservoir
Jack Hole Flat
North Side Moss
Lily Green
Great Scar
MALHAM COVE
GORDALE SCAR
NEW HOUSE FARM MALHAM
Lower Height
Grysedale Ho
Threshfield
UPPER WHARFEDALE MUS
Scar Top Ho
Scar Side Ho
Hartlington Pasture
Grimwith Fell
Nussey House Fm
Craven Moor
Rye Loaf Hill 547
Pikedaw Hill
Field Barns
Shorkley Hill
Park Ho
Lane Head
Threshfield Moor
Bow Br
VISITOR CENTRE
Garnshaw Ho
Edge Ho
Dibbles Br
Fancarl Ho
Keld Houses
Kirkby Fell
MALHAM
Malham
Scosthrop High Moor
Longlands Barn
Aire Head
Hanlith Moor
Brown Hill
Hetton Common
Lainger Ho
Linton
Lythe Ho
Hebden
Holes Beck Ho
Langerton Hill
Fancarl Crag
STUMP CROSS CAVERNS
High Crag
Black Hill
Low Bucker Ho
High Bucker Ho
Boss Moor
Ings Ho
Ranelands Fm
Loup Scar
278
Raikes Fm
Appletreewick Pasture
Scosthrop Moor
Kirkby Beck
Kirkby Malham
Hanlith
Calton Moor
Winterburn Moor
High Cow Ho
Swinden Quarry
Linton Moor
Thorpe
Escoe Ho
Elbolton
Kail Hill
Burnsall
Hartlington
Parcevall Hall
PARCEVALL HALL GDNS
Eller Edge Nook
Pock Stones Moor
High Barn
Crake Moor
Holgate Head
Way Gill
Winterburn Reservoir
Fleets
Langerton Fm
Threapland
Stebden Hill
Numberstones End
Air Scar Crags
Appletreewick
Skyreholme
Little Simon's Seat
Great Pock Stones
Cracoe
Skelterton Hill
Burnsall and Thorpe Fell
Low Hall
Simon's Seat 485
Lord's Seat
Black Crag
Bookilber Barn
Airton Green
Low Scarth Barn
River Aire
Calton
Horse Holme Wood
In Fell
506 Thorpe Fell Top
Gill Beck Head
Lake Plantn
Drebley
Howgill
Hen Stones
Gt Agill Head
Newton Moor 291
Otterburn Beck
Park Ho
Airton
Cowper Cote
Winterburn
Hetton
Manor Ho
Rylstone
Hole Ho
Simm Bottom
Barden Fell
Hellifield Moor
Otterburn
Skeld Gate
Hall Fell
Water Crag
Upper Barden Reservoir
Standard Flat
Nelly Park Wood
Club Nook Fm
Lower Fell Plantn
Earl Seat 448
Rocking Stone
Middle Tongue
Brown Bank Head
Little Newton
A684
B6160
B6265
B6255
223
204
205
214

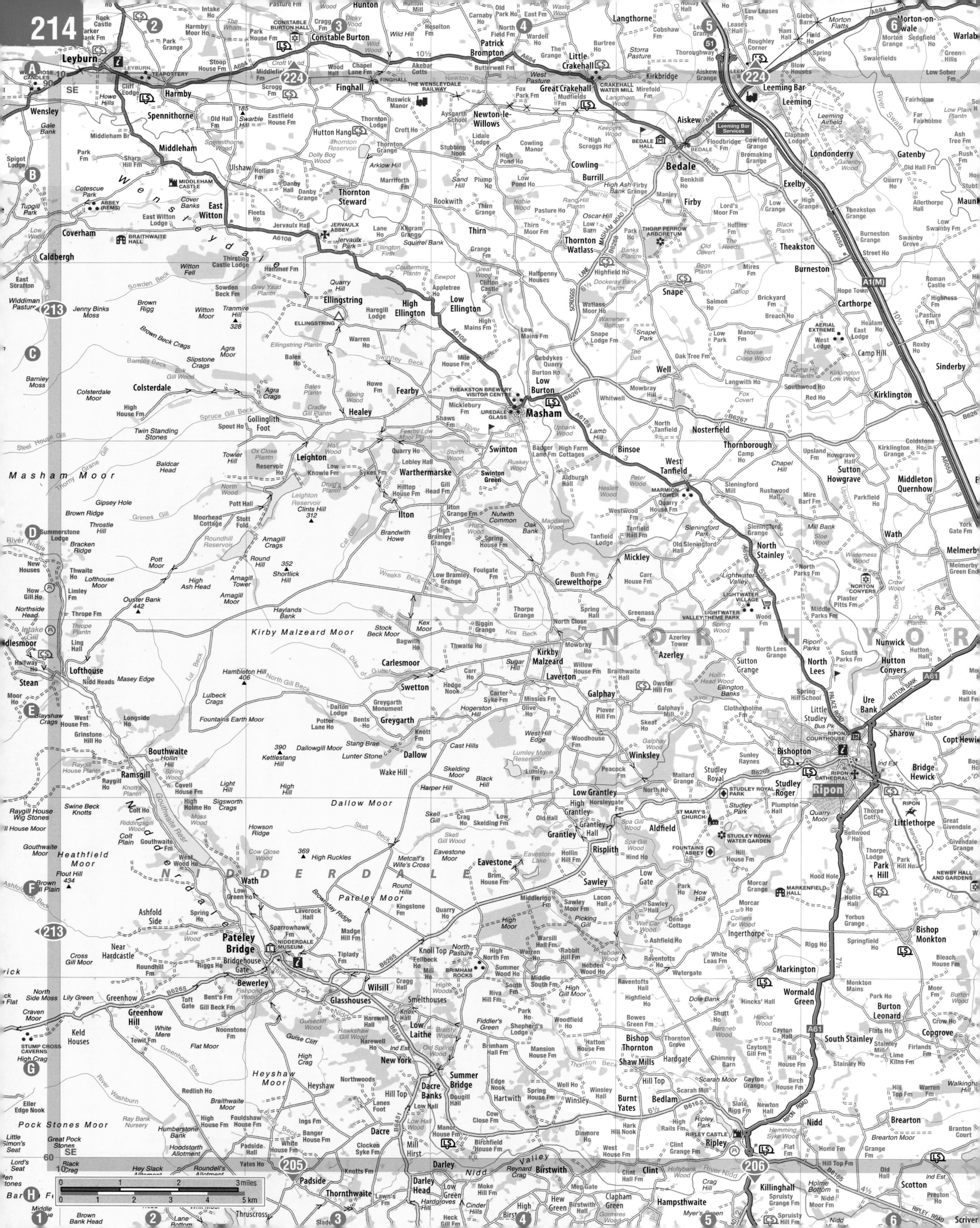
Leyburn
Constable Burton
Patrick Brompton
Langthorne
Little Crakehall
Great Crakehall
Kirkbridge
Leeming Bar
Leeming
Harmby
Finghall
Wensley
Spennithorne
Middleham
Newton-le-Willows
Aiskew
Bedale
Leeming Bar Services
Londonderry
Gatenby
Exelby
Firby
Burrill
Cowling
Thornton Steward
East Witton
Coverham
Caldbergh
Jervaulx Abbey
Thirn
Thornton Watlass
Snape
Theakston
Burneston
Carthorpe
Ellingstring
High Ellington
Low Ellington
Well
Sinderby
Kirklington
Colsterdale
Fearby
Healey
Masham
Low Burton
Nosterfield
Thornborough
Binsoe
West Tanfield
Leighton
Warthermarske
Swinton
Sutton Howgrave
Middleton Quernhow
Masham Moor
Ilton
Wath
North Stainley
Mickley
Grewelthorpe
Kirby Malzeard Moor
Kirkby Malzeard
Laverton
Azerley
Carlesmoor
Swetton
Galphay
North Lees
Nunwick
Hutton Conyers
Lofthouse
Stean
Ure Bank
Sharow
Greygarth
Dallow
Winksley
Bishopton
Ripon
Bridge Hewick
Ramsgill
Bouthwaite
Studley Roger
Low Grantley
High Grantley
Grantley
Risplith
Aldfield
Fountains Abbey
Littlethorpe
Dallow Moor
Nidderdale
Eavestone
Sawley
Pateley Moor
Heathfield Moor
Pateley Bridge
Ingerthorpe
Bishop Monkton
Markington
Wormald Green
Bewerley
Wilsill
Glasshouses
Greenhow Hill
Low Laithe
New York
Summer Bridge
Dacre Banks
Bishop Thornton
Shaw Mills
South Stainley
Burton Leonard
Copgrove
Heyshaw Moor
Heyshaw
Hartwith
Burnt Yates
Bedlam
Nidd
Brearton
Pock Stones Moor
Dacre
Ripley
Padside
Darley
Birstwith
Clint
Killinghall
Thornthwaite
Hampsthwaite
Scotton
NORTH YORKSHIRE
A1(M)
A61
A6108
A684
B6265
224
213
205
206
0 1 2 3 miles
0 1 2 3 4 5 km

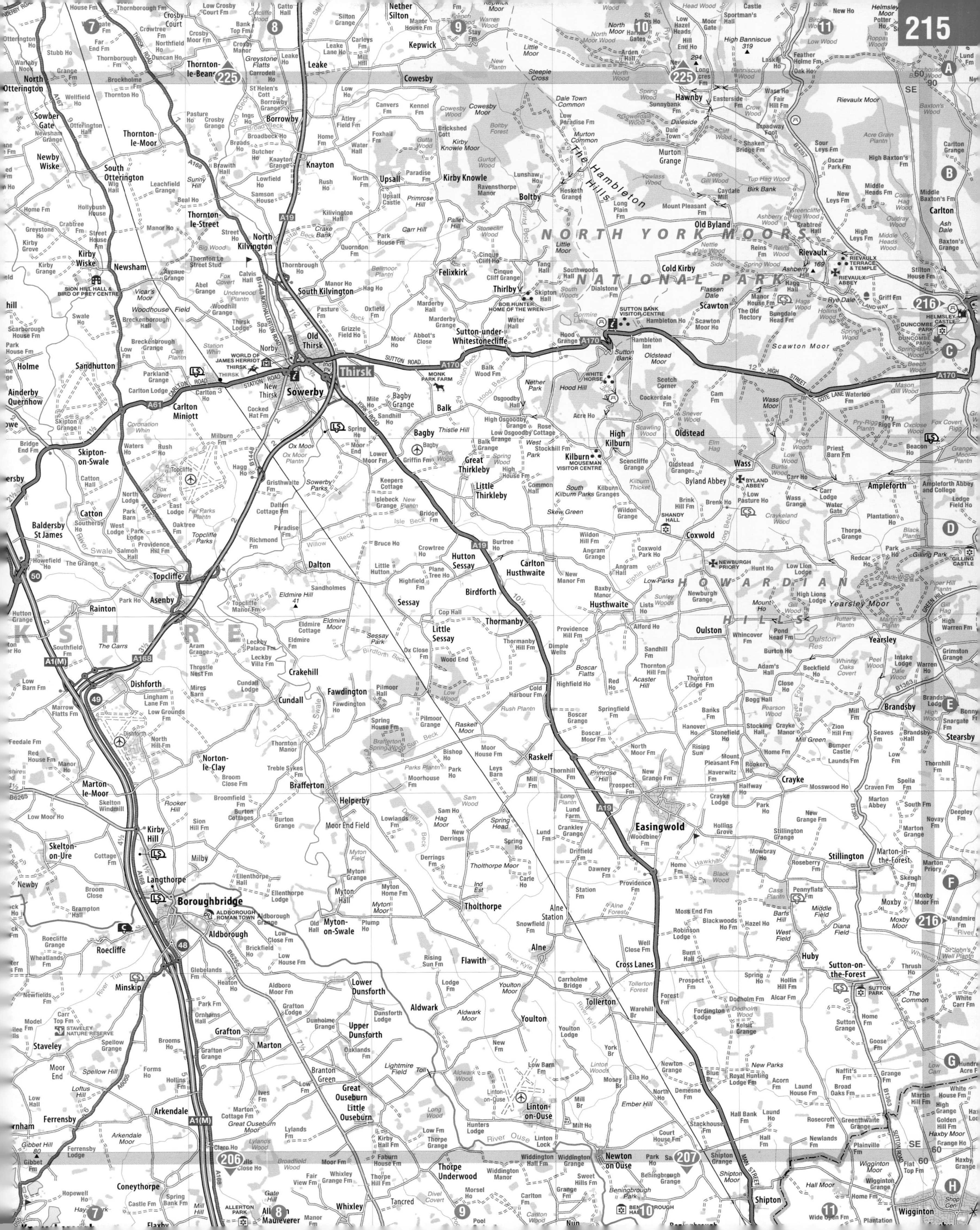
NORTH YORK MOORS NATIONAL PARK
HOWARDIAN HILLS
The Hambleton Hills
YORKSHIRE
Thirsk
Sowerby
Easingwold
Boroughbridge
Aldborough
Helmsley
Rievaulx
Coxwold
Ampleforth
Topcliffe
Dishforth
Helperby
Brafferton
Tollerton
Alne
Huby
Sutton-on-the-Forest
Stillington
Crayke
Brandsby
Shipton
Wigginton
Linton-on-Ouse
Newton on Ouse
Kilburn
Sutton-under-Whitestonecliffe
Felixkirk
Kirby Knowle
Cowesby
Kepwick
Leake
Thornton-le-Beans
North Otterington
South Otterington
Thornton-le-Moor
Thornton-le-Street
North Kilvington
South Kilvington
Newsham
Kirby Wiske
Sandhutton
Carlton Miniott
Skipton-on-Swale
Baldersby St James
Catton
Asenby
Rainton
Dalton
Sessay
Hutton Sessay
Birdforth
Thormanby
Husthwaite
Oulston
Yearsley
Raskelf
Great Ouseburn
Little Ouseburn
Upper Dunsforth
Lower Dunsforth
Aldwark
Youlton
Flawith
Tholthorpe
Myton-on-Swale
Marton
Grafton
Minskip
Roecliffe
Langthorpe
Kirby Hill
Milby
Norton-le-Clay
Cundall
Crakehill
Fawdington
Marton-le-Moor
Skelton-on-Ure
Staveley
Ferrensby
Arkendale
Coneythorpe
Whixley
Tholthorpe
Thorpe Underwood
Cross Lanes
Hawnby
Boltby
Thirlby
Scawton
Old Byland
Cold Kirby
Wass
Byland Abbey
Oldstead
High Kilburn
Bagby
Balk
Great Thirkleby
Little Thirkleby
Carlton Husthwaite
Carlton
A1(M)
A19
A61
A168
A170
B1363
B1448
River Ouse
River Swale
River Kyle
206
207
216
225

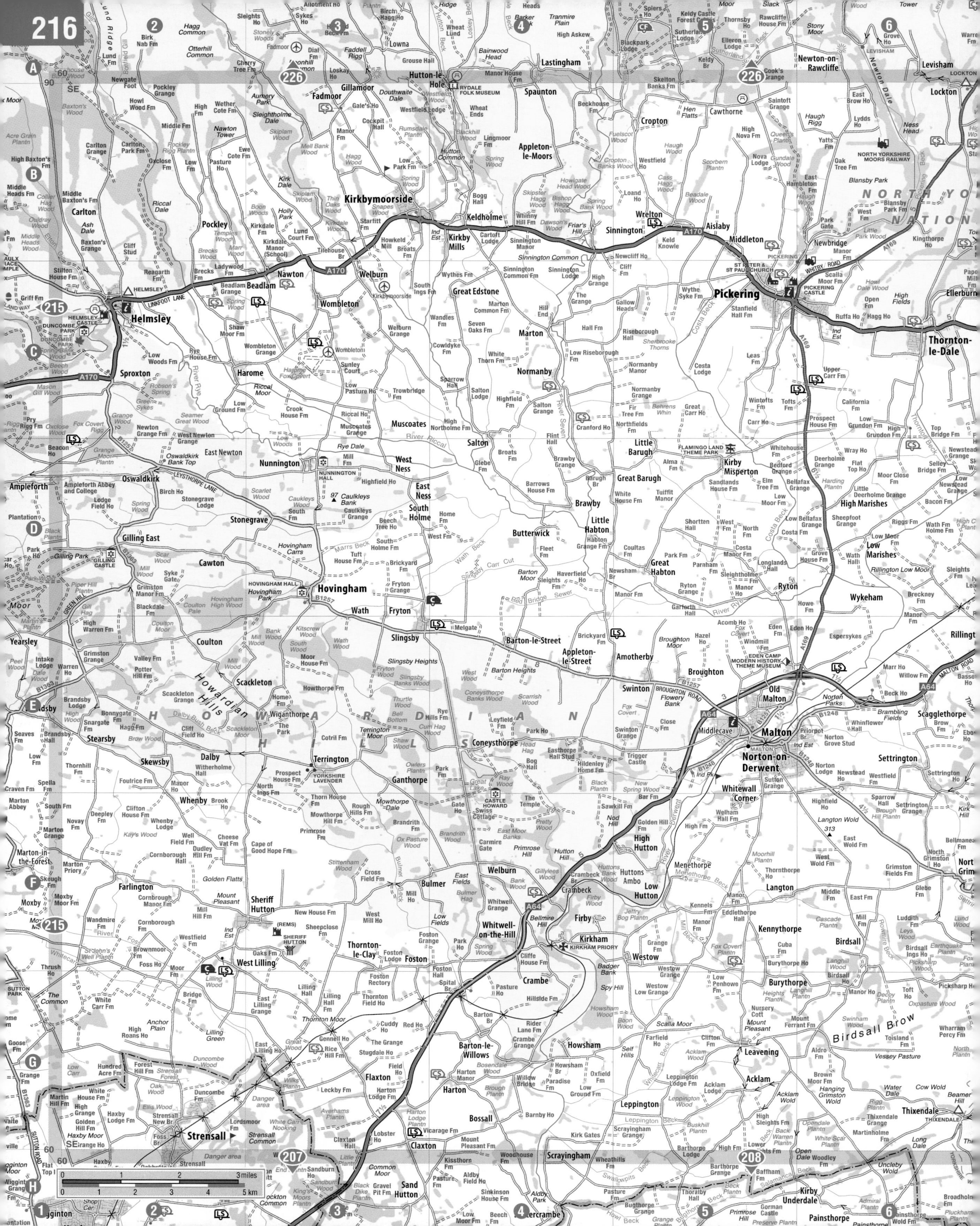
Helmsley
Kirkbymoorside
Pickering
Malton
Norton-on-Derwent
Old Malton
Thornton-le-Dale
Hovingham
Slingsby
Strensall
Sheriff Hutton
Terrington
Castle Howard
Kirkham Priory
Lastingham
Hutton-le-Hole
Ryedale Folk Museum
Appleton-le-Moors
Cropton
Sinnington
Nawton
Beadlam
Wombleton
Welburn
Harome
Nunnington
Oswaldkirk
Ampleforth
Gilling East
Stonegrave
Coulton
Yearsley
Scackleton
Dalby
Stearsby
Skewsby
Whenby
Farlington
West Lilling
Foston
Thornton-le-Clay
Bulmer
Whitwell-on-the-Hill
Crambe
Firby
Westow
Barton-le-Willows
Howsham
Flaxton
Harton
Bossall
Claxton
Sand Hutton
Leppington
Scrayingham
Acklam
Leavening
Burythorpe
Kennythorpe
Langton
Birdsall
Settrington
Scagglethorpe
Rillington
Wykeham
High Marishes
Low Marishes
Ryton
Kirby Misperton
Great Habton
Little Habton
Brawby
Butterwick
Marton
Normanby
Salton
Muscoates
Great Edstone
Keldholme
Kirkby Mills
Middleton
Aislaby
Wrelton
Newton-on-Rawcliffe
Levisham
Lockton
Spaunton
Gillamoor
Fadmoor
Pockley
Carlton
Sproxton
Amotherby
Swinton
Broughton
Appleton-le-Street
Barton-le-Street
Coneysthorpe
Ganthorpe
Fryton
Wath
Cawton
Huttons Ambo
Low Hutton
High Hutton
Menethorpe
Thixendale
Kirby Underdale
Howardian Hills
North York Moors National Park
North Yorkshire Moors Railway
Flamingo Land Theme Park
Eden Camp Modern History Theme Museum
Yorkshire Lavender
Duncombe Park
Helmsley Castle
Nunnington Hall
Hovingham Hall
Gilling Castle
Birdsall Brow
Danger area
A170
A169
A64
B1257
B1363
B1248
215
226
207
208
0 1 2 3 miles
0 1 2 3 4 5 km

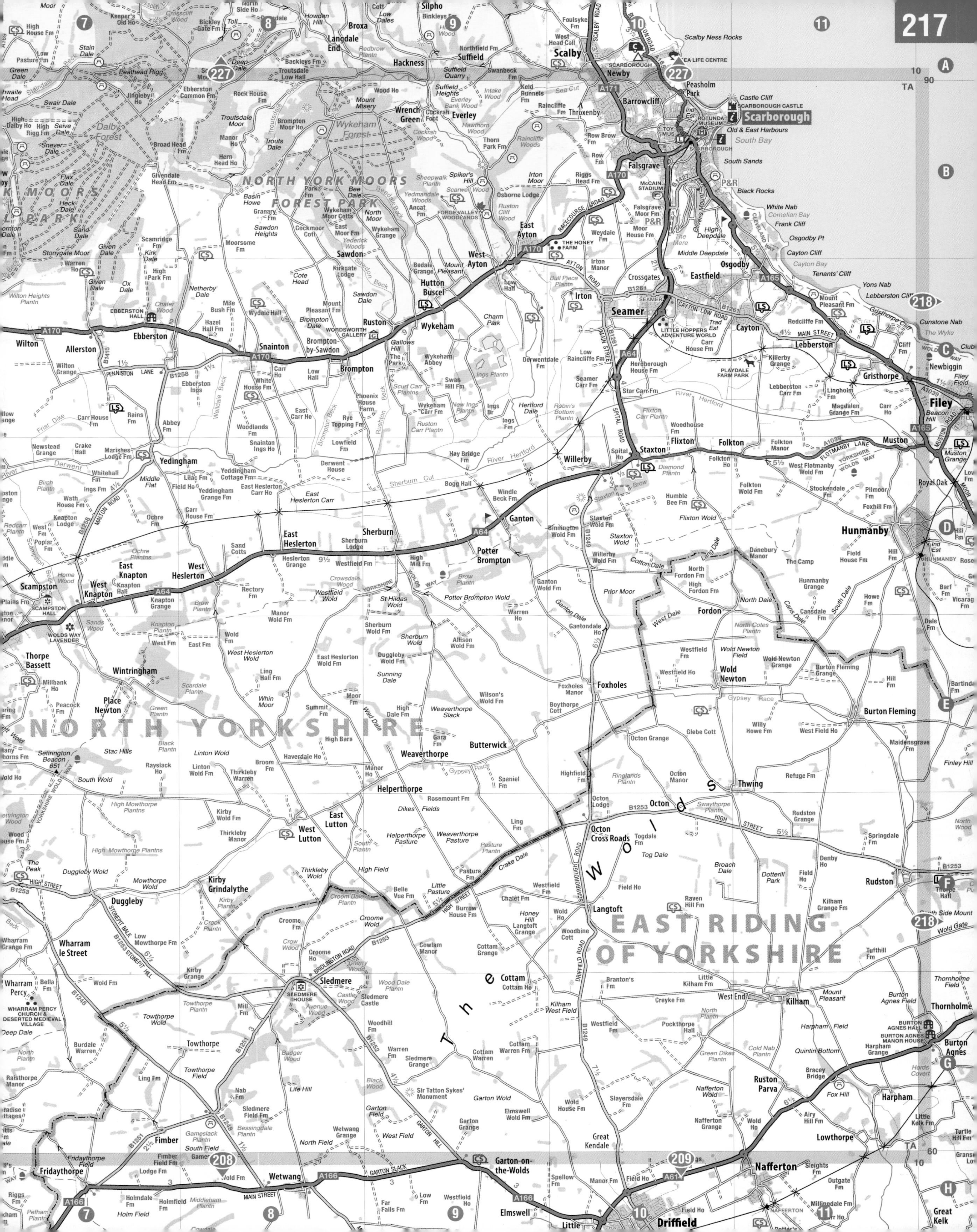
Scarborough
Scalby
Newby
Barrowcliff
Falsgrave
Seamer
Cayton
Osgodby
Eastfield
Filey
Gristhorpe
Lebberston
Hunmanby
Muston
Folkton
Flixton
Staxton
Willerby
Ganton
Sherburn
East Heslerton
West Heslerton
West Knapton
East Knapton
Scampston
Yedingham
Ebberston
Allerston
Wilton
Snainton
Brompton
Wykeham
Ruston
Hutton Buscel
West Ayton
East Ayton
Hackness
Suffield
Everley
Broxa
Langdale End
Silpho
Wrench Green
Potter Brompton
Foxholes
Wold Newton
Fordon
Burton Fleming
Thwing
Octon
Butterwick
Weaverthorpe
Helperthorpe
East Lutton
West Lutton
Kirby Grindalythe
Duggleby
Wintringham
Thorpe Bassett
Place Newton
Wharram le Street
Wharram Percy
Sledmere
Cottam
Langtoft
Rudston
Kilham
Thornholme
Burton Agnes
Harpham
Ruston Parva
Lowthorpe
Nafferton
Driffield
Garton-on-the-Wolds
Wetwang
Fimber
Fridaythorpe
Towthorpe
Elmswell
Great Kendale
Great Kelk
NORTH YORKSHIRE
EAST RIDING OF YORKSHIRE
NORTH YORK MOORS FOREST PARK
The Wolds
Dalby Forest
Wykeham Forest
SCARBOROUGH CASTLE
SEA LIFE CENTRE
ROTUNDA MUSEUM
LITTLE HOPPERS ADVENTURE WORLD
PLAYDALE FARM PARK
WORDSWORTH GALLERY
EBBERSTON HALL
SCAMPSTON HALL
SLEDMERE HOUSE
BURTON AGNES HALL
WHARRAM PERCY CHURCH & DESERTED MEDIEVAL VILLAGE
WOLDS WAY LAVENDER
Sir Tatton Sykes' Monument
A170
A64
A165
A171
A166
A614
A1039
B1253
B1249
B1248
B1251
B1252
B1258
B1261
B1415
218
227
208
209

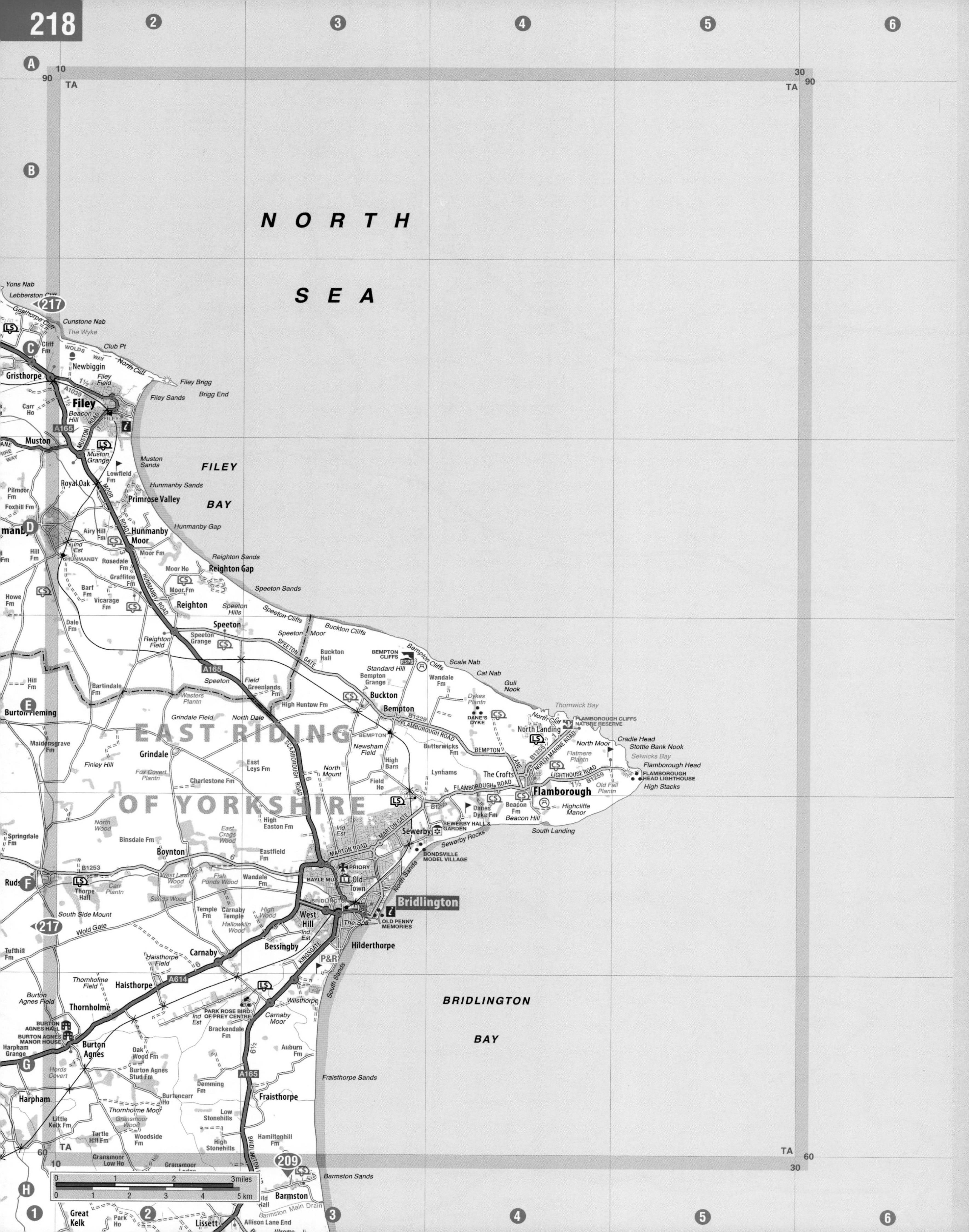
NORTH SEA
FILEY BAY
BRIDLINGTON BAY
EAST RIDING OF YORKSHIRE
Filey
Bridlington
Flamborough
Flamborough Head
Bempton
Buckton
Speeton
Reighton
Hunmanby Moor
Primrose Valley
Muston
Gristhorpe
Sewerby
Hilderthorpe
Bessingby
Carnaby
Boynton
Grindale
Haisthorpe
Thornholme
Burton Agnes
Harpham
Fraisthorpe
Barmston
3 miles
5 km

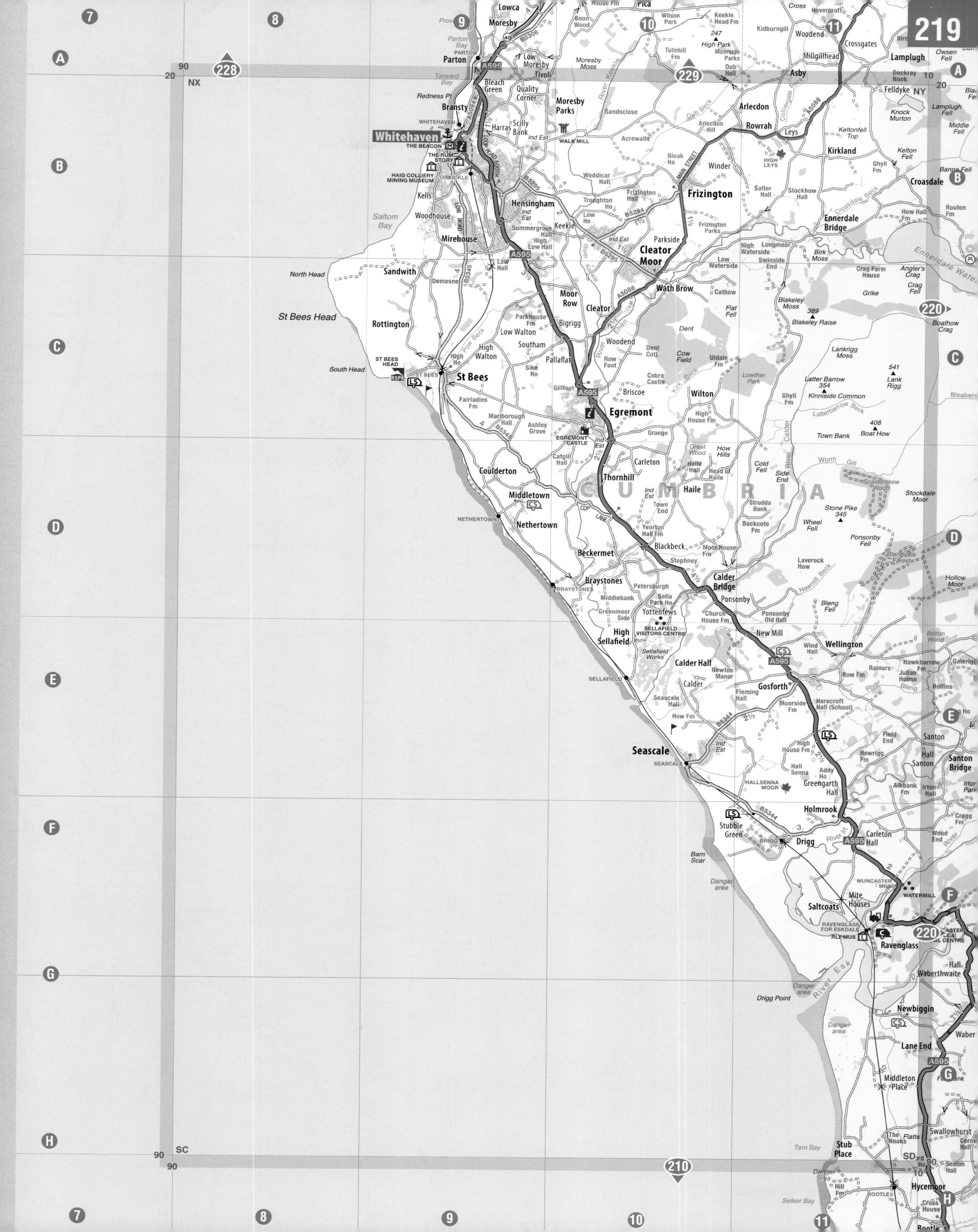

Whitehaven
Parton
Bransty
Moresby
Lowca
Hensingham
Mirehouse
Kells
Woodhouse
Sandwith
St Bees Head
North Head
South Head
Rottington
St Bees
Egremont
Cleator Moor
Cleator
Frizington
Moor Row
Bigrigg
Wath Brow
Thornhill
Haile
Wilton
Coulderton
Middletown
Nethertown
Beckermet
Braystones
Calder Bridge
Ponsonby
High Sellafield
Calder Hall
Gosforth
Seascale
Holmrook
Drigg
Saltcoats
Ravenglass
Waberthwaite
Newbiggin
Lane End
Stub Place
Hycemoor
Wellington
Santon Bridge
Kirkland
Lamplugh
Arlecdon
Rowrah
Asby
Crossgates
Croasdale
Ennerdale Bridge
C U M B R I A
A595
B5345
B5344
B5295
B5294
A5086
A5094
228
229
220
210

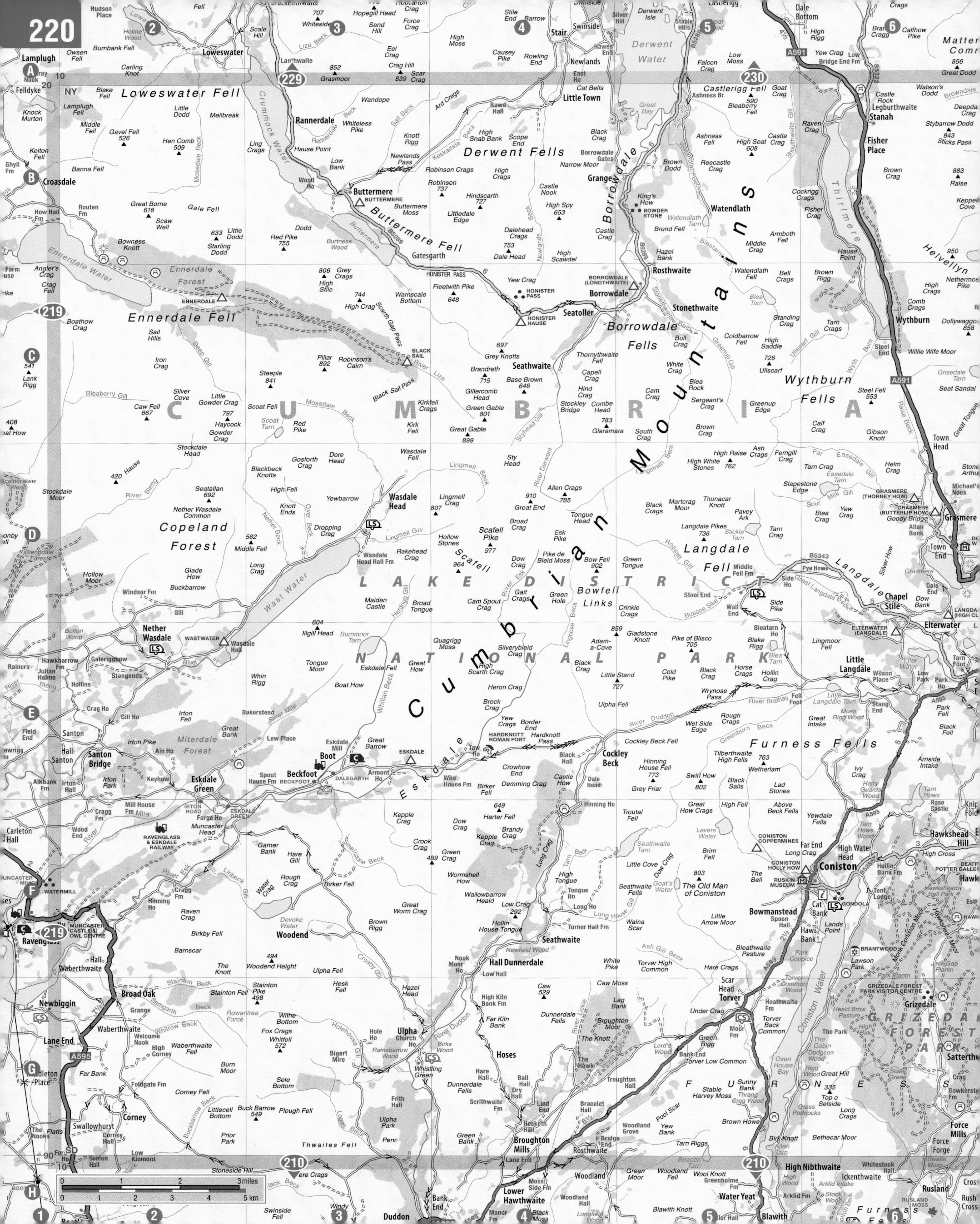
A
B
C
D
E
F
G
H
1
2
3
4
5
6
NY
SD
229
230
219
210
Lamplugh
Loweswater
Loweswater Fell
Felldyke
Knock Murton
Kelton Fell
Croasdale
Ennerdale Water
Ennerdale Forest
Ennerdale Fell
Cumbria
Lake District National Park
Cumbrian Mountains
Crummock Water
Rannerdale
Hause Point
Buttermere
Buttermere Fell
Gatesgarth
Honister Pass
Derwent Fells
Derwent Water
Stair
Swinside
Newlands
Little Town
Grange
Borrowdale
Borrowdale Fells
Rosthwaite
Stonethwaite
Seatoller
Seathwaite
Watendlath
Castlerigg Fell
Legburthwaite
Stanah
Fisher Place
Thirlmere
Helvellyn
Wythburn
Wythburn Fells
A591
Grasmere
Town End
Langdale Fell
Langdale Pikes
Chapel Stile
Elterwater
Little Langdale
Great Gable
Kirk Fell
Pillar
Black Sail Pass
Wasdale Head
Wast Water
Nether Wasdale
Copeland Forest
Scafell Pike
Scafell
Bow Fell
Bowfell Links
Esk Pike
Crinkle Crags
Eskdale
Eskdale Green
Boot
Beckfoot
Miterdale Forest
Santon Bridge
Santon
Irton Pike
Hardknott Pass
Cockley Beck
Wrynose Pass
River Duddon
Furness Fells
Wetherlam
Coniston
The Old Man of Coniston
Coniston Water
Torver
Seathwaite
Hall Dunnerdale
Ulpha
Woodend
Hoses
Broughton Mills
Lower Hawthwaite
Ravenglass
Waberthwaite
Broad Oak
Newbiggin
Lane End
Corney
Swallowhurst
A595
Hawkshead Hill
Grizedale
Grizedale Forest Park
High Nibthwaite
Rusland
Force Mills
Water Yeat
Blawith
Duddon
Thwaites Fell
Dunnerdale Fells
3 miles
5 km

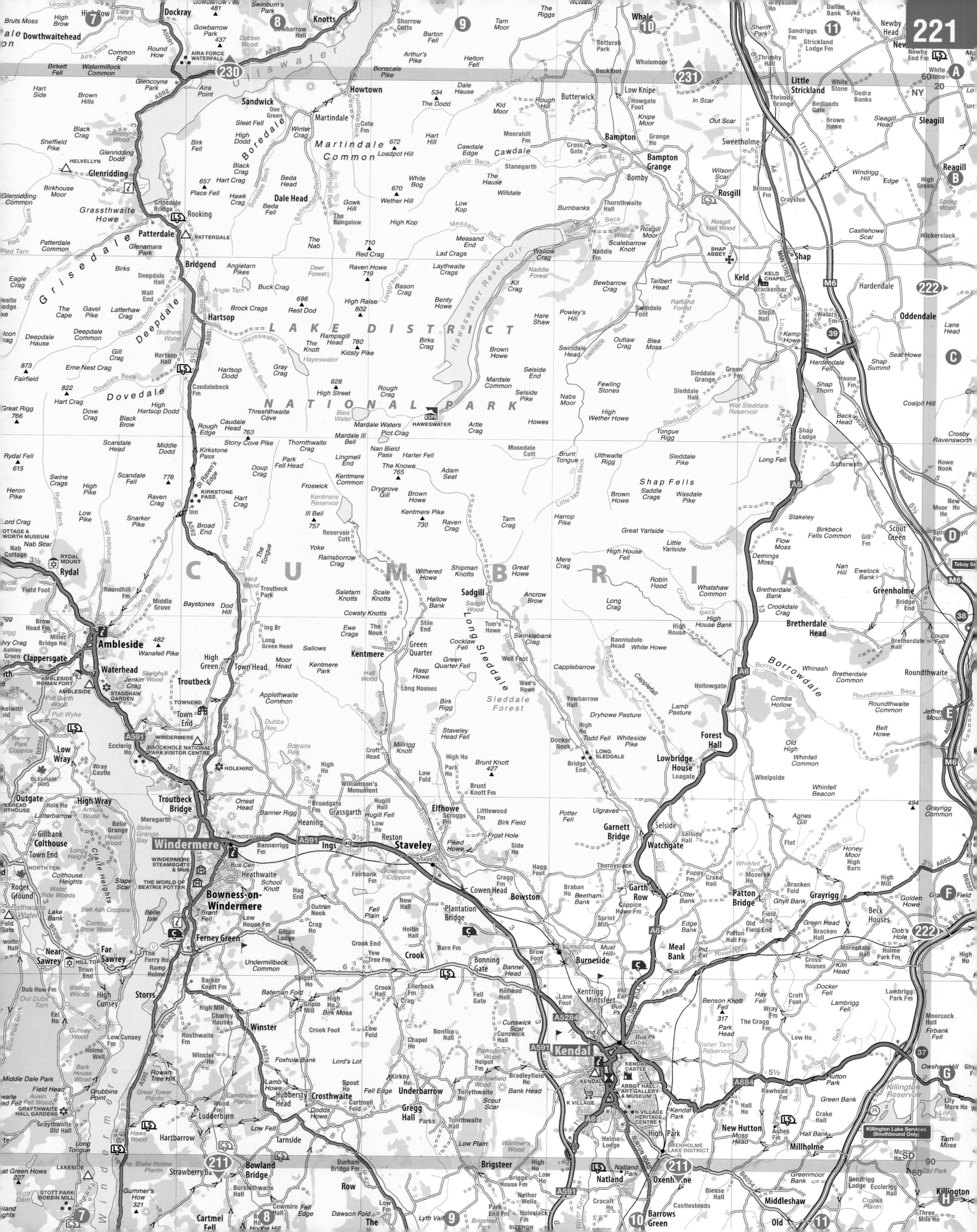

Bruts Moss
High Row
High Brow
Dowthwaitehead
Dockray
Gowbarrow Park
437
Aira Force Waterfall
Knotts
Sharrow Cotts
Barton Fell
The Riggs
Tarn Moor
Whale
Sheriff Park
Sandriggs Fm
Strickland Lodge Fm
Dallan Bank
Syke Ho
Newby Head
Common Fell
Round How
Aira Beck
Birkett Fell
Watermillock Common
Ullswater
230
Arthur's Pike
Helton Fell
Setterah Park
Whalemoor
231
Thrimby Hall
Bonscale Pike
Beckfoot
Little Strickland
White Stone
Dedra Banks
Glencoyne Park
Aira Point
Hart Side
Brown Hills
Sandwick
Howtown
534
The Dodd
Dale Hause
Kid Moor
Rough Hill
Butterwick
Low Knipe
Howgate Foot
Knipe Moor
In Scar
Thrimby Grange
Bedlands Gate
Brown Howe
Sleagill Head
Sleagill
Doe Green
Sleet Fell
Martindale
Cote Fm
Winter Crag
Boredale
High Dodd
Out Scar
Black Crag
Sheffield Pike
Glencoyne Wood
Glenridding Dodd
Helvellyn
Glenridding
Birk Fell
Martindale Common
672
Loadpot Hill
Hart Hill
Cawdale Edge
Cawdale
Moorahill Fm
Cross Gate
Bampton
Grange Ho
Sweetholme
Bampton Grange
Stanegarth
Cawdale Beck
Black Crag
Hart Crag
657
Place Fell
Beda Head
White Bog
670
Wether Hill
The Hause
Willdale
Bomby
Wilson Scar
Windrigg Hill
Edge
Reagill
High Green
Birkhouse Moor
Glenridding Common
Dale Head
Hawk Crag
Beda Fell
Gowk Hill
The Bungalow
Low Kop
High Kop
Burnbanks
Thornthwaite Hall
Rosgill
Brunns Fm
Crayston
Grassthwaite Howe
Grisedale Bridge
Rooking
Patterdale
Measand Beck
Rosgill Moor
Rosgill Hall Wood
Spring Wood
Red Tarn
Patterdale Common
Glenamara Park
The Nab
710
Red Crag
Measand End
Lad Crags
Frith Wood
Scalebarrow Knott
Naddle Fm
Wallow Crag
Shap Abbey
Shap
Castlehowe Scar
Wickerslack
Bridgend
Grisedale
Birks
Angletarn Pikes
Deer Forest
Raven Howe
719
Laythwaite Crags
Haweswater Reservoir
Naddle Forest
Keld
Keld Chapel
Hardendale
222
Eagle Crag
Deepdale Hall
Angle Tarn
Buck Crag
Bason Crag
Kit Crag
Bewbarrow Crag
Tailbert Head
Brackenber Lo
Wall End
Deepdale
696
Rest Dod
High Raise
802
Benty Howe
Ralfland Forest
Swindale Foot
The Cape
Gavel Pike
Latterhaw Crag
Brock Crags
Hartsop
Lake District
Hare Shaw
Powley's Hill
Steps Hall
Waters Fm
Oddendale
Lane Head
Deepdale Common
Brothers Water
Hayeswater Gill
Rampsgill Head
The Knott
780
Kidsty Pike
Birks Crag
Swindale
Outlaw Crag
Blea Moss
Kemp Howe
39
Deepdale Hause
Gill Crag
Hartsop Hall
Hayeswater
Brown Howe
Swindale Head
Hardendale Fell
Shap Summit
Seal Howe
873
Erne Nest Crag
Gray Crag
Selside End
Green Fm
Fairfield
Hartsop Dodd
Pasture Beck
828
High Street
Mardale Common
Fewling Stones
Sleddale Grange
Shap Thorn
Hause Fm
822
Hart Crag
Dovedale
Caudalebeck Fm
Rough Crag
Selside Pike
Nabs Moor
Sleddale Hall
Wet Sleddale Reservoir
Coalpit Hill
Great Rigg
766
Dove Crag
High Hartsop Dodd
Black Brow
National Park
Threshthwaite Cove
Blea Water
Mardale Waters
Haweswater
Howes
High Wether Howe
Beck Head
Rough Edge
Caudale Head
763
Stony Cove Pike
Mardale III Bell
Piot Crag
Artle Crag
Tongue Rigg
Shap Lodge
Crosby Ravensworth
Scandale Head
Middle Dodd
Thornthwaite Crag
Nan Bield Pass
Harter Fell
Mosedale Cott
Brunt Tongue
Ulthwaite Rigg
Sleddale Pike
Long Fell
Rydal Fell
615
Kirkstone Pass
Park Fell Head
Lingmell End
The Knowe
765
Adam Seat
Satterwaith
Howe Nook
Scandale Fell
776
Doup Crag
Kentmere Common
Shap Fells
Saddle Crags
Wasdale Pike
Swine Crags
High Pike
Heron Pike
St Raven's Edge
Kirkstone Pass
Froswick
Drygrove Gill
Brown Howe
Raven Crag
Hart Crag
Kentmere Reservoir
Kentmere Pike
730
Harrop Pike
Low Pike
Snarker Pike
Inn
Broad End
Ill Bell
757
Raven Crag
Tarn Crag
Stakeley
Birkbeck Fells Common
Moor Ho
Lord Crag
Cottage & Worth Museum
Nab Scar
Nab Cottage
Reservoir Cott
Great Yarlside
Flow Moss
Gill Fm
Scout Green
Rydal Mount
Rydal
The Tongue
Yoke
Rainsborrow Crag
Little Yarlside
Demings Moss
High House Fell
Mere Crag
Nan Hill
Ewelock Bank
Cumbria
Withered Howe
Shipman Knotts
Great Howe
Robin Hood
Whatshaw Common
Bretherdale Bank
Greenholme
Field Foot
Roundhill Fm
Baystones
Dod Hill
Troutbeck Park
Hird Wood
Saletarn Knotts
Scale Knotts
Hallow Bank
Sadgill
Sadgill Wood
Ancrow Brow
Long Crag
Crookdale Crag
Bridge End
Middle Grove
Cowsty Knotts
Long Sleddale
Brow Head Fm
Miller Bridge Ho
Ambleside
482
Wansfell Pike
Ing Br
Long Green Head
Ewe Crags
The Nook
Stile End
Tom's Howe
Swinklebank Crag
Bannisdale Head
White Howe
High House
High House Bank
Bretherdale Head
Bretherdale Hall
Loups Fell
Clappersgate
Waterhead
High Green
Town Head
Sallows
Kentmere
Green Quarter
Cocklaw Fell
Well Foot
Capplebarrow
Moor Head
Kentmere Park
Green Quarter Fell
Borrowdale
Whinash
Bretherdale Common
Roundthwaite
Ambleside Roman Fort
Skelghyll Wood
Jenkin Crag
Stagshaw Garden
Troutbeck
Hall Wood
Rasp Howe
Wad's Howe
Hollowgate
Long Houses
Applethwaite Common
Yewbarrow Hall
Cappleall
Combs Hollow
Roundthwaite Beck
Roundthwaite Common
Townend
Town End
Birk Rigg
Sleddale Forest
Dryhowe Pasture
Lamb Pasture
Pull Wyke
Dubbs Res
Staveley Head Fell
High Ho
Todd Fell
Whiteside Pike
Forest Hall
Belt Howe
Windermere
Brockhole National Park Visitor Centre
Millrigg Knott
Docker Nook
Long Sleddale
Old High
Whinfell Common
Low Wray
Ecclerig Ho
Holehird
Croft Head
High Park Ho
Brunt Knott
427
Bridge End
Lowbridge House
Leagate
Wray Castle
Blelham Bog
Borrans Res
High Ho
Low Fold
Whelpside
Outgate
High Wray
Williamson's Monument
Brunt Knott Fm
Whinfell Beacon
Troutbeck Bridge
Meregarth
Orrest Head
Banner Rigg
Broadgate
Grassgarth
Hugill Hall
Hugill Fell
Elfhowe
Scroggs
Littlewood Fm
Birk Field
Potter Fell
Ulgraves
494
Grayrigg Common
Latterbarrow
Belle Grange
Heald Wood
Heaning
Low Ho
Reston
Agnes Gill
Gillbank
Colthouse
Town End
Belle Grange Bay
Windermere
Bannerrigg Fm
Ings
Staveley
Frost Hole
Side Ho
Garnett Bridge
Selside
Selside Hall
Flat
Honey Moor
High Barn
Claife Heights
Windermere Steamboats & Mus
Heathwaite
Fairbank Fm
Piked Howe
Brownspring Coppice
Thornyslack Fm
Watchgate
North Fen
Colthouse Heights
The World of Beatrix Potter
School Knott
Bowness-on-Windermere
Hag End
Cowen Head
Cragg Fm
Hagg Foot
Bowston
Braban Ho
Beetham Bank
Garth Row
Poppy Fm
Crake Hall
Mozergh
Patton Bridge
Bracken Fold
Grayrigg
High Mill
Roger Ground
Esthwaite Water
Slape Scar
Belt Ash Coppice
Outrun Nook
New Hall
Fell Plain
Plantation Bridge
Coppice Howe Fm
Otter Bank
Ghyll Bank
Beck Houses
Golden Howe
Lake Bank
Belle Isle
Brant Fell
Cuckoo Brow Wood
Low House Fm
Crag Ho
Gilpin Lodge
Hollin Hall
Sprint Mill
Edge Bank
Field End
Old Field End
Green Head
Bracken Hall
Dob's Hole
222
Ferney Green
Crook End
Barn Fm
Burneside
Must Hill
Meal Bank
Patton Hall Fm
Ind Est
River Mint
Moresdale Hall
Holme Park Fm
High Ho
Near Sawrey
Hill Top
Far Sawrey
The Ferry Ho
Ramp Holme
Town End
Undermillbeck Common
Yew Tree Fm
Crook
Bonning Gate
Bannel Head
Brow Foot
Burneside
Cross Houses
Kiln Head
Dub How Fm
Out Dubs Tarn
Bishop Woods
High Cunsey
Storrs
Barker Knott Fm
Bateman Fold
Spigot Ho
Crook Hall
Ellerbeck Fm
Fell Gate
Halhead Hall
Lane Foot
Kentrigg
Mintsfeet
Ind Est
Bus Pk
Shap Road
Benson Knott Fell
317
Hay Fell
Wray Fm
Croft Foot
Docker Fell
Lambrigg Fell
Lambrigg Park Fm
Eel Ho
High Mill
Charley Houses
Gilpin Mill
High Ho
Birk Moss
Crook Foot
Low Fold
Cunswick Scar
Cunswick Hall
The Cragg Fm
Park Head
Moorcock Hall
Firbank Fell
Cunsey Wood
Low Cunsey
Rosthwaite Fm
Winster
Bonfire Hall
Kendal
Bus Pk
Fisher Tarn Reservoir
Low Ho
Holme Well
Winster Ho
Chapel Ho
Parkspring Wood
Helpot Fm
Kendal Castle
Owshaw Hill
Bark House Wood
Rowan Tree Hill
Foxhole Bank
Lord's Lot
Barrowfield Wood
Bradleyfield Ho
Abbot Hall Art Gallery & Museum
Kendal
Hutton Park
Middle Dale Park
Field Head
Grubbins Point
Great Tower Plantn
Lambhowe Plantn
Lamb Howe
Spout Ho
Kirkby Ho
Underbarrow
Tullythwaite Ho
Bank Head
Rawhead Fm
Green Bank
Killington Reservoir
Graythwaite Hall Gardens
Wood Fm
Ludderburn
Hubbersty Head
Crosthwaite
Fell Edge
Cartmel Fold
Scout Scar
K Village
K Village Heritage Centre
Hall Ho
Kendal Park
Crake Hall
Lily Mere Ho
Graythwaite Old Hall
Gregg Hall
Tullithwaite Hall
New Hutton
Moss Head
Ashes Fm
Hall Bank
Killington Lake Services (Southbound Only)
Haws Wood
Hartbarrow
Dodds Howe
Low Fell
Parks
High Park
Millholme
Long Tongue
Tarnside
Low Plain
Warriner's Wood
Helme Lodge
Oxenholme Lake District
Burton Road
Tarn Moss
Lakeside
Blake Holme Plantn
Strawberry Bank
211
Bowland Bridge
Durham Bridge Fm
Brigsteer
High Ho
Natland
Natland Park
Oxenholme
Greenmoor Bank
Mutton Hall
Old Park
Great Green Hows
227
High Dam
Stott Park Bobbin Mill
Gummer's How
321
Burblethwaite Hall
Row
Low Ho
Briggs House Fm
Nether Wells
Holeslack Fm
Park End Fm
Cracalt Ho
Blease Hall
Castlesteads
Middleshaw
Bendrigg Lodge
Eccleriggs Hall
Crooks Plantn
Killington
Cartmel Fell
Cowmire Hall
Fell Edge
Dawson Fold
Lyth Valley
Sizergh
Barrows Green
Old
Three Mile Ho
The

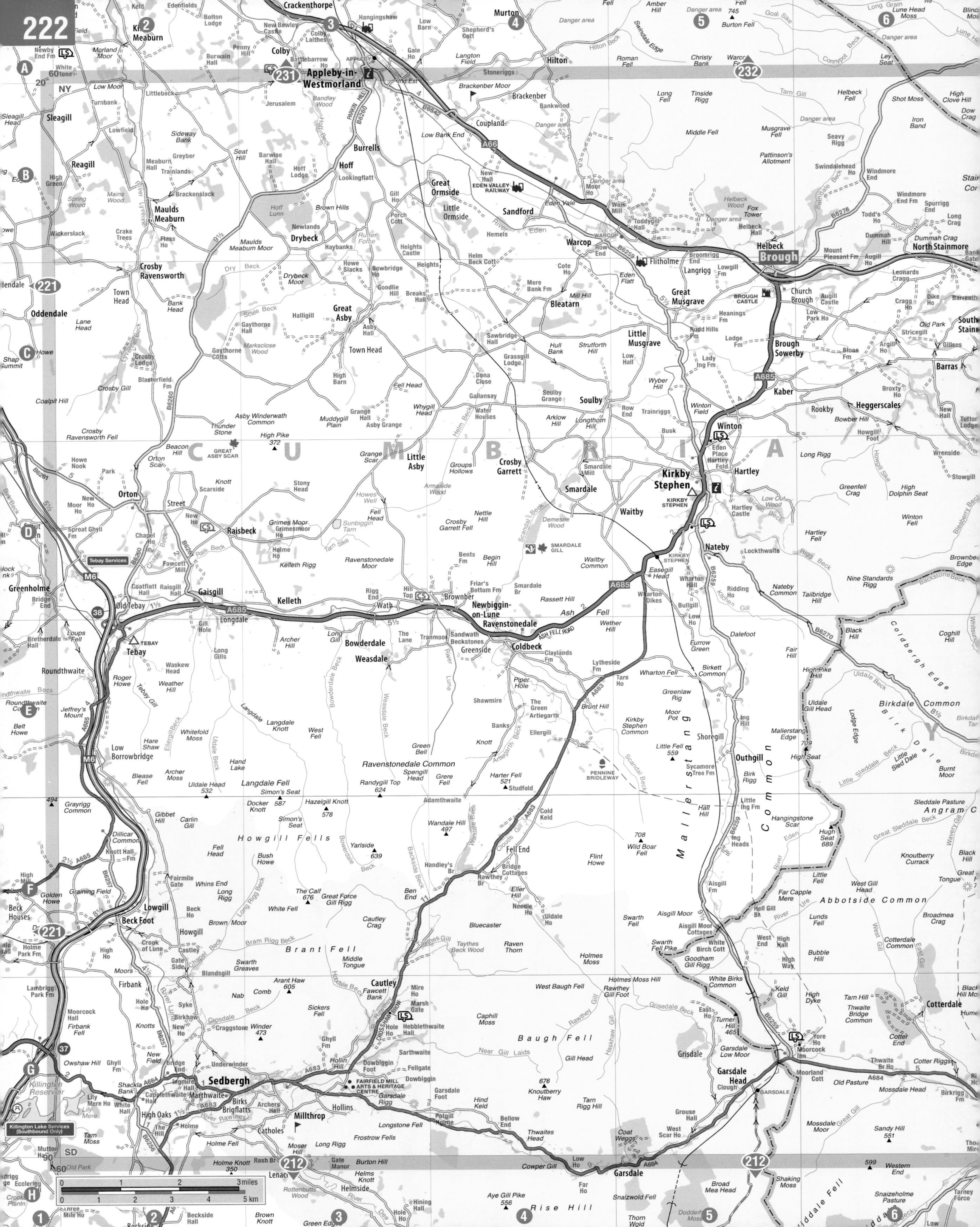

Appleby-in-Westmorland
Kirkby Stephen
Brough
Sedbergh
Tebay
Orton
Crosby Ravensworth
Warcop
Great Asby
Newbiggin-on-Lune
Ravenstonedale
Garsdale Head
Garsdale
Howgill Fells
Baugh Fell
Mallerstang Common
Abbotside Common
Birkdale Common
Ravenstonedale Common
CUMBRIA
Tebay Services
Killington Lake Services (Southbound Only)

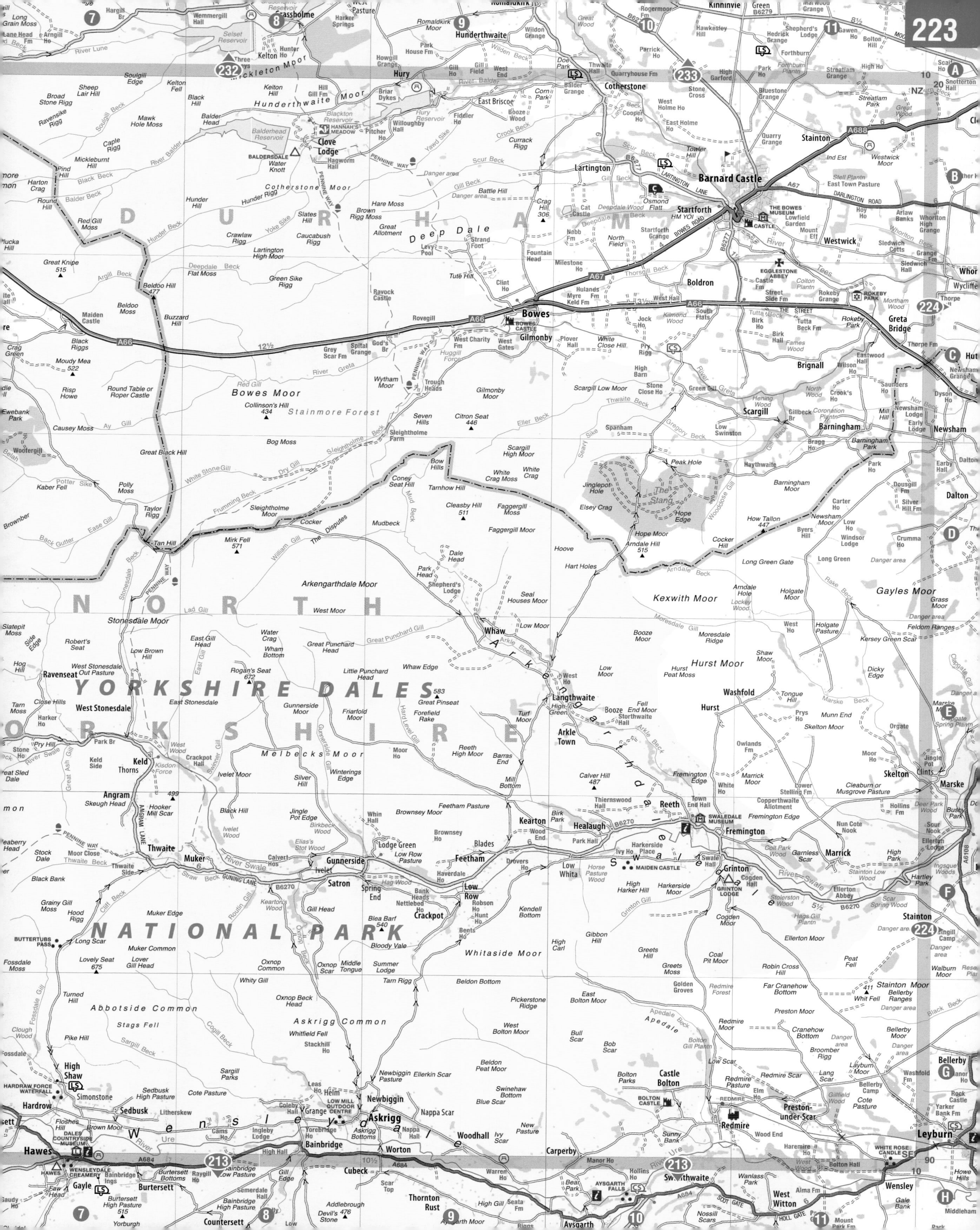

223
D U R H A M
N O R T H
Y O R K S H I R E
YORKSHIRE DALES
NATIONAL PARK
Barnard Castle
Startforth
Bowes
Gilmonby
Lartington
Cotherstone
Boldron
Westwick
Stainton
Greta Bridge
Brignall
Scargill
Barningham
Newsham
Dalton
Kelton
Hury
Hunderthwaite
Clove Lodge
Hunderthwaite Moor
Cotherstone Moor
Deep Dale
Bowes Moor
Stainmore Forest
Tan Hill
Arkengarthdale Moor
Whaw
Langthwaite
Arkle Town
Reeth
Healaugh
Fremington
Grinton
Marrick
Marske
Skelton
Hurst
Washfold
Kexwith Moor
Hurst Moor
Gayles Moor
Stonesdale Moor
Ravenseat
West Stonesdale
Keld
Thorns
Angram
Thwaite
Muker
Gunnerside
Ivelet
Satron
Feetham
Kearton
Low Row
Crackpot
Melbecks Moor
Whitaside Moor
Askrigg Common
Abbotside Common
Stags Fell
High Shaw
Simonstone
Hardrow
Sedbusk
Hawes
Gayle
Burtersett
Bainbridge
Askrigg
Newbiggin
Nappa Scar
Woodhall
Carperby
Castle Bolton
Redmire
Preston-under-Scar
Leyburn
Wensley
West Witton
Swinithwaite
Aysgarth
Thornton Rust
Cubeck
Worton
Countersett
Wensleydale
Swaledale
Arkengarthdale
THE BOWES MUSEUM
EGGLESTONE ABBEY
ROKEBY PARK
BOWES CASTLE
SWALEDALE MUSEUM
MAIDEN CASTLE
BOLTON CASTLE
BUTTERTUBS PASS
HARDRAW FORCE WATERFALL
DALES COUNTRYSIDE MUSEUM
WENSLEYDALE CREAMERY
AYSGARTH FALLS
A66
A67
A688
A684
B6270
B6277
B6279
PENNINE WAY
Great Knipe 515
Mirk Fell 571
Collinson's Hill 434
Citron Seat 446
Cleasby Hill 511
Arndale Hill 515
How Tallon 447
Rogan's Seat 672
Great Pinseat 583
Calver Hill 487
Blea Barf 540
Lovely Seat 675
Stainton Moor

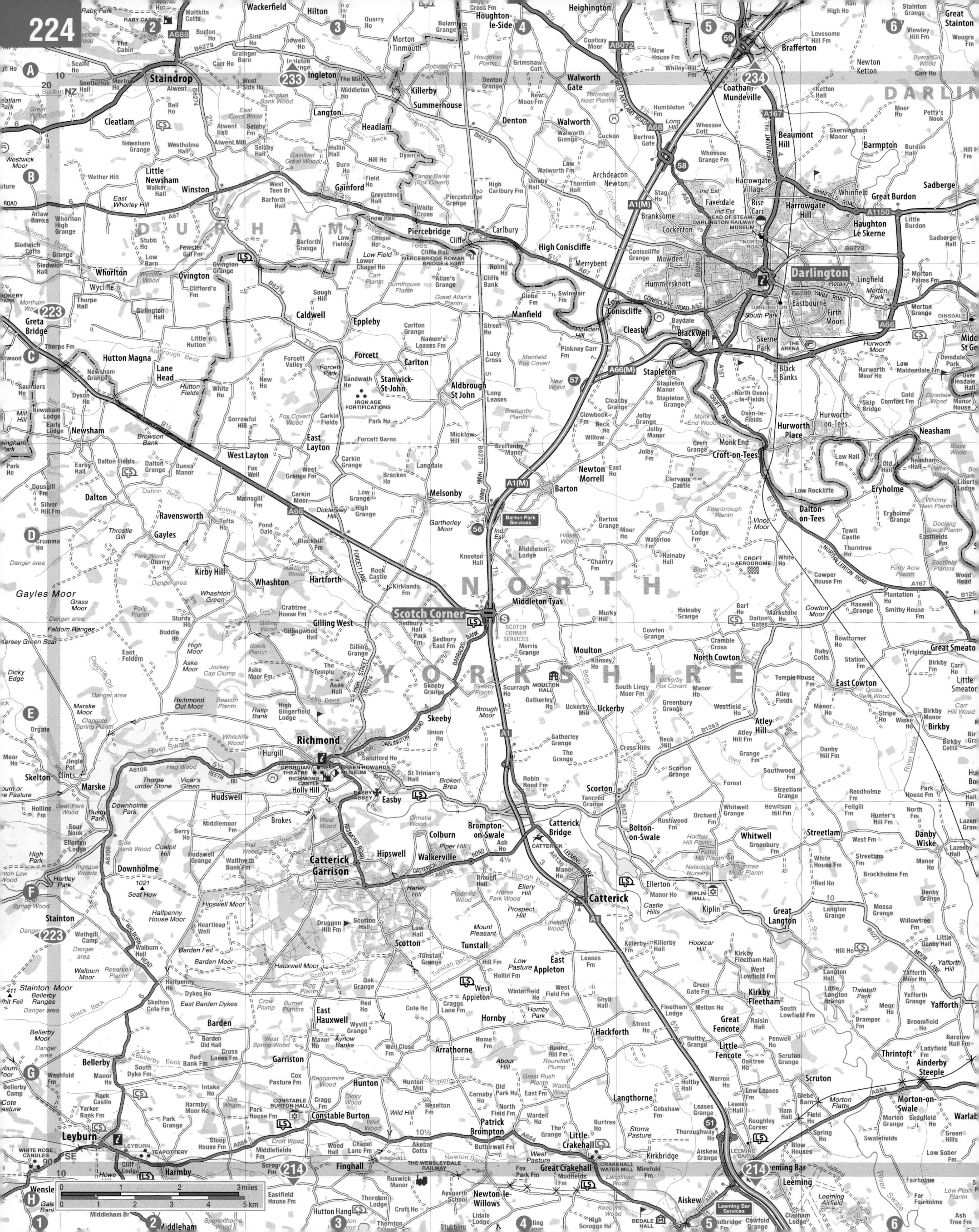
Raby Park
Wackerfield
Hilton
Heighington
Great Stainton
Houghton-le-Side
Brafferton
Staindrop
Ingleton
Killerby
Summerhouse
Langton
Headlam
Denton
Walworth Gate
Walworth
Coatham Mundeville
DARLIN
Cleatlam
Beaumont Hill
Barmpton
Little Newsham
Winston
Gainford
Archdeacon Newton
Harrowgate Village
Faverdale
Whinfield
Great Burdon
Sadberge
Harrowgate Hill
Haughton Le Skerne
D U R H A M
Piercebridge
Cliffe
Carlbury
High Coniscliffe
Cockerton
Merrybent
Mowden
Hummersknott
Darlington
Lingfield
Whorlton
Wycliffe
Ovington
Greta Bridge
Caldwell
Eppleby
Manfield
Low Coniscliffe
Cleasby
Blackwell
Eastbourne
Firth Moor
Forcett
Carlton
Hutton Magna
Lane Head
Stanwick-St-John
Aldbrough St John
Stapleton
Newsham
East Layton
West Layton
Hurworth Place
Hurworth-on-Tees
Neasham
Croft-on-Tees
Melsonby
Newton Morrell
Barton
Dalton
Ravensworth
Gayles
Eryholme
Dalton-on-Tees
Kirby Hill
Whashton
Hartforth
Gayles Moor
N O R T H
Middleton Tyas
Scotch Corner
Gilling West
Moulton
North Cowton
Y O R K S H I R E
East Cowton
Great Smeaton
Skeeby
Uckerby
Atley Hill
Birkby
Richmond
Hurgill
Marske
Skelton
Hudswell
Easby
Scorton
Catterick Bridge
Brompton-on-Swale
Bolton-on-Swale
Whitwell
Streetlam
Danby Wiske
Catterick Garrison
Downholme
Hipswell
Colburn
Walkerville
Catterick
Ellerton
Kiplin
Great Langton
Stainton
Scotton
Tunstall
East Appleton
West Appleton
Kirkby Fleetham
Yafforth
East Hauxwell
Barden
Hornby
Hackforth
Great Fencote
Little Fencote
Bellerby
Garriston
Arrathorne
Thrintoft
Ainderby Steeple
Scruton
Hunton
Langthorne
Morton-on-Swale
Constable Burton
Patrick Brompton
Leyburn
Harmby
Little Crakehall
Great Crakehall
Kirkbridge
Finghall
Newton-le-Willows
Aiskew
Leeming Bar
Leeming
Middleham
Scotch Corner Services
Barton Park Services
Leeming Bar Services
A1(M)
A1
A66
A66(M)
A67
A68
A167
A684
A6108
A6136
B6275
B6274
B6279
B6271
B6280
B1263
233
234
223
214
0 1 2 3 miles
0 1 2 3 4 5 km

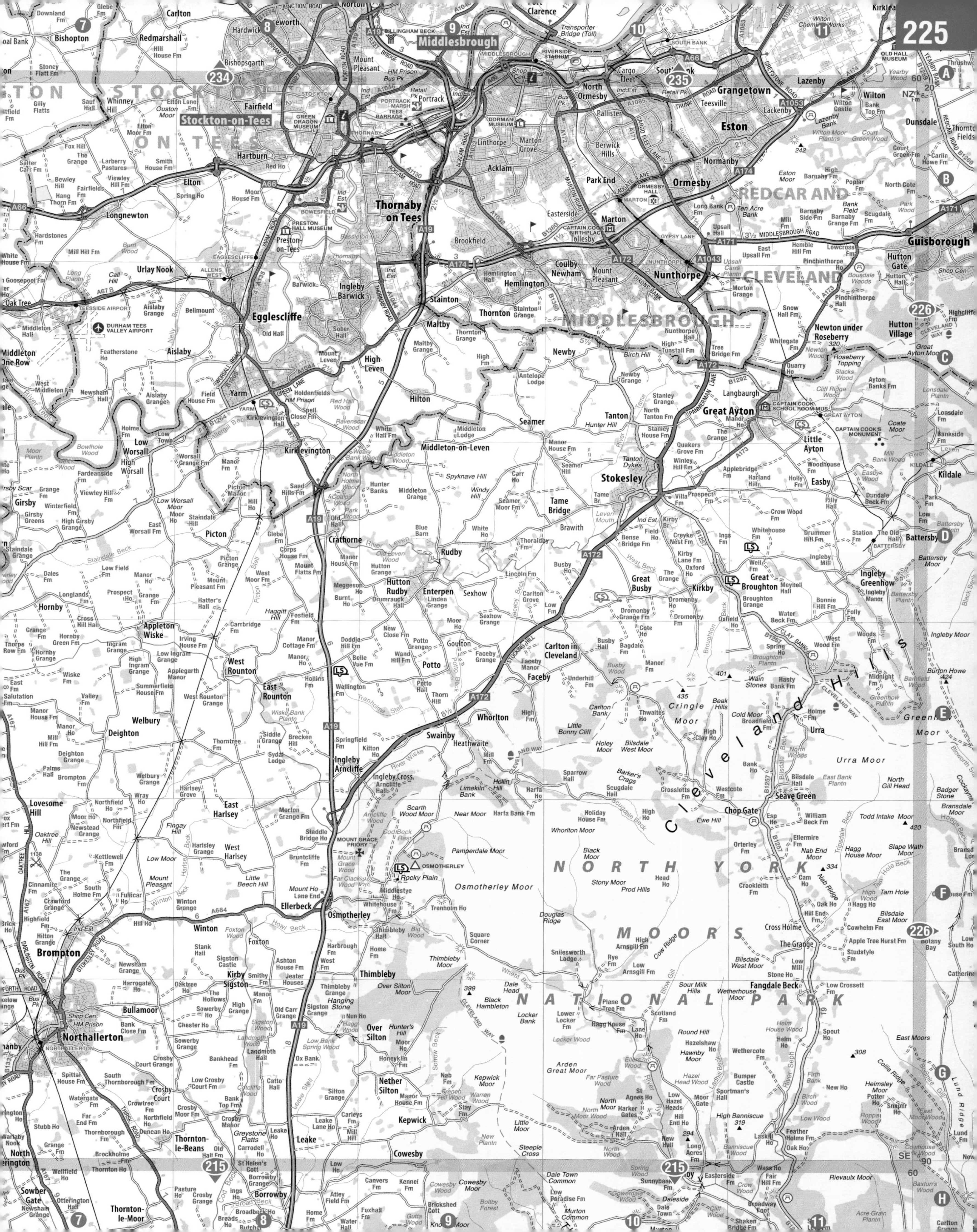

Middlesbrough
Stockton-on-Tees
STOCKTON ON TEES
REDCAR AND CLEVELAND
MIDDLESBROUGH
NORTH YORK MOORS NATIONAL PARK
Cleveland Hills
Bishopton
Carlton
Redmarshall
Bishopsgarth
Fairfield
Hartburn
Elton
Longnewton
Thornaby on Tees
Preston-on-Tees
Egglescliffe
Urlay Nook
Aislaby
Yarm
Kirklevington
Low Worsall
High Worsall
Girsby
Picton
Appleton Wiske
Hornby
West Rounton
East Rounton
Welbury
Deighton
Lovesome Hill
East Harlsey
West Harlsey
Brompton
Northallerton
Winton
Foxton
Kirby Sigston
Bullamoor
Thornton-le-Beans
Thornton-le-Moor
Borrowby
Leake
Cowesby
Kepwick
Nether Silton
Over Silton
Thimbleby
Osmotherley
Ellerbeck
Ingleby Arncliffe
Swainby
Whorlton
Potto
Hutton Rudby
Rudby
Enterpen
Crathorne
Middleton-on-Leven
Hilton
High Leven
Maltby
Stainton
Thornton
Hemlington
Coulby Newham
Acklam
Linthorpe
Marton
Nunthorpe
Ormesby
Eston
Grangetown
Lazenby
Wilton
Guisborough
Hutton Gate
Hutton Village
Newton under Roseberry
Great Ayton
Little Ayton
Stokesley
Tame Bridge
Seamer
Newby
Tanton
Easby
Kildale
Battersby
Ingleby Greenhow
Great Broughton
Kirkby
Great Busby
Faceby
Carlton in Cleveland
Chop Gate
Seave Green
Urra
Fangdale Beck
Cringle Moor
Urra Moor
Osmotherley Moor
Middlesbrough Teesside Airport
DURHAM TEES VALLEY AIRPORT
A66
A19
A172
A174
A171
A173
A684
A167
226
234
235
215

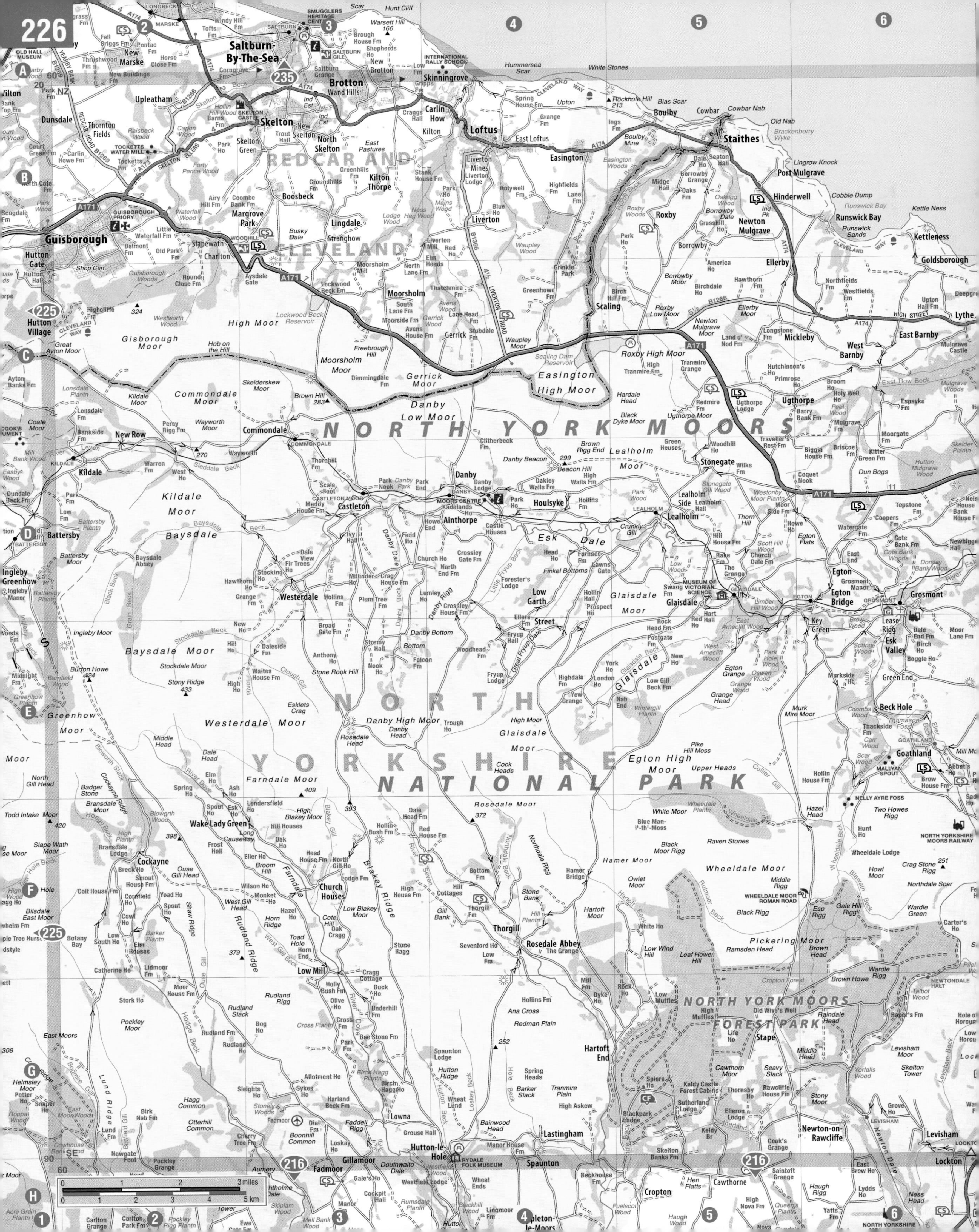

Saltburn-By-The-Sea
New Marske
Upleatham
Skelton
North Skelton
Brotton
Skinningrove
Carlin How
Loftus
Easington
Boulby
Staithes
Port Mulgrave
Hinderwell
Runswick Bay
Kettleness
Goldsborough
Lythe
East Barnby
West Barnby
Mickleby
Ellerby
Newton Mulgrave
Roxby
Scaling
Liverton
Lingdale
Margrove Park
Boosbeck
Kilton Thorpe
Moorsholm
Gerrick
Charlton
Guisborough
Hutton Gate
Hutton Village
Dunsdale
REDCAR AND CLEVELAND
NORTH YORK MOORS
NORTH YORKSHIRE NATIONAL PARK
High Moor
Gisborough Moor
Commondale Moor
Commondale
Danby Low Moor
Moorsholm Moor
Gerrick Moor
Easington High Moor
Roxby High Moor
Ugthorpe
New Row
Kildale
Kildale Moor
Baysdale
Battersby
Ingleby Greenhow
Castleton
Danby
Ainthorpe
Houlsyke
Lealholm
Stonegate
Esk Dale
Glaisdale
Egton
Egton Bridge
Grosmont
Esk Valley
Westerdale
Low Garth
Street
Baysdale Moor
Westerdale Moor
Danby High Moor
Glaisdale Moor
Egton High Moor
Farndale Moor
Wake Lady Green
Cockayne
Church Houses
Low Mill
Rosedale Abbey
Thorgill
Goathland
Beck Hole
Wheeldale Moor
Pickering Moor
NORTH YORK MOORS FOREST PARK
Stape
Hartoft End
Lastingham
Hutton-le-Hole
Gillamoor
Fadmoor
Spaunton
Cropton
Cawthorne
Newton-on-Rawcliffe
Levisham
Lockton
Lowna
Rudland Rigg
Blakey Ridge
Lund Ridge
NORTH YORKSHIRE MOORS RAILWAY
235
225
216
0 1 2 3 miles
0 1 2 3 4 5 km

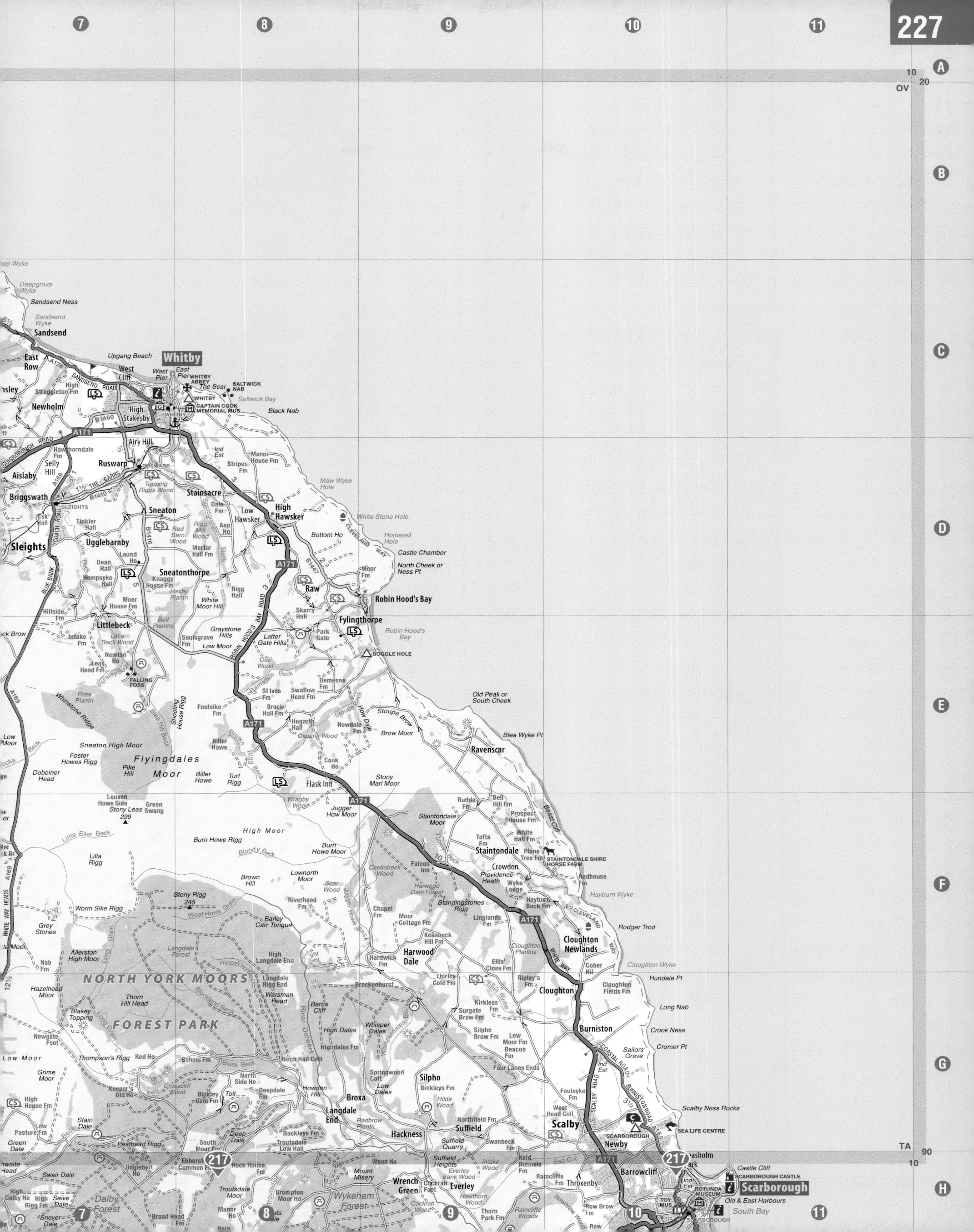
Whitby
Sandsend
Sandsend Ness
East Row
Newholm
Ruswarp
Aislaby
Briggswath
Sleights
Sneaton
Ugglebarnby
Sneatonthorpe
Littlebeck
Stainsacre
High Hawsker
Low Hawsker
Raw
Robin Hood's Bay
Fylingthorpe
Robin Hood's Bay
Boggle Hole
Ravenscar
Flask Inn
Flyingdales Moor
Staintondale
Cloughton Newlands
Cloughton
Burniston
Harwood Dale
Silpho
Suffield
Hackness
Broxa
Langdale End
Scalby
Newby
Barrowcliff
Throxenby
Everley
Wrench Green
Scarborough
NORTH YORK MOORS FOREST PARK
Dalby Forest
Wykeham Forest
A171
A169
A174
A165
B1416
B1447
B1460
B1410
CLEVELAND WAY
WHITE WAY HEADS
SCARBOROUGH CASTLE
SEA LIFE CENTRE
WHITBY ABBEY
CAPTAIN COOK MEMORIAL MUS
ROTUNDA MUSEUM
STAINTONDALE SHIRE HORSE FARM
South Bay
Castle Cliff
Old & East Harbours
Saltwick Bay
Black Nab
Hayburn Wyke
Cloughton Wyke
Scalby Ness Rocks
217

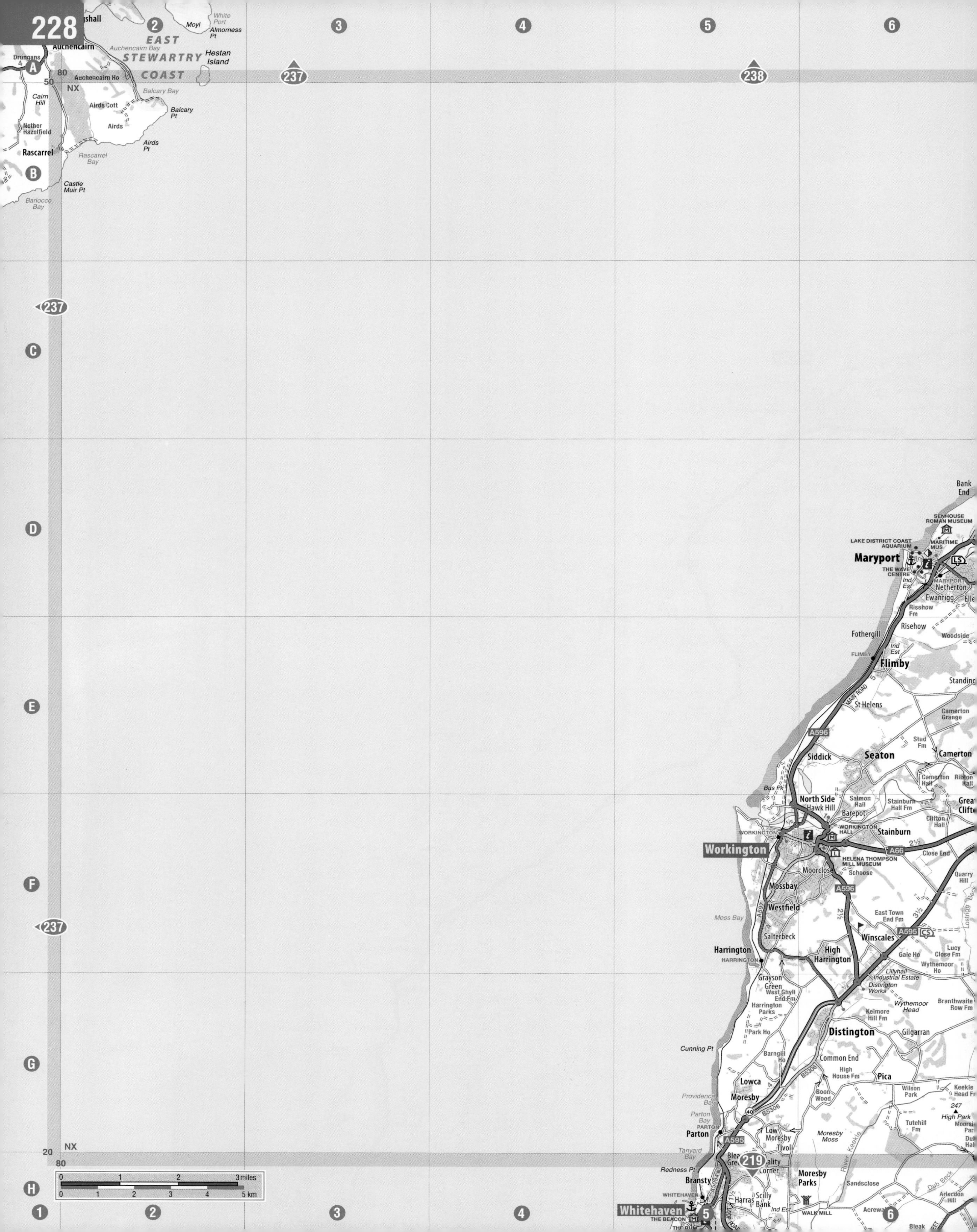

EAST
STEWARTRY
COAST

Drungans
Auchencairn
Auchencairn Bay
Auchencairn Ho

shall
Moyl
White
Port
Almorness
Pt
Hestan
Island

NX
80
50

Cairn
Hill

Nether
Hazelfield

Rascarrel

Airds Cott
Airds
Airds
Pt

Balcary Bay
Balcary
Pt

Rascarrel
Bay

Castle
Muir Pt

Barlocco
Bay

237

237

237

Bank
End

SENHOUSE
ROMAN MUSEUM

LAKE DISTRICT COAST
AQUARIUM

MARITIME
MUS.

Maryport

THE WAVE
CENTRE

Ind
Est

MARYPORT
Ind
Est

Netherton

Ewanrigg

Elle

Risehow
Fm

Fothergill

Risehow

Woodside

FLIMBY

Ind
Est

Flimby

Standing

St Helens

Camerton
Grange

A596

Stud
Fm

Siddick

Seaton

Camerton

Camerton
Hall

Ribton
Hall

Bus Pk

North Side
Hawk Hill

Salmon
Hall

Barepot

Stainburn
Hall Fm

Clifton
Hall

Grea
Clifte

WORKINGTON

WORKINGTON
HALL

Stainburn

Workington

HELENA THOMPSON
MILL MUSEUM

A66

2½

Close End

Moorclose

Schoose

Quarry
Hill

Mossbay

A596

Westfield

Moss Bay

Salterbeck

East Town
End Fm

2½

3½

Lostrigg Beck

Harrington

HARRINGTON

High
Harrington

Winscales

A595

Gale Ho

Lucy
Close
Fm

Wythemoor
Ho

Grayson
Green

West Ghyll
End Fm

Lillyhall
Industrial Estate

Distington
Works

Wythemoor
Head

Branthwaite
Row Fm

Harrington
Parks

Park Ho

Kelmore
Head

Kelmore
Hill Fm

Distington

Gilgarran

Cunning Pt

Barngill
Ho

Common End

High
House Fm

Pica

Wilson
Park

Keekle
Head Fm

247

Providence
Bay

Lowca

Moresby

Boon
Wood

High Park
Moorsi
Par

Tutehill
Fm

Dut
Hall

Parton
Bay
PARTON

Low
Moresby

Tivoli

Moresby
Moss

River Keekle

Tanyard
Bay

Parton

A595

Blea
Gree

ality

219

Moresby
Parks

Sandsclose

Redness Pt

Bransty

Corner

Dub Beck

WHITEHAVEN

Whitehaven

THE BEACON

Harras

Scilly
Bank

Ind Est

WALK MILL

Acrewa

Bleak

THE R

A

B

C

D

E

F

G

H

1

2

3

4

5

6

0   1   2   3 miles
0   1   2   3   4   5 km

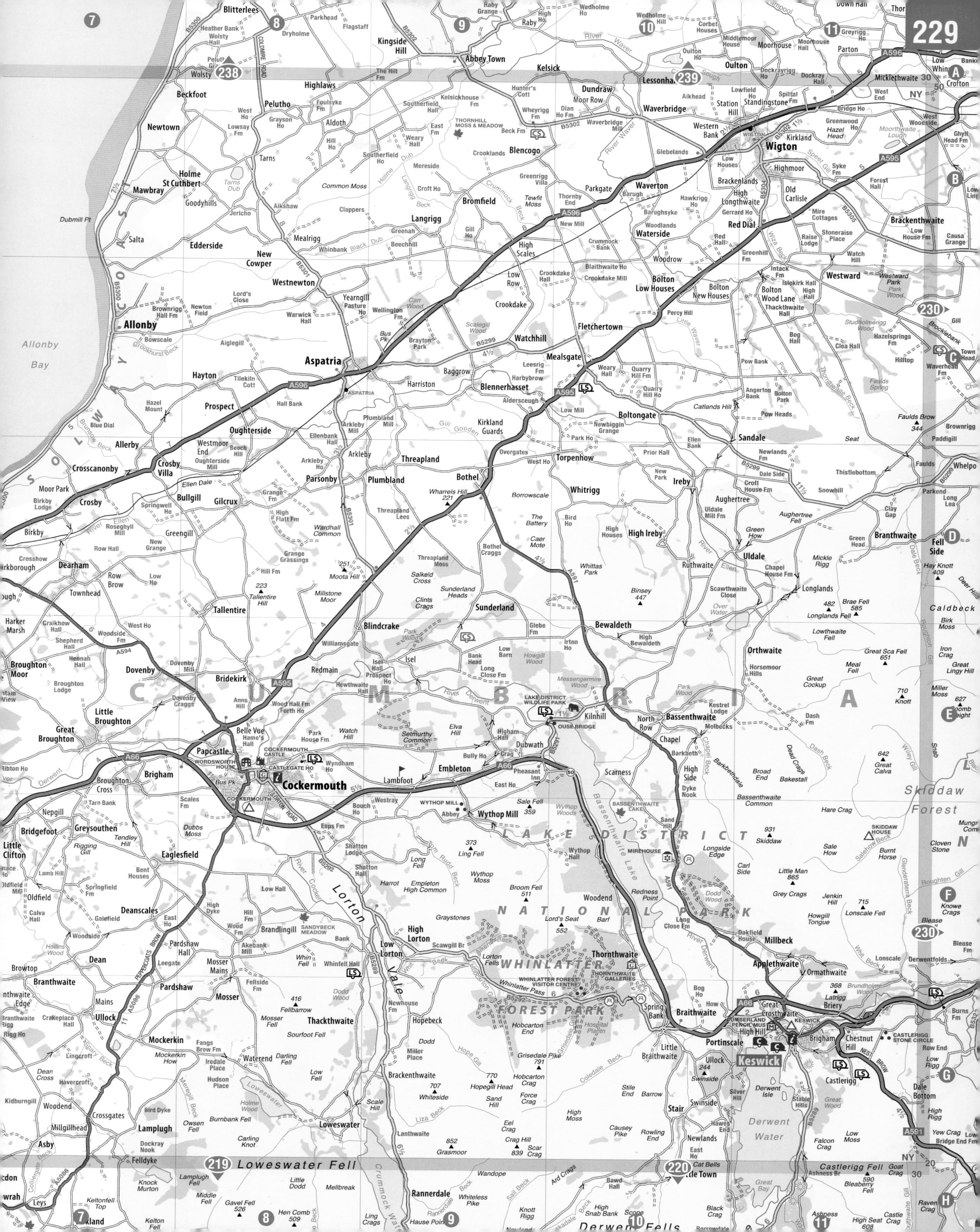
Blitterlees
Heather Bank
Wolsty Hall
Wolsty
Beckfoot
Newtown
Mawbray
Holme St Cuthbert
Goodyhills
Dubmill Pt
Salta
Edderside
Allonby
Allonby Bay
Hayton
Prospect
Oughterside
Allerby
Crosscanonby
Crosby Villa
Moor Park
Crosby
Birkby
Bullgill
Gilcrux
Dearham
Tallentire
Broughton Moor
Dovenby
Bridekirk
Little Broughton
Great Broughton
Papcastle
Brigham
Broughton Cross
Cockermouth
Nepgill
Bridgefoot
Greysouthen
Little Clifton
Eaglesfield
Oldfield
Deanscales
Dean
Branthwaite
Ullock
Mockerkin
Lamplugh
Asby
Pelutho
Highlaws
Aspatria
Westnewton
New Cowper
Mealrigg
Langrigg
Bromfield
Abbey Town
Kingside Hill
Kelsick
Aldoth
Blencogo
Dundraw
Moor Row
Waverbridge
Lessonhall
Oulton
Wigton
Waverton
Parkgate
Waterside
Red Dial
Brackenthwaite
Westward
Bolton Low Houses
Bolton New Houses
Fletchertown
Watchhill
Mealsgate
Baggrow
Blennerhasset
Crookdake
Boltongate
Sandale
Torpenhow
Ireby
Whitrigg
High Ireby
Uldale
Aughertree
Branthwaite
Fell Side
Threapland
Plumbland
Parsonby
Arkleby
Bothel
Sunderland
Blindcrake
Isel
Redmain
Bewaldeth
Orthwaite
Longlands
Caldbeck
Bassenthwaite
Kilnhill
Embleton
Dubwath
Wythop Mill
Lorton Vale
High Lorton
Low Lorton
Thornthwaite
Braithwaite
Portinscale
Keswick
Millbeck
Applethwaite
Ormathwaite
Castlerigg
Brigham
Chestnut Hill
Mosser
Pardshaw
Thackthwaite
Loweswater
Rannerdale
Stair
Newlands
Swinside
Derwent Water
Bassenthwaite Lake
Skiddaw Forest
Skiddaw 931
Lord's Seat 552
Grisedale Pike 791
WHINLATTER FOREST PARK
LAKE DISTRICT NATIONAL PARK
CUMBRIA
SOLWAY COAST
Loweswater Fell
Castlerigg Fell
Derwent Fells
A596
A595
A594
A591
A66
A5086
B5300
B5301
B5302
B5292
B5289

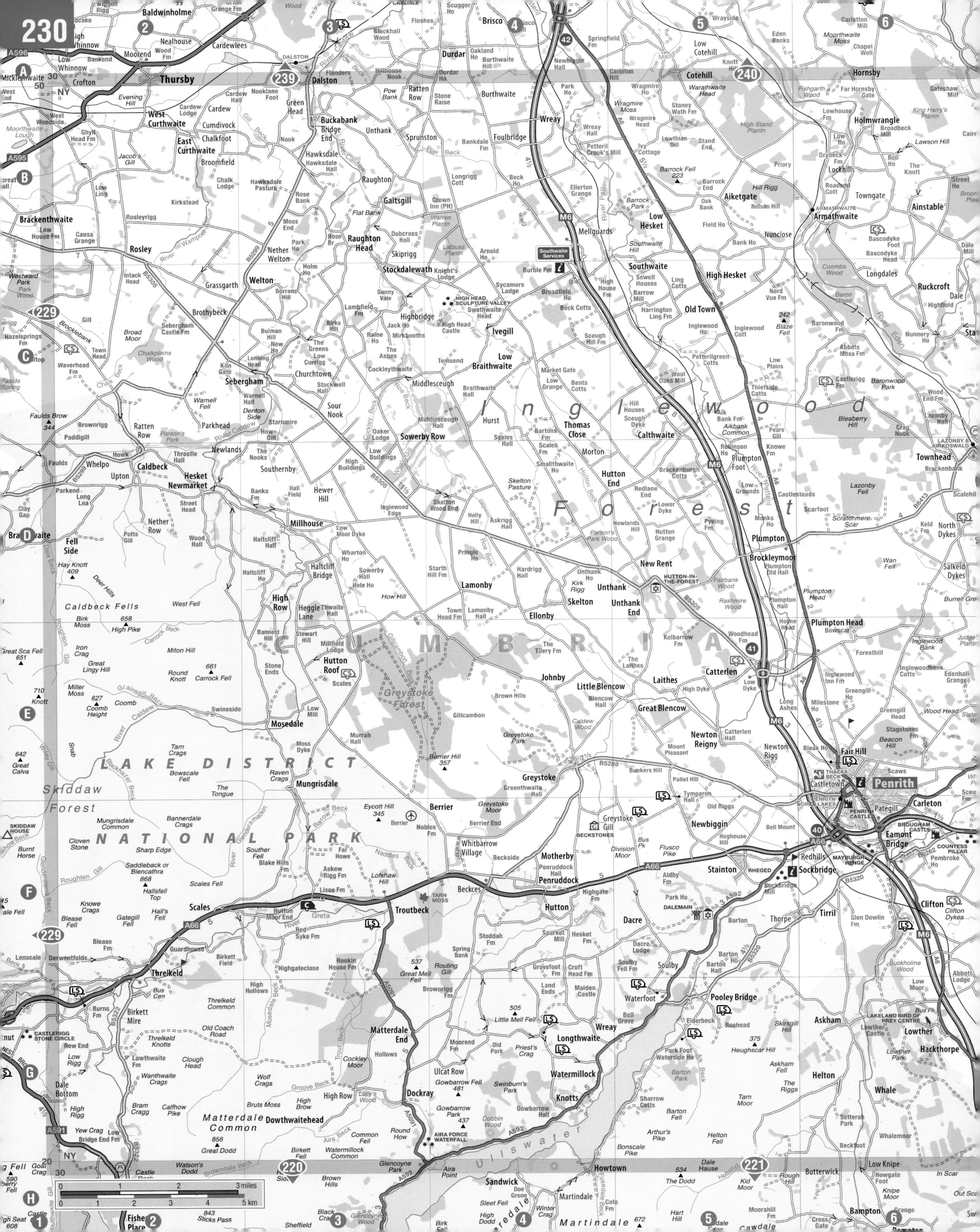

230
Baldwinholme
Nealhouse
Cardewlees
Moorend
Thursby
Dalston
Crofton
Evening Hill
West Curthwaite
East Curthwaite
Cardew
Cumdivock
Chalkfoot
Broomfield
Buckabank
Green Head
Hawksdale
Raughton
Gaitsgill
Raughton Head
Stockdalewath
Rosley
Welton
Brackenthwaite
Brothybeck
Sebergham
Churchtown
Highbridge
Ivegill
Low Braithwaite
Middlesceugh
Sowerby Row
Caldbeck
Hesket Newmarket
Whelpo
Upton
Millhouse
Fell Side
Lamonby
Skelton
Ellonby
Unthank
Unthank End
Hutton Roof
Mosedale
Mungrisdale
Berrier
Greystoke
Johnby
Little Blencow
Great Blencow
Newton Reigny
Penruddock
Motherby
Hutton
Dacre
Stainton
Sockbridge
Tirril
Scales
Troutbeck
Threlkeld
Matterdale End
Dockray
Dowthwaitehead
Watermillock
Wreay
Longthwaite
Pooley Bridge
Waterfoot
Soulby
Askham
Lowther
Hackthorpe
Helton
Whale
Sandwick
Martindale
Howtown
Bampton
Butterwick
Clifton
Eamont Bridge
Carleton
Penrith
Fair Hill
Castletown
Catterlen
Laithes
Plumpton Head
Plumpton
Brockleymoor
New Rent
Hutton End
Thomas Close
Calthwaite
Morton
Southwaite
Low Hesket
High Hesket
Old Town
Aiketgate
Armathwaite
Ainstable
Ruckcroft
Longdales
Cotehill
Hornsby
Holmwrangle
Durdar
Brisco
Wreay
Foulbridge
Sprunston
Unthank
Townhead
North Dykes
Salkeld Dykes
Inglewood Forest
CUMBRIA
LAKE DISTRICT NATIONAL PARK
Skiddaw Forest
Caldbeck Fells
Matterdale Common
Greystoke Forest
Ullswater
Southwaite Services
HIGH HEAD SCULPTURE VALLEY
HUTTON-IN-THE-FOREST
DALEMAIN
RHEGED
AIRA FORCE WATERFALL
CASTLERIGG STONE CIRCLE
LAKELAND BIRD OF PREY CENTRE
BROUGHAM CASTLE
PENRITH CASTLE
COUNTESS PILLAR
MAYBURGH HENGE
BECKSTONES
SKIDDAW HOUSE
High Pike 658
Carrock Fell 661
Great Calva 642
Knott 710
Great Sca Fell 651
Blencathra 868
Great Mell Fell 537
Little Mell Fell 505
Gowbarrow Fell 481
Great Dodd 856
Heughscar Hill 375
Barrock Fell 223
Blaze Fell 242
Fauld Brow 344
Hay Knott 409
Eycott Hill 345
Berrier Hill 357
Sticks Pass 843
M6
A6
A66
A591
A592
A5091
B5305
B5299
B5288
B5320
A596
A595
229
239
240
220
221
0 1 2 3 miles
0 1 2 3 4 5 km

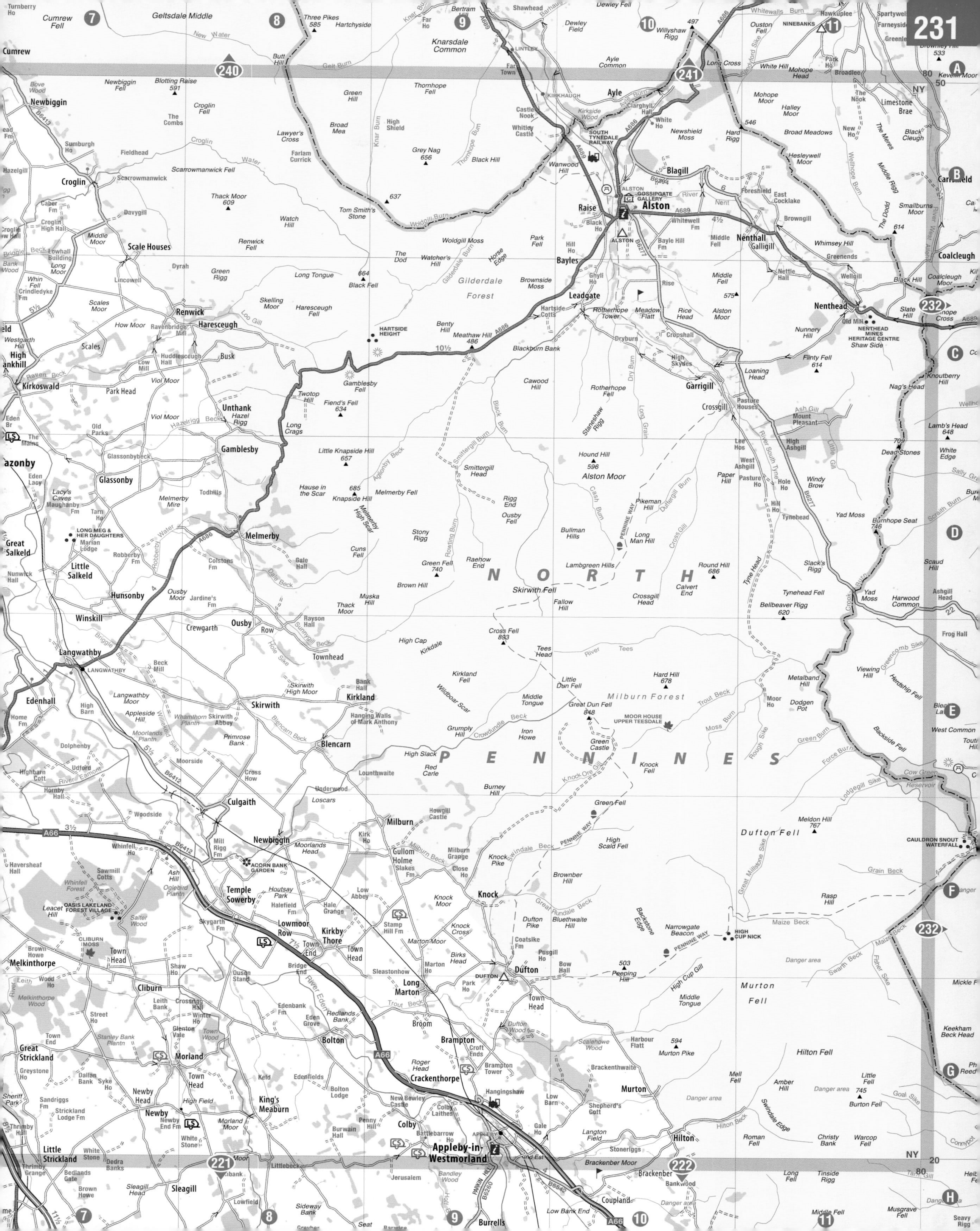

Turnberry Ho
Cumrew Fell
Geltsdale Middle
Three Pikes 585
Hartchyside
Bertram Hill
Far Ho
Knarsdale Common
Shawhead
Dewley Fell
Dewley Field
Willyshaw Rigg
497
Whitewalls Burn
Ouston Fell
NINEBANKS
Hawkuplee
Spartywell
Farneyside
Greenley
Cumrew
New Water
Butt Hill
Gelt Burn
LINTLEY
Far Town
Ayle Common
Long Cross
White Hill
Mohope Head
Park Ho
Broadlee
Brownley Hill 533
Kevelin Moor
NY
50
80
Bove Wood
Newbiggin Fell
Blotting Raise 591
Newbiggin
Croglin Fell
The Combs
Green Hill
Thornhope Fell
Broad Mea
High Shield
Lawyer's Cross
Farlam Currick
Knar Burn
Thornhope Burn
Grey Nag 656
Black Hill
KIRKHAUGH
Castle Nook
Whitley Castle
Ayle
Ayle Burn
Clarghyll Hall
Kirkside Wood
White Ho
SOUTH TYNEDALE RAILWAY
Newshield Moss
Hard Rigg
546
Mohope Moor
Halley Moor
The Nook
Limestone Brae
Broad Meadows
New Ho
The Meres
Black Cleugh
Hesleywell Moor
Middle Rigg
Sumburgh Ho
Fieldhead
Croglin
Hazelgill
Croglin
Scarrowmanwick
Scarrowmanwick Fell
Water
Wanwood Hill
Blagill
Carrshield
Thack Moor 609
637
Tom Smith's Stone
Woldgill Burn
ALSTON
GOSSIPGATE GALLERY
Alston
River
Nent
Foreshield
East Cocklake
Smallburns Moor
The Dodd
Caber Fm
Croglin High Hall
Davygill
Middle Moor
Watch Hill
Raise
Black Ho
Whitewell Fm
Browngill
614
Renwick Fell
Woldgill Moss
Park Fell
Hill Ho
Bayle Hill Fm
Middle Fell
Nenthall
Galligill
Whimsey Hill
Coalcleugh
Lowhall Building
Long Moor
Scale Houses
The Dod
Watcher's Hill
Horse Edge
Bayles
Greenends
Whin Fell
Crindledyke Fm
Dyrah
Lincowell
Green Rigg
Long Tongue
664
Black Fell
Gilderdale Forest
Brownside Moss
Ghyll Ho
Rise
Nettle Hall
Wellgill
Black Hill
Coalcleugh Moor
Scales Moor
Skelling Moor
Harescuegh Fell
Leadgate
Middle Fell
575
Renwick
Hartside Cotts
Rotherhope Tower
Meadow Flatt
Rice Head
Alston Moor
Nenthead
Slate Hill
Old Mill
NENTHEAD MINES HERITAGE CENTRE
Shaw Side
How Moor
Ravenbridge Mill
Harescuegh
Loo Gill
HARTSIDE HEIGHT
Benty Hill
Meathaw Hill 486
Blackburn Bank
Dryburn
Cropshall
Nunnery Hill
Westgarth Hill
High Bankhill
Scales
Huddlescough Hall
Busk
Low Mill
Viol Moor
10½
Gamblesby Fell
Dry Burn
High Skydes
Loaning Head
Flinty Fell 614
Knoutberry Hill
Nag's Head
Raven Beck
Kirkoswald
Park Head
Twotop Hill
Fiend's Fell 634
Cawood Hill
Rotherhope Fell
Garrigill
Crossgill
Pasture Houses
Ash Gill
Mount Pleasant
Eden Br
Viol Moor
Unthank
Hazel Rigg
Hazelrigg Beck
Long Crags
Black Burn
Staneshaw Rigg
Long Grain
Lamb's Head 648
Old Parks
The Mains
Gamblesby
Little Knapside Hill 657
Aglionby Beck
Smittergill Burn
Hound Hill 596
Alston Moor
Lee Hos
High Ashgill
709
Dead Stones
White Edge
Glassonbybeck
West Ashgill
Kirkoswald
Eden Lacy
Glassonby
Hause in the Scar
685
Knapside Hill
Melmerby Fell
Smittergill Head
Paper Hill
Pasture Ho
Hole Ho
Windy Brow
Lacy's Caves
Maughanby Fm
Melmerby Mire
Todhills
Melmerby High Scar
Rigg End
Ousby Fell
Pikeman Hill
Dufton Ghyll Burn
Hill Ho
Tynehead
Yad Moss
Burnhope Seat 746
Tarn Ho
LONG MEG & HER DAUGHTERS
Marian Lodge
Melmerby
Stony Rigg
Bullman Hills
PENNINE WAY
Long Man Hill
Cross Gill
Great Salkeld
Robberby Fm
Colstons Fm
Gale Hall
Cuns Fell
Rowling Burn
Green Fell 740
Raehow End
Lambgreen Hills
Round Hill 686
Slack's Rigg
Scaud Hill
Nunwick Hall
Little Salkeld
Dale Beck
Brown Hill
N O R T H
Skirwith Fell
Calvert End
Tyne Head
Tynehead Fell
Yad Moss
Harwood Common
Ashgill Head
Hunsonby
Ousby Moor
Jardine's Fm
Muska Hill
Thack Moor
Fallow Hill
Crossgill Head
Bellbeaver Rigg 620
Winskill
Crewgarth
Ousby
Rayson Hall
Row
Frog Hall
Langwathby
LANGWATHBY
Beck Mill
Hole Sike
Townhead
High Cap
Kirkdale
Cross Fell 893
Tees Head
River Tees
Edenhall
High Barn
Langwathby Moor
Skirwith High Moor
Bank Hall
Kirkland
Kirkland Fell
Wildboar Scar
Little Dun Fell
Hard Hill 678
Metalband Hill
Viewing Hill
Greencomb Sike
Herdship Fell
Home Fm
Appleside Hill
Whamthorn Plantn
Skirwith
Skirwith Abbey
Hanging Walls of Mark Anthony
Middle Tongue
Great Dun Fell 848
Milburn Forest
Trout Beck
MOOR HOUSE UPPER TEESDALE
Moor Ho
Dodgen Pot
West Common
Dolphenby
Moorlands Plantn
Primrose Bank
Blencarn Beck
Blencarn
Grumply Hill
Crowdundle Beck
Iron Howe
Green Castle
Moss Burn
Backside Fell
Udford
Moorside
Highbarn Cott
River Eamont
High Slack
P E N N I N E S
Red Carle
Knock Fell
Cross How
Lounthwaite
Rough Sike
Green Burn
Force Burn
Cow Green Reservoir
Hornby Hall
B6412
Underwood
Loscars
Burney Hill
Knock Ore Gill
Lodgegill Sike
Culgaith
Woodside
A66
3½
Howgill Castle
Green Fell
Meldon Hill 767
Milburn
Dufton Fell
Whinfell Ho
Newbiggin
Moorlands Head
Kirk Ho
Gullom Holme
Milburn Beck
Milburn Grange
Swindale Beck
High Scald Fell
CAULDRON SNOUT WATERFALL
Haversheaf Hall
Mill Rigg Fm
ACORN BANK GARDEN
Slakes Fm
Close Ho
Knock Pike
Brownber Hill
Grain Beck
Sawmill Cotts
Whinfell Forest
Ash Hill
Oglebird Plantn
Temple Sowerby
Houtsay Park
Low Abbey
Knock
Great Rundale Beck
Great Millstone Beck
Rasp Hill
Leacet Hill
OASIS LAKELAND FOREST VILLAGE
Halefield Fm
Hale Grange
Knock Moor
Dufton Pike
Bluethwaite Hill
Backstone Edge
Narrowgate Beacon
HIGH CUP NICK
Maize Beck
Salter Wood
Skygarth Fm
Lowmoor Row
Kirkby Thore
Stamp Hill Fm
Knock Cross
Coatsike Fm
PENNINE WAY
CLIBURN MOSS
Town End
Town Head
Marton Moor
Birks Head
Pusgill Ho
Bow Hall
Danger area
Swarth Beck
Fisher Sike
Brown Howe
Town Head
Shaw Ho
Ousen Stand
Bridge End
Sleastonhow
Marton Ho
DUFTON
Dufton
503
Peeping Hill
High Cup Gill
Murton Fell
Melkinthorpe
Leith
Wood Ho
Cliburn
Crossrigg Hall
River Eden
Long Marton
Park Ho
Town Head
Middle Tongue
Mickle Fell
Melkinthorpe Wood
Leith Bank
Winter Ho
Edenbank Fm
Redlands Bank
Trout Beck
Street Ho
Glenton Vale
Town Wood
Eden Grove
Broom
Dufton Wood
Scalehowe Wood
Harbour Flatt
594
Murton Pike
Hilton Fell
Keekham Beck Head
Town End
Stanley Bank Plantn
Bolton
Brampton
Croft Ends
Great Strickland
Morland
Greystone Ho
Dallan Bank
Syke Ho
Town Head
Keld
Edenfields
Roger Head
Crackenthorpe
Brampton Tower
Brackenthwaite
Mell Fell
Amber Hill
Danger area
Little Fell
745
Burton Fell
Goal Sike
Sheriff Park
Sandriggs Fm
Strickland Lodge Fm
Newby Head
High Field
Bolton Lodge
King's Meaburn
New Bewley Castle
Colby Laithes
Hangingshaw
Low Barn
Murton
Shepherd's Gott
Danger area
Swindale Edge
Thrimby Hall
Newby
Newby End Fm
Morland Moor
Burwain Hall
Penny Hill
Colby
Battlebarrow Ho
APPLEBY
Gale Ho
Langton Field
Hilton Beck
Hilton
Roman Fell
Christy Bank
Warcop Fell
Little Strickland
White Stone
Dedra Banks
White Stone
Appleby-in-Westmorland
Stoneriggs
Brackenber Moor
NY
80
20
Thrimby Grange
Bedlands Gate
Moor
Littlebeck
Jerusalem
Bandley Wood
Brackenber
Bankwood
Long Fell
Tinside Rigg
Brown Howe
Sleagill Head
Sleagill
Lowfield
Sideway Bank
PARKIN HILL
B6260
B6542
Coupland
Low Bank End
Burrells
Middle Fell
Musgrave Fell
Seavy Rigg
11½
240
241
221
222
232
7
8
9
10
11
A
B
C
D
E
F
G
H

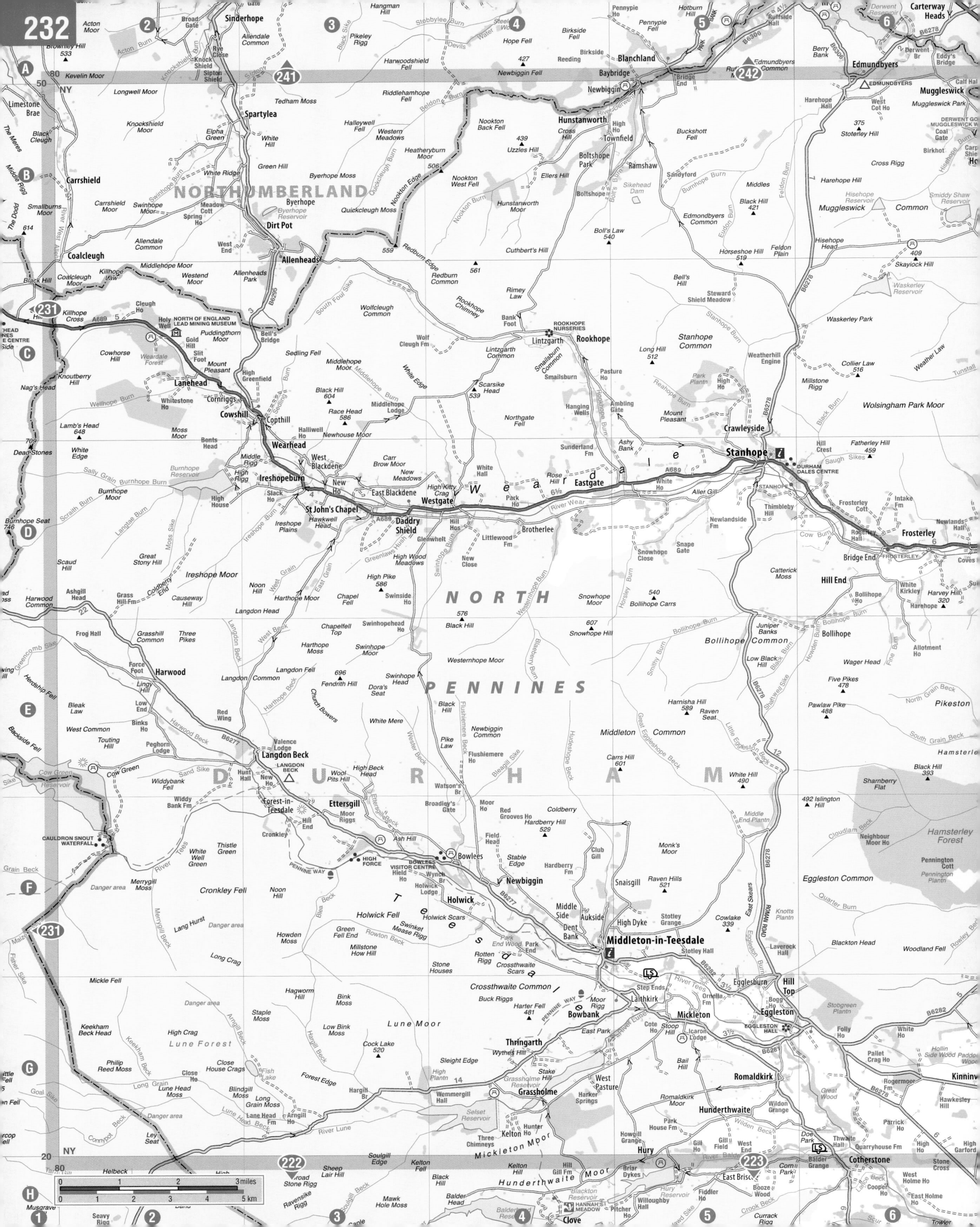

Acton Moor
Broad Gate
Sinderhope
Allendale Common
Hangman Hill
Stobbylee Burn
Pikeley Rigg
Pennypie Ho
Pennypie Fell
Hotburn Hill
Ruffside Hall
Derwent Reservoir
Carterway Heads
Brownley Hill 533
Acton Burn
Knock Shield
Rye Close
Harwoodshield Fell
Hope Fell
Birkside Fell
Birkside
Blanchland
Berry Bank
Derwent Br
Eddy's Bridge
Kevelin Moor
Sipton Shield
241
Newbiggin Fell
Reeding
Baybridge
Bridge End
242
Edmundbyers Common
Edmundbyers
Limestone Brae
Longwell Moor
Riddlehamhope Fell
Newbiggin
EDMUNDBYERS
Muggleswick
Tedham Moss
Spartylea
Nookton Back Fell
Hunstanworth
Harehope Hall
West Cot Ho
Muggleswick Park
The Meres
Black Cleugh
Knockshield Moor
Elpha Green
White Hill
Halleywell Fell
Western Meadows
Heatheryburn Moor
Uzzles Hill
Cross Hill
High Townfield
Buckshott Fell
Storerley Hill
Coal Gate
Birkhot
Middle Rigg
Carrshield
Green Hill
White Ridge
Byerhope Moss
Nookton Edge
Nookton West Fell
Ellers Hill
Boltshope Park
Ramshaw
Sandyford
Cross Rigg
Harehope Hill
NORTHUMBERLAND
Middles
Hisehope Reservoir
Smiddy Shaw Reservoir
Smalburns Moor
Carrshield Moor
Swinhope Moor
Meadow Cott
Byerhope
Byerhope Reservoir
Quickcleugh Moss
Hunstanworth Moor
Boltshope
Sikehead Dam
Black Hill 421
Muggleswick
Common
The Dodd
Spring Ho
Dirt Pot
Edmondbyers Common
614
Allendale Common
West End
Allenheads
Bolt's Law 540
Coalcleugh
Redburn Edge
Cuthbert's Hill
Horseshoe Hill 519
Feldon Plain
Hisehope Head
409
Skyiack Hill
Middlehope Moor
Westend Moor
Redburn Common
561
Bell's Hill
Waskerley Reservoir
Black Hill
Coalcleugh Moor
Killhope Law
Allenheads Park
Rimey Law
Steward Shield Meadow
231
Killhope Cross
Cleugh Ho
Wolfcleugh Common
Rookhope Chimney
Bank Foot
Waskerley Park
Holy Well
NORTH OF ENGLAND LEAD MINING MUSEUM
ROOKHOPE NURSERIES
Puddingthorn Moor
Bell's Bridge
Lintzgarth
Rookhope
Stanhope Common
Cowhorse Hill
Gold Hill
Weardale Forest
Wolf Cleugh Fm
Long Hill 512
Slit Foot
Sedling Fell
Lintzgarth Common
Weatherhill Engine
Collier Law 516
Mount Pleasant
Middlehope Moor
Smallsburn Common
Smailsburn
Pasture Ho
Millstone Rigg
Knoutberry Hill
Nag's Head
Lanehead
High Greenfield
White Edge
Scarsike Head
Park Plantn
High Ho
Weather Law
Tunstall
Black Hill 604
539
Wolsingham Park Moor
Whitestone Ho
Cornriggs
Middlehope Lodge
Hanging Wells
Ambling Gate
Mount Pleasant
Cowshill
Copthill
Race Head 586
Northgate Fell
Crawleyside
Lamb's Head 648
Halliwell Ho
Newhouse Moor
Moss Moor
Wearhead
Sunderland Fm
Ashy Bank
Hill Crest
Fatherley Hill 459
Bents Head
709
Dead Stones
White Edge
West Blackdene
Carr Brow Moor
Stanhope
DURHAM DALES CENTRE
Saugh Sikes
Burnhope Reservoir
Middle Rigg
White Hall
Rose Hill
Weardale
High Rigg
Ireshopeburn
New Meadows
High Kitty Crag
Eastgate
White Ho
A689
Burnhope Burn
Burnhope Moor
Slack Ho
New Ho
East Blackdene
Westgate
Aller Gill
STANHOPE
High House
St John's Chapel
Park Ho
River Wear
Thimbleby Hill
Frosterley Cott
Intake Fm
Hawkwell Head
Daddry Shield
Hill Hos
Newlandside Fm
Ireshope Plains
Brotherlee
Burnhope Seat 746
Glenwhelt
Littlewood Fm
Snape Gate
Ruskerley Hall
Frosterley
Newlands Hall
Snowhope Close
Bridge End
FROSTERLEY
Great Stony Hill
High Wood Meadows
New Close
Catterick Moss
Coves
Scaud Hill
Ireshope Moor
Hill End
White Kirkley
Harvey Hill 320
Noon Hill
High Pike 586
Swinside Ho
NORTH
Snowhope Moor
540
Bollihope Carrs
Bollihope Ho
Harehope
Ashgill Head
Grass Hill Fm
Coldberry End
Causeway Hill
Harthope Moor
Chapel Fell
Harwood Common
Langdon Head
576
Black Hill
607
Snowhope Hill
Frog Hall
Grasshill Common
Three Pikes
Chapelfell Top
Swinhopehead Ho
Juniper Banks
Bollihope
Bollihope Common
Allotment Ho
Harthope Moss
Swinhope Moor
Westernhope Moor
Low Black Hill
Wager Head
Force Foot
Harwood
Langdon Common
Langdon Fell
696
Fendrith Hill
Swinhope Head
Dora's Seat
Five Pikes 478
Lingy Hill
PENNINES
Herdship Fell
Bleak Law
Low End
Church Bowers
Black Hill
Hamisha Hill 589
Raven Seat
Pawlaw Pike 488
Pikeston
Binks Ho
Red Wing
White Mere
Newbiggin Common
Middleton Common
West Common
Touting Hill
Peghorn Lodge
Valence Lodge
Pike Law
South Grain Beck
Hamsterley
Backside Fell
Langdon Beck
LANGDON BECK
Flushiemere Ho
Carrs Hill 601
Black Hill 393
Cow Green
Cow Green Reservoir
Widdybank Fell
Hunt Hall
New Ho
Wool Pits Hill
High Beck Head
DURHAM
White Hill 490
Sharnberry Flat
Widdy Bank Fm
Forest-in-Teesdale
Ettersgill
Watson's Br
Broadley's Gate
Moor Ho
Red Grooves Ho
Coldberry
Hardberry Hill 529
Middle End Plantn
492 Islington Hill
Hamsterley Forest
Moor Riggs
Hill End
Cronkley
Ash Hill
Field Head
Club Gill
Monk's Moor
Neighbour Moor Ho
CAULDRON SNOUT WATERFALL
Thistle Green
White Well Green
HIGH FORCE
BOWLEES VISITOR CENTRE
Bowlees
Stable Edge
Hardberry Fm
Pennington Cott
Pennington Plantn
PENNINE WAY
Hield Ho
Wynch Br
Newbiggin
Snaisgill
Raven Hills 521
Eggleston Common
Grain Beck
Danger area
Merrygill Moss
Cronkley Fell
Noon Hill
Holwick Lodge
Holwick
Teesdale
Quarter Burn
Knotts Plantn
Middle Side
Aukside
Cowlake 339
High Dyke
Stotley Grange
Holwick Fell
Holwick Scars
Swinket Mease Rigg
231
Lang Hurst
Danger area
Howden Moss
Green Fell End
Millstone How Hill
Rowton Beck
Dent Bank
Middleton-in-Teesdale
Stotley Hall
Blackton Head
Woodland Fell
Laverock Hall
Long Crag
Park End Wood
Park End
Rotten Rigg
Crossthwaite Scars
Stone Houses
Egglesburn
Hill Top
Mickle Fell
Crossthwaite Common
Step Ends
Laithkirk
Ornella Fm
Bogg Ho
Eggleston
Stobgreen Plantn
Danger area
Hagworm Hill
Bink Moss
Buck Riggs
Harter Fell 481
Moor Rigg
Bowbank
Mickleton
EGGLESTON HALL
Folly Ho
White Ho
Staple Moss
Low Bink Moss
Lune Moor
East Park
Cote Ho
Stoop Hill
Icaron Lodge
Keekham Beck Head
High Crag
Lune Forest
Cock Lake 520
Thringarth
Wythes Hill
Hollin Side Wood
Pallet Crag Ho
Philip Reed Moss
Close House Crags
Fish Lake
Sleight Edge
Bail Hill
Romaldkirk
Kinninvie
Close Ho
Forest Edge
High Plantn
Grassholme Reservoir
Stake Hill
West Pasture
Rogermoor Fm
Long Grain
Lune Head Moss
Blindgill Moss
Hargill Br
Wemmergill Hall
Grassholme
Harker Springs
Romaldkirk Moor
Great Wood
Hawkesley Hill
Long Grain Moss
Lane Head Fm
Arngill Ho
Selset Reservoir
Hunderthwaite
Wilden Grange
Danger area
River Lune
Hunter Ho
Park House Fm
Parrick Ho
Ley Seat
Connypot Beck
Three Chimneys
Kelton Ho
Howgill Grange
Gill Ho
Gill Field
West End
Doe Park
Thwaite Hall
Quarryhouse Fm
High Ho
High Garford
NY
Mickleton Moor
Hury
223
Balder Grange
Cotherstone
Stone Cross
222
Soulgill Edge
Kelton Fell
Kelton Hill
Hill Gill Fm
Briar Dykes
East Briscoe
Corn Park
West Holme Ho
Helbeck
Broad Stone Rigg
Sheep Lair Hill
Black Hill
Hunderthwaite Moor
Blackton Reservoir
Hury Reservoir
Fiddler Ho
Booze Wood
Cooper Ho
East Holme Ho
Ravensike Rigg
Mawk Hole Moss
Balder Head
HANNAH'S MEADOW
Willoughby Hall
Pitcher Ho
Crook Beck
Musgrave
Seavy Rigg
Balderhead Reservoir
Clove
Currack Rigg
Towler
0 1 2 3 miles
0 1 2 3 4 5 km

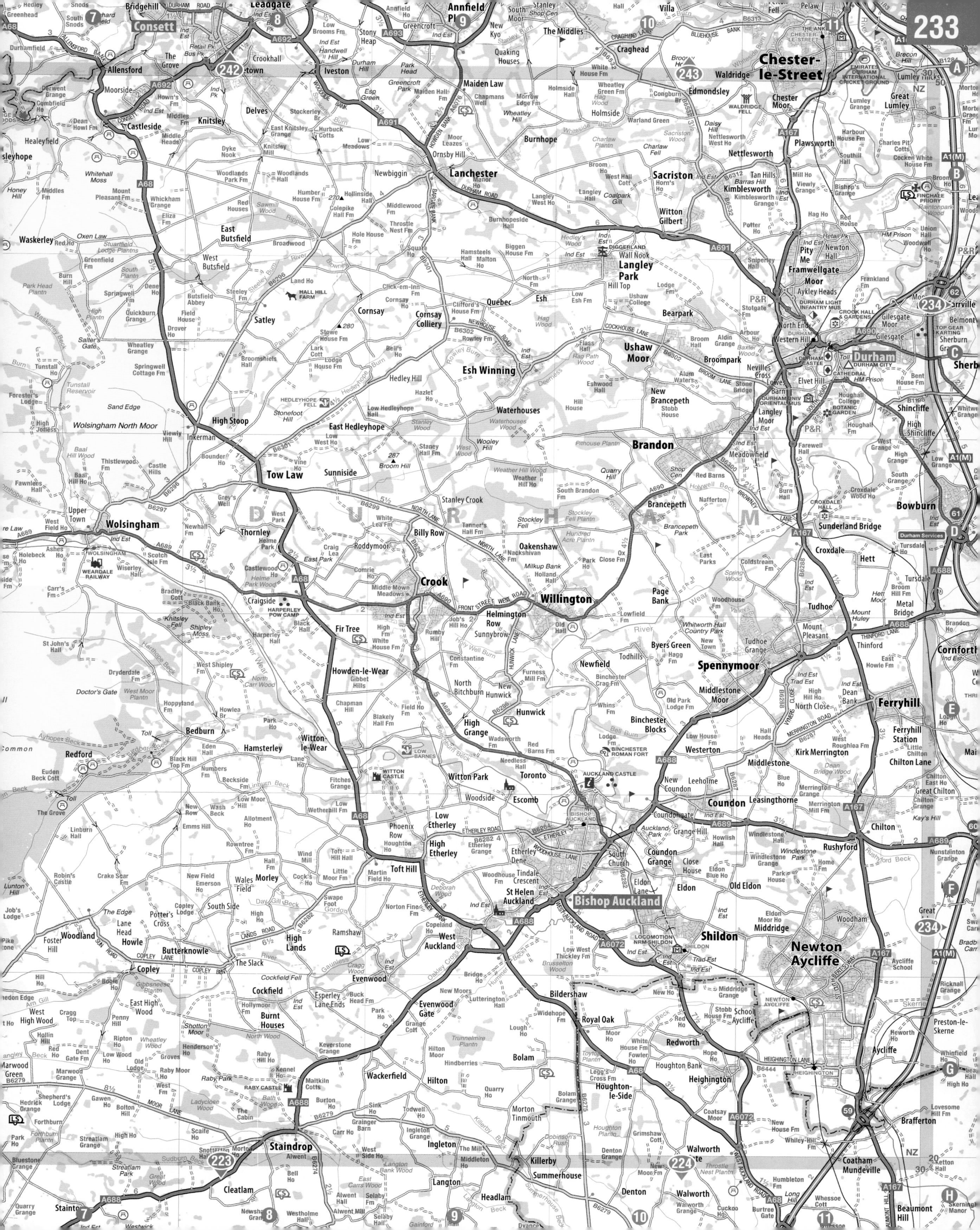
Consett
Leadgate
Annfield Plain
Chester-le-Street
Allensford
Castleside
Knitsley
Delves
Iveston
Maiden Law
Lanchester
Burnhope
Craghead
Edmondsley
Sacriston
Kimblesworth
Witton Gilbert
Langley Park
Esh
Quebec
Cornsay
Cornsay Colliery
Satley
Esh Winning
Ushaw Moor
Bearpark
Durham
Brandon
Waskerley
Tow Law
Wolsingham
Thornley
Crook
Willington
Billy Row
Brancepeth
Shincliffe
Bowburn
Sunderland Bridge
Tudhoe
Spennymoor
Ferryhill
Fir Tree
Howden-le-Wear
Hamsterley
Witton-le-Wear
Bedburn
Redford
Hunwick
Witton Park
Toronto
Escomb
Bishop Auckland
Coundon
Shildon
Newton Aycliffe
Chilton
Rushyford
Middlestone
Kirk Merrington
West Auckland
Toft Hill
Woodland
Copley
Cockfield
Evenwood
Staindrop
Raby Castle
Hilton
Wackerfield
Heighington
Redworth
Aycliffe
Ingleton
Killerby
Summerhouse
Walworth
Denton
Headlam
Langton
Cleatlam
Bolam
Houghton-le-Side
Coatham Mundeville
Brafferton
DURHAM
Durham Services
242
243
234
223
224
A68
A689
A690
A691
A692
A167
A688
A6072
A1(M)

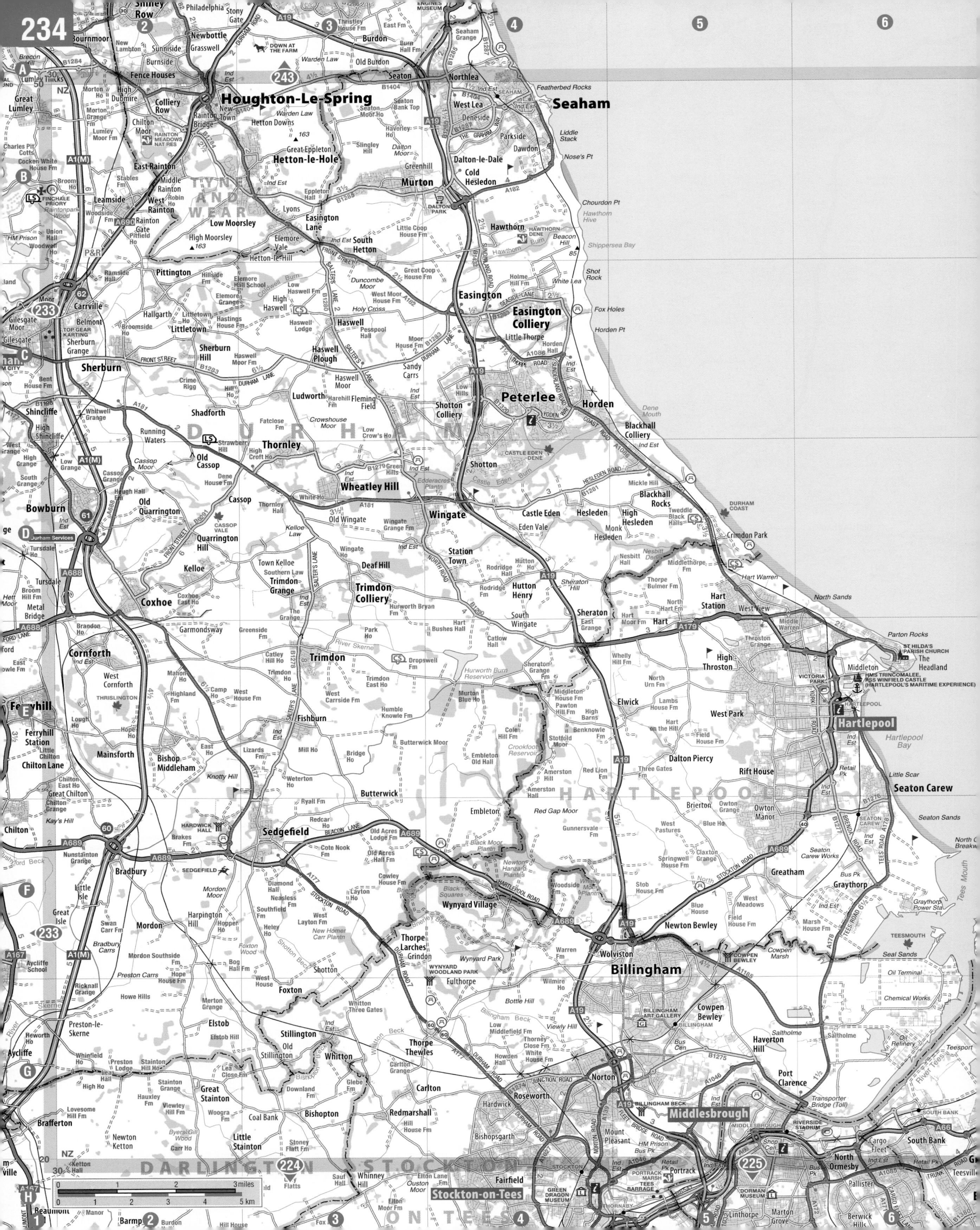
Houghton-Le-Spring
Seaham
Hetton-le-Hole
Murton
Seaton
Northlea
West Lea
Deneside
Parkside
Dawdon
Dalton-le-Dale
Cold Hesledon
Hawthorn
Easington
Easington Colliery
Little Thorpe
Peterlee
Horden
Blackhall Colliery
Shotton Colliery
Shotton
Castle Eden
Hesleden
High Hesleden
Monk Hesleden
Blackhall Rocks
Crimdon Park
Wingate
Wheatley Hill
Thornley
Ludworth
Haswell
Haswell Plough
South Hetton
Easington Lane
Pittington
Littletown
Sherburn
Sherburn Hill
Shadforth
Carrville
Belmont
Gilesgate
Shincliffe
High Shincliffe
Bowburn
Cassop
Old Cassop
Old Quarrington
Quarrington Hill
Kelloe
Coxhoe
Cornforth
West Cornforth
Ferryhill
Ferryhill Station
Chilton Lane
Mainsforth
Bishop Middleham
Chilton
Great Chilton
Bradbury
Little Isle
Great Isle
Mordon
Preston-le-Skerne
Aycliffe
Brafferton
Newton Ketton
Great Stainton
Little Stainton
Stillington
Old Stillington
Whitton
Bishopton
Redmarshall
Carlton
Thorpe Thewles
Foxton
Sedgefield
Butterwick
Fishburn
Trimdon
Trimdon Colliery
Trimdon Grange
Deaf Hill
Station Town
Hutton Henry
Sheraton
Hart
Hart Station
West View
Middle Warren
High Throston
Hartlepool
The Headland
Seaton Carew
Owton Manor
Rift House
Dalton Piercy
Elwick
West Park
Greatham
Graythorp
Newton Bewley
Wolviston
Billingham
Cowpen Bewley
Haverton Hill
Port Clarence
Norton
Roseworth
Hardwick
Bishopsgarth
Fairfield
Stockton-on-Tees
Middlesbrough
North Ormesby
South Bank
Cargo Fleet
Wynyard Village
Thorpe Larches
Grindon
Embleton
DURHAM
HARTLEPOOL
DARLINGTON
STOCKTON-ON-TEES
TYNE AND WEAR
A19
A1(M)
A179
A689
A177
A181
A688
A167
243
233
224
225
0 1 2 3 miles
0 1 2 3 4 5 km

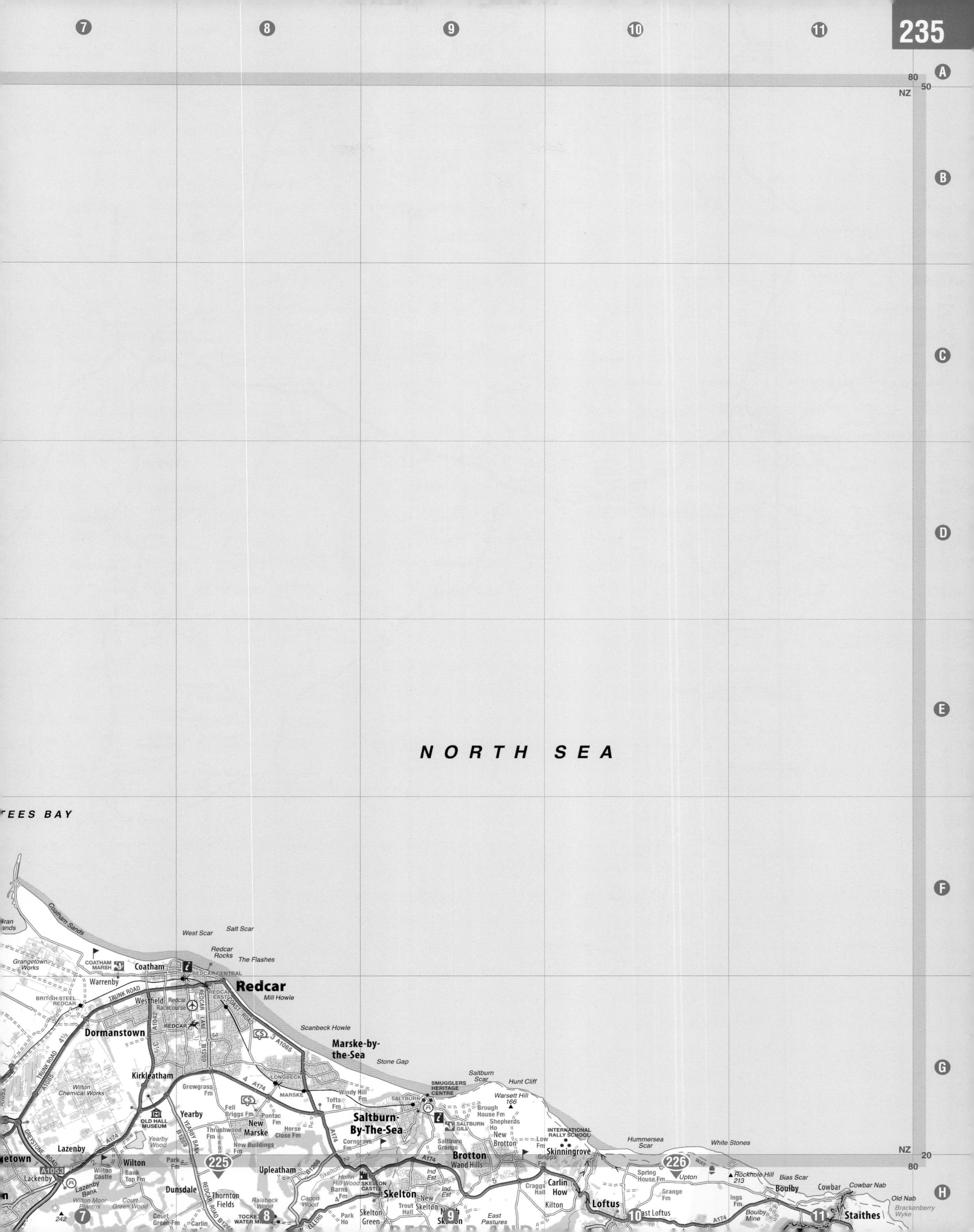

NORTH SEA
TEES BAY
Coatham Sands
West Scar
Salt Scar
Redcar Rocks
The Flashes
Grangetown Works
COATHAM MARSH
Coatham
Warrenby
REDCAR CENTRAL
Redcar
Mill Howle
BRITISH STEEL REDCAR
TRUNK ROAD
Westfield
Redcar Racecourse
REDCAR EAST
COAST ROAD
REDCAR LANE
Dormanstown
Scanbeck Howle
Marske-by-the-Sea
Stone Gap
Kirkleatham
Wilton Chemical Works
LONGBECK
MARSKE
Grewgrass Fm
Windy Hill Fm
Saltburn Scar
Hunt Cliff
SMUGGLERS HERITAGE CENTRE
SALTBURN
Warsett Hill 166
OLD HALL MUSEUM
Yearby
Fell Briggs Fm
Pontac Fm
New Marske
Tofts Fm
Saltburn-By-The-Sea
SALTBURN GILL
Brough House Fm
Shepherds Ho
New Brotton
INTERNATIONAL RALLY SCHOOL
Skinningrove
Hummersea Scar
White Stones
Thrushwood Fm
Horse Close Fm
Corngrave Fm
Saltburn Grange
Brotton
Wand Hills
Low Fm
Gripps Fm
Lazenby
Yearby Wood
New Buildings Fm
YEARBY BANK
Wilton
Park Fm
225
Upleatham
226
Spring House Fm
Upton
Rockhole Hill 213
Bias Scar
Boulby
Cowbar
Cowbar Nab
Old Nab
Brackenberry Wyke
Lackenby
Wilton Castle
Bank Top Fm
Lazenby Bank
Wilton Moor Plantns
Court Green Wood
Dunsdale
Thornton Fields
Raisbeck Wood
Hollin Hill Wood
Barns Fm
SKELTON CASTLE
Skelton
New Skelton
Ind Est
Craggs Hall
Carlin How
Kilton
Loftus
East Loftus
Grange Fm
Ings Fm
Boulby Mine
Staithes
Capon Wood
Park Ho
Skelton Green
Trout Hall
North Skelton
East Pastures
Court Green Fm
Carlin
TOCKETTS WATER MILL
242
A1053
A1085
A174
A1042
B1269
A174
B1268
GREYSTONE ROAD
REDCAR ROAD
NZ
80
50
20

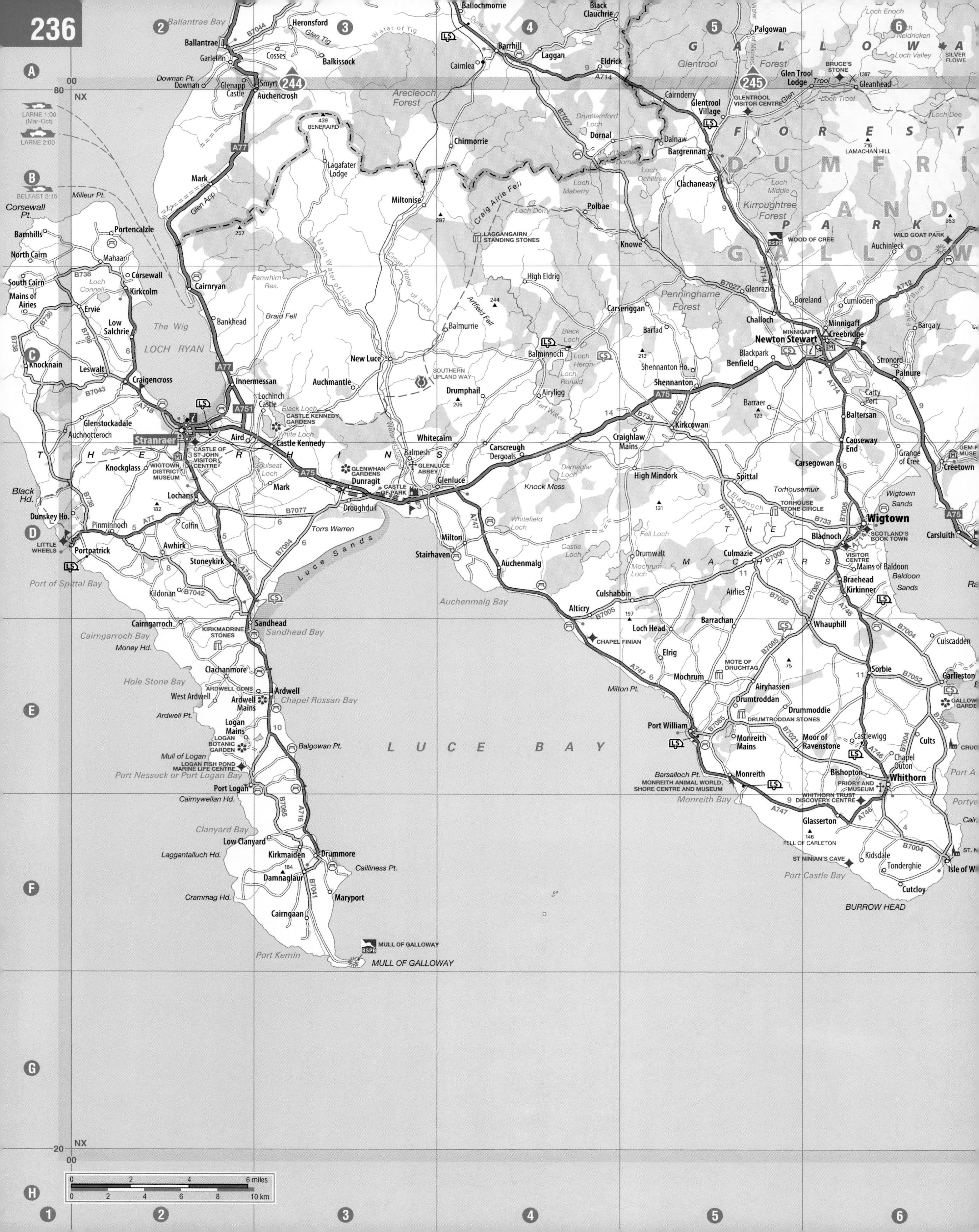
Ballantrae Bay
Ballantrae
Garleffin
Heronsford
Glen Tig
Cosses
Balkissock
Water of Tig
Ballochmorrie
Barrhill
Cairnlea
Laggan
Black Clauchrie
Eldrick
Palgowan
Glentrool
Forest
Glen Trool Lodge
Trool
Loch Trool
Gleanhead
BRUCE'S STONE
Loch Enoch
Loch Valley
SILVER FLOWE
G A L L O W A Y
F O R E S T
D U M F R I
P A R K
G A L L O W
Downan Pt.
Downan
Glenapp Castle
Smyrt
Auchencrosh
244
245
Arecleoch Forest
439 BENERAIRD
Cairnderry
Glentrool Village
GLENTROOL VISITOR CENTRE
Drumlamford Loch
Dornal
Dalnaw
Bargrennan
Loch Dee
716 LAMACHAN HILL
LARNE 1:00 (Mar-Oct)
LARNE 2:00
BELFAST 2:15
NX
80
00
A77
Mark
Glen App
Lagafater Lodge
Chirmorrie
Miltonise
Loch Ochiltree
Loch Maberry
Clachaneasy
Loch Middle
Kirroughtree Forest
Corsewall Pt.
Milleur Pt.
Barnhills
Portencalzie
North Cairn
Mahaar
South Cairn
Corsewall
Loch Connell
Kirkcolm
Mains of Airies
Ervie
Low Salchrie
The Wig
LOCH RYAN
Cairnryan
Bankhead
Penwhirn Res.
Braid Fell
Main Water of Luce
Cross Water of Luce
Craig Airie Fell
Loch Derry
Polbae
LAGGANGAIRN STANDING STONES
Knowe
WOOD OF CREE
WILD GOAT PARK
Auchinleck
High Eldrig
Arfield Fell
Carseriggan
Penninghame Forest
B7027
Glenrazie
Boreland
Cumloden
Challoch
Newton Stewart
MINNIGAFF
Minnigaff
Creebridge
Bargaly
Balmurrie
Black Loch
Balminnoch
Loch Heron
Loch Ronald
Barfad
Shennanton Ho.
Blackpark
Benfield
Shennanton
Stronord
Palnure
Knocknain
Leswalt
Craigencross
B7043
Innermessan
A751
New Luce
Auchmantle
SOUTHERN UPLAND WAY
Drumphail
Airyligg
Tarf Water
Lochinch Castle
Black Loch
CASTLE KENNEDY GARDENS
White Loch
Glenstockadale
Auchnotteroch
Stranraer
Aird
Castle Kennedy
CASTLE OF ST JOHN VISITOR CENTRE
WIGTOWN DISTRICT MUSEUM
Whitecairn
Balmesh
GLENLUCE ABBEY
Carscreugh
Dergoals
Craighlaw Mains
Kirkcowan
A75
B733
B735
Barraer
Carty Port
Baltersan
Causeway End
Grange of Cree
Creetown
Knockglass
Soulseat Loch
T H E R H I N S
GLENWHAN GARDENS
Dunragit
CASTLE OF PARK
Glenluce
Dernaglar Loch
Knock Moss
High Mindork
Spittal
Torhousemuir
Carsegowan
TORHOUSE STONE CIRCLE
Wigtown Sands
Wigtown
Black Hd.
Lochans
Mark
Droughduil
B7077
Dunskey Ho.
Pinminnoch
Colfin
Torrs Warren
Whitefield Loch
Fell Loch
Bladnoch
SCOTLAND'S BOOK TOWN
Carsluith
LITTLE WHEELS
Portpatrick
Awhirk
Stoneykirk
B7084
Milton
Stairhaven
A747
Auchenmalg
Castle Loch
Drumwalt
Mochrum Loch
T H E M A C H A R S
Culmazie
B7005
VISITOR CENTRE
Mains of Baldoon
Baldoon Sands
Port of Spittal Bay
Kildonan
B7042
Luce Sands
Auchenmalg Bay
Culshabbin
Airlies
Braehead
Kirkinner
Cairngarroch
Cairngarroch Bay
KIRKMADRINE STONES
Sandhead
Sandhead Bay
Alticry
Loch Head
Barrachan
Whauphill
CHAPEL FINIAN
Money Hd.
Elrig
B7004
Culscadden
Hole Stone Bay
Clachanmore
ARDWELL GDNS
Ardwell
Ardwell Mains
West Ardwell
Chapel Rossan Bay
Ardwell Pt.
MOTE OF DRUCHTAG
Mochrum
Airyhassen
Sorbie
Garlieston
Milton Pt.
Drumtroddan
Drummoddie
DRUMTRODDAN STONES
Logan Mains
LOGAN BOTANIC GARDEN
Balgowan Pt.
L U C E B A Y
Port William
Monreith Mains
Moor of Ravenstone
Castlewigg
Cults
Mull of Logan
LOGAN FISH POND MARINE LIFE CENTRE
Port Nessock or Port Logan Bay
Port Logan
Cairnywellan Hd.
B7065
A716
Barsalloch Pt.
MONREITH ANIMAL WORLD, SHORE CENTRE AND MUSEUM
Monreith
Monreith Bay
Bishopton
Chapel Outon
PRIORY AND MUSEUM
Whithorn
WHITHORN TRUST DISCOVERY CENTRE
Clanyard Bay
Low Clanyard
Glasserton
146 FELL OF CARLETON
Laggantalluch Hd.
Kirkmaiden
Drummore
Damnaglaur
Cailliness Pt.
ST NINIAN'S CAVE
Kidsdale
Tonderghie
Isle of Whithorn
Crammag Hd.
B7041
Maryport
Port Castle Bay
Cutcloy
BURROW HEAD
Cairngaan
MULL OF GALLOWAY
Port Kemin
NX
20
00
0 2 4 6 miles
0 2 4 6 8 10 km
A B C D E F G H
1 2 3 4 5 6

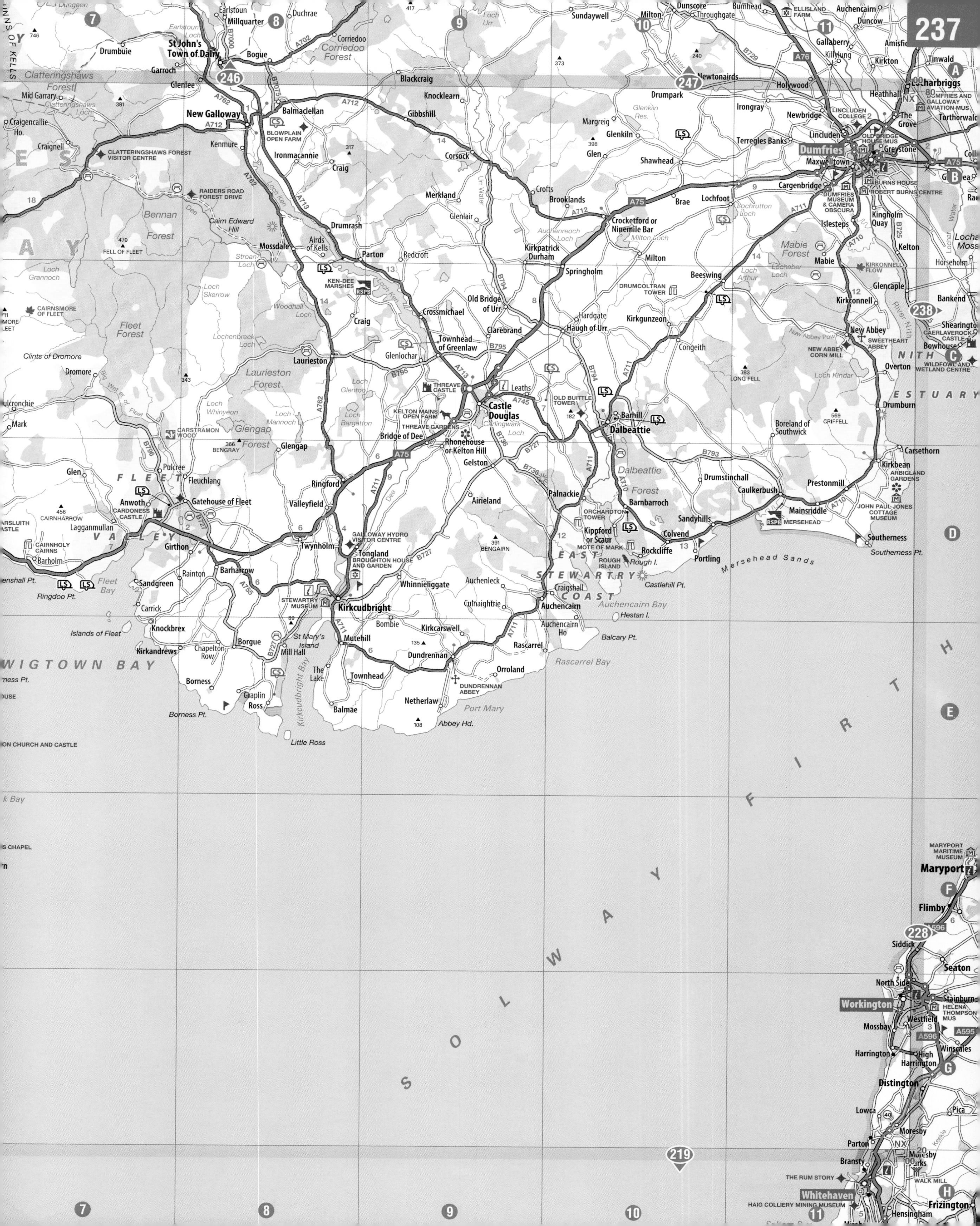
Earlstoun
Millquarter
Duchrae
Corriedoo
Corriedoo Forest
St John's Town of Dalry
Drumbuie
Clatteringshaws Forest
Garroch
Glenlee
Bogue
Blackcraig
Knocklearn
Gibbshill
Balmaclellan
Mid Garrary
New Galloway
Craigencallie Ho.
Craignell
Clatteringshaws Forest Visitor Centre
Kenmure
Blowplain Open Farm
Ironmacannie
Craig
Corsock
Raiders Road Forest Drive
Bennan Forest
Cairn Edward Hill
Fell of Fleet
Mossdale
Airds of Kells
Drumrash
Parton
Redcroft
Merkland
Glenlair
Loch Grannoch
Loch Skerrow
Ken-Dee Marshes
Woodhall Loch
Cairnsmore of Fleet
Fleet Forest
Lochenbreck Loch
Craig
Crossmichael
Townhead of Greenlaw
Glenlochar
Laurieston
Clints of Dromore
Dromore
Laurieston Forest
Threave Castle
Kelton Mains Open Farm
Threave Gardens
Castle Douglas
Carlingwark Loch
Leaths
Loch Whinyeon
Glengap Forest
Carstramon Wood
Bengray
Glengap
Bridge of Dee
Rhonehouse or Kelton Hill
Gelston
Glen
Pulcree
Fleuchlang
Anwoth
Cardoness Castle
Gatehouse of Fleet
Ringford
Valleyfield
Airieland
Palnackie
Cairnholy Cairns
Barholm
Lagganmullan
Girthon
Twynholm
Galloway Hydro Visitor Centre
Tongland
Broughton House and Garden
Rainton
Barharrow
Sandgreen
Fleet Bay
Ringdoo Pt.
Carrick
Knockbrex
Islands of Fleet
Stewartry Museum
Kirkcudbright
Whinnieliggate
Auchenleck
Culnaightrie
Bombie
Kirkcarswell
Mutehill
Borgue
Chapelton Row
Kirkandrews
St Mary's Island
Mill Hall
Dundrennan
Dundrennan Abbey
Townhead
The Lake
Balmae
Netherlaw
Port Mary
Abbey Hd.
Borness
Borness Pt.
Graplin
Ross
Little Ross
Kirkcudbright Bay
WIGTOWN BAY
FLEET VALLEY
Sundaywell
Milton
Dunscore
Throughgate
Burnhead
Ellisland Farm
Auchencairn
Duncow
Gallaberry
Killylung
Amisfield
Kirkton
Tinwald
Newtonairds
Drumpark
Holywood
Locharbriggs
Heathhall
Dumfries and Galloway Aviation Mus
Irongray
Newbridge
Lincluden College
Lincluden
The Grove
Torthorwald
Margreig
Glenkiln Res.
Glenkiln
Glen
Terregles Banks
Shawhead
Old Bridge House Mus
Dumfries
Maxwelltown
Greystone
Cargenbridge
Burns House
Robert Burns Centre
Dumfries Museum & Camera Obscura
Crofts
Brooklands
Brae
Lochfoot
Lochrutton Loch
Crocketford or Ninemile Bar
Auchenreoch Loch
Milton Loch
Kirkpatrick Durham
Milton
Islesteps
Kingholm Quay
Kelton
Mabie Forest
Mabie
Lochaber Loch
Loch Arthur
Beeswing
Springholm
Drumcoltran Tower
Kirkconnell Flow
Horseholm
Glencaple
Kirkconnell
Bankend
Old Bridge of Urr
Hardgate
Haugh of Urr
Kirkgunzeon
Clarebrand
Congeith
New Abbey
Sweetheart Abbey
New Abbey Corn Mill
Caerlaverock Castle
Bowhouse
Wildfowl and Wetland Centre
Overton
Long Fell
Loch Kindar
NITH ESTUARY
Old Buittle Tower
Barhill
Dalbeattie
Drumburn
Criffel
Boreland of Southwick
Carsethorn
Kirkbean
Arbigland Gardens
Dalbeattie Forest
Drumstinchall
Caulkerbush
Prestonmill
Barnbarroch
Mainsriddle
John Paul Jones Cottage Museum
Mersehead
Orchardton Tower
Sandyhills
Kippford or Scaur
Colvend
Southerness
Southerness Pt.
Mote of Mark
Rockcliffe
Portling
Rough Island
Rough I.
Bengairn
EAST STEWARTRY COAST
Mersehead Sands
Castlehill Pt.
Craigshall
Auchencairn
Auchencairn Bay
Hestan I.
Auchencairn Ho
Balcary Pt.
Rascarrel
Rascarrel Bay
Orroland
SOLWAY FIRTH
Maryport Maritime Museum
Maryport
Flimby
Siddick
Seaton
North Side
Workington
Stainburn
Helena Thompson Mus
Westfield
Mossbay
Winscales
Harrington
High Harrington
Distington
Lowca
Pica
Moresby
Parton
Bransty
Moresby Parks
The Rum Story
Walk Mill
Whitehaven
Haig Colliery Mining Museum
Frizington
Hensingham

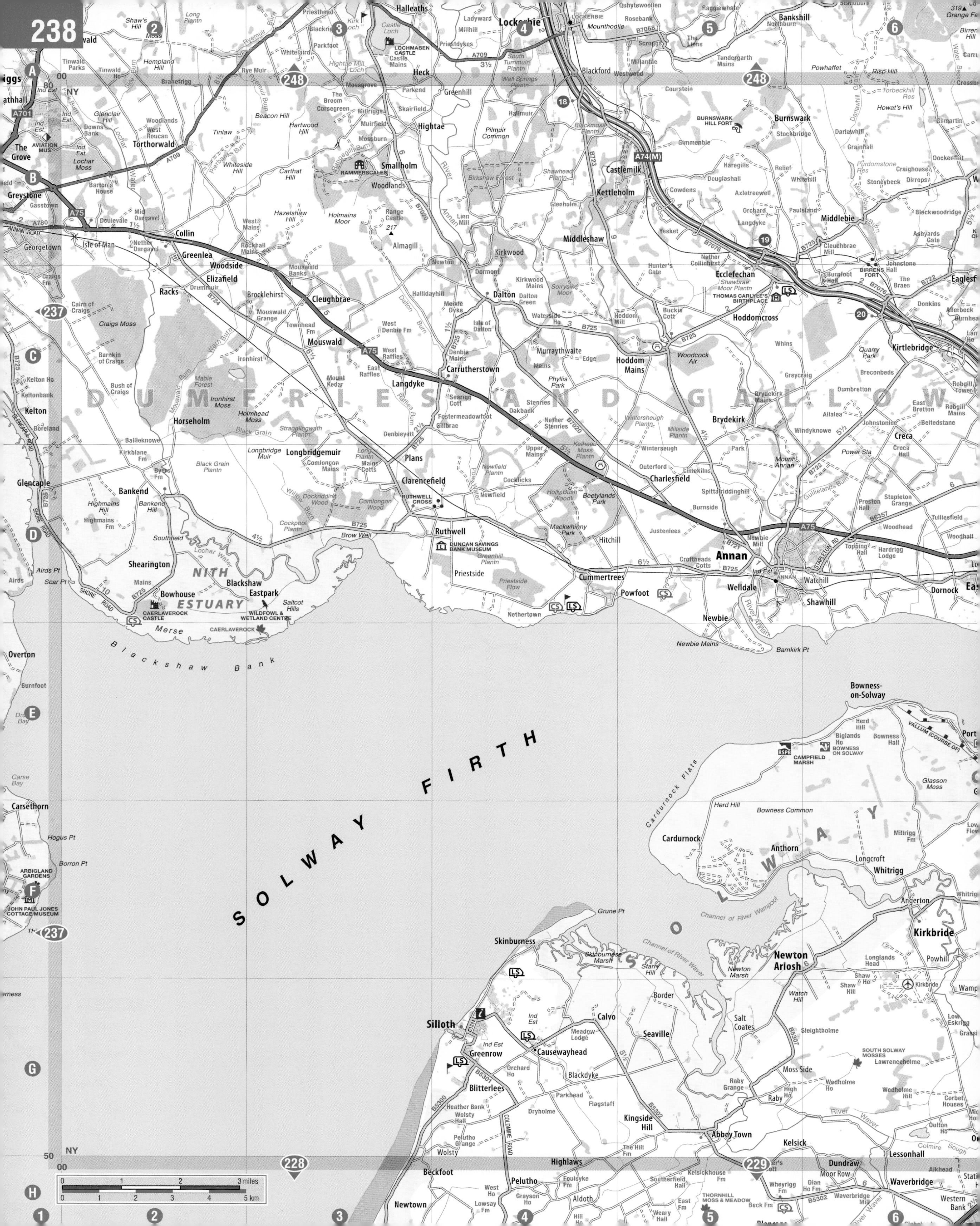

Lockerbie
Halleaths
Lochmaben Castle
Heck
Hightae
Smallholm
Rammerscales
Woodlands
Torthorwald
Collin
Greenlea
Woodside
Elizafield
Racks
Cleughbrae
Mouswald
Langdyke
Carrutherstown
Dalton
Kirkwood
Middleshaw
Castlemilk
Kettleholm
Ecclefechan
Thomas Carlyle's Birthplace
Hoddomcross
Hoddom Mains
Burnswark
Burnswark Hill Fort
Middlebie
Kirtlebridge
Brydekirk
Creca
Charlesfield
Annan
Welldale
Shawhill
Watchill
Dornock
Newbie
Cummertrees
Powfoot
Ruthwell
Duncan Savings Bank Museum
Clarencefield
Plans
Longbridgemuir
Bankend
Horseholm
Glencaple
Kelton
Shearington
Bowhouse
Blackshaw
Eastpark
Caerlaverock Castle
Wildfowl & Wetland Centre
Nith Estuary
Blackshaw Bank
Greystone
Georgetown
Isle of Man
The Grove
DUMFRIES AND GALLOWAY
SOLWAY FIRTH
Bowness-on-Solway
Campfield Marsh
Vallum (course of)
Cardurnock
Anthorn
Whitrigg
Kirkbride
Newton Arlosh
Skinburness
Silloth
Greenrow
Causewayhead
Calvo
Seaville
Blitterlees
Kingside Hill
Abbey Town
Kelsick
Dundraw
Lessonhall
Waverbridge
Beckfoot
Pelutho
Newtown
South Solway Mosses
Carsethorn
Arbigland Gardens
John Paul Jones Cottage Museum
Overton
A75
A74(M)
A709
A701
B725
248
237
228
229
0 1 2 3 miles
0 1 2 3 4 5 km

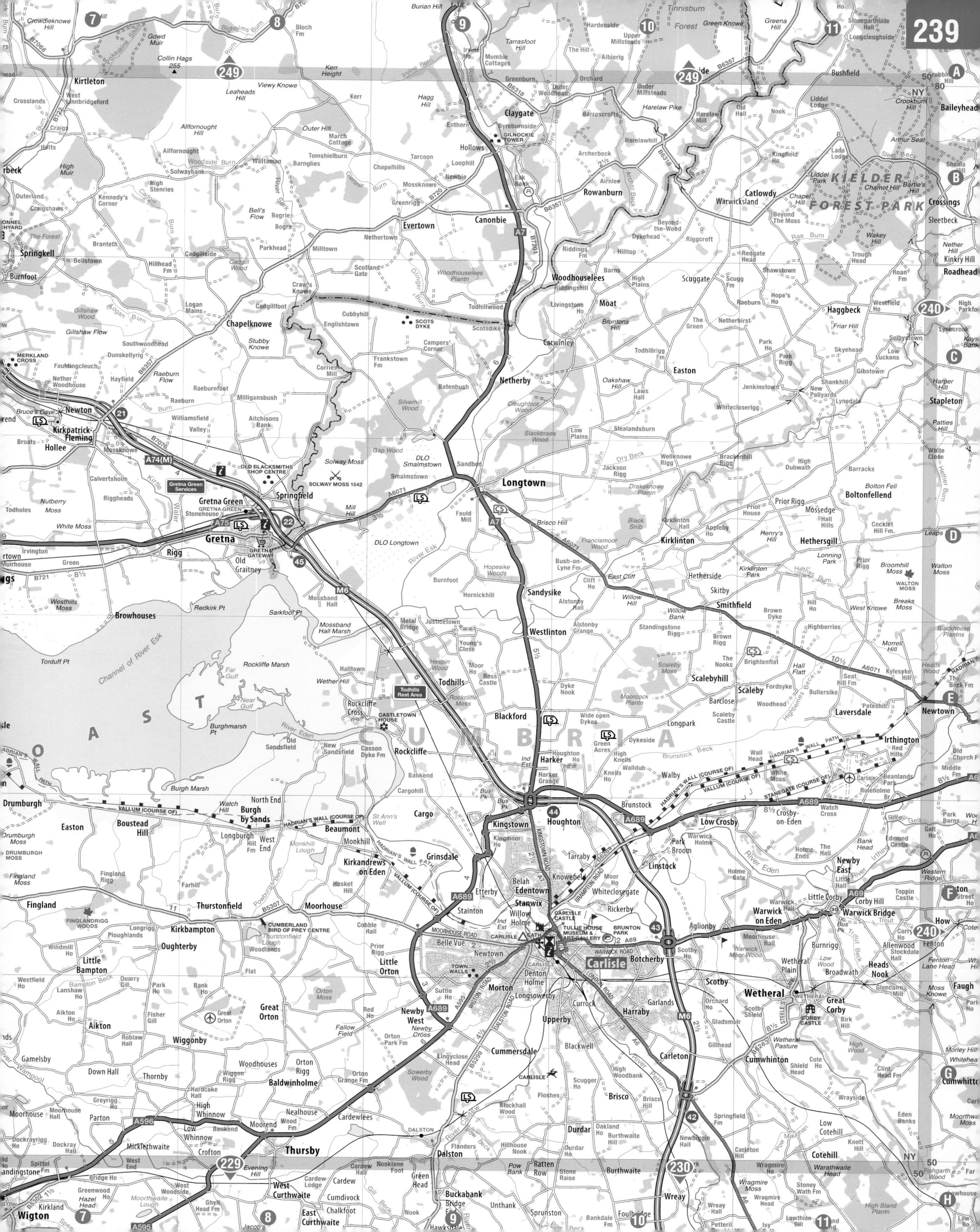

Crowdieknowe Hill
Kirtleton
Crosslands
West Linnbridgeford
Craigs
Hatts
High Muir
Allfornought
Solwaybank
Woodside Burn
Wattaman
Barnglies
Tomshielburn
Outer Hill
March Cottage
Kerr
Kerr Height
Hagg Hill
Leaheads Hill
Viewy Knowe
Collin Hags 255
Gowd Muir
Bigholms Burn
Bloch Fm
Burian Hill
Irvine Ho
Mumbie Cottages
Tarrasfoot Hill
Greenburn
Claygate
Byreburnside
GILNOCKIE TOWER
Enthorn
Hollows
Loophill
Newbie
Tarcoon
Chapelhills
Mossknowe
Greenrigg
Evertown
Canonbie
Eskbank
Rowanburn
Hardenside
Upper Millsteads
Albierig
The Hill
Orchard
Outer Woodhead
Under Millsteads
Barrascrofts
Harelaw Pike
Harelaw Mill
Harelawhill
Archerbeck
Airnlee
Tinnisburn Forest
Green Knowe
Greena Hill
Stonegarthside Hall
Longcleughside
Bushfield
Crookburn Hill
Baileyhead
Old Hall
Nook
Liddel Lodge
Arthur Seat
Kingfield Ho
Lads Lodge
Liddel Park
KIELDER FOREST PARK
Chamot Hill
Bartie's Hill
Sheala Hill
Crossings
Sleetbeck
Catlowdy
Warwicksland
Chapel Hill
Beyond The Moss
Beyond-the-Wood
Riggcroft
Dykehead
Rae Burn
Wakey Hill
Trough Head
Nether Hill
Kinkry Hill
Roadhead
Roan Fm
Westfield Ho
Haggbeck
Friar Hill
High Parkfoot
Lynecrook
Selbystown
Low Luckens
Skyehead
Gibbstown
Shankhill
New Pallyards
Lynedale
Jenkinstown
Harper Hill
Stapleton
Patties Hill
White Close
Springkell
Bellstown
Burnfoot
Branteth
The Forest
Cadgillside
Hillhead Fm
Cadgill Wood
Parkhead
Milltown
Nethertown
Scotland Gate
Woodhouselees Plantn
Bell's Flow
Bogrie
Bogra
Gillshaw Wood
Gillshaw Flow
Logan Mains
Cadgillfoot
Chapelknowe
Stubby Knowe
Southwoodhead
Dunskellyrig
MERKLAND CROSS
Fauldingcleugh
Nether Woodhouse
Hayfield
Raeburn Flow
Raeburnfoot
Raeburn
Milligansbush
Williamsfield
Valley
Aitchisons Bank
Bruce's Cave
Newton
Kirkpatrick-Fleming
Hollee
Broats
Mossknowe
Calvertsholm
Riggheads
Nutberry Moss
Todholes
White Moss
Gretna Green Services
OLD BLACKSMITHS SHOP CENTRE
Gretna Green
GRETNA GREEN
Stonehouse
Springfield
Gretna
GRETNA GATEWAY
Rigg
Irvington
Muirhouse
Green
Old Graitney
Westhills Moss
Browhouses
Redkirk Pt
Torduff Pt
Channel of River Esk
Craw's Knowe
Cubbyhill
Englishtown
SCOTS DYKE
Scotsdike
Todhillwood
Campers' Corner
Frankstown Fm
Corries Mill
Batenbush
Silverhill Wood
Solway Moss
SOLWAY MOSS 1542
Gap Wood
DLO Smalmstown
Smalmstown
Mill Hill
DLO Longtown
River Esk
Sandbed
Longtown
Fauld Mill
Netherby
Woodhouselees
Riddingshill
Riddings Fm
Hilltop
Barns
High Plains
Livingstone Ho
Moat
Bruntons Hill
Carwinley
Cleughfoot Wood
Slackbraes Wood
Low Plains
Stealandsburn
Oakshaw Hill
Laws Hall
Scuggate
Scugg Fm
Raeburn
Hope's Ho
The Green
Netherhirst
Tod hillrigg Fm
Easton
Park Ho
Park Rigg
Whiteclosrigg
Redgate Head
Shawstown
Dry Beck
Jackson Rigg
Wellknowe Rigg
Brackenhill Rigg
Drakeknowe Plantn
High Dubwath
Barracks
Bolton Fell
Boltonfellend
Prior Rigg
Mossedge
Prior House
Black Snib
Kirklinton Hall
Appleby Ho
Henry's Hill
Cocklet Hill Fm
Hethersgill
Kirklinton
Brisco Hill
Francismoor Wood
Lonning Park
Prior Rigg
Broomhill Moss
Leaps
Walton Moss
WALTON MOSS
Bush-on-Lyne Fm
East Cliff
Hetherside
Kirklinton Park
Skitby
Smithfield
Hill Ho
Brown Dyke
West Knowe
Breaks Moss
Hopesike Woods
Burnfoot
Hornickhill
Sandysike
Clift Ho
Alstonby Hall
Willow Hill
Willow Bank
Westlinton
Alstonby Grange
Standingstone Rigg
Highberries
Blackhouse Plantns
Morrell Hill
Mossband Hall
Sarkfoot Pt
Mossband Hall Marsh
Metal Bridge
Justicetown
Young's Close
Hespin Wood
Moor Ho
Ross Castle
Todhills
Todhills Rest Area
Rockcliffe Moss
Halltown
Wether Hill
Rockcliffe Marsh
Far Gulf
Near Gulf
Burghmarsh Pt
Rockcliffe Cross
CASTLETOWN HOUSE
Rockcliffe
Sandsfield
Old Sandsfield
New Sandsfield
Casson Dyke Fm
River Eden
Brown Rigg
The Nooks
Brightenflat
Hall Flatt
Scaleby Moss
Scalebyhill
Scaleby
Fordsyke
Bullersike
Seat Hill Fm
Kylesyke Hill
Heads Wood
The Beck Fm
Newtown
Laversdale
Pateshill
Woodhead
Barclose
Scaleby Castle
Longpark
Dyke Nook
Moorcock Plantn
Blackford
Wide open Dykes
Green Acres
Dykeside
Harker
Houghton Ho
Ind Est
Harker Grange
High Knells
Walldub
Knells Ho
Walby
Brunstock Beck
Wall Head
White Moss
Irthington
Red Hills
Old Church Fm
Middle Fm
Beanlands Park
Ruleholme
HADRIAN'S WALL PATH
HADRIAN'S WALL (COURSE OF)
VALLUM (COURSE OF)
STANEGATE (COURSE OF)
CUMBRIA
Bankend
Cargohill
Cargo
Bus Pk
Kingstown
Houghton
Brunstock
Low Crosby
Crosby-on-Eden
Watch Cross
Park Barns
Gelt Ho
Edmond Castle
Bank Head
Warwick Holme
Park Broom
Holme Ends
The Hall
Newby East
Little Corby
Toppin Castle
Corby Hill
Warwick Bridge
Warwick on Eden
Western Ridge
Burgh Marsh
Drumburgh
Easton
Drumburgh Moss
DRUMBURGH MOSS
Boustead Hill
Watch Hill
North End
Burgh by Sands
Longburgh
West End
Hill Fm
Beaumont
St Ann's Well
Monkhill
Monkhill Lough
Kirkandrews on Eden
Grinsdale
Fingland Moss
Fingland Rigg
Farhill
Hosket Hill
Fingland
Thurstonfield
Moorhouse
FINGLANDRIGG WOODS
Longrigg
Ploughlands
Kirkbampton
CUMBERLAND BIRD OF PREY CENTRE
Thurstonfield Lough
Woodlands
Cobble Hall
Prior Rigg
Windmill Ho
Oughterby
Little Bampton
Little Orton
Etterby
Stainton
Kingmoor Ind Est
Belah
Edentown
Stanwix
Willow Holme
Ind Est
CARLISLE CASTLE
TULLIE HOUSE MUSEUM & ART GALLERY
BRUNTON PARK
Tarraby
Knowefield
Moor Ho
Whiteclosegate
Rickerby
Linstock
Aglionby
Belle Vue
Newtown
CARLISLE
Carlisle
Botcherby
Scotby Ho
TOWN WALLS
Denton Holme
Moorhouse Hall
Warwick Moor Wood
Burnrigg
Wetheral Plain
Low Wood
Broadwath
Allenwood
Stockdale Hall
Heads Nook
Fenton
Fenton Lane Head
Glencairn Mill
Moss Knowe
Faugh
Westfield Ho
Bampton Beck
Lanshaw Ho
Quarry Gill
Park Ho
Flat
Bank Ho
Orton Moss
Suttle Ho
Morton
Longsowerby
Currock
Harraby
Garlands
Scotby
Orchard Ho
Scotby Shield
Wetheral
WETHERAL
Great Corby
CORBY CASTLE
Birk Hill
Aikton Ho
Aikton
Fisher Gill
Roblaw Hall
Great Orton
Red Ho
Fallow Field
Newby West
Newby Cross
Orton Park Fm
Upperby
Gladsmuir
Gillhead
Wetheral Pasture
High Wood
Wiggonby
Cummersdale
Blackwell
Carleton
Cumwhinton
Shield Head
Cote Ho
Clint Head Fm
Morley Hill
Gamelsby
Down Hall
Thornby
Woodhouses
Wiggon Rigg
Orton Rigg
Baldwinholme
Orton Grange Fm
Lingyclose Head
Sowerby Wood
High Woodbank
Scugger Ho
Brisco
Brisco Hill
Wrayside
Hardcake Hall
Greyrigg Ho
Moorhouse
Moorhouse Hall
Parton
High Whinnow
Nealhouse
Cardewlees
Flashes
Blackhall Wood
Springfield Ho
Eden Banks
Moorthwaite Moss
Dockrayrigg Ho
Dockray Hall
Mickle thwaite
Low Whinnow
Bankend
Crofton
Moorend
Wood Fm
Thursby
DALSTON
Dalston
Flanders
Hillhouse Nook
Durdar
Oakland Ho
Burthwaite Hill
Newbiggin Hall
Low Cotehill
Knott Hill
Carleton Ho
Cotehill
Spittal Fm
Waddingstone
Bridge Ho
West End Fm
Evening Hill
Cardew Hall
Nooklane Foot
Green Head
Pow Bank
Ratten Row
Stone Raise
Burthwaite
Wragmire Ho
Wragmire Moss
Warathwaite Head
Stoney Wath Fm
Wragmire Head
Fenton Lane Head
Greenwood Ho
Hazel Head
Moorthwaite Lough
West Woodside
Ghyll Head Fm
West Curthwaite
Cardew Lodge
Cardew
Cumdivock
Chalkfoot
East Curthwaite
Buckabank
Bridge End
Unthank
Sprunston
Bankdale Fm
Foulbridge
Wreay
Wreay Hall
High Stand Plantn
Wigton
Kirkland
Petteril
Lowthian Gill
Nook
Jacob's
Hawksdale
Hallsteads
RIVER CALDEW
River Petteril
A74(M)
A75
A7
A6071
A689
A69
A595
A596
A6
M6
B7068
B6357
B6318
B720
B7076
B721
B5307
B5299
B6263
B6413
KINGSTOWN ROAD
MOORHOUSE ROAD
WARWICK ROAD
LONDON ROAD
WIGTON ROAD
DALSTON ROAD
BRAMPTON ROAD
249
240
229
230
NY
50
80

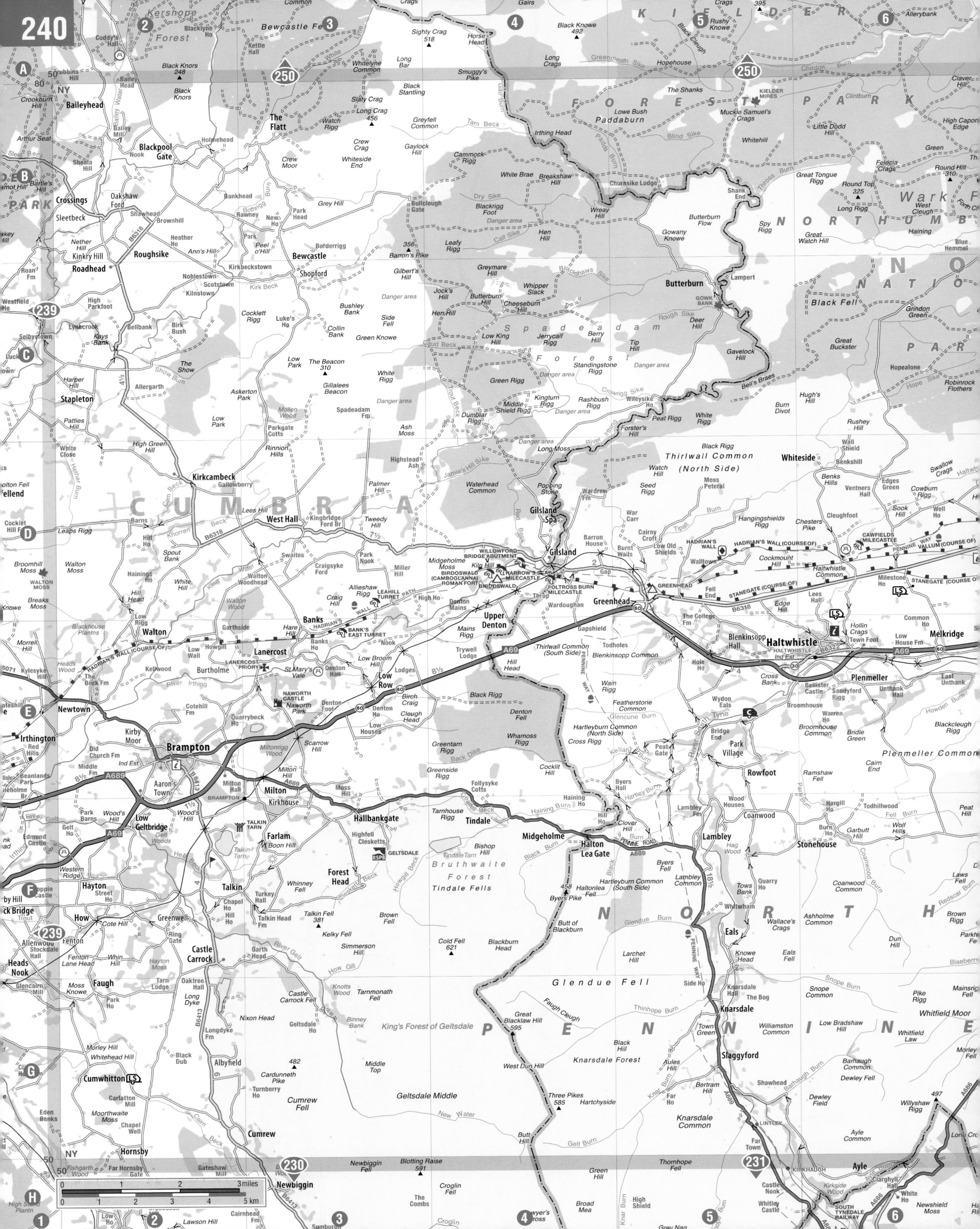
Kershope Forest
Bewcastle Fell
Kielder Forest Park
Sighty Crag 518
Black Knowe 492
Horse Head
Long Crags
Hopehouse
Allerybank
Black Knors 248
Whitelyne Common
Smuggy's Pike
Baileyhead
Black Stantling
Kielder Mires
Lowe Bush Paddaburn
Muckle Samuel's Crags
The Flatt
Slaty Crag
Long Crag 456
Greyfell Common
Blackpool Gate
Irthing Head
Whitehill
Crew Moor
Whiteside End
Gaylock Hill
Cammock Rigg
White Brae
Breakshaw Rill
Churnsike Lodge
Great Tongue Rigg
Round Top 325
Round Hill 310
Crossings
Oakshaw Ford
Bankhead
Grey Hill
Bullcleugh Gate
Blackrigg Foot
Shank End
Wreay Hill
Butterburn Flow
Spy Rigg
Long Rigg
Northumberland National Park
Roughsike
Kinkry Hill
Roadhead
Bewcastle
Borderrigg
Shopford
Barron's Pike
Leafy Rigg
Hen Hill
Gowany Knowe
Great Watch Hill
Gilbert's Hill
Greymare Hill
Butterburn
Lampert
Gowk Bank
Whipper Slack
Black Fell
Cocklett Rigg
Luke's Ho
Bushley Bank
Jock's Hill
Butterburn Hill
Cheeseburn Hill
Side Fell
Grindon Green
Collin Bank
Green Knowe
Low King Hill
Jerrycalf Rigg
Berry Hill
Deer Hill
Spadeadam Forest
Tip Hill
Great Buckster
Gavelock Hill
Stapleton
The Show
Low Park
The Beacon 310
Gillalees Beacon
White Rigg
Green Rigg
Standingstone Rigg
Hopealone
Robinrock Flothers
Allergarth
Askerton Park
Spadeadam Fm
Middle Shield Rigg
Kingturn Rigg
Rashbush Rigg
Wileysike
Hugh's Hill
Bell's Braes
Patties Hill
Parkgate Cotts
Ash Moss
Dumblar Rigg
Peat Rigg
White Rigg
Burn Divot
High Green Hill
Rinnion Hills
Forster's Hill
Black Rigg
Thirlwall Common (North Side)
Whiteside
Long Moss
Highstead Ash
Watch Hill
Seed Rigg
Moss Peteral
Benkshill
Swallow Crags
Kirkcambeck
Palmer Hill
Waterhead Common
Popping Stone
Wardrew Fm
Benks Hills
Ventners Hall
Edges Green
Cowburn Rigg
CUMBRIA
West Hall
Kingbridge Ford Br
Tweedy Hill
Gilsland Spa
War Carr
Hangingshields Rigg
Chesters Pike
Cleughfoot
Sook Hill
Well Ho
Leaps Rigg
B6318
Cairny Croft
Gilsland
Barron House
Burnt Walls
Low Old Shields
Hadrian's Wall
Cawfields Milecastle
Pennine Way
Vallum (course of)
Walton Moss
Spout Bank
Swaites
Craigsyke Ford
Park Nook
Miller Hill
Midgeholme Moss
Willowford Bridge Abutment
Harrow's Scar Milecastle
Birdoswald
Gap
Greenhead
Walltown
Cockmount Hill
Haltwhistle Common
Milestone Ho
Stanegate (course of)
Walton Woodhead
Allieshaw Rigg
Leahill Turret
Poltross Burn Milecastle
Thirlwall Castle
Fell End
Lees Hall
Craig Hill
High Ho
Denton Mains
Upper Denton
Throp
Wardoughan
Edge Hill
Common Ho
Walton
Banks
Banks East Turret
Hare Hill
Mains Rigg
Gapshield
The College Fm
Blenkinsopp Hall
Haltwhistle
Hollin Crags
Town Foot
Melkridge
Low House Fm
Lanercost
Lanercost Priory
Howgill
Low Wall
Banks Ho
Nook
Trywell Lodge
Thirlwall Common (South Side)
Todholes
Blenkinsopp Common
A69
Burtholme
St Mary's Vale
Denton Hall
Low Broom Hill
Lodges
Hill Head
Hole Ho
Plenmeller
East Unthank
Kylesyke Hill
The Beck Fm
Low Row
Naworth Castle
Naworth Park
Birch Craig
Black Rigg
Wain Rigg
Cross Bank
Bellister Castle
Sandyford Rigg
Unthank Hall
Newtown
Cotehill Fm
Quarrybeck Ho
Denton Foot
Denton Ho
Cleugh Head
Denton Fell
Featherstone Common
Wydon Eals
Broomhouse
Irthington
Kirby Moor
Brampton
Scarrow Hill
Low Houses
Whamoss Rigg
Hartleyburn Common (North Side)
Cross Rigg
Bridge End
Park Village
Broomhouse Common
Bridle Green
Blackcleugh Rigg
Greentarn Rigg
Peat Gate
Plenmeller Common
Aaron's Town
Milton
Milton Hill
Greenside Rigg
Follysyke Cotts
Cocklit Hill
Byers Hall
Rowfoot
Ramshaw Fell
Cairn End
Kirkhouse
Moss Ho
Hallbankgate
Tarnhouse Rigg
Tindale
Haining Ho
Lambley Fm
Wood Houses
Coanwood
Hargill Ho
Todhillwood
Peat Hill
Low Geltbridge
Talkin Tarn
Farlam
Midgeholme
Halton Lea Gate
Clover Hill
Lambley
Burn Ho
Garbutt Hill
Wolf Hills
Stonehouse
Highfell
Clesketts
Geltsdale
Bishop Hill
Tindale Tarn
Bruthwaite Forest
Tindale Fells
Hayton
Forest Head
Whinney Fell
Turkey Hall
Byers Fell
Lambley Common
Quarry Ho
Coanwood Common
Laws Fell
How
Cote Hill
Talkin
Greenwell
Talkin Head Fm
Talkin Fell 381
Brown Fell
Byers Pike
Haltonlea Fell
Hartleyburn Common (South Side)
Whitwham
Ashholme Common
Brown Rigg
Fenton
Kelky Fell
Cold Fell 621
Blackburn Head
Butt of Blackburn
Eals
Wallace's Crags
Dun Hill
Heads Nook
Castle Carrock
Garth Head
Simmerson Hill
Larchet Hill
Knowe Head
Eals Fell
Faugh
Tarn Lodge
Oaktree Hall
Glendue Fell
Side Ho
Snope Common
Pike Rigg
Tarnmonath Fell
Castle Carrock Fell
Knarsdale Hall
The Bog
Knarsdale
Long Dyke
Nixon Head
Binney Bank
King's Forest of Geltsdale
Great Blacklaw Hill 595
PENNINES
Town Green
Williamston Common
Low Bradshaw Hill
Whitfield Moor
Whitfield Law
Longdyke Fm
Black Hill
Knarsdale Forest
Slaggyford
Black Dub
Albyfield
Cardunneth Pike 482
Middle Top
West Dun Hill
Aules Hill
Barhaugh Common
Dewley Fell
Cumwhitton
Turnberry Ho
Bertram Hill
Shawhead
Dewley Field
Willyshaw Rigg
Cumrew Fell
Geltsdale Middle
Three Pikes 585
Hartchyside
Far Ho
Knarsdale Common
Cumrew
Butt Hill
Lintley
Ayle Common
Hornsby
Far Town
Newbiggin Fell
Blotting Raise 591
Croglin Fell
Green Hill
Thornhope Fell
Ayle
Clarghyll Hall
Newbiggin
Castle Nook
Kirkhaugh
White Ho
Newshield Moss
The Combs
Broad Mea
High Shield
Whitley Castle
South Tynedale Railway
Lawson Hill
3 miles
5 km

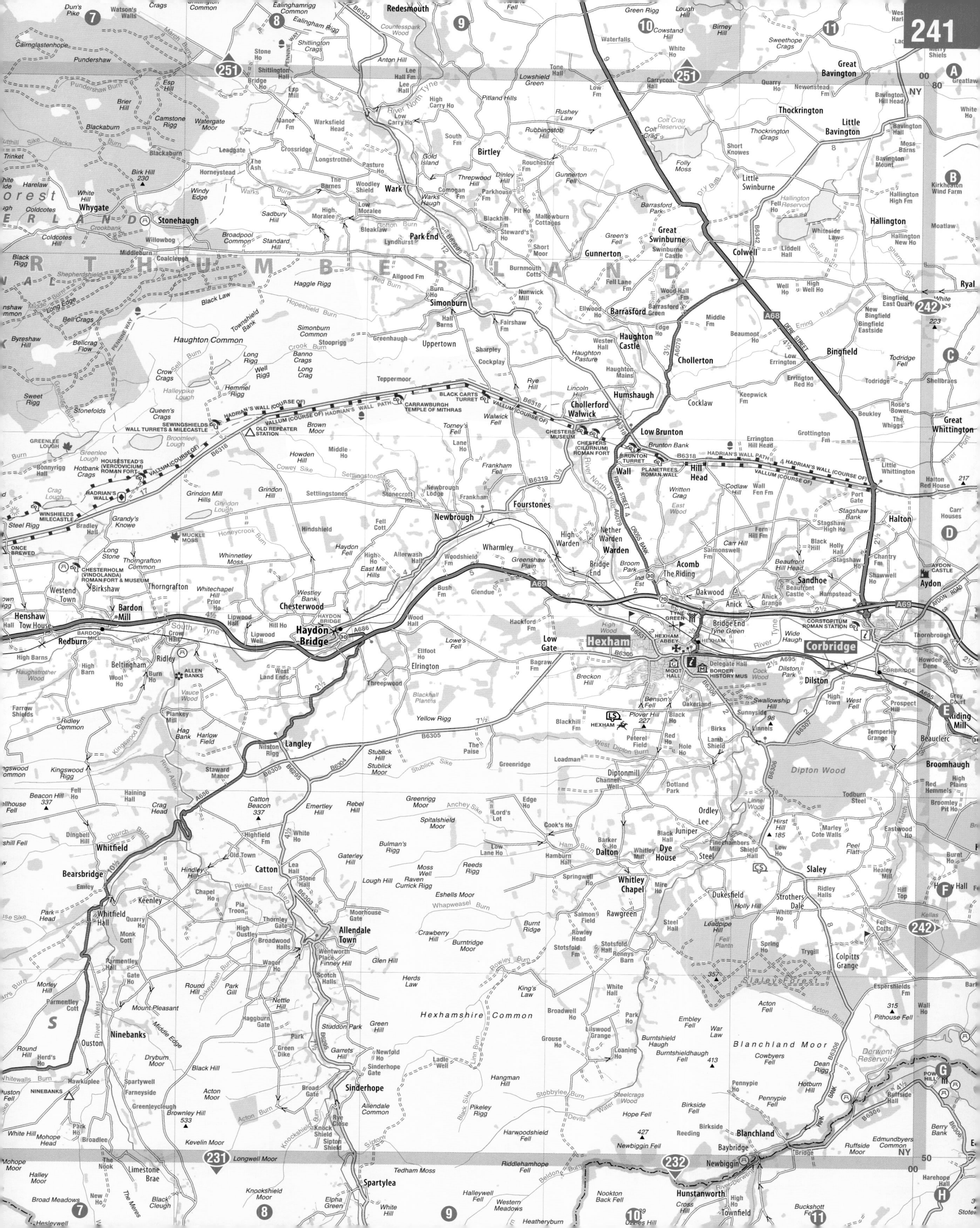

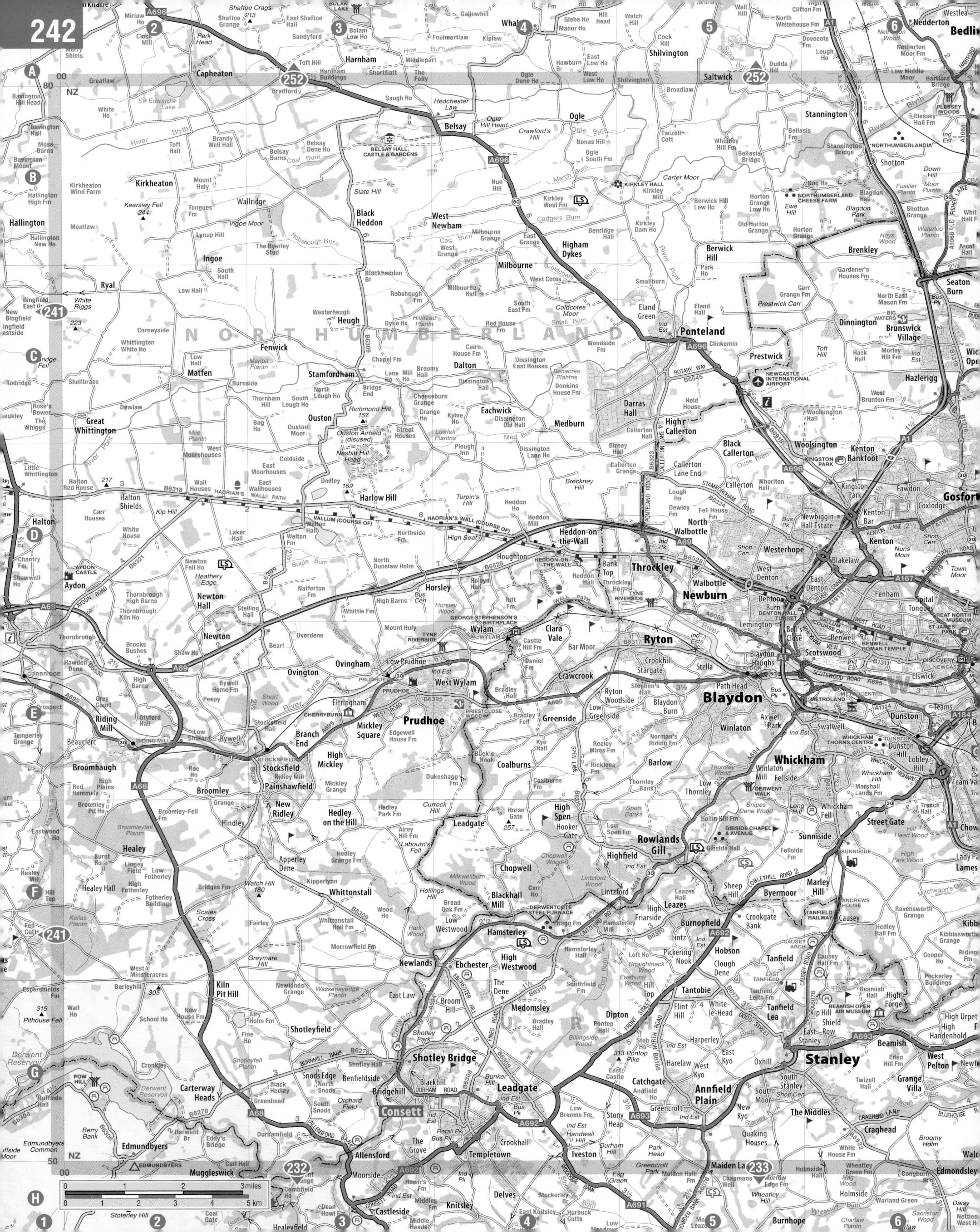
NORTHUMBERLAND
DURHAM
Belsay
Ponteland
Stamfordham
Heddon-on-the-Wall
Throckley
Newburn
Ryton
Blaydon
Prudhoe
Wylam
Whickham
Stanley
Consett
Shotley Bridge
Leadgate
Annfield Plain
Rowlands Gill
Kingston Park
Dinnington
Stannington
Ovingham
Riding Mill
Stocksfield
Ebchester
Tantobie
Dunston
Gosforth
Edmundbyers
Muggleswick
Newcastle International Airport
Belsay Hall, Castle & Gardens
Northumberlandia
Kirkley Hall
Beamish Open Air Museum
Gibside Chapel & Avenue
Derwentcote Steel Furnace
Tanfield Railway
Hadrian's Wall (course of)
Derwent Reservoir
River Tyne
A696
A69
A68
A692
A693
A694
A695
A1
0 1 2 3 miles
0 1 2 3 4 5 km

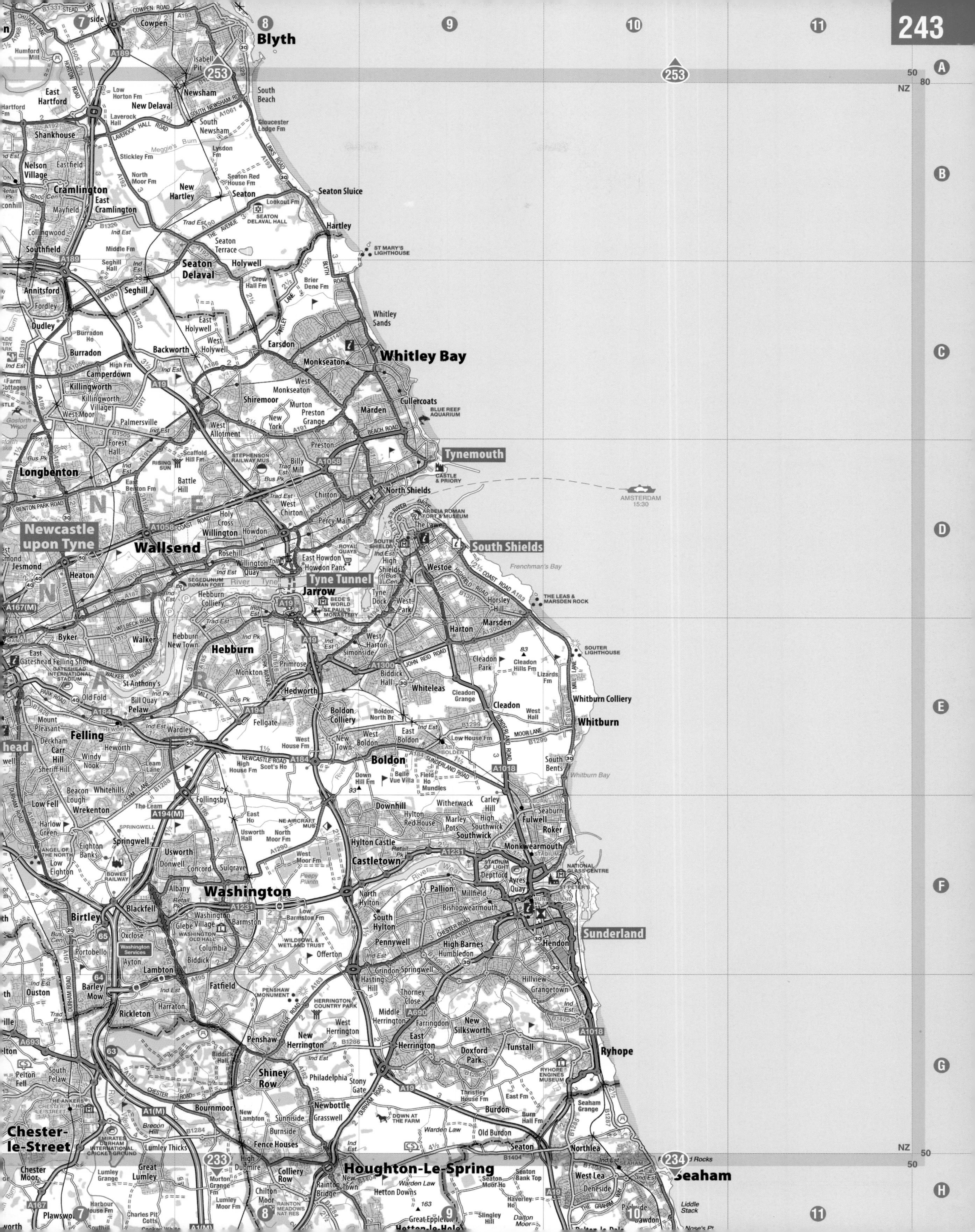
Blyth
Cowpen
Newsham
South Beach
New Delaval
South Newsham
Cramlington
East Cramlington
Seaton Sluice
Hartley
Seaton Delaval
Holywell
Seghill
Annitsford
Whitley Bay
Monkseaton
Earsdon
Backworth
Killingworth
Shiremoor
Cullercoats
Tynemouth
North Shields
Longbenton
Wallsend
Newcastle upon Tyne
South Shields
Tyne Tunnel
Jarrow
Hebburn
Felling
Boldon
Whitburn
Cleadon
Washington
Castletown
Sunderland
Hendon
Roker
Ryhope
Birtley
Chester-le-Street
Shiney Row
Houghton-Le-Spring
Seaham
AMSTERDAM 15:30

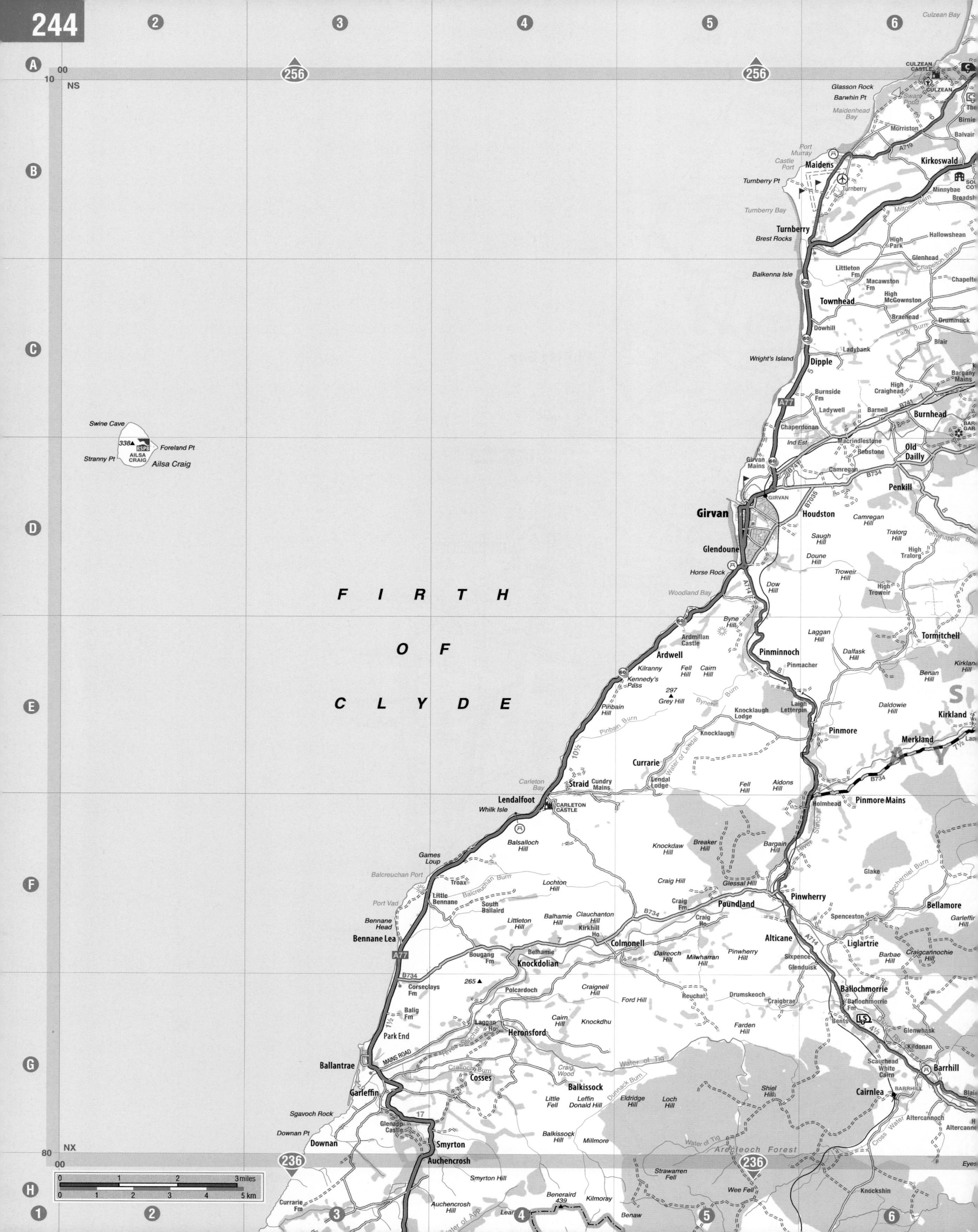
FIRTH OF CLYDE
Ailsa Craig
Swine Cave
Foreland Pt
Stranny Pt
Culzean Bay
Culzean Castle
Glasson Rock
Barwhin Pt
Maidenhead Bay
Morriston
Kirkoswald
Maidens
Port Murray
Castle Port
Turnberry Pt
Turnberry Bay
Turnberry
Brest Rocks
Balkenna Isle
Townhead
Dowhill
Wright's Island
Dipple
Ladybank
Burnside Fm
Ladywell
Barneil
Burnhead
Chaperdonan
Ind Est
Macrindlestone
Robstone
Old Dailly
Girvan Mains
Camregan
Penkill
Girvan
Houdston
Camregan Hill
Glendoune
Horse Rock
Saugh Hill
Doune Hill
Tralorg Hill
High Tralorg
Woodland Bay
Dow Hill
Troweir Hill
High Troweir
Byne Hill
Ardmillan Castle
Ardwell
Pinminnoch
Laggan Hill
Dalfask Hill
Tormitchell
Kilranny
Kennedy's Pass
Fell Hill
Cairn Hill
Pinmacher
Grey Hill
Pinbain Hill
Knocklaugh Lodge
Laigh Letterpin
Benan Hill
Daldowie Hill
Kirkland
Knocklaugh
Pinmore
Merkland
Currarie
Carleton Bay
Straid
Cundry Mains
Lendal Lodge
Fell Hill
Aldons Hill
Lendalfoot
Whilk Isle
Carleton Castle
Holmhead
Pinmore Mains
Balsalloch Hill
Knockdaw Hill
Breaker Hill
Bargain Hill
Games Loup
Balcreuchan Port
Troax
Little Bennane
Lochton Hill
Craig Hill
Glessal Hill
Glake
Port Vad
South Ballaird
Craig Fm
Poundland
Pinwherry
Bellamore
Bennane Head
Bennane Lea
Littleton Hill
Balhamie Hill
Clauchanton Hill
Kirkhill Ho
Craig Ho
Spenceston
Altican e
Liglartrie
Colmonell
Bougang Fm
Bellamie
Knockdolian
Dalreoch Hill
Milwharran Hill
Pinwherry Hill
Sixpence
Glenduisk
Barbae Hill
Craigcannochie Hill
Corseclays Fm
265
Polcardoch
Craigneil Hill
Ford Hill
Reuchal
Drumskeoch
Craigbrae
Ballochmorrie
Balig Fm
Cairn Hill
Knockdhu
Bents
Laggan Ho
Heronsford
Farden Hill
Park End
Glenwhask
Kildonan
Ballantrae
Mains Road
Water of Tig
Craig Wood
Cosses
Scaurhead
White Cairn
Barrhill
Garleffin
Balkissock
Little Fell
Leffin Donald Hill
Eldridge Hill
Loch Hill
Shiel Hill
Cairnlea
Sgavoch Rock
Glenapp Castle
Downan Pt
Downan
Balkissock Hill
Millmore
Altercannoch
Smyrton
Auchencrosh
Arecleoch Forest
Smyrton Hill
Strawarren Fell
Wee Fell
Knockshin
Currarie Fm
Auchencrosh Hill
Benerairy 439
Kilmoray
Benaw
A77
A714
B734
B741
B7035
A719
256
236
NS
3 miles
5 km

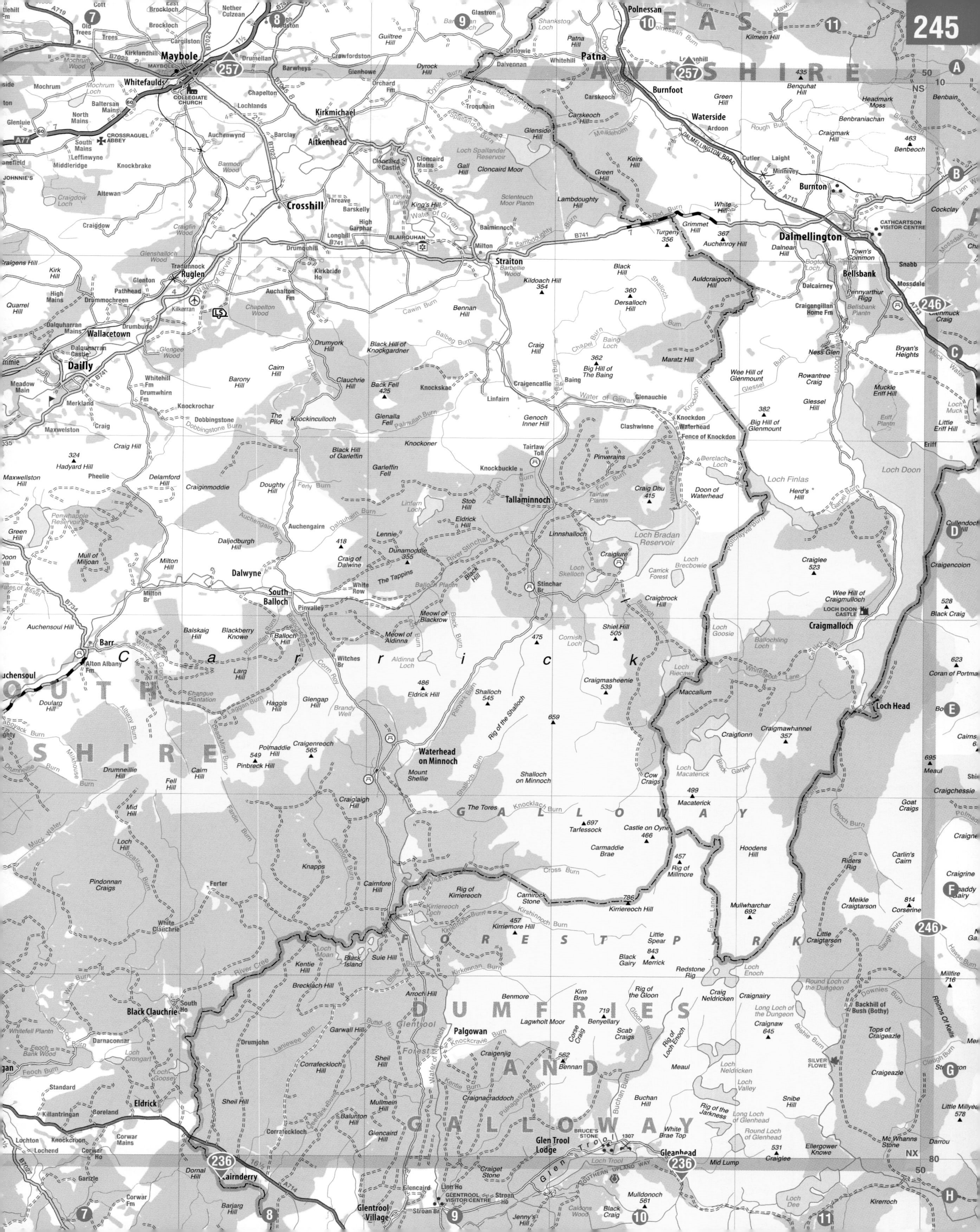
EAST AYRSHIRE
SOUTH AYRSHIRE
Carrick
GALLOWAY FOREST PARK
DUMFRIES AND GALLOWAY
Maybole
Whitefaulds
Collegiate Church
Crossraguel Abbey
Kirkmichael
Aitkenhead
Crosshill
Blairquhan
Straiton
Ruglen
Kilkerran
Wallacetown
Dailly
Barr
Patna
Polnessan
Burnfoot
Waterside
Dalmellington Road
Burnton
Dalmellington
Cathcartson Visitor Centre
Bellsbank
Loch Doon
Loch Doon Castle
Craigmalloch
Loch Head
Loch Bradan Reservoir
Loch Finlas
Tallaminnoch
Stinchar Br
South Balloch
Pinvalley
Waterhead on Minnoch
Mount Shellie
Shalloch on Minnoch
Tarfessock
Kirriereoch Hill
Merrick
Benyellary
Black Clauchrie
Eldrick
Palgowan
Glentrool
Glen Trool Lodge
Bruce's Stone
Loch Trool
Glenhead
Southern Upland Way
Glentrool Visitor Centre
Glentrool Village
Cairnderry
Mulldonoch
Silver Flowe
Backhill of Bush (Bothy)
Rhinns Of Kells
Corserine
Meaul
Coran of Portmark
Black Craig
Craigencolon
Mullwharchar
Craignaw
Loch Enoch
Loch Neldricken
Loch Valley
Round Loch of Glenhead
Long Loch of Glenhead
Craiglee
Water of Girvan
River Stinchar
River Cree
Water of Minnoch
A77
A713
A714
B741
B734
B7023
B7024
B7045
B7027
257
246
236
7
8
9
10
11
A
B
C
D
E
F
G
H
NS
NX
50
10
80

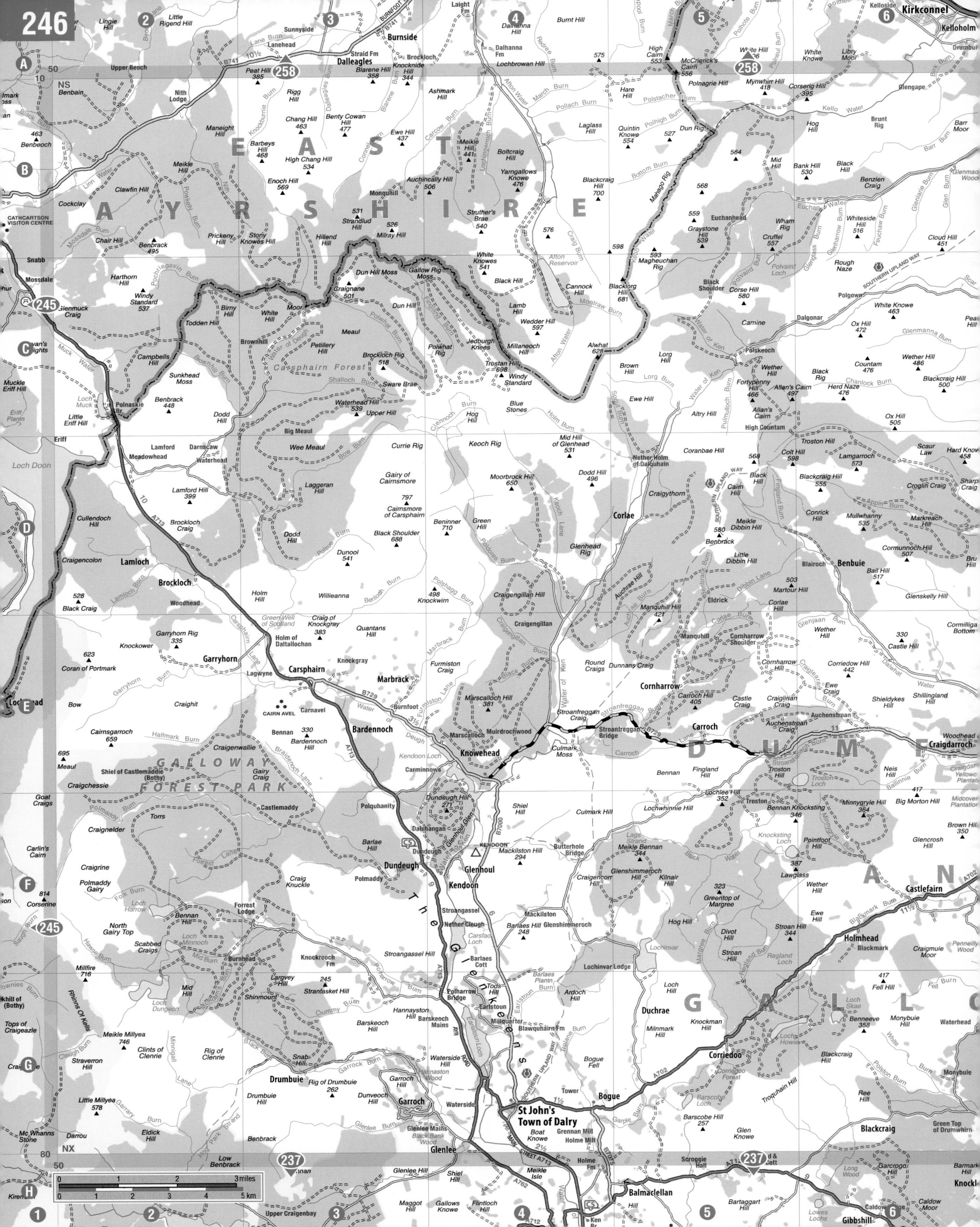

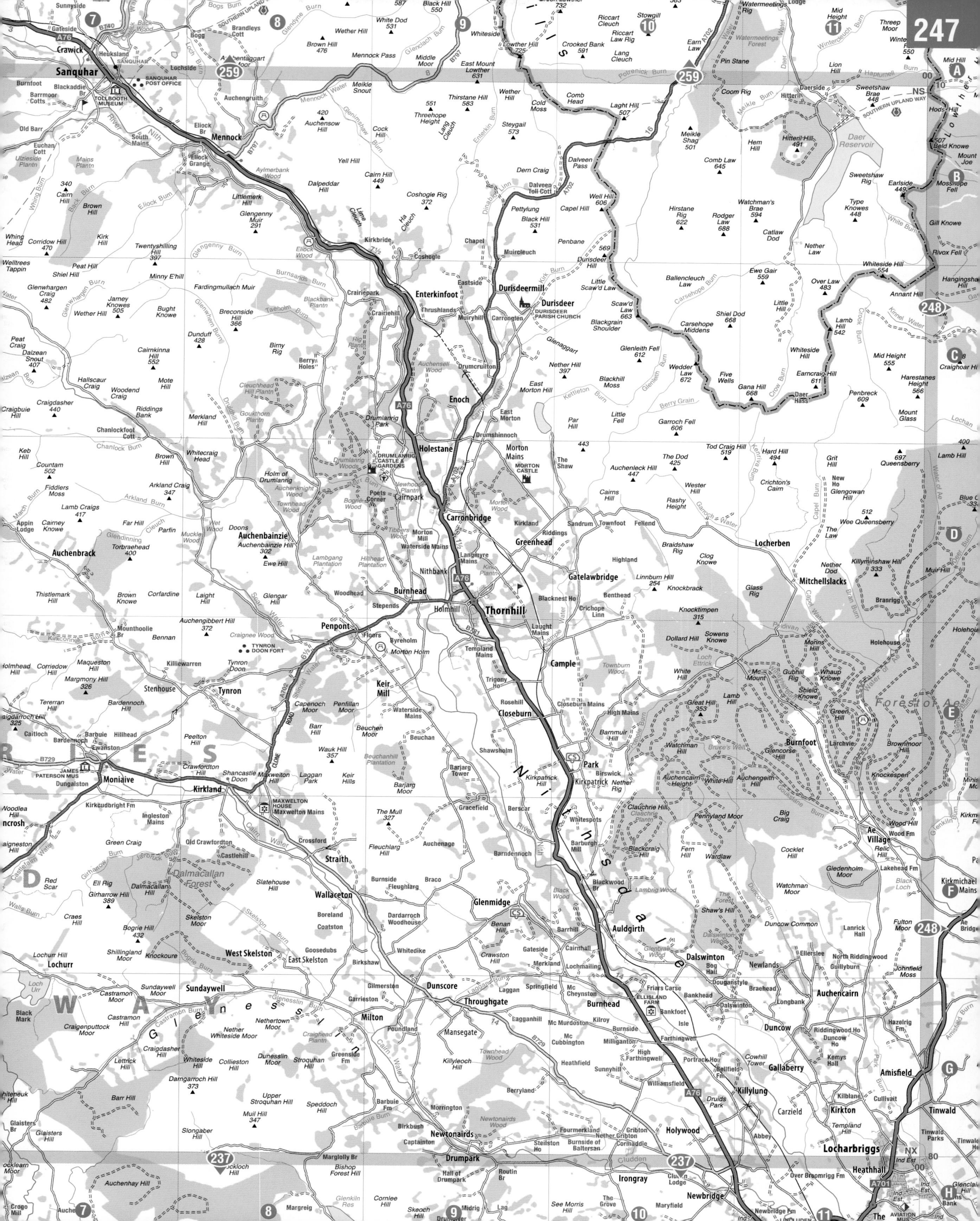
Sunnyside
Gateside
Crawick
Sanquhar
Heuksland
SANQUHAR POST OFFICE
TOLLBOOTH MUSEUM
Burnfoot
Blackaddie
Barrmoor Cotts
Lochside
Auchengruith
Mennock
Elliock Br
Old Barr
South Mains
Euchan Cott
Ulzieside Plantn
Mains Plantn
Elliock Grange
Aylmerbank Wood
Brandleys Cott
Bogg
Wether Hill
Brown Hill 476
Mennock Pass
Middle Moor
White Dod 531
Whiteside
East Mount Lowther 631
Meikle Snout
Thirstane Hill 583
Threehope Height
Lang Cleuch
Auchensow Hill
Cock Hill
Yell Hill
Steygail 573
Wether Hill
Cold Moss
Comb Head
Laght Hill 507
Lowther Hill 725
Crooked Bank 591
Riccart Cleuch
Riccart Law Rig
Lang Cleuch
Stowgill
Watermeetings Rig
Watermeetings Forest
Earn Law
Pin Stane
Mid Height
Threep Moor
Lion Hill
Mid Hill
Coom Rig
Daerside
Hitterill
Sweetshaw Brae 448
SOUTHERN UPLAND WAY
Hods Hill
Beld Knowe
Mount Joe
Daer Reservoir
Meikle Shag 501
Hem Hill
Hitterill Hill 491
Comb Law 645
Sweetshaw Rig
Earlside 449
Mosshope Fell
Dalveen Pass
Dern Craig
Dalveen Toll Cott
Well Hill 606
Capel Hill
Pettylung
Black Hill 531
Penbane
Hirstane Rig 622
Rodger Law 688
Watchman's Brae 594
Catlaw Dod
Type Knowes 448
Gill Knowe
Rivox Fell
Nether Law
Dalpeddar Hill
Cairn Hill 449
Coshogle Rig 372
Lime Cleuch
Ha Cleuch
Kirkbride
Coshogle
Chapel
Muircleuch
Durisdeer Hill
Little Scaw'd Law
Ballencleuch Law
Ewe Gair 559
Over Law 483
Whiteside Hill 554
Hangingshaw Hill
Annant Hill
Cairn Hill
Brown Hill
Littlemerk Hill
Glengenny Muir 291
Whing Head
Corridow Hill 470
Kirk Hill
Twentyshilling Hill 397
Elliock Wood
Welltrees Tappin
Peat Hill
Shiel Hill
Minny E'hill
Glenwhargen Craig 482
Fardingmullach Muir
Crairiepark
Enterkinfoot
Eastside
Durisdeermill
Durisdeer
DURISDEER PARISH CHURCH
Scaw'd Law 663
Shiel Dod 668
Little Hill
Lamb Hill 542
Jarney Knowes 505
Wether Hill
Bught Knowe
Breconside Hill 366
Crairiehill
Thrushlands
Muiryhill
Carronglen
Blackgrain Shoulder
Carsehope Middens
Whiteside Hill
Glenaggart
Glenleith Fell 612
Mid Height 555
Peat Craig
Dalzean Snout 407
Cairnkinna Hill 552
Dunduff 428
Birny Rig
Berry Holes
Rig Plantn
Auchensell Wood
Drumcruilton
Nether Hill 397
Blackhill Moss
Wedder Law 672
Five Wells
Earncraig Hill 611
Harestanes Height 566
Hallscaur Craig
Woodend Craig
Mote Hill
Cleuchhead Hill Plantn
East Morton Hill
Gana Hill 668
Daer Hass
Penbreck 609
Enoch
East Morton
Craigbuie Hill
Craigdasher Hill 440
Riddings Bank
Merkland Hill
Goukthorn Plantn
Drumlanrig Park
Par Hill
Little Fell
Garroch Fell 606
Mount Glass
Chanlockfoot Cott
Holestane
Drumshinnoch
Keb Hill
Countam 502
Brown Hill
Whitecraig Head
DRUMLANRIG CASTLE & GARDENS
Drumlanrig Woods
Morton Mains
MORTON CASTLE
The Shaw
Tod Craig Hill 519
The Dod 425
Auchenleck Hill 447
Hard Hill 494
Grit Hill
Queensberry 697
Lamb Hill
Fiddlers Moss
Arkland Craig 347
Holm of Drumlanrig
Auchenknight Wood
Poets Corner
Cairnpark
Newhouse Plantn
Crichton's Cairn
New Ho
Glengowan Hill
Lamb Craigs 417
Townhead Wood
Bogrie Wood
Morton Wood
Cairns Hill
Wester Hill
Rashy Height
512
Wee Queensberry
Appin Lodge
Cairney Knowe
Far Hill
Parfin
Wet Wood
Doons
Carronbridge
Kirkland
Sandrum
Townfoot
Fellend
Riddings
The Law
Auchenbrack
Glendinning
Torbraehead 400
Muckle Wood
Auchenbainzie
Auchenbainzie Hill 302
Ewe Hill
Tibbers Wood
Morton Mill
Waterside Mains
Lambgang Plantation
Hillhead Plantation
Langmyre Mains
Greenhead
Braidshaw Rig
Clog Knowe
Locherben
Nether Dod
Killyminshaw Hill 333
Mitchellslacks
Highland
Gatelawbridge
Linnburn Hill 254
Knockbrack
Glass Rig
Thistlemark Hill
Brown Knowe
Corfardine
Laight Hill
Glengar Hill
Woodhead
Burnhead
Nithbank
Kirk Plantn
Stepends
Holmhill
Thornhill
Blacknest Ho
Benthead
Crichope Linn
Knocktimpen 315
Branrigg
Muir Hill
Mounthoolie Br
Auchengibbert Hill 372
Bennan
Craignee Wood
Penpont
Floors
Byreholm
Morton Holm
Laught Mains
Dollard Hill
Sowens Knowe
Holehouse
TYNRON DOON FORT
Templand Mains
Cample
Townburn Wood
Loch Ettrick
White Hill
Mc Mount
Gubhill Rig
Morins Hill
Whaup Knowe
Holmhead
Corriedow Hill
Maqueston Hill
Killiewarren
Tynron Doon
Margmony Hill 326
Stenhouse
Tynron
Keir Mill
Trigony Ho
Rosehill
Closeburn Mains
High Mains
Lamb Hill
Great Hill 353
Shield Knowe
Green Hill
Forest of Ae
Tererran Hill
Bardennoch Hill
Capenoch Moor
Penfillan Moor
Waterside Mains
Closeburn
Barnmuir Hill
Burnfoot
Larchvie
Brownmoor Hill
Caitloch
Barbuie
Hillhead
Bardennoch
Ewanston
Barr Hill
Beuchen Moor
Beuchan
Peelton Hill
Wauk Hill 357
Shawsholm
Watchman Hill
Bruce's Well
Glencorse Hill
JAMES PATERSON MUS
Dungalston
Moniaive
Crawfordton Hill
Kirkland
Shancastle Doon
Maxwelton Hill
Laggan Park
Keir Hills
Beuchanhill Plantation
Barjarg Tower
Barjarg Moor
Park
Birswick
Kirkpatrick
Kirkpatrick Hill
Nether Rig
Auchencairn Height
White Hill
Auchengeith Hill
Knockespen
Kirkcudbright Fm
MAXWELTON HOUSE
Maxwelton Mains
Ingleston Mains
Woodlea Hill
The Mull 327
Gracefield
Berscar
Clauchrie Hill
Clauchrie Plantn
Pennyland Moor
Big Craig
Ae Village
Wood Hill
Wood Fm
Relic Hill
Lakehead Fm
Green Craig
Old Crawfordton
Castlehill
Crossford
Auchenage
Fleuchlarg Hill
Barndennoch
Barburgh Mill
Blackcraig Hill
Whitespots
Wardlaw
Fern Hill
Cocklet Hill
Dalmacallan Forest
Dalmacallan Hill
Straith
Red Scar
Ell Rig
Girharrow Hill 389
Slatehouse Hill
Wallaceton
Burnside
Fleughlarg
Braco
Glenmidge
Black Wood
Blackwood Br
Lambrig Wood
Gledenholm Moor
Watchman Moor
Black Loch
Kirkmichael Mains
Craes Hill
Skelston Moor
Boreland
Coatston
Dardarroch Woodhouse
Shaw's Hill
Duncow Common
Lanrick Hall
Fulton Moor
Ae Bridge
Bogrie Hill 432
Shillingland Moor
Knockoure
West Skelston
East Skelston
Goosedubs
Whitedike
Birkshaw
Benan Hill
Crawston Hill
Gateside
Merkland
Barrhill
Cairnhall
Auldgirth
Glenrae Wood
Dalswinton
Bog Hall
Ellerslee
North Riddingwood
Guillyburn
Johnfield Moss
Lochurr Hill
Lochurr
Loch Urr
Sundaywell Moor
Sundaywell
Castramon Moor
Gilmerston
Garrieston
Dunscore
Laggan
Springfield
Lochmailing
Mc Cheynston
Burnhead
Friars Carse
ELLISLAND FARM
Bankhead
Douganstyle
Braehead
Newlands
Auchencairn
Black Mark
Castramon Hill
Craigenputtock Moor
Nether Whiteside Moor
Nethertown Moor
Milton
Throughgate
Poundland
Mansegate
Lagganhill
Mc Murdoston
Kilroy
Burnside
Bankfoot
Isle
Dalswinton
Longbank
Duncow
Riddingwood Ho
Duncow Ho
Hazelrig Fm
Craigdasher Hill
Craighead Plantn
Greenside Fm
Mc Cubbington
Milliganton
High Farthingwell
Farthingwell
Portrack Ho
Cowhill Tower
Kemys Hall
Gallaberry
Amisfield
Lettrick Hill
Whiteside Hill
Collieston Hill
Dunesslin Moor
Stroquhan Hill
Killyleoch Hill
Townhead Wood
Heathfield
Sunnyhill
Bellfield Fm
Darngarroch Hill 373
Williamsfield
Killylung
Berryland
Druids Park
Kilblane
Cullivait
Kirkton
Tinwald
Upper Stroquhan Hill
Barr Hill
Speddoch Hill
Barbuie Fm
Morrington
Carzield
Templand Fm
Tinwald Parks
Glaisters Br
Glaisters Hill
Muil Hill 347
Slongaber Hill
Birkbush
Captainton
Newtonairds
Newtonairds Wood
Fourmerkland
Nether Gribton
Gribton
Cormaddie
Holywood
Abbey
Steilston Ho
Burnside of Baltersan
Locharbriggs
Cockloch Hill
Marglolly Br
Bishop Forest Hill
Drumpark
Hall of Drumpark
Routin Br
Cluden
Irongray
Cluden Lodge
Over Broomrigg Fm
Heathhall
Ind Est
Auchenhay Hill
Crogo Mill
Margreig
Glenkiln Res
Cornlee Hill
Skeoch Hill
Midrig
Lag
See Morris Hill
The Grove
Maryfield
Newbridge
Newbridge Fm
AVIATION MUS
Glenclair Hill
Bank
Nithsdale
Glenesslin
Lowther Hills
A76
A702
B740
B797
B729
B731
CLONE ROAD
259
248
237
NS
NX
00
80

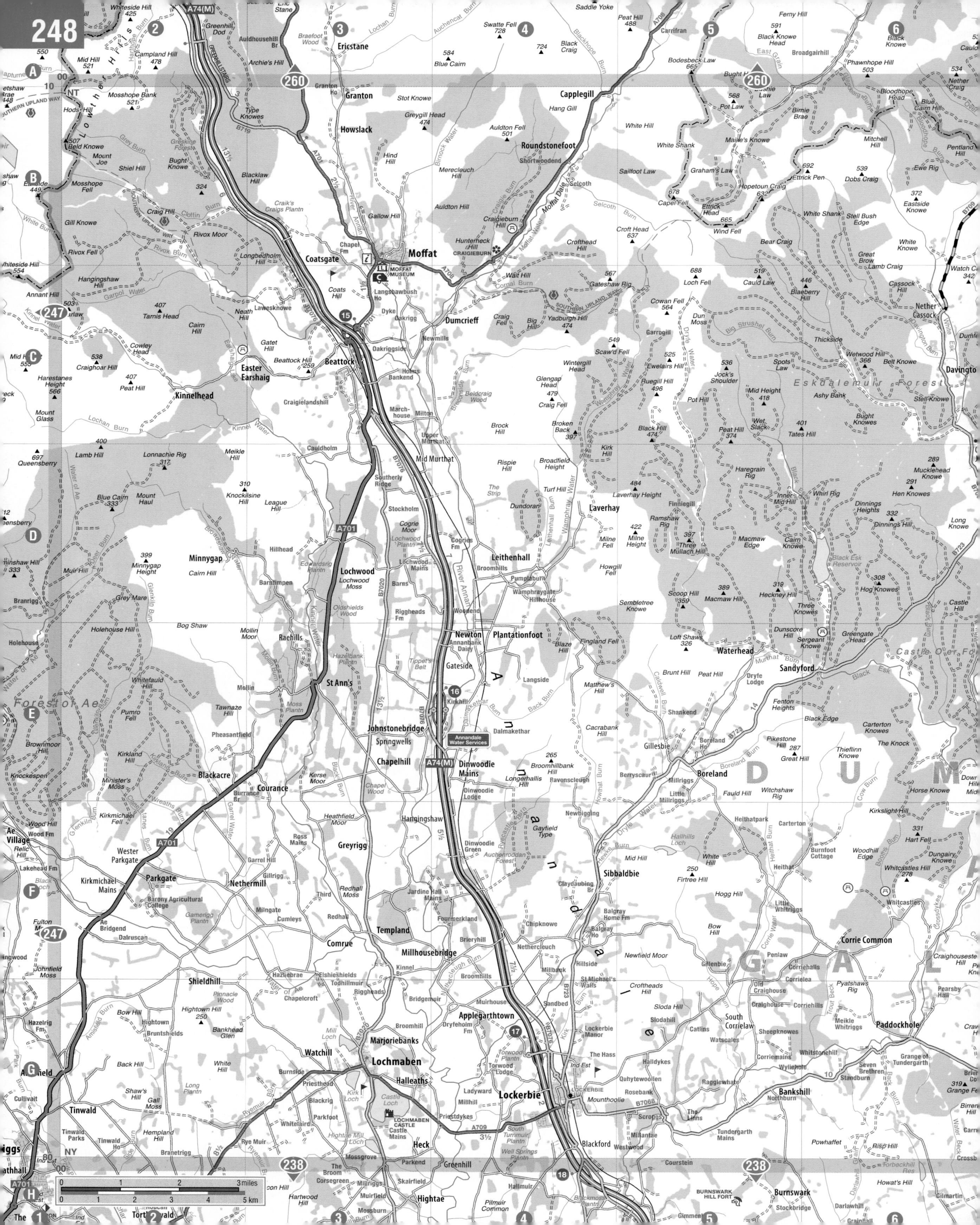

A74(M)
Moffat
Moffat Museum
Beattock
Coatsgate
Granton
Howslack
Ericstane
Capplegill
Roundstonefoot
Shortwoodend
Craigieburn
Dumcrieff
Easter Earshaig
Kinnelhead
Minnygap
Lochwood
Leithenhall
Laverhay
Newton
Plantationfoot
Gateside
St Ann's
Johnstonebridge
Springwells
Chapelhill
Dinwoodie Mains
Annandale Water Services
Blackacre
Courance
Parkgate
Wester Parkgate
Kirkmichael Mains
Nethermill
Greyrigg
Templand
Comrue
Millhousebridge
Shieldhill
Applegarthtown
Marjoriebanks
Lochmaben
Lochmaben Castle
Halleaths
Watchill
Tinwald
Heck
Lockerbie
Blackford
Greenhill
Hightae
Sibbaldbie
Boreland
Gillesbie
Waterhead
Sandyford
Corrie Common
Paddockhole
Bankshill
Burnswark
Burnswark Hill Fort
Eskdalemuir Forest
Forest of Ae
Ae Village
Annandale
Dumfries and Galloway
Southern Upland Way
Lowther Hills
Black Esk Reservoir
River Annan
Kinnel Water
Moffat Water
Wamphray Water
Dryfe Water
Water of Ae
A701
A708
A709
B7076
B7020
B7068
B723
B719
247
260
238
NT
NY
0 1 2 3 miles
0 1 2 3 4 5 km

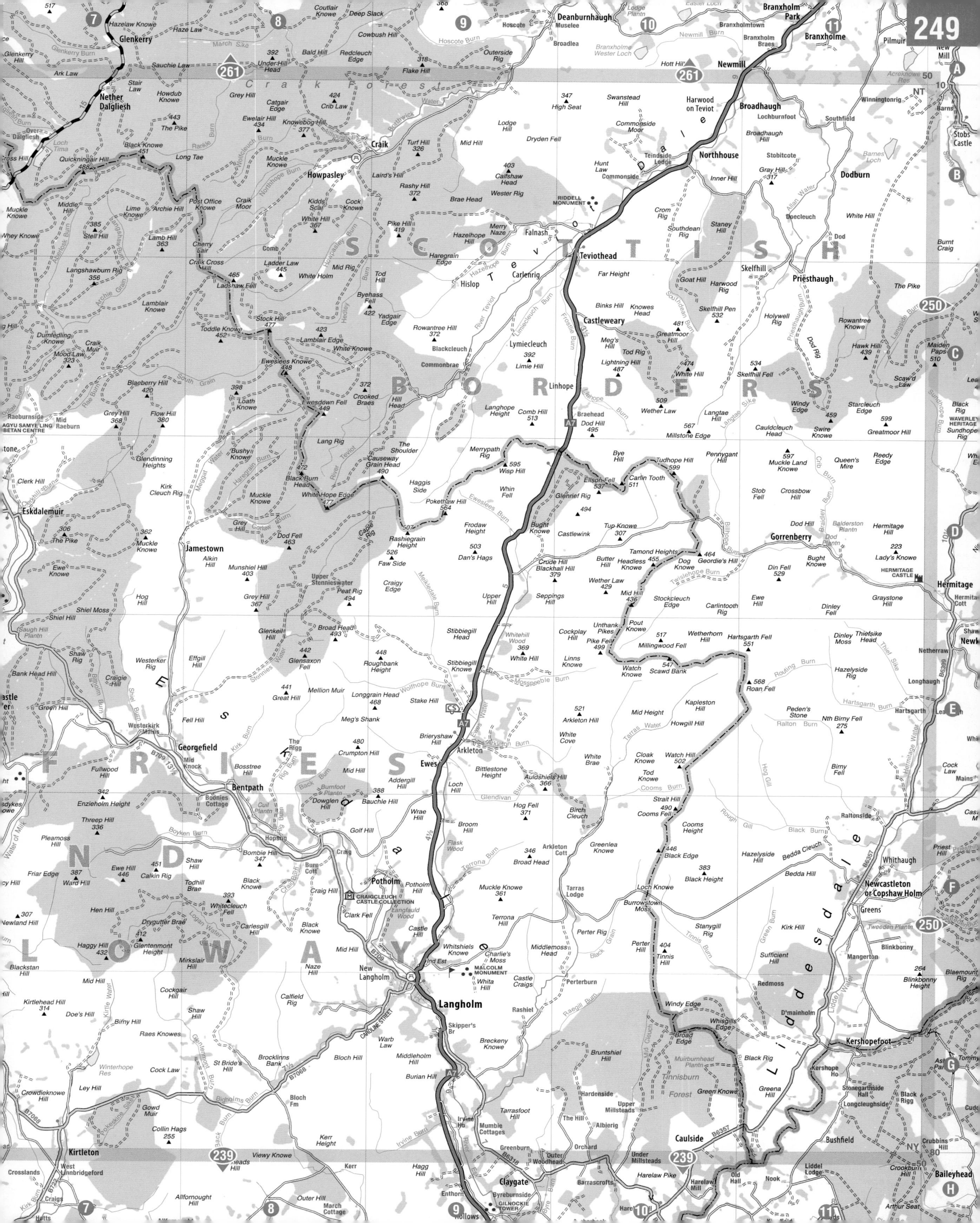

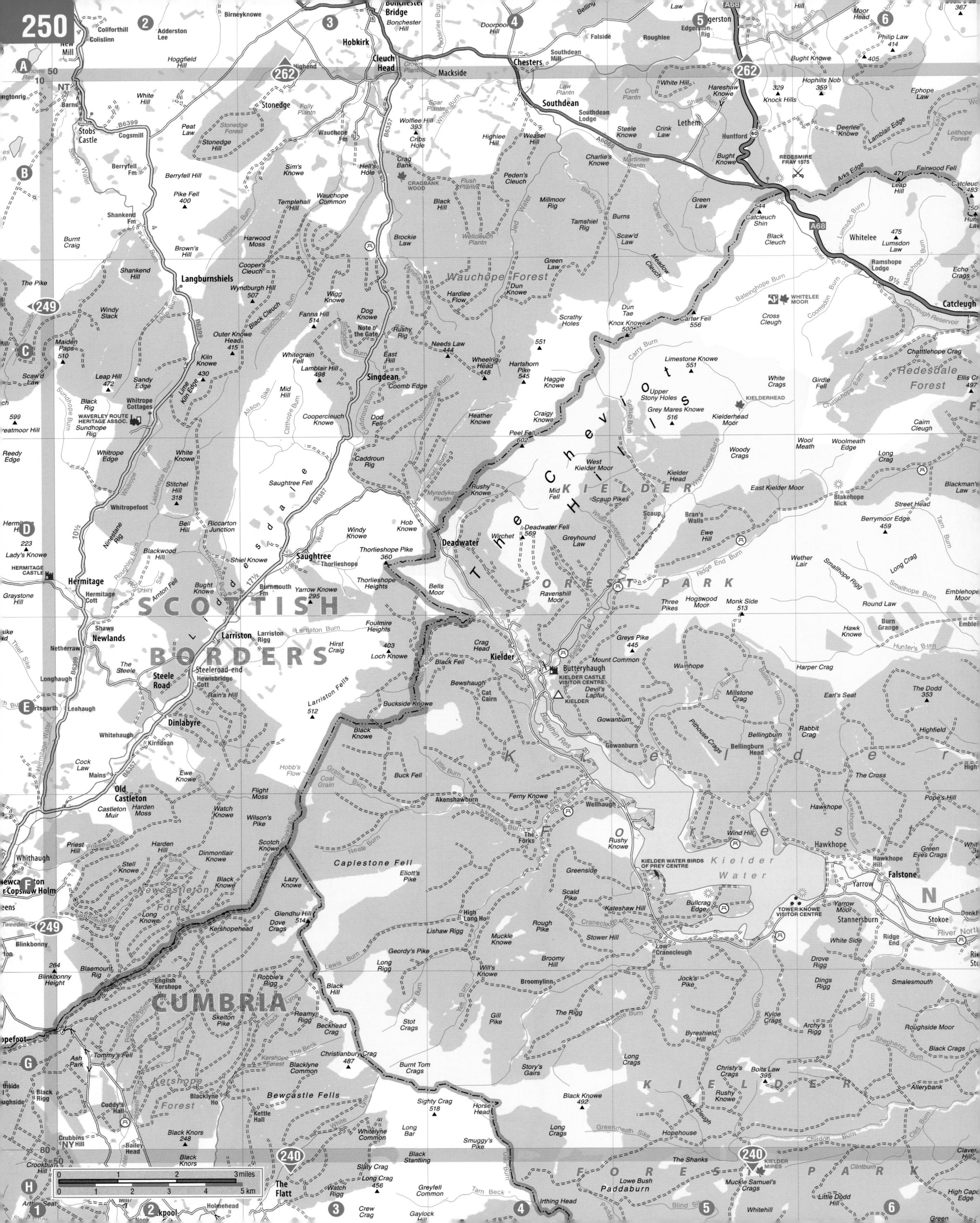

SCOTTISH
BORDERS
CUMBRIA
The Cheviot Hills
KIELDER FOREST PARK
Kielder Forest
Liddesdale
Wauchope Forest
Redesdale Forest
Newcastleton Forest
Kershope Forest
Kielder Water
Bewcastle Fells
Caplestone Fell
Bonchester Bridge
Bonchester Hill
Hobkirk
Cleuch Head
Mackside
Chesters
Southdean
Southdean Mill
Falside
Roughlee
Edgerston
Birneyknowe
Adderston Lee
Coliforthill
Colislinn
New Mill
Hoggfield Hill
Highend
Doorpool Hill
Bellion
Law
Moor Head
Philip Law
414
405
Bught Knowe
Hophills Nob
359
329
Knock Hills
Ephope Law
Lethem
Hareshaw Knowe
White Hill
Law Plantn
Croft Plantn
Southdean Lodge
Steele Knowe
Crink Law
Huntford
Bught Knowe
Deerlee Knowe
Lamblair Edge
Leithope Forest
REDESMIRE FRAY 1575
Arks Edge
471
Leap Hill
Fairwood Fell
Catcleuch
483
Stobs Castle
Cogsmill
B6399
Barns
White Hill
Stonedge
Folly Plantn
Stonedge Forest
Stonedge Hill
Peat Law
Wolflee Hill
393
Cribs Hole
Wauchope Fm
Spar Plantn
White Burn
Highlee Hill
Weasel Hill
A6088
Charlie's Knowe
Martinlee Plantn
Berryfell Fm
Berryfell Hill
Sim's Knowe
Hell's Hole
Crag Bank
CRAGBANK WOOD
Flush Plantn
Peden's Cleuch
Pike Fell
400
Templehall Hill
Wauchope Common
Black Hill
Millmoor Rig
Green Law
Catcleuch Shin
544
A68
Shankend
Burnt Craig
Harwood Moss
Brockie Law
Wellcleuch Plantn
Tamshiel Rig
Burns
Scaw'd Law
Black Cleuch
Whitelee
475
Lumsdon Law
Ramshope Lodge
Echo Crags
Brown's Hill
Cooper's Cleuch
Shankend Hill
Langburnshiels
Wyndburgh Hill
507
Wigg Knowe
Green Law
Meadow Cleuch
Dun Knowe
Hardlee Flow
The Pike
Windy Slack
Black Cleuch
Fanna Hill
514
Dog Knowe
Note o' the Gate
Rushy Rig
Dun Tae
Knox Knowe
500
Carter Fell
556
WHITELEE MOOR
Cross Cleugh
Catcleugh Reservoir
Catcleugh
Bateinghope Burn
Scrathy Holes
551
Maiden Paps
510
Outer Knowe Head
415
Kiln Knowe
430
Whitegrain Fell
Lamblair Hill
498
East Hill
Needs Law
444
Wheeling Head
448
Hartshorn Pike
545
Limestone Knowe
551
Chattlehope Crag
Scaw'd Law
Leap Hill
472
Sandy Edge
Lime Kiln Edge
Singdean
Coomb Edge
Haggie Knowe
Upper Stony Holes
White Crags
Girdle Fell
Ellis Crag
497
Black Rig
Whitrope Cottages
WAVERLEY ROUTE HERITAGE ASSOC.
Sundhope Rig
Sundhope Burn
Mid Hill
Coopercleuch Knowe
Dod Fell
Heather Knowe
Craigy Knowe
Grey Mares Knowe
516
KIELDERHEAD
Kielderhead Moor
Cairn Cleugh
599
Greatmoor Hill
Reedy Edge
Whitrope Edge
White Knowe
Caddroun Rig
Peel Fell
602
Wool Meath
Woolmeath Edge
Woody Crags
Long Crag
West Kielder Moor
Kielder Head
Stitchel Hill
318
Saughtree Fell
Rushy Knowe
Myredykes Plantn
Mid Fell
Scaup Pikes
East Kielder Moor
Blakehope Nick
Blackman's Law
Street Head
Whitropefoot
Bell Hill
Riccarton Junction
Hob Knowe
Windy Knowe
Deadwater
Wirchet
Deadwater Fell
569
Greyhound Law
Scaup
Bran's Walls
Ewe Hill
Berrymoor Edge
459
Hermitage Hill
223
Lady's Knowe
HERMITAGE CASTLE
Hermitage
Hermitage Cott
Blackwood Hill
Ninestane Rig
Shiel Knowe
Saughtree
Thorlieshope
Thorlieshope Pike
360
Wether Lair
Smallhope Rigg
Long Crag
Graystone Hill
Amton Fell
Bught Knowe
Burnmouth Fm
Yarrow Knowe
295
Thorlieshope Heights
Bells Moor
Ravenshill Moor
Three Pikes
Hogswood Moor
Monk Side
513
Round Law
Emblehope Moor
Shaws
Newlands
Netherraw
Larriston
Larriston Rigg
Larriston Burn
Foulmire Heights
Hirst Craig
403
Loch Knowe
Crag Head
Greys Pike
445
Hawk Knowe
Burn Grange
Kielder
Mount Common
Butteryhaugh
KIELDER CASTLE VISITOR CENTRE
Devil's Lapful
KIELDER
Wainhope
Harper Crag
The Steele
Steele Road
Steeleroad-end
Hewisbridge Cott
Rain's Hill
Longhaugh
Black Fell
Bewshaugh
Cat Cairn
Millstone Crag
Earl's Seat
The Dodd
353
Larriston Fells
512
Buckside Knowe
Gowanburn
Highfield
Ertsgarth
Leahaugh
Dinlabyre
Whitehaugh
Kirndean
Black Knowe
Bakethin Res
Pithouse Crags
Bellingburn
Bellingburn Head
Rabbit Crag
Cock Law
Mains
Ewe Knowe
Hobb's Flow
Coal Grain
Buck Fell
The Cross
Old Castleton
Castleton Muir
Harden Moss
Flight Moss
Watch Knowe
Wilson's Pike
Akenshawburn
Ferny Knowe
Wellhaugh
Hawkhope
Pope's Hill
Priest Hill
Harden Hill
Dinmontlair Knowe
Scotch Knowe
The Forks
Rushy Knowe
Wind Hill
Hawkhope
Green Eyes Crags
Whithaugh
Stell Knowe
Black Knowe
Lazy Knowe
Elliott's Pike
Greenside
KIELDER WATER BIRDS OF PREY CENTRE
Hawkhope Hill
Falstone
Newcastleton
Copshaw Holm
Yarrow
Scald Pike
Kateshaw Hill
Bullcrag Edge
TOWER KNOWE VISITOR CENTRE
Yarrow Moor
Stannersburn
Stokoe
Donkleywood
Long Knowe
Kershopehead
Glendhu Hill
514
Dove Crags
High Long Ho
Lishaw Rigg
Rough Pike
Stower Hill
Low Cranecleugh
White Side
Ridge End
River North Tyne
Blinkbonny
Geordy's Pike
Muckle Knowe
Drove Rigg
Blinkbonny Height
264
Blaemount Rig
Robbie's Rigg
Long Rigg
Will's Knowe
Broomy Hill
Broomylinn
Jock's Pike
Dings Rigg
Smalesmouth
English Kershope
Black Hill
Reamy Rigg
Skelton Pike
Beckhead Crag
Stot Crags
Gill Pike
The Rigg
Byreshield Hill
Kyloe Crags
Archy's Rigg
Roughside Moor
Black Crags
Penton
Tommy's Fell
Ash Park
Christianbury Crag
487
Burnt Tom Crags
Blacklyne Common
Long Crags
Story's Gairs
Christy's Crags
Bolts Law
395
Allerybank
Black Rigg
Cuddy's Hall
Blacklyne Ho
Kettle Hall
Sighty Crag
518
Horse Head
Black Knowe
492
Rushy Knowe
Black Cleugh
Long Bar
Whitelyne Common
Smuggy's Pike
Long Crags
Greenmeath Sike
Hopehouse
Chirdon Burn
Crubbins Hill
Bailey Head
Black Knors
248
Black Knors
Black Stantling
The Shanks
KIELDER MIRES
Claver Hill
Crookburn Hill
Slaty Crag
Lamoul Crag
456
Watch Rigg
Greyfell Common
Tarn Beck
Lowe Bush
Paddaburn
Muckle Samuel's Crags
Little Dodd Hill
High Cape Edge
The Flatt
Arthur's Seat
Holmehead
Crew Crag
Gaylock Hill
Irthing Head
Whitehill
Blind Sike
Green
0 1 2 3 miles
0 1 2 3 4 5 km
249
262
240

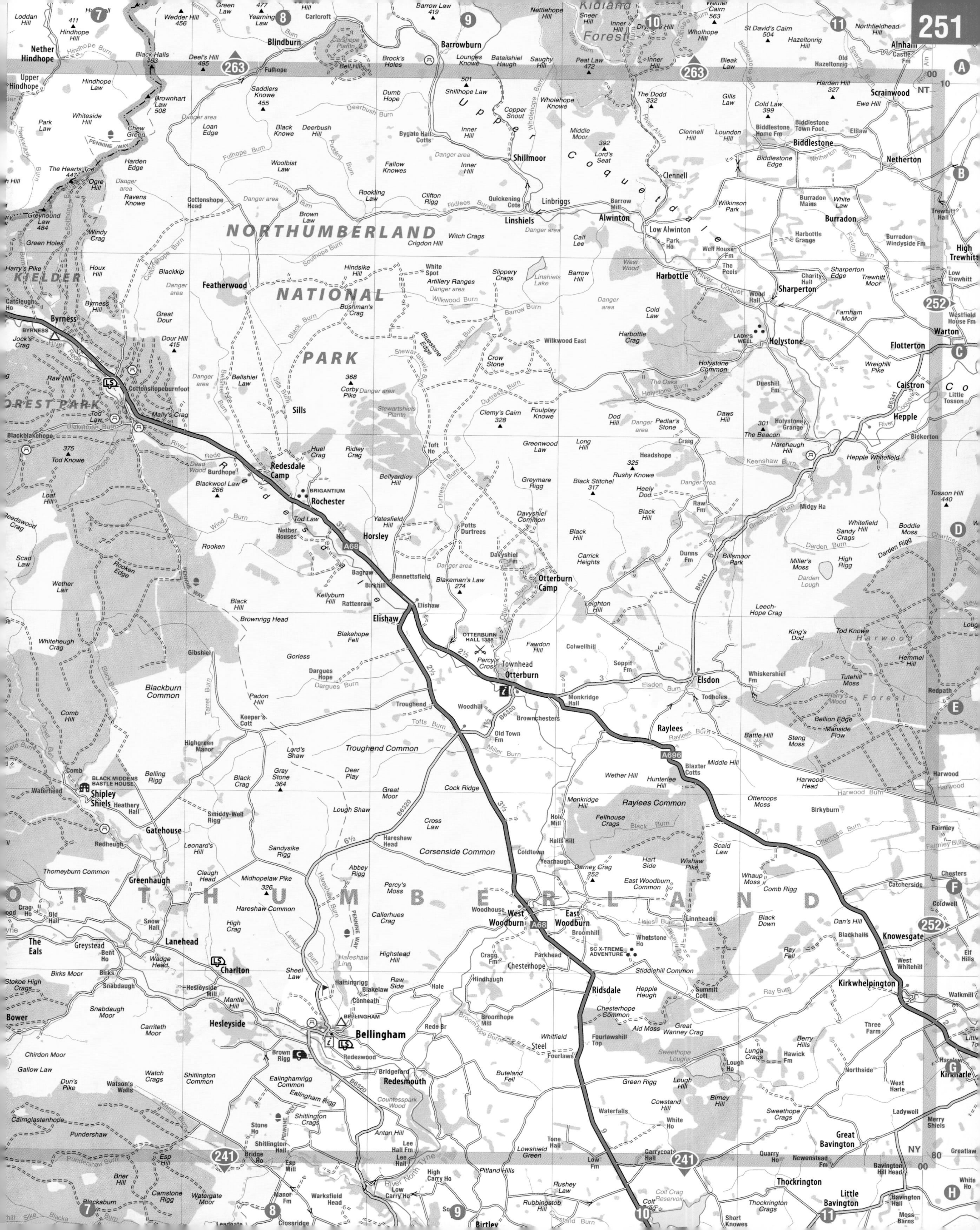

NORTHUMBERLAND
NATIONAL
PARK
KIELDER
FOREST PARK
Upper Coquetdale
Kidland Forest
NORTHUMBERLAND
263
252
241
A68
A696
B6320
B6341
Nether Hindhope
Upper Hindhope
Hindhope Law
Whiteside Hill
Park Law
Loddan Hill
Black Halls 463
Brownhart Law 508
Chew Green
PENNINE WAY
Harden Edge
The Hearts Toe 447
Ogre Hill
Ravens Knowe
Greyhound Law 484
Green Holes
Windy Crag
Harry's Pike
Houx Hill
Catcleugh Ho
Byrness
Byrness Hill
Jock's Crag
Raw Hill
Cottonshopeburnfoot
Tod Law
Mally's Crag
Blackblakehope
Blakehope Burn
375 Tod Knowe
Dead Wood
Burdhope
Blackwool Law 266
Loaf Hill
Reedswood Crag
Scad Law
Wether Lair
Whiteheugh Crag
Comb Hill
Comb
BLACK MIDDENS BASTLE HOUSE
Shipley Shiels
Waterhead
Heathery Hall
Redheugh
Thorneyburn Common
Greenhaugh
Gatehouse
Crag Ho
Old Hall
The Eals
Greystead
Bent Ho
Birks Moor
Birks
Snabdaugh
Snabdaugh Moor
Stokoe High Crags
Bower
Chirdon Moor
Gallow Law
Dun's Pike
Watson's Walls
Cairnglastenhope
Pundershaw
Pundershaw Burn
Blackaburn
Brier Hill
Camstone Rigg
Watergate Moor
Esp Hill
Wedder Hill 456
Deel's Hill 495
Green Law
Yearning Law 477
Blindburn
Carlcroft
Fulhope
Carshope Plantn
Bell Hill
Barrowburn
Barrow Law 419
Brock's Holes
Lounges Knowe
Bataishiel Haugh
Saughy Hill
Peat Law 472
Nettlehope Hill
Sneer Hill
Inner Hill
Dryhope Hill
Wether Cairn 563
Wholhope Hill
Bleak Law
St David's Cairn 504
Hazeltonrig Hill
Northfieldhead Hill
Alnham
Castle Fm
Old Hazeltonrig
Saddlers Knowe 455
Loan Edge
Dumb Hope
501 Shillhope Law
Copper Snout
Wholehope Knowe
The Dodd 332
Gills Law
Harden Hill 327
Cold Law 399
Scrainwood
Ewe Hill
Black Knowe
Deerbush Hill
Bygate Hall Cotts
Inner Hill
Middle Moor
392 Lord's Seat
Clennell Hill
Loundon Hill
Biddlestone Home Fm
Biddlestone Town Foot
Biddlestone
Ellilaw
Woolbist Law
Fallow Knowes
Shillmoor
Clennell
Biddlestone Edge
Netherton
Cottonshope Head
Rookling Law
Clifton Rigg
Quickening Cote
Linbriggs
Linshiels
Barrow Mill
Alwinton
Low Alwinton
Wilkinson Park
Burradon Mains
White Law
Burradon
Trewhitt Hall
Brown Law
Witch Crags
Crigdon Hill
Calf Lee
Park Ho
Well House Fm
Harbottle Grange
Burradon Windyside Fm
High Trewhitt
Low Trewhitt
Blackkip
Featherwood
Hindsike Hill
White Spot
Artillery Ranges
Slippery Crags
Linshiels Lake
Barrow Hill
West Wood
Harbottle
The Peels
Charity Hall
Sharperton Edge
Trewhitt Moor
Sharperton
Wood Hall
Great Dour
Dour Hill 415
Bushman's Crag
Cold Law
Harbottle Crag
LADY'S WELL
Holystone
Farnham Moor
Westfield House Fm
Warton
Flotterton
Wilkwood East
Holystone Common
Crow Stone
Wreighill Pike
368 Corby Pike
Bellshiel Law
Sills
Stewartshiels Plantn
The Oaks
Dueshill Fm
Caistron
Little Tosson
Clemy's Cairn 328
Foulplay Knowe
Dod Hill
Pedlar's Stone
Daws Hill
301 The Beacon
Holystone Grange
Hepple
Bickerton
Huel Crag
Ridley Crag
Toft Ho
Greenwood Law
Long Hill
Craig
Harehaugh Hill
Hepple Whitefield
Redesdale Camp
BRIGANTIUM
Rochester
Bellyardley Hill
325 Rushy Knowe
Headshope
Greymare Rigg
Black Stitchel 317
Heely Dod
Tosson Hill 440
Midgy Ha
Yatesfield Hill
Potts Durtrees
Davyshiel Common
Black Hill
Raw Fm
Whitefield Hill
Boddle Moss
Sandy Crags
Darden Rigg
Tod Law
Nether Houses
Horsley
Rooken
Rooken Edge
Black Hill
Carrick Heights
Dunns Fm
Billsmoor Park
Miller's Moss
High Rigg
Darden Lough
Bagraw
Birkhill
Bennettsfield
Davyshiel Fm
Blakeman's Law 274
Otterburn Camp
Kellyburn Hill
Rattenraw
Elishaw
Leighton Hill
Leech-Hope Crag
Brownrigg Head
Blakehope Fell
OTTERBURN HALL 1388
Fawdon Hill
Colwellhill
King's Dod
Tod Knowe
Harwood
Hemmel Hill
Gorless
Percy's Cross
Townhead
Otterburn
Soppit Fm
Elsdon
Whiskershiel Fm
Tutehill Moss
Gibshiel
Dargues Hope
Redpath
Blackburn Common
Padon Hill
Troughend
Woodhill
Monkridge Hall
Todholes
Harry's Wood
Bellion Edge
Manside Flow
Keeper's Cott
Brownchesters
Old Town Fm
Raylees
Battle Hill
Steng Moss
Highgreen Manor
Lord's Shaw
Troughend Common
Blaxter Cotts
Middle Hill
Belling Rigg
Black Crag
Gray Stone 364
Deer Play
Great Moor
Cock Ridge
Wether Hill
Hunterlee Hill
Harwood Head
Smiddy-Well Rigg
Lough Shaw
Monkridge Hill
Raylees Common
Ottercops Moss
Birkyburn
Cross Law
Hole Mill
Fellhouse Crags
Fairnley
Leonard's Hill
Sandysike Rigg
Hareshaw Head
Corsenside Common
Halls Hill
Coldtown
Yearhaugh
Scald Law
Abbey Rigg
Cleugh Head
Midhopelaw Pike 326
Percy's Moss
Darney Crag 252
Hart Side
Wishaw Pike
East Woodburn Common
Whaup Moss
Comb Rigg
Chesters
Catcheside
Coldwell
Hareshaw Common
Callerhues Crag
Woodhouse
West Woodburn
East Woodburn
Broomhill
Linnheads
Black Down
Dan's Hill
Blackhalls
Knowesgate
Snow Hall
High Crag
Whetstone Ho
SC X-TREME ADVENTURE
Lanehead
Wadge Head
Charlton
Highstead Hill
Cragg Ho
Parkhead
Chesterhope
Ray Fell
West Whitehill
Elf Hills
Hesleyside Mill
Sheel Law
Hainingrigg
Blakelaw
Raw Side
Hole
Hindhaugh
Ridsdale
Hepple Heugh
Stiddlehill Common
Summit Cott
Kirkwhelpington
Walkmill
Mantle Hill
Conheath
BELLINGHAM
Bellingham
Carriteth Moor
Hesleyside
Broomhope Mill
Chesterhope Common
Aid Moss
Great Wanney Crag
Three Farm
Rede Br
Whitfield
Steel
Fourlaws
Fourlawshill Top
Sweethope Loughs
Berry Hills
Hawick Fm
Brown Rigg
Redeswood
Watch Crags
Shitlington Common
Bridgeford
Redesmouth
Buteland Fell
Lunga Crags
Lough Ho
Lough Hill
Green Rigg
Northside
West Harle
Kirkharle
Ealinghamrigg Common
Ealingham Rigg
Countesspark Wood
Cowstand Hill
Birney Hill
Sweethope Crags
Ladywell
Merry Shiels
Shitlington Crags
Stone Ho
Shitlington Hall
Waterfalls
White Ho
Great Bavington
Anton Hill
Lee Hall Fm
Lee Hall
Tone Hall
Lowshield Green
Carrycoats Hall
Quarry Ho
Newonstead Fm
Greatlaw
Bridge Ho
Esp Mill
River North Tyne
High Carry Ho
Low Carry Ho
Pitland Hills
Rushey Law
Low Fm
Bavington Hill Head
Bavington Hall
White Ho
Manor Fm
Warksfield Head
Rubbingstob Hill
Colt Crag Reservoir
Colt Crag
Thockrington
Thockrington Crags
Little Bavington
Short Knowes
Moss Barns
Leadgate
Crossridge
Birtley

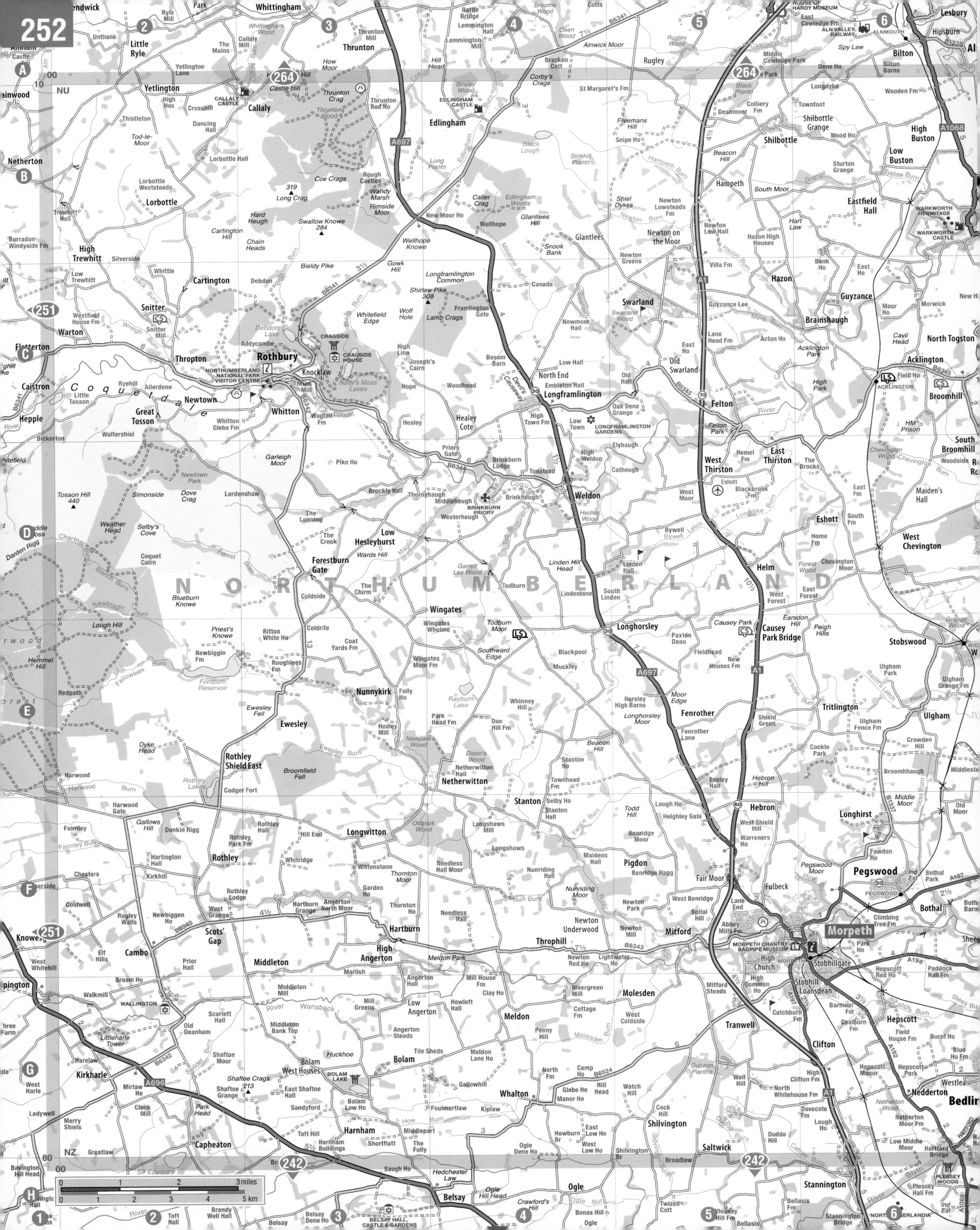

NORTHUMBERLAND
Rothbury
Morpeth
Whittingham
Thrunton
Little Ryle
Yetlington
Callaly
Callaly Castle
Castle Hill
Edlingham
Edlingham Castle
Rugley
Lesbury
Hipsburn
Alnmouth
Aln Valley Railway
Bilton
Shilbottle
High Buston
Low Buston
Hampeth
Netherton
Lorbottle
Lorbottle Hall
High Trewhitt
Cartington
Snitter
Warton
Thropton
Cragside
Cragside House
Northumberland National Park Visitor Centre
Knocklaw
Newtown
Whitton
Great Tosson
Hepple
Caistron
Little Tosson
Coquetdale
Tosson Hill 440
Swarland
Old Swarland
Felton
Longframlington
Longframlington Gardens
Brinkburn Priory
Weldon
West Thirston
East Thirston
Eshott
Acklington
Warkworth Hermitage
Warkworth Castle
Hazon
Guyzance
Brainshaugh
North Togston
Broomhill
South Broomhill
West Chevington
Helm
Longhorsley
Causey Park Bridge
Stobswood
Forestburn Gate
Low Hesleyhurst
Wingates
Nunnykirk
Ewesley
Rothley Shield East
Netherwitton
Stanton
Fenrother
Tritlington
Ulgham
Hebron
Longhirst
Pegswood
Bothal
Longwitton
Rothley
Pigdon
Fulbeck
Mitford
Hartburn
Scots' Gap
Cambo
Wallington
Middleton
High Angerton
Throphill
Newton Underwood
Meldon
Molesden
Tranwell
Kirkharle
Capheaton
Bolam
Bolam Lake
Harnham
Whalton
Shilvington
Saltwick
Clifton
Hepscott
Nedderton
Stannington
Belsay
Belsay Hall, Castle & Gardens
Ogle
Plessey Woods
Morpeth Chantry Bagpipe Museum
Stobhillgate
Simonside
Fontburn Reservoir
A697
A1
A696
A68
B6341
B6342
B6343
B6344
B6345
B6524
NU
NZ
264
251
242
0 1 2 3 miles
0 1 2 3 4 5 km

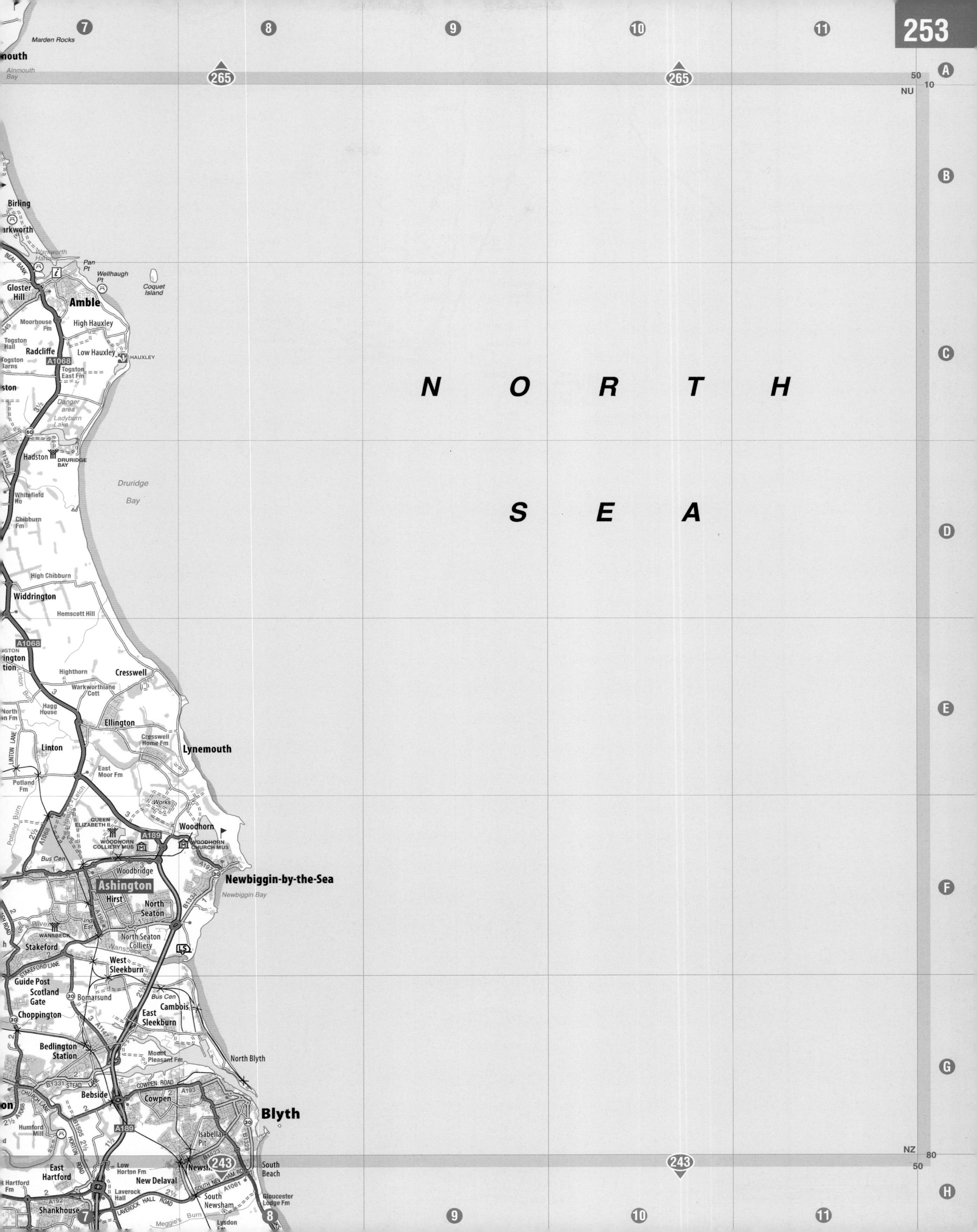

Marden Rocks

7   8   9   10   11

mouth

Alnmouth
Bay

265   265

50
10

NU

A

B

Birling

rkworth

Warkworth
Harbour

Beal
Bank

Pan
Pt

Wellhaugh
Pt

Coquet
Island

Gloster
Hill

Amble

Moorhouse
Fm

High Hauxley

Togston
Hall

Radcliffe

Low Hauxley

HAUXLEY

A1068

Togston
Barns

Togston
East Fm

ston

Danger
area
Ladyburn
Lake

N O R T H

C

Hadston

DRURIDGE
BAY

B1330

Druridge
Bay

Whitefield
Ho

S E A

Chibburn
Fm

D

High Chibburn

Widdrington

Hemscott Hill

A1068

NGTON

ington
tion

Highthorn

Cresswell

Warkworthlane
Cott

North
n Fm

Hagg
House

E

LINTON LANE

Ellington

Cresswell
Home Fm

Linton

Lynemouth

East
Moor Fm

Potland
Fm

Polland Burn

Works

QUEEN
ELIZABETH II

A189

Woodhorn

WOODHORN
COLLIERY MUS

WOODHORN
CHURCH MUS

Bus Cen

A197

Woodbridge

A197

F

Ashington

Hirst

Newbiggin-by-the-Sea

Newbiggin Bay

North
Seaton

River

WANSBECK

North Seaton
Colliery

h

Wansbeck

L5

Stakeford

Guide Post

West
Sleekburn

STAKEFORD LANE

Scotland
Gate

Bomarsund

Bus Cen

Cambois

Choppington

East
Sleekburn

Bedlington
Station

Mount
Pleasant Fm

North Blyth

G

B1331 STEAD LANE

COWPEN ROAD

A193

Bebside

Cowpen

A193

Humford
Mill

CHURCH LANE

HORTON ROAD

B1331

A189

Blyth

on

Isabella
Pit

NZ
80
50

B1505

243

South
Beach

East
Hartford

Low
Horton Fm

Newsh

SOUTH NEWSHAM RD

New Delaval

Laverock
Hall

South
Newsham

A1061

Gloucester
Lodge Fm

H

Hartford
Hall

Shankhouse

A192

7   8   9   10   11

Meggie's Burn

LAVEROCK HALL ROAD

Lysdon

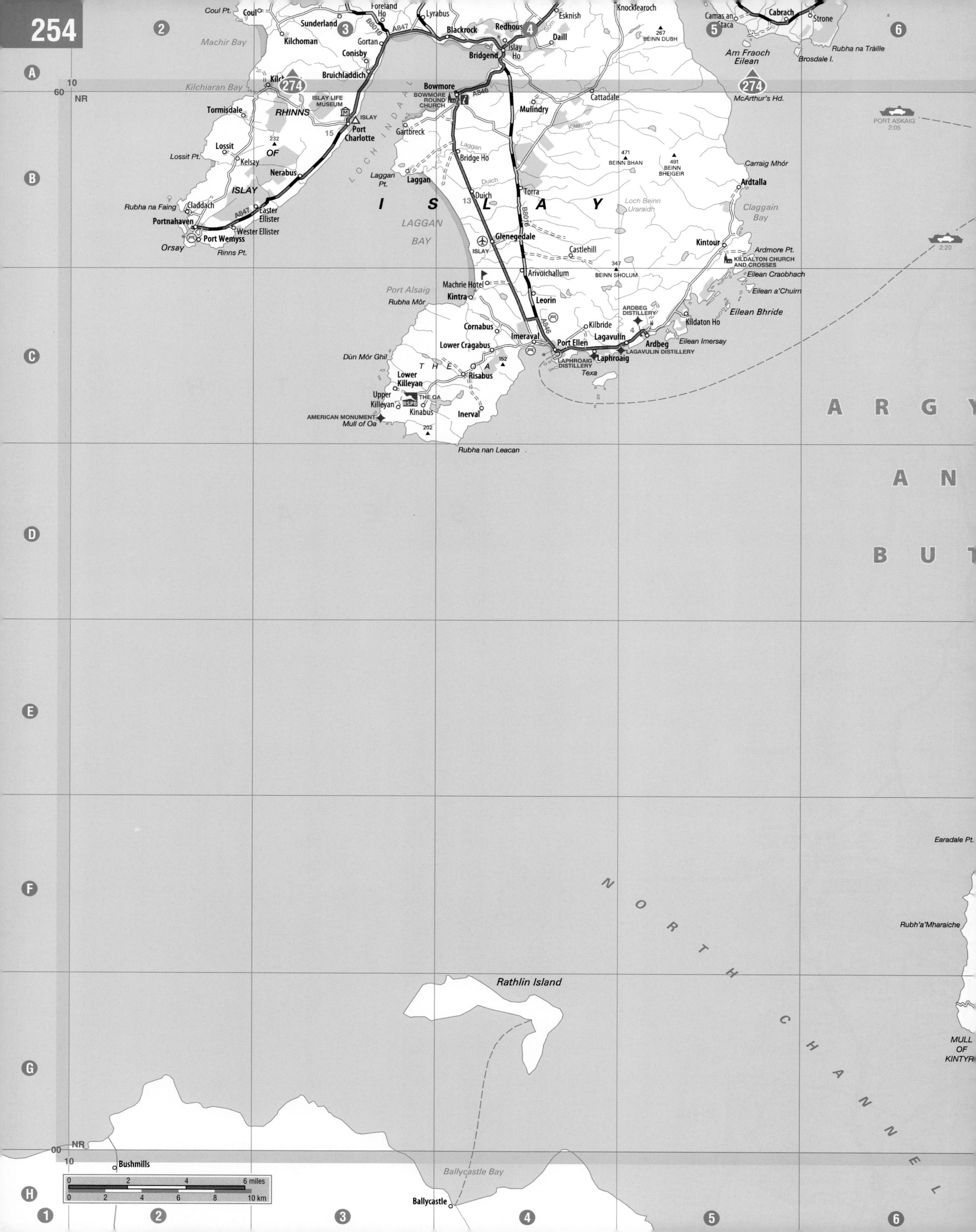

A B C D E F G H

1 2 3 4 5 6

ISLAY

Coul Pt.
Coul
Foreland Ho
Lyrabus
Esknish
Knockfearoch
Camas an
taca
Cabrach
Strone

Sunderland
Kilchoman
Gortan
Conisby
Blackrock
Redhous
Daill
BEINN DUBH
267
Rubha na Tràille
Brosdale I.

Bridgend
Islay
Ho
Am Fraoch
Eilean

Machir Bay
Kilchiaran Bay

Bruichladdich
ISLAY LIFE MUSEUM
Bowmore
BOWMORE
ROUND
CHURCH
A846
Cattadale
McArthur's Hd.
PORT ASKAIG
2:05

Tormisdale
RHINNS
Port Charlotte
Mulindry

Lossit
Lossit Pt.
232
Kelsay
OF
15
Gartbreck
Laggan
Bridge Ho
Laggan
Duich
BEINN BHAN
471
BEINN
BHEIGEIR
491
Carraig Mhòr

Nerabus
ISLAY
Laggan
Pt.
Laggan
Torra
B8016
Loch Beinn
Uraraidh
Ardtalla

Rubha na Faing
Claddach
ISLAY
LAGGAN
BAY
Duich
Claggain
Bay

Portnahaven
Easter
Ellister
Wester Ellister
A847
Glenegedale
ISLAY
Castlehill
347
Kintour
Ardmore Pt.
KILDALTON CHURCH
AND CROSSES
2:20

Port Wemyss
Orsay
Rinns Pt.
Arivoichallum
BEINN SHOLUM
Eilean Craobhach
Eilean a'Chuirn

Port Alsaig
Rubha Mòr
Machrie Hotel
Kintra
Leorin
ARDBEG
DISTILLERY
Kildaton Ho
Eilean Bhride

Dùn Mòr Ghil
Cornabus
Lower Cragabus
Imeraval
A846
Kilbride
Lagavulin
Ardbeg
Kildalton Ho
Eilean Imersay

THE OA
Risabus
152
Port Ellen
LAGAVULIN DISTILLERY
Laphroaig
Texa

Lower
Killeyan
Upper
Killeyan
RSPB
THE OA
Kinabus
Inerval
LAPHROAIG
DISTILLERY

AMERICAN MONUMENT
Mull of Oa
202

Rubha nan Leacan

A R G Y
A N
B U T

N O R T H
C H A N N E L

Earadale Pt.

Rubh'a'Mharaiche

Rathlin Island

MULL
OF
KINTYRE

Bushmills

Ballycastle Bay

0 2 4 6 miles
0 2 4 6 8 10 km

Ballycastle

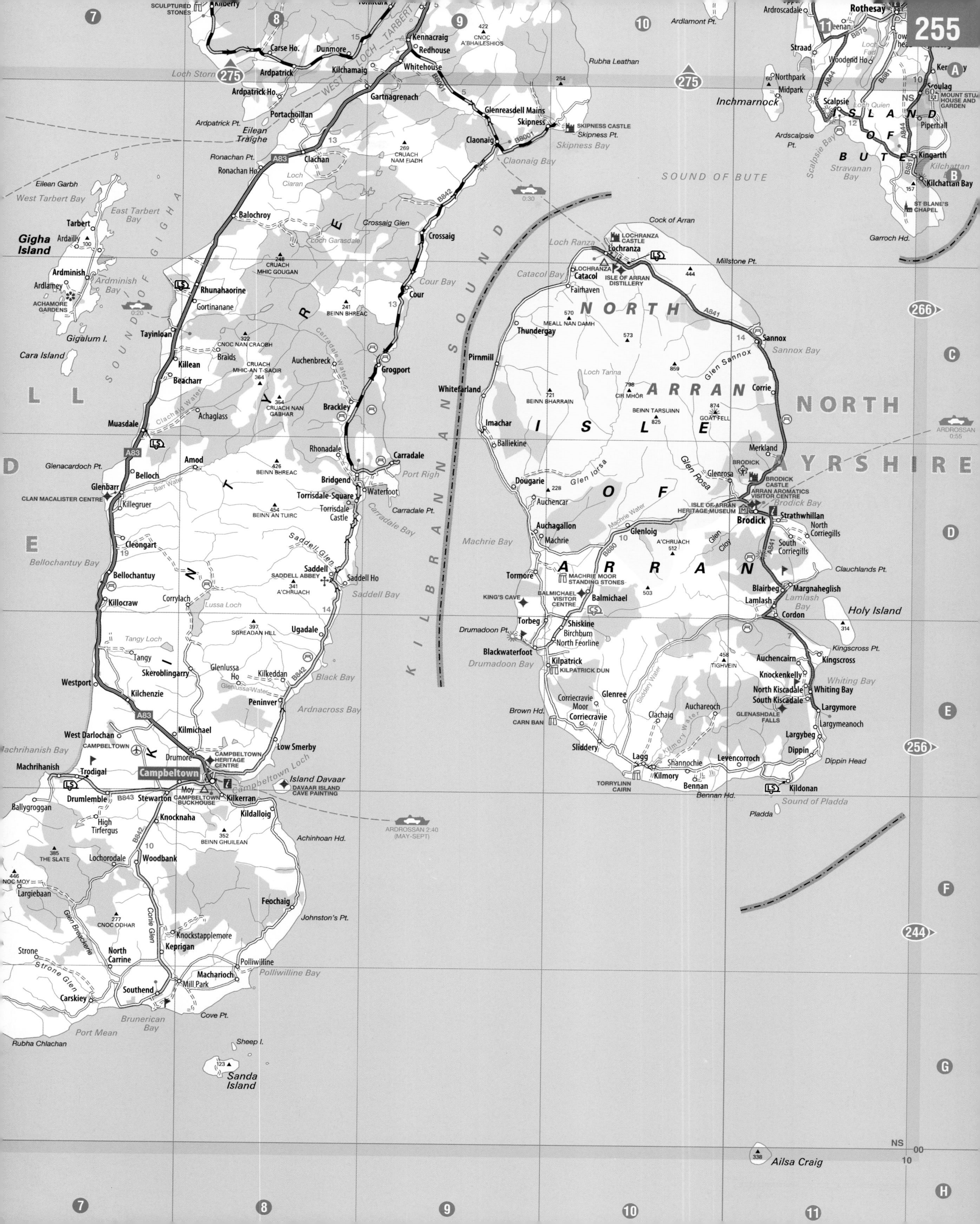
Kintyre
Isle of Arran
North Ayrshire
Isle of Bute
Kilbrannan Sound
Sound of Gigha
Sound of Bute
Gigha Island
Campbeltown
Brodick
Lochranza
Tarbert
Ardminish
Carradale
Saddell
Lamlash
Whiting Bay
Blackwaterfoot
Machrihanish
Southend
Sanda Island
Holy Island
Ailsa Craig
Inchmarnock
Rothesay
Kingarth
Goat Fell
Cir Mhòr
Beinn Tarsuinn
Beinn Bharrain
Skipness Castle
Brodick Castle
Lochranza Castle
Isle of Arran Distillery
Isle of Arran Heritage Museum
Machrie Moor Standing Stones
King's Cave
Davaar Island Cave Painting
Achamore Gardens
Saddell Abbey
Clan Macalister Centre
Campbeltown Heritage Centre
Ardrossan 2:40 (May-Sept)
Ardrossan 0:55
A83
B842
A841
B880
275
266
256
244

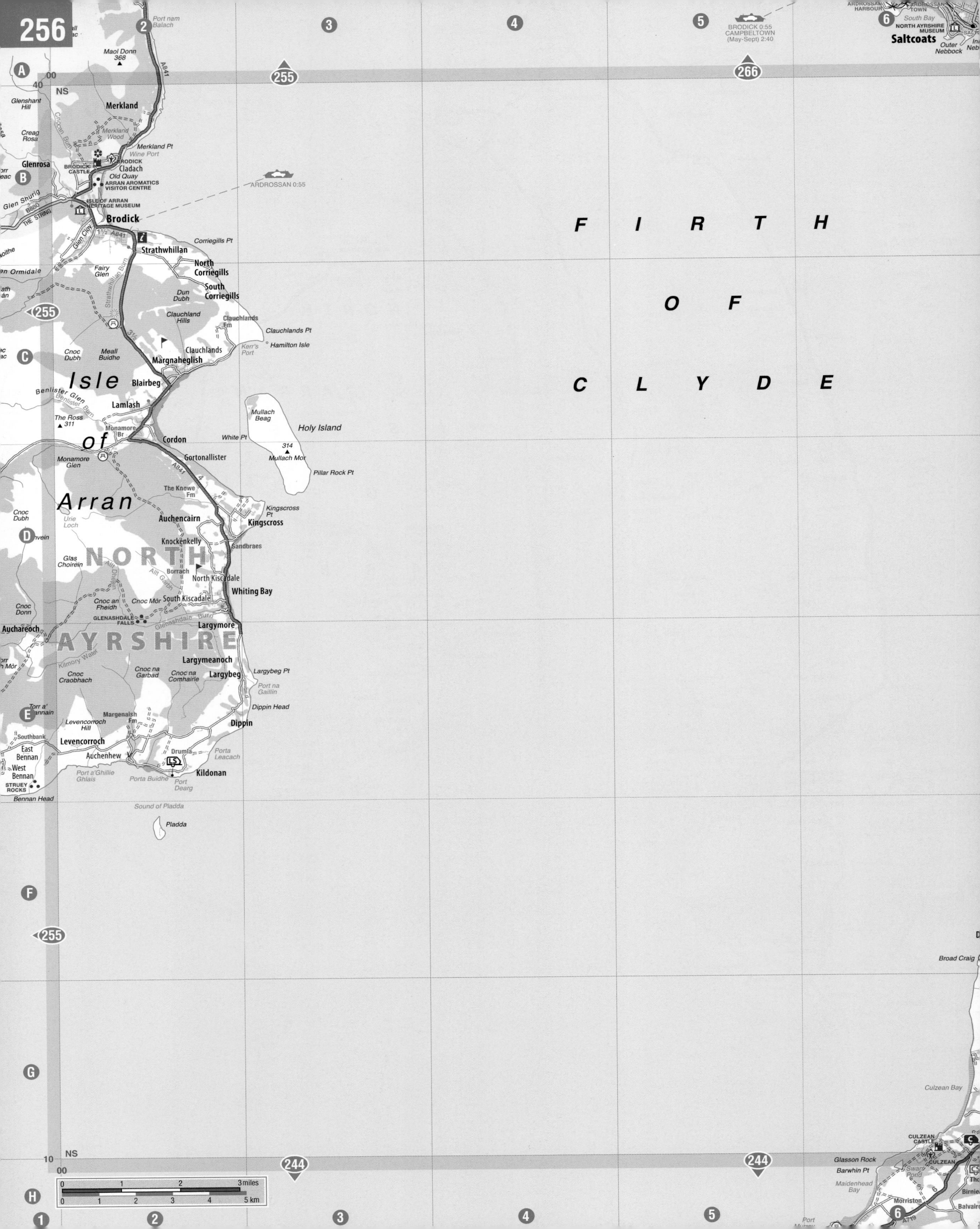

FIRTH OF CLYDE
Isle of Arran
NORTH AYRSHIRE
Brodick
Merkland
Merkland Pt
Wine Port
Brodick Castle
Cladach
Old Quay
Arran Aromatics Visitor Centre
Isle of Arran Heritage Museum
Glenrosa
Glen Shurig
The String
Maol Donn 368
Port nam Balach
Glenshant Hill
Creag Rosa
Merkland Wood
Glen Cloy
Strathwhillan
Corriegills Pt
North Corriegills
South Corriegills
Fairy Glen
Dun Dubh
Clauchland Hills
Clauchlands Fm
Clauchlands Pt
Hamilton Isle
Kerr's Port
Clauchlands
Margnaheglish
Cnoc Dubh
Meall Buidhe
Blairbeg
Lamlash
Benlister Glen
The Ross 311
Monamore Br
Cordon
Monamore Glen
White Pt
Holy Island
Mullach Beag
314 Mullach Mor
Pillar Rock Pt
Gortonallister
The Knowe Fm
Auchencairn
Kingscross Pt
Kingscross
Urie Loch
Cnoc Dubh
Knockenkelly
Sandbraes
Glas Choirein
Borrach
North Kiscadale
Whiting Bay
Cnoc an Fheidh
Cnoc Mor
South Kiscadale
Cnoc Donn
Glenashdale Falls
Glenashdale Burn
Largymore
Auchareoch
Kilmory Water
Largymeanoch
Cnoc Craobhach
Cnoc na Garbad
Cnoc na Comhairle
Largybeg
Largybeg Pt
Port na Gaillin
Dippin Head
Dippin
Torr a' Chruinn
Margenaish Fm
Levencorroch Hill
Levencorroch
Southbank
East Bennan
West Bennan
Struey Rocks
Bennan Head
Auchenhew
Drumla
Porta Leacach
Kildonan
Port a'Ghillie Ghlais
Porta Buidhe
Port Dearg
Sound of Pladda
Pladda
A841
B880
ARDROSSAN 0:55
BRODICK 0:55 CAMPBELTOWN (May-Sept) 2:40
Ardrossan Harbour
Ardrossan Town
South Bay
North Ayrshire Museum
Saltcoats
Outer Nebbock
Broad Craig
Culzean Bay
Culzean Castle
Culzean
Glasson Rock
Barwhin Pt
Swan Pond
Maidenhead Bay
Morriston
Birnie
Balvaird
A719
NS
255
266
244
0 1 2 3 miles
0 1 2 3 4 5 km

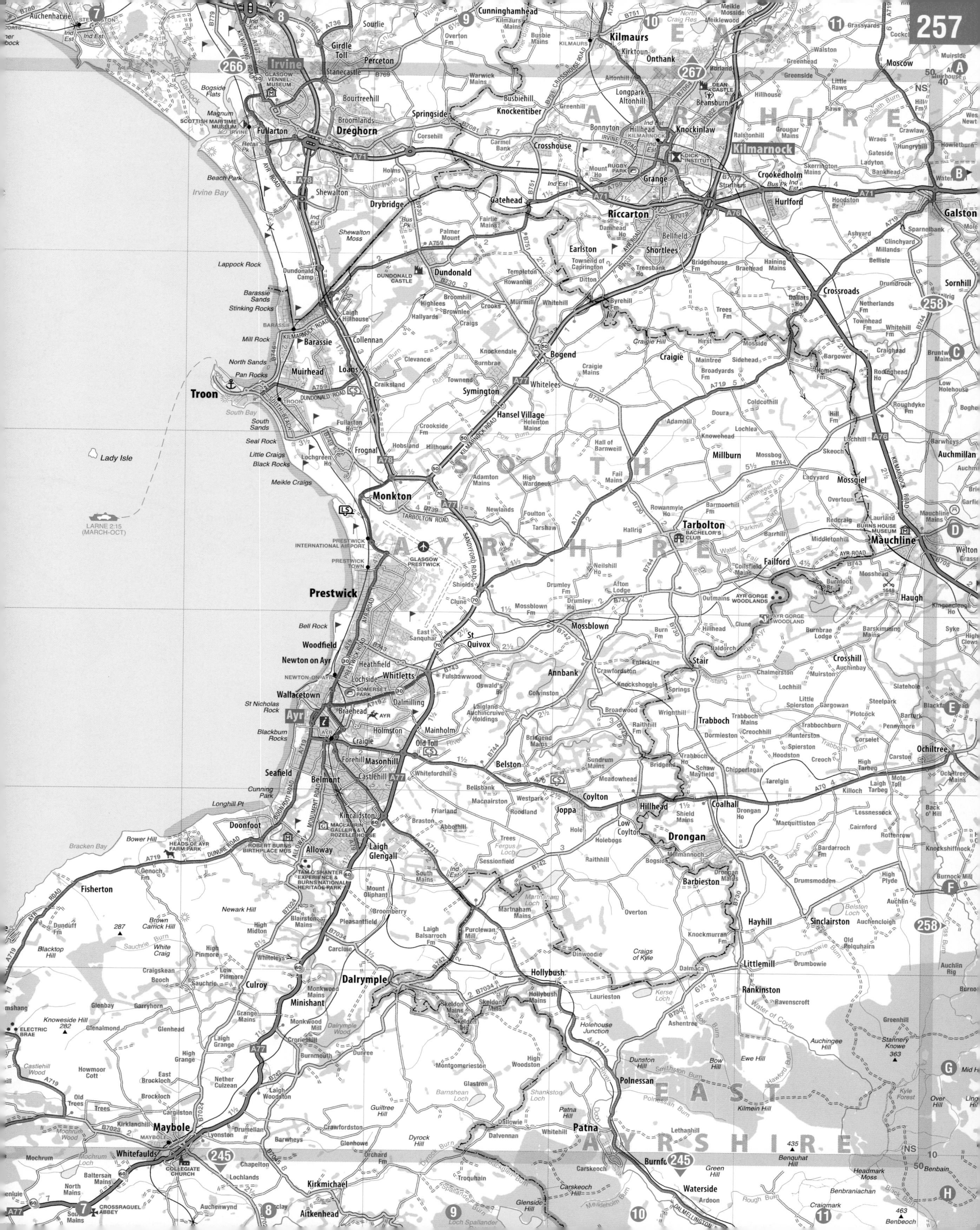
EAST AYRSHIRE
SOUTH AYRSHIRE
Kilmarnock
Irvine
Ayr
Troon
Prestwick
Maybole
Galston
Mauchline
Kilmaurs
Dreghorn
Fullarton
Girdle Toll
Perceton
Stanecastle
Bourtreehill
Broomlands
Springside
Crosshouse
Knockentiber
Busbiehill
Cunninghamhead
Onthank
Kirktoun
Knockinlaw
Beansburn
Bonnyton
Hillhead
Grange
Riccarton
Bellfield
Shortlees
Crookedholm
Hurlford
Gatehead
Drybridge
Shewalton
Dundonald
DUNDONALD CASTLE
Barassie
Muirhead
Loans
Symington
Hansel Village
Bogend
Craigie
Monkton
Tarbolton
BACHELOR'S CLUB
Failford
Crossroads
Mossgiel
BURNS HOUSE MUSEUM
Haugh
Mossblown
Annbank
St Quivox
Whitletts
Heathfield
Lochside
Newton on Ayr
Woodfield
Wallacetown
Dalmilling
Braehead
Holmston
Craigie
Forehill
Masonhill
Castlehill
Belmont
Seafield
Kincaidston
Doonfoot
Alloway
Laigh Glengall
Belston
Coylton
Joppa
Hillhead
Coalhall
Drongan
Barbieston
Stair
Trabboch
Ochiltree
Sinclairston
Hayhill
Littlemill
Rankinston
Hollybush
Dalrymple
Minishant
Culroy
Polnessan
Patna
Waterside
Burnfoot
Kirkmichael
Aitkenhead
Whitefaulds
Mochrum
Fisherton
Heads of Ayr
Lady Isle
Irvine Bay
South Bay
Bracken Bay
LARNE 2:15 (MARCH-OCT)
PRESTWICK INTERNATIONAL AIRPORT
GLASGOW PRESTWICK
SCOTTISH MARITIME MUSEUM
GLASGOW VENNEL MUSEUM
DEAN CASTLE
DICK INSTITUTE
ROBERT BURNS BIRTHPLACE MUS
HEADS OF AYR FARM PARK
TAM O'SHANTER EXPERIENCE & BURNS NATIONAL HERITAGE PARK
MACLAURIN GALLERY & ROZELLE HOUSE
COLLEGIATE CHURCH
CROSSRAGUEL ABBEY
AYR GORGE WOODLANDS
Benquhat Hill 435
Benbeoch 463
Stannery Knowe 363
266
267
258
245
A71
A76
A77
A78
A70
A719
A713
A759
A736
A735
A79
B730
B744
B742
B7034
B7024
B7023
B7045
DALMELLINGTON

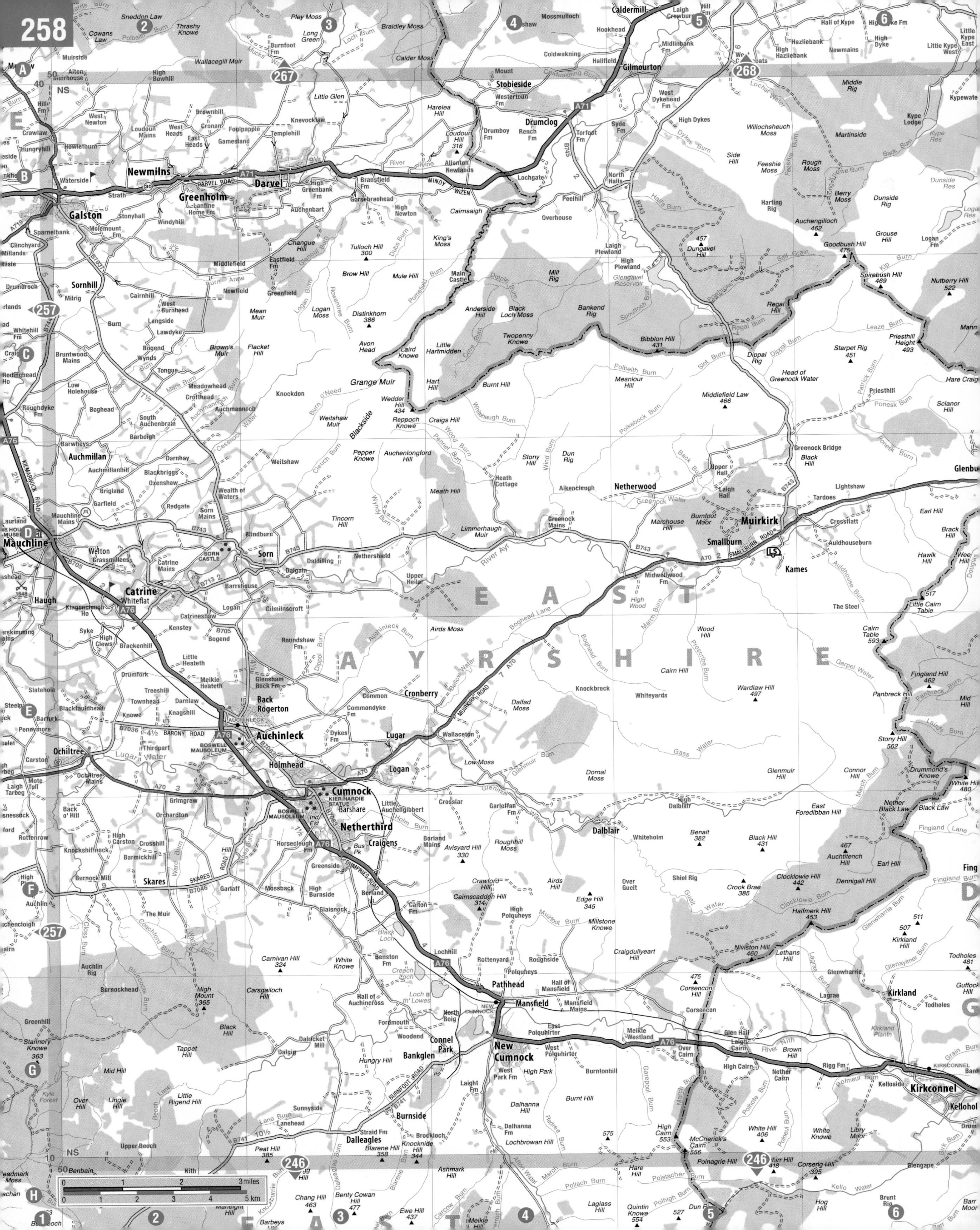
Sneddon Law
Cowans Law
Thrashy Knowe
Pley Moss
Long Green
Braidley Moss
Mossmulloch
Caldermill
Laigh Crewburn
Hill Fm
Hall of Kype
Little Kype
Little Kype East
Little Kype West
Muirside
Burnfoot Rm
Wallacegill Muir
Calder Moss
Hookhead
Midlinbank Fm
Hazliebank
High Dyke
High Hazliebank
Newmains
Alton Muirhouse
High Bowhill
Mount
Stobieside
Westertoun Fm
Coldwakning
Hallfield
Gilmourton
Middle Rig
Kypewater
NS
Little Glen
Harelea Hill
West Dykehead Fm
West Newton
Brownhill
Knevocklaw
Drumclog
High Dykes
Willochsheuch Moss
Martinside
Kype Lodge
Crawlaw
Hungryhill
Howletburn
Loudoun Mains
West Heads
East Heads
Foulpapple
Gamesland
Templehill
Loudoun Hill 316
Drumboy Fm
Rench Fm
Torfoot Fm
Syde Fm
Side Hill
Feeshie Moss
Rough Moss
Newmilns
Darvel
Allanton Newlands
North Halls
Waterside
Greenholm
Darvel Road
Bransfield Fm
Windy Wizen
Lochgate
Dunside Res
Strath
Lanfine Home Fm
High Greenbank Fm
Gorsebraehead
Peelhill
Galston
Stonyhall
Windyhill
Auchenbart
High Newton
Cairnsaigh
Overhouse
Harting Rig
Berry Moss
Dunside Rig
Sparnelbank
Molemount Fm
King's Moss
Auchengilloch 462
Grouse Hill
Logan Fm
Clinchyard
Millands
Changue Hill
Tulloch Hill 300
Dungavel Hill 457
Goodbush Hill 475
Laigh Plewland
Middlefield
Eastfield Fm
Brow Hill
Mule Hill
Main Castle
Mill Rig
High Plewland
Glengavel Reservoir
Spirebush Hill 469
Nutberry Hill 522
Sornhill
Drumdroch
Newfield
Milrig
Cairnhill
West Burnhead
Greenfield
Anderside Hill
Black Loch Moss
Bankend Rig
Regal Hill
257
Mean Muir
Logan Moss
Distinkhorn 386
Whitehill Fm
Burn
Langside
Lawdyke
Avon Head
Laird Knowe
Little Hartmidden
Twopenny Knowe
Bibblon Hill 431
Leaze Burn
Priesthill Height 493
Bogend
Brown's Muir
Flacket Hill
Starpet Rig 451
Dippal Rig
Head of Greenock Water
Bruntwood Mains
Wynds
Tongue
Grange Muir
Hart Hill
Burnt Hill
Meanlour Hill
Hare Craig
Rodinghead
Low Holehouse
Meadowhead
Crofthead
Knockdon
Wedder Hill 434
Middlefield Law 466
Priesthill
Roughdyke Fm
Boghead
Auchmannoch
South Auchenbrain
Weitshaw Muir
Reppoch Knowe
Craigs Hill
Sclanor Hill
Blackside
Barboigh
Barwheys
Auchmillan
Darnhay
Weitshaw
Pepper Knowe
Auchenlongford Hill
Stony Hill
Dun Rig
Greenock Bridge
Black Hill
Glenbu
Auchmillanhill
Blackbriggs
Oxenshaw
Upper Hall
A76
Kilmarnock Road
Brigland
Wealth of Waters
Heath Cottage
Aikencleugh
Netherwood
Lightshaw
Laigh Hall
Tardoes
Garfield
Redgate
Meath Hill
Earl Hill
Mauchline Mains
Sorn Mains
Tincorn Hill
Limmerhaugh Muir
Greenock Mains
Marchouse Hill
Burnfoot Moor
Muirkirk
Crossflatt
Brack Hill
Lauriand
Burns House Museum
Blindburn
Mauchline
Welton
Grassmillees
Catrine Mains
Sorn Castle
Sorn
Nethershield
Daldilling
Dalgain
River Ayr
Smallburn
Smallburn Road
Auldhouseburn
Hawlk Hill
Wee Hill
Kames
Catrine
Whiteflat
Barrshouse
Upper Heilar
Midwellwood Fm
Haugh
Kingencleugh Ho
Logan
Gilmilnscroft
High Wood
EAST
Little Cairn Table
The Steel
Catrineshaw
Kenstey
Bogend
Airds Moss
Boghead Lane
Wood Hill
Syke
High Clews
Brackenhill
Roundshaw Fm
Cairn Table 593
Little Heateth
AYRSHIRE
Drumfork
Meikle Heateth
Glensham Rock Fm
Cairn Hill
Garpel Water
Slatehole
Treeshill
Townhead
Darnlaw
Back Rogerton
Common
Cronberry
Dalfad Moss
Knockbreck
Whiteyards
Wardlaw Hill 497
Fingland Hill 462
Panbreck Hill
Blackfauldhead
Knowe
Knagshill
Commondyke Fm
Muirkirk Road
Mid Hill
Barfurk
Pennymore
B7036
Baronty Road
Auchinleck
Dykes Fm
Lugar
Wallaceton
Lairds Burn
Thirdpart
Boswell Mausoleum
Stony Hill 562
Ochiltree
Lugar Water
Holmhead
Gass Water
Carston
Logan
Low Moss
Dornal Moss
Glenmuir Hill
Connor Hill
Drummond's Knowe
White Hill 480
Mote Toll
Ochiltree Mains
Laigh Tarbeg
Grimgrow
Cumnock
Kier Hardie Statue
Barshare
Little Auchengibbert
Crosslar
Garleffan Fm
High Dalblair
East Foredibban Hill
Nether Black Law
Black Law
Back o' Hill
Orchardton
Netherthird
Dalblair
Fingland Lane
High Carston
Crosshill
Horsecleugh Fm
Craigens
Borland Mains
Avisyard Hill 330
Roughhill Moss
Whiteholm
Benalt 382
Black Hill 431
Auchtitench Hill 467
Earl Hill
Rottenrow
Knockshiffnock
Barmickhill
Bus Pk
Burnock Mill
Skares
Skares Road
Greenside
Dumfries Road
Crawford Hill
Airds Hill
Over Guelt
Shiel Rig
Crook Brae 385
Clocklowie Hill 442
Dennigall Hill
Fing
Fingland Burn
Garlaff
Mossback
High Burnside
Berland
Cairnscadden Hill 314
Edge Hill 345
Auchlin
The Muir
Glaisnock
Calton Fm
High Polquheys
Millstone Knowe
Halfmerk Hill 453
511
507
Kirkland Hill
Black Loch
Carnivan Hill 324
White Knowe
Benston Fm
Lochhill
Rottenyard
Roughside
Craigdullyeart Hill
Niviston Hill 460
Lethans Hill
Todholes 481
Auchlin Rig
Polquheys
Glenwharrie
Burnockhead
High Mount 365
Carsgailoch Hill
Hall of Auchincross
Loch o' th' Lowes
Pathhead
Hall of Mansfield
Corsencon Hill 475
Lagrae
Kirkland
Guffock Hill
Todholes
Mansfield
New Cumnock
Greenhill
Fordmouth
North Boig
Mansfield Mains
Corsencon
Black Hill
Woodend
Connel Park
East Polquhirter
Meikle Westland
Glen Hall
Laigh Cairn
Kirkland Plantn
Stannery Knowe 363
Tappet Hill
Dalricket Mill
Dalgig
Bankglen
West Polquhirter
Over Cairn
River Nith
Brown Hill
Mid Hill
Hungry Hill
West Park Fm
High Park
Burntonhill
High Cairn
Rigg Fm
Nether Cairn
Kelloside
Kirkconnel
Kelloholm
Over Hill
Lingie Hill
Little Rigend Hill
Laight Fm
Burnt Hill
Polhote Burn
Dalhanna Hill
Sunnyside
Burnfoot Road
Burnside
Lanehead
Dalhanna Fm
White Hill 406
White Knowe
Libry Moor
Upper Beoch
Straid Fm
Dalleagles
Brockloch
Knocknide Hill 344
Lochbrowan Hill
575
High Cairn 553
McCrierick's Cairn 556
Peat Hill 385
Blarene Hill 358
Polnagrie Hill
Corserig Hill 395
Glengape
NS
Benbain
Nith
Ashmark Hill
Hare Hill
Polstacher Burn
Polnagrie Hill 418
246
Chang Hill 463
Benty Cowan Hill 477
Ewe Hill 437
Laglass Hill
Quintin Knowe 554
527
Hog Hill
Brunt Rig
Barr Moor
Barbeys
0 1 2 3 miles
0 1 2 3 4 5 km
267
268

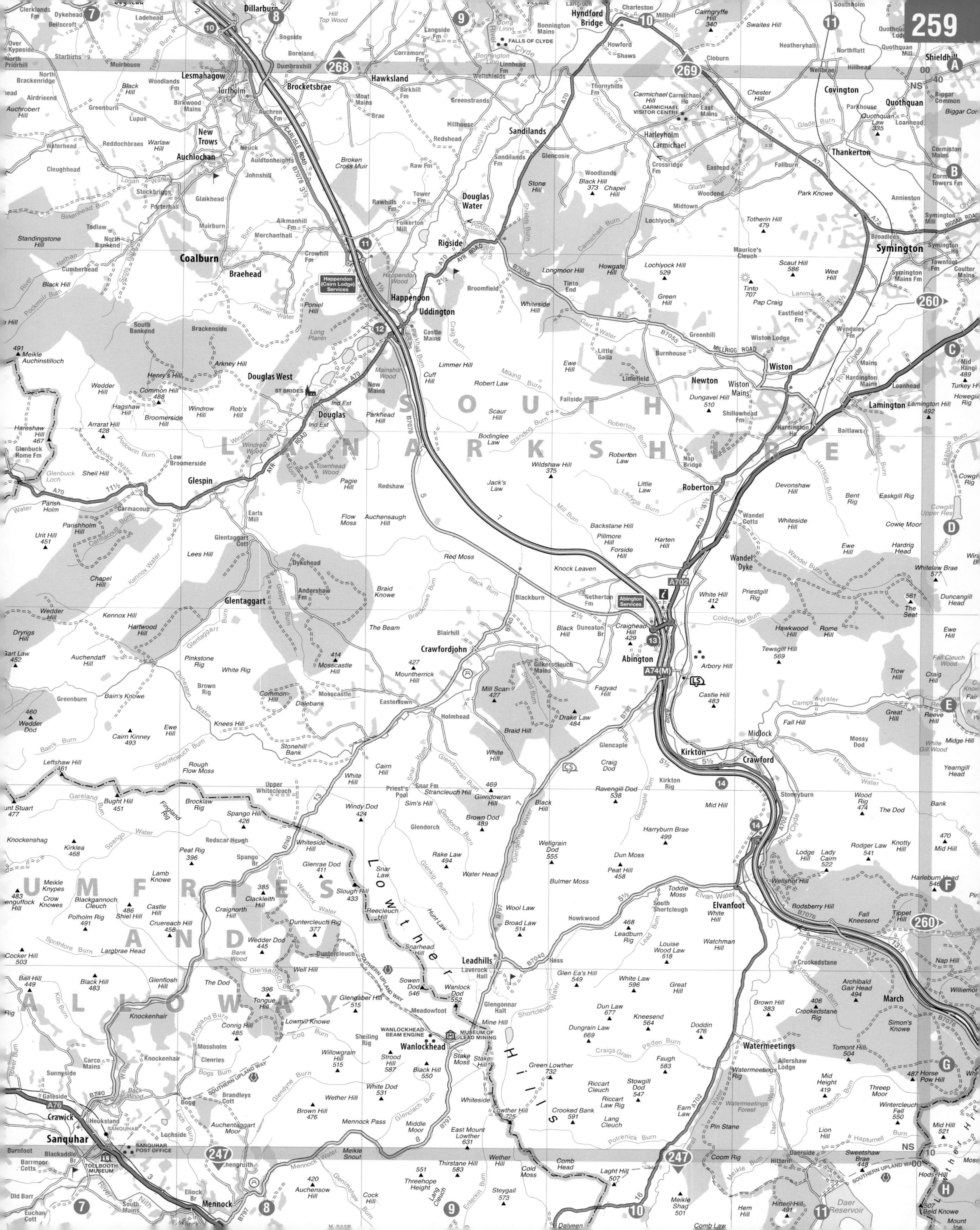

SOUTH LANARKSHIRE
DUMFRIES AND GALLOWAY
Lowther Hills
Dillarburn
Hyndford Bridge
Charleston
Millhill
Cairngryffe Hill 340
Swaites Hill
Heatheryhall
Northflatt
Shieldhill
Lesmahagow
Turfholm
Brocketsbrae
Hawksland
Dumbraxhill
Corramore Fm
Linnhead Fm
Wellshields
FALLS OF CLYDE
Bonnington Mains
Howford
Shaws
Cloburn
Wellbrae
Covington
Quothquan
Biggar Common
Chester Hill
Carmichael Hill
CARMICHAEL VISITOR CENTRE
East Mains
Sandilands
Harleyholm
Carmichael
Thankerton
New Trows
Auchlochan
Auldtonheights
Broken Cross Muir
Greenstrands
Redshead
Glencosie
Crossridge Fm
Eastend
Woodlands
Black Hill 373
Chapel Hill
Stone Hill
Woodend
Park Knowe
Annieston
Douglas Water
Rawhills Fm
Tower Mains
Folkerton Mill
Rigside
Midtown
Lochlyoch
Totherin Hill 479
Symington
Coalburn
Braehead
Merchanthall
Crowhill Fm
Happendon (Cairn Lodge) Services
Happendon
Uddington
Longmoor Hill
Howgate Hill
Lochlyock Hill 529
Scaut Hill 586
Tinto 707
Wee Hill
Pap Craig
Green Hill
Tinto End
Broomfield
Whiteside Hill
Eastfield Fm
Wyndales Fm
Brackenside
South Bankend
Poniel Hill
Long Plantn
Castle Mains
Limmer Hill
Cuff Hill
Greenhill
Wiston Lodge
Burnhouse
Wiston
Meikle Auchinstilloch 491
Arkney Hill
Henry's Hill
Common Hill 488
Douglas West
ST BRIDES
Douglas
New Mains
Robert Law
Ewe Hill
Little Galla
Limefield
Newton
Wiston Mains
Dungavel Hill 510
Shillowhead Fm
Lamington
Lamington Hill 492
Wedder Hill
Hagshaw Hill
Windrow Hill
Rob's Hill
Broomerside Hill
Parkhead Hill
Scaur Hill
Fallside
Hardington Ho
Baitlaws
Hareshaw Hill 467
Arrarat Hill 428
Glenbuck Home Fm
Low Broomerside
Townhead Wood
Bodinglee Law
Wildshaw Hill 375
Roberton Law
Nap Bridge
Sheil Hill
Glespin
Pagie Hill
Redshaw
Jack's Law
Little Law
Roberton
Devonshaw Hill
Bent Rig
Easkgill Rig
Parish Holm
Carmacoup
Earls Mill
Flow Moss
Auchensaugh Hill
Backstane Hill
Pillmore Hill
Forside Hill
Harten Hill
Wandel Cotts
Whiteside Hill
Cowie Moor
Parishholm Hill
Urit Hill 451
Glentaggart Cott
Lees Hill
Red Moss
Knock Leaven
Wandel Dyke
Ewe Hill
Hardrig Head
Chapel Hill
Dykehead
Andershaw Fm
Braid Knowe
Blackburn
Netherton Fm
Abington Services
White Hill 412
Priestgill Rig
Whitelaw Brae 577
Duncangill Head
The Seat 561
Glentaggart
Wedder Hill
Kennox Hill
Hartwood Hill
The Beam
Blairhill
Black Hill
Duneaton Br
Craighead Hill 429
Hawkwood Hill
Rome Hill
Ewe Hill
Drygrigs Hill
Gart Law 452
Auchendaff Hill
Pinkstone Rig
White Rig
Mosscastle Hill 414
Crawfordjohn
Mountherrick Hill 427
Gilkerscleuch Mains
Abington
Arbory Hill
Tewsgill Hill 569
Brown Rig
Common Hill
Mosscastle
Dalebank
Eastertown
Mill Scar 427
Fagyad Hill
Castle Hill 483
Trow Hill
Craig Hill
Bain's Knowe
Greenburn
Cairn Kinney 493
Ewe Hill
Knees Hill
Holmhead
Braid Hill
Drake Law 484
Great Hill
Reeve Hill
Wedder Dod 460
Stonehill Bank
Glencaple
Midlock
Fall Hill
Mossy Dod
Midge Hill
Leftshaw Hill 461
Rough Flow Moss
White Hill
Cairn Hill
White Hill
Craig Dod
Kirkton
Crawford
Yearngill Head
Bught Hill 451
Brocklaw Rig
Upper Whitecleuch
Priest's Pool
Snar Fm
Strancleuch Hill
Glendowran Hill 469
Ravengill Dod 538
Kirkton Rig
Stoneyburn
Wood Rig 474
The Dod
Bank
Spango Hill 426
Windy Dod 424
Sim's Hill
Brown Dod 489
Black Hill
Mid Hill
Knockenshag
Kirklea 468
Redscar Heugh
Whiteside Hill
Glendorch
Harryburn Brae 499
Rodger Law 541
Knotty Hill
Mid Hill 470
Peat Rig 396
Spango Br
Rake Law 494
Wellgrain Dod 555
Dun Moss
Lodge Hill
Lady Cairn 522
Lamb Knowe
Glenrae Dod 411
Snar Law
Water Head
Peat Hill 458
Bulmer Moss
Wellshot Hill
Harleburn Head 546
Meikle Knypes
Crow Knowes
Blackgannoch Cleuch
Clackleith Hill 385
Slough Hill 433
Toddle Moss
South Shortcleugh
Elvanfoot
Bodsberry Hill
Polholm Rig 491
Shiel Hill 486
Castle Hill
Craignorth Hill
Reecleuch Hill
Wool Law
Howkwood
White Hill
Fall Kneesend
Tippet Hill
Cruereach Hill 458
Duntercleuch Rig 377
Broad Law 514
Leadburn Rig 468
Louise Wood Law 618
Watchman Hill
Cocker Hill 503
Largbrae Head
Wedder Dod 445
Bank Wood
Duntercleuch
Snarhead Hill
Leadhills
Hass
Crookedstane
Nap Hill
Ball Hill 449
Black Hill 483
Glenflosh Hill
The Dod
Well Hill
Sowen Dod 546
Wanlock Dod 552
Laverock Hall
Glen Ea's Hill 549
White Law 596
Great Hill
Archibald Gair Head 494
March
Williemor
Tongue Hill 396
Glengaber Hill 515
Glengonnar Halt
Dun Law 677
Brown Hill 383
Crookedstane Rig 406
Knockenhair
Lowmill Knowe
Meadowfoot
Mine Hill
Kneesend 564
Dungrain Law 669
Doddin 476
Simon's Knowe
Conrig Hill 485
WANLOCKHEAD BEAM ENGINE
MUSEUM OF LEAD MINING
Sheiling Rig
Wanlockhead
Mossholm
Carco Mains
Clenries
Willowgrain Hill 515
Stroud Hill 587
Black Hill 550
Stake Moss
Stake Hill
Faugh 583
Watermeetings
Tomont Hill 504
Knockenhair
Sunnyside
Bogs Burn
Green Lowther 732
Allershaw Lodge
Horse Pow Hill 487
Gateside
Back Wood
Brandleys Cott
Wether Hill
White Dod 531
Whiteside
Riccart Cleuch
Stowgill Dod 547
Watermeetings Rig
Mid Height 419
Threep Moor
Crawick
Heuksland
SANQUHAR
Bogg
Lochside
Brown Hill 476
Lowther Hill 725
Crooked Bank 591
Riccart Law Rig
Lang Cleuch
Earn Law
Watermeetings Forest
Wintercleuch Fell 550
Sanquhar
Auchentaggart Moor
Mennock Pass
Middle Moor
East Mount Lowther 631
Pin Stane
Lion Hill
Mid Hill 521
Burnfoot
Blackaddie Br
SANQUHAR POST OFFICE
TOLLBOOTH MUSEUM
Chengruith
Meikle Snout
Thirstane Hill 583
Wether Hill
Cold Moss
Comb Head
Laght Hill 507
Coom Rig
Hitteril
Daerside
Sweetshaw Brae 448
Hods Hill
Barrmoor Cotts
Threehope Height 551
Steygail 573
Old Barr
Elioch Br
Auchensow Hill 420
Cock Hill
Lang Cleuch
Meikle Shag 501
Hem Hill
Hitteril Hill 491
Daer Reservoir
Beld Knowe 507
Euchan Cott
South Mains
Mennock
Dalveen
Comb Law
SOUTHERN UPLAND WAY
A70
A73
A72
A702
A74(M)
A76
B7078
B7055
B740
B797
B7040
B7076
CARLISLE ROAD
AYR ROAD
MILLRIGG ROAD
BIGGAR ROAD
NS
00
40
10
268
269
260
247

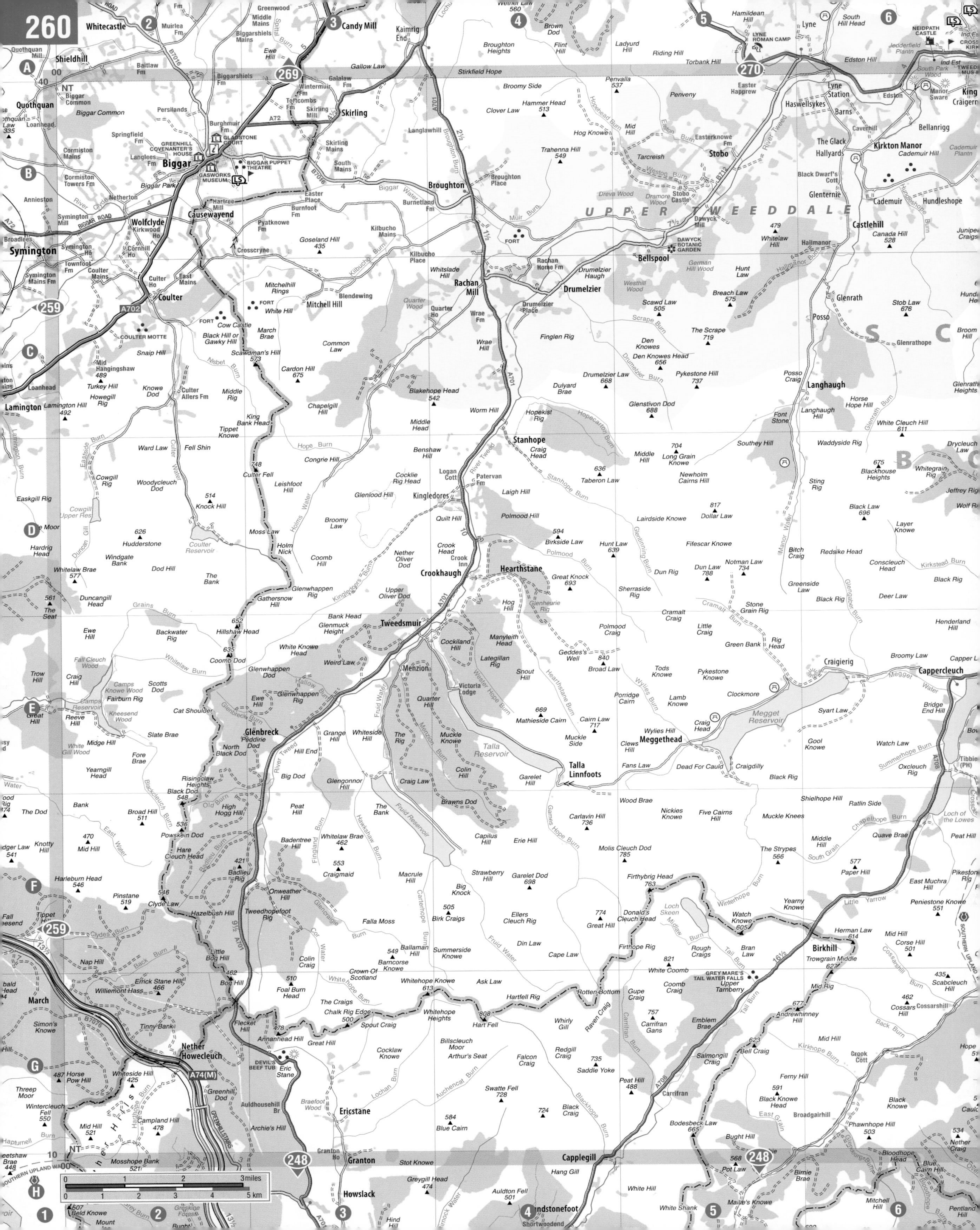

Whitecastle
Candy Mill
Kaimrig End
Broughton Heights
Flint Hill
Ladyurd Hill
Riding Hill
Hamildean Hill
Lyne
Lyne Roman Camp
South Hill Head
Neidpath Castle
Quothquan Mill
Shieldhill
Muirlea Fm
Greenwood
Middle Mains
Biggarshiels Mains
Ewe Hill
Gallow Law
Stirkfield Hope
Torbank Hill
Edston Hill
Baitlaw Fm
Biggarshiels Fm
Galalaw Fm
Wintermuir Fm
Toftcombs Fm
Skirling Mill
Skirling
Broomy Side
Penvalla 537
Easter Happrew
Lyne Station
Haswellsykes
Barns
Edston
Manor Sware
Quothquan
Biggar Common
Persilands
Clover Law
Hammer Head 513
Penveny
Caverhill
Bellanrigg
Burghmuir Fm
Springfield Fm
Greenhill Covenanter's House
Gladstone Court
Langlawhill
Broughton Burn
Hopehead Burn
Mid Hill
Hog Knowe
Easterknowe Fm
The Glack
Hallyards
Kirkton Manor
Cademuir Hill
Cormiston Mains
Langlees Fm
Biggar
Biggar Puppet Theatre
Gasworks Museum
Skirling Mains
South Mains
Trahenna Hill 549
Tarcreish
Stobo
Cormiston Towers Fm
Biggar Park
Broughton
Broughton Place
Weston Burn
Black Dwarf's Cott
Glenternie
Cademuir
Hundleshope
Annieston
Netherton
Hartree Mill
Easter Place
Burnetland Fm
Dreva Wood
Dramore Wood
Stobo Castle
Symington Mill
Wolfclyde
Kirkwood Ho
Causewayend
Burnfoot Fm
Pyatknowe Fm
Upper Tweeddale
Dawyck Mill
479 Whitelaw Hill
Castlehill
Canada Hill 528
Symington
Symington Ho
Cornhill Ho
Crosscryne
Goseland Hill 435
Kilbucho Mains
Fort
Dawyck Botanic Garden
Bellspool
Hallmanor
Townfoot Fm
Coulter Mains
Kilbucho Place
Whitslade Hill
Rachan Home Fm
Drumelzier Haugh
German Hill Wood
Hunt Law
Symington Mains Fm
Culter Ho
East Mains
Mitchellhill Rings
Rachan Mill
Drumelzier
Westhill Wood
Breach Law 575
Glenrath
Coulter
Blendewing
Mitchell Hill
Quarter Wood
Quarter Ho
Drumelzier Place
Scawd Law 505
Stob Law 676
Fort
White Hill
Wrae Fm
Scrape Burn
Posso
Coulter Motte
Cow Castle
Black Hill or Gawky Hill
March Brae
Wrae Hill
Finglen Rig
The Scrape 719
Den Knowes
Glenrathope
Broom Hill
Snaip Hill
Common Law
Den Knowes Head 656
Nisbet Burn
Scawdman's Hill 573
Mid Hangingshaw 489
Cardon Hill 675
Drumelzier Law 668
Pykestone Hill 737
Posso Craig
Langhaugh
Turkey Hill
Howegill Rig
Knowe Dod
Culter Allers Fm
Middle Rig
Blakehope Head 542
Dulyard Brae
Horse Hope Hill
Loanhead
Lamington
Lamington Hill 492
Chapelgill Hill
King Bank Head
Worm Hill
Hopekist Rig
Glenstivon Dod 688
Font Stone
Langhaugh Hill
Middle Head
Tippet Knowe
Hopecarton Burn
White Cleuch Hill 611
Ward Law
Fell Shin
Hope Burn
Benshaw Hill
Stanhope
Craig Head
Middle Hill
704 Long Grain Knowe
Southey Hill
Waddyside Rig
Drycleuch Law
Congrie Hill
748 Culter Fell
Logan Cott
River Tweed
Patervan Fm
Taberon Law 636
Newholm Cairns Hill
Blackhouse Heights 675
Whitegrain Rig
Cowgill Rig
Woodycleuch Dod
Leishfoot Hill
Cocklie Rig Head
Glenlood Hill
Kingledores
Laigh Hill
Stanhope Burn
Sting Rig
Jeffrey Rig
514 Knock Hill
Easkgill Rig
Cowgill Upper Res
Quilt Hill
Polmood Hill
817 Dollar Law
Lairdside Knowe
Black Law 696
Wolf Rig
Broomy Law
Layer Knowe
De Moor
626 Hudderstone
Moss Law
594 Birkside Law
Fifescar Knowe
Hardrig Head
Coulter Reservoir
Holm Nick
Crook Head
Nether Oliver Dod
Crook Inn
Hunt Law 639
Polmood Burn
Bitch Craig
Redsike Head
Consclecuch Head
Kirkstead Burn
Windgate Bank
Coomb Hill
Hearthstane
Whitelaw Brae 577
Dod Hill
The Bank
Crookhaugh
Great Knock 693
Dun Rig
Dun Law 788
Notman Law 734
Black Rig
Glenwhappen Rig
Sherraside Rig
Greenside Law
Upper Oliver Dod
Duncangill Head
561 The Seat
Gathersnow Hill
Hog Hill
Glenheurie Rig
Stone Grain Rig
Black Rig
Deer Law
Grains Burn
Bank Head
Glenmuck Height
Cramalt Craig
Backwater Rig
652 Hillshaw Head
Tweedsmuir
Polmood Craig
Little Craig
Henderland Hill
Ewe Hill
Manyleith Head
Rig Head
Green Bank
White Knowe Head
Cockiland Hill
635 Coomb Dod
Lategillan Rig
Geddes's Well
840 Broad Law
Broomy Law
Capper Law
Fall Cleuch Wood
Whitelaw Burn
Weird Law
Menzion
Craigierig
Cappercleuch
Craig Hill
Glenwhappen Dod
Snout Hill
Tods Knowe
Pykestone Knowe
Megget Water
Trow Hill
Camps Knowe Wood
Scotts Dod
Glenwhappen Rig
Victoria Lodge
Quarter Hill
Porridge Cairn
Clockmore
Lamb Knowe
Syart Law
Bridge End Hill
Fairburn Rig
Ewe Hill
Cat Shoulder
Camps Reservoir
Kneesend Wood
Great Hill
Reeve Hill
Slate Brae
Glenbreck
Peddirie Dod
Grange Hill
Whiteside Hill
The Rig
Muckle Knowe
669 Mathieside Cairn
Cairn Law 717
Craig Head
Megget Reservoir
Wylies Hill
Meggethead
Clews Hill
Gool Knowe
Watch Law
White Gill Wood
Midge Hill
Fore Brae
North Black Dod
Hill End
Talla Reservoir
Muckle Side
Fans Law
Talla Linnfoots
Dead For Cauld
Craigdilly
Summerhope Burn
Oxcleuch Rig
Tibbie (PH)
Yearngill Head
Risingclaw Heights
Big Dod
Glengonnor Hill
Craig Law
Colin Hill
Garelet Hill
Black Rig
Black Dod 548
Wood Brae
Shielhope Hill
Ratlin Side
Bank
The Dod
High Hogg Hill
Broad Hill 511
Peat Hill
The Bank
Fruid Reservoir
Brawns Dod
Carlavin Hill 736
Nickies Knowe
Five Cairns Hill
Muckle Knees
Loch of the Lowes
536 Powskein Dod
Badentree Hill
Whitelaw Brae 462
Capilus Hill
Erie Hill
Games Hope Burn
Chapelhope Burn
Middle Hill
Quave Brae
Peat Hill
470 Mid Hill
Knotty Hill
Hare Cleuch Head
Molis Cleuch Dod 785
The Strypes 566
Law 541
421 Badlieu Rig
553 Craigmaid
Macrule Hill
Strawberry Hill
Garelet Dod 698
Firthybrig Head 763
577 Paper Hill
East Muchra Hill
Pikestone Rig
Harleburn Head 546
Pinstane 519
546 Clyde Law
Onweather Hill
Big Knock
Winterhope Burn
Little Yarrow
Yearny Knowe
Peniestone Knowe 551
Hazelbush Hill
Tweedhopefoot Rig
505 Birk Craigs
Falla Moss
Ellers Cleuch Rig
774 Great Hill
Donald's Cleuch Head
Loch Skeen
Watch Knowe 605
Herman Law 614
Mid Hill
Corse Hill 501
Tippet Hill
Clydes Burn
Little Bog Hill
Colin Craig
Ballaman Hill
549 Barncorse Knowe
Summerside Knowe
Din Law
Cape Law
Firthope Rig
Rough Craigs
Bran Law
Birkhill
Trowgrain Middle 627
Nap Hill
Errick Stane Hill 466
462 Bog Hill
Crown Of Scotland
510 Foal Burn Head
Whitehope Knowe 613
Ask Law
821 White Coomb
Grey Mare's Tail Waterfalls
Upper Tamberry
435 Scabcleuch Hill
March
Williemont Hass
The Craigs
Chalk Rig Edge 500
Whitehope Heights
Hartfell Rig
Rotten Bottom
Gupe Craig
Coomb Craig
Mid Rig
462 Cossars Hill
Cossarshill
Simon's Knowe
Tinny Bank
Flecket Hill
478 Annanhead Hill
Spout Craig
808 Hart Fell
Whirly Gill
Raven Craig
757 Carrifran Gans
Emblem Brae
677 Andrewhinney Hill
Nether Howecleuch
Great Hill
Billscleuch Moor
Arthur's Seat
Redgill Craig
735 Saddle Yoke
Salmongill Craig
623 Bell Craig
Mid Hill
Crook Cott
Hope
Devil's Beef Tub
Eric Stane
Cocklaw Knowe
Falcon Craig
Peat Hill 488
Ferny Hill
487 Horse Pow Hill
Whiteside Hill 425
Greenhill Dod
Swatte Fell 728
Carrifran
591 Black Knowe Head
Black Knowe
Threep Moor
Wintercleuch Fell 550
Auldhousehill Br
Braefoot Wood
Ericstane
724
Black Craig
Broadgairhill
Campland Hill 478
584 Blue Cairn
Bodesbeck Law 665
Phawnhope Hill 503
Mid Hill 521
Archie's Hill
Bught Hill
534 Nether Craig
Mosshope Bank 521
Granton Ho
Granton
Stot Knowe
Capplegill
568 Pot Law
Bloodhope Head
Blue Cairn Hill
Southern Upland Way
Greygill Head 474
Hang Gill
Birnie Brae
Howslack
Auldton Fell 501
White Hill
White Shank
Maiden's Knowe
Mitchell Hill
Pentland Hill
507 Beld Knowe
Mount
Shortwoodend
Hind Hill
A701
A702
A72
A708
A74(M)
B7016
B712
B7076
269
270
259
248
0 1 2 3 miles
0 1 2 3 4 5 km

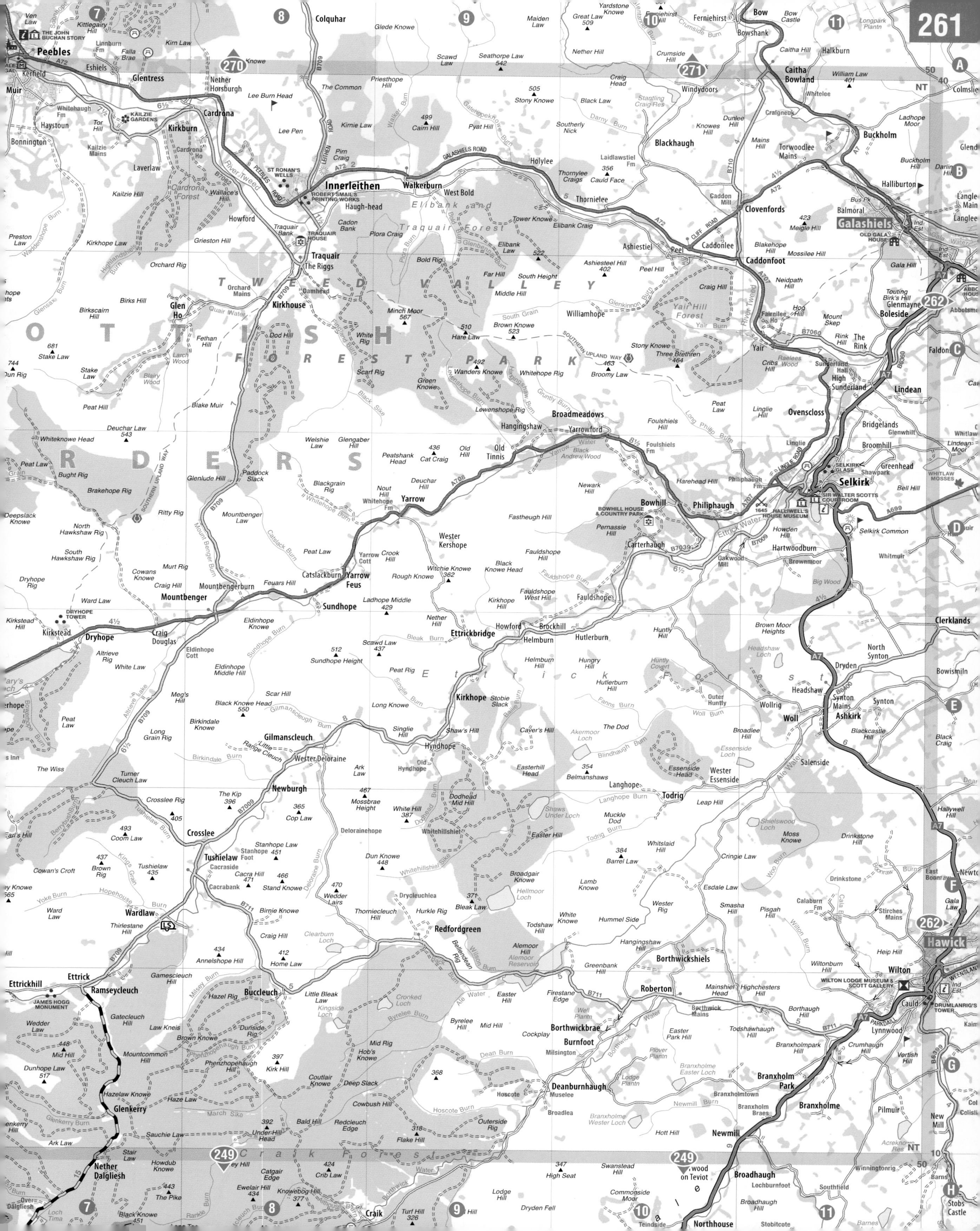

Peebles
Innerleithen
Walkerburn
Galashiels
Selkirk
Hawick
Traquair
Yarrow
Ettrickbridge
Tweed Valley Forest Park
Scottish Borders
Ettrick Forest
Craik Forest
Clovenfords
Caddonfoot
Ashkirk
Roberton
Ettrick
Wilton

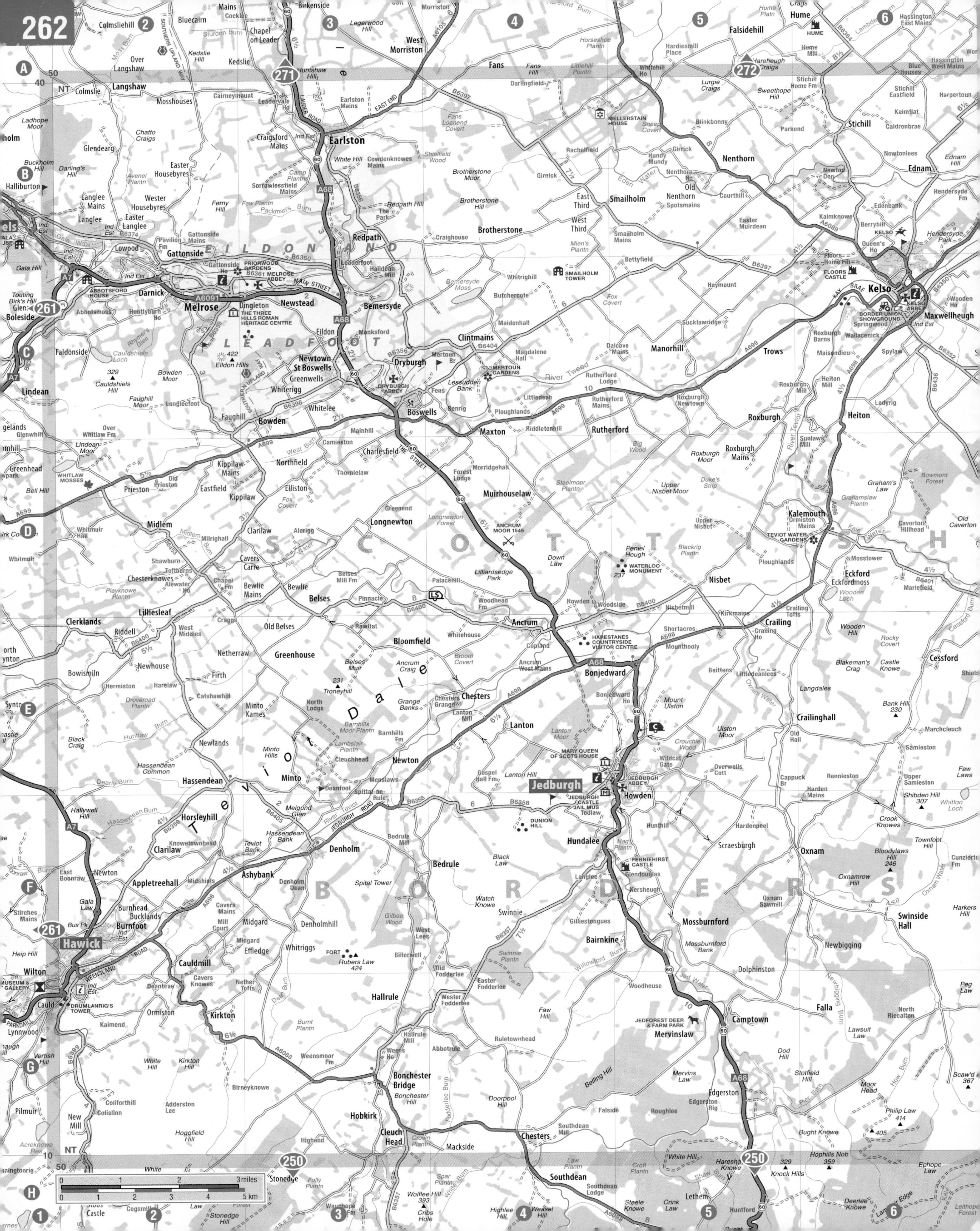
Colmsliehill
Bluecairn
Mains
Cocklee
Chapel on Leader
Birkenside
Legerwood Hill
Morriston
West Morriston
Hume
Falsidehill
HUME
Hassington East Mains
Over Langshaw
Kedslie Hill
Kedslie
Huntshaw Hill
271
Fans
Fans Hill
Horseshoe Plantn
Hardiesmill Place
Hume Mill
Harehaugh Craigs
272
Whitehill Ho
Littlefield Plantn
Hassington West Mains
Blue Houses
Colmslie
Langshaw
Cairneymount
Leadervale Ho
LAUDER ROAD
Darlingfield
Lurgie Craigs
Stichill Home Fm
Sweethope Hill
Stichill Eastfield
Harpertoun
Mosshouses
Earlston Mains
EAST END
B6397
Fans Loanend Covert
MELLERSTAIN HOUSE
Sneep Covert
Blinkbonny
Stichill
Kaimflat
Caldronbrae
Ladhope Moor
Chatto Craigs
Craigsford Mains
Ind Est
Earlston
Parkend
Glendearg
White Hill
Cowdenknowes Mains
Shielfield Wood
Rachelfield
Hundy Mundy
Girrick
Nenthorn
Newtonlees
Ednam Hill
Buckholm Hill
Darling's Hill
Easter Housebyres
Avenel Plantn
Camp Plantns
Brotherstone Moor
Girnick
Eden Water
Nenthorn Ho
Old Nenthorn
Newton Don
Ednam
Halliburton
Sorrowlessfield Mains
Redpath Hill
Brotherstone Hill
East Third
Smailholm
Spotsmains
Courthill
Hendersyde Fm
Langlee Mains
Wester Housebyres
Ferny Hill
Faw Plantn
Packman's Burn
The Park
Edenbank
Langlee
Easter Langlee
West Third
Easter Muirdean
Kaimknowe
Berryhill
Ind Est
Gattonside Mains
Redpath
Craighouse
Brotherstone
Smailholm Mains
KELSO
Hendersyde Park
Pavilion Fm
Lowood
Gattonside
EILDON AND
Mien's Plantn
Queen's Ho
Floors Home Fm
Gala Hill
Ind Est
PRIORWOOD GARDENS
Leaderfoot
Bettyfield
B6397
FLOORS CASTLE
MELROSE ABBEY
Halidean Mill
SMAILHOLM TOWER
Whitrighill
Haymount
Kelso
Wooden Ho
Touting Birk's Hill
ABBOTSFORD HOUSE
Darnick
MAIN STREET
Bemersyde Moss
Butchercote
Fox Covert
BORDER UNION SHOWGROUND
Springwood
Maxwellheugh
Glen
261
Boleside
Melrose
A6091
Dingleton
Newstead
THE THREE HILLS ROMAN HERITAGE CENTRE
Bemersyde
Maidenhall
Sucklawridge
Wallacenick
Ind Est
Abbotsmoss
Huntlyburn Ho
Eildon
Monksford
Clintmains
Dalcove Mains
Manorhill
Trows
Roxburgh Barns
Maisondieu
Spylaw
Faldonside
Cauldshiels Loch
LEADFOOT
Newtown St Boswells
Dryburgh
Mertoun Br
Magdalene Hall
MERTOUN GARDENS
River Tweed
Rutherford Lodge
329 Cauldshiels Hill
422 Eildon Hills
Bowden Moor
Greenwells
DRYBURGH ABBEY
Lessudden Bank
Fens
Littledean
Roxburgh Mill
Heiton Mill
Lindean
Whiterigg
Faughill Moor
Longleefoot
St Boswells
Benrig
Ploughlands
Rutherford Mains
Roxburgh Newtown
Roxburgh
Heiton
Ladyrig
Faughill
Bowden
Whitelee
Riddletonhill
Maxton
Rutherford
Over Whitlaw Fm
Mainhill
Camieston
Charlesfield
THE STREET
Kelly Burn
Big Wood
Roxburgh Moor
Roxburgh Mains
Sunlaws Mill
Lindean Moor
West Burn
Northfield
Kippilaw Mains
Morridgehall
Greenhead
Thornielaw
Forest Lodge
Steelmoor Plantn
Upper Nisbet Moor
Duke's Strip
Graham's Law
Bowmont Forest
WHITLAW MOSSES
Old Prieston
Prieston
Eastfield
Elliston
Muirhouselaw
Grahamslaw Plantn
Bell Hill
Kippilaw
Fox Covert
Greenend
Kalemouth
Ormiston Mains
Old Caverton
Caverton Hillhead
Whitmuir Hall
Midlem
Longnewton
Longnewton Forest
ANCRUM MOOR 1545
Upper Nisbet
TEVIOT WATER GARDENS
Milrighall
Clarilaw
Alerigg
SCOTTISH
Down Law
Peniel Heugh
Blackrig Plantn
Whitmuir
Shawburn
Cavers Carre
Ale Water
WATERLOO MONUMENT
Ploughlands
Mosstower
Toftbarns
237
Eckford
Eckfordmoss
Marlefield
Chesterknowes
Alewater Ho
Chapel Fm
Bewlie Mains
Bewlie
Belses Mill Fm
Palacehill
Lilliardsedge Park
Nisbet
Wooden Loch
Playknowe Plantn
Belses
Pinnacle
Woodhead Fm
Howden
Woodside
B6400
Nisbetmill
Lilliesleaf
Kirkmains
Crailing Tofts
Clerklands
Cragss
Old Belses
Rawflat
Ancrum
Crailing
Riddell
West Middles
Whitehouse
HARESTANES COUNTRYSIDE VISITOR CENTRE
Shortacres
Crailing Ho
Wooden Hill
Rocky Covert
Cessford
Netherraw
Greenhouse
Bloomfield
Copland
Mounthooly
Newhouse
Belses Muir
Ancrum Craig
Broom Covert
Ancrum West Mains
Bonjedward
Baittens
Littledeanlees
Blakeman's Crag
Castle Knowe
Bowismiln
Firth
231 Troneyhill
Dale
Bonjedward Ho
Langdales
Hermiston
Harelaw
Catshawhill
Minto Kames
North Lodge
Grange Banks
Chesters Grange
Chesters
Mount Ulston
Oxnam Water
Bank Hill 230
Droveroad Plantn
Lanton Mill
Lanton
Crailinghall
Black Craig
Huntlaw
Bamhills Moor Plantn
Barnhills Fm
Lanton Moor
Ulston Moor
Old Hall
Marchcleuch
Newlands
Minto Hills
Lambslair Plantn
Crouchie Wood
Samieston
Hassendean Common
Cleuchhead
Newton
MARY QUEEN OF SCOTS HOUSE
Wildcat Gate
Overwells Cott
Faw Laws
Dearly Burn
Hassendean
Minto
Deanfoot
Menslaws
Gospel Hall Fm
Lanton Hill
Cappuck Br
Rennieston
Upper Samieston
Teviot
Spittal-on-Rule
Jedburgh
JEDBURGH ABBEY
Howden
Harden Mains
Shibden Hill 307
Whitton Loch
Hallywell Hill
Hassendean Burn
Horsleyhill
Melgund Glen
River Teviot
JEDBURGH ROAD
B6358
JEDBURGH CASTLE JAIL MUS
Todlaw
DUNION HILL
Hunthill
Hardenpeel
Crook Knowes
Knowetownhead
Hassendean Bank
Teviot Bank
Denholm
Bedrule Mill
Hundalee
Scraesburgh
Townfoot Hill
Clarilaw
Oxnam
Bloodylaws Hill 246
Cunzierton Fm
East Boonraw
Newton
Appletreehall
Midshiels
Ashybank
Denholm Dean
BORDERS
Bedrule
Black Law
FERNIEHIRST CASTLE
Glendouglas
Oxnamrow Hill
Spital Tower
Langlee
Kersheugh
Stirches Mains
Gala Law
Burnhead
Bucklands
Cavers Mains
Watch Knowe
Swinnie
Oxnam Sawmill
Swinside Hall
Harkers Hill
Bus Pk
Burnfoot
Mill Court
Midgard
Denholmhill
Gilboa Wood
West Lees
Gilliestongues
Mossburnford
261
Hawick
Ind Est
Midgard
Effledge
Whitriggs
FORT
Rubers Law 424
Billerwell
Swinnie Plantn
Bairnkine
Mossburnford Bank
Newbigging
Heip Hill
Wilton
WEENSLAND
Cauldmill
Willowford Burn
Dolphinston
MUSEUM & GALLERY
Ind Est
Cavers Knowes
Nether Tofts
Old Fodderlee
Easter Fodderlee
Woodhouse
Peg Law
Cauld
Deanbrae
Hallrule
Wester Fodderlee
Newbigging Burn
DRUMLANRIG'S TOWER
Ormiston
Kirkton
Burnt Plantn
Faw Hill
JEDFOREST DEER & FARM PARK
Mervinslaw
Camptown
Falla
North Riccalton
Parkdail
Lynnwood
Kaimend
Hallrule Mill
Abbotrule
Ruletownhead
Lawsuit Law
Vertish Hill
White Hill
Kirkton Hill
Weens Ho
Weensmoor Fm
Dod Hill
Bonchester Bridge
Belling Hill
Mervins Law
Stotfield Hill
Scaw'd 367
Moor Head
Colliforthill
Colislinn
Adderston Lee
Birneyknowe
Bonchester Hill
Doorpool Hill
Falside
Roughlee
Edgerston
Edgerston Rig
Philip Law 414
Pilmuir
New Mill
Hoggfield Hill
Hobkirk
Cleuch Head
Highend
Crown Plantn
Mackside
Chesters
Southdean Mill
405
Bught Knowe
Acreknowe Res
White Hill
Law Plantn
Croft Plantn
Hareshaw Knowe
329 Knock Hills
Hophills Nob 359
250
Ephope Law
Stonedge
Folly Plantn
Spar Plantn
Southdean
Southdean Lodge
Shaw Burn
Stobs Castle
Cogsmill
Stonedge Hill
Wauchope Fm
Wolfiee Hill 393
Cribs Hole
Highlee Hill
Weasel Hill
Steele Knowe
Crink Law
Lethem
Huntford
Deerlee Knowe
Leithope Forest
0 1 2 3 miles
0 1 2 3 4 5 km

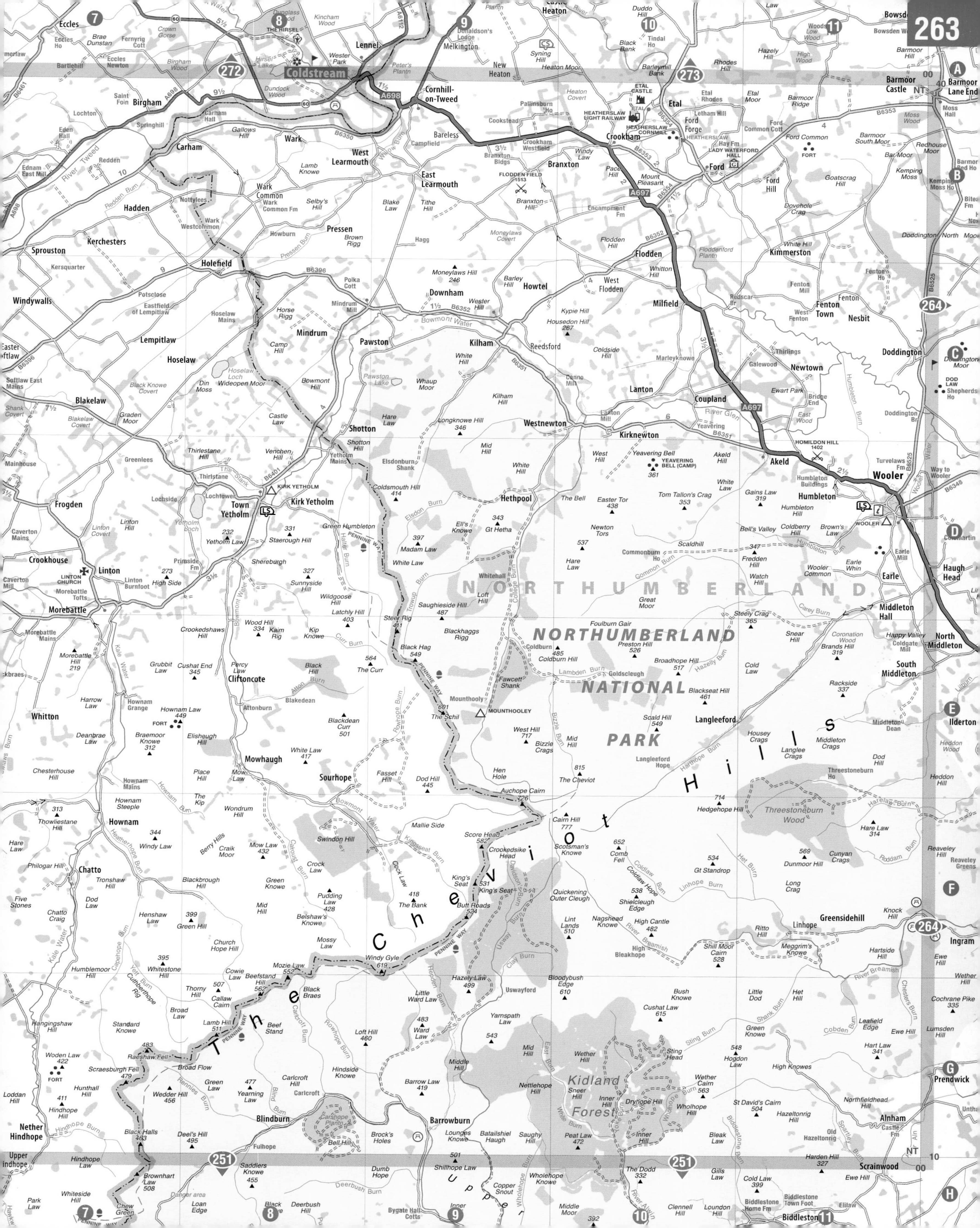
Eccles
Birgham
Coldstream
Lennel
Melkington
Cornhill-on-Tweed
New Heaton
Castle Heaton
Carham
Wark
West Learmouth
East Learmouth
Bareless
Campfield
Crookham
Etal
Etal Castle
Heatherslaw Light Railway
Ford
Ford Forge
Lady Waterford Hall
Branxton
Flodden Field 1513
Pallinsburn Ho
Hadden
Wark Common
Pressen
Sprouston
Kerchesters
Holefield
Windywalls
Mindrum
Pawston
Kilham
Downham
Howtel
West Flodden
Flodden
Milfield
Kimmerston
Fenton Town
Nesbit
Doddington
Newtown
Lanton
Coupland
Westnewton
Kirknewton
Akeld
Homildon Hill 1402
Wooler
Humbleton
Earle
Haugh Head
Middleton Hall
North Middleton
South Middleton
Ilderton
Lempitlaw
Hoselaw
Blakelaw
Shotton
Kirk Yetholm
Town Yetholm
Frogden
Crookhouse
Linton
Morebattle
Clifton Cote
Mowhaugh
Sourhope
Hownam
Chatto
Whitton
Hethpool
Yeavering Bell 361
Langleeford
Greensidehill
Linhope
Ingram
Prendwick
Alnham
Scrainwood
Barrowburn
Blindburn
Nether Hindhope
Biddlestone
Northumberland
Northumberland National Park
The Cheviot Hills
The Cheviot 815
Hedgehope Hill 714
Windy Gyle 619
Auchope Cairn 726
The Schil 601
Cairn Hill 777
Kidland Forest
Threestoneburn Wood
Pennine Way
A697
A698
A6112
B6350
B6352
B6396
B6351
B6401
B6353
B6354
B6525
B6348
A1
A
B
C
D
E
F
G
H
272
273
264
251
7
8
9
10
11

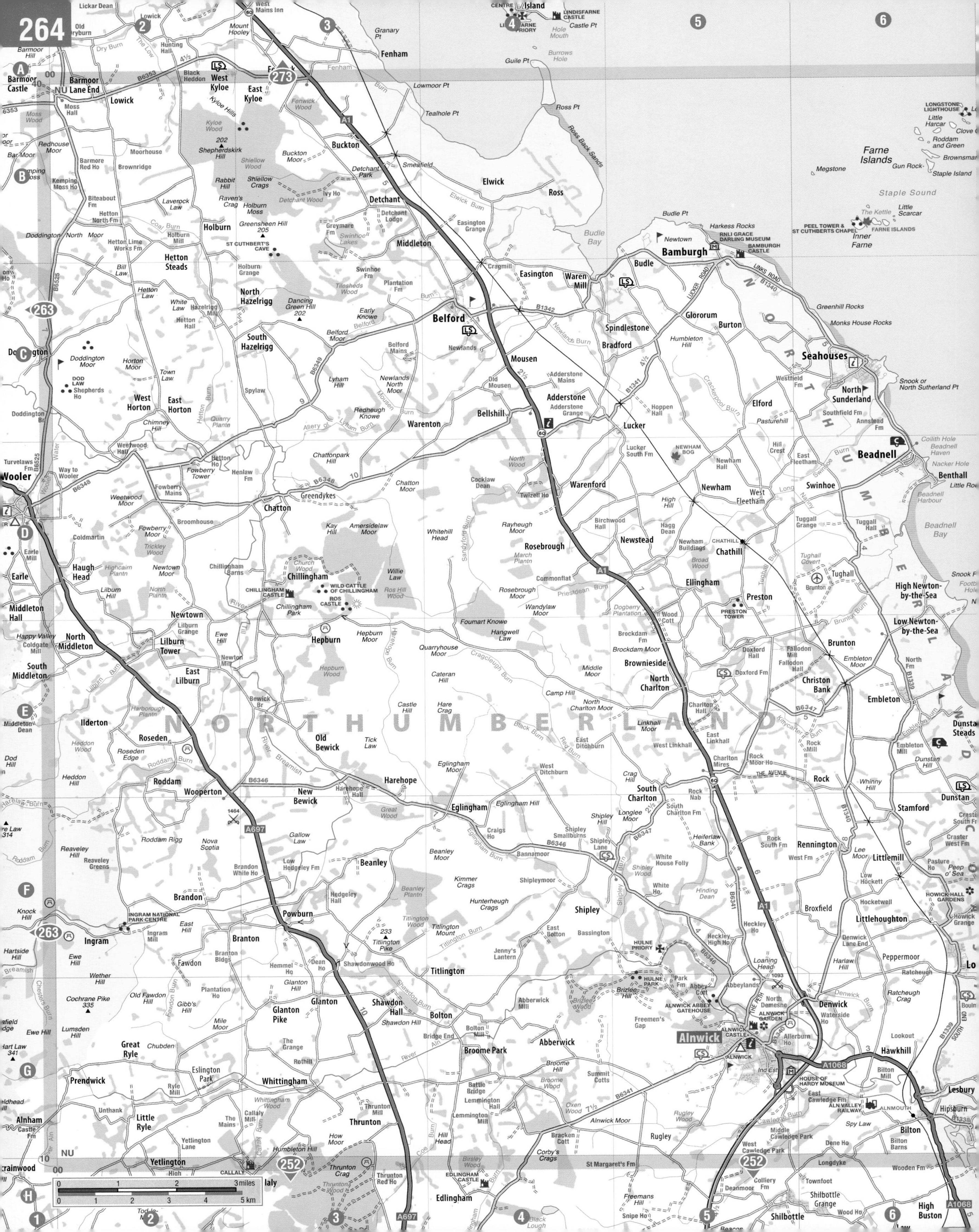

Lickar Dean
Old Dryburn
Lowick
West Mains Inn
Mount Hooley
Granary Pt
Fenham
Centre
Island
Lindisfarne Castle
Castle Pt
Lindisfarne Priory
Hole Mouth
Burrows Hole
Guile Pt
Barmoor Hill
Barmoor Castle
Barmoor Lane End
Dry Burn
Hunting Hall
Black Heddon
West Kyloe
East Kyloe
B6353
Fenham
Lowmoor Pt
Moss Hall
Moss Wood
Fenwick Wood
Tealhole Pt
Ross Pt
Kyloe Wood
Kyloe Hills
202
Shepherdskirk Hill
Buckton
Ross Back Sands
Redhouse Moor
Moorhouse
Bar Moor
Barmore Red Ho
Brownridge
Shiellow Wood
Buckton Moor
Smeafield
Kemping Moss
Kemping Moss Ho
Rabbit Hill
Shiellow Crags
Detchant Park
Elwick
Ross
Biteabout Fm
Raven's Crag
Detchant Wood
Ivy Ho
Detchant
Laverock Law
Holburn Moss
Detchant Lodge
Elwick Burn
Hetton North Fm
Coal Burn
Greymare Fm
Easington Grange
Doddington
North Moor
Holburn Mill
Holburn
Greensheen Hill
205
Swinhoe Lakes
Middleton
Bludle Pt
Budle Bay
Hetton Lime Works Fm
Hetton Steads
St Cuthbert's Cave
Cragmill
Easington
Waren Mill
Budle
Bamburgh
Newtown
Harkess Rocks
RNLI Grace Darling Museum
Bamburgh Castle
Links Road
B1340
Bill Law
Holburn Grange
Swinhoe Fm
Tileshed Wood
Plantation Fm
Hetton Law
North Hazelrigg
Early Knowe
Belford
B1342
Lucker Road
Glororum
Burton
B6525
White Law
Hazelrigg Mill
Dancing Green Hill
202
Hetton Hall
South Hazelrigg
Belford Moor
Newlands
Spindlestone
Bradford
Newlands Burn
Humbleton Hill
Greenhill Rocks
Monks House Rocks
Seahouses
Doddington Moor
Horton Moor
Belford Mains
Mousen
Adderstone Mains
Westfield Fm
North Sunderland
Snook or North Sutherland Pt
Dod Law
Shepherds Ho
Town Law
Spylaw
B6349
Lyham Hill
Newlands North Moor
Old Mousen
Adderstone
Adderstone Grange
B1341
Hoppen Hall
Crackerpool Burn
Elford
Southfield Fm
Doddington Br
West Horton
East Horton
Redheugh Knowe
Warenton
Bellshill
Lucker
Pasturehill
Annstead Fm
Chimney Hill
Quarry Plantn
Hetton Burn
Allery
Lyham Burn
Lucker South Fm
Newham Bog
Hill Crest
East Fleetham
Beadnell
Coilth Hole
Beadnell Haven
Nacker Hole
Turvelaws Fm
Way to Wooler
Weetwood Hall
Hetton Ho
Fowberry Tower
Henlaw Fm
Chattonpark Hill
North Wood
Newham Hall
Benthall
Little Rock
Wooler
B6348
B6346
Fowberry Mains
Greendykes
Chatton Moor
Cocklaw Dean
Twizell Ho
Warenford
Newham
West Fleetham
Swinhoe
Beadnell Harbour
Weetwood Moor
Chatton
High Hill
Birchwood Hall
Tuggall Grange
Tuggall Hall
Beadnell Bay
Coldmartin
Broomhouse
Fowberry Moor
Trickley Wood
Kay Hill
Amersidelaw Moor
Whitehill Head
Rayheugh Moor
Rosebrough
Hagg Dean
Newstead
Newham Buildings
Chathill
Broad Wood
Tughall Covert
Earle Mill
Haugh Head
Highcairn Plantn
Newtown Moor
Chillingham Barns
Church Wood
Chillingham
Willie Law
March Plantn
Commonflat
Ellingham
Tughall
Brunton
Snook Fox
Earle
Lilburn Hill
North Plantn
Chillingham Castle
Wild Cattle of Chillingham
Ros Castle
Ros Hill Wood
Rosebrough Moor
Priestdean Burn
Preston
Preston Tower
High Newton-by-the-Sea
Middleton Hall
Newtown
Chillingham Park
Wandylaw Moor
Dogberry Plantation
Wood Cott
Low Newton-by-the-Sea
Happy Valley
Coldgate Mill
North Middleton
Lilburn Grange
Lilburn Tower
Ewe Hill
Hepburn
Hepburn Moor
Foumart Knowe
Hangwell Law
Brockdam Fm
Brockdam Moor
Brunton
Quarryhouse Moor
Doxford Hall
Fallodon Mill
Fallodon Hall
Embleton Moor
North Fm
South Middleton
East Lilburn
Newton Mill
Hepburn Wood
Cateran Hill
Craglough Burn
Middle Moor
Brownieside
North Charlton
Doxford Fm
Christon Bank
Embleton
B1339
Castle Hill
Hare Crag
Camp Hill
North Charlton Moor
Charlton Hall
B6347
Dunstan Steads
Middleton Dean
Ilderton
Harborough Plantn
Roseden
Bewick Br
Old Bewick
Tick Law
Black Burn
Linkhall Moor
East Linkhall
West Linkhall
Rock Mill
Embleton Mill
Heddon Wood
Roseden Edge
Roddam Burn
River Breamish
Red Burn
East Ditchburn
Charlton Mires
Rock Moor Ho
The Avenue
Dunstan Hill
Dod Hill
Heddon Hill
Roddam
Wooperton
B6346
New Bewick
Harehope
Harehope Hall
Eglingham Moor
West Ditchburn
Crag Hill
South Charlton
Rock Nab
Rock
Whinny Hill
Dunstan
Harelaw Burn
1464
A697
Eglingham
Eglingham Hill
Shipley Hill
Longlee Moor
South Charlton Fm
Stamford
Craster South Fm
Great Wood
Craigs Ho
Shipley Smallburns
B1340
Hare Law 314
Roddam Rigg
Nova Scotia
Gallow Law
B6346
Shipley Lane
Heiferlaw Bank
Rock South Fm
Rennington
Craster West Fm
Reaveley Hill
Reaveley Greens
Low Hedgeley Fm
Beanley
Beanley Moor
Bannamoor
West Fm
White House Folly
Lee Moor
Littlemill
Pasture Ho
Peep o' Sea
Brandon White Ho
Kimmer Crags
Shipleymoor
Shipley Wood
White Ho
Hinding Dean
Low Hocket
Howick Hall Gardens
Hedgeley Hall
Beanley Plantn
Hunterheugh Crags
Hocketwell
Brandon
Shipley
B6341
Broxfield
Littlehoughton
Knock Hill
Ingram National Park Centre
Powburn
Tillington Wood
A1
Howick Grange
East Hill
Ingram Mill
Branton
233 Titlington Pike
Titlington Mount
Titlington Burn
East Bolton
Bassington
Heckley Ho
Heckley High Ho
Denwick Lane End
Peppermoor
Ingram
Hartside Hill
Ewe Hill
Branton Bldgs
Jenny's Lantern
Hulne Priory
Loaning Head
Harlaw Hill
Lo
Breamish
Fawdon
Hemmel Ho
Dean Ho
Shawdonwood Ho
Titlington
Hulne Park
Park Fm
Abbey Cott
Abbeylands
1093
Ratcheugh
Wether Hill
Plantation Ho
Glanton Hill
Shawdon Burn
Brizlee Hill
Brizlee Wood
Denwick
Ratcheugh Crag
Cochrane Pike 335
Old Fawdon Hill
Fawdon Burn
Gibb's Hill
Glanton
Glanton Pike
Shawdon Hall
Shawdon Hill
Bolton
Abberwick Mill
Alnwick Abbey Gatehouse
The Peth
North Demesne
Alnwick Garden
Waterside Ho
Boulmer
Mile Moor
Freemen's Gap
Allerburn Ho
Lookout
Chesters Burn
Lumsden Hill
Ewe Hill
Bridge End
Bolton Mill
Alnwick
Alnwick Castle
B1339
Hart Law 341
Great Ryle
Chubden
The Grange
River Aln
Broome Park
Abberwick
Hawkhill
Rothill
Alnwick
Ind Est
A1068
Prendwick
Eslington Park
Whittingham
Broome Hill
Battle Bridge
Broome Wood
Summit Cotts
House of Hardy Museum
Bilton Mill
Lesbury
Eldhead
Unthank
Ryle Mill
Whittingham Wood
Lemmington Hall
B6341
East Cawledge Fm
Aln Valley Railway
Alnmouth
Hipsburn
Alnham
Alnham Castle Fm
Little Ryle
The Mains
Callaly Mill
Thrunton Mill
Thrunton Wood
Thrunton
Lemmington Mill
Oxen Wood
Alnwick Moor
Rugley Wood
Cawledge Burn
Spy Law
Bilton
B1338
NU
Yetlington Lane
How Moor
Hill Head
Bracken Cott
Rugley
Middle Cawledge Park
Dene Ho
Bilton Barns
Humbleton Hill
Corby's Crags
West Cawledge Park
Crainwood
Yetlington
Callaly
Thrunton Crag
Thrunton Red Ho
Coe Burn
Birsley Wood
Edlingham Castle
St Margaret's Fm
Longdyke
Wooden Fm
High
Callaly
Colliery Fm
Townfoot
0 1 2 3 miles
0 1 2 3 4 5 km
Edlingham
Freemans Hill
Deanmoor
Shilbottle Grange
High Buston
A1068
A697
Tod Le
Black Lough
Snipe Ho
Shilbottle
Wood Ho
Beacon
Longstone Lighthouse
Little Harcar
Clove
Roddam and Green
Brownsman
Farne Islands
Megstone
Gun Rock
Staple Island
Staple Sound
The Kettle
Little Scarcar
Peel Tower & St Cuthberts Chapel
Farne Islands
Inner Farne
NORTHUMBERLAND
273
263
252

7　　8　　9　　10　　11

A
50
40
NU

B

C

D

N O R T H

S E A

E

Castle Pt
DUNSTANBURGH CASTLE
Queen Margaret's Cove

mbleton Bay

stone

n Pt

Craster

Cullernose Pt

wick

Rumbling Kern

Howick Haven
ed ead

Sugar Sands

Low Stead

Howdiemont Sands

oughton

Red Ends

F

Boulmer

Boulmer Haven
ld

Seaton Pt

G

Marden Rocks

mouth

Alnmouth Bay

NU
10
50

253　　253

H

7　　8　　9　　10　　11

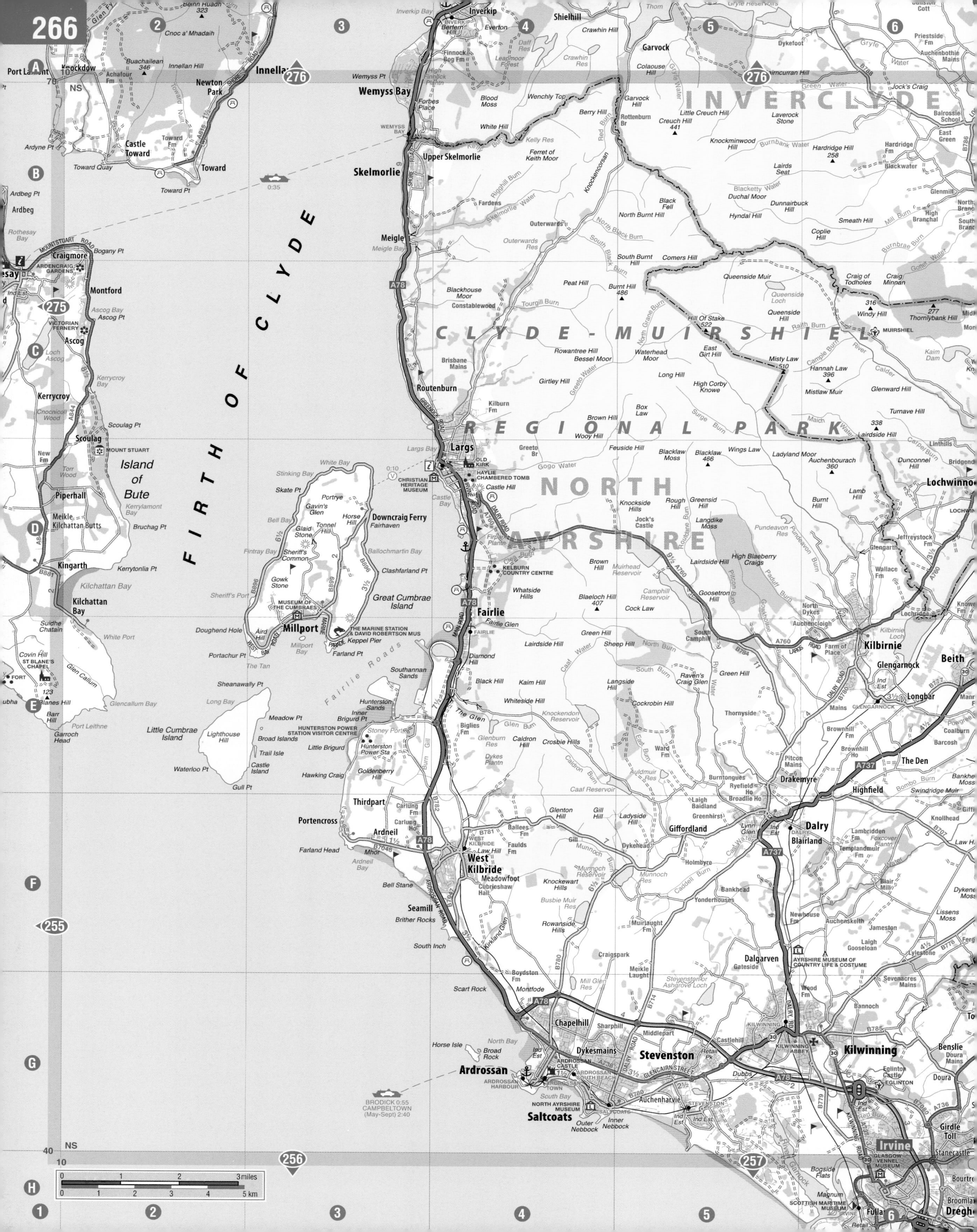
FIRTH OF CLYDE
CLYDE-MUIRSHIEL REGIONAL PARK
NORTH AYRSHIRE
INVERCLYDE
Island of Bute
Great Cumbrae Island
Little Cumbrae Island
Wemyss Bay
Skelmorlie
Largs
Fairlie
Millport
West Kilbride
Ardrossan
Saltcoats
Stevenston
Kilwinning
Irvine
Dalry
Kilbirnie
Beith
Inverkip
Innellan
Toward
Kingarth
Kilchattan Bay
Ascog
Craigmore
276
275
255
256
257
BRODICK 0:55
CAMPBELTOWN
(May-Sept) 2:40
3 miles
5 km

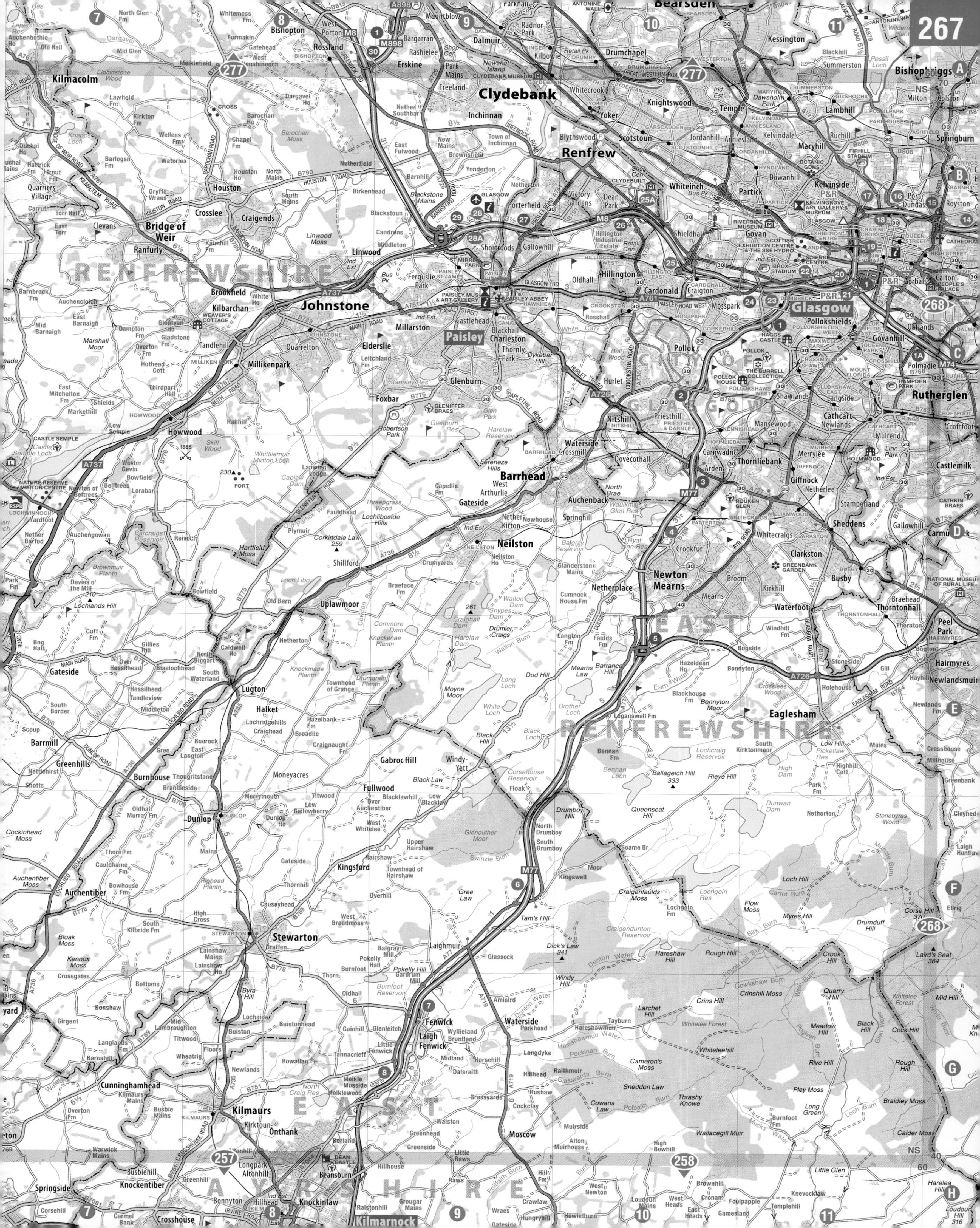

Bearsden
Kilmacolm
Bishopton
Rossland
Erskine
Dalmuir
Drumchapel
Kessington
Bishopbriggs
Clydebank
Inchinnan
Knightswood
Temple
Lambhill
Milton
Springburn
Renfrew
Scotstoun
Jordanhill
Anniesland
Kelvindale
Maryhill
Ruchill
Kelvinside
Partick
Whiteinch
Houston
Crosslee
Craigends
Bridge of Weir
Ranfurly
Linwood
Govan
Shieldhall
Hillington
Cardonald
Craigton
Mosspark
RENFREWSHIRE
Johnstone
Kilbarchan
Brookfield
Paisley
Glasgow
Pollokshields
Govanhill
Millarston
Elderslie
Quarrelton
Castlehead
Charleston
Tandlehill
Millikenpark
Glenburn
Foxbar
Pollok
CITY OF GLASGOW
Rutherglen
Shawlands
Cathcart
Newlands
Nitshill
Priesthill
Howwood
Barrhead
Waterside
Crossmill
Dovecothall
Thornliebank
Giffnock
Merrylee
Castlemilk
Arden
Carnwadric
Auchenback
Gateside
Neilston
Springhill
Netherlee
Stamperland
Sheddens
Whitecraigs
Clarkston
Crookfur
Newton Mearns
Broom
Busby
Mearns
Kirkhill
Uplawmoor
Shillford
Netherplace
Waterfoot
Thorntonhall
Peel Park
EAST
Hairmyres
Newlandsmuir
Lugton
Gateside
Halket
Eaglesham
RENFREWSHIRE
Barrmill
Greenhills
Burnhouse
Gabroc Hill
Fullwood
Dunlop
Kingsford
Auchentiber
Stewarton
Fenwick
Laigh Fenwick
Waterside
Cunninghamhead
Kilmaurs
EAST
Onthank
Moscow
AYRSHIRE
Springside
Knockentiber
Crosshouse
Knockinlaw
Kilmarnock
M8
M77
M74
A737
A726
A736
A77

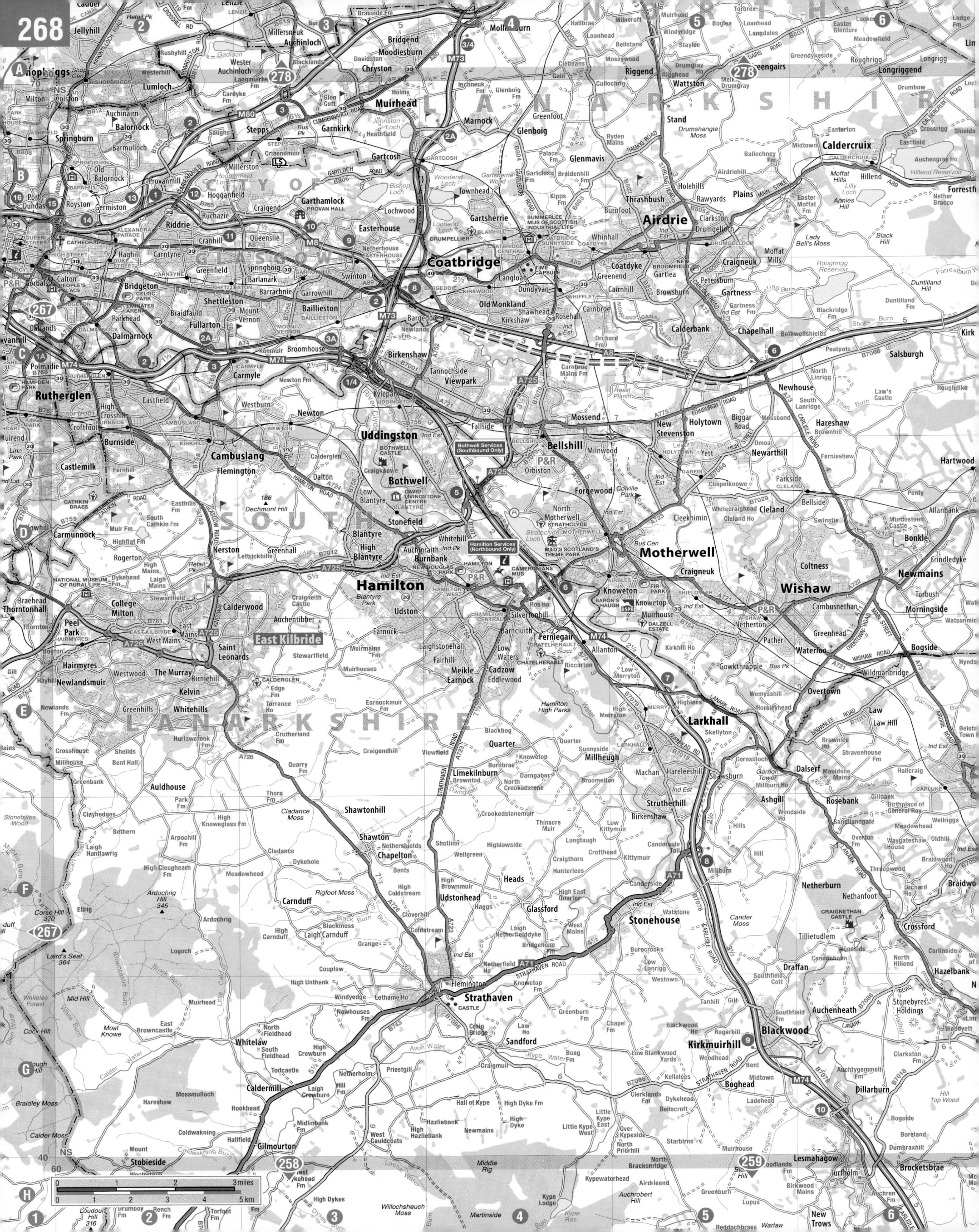

NORTH
LANARKSHIRE
CITY OF GLASGOW
SOUTH LANARKSHIRE
Bishopbriggs
Springburn
Balornock
Stepps
Muirhead
Chryston
Moodiesburn
Bridgend
Mollinsburn
Riggend
Glenboig
Marnock
Glenmavis
Caldercruix
Plains
Airdrie
Coatbridge
Gartsherrie
Easterhouse
Garthamlock
Riddrie
Provanmill
Royston
Haghill
Carntyne
Shettleston
Bridgeton
Parkhead
Dalmarnock
Baillieston
Garrowhill
Barrachnie
Old Monkland
Kirkshaw
Coatdyke
Greenend
Calderbank
Chapelhall
Salsburgh
Newhouse
Holytown
New Stevenston
Mossend
Bellshill
Viewpark
Tannochside
Birkenshaw
Uddingston
Bothwell
Carmyle
Rutherglen
Cambuslang
Burnside
Castlemilk
Carmunnock
Blantyre
High Blantyre
Stonefield
Hamilton
Motherwell
Wishaw
Newmains
Cleland
Bonkle
Craigneuk
Knowetop
Ferniegair
Larkhall
Overtown
Dalserf
Rosebank
Ashgill
Netherburn
Crossford
Hazelbank
Quarter
Millheugh
Stonehouse
Glassford
Strathaven
Chapelton
Shawton
Sandford
Kirkmuirhill
Blackwood
Boghead
Lesmahagow
Auchenheath
East Kilbride
Calderwood
Nerston
Peel Park
College Milton
Hairmyres
Newlandsmuir
The Murray
Kelvin
Whitehills
Greenhills
Saint Leonards
Auldhouse
Caldermill
Gilmourton
Stobieside
Earnock
Meikle Earnock
Fairhill
Udston
Silvertonhill
Bothwell Services (Southbound Only)
Hamilton Services (Northbound Only)
M&D'S SCOTLAND'S THEME PARK
STRATHCLYDE
M8
M73
M74
M80
A71
A725
A726
A723
278
267
258
259
0 1 2 3 miles
0 1 2 3 4 5 km

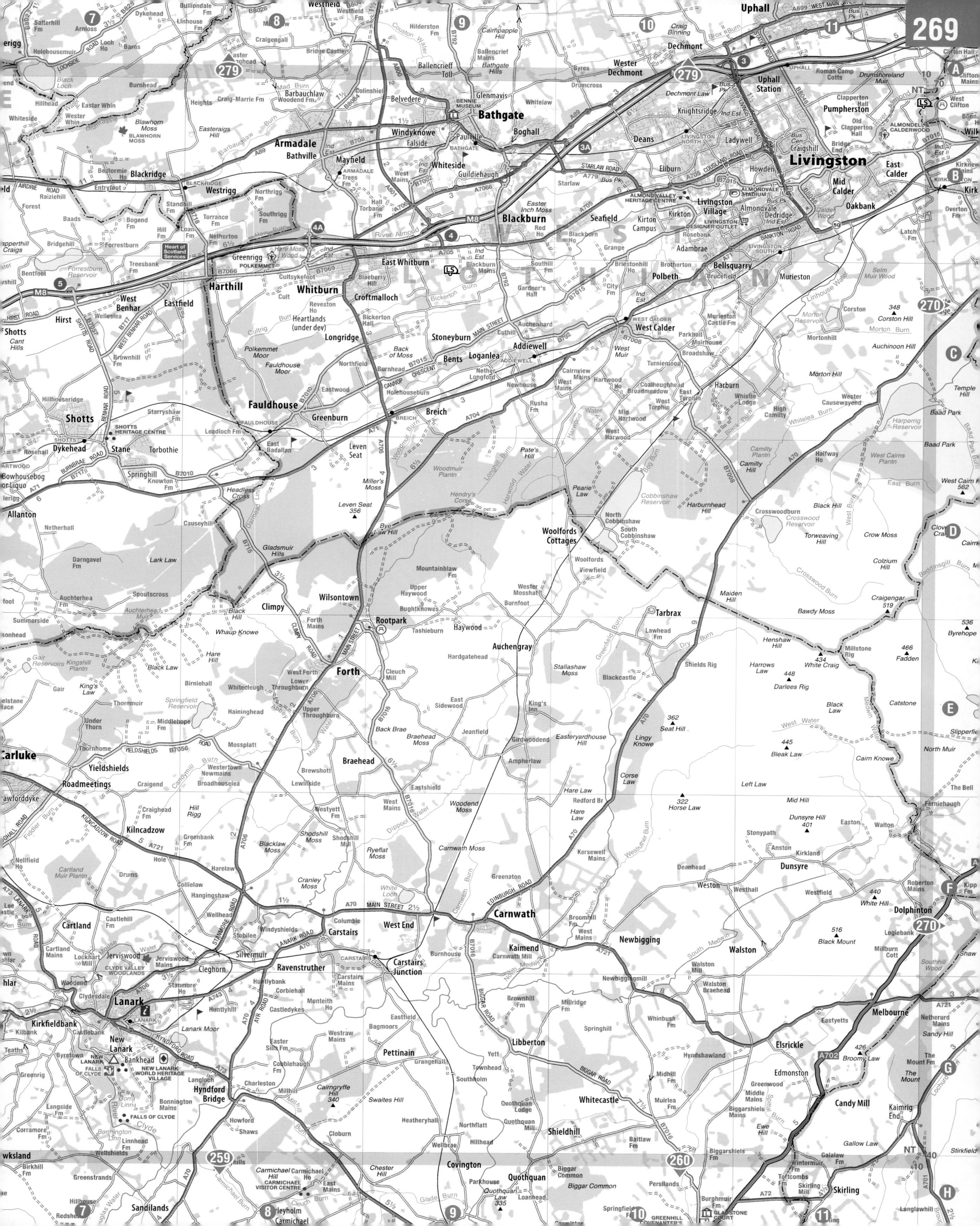

Uphall
Dechmont
Wester Dechmont
Uphall Station
Pumpherston
Livingston
East Calder
Mid Calder
Oakbank
Kirknewton
Bathgate
Boghall
Glenmavis
Belvedere
Windyknowe
Armadale
Bathville
Mayfield
Whiteside
Blackridge
Westrigg
Blackburn
Seafield
Livingston Village
Almondvale
Dedridge
Kirkton Campus
Knightsridge
Ladywell
Deans
Eliburn
Howden
Craigshill
Starlaw
Adambrae
Bellsquarry
Murieston
Polbeth
West Calder
Addiewell
Loganlea
Bents
Stoneyburn
Longridge
Whitburn
East Whitburn
Croftmalloch
Harthill
Greenrigg
Polkemmet
West Benhar
Eastfield
Hirst
Shotts
Dykehead
Stane
Torbothie
Fauldhouse
Greenburn
Breich
Harburn
West Torphin
Woolfords Cottages
Tarbrax
Auchengray
Wilsontown
Climpy
Rootpark
Forth
Braehead
Carluke
Yieldshields
Roadmeetings
Kilncadzow
Cartland
Carstairs
Carstairs Junction
Carnwath
West End
Kaimend
Newbigging
Walston
Dunsyre
Dolphinton
Ravenstruther
Lanark
Kirkfieldbank
New Lanark
Hyndford Bridge
Pettinain
Libberton
Whitecastle
Shieldhill
Covington
Quothquan
Elsrickle
Melbourne
Candy Mill
Skirling
Sandilands
Allanton
Leven Seat 356
Seat Hill 362
Horse Law 322
Dunsyre Hill 401
Black Mount 516
White Hill 440
Craigengar 519
White Craig 434
Bleak Law 445
Darlees Rig 448
LOTHIAN
Heart of Scotland Services
NEW LANARK WORLD HERITAGE VILLAGE
FALLS OF CLYDE
CARMICHAEL VISITOR CENTRE
GREENHILL COVENANTER'S
GLADSTONE COURT
279
270
259
260

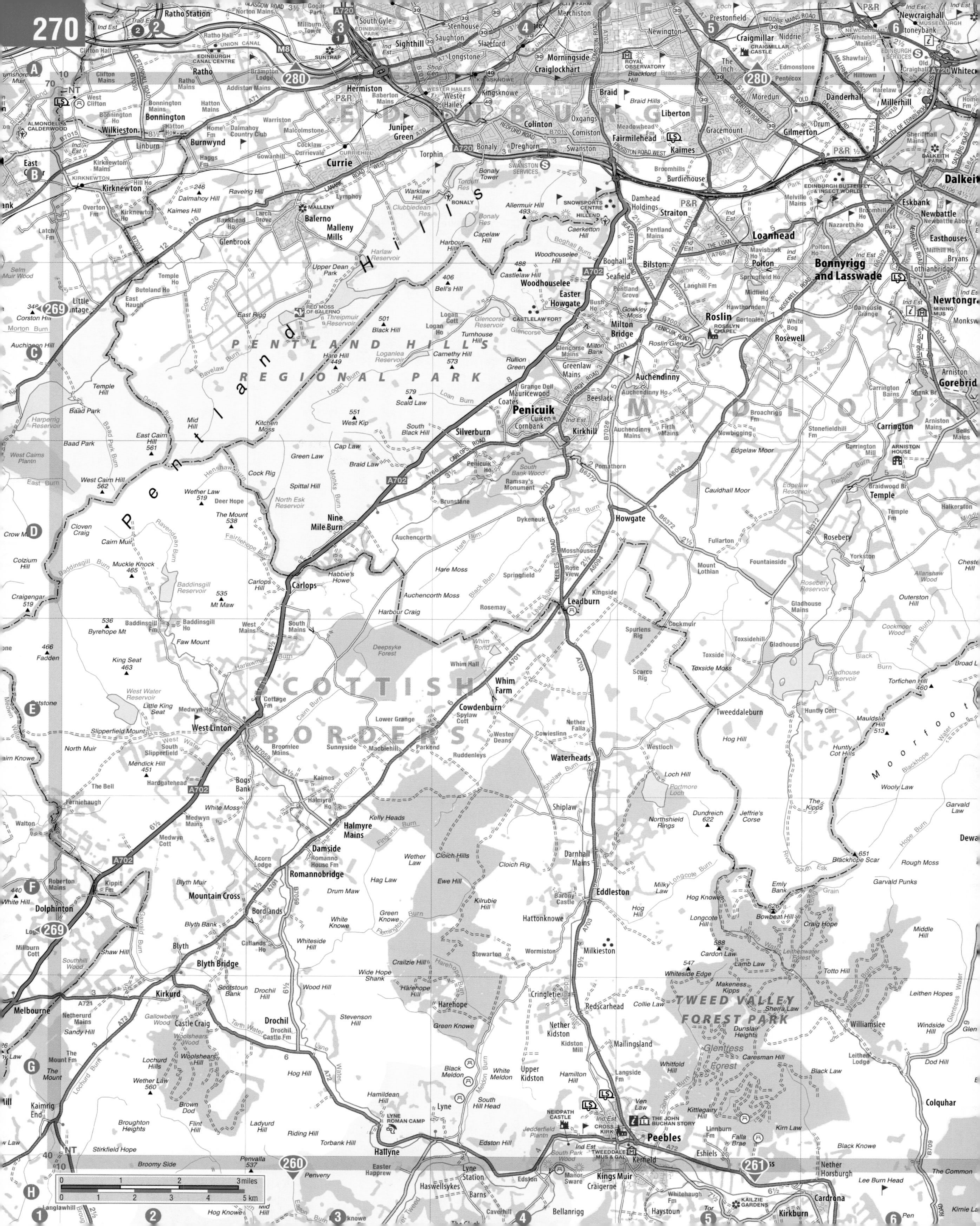
Ratho Station
Ratho
Ratho Hall
Union Canal
Edinburgh Canal Centre
Clifton Hall
Clifton Mains
West Clifton
Bonnington Mains
Bonnington
Wilkieston
Almondell & Calderwood
Linburn
Burnwynd
Hatton Mains
Dalmahoy Country Club
Addiston Mains
Warriston
Malcolmstone
Cocklaw
Currievale
Gowanhill
Haggs Fm
East Calder
Kirknewton
Kirknewton Mains
Overton Fm
Dalmahoy Hill
Ravelrig Hill
Kaimes Hill
Lymphoy
Balerno
Malleny
Malleny Mills
Bankhead Ho
Larch Grove
Glenbrook
Latch Fm
Temple Ho
Buteland Ho
East Haugh
Little Vantage
Corston Hill
Morton Burn
Auchinoon Hill
Currie
Hermiston
Juniper Green
Torphin
Colinton
Bonaly
Dreghorn
Swanston
Oxgangs
Comiston
Fairmilehead
Kaimes
Liberton
Gracemount
Gilmerton
Braid
Braid Hills
Moredun
Danderhall
Millerhill
Drum
Sighthill
South Gyle
Stenhouse
Saughton
Slateford
Longstone
Kingsknowe
Wester Hailes
Baberton Mains
Morningside
Craiglockhart
Merchiston
Newington
Royal Observatory
Blackford Hill
Prestonfield
Craigmillar
Craigmillar Castle
Niddrie
Newcraighall
Stoneybank
Edmonstone
The Inch
Shawfair
Hilltown
Whitecraig
Edinburgh
Dalkeith
Dalkeith Park
Sheriffhall Mains
Burdiehouse
Broomhills
Damhead Holdings
Straiton
Loanhead
Pentland Mains
Bilston
Boghall
Seafield
Pentland Grove
Roslin
Rosslyn Chapel
Roslin Glen
Polton
Mavisbank
Bonnyrigg and Lasswade
Eskbank
Newbattle
Newbattle Abbey
Easthouses
Lothianbridge
Nazareth Ho
Hawthornden
Gorton Lee
Rosewell
White Bog
Newtongrange
Mining Museum
Gorebridge
Arniston
Arniston House
Carrington
Carrington Barns
Carrington Mill
Edinburgh Butterfly & Insect World
Snowsports Centre
Hillend
Allermuir Hill 493
Caerketton Hill
Capelaw Hill
Bonaly Tower
Bonaly Res
Clubbiedean Res
Torduff Res
Harlaw Reservoir
Threipmuir Reservoir
Red Moss of Balerno
Upper Dean Park
Harbour Hill
Bell's Hill 406
Castlelaw Hill 488
Woodhouselee Hill
Woodhouselee
Easter Howgate
Castlelaw Fort
Glencorse Reservoir
Logan Cott
Logan Ho
Turnhouse Hill
Black Hill 501
Loganlea Reservoir
Carnethy Hill 573
Hare Hill 449
Scald Law 579
West Kip 551
South Black Hill
Rullion Green
Milton Bridge
Gowkley Moss
Glencorse Mains
Milton Bank
Greenlaw Mains
Auchendinny
Auchendinny Ho
Auchendinny Mains
Penicuik
Cuiken
Cornbank
Kirkhill
Beeslack
Mauricewood
Coates
Grange Dell
Firth Mains
Broachrigg Fm
Newbigging
Stonefieldhill Fm
Edgelaw Moor
Edgelaw Reservoir
Cauldhall Moor
Temple
Braidwood Br
Pomathorn
Silverburn
Penicuik Ho
South Bank Wood
Ramsay's Monument
Brunstane
Howgate
Dykeneuk
Auchencorth
Hare Moss
Springfield
Auchencorth Moss
Rosemay
Mosshouses
Rose View
Kingside
Leadburn
Cockmuir
Spurlens Rig
Fullarton
Mount Lothian
Fountainside
Rosebery
Rosebery Reservoir
Yorkston
Gladhouse Mains
Gladhouse
Gladhouse Reservoir
Toxsidehill
Toxside
Toxside Moss
Outerston Hill
Cockmoor Wood
Allanshaw Wood
Torfichen Hill 460
Mauldslie Hill 513
Huntly Cot Hills
Moorfoot
Pentland Hills Regional Park
Pentland Hills
Temple Hill
Baad Park
Harperrig Reservoir
West Cairns Plantn
East Cairn Hill 561
West Cairn Hill 562
Mid Hill
Kitchen Moss
Green Law
Cap Law
Braid Law
Cock Rig
Spittal Hill
North Esk Reservoir
Wether Law 519
Deer Hope
The Mount 538
Nine Mile Burn
Cloven Craig
Cairn Muir
Muckle Knock 465
Baddinsgill Reservoir
Carlops Hill
Carlops
Habbie's Howe
Mt Maw 535
Byrehope Mt 536
Baddinsgill Fm
Baddinsgill Ho
West Mains
South Mains
Faw Mount
Harbour Craig
Deepsyke Forest
Whim Pond
Whim Hall
Whim Farm
Fadden 466
King Seat 463
West Water Reservoir
Little King Seat
Medwyn Ho
West Linton
Cottage Fm
Scottish Borders
Lower Grange
Cowdenburn
Spylaw Cott
Wester Deans
Cowieslinn
Nether Falla
Waterheads
Westloch
Tweeddaleburn
Hog Hill
Huntly Cott
Slipperfield Mount
North Muir
West Slipperfield
South Slipperfield
Mendick Hill 451
Broomlee Mains
Sunnyside
Macbiehill
Parkend
Ruddenleys
The Bell
Hardgatehead
Bogs Bank
Kaimes
Halmyre Ho
White Moss
Ferniehaugh
Medwyn Mains
Kelly Heads
Halmyre Mains
Damside
Romanno House Fm
Romannobridge
Loch Hill
Portmore Loch
Shiplaw
Northshield Rings
Dundreich 622
Jeffrie's Corse
The Kipps
Wooly Law
Garvald Law
Blackhope Scar 651
Rough Moss
Garvald Punks
Walton
Medwyn Cott
Acorn Lodge
Wether Law
Cloich Hills
Cloich Rig
Darnhall Mains
Robertson Mains
White Hill
Dolphinton
Kippit Fm
Blyth Muir
Mountain Cross
Hag Law
Ewe Hill
Drum Maw
Kilrubie Hill
Barony Castle
Eddleston
Milky Law
Hog Knowe
Emly Bank
Bowbeat Hill 626
Longcote Hill
Craig Hope
Middle Hill
Blyth Bank
Bordlands
White Knowe
Green Knowe
Hog Hill
Hattonknowe
Cardon Law 588
Millburn Cott
Southhill Wood
Shaw Hill
Blyth
Callands Ho
Whiteside Hill
Stewarton
Wormiston
Milkieston
Lamb Law
Totto Hill
Blyth Bridge
Wide Hope Shank
Crailzie Hill
Harehope Hill
Harehope
Whiteside Edge 547
Makeness Kipps
Leithen Hopes
Melbourne
Kirkurd
Scotstoun Bank
Drochil Hill
Wood Hill
Cringletie
Redscarhead
Collie Law
Tweed Valley Forest Park
Shiel Law
Williamslee
Windside Hill
Netherurd Mains
Sandy Hill
Gallowberry Wood
Castle Craig
Woolshears Wood
Drochil
Drochil Castle Fm
Stevenson Hill
Green Knowe
Nether Kidston
Kidston Mill
Mailingsland
Dunslair Heights
Glentress Forest
Caresman Hill
Leithen Lodge
Dod Hill
Mount Fm
The Mount
Lochurd Hills
Woolshears Hill
Wether Law 560
Hog Hill
Black Meldon
White Meldon
Upper Kidston
Hamilton Hill
Langside Fm
Whitfold Hill
Black Law
Colquhar
Kaimrig End
Brown Dod
Broughton Heights
Flint Hill
Ladyurd Hill
Hamildean Hill
Lyne Roman Camp
Lyne
South Hill Head
Neidpath Castle
Jedderfield Plantn
Ven Law
The John Buchan Story
Kittlegairy Hill
Kirn Law
Peebles
Cross Kirk
Linnburn Fm
Falla Brae
Eshiels
Black Knowe
Stirkfield Hope
Riding Hill
Torbank Hill
Hallyne
Edston Hill
South Park Wood
Tweeddale Mus & Gal
Kerfield
Broomy Side
Penvalla 537
Penveny
Easter Happrew
Lyne Station
Edston
Manor Sware
Kings Muir
Craigerne
Nether Horsburgh
Lee Burn Head
The Common
Haswellsykes
Barns
Caverhill
Bellanrigg
Whitehaugh Fm
Haystoun
Kailzie Gardens
Kirkburn
Cardrona
Langlawhill
Hog Knowe
0 1 2 3 miles
0 1 2 3 4 5 km

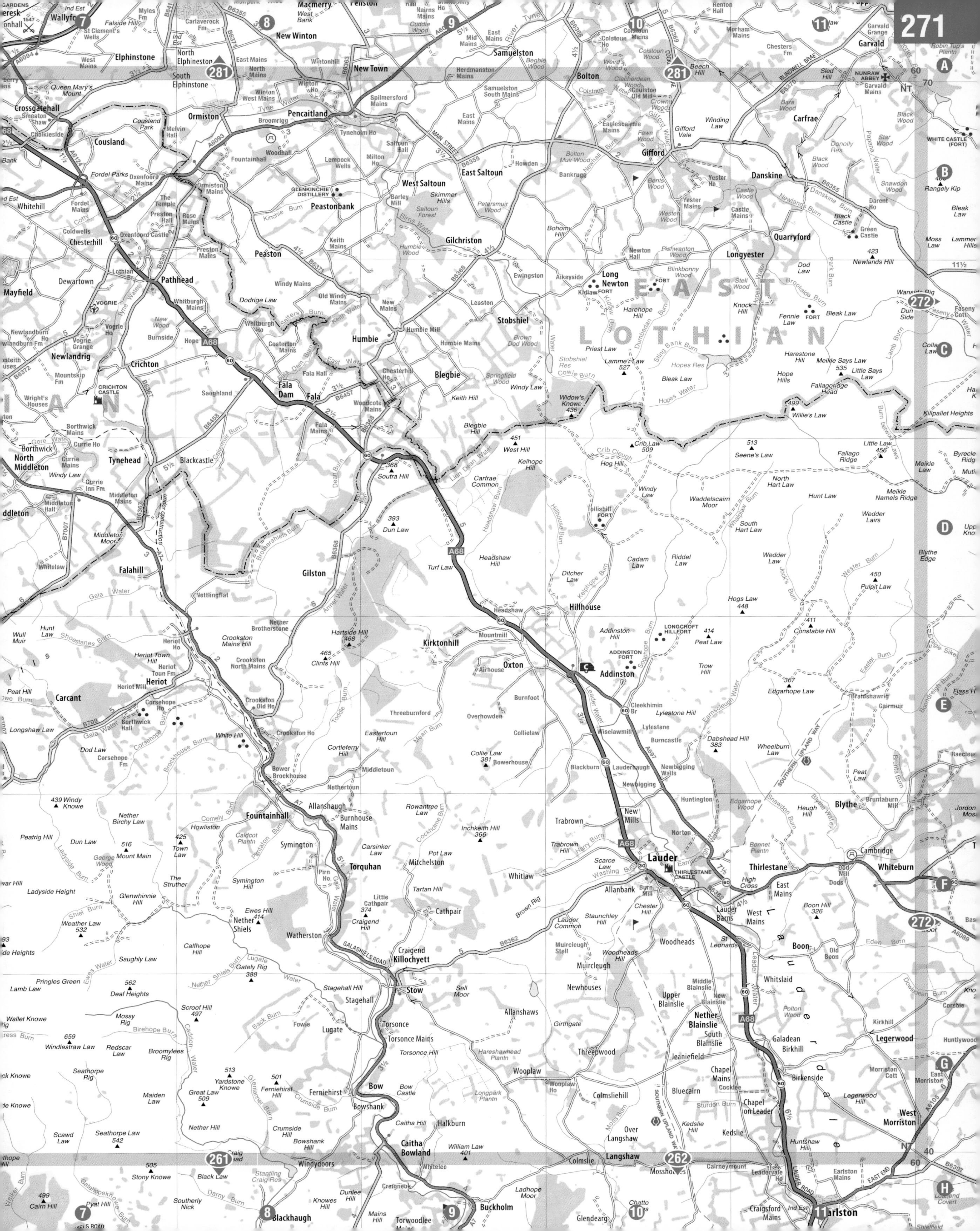

Wallyford
Elphinstone
North Elphinstone
South Elphinstone
Macmerry
New Winton
New Town
Samuelston
Bolton
Garvald
Nunraw Abbey
Crossgatehall
Ormiston
Pencaitland
Cousland
Fordel Parks
Oxenfoord Mains
Ormiston Mains
Glenkinchie Distillery
Peastonbank
West Saltoun
East Saltoun
Gifford
Danskine
Carfrae
White Castle (Fort)
Whitehill
Chesterhill
Mayfield
Dewartown
Pathhead
Peaston
Gilchriston
Longyester
Quarryford
Newlands Hill
Long Newton
EAST LOTHIAN
Newlandrig
Crichton
Crichton Castle
Humbie
Stobshiel
Fala Dam
Fala
Blegbie
Lammer Law 527
Widow's Knowe 436
Willie's Law
Killpallet Heights
Borthwick
North Middleton
Tynehead
Blackcastle
Soutra Hill
Crib Law 509
Seene's Law
Little Law 456
Middleton
Falahill
Gilston
Dun Law 393
Headshaw Hill
Turf Law
Hillhouse
Tollishill Fort
Riddel Law
Hogs Law 448
Pulpit Law 450
Heriot
Carcant
Crookston
Kirktonhill
Oxton
Addinston
Longcroft Hillfort
Peat Law 414
Constable Hill 411
Edgarhope Law 367
Fountainhall
Allanshaugh
Burnhouse Mains
Symington
Torquhan
Trabrown
New Mills
Lauder
Thirlestane Castle
Thirlestane
Cambridge
Whiteburn
Blythe
Southern Upland Way
Dabshead Hill 383
Collie Law 381
Inchkeith Hill 366
Mitchelston
Cathpair
Craigend Killochyett
Galashiels Road
Stow
Stagehall
Nether Shiels
Watherston
Lugate
Torsonce
Torsonce Mains
Allanshaws
Girthgate
Newhouses
Upper Blainslie
Nether Blainslie
South Blainslie
Threepwood
Wooplaw
Colmslie
Colmsliehill
Bluecairn
Chapel on Leader
Kedslie
Legerwood
Birkenside
West Morriston
Boon
Whitslaid
Galadean
Lauderdale
Gately Rig 388
Deaf Heights 562
Windlestraw Law 659
Weather Law 532
Scroof Hill 497
Yardstone Knowe 513
Great Law 509
Ferniehirst 501
Seathorpe Law 542
Stony Knowe 505
Cairn Hill 499
Bow
Bowshank
Caitha Bowland
Windydoors
Langshaw
Mossilee
Blackhaugh
Buckholm
Earlston
William Law 401
A68
A7
A697
B6355
B6368
B6362
281
272
261
262

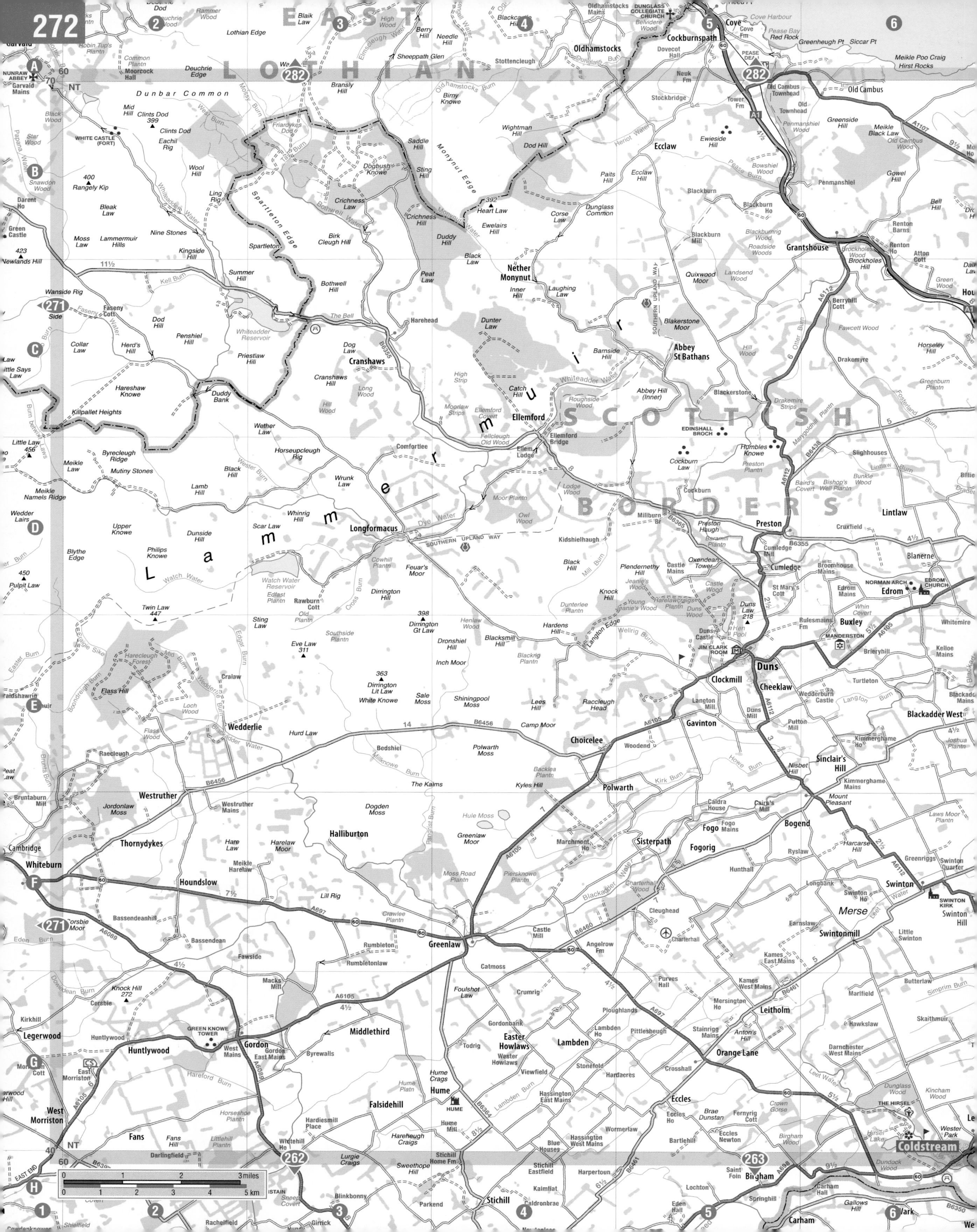

EAST LOTHIAN
SCOTTISH BORDERS
Lammermuir
Dunbar Common
Oldhamstocks
Cockburnspath
Cove
Grantshouse
Ecclaw
Abbey St Bathans
Cranshaws
Ellemford
Longformacus
Preston
Duns
Lintlaw
Edrom
Buxley
Cumledge
Gavinton
Choicelee
Polwarth
Westruther
Wedderlie
Thornydykes
Houndslow
Whiteburn
Halliburton
Greenlaw
Fogo
Fogorig
Sisterpath
Bogend
Sinclair's Hill
Swinton
Swintonmill
Leitholm
Orange Lane
Eccles
Hume
Falsidehill
Gordon
Huntlywood
Legerwood
West Morriston
Lambden
Easter Howlaws
Middlethird
Stichill
Coldstream
Birgham
Carham
Blackadder West
Twin Law 447
Spartleton Edge
Monynut Edge
Whiteadder Reservoir
Watch Water Reservoir
Southern Upland Way
Merse
282
271
262
263
A1
A6105
A697
A6112
A6089
B6355
B6456
B6460

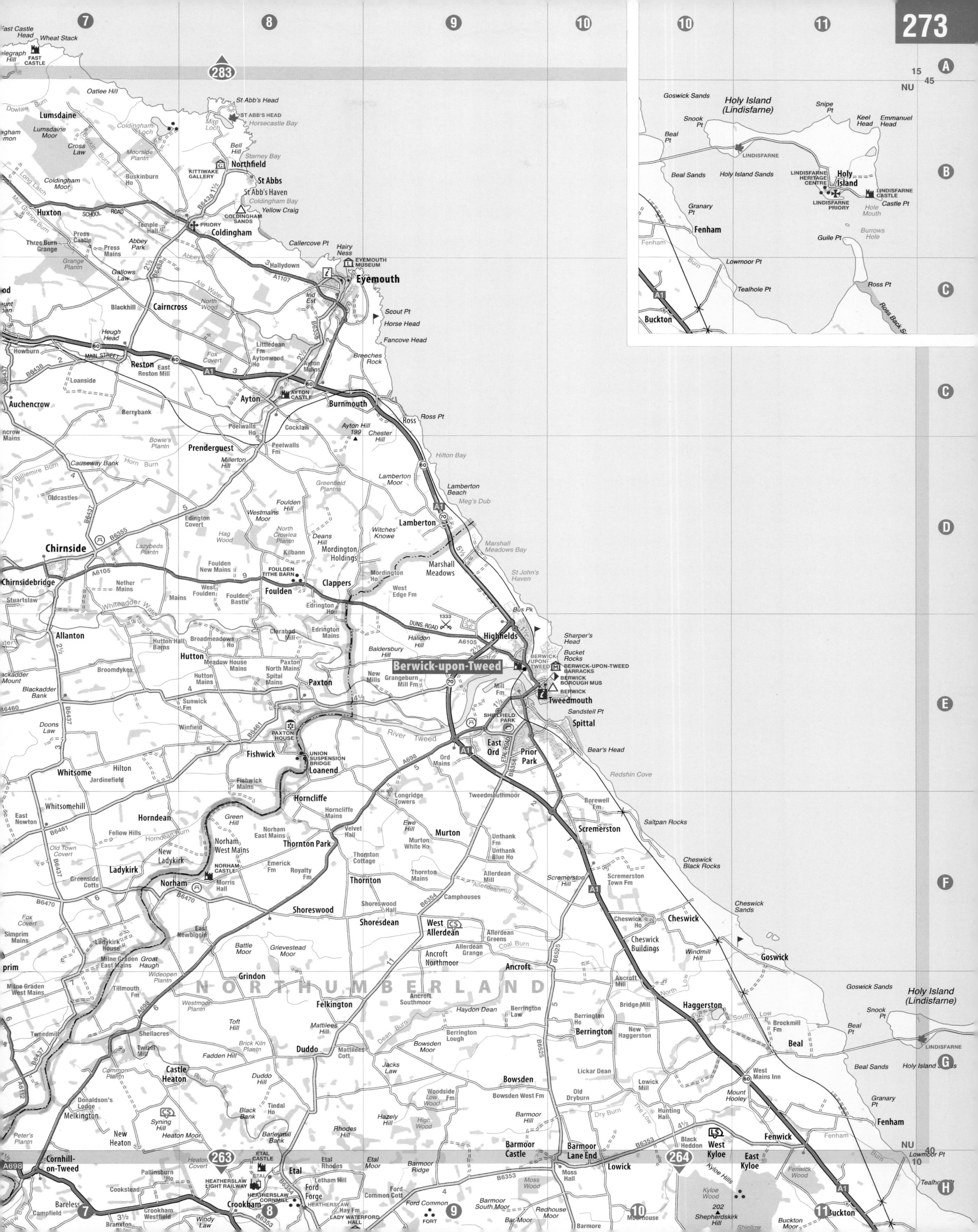

283
263
264
Fast Castle Head
Wheat Stack
Fast Castle
Oatlee Hill
St Abb's Head
Lumsdaine
Lumsdaine Moor
Coldingham Loch
Cross Law
Northfield
St Abbs
St Abb's Haven
Kittiwake Gallery
Coldingham Bay
Yellow Craig
Coldingham Sands
Huxton
Coldingham
Priory
Coldingham Moor
Press Castle
Three Burn Grange
Callercove Pt
Hairy Ness
Eyemouth Museum
Eyemouth
Hallydown
Cairncross
Blackhill
Scout Pt
Horse Head
Fancove Head
Breeches Rock
Heugh Head
Howburn
Reston
East Reston Mill
Loanside
Auchencrow
Ayton
Ayton Castle
Burnmouth
Ross
Ross Pt
Berrybank
Peelwalls Ho
Cocklaw
Ayton Hill 199
Chester Hill
Prenderguest
Hilton Bay
Lamberton Moor
Lamberton Beach
Meg's Dub
Causeway Bank
Oldcastles
Lamberton
Chirnside
Chirnsidebridge
Edington Covert
Westmains Moor
Foulden Hill
Mordington Holdings
Marshall Meadows
Marshall Meadows Bay
St John's Haven
Foulden Tithe Barn
Foulden
Clappers
Mordington Ho
West Edge Fm
Stuartslaw
Allanton
Hutton
Highfields
Bus Pk
Sharper's Head
Bucket Rocks
Berwick-upon-Tweed
Berwick-upon-Tweed Barracks
Berwick Borough Mus
Tweedmouth
Spittal
Sandstell Pt
Paxton
Paxton House
Union Suspension Bridge
Fishwick
Loanend
Horncliffe
East Ord
Prior Park
Bear's Head
Redshin Cove
Whitsome
Hilton
Whitsomehill
Horndean
Ladykirk
Norham
Norham Castle
Thornton Park
Murton
Tweedmouthmoor
Scremerston
Saltpan Rocks
Cheswick Black Rocks
Thornton
Shoreswood
Shoresdean
West Allerdean
Cheswick
Cheswick Sands
Goswick
Ancroft
Grindon
Felkington
Haggerston
N O R T H U M B E R L A N D
Duddo
Berrington
Beal
Castle Heaton
Bowsden
Fenwick
Melkington
Cornhill-on-Tweed
Etal
Etal Castle
Heatherslaw Light Railway
Heatherslaw Cornmill
Crookham
Ford
Ford Forge
Barmoor Castle
Barmoor Lane End
Lowick
West Kyloe
East Kyloe
Kyloe Wood
Shepherdskirk Hill 202
Buckton
Holy Island (Lindisfarne)
Goswick Sands
Snook Pt
Snipe Pt
Keel Head
Emmanuel Head
Beal Sands
Holy Island Sands
Lindisfarne
Lindisfarne Heritage Centre
Holy Island
Lindisfarne Castle
Lindisfarne Priory
Castle Pt
Granary Pt
Fenham
Hole Mouth
Burrows Hole
Guile Pt
Lowmoor Pt
Tealhole Pt
Ross Pt
Ross Back Sands

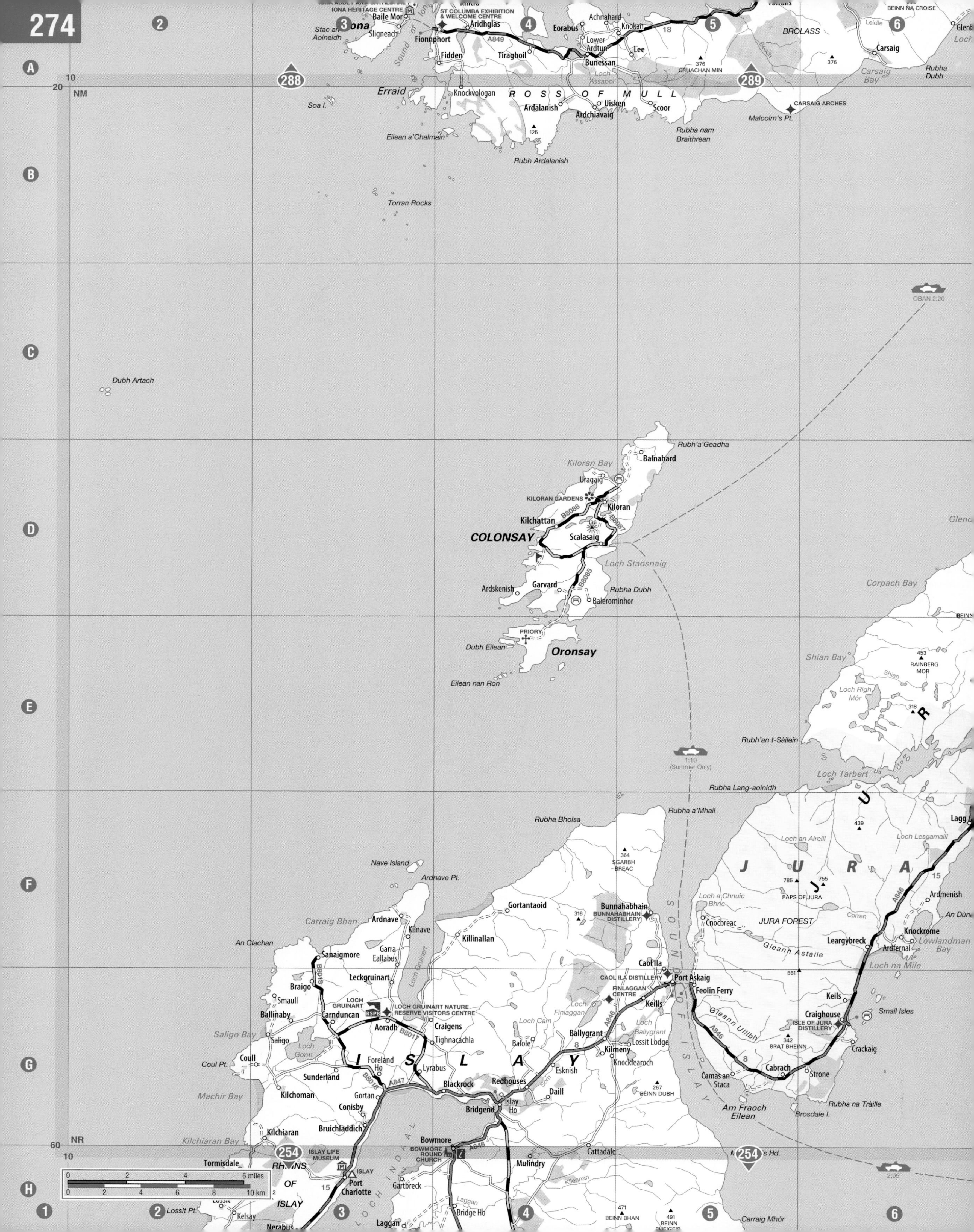

A
B
C
D
E
F
G
H

1 2 3 4 5 6

IONA ABBEY AND BATTLEFIELD
IONA HERITAGE CENTRE
ST COLUMBA EXHIBITION
& WELCOME CENTRE
Achnahard
Knokan
BEINN NA CROISE
Iona
Baile Mor
Aridhglas
Eorabus
Leidle
Glen
Slioneach
Fionnphort
A849
Lower
Lee
18
Carsaig
Fidden
Tiraghoil
Ardtun
Bunessan
BROLASS
Stac an
Aoineidh
Loch
Assapol
376
376
Rubha
Dubh
10
CRUACHAN MIN
289
Carsaig
20
Erraid
Knockvologan
ROSS OF MULL
Bay
NM
Soa I.
Ardalanish
Uisken
Scoor
CARSAIG ARCHES
288
125
Malcolm's Pt.
CARSAIG ARCHES
Eilean a'Chalmain
Ardchiavaig
Rubha nam
Braithrean
Rubh Ardalanish

Torran Rocks

OBAN 2:20

Dubh Artach

Rubh'a'Geadha
Kiloran Bay
Balnahard
Uragaig
KILORAN GARDENS
Kiloran
Glen
Kilchattan
B8086
COLONSAY
Scalasaig
Corpach Bay
Loch Staosnaig
BEINN
Ardskenish
Garvard
Rubha Dubh
Shian Bay
453
RAINBERG
MOR
Balerominhor
Shian
DUBH EILEAN
PRIORY
318
R
Dubh Eilean
Oronsay
Rubh'an t-Sàilein
Eilean nan Ron
Loch Righ
Môr
Loch Tarbert
1:10
(Summer Only)
Rubha Lang-aoinidh
J
U
Rubha Bholsa
Rubha a'Mhail
439
Lagg
Nave Island
Ardnave Pt.
364
SGARBH
BREAC
785
755
JURA
15
PAPS OF JURA
J
Ardmenish
Carraig Bhan
Ardnave
Gortantaoid
316
Loch a'Chnuic
Bhric
JURA FOREST
An Dùna
Kilnave
Killinallan
BUNNAHABHAIN
Cnocbreac
An Clachan
BUNNAHABHAIN
DISTILLERY
Corran
Sanaigmore
Garra
Eallabus
Gleann Astaile
Knockrome
Leckgruinart
Loch Gruinart
Caol Ila
Leargybreck
Lowlandman
Bay
Braigo
CAOL ILA DISTILLERY
Ardfernal
561
Loch na Mile
Smaull
LOCH
GRUINART
FINLAGGAN
CENTRE
Port Askaig
Ballinaby
Carnduncan
RSPB
LOCH GRUINART NATURE
RESERVE VISITORS CENTRE
Keills
Feolin Ferry
Keils
Saligo Bay
Aoradh
Craigens
Loch
Finlaggan
Craighouse
Small Isles
Saligo
Tighnacachla
Balole
Loch
Ballygrant
ISLE OF JURA
DISTILLERY
Loch
Gorm
8
Ballygrant
342
BRAT BHEINN
Coul Pt.
Coull
ISLAY
Foreland
Ho
Lyrabus
Kilmeny
Gleann Ullibh
Cabrach
Crackaig
Sunderland
Knockfearoch
Camas an
Staca
Strone
Machir Bay
Blackrock
Redhouses
Esknish
8
Rubha na Tràille
Kilchoman
Gortan
Bridgend
Daill
267
BEINN DUBH
Am Fraoch
Eilean
Brosdale I.
Conisby
Islay
Ho
60
Bruichladdich
NR
Kilchiaran
Cattadale
254
Kilchiaran Bay
Bowmore
ISLAY LIFE
MUSEUM
RHINS
BOWMORE
ROUND CHURCH
A846
s Hd.
254
10
Tormisdale
OF
Mulindry
2:05
ISLAY
Port
Charlotte
ISLAY
15
0 2 4 6 miles
Lossit Pt.
Gartbreck
Laggan
0 2 4 6 8 10 km
Kelsay
Nerabus
Bridge Ho
471
BEINN BHAN
491
BEINN
Carraig Mhôr

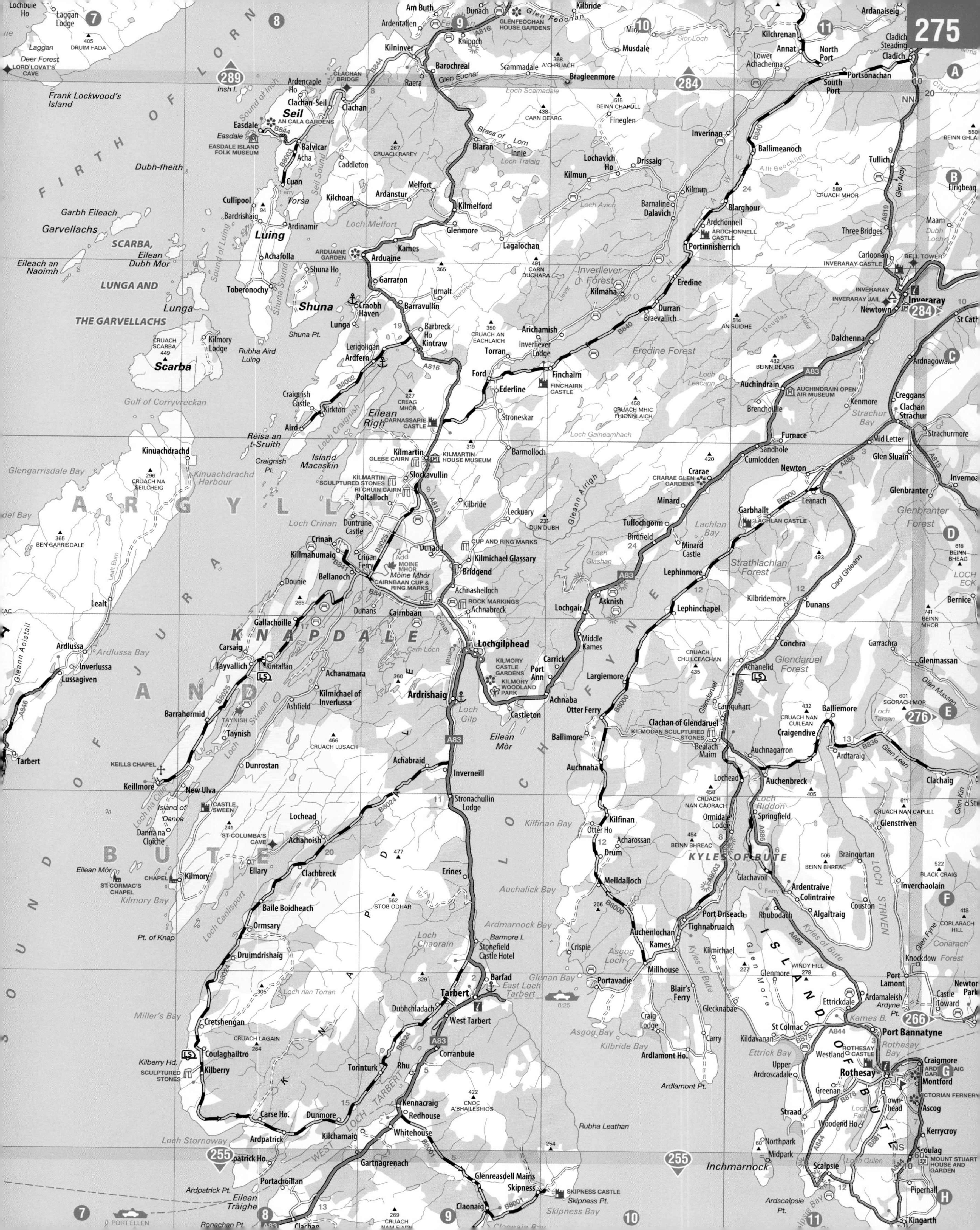

FIRTH OF LORN
ARGYLL
KNAPDALE
AND BUTE
SOUND OF JURA
LOCH FYNE
KYLES OF BUTE
ISLAND OF BUTE
Lochgilphead
Inveraray
Tarbert
Rothesay
Ardrishaig
Kilmartin
Seil
Luing
Shuna
Scarba
Garvellachs
Inchmarnock

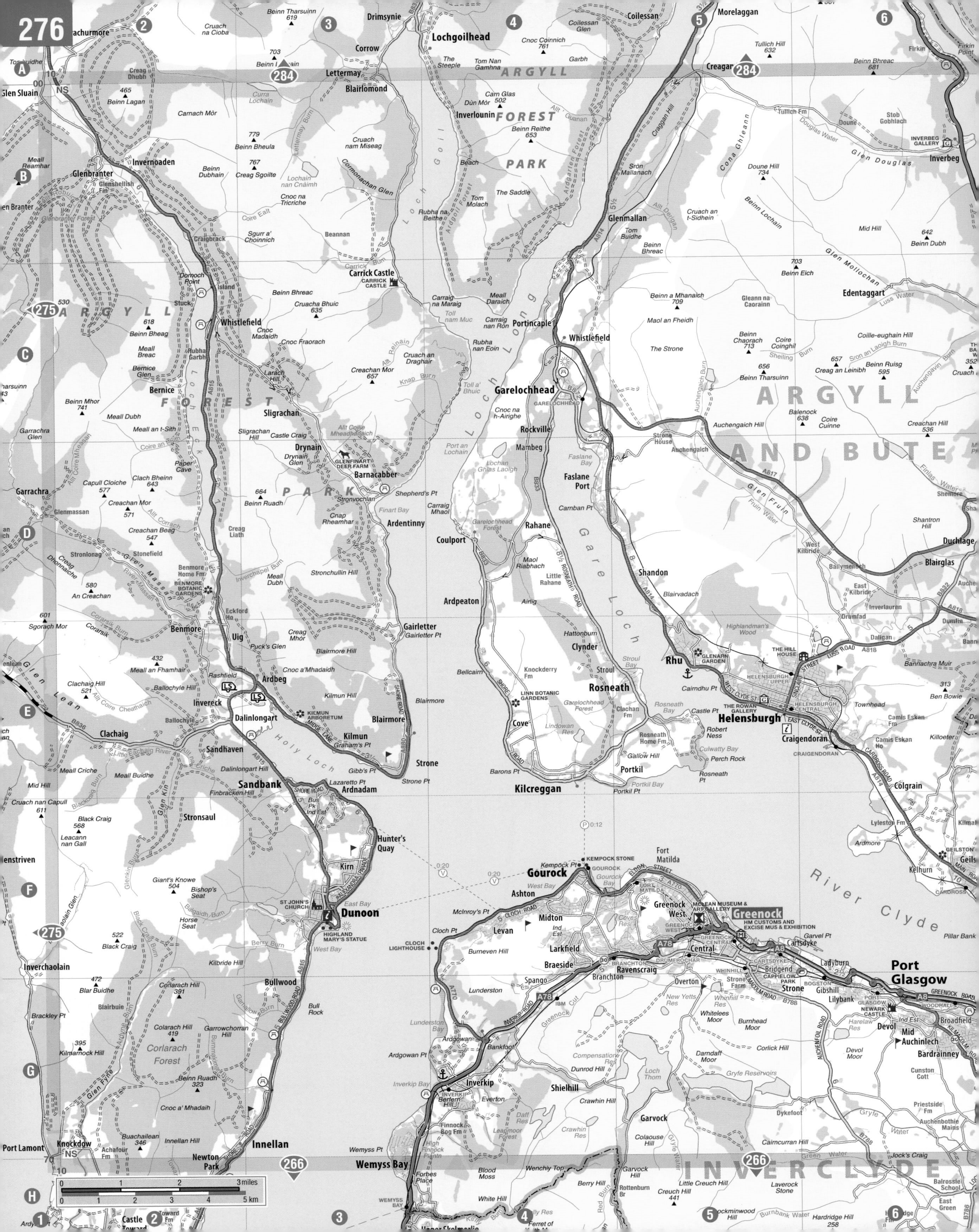
ARGYLL
FOREST
PARK
ARGYLL AND BUTE
INVERCLYDE
River Clyde
Loch Long
Gare Loch
Holy Loch
Loch Eck
Loch Goil
Lochgoilhead
Drimsynie
Corrow
Lettermay
Blairlomond
Inverlounin
Beinn Tharsuinn 619
Cruach na Cioba
Coilessan
Coilessan Glen
Cnoc Coinnich 761
Tom Nan Gamhna
The Steeple
Garbh
Morelaggan
Tullich Hill 632
Beinn Bhreac 681
Firkin
Firkin Point
Creagan
Carn Glas 502
Dùn Mòr
Beinn Reithe 653
Glen Sluain
Beinn Lagan
Creag Dhubh
Curra Lochain
Carnach Mòr
Glenbranter
Invernoaden
Beinn Bheula
Creag Sgoilte
Beinn Dubhain
Lochain nan Cnàimh
Cormonachan Glen
Cnoc na Tricriche
Sgurr a' Choinnich
Beannan
Rubha na Beithe
Beach
The Saddle
Tom Molach
Glenmallan
Tom Buidhe
Beinn Bhreac
Sròn Mallanach
Cona Ghleann
Doune Hill 734
Inverbeg
Inverbeg Gallery
Glen Douglas
Douglas Water
Tullich Fm
Doune
Stob Gobhlach
Beinn Lochain
Cruach an t-Sidhein
Mid Hill
Beinn Dubh 642
Glen Mollochan
Beinn Eich 703
Edentaggart
Luss Water
Craigbrack
Dornoch Point
Island
Stuck
Whistlefield
Carrick Castle
Beinn Bhreac
Cruacha Bhuic 635
Carraig na Maraig
Toll nam Muc
Meall Daraich
Carraig nan Ròn
Portincaple
Rubha nan Eoin
Beinn a Mhanaich 709
Gleann na Caorainn
Maol an Fheidh
The Strone
Beinn Chaorach 713
Coire Coinghil
Beinn Tharsuinn 656
Creag an Leinibh 657
Beinn Ruisg 595
Coille-eughain Hill
Beinn Bheag 618
Meall Breac
Bernice Glen
Bernice
Rubha Garbh
Cnoc Madaidh
Cnoc Fraorach
Larach Hill
Cruach an Draghair
Creachan Mor 657
Knap Burn
Toll a' Bhuic
Garelochhead
Cnoc na h-Airighe
Rockville
Mambeg
Faslane Bay
Faslane Port
Auchengaich
Auchengaich Hill
Balenock 638
Coire Cuinne
Creachan Hill 536
Beinn Mhor 741
Meall Dubh
Meall an t-Sìth
Garrachra Glen
Paper Cave
Sligrachan
Sligrachan Hill
Castle Craig
Drynain
Drynain Glen
Glenfinart Deer Farm
Barnacabber
Port an Lochain
Lochan Ghlas Laoigh
Shepherd's Pt
Stronvochlan
Finart Bay
Carraig Mhaol
Ardentinny
Garelochhead Forest
Rahane
Carnban Pt
Glen Fruin
Fruin Water
Shantron Hill
Duchlage
Garrachra
Capull Cloiche 577
Clach Bheinn 643
Beinn Ruadh 664
Creachan Mor 571
Glenmassan
Creachan Beag 547
Creag Liath
Cnap Rheamhar
Coulport
Maol Riabhach
Little Rahane
West Kilbride
Blairglas
Shandon
Stronlonag
Stonefield
Benmore Home Fm
Benmore Botanic Gardens
Stronchullin Hill
Meall Dubh
An Creachan
Ardpeaton
Airlig
Blairvadach
East Kilbride
Inverlauren
Sgorach Mor 601
Corarsik
Eckford Ho
Benmore
Uig
Creag Mhor
Gairletter
Gairletter Pt
Blairmore Hill
Hattonburn
Clynder
Highlandman's Wood
The Hill House
Daligan
Glen Lean
Meall an Fhamhair 432
Clachaig Hill 521
Ballochyle Hill
Rashfield
Puck's Glen
Ardbeg
Cnoc a'Mhadaidh
Bellcairn
Knockderry Fm
Stroul
Stroul Bay
Rhu
Glenarn Garden
Cairndhu Pt
Helensburgh
Helensburgh Upper
Bannachra Muir
Ben Bowie 313
Invereck
Dalinlongart
Kilmun Arboretum
Kilmun Hill
Blairmore
Linn Botanic Gardens
Rosneath
Garelochhead Forest
Clachan Fm
Rosneath Bay
Castle Pt
The Rowan Gallery
Townhead
Clachaig
Ballochyle
Kilmun
Graham's Pt
Cove
Lindowan Res
Robert Ness
Craigendoran
Camis Eskan Fm
Killoeter
Sandhaven
Dalinlongart Hill
Strone
Strone Pt
Gibb's Pt
Barons Pt
Rosneath Home Fm
Gallow Hill
Culwatty Bay
Perch Rock
Rosneath Pt
Meall Criche
Meall Buidhe
Mid Hill
Sandbank
Lazaretto Pt
Ardnadam
Finbracken Hill
Kilcreggan
Portkil
Portkil Bay
Portkil Pt
Colgrain
Cruach nan Capull 611
Black Craig 568
Leacann nan Gall
Stronsaul
Hunter's Quay
Lyleston Fm
Ardmore
Kelhurn
Benstriven
Kirn
Fort Matilda
Kempock Stone
Gourock
Gourock Bay
Ashton
West Bay
Giant's Knowe 504
Bishop's Seat
Horse Seat
St John's Church
Dunoon
East Bay
Highland Mary's Statue
McInroy's Pt
Cloch Road
Midton
Greenock West
McLean Museum & Art Gallery
Greenock
HM Customs and Excise Mus & Exhibition
Garvel Pt
Pillar Bank
Black Craig 522
Berry Burn
West Bay
Cloch Pt
Cloch Lighthouse
Levan
Burneven Hill
Larkfield
Central
Cartsdyke
Inverchaolain
Kilbride Hill
Braeside
Ravenscraig
Branchton
Spango
Overton
Bridgend
Strone
Ladyburn
Port Glasgow
Gibshill
Lilybank
Newark Castle
Broadfield
Blar Buidhe 472
Corlarach Hill 391
Bullwood
Bull Rock
Lunderston
Lunderston Bay
New Yetts Res
Whitelees Moor
Burnhead Moor
Harelaw Res
Devol
Mid Auchinlech
Bardrainney
Devol Moor
Brackley Pt
Blairbuie
Colarach Hill 419
Garrowchorran Hill
Corlarach Forest
Kilmarnock Hill 395
Ardgowan
Bankfoot
Ardgowan Pt
Compensation Res
Dunrod Hill
Darndaff Moor
Corlick Hill
Loch Thom
Gryfe Reservoirs
Cunston Cott
Beinn Ruadh 323
Cnoc a' Mhadaidh
Inverkip
Inverkip Bay
Everton
Shielhill
Crawhin Hill
Garvock
Colaouse Hill
Dykefoot
Priestside Fm
Auchenbothie Mains
Buachailean 346
Innellan Hill
Innellan
Finnock Bog Fm
Daff Res
Leapmoor Forest
Crawhin Res
Caimcurran Hill
Jock's Craig
Port Lamont
Knockdow
Achafour Fm
Newton Park
Wemyss Pt
Wemyss Bay
Forbes Place
Blood Moss
Wenchly Top
Berry Hill
Garvock Hill
Rottenburn Br
Little Creuch Hill
Creuch Hill 441
Laverock Stone
Balrossie School
White Hill
Hardridge Hill 258
East Green
Castle Toward
Toward Fm
0 1 2 3 miles
0 1 2 3 4 5 km

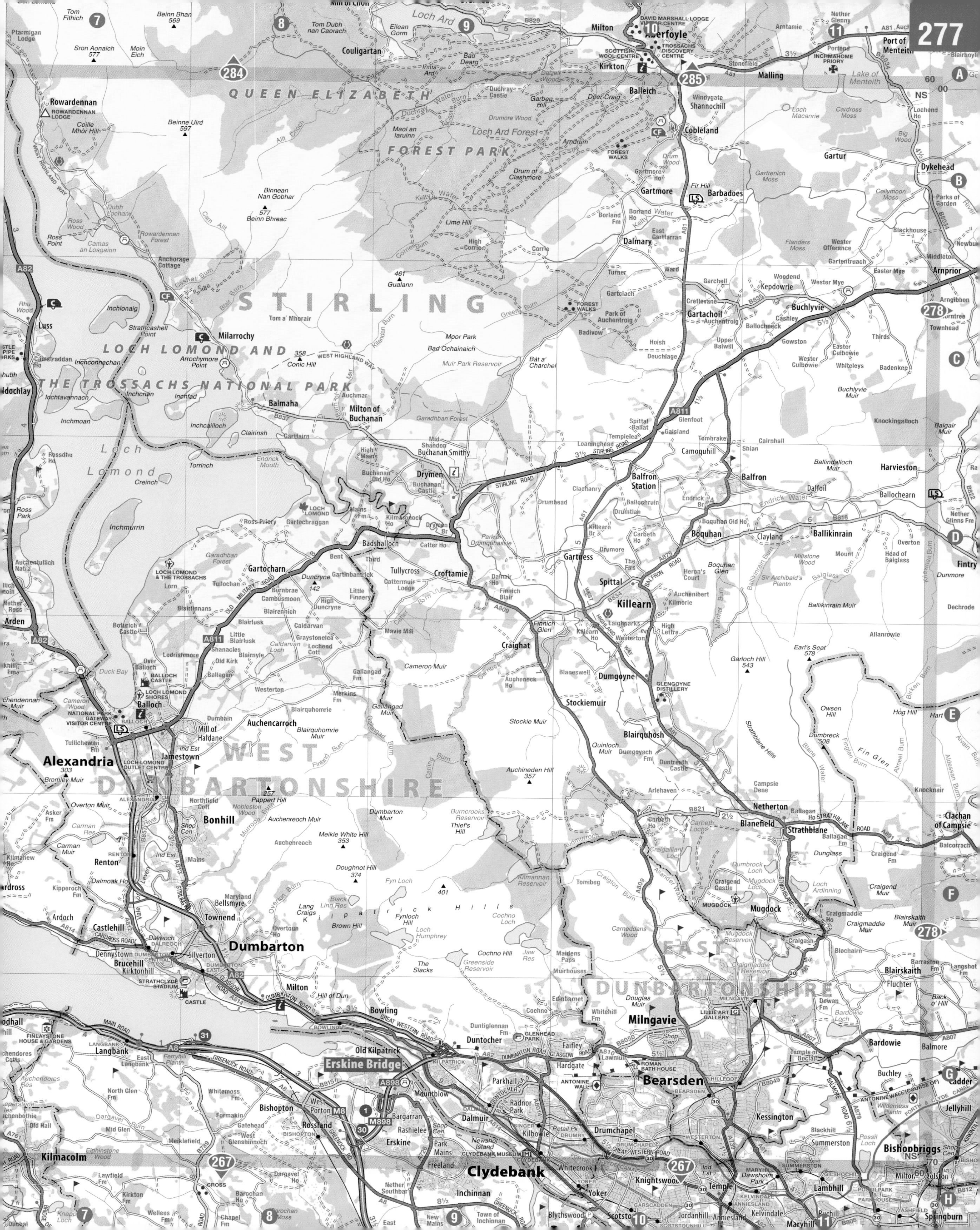

Tom Fithich
Ptarmigan Lodge
Beinn Bhan 569
Sron Aonaich 577
Moin Eich
Tom Dubh nan Caorach
Loch Ard
Eilean Gorm
Couligartan
Milton
DAVID MARSHALL LODGE VISITOR CENTRE
Aberfoyle
SCOTTISH WOOL CENTRE
TROSSACHS DISCOVERY CENTRE
Kirkton
Arntamie
Nether Glenny
Port of Menteith
INCHMAHOME PRIORY
Lake of Menteith
Malling
Stonefield
QUEEN ELIZABETH
FOREST PARK
Rowardennan
ROWARDENNAN LODGE
Coille Mhòr Hill
Beinne Uird 597
Bad Dearg
Innis Ard
Duchray Castle
Garbeg Hill
Deer Craig
Balleich
Windygate
Shannochill
Drumore Wood
Maol an Iaruinn
Loch Ard Forest
Arndrum
Cobleland
FOREST WALKS
Loch Macanrie
Cardross Moss
Gartur
Big Wood
Lochend Ho
Dykehead
Parks of Garden
Drum of Clashmore
Gartmore
Fir Hill
Barbadoes
Gartrenich Moss
Collymoon Moss
WEST HIGHLAND WAY
Binnean Nan Gobhar
577 Beinn Bhreac
Dubh Lochan
Ross Wood
Ross Point
Camas an Losgainn
Rowardennan Forest
Kelty Water
Lime Hill
Borland Fm
Bortand Ho
East Gartfarran
Dalmary
Flanders Moss
Wester Offerance
Blackhouse
Middleton
Gartentruach
Corrie
High Corrie
Anchorage Cottage
A82
Arnprior
Easter Mye
461 Gualann
Ward
Turner
Garchell
Woodend
Kepdowrie
Wester Mye
Arngibbon
Gartclach
Crettevane
Rhu Wood
Inchlonaig
STIRLING
Forest Walks
Park of Auchentroig
Gartachoil
Buchlyvie
Cashley
Ballochneck
Townhead
Luss
Strathcashell Point
Milarrochy
Tom a' Mhorair
Moor Park
Bad Ochainaich
Badivow
Hoish
Upper Balwill
Gowston
Thirds
LOCH LOMOND AND
THE TROSSACHS NATIONAL PARK
Camstraddan Ho
Inchconnachan
Arrochymore Point
358 Conic Hill
Muir Park Reservoir
Bàt a' Charchel
Douchlage
Wester Culbowie
Easter Culbowie
Whiteleys
Badenkep
Inchtavannach
Inchcruin
Inchfad
Auchmar
Balmaha
Milton of Buchanan
Buchlyvie Muir
Inchmoan
Inchcailloch
Clairinsh
Garadhban Forest
A811
Glenfoot
Knockingalloch
Balgair Muir
Gartfairn
Spittal Ballat
Templelea
Gaisland
Loch Lomond
Rossdhu Ho
Creinch
Torrinch
Endrick Mouth
High Mains
Mid Shandon
Buchanan Smithy
Loaninghead
STIRLING ROAD
Tombrake
Camoquhill
Cairnhall
Shian
Ballindalloch Muir
Harvieston
Drymen
Buchanan Old Ho
Buchanan Castle
Balfron Station
Balfron
Clachanry
Drumhead
Ballochruin
Drumtian
Endrick Ho
Endrick Water
Dalfoil
Ballochearn
Ross Park
Inchmurrin
Ross Priory
Gartochraggan
LOCH LOMOND
Mains Fm
Kilmaronock
Drymen Br
Killearn Br
Carbeth Ho
Boquhan Old Ho
Boquhan
Clayland
Ballikinrain
Nether Glinns Fm
Auchentullich
Badshalloch
Catter Ho
Park of Drumquhassle
Drumore
Gartness
The Firs
Boquhan Glen
Mount
Overton
Head of Balglass
Fintry
Millstone Wood
Bent
Third
Gartocharn
Gartinbantrick
Tullycross
Croftamie
LOCH LOMOND & THE TROSSACHS
Tullochan
Lorn
Duncryne 142
Cattermuir Lodge
Dalnair Ho
Finnich Blair
Spittal
Killearn
Heron's Court
Auchenibert
Kilmorie
Sir Archibald's Plantn
Ballikinrain Muir
Dunmore
Dechrode
Burnbrae
Cambusmoon
Little Finnery
High Duncryne
Blairennich
Blairlinnans
A809
Finnich Glen
Laighparks
Westerton
High Lettre
Arden
Boturich Castle
Blairlusk
Caldarvan
Little Blairlusk
Mavie Mill
Allanrowie
Graystonelea
Lochend Cott
Caldarvan Loch
Craighat
Earl's Seat 578
Garloch Hill 543
Ledrishmore
Shanacles
Old Kirk
Blairnyle
Cameron Muir
Over Balloch
BALLOCH CASTLE
Ballagan
Gallangad Fm
Duck Bay
Blaneswell
Dumgoyne
Auchencck Ho
Westerton
Merkins Fm
GLENGOYNE DISTILLERY
LOCH LOMOND SHORES
Balloch
Cameron Wood
NATIONAL PARK GATEWAY VISITOR CENTRE
Gallangad Muir
Stockiemuir
Stockie Muir
Owsen Hill
Hog Hill
Dumbain
Auchencarroch
Blairquhomrie
Mill of Haldane
Blairquhosh
Strathblane Hills
Dumbreck 508
Fin Glen
Tullichewan Fm
Ind Est
Jamestown
Alexandria
303 Bromley Muir
LOCH LOMOND OUTLET CENTRE
WEST
DUNBARTONSHIRE
Quinloch Muir
Dumgoyach Fm
Duntreath Castle
Auchineden Hill 357
257 Pappert Hill
Northfield Cott
Nobleston Wood
Campsie Dene
Arlehaven
Knocknair
Overton Muir
Asker Fm
Carman Res
Bonhill
Auchenreoch Muir
Dumbarton Muir
Burncrooks Reservoir
Thief's Hill
Netherton
Blanefield
Strathblane
Ballagan Fm
Clachan of Campsie
Balcorrach
Carman Muir
Renton
Meikle White Hill 353
Auchenreoch
Carbeth Loch
Craigallian Loch
Dunglass
Craigend Fm
Dalmoak Ho
Kipperoch Fm
Maryland
Bellsmyre
Doughnot Hill 374
Fyn Loch
401
Kilmannan Reservoir
Tomibeg
Dumbrock Loch
Craigend Castle
Mugdock Loch
Loch Ardinning
Craigend Muir
Lang Craigs
Black Linn Res
Kilpatrick Hills
Cochno Loch
Ardoch
Castlehill
Townend
Fynloch Hill
Brown Hill
Carneddans Wood
MUGDOCK
Mugdock
Craigmaddie Ho
Craigmaddie Muir
Blairskaith Muir
CARDROSS ROAD
Dalreoch
Overtoun Ho
Loch Humphrey
Mugdock Reservoir
Craigash
Dennystown
Brucehill
Kirktonhill
Silverton
Dumbarton
Cochno Hill
Jaw Res
Maidens Paps
Muirhouses
EAST
Blochairn
Blairskaith
Barraston Fm
Langshot Fm
STRATHCLYDE STADIUM
The Slacks
Greenside Reservoir
Craigmaddie Reservoir
Fluchter
CASTLE
Milton
Hill of Dun
Edinbarnet
DUNBARTONSHIRE
Dowan Fm
Back o' Hill
Bowling
Cochno
Whitehill Fm
Douglas Muir
Milngavie
LILLIE ART GALLERY
Bardowie Loch
Bardowie
Balmore
FINLAYSTONE HOUSE & GARDENS
Langbank
Duntiglennan Fm
GLENHEAD PARK
Duntocher
Faifley
Temple of Boclair
Old Kilpatrick
Erskine Bridge
Hardgate
ROMAN BATH HOUSE
Buchley
Cadder
Achendores Res
Parkhall
ANTONINE WALL
Bearsden
ANTONINE WALL (COURSE OF)
Mountblow
North Glen Fm
Whitemoss Fm
West Porton
Bishopton
Radnor Park
Kessington
Jellyhill
Wilderness Plantn
Bargarran
Rashielee
Dalmuir
Blackhill
Formakin
Rossland
Kilbowie
Drumchapel
Summerston
Possil Loch
Bishopbriggs
Mid Glen
Erskine
Park Mains
Newshot Island
Meiklefield
West Glenshinnoch
Kilmacolm
Elphinstone Wood
CLYDEBANK MUSEUM
Whitecrook
Knightswood
Freeland
Clydebank
Temple
Dawsholm Park
Lambhill
Milton
Colston
Lawfield Fm
Dargavel Ho
CROSS
Nether Southbar
Yoker
Kirkton Fm
Barochan Ho
Inchinnan
Kelvindale
Springburn
Wellees Fm
Chapel Fm
Barochan Moss
Town of Inchinnan
Blythswood
Scotstoun
Jordanhill
Anniesland
Maryhill
Ruchill
New Mains
East

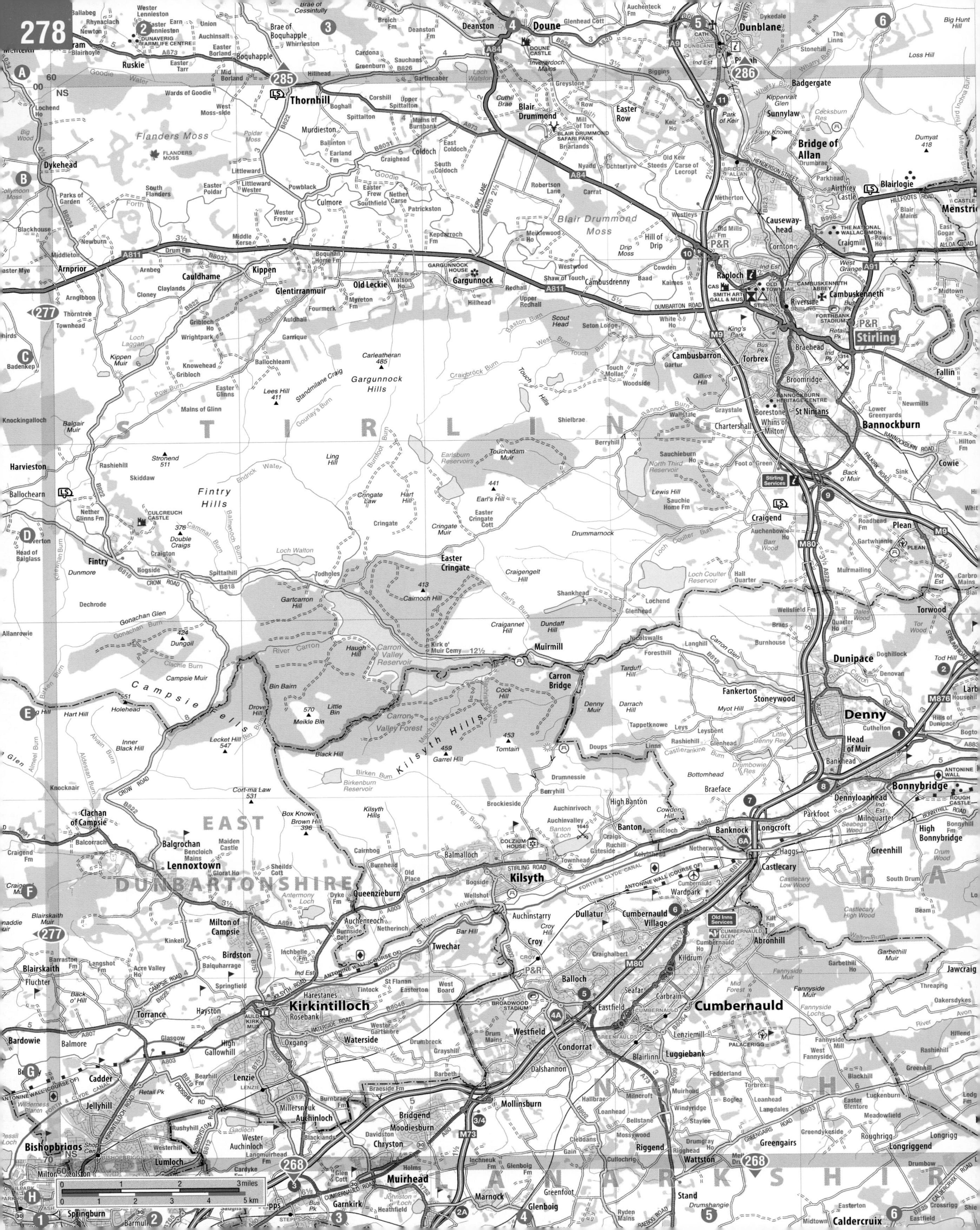

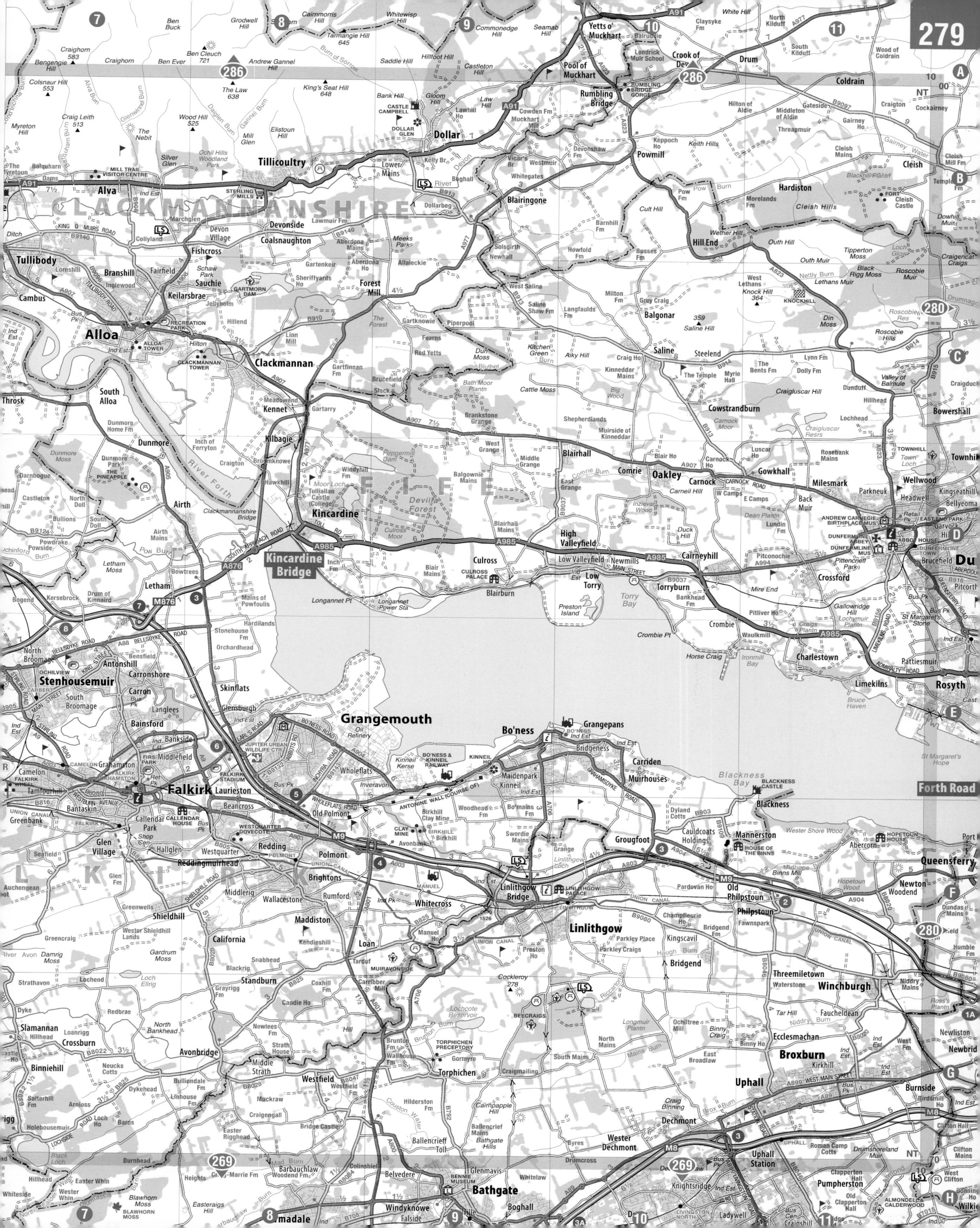
CLACKMANNANSHIRE
FIFE
Kincardine Bridge
Forth Road
Yetts o' Muckhart
Pool of Muckhart
Rumbling Bridge
Crook of Devon
Drum
Coldrain
Cleish
Hardiston
Cleish Hills
Dollar
Tillicoultry
Alva
Devon Village
Devonside
Coalsnaughton
Fishcross
Sauchie
Tullibody
Cambus
Alloa
Clackmannan
Kennet
Kilbagie
South Alloa
Dunmore
Airth
Kincardine
Tulliallan Castle (College)
Blairingone
Powmill
Hill End
Forest Mill
Saline
Steelend
Balgonar
Knockhill
Oakley
Comrie
Carnock
Blairhall
Gowkhall
Milesmark
Cowstrandburn
Dunfermline
Wellwood
Headwell
Cairneyhill
Crossford
High Valleyfield
Low Valleyfield
Newmills
Culross
Low Torry
Torryburn
Blairburn
Crombie
Charlestown
Limekilns
Rosyth
Torry Bay
Preston Island
Longannet Pt
Crombie Pt
Stenhousemuir
Carron
Carronshore
Larbert
Skinflats
Grangemouth
Bo'ness
Grangepans
Carriden
Muirhouses
Blackness
Blackness Bay
Mannerston
Abercorn
Queensferry
Falkirk
Laurieston
Camelon
Tamfourhill
Bantaskin
Callendar Park
Glen Village
Westquarter
Redding
Reddingmuirhead
Polmont
Brightons
Rumford
Wallacestone
Maddiston
Whitecross
Linlithgow Bridge
Linlithgow
Linlithgow Palace
Philpstoun
Old Philpstoun
Newton
Woodend
Grougfoot
Bridgend
Winchburgh
Threemiletown
Kingscavil
Shieldhill
California
Standburn
Avonbridge
Slamannan
Crossburn
Binniehill
Westfield
Torphichen
Broxburn
Uphall
Uphall Station
Dechmont
Wester Dechmont
Pumpherston
Bathgate
Boghall
Armadale
Blackburn
Kirkhill
Burnside
Newliston
River Forth
Union Canal
Antonine Wall (course of)
M9
M8
M876
A91
A907
A985
A904
A803
A706
A801
A89
A899
280
286
269

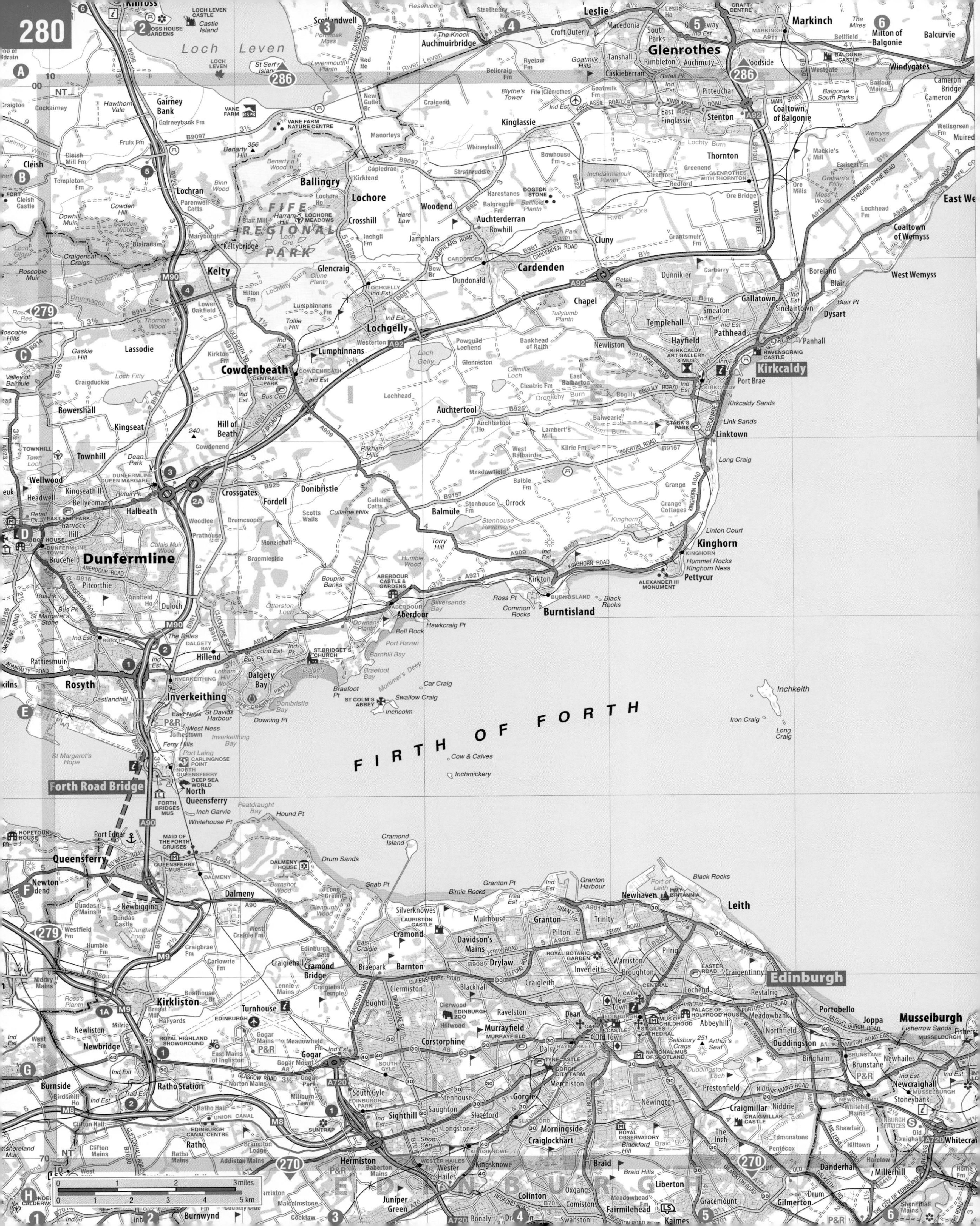
Kinross
Loch Leven
Scotlandwell
Leslie
Glenrothes
Markinch
Milton of Balgonie
Balcurvie
Windygates
Cameron Bridge
Coaltown of Balgonie
Kinglassie
Thornton
Ballingry
Lochore
Lochore Meadows
Fife Regional Park
Lochran
Kelty
Cardenden
Auchterderran
Cluny
Dysart
Gallatown
Sinclairtown
Pathhead
Kirkcaldy
Linktown
Kinghorn
Pettycur
Burntisland
Aberdour
Dalgety Bay
Inverkeithing
Rosyth
Dunfermline
Cowdenbeath
Lochgelly
Auchtertool
Crossgates
Hill of Beath
Halbeath
Lumphinnans
East Wemyss
Coaltown of Wemyss
West Wemyss
FIFE
FIRTH OF FORTH
Inchkeith
Inchcolm
North Queensferry
Forth Road Bridge
Queensferry
Dalmeny
Kirkliston
Newbridge
Ratho
Turnhouse
Cramond
Barnton
Davidson's Mains
Granton
Newhaven
Leith
Trinity
Edinburgh
Portobello
Musselburgh
Joppa
Duddingston
Corstorphine
Murrayfield
Gorgie
Colinton
Liberton
Gilmerton
Craigmillar
Danderhall
Millerhill
Newcraighall
Wester Hailes
Juniper Green
Sighthill
Hermiston
1 2 3 miles
0 1 2 3 4 5 km

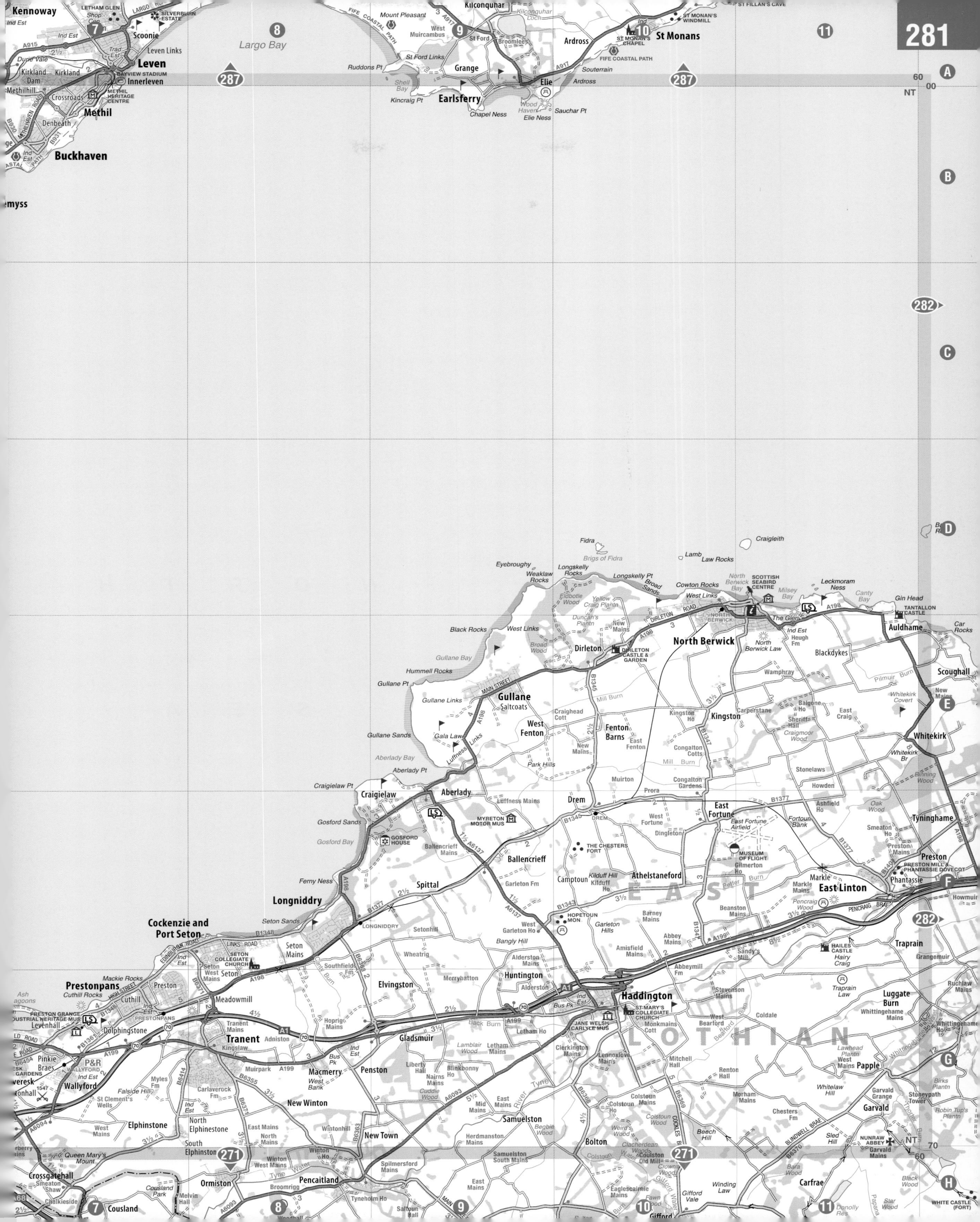
Kennoway
Leven
Innerleven
Methil
Buckhaven
Scoonie
Leven Links
Largo Bay
Kilconquhar
St Monans
Ardross
Elie
Earlsferry
Grange
St Ford
Mount Pleasant
West Muircambus
Broomlees
Chapel Ness
Elie Ness
Saucher Pt
Kincraig Pt
Ruddons Pt
Shell Bay
FIFE COASTAL PATH
287
282
271
Fidra
Craigleith
Lamb
Law Rocks
Eyebroughy
North Berwick
SCOTTISH SEABIRD CENTRE
TANTALLON CASTLE
Auldhame
Scoughall
Dirleton
DIRLETON CASTLE & GARDEN
Gullane
Saltcoats
Gullane Bay
Gullane Sands
Aberlady Bay
Aberlady
Craigielaw
Gosford Sands
Gosford Bay
GOSFORD HOUSE
MYRETON MOTOR MUS
Kingston
Fenton Barns
West Fenton
Drem
East Fortune
MUSEUM OF FLIGHT
Whitekirk
Tyninghame
Preston
PRESTON MILL & PHANTASSIE DOVECOT
Phantassie
East Linton
Athelstaneford
Ballencrieff
THE CHESTERS FORT
Spittal
Longniddry
Cockenzie and Port Seton
SETON COLLEGIATE CHURCH
Prestonpans
Tranent
Meadowmill
Elvingston
Huntington
Haddington
ST MARY'S COLLEGIATE CHURCH
JANE WELSH CARLYLE MUS
HAILES CASTLE
Traprain
Traprain Law
Luggate Burn
Gladsmuir
Macmerry
Penston
Wallyford
Elphinstone
New Winton
Samuelston
New Town
Pencaitland
Ormiston
Bolton
Gifford
Garvald
NUNRAW ABBEY
Papple
Carfrae
Crossgatehall
Cousland
EAST
LOTHIAN

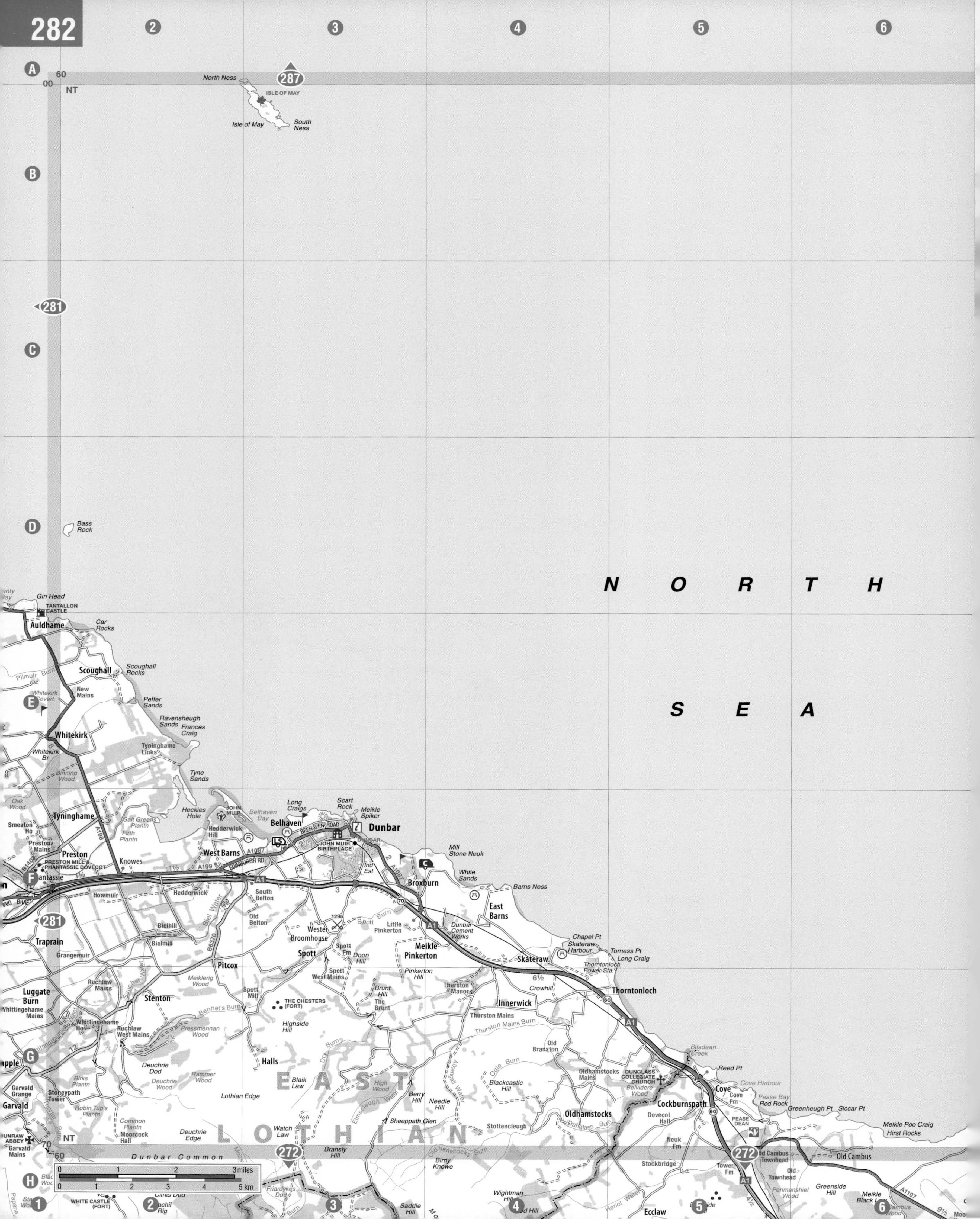

NORTH SEA

Isle of May

North Ness
South Ness

Bass Rock

Gin Head
TANTALLON CASTLE
Auldhame
Car Rocks
Scoughall
Scoughall Rocks
New Mains
Whitekirk Covert
Peffer Sands
Ravensheugh Sands
Frances Craig
Whitekirk
Whitekirk Br
Tyninghame Links
Blinning Wood
Tyne Sands
Oak Wood
Pilmuir Burn
Tyninghame
Salt Greens Plantn
Pleth Plantn
Smeaton Ho
Preston Mains
Preston
Knowes
Heckies Hole
JOHN MUIR
Belhaven Bay
Long Craigs
Scart Rock
Meikle Spiker
Dunbar
Belhaven
Hedderwick Hill
West Barns
JOHN MUIR BIRTHPLACE
Mill Stone Neuk
White Sands
Barns Ness
Ind Est
Broxburn
East Barns
PRESTON MILL
PHANTASSIE DOVECOT
Phantassie
Howmuir
Hedderwick
South Belton
Dunbar Cement Works
Chapel Pt
Skateraw Harbour
Torness Pt
Long Craig
Thorntonloch Power Sta
Bielhill
Old Belton
Little Pinkerton
Wester Broomhouse
Spott Fm
Meikle Pinkerton
Skateraw
Traprain
Bielmill
Spott
Doon Hill
Pinkerton Hill
Grangemuir
Pitcox
Spott West Mains
Thurston Manor
Crowhill
Thorntonloch
Meiklerig Wood
Spott Mill
Brunt Hill
The Brunt
Thurston Mains
Innerwick
Ruchlaw Mains
Luggate Burn
Stenton
THE CHESTERS (FORT)
Thurston Mains Burn
Whittinghame Mains
Whittinghame Ho
Ruchlaw West Mains
Pressmennan Wood
Highside Hill
Bennet's Burn
Old Branxton
Bilsdean Creek
Reed Pt
Deuchrie Dod
Rammer Wood
Blaik Law
High Wood
Berry Hill
Blackcastle Hill
Oldhamstocks Mains
DUNGLASS COLLEGIATE CHURCH
Belvidere Wood
Cove Harbour
Cove
Halls
Cove Fm
Pease Bay
Red Rock
Birks Plantn
Deuchrie Wood
Lothian Edge
Needle Hill
Oldhamstocks
Dovecot Hall
Greenheugh Pt
Siccar Pt
Garvald Grange
Stoneypath Tower
Robin Tup's Plantn
Watch Law
PEASE DEAN
Garvald
Garvald Mains
DUNRAW ABBEY
Common Plantn
Moorcock Hall
Deuchrie Edge
Blackcastle Hill
Stottencleugh
Dunlaw's Burn
Neuk Fm
Meikle Poo Craig
Hirst Rocks
Dunbar Common
Bransly Hill
Birny Knowe
Old Cambus Townhead
Old Cambus
Black Wood
White Castle (Fort)
Achil Rig
Clints Dod
Friardykes Dod
Wightman Hill
Saddle Hill
Stockbridge
Tower Fm
Ecclaw
Penmanshiel Wood
Greenside Wood
Meikle Black

EAST LOTHIAN

0   1   2   3 miles
0   1   2   3   4   5 km

7 8 9 10 11

A

10
00
NT

B

C

D

E

F

G

Fast Castle
Head — Wheat Stack

elegraph
Hill   FAST
CASTLE

NT
70
10

Oatlee Hill

Dowlaw
Burn

Lumsdaine

Lumsdaine
Moor

Coldingham
Loch

Mire
Loch

St Abb's Head

ST ABB'S HEAD

Horsecastle Bay

273

273

Bell

ngham
mon

Cross

7 8 9 10 11

H

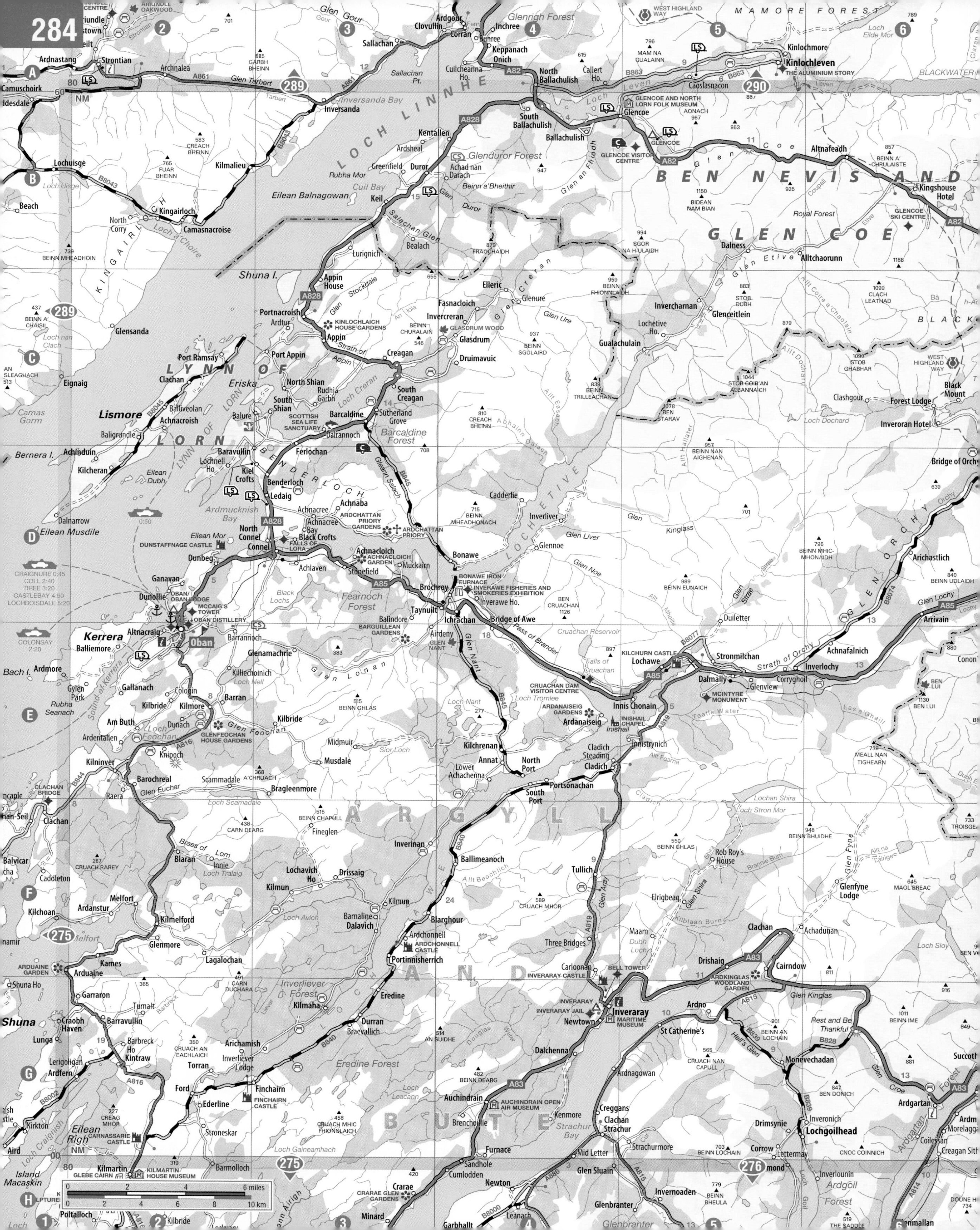

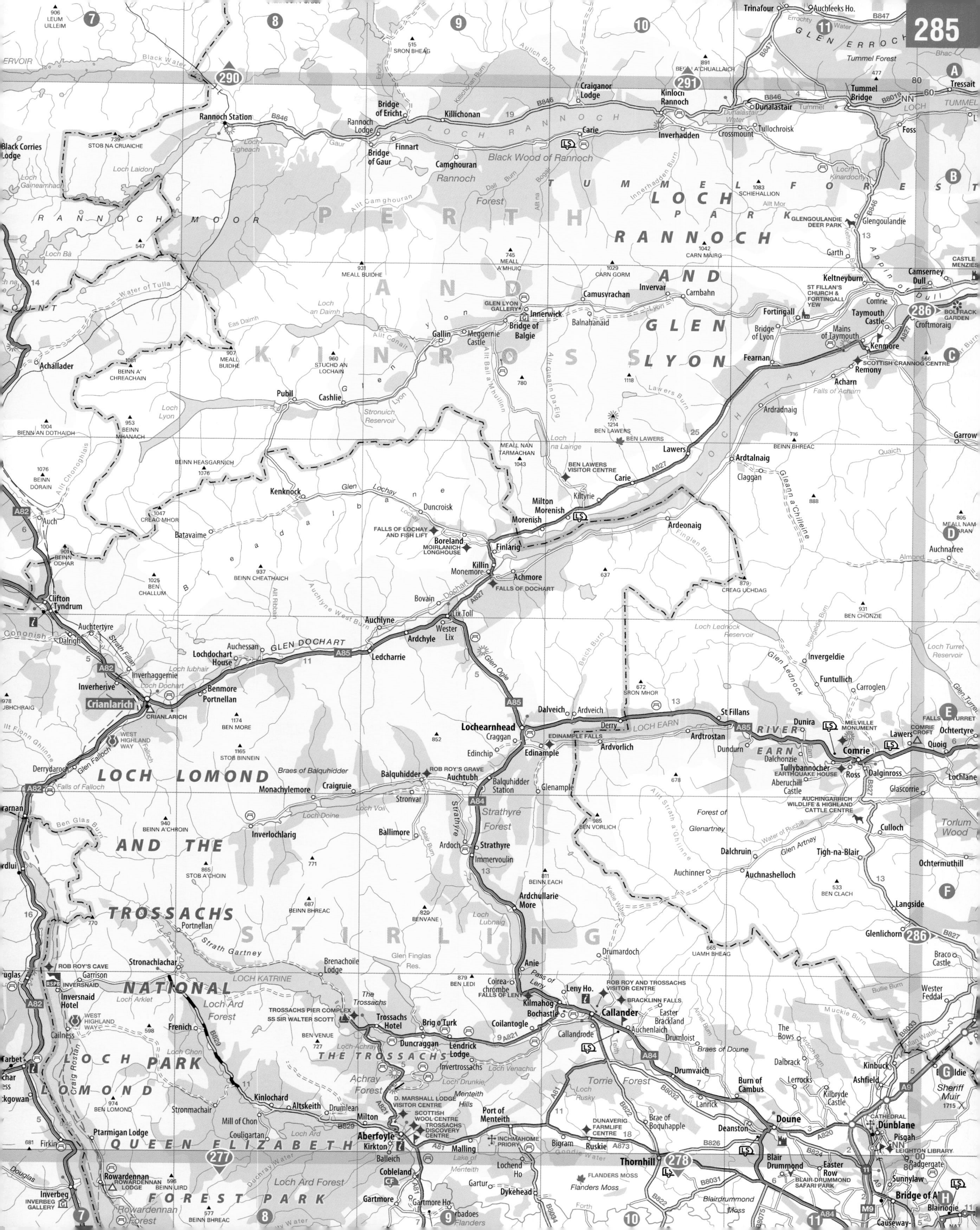
Trinafour
Auchleeks Ho.
B847
GLEN ERROCH
Tummel Forest
Tressait
Tummel Bridge
Dunalastair
Kinloch Rannoch
Craiganor Lodge
Bridge of Ericht
Killichonan
LOCH RANNOCH
Rannoch Station
Rannoch Lodge
Bridge of Gaur
Finnart
Carie
Inverhadden
Crossmount
Tullochroisk
Foss
Black Corries Lodge
STOB NA CRUAICHE
Loch Laidon
Camghouran
Black Wood of Rannoch
Rannoch Forest
RANNOCH MOOR
PERTH AND KINROSS
TUMMEL FOREST
LOCH RANNOCH AND GLEN LYON
SCHIEHALLION
Glengoulandie
GLENGOULANDIE DEER PARK
CARN MAIRG
Garth
Keltneyburn
Camserney
Dull
CASTLE MENZIES
MEALL BUIDHE
CARN GORM
Invervar
Carnbahn
Camusvrachan
GLEN LYON GALLERY
Innerwick
Bridge of Balgie
Balnahanaid
Gallin
Meggernie Castle
Fortingall
ST FILLAN'S CHURCH & FORTINGALL YEW
Bridge of Lyon
Mains of Taymouth
Taymouth Castle
Comrie
BOLFRACKS GARDEN
Croftmoraig
Kenmore
Fearnan
SCOTTISH CRANNOG CENTRE
Remony
Acharn
Falls of Acharn
Achallader
BEINN A' CHREACHAIN
MEALL BUIDHE
STUCHD AN LOCHAIN
Pubil
Cashlie
Loch Lyon
Stronuich Reservoir
BEINN MHANACH
BIENN AN DOTHAIDH
BEN LAWERS
Ardradnaig
Lawers
LOCH TAY
BEINN BHREAC
Garrow
Ardtalnaig
Claggan
MEALL NAN TARMACHAN
BEN LAWERS VISITOR CENTRE
Carie
Kiltyrie
Milton Morenish
Morenish
Ardeonaig
BEINN HEASGARNICH
BEINN DÒRAIN
Kenknock
Glen Lochay
Duncroisk
CREAG MHOR
Auch
Batavaime
FALLS OF LOCHAY AND FISH LIFT
Boreland
MOIRLANICH LONGHOUSE
Finlarig
Killin
Monemore
Achmore
FALLS OF DOCHART
BEINN ODHAR
BEINN CHEATHAICH
BEN CHALLUM
Breadalbane
Clifton
Tyndrum
Bovain
Lix Toll
Wester Lix
Auchlyne
Ardchyle
CREAG UCHDAG
BEN CHONZIE
Auchtertyre
Dalrigh
Strath Fillan
Auchessan
GLEN DOCHART
Lochdochart House
Ledcharrie
A85
Glen Ogle
Loch Lednock Reservoir
Glen Lednock
Invergeldie
Loch Turret Reservoir
Funtullich
Carroglen
Inverhaggernie
Inverherive
Crianlarich
Benmore
Portnellan
BEN MORE
STOB BINNEIN
WEST HIGHLAND WAY
Derrydaroch
Glen Falloch
Falls of Falloch
SRON MHOR
Dalveich
Ardveich
St Fillans
Lochearnhead
Craggan
Edinchip
LOCH EARN
EDINAMPLE FALLS
Edinample
Ardvorlich
Ardtrostan
Dundurn
Dunira
RIVER EARN
MELVILLE MONUMENT
COMRIE CROFT
Lawers
Ochtertyre
Quoig
Comrie
Dalchonzie
Tullybannocher
EARTHQUAKE HOUSE
Ross
Dalginross
Lochlane
Aberuchill Castle
Glascorrie
AUCHINGARRICH WILDLIFE & HIGHLAND CATTLE CENTRE
Braes of Balquhidder
Balquhidder
ROB ROY'S GRAVE
Auchtubh
Balquhidder Station
Glenample
Monachylemore
Craigruie
Stronvar
Loch Voil
Loch Doine
LOCH LOMOND AND THE TROSSACHS NATIONAL PARK
Inverlochlarig
Ballimore
Strathyre
Strathyre Forest
Ardoch
Immervoulin
BEN VORLICH
Forest of Glenartney
Culloch
Torlum Wood
Dalchruin
Glen Artney
Tigh-na-Blair
Auchinner
Auchnashelloch
Ochtermuthill
BEINN A' CHROIN
STOB A' CHOIN
BEINN EACH
BEN CLACH
BEINN BHREAC
BENVANE
Loch Lubnaig
Ardchullarie More
Langside
Portnellan
Strath Gartney
Glen Finglas Res.
Drumardoch
UAMH BHEAG
Glenlichorn
Braco Castle
Stronachlachar
ROB ROY'S CAVE
Garrison
INVERSNAID
Inversnaid Hotel
LOCH KATRINE
Loch Arklet
Loch Ard Forest
Brenachoile Lodge
BEN LEDI
Anie
Pass of Leny
Coirea-chrombe
FALLS OF LENY
Leny Ho.
ROB ROY AND TROSSACHS VISITOR CENTRE
BRACKLINN FALLS
Kilmahog
Bochastle
Callander
Wester Feddal
The Trossachs
TROSSACHS PIER COMPLEX
SS SIR WALTER SCOTT
Trossachs Hotel
Brig o'Turk
Coilantogle
Easter Brackland
Auchenlaich
Drumloist
Braes of Doune
The Bows
Cailness
Frenich
BEN VENUE
Duncraggan
Lendrick Lodge
Callandrode
THE TROSSACHS
Invertrossachs
Loch Venachar
Loch Drunkie
Achray Forest
Torrie Forest
Drumvaich
Burn of Cambus
Dalbrack
Lerrocks
Kinbuck
Ashfield
Sheriff Muir
Tarbet
LOCH LOMOND
BEN LOMOND
Kinlochard
Altskeith
Drumlean
D. MARSHALL LODGE VISITOR CENTRE
Menteith Hills
Port of Menteith
Lanrick
Kilbryde Castle
Stronmachair
Mill of Chon
Milton
SCOTTISH WOOL CENTRE
TROSSACHS DISCOVERY CENTRE
DUNAVERIG FARMLIFE CENTRE
Brae of Boquhapple
Deanston
Doune
CATHEDRAL
Dunblane
Ptarmigan Lodge
Couligartan
Aberfoyle
Kirkton
INCHMAHOME PRIORY
Malling
Bigram
Ruskie
Pisgah
LEIGHTON LIBRARY
QUEEN ELIZABETH FOREST PARK
Balleich
Lake of Menteith
Lochend Ho
Thornhill
Blair Drummond
Easter Row
Badgergate
Sunnylaw
Rowardennan
ROWARDENNAN LODGE
BEINN UIRD
Cobleland
Gartur
Dykehead
FLANDERS MOSS
Flanders Moss
Blairdrummond Moss
BLAIR DRUMMOND SAFARI PARK
Bridge of Allan
Inverbeg
INVERBEG GALLERY
Rowardennan Forest
Gartmore
Gartmore Ho
Forth
BEINN BHREAC
Blairlogie
Causeway-

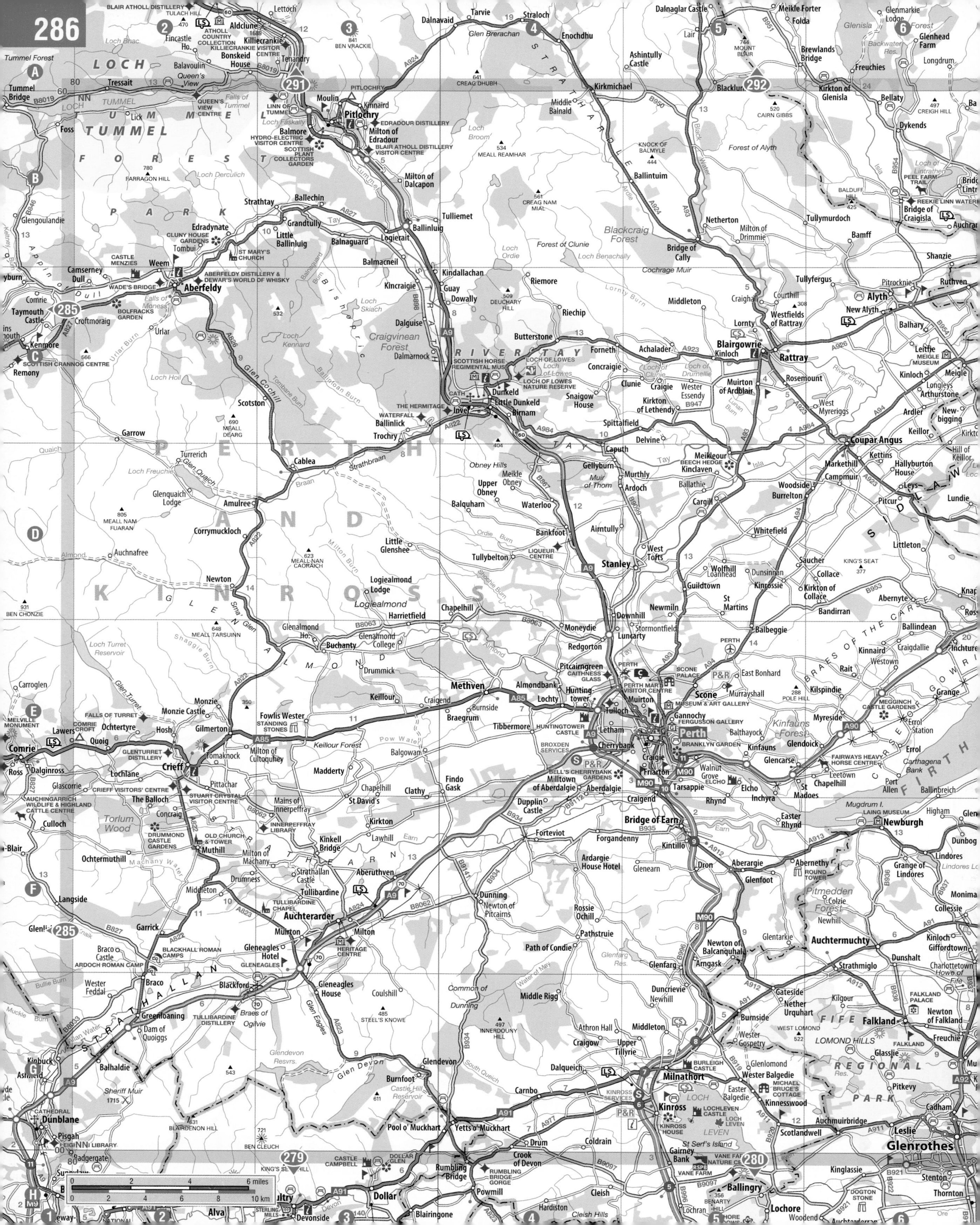

BLAIR ATHOLL DISTILLERY
TULACH HILL
Lettoch
Aldclune
Killiecrankie
Fincastle Ho.
Loch Bhac
Tummel Forest
LOCH
Bonskeid House
Balavoulin
Queen's View
Tenandry
Tummel Bridge
Tressait
LOCH TUMMEL
Lick
Foss
Moulin
PITLOCHRY
Kinnaird
Pitlochry
EDRADOUR DISTILLERY
Milton of Edradour
Balmore
HYDRO-ELECTRIC VISITOR CENTRE
SCOTTISH PLANT COLLECTORS GARDEN
BLAIR ATHOLL DISTILLERY VISITOR CENTRE
TUMMEL FOREST PARK
780 FARRAGON HILL
Loch Derculich
Milton of Dalcapon
Dalnavaid
Tarvie
Straloch
Enochdhu
Glen Brerachan
641 CREAG DHUBH
Kirkmichael
Middle Balnald
Ashintully Castle
Dalnaglar Castle
Lair
Meikle Forter
Folda
Glenmarkie Lodge
Glenisla
Glenhead Farm
Brewlands Bridge
Freuchies
Longdrum
Blacklunans
520 CAIRN GIBBS
Kirkton of Glenisla
Bellaty
497 CREIGH HILL
Dykends
Forest of Alyth
KNOCK OF BALMYLE
Loch Broom
534 MEALL REAMHAR
561 CREAG NAM MIAL
Ballintuim
Loch of Lintrathen
PEEL FARM TRAIL
BALDUFF HILL
REEKIE LINN WATERFALL
Bridge of Craigisla
Auchrannie
Strathtay
Ballechin
Glengoulandie
Edradynate
CLUNY HOUSE GARDENS
Grandtully
Little Ballinluig
Tombui
ST MARY'S CHURCH
Ballinluig
Tulliemet
Logierait
Balnaguard
Netherton
Milton of Drimmie
Tullymurdoch
Bamff
Blackcraig Forest
Forest of Clunie
Loch Ordie
Loch Benachally
Bridge of Cally
Cochrage Muir
Shanzie
CASTLE MENZIES
Weem
Camserney
Dull
Aberfeldy
ABERFELDY DISTILLERY & DEWAR'S WORLD OF WHISKY
WADE'S BRIDGE
Falls of Moness
Comrie
Taymouth Castle
Kenmore
BOLFRACKS GARDEN
Croftmoraig
Urlar
SCOTTISH CRANNOG CENTRE
Remony
Balmacneil
Kindallachan
Kincraigie
Guay
Dowally
Loch Skiach
509 DEUCHARY HILL
Riemore
Riechip
Tullyfergus
Pitrocknie
Ruthven
Alyth
New Alyth
Courthill
Craighall
Westfields of Rattray
Middleton
Dalguise
Craigvinean Forest
Dalmarnock
Loch Kennard
Butterstone
Forneth
Achalader
Blairgowrie
Kinloch
Rattray
Lornty
Balhary
RIVER TAY
SCOTTISH HORSE REGIMENTAL MUSEUM
LOCH OF LOWES VISITOR CENTRE
LOCH OF LOWES NATURE RESERVE
Dunkeld
Little Dunkeld
Birnam
Concraigie
Clunie
Craigie
Kirkton of Lethendy
Wester Essendy
Muirton of Ardblair
Rosemount
Meigle Museum
Meigle
Longleys
Arthurstone
Loch Hoil
Scotston
Glen Cochill
690 MEALL DEARG
THE HERMITAGE
Inver
Ballinlick
Trochry
Snaigow House
Spittalfield
Delvine
West Myreriggs
Ardler
New-bigging
Coupar Angus
Keillor
Garrow
Turrerich
Glen Quaich
Loch Freuchie
Cablea
Strathbraan
Obney Hills
Caputh
Meikleour
BEECH HEDGE
Kinclaven
Ballathie
Gellyburn
Murthly
Ardoch
Muir of Thorn
Markethill
Campmuir
Kettins
Hallyburton House
Hill of Keillor
Glenquaich Lodge
Amulree
805 MEALL NAM FUARAN
Upper Obney
Meikle Obney
Balquharn
Waterloo
Cargill
Woodside
Burrelton
Pitcur
Lundie
Corrymuckloch
Auchnafree
Almond
Little Glenshee
623 MEALL NAN CAORAICH
Bankfoot
LIQUEUR CENTRE
Tullybelton
Airntully
West Tofts
Stanley
Whitefield
Littleton
Wolfhill
Loanhead
Dunsinnan
Saucher
Collace
KING'S SEAT
Kirkton of Collace
Guildtown
Kinrossie
St Martins
Abernyte
Bandirran
Newton
931 BEN CHONZIE
PERTH AND KINROSS
Logiealmond Lodge
Logiealmond
Harrietfield
Chapelhill
Downhill
Newmiln
Stormontfield
Balbeggie
Ballindean
648 MEALL TARSUINN
Glenalmond Ho.
Buchanty
Glenalmond College
Moneydie
Luncarty
Redgorton
PERTH
Kinnaird
Craigdallie
Inchture
Loch Turret Reservoir
GLEN ALMOND
Drummick
Pitcairngreen
CAITHNESS GLASS
SCONE PALACE
East Bonhard
Rait
Westown
BRAES OF THE CARSE
Carroglen
Monzie
Monzie Castle
FALLS OF TURRET
COMRIE CROFT
Ochtertyre
Hosh
Gilmerton
Fowlis Wester
STANDING STONES
Keillour
Methven
Craigend
Almondbank
Huntingtower
Lochty
PERTH MART VISITOR CENTRE
Muirton
Scone
Murrayshall
288 POLE HILL
Kilspindie
MEGGINCH CASTLE GARDENS
Grange
Lawers
Quoig
Comrie
GLENTURRET DISTILLERY
Crieff
Tomaknock
Milton of Cultoquhey
Keillour Forest
Burnside
Braegrum
Tibbermore
HUNTINGTOWER CASTLE
Tulloch
MUSEUM & ART GALLERY
Gannochy
FERGUSSON GALLERY
Balthayock
Kinfauns Forest
Myreside
Errol Station
Ross
Dalginross
Glascorrie
CRIEFF VISITORS' CENTRE
Pittachar
STUART CRYSTAL VISITOR CENTRE
Lochlane
Madderty
Balgowan
Findo Gask
Letham
Cherrybank
BROXDEN SERVICES
Perth
BRANKLYN GARDEN
Kinfauns
Glendoick
Errol
AUCHINGARRICH WILDLIFE & HIGHLAND CATTLE CENTRE
The Balloch
Concraig
Torlum Wood
Mains of Innerpeffray
Chapelhill
Clathy
St David's
BELL'S CHERRYBANK GARDENS
Milltown of Aberdalgie
Aberdalgie
Craigie
Friarton
Walnut Grove
ELCHO
Elcho
Tarsappie
Glencarse
FAIRWAYS HEAVY HORSE CENTRE
Leetown
Chapelhill
St Madoes
Carthagena Bank
Port Allen
Ballinbreich
FIRTH OF TAY
Culloch
DRUMMOND CASTLE GARDENS
OLD CHURCH & TOWER
INNERPEFFRAY LIBRARY
Kirkton
Dupplin Castle
Craigend
Rhynd
Easter Rhynd
Mugdrum I.
LAING MUSEUM
Newburgh
Higham
Muthill
Milton of Machany
Kinkell Bridge
Lawhill
Forteviot
Forgandenny
Bridge of Earn
Kintillo
Dunbog
Lindores
Ochtermuthill
Machany Water
Strathallan Castle
Aberuthven
Ardargie House Hotel
Glenearn
Dron
Aberargie
Abernethy
ROUND TOWER
Grange of Lindores
Drumness
Tullibardine
Glenfoot
Middleton
Langside
TULLIBARDINE CHAPEL
Auchterarder
Dunning
Newton of Pitcairns
Rossie Ochill
Pitmedden Forest
Colzie
Newhill
Collessie
Garrick
Muirton
Milton
HERITAGE CENTRE
Pathstruie
Glentarkie
Auchtermuchty
Kinloch
Giffordtown
Braco Castle
BLACKHALL ROMAN CAMPS
ARDOCH ROMAN CAMP
Gleneagles Hotel
GLENEAGLES
Path of Condie
Glenfarg Res.
Newton of Balcanquhal
Glenfarg
Arngask
Strathmiglo
Dunshalt
Charlottetown
Howe of Fife
Wester Feddal
Braco
Blackford
Gleneagles House
Coulshill
Common of Dunning
Water of May
Middle Rigg
Duncrievie
Newhill
Gateside
Nether Urquhart
Kilgour
FALKLAND PALACE
Greenloaning
TULLIBARDINE DISTILLERY
Braes of Ogilvie
STRATHALLAN
Glen Eagles
485 STEEL'S KNOWE
497 INNERDOUNY HILL
Athron Hall
Middleton
Burnside
Wester Gospetry
WEST LOMOND
FIFE
Falkland
Newton of Falkland
Freuchie
Dam of Quoiggs
Kinbuck
Ashfield
Balhaldie
543
Glendevon Resvrs.
Glen Devon
Glendevon
South Queich
Craigow
Upper Tillyrie
LOMOND HILLS
FALKLAND
Glasslie
REGIONAL PARK
Sheriff Muir
1715
Burnfoot
Castlehill Reservoir
611
Dalqueich
Milnathort
BURLEIGH CASTLE
Glenlomond
Wester Balgedie
Easter Balgedie
MICHAEL BRUCE'S COTTAGE
Kinnesswood
Pitkevy
Carnbo
KINROSS SERVICES
Kinross
LOCHLEVEN CASTLE
LOCH LEVEN
KINROSS HOUSE
Cadham
CATHEDRAL
Dunblane
831 BLAIRDENON HILL
Pool o' Muckhart
Yetts o' Muckhart
Drum
Coldrain
St Serf's Island
Auchmuirbridge
Scotlandwell
Leslie
Glenrothes
Pisgah
LIBRARY
Radgergate
721 BEN CLEUCH
KING'S SEAT HILL
CASTLE CAMPBELL
DOLLAR GLEN
Rumbling Bridge
RUMBLING BRIDGE GORGE
Crook of Devon
Gairney Bank
VANE FARM NATURE CENTRE
Kinglassie
Stenton
Thornton
Powmill
Dollar
Blairingone
Hardiston
Cleish
Cleish Hills
Ballingry
356 BENARTY HILL
Lochore
Lochran
DOGTON STONE
Woodend
Alva
Devonside
0 2 4 6 miles
0 2 4 6 8 10 km

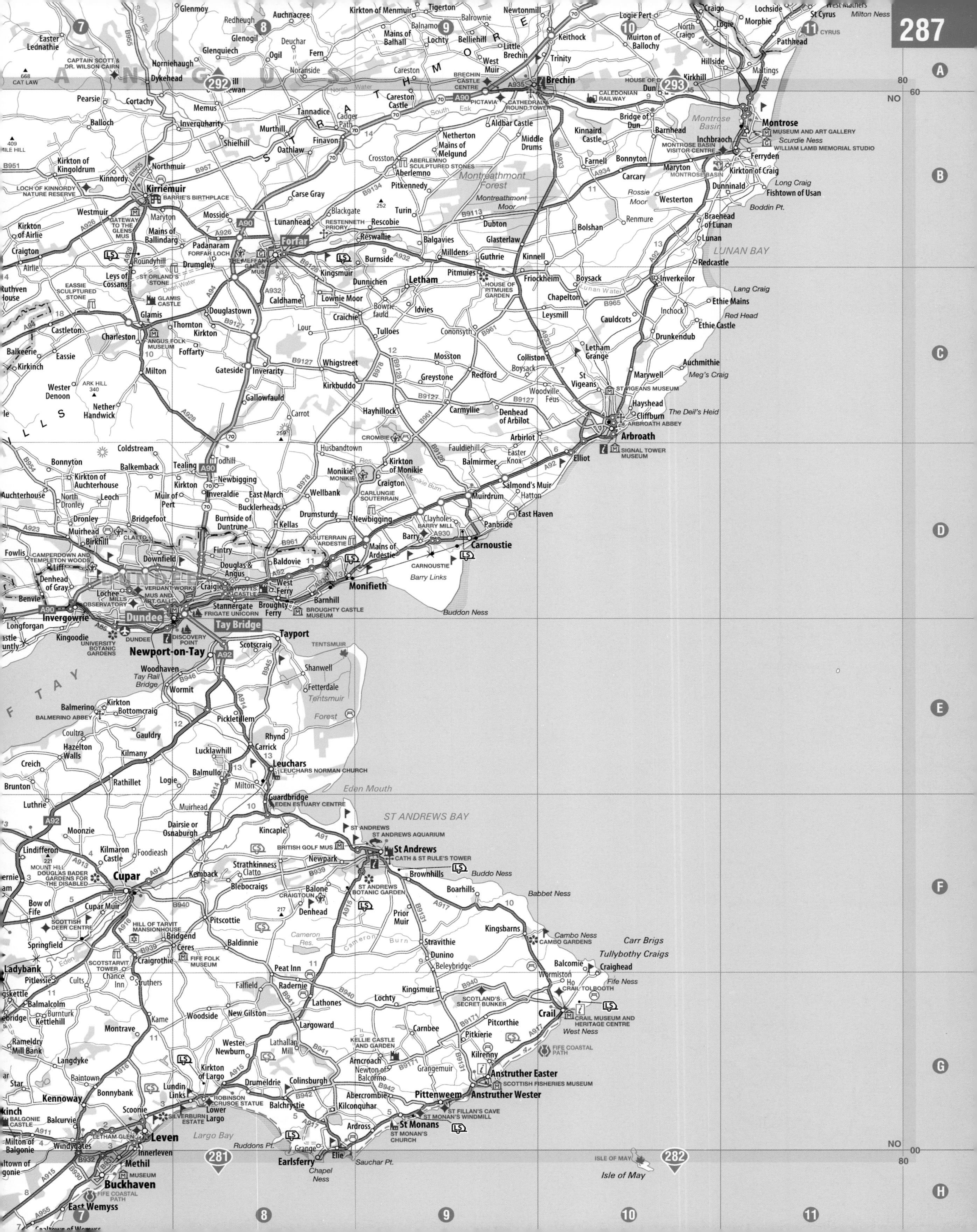
Montrose
Arbroath
Forfar
Brechin
Kirriemuir
Dundee
Carnoustie
Monifieth
Newport-on-Tay
Tayport
Leuchars
St Andrews
Cupar
Crail
Anstruther Easter
Anstruther Wester
Pittenweem
St Monans
Leven
Methil
Buckhaven
Elie
Earlsferry
Isle of May
Tay Bridge
LUNAN BAY
ST ANDREWS BAY
Largo Bay
Montrose Basin
Tentsmuir Forest
Barry Links
Buddon Ness
Eden Mouth
Fife Ness
Carr Brigs
Tullybothy Craigs

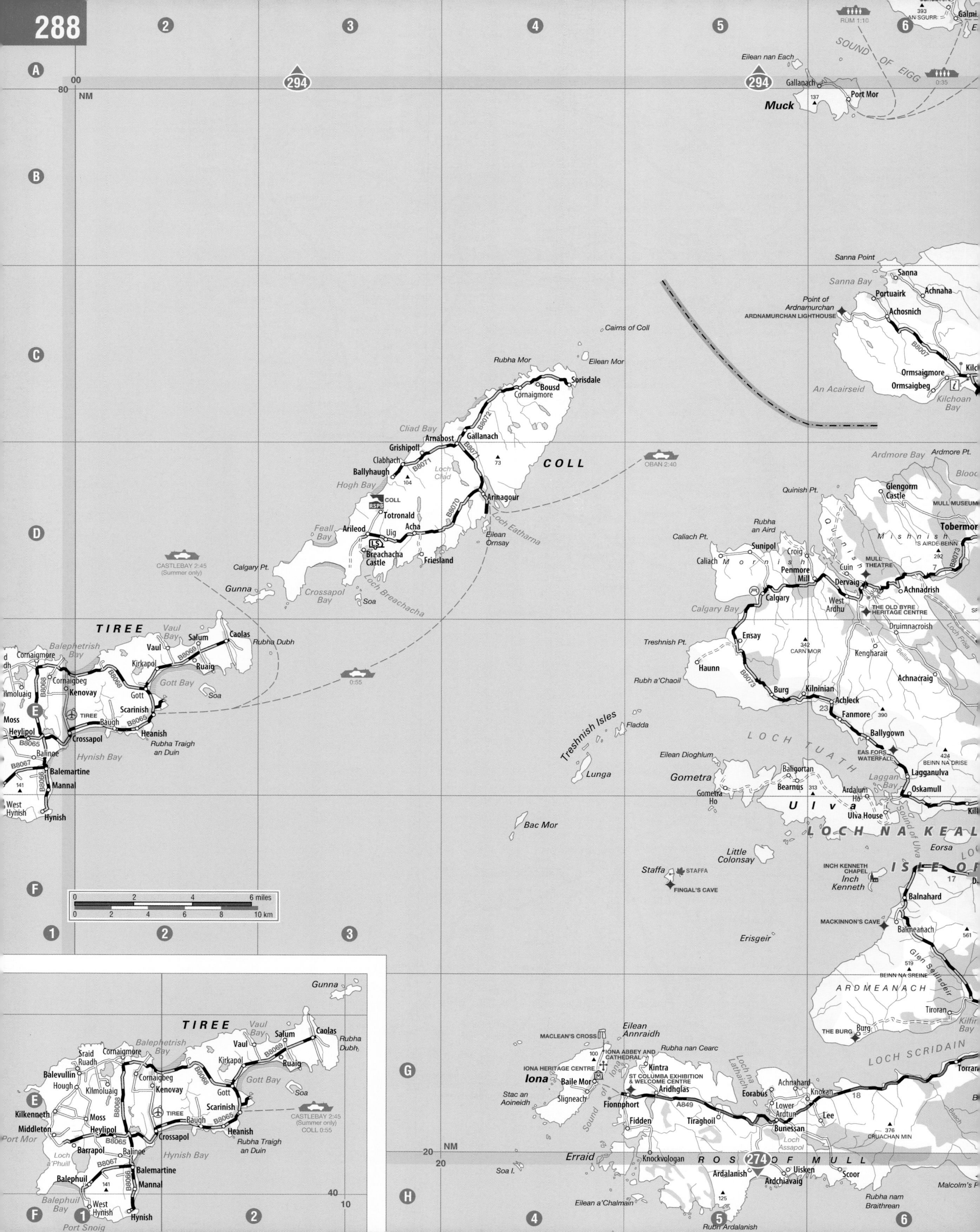

294
294
274
Muck
Gallanach
Port Mor
Eilean nan Each
SOUND OF EIGG
RÙM 1:10
AN SGURR
Galmi
Sanna Point
Sanna Bay
Sanna
Portuairk
Achnaha
Point of Ardnamurchan
ARDNAMURCHAN LIGHTHOUSE
Achosnich
Ormsaigmore
Ormsaigbeg
Kilchoan Bay
An Acairseid
Cairns of Coll
Eilean Mor
Rubha Mor
Sorisdale
Bousd
Cornaigmore
Cliad Bay
Arnabost
Gallanach
Grishipoll
Clabhach
Ballyhaugh
Hogh Bay
COLL
Loch Cliad
Arinagour
OBAN 2:40
Totronald
Feall Bay
Arileod
Uig
Acha
Breachacha Castle
Friesland
Eilean Ornsay
Loch Eatharna
Calgary Pt.
Gunna
Crossapol Bay
Soa
Loch Breachacha
CASTLEBAY 2:45 (Summer only)
TIREE
Vaul Bay
Salum
Caolas
Rubha Dubh
Balephetrish Bay
Cornaigmore
Vaul
Kirkapol
Ruaig
Gott Bay
Cornaigbeg
Kenovay
Gott
Soa
Scarinish
Moss
Heylipol
Baugh
Crossapol
Heanish
Rubha Traigh an Duin
Balinoe
Hynish Bay
Balemartine
Mannal
West Hynish
Hynish
0:55
Ardmore Bay
Ardmore Pt.
Quinish Pt.
Glengorm Castle
MULL MUSEUM
Tobermory
Rubha an Aird
Caliach Pt.
Sunipol
Caliach
Croig
Penmore Mill
Mishnish
Cuin
MULL THEATRE
Dervaig
Achnadrish
Calgary
Calgary Bay
West Ardhu
THE OLD BYRE HERITAGE CENTRE
Treshnish Pt.
Ensay
CARN MOR
Druimnacroish
Kengharair
Haunn
Rubh a'Chaoil
Burg
Kilninian
Achnacraig
Achleck
Fanmore
Treshnish Isles
Fladda
LOCH TUATH
Ballygown
EAS FORS WATERFALL
BEINN NA DRISE
Eilean Dioghlum
Lunga
Gometra
Baligortan
Bearnus
Gometra Ho
Ulva
Ardalum Ho
Laggan Bay
Lagganulva
Oskamull
Ulva House
Bac Mor
LOCH NA KEAL
Eorsa
Little Colonsay
Staffa
STAFFA
FINGAL'S CAVE
INCH KENNETH CHAPEL
Inch Kenneth
ISLE OF
Balnahard
MACKINNON'S CAVE
Balmeanach
Erisgeir
Glen Seilisdeir
BEINN NA SREINE
ARDMEANACH
Tiroran
Kilfinichen Bay
THE BURG
Burg
LOCH SCRIDAIN
Eilean Annraidh
MACLEAN'S CROSS
IONA ABBEY AND CATHEDRAL
Rubha nan Cearc
IONA HERITAGE CENTRE
Iona
Kintra
ST COLUMBA EXHIBITION & WELCOME CENTRE
Baile Mor
Stac an Aoineidh
Sligneach
Fionnphort
Aridhglas
Loch na Lathaich
Eorabus
Achnahard
Knokan
Lower Ardtun
Lee
Fidden
Tiraghoil
Bunessan
CRUACHAN MIN
Sound of Iona
Loch Assapol
Erraid
Knockvologan
ROSS OF MULL
Soa I.
Ardalanish
Uisken
Ardchiavaig
Scoor
Malcolm's Point
Eilean a'Chalmain
Rubh Ardalanish
Rubha nam Braithrean
Torranuachdrach
0 2 4 6 miles
0 2 4 6 8 10 km
TIREE
Gunna
Vaul Bay
Salum
Caolas
Rubha Dubh
Balephetrish Bay
Sraid Ruadh
Cornaigmore
Vaul
Balevullin
Kirkapol
Ruaig
Hough
Cornaigbeg
Kilmoluaig
Kenovay
Gott Bay
Soa
Gott
Scarinish
Kilkenneth
Moss
TIREE
CASTLEBAY 2:45 (Summer only) COLL 0:55
Baugh
Middleton
Heylipol
Crossapol
Heanish
Port Mor
Barrapol
Balinoe
Hynish Bay
Rubha Traigh an Duin
Loch a'Phuill
Balemartine
Balephuil
Mannal
Balephuil Bay
West Hynish
Hynish
Port Snoig
NM

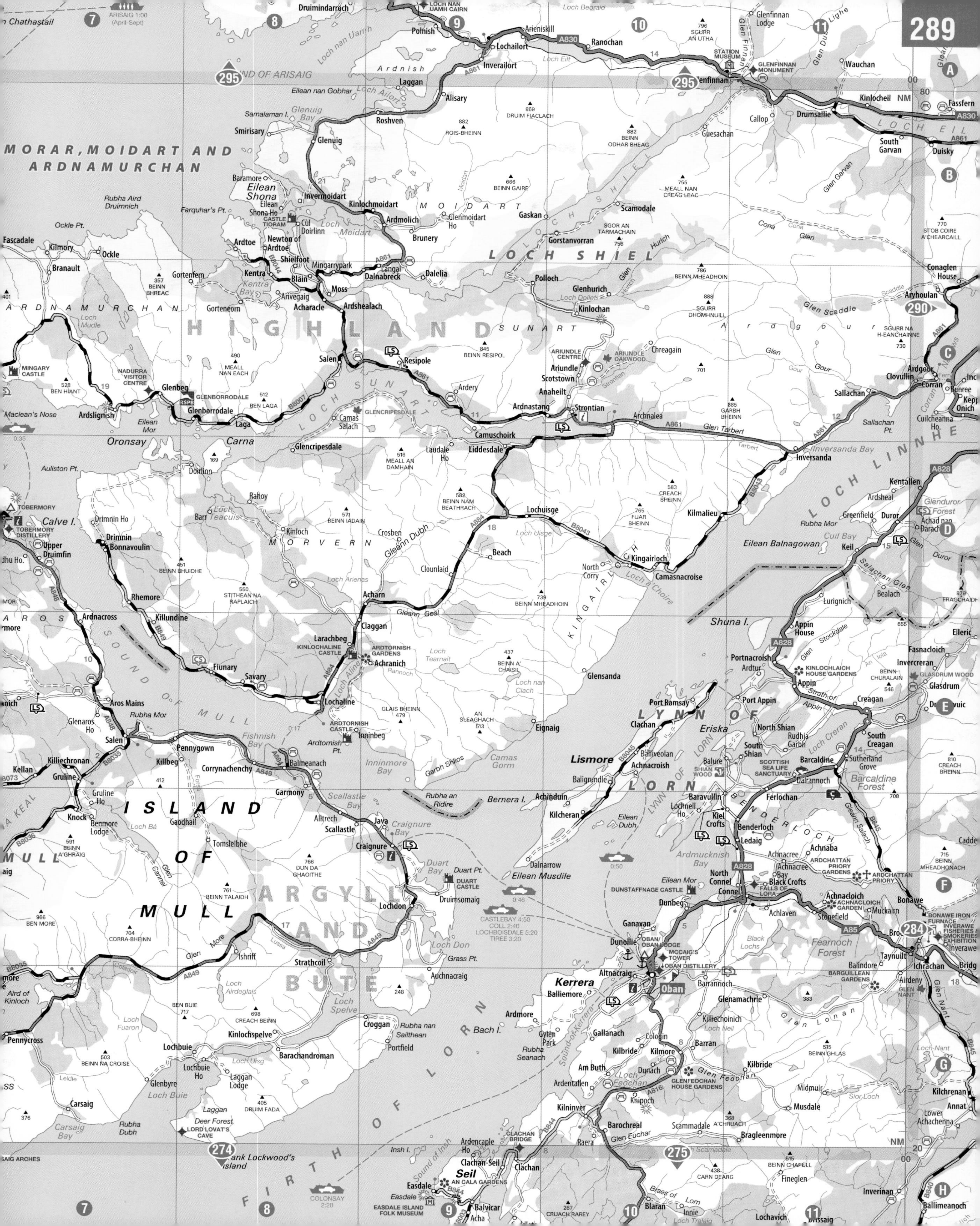
MORAR, MOIDART AND ARDNAMURCHAN
HIGHLAND
ISLAND OF MULL
ARGYLL AND BUTE
LOCH SHIEL
MOIDART
SUNART
LOCH SUNART
MORVERN
SOUND OF MULL
LYNN OF LORN
FIRTH OF LORN
LOCH LINNHE
Ardgour
Kingairloch
Benderloch
Lismore
Kerrera
Seil
Oban
Glenfinnan
Lochailort
Arisaig
Acharacle
Salen
Strontian
Lochaline
Craignure
Tobermory
Appin
Connel
Taynuilt
Kilninver
Ardnamurchan
Corran
Duror
Easdale

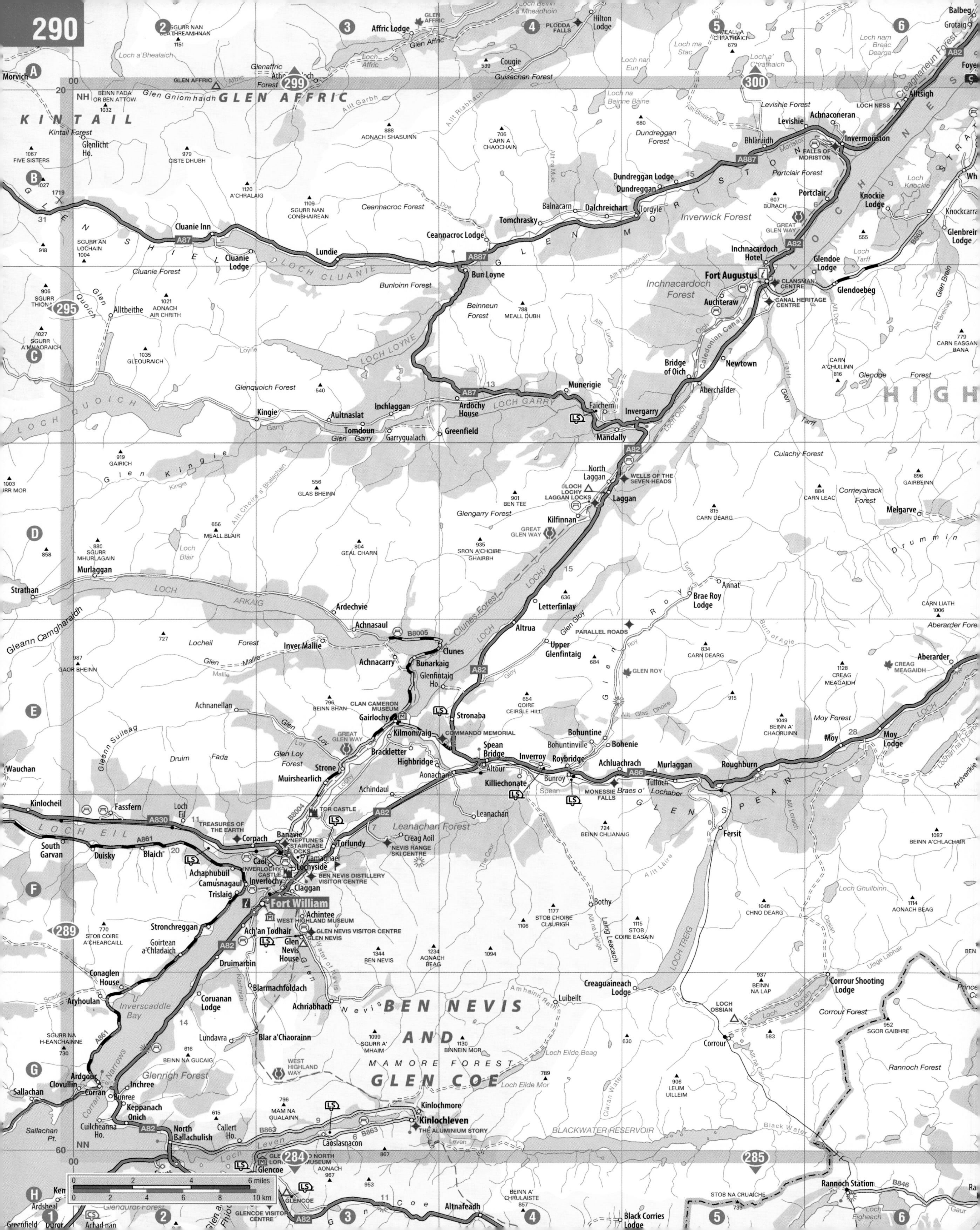
GLEN AFFRIC
Affric Lodge
Glen Affric
Loch a' Bhealaich
SGURR NAN CEATHREAMHNAN
1151
Hilton Lodge
PLODDA FALLS
Balbeg
Grotaig
MEALL A' CHRATHAICH
679
Loch ma Stac
Loch nam Breac Dearga
Creag nan Eun Forest
A82
Morvich
Cougie
Guisachan Forest
Loch nan Eun
Loch a' Chrathaich
Glenaffric
Athnamulloch
Forest
299
300
GLEN AFFRIC
NH
BEINN FADA OR BEN ATTOW
1032
Glen Gniomhaidh
Allt Garbh
Allt Riabhach
Loch na Beinne Bàine
Levishie Forest
Alltsigh
LOCH NESS
Levishie
Achnaconeran
Invermoriston
KINTAIL
Kintail Forest
Glenlicht Ho.
888
AONACH SHASUINN
706
CARN A' CHAOCHAIN
680
Dundreggan Forest
Bhlàraidh
FALLS OF MORISTON
1067
FIVE SISTERS
979
CISTE DHUBH
A887
Portclair Forest
Dundreggan Lodge
Dundreggan
Portclair
Knockie Lodge
Loch Knockie
Knockcarra
1027
1719
1120
A' CHRALAIG
1109
SGURR NAN CONBHAIREAN
Ceannacroc Forest
Balnacarn
Dalchreichart
Torgyle
607
BURACH
Inverwick Forest
GREAT GLEN WAY
GLEN SHIEL
Cluanie Inn
A87
Ceannacroc Lodge
Tomchrasky
GLEN MORISTON
555
Glenbreirn Lodge
SGURR AN LOCHAIN
1004
918
Cluanie Lodge
Lundie
LOCH CLUANIE
A887
Inchnacardoch Hotel
Glendoe Lodge
Loch Tarff
B862
Cluanie Forest
Bun Loyne
Bunloinn Forest
Allt Phocaichain
Inchnacardoch Forest
Fort Augustus
CLANSMAN CENTRE
CANAL HERITAGE CENTRE
Glendoebeg
906
SGURR THIONAIL
295
Glen Quoich
Alltbeithe
1021
AONACH AIR CHRITH
Beinneun Forest
788
MEALL DUBH
Auchteraw
1027
SGURR A' MHAORAICH
1035
GLEOURAICH
LOCH LOYNE
Caledonian Canal
779
CARN EASGANN BANA
Bridge of Oich
Newtown
CARN A' CHUILINN
816
Glendoe Forest
HIGHLAND
Glenquoich Forest
540
13
Munerigie
Aberchalder
LOCH QUOICH
Kingie
Aultnaslat
Inchlaggan
Ardochy House
LOCH GARRY
Faichem
Invergarry
Tomdoun
Glen Garry
Garrygualach
Greenfield
Mandally
A82
Culachy Forest
919
GAIRICH
Glen Kingie
1003
556
GLAS BHEINN
North Laggan
WELLS OF THE SEVEN HEADS
LOCH LOCHY
LAGGAN LOCKS
Laggan
901
BEN TEE
896
GAIRBEINN
884
CARN LEAC
Corrieyairack Forest
Melgarve
815
CARN DEARG
Glengarry Forest
Kilfinnan
656
MEALL BLAIR
GREAT GLEN WAY
880
SGURR MHURLAGAIN
858
Loch Blàir
804
GEAL CHARN
935
SRON A' CHOIRE GHAIRBH
Drummin
Murlaggan
15
Strathan
LOCH ARKAIG
636
Annat
Brae Roy Lodge
Ardechvie
Letterfinlay
CARN LIATH
1006
Gleann Camgharaidh
Achnasaul
B8005
Clunes Forest
Altrua
Glen Gloy
PARALLEL ROADS
Aberarder Forest
727
Locheil Forest
Inver Mallie
Clunes
Upper Glenfintaig
834
CARN DEARG
987
GAOR BHEINN
Glen Mallie
Achnacarry
Bunarkaig
684
GLEN ROY
1128
CREAG MEAGAIDH
Aberarder
CREAG MEAGAIDH
Glenfintaig Ho.
Burn of Agie
Achnanellan
796
BEINN BHAN
CLAN CAMERON MUSEUM
Gairlochy
654
COIRE CEIRSLE HILL
915
Stronaba
Moy Forest
1049
BEINN A' CHAORUINN
Glen Loy
GREAT GLEN WAY
Kilmonivaig
COMMANDO MEMORIAL
Bohuntine
Bohuntinville
Bohenie
Moy
Moy Lodge
28
Gleann Sulleag
Druim Fada
Glen Loy Forest
Brackletter
Highbridge
Spean Bridge
Inverroy
Roybridge
Achluachrach
Murlaggan
Roughburn
Wauchan
Strone
Muirshearlich
Aonachan
Altour
Killiechonate
Bunroy
A86
Tulloch
Lochaber
Braes o' Lochaber
MONESSIE FALLS
Achindaul
Spean
Kinlocheil
Fassfern
Loch Eil
A830
TOR CASTLE
B8004
A82
Leanachan
GLEN SPEAN
LOCH EIL
TREASURES OF THE EARTH
Corpach
Banavie
NEPTUNE'S STAIRCASE LOCKS
Leanachan Forest
724
BEINN CHLIANAIG
South Garvan
Duisky
A861
Blaich
20
Caol
Camaghael
Torlundy
Creag Aoil
NEVIS RANGE SKI CENTRE
Fersit
1087
BEINN A' CHLACHAIR
Achaphubuil
INVERLOCHY CASTLE
Lochyside
BEN NEVIS DISTILLERY VISITOR CENTRE
Camusnagaul
Inverlochy
Claggan
Allt Laire
Loch Ghuilbinn
Trislaig
Fort William
Bothy
1046
CHNO DEARG
1114
AONACH BEAG
Achintee
WEST HIGHLAND MUSEUM
1177
STOB CHOIRE CLAURIGH
1106
1115
STOB COIRE EASAIN
289
770
STOB COIRE A' CHEARCAILL
Stronchreggan
Ach'an Todhair
GLEN NEVIS VISITOR CENTRE
Glen Nevis House
Goirtean a' Chladaich
A82
1344
BEN NEVIS
1234
AONACH BEAG
1094
Lairig Leacach
LOCH TREIG
Druimarbin
Water of Nevis
Conaglen House
Blarmachfoldach
Creaguaineach Lodge
937
BEINN NA LAP
Corrour Shooting Lodge
Aryhoulan
Coruanan Lodge
Achriabhach
BEN NEVIS AND GLEN COE
Luibeilt
LOCH OSSIAN
Corrour Forest
Inverscaddle Bay
14
Lundavra
Blar a' Chaorainn
1099
SGURR A' MHAIM
1130
BINNEIN MOR
630
Corrour
583
952
SGOR GAIBHRE
SGURR NA H-EANCHAINNE
730
616
BEINN NA GUCAIG
Loch Eilde Beag
WEST HIGHLAND WAY
MAMORE FOREST
Rannoch Forest
Ardgour
Clovullin
Corran
Glenrigh Forest
Inchree
Corran Narrows
789
Loch Eilde Mor
906
LEUM UILLEIM
Sallachan
Bunree
796
MAM NA GUALAINN
Kinlochmore
Kinlochleven
Keppanach
Onich
615
THE ALUMINIUM STORY
Cuilcheanna Ho.
A82
North Ballachulish
Callert Ho.
B863
Caolasnacon
BLACKWATER RESERVOIR
Black Water
Sallachan Pt.
NN
60
00
Loch Leven
GLENCOE NORTH LORN FOLK MUSEUM
284
867
285
AONACH
967
Glencoe
Rannoch Station
B846
953
BEINN A' CHRULAISTE
857
STOB NA CRUAICHE
739
GLENCOE
GLENCOE VISITOR CENTRE
Glen Coe
Altnafeadh
Black Corries Lodge
Loch Eigheach
Gaur
Kentallen
Ardsheal
Glenduror Forest
Achadnan
Greenfield
Duror
A82
0 2 4 6 miles
0 2 4 6 8 10 km

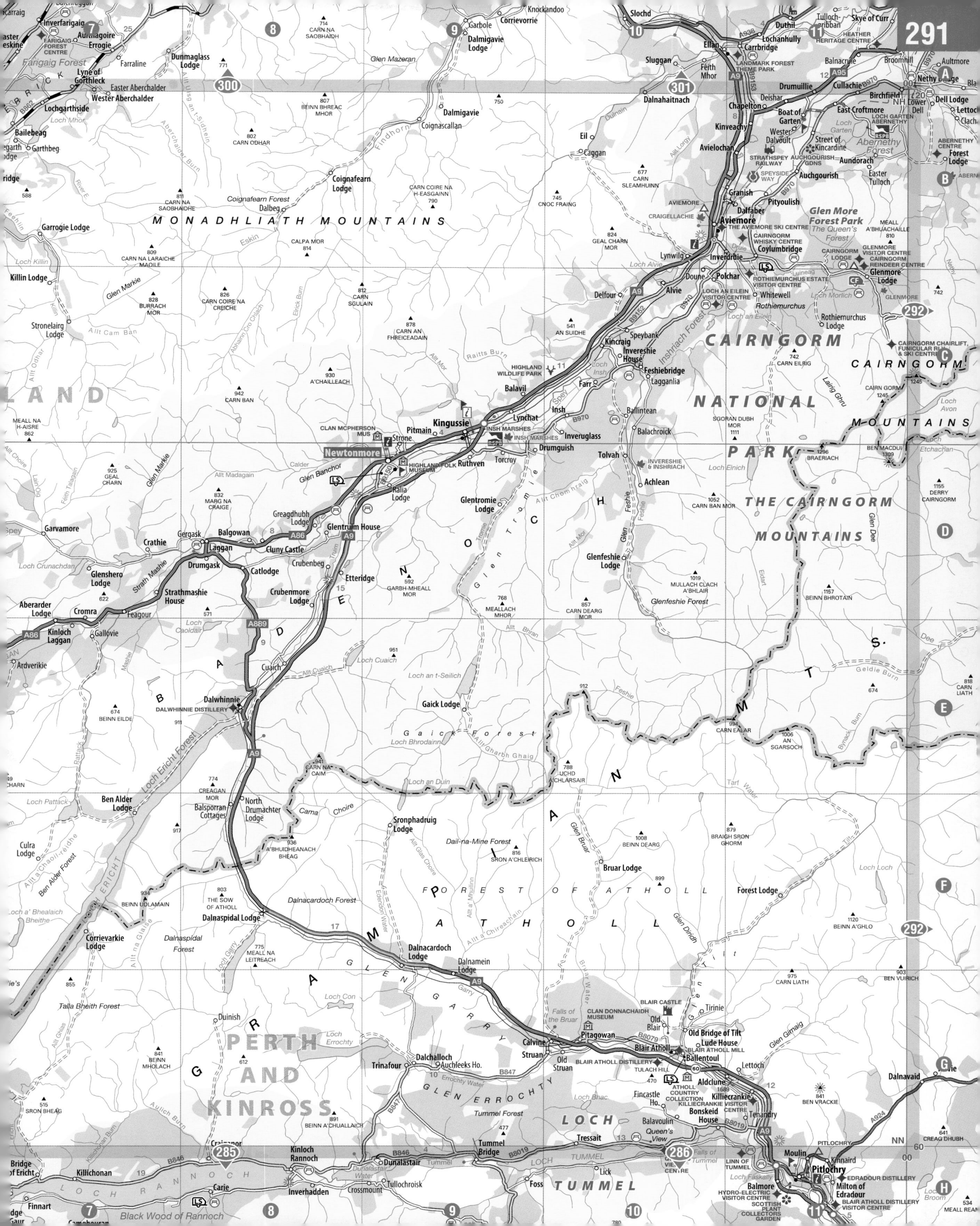
MONADHLIATH MOUNTAINS
CAIRNGORM NATIONAL PARK
THE CAIRNGORM MOUNTAINS
CAIRNGORM MOUNTAINS
FOREST OF ATHOLL
PERTH AND KINROSS
LOCH TUMMEL
LOCH RANNOCH
GLEN GARRY
GLEN ERROCHTY
Kingussie
Newtonmore
Aviemore
Pitlochry
Dalwhinnie
Blair Atholl
Carrbridge
Kincraig
Laggan
Glen More Forest Park
Gaick Forest
Coignafearn Forest
Loch Ericht Forest
Dalnacardoch Forest
Dail-na-Mine Forest
Glenfeshie Forest
Tummel Forest
Talla Bheith Forest
Black Wood of Rannoch
A9
A86
A889
A95
A924
B847
B846
B8019
B970
B9152

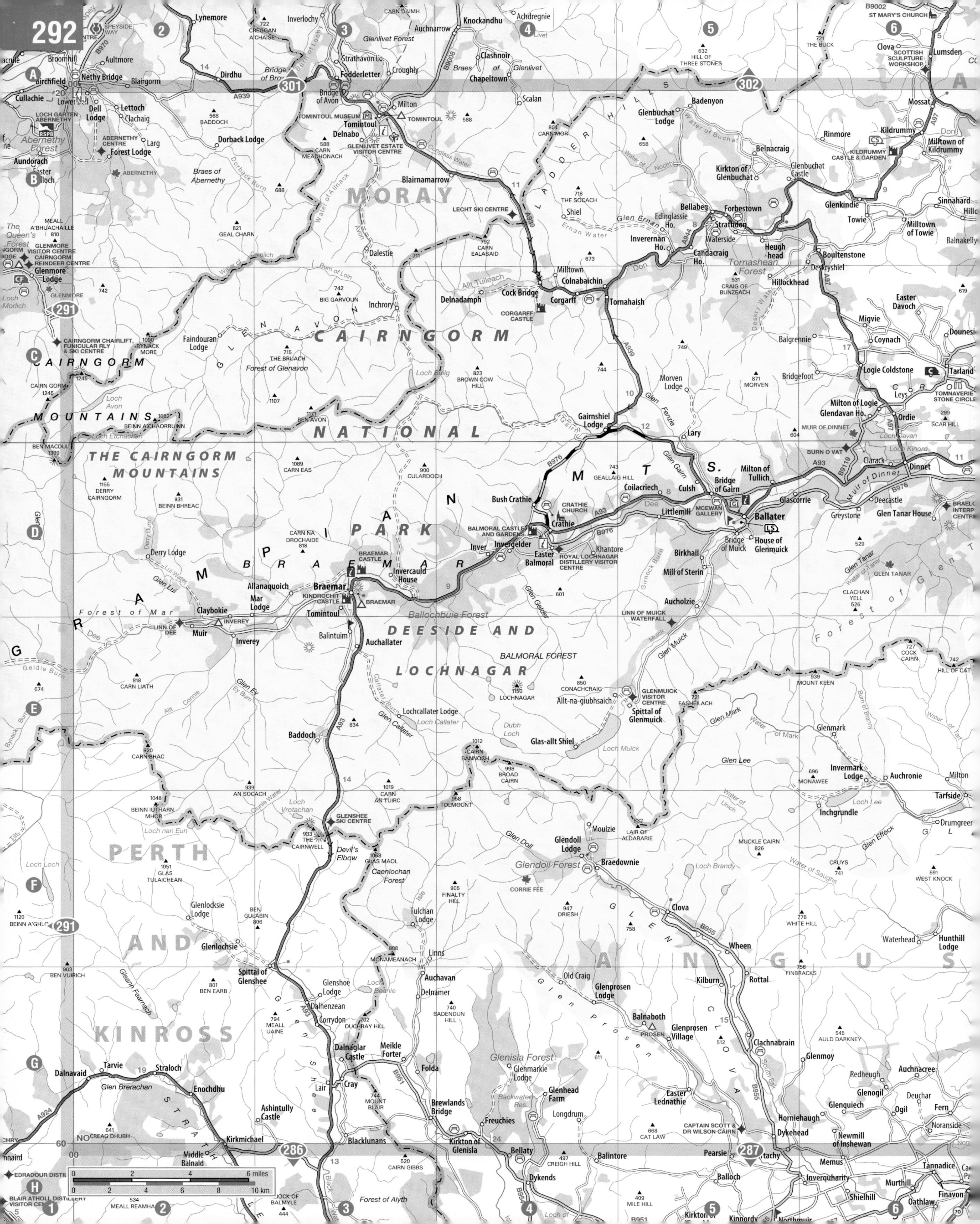
MORAY
CAIRNGORM NATIONAL PARK
CAIRNGORM MOUNTAINS
THE CAIRNGORM MOUNTAINS
GRAMPIAN MTS.
BRAEMAR
DEESIDE AND LOCHNAGAR
BALMORAL FOREST
LADDER HILLS
PERTH AND KINROSS
ANGUS
GLEN CLOVA
GLEN PROSEN
STRATH
Lynemore
Inverlochy
Achdregnie
Knockandhu
Auchnarrow
Glenlivet Forest
Braes of Glenlivet
Clashnoir
Chapeltown
Scalan
Strathavon Lo.
Fodderletter
Croughly
Bridge of Avon
Milton
Tomintoul
Delnabo
TOMINTOUL MUSEUM
GLENLIVET ESTATE VISITOR CENTRE
Nethy Bridge
Broomhill
Aultmore
Dirdhu
Birchfield
Blairgorm
Cullachie
Lower Dell
Dell Lodge
Lettoch
Clachaig
LOCH GARTEN ABERNETHY
RSPB
Abernethy Forest
Forest Lodge
Larg
Dorback Lodge
Braes of Abernethy
Aundorach
Blairnamarrow
Glenbuchat Lodge
Badenyon
Belnacraig
Kirkton of Glenbuchat
Glenbuchat Castle
Rinmore
Kildrummy
Milltown of Kildrummy
KILDRUMMY CASTLE & GARDEN
Mossat
Lumsden
Clova
SCOTTISH SCULPTURE WORKSHOP
ST MARY'S CHURCH
Glenkindie
Towie
Sinnahard
Milltown of Towie
Balnakelly
Bellabeg
Forbestown
Edinglassie Ho.
Strathdon
Waterside
Inverernan Ho.
Candacraig Ho.
Heugh-head
Boultenstone
Deskryshiel
Tornashean Forest
Hillockhead
LECHT SKI CENTRE
Shiel
THE SOCACH
Glen Ernan
Milltown
Colnabaichin
Corgarff
Tornahaish
Cock Bridge
Delnadamph
CORGARFF CASTLE
Dalestie
Inchrory
BIG GARVOUN
CARN EALASAID
GLENMORE VISITOR CENTRE
CAIRNGORM REINDEER CENTRE
Glenmore Lodge
Loch Morlich
CAIRNGORM CHAIRLIFT, FUNICULAR RLY & SKI CENTRE
Faindouran Lodge
GLEN AVON
THE BRUACH
Forest of Glenavon
Loch Builg
BROWN COW HILL
CAIRN GORM
Loch Avon
BEINN A'CHAORRUINN
BEN AVON
Loch Etchachan
BEN MACDUI
CARN EAS
CULARDOCH
DERRY CAIRNGORM
BEINN BHREAC
CARN NA DROCHAIDE
Derry Lodge
Glen Lui
Allanaquoich
Mar Lodge
Claybokie
Forest of Mar
LINN OF DEE
Muir
INVEREY
Inverey
Braemar
KINDROCHIT CASTLE
BRAEMAR CASTLE
Invercauld House
Tomintoul
Ballochbuie Forest
Balintuim
Auchallater
Easter Davoch
Migvie
Coynach
Balgrennie
Logie Coldstone
Tarland
TOMNAVERIE STONE CIRCLE
Leys
Bridgefoot
MORVEN
Morven Lodge
Milton of Logie
Glendavan Ho.
Ordie
MUIR OF DINNET
SCAR HILL
BURN O VAT
Clarack
Dinnet
Gairnshiel Lodge
Glen Fenzie
Lary
Glen Gairn
GEALLAIG HILL
Milton of Tullich
Bridge of Gairn
Coilacriech
Culsh
Bush Crathie
CRATHIE CHURCH
Crathie
Littlemill
MCEWAN GALLERY
Ballater
Glascorrie
Deecastle
Greystone
Glen Tanar House
BALMORAL CASTLE AND GARDENS
Inver
Invergelder
Easter Balmoral
ROYAL LOCHNAGAR DISTILLERY VISITOR CENTRE
Khantore
Birkhall
Bridge of Muick
House of Glenmuick
Mill of Sterin
Aucholzie
Glen Gelder
GLEN TANAR
CLACHAN YELL
Forest of Glen Tanar
LINN OF MUICK WATERFALL
Glen Muick
COCK CAIRN
HILL OF CAT
MOUNT KEEN
CONACHCRAIG
LOCHNAGAR
Allt-na-giubhsaich
GLENMUICK VISITOR CENTRE
Spittal of Glenmuick
FASHEILACH
Glen Mark
Glenmark
Lochcallater Lodge
Loch Callater
Glen Callater
Baddoch
Dubh Loch
Glas-allt Shiel
Loch Muick
CARN LIATH
CAIRN BANNOCH
BROAD CAIRN
CARN AN TUIRC
TOLMOUNT
CARN BHAC
AN SOCACH
BEINN IUTHARN MHOR
Loch Vrotachan
GLENSHEE SKI CENTRE
THE CAIRNWELL
Loch nan Eun
Devil's Elbow
GLAS MAOL
Caenlochan Forest
Glen Lee
MONAWEE
Invermark Lodge
Auchronie
Milton
Tarfside
Loch Lee
Inchgrundle
Drumgreer
Glen Doll
Moulzie
LAIR OF ALDARARIE
Glendoll Lodge
Braedownie
Glendoll Forest
CORRIE FEE
MUCKLE CAIRN
Loch Brandy
CRUYS
WEST KNOCK
Glen Effock
Loch Loch
GLAS TULAICHEAN
Glenlocksie Lodge
BEN GULABIN
BEINN A'GHLO
Glenlochsie
FINALTY HILL
Tulchan Lodge
DRIESH
Clova
WHITE HILL
Waterhead
Hunthill Lodge
Wheen
MONAMEANACH
Linns
BEN VUIRICH
Spittal of Glenshee
BEN EARB
Glenshoe Lodge
Loch Beanie
Auchavan
Delnamer
Old Craig
Glenprosen Lodge
Kilburn
Rottal
FINBRACKS
Dalhenzean
Corrydon
DUCHRAY HILL
BADENDUN HILL
Balnaboth
PROSEN
Glenprosen Village
Clachnabrain
AULD DARKNEY
MEALL UAINE
Dalnaglar Castle
Meikle Forter
Glenisla Forest
Glenmarkie Lodge
Glenhead Farm
Backwater Res.
Glenmoy
Redheugh
Auchnacree
Glenogil
Glenquiech
Deuchar
Ogil
Fern
Noranside
Dalnavaid
Tarvie
Straloch
Glen Brerachan
Enochdhu
Cray
Lair
Folda
MOUNT BLAIR
Brewlands Bridge
Easter Lednathie
Longdrum
Ashintully Castle
Freuchies
CREAG DHUBH
Kirkmichael
Middle Balnald
Blacklunans
Kirkton of Glenisla
CAT LAW
CAPTAIN SCOTT & DR WILSON CAIRN
Horniehaugh
Dykehead
Newmill of Inshewan
Bellaty
Balintore
Pearsie
Memus
Tannadice
CAIRN GIBBS
CREIGH HILL
Dykends
Balloch
Inverquharity
Murthill
Shielhill
Oathlaw
Finavon
EDRADOUR DISTILLERY
BLAIR ATHOLL DISTILLERY VISITOR CENTRE
MEALL REAMHAR
HOCK OF BALMYLE
Forest of Alyth
MILE HILL
Kirkton
Kinnordy
Northmuir
0 2 4 6 miles
0 2 4 6 8 10 km
291
301
302
286
287

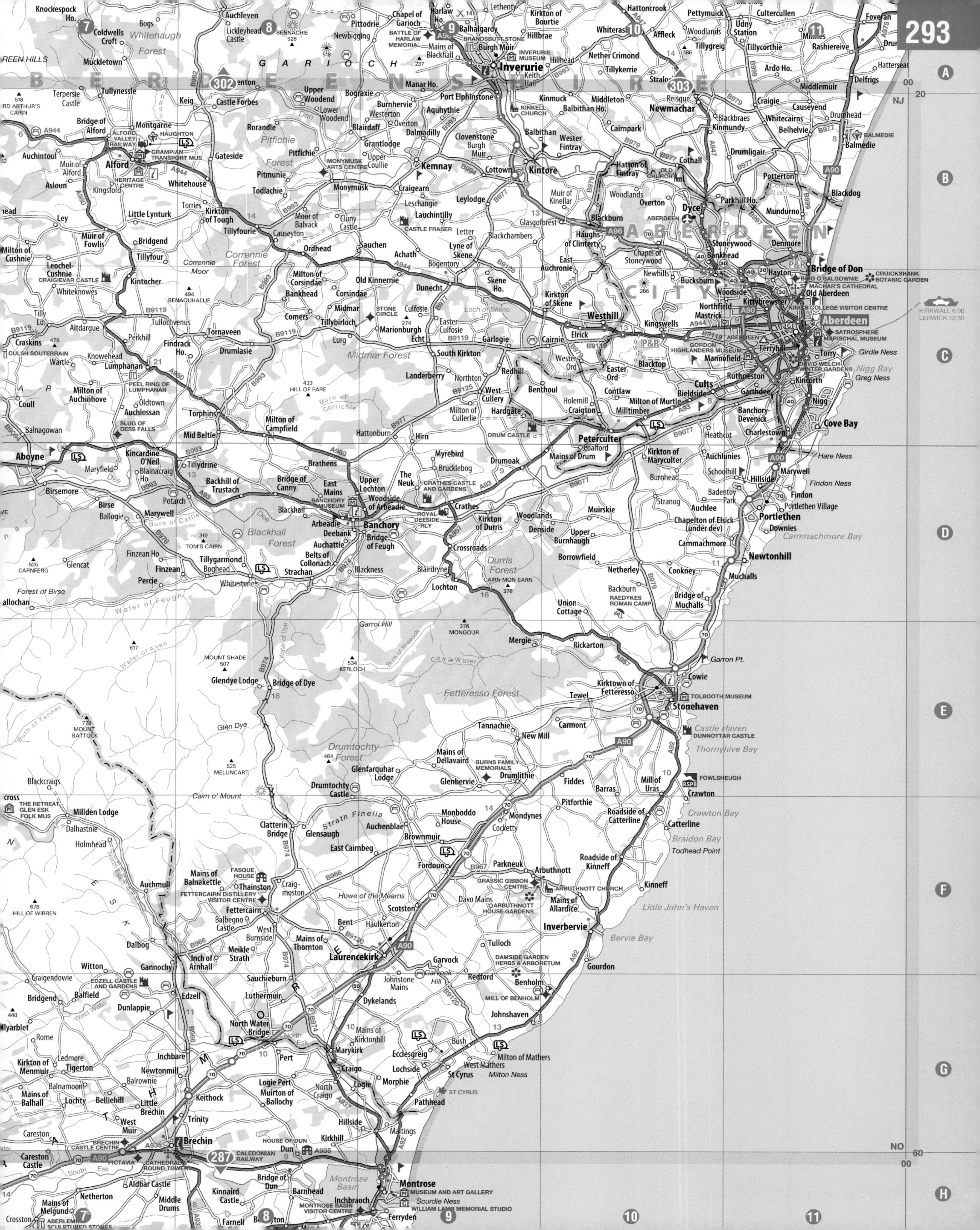

ABERDEENSHIRE
GARIOCH
ABERDEEN CITY
Knockespock Ho.
Coldwells Croft
Bogs
Whitehaugh Forest
Auchleven
Lickleyhead Castle
Bennachie
Pittodrie
Newbigging
Chapel of Garioch
Harlaw Ho.
Battle of Harlaw Memorial
Mains of Blackhall
Balhalgardy
Brandsbutt Stone
Burgh Muir
Inverurie
Inverurie Museum
Keith Hall
Lethenty
Kirkton of Bourtie
Hillbrae
Hillhead
Hattoncrook
Whiterashes
Affleck
Pettymuick
Woodlands
Tillygreig
Udny Station
Cultercullen
Tillycorthie
Foveran
Mintlaw
Rashiereive
Muckletown
Nether Crimond
Tillykerrie
Straloch
Ardo Ho.
Hatterseat
Delfrigs
Middlemuir
Terpersie Castle
Tullynessle
Keig
Castle Forbes
Upper Woodend
Lower Woodend
Bograxie
Burnhervie
Westerton
Overton
Manar Ho.
Port Elphinstone
Aquhythie
Kinkell Church
Kinmuck
Balbithan Ho.
Middleton
Reisque
Newmachar
Craigie
Causeyend
Whitecairns
Belhelvie
Blackbraes
Kinmundy
Drumhead
Balmedie
Bridge of Alford
Montgarrie
Alford Valley Railway
Haughton
Grampian Transport Mus
Alford
Heritage Centre
Auchintoul
Muir of Alford
Asloun
Kingsford
Gateside
Whitehouse
Rorandle
Pitfichie Forest
Pitfichie
Monymusk Arts Centre
Upper Coullie
Blairdaff
Grantlodge
Dalmadilly
Kemnay
Clovenstone
Burgh Muir
Cottown
Balbithan
Kintore
Wester Fintray
Cairnpark
Hatton of Fintray
Old Church
Cothall
Drumligair
Potterton
Corby Loch
Blackdog
Pitmunie
Todlachie
Monymusk
Craigearn
Leschangie
Leylodge
Muir of Kinellar
Woodlands
Overton
Dyce
Parkhill Ho.
Mundurno
Ley
Little Lynturk
Torries
Kirkton of Tough
Tillyfourie
Moor of Balvack
Cluny Castle
Lauchintilly
Castle Fraser
Glasgoforest
Blackburn
Aberdeen Airport
Muir of Fowlis
Bridgend
Causeyton
Tillyfour
Corrennie Forest
Corrennie Moor
Ordhead
Sauchen
Letter
Lyne of Skene
Achath
Bogentory
Blackchambers
Haughs of Clinterty
Chapel of Stoneywood
Stoneywood
Bankhead
Denmore
Bridge of Don
Cruickshank Botanic Garden
Milton of Cushnie
Leochel-Cushnie
Craigievar Castle
Kintocher
Whiteknowes
Milton of Corsindae
Corsindae
Bankhead
Old Kinnernie
Dunecht
Skene Ho.
East Auchronie
Newhills
Bucksburn
Hayton
Brig o' Balgownie
St Machar's Cathedral
Old Aberdeen
Woodside
Kittybrewster
King's College Visitor Centre
Kirkton of Skene
Westhill
Northfield
Mastrick
Kingswells
Aberdeen
Satrosphere
Marischal Museum
Kirkwall 6:00
Lerwick 12:30
Tilly Lo.
Altdargue
Perkhill
Tullochvenus
Tornaveen
Comers
Midmar
Stone Circle
Tillybirloch
Cullfosie
Marionburgh
Easter Cullfosie
Echt
Loch of Skene
Elrick
Craskins
Culsh Souterrain
Wartle
Knowehead
Lumphanan
Peel Ring of Lumphanan
Findrack Ho.
Drumlasie
Lurg
Midmar Forest
South Kirkton
Garlogie
Cairnie
Wester Ord
Easter Ord
Gordon Highlanders Museum
Blacktop
Mannofield
Ferryhill
Torry
Girdle Ness
David Welch Winter Gardens
Nigg Bay
Greg Ness
Coull
Milton of Auchinhove
Oldtown
Auchlossan
Slug of Dess Falls
Hill of Fare
Burn of Corrichie
Landerberry
Northton
Redhill
West Cullery
Hardgate
Milton of Cullerlie
Benthoul
Holemill
Craigton
Contlaw
Milltimber
Milton of Murtle
Bieldside
Cults
Ruthrieston
Garthdee
Kincorth
Nigg
Balnagowan
Torphins
Mid Beltie
Milton of Campfield
Hattonburn
Hirn
Drum Castle
Peterculter
Coalford
Mains of Drum
Kirkton of Maryculter
Banchory-Devenick
Heathcot
Charleston
Cove Bay
Aboyne
Maryfield
Kincardine O'Neil
Blainacraig Ho
Tillydrine
Backhill of Trustach
Brathens
Bridge of Canny
East Mains
Upper Lochton
The Neuk
Myrebird
Brucklebog
Crathes Castle and Gardens
Drumoak
Auchlunies
Schoolhill
Hare Ness
Marywell
Hillside
Findon Ness
Findon
Birsemore
Birse
Ballogie
Potarch
Marywell
Burn of Cattie
Banchory Museum
Woodside of Arbeadie
Blackhall
Arbeadie
Banchory
Royal Deeside Rly
Crathes
Kirkton of Durris
Woodlands
Denside
Burnhead
Strangg
Badentoy Park
Auchlee
Portlethen Village
Portlethen
Chapelton of Elsick (under dev)
Downies
Cammachmore Bay
Tom's Cairn
Blackhall Forest
Deebank
Bridge of Feugh
Auchattie
Upper Burnhaugh
Cammachmore
Carnferg
Glencat
Finzean Ho
Finzean
Tillygarmond
Boghead
Belts of Collonach
Strachan
Blackness
Blairdryne
Crossroads
Durris Forest
Borrowfield
Netherley
Cookney
Newtonhill
Muchalls
Forest of Birse
Percie
Whitestone
Lochton
Cairn-mon Earn
Backburn
Raedykes Roman Camp
Bridge of Muchalls
Allochan
Water of Feugh
Union Cottage
Garrol Hill
Mongour
Mergie
Rickarton
Water of Aven
Mount Shade
Kerloch
Burn of Sheeoch
Cowie Water
Garron Pt.
Cowie
Glendye Lodge
Bridge of Dye
Water of Dye
Kirktown of Fetteresso
Fetteresso Forest
Tewel
Tolbooth Museum
Stonehaven
Burn of Tennet
Mount Battock
Glen Dye
Tannachie
New Mill
Carmont
Castle Haven
Dunnottar Castle
Thornyhive Bay
Drumtochty Forest
Melluncart
Mains of Dellavaird
Burns Family Memorials
Drumlithie
Glenfarquhar Lodge
Glenbervie
Fiddes
Barras
Mill of Uras
Fowlsheugh
Crawton
Blackcraigs
Cairn o' Mount
Drumtochty Castle
Strath Finella
Pitforthie
Mondynes
Cocketty
Roadside of Catterline
Crawton Bay
Catterline
The Retreat Glen Esk Folk Mus
Millden Lodge
Dalhastnie
Clatterin Bridge
Glensaugh
Auchenblae
Monboddo House
Brownmuir
Braidon Bay
Todhead Point
Holmhead
East Cairnbeg
Fordoun
Parkneuk
Arbuthnott
Roadside of Kinneff
Mains of Balnakettle
Fasque House
Thainston
Craigmoston
Grassic Gibbon Centre
Arbuthnott Church
Kinneff
Auchmull
Fettercairn Distillery Visitor Centre
Howe of the Mearns
Davo Mains
Arbuthnott House Gardens
Mains of Allardice
Little John's Haven
Hill of Wirren
Fettercairn
Balbegno Castle
Scotston
Bent
Haulkerton
Inverbervie
Bervie Bay
Dalbog
West Burnside
Meikle Strath
Mains of Thornton
Tulloch
Inch of Arnhall
Laurencekirk
Garvock
Garvock Hill
Damside Garden Herbs & Arboretum
Gourdon
Witton
Gannochy
Edzell Castle and Gardens
Sauchieburn
Johnstone Mains
Redford
Benholm
Craigendowie
Luthermuir
Dykelands
Mill of Benholm
Bridgend
Balfield
Dunlappie
Edzell
West Water
Johnshaven
North Water Bridge
Mains of Kirktonhill
Nlyarblet
Rome
Inchbare
Pert
Marykirk
Ecclesgreig
Bush
Milton of Mathers
Kirkton of Menmuir
Ledmore
Tigerton
Newtonmill
Craigo
Lochside
West Mathers
Balnamoon
Balrownie
Logie Pert
Logie
Morphie
St Cyrus
Milton Ness
Mains of Balhall
Lochty
Belliehill
Little Brechin
Keithock
Muirton of Ballochy
North Craigo
Pathhead
St Cyrus
West Muir
Trinity
Hillside
Caresten
Brechin Castle Centre
Brechin
House of Dun
Dun
Kirkhill
Maltings
Careston Castle
Pictavia
Cathedral Round Tower
Caledonian Railway
South Esk
Montrose Basin
Montrose
Museum and Art Gallery
Aldbar Castle
Bridge of Dun
Netherton
Middle Drums
Kinnaird Castle
Barnhead
Inchbraoch
Scurdie Ness
Montrose Basin Visitor Centre
William Lamb Memorial Studio
Mains of Melgund
Crosston
Aberlemno Sculptured Stones
Farnell
Ferryden

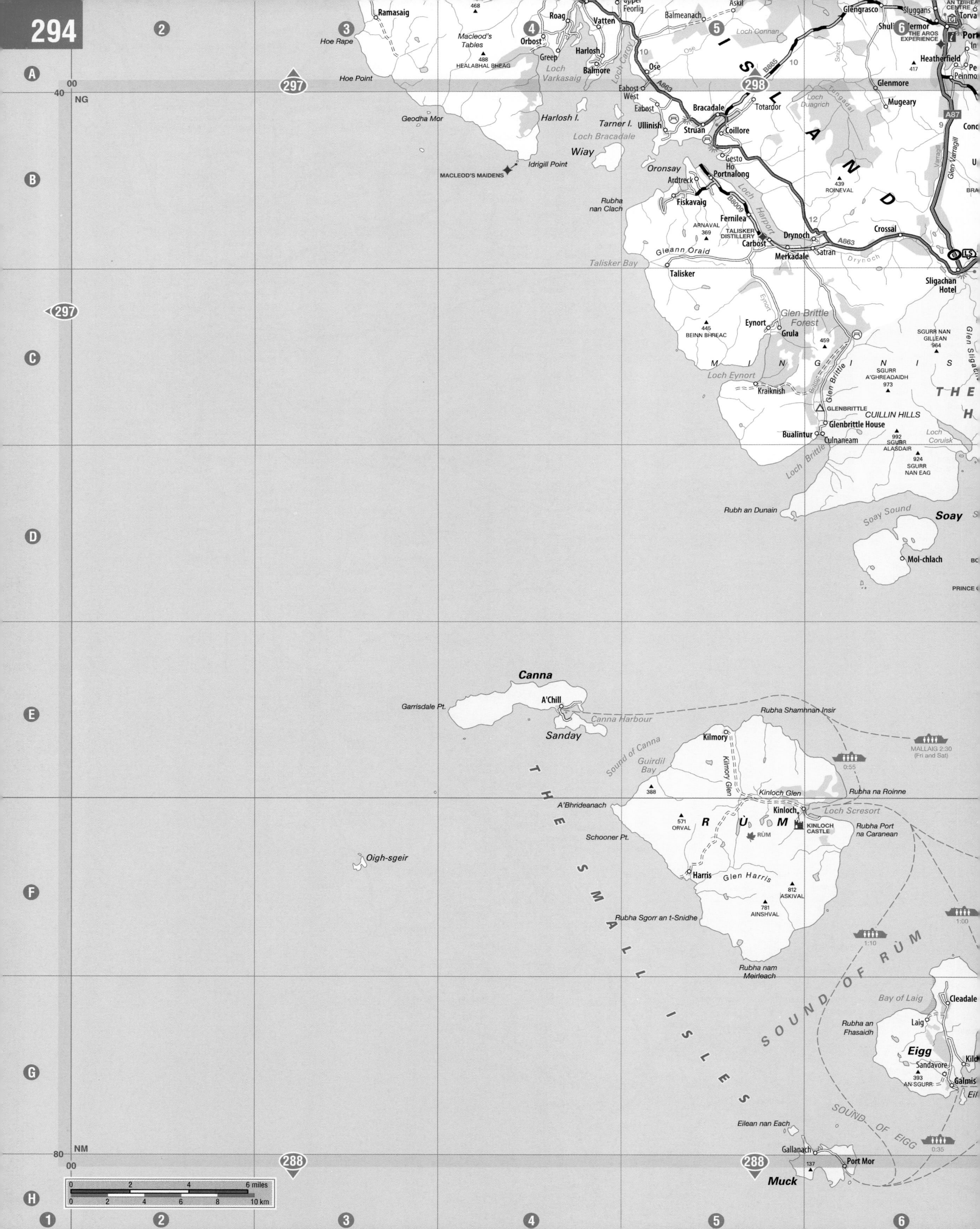
Ramasaig
Hoe Rape
Hoe Point
Macleod's Tables
488 HEALABHAL BHEAG
Roag
Orbost
Vatten
Harlosh
Greep
Balmore
Loch Varkasaig
Feorlig
Balmeanach
Askil
Loch Connan
Ose
Eabost West
Eabost
Bracadale
Totardor
Ullinish
Struan
Coillore
Glengrasco
Sluggans
Glenmore
Mugeary
Heatherfield
THE AROS EXPERIENCE
Geodha Mor
Harlosh I.
Tarner I.
Loch Bracadale
Wiay
MACLEOD'S MAIDENS
Idrigill Point
Oronsay
Gesto
Portnalong
Ardtreck
Fiskavaig
Rubha nan Clach
Fernilea
ARNAVAL 369
TALISKER DISTILLERY
Carbost
Loch Harport
Drynoch
Crossal
Merkadale
Satran
439 ROINEVAL
Gleann Oraid
Talisker Bay
Talisker
Sligachan Hotel
Glen Varragill
Eynort
Grula
Glen Brittle Forest
445 BEINN BHREAC
459
SGURR NAN GILLEAN 964
SGURR A'GHREADAIDH 973
Loch Eynort
Kraiknish
GLENBRITTLE
CUILLIN HILLS
Glenbrittle House
Bualintur
Culnaneam
992 SGURR ALASDAIR
924 SGURR NAN EAG
Loch Coruisk
Loch Brittle
Rubh an Dunain
Soay Sound
Soay
Mol-chlach
ISLAND
MINGINIS
Canna
A'Chill
Garrisdale Pt.
Canna Harbour
Sanday
Sound of Canna
Rubha Shamhnan Insir
Kilmory
Guirdil Bay
388
Kilmory Glen
MALLAIG 2:30 (Fri and Sat)
0:55
Kinloch Glen
Rubha na Roinne
A'Bhrideanach
Kinloch
Loch Scresort
571 ORVAL
RÙM
KINLOCH CASTLE
Rubha Port na Caranean
Schooner Pt.
Oigh-sgeir
Harris
Glen Harris
812 ASKIVAL
781 AINSHVAL
Rubha Sgorr an t-Snidhe
1:00
1:10
Rubha nam Meirleach
THE SMALL ISLES
SOUND OF RÙM
Bay of Laig
Cleadale
Laig
Rubha an Fhasaidh
Eigg
Sandavore
393 AN SGURR
Galmis
SOUND OF EIGG
0:35
Eilean nan Each
Gallanach
137
Port Mor
Muck
297
298
288
0 2 4 6 miles
0 2 4 6 8 10 km

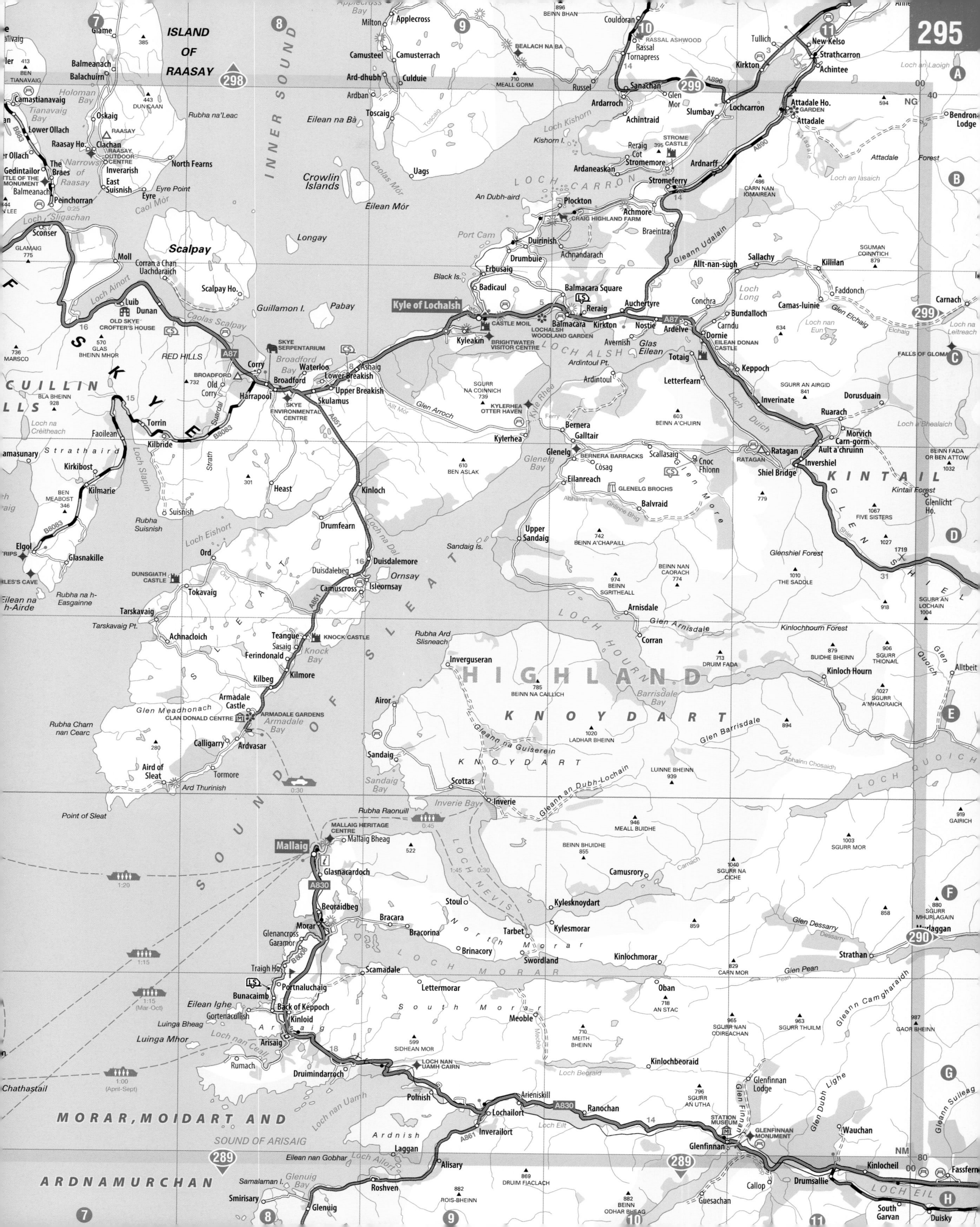

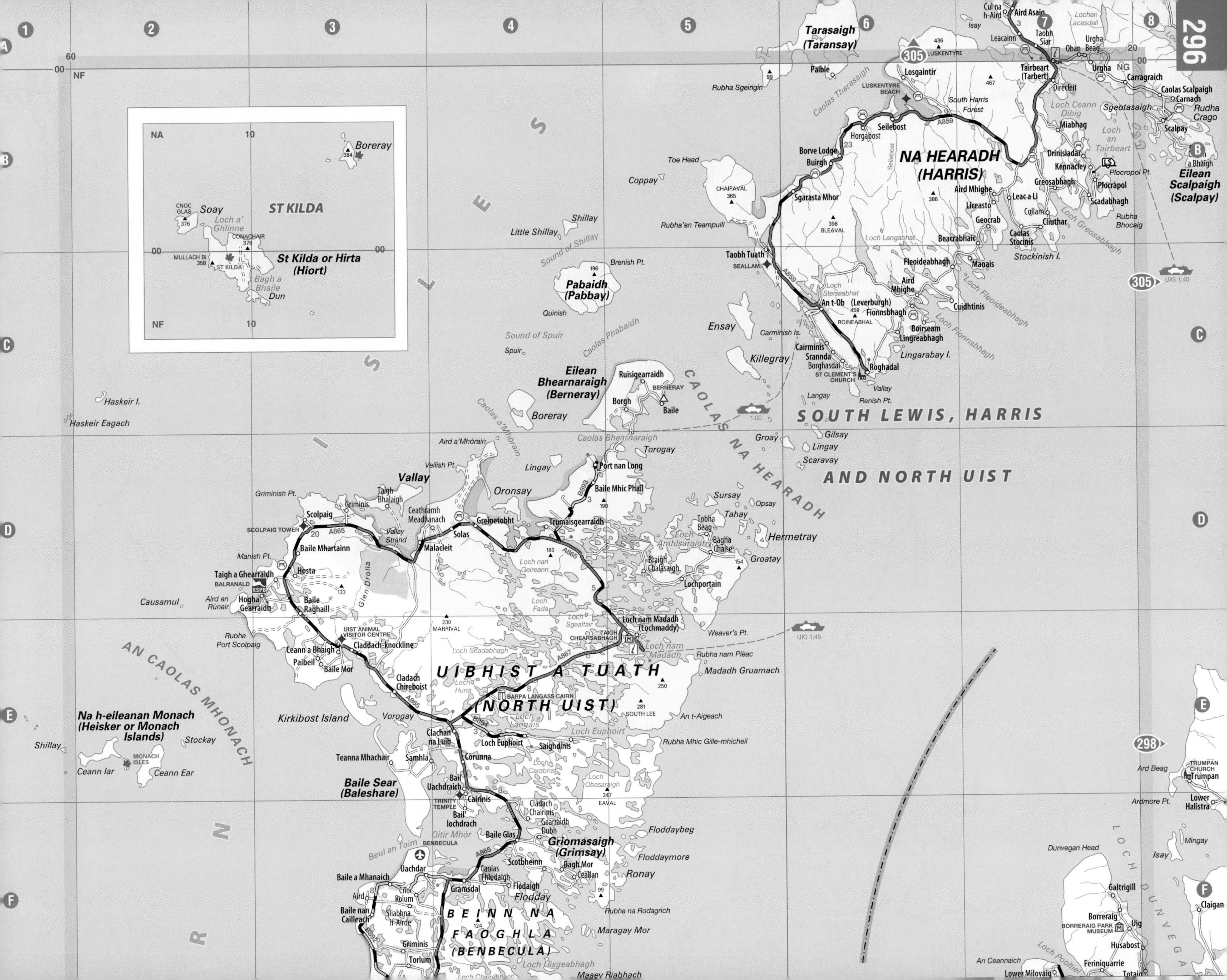

SOUTH LEWIS, HARRIS

AND NORTH UIST

NA HEARADH
(HARRIS)

Tarasaigh
(Taransay)

South Harris
Forest

CAOLAS NA HEARADH

ST KILDA

St Kilda or Hirta
(Hiort)

Soay

Na h-eileanan Monach
(Heisker or Monach Islands)

Pabaidh
(Pabbay)

Eilean
Bhearnaraigh
(Berneray)

UIBHIST A TUATH

NORTH UIST

Valley

Oronsay

Baile Sear
(Baleshare)

Kirkibost Island

AN CAOLAS MHONACH

Griomasaigh
(Grimsay)

BEINNA

FAOGHLA

BENBECULA

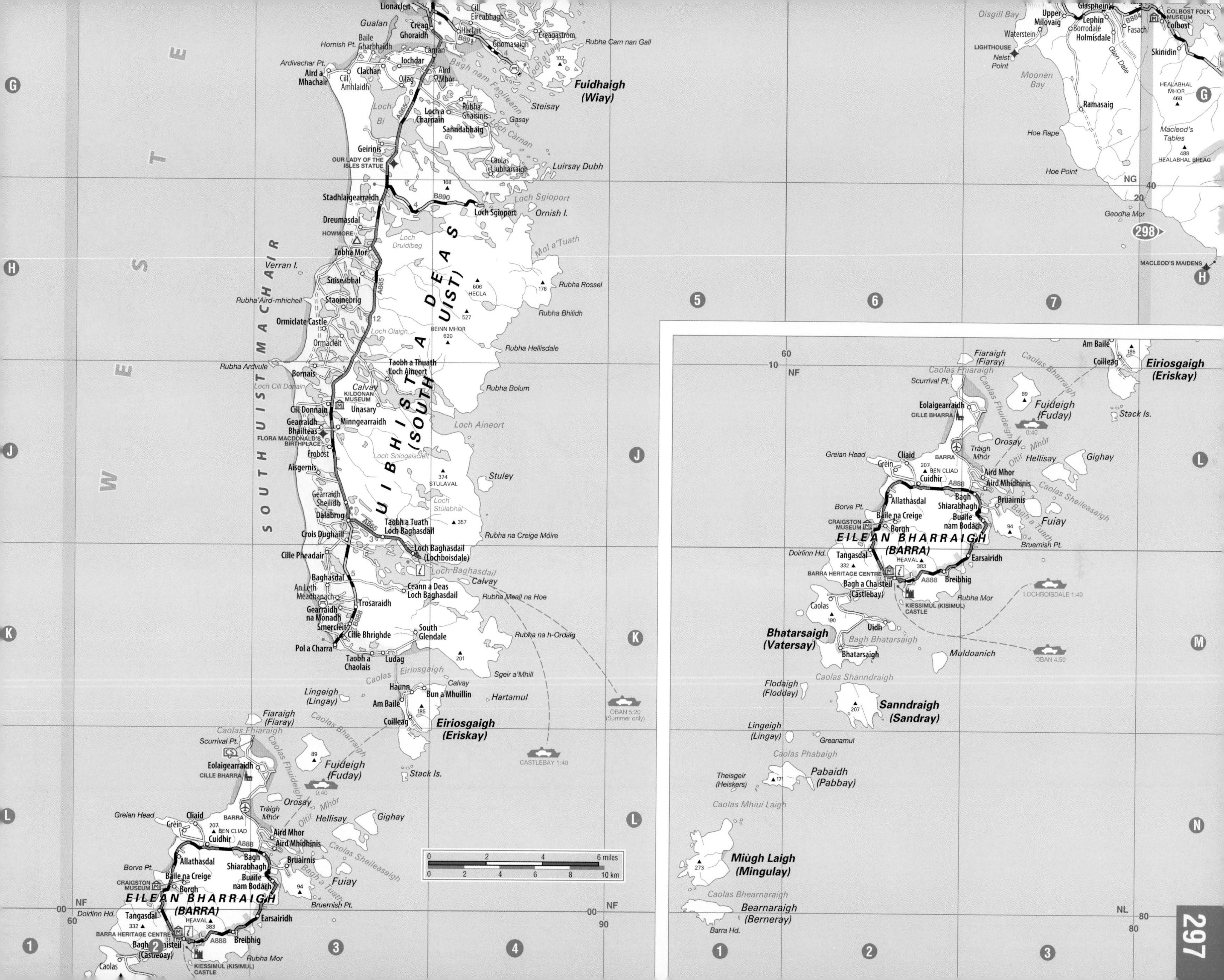

WEST
SOUTH UIST MACHAIR
UIBHIST A DEAS (SOUTH UIST)
Lionacleit
Gualan
Creag Ghoraidh
Cill Eireabhagh
Haclait
Creagastrom
Griomasaigh
Rubha Cam nan Gall
Baile Gharbhaidh
Hornish Pt.
Càrnan
Iochdar
Ardivachar Pt.
Aird a Mhachair
Cill Amhlaidh
Clachan
Ollag
Aird Mhòr
Bagh nam Faoileann
Loch Bi
Loch a Chàrnain
Rubha Ghaisinis
Gasay
Steisay
Fuidhaigh (Wiay)
Sanndabhaig
Loch Càrnan
Geirinis
OUR LADY OF THE ISLES STATUE
Caolas Liubharsaigh
Luirsay Dubh
Stadhlaigearraidh
Loch Sgioport
Ornish I.
Dreumasdal
HOWMORE
Loch Druidibeg
Tobha Mor
Mol a'Tuath
Verran I.
Sniseabhal
HECLA
606
176
Rubha Rossel
Rubha'Aird-mhicheil
Staoinebrig
Rubha Bhilidh
Ormiclate Castle
Loch Olaigh
BEINN MHOR
620
Ormacleit
Rubha Hellisdale
Rubha Ardvule
Bornais
Loch Cill Donain
Taobh a Thuath Loch Aineort
Calvay
KILDONAN MUSEUM
Rubha Bolum
Cill Donnain
Unasary
Gearraidh Bhailteas
Minngearraidh
FLORA MACDONALD'S BIRTHPLACE
Loch Aineort
Frobost
Loch Sniogaisclett
Aisgernis
STULAVAL
374
Stuley
Gearraidh Sheilidh
Loch Stùlabhal
357
Dalabrog
Taobh a Tuath Loch Baghasdail
Crois Dughaill
Rubha na Creige Mòire
Cille Pheadair
Loch Baghasdail (Lochboisdale)
Loch Baghasdail
Calvay
Baghasdal
Ceann a Deas Loch Baghasdail
An Leth Meadhanach
Rubha Meall na Hoe
Trosaraidh
Gearraidh na Monadh
Smercleit
Cille Bhrighde
South Glendale
Rubha na h-Ordaig
Pol a Charra
Taobh a Chaolais
Ludag
201
Caolas Eiriosgaigh
Sgeir a'Mhill
Calvay
Lingeigh (Lingay)
Haunn
Bun a'Mhuillin
Hartamul
Am Baile
185
OBAN 5:20 (Summer only)
Fiaraigh (Fiaray)
Coilleag
Eiriosgaigh (Eriskay)
Caolas Fhiaraigh
Caolas Bharraigh
Scurrival Pt.
Caolas Fhuideigh
89
Fuideigh (Fuday)
CASTLEBAY 1:40
Eolaigearraidh
CILLE BHARRA
0:40
Stack Is.
Orosay
Tràigh Mhòr
Oltir Mhòr
Hellisay
Gighay
Greian Head
Cliaid
BARRA
Grèin
207
BEN CLIAD
Cuidhir
Aird Mhor
Aird Mhidhinis
Allathasdal
Bagh Shiarabhagh
Caolas Sheileasaigh
Bruairnis
Borve Pt.
Baile na Creige
CRAIGSTON MUSEUM
Borgh
Buaile nam Bodach
Fuiay
Bagh a Tuath
94
EILEAN BHARRAIGH (BARRA)
Bruernish Pt.
Doirlinn Hd.
Tangasdal
332
HEAVAL
383
Earsairidh
BARRA HERITAGE CENTRE
Bagh a Chaisteil (Castlebay)
Breibhig
Caolas
KIESSIMUL (KISIMUL) CASTLE
Rubha Mor
0 2 4 6 miles
0 2 4 6 8 10 km
NF 00 60
NF 00 90
Oisgill Bay
Upper Milovaig
Glaspheinn
Lephin
Borrodale
Holmisdale
Fasach
COLBOST FOLK MUSEUM
Colbost
Waterstein
LIGHTHOUSE
Neist Point
Glen Dale
Hamara
Skinidin
Moonen Bay
HEALABHAL MHOR
468
Ramasaig
Hoe Rape
Macleod's Tables
488
HEALABHAL BHEAG
Hoe Point
NG 40 20
Geodha Mor
298
MACLEOD'S MAIDENS
Am Baile
185
Coilleag
Eiriosgaigh (Eriskay)
NF 60 10
Fiaraigh (Fiaray)
Caolas Fhiaraigh
Caolas Bharraigh
Scurrival Pt.
89
Fuideigh (Fuday)
Eolaigearraidh
CILLE BHARRA
Caolas Fhuideigh
Stack Is.
0:40
Orosay
Tràigh Mhòr
Oltir Mhòr
Hellisay
Gighay
Greian Head
Cliaid
BARRA
Grèin
207
BEN CLIAD
Cuidhir
Aird Mhor
Aird Mhidhinis
Caolas Sheileasaigh
Borve Pt.
Allathasdal
Bagh Shiarabhagh
Bruairnis
CRAIGSTON MUSEUM
Baile na Creige
Borgh
Buaile nam Bodach
Fuiay
94
Bagh a Tuath
EILEAN BHARRAIGH (BARRA)
Bruernish Pt.
Doirlinn Hd.
Tangasdal
332
HEAVAL
383
Earsairidh
BARRA HERITAGE CENTRE
Bagh a Chaisteil (Castlebay)
Breibhig
LOCHBOISDALE 1:40
Caolas
190
KIESSIMUL (KISIMUL) CASTLE
Rubha Mor
Bhatarsaigh (Vatersay)
Uidh
Bagh Bhatarsaigh
Bhatarsaigh
Muldoanich
OBAN 4:50
Caolas Shanndraigh
Flodaigh (Flodday)
207
Sanndraigh (Sandray)
Lingeigh (Lingay)
Greanamul
Caolas Phabaigh
Theisgeir (Heiskers)
17
Pabaidh (Pabbay)
Caolas Mhiui Laigh
273
Miùgh Laigh (Mingulay)
Caolas Bhearnaraigh
Bearnaraigh (Berneray)
Barra Hd.
NL 80 80

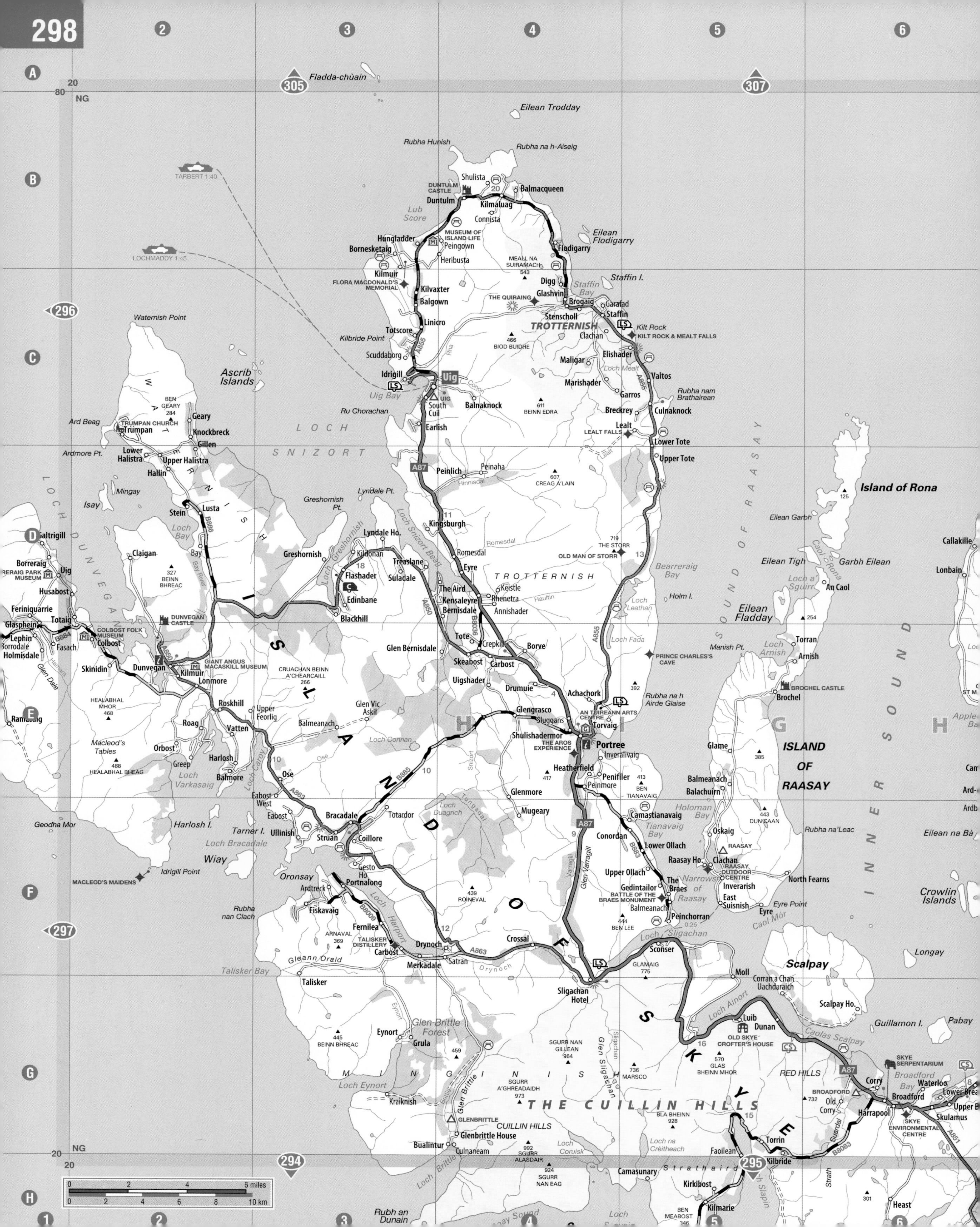
2
3
4
5
6
A
B
C
D
E
F
G
H
1
305
307
294
295
296
297
20
80
NG
Fladda-chùain
Eilean Trodday
Rubha Hunish
Rubha na h-Aiseig
TARBERT 1:40
LOCHMADDY 1:45
Shulista
DUNTULM CASTLE
Duntulm
Balmacqueen
Kilmaluag
Connista
Lub Score
Eilean Flodigarry
Hungladder
MUSEUM OF ISLAND LIFE
Peingown
Borneskètaig
Heribusta
Flodigarry
MEALL NA SUIRAMACH 543
Kilmuir
FLORA MACDONALD'S MEMORIAL
Digg
Staffin Bay
Staffin I.
Kilvaxter
THE QUIRAING
Glashvin
Balgown
Brogaig
Garafad
Staffin
Waternish Point
Stenscholl
TROTTERNISH
Kilt Rock
KILT ROCK & MEALT FALLS
Linicro
Clachan
Totscore
Kilbride Point
466 BIOD BUIDHE
Elishader
Scuddaborg
Maligar
Loch Mealt
Ascrib Islands
Idrigill
Uig
Valtos
Uig Bay
UIG
South Cuil
Marishader
Conon
Balnaknock
Rubha nam Brathairean
Garros
611 BEINN EDRA
Ru Chorachan
Breckrey
Culnaknock
BEN GEARY 284
Geary
Ard Beag
TRUMPAN CHURCH
Trumpan
LOCH
Earlish
Lealt
Knockbreck
LEALT FALLS
Lower Tote
Gillen
SNIZORT
Ardmore Pt.
Lower Halistra
Upper Halistra
Upper Tote
Hallin
A87
Peinlich
Peinaha
Hinnisdal
607 CREAG A'LAIN
Island of Rona
Mingay
Lyndale Pt.
Isay
Greshornish Pt.
125
Lusta
Stein
Loch Bay
Kingsburgh
Eilean Garbh
Galtrigill
Claigan
Bay
Lyndale Ho.
Loch Snizort Beag
719 THE STORR
Callakille
Borreraig
Greshornish
Kildonan
Romesdal
OLD MAN OF STORR
Eilean Tigh
Garbh Eilean
MUSEUM
Uig
327 BEINN BHREAC
Loch Greshornish
Treaslane
Eyre
TROTTERNISH
Bearreraig Bay
Lonbain
Husabost
Flashader
Suladale
Keistle
Loch a' Sguirr
An Caol
Feriniquarrie
Edinbane
The Aird
Kensaleyre
Rhenetra
Haultin
Holm I.
Eilean Fladday
Totaig
DUNVEGAN CASTLE
Blackhill
Bernisdale
Annishader
Loch Leathan
254
Glasphein
COLBOST FOLK MUSEUM
Colbost
Lephin
Borrodale
Fasach
Holmisdale
Tote
Crepkill
Loch Fada
Torran
Glen Bernisdale
Borve
Manish Pt.
Loch Arnish
Arnish
Skinidin
Dunvegan
GIANT ANGUS MACASKILL MUSEUM
Kilmuir
Skeabost
Carbost
PRINCE CHARLES'S CAVE
Glen Dale
CRUACHAN BEINN A'CHEARCAILL 266
Lonmore
Uigshader
392
BROCHEL CASTLE
HEALABHAL MHOR 468
Drumuie
Brochel
Achachork
Rubha na h Airde Glaise
Roskhill
Upper Feorlig
Glen Vic Askil
Glengrasco
AN TUIREANN ARTS CENTRE
Torvaig
Ramasaig
Sluggans
Roag
Vatten
Balmeanach
Shulishadermor
THE AROS EXPERIENCE
Portree
Glame
ISLAND OF RAASAY
Loch Connan
Macleod's Tables
Orbost
Inveralivaig
385
Greep
Harlosh
488 HEALABHAL BHEAG
Loch Varkasaig
Loch Caroy
Ose
B885
Heatherfield
417
Penifiler
413 BEN TIANAVAIG
Peinmore
Balmeanach
Balachuirn
Balmore
Glenmore
Eabost West
Eabost
Loch Duagrich
Mugeary
Camastianavaig
Holoman Bay
443 DUN CAAN
Geodha Mor
Harlosh I.
Tarner I.
Ullinish
Bracadale
Totardor
Tianavaig Bay
Oskaig
Rubha na'Leac
Eilean na Bà
Loch Bracadale
Struan
Coillore
Conordan
RAASAY
Lower Ollach
Wiay
Raasay Ho.
Clachan
RAASAY OUTDOOR CENTRE
Idrigill Point
Gesto Ho
Upper Ollach
The Braes
Narrows of Raasay
North Fearns
MACLEOD'S MAIDENS
Oronsay
Portnalong
Glen Varragill
Gedintailor
Inverarish
Crowlin Islands
Ardtreck
BATTLE OF THE BRAES MONUMENT
Balmeanach
East Suisnish
Eyre Point
Rubha nan Clach
Fiskavaig
439 ROINEVAL
Peinchorran
Eyre
Loch Harport
444 BEN LEE
Caol Mòr
Fernilea
Loch Sligachan
ARNAVAL 369
TALISKER DISTILLERY
Drynoch
Crossal
Sconser
Longay
Carbost
A863
Gleann Oraid
Merkadale
Satran
Drynoch
GLAMAIG 775
Scalpay
Talisker Bay
Moll
Corran a Chan Uachdaraich
Talisker
Sligachan Hotel
Eynort
Glen Brittle Forest
Scalpay Ho.
Loch Ainort
Luib
Dunan
Guillamon I.
Pabay
445 BEINN BHREAC
Eynort
Grula
459
SGURR NAN GILLEAN 964
OLD SKYE CROFTER'S HOUSE
Caolas Scalpay
Glen Sligachan
570 GLAS BHEINN MHOR
SKYE SERPENTARIUM
736 MARSCO
RED HILLS
Broadford Bay
MINGINISH
Loch Eynort
SGURR A'GHREADAIDH 973
Corry
Waterloo
BROADFORD
Broadford
Lower Breakish
Kraiknish
THE CUILLIN HILLS
732
Old Corry
Harrapool
Upper Breakish
SKYE
Glen Brittle
GLENBRITTLE
CUILLIN HILLS
BLA BHEINN 928
SKYE ENVIRONMENTAL CENTRE
Skulamus
Loch na Crèitheach
Torrin
Suardal
Bualintur
Glenbrittle House
Loch Coruisk
992 SGURR ALASDAIR
Faoilean
B8083
Culnaneam
Kilbride
924 SGURR NAN EAG
Camasunary
Strathaird
Strath
Loch Brittle
Kirkibost
301
Heast
Kilmarie
BEN MEABOST 346
Rubh an Dunain
0 2 4 6 miles
0 2 4 6 8 10 km

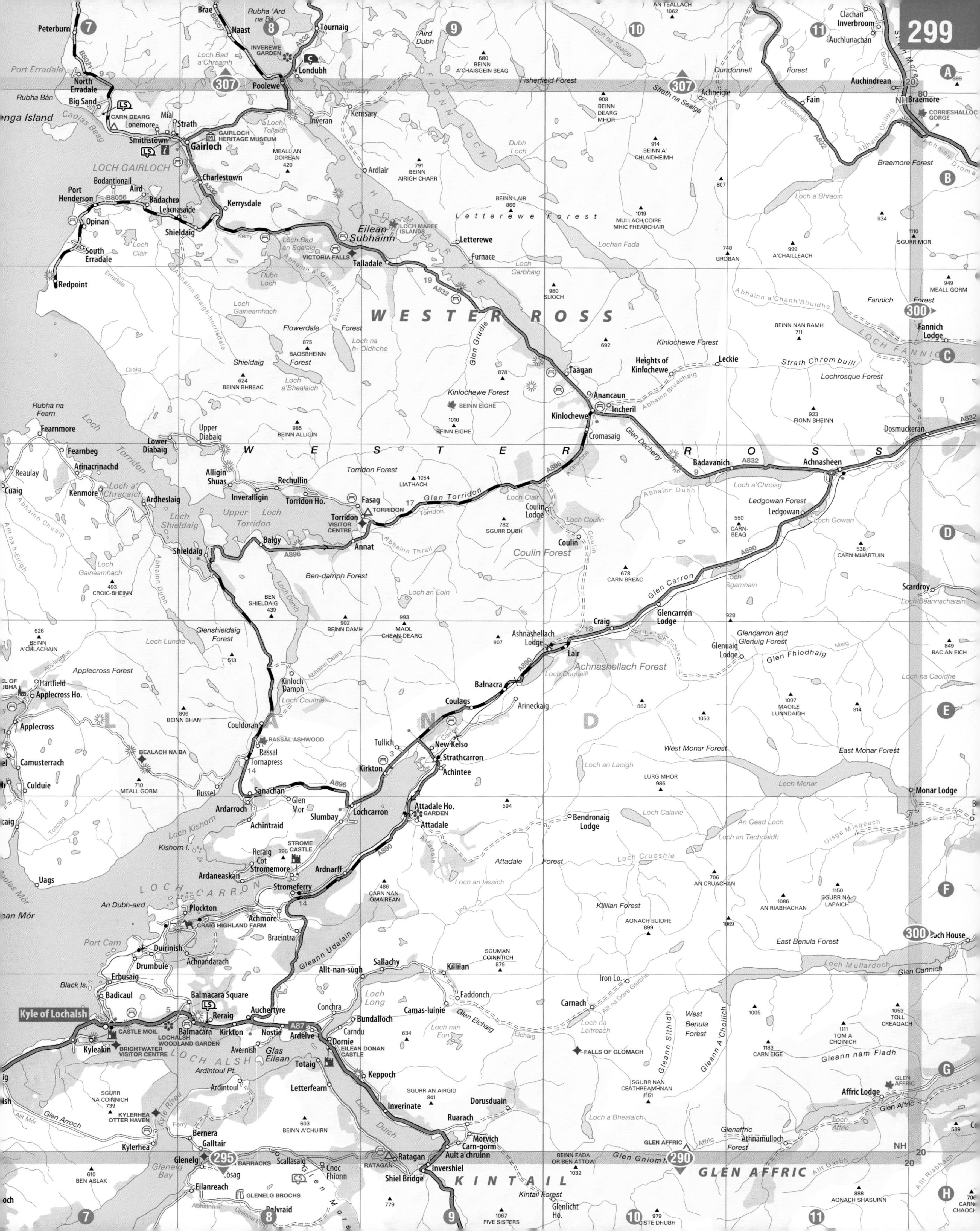
Peterburn
Brae
Rubha 'Ard na Bà
Naast
Tournaig
Aird Dubh
AN TEALLACH 1062
Loch na Sealga
Clachan
Inverbroom
Auchlunachan
Port Erradale
North Erradale
Loch Bad a' Chreamh
INVEREWE GARDEN
Londubh
680 BEINN A'CHAISGEIN BEAG
Dundonnell
Forest
Auchindrean
Rubha Bàn
Big Sand
Poolewe
Fisherfield Forest
Strath na Sealga
Achneigie
Fain
Braemore
CORRIESHALLOCH GORGE
Caolas Beag
CARN DEARG
Lonemore
Mial
Strath
Inveran
Kernsary
908 BEINN DEARG MHOR
Smithstown
GAIRLOCH HERITAGE MUSEUM
Gairloch
Loch Tollaidh
FINN LOCH
Dubh Loch
914 BEINN A' CHLAIDHEIMH
LOCH GAIRLOCH
MEALL AN DOIREAN 420
Ardlair
791 BEINN AIRIGH CHARR
Braemore Forest
Bodantionail
Port Henderson
Aird
Charlestown
Badachro
Leacnasaide
Kerrysdale
807
Loch a' Bhraoin
BEINN LAIR 860
Opinan
Letterewe Forest
1019 MULLACH COIRE MHIC FHEARCHAIR
934
Shieldaig
Kerry
LOCH MAREE ISLANDS
Eilean Subhainn
Letterewe
Loch Clàir
South Erradale
Loch Bad an Sgalaig
VICTORIA FALLS
Talladale
Furnace
Lochan Fada
748 GROBAN
999 A'CHAILLEACH
1110 SGURR MOR
Redpoint
Dubh Loch
Loch Garbhaig
980 SLIOCH
949 MEALL GORM
Abhainn a'Chadh'Bhuidhe
Fannich
Forest
Loch Gaineamhach
WESTER ROSS
Fannich Lodge
Flowerdale
Forest
Loch na h- Oidhche
BEINN NAN RAMH 711
875 BAOSBHEINN Forest
Glen Grudie
692
Kinlochewe Forest
LOCH FANNICH
Heights of Kinlochewe
Leckie
Strath Chrombuill
Shieldaig
624 BEINN BHREAC
Loch a'Bhealaich
878
Taagan
Lochrosque Forest
Kinlochewe Forest
Anancaun
BEINN EIGHE
Incheril
Rubha na Fearn
Kinlochewe
933 FIONN BHEINN
1010 BEINN EIGHE
Fearnmore
Upper Diabaig
985 BEINN ALLIGIN
Cromasaig
Glen Docherty
Dosmuckeran
Lower Diabaig
Fearnbeg
WESTER ROSS
Badavanich
Achnasheen
Arinacrinachd
Torridon Forest
1054 LIATHACH
Reaulay
Alligin Shuas
Rechullin
Loch a'Chroisg
Cuaig
Kenmore
Loch a' Chracaich
Inveralligin
Torridon Ho.
Fasag
Glen Torridon
Loch Clair
Ledgowan Forest
Ardheslaig
TORRIDON
Coulin Lodge
Ledgowan
Loch Shieldaig
Upper Loch Torridon
Torridon VISITOR CENTRE
782 SGURR DUBH
Loch Coulin
550 CARN-BEAG
Loch Gowan
Balgy
Annat
Coulin
Shieldaig
Coulin Forest
538 CARN MHARTUIN
Loch Gaineamhach
493 CROIC-BHEINN
Ben-damph Forest
678 CARN BREAC
Glen Carron
Loch Sgamhain
Scardroy
Loch an Eoin
Loch Beannacharain
BEN SHIELDAIG 439
Craig
Glencarron Lodge
626 BEINN A'CHLACHAIN
902 BEINN DAMH
993 MAOL CHEAN-DEARG
Ashnashellach Lodge
928
Glencarron and Glenuig Forest
Glenshieldaig Forest
Loch Lundie
907
Lair
Glenuaig Lodge
Glen Fhiodhaig
849 BAC AN EICH
Applecross Forest
513
Achnashellach Forest
Loch Dughaill
Loch na Caoidhe
Hartfield
Kinloch Damph
Balnacra
Applecross Ho.
Loch Coultrie
Coulags
Arineckaig
862
1007 MAOILE LUNNDAIDH
814
1053
Applecross
896 BEINN BHAN
Couldoran
LAND
RASSAL ASHWOOD
Tullich
New Kelso
West Monar Forest
East Monar Forest
BEALACH NA BA
Rassal
Strathcarron
Camusterrach
Tornapress
Kirkton
Achintee
Loch an Laoigh
LURG MHOR 986
Culduie
710 MEALL GORM
Russel
Sanachan
Loch Monar
Monar Lodge
Glen Mor
Slumbay
Lochcarron
Attadale Ho. GARDEN
Ardarroch
594
Bendronaig Lodge
Loch Calavie
Achintraid
Attadale
An Gead Loch
Loch Kishorn
Loch an Tachdaidh
Uisge Misgeach
STROME CASTLE
Kishorn I.
Reraig
Cot
395
Attadale
Forest
Loch Cruoshie
Ardaneaskan
Stromemore
Ardnarff
Uags
Stromeferry
486 CARN NAN IOMAIREAN
Loch an Iasaich
706 AN CRUACHAN
1150 SGURR NA LAPAICH
LOCH CARRON
An Dubh-aird
Plockton
1086 AN RIABHACHAN
Killilan Forest
Achmore
CRAIG HIGHLAND FARM
AONACH BUIDHE 899
1069
Braeintra
East Benula Forest
Loch House
Port Cam
Duirinish
SGUMAN COINNTICH 879
Drumbuie
Achnandarach
Gleann Udalain
Loch Mullardoch
Glen Cannich
Allt-nan-sùgh
Sallachy
Killilan
Iron Lo.
Erbusaig
Black Is.
Badicaul
Balmacara Square
Loch Long
Faddonch
Carnach
West Benula Forest
1005
1053 TOLL CREAGACH
Kyle of Lochalsh
Reraig
Auchertyre
Conchra
Camas-luinie
Glen Elchaig
Loch na Leitreach
CASTLE MOIL
Balmacara
LOCHALSH WOODLAND GARDEN
Kirkton
Nostie
Ardelve
Bundalloch
Gleann Sithidh
Gleann A'Chollich
1111 TOM A CHOINICH
Kyleakin
BRIGHTWATER VISITOR CENTRE
Carndu
634
Loch nan Eun
Elchaig
Avernish
Dornie
EILEAN DONAN CASTLE
FALLS OF GLOMACH
1183 CARN EIGE
Gleann nam Fiadh
LOCH ALSH
Glas Eilean
Ardintoul Pt.
Totaig
Keppoch
Ardintoul
Letterfearn
SGURR NAN CEATHREAMHNAN 1151
SGURR NA COINNICH 739
SGURR AN AIRGID 841
GLEN AFFRIC
Affric Lodge
Glen Arroch
Kyle Rhea
KYLERHEA OTTER HAVEN
Inverinate
Dorusduain
Glen Affric
Loch Duich
Ruarach
Loch a'Bhealaich
Loch Affric
Allt Mòr
Ferry
603 BEINN A'CHUIRN
Bernera
Morvich
Glenaffric
Athnamulloch
Kylerhea
Galltair
Carn-gorm
GLEN AFFRIC
Forest
539
Glenelg
BARRACKS
Scallasaig
Ratagan
Ault a'chruinn
BEINN FADA OR BEN ATTOW 1032
Glen Gniomh
GLEN AFFRIC
Allt Garbh
Allt Riabhach
610 BEN ASLAK
Glenelg Bay
Cosag
Cnoc Fhionn
RATAGAN
Shiel Bridge
Inversheil
KINTAIL
Kintail Forest
888 AONACH SHASUINN
706 CARN CHAOCH
Eilanreach
GLENELG BROCHS
Glen More
Balvraid
Gleann Beag
779
1067 FIVE SISTERS
Glenlicht Ho.
979 CISTE DHUBH
Loch
A832
A896
A890
A87
B8021
B8057
B8056
NH
20
80

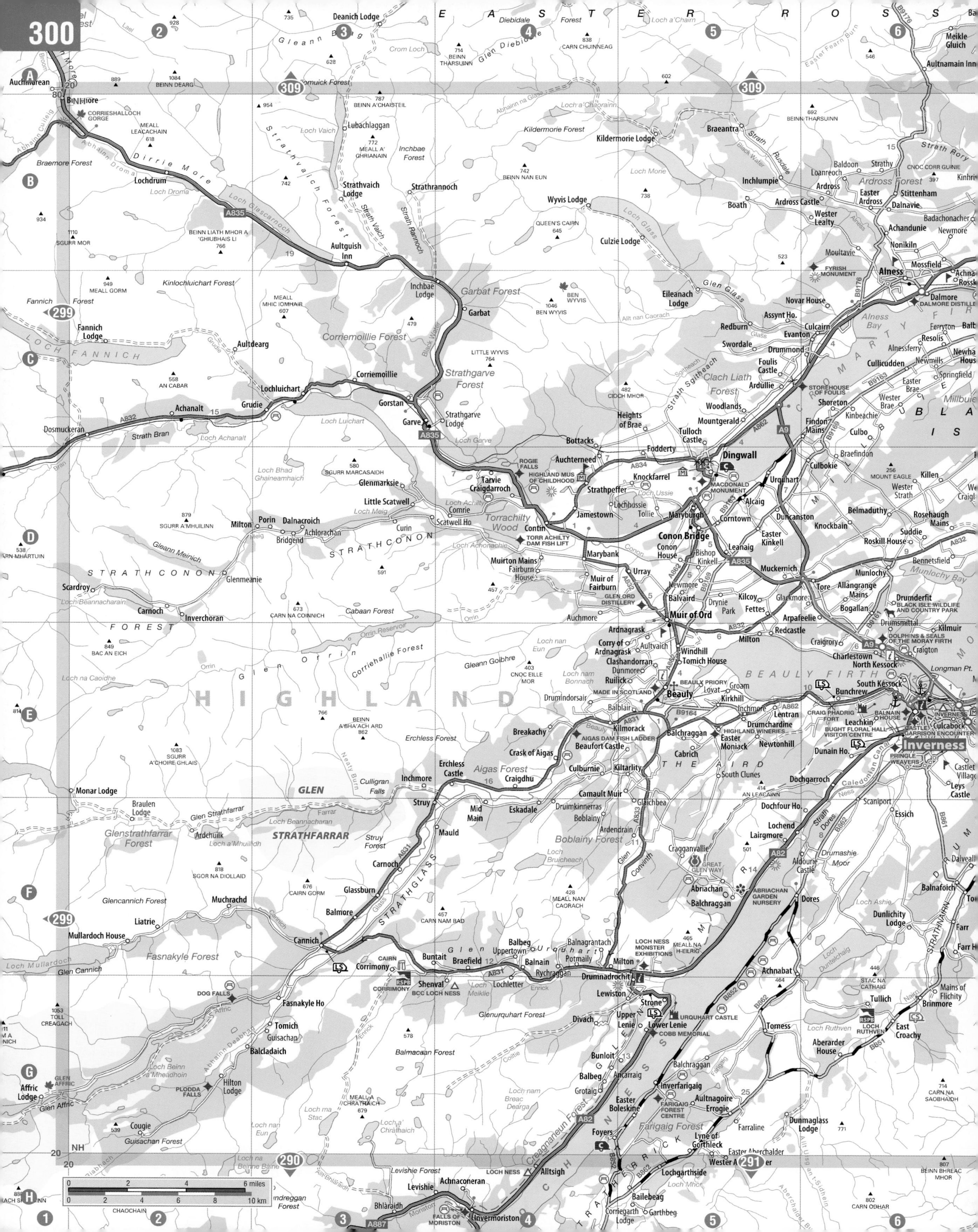

EASTER ROSS
HIGHLAND
309
299
290
291
Deanich Lodge
Diebidale
Forest
Loch a'Chàirn
Meikle Gluich
Aultnamain Inn
Auchmarean
Braemore
Corrieshalloch Gorge
Beinn Dearg
1084
Beinn Tharsuinn
Glen Diebidale
Carn Chuinneag
838
Gleann Beag
Crom Loch
Alladale Lodge
Inverlael Forest
Freevater Forest
Beinn a'Chaisteil
787
Abhainn na Glasa
Loch a'Chàrrainn
Kildermorie Forest
Kildermorie Lodge
Braeantra
Strath Rory
Strath Rusdale
Black Water
Loch Vaich
Lubachlaggan
Meall a' Ghrianain
772
Inchbae Forest
Strathvaich Forest
Meall Leacachain
618
Braemore Forest
Dirrie More
Abhainn Droma
Lochdrum
Loch Droma
Loch Glascarnoch
A835
Beinn Nan Eun
742
Loch Morie
Inchlumpie
Baldoon
Strathy
Loanreoch
Ardross Forest
Cnoc Corr Guinie
Ardross
Ardross Castle
Easter Ardross
Stittenham
Dalnavie
Boath
Wester Lealty
Badachonacher
Strathvaich Lodge
Strathrannoch
Strath Vaich
Strath Rannoch
Wyvis Lodge
Loch Glass
Queen's Cairn
645
Culzie Lodge
Achandunie
Newmore
Nonikiln
Mossfield
Sgurr Mor
1110
934
Beinn Liath Mhor a' Ghiubhais Li
766
Aultguish Inn
Moultavie
Fyrish Monument
Alness
Kinlochluichart Forest
Meall Gorm
949
Inchbae Lodge
Garbat Forest
Garbat
Ben Wyvis
1046
Glen Glass
Eileanach Lodge
Novar House
Dalmore
Dalmore Distillery
Fannich Forest
Fannich Lodge
Loch Fannich
Meall Mhic Iomhair
607
Corriemoillie Forest
Aultdearg
Allt nan Caorach
Assynt Ho.
Culcairn
Evanton
Redburn
Swordale
Drummond
Alness Bay
Ferryton
Resolis
Alnessferry
Cullicudden
Newmills
Springfield
Foulis Castle
Clach Liath Forest
Strath Sgitheach
Ardullie
Storehouse of Foulis
Cromarty Firth
Easter Brae
Wester Brae
Shoreton
Kinbeachie
Findon Mains
Culbo
Black Isle
Little Wyvis
764
Strathgarve Forest
An Cabar
558
Lochluichart
Corriemoillie
Gorstan
Garve
Strathgarve Lodge
Cioch Mhor
482
Heights of Brae
Woodlands
Mountgerald
Tulloch Castle
Achanalt
Grudie
Loch Luichart
Dosmuckeran
A832
Strath Bran
Loch Achanalt
Loch Garve
Bottacks
Auchterneed
Fodderty
Dingwall
Braefindon
Culbokie
Mount Eagle
Killen
Sgurr Marcasaidh
580
Loch Bhad Ghaineamhaich
Glenmarksie
Rogie Falls
Highland Mus of Childhood
Tarvie
Craigdarroch
Strathpeffer
Knockfarrel
Loch Ussie
MacDonald Monument
Urquhart
Wester Strath
Little Scatwell
Loch Achilty
Comrie
Loch Meig
Scatwell Ho
Torrachilty Wood
Contin
Lochussie
Jamestown
Tollie
Maryburgh
Alcaig
Corntown
Duncanston
Belmaduthy
Rosehaugh Mains
Knockbain
Sgurr a' Mhuilinn
879
Milton
Porin
Dalnacroich
Achlorachan
Bridgend
Curin
Strathconon
Loch Achonachie
Torr Achilty Dam Fish Lift
Conon Bridge
Conon House
Easter Kinkell
Suddie
Roskill House
Gleann Meinich
Glenmeanie
Muirton Mains
Fairburn House
Marybank
Bishop Kinkell
Leanaig
Muckernich
Bennetsfield
Munlochy
Munlochy Bay
Urray
Muir of Fairburn
Newmore
Tore
Allangrange Mains
Drumderfit
Black Isle Wildlife and Country Park
Scardroy
Loch Beannacharain
Carnoch
Inverchoran
Carn na Coinnich
673
Cabaan Forest
Glen Ord Distillery
Auchmore
Balvaird
Drynie Park
Kilcoy
Glackmore
Fettes
Bogallan
Muir of Ord
Arpafeelie
Drumsmittal
Kilmuir
Orrin
Orrin Reservoir
Bac an Eich
849
Glen Orrin
Corriehallie Forest
Gleann Goibhre
Loch nan Eun
Ardnagrask
Corry of Ardnagrask
Aultvaich
Windhill
Tomich House
Redcastle
Milton
Craigrory
Dolphins & Seals of the Moray Firth
Craigton
Charlestown
North Kessock
Longman Pt.
Clashandorran
Dunmore
Ruilick
Cnoc Eille Mor
403
Loch nam Bonnach
Loch na Caoidhe
Beauly Firth
Beauly Priory
Groam
Lovat
Kirkhill
Bunchrew
South Kessock
Drumindorsair
Made in Scotland
Beauly
Balblair
Inchmore
Lentran
Craig Phadrig Fort
Drumchardine
Leachkin
Balnain House
Inverness
Culcabock
Castle Garrison Encounter
Bught Floral Hall Visitor Centre
Beinn a' Bha'ach Ard
862
766
Kilmorack
Balchraggan
Highland Wineries
Easter Moniack
Newtonhill
Dunain Ho.
Breakachy
Aigas Dam Fish Ladder
Beaufort Castle
Crask of Aigas
Cabrich
The Aird
Sgurr a' Choire Ghlais
1083
Erchless Forest
Erchless Castle
Aigas Forest
Culburnie
Kiltarlity
South Clunes
Pringle Weavers
Castle Village
Leys Castle
Monar Lodge
Culligran Falls
Inchmore
Craigdhu
Glen
An Leacainn
414
Dochgarroch
Caledonian Canal
Braulen Lodge
Glen Strathfarrar
Loch Beannacharan
Farrar
Struy
Mid Main
Eskadale
Camault Muir
Druimkinnerras
Glaichbea
Dochfour Ho.
Scaniport
Essich
Glenstrathfarrar Forest
Ardchuilk
Loch a' Mhuillidh
Strathfarrar
Struy Forest
Mauld
Boblainy
Ardendrain
Boblainy Forest
Lochend
Lairgmore
Strath Dores
B862
B861
Sgor na Diollaid
818
Carnoch
A831
Loch Bruicheach
Glen Convinth
Cragganvallie
Great Glen Way
Aldourie Castle
Drumashie Moor
Dalveallan
Cairn Gorm
676
Glassburn
Strathglass
Abriachan
Abriachan Garden Nursery
Balnafoich
Glencannich Forest
Muchrachd
Balmore
Meall nan Caorach
428
Balchraggan
Dores
Loch Ashie
Dunlichity Lodge
Strathnairn
Liatrie
Carn nam Bad
457
Mullardoch House
Cannich
Glen Urquhart
Balbeg
Uppertown
Balnagrantach
Loch Ness Monster Exhibitions
Meall na h-Eilrig
465
Farr
Farr House
Loch Mullardoch
Glen Cannich
Fasnakyle Forest
Cairn
Corrimony
Buntait
Braefield
Balnain
Polmaily
Rychraggan
Milton
Loch Duntelchaig
Achnabat
Stac na Cathaig
446
Mains of Flichity
Brinmore
Toll Creagach
1053
Dog Falls
Affric
Fasnakyle Ho
Shenval
BCC Loch Ness
Corrimony
Loch Meiklie
Lochletter
Enrick
Drumnadrochit
Lewiston
Strone
Urquhart Castle
Tullich
Tomich
Guisachan
Glenurquhart Forest
Divach
Upper Lenie
Lower Lenie
Cobb Memorial
Torness
Loch Ruthven
East Croachy
Balcladaich
Abhainn Deabhag
578
Balmacaan Forest
Coiltie
Bunloit
Aberarder House
Loch Beinn a' Mheadhoin
Glen Affric
Affric Lodge
Plodda Falls
Hilton Lodge
Balbeg
Ancarraig
Balchraggan
Farigaig
Inverfarigaig
Grotaig
Loch nam Breac Dearga
Easter Boleskine
Farigaig Forest Centre
Aultnagoire
Errogie
Carn na Saobhaidh
714
Meall a' Chrathaich
679
Loch ma Stac
Loch a' Chràthaich
Cougie
539
Guisachan Forest
Loch nan Eun
Creagnaneun Forest
A82
Foyers
Farigaig Forest
Lyne of Gorthleck
Farraline
Dunmaglass Lodge
771
NH
20
Loch na Beinne Baine
Levishie Forest
Loch Ness
Alltsigh
Stratherrick
Easter Aberchalder
Wester Aberchalder
Beinn Bhreac Mhor
807
Achnaconeran
Levishie
Invermoriston
Falls of Moriston
Bhlàraidh
A887
Lochgarthside
Loch Mhòr
Bailebeag
Corriegarth Lodge
Garthbeg
Carn Odhar
802
Chaochain
Ruadh Creag
0 2 4 6 miles
0 2 4 6 8 10 km

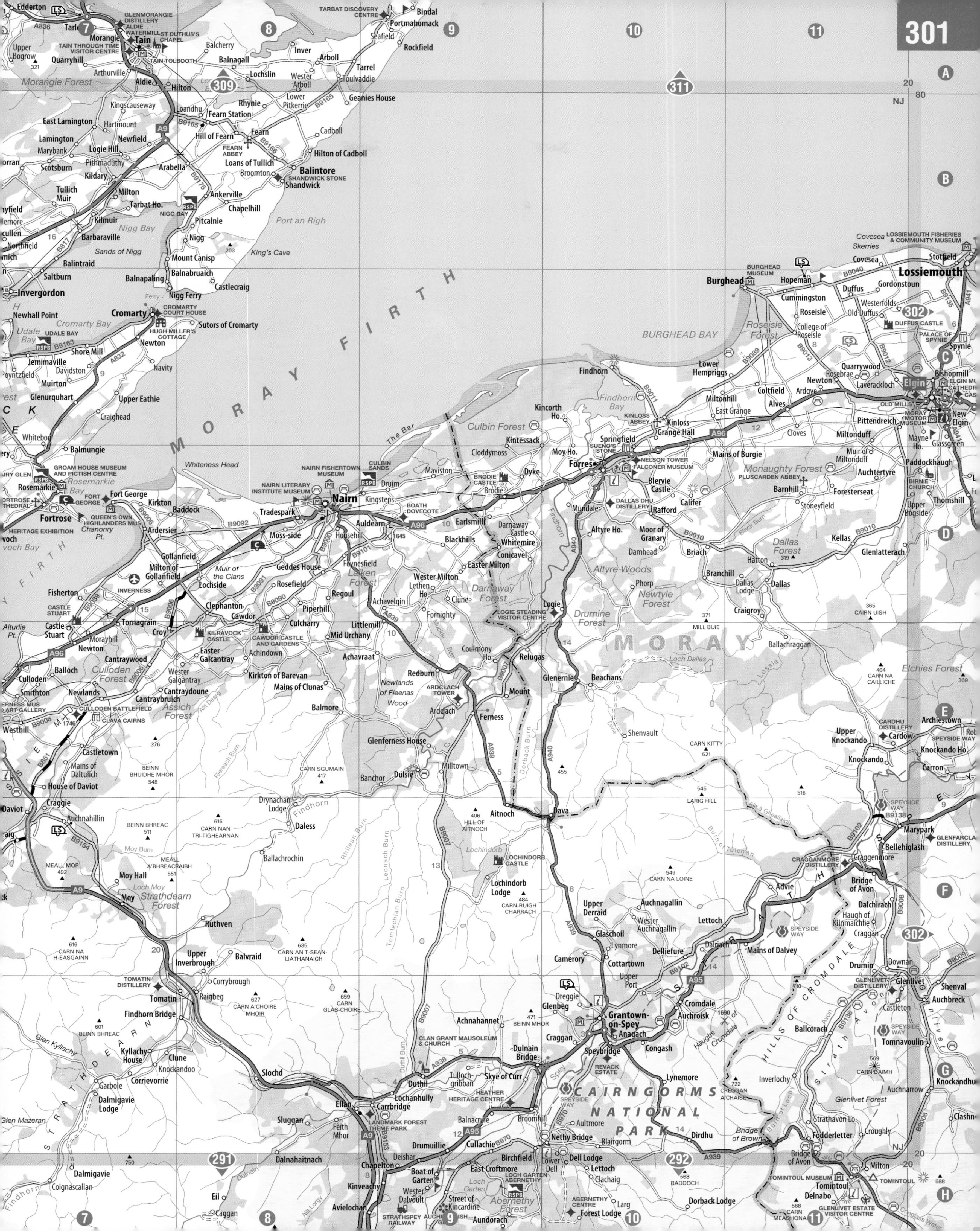
MORAY FIRTH
MORAY
Burghead Bay
Nigg Bay
Cromarty Bay
Port an Righ
Tain
Invergordon
Cromarty
Fortrose
Nairn
Forres
Burghead
Lossiemouth
Elgin
Grantown-on-Spey
Tomintoul
Carrbridge
CAIRNGORMS NATIONAL PARK
HILLS OF CROMDALE
Culbin Forest
Darnaway Forest
Lochindorb
Dava
Ardersier
Fort George
Balintore
Portmahomack
Kinloss
Alves
Dallas
Glenlivet
Dulnain Bridge
Nethy Bridge
Boat of Garten
Aviemore
Tomatin
Moy
Culloden
Cawdor
Auldearn
Findhorn
Hopeman
Duffus
Rothes
Knockando
Marypark
Advie
Cromdale
Tomnavoulin
Balmungie
Rosemarkie
Kirkton
Croy
Tornagrain
Newton
Dalcross
Glenferness House
Ferness
Relugas
Logie
Dunphail
Edinkillie
Spey
Findhorn
Nairn
Lossie
Divie
Dorback Burn
Dulnain
Nethy
Avon
Livet
A9
A96
A939
A940
A95
B9007
B9102
B9006
B9011
B9013
B9010
B9012
B9089
B9091
B9090
B9101
B9165
B9175
B9163
B9153
B9008
B9136
B9009
B8970
302
309
311
291
292
7
8
9
10
11
A
B
C
D
E
F
G
H
NJ

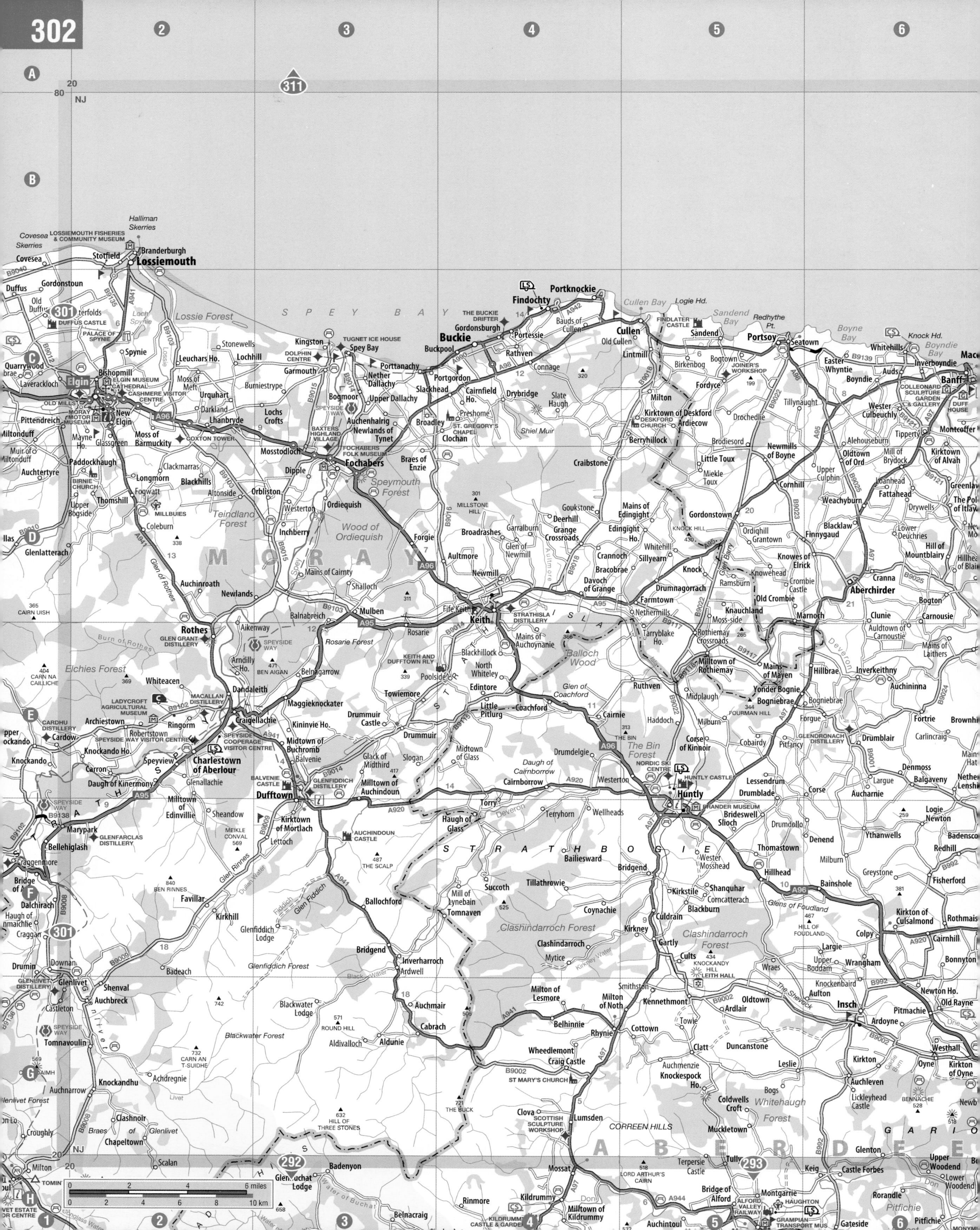

2
3
4
5
6
A
B
311
NJ
Halliman Skerries
Covesea Skerries
LOSSIEMOUTH FISHERIES & COMMUNITY MUSEUM
Branderburgh
Stotfield
Lossiemouth
Covesea
Duffus
Gordonstoun
Old Duffus
301
DUFFUS CASTLE
Loch Spynie
Lossie Forest
PALACE OF SPYNIE
Spynie
Quarrywood
Laverackloch
Elgin
Bishopmill
ELGIN MUSEUM
CATHEDRAL
CASHMERE VISITOR CENTRE
OLD MILLS
MORAY MOTOR MUSEUM
New Elgin
Pittendreich
Mayne Ho.
Glassgreen
Moss of Barmuckity
COXTON TOWER
Lhanbryde
Darkland
Urquhart
Moss of Meft
Leuchars Ho.
Stonewells
Lochhill
Burniestrype
Lochs Crofts
Mosstodloch
S P E Y B A Y
Kingston
TUGNET ICE HOUSE
Spey Bay
DOLPHIN CENTRE
Garmouth
Porttanachy
Nether Dallachy
Upper Dallachy
Bogmoor
SPEYSIDE WAY
Auchenhalrig
Newlands of Tynet
BAXTERS HIGHLAND VILLAGE
FOCHABERS FOLK MUSEUM
Fochabers
Speymouth Forest
Dipple
Orbliston
Westerton
Ordiequish
Wood of Ordiequish
Inchberry
Mains of Cairnty
Shalloch
Paddockhaugh
BIRNIE CHURCH
Longmorn
Fogwatt
Blackhills
Clackmarras
Altonside
Thomshill
Upper Bogside
MILLBUIES
Teindland Forest
Coleburn
338
Glenlatterach
M O R A Y
Glen of Rothes
Auchinroath
Newlands
365 CAIRN UISH
Rothes
GLEN GRANT DISTILLERY
Burn of Rothes
Aikenway
SPEYSIDE WAY
Arndilly Ho.
471 BEN AIGAN
Elchies Forest
404 CARN NA CAILLICHE
369
Whiteacen
LADYCROFT AGRICULTURAL MUSEUM
MACALLAN DISTILLERY
Dandaleith
Craigellachie
CARDHU DISTILLERY
Archiestown
Cardow
Robertstown
Ringorm
SPEYSIDE COOPERAGE VISITOR CENTRE
SPEYSIDE WAY VISITOR CENTRE
Knockando Ho.
Knockando
Carron
Speyview
Charlestown of Aberlour
Glenallachie
Daugh of Kinermony
Milltown of Edinvillie
Sheandow
MEIKLE CONVAL 569
Marypark
GLENFARCLAS DISTILLERY
Bellehiglash
Craggenmore
Bridge of Avon
Dalchirach
Haugh of Urnachie
Craggan
840 BEN RINNES
Favillar
Glen Rinnes
Kirkhill
Glenfiddich Lodge
Glenfiddich Forest
Drumin
Downan
Glenlivet
GLENLIVET DISTILLERY
Shenval
Auchbreck
Castleton
Badeach
742
Blackwater Lodge
571 ROUND HILL
Aldivalloch
Aldunie
Blackwater Forest
SPEYSIDE WAY
Tomnavoulin
732 CARN AN T-SUIDHE
569 CAIRN EL...
Auchnarrow
Knockandhu
Achdregnie
Livet
Glenlivet Forest
Clashnoir
Braes of Glenlivet
Chapeltown
Croughly
Scalan
Milton
TOMIN
632 HILL OF THREE STONES
292
Glenbuchat Lodge
Badenyon
Belnacraig
658
Water of Buchat
THE BUCKIE DRIFTER
Findochty
Portknockie
Gordonsburgh
Buckie
Portessie
Bauds of Cullen
Cullen Bay
Logie Hd.
FINDLATER CASTLE
Cullen
Old Cullen
Lintmill
Sandend Bay
Redhythe Pt.
Sandend
Portsoy
Seatown
Boyne Bay
Knock Hd.
Boyndie Bay
Buckpool
Rathven
Connage
Portgordon
Slackhead
Cairnfield Ho.
Drybridge
Slate Haugh
Preshome
Broadley
ST. GREGORY'S CHAPEL
Clochan
Shiel Muir
Braes of Enzie
301 MILLSTONE HILL
Forgie
Broadrashes
Aultmore
Newmill
Fife Keith
Keith
STRATHISLA DISTILLERY
Mulben
Balnabreich
Rosarie
Rosarie Forest
KEITH AND DUFFTOWN RLY
Poolside
Blackhillock
North Whiteley
Edintore
Towiemore
Belnagarrow
Maggieknockater
Kininvie Ho.
Drummuir Castle
Drummuir
Midtown of Buchromb
Balvenie
Glack of Midthird
Slogan
Midtown of Glass
Milltown of Auchindoun
417
BALVENIE CASTLE
GLENFIDDICH DISTILLERY
Dufftown
Kirktown of Mortlach
Lettoch
AUCHINDOUN CASTLE
487 THE SCALP
Glen Fiddich
Ballochford
Bridgend
Inverharroch
Ardwell
Auchmair
Cabrach
Torry
Haugh of Glass
Deveron
S T R A T H B O G I E
Mill of Lynebain
Tomnaven
Succoth
525
Tillathrowie
Clashindarroch Forest
Clashindarroch
Mytice
Milton of Lesmore
Belhinnie
Rhynie
Wheedlemont
Craig Castle
B9002
ST MARY'S CHURCH
721 THE BUCK
Clova
SCOTTISH SCULPTURE WORKSHOP
Lumsden
Mossat
Kildrummy
Milltown of Kildrummy
Rinmore
KILDRUMMY CASTLE & GARDEN
Mains of Auchoynanie
366
Balloch Wood
Glen of Coachford
Little Pitlurg
Coachford
Cairnie
313 THE BIN
The Bin Forest
Drumdelgie
Daugh of Cairnborrow
Cairnborrow
Westerton
NORDIC SKI CENTRE
HUNTLY CASTLE
Huntly
BRANDER MUSEUM
Terryhorn
Wellheads
Bailiesward
Bridgend
Goukstone
Deerhill
Garralburn
Grange Crossroads
Glen of Newmill
Craibstone
Mains of Edingight
Edingight Ho.
Crannoch
Bracobrae
Davoch of Grange
Sillyearn
Whitehill
Knock
Drumnagorrach
Farmtown
Nethermills
Tarryblake Ho.
Isla
Ruthven
Haddoch
Corse of Kinnoir
Milltown of Rothiemay
Rothiemay Crossroads
Moss-side
265
Midplaugh
Milburn
Milton
Kirktown of Deskford
DESKFORD CHURCH
Ardiecow
Berryhillock
Birkenbog
Bogtown
JOINER'S WORKSHOP
199
Fordyce
Little Toux
Miekle Toux
Brodiesord
Drochedlie
Gordonstown
KNOCK HILL 430
Ordiqhill
Grantown
Glen Barry
Knowehead
Ramsburn
Crombie Castle
Old Crombie
Knauchland
Newmills of Boyne
Cornhill
Upper Culphin
Finnygaud
Blacklaw
Knowes of Elrick
Mains of Mayen
Yonder Bognie
Bogniebrae
344 FOURMAN HILL
Cobairdy
Pitfancy
Forgue
GLENDRONACH DISTILLERY
Marnoch
Hillbrae
Deveron
Inverkeithny
Auchininna
Fortrie
Drumblair
Carlincraig
Brownhill
Denmoss
Balgaveny
Largue
Lessendrum
Drumblade
Corse
Aucharnie
Brideswell
Slioch
Drumdollo
Denend
Ythanwells
Logie Newton
Badenscoth
Redhill
Wester Mosshead
Thomastown
Milburn
Hillhead
Greystone
Bainshole
381
Fisherford
Kirkstile
Shanquhar
Corncatterach
Blackburn
Coynachie
Culdrain
Kirkney
Gartly
Cults
Clashindarroch Forest
434 KNOCKANDY HILL
LEITH HALL
Glens of Foudland
467 HILL OF FOUDLAND
Kirkton of Culsalmond
Rothmaise
Colpy
Cairnhill
Largie
Upper Boddam
Wrangham
Bonnyton
Wraes
Smithston
Milton of Noth
Kennethmont
Knockenbaird
Aulton
Oldtown
Ardlair
The Shevock
Insch
Newton Ho.
Old Rayne
Pitmachie
Ardoyne
Towie
Cottown
Clatt
Duncanstone
Auchmenzie
Knockespock Ho.
Leslie
Kirkton
Oyne
Kirkton of Oyne
Westhall
Coldwells Croft
Whitehaugh Forest
Auchleven
Lickleyhead Castle
BENNACHIE 528
518
Muckletown
CORREEN HILLS
G A R I O
A B E R D E E
Glenton
Tullynessle
293
Terpersie Castle
518 LORD ARTHUR'S CAIRN
Bridge of Alford
ALFORD VALLEY RAILWAY
GRAMPIAN TRANSPORT MUS
Montgarrie
HAUGHTON
Castle Forbes
Keig
Upper Woodend
Lower Woodend
Rorandle
Pitfichie
Gateside
Auchintoul
Whitehills
Easter Whyntie
Auds
Inverboyndie
Banff
Boyndie
COLLEONARD SCULPTURE GARDEN & GALLERY
DUFF HOUSE
Tillynaught
Wester Culbeuchly
Montcoffer
Tipperty
Alehouseburn
Oldtown of Ord
Mill of Brydock
Kirktown of Alvah
Loanhead
Fattahead
Greenlaw
The Pole of Itlaw
Weachyburn
Drywells
Lower Deuchries
Hill of Mountblairy
Cranna
Aberchirder
Bogton
Clunie
Carnousie
Auldtown of Carnoustie
Mains of Laithers
A96
A95
A941
A920
A97
A98
A942
A990
A944
B9040
B9012
B9135
B9103
B9015
B9014
B9016
B9018
B9022
B9023
B9025
B9117
B9118
B9115
B9102
B9138
B9008
B9009
B9136
B9139
B9121
B9024
B9001
B992
B9002
Scale
0 2 4 6 miles
0 2 4 6 8 10 km

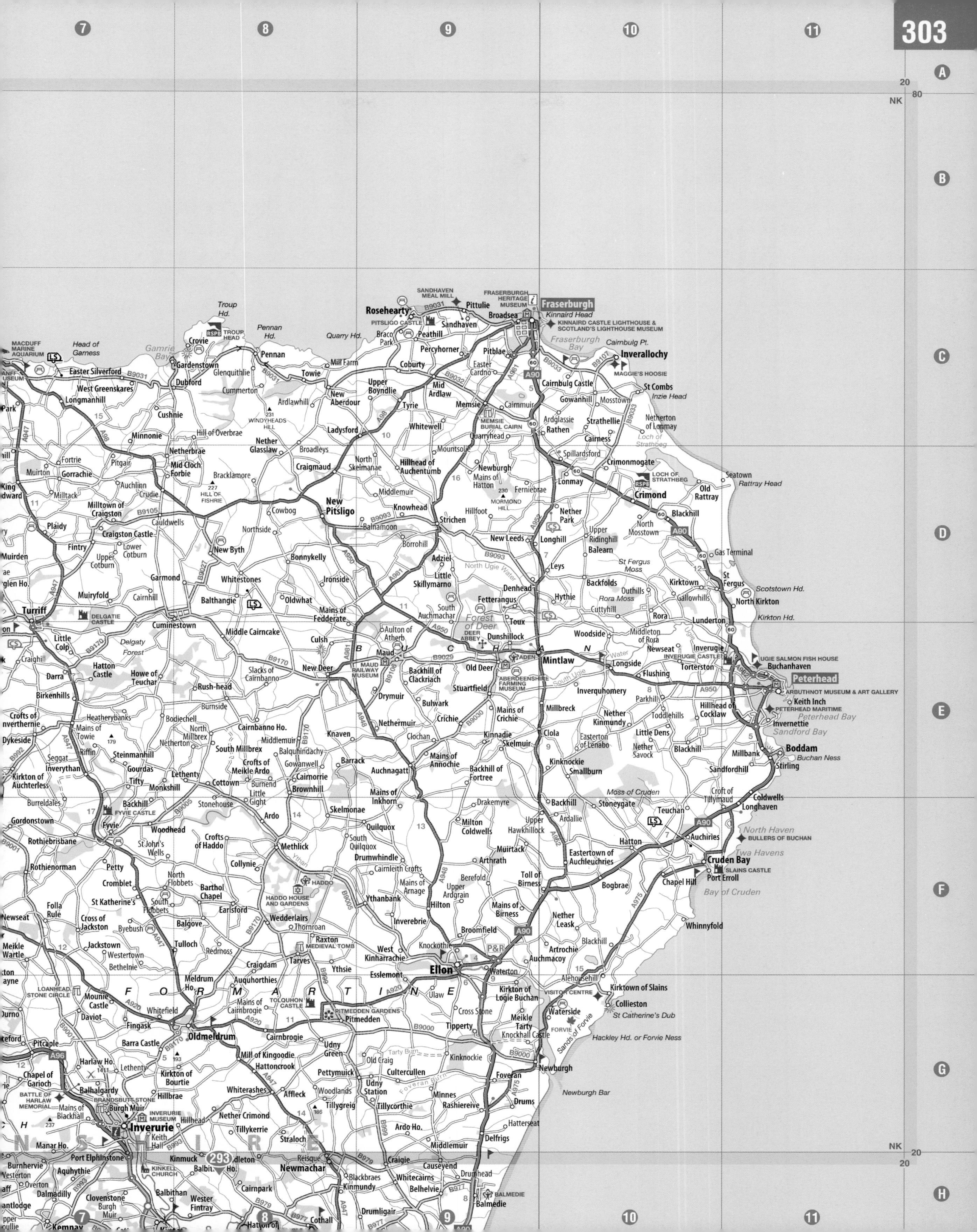
7
8
9
10
11
A
B
C
D
E
F
G
H
NK
20
80
Troup Hd.
Pennan Hd.
Quarry Hd.
SANDHAVEN MEAL MILL
FRASERBURGH HERITAGE MUSEUM
Fraserburgh
Kinnaird Head
KINNAIRD CASTLE LIGHTHOUSE & SCOTLAND'S LIGHTHOUSE MUSEUM
Rosehearty
Pittulie
Broadsea
PITSLIGO CASTLE
Sandhaven
Braco Park
Peathill
Percyhorner
Pitblae
Fraserburgh Bay
Cairnbulg Pt.
Inverallochy
MAGGIE'S HOOSIE
MACDUFF MARINE AQUARIUM
Head of Garness
Gamrie Bay
RSPB
TROUP HEAD
Crovie
Gardenstown
Pennan
Mill Farm
Coburty
Easter Cardno
Cairnbulg Castle
St Combs
Inzie Head
Easter Silverford
Dubford
Glenquithlie
Towie
Upper Boyndlie
Mid Ardlaw
Gowanhill
Mosstown
West Greenskares
Cummerton
New Aberdour
Ardlawhill
Tyrie
Memsie
Cairnmuir
Longmanhill
Cushnie
WINDYHEADS HILL
Whitewell
MEMSIE BURIAL CAIRN
Ardglassie
Rathen
Strathellie
Netherton of Lonmay
Minnonie
Hill of Overbrae
Ladysford
Quarryhead
Cairness
Loch of Strathbeg
Netherbrae
Nether Glasslaw
Broadleys
Mountsolie
Spillardsford
Fortrie
Pitgair
Mid Cloch Forbie
Craigmaud
North Skelmanae
Hillhead of Auchentumb
Newburgh
Crimonmogate
Seatown
Rattray Head
Muirton
Gorrachie
Bracklamore
Mains of Hatton
Ferniebrae
Lonmay
LOCH OF STRATHBEG
Crimond
Old Rattray
King Edward
Milltack
Auchlinn
Crudie
HILL OF FISHRIE
Middlemuir
MORMOND HILL
Milltown of Craigston
Cowbog
New Pitsligo
Knowhead
Hillfoot
Nether Park
Blackhill
Cauldwells
Northside
Balnamoon
Strichen
Plaidy
Craigston Castle
New Leeds
Longhill
Upper Ridinghill
North Mosstown
Fintry
Lower Cotburn
Upper Cotburn
New Byth
Borrohill
Balearn
Gas Terminal
Muirden
Bonnykelly
Adziel
North Ugie Water
Leys
St Fergus Moss
Garmond
Whitestones
Ironside
Little Skillymarno
Backfolds
Kirktown
St Fergus
Scotstown Hd.
Denhead
Muiryfold
Cairnhill
Balthangie
Oldwhat
Mains of Fedderate
South Auchmachar
Fetterangus
Hythie
Outhills
Rora Moss
Gallowhills
North Kirkton
Turriff
DELGATIE CASTLE
Cuminestown
Forest of Deer
Toux
Cuttyhill
Rora
Lunderton
Kirkton Hd.
Little Colp
Middle Cairncake
Aulton of Atherb
DEER ABBEY
Dunshillock
Woodside
Middleton of Rora
Delgaty Forest
Culsh
Maud
BUCHAN
Mintlaw
Newseat
Inverugie
UGIE SALMON FISH HOUSE
Craighill
Hatton Castle
Slacks of Cairnbanno
New Deer
MAUD RAILWAY MUSEUM
Backhill of Clackriach
Old Deer
ADEN
Longside
INVERUGIE CASTLE
Torterston
Buchanhaven
Darra
Howe of Teuchar
ABERDEENSHIRE FARMING MUSEUM
Flushing
Peterhead
Birkenhills
Rush-head
Drymuir
Stuartfield
Inverquhomery
Parkhill
ARBUTHNOT MUSEUM & ART GALLERY
Keith Inch
Burnside
Bulwark
Millbreck
Hillhead of Cocklaw
PETERHEAD MARITIME
Crofts of Invertherrie
Heatherybanks
Bodiechell
Nethermuir
Crichie
Mains of Crichie
Nether Kinmundy
Toddlehills
Peterhead Bay
Mains of Towie
North Millbrex
Cairnbanno Ho.
Invernettie
Sandford Bay
Dykeside
Netherton
Middlemuir
Knaven
Clochan
Kinnadie
Clola
Easterton of Lenabo
Little Dens
Blackhill
Millbank
Boddam
Seggat
Riffin
Steinmanhill
South Millbrex
Balquhindachy
Skelmuir
Nether Savock
Buchan Ness
Inverythan
Gourdas
Crofts of Meikle Ardo
Gowanwell
Barrack
Mains of Annochie
Kinknockie
Stirling
Kirkton of Auchterless
Tifty
Lethenty
Cairnorrie
Auchnagatt
Backhill of Fortree
Smallburn
Sandfordhill
Monkshill
Cottown
Burnend
Brownhill
Moss of Cruden
Croft of Tillymaud
Burreldales
Backhill
Little Gight
Mains of Inkhorn
Drakemyre
Backhill
Stoneygate
Coldwells
FYVIE CASTLE
Stonehouse
Longhaven
Gordonstown
Fyvie
Ardo
Skelmonae
Upper Hawkhillock
Teuchan
Milton Coldwells
Ardallie
Woodhead
Quilquox
Rothiebrisbane
St John's Wells
Crofts of Haddo
Methlick
South Quilquox
Hatton
Auchiries
North Haven
BULLERS OF BUCHAN
Muirtack
Eastertown of Auchleuchries
Drumwhindle
Arthrath
Two Havens
Cruden Bay
Rothienorman
Petty
Collynie
Ythan
Cairnleith Crofts
SLAINS CASTLE
Port Erroll
Cromblet
North Flobbets
HADDO
Mains of Arnage
Berefold
Toll of Birness
Chapel Hill
Barthol Chapel
Upper Ardgrain
Bogbrae
Bay of Cruden
Folla Rule
St Katherine's
South Flobbets
HADDO HOUSE AND GARDENS
Ythanbank
Hilton
Mains of Birness
Earlsford
Newseat
Cross of Jackston
Byebush
Balgove
Wedderlairs
Inverebrie
Nether Leask
Whinnyfold
Thornroan
Broomfield
Jackstown
Tulloch
Raxton
MEDIEVAL TOMB
Blackhill
Meikle Wartle
Westertown
Bethelnie
Redmoss
West Kinharrachie
Knockothie
P&R
Artrochie
Craigdam
Tarves
Ythsie
Auchmacoy
Esslemont
Ellon
Waterton
Alehousehill
LOANHEAD STONE CIRCLE
Meldrum Ho.
Auquhorthies
FORMARTINE
Kirkton of Logie Buchan
Kirktown of Slains
Mounie Castle
Whitefield
Mains of Cairnbrogie
TOLQUHON CASTLE
Ulaw
VISITOR CENTRE
Collieston
Daviot
Fingask
PITMEDDEN GARDENS
Pitmedden
Cross Stone
Waterside
St Catherine's Dub
Tipperty
Meikle Tarty
FORVIE
Sands of Forvie
Oldmeldrum
Knockhall Castle
Hackley Hd. or Forvie Ness
Barra Castle
Cairnbrogie
Udny Green
Pitcaple
Mill of Kingoodie
Tarty Burn
Old Craig
Kinknockie
Newburgh
Harlaw Ho.
Lethenty
Hattoncroak
Pettymuick
Cultercullen
Foveran
Chapel of Garioch
Kirkton of Bourtie
Udny Station
Foveran Burn
BATTLE OF HARLAW MEMORIAL
Balhalgardy
BRANDSBUTT STONE
Hillbrae
Whiterashes
Affleck
Woodlands
Minnes
Drums
Newburgh Bar
Mains of Blackhall
Burgh Muir
INVERURIE MUSEUM
Hillhead
Nether Crimond
Tillygreig
Tillycorthie
Rashiereive
Inverurie
Tillykerrie
Ardo Ho.
Hatterseat
Manar Ho.
Keith Hall
Straloch
Middlemuir
Delfrigs
Port Elphinstone
Kinmuck
Reisque
Craigie
Burnhervie
Westerton
KINKELL CHURCH
Newmachar
Causeyend
Aquhythie
Overton
Blackbraes
Whitecairns
Drumhead
Dalmadilly
Clovenstone
Burgh Muir
Balbithan
Wester Fintray
Cairnpark
Kinmundy
Belhelvie
BALMEDIE
Balmedie
Kemnay
Drumligair
Cothall
Hatton of

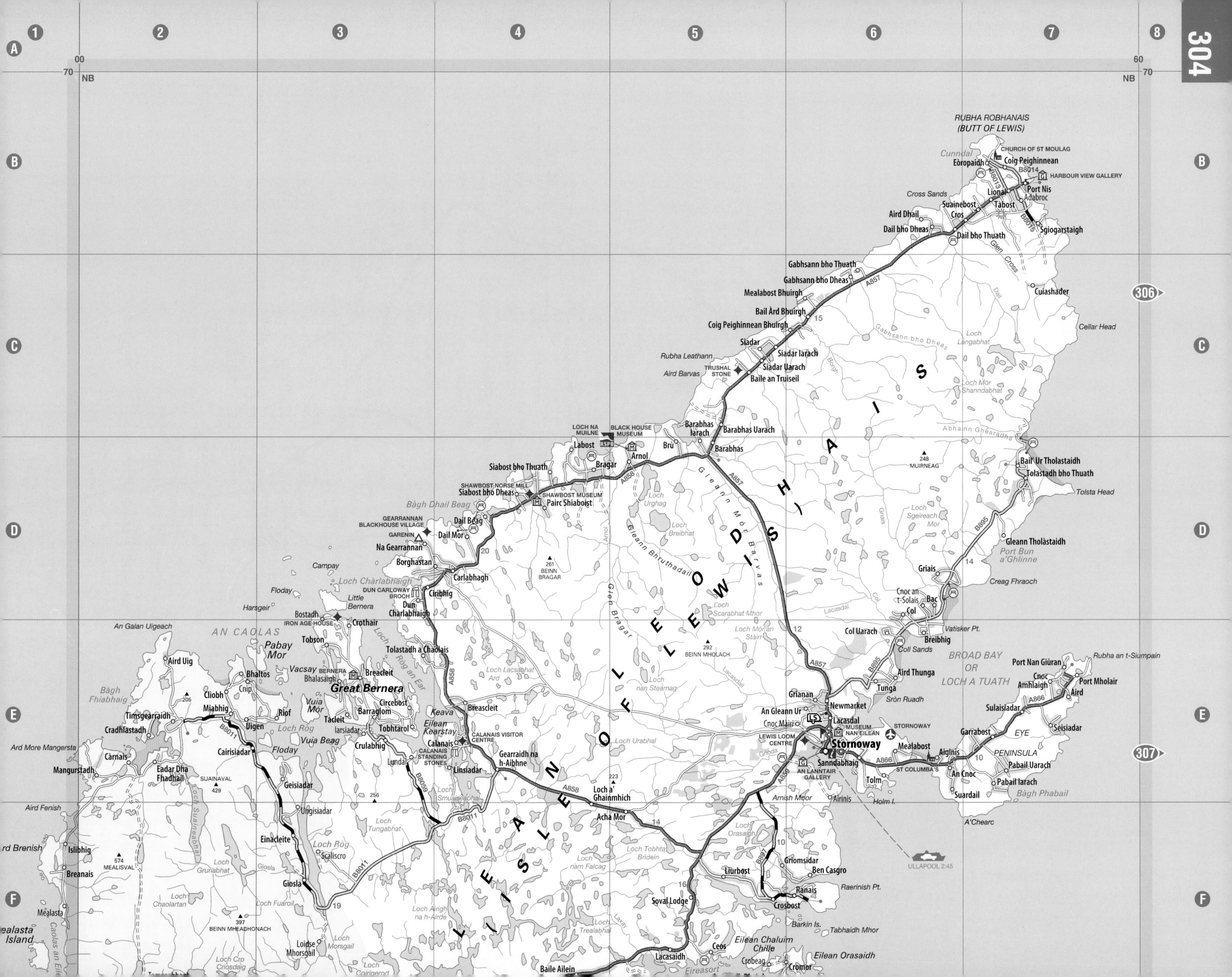
A
B
C
D
E
F
1
2
3
4
5
6
7
8
NB
306
307
RUBHA ROBHANAIS
(BUTT OF LEWIS)
CHURCH OF ST MOULAG
HARBOUR VIEW GALLERY
Eòropaidh
Coig Peighinnean
Port Nis
Adabroc
Sgiogarstaigh
Lional
Tabost
Suainebost
Cros
Dail bho Thuath
Dail bho Dheas
Aird Dhail
Cross Sands
Cunndal
Glen Cross
Culashader
Cellar Head
Tolsta Head
Tolastadh bho Thuath
Bail' Ur Tholastaidh
Gleann Tholàstaidh
Port Bun a' Ghlinne
Creag Fhraoch
Loch Langabhat
Loch Mòr Shanndabhat
Abhainn Ghearadha
Gabhsann bho Dheas
Gabhsann bho Thuath
Mealabost Bhuirgh
Bail Àrd Bhuirgh
Coig Peighinnean Bhuirgh
Siadar
Siadar Iarach
Siadar Uarach
Baile an Truiseil
TRUSHAL STONE
Barabhas Uarach
Barabhas
Barabhas Iarach
Rubha Leathann
Aird Barvas
Brù
Arnol
BLACK HOUSE MUSEUM
LOCH NA MUILNE
Labost
Bragar
SHAWBOST MUSEUM
Pairc Shiaboist
Siabost bho Thuath
Siabost bho Dheas
SHAWBOST NORSE MILL
Dail Beag
Dail Mòr
Bàgh Dhail Beag
Carlabhagh
GEARRANNAN BLACKHOUSE VILLAGE
GARENIN
Na Gearrannan
Borghastan
Loch Chàrlabhaigh
DUN CARLOWAY BROCH
Dùn Charlabhaigh
Cìrbhig
Tolastadh a' Chaolais
MUIRNEAG
BEINN MHOLACH
BEINN BRAGAR
Gleann Mòr Barvas
Gleann Bhruthadail
Glen Bragar
ISLE OF LEWIS
Griais
Bac
Col
Cnoc an t-Solais
Breibhig
Vatisker Pt.
Coll Sands
BROAD BAY OR LOCH A TUATH
Aird Thunga
Tunga
Sròn Ruadh
Col Uarach
Newmarket
Lacasdal
MUSEUM NAN EILEAN
Stornoway
STORNOWAY
Sanndabhaig
AN LANNTAIR GALLERY
Grianan
An Gleann Ùr
Cnoc Màiri
LEWIS LOOM CENTRE
Mealabost
Aiginis
ST COLUMBA'S
Tolm
Holm I.
Àirinis
Arnish Moor
ULLAPOOL 2:45
Rubha an t-Siumpain
Port Mholair
Aird
Port Nan Giùran
Cnoc Amhlaigh
Seisiadar
Sulaisiadar
EYE PENINSULA
Garrabost
Pabail Uarach
Pabail Iarach
Bàgh Phabail
An Cnoc
Suardail
A' Chearc
Griomsidar
Ben Casgro
Raerinish Pt.
Ranais
Crosbost
Liurbost
Barkin Is.
Tabhaidh Mhor
Eilean Chaluim Chille
Crobeag
Cromor
Ceos
Eilean Orasaidh
Eireasort
Lacasaidh
Soval Lodge
Loch a' Ghainmhich
Acha Mor
Baile Ailein
Gearraidh na h-Aibhne
CALANAIS VISITOR CENTRE
Calanais
CALANAIS STANDING STONES
Breascleit
Linsiadar
Keava
Eilean Kearstay
Lundal
Tobhtarol
Circebost
Great Bernera
Breacleit
Barraglom
Crulabhig
Tacleit
Iarsiadar
Crothair
Little Bernera
Bostadh
IRON AGE HOUSE
Tobson
Bhalasaigh
BERNERA MUSEUM
Campay
Floday
Vacsay
Pabay Mor
Vuia Mòr
Vuia Beag
Loch Ròg
Loch Rog an Ear
Harsgeir
AN CAOLAS
Bhaltos
Cnip
Riof
Uigen
Cliobh
Miabhig
Cairisiadar
Aird Uig
Ungisiadar
Geisiadar
Einacleite
Giosla
Scaliscro
Loidse Mhorsgail
SUAINAVAL
Loch Suaineabhal
BEINN MHEADHONACH
Eadar Dha Fhadhail
Timsgearraidh
Cradhlastadh
Càrnais
Bàgh Fhiabhaig
An Galan Uigeach
MEALISVAL
Mangurstadh
Islibhig
Breanais
Ard More Mangersta
Aird Fenish
Mealasta
Caolas an Eile
A857
A858
A859
A866
B8011
B8013
B8014
B8015
B895
B897
B8059

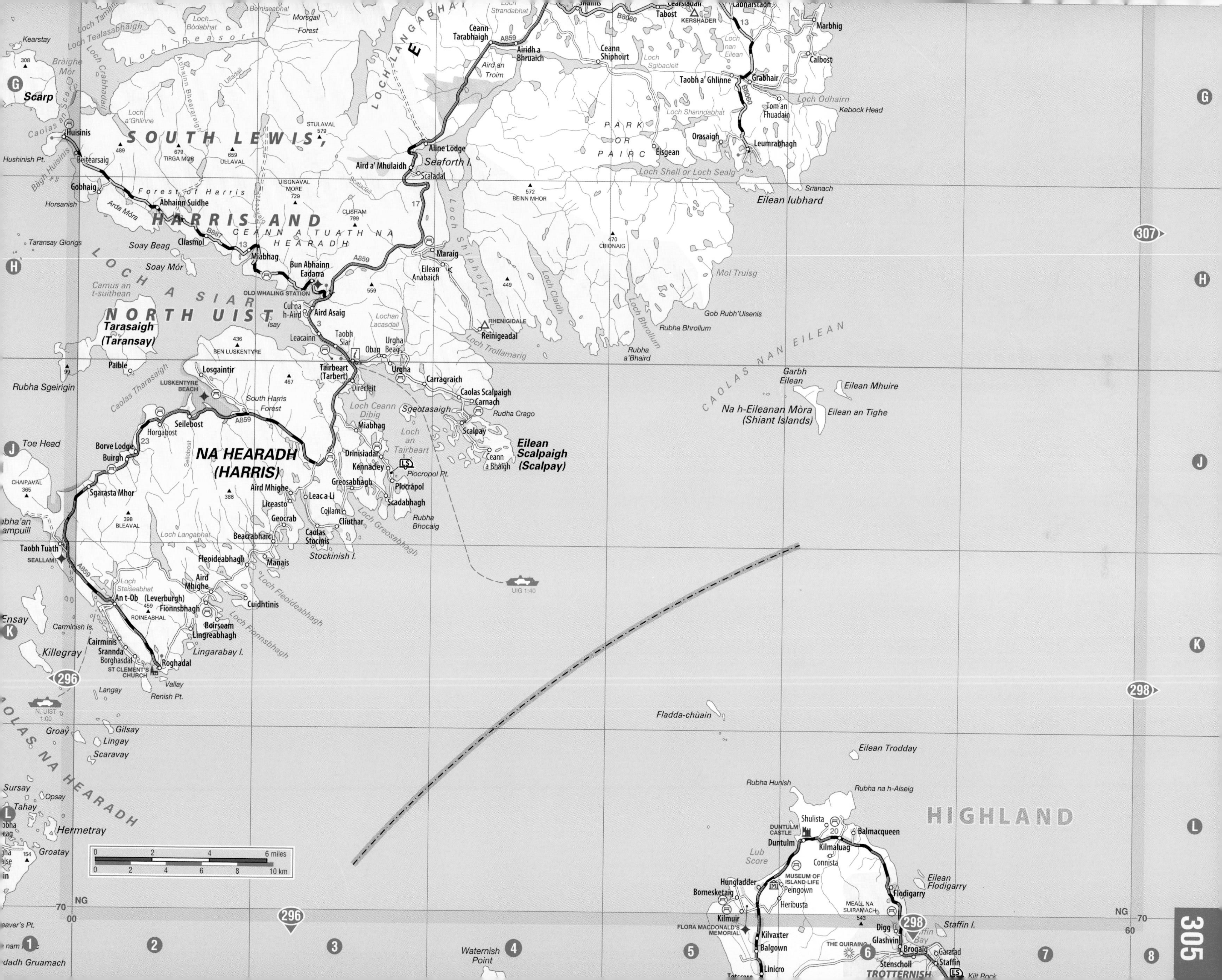

HIGHLAND
SOUTH LEWIS,
HARRIS AND
NORTH UIST
NA HEARADH (HARRIS)
CEANN A TUATH NA HEARADH
LOCH A SIAR
CAOLAS NAN EILEAN
CAOLAS NA HEARADH
TROTTERNISH
Na h-Eileanan Mòra (Shiant Islands)
Eilean Scalpaigh (Scalpay)
Tarasaigh (Taransay)
Eilean Iubhard
Eilean Mhuire
Eilean an Tighe
Garbh Eilean
Eilean Trodday
Eilean Flodigarry
Fladda-chùain
Staffin I.
Seaforth I.
Stockinish I.
Lingarabay I.
Killegray
Ensay
Scarp
Soay Mòr
Soay Beag
Groay
Gilsay
Lingay
Scaravay
Hermetray
Groatay
Opsay
Tahay
Sursay
Langay
Rubha Hunish
Rubha na h-Aiseig
Waternish Point
Toe Head
Rubha Sgeirigin
Hushinish Pt.
Renish Pt.
Kebock Head
Rubha Bhrollum
Rubha Bhocaig
Gob Rubh'Uisenis
Mol Truisg
Loch Shell or Loch Sealg
Loch Shiphoirt
Loch Claidh
Loch Bhrollum
Loch Trollamarig
Loch Odhairn
Loch Langabhat
Loch Tealasabhaigh
Loch Crabhadail
Loch Reasort
Loch Fleoideabhagh
Loch Fionnsbhagh
Loch Greosabhagh
Loch Ceann Dibig
Loch an Tairbeart
Caolas Tharasaigh
Bagh Huisinis
Camus an t-Suithean
Forest of Harris
South Harris Forest
PARK OR PAIRC
Tairbeart (Tarbert)
An t-Ob (Leverburgh)
Aline Lodge
Ceann Tarabhaigh
Airidh a Bhruaich
Ceann Shiphoirt
Tabost
Taobh a' Ghlinne
Grabhair
Leumrabhagh
Orasaigh
Eisgean
Calbost
Marbhig
Tom an Fhuadain
Maraig
Reinigeadal
Caolas Scalpaigh
Carragraich
Urgha
Sgeotasaigh
Scalpay
Ceann a Bhaigh
Plocrapol
Scadabhagh
Drinisiadar
Kennacley
Miabhag
Greosabhagh
Cluthar
Caolas Stocinis
Leac a Li
Geocrab
Manais
Beacrabhaic
Aird Mhighe
Fleoideabhagh
Cuidhtinis
Fionnsbhagh
Lingreabhagh
Roghadal
Borghasdal
Srannda
Cairminis
Sgarasta Mhor
Borve Lodge
Buirgh
Horgabost
Seilebost
Losgaintir
Taobh Tuath
Aird Asaig
Bun Abhainn Eadarra
Cliasmol
Abhainn Suidhe
Huisinis
Beitearsaig
Gobhaig
Aird a' Mhulaidh
Scaladal
Leacainn
Taobh Siar
Oban
Direcleit
OLD WHALING STATION
LUSKENTYRE BEACH
ST CLEMENT'S CHURCH
SEALLAM!
Digg
Flodigarry
Balmacqueen
Kilmaluag
Connista
Shulista
Duntulm
DUNTULM CASTLE
MUSEUM OF ISLAND LIFE
Peingown
Heribusta
Hungladder
Kilmuir
Bornesketaig
FLORA MACDONALD'S MEMORIAL
Kilvaxter
Balgown
Linicro
Glashvin
Brogaig
Stenscholl
Staffin
Garafad
THE QUIRAING
MEALL NA SUIRAMACH
Lub Score
Kilt Rock
RHENIGIDALE
KERSHADER
UIG 1:40
N. UIST 1:00
A859
B8060
B887
NG

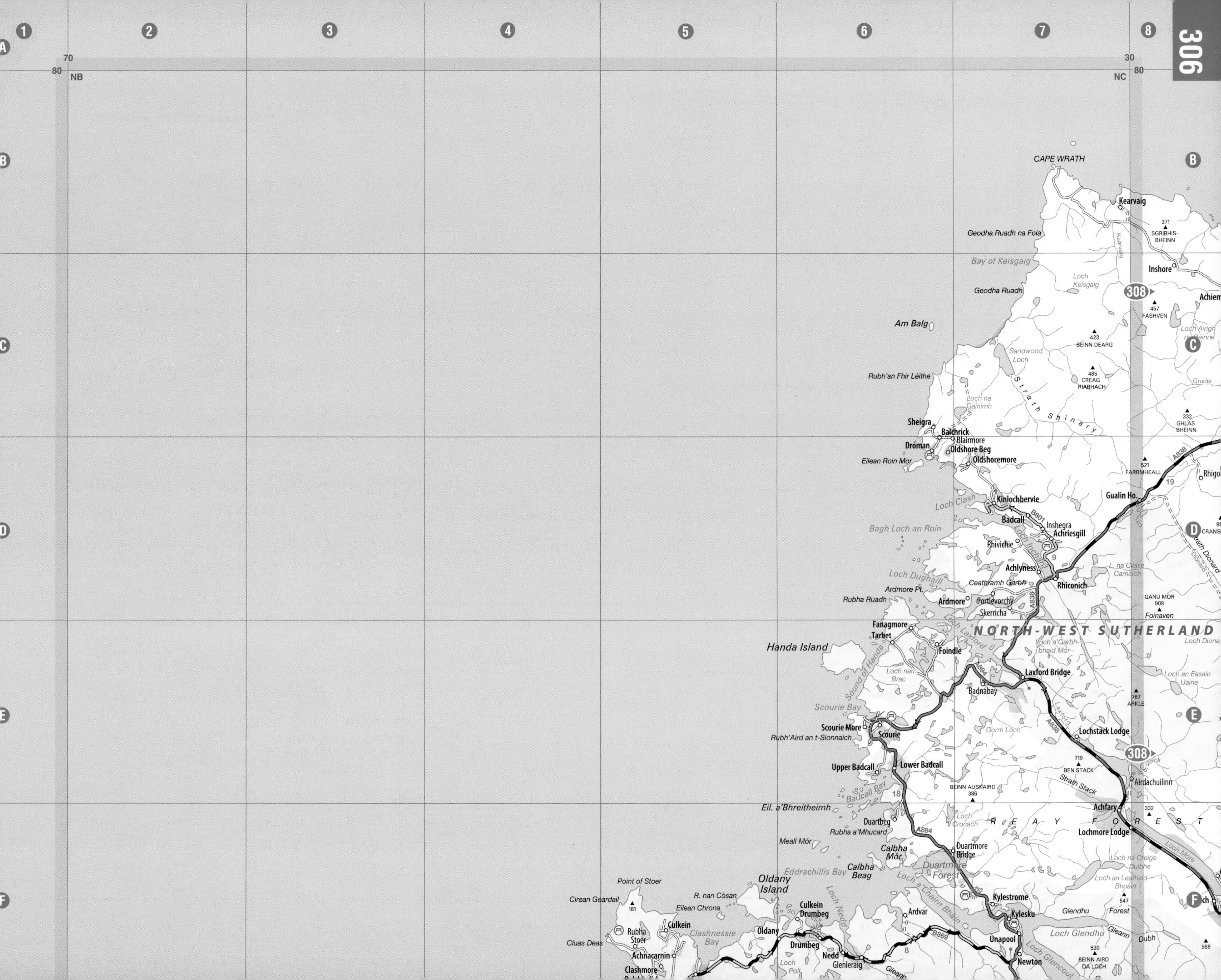
CAPE WRATH
Kearvaig
371 SGRIBHIS-BHEINN
Geodha Ruadh na Fola
Bay of Keisgaig
Inshore
Loch Keisgaig
Geodha Ruadh
308
457 FASHVEN
Achien
Am Balg
423 BEINN DEARG
Loch Airigh na Beinne
Sandwood Loch
485 CREAG RIABHACH
Grudie
Rubh'an Fhir Léithe
Loch na Gainimh
Strath Shinary
332 GHLAS BHEINN
Sheigra
Balchrick
Blairmore
Droman
Oldshore Beg
Oldshoremore
Eilean Roin Mor
A838
521 FARRMHEALL
Rhigo
19
Loch Clash
Kinlochbervie
Gualin Ho.
B801
Badcall
Inshegra
Achriesgill
Bagh Loch an Roin
Loch Inchard
Rhivichie
Strath Dionard
Achlyness
Loch Dughaill
Ceathramh Garbh
Rhiconich
L. na Claise Carnaich
Ardmore Pt.
Rubha Ruadh
Ardmore
Portlevorchy
Skerricha
GANU MOR 908
Foinaven
Fanagmore
Tarbet
NORTH-WEST SUTHERLAND
Loch Laxford
Loch Diona
Handa Island
Foindle
Loch a'Garbh-bhaid Mòr
Sound of Handa
Loch nam Brac
Laxford Bridge
Loch an Easain Uaine
Badnabay
787 ARKLE
Scourie Bay
Laxford
Scourie More
Gorm Loch
Lochstack Lodge
Rubh'Aird an t-Sionnaich
Scourie
Upper Badcall
Lower Badcall
719 BEN STACK
Airdachuilinn
Strath Stack
Badcall Bay
BEINN AUSKAIRD 386
Eil. a'Bhreitheimh
Achfary
332
Loch Crocach
REAY FOREST
Duartbeg
Lochmore Lodge
Rubha a'Mhucard
A894
Meall Mór
Duartmore Bridge
Loch More
Calbha Mór
Loch na Creige Duibhe
Eddrachillis Bay
Calbha Beag
Duartmore Forest
Loch an Leathaid Bhuain
Point of Stoer
Oldany Island
Loch a'Chairn Bhain
Loch Nedd
R. nan Còsan
Cirean Geardail
Culkein Drumbeg
Kylestrome
547 Forest
161
Eilean Chrona
Ardvar
Glendhu
Kylesku
Rubha Stoer
Culkein
Clashnessie Bay
Oldany
B869
Loch Glendhu
Gleann Dubh
Cluas Deas
Achnacarnin
Drumbeg
Unapool
8
530 BEINN AIRD DA LOCH
Loch Glencoul
566
Clashmore
Nedd
Glenleraig
Newton
Loch Poll
NB
NC
70
80
30

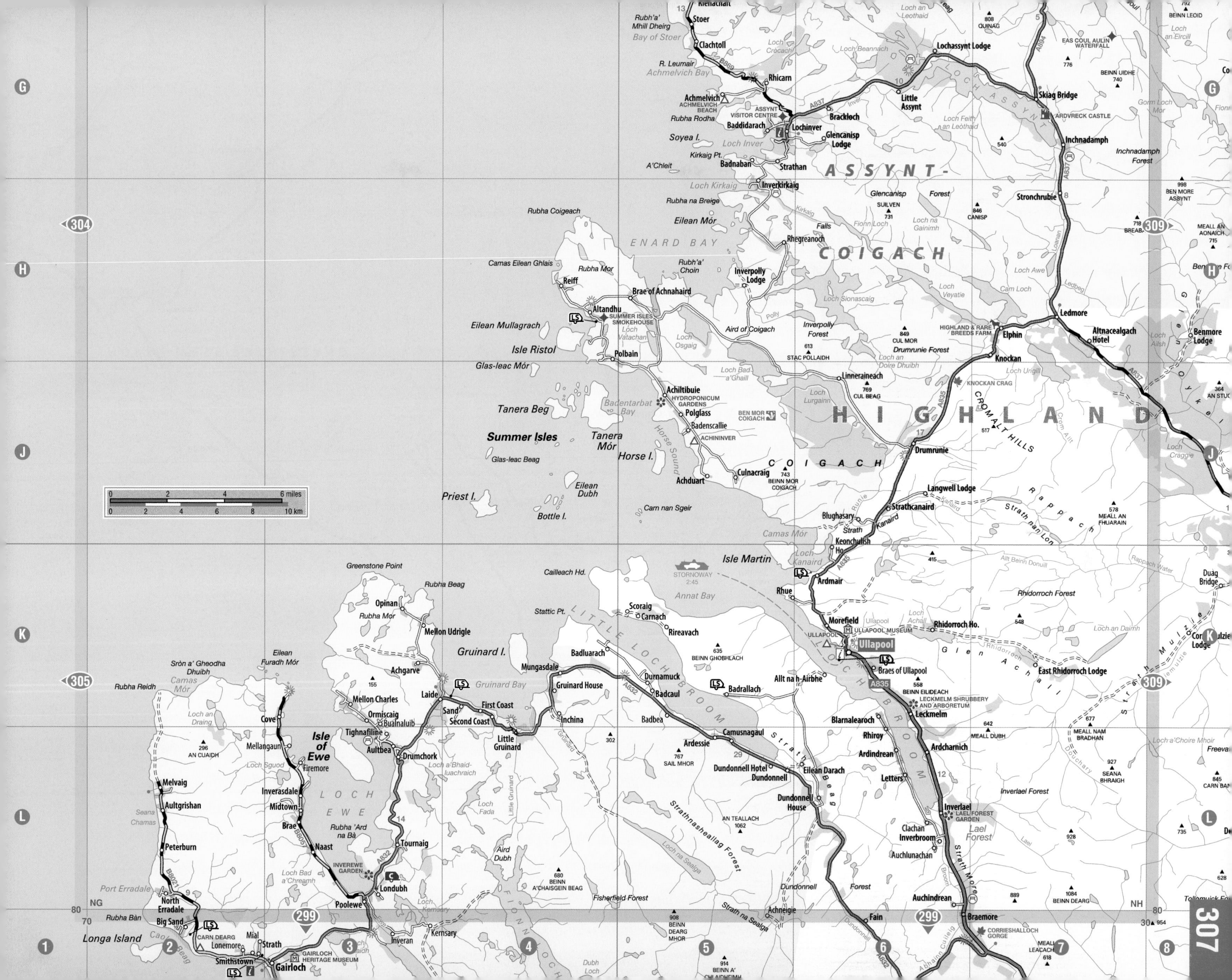

Stoer
Clachtoll
Rubh'a' Mhill Dheirg
Bay of Stoer
R. Leumair
Achmelvich Bay
Rhicarn
Achmelvich
ACHMELVICH BEACH
ASSYNT VISITOR CENTRE
Rubha Rodha
Baddidarach
Lochinver
Soyea I.
Loch Inver
Kirkaig Pt.
Badnaban
Strathan
A'Chleit
Loch Kirkaig
Inverkirkaig
Rubha na Breige
Eilean Mór
ENARD BAY
Rubha Coigeach
Camas Eilean Ghlais
Rubha Mor
Reiff
Brae of Achnahaird
Rubh'a' Choin
Inverpolly Lodge
Altandhu
SUMMER ISLES SMOKEHOUSE
Eilean Mullagrach
Isle Ristol
Polbain
Glas-leac Mór
Aird of Coigach
Achiltibuie
HYDROPONICUM GARDENS
Polglass
Badentarbat Bay
Tanera Beg
Badenscallie
ACHININVER
Summer Isles
Tanera Mór
Horse I.
Horse Sound
Glas-leac Beag
Culnacraig
Achduart
Eilean Dubh
Priest I.
Bottle I.
Carn nan Sgeir
Little Assynt
Lochassynt Lodge
LOCH ASSYNT
Brackloch
Glencanisp Lodge
Skiag Bridge
ARDVRECK CASTLE
Inchnadamph
Inchnadamph Forest
EAS COUL AULIN WATERFALL
ASSYNT-
COIGACH
Glencanisp Forest
SUILVEN 731
846 CANISP
Stronchrubie
Rhegreanoch
Falls
Inverpolly Forest
613 STAC POLLAIDH
849 CUL MOR
Drumrunie Forest
HIGHLAND & RARE BREEDS FARM
Elphin
Knockan
KNOCKAN CRAG
Ledmore
Altnacealgach Hotel
Benmore Lodge
Linneraineach
769 CUL BEAG
BEN MOR COIGACH
HIGHLAND
CROMALT HILLS
Drumrunie
COIGACH
743 BEINN MOR COIGACH
Langwell Lodge
Strathcanaird
Strath nan Lon
Rappach
578 MEALL AN FHUARAIN
Blughasary
Strath Kanaird
Keonchulish
Camas Mór
Loch Kanaird
Isle Martin
STORNOWAY 2:45
Ardmair
Rhue
Annat Bay
Rhidorroch Forest
Morefield
ULLAPOOL MUSEUM
Rhidorroch Ho.
Ullapool
Glen Achall
Braes of Ullapool
East Rhidorroch Lodge
LECKMELM SHRUBBERY AND ARBORETUM
Leckmelm
LOCH BROOM
Duag Bridge
Greenstone Point
Rubha Beag
Cailleach Hd.
Opinan
Rubha Mor
Mellon Udrigle
Static Pt.
Scoraig
Carnach
Rireavach
635 BEINN GHOBHLACH
LITTLE LOCH BROOM
Gruinard I.
Badluarach
Mungasdale
Gruinard House
Gruinard Bay
Achgarve
Laide
Sand
First Coast
Second Coast
Mellon Charles
Ormiscaig
Bualnaluib
Tighnafiline
Aultbea
Inchina
Little Gruinard
Durnamuck
Badcaul
Badbea
Badrallach
Allt na h-Airbhe
Blarnalearoch
Rhiroy
Ardindrean
Ardcharnich
Letters
Camusnagaul
Ardessie
767 SAIL MHOR
Dundonnell Hotel
Dundonnell
Eilean Darach
Strath Beag
Dundonnell House
AN TEALLACH 1062
Strathnasheallag Forest
Inverlael
LAEL FOREST GARDEN
Lael Forest
Inverlael Forest
Clachan
Inverbroom
Auchlunachan
Strath More
Auchindrean
Braemore
CORRIESHALLOCH GORGE
1084 BEINN DEARG
Srón a' Gheodha Dhubh
Rubha Reidh
Camas Mór
Eilean Furadh Mór
Cove
Isle of Ewe
Mellangaun
Firemore
Drumchork
Loch Sguod
296 AN CUAIDH
Melvaig
Aultgrishan
Inverasdale
Midtown
Brae
LOCH EWE
Rubha 'Ard na Bà
Naast
Tournaig
Peterburn
INVEREWE GARDEN
Londubh
Poolewe
Port Erradale
North Erradale
Rubha Bàn
Big Sand
Longa Island
CARN DEARG
Lonemore
Mial
Strath
Smithstown
Gairloch
GAIRLOCH HERITAGE MUSEUM
Inveran
Kernsary
680 BEINN A'CHAISGEIN BEAG
Fisherfield Forest
908 BEINN DEARG MHOR
Strath na Sealga
Achneigie
Dundonnell Forest
Fain
Loch na Sealga
A837
A835
A832
A894
B869
B8021
B8057
304
305
309
299
0 2 4 6 miles
0 2 4 6 8 10 km

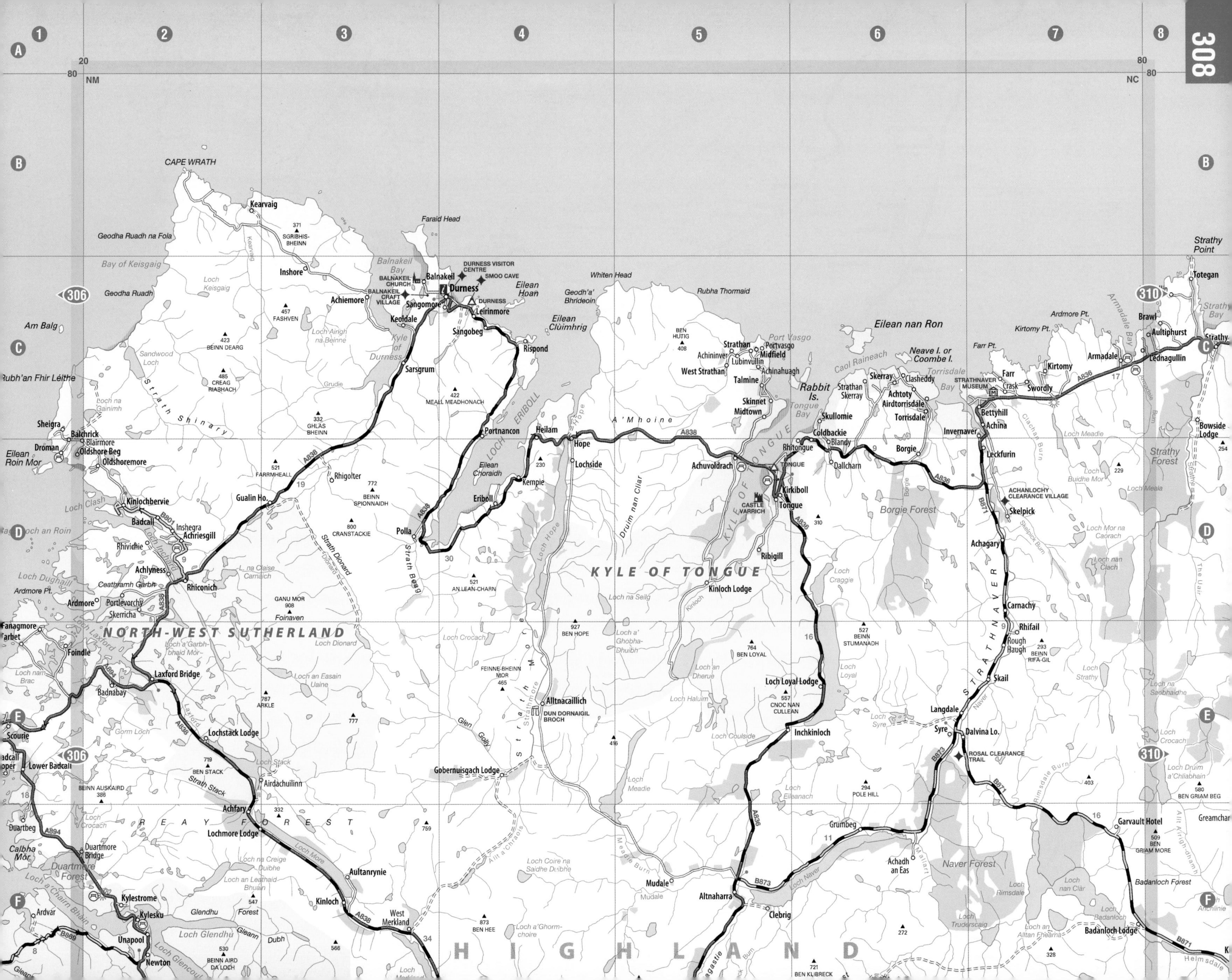

CAPE WRATH
Kearvaig
Geodha Ruadh na Fola
Bay of Keisgaig
Geodha Ruadh
Am Balg
Inshore
Achiemore
Faraid Head
Balnakeil Bay
Balnakeil
Balnakeil Church
Balnakeil Craft Village
Durness Visitor Centre
Smoo Cave
Durness
Sangomore
Leirinmore
Keoldale
Kyle of Durness
Sangobeg
Eilean Hoan
Eilean Clùimhrig
Rispond
Whiten Head
Geodh'a' Bhrideoin
Rubha Thormaid
Sarsgrum
Loch Eriboll
Portnancon
Heilam
Hope
Lochside
A'Mhoine
Eilean Choraidh
Kempie
Eriboll
Polla
Strath Beag
Strath Dionard
Rhigolter
Gualin Ho.
Sandwood Loch
Strath Shinary
Sheigra
Balchrick
Blairmore
Droman
Oldshore Beg
Oldshoremore
Eilean Roin Mor
Kinlochbervie
Badcall
Inshegra
Achriesgill
Rhivichie
Achlyness
Rhiconich
Ardmore
Portlevorchy
Skerricha
Fanagmore
Foindle
NORTH-WEST SUTHERLAND
Laxford Bridge
Badnabay
Lochstack Lodge
Ben Stack
Strath Stack
Airdachuilinn
Achfary
Lochmore Lodge
REAY FOREST
Scourie
Lower Badcall
Duartbeg
Duartmore Bridge
Duartmore Forest
Kylestrome
Kylesku
Unapool
Newton
Ardvar
Aultanrynie
Kinloch
West Merkland
Foinaven
Arkle
Ben Hope
Alltnacaillich
Dun Dornaigil Broch
Strathmore
Gobernuisgach Lodge
Glen Golly
Ben Hee
KYLE OF TONGUE
Strathan
West Strathan
Achininver
Portvasgo
Midfield
Lubinvullin
Achinahuagh
Talmine
Skinnet
Midtown
Rabbit Is.
Tongue Bay
Achuvoldrach
Castle Varrich
Tongue
Kirkiboll
Rhitongue
Ribigill
Kinloch Lodge
Ben Loyal
Loch Loyal Lodge
Cnoc nan Cullean
Inchkinloch
Mudale
Altnaharra
Clebrig
Ben Klibreck
Skullomie
Coldbackie
Blandy
Dallcharn
Strathan Skerray
Skerray
Achtoty
Clashеddy
Airdtorrisdale
Torrisdale
Borgie
Eilean nan Ron
Neave I. or Coombe I.
Caol Raineach
Borgie Forest
Beinn Stumanadh
Pole Hill
Grumbeg
Achadh an Eas
Farr Pt.
Farr
Crask
Strathnaver Museum
Bettyhill
Achina
Invernaver
Leckfurin
Achanlochy Clearance Village
Skelpick
Achagary
Carnachy
Rhifail
Rough Haugh
Skail
Langdale
Syre
Dalvina Lo.
Rosal Clearance Trail
STRATHNAVER
Naver Forest
Kirtomy Pt.
Kirtomy
Swordly
Ardmore Pt.
Armadale
Armadale Bay
Brawl
Aultiphurst
Lednagullin
Strathy Point
Totegan
Strathy
Strathy Bay
Bowside Lodge
Strathy Forest
Garvault Hotel
Ben Griam More
Ben Griam Beg
Badanloch Forest
Badanloch Lodge
HIGHLAND

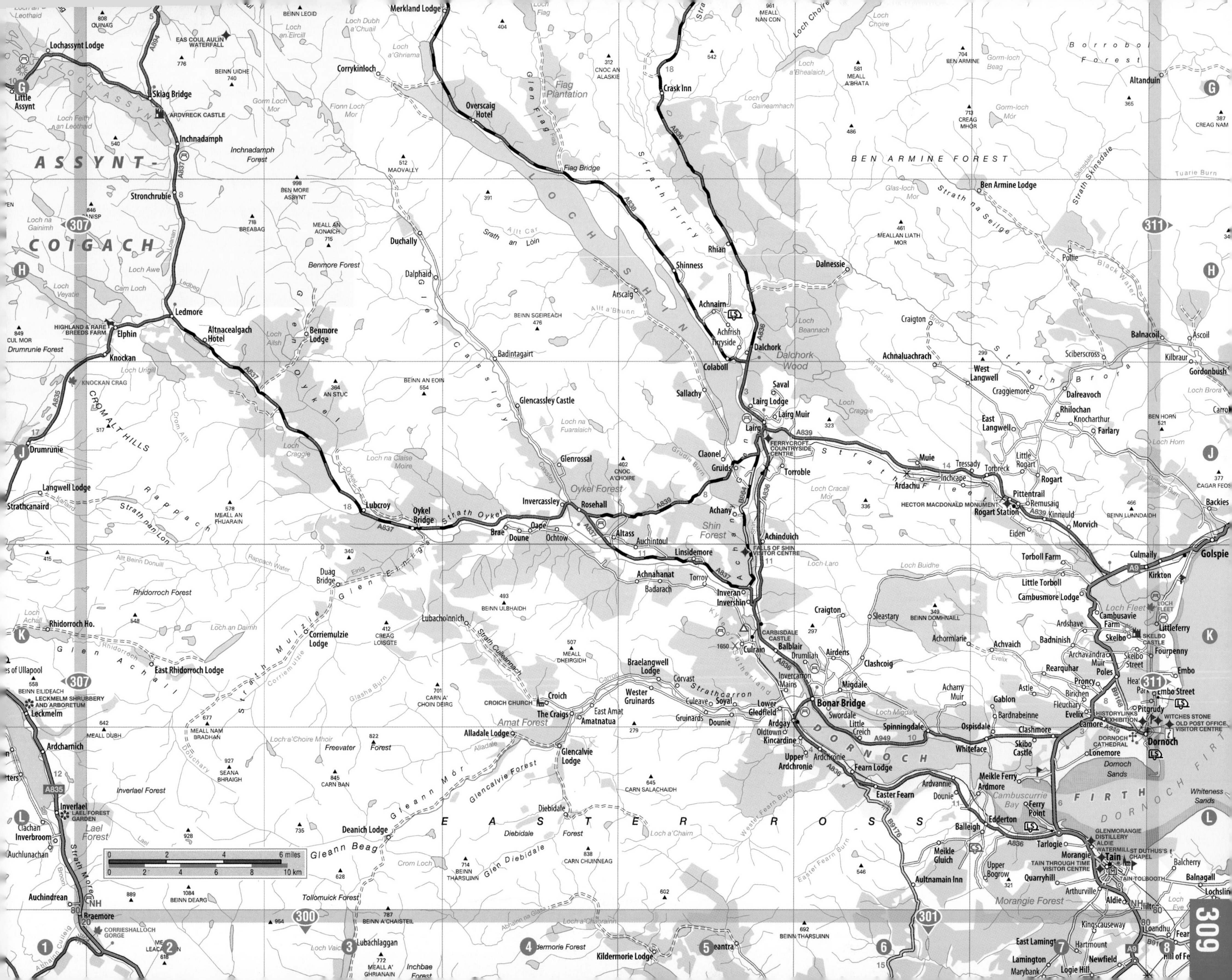
Golspie
Dornoch
Dornoch Firth
Tain
Bonar Bridge
Lairg
Loch Shin
Ben Armine Forest
Strath Brora
Strath Fleet
Rogart
Edderton
Ardgay
Invershin
Shin Forest
Oykel Bridge
Glen Oykel
Glen Cassley
Rosehall
Inchnadamph
Ledmore
Elphin
Knockan
Drumrunie
Cromalt Hills
Assynt
Coigach
Easter Ross
Glen Einig
Amat Forest
Strath Mulzie
Crask Inn
Overscaig Hotel
Altnacealgach Hotel
Skiag Bridge
Ardvreck Castle
Leckmelm
Braemore
Strath More
Inverlael
Dornoch Cathedral
Glenmorangie Distillery
Falls of Shin Visitor Centre
Carbisdale Castle

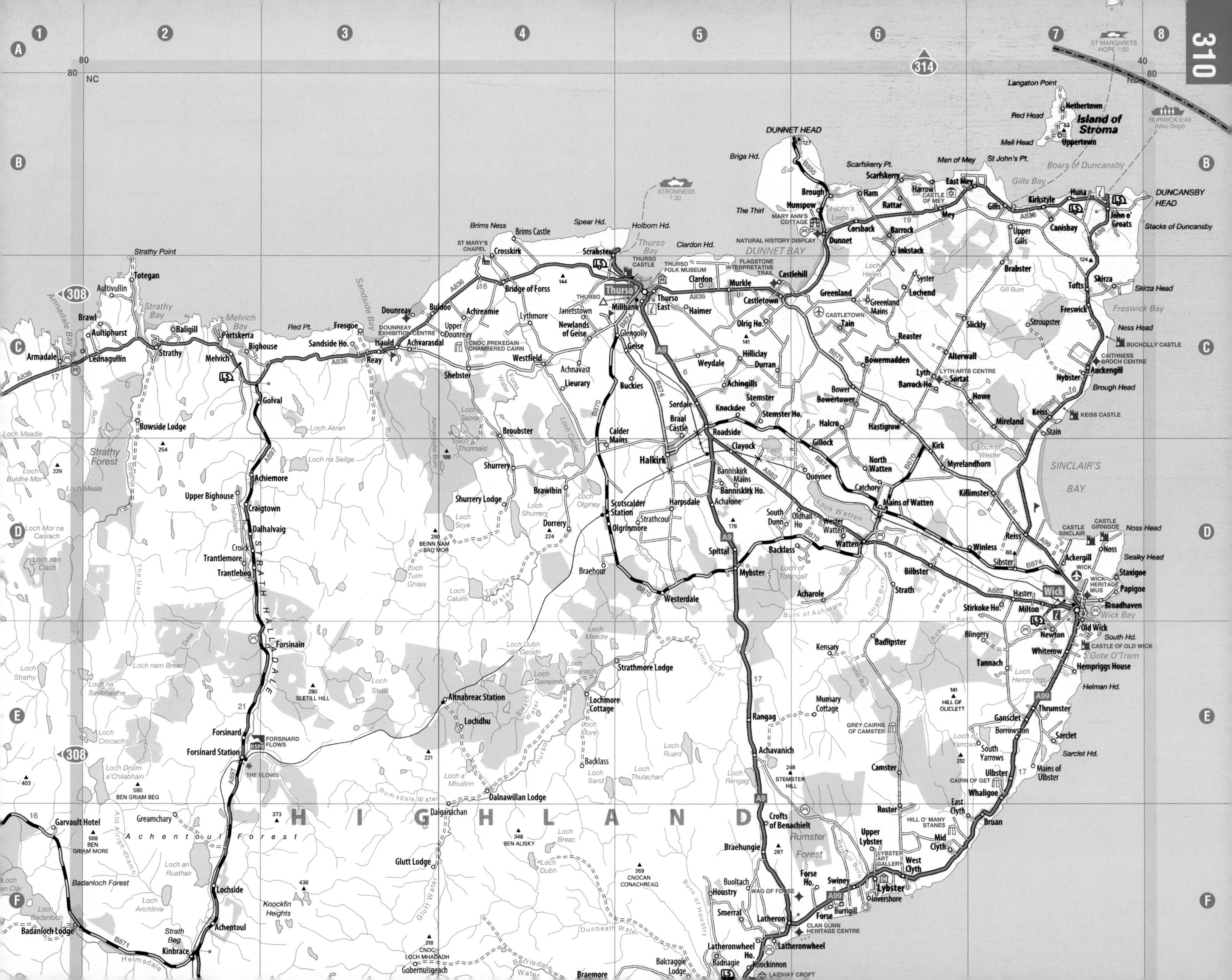

DUNCANSBY HEAD
Stacks of Duncansby
Island of Stroma
John o' Groats
Freswick Bay
Skirza Head
Ness Head
Noss Head
Wick
Wick Bay
SINCLAIR'S BAY
Keiss
Castletown
DUNNET HEAD
DUNNET BAY
Dunnet
Men of Mey
Thurso
Thurso Bay
Scrabster
Halkirk
Watten
Loch Watten
Lybster
Latheron
Dunbeath Water
Reay
Dounreay
Sandside Bay
Melvich
Melvich Bay
Strathy
Strathy Point
Strathy Bay
Strathy Forest
Armadale
Armadale Bay
Forsinard
STRATH HALLADALE
Kinbrace
Badanloch Lodge
Garvault Hotel
HIGHLAND
Achentoul Forest
Rumster Forest
Badanloch Forest

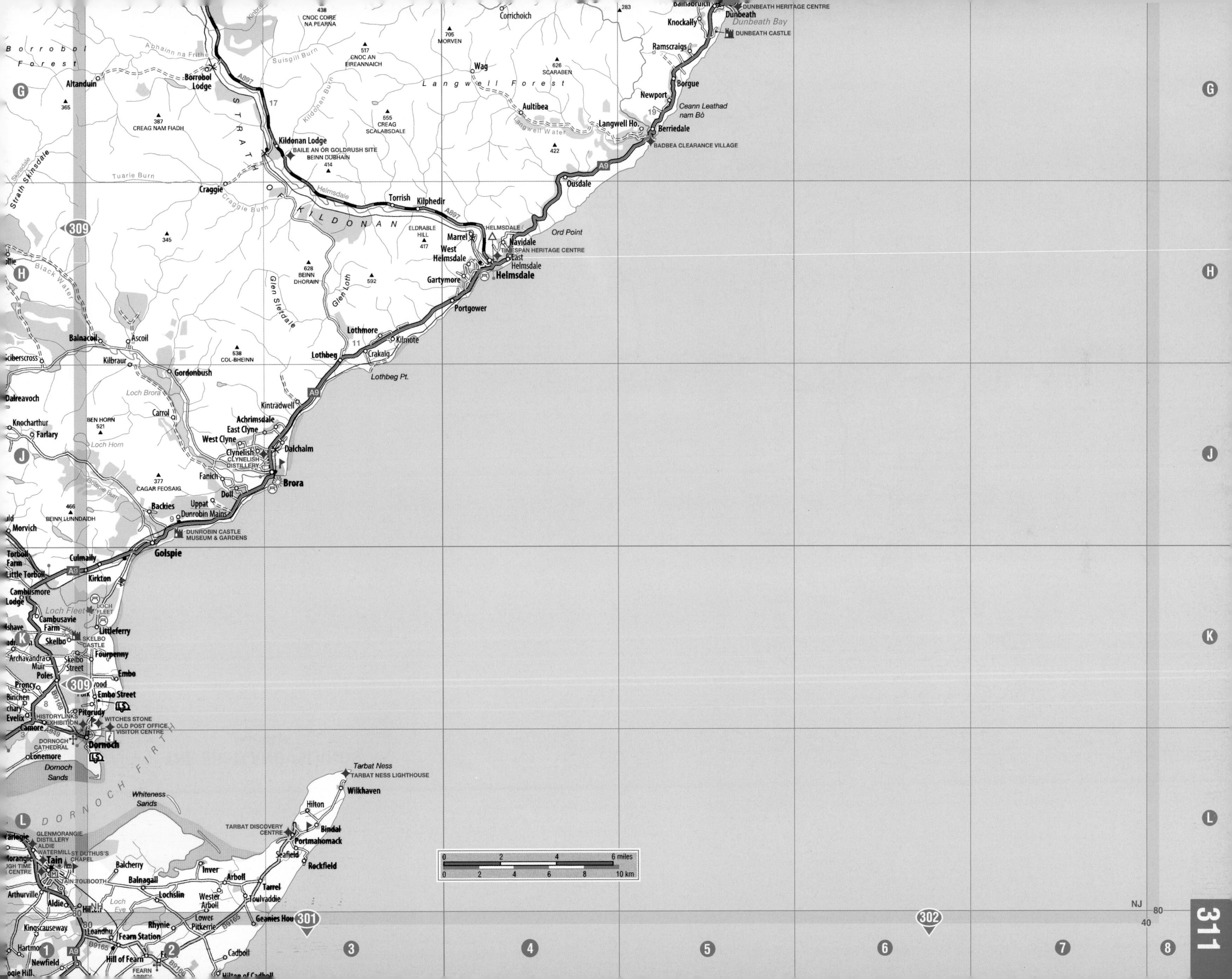
Borrobol Forest
Altanduin
Borrobol Lodge
Abhainn na Frithe
Suisgill Burn
Kildonan Burn
CNOC COIRE NA PEARNA 438
CNOC AN EIREANNAICH 517
MORVEN 705
Corrichoich
Wag
Langwell Forest
SCARABEN 626
CREAG SCALABSDALE 555
Aultibea
Langwell Water
Langwell Ho.
Knockally
Ramscraigs
Dunbeath
DUNBEATH HERITAGE CENTRE
Dunbeath Bay
DUNBEATH CASTLE
Borgue
Newport
Ceann Leathad nam Bò
Berriedale
BADBEA CLEARANCE VILLAGE
CREAG NAM FIADH 387
365
STRATH OF KILDONAN
Kildonan Lodge
BAILE AN OR GOLDRUSH SITE
BEINN DUBHAIN 414
Helmsdale
Tuarie Burn
Strath Skinsdale
Craggie
Craggie Burn
Torrish
Kilphedir
A897
A9
Ousdale
Ord Point
HELMSDALE
Navidale
TIMESPAN HERITAGE CENTRE
East Helmsdale
Helmsdale
Marrel
West Helmsdale
ELDRABLE HILL 417
Gartymore
Portgower
345
BEINN DHORAIN 628
592
Glen Loth
Glen Sletdale
Black Water
Lothmore
Kilmote
Crakaig
Lothbeg
Lothbeg Pt.
Balnacoil
Ascoil
Kilbraur
Gordonbush
COL-BHEINN 538
Loch Brora
Carrol
Kintradwell
Achrimsdale
East Clyne
West Clyne
Clynelish
CLYNELISH DISTILLERY
Dalchalm
Brora
Fanich
Doll
Uppat
Dunrobin Mains
DUNROBIN CASTLE MUSEUM & GARDENS
Golspie
Backies
CAGAR FEOSAIG 377
BEN HORN 521
Loch Horn
Knocharthur
Farlary
Dalreavoch
Morvich
BEINN LUNNDAIDH 466
Culmaily
Kirkton
Little Torboll
Cambusmore Lodge
Loch Fleet
LOCH FLEET
Cambusavie Farm
Skelbo
SKELBO CASTLE
Littleferry
Fourpenny
Archavandra Muir
Skelbo Street
Poles
Embo
Embo Street
Proncy
Birichen
Evelix
Pitgrudy
HISTORYLINKS EXHIBITION
WITCHES STONE
OLD POST OFFICE VISITOR CENTRE
Camore
DORNOCH CATHEDRAL
Dornoch
Lonemore
Dornoch Sands
DORNOCH FIRTH
Whiteness Sands
Tarbat Ness
TARBAT NESS LIGHTHOUSE
Wilkhaven
Hilton
TARBAT DISCOVERY CENTRE
Bindal
Portmahomack
Seafield
Rockfield
GLENMORANGIE DISTILLERY
ALDIE WATERMILL
ST DUTHUS'S CHAPEL
Tain
TAIN TOLBOOTH
Balcherry
Balnagall
Inver
Arboll
Tarrel
Lochslin
Wester Arboll
Toulvaddie
Arthurville
Aldie
Loch Eye
Kingscauseway
Lower Pitkerrie
Geanies Hou
Rhynie
Fearn Station
Loandhu
Newfield
Hill of Fearn
FEARN ABBEY
Cadboll
B9165
B9166
A949
NJ
80
40
0 2 4 6 miles
0 2 4 6 8 10 km
G H J K L
1 2 3 4 5 6 7 8
309
301
302

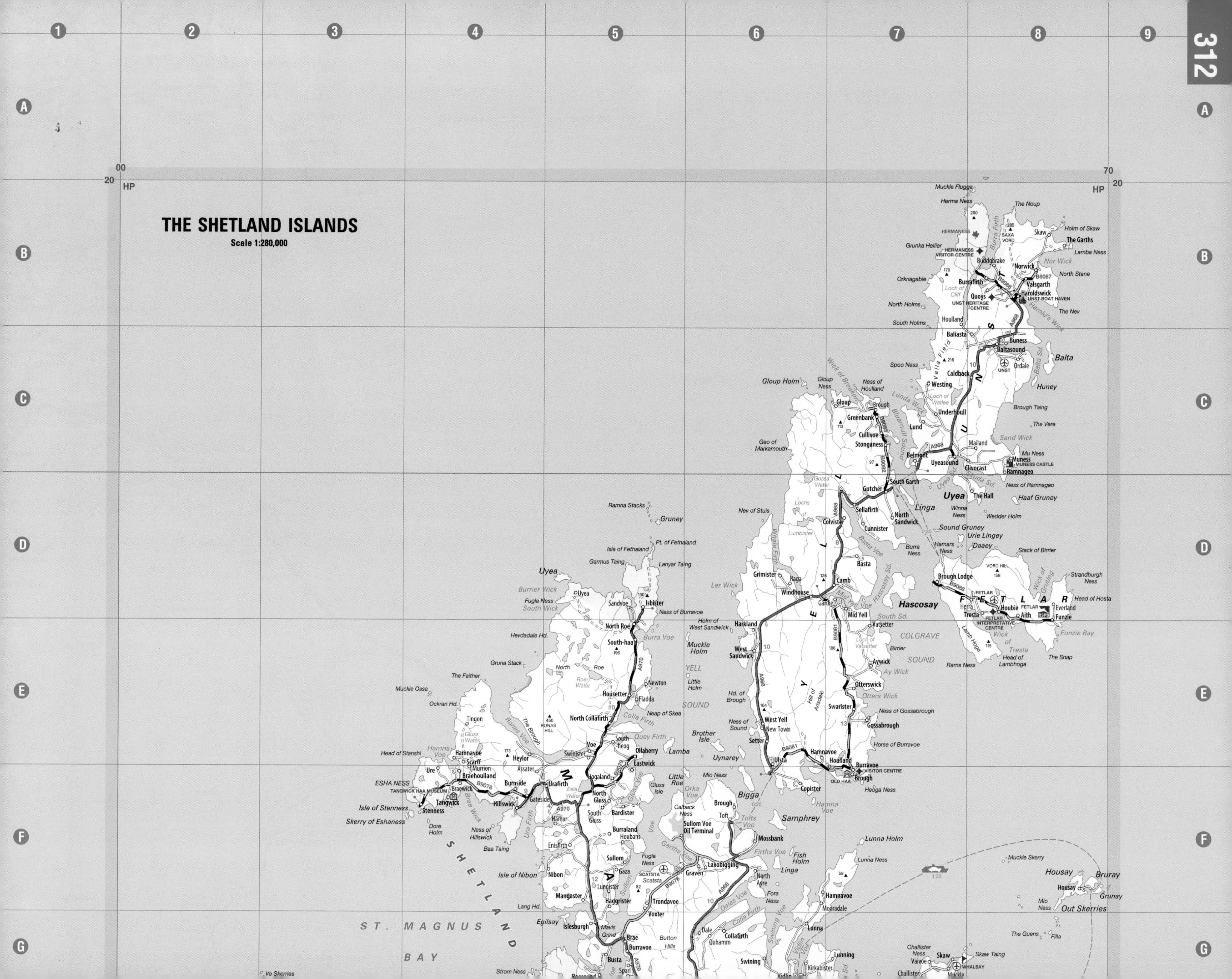
THE SHETLAND ISLANDS
Scale 1:280,000
UNST
YELL
FETLAR
MAINLAND
Muckle Flugga
Herma Ness
The Noup
Holm of Skaw
Skaw
The Garths
Lamba Ness
Norwick
Valsgarth
Haroldswick
UNST BOAT HAVEN
Burrafirth
Buddabrake
Quoys
UNST HERITAGE CENTRE
HERMANESS VISITOR CENTRE
Houlland
Baliasta
Buness
Baltasound
Ordale
Balta
Huney
Caldback
Westing
Underhoull
Lund
Belmont
Uyeasound
Clivocast
Mailand
Muness
MUNESS CASTLE
Ramnageo
Uyea
The Hall
Haaf Gruney
Linga
Bluemull Sound
Gloup Holm
Gloup
Greenbank
Cullivoe
Stonganess
Brough
South Garth
Gutcher
Sellafirth
North Sandwick
Cunnister
Colvister
Basta
Camb
Gardie
Mid Yell
Windhouse
Grimister
Hascosay
Brough Lodge
Houbie
Tresta
Aith
Everland
Funzie
Funzie Bay
Strandburgh Ness
Head of Hosta
Lamb Hoga
Rams Ness
The Snap
COLGRAVE SOUND
Vatsetter
Aywick
Otterswick
Swarister
Gossabrough
Burravoe
Hamnavoe
Houlland
OLD HAA
Heoga Ness
Copister
Ulsta
Setter
West Yell
New Town
West Sandwick
Harkland
Whale Firth
YELL SOUND
Samphrey
Bigga
Brother Isle
Uynarey
Lamba
Little Roe
Brough
Toft
Sullom Voe Oil Terminal
Mossbank
Firths Voe
Fish Holm
Lunna Holm
Lunna Ness
Hamnavoe
Lunna
Lunning
Vidlin
Skaw
WHALSAY
Housay
Bruray
Grunay
Out Skerries
Ramna Stacks
Gruney
Isle of Fethaland
Pt. of Fethaland
Isbister
Sandvoe
North Roe
South-haa
Burra Voe
Uyea
Newton
Housetter
Fladda
Colla Firth
North Collafirth
RONAS HILL
Voe
Ollaberry
Eastwick
Swinister
Hogaland
North Gluss
South Gluss
Bardister
Burraland
Sullom
Gaza
Lunnister
Haggrister
Graven
Laxobigging
Trondavoe
Voxter
Mangaster
Nibon
Isle of Nibon
Eriksfirth
Hamar
Urafirth
Gateside
Hillswick
Burnside
Heylor
The Brough
Ronas Voe
Tingon
Hamnavoe
Scarff
Braehoulland
Braewick
Tangwick
TANGWICK HAA MUSEUM
Stenness
Ure
ESHA NESS
Isle of Stenness
Skerry of Eshaness
Dore Holm
Ness of Hillswick
The Faither
Muckle Ossa
Isfesburgh
Mavis Grind
Brae
Burravoe
Busta
Egilsay
Lang Hd.
Strom Ness
Ve Skerries
ST. MAGNUS BAY
SHETLAND
Dale
Collafirth
Swining

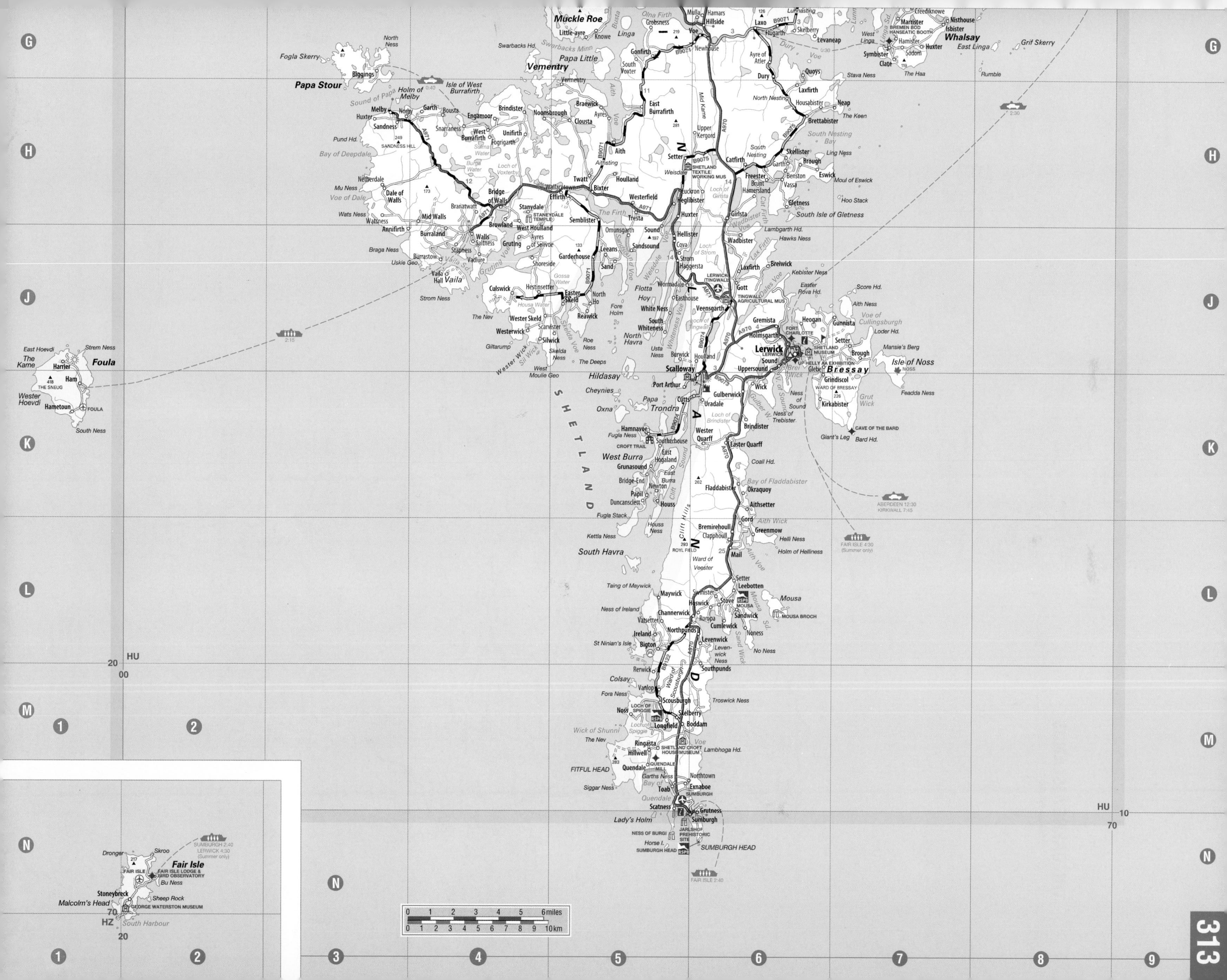
SHETLAND
Lerwick
Bressay
Isle of Noss
Whalsay
Papa Stour
Foula
Fair Isle
Mousa
West Burra
Trondra
South Havra
Vaila
Vementry
Papa Little
Muckle Roe
Scalloway
Sumburgh
SUMBURGH HEAD
FITFUL HEAD
Walls
Sandness
Aith
Voe
Tingwall
Sandwick
Levenwick
Bridge of Walls
Gulberwick
Easter Quarff
Hamnavoe
Weisdale
Laxo
Gott
Girlsta
Catfirth
Skellister
Boddam
Channerwick
Bigton
Toab
Grutness
Hildasay
Oxna
A970
A971
B9074
B9071
0 1 2 3 4 5 6 miles
0 1 2 3 4 5 6 7 8 9 10 km

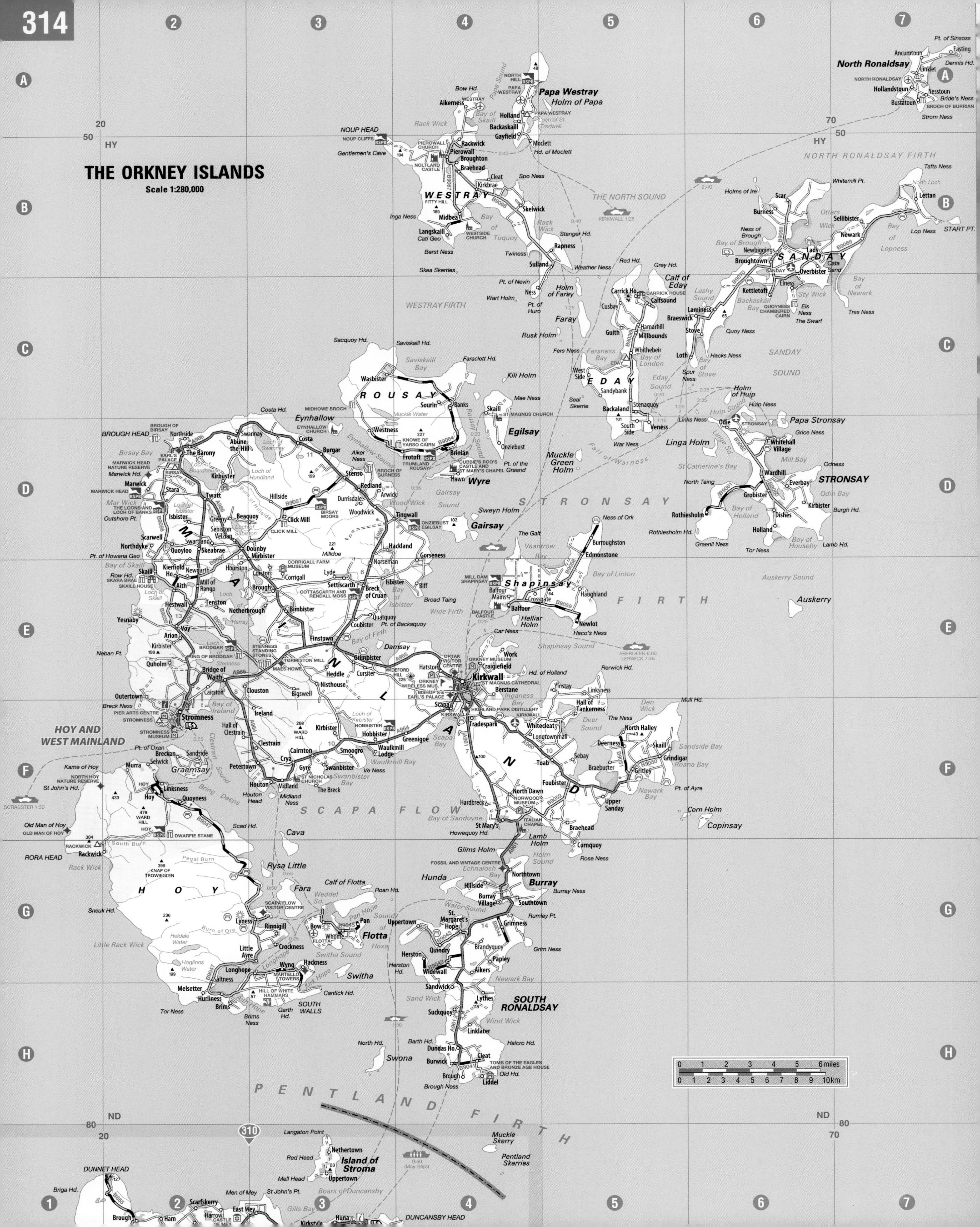
THE ORKNEY ISLANDS
Scale 1:280,000
HY
ND
North Ronaldsay
NORTH RONALDSAY FIRTH
Papa Westray
Holm of Papa
WESTRAY
WESTRAY FIRTH
THE NORTH SOUND
SANDAY
SANDAY SOUND
Calf of Eday
EDAY
Faray
Holm of Faray
ROUSAY
Eynhallow
Egilsay
Wyre
Gairsay
Muckle Green Holm
STRONSAY
Papa Stronsay
Linga Holm
Auskerry
Auskerry Sound
Shapinsay
Helliar Holm
FIRTH
MAINLAND
Kirkwall
Stromness
Finstown
HOY AND WEST MAINLAND
Graemsay
SCAPA FLOW
Cava
Rysa Little
Fara
Calf of Flotta
Flotta
Switha
HOY
SOUTH WALLS
Burray
Hunda
Lamb Holm
Glims Holm
Copinsay
Corn Holm
SOUTH RONALDSAY
Swona
PENTLAND FIRTH
Muckle Skerry
Pentland Skerries
Island of Stroma
DUNNET HEAD
DUNCANSBY HEAD
NOUP HEAD
BROUGH HEAD
MARWICK HEAD
Old Man of Hoy
RORA HEAD
START PT.
Sacquoy Hd.
Costa Hd.
Brough
Dunnet
Kirkwall
ABERDEEN 6:00
LERWICK 7:45
SCRABSTER 1:30
0 1 2 3 4 5 6 miles
0 1 2 3 4 5 6 7 8 9 10 km

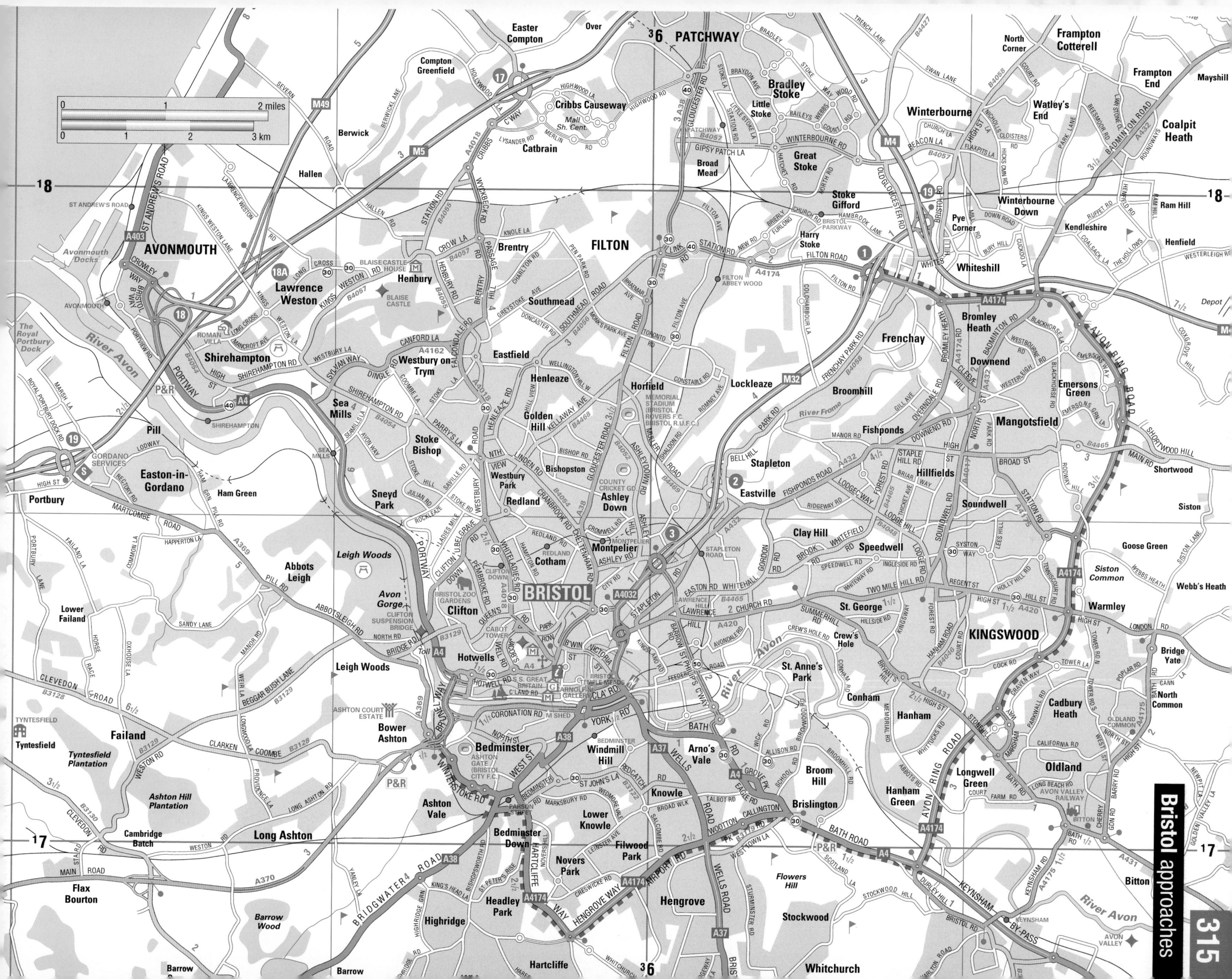
BRISTOL
AVONMOUTH
FILTON
KINGSWOOD
PATCHWAY
Avonmouth Docks
The Royal Portbury Dock
River Avon
Shirehampton
Lawrence Weston
Henbury
Westbury on Trym
Sea Mills
Stoke Bishop
Sneyd Park
Clifton
Hotwells
Bedminster
Southmead
Horfield
Henleaze
Golden Hill
Bishopston
Redland
Cotham
Montpelier
Ashley Down
Eastville
Stapleton
Lockleaze
Frenchay
Fishponds
Hillfields
Speedwell
St. George
Crew's Hole
Conham
Hanham
Hanham Green
St. Anne's Park
Broom Hill
Brislington
Stockwood
Whitchurch
Knowle
Windmill Hill
Arno's Vale
Lower Knowle
Filwood Park
Hengrove
Novers Park
Hartcliffe
Bedminster Down
Headley Park
Highridge
Ashton Vale
Bower Ashton
Leigh Woods
Abbots Leigh
Long Ashton
Failand
Lower Failand
Tyntesfield
Flax Bourton
Cambridge Batch
Barrow
Easton-in-Gordano
Pill
Portbury
Ham Green
Mangotsfield
Downend
Bromley Heath
Emersons Green
Soundwell
Warmley
Siston Common
Oldland
Cadbury Heath
Longwell Green
Bitton
Bridge Yate
North Common
Goose Green
Webb's Heath
Siston
Shortwood
Winterbourne
Winterbourne Down
Frampton Cotterell
Coalpit Heath
Frampton End
Watley's End
North Corner
Kendleshire
Henfield
Ram Hill
Mayshill
Whiteshill
Pye Corner
Stoke Gifford
Great Stoke
Harry Stoke
Bradley Stoke
Little Stoke
Broad Mead
Brentry
Eastfield
Cribbs Causeway
Catbrain
Easter Compton
Compton Greenfield
Over
Berwick
Hallen
Flowers Hill
Avon Gorge
AVON RING ROAD
PORTWAY
BRISTOL PARKWAY
GORDANO SERVICES
CLIFTON SUSPENSION BRIDGE
ASHTON COURT ESTATE
BLAISE CASTLE
MEMORIAL STADIUM (BRISTOL ROVERS F.C. BRISTOL R.U.F.C.)
ASHTON GATE (BRISTOL CITY F.C.)
COUNTY CRICKET GD
BRISTOL ZOO GARDENS
2 miles
3 km

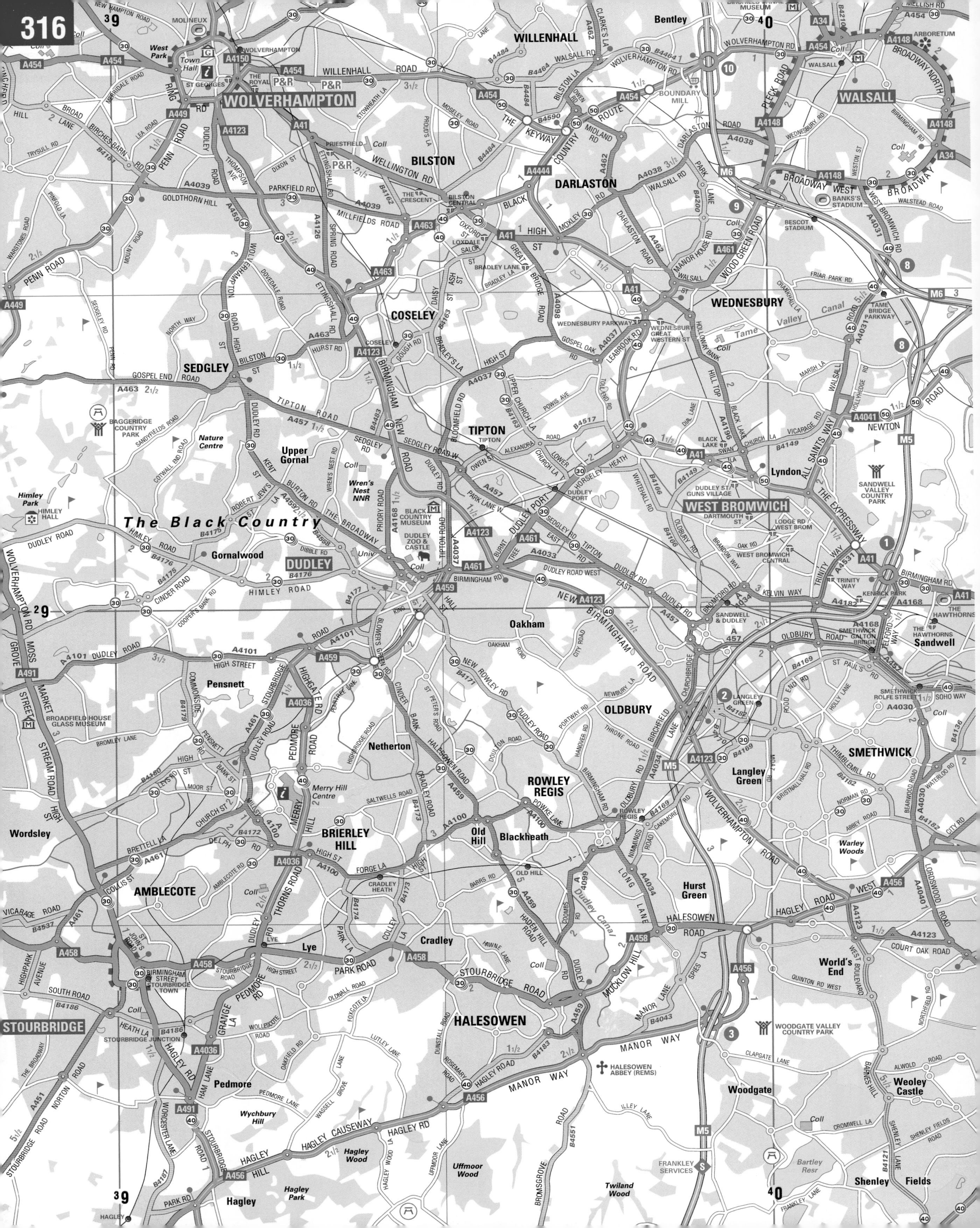

WOLVERHAMPTON
WALSALL
Bentley
WILLENHALL
BILSTON
DARLASTON
COSELEY
WEDNESBURY
SEDGLEY
TIPTON
Upper Gornal
WEST BROMWICH
Lyndon
Newton
Sandwell Valley Country Park
The Black Country
Gornalwood
DUDLEY
Black Country Museum
Dudley Zoo & Castle
Oakham
Himley Park
Himley Hall
Baggeridge Country Park
Pensnett
Broadfield House Glass Museum
Netherton
OLDBURY
SMETHWICK
Sandwell
Merry Hill Centre
ROWLEY REGIS
Langley Green
Wordsley
BRIERLEY HILL
Old Hill
Blackheath
AMBLECOTE
Hurst Green
Warley Woods
Cradley
Lye
World's End
STOURBRIDGE
HALESOWEN
Woodgate Valley Country Park
Halesowen Abbey (rems)
Pedmore
Wychbury Hill
Woodgate
Weoley Castle
Hagley Wood
Uffmoor Wood
Frankley Services
Bartley Resr
Hagley Park
Hagley
Twiland Wood
Shenley Fields

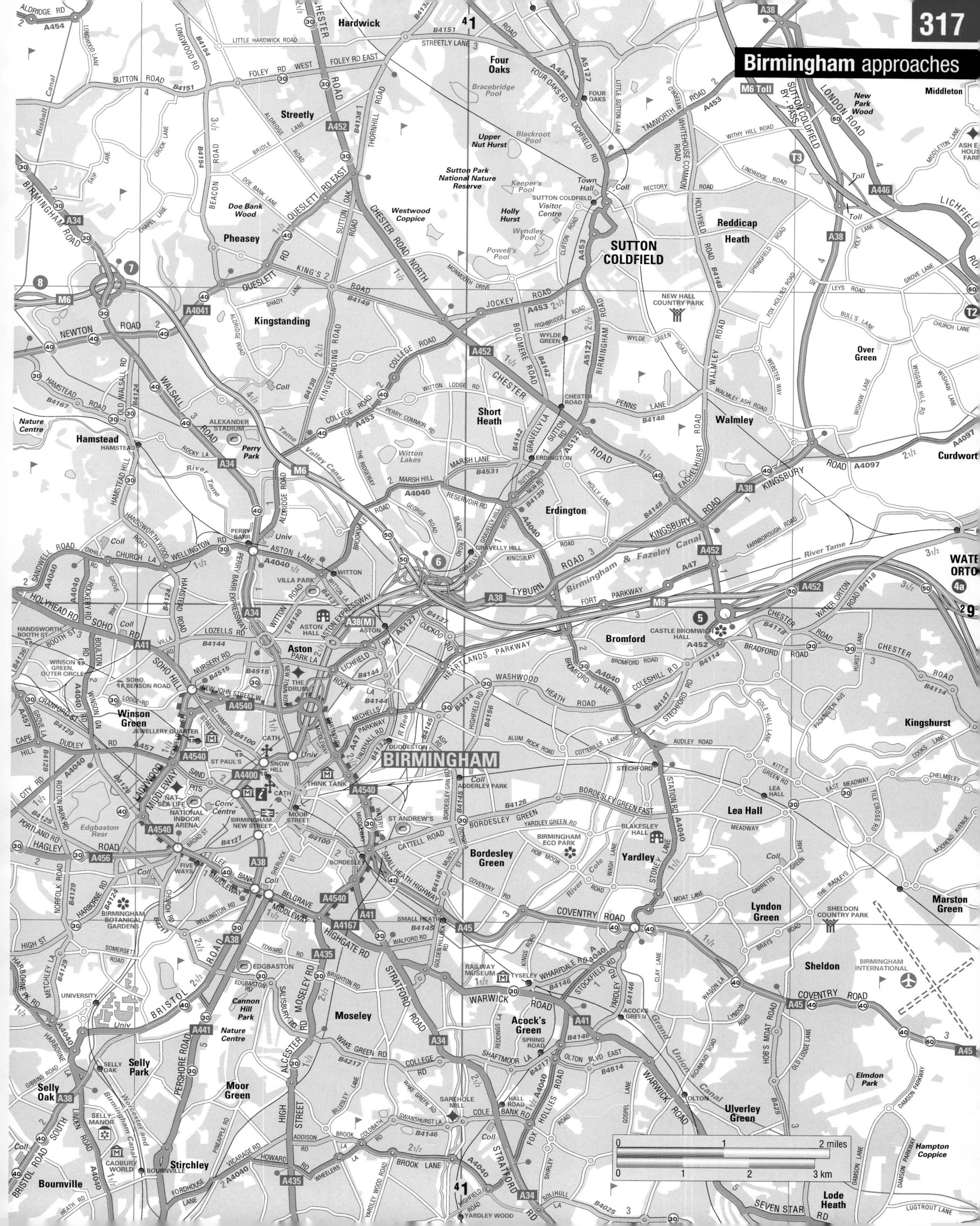
Hardwick
Four Oaks
Bracebridge Pool
Streetly
Upper Nut Hurst
Blackroot Pool
Sutton Park National Nature Reserve
Keeper's Pool
Westwood Coppice
Holly Hurst
Doe Bank Wood
Pheasey
Town Hall
Sutton Coldfield Visitor Centre
Wyndley Pool
Powell's Pool
SUTTON COLDFIELD
Reddicap Heath
New Park Wood
Middleton
Kingstanding
New Hall Country Park
Over Green
Short Heath
Walmley
Nature Centre
Hamstead
Alexander Stadium
Perry Park
Witton Lakes
Erdington
Curdworth
Villa Park
Aston Hall
Aston
Bromford
Castle Bromwich Hall
Kingshurst
Winson Green
Jewellery Quarter
BIRMINGHAM
Think Tank
Nat Sea Life
National Indoor Arena
Edgbaston Resr
Birmingham New Street
Moor Street
St Andrew's
Bordesley Green
Birmingham Eco Park
Blakesley Hall
Yardley
Lea Hall
Marston Green
Lyndon Green
Sheldon Country Park
Birmingham Botanical Gardens
Edgbaston
Railway Museum
Sheldon
Birmingham International
University
Cannon Hill Park
Moseley
Acock's Green
Nature Centre
Selly Park
Selly Oak
Moor Green
Elmdon Park
Sarehole Mill
Ulverley Green
Selly Manor
Cadbury World
Stirchley
Bournville
Hampton Coppice
Lode Heath
0 1 2 miles
0 1 2 3 km
M6
M6 Toll
A38(M)
A452
A34
A38
A45
A4040
A4540
A41
A435
A441
A456
A47
A5127
A453
A4097

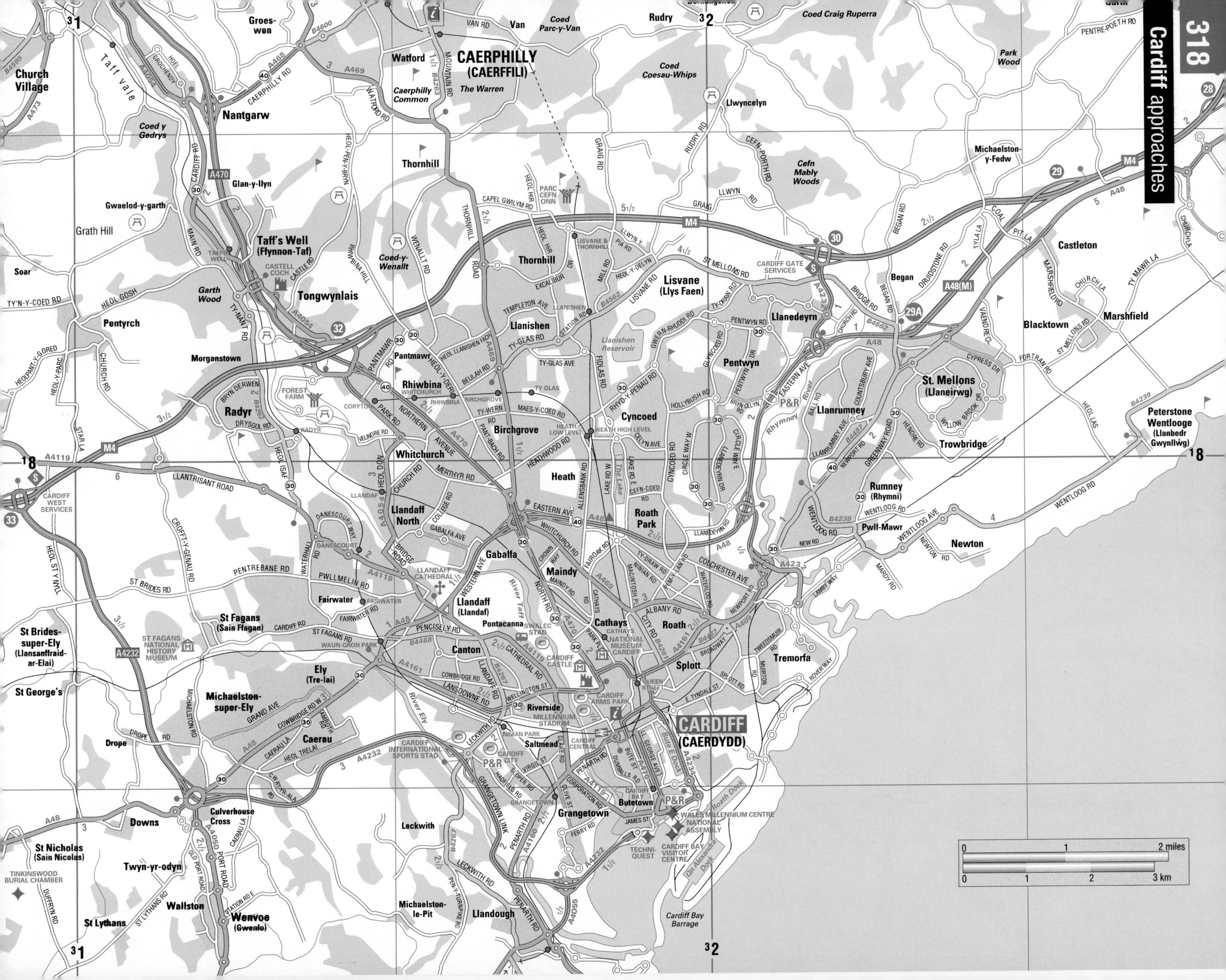
CARDIFF (CAERDYDD)
CAERPHILLY (CAERFFILI)
Castleton
Marshfield
Peterstone Wentlooge (Llanbedr Gwynllŵg)
Blacktown
Michaelston-y-Fedw
Park Wood
St. Mellons (Llaneirwg)
Trowbridge
Newton
Began
Rumney (Rhymni)
Pwll-Mawr
Llanrumney
Llanedeyrn
Pentwyn
Tremorfa
Cefn Mably Woods
Coed Craig Ruperra
Llwyncelyn
Rudry
Coed Coesau-Whips
Lisvane (Llys Faen)
Cyncoed
Roath Park
Roath
Splott
Cathays
Heath
Maindy
Thornhill
Llanishen
Birchgrove
Coed Parc-y-Van
Van
The Warren
Watford
Caerphilly Common
Rhiwbina
Pantmawr
Whitchurch
Llandaff North
Gabalfa
Llandaff (Llandaf)
Pontacanna
Canton
Riverside
Butetown
Grangetown
Saltmead
Llandough
Leckwith
Michaelston-le-Pit
Fairwater
Ely (Tre-lai)
Caerau
Tongwynlais
Taff's Well (Ffynnon-Taf)
Glan-y-llyn
Groes-wen
Nantgarw
Radyr
Morganstown
Garth Wood
Coed y Gedrys
Gwaelod-y-garth
Taff vale
Grath Hill
Pentyrch
Soar
Church Village
St Fagans (Sain Ffagan)
ST FAGANS NATIONAL HISTORY MUSEUM
Michaelston-super-Ely
Culverhouse Cross
Wenvoe (Gwenfô)
Wallston
Twyn-yr-odyn
Downs
Drope
St Lythans
St Nicholas (Sain Nicolas)
TINKINSWOOD BURIAL CHAMBER
St Brides-super-Ely (Llansanffraid-ar-Elai)
St George's
CARDIFF WEST SERVICES
CARDIFF GATE SERVICES
Llanishen Reservoir
The Lake
River Taff
River Ely
Rhymney River
Roath Dock
Bute E Dock
Queen Alexandra Dock
Cardiff Bay Barrage
WALES MILLENNIUM CENTRE
NATIONAL ASSEMBLY
CARDIFF BAY VISITOR CENTRE
TECHNIQUEST
MILLENNIUM STADIUM
CARDIFF ARMS PARK
CARDIFF CASTLE
NATIONAL MUSEUM CARDIFF
LLANDAFF CATHEDRAL
CASTELL COCH
CARDIFF CITY STAD
CARDIFF INTERNATIONAL SPORTS STAD
PARC CEFN ONN
FOREST FARM
M4
A48(M)
A48
A470
A469
A4232
A4119
A4161
A4160
A4055
A4050
A4054
A4234
A473
B4263
B4262
B4267
B4239
B4487
B4562
2 miles
3 km

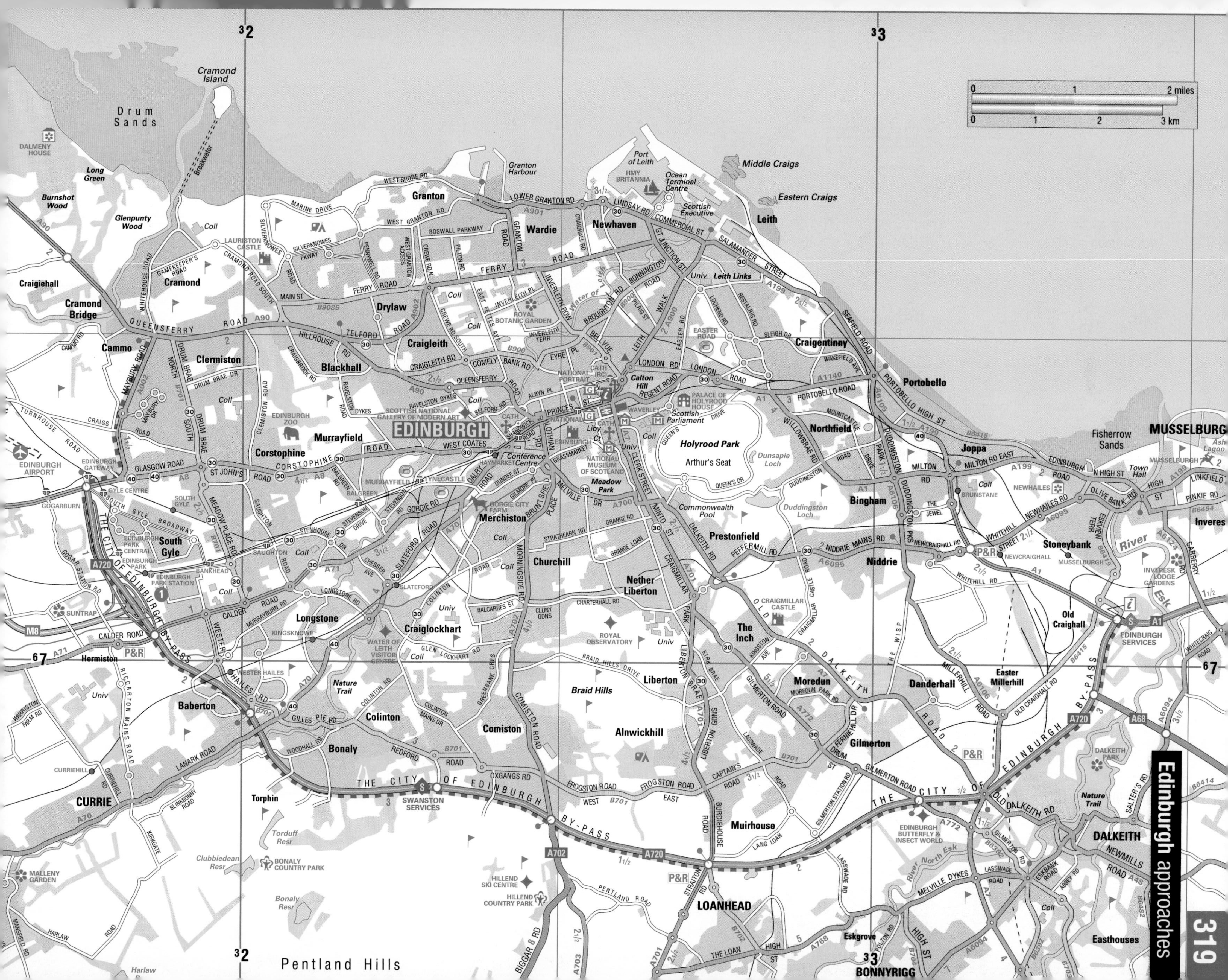

Edinburgh approaches

0 1 2 miles
0 1 2 3 km
32
33
67
Cramond Island
Drum Sands
DALMENY HOUSE
Long Green
Burnshot Wood
Glenpunty Wood
Craigiehall
Cramond Bridge
Cramond
Cammo
Clermiston
Granton
Granton Harbour
Wardie
Newhaven
Port of Leith
HMY BRITANNIA
Ocean Terminal Centre
Scottish Executive
Leith
Leith Links
Middle Craigs
Eastern Craigs
Drylaw
Craigleith
Blackhall
ROYAL BOTANIC GARDEN
Craigentinny
Portobello
Calton Hill
PALACE OF HOLYROODHOUSE
Scottish Parliament
Holyrood Park
Arthur's Seat
Dunsapie Loch
Northfield
SCOTTISH NATIONAL GALLERY OF MODERN ART
EDINBURGH ZOO
Murrayfield
Corstophine
EDINBURGH AIRPORT
EDINBURGH GATEWAY
GYLE CENTRE
South Gyle
EDINBURGH PARK STATION
SUNTRAP
Conference Centre
NATIONAL MUSEUM OF SCOTLAND
Meadow Park
GORGIE CITY FARM
Merchiston
Commonwealth Pool
Duddingston Loch
Bingham
Joppa
Fisherrow Sands
MUSSELBURGH
Town Hall
NEWHAILES
Stoneybank
River Esk
INVERESK LODGE GARDENS
Old Craighall
EDINBURGH SERVICES
Prestonfield
Niddrie
Churchill
Nether Liberton
CRAIGMILLAR CASTLE
The Inch
Longstone
Craiglockhart
WATER OF LEITH VISITOR CENTRE
ROYAL OBSERVATORY
Hermiston
Liberton
Moredun
Danderhall
Easter Millerhill
Braid Hills
Baberton
Nature Trail
Colinton
Comiston
Alnwickhill
Gilmerton
Bonaly
CURRIE
Torphin
SWANSTON SERVICES
Muirhouse
EDINBURGH BUTTERFLY & INSECT WORLD
DALKEITH
Torduff Resr
Clubbiedean Resr
BONALY COUNTRY PARK
Bonaly Resr
MALLENY GARDEN
HILLEND SKI CENTRE
HILLEND COUNTRY PARK
LOANHEAD
Eskgrove
BONNYRIGG
Easthouses
Harlaw
Pentland Hills
THE CITY OF EDINBURGH BY-PASS
A1
A7
A8
A68
A70
A71
A90
A199
A701
A702
A703
A720
A772
A6106
M8

Glasgow approaches

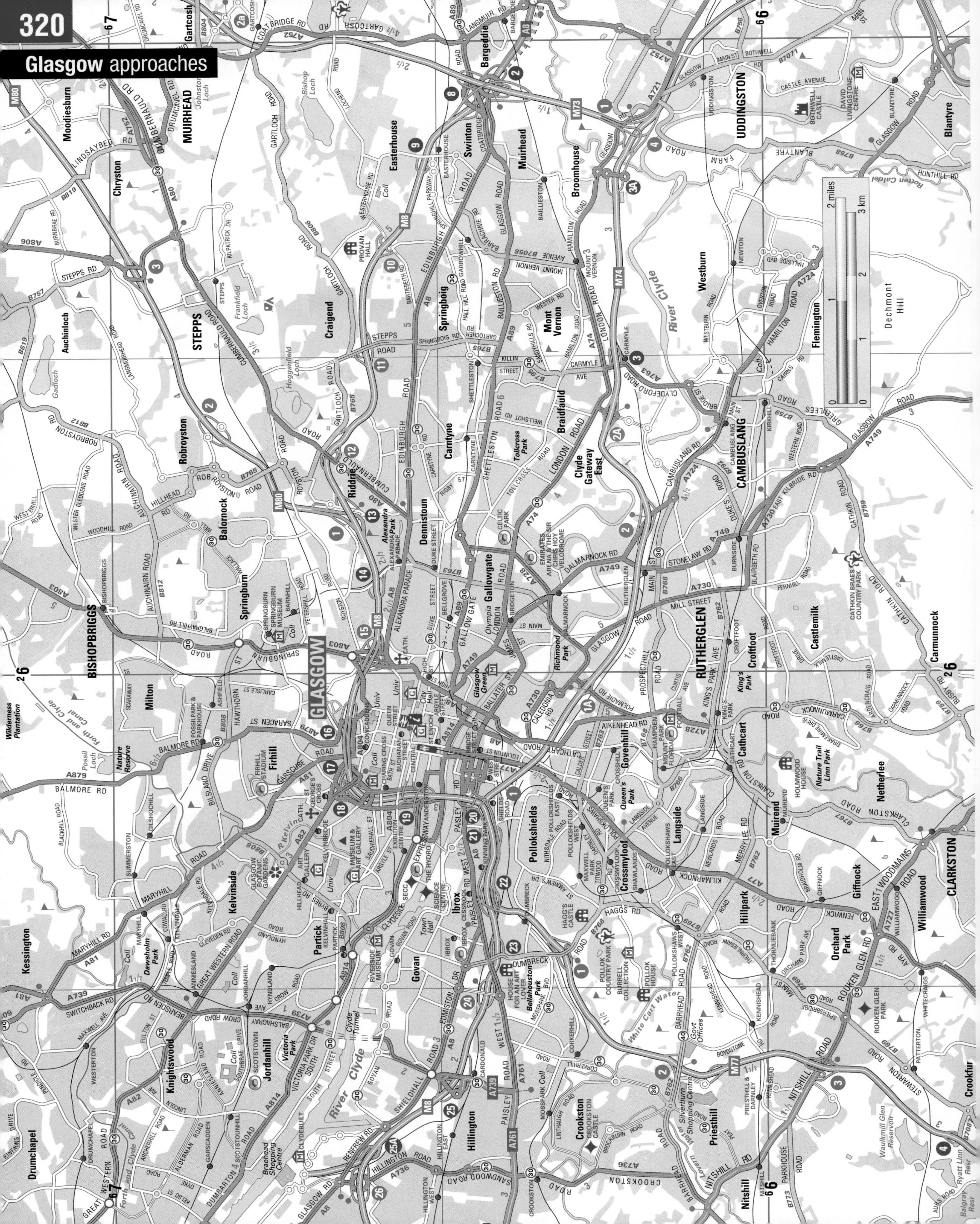

Gartcosh
Bargeddie
Moodiesburn
MUIRHEAD
Chryston
Easterhouse
Swinton
Muirhead
Broomhouse
UDDINGSTON
Blantyre
Bothwell Castle
David Livingstone Centre
Provan Hall
Craigend
Springboig
Mont Vernon
Westburn
Flemington
Dechmont Hill
Auchinloch
STEPPS
Robroyston
Riddrie
Carntyne
Braidfauld
Tollcross Park
Clyde Gateway East
CAMBUSLANG
Balornock
Dennistoun
Alexandra Park
Gallowgate
Celtic Park
Emirates Arena & the Sir Chris Hoy Velodrome
BISHOPBRIGGS
Springburn
Springburn Museum
Milton
Richmond Park
RUTHERGLEN
Croftfoot
Castlemilk
Cathkin Braes Country Park
Carmunnock
Glasgow Green
King's Park
Firhill
Firhill Stadium
Nature Reserve
Possil Loch
Wilderness Plantation
Forth and Clyde Canal
Govanhill
Cathcart
Netherlee
Linn Park
Holmwood House
Pollokshields
Queen's Park
Langside
Muirend
Crossmyloof
Kelvinside
Glasgow Botanic Gardens
Art Gallery
Museum & Art Gallery
The Hydro
Science Centre
SECC
Kessington
Dawsholm Park
Partick
Riverside Museum
Govan
Ibrox
Town Hall
Hillpark
Giffnock
CLARKSTON
Williamwood
Orchard Park
Haggs Castle
Pollok Country Park
Burrell Collection
Pollok House
Dumbreck
House for an Art Lover
Bellahouston Park
White Cart Water
Rouken Glen Park
Knightswood
Jordanhill
Victoria Park
Clyde Tunnel
River Clyde
Drumchapel
Braehead Shopping Centre
Hillington
Crookston
Crookston Castle
Priesthill
Silverburn Shopping Centre
Nitshill
Crookfur
Waulkmill Glen Reservoir
Ryatt Linn Resr
Balgray Resr

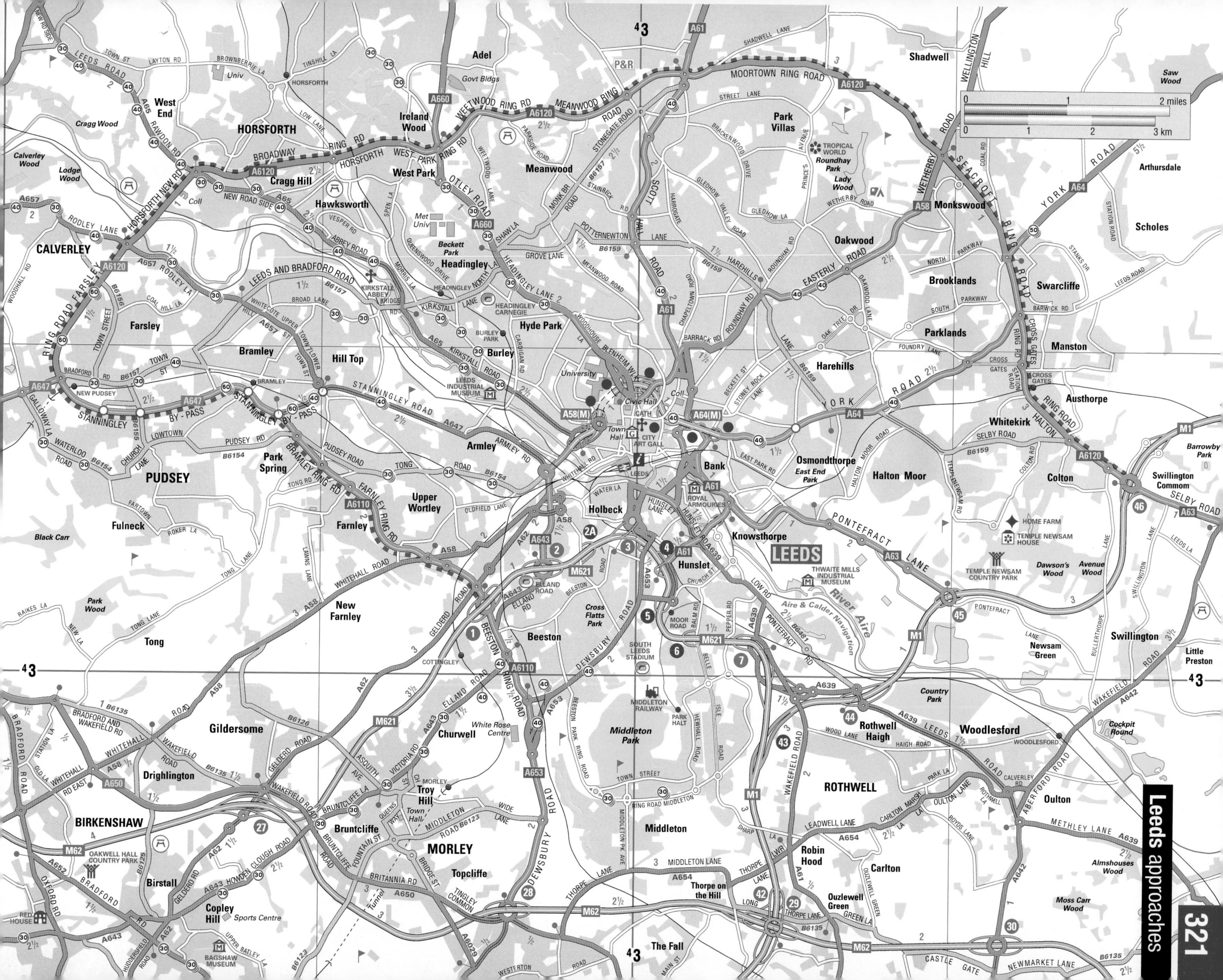

Adel
Shadwell
Saw Wood
2 miles
3 km
MOORTOWN RING ROAD
SHADWELL LANE
Govt Bldgs
P&R
West End
HORSFORTH
Ireland Wood
Park Villas
TROPICAL WORLD
Roundhay Park
Lady Wood
Arthursdale
Scholes
Cragg Wood
Calverley Wood
Lodge Wood
Cragg Hill
West Park
Meanwood
Monkswood
Hawksworth
Met Univ
Beckett Park
Headingley
Oakwood
CALVERLEY
Brooklands
Swarcliffe
Farsley
Hyde Park
Parklands
Manston
Bramley
Hill Top
Burley
LEEDS INDUSTRIAL MUSEUM
University
Harehills
Civic Hall
Austhorpe
Whitekirk
Armley
Osmondthorpe
East End Park
Halton Moor
Colton
Barrowby Park
Swillington Common
PUDSEY
Park Spring
Bank
ROYAL ARMOURIES
Upper Wortley
Holbeck
HOME FARM
TEMPLE NEWSAM HOUSE
TEMPLE NEWSAM COUNTRY PARK
Fulneck
Black Carr
Farnley
Knowsthorpe
LEEDS
Hunslet
THWAITE MILLS INDUSTRIAL MUSEUM
Dawson's Wood
Avenue Wood
River Aire
Aire & Calder Navigation
New Farnley
Park Wood
Tong
Beeston
Cross Flatts Park
SOUTH LEEDS STADIUM
Newsam Green
Swillington
Little Preston
MIDDLETON RAILWAY
PARK HALT
Middleton Park
Country Park
Woodlesford
Cockpit Round
Gildersome
White Rose Centre
Churwell
Rothwell Haigh
Drighlington
ROTHWELL
Oulton
Troy Hill
Town Hall
BIRKENSHAW
Bruntcliffe
MORLEY
Middleton
Robin Hood
Carlton
Almshouses Wood
OAKWELL HALL COUNTRY PARK
Birstall
Topcliffe
TINGLEY COMMON
Thorpe on the Hill
Ouzlewell Green
Moss Carr Wood
Copley Hill
Sports Centre
RED HOUSE
BAGSHAW MUSEUM
The Fall
BRADFORD ROAD
OXFORD RD
STANNINGLEY BY-PASS
GALLOWAY LA
WATERLOO ROAD
DEWSBURY ROAD
PONTEFRACT LANE
YORK ROAD
WAKEFIELD ROAD

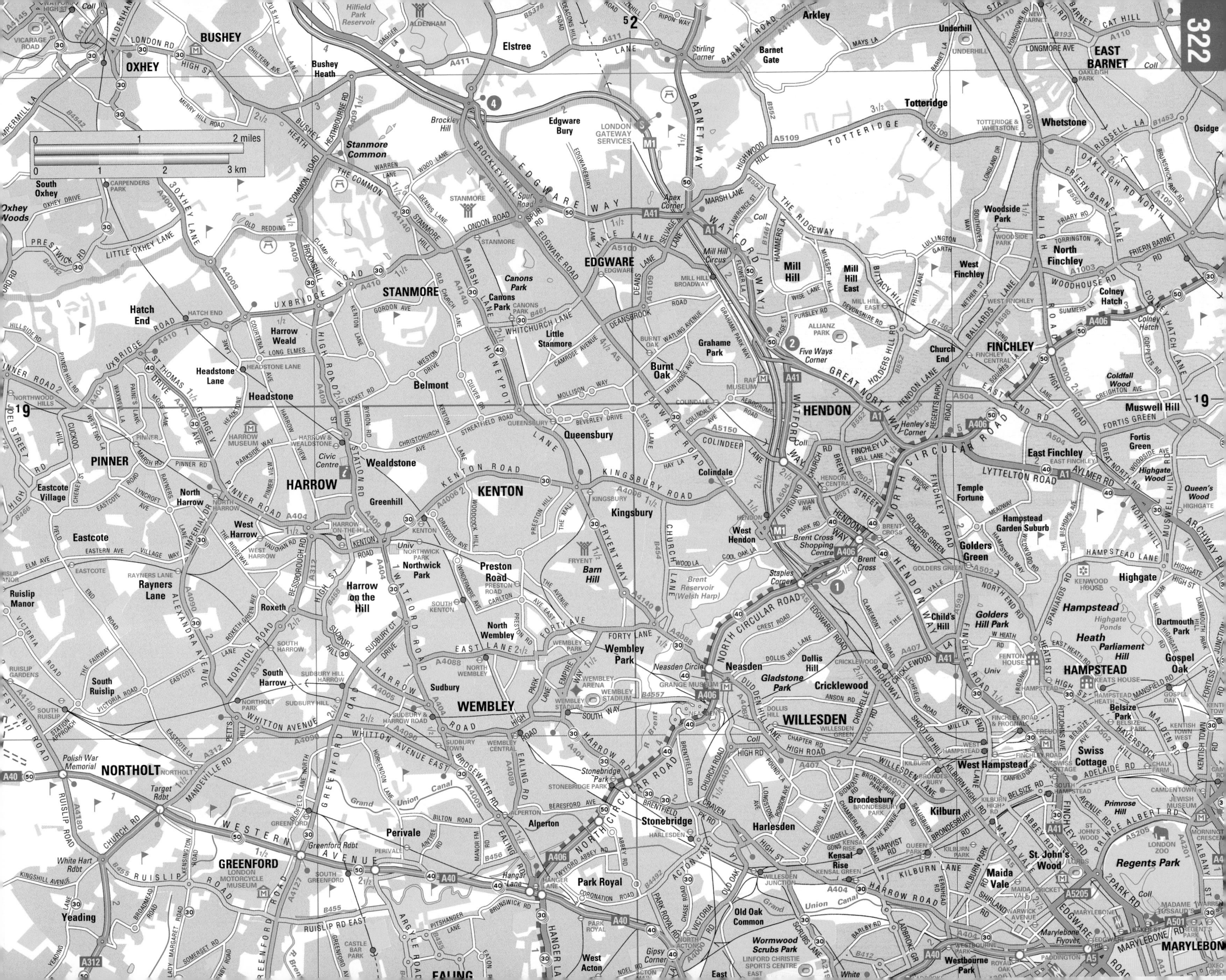
BUSHEY
OXHEY
Bushey Heath
Elstree
Arkley
Barnet Gate
Underhill
EAST BARNET
Totteridge
Whetstone
Osidge
Stanmore Common
Brockley Hill
Edgware Bury
LONDON GATEWAY SERVICES
South Oxhey
Oxhey Woods
Woodside Park
North Finchley
West Finchley
Mill Hill
Mill Hill East
Colney Hatch
EDGWARE
STANMORE
Canons Park
Little Stanmore
Hatch End
Harrow Weald
Grahame Park
Burnt Oak
Five Ways Corner
Church End
FINCHLEY
Coldfall Wood
Muswell Hill
Headstone Lane
Headstone
Belmont
HENDON
PINNER
Queensbury
Fortis Green
East Finchley
Wealdstone
HARROW
KENTON
Colindale
Temple Fortune
Highgate Wood
Queen's Wood
Eastcote Village
North Harrow
Greenhill
Kingsbury
Hampstead Garden Suburb
West Harrow
Eastcote
West Hendon
Brent Cross Shopping Centre
Golders Green
Highgate
Rayners Lane
Ruislip Manor
Harrow on the Hill
Northwick Park
Preston Road
Barn Hill
Brent Reservoir (Welsh Harp)
Staples Corner
Hampstead
Roxeth
North Wembley
Wembley Park
Child's Hill
Golders Hill Park
Dartmouth Park
Heath
Parliament Hill
South Ruislip
South Harrow
Neasden
Dollis Hill
Gladstone Park
Cricklewood
HAMPSTEAD
Gospel Oak
Sudbury
WEMBLEY
WILLESDEN
Belsize Park
Swiss Cottage
West Hampstead
NORTHOLT
Polish War Memorial
Target Rbdt
Stonebridge Park
Brondesbury
Kilburn
Primrose Hill
Perivale
Alperton
Stonebridge
Harlesden
Kensal Rise
St. John's Wood
Regents Park
White Hart Rbdt
GREENFORD
Greenford Rbdt
Hangar Lane
Park Royal
Maida Vale
Yeading
Old Oak Common
Wormwood Scrubs Park
West Acton
Gipsy Corner
Westbourne Park
Marylebone Flyover
MARYLEBONE
EALING
2 miles
3 km

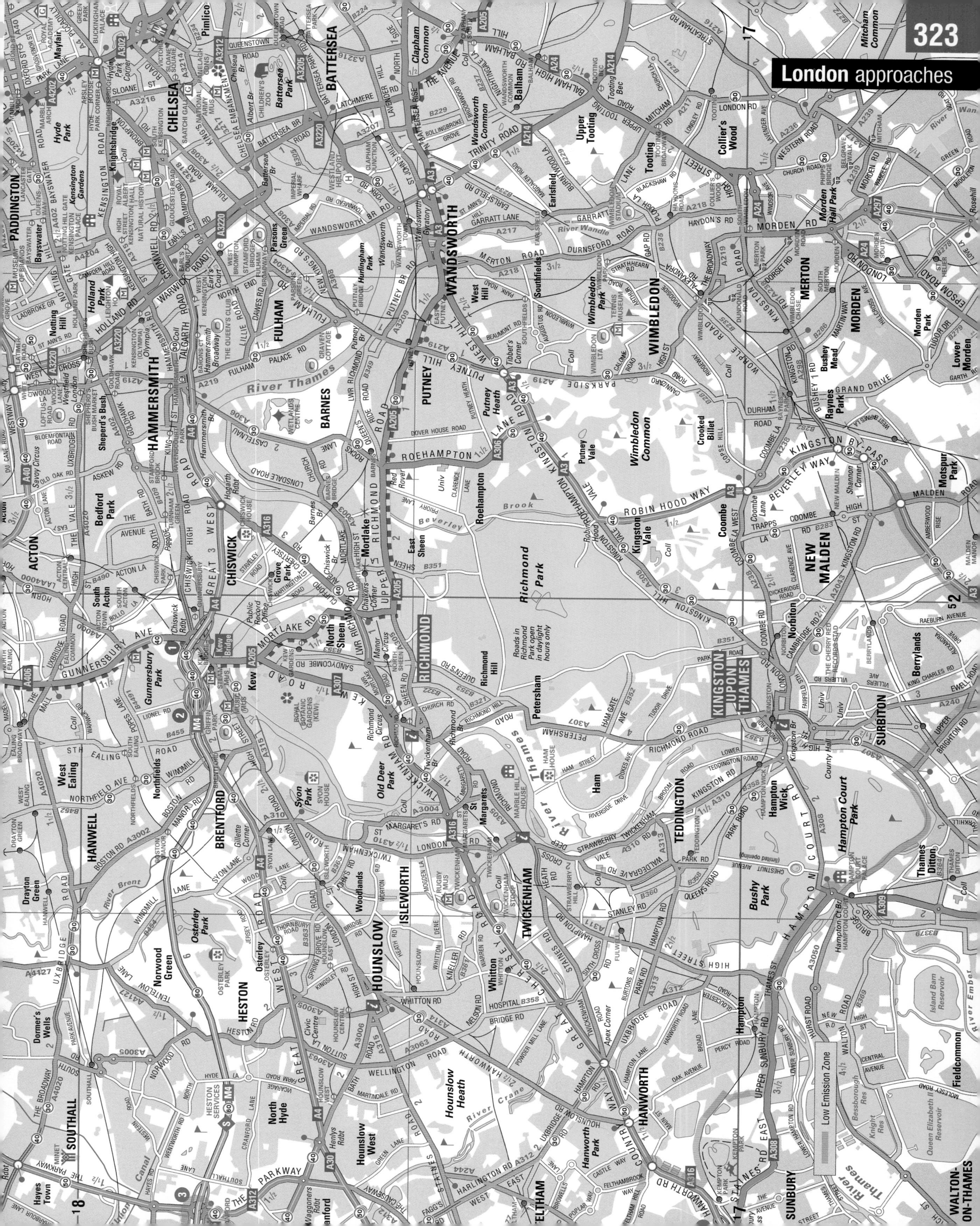
PADDINGTON
Bayswater
Notting Hill
Holland Park
Kensington Gardens
Hyde Park
Mayfair
Knightsbridge
CHELSEA
Pimlico
BATTERSEA
Battersea Park
Clapham Common
Balham
Upper Tooting
Tooting Bec
Tooting
Collier's Wood
Mitcham Common
FULHAM
Parsons Green
Hurlingham Park
Wandsworth Common
WANDSWORTH
Earlsfield
Southfields
West Hill
WIMBLEDON
Wimbledon Park
MERTON
Morden Hall Park
MORDEN
Morden Park
Lower Morden
HAMMERSMITH
Shepherd's Bush
BARNES
PUTNEY
Putney Heath
Wimbledon Common
Putney Vale
Crooked Billet
Raynes Park
Bushey Mead
Motspur Park
ACTON
Bedford Park
CHISWICK
South Acton
Roehampton
East Sheen
Mortlake
Richmond Park
Kingston Vale
Coombe
NEW MALDEN
Norbiton
Berrylands
Gunnersbury Park
Kew
RICHMOND
Richmond Hill
Roads in Richmond Park open in daylight hours only
Petersham
KINGSTON UPON THAMES
SURBITON
Ham
Royal Botanic Gardens (Kew)
West Ealing
Northfields
BRENTFORD
Syon Park
Old Deer Park
Margarets
TEDDINGTON
Hampton Wick
Hampton Court Park
HANWELL
Drayton Green
Osterley Park
Norwood Green
ISLEWORTH
Woodlands
TWICKENHAM
Bushy Park
Thames Ditton
HESTON
HOUNSLOW
Whitton
Hampton
Dormer's Wells
SOUTHALL
North Hyde
Hounslow West
Hounslow Heath
HANWORTH
Hanworth Park
SUNBURY
Fieldcommon
WALTON-ON-THAMES
Hayes Town
River Thames
Low Emission Zone

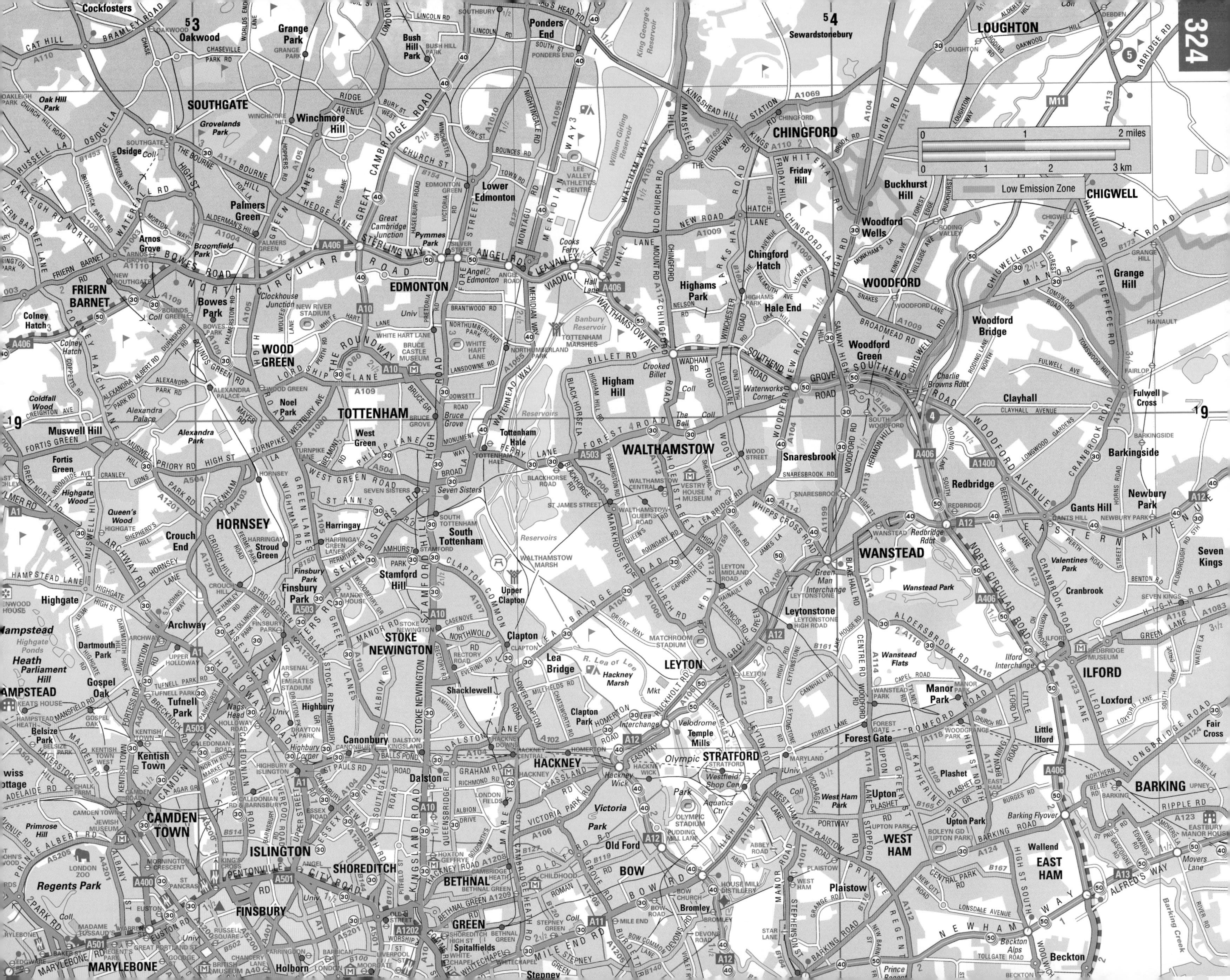

Cockfosters
Oakwood
Grange Park
Bush Hill Park
Ponders End
Sewardstonebury
Loughton
Oak Hill Park
Southgate
Grovelands Park
Winchmore Hill
Chingford
Friday Hill
Buckhurst Hill
Chigwell
Osidge
Palmers Green
Lower Edmonton
Woodford Wells
Arnos Grove
Broomfield Park
Chingford Hatch
Woodford
Grange Hill
Friern Barnet
Bowes Park
Edmonton
Highams Park
Hale End
Woodford Bridge
Colney Hatch
Wood Green
Noel Park
Tottenham
Higham Hill
Woodford Green
Clayhall
Fulwell Cross
Muswell Hill
Alexandra Palace
Alexandra Park
West Green
Tottenham Hale
Walthamstow
Snaresbrook
Barkingside
Fortis Green
Redbridge
Newbury Park
Highgate Wood
Queen's Wood
Gants Hill
Hornsey
Crouch End
Stroud Green
Harringay
South Tottenham
Seven Sisters
Wanstead
Seven Kings
Finsbury Park
Stamford Hill
Upper Clapton
Valentines Park
Cranbrook
Highgate
Wanstead Park
Archway
Leytonstone
Hampstead
Stoke Newington
Clapton
Dartmouth Park
Heath
Parliament Hill
Lea Bridge
Hackney Marsh
Leyton
Ilford
Gospel Oak
Tufnell Park
Shacklewell
Highbury
Wanstead Flats
Manor Park
Loxford
Kentish Town
Belsize Park
Clapton Park
Temple Mills
Little Ilford
Fair Cross
Canonbury
Forest Gate
Dalston
Hackney
Stratford
Hackney Wick
Barking
Plashet
West Ham Park
Upton
Camden Town
Victoria Park
Upton Park
Primrose Hill
Islington
Old Ford
West Ham
Wallend
Shoreditch
Bethnal
Bow
East Ham
Plaistow
Regents Park
Finsbury
Bromley
Green
Spitalfields
Marylebone
Holborn
Stepney
Beckton

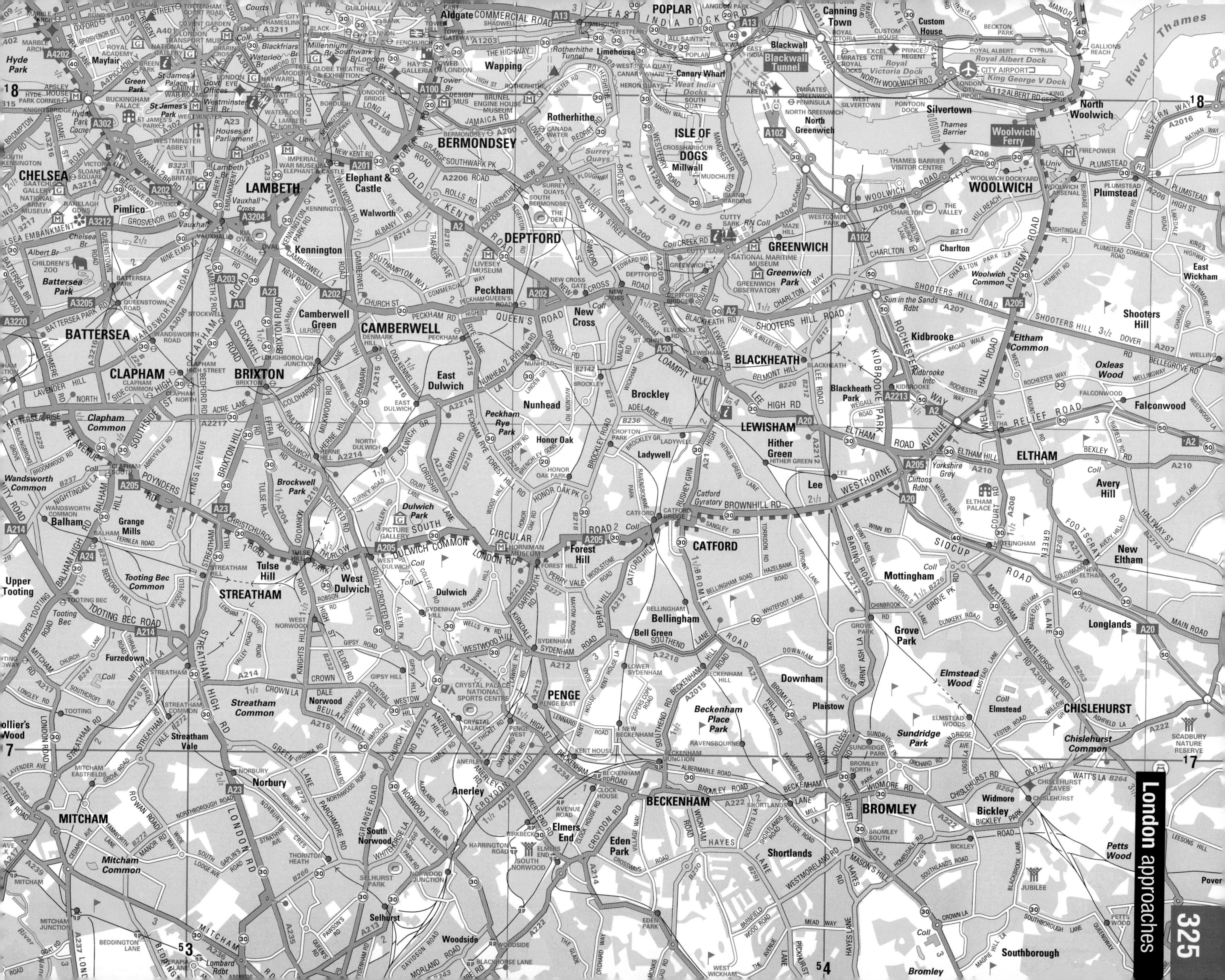
Hyde Park
Mayfair
Green Park
CHELSEA
Pimlico
Battersea Park
BATTERSEA
CLAPHAM
Clapham Common
Wandsworth Common
Balham
Grange Mills
Upper Tooting
Tooting Bec Common
Furzedown
Streatham Vale
MITCHAM
Mitcham Common
LAMBETH
Elephant & Castle
Walworth
Kennington
BRIXTON
Camberwell Green
CAMBERWELL
East Dulwich
Tulse Hill
STREATHAM
West Dulwich
Dulwich
Streatham Common
Norbury
BERMONDSEY
Wapping
Aldgate
Rotherhithe
DEPTFORD
Peckham
New Cross
Nunhead
Honor Oak
Brockley
Ladywell
Forest Hill
PENGE
Anerley
Elmers End
South Norwood
Selhurst
Woodside
POPLAR
Limehouse
Canary Wharf
ISLE OF DOGS
Millwall
Canning Town
Custom House
Blackwall
North Greenwich
Silvertown
North Woolwich
WOOLWICH
Plumstead
GREENWICH
Charlton
BLACKHEATH
LEWISHAM
Hither Green
Lee
Kidbrooke
Shooters Hill
East Wickham
Falconwood
ELTHAM
Avery Hill
New Eltham
Mottingham
CATFORD
Bellingham
Bell Green
Grove Park
Longlands
Downham
Plaistow
Elmstead Wood
Sundridge Park
CHISLEHURST
Chislehurst Common
BECKENHAM
Eden Park
Shortlands
BROMLEY
Widmore
Bickley
Petts Wood
Southborough
River Thames

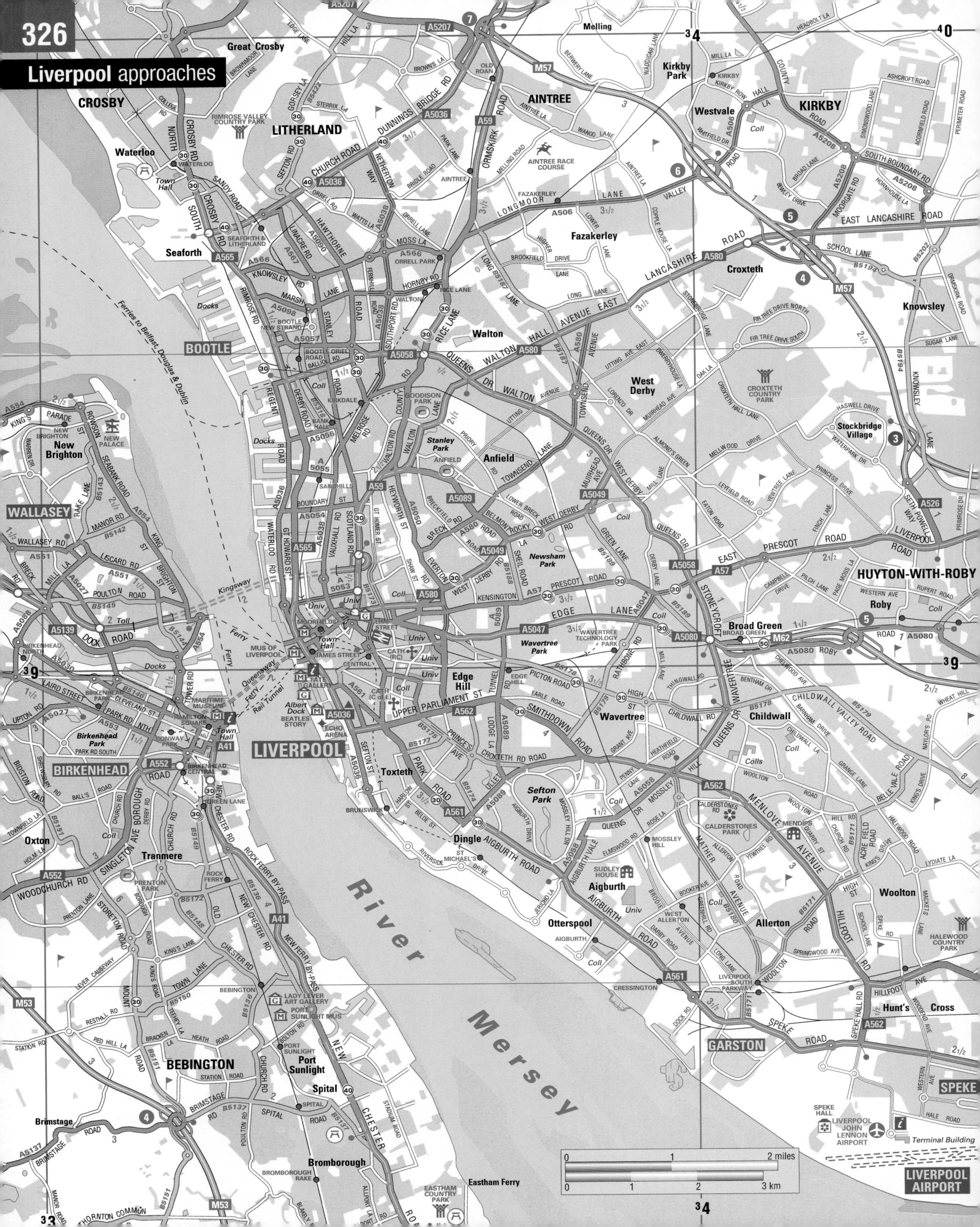

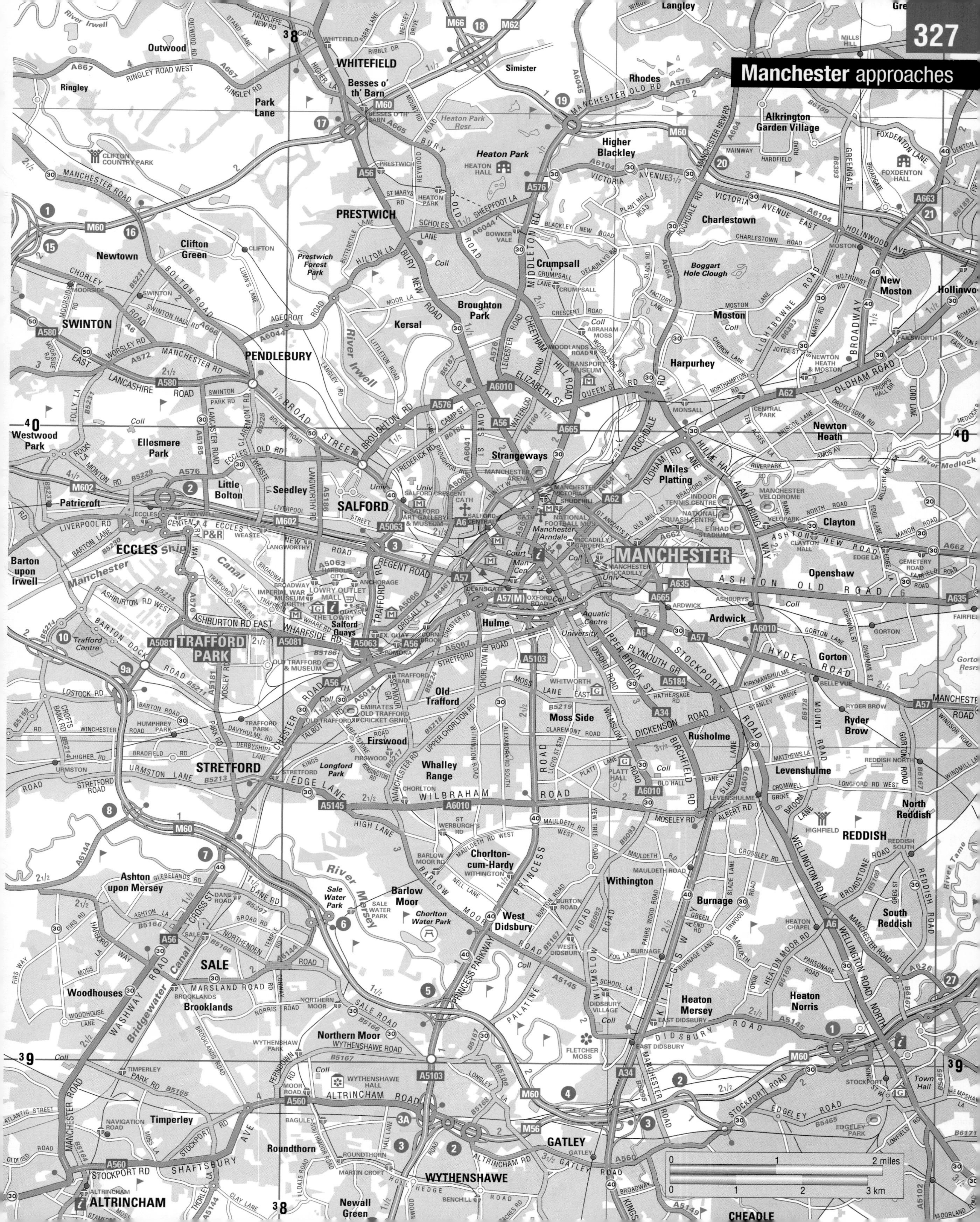
MANCHESTER
SALFORD
WHITEFIELD
PRESTWICH
PENDLEBURY
SWINTON
ECCLES
TRAFFORD PARK
STRETFORD
SALE
ALTRINCHAM
WYTHENSHAWE
GATLEY
CHEADLE
REDDISH
Timperley
Brooklands
Woodhouses
Ashton upon Mersey
Chorlton-cum-Hardy
Withington
Didsbury
Levenshulme
Rusholme
Moss Side
Hulme
Ardwick
Openshaw
Gorton
Clayton
Miles Platting
Harpurhey
Moston
Crumpsall
Charlestown
Higher Blackley
Heaton Park
Kersal
Broughton Park
Strangeways
Old Trafford
Whalley Range
Firswood
Newall Green
Northern Moor
Roundthorn
Heaton Mersey
Heaton Norris
Burnage
Ryder Brow
Newton Heath
New Moston
Alkrington Garden Village
Rhodes
Simister
Besses o' th' Barn
Outwood
Ringley
Clifton Green
Newtown
Ellesmere Park
Little Bolton
Seedley
Patricroft
Barton upon Irwell
Westwood Park
Salford Quays
Manchester Ship Canal
River Irwell
River Mersey
Bridgewater Canal
0 1 2 miles
0 1 2 3 km

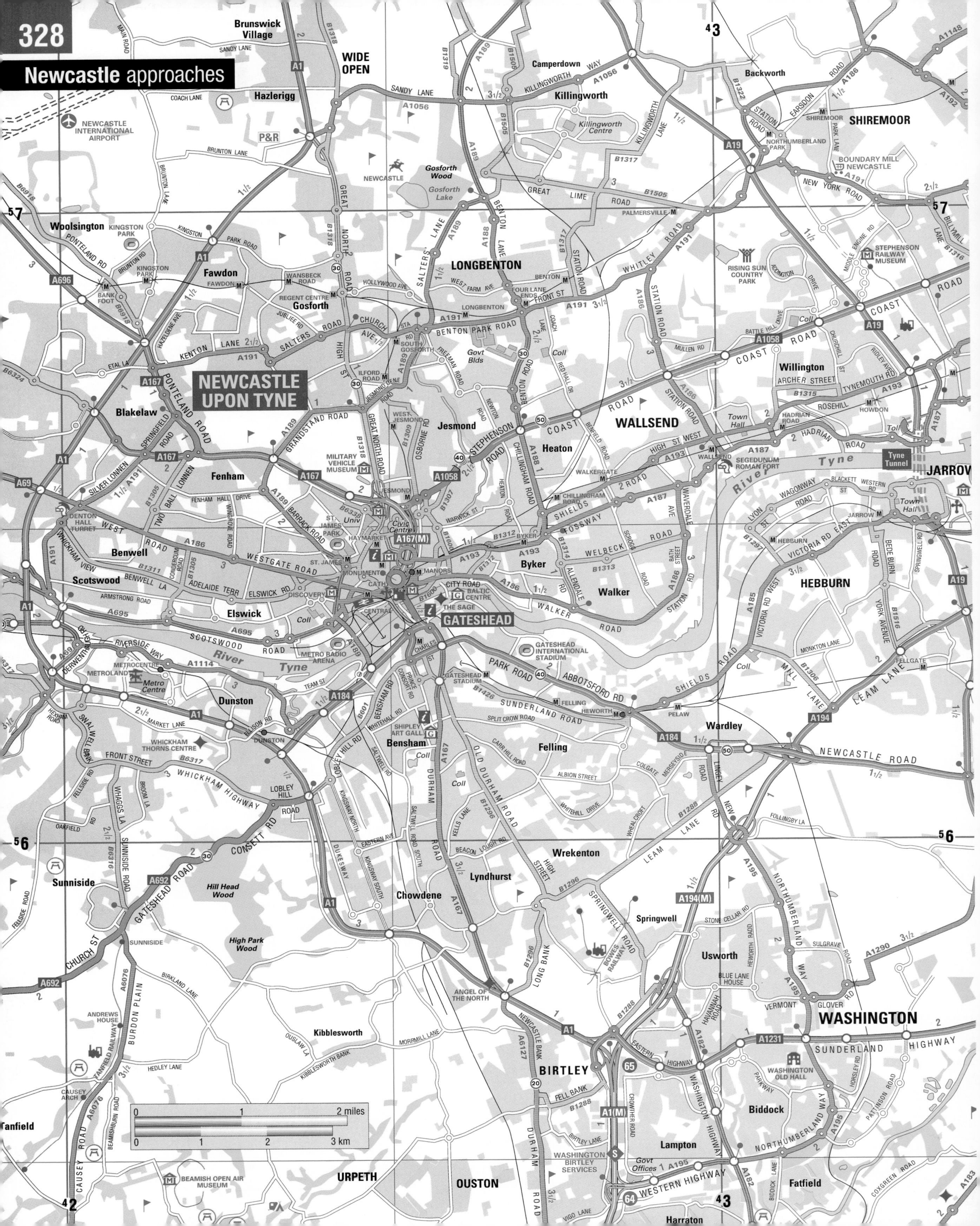
Brunswick Village
WIDE OPEN
Hazlerigg
Camperdown
Killingworth
Killingworth Centre
Backworth
SHIREMOOR
NEWCASTLE INTERNATIONAL AIRPORT
P&R
Gosforth Wood
Gosforth Lake
NEWCASTLE
BOUNDARY MILL NEWCASTLE
Woolsington
KINGSTON PARK
Fawdon
Gosforth
LONGBENTON
RISING SUN COUNTRY PARK
STEPHENSON RAILWAY MUSEUM
Govt Blds
NEWCASTLE UPON TYNE
Blakelaw
Jesmond
WALLSEND
Willington
Town Hall
HOWDON
Tyne Tunnel
JARROW
Heaton
SEGEDUNUM ROMAN FORT
MILITARY VEHICLE MUSEUM
Fenham
Civic Centre
Benwell
Scotswood
Byker
Walker
HEBBURN
Elswick
GATESHEAD
BALTIC CENTRE
THE SAGE
GATESHEAD INTERNATIONAL STADIUM
METRO RADIO ARENA
River Tyne
METROCENTRE
METROLAND
Dunston
WHICKHAM THORNS CENTRE
SHIPLEY ART GALL
Bensham
Felling
Wardley
Sunniside
Hill Head Wood
Wrekenton
Lyndhurst
Chowdene
Springwell
High Park Wood
Usworth
BLUE LANE HOUSE
ANGEL OF THE NORTH
WASHINGTON
ANDREWS HOUSE
Kibblesworth
BIRTLEY
WASHINGTON OLD HALL
CAUSEY ARCH
Biddock
Tanfield
Lampton
WASHINGTON BIRTLEY SERVICES
BEAMISH OPEN AIR MUSEUM
URPETH
OUSTON
Fatfield
Harraton
0 1 2 miles
0 1 2 3 km

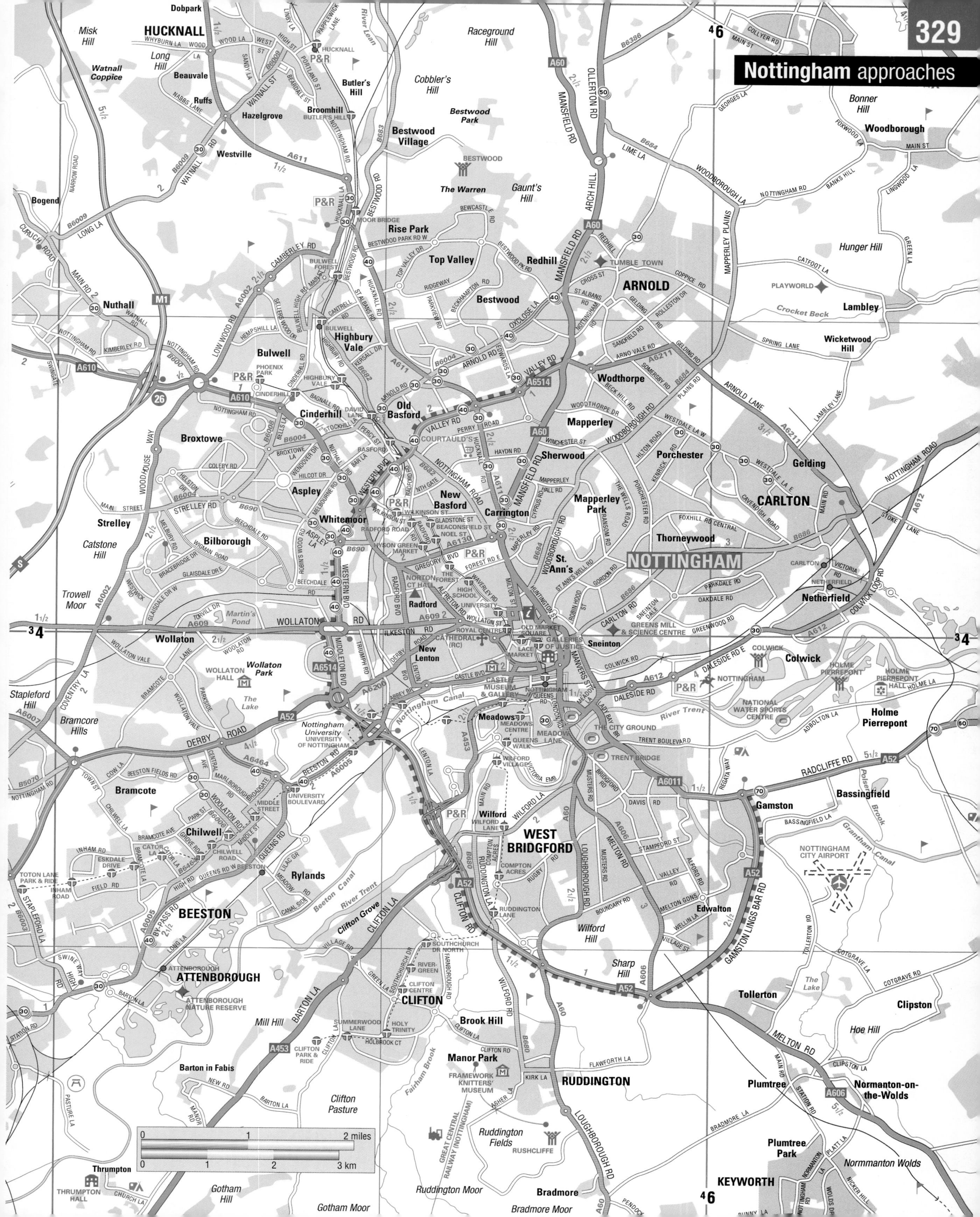
HUCKNALL
Dobpark
Misk Hill
Watnall Coppice
Long Hill
Beauvale
Ruffs
Hazelgrove
Westville
Bogend
Nuthall
Butler's Hill
Broomhill
Raceground Hill
Cobbler's Hill
Bestwood Park
Bestwood Village
BESTWOOD
The Warren
Gaunt's Hill
Rise Park
Top Valley
Redhill
Bestwood
ARNOLD
TUMBLE TOWN
Bonner Hill
Woodborough
Hunger Hill
PLAYWORLD
Lambley
Crocket Beck
Wicketwood Hill
Bulwell
Highbury Vale
Cinderhill
Old Basford
Wodthorpe
Mapperley
Broxtowe
Sherwood
Porchester
Gelding
Aspley
New Basford
Carrington
Mapperley Park
CARLTON
Strelley
Whitemoor
Thorneywood
Bilborough
Catstone Hill
St. Ann's
NOTTINGHAM
Netherfield
Trowell Moor
Radford
Martin's Pond
Wollaton
WOLLATON
Sneinton
Colwick
Wollaton Park
WOLLATON HALL
New Lenton
The Lake
HOLME PIERREPONT
Stapleford Hill
Bramcore Hills
Nottingham University
UNIVERSITY OF NOTTINGHAM
Meadows
THE CITY GROUND
River Trent
NATIONAL WATER SPORTS CENTRE
Holme Pierrepont
TRENT BRIDGE
Bramcote
Chilwell
Wilford
WEST BRIDGFORD
Gamston
Bassingfield
NOTTINGHAM CITY AIRPORT
Rylands
BEESTON
Beeston Canal
Clifton Grove
Wilford Hill
Edwalton
ATTENBOROUGH
ATTENBOROUGH NATURE RESERVE
Sharp Hill
CLIFTON
Tollerton
Clipston
Mill Hill
Brook Hill
Hoe Hill
Manor Park
FRAMEWORK KNITTERS' MUSEUM
RUDDINGTON
Plumtree
Normanton-on-the-Wolds
Barton in Fabis
Clifton Pasture
Ruddington Fields
RUSHCLIFFE
Plumtree Park
Normmanton Wolds
KEYWORTH
Thrumpton
THRUMPTON HALL
Gotham Hill
Ruddington Moor
Bradmore
Gotham Moor
Bradmore Moor
0 1 2 miles
0 1 2 3 km

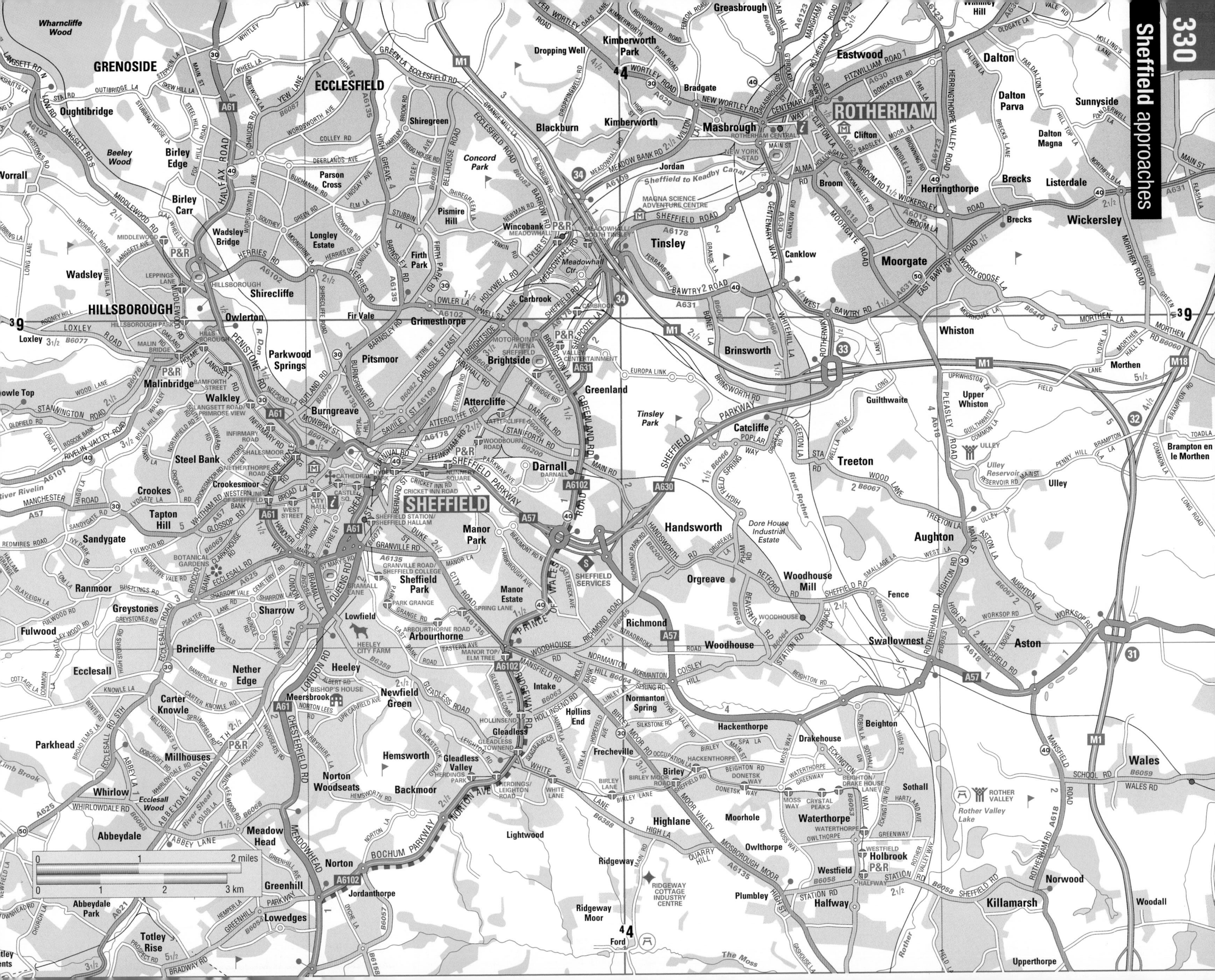
ROTHERHAM
SHEFFIELD
HILLSBOROUGH
ECCLESFIELD
GRENOSIDE
Sunnyside
Wickersley
Listerdale
Dalton Magna
Dalton Parva
Dalton
Brecks
Herringthorpe
Moorgate
Eastwood
Clifton
Broom
Canklow
Masbrough
Greasbrough
Bradgate
Kimberworth Park
Kimberworth
Jordan
Tinsley
Brinsworth
Whiston
Upper Whiston
Ulley
Morthen
Brampton en le Morthen
Wales
Woodall
Aston
Aughton
Swallownest
Norwood
Killamarsh
Upperthorpe
Rother Valley Lake
Treeton
Guilthwaite
Catcliffe
Woodhouse Mill
Fence
Beighton
Sothall
Holbrook
Drakehouse
Waterthorpe
Westfield
Halfway
Hackenthorpe
Moorhole
Owlthorpe
Plumbley
Woodhouse
Orgreave
Handsworth
Tinsley Park
Greenland
Richmond
Normanton Spring
Birley
Highlane
Ridgeway
Ridgeway Moor
Ford
Frecheville
Hollins End
Intake
Lightwood
Gleadless
Gleadless Townend
Gleadless Valley
Manor Estate
Manor Park
Darnall
Attercliffe
Brightside
Carbrook
Wincobank
Blackburn
Dropping Well
Concord Park
Pismire Hill
Shiregreen
Firth Park
Grimesthorpe
Pitsmoor
Fir Vale
Burngreave
Parson Cross
Longley Estate
Shirecliffe
Parkwood Springs
Owlerton
Wadsley Bridge
Birley Edge
Birley Carr
Beeley Wood
Oughtibridge
Wharncliffe Wood
Wadsley
Malinbridge
Walkley
Crookesmoor
Steel Bank
Crookes
Tapton Hill
Sandygate
Ranmoor
Fulwood
Greystones
Ecclesall
Brincliffe
Nether Edge
Sharrow
Heeley
Lowfield
Sheffield Park
Arbourthorne
Newfield Green
Hemsworth
Backmoor
Norton Woodseats
Meersbrook
Norton
Jordanthorpe
Meadow Head
Greenhill
Lowedges
Carter Knowle
Millhouses
Abbeydale
Abbeydale Park
Whirlow
Parkhead
Totley Rise
Loxley
Sheffield Services
River Rother
R. Don
River Rivelin
Dore House Industrial Estate
Ridgeway Cottage Industry Centre
Magna Science Adventure Centre
Meadowhall Ctr
Botanical Gardens
Heeley City Farm
Bishop's House
Ulley Reservoir
Sheffield to Keadby Canal
M1
M18
A61
A57
A630
A631
A618
A6102
A6135
A6178
2 miles
3 km

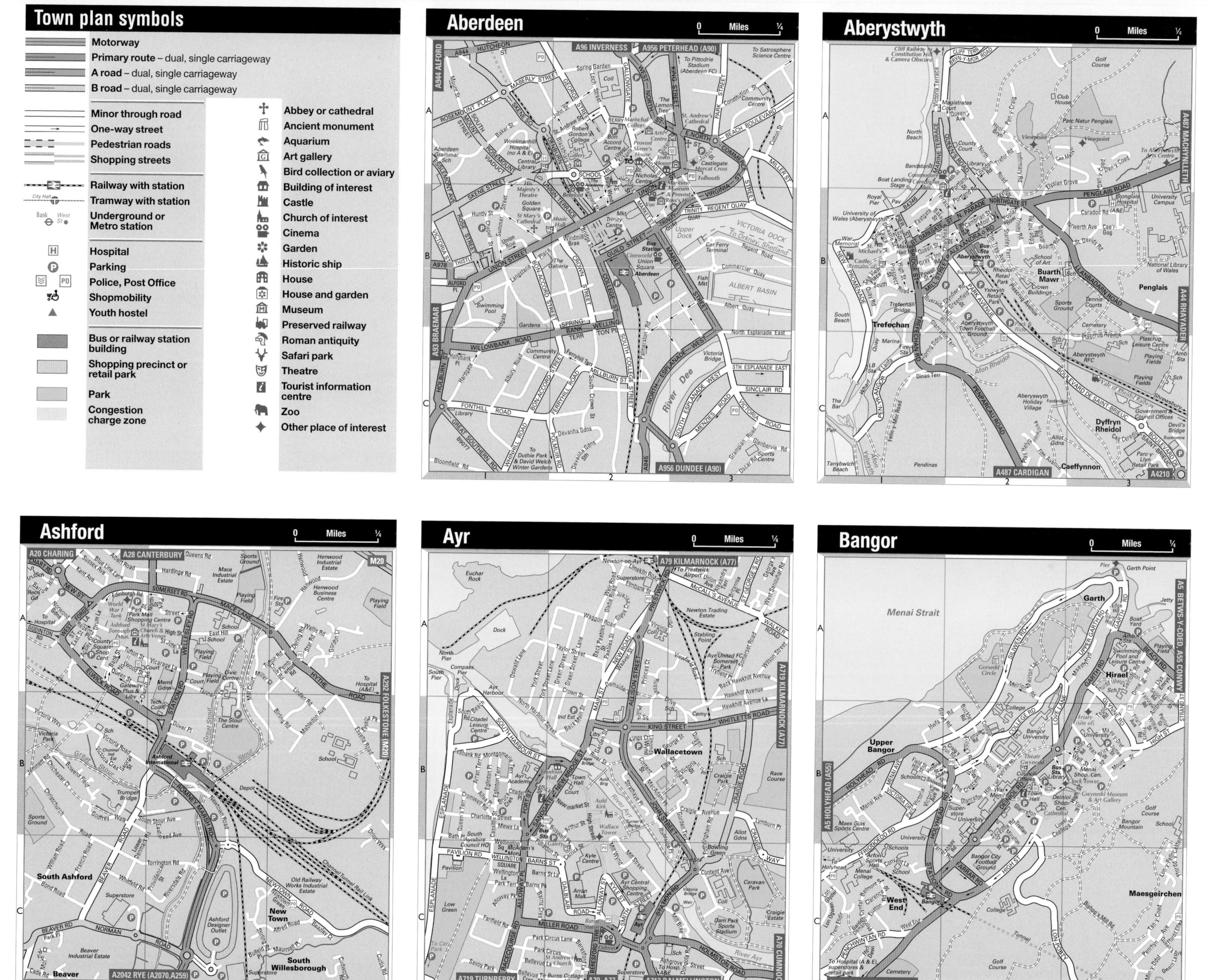

Town plan symbols

Motorway

Primary route – dual, single carriageway

A road – dual, single carriageway

B road – dual, single carriageway

Minor through road

One-way street

Pedestrian roads

Shopping streets

Railway with station

Tramway with station

Underground or Metro station

Hospital

Parking

Police, Post Office

Shopmobility

Youth hostel

Bus or railway station building

Shopping precinct or retail park

Park

Congestion charge zone

Abbey or cathedral

Ancient monument

Aquarium

Art gallery

Bird collection or aviary

Building of interest

Castle

Church of interest

Cinema

Garden

Historic ship

House

House and garden

Museum

Preserved railway

Roman antiquity

Safari park

Theatre

Tourist information centre

Zoo

Other place of interest

Aberystwyth

Bangor

Aberdeen

Ayr

Ashford

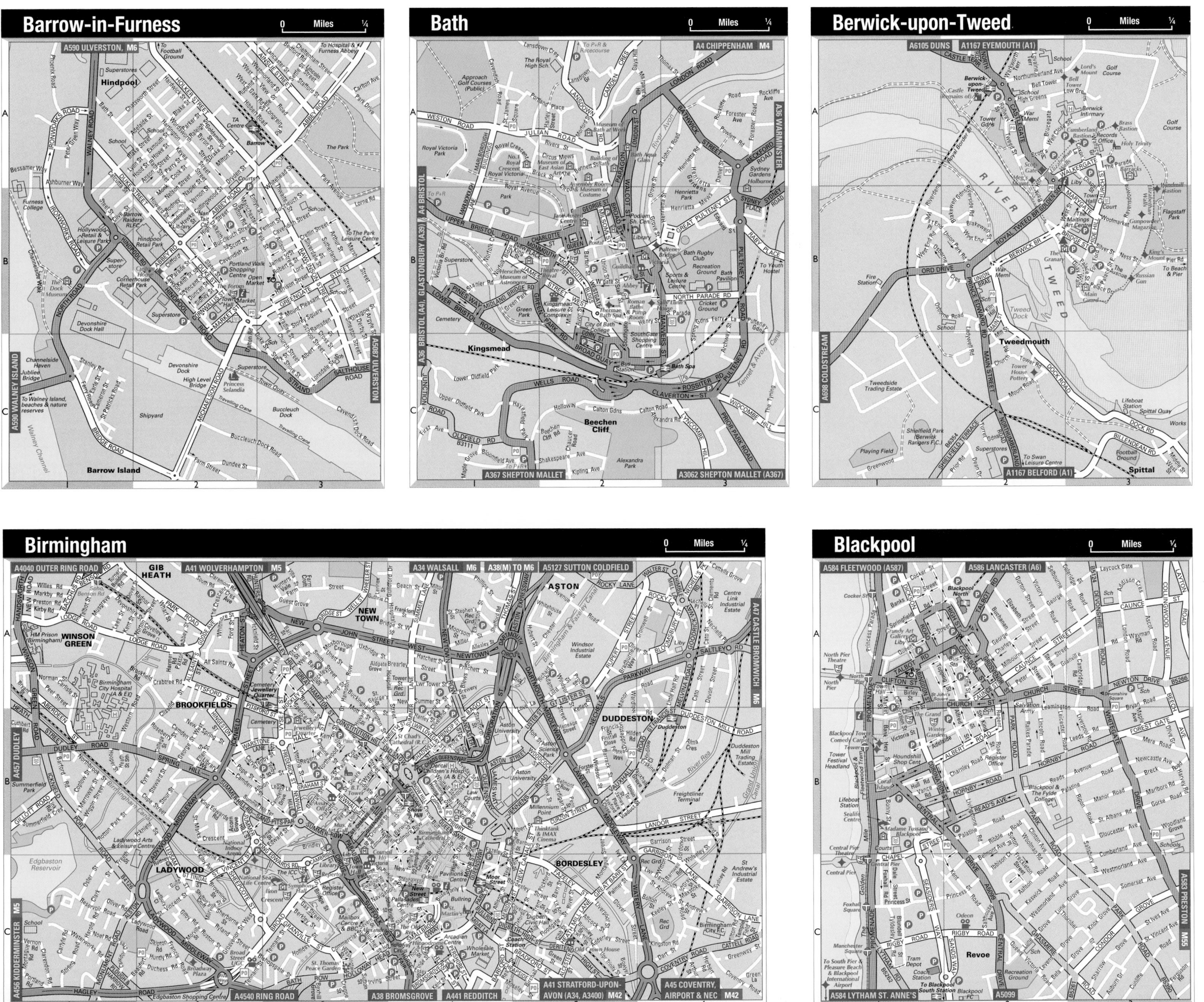
Barrow-in-Furness
Bath
Berwick-upon-Tweed
Birmingham
Blackpool

Bournemouth page 19 • **Bradford** page 205 • **Brighton** page 36 • **Bristol** page 60 • **Bury St Edmunds** page 125

333

Brighton

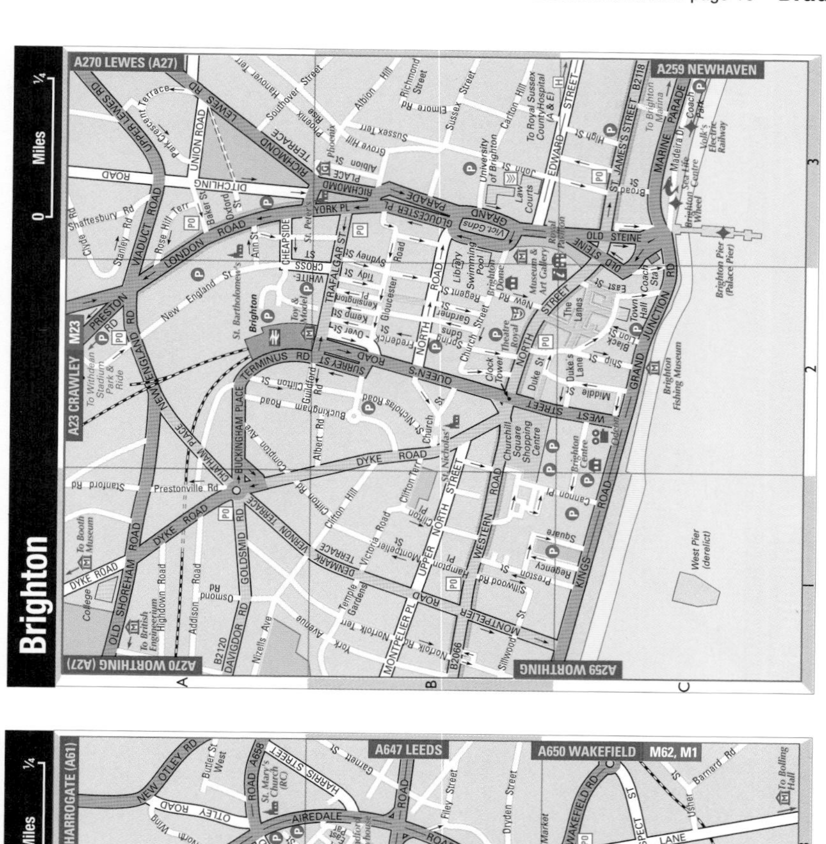

Bury St Edmunds

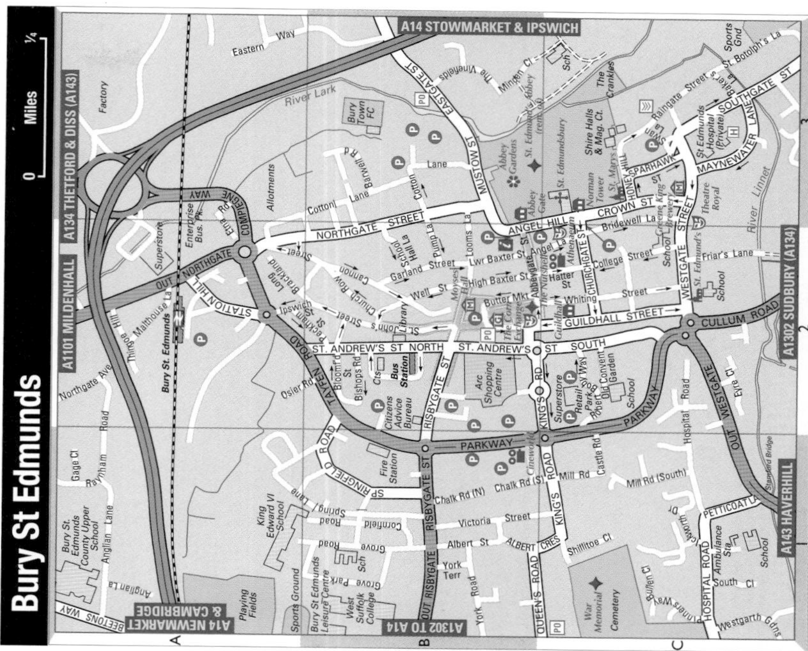

Bradford

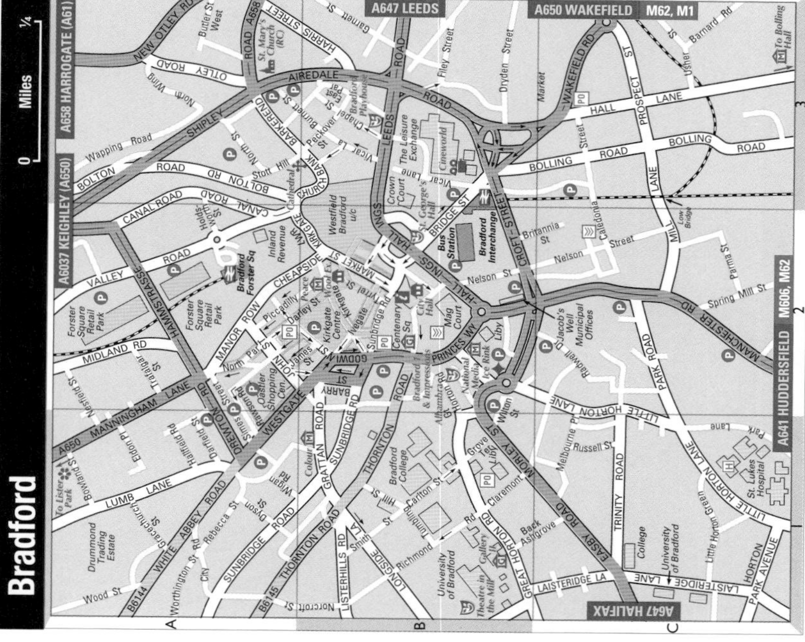

Bristol

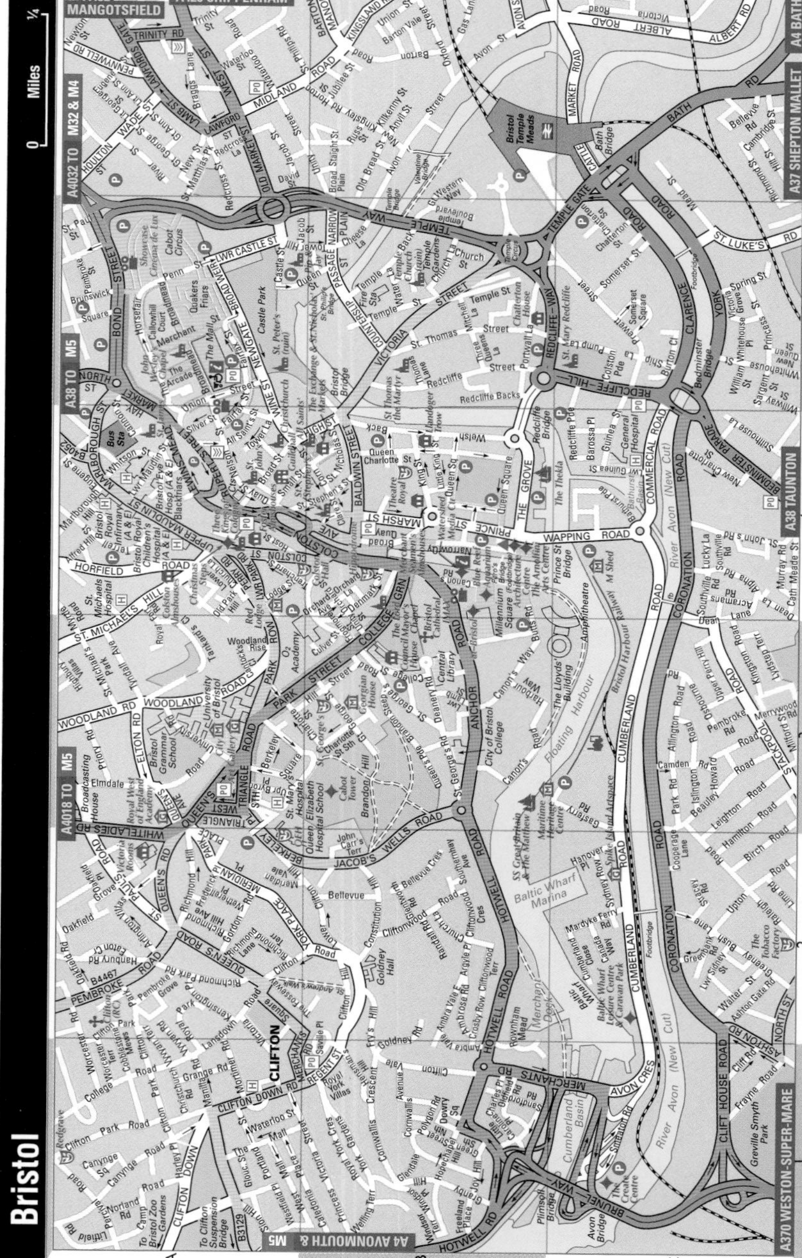

Bournemouth

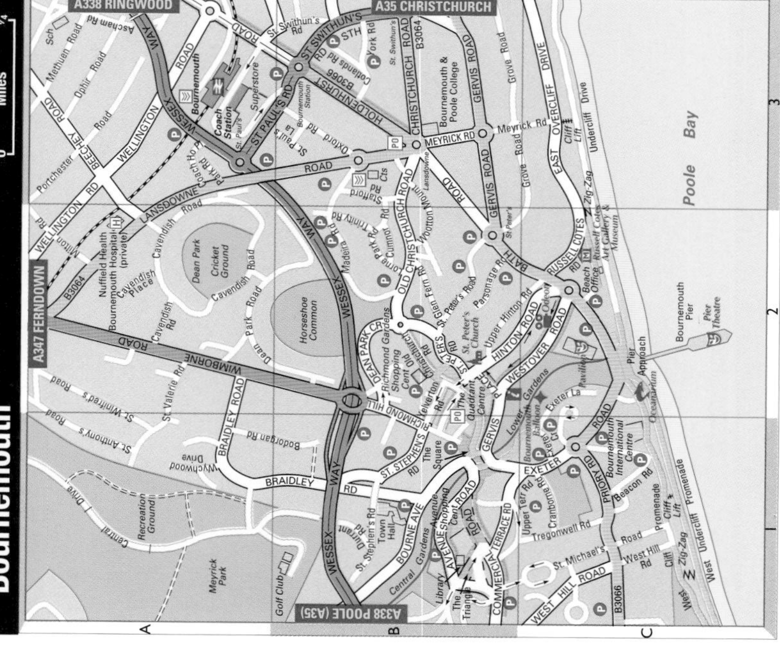

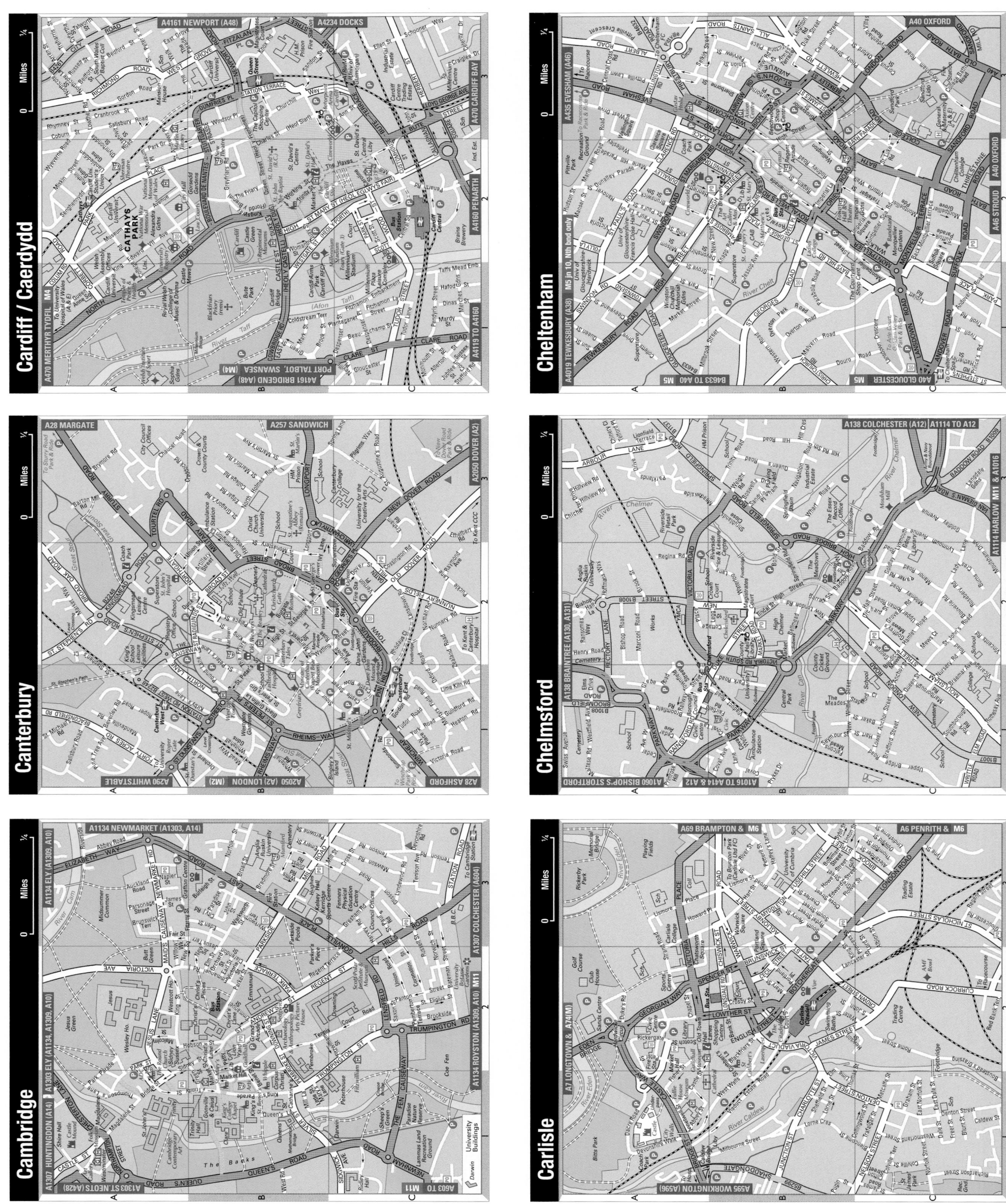
Cardiff / Caerdydd
Cheltenham
Canterbury
Chelmsford
Cambridge
Carlisle

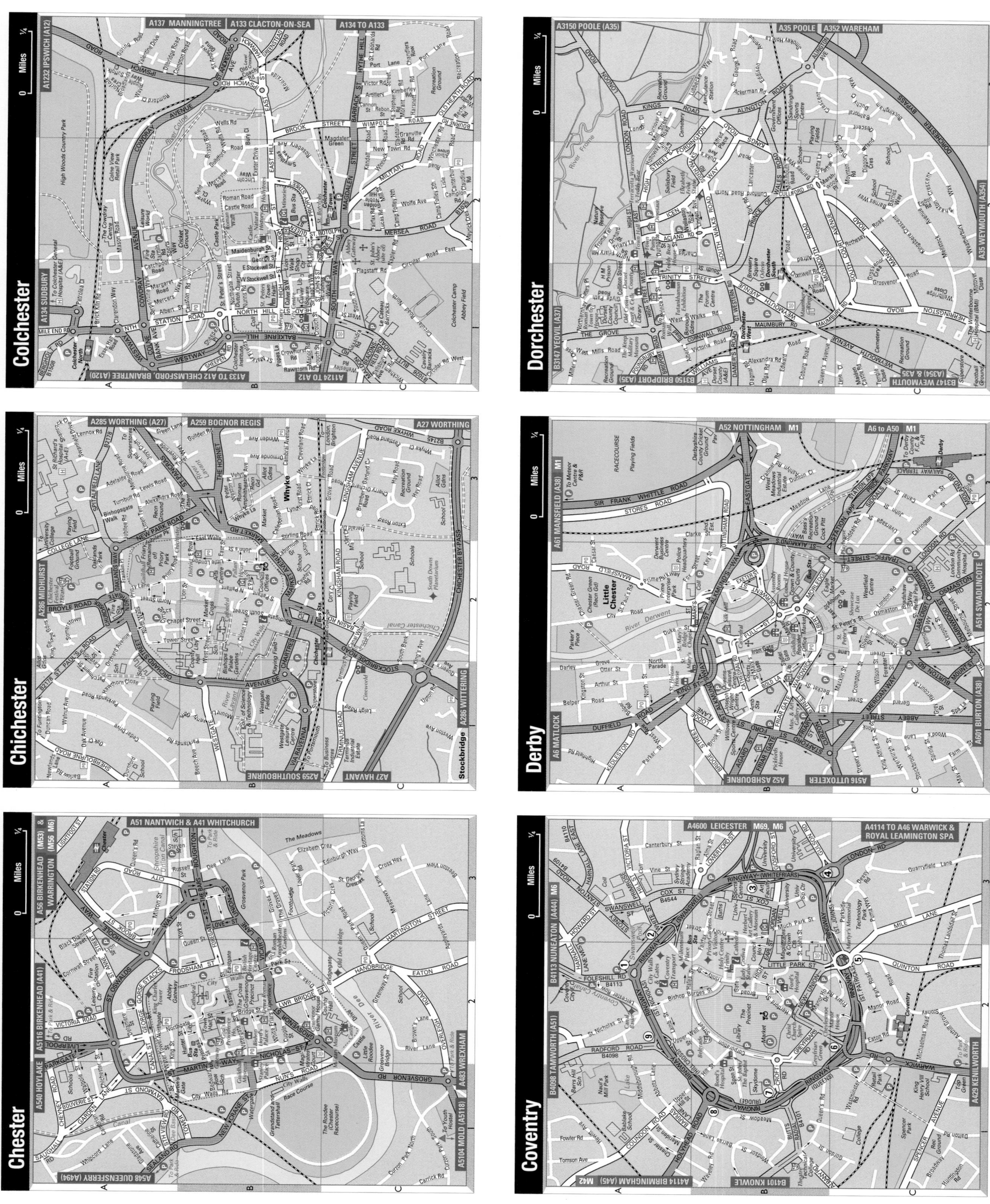
Colchester
A137 MANNINGTREE
A133 CLACTON-ON-SEA
A134 TO A133
A1232 IPSWICH (A12)
A134 SUDBURY
A133 TO A12 CHELMSFORD, BRAINTREE (A120)
A1124 TO A12
Dorchester
A3150 POOLE (A35)
A35 POOLE
A352 WAREHAM
A35 WEYMOUTH (A354)
B3147 WEYMOUTH (A354) & A35
B3150 BRIDPORT (A35)
B3147 YEOVIL (A37)
Chichester
A285 WORTHING (A27)
A259 BOGNOR REGIS
A27 WORTHING
A286 MIDHURST
A286 WITTERING
A27 HAVANT
A259 SOUTHBOURNE
Derby
A52 NOTTINGHAM M1
A6 to A50 M1
A61 MANSFIELD (A38) M1
A514 SWADLINCOTE
A601 BURTON (A38)
A6 MATLOCK
A516 UTTOXETER
A52 ASHBOURNE
Chester
A51 NANTWICH & A41 WHITCHURCH
A56 BIRKENHEAD (M53) & WARRINGTON (M56 M6)
A5116 BIRKENHEAD (A41)
A540 HOYLAKE
A548 QUEENSFERRY (A494)
A5104 MOLD (A5118)
A483 WREXHAM
Coventry
A4600 LEICESTER M69, M6
A4114 TO A46 WARWICK & ROYAL LEAMINGTON SPA
B4113 NUNEATON (A444) M6
B4098 TAMWORTH (A51)
A429 KENILWORTH
A4114 BIRMINGHAM (A45) M42
B4101 KNOWLE
Miles
0
¼

Durham

A691 CONSETT
A690 SUNDERLAND A1 (M)
A177 STOCKTON A1 (M)
A177 TO A167
A167 DARLINGTON A1 (M)
A690 WILLINGTON A167 NEWCASTLE A1 (M)
0 Miles ¼

Dundee

A929 FORFAR (A90)
A92 ABERDEEN (A90)
A92 EDINBURGH
A85 & PERTH (A90)
A923 COUPAR ANGUS
FIRTH OF TAY
0 Miles ¼

Dumfries

A76 KILMARNOCK
A701 MOFFAT
A709 LOCKERBIE
A780 ANNAN (A75)
A710 DALBEATTIE
A711 DALBEATTIE A780 STRANRAER (A75)
0 Miles ¼

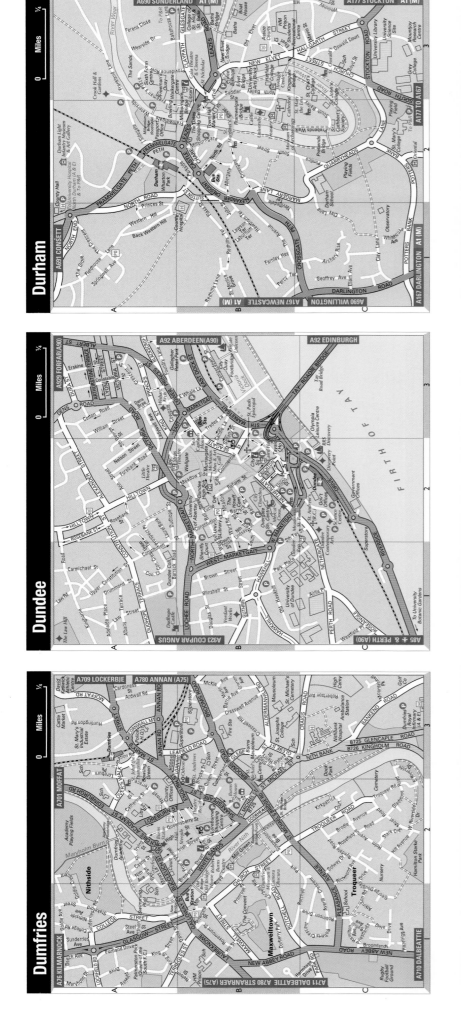

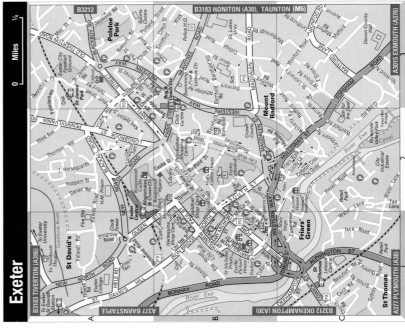

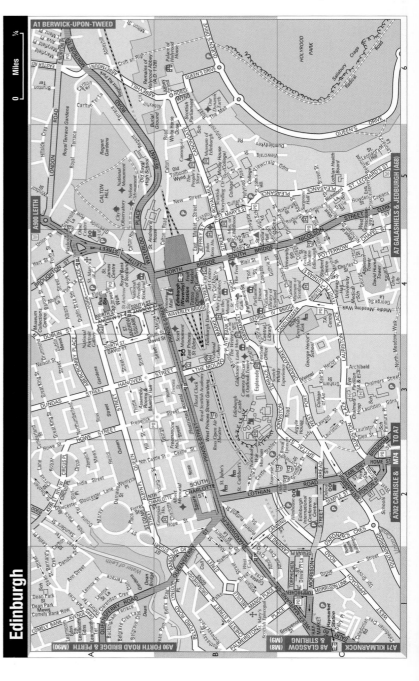

Fort William page 290 • **Glasgow** page 267 • **Gloucester** page 80 • **Grimsby** page 201 • **Hanley (Stoke-on-Trent)** page 168

337

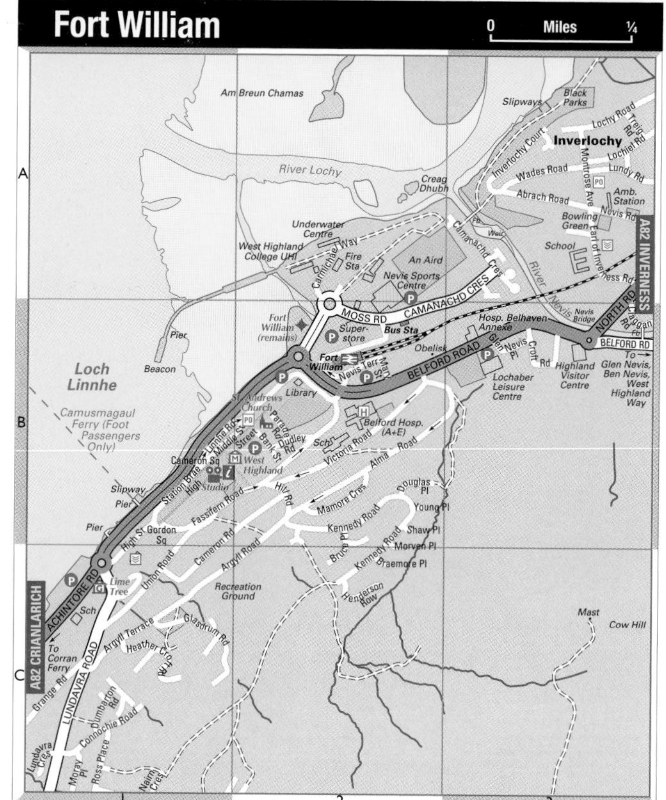

Hanley (Stoke-on-Trent)

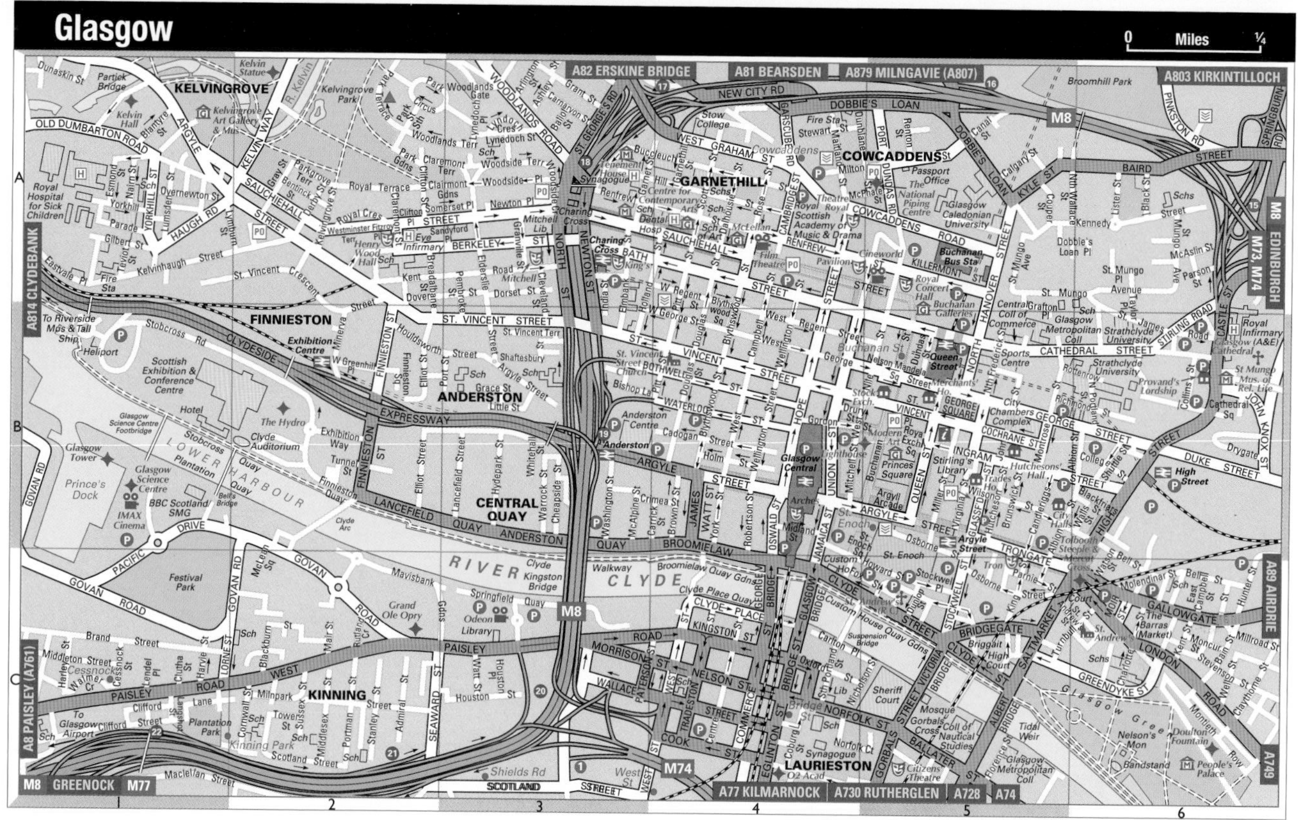

Glasgow

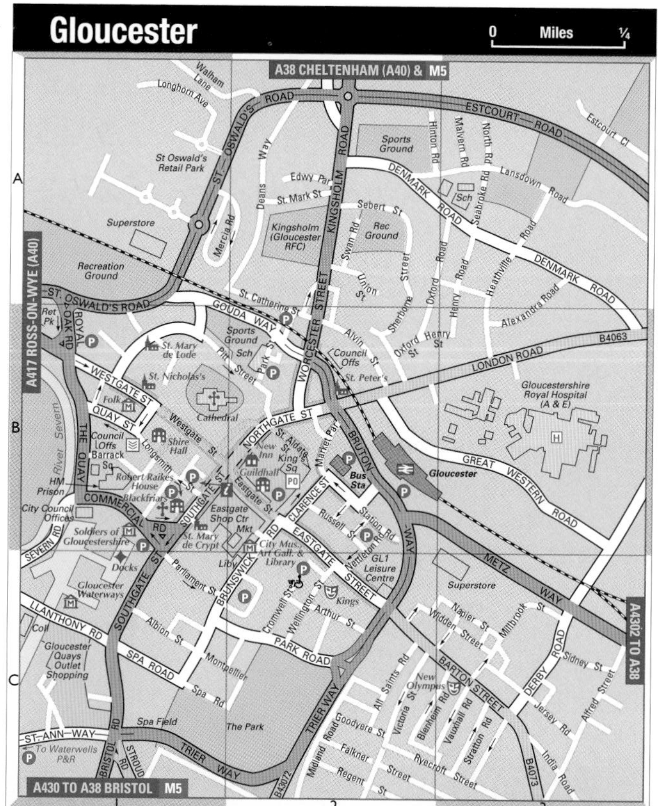

Grimsby

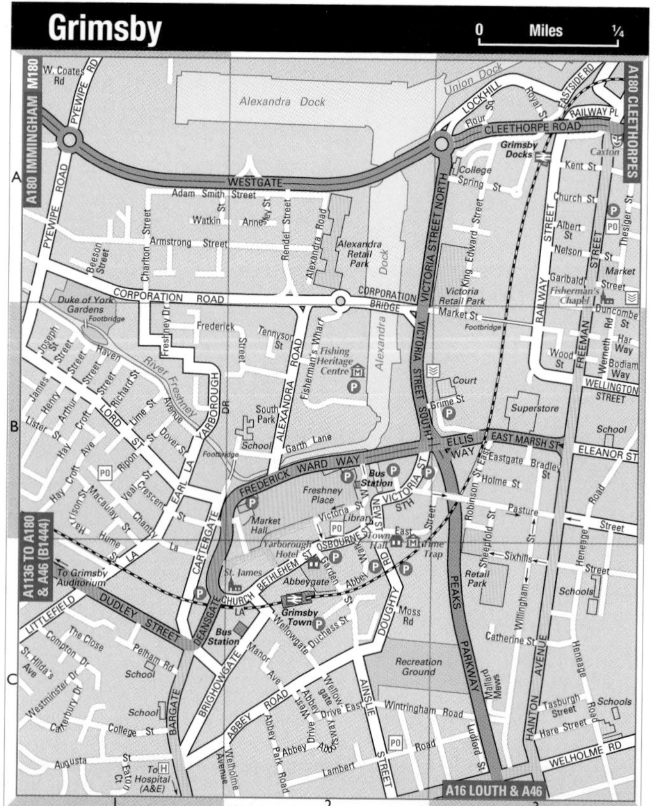

Fort William

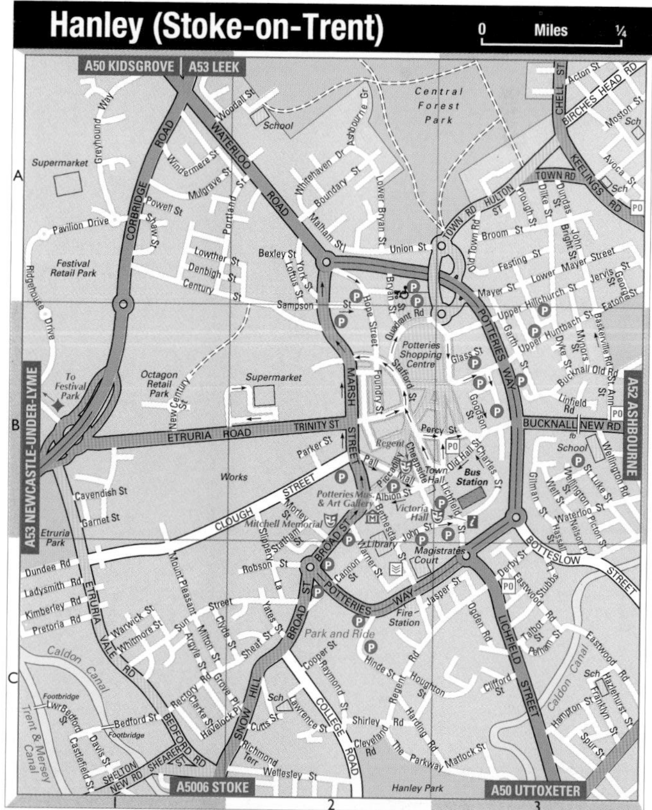

Gloucester

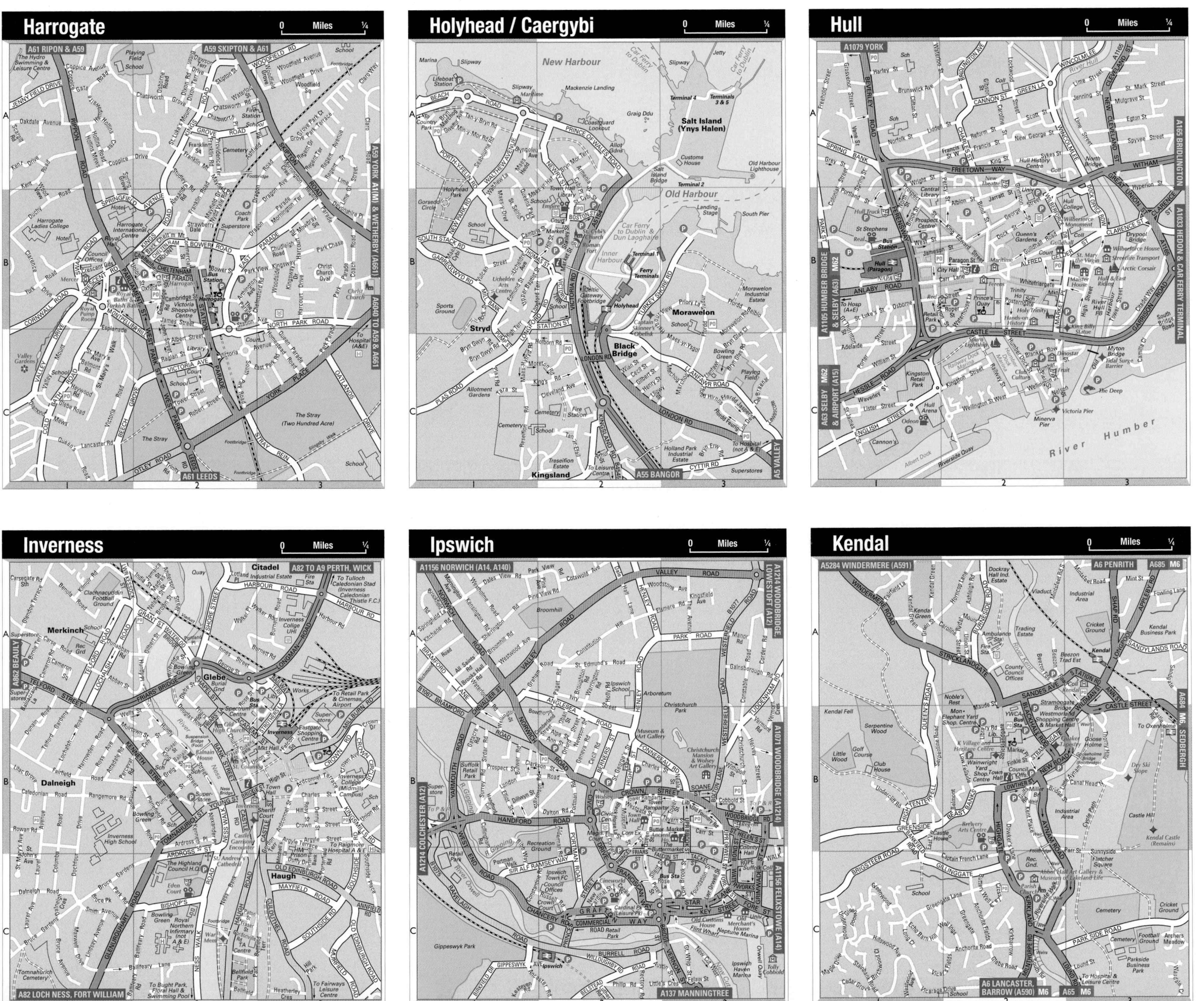
Harrogate
A61 RIPON & A59
A59 SKIPTON & A61
A59 YORK A1(M) & WETHERBY (A661)
A6040 TO A59 & A661
A61 LEEDS
The Stray (Two Hundred Acre)
Holyhead / Caergybi
New Harbour
Salt Island (Ynys Halen)
Old Harbour
A55 BANGOR
A5 VALLEY
Hull
A1079 YORK
A165 BRIDLINGTON
A1033 HEDON & CAR FERRY TERMINAL
A1105 HUMBER BRIDGE & SELBY (A63) M62
A63 SELBY M62 & AIRPORT (A15)
River Humber
Inverness
A82 TO A9 PERTH, WICK
A862 BEAULY
A82 LOCH NESS, FORT WILLIAM
Ipswich
A1156 NORWICH (A14, A140)
A1214 WOODBRIDGE, LOWESTOFT (A12)
A1071 WOODBRIDGE (A1214)
A1156 FELIXSTOWE (A14)
A1214 COLCHESTER (A12)
A137 MANNINGTREE
Kendal
A5284 WINDERMERE (A591)
A6 PENRITH
A685 M6
A684 M6, SEDBERGH
A6 LANCASTER, BARROW (A590) M6
A65 M6
Miles

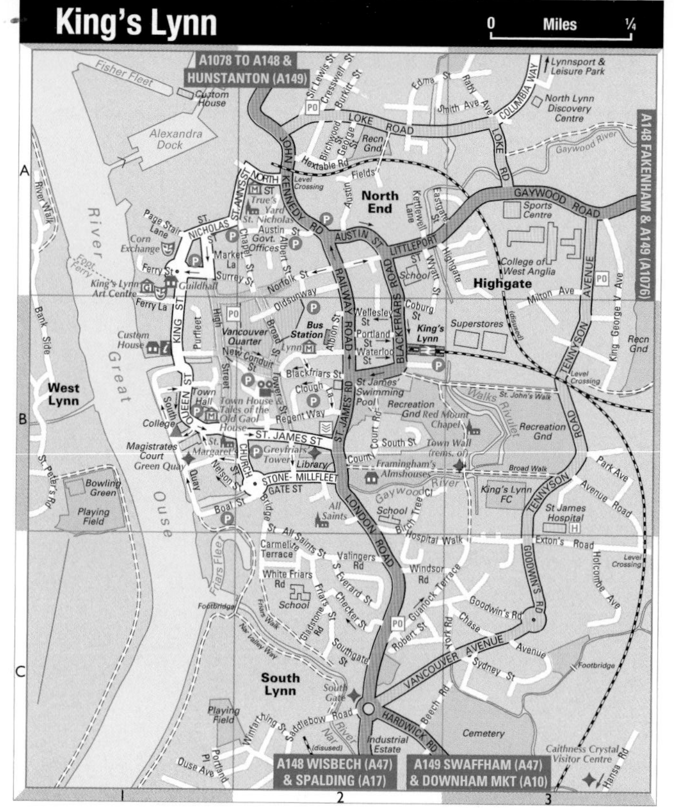

Leeds

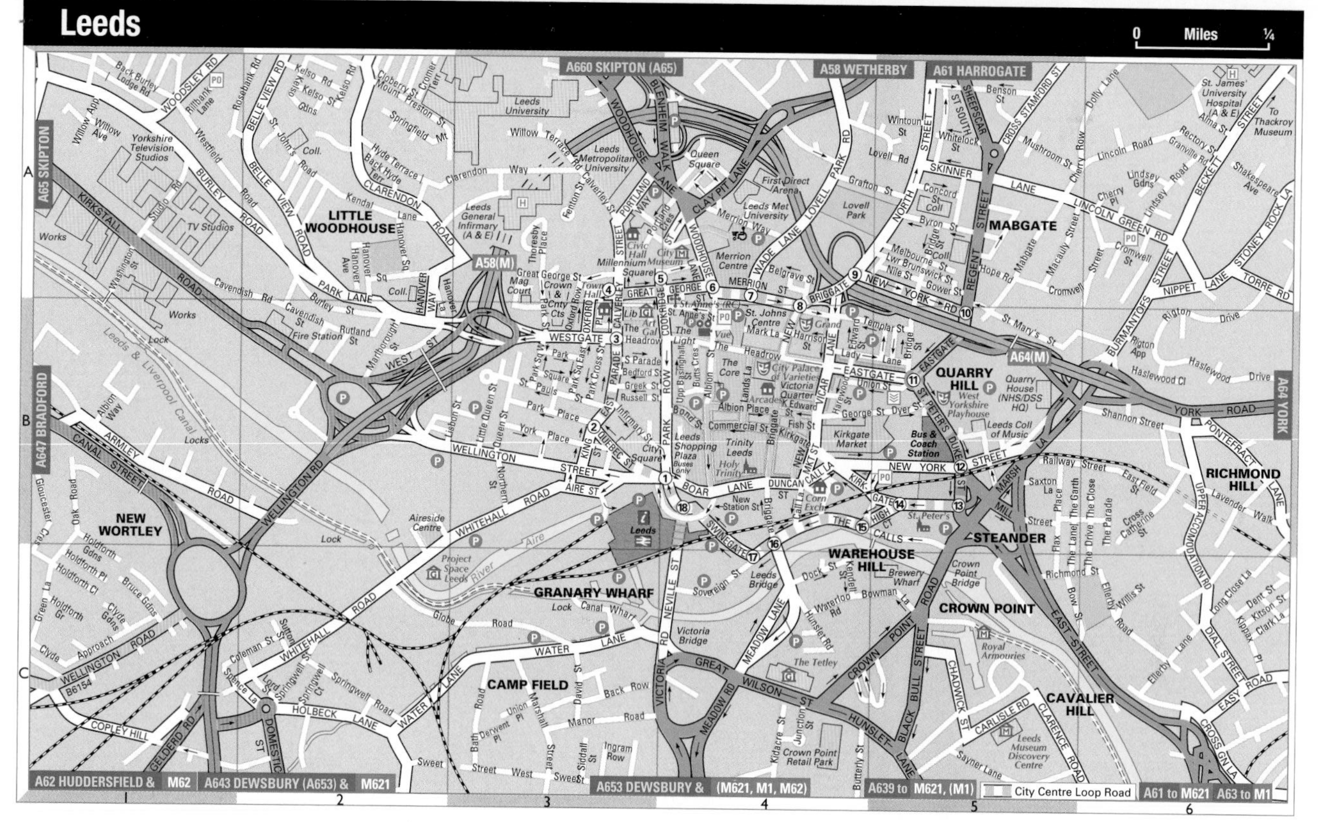

Lewes

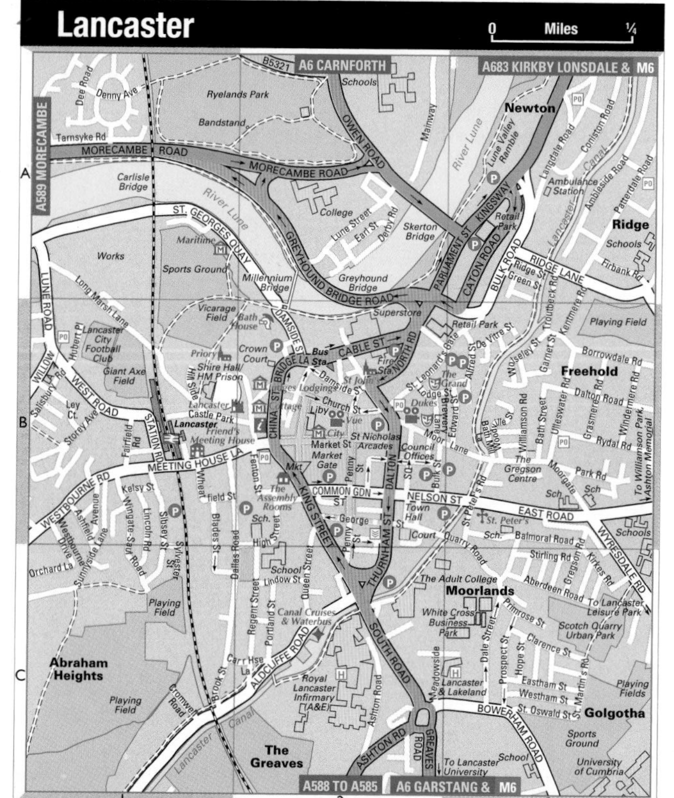

Leicester

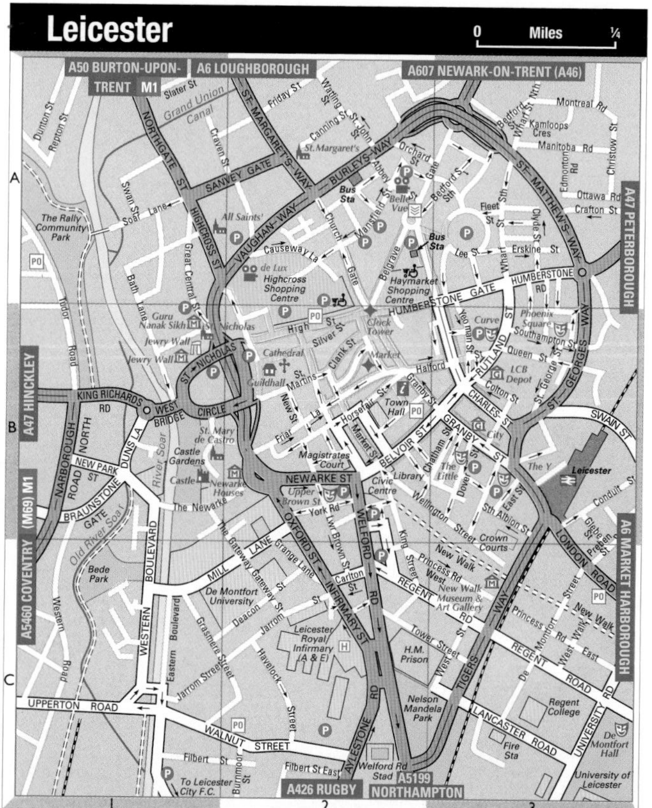

King's Lynn

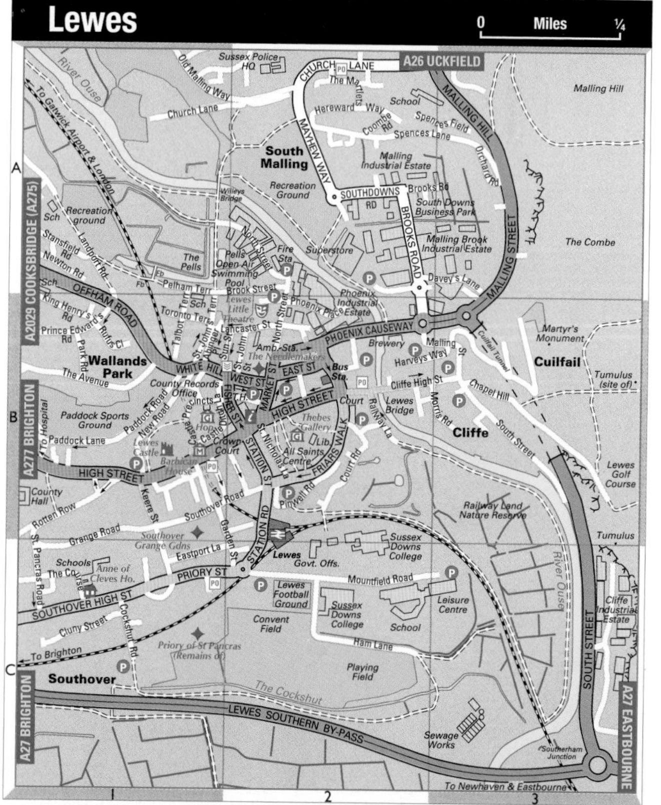

Lancaster

340
London streets
ST. JOHN'S WOOD
REGENT'S PARK
SOMERS TOWN
LISSON GREEN
PADDINGTON
FITZROVIA
BLOOMSBURY
SOHO
MAYFAIR
HYDE PARK
KENSINGTON GARDENS
THE SERPENTINE
GREEN PARK
ST. JAMES'S
ST. JAMES'S PARK
KNIGHTSBRIDGE
BROMPTON
WESTMINSTER
PIMLICO
Euston
Marylebone
Paddington
Victoria
Buckingham Palace
British Museum
Marble Arch
Hyde Park Corner

HOXTON
FINSBURY
SHOREDITCH
CLERKENWELL
HOLBORN
THE CITY
SOUTHWARK
SOUTH BANK
BERMONDSEY
NEWINGTON
LAMBETH
RIVER
THAMES
The Barbican
St Paul's Cathedral
Liverpool Street
London Bridge
Waterloo
Elephant & Castle
Tate Modern
The Tower of London
Imperial War Museum
Lincoln's Inn Fields
Miles
0
1/2
5
6
7
8
B
C
D
E
F

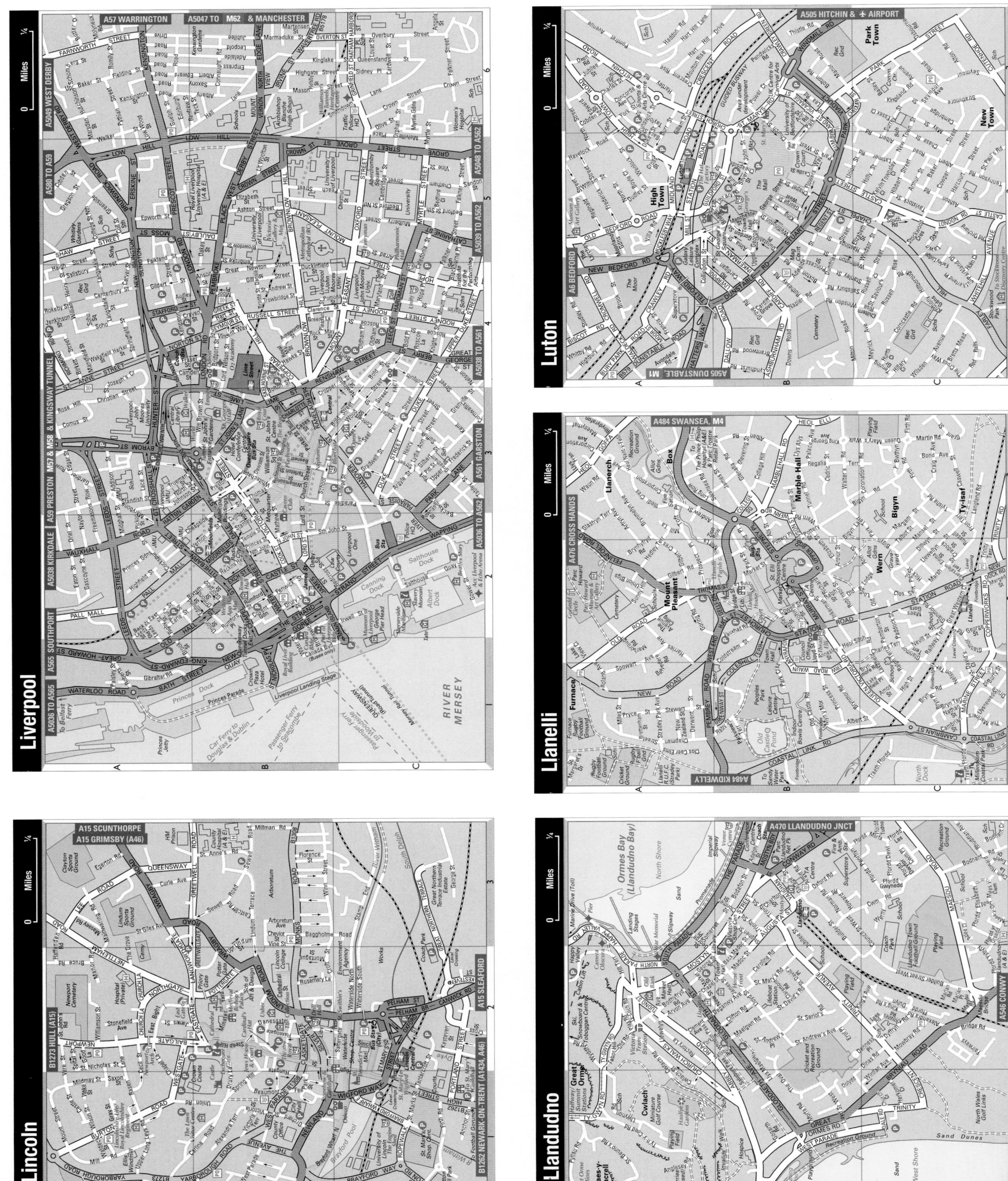

Liverpool

Luton

Llanelli

Lincoln

Llandudno

Macclesfield
Manchester
Maidstone
Merthyr Tydfil / Merthyr Tudful
Middlesbrough

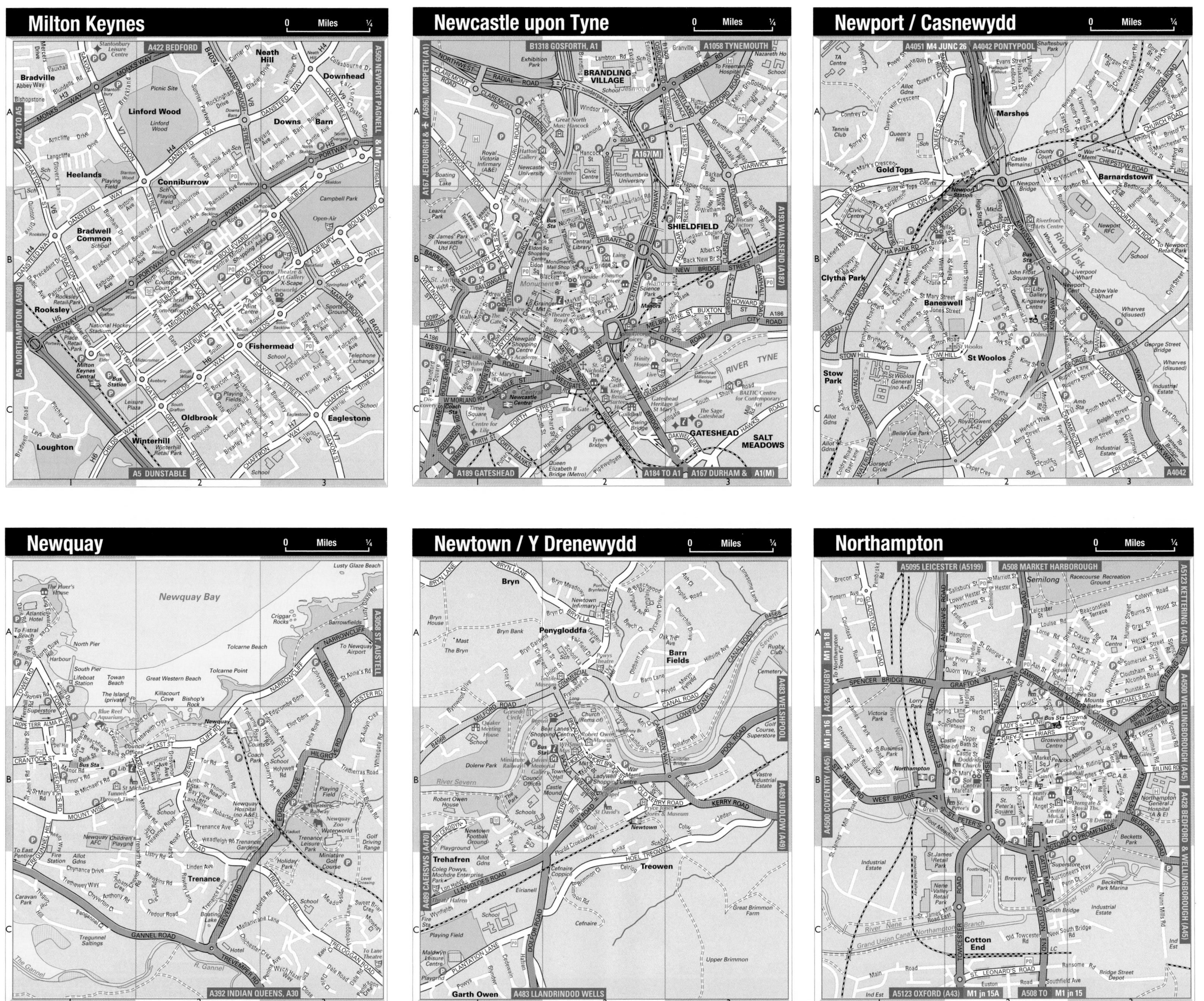
Milton Keynes
Newcastle upon Tyne
Newport / Casnewydd
Newquay
Newtown / Y Drenewydd
Northampton

Norwich
A1067 CROMER (A140)
A1151 WROXHAM
A1242 GREAT YARMOUTH (A47)
A1074 SWAFFHAM (A47)
A11 THETFORD
A1056 IPSWICH (A140)
A147 LOWESTOFT (A146)
Nottingham
A60 MANSFIELD
A612 NEWARK-ON-TRENT
A609 A610 to M1
A52 DERBY & M1
A6005 LONG EATON
A453 TAMWORTH & M1
A6008
A60 LOUGHBOROUGH
Oban
A85 CRIANLARICH (A82)
A816 LOCHGILPHEAD
Oban Bay
Soroba
Oxford
A4144 CHELTENHAM (A40)
A4165 BANBURY (A4260)
University Buildings
A420 LONDON (A40, M40)
A4158 MAIDENHEAD (A4074)
A420 SWINDON
A4144 NEWBURY (A34)
Perth
A85 CRIEFF
A912 PITLOCHRY (A9)
A93 BLAIRGOWRIE
A94 COUPAR ANGUS
A85 DUNDEE (A90)
A93 STIRLING (A9)
A912 EDINBURGH (M90)
River Tay
Peterborough
A15 SLEAFORD
A1139 TO A15, A47, A16
A1179 LEICESTER (A47)
A605 TO A1
A15 HUNTINGTON A1(M)
A605 WHITTLESEY
A1139 TO A1(M)
Eastgate
New Fletton

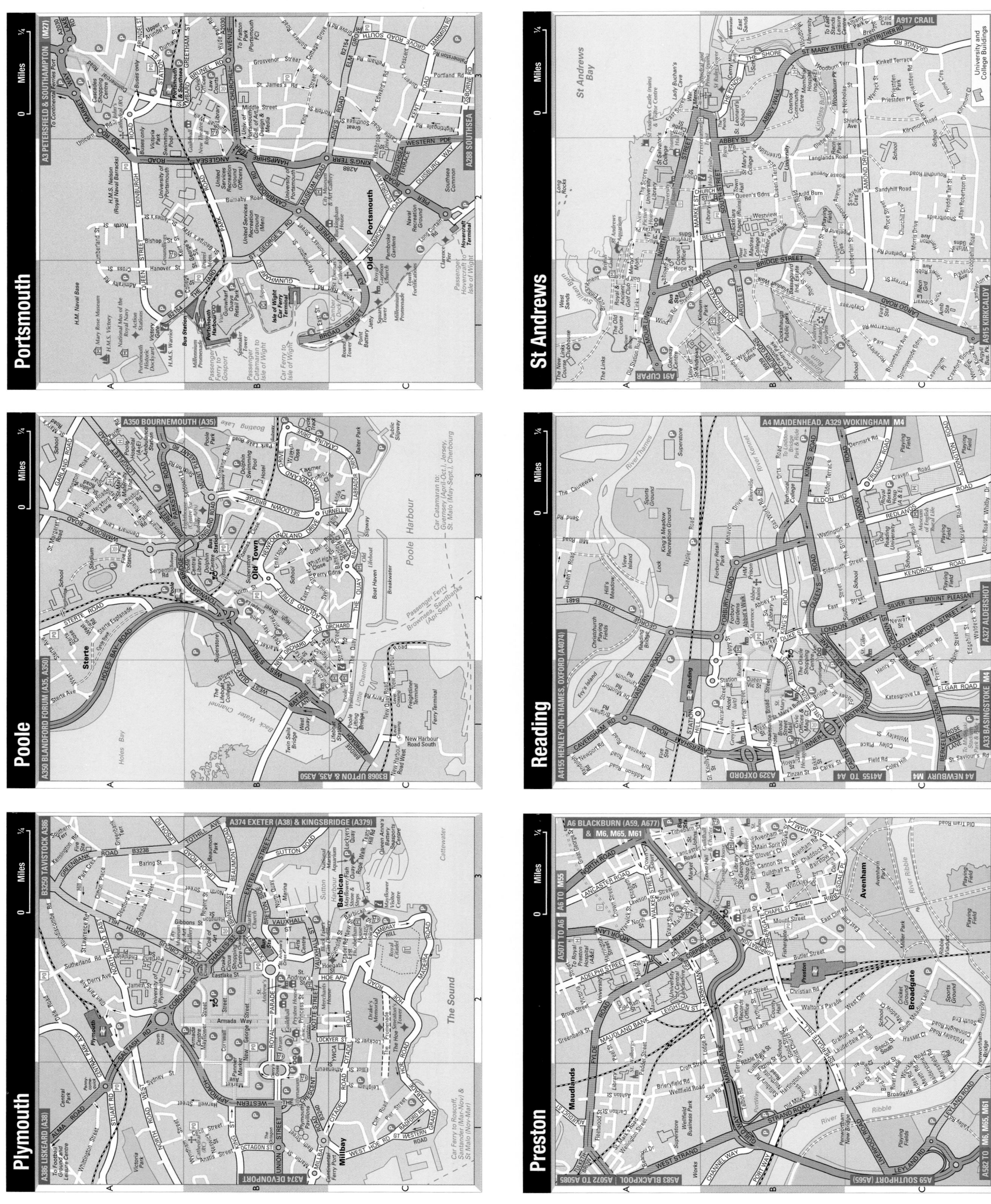
Portsmouth
St Andrews
Poole
Reading
Plymouth
Preston

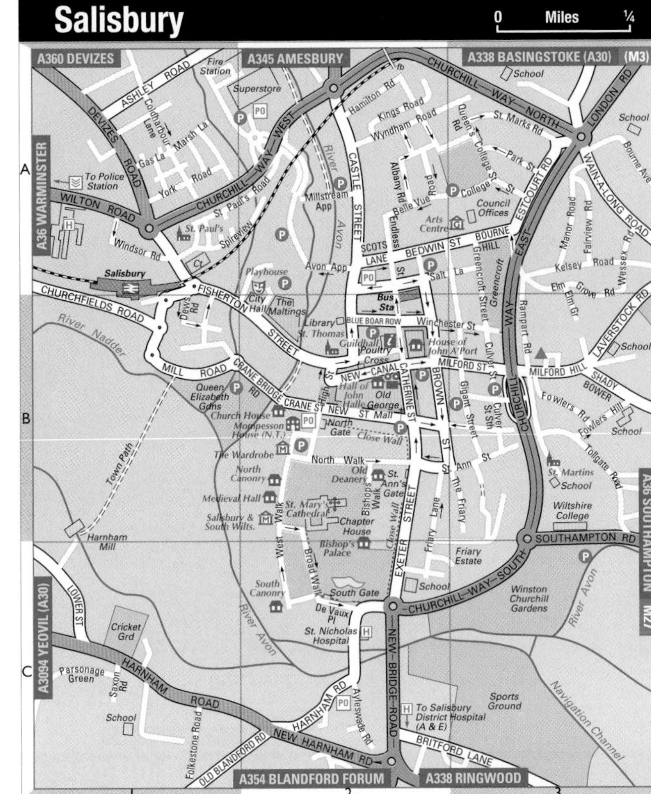
Salisbury
0 Miles 1/4
A360 DEVIZES
A345 AMESBURY
A338 BASINGSTOKE (A30) (M3)
A36 WARMINSTER
A36 SOUTHAMPTON M27
A3094 YEOVIL (A30)
A354 BLANDFORD FORUM
A338 RINGWOOD

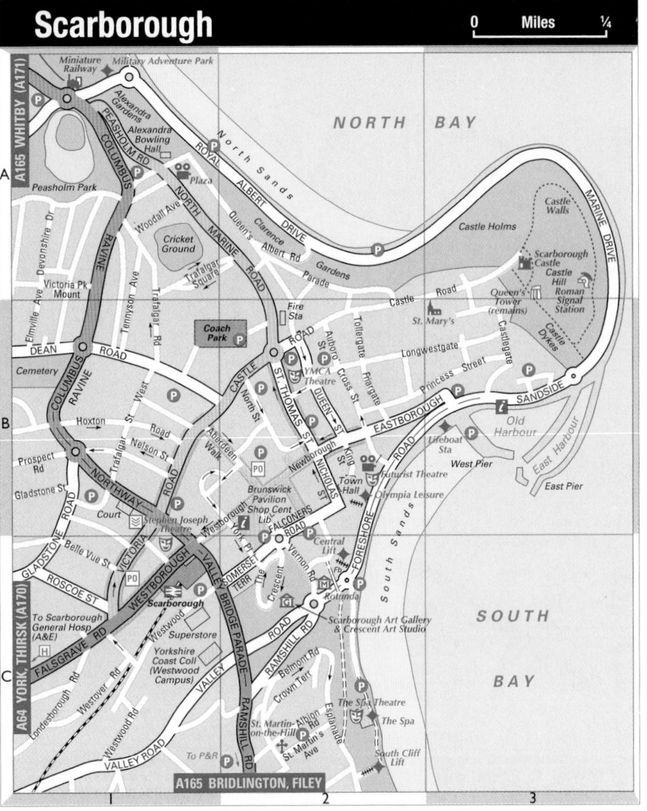
Scarborough
0 Miles 1/4
NORTH BAY
SOUTH BAY
A165 WHITBY (A171)
A64 YORK, THIRSK (A170)
A165 BRIDLINGTON, FILEY

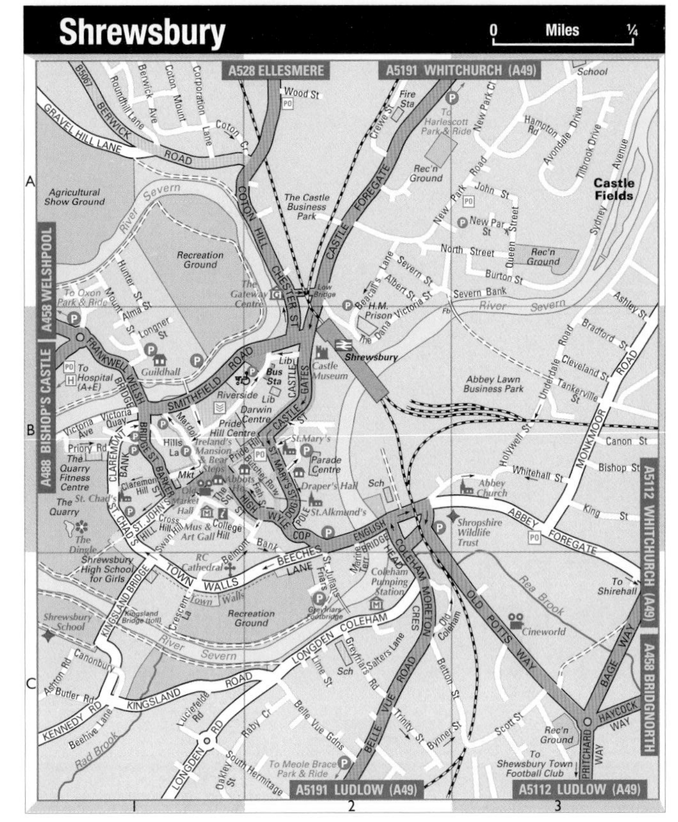
Shrewsbury
0 Miles 1/4
A528 ELLESMERE
A5191 WHITCHURCH (A49)
A458 WELSHPOOL
A488 BISHOP'S CASTLE
A5112 WHITCHURCH (A49)
A458 BRIDGNORTH
A5191 LUDLOW (A49)
A5112 LUDLOW (A49)

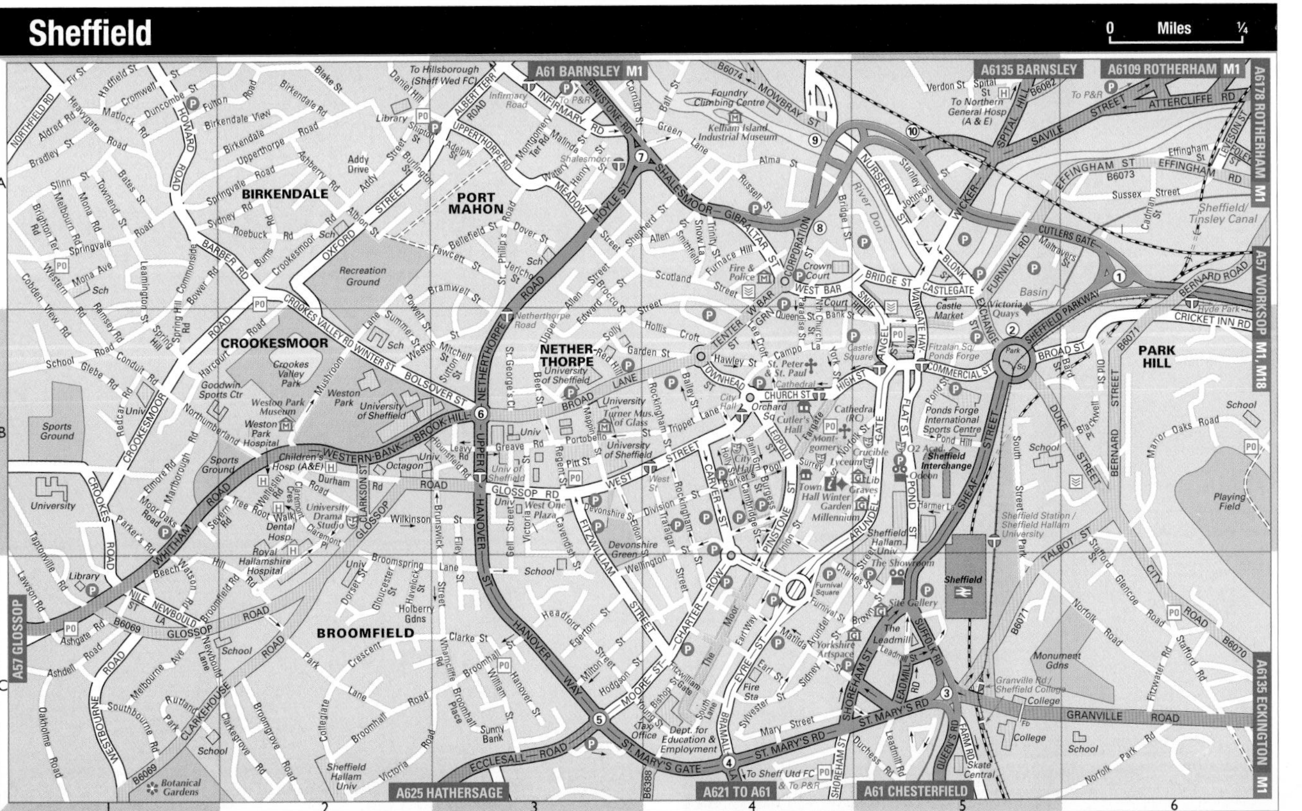
Sheffield
0 Miles 1/4
A61 BARNSLEY M1
A6135 BARNSLEY
A6109 ROTHERHAM M1
A6178 ROTHERHAM M1
A57 WORKSOP M1, M18
A6135 ECKINGTON M1
A57 GLOSSOP
A625 HATHERSAGE
A621 TO A61
A61 CHESTERFIELD
BIRKENDALE
PORT MAHON
CROOKESMOOR
NETHER-THORPE
PARK HILL
BROOMFIELD

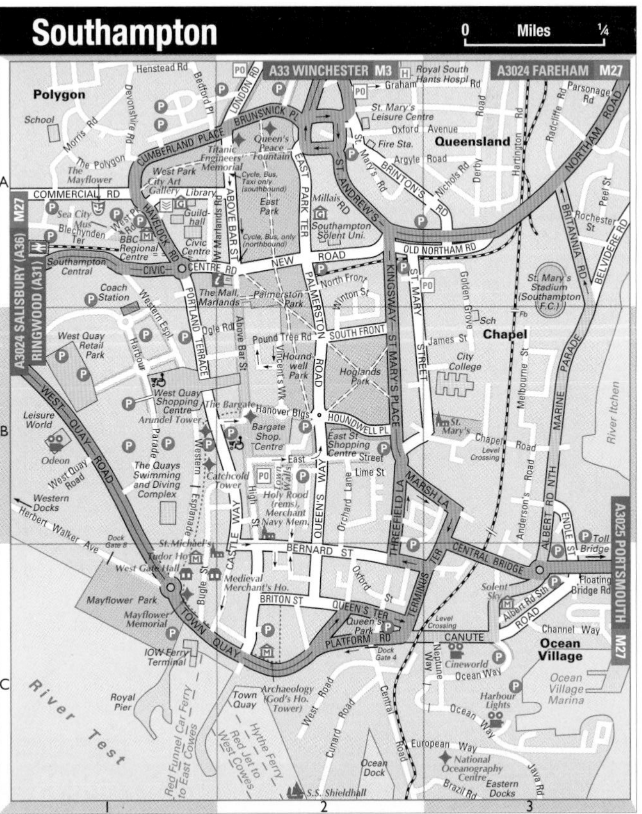
Southampton
0 Miles 1/4
A33 WINCHESTER M3
A3024 FAREHAM M27
A3024 SALISBURY (A36) M27
RINGWOOD (A31)
A3025 PORTSMOUTH M27
Polygon
Queensland
Chapel
Ocean Village
River Test

348

Southend page 69 • **Stirling** page 278 • **Stoke** page 168 • **Stratford-upon-Avon** page 118 • **Sunderland** page 243 • **Swansea** page 56

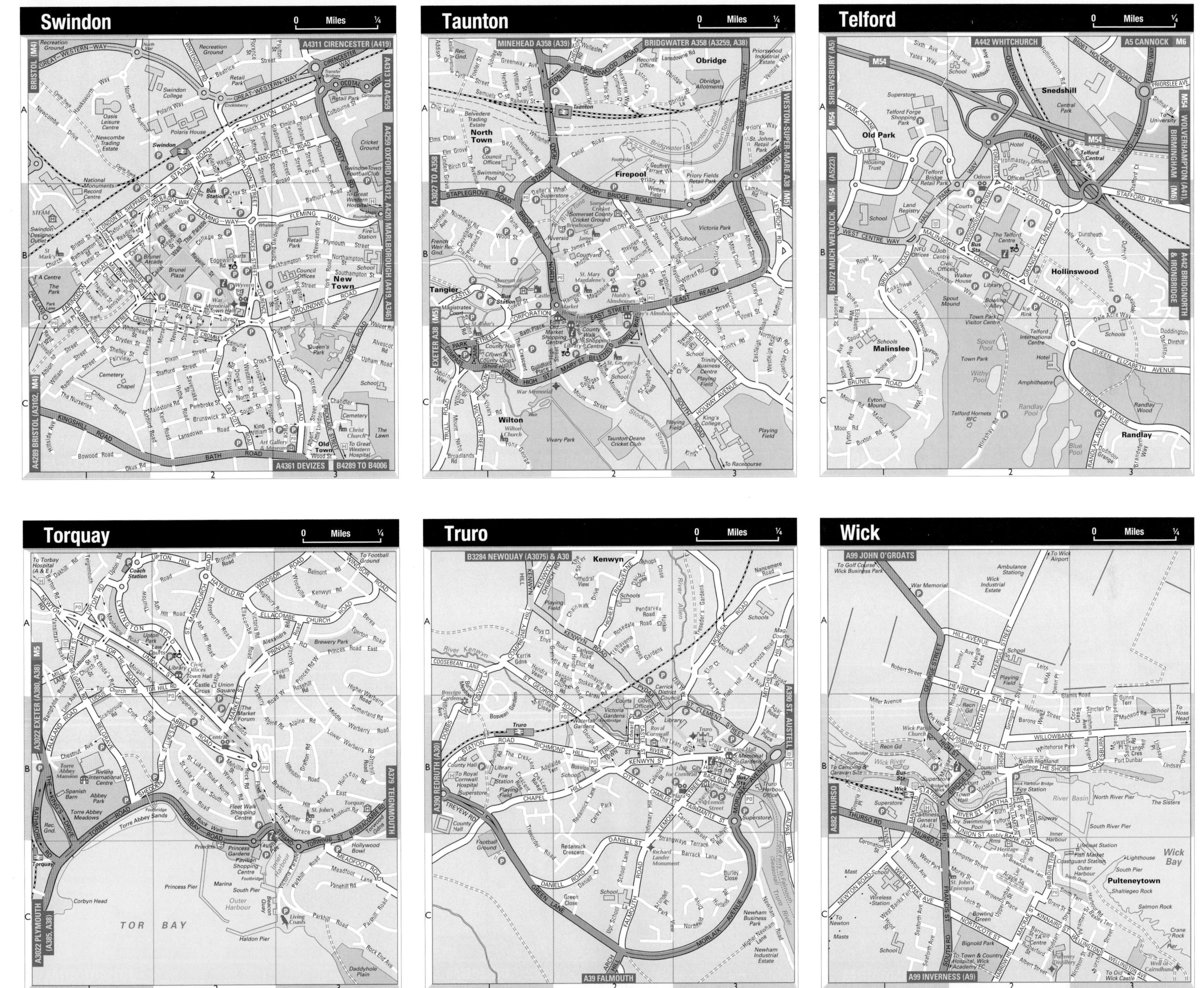
Swindon
Taunton
Telford
Torquay
Truro
Wick

350

Winchester page 33 • **Windsor** page 66 • **Wolverhampton** page 133 • **Worcester** page 117 • **Wrexham** page 166 • **York** page 207

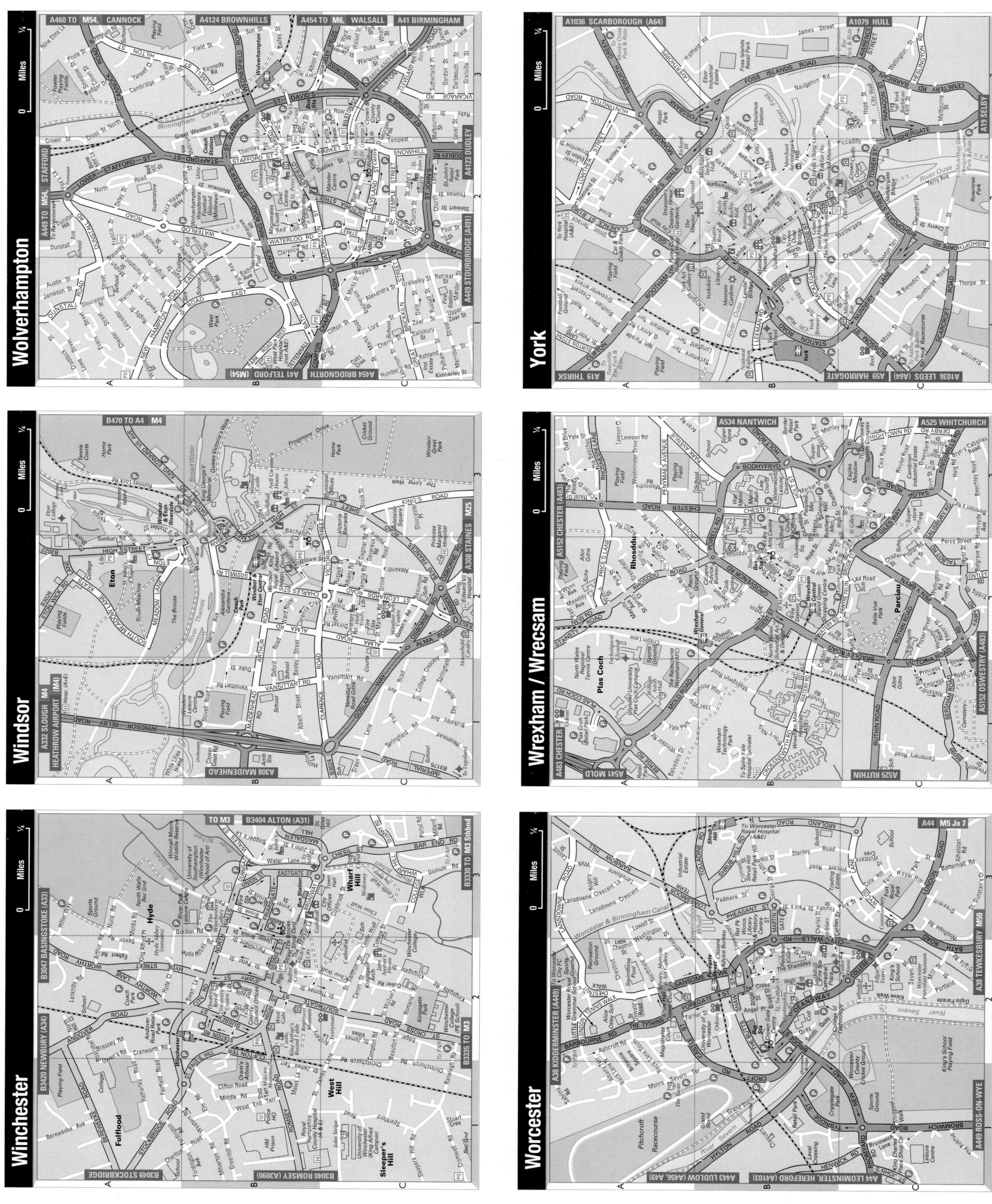

Wolverhampton

York

Windsor

Wrexham / Wrecsam

Winchester

Worcester

Town plan indexes

Bacchus Rd A1
Bagot St B4
Banbury St B5
Barford Rd B1
Barford St C4
Barn St C5
Barnwell Rd C6
Barr St A3
Barrack St B5
Bartholomew St C4
Barwick St B4
Bath Row C3
Beaufort Rd C1
Belmont Row B5
Benson Rd A1
Berkley St C3
Bexhill Gr C3
Birchall St C5
Birmingham City FC C6
Birmingham City Hospital (A&E) A1
Bishopsgate St C3
Blews St A4
Bloomsbury St A6
Blucher St C3
Bordesley St C4
Bowyer St C5
Bradburne Way A5
Bradford St C5
Branston St A3
Brearley St A4
Brewery St A4
Bridge St A3
Bridge St C3
Bridge St West A4
Brindley Dr B3
Broad St C3
Broad St UGC C2
Broadway Plaza C2
Bromley St C5
Bromsgrove St C4
Brookfield Rd A2
Browning St C2
Bryant St A1
Buckingham St A3
Bullring C4
Bull St B4
Cambridge St C3
Camden Dr B3
Camden St B2
Cannon St C4
Cardigan St B5
Carlisle St A1
Carlyle Rd C1
Caroline St B3
Carver St B2
Cato St A6
Cattell Rd C6
Cattells Gr A6
Cawdor Cr C1
Cecil St B4
Cemetery A2/B2
Cemetery La A2
Ctr Link Industrial Est A6
Charlotte St B3
Cheapside C4
Chester St A5
Children's Hospital (A&E) B4
Church St B4
Claremont Rd A2
Clarendon Rd C1
Clark St C1
Clement St B3
Clissold St B2
Cliveland St B4
Coach Station C5
College St B2
Colmore Circus B4
Colmore Row B4
Commercial St C3
Constitution Hill B3
Convention Ctr, The C3
Cope St B2
Coplow St B1
Corporation St B4
Council House B3
County Court B4
Coveley Gr A2
Coventry Rd C6
Coventry St C5
Cox St B3
Crabtree Rd A2
Cregoe St C3
Crescent Ave A2
Crescent Theatre C3
Cromwell St A6
Cromwell St B3
Curzon St B5
Cuthbert Rd B1
Dale End B4
Dart St C6
Dartmouth Circus A4
Dartmouth Middleway A5
Dental Hospital B4
Deritend C5
Devon St A6
Devonshire St A1
Digbeth Civic Hall C5
Digbeth High St C4
Dolman St B6
Dover St A1
Duchess Rd C2
Duddeston B6
Duddeston Manor Rd B5
Duddeston Mill Rd B6
Duddeston Mill Trading Estate B6
Dudley Rd B1
Edgbaston Sh Ctr C2
Edmund St B3
Edward St B3
Elkington St A4
Ellen St B2
Ellis St C3
Erskine St B6
Essex St C4
Eyre St B2
Farm Croft A3
Farm St A3
Fazeley St B4/C5
Felstead Way B5
Finstall Cl B5
Five Ways C2
Fleet St B3
Floodgate St C5
Ford St A2
Fore St C4
Forster St B5
Francis Rd C2
Francis St B5
Frankfort St A4
Frederick St B3
Freeth St C1
Freightliner Terminal B6
Garrison La C6
Garrison St B6
Gas St C3
Geach St A4
George St B3
George St West B2
Gibb St C5
Gillott Rd B1
Gilby Rd C2
Glover St C5
Goode Ave A2
Goodrick Way A6
Gordon St B6
Graham St B3
Granville St C3
Gray St C6
Great Barr St C5
Great Charles St B3
Great Francis St B6
Great Hampton Row A3
Great Hampton St A3
Great King St A3
Great Lister St A5
Great Tindal St C2
Green La C6
Green St C5
Greenway St C6
Grosvenor St West C2
Guest Gr A3
Guild Cl C2
Guildford Dr A4
Guthrie Cl A3
Hagley Rd C1
Hall St B3
Hampton St A3
Handsworth New Rd A1
Hanley St B4
Harford St A3
Harmer Rd A2
Harold Rd C1
Hatchett St A4
Heath Mill La C5
Heath St B1
Heath St South B1
Heaton St A2
Heneage St B5
Henrietta St B4
Herbert Rd C6
High St C4
High St C5
Hilden Rd B5
Hill St C3/C4
Hindlow Cl B6
Hingeston St B2
Hippodrome Theatre C4
HM Prison A1
Hockley Circus A2
Hockley Hill A3
Hockley St A3
Holliday St C3
Holloway Circus C4
Holloway Head C3
Holt St B5
Hooper St B1
Horse Fair C4
Hospital St A4
Howard St B3
Howe St B5
Hubert St A5
Hunters Rd A2
Hunters Vale A3
Huntly Rd C2
Hurst St C4
Icknield Port Rd B1
Icknield Sq B2
Icknield St A2/B2
Ikon Gallery C3
Information Ctr C4
Inge St C4
Irving St C3
Ivy La C5
James Watt Queensway B4
Jennens Rd B5
Jewellery Quarter A3
Jewellery Quarter Museum B3
John Bright St C4
Keeley St C6
Kellett Rd B5
Kent St C4
Kenyon St B3
Key Hill A3
Kilby Ave C2
King Edwards Rd B2
King Edwards Rd C3
Kingston Rd C6
Kirby Rd A1
Ladywood Arts & Ctr B1
Ladywood Middleway C2/C3
Ladywood Rd C1
Lancaster St B4
Landor St B6
Law Courts B4
Lawford Cl B5
Lawley Middleway B5
Ledbury Cl C2
Ledsam St B2
Lees St A1
Legge La B3
Lennox St A3
Library A6/C3
Library Walk B2
Lighthorne Ave B2
Link Rd B1
Lionel St B3
Lister St B5
Little Ann St C5
Little Hall Rd A6
Liverpool St C5
Livery St B3/B4
Lodge Rd A1
Lord St A5
Love La A5
Loveday St B4
Lower Dartmouth St C6
Lower Loveday St B4
Lower Tower St A4
Lower Trinty St C5
Ludgate Hill B3
Mailbox Centre & BBC C3
Margaret St B3
Markby Rd A1
Marroway St B1
Maxstoke St C6
Melvina Rd A6
Meriden St C4
Metropolitan (RC) B4
Midland St B6
Milk St C5
Mill St A5
Millennium Point B5
Miller St A4
Milton St A4
Moat La C4
Montague Rd C1
Montague St C5
Monument Rd C1
Moor Street C4
Moor St Queensway C4
Moorsom St A4
Morville St C2
Mosborough Cr A3
Moseley St C4
Mott St B3
Mus & Art Gallery B3
Musgrave Rd A1
National Indoor Arena C2
National Sea Life Centre C3
Navigation St C3
Nechell's Park Rd A6
Nechells Parkway B5
Nechells Pl A6
New Bartholomew St C4
New Canal St C5
New John St West A3
New Spring St B2
New St C4
New Street C4
New Summer St A4
New Town Row A4
Newhall Hill B3
Newhall St B3
Newton St B4
Newtown A4
Noel Rd C1
Norman St A1
Northbrook St B1
Northwood St B3
Norton St A2
Old Crown House C5
Old Rep Theatre, The C4
Old Snow Hill B4
Oliver Rd C1
Oliver St A5
Osler St C1
Oxford St C5
Pallasades Centre C4
Palmer St C5
Paradise Circus C3
Paradise St C3
Park Rd A2
Park St C4
Pavilions Centre C4
Paxton Rd A2
Peel St A1
Penn St B5
Pershore St C4
Phillips St A4
Pickford St C5
Pinfold St C4
Pitsford St A2
Plough & Harrow Rd C1
Police Station A4/B1/B4/C2/C4
Pope St B2
Portland Rd C1
Post Office A3/A5/B1/B3/B4/B5/C2/C3/C5
Preston Rd A1
Price St B4
Princip St B4
Printing House St B4
Priory Queensway B4
Pritchett St A4
Proctor St A5
Queensway B3
Radnor St A2
Rea St C4
Regent Pl B3
Register Office C3
Repertory Theatre C3
Reservoir Rd C1
Richard St A5
River St C5
Rocky La A5/A6
Rodney Cl C2
Roseberry St B2
Rotton Park St B1
Rupert St A5
Ruston St C2
Ryland St C2
St Andrew's Ind Est C6
St Andrew's Rd C6
St Andrew's St C6
St Bolton St C6
St Chads Queensway B4
St Clements Rd A6
St George's St A3
St James Pl B5
St Marks Cr B2
St Martin's C4
St Paul's B3
St Paul's B3
St Paul's Sq B3
St Philip's B4
St Stephen's St A4
St Thomas' Peace Garden C3
St Vincent St C2
Saltley Rd A6
Sand Pits Pde B3
Severn St C3
Shadwell St B4
Sheepcote St C2
Shefford Rd A4
Sherborne St C2
Shylton's Croft C2
Skipton Rd C2
Smallbrook Queensway C4
Smith St A3
Snow Hill B4
Snow Hill Queensway B4
Soho, Benson Rd A1
South Rd A2
Spencer St B3
Spring Hill B2
Staniforth St B4
Station St C4
Steelhouse La B4
Stephenson St C4
Steward St B2
Stirling Rd C1
Stour St B2
Suffolk St C3
Summer Hill Rd B2
Summer Hill St B2
Summer Hill Terr B2
Summer La A4
Summer Row B3
Summerfield Cr B1
Summerfield Park B1
Sutton St C3
Swallow St C3
Sydney Rd C6
Symphony Hall C3
Talbot St A1
Temple Row C4
Temple St C4
Templefield St C6
Tenby St B3
Tenby St North B2
Tennant St C2/C3
The Crescent A2
Thimble Mill La A6
Thinktank (Science & Discovery) B5
Thomas St A4
Thorpe St C4
Tilton Rd C6
Tower St A4
Town Hall C3
Trent St C5
Turner's Buildings A1
Unett St A3
Union Terr B5
Upper Trinity St C5
Uxbridge St A3
Vauxhall Gr B5
Vauxhall Rd B5
Vernon Rd C1
Vesey St B4
Viaduct St B5
Victoria Sq C3
Villa St A3
Vittoria St B3
Vyse St B3
Walter St A6
Wardlow Rd A5
Warstone La B2
Washington St C3
Water St B3
Waterworks Rd C1
Watery La C5
Well St A3
Western Rd B1
Wharf St A2
Wheeler St A3
Whitehouse St A5
Whitmore St A2
Whittall St B4
Wholesale Market C4
Wiggin St B1
Willes Rd A1
Windsor Industrial Est A5
Windsor St A5
Windsor St B5
Winson Green Rd A1
Witton St C6
Wolseley St C6
Woodcock St B5

Blackpool 332

Abingdon St A1
Addison Cr A3
Adelaide St B1
Albert Rd B2
Alfred St B2
Ascot Rd A3
Ashton Rd C2
Auburn Gr C3
Bank Hey St B1
Banks St A1
Beech Ave A3
Bela Gr C2
Belmont Ave B2
Birley St A1
Blackpool & Fleetwood Tram B1
Blackpool & The Fylde College B2
Blackpool FC C2
Blackpool North A2
Blackpool Tower B1
Blundell St C1
Bonny St B1
Breck Rd B3
Bryan Rd A3
Buchanan St A2
Bus Station A2
Cambridge Rd A3
Caunce St A2/A3
Central Dr B1/C2
Central Pier C1
Central Pier C1
Central Pier Theatre C1
Chapel St C1
Charles St A2
Charnley Rd B2
Church St A1/A2
Clinton Ave B2
Coach Station A2/C1
Cocker St A1
Cocker St A1
Coleridge Rd A3
Collingwood Ave A3
Comedy Carpet B1
Condor Gr C3
Cookson St A2
Coronation St B1
Corporation St A1
Courts B1
Cumberland Ave B3
Cunliffe Rd C3
Dale St C1
Devonshire Rd A3
Devonshire Sq A3
Dickson Rd A1
Elizabeth St A2
Ferguson Rd C3
Forest Gate B3
Foxhall Rd C1
Foxhall Sq C1
Freckleton St C2
George St A2
Gloucester Ave B3
Golden Mile, The C1
Gorse Rd B3
Gorton St A2
Grand Theatre, The B1
Granville Rd A2
Grasmere Rd C2
Grosvenor St A2
Grundy Art Gallery A1
Harvey Rd B3
Hornby Rd B2
Houndshill Sh Ctr B1
Hull Rd B1
Ibbison Ct C2
Information Ctr A1
Kent Rd C2
Keswick Rd C2
King St A2
Knox Gr C3
Laycock Gate A3
Layton Rd A3
Leamington Rd B2
Leeds Rd B3
Leicester Rd B2
Levens Gr C2
Library A1
Lifeboat Station B1
Lincoln Rd B2
Liverpool Rd B3
Livingstone Rd B2
London Rd A3
Lune Gr C2
Lytham Rd C1
Madame Tussaud's Blackpool B1
Manchester Sq C1
Manor Rd B3
Maple Ave B3
Market St A1
Marlboro Rd B3
Mere Rd B3
Milbourne St A2
Newcastle Ave B3
Newton Dr A3
North Pier A1
North Pier A1
North Pier Theatre A1
Odeon C2
Olive Gr B3
Palatine Rd B2
Park Rd B2/C3
Peter St A2
Police Station B1
Post Office A1/A3B1/B2/B3
Princess Pde A1
Princess St C1/C2
Promenade A1/C1
Queen St A1
Queen Victoria Rd C2
Raikes Pde B2
Reads Ave B2
Regent Rd B2
Register Office B2
Ribble Rd B2
Rigby Rd C1/C2
Ripon Rd B3
St Albans Rd B3
St John's Square A1
St Ives Ave C3
St Vincent Ave C3
Salisbury Rd B3
Salthouse Ave C2
Salvation Army Centre A2
Sands Way C2
Sealife Centre B1
Seasiders Way C1
Selbourne Rd A2
Sharrow Gr C3
Somerset Ave C3
Springfield Rd A1
South King St B2
Sutton Pl B2
Talbot Rd A1/A2
Thornber Gr C2
Topping St A1
Tower B1
Town Hall A1
Tram Depot C1
Tyldesley Rd C1
Vance Rd B1
Victoria St B1
Victory Rd A2
Wayman Rd A3
Westmorland Ave C2/C3
Whitegate Dr B3
Winter Gardens Theatre B1
Woodland Gr B3
Woolman Rd B2

Bournemouth 333

Ascham Rd A3
Avenue Rd B1
Ave Shopping Centre B1
Bath Rd C2
Beacon Rd C1
Beach Office C2
Beechey Rd A3
Bodorgan Rd B1
Bourne Ave B1
Bournemouth A3
Bournemouth & Poole College B3
Bournemouth Balloon C2
Bournemouth Int Ctr C1
Bournemouth Pier C2
Bournemouth Sta B3
Braidley Rd A1
Cavendish Place A2
Cavendish Rd A2
Central Drive A1
Central Gdns B1
Christchurch Rd B3
Cliff Lift C1/C3
Coach House Pl A3
Coach Station A3
Commercial Rd B1
Cotlands Rd B3
Courts B3
Cranborne Rd C1
Cricket Ground A2
Cumnor Rd B2
Dean Park A2
Dean Park Cr B2
Dean Park Rd A2
Durrant Rd B1
East Overcliff Dr C3
Exeter Cr C1
Exeter La C2
Exeter Rd C1
Gervis Place B1
Gervis Rd B3
Glen Fern Rd B2
Golf Club B1
Grove Rd B3
Hinton Rd C2
Holdenhurst Rd B3
Horseshoe Common B2
Nuffield Health Bournemouth Hospital (private) A2
Information Ctr B2
Lansdowne B3
Lansdowne Rd A2
Lorne Park Rd B2
Lower Gdns B1/C2
Madeira Rd B2
Methuen Rd A3
Meyrick Park A1
Meyrick Rd B3
Milton Rd A2
Oceanarium C2
Odeon Cinema C2
Old Christchurch Rd B2
Ophir Rd A3
Oxford Rd B3
Park Rd A3
Parsonage Rd B2
Pavilion C2
Pier Approach C2
Pier Theatre C2
Police Station A3/B3
Portchester Rd A3
Post Office B1/B3
Priory Rd C1
Quadrant, The B2
Recreation Ground A1
Richmond Gardens Shopping Centre B2
Richmond Hill Rd B1
Russell Cotes Art Gallery & Museum C2
Russell Cotes Rd C2
St Anthony's Rd A1
St Michael's Rd C1
St Paul's A3
St Paul's La B3
St Paul's Rd A3
St Peter's B2
St Peter's B2
St Peter's Rd B2
St Stephen's Rd B1/B2
St Swithun's B3
St Swithun's Rd B3
St Swithun's Rd South B3
St Valerie Rd A2
St Winifred's Rd A2
Stafford Rd B3
Terrace Rd B1
The Square B1
The Triangle B1
Town Hall B1
Tregonwell Rd C1
Trinity Rd B2
Undercliff Drive C3
Upper Hinton Rd B2
Upper Terr Rd C1
Wellington Rd A2/A3
Wessex Way A3/B1/B2
West Cliff Promenade C1
West Hill Rd C1
West Undercliff Prom C1
Westover Rd B2
Wimborne Rd A2
Wootton Mount B2
Wychwood Dr A1
Yelverton Rd B2
York Rd B3
Zig-Zag Walks C1/C3

Bradford 333

Alhambra B2
Back Ashgrove B1
Barkerend Rd A3
Barnard Rd C3
Barry St B2
Bolling Rd C3
Bolton Rd A3
Bowland St A1
Bradford 1 B2
Bradford College B1
Bradford Forster Sq A2
Bradford Interchange B3
Bradford Playhouse B3
Bridge St B2
Britannia St B2
Burnett St B3
Bus Station B2
Butler St West A3
Caledonia St C2
Canal Rd A2
Carlton St B1
Cathedral A3
Centenary Sq B2
Chapel St B3
Cheapside A2
Church Bank B3
Cineworld B3
City Hall B2
City Rd A1
Claremont B1
Colour Museum B1
Croft St B2
Crown Court B3
Darfield St A1
Darley St A2
Drewton Rd A1
Drummond Trading Estate A1
Dryden St B3
Dyson St A1
Easby Rd C1
East Parade B3
Eldon Pl A1
Filey St B3
Forster Square Ret Pk A2
Gallery II B1
Garnett St B3
Godwin St B2
Gracechurch St A1
Grattan Rd B1
Great Horton Rd B1/B2
Grove Terr B1
Hall Ings B2
Hall La C3
Hallfield Rd A1
Hammstrasse A2
Harris St B3
Holdsworth St A2
Ice Rink B2
Impressions B2
Information Ctr B2
Ivegate B2
Inland Revenue A2
Jacob's Well Municipal Offices B2
James St A2
John St A2
Kirkgate B2
Kirkgate Centre B2
Laisteridge La C1
Leeds Rd B3
Library B1/B2
Listerhills Rd B1
Little Horton La C1
Little Horton Gn C1
Longside La B1
Lower Kirkgate B2
Lumb La A1
Magistrates Court B2
Manchester Rd C2
Manningham La A1
Manor Row A2
Market C3
Market St B2
Melbourne Place C1
Midland Rd A2
Mill La C2
Morley St B1
National Media B2
Nelson St B2/C2
Nesfield St A2
New Otley Rd A3
Norcroft St B1
North Parade A2
North St A3
North Wing A3
Oastler Shopping Ctr A2
Otley Rd A3
Park Ave C1
Park La C1
Park Rd C2
Parma St C2
Peace Museum B2
Peckover St B3
Piccadilly A2
Police Station B2/C2
Post Office A2/B1/B2/C3
Princes Way B2
Prospect St C3
Radwell Drive C2
Rawson Rd A1
Rebecca St A1
Richmond Rd B1
Russell St C1
St George's Hall B2
St Lukes Hospital C1
St Mary's A3
Shipley Airedale Rd A3/B3
Simes St A1
Smith St B1
Spring Mill St C2
Stott Hill A3
Sunbridge Rd A1/B1/B2
The Leisure Exchange B3
Theatre in the Mill B1
Thornton Rd A1/B1
Trafalgar St A2
Trinity Rd C1
Tumbling Hill St B1
Tyrrel St B2
Univ of Bradford B1/C1
Usher St C3
Valley Rd A2
Vicar La B3
Wakefield Rd C3
Wapping Rd A3
Westgate A1
White Abbey Rd A1
Wigan Rd A1
Wilton St B1
Wood St A1
Wool Exchange B2
Worthington St A1

Brighton 333

Addison Rd A1
Albert Rd B2
Albion Hill B3
Albion St B3
Ann St A3
Baker St A3
Black Lion St C2
Brighton A2
Brighton Centre C2
Brighton Fishing Museum C2
Brighton Pier (Palace Pier) C3
Brighton Wheel C3
Broad St C3
Buckingham Pl A2
Buckingham Rd B2
Cannon Pl C1
Carlton Hill B3
Chatham Pl A1
Cheapside A3
Church St B2
Churchill Sq Sh Ctr B2
Clifton Hill B1
Clifton Pl B1
Clifton Rd B1
Clifton St A2
Clifton Terr B1
Clock Tower B2
Coach Station C3
Coach Park C3
Compton Ave A2
Davigdor Rd A1
Denmark Terr B1
Ditchling Rd A3
Dome B2
Duke St B2
Duke's La C2
Dyke Rd A1/B2
East St C2
Edward St B3
Elmore Rd B3
Frederick St B2
Gardner St B2
Gloucester Pl B3
Gloucester Rd B2
Goldsmid Rd A1
Grand Junction Rd C2
Grand Pde B3
Grove Hill B3
Guildford St A2
Hampton Pl B1
Hanover Terr A3
High St C3
Highdown Rd A1
Information Ctr C2
John St B3
Kemp St B2
Kensington Pl B2
Kings Rd C1
Law Courts B3
Lewes Rd A3
Library B2
London Rd A3
Madeira Dr C3
Marine Pde C3
Middle St C2
Montpelier Pl B1
Montpelier Rd B1
Montpelier St B1
Mus & Art Gallery B3
New England Rd A2
New England St A2
New Rd B2
Nizells Ave A1
Norfolk Rd B1
Norfolk Terr B1
North Rd B2
North St B2
Odeon C2
Old Shoreham Rd A1
Old Steine C3
Osmond Rd A1
Over St B2
Oxford St A3
Park Crescent Terr A3
Phoenix Art Gallery B3
Phoenix Rise A3
Police Station B3
Post Office A1/A2/A3/B1/B2/B3/C3
Preston Rd A2
Preston St B1
Prestonville Rd A1
Queen's Rd B2
Regency Sq C1
Regent St B2
Richmond Pl B3
Richmond St B3
Richmond Terr A3
Rose Hill Terr A3
Royal Alexandra Hospital B1
Royal Pavilion B2
St Bartholomew's A3
St James's St C3
St Nicholas Rd B2
St Nicholas' B2
St Peter's A3
Sea Life Centre C3
Shaftesbury Rd A3
Ship St C2
Sillwood Rd B1
Sillwood St B1
Southover St A3
Spring Gdns B2
Stanford Rd A1
Stanley Rd A3
Surrey St B2
Sussex St B3
Sussex Terr B3
Swimming Pool B3
Sydney St B3
Temple Gdns B1
Terminus Rd A2
The Lanes C2
Theatre Royal B2
Tidy St B2
Town Hall C2
Toy & Model Mus A2
Trafalgar St B2
Union Rd A3
University of Brighton B3
Upper Lewes Rd A3
Upper North St B1
Viaduct Rd A3
Victoria Gdns B3
Victoria Rd B1
Volk's Electric Railway C3
West Pier (derelict) C1
West St C2
Western Rd B1
Whitecross St B2
York Ave B1
York Pl B3

Bristol 333

Acramans Rd C4
Albert Rd C6
Alfred Hill A4
All Saint's St A4
All Saints' B4
Allington Rd C3
Alpha Rd C4
Ambra Vale B1
Ambra Vale East B2
Ambrose Rd B2
Amphitheatre C3
Anchor Rd B3
Anvil St B6
Architecture Ctr B4
Argyle Pl B2
Arlington Villas A2
Arnolfini Arts Centre, The B4
Art Gallery A3
Ashton Gate Rd C2
Ashton Rd C1
at-Bristol B3
Avon Bridge C1
Avon Cr C1
Avon St B6
Baldwin St B4
Baltic Wharf C2
Baltic Wharf L Ctr & Caravan Pk C2
Baltic Wharf Marina C2
Barossa Pl C4
Barton Manor B6
Barton Rd B6
Barton Vale B6
Bath Rd C6
Bathurst Basin C4
Bathurst Parade C4
Beauley Rd C3
Bedminster Bridge C5
Bedminster Parade C4
Bellevue B2
Bellevue Cr B2
Bellevue Rd C6
Berkeley Pl A2
Berkeley Sq A3
Birch Rd C2
Blackfriars A4
Bond St A5
Braggs La A6
Brandon Hill B3
Brandon Steep B3
Bristol Bridge B5
Bristol Cath (CE) B3
Bristol Eye Hospital (A&E) A4
Bristol Grammar School A3
Bristol Harbour Railway C3
Bristol Royal Children's Hospital A4
Bristol Royal Infirmary (A&E) A4
Bristol Temple Meads Station B6
Broad Plain B6
Broad Quay B4
Broad St A4
Broad Weir A5
Broadcasting House A3
Broadmead A5
Brunel Way C1
Brunswick Sq A5
Burton Cl C5
Bus Station A4
Butts Rd B3
Cabot Circus A5
Cabot Tower B3
Caledonia Pl B1
Callowhill Ct A5
Cambridge St C6
Camden Rd C3
Camp Rd A1
Canada Way C2
Cannon St A4
Canon's Rd B3/B4
Canon's Way B3

Bury St Edmunds • Cambridge • Canterbury • Cardiff • Carlisle 353

Cantock's Cl A3
Canynge Rd A1
Canynge Sq A1
Castle Park A5
Castle St A5
Catherine Meade St C4
Cattle Market Rd C6
Central Library B3
Charles Pl B1
Charlotte St B3
Charlotte St South B3
Chatterton House B5
Chatterton Sq C5
Chatterton St C5
Cheese La B5
Christchurch A4
Christchurch Rd A1
Christmas Steps ✦ A4
Church La B2/B5
Church St B5
City Museum A3
City of Bristol College B3
Clare St B4
Clarence Rd C5
Cliff Rd C1
Clift House Rd C1
Clifton Cath (RC) + A2
Clifton Down A1
Clifton Down Rd A1
Clifton Hill B2
Clifton Park A1/A2
Clifton Park Rd A1
Clifton Rd A2
Cliftonwood Cr B2
Cliftonwood Rd B2
Cliftonwood Terr B2
Clifton Vale B1
Cobblestone Mews A1
College Green B3
College Rd A1
College St B3
Colston Almshouses A4
Colston Ave B4
Colston Hall B4
Colston Parade C5
Colston St A4
Commercial Rd C4
Commonwealth Museum B5
Constitution Hill B2
Cooperage La C2
Corn St B4
Cornwallis Ave B1
Cornwallis Cr B1
Coronation Rd C2/C4
Council House B3
Counterslip B5
Courts A4
Create Centre, The ✦ C1
Crosby Row B2
Culver St B3
Cumberland Basin C1
Cumberland Cl C2
Cumberland Rd C2/C3
David St A6
Dean La C4
Deanery Rd B3
Denmark St B4
Dowry Sq B1
Eaton Cr A2
Elmdale Rd A3
Elton Rd A3
Eugene St A4/A6
Exchange, The and St Nicholas' Mkts B4
Fairfax St A4
Fire Station B5
Floating Harbour C3
Foster Almshouses A4
Frayne Rd C1
Frederick Pl A2
Freeland Pl B1
Frogmore St B3
Fry's Hill B2
Gas La B6
Gasferry Rd C3
General Hospital C4
Georgian House B3
Glendale B1
Glentworth Rd B2
Gloucester St A1
Goldney Hall B2
Goldney Rd B1
Gordon Rd A2
Granby Hill B1
Grange Rd A1
Great Ann St A6
Great George St A6/B3
Great George Rd B3
Great Western Way B6
Green St North B1
Green St South B1
Greenay Bush La C2
Greenbank Rd C2
Greville Smyth Park C1
Guildhall A4
Guinea St C4
Hamilton Rd C3
Hanbury Rd A2
Hanover Pl C2
Harbour Way B3
Harley Pl A1
Haymarket A5
Hensman's Hill B1
High St B4
Highbury Villas A3
Hill St B3
Hill St C6
Hippodrome B4
Hopechapel Hill B1
Horfield Rd A4
Horton St B6
Host St A4
Hotwell Rd B1/B2
Houlton St A6
Howard Rd C3
IMAX Cinema B4
Information Ctr B4
Islington Rd C3
Jacob St A5/A6
Jacob's Wells Rd B2
John Carr's Terr B2
John Wesley's Chapel A5
Joy Hill B1
Jubilee St B6
Kensington Pl A2
Kilkenny St B6
King St B4
Kingsland Rd B6
Kingston Rd C3
Lamb St A6
Lansdown Rd A2
Lawford St A6
Lawfords Gate A6
Leighton Rd C3
Lewins Mead A4
Lime Rd C2
Little Ann St A6
Little Caroline Pl B1
Little George St A6
Little King St B4
Litfield Rd A1
Llandoger Trow B4
Lloyds' Building, The C3
Lodge St A4
Lord Mayor's Chapel, The B4
Lower Castle St A5
Lower Church La A4
Lower Clifton Hill B2
Lower Guinea St C4
Lower Lamb St B3
Lower Maudlin St A4
Lower Park Rd A4
Lower Sidney St C2
Lucky La C4
Lydstep Terr C3
Mall (Galleries Shopping Centre), The A5
Manilla Rd A1
Mardyke Ferry Rd C2
Maritime Heritage Centre B3
Marlborough Hill A4
Marlborough St A4
Marsh St B4
Mead St C5
Merchant Dock B2
Merchant Seamen's Almshouses B4
Merchant St A5
Merchants Rd A1
Merchants Rd C1
Meridian Pl A2
Meridian Vale A2
Merrywood Rd C3
Midland Rd A6
Milford St C3
Millennium Sq B3
Mitchell La B5
Mortimer Rd A1
M Shed C4
Murray Rd C4
Myrtle Rd A3
Narrow Plain B5
Narrow Quay B4
Nelson St A4
New Charlotte St C4
New Kingsley Rd B6
New Queen St C5
New St A6
Newgate A5
Newton St A6
Norland Rd A1
North St C2
O2 Academy B3
Oakfield Gr A2
Oakfield Pl A2
Oakfield Rd A2
Old Bread St B6
Old Market St A6
Old Park Hill A4
Oldfield Rd B1
Orchard Ave B4
Orchard La B4
Orchard St B4
Osbourne Rd C3
Oxford St B6
Park Pl A2
Park Rd C3
Park Row A4
Park St A3
Passage St B5
Pembroke Gr A2
Pembroke Rd A2
Pembroke Rd C3
Pembroke St A5
Penn St A5
Pennywell Rd A6
Percival Rd A1
Pero's Bridge B4
Perry Rd A4
Pip & Jay A5
Plimsoll Bridge B1
Polygon Rd B1
Portland St A1
Portwall La B5
Post Office A1/A3/A4/A5/A6/B1/B4/C4/C5
Prewett St C5
Prince St B4
Prince St Bridge C4
Princess St C5
Princess Victoria St B1
Priory Rd A3
Pump La C5
QEH Theatre A2
Queen Charlotte St B4
Quakers Friars A5
Quay St A4
Queen Elizabeth Hospital School B2
Queen Sq B4
Queen St A5
Queen's Ave A3
Queen's Parade B3
Queen's Rd A2/A3
Raleigh Rd C2
Randall Rd B2
Redcliffe Backs B5
Redcliffe Bridge B4
Redcliffe Hill C5
Redcliffe Parade C4
Redcliffe St B5
Redcliffe Way B5
Redcross St A6
Redgrave Theatre A1
Red Lodge A4
Regent St B1
Richmond Hill A2
Richmond Hill Ave A2
Richmond La A2
Richmond Park Rd A2
Richmond St C6
Richmond Terr A2
River St A6
Rownham Mead B2
Royal Fort Rd A3
Royal Park A2
Royal West of England Academy A3
Royal York Cr B1
Royal York Villas B1
Rupert St A4
Russ St B6
St Andrew's Walk B2
St George's B3
St George's Rd B3
St James A4
St John's A4
St John's Rd C4
St Luke's Rd C5
St Mary Redcliffe C5
St Mary's Hospital A3
St Matthias Park A6
St Michael's Hill A3
St Michael's Hospl A4
St Michael's Park A3
St Nicholas St B4
St Paul St A5
St Paul's Rd A2
St Peter's (ruin) A5
St Philip's Bridge B5
St Philips Rd A6
St Stephen's B4
St Stephen's St B4
St Thomas St B5
St Thomas the Martyr B5
Sandford Rd B1
Sargent St C5
Saville Pl B1
Ship La C5
Showcase Cinema de Lux A5
Silver St A4
Sion Hill A1
Small St A4
Smeaton Rd C1
Somerset Sq C5
Somerset St C5
Southernhay Ave B2
Southville Rd C4
Spike Island Artspace C2
Spring St C5
SS Great Britain and The Matthew B2
Stackpool Rd C3
Staight St B6
Stillhouse La C4
Stracey Rd C2
Sydney Row C2
Tankard's Cl A3
Temple Back B5
Temple Boulevard B5
Temple Bridge B5
Temple Church B5
Temple Circus B5
Temple Gate C5
Temple St B5
Temple Way B5
Terrell St A4
The Arcade A5
The Fosseway A2
The Grove B4
The Horsefair A5
The Mall A1
Theatre Royal B4
Thekla The B4
Thomas La B5
Three Kings of Cologne A4
Three Queens La B5
Tobacco Factory, The C2
Tower Hill B5
Tower La A4
Trenchard St A4
Triangle South A3
Triangle West A3
Trinity Rd A6
Trinity St A6
Tyndall Ave A3
Union St A5
Union St B6
Unity St A6
Unity St B3
University of Bristol A3
University Rd A3
Upper Maudlin St A4
Upper Perry Hill C3
Upper Byron Pl A3
Upton Rd C2
Valentine Bridge B6
Victoria Gr C5
Victoria Rd C6
Victoria Rooms A2
Victoria Sq A2
Victoria St B5
Vyvyan Rd A1
Vyvyan Terr A1
Wade St A6
Walter St C2
Wapping Rd C4
Water La B5
Waterloo Rd A6
Waterloo St A1
Waterloo St A6
Watershed Media Centre ✦ B4
Welling Terr B1
Welsh Back B4
West Mall A1
West St A6
Westfield Pl A1
Wetherell Pl A2
Whitehouse Pl C5
Whitehouse St C5
Whiteladies Rd A2
Whitson St A4
William St C5
Willway St C5
Windsor Pl B1
Windsor Terr B1
Wine St A4
Woodland Rise A3
Woodland Rd A3
Worcester Rd A1
Worcester Terr A1
YHA B4
York Gdns B1
York Pl A2
York Rd C5

Bury St Edmunds 333

Abbey Gardens B3
Abbey Gate B3
Abbeygate St B2
Albert Cr B1
Albert St B1
Ambulance Sta C1
Angel Hill B2
Angel La B2
Anglian Lane A1
Arc Shopping Centre B2
Athenaeum C2
Baker's La C3
Barwell Rd B3
Beetons Way A1
Bishops Rd B2
Bloomfield St B2
Bridewell La C2
Bullen Cl C1
Bury St Edmunds ≋ A2
Bury St Edmunds County Upper School A1
Bury St Edmunds L Ctr B1
Bury Town FC B3
Bus Station B2
Butter Mkt B2
Cannon St B2
Castle Rd C1
Cemetery C1
Chalk Rd (N) B1
Chalk Rd (S) B1
Church Row B2
Churchgate St C2
Cineworld B1
Citizens Advice Bureau B2
College St C2
Compiegne Way A3
Corn Exchange, The B2
Cornfield Rd B1
Cotton Lane B3
Courts B2
Covent Garden C2
Crown St C3
Cullum Rd C2
Eastern Way A3
Eastgate St B3
Enterprise Bsns Park A2
Etna Rd A2
Eyre Cl C2
Fire Station B1
Friar's Lane C2
Gage Cl A1
Garland St B2
Greene King Brewery C3
Grove Park B1
Grove Rd B1
Guildhall C2
Guildhall St C2
Hatter St C2
High Baxter St B2
Honey Hill C3
Hospital Rd C1/C2
Ickworth Dr C1
Information Ctr B2
Ipswich St A2
King Edward VI Sch A1
King's Rd C1/B2
Library B2
Long Brackland A2
Looms La B2
Lwr Baxter St B2
Malthouse La A2
Maynewater La C3
Mill Rd C1
Mill Rd (South) C1
Minden Close B3
Moyses Hall B2
Mustow St B3
Norman Tower C3
Northgate Ave A2
Northgate St B2
Nutshell, The B2
Osier Rd A2
Out Northgate A2
Out Risbygate B1
Out Westgate C2
Parkway B1/C2
Peckham St B2
Petticoat La C1
Phoenix Day Hospital C1
Pinners Way C1
Police Station C3
Post Office B2/B3
Pump La B2
Queen's Rd B1
Raingate St C3
Raynham Rd A1
Retail Park C2
Risbygate St B1/B2
Robert Boby Way C2
St Andrew's St North B2
St Andrew's St South B2
St Botolph's La C3
St Edmunds Hospital (private) C3
St Edmund's C2
St Edmund's Abbey (Remains) ✦ B3
St Edmundsbury + C3
St John's St B2
St Marys C3
School Hall La B2
Shillitoe Cl C1
Shire Halls & Magistrates Ct C3
South Cl C1
Southgate St C3
Sparhawk St C3
Spring Lane B1
Springfield Rd B1
Station Hill A2
Swan La C3
Tayfen Rd B2
The Vinefields B3
Theatre Royal C3
Thingoe Hill A2
Victoria St B1
War Memorial ✦ C1
Well St B2
West Suffolk College B1
Westgarth Gdns C1
Westgate St C2
Whiting St C2
York Rd B1
York Terr B1

Cambridge 334

Abbey Rd A3
ADC A2
Anglia Ruskin University B3
Archaeology & Anthropology B2
Art Gallery A1
Arts Picture House B2
Arts Theatre B1
Auckland Rd A3
Bateman St C2
BBC C3
Benet St B1
Bradmore St B3
Bridge St A1
Broad St B3
Brookside C2
Brunswick Terr A3
Burleigh St B3
Bus Station B2
Butt Green A2
Cambridge Contemporary Art Gallery B1
Castle Mound A1
Castle St A1
Cemetery B3
Chesterton La A1
Christ's (Coll) B2
Christ's Lane B2
Christ's Pieces B2
City Rd B3
Clare (Coll) B1
Clarendon St B2
Coe Fen C2
Coronation St C2
Corpus Christi (Coll) B1
Council Offices C3
Cross St C3
Crusoe Bridge C1
Darwin (Coll) C1
Devonshire Rd C3
Downing (Coll) C2
Downing St B2
Earl St B2
East Rd B3
Eden St B3
Elizabeth Way A3
Elm St B2
Emery St B3
Emmanuel (Coll) B2
Emmanuel Rd B2
Emmanuel St B2
Fair St A3
Fenners Physical Education Centre C3
Fire Station B3
Fitzroy St A3
Fitzwilliam Museum C2
Fitzwilliam St C2
Folk Museum A1
Glisson Rd C3
Gonville & Caius (Coll) B1
Gonville Place C2
Grafton Centre A3
Grand Arcade B2
Gresham Rd C3
Green St B1
Guest Rd B3
Guildhall B2
Harvey Rd C3
Hills Rd C3
Hobson St B2
Hughes Hall (Coll) B3
Information Ctr B2
James St A3
Jesus (Coll) A2
Jesus Green A2
Jesus La A2
Jesus Terr B3
John St B3
Kelsey Kerridge Sports Centre B3
King St A2
King's (Coll) B1
King's College Chapel B1
King's Parade B1
Lammas Land Rec Gd C1
Lensfield Rd C2
Library B2
Lion Yard B2
Little St Mary's La B1
Lyndewod Rd C3
Magdalene (Coll) A1
Magdalene St A1
Maid's Causeway A3
Malcolm St A2
Market Hill B1
Market St B1
Mathematical Bridge B1
Mawson Rd C3
Midsummer Common A3
Mill La B1
Mill Rd B3
Mill St C3
Mumford B3
Napier St A3
New Square A2
Newmarket Rd A3
Newnham Rd C1
Norfolk St B3
Northampton St A1
Norwich St C2
Orchard St B2
Panton St C2
Paradise Nature Reserve C1
Paradise St B3
Park Parade A1
Park St A2
Park Terr B2
Parker St B2
Parker's Piece B2
Parkside B3
Parkside Pools B3
Parsonage St A3
Pemberton Terr C2
Pembroke (Coll) B2
Pembroke St B1
Perowne St B3
Peterhouse (Coll) C1
Petty Cury B2
Police Station B3
Post Office A1/A3/B2/B3/C1/C2/C3
Queens' (Coll) B1
Queen's La B1
Queen's Rd B1
Regent St B2
Regent Terr B2
Ridley Hall (Coll) C1
Riverside A3
Round Church, The A1
Russell St C2
St Andrew's St B2
St Benet's B1
St Catharine's (Coll) B1
St Eligius St C2
St John's (Coll) A1
St Mary's B1
St Paul's Rd C3
Saxon St C2
Scott Polar Institute & Museum C2
Sedgwick Museum B2
Sheep's Green C1
Shire Hall A1
Sidgwick Ave C1
Sidney St A2
Sidney Sussex (Coll) A2
Silver St B1
Station Rd C3
Tenison Ave C3
Tenison Rd C3
Tennis Court Rd B2
The Backs B1
The Fen Causeway C1
Thompson's La A1
Trinity (Coll) A1
Trinity Hall (Coll) B1
Trinity St B1
Trumpington Rd C2
Trumpington St B1
Union Rd C2
University Botanic Gardens C2
Victoria Ave A2
Victoria St B2
Warkworth St B3
Warkworth Terr B3
Wesley House (Coll) A2
West Rd B1
Westcott House (Coll) A2
Westminster (Coll) A1
Whipple B2
Willis Rd B3
Willow Walk A2

Canterbury 334

Artillery St B2
Barton Mill Rd A3
Beaconsfield Rd A1
Beaney The B2
Beverley Rd A1
Bingley's Island B1
Black Griffin La B1
Broad Oak Rd A2
Broad St B2
Brymore Rd A3
Burgate B2
Bus Station C2
Canterbury College C3
Canterbury East ≋ C1
Canterbury Tales, The ✦ B2
Canterbury West ≋ A1
Castle C1
Castle Row C1
Castle St C1
Cathedral + B2
Chaucer Rd A3
Christ Church Univ B3
Christchurch Gate ✦ B2
City Council Offices A3
City Wall B2
Coach Park A2
College Rd B3
Cossington Rd C2
Court B2
Craddock Rd A3
Crown & County Courts B3
Dane John Gdns C2
Dane John Mound ✦ C1
Deanery B2
Dover St C2
Duck La B2
Eastbridge Hospl B1
Edgar Rd B3
Ersham Rd C3
Ethelbert Rd C3
Fire Station C2
Forty Acres Rd A1
Gordon Rd C1
Greyfriars ✦ B1
Guildford Rd C1
Havelock St B2
Heaton Rd C1
High St B2
HM Prison B3
Information Ctr A2/B2
Ivy La B2
Ivy Pl C1
King St B2
King's School B2/B3
King's School Leisure Facilities A2
Kingsmead L Ctr A2
Kingsmead Rd A2
Kirby's La B1
Lansdown Rd C2
Lime Kiln Rd C1
Longport B3
Lower Chantry La C3
Mandeville Rd A1
Market Way A2
Marlowe Arcade B2
Marlowe Ave C2
Marlowe Theatre B2
Martyrs Field Rd C1
Mead Way B1
Military Rd B2
Monastery St B2
Museum of Canterbury (Rupert Bear Museum) B1
New Dover Rd C3
Norman Rd C2
North Holmes Rd B3
North La B1
Northgate A2
Nunnery Fields C2
Nunnery Rd C2
Oaten Hill C2
Odeon Cinema C2
Old Dover Rd C2
Old Palace B2
Old Ruttington La B2
Old Weavers B2
Orchard St B1
Oxford Rd C1
Palace St B2
Pilgrims Way C3
Pin Hill C1
Pine Tree Ave A1
Police Station C2
Post Office B2/C1/C2
Pound La B1
Puckle La C2
Raymond Ave C2
Registry Office A2
Rheims Way B1
Rhodaus Cl C2
Rhodaus Town C2
Roman Museum B2
Roper Gateway A1
Roper Rd A1
Rose La B2
St Augustine's Abbey (remains) + B3
St Augustine's Rd C3
St Dunstan's A1
St Dunstan's St A1
St George's Pl C2
St George's St B2
St George's Tower ✦ B2
St Gregory's Rd B3
St John's Hospital A2
St Margaret's St B2
St Martin's B3
St Martin's Ave B3
St Martin's Rd B3
St Michael's Rd A1
St Mildred's C1
St Peter's Gr B1
St Peter's La B2
St Peter's Pl B1
St Peter's St B1
St Radigunds St B2
St Stephen's Ct A1
St Stephen's Path A1
St Stephen's Rd A2
Salisbury Rd A1
Simmonds Rd C1
Spring La C3
Station Rd West B1
Stour St B1
Sturry Rd A3
The Causeway A2
The Friars B2
Tourtel Rd A3
Tudor Rd C1
Union St B2
University for the Creative Arts C3
Vernon Pl C2
Victoria Rd C1
Watling St B2
Westgate Gdns B1
Westgate Towers B1
Whitefriars B2
Whitehall Gdns B1
Whitehall Rd B1
Wincheap C1
York Rd C1
Zealand Rd C2

Cardiff Caerdydd 334

Adam St B3
Alexandra Gdns A2
Allerton St C1
Arran St A3
ATRiuM (Univ of Glamorgan) C3
Beauchamp St C1
Bedford St A3
Blackfriars Priory (rems) + B1
Boulevard De Nantes B2
Brains Brewery C2
Brook St B1
Bus Station C2
Bute Park B1
Bute St C2
Bute Terr C3
Callaghan Sq C2/C3
Capitol Sh Ctr, The B3
Cardiff Arms Park (Cardiff RFC) B1
Cardiff Bridge B1
Cardiff Castle B2
Cardiff Central Sta ≋ C2
Cardiff Ctr Trading Est C3
Cardiff Univ A1/A2/B3
Cardiff University Student's Union A2
Caroline St C2
Castle Green B2
Castle Mews A1
Castle St (Heol y Castell) B1
Cathays Station ≋ A2
Celerity Drive C3
Central Library C2
Central Sq C2
Charles St (Heol Siarl) B3
Churchill Way B3
City Hall A2
City Rd A3
Clare Rd C1
Clare St C1
Coburn St A3
Coldstream Terr B1
College Rd A1
Colum Rd A1
Court C2
Court Rd C1
Craiglee Drive C3
Cranbrook St A3
Customhouse St C2
Cyfartha St A3
Despenser Place C1
Despenser St C1
Dinas St C1
Duke St (Heol y Dug) B2
Dumfries Place B3
East Grove A3
Ellen St C3
Fire Station B3
Fitzalan Place B3
Fitzhamon Emb C1
Fitzhamon La C1
g39 C2
Gloucester St C1
Glynrhondda St A2
Gordon Rd A3
Gorsedd Gdns B2
Green St B1
Greyfriars Rd B2
HM Prison B3
Hafod St C1
Herbert St C3
High St B2
Industrial Estate C3
John St C3
Jubilee St C1
King Edward VII Ave A1
Kingsway (Ffordd y Brenin) B2
Knox Rd B3
Law Courts B2
Llanbleddian Gdns A2
Llantwit St A2
Lloyd George Ave C3
Lower Cathedral Rd B1
Lowther Rd A3
Magistrates Court B3
Mansion House A3
Mardy St C1
Mark St B1
Market B2
Mary Ann St C3
Merches Gdns C1
Mill La C2
Millennium Bridge B1
Millennium Plaza Leisure Complex C1
Millennium Stadium C1
Millennium Stadium Tours (Gate 3) ✦ B2
Miskin St A2
Monmouth St C1
Motorpoint Arena Cardiff ✦ C3
Museum Ave A2
Museum Place A2
National Museum of Wales A2
National War Meml ✦ A2
Neville Place C1
New Theatre B2
Newport Rd B3
Northcote La A3
Northcote St A3
Park Grove A4
Park Place A2
Park St C2
Penarth Rd C2
Pendyris St C1
Plantaganet St C1
Quay St B2
Queen Anne Sq A1
Queen St (Heol y Frenhines) B2
Queen St Station ≋ B3
Regimental Museums B2
Rhymney St A3
Richmond Rd A3
Royal Welsh College of Music and Drama A1
Russell St A3
Ruthin Gdns A2
St Andrews Place A2
St David's + B2
St David's 2 C2
St David's Centre B2
St David's Hall ✦ B2
St John The Baptist B2
St Mary St (Heol Eglwys Fair) B2
St Peter's St A3
Salisbury Rd A3
Sandon St B3
Schooner Way C3
Scott Rd C2
Scott St C2
Senghennydd Rd A2
Sherman Theatre A2
Sophia Gardens A1
South Wales Baptist College A3
Stafford Rd C1
Station Terr B3
Stuttgarter Strasse B2
Sussex St C1
Taffs Mead Emb C1
Talworth St A3
Temple of Peace & Health ✦ A1
The Cardiff Story B2
The Friary B2
The Hayes B2
The Parade A3
The Walk A3
Treharris St A3
Trinity St B2
Tudor La C1
Tudor St C1
Welsh Assembly Offices A1
Welsh Inst of Sport ✦ A1
West Grove A3
Westgate St (Heol y Porth) B2
Windsor Place B3
Womanby St B2
Wood St C2
Working St B2
Wyeverne Rd A2

Carlisle 334

Abbey St A1
Aglionby St B3
Albion St C3
Alexander St C3
AMF Bowl ✦ C2
Annetwell St A1
Bank St B2
Bitts Park A1
Blackfriars St B2
Blencome St C1
Blunt St C1
Botchergate B2
Boustead's Grassing C2
Bowman St B3
Broad St B3
Bridge St A1
Brook St C3
Brunswick St B2
Bus Station B2
Caldew Bridge A1
Caldew St C1
Carlisle (Citadel) Station B2
Carlisle College A2
Castle A1
Castle St A1
Castle Way A1
Cathedral + A1
Cecil St B2
Chapel St A2
Charles St B3
Charlotte St B1
Chatsworth Square A2
Chiswick St B2
Citadel, The ✦ B2
City Walls A1
Civic Centre A2
Clifton St C1
Close St B3
Collingwood St C1
Colville St C1
Colville Terr C1
Court B2
Court St B2
Crosby St B2
Crown St C2
Currock Rd C2
Dacre Rd A1
Dale St C1
Denton St C1
Devonshire Walk A1
Duke's Rd A2
East Dale St C1
East Norfolk St C1
Eden Bridge A2
Edward St B3
Elm St B1
English St B2
Fire Station A2
Fisher St A1
Flower St B3
Freer St C1
Fusehill St B3
Georgian Way A2
Gloucester Rd C3
Golf Course A2
Graham St C1
Grey St B3
Guildhall Museum A2
Halfey's La B3
Hardwicke Circus A2
Hart St B3

354 Chelmsford • Cheltenham • Chester • Chichester • Colchester • Coventry • Derby • Dorchester

Hewson St C2
Howard Pl A3
Howe St B3
Information Ctr A2
James St B2
Junction St B1
King St B2
Lancaster St B2
Lanes Shopping Ctr B2
Laserquest ✦ B2
Library A2/B1
Lime St B1
Lindisfarne St C3
Linton St B3
Lismore Pl A3
Lismore St B3
London Rd C3
Lonsdale Rd B2
Lord St C3
Lorne Cres B1
Lorne St B1
Lowther St B2
Market Hall A2
Mary St B2
Memorial Bridge A3
Metcalfe St C1
Milbourne St B1
Myddleton St B3
Nelson St C1
Norfolk St C1
Old Town Hall A2
Oswald St C3
Peter St A2
Petteril St B3
Police Station A2
Portland Pl B2
Portland Sq B2
Post Office A2/B2/B3/C1/C3
Princess St C2
Pugin St B1
Red Bank Terr C2
Regent St C3
Richardson St C1
Rickerby Park A3
Rickergate A2
River St B3
Rome St C2
Rydal St B3
St Cuthbert's B2
St Cuthbert's La B2
St James' Park C1
St James' Rd C1
St Nicholas St C3
Sands Centre A2
Scotch St A2
Shaddongate B1
Sheffield St B1
South Henry St B3
South John St C2
South St B3
Spencer St B2
Sports Centre A2
Strand Rd A2
Swimming Baths B2
Sybil St B3
Tait St B2
Thomas St B1
Thomson St C3
Trafalgar St C1
Tullie Ho Museum A1
Tyne St C3
University of Cumbria B3
Viaduct Estate Rd B1
Victoria Pl A2
Victoria Viaduct B2
Vue B2
Warwick Rd B2
Warwick Sq B3
Water St B2
West Walls B1
Westmorland St C1

Chelmsford 334

Ambulance Station B1
Anchor St C1
Anglia Ruskin Univ A2
Arbour La A3
Baddow Rd B2/C3
Baker St C1
Barrack Sq B2
Bellmead B2
Bishop Hall La A2
Bishop Rd A2
Bond St B2
Boswells Dr B3
Boudicca Mews C2
Bouverie Rd C2
Bradford St C1
Braemar Ave C1
Brook St A2
Broomfield Rd A1
Burns Cres C2
Bus Station B1
Can Bridge Way B2
Cedar Ave A1
Cedar Ave West A1
Cemetery A1
Cemetery A2
Cemetery C1
Central Park B1
Chelmsford ✝ B2
Chelmsford A1
Chichester Dr A3
Chinery Cl A3
Cinema B2
Civic Centre A1
Civic Theatre B1
College C1
Cottage Pl A2
County Cricket Gd B2
County Hall B2
Coval Ave B1
Coval La B1
Coval Wells B1
Crown Court B2
Duke St B2
Elm Rd C1
Elms Dr A1
Essex Record Office, The B3
Fairfield Rd B1
Falcons Mead B1
George St C2
Glebe Rd A1
Godfrey's Mews C2
Goldlay Ave C3
Goldlay Rd C2
Grove Rd C2
HM Prison A3
Hall St C2
Hamlet Rd C2
Hart St C1
Henry Rd A2
High Bridge Rd B2
High Chelmer Sh Ctr B2
High St B2
Hill Cres B3
Hill Rd Sth B3
Hill Rd B3
Hillview Rd A3
Hoffmans Way A2
Hospital [H] B2
Lady La C2
Langdale Gdns C3
Legg St B2
Library B2
Library C2
Lionfield Terr A3
Lower Anchor St C1
Lynmouth Ave C2
Lynmouth Gdns C3
Magistrates Court B2
Maltese Rd A1
Manor Rd C2
Marconi Rd A2
Market B2
Market Rd B2
Marlborough Rd C1
Meadows Sh Ctr, The B2
Meadowside A3
Mews Ct C2
Mildmay Rd C2
Moulsham Dr C2
Moulsham Mill ✦ C3
Moulsham St C1/C2
Navigation Rd B3
New London Rd B2/C1
New St A2/B2
New Writtle St C1
Nursery Rd C2
Orchard St C2
Park Rd B1
Parker Rd C2
Parklands Dr A3
Parkway A1/B1/B2
Police Station A2
Post Office A3/B2/C2
Primrose Hill A1
Prykes Dr B1
Queen St C1
Queen's Rd B3
Railway St A1
Rainsford Rd A1
Ransomes Way A2
Rectory La A2
Regina Rd A2
Riverside Ice & L Ctr B2
Riverside Retail Park A3
Rosebery Rd C2
Rothesay Ave C1
St John's Rd C2
Sandringham Pl B3
Seymour St B1
Shrublands Cl B3
Southborough Rd C1
Springfield Basin B3
Springfield Rd A3/B2/B3
Stapleford Cl C1
Swiss Ave A1
Telford Pl A3
The Meades B1
Tindal St B2
Townfield St A1
Trinity Rd B3
University B1
Upper Bridge Rd C1
Upper Roman Rd C2
Van Dieman's Rd C3
Viaduct Rd B1
Vicarage Rd C1
Victoria Rd A2
Victoria Rd South B2
Vincents Rd C2
Waterloo La B2
Weight Rd B3
Westfield Ave A1
Wharf Rd B3
Writtle Rd C1
YMCA A2
York Rd C1

Cheltenham 334

Albert Rd A3
Albion St B3
All Saints Rd B3
Ambrose St B2
Andover Rd C1
Art Gallery & Mus B2
Axiom Centre B3
Back Montpellier Terr C2
Bandstand ✦ C2
Bath Pde B2
Bath Rd C2
Bays Hill Rd C1
Beechwood Sh Ctr B3
Bennington St B2
Berkeley St B3
Brewery The A2
Brunswick St South A2
Bus Station B2
CAB B2
Carlton St B3
Central Cross Road A3
Cheltenham College C2
Cheltenham FC A3
Cheltenham General (A&E) [H] C3
Christchurch Rd B1
Cineworld A2
Clarence Rd A2
Clarence Sq A2
Clarence St B2
Cleeveland St A1
Coach Park A2
College Baths Road C3
College Rd C2
Colletts Dr A1
Corpus St C3
Devonshire St A2
Douro Rd B1
Duke St B3
Dunalley Pde A2
Dunalley St A2
Everyman B2
Evesham Rd A3
Fairview Rd B3
Fairview St B3
Fire Station C3
Folly La A2
Gloucester Rd A1
Grosvenor St B3
Grove St A1
Gustav Holst A3
Hanover St A2
Hatherley St C1
Henrietta St A2
Hewlett Rd B3
High St B2/B3
Hudson St A2
Imperial Gdns C2
Imperial La B2
Imperial Sq C2
Information Ctr B2
Keynsham Rd C3
King St A2
Knapp Rd B2
Ladies College B2
Lansdown Cr C1
Lansdown Rd C1
Leighton Rd B3
Library B2
London Rd C3
Lypiatt Rd C1
Malvern Rd B1
Manser St A2
Market St A1
Marle Hill Pde A2
Marle Hill Rd A2
Millbrook St A1
Milsom St A2
Montpellier Gdns C2
Montpellier Gr C2
Montpellier Pde C2
Montpellier Spa Rd C2
Montpellier St C1
Montpellier Terr C2
Montpellier Walk C2
New St B2
North Pl B2
Old Bath Rd C3
Oriel Rd B2
Overton Park Rd B1
Overton Rd B1
Oxford St C3
Parabola Rd B1
Park Pl C1
Park St A1
Pittville Circus A3
Pittville Cr A3
Pittville Lawn A3
Pittville Park A2
Playhouse B2
Police Station B1/C1
Portland St B3
Post Office B2/C2
Prestbury Rd A3
Prince's Rd C1
Priory St B3
Promenade B2
Queen St A1
Recreation Ground A2
Regent Arcade B2
Regent St B2
Rodney Rd B2
Royal Cr B2
Royal Wells Rd B2
St George's Pl B2
St Georges Rd B1
St Gregory's B2
St James St B3
St John's Ave B3
St Luke's Rd C2
St Margarets Rd A2
St Mary's B2
St Matthew's B2
St Paul's La A2
St Paul's Rd A2
St Paul's St A2
St Stephen's Rd C1
Sandford Lido C3
Sandford Mill Road C3
Sandford Park C3
Sandford Rd C2
Selkirk St A3
Sherborne Pl B3
Sherborne St B3
Suffolk Pde C2
Suffolk Rd C1
Suffolk Sq C1
Sun St A1
Swindon Rd B2
Sydenham Villas Rd C3
Tewkesbury Rd A1
The Courtyard B1
Thirlstaine Rd C2
Tivoli Rd C1
Tivoli St C1
Town Hall & Theatre B2
Townsend St A1
Trafalgar St C2
Union St B3
Univ of Gloucestershire (Francis Cl Hall) A2
Univ of Gloucestershire (Hardwick) A1
Victoria Pl B3
Victoria St A2
Vittoria Walk C2
Wel Pl B2
Wellesley Rd A2
Wellington Rd A3
Wellington Sq A3
Wellington St B2
West Drive A3
Western Rd B1
Winchcombe St B3
Winston Churchill Memorial Gardens A1

Chester 335

Abbey Gateway A2
Appleyards La C3
Bedward Row B1
Beeston View C3
Bishop Lloyd's Pal B2
Black Diamond St A2
Bottoms La C3
Boughton B3
Bouverie St A1
Bridge St B2
Bridgegate C2
British Heritage Ctr B2
Brook St A3
Brown's La C2
Bus Station B2
Cambrian Rd A1
Canal St A2
Carrick Rd C1
Castle C2
Castle Dr C2
Cathedral ✝ B2
Catherine St A1
Chester A3
Cheyney Rd A1
Chichester St A1
City Rd A3
City Walls B1/B2
City Walls Rd B1
Cornwall St A2
County Hall C2
Cross Hey C3
Cuppin St B2
Curzon Park North C1
Curzon Park South C1
Dee Basin A1
Dee La B3
Delamere St A2
Dewa Roman Experience B2
Duke St B2
Eastgate B2
Eastgate St B2
Eaton Rd C2
Edinburgh Way C3
Elizabeth Cr B3
Fire Station A2
Foregate St B2
Frodsham St B2
Gamul House B2
Garden La A1
Gateway Theatre B2
George St A2
Gladstone Ave A1
God's Providence House B2
Gorse Stacks A2
Greenway St C2
Grosvenor Bridge C1
Grosvenor Museum B2
Grosvenor Park B3
Grosvenor Precinct B2
Grosvenor Rd C1
Grosvenor St B2
Groves Rd B3
Guildhall Museum B1
Handbridge C2
Hartington St C3
Hoole Way A2
Hunter St B2
Information Ctr B2
King Charles' Tower ✦ A2
King St A2
Leisure Centre A2
Library B2
Lightfoot St A3
Little Roodee C2
Liverpool Rd A2
Love St B3
Lower Bridge St B2
Lower Park Rd B3
Lyon St A2
Magistrates Court B2
Meadows La C3
Military Museum C2
Milton St A3
New Crane St B1
Nicholas St B2
Northgate A2
Northgate St A2
Nun's Rd B1
Old Dee Bridge ✦ C2
Overleigh Rd C2
Park St B2
Police Station B2
Post Office A2/A3/B2/C2
Princess St B2
Queen St B2
Queen's Park Rd C3
Queen's Rd A3
Race Course B1
Raymond St A1
River La C2
Roman Amphitheatre & Gardens B2
Roodee, The (Chester Racecourse) B1
Russell St A3
St Anne St A2
St George's Cr C3
St Martin's Gate A1
St Martin's Way B1
St Oswalds Way A2
Saughall Rd A1
Sealand Rd A1
South View Rd A1
Stanley Palace B1
Station Rd A3
Steven St A3
The Bars B3
The Cross B2
The Groves B3
The Meadows B3
Tower Rd B1
Town Hall B2
Union St B3
Vicar's La B2
Victoria Cr C3
Victoria Rd A2
Walpole St A1
Water Tower St A1
Watergate B1
Watergate St B2
Whipcord La A1
White Friars B2
York St B3

Chichester 335

Adelaide Rd A3
Alexandra Rd A3
Arts Centre B2
Ave de Chartres B1/B2
Barlow Rd A1
Basin Rd C2
Beech Ave B1
Bishops Pal Gardens B2
Bishopsgate Walk A3
Bramber Rd C3
Broyle Rd A2
Bus Station B2
Caledonian Rd B3
Cambrai Ave B3
Canal Wharf C2
Canon La B2
Cathedral ✝ B2
Cavendish St A1
Cawley Rd B2
Cedar Dr A1
Chapel St A2
Cherry Orchard Rd C3
Chichester By-Pass C2/C3
Chichester Cinema B3
Chichester Festival A2
Chichester B2
Churchside A2
Cineworld C1
City Walls B2
Cleveland Rd B3
College La A2
Coll of Science & Technology B1
Cory Cl C2
Council Offices B2
County Hall B2
Courts B2
District B2
Duncan Rd A1
Durnford Cl A1
East Pallant B2
East Row B2
East St B2
East Walls B3
Eastland Rd C3
Ettrick Cl B3
Ettrick Rd B3
Exton Rd C3
Fire Station A2
Football Ground A2
Franklin Pl A2
Friary (Rems of) A2
Garland Cl C3
Green La A3
Grove Rd C3
Guilden Rd B3
Guildhall A2
Hawthorn Cl A1
Hay Rd C3
Henty Gdns B1
Herald Dr C3
Information Ctr B2
John's St B2
Joys Croft A3
Jubilee Pk A3
Jubilee Rd A3
Juxon Cl B1
Kent Rd A3
King George Gdns A2
King's Ave C2
Kingsham Ave C3
Kingsham Rd C2
Laburnum Gr B3
Leigh Rd C1
Lennox Rd A3
Lewis Rd A3
Library B2
Lion St B2
Litten Terr A3
Little London B2
Lyndhurst Rd B3
Market B3
Market Ave B2
Market Cross B2
Market Rd B3
Martlet Cl C2
Melbourne Rd A3
Mount La B1
New Park Rd A3
Newlands La A1
North Pallant B2
North St A2
North Walls A2
Northgate A2
Oak Ave A1
Oak Cl A1
Oaklands Park A2
Oaklands Way A2
Orchard Ave A1
Orchard St A1
Ormonde Ave B3
Pallant House B2
Parchment St A1
Parklands Rd A1/B1
Peter Weston Pl B3
Police Station C2
Post Office A1/B2/B3
Priory La A2
Priory Park A2
Priory Rd A2
Queen's Ave C1
Riverside A3
Roman Amphitheatre B3
St Cyriacs A2
St Pancras A3
St Paul's Rd A2
St Richard's Hospital (A&E) [H] A3
Shamrock Cl A3
Sherbourne Rd A1
Somerstown A2
South Bank C2
South Downs Planetarium ✦ C2
South Pallant B2
South St B2
Southgate B2
Spitalfield La A3
Stirling Rd B3
Stockbridge Rd C1/C2
Swanfield Dr A3
Terminus Ind Est C1
Terminus Rd C1
The Hornet B3
The Litten A3
Tower St A2
Tozer Way A3
Turnbull Rd A3
Upton Rd C1
Velyn Ave B3
Via Ravenna B1
Walnut Ave A1
West St B2
Westgate B1
Westgate Fields B1
Westgate Leisure Ctr B1
Weston Ave C1
Whyke Cl C3
Whyke La B3
Whyke Rd C3
Winden Ave B3

Colchester 335

Abbey Gateway ✝ C2
Albert St A1
Albion Grove C2
Alexandra Rd C1
Artillery St C3
Arts Centre B1
Balkerne Hill B1
Barrack St C3
Beaconsfield Rd C1
Beche Rd C3
Bergholt Rd A1
Bourne Rd C3
Brick Kiln Rd A1
Bristol Rd B2
Broadlands Way A3
Brook St B3
Bury Cl B2
Bus Sta B2
Butt Rd C1
Camp Folley North C2
Camp Folley South C2
Campion Rd C2
Cannon St C3
Canterbury Rd C2
Castle B2
Castle Park B2
Castle Rd B2
Catchpool Rd A1
Causton Rd B1
Cavalry Barracks C1
Chandlers Row C3
Circular Rd East C2
Circular Rd North C1
Circular Rd West C1
Clarendon Way A1
Claudius Rd C2
Colchester Camp Abbey Field C1
Colchester Institute B1
Colchester A1
Colchester Town C2
Colne Bank Ave A1
Colne View Retail Park A2
Compton Rd A3
Cowdray Ave A1/A2
Cowdray Centre, The A2
Crouch St B1
Crowhurst Rd B1
Culver Square Sh Ctr B1
Culver St East B2
Culver St West B1
Dilbridge Rd A3
East Hill B2
East St B3
East Stockwell St B1
Eld La B1
Essex Hall Rd A1
Exeter Dr B2
Fairfax Rd C2
Fire Station A2
Flagstaff Rd C1
George St B2
Gladstone Rd C2
Golden Noble Hill C2
Goring Rd A3
Granville Rd C3
Greenstead Rd B3
Guildford Rd B2
Harsnett Rd C3
Harwich Rd B3
Head St B1
High St B1/B2
High Woods Ctry Park A2
Hollytrees B2
Hythe Hill C3
Information Ctr B2
Ipswich Rd A3
Jarmin Rd A2
Kendall Rd C2
Kimberley Rd C3
King Stephen Rd C3
Le Cateau Barracks C1
Leisure World A2
Library B1
Lincoln Way B2
Lion Walk Sh Ctr B1
Lisle Rd C2
Lucas Rd C2
Magdalen Green C3
Magdalen St C2
Maidenburgh St B2
Maldon Rd C1
Manor Rd B1
Margaret Rd A1
Mason Rd A2
Mercers Way A1
Mercury B1
Mersea Rd C2
Meyrick Cr C2
Mile End Rd A1
Military Rd C2
Mill St C2
Minories B2
Moorside B3
Morant Rd C3
Napier Rd C2
Natural History B2
New Town Rd C2
Norfolk Cr A3
North Hill B1
North Station Rd A1
Northgate St B1
Nunns Rd B1
Odeon B1
Old Coach Rd B3
Old Heath Rd C3
Osborne St B2
Petrolea Cl A1
Police Station C1
Popes La B1
Port La C3
Post Office B1/B2/C2
Priory St B2
Queen St B2
Rawstorn Rd B1
Rebon St C3
Recreation Rd C3
Ripple Way A3
Roman Rd B2
Roman Wall B2
Romford Cl A3
Rosebery Ave B2
St Andrews Ave B3
St Andrews Gdns B3
St Botolph St B2
St Botolphs B2
St John's Abbey (site of) ✝ C2
St John's St B1
St Johns Walk Sh Ctr B1
St Leonards Rd C3
St Marys Fields B1
St Peters B1
St Peter's St B1
Salisbury Ave C1
Serpentine Walk A1
Sheepen Pl B1
Sheepen Rd B1
Sir Isaac's Walk B1
Smythies Ave B2
South St C1
South Way C1
Sports Way A2
Suffolk Cl A3
Town Hall B1
Valentine Dr A3
Victor Rd C3
Wakefield Cl B2
Wellesley Rd C1
Wells Rd B2/B3
West St C1
West Stockwell St B1
Weston Rd C3
Westway A1
Wickham Rd C1
Wimpole Rd C3
Winchester Rd C2
Winnock Rd C2
Wolfe Ave C2
Worcester Rd B2

Coventry 335

Abbots La A1
Albany Rd B1
Alma St B3
Art Faculty B3
Asthill Grove C2
Bablake School A1
Barras La A1/B1
Barrs Hill School A1
Belgrade B2
Bishop Burges St A2
Bond's Hospital B1
Broad Gate B2
Broadway C1
Bus Station A3
Butts Radial B1
Canal Basin ✦ A2
Canterbury St A3
Cathedral ✝ B3
Chester St A1
Cheylesmore Manor House B2
Christ Church Spire ✦ B2
City Walls & Gates ✦ A2
Corporation St B2
Council House B2
Coundon Rd A1
Coventry Station C2
Coventry Transport Museum A2
Cox St A3
Croft Rd B1
Dalton Rd C1
Deasy Rd C3
Earl St B2
Eaton Rd C2
Fairfax St B2
Foleshill Rd A2
Ford's Hospital B2
Fowler Rd A1
Friars Rd C2
Gordon St C1
Gosford St B3
Greyfriars Green ✦ B2
Greyfriars Rd B2
Gulson Rd B3
Hales St A2
Harnall Lane East A3
Harnall Lane West A2
Herbert Art Gallery & Museum B3
Hertford St B2
Hewitt Ave A1
High St B2
Hill St B1
Holy Trinity B2
Holyhead Rd A1
Howard St A3
Huntingdon Rd C1
Information Ctr B3
Jordan Well B3
King Henry VIII Sch C1
Lady Godiva Statue ✦ B2
Lamb St A2
Leicester Row A2
Library B2
Little Park St B2
London Rd C3
Lower Ford St B3
Magistrates & Crown Courts B2
Manor House Drive B2
Manor Rd C2
Market B2
Martyr's Memorial ✦ C2
Meadow St B1
Meriden St A1
Michaelmas Rd C2
Middleborough Rd A1
Mile La C3
Millennium Place ✦ A2
Much Park St B3
Naul's Mill Park A1
New Union B2
Park Rd C2
Parkside C3
Post Office B2
Primrose Hill St A3
Priory Gardens & Visitor Centre B2
Priory St B3
Puma Way C3
Quarryfield La C3
Queen's Rd B1
Quinton Rd C2
Radford Rd A2
Raglan St B3
Retail Park C1
Ringway (Hill Cross) A1
Ringway (Queens) B1
Ringway (Rudge) B1
Ringway (St Johns) B3
Ringway (St Nicholas) A2
Ringway (St Patricks) C2
Ringway (Swanswell) A2
Ringway (Whitefriars) B3
St John St B2
St John The Baptist B2
St Nicholas St A2
Skydome B1
Spencer Ave C1
Spencer Park C1
Spon St B1
Sports Centre B3
Stoney Rd C2
Stoney Stanton Rd A3
Swanswell Pool A3
Sydney Stringer Acad A3
Technical College B1
Technology Park C3
The Precinct B2
Theatre B1
Thomas Landsdail St C2
Tomson Ave A1
Top Green C2
Trinity St B2
University B3
University Sports Ctr B3
Upper Hill St A1
Upper Well St A2
Victoria St A3
Vine St A3
Warwick Rd C2
Waveley Rd B1
Westminster Rd C1
White St A3
Windsor St B1

Derby 335

Abbey St C1
Agard St B1
Albert St B2
Albion St B2
Ambulance Station B1
Arthur St A1
Ashlyn Rd B3
Assembly Rooms B2
Babington La C2
Becket St B1
Belper Rd A1
Bold La B1
Bradshaw Way C2
Bradshaw Way Ret Pk C2
Bridge St B1
Brook St B1
Burton Rd C1
Bus Station B2
Caesar St A2
Canal St C3
Carrington St C3
Cathedral ✝ B2
Cathedral Rd B1
Charnwood St C2
Chester Green Rd A2
City Rd A2
Clarke St A3
Cock Pitt B3
Council House B2
Courts B1
Cranmer Rd B3
Crompton St C1
Crown & County Courts B2
Curzon St B1
Darley Grove A1
Derby C3
Derbyshire County Cricket Ground B3
Derwent Bsns Centre A2
Derwent St B2
Drewry La C1
Duffield Rd A1
Duke St A2
Dunton Cl B3
Eagle Market C2
Eastgate B3
East St B2
Exeter St B2
Farm St C1
Ford St B1
Forester St C1
Fox St A2
Friar Gate B1
Friary St B1
Full St B2
Gerard St C1
Gower St C2
Green La C2
Grey St C1
Guildhall B2
Harcourt St C1
Highfield Rd A1
Hill La C2
Information Ctr B2
Iron Gate B2
John St C3
Joseph Wright Centre B1
Kedleston Rd A1
Key St B2
King Alfred St C1
King St A1
Kingston St A1
Lara Croft Way C2
Leopold St C2
Library B1
Liversage St C3
Lodge La B1
London Rd C2
London Rd Community Hospital [H] C2
Macklin St C1
Mansfield Rd A2
Market B2
Market Pl B2
May St C1
Meadow La B3
Melbourne St C2
Mercian Way C1
Midland Rd C3
Monk St C1
Morledge B2
Mount St C1
Mus & Art Gallery B1
Noble St C3
North Parade A1
North St A1
Nottingham Rd B3
Osmaston Rd C2
Otter St A1
Park St C3
Parker St A1
Pickfords House B1
Playhouse C2
Police HQ A2
Police Station B2
Post Office A1/A2/B1/B2/C2/C3
Prime Enterprise Park A2
Pride Parkway C3
Prime Parkway A2
Queens Leisure Centre B1
Racecourse A3
Railway Terr C3
Register Office B2
Sadler Gate B1
St Alkmund's Way B1/B2
St Helens House ✦ A1
St Mary's A1
St Mary's Bridge A2
St Mary's Bridge Chapel A2
St Mary's Gate B1
St Paul's Rd A2
St Peter's C2
St Peter's St C2
Showcase De Lux C2
Siddals Rd C3
Silk Mill B2
Sir Frank Whittle Rd A3
Spa La C1
Spring St C1
Stafford St B1
Station Approach C3
Stockbrook St C1
Stores Rd A3
Traffic St C2
Wardwick B1
Werburgh St C1
West Ave A1
Westfield Centre C2
West Meadows Ind Est B3
Wharf Rd A2
Wilmot St C2
Wilson St C1
Wood's La C1

Dorchester 335

Ackerman Rd B3
Acland Rd A2
Albert Rd A1
Alexandra Rd B1
Alfred Place B3
Alfred Rd B2
Alington Ave B3
Alington Rd B3
Ambulance Station B3
Ashley Rd B1

Carmichael Way A2
Claggan Rd B3
Connochie Rd C1
Cow Hill C3
Creag Dhubh A2
Croft Rd B3
Douglas Pl B2
Dudley Rd B2
Dumbarton Rd C1
Earl of Inverness Rd A3
Fassifern Rd B1
Fire Station A2
Fort William ≋ B2
Fort William (Remains) ✦ B2
Glasdrum Rd C1
Glen Nevis Pl B3
Gordon Sq B1
Grange Rd C1
Heather Croft Rd C1
Henderson Row C2
High St B1
Highland Visitor Ctr B3
Hill Rd B2
Hospital Belhaven Annexe B3
Information Ctr A3
Inverlochy Ct A3
Kennedy Rd B2/C2
Library B2
Lime Tree Gallery ✦ C1
Linnhe Rd B1
Lochaber Leisure Ctr B3
Lochiel Rd A3
Lochy Rd A3
Lundavra Cres C1
Lundavra Rd C1
Lundy Rd A3
Mamore Cr B2
Mary St B2
Middle St B1
Montrose Ave A3
Moray Pl C1
Morven Pl C2
Moss Rd B2
Nairn Cres C1
Nevis Bridge B3
Nevis Rd A3
Nevis Sports Centre A2
Nevis Terr B2
North Rd B3
Obelisk B2
Parade Rd B2
Police Station A3/C1
Post Office A3/B2
Ross Pl C1
St Andrews B2
Shaw Pl B2
Station Brae B1
Studio B1
Treig Rd A3
Underwater Centre A2
Union Rd C1
Victoria Rd B2
Wades Rd A3
West Highland B2
West Highland College UHI A2
Young Pl B2

Glasgow 337

Admiral St C2
Albert Bridge C5
Albion St B5
Anderston ≋ B3
Anderston Centre B3
Anderston Quay B3
Arches B4
Argyle St A1/A2/B3/B4/B5
Argyle Street ≋ B5
Argyll Arcade B5
Arlington St A3
Arts Centre B3
Ashley St A3
Bain St C6
Baird St A6
Baliol St A3
Ballater St C5
Barras, The (Market) C6
Bath St A3
BBC Scotland/SMG B1
Bell St C6
Bell's Bridge B1
Bentinck St A2
Berkeley St A3
Bishop La B3
Black St A6
Blackburn St C2
Blackfriars St B6
Blantyre St A1
Blythswood Sq A4
Blythswood St B4
Bothwell St B4
Brand St C1
Breadalbane St A2
Bridge St C4
Bridge St Ⓜ C4
Bridgegate C5
Briggait C5
Broomhill Park A6
Broomielaw B4
Broomielaw Quay Gdns B3
Brown St B4
Brunswick St B5
Buccleuch St A3
Buchanan Bus Station A5
Buchanan Galleries A5
Buchanan St B5
Buchanan St Ⓜ B5
Cadogan St B4
Caledonian University A5
Calgary St A5
Cambridge St A4
Canal St A5
Candleriggs B5
Carlton Pl C4
Carnarvon St A3
Carrick St B4
Castle St B6
Cathedral Sq B6
Cathedral St B5
Central College of Commerce B5
Ctr for Contemporary Arts A4
Centre St C4
Cessnock Ⓜ C1
Cessnock St C1
Charing Cross ≋ A3
Charlotte St C6
Cheapside St B3
Cineworld A5
Citizens' Theatre C5
City Chambers Complex B5
City Halls B5
Clairmont Gdns A2
Claremont St A2
Claremont Terr A2
Claythorne St C6
Cleveland St A3
Clifford La C1
Clifford St C1
Clifton Pl A2
Clifton St A2
Clutha St C1
Clyde Arc B2
Clyde Auditorium B2
Clyde Pl C4
Clyde Place Quay C4
Clyde St C5
Clyde Walkway C3
Clydeside Expressway B2
Coburg St C4
Cochrane St B5
College of Nautical Studies C5
College St B6
Collins St B6
Commerce St C4
Cook St C4
Cornwall St C2
Couper St A5
Cowcaddens Ⓜ A4
Cowcaddens Rd A4
Crimea St B3
Custom House C4
Custom Ho Quay Gdns C4
Dalhousie St A4
Dental Hospital A4
Derby St A2
Dobbie's Loan A4/A5
Dobbie's Loan Pl A5
Dorset St A3
Douglas St B4
Doulton Fountain ✦ C6
Dover St A2
Drury St B4
Drygate B6
Duke St B6
Dunaskin St A1
Dunblane St A4
Dundas St B5
Dunlop St C5
East Campbell St C6
Eastvale Pl A1
Eglinton St C4
Elderslie St A3
Elliot St B2
Elmbank St A3
Esmond St A1
Exhibition Centre ≋ B2
Exhibition Way B2
Eye Infirmary A2
Festival Park C1
Film Theatre A4
Finnieston Quay B2
Finnieston St B2
Fitzroy Pl A2
Florence St C5
Fox St C5
Gallowgate C6
Garnet St A3
Garnethill St A4
Garscube Rd A4
George Sq B5
George St B5
George V Bridge C4
Gilbert St A1
Glasgow Bridge C4
Glasgow Cathedral ✝ B6
Glasgow Central ≋ B4
Glasgow Green C6
Glasgow Metropolitan College B5/C5
Glasgow Tower ✦ B1
Glasgow Science Centre ✦ B1
Glasgow Science Centre Footbridge B1
Glassford St B5
Glebe St A6
Gorbals Cross C5
Gorbals St C5
Gordon St B4
Govan Rd B1/C1/C2
Grace St B3
Grand Ole Opry ✦ C2
Grafton Pl A5
Grant St A3
Granville St A3
Gray St A2
Greendyke St C6
Grey Eagle St B7
Harley St C1
Harvie St C1
Haugh Rd A1
Heliport B1
Henry Wood Hall A2
High Court C5
High St B6
High Street ≋ B6
Hill St A3
Holland St A3
Holm St B4
Hope St A5
Houldsworth St B2
Houston Pl C3
Houston St C3
Howard St C5
Hunter St C6
Hutcheson St B5
Hutchesons Hall B5
Hydepark St B3
Hydro The B2
Imax Cinema B1
India St A3
Information Ctr B5
Ingram St B5
Jamaica St B4
James Watt St B4
John Knox St B6
John St B5
Kelvin Hall ✦ A1
Kelvin Statue ✦ A2
Kelvin Way A2
Kelvingrove Art Gallery & Museum A1
Kelvingrove Park A2
Kelvingrove St A2
Kelvinhaugh St A1
Kennedy St A6
Kent Rd A2
Killermont St A5
King St B5
King's A3
Kingston Bridge C3
Kingston St C4
Kinning Park Ⓜ C2
Kyle St A5
Lancefield Quay B2
Lancefield St B3
Langshot St C1
Lendel Pl C1
Lighthouse ✦ B4
Lister St A6
Little St B3
London Rd C6
Lorne St C1
Lower Harbour B1
Lumsden St A1
Lymburn St A1
Lyndoch Cr A3
Lynedoch Pl A3
Lynedoch St A3
Maclellan St C1
Mair St C2
Maitland St A4
Mansell St C7
Mavisbank Gdns C2
Mcalpine St B3
Mcaslin St A6
McLean Sq C2
McLellan Gallery A4
McPhater St A4
Merchants' House B5
Middlesex St C2
Middleton St C1
Midland St B4
Miller St B5
Millroad St C6
Milnpark St C2
Milton St A4
Minerva St B2
Mitchell Library A3
Mitchell St West B4
Mitchell Theatre A3
Modern Art Gallery B5
Moir St C6
Molendinar St C6
Moncur St C6
Montieth Row C6
Montrose St B5
Morrison St C3
Mosque C5
Nairn St A1
Nelson Mandela Sq B5
Nelson St C4
Nelson's Monument C6
New City Rd A4
Newton St A3
Newton Pl A3
Nicholson St C4
Nile St B5
Norfolk Court C4
Norfolk St C4
North Frederick St B5
North Hanover St B5
North Portland St B6
North St A3
North Wallace St A5
O2 Academy ✦ C4
Odeon C3
Old Dumbarton Rd A1
Osborne St B5/C5
Oswald St B4
Overnewton St A1
Oxford St C4
Pacific Dr B1
Paisley Rd C3
Paisley Rd West C1
Park Circus A2
Park Gdns A2
Park St South A2
Park Terr A2
Parkgrove Terr A2
Parnie St C5
Parson St A6
Partick Bridge A1
Passport Office A5
Pavilion Theatre A4
Pembroke St A3
People's Palace C6
Pinkston Rd A6
Piping Centre, The National ✦ A5
Pitt St A4/B4
Plantation Park C1
Plantation Quay B1
Police Sta A4/A6/B5
Port Dundas Rd A5
Port St B2
Portman St C2
Prince's Dock B1
Princes Sq B5
Provand's Lordship B6
Queen St B5
Queen Street ≋ B5
Renfrew St A3/A4
Renton St A5
Richmond St B5
Robertson St B4
Rose St A4
Rottenrow B5
Royal Concert Hall A5
Royal Cr A2
Royal Exchange Sq B5
Royal Highland Fusiliers Museum A3
Royal Hospital For Sick Children A1
Royal Infirmary B6
Royal Scottish Academy of Music & Drama A4
Royal Terr A2
Rutland Cr C2
St Kent St C6
St Andrew's (RC) ✝ C5
St Andrew's C6
St Andrew's St C5
St Enoch Ⓜ B5
St Enoch Shopping Ctr B5
St Enoch Sq B4
St George's Rd A3
St James Rd B6
St Mungo Ave A5/A6
St Mungo Museum of Religious Life B6
St Mungo Pl A6
St Vincent Cr A2
St Vincent Pl B5
St Vincent St B3/B4
St Vincent Street Church B4
St Vincent Terr B3
Saltmarket C5
Sandyford Pl A3
Sauchiehall St A2/A4
School of Art A4
Sclater St B7
Scotland St C2
Scott St A4
Scottish Exhibition & Conference Centre B1
Seaward St C2
Shaftesbury St B3
Sheriff Court C5
Shields Rd Ⓜ C3
Shuttle St B6
Somerset Pl A2
South Portland St C4
Springburn Rd A6
Springfield Quay C3
Stanley St C2
Stevenson St C6
Stewart St A4
Stirling Rd B6
Stirling's Library B5
Stobcross Quay B1
Stobcross Rd B1
Stock Exchange B5
Stockwell Pl C5
Stockwell St B5
Stow College A4
Strathclyde University B6
Sussex St C2
Synagogues A3/C4
Taylor Pl A6
Tenement House A3
Teviot St A1
Theatre Royal A4
Tolbooth Steeple & Mercat Cross ✦ C6
Tower St C2
Trades House B5
Tradeston St C4
Transport Museum A1
Tron C5
Trongate B5
Tunnel St B2
Turnbull St C5
Union St B4
Victoria Bridge C5
Virginia St B5
West Greenhill Pl B2
West Regent St A4
Wallace St C3
Walls St B6
Walmer Cr C1
Warrock St B3
Washington St B3
Waterloo St B4
Watson St B6
Watt St C3
Wellington St B4
West Campbell St B4
West George St B4
West Graham St A4
West Regent St B4
West St C4
West St Ⓜ C4
Westminster Terr A2
Whitehall St B3
Wilkes St C7
Wilson St B5
Woodlands Gate A3
Woodlands Rd A3
Woodlands Terr A2
Woodside Cr A3
Woodside Pl A3
Woodside Terr A3
York St B4
Yorkhill Pde A1
Yorkhill St A1

Gloucester 337

Albion St C1
Alexandra Rd B3
Alfred St C3
All Saints Rd C2
Alvin St B2
Arthur St C2
Barton St C2
Barrack Square B1
Blackfriars ✝ B1
Blenheim Rd C2
Bristol Rd C1
Brunswick Rd C2
Bruton Way B2
Bus Station B2
City Council Offices B1
City Mus, Art Gall & Library B2
Clarence St B2
Commercial Rd B1
Cromwell St C2
Deans Way A2
Denmark Rd A3
Derby Rd C3
Docks ✦ C1
Eastgate Shopping Ctr B1
Eastgate St B2
Edwy Pde A2
Estcourt Cl A3
Estcourt Rd A3
Falkner St C2
Folk Museum B1
GL1 Leisure Centre C2
Gloucester Cath ✝ B1
Gloucester Quays Outlet Shopping C1
Gloucester Station ≋ B2
Gloucestershire Royal Hospital (A&E) B3
Gloucester Waterways C1
Goodyere St C2
Gouda Way A1
Great Western Rd B3
Guildhall B2
Heathville Rd A3
Henry Rd B3
Henry St B2
Hinton Rd A2
HM Prison B1
India Rd C3
Information Ctr B1
Jersey Rd C3
King's C2
King's Sq B2
Kingsholm (Gloucester RFC) A2
Kingsholm Rd A2
Lansdown Rd A3
Library C2
Llanthony Rd C1
London Rd B3
Longhorn Ave A1
Longsmith St B1
Malvern Rd A3
Market Pde B2
Mercia Rd A1
Metz Way C3
Midland Rd C2
Millbrook St C3
Market B2
Montpellier C1
Napier St C3
Nettleton Rd C2
New Inn B2
New Olympus C3
North Rd A3
Northgate St B2
Oxford Rd A2
Oxford St B2
Pk & Ride Gloucester A1
Park Rd C2
Park St B2
Parliament St C1
Pitt St B1
Police Station B1
Post Office B2
Quay St B1
Recreation Gd A1/A2
Regent St C2
Robert Raikes Ho B1
Royal Oak Rd B1
Russell St B2
Ryecroft St C2
St Aldate St B2
St Ann Way C1
St Catherine St A2
St Mark St A2
St Mary de Crypt B1
St Mary de Lode B1
St Nicholas's B1
St Oswald's Rd A1
St Oswald's Retail Park A1
St Peter's B2
Seabroke Rd A3
Sebert St A2
Severn Rd C1
Sherborne St B2
Shire Hall B1
Sidney St C3
Soldiers of Gloucestershire B1
Southgate St B1/C1
Spa Field C1
Spa Rd C1
Sports Ground A2/B2
Station Rd B2
Stratton Rd C3
Stroud Rd C1
Superstore A1
Swan Rd A2
The Park C2
The Quay B1
Trier Way C1/C2
Union St A2
Vauxhall Rd C3
Victoria St C2
Walham Lane A1
Wellington St C2
Westgate Retail Park B1
Westgate St B1
Widden St C2
Worcester St B2

Grimsby 337

Abbey Drive East C2
Abbey Drive West C2
Abbey Park Rd C2
Abbey Rd C2
Abbey Walk C2
Abbeygate Sh Ctr C2
Abbotsway C2
Adam Smith St A1/A2
Ainslie St C2
Albert St A3
Alexandra Dock A2/B2
Alexandra Retail Park A2
Alexandra Rd A2/B2
Annesley St A2
Armstrong St A1
Arthur St B1
Augusta St C1
Bargate C1
Beeson St A1
Bethlehem St C2
Bodiam Way B3
Bradley St B3
Brighowgate C1/C2
Bus Station B2/C2
Canterbury Dr C1
Cartergate B1/C1
Catherine St C3
Caxton A3
Chantry La B1
Charlton St A1
Church La C2
Church St A3
Cleethorpe Rd A3
College A3
College St C1
Compton Dr C1
Corporation Bridge A2
Corporation Rd A1
Court B3
Crescent St B1
Deansgate C1
Doughty Rd C2
Dover St B1
Duchess St C2
Dudley St C1
Duke of York Gardens B1
Duncombe St B3
Earl La B1
East Marsh St B3
East St B2
Eastgate B3
Eastside Rd A3
Eaton Ct C1
Eleanor St B3
Ellis Way B3
Fisherman's Chapel A3
Fisherman's Wharf B2
Fishing Heritage Centre B2
Flour Sq A3
Frederick St B1
Frederick Ward Way B2
Freeman St A3/B3
Freshney Dr B1
Freshney Pl B2
Garden St C2
Garibaldi St A3
Garth La B2
Grime St B3
Grimsby Docks Sta ≋ A3
Grimsby Town Sta ≋ C2
Hainton Ave C3
Har Way B3
Hare St C3
Harrison St B1
Haven Ave B1
Hay Croft Ave B1
Hay Croft St B1
Heneage Rd B3/C3
Henry St B1
Holme St B3
Hume St C1
James St B1
Joseph St B1
Kent St A3
King Edward St A3
Lambert Rd C2
Library B2
Lime St B1
Lister St B1
Littlefield La C1
Lockhill A3
Lord St B1
Ludford St C3
Macaulay St B1
Mallard Mews C3
Manor Ave C2
Market A3
Market Hall B2
Market St B3
Moss Rd C2
Nelson St A3
New St B2
Osbourne St B2
Pasture St B3
Peaks Parkway C3
Pelham Rd C1
Police Station A3
Post Office B1/B2/C2
Pyewipe Rd A1
Railway Pl A3
Railway St A3
Recreation Ground C2
Rendel St A2
Retail Park A2
Richard St B1
Ripon St B1
Robinson St East B3
Royal St A3
St Hilda's Ave C1
St James C2
Sheepfold St B3/C3
Sixhills St C3
South Park B2
Spring St A3
Superstore B3
Tasburgh St C3
Tennyson St B2
The Close C1
Thesiger St A3
Time Trap C2
Town Hall B2
Veal St B1
Victoria Retail Park A3
Victoria St North A2
Victoria St South B2
Victoria St West B2
Watkin St A1
Welholme Ave C2
Welholme Rd C3
Wellington St B3
Wellowgate C2
Werneth Rd B3
West Coates Rd A1
Westgate A2
Westminster Dr C1
Willingham St C3
Wintringham Rd C2
Wood St B3
Yarborough Dr B1
Yarborough Hotel C2

Hanley 337

Acton St A3
Albion St B2
Argyle St C1
Ashbourne Gr A2
Avoca St A3
Baskerville Rd B3
Bedford Rd C1
Bedford St C1
Bethesda St B2
Bexley St A2
Birches Head Rd A3
Botteslow St C3
Boundary St A2
Broad St C2
Broom St A3
Bryan St A2
Bucknall New Rd B3
Bucknall Old Rd B3
Bus Station B3
Cannon St C2
Castlefield St C1
Hanley Park C2
Cavendish St B1
Central Forest Pk A2
Charles St B3
Cheapside B2
Chell St A3
Clarke St C1
Cleveland Rd C2
Clifford St C3
Clough St B2
Clyde St C1
College Rd C2
Cooper St C2
Corbridge Rd A1
Cutts St C2
Davis St C1
Denbigh St A1
Derby St C3
Dilke St A3
Dundas St A3
Dundee Rd C1
Dyke St B3
Eastwood Rd C3
Eaton St A3
Etruria Park B1
Etruria Rd B1
Etruria Vale Rd C1
Festing St A3
Festival Retail Park A1
Fire Station C2
Foundry St B2
Franklyn St C3
Garnet St B1
Garth St B3
George St A3
Gilman St B3
Glass St B3
Goodson St B3
Greyhound Way A1
Grove Pl C1
Hampton St C3
Hanley Park C2
Harding Rd C2
Hassall St B3
Havelock Pl C1
Hazlehurst St C3
Hinde St C2
Hope St B2
Houghton St C2
Hulton St A3
Information Ctr B3
Jasper St C2
Jervis St A3
John Bright St A3
John St B2
Keelings Rd A3
Kimberley Rd C1
Ladysmith Rd C1
Lawrence St C2
Leek Rd C3
Library C2
Lichfield St C3
Linfield Rd B3
Loftus St A2
Lower Bedford St C1
Lower Bryan St A2
Lower Mayer St A3
Lowther St A1
Magistrates Court C2
Malham St A2
Marsh St B2
Matlock St C3
Mayer St A3
Milton St C1
Mitchell Memorial Theatre B2
Morley St B2
Moston St A3
Mount Pleasant C1
Mulgrave St A1
Mynors St B3
Nelson Pl B3
New Century St B1
Octagon Retail Park B1
Ogden Rd C3
Old Hall St B3
Old Town Rd A3
Pall Mall B2
Palmerston St C3
Park and Ride C2
Parker St B2
Pavilion Dr A1
Pelham St C3
Percy St B2
Piccadilly B2
Picton St B3
Plough St A3
Police Station C2
Portland St A1
Post Office A3/B3/C3
Potteries Museum & Art Gallery B2
Potteries Sh Ctr B2
Potteries Way C2
Powell St A1
Pretoria Rd C1
Quadrant Rd B2
Ranelagh St C2
Raymond St C2
Rectory Rd C1
Regent Rd C2
Regent Theatre B2
Richmond Terr C2
Ridgehouse Dr A1
Robson St C2
St Ann St B3
St Luke St B3
Sampson St B2
Shaw St A1
Sheaf St C3
Shearer St C1
Shelton New Rd C1
Shirley Rd C2
Slippery La B2
Snow Hill C2
Spur St C3
Stafford St B2
Statham St B2
Stubbs La C3
Sun St C1
Supermarket A1/B2
Talbot St C3
The Parkway C2
Town Hall B2
Town Rd A3
Trinity St B2
Union St A2
Upper Hillchurch St A3
Upper Huntbach St B3
Victoria Hall Theatre B3
Warner St C2
Warwick St C1
Waterloo Rd A1
Waterloo St B3
Well St B3
Wellesley St C2
Wellington Rd B3
Wellington St B3
Whitehaven Dr A2
Whitmore St C1
Windermere St A1
Woodall St A1
Yates St C2
York St A2

Harrogate 338

Albert St C2
Alexandra Rd B2
Arthington Ave B2
Ashfield Rd A2
Back Cheltenham Mount B2
Beech Grove C1
Belmont Rd C1
Bilton Dr A2
Bower Rd B2
Bower St B2
Bus Station B2
Cambridge Rd B2
Cambridge St B2
Cemetery A2
Chatsworth Pl A2
Chatsworth Grove A2
Chatsworth Rd A2
Chelmsford Rd B3
Cheltenham Cr B2
Cheltenham Mt B2
Cheltenham Pde B2
Christ Church B3
Christ Church Oval B3
Chudleigh Rd B3
Clarence Dr B1
Claro Rd A3
Claro Way A3
Coach Park B2
Coach Rd B3
Cold Bath Rd C1
Commercial St B2
Coppice Ave A1
Coppice Dr A1
Coppice Gate A1
Cornwall Rd B1
Council Offices B1
Court C3
Crescent Gdns B1
Crescent Rd B1
Dawson Terr A2
Devonshire Pl B3
Diamond Mews C1
Dixon Rd A2
Dixon Terr A2
Dragon Ave B3
Dragon Parade B2
Dragon Rd B2
Duchy Rd B1
East Parade B2
East Park Rd C3
Esplanade B1
Fire Station A2
Franklin Mount A2
Franklin Rd B2
Franklin Square A2
Glebe Rd C1
Grove Park Ct A3
Grove Park Terr A3
Grove Rd A2
Hampswaite Rd A1
Harcourt Dr B3
Harcourt Rd B3
Harrogate ≋ B2
Harrogate Int Ctr B1
Harrogate Ladies Coll B1
Harrogate Theatre B2
Heywood Rd C1
Hollins Cr A1
Hollins Mews A1
Hollins Rd A1
Homestead Rd C3
Hydro Leisure Ctr, The A1
Information Ctr B1
James St B2
Jenny Field Dr A1
John St B2
Kent Dr A1
Kent Rd A1
Kings Rd A2
Kingsway B3
Kingsway Dr B3
Lancaster Rd C1
Leeds Rd C2
Lime Grove B3
Lime St A3
Mayfield Grove B2
Mayfield Pl A2
Mercer B1
Montpellier Hill B1
Mornington Cr A3
Mornington Terr B3
Mowbray Sq B3
North Park Rd B3
Nydd Vale Rd B2
Oakdale Ave A1
Oatlands Dr C3
Odeon B2
Osborne Rd A2
Otley Rd C2
Oxford St B2
Park Chase B3
Park Parade B3
Park View B2
Parliament St B1
Police Station B3
Post Office B2/C1
Providence Terr A2
Queen Parade C3
Queen's Rd C1
Raglan St C2
Regent Ave A3
Regent Grove A3
Regent Parade A3
Regent St A3
Regent Terr A3
Rippon Rd A1
Robert St C2
Royal Baths & Turkish Baths B1
Royal Pump Room B1
St Luke's Mount A2
St Mary's Ave C1
St Mary's Walk C1
Scargill Rd A1
Skipton Rd A3
Skipton St A2
Slingsby Walk C3
South Park Rd C2
Spring Grove A1
Springfield Ave B1
Station Ave B2
Station Parade B2
Strawberry Dale B2
Stray Rein C3
Studley Rd A2
Superstore B2
Swan Rd B1
The Parade B2
The Stray C2/C3
Tower St C2
Trinity Rd C2
Union St B2
Valley Dr C1
Valley Gardens C1
Valley Mount C1
Victoria Ave C2
Victoria Rd C1
Victoria Shopping Ctr B2
Waterloo St A2
West Park C2
West Park St C2
Wood View A1
Woodfield Ave A3
Woodfield Dr A3
Woodfield Grove A3
Woodfield Rd A3
Woodfield Square A3
Woodside B3
York Pl C3
York Rd B1

Holyhead Caergybi 338

Armenia St A2
Arthur St C2
Beach Rd A1
Boston St B2
Bowling Green C3
Bryn Erw Rd C3
Bryn Glas Cl C3
Bryn Glas Rd C3
Bryn Gwyn Rd C1
Bryn Marchog A1
Bryn Mor Terr A2
Bryngoleu Ave A1
Cae Braenar C3
Cambria St B1
Captain Skinner's Obelisk ✦ B2
Cecil St C2
Celtic Gateway Footbridge B2
Cemetery C1/C2
Cleveland Ave C2
Coastguard Lookout A2
Court B2
Customs House A3
Cybi Pl A2

Cyttir Rd C3
Edmund St B1
Empire B2
Ferry Terminals B2
Ffordd Beibio B3
Ffordd Feurig C3
Ffordd Hirnos C3
Ffordd Jasper C3
Ffordd Tudur B3
Fire Station C2
Garreglwyd Rd B1
Gilbert St C2
Gorsedd Circle B1
Gwelfor Ave A1
Harbour View B3
Henry St C2
High Terr C1
Hill St B2
Holborn Rd C2
Holland Park Industrial Estate C3
Holyhead Park B1
Holyhead Station B2
Information Ctr B2
King's Rd C2
Kingsland Rd C2
Lewascote C3
Library B2
Lifeboat Station A1
Llanfawr Cl C3
Llanfawr Rd C3
Lligwy St C2
Lon Deg C3
London Rd C3
Longford Rd B1
Longford Terr B1
Maes Cybi B1
Maes Hedd A1
Maes-Hyfryd Rd C1
Maes-y-Dref B1
Maes-yr-Haf A2/B1
Maes-yr-Ysgol C3
Marchog C3
Marina A1
Maritime Museum A1
Market B2
Market St B2
Mill Bank B1
Min-y-Mor Rd A1
Morawelon Ind Est B3
Morawelon Rd B3
Moreton Rd C1
New Park Rd B1
Newry St A2
Old Harbour Lighthouse A3
Plas Rd C1
Police Station B2
Porth-y-Felin Rd A1
Post Office A1/B1/B2/B3/C2/C3
Prince of Wales Rd A2
Priory La B3
Pump St C1
Queens Park B1
Reseifion Rd C1
Rock St B1
Roman Fort B2
St Cybi St B2
St Cybi's Church B2
St Seiriol's Cl B1
Salt Island Bridge A2
Seabourne Rd A1
South Stack Rd B1
Sports Ground B1
Stanley St B2
Station St B2
Tan-y-Bryn Rd A1
Tan-yr-Efail C2
Tara St C1
Thomas St B1
Town Hall A2
Treseifion Estate C2
Turkey Shore Rd B2
Ucheldre Arts Centre B1
Ucheldre Ave B1
Upper Baptist St B1
Victoria Rd B2
Victoria Terr B2
Vulcan St B1
Walthew Ave A1
Walthew La A1
Wian St C2

Hull 338

Adelaide St C1
Albert Dock C1
Albion St B2
Alfred Gelder St B2
Anlaby Rd B1
Arctic Corsair B3
Beverley Rd A1
Blanket Row C2
Bond St B2
Bridlington Ave A2
Brook St B1
Brunswick Ave A1
Bus Station B1
Camilla Cl C3
Cannon St A2
Cannon's C1
Caroline St A2
Carr La B2
Castle St C2
Central Library B1
Charles St A2
Citadel Way B3
City Hall B2
City Hall Theatre B2
Clarence St B3
Cleveland St A3
Clifton St A1
Club Culture C2
Colonial St B1
Court B2
Deep, The C3
Dock Office Row B3
Dock St B2
Dinostar C2
Drypool Bridge B3
Egton St A3
English St C1
Ferens Gallery B2
Ferensway B1
Francis St A2
Francis St West A2
Freehold St A1
Freetown Way A2
Fruit Theatre C2
Garrison Rd B3
George St B2
Gibson St A2
Great Thornton St B1
Great Union St A3
Green La A2
Grey St A1
Grimston St B2
Grosvenor St A1
Guildhall B2
Guildhall Rd B2
Hands-on History B2
Harley St A1
Hessle Rd C1
High St B3
Holy Trinity B2
Hull & East Riding Museum B3
Hull Arena C1
Hull College B3
Hull History Centre A2
Hull (Paragon) Station B1
Hull Truck Theatre B1
Humber Dock Marina C2
Humber Dock St C2
Humber St C2
Hyperion St A3
Information Ctr B2
Jameson St B1
Jarratt St B2
Jenning St A3
King Billy Statue C2
King Edward St B2
King St A2
Kingston Retail Park C1
Kingston St C2
Liddell St A1
Lime St A3
Lister St C1
Lockwood St A2
Maister House B3
Maritime Museum B2
Market B2
Market Place B2
Minerva Pier C2
Mulgrave St A3
Myton Bridge C3
Myton St B1
NAPA (Northern Acad of Performing Arts) B1
Nelson St C2
New Cleveland St A3
New George St A2
New Theatre A2
Norfolk St A1
North Bridge A3
North St B1
Odeon C1
Old Harbour C3
Osborne St B1
Paragon St B2
Park St B1
Percy St A2
Pier St C2
Police Station B1
Post Office A1/B1/B2
Porter St C1
Portland St B1
Posterngate B2
Prince's Quay B2
Prospect Centre B1
Prospect St B1
Queen's Gdns B2
Railway Dock Marina C2
Railway St C2
Real B1
Red Gallery B1
Reform St A2
Retail Park B1
River Hull Footbridge B3
Riverside Quay C2
Roper St B2
St James St C1
St Luke's St B1
St Mark St A3
St Mary the Virgin B3
St Stephens Sh Ctr B1
Scott St A2
South Bridge Rd B3
Spring Bank A1
Spring St B1
Spurn Lightship C2
Spyvee St A3
Streetlife Transport Museum B3
Sykes St A2
Tidal Surge Barrier C3
Tower St B3
Trinity House B2
University B2
Vane St A1
Victoria Pier C2
Waterhouse La B2
Waterloo St A1
Waverley St C1
Wellington St C2
Wellington St West C2
West St B1
Whitefriargate B2
Wilberforce Dr B2
Wilberforce House B3
Wilberforce Monument B3
William St C1
Wincolmlee A3
Witham A3
Wright St A1

Inverness 338

Abban St A1
Academy St B2
Alexander Pl B2
Anderson St A2
Annfield Rd C3
Ardconnel St B3
Ardconnel Terr B3
Ardross Pl B2
Ardross St B2
Argyle St B3
Argyle Terr B3
Attadale Rd B1
Ballifeary La C2
Ballifeary Rd C1/C2
Balnacraig La A1
Balnain House B2
Balnain St B2
Bank St B2
Bellfield Park C2
Bellfield Terr C3
Benula Rd A1
Birnie Terr A1
Bishop's Rd C2
Bowling Green A2
Bowling Green B2
Bowling Green C2
Bridge St B2
Brown St A2
Bruce Ave C1
Bruce Gdns C1
Bruce Pk C1
Burial Ground A2
Burnett Rd A3
Bus Station B3
Caledonian Rd B1
Cameron Rd A1
Cameron Sq A1
Carse Rd A1
Carsegate Rd Sth A1
Castle Garrison Encounter B2
Castle Rd B2
Castle St B3
Celt St B2
Chapel St A2
Charles St B3
Church St B2
Clachnacuddin Football Ground A1
Columba Rd B1/C1
Crown Ave B3
Crown Circus B3
Crown Dr B3
Crown Rd B3
Crown St B3
Culduthel Rd C3
Dalneigh Cres C1
Dalneigh Rd C1
Denny St B3
Dochfour Dr B1/C1
Douglas Row B2
Duffy Dr C3
Dunabban Rd A1
Dunain Rd B1
Duncraig St B2
Eastgate Shopping Ctr B3
Eden Court C2
Fairfield Rd B1
Falcon Sq B3
Fire Station A3
Fraser St B2
Fraser St C2
Friars' Bridge A2
Friars' La B2
Friars' St A2
George St A2
Gilbert St A2
Glebe St A2
Glendoe Terr A1
Glenurquhart Rd C1
Gordon Terr B3
Gordonville Rd C2
Grant St A2
Greig St B2
HM Prison B3
Harbour Rd A3
Harrowden Rd B1
Haugh Rd C2
Heatherley Cres C3
High St B3
Highland Council HQ, The C2
Hill Park C3
Hill St B3
Huntly Pl A2
Huntly St B2
India St A2
Industrial Estate A3
Information Ctr B2
Innes St A2
Inverness B3
Inverness College (Midmills Campus) B3
Inverness College UHI A3
Inverness High School B1
Inverness Museum B2
Jamaica St A2
Kenneth St B2
Kilmuir Rd A1
King St B2
Kingsmills Rd B3
Laurel Ave B1/C1
Library A3
Lilac Gr B1
Lindsay Ave C1
Lochalsh Rd A1/B1
Longman Rd A3
Lotland Pl A2
Lower Kessock St A1
Madras St A2
Market Hall B3
Maxwell Dr C1
Mayfield Rd C3
Millburn Rd B3
Mitchell's La C3
Montague Row B2
Muirfield Rd C3
Muirtown St B1
Nelson St A2
Ness Bank C2
Ness Bridge B2
Ness Walk B2/C2
Old Edinburgh Rd C3
Old High Church B2
Park Rd C1
Paton St C2
Perceval Rd B1
Planefield Rd B2
Police Station A3
Porterfield Bank C3
Porterfield Rd C3
Portland Pl A2
Post Office A2/B1/B2/B3
Queen St B2
Queensgate B2
Railway Terr A3
Rangemore Rd B1
Reay St B3
Riverside St A2
Rose St A2
Ross Ave B1
Rowan Rd B1
Royal Northern Infirmary C2
St Andrew's Cathedral C2
St Columba B2
St John's Ave C1
St Mary's Ave C1
Sheriff Court B3
Shore St A2
Smith Ave C1
Southside Pl C3
Southside Rd C3
Spectrum Centre B2
Strothers La B3
Superstore B2
TA Centre C2
Telford Gdns B1
Telford Rd A1
Telford St A1
Tomnahurich Cemetery C1
Tomnahurich St B2
Town Hall B3
Union Rd B3
Union St B3
Walker Pl A2
Walker Rd A3
War Memorial C2
Waterloo Bridge A2
Wells St B1
Young St B2

Ipswich 338

Alderman Rd B2
All Saints' Rd A1
Alpe St B2
Ancaster Rd C1
Ancient House B3
Anglesea Rd B2
Ann St B2
Arboretum A2
Austin St C2
Belstead Rd C2
Berners St B2
Bibb Way B1
Birkfield Dr C1
Black Horse La B2
Bolton La B3
Bond St C3
Bowthorpe Cl B2
Bramford La A1
Bramford Rd A1
Bridge St C2
Brookfield Rd A1
Brooks Hall Rd A1
Broomhill A2
Broomhill Rd A1
Broughton Rd A2
Bulwer Rd B1
Burrell Rd C2
Butter Market B2
Buttermarket Shopping Centre, The B3
Cardinal Park Leisure Park C2
Carr St B3
Cecil Rd B2
Cecilia St C2
Chancery Rd C2
Charles St B2
Chevallier St A1
Christchurch Mansion & Wolsey Art Gallery B3
Christchurch Park A3
Christchurch St B3
Cineworld C2
Civic Centre B2
Civic Dr B2
Clarkson St B1
Cobbold St B3
Commercial Rd C2
Constable Rd A3
Constantine Rd C1
Constitution Hill A2
Corder Rd A3
Corn Exchange B2
Cotswold Ave A2
Council Offices C2
County Hall B3
Crown Court C2
Crown St B2
Cullingham Rd B1
Cumberland St B2
Curriers La B2
Dale Hall La A2
Dales View Rd A1
Dalton Rd B2
Dillwyn St B1
Elliot St B1
Elm St B2
Elsmere Rd A3
Falcon St C2
Felaw St C3
Flint Wharf C3
Fonnereau Rd B2
Fore St C3
Foundation St C3
Franciscan Way C2
Friars St C2
Gainsborough Rd A3
Gatacre Rd B1
Geneva Rd B2
Gippeswyk Ave C1
Gippeswyk Park C1
Grafton Way C2
Graham Rd A1
Grimwade St C3
Great Whip St C3
Handford Cut B1
Handford Rd B1
Henley Rd A2
Hervey St B3
High St B2
Holly Rd A2
Information Ctr B3
Ipswich Haven Marina C3
Ipswich School A2
Ipswich Station C2
Ipswich Town FC (Portman Road) C2
Ivry St A2
Kensington Rd A1
Kesteven Rd C1
Key St C3
Kingsfield Ave A3
Kitchener Rd A1
Magistrates Court B2
Little's Cr C2
London Rd B1
Low Brook St C3
Lower Orwell St C3
Luther Rd C2
Manor Rd A3
Mornington Ave A1
Museum & Art Gallery B2
Museum St B2
Neale St B3
New Cardinal St C2
New Cut East C3
New Cut West C3
New Wolsey B2
Newson St B2
Norwich Rd A1/B1
Oban St B2
Old Customs House C3
Old Foundry Rd B3
Old Merchant's House C3
Orford St B2
Paget Rd A2
Park Rd A3
Park View Rd A2
Peter's St C2
Philip Rd C2
Pine Ave A2
Pine View Rd A2
Police Station B2
Portman Rd B2
Portman Walk C1
Post Office B2/B3
Princes St C2
Prospect St B1
Queen St B2
Ranelagh Rd C1
Recreation Ground B1
Rectory Rd C2
Regent Theatre B3
Retail Park C1
Retail Park C2
Richmond Rd A1
Rope Walk C3
Rose La C3
Russell Rd C2
St Edmund's Rd A2
St George's St B2
St Helen's St B3
Sherrington Rd A1
Silent St C2
Sir Alf Ramsey Way C1
Sirdar Rd B1
Soane St B3
Springfield La A1
Star La C3
Stevenson Rd B1
Suffolk College C3
Suffolk Retail Park B1
Superstore B1
Surrey Rd B1
Tacket St C3
Tavern St B3
The Avenue A3
Tolly Cobbold Museum C3
Tower Ramparts B2
Tower Ramparts Shopping Centre B2
Tower St B3
Town Hall B2
Tuddenham Rd A3
Upper Brook St B3
Upper Orwell St B3
University C3
Valley Rd A2
Vermont Cr B3
Vermont Rd B3
Vernon St C3
Warrington Rd A2
Waterloo Rd A1
Waterworks St C3
Wellington St B1
West End Rd B1
Westerfield Rd A3
Westgate St B2
Westholme Rd A1
Westwood Ave A1
Willoughby Rd C2
Withipoll St B3
Woodbridge Rd B3
Woodstone Ave A3
Yarmouth Rd B1

Kendal 338

Abbot Hall Art Gallery & Museum of Lakeland Life C2
Ambulance Station A2
Anchorite Fields C2
Anchorite Rd C2
Ann St A3
Appleby Rd A3
Archers Meadow C3
Ashleigh Rd A2
Aynam Rd B2
Bankfield Rd B1
Beast Banks B2
Beezon Fields A2
Beezon Rd A2
Beezon Trad Est A3
Belmont B2
Birchwood Cl C1
Blackhall Rd B2
Brewery Arts Ctr B2
Bridge St B2
Brigsteer Rd C1
Burneside Rd A2
Bus Station B2
Buttery Well La C2
Canal Head North B3
Captain French La C2
Caroline St A2
Castle Hill B3
Castle Howe B2
Castle Rd B3
Castle St A3/B3
Cedar Gr C1
Council Offices B2
County Council Offices A2
Cricket Ground A3
Cricket Ground C3
Cross La C2
Dockray Hall Ind Estate A2
Dowker's La B2
Dry Ski Slope B3
East View B1
Echo Barn Hill C1
Elephant Yard Shopping Centre B2
Fairfield La A1
Finkle St B2
Fire Station A2
Fletcher Square C3
Football Ground C3
Fowling La A3
Gillinggate C2
Glebe Rd C2
Golf Course B1
Goose Holme B3
Gooseholme Bridge B3
Green St A1
Greengate C2
Greengate La C1/C2
Greenside B1
Greenwood C1
Gulfs Rd B2
High Tenterfell B1
Highgate B2
Hillswood Ave C1
Horncop La A2
Information Ctr B2
K Village and Heritage Centre C2
Kendal Business Park A3
Kendal Castle (Remains) B3
Kendal Fell B1
Kendal Green A1
Kendal A2
Kendal Station A3
Kent Pl B2
Kirkbarrow C2
Kirkland C2
Library B2
Library Rd B2
Little Aynam B3
Little Wood B1
Long Cl C1
Longpool A3
Lound Rd C3
Lound St C3
Low Fellside B2
Lowther St B2
Maple Dr C1
Market Pl B2
Maude St B2
Miller Bridge B2
Milnthorpe Rd C2
Mint St A3
Mintsfeet Rd A3
Mintsfeet Rd South A2
New Rd B2
Noble's Rest B2
Parish Church C2
Park Side Rd C3
Parkside Business Park C3
Parr St B3
Police Station A2
Post Office A3/B2/C2
Quaker Tapestry B2
Queen's Rd B1
Riverside Walk C2
Rydal Mount A2
Sandes Ave A2
Sandgate A3
Sandylands Rd A3
Serpentine Rd B1
Serpentine Wood B1
Shap Rd A3
South Rd C2
Stainbank Rd C1
Station Rd A3
Stramongate B2
Stramongate Bridge B2
Stricklandgate A2/B2
Sunnyside C3
Thorny Hills B3
Town Hall B2
Undercliff Rd B1
Underwood C1
Union St A2
Vicar's Fields C2
Vicarage Dr C1/C2
Wainwright Yd Sh Ctr B2
Wasdale Cl C3
Well Ings C2
Westmorland Shopping Centre & Market Hall B2
Westwood Ave C1
Wildman St A3
Windermere Rd A1
YHA B2
YWCA B2

King's Lynn 339

Albert St A2
Albion St B2
All Saints B2
All Saints St B2
Austin Fields A2
Austin St A2
Avenue Rd B3
Bank Side B1
Beech Rd C2
Birch Tree Cl B2
Birchwood St A2
Blackfriars Rd B2
Blackfriars St B2
Boal St B1
Bridge St B2
Broad St B2
Broad Walk B3
Burkitt St A2
Bus Station A2
Carmelite Terr C2
Chapel St A2
Chase Ave C3
Checker St C2
Church St B2
Clough La B2
Coburg St B2
College of West Anglia A3
Columbia Way A3
Corn Exchange A1
County Court Rd B2
Cresswell St A2
Custom House A1
Eastgate St A2
Edma St A2
Exton's Rd C3
Ferry La B1
Ferry St A1
Framingham's Almshouses B2
Friars St C2
Friars Walk C2
Gaywood Rd A3
George St A2
Gladstone Rd C2
Goodwin's Rd C3
Green Quay B1
Greyfriars' Tower B2
Guanock Terr C2
Guildhall A1
Hansa Rd C3
Hardwick Rd C2
Hextable Rd A2
High St B1
Holcombe Ave C3
Hospital Walk C2
Information Ctr B1
John Kennedy Rd A2
Kettlewell Lane A2
King George V Ave B3
King's Lynn Art Centre A1
King's Lynn FC B3
King's Lynn Station B2
King St B1
Library B2
Littleport St A2
Loke Rd A2
London Rd B2
Lynn Museum B2
Majestic B2
Magistrates Court B1
Market La A1
Millfleet B2
Milton Ave A3
Nar Valley Walk C2
Nelson St B1
New Conduit St B2
Norfolk St A2
North Lynn Discovery Centre A3
North St A2
Oldsunway B2
Ouse Ave C1
Page Stair Lane A1
Park Ave B3
Police Station B2
Portland Pl C1
Portland St B2
Post Office A3/C2
Purfleet B1
Queen St B1
Raby Ave A3
Railway Rd A2
Red Mount Chapel B3
Regent Way B2
River Walk A1
Robert St C2
Saddlebow Rd C2
St Ann's St A1
St James' Rd B2
St James' Swimming Pool B2
St James St B2
St John's Walk B3
St Margaret's B1
St Nicholas A2
St Nicholas St A1
St Peter's Rd B1
Sir Lewis St A2
Smith Ave A3
South Everard St C2
South Gate C2
South Quay B1
South St B2
Southgate St C2
Stonegate St B2
Surrey St A1
Sydney St C3
Tennyson Ave B3
Tennyson Rd B3
Tower St B2
Town Hall B1
Town House & Tales of The Old Gaol House B1
Town Wall (Remains) B3
True's Yard Museum A2
Valingers Rd C2
Vancouver Ave C2
Vancouver Quarter B2
Waterloo St B2
Wellesley St B2
White Friars Rd C2
Windsor Rd C2
Winfarthing St C2
Wyatt St A2
York Rd C3

Lancaster 339

Aberdeen Rd C3
Adult College, The C3
Aldcliffe Rd C2
Alfred St B3
Ambleside Rd A3
Ambulance Sta A3
Ashfield Ave B1
Ashton Rd C2
Assembly Rooms, The B2
Balmoral Rd B3
Bath House B2
Bath Mill La B3
Bath St B3
Blades St B1
Borrowdale Rd B3
Bowerham Rd C3
Brewery La B2
Bridge La B2
Brook St C1
Bulk Rd A3
Bulk St B2
Bus Station B2
Cable St B2
Canal Cruises & Waterbus C2
Carlisle Bridge A1
Carr House La C2
Castle B1
Castle Park B1
Caton Rd A3
China St B2
Church St B2
City Museum B2
Clarence St C3
Common Gdn St B2
Coniston Rd A3
Cottage Museum B2
Council Offices B2
Court B2
Cromwell Rd C1
Crown Court B1
Dale St C3
Dallas Rd B1/C1
Dalton Rd B3
Dalton Sq B2
Damside St B2
De Vitre St B3
Dee Rd A1
Denny Ave A1
Derby Rd A2
Dukes B2
Earl St A2
East Rd B3
Eastham St C3
Edward St B3
Fairfield Rd B1
Fenton St B2
Firbank Rd A3
Fire Station B2
Friend's Meeting House B1
Garnet St B3
George St B2
Giant Axe Field B1
Grand, The B2
Grasmere Rd B3
Greaves Rd C2
Green St A3
Gregson Centre, The B3
Gregson Rd C3
Greyhound Bridge A2
Greyhound Bridge Rd A2
High St B2
Hill Side B1
Hope St C3
Hubert Pl B1
Information Ctr B2
Judges Lodgings B2
Kelsy St B1
Kentmere Rd B3
King St B2
Kingsway A3
Kirkes Rd C3
Lancaster & Lakeland H C3
Lancaster City Football Club B1
Lancaster Station B1
Langdale Rd A3
Ley Ct B1
Library B2
Lincoln Rd B1
Lindow St C2
Lodge St B2
Long Marsh La B1
Lune Rd A1
Lune St A2
Lune Valley Ramble A3
Mainway A2
Maritime Museum A1
Market St B2
Mkt Gate Shopping Ctr B2
Meadowside C2
Meeting House La B1
Millennium Bridge A2
Moor La B2
Moorgate B3
Morecambe Rd A1/A2
Nelson St B2
North Rd B2
Orchard La C1
Owen Rd A2
Park Rd B3
Parliament St A3
Patterdale Rd A3
Penny St B2
Police Station B2
Portland St C2
Post Office A3/B1/B2/B3/C3
Primrose St C3
Priory B1
Prospect St C3
Quarry Rd B3
Queen St C2
Regent St C2
Ridge La A3
Ridge St A3
Royal Lancaster Infirmary (A&E) C2
Rydal Rd B3
Ryelands Park A1
St Georges Quay A1
St John's B2
St Leonard's Gate B2
St Martin's Rd C3
St Nicholas Arcades Shopping Centre B2
St Oswald St C3
St Peter's B3
St Peter's Rd B3
Salisbury Rd B1
Scotch Quarry Urban Park C3
Shire Hall/HM Prison B1
Sibsey St B1
Skerton Bridge A2
South Rd C2
Station Rd B1
Stirling Rd C3
Storey Ave B1
Sunnyside La C1
Sylvester St C1
Tarnsyke Rd A1
Thurnham St C2
Town Hall B2
Troutbeck Rd B3
Ulleswater Rd B3
University of Cumbria C3
Vicarage Field B1
Vue B2
West Rd B1
Westbourne Dr C1
Westbourne Rd B1
Westham St C3
White Cross Business Park C2
Wheatfield St B1
Williamson Rd B3
Willow La B1
Windermere Rd B3
Wingate-Saul Rd B1
Wolseley St B3
Woodville St B3
Wyresdale Rd C3

Leeds 339

Aire St B3
Aireside Centre B2
Albion Pl B4
Albion St B4
Albion Way B1
Alma St A6
Arcades B4
Armley Rd B1
Back Burley Lodge Rd A1
Back Hyde Terr A2
Back Row C3
Bath Rd C3
Beckett St A6
Bedford St B3
Belgrave St A4
Belle View Rd A2
Benson St A5
Black Bull St C5
Blenheim Walk A3
Boar La B4
Bond St B4
Bow St C5
Bowman La C4
Brewery C4
Bridge St A5/B5
Briggate B4
Bruce Gdns C1
Burley Rd A1
Burley St B1
Burmantofs St B6
Bus & Coach Station B5
Butterly St C4
Butts Cr B4
Brewery Wharf C5
Byron St A5
Call La B4
Calverley St A3/B3
Canal St B1
Canal Wharf C3
Carlisle Rd C5
Cavendish Rd A1
Cavendish St A2
Chadwick St C5
Cherry Pl A6
Cherry Row A5
City Museum A4
City Palace of Varieties B4
City Sq B3
Civic Hall A3
Clarence Road C5
Clarendon Rd A2

Clarendon Way A3
Clark La C4
Clay Pit La A4
Cloberry St A2
Clyde Approach C1
Clyde Gdns C1
Coleman St C2
Commercial St B4
Concord St A5
Cookridge St A4
Copley Hill C1
Corn Exchange B4
Cromer Terr A2
Cromwell St A5
Cross Catherine St B6
Cross Green La C6
Cross Stamford St A5
Crown & County Courts A3
Crown Point Bridge C5
Crown Point Retail Park C4
Crown Point Rd C4
David St C3
Dent St C6
Derwent Pl C3
Dial St C6
Dock St C4
Dolly La A6
Domestic St C2
Duke St B5
Duncan St B4
Dyer St B5
East Field St B6
East Pde B3
East St C5
Eastgate B5
Easy Rd C6
Edward St B4
Ellerby La C6
Ellerby Rd C6
Fenton St A3
Fire Station B2
First Direct Arena A4
Fish St B4
Flax Pl B5
Gelderd Rd C1
George St B4
Globe Rd C2
Gloucester Cr B1
Gower St A5
Grafton St A4
Grand Theatre B4
Granville Rd A6
Great George St A3
Great Wilson St C4
Greek St B3
Green La C1
Hanover Ave A2
Hanover La A2
Hanover Sq A2
Hanover Way A2
Harewood St B4
Harrison St B4
Haslewood Cl B6
Haslewood Drive B6
High Court B5
Holbeck La C2
Holdforth Cl C1
Holdforth Gdns B1
Holdforth Gr C1
Holdforth Pl C1
Holy Trinity B4
Hope Rd A5
Hunslet La C4
Hunslet Rd C4
Hyde Terr A2
Infirmary St B3
Information Ctr B3
Ingram Row C3
Junction St C4
Kelso Gdns A2
Kelso Rd A2
Kelso St A2
Kendal La A2
Kendell St C4
Kidacre St C4
King Edward St B4
King St B3
Kippax Pl C6
Kirkgate B4
Kirkgate Market B4
Kirkstall Rd A1
Kitson St C6
Lady La B4
Lands La B4
Lavender Walk B6
Leeds Art Gallery B3
Leeds Bridge C4
Leeds College of Music B5
Leeds General Infirmary (A&E) A3
Leeds Metropolitan University A3/A4
Leeds Museum Discovery Centre C5
Leeds Shopping Plaza B4
Leeds Station B3
Leeds University A3
Library B3
Lincoln Green Rd A6
Lincoln Rd A6
Lindsey Gdns A6
Lindsey Rd A6
Lisbon St B3
Little Queen St B3
Long Close La C6
Lord St C2
Lovell Park A4
Lovell Park Rd A4
Lovell Rd A5
Lower Brunswick St A5
Mabgate A5
Macauly St A5
Magistrates Court A3
Manor Rd C3
Mark La B4
Marlborough St B2
Marsh La B5
Marshall St C3
Meadow La C4
Meadow Rd C4
Melbourne St A5
Merrion Centre A4
Merrion St A4
Merrion Way A4
Mill St B5
Millennium Sq A3
Mount Preston St A2
Mushroom St A5
Neville St C4
New Briggate A4/B4
New Market St B4
New Station St B4
New York Rd A5
New York St B5
Nile St A5
Nippet La A6
North St A4
Northern St B3
Oak Rd B1
Oxford Pl B3
Oxford Row A3
Park Cross St B3
Park La A2
Park Pl B3
Park Row B4
Park Sq B3
Park Sq East B3
Park Sq West B3
Park St B3
Police Station B5
Pontefract La B6
Portland Cr A3
Portland Way A3
Post Office B4/B5
Project Space Leeds C2
Quarry House (NHS/DSS Headquarters) B5
Quebec St B3
Queen St B3
Railway St B5
Rectory St A6
Regent St A5
Richmond St C5
Rigton Approach B6
Rigton Dr B6
Rillbank La A1
Rosebank Rd A1
Royal Armouries C5
Russell St B3
Rutland St B2
St Anne's Cathedral (RC) A4
St Anne's St B4
St James' Hospital A6
St Johns Centre B4
St John's Rd A2
St Mary's St B5
St Pauls St B3
St Peter's B5
Saxton La B5
Sayner La C5
Shakespeare Ave A6
Shannon St B6
Sheepscar St South A5
Siddall St C3
Skinner La A5
South Pde B3
Sovereign St C4
Spence La C2
Springfield Mount A2
Springwell Ct C2
Springwell Rd C2
Springwell St C2
Stoney Rock La A6
Studio Rd A1
Sutton St C2
Sweet St C3
Sweet St West C3
Swinegate B4
Templar St B5
The Calls B5
The Close B6
The Core B4
The Drive B6
The Garth B5
The Headrow B3/B4
The Lane B5
The Light B4
The Parade B6
Thoresby Pl A3
Torre Rd A6
Town Hall A3
Union Pl C3
Union St B5
Upper Accomodation Rd B6
Upper Basinghall St B4
Vicar La B4
Victoria Bridge C4
Victoria Quarter B4
Victoria Rd C4
Vue B4
Wade La A4
Washington St A1
Water La C3
Waterloo Rd C4
Wellington Rd B2/C1
Wellington St B3
West St B2
West Yorkshire Playhouse B5
Westfield Rd A1
Westgate B3
Whitehall Rd B3/C2
Whitelock St A5
Willis St C6
Willow Approach A1
Willow Ave A1
Willow Terrace Rd A3
Wintoun St A5
Woodhouse La A3/A4
Woodsley Rd A1
York Pl B3
York Rd B6
Yorkshire Television Studios A1

Leicester 339

Abbey St A2
All Saints' A1
Aylestone Rd C2
Bath La A1
Bede Park C1
Bedford St A3
Bedford St South A3
Belgrave Gate A2
Belle Vue A2
Belvoir St B2
Braunstone Gate B1
Burleys Way A2
Burnmoor St C2
Bus Station A2
Canning St A2
Carlton St C2
Castle B1
Castle Gardens B1
Cathedral B2
Causeway La A2
Charles St B3
Chatham St B2
Christow St A3
Church Gate A2
City Gallery B3
Civic Centre B2
Clank St B2
Clock Tower B2
Clyde St A3
Colton St B3
Conduit St B3
Crafton St A3
Craven St A1
Crown Courts B3
Curve B3
De Lux A2
De Montfort Hall C3
De Montfort St C3
De Montfort University C1
Deacon St C2
Dover St B3
Duns La B1
Dunton St A1
East St B3
Eastern Boulevard C1
Edmonton Rd A3
Erskine St A3
Filbert St C1
Filbert St East C2
Fire Station C3
Fleet St A3
Friar La B2
Friday St A2
Gateway St C2
Glebe St B3
Granby St B3
Grange La C2
Grasmere St C1
Great Central St A1
Guildhall B2
Guru Nanak Sikh Museum B1
Halford St B2
Havelock St C2
Haymarket Sh Ctr A2
High St A2
Highcross St A1
Highcross Sh Ctr A2
HM Prison C2
Horsefair St B2
Humberstone Gate B2
Humberstone Rd A3
Infirmary St C2
Information Ctr B2
Jarrom St C2
Jewry Wall B1
Kamloops Cr A3
King Richards Rd B1
King St B2
Lancaster Rd C3
LCB Depot B3
Lee St A3
Leicester Royal Infirmary (A&E) C2
Leicester Station B3
Library B2
Little Theatre, The B3
London Rd C3
Lower Brown St B2
Magistrates Court B2
Manitoba Rd A3
Mansfield St A2
Market B2
Market St B2
Mill La C2
Montreal Rd A3
Narborough Rd North B1
Nelson Mandela Park C2
New Park St B1
New St B2
New Walk C3
New Walk Museum & Art Gallery C3
Newarke Houses B2
Newarke St B2
Northgate St A1
Orchard St A2
Ottawa Rd A3
Oxford St C2
Upper Brown St B2
Phoenix Square B3
Police Station A3
Post Office A1/B2/C2/C3
Prebend St C3
Princess Rd East C3
Princess Rd West C3
Queen St B3
Regent College C3
Regent Rd C2/C3
Repton St A1
Rutland St B3
St George St B3
St Georges Way B3
St John St A2
St Margaret's A2
St Margaret's Way A2
St Martins B2
St Mary de Castro B1
St Matthew's Way A3
St Nicholas B1
St Nicholas Circle B1
Sanvey Gate A2
Silver St B2
Slater St A1
Soar La A1
South Albion St B3
Southampton St B3
Swain St B3
Swan St A1
The Gateway C2
The Newarke B1
The Rally Com Park A2
Tigers Way C3
Tower St C3
Town Hall B2
Tudor Rd B1
University of Leicester C3
University Rd C3
Upperton Rd C1
Vaughan Way A2
Walnut St C2
Watling St A2
Welford Rd B2
Welford Rd Stadium C2
Wellington St B2
West Bridge B1
West St C3
West Walk C3
Western Boulevard C1
Western Rd C1
Wharf St North A3
Wharf St South A3
Y' Theatre, The B3
Yeoman St B3
York Rd B2

Lewes 339

Abinger Pl B1
All Saints Centre B2
Ambulance Station B2
Anne of Cleves House C1
Barbican House Museum B1
Brewery B2
Brook St A2
Brooks Rd A2
Bus Station B2
Castle Ditch La B1
Castle Precincts B1
Chapel Hill B3
Church La A1/A2
Cliffe High St B2
Cliffe Industrial Est C3
Cluny St C1
Cockshut Rd C1
Convent Field C2
Coombe Rd A2
County Hall B1
County Records Office B1
Court B2
Court Rd B2
Crown Court B2
Cuilfail Tunnel B3
Davey's La A3
East St B2
Eastport La C1
Fire Station A2
Fisher St B2
Friars Walk B2
Garden St B1
Government Offices C2
Grange Rd B1
Ham La C2
Harveys Way B2
Hereward Way A2
High St B1/B2
Hop Gallery B2
Information Ctr B2
Keere St B1
King Henry's Rd B1
Lancaster St B2
Landport Rd A1
Leisure Centre C3
Lewes Bridge B2
Lewes Castle B1
Lewes Football Ground C2
Lewes Golf Course B3
Lewes Southern By-Pass C2
Lewes Station B2
Library B2
Malling Ind Est A2
Malling Brook Ind Est A3
Malling Hill A3
Malling St A3/B3
Market St B2
Martyr's Monument B3
Mayhew Way A2
Morris Rd B3
Mountfield Rd C2
New Rd B1
Newton Rd A1
North St A2/B2
Offham Rd B1
Old Malling Way A1
Orchard Rd A3
Paddock La B1
Paddock Rd B1
Paddock Sports Ground B1
Park Rd B1
Pelham Terr A1
Pells Open Air Swimming Pool A1
Phoenix Causeway B2
Phoenix Ind Est B2
Phoenix Pl B2
Pinwell Rd B2
Police Station B1
Post Office A2/B1/B2/C1
Prince Edward's Rd B1
Priory St C1
Priory of St Pancras (remains of) C1
Railway La B2
Railway Land Nature Reserve B3
Rotten Row B1
Rufus Cl B1
St Pancras Rd C1
St John St B2
St John's Terr B1
St Nicholas La B2
Sewage Works C3
South Downs Business Park A3
South St B3/C3
Southdowns Rd A2
Southerham Junction C3
Southover Grange Gdns B1
Southover High St C1
Southover Rd B1
Spences Field A3
Spences La A2
Stansfield Rd A1
Station Rd B2
Station St B2
Sun St B1
Sussex Downs College C2
Sussex Police HQ A2
Talbot Terr B1
The Avenue B1
The Course C1
The Martlets A2
The Needlemakers B2
The Pells A1
Thebes Gallery B2
Toronto Terr B1
Town Hall B2
West St B2
White Hill B1
Willeys Bridge A1

Lincoln 342

Alexandra Terr B1
Anchor St C1
Arboretum B3
Arboretum Ave B3
Baggholme Rd B3
Bailgate A2
Beaumont Fee B1
Brayford Way C1
Brayford Wharf East C1
Brayford Wharf North B1
Bruce Rd A2
Burton Rd A1
Bus Station (City) C2
Canwick Rd C2
Cardinal's Hat B2
Carline Rd B1
Castle B1
Castle St A1
Cathedral B2
Cathedral St B2
Cecil St A2
Chapel La A2
Cheviot St B3
Church La A2
City Hall B1
Clasketgate B2
Clayton Sports Ground A3
Coach Park C2
Collection, The B2
County Hospital (A&E) B3
County Office B1
Courts C1
Croft St B2
Cross St C2
Crown Courts B1
Curle Ave A3
Danesgate B2
Drill Hall B2
Drury La B1
East Bight A2
East Gate A2
Eastcliff Rd B3
Eastgate B2
Egerton Rd A3
Ellis Windmill A1
Engine Shed, The C1
Environment Agency C2
Exchequer Gate B2
Firth Rd C1
Flaxengate B2
Florence St B3
George St C3
Good La A2
Gray St A1
Great Northern Terr C3
Great Northern Terrace Industrial Estate C3
Greetwell Rd B3
Greetwellgate B3
Haffenden Rd A2
High St B2/C1
HM Prison A3
Hospital (Private) A2
Hungate B2
James St A2
Jews House & Court B2
Kesteven St C2
Langworthgate A2
Lawn Visitor Centre, The B1
Lee Rd A3
Library B2
Lincoln College B2
Lincoln Central Station C2
Lincolnshire Life/Royal Lincolnshire Regiment Museum A1
Lindum Rd B2
Lindum Sports Ground A3
Lindum Terr B3
Mainwaring Rd A3
Manor Rd A2
Market C2
Massey Rd A3
Medieval Bishop's Palace B2
Mildmay St A1
Mill Rd A1
Millman Rd B3
Minster Yard B2
Monks Rd B3
Montague St B2
Mount St A1
Nettleham Rd A2
Newland B1
Newport A2
Newport Arch A2
Newport Cemetery A2
Northgate A2
Odeon C1
Orchard St B1
Oxford St C2
Park St B1
Pelham Bridge C2
Pelham St C2
Police Station B1
Portland St C2
Post Office A1/A2/B1/B3/C2
Potter Gate B2
Priory Gate B2
Queensway A3
Rasen La A1
Ropewalk C1
Rosemary La B2
St Anne's Rd B3
St Benedict's C1
St Giles Ave A3
St John's Rd A2
St Marks St C1
St Mark's Sh Ctr C1
St Mary-Le-Wigford C1
St Mary's St C2
St Nicholas St A2
St Swithin's B2
Saltergate C1
Saxon St A1
Sch of Art & Design B2
Sewell Rd B3
Silver St B2
Sincil St C2
Spital St A2
Spring Hill B1
Stamp End C3
Steep Hill B2
Stonebow & Guildhall C2
Stonefield Ave A2
Tentercroft St C1
The Avenue B1
The Grove A3
Theatre Royal B2
Tritton Retail Park C1
Tritton Rd C1
Union Rd B1
University of Lincoln C1
Upper Lindum St B3
Upper Long Leys Rd A1
Usher B2
Vere St A2
Victoria St B1
Victoria Terr B1
Vine St B3
Wake St A1
Waldeck St A1
Waterside Sh Ctr C2
Waterside North C2
Waterside South C2
West Pde B1
Westgate A2
Wigford Way C1
Williamson St A2
Wilson St A1
Winn St B3
Wragby Rd A3
Yarborough Rd A1

Liverpool 342

Abercromby Sq C5
Acc Liverpool C2
Addison St A3
Adelaide Rd B6
Ainsworth St B4
Albany Rd B6
Albert Dock C2
Albert Edward Rd B6
Angela St C6
Anson St B4
Archbishop Blanche High School B6
Argyle St C3
Arrad St C4
Ashton St B5
Audley St A4
Back Leeds St A2
Basnett St B3
Bath St A1
Beatles Story C2
Beckwith St C3
Bedford Close C5
Bedford St North C5
Bedford St South C5
Benson St C4
Berry St C4
Birkett St A4
Bixteth St B2
Blackburne Place C4
Bluecoat B3
Bold Place C4
Bold St C4
Bolton St B3
Bridport St B4
Bronte St B4
Brook St A1
Brownlow Hill B4/B5
Brownlow St B5
Brunswick Rd A5
Brunswick St B1
Bus Station C2
Butler Cr A6
Byrom St A3
Caledonia St C4
Cambridge St C5
Camden St A4
Canada Blvd B1
Canning Dock C2
Canterbury St A4
Cardwell St C6
Carver St A4
Cases St B3
Castle St B2
Catherine St C5
Cavern Club B3
Central Library A3
Central Station B3
Chapel St B2
Charlotte St B3
Chatham Place C6
Chatham St C5
Cheapside B2
Chestnut St C5
Christian St A3
Church St B3
Churchill Way North A3
Churchill Way South B3
Clarence St B4
Coach Station A4
Cobden St A5
Cockspur St A2
College St C3
College St North A5
College St South A5
Colquitt St C4
Comus St A3
Concert St C3
Connaught Rd B6
Cook St B2
Copperas Hill B4
Cornwallis St C3
Covent Garden B2
Craven St A4
Cropper St B3
Crown St B5/C6
Cumberland St B2
Cunard Building B1
Dale St B2
Dansie St B4
Daulby St B5
Dawson St B3
Derby Sq B2
Drury La B2
Duckinfield St B4
Duke St C3
Earle St A2
East St A2
Eaton St A2
Edgar St A3
Edge La B6
Edinburgh Rd A6
Edmund St B2
Elizabeth St B5
Elliot St B3
Empire Theatre B4
Empress Rd B6
Epworth St A5
Erskine St A5
Everyman Theatre C5
Exchange St East B2
Fact Centre, The C4
Falkland St A5
Falkner St C5/C6
Farnworth St A6
Fenwick St B2
Fielding St A6
Fleet St C3
Fraser St A4
Freemasons Row A2
Gardner Row A3
Gascoyne St A2
George Pier Head C1
George St B2
Gibraltar Road A1
Gilbert St C3
Gildart St A4
Gill St B4
Goree B2
Gower St C2
Gradwell St C3
Great Crosshall St A3
Great George St C4
Great Howard St A1
Great Newton St B4
Greek St B4
Green La B4
Greenside A5
Greetham St C3
Gregson St A5
Grenville St C3
Grinfield St C6
Grove St C5
Guelph St A6
Hackins Hey B2
Haigh St A4
Hall La B6
Hanover St B3
Harbord St C6
Hardman St C4
Harker St A4
Hart St B4
Hatton Garden A2
Hawke St B4
Helsby St B6
Henry St C3
HM Customs & Excise National Museum C2
Highfield St A2
Highgate St B6
Hilbre St B4
Hope Place C4
Hope St C4
Houghton St B3
Hunter St A3
Hutchinson St A6
Information Ctr C2
Institute For The Performing Arts C4
Irvine St B6
Irwell St B2
Islington A4
James St B2
James St Station B2
Jenkinson St A4
Johnson St A3
Jubilee Drive B6
Kempston St A4
Kensington A6
Kensington Gdns B6
Kensington St A6
Kent St C3
King Edward St A1
Kinglake St B6
Knight St C4
Lace St A3
Langsdale St A4
Law Courts C2
Leece St C4
Leeds St A2
Leopold Rd B6
Lime St B3
Lime St Station B4
Little Woolton St B5
Liver St C2
Liverpool John Moores University A3/B4/C4
Liverpool Landing Stage B1
Liverpool One C2
London Rd A4/B4
Lord Nelson St B4
Lord St B2
Lovat St C6
Low Hill A5
Low Wood St A6
Lydia Ann St C3
Mansfield St A4
Marmaduke St B6
Marsden St A6
Martensen St B6
Marybone A3
Maryland St C4
Mason St B6
Mathew St B2
May St B4
Melville Place C6
Merseyside Maritime Museum C2
Metquarter B3
Metropolitan Cathedral (RC) B5
Midghall St A2
Molyneux Rd A6
Moor Place B4
Moorfields B2
Moorfields Station B2
Moss St A5
Mount Pleasant B4/B5
Mount St C4
Mount Vernon B6
Mulberry St C5
Municipal Buildings B2
Mus of Liverpool C2
Myrtle Gdns C6
Myrtle St C5
Naylor St A2
Nelson St C4
Neptune Theatre B3
New Islington A4
New Quay B1
Newington St C3
North John St B2
North St A3
North View B6
Norton St A4
Oakes St B5
O2 Academy
Odeon B4
Old Hall St A1
Old Leeds St A2
Oldham Place C4
Oldham St C4
Olive St C6
Open Eye Gallery C3
Oriel St A2
Ormond St B2
Orphan St C6
Overbury St C6
Overton St B6
Oxford St C5
Paisley St A1
Pall Mall A2
Paradise St C3
Park La C3
Parker St B3
Parr St C3
Peach St B5
Pembroke Place B4
Pembroke St B5
Philharmonic Hall C5
Pickop St A2
Pilgrim St C4
Pitt St C3
Playhouse Theatre B3
Pleasant St B4
Police Headquarters C2
Police Station A4/B4
Pomona St B4
Port of Liverpool Building B2
Post Office A2/A4/A5/A6/B2/B3/B4/C4
Pownall St C2
Prescot St A5
Preston St B3
Princes Dock A1
Princes Gdns A2
Princes Jetty A1
Princes Pde B1
Princes St B2
Pythian St A6
Queen Sq Bus Station B3
Queensland St C6
Queensway Tunnel (Docks exit) B1
Queensway Tunnel (Entrance) B3
Radio City B2
Ranelagh St B3
Redcross St B2
Renfrew St B6
Renshaw St B4
Richmond Row A4
Richmond St B3
Rigby St A2
Roberts St A1
Rock St B4
Rodney St C4
Rokeby St A4
Romily St A6
Roscoe La C4
Roscoe St C4
Rose Hill A3
Royal Court Theatre B3
Royal Liver Building B1
Royal Liverpool Hospital (A&E) B5
Royal Mail St B4
Rumford Place B2
Rumford St B2
Russell St B4
St Andrew St B4
St Anne St A4
St Georges Hall B3
St John's Centre B3
St John's Gdns B3
St John's La B3
St Joseph's Cr A4
St Minishull St B5
St Nicholas Place B1
St Paul's Sq A2
St Vincent Way B4
Salisbury St A4
Salthouse Dock C2
Salthouse Quay C2
Sandon St C5
Saxony Rd B6
Schomberg St A6
School La B2
Seel St C3
Seymour St B4
Shaw St A5
Sidney Place C6
Sir Thomas St B3
Skelhorne St B4
Slater St C3
Slavery Museum C2
Smithdown La B6
Soho Sq A4
Soho St A4
South John St B2
Springfield A4
Stafford St A4
Standish St A3
Stanley St B2
Strand St C2
Suffolk St C3
Tabley St C3
Tarleton St B3
Tate Gallery C2
Teck St B6
Temple St B2
The Beacon B3
The Strand B2
Tithebarn St B2
Town Hall B2
Traffic Police HQ C6
Trowbridge St B4
Trueman St A3
Union St B2
Unity Theatre C4
University C5
Univ of Liverpool B5
Upper Duke St C4
Upper Frederick St C3
Upper Baker St A6
Vauxhall Rd A2
Vernon St B2
Victoria Gallery & Museum B5
Victoria St B2
Vine St C5
Wakefield St A4
Walker Art Gallery A3
Walker St A6
Wapping C2
Water St B1/B2
Waterloo Rd A1
Wavertree Rd B6
West Derby Rd A6
West Derby St B5
Whitechapel B3
Western Approaches War Museum B2
Whitley Gdns A5
William Brown St B3
William Henry St A4
Williamson Sq B3
Williamson St B3
Williamson's Tunnels Heritage Centre C6
Women's Hospital C6
Wood St B3
World Museum, Liverpool A3
York St C3

Llandudno 342

Abbey Pl B1
Abbey Rd B1
Adelphi St B3
Alexandra Rd C2
Anglesey Rd A1
Argyll Rd B3
Arvon Ave A2
Atlee Cl C3
Augusta St B3
Back Madoc St B2
Bodafon St B3
Bodhyfryd Rd A2
Bodnant Cr C3
Bodnant Rd C3
Bridge Rd C2
Bryniau Rd C1
Builder St B3
Builder St West C2
Cabin Lift A2

Regency St F4
Regent Sq B5
Regent St C4
Regent's Park B3
Richmond Terr E5
Ridgmount St C4
Riley Rd E8
Rivington St B8
Robert St B3
Rochester Row F4
Rockingham St E7
Rodney Rd F7
Rolls Rd F8
Ropemaker St C7
Rosebery Ave B6
Rossmore Rd B2
Rothsay St E8
Rotten Row E2
Roupell St D6
Royal Academy of Arts D4
Royal Academy of Dramatic Art B4
Royal Academy of Music B3
Royal Albert Hall E1
Royal Artillery Memorial E2
Royal Brompton Hosp F1
Royal Brompton Hospital F2
Royal College of Nursing C3
Royal Coll of Surgeons C5
Royal Festival Hall D5
Royal London Hospital for Integrated Medicine C5
Royal Marsden Hospital F1
Royal National Theatre D6
Royal National Throat, Nose and Ear Hospital B5
Royal Opera House D5
Rushworth St E6
Russell Sq B4
Russell Square B5
Rutland Gate E2
Sackville St D4
Sadlers Wells B6
Saffron Hill C6
Sale Pl C2
Sancroft St F5
Savile Row D4
Savoy Pl D5
Savoy St D5
School of Hygiene & Tropical Medicine C4
Science Mus E1
Scrutton St B8
Sekforde St B6
Serpentine Gallery E1
Serpentine Rd D2
Seven Dials C5
Seward St B6
Seymour Pl C2
Seymour St C2
Shad Thames D8/E8
Shaftesbury Ave D4
Shakespeare's Globe Theatre D7
Shepherd Market D3
Sherwood St D4
Shoe La C6
Shoreditch High St B8
Shoreditch High St B8
Shorts Gdns C5
Shouldham St C2
Sidmouth St B5
Silk St C7
Sir John Soane's Museum C5
Skinner St B6
Sloane Ave F2
Sloane Sq F2
Sloane Square F3
Sloane St E2
Snow Hill C6
Soho Sq C4
Somerset House D5
South Audley St D3
South Carriage Dr E2
South Eaton Pl F3
South Kensington F1
South Molton St C3
South Parade F1
South Pl C7
South St D3
South Terr F2
South Wharf Rd C1
Southampton Row C5
Southampton St D5
Southwark D6
Southwark Bridge D7
Southwark Bridge Rd D7
Southwark Cath D7
Southwark Park Rd F8
Southwark St D7
Spa Rd E8
Speakers' Corner D2
Spencer St B6
Spital Sq C8
Spring St C1
St Alban's St D4
St Andrew St C6
St Barnabas St F3
St Bartholomew's Hospital C6
St Botolph St C8
St Bride St C6
St George's Circus F6
St George's Dr F4
St George's Rd E6
St George's Sq F4
St Giles High St C4
St James's Palace D4
St James's Park E4
St James's St D4
St John St B6
St John's Wood Rd B1
St Margaret St E5
St Mark's Hosp A6
St Martin's La D5
St Martin's Le Grand C7
St Mary Axe C8
St Mary's Hosp C1
St Pancras International A5
St Paul's C7
St Paul's Cath C7
St Paul's Churchyard C6
St Thomas' Hosp E5
St Thomas St D7
Stamford St D6
Stanhope St B4
Stanhope Terr D1
Stephenson Way B4
Stock Exchange C6
Stoney St D7
Strand C6
Strathearn Pl D2
Stratton St D3
Sumner St D6
Sussex Gdns C1
Sussex Pl C1
Sussex Sq D1
Sussex St F3
Sutton's Way B7
Swan St E7
Swanfield St B8
Swinton St B5
Sydney Pl F1
Sydney St F2
Tabard St E7
Tabernacle St B7
Tachbrook St F4
Tanner St E8
Tate Britain F5
Tate Modern D7
Tavistock Pl B5
Tavistock Sq B4
Tea & Coffee Museum D7
Temple D6
Temple Ave D6
Temple Pl D5
Terminus Pl E3
Thayer St C3
The Barbican Centre for Arts C7
The Brunswick Shopping Centre B5
The Cut E6
The Mall E4
Theobald's Rd C5
Thorney St F5
Threadneedle St C7
Throgmorton St C7
Thurloe Pl F1
Thurloe Sq F2
Tonbridge St B5
Tooley St D8
Torrington Pl B4
Tothill St E4
Tottenham Court Rd B4
Tottenham Court Rd C4
Tottenham St C4
Tower Bridge D8
Tower Bridge App D8
Tower Bridge Rd E8
Tower Hill D8
Tower Hill D8
Tower of London, The D8
Toynbee St C8
Trafalgar Square D4
Trinity Sq D8
Trinity St E7
Trocadero Centre D4
Tudor St D6
Turin St B9
Turnmill St C6
Tyers St F5
Ufford St E6
Union St D6
Univ Coll Hospl B4
University of London C4
Univ of Westminster C3
University St B4
Upper Belgrave St E3
Upper Berkeley St C2
Upper Brook St D3
Upper Grosvenor St D3
Upper Ground D6
Upper Montague St C2
Upper St Martin's La D5
Upper Thames St D7
Upper Wimpole St C3
Upper Woburn Pl B4
Vauxhall Bridge Rd F4
Vauxhall St F5
Vere St C3
Vernon Pl C5
Vestry St B7
Victoria E3
Victoria and Albert Museum E1
Victoria Coach Station F3
Victoria Embankment D5
Victoria Place Shopping Centre F3
Victoria St E4
Villiers St D5
Vincent Sq F4
Vinopolis City of Wine D7
Virginia Rd B8
Wakley St B6
Walbrook C7
Walcot Sq F6
Wallace Collection C3
Walnut Tree Walk F6
Walton St F2
Walworth Rd F7
Wardour St C4/D4
Warner St B6
Warren St B4
Warren St B4
Warwick Sq F4
Warwick Way F3
Waterloo E6
Waterloo Bridge D5
Waterloo East D6
Waterloo Rd E6
Watling St C7
Webber St E6
Welbeck St C3
Wellington Arch E3
Wellington Mus E3
Wellington Rd B2
Wellington Row B9
Wells St C4
Wenlock St A7
Wentworth St C8
West Carriage Dr D2
West Smithfield C6
West Sq E6
Westbourne St D1
Westbourne Terr C1
Westminster E5
Westminster Abbey E5
Westminster Bridge E5
Westminster Bridge Rd E6
Westminster Cathedral (RC) E4
Westminster City Hall E4
Westminster Hall E5
Weston St E7
Weymouth St C3
Wharf Rd A7
Wharton St B5
Whitcomb St D4
White Cube B8
White Lion Hill D6
White Lion St A6
Whitechapel Rd C9
Whitecross St B7
Whitefriars St C6
Whitehall D5
Whitehall Pl D5
Wigmore Hall C3
Wigmore St C3
William IV St D5
Willow Walk F8
Wilmington Sq B6
Wilson St C7
Wilton Cres E3
Wilton Rd F4
Wimpole St C3
Winchester St F3
Wincott St F6
Windmill Walk D6
Woburn Pl B4
Woburn Sq B4
Wood St C7
Woodbridge St B6
Wootton St D6
Wormwood St C8
Worship St B7
Wren St B5
Wynyatt St B6
York Rd E5
York St C2
York Terrace East B3
York Terrace West B3

Luton 342

Adelaide St B1
Albert Rd C2
Alma St B2
Alton Rd C3
Anthony Gdns C1
Arthur St C2
Ashburnham Rd B1
Ashton Rd C2
Avondale Rd A1
Back St A2
Bailey St C3
Baker St C2
Biscot Rd A1
Bolton Rd B3
Boyle Cl A2
Brantwood Rd B1
Bretts Mead C1
Bridge St B2
Brook St A1
Brunswick St A3
Burr St A3
Bury Park Rd A1
Bute St B2
Buxton Rd B2
Cambridge St C3
Cardiff Grove B1
Cardiff Rd B1
Cardigan St A2
Castle St B2/C2
Chapel St C2
Charles St A3
Chase St C2
Cheapside B2
Chequer St C3
Chiltern Rise C1
Church St B2/B3
Cinema A2
Cobden St A3
Collingdon St A1
Community Centre C3
Concorde Ave A3
Corncastle Rd C1
Cowper St C2
Crawley Green Rd B3
Crawley Rd A1
Crescent Rise A3
Crescent Rd A3
Cromwell Rd A1
Cross St A2
Crown Court B2
Cumberland St B2
Cutenhoe Rd C3
Dallow Rd B1
Downs Rd B1
Dudley St A2
Duke St A2
Dumfries St B1
Dunstable Place B2
Dunstable Rd A1/B1
Edward St A3
Elizabeth St C2
Essex Cl C3
Farley Hill C1
Farley Lodge C1
Flowers Way B2
Francis St A1
Frederick St A2
Galaxy L Complex A2
George St B2
George St West B2
Gillam St A3
Gordon St B2
Grove Rd B1
Guildford St A2
Haddon Rd A3
Harcourt St C2
Hart Hill Drive A3
Hart Hill Lane A3
Hartley Rd A3
Hastings St B2
Hat Factory, The B2
Hatters Way A1
Havelock Rd A2
Hibbert St C2
High Town Rd A3
Highbury Rd A1
Hightown Community Sports & Arts Centre A3
Hillary Cres C1
Hillborough Rd C1
Hitchin Rd A3
Holly St C2
Holm C1
Hucklesby Way A2
Hunts Cl C1
Information Ctr B2
Inkerman St A2
John St B2
Jubilee St A3
Kelvin Cl C2
King St B2
Kingsland Rd C3
Latimer Rd C2
Lawn Gdns C2
Lea Rd B3
Library B2
Library Rd B2
Liverpool Rd B1
London Rd C2
Luton Station A2
Lyndhurst Rd B1
Magistrates Court B2
Mall, The B2
Manchester St B2
Manor Rd B3
May St C3
Meyrick Ave C1
Midland Rd A2
Mill St A2
Milton Rd B1
Moor St A1
Moor, The A1
Moorland Gdns A2
Moulton Rise A3
Museum & Art Gallery A2
Napier Rd B1
New Bedford Rd A1
New Town St C2
North St A3
Old Bedford Rd A2
Old Orchard C2
Osbourne Rd C3
Oxen Rd A3
Park Sq B2
Park St B3/C3
Park St West B2
Park Viaduct B3
Parkland Drive C1
Police Station B1
Pomfret Ave A3
Pondwicks Rd B3
Post Office A1/A2/B2/C3
Power Court B3
Princess St B1
Red Rails C1
Regent St B2
Reginald St A2
Rothesay Rd B1
Russell Rise C1
Russell St C1
St Ann's Rd B3
St George's B2
St George's Square B2
St Mary's B3
St Marys Rd B3
St Paul's Rd C2
St Saviour's Cres C1
Salisbury Rd B1
Seymour Ave C3
Seymour Rd C3
Silver St B2
South Rd C2
Stanley St B1
Station Rd A2
Stockwood Cres C2
Stockwood Park C1
Strathmore Ave C2
Stuart St B2
Studley Rd A1
Surrey St C3
Sutherland Place C1
Tavistock St C2
Taylor St A3
Telford Way A1
Tennyson Rd C2
Tenzing Grove C1
The Cross Way C1
The Larches A2
Thistle Rd B3
Town Hall B2
Townsley Cl C2
UK Centre for Carnival Arts B3
Union St B2
Univ of Bedfordshire B3
Upper George St B2
Vicarage St B3
Villa Rd A2
Waldeck Rd A1
Wellington St B1/B2
Wenlock St A2
Whitby Rd A1
Whitehill Ave C1
William St A2
Wilsden Ave C1
Windmill Rd B3
Windsor St C2
Winsdon Rd B1
York St A3

Macclesfield 343

108 Steps B2
Abbey Rd A1
Alton Dr A3
Armett St C1
Athey St B1
Bank St C3
Barber St C3
Barton St C1
Beech La A2
Beswick St B1
Black La A2
Black Rd C3
Blakelow Gardens C3
Blakelow Rd C3
Bond St B1/C1
Bread St C1
Bridge St B1
Brock St A2
Brocklehurst Ave A3
Brook St B3
Brookfield La B3
Brough St West C1
Brown St C1
Brynton Rd A2
Buckley St C2
Bus Station B2
Buxton Rd B3
Byrons St C2
Canal St B3
Carlsbrook Ave A3
Castle St B2
Catherine St B1
Cemetery A1
Chadwick Terr A3
Chapel St C2
Charlotte St B2
Chester Rd B1
Chestergate B1
Christ Church B1
Churchill Way B2
Coare St A1
Commercial Rd B2
Conway Cres A3
Copper St C3
Cottage St B1
Court A2
Court B2
Crematorium A1
Crew Ave A3
Crompton Rd B1/C1
Cross St C2
Crossall St C1
Cumberland St A1/B1
Dale St B3
Duke St B2
Eastgate B3
Exchange St B2
Fence Ave B3
Fence Ave Ind Est A3
Flint St B3
Foden St A2
Fountain St B3
Gateway Gallery B1
Garden St A3
Gas Rd B2
George St B2
Glegg St B3
Golf Course C3
Goodall St B3
Grange Rd C1
Great King St B1
Green St B3
Grosvenor Sh Ctr B2
Gunco La C3
Half St C2
Hallefield Rd B3
Hatton St C1
Hawthorn Way A3
Heapy St C3
Henderson St B1
Heritage Centre & Silk Museum B2
Hibel Rd A2
High St C2
Hobson St C2
Hollins Rd C3
Hope St West B1
Horseshoe Dr B1
Hurdsfield Rd A3
Information Ctr B2
James St C2
Jodrell St B3
John St C2
Jordangate A2
King Edward St B2
King George's Field C3
King St B2
King's School A1
Knight Pool C3
Knight St C3
Lansdowne St A3
Library B2
Lime Gr B3
Little Theatre C2
Loney St B1
Longacre St B1
Lord St C2
Lowe St C2
Lowerfield Rd A3
Lyon St B1
Macclesfield College C1
Macclesfield Sta B2
Marina B3
Market B2
Market Pl B2
Masons La A3
Mill La C2
Mill Rd C2
Mill St B2
Moran Rd C1
New Hall St A2
Newton St C1
Nicholson Ave A3
Nicholson Cl A3
Northgate Ave A2
Old Mill La C2
Paradise Mill C2
Paradise St B1
Park Green B2
Park La C1
Park Rd C1
Park St C2
Park Vale Rd C1
Parr St B1
Peel St C2
Percyvale St A3
Peter St C1
Pickford St B2
Pierce St B1
Pinfold St B1
Pitt St C2
Police Station B2
Pool St C2
Poplar Rd C2
Post Office B1/B2/B3
Pownall St A2
Prestbury Rd A1/B1
Queen Victoria St B2
Queen's Ave A3
Registrar B2
Richmond Hill C3
Riseley St B1
Roan Ct B3
Roe St B2
Rowan Way A3
Ryle St C2
Ryle's Park Rd C1
St George's St C2
St Michael's B2
Samuel St B2
Saville St C3
Shaw St B1
Slater St C1
Snow Hill C3
South Park C1
Spring Gdns A2
Statham St C2
Station St A2
Steeple St A3
Sunderland St B2
Superstore A1/A2/C2
Swettenham St B3
The Silk Rd A2/B2
Thistleton Cl C2
Thorp St B2
Town Hall B2
Townley St B2
Turnock St C3
Union Rd B3
Union St B2
Victoria Park B3
Vincent St C2
Waters Green B2
Waterside C2
West Bond St B1
West Park A1
West Park Museum A1
Westbrook Dr A1
Westminster Rd A1
Whalley Hayes B1
Windmill St C3
Withyfold Dr A2
York St B3

Maidstone 343

Albion Pl B3
All Saints B2
Allen St A3
Amphitheatre C2
Archbishop's Pal B2
Bank St B2
Barker Rd C2
Barton Rd C3
Beaconsfield Rd C1
Bedford Pl B1
Bentlif Art Gallery B2
Bishops Way B2
Bluett St A3
Bower La C1
Bower Mount Rd B1
Bower Pl C1
Bower St B1
Bowling Alley B3
Boxley Rd A3
Brenchley Gardens A2
Brewer St A3
Broadway B2
Broadway Sh Ctr B2
Brunswick St C3
Buckland Hill A1
Buckland Rd B1
Bus Station B3
Campbell Rd C3
Carriage Museum B2
Church Rd C1
Church St B3
Cinema C2
College Ave C2
College Rd C2
Collis Memorial Gdn C3
Cornwallis Rd B1
Corpus Christi Hall B2
County Hall A2
County Rd A3
Crompton Gdns C3
Crown & County Courts B2
Curzon Rd A3
Dixon Cl C2
Douglas Rd C1
Earl St B2
Eccleston Rd C2
Fairmeadow B2
Fisher St A2
Florence Rd C1
Foley St A3
Foster St C3
Fremlin Walk Sh Ctr B2
Gabriel's Hill B3
George St C3
Grecian St A3
Hardy St A3
Hart St C2
Hastings Rd C3
Hayle Rd C3
Hazlitt Theatre B2
Heathorn St A3
Hedley St A3
High St B2
HM Prison A3
Holland Rd A3
Hope St A2
Information Ctr B2
James St A3
James Whatman Way A2
Jeffrey St A3
Kent County Council Offices A2
Kent History & Liby Ctr A2
King Edward Rd C2
King St B3
Kingsley Rd C3
Knightrider St B3
Launder Way C1
Lesley Pl A1
Little Buckland Ave A1
Lockmeadow Leisure Complex C2
London Rd B1
Lower Boxley Rd A2
Lower Fant Rd C1
Magistrates Court B3
Maidstone Barracks Station A1
Maidstone Borough Council Offices B1
Maidstone East Sta A2
Maidstone Museum B2
Maidstone West Sta B2
Market C2
Market Buildings B2
Marsham St B3
Medway St B2
Medway Trading Est C2
Melville Rd C3
Mill St B2
Millennium Bridge C2
Mote Rd B3
Muir Rd C3
Old Tovil Rd C2
Palace Ave B3
Perryfield St A2
Police Station B3
Post Office A2/B2/B3/C3
Priory Rd C3
Prospect Pl C1
Pudding La B2
Queen Anne Rd B3
Queens Rd A1
Randall St A2
Rawdon Rd C3
Reginald Rd C1
Rock Pl B1
Rocky Hill B1
Romney Pl B3
Rose Yard B2
Rowland Cl C1
Royal Engineers' Rd A2
Royal Star Arcade B2
St Annes Ct B1
St Faith's St B2
St Luke's Rd A3
St Peter's Br B2
St Peter's Wharf Retail Park B2
St Peter St B2
St Philip's Ave C3
Salisbury Rd A3
Sandling Rd A2
Scott St A2
Scrubs La B1
Sheal's Cres C3
Somerfield La B1
Somerfield Rd B1
Staceys St A2
Station Rd A2
Superstore A1/B2/B3
Terrace Rd B1
The Mall B3
The Somerfield Hospital A1
Tonbridge Rd C1
Tovil Rd C2
Town Hall B2
Trinity Park A3
Tufton St B3
Union St B3
Upper Fant Rd C1
Upper Stone St C3
Victoria St B1
Visitor Centre A1
Warwick Pl B1
Wat Tyler Way B3
Waterloo St C3
Waterlow Rd A3
Week St B2
Well Rd A3
Westree Rd C1
Wharf Rd C1
Whatman Park A1
Wheeler St A3
Whitchurch Cl B1
Woodville Rd C3
Wyatt St B3
Wyke Manor Rd B3

Manchester 343

Adair St B6
Addington St A5
Adelphi St A1
Air & Space Gallery B2
Albert Sq B3
Albion St C3
AMC Great Northern B3
Ancoats Gr B6
Ancoats Gr North B6
Angela St C2
Aquatic Centre C4
Ardwick Green Park C5
Ardwick Green North C5
Ardwick Green South C5
Arlington St A2
Artillery St B3
Arundel St C2
Atherton St B2
Atkinson St B3
Aytoun St B4
Back Piccadilly A4
Baird St B5
Balloon St A4
Bank Pl A1
Baring St B5
Barrack St C1
Barrow St A1
BBC TV Studios C4
Bendix St A5
Bengal St A5
Berry St C5
Blackfriars Rd A3
Blackfriars St A3
Blantyre St C2
Bloom St B4
Blossom St A5
Boad St B5
Bombay St B4
Booth St A3
Booth St B4
Bootle St B3
Brazennose St B3
Brewer St A5
Bridge St A3
Bridgewater Hall B3
Bridgewater Pl A4
Bridgewater St B2
Brook St C4
Brotherton Dr A2
Brown St A3
Brown St B4
Brunswick St C6
Brydon Ave C6
Buddhist Centre A4
Bury St A2
Bus & Coach Station B4
Bus Station B4
Butler St A6
Buxton St C5
Byrom St B3
Cable St A5
Calder St B1
Cambridge St C3/C4
Camp St B3
Canal St B4
Cannon St A1
Cannon St A4
Cardroom Rd A6
Carruthers St A6
Castle St C2
Cateaton St A3
Cathedral A3
Cathedral St A3
Cavendish St C4
Chapel St A1/A3
Chapeltown St B5
Charles St C4
Charlotte St B4
Chatham St B4
Cheapside A3
Chepstow St B3
Chester Rd C1/C2
Chester St C4
Chetham's (Dept Store) A3
China La B5
Chippenham Rd A6
Chorlton Rd C2
Chorlton St B4
Church St A2
Church St A4
City Park A4
City Rd C3
Civil Justice Centre B2
Cleminson St A2
Clowes St A3
College Land A3
Coll of Adult Ed C4
Collier St B2
Commercial St C3
Conference Centre C4
Cooper St B4
Copperas St A4
Cornbrook C1
Cornell St A5
Cornerhouse C4
Corporation St A4
Cotter St C6
Cotton St A5
Cow La B1
Cross St B3
Crown Court B4
Crown St C2
Cube Gallery B4
Dalberg St C6
Dale St A4/B5
Dancehouse, The C4
Dantzic St A4
Dark La C6
Dawson St C2
Dean St A5
Deansgate A3/B3
Deansgate Station C3
Dolphin St C6
Downing St C5
Ducie St B5
Duke Pl B2
Duke St B2
Durling St C6
East Ordsall La A2/B1
Edge St A4
Egerton St C2
Ellesmere St C1
Everard St C1
Every St B6
Fairfield St B5
Faulkner St B4
Fennel St A3
Ford St A2
Ford St C6
Fountain St B4
Frederick St A2
Gartside St B2
Gaythorne St A1
George Leigh St A5
George St A1
George St B4
G-Mex C3
Goadsby St A4
Gore St A2
Goulden St A5
Granada TV Centre B2
Granby Row B4
Gravel St A3
Great Ancoats St A5
Great Bridgewater St B3
Great George St A1
Great Jackson St C2
Great Marlborough St C4
Greengate A3
Green Room, The C4
Grosvenor St C5
Gun St A5
Hadrian Ave B6
Hall St B3
Hampson St B1
Hanover St A4
Hanworth Cl C5
Hardman St B3
Harkness St C6
Harrison St B6
Hart St B4
Helmet St B6
Henry St A5
Heyrod St B6
High St A4
Higher Ardwick C6
Hilton St A4/A5
Holland St A6
Hood St A5
Hope St B1
Hope St B4
Houldsworth St A5
Hoyle St C6
Hulme Hall Rd C1
Hulme St A1
Hulme St C3
Hyde Rd C6
Information Ctr B3
Irwell St A2
Islington St A2
Jackson Cr C2
Jackson's Row B3
James St A1
Jenner Cl C2
Jersey St A5
John Dalton St A1
John Dalton St B3
John Ryland's Liby B3
John St A2
Kennedy St B3
Kincardine Rd C5
King St A3
King St West A3
Law Courts B3
Laystall St B5
Lever St A5
Library B3
Linby St C2
Little Lever St A4
Liverpool Rd B2
Liverpool St B1
Lloyd St B3
Lockton Cl C5
London Rd B5
Long Millgate A3
Longacre St B6
Loom St A5
Lower Byrom St B2
Lower Mosley St B3
Lower Moss La C2
Lower Ormond St C4
Loxford La C4
Luna St A5
Major St B4
Manchester Arndale A4
Manchester Art Gallery B4
Manchester Central Convention Complex B3
Manchester Metropolitan University B4/C4
Manchester Piccadilly Station B5
Manchester Technology Centre C4
Mancunian Way C3
Manor St C5
Marble St A4
Market St A2
Market St A4
Market St A4
Marsden St A3
Marshall St A5
Mayan Ave A2
Medlock St C3
Middlewood St B1
Miller St A4
Minshull St B4
Mosley St A4
Mount St B3
Mulberry St B3
Murray St A5
Museum of Science & Industry (MOSI) B2
Nathan Dr A2
National Football Mus A4
Naval St A5
New Bailey St A2
New Elm Rd B2
New Islington A6

Bear Lanes Sh Ctr B2
Beech Cl A2
Beechwood Dr A2
Brimmon Cl C2
Brimmon Rd C2
Broad St B2
Bryn Bank A1
Bryn Cl A2
Bryn Gdns A1
Bryn House A1
Bryn La A1/A2
Bryn Meadows A2
Bryn St A2
Brynglais Ave A2
Brynglais Cl A2
Bus Station B2
Byrnwood Dr A1
Cambrian Bridge B3
Cambrian Gdns B2
Cambrian Way B2
Canal Rd A3
Castle Mound B2
Cedewain C1
Cefnaire C2
Cefnaire Coppice C2
Ceiriog C2
Cemetery A3
Church (Remains of) B2
Churchill Dr A3
Cledan B3
Colwyn B3
Commercial St A2
Council Offices B1
Crescent St A1
Cwm Llanfair A2
Davies Memorial Gallery B2
Dinas B2
Dolafon Rd B3
Dolerw Park B1
Dolfor Rd C1
Eirianell C1
Fairfield Dr A2
Ffordd Croesawdy B2
Fire Station C1
Frankwell St A2
Frolic St B2
Fron La A1
Garden La A2
Gas St B2
Glyndŵr C1
Golwgydre La B2
Gorsedd Circle B1
Great Brimmon Farm C3
Hafren C1
Halfpenny Bridge B2
High St B2
Hillside Ave A3
Hoel Treowen C2
Information Ctr B2
Kerry Rd B3
Ladywell Shopping Ctr B2
Library B1
Llanfair Rd A2
Llanidloes Rd C1
Llys Ifor A2
Lon Cerddyn B1
Lonesome La A3
Long Bridge A2
Lon Helyg C1
Lower Canal Rd B3
Maldwyn Leisure Ctr C1
Market B2
Market St B2
Milford Rd B1
Mill Cl B2
Miniature Railway B1
Mwyn Fynydd A3
New Church St B2
New Rd B2
Newtown Football Gd B1
Newtown Infirmary A2
Newtown Station B2
Oak Tree Ave A3
Old Kerry Rd B2
Oldbarn La A2
Park Cl B1
Parklands B1
Park La B1
Park St B2
Pavillion Ct C1
Plantation La C1
Police Station B1
Pont Brynfedw A2
Pool Rd B3
Poplar Rd A3
Post Office B2/C1
Powys C1
Powys Theatre A2
Pryce Jones Stores & Museum B2
Quaker Meeting Ho B1
Regent B2
Robert Owen House B1
Robert Owen Mus B2
Rugby Club A3
St David's B2
School La A2
Sheaf St B3
Short Bridge St B2
Stone St B2
Sycamore Dr A2
Textile Museum A2
The Bryn A1
The Park B1
Town Hall B2
Union St A2
Upper Brimmon C3
Vastre Industrial Est B3
War Memorial B2
WHSmith Museum B2
Wynfields C1
Y Ffrydd A3

Northampton 344

78 Derngate B3
Abington Sq B3
Abington St B3
Alcombe St A3
All Saints' B2
Ambush St B1
Angel St B2
Arundel St A2
Ash St A2
Auctioneers Way C2
Bailiff St A2
Barrack Rd A2
Beaconsfield Terr A3
Becketts Park C3
Becketts Park Marina C3
Bedford Rd B3
Billing Rd B3
Brecon St A1
Brewery C2
Bridge St C2
Broad St B2
Burns St A3
Bus Station B2
Campbell St A2
Castle (Site of) B2
Castle St B2
Cattle Market Rd C2
Central Museum & Art Gallery B2
Charles St A3
Cheyne Walk B3
Church La A2
Clare St A3
Cloutsham St A3
College St B2
Colwyn Rd A3
Cotton End C2
Countess Rd A1
County Hall B2
Court A2
Craven St A3
Crown & County Cts B3
Denmark Rd B3
Derngate B3
Derngate & Royal Theatres B3
Doddridge Church B2
Duke St A3
Dunster St A3
Earl St A3
Euston Rd C2
Fire Station A3
Foot Meadow B2
Gladstone Rd A1
Gold St B2
Grafton St A2
Gray St A3
Green St B1
Greenwood Rd B1
Greyfriars B2
Grosvenor Centre B2
Grove Rd A3
Guildhall B2
Hampton St A2
Harding Terr A2
Hazelwood Rd B3
Herbert St B2
Hervey St A3
Hester St A2
Holy Sepulchre A2
Hood St A3
Horse Market B2
Hunter St A3
Information Ctr B1
Kettering Rd A3
Kingswell St B2
Lady's La B2
Leicester St A2
Leslie Rd A2
Library B3
Lorne Rd A2
Lorry Park A1
Louise Rd A2
Lower Harding St A2
Lower Hester St A2
Lower Mounts B3
Lower Priory St A2
Main Rd C1
Marefair B2
Market Sq B2
Marlboro Rd B1
Marriott St A2
Military Rd A3
Mounts Baths L Ctr A3
Nene Valley Retail Pk C1
New South Bridge Rd C2
Northampton General Hospital (A&E) B3
Northampton Sta B1
Northcote St A2
Nunn Mills Rd C3
Old Towcester Rd C2
Overstone Rd A3
Peacock Pl B2
Pembroke Rd A1
Penn Court C2
Police Station B3
Post Office A1/A2/B3/C2
Quorn Way A2
Ransome Rd C3
Regent Sq A2
Robert St A2
St Andrew's Rd B1
St Andrew's St A2
St Edmund's Rd B3
St George's St A2
St Giles B3
St Giles St B3
St Giles' Terr B3
St James' Mill Rd B1
St James' Mill Rd East C1
St James Park Rd B1
St James Retail Park C1
St James Rd B1
St Leonard's Rd C2
St Mary's St B2
St Michael's Rd A3
St Peter's B2
St Peter's Sq Sh Prec B2
St Peter's Way B2
Salisbury St A2
Scarletwell St B2
Semilong Rd A2
Sheep St B2
Sol Central (L Ctr) B2
Somerset St A3
South Bridge C2
Southfield Ave C2
Spencer Bridge Rd A1
Spencer Rd A3
Spring Gdns B3
Spring La B2
Swan St B3
TA Centre A3
Tanner St B2
The Drapery B2
The Ridings B3
Tintern Ave A1
Towcester Rd C2
Upper Bath St B2
Upper Mounts A2
Victoria Park A1
Victoria Promenade B2
Victoria Rd A3
Victoria St A2
Wellingborough Rd A3
West Bridge B1
York Rd B3

Norwich 345

Albion Way C3
All Saints Green C2
Anchor Cl A3
Anchor St A3
Anglia Sq A2
Argyle St C3
Arts Centre B1
Ashby St C2
Assembly House B1
Bank Plain B2
Barker St A1
Barn Rd A1
Barrack St A3
Ber St C2
Bethel St B1
Bishop Bridge A3
Bishopbridge Rd A3
Bishopgate A3
Blackfriars St A2
Botolph St A2
Bracondale C3
Brazen Gate C2
Bridewell B2
Brunswick Rd C1
Bull Close Rd A2
Bus Station C2
Calvert St A2
Cannell Green A3
Carrow Rd C3
Castle Mall B2
Castle Meadow B2
Castle & Museum B2
Cathedral B2
Cathedral Retail Park A1
Cattlemarket St B2
Chantry Rd C1
Chapel Loke C2
Chapelfield East B1
Chapelfield Gdns B1
Chapelfield North B1
Chapelfield Rd B1
Chapelfield Sh Ctr C1
City Hall B1
City Rd C2
City Wall C1/C3
Colegate A2
Coslany St B1
Cow Hill B1
Cow Tower A3
Cowgate A2
Crown & Magistrates Courts A2
Dragon Hall Heritage Centre C3
Duke St A1
Edward St A2
Elm Hill B2
Erpingham Gate B2
Fire Station B1
Fishergate A2
Foundry Bridge B3
Fye Bridge A2
Garden St C2
Gas Hill B3
Grapes Hill B1
Great Hospital Halls, The A3
Grove Ave C1
Grove Rd C1
Guildhall B1
Gurney Rd A3
Hall Rd C2
Heathgate A3
Heigham St A1
Horn's La C2
Information Ctr B1
Ipswich Rd C1
James Stuart Gdns B3
King Edward VI School B2
King St B2
King St C3
Koblenz Ave C3
Library B1
London St B2
Lower Clarence Rd B3
Lower Cl B3
Maddermarket B1
Magdalen St A2
Mariners La C2
Market B2
Market Ave B2
Mountergate B3
Mousehold St A3
Newmarket Rd C1
Norfolk Gallery B2
Norfolk St C1
Norwich City FC C3
Norwich Station B3
Oak St A1
Palace St A2
Pitt St A1
Playhouse B2
Post Office A2/B2/C2
Pottergate B1
Prince of Wales Rd B2
Princes St B2
Pull's Ferry B3
Puppet Theatre A2
Quebec Rd B3
Queen St B2
Queens Rd C2
RC Cathedral B1
Recorder Rd B3
Riverside Ent Ctr C3
Riverside Swimming Centre C3
Riverside Retail Park C3
Riverside Rd B3
Rosary Rd B3
Rose La B2
Rouen Rd C2
Royal Norfolk Regiment Museum B2
St Andrew's & Blackfriars Hall B2
St Andrews St B2
St Augustines St A1
St Benedicts St B1
St Ethelbert's Gate B2
St Faiths La B3
St Georges St A2
St Giles St B1
St James Cl A3
St Julians C2
St Martin's La A1
St Peter Mancroft B2
St Peters St B1
St Stephens Rd C1
St Stephens St C1
Silver Rd A2
Silver St A2
Southwell Rd C2
Strangers Hall B1
Superstore C2
Surrey St C2
Sussex St A1
The Close B3
The Forum B1
The Walk B2
Theatre Royal B1
Theatre St B1
Thorn La C2
Thorpe Rd B3
Tombland B2
Union St C1
Vauxhall St B1
Victoria St C1
Walpole St B1
Wensum St A2
Wessex St C1
Westwick St A1
Wherry Rd C3
Whitefriars A2
Willow La B1
Yacht Station B3

Nottingham 345

Abbotsford Dr A3
Addison St A1
Albert Hall B1
Alfred St South A3
Alfreton Rd B1
All Saints Rd A1
Annesley Gr A2
Arboretum A1
Arboretum St A1
Arthur St A1
Arts Theatre B3
Ashforth St A3
Balmoral Rd A1
Barker Gate B3
Bath St B3
Belgrave Centre B1
Bellar Gate B3
Belward St B3
Blue Bell Hill Rd B3
Brewhouse Yard C2
Broad Marsh Bus Sta C2
Broad Marsh Precinct C2
Broad St B3
Brook St B3
Burns St A1
Burton St B2
Bus Station A2
Canal St C2
Carlton St B3
Carrington St C2
Castle Blvd C1
Castle C2
Castle Gate C2
Castle Mdw Retail Pk C1
Castle Meadow Rd C1
Castle Museum & Gallery C2
Castle Rd C2
Castle Wharf C2
Cavendish Rd East C1
Cemetery B1
Chaucer St B1
Cheapside B2
Church Rd A3
City Link C3
City of Caves C2
Clarendon St B1
Cliff Rd C3
Clumber Rd East C1
Clumber St B2
College St B1
Collin St C2
Conway Cl A2
Council House B2
Court B2
Cranbrook St B3
Cranmer St A2
Cromwell St B1
Curzon St B3
Derby Rd B1
Dryden St A2
Exchange Arcade B2
Fishpond Dr C1
Fletcher Gate B3
Forest Rd East A1
Forest Rd West A1
Friar La C2
Galleries of Justice C3
Gedling Gr A1
Gedling St B3
George St B3
Gill St A2
Glasshouse St B2
Goldsmith St B2
Goose Gate B3
Great Freeman St A2
Guildhall B2
Hamilton Dr C1
Hampden St A1
Heathcote St B3
High Pavement C3
High School A1
Holles Cr C1
Hope Dr C1
Hungerhill Rd A3
Huntingdon Dr C1
Huntingdon St A2
Information Ctr B2
Instow Rise A3
International Com Ctr A2
Kent St B3
King St B2
Lace Centre, The C2
Lace Market B3
Lace Mkt Theatre C3
Lamartine St B3
Lenton Rd C1
Lewis Cl A3
Lincoln St B2
London Rd C3
Long Row B2
Low Pavement C2
Lower Parliament St B3
Magistrates Court C2
Maid Marian Way B2
Mansfield Rd A2/B2
Middle Hill C2
Milton St B2
Mount St B2
National Ice Centre C3
Newcastle Dr B1
Newstead Gr A2
North Sherwood St A2
Nottingham Arena C3
Nottingham Station C3
Nottingham Trent University A2/B2
Old Market Square B2
Oliver St A1
Park Dr C1
Park Row C1
Park Terr B1
Park Valley C1
Peas Hill Rd A3
Peel St A1
Pelham St B2
Peveril Dr C1
Plantagenet St A3
Playhouse Theatre B1
Plumptre St C3
Police Station B2
Poplar St C3
Portland Rd B1
Post Office B2
Queen's Rd C3
Raleigh St A1
Regent St B1
Rick St B3
Robin Hood Statue C2
Robin Hood St B3
Royal Centre B2
Royal Children Inn C2
Royal Concert Hall B2
St Ann's Hill Rd A2
St Ann's Way A2
St Ann's Well Rd A3
St Barnabas B1
St James' St B2
St Mark's St B3
St Mary's Gdn of Rest B3
St Mary's Gate B3
St Nicholas C2
St Peter's C2
St Peter's Gate B2
Salutation Inn C2
Shakespeare St B2
Shelton St A2
South Pde B2
South Rd C1
South Sherwood St B2
Station St C3
Station Street C3
Stoney St B3
Talbot St B1
Tattershall Dr C1
Tennis Dr B1
Tennyson St A1
The Park C1
The Ropewalk B1
Theatre Royal B2
Trent St C3
Trent University B2
Trinity Square Sh Ctr B2
Trip To Jerusalem Inn C2
Union Rd B3
Upper Parliament St B2
Victoria Centre B2
Victoria Leisure Ctr B3
Victoria Park B3
Victoria St B2
Walter St A1
Warser Gate B3
Watkin St A2
Waverley St A1
Wheeler Gate B2
Wilford Rd C2
Wilford St C2
Willoughby House C2
Wollaton St B1
Woodborough Rd A2
Woolpack La B3
York St A2

Oban 345

Aird's Cres B2
Albany St B2
Albert La A2
Albert Rd A2
Alma Cres B1
Ambulance Station C2
Angus Terr C3
Ardconnel Rd A2
Ardconnel Terr B2
Argyll Sq B2
Argyll St B2
Atlantis Leisure Ctr A2
Bayview Rd A1
Benvoulin Rd A2
Bowling Green A2
Breadalbane St A2
Bus Station B2
Campbell St B2
College B2
Colonsay Terr C3
Columba Building B2
Combie St B2
Corran Brae A1
Corran Esplanade A1/A2
Corran Halls A2
Court B2
Crannaig-a-Mhinisteir B1
Crannog La C2
Croft Ave A2
Dalintart Dr C3
Dalriach Rd A2
Distillery B2
Drummore Rd C2
Duncraggan Rd A2
Dunollie Rd A2
Dunuaran Rd B1
Feochan Gr C3
Ferry Terminal B1
Gallanach Rd B1
George St A2
Glencruitten Dr C3
Glencruitten Rd B3
Glenmore Rd C1
Glenshellach Rd C1
Glenshellach Terr B2
Harbour Bowl B2
Hazeldean Cres A3
High St B2
Highland Theatre Cinema A2
Hill St B2
Industrial Estate C2
Information Ctr B2
Islay Rd C3
Jacob's Ladder B2
Jura Rd C3
Knipoch Pl C3
Laurel Cres A2
Laurel Rd A2/A3
Library A1
Lifeboat Station B1
Lighthouse Pier B1
Lismore Cres A2
Lochavullin Dr B2
Lochavullin Rd C2
Lochside St B2
Longsdale Cres A3
Longsdale Rd A2/A3
Longsdale Terr A3
Lunga Rd C3
Lynn Rd C2
Market St B2
McCaig Rd C3
McCaig's Tower A2
Mill La C2
Miller Rd C2
Millpark Ave C2
Millpark Rd C2
Mossfield Ave B3
Mossfield Dr B3
Mossfield Stadium B3
Nant Dr C3
Nelson Rd C2
North Pier B2
Nursery La A2
Oban B2
Police Station B2
Polvinister Rd C3
Post Office A2/B2
Pulpit Dr C1
Pulpit Hill C1
Pulpit Hill Viewpoint B1
Quarry Rd C2
Queen's Park Pl B2
Railway Quay B2
Rockfield Rd B2
St Columba's A1
St John's A2
Scalpay Terr C3
Shore St B1
Shuna Terr C3
Sinclair Dr C2
Soroba Rd B2/C2
South Pier B2
Stevenson St B2
Tweedale St B2
Ulva Rd C2
Villa Rd B1
War & Peace A2

Oxford 345

Adelaide St A1
Albert St A1
All Souls (Coll) B2
Ashmolean Mus B2
Balliol (Coll) B2
Banbury Rd A2
Bate Collection of Musical Instruments C2
Beaumont St B1
Becket St B1
Blackhall Rd A2
Blue Boar St B2
Bodleian Library B2
Botanic Garden B3
Brasenose (Coll) B2
Brewer St C2
Broad St B2
Burton-Taylor Theatre B2
Bus Station B1
Canal St A1
Cardigan St A1
Carfax Tower B2
Castle B1
Castle St B1
Catte St B2
Cemetery C1
Christ Church (Coll) B2
Christ Church Cath C2
Christ Church Mdw C2
Clarendon Centre B2
Coach & Lorry Park C1
College B3
Coll of Further Ed C1
Cornmarket St B2
Corpus Christi (Coll) B2
County Hall B1
Covered Market B2
Cowley Pl C3
Cranham St A1
Cranham Terr A1
Cricket Ground B1
Crown & County Courts C2
Deer Park B3
Exeter (Coll) B2
Folly Bridge C2
George St B1
Great Clarendon St A1
Hart St A1
Hertford (Coll) B2
High St B3
Hollybush Row B1
Holywell St B2
Hythe Bridge St B1
Ice Rink C1
Information Ctr B2
Jericho St A1
Jesus (Coll) B2
Jowett Walk B3
Juxon St A1
Keble (Coll) A2
Keble Rd A2
Library B2
Linacre (Coll) A3
Lincoln (Coll) B2
Little Clarendon St A1
Longwall St B3
Magdalen (Coll) B3
Magdalen Bridge B2
Magdalen St B2
Magistrate's Court C2
Manchester (Coll) B2
Manor Rd B3
Mansfield (Coll) A2
Mansfield Rd A3
Market B1
Marlborough Rd C2
Martyrs' Memorial B2
Merton Field B3
Merton (Coll) B3
Merton St B2
Mus of Modern Art B2
Museum of Oxford B2
Museum Rd A2
New College (Coll) B3
New Inn Hall St B2
New Rd B1
New Theatre B2
Norfolk St C1
Nuffield (Coll) B1
Observatory A1
Observatory St A1
Odeon B1/B2
Old Fire Station B1
Old Greyfriars St C2
Oriel (Coll) B2
Oxford Station B1
Oxford Story, The B2
Oxford University Research Centres A1
Oxpens Rd C1
Paradise Sq C1
Paradise St B1
Park End St B1
Parks Rd A2/B2
Pembroke (Coll) C2
Phoenix A1
Picture Gallery C2
Plantation Rd A1
Playhouse B2
Police Station C2
Post Office A1/B2
Pusey St B1
Queen's La B3
Queen's (Coll) B3
Radcliffe Camera B2
Rewley Rd B1
Richmond Rd A1
Rose La B3
Ruskin (Coll) B1
Saïd Business School B1
St Aldates C2
St Anne's (Coll) A1
St Antony's (Coll) A1
St Bernard's Rd A1
St Catherine's (Coll) B3
St Cross Building A3
St Cross Rd A3
St Edmund Hall (Coll) B3
St Giles St A2
St Hilda's (Coll) C3
St John St B2
St John's (Coll) B2
St Mary the Virgin B2
St Michael at the Northgate B2
St Peter's (Coll) B1
St Thomas St B1
Science Area A2
Science Museum B2
Sheldonian Theatre B2
Somerville (Coll) A1
South Parks Rd A2
Speedwell St C2
Sports Ground C3
Thames St C2
Town Hall B2
Trinity (Coll) B2
Turl St B2
University Coll (Coll) B3
Univ Mus & Pitt Rivers Mus A2
University Parks A2
Wadham (Coll) B2
Walton Cr A1
Walton St A1
Western Rd C2
Westgate Sh Ctr B2
Woodstock Rd A1
Worcester (Coll) B1

Perth 345

A K Bell Library B2
Abbot Cres C1
Abbot St C1
Albany Terr A1
Albert Monument A3
Alexandra St B2
Atholl St A2
Balhousie Ave A2
Balhousie Castle Black Watch Museum A2
Balhousie St A2
Ballantine Pl A1
Barossa Pl A2
Barossa St A2
Barrack St A2
Bell's Sports Centre A2
Bellwood B3
Blair St B1
Burn Park C1
Bus Station B2
Caledonian Rd B2
Canal Cres B2
Canal St B3
Cavendish Ave C1
Charles St B2
Charlotte Pl A2
Charlotte St A3
Church St A1
City Hall B3
Club House C3
Clyde Pl C1
Commercial St A3
Concert Hall B3
Council Chambers B3
County Pl B2
Court B3
Craigie Pl C2
Crieff Rd A1
Croft Park C2
Cross St B2
Darnhall Cres C1
Darnhall Dr C1
Dewars Centre B1
Dundee Rd B3
Dunkeld Rd A1
Earl's Dykes B1
Edinburgh Rd C3
Elibank St B1
Fair Maid's House A3
Fergusson B3
Feus Rd A1
Fire Station A1
Fitness Centre B3
Foundary La A2
Friar St C1
George St B3
Glamis Pl C1
Glasgow Rd B1
Glenearn Rd C2
Glover St B1/C1
Golf Course A2
Gowrie St A3
Gray St B1
Graybank Rd B1
Greyfriars Burial Ground B3
Hay St A2
High St B2/B3
Hotel B2
Inchaffray St A1
Industrial/Retail Park B1
Information Ctr B2
Isla Rd A3
James St B2
Keir St A3
King Edward St B3
King James VI Golf Course C3
King St B2
Kings Pl C2
Kinnoull Causeway B2
Kinnoull Aisle 'Monument' B3
Kinnoull St B2
Knowelea Pl C1
Knowelea Terr C1
Ladeside Bsns Centre A1
Leisure Pool B1
Leonard St B2
Lickley St B2
Lochie Brae A3
Long Causeway A1
Low St A2
Main St A3
Marshall Pl C3
Melville St A2
Mill St B3
Milne St B2
Murray Cres C1
Murray St B2
Needless Rd C1
New Rd B2
North Inch A3
North Methven St A2
Park Pl C1
Perth B2
Perth Bridge A3
Perth Business Park B1
Perth Museum & Art Gallery B3
Perth Station C2
Pickletulllum Rd B1
Pitheavlis Cres C1
Playhouse B2
Police Station A2
Pomarium St B2
Post Office A3/B2/C2
Princes St B3
Priory Pl C2
Queen St C1
Queen's Bridge B3
Riggs Rd B1
Riverside B3
Riverside Park B3
Rodney Park B3
Rose Terr A2
St Catherines Ret Pk A1
St Catherine's Rd A1/A2
St John St B3
St John's Kirk B3
St John's Shopping Centre B2
St Leonards Bridge C2
St Ninians Cath A2
Scott Monument C2
Scott St B2
Sheriff Court B3
Shore Rd C3
Skate Park C3
South Inch C2
South Inch Bsns Ctr C3
South Inch Park C2
South Inch View C2
South Methven St B2
South St B3
South William St B2
Stormont St A2
Strathmore St A3
Stuart Ave C1
Tay St B3
The Stables A1
The Stanners B3
Union La A2
Victoria St B2
Watergate B3
Wellshill Cemetery A1
West Bridge St A3
West Mill St B2
Whitefriers Cres B1
Whitefriers St B1
Wilson St C1
Windsor Terr C1
Woodside Cres C1
York Pl B2
Young St C1

Peterborough 345

Athletics Arena B3
Bishop's Palace B2
Bishop's Rd B2/B3
Boongate A3
Bourges Boulevard A1
Bourges Retail Pk B1/B2
Bridge House (Council Offices) C2
Bridge St B2
Bright St A1
Broadway A2
Broadway A2
Brook St A2
Burghley Rd A2
Bus Station B2
Cavendish St A3
Charles St A3
Church St B2
Church Walk A2
Cobden Ave A1
Cobden St A1
Cowgate B2
Craig St A2
Crawthorne Rd A2
Cripple Sidings La C2
Cromwell Rd A1
Dickens St A3
Eastfield Rd A3
Eastgate B3
Fire Station A1
Fletton Ave C2
Frank Perkins Parkway C3
Geneva St A2
George St C1
Gladstone St A1
Glebe Rd C2
Gloucester Rd C3
Granby St B3
Grove St C1
Guildhall B2
Hadrians Ct C3
Henry St A2
Hereward Cross (Sh) B2
Hereward Rd B3
Information Ctr B2
Jubilee St C1
Key Theatre C2
Kent Rd B1
Kirkwood Cl B1
Lea Gdns B1
Library A2
Lincoln Rd A2
London Rd C2
Long Causeway B2
Lower Bridge St C2
Magistrates Court B2
Manor House St A2
Mayor's Walk A1
Midland Rd A1
Monument St A2
Morris St A3
Mus & Art Gallery B2
Nene Valley Railway C1
New Rd A2
New Rd C1
Northminster A2
Old Customs House C2
Oundle Rd C1
Padholme Rd A3

Palmerston Rd C1
Park Rd A2
Passport Office B2
Peterborough District Hospital (A&E) B1
Peterborough Sta B1
Peterborough Nene Valley C1
Peterborough United FC C2
Police Station B2
Post Office A3/B1/B2/B3/C1
Priestgate B2
Queen's Walk C2
Queensgate Centre B2
Railworld C1
Regional Swimming & Fitness Centre B3
River La B1
Rivergate Sh Ctr B2
Riverside Mead C3
Russell St A1
St John's B2
St John's St A3
St Marks St A2
St Peter's B2
St Peter's Rd B2
Saxon Rd A3
Spital Bridge A1
Stagshaw Dr C3
Star Rd B3
Thorpe Lea Rd B1
Thorpe Rd B1
Thorpe's Lea Rd B1
Tower St A2
Town Hall B2
Viersen Platz B2
Vineyard Rd B3
Wake Rd B3
Wellington St A3
Wentworth St B2
Westgate B2
Whalley St A3
Wharf Rd C1
Whitsed St A3
YMCA A3

Plymouth 346

Alma Rd A1
Anstis St B1
Armada Centre B2
Armada St A3
Armada Way B2
Arts Centre B2
Athenaeum B1
Athenaeum St C1
Barbican C3
Barbican C3
Baring St A3
Bath St B1
Beaumont Park B3
Beaumont Rd B3
Black Friars Gin Distillery C2
Breton Side B3
Bus Station B2
Castle St C3
Cathedral (RC) B1
Cecil St B1
Central Park A1
Central Park Ave A2
Charles Church B3
Charles Cross B3
Charles St B2
City Museum & Art Gallery B2
Citadel Rd C2
Citadel Rd East C2
Civic Centre B2
Cliff Rd C1
Clifton Pl A3
Cobourg St A2
College of Art B2
Continental Ferry Port B1
Cornwall St B2
Dale Rd A2
Deptford Pl A3
Derry Ave A2
Derry's Cross B1
Drake Circus B2
Drake Cir Sh Ctr B2
Drake's Memorial C2
Drum B2
Eastlake St B2
Ebrington St B3
Elizabethan House C3
Elliot St C1
Endsleigh Pl A2
Exeter St B3
Fire Station A3
Fish Quay C3
Gibbons St A3
Glen Park Ave A2
Grand Pde C1
Great Western Rd C1
Greenbank Rd A3
Greenbank Terr A3
Guildhall B2
Hampton St B3
Harwell St B1
Hill Park Cr A3
Hoe Approach B2
Hoe Rd C2
Hoegate St C2
Houndiscombe Rd A2
Information Ctr C3
James St A2
Kensington Rd A3
King St B1
Lambhay Hill C3
Leigham St C1
Library B2
Lipson Rd A3/B3
Lockyer St C2
Lockyers Quay C3
Madeira Rd C2
Marina B3
Market Ave B1
Martin St B1
Mayflower Stone & Steps C3
Mayflower St B2
Mayflower Visitor Centre C3
Merchants House B2
Millbay Rd B1
National Marine Aquarium C3
Neswick St B1
New George St B2
New St C3
North Cross A2
North Hill A3
North Quay B2
North Rd East A2
North Rd West A1
North St B3
Notte St B2
Octagon St B1
Pannier Market B1
Pennycomequick A1
Pier St C1
Plymouth Pavilions B1
Plymouth Station A2
Police Station B3
Portland Sq A2
Post Office A1/B1/B2
Princess St B2
Prysten House B2
Queen Anne's Battery Seasports Centre C3
Radford Rd C1
Regent St B3
Rope Walk C3
Royal Citadel C2
Royal Pde B2
St Andrew's B2
St Andrew's Cross B2
St Andrew's St B2
St Lawrence Rd A2
Saltash Rd A2
Smeaton's Tower C2
Southern Terr A3
Southside St C2
Stuart Rd A1
Sutherland Rd A2
Sutton Rd B3
Sydney St A1
Teats Hill Rd C3
The Crescent B1
The Hoe C2
The Octagon B1
The Promenade C2
Tothill Ave B3
Union St B1
Univ of Plymouth A2
Vauxhall St B2/3
Victoria Park A1
West Hoe Rd C1
Western Approach B1
Whittington St A1
Wyndham St B1
YMCA B2
YWCA C2

Poole 346

Ambulance Station A3
Baiater Gdns C2
Baiter Park C3
Ballard Cl C2
Ballard Rd C2
Bay Hog La B1
Bridge Approach C1
Bus Station B2
Castle St B2
Catalina Dr B3
Chapel La B2
Church St B1
Cinnamon La B1
Colborne Cl B3
Dear Hay La B2
Denmark La A3
Denmark Rd A3
East St B2
Elizabeth Rd A3
Emerson Rd B2
Ferry Rd C1
Ferry Terminal C1
Fire Station A2
Freightliner Terminal C1
Furnell Rd B3
Garland Rd A3
Green Rd B2
Heckford La A3
Heckford Rd A3
High St B2
High St North A3
Hill St B2
Holes Bay Rd A1
Hospital (A&E) A3
Information Ctr C2
Kingland Rd B3
Kingston Rd A3
Labrador Dr C3
Lagland St B2
Lander Cl C3
Old Lifeboat C2
Lighthouse – Poole Centre for the Arts B3
Longfleet Rd A3
Maple Rd A3
Market Cl B2
Market St B2
Mount Pleasant Rd B3
New Harbour Rd C1
New Harbour Rd South C1
New Harbour Rd West C1
New Orchard B1
New Quay Rd C1
New St B2
Newfoundland Dr B2
North St B2
Old Orchard B2
Parish Rd A3
Park Lake Rd B3
Parkstone Rd A3
Perry Gdns B2
Pitwines Cl B2
Police Station A2
Poole Central Library B2
Poole Lifting Bridge C1
Poole Park B2
Poole Station A2
Poole Waterfront Museum C1
Post Office A2/B2
St John's Rd A3
St Margaret's Rd A2
St Mary's Maternity Unit A3
St Mary's Rd A3
Seldown Bridge B3
Seldown La B3
Seldown Rd B3
Serpentine Rd A2
Shaftesbury Rd A3
Skinner St B2
Slipway B1
Stanley Rd C2
Sterte Ave A2
Sterte Ave West A1
Sterte Cl A2
Sterte Esplanade A2
Sterte Rd A2
Strand St C2
Swimming Pool B3
Taverner Cl B3
Thames St B1
The Lifeboat College B2
The Quay C2
Towngate Bridge B2
Vallis Cl C3
Waldren Cl B3
West Quay B1
West Quay Rd B1
West St B1
West View Rd A2
Whatleigh Cl B2
Wimborne Rd A3

Portsmouth 346

Action Stations C1
Admiralty Rd A1
Alfred Rd A2
Anglesea Rd B2
Arundel St B3
Aspex B1
Bishop St A2
Broad St C1
Buckingham House C2
Burnaby Rd B2
Bus Station B1
Camber Dock C1
Cambridge Rd B2
Car Ferry to Isle of Wight B1
Cascades Sh Ctr A3
Castle Rd C3
City Museum & Art Gallery B2
Civic Offices B3
Clarence Pier C2
College St B1
Commercial Rd A3
Cottage Gr B3
Cross St A1
Cumberland St A2
Duisburg Way C2
Durham St A3
East St B1
Edinburgh Rd A2
Elm Gr C3
Great Southsea St C3
Green Rd B3
Greetham St B3
Grosvenor St B3
Groundlings A2
Grove Rd North C3
Grove Rd South C3
Guildhall B3
Guildhall Walk B3
Gunwharf Quays Retail Park B1
Gunwharf Rd B1
Hambrook St C2
Hampshire Terr B2
Hanover St A1
High St C2
HM Naval Base A1
HMS Nelson (Royal Naval Barracks) A2
HMS Victory A1
HMS Warrior A1
Hovercraft Terminal C2
Hyde Park Rd B3
Information Ctr A1/B3
Isambard Brunel Rd B3
Isle of Wight Car Ferry Terminal B1
Kent Rd C3
Kent St A2
King St B3
King's Rd C3
King's Terr C2
Lake Rd A3
Law Courts B3
Library B3
Long Curtain Rd C2
Market Way A3
Marmion Rd C3
Mary Rose Museum A1
Middle St B3
Millennium Prom B1/C1
Museum Rd B2
National Museum of the Royal Navy A1
Naval Recreation Gd C2
Nightingale Rd C3
Norfolk St B3
North St A2
Osborne Rd C3
Park Rd B2
Passenger Catamaran to Isle of Wight B1
Passenger Ferry to Gosport B1
Pelham Rd C3
Pembroke Gdns C2
Pier Rd C2
Point Battery C1
Police Station B3
Portsmouth & Southsea A3
Portsmouth Harbour B1
Portsmouth Historic Dockyard A1
Post Office A2/A3/B1/B3/C3
Queen St A1
Queen's Cr C3
Round Tower C1
Royal Garrison Church C1
St Edward's Rd C3
St George's Rd B2
St George's Sq B1
St George's Way B2
St James's Rd B3
St James's St A2
St John's Cath (RC) A3
St Thomas's Cath C1
St Thomas's St B2
Somers Rd B3
Southsea Common C2
Southsea Terr C2
Spinnaker Tower B1
Square Tower C1
Station St A3
Swimming Pool A2
The Hard B1
Town Fortifications C1
Unicorn Rd A2
United Services Recreation Ground B2
University of Portsmouth A2/B2
Univ of Portsmouth – College of Art, Design & Media B3
Upper Arundel St A3
Victoria Ave C2
Victoria Park A2
Victory Gate A1
Vue B1
Warblington St B1
Western Pde C2
White Hart Rd C1
Winston Churchill Ave B3

Preston 346

Adelphi St A2
Anchor Ct B3
Aqueduct St A1
Ardee Rd C1
Arthur St B2
Ashton St A1
Avenham La B3
Avenham Park C3
Avenham Rd B3
Avenham St B3
Bairstow St B3
Balderstone Rd C1
Beamont Dr A1
Beech St South C2
Bird St C1
Bow La B2
Brieryfield Rd A1
Broadgate C1
Brook St A2
Bus Station A3
Butler St B2
Cannon St B3
Carlton St A1
Chaddock St B3
Channel Way B1
Chapel St B3
Christ Church St B2
Christian Rd B2
Cold Bath St A2
Coleman Ct C1
Connaught Rd C2
Corn Exchange B3
Corporation St A2/B2
County Hall B2
County Records Office B2
Court A3
Court B3
Cricket Ground C2
Croft St A1
Cross St B3
Crown Court A3
Crown St A3
East Cliff C3
East Cliff Rd B3
Edward St A2
Elizabeth St A3
Euston St B1
Fishergate B2/B3
Fishergate Hill B2
Fishergate Sh Ctr B2
Fitzroy St B1
Fleetwood St A1
Friargate A3
Fylde Rd A1/A2
Gerrard St B2
Glover's Ct B3
Good St B2
Grafton St B2
Great George St A3
Great Shaw St A3
Greenbank St A2
Guild Way B1
Guildhall & Charter B3
Guildhall St B3
Harrington St A2
Harris Museum B3
Hartington Rd B1
Hasset Cl C2
Heatley St B2
Hind St C2
Information Ctr B3
Kilruddery Rd C1
Lancaster Rd A3/B3
Latham St B3
Lauderdale St C2
Lawson St A3
Leighton St A2
Leyland Rd C1
Library A1
Library B3
Liverpool Rd C1
Lodge St B2
Lune St B3
Main Sprit West B3
Maresfield Rd C1
Market St West A3
Marsh La B1/B2
Maudland Bank A2
Maudland Rd A2
Meadow Ct C2
Meath Rd C1
Mill Hill A2
Miller Arcade B3
Miller Park C3
Moor La A3
Mount St B3
North Rd A3
North St A3
Northcote Rd B1
Old Milestones B1
Old Tram Rd C3
Pedder St A1/A2
Peel St A2
Penwortham Bridge C2
Penwortham New Bridge C1
Pitt St B2
Playhouse A3
Police Station A3
Port Way B1
Post Office B3
Preston Station B2
Ribble Bank St B2
Ribble Viaduct C2
Ribblesdale Pl B3
Ringway B3
River Parade C1
Riverside C2
St Georges B3
St George's Sh Ctr B3
St Johns B3
St Johns Shopping Ctr A3
St Mark's Rd A1
St Walburges A1
Salisbury Rd B1
Sessions House B3
Snow Hill A3
South End C2
South Meadow La C2
Spa Rd B1
Sports Ground C2
Strand Rd B1
Syke St B3
Talbot Rd B1
Taylor St C1
Tithebarn St A3
Town Hall B3
Tulketh Brow A1
University of Central Lancashire A2
Valley Rd C1
Victoria St A2
Walker St A3
Walton's Parade B2
Warwick St A3
Wellfield Bsns Park A1
Wellfield Rd A1
Wellington St A1
West Cliff C2
West Strand A1
Winckley Rd C1
Winckley Square B3
Wolseley Rd C2

Reading 346

Abbey Ruins B2
Abbey Sq B2
Abbey St B2
Abbot's Walk B2
Acacia Rd C2
Addington Rd C3
Addison Rd A1
Allcroft Rd C3
Alpine St C2
Baker St B1
Berkeley Ave C1
Bridge St B1
Brigham Rd A1
Broad St B1
Broad Street Mall B1
Carey St B1
Castle Hill C1
Castle St B1
Caversham Rd A1
Christchurch Playing Fields A2
Civic Offices & Magistrate's Court B1
Coley Hill C1
Coley Pl C1
Craven Rd C3
Crown St C2
De Montfort Rd A1
Denmark Rd C3
Duke St B2
East St B2
Edgehill St C2
Eldon Rd B3
Eldon Terr B3
Elgar Rd C1
Erleigh Rd C3
Field Rd C1
Fire Station A1
Fobney St B1
Forbury Gdns B2
Forbury Retail Park B2
Forbury Rd B2
Francis St C1
Friar St B1
Garrard St B1
Gas Works Rd B3
George St A2
Great Knollys St B1
Greyfriars B1
Gun St B1
Henry St C1
Hexagon Theatre, The B1
Hill's Meadow A2
HM Prison B2
Howard St B1
Information Ctr B1
Inner Distribution Rd B1
Katesgrove La C1
Kenavon Dr B2
Kendrick Rd C2
King's Meadow Recreation Ground A2
King's Rd B2
Library B2
London Rd C3
London St B2
Lynmouth Rd A1
Market Pl B2
Mill La B2
Mill Rd A2
Minster St B1
Morgan Rd C3
Mount Pleasant C2
Museum of English Rural Life C3
Napier Rd A2
Newark St C2
Newport Rd A1
Old Reading Univ C3
Oracle Sh Ctr, The B1
Orts Rd B3
Pell St C1
Queen Victoria St B1
Queen's Rd A2
Queen's Rd B2
Police Station B1
Post Office B2
Randolph Rd A1
Reading Bridge A2
Reading Station A1
Redlands Rd C3
Renaissance Hotel B1
Riverside Museum B3
Rose Kiln La C1
Royal Berks Hospital (A&E) C3
St Giles C2
St Laurence B2
St Mary's B1
St Mary's Butts B1
St Saviour's Rd C1
Send Rd A3
Sherman Rd C2
Sidmouth St B2
Silver St C2
South St B2
Southampton St C2
Station Hill A1
Station Rd B1
Superstore A3
Swansea Rd A1
Technical College B3
The Causeway A3
The Grove B2
Valpy St B2
Vastern Rd A1
Vue B2
Waldeck St C2
Watlington St B3
West St B1
Whitby Dr C3
Wolseley St C1
York Rd A1
Zinzan St B1

St Andrews 346

Abbey St B2
Abbey Walk B3
Abbotsford Cres A1
Albany Pk C3
Allan Robertson Dr C2
Ambulance Station C1
Anstruther Rd C3
Argyle St B1
Argyll Business Park C1
Auld Burn Rd B2
Bassaguard Ind Est B1
Bell St B2
Blackfriars Chapel (Ruins) B2
Boase Ave B2
Braid Cres C3
Brewster Pl C3
Bridge St B1
British Golf Mus A1
Broomfaulds Ave C1
Bruce Embankment A1
Bruce St C2
Bus Station A1
Byre B2
Canongate C1
Cathedral and Priory (Ruins) B3
Cemetery B3
Chamberlain St C1
Church St B2
Churchill Cres C2
City Rd A1
Claybraes C1
Cockshaugh Public Pk B1
Cosmos Com Centre B3
Council Office A2
Crawford Gdns C1
Doubledykes Rd B1
Drumcarrow Rd C1
East Sands B3
East Scores A3
Fire Station C1
Forrest St C1
Fraser Ave C1
Freddie Tait St C2
Gateway Centre A1
Glebe Rd B2
Golf Pl A1
Grange Rd C3
Greenside Pl B2
Greyfriars Gdns A2
Hamilton Ave C2
Hepburn Gdns B1
Holy Trinity B2
Horseleys Park C1
Information Ctr B2
Irvine Cres C3
James Robb Ave C1
James St B1
John Knox Rd C1
Kennedy Gdns B1
Kilrymont Cl C3
Kilrymont Pl C3
Kilrymont Rd C3
Kinburn Park B1
Kinkell Terr C3
Kinnesburn Rd B2
Ladebraes Walk B2
Lady Buchan's Cave A3
Lamberton Pl C1
Lamond Dr C2
Langlands Rd B2
Largo Rd C1
Learmonth Pl C1
Library B2
Links Clubhouse A1
Links, The A1
Livingstone Cres B2
Long Rocks A2
Madras College B2
Market St A2
Martyr's Monument A1
Memorial Hospital (No A&E) B3
Murray Pk A2
Murray Pl A2
Nelson St B2
New Course, The A1
New Picture House A2
North Castle St A3
North St A2
Old Course, The A1
Old Station Rd A1
Pends, The B3
Pilmour Links A1
Pipeland Rd B2/C2
Police Station A2
Post Office B2
Preservation Trust B3
Priestden Pk C3
Priestden Pl C3
Priestden Rd C3
Queen's Gdns B2
Queen's Terr B2
Roundhill Rd C2
Royal & Ancient Golf Club A1
St Andrews B1
St Andrews Aquarium A2
St Andrews Botanic Garden B1
St Andrews Castle (Ruins) & Visitor Centre A2
St Leonard's School B3
St Mary St B3
St Mary's College B2
St Nicholas St C3
St Rules Tower B3
St Salvator's College A2
Sandyhill Cres C2
Sandyhill Rd C2
Scooniehill Rd C2
Shields Ave C3
Shoolbraids C2
Sloan St B1
South St B2
Spottiswoode Gdns C1
Station Rd A1
Swilcen Bridge A1
The Scores A2
The Shore B3
Tom Morris Dr C2
Tom Stewart La C1
Town Hall B2
Union St A2
University Chapel A2
University Library A2
Univ of St Andrews A1
Viaduct Walk B1
War Memorial A3
Wardlaw Gdns B1
Warrack St C3
Watson Ave B2
West Port B2
West Sands A1
Westview B2
Windmill Rd A1
Winram Pl C1
Wishart Gdns C2
Woodburn Pk B3
Woodburn Pl B3
Woodburn Terr B3
Younger Hall A2

Salisbury 347

Albany Rd A2
Arts Centre A3
Ashley Rd A1
Avon Approach A2
Ayleswade Rd C2
Bedwin St A2
Belle Vue A2
Bishop's Palace C2
Bishops Walk B2
Blue Boar Row B2
Bourne Ave A3
Bourne Hill A3
Britford La C2
Broad Walk C2
Brown St B2
Bus Station B2
Castle St A2
Catherine St B2
Chapter House B2
Church House B2
Churchfields Rd B1
Churchill Way East B3
Churchill Way North A3
Churchill Way South C2
Churchill Way West A1
City Hall B2
Close Wall B2
Coldharbour La A1
College St A3
Council Offices A3
Court A1
Crane Bridge Rd B2
Crane St B2
Cricket Ground C1
Culver St South B3
De Vaux Pl C2
Devizes Rd A1
Dews Rd B1
Elm Grove B3
Elm Grove Rd A3
Endless St A2
Estcourt Rd A3
Exeter St C2
Fairview Rd A3
Fire Station A1
Fisherton St A1
Folkestone Rd C1
Fowlers Hill B3
Fowlers Rd B3
Friary Estate C3
Friary La B2
Gas La A1
Gigant St B3
Greencroft B3
Greencroft St A3
Guildhall B2
Hall of John Halle B2
Hamilton Rd A2
Harnham Mill B1
Harnham Rd C1/C2
High St B2
Hospital A1
Ho of John A'Port B2
Information Ctr B2
Kelsey Rd A3
King's Rd A2
Laverstock Rd B3
Library B2
London Rd A3
Lower St C1
Maltings, The B2
Manor Rd A3
Marsh La A1
Medieval Hall B2
Milford Hill B3
Milford St B3
Mill Rd B1
Millstream Approach A2
Mompesson House (NT) B2
New Bridge Rd C2
New Canal B2
New Harnham Rd C2
New St B2
North Canonry B2
North Gate B2
North Walk B2
Old George Hall B2
Old Blandford Rd C1
Old Deanery B2
Park St A3
Parsonage Green C1
Playhouse Theatre A2
Post Office A2/B2/C2
Poultry Cross B2
Queen Elizabeth Gdns B1
Queen's Rd A3
Rampart Rd B3
St Ann's Gate B2
St Ann St B2
St Marks Rd A3
St Martins B3
St Mary's Cathedral B2
St Nicholas Hospl C2
St Paul's A1
St Paul's Rd A1
St Thomas B2
Salisbury & South Wiltshire Museum B2
Salisbury General Hospital (A&E) C2
Salisbury Station A1
Salt La A3
Saxon Rd C1
Scots La A2
Shady Bower B3
South Canonry C2
South Gate C2
Southampton Rd B2
Spire View A1
Sports Ground C3
The Friary B3
Tollgate Rd B3
Town Path B1
Wain-a-Long Rd A3
Wardrobe, The B2
Wessex Rd A3
West Walk C2
Wilton Rd A1
Wiltshire College B3
Winchester St B3
Windsor Rd A1
Winston Churchill Gdns C3
Wyndham Rd A2
YHA B3
York Rd A1

Scarborough 347

Aberdeen Walk B2
Albert Rd A2
Albion Rd C2
Alexandra Bowling Hall A1
Alexandra Gardens A1
Auborough St B2
Belle Vue St C1
Belmont Rd C2
Brunswick Pavilion Shopping Centre B2
Castle Dykes B3
Castlegate B3
Castle Holms A3
Castle Hill A3
Castle Rd B2
Castle Walls A3
Cemetery B1
Central Lift C2
Clarence Gardens A2
Coach Park B1
Columbus Ravine A1
Court B1
Cricket Ground A1
Cross St B2
Crown Terr C2
Dean Rd B1
Devonshire Dr A1
East Harbour B3
East Pier B3
Eastborough B2
Elmville Ave B1
Esplanade C2
Falconers Rd B2
Falsgrave Rd C1
Fire Station B2
Foreshore Rd B2
Friargate B2
Futurist Theatre B2
Gladstone Rd B1
Gladstone St B1
Hoxton Rd B1
Information Ctr B2/B3
King St B2
Library B2
Lifeboat Station B3
Londesborough Rd C1
Longwestgate B3
Marine Dr A3
Military Adventure Pk A1
Miniature Railway A1
Nelson St B1
Newborough B2
Nicolas St B2
North Marine Rd A1
North St B2
Northway B1
Old Harbour B3
Olympia Leisure B2
Peasholm Park A1
Peasholm Rd A1
Plaza A1
Police Station B1
Post Office B2/C1
Princess St B3
Prospect Rd B1
Queen St B2
Queen's Parade A2
Queen's Tower (Remains) A3
Ramshill Rd C2
Roman Signal Sta A3
Roscoe St C1
Rotunda Museum C2
Royal Albert Dr A2
St Martin-on-the-Hill C2
St Martin's Ave C2
St Mary's B3
St Thomas St B2
Sandside B3
Scarborough Art Gallery and Crescent Art Studio C2
Scarborough Castle A3
Scarborough C1
Somerset Terr C2
South Cliff Lift C2
Spa, The C2
Spa Theatre, The C2
Stephen Joseph Theatre B1
Tennyson Ave B1
The Crescent C2
Tollergate B2
Town Hall B2
Trafalgar Rd B1
Trafalgar Square A1
Trafalgar St West B1
Valley Bridge Parade C2
Valley Rd C1
Vernon Rd C2
Victoria Park Mount A1
Victoria Rd B1
West Pier B3
Westborough C1
Westover Rd C1
Westwood C1
Woodall Ave A1
YMCA Theatre B2
York Pl B2
Yorkshire Coast College (Westwood Campus) C1

Sheffield 347

Addy Dr A2
Addy St A2
Adelphi St A3
Albert Terrace Rd A3
Albion St A2
Aldred Rd A1
Allen St A4
Alma St A4
Angel St B5
Arundel Gate B5
Arundel St C4
Ashberry Rd A2
Ashdell Rd C1
Ashgate Rd C1
Athletics Centre B2
Attercliffe Rd A6
Bailey St B4
Ball St A4
Balm Green B4
Bank St B4
Barber Rd A2
Bard St B5
Barker's Pool B4

Bates St A1
Beech Hill Rd C1
Beet St B3
Bellefield St A3
Bernard Rd A6
Bernard St B6
Birkendale A2
Birkendale Rd A2
Birkendale View A1
Bishop St C4
Blackwell Pl B6
Blake St A2
Blonk St A5
Bolsover St B2
Botanical Gdns C1
Bower Rd A1
Bradley St A1
Bramall La C4
Bramwell St A3
Bridge St A4/A5
Brighton Terrace Rd A1
Broad La B3
Broad St B6
Brocco St A3
Brook Hill B3
Broomfield Rd C1
Broomgrove Rd C2
Broomhall Pl C3
Broomhall Rd C2
Broomhall St C3
Broomspring La C2
Brown St C5
Brunswick St B3
Burgess St B4
Burlington St A2
Burns Rd A2
Cadman St A6
Cambridge St B4
Campo La B4
Carver St B4
Castle Market B5
Castle Square B5
Castlegate A5
Cathedral (RC) ✝ B4
Cathedral B4
Cavendish St B3
Charles St C4
Charter Row C4
Children's Hospital (A&E) B2
Church St B4
City Hall B4
City Hall B4
City Rd C6
Claremont Cr B2
Claremont Pl B2
Clarke St C3
Clarkegrove Rd C2
Clarkehouse Rd C1
Clarkson St B2
Cobden View Rd A1
Collegiate Cr C2
Commercial St B5
Commonside A1
Conduit Rd B1
Cornish St A3
Corporation St A4
Court B4
Cricket Inn Rd B6
Cromwell St A1
Crookes Rd B1
Crookes Valley Park B2
Crookes Valley Rd B2
Crookesmoor Rd A2
Crown Court A4
Crucible Theatre B5
Cutlers Gate A6
Cutler's Hall B4
Daniel Hill A2
Dental Hospital B2
Dept for Education & Employment C4
Devonshire Green B3
Devonshire St B3
Division St B4
Dorset St C2
Dover St A3
Duchess Rd C5
Duke St B5
Duncombe St A1
Durham Rd B2
Earl St C4
Earl Way C4
Ecclesall Rd C3
Edward St B3
Effingham Rd A6
Effingham St A6
Egerton St C3
Eldon St B3
Elmore Rd B1
Exchange St B5
Eyre St C4
Fargate B4
Farm Rd C5
Fawcett St A3
Filey St B3
Fire & Police Mus A4
Fire Station C4
Fir St A1
Fitzalan Sq/ Ponds Forge B5
Fitzwater Rd C6
Fitzwilliam Gate C4
Fitzwilliam St B3
Flat St B5
Foley St A6
Foundry Climbing Ctr A4
Fulton Rd A1
Furnace Hill A4
Furnival Rd A5
Furnival Sq C4
Furnival St C4
Garden St B3
Gell St B3
Gibraltar St A4
Glebe Rd B1
Glencoe Rd C6
Glossop Rd B2/B3/C1
Gloucester St C2
Granville Rd C6
Granville Rd/ Sheffield College C5
Graves Gallery B5
Greave Rd B3
Green La A4
Hadfield St A1
Hanover St C3
Hanover Way C3
Harcourt Rd B1
Harmer La B5
Havelock St C2
Hawley St B4
Haymarket B5
Headford St C3
Heavygate Rd A1
Henry St A3
High St B4
Hodgson St C3
Holberry Gdns C2
Hollis Croft B4
Holly St B4
Hounsfield Rd B3
Howard Rd A1
Hoyle St A3
Hyde Park A6
Infirmary Rd A3
Infirmary Rd A3
Information Ctr B4
Jericho St A3
Johnson St A5
Kelham Island Industrial Mus A4
Lawson Rd C1
Leadmill Rd C5
Leadmill St C5
Leadmill, The C5
Leamington St A1
Leavy Rd B3
Lee Croft B4
Leopold St B4
Leveson St A6
Library A2
Library B5
Library C1
Lyceum Theatre B5
Malinda St A3
Maltravers St A5
Manor Oaks Rd B6
Mappin St B3
Marlborough Rd B1
Mary St C4
Matilda St C4
Matlock Rd A1
Meadow St A3
Melbourn Rd A1
Melbourne Ave C1
Millennium Galleries B5
Milton St C3
Mitchell St B3
Mona Ave A1
Mona Rd A1
Montgomery Terr Rd A3
Montgomery Theatre B4
Monument Gdns C6
Moor Oaks Rd B1
Moore St C3
Mowbray St A4
Mushroom La B2
Netherthorpe Rd B3
Netherthorpe Rd B3
Newbould La C1
Nile St C1
Norfolk Park Rd C6
Norfolk Rd C6
Norfolk St B4
North Church St B4
Northfield Rd A1
Northumberland Rd B1
Nursery St A5
O2 Academy B5
Oakholme Rd C1
Octagon B2
Odeon B5
Old St B6
Orchard Square B4
Oxford St A2
Paradise St B4
Park La C2
Park Sq B5
Parker's Rd B1
Pearson Building (Univ) C2
Penistone Rd A3
Pinstone St B4
Pitt St B3
Police Station A4/B5
Pond Hill B5
Pond St B5
Ponds Forge Int Sports Ctr B5
Portobello St B3
Post Office A1/A2/B3/B4/B5/B6/C1/C3/C4/C6
Powell St A2
Queen St B4
Queen's Rd C5
Ramsey Rd B1
Red Hill B3
Redcar Rd B1
Regent St B3
Rockingham St B4
Roebuck Rd A2
Royal Hallamshire Hospital C2
Russell St A4
Rutland Park C1
St George's Cl B3
St Mary's Gate C3
St Mary's Rd C4/C5
St Peter & St Paul Cathedral ✝ B4
St Philip's Rd A3
Savile St A5
School Rd B1
Scotland St A4
Severn Rd B1
Shalesmoor A4
Shalesmoor A3
Sheaf St B5
Sheffield Hallam Univ B5
Sheffield Ice Sports Ctr – Skate Central C5
Sheffield Interchange B5
Sheffield Parkway A6
Sheffield Station C5
Sheffield Sta/ Sheffield Hallam Univ B5
Sheffield University B2
Shepherd St A3
Shipton St A2
Shoreham St C4
Showroom, The C5
Shrewsbury Rd C5
Sidney St C4
Site Gallery C5
Slinn St A1
Smithfield A4
Snig Hill A5
Snow La A4
Solly St B3
Southbourne Rd C1
South La C4
South Street Park B5
Spital Hill A5
Spital St A5
Spring Hill B1
Spring Hill Rd B1
Springvale Rd A1
Stafford Rd C6
Stafford St B6
Stanley St A5
Suffolk Rd C5
Summer St B2
Sunny Bank C3
Surrey St B4
Sussex St A6
Sutton St B3
Sydney Rd A2
Sylvester St C4
Talbot St B6
Taptonville Rd B1
Tax Office C4
Tenter St B4
The Moor C4
Town Hall B4
Townend St A1
Townhead St B4
Trafalgar St B4
Tree Root Walk B2
Trinity St A4
Trippet La B4
Turner Mus of Glass B3
Union St B4
Univ Drama Studio B2
Univ of Sheffield B3
Upper Allen St A3
Upper Hanover St B3
Upperthorpe Rd A2/A3
Verdon St A5
Victoria Quays ✦ B5
Victoria Rd C2
Victoria St B3
Waingate B5
Watery St A3
Watson Rd C1
Wellesley Rd B2
Wellington St C3
West Bar A4
West Bar Green A4
West One Plaza B3
West St B3
West St B4
Westbourne Rd C1
Western Bank B2
Western Rd A1
Weston Park B2
Weston Park Hospl B2
Weston Park Mus B2
Weston St A2
Wharncliffe Rd C3
Whitham Rd B1
Wicker A5
Wilkinson St B2
William St C3
Winter Garden ✦ B4
Winter St B2
York St B4
Yorkshire Artspace C5
Young St C4

Shrewsbury 347

Abbey Church B3
Abbey Foregate B3
Abbey Lawn Bsns Park B3
Abbots House B2
Agricultural Show Gd A1
Albert St A2
Alma St B1
Ashley St A3
Ashton Rd C1
Avondale Dr A3
Bage Way C3
Barker St B1
Beacall's La A2
Beeches La C2
Beehive La C1
Belle Vue Gdns C2
Belle Vue Rd C2
Belmont Bank C1
Berwick Ave A1
Berwick Rd A1
Betton St C2
Bishop St C3
Bradford St B3
Bridge St B1
Bus Station B2
Butcher Row B2
Burton St A3
Butler Rd C1
Bynner St C2
Canon St B3
Canonbury C1
Castle Bsns Park, The A2
Castle Foregate A2
Castle Gates B2
Castle Museum B2
Castle St B2
Cathedral (RC) ✝ C1
Chester St A2
Cineworld C3
Claremont Bank B1
Claremont Hill B1
Cleveland St B3
Coleham Head B2
Coleham Pumping Station C2
College Hill B1
Corporation La A1
Coton Cres A1
Coton Hill A2
Coton Mount A1
Crescent La C1
Crewe St A2
Cross Hill B1
Darwin Centre B2
Dingle, The B1
Dogpole B2
Draper's Hall B2
English Bridge B2
Fish St B2
Frankwell B1
Gateway Ctr, The A2
Gravel Hill La A1
Greyfriars Rd C2
Guildhall B1
Hampton Rd A3
Haycock Way C3
HM Prison B2
High St B1
Hills La B1
Holywell St B3
Hunter St A1
Information Ctr B1
Ireland's Mansion & Bear Steps B1
John St A3
Kennedy Rd C1
King St B3
Kingsland Bridge C1
Kingsland Bridge (toll) C1
Kingsland Rd C1
Library B2
Lime St C2
Longden Coleham C2
Longden Rd C1
Longner St B1
Luciefelde Rd C1
Mardol B1
Market B1
Marine Terr C2
Monkmoor Rd B3
Moreton Cr C2
Mount St A1
New Park Cl A3
New Park Rd A2
New Park St A3
North St A2
Oakley St C1
Old Coleham C2
Old Market Hall B1
Old Potts Way C3
Parade Centre B2
Police Station B1
Post Office A2/B1/B2/B3
Pride Hill B1
Pride Hill Centre B1
Priory Rd B1
Pritchard Way C3
Queen St A3
Raby Cr C2
Rad Brook C1
Rea Brook C3
Riverside B1
Roundhill La A1
St Alkmund's B2
St Chad's B1
St Chad's Terr B1
St John's Hill B1
St Julians Friars C2
St Mary's B2
St Mary's St B2
Salters La C2
Scott St C3
Severn Bank A3
Severn St A2
Shrewsbury B2
Shrewsbury High School for Girls C1
Shrewsbury Mus & Art Gall B1
Shrewsbury School ✦ C1
Shropshire Wildlife Trust ✦ B3
Smithfield Rd B1
South Hermitage C1
Swan Hill C1
Sydney Ave A3
Tankerville St B3
The Dana B2
The Quarry B1
The Square B1
Tilbrook Dr A3
Town Walls C1
Trinity St C2
Underdale Rd B3
Victoria Ave B1
Victoria Quay B1
Victoria St B2
Welsh Bridge B1
Whitehall St B3
Wood St A2
Wyle Cop B2

Southampton 347

Above Bar St A2
Albert Rd North B3
Albert Rd South C3
Anderson's Rd B3
Archaeology Mus (God's Ho Tower) C2
Argyle Rd A2
Arundel Tower B1
Bargate, The ✦ B2
Bargate Shopping Ctr B2
BBC Regional Centre A1
Bedford Pl A1
Belvidere Rd A3
Bernard St C2
Blechynden Terr A1
Brazil Rd C3
Brinton's Rd A2
Britannia Rd A3
Briton St C2
Brunswick Pl A2
Bugle St C1
Canute Rd C3
Castle Way C2
Catchcold Tower ✦ B1
Central Bridge C3
Central Rd C2
Channel Way C3
Chapel Rd B3
Cineworld C3
City Art Gallery A1
City College B3
Civic Centre A1
Civic Centre Rd A1
Coach Station B1
Commercial Rd A1
Cumberland Pl A1
Cunard Rd C2
Derby Rd A3
Devonshire Rd A1
Dock Gate 4 C2
Dock Gate 8 B1
East Park A2
East Park Terr A2
East St B2
East St Shopping Ctr B2
Endle St B3
European Way C2
Fire Station A2
Floating Bridge Rd C3
Golden Gr A3
Graham Rd A2
Guildhall A1
Hanover Bldgs B2
Harbour Lights C3
Harbour Pde B1
Hartington Rd A3
Havelock Rd A1
Henstead Rd A1
Herbert Walker Ave B1
High St B2
Hoglands Park B2
Holy Rood (Rems), Merchant Navy Memorial B2
Houndwell Park B2
Houndwell Pl B2
Hythe Ferry C2
Information Ctr A1
Isle of Wight Ferry Terminal C1
James St B3
Java Rd C2
Kingsway A2
Leisure World B1
Library A1
Lime St B2
London Rd A2
Marine Pde B3
Marsh La B2
Mayflower Meml ✦ C1
Mayflower Park C1
Mayflower Theatre, The A1
Medieval Merchant's House C1
Melbourne St B3
Millais A2
Morris Rd A1
National Oceanography Centre C3
Neptune Way C3
New Rd A2
Nichols Rd A3
North Front A2
Northam Rd A3
Ocean Dock C2
Ocean Village Marina C3
Ocean Way C3
Odeon B1
Ogle Rd B1
Old Northam Rd A2
Orchard La B2
Oxford Ave A2
Oxford St C2
Palmerston Park A2
Palmerston Rd A2
Parsonage Rd A3
Peel St A3
Platform Rd C2
Police Station A1
Portland Terr B1
Post Office A2/A3/B2
Pound Tree Rd B2
Quays Swimming & Diving Complex, The B1
Queen's Park C2
Queen's Peace Fountain ✦ A2
Queen's Terr C2
Queen's Way B2
Radcliffe Rd A3
Rochester St A3
Royal Pier C1
Royal South Hants Hospital A2
Sea City Mus A1
St Andrew's Rd A2
St Mary St A2
St Mary's B3
St Mary's Leisure Ctr A2
St Mary's Pl B2
St Mary's Rd A2
St Mary's Stadium (Southampton FC) A3
St Michael's C1
Solent Sky C3
South Front B2
Southampton Central Station A1
Southampton Solent University A2
SS Shieldhall C2
Terminus Terr C2
The Mall, Marlands A1
The Polygon A1
Threefield La B2
Titanic Engineers' Memorial ✦ A2
Town Quay C1
Town Walls B2
Tudor House C1
Vincent's Walk B2
West Gate Hall C1
West Marlands Rd A1
West Park A1
West Park Rd A1
West Quay Rd B1
West Quay Retail Park B1
West Quay Sh Ctr B1
West Rd C2
Western Esplanade B1
Winton St A2

Southend-on-Sea 348

Adventure Island ✦ C3
Albany Ave A1
Albert Rd C3
Alexandra Rd C2
Alexandra St C2
Alexandra Yacht Club ✦ C2
Ashburnham Rd B2
Ave Rd B1
Avenue Terr B1
Balmoral Rd B1
Baltic Ave B3
Baxter Ave A2/B2
Beecroft Art Gallery C1
Bircham Rd A2
Boscombe Rd B3
Boston Ave A1/B2
Bournemouth Park Rd A3
Browning Ave A3
Bus Station C3
Byron Ave A3
Cambridge Rd C1/C2
Canewdon Rd B1
Carnarvon Rd A2
Central Ave A3
Chelmsford Ave A1
Chichester Rd B2
Church Rd C3
Civic Centre A2
Clarence Rd C2
Clarence St C2
Cliff Ave B1
Cliffs Pavilion C1
Clifftown Parade C2
Clifftown Rd C2
Colchester Rd A1
College Way B2
Coleman St B3
County Court B3
Cromer Rd B3
Crowborough Rd A2
Dryden Ave A3
East St A2
Elmer App B2
Elmer Ave B2
Gainsborough Dr A1
Gayton Rd A2
Glenhurst Rd A2
Gordon Pl B2
Gordon Rd B2
Grainger Rd A2
Greyhound Way A3
Guildford Rd B3
Hamlet Ct Rd B1
Hamlet Rd C1
Harcourt Ave A1
Hartington Rd C3
Hastings Rd B3
Herbert Gr C3
Heygate Ave C3
High St B2/C2
Information Ctr C3
Kenway A2
Kilworth Ave B3
Lancaster Gdns B3
Library B2
London Rd B1
Lucy Rd C3
MacDonald Ave A1
Magistrates Court A2
Maldon Rd A2
Maine Ave C1
Marine Rd C1
Marine Parade C3
Milton Rd B1
Milton St B2
Napier Ave B2
North Ave A3
North Rd A1/B1
Odeon B2
Osborne Rd B1
Park Cres B1
Park Rd B1
Park St B1
Park Terr B1
Pier Hill C3
Pleasant Rd C3
Police Station A2
Post Office B2/B3
Princes St B2
Queens Rd B2
Queensway B2/B3/C3
Rayleigh Ave A1
Redstock Rd A2
Rochford Ave A1
Royal Mews C2
Royal Terr C2
Royals Sh Ctr, The C3
Ruskin Ave A3
St Ann's Rd B3
St Helen's Rd B1
St John's Rd B1
St Leonard's Rd C3
St Lukes Rd A3
St Vincent's Rd C1
Salisbury Ave A1/B1
Scratton Rd C2
Shakespeare Dr A1
Short St A2
South Ave A3
Southchurch Rd B3
South Essex College B2
Southend Central B2
Southend Pier Railway C3
Southend Radio C2
Southend United FC A1
Southend Victoria B2
Stadium Rd A2
Stanfield Rd A2
Stanley Rd C3
Sutton Rd A3/B3
Swanage Rd B3
Sweyne Ave A1
Sycamore Gr A3
Tennyson Ave A3
The Grove A3
Tickfield Ave A2
Tudor Rd A1
Tunbridge Rd A2
Tylers Ave B3
Tyrrel Dr B3
Univ of Essex B2/C2
Vale Ave A2
Victoria Ave A2
Victoria Sh Ctr, The B2
Warrior Sq B3
Wesley Rd C3
West Rd A1
West St A1
Westcliff Ave C1
Westcliff Parade C1
Western Esplanade C1
Weston Rd C2
Whitegate Rd B3
Wilson Rd C1
Wimborne Rd B3
York Rd C3

Stirling 348

Abbey Rd A3
Abbotsford Pl A3
Abercromby Pl C1
Albert Halls B1
Albert Pl B1
Alexandra Pl A3
Allan Park C2
Ambulance Station A2
AMF Ten Pin Bowling ✦ B2
Argyll Ave A3
Argyll's Lodging ✦ B1
Back O' Hill Ind Est A1
Back O' Hill Rd A1
Baker St C2
Ballengeich Pass A1
Balmoral Pl B1
Barn Rd B1
Barnton St B2
Bow St B1
Bruce St A2
Burghmuir Ind Est C2
Burghmuir Rd A2/B2/C2
Bus Station B2
Cambuskenneth Bridge A3
Carlton C2
Castle Ct B1
Causewayhead Rd A2
Cemetery A1
Church of the Holy Rude B1
Clarendon Pl C1
Club House B1
Colquhoun St C3
Corn Exchange B2
Council Offices C2
Court B2
Cowane A2
Cowane St A2
Cowane's Hospital B1
Crawford Sh Arc B2
Crofthead Rd A1
Dean Cres A3
Douglas St A2
Drip Rd A1
Drummond La C1
Drummond Pl C1
Drummond Pl La C1
Dumbarton Rd C2
Eastern Access Rd B2
Edward Ave A3
Edward Rd A2
Forrest Rd A2
Fort A1
Forth Cres B2
Forth St A2
Gladstone Pl C1
Glebe Ave C1
Glebe Cres C1
Golf Course C1
Goosecroft Rd B2
Gowanhill A1
Greenwood Ave B1
Harvey Wynd A1
Information Ctr B1
Irvine Pl B2
James St A2
John St B1
Kerse Rd C3
King's Knot ✦ B1
King's Park C1
King's Park Rd C1
Laurencecroft Rd A2
Leisure Pool B2
Library B2
Linden Ave C2
Lovers Wk A2
Lower Back Walk B1
Lower Bridge St A2
Lower Castlehill A1
Mar Pl B1
Meadow Pl A3
Meadowforth Rd C3
Middlemuir Rd C3
Millar Pl A3
Morris Terr B2
Mote Hill A1
Murray Pl B2
Nelson Pl C2
Old Town Cemetery B1
Old Town Jail ✦ B1
Orchard House Hospital (No A&E) A2
Park Terr C1
Phoenix Industrial Est C3
Players Rd C3
Port St C2
Princes St B2
Queen St B2
Queen's Rd B1
Queenshaugh Dr A3
Rainbow Slides B2
Ramsay Pl A2
Riverside Dr A3
Ronald Pl A1
Rosebery Pl A2
Royal Gardens B1
Royal Gdns B1
St Mary's Wynd B1
St Ninian's Rd C2
Scott St A2
Seaforth Pl B2
Shore Rd B2
Smith Art Gallery & Museum B1
Snowdon Pl C1
Snowdon Pl La C1
Spittal St B2
Springkerse Ind Est C3
Springkerse Rd C3
Stirling Bsns Centre C2
Stirling Castle A1
Stirling County Rugby Football Club A3
Stirling Enterprise Pk B3
Stirling Old Bridge A2
Stirling Station B2
Superstore A2
Sutherland Ave A3
TA Centre C3
Tannery La A2
The Bastion ✦ C2
The Changing Room B1
Thistle Industrial Est C3
Thistles Sh Ctr, The B2
Tollbooth, The ✦ B1
Town Wall B1
Union St A2
Upper Back Walk B1
Upper Bridge St A1
Upper Castlehill B1
Upper Craigs C2
Victoria Pl C1
Victoria Rd B1
Victoria Sq B1/C1
Vue B2
Wallace St A2
Waverley Cres A3
Wellgreen Rd C2
Windsor Pl C1
YHA ▲ B1

Stoke 348

Ashford St A3
Avenue Rd A3
Aynsley Rd A2
Barnfield C1
Bath St C2
Beresford St A3
Bilton St C2
Boon Ave C2
Booth St C2
Boothen Rd C2/C3
Boughey St C2
Boughey Rd B3
Brighton St B1
Campbell Rd C2
Carlton Rd B3
Cauldon Rd A3
Cemetery A2
Cemetery Rd A2
Chamberlain Ave C1
Church (RC) B2
Church St C2
City Rd C3
Civic Centre & King's Hall B3
Cliff Vale Pk A1
College Rd A3
Convent Cl B2
Copeland St B2
Cornwallis St C3
Corporation St C2
Crowther St A3
Dominic St B1
Elenora St B2
Elgin St B2
Epworth St A3
Etruscan St A1
Film Theatre B3
Fleming Rd C2
Fletcher Rd C2
Floyd St B2
Foden St C2
Frank St C2
Franklin Rd C1
Frederick Ave B1
Garden St C1
Garner St A1
Gerrard St B2
Glebe St B3
Greatbach Ave B1
Hanley Park A3
Harris St B1
Hartshill Rd B1
Hayward St A2
Hide St B2
Higson Ave B2
Hill St B2
Honeywall B2
Hunters Dr C1
Hunters Way C1
Keary St C2
Kingsway B2
Leek Rd B3
Library C2
Lime St C2
Liverpool Rd B2
London Rd C2
Lonsdale St C2
Lovatt St B2
Lytton St B3
Market C2
Newcastle La C1
Newlands St A2
Norfolk St A2
North St A1/B2
North Staffordshire Royal Infirmary (A&E) B1
Northcote Ave B2
Oldmill St C3
Oriel St B1
Oxford St B1
Penkhull New Rd C1
Penkhull St C1
Police Station C2
Portmeirion Pottery ✦ C2
Post Office A3/B1/B3/C1/C2
Prince's Rd B1
Pump St B2
Quarry Ave B1
Quarry Rd B1
Queen Anne St A3
Queen's Rd C1
Queensway A1/B2/C3
Richmond St B1
Rothwell St C1
St Peter's B3
St Thomas Pl C1
Scrivenor Rd A1
Seaford St A3
Selwyn St C3
Shelton New Rd A1
Shelton Old Rd B2
Sheppard St C2
Spark St C2
Spencer Rd B3
Spode St C2
Squires View B3
Staffordshire Univ B3
Stanley Matthews Sports Centre B3
Station Rd B3
Stoke Business Park C3
Stoke Recreation Ctr C2
Stoke Rd A2
Stoke-on-Trent Coll A3
Stoke-on-Trent Sta B3
Sturgess St C2
The Villas C1
Thistley Hough C1
Thornton Rd B3
Tolkien Way B1
Trent Valley Rd C1
Vale St B2
Watford St A3
Wellesley St A3
West Ave B1
Westland St B1
Yeaman St C2
Yoxall Ave B1

Stratford-upon-Avon 348

Albany Rd B1
Alcester Rd B1
Ambulance Station B1
Arden St B2
Avenue Farm A1
Ave Farm Ind Est A1
Avenue Rd A1
Avon Industrial Estate A2
Baker Ave A1
Bandstand C3
Benson Rd A3
Birmingham Rd A2
Boat Club B3
Borden Pl C1
Brass Rubbing Ctr ✦ C2
Bridge St B2
Bridgetown Rd C3
Bridgeway B3
Broad St C2
Broad Walk C2
Brookvale Rd C1
Bull St C2
Bus Station B2
Butterfly Farm ✦ C3
Cemetery C1
Chapel La B2
Cherry Orchard C1
Chestnut Walk B2
Children's Playground C3
Church St C2
Civic Hall B2
Clarence Rd B1
Clopton Bridge ✦ B3
Clopton Rd A2
Coach Terminal & Park B3
College B1
College La C2
College St C2
Com Sports Centre B1
Council Offices (District) B2
Courtyard C2
Cox's Yard ✦ B3
Cricket Ground C3
Ely Gdns B2
Ely St B2
Evesham Rd C1
Fire Station B1
Foot Ferry C3

Fordham Ave A2
Gallery, The B3
Garrick Way C1
Gower Memorial ✦ B3
Great William St B2
Greenhill St B2
Grove Rd B2
Guild St B2
Guildhall & School B2
Hall's Croft C2
Hartford Rd C1
Harvard House B2
Henley St B2
High St B2
Holton St C2
Holy Trinity C2
Information Ctr B3
Jolyffe Park Rd A2
Kipling Rd C3
Leisure & Visitor Ctr B3
Library B2
Lodge Rd B1
Maidenhead Rd A3
Mansell St B2
Masons Court B2
Masons Rd A1
Maybird Shopping Pk A2
Maybrook Rd A1
Mayfield Ave A2
Meer St B2
Mill La C2
Moat House Hotel B3
Narrow La C2
Nash's Ho & New Pl B2
New St C2
Old Town C2
Orchard Way C1
Paddock La C1
Park Rd A1
Payton St B2
Percy St A2
Police Station B2
Post Office B2/B3
Recreation Ground C2
Regal Road A2
Rother St B2
Rowley Cr A3
Royal Shakespeare Theatres B3
Ryland St C2
Saffron Meadow C2
St Andrew's Cr B1
St Gregory's A3
St Gregory's Rd A3
St Mary's Rd A2
Sanctus Dr C2
Sanctus St C1
Sandfield Rd C2
Scholars La B2
Seven Meadows Rd C2
Shakespeare Ctr ✦ B2
Shakespeare Institute C2
Shakespeare St B2
Shakespeare's Birthplace ✦ B2
Sheep St B2
Shelley Rd C3
Shipston Rd C3
Shottery Rd C1
Slingates Rd A2
Southern La C2
Station Rd B1
Stratford Healthcare B2
Stratford Hospital B2
Stratford Sports Club B1
Stratford-upon-Avon Station B1
Swan's Nest La B3
Swan Theatre B3
Talbot Rd A2
The Greenway C2
The Willows B1
The Willows North B1
Tiddington Rd B3
Timothy's Bridge Industrial Estate A1
Timothy's Bridge Rd A1
Town Hall & Council Offices B2
Town Sq B2
Trinity St C2
Tyler St B2
War Memorial Gdns B3
Warwick Rd B3
Waterside B3
Welcombe Rd A3
West St C2
Western Rd A2
Wharf Rd A2
Wood St B2

Sunderland 348

Albion Pl C2
Alliance Pl B1
Argyle St C2
Ashwood St C1
Athenaeum St B2
Azalea Terr C2
Beach St A1
Bede Theatre C3
Bedford St B2
Beechwood Terr C1
Belvedere Rd C2
Blandford St B2
Borough Rd B3
Bridge Cr B2
Bridge St B2
Brooke St A2
Brougham St B2
Burdon Rd C2
Burn Park C1
Burn Park Rd C1
Burn Park Tech Park C1
Carol St B1
Charles St A3
Chester Rd C1
Chester Terr B1
Church St A3
Civic Centre C2
Cork St B3
Coronation St B3
Cowan Terr C2
Crowtree Rd B2
Dame Dorothy St A2
Deptford Rd B1
Deptford Terr A1
Derby St C2
Derwent St C2
Dock St A3
Dundas St A2
Durham Rd C1
Easington St A2
Egerton St C3
Empire B3
Empire Theatre B2
Farringdon Row B1
Fawcett St B2
Fox St C1
Foyle St B3
Frederick St B3
Gill Rd B2
Hanover Pl A1
Havelock Terr C1
Hay St A2
Headworth Sq B3
Hendon Rd B3
High St East B3
High St West B2/B3
Holmeside B2
Hylton Rd B1
Information Ctr B2
John St B3
Kier Hardie Way A2
Lambton St B3
Laura St C3
Lawrence St B3
Leisure Centre B2
Library & Arts Centre B3
Lily St B1
Lime St B1
Livingstone Rd B2
Low Row B2
Matamba Terr B1
Millburn St B1
Millennium Way A2
Minster B2
Monkwearmouth Station Museum A2
Mowbray Park C3
Mowbray Rd C3
Murton St C3
National Glass Ctr ✦ A3
New Durham Rd C1
Newcastle Rd A2
Nile St B3
Norfolk St B3
North Bridge St A2
Northern Gallery for Contemporary Art B3
Otto Terr C1
Park La C2
Park Lane Ⓜ C2
Park Rd C2
Paul's Rd B3
Peel St C3
Police Station B2
Post Office B2
Priestly Cr A1
Queen St B2
Railway Row B1
Retail Park B1
Richmond St A2
Roker Ave A2
Royalty Theatre C1
Ryhope Rd C2
St Mary's Way B2
St Michael's Way B2
St Peter's A3
St Peter's Ⓜ A2
St Peter's Way A3
St Vincent St C3
Salem Rd C3
Salem St C3
Salisbury St C3
Sans St B3
Silkworth Row B1
Southwick Rd A2
Stadium of Light (Sunderland AFC) A2
Stadium Way A2
Stobart St A2
Stockton Rd C2
Suffolk St C3
Sunderland Aquatic Centre A2
Sunderland Ⓜ B2
Sunderland Mus C3
Sunderland Station B2
Sunderland St B3
Tatham St C3
Tavistock Pl B3
The Bridges B2
The Place B3
The Royalty C1
Thelma St C1
Thomas St North A2
Thornholme Rd C1
Toward Rd C3
Transport Interchange C2
Trimdon St Way B1
Tunstall Rd C2
University Ⓜ C1
University Library C1
University of Sunderland (City Campus) B1
University of Sunderland (Sir Tom Cowie at St Peter's Campus) A3
Vaux Brewery Way A2
Villiers St B3
Villiers St South B3
Vine Pl C2
Violet St B1
Walton La B3
Waterworks Rd B1
Wearmouth Bridge B2
Wellington La A1
West Sunniside B3
West Wear St B3
Westbourne Rd B1
Western Hill C1
Wharncliffe B1
Whickham St A3
White House Rd C3
Wilson St North A2
Winter Gdns C3
Wreath Quay A1

Swansea 348
Abertawe

Adelaide St C3
Albert Row C3
Alexandra Rd B3
Argyle St C1
Baptist Well Pl A2
Beach St C1
Belle Vue Way B3
Berw Rd A1
Berwick Terr A2
Bond St C1
Brangwyn Concert Hall C1
Bridge St A3
Brookands Terr B1
Brunswick St C1
Bryn-Syfi Terr A2
Bryn-y-Mor Rd C1
Bullins La B1
Burrows Rd C1
Bus/Rail link A3
Bus Station C2
Cadfan Rd A1
Cadrawd Rd A1
Caer St B3
Carig Cr A1
Carlton Terr B2
Carmarthen Rd A3
Castle Square B3
Castle St B3
Catherine St C1
Cinema C3
Civic Centre & Library C2
Clarence St C2
Colbourne Terr A2
Constitution Hill B1
Court B3
Creidiol Rd A2
Cromwell St B2
Duke St B1
Dunvant Pl C2
Dyfatty Park A3
Dyfatty St A3
Dyfed Ave A1
Dylan Thomas Ctr ✦ B3
Dylan Thomas Theatre C3
Eaton Cr C1
Eigen Cr A1
Elfed Rd A1
Emlyn Rd A1
Evans Terr A3
Fairfield Terr B1
Ffynone Dr B1
Ffynone Rd B1
Fire Station B3
Firm St A2
Fleet St C1
Francis St C1
Fullers Row B2
George St B2
Glamorgan St C2
Glyndŵr Pl A1
Graig Terr A3
Grand Theatre C2
Granogwen Rd A2
Guildhall C1
Guildhall Rd South C1
Gwent Rd A1
Gwynedd Ave A1
Hafod St A3
Hanover St B1
Harcourt St B2
Harries St A2
Heathfield B2
Henrietta St B1
Hewson St B2
High St A3/B3
High View A2
Hill St A2
Historic Ships Berth C3
HM Prison C2
Information Ctr C2
Islwyn Rd A1
King Edward's Rd C1
Law Courts C1
Long Ridge A2
Madoc St C2
Mansel St B2
Maritime Quarter C3
Market B3
Mayhill Gdns B1
Mayhill Rd A1
Mega Bowl ✦ B3
Milton Terr A2
Mission Gallery C3
Montpellier Terr B1
Morfa Rd A3
Mount Pleasant B2
National Waterfront Museum C3
Nelson St C2
New Cut Rd A3
New St A3
Nicander Pde A2
Nicander Pl A2
Nicholl St B2
Norfolk St B2
North Hill Rd A2
Northampton La B2
Orchard St B3
Oxford St B2
Oystermouth Rd C1
Page St B2
Pant-y-Celyn Rd B1
Parc Tawe Link B3
Parc Tawe North B3
Parc Tawe Sh & L Ctr B3
Patti Pavilion C1
Paxton St C2
Penmaen Terr B1
Pen-y-Graig Rd A1
Phillips Pde C1
Picton Terr B2
Plantasia B3
Police Station B2
Post Office A1/A2/B2/C1
Powys Ave A1
Primrose St B2
Princess Way B3
Promenade B2
Pryder Gdns A1
Quadrant Centre C2
Quay Park B3
Rhianfa La B1
Rhondda St B2
Richardson St C2
Rodney St C1
Rose Hill B1
Rosehill Terr B1
Russell St B1
St Helen's Ave C1
St Helen's Cr C1
St Helen's Rd C1
St James Gdns B1
St James's Cr B1
St Mary's B3
Sea View Terr A3
Singleton St C2
South Dock C3
Stanley Pl B2
Strand B3
Swansea Castle B3
Swansea Coll Arts Ctr C1
Swansea Metropolitan University B2
Swansea Museum C3
Swansea Station A3
Taliesyn Rd B1
Tan y Marian Rd A1
Tegid Rd A2
Teilo Cr A1
Terrace Rd B1/B2
The Kingsway B2
The LC C3
Tontine St A3
Tower of Eclipse ✦ C3
Townhill Rd A1
Tramshed The C3
Trawler Rd C3
Union St B2
Upper Strand A3
Vernon St A3
Victoria Quay C3
Victoria Rd B3
Vincent St C1
Walter Rd B1
Watkin St A2
Waun-Wen Rd A2
Wellington St C2
Westbury St C1
Western St C1
Westway C2
William St C2
Wind St B3
Woodlands Terr B1
YMCA B2
York St C3

Swindon 349

Albert St C3
Albion St C1
Alfred St A2
Alvescot Rd C3
Art Gallery & Museum C3
Ashford Rd C1
Aylesbury St A2
Bath Rd C2
Bathampton St B1
Bathurst Rd B3
Beatrice St A2
Beckhampton St B3
Bowood Rd C1
Bristol St B1
Broad St A3
Brunel Arcade B2
Brunel Plaza B2
Brunswick St C2
Bus Station B2
Cambria Bridge Rd B1
Cambria Place B1
Canal Walk B2
Carfax St B2
Carr St B1
Cemetery C1/C3
Chandler Cl C3
Chapel C1
Chester St B1
Christ Church C3
Church Place B1
Cirencester Way A3
Clarence St B2
Clifton St C1
Cockleberry A2
Colbourne A3
Colbourne St A3
College St B2
Commercial Rd B2
Corporation St A2
Council Offices B3
County Rd A3
Courts B2
Cricket Ground A3
Cricklade Street C3
Crombey St B1/C2
Cross St C2
Curtis St B1
Deacon St C1
Designer Outlet (Great Western) B1
Dixon St C2
Dover St C2
Dowling St C2
Drove Rd C3
Dryden St C1
Durham St C3
East St B1
Eastcott Hill C2
Eastcott Rd C2
Edgeware Rd B2
Edmund St C2
Elmina Rd A3
Emlyn Square B1
Euclid St B3
Exeter St B1
Fairview C1
Faringdon Rd B1
Farnsby St B1
Fire Station B3
Fleet St B2
Fleming Way B2/B3
Florence St A2
Gladstone St A3
Gooch St A2
Graham St A3
Great Western Way A1/A2
Groundwell Rd B3
Hawksworth Way A1
Haydon St A2
Henry St B2
Hillside Ave C1
Holbrook Way B2
Hunt St C3
Hydro B1
Hythe Rd C2
Information Ctr B2
Joseph St C1
Kent Rd C2
King William St C2
Kingshill Rd C1
Lansdown Rd C2
Leicester St B3
Library B2
Lincoln St B3
Little London C3
London St B1
Magic B3
Maidstone Rd C2
Manchester Rd A3
Maxwell St B1
Milford St B2
Milton Rd B1
Morse St C2
National Monuments Record Centre B1
Newcastle St B3
Newcombe Drive A1
Newcombe Trading Estate A1
Newhall St C2
North St C2
North Star Ave A1
North Star A1
Northampton St B3
Oasis Leisure Centre A1
Ocotal Way A3
Okus Rd C1
Old Town C3
Oxford St B1
Park Lane B1
Park Lane B1
Pembroke St C2
Plymouth St B3
Polaris House A2
Polaris Way A2
Police Station B2
Ponting St A2
Post Office B1/B2/C1/C3
Poulton St A3
Princes St B2
Prospect Hill C2
Prospect Place C2
Queen St B2
Queen's Park C3
Radnor St C1
Read St C1
Reading St B1
Regent St B2
Retail Park A2/A3/B3
Rosebery St A3
St Mark's B1
Salisbury St A3
Savernake St C2
Shelley St C1
Sheppard St B1
South St C2
Southampton St B3
Spring Gardens B3
Stafford Street C2
Stanier St C2
Station Road A2
STEAM B1
Swindon College A2
Swindon Rd C2
Swindon Station A2
Swindon Town Football Club A3
TA Centre B1
Tennyson St B1
The Lawn C3
The Nurseries C1
The Parade B2
The Park B1
Theobald St B1
Town Hall B2
Transfer Bridges A3
Union St C2
Upham Rd C3
Victoria Rd C3
Walcot Rd B3
War Memorial ✦ B2
Wells St B3
Western St C2
Westmorland Rd B3
Whalebridge B2
Whitehead St C1
Whitehouse Rd A2
William St C1
Wood St C3
Wyvern Theatre & Arts Centre B2
York Rd B3

Taunton 349

Addison Gr A1
Albemarle Rd A1
Alfred St B3
Alma St C2
Bath Pl C1
Belvedere Rd A1
Billet St B2
Billetfield C2
Birch Gr A1
Brewhouse Theatre B2
Bridge St B1
Bridgwater & Taunton Canal A2
Broadlands Rd C1
Burton Pl C1
Bus Station B1
Canal Rd A2
Cann St C1
Canon St B2
Castle B1
Castle St B1
Cheddon Rd A2
Chip Lane A1
Clarence St B1
Cleveland St B1
Clifton Terr A2
Coleridge Cres C3
Compass Hill C1
Compton Cl A2
Corporation St B1
Council Offices A1
County Walk Sh Ctr C2
Courtyard B2
Cranmer Rd B2
Critchard Way B3
Cyril St A1
Deller's Wharf B1
Duke St B2
East Reach B3
East St B3
Eastbourne Rd B2
Eastleigh Rd C3
Eaton Cres A2
Elm Gr A1
Elms Cl A1
Fons George C1
Fore St B2
Fowler St A1
French Weir Rec Grd B1
Geoffrey Farrant Wk A2
Gray's Almshouses B2
Grays Rd B3
Greenway Ave A1
Guildford Pl C1
Hammet St B2
Haydon Rd B3
Heavitree Way A2
Herbert St A1
High St C2
Holway Ave C3
Hugo St B3
Huish's Almshouses B2
Hurdle Way C2
Information Ctr C2
Jubilee St A1
King's College C3
Kings Cl C3
Laburnum St B2
Lambrook Rd B3
Lansdowne Rd A3
Leslie Ave A1
Leycroft Rd B3
Library C2
Linden Gr A1
Magdalene St B2
Magistrates Court B1
Malvern Terr A2
Market House B2
Mary St C2
Middle St B2
Midford Rd B3
Mitre Court B3
Mount Nebo C1
Mount St C2
Mountway C2
Mus of Somerset B1
North St B2
Northfield Ave B1
Northfield Rd B1
Northleigh Rd C3
Obridge Allotments A3
Obridge Lane A3
Obridge Rd A3
Obridge Viaduct A3
Old Mkt Shopping Ctr C2
Osborne Way C1
Park St C1
Paul St C2
Plais St A2
Playing Field C3
Police Station C1
Portland St B1
Post Office B1/B2/C1
Priorswood Ind Est A3
Priorswood Rd A2
Priory Ave B2
Priory Bridge Rd B2
Priory Fields Retail Pk A3
Priory Park A2
Priory Way A3
Queen St B3
Railway St A1
Records Office A2
Recreation Grd A1
Riverside Place B2
St Augustine St B2
St George's C2
St Georges Sq C2
St James B2
St James St B2
St John's C1
St John's Rd B1
St Josephs Field C2
St Mary Magdalene B2
Samuels Ct A1
Shire Hall & Law Courts C1
Somerset County Cricket Ground B2
Somerset County Hall C1
Somerset Cricket B2
South Rd C3
South St C3
Staplegrove Rd B1
Station Rd A1
Stephen St B2
Swimming Pool A1
Tancred St B2
Tauntfield Cl C3
Taunton Deane Cricket Club C2
Taunton Station A2
The Avenue A1
The Crescent C1
The Mount C2
Thomas St A1
Toneway A3
Tower St B1
Trevor Smith Pl C3
Trinity Bsns Centre C3
Trinity Rd C3
Trinity St B3
Trull Rd C1
Tudor House B2
Upper High St C1
Venture Way A3
Victoria Gate B3
Victoria Park B3
Victoria St B3
Viney St B3
Vivary Park C2
Vivary Rd C1
War Memorial ✦ C1
Wellesley St A2
Wheatley Cres A3
Whitehall A1
Wilfred Rd B3
William St A1
Wilton Church C1
Wilton Cl C1
Wilton Gr C1
Wilton St C1
Winchester St B2
Winters Field B2
Wood St B1
Yarde Pl B1

Telford 349

Alma Ave C1
Amphitheatre C2
Bowling Alley B2
Brandsfarm Way C3
Brunel Rd B1
Bus Station B2
Buxton Rd C1
Central Park A2
Civic Offices B2
Coach Central B2
Coachwell Cl B1
Colliers Way A1
Courts B2
Dale Acre Way B3
Darliston C3
Deepdale B3
Deercote B2
Dinthill C3
Doddington C3
Dodmoor Grange C3
Downemead B3
Duffryn B3
Dunsheath B3
Euston Way A3
Eyton Mound C1
Eyton Rd C1
Forgegate A2
Grange Central B2
Hall Park Way B1
Hinkshay Rd C2
Hollinsworth Rd A2
Holyhead Rd A3
Housing Trust A1
Ice Rink B2
Information Ctr B2
Ironmasters Way A2
Job Centre B1
Land Registry B1
Lawn Central B2
Lawnswood C1
Library B2
Malinsgate B1
Matlock Ave C1
Moor Rd C1
Mount Rd C1
NFU Offices B1
Odeon B2
Park Lane A1
Police Station B1
Priorslee Ave A3
Queen Elizabeth Ave C3
Queen Elizabeth Way B1
Queensway A2/B3
Rampart Way A2
Randlay Ave C3
Randlay Wood C3
Rhodes Ave C1
Royal Way B1
St Leonards Rd B1
St Quentin Gate B2
Shifnal Rd A3
Sixth Ave A1
Southwater Way B1
Spout Lane C1
Spout Mound B1
Spout Way C1
Stafford Court B3
Stafford Park B3
Stirchley Ave C3
Stone Row C1
Telford Bridge Ret Pk A1
Telford Central Sta A3
Telford Centre, The B2
Telford Forge Sh Pk A1
Telford Hornets RFC C2
Telford Int Ctr C2
Telford Way A3
Third Ave A2
Town Park C2
Town Park Visitor Ctr B2
Walker House B2
Wellswood Ave A2
West Centre Way B1
Withywood Drive C1
Woodhouse Central B2
Yates Way A1

Torquay 349

Abbey Rd B2
Alexandra Rd A2
Alpine Rd B3
Ash Hill Rd A2
Babbacombe Rd B3
Bampfylde Rd B1
Barton Rd A1
Beacon Quay C2
Belgrave Rd A1/B1
Belmont Rd A3
Berea Rd A3
Braddons Hill Rd East B3
Brewery Park A3
Bronshill Rd A2
Castle Circus A2
Castle Rd A2
Cavern Rd A3
Central B2
Chatsworth Rd A2
Chestnut Ave B1
Church St A1
Civic Offices A2
Coach Station A1
Corbyn Head C1
Croft Hill B1
Croft Rd B1
Daddyhole Plain C3
East St A1
Egerton Rd A3
Ellacombe Church Rd A3
Ellacombe Rd A2
Falkland Rd B1
Fleet St B2
Fleet Walk Sh Ctr B2
Grafton Rd B3
Haldon Pier C2
Hatfield Rd A2
Highbury Rd A2
Higher Warberry Rd A3
Hillesdon Rd B3
Hollywood Bowl C3
Hoxton Rd A3
Hunsdon Rd B3
Information Ctr B2
Inner Harbour C3
Kenwyn Rd A3
Laburnum St A1
Law Courts A2
Library A2
Lime Ave B1
Living Coasts C3
Lower Warberry Rd B3
Lucius St B1
Lymington Rd A1
Magdalene Rd A1
Marina C2
Market Forum The B2
Market St B2
Meadfoot Lane C3
Meadfoot Rd C3
Melville St B2
Middle Warberry Rd B3
Mill Lane A1
Montpellier Rd B3
Morgan Ave A1
Museum Rd B3
Newton Rd A1
Oakhill Rd A1
Outer Harbour C2
Parkhill Rd C3
Pavilion Shopping Ctr C2
Pimlico B2
Police Station A1
Post Office A1/B2
Princes Rd A3
Princes Rd East A3
Princes Rd West A3
Princess Gdns C2
Princess Pier C2
Princess Theatre C2
Rathmore Rd B1
Recreation Grd B1
Riviera Int Ctr B1
Rock End Ave C3
Rock Rd B2
Rock Walk B2
Rosehill Rd A3
St Efride's Rd A1
St John's B3
St Luke's Rd B2
St Luke's Rd North B2
St Luke's Rd South B2
St Marychurch Rd A2
Scarborough Rd B1
Shedden Hill B2
South Pier C2
South St A1
Spanish Barn B1
Stitchill Rd B3
Strand B3
Sutherland Rd B3
Teignmouth Rd A1
Temperance St B2
The King's Drive B1
The Terrace B3
Thurlow Rd A1
Tor Bay B1
Tor Church Rd A1
Tor Hill Rd A1
Torbay Rd B2
Torquay Museum B3
Torquay Station C1
Torre Abbey Mansion B1
Torre Abbey Meadows B1
Torre Abbey Sands B1
Torwood Gdns B3
Torwood St C3
Town Hall A2
Union Square A2
Union St A1
Upton Hill A2
Upton Park A1
Upton Rd A1
Vanehill Rd C3
Vansittart Rd A1
Vaughan Parade C2
Victoria Parade C3
Victoria Rd A2
Warberry Rd West B2
Warren Rd B2
Windsor Rd A2/A3
Woodville Rd A3

Truro 349

Adelaide Ter B1
Agar Rd B3
Arch Hill C2
Arundell Pl C2
Avondale Rd B1
Back Quay B3
Barrack La C3
Barton Meadow A1
Benson Rd A2
Bishops Cl A2
Bosvean Gdns B1
Bosvigo Gardens B1
Bosvigo La A1
Bosvigo Rd B2
Broad St A3
Burley Cl C3
Bus Station B3
Calenick St B2
Campfield Hill B3
Carclew St B3
Carew Rd A2
Carey Park B2
Carlyon Rd A2
Carvoza Rd A3
Castle St B2
Cathedral View A2
Chainwalk Dr A2
Chapel Hill B1
Charles St B2
City Hall B3
City Rd B2
Coinage Hall B3
Comprigney Hill A1
Coosebean La A1
Copes Gdns A2
County Hall B1
Courtney Rd A2
Crescent Rd B1
Crescent Rise B1
Daniell Court C2
Daniell Rd C2
Daniell St C2
Daubuz Cl A2
Dobbs La B1
Edward St B2
Eliot Rd A2
Elm Court A3
Enys Cl A1
Enys Rd A1
Fairmantle St B3
Falmouth Rd C2
Ferris Town B2
Fire Station B1
Frances St B2
George St B2
Green Cl C2
Green La C1
Grenville Rd A2
Hall For Cornwall B3
Hendra Rd A2
Hendra Vean A1
High Cross B3
Higher Newham La C3
Higher Trehaverne A2
Hillcrest Ave B1
Hospital B2
Hunkin Cl A2
Hurland Rd C3
Infirmary Hill B2
James Pl B3
Kenwyn Church Rd A1
Kenwyn Hill A1
Kenwyn Rd A2
Kenwyn St B2
Kerris Gdns A1
King St B3
Lemon Quay B3
Lemon St Gallery B3
Library B1/B3
Malpas Rd B3
Market B3
Memorial Gdns B3
Merrifield Close B1
Mitchell Hill A3
Moresk Cl A3
Moresk Rd A3
Morlaix Ave C3
Nancemere Rd A3
Newham Bsns Park C3
Newham Industrial Est C3
Newham Rd C3
Northfield Dr C3
Oak Way A3
Old County Hall B1
Pal's Terr A3
Park View C2
Pendarves Rd A2
Plaza Cinema B3
Police Station B3
Post Office B2/B3
Prince's St B3
Pydar St A2
Quay St B3
Redannick Cres C2
Redannick La B2
Richard Lander Monument ✦ C2
Richmond Hill B1
River St B2
Rosedale Rd A1
Royal Cornwall Mus B2
St Aubyn Rd C3
St Clement St B3

St George's Rd A1
School La C2
Station Rd B1
Stokes Rd A2
Strangways Terr C3
Tabernacle St B3
The Avenue A3
The Crescent B1
The Leats B2
The Spires A2
Trehaverne La A2
Tremayne Rd A2
Treseder's Gdns A3
Treworder Rd B1
Treyew Rd B1
Truro Cathedral + B3
Truro Harbour Office B3
Truro Station ≥ B3
Union St B2
Upper School La C2
Victoria Gdns B2
Waterfall Gdns B2

Wick 349

Ackergill Cres A2
Ackergill St A2
Albert St C2
Ambulance Station A2
Argyle Sq C2
Assembly Rooms C2
Bank Row C2
Bankhead B1
Barons Well B2
Barrogill St C2
Bay View B3
Bexley Terr C3
Bignold Park C2
Bowling Green C2
Breadalbane Terr C2
Bridge of Wick B1
Bridge St B2
Brown Pl C2
Burn St B2
Bus Station B1
Caithness General Hospital (A&E) B1
Cliff Rd B1
Coach Rd B2
Coastguard Station C3
Corner Cres B3
Coronation St C1
Council Offices B2
Court B2
Crane Rock C3
Dempster St C2
Dunnet Ave A2
Fire Station B2
Fish Market C3
Francis St C1
George St A1
Girnigoe St B2
Glamis Rd B2
Gowrie Pl B1
Grant St C2
Green Rd B2
Gunns Terr B3
Harbour Quay B2
Harbour Rd C3
Harbour Terr C2
Harrow Hill C2
Henrietta St A2/B2
Heritage Museum C2
High St B2
Hill Ave A2
Hillhead Rd B3
Hood St C1
Huddart St C2
Information Ctr B2
Kenneth St C1
Kinnaird St C2
Kirk Hill B1
Langwell Cres B3
Leishman Ave B3
Leith Walk A2
Library B2
Lifeboat Station C3
Lighthouse C3
Lindsay Dr B3
Lindsay Pl B3
Loch St C2
Louisburgh St B2
Lower Dunbar St C2
Macleay La B1
Macleod Rd B3
MacRae St C2
Martha Terr B2
Miller Ave B1
Miller La B1
Moray St C2
Mowat Pl B3
Murchison St C3
Newton Ave C1
Newton Rd C1
Nicolson St C3
North Highland Coll B2
North River Pier B3
Northcote St C2
Owen Pl A2
Police Station B1
Port Dunbar B3
Post Office B2/C2
Pulteney Distillery C2
River St B2
Robert St A1
Rutherford St C2
St John's Episcopal C2
Sandigoe Rd B3
Scalesburn B3
Seaforth Ave C1
Shore La B2
Sinclair Dr B3
Sinclair Terr C2
Smith Terr C3
South Pier C3
South Quay C3
South Rd C1
South River Pier B3
Station Rd B1
Swimming Pool B2
TA Centre C2
Telford St B2
The Shore B2
Thurso Rd B1
Thurso St B1
Town Hall B2
Union St B2
Upper Dunbar St C2
Vansittart St C3
Victoria Pl B2
War Memorial A1
Well of Cairndhuna C3
Wellington Ave C3
Wellington St C3
West Banks Ave C1
West Banks Terr C1
West Park C1
Whitehorse Park B2
Wick Harbour Bridge B2
Wick Industrial Estate A2
Wick Parish Church B1
Wick Station ≥ B1
Williamson St B2
Willowbank B2

Winchester 350

Andover Rd A2
Andover Rd Retail Pk A2
Archery La C2
Arthur Rd A2
Bar End Rd C3
Beaufort Rd C2
Beggar's La B3
Bereweeke Ave A1
Bereweeke Rd A1
Boscobel Rd A2
Brassey Rd A2
Broadway B3
Brooks Sh Ctr, The B3
Bus Station B3
Butter Cross B2
Canon St C2
Castle Wall C2/C3
Castle, King Arthur's Round Table B2
Cathedral + C2
Cheriton Rd A1
Chesil St C3
Chesil Theatre C3
Christchurch Rd C1
City Mill B3
City Museum B2
City Offices C3
City Rd B2
Clifton Rd B1
Clifton Terr B2
Close Wall C2/C3
Coach Park A2
Colebrook St C3
College St C2
College Walk C3
Compton Rd C2
County Council Offices B2
Cranworth Rd A2
Cromwell Rd C1
Culver Rd C2
Domum Rd C3
Durngate Pl B3
Eastgate St B3
Edgar Rd C2
Egbert Rd A2
Elm Rd B1
Everyman C2
Fairfield Rd A1
Fire Station B3
Fordington Ave B1
Fordington Rd A1
Friarsgate B3
Gordon Rd B3
Greenhill Rd B1
Guildhall B3
HM Prison B1
Hatherley Rd A1
High St B2
Hillier Way A3
Hyde Abbey (Remains) + A2
Hyde Abbey Rd B2
Hyde Cl A2
Hyde St A2
Information Ctr B3
Jane Austen's Ho C2
Jewry St B2
John Stripe Theatre C1
King Alfred Pl A2
Kingsgate Arch C2
Kingsgate Park C2
Kingsgate Rd C2
Kingsgate St C2
Lankhills Rd A2
Library B2
Lower Brook St B3
Magdalen Hill B3
Market La B2
Mews La B1
Middle Brook St B3
Middle Rd B1
Military Museums B2
Milland Rd C3
Milverton Rd B1
Monks Rd A3
North Hill Cl A2
North Walls B2
North Walls Rec Gnd A3
Nuns Rd A3
Oram's Arbour B1
Owen's Rd A2
Parchment St B2
Park & Ride C3
Park Ave B3
Playing Field A1
Police HQ B1
Police Station B3
Portal Rd C3
Post Office B2/C1
Quarry Rd C3
Ranelagh Rd C1
Regiment Museum B2
River Park Leisure Ctr B3
Romans' Rd C2
Romsey Rd B1
Royal Hampshire County Hospital (A&E) B1
St Cross Rd C2
St George's St B2
St Giles Hill C3
St James' La B1
St James' Terr B1
St James Villas C2
St John's B3
St John's St B3
St Michael's Rd C2
St Paul's Hill B1
St Peter St B2
St Swithun St C2
St Thomas St C2
Saxon Rd A2
School of Art B3
Sleepers Hill Rd C1
Southgate St B2
Sparkford Rd C1
Staple Gdns B2
Station Rd B2
Step Terr B1
Stockbridge Rd A1
Stuart Cres C1
Sussex St B2
Swan Lane B2
Tanner St B3
The Square B2
The Weirs C3
The Winchester Gallery B3
Theatre Royal B2
Tower St B2
Town Hall C3
Union St B3
Univ of Southampton (Winchester School of Art) B3
Univ of Winchester (King Alfred Campus) C1
Upper Brook St B2
Wales St B3
Water Lane B3
West End Terr B1
West Gate B2
Western Rd B1
Wharf Hill C3
Winchester College C2
Winchester Station ≥ A2
Winnall Moors Wildlife Reserve A3
Wolvesey Castle C3
Worthy Lane A2
Worthy Rd A2

Windsor 350

Adelaide Sq C3
Albany Rd C2
Albert St B1
Alexandra Gdns B2
Alexandra Rd C2
Alma Rd B2
Ambulance Station B1
Arthur Rd B2
Bachelors Acre B3
Barry Ave B2
Beaumont Rd C2
Bexley St B1
Boat House B2
Brocas St B2
Brook St C3
Bulkeley Ave C1
Castle Hill B3
Charles St B2
Claremont Rd C2
Clarence Cr B2
Clarence Rd B1
Clewer Court Rd B1
Coach Park B2
College Cr C1
Courts C2
Cricket Ground C3
Dagmar Rd C2
Datchet Rd B3
Devereux Rd C2
Dorset Rd C2
Duke St B1
Elm Rd C1
Eton College A3
Eton Ct A2
Eton Sq A2
Eton Wick Rd A2
Fire Station C2
Farm Yard B3
Frances Rd C2
Frogmore Dr B3
Gloucester Pl C3
Goslar Way C1
Goswell Hill B2
Goswell Rd B2
Green La C1
Grove Rd C2
Guildhall B3
Helena Rd C2
Helston La B1
High St A2/B3
Holy Trinity C2
Hospital (Private) C2
Household Cavalry C2
Imperial Rd C1
Information Ctr B2/B3
Keats La A2
King Edward Ct B2
King Edward VII Ave A3
King Edward VII Hospital C2
King George V Memorial B3
King's Rd C3
King Stable St A2
Library C2
Maidenhead Rd B1
Meadow La A2
Municipal Offices C3
Nell Gwynne's Ho B3
Osborne Rd C2
Oxford Rd B1
Park St B3
Peascod St B2
Police Station C2
Post Office A2
Princess Margaret Hospital C2
Queen Victoria's Walk B3
Queen's Rd C2
River St B2
Romney Island A3
Romney Lock A3
Romney Lock Rd A3
Russell St C2
St John's B3
St John's Chapel A2
St Leonards Rd C2
St Mark's Rd C2
Sheet St C3
South Meadow A2
South Meadow La A2
Springfield Rd C1
Stovell Rd B1
Sunbury Rd A2
Tangier La A2
Tangier St A3
Temple Rd C2
Thames St B3
The Brocas A2
The Home Park A3/C3
The Long Walk C3
Theatre Royal B3
Trinity Pl C2
Vansittart Rd B1/C1
Vansittart Rd Gdns C1
Victoria Barracks C2
Victoria St C2
Ward Royal B2
Westmead C1
White Lilies Island A1
William St B2
Windsor Arts Ctr C2
Windsor Castle B3
Windsor & Eton Central ≥ B2
Windsor & Eton Riverside ≥ A3
Windsor Bridge B3
Windsor Great Park C3
Windsor Leisure Ctr B1
Windsor Relief Rd A1
Windsor Royal Sh B2
York Ave C1
York Rd C1

Wolverhampton 350

Albion St B3
Alexandra St C1
Arena C2
Arts Gallery B2
Ashland St C1
Austin St A1
Badger Dr A3
Bailey St B3
Bath Ave B1
Bath Rd B1
Bell St C2
Berry St B3
Bilston Rd C3
Bilston St C3
Birmingham Canal A3
Bone Mill La A2
Brewery Rd B1
Bright St A1
Burton Cres B3
Bus Station B3
Cambridge St A3
Camp St B2
Cannock Rd A3
Castle St C2
Chapel Ash C1
Cherry St C1
Chester St A1
Church La C2
Church St C2
Civic Centre B2
Clarence Rd B2
Cleveland St C2
Clifton St C1
Coach Station B2
Compton Rd B1
Corn Hill B3
Coven St A3
Craddock St A1
Cross St North A2
Crown & County Courts C3
Crown St A2
Culwell St B3
Dale St C1
Darlington St C1
Dartmouth St C3
Devon Rd A1
Drummond St B2
Dudley Rd C2
Dudley St B2
Duke St C3
Dunkley St B2
Dunstall Ave A2
Dunstall Hill A2
Dunstall Rd A1/A2
Evans St A1
Fawdry St A1
Field St B3
Fire Station C1
Fiveways A2
Fowler Playing Fields A3
Fox's La A2
Francis St A2
Fryer St B3
Gloucester St A1
Gordon St C3
Graiseley St C1
Grand B3
Granville St C3
Great Brickkiln St C1
Great Hampton St A1
Great Western St A2
Grimstone St B3
Harrow St A1
Hilton St A3
Horseley Fields C3
Humber Rd C1
Jack Hayward Way A2
Jameson St A1
Jenner St C3
Kennedy Rd B3
Kimberley St C1
King St B2
Laburnum St C1
Lansdowne Rd B1
Leicester St A1
Lever St C3
Library C3
Lichfield St B2
Light House B3
Little's La B3
Lock St B3
Lord St C1
Lowe St A1
Lower Stafford St A2
Magistrates Court B2
Mander Centre C2
Mander St C1
Market St B2
Market C2
Melbourne St C3
Merridale St C1
Middlecross C3
Molineux St B2
Mostyn St A1
New Hampton Rd East A1
Nine Elms La A3
North Rd A2
Oaks Cres C1
Oxley St A2
Paget St A1
Park Ave B1
Park Road East A1
Park Road West B1
Paul St C2
Pelham St C1
Penn Rd C2
Piper's Row B3
Pitt St C2
Police Station C3
Pool St C2
Poole St A3
Post Office A1/A2/B2/B2
Powlett St C3
Queen St B2
Raby St C3
Raglan St C1
Railway Dr B3
Red Hill St A2
Red Lion St B2
Retreat St C1
Ring Rd B2
Rugby St A1
Russell St C1
St Andrew's B1
St David's B3
St George's C3
St George's Pde C2
St James St C3
St John's C2
St John's C2
St John's Retail Park C2
St John's Square C2
St Mark's C1
St Marks Rd C1
St Marks St C1
St Patrick's B2
St Peter's B2
St Peter's B2
Salisbury St C1
Salop St C2
School St C2
Sherwood St A2
Smestow St A3
Snowhill C2
Springfield Rd A3
Stafford St B2
Staveley Rd A1
Steelhouse La C3
Stephenson St C1
Stewart St C2
Sun St B3
Sutherland Pl C3
Tempest St C2
Temple St C2
Tettenhall Rd B1
The Maltings B2
The Royal C3
Thomas St C2
Thornley St B2
Tower St C2
University B2
Upper Zoar St C1
Vicarage Rd C3
Victoria St C2
Walpole St A1
Walsall St C3
Ward St C3
Warwick St C3
Water St A3
Waterloo Rd B2
Wednesfield Rd B3
West Pk (not A&E) B1
West Park Swimming Pool B1
Wharf St C3
Whitmore Hill B2
Wolverhampton ≥ B3
Wolverhampton St George's C2
Wolverhampton Wanderers Football Gnd (Molineux) B2
Worcester St C2
Wulfrun Centre C2
Yarwell Cl A3
York St C3
Zoar St C1

Worcester 350

Albany Terr A1
Alice Otley School A2
Angel Pl B2
Angel St B2
Ashcroft Rd A2
Athelstan Rd C3
Back Lane North A1
Back Lane South A1
Barbourne Rd A2
Bath Rd C2
Battenhall Rd C3
Bridge St B2
Britannia Sq A1
Broad St B2
Bromwich La C1
Bromwich Rd C1
Bromyard Rd C1
Bus Station B2
Carden St B3
Castle St A2
Cathedral + C2
Cathedral Plaza B2
Charles St B3
Chequers La B1
Chestnut St A2
Chestnut Walk A2
Citizens' Advice Bureau B2
City Walls Rd B2
Cole Hill C3
College of Technology B2
College St C2
Commandery C3
Cripplegate Park B1
Croft Rd B1
Cromwell St B3
CrownGate Centre B2
Deansway B2
Diglis Pde C2
Diglis Rd C2
Edgar Tower C2
Farrier St A2
Fire Station B2
Foregate St B2
Foregate Street ≥ B2
Fort Royal Hill C3
Fort Royal Park C3
Foundry St B3
Friar St C2
George St B3
Grand Stand Rd B1
Greenhill C3
Greyfriars B2
Guildhall B2
Henwick Rd B1
High St B2
Hill St B3
Huntingdon Hall B2
Hylton Rd B1
Information Ctr B2
King Charles Pl Sh Ctr C1
King's School C2
King's School Playing Field C2
Kleve Walk C2
Lansdowne Cr A3
Lansdowne Rd A3
Lansdowne Walk A3
Laslett St A3
Leisure Centre A3
Library, Museum & Art Gallery A2
Little Chestnut St A2
Little London A2
London Rd C3
Lowell St A3
Lowesmoor B2
Lowesmoor Terr A3
Lowesmoor Wharf A3
Magistrates Court A2
Midland Rd B3
Mill St C2
Moors Severn Terr A1
New Rd C1
New St B2
Northfield St A2
Odeon B2
Padmore St B3
Park St C3
Pheasant St B3
Pitchcroft Racecourse A1
Police Station A2
Portland St C2
Post Office B2
Quay St B2
Queen St B2
Rainbow Hill A3
Recreation Ground A2
Reindeer Court B2
Rogers Hill A3
Sabrina Rd A1
St Dunstan's Cr C3
St John's C1
St Martin's Gate B3
St Oswald's Rd A2
St Paul's St B3
St Swithin's Church B2
St Wulstans Cr C3
Sansome Walk A2
Severn St C2
Shaw St B2
Shire Hall Crown Ct A2
Shrub Hill ≥ B3
Shrub Hill Retail Park B3
Shrub Hill Rd B3
Slingpool Walk C1
South Quay B2
Southfield St A2
Sports Ground A2/C1
Stanley Rd B3
Swan, The A1
Swimming Pool A2
Tallow Hill B3
Tennis Walk A2
The Avenue C1
The Butts B2
The Cross B2
The Shambles B2
The Tything A2
Tolladine Rd B3
Tudor House B2
Tybridge St B1
Univ of Worcester B2
Vincent Rd B3
Vue C2
Washington St A3
Woolhope Rd C3
Worcester Bridge B2
Worcester County Cricket Ground C1
Worcester Library & History Centre B3
Worcester Porcelain Museum C2
Worcester Royal Grammar School A2
Wylds La C3

Wrexham Wrecsam 350

Abbot St B2
Acton Rd A3
Albert St C3
Alexandra Rd C1
Aran Rd A3
Barnfield C3
Bath Rd C2
Beechley Rd C3
Belgrave Rd C2
Belle Vue Park C2
Belle Vue Rd C2
Belvedere Dr A1
Bennion's Rd C3
Berse Rd A1
Bersham Rd C1
Birch St C3
Bodhyfryd B3
Border Retail Park B3
Bradley Rd C2
Bright St B1
Bron-y-Nant B1
Brook St C2
Bryn-y-Cabanau Rd C3
Bury St C1
Bus Station B2
Butchers Market B3
Caia Rd C3
Cambrian Ind Est C3
Caxton Pl B2
Cemetery C1
Centenary Rd C1
Chapel St C2
Charles St B3
Chester Rd A3
Chester St B3
Cilcen Gr A3
Citizens Advice Bureau B2
Cobden Rd B1
Council Offices B3
County C2
Crescent Rd B3
Crispin La A2
Croesnewyth Rd B1
Cross St A2
Cunliffe St A2
Derby Rd C3
Dolydd Rd B1
Duke St B2
Eagles Meadow C3
Earle St C2
East Ave A2
Edward St C2
Egerton St B2
Empress Rd C1
Erddig Rd C2
Fairy Rd C2
Fire Station B2
Foster Rd A3
Foxwood Dr C1
Garden Rd A2
General Market B3
Gerald St B2
Gibson St C1
Glyndŵr University Plas Coch Campus A1
Greenbank St C3
Greenfield A2
Grosvenor Rd B2
Grove Park B2
Grove Park Rd B3
Grove Rd A3
Guildhall B2
Haig Rd C3
Hampden Rd C2
Hazel Gr A3
Henblas St B3
High St B3
Hightown Rd C3
Hill St B2
Holt Rd B3
Holt St B3
Hope St B2
Huntroyde Ave C3
Information Ctr B3
Island Gn Sh Ctr B2
Job Centre B2
Jubilee Rd B2
King St B2
Kingsmills Rd C3
Lambpit St B3
Law Courts B3
Lawson Cl A3
Lawson Rd A3
Lea Rd C2
Library & Arts Centre B2
Lilac Way B1
Llys David Lord B1
Lorne St A2
Maesgwyn Rd B1
Maesydre Rd A3
Manley Rd B3
Market St B3
Mawddy Ave A2
Mayville Ave A2
Memorial Gallery B2
Memorial Hall B3
Mold Rd A1
Mount St C3
Neville Cres A3
New Rd A2
North Wales Regional Tennis Centre A1
North Wales School of Art & Design B2
Oak Dr A3
Park Ave A3
Park St A2
Peel St C1
Pentre Felin C2
Pen y Bryn C2
Penymaes Ave A3
Peoples Market B3
Percy St C2
Plas Coch Retail Park A1
Plas Coch Rd A1
Police Station B3
Poplar Rd C2
Post Office A2/B2/C2/C3
Powell Rd B3
Poyser St C2
Price's La A2
Primose Way B1
Princess St C1
Queen St B3
Queens Sq B2
Regent St B2
Rhosddu Rd A2/B2
Rhosnesni La A3
Rivulet Rd C3
Ruabon Rd C2
Ruthin Rd C1/C2
St Giles C3
St Giles Way C3
St James Ct A2
St Mary's + B2
Salisbury Rd C3
Salop Rd C3
Sontley Rd C2
Spring Rd A2
Stanley St C3
Stansty Rd A2
Station Approach B2
Studio B2
Talbot Rd C2
Techniquest Glyndŵr A2
The Beeches A3
The Pines A3
Town Hill C2
Trevor St C2
Trinity St B2
Tuttle St C3
Vale Park A1
Vernon St B2
Vicarage Hill B2
Victoria Rd C2
Walnut St A2
War Memorial B3
Waterworld L Ctr B3
Watery Rd B1/B2
Wellington Rd C2
Westminster Dr A3
William Aston Hall A1
Windsor Rd A1
Wrexham AFC A1
Wrexham Central ≥ B2
Wrexham General ≥ B2
Wrexham Maelor Hospital (A&E) B1
Wrexham Technology Park B1
Wynn Ave A2
Yale College B3
Yale Gr A3
Yorke St C3

York 350

Aldwark B2
Ambulance Station B3
Barbican Rd C3
Barley Hall B2
Bishopgate St C2
Bishopthorpe Rd C2
Blossom St C1
Bootham A1
Bootham Cr A1
Bootham Terr A1
Bridge St B2
Brook St A2
Brownlow St A2
Burton Stone La A1
Castle Museum C2
Castlegate B2
Cemetery Rd C3
Cherry St C2
City Screen B2
City Wall A2/B1/C3
Clarence St A2
Clementhorpe C2
Clifford St B2
Clifford's Tower B2
Clifton A1
Coach park A2
Coney St B2
Cromwell Rd C2
Crown Court C2
Davygate B2
Deanery Gdns A2
DIG B2
Ebor Industrial Estate B3
Fairfax House B2
Fishergate C3
Foss Islands Retail Pk B3
Foss Islands Rd B3
Fossbank A3
Garden St A2
George St C3
Gillygate A2
Goodramgate B2
Grand Opera House B2
Grosvenor Terr A1
Guildhall B2
Hallfield Rd A3
Heslington Rd C3
Heworth Green A3
Holy Trinity B2
Hope St C3
Huntington Rd A3
Information Ctr B2
James St B3
Jorvik Viking Ctr B2
Kent St C3
Lawrence St C3
Layerthorpe A3
Leeman Rd B1
Lendal B2
Lendal Bridge B1
Library B1
Longfield Terr A1
Lord Mayor's Walk A2
Lower Eldon St A2
Lowther St A2
Mansion House B2
Margaret St C3
Marygate A1
Melbourne St C3
Merchant Adventurer's Hall B2
Merchant Taylors' Hall B2
Micklegate B1
Micklegate Bar C1
Minster, The + A2
Monkgate A2
Moss St C1
Museum Gdns B1
Museum St B1
National Railway Museum B1
Navigation Rd B3
Newton Terr C2
North Pde A1
North St B2
Nunnery La C1
Nunthorpe Rd C1
Ouse Bridge B2
Paragon St C3
Park Gr A3
Park St C1
Parliament St B2
Peasholme Green B3
Penley's Grove St A2
Piccadilly B2
Police Station B2
Post Office B1/B2/C3
Priory St B1
Purey Cust Nuffield Hospital, The A2
Queen Anne's Rd A1
Quilt Museum B3
Reel C1
Regimental Mus B2
Richard III Museum A2
Roman Bath B2
Rowntree Park C2
St Andrewgate B2
St Benedict Rd C1
St John St A2
St Olave's Rd A1
St Peter's Gr A1
St Saviourgate B2
Scarcroft Hill C1
Scarcroft Rd C1
Skeldergate C2
Skeldergate Bridge C2
Station Rd B1
Stonegate B2
Sycamore Terr A1
Terry Ave C2
The Shambles B2
The Stonebow B2
Theatre Royal B2
Thorpe St C1
Toft Green B1
Tower St C2
Townend St A2
Treasurer's House A2
Trinity La B1
Undercroft Mus A2
Union Terr A2
Victor St C2
Vine St C2
Walmgate B3
Wellington St C3
York Art Gallery A1
York Barbican C3
York Brewery B1
York Dungeon, The B2
York Station ≥ B1

Abbreviations used in the index

Aberdeen **Aberdeen City**
Aberds **Aberdeenshire**
Ald **Alderney**
Anglesey **Isle of Anglesey**
Angus **Angus**
Argyll **Argyll and Bute**
Bath **Bath and North East Somerset**
Bedford **Bedford**
Bl Gwent **Blaenau Gwent**
Blackburn **Blackburn with Darwen**
Blackpool **Blackpool**
Bmouth **Bournemouth**
Borders **Scottish Borders**
Brack **Bracknell**
Bridgend **Bridgend**
Brighton **City of Brighton and Hove**
Bristol **City and County of Bristol**
Bucks **Buckinghamshire**
C Beds **Central Bedfordshire**
Caerph **Caerphilly**
Cambs **Cambridgeshire**
Cardiff **Cardiff**
Carms **Carmarthenshire**
Ceredig **Ceredigion**
Ches E **Cheshire East**
Ches W **Cheshire West and Chester**
Clack **Clackmannanshire**
Conwy **Conwy**
Corn **Cornwall**
Cumb **Cumbria**
Darl **Darlington**
Denb **Denbighshire**
Derby **City of Derby**
Derbys **Derbyshire**
Devon **Devon**
Dorset **Dorset**
Dumfries **Dumfries and Galloway**
Dundee **Dundee City**
Durham **Durham**
E Ayrs **East Ayrshire**
E Dunb **East Dunbartonshire**
E Loth **East Lothian**
E Renf **East Renfrewshire**
E Sus **East Sussex**
E Yorks **East Riding of Yorkshire**
Edin **City of Edinburgh**
Essex **Essex**
Falk **Falkirk**
Fife **Fife**
Flint **Flintshire**
Glasgow **City of Glasgow**
Glos **Gloucestershire**
Gtr Man **Greater Manchester**
Gwyn **Gwynedd**
Halton **Halton**
Hants **Hampshire**
Hereford **Herefordshire**
Herts **Hertfordshire**
Highld **Highland**
Hrtlpl **Hartlepool**
Hull **Hull**
IoM **Isle of Man**
IoW **Isle of Wight**
Invclyd **Inverclyde**
Kent **Kent**
Lancs **Lancashire**
Leicester **City of Leicester**
Leics **Leicestershire**
Lincs **Lincolnshire**
London **Greater London**
Luton **Luton**
M Keynes **Milton Keynes**
M Tydf **Merthyr Tydfil**
Mbro **Middlesbrough**
Medway **Medway**
Mers **Merseyside**
Midloth **Midlothian**
Mon **Monmouthshire**
Moray **Moray**
N Ayrs **North Ayrshire**
N Lincs **North Lincolnshire**
N Lanark **North Lanarkshire**
N Som **North Somerset**
N Yorks **North Yorkshire**
NE Lincs **North East Lincolnshire**
Neath **Neath Port Talbot**
Newport **City and County of Newport**
Norf **Norfolk**
Northants **Northamptonshire**
Northumb **Northumberland**
Nottingham **City of Nottingham**
Notts **Nottinghamshire**
Orkney **Orkney**
Oxon **Oxfordshire**
Pboro **Peterborough**
Pembs **Pembrokeshire**
Perth **Perth and Kinross**
Plym **Plymouth**
Poole **Poole**
Powys **Powys**
Ptsmth **Portsmouth**
Reading **Reading**
Redcar **Redcar and Cleveland**
Renfs **Renfrewshire**
Rhondda **Rhondda Cynon Taff**
Rutland **Rutland**
S Ayrs **South Ayrshire**
S Glos **South Gloucestershire**
S Lanark **South Lanarkshire**
S Yorks **South Yorkshire**
Scilly **Scilly**
Shetland **Shetland**
Shrops **Shropshire**
Slough **Slough**
Som **Somerset**
Soton **Southampton**
Staffs **Staffordshire**
Southend **Southend-on-Sea**
Stirling **Stirling**
Stockton **Stockton-on-Tees**
Stoke **Stoke-on-Trent**
Suff **Suffolk**
Sur **Surrey**
Swansea **Swansea**
Swindon **Swindon**
T&W **Tyne and Wear**
Telford **Telford & Wrekin**
Thurrock **Thurrock**
Torbay **Torbay**
Torf **Torfaen**
V Glam **The Vale of Glamorgan**
W Berks **West Berkshire**
W Dunb **West Dunbartonshire**
W Isles **Western Isles**
W Loth **West Lothian**
W Mid **West Midlands**
W Sus **West Sussex**
W Yorks **West Yorkshire**
Warks **Warwickshire**
Warr **Warrington**
Wilts **Wiltshire**
Windsor **Windsor and Maidenhead**
Wokingham **Wokingham**
Worcs **Worcestershire**
Wrex **Wrexham**
York **City of York**

Index to road maps of Britain

How to use the index

Example **Blatherwycke** Northants **137** D9

- D9 — grid square
- 137 — page number
- Northants — county or unitary authority

A

Aaron's Hill Sur 50 E3
Aaron's Town Cumb 240 E2
Abbas Combe Som 30 C2
Abberley Worcs 116 D5
Abberton Essex 89 B8
Worcs 117 G9
Abberwick Northumb 264 G4
Abbess End Essex 87 C9
Abbess Roding Essex 87 C9
Abbey Devon 27 E10
Abbeycwmhir Powys 113 C11
Abbey-cwm-hir Powys 113 C11
Abbeydale Glos 80 B5
S Yorks 186 E4
Abbeydale Park S Yorks 186 E4
Abbey Dore Hereford 97 E7
Abbey Field Essex 107 G9
Abbey Gate Kent 53 B9
Abbey Green Shrops 149 C10
Staffs 169 D7
Abbey Hey Gtr Man 184 B5
Abbeyhill Edin 280 G5
Abbey Hulton Stoke 168 F6
Abbey Mead Sur 66 F4
Abbey St Bathans Borders 272 C5
Abbeystead Lancs 203 C7
Abbey Town Cumb 238 G5
Abbey Village Lancs 194 C6
Abbey Wood London 68 D3
Abbots Bickington Devon 24 E5
Abbots Bromley Staffs 151 E11
Abbotsbury Dorset 17 D7
Abbotsford W Sus 36 C4
Abbotsham Devon 24 B6
Abbotskerswell Devon 9 B7
Abbots Langley Herts 85 E9
Abbotsleigh Devon 8 F6
Abbots Leigh N Som 60 E4
Abbotsley Cambs 122 F4
Abbot's Meads Ches W 166 B5
Abbots Morton Worcs 117 F10
Abbots Ripton Cambs 122 B4
Abbots Salford Warks 117 G11
Abbotstone Hants 48 G5
Abbotswood Hants 32 C5
Sur 50 C4
Abbots Worthy Hants 48 G3
Abbotts Ann Hants 47 E10
Abcott Shrops 115 B7
Abdon Shrops 131 F11
Abdy S Yorks 186 B6
Aber Ceredig 93 B9
Aberaeron Ceredig 111 E9
Aberaman Rhondda 77 E8
Aberangell Gwyn 146 G6
Aber-Arad Carms 92 D6
Aberarder Highld 290 E6
Aberarder House Highld 300 G6
Aberarder Lodge Highld 291 E7
Aberargie Perth 286 F5
Aberarth Ceredig 111 E9
Aberavon Neath 57 C8
Aber-banc Ceredig 93 C7
Aberbargoed Caerph 77 E11
Aberbechan Powys 130 E2
Aberbeeg Bl Gwent 78 E2
Aberbran Powys 95 F9
Abercanaid M Tydf 77 E9
Abercarn Caerph 78 G2
Abercastle Pembs 91 E7
Abercegir Powys 128 C6
Aberchalder Highld 290 C5
Aberchirder Aberds 302 D6
Abercorn W Loth 279 F11
Aber Cowarch Gwyn 147 F7
Abercraf Powys 76 C4
Abercregan Neath 57 B11
Abercrombie Fife 287 G9
Abercwmboi Rhondda 77 F8
Abercych Pembs 92 C4
Abercynafon Powys 77 B9
Abercynffig / Aberkenfig Bridgend 57 E11
Abercynon Rhondda 77 F9
Aberdalgie Perth 286 E4
Aberdâr / Aberdare Rhondda 77 E7
Aberdare / Aberdâr Rhondda 77 E7
Aberdaron Gwyn 144 D3
Aberdeen Aberdeen 293 C11
Aberdesach Gwyn 162 E6
Aberdour Fife 280 D3
Aberdovey / Aberdyfi Gwyn 128 D2
Aberdulais Neath 76 E3
Aberdyfi / Aberdovey Gwyn 128 D2
Aberedw Powys 95 B11
Abereiddy Pembs 90 E5
Abererch Gwyn 145 B7
Aberfan M Tydf 77 E9
Aberfeldy Perth 286 C2
Aberffraw Anglesey 162 B5
Aberffrwd Ceredig 112 B3
Mon 78 D5
Aberford W Yorks 206 F4
Aberfoyle Stirl 285 G9
Abergarw Bridgend 58 C2
Abergarwed Neath 76 E4
Abergavenny Mon 78 C3
Abergele Conwy 180 F6
Aber-Giâr Carms 93 C10
Abergorlech Carms 93 E11
Abergwaun / Fishguard Pembs 91 D9
Abergwesyn Powys 113 G7
Abergwili Carms 93 G8
Abergwynant Gwyn 146 F3
Abergwynfi Neath 57 B11
Aber-gwynfi Neath 57 B11
Abergwyngregyn Gwyn 179 G11
Abergynolwyn Gwyn 128 B3
Aber-Hirnant Gwyn 147 C9
Aberhosan Powys 128 D6
Aberkenfig / Abercynffig Bridgend 57 E11
Aberlady E Loth 281 E9
Aberlemno Angus 287 B9
Aberlerry Ceredig 128 E2
Aberllefenni Gwyn 128 B5
Aberllydan / Broad Haven Pembs 72 C5
Aberllynfi / Three Cocks Powys 96 D3
Abermagwr Ceredig 112 C3
Abermaw / Barmouth Gwyn 146 F2
Abermeurig Ceredig 111 F11
Aber miwl / Abermule Powys 130 E3
Abermorddu Flint 166 D4
Abermule / Aber-miwl Powys 130 E3
Abernaint Powys 148 E2
Abernant Carms 92 G6
Powys 130 D3
Aber-nant Rhondda 77 E8
Abernethy Perth 286 F5
Abernyte Perth 286 D6
Aber-oer Wrex 166 F3
Aberogwr / Ogmore by Sea V Glam 57 F11
Aberpennar / Mountain Ash Rhondda 77 F8
Aberporth Ceredig 110 G5
Ach'an Todhair Highld 290 F2
Aber-Rhiwlech Gwyn 147 E8
Aberriw / Berriew Powys 130 C3
Abersoch Gwyn 144 D6
Abersychan Torf 78 E3
Abertawe / Swansea Swansea 56 C6
Aberteifi / Cardigan Ceredig 92 B3
Aberthin V Glam 58 D4
Abertillery Bl Gwent 78 E2
Abertridwr Caerph 58 B6
Powys 147 F10
Abertrinant Gwyn 128 B2
Abertysswg Caerph 77 D10
Aberuchill Castle Perth 285 E11
Aberuthven Perth 286 F3
Aber-Village Powys 96 G2
Aberyscir Powys 95 F9
Aberystwyth Ceredig 111 A11
Abhainn Suidhe W Isles 305 H2
Abingdon Oxon 83 F7
Abinger Common Sur 50 D6
Abinger Hammer Sur 50 D5
Abington Northants 120 E5
S Lnrk 259 E10
Abington Pigotts Cambs 104 C6
Abington Vale Northants 120 E5
Abingworth W Sus 35 D10
Ab Kettleby Leics 154 E4
Ab Lench Worcs 117 G10
Ablington Glos 81 D10
Wilts 47 D7
Abney Derbys 185 F11
Aboyne Aberds 293 D7
Abraham Heights Lancs 211 G9
Abram Gtr Man 194 G6
Abriachan Highld 300 F5
Abridge Essex 87 F7
Abronhill N Lnrk 278 F5
Abshot Hants 33 F8
Abson S Glos 61 E8
Abthorpe Northants 102 B2
Abune-the-Hill Orkney 314 D2
Aby Lincs 190 F6
Acaster Malbis York 207 D7
Acaster Selby N Yorks 207 E7
Accrington Lancs 195 B9
Acha Argyll 275 B8
Argyll 288 D3
Achabraid Argyll 275 E9
Achachork Highld 298 E4
Achadh an Eas Highld 308 F6
Achad nan Darach Highld 284 B4
Achadunan Argyll 284 F5
Achafolla Argyll 275 B8
Achagary Highld 308 D7
Achaglass Argyll 255 C8
Achahoish Argyll 275 F8
Achalader Perth 286 C5
Achallader Argyll 285 C7
Achalone Highld 310 D5
Acha Mor W Isles 304 F5
Achanalt Highld 300 C2
Achanamara Argyll 275 E8
Achandunie Highld 300 B6
Achanelid Argyll 275 E11
Achany Highld 309 J5
Achaphubuil Highld 290 F2
Acharacle Highld 289 C8
Acharn Highld 289 D9
Perth 285 C11
Acharole Highld 310 D6
Acharossan Argyll 275 F10
Acharry Muir Highld 309 K6
Achath Aberds 293 B9
Achavanich Highld 310 E5
Achavelgin Highld 301 D9
Achavraat Highld 301 E9
Achddu Carms 74 E6
Achdregnie Moray 302 G2
Achduart Highld 307 J5
Achentoul Highld 310 F2
Achfary Highld 306 F7
Achfrish Highld 309 H5
Achgarve Highld 307 K3
Achiemore Highld 308 C3
Highld 310 D2
A'Chill Highld 294 E4
Achiltibuie Highld 307 J5
Achina Highld 308 C7
Achinahuagh Highld 308 C5
Achindaul Highld 290 E3
Achindown Highld 301 E8
Achinduich Highld 309 J5
Achinduin Argyll 289 F10
Achingills Highld 310 C5
Achininver Highld 308 C5
Achintee Highld 290 F3
Highld 299 E9
Achintraid Highld 295 B10
Achlaven Argyll 289 F11
Achlean Highld 291 D10
Achleck Argyll 288 E6
Achlorachan Highld 300 D3
Achluachrach Highld 290 E4
Achlyness Highld 306 D7
Achmelvich Highld 307 G5
Achmore Highld 295 B10
Stirl 285 D9
Achnaba Argyll 275 E10
Argyll 289 F11
Achnabat Highld 300 F5
Achnabreck Argyll 275 D9
Achnacarnin Highld 306 F5
Achnacarry Highld 290 E3
Achnacloich Argyll 289 F11
Highld 295 E7
Achnaconeran Highld 290 B6
Achnacraig Argyll 288 E6
Achnacree Argyll 289 F11
Achnacree Bay Argyll 289 F11
Achnacroish Argyll 289 E10
Achnadrish Argyll 288 D6
Achnafalnich Argyll 284 E6
Achnagarron Highld 300 C6
Achnaha Highld 288 C6
Achnahanat Highld 309 K5
Achnahannet Highld 301 G9
Achnahard Argyll 288 G5
Achnairn Highld 309 H5
Achnaluachrach Highld 309 J6
Achnandarach Highld 295 B10
Achnanellan Highld 290 E2
Achnasaul Highld 290 E3
Achnasheen Highld 299 D11
Achnashelloch Argyll 275 D9
Achnavast Highld 310 C4
Achneigie Highld 299 B10
Achormlarie Highld 309 K6
Achorn Highld 310 F5
Achosnich Highld 288 C6
Achranich Highld 289 E9
Achreamie Highld 310 C4
Achriabhach Highld 290 G3
Achriesgill Highld 306 D7
Achrimsdale Highld 311 J3
Achtoty Highld 308 C6
Achurch Northants 137 G10
Achuvoldrach Highld 308 D5
Achvaich Highld 309 K7
Achvarasdal Highld 310 C3
Ackenthwaite Cumb 211 C10
Ackergill Highld 310 D7
Acklam Mbro 225 B9
N Yorks 216 G5
Ackleton Shrops 132 D5
Acklington Northumb 252 C6
Ackton W Yorks 198 C2
Ackworth Moor Top W Yorks 198 D2
Acle Norf 161 G8
Acock's Green W Mid 134 G2
Acol Kent 71 F10
Acomb Northumb 241 D10
York 207 C7
Acre Gtr Man 196 F2
Lancs 195 C9
Acrefair Wrex 166 G3
Acres Nook Staffs 168 E4
Acre Street W Sus 21 B11
Acton Ches E 167 E10
Dorset 18 F5
London 67 C8
Shrops 130 G6
Staffs 168 G4
Suff 107 C7
Worcs 116 D6
Wrex 166 E4
Acton Beauchamp Hereford 116 G3
Acton Bridge Ches W 183 F9
Acton Burnell Shrops 131 C10
Acton Green Hereford 116 G3
London 67 D8
Acton Pigott Shrops 131 C10
Acton Place Suff 107 B7
Acton Reynald Shrops 149 E10
Acton Round Shrops 132 D2
Acton Scott Shrops 131 F9
Acton Trussell Staffs 151 F8
Acton Turville S Glos 61 C10
Adabroc W Isles 304 B7
Adambrae W Loth 269 A10
Adam's Green Dorset 29 F8
Adbaston Staffs 150 D5
Adber Dorset 29 C9
Adbolton Notts 154 B2
Adderbury Oxon 101 D9
Adderley Shrops 150 B3
Adderley Green Stoke 168 G6
Adderstone Northumb 264 C4
Addiewell W Loth 269 C9
Addingham W Yorks 205 D7
Addingham Moorside W Yorks 205 D7
Addington Bucks 102 F4
Corn 6 B5
Kent 53 B7
London 67 G11
Addinston Borders 271 E10
Addiscombe London 67 F10
Addlestone Sur 66 G5
Addlestonemoor Sur 66 F4
Addlethorpe Lincs 175 B8
Adel W Yorks 205 F11
Adeney Telford 150 F4
Adeyfield Herts 85 D9
Adfa Powys 129 C11
Adforton Hereford 115 C8
Adgestone IoW 21 D7
Adisham Kent 55 C8
Adlestrop Glos 100 F4
Adlingfleet E Yorks 199 C10
Adlington Ches E 184 E6
Lancs 194 E6
Adlington Park Lancs 194 E5
Admaston Staffs 151 E10
Telford 150 G2
Admington Warks 100 B4
Adpar Ceredig 92 C6
Adsborough Som 28 B3
Adscombe Som 43 F7
Adstock Bucks 102 E4
Adstone Northants 119 G11
Adswood Gtr Man 184 D5
Adversane W Sus 35 C9
Advie Highld 301 F11
Adwalton W Yorks 197 B8
Adwell Oxon 83 F11
Adwick le Street S Yorks 198 F4
Adwick upon Dearne S Yorks 198 G3
Adziel Aberds 303 D9
Ae Dumfries 247 F11
Ae Village Dumfries 247 F11
Affetside Gtr Man 195 E9
Affleck Aberds 303 G8
Affpuddle Dorset 18 C2
Affric Lodge Highld 299 G11
Afon Eitha Wrex 166 F3
Afon-wen Flint 181 G10
Afon Wen Gwyn 145 B8
Afton IoW 20 D2
Agar Nook Leics 153 G9
Agbrigg W Yorks 197 D10
Aggborough Worcs 116 B6
Agglethorpe N Yorks 213 B11
Aglionby Cumb 239 F10
Agneash IoM 192 D5
Aifft Denb 165 B10
Aigburth Mers 182 D5
Aiginis W Isles 304 E6
Aike E Yorks 209 D7
Aikenway Moray 302 E2
Aikerness Orkney 314 A4
Aikers Orkney 314 G4
Aiketgate Cumb 230 B5
Aikton Cumb 239 G7
Ailby Lincs 190 F6
Ailey Hereford 96 B6
Ailstone Warks 118 G4
Ailsworth Pboro 138 D2
Aimes Green Essex 86 E5
Ainderby Quernhow N Yorks 215 C7
Ainderby Steeple N Yorks 224 G6
Aingers Green Essex 108 G2
Ainley Top W Yorks 196 D6
Ainsdale Mers 193 E10
Ainsdale-on-Sea Mers 193 E9
Ainstable Cumb 230 B6
Ainsworth Gtr Man 195 E9
Ainthorpe N Yorks 226 D4
Aintree Mers 182 B5
Aird Argyll 275 C8
Dumfries 236 C2
Highld 299 B7
W Isles 296 F3
W Isles 304 E7
Airdachuilinn Highld 306 E7
Aird a Mhachair W Isles 297 G3
Aird a' Mhulaidh W Isles 305 G3
Aird Asaig W Isles 305 H3
Aird Dhail W Isles 304 B6
Airdens Highld 309 K6
Airdeny Argyll 289 G11
Aird Mhidhinis W Isles 297 L3
Aird Mhighe W Isles 296 C6
W Isles 305 J3
Aird Mhòr W Isles 297 G4
Aird Mhor W Isles 297 L3
Aird of Sleat Highld 295 E7
Airdrie N Lnrk 268 B5
Airds of Kells Dumfries 237 B8
Aird Thunga W Isles 304 E6
Airdtorrisdale Highld 308 C6
Aird Uig W Isles 304 E2
Airedale W Yorks 198 B3
Aire View N Yorks 204 D5
Airidh a Bhruaich W Isles 305 G4
Airieland Dumfries 237 D9
Airinis W Isles 304 E6
Airlie Angus 287 B7
Airlies Dumfries 236 D5
Airmyn E Yorks 199 B8
Airntully Perth 286 D4
Airor Highld 295 E9
Airth Falk 279 D7
Airthrey Castle Stirl 278 B6
Airton N Yorks 204 B4
Airyhassen Dumfries 236 E5
Airy Hill N Yorks 227 D7
Airyligg Dumfries 236 C4
Aisby Lincs 155 B10
Lincs 188 C5
Aisgernis W Isles 297 J3
Aish Devon 8 C3
Devon 8 D6
Aisholt Som 43 F7
Aiskew N Yorks 214 B5
Aislaby N Yorks 216 B5
N Yorks 227 D7
Stockton 225 C8
Aisthorpe Lincs 188 E6
Aith Orkney 314 E2
Shetland 312 D8
Shetland 313 H5
Aithnen Powys 148 E4
Aithsetter Shetland 313 K6
Aitkenhead S Ayrs 245 B8
Aitnoch Highld 301 F9
Akeld Northumb 263 D11
Akeley Bucks 102 D4
Akenham Suff 108 B2
Albany T&W 243 F7
Albaston Corn 12 G4
Alberbury Shrops 149 G7
Albert Town Pembs 72 B6
Albert Village Leics 152 F6
Albourne W Sus 36 D3
Albourne Green W Sus 36 D3
Albrighton Shrops 132 C6
Shrops 149 F9
Albro Castle Ceredig 92 B3
Alburgh Norf 142 F5
Albury Herts 105 G8
Sur 50 D5
Albury End Herts 105 G8
Albury Heath Sur 50 D5
Albyfield Cumb 240 G2
Alby Hill Norf 160 C3
Alcaig Highld 300 D5
Alcaston Shrops 131 F9
Alcester Dorset 30 C5
Warks 117 F11
Alcester Lane's End W Mid 133 G11
Alciston E Sus 23 D8
Alcombe Som 42 D3
Wilts 61 F10
Alconbury Cambs 122 B3
Alconbury Weston Cambs 122 B3
Aldbar Castle Angus 287 B9
Aldborough Norf 160 C3
N Yorks 215 F8
Aldborough Hatch London 68 B3
Aldbourne Wilts 63 D9
Aldbrough E Yorks 209 F10
Aldbrough St John N Yorks 224 C4
Aldbury Herts 85 C7
Aldcliffe Lancs 211 G9
Aldclune Perth 291 G11
Aldeburgh Suff 127 F9
Aldeby Norf 143 E8
Aldenham Herts 85 F10
Alderbrook E Sus 37 B8
Alderbury Wilts 31 B11
Aldercar Derbys 170 F6
Alderford Norf 160 F2
Alder Forest Gtr Man 184 B3
Alderholt Dorset 31 E10
Alderley Glos 80 G3
Alderley Edge Ches E 184 F4
Alderman's Green W Mid 135 G7
Aldermaston W Berks 64 F5
Aldermaston Soke W Berks 64 G6
Aldermaston Wharf W Berks 64 F6
Alderminster Warks 100 B4
Aldermoor Soton 32 D5
Alder Moor Staffs 152 D4

370 Bar–Ber

Barbreck Ho Argyll 275 C9
Barbridge Ches E 167 D10
Barbrook Devon 41 D8
Barby Northants 119 C10
Barby Nortoft Northants 119 C11
Barcaldine Argyll 289 E11
Barcelona Corn 6 E4
Barcheston Warks 100 D5
Barclose Cumb 239 E10
Barcombe E Sus 36 E6
Barcombe Cross E Sus 36 D6
Barcroft W Yorks 204 F6
Barden N Yorks 224 G2
Bardennoch Dumfries 246 E3
Barden Park Kent 52 D5
Barden Scale N Yorks 205 B7
Bardfield End Green Essex 106 E2
Bardfield Saling Essex 106 F3
Bardister Shetland 312 F5
Bardnabeinne Highld 309 K7
Bardney Lincs 173 B10
Bardon Leics 153 G8
Bardon Mill Northumb 241 E7
Bardowie E Dunb 277 G11
Bardown E Sus 37 B11
Bardrainney Invclyd 276 G6
Bardrishaig Argyll 275 B8
Bardsea Cumb 210 E6
Bardsey W Yorks 206 E3
Bardsley Gtr Man 196 G2
Bardwell Suff 125 C8
Bare Lancs 211 G9
Bare Ash Som 43 F9
Bareless Northumb 263 B9
Bar End Hants 33 B7
Barepot Cumb 228 F6
Bareppa Corn 3 D7
Barfad Argyll 275 G9
Dumfries 236 C5
Barford Norf 142 B2
Sur 49 F11
Warks 118 E5
Barford St John Oxon 101 E8
Barford St Martin Wilts 46 G5
Barford St Michael Oxon 101 E8
Barfrestone Kent 55 C9
Bargaly Dumfries 236 C6
Bargarran Renfs 277 G9
Bargate Derbys 170 F5
Bargeddie N Lnrk 268 C4
Bargoed Caerph 77 F10
Bargrennan Dumfries 236 B5
Barham Cambs 122 B2
Kent 55 C8
Suff 126 G2
Barharrow Dumfries 237 D8
Barhill Dumfries 237 C10
Bar Hill Cambs 123 E7
Staffs 168 G3
Barholm Dumfries 237 D7
Lincs 155 G11
Barkby Leics 136 B2
Barkby Thorpe Leics 136 B2
Barkers Green Shrops 149 D10
Barkers Hill Wilts 30 B6
Barkestone-le-Vale Leics 154 C5
Barkham Wokingham 65 F9
Barking London 68 C2
Suff 125 G11
Barkingside London 68 B2
Barking Tye Suff 125 G11
Barkisland W Yorks 196 D5
Barkla Shop Corn 4 E4
Barkston Lincs 172 G6
N Yorks 206 F5
Barkston Ash N Yorks 206 F5
Barkway Herts 105 D7
Barlake Som 45 D7
Barlanark Glasgow 268 C3
Barland Powys 114 E5
Barland Common Swansea 56 D5
Barlaston Staffs 151 B7
Barlavington W Sus 35 D7
Barlborough Derbys 187 F7
Barlby N Yorks 207 G8
Barlestone Leics 135 B8
Barley Herts 105 D7
Lancs 204 E2
Barleycroft End Herts 105 F8
Barley End Bucks 85 C7
Barley Green Lancs 204 E2
Barley Mow T&W 243 G7
Barleythorpe Rutland 136 B6
Barling Essex 70 B2
Barlings Lincs 189 G9
Barlow Derbys 186 G4
N Yorks 198 B6
T&W 242 E5
Barlow Moor Gtr Man 184 C4
Barmby Moor E Yorks 207 D11
Barmby on the Marsh E Yorks 199 B7
Barmer Norf 158 C6
Barming Heath Kent 53 B8
Barmolloch Argyll 275 D9
Bar Moor T&W 242 E4
Barmoor Castle Northumb 263 B11
Barmoor Lane End Northumb 264 B2
Barmouth / Abermaw Gwyn 146 F2
Barmpton Darl 224 B6
Barmston E Yorks 209 B9
T&W 243 F8
Barmulloch Glasgow 268 B2
Barnaby Green Suff 127 B9
Barnacabber Argyll 276 D3
Barnack Pboro 137 B11
Barnacle Warks 135 G7
Barnaline Argyll 275 B10
Barnard Castle Durham 223 B11
Barnard Gate Oxon 82 C6
Barnardiston Suff 106 B4
Barnard's Green Worcs 98 B5
Barnardtown Newport 59 B10
Barnbarroch Dumfries 237 D10
Barnbow Carr W Yorks 206 F3
Barnburgh S Yorks 198 G3
Barnby Suff 143 F9
Barnby Dun S Yorks 198 F6
Barnby in the Willows Notts 172 E5
Barnby Moor Notts 187 E11
Barncluith S Lnrk 268 E4
Barndennoch Dumfries 247 F9
Barne Barton Plym 7 D8
Barnehurst London 68 D4
Barnes Cray London 68 D4
Barnes Hall S Yorks 186 B4
Barnes Street Kent 52 D6
Barnet London 86 F2
Barnetby le Wold N Lincs 200 F5
Barnet Gate London 86 F2
Barnettbrook Worcs 117 B7
Barnett Brook Ches E 167 G10
Barney Norf 159 C9
Barnfield Kent 54 D2
Barnfields Hereford 97 C9
Staffs 169 D7
Barnham Suff 125 B7
W Sus 35 G7
Barnham Broom Norf 141 B11
Barnhead Angus 287 B10
Barnhill Ches W 167 E7
Dundee 287 D8
Moray 301 D11
Barnhills Dumfries 236 B1
Barningham Durham 223 C11
Suff 125 B9
Barningham Green Norf 160 C2
Barnmoor Green Warks 118 E3
Barnoldby le Beck NE Lincs 201 G8
Barnoldswick Lancs 204 D3
N Yorks 212 E3
Barns Borders 260 B6
Barnsbury London 67 C10
Barnsdale Rutland 137 B8
Barns Green W Sus 35 B10
Barnside W Yorks 197 F7
Barnsley Glos 81 D9
Shrops 132 E5
S Yorks 197 F10
Barnsole Kent 55 B9
Barnstaple Devon 40 G5
Barnston Essex 87 B10
Mers 182 E3
Barnstone Notts 154 B4
Barnt Green Worcs 117 C10
Barnton Ches W 183 F10
Edin 280 F3
Barnwell Northants 137 G10
Barnwell All Saints Northants 137 G10
Barnwell St Andrew Northants 137 F10
Barnwood Glos 80 B5
Barochreal Argyll 289 G10
Barons Cross Hereford 115 F9
Barr Highld 289 D8
S Ayrs 245 E7
Som 27 C11
Barra Castle Aberds 303 G7
Barrachan Dumfries 236 E5
Barrachnie Glasgow 268 C3
Barrack Aberds 303 E8
Barrack Hill Newport 59 B10
Barraer Dumfries 236 C5
Barraglom W Isles 304 E3
Barrahormid Argyll 275 E8
Barran Argyll 289 G10
Barranrioch Argyll 289 G10
Barrapol Argyll 288 E1
Barras Aberds 293 E10
Cumb 222 C6
Barrasford Northumb 241 C10
Barravullin Argyll 275 C9
Barr Common W Mid 133 D11
Barregarrow IoM 192 D4
Barrets Green Ches E 167 D9
Barrhead E Renf 267 D9
Barrhill S Ayrs 244 G6
Barrington Cambs 105 B7
Som 28 D5
Barripper Corn 2 B4
Barrmill N Ayrs 267 E7
Barrock Highld 310 B6
Barrock Ho Highld 310 C6
Barrow Glos 99 G7
Lancs 203 F10
Rutland 155 F7
Shrops 132 C3
Som 44 E5
Suff 124 E5
S Yorks 186 B5
Barroway Drove Norf 139 C11
Barrow Bridge Gtr Man 195 E7
Barrowburn Northumb 263 G9
Barrow Burn Northumb 263 G9
Barrowby Lincs 155 B7
Barrowcliff N Yorks 217 B10
Barrow Common N Som 60 F4
Barrowden Rutland 137 C8
Barrowford Lancs 204 F3
Barrow Green Kent 70 G3
Barrow Gurney N Som 60 F4
Barrow Hann N Lincs 200 C5
Barrow Haven N Lincs 200 C5
Barrowhill Kent 54 F6
Barrow Hill Derbys 186 F6
Dorset 18 B5
Barrow-in-Furness Cumb 210 F4
Barrow Island Cumb 210 F3
Barrowmore Estate Ches W 167 B7
Barrow Nook Lancs 194 G2
Barrows Green Ches E 167 D11
Cumb 211 B10
Notts 171 E7
Barrow's Green Mers 183 D8
Barrow Street Wilts 45 G10
Barrow upon Humber N Lincs 200 C5
Barrow upon Soar Leics 153 F11
Barrow upon Trent Derbys 153 D7
Barrow Vale Bath 60 G6
Barrow Wake Glos 80 B6
Barry Angus 287 D9
V Glam 58 F6
Barry Dock V Glam 58 F6
Barry Island V Glam 58 F6
Barsby Leics 154 G3
Barsham Suff 143 F7
Barshare E Ayrs 258 F3
Barstable Essex 69 B8
Barston W Mid 118 B4
Bartestree Hereford 97 C11
Barthol Chapel Aberds 303 F8
Bartholomew Green Essex 106 G4
Barthomley Ches E 168 E3
Bartington Ches W 183 F10
Bartley Hants 32 E4
Bartley Green W Mid 133 G10
Bartlow Cambs 105 B11
Barton Cambs 123 F8
Ches W 166 E6
Glos 80 B4
Glos 99 F11
IoW 20 D6
Lancs 193 F11
Lancs 202 F6
N Som 43 B11
N Yorks 224 D4
Oxon 83 D9
Torbay 9 B8
Warks 118 G2
Barton Abbey Oxon 101 G9
Barton Bendish Norf 140 B4
Barton Court Hereford 98 C4
Barton End Glos 80 F4
Barton Gate Devon 41 E7
Staffs 152 F3
Barton Green Staffs 152 F3
Barton Hartshorn Bucks 102 E2
Barton Hill Bristol 60 E6
N Yorks 216 G4
Barton in Fabis Notts 153 C10
Barton in the Beans Leics 135 B7
Barton-le-Clay C Beds 103 E11
Barton-le-Street N Yorks 216 E4
Barton-le-Willows N Yorks 216 G4
Barton Mills Suff 124 C4
Barton on Sea Hants 19 C10
Barton on the Heath Warks 100 E5
Barton St David Som 44 G4
Barton Seagrave Northants 121 B7
Bartonsham Hereford 97 D10
Barton Stacey Hants 48 E2
Barton Town Devon 41 E7
Barton Turf Norf 161 E7
Barton Turn Staffs 152 F4
Barton-under-Needwood Staffs 152 F3
Barton-upon-Humber N Lincs 200 C4
Barton Upon Irwell Gtr Man 184 B3
Barton Waterside N Lincs 200 C4
Barugh S Yorks 197 F10
Barugh Green S Yorks 197 F10
Barway Cambs 123 B10
Barwell Leics 135 D8
London 67 G7
Barwick Devon 25 F9
Herts 86 B5
Som 29 E9
Barwick in Elmet W Yorks 206 F3
Baschurch Shrops 149 E8
Bascote Warks 119 E8
Bascote Heath Warks 119 E7
Base Green Suff 125 E10
Basford Shrops 131 F7
Staffs 168 F5
Basford Green Staffs 169 E7
Bashall Eaves Lancs 203 E9
Bashley Hants 19 B10
Bashley Park Hants 19 B10
Basildon Essex 69 B8
Basingstoke Hants 48 C6
Baslow Derbys 186 G3
Bason Bridge Som 43 D10
Bassaleg Newport 59 B9
Bassenthwaite Cumb 229 E10
Bassett Soton 32 D6
S Yorks 186 E3
Bassett Green Soton 32 D6
Bassingbourn Cambs 104 C6
Bassingfield Notts 154 B2
Bassingham Lincs 172 C6
Bassingthorpe Lincs 155 D9
Bassus Green Herts 104 F6
Basta Shetland 312 D7
Basted Kent 52 B6
Baston Lincs 156 G2
Bastonford Worcs 116 G6
Bastwick Norf 161 F8
Baswich Staffs 151 E8
Baswick Steer E Yorks 209 D7
Batavaime Stirl 285 D8
Batch Som 43 B10
Batchcott Shrops 115 C9
Batchfields Hereford 98 B3
Batchley Worcs 117 D10
Batchworth Herts 85 G9
Batchworth Heath Herts 85 G9
Batcombe Dorset 29 G10
Som 45 F7
Bate Heath Ches E 183 F11
Bateman's Green Worcs 117 B11
Bateman's Hill Pembs 73 E8
Batemoor S Yorks 186 E5
Batford Herts 85 B10
Bath Bath 61 F8
Bathampton Bath 61 F9
Bathealton Som 27 C9
Batheaston Bath 61 F9
Bathford Bath 61 F9
Bathgate W Loth 269 B9
Bathley Notts 172 D3
Bathpool Corn 11 G11
Som 28 B3
Bath Side Essex 108 E5
Bath Vale Ches E 168 C5
Bathville W Loth 269 B8
Bathway Som 44 C5
Bathwick Bath 61 F9
Batlers Green Herts 85 F11
Batley W Yorks 197 C8
Batley Carr W Yorks 197 C8
Batsford Glos 100 E3
Batson Devon 9 G9
Batsworthy Devon 26 D4
Batten's Green Som 28 D3
Battenton Green Worcs 116 D6
Battersby N Yorks 225 D11
Battersea London 67 D9
Battisborough Cross Devon 7 F11
Battisford Suff 125 G11
Battisford Tye Suff 125 G10
Battle E Sus 38 D2
Powys 95 E10
Battledown Glos 99 G9
Battledown Cross Devon 25 F7
Battlefield Shrops 149 F10
Battle Hill T&W 243 D8
Battlesbridge Essex 88 G3
Battlescombe Glos 80 D6
Battlesden C Beds 103 F9
Battlesea Green Suff 126 B4
Battleton Som 26 B6
Battlies Green Suff 125 E7
Battram Leics 135 B8
Battramsley Hants 20 B2
Battramsley Cross Hants 20 B2
Batt's Corner Hants 49 E10
Battyeford W Yorks 197 C7
Batworthy Devon 13 D10
Bauds of Cullen Moray 302 C4
Baugh Argyll 288 E2
Baughton Worcs 99 C7
Baughurst Hants 48 B5
Baulking Oxon 82 G4
Baumber Lincs 190 G2
Baunton Glos 81 E8
Baverstock Wilts 46 G4
Bawburgh Norf 142 B3
Bawdeswell Norf 159 E10
Bawdrip Som 43 F10
Bawdsey Suff 108 C6
Bawsey Norf 158 F3
Bawtry S Yorks 187 C11
Baxenden Lancs 195 B9
Baxterley Warks 134 D5
Baxter's Green Suff 124 F5
Bay Dorset 30 B4
Highld 298 D2
Baybridge Hants 33 C8
Northumb 241 G11
Baycliff Cumb 210 E5
Baydon Wilts 63 D9
Bayford Herts 86 D4
Som 30 B2
Bay Gate Lancs 203 D11
Bay Horse Lancs 202 C5
Bayles Cumb 231 C10
Bayley's Hill Kent 52 C4
Baylham Suff 126 G2
Baylis Green Worcs 117 C11
Baynard's Green Oxon 101 F10
Baynhall Worcs 99 B7
Baysham Hereford 97 F11
Bayston Hill Shrops 131 B9
Bayswater London 67 C9
Baythorne End Essex 106 C4
Baythorpe Lincs 174 G2
Bayton Worcs 116 C3
Bayton Common Worcs 116 C4
Bay View Kent 70 E4
Bayworth Oxon 83 E8
Beach Highld 289 D9
S Glos 61 E8
Beachampton Bucks 102 D5
Beachamwell Norf 140 B5
Beachans Moray 301 E10
Beacharr Argyll 255 C7
Beachborough Kent 55 F7
Beach Hay Worcs 116 C4
Beachlands E Sus 23 E11
Beachley Glos 79 G9
Beacon Corn 2 B5
Devon 27 F11
Devon 28 F2
Beacon Down E Sus 37 C9
Beacon End Essex 107 G9
Beaconhill Northumb 243 B7
Beacon Hill Bath 61 F9
Bucks 84 G6
Cumb 210 E4
Dorset 18 C5
Essex 88 C5
Kent 53 G10
Notts 172 E4
Suff 108 B4
Sur 49 F11
Beacon Lough T&W 243 F7
Beacon's Bottom Bucks 84 F3
Beaconsfield Bucks 66 B2
Beaconside Staffs 151 E8
Beacrabhaic W Isles 305 J3
Beadlam N Yorks 216 C3
Beadlow C Beds 104 D2
Beadnell Northumb 264 D6
Beaford Devon 25 E9
Beal Northumb 273 G11
N Yorks 198 B4
Bealach Highld 289 D11
Bealach Maim Argyll 275 E10
Bealbury Corn 7 B7
Beal's Green Kent 53 G9
Bealsmill Corn 12 F3
Beambridge Shrops 131 F10
Beam Bridge Som 27 D10
Beam Hill Staffs 152 D4
Beamhurst Staffs 151 B11
Beamhurst Lane Staffs 151 B11
Beaminster Dorset 29 G7
Beamish Durham 242 G6
Beamond End Bucks 84 F6
Beamsley N Yorks 205 C7
Bean Kent 68 E5
Beanacre Wilts 62 F2
Beancross Falk 279 F8
Beanhill M Keynes 103 D7
Beanley Northumb 264 F3
Beansburn E Ayrs 257 B10
Beanthwaite Cumb 210 C4
Beaquoy Orkney 314 D3
Bear Cross Bmouth 19 B7
Beard Hill Som 44 E6
Beardly Batch Som 44 E6
Beardwood Blkburn 195 B7
Beare Devon 27 G7
Beare Green Sur 51 E7
Bearley Warks 118 E3
Bearley Cross Warks 118 E3
Bearnus Argyll 288 E5
Bearpark Durham 233 C10
Bearsbridge Northumb 241 F7
Bearsden E Dunb 277 G10
Bearsted Kent 53 B9
Bearstone Shrops 150 B4
Bearwood Hereford 115 F7
Poole 18 B6
W Mid 133 F10
Beasley Staffs 168 F4
Beattock Dumfries 248 C3
Beauchamp Roding Essex 87 C9
Beauchief S Yorks 186 E4
Beauclerc Northumb 242 E2
Beaudesert Warks 118 D3
Beaufort Bl Gwent 77 C11
Beaufort Castle Highld 300 E5
Beaulieu Hants 32 G5
Beaulieu Wood Dorset 30 F2
Beauly Highld 300 E5
Beaumaris Anglesey 179 F10
Beaumont Cumb 239 F8
Essex 108 G3
Windsor 66 E3
Beaumont Hill Darl 224 B5
Beaumont Leys Leicester 135 B11
Beausale Warks 118 C4
Beauvale Notts 171 F8
Beauworth Hants 33 B9
Beavan's Hill Hereford 98 G3
Beaworthy Devon 12 B5
Beazley End Essex 106 F4
Bebington Mers 182 E4
Bebside Northumb 253 G7
Beccles Suff 143 E8
Becconsall Lancs 194 C2
Beck Bottom Cumb 210 C5
W Yorks 197 C10
Beckbury Shrops 132 C5
Beckces Cumb 230 F4
Beckenham London 67 F11
Beckermet Cumb 219 D10
Beckermonds N Yorks 213 C7
Beckery Som 44 F3
Beckett End Norf 140 D5
Beckfoot Cumb 220 E3
Cumb 229 B7
Beck Foot Cumb 222 F2
W Yorks 205 F8
Beckford Worcs 99 D9
Beckhampton Wilts 62 F5
Beck Head Cumb 211 C8
Beck Hole N Yorks 226 E6
Beck Houses Cumb 221 F11
Beckingham Lincs 172 E5
Notts 188 D3
Beckington Som 45 C10
Beckjay Shrops 115 B7
Beckley E Sus 38 C5
Hants 19 B10
Oxon 83 C9
Beckley Furnace E Sus 38 C4
Beck Row Suff 124 B3
Beckside Cumb 212 B2
Beck Side Cumb 210 C4
Cumb 211 C7
Beckton London 68 C2
Beckwith N Yorks 205 C11
Beckwithshaw N Yorks 205 C11
Becontree London 68 B3
Bedale N Yorks 214 B5
Bedburn Durham 233 E8
Bedchester Dorset 30 D5
Beddau Rhondda 58 B5
Beddgelert Gwyn 163 F9
Beddingham E Sus 36 F6
Beddington London 67 G10
Beddington Corner London 67 F9
Bedfield Suff 126 D4
Bedford Beds 121 G11
Gtr Man 183 B11
Bedford Park London 67 D8
Bedgebury Cross Kent 53 G8
Bedgrove Bucks 84 C4
Bedham W Sus 35 C8
Bedhampton Hants 22 B2
Bedingfield Suff 126 D3
Bedingham Green Norf 142 E5
Bedlam N Yorks 214 G5
Som 45 D9
Bedlam Street W Sus 36 D3
Bedlar's Green Essex 105 G10
Bedlington Northumb 253 G7
Bedlington Station Northumb 253 G7
Bedlinog M Tydf 77 E9
Bedminster Bristol 60 E5
Bedminster Down Bristol 60 F5
Bedmond Herts 85 E9
Bednall Staffs 151 F9
Bednall Head Staffs 151 F9
Bedrule Borders 262 F4
Bedstone Shrops 115 B7
Bedwas Caerph 59 B7
Bedwell Herts 104 G4
Wrex 166 F5
Bedwellty Caerph 77 E11
Bedwellty Pits Bl Gwent 77 D11
Bedwlwyn Wrex 148 B4
Bedworth Warks 135 F7
Bedworth Heath Warks 134 F6
Bedworth Woodlands Warks 134 F6
Bed-y-coedwr Gwyn 146 D4
Beeby Leics 136 B3
Beech Hants 49 F7
Staffs 151 B7
Beechcliff Staffs 151 B7
Beechcliffe W Yorks 205 E7
Beechen Cliff Bath 61 G9
Beech Hill Gtr Man 194 F5
W Berks 65 G7
Beechingstoke Wilts 46 B5
Beech Lanes W Mid 133 F10
Beechwood Halton 183 E8
Newport 59 B10
W Mid 118 B5
W Yorks 206 F2
Beecroft C Beds 103 G10
Beedon W Berks 64 D3
Beedon Hill W Berks 64 D3
Beeford E Yorks 209 C8
Beeley Derbys 170 B3
Beelsby NE Lincs 201 G8
Beenham W Berks 64 F5
Beenham's Heath Windsor 65 D10
Beenham Stocks W Berks 64 F5
Beeny Corn 11 C8
Beer Devon 15 D10
Som 44 G2
Beercrocombe Som 28 C4
Beer Hackett Dorset 29 E9
Beesands Devon 8 G6
Beesby Lincs 191 E7
Beeslack Midloth 270 C4
Beeson Devon 8 G6
Beeston C Beds 104 B3
Ches W 167 D8
Norf 159 F8
Notts 153 B10
W Yorks 205 G11
Beeston Hill W Yorks 205 G11
Beeston Park Side W Yorks 197 B9
Beeston Regis Norf 177 E11
Beeston Royds W Yorks 205 G11
Beeston St Lawrence Norf 160 E6
Beeswing Dumfries 237 C10
Beetham Cumb 211 D9
Som 28 E3
Beetley Norf 159 F9
Beffcote Staffs 150 F6
Began Cardiff 59 C8
Begbroke Oxon 83 C7
Begdale Cambs 139 B9
Begelly Pembs 73 D10
Beggar Hill Essex 87 E10
Beggarington Hill W Yorks 197 C9
Beggars Ash Hereford 98 D4
Beggars Bush W Sus 35 F11
Beggar's Bush Powys 114 E5
Beggars Pound V Glam 58 F4
Beggearn Huish Som 42 F4
Beguildy Powys 114 B3
Beighton Norf 143 B7
S Yorks 186 E6
Beighton Hill Derbys 170 E3
Beili-glas Mon 78 C4
Beitearsaig W Isles 305 G1
Beith N Ayrs 266 E6
Bekesbourne Kent 55 B7
Bekesbourne Hill Kent 55 B7
Belah Cumb 239 F9
Belan Powys 130 C4
Belaugh Norf 160 F5
Belbins Hants 32 C5
Belbroughton Worcs 117 B8
Belchalwell Dorset 30 F3
Belchalwell Street Dorset 30 F3
Belchamp Otten Essex 106 C6
Belchamp St Paul Essex 106 C5
Belchamp Walter Essex 106 C6
Belcher's Bar Leics 135 B8
Belchford Lincs 190 F3
Beleybridge Fife 287 F9
Belfield Gtr Man 196 E2
Belford Northumb 264 C4
Belgrano Conwy 181 F7
Belgrave Ches W 166 C5
Leicester 135 B11
Staffs 134 C4
Belgravia London 67 D9
Belhaven E Loth 282 F3
Belhelvie Aberds 293 B11
Belhinnie Aberds 302 G4
Bellabeg Aberds 292 B5
Bellamore S Ayrs 244 F6
Bellanoch Argyll 275 D8
Bellanrigg Borders 260 B6
Bellasize E Yorks 199 B10
Bellaty Angus 286 B6
Bell Bar Herts 86 D3
Bell Busk N Yorks 204 B4
Bell Common Essex 86 E6
Belleau Lincs 190 F6
Belle Eau Park Notts 171 D11
Belle Green S Yorks 197 F11
Bellehiglash Moray 301 F11
Belle Isle W Yorks 197 B10
Bell End Worcs 117 B8
Bellerby N Yorks 224 G2
Belle Vale Mers 182 D6
W Mid 133 G9
Bellever Devon 13 F9
Bellevue Worcs 117 C9
Belle Vue Cumb 229 E8
Cumb 239 F9
Gtr Man 184 B5
Shrops 149 G9
S Yorks 198 G5
W Yorks 197 D10
Bellfield E Ayrs 257 B10
Bellfields Sur 50 C3
Bell Green London 67 E11
W Mid 135 G7
Bell Heath Worcs 117 B9
Bell Hill Hants 34 C2
Belliehill Angus 293 G7
Bellingdon Bucks 84 D6
Bellingham London 67 E11
Northumb 251 G8
Bellmount Norf 157 E10
Belloch Argyll 255 D7
Bellochantuy Argyll 255 D7
Bell o' th' Hill Ches W 167 F8
Bellsbank E Ayrs 245 C11
Bell's Close T&W 242 E5
Bell's Corner Suff 107 D9
Bellshill N Lnrk 268 C4
Northumb 264 C4
Bellside N Lnrk 268 D6
Bellsmyre W Dunb 277 F8
Bellspool Borders 260 B5
Bellsquarry W Loth 269 C10
Bells Yew Green E Sus 52 F6
Belluton Bath 60 G6
Bellyeoman Fife 280 D2
Belmaduthy Highld 300 D6
Belmesthorpe Rutland 155 G10
Belmont Blkburn 195 D7
Durham 234 C2
E Sus 38 E4
Harrow 67 G9
Oxon 63 B11
S Ayrs 257 E8
Shetland 312 C7
Sutton 85 G11
Belnacraig Aberds 292 B5
Belnagarrow Moray 302 E3
Belnie Lincs 156 C5
Belowda Corn 5 C9
Belper Derbys 170 F4
Belper Lane End Derbys 170 F4
Belph Derbys 187 F8
Belsay Northumb 242 B4
Belses Borders 262 D3
Belsford Devon 8 D5
Belsize Herts 85 E8
Belstead Suff 108 C2
Belston S Ayrs 257 E9
Belstone Devon 13 C8
Belstone Corner Devon 13 B8
Belthorn Blkburn 195 C8
Beltinge Kent 71 F7
Beltingham Northumb 241 E7
Beltoft N Lincs 199 F10
Belton Leics 153 E8
Lincs 155 B8
N Lincs 199 F9
Norf 143 C9
Belton in Rutland Rutland 136 C6
Beltring Kent 53 D7
Belts of Collonach Aberds 293 D8
Belvedere London 68 D3
W Loth 269 B9
Belvoir Leics 154 C6
Bembridge IoW 21 D8
Bemersyde Borders 262 C3
Bemerton Wilts 46 G6
Bemerton Heath Wilts 46 G6
Bempton E Yorks 218 E3
Benacre Suff 143 G10
Ben Alder Lodge Highld 291 F7
Ben Armine Lodge Highld 309 H7
Benbuie Dumfries 246 D6
Ben Casgro W Isles 304 F6
Benchill Gtr Man 184 D4
Bencombe Glos 80 F3
Benderloch Argyll 289 F11
Bendish Herts 104 G3
Bendronaig Lodge Highld 299 F10
Benenden Kent 53 G10
Benfield Dumfries 236 C5
Benfieldside Durham 242 G3
Bengal Pembs 91 E9
Bengate Norf 160 D6
Bengeo Herts 86 C4
Bengeworth Worcs 99 C10
Bengrove Glos 99 E9
Benhall Glos 99 G8
Benhall Green Suff 127 E7
Benhall Street Suff 127 E7
Benhilton London 67 F9
Benholm Aberds 293 G10
Beningbrough N Yorks 206 B6
Benington Herts 104 G5
Lincs 174 F5
Benington Sea End Lincs 174 F6
Benllech Anglesey 179 E8
Benmore Argyll 276 E2
Stirl 285 E8
Benmore Lodge Argyll 289 F7
Highld 309 H3
Bennacott Corn 11 C11
Bennah Devon 14 E2
Bennan N Ayrs 255 E10
Bennane Lea S Ayrs 244 F3
Bennetland E Yorks 199 B10
Bennetsfield Highld 300 D6
Bennett End Bucks 84 F3
Bennetts End Herts 85 D9
Benniworth Lincs 190 E2
Benover Kent 53 D8
Ben Rhydding W Yorks 205 D8
Bensham T&W 242 E6
Benslie N Ayrs 266 G6
Benson Oxon 83 G10
Benston Shetland 313 H6
Bent Aberds 293 F8
Benter Som 44 D6
Bentfield Bury Essex 105 F9
Bentfield Green Essex 105 F10
Bentgate Gtr Man 196 E2
Bent Gate Lancs 195 C9
Benthall Northumb 264 D6
Shrops 132 C3
Bentham Glos 80 B6
Benthoul Aberdeen 293 C10
Bentilee Stoke 168 F6
Bentlass Pembs 73 E7
Bentlawnt Shrops 130 C6
Bentley Essex 87 F9
E Yorks 208 F6
Hants 49 E9
Suff 108 D2
S Yorks 198 F5
Warks 134 D5
W Mid 133 D9
Worcs 117 D9
Bentley Common Warks 134 D5
Bentley Heath Herts 86 F2
W Mid 118 B3
Bentley Rise S Yorks 198 G5
Benton Devon 41 F7
Benton Green W Mid 118 B5
Bentpath Dumfries 249 E8
Bents W Loth 269 C9
Bents Head W Yorks 205 F7
Bentwichen Devon 41 G8
Bentworth Hants 49 E7
Benvie Dundee 287 D7
Benville Dorset 29 G8
Benwell T&W 242 E6
Benwick Cambs 138 E6
Beobridge Shrops 132 E5
Beoley Worcs 117 D11
Beoraidbeg Highld 295 F8
Bepton W Sus 34 D5
Berden Essex 105 F9
Bere Alston Devon 7 B8
Berechurch Essex 107 G9
Bere Ferrers Devon 7 C9
Berefold Aberds 303 F9
Berepper Corn 2 E5
Bere Regis Dorset 18 C2
Bergh Apton Norf 142 C6
Berghers Hill Bucks 66 B2
Berhill Som 44 F2
Berinsfield Oxon 83 F9
Berkeley Glos 79 F11
Berkeley Heath Glos 79 F11
Berkeley Road Glos 80 E2

Berkeley Towers
Ches E 167 E11
Berkhamsted Herts 85 D7
Berkley Som 45 D10
Berkley Down Som 45 D9
Berkley Marsh Som 45 D10
Berkswell W Mid 118 B4
Bermondsey London 67 D10
Bermuda Warks 135 F7
Bernards Heath
Herts 85 D11
Bernera Highld 295 C10
Berner's Cross
Devon 25 F10
Berner's Hill E Sus 53 G8
Berners Roding
Essex 87 D10
Bernice Argyll 276 C2
Bernisdale Highld 298 D4
Berrick Salome
Oxon 83 G10
Berriedale Highld 311 G5
Berrier Cumb 230 F3
Berriew / Aberriw
Powys 130 C3
Berrington
Northumb 273 G10
Shrops 131 B10
Worcs 115 D11
Berrington Green
Worcs 115 D11
Berriowbridge Corn 11 F11
Berrow Som 43 C10
Worcs 98 E5
Berrow Green
Worcs 116 F4
Berry Swansea 56 D3
Berry Brow
W Yorks 196 E6
Berry Cross Devon 25 E7
Berry Down Cross
Devon 40 E5
Berryfield Wilts 61 G11
Berrygate Hill
E Yorks 201 C8
Berry Hill Glos 79 C9
Pembs 91 C11
Stoke 168 F6
Worcs 117 E7
Berryhillock Moray 302 C5
Berrylands London 67 F7
Berry Moor S Yorks 197 G9
Berrynarbor Devon 40 D5
Berry Pomeroy Devon 8 C6
Berrysbridge Devon 26 G6
Berry's Green London 52 B2
Bersham Wrex 166 F4
Berstane Orkney 314 E4
Berth-ddu Flint 166 B2
Berthengam Flint 181 F10
Berwick E Sus 23 D8
Kent 54 F6
S Glos 60 C5
Berwick Bassett
Wilts 62 E5
Berwick Hill
Northumb 242 B5
Berwick Hills Mbro 225 B10
Berwick St James
Wilts 46 F5
Berwick St John
Wilts 30 C6
Berwick St Leonard
Wilts 46 G2
Berwick-upon-Tweed
Northumb 273 E9
Berwick Wharf
Shrops 149 G10
Berwyn Denb 165 G11
Bescaby Leics 154 D6
Bescar Lancs 193 E11
Bescot W Mid 133 D10
Besford Shrops 149 E11
Worcs 99 C8
Bessacarr S Yorks 198 G6
Bessels Green Kent 52 B4
Bessels Leigh Oxon 83 E7
Besses o' th' Barn
Gtr Man 195 F10
Bessingby E Yorks 218 F3
Bessingham Norf 160 B3
Best Beech Hill
E Sus 52 G6
Besthorpe Norf 141 D11
Notts 172 C4
Bestwood
Nottingham 171 G9
Bestwood Village
Notts 171 F9
Beswick E Yorks 208 D6
Gtr Man 184 B5
Betchcott Shrops 131 D8
Betchton Heath
Ches E 168 C3
Betchworth Sur 51 D8
Bethania Ceredig 111 E11
Gwyn 163 E10
Gwyn 164 F2
Bethany Corn 6 D6
Bethel Anglesey 178 G5
Corn 5 E10
Gwyn 147 B9
Gwyn 163 B8
Bethelnie Aberds 303 F7
Bethersden Kent 54 E2
Bethesda Gwyn 163 B10
Pembs 73 B9
Bethlehem Carms 94 F3
Bethnal Green
London 67 C10
Betley Staffs 168 F3
Betley Common
Staffs 168 F2
Betsham Kent 68 E6
Betteshanger Kent 55 C10
Bettiscombe Dorset 16 B3
Bettisfield Wrex 149 B9
Betton Shrops 130 C6
Shrops 150 B3
Betton Strange
Shrops 131 B10
Bettws Bridgend 58 B2
Mon 78 B3
Newport 78 G3
Bettws Cedewain
Powys 130 D2
Bettws Gwerfil Goch
Denb 165 F8
Bettws Ifan Ceredig 92 B6
Bettws Newydd Mon 78 D5
Bettws-y-crwyn
Shrops 130 G4
Bettyhill Highld 308 C7
Betws Bridgend 57 D11
Carms 75 C10
Betws Bledrws
Ceredig 111 G11
Betws-Garmon
Gwyn 163 D8
Betws Ifan Ceredig 92 B6
Betws-y-Coed
Conwy 164 D4
Betws-yn-Rhos
Conwy 180 G6
Beulah Ceredig 92 B5
Powys 113 G8
Bevendean Brighton 36 F4
Bevercotes Notts 187 G11
Bevere Worcs 116 F6
Beverley E Yorks 208 F6
Beverston Glos 80 G5
Bevington Glos 79 F11
Bewaldeth Cumb 229 E10
Bewbush W Sus 51 F8
Bewcastle Cumb 240 C3
Bewdley Worcs 116 B5
Bewerley N Yorks 214 G3
Bewholme E Yorks 209 C9
Bewley Common
Wilts 62 F2
Bewlie Borders 262 D3
Bewlie Mains
Borders 262 D3
Bewsey Warr 183 D9
Bexfield Norf 159 D10
Bexhill E Sus 38 F2
Bexley London 68 E3
Bexleyheath London 68 D3
Bexleyhill W Sus 34 B6
Bexon Kent 53 B11
Bexwell Norf 140 C2
Beyton Suff 125 E8
Beyton Green Suff 125 E8
Bhalasaigh W Isles 304 E3
Bhaltos W Isles 304 E2
Bhatarsaigh
W Isles 297 M2
Bhlàraidh Highld 290 B5
Bibstone S Glos 79 G11
Bibury Glos 81 D10
Bicester Oxon 101 G11
Bickenhall Som 28 D3
Bickenhill W Mid 134 G3
Bicker Lincs 156 B4
Bicker Bar Lincs 156 B4
Bicker Gauntlet
Lincs 156 B4
Bickershaw
Gtr Man 194 G6
Bickerstaffe Lancs 194 G2
Bickerton Ches E 167 E8
Devon 9 G11
N Yorks 206 C5
Bickford Staffs 151 G7
Bickham Som 42 E3
Bickingcott Devon 26 B3
Bickington Devon 13 G11
Devon 40 G4
Bickleigh Devon 7 C10
Devon 26 F6
Bickleton Devon 40 G4
Bickley Ches W 167 F8
London 68 F2
Worcs 116 C2
Bickley Moss
Ches W 167 F8
Bickley Town
Ches W 167 F8
Bickleywood
Ches W 167 F8
Bickmarsh Warks 100 B2
Bicknacre Essex 88 E3
Bicknoller Som 42 F6
Bicknor Kent 53 B11
Bickton Hants 31 E11
Bicton Hereford 115 E9
Pembs 72 D4
Shrops 130 G5
Shrops 149 F8
Bicton Heath
Shrops 149 G9
Bidborough Kent 52 E5
Bidden Hants 49 D8
Biddenden Kent 53 F11
Biddenden Green
Kent 53 E11
Biddenham Beds 103 B10
Biddestone Wilts 61 E11
Biddick T&W 243 F8
Biddick Hall T&W 243 E9
Biddisham Som 43 C11
Biddlesden Bucks 102 C2
Biddlestone
Northumb 251 B11
Biddulph Staffs 168 D5
Biddulph Moor
Staffs 168 D6
Bideford Devon 25 B7
Bidford-on-Avon
Warks 118 G2
Bidlake Devon 12 D5
Bidston Mers 182 C3
Bidston Hill Mers 182 D3
Bidwell C Beds 103 G10
Bielby E Yorks 207 E11
Bieldside Aberdeen 293 C10
Bierley IoW 20 F6
W Yorks 205 G9
Bierton Bucks 84 B4
Bigbury Devon 8 F3
Bigbury-on-Sea
Devon 8 G3
Bigby Lincs 200 F5
Bigfrith Windsor 65 C11
Biggar Cumb 210 F3
S Lnrk 260 B2
Biggar Road N Lnrk 268 C5
Biggin Derbys 169 D11
Derbys 170 F3
N Yorks 206 F6
Thurrock 69 D7
Biggings Shetland 313 G3
Biggin Hill London 52 B2
Biggleswade
C Beds 104 C3
Bighouse Highld 310 C2
Bighton Hants 48 G6
Biglands Cumb 239 G7
Big Mancot Flint 166 B4
Bignall End Staffs 168 E4
Bignor W Sus 35 E7
Bigods Essex 106 G2
Bigram Stirl 285 G10
Bigrigg Cumb 219 C10
Big Sand Highld 299 B7
Bigswell Orkney 314 E3
Bigton Shetland 313 L5
Bilberry Corn 5 C10
Bilborough
Nottingham 171 G8
Bilbrook Som 42 E4
Staffs 133 C7
Bilbrough N Yorks 206 D6
Bilbster Highld 310 D6
Bilby Notts 187 E10
Bildershaw
Durham 233 G10
Bildeston Suff 107 B9
Billacombe Plym 7 E10
Billacott Corn 11 C11
Billericay Essex 87 G11
Billesdon Leics 136 C4
Billesley Warks 118 F2
W Mid 133 G11
Billesley Common
W Mid 133 G11
Billingborough
Lincs 156 C2
Billinge Mers 194 G4
Billingford Norf 126 B3
Norf 159 E10
Billingham Stockton 234 G5
Billinghay Lincs 173 E11
Billingley S Yorks 198 G2
Billingshurst W Sus 35 B9
Billingsley Shrops 132 F4
Billington C Beds 103 G8
Lancs 203 F10
Staffs 151 E7
Billockby Norf 161 G8
Bill Quay T&W 243 E7
Billy Mill T&W 243 D8
Billy Row Durham 233 D9
Bilmarsh Shrops 149 D9
Bilsborrow Lancs 202 F6
Bilsby Lincs 191 F7
Bilsby Field Lincs 191 F7
Bilsdon Devon 14 C2
Bilsham W Sus 35 G7
Bilsington Kent 54 G4
Bilson Green Glos 79 C11
Bilsthorpe Notts 171 C10
Bilsthorpe Moor
Notts 171 D11
Bilston Midloth 270 C5
W Mid 133 D9
Bilstone Leics 135 B7
Bilting Kent 54 D5
Bilton E Yorks 209 G9
Northumb 264 G6
N Yorks 206 B2
Warks 119 C9
Bilton Haggs
N Yorks 206 D5
Bilton in Ainsty
N Yorks 206 D5
Bimbister Orkney 314 E3
Binbrook Lincs 190 C2
Binchester Blocks
Durham 233 E10
Bincombe Dorset 17 E9
Som 43 F7
Bindal Highld 311 L3
Bindon Som 27 C10
Binegar Som 44 D6
Bines Green W Sus 35 D11
Binfield Brack 65 E10
Binfield Heath Oxon 65 D8
Bingfield Northumb 241 C11
Bingham Edin 280 G6
Notts 154 B4
Bingley W Yorks 205 F8
Bings Heath
Shrops 149 F10
Binham Norf 159 B9
Binley Hants 48 C2
W Mid 119 B7
Binley Woods
Warks 119 B7
Binnegar Dorset 18 D3
Binniehill Falk 279 G7
Binscombe Sur 50 D3
Binsey Oxon 83 D7
Binsoe N Yorks 214 D4
Binstead Hants 49 E9
IoW 21 C7
Binsted Hants 49 E9
W Sus 35 F7
Binton Warks 118 G2
Bintree Norf 159 E10
Binweston Shrops 130 C6
Birch Essex 88 B6
Gtr Man 195 F11
Birch Acre Worcs 117 C11
Birchall Hereford 98 D3
Staffs 169 E7
Bircham Newton
Norf 158 C5
Bircham Tofts Norf 158 C5
Birchan Coppice
Worcs 116 C6
Birchanger Essex 105 G10
Birch Berrow Worcs 116 E4
Birchburn N Ayrs 255 E10
Birch Cross Staffs 152 C2
Birchden E Sus 52 F4
Birchencliffe
W Yorks 196 D6
Birchend Hereford 98 C3
Birchendale Staffs 151 B11
Bircher Hereford 115 D9
Birches Green
W Mid 134 E2
Birches Head Stoke 168 F5
Birchett's Green
E Sus 53 G7
Birchfield Highld 301 G9
W Mid 133 E11
Birch Green Essex 88 B6
Herts 86 C3
Lancs 194 F3
Worcs 99 B7
Birchgrove Cardiff 59 D7
E Sus 36 B6
Swansea 57 B8
Birchhall Corner
Essex 107 E10
Birch Heath
Ches W 167 C8
Birch Hill Brack 65 F11
Ches W 183 G8
Birchill Devon 28 G4
Birchills W Mid 133 D10
Birchington Kent 71 F9
Birchley Heath
Warks 134 E5
Birchmoor Warks 134 C5
Birchmoor Green
C Beds 103 E8
Bircholt Forstal Kent 54 E5
Birchover Derbys 170 C2
Birch Vale Derbys 185 D8
Birchwood Herts 86 D2
Lincs 172 B6
Som 28 E2
Warr 183 C10
Birchy Hill Hants 19 B11
Bircotes Notts 187 C10
Birdbrook Essex 106 C4
Birdbush Wilts 30 C6
Birdfield Argyll 275 D10
Birdforth N Yorks 215 D9
Birdham W Sus 22 D4
Birdholme Derbys 170 B5
Birdingbury Warks 119 D8
Birdlip Glos 80 C6
Birdsall N Yorks 216 F6
Birds Edge W Yorks 197 F8
Birds End Suff 124 E5
Birdsgreen Shrops 132 F5
Birds Green Essex 87 D9
Birdsmoorgate
Dorset 28 G5
Birdston E Dunb 278 F3
Bird Street Suff 125 G10
Birdwell S Yorks 197 G10
Birdwood Glos 80 B2
Birgham Borders 263 B7
Birichen Highld 309 K7
Birkacre Lancs 194 D5
Birkby Cumb 229 D7
N Yorks 224 E6
W Yorks 196 D6
Birkdale Mers 193 D10
Birkenbog Aberds 302 C5
Birkenhead Mers 182 D4
Birkenhills Aberds 303 E7
Birkenshaw N Lnrk 268 C3
S Lnrk 268 F5
W Yorks 197 B8
Birkenshaw Bottoms
W Yorks 197 B8
Birkenside Borders 271 G11
Birkett Mire Cumb 230 G2
Birkhall Aberds 292 D5
Birkhill Angus 287 D7
Borders 260 F6
Borders 271 G11
Birkholme Lincs 155 E9
Birkhouse W Yorks 197 C7
Birkin N Yorks 198 B4
Birks Cumb 222 G3
W Yorks 197 B9
Birkshaw Northumb 241 D7
Birley Hereford 115 G9
Birley Carr S Yorks 186 C4
Birley Edge S Yorks 186 C4
Birleyhay Derbys 186 E5
Birling Kent 69 G7
Northumb 252 B6
Birling Gap E Sus 23 F9
Birlingham Worcs 99 C8
Birmingham
W Mid 133 F11
Birnam Perth 286 C4
Birniehill S Lnrk 268 E2
Birse Aberds 293 D7
Birsemore Aberds 293 D7
Birstall Leics 135 B11
W Yorks 197 B8
Birstall Smithies
W Yorks 197 B8
Birstwith N Yorks 205 B10
Birthorpe Lincs 156 C2
Birtle Gtr Man 195 E10
Birtley Hereford 115 D7
Northumb 241 B9
Shrops 131 E9
T&W 243 F7
Birtley Green Sur 50 E4
Birtsmorton Worcs 98 D6
Birts Street Worcs 98 D5
Bisbrooke Rutland 137 D7
Biscathorpe Lincs 190 D2
Biscombe Som 27 E11
Biscot Luton 103 G11
Biscovey Corn 5 E11
Bisham Windsor 65 C10
Bishampton Worcs 117 G9
Bish Mill Devon 26 B2
Bishon Common
Hereford 97 C8
Bishop Auckland
Durham 233 F10
Bishopbridge Lincs 189 C8
Bishopbriggs
E Dunb 278 G2
Bishop Burton
E Yorks 208 F5
Bishopdown Wilts 47 G7
Bishop Kinkell
Highld 300 D5
Bishop Middleham
Durham 234 E2
Bishopmill Moray 302 C2
Bishop Monkton
N Yorks 214 F6
Bishop Norton Lincs 189 C7
Bishopsbourne Kent 55 C7
Bishops Cannings
Wilts 62 G4
Bishop's Castle
Shrops 130 F6
Bishop's Caundle
Dorset 29 E11
Bishop's Cleeve Glos 99 F9
Bishop's Down
Dorset 29 E11
Bishops Frome
Hereford 98 B3
Bishopsgarth
Stockton 234 G4
Bishopsgate Sur 66 E3
Bishops Green Essex 87 B5
Bishop's Green
W Berks 64 G4
Bishop's Hull Som 28 C2
Bishop's Itchington
Warks 119 F7
Bishops Lydeard
Som 27 B11
Bishop's Norton Glos 98 G6
Bishops Nympton
Devon 26 C3
Bishop's Offley
Staffs 150 D5
Bishop's Quay Corn 2 D6
Bishop's Stortford
Herts 105 G9
Bishop's Sutton
Hants 48 G6
Bishop's Tachbrook
Warks 118 E6
Bishops Tawton
Devon 40 G5
Bishopsteignton
Devon 14 G4
Bishopstoke Hants 33 D7
Bishopston Bristol 60 D5
Swansea 56 D5
Bishopstone Bucks 84 C4
E Sus 23 E7
Hereford 97 C8
Kent 71 F8
Swindon 63 C8
Wilts 31 B9
Bishopstrow Wilts 45 E11
Bishop Sutton Bath 44 B5
Bishop's Waltham
Hants 33 D9
Bishopswood Som 28 E3
Bishop's Wood
Staffs 132 B6
Bishopsworth Bristol 60 F5
Bishop Thornton
N Yorks 214 G5
Bishopthorpe York 207 D7
Bishopton Darl 234 G3
Dumfries 236 E6
N Yorks 214 E6
Renfs 277 G8
Warks 118 F3
Bishopwearmouth
T&W 243 F9
Bishop Wilton
E Yorks 207 B11
Bishpool Newport 59 B10
Bishton Newport 59 B11
Staffs 151 E10
Bisley Glos 80 D6
Sur 50 B3
Bisley Camp Sur 50 B2
Bispham Blkpool 202 E2
Bispham Green
Lancs 194 E3
Bissoe Corn 4 G5
Bissom Corn 3 C7
Bisterne Hants 31 G10
Bisterne Close Hants 32 G2
Bitchet Green Kent 52 C5
Bitchfield Lincs 155 D9
Bittadon Devon 40 E4
Bittaford Devon 8 D3
Bittering Norf 159 F8
Bitterley Shrops 115 B11
Bitterne Soton 33 E7
Bitterne Park Soton 32 E6
Bitterscote Staffs 134 C4
Bitteswell Leics 135 F10
Bittles Green Dorset 30 C5
Bitton S Glos 61 F7
Bix Oxon 65 B8
Bixter Shetland 313 H5
Blaby Leics 135 D11
Blackacre Dumfries 248 E2
Blackadder West
Borders 272 E6
Blackawton Devon 8 E6
Black Bank Cambs 139 F10
Warks 135 F7
Black Banks Darl 224 C5
Black Barn Lincs 157 D8
Blackbeck Cumb 219 D10
Blackbird Leys Oxon 83 E9
Blackborough Devon 27 F9
Norf 158 G3
Blackborough End
Norf 158 G3
Black Bourton Oxon 82 E3
Blackboys E Sus 37 C8
Blackbraes Aberds 293 B10
Blackbrook Derbys 170 F4
Derbys 185 E9
Mers 183 B8
Staffs 150 B5
Sur 51 D7
Blackburn Aberds 293 B10
Aberds 302 F5
Blkburn 195 B7
S Yorks 186 C5
W Loth 269 B9
Black Callerton
T&W 242 D5
Black Carr Norf 141 D11
Blackcastle Midloth 271 D8
Blackchambers
Aberds 293 B9
Black Clauchrie
S Ayrs 245 G7
Black Corner W Sus 51 F9
Black Corries Lodge
Highld 284 B6
Blackcraig Dumfries 246 G6
Blackcraigs Angus 293 E7
Black Crofts Argyll 289 F11
Black Cross Corn 5 C8
Black Dam Hants 48 C6
Blackden Heath
Ches E 184 G3
Blackditch Oxon 82 D6
Blackdog Aberds 293 B11
Black Dog Devon 26 F4
Blackdown Dorset 28 G5
Hants 33 C8
Warks 118 D6
Blackdyke Cumb 238 G4
Blackdykes E Loth 281 E11
Blacker Hill
S Yorks 197 G11
Blacketts Kent 70 F2
Blackfell T&W 243 F7
Blackfen London 68 E3
Blackfield Hants 32 G6
Blackford Cumb 239 E9
Dumfries 248 G4
Perth 286 G2
Shrops 131 G11
Som 29 B11
Som 42 D2
Som 44 D2
Blackford Bridge
Gtr Man 195 F10
Blackfordby Leics 152 F6
Blackfords Staffs 151 G9
Blackgang IoW 20 F5
Blackgate Angus 287 B8
Blackhall Aberds 293 D8
Edin 280 G4
Renfs 267 C9
Blackhall Colliery
Durham 234 D5
Blackhall Mill T&W 242 F4
Blackhall Rocks
Durham 234 D5
Blackham E Sus 52 F3
Blackhaugh
Borders 261 B10
Blackheath Essex 107 G10
London 67 D11
Suff 127 C8
Sur 50 D4
W Mid 133 F9
Blackheath Park
London 68 D2
Black Heddon
Northumb 242 B3
Blackhill Aberds 303 D10
Aberds 303 E10
Aberds 303 F10
Durham 242 G3
Hants 32 D4
Highld 298 D3
Black Hill W Yorks 204 E6
Blackhillock Moray 302 E4
Blackhills Highld 301 D9
Moray 302 D2
Swansea 56 C5
Blackhorse Devon 14 C5
S Glos 61 D7
Black Horse Drove
Cambs 139 E11
Blackjack Lincs 156 B5
Black Lake W Mid 133 E9
Blackland Wilts 62 F4
Blacklands E Sus 38 E4
Hereford 98 C2
Black Lane Gtr Man 195 F9
Blacklaw Aberds 302 D6
Blackleach Lancs 202 G5
Blackley Gtr Man 195 G11
W Yorks 196 D6
Blacklunans Perth 292 G3
Black Marsh Shrops 130 D6
Blackmarstone
Hereford 97 D10
Blackmill Bridgend 58 B2
Blackminster Worcs 99 C11
Blackmoor Bath 60 G5
Gtr Man 195 G7
Hants 49 G9
N Som 60 G3
Som 27 D11
Black Moor Lancs 194 E3
W Yorks 205 F11
Blackmoorfoot
W Yorks 196 E5
Blackmoor Gate
Devon 41 E7
Blackmore Essex 87 E10
Shrops 130 B6
Blackmore End
Essex 106 E4
Herts 85 B11
Worcs 98 C6
Black Mount Argyll 284 C6
Blackness Aberds 293 D8
E Sus 52 G4
Falk 279 F11
Blacknest Hants 49 E9
Windsor 66 F3
Blacknoll Dorset 18 D2
Black Notley Essex 106 G5
Blacko Lancs 204 E3
Blackoe Shrops 149 B10
Blackpark Dumfries 236 C5
Black Park Wrex 166 G4
Black Pill Swansea 56 C6
Blackpole Worcs 117 F7
Black Pole Lancs 202 F5
Blackpool Blkpool 202 F2
Devon 7 E11
Devon 9 F7
Devon 14 G2
Pembs 73 C9
Blackpool Gate
Cumb 240 B2
Blackridge W Loth 269 B7
Blackrock Argyll 274 G4
Bath 60 F6
Mon 78 C2
Black Rock Brighton 36 G4
Corn 2 C5
Blackrod Gtr Man 194 E6
Blackshaw Dumfries 238 D2
Blackshaw Head
W Yorks 196 B3
Blackshaw Moor
Staffs 169 D8
Blacksmith's Corner
Suff 108 C2
Blacksmith's Green
Suff 126 D2
Blacksnape Blkburn 195 C8
Blackstone Worcs 116 C5
W Sus 36 D2
Black Street Suff 143 F10
Black Tar Pembs 73 D7
Blackthorn Oxon 83 B10
Blackthorpe Suff 125 E8
Blacktoft E Yorks 199 C10
Blacktop Aberdeen 293 C10
Black Torrington
Devon 25 F7
Blacktown Newport 59 C9
Black Vein Caerph 78 G2
Blackwall Derbys 170 F3
London 67 C11
Blackwall Tunnel
London 67 C11
Blackwater Corn 4 F4
Dorset 19 B8
Hants 49 B11
IoW 20 D6
Norf 159 E11
Som 28 D3
Blackwaterfoot
N Ayrs 255 E9
Blackwater Lodge
Moray 302 G3
Blackweir Cardiff 59 D7
Blackwell Cumb 239 G10
Darl 224 C5
Derbys 170 D6
Derbys 185 G10
Devon 27 B8
Warks 100 C4
Worcs 117 C9
W Sus 51 F11
Blackwood Caerph 77 F11
S Lnrk 268 G5
Warr 183 C10
Blackwood Hill
Staffs 168 D6
Blacon Ches W 166 B5
Bladbean Kent 55 D7
Blades N Yorks 223 F9
Bladnoch Dumfries 236 D6
Bladon Oxon 82 C6
Blaenannerch
Ceredig 92 B4
Blaenau Carms 75 C10
Flint 166 D2
Blaenau Dolwyddelan
Conwy 164 E2
Blaenau Ffestiniog
Gwyn 164 F2
Blaenau-Gwent
Bl Gwent 78 E2
Blaenavon Torf 78 D3
Blaenbedw Fawr
Ceredig 111 G7
Blaencaerau
Bridgend 57 C11
Blaencelyn Ceredig 111 G7
Blaen-Cil-Llech
Ceredig 92 C6
Blaen Clydach
Rhondda 77 G7
Blaencwm Rhondda 76 F6
Blaendulais / Seven
Sisters Neath 76 D4
Blaendyryn Powys 95 D8
Blaenffos Pembs 92 D3
Blaengarw Bridgend 76 G6
Blaengwrach Neath 76 D5
Blaengwynfi Neath 57 B11
Blaen-gwynfi Neath 57 B11
Blaenllechau
Rhondda 77 F8
Blaen-pant Ceredig 92 C5
Blaenpennal
Ceredig 112 E2
Blaenplwyf Ceredig 111 B11
Blaenporth Ceredig 92 B5
Blaenrhondda
Rhondda 76 E6
Blaenwaun Carms 92 F4
Blaen-waun Carms 92 F4
Ceredig 111 G7
Blaen-y-coed Carms 92 F6
Blaenycwm Ceredig 112 B6
Blaen-y-cwm
Bl Gwent 77 C10
Denb 147 C10
Gwyn 146 E4
Powys 147 E11
Blagdon N Som 44 B4
Torbay 9 C7
Blagdon Hill Som 28 D2
Blagill Cumb 231 B10
Blaguegate Lancs 194 F3
Blaich Highld 290 F2
Blain Highld 289 C8
Blaina Bl Gwent 78 D2
Blainacraig Ho
Aberds 293 D7
Blair Fife 280 C6
Blair Atholl Perth 291 G10
Blairbeg N Ayrs 256 C2
Blairburn Fife 279 D9
Blairdaff Aberds 293 B8
Blair Drummond
Stirl 278 B4
Blairdryne Aberds 293 D9
Blairglas Argyll 276 D6
Blairgorm Highld 301 G10
Blairgowrie Perth 286 C5
Blairhall Fife 279 D10
Blairhill N Lnrk 268 B4
Blairingone Perth 279 B9
Blairland N Ayrs 266 F6
Blairlinn N Lnrk 278 G5
Blairlogie Stirl 278 B6
Blairlomond Argyll 276 B3
Blairmore Argyll 276 E3
Highld 306 D6
Blairnamarrow
Moray 292 B4
Blairquhosh Stirl 277 E10
Blair's Ferry Argyll 275 G10
Blairskaith E Dunb 277 F11
Blaisdon Glos 80 B2
Blaise Hamlet Bristol 60 D5
Blakebrook Worcs 116 B6
Blakedown Worcs 117 B7
Blake End Essex 106 G4
Blakelands
M Keynes 103 C7
Blakelaw Borders 263 C7
T&W 242 D6
Blakeley Staffs 133 E7
Blakeley Lane Staffs 169 F7
Blakelow Ches E 167 E11
Blakemere Hereford 97 C7
Blakenall Heath
W Mid 133 C10
Blakeney Glos 79 D11
Norf 177 E8
Blakenhall Ches E 168 F2
W Mid 133 D8
Blakeshall Worcs 132 G6
Blakesley Northants 120 G2
Blanchland
Northumb 241 G11
Blandford Camp
Dorset 30 F6
Blandford Forum
Dorset 30 F5
Blandford St Mary
Dorset 30 F5
Bland Hill N Yorks 205 C10
Blandy Highld 308 D6
Blanefield Stirl 277 F11
Blanerne Borders 272 D6
Blank Bank Staffs 168 F4
Blankney Lincs 173 C9
Blantyre S Lnrk 268 D3
Blar a'Chaorainn
Highld 290 G3
Blaran Argyll 275 B9
Blarghour Argyll 275 B10
Blarmachfoldach
Highld 290 G2
Blarnalearoch
Highld 307 K6
Blasford Hill Essex 88 C2
Blashford Hants 31 F11
Blaston Leics 136 D6
Blatchbridge Som 45 D9
Blatherwycke
Northants 137 D9
Blawith Cumb 210 B5
Blaxhall Suff 127 F7
Blaxton S Yorks 199 G7
Blaydon T&W 242 E5
Blaydon Burn T&W 242 E5
Blaydon Haughs
T&W 242 E5
Bleach Green Cumb 219 B9
Suff 126 B4
Bleadney Som 44 D3
Bleadon N Som 43 B10
Bleak Acre Hereford 98 B2
Bleak Hall
M Keynes 103 D7
Bleak Hey Nook
Gtr Man 196 F4
Bleak Hill Hants 31 E10
Blean Kent 70 G6
Bleasby Lincs 189 E10
Notts 172 F2
Bleasby Moor
Lincs 189 E10
Bleasdale Lancs 203 D7
Bleatarn Cumb 222 C4
Blebocraigs Fife 287 F8
Bleddfa Powys 114 D4
Bledington Glos 100 G4
Bledlow Bucks 84 E3
Bledlow Ridge Bucks 84 F3
Bleet Wilts 45 B11
Blegbie E Loth 271 C9
Blegbury Devon 24 B2
Blencarn Cumb 231 E8
Blencogo Cumb 229 B9
Blendworth Hants 34 E2
Blenheim Oxon 83 D9
Oxon 83 E9
Blenheim Park Norf 158 C6
Blenkinsopp Hall
Northumb 240 E5
Blennerhasset
Cumb 229 C9
Blervie Castle
Moray 301 D10
Bletchingdon Oxon 83 B8
Bletchingley Sur 51 C10
Bletchley M Keynes 103 E7
Shrops 150 C2
Bletherston Pembs 91 G11
Bletsoe Beds 121 F10
Blewbury Oxon 64 B4
Bliby Kent 54 F4
Blickling Norf 160 D3
Blidworth Notts 171 D9
Blidworth Bottoms
Notts 171 E9
Blidworth Dale
Notts 171 E9
Blindburn Northumb 263 G8
Blindcrake Cumb 229 E8
Blindley Heath Sur 51 D11
Blindmoor Som 28 E3
Blingery Highld 310 E7
Blisland Corn 11 G8
Blissford Hants 31 E11
Bliss Gate Worcs 116 C4
Blisworth Northants 120 G4
Blithbury Staffs 151 E11
Blitterlees Cumb 238 G4
Blockley Glos 100 D3
Blofield Norf 142 B6
Blofield Heath Norf 160 G6
Blo' Norton Norf 125 B10
Bloodman's Corner
Suff 143 D10
Bloomfield Bath 45 B7
Bath 61 G8
Borders 262 E3
W Mid 133 E9
Bloomsbury London 67 C10
Blore Staffs 150 C4
Staffs 169 F10
Bloreheath Staffs 150 B4
Blossomfield
W Mid 118 B2
Blount's Green
Staffs 151 C11
Blowick Mers 193 D11
Blowinghouse Corn 4 E4
Bloxham Oxon 101 D8
Bloxholm Lincs 173 E9
Bloxwich W Mid 133 C9
Bloxworth Dorset 18 C3
Blubberhouses
N Yorks 205 B9
Blue Anchor Corn 5 D8
Som 42 E4
Swansea 56 B4
Bluebell Telford 149 G11
Blue Bell Hill Kent 69 G8

Bluecairn Borders.. 271 G10
Blue Hill Herts...... 104 G5
Blue Row Essex.......89 C8
Bluetown Kent........54 B2
Blue Town Kent.......70 D2
Blue Vein Wilts......61 F10
Bluewater Kent.......68 E5
Blughasary Highld ...307 J6
Blundellsands Mers..182 B4
Blundeston Suff ... 143 D10
Blundies Staffs 132 F6
Blunham C Beds 122 G3
Blunsdon St Andrew
Swindon............62 B6
Bluntington Worcs...117 C7
Bluntisham Cambs ...123 C7
Blunts Corn............6 C6
Blunt's Green
Warks 118 D2
Blurton Stoke........ 168 G5
Blyborough Lincs 188 C6
Blyford Suff 127 B8
Blymhill Staffs...... 150 G6
Blymhill Lawns
Staffs............ 150 G6
Blyth Borders........270 F2
Northumb 253 G8
Notts............187 D10
Blyth Bridge
Borders............270 F2
Blythburgh Suff......127 B9
Blythe Borders......271 F11
Blythe Bridge Staffs. 169 G7
Blythe Marsh Staffs . 169 G7
Blyth End Warks 134 E4
Blythswood Renfs...267 B10
Blyton Lincs 188 C5
Boarhills Fife........287 F9
Boarhunt Hants.......33 F10
Boarsgreave Lancs. 195 C10
Boarshead E Sus.......52 G4
Boars Hill Oxon 83 E7
Boarstall Bucks 83 C10
Boasley Cross Devon ..12 C5
Boath Highld........300 B5
Boat of Garten
Highld 291 B11
Bobbing Kent........69 F11
Bobbington Staffs ...132 E6
Bobbingworth Essex..87 D8
Bobby Hill Suff 125 C10
Boblainy Highld 300 F4
Bocaddon Corn.........6 D3
Bochastle Stirl..... 285 G10
Bockhanger Kent......54 E4
Bocking Essex...... 106 G5
Bocking Churchstreet
Essex............106 F5
Bocking's Elm Essex .89 B11
Bockleton Worcs ...115 E11
Bockmer End Bucks ..65 B10
Bocombe Devon 24 C5
Bodantionail Highld..299 B7
Boddam Aberds.....303 E11
Shetland 313 M5
Bodden Som.........44 E6
Boddington Glos......99 F7
Bodedern Anglesey...178 E4
Bodellick Corn........10 G5
Bodelva Corn..........5 E11
Bodelwyddan Denb ..181 F8
Bodenham
Hereford 115 G10
Wilts 31 B11
Bodenham Bank
Hereford 98 E2
Bodenham Moor
Hereford 115 G10
Bodermid Gwyn 144 D3
Bodewryd Anglesey ..178 C5
Bodfari Denb....... 181 G9
Bodffordd Anglesey ..178 F6
Bodham Norf.......177 E10
Bodiam E Sus.........38 B3
Bodicote Oxon...... 101 D9
Bodiechell Aberds ...303 E7
Bodieve Corn..........10 G5
Bodiggo Corn..........5 D10
Bodilly Corn...........2 C5
Bodinnick Corn........6 E2
Bodle Street Green
E Sus 23 C11
Bodley Devon.........41 D7
Bodmin Corn..........5 B11
Bodmiscombe
Devon 27 F10
Bodney Norf......... 140 D6
Bodorgan Anglesey...162 B5
Bodsham Kent........54 D6
Boduan Gwyn.........144 B6
Boduel Corn...........6 C4
Bodwen Corn.........5 C10
Bodymoor Heath
Warks 134 D4
Bofarnel Corn 6 C2
Bogallan Highld.....300 D6
Bogbrae Aberds.....303 F10
Bogend Borders 272 F5
Notts 171 F7
S Ayrs 257 C9
Bogentory Aberds....293 C9
Boghall Midloth 270 B4
W Loth........... 269 B9
Boghead Aberds 293 D8
S Lnrk 268 G5
Bogmoor Moray 302 C3
Bogniebrae Aberds ..302 E5
Aberds........... 302 E6
Bognor Regis W Sus ..22 D6
Bograxie Aberds 293 B9
Bogs Aberds 302 G5
Bogs Bank Borders...270 E3
Bogside N Lnrk.......268 E6
Bogthorn W Yorks....204 F6
Bogton Aberds...... 302 D6
Bogtown Aberds......302 C5
Bogue Dumfries......246 G4
Bohemia E Sus........38 E4
Wilts 32 D2
Bohenie Highld 290 E4
Bohetherick Corn......7 B8
Bohortha Corn.........3 C9
Bohuntine Highld 290 E4
Bohuntinville Highld .290 E4
Boirseam W Isles 296 C6
Bojewyan Corn 1 C3
Bokiddick Corn.........5 C11
Bolahaul Fm Carms ...74 B6
Bolam Durham....... 233 G9
Northumb 252 G3
Bolam West Houses
Northumb 252 G3
Bolas Heath Telford ..150 E3
Bolberry Devon.........9 G8
Bold Heath Mers.... 183 D8
Boldmere W Mid......134 E2
Boldon T&W..........243 E9
Boldon Colliery
T&W 243 E8
Boldre Hants 20 B2
Boldron Durham ... 223 C10
Bole Notts.......... 188 D3
Bolehall Staffs.......134 C4
Bolehill Derbys 170 E3
Derbys........... 186 G6
S Yorks............ 186 E5
Bole Hill Derbys..... 186 G4
Bolenowe Corn 2 B5
Boleside Borders.... 261 C11
Boley Park Staffs 134 B2
Bolham Devon.........27 E7
Notts 188 E2
Bolham Water
Devon 27 E11
Bolholt Gtr Man 195 E9
Bolingey Corn 4 E5
Bolitho Corn...........2 C5
Bollihope Durham.....232 E6
Bollington Ches E 184 F6
Bollington Cross
Ches E 184 F6
Bolney W Sus 36 C3
Bolnhurst Beds......121 F11
Bolnore W Sus.........36 C4
Bolshan Angus......287 B10
Bolsover Derbys 187 G7
Bolsterstone
S Yorks 186 B3
Bolstone Hereford.....97 E11
Boltby N Yorks 215 B9
Bolter End Bucks......84 G3
Bolton Cumb 231 G8
E Loth 281 G10
E Yorks........... 207 C11
Gtr Man...........195 F8
Northumb 264 G4
W Yorks...........205 F9
Bolton Abbey
N Yorks 205 C7
Bolton Bridge
N Yorks 205 C7
Bolton-by-Bowland
Lancs............ 203 D11
Boltonfellend
Cumb............ 239 D11
Boltongate Cumb .. 229 C10
Bolton Green Lancs . 194 D5
Bolton Houses
Lancs............. 202 G4
Bolton-le-Sands
Lancs.............211 F9
Bolton Low Houses
Cumb............ 229 C10
Bolton New Houses
Cumb............ 229 C10
Bolton-on-Swale
N Yorks 224 F5
Bolton Percy
N Yorks 206 E6
Bolton Town End
Lancs.............211 F9
Bolton upon Dearne
S Yorks 198 G3
Bolton Wood Lane
Cumb............ 229 C11
Bolton Woods
W Yorks...........205 F9
Boltshope Park
Durham...........232 B4
Bolventor Corn 11 F9
Bomarsund
Northumb 253 G7
Bombie Dumfries..... 237 D9
Bomby Cumb 221 B10
Bomere Heath
Shrops.............149 F9
Bonaly Edin 270 B4
Bonar Bridge Highld. .309 K6
Bonawe Argyll 284 D4
Bonby N Lincs....... 200 D4
Boncath Pembs 92 D4
Bonchester Bridge
Borders 262 G3
Bonchurch IoW 21 F7
Bondend Glos 80 B5
Bond End Staffs......152 F2
Bondleigh Devon 25 G11
Bondman Hays
Leics 135 B9
Bonds Lancs..........202 E5
Bondstones Devon 25 F9
Bonehill Devon 13 F10
Staffs............ 134 C3
Bo'ness Falk.........279 E9
Bonhill W Dunb 277 F7
Boningale Shrops 132 C6
Bonjedward Borders .262 E5
Bonkle N Lnrk........ 268 D6
Bonnavoulin Highld . 289 D7
Bonning Gate Cumb..221 F9
Bonnington Borders. .261 B7
Edin 270 B2
Kent...............54 F5
Bonnybank Fife...... 287 G7
Bonnybridge Falk....278 E6
Bonnykelly Aberds .. 303 D8
Bonnyrigg and Lasswade
Midloth 270 B6
Bonnyton Aberds 302 F6
Angus 287 B10
Angus 287 D7
E Ayrs 257 B10
Bonsall Derbys....... 170 D3
Bonskeid House
Perth 291 G10
Bonson Som.......... 43 E8
Bont Mon 78 B5
Bontddu Gwyn.......146 F3
Bont-Dolgadfan
Powys 129 C7
Bont Fawr Carms 94 F4
Bont goch / Elerch
Ceredig 128 F3
Bonthorpe Lincs 191 G7
Bontnewydd
Ceredig 112 D2
Gwyn 163 D7
Bont-newydd
Conwy 181 G8
Bont Newydd Gwyn ..146 E5
Gwyn 164 G2
Bontuchel Denb 165 D9
Bonvilston / Tresimwn
V Glam.............58 E5
Bon-y-maen
Swansea 57 B7
Boode Devon 40 F4
Booker Bucks.........84 G4
Bookham Dorset......30 G2
Booleybank
Shrops........... 149 D11
Boon Borders 271 F11
Boon Hill Staffs......168 E4
Boorley Green Hants .33 E8
Boosbeck Redcar 226 B3
Boose's Green
Essex.............106 E6
Boot Cumb 220 E3
Booth Staffs....... 151 D10
W Yorks...........196 B4
Booth Bank Ches E .. 184 D2
Booth Bridge Lancs . 204 D4
Boothby Graffoe
Lincs 173 D7
Boothby Pagnell
Lincs 155 C9
Boothen Stoke....... 168 G5
Boothferry E Yorks ...199 B8
Boothgate Derbys.....170 F5
Booth Green
Ches E 184 E6
Boothroyd W Yorks...197 C8
Boothsdale Ches W ..167 B8
Boothstown
Gtr Man 195 G8
Boothtown W Yorks ..196 B5
Boothville Northants..120 E5
Booth Wood
W Yorks.......... 196 D4
Bootle Cumb.........210 B2
Mers 182 B4
Booton Norf..........160 E2
Boots Green
Ches W 184 G3
Boot Street Suff 108 B4
Booze N Yorks 223 E10
Boquhan Stirl...... 277 D10
Boquio Corn...........2 C5
Boraston Shrops 116 D2
Boraston Dale
Shrops............116 C2
Borden Kent.........69 G11
W Sus 34 C4
Border Cumb 238 G5
Bordesley W Mid....133 F11
Bordesley Green
W Mid 134 F2
Bordlands Borders ...270 F3
Bordley N Yorks 213 G8
Bordon Hants.........49 F10
Bordon Camp Hants ..49 F9
Boreham Essex.......88 D3
Wilts 45 E11
Boreham Street
E Sus 23 C11
Borehamwood
Herts..............85 F11
Boreland Dumfries ...236 C5
Dumfries 248 E5
Fife 280 C6
Stirl 285 D9
Boreland of Southwick
Dumfries 237 C11
Boreley Worcs....... 116 D6
Borestone Stirl 278 C5
Borgh W Isles 296 C5
W Isles 297 L2
Borghasdal W Isles ..296 C6
Borghastan W Isles . 304 D4
Borgie Highld....... 308 D6
Borgue Dumfries......237 E8
Highld 311 G5
Borley Essex.........106 C6
Borley Green Essex .106 C6
Suff 125 E9
Bornais W Isles......297 J3
Bornesketaig Highld .298 B3
Borness Dumfries....237 E8
Borough Scilly 1 G3
Boroughbridge
N Yorks 215 F7
Borough Green Kent . 52 B6
Borough Marsh
Wokingham.........65 D9
Borough Park Staffs .134 B4
Borough Post Som....28 C4
Borras Wrex.........166 E4
Borras Head Wrex ...166 E5
Borreraig Highld 296 F7
Borrobol Lodge
Highld 311 G2
Borrodale Highld.... 297 G7
Borrohill Aberds 303 D9
Borrowash Derbys ...153 C8
Borrowby N Yorks....215 B8
N Yorks 226 B5
Borrowdale Cumb....220 C5
Borrowfield
Aberds........... 293 D10
Borrowston Highld ...310 E7
Borrowstoun Mains
Falk..............279 E9
Borstal Medway.......69 F8
Borthwick Midloth ... 271 D7
Borthwickbrae
Borders 261 G10
Borthwickshiels
Borders 261 F10
Borth / Y Borth
Ceredig 128 E2
Borth-y-Gest
Gwyn.............145 B11
Borve Highld.........298 E4
Borve Lodge
W Isles 305 J2
Borwick Lancs.......211 E10
Borwick Rails Cumb. 210 D3
Bosavern Corn.........1 C3
Bosbury Hereford 98 C3
Boscadjack Corn........2 C5
Boscastle Corn 11 C8
Boscean Corn 1 C3
Boscombe Bmouth 19 C8
Wilts 47 F8
Boscomoor Staffs.... 151 G8
Boscoppa Corn 5 E10
Boscreege Corn 2 C3
Bosham W Sus........22 C4
Bosham Hoe W Sus ...22 C4
Bosherston Pembs....73 G7
Boskednan Corn.......1 C4
Boskenna Corn 1 E4
Bosleake Corn.........4 G3
Bosley Ches E 168 B6
Boslowick Corn........3 C7
Boslymon Corn 5 C11
Bosoughan Corn.......5 C7
Bosporthennis Corn ...1 B4
Bossall N Yorks 216 G4
Bossiney Corn 11 D7
Bossingham Kent.....54 D6
Bossington Hants....47 G10
Kent...............55 B8
Som............... 41 D11
Bostadh W Isles 304 D3
Bostock Green
Ches W 167 B11
Boston Lincs........ 174 G4
Boston Long Hedges
Lincs 174 F5
Boston Spa
W Yorks.......... 206 D4
Boston West Lincs ...174 F3
Boswednack Corn 1 B4
Boswin Corn..........2 C5
Boswinger Corn 5 G9
Boswyn Corn 2 B5
Botallack Corn.........1 C3
Botany Bay London 86 F3
Mon...............79 E8
Botcherby Cumb 239 F10
Botcheston Leics 135 B9
Botesdale Suff......125 B10
Bothal Northumb 252 F6
Bothampstead
W Berks...........64 D4
Bothamsall Notts .. 187 G11
Bothel Cumb....... 229 D9
Bothenhampton
Dorset.............16 C5
Bothwell S Lnrk 268 D4
Bothy Highld.........290 F4
Botley Bucks..........85 E7
Hants..............33 E8
Oxon 83 D7
Botloe's Green Glos... 98 F4
Botolph Claydon
Bucks............ 102 G4
Botolphs W Sus.......35 F11
Bottacks Highld 300 C4
Botternell Corn 11 G11
Bottesford Leics 154 B6
N Lincs.......... 199 F11
Bottisham Cambs ...123 E10
Bottlesford Wilts 46 B6
Bottom Boat
W Yorks.......... 197 C11
Bottomcraig Fife 287 E7
Bottom House
Staffs.............169 E8
Bottomley W Yorks .. 196 D5
Bottom of Hutton
Lancs.............194 B3
Bottom o' th' Moor
Gtr Man...........195 E7
Bottom Pond Kent 53 B11
Bottoms Corn...........1 E3
Bottreaux Mill Devon . 26 B4
Bottrells Close Bucks .85 G7
Botts Green Warks....134 E4
Botusfleming Corn.....7 C8
Botwnnog Gwyn 144 C5
Bough Beech Kent 52 D3
Boughrood Powys 96 D2
Boughrood Brest
Powys 96 D2
Boughspring Glos 79 F9
Boughton Ches W 166 B6
Lincs 173 F10
Norf.............. 140 C3
Northants 120 D5
Notts............ 171 B11
Boughton Aluph
Kent...............54 D4
Boughton Corner
Kent...............54 D4
Boughton Green
Kent...............53 C9
Boughton Heath
Ches W 166 B6
Boughton Lees Kent ..54 D4
Boughton Malherbe
Kent..............53 D11
Boughton Monchelsea
Kent...............53 C9
Boughton Street
Kent...............54 B5
Bougton End
C Beds 103 D9
Boulby Redcar 226 B5
Bould Oxon......... 100 G4
Boulden Shrops 131 F10
Boulder Clough
W Yorks...........196 C4
Bouldnor IoW 20 D3
Bouldon Shrops 131 F10
Boulmer Northumb .. 265 G7
Boulsdon Glos.........98 G4
Boulston Pembs 73 C7
Boultenstone
Aberds............292 B6
Boultham Lincs......173 B7
Boultham Moor
Lincs 173 B7
Boulton Derbys 153 C7
Boulton Moor
Derbys............153 C7
Boundary Leics 152 F6
Staffs............ 169 G7
Boundstone Sur 49 E10
Bountis Thorne
Devon 24 D5
Bourn Cambs 122 F6
Bournbrook
W Mid 133 G10
Bourne Lincs 155 E11
N Som 44 B3
Bourne End Beds ...121 E10
Bucks..............65 B11
C Beds 103 C9
Herts 85 D8
Bournemouth
Bmouth 19 C7
Bournes Green Glos .. 80 E6
Sthend.............70 B2
Worcs 117 C8
Bourne Vale
W Mid 133 D11
Bourne Valley Poole ..19 C7
Bournheath Worcs...117 C9
Bournmoor Durham. 243 G8
Bournside Glos.......99 G8
Bournstream Glos 80 G2
Bournville W Mid ... 133 G10
Bourton Bucks........102 E4
Dorset............ 45 G9
N Som 59 G11
Oxon 63 B8
Shrops........... 131 D11
Wilts 62 G4
Bourton on Dunsmore
Warks 119 C8
Bourton-on-the-Hill
Glos..............100 E3
Bourton-on-the-Water
Glos.............. 100 G3
Bourtreehill N Ayrs ..257 B8
Bousd Argyll........288 C4
Bousta Shetland..... 313 H4
Boustead Hill Cumb . 239 F7
Bouth Cumb 210 B6
Bouthwaite N Yorks ..214 E2
Bouts Worcs.........117 F10
Bovain Stirl......... 285 D9
Boveney Bucks.......66 D2
Boveridge Dorset 31 E9
Boverton V Glam 58 F3
Bovey Tracey Devon... 14 F2
Bovingdon Herts......85 E8
Bovingdon Green
Bucks..............65 B10
Herts 85 E8
Bovinger Essex 87 D8
Bovington Camp
Dorset.............18 D2
Bow Borders........ 271 G9
Devon 8 D6
Devon 26 G2
Orkney........... 314 G3
Oxon 82 G4
Bowbank Durham ... 232 G4
Bowbeck Suff 125 B8
Bow Brickhill
M Keynes..........103 E8
Bowbridge Glos 80 E5
Bowbrook Shrops ... 149 G9
Bow Broom S Yorks . 187 B7
Bowburn Durham ... 234 D2
Bowcombe IoW 20 D5
Bow Common
London............67 C11
Bowd Devon 15 C8
Bowden Borders 262 C3
Devon 8 F6
Dorset.............30 C3
Bowden Hill Wilts.....62 F2
Bowdens Som.........28 B6
Bowderdale Cumb ...222 E3
Bowdon Gtr Man 184 D3
Bower Highld 310 C6
Northumb 251 G7
Bower Ashton Bristol. .60 E5
Bowerchalke Wilts....31 C8
Bower Heath Herts ..85 B10
Bowerhill Wilts 62 G2
Bower Hinton Som....29 D7
Bowerhope Borders ..261 E7
Bower House Tye
Suff 107 C9
Bowermadden
Highld 310 C6
Bowers Staffs........150 B6
Bowers Gifford Essex . 69 B9
Bowershall Fife.... 279 C11
Bowertower Highld ..310 C6
Bowes Durham.......223 C9
Bowes Park London ...86 G4
Bowgreave Lancs ...202 E5
Bowgreen Gtr Man .. 184 D3
Bowhill Borders.... 261 D10
Fife 280 B4
Bowhouse Dumfries . 238 D2
Bowhousebog or Liquo N
Lnrk............ 269 D7
Bowing Park Mers .. 182 D6
Bowismiln Borders...262 E2
Bowithick Corn.......11 E9
Bowker's Green
Lancs............ 194 G2
Bowland Bridge
Cumb.............211 B8
Bowldown Wilts 62 D2
Bowlee Gtr Man......195 F10
Bowlees Durham.....232 F4
Bowler's Town E Sus ..38 C6
Bowley Hereford ... 115 G10
Bowley Lane
Hereford 98 C3
Bowley Town
Hereford 115 G10
Bowlhead Green Sur.. 50 F2
Bowling W Dunb 277 G9
W Yorks.......... 205 G9
Bowling Alley Hants...49 D9
Bowling Bank Wrex..166 F5
Bowling Green Corn ..5 D10
Corn.............. 12 G3
Glos...............81 E8
Hants..............19 B11
Shrops........... 150 D2
W Mid 133 F8
Worcs 116 G6
Bowlish Som 44 E6
Bowmans Kent 68 E4
Bowmanstead Cumb . 220 F6
Bowmore Argyll 254 B4
Bowness-on-Solway
Cumb.............238 E6
Bowness-on-
Windermere Cumb . 221 F8
Bow of Fife Fife......287 F7
Bowridge Hill Dorset...30 B4
Bowrie-fauld Angus .287 C9
Bowsden Northumb.. 273 G9
Bowsey Hill Windsor .65 C10
Bowshank Borders .. 271 G9
Bowside Lodge
Highld 310 C2
Bowston Cumb.......221 F9
Bow Street Ceredig . 128 G2
Norf.............. 141 D10
Bowthorpe Norf 142 B3
Bowyer's Common
Hants..............34 B3
Box Glos 80 E5
Wilts 61 F10
Boxbush Glos.........80 C2
Glos.............. 98 G3
Box End Beds.......103 B10
Boxford Suff........107 C9
W Berks 64 E2
Boxgrove W Sus 22 B6
Box Hill Sur 51 C7
Wilts 61 F10
Boxley Kent 53 B9
Boxmoor Herts 85 D9
Box's Shop Corn 24 G2
Boxted Essex 107 E9
Suff 124 G6
Boxted Cross
Essex.............107 E10
Boxted Heath
Essex.............107 E10
Box Trees W Mid.....118 C2
Boxwell Glos 80 G4
Boxworth Cambs.....122 E6
Boxworth End
Cambs 123 D7
Boyatt Wood Hants ...32 C6
Boyden End Suff.....124 F4
Boyden Gate Kent..... 71 F8
Boyland Common
Norf.............. 141 G11
Boylestone Derbys ...152 B3
Boylestonfield
Derbys............152 B3
Boyndie Aberds......302 C6
Boyn Hill Windsor 65 C11
Boynton E Yorks.....218 F2
Boysack Angus 287 C9
Angus 287 C10
Boys Hill Dorset.......29 E11
Boys Village V Glam....58 F4
Boythorpe Derbys... 186 G5
Boyton Corn..........12 C2
Suff 109 B7
Wilts 46 F3
Boyton Cross Essex . 87 D10
Boyton End Essex....106 E2
Suff 106 C4
Bozeat Northants.....121 F8
Bozen Green Herts....105 F8
Braaid IoM..........192 E4
Braal Castle Highld...310 C5
Brabling Green Suff. .126 E5
Brabourne Kent 54 E5
Brabourne Lees Kent . 54 E5
Brabster Highld 310 C7
Bracadale Highld.....294 B5
Bracara Highld.......295 F9
Braceborough
Lincs 155 G11
Bracebridge Lincs ...173 B7
Bracebridge Heath
Lincs 173 B7
Bracebridge Low Fields
Lincs 173 B7
Braceby Lincs.......155 B10
Bracewell Lancs 204 D3
Bracken Bank
W Yorks...........204 F6
Brackenber Cumb ...222 B4
Brackenbottom
N Yorks 212 E6
Brackenfield Derbys 170 D5
Brackenhall
W Yorks.......... 197 D7
Bracken Hill
W Yorks...........197 C7
Brackenlands
Cumb.............229 B11
Bracken Park
W Yorks...........206 E3
Brackenthwaite
Cumb............ 229 B11
Cumb............ 229 G9
N Yorks 205 C11
Brackla / Bragle
Bridgend 58 D2
Bracklamore
Aberds........... 303 D8
Bracklesham W Sus...22 D4
Brackletter Highld ...290 E3
Brackley Argyll 255 C8
Northants 101 D11
Brackloch Highld.... 307 G6
Bracknell Brack......65 F11
Braco Perth 286 G2
Bracobrae Moray 302 D5
Braco Castle Perth ...286 F2
Bracon N Lincs.......199 F9
Bracon Ash Norf..... 142 D3
Braco Park Aberds ...303 C9
Bracorina Highld.....295 F9
Bradaford Devon......12 C3
Bradbourne Derbys ..170 E2
Bradbury Durham 234 F2
Bradda IoM 192 F2
Bradden Northants ...102 B2
Braddock Corn 6 C3
Braddocks Hay
Staffs............ 168 D5
Bradeley Stoke 168 E5
Bradeley Green
Ches E 167 G8
Bradenham Bucks 84 F4
Norf.............. 141 B8
Bradenstoke Wilts....62 D4
Brades Village
W Mid 133 E9
Bradfield Devon 27 F9
Essex............. 108 E2
Norf.............. 160 C5
W Berks 64 E6
Bradfield Combust
Suff 125 F7
Bradfield Green
Ches E 167 D11
Bradfield Heath
Essex.............108 F2
Bradfield St Clare
Suff 125 F8
Bradfield St George
Suff 125 E8
Bradford Corn 11 F8
Derbys........... 170 C2
Devon 24 F6
Gtr Man........... 184 B5
Northumb 264 C5
W Yorks.......... 205 G9
Bradford Abbas
Dorset.............29 E9
Bradford Leigh
Wilts 61 G10
Bradford-on-Avon
Wilts 61 G10
Bradford-on-Tone
Som...............27 C11
Bradford Peverell
Dorset.............17 C9
Bradgate S Yorks....186 C6
Bradiford Devon 40 F5
Brading IoW 21 D8
Bradley Derbys 170 F2
Glos.............. 80 G3
Hants..............48 E6
NE Lincs..........201 F8
Staffs.............151 F7
W Mid 133 D8
Wrex 166 E4
W Yorks.......... 197 C7
Bradley Cross Som.... 44 C3
Bradley Fold
Gtr Man...........195 F9
Bradley Green
Ches W 167 F8
Glos.............. 80 G2
Som...............43 F9
Warks 134 C5
Worcs 117 E9
Bradley in the Moors
Staffs............ 169 G9
Bradley Mills
W Yorks.......... 197 D7
Bradley Mount
Ches E 184 F6
Bradley Stoke S Glos .. 60 C6
Bradlow Hereford 98 D4
Bradmore Notts 153 C11
W Mid 133 D7
Bradney Shrops 132 D5
Som...............43 F10
Bradninch Devon 27 G8
Bradnock's Marsh
W Mid 118 B4
Bradnop Staffs 169 D8
Bradnor Green
Hereford 114 F5
Bradpole Dorset 16 C5
Bradshaw Gtr Man ...195 E8
Staffs............ 168 D6
W Yorks.......... 196 E5
W Yorks.......... 205 G7
Bradstone Devon 12 E3
Bradville M Keynes ..102 C6
Bradwall Green
Ches E 168 C3
Bradway S Yorks 186 E4
Bradwell Derbys 185 E11
Devon 40 E3
Essex............ 106 G6
M Keynes......... 102 D6
Norf............. 143 C10
Staffs.............168 F4
Bradwell Common
M Keynes......... 102 D6
Bradwell Grove Oxon .82 D2
Bradwell Hills
Derbys............185 E11
Bradwell on Sea
Essex..............89 D8
Bradwell Waterside
Essex..............89 D7
Bradworthy Devon 24 E4
Bradworthy Cross
Devon 24 E4
Brae Dumfries.......237 B10
Highld 307 L3
Highld 309 J4
Shetland 312 G5
Braeantra Highld.....300 B5
Braebuster Orkney ...314 F5
Braedownie Angus....292 F4
Braeface Falk 278 E5
Braefield Highld 300 F4
Braefindon Highld ... 300 D6
Braegrum Perth 286 E4
Braehead Dumfries.. 236 D6
Orkney........... 314 B4
Orkney...........314 F5
S Ayrs 257 E8
S Lnrk 259 C8
S Lnrk 267 D11
S Lnrk 269 E9
Stirl 278 C6
Braehead of Lunan
Angus 287 B10
Braehoulland
Shetland 312 F4
Braehour Highld 310 D4
Braehungie Highld ...310 F5
Braeintra Highld 295 B10
Braelangwell Lodge
Highld 309 K5
Braemar Aberds 292 D3
Braemore Highld.....299 B11
Highld 310 F4
Brae of Achnahaird
Highld 307 H5
Brae of Boquhapple
Stirl 285 G10
Braepark Edin 280 F3
Brae Roy Lodge
Highld 290 D5
Braeside Invclyd 276 F4
Braes of Enzie
Moray 302 D3
Braes of Ullapool
Highld 307 K6
Braeswick Orkney....314 C6
Braevallich Argyll .. 275 C10
Braewick Shetland ...312 F4
Shetland 313 H5
Brafferton Darl 233 G11
N Yorks 215 E8
Brafield-on-the-Green
Northants 120 F6
Bragar W Isles....... 304 D4
Bragbury End Herts . 104 G5
Bragenham Bucks ...103 F8
Bragle / Brackla
Bridgend 58 D2
Bragleenmore
Argyll............ 289 G11
Braichmelyn Gwyn..163 B10
Braichyfedw Powys ..129 E7
Braid Edin 280 G4
Braides Lancs....... 202 C4
Braidfauld Glasgow ..268 C2
Braidley N Yorks ... 213 C10
Braids Argyll..........255 C8
Braidwood S Lnrk 268 F6
Braigh Chalasaigh
W Isles 296 D5
Braigo Argyll 274 G3
Brailsford Derbys ... 170 G3
Brailsford Green
Derbys............ 170 G3
Braingortan Argyll ..275 F11
Brain's Green Glos... 79 D11
Brainshaugh
Northumb 252 C6
Braintree Essex..... 106 G5
Braiseworth Suff 126 C2
Braishfield Hants 32 B5
Braiswick Essex 107 F9
Braithwaite Cumb.. 229 G10
S Yorks........... 198 E6
W Yorks.......... 204 E6
Braithwell S Yorks....187 C8
Brakefield Green
Norf..............141 B10
Brakenhill W Yorks .. 198 D2
Bramber W Sus.......35 E11
Bramblecombe
Dorset.............30 G3
Brambridge Hants 33 C7
Bramcote Notts.....153 B10
Warks 135 F8
Bramcote Hills
Notts 153 B10
Bramcote Mains
Warks 135 F8
Bramdean Hants......33 B10
Bramerton Norf 142 C5
Bramfield Herts 86 B3
Suff 127 C7
Bramford Suff.......108 B2
W Mid 133 E8
Bramhall Gtr Man ... 184 D5
Bramhall Moor
Gtr Man.......... 184 D6
Bramhall Park
Gtr Man.......... 184 D5
Bramham W Yorks ...206 E4
Bramhope
W Yorks...........205 E11
Bramley Derbys......186 F6
Hants..............48 B6
Sur............... 50 D4
S Yorks........... 187 C7
W Yorks.......... 205 F10
Bramley Corner
Hants..............48 B6
Bramley Green Hants . 49 B7
Bramley Head
N Yorks 205 B8
Bramley Vale
Derbys............171 B7
Bramling Kent........55 B8
Brampford Speke
Devon 14 B4
Brampton Cambs 122 C4
Cumb............ 231 G9
Cumb............ 240 E2
Derbys........... 186 G5
Hereford 97 D8
Lincs 188 F4
Norf.............. 160 E4
Suff 143 G8
S Yorks........... 198 G2
Brampton Abbotts
Hereford 98 F2
Brampton Ash
Northants 136 F5
Brampton Bryan
Hereford 115 C7
Brampton en le Morthen
S Yorks 187 D7
Brampton Park
Cambs 122 C4
Brampton Street
Suff 143 G8
Bramshall Staffs.... 151 C11
Bramshaw Hants......32 D3
Bramshill Hants 65 G8
Bramshott Hants.....49 G10
Bramwell Som.........28 B6
Branatwatt Shetland. 313 H4
Branault Highld 289 C7
Branbridges Kent......53 D7
Brancaster Norf 176 E3
Brancaster Staithe
Norf...............176 E3
Brancepeth
Durham.......... 233 D10
Branch End
Northumb 242 E3
Branchill Moray.... 301 D10
Branchton Invclyd....276 F4
Brand End Lincs 174 F5
Branderburgh
Moray 302 B2
Brandesburton
E Yorks 209 D8
Brandeston Suff 126 E4
Brand Green Glos.....98 F4
Hereford 98 C5
Brandhill Shrops 115 B8
Brandis Corner
Devon 24 G6
Brandish Street Som... 42 D2
Brandiston Norf 160 E2
Brandlingill Cumb... 229 F8
Brandon Durham.... 233 D10
Lincs 172 F6
Northumb 264 F2
Suff 140 F5
Warks 119 B8
Brandon Bank
Cambs 140 F2
Brandon Creek Norf .140 E2

Warks 134 E4
Warks 134 E5
Wilts 62 D4
W Mid 119 B7
Worcs 98 C6
Church Enstone
Oxon 101 G7
Churches Green
E Sus 23 B10
Church Fenton
N Yorks 206 F6
Churchfield Hereford 98 B4
W Mid 133 E10
Churchfields Wilts 31 B10
Churchgate Herts 86 E4
Churchgate Street
Essex 87 C7
Church Green Devon 15 B9
Norf 141 E11
Church Gresley
Derbys 152 F5
Church Hanborough
Oxon 82 C6
Church Hill
Ches W 167 C10
Pembs 73 C7
Staffs 151 G10
W Mid 133 D9
Worcs 117 D11
Church Hougham
Kent 55 E9
Church Houses
N Yorks 226 F3
Churchill Devon 28 G4
Devon 40 E5
N Som 44 B2
Oxon 100 G5
Worcs 117 B7
Worcs 117 G8
Churchill Green
N Som 60 G2
Churchinford Som 28 E2
Church Knowle
Dorset 18 E4
Church Laneham
Notts 188 F4
Church Langton
Leics 136 E4
Church Lawford
Warks 119 B8
Church Lawton
Ches E 168 D4
Church Leigh
Staffs 151 B10
Church Lench
Worcs 117 G10
Church Mayfield
Staffs 169 G11
Church Minshull
Ches E 167 C11
Churchmoor Rough
Shrops 131 F8
Church Norton
W Sus 22 D5
Church Oakley Hants 48 C5
Churchover Warks 135 G10
Church Preen
Shrops 131 D10
Church Pulverbatch
Shrops 131 C8
Churchstanton Som 27 E11
Churchstoke Powys 130 E5
Churchstow Devon 8 F4
Church Stowe
Northants 120 F2
Church Street
Essex 106 C5
Kent 69 E8
Church Stretton
Shrops 131 E9
Churchtown Pembs 73 D10
Churchtown Corn 11 F7
Cumb 230 C3
Derbys 170 C3
Devon 24 G3
Devon 41 E7
IoM 192 C5
Lancs 202 E5
Mers 193 D11
Shrops 130 F5
Som 42 F3
Church Town Corn 4 G3
Leics 153 F7
N Lincs 199 F9
Sur 51 C11
Church Village
Rhondda 58 B5
Church Warsop
Notts 171 B9
Church Westcote
Glos 100 G4
Church Whitfield
Kent 55 D10
Church Wilne
Derbys 153 C8
Churchwood W Sus 35 D8
Churnet Grange
Staffs 169 E7
Churnsike Lodge
Northumb 240 B5
Churscombe Torbay 9 C7
Churston Ferrers
Torbay 9 D8
Churt Sur 49 F11
Churton Ches W 166 D6
Churwell W Yorks 197 B9
Chute Cadley Wilts 47 C10
Chute Standen
Wilts 47 C10
Chweffordd Conwy 180 G4
Chwilog Gwyn 145 B8
Chwitffordd / Whitford
Flint 181 F10
Chyandour Corn 1 C5
Chyanvounder Corn 2 E5
Chycoose Corn 3 B8
Chynhale Corn 2 C4
Chynoweth Corn 2 C2
Chyvarloe Corn 2 E5
Cicelyford Mon 79 E8
Cilan Uchaf Gwyn 144 E5
Cilau Pembs 91 D8
Cilcain Flint 165 B11
Cilcennin Ceredig 111 E10
Cilcewydd Powys 130 C4
Cilfor Gwyn 146 B2
Cilfrew Neath 76 E3
Cilfynydd Rhondda 77 G9
Cilgerran Pembs 92 C3
Cilgwyn Carms 94 F4
Ceredig 92 C6
Gwyn 163 E7
Pembs 91 D11
Ciliau Aeron Ceredig 111 F9
Cill Amhlaidh
W Isles 297 G3
Cill Donnain
W Isles 297 J3
Cille Bhrighde
W Isles 297 K3
Cill Eireabhagh
W Isles 297 G4
Cille Pheadair
W Isles 297 K3
Cilmaengwyn Neath 76 D2
Cilmery Powys 113 G10
Cilsan Carms 93 G11
Ciltalgarth Gwyn 164 G5
Ciltwrch Powys 96 C3
Cilybebyll Neath 76 E2
Cil y coed / Caldicot
Mon 60 B3
Cilycwm Carms 94 D5
Cimla Neath 57 B9
Cinderford Glos 79 C11
Cinderhill Derbys 170 F5
Nottingham 171 G8
Cinder Hill Gtr Man 195 F9
Kent 52 D4
W Mid 133 E8
W Sus 36 B5
Cinnamon Brow
Warr 183 C10
Cippenham Slough 66 C2
Cippyn Pembs 92 B2
Circebost W Isles 304 E3
Cirencester Glos 81 E8
Ciribhig W Isles 304 D3
City London 67 C10
Powys 130 F4
V Glam 58 D3
City Dulas Anglesey 179 D7
Clabhach Argyll 288 D3
Clachaig Argyll 276 E2
Highld 292 B2
N Ayrs 255 E10
Clachan Argyll 255 B8
Argyll 275 B8
Argyll 284 F5
Argyll 289 E10
Highld 295 B7
Highld 298 C4
Highld 307 L6
W Isles 297 G3
Clachaneasy
Dumfries 236 B5
Clachanmore
Dumfries 236 E2
Clachan na Luib
W Isles 296 E4
Clachan of Campsie
E Dunb 278 F2
Clachan of Glendaruel
Argyll 275 E10
Clachan-Seil Argyll 275 B8
Clachan Strachur
Argyll 284 G4
Clachbreck Argyll 275 F8
Clachnabrain Angus 292 G5
Clachtoll Highld 307 G5
Clackmannan Clack 279 C8
Clackmarras Moray 302 D2
Clacton-on-Sea
Essex 89 B11
Cladach N Ayrs 256 B2
Cladach Chairinis
W Isles 296 F4
Cladach Chireboist
W Isles 296 E3
Claddach Argyll 254 B2
Claddach-knockline
W Isles 296 E3
Cladich Argyll 284 E4
Cladich Steading
Argyll 284 E4
Cladswell Worcs 117 F10
Claggan Highld 289 E8
Highld 290 F3
Perth 285 D11
Claigan Highld 298 D2
Claines Worcs 117 F7
Clandown Bath 45 B7
Clanfield Hants 33 D11
Oxon 82 E3
Clanking Bucks 84 D4
Clanville Hants 47 D10
Som 44 G6
Wilts 62 D2
Claonaig Argyll 255 B9
Claonel Highld 309 J5
Clapgate Dorset 31 G8
Herts 105 G8
Clapham Beds 121 G10
Devon 14 D3
London 67 D9
N Yorks 212 F4
W Sus 35 F9
Clapham Green
Beds 121 G10
N Yorks 205 B10
Clapham Hill Kent 70 G6
Clapham Park London 67 E9
Clap Hill Kent 54 F5
Clapper Corn 10 G6
Clapper Hill Kent 53 F10
Clappers Borders 273 D8
Clappersgate Cumb 221 E7
Clapphoull Shetland 313 L6
Clapton Som 28 F6
Som 44 C6
W Berks 63 E11
Clapton in Gordano
N Som 60 E3
Clapton-on-the-Hill
Glos 81 B11
Clapton Park
London 67 B11
Clapworthy Devon 25 C11
Clarach Ceredig 128 G2
Clarack Aberds 292 D6
Clara Vale T&W 242 E4
Clarbeston Pembs 91 G10
Clarbeston Road
Pembs 91 G10
Clarborough Notts 188 E2
Clardon Highld 310 C5
Clare Oxon 83 F11
Suff 106 B5
Clarebrand
Dumfries 237 C9
Claregate W Mid 133 C7
Claremont Park Sur 66 G6
Claremount
W Yorks 196 B5
Clarencefield
Dumfries 238 D3
Clarence Park
N Som 59 G10
Clarendon Park
Leicester 135 C11
Clareston Pembs 73 C7
Clarilaw Borders 262 D3
Borders 262 F2
Clarken Green Hants 48 C5
Clark Green Ches E 184 F6
Clarksfield Gtr Man 196 G2
Clark's Green Sur 51 F7
Clark's Hill Lincs 157 E7
Clarkston E Renf 267 D11
N Lnrk 268 B5
Clase Swansea 57 B7
Clashandorran
Highld 300 E5
Clashcoig Highld 309 K6
Clasheddy Highld 308 C6
Clashgour Argyll 284 C6
Clashindarroch
Aberds 302 F4
Clashmore Highld 306 F5
Highld 309 L7
Clashnessie Highld 306 F5
Clashnoir Moray 302 G2
Clate Shetland 313 G7
Clatford Wilts 63 F7
Clatford Oakcuts
Hants 47 F10
Clathy Perth 286 F3
Clatt Aberds 302 G5
Clatter Powys 129 E9
Clatterford IoW 20 D5
Clatterford End
Essex 87 C10
Essex 87 D9
Essex 87 E8
Clatterin Bridge
Aberds 293 F8
Clatto Fife 287 F8
Clatworthy Som 42 G5
Clauchlands N Ayrs 256 C2
Claughton Lancs 202 E6
Lancs 211 F11
Mers 182 D4
Clavelshay Som 43 G9
Claverdon Warks 118 E3
Claverham N Som 60 F2
Claverhambury Essex 86 E6
Clavering Essex 105 E9
Claverley Shrops 132 E5
Claverton Bath 61 G9
Claverton Down Bath 61 G9
Clawdd-côch
V Glam 58 D5
Clawdd-newydd
Denb 165 E9
Clawdd Poncen
Denb 165 G9
Clawthorpe Cumb 211 D10
Clawton Devon 12 B3
Claxby Lincs 189 C10
Lincs 191 G7
Claxby St Andrew
Lincs 191 G7
Claxton Norf 142 C6
N Yorks 216 G3
Claybokie Aberds 292 D2
Claybrooke Magna
Leics 135 F9
Claybrooke Parva
Leics 135 F9
Clay Common Suff 143 G9
Clay Coton
Northants 119 B11
Clay Cross Derbys 170 C5
Claydon Glos 99 E8
Oxon 119 G9
Suff 126 G2
Clay End Herts 104 F6
Claygate Dumfries 239 B9
Kent 52 C6
Kent 53 E8
Sur 67 G7
Claygate Cross Kent 52 B6
Clayhall Hants 21 B8
London 86 G6
Clayhanger Devon 27 C8
Som 28 E4
W Mid 133 C10
Clayhidon Devon 27 D11
Clayhill E Sus 38 C4
Hants 32 F4
Clay Hill Bristol 60 E6
London 86 F4
W Berks 64 E5
Clayhithe Cambs 123 E10
Clayholes Angus 287 D9
Clay Lake Lincs 156 E5
Clayland Stirl 277 D11
Clay Mills Derbys 152 D5
Clayock Highld 310 D5
Claypit Hill Cambs 123 G7
Claypits Devon 27 B7
Glos 80 D3
Kent 55 B9
Suff 140 G4
Claypole Lincs 172 F5
Clays End Bath 61 G8
Claythorpe Lincs 190 F6
Clayton Gtr Man 184 B5
Staffs 168 G5
S Yorks 198 F3
W Sus 36 E3
W Yorks 205 G8
Clayton Brook
Lancs 194 C5
Clayton Green
Lancs 194 C5
Clayton Heights
W Yorks 205 G8
Clayton-le-Dale
Lancs 203 G9
Clayton-le-Moors
Lancs 203 G10
Clayton-le-Woods
Lancs 194 C5
Clayton West
W Yorks 197 E9
Clayworth Notts 188 D2
Cleadale Highld 294 G6
Cleadon T&W 243 E9
Cleadon Park T&W 243 E9
Clearbrook Devon 7 B10
Clearwell Glos 79 D9
Newport 59 B9
Clearwood Wilts 45 D10
Cleasby N Yorks 224 C5
Cleat Orkney 314 B4
Orkney 314 H4
Cleatlam Durham 224 B2
Cleator Cumb 219 C10
Cleator Moor
Cumb 219 B10
Cleave Devon 28 G2
Clebrig Highld 308 F5
Cleckheaton
W Yorks 197 B7
Cleddon Mon 79 E8
Cleedownton
Shrops 131 G11
Cleehill Shrops 115 B11
Cleekhimin N Lnrk 268 D5
Cleemarsh Shrops 131 G11
Clee St Margaret
Shrops 131 G11
Cleestanton
Shrops 115 B11
Cleethorpes
NE Lincs 201 F10
Cleeton St Mary
Shrops 116 B2
Cleeve Glos 80 C2
N Som 60 F3
Oxon 64 C6
Cleeve Hill Glos 99 F9
Cleeve Prior Worcs 99 B11
Cleghorn S Lnrk 269 F8
Clegyrnant Powys 129 B8
Clehonger Hereford 97 D9
Cleirwy / Clyro
Powys 96 C4
Cleish Perth 279 B11
Cleland N Lnrk 268 D5
Clements End Glos 79 D9
Clement's End
C Beds 85 B8
Clement Street Kent 68 E4
Clench Wilts 63 G7
Clench Common
Wilts 63 F7
Clencher's Mill
Hereford 98 D4
Clenchwarton Norf 157 E11
Clennell Northumb 251 B10
Clent Worcs 117 B8
Cleobury Mortimer
Shrops 116 B3
Cleobury North
Shrops 132 F2
Cleongart Argyll 255 D7
Clephanton Highld 301 D8
Clerkenwater Corn 5 B11
Clerkenwell London 67 C10
Clerk Green
W Yorks 197 C8
Clerklands Borders 262 E2
Clermiston Edin 280 G3
Clestrain Orkney 314 F3
Cleuch Head
Borders 262 G3
Cleughbrae
Dumfries 238 C3
Clevancy Wilts 62 D5
Clevans Renfs 267 B7
Clevedon N Som 60 E2
Cleveley Oxon 101 G7
Cleveleys Lancs 202 E2
Cleverton Wilts 62 B3
Clevis Bridgend 57 F10
Clewer Som 44 C2
Clewer Green
Windsor 66 D2
Clewer New Town
Windsor 66 D3
Clewer Village
Windsor 66 D3
Cley next the Sea
Norf 177 E8
Cliaid W Isles 297 L2
Cliasmol W Isles 305 H2
Cliburn Cumb 231 G7
Click Mill Orkney 314 D3
Cliddesden Hants 48 D6
Cliff Derbys 185 D8
Warks 134 D4
Cliffburn Angus 287 C10
Cliffe Lancs 203 G10
Medway 69 D8
N Yorks 207 G9
N Yorks 224 B4
Cliff End E Sus 38 E5
W Yorks 196 D6
Cliffe Woods Medway 69 E8
Clifford Devon 24 C4
Hereford 96 B4
W Yorks 206 E4
Clifford Chambers
Warks 118 G3
Clifford's Mesne
Glos 98 G4
Cliffs End Kent 71 G10
Clifftown Sthend 69 B11
Clifton Bristol 60 E5
C Beds 104 D3
Ches W 183 F8
Cumb 230 F6
Derbys 169 G11
Devon 40 E5
Gtr Man 195 G9
Lancs 202 G5
Northumb 252 G6
Nottingham 153 C11
N Yorks 205 D9
Oxon 101 E9
Stirl 285 D7
S Yorks 186 C6
S Yorks 187 B8
Worcs 98 B6
W Yorks 197 C7
York 207 C7
Clifton Campville
Staffs 152 G5
Cliftoncote Borders 263 E8
Clifton Green
Gtr Man 195 G9
Clifton Hampden
Oxon 83 F8
Clifton Junction
Gtr Man 195 G9
Clifton Manor
C Beds 104 D3
Clifton Maybank
Dorset 29 E9
Clifton Moor York 207 B7
Clifton Reynes
M Keynes 121 G8
Clifton upon Dunsmore
Warks 119 B10
Clifton upon Teme
Worcs 116 E4
Cliftonville Kent 71 E11
N Lnrk 268 B4
Norf 160 B6
Climping W Sus 35 G8
Climpy S Lnrk 269 D8
Clink Som 45 D9
Clinkham Wood
Mers 183 B8
Clint N Yorks 205 B11
Clint Green Norf 159 G10
Clintmains Borders 262 C4
Clints N Yorks 224 E2
Cliobh W Isles 304 E2
Clipiau Gwyn 146 G6
Clippesby Norf 161 G8
Clippings Green
Norf 159 G10
Clipsham Rutland 155 F9
Clipston Northants 136 G4
Notts 154 C2
Clipstone C Beds 103 F8
Clitheroe Lancs 203 E10
Cliuthar W Isles 305 J3
Clive Ches W 167 B11
Shrops 149 E10
Clive Green
Ches W 167 C11
Clive Vale E Sus 38 E4
Clivocast Shetland 312 C8
Clixby Lincs 200 G6
Cloatley Wilts 81 G7
Cloatley End Wilts 81 G7
Clocaenog Denb 165 E9
Clochan Aberds 303 E9
Moray 302 C4
Clock Face Mers 183 C8
Clock House London 67 G9
Clockmill Borders 272 E5
Clock Mills Hereford 96 B5
Cloddiau Powys 130 B4
Cloddymoss Moray 301 D9
Clodock Hereford 96 F6
Cloford Som 45 E8
Cloford Common
Som 45 E8
Cloigyn Carms 74 C6
Clola Aberds 303 E10
Clophill C Beds 103 D11
Clopton Northants 137 G11
Suff 126 G4
Clopton Corner
Suff 126 G4
Clopton Green Suff 124 G5
Suff 125 E9
Closeburn Dumfries 247 E9
Close Clark IoM 192 E3
Close House
Durham 233 F10
Closworth Som 29 E9
Clothall Herts 104 E5
Clothall Common
Herts 104 E5
Clotton Ches W 167 C8
Clotton Common
Ches W 167 C8
Cloudesley Bush
Warks 135 F9
Clouds Hereford 97 D11
Cloud Side Staffs 168 C6
Clough Gtr Man 196 D2
Gtr Man 196 F2
W Yorks 196 E5
Clough Dene
Durham 242 F5
Cloughfold Lancs 195 C10
Clough Foot
W Yorks 196 C2
Clough Hall Staffs 168 E4
Clough Head
W Yorks 196 C5
Cloughton
N Yorks 227 G10
Cloughton Newlands
N Yorks 227 F10
Clounlaid Highld 289 D9
Clousta Shetland 313 H5
Clouston Orkney 314 E2
Clova Aberds 302 G4
Angus 292 F5
Clovelly Devon 24 C4
Clove Lodge
Durham 223 B8
Clovenfords
Borders 261 B10
Clovenstone Aberds 293 B9
Cloves Moray 301 C11
Clovullin Highld 290 G2
Clowance Wood Corn 2 C4
Clow Bridge Lancs 195 B10
Clowne Derbys 187 F7
Clows Top Worcs 116 C4
Cloy Wrex 166 G5
Cluanie Inn Highld 290 B2
Cluanie Lodge
Highld 290 B2
Clubmoor Mers 182 C5
Clubworthy Corn 11 C11
Cluddley Telford 150 G2
Clun Shrops 130 G6
Clunbury Shrops 131 G7
Clunderwen Carms 73 B10
Clune Highld 301 D9
Highld 301 G7
Clunes Highld 290 E4
Clungunford Shrops 115 B7
Clunie Aberds 302 D6
Perth 286 C5
Clunton Shrops 130 G6
Cluny Fife 280 B4
Cluny Castle Aberds 293 B8
Highld 291 D8
Clutton Bath 44 B6
Ches W 167 E7
Clutton Hill Bath 44 B6
Clwt-grugoer
Conwy 165 C7
Clwt-y-bont Gwyn 163 C9
Clwydyfagwyr
M Tydf 77 D8
Clydach Mon 78 C2
Swansea 75 E11
Clydach Terrace
Powys 77 C11
Clydach Vale
Rhondda 77 G7
Clydebank W Dunb 277 G9
Clyffe Pypard Wilts 62 D5
Clynder Argyll 276 E4
Clyne Neath 76 E4
Clynelish Highld 311 J2
Clynnog-fawr Gwyn 162 F6
Clyro / Cleirwy
Powys 96 C4
Clyst Honiton Devon 14 C5
Clyst Hydon Devon 27 G8
Clyst St George
Devon 14 D5
Clyst St Lawrence
Devon 27 G8
Clyst St Mary Devon 14 C5
Cnip W Isles 304 E2
Cnoc Amhlaigh
W Isles 304 E7
Cnoc an t-Solais
W Isles 304 D6
Cnocbreac Argyll 274 F5
Cnoc Fhionn
Highld 295 D10
Cnoc Màiri W Isles 304 E6
Cnoc Rolum
W Isles 296 F3
Cnwch-coch
Ceredig 112 B3
Coachford Aberds 302 E4
Coad's Green Corn 11 F11
Coal Aston Derbys 186 F5
Coal Bank Darl 234 G3
Coalbrookdale
Telford 132 C3
Coalbrookvale
Bl Gwent 77 D11
Coalburn S Lnrk 259 C8
Coalburns T&W 242 E4
Coalcleugh
Northumb 232 B2
Coaley Glos 80 E3
Coaley Peak Glos 80 E3
Coalford Aberds 293 D10
Coalhall E Ayrs 257 F10
Coalhill Essex 88 F3
Coalmoor Telford 132 B3
Coalpit Field Warks 135 F7
Coalpit Heath S Glos 61 C7
Coalpit Hill Staffs 168 E4
Coal Pool W Mid 133 C10
Coalport Telford 132 C3
Coalsnaughton
Clack 279 B8
Coaltown of Balgonie
Fife 280 B5
Coaltown of Wemyss
Fife 280 B6
Coalville Leics 153 G8
Coalway Glos 79 C9
Coanwood Northumb 240 F5
Coarsewell Devon 8 E4
Coat Som 29 C7
Coatbridge N Lnrk 268 C4
Coatdyke N Lnrk 268 C5
Coate Swindon 63 C7
Wilts 62 G4
Coates Cambs 138 D6
Glos 81 E7
Lancs 204 D3
Lincs 188 E6
Midloth 270 C4
Notts 188 E4
W Sus 35 D7
Coatham Redcar 235 F7
Coatham Mundeville
Darl 233 G11
Coatsgate Dumfries 248 B3
Cobairdy Aberds 302 E5
Cobbaton Devon 25 B10
Cobbler's Corner
Worcs 116 F5
Cobbler's Green
Norf 142 E5
Cobbler's Plain Mon 79 E7
Cobbs Warr 183 D10
Cobb's Cross Glos 98 E5
Cobbs Fenn Essex 106 E5
Cobby Syke N Yorks 205 B9
Coberley Glos 81 B7
Cobhall Common
Hereford 97 D9
Cobham Kent 69 F7
Sur 66 G6
Cobleland Stirl 277 B10
Cobler's Green
Essex 87 B11
Cobley Dorset 31 C8
Cobley Hill Worcs 117 C10
Cobnash Hereford 115 E9
Cobridge Stoke 168 F5
Cobscot Shrops 150 B3
Coburty Aberds 303 C9
Cockadilly Glos 80 E4
Cock Alley Derbys 186 G6
Cock and End Suff 124 G4
Cockayne N Yorks 226 F2
Cock Bank Wrex 166 F5
Cock Bevington
Warks 117 G11
Cock Bridge Aberds 292 C4
Cockburnspath
Borders 282 G5
Cock Clarks Essex 88 E4
Cockden Lancs 204 G3
Cockenzie and Port
Seton E Loth 281 F8
Cocker Bar Lancs 194 C4
Cockerham Lancs 202 C5
Cockermouth Cumb 229 E8
Cockernhoe Herts 104 G2
Cockernhoe Green
Herts 104 G2
Cockersdale
W Yorks 197 B8
Cockerton Darl 224 B5
Cockett Swansea 56 C6
Cocketty Aberds 293 F9
Cockfield Durham 233 G8
Suff 125 G8
Cockfosters London 86 F3
Cock Gate Hereford 115 D9
Cock Green Essex 87 B11
Cockhill Som 44 G6
Cock Hill N Yorks 206 B6
Cocking W Sus 34 D5
Cocking Causeway
W Sus 34 D5
Cockington Torbay 9 C7
Cocklake Som 44 D2
Cocklaw Northumb 241 C10
Cockleford Glos 81 C7
Cockley Beck Cumb 220 E4
Cockley Cley Norf 140 C5
Cockley Hill
W Yorks 197 D7
Cock Marling E Sus 38 D5
Cocknowle Dorset 18 E4
Cockpole Green
Wokingham 65 C9
Cocks Corn 4 E5
Cocks Green Suff 125 F7
Cockshead Ceredig 112 F2
Cockshoot Hereford 97 D11
Cockshutford
Shrops 131 F11
Cockshutt Shrops 132 G4
Shrops 149 D8
Cock Street Kent 53 C9
Suff 107 D9
Cockthorpe Norf 177 E7
Cockwells Corn 2 C2
Cockwood Devon 14 E5
Som 43 E8
Cockyard Derbys 185 F8
Hereford 97 E8
Codda Corn 11 F9
Coddenham Suff 126 G2
Coddenham Green
Suff 126 F2
Coddington
Ches W 167 D7
Hereford 98 C4
Notts 172 E4
Codford St Mary
Wilts 46 F3
Codford St Peter
Wilts 46 F3
Codicote Herts 86 B2
Codicote Bottom
Herts 86 B2
Codmore Bucks 85 E7
Codmore Hill W Sus 35 C9
Codnor Derbys 170 F6
Codnor Breach
Derbys 170 F6
Codnor Gate Derbys 170 E6
Codnor Park Derbys 170 E6
Codrington S Glos 61 D8
Codsall Staffs 133 C7
Codsall Wood Staffs 132 B6
Codsend Som 41 F11
Coedcae Bl Gwent 77 D11
Torf 78 D3
Coed Cwnwr Mon 78 F6
Coedely Rhondda 58 B4
Coed Eva Torf 78 G3
Coedkernew Newport 59 C9
Coed Llai / Leeswood
Flint 166 D3
Coed Mawr Gwyn 179 G9
Coed Morgan Mon 78 C5
Coedpoeth Wrex 166 E3
Coed-Talon Flint 166 D3
Coedway Powys 148 G6
Coed-y-bryn Ceredig 93 C7
Coed-y-caerau
Newport 78 G5
Coed-y-fedw Mon 78 D6
Coed y Garth
Ceredig 128 E3
Coed y go Shrops 148 D5
Coed-y-paen Mon 78 F4
Coed-y-parc Gwyn 163 B10
Coed-yr-ynys Powys 96 G3
Coed Ystumgwern
Gwyn 145 E11
Coed-y-wlad Powys 130 B4
Coelbren Powys 76 C4
Coffee Hall
M Keynes 103 D7
Coffinswell Devon 9 B7
Cofton Devon 14 E5
Cofton Common
W Mid 117 B10
Cofton Hackett
Worcs 117 B10
Cog V Glam 59 F7
Cogan V Glam 59 E7
Cogenhoe Northants 120 E6
Cogges Oxon 82 D5
Coggeshall Essex 106 G6
Coggeshall Hamlet
Essex 107 G7
Coggins Mill E Sus 37 B9
Coignafearn Lodge
Highld 291 B8
Coignascallan
Highld 291 B9
Coig Peighinnean
W Isles 304 B7
Coig Peighinnean
Bhuirgh W Isles 304 C6
Coilacriech Aberds 292 D5
Coilantogle Stirl 285 G9
Coilessan Argyll 284 G6
Coilleag W Isles 297 K3
Coillemore Highld 300 B6
Coillore Highld 294 B5
Coirea-chrombe
Stirl 285 G9
Coisley Hill S Yorks 186 E6
Coity Bridgend 58 C2
Cokenach Herts 105 D7
Cokhay Green
Derbys 152 D5
Col W Isles 304 D6
Colaboll Highld 309 H5
Colan Corn 5 C7
Colaton Raleigh
Devon 15 D7
Colbost Highld 298 E2
Colburn N Yorks 224 F3
Colby Cumb 231 G9
IoM 192 E3
Norf 160 C4
Colchester Essex 107 F10
Colchester Green
Suff 125 F8
Colcot V Glam 58 F6
Cold Ash W Berks 64 F4
Cold Ashby
Northants 120 B3
Cold Ash Hill Hants 49 G10
Cold Ashton S Glos 61 E9
Cold Aston Glos 81 B10
Coldbackie Highld 308 D6
Coldbeck Cumb 222 E4
Coldblow London 68 E4
Cold Blow Pembs 73 C10
Cold Brayfield
M Keynes 121 G8
Coldbrook Powys 96 D3
Cold Christmas Herts 86 B5
Cold Cotes N Yorks 212 E4
Coldean Brighton 36 F4
Coldeast Devon 14 G2
Coldeaton Derbys 169 D10
Cold Elm Glos 98 E6
Colden W Yorks 196 B3
Colden Common
Hants 33 C7
Coldfair Green Suff 127 E8
Coldham Cambs 139 C8
Staffs 133 B7
Coldham's Common
Cambs 123 F9
Cold Hanworth
Lincs 189 E8
Coldharbour Corn 4 F5
Devon 27 E9
Dorset 17 E9
Glos 79 E9
Kent 52 C5
London 68 D4
Sur 50 E6
Cold Harbour Dorset 18 D4
Herts 85 B10
Kent 69 G11
Lincs 155 C9
Oxon 64 D6
Wilts 45 B11
Wilts 45 D11
Windsor 65 D10
Cold Hatton Telford 150 E2
Cold Hatton Heath
Telford 150 E2
Cold Hesledon
Durham 234 B4
Cold Hiendley
W Yorks 197 E11
Cold Higham
Northants 120 G3
Coldingham Borders 273 B8
Cold Inn Pembs 73 D10
Cold Kirby N Yorks 215 C10
Coldmeece Staffs 151 C7
Cold Moss Heath
Ches E 168 C3
Cold Newton Leics 136 B4
Cold Northcott
Corn 11 D10
Cold Norton Essex 88 E4
Coldoch Stirl 278 B3
Cold Overton Leics 154 G6
Coldra Newport 59 B11
Coldrain Perth 286 G4
Coldred Kent 55 D9
Coldridge Devon 25 F11
Cold Row Lancs 202 E3
Coldstream Angus 287 D7
Borders 263 B8
Coldvreath Corn 5 D9
Coldwaltham W Sus 35 D8
Cold Well Staffs 151 G11
Coldwells Aberds 303 E11
Coldwells Croft
Aberds 302 G5
Cole Som 45 G7
Colebatch Shrops 130 F6
Colebrook Devon 27 F8
Colebrooke Devon 13 B11
Coleburn Moray 302 D2
Coleby Lincs 173 C7
N Lincs 199 D11
Cole End Essex 105 D11
Warks 134 F3
Coleford Devon 26 G3
Glos 79 C9
Som 45 D7
Coleford Water Som 42 G6
Colegate End Norf 142 F3
Cole Green Herts 86 C3
Herts 105 E8
Colehall W Mid 134 F2
Cole Henley Hants 48 C3
Colehill Dorset 31 G8
Coleman Green
Herts 85 C11
Coleman's Hatch
E Sus 52 G3
Colemere Shrops 149 C8
Colemore Hants 49 G8
Colemore Green
Shrops 132 D4
Coleorton Leics 153 F8
Coleorton Moor
Leics 153 F8
Cole Park London 67 E7
Colerne Wilts 61 E10
Colesbourne Glos 81 C7
Colesbrook Dorset 30 B4
Cole's Cross Dorset 28 G5
Colesden Beds 122 F2
Coles Green Suff 107 C11
Worcs 116 G5
Cole's Green Suff 126 E5
Coleshill Bucks 85 F7
Oxon 82 G2
Warks 134 F4

Cwmsychpant
Ceredig 93 B9
Cwmsyfiog Caerph 77 E11
Cwmsymlog Ceredig 128 G4
Cwmtillery Bl Gwent 78 D2
Cwm-twrch Isaf
Powys 76 C3
Cwm-twrch Uchaf
Powys 76 C3
Cwmwdig Water
Pembs 90 E6
Cwmwysg Powys 95 F7
Cwm-y-glo Carms 75 C9
Gwyn 163 C8
Cwmynyscoy Torf 78 F3
Cwmyoy Mon 96 G5
Cwmystwyth
Ceredig 112 C5
Cwrt Gwyn 128 C3
Cwrt-newydd Ceredig 93 B9
Cwrt-y-cadno Carms 94 C3
Cwrt-y-gollen Powys 78 B2
Cydweli / Kidwelly
Carms 74 D6
Cyffordd Llandudno /
Llandudno Junction
Conwy 180 F3
Cyffylliog Denb 165 D9
Cyfronydd Powys 130 B2
Cymau Flint 166 D3
Cymdda Bridgend 58 C2
Cymer Neath 57 B11
Cymmer Rhondda 77 G8
Cyncoed Cardiff 59 C7
Cynghordy Carms 94 C6
Cynheidre Carms 75 D7
Cynonville Neath 57 B10
Cyntwell Cardiff 58 D6
Cynwyd Denb 165 G9
Cynwyl Elfed Carms 93 F7
Cywarch Gwyn 147 F7

D

Daccombe Devon 9 B8
Dacre Cumb 230 F5
N Yorks 214 G3
Dacre Banks
N Yorks 214 G3
Daddry Shield
Durham 232 D3
Dadford Bucks 102 D3
Dadlington Leics 135 D8
Dafarn Faig Gwyn 163 F7
Dafen Carms 75 E8
Daffy Green Norf 141 B9
Dagdale Staffs 151 C11
Dagenham London 68 C3
Daggons Dorset 31 E10
Daglingworth Glos 81 D7
Dagnall Bucks 85 B7
Dagtail End Worcs 117 E10
Dagworth Suff 125 E10
Dail Beag W Isles 304 D4
Dail bho Dheas
W Isles 304 B6
Dail bho Thuath
W Isles 304 B6
Daill Argyll 274 G4
Dailly S Ayrs 245 C7
Dail Mor W Isles 304 D4
Dainton Devon 9 B7
Dairsie or Osnaburgh
Fife 287 F8
Daisy Green Suff 125 D10
Suff 125 D11
Daisy Hill Gtr Man 195 G7
W Yorks 197 B9
W Yorks 205 G8
Daisy Nook
Gtr Man 196 G2
Dalabrog W Isles 297 J3
Dalavich Argyll 275 B10
Dalbeattie
Dumfries 237 C10
Dalbeg Highld 291 B8
Dalblair E Ayrs 258 F4
Dalbog Angus 293 F7
Dalbrack Stirl 285 G11
Dalbury Derbys 152 C5
Dalby IoM 192 E3
Lincs 190 G6
N Yorks 216 E2
Dalchalloch Perth 291 G9
Dalchalm Highld 311 J3
Dalchenna Argyll 284 G4
Dalchirach Moray 301 F11
Dalchonzie Perth 285 E11
Dalchork Highld 309 H5
Dalchreichart
Highld 290 B4
Dalchruin Perth 285 F11
Dalderby Lincs 174 B2
Dale Cumb 230 C6
Gtr Man 196 F3
Pembs 72 D4
Shetland 312 G6
Dale Abbey Derbys 153 B8
Dalebank Derbys 170 C5
Dale Bottom Cumb 229 G11
Dale Brow Ches E 184 F6
Dale End Derbys 170 C2
N Yorks 204 D5
Dale Head Cumb 221 B8
Dale Hill E Sus 53 G7
E Sus 53 G8
Dalelia Highld 289 C9
Dale Moor Derbys 153 B8
Dale of Walls
Shetland 313 H3
Dales Brow
Gtr Man 195 G9
Dales Green Staffs 168 D5
Daless Highld 301 F8
Dalestie Moray 292 B3
Dalestorth Notts 171 C8
Dalfaber Highld 291 B11
Dalfoil Stirl 277 D11
Dalganachan Highld 310 E4
Dalgarven N Ayrs 266 F5
Dalgety Bay Fife 280 E3
Dalginross Perth 285 E11
Dalguise Perth 286 C3
Dalhalvaig Highld 310 D2
Dalham Suff 124 E4
Dalhastnie Angus 293 F7
Dalhenzean Perth 292 G3
Dalinlongart Argyll 276 E2
Dalkeith Midloth 270 B6
Dallam Warr 183 C9
Dallas Moray 301 D11
Dallas Lodge
Moray 301 D11
Dallcharn Highld 308 D6
Dalleagles E Ayrs 258 G3
Dallicott Shrops 132 E5
Dallimores IoW 20 C6
Dallinghoo Suff 126 G5
Dallington E Sus 23 B11
Northants 120 E4
Dallow N Yorks 214 E3
Dalmadilly Aberds 293 B9
Dalmally Argyll 284 E5
Dalmarnock
Glasgow 268 C2
Perth 286 C3
Dalmary Stirl 277 B10
Dalmellington
E Ayrs 245 B11
Dalmeny Edin 280 F2
Dalmigavie Highld 291 B9
Dalmigavie Lodge
Highld 301 G7
Dalmilling S Ayrs 257 E9
Dalmore Highld 300 C6
Dalmuir W Dunb 277 G9
Dalnabreck Highld 289 C8
Dalnacardoch Lodge
Perth 291 F9
Dalnacroich Highld 300 D3
Dalnaglar Castle
Perth 292 G3
Dalnahaitnach
Highld 301 G8
Dalnamein Lodge
Perth 291 G9
Dalnarrow Argyll 289 F9
Dalnaspidal Lodge
Perth 291 F8
Dalnavaid Perth 292 G2
Dalnavie Highld 300 B6
Dalnaw Dumfries 236 B5
Dalnawillan Lodge
Highld 310 E4
Dalness Highld 284 B5
Dalnessie Highld 309 H6
Dalphaid Highld 309 H3
Dalqueich Perth 286 G4
Dalrannoch Argyll 289 E11
Dalreavoch Highld 309 J7
Dalriach Highld 301 F10
Dalrigh Stirl 285 E7
Dalry Edin 280 G4
N Ayrs 266 F5
Dalrymple E Ayrs 257 G9
Dalscote Northants 120 G3
Dalserf S Lnrk 268 E6
Dalshannon N Lnrk 278 G4
Dalston Cumb 239 G9
London 67 C10
Dalswinton
Dumfries 247 F10
Dalton Cumb 211 D10
Dumfries 238 C4
Lancs 194 F3
Northumb 241 F10
Northumb 242 C4
N Yorks 215 D8
N Yorks 224 D2
S Lnrk 268 D3
S Yorks 187 C7
W Yorks 197 D7
Dalton-in-Furness
Cumb 210 E4
Dalton-le-Dale
Durham 234 B4
Dalton Magna
S Yorks 187 C7
Dalton-on-Tees
N Yorks 224 D5
Dalton Parva
S Yorks 187 C7
Dalton Piercy Hrtlpl 234 E5
Dalveallan Highld 300 F6
Dalveich Stirl 285 E10
Dalvina Lo Highld 308 E6
Dalwey Telford 132 B3
Dalwhinnie Highld 291 E8
Dalwood Devon 28 G3
Dalwyne S Ayrs 245 D8
Damask Green
Herts 104 F5
Damems W Yorks 204 F6
Damerham Hants 31 D10
Damery Glos 80 G2
Damgate Norf 143 B8
Norf 161 F9
Dam Green Norf 141 F11
Damhead Moray 301 D10
Dam Head W Yorks 196 B6
Damhead Holdings
Midloth 270 B5
Dam Mill Staffs 133 C7
Damnaglaur
Dumfries 236 F3
Dam of Quoiggs
Perth 286 G2
Damside Borders 270 F3
Dam Side Lancs 202 D4
Danaway Kent 69 G11
Danbury Essex 88 E3
Danbury Common
Essex 88 E3
Danby N Yorks 226 D4
Danby Wiske
N Yorks 224 F6
Dan Caerlan Rhondda 58 C5
Dancers Hill Herts 86 F2
Dancing Green
Hereford 98 G2
Dandaleith Moray 302 E2
Danderhall Midloth 270 B6
Dandy Corner Suff 125 D11
Danebank Ches E 185 E7
Dane Bank Gtr Man 184 B6
Danebridge Ches E 169 B7
Dane End Herts 104 G6
Danegate E Sus 52 G5
Danehill E Sus 36 B6
Dane in Shaw
Ches E 168 C5
Danemoor Green
Norf 141 B11
Danesbury Herts 86 B2
Danesfield Bucks 65 C10
Danesford Shrops 132 E4
Daneshill Hants 49 C7
Danesmoor Derbys 170 C6
Danes Moss Ches E 184 G6
Dane Street Kent 54 C5
Daneway Glos 80 E6
Dangerous Corner
Gtr Man 195 G7
Lancs 194 E4
Daniel's Water Kent 54 E3
Danna na Cloiche
Argyll 275 F7
Dannonchapel Corn 10 E6
Danskine E Loth 271 B11
Danthorpe E Yorks 209 G10
Danygraig Caerph 78 G2
Danzey Green
Warks 118 D2
Dapple Heath
Staffs 151 D10
Darby End W Mid 133 F9
Darby Green Hants 65 G10
Darbys Green
Worcs 116 F4
Darby's Hill W Mid 133 F9
Darcy Lever
Gtr Man 195 F8
Dardy Powys 78 B2
Darenth Kent 68 E5
Daresbury Halton 183 E9
Daresbury Delph
Halton 183 E9
Darfield S Yorks 198 G2
Darfoulds Notts 187 F9
Dargate Kent 70 G5
Dargate Common
Kent 70 G5
Darite Corn 6 B5
Darkland Moray 302 C2
Darland Wrex 166 D5
Darlaston W Mid 133 D9
Darlaston Green
W Mid 133 D9
Darley N Yorks 205 B10
Shrops 132 D3
Darley Abbey Derby 153 B7
Darley Bridge
Derbys 170 C3
Darley Dale Derbys 170 C3
Darleyford Corn 11 G11
Darley Green Warks 118 C3
Darleyhall Herts 104 G2
Darley Head
N Yorks 205 B9
Darley Hillside
Derbys 170 C3
Darlingscott Warks 100 C4
Darlington Darl 224 C5
Darliston Shrops 149 C11
Darlton Notts 188 G3
Darmsden Suff 125 G11
Darnall S Yorks 186 D5
Darnaway Castle
Moray 301 D9
Darnford Staffs 134 B2
Darnhall Ches W 167 C10
Darnhall Mains
Borders 270 F4
Darn Hill Gtr Man 195 E10
Darnick Borders 262 C2
Darowen Powys 128 C6
Darra Aberds 303 E7
Darracott Devon 24 D2
Devon 40 F3
Darras Hall
Northumb 242 C5
Darrington W Yorks 198 D3
Darrow Green Norf 142 F5
Darsham Suff 127 D8
Darshill Som 44 E6
Dartford Kent 68 E4
Dartford Crossing
Kent 68 D5
Dartington Devon 8 C5
Dartmeet Devon 13 G9
Dartmouth Devon 9 E7
Dartmouth Park
London 67 B9
Darton S Yorks 197 F10
Darvel E Ayrs 258 B3
Darvillshill Bucks 84 F4
Darwell Hole E Sus 23 B11
Darwen Blkburn 195 C7
Dassels Herts 105 F7
Datchet Windsor 66 D3
Datchet Common
Windsor 66 D3
Datchworth Herts 86 B3
Datchworth Green
Herts 86 B3
Daubhill Gtr Man 195 F8
Daugh of Kinermony
Moray 302 E2
Dauntsey Wilts 62 C3
Dauntsey Lock Wilts 62 C3
Dava Moray 301 F10
Davenham
Ches W 183 G11
Davenport Ches E 168 B4
Gtr Man 184 D5
Davenport Green
Ches E 184 F4
Gtr Man 184 D4
Daventry Northants 119 E11
Davidson's Mains
Edin 280 F4
Davidston Highld 301 C7
Davidstow Corn 11 D9
David Street Kent 68 G6
David's Well Powys 113 B11
Davington Dumfries 248 C6
Kent 70 G4
Daviot Aberds 303 G7
Highld 301 F7
Davis's Town E Sus 23 B8
Davoch of Grange
Moray 302 D4
Davo Mains Aberds 293 F9
Davyhulme Gtr Man 184 B3
Daw Cross
N Yorks 205 C11
Dawdon Durham 234 B4
Daw End W Mid 133 C10
Dawesgreen Sur 51 D8
Dawker Hill N Yorks 207 F7
Dawley Telford 132 B3
Dawley Bank Telford 132 B3
Dawlish Devon 14 F5
Dawlish Warren
Devon 14 F5
Dawn Conwy 180 G5
Daw's Cross Essex 107 E7
Daw's Green Som 27 C11
Daws Heath Essex 69 B10
Dawshill Worcs 116 G6
Daw's House Corn 12 E2
Dawsmere Lincs 157 C8
Daybrook Notts 171 F9
Day Green Ches E 168 D3
Dayhills Staffs 151 C9
Dayhouse Bank
Worcs 117 B9
Daylesford Glos 100 F4
Daywall Shrops 148 C5
Ddol Flint 181 G10
Ddôl Cownwy
Powys 147 F10
Ddrydwy Anglesey 178 G5
Deacons Hill Herts 85 F11
Deadman's Cross
C Beds 104 C2
Deadman's Green
Staffs 151 B10
Deadwater Hants 49 F10
Northumb 250 D4
Deaf Hill Durham 234 D3
Deal Hall Essex 89 F8
Kent 55 C11
Dean Cumb 229 F7
Devon 8 C4
Devon 40 D6
Devon 40 E4
Devon 41 D8
Dorset 31 D7
Edin 280 G4
Hants 33 D9
Hants 48 G2
Lancs 195 B11
Oxon 100 G6
Som 45 E7
Dean Bank Durham 233 E11
Deanburnhaugh
Borders 261 G9
Dean Court Oxon 83 D7
Dean Cross Devon 40 E4
Deane Gtr Man 195 F7
Hants 48 C4
Deanend Dorset 31 D7
Dean Head S Yorks 197 G9
Deanich Lodge
Highld 309 L3
Deanland Dorset 31 D7
Deanlane End W Sus 34 E2
Dean Lane Head
W Yorks 205 G7
Dean Park Renfs 267 B10
Dean Prior Devon 8 C4
Dean Row Ches E 184 E5
Deans W Loth 269 B10
Deans Bottom Kent 69 G11
Deanscales Cumb 229 F7
Deansgreen
Ches E 183 D11
Dean's Green
Warks 118 D2
Deanshanger
Northants 102 D5
Deans Hill Kent 69 G11
Deanston Stirl 285 G11
Dean Street Kent 53 C8
Dearham Cumb 229 D7
Dearnley Gtr Man 196 D2
Debach Suff 126 G4
Debdale Gtr Man 184 B5
Debden Essex 86 F6
Essex 105 E11
Debden Cross
Essex 105 E11
Debden Green Essex 86 F6
Essex 105 E11
De Beauvoir Town
London 67 C10
Debenham Suff 126 E3
Deblin's Green Worcs 98 B6
Dechmont W Loth 279 G10
Deckham T&W 243 E7
Deddington Oxon 101 E9
Dedham Essex 107 E11
Dedham Heath
Essex 107 E11
Dedridge W Loth 269 B11
Dedworth Windsor 66 D2
Deebank Aberds 293 D8
Deecastle Aberds 292 D6
Deene Northants 137 E8
Deenethorpe
Northants 137 E9
Deepcar S Yorks 186 B3
Deepclough Derbys 185 B8
Deepcut Sur 50 B2
Deepdale C Beds 104 B4
Cumb 212 C4
N Yorks 213 D7
Deepdene Sur 51 D7
Deepfields W Mid 133 E8
Deeping Gate Lincs 138 B2
Deeping St James
Lincs 138 B3
Deeping St Nicholas
Lincs 156 F4
Deepthwaite Cumb 211 C10
Deepweir Mon 60 B3
Deerhill Moray 302 D4
Deerhurst Glos 99 F7
Deerhurst Walton
Glos 99 F7
Deerland Pembs 73 C7
Deerness Orkney 314 F5
Deer's Green Essex 105 E9
Deerstones N Yorks 205 C7
Deerton Street Kent 70 G3
Defford Worcs 99 C8
Defynnog Powys 95 F8
Deganwy Conwy 180 F3
Degar V Glam 58 D4
Degibna Corn 2 D5
Deighton N Yorks 225 E7
W Yorks 197 D7
York 207 E8
Deiniolen Gwyn 163 C9
Deishar Highld 291 B11
Delabole Corn 11 E7
Delamere Ches W 167 B9
Delfour Highld 291 C10
Delfrigs Aberds 303 G9
Delliefure Highld 301 F10
Dell Lodge Highld 292 B2
Dell Quay W Sus 22 C4
Delly End Oxon 82 C5
Delnabo Moray 292 B3
Delnadamph Aberds 292 C4
Delnamer Angus 292 G3
Delph Gtr Man 196 F3
Delves Durham 233 B8
Delvine Perth 286 C5
Delvin End Essex 106 D5
Dembleby Lincs 155 B10
Demelza Corn 5 C9
Denaby Main
S Yorks 187 B7
Denbeath Fife 281 B7
Denbigh Denb 165 B9
Denbury Devon 8 B6
Denby Derbys 170 F5
Denby Bottles
Derbys 170 F5
Denby Common
Derbys 170 F6
Denby Dale
W Yorks 197 F8
Denchworth Oxon 82 G5
Dendron Cumb 210 E4
Denel End C Beds 103 D10
Denend Aberds 302 F6
Dene Park Kent 52 C5
Deneside Durham 234 B4
Denford Northants 121 B9
Staffs 169 E7
Dengie Essex 89 E7
Denham Bucks 66 B4
Bucks 102 G5
Suff 124 E5
Suff 126 C3
Denham Corner
Suff 126 C3
Denham End Suff 124 E5
Denham Green Bucks 66 B4
Denham Street Suff 126 C3
Denhead Aberds 303 D9
Fife 287 F8
Denhead of Arbilot
Angus 287 C9
Denhead of Gray
Dundee 287 D7
Denholm Borders 262 F3
Denholme W Yorks 205 G7
Denholme Clough
W Yorks 205 G7
Denholme Edge
W Yorks 205 G7
Denholme Gate
W Yorks 205 G7
Denholmhill Borders 262 F3
Denio Gwyn 145 B7
Denmead Hants 33 E11
Denmore Aberdeen 293 B11
Denmoss Aberds 302 E6
Dennington Suff 126 D5
Dennington Corner
Suff 126 D5
Dennington Hall
Suff 126 D5
Denny Falk 278 E6
Denny Bottom Kent 52 F5
Denny End Cambs 123 D9
Dennyloanhead
Falk 278 E6
Denny Lodge Hants 32 F4
Dennystown
W Dunb 277 F7
Denshaw Gtr Man 196 E3
Denside Aberds 293 D10
Densole Kent 55 E8
Denston Suff 124 G5
Denstone Staffs 169 G9
Denstroude Kent 70 G6
Dent Cumb 212 B4
Dent Bank Durham 232 F4
Denton Cambs 138 F2
Darl 224 B4
E Sus 23 E7
Gtr Man 184 B6
Kent 55 D8
Kent 69 E7
Lincs 155 C7
Norf 142 F5
Northants 120 F6
N Yorks 205 D8
Oxon 83 E9
Denton Burn T&W 242 D5
Denton Holme
Cumb 239 G10
Denton's Green
Mers 183 B7
Denver Norf 140 C2
Denvilles Hants 22 B2
Denwick Northumb 264 G6
Deopham Norf 141 C11
Deopham Green
Norf 141 D10
Deopham Stalland
Norf 141 D10
Depden Suff 124 F5
Depden Green Suff 124 F5
Deppers Bridge
Warks 119 F7
Deptford London 67 D11
T&W 243 F9
Wilts 46 F4
Derby Derbys 153 B7
Devon 40 G5
Derbyhaven IoM 192 F3
Derbyshire Hill
Mers 183 C8
Dereham Norf 159 G9
Dergoals Dumfries 236 D4
Deri Caerph 77 E10
Derriford Plym 7 D9
Derril Devon 24 G4
Derringstone Kent 55 D8
Derrington Shrops 132 E2
Staffs 151 E7
Derriton Devon 24 G4
Derry Stirl 285 E10
Derrydaroch Stirl 285 E7
Derry Downs London 68 F3
Derry Fields Wilts 81 G8
Derryguaig Argyll 288 F6
Derry Hill Wilts 62 E3
Derry Lodge Aberds 292 D2
Derrythorpe
N Lincs 199 F10
Dersingham Norf 158 C3
Dertfords Wilts 45 D10
Dervaig Argyll 288 D6
Derwen Bridgend 58 C2
Denb 165 E9
Derwenlas Powys 128 D4
Desborough
Northants 136 G6
Desford Leics 135 C9
Deskryshiel Aberds 292 B6
Detchant Northumb 264 B3
Detling Kent 53 B9
Deuchar Angus 292 G6
Deuddwr Powys 148 F4
Deuxhill Shrops 132 F3
Devauden Mon 79 F7
Deveral Corn 2 B3
Devil's Bridge /
Pontarfynach
Ceredig 112 B4
Devitts Green
Warks 134 E5
Devizes Wilts 62 G4
Devol Invclyd 276 G6
Devonport Plym 7 E9
Devonside Clack 279 B8
Devon Village Clack 279 B8
Devoran Corn 3 B7
Dewar Borders 270 F6
Dewartown Midloth 271 C7
Dewes Green Essex 105 E9
Dewlands Common
Dorset 31 F9
Dewlish Dorset 17 B11
Dewsbury W Yorks 197 C8
Dewsbury Moor
W Yorks 197 C8
Dewshall Court
Hereford 97 E9
Dhoon IoM 192 D5
Dhoor IoM 192 C5
Dhowin IoM 192 B5
Dhustone Shrops 115 B11
Dial Green W Sus 34 B6
Dial Post W Sus 35 D11
Dibberford Dorset 29 G7
Dibden Hants 32 F6
Dibden Purlieu Hants 32 F6
Dickens Heath
W Mid 118 B2
Dickleburgh Norf 142 G3
Dickleburgh Moor
Norf 142 G3
Dickon Hills Lincs 174 D6
Didbrook Glos 99 E11
Didcot Oxon 64 B4
Diddington Cambs 122 D3
Diddlebury Shrops 131 F10
Diddywell Devon 25 B7
Didley Hereford 97 E9
Didling W Sus 34 D4
Didlington Norf 140 D5
Didmarton Glos 61 B10
Didsbury Gtr Man 184 C4
Didworthy Devon 8 C3
Diebidale Highld 309 L4
Digbeth W Mid 133 F11
Digby Lincs 173 E9
Digg Highld 298 C4
Diggle Gtr Man 196 F4
Diglis Worcs 116 G6
Digmoor Lancs 194 F3
Digswell Herts 86 B3
Digswell Park Herts 86 C2
Digswell Water Herts 86 C3
Dihewyd Ceredig 111 F9
Dilham Norf 160 D6
Dilhorne Staffs 169 G7
Dillarburn S Lnrk 268 G6
Dill Hall Lancs 195 B8
Dillington Cambs 122 D2
Som 28 D5
Dilston Northumb 241 E11
Dilton Marsh Wilts 45 D11
Dilwyn Hereford 115 G8
Dimlands V Glam 58 F3
Dimmer Som 44 G6
Dimple Derbys 170 C3
Gtr Man 195 D8
Dimsdale Staffs 168 F4
Dimson Corn 12 G4
Dinas Carms 92 E5
Corn 10 G4
Gwyn 144 B5
Gwyn 163 D7
Dinas Cross Pembs 91 D10
Dinas Dinlle Gwyn 162 D6
Dinas-Mawddwy
Gwyn 147 G7
Dinas Mawr Conwy 164 E4
Dinas Powys V Glam 59 E7
Dinbych y Pysgod /
Tenby Pembs 73 E10
Dinckley Lancs 203 F9
Dinder Som 44 E5
Dinedor Hereford 97 D10
Dinedor Cross
Hereford 97 D10
Dines Green Worcs 116 F6
Dingestow Mon 79 C7
Dinghurst N Som 44 B2
Dingle Mers 182 D5
Dingleden Kent 53 G10
Dingleton Borders 262 C2
Dingley Northants 136 F5
Dingwall Highld 300 D5
Dinlabyre Borders 250 E2
Dinmael Conwy 165 G8
Dinnet Aberds 292 D6
Dinnington Som 28 E6
S Yorks 187 D8
T&W 242 C6
Dinorwic Gwyn 163 C9
Dinton Bucks 84 C3
Wilts 46 G4
Dinwoodie Mains
Dumfries 248 E4
Dinworthy Devon 24 D4
Dipford Som 28 C2
Dipley Hants 49 B8
Dippenhall Sur 49 D10
Dippertown Devon 12 E4
Dippin N Ayrs 256 E2
Dipple Devon 24 D4
Moray 302 D3
S Ayrs 244 C6
Diptford Devon 8 D4
Dipton Durham 242 G5
Diptonmill
Northumb 241 E10
Dirdhu Highld 301 G10
Direcleit W Isles 305 J3
Dirleton E Loth 281 E10
Dirt Pot Northumb 232 B3
Discoed Powys 114 E5
Discove Som 45 G7
Diseworth Leics 153 E9
Dishes Orkney 314 D6
Dishforth N Yorks 215 E7
Dishley Leics 153 E10
Disley Ches E 185 E7
Diss Norf 126 B2
Disserth Powys 113 F10
Distington Cumb 228 G6
Ditchampton Wilts 46 G5
Ditcheat Som 44 F6
Ditchfield Bucks 84 G4
Ditchford Hill
Worcs 100 D4
Ditchingham Norf 142 E6
Ditchling E Sus 36 D4
Ditherington
Shrops 149 G10
Ditteridge Wilts 61 F10
Dittisham Devon 9 E7
Ditton Halton 183 D7
Kent 53 B8
Ditton Green Cambs 124 F3
Ditton Priors Shrops 132 F2
Dittons E Sus 23 E10
Divach Highld 300 G4
Divlyn Carms 94 D5
Dixton Glos 99 E9
Mon 79 C8
Dizzard Corn 11 B9
Dobcross Gtr Man 196 F3
Dobs Hill Flint 166 C4
Dobson's Bridge
Shrops 149 C9
Dobwalls Corn 6 C4
Doccombe Devon 13 D11
Dochfour Ho Highld 300 F6
Dochgarroch Highld 300 E6
Dockeney Norf 143 E7
Dockenfield Sur 49 E10
Docker Lancs 211 E11
Docking Norf 158 B5
Docklow Hereford 115 F11
Dockray Cumb 230 G3
Dockroyd W Yorks 204 F6
Doc Penfro / Pembroke
Dock Pembs 73 E7
Docton Devon 24 C2
Dodbrooke Devon 8 G4
Dodburn Borders 249 B11
Doddenham Worcs 116 F5
Doddinghurst Essex 87 F9
Doddington Cambs 139 E7
Kent 54 B2
Lincs 188 G6
Northumb 263 C11
Shrops 116 B2
Doddiscombsleigh
Devon 14 D3
Doddshill Norf 158 C3
Doddycross Corn 6 C6
Dodford Northants 120 E2
Worcs 117 C8
Dodington S Glos 61 C9
Som 43 E7
Dodleston Ches W 166 C5
Dodmarsh Hereford 97 C11
Dodscott Devon 25 D8
Dods Leigh Staffs 151 C10
Dodworth S Yorks 197 F10
Dodworth Bottom
S Yorks 197 G10
Dodworth Green
S Yorks 197 G10
Doe Bank W Mid 134 D2
Doe Green Warr 183 D9
Doehole Derbys 170 D5
Doe Lea Derbys 171 B7
Doffcocker Gtr Man 195 E7
Dogdyke Lincs 174 D2
Dog & Gun Mers 182 B5
Dog Hill Gtr Man 196 F3
Dogingtree Estate
Staffs 151 G9
Dogley Lane
W Yorks 197 E7
Dogmersfield Hants 49 C9
Dogridge Wilts 62 B5
Dogsthorpe Pboro 138 C3
Dog Village Devon 14 B5
Doirlinn Highld 289 D8
Dolanog Powys 147 G11
Dolau Powys 114 D2
Rhondda 58 C3
Dolbenmaen Gwyn 163 G8
Dole Ceredig 128 F2
Dolemeads Bath 61 G9
Doley Staffs 150 D4
Dolfach Powys 129 C8
Dol-ffanog Gwyn 146 G4
Dolfor Powys 130 F2
Dol-fôr Powys 128 B6
Dolgarrog Conwy 164 B3
Dolgellau Gwyn 146 F4
Dolgerdd Ceredig 111 G8
Dolgoch Gwyn 128 C3
Dolgran Carms 93 E8
Dolhelfa Powys 113 C8
Dolhendre Gwyn 147 C7
Doll Highld 311 J2
Dollar Clack 279 B9
Dolley Green Powys 114 D5
Dollis Hill London 67 B8
Dollwen Ceredig 128 G3
Dolphin Flint 181 G11
Dolphingstone
E Loth 281 G7
Dolphinholme
Lancs 202 C6
Dolphinston Borders 262 F5
Dolphinton S Lnrk 270 F2
Dolton Devon 25 E9
Dolwen Conwy 180 G5
Powys 129 B9
Dolwyd Conwy 180 F4
Dolwyddelan Conwy 164 E2
Dôl-y-Bont Ceredig 128 F2
Dol-y-cannau Powys 96 B3
Dolydd Gwyn 163 D7
Dolyhir Powys 114 F4
Dolymelinau
Powys 129 D11
Dolywern Wrex 148 B4
Domewood Sur 51 E10
Domgay Powys 148 F5
Dommett Som 28 E3
Doncaster S Yorks 198 G5
Doncaster Common
S Yorks 198 G6
Dones Green
Ches W 183 F10
Donhead St Andrew
Wilts 30 C6
Donhead St Mary
Wilts 30 C6
Donibristle Fife 280 D3
Doniford Som 42 E5
Donington Lincs 156 B4
Shrops 132 C6
Donington Eaudike
Lincs 156 B4
Donington le Heath
Leics 153 G8
Donington on Bain
Lincs 190 E2
Donington South Ing
Lincs 156 C4
Donisthorpe Leics 152 G6
Don Johns Essex 106 F6
Donkey Street Kent 54 G6
Donkey Town Sur 66 G2
Donna Nook Lincs 190 B6
Donnington Glos 100 F3
Hereford 98 E4
Shrops 131 B11
Telford 150 G4
W Berks 64 F3
W Sus 22 C5
Donnington Wood
Telford 150 G4
Donwell T&W 243 F7
Donyatt Som 28 E4
Doomsday Green
W Sus 35 B11
Doonfoot S Ayrs 257 F8
Dora's Green Hants 49 D10
Dorback Lodge
Highld 292 B2
Dorcan Swindon 63 C7
Dorchester Dorset 17 C9
Oxon 83 G9
Dordale Worcs 117 C8
Dordon Warks 134 C5
Dore S Yorks 186 E4
Dores Highld 300 F5
Dorking Sur 51 D7
Dorking Tye Suff 107 D8
Dorley's Corner
Suff 127 D7
Dormansland Sur 52 E2
Dormans Park Sur 51 E11
Dormanstown
Redcar 235 G7
Dormer's Wells
London 66 C6
Dormington
Hereford 97 C11
Dormston Worcs 117 F9
Dorn Glos 100 E4
Dornal S Ayrs 236 B4
Dorney Bucks 66 D2
Dorney Reach Bucks 66 D2
Dorn Hill Worcs 100 E3
Dornie Highld 295 C10
Dornoch Highld 309 L7
Dornock Dumfries 238 D6
Dorrery Highld 310 D4
Dorridge W Mid 118 B3
Dorrington Lincs 173 E9
Shrops 131 C9
Dorsington Warks 100 B2
Dorstone Hereford 96 C6
Dorton Bucks 83 C11
Dorusduain Highld 295 C11
Doseley Telford 132 B3
Dosmuckeran
Highld 300 C2
Dosthill Staffs 134 C4
Staffs 134 D4
Dothan Anglesey 178 G5
Dothill Telford 150 G2
Dottery Dorset 16 B5
Doublebois Corn 6 C3
Double Hill Bath 45 B8
Dougarie N Ayrs 255 D9
Doughton Glos 80 G5
Norf 159 D7
Douglas IoM 192 E4
S Lnrk 259 C8
Douglas & Angus
Dundee 287 D8
Douglastown Angus 287 C8
Douglas Water S
Lnrk 259 B9
Douglas West S
Lnrk 259 C8
Doulting Som 44 E6
Dounby Orkney 314 D2
Doune Highld 291 C10
Highld 309 J4
Stirl 285 G11
Doune Park Aberds 303 C7
Douneside Aberds 292 C6
Dounie Argyll 275 D8
Highld 309 K5
Highld 309 L6
Dounreay Highld 310 C3
Doura N Ayrs 266 G6
Dousland Devon 7 B10
Dovaston Shrops 149 E7
Dovecot Mers 182 C6
Dovecothall
Glasgow 267 D10
Dove Green Notts 171 E7
Dove Holes Derbys 185 F9
Dovenby Cumb 229 E7
Dovendale Lincs 190 E4
Dove Point Mers 182 C2
Dover Gtr Man 194 G6

Kent 55 E10
Dovercourt Essex 108 E5
Doverdale Worcs 117 D7
Doverhay Som 41 D11
Doveridge Derbys 152 C2
Doversgreen Sur 51 D9
Dowally Perth 286 C4
Dowanhill Glasgow 267 B11
Dowbridge Lancs 202 G4
Dowdeswell Glos 81 B7
Dowe Hill Norf 161 F10
Dowlais M Tydf 77 D10
Dowlais Top M Tydf 77 D9
Dowland Devon 25 E9
Dowles Worcs 116 B5
Dowlesgreen
  Wokingham 65 F10
Dowlish Ford Som 28 E5
Dowlish Wake Som 28 E5
Downall Green
  Gtr Man 194 G5
Down Ampney Glos 81 F10
Downan Moray 301 F11
  S Ayrs 244 G3
Downcraig Ferry
  N Ayrs 266 D3
Downderry Corn 6 E6
Downe London 68 G2
Downend Glos 80 F4
  IoW 20 D6
  S Glos 60 D6
  W Berks 64 D3
Down End Som 43 E10
Downfield Dundee 287 D7
Down Field Cambs 124 C2
Downgate Corn 11 G11
  Corn 12 G3
Down Hall Cumb 239 G7
Downham Essex 88 F2
  Lancs 203 E11
  London 67 E11
  Northumb 263 C9
Downham Market
  Norf 140 C2
Down Hatherley Glos 99 G7
Downhead Som 29 B9
  Som 45 D7
Downhead Park
  M Keynes 103 C7
Downhill Corn 5 B7
  Perth 286 D4
  T&W 243 F9
Downholland Cross
  Lancs 193 F11
Downholme
  N Yorks 224 F2
Downicary Devon 12 C3
Downies Aberds 293 D11
Downinney Corn 11 C10
Downley Bucks 84 G4
Down Park W Sus 51 F10
Downs V Glam 58 E6
Down St Mary Devon 26 G2
Downside C Beds 103 G10
  E Sus 23 E9
  N Som 60 F3
  Som 44 D6
  Som 50 B6
  Sur 51 B7
Down Street E Sus 36 C6
Down Thomas Devon 7 E10
Downton Hants 19 C11
  Powys 114 E4
  Shrops 149 G10
  Wilts 31 C11
Downton on the Rock
  Hereford 115 C8
Dowsby Lincs 156 D2
Dowsdale Lincs 156 G5
Dowslands Som 28 C2
Dowthwaitehead
  Cumb 230 G3
Doxey Staffs 151 E8
Doxford Park T&W 243 G9
Doynton S Glos 61 E8
Drabblegate Norf 160 D4
Draethen Newport 59 B8
Draffan S Lnrk 268 F5
Dragley Beck Cumb 210 D5
Dragonby N Lincs 200 E2
Dragons Green
  W Sus 35 C10
Drakehouse
  S Yorks 186 E6
Drakeland Corner
  Devon 7 D11
Drakelow Worcs 132 G6
Drakemyre Aberds 303 F9
  N Ayrs 266 E5
Drake's Broughton
  Worcs 99 B8
Drakes Cross
  Worcs 117 B11
Drakestone Green
  Suff 107 B9
Drakewalls Corn 12 G4
Draughton
  Northants 120 B5
  N Yorks 204 C6
Drawbridge Corn 6 B3
Drax N Yorks 199 B7
Draycot Oxon 83 D10
Draycot Cerne Wilts 62 D2
Draycote Warks 119 C8
Draycot Fitz Payne
  Wilts 62 G6
Draycot Foliat
  Swindon 63 D7
Draycott Derbys 153 C8
  Glos 80 E2
  Glos 100 D3
  Shrops 132 E6
  Som 29 C8
  Som 44 C3
  Worcs 99 B7
Draycott in the Clay
  Staffs 152 D3
Draycott in the Moors
  Staffs 169 G7
Drayford Devon 26 E3
Drayton Leics 136 E6
  Lincs 156 B4
  Norf 160 G3
  Northants 119 E11
  Oxon 83 G7
  Oxon 101 C8
  Ptsmth 33 F11
  Som 28 C6
  Som 29 D7
  Warks 118 F3
  Worcs 117 B8
Drayton Bassett
  Staffs 134 C3
Drayton Beauchamp
  Bucks 84 C6
Drayton Parslow
  Bucks 102 F6
Drayton St Leonard
  Oxon 83 F10
Drebley N Yorks 205 B7
Dreemskerry IoM 192 C5
Dreenhill Pembs 72 C6
Drefach Carms 75 C8
  Carms 92 G5
  Carms 93 D7
Dre-fach Carms 75 B11
  Ceredig 93 B10
Drefelin Carms 93 D7
Dreggie Highld 301 G10
Dreghorn Edin 270 B4
  N Ayrs 257 B9
Dre-gôch Denb 165 B10
Drellingore Kent 55 E8
Drem E Loth 281 F10
Dresden Stoke 168 G6
Dreumasdal
  W Isles 297 H3
Drewsteignton
  Devon 13 C10
Driby Lincs 190 G5
Driffield E Yorks 208 B6
  Glos 81 F9
Drift Corn 1 D4
Drigg Cumb 219 F11
Drighlington
  W Yorks 197 B8
Drimnin Highld 289 D7
Drimnin Ho Highld 289 D7
Drimpton Dorset 28 F6
Drimsynie Argyll 284 G5
Dringhoe E Yorks 209 C9
Dringhouses York 207 D7
Drinisiadar W Isles 305 J3
Drinkstone Suff 125 E9
Drinkstone Green
  Suff 125 E9
Drishaig Argyll 284 F5
Drissaig Argyll 275 B10
Drive End Dorset 29 F9
Driver's End Herts 86 B2
Drochedlie Aberds 302 C5
Drochil Borders 270 G3
Drointon Staffs 151 D10
Droitwich Spa
  Worcs 117 E7
Droman Highld 306 D6
Dromore Dumfries 237 C7
Dron Perth 286 F5
Dronfield Derbys 186 F5
Dronfield Woodhouse
  Derbys 186 F4
Drongan E Ayrs 257 F10
Dronley Angus 287 D7
Droop Dorset 30 F3
Drope Cardiff 58 D6
Dropping Well
  S Yorks 186 C5
Droughduil
  Dumfries 236 D3
Droxford Hants 33 D10
Droylsden Gtr Man 184 B6
Drub W Yorks 197 B7
Druggers End Worcs 98 D5
Druid Denb 165 G8
Druidston Pembs 72 B5
Druim Highld 301 D9
Druimarbin Highld 290 F2
Druimavuic Argyll 284 C4
Druimdrishaig
  Argyll 275 F8
Druimindarroch
  Highld 295 G8
Druimkinnerras
  Highld 300 F4
Druimnacroish
  Argyll 288 E6
Druimsornaig Argyll 289 F9
Druimyeon More
  Argyll 255 B7
Drum Argyll 275 F10
  Edin 270 B6
  Perth 286 G4
Drumardoch Stirl 285 F10
Drumbeg Highld 306 F6
Drumblade Aberds 302 E5
Drumblair Aberds 302 E6
Drumbuie Dumfries 246 G3
  Highld 295 B9
Drumburgh Cumb 239 F7
Drumburn
  Dumfries 237 C11
Drumchapel
  Glasgow 277 G10
Drumchardine
  Highld 300 E5
Drumchork Highld 307 L3
Drumclog S Lnrk 258 B4
Drumdelgie Aberds 302 E4
Drumderfit Highld 300 D6
Drumdollo Aberds 302 F6
Drumeldrie Fife 287 G8
Drumelzier Borders 260 C4
Drumfearn Highld 295 D8
Drumgask Highld 291 D8
Drumgelloch N Lnrk 268 B5
Drumgley Angus 287 B8
Drumgreen Angus 292 F6
Drumguish Highld 291 D9
Drumhead Aberds 293 B11
Drumin Moray 301 F11
Drumindorsair
  Highld 300 E4
Drumlasie Aberds 293 C8
Drumlean Stirl 285 G8
Drumlemble Argyll 255 F7
Drumliah Highld 309 K6
Drumligair Aberds 293 B11
Drumlithie Aberds 293 E9
Drumloist Stirl 285 G10
Drummersdale
  Lancs 193 E11
Drummick Perth 286 E3
Drummoddie
  Dumfries 236 E5
Drummond Highld 300 C6
Drummore Dumfries 236 F3
Drummuir Moray 302 E3
Drummuir Castle
  Moray 302 E3
Drumnadrochit
  Highld 300 G5
Drumnagorrach
  Moray 302 D5
Drumness Perth 286 F2
Drumoak Aberds 293 D9
Drumore Argyll 255 E8
Drumpark Dumfries 247 G9
Drumpellier N Lnrk 268 B4
Drumphail Dumfries 236 C4
Drumrash Dumfries 237 B8
Drumrunie Highld 307 J6
Drumry W Dunb 277 G10
Drums Aberds 303 G9
Drumsallie Highld 289 B11
Drumsmittal Highld 300 E6
Drumstinchall
  Dumfries 237 D10
Drumsturdy Angus 287 D8
Drumtochty Castle
  Aberds 293 F8
Drumtroddan
  Dumfries 236 E5
Drumuie Highld 298 E4
Drumuillie Highld 301 G9
Drumvaich Stirl 285 G10
Drumwalt Dumfries 236 D5
Drumwhindle
  Aberds 303 F9
Drunkendub Angus 287 C10
Drury Flint 166 C3
Drurylane Norf 141 C8
Drury Lane Wrex 167 G7
Drury Square Norf 159 F8
Drybeck Cumb 222 B3
Drybridge Moray 302 C4
  N Ayrs 257 B9
Drybrook Glos 79 B10
Dryburgh Borders 262 C3
Dryden Borders 261 E11
Dry Doddington
  Lincs 172 F4
Dry Drayton Cambs 123 E7
Dryhill Kent 52 B3
Dry Hill Hants 49 F7
Dryhope Borders 261 E7
Drylaw Edin 280 F4
Drym Corn 2 C4
Drymen Stirl 277 D9
Drymere Norf 140 B5
Drymuir Aberds 303 E9
Drynachan Lodge
  Highld 301 F8
Drynain Argyll 276 D3
Drynham Wilts 45 B11
Drynie Park Highld 300 D5
Drynoch Highld 294 B6
Dry Sandford Oxon 83 E7
Dryslwyn Carms 93 G11
Dry Street Essex 69 B7
Dryton Shrops 131 B11
Drywells Aberds 302 D6
Duag Bridge Highld 309 K3
Duartbeg Highld 306 F6
Duartmore Bridge
  Highld 306 F6
Dubbs Cross Devon 12 C3
Dubford Aberds 303 C8
Dubhchladach
  Argyll 275 G9
Dublin Suff 126 D3
Dubton Angus 287 B9
Dubwath Cumb 229 E9
Duchally Highld 309 H3
Duchlage Argyll 276 D6
Duchrae Dumfries 246 G5
Duck Corner Suff 109 C7
Duck End Beds 103 C11
  Beds 121 G9
  Bucks 102 F5
  Cambs 122 E4
  Essex 105 G10
  Essex 106 E3
  Essex 106 F3
Duckend Green
  Essex 106 G4
Duckhole S Glos 79 G10
Duckington Ches W 167 E7
Ducklington Oxon 82 D5
Duckmanton Derbys 186 G6
Duck's Cross Beds 122 F2
Ducks Island London 86 F2
Duckswich Worcs 98 D6
Dudbridge Glos 80 E4
Dudden Hill London 67 B8
Duddenhoe End
  Essex 105 D9
Duddingston Edin 280 G5
Duddington
  Northants 137 C9
Duddlestone Som 28 C2
Duddleswell E Sus 37 B7
Duddlewick Shrops 132 G3
Duddo Northumb 273 G8
Duddon Ches W 167 C8
Duddon Bridge
  Cumb 210 B3
Duddon Common
  Ches W 167 B8
Dudleston Shrops 148 B6
Dudleston Grove
  Shrops 149 B7
Dudleston Heath
  (Criftins) Shrops 149 B7
Dudley T&W 243 C7
  W Mid 133 E8
Dudley Hill W Yorks 205 G9
Dudley Port W Mid 133 E9
Dudley's Fields
  W Mid 133 C9
Dudley Wood
  W Mid 133 F8
Dudlows Green
  Warr 183 E10
Dudsbury Dorset 19 B7
Dudswell Herts 85 D7
Dudwells Pembs 91 G8
Duerdon Devon 24 D4
Duffield Derbys 170 G4
Duffieldbank
  Derbys 170 G5
Duffryn Neath 57 B10
  Newport 59 B9
  Shrops 130 G4
Dufftown Moray 302 F3
Duffus Moray 301 C11
Dufton Cumb 231 F9
Duggleby N Yorks 217 F7
Duich Argyll 254 B4
Duiletter Argyll 284 D5
Duinish Perth 291 G8
Duirinish Highld 295 B9
Duisdalebeg Highld 295 D8
Duisdalemore
  Highld 295 D9
Duisky Highld 290 F2
Duke End Warks 134 F4
Dukesfield
  Northumb 241 F10
Dukestown
  Bl Gwent 77 C10
Dukinfield Gtr Man 184 B6
Dulas Anglesey 179 D7
Dulcote Som 44 E5
Dulford Devon 27 F9
Dull Perth 286 C2
Dullatur N Lnrk 278 F4
Dullingham Cambs 124 F2
Dullingham Ley
  Cambs 124 F2
Dulnain Bridge
  Highld 301 G9
Duloch Fife 280 D2
Duloe Beds 122 E3
  Corn 6 D4
Dulsie Highld 301 E9
Dulverton Som 26 B6
Dulwich London 67 E10
Dulwich Village
  London 67 E10
Dumbarton W Dunb 277 F7
Dumbleton Glos 99 D10
Dumcrieff Dumfries 248 C4
Dumfries Dumfries 237 B11
Dumgoyne Stirl 277 E10
Dummer Hants 48 D5
Dumpford W Sus 34 C4
Dumpinghill Devon 24 F6
Dumpling Green
  Norf 159 G10
Dumplington
  Gtr Man 184 B3
Dumpton Kent 71 F11
Dun Angus 287 B10
Dunach Argyll 289 G10
Dunadd Argyll 275 D9
Dunain Ho Highld 300 E6
Dunalastair Perth 285 B11
Dunan Highld 295 C7
Dunans Argyll 275 D9
  Argyll 275 D11
Dunball Som 43 E10
Dunbar E Loth 282 F3
Dunbeath Highld 311 G5
Dunbeg Argyll 289 F10
Dunblane Stirl 285 G11
Dunbog Fife 286 F6
Dunbridge Hants 32 B4
Duncansclett
  Shetland 313 K5
Duncanston Highld 300 D5
Duncanstone
  Aberds 302 G5
Dun Charlabhaigh
  W Isles 304 D3
Dunchideock Devon 14 D3
Dunchurch Warks 119 C9
Duncombe Lancs 202 F6
Duncote Northants 120 G3
Duncow Dumfries 247 G11
Duncraggan Stirl 285 G9
Duncrievie Perth 286 G5
Duncroisk Stirl 285 D9
Duncton W Sus 35 D7
Dundas Ho Orkney 314 H4
Dundee Dundee 287 D8
Dundeugh Dumfries 246 F3
Dundon Som 44 G3
Dundonald Fife 280 C4
  S Ayrs 257 C9
Dundon Hayes Som 44 G3
Dundonnell Highld 307 L5
Dundonnell Hotel
  Highld 307 L5
Dundonnell House
  Highld 307 L6
Dundraw Cumb 229 B10
Dundreggan Highld 290 B5
Dundreggan Lodge
  Highld 290 B5
Dundrennan
  Dumfries 237 E9
Dundridge Hants 33 D9
Dundry N Som 60 F5
Dundurn Perth 285 E11
Dundyvan N Lnrk 268 C4
Dunecht Aberds 293 C9
Dunfermline Fife 279 D11
Dunfield Glos 81 F10
Dunford Bridge
  S Yorks 197 G7
Dungate Kent 54 B2
Dunge Wilts 45 C11
Dungeness Kent 39 D9
Dungworth S Yorks 186 D3
Dunham Notts 188 G4
Dunham-on-the-Hill
  Ches W 183 G7
Dunham on Trent
  Notts 188 G4
Dunhampstead
  Worcs 117 E8
Dunhampton Worcs 116 D6
Dunham Town
  Gtr Man 184 D2
Dunham Woodhouses
  Gtr Man 184 D2
Dunholme Lincs 189 F8
Dunino Fife 287 F9
Dunipace Falk 278 E6
Dunira Perth 285 E11
Dunkeld Perth 286 C4
Dunkerton Bath 45 B8
Dunkeswell Devon 27 F10
Dunkeswick
  N Yorks 206 D2
Dunkirk Cambs 139 F10
  Ches W 182 G5
  Kent 54 B5
  Norf 160 D4
  Nottingham 153 B11
  S Glos 61 B9
  Staffs 168 E4
  Wilts 62 G3
Dunk's Green Kent 52 C6
Dunlappie Angus 293 G7
Dunley Hants 48 C3
  Worcs 116 D5
Dunlichity Lodge
  Highld 300 F6
Dunlop E Ayrs 267 F8
Dunmaglass Lodge
  Highld 300 G5
Dunmere Corn 5 B10
Dunmore Argyll 275 G8
  Falk 279 D7
  Highld 300 E5
Dunnerholme Cumb 210 D4
Dunnet Highld 310 B6
Dunnichen Angus 287 C9
Dunnikier Fife 280 C5
Dunninald Angus 287 B11
Dunning Perth 286 F4
Dunnington
  E Yorks 209 C9
  Warks 117 G11
  York 207 C9
Dunningwell Cumb 210 C3
Dunnockshaw
  Lancs 195 B10
Dunnose IoW 21 F7
Dunnsheath Shrops 149 F9
Dunn Street Kent 54 D3
  Kent 69 G9
Dunollie Argyll 289 F10
Dunoon Argyll 276 F3
Dunragit Dumfries 236 D3
Dunrobin Mains
  Highld 311 J2
Dunrostan Argyll 275 E8
Duns Borders 272 E5
Dunsa Derbys 186 G2
Dunsby Lincs 156 D2
Dunscar Gtr Man 195 E8
Dunscore Dumfries 247 G9
Dunscroft S Yorks 199 F7
Dunsdale Redcar 226 B2
Dunsden Green Oxon 65 D8
Dunsfold Sur 50 F4
Dunsfold Common
  Sur 50 F4
Dunsfold Green Sur 50 F4
Dunsford Devon 14 D2
  Sur 50 F4
Dunshalt Fife 286 F6
Dunshillock Aberds 303 E9
Dunsill Notts 171 C7
Dunsinnan Perth 286 D5
Dunskey Ho
  Dumfries 236 D2
Dunslea Corn 11 G11
Dunsley N Yorks 227 C7
  Staffs 133 G7
Dunsmore Bucks 84 D5
  Warks 119 B10
Dunsop Bridge
  Lancs 203 C9
Dunstable C Beds 103 G10
Dunstall Staffs 151 D11
Dunstall Staffs 152 E3
Dunstall Common
  Worcs 99 C7
Dunstall Green Suff 124 E4
Dunstall Hill W Mid 133 C8
Dunstan Northumb 265 F7
Dunstan Steads
  Northumb 264 E6
Dunster Som 42 E3
Duns Tew Oxon 101 F9
Dunston Derbys 186 G5
  Lincs 173 C9
  Norf 142 C4
  Staffs 151 F8
  T&W 242 E6
Dunstone Devon 7 E11
  Devon 8 G5
Dunston Heath
  Staffs 151 F8
Dunston Hill T&W 242 E6
Dunsville S Yorks 198 F6
Dunswell E Yorks 209 F7
Dunsyre S Lnrk 269 F11
Dunterton Devon 12 F3
Dunthrop Oxon 101 F7
Duntisbourne Abbots
  Glos 81 D7
Duntisbourne Leer
  Glos 81 D7
Duntisbourne Rouse
  Glos 81 D7
Duntish Dorset 29 F11
Duntocher W Dunb 277 G9
Dunton Bucks 102 G6
  C Beds 104 C4
  Norf 159 C7
Dunton Bassett
  Leics 135 E10
Dunton Green Kent 52 B4
Dunton Patch Norf 159 C7
Dunton Wayletts
  Essex 87 G11
Duntrune Castle
  Argyll 275 D8
Duntulm Highld 298 B4
Dunure S Ayrs 257 F7
Dunvant / Dynfant
  Swansea 56 C5
Dunvegan Highld 298 E2
Dunveth Corn 10 G5
Dunwear Som 43 F10
Dunwich Suff 127 C9
Dunwood Staffs 168 D6
Dupplin Castle
  Perth 286 F4
Durdar Cumb 239 G10
Durgan Corn 3 D7
Durgates E Sus 52 G6
Durham Durham 233 C11
Durisdeer Dumfries 247 C9
Durisdeermill
  Dumfries 247 C9
Durkar W Yorks 197 D10
Durleigh Som 43 F9
Durleighmarsh
  W Sus 34 C3
Durley Hants 33 D8
  Wilts 63 G8
Durley Street Hants 33 D8
Durlock Kent 55 B9
Durlow Common
  Hereford 98 D2
Durn Gtr Man 196 D2
Durnamuck Highld 307 K5
Durness Highld 308 C4
Durnfield Som 29 C7
Durno Aberds 303 G7
Durns Town Hants 19 B11
Duror Highld 289 D11
Durran Argyll 275 C10
  Highld 310 C5
Durrant Green Kent 53 F11
Durrants Hants 22 B2
Durrington Wilts 47 E7
  W Sus 35 F10
Durrisdale Orkney 314 D3
Dursley Glos 80 F3
  Wilts 45 C11
Dursley Cross Glos 98 G3
Durston Som 28 B3
Durweston Dorset 30 F5
Dury Shetland 313 G6
Duryard Devon 14 C4
Duston Northants 120 E4
Dutch Village Essex 69 C9
Duthil Highld 301 G9
Dutlas Powys 114 B4
Duton Hill Essex 106 F2
Dutson Corn 12 D2
Dutton Ches W 183 F9
Duxford Cambs 105 B9
  Oxon 82 F5
Duxmoor Shrops 115 B8
Dwygyfylchi Conwy 180 F2
Dwyran Anglesey 162 B6
Dwyrhiw Powys 129 C11
Dyce Aberdeen 293 B10
Dyche Som 43 E7
Dye House
  Northumb 241 F10
Dyer's Common
  S Glos 60 C5
Dyer's Green Cambs 105 B7
Dyffryn Bridgend 57 C11
  Carms 92 G6
  Ceredig 110 G5
  Pembs 91 D8
Dyffryn Ardudwy
  Gwyn 145 E11
Dyffryn-bern
  Ceredig 110 G5
Dyffryn Castell
  Ceredig 128 G5
Dyffryn Ceidrych
  Carms 94 F4
Dyffryn Cellwen
  Neath 76 D5
Dyke Lincs 156 E2
  Moray 301 D9
Dykehead Angus 292 G5
  N Lnrk 269 D7
  Stirl 277 B11
Dykelands Aberds 293 G9
Dykends Angus 286 B6
Dykeside Aberds 303 E7
Dykesmains N Ayrs 266 G5
Dylife Powys 129 E7
Dymchurch Kent 39 B9
Dymock Glos 98 E4
Dynfant / Dunvant
  Swansea 56 C5
Dyrham S Glos 61 D8
Dysart Fife 280 C6
Dyserth Denb 181 F9

E

Eabost Highld 294 B5
Eabost West Highld 298 E3
Each End Kent 55 B10
Eachway Worcs 117 B9
Eachwick Northumb 242 C4
Eadar Dha Fhadhail
  W Isles 304 E2
Eagland Hill Lancs 202 D4
Eagle Lincs 172 B5
Eagle Barnsdale
  Lincs 172 B5
Eagle Moor Lincs 172 B5
Eaglesfield Cumb 229 F7
  Dumfries 238 C6
Eaglesham E Renf 267 E11
Eaglestone
  M Keynes 103 D7
Eaglethorpe
  Northants 137 E11
Eagle Tor Derbys 170 C2
Eagley Gtr Man 195 E8
Eairy IoM 192 E3
Eakley Lanes
  M Keynes 120 G6
Eakring Notts 171 C11
Ealand N Lincs 199 E9
Ealing London 67 C7
Eals Northumb 240 F5
Eamont Bridge
  Cumb 230 F6
Earby Lancs 204 D3
Earcroft Blkburn 195 C7
Eardington Shrops 132 E4
Eardisland Hereford 115 F8
Eardisley Hereford 96 B6
Eardiston Shrops 149 D7
  Worcs 116 D3
Earith Cambs 123 C7
Earle Northumb 263 D11
Earlestown Mers 183 B9
Earley Wokingham 65 E9
Earlham Norf 142 B4
Earlish Highld 298 C3
Earls Barton
  Northants 121 E7
Earls Colne Essex 107 F7
Earl's Common
  Worcs 117 F9
Earl's Court London 67 D9
Earl's Croome Worcs 99 C7
Earlsdon W Mid 118 B6
Earl's Down E Sus 23 B10
Earlsferry Fife 281 B9
Earlsfield Lincs 155 B8
  London 67 E9
Earlsford Aberds 303 F8
Earl's Green Suff 125 D10
Earlsheaton
  W Yorks 197 C9
Earl Shilton Leics 135 D9
Earlsmill Moray 301 D9
Earl Soham Suff 126 E4
Earl Sterndale
  Derbys 169 B9
Earlston Borders 262 B3
  E Ayrs 257 B10
Earlstone Common
  Hants 64 G3
Earl Stoneham Suff 126 F2
Earl Stonham Suff 126 F2
Earlstoun Dumfries 246 G4
Earlswood Mon 79 F7
  Sur 51 D9
  Warks 118 C2
Earnley W Sus 22 D4
Earnock S Lnrk 268 E3
Earnshaw Bridge
  Lancs 194 C4
Earsairidh W Isles 297 M3
Earsdon T&W 243 C8
Earsham Norf 142 F6
Earsham Street Suff 126 B4
Earswick York 207 B8
Eartham W Sus 22 B6
Earthcott Green
  S Glos 61 B7
Easby N Yorks 224 E3
  N Yorks 225 D11
Easdale Argyll 275 B8
Easebourne W Sus 34 C5
Easenhall Warks 119 B9
Eashing Sur 50 E2
Easington Bucks 83 C11
  Durham 234 C4
  E Yorks 201 D11
  Lancs 203 C10
  Northumb 264 C4
  Oxon 83 F11
  Oxon 101 D9
  Redcar 226 B4
Easington Colliery
  Durham 234 C4
Easington Lane
  T&W 234 B3
Easingwold
  N Yorks 215 F10
Easole Street Kent 55 C9
Eason's Green E Sus 23 B8
Eassie Angus 287 C7
East Aberthaw
  V Glam 58 F4
Eastacombe Devon 25 B8
  Devon 25 C9
Eastacott Devon 25 C10
East Acton London 67 C8
East Adderbury
  Oxon 101 D9
East Allington Devon 8 F5
East Amat Highld 309 K4
East Anstey Devon 26 B5
East Anton Hants 47 D11
East Appleton
  N Yorks 224 F4
East Ardsley
  W Yorks 197 B10
East Ashling W Sus 22 B4
East Aston Hants 48 D2
East Auchronie
  Aberds 293 C10
East Ayton N Yorks 217 B9
East Bank Bl Gwent 78 D2
East Barkwith
  Lincs 189 E11
East Barming Kent 53 C8
East Barnby
  N Yorks 226 C6
East Barnet London 86 F3
East Barns E Loth 282 F4
East Barsham Norf 159 C8
East Barton Suff 125 D8
East Beach W Sus 22 E5
East Beckham
  Norf 177 E11
East Bedfont London 66 E5
East Bergholt Suff 107 D11
East Bierley
  W Yorks 197 B7
East Bilney Norf 159 F9
East Blackdene
  Durham 232 D3
East Blatchington
  E Sus 23 E7
East Bloxworth
  Dorset 18 C3
East Boldon T&W 243 E9
East Boldre Hants 32 G5
East Bonhard Perth 286 E5
Eastbourne Darl 224 C6
  E Sus 23 F10
East Bower Som 43 F10
East Brent Som 43 C11
Eastbridge Suff 127 D9
East Bridgford
  Notts 171 G11
East Briscoe
  Durham 223 B9
Eastbrook Som 28 C2
  V Glam 59 E7
East Buckland Devon 41 G7
East Budleigh Devon 15 E7
Eastburn E Yorks 208 B5
  W Yorks 204 E6
Eastburn Br
  W Yorks 204 E6
East Burnham Bucks 66 C3
East Burrafirth
  Shetland 313 H5
East Burton Dorset 18 D2
Eastbury London 85 G9
  W Berks 63 D10
East Butsfield
  Durham 233 B8
East Butterleigh
  Devon 27 F7
East Butterwick
  N Lincs 199 F10
Eastby N Yorks 204 C6
East Cairnbeg
  Aberds 293 F9
East Calder
  W Loth 269 B11
East Carleton Norf 142 C3
East Carlton
  Northants 136 F6
  W Yorks 205 E10
East Chaldon or Chaldon
  Herring Dorset 17 E11
East Challow Oxon 63 B11
East Charleton Devon 8 G5
East Chelborough
  Dorset 29 F9
East Chiltington
  E Sus 36 D5
East Chinnock Som 29 E7
East Chisenbury
  Wilts 46 C6
East Cholderton
  Hants 47 D9
Eastchurch Kent 70 E3
East Clandon Sur 50 C5
East Claydon Bucks 102 F4
East Clevedon
  N Som 60 E2
East Clyne Highld 311 J3
East Clyth Highld 310 F7
East Coker Som 29 E8
Eastcombe Glos 80 E5
East Combe Som 43 G7
East Common
  N Yorks 207 G8
East Compton Dorset 30 D5
  Som 44 E6
East Cornworthy
  Devon 8 D6
Eastcote London 66 B6
  Northants 120 G3
  W Mid 118 B3
Eastcote Village
  London 66 B6
Eastcott Corn 24 D3
  Wilts 46 B4
East Cottingwith
  E Yorks 207 E10
Eastcotts Beds 103 B11
Eastcourt Wilts 63 G8
  Wilts 81 G7
East Cowes IoW 20 B6
East Cowick
  E Yorks 199 C7
East Cowton
  N Yorks 224 E6
East Cramlington
  Northumb 243 B7
East Cranmore Som 45 E7
East Creech Dorset 18 E4
East Croachy Highld 300 G6
East Croftmore
  Highld 291 B11
East Curthwaite
  Cumb 230 B2
East Dean E Sus 23 F9
  Glos 98 G3
  Hants 32 B3
  W Sus 34 E6
East Dene S Yorks 186 C6
East Denton T&W 242 D6
East Didsbury
  Gtr Man 184 C5
Eastdon Devon 14 F5
Eastdown Devon 8 F6
East Down Devon 40 E6
East Drayton Notts 188 F3
East Dulwich
  London 67 E10
East Dundry N Som 60 F5
East Ella Hull 200 B5
Eastend Essex 86 C6
  Oxon 100 G6
East End Beds 122 F2
  Bucks 84 B4
  C Beds 103 C9
  Dorset 18 B5
  Essex 89 D8
  E Yorks 201 B9
  E Yorks 209 B9
  E Yorks 209 G9
  Glos 81 E11
  Hants 20 B3
  Hants 33 C11
  Hants 64 G2
  Herts 105 F9
  Kent 53 E11
  Kent 53 F10
  Kent 70 E3
  M Keynes 103 C8
  N Som 60 E3
  Oxon 82 C5
  Oxon 101 D9
  Oxon 101 E7
  S Glos 61 E9
  Som 29 B10
  Som 44 C5
  Som 45 D7
  Suff 108 E2
  Suff 126 F3
East End Green Herts 86 C3
Easter Aberchalder
  Highld 291 B7
Easter Ardross
  Highld 300 B6
Easter Balgedie
  Perth 286 G5
Easter Balmoral
  Aberds 292 D4
Easter Boleskine
  Highld 300 G5
Easter Brackland
  Stirl 285 G10
Easter Brae Highld 300 C6
Easter Cardno
  Aberds 303 C9
Easter Compton
  S Glos 60 C5
Easter Cringate
  Stirl 278 D4
Easter Culfosie
  Aberds 293 C9
Easter Davoch
  Aberds 292 C6
Easter Earshaig
  Dumfries 248 C2
Easter Ellister Argyll 254 B3
Easter Fearn Highld 309 L6
Easter Galcantray
  Highld 301 E8
Eastergate W Sus 22 B6

Grasmere Cumb 220 D6
Grasscroft Gtr Man 196 G3
Grassendale Mers 182 D5
Grassgarth Cumb 221 F8
Cumb 230 C2
Grass Green Essex 106 D4
Grassholme Durham 232 G4
Grassington
N Yorks 213 G10
Grassmoor Derbys 170 B6
Grassthorpe Notts 172 B3
Grasswell T&W 243 G8
Grateley Hants 47 E9
Gratton Devon 24 E5
Gratwich Staffs 151 C10
Gravel Ches W 167 B11
Gravel Castle Kent 55 D8
Graveley Cambs 122 E4
Herts 104 F4
Gravelhill Shrops 149 G9
Gravel Hill Bucks 85 G8
Gravel Hole
Gtr Man 196 F2
Shrops 149 B7
Gravelly Hill W Mid 134 E2
Gravels Shrops 130 D6
Gravelsbank Shrops 130 C6
Graven Shetland 312 F6
Graveney Kent 70 G5
Gravenhunger Moss
Shrops 168 G2
Gravesend Herts 105 F8
Kent 68 E6
Grayingham Lincs 188 B6
Grayrigg Cumb 221 F11
Grays Thurrock 68 D6
Grayshott Hants 49 F11
Grayson Green
Cumb 228 F5
Grayswood Sur 50 G2
Graythorp Hrtlpl 234 F6
Grazeley Wokingham 65 F7
Grazeley Green
W Berks 65 F7
Greagdhubh Lodge
Highld 291 D8
Greamchary Highld 310 F2
Greasbrough
S Yorks 186 B6
Greasby Mers 182 D3
Greasley Notts 171 F7
Great Abington
Cambs 105 B10
Great Addington
Northants 121 B9
Great Alne Warks 118 F2
Great Altcar Lancs 193 F10
Great Amwell Herts 86 C5
Great Asby Cumb 222 C3
Great Ashfield Suff 125 D9
Great Ashley Wilts 61 G10
Great Ayton
N Yorks 225 C11
Great Baddow Essex 88 E2
Great Bardfield
Essex 106 E3
Great Barford Beds 122 G2
Great Barrington
Glos 82 C2
Great Barrow
Ches W 167 B7
Great Barton Suff 125 D7
Great Barugh
N Yorks 216 D4
Great Bavington
Northumb 251 G11
Great Bealings Suff 108 B4
Great Bedwyn Wilts 63 G9
Great Bentley Essex 108 G2
Great Berry Essex 69 B7
Great Billing
Northants 120 E6
Great Bircham Norf 158 C5
Great Blakenham
Suff 126 G2
Great Blencow
Cumb 230 E5
Great Bolas Telford 150 E2
Great Bookham Sur 50 C6
Great Bosullow Corn 1 C4
Great Bourton Oxon 101 B9
Great Bowden Leics 136 F4
Great Bower Kent 54 C4
Great Bradley Suff 124 G3
Great Braxted Essex 88 C5
Great Bricett Suff 125 G10
Great Brickhill
Bucks 103 E8
Great Bridge W Mid 133 E9
Great Bridgeford
Staffs 151 D7
Great Brington
Northants 120 D3
Great Bromley
Essex 107 F11
Great Broughton
Cumb 229 E7
N Yorks 225 D10
Great Buckland Kent 69 G7
Great Budworth
Ches W 183 F11
Great Burdon Darl 224 B6
Great Burgh Sur 51 B8
Great Burstead
Essex 87 G11
Great Busby
N Yorks 225 D10
Great Canfield Essex 87 B9
Great Carlton Lincs 190 D6
Great Casterton
Rutland 137 B9
Rutland 137 B10
Great Cellws
Powys 113 E11
Great Chalfield
Wilts 61 G11
Great Chart Kent 54 E3
Great Chatwell
Staffs 150 G5
Great Chell Stoke 168 E5
Great Chesterford
Essex 105 C10
Great Cheveney Kent 53 E8
Great Cheverell Wilts 46 C3
Great Chilton
Durham 233 E11
Great Chishill
Cambs 105 D8
Great Clacton Essex 89 B11
Great Claydons Essex 88 E3
Great Cliff
W Yorks 197 D10
Great Clifton Cumb 228 F6
Great Coates
NE Lincs 201 F8
Great Comberton
Worcs 99 C9
Great Common Suff 143 F7
W Sus 35 B8
Great Corby Cumb 239 G11
Great Cornard Suff 107 C7
Great Cowden
E Yorks 209 E10
Great Coxwell Oxon 82 G3
Great Crakehall
N Yorks 224 G4
Great Cransley
Northants 120 B6
Great Cressingham
Norf 141 C7
Great Crosby Mers 182 B4
Great Crosthwaite
Cumb 229 G11
Great Cubley Derbys 152 B3
Great Dalby Leics 154 G4
Great Denham
Beds 103 B10
Great Doddington
Northants 121 E7
Great Doward
Hereford 79 B9
Great Dunham Norf 159 G7
Great Dunmow
Essex 106 G2
Great Durnford Wilts 46 F6
Great Easton Essex 106 F2
Leics 136 E6
Great Eccleston
Lancs 202 E4
Great Edstone
N Yorks 216 C4
Great Ellingham
Norf 141 D10
Great Elm Som 45 D8
Great Eppleton
T&W 234 B3
Greater Doward
Hereford 79 B9
Great Eversden
Cambs 123 G7
Great Fencote
N Yorks 224 G5
Greatfield Wilts 62 B5
Great Finborough
Suff 125 F10
Greatford Lincs 155 G11
Great Fransham
Norf 159 G7
Great Gaddesden
Herts 85 C8
Greatgap Bucks 84 B6
Greatgate Staffs 169 G9
Great Gate Staffs 169 G9
Great Gidding
Cambs 138 G2
Great Givendale
E Yorks 208 C2
Great Glemham
Suff 126 E6
Great Glen Leics 136 D3
Great Gonerby Lincs 155 B7
Great Gransden
Cambs 122 F5
Great Green Cambs 104 C5
Norf 142 F5
Suff 125 B11
Suff 125 F8
Suff 126 B2
Great Habton
N Yorks 216 D5
Great Hale Lincs 173 G10
Great Hallingbury
Essex 87 B8
Greatham Hants 49 G9
Hrtlpl 234 F5
W Sus 35 D8
Great Hampden
Bucks 84 E4
Great Harrowden
Northants 121 C7
Great Harwood
Lancs 203 G10
Great Haseley Oxon 83 E10
Great Hatfield
E Yorks 209 E9
Great Haywood
Staffs 151 E9
Staffs 151 E10
Great Heath W Mid 134 G6
Great Heck N Yorks 198 C5
Great Henny Essex 107 D7
Great Hinton Wilts 46 B2
Great Hivings Bucks 85 E7
Great Hockham
Norf 141 E9
Great Holcombe
Oxon 83 F10
Great Holland Essex 89 B12
Great Hollands
Brack 65 F11
Great Holm
M Keynes 102 D6
Great Honeyborough
Pembs 73 D7
Great Horkesley
Essex 107 E9
Great Hormead
Herts 105 F7
Great Horton
W Yorks 205 G8
Great Horwood
Bucks 102 E5
Great Houghton
Northants 120 F5
S Yorks 198 F2
Great Howarth
Gtr Man 196 D2
Great Hucklow
Derbys 185 F11
Great Job's Cross
Kent 38 B4
Great Kelk E Yorks 209 B8
Great Kendale
E Yorks 217 G10
Great Kimble Bucks 84 D4
Great Kingshill Bucks 84 F5
Great Langton
N Yorks 224 F5
Great Lea Common
Reading 65 F8
Great Leighs Essex 88 B2
Great Lever
Gtr Man 195 F8
Great Limber Lincs 200 F6
Great Linford
M Keynes 103 C7
Great Livermere
Suff 125 C7
Great Longstone
Derbys 186 G2
Great Lumley
Durham 233 B11
Great Lyth Shrops 131 B9
Great Malgraves
Thurrock 69 C7
Great Malvern Worcs 98 B5
Great Maplestead
Essex 106 E6
Great Marton
Blkpool 202 F2
Great Marton Moss
Blkpool 202 G2
Great Massingham
Norf 158 E5
Great Melton Norf 142 B2
Great Milton Oxon 83 E10
Great Missenden
Bucks 84 E5
Great Mitton Lancs 203 F10
Great Mongeham
Kent 55 C10
Greatmoor Bucks 102 G4
Great Moor
Gtr Man 184 D6
Staffs 132 D6
Great Moulton Norf 142 E3
Great Munden
Herts 105 G7
Great Musgrave
Cumb 222 C5
Greatness Kent 52 B4
Great Ness Shrops 149 F7
Great Notley Essex 106 G4
Great Oak Mon 78 D5
Great Oakley Essex 108 F3
Northants 137 F7
Great Offley Herts 104 F2
Great Ormside
Cumb 222 B4
Great Orton Cumb 239 G8
Great Ouseburn
N Yorks 215 G8
Great Oxendon
Northants 136 G4
Great Oxney Green
Essex 87 D11
Great Palgrave Norf 158 G6
Great Parndon Essex 86 D6
Great Pattenden
Kent 53 E8
Great Paxton Cambs 122 E4
Great Plumpton
Lancs 202 G3
Great Plumstead
Norf 160 G6
Great Ponton Lincs 155 C8
Great Preston
W Yorks 198 B2
Great Purston
Northants 101 D10
Great Raveley
Cambs 138 G5
Great Rissington
Glos 81 B11
Great Rollright
Oxon 100 E6
Great Ryburgh Norf 159 D9
Great Ryle
Northumb 264 G2
Great Ryton Shrops 131 C9
Great Saling Essex 106 F4
Great Salkeld Cumb 231 D7
Great Sampford
Essex 106 D2
Great Sankey Warr 183 D9
Great Saredon
Staffs 133 B9
Great Saxham Suff 124 E5
Great Shefford
W Berks 63 E11
Great Shelford
Cambs 123 G9
Great Shoddesden
Hants 47 D9
Great Smeaton
N Yorks 224 E6
Great Snoring Norf 159 C8
Great Somerford
Wilts 62 C3
Great Stainton Darl 234 G2
Great Stambridge
Essex 88 G5
Great Staughton
Cambs 122 E2
Great Steeping
Lincs 174 C6
Great Stoke S Glos 60 C6
Great Stonar Kent 55 B10
Greatstone-on-Sea
Kent 39 C9
Great Stretton Leics 136 C3
Great Strickland
Cumb 231 G7
Great Stukeley
Cambs 122 C4
Great Sturton Lincs 190 F2
Great Sutton
Ches W 182 F5
Shrops 131 G10
Great Swinburne
Northumb 241 B10
Great Tew Oxon 101 F7
Great Tey Essex 107 F7
Great Thirkleby
N Yorks 215 D9
Great Thurlow Suff 124 G3
Great Torrington
Devon 25 D7
Great Tosson
Northumb 252 C2
Great Totham Essex 88 C5
Great Tows Lincs 190 C2
Great Tree Corn 6 D5
Great Urswick
Cumb 210 E5
Great Wakering
Essex 70 B2
Great Waldingfield
Suff 107 C8
Great Walsingham
Norf 159 B8
Great Waltham
Essex 87 C11
Great Warley Essex 87 G9
Great Washbourne
Glos 99 E9
Great Weeke Devon 13 D10
Great Weldon
Northants 137 F8
Great Welnetham
Suff 125 F7
Great Wenham
Suff 107 D11
Great Whittington
Northumb 242 C2
Great Wigborough
Essex 89 C7
Great Wilbraham
Cambs 123 F10
Great Wilne Derbys 153 C8
Great Wishford Wilts 46 F5
Great Witchingham
Norf 160 E2
Great Witcombe
Glos 80 C6
Great Witley Worcs 116 D5
Great Wolford
Warks 100 E4
Greatworth
Northants 101 C11
Great Wratting Suff 106 B3
Great Wymondley
Herts 104 F4
Great Wyrley Staffs 133 B9
Great Wytheford
Shrops 149 F11
Great Yarmouth
Norf 143 B10
Great Yeldham
Essex 106 D5
Greave Gtr Man 184 C6
Lancs 195 C11
Grebby Lincs 174 B6
Greeba IoM 192 D4
Green Denb 165 B9
Pembs 73 E7
Powys 130 E5
Greenacres Gtr Man 196 F2
Greenan Argyll 275 G11
Greenbank
Ches W 183 G10
Falk 279 F7
Shetland 312 C7
Green Bank Cumb 211 C7
Green Bottom Corn 4 F5
Glos 79 B11
Greenburn W Loth 269 C8
Green Close
N Yorks 212 F4
Green Clough
W Yorks 205 G7
Green Crize
Hereford 97 D10
Greencroft Durham 242 G5
Green Cross Sur 49 F11
Greendale Ches E 184 F5
Greendikes
Northumb 264 D3
Greendown Som 44 C5
Green Down Devon 28 G3
Greendykes
Northumb 264 D3
Greenend N Lnrk 268 C4
Oxon 100 G6
Green End Beds 103 B10
Beds 121 E11
Beds 122 E2
Beds 122 G2
Bucks 84 F4
Bucks 103 E8
Cambs 122 C4
Cambs 123 F7
C Beds 103 D11
Herts 85 D8
Herts 104 E5
Herts 104 E6
Herts 104 G6
Herts 105 F7
Lancs 204 D4
N Yorks 226 E6
Warks 134 F5
Greenfaulds N Lnrk 278 G5
Greenfield C Beds 103 E11
Glasgow 268 C2
Gtr Man 196 G3
Highld 289 D11
Highld 290 C4
Oxon 84 G2
Greenfield / Maes-Glas
Flint 181 F11
Greenfoot N Lnrk 268 B4
Greenford London 66 C6
Greengairs N Lnrk 278 G5
Greengarth Hall
Cumb 219 E11
Greengate Gtr Man 196 D2
Norf 159 F10
Green Gate Devon 27 D8
Greengates
W Yorks 205 F9
Greengill Cumb 229 D8
Green Hailey Bucks 84 E4
Greenhalgh Lancs 202 F4
Greenhall S Lnrk 268 D3
Greenham Dorset 28 G6
Som 27 C9
W Berks 64 F3
Green Hammerton
N Yorks 206 B5
Greenhaugh
Northumb 251 F7
Green Haworth
Lancs 195 B9
Greenhead
Borders 261 D11
Dumfries 247 D9
N Lnrk 268 E6
Northumb 240 D5
Staffs 169 F7
Green Head Cumb 230 B3
Green Heath Staffs 151 G9
Greenheys Gtr Man 195 G8
Greenhill Dumfries 238 B4
Durham 234 B3
Falk 278 F6
Hereford 98 B4
Kent 71 F7
Leics 153 G8
London 67 B7
S Yorks 186 E4
Worcs 99 B10
Worcs 116 B6
Green Hill Kent 53 C9
Lincs 155 B8
Wilts 62 B5
W Yorks 206 F4
Greenhill Bank
Shrops 149 B7
Greenhillocks
Derbys 170 F6
Greenhills N Ayrs 267 E7
S Lnrk 268 E2
Greenhithe Kent 68 E5
Greenholm E Ayrs 258 B2
Greenholme Cumb 221 D11
Greenhouse Borders 262 E3
Greenhow N Yorks 214 G2
Greenhow Hill
N Yorks 214 G2
Greenigoe Orkney 314 F4
Greenland Highld 310 C6
S Yorks 186 D5
Greenland Mains
Highld 310 C6
Greenlands Bucks 65 B9
Worcs 117 D11
Green Lane Devon 13 F11
Hereford 98 B2
Powys 130 D3
Warks 117 E11
Warks 118 B6
Greenlaw Aberds 302 D6
Borders 272 F4
Greenlaw Mains
Midloth 270 C4
Greenlea Dumfries 238 B2
Greenley M Keynes 102 C6
Greenloaning Perth 286 G2
Greenlooms
Ches W 167 C7
Greenman's Lane
Wilts 62 C3
Greenmeadow
Swindon 62 B6
Torf 78 F3
Green Moor
S Yorks 186 B3
Greenmount
Gtr Man 195 E9
Greenmow Shetland 313 L6
Greenoak E Yorks 199 B10
Greenock Invclyd 276 F5
Greenock West
Invclyd 276 F5
Greenodd Cumb 210 C6
Green Ore Som 44 C5
Green Parlour Bath 45 C8
Green Quarter
Cumb 221 E9
Greenrigg W Loth 269 C8
Greenrow Cumb 238 G4
Greens Borders 249 F11
Green St Green
London 68 G3
Greensforge Staffs 133 F7
Greensgate Norf 160 F2
Greenside Cumb 222 E4
Derbys 186 F5
Gtr Man 184 B6
T&W 242 E4
W Yorks 197 D7
Green Side W Yorks 197 E7
W Yorks 205 G11
Greensidehill
Northumb 263 F11
Greens Norton
Northants 102 B3
Greensplat Corn 5 D9
Greenstead Essex 107 F10
Greenstead Green
Essex 106 F6
Greensted Essex 87 E8
Greensted Green
Essex 87 E8
Green Street Essex 87 F10
E Sus 38 E3
Glos 80 B5
Glos 80 E3
Herts 85 F11
Herts 105 G9
Worcs 99 B7
Worcs 99 C7
W Sus 35 C10
Greenstreet Green
Suff 107 B10
Green Street Green
Kent 68 E5
London 68 G3
Green Tye Herts 86 B6
Greenway Hereford 98 E4
Pembs 91 E11
Som 27 B11
V Glam 58 E5
Worcs 116 C4
Greenwell Cumb 240 F2
Greenwells Borders 262 C3
Greenwich London 67 D11
Suff 108 C3
Wilts 46 G2
Greenwith Common
Corn 4 G5
Greenwoods Essex 87 F11
Greeny Orkney 314 D2
Greep Highld 298 E2
Greet Glos 99 E10
Kent 54 B2
Greete Shrops 115 C11
Greetham Lincs 190 G4
Rutland 155 G8
Greetland W Yorks 196 C5
Greetland Wall Nook
W Yorks 196 C5
Greetwell N Lincs 200 G2
Gregg Hall Cumb 221 G9
Gregson Lane Lancs 194 B5
Gregynog Powys 129 D11
Grèin W Isles 297 L2
Greinetobht
W Isles 296 D4
Greinton Som 44 F2
Gremista Shetland 313 J6
Grenaby IoM 192 E3
Grendon Northants 121 E7
Warks 134 C5
Grendon Bishop
Hereford 115 F11
Grendon Common
Warks 134 D5
Grendon Green
Hereford 115 F11
Grendon Underwood
Bucks 102 G3
Grenofen Devon 12 G5
Grenoside S Yorks 186 C4
Greosabhagh
W Isles 305 J3
Gresford Wrex 166 E5
Gresham Norf 160 B3
Greshornish Highld 298 D3
Gressenhall Norf 159 F9
Gressingham
Lancs 211 F11
Gresty Green
Ches E 168 E2
Greta Bridge
Durham 223 C11
Gretna Dumfries 239 D8
Gretna Green
Dumfries 239 D8
Gretton Glos 99 E10
Northants 137 E7
Shrops 131 D10
Gretton Fields Glos 99 E10
Grewelthorpe
N Yorks 214 D4
Greyfield Bath 44 B6
Greygarth N Yorks 214 E3
Grey Green N Lincs 199 F9
Greylake Som 43 G11
Greylake Fosse Som 44 F2
Greynor Carms 75 D9
Greynor-isaf Carms 75 D9
Greyrigg Dumfries 248 F3
Greys Green Oxon 65 C8
Greysouthen Cumb 229 F7
Greystead Northumb 251 F7
Greystoke Cumb 230 E4
Greystoke Gill Cumb 230 F4
Greystone Aberds 292 D6
Aberds 302 F6
Angus 287 C9
Cumb 211 D10
Dumfries 237 B11
Greystonegill
N Yorks 212 F3
Greystones S Yorks 186 D4
Warks 99 B11
Greytree Hereford 97 F11
Greywell Hants 49 C8
Griais W Isles 304 D6
Grianan W Isles 304 E6
Gribb Dorset 28 G5
Gribthorpe E Yorks 207 F11
Gridley Corner Devon 12 C3
Griff Warks 135 F7
Griffins Hill
W Mid 133 G10
Griffithstown Torf 78 F3
Griffydam Leics 153 F8
Grigg Kent 53 E11
Griggs Green Hants 49 G10
Grillis Corn 2 B5
Grilstone Devon 26 C2
Grimbister Orkney 314 E3
Grimblethorpe
Lincs 190 D2
Grimeford Village
Lancs 194 E6
Grimes Hill Worcs 117 B11
Grimesthorpe
S Yorks 186 C5
Grimethorpe
S Yorks 198 F2
Griminis W Isles 296 D3
W Isles 296 F3
Grimister Shetland 312 D6
Grimley Worcs 116 E6
Grimness Orkney 314 G4
Grimoldby Lincs 190 D5
Grimpo Shrops 149 D7
Grimsargh Lancs 203 G7
Grimsbury Oxon 101 C9
Grimsby NE Lincs 201 E9
Grimscote Northants 120 G3
Grimscott Corn 24 F3
Grimshaw Blkburn 195 C8
Grimshaw Green
Lancs 194 E3
Grimsthorpe Lincs 155 E10
Grimston E Yorks 209 F11
Leics 154 E3
Norf 158 E4
York 207 C8
Grimstone Dorset 17 C8
Grimstone End Suff 125 D8
Grinacombe Moor
Devon 12 C4
Grindale E Yorks 218 E2
Grindigar Orkney 314 F5
Grindiscol Shetland 313 K6
Grindle Shrops 132 C5
Grindleford Derbys 186 F2
Grindleton Lancs 203 D11
Grindley Staffs 151 D10
Grindley Brook
Shrops 167 G8
Grindlow Derbys 185 F11
Grindon Northumb 273 G8
Staffs 169 E9
Stockton 234 F3
T&W 243 G9
Grindonmoor Gate
Staffs 169 E9
Grindsbrook Booth
Derbys 185 D10
Gringley on the Hill
Notts 188 C2
Grinsdale Cumb 239 F9
Grinshill Shrops 149 E10
Grinstead Hill Suff 125 G11
Grinton N Yorks 223 F10
Griomasaigh
W Isles 297 G4
Griomsidar W Isles 304 F5
Grisdale Cumb 222 G5
Grishipoll Argyll 288 D3
Grisling Common
E Sus 36 C6
Gristhorpe
N Yorks 217 C11
Griston Norf 141 D8
Gritley Orkney 314 F5
Grittenham Wilts 62 C4
Grittlesend Hereford 98 B4
Grittleton Wilts 61 C11
Grizebeck Cumb 210 C4
Grizedale Cumb 220 G6
Groam Highld 300 E5
Grobister Orkney 314 D6
Grobsness Shetland 313 G5
Groby Leics 135 B10
Groes Conwy 165 C8
Neath 57 D9
Groes Efa Denb 165 B10
Groes-faen Rhondda 58 C5
Groes-fawr Denb 165 B10
Groesffordd Gwyn 144 B5
Powys 95 F11
Groesffordd Marli
Denb 181 G8
Groeslon Gwyn 163 C8
Gwyn 163 D7
Groes-lwyd Mon 96 G6
Powys 148 G4
Groespluan Powys 130 B4
Groes-wen Caerph 58 B6
Grogport Argyll 255 C9
Gromford Suff 127 F7
Gronant Flint 181 E9
Gronwen Shrops 148 D5
Groombridge E Sus 52 F4
Grosmont Mon 97 G8
N Yorks 226 D6
Gross Green Warks 119 F7
Grotaig Highld 300 G4
Groton Suff 107 C9
Grotton Gtr Man 196 G3
Grougfoot Falk 279 F10
Grove Bucks 103 G8
Dorset 17 G10
Hereford 98 C2
Kent 71 G8
Notts 188 F2
Oxon 82 G6
Pembs 73 E7
Grove End Kent 69 G11
Warks 100 D6
Warks 134 D3
Grove Green Kent 53 B9
Grovehill E Yorks 208 F6
Herts 85 D9
Grove Hill E Sus 23 C10
Kent 71 G8
Grove Park London 67 D8
London 68 E2
Groves Kent 55 B9
Grovesend Swansea 75 E9
Grove Town
W Yorks 198 C3
Grove Vale W Mid 133 E10
Grubb Street Kent 68 F5
Grub Street Staffs 150 D5
Grudie Highld 300 C3
Gruids Highld 309 J5
Gruinard House
Highld 307 K4
Gruinards Highld 309 K5
Grula Highld 294 C5
Gruline Argyll 289 E7
Gruline Ho Argyll 289 F7
Grumbeg Highld 308 F6
Grumbla Corn 1 D4
Grunasound
Shetland 313 K5
Grundisburgh Suff 126 G4
Grunsagill Lancs 203 C11
Gruting Shetland 313 J4
Grutness Shetland 313 N6
Gryn Goch Gwyn 162 F6
Gualachulain Highld 284 C5
Gualin Ho Highld 308 D3
Guardbridge Fife 287 F8
Guard House
W Yorks 204 E6
Guarlford Worcs 98 B6
Guay Perth 286 C4
Gubbion's Green
Essex 88 B2
Gubblecote Herts 84 C6
Guesachan Highld 289 B10
Guestling Green
E Sus 38 E5
Guestling Thorn
E Sus 38 D4
Guestwick Norf 159 D11
Guestwick Green
Norf 159 D11
Guide Blkburn 195 B8
Guide Bridge
Gtr Man 184 B6
Guide Post
Northumb 253 F7
Guilden Morden
Cambs 104 C5
Guilden Sutton
Ches W 166 B6
Guildford Sur 50 D3
Guildford Park Sur 50 D3
Guildiehaugh
W Loth 269 B9
Guildtown Perth 286 D5
Guilford Pembs 73 D7
Guilsborough
Northants 120 C3
Guilsfield / Cegidfa
Powys 148 G4
Guilthwaite S Yorks 187 D7
Guilton Kent 55 B9
Guineaford Devon 40 F5
Guisachan Highld 300 G3
Guisborough Redcar 226 B2
Guiseley W Yorks 205 E9
Guist Norf 159 D9
Guith Orkney 314 C5
Guiting Power Glos 99 G11
Gulberwick Shetland 313 K6
Gullane E Loth 281 E9
Guller's End Worcs 99 D7
Gulling Green Suff 124 F6
Gullom Holme
Cumb 231 F9
Gulval Corn 1 C5
Gulworthy Devon 12 G4
Gumfreston Pembs 73 E10
Gumley Leics 136 E3
Gummow's Shop Corn 5 D7
Gunby E Yorks 207 F10
Lincs 155 E8
Lincs 175 B7
Gundenham Som 27 C10
Gundleton Hants 48 G6
Gun Green Kent 53 G9
Gun Hill E Sus 23 C9
Gunn Devon 40 G6
Gunnersbury London 67 D7
Gunnerside N Yorks 223 F9
Gunnerton
Northumb 241 C10
Gunness N Lincs 199 E10
Gunnislake Corn 12 G4
Gunnista Shetland 313 J7
Gunstone Staffs 133 C7
Guns Village W Mid 133 E9
Gunter's Bridge
W Sus 35 C7
Gunthorpe Lincs 188 B4
Norf 159 C10
Notts 171 G11
Pboro 138 C3
Rutland 137 B7
Gunton Suff 143 D10
Gunville IoW 20 D5
Gunwalloe Corn 2 E5
Gunwalloe Fishing Cove
Corn 2 E5
Gupworthy Som 42 F3
Gurnard IoW 20 B5
Gurnett Ches E 184 G6
Gurney Slade Som 44 D6
Gurnos M Tydf 77 D8
Powys 76 D3
Gushmere Kent 54 B4
Gussage All Saints
Dorset 31 E8
Gussage St Andrew
Dorset 31 E7
Gussage St Michael
Dorset 31 E7
Gustard Wood Herts 85 B11
Guston Kent 55 E10
Gutcher Shetland 312 D7
Guthram Gowt Lincs 156 E3
Guthrie Angus 287 B9
Guyhirn Cambs 139 C7
Guyhirn Gull Cambs 139 C7
Guy's Cliffe Warks 118 D5
Guy's Head Lincs 157 D9
Guy's Marsh Dorset 30 C4
Guyzance Northumb 252 C6
Gwaelod-y-garth
Cardiff 58 C6
Gwaenysgor Flint 181 E9
Gwalchmai Anglesey 178 F5
Gwalchmai Uchaf
Anglesey 178 F5
Gwallon Corn 2 C2
Gwastad Pembs 91 G10
Gwastadgoed
Gwyn 145 G11
Gwastadnant
Gwyn 163 D10
Gwaun-Cae-Gurwen
Neath 76 C2
Gwaun-Leision
Neath 76 C2
Gwavas Corn 2 D5
Corn 2 G6
Gwbert Ceredig 92 B3
Gwedna Corn 2 C4
Gweek Corn 2 D6
Gwehelog Mon 78 E5
Gwenddwr Powys 95 C11
Gwennap Corn 2 B6
Gwenter Corn 2 F6
Gwernaffield-y-Waun
Flint 166 C2
Gwernafon Powys 129 E8
Gwerneirin Powys 129 F10
Powys 130 G3
Gwernesney Mon 78 E6
Gwernogle Carms 93 E10
Gwernol Denb 166 E2
Gwern y brenin
Shrops 148 D6
Gwernydd Powys 129 C11
Gwernymynydd
Flint 166 C2
Gwern-y-Steeple
V Glam 58 D5
Gwersyllt Wrex 166 E4
Gwespyr Flint 181 E10
Gwills Corn 4 D6
Gwinear Corn 2 B3
Gwinear Downs Corn 2 C4
Gwithian Corn 2 A3
Gwredog Anglesey 178 D6
Gwrhay Caerph 77 F11
Gwyddelwern Denb 165 F9
Gwyddgrug Carms 93 D9
Gwynfryn Wrex 166 E3
Gwystre Powys 113 D11
Gwytherin Conwy 164 C5
Gyfelia Wrex 166 F4
Gyffin Conwy 180 F3
Gylen Park Argyll 289 G10
Gyre Orkney 314 F3
Gyrn Denb 165 D11
Gyrn-goch Gwyn 162 F6

H

Habberley Shrops 131 C7
Worcs 116 B6
Habergham Lancs 204 G2
Habertoft Lincs 175 B8
Habin W Sus 34 C4
Habrough NE Lincs 200 E6
Haccombe Devon 14 G3
Haceby Lincs 155 B10
Hacheston Suff 126 F6
Hackbridge London 67 F9

Hackenthorpe
S Yorks 186 E6
Hackford Norf 141 C11
Hackforth N Yorks 224 G4
Hack Green
Ches E 167 F10
Hackland Orkney 314 D3
Hackleton Northants 120 F6
Hacklinge Kent 55 C10
Hackman's Gate
Worcs 117 B7
Hackness N Yorks 227 G9
Orkney 314 G3
Som 43 D10
Hackney London 67 C10
Hackney Wick
London 67 C11
Hackthorn Lincs 189 E7
Wilts 47 D7
Hackthorpe Cumb 230 G6
Haclait W Isles 297 G4
Haconby Lincs 156 D2
Hacton London 68 B4
Haddacott Devon 25 C8
Hadden Borders 263 B7
Haddenham Bucks 84 D2
Cambs 123 B9
Haddenham End Field
Cambs 123 B9
Haddington
E Loth 281 G10
Lincs 172 C6
Haddiscoe Norf 143 D8
Haddoch Aberds 302 E5
Haddon Cambs 138 E2
Ches E 169 B7
Hade Edge W Yorks 196 F6
Hademore Staffs 134 B3
Haden Cross W Mid 133 F9
Hadfield Derbys 185 B8
Hadham Cross Herts 86 B6
Hadham Ford Herts 105 G8
Hadleigh Essex 69 B10
Suff 107 C10
Hadleigh Heath
Suff 107 C9
Hadley London 86 F2
Telford 150 G3
Worcs 117 E7
Hadley Castle
Telford 150 G3
Hadley End Staffs 152 E2
Hadley Wood London 86 F3
Hadlow Kent 52 D6
Hadlow Down E Sus 37 C8
Hadlow Stair Kent 52 D6
Hadnall Shrops 149 F10
Hadspen Som 45 G7
Hadstock Essex 105 C11
Hadston Northumb 253 D7
Hady Derbys 186 G5
Hadzor Worcs 117 E8
Haffenden Quarter
Kent 53 E11
Hafod Swansea 57 C7
Hafod-Dinbych
Conwy 164 E5
Hafod Grove Pembs 92 C2
Hafodiwan Ceredig 111 G7
Hafod-lom Conwy 180 G5
Hafod-y-Green
Denb 181 G8
Hafodyrynys
Bl Gwent 78 F2
Hag Fold Gtr Man 195 G7
Haggate Gtr Man 196 F2
Lancs 204 F3
Haggbeck Cumb 239 C11
Haggersta Shetland 313 J5
Haggerston London 67 C10
Northumb 273 G10
Hagginton Hill Devon 40 D5
Haggrister Shetland 312 F5
Haggs Falk 278 F5
Haghill Glasgow 268 B2
Hagley Hereford 97 C11
Worcs 133 G8
Hagloe Glos 79 D11
Hagmore Green
Suff 107 D9
Hagnaby Lincs 174 C4
Lincs 191 F7
Hagnaby Lock Lincs 174 D4
Hague Bar Derbys 185 D7
Hagworthingham
Lincs 174 B4
Haigh Gtr Man 194 F6
S Yorks 197 E9
Haigh Moor
W Yorks 197 C9
Haighton Green
Lancs 203 G7
Haighton Top Lancs 203 G7
Haile Cumb 219 D10
Hailes Glos 99 E10
Hailey Herts 86 C5
Oxon 64 B6
Oxon 82 C5
Hailsham E Sus 23 D9
Hailstone Hill Wilts 81 G9
Hail Weston Cambs 122 E3
Haimer Highld 310 C5
Haimwood Powys 148 F6
Hainault London 87 G7
Haine Kent 71 F11
Hainford Norf 160 F4
Hains Dorset 30 D3
Hainton Lincs 189 E11
Hainworth W Yorks 205 F7
Hainworth Shaw
W Yorks 205 F7
Hairmyres S Lnrk 268 E2
Haisthorpe E Yorks 218 G2
Hakeford Devon 40 F6
Hakin Pembs 72 D5
Halabezack Corn 2 C6
Halam Notts 171 E11
Halamanning Corn 2 C3
Halbeath Fife 280 D2
Halberton Devon 27 E8
Halcon Som 28 B2
Halcro Highld 310 C6
Haldens Herts 86 C2
Hale Cumb 211 D10
Gtr Man 184 D3
Halton 183 E7
Hants 31 D11
Kent 71 F9
Medway 69 F9
Som 30 B3
Sur 49 D10
Hale Bank Halton 183 E7
Hale Barns Gtr Man 184 D3
Halecommon W Sus 34 C4
Hale Coombe N Som 44 B2
Hale End London 86 G5
Hale Green E Sus 23 C9
Hale Mills Corn 4 G5
Hale Nook Lancs 202 E3
Hales Norf 143 D7
Staffs 150 C4
Hales Bank
Hereford 116 G2
Halesfield Telford 132 C4
Halesgate Lincs 156 D6
Hales Green
Derbys 169 G11
Norf 143 D7
Halesowen W Mid 133 G9
Hales Park Worcs 116 B5
Hales Place Kent 54 B6
Hales Street Norf 142 F3
Hale Street Kent 53 D7
Hales Wood Hereford 98 E2
Halesworth Suff 127 B7
Halewood Mers 183 D7
Half Moon Village
Devon 14 B3
Halford Shrops 131 G8
Warks 100 B5
Halfpenny Cumb 211 B10
Halfpenny Furze
Carms 74 C3
Halfpenny Green
Staffs 132 E6
Halfway Carms 75 E8
Carms 94 E2
Carms 94 E6
S Yorks 186 E6
W Berks 64 F2
Wilts 45 D11
Halfway Bridge
W Sus 34 C6
Halfway House
Shrops 148 G6
Halfway Houses
Gtr Man 195 F9
Kent 70 E2
Halfway Street Kent 55 D9
Halgabron Corn 11 D7
Halifax W Yorks 196 B5
Halkburn Borders 271 G9
Halket E Ayrs 267 E8
Halkirk Highld 310 D5
Halkyn / Helygain
Flint 182 G2
Halkyn Mountain
Flint 182 G2
Hallam Fields
Derbys 153 B9
Halland E Sus 23 B8
Hallaton Leics 136 D5
Hallatrow Bath 44 B6
Hallbankgate Cumb 240 F3
Hall Bower W Yorks 196 E6
Hall Broom S Yorks 186 D3
Hall Cross Lancs 202 G4
Hall Dunnerdale
Cumb 220 F4
Halleaths Dumfries 248 G3
Hallen S Glos 60 C5
Hallend Warks 118 D2
Hall End Beds 103 B10
C Beds 103 D11
Lincs 174 E6
S Glos 61 B8
Warks 134 C5
Hallew Corn 5 D10
Hallfield Gate
Derbys 170 D5
Hall Flat Worcs 117 C9
Hallgarth Durham 234 C2
Hall Garth York 207 C9
Hallglen Falk 279 F7
Hall Green Ches E 168 D4
Essex 106 D5
Lancs 194 C3
Lancs 194 F4
W Mid 133 E10
W Mid 134 G2
W Mid 135 G7
Wrex 167 G7
W Yorks 197 D10
Hall Grove Herts 89 C8
Halliburton
Borders 261 B11
Borders 272 F3
Hallin Highld 298 D2
Halling Medway 69 G8
Hallingbury Street
Essex 87 B8
Hallington Lincs 190 D4
Northumb 241 B11
Hall i' th' Wood
Gtr Man 195 E8
Halliwell Gtr Man 195 E8
Hall of Clestrain
Orkney 314 F2
Hall of Tankerness
Orkney 314 F5
Hall of the Forest
Shrops 130 G4
Hallon Shrops 132 D5
Hallonsford Shrops 132 D5
Halloughton Notts 171 E11
Hallow Worcs 116 F6
Hallowes Derbys 186 F5
Hallow Heath Worcs 116 F6
Hallowsgate
Ches W 167 B8
Hallrule Borders 262 G3
Halls E Loth 282 G3
Hallsands Devon 9 G11
Hall Santon Cumb 220 E2
Hall's Cross E Sus 23 D11
Hallsford Bridge
Essex 87 E9
Halls Green Essex 86 D6
Hall's Green Herts 104 F5
Kent 52 D4
Hallspill Devon 25 C7
Hallthwaites Cumb 210 B3
Hall Waberthwaite
Cumb 220 F2
Hallwood Green Glos 98 E3
Hallworthy Corn 11 D9
Hallyards Borders 260 B6
Hallyburton House
Perth 286 D6
Hallyne Borders 270 G3
Halmer End Staffs 168 F3
Halmond's Frome
Hereford 98 B3
Halmore Glos 79 E11
Halmyre Mains
Borders 270 F3
Halnaker W Sus 22 B6
Halsall Lancs 193 E11
Halse Northants 101 C11
Som 27 B10
Halsetown Corn 2 B2
Halsfordwood Devon 14 C3
Halsham E Yorks 201 B9
Halsinger Devon 40 F4
Halstead Essex 106 E6
Kent 68 G3
Leics 136 B4
Halstock Dorset 29 F8
Halsway Som 42 F6
Haltcliff Bridge
Cumb 230 D3
Halterworth Hants 32 C5
Haltham Lincs 174 C2
Haltoft End Lincs 174 F5
Halton Bucks 84 C5
Halton 183 E8
Lancs 211 G10
Northumb 241 D11
Wrex 148 B6
W Yorks 206 G2
Halton Barton Corn 7 B8
Halton Brook Halton 183 E8
Halton East N Yorks 204 C6
Halton Fenside
Lincs 174 C6
Halton Gill N Yorks 213 D7
Halton Green
Lancs 211 F10
Halton Holegate
Lincs 174 B6
Halton Lea Gate
Northumb 240 F5
Halton Moor
W Yorks 206 G2
Halton Shields
Northumb 242 D2
Halton View Halton 183 D8
Halton West
N Yorks 204 C2
Haltwhistle
Northumb 240 E6
Halvergate Norf 143 B8
Halvosso Corn 2 C6
Halwell Devon 8 E5
Halwill Devon 12 B4
Halwill Junction
Devon 24 G6
Halwin Corn 2 C5
Ham Devon 28 G2
Glos 79 F11
Glos 99 G9
Highld 310 B6
Kent 55 C10
London 67 E7
Plym 7 D9
Shetland 313 K1
Som 27 C11
Som 28 B3
Som 28 E3
Som 45 D7
Wilts 63 G10
Hamar Shetland 312 F5
Hamarhill Orkney 314 C5
Hamars Shetland 313 G6
Hambleden Bucks 65 B9
Hambledon Hants 33 E10
Sur 50 F3
Hamble-le-Rice
Hants 33 F7
Hambleton Lancs 202 E3
N Yorks 205 C7
N Yorks 207 G7
Hambleton Moss Side
Lancs 202 E3
Hambridge Som 28 C5
Hambrook S Glos 60 D6
W Sus 22 B3
Ham Common Dorset 30 B4
Hameringham Lincs 174 B4
Hamerton Cambs 122 B2
Hametoun Shetland 313 K1
Ham Green Bucks 83 B11
Hants 48 G2
Hereford 98 C4
Kent 38 B5
Kent 69 F10
N Som 60 D4
Wilts 61 G11
Worcs 117 E10
Ham Hill Kent 69 G8
Hamilton S Lnrk 268 D3
Hamister Shetland 313 G7
Hamlet Dorset 29 F9
Hammer W Sus 49 G11
Hammer Bottom
Hants 49 G11
Hammerfield Herts 85 D8
Hammerpot W Sus 35 F9
Hammersmith
Derbys 170 E5
London 67 D8
Hammerwich
Staffs 133 B11
Hammerwood E Sus 52 F2
Hammill Kent 55 B9
Hammond Street
Herts 86 E4
Hammoon Dorset 30 E4
Ham Moor Sur 66 G5
Hamnavoe Shetland 312 E4
Shetland 312 E6
Shetland 312 F6
Shetland 313 K5
Hamnish Clifford
Hereford 115 F10
Hamp Som 43 F10
Hampden Park
E Sus 23 E10
Hampen Glos 81 B9
Hamperden End
Essex 105 E11
Hamperley Shrops 131 F8
Hampers Green
W Sus 35 C7
Hampeth Northumb 252 B5
Hampnett Glos 81 B10
Hampole S Yorks 198 E4
Hampreston Dorset 19 B7
Hampsfield Cumb 211 C8
Hampson Green
Lancs 202 C5
Hampstead London 67 B9
Hampstead Garden
Suburb London 67 B9
Hampstead Norreys
W Berks 64 D4
Hampsthwaite
N Yorks 205 B11
Hampton Kent 71 F7
London 66 F6
Shrops 132 F4
Swindon 81 G11
Worcs 99 C10
Hampton Bank
Shrops 149 C9
Hampton Beech
Shrops 130 B6
Hampton Bishop
Hereford 97 D11
Hampton Fields Glos 80 F5
Hampton Gay Oxon 83 B7
Hampton Green
Ches W 167 F8
Glos 80 E5
Hampton Hargate
Pboro 138 E3
Hampton Heath
Ches W 167 F7
Hampton Hill London 66 E6
Hampton in Arden
W Mid 134 G4
Hampton Loade
Shrops 132 F5
Hampton Lovett
Worcs 117 D7
Hampton Lucy
Warks 118 F5
Hampton Magna
Warks 118 D5
Hampton on the Hill
Warks 118 E5
Hampton Park
Hereford 97 D10
Soton 32 D6
Hampton Poyle Oxon 83 B8
Hamptons Kent 52 C6
Hampton Wick
London 67 F7
Hamptworth Wilts 32 D2
Hamrow Norf 159 E8
Hamsey E Sus 36 E6
Hamsey Green
London 51 B10
Hamshill Glos 80 E3
Hamstall Ridware
Staffs 152 F2
Hamstead IoW 20 C4
W Mid 133 E10
Hamstead Marshall
W Berks 64 F2
Hamsterley Durham 233 E8
Durham 242 F4
Hamstreet Kent 54 G4
Ham Street Som 44 G5
Hamworthy Poole 18 C5
Hanbury Staffs 152 D3
Worcs 117 E9
Hanbury Woodend
Staffs 152 D3
Hanby Lincs 155 C10
Hanchett Village
Suff 106 B3
Hanchurch Staffs 168 G4
Handbridge Ches W 166 B6
Handcross W Sus 36 B3
Handforth Ches E 184 E5
Hand Green
Ches W 167 C8
Handless Shrops 131 E7
Handley Ches W 167 D7
Derbys 170 C5
Handley Green
Essex 87 E11
Handsacre Staffs 151 F11
Handside Herts 86 C2
Handsworth
S Yorks 186 D6
W Mid 133 E10
Handsworth Wood
W Mid 133 E11
Handy Cross Bucks 84 G5
Devon 24 B6
Som 42 G6
Hanford Dorset 30 E4
Stoke 168 G5
Hangersley Hants 31 F11
Hanging Bank Kent 52 C3
Hanging Heaton
W Yorks 197 C9
Hanging Houghton
Northants 120 C5
Hanging Langford
Wilts 46 F4
Hangingshaw
Borders 261 C9
Dumfries 248 F4
Hangleton Brighton 36 F3
W Sus 35 G9
Hangsman Hill
S Yorks 199 E7
Hanham S Glos 60 E6
Hanham Green
S Glos 60 E6
Hankelow Ches E 167 F11
Hankerton Wilts 81 G7
Hankham E Sus 23 D10
Hanley Stoke 168 F5
Hanley Castle Worcs 98 C6
Hanley Child Worcs 116 E3
Hanley Swan Worcs 98 C6
Hanley William
Worcs 116 D3
Hanlith N Yorks 213 G8
Hanmer Wrex 149 B9
Hannaford Devon 25 B10
Hannafore Corn 6 E5
Hannah Lincs 191 F8
Hanningfields Green
Suff 125 G7
Hannington Hants 48 B4
Northants 120 C6
Swindon 81 G11
Hannington Wick
Swindon 81 F11
Hanscombe End
C Beds 104 E2
Hansel Devon 8 F6
Hansel Village
S Ayrs 257 C9
Hansley Cross
Staffs 169 G9
Hanslope M Keynes 102 B6
Hanthorpe Lincs 155 E11
Hanwell London 67 C7
Oxon 101 C8
Hanwood Shrops 131 B8
Hanwood Bank
Shrops 149 G8
Hanworth Brack 65 F11
London 66 E6
Norf 160 B3
Happendon S Lnrk 259 C9
Happisburgh Norf 161 C7
Happisburgh Common
Norf 161 D7
Hapsford Ches W 183 G7
Som 45 D9
Hapton Lancs 203 G11
Norf 142 D3
Hararden / Penarlâg
Flint 166 B4
Harberton Devon 8 D5
Harbertonford Devon 8 D5
Harbledown Kent 54 B6
Harborne W Mid 133 G10
Harborough Magna
Warks 119 B9
Harborough Parva
Warks 119 B9
Harbottle
Northumb 251 C10
Harbour Heights
E Sus 36 G6
Harbourland Kent 53 B9
Harbourneford Devon 8 C4
Harbours Hill
Worcs 117 D9
Harbour Village
Pembs 91 D8
Harbridge Hants 31 E10
Harbridge Green
Hants 31 E10
Harburn W Loth 269 C10
Harbury Warks 119 F7
Harby Leics 154 C4
Notts 188 G5
Harcombe Devon 14 E3
Devon 15 C9
Harcourt Corn 3 B8
Harcourt Hill Oxon 83 E7
Hardbreck Orkney 314 F4
Hardeicke Glos 80 C4
Harden S Yorks 197 G7
W Mid 133 C10
W Yorks 205 F7
Hardendale Cumb 221 C11
Hardenhuish Wilts 62 E2
Harden Park Ches E 184 F4
Hardgate Aberds 293 C9
Dumfries 237 C10
N Yorks 214 G5
W Dunb 277 G10
Hardham W Sus 35 D8
Hardhorn Lancs 202 F3
Hardingham Norf 141 C10
Hardings Booth
Staffs 169 C9
Hardingstone
Northants 120 F5
Hardings Wood
Staffs 168 E4
Hardington Som 45 C8
Hardington Mandeville
Som 29 E8
Hardington Marsh
Som 29 F8
Hardington Moor
Som 29 E8
Hardiston Perth 279 B11
Hardisworthy Devon 24 C2
Hardley Hants 32 G6
Hardley Street Norf 143 C7
Hardmead
M Keynes 103 B8
Hardrow N Yorks 223 G7
Hardstoft Derbys 170 C6
Hardstoft Common
Derbys 170 C6
Hardway Hants 33 G10
Som 45 G8
Hardwick Bucks 84 B4
Cambs 122 D3
Cambs 123 F7
Norf 142 F4
Norf 158 F2
Northants 121 D7
Oxon 82 D5
Oxon 101 C8
Oxon 101 F11
Shrops 131 E7
Stockton 234 G4
S Yorks 187 D7
W Mid 133 D11
Hardwicke Glos 80 C3
Glos 99 F8
Hereford 96 C5
Hardwick Green
Worcs 98 E6
Hardwick Village
Notts 187 F10
Hardy's Green
Essex 107 G8
Hare Som 28 D3
Hare Appletree
Lancs 202 B6
Hareby Lincs 174 B4
Harecroft W Yorks 205 F7
Hareden Lancs 203 C8
Hare Edge Derbys 186 G4
Harefield London 85 G9
Soton 33 E7
Harefield Grove
London 85 G9
Haregate Staffs 169 D7
Hare Green Essex 107 G11
Hare Hatch
Wokingham 65 D10
Harehill Derbys 152 B3
Harehills W Yorks 206 G2
Harehope Borders 270 G4
Northumb 264 E3
Harelaw Durham 242 G5
Hareleeshill S Lnrk 268 E5
Hareplain Kent 53 F10
Haresceugh Cumb 231 C8
Harescombe Glos 80 C4
Haresfield Glos 80 C4
Swindon 82 G2
Haresfinch Mers 183 B8
Hareshaw N Lnrk 268 C6
Hareshaw Head
Northumb 251 F9
Harestanes E Dunb 278 G3
Harestock Hants 48 G3
Hare Street Essex 86 D6
Herts 104 F6
Herts 105 F7
Harewood W Yorks 206 D2
Harewood End
Hereford 97 F10
Harewood Hill
W Yorks 204 F6
Harford Carms 94 C2
Devon 8 D2
Devon 40 G6
Hargate Norf 142 E2
Hargate Hill Derbys 185 C8
Hargatewall
Derbys 185 F10
Hargrave Ches W 167 C7
Northants 121 C10
Suff 124 F5
Harker Cumb 239 E9
Harker Marsh Cumb 229 E7
Harkland Shetland 312 E6
Harknett's Gate
Essex 86 D6
Harkstead Suff 108 E3
Harlaston Staffs 152 G4
Harlaw Ho Aberds 303 G7
Harlaxton Lincs 155 C7
Harlech Gwyn 145 C11
Harlequin Notts 154 B3
Harlescott Shrops 149 F10
Harlesden London 67 C8
Harlesthorpe
Derbys 187 F7
Harleston Devon 8 F5
Norf 142 G4
Suff 125 F10
Harlestone
Northants 120 E4
Harle Syke Lancs 204 F3
Harley Shrops 131 C11
S Yorks 186 B5
Harleyholm S Lnrk 259 B10
Harley Shute E Sus 38 F3
Harleywood Glos 80 F4
Harling Road Norf 141 F9
Harlington C Beds 103 E10
London 66 D5
S Yorks 198 G3
Harlosh Highld 298 E2
Harlow Essex 86 C6
Harlow Carr
N Yorks 205 C11
Harlow Green T&W 243 F7
Harlow Hill
Northumb 242 D3
N Yorks 205 C11
Harlthorpe E Yorks 207 F10
Harlton Cambs 123 G7
Harlyn Corn 10 F3
Harman's Corner
Kent 69 G11
Harman's Cross
Dorset 18 E5
Harmans Water
Brack 65 F11
Harmby N Yorks 214 B2
Harmer Green Herts 86 B3
Harmer Hill Shrops 149 E9
Harmondsworth
London 66 D5
Harmston Lincs 173 C7
Harnage Shrops 131 C11
Harnham Northumb 242 B3
Wilts 31 B10
Wilts 31 B11
Harnhill Glos 81 E9
Harold Hill London 87 G8
Harold Park London 87 G9
Haroldston West
Pembs 72 B5
Haroldswick
Shetland 312 B8
Harold Wood London 87 G8
Harome N Yorks 216 C2
Harpenden Herts 85 C10
Harpenden Common
Herts 85 C10
Harper Green
Gtr Man 195 F8
Harperley Durham 242 G5
Harper's Gate Staffs 169 D7
Harper's Green Norf 159 E8
Harpford Devon 15 C7
Harpham E Yorks 217 G11
Harpley Norf 158 D5
Worcs 116 E3
Harpole Northants 120 E3
Harpsdale Highld 310 D5
Harpsden Oxon 65 C9
Harpsden Bottom
Oxon 65 C9
Harpswell Lincs 188 D6
Harpton Powys 114 F4
Harpurhey
Gtr Man 195 G11
Harpur Hill Derbys 185 G9
Harraby Cumb 239 G10
Harracott Devon 25 B9
Harrapool Highld 295 C8
Harras Cumb 219 B9
Harraton T&W 243 G7
Harrier Shetland 313 J1
Harrietfield Perth 286 E3
Harrietsham Kent 53 C11
Harringay London 67 B10
Harrington Cumb 228 F5
Lincs 190 G5
Northants 136 G5
Harringworth
Northants 137 D8
Harris Highld 294 F5
Harriseahead Staffs 168 D5
Harriston Cumb 229 C9
Harrogate N Yorks 206 C2
Harrold Beds 121 F8
Harrop Dale
Gtr Man 196 F4
Harrow Highld 310 B6
London 67 B7
Harrowbarrow Corn 7 B7
Harrowbeer Devon 7 B10
Harrowby Lincs 155 B8
Harrowden Beds 103 B11
Harrowgate Hill
Darl 224 B5
Harrowgate Village
Darl 224 B5
Harrow Green Suff 125 G7
Harrow Hill Glos 79 B10
Harrow on the Hill
London 67 B7
Harrow Street Suff 107 D9
Harrow Weald
London 85 G11
Harry Stoke S Glos 60 D6
Harston Cambs 123 G8
Leics 154 C6
Harswell E Yorks 208 E2
Hart Hrtlpl 234 E5
Hartbarrow Cumb 221 G8
Hartburn Northumb 252 F3
Stockton 225 B8
Hartcliffe Bristol 60 F5
Hart Common
Gtr Man 194 F6
Hartest Suff 124 G6
Hartest Hill Suff 124 G6
Hartfield E Sus 52 F3
Highld 299 E7
Hartford Cambs 122 C5
Ches W 183 G10
Som 27 B7
Hartfordbeach
Ches W 183 G10
Hartfordbridge Hants 49 B9
Hartford End Essex 87 B11
Hartforth N Yorks 224 D3
Hartgrove Dorset 30 D4
Hartham Herts 86 C4
Harthill Ches W 167 D8
N Lnrk 269 C8
S Yorks 187 E7
Hart Hill Luton 104 G2
Hartington Derbys 169 C10
Hartland Devon 24 C3
Hartle Worcs 117 B8
Hartlebury Shrops 132 D4
Worcs 116 C6
Hartlebury Common
Worcs 116 C6
Hartlepool Hrtlpl 234 E6
Hartley Cumb 222 D5
Kent 53 G9
Kent 68 F6
Northumb 243 B8
Plym 7 D9
Hartley Green Kent 68 F6
Staffs 151 D9
Hartley Mauditt
Hants 49 F8
Hartley Westpall
Hants 49 B7
Hartley Wintney
Hants 49 B9
Hartlington
N Yorks 213 G10
Hartlip Kent 69 G10
Hartmoor Dorset 30 C3
Hartmount Highld 301 B7
Hartoft End
N Yorks 226 G5
Harton N Yorks 216 G4
Shrops 131 F9
T&W 243 E9
Hartpury Glos 98 F5
Hartsgreen Shrops 132 G5
Hart's Green Suff 125 F7
Hartshead W Yorks 197 C7
Hartshead Green
Gtr Man 196 G3
Hartshead Moor Side
W Yorks 197 C7
Hartshead Moor Top
W Yorks 197 B7
Hartshead Pike
Gtr Man 196 G3
Hartshill Stoke 168 F5
Warks 134 E6
Hart's Hill W Mid 133 F8
Hartshill Green
Warks 134 E6
Hartshorne Derbys 152 E6
Hartsop Cumb 221 C8
Hart Station Hrtlpl 234 D5
Hartswell Som 27 B9
Hartwell Northants 120 G5
Staffs 151 B8
Hartwith N Yorks 214 G4
Hartwood Lancs 194 D5
N Lnrk 268 D6
Hartwoodburn
Borders 261 D11
Harvel Kent 68 G6
Harvest Hill W Mid 134 G5
Harvieston Stirl 277 D11
Harvills Hawthorn
W Mid 133 E9
Harvington Worcs 99 B11
Worcs 117 C7
Harvington Cross
Worcs 99 B11
Harvington Hill
Worcs 99 B10
Harwell Notts 187 C11
Oxon 64 B3
Harwich Essex 108 E5
Harwood Durham 232 E2
Gtr Man 195 E8
Harwood Dale
N Yorks 227 F9
Harwood Lee
Gtr Man 195 E8
Harwood on Teviot
Borders 249 B10
Harworth Notts 187 C10
Hasbury W Mid 133 G9
Hascombe Sur 50 E3
Haselbech Northants 120 B4
Haselbury Plucknett
Som 29 E7
Haseley Warks 118 D4
Haseley Green
Warks 118 D4
Haseley Knob
Warks 118 C4
Haselor Warks 118 F2
Hasfield Glos 98 F6
Hasguard Pembs 72 D5
Haskayne Lancs 193 F11
Hasketon Suff 126 G4
Hasland Derbys 170 B5
Haslemere Sur 50 G2
Haslingbourne
W Sus 35 C7
Haslingden Lancs 195 C9
Haslingfield Cambs 123 G8
Haslington Ches E 168 D2
Hasluck's Green
W Mid 118 B2
Hassall Ches E 168 D3
Hassall Green
Ches E 168 D3
Hassell Street Kent 54 D5
Hassendean Borders 262 E2
Hassingham Norf 143 B7
Hassocks W Sus 36 D3
Hassop Derbys 186 G2
Haster Highld 310 D7
Hasthorpe Lincs 175 B7
Hastigrow Highld 310 C6
Hasting Hill T&W 243 G9
Hastingleigh Kent 54 E5
Hastings E Sus 38 F4
Som 28 D4
Hastingwood Essex 87 D7
Hastoe Herts 84 D6
Haston Shrops 149 E10
Haswell Durham 234 C3
Haswell Moor
Durham 234 C3
Haswell Plough
Durham 234 C3
Haswellsykes
Borders 260 B6
Hatch C Beds 104 B3
Devon 8 F4
Hants 49 C7
Wilts 30 B6
Hatch Beauchamp
Som 28 C4
Hatch Bottom Hants 33 E7
Hatch End Beds 121 E11
London 85 G10
Hatchet Gate Hants 32 G5
Hatchet Green
Hants 31 D11
Hatch Farm Hill
W Sus 34 B6
Hatch Green Som 28 D4
Hatching Green
Herts 85 C10
Hatchmere Ches W 183 G9
Hatch Warren Hants 48 D6
Hatcliffe NE Lincs 201 G8
Hateley Heath
W Mid 133 E10
Hatfield Hereford 115 F11
Herts 86 D2
S Yorks 199 F7
Worcs 117 G7
Hatfield Broad Oak
Essex 87 B8
Hatfield Chase
S Yorks 199 E8
Hatfield Garden Village
Herts 86 D2
Hatfield Heath Essex 87 B8
Hatfield Hyde Herts 86 C2
Hatfield Peverel
Essex 88 C3
Hatfield Woodhouse
S Yorks 199 F7
Hatford Oxon 82 G4
Hatherden Hants 47 C10
Hatherleigh Devon 25 G8
Hatherley Glos 99 G8
Hathern Leics 153 E9
Hatherop Glos 81 D11
Hathersage Derbys 186 E2
Hathersage Booths
Derbys 186 E2
Hathershaw
Gtr Man 196 G2
Hatherton Ches E 167 F11
Staffs 151 G9
Hatley St George
Cambs 122 G5
Hatston Orkney 314 E4
Hatt Corn 7 C7
Hatterseat Aberds 303 G9
Hattersley Gtr Man 185 C7
Hatt Hill Hants 32 B4
Hattingley Hants 48 F6
Hatton Aberds 303 F10
Angus 287 D9
Derbys 152 D4
Lincs 189 F11
London 66 D5
Moray 301 D11
Shrops 131 E9
Warks 118 D4
Warr 183 E9
Hattonburn Aberds 293 C9
Hatton Castle
Aberds 303 E7
Hattoncrook Aberds 303 G8
Hatton Grange
Shrops 132 C5
Hatton Heath
Ches W 167 C7
Hatton Hill Sur 66 G2
Hattonknowe
Borders 270 F4
Hatton of Fintray
Aberds 293 B10
Hatton Park
Northants 121 D7

Hig–Hoo 389

Higher Hurdsfield
Ches E 184 G6
Higher Kingcombe
Dorset 16 B6
Higher Kinnerton
Flint 166 C4
Higher Land Corn 12 G3
Higher Marsh Som 30 C2
Higher Melcombe
Dorset 30 G2
Higher Menadew
Corn 5 D10
Higher Molland
Devon 41 G8
Higher Muddiford
Devon 40 F5
Higher Nyland Dorset 30 C2
Higher Penwortham
Lancs 194 B4
Higher Pertwood
Wilts 45 F11
Higher Porthpean
Corn 5 E10
Higher Poynton
Ches E 184 E6
Higher Prestacott
Devon 12 B3
Higher Rads End
C Beds 103 E9
Higher Ridge
Shrops 149 C7
Higher Rocombe Barton
Devon 9 B8
Higher Row Dorset 31 G8
Higher Runcorn
Halton 183 E8
Higher Sandford
Dorset 29 C10
Higher Shotton
Flint 166 B4
Higher Shurlach
Ches W 183 G11
Higher Slade Devon 40 D4
Higher Street Som 42 E6
Higher Tale Devon 27 G9
Higher Tolcarne Corn 5 B7
Higher Totnell
Dorset 29 F10
Highertown Corn 4 G6
Corn 11 E8
Higher Town Corn 5 C10
Scilly 1 F4
Som 42 D3
Higher Tremarcoombe
Corn 6 B5
Higher Vexford Som 42 F6
Higher Walreddon
Devon 12 G5
Higher Walton
Lancs 194 B5
Warr 183 D9
Higher Wambrook
Som 28 F3
Higher Warcombe
Devon 40 D3
Higher Weaver
Devon 27 G9
Higher Whatcombe
Dorset 30 G4
Higher Wheelton
Lancs 194 C6
Higher Whitley
Ches W 183 E10
Higher Wincham
Ches W 183 F11
Higher Woodsford
Dorset 17 D11
Higher Wraxall
Dorset 29 G9
Higher Wych
Ches W 167 G7
High Etherley
Durham 233 F9
High Ferry Lincs 174 F5
Highfield E Yorks 207 F10
Glos 79 E10
Gtr Man 194 G5
Gtr Man 195 F8
Herts 85 D9
N Ayrs 266 E6
Oxon 101 G11
Soton 32 E6
S Yorks 186 D5
T&W 242 F4
High Field Lancs 203 C10
Highfields Cambs 123 F7
Derbys 170 B6
Essex 88 B5
Glos 80 F3
Leicester 136 C2
Northumb 273 E9
Staffs 151 E8
S Yorks 198 F4
High Flatts W Yorks 197 F8
High Forge Durham 242 G6
High Friarside
Durham 242 F5
High Gallowhill
E Dunb 278 G2
High Garrett Essex 106 F5
Highgate E Sus 52 G2
Kent 53 G9
London 67 B9
Powys 130 D2
S Yorks 198 G3
W Mid 133 F11
High Grange
Durham 233 E9
High Grantley
N Yorks 214 F4
High Green Cumb 221 E8
Norf 141 B8
Norf 142 B2
Norf 159 G8
Shrops 132 G4
Suff 125 E7
S Yorks 186 B4
Worcs 99 B7
W Yorks 197 E7
High Halden Kent 53 F11
High Halstow
Medway 69 D9
High Ham Som 44 G2
High Handenhold
Durham 242 G6
High Harrington
Cumb 228 F6
High Harrogate
N Yorks 206 B2
High Haswell
Durham 234 C3
High Hatton Shrops 150 E2
High Hauxley
Northumb 253 C7
High Hawsker
N Yorks 227 D8
High Heath Shrops 150 D3
W Mid 133 C10
High Hesket Cumb 230 C5
High Hesleden
Durham 234 D5
High Hill Cumb 229 G11
High Houses Essex 87 C11
High Hoyland
S Yorks 197 E9
High Hunsley
E Yorks 208 F4
High Hurstwood
E Sus 37 B7
High Hutton
N Yorks 216 F5
High Ireby Cumb 229 D10
High Kelling Norf 177 E10
High Kilburn
N Yorks 215 D10
High Lands Durham 233 F8
Highlane Ches E 168 B5
Derbys 186 E6
High Lane Gtr Man 185 D7
Worcs 116 E3
Highlanes Corn 10 G4
Staffs 150 C5
High Lanes Corn 2 B3
High Laver Essex 87 D8
Highlaws Cumb 229 B8
Highleadon Glos 98 G5
High Legh Ches E 184 E2
Highleigh W Sus 22 D4
High Leven Stockton 225 C8
Highley Shrops 132 G4
High Littleton Bath 44 B6
High Longthwaite
Cumb 229 B11
High Lorton Cumb 229 F9
High Marishes
N Yorks 216 D6
High Marnham
Notts 188 G4
High Melton
S Yorks 198 G4
High Mickley
Northumb 242 E3
High Mindork
Dumfries 236 D5
Highmoor Cumb 229 B11
Oxon 65 B8
High Moor Derbys 187 E7
Lancs 194 E4
Highmoor Cross
Oxon 65 C8
Highmoor Hill Mon 60 B3
High Moorsley T&W 234 B2
Highnam Glos 80 B3
Highnam Green Glos 98 G5
High Nash Glos 79 C9
High Newton Cumb 211 C8
High Newton-by-the-Sea Northumb 264 D6
High Nibthwaite
Cumb 210 B5
Highoak Norf 141 C11
High Oaks Cumb 222 G2
High Offley Staffs 150 D5
High Ongar Essex 87 E9
High Onn Staffs 150 F6
High Onn Wharf
Staffs 150 F6
High Park Cumb 221 G10
Mers 193 D11
Highridge Bristol 60 F5
High Risby N Lincs 200 E2
Highroad Well Moor
W Yorks 196 B5
High Roding Essex 87 B10
High Rougham Suff 125 E8
High Row Cumb 230 D3
Cumb 230 G3
High Salvington
W Sus 35 F10
High Scales Cumb 229 B9
High Sellafield
Cumb 219 E10
High Shaw N Yorks 223 G7
High Shields T&W 243 D9
High Shincliffe
Durham 233 C11
High Side Cumb 229 E10
High Southwick
T&W 243 F9
High Spen T&W 242 F4
High Stakesby
N Yorks 227 C7
Highstead Kent 71 F8
Highsted Kent 70 G2
High Stoop Durham 233 C8
Highstreet Kent 70 G5
High Street Corn 5 E9
Kent 53 G8
Pembs 73 B11
Suff 107 B7
Suff 127 C8
Suff 127 F8
Suff 143 G7
Highstreet Green
Essex 106 E5
Sur 50 F3
High Street Green
Suff 125 F10
High Sunderland
Borders 261 C11
Hightae Dumfries 238 B3
Highter's Heath
W Mid 117 B11
High Throston
Hrtlpl 234 E5
High Tirfergus
Argyll 255 F7
Hightown Ches E 168 C5
Hants 31 G11
Mers 193 G10
Soton 33 E7
Wrex 166 F4
W Yorks 197 C7
High Town Luton 103 G11
Shrops 132 E4
Staffs 151 G9
Hightown Green
Suff 125 F9
Hightown Heights
W Yorks 197 C7
High Toynton Lincs 174 B3
High Trewhitt
Northumb 252 B2
High Urpeth
Durham 242 G6
High Valleyfield
Fife 279 D10
High Walton Cumb 219 C9
High Warden
Northumb 241 D10
High Water Head
Cumb 220 F6
Highway Corn 4 G4
Hereford 97 B9
Som 29 C7
Wilts 62 E4
Windsor 65 C11
Highweek Devon 14 G2
High Westwood
Durham 242 F4
High Whinnow
Cumb 239 G8
Highwood Devon 27 F10
Dorset 18 D3
Essex 87 E10
Hants 31 F11
Worcs 116 D3
Highwood Hill
London 86 G2
High Woolaston Glos 79 F9
High Worsall
N Yorks 225 D7
Highworth Swindon 82 G2
High Wray Cumb 221 F7
High Wych Herts 87 C7
High Wycombe
Bucks 84 G5
Hilborough Norf 140 C6
Hilborough Ho Norf 140 C6
Hilcot Glos 81 B7
Hilcote Derbys 171 D7
Hilcot End Glos 81 E9
Hilcott Wilts 46 B6
Hildenborough Kent 52 D5
Hilden Park Kent 52 D5
Hildersham Cambs 105 B10
Hildersley Hereford 98 G2
Hilderstone Staffs 151 C8
Hilderthorpe
E Yorks 218 F3
Hilfield Dorset 29 F10
Hilgay Norf 140 D2
Hill S Glos 79 G10
Warks 119 D9
W Mid 134 D2
Hillam N Yorks 198 B4
Hillbeck Cumb 222 B5
Hillblock Pembs 73 B8
Hillborough Kent 71 F8
Hill Bottom Oxon 64 D6
Hillbourne Poole 18 C6
Hillbrae Aberds 302 E6
Aberds 303 G7
Hill Brow W Sus 34 B3
Hillbutts Dorset 31 G7
Hill Chorlton Staffs 150 B5
Hillcliffe Warr 183 D10
Hillclifflane Derbys 170 F3
Hillcommon Som 27 B11
Hill Common Norf 161 E8
Hill Corner Som 45 D10
Hill Croome Worcs 99 C7
Hillcross Derbys 152 C6
Hill Dale Lancs 194 E3
Hill Deverill Wilts 45 E11
Hilldyke Lincs 174 F4
Hill Dyke Lincs 174 F4
Hillend Fife 280 E2
N Lnrk 268 B6
N Som 43 B11
Shrops 132 E6
Swansea 56 C2
Hill End Durham 232 D6
Fife 279 B10
Glos 99 D8
London 85 G8
N Yorks 205 C7
Som 29 E8
Worcs 117 E8
Hillend Green Glos 98 F4
Hillersland Glos 79 C9
Hillerton Devon 13 B10
Hillesden Bucks 102 F3
Hillesden Hamlet
Bucks 102 E3
Hillesley Glos 61 B9
Hillfarance Som 27 C11
Hillfarrance Som 27 C11
Hillfield Devon 8 E6
W Mid 118 B2
Hillfields S Glos 60 D6
W Mid 118 B6
Hillfoot Aberds 303 D9
W Yorks 205 G10
Hillfoot End C Beds 104 E2
Hill Furze Worcs 99 B9
Hill Gate Hereford 97 F9
Hillgreen W Berks 64 D3
Hill Green Essex 105 E9
Kent 69 G10
Hillgrove W Sus 34 B6
Hillhampton
Hereford 97 B11
Hillhead Aberds 302 F5
Aberds 303 G8
Corn 5 C11
Devon 9 E8
E Ayrs 257 B10
S Ayrs 257 F10
Hill Head Hants 33 G8
Northumb 241 D10
Hillhead of Auchentumb
Aberds 303 D9
Hillhead of Blairy
Aberds 302 D6
Hillhead of Cocklaw
Aberds 303 E10
Hill Hoath Kent 52 E3
Hill Hook W Mid 134 C2
Hillhouse Borders 271 D10
Hill Houses Shrops 116 B2
Hilliard's Cross
Staffs 152 G3
Hilliclay Highld 310 C5
Hillingdon London 66 C5
Hillingdon Heath
London 66 C5
Hillington Glasgow 267 C10
Norf 158 D4
Hillis Corner IoW 20 C5
Hillmoor Devon 27 E10
Hillmorton Warks 119 C10
Hill Mountain Pembs 73 D7
Hillockhead Aberds 292 B6
Aberds 292 C5
Hillock Vale Lancs 195 B9
Hill of Beath Fife 280 C3
Hill of Drip Stirl 278 B5
Hill of Fearn Highld 301 B8
Hill of Keillor Angus 286 C6
Hill of Mountblairy
Aberds 302 D6
Hill of Overbrae
Aberds 303 C8
Hill Park Hants 33 F9
Kent 52 B2
Hillpool Worcs 117 B7
Hillpound Hants 33 D9
Hill Ridware Staffs 151 F11
Hillsborough
S Yorks 186 C4
Hillside Aberds 293 D11
Angus 293 G9
Devon 8 C4
Devon 27 F11
Hants 49 C9
Mers 193 E10
Orkney 314 D3
Orkney 314 G4
Shetland 313 G6
Shrops 131 F11
Wilts 81 G9
Hill Side Hants 34 B3
S Yorks 197 G8
Worcs 116 E5
W Yorks 197 D7
Hill Somersal
Derbys 152 C2
Hills Town Derbys 171 B7
Hillstreet Hants 32 D4
Hill Street Kent 54 D6
Hillswick Shetland 312 F4
Hilltop Bl Gwent 77 D11
Bucks 85 E7
Derbys 170 C4
Hill Top Derbys 186 F5
Durham 232 G5
Durham 233 C10
Durham 242 G5
Gtr Man 195 G8
Hants 32 G6
Notts 171 F7
N Yorks 214 G3
N Yorks 214 G5
Staffs 133 B7
S Yorks 186 C5
S Yorks 186 D3
S Yorks 187 B7
S Yorks 197 F9
Warks 134 E5
Warks 135 E7
W Mid 133 E9
W Sus 34 C5
W Yorks 196 E5
W Yorks 197 D10
W Yorks 205 G7
W Yorks 205 G11
Hillview T&W 243 G9
Hill View Dorset 18 B5
Hillway IoW 21 D8
Hillwell Shetland 313 M5
Hill Wood W Mid 134 C2
Hill Wootton Warks 118 D6
Hillyfields Hants 32 D5
Hilmarton Wilts 62 D4
Hilperton Wilts 45 B11
Hilperton Marsh
Wilts 45 B11
Hilsea Ptsmth 33 G11
Hilston E Yorks 209 G11
Hiltingbury Hants 32 C6
Hilton Aberds 303 F9
Borders 273 E7
Cambs 122 D5
Cumb 231 G10
Derbys 152 C4
Dorset 30 G3
Durham 233 G9
Highld 309 L7
Highld 311 L3
Shrops 132 D5
Staffs 133 B11
Stockton 225 C9
Hilton House
Gtr Man 194 F6
Hilton Lodge Highld 300 G2
Hilton of Cadboll
Highld 301 B8
Hilton Park
Gtr Man 195 G10
Himbleton Worcs 117 F8
Himley Staffs 133 E7
Hincaster Cumb 211 C10
Hinchley Wood Sur 67 F7
Hinchliffe Mill
W Yorks 196 F6
Hinchwick Glos 100 E2
Hinckley Leics 135 E8
Hinderclay Suff 125 B10
Hinderton Ches W 182 F4
Hinderwell N Yorks 226 B5
Hindford Shrops 148 C6
Hindhead Sur 49 F11
Hindle Fold Lancs 203 G10
Hindley Gtr Man 194 G6
Northumb 242 F2
Hindley Green
Gtr Man 194 G6
Hindlip Worcs 117 F7
Hindolveston Norf 159 D10
Hindon Wilts 46 G2
Hindpool Cumb 210 F3
Hindringham Norf 159 B9
Hindsford Gtr Man 195 G7
Hingham Norf 141 C10
Hinstock Shrops 150 D3
Hintlesham Suff 107 C11
Hinton Glos 79 E11
Hants 19 B10
Hereford 96 D6
Northants 119 G10
S Glos 61 D8
Shrops 131 B8
Som 29 C9
Hinton Ampner
Hants 33 B9
Hinton Blewett Bath 44 B5
Hinton Charterhouse
Bath 45 B9
Hinton Cross Worcs 99 C10
Hinton-in-the-Hedges
Northants 101 D11
Hinton Martell Dorset 31 F8
Hinton on the Green
Worcs 99 C10
Hinton Parva Dorset 31 G7
Swindon 63 C8
Hinton St George
Som 28 E6
Hinton St Mary
Dorset 30 D3
Hinton Waldrist Oxon 82 F5
Hints Shrops 116 C2
Staffs 134 C3
Hinwick Beds 121 E8
Hinwood Shrops 131 B7
Hinxhill Kent 54 E5
Hinxton Cambs 105 B9
Hinxworth Herts 104 C4
Hipperholme
W Yorks 196 B6
Hipplecote Worcs 116 F4
Hipsburn Northumb 264 G6
Hipswell N Yorks 224 F3
Hirael Gwyn 179 G9
Hiraeth Carms 92 G3
Hirn Aberds 293 C9
Hirnant Powys 147 E11
Hirst N Lnrk 269 C7
Northumb 253 F7
Hirst Courtney
N Yorks 198 C6
Hirwaen Denb 165 C10
Hirwaun Rhondda 77 D7
Hirwaun Common
Bridgend 58 C2
Hiscott Devon 25 B8
Hislop Borders 249 C9
Hismoley Wilts 45 D11
Histon Cambs 123 E8
Hitcham Suff 125 G9
Hitchill Dumfries 238 D4
Hitchin Herts 104 F3
Hitchin Hill Herts 104 F3
Hitcombe Bottom
Wilts 45 E10
Hither Green London 67 E11
Hittisleigh Devon 13 C10
Hittisleigh Barton
Devon 13 B10
Hive E Yorks 208 G2
Hixon Staffs 151 D10
Hoaden Kent 55 B9
Hoar Cross Staffs 152 E2
Hoarwithy Hereford 97 F10
Hoath Kent 71 G8
Hoath Corner Kent 52 E3
Hobarris Shrops 114 B6
Hobbister Orkney 314 F3
Hobble End Staffs 133 B10
Hobbles Green Suff 124 G4
Hobbs Cross Essex 87 C7
Essex 87 F7
Hobbs Wall Bath 61 G7
Hob Hill Ches W 167 E7
Hobkirk Borders 262 G3
Hobroyd Derbys 185 C8
Hobson Durham 242 F5
Hoby Leics 154 F3
Hoccombe Som 27 B10
Hockenden London 68 F3
Hockerill Herts 105 G9
Hockering Norf 159 G11
Hockering Heath
Norf 159 G11
Hockerton Notts 172 D2
Hockholler Som 27 C11
Hockholler Green
Som 27 C11
Hockley Ches E 184 E6
Essex 88 G4
Kent 54 B3
Staffs 134 C4
W Mid 118 B5
Hockley Heath
W Mid 118 C3
Hockliffe C Beds 103 F9
Hockwold cum Wilton
Norf 140 F4
Hockworthy Devon 27 D8
Hocombe Hants 32 C6
Hoddesdon Herts 86 D5
Hoddlesden Blkburn 195 C8
Hoddomcross
Dumfries 238 C5
Hoddom Mains
Dumfries 238 C5
Hoden Worcs 99 B11
Hodgefield Staffs 168 E6
Hodgehill Ches E 168 B4
W Mid 134 F2
Hodgeston Pembs 73 F8
Hodley Powys 130 E3
Hodnet Shrops 150 D2
Hodnetheath
Shrops 150 D2
Hodsock Notts 187 D10
Hodsoll Street Kent 68 G6
Hodson Swindon 63 C7
Hodthorpe Derbys 187 F8
Hoe Hants 33 D9
Norf 159 F9
Sur 50 D5
Hoe Benham
W Berks 64 F2
Hoe Gate Hants 33 E10
Hoff Cumb 222 B3
Hoffleet Stow Lincs 156 B4
Hogaland Shetland 312 F5
Hogben's Hill Kent 54 B4
Hogganfield
Glasgow 268 B2
Hoggard's Green
Suff 125 F7
Hoggeston Bucks 102 G6
Hoggington Wilts 45 B10
Hoggrill's End
Warks 134 E4
Hogha Gearraidh
W Isles 296 D3
Hog Hatch Sur 49 D10
Hoghton Lancs 194 B6
Hoghton Bottoms
Lancs 194 B6
Hogley Green
W Yorks 196 F6
Hognaston Derbys 170 E2
Hogpits Bottom
Herts 85 E8
Hogsthorpe Lincs 191 G8
Hogstock Dorset 31 F7
Holbeach Lincs 157 E7
Holbeach Bank
Lincs 157 D7
Holbeach Clough
Lincs 156 D6
Holbeach Drove
Lincs 156 G6
Holbeache Worcs 116 B5
Holbeach Hurn
Lincs 157 D7
Holbeach St Johns
Lincs 156 F6
Holbeach St Marks
Lincs 157 C7
Holbeach St Matthew
Lincs 157 C8
Holbeck Notts 187 G8
W Yorks 205 G11
Holbeck Woodhouse
Notts 187 G8
Holberrow Green
Worcs 117 F10
Holbeton Devon 8 E2
Holborn London 67 C10
Holborough Kent 69 G8
Holbrook Derbys 170 G5
Suff 108 D3
S Yorks 186 E6
Holbrook Common
S Glos 61 E7
Holbrook Moor
Derbys 170 F5
Holbrooks W Mid 134 G6
Holburn Northumb 264 B2
Holbury Hants 32 G6
Holcombe Devon 14 G5
Gtr Man 195 D9
Som 45 D7
Holcombe Brook
Gtr Man 195 E9
Holcombe Rogus
Devon 27 D9
Holcot Northants 120 D5
Holdbrook London 86 F5
Holden Lancs 203 D11
Holdenby Northants 120 D3
Holden Fold
Gtr Man 196 F2
Holdenhurst Bmouth 19 B8
Holder's Green
Essex 106 F2
Holders Hill London 86 G2
Holdfast Worcs 99 D7
Holdgate Shrops 131 F11
Holdingham Lincs 173 F9
Holditch Dorset 28 G4
Holdsworth
W Yorks 196 B5
Holdworth S Yorks 186 C3
Hole Devon 24 D4
W Yorks 204 F6
Hole Bottom
W Yorks 196 C2
Holefield Borders 263 C8
Holehills N Lnrk 268 B5
Holehouse Derbys 185 C8
Holehouses Ches E 184 F2
Hole-in-the-Wall
Hereford 98 F2
Holemill Aberdeen 293 C10
Holemoor Devon 24 F6
Hole's Hole Devon 7 B8
Holestane Dumfries 247 D9
Holestone Derbys 170 C4
Hole Street W Sus 35 E10
Holewater Devon 41 F8
Holford Som 43 E7
Holgate York 207 C7
Holker Cumb 211 D7
Holkham Norf 176 E5
Hollacombe Devon 24 G5
Devon 26 G4
Hollacombe Hill
Devon 7 E10
Holland Orkney 314 A4
Orkney 314 D6
Sur 52 C2
Holland Fen Lincs 174 F2
Holland Lees Lancs 194 F4
Holland-on-Sea
Essex 89 B12
Hollands Som 29 D9
Hollandstoun
Orkney 314 A7
Hollee Dumfries 239 D7
Hollesley Suff 109 C7
Hollicombe Torbay 9 C7
Hollies Common
Staffs 150 E6
Hollinfare Warr 183 C11
Hollingbourne Kent 53 B10
Hollingbury Brighton 36 F4
Hollingdean Brighton 36 F4
Hollingdon Bucks 103 F7
Hollingrove E Sus 37 C11
Hollingthorpe
W Yorks 197 D10
Hollington Derbys 152 B4
E Sus 38 E3
Hants 48 B2
Staffs 151 B11
Hollington Cross
Hants 48 B2
Hollington Grove
Derbys 152 B4
Hollingwood Derbys 186 G6
Hollingworth
Gtr Man 185 B8
Hollin Hall Lancs 204 F4
Hollin Park W Yorks 206 F2
Hollins Cumb 222 G3
Derbys 186 G4
Gtr Man 195 F8
Gtr Man 195 F10
Gtr Man 195 F11
Staffs 168 D6
Staffs 168 E4
Staffs 169 F7
Hollinsclough Staffs 169 B9
Hollins End S Yorks 186 E5
Hollinsgreen
Ches E 168 C2
Hollins Green
Warr 183 C11
Hollins Lane Lancs 202 C5
Shrops 149 B10
Hollinswood Telford 132 B4
Hollinthorpe
W Yorks 206 G3
Hollinwood
Gtr Man 196 G2
Shrops 149 B10
Hollis Green Devon 27 F9
Hollis Head Devon 27 G7
Hollocombe Devon 25 E10
Hollocombe Town
Devon 25 E10
Holloway Derbys 170 D4
Wilts 45 G11
Windsor 65 C10
Holloway Hill Sur 50 E3
Hollow Brook Bath 60 G5
Hollowell Northants 120 C3
Hollow Meadows
S Yorks 186 D2
Hollowmoor Heath
Ches W 167 B7
Hollow Oak Dorset 18 C2
Hollows Dumfries 239 B9
Hollow Street Kent 71 G8
Holly Bank W Mid 133 C11
Hollyberry End
W Mid 134 G5
Holly Brook Som 44 D4
Hollybush Caerph 77 E11
E Ayrs 257 G9
Stoke 168 G5
Torf 78 G3
Worcs 98 D5
Holly Bush Wrex 166 G6
Hollybush Corner
Bucks 66 B3
Suff 125 F8
Hollybushes Kent 54 B2
Hollybush Hill Bucks 66 C3
Essex 89 B10
Hollycroft Leics 135 E8
Holly Cross Windsor 65 C10
Holly End Norf 139 B9
Holly Green Bucks 84 E3
Worcs 99 C7
Holly Hill N Yorks 224 E3
Hollyhurst Shrops 131 D9
Warks 135 F7
Hollym E Yorks 201 B10
Hollywaste Shrops 116 B2
Hollywater Hants 49 G10
Hollywood Worcs 117 B11
Holmacott Devon 25 B8
Holman Clavel Som 28 D2
Holmbridge
W Yorks 196 F6
Holmbury St Mary
Sur 50 E6
Holmbush Corn 5 E10
Dorset 28 G5
Holmcroft Staffs 151 D8
Holme Cambs 138 F3
C Beds 104 C3
Cumb 211 D10
N Lincs 200 F2
Notts 172 D4
N Yorks 215 C7
W Yorks 196 F6
W Yorks 205 G9
Holmebridge Dorset 18 D3
Holme Chapel
Lancs 195 B11
Holme Green
C Beds 104 C3
N Yorks 207 E7
Wokingham 65 F10
Holme Hale Norf 141 B7
Holme Hill NE Lincs 201 F9
Holme Lacy
Hereford 97 D11
Holme Lane Notts 154 B2
Holme Marsh
Hereford 114 G6
Holme Mills Cumb 211 D10
Holme next the Sea
Norf 176 E2
Holme-on-Spalding-Moor E Yorks 208 F2
Holme on the Wolds
E Yorks 208 D5
Holme Pierrepont
Notts 154 B2
Holmer Hereford 97 C10
Holmer Green Bucks 84 F6
Holmes Lancs 194 D2
Holme St Cuthbert
Cumb 229 B8
Holmes Chapel
Ches E 168 B3
Holmesdale Derbys 186 F5
Holmesfield Derbys 186 F4
Holme Slack Lancs 203 G7
Holme's Hill E Sus 23 C8
Holmeswood Lancs 194 D2
Holmethorpe Sur 51 C9
Holmewood Derbys 170 B6
Holme Wood
W Yorks 205 G9
Holmfield W Yorks 196 B5
Holmfirth W Yorks 196 F6
Holmhead Angus 293 F7
Dumfries 246 F6
E Ayrs 258 E3
Holmhill Dumfries 247 D9
Holmisdale Highld 297 G7
Holmley Common
Derbys 186 F5
Holmpton E Yorks 201 C11
Holmrook Cumb 219 F11
Holmsgarth
Shetland 313 J6
Holmside Durham 233 B10
Holmsleigh Green
Devon 28 G2
Holmston S Ayrs 257 E9
Holmwood Corner
Sur 51 E7
Holmwrangle Cumb 230 B6
Holne Devon 8 B4
Holnest Dorset 29 E11
Holnicote Som 42 D2
Holsworthy Devon 24 G4
Holsworthy Beacon
Devon 24 F5
Holt Dorset 31 G8
Hants 49 C8
Mers 183 C7
Norf 159 B11
Wilts 61 G11
Worcs 116 E6
Wrex 166 E6
Holtby York 207 C9
Holt End Hants 49 F7
Worcs 117 D11
Holt Fleet Worcs 116 E6
Holt Green Lancs 193 G11
Holt Head W Yorks 196 E5
Holt Heath Dorset 31 G9
Worcs 116 E6
Holt Hill Kent 53 B8
Staffs 152 D2
Holton Oxon 83 D10
Som 29 B11
Suff 127 B7
Holton cum Beckering
Lincs 189 E10
Holton Heath Dorset 18 C4
Holton le Clay Lincs 201 G9
Holton le Moor
Lincs 189 B9
Holton St Mary
Suff 107 D11
Holt Park W Yorks 205 E11
Holt Pound Hants 49 E10
Holts Gtr Man 196 G3
Holtspur Bucks 84 G6
Holt Wood Dorset 31 F8
Holtye E Sus 52 F3
Holway Dorset 28 G5
Dorset 29 C10
Flint 181 F11
Som 28 C2
Holwell Dorset 30 E2
Herts 104 E3
Leics 154 E4
Oxon 82 D2
Som 45 D8
Holwellbury C Beds 104 E3
Holwick Durham 232 F4
Holworth Dorset 17 E11
Holybourne Hants 49 E8
Holy City Devon 28 G3
Holy Cross T&W 243 D8
Worcs 117 B8
Holyfield Essex 86 E5
Holyhead / Caergybi
Anglesey 178 E2
Holy Island
Northumb 273 B11
Holylee Borders 261 B9
Holymoorside
Derbys 170 B4
Holyport Windsor 65 D11
Holystone
Northumb 251 C11
Holytown N Lnrk 268 C5
Holy Vale Scilly 1 G4
Holywell Cambs 122 C6
C Beds 85 B8
Corn 4 D5
Dorset 29 G9
E Sus 23 F9
Glos 80 G3
Hereford 97 C7
Herts 85 F9
Northumb 243 C8
Som 29 E8
Warks 118 D3
Holywell Green
W Yorks 196 D5
Holywell Lake Som 27 C10
Holywell Row Suff 124 B4
Holywell / Treffynnon
Flint 181 F11
Holywood
Dumfries 247 G10
Homedowns Glos 99 E8
Homer Shrops 132 C2
Homer Green
Mers 193 G10
Homersfield Suff 142 F5
Homerton London 67 B11
Hom Green
Hereford 97 G11
Homington Wilts 31 B10
Honeybourne
Worcs 100 C2
Honeychurch Devon 25 G10
Honeydon Beds 122 F2
Honey Hall N Som 60 G2
Honeyhill
Wokingham 65 F10
Honey Hill Kent 70 G6
Honeystreet Wilts 62 G6
Honey Street Wilts 62 G6
Honey Tye Suff 107 D9
Honeywick C Beds 103 G9
Honicknowle Plym 7 D9
Honiley Warks 118 C4
Honing Norf 160 D6
Honingham Norf 160 G2
Honington Lincs 172 G6
Suff 125 C8
Warks 100 C5
Honiton Devon 27 G11
Honkley Wrex 166 D4
Honley W Yorks 196 E6
Honley Moor
W Yorks 196 E6
Honnington Telford 150 F4
Honor Oak London 67 E11
Honor Oak Park
London 67 E11
Honresfeld Gtr Man 196 D2
Hoo Kent 71 G9

Lan–Lit 393

Langford Green
Devon 27 G8
N Som 44 B3
Langham Dorset 30 B3
Essex 107 E10
Norf 177 E8
Rutland 154 G6
Som 28 E4
Suff 125 C9
Langhaugh Borders 260 C6
Langho Lancs 203 G10
Langholm Dumfries 249 G9
Langholme N Lincs 188 B3
Langhope Borders 261 E10
Langland Swansea 56 D6
Langlee Borders 262 B2
Langleeford
Northumb 263 E10
Langlee Mains
Borders 262 B2
Langlees Falk 279 E7
Langley Ches E 184 G6
Derbys 170 F6
Essex 105 D8
Glos 99 F10
Gtr Man 195 F11
Hants 32 G6
Herts 104 G4
Kent 53 C10
Northumb 241 E8
Oxon 82 B4
Slough 66 D4
Som 27 B9
Warks 118 E3
W Mid 133 F9
W Sus 34 B4
Langley Burrell Wilts 62 D2
Langleybury Herts 85 E9
Langley Common
Derbys 152 B5
Wokingham 65 F9
Langley Corner
Bucks 66 C4
Langley Green
Derbys 152 B5
Essex 107 G7
Warks 118 E3
W Mid 133 F9
W Sus 51 F9
Langley Heath Kent 53 C10
Langley Marsh Som 27 B9
Langley Mill Derbys 170 F6
Langley Moor
Durham 233 C11
Langley Park
Durham 233 C10
Langley Street Norf 143 C7
Langley Vale Sur 51 B8
Langloan N Lnrk 268 C4
Langney E Sus 23 E10
Langold Notts 187 D9
Langore Corn 12 D2
Langport Som 28 B6
Langrick Lincs 174 F3
Langrick Bridge
Lincs 174 F3
Langridge Bath 61 F8
Langridge Ford
Devon 25 C9
Langrigg Cumb 222 C5
Cumb 229 B9
Langrish Hants 34 C2
Langsett S Yorks 197 G8
Langshaw Borders 262 B2
Langside Glasgow 267 C11
Perth 285 F11
Langskaill Orkney 314 B4
Langstone Devon 13 E10
Hants 22 C2
Newport 78 G5
Langthorne N Yorks 224 G5
Langthorpe N Yorks 215 F7
Langthwaite
N Yorks 223 E10
Langtoft E Yorks 217 F10
Lincs 156 G2
Langton Durham 224 B3
Lincs 174 B2
Lincs 190 G5
N Yorks 216 F5
Langton by Wragby
Lincs 189 F11
Langton Green Kent 52 F4
Suff 126 C2
Langton Herring
Dorset 17 E8
Langton Long Blandford
Dorset 30 F5
Langton Matravers
Dorset 18 F6
Langtree Devon 25 D7
Langtree Week
Devon 25 D7
Langwathby Cumb 231 E7
Langwell Ho Highld 311 G5
Langwell Lodge
Highld 307 J6
Langwith Derbys 171 B8
Langwith Junction
Derbys 171 B8
Langworth Lincs 189 F9
Lanham Green
Essex 106 G5
Lanivet Corn 5 C10
Lanjeth Corn 5 E9
Lanjew Corn 5 C9
Lank Corn 11 F7
Lanlivery Corn 5 D11
Lanner Corn 2 B6
Lanreath Corn 6 D3
Lanrick Stirl 285 G10
Lansallos Corn 6 E3
Lansbury Park
Caerph 59 B7
Lansdown Bath 61 F8
Glos 99 G8
Lanstephan Corn 12 D2
Lanteglos Corn 11 E7
Lanteglos Highway
Corn 6 E3
Lanton Borders 262 E4
Northumb 263 C10
Lantuel Corn 5 B9
Lantyan Corn 6 D2
Lapal W Mid 133 G9
Lapford Devon 26 F2
Lapford Cross Devon 26 F2
Laphroaig Argyll 254 C4
Lapley Staffs 151 G7
Lapworth Warks 118 C3
Larachbeg Highld 289 E8
Larbert Falk 279 E7
Larbreck Lancs 202 E4
Larches Lancs 202 G6
Larden Green
Ches E 167 E9
Larg Highld 292 B2
Largie Aberds 302 F6
Largiebaan Argyll 255 F7
Largiemore Argyll 275 E10
Largoward Fife 287 G8
Largs N Ayrs 266 D4
Largue Aberds 302 E6
Largybeg N Ayrs 256 E3
Largymeanoch
N Ayrs 256 E2
Largymore N Ayrs 256 E2
Larkfield Invclyd 276 F4
Kent 53 B8
W Yorks 205 F10
Larkhall Bath 61 F9
S Lnrk 268 E5
Larkhill Wilts 46 E6
Lark Hill Gtr Man 195 G7
Larklands Derbys 171 G7
Larks' Hill Suff 108 B3
Larling Norf 141 F9
Larport Hereford 97 D11
Larrick Corn 12 F2
Larriston Borders 250 E2
Lartington Durham 223 B10
Lary Aberds 292 C5
Lasborough Glos 80 G4
Lasham Hants 49 E7
Lashenden Kent 53 E10
Lask Edge Staffs 168 D6
Lassington Glos 98 G5
Lassodie Fife 280 C2
Lastingham
N Yorks 226 G4
Latcham Som 44 D2
Latchbrook Corn 7 D8
Latchford Herts 105 G7
Oxon 83 E11
Warr 183 D10
Latchingdon Essex 88 E5
Latchley Corn 12 G4
Latchmere Green
Hants 64 G6
Latchmore Bank
Essex 87 B7
Lately Common
Warr 183 B11
Lathallan Mill Fife 287 G8
Lathbury M Keynes 103 B7
Latheron Highld 310 F5
Latheronwheel
Highld 310 F5
Latheronwheel Ho
Highld 310 F5
Lathom Lancs 194 E3
Lathones Fife 287 G8
Latimer Bucks 85 F8
Latteridge S Glos 61 C7
Lattiford Som 29 B11
Lattinford Hill Suff 107 D11
Latton Wilts 81 F9
Latton Bush Essex 87 D7
Lauchintilly Aberds 293 B9
Laudale Ho Highld 289 D9
Lauder Borders 271 F10
Lauder Barns
Borders 271 F10
Laugharne / Talacharn
Carms 74 C4
Laughern Hill Worcs 116 F5
Laughterton Lincs 188 F4
Laughton E Sus 23 C8
Leics 136 F3
Lincs 155 C11
Lincs 188 B4
Laughton Common
E Sus 23 C7
S Yorks 187 D8
Laughton en le Morthen
S Yorks 187 D8
Launcells Corn 24 F2
Launcells Cross Corn 24 F3
Launceston Corn 12 D2
Launcherley Som 44 E4
Laund Lancs 195 C10
Launton Oxon 102 G2
Laurencekirk
Aberds 293 F9
Laurieston Dumfries 237 C8
Falk 279 F8
Lavendon M Keynes 121 G8
Lavenham Suff 107 B8
Laverackloch
Moray 301 C11
Laverhay Dumfries 248 D4
Laverlaw Borders 261 B7
Laverley Som 44 F5
Lavernock V Glam 59 F7
Laversdale Cumb 239 E11
Laverstock Wilts 47 G7
Laverstoke Hants 48 D3
Laverton Glos 99 D11
N Yorks 214 E4
Som 45 C9
Lavington Sands
Wilts 46 B4
Lavister Wrex 166 D5
Lavrean Corn 5 D10
Lawers Perth 285 D10
Perth 285 E11
Lawford Essex 107 E11
Som 42 F6
Lawford Heath
Warks 119 C9
Lawhill Perth 286 F3
Law Hill S Lnrk 268 E6
Lawhitton Corn 12 E3
Lawkland N Yorks 212 F5
Lawkland Green
N Yorks 212 F5
Lawley Telford 132 B3
Lawn Swindon 63 C7
Lawnhead Staffs 150 E6
Lawns W Yorks 197 C10
Lawnswood
W Yorks 205 F11
Lawnt Denb 165 B8
Lawrence Hill
Newport 59 B10
Lawrence Weston
Bristol 60 D4
Lawrenny Pembs 73 D8
Lawrenny Quay
Pembs 73 D8
Lawshall Suff 125 G7
Lawshall Green
Suff 125 G7
Lawton Hereford 115 F8
Shrops 131 G10
Lawton-gate
Ches E 168 D4
Lawton Heath End
Ches E 168 D3
Laxey IoM 192 D5
Laxfield Suff 126 C5
Laxfirth Shetland 313 H6
Shetland 313 J6
Laxford Bridge
Highld 306 E7
Laxo Shetland 313 G6
Laxobigging
Shetland 312 F6
Laxton E Yorks 199 B9
Northants 137 D8
Notts 172 B2
Laycock W Yorks 204 E6
Layer Breton Essex 88 B6
Layer de la Haye
Essex 89 B7
Layer Marney Essex 88 B6
Layerthorpe York 207 C8
Layham Suff 107 C10
Laymore Dorset 28 G5
Layters Green Bucks 85 G7
Laytham E Yorks 207 F10
Layton Blkpool 202 F2
Lazenby Redcar 225 B11
Lazonby Cumb 230 D6
Lea Derbys 170 D4
Hereford 98 G3
Lancs 202 G5
Lincs 188 D4
Shrops 131 B8
Shrops 131 F7
Wilts 62 B3
Lea Bridge London 67 B11
Leabrooks Derbys 170 E6
Lea by Backford
Ches W 182 G5
Leacainn W Isles 305 H3
Leac a Li W Isles 305 J3
Leachkin Highld 300 E6
Leacnasaide Highld 299 B7
Leadburn Midloth 270 D4
Leadendale Staffs 151 B8
Leadenham Lincs 173 E7
Leaden Roding Essex 87 C9
Leadgate Cumb 231 C10
Durham 242 G4
T&W 242 F4
Leadhills S Lnrk 259 G9
Leadingcross Green
Kent 53 C11
Leadmill Derbys 186 E2
Flint 166 C2
Lea End Worcs 117 B10
Leafield Oxon 82 B4
Wilts 61 F11
Lea Forge Ches E 168 F2
Leagrave Luton 103 G10
Leagreen Hants 19 C11
Lea Green Mers 183 C8
Lea Hall W Mid 134 F2
Lea Heath Staffs 151 D10
Leake Lincs 174 F6
N Yorks 225 G8
Leake Commonside
Lincs 174 E5
Leake Fold Hill
Lincs 174 E6
Lealholm N Yorks 226 D5
Lealholm Side
N Yorks 226 D5
Lea Line Hereford 98 G3
Lealt Argyll 275 D7
Highld 298 C5
Leam Derbys 186 F2
Lea Marston Warks 134 E4
Leamington Hastings
Warks 119 D8
Leamoor Common
Shrops 131 F8
Leamore W Mid 133 C9
Leamside Durham 234 B2
Leanach Argyll 275 D11
Leanachan Highld 290 F4
Leanaig Highld 300 D5
Leapgate Worcs 116 C6
Leargybreck Argyll 274 F6
Lease Rigg N Yorks 226 E6
Leasey Bridge Herts 85 C11
Leasgill Cumb 211 C9
Leasingham Lincs 173 F9
Leasingthorne
Durham 233 F11
Leason Swansea 56 C3
Leasowe Mers 182 C3
Leatherhead Sur 51 B7
Leatherhead Common
Sur 51 B7
Leathern Bottle Glos 80 E2
Leathley N Yorks 205 D10
Leaths Dumfries 237 C9
Leaton Shrops 149 F9
Telford 150 G2
Leaton Heath
Shrops 149 F9
Lea Town Lancs 202 G5
Lea Valley Herts 85 B11
Leaveland Kent 54 C4
Leavenheath Suff 107 D9
Leavening N Yorks 216 G5
Leavesden Green
Herts 85 E9
Leaves Green London 68 G2
Lea Yeat Cumb 212 B5
Leazes Durham 242 F5
Lebberston
N Yorks 217 C11
Leburnick Corn 12 E3
Lechlade-on-Thames
Glos 82 F2
Leck Lancs 212 D2
Leckford Hants 47 F11
Leckfurin Highld 308 D7
Leckgruinart Argyll 274 G3
Leckhampstead
Bucks 102 D4
W Berks 64 D2
Leckhampstead Thicket
W Berks 64 D2
Leckhampton Glos 80 B6
Leckie Highld 299 C10
Leckmelm Highld 307 K6
Leckuary Argyll 275 D9
Leckwith V Glam 59 E7
Leconfield E Yorks 208 E6
Ledaig Argyll 289 F11
Ledburn Bucks 103 G8
Ledbury Hereford 98 D4
Ledcharrie Stirl 285 E9
Leddington Glos 98 E3
Ledgemoor
Hereford 115 G8
Ledgowan Highld 299 D11
Ledicot Hereford 115 E8
Ledmore Angus 293 G7
Highld 307 H7
Lednagullin Highld 308 C7
Ledsham Ches W 182 G5
W Yorks 198 B3
Ledston W Yorks 198 B2
Ledstone Devon 8 F4
Ledston Luck
W Yorks 206 G4
Ledwell Oxon 101 F8
Lee Argyll 288 G6
Devon 40 D3
Devon 40 D5
Hants 32 D5
Lancs 203 B7
London 67 E11
Northumb 241 F10
Shrops 149 C8
Leeans Shetland 313 J5
Lee Bank W Mid 133 F11
Leebotten Shetland 313 L6
Leebotwood Shrops 131 D9
Lee Brockhurst
Shrops 149 D10
Leece Cumb 210 F4
Lee Chapel Essex 69 B7
Leechpool Mon 60 B4
Lee Clump Bucks 84 E6
Lee Common Bucks 84 E6
Leeds Kent 53 C10
W Yorks 205 G11
Leedstown Corn 2 C4
Leeford Devon 41 D9
Lee Gate Bucks 84 D5
Leegomery Telford 150 G3
Lee Ground Hants 33 F8
Lee Head Derbys 185 C8
Leeholme Durham 233 E10
Leek Staffs 169 D7
Leekbrook Staffs 169 E7
Leek Wootton
Warks 118 D5
Lee Mill Devon 8 D2
Leeming N Yorks 214 B5
W Yorks 204 G6
Leeming Bar
N Yorks 224 G5
Leemings Lancs 203 D10
Lee Moor Devon 7 C11
W Yorks 197 B10
Lee-on-the-Solent
Hants 33 G9
Lee-over-Sands
Essex 89 C10
Lees Derbys 152 B5
Gtr Man 196 G3
W Yorks 204 F6
Leesthorpe Leics 154 G5
Leeswood / Coed-Llai
Flint 166 D3
Leetown Perth 286 E6
Leftwich Ches W 183 G11
Legar Powys 78 B2
Legbourne Lincs 190 E5
Legburthwaite
Cumb 220 B6
Legerwood
Borders 271 G11
Leggatt Hill W Sus 34 C6
Legsby Lincs 189 D10
Leicester Leicester 135 C11
Leicester Forest East
Leics 135 C10
Leicester Grange
Warks 135 E8
Leigh Devon 26 E2
Dorset 18 B6
Dorset 29 F10
Dorset 30 F3
Glos 99 F7
Gtr Man 195 G7
Kent 52 D4
Shrops 130 C6
Sur 51 D8
Wilts 81 G9
Worcs 116 G5
Leigham Plym 7 D10
Leigh Beck Essex 69 C10
Leigh Common Som 30 B2
Leigh Delamere
Wilts 61 D11
Leigh Green Kent 54 G2
Leighland Chapel
Som 42 F4
Leigh-on-Sea
Sthend 69 B10
Leigh Park Hants 22 B2
Leigh Sinton Worcs 116 G5
Leighswood
W Mid 133 C11
Leighterton Glos 80 G4
Leighton N Yorks 214 D3
Shrops 132 B2
Som 45 E8
Leighton Bromswold
Cambs 122 B2
Leighton Buzzard
C Beds 103 F8
Leighton / Tre'r llai
Powys 130 B4
Leigh upon Mendip
Som 45 D7
Leigh Woods N Som 60 E5
Leinthall Earls
Hereford 115 D8
Leinthall Starkes
Hereford 115 D8
Leintwardine
Hereford 115 C8
Leire Leics 135 E10
Leirinmore Highld 308 C4
Leiston Suff 127 E8
Leitfie Perth 286 C6
Leith Edin 280 F5
Leithenhall
Dumfries 248 D4
Leitholm Borders 272 G5
Lelant Corn 2 B2
Lelant Downs Corn 2 B2
Lelley E Yorks 209 G10
Lem Hill Worcs 116 C4
Lemington T&W 242 E5
Lemmington Hall
Northumb 264 G4
Lempitlaw Borders 263 C7
Lemsford Herts 86 C2
Lenacre Cumb 212 B3
Lenborough Bucks 102 E3
Lenchwick Worcs 99 B10
Lendalfoot S Ayrs 244 F4
Lendrick Lodge
Stirl 285 G9
Lenham Kent 53 C11
Lenham Forstal Kent 54 C2
Lenham Heath Kent 54 D2
Lennel Borders 273 G7
Lennoxtown E Dunb 278 F2
Lent Bucks 66 C2
Lenten Pool Denb 165 B8
Lenton Lincs 155 C10
Nottingham 153 B11
Lenton Abbey
Nottingham 153 B10
Lentran Highld 300 E5
Lent Rise Bucks 66 C2
Lenwade Norf 159 F11
Leny Ho Stirl 285 G10
Lenzie E Dunb 278 G3
Lenziemill N Lnrk 278 G5
Leoch Angus 287 D7
Leochel-Cushnie
Aberds 293 B7
Leominster Hereford 115 F9
Leomonsley Staffs 134 B2
Leonard Stanley Glos 80 E4
Leonardston Pembs 72 D6
Leorin Argyll 254 C4
Lepe Hants 20 B5
Lephin Highld 297 G7
Lephinchapel
Argyll 275 D10
Lephinmore Argyll 275 D10
Leppington N Yorks 216 G5
Lepton W Yorks 197 D8
Lepton Edge
W Yorks 197 D8
Lerigoligan Argyll 275 C9
Lerrocks Stirl 285 G11
Lerryn Corn 6 D2
Lerwick Shetland 313 J6
Lesbury Northumb 264 G6
Leschangie Aberds 293 B9
Le Skerne Haughton
Darl 224 B6
Leslie Aberds 302 G5
Fife 286 G6
Lesmahagow S Lnrk 259 B8
Lesnewth Corn 11 C8
Lessendrum Aberds 302 E5
Lessingham Norf 161 D7
Lessness Heath
London 68 D3
Lessonhall Cumb 238 G6
Leswalt Dumfries 236 C2
Letchmore Heath
Herts 85 F11
Letchworth Herts 104 E4
Letcombe Bassett
Oxon 63 B11
Letcombe Regis
Oxon 63 B11
Letham Angus 287 C9
Falk 279 D7
Fife 287 F7
Perth 286 E4
Letham Grange
Angus 287 C10
Lethem Borders 250 B5
Lethen Ho Highld 301 D9
Lethenty Aberds 303 E8
Aberds 303 G7
Letheringham Suff 126 F5
Letheringsett Norf 159 B11
Lettaford Devon 13 E10
Lettan Orkney 314 B7
Letter Aberds 293 B9
Letterewe Highld 299 B9
Letterfearn Highld 295 C10
Letterfinlay Highld 290 D4
Lettermay Argyll 284 G5
Lettermorar Highld 295 G9
Lettermore Argyll 288 E6
Letters Highld 307 L6
Letterston / Treletert
Pembs 91 F8
Lettoch Highld 292 B2
Highld 301 F10
Moray 302 F3
Perth 291 G11
Letton Hereford 96 B6
Hereford 115 C7
Letton Green Norf 141 B9
Lett's Green Kent 52 B3
Letty Brongu
Bridgend 57 D11
Letty Green Herts 86 C3
Letwell S Yorks 187 D9
Leuchars Fife 287 E8
Leuchars Ho Moray 302 C2
Leumrabhagh
W Isles 305 G5
Levalsa Meor Corn 5 F10
Levan Invclyd 276 F4
Levaneap Shetland 313 G6
Levedale Staffs 151 F7
Level of Mendalgief
Newport 59 B10
Level's Green Essex 105 G9
Leven E Yorks 209 D8
Fife 287 G7
Levencorroch
N Ayrs 256 E2
Levenhall E Loth 281 G7
Levens Cumb 211 B9
Leven Seat W Loth 269 D8
Levens Green Herts 105 G7
Levenshulme
Gtr Man 184 C5
Leventhorpe
W Yorks 205 G8
Levenwick Shetland 313 L6
Lever-Edge
Gtr Man 195 F8
Leverington Cambs 157 G8
Leverington Common
Cambs 157 G8
Leverstock Green
Herts 85 D9
Leverton Lincs 174 F6
W Berks 63 E10
Leverton Highgate
Lincs 174 F6
Leverton Lucasgate
Lincs 174 F6
Leverton Outgate
Lincs 174 F6
Levington Suff 108 D4
Levisham N Yorks 226 G6
Levishie Highld 290 B6
Lew Oxon 82 D4
Lewannick Corn 11 E11
Lewcombe Dorset 29 F9
Lewdown Devon 12 D4
Lewes E Sus 36 E6
Leweston Pembs 91 G8
Lewisham London 67 D11
Lewiston Highld 300 G5
Lewistown Bridgend 58 B2
Lewknor Oxon 84 F2
Leworthy Devon 24 G4
Devon 41 F7
Lewson Street Kent 70 G3
Lewth Lancs 202 F5
Lewthorn Cross
Devon 13 F11
Lewtrenchard Devon 12 D5
Lexden Essex 107 G9
Ley Aberds 293 B7
Corn 6 B3
Som 41 F10
Leybourne Kent 53 B7
Leyburn N Yorks 224 G2
Leycett Staffs 168 F3
Leyfields Staffs 134 B4
Ley Green Herts 104 G3
Ley Hey Park
Gtr Man 185 D7
Leyhill Bucks 85 E7
S Glos 79 G11
Ley Hill W Mid 134 D2
Leyland Lancs 194 C4
Leylodge Aberds 293 B9
Leymoor W Yorks 196 D6
Leys Aberds 292 C6
Aberds 303 D10
Cumb 219 B11
Perth 286 D6
Staffs 169 F8
Leys Castle Highld 300 E6
Leysdown-on-Sea
Kent 70 E4
Leys Hill Hereford 79 B9
Leysmill Angus 287 C10
Leys of Cossans
Angus 287 C7
Leysters Hereford 115 E11
Leysters Pole
Hereford 115 E11
Leyton London 67 B11
Leytonstone London 67 B11
Lezant Corn 12 F2
Lezerea Corn 2 C5
Leziate Norf 158 F3
Lhanbryde Moray 302 C2
Liatrie Highld 300 F2
Libanus Powys 95 F9
Libberton S Lnrk 269 G9
Libbery Worcs 117 F9
Liberton Edin 270 B5
Liceasto W Isles 305 J3
Lichfield Staffs 134 B2
Lick Perth 286 B2
Lickey Worcs 117 B9
Lickey End Worcs 117 C9
Lickfold W Sus 34 B6
Lickhill Worcs 116 C6
Lickleyhead Castle
Aberds 302 G6
Liddaton Devon 12 E5
Liddel Orkney 314 H4
Liddesdale Highld 289 D9
Liddeston Pembs 72 D5
Liddington Swindon 63 C8
Liden Swindon 63 C7
Lidgate Suff 124 F4
Lidget S Yorks 199 G7
Lidget Green
W Yorks 205 G8
Lidgett Notts 171 B10
Lidgett Park
W Yorks 206 F2
Lidham Hill E Sus 38 D4
Lidlington C Beds 103 D9
Lidsey W Sus 22 C6
Lidsing Kent 69 G9
Lidstone Oxon 101 G7
Lieurary Highld 310 C4
Liff Angus 287 D7
Lifford W Mid 117 B11
Lifton Devon 12 D3
Liftondown Devon 12 D3
Lightcliffe W Yorks 196 B6
Lighteach Shrops 149 C10
Lightfoot Green
Lancs 202 G6
Lighthorne Warks 118 F6
Lighthorne Heath
Warks 119 F7
Lighthorne Rough
Warks 118 F6
Lightmoor Telford 132 B3
Light Oaks Staffs 168 E6
Lightpill Glos 80 E4
Lightwater Sur 66 G2
Lightwood Shrops 132 E2
Shrops 150 D3
Staffs 169 G8
Stoke 168 G6
S Yorks 186 E5
Lightwood Green
Ches E 167 G10
Wrex 166 G5
Liglartrie S Ayrs 244 F6
Lilbourne
Northants 119 B11
Lilburn Tower
Northumb 264 E2
Lilford Gtr Man 195 G7
Lillesdon Som 28 C4
Lilleshall Telford 150 F4
Lilley Herts 104 F2
W Berks 64 D2
Lilliesleaf Borders 262 E2
Lillingstone Dayrell
Bucks 102 D4
Lillingstone Lovell
Bucks 102 C4
Lillington Dorset 29 E10
Warks 118 D6
Lilliput Poole 18 C6
Lilstock Som 43 E7
Lilybank Invclyd 276 G6
Lilyhurst Shrops 150 G4
Lilyvale Kent 54 F5
Limbrick Lancs 194 D6
Limbury Luton 103 G11
Limebrook Hereford 115 D7
Limefield Gtr Man 195 E10
Limehouse London 67 C11
Limehurst Gtr Man 196 G2
Limekilnburn S Lnrk 268 E4
Limekiln Field
Derbys 187 G7
Limekilns Fife 279 E11
Limerigg Falk 279 G7
Limerstone IoW 20 E4
Lime Side Gtr Man 196 G2
Limestone Brae
Northumb 231 B11
Lime Street Worcs 98 E6
Lime Tree Park
W Mid 118 B5
Limington Som 29 C8
Limpenhoe Norf 143 C7
Limpenhoe Hill
Norf 143 C8
Limpers Hill Wilts 45 G10
Limpley Stoke Wilts 61 G9
Limpsfield Sur 52 C2
Limpsfield Chart Sur 52 C2
Limpsfield Common
Sur 52 C2
Linbriggs Northumb 251 B9
Linburn W Loth 270 B2
Linby Notts 171 E8
Linchmere W Sus 49 G11
Lincluden Dumfries 237 B11
Lincoln Lincs 189 G7
Lincomb Worcs 116 D6
Lincombe Devon 8 D4
Devon 40 D3
Lindale Cumb 211 C8
Lindal in Furness
Cumb 210 D5
Lindean Borders 261 C11
Linden Glos 80 B4
Lindfield W Sus 36 B4
Lindford Hants 49 F10
Lindifferon Fife 287 F7
Lindley N Yorks 205 D10
W Yorks 196 D6
Lindley Green
N Yorks 205 D10
Lindores Fife 286 F6
Lindow End Ches E 184 F4
Lindrick Dale
S Yorks 187 E8
Lindridge Worcs 116 D3
Lindsell Essex 106 F2
Lindsey Suff 107 C9
Lindsey Tye Suff 107 B9
Lindwell W Yorks 196 C5
Lineholt Worcs 116 D6
Lineholt Common
Worcs 116 D6
Liney Som 43 F11
Linfitts Gtr Man 196 F3
Linford Hants 31 F11
Thurrock 69 D7
Lingague IoM 192 E3
Lingards Wood
W Yorks 196 E5
Lingbob W Yorks 205 F7
Lingdale Redcar 226 B3
Lingen Hereford 115 D7
Lingfield Darl 224 C6
Sur 51 E11
Lingfield Common
Sur 51 E11
Lingley Green Warr 183 D9
Lingley Mere Warr 183 D10
Lingreabhagh
W Isles 296 C6
Lingwood Norf 143 B7
Linhope Borders 249 C10
Northumb 263 F11
Linicro Highld 298 C3
Link N Som 44 B3
Linkend Worcs 98 E6
Linkenholt Hants 47 B11
Linkhill Kent 38 B4
Linkinhorne Corn 12 G2
Linklater Orkney 314 H4
Linklet Orkney 314 A7
Linksness Orkney 314 E5
Orkney 314 F2
Linktown Fife 280 C5
Linley Shrops 131 E7
Shrops 132 D3
Linley Brook Shrops 132 D3
Linleygreen Shrops 132 D3
Linley Green
Hereford 116 G3
Linlithgow W Loth 279 F10
Linlithgow Bridge
W Loth 279 F9
Linndhu Ho Argyll 289 D7
Linneraineach
Highld 307 J6
Linns Angus 292 F3
Linnyshaw Gtr Man 195 G8
Linshiels Northumb 251 B9
Linsiadar W Isles 304 E4
Linsidemore Highld 309 K5
Linslade C Beds 103 F8
Linstead Parva Suff 126 B6
Linstock Cumb 239 F10
Linthorpe Mbro 225 B9
Linthurst Worcs 117 C9
Linthwaite W Yorks 196 E6
Lintlaw Borders 272 D6
Lintmill Moray 302 C5
Linton Borders 263 D7
Cambs 105 B11
Derbys 152 F5
Hereford 98 F3
Kent 53 D9
Northumb 253 E7
N Yorks 213 G9
W Yorks 206 D3
Linton Heath Derbys 152 F5
Linton Hill Hereford 98 G3
Linton-on-Ouse
N Yorks 215 G9
Lintridge Glos 98 E4
Lintz Durham 242 F5
Lintzford T&W 242 F4
Lintzgarth Durham 232 C4
Linwood Hants 31 F11
Lincs 189 D10
Renfs 267 C8
Lionacleit W Isles 297 G3
Lional W Isles 304 B7
Lions Green E Sus 23 B9
Liphook Hants 49 G10
Lipley Shrops 150 C4
Lippitts Hill Essex 86 F5
Liquo or Bowhousebog N
Lnrk 269 D7
Liscard Mers 182 C4
Liscombe Som 41 G11
Liskeard Corn 6 C5
Liss Hants 34 B3
Lissett E Yorks 209 B8
Liss Forest Hants 34 B3
Lissington Lincs 189 E10
Lisson Grove London 67 C9
Listerdale S Yorks 187 C7
Listock Som 28 C4
Listoft Lincs 191 G8
Liston Essex 107 C7
Liston Garden Essex 106 B6
Lisvane Cardiff 59 C7
Liswerry Newport 59 B10
Litcham Norf 159 F7
Litchard Bridgend 58 C2
Litchborough
Northants 120 G2
Litchfield Hants 48 C3
Litchurch Derbys 153 B7
Litherland Mers 182 B4
Litlington Cambs 104 C6
E Sus 23 E8
Litmarsh Hereford 97 B10
Little Abington
Cambs 105 B10
Little Addington
Northants 121 C9
Little Airmyn
E Yorks 199 B8
Little Almshoe
Herts 104 F3
Little Alne Warks 118 E2
Little Altcar Mers 193 F10
Little Ann Hants 47 E10
Little Arowry Wrex 167 G7
Little Asby Cumb 222 D3
Little Ashley Wilts 61 G10
Little Assynt Highld 307 G6
Little Aston Staffs 133 C11
Little Atherfield IoW 20 E5
Little Ayre Orkney 314 G3
Little-ayre Shetland 313 G5
Little Ayton
N Yorks 225 C11
Little Baddow Essex 88 D3
Little Badminton
S Glos 61 C10
Little Ballinluig
Perth 286 B3
Little Bampton
Cumb 239 F7
Little Bardfield
Essex 106 E3
Little Barford Beds 122 F3
Little Barningham
Norf 160 C2
Little Barrington
Glos 82 C2
Little Barrow
Ches W 183 G7
Little Barugh
N Yorks 216 D5
Little Bavington
Northumb 241 B11
Little Bayham E Sus 52 F6
Little Bealings Suff 108 B4
Littlebeck N Yorks 227 D7
Little Beckford Glos 99 E9
Little Bedwyn Wilts 63 F9
Little Bentley Essex 108 F2
Little Berkhamsted
Herts 86 D3
Little Billing
Northants 120 E6
Little Billington
C Beds 103 G8
Little Birch Hereford 97 E10
Little Bispham
Blkpool 202 E2
Little Blakenham
Suff 108 B2
Little Blencow
Cumb 230 E5
Little Bloxwich
W Mid 133 C10
Little Bognor W Sus 35 C8
Little Bolehill
Derbys 170 E3
Little Bollington
Ches E 184 D2
Little Bolton
Gtr Man 184 B3
Little Bookham Sur 50 C6
Littleborough Devon 26 E4
Gtr Man 196 D2
Notts 188 E4
Little Bosullow Corn 1 C4
Littlebourne Kent 55 B8
Little Bourton Oxon 101 C9

Mansewood
Glasgow 267 C11
Mansfield E Ayrs 258 G4
Notts 171 C8
Mansfield Woodhouse
Notts 171 C8
Manson Green
Norf 141 C10
Mansriggs Cumb 210 C5
Manston Dorset 30 D4
Kent 71 F10
W Yorks 206 F3
Manswood Dorset 31 F7
Manthorpe Lincs 155 B8
Lincs 155 F11
Mantles Green Bucks 85 F7
Manton N Lincs 200 G2
Notts 187 F9
Rutland 137 C7
Wilts 63 F7
Manton Warren
N Lincs 200 F2
Manuden Essex 105 F9
Manwood Green
Essex 87 C8
Manywells Height
W Yorks 205 F7
Maperton Som 29 B11
Maplebeck Notts 172 C2
Maple Cross Herts 85 G8
Mapledurham Oxon 65 D7
Mapledurwell Hants 49 C7
Maple End Essex 105 D11
Maplehurst W Sus 35 C11
Maplescombe Kent 68 G5
Mapleton Derbys 169 F11
Mapperley Derbys 170 G6
Nottingham 171 G9
Mapperley Park
Nottingham 171 G9
Mapperton Dorset 16 B6
Dorset 18 B4
Mappleborough Green
Warks 117 D11
Mappleton E Yorks 209 E10
Mapplewell
S Yorks 197 F10
Mappowder Dorset 30 F2
Maraig W Isles 305 H3
Marazanvose Corn 4 E6
Marazion Corn 2 C2
Marbhig W Isles 305 G6
Marbrack Dumfries 246 E3
Marbury Ches E 167 F9
March Cambs 139 D8
S Lnrk 259 G11
Marcham Oxon 83 F7
Marchamley
Shrops 149 D11
Marchamley Wood
Shrops 149 C11
Marchington Staffs 152 C2
Marchington Woodlands
Staffs 152 D2
Marchroes Gwyn 144 D6
Marchwiel Wrex 166 F5
Marchwood Hants 32 E5
Marcross V Glam 58 F2
Marden Hereford 97 B10
Kent 53 E8
T&W 243 C9
Wilts 46 B5
Marden Ash Essex 87 E9
Marden Beech Kent 53 E8
Marden's Hill E Sus 52 G3
Marden Thorn Kent 53 E9
Mardleybury Herts 86 B3
Mardu Shrops 130 G5
Mardy Mon 78 B4
Shrops 148 C5
Marefield Leics 136 B4
Mareham le Fen
Lincs 174 C3
Mareham on the Hill
Lincs 174 B3
Marehay Derbys 170 F5
Marehill W Sus 35 D9
Maresfield E Sus 37 C7
Maresfield Park
E Sus 37 C7
Marfleet Hull 200 B6
Marford Wrex 166 D5
Margam Neath 57 D9
Margaret Marsh
Dorset 30 D4
Margaret Roding
Essex 87 C9
Margaretting Essex 87 E11
Margaretting Tye
Essex 87 E11
Margate Kent 71 E11
Margery Sur 51 C9
Margnaheglish
N Ayrs 256 C2
Margreig Dumfries 237 B10
Margrove Park
Redcar 226 B3
Marham Norf 158 G4
Marhamchurch Corn 24 G2
Marholm Pboro 138 C2
Marian Flint 181 F9
Marian Cwm Denb 181 F9
Mariandyrys
Anglesey 179 E10
Marianglas Anglesey 179 E8
Marian-glas
Anglesey 179 E8
Mariansleigh Devon 26 C2
Marian y de / South
Beach Gwyn 145 C7
Marian y mor / West
End Gwyn 145 C7
Marine Town Kent 70 E2
Marionburgh
Aberds 293 C9
Marishader Highld 298 C4
Marjoriebanks
Dumfries 248 G3
Mark Dumfries 236 D3
Dumfries 237 C7
S Ayrs 236 B2
Som 43 D11
Markbeech Kent 52 E3
Markby Lincs 191 F7
Mark Causeway
Som 43 D11
Mark Cross E Sus 23 C7
E Sus 52 G5
Markeaton Derbys 152 B6
Market Bosworth
Leics 135 C8
Market Deeping
Lincs 138 B2
Market Drayton
Shrops 150 C3
Market Harborough
Leics 136 F4
Markethill Perth 286 D6
Market Lavington
Wilts 46 C4
Market Overton
Rutland 155 F7
Market Rasen
Lincs 189 D10
Market Stainton
Lincs 190 F2
Market Warsop
Notts 171 B9
Market Weighton
E Yorks 208 E3
Market Weston Suff 125 B9
Markfield Leics 153 G9
Mark Hall North
Essex 87 C7
Mark Hall South
Essex 87 C7
Markham Caerph 77 E11
Markham Moor
Notts 188 G2
Markinch Fife 286 G6
Markington N Yorks 214 F5
Markland Hill
Gtr Man 195 F7
Markle E Loth 281 F11
Marksbury Bath 61 G7
Mark's Corner IoW 20 C5
Marks Gate London 87 G7
Marks Tey Essex 107 G8
Markyate Herts 85 B9
Marland Gtr Man 195 E11
Marlas Hereford 97 F8
Marl Bank Worcs 98 C5
Marlborough Wilts 63 F7
Marlbrook
Hereford 115 G10
Worcs 117 C9
Marlcliff Warks 117 G11
Marldon Devon 9 C7
Marle Green E Sus 23 B9
Marle Hill Glos 99 G9
Marlesford Suff 126 F6
Marley Kent 55 C7
Kent 55 C10
Marley Green
Ches E 167 F9
Marley Heights
W Sus 49 G11
Marley Hill T&W 242 F6
Marley Pots T&W 243 F9
Marlingford Norf 142 B2
Mar Lodge Aberds 292 D2
Marloes Pembs 72 D3
Marlow Bucks 65 B10
Hereford 115 B8
Marlow Bottom
Bucks 65 B11
Marlow Common
Bucks 65 B10
Marlpit Hill Kent 52 D2
Marlpits E Sus 38 E2
Marlpool Derbys 170 F6
Marnhull Dorset 30 D3
Marnoch Aberds 302 D5
Marnock N Lnrk 268 B4
Marple Gtr Man 185 D7
Marple Bridge
Gtr Man 185 D7
Marpleridge
Gtr Man 185 D7
Marr S Yorks 198 F4
Marrel Highld 311 H4
Marr Green Wilts 63 G8
Marrick N Yorks 223 F11
Marrister Shetland 313 G7
Marros Carms 74 D2
Marsden T&W 243 E9
W Yorks 196 E4
Marsden Height
Lancs 204 F3
Marsett N Yorks 213 B8
Marsh Bucks 84 D4
Devon 28 E3
W Yorks 196 D6
W Yorks 204 F6
Marshall Meadows
Northumb 273 D9
Marshall's Cross
Mers 183 C8
Marshall's Elm Som 44 G3
Marshall's Heath
Herts 85 B11
Marshalsea Dorset 28 G5
Marshalswick Herts 85 D11
Marsham Norf 160 E3
Marshaw Lancs 203 C7
Marsh Baldon Oxon 83 F9
Marsh Benham
W Berks 64 F2
Marshborough Kent 55 B10
Marshbrook Shrops 131 F8
Marshchapel Lincs 190 B5
Marsh Common
S Glos 60 C5
Marsh End Worcs 98 D6
Marshfield Newport 59 C9
S Glos 61 E9
Marshfield Bank
Ches E 167 D11
Marshgate Corn 11 C9
Marsh Gate
W Berks 63 F10
Marsh Gibbon
Bucks 102 G2
Marsh Green
Ches W 183 F8
Devon 14 C6
Gtr Man 194 F5
Kent 52 E2
Staffs 168 D5
Telford 150 G2
Marsh Houses
Lancs 202 C5
Marshland St James
Norf 139 B10
Marsh Lane Derbys 186 F6
Glos 79 D9
Marsh Mills Som 43 F7
Marshmoor Herts 86 D2
Marshside Kent 71 F8
Mers 193 D11
Marsh Side Norf 176 E3
Marsh Street Som 42 E3
Marshwood Dorset 16 B3
Marske N Yorks 224 E2
Marske-by-the-Sea
Redcar 235 G8
Marston Ches W 183 F11
Hereford 115 F7
Lincs 172 G5
Oxon 83 D8
Staffs 150 G6
Staffs 151 D8
Warks 119 B8
Warks 134 E4
Wilts 46 B3
Marston Bigot Som 45 E9
Marston Doles
Warks 119 F9
Marston Gate Som 45 D9
Marston Green
W Mid 134 F3
Marston Hill Glos 81 F10
Marston Jabbett
Warks 135 F7
Marston Magna Som 29 C9
Marston Meysey
Wilts 81 F10
Marston Montgomery
Derbys 152 B2
Marston Moretaine
C Beds 103 C9
Marston on Dove
Derbys 152 D4
Marston St Lawrence
Northants 101 C10
Marston Stannett
Hereford 115 F11
Marston Trussell
Northants 136 F3
Marstow Hereford 79 B9
Marsworth Bucks 84 C6
Marten Wilts 47 B9
Marthall Ches E 184 F4
Martham Norf 161 F9
Marthwaite Cumb 222 G2
Martin Hants 31 D9
Kent 55 D10
Lincs 173 D10
Lincs 174 B2
Martindale Cumb 221 B8
Martin Dales Lincs 173 C11
Martin Drove End
Hants 31 C9
Martinhoe Devon 41 D7
Martinhoe Cross
Devon 41 D7
Martin Hussingtree
Worcs 117 E7
Martin Mill Kent 55 D10
Martin Moor Lincs 174 C2
Martinscroft Warr 183 D11
Martin's Moss
Ches E 168 C4
Martinstown Dorset 17 D8
Martinstown or
Winterbourne St
Martin Dorset 17 D8
Martlesham Suff 108 B4
Martlesham Heath
Suff 108 B4
Martletwy Pembs 73 C8
Martley Worcs 116 E5
Martock Som 29 D7
Marton Ches E 168 B5
Ches W 167 B10
Cumb 210 D4
E Yorks 209 F9
E Yorks 209 F11
Lincs 188 E4
Mbro 225 B10
N Yorks 215 G8
N Yorks 216 C4
Shrops 130 C5
Shrops 149 E8
Warks 119 D8
Marton Green
Ches W 167 B10
Marton Grove Mbro 225 B9
Marton-in-the-Forest
N Yorks 215 F11
Marton-le-Moor
N Yorks 215 E7
Marton Moor Warks 119 D8
Marton Moss Side
Blkpool 202 G2
Martyr's Green Sur 50 B5
Martyr Worthy Hants 48 G4
Marwick Orkney 314 D2
Marwood Devon 40 F4
Marybank Highld 300 D4
Highld 301 B7
Maryburgh Highld 300 D5
Maryfield Aberds 293 D7
Corn 7 D8
Maryhill Glasgow 267 B11
Marykirk Aberds 293 G8
Maryland Mon 79 D8
Marylebone
Gtr Man 194 F5
Marypark Moray 301 F11
Maryport Cumb 228 D6
Dumfries 236 F3
Mary Tavy Devon 12 F6
Maryton Angus 287 B8
Angus 287 B10
Marywell Aberds 293 D7
Aberds 293 D11
Angus 287 C10
Masbrough S Yorks 186 C6
Mascle Bridge
Pembs 73 D7
Masham N Yorks 214 C4
Mashbury Essex 87 C11
Masongill N Yorks 212 D3
Masonhill S Ayrs 257 E9
Mastin Moor Derbys 187 F7
Mastrick Aberdeen 293 C10
Matchborough
Worcs 117 D11
Matching Essex 87 C8
Matching Green
Essex 87 C8
Matching Tye Essex 87 C8
Matfen Northumb 242 C2
Matfield Kent 53 E7
Mathern Mon 79 G8
Mathon Hereford 98 B4
Mathry Pembs 91 E7
Matlaske Norf 160 C3
Matley Gtr Man 185 B7
Matlock Derbys 170 C3
Matlock Bank
Derbys 170 C3
Matlock Bath
Derbys 170 D3
Matlock Bridge
Derbys 170 D3
Matlock Cliff
Derbys 170 D4
Matlock Dale
Derbys 170 D3
Matshead Lancs 202 E6
Matson Glos 80 B4
Matterdale End
Cumb 230 G3
Mattersey Notts 187 D11
Mattersey Thorpe
Notts 187 D11
Matthewsgreen
Wokingham 65 F10
Mattingley Hants 49 B8
Mattishall Norf 159 G11
Mattishall Burgh
Norf 159 G11
Mauchline E Ayrs 257 D11
Maud Aberds 303 E9
Maudlin Corn 5 C11
Dorset 28 F5
W Sus 22 B5
Maudlin Cross Dorset 28 F5
Maugersbury Glos 100 F4
Maughold IoM 192 C5
Mauld Highld 300 F4
Maulden C Beds 103 D11
Maulds Meaburn
Cumb 222 B2
Maunby N Yorks 215 B7
Maund Bryan
Hereford 115 G11
Maundown Som 27 B9
Mauricewood
Midloth 270 C4
Mautby Norf 161 G9
Mavesyn Ridware
Staffs 151 F11
Mavis Enderby Lincs 174 B5
Maviston Highld 301 D9
Mawbray Cumb 229 B7
Mawdesley Lancs 194 E3
Mawdlam Bridgend 57 E10
Mawgan Corn 2 D6
Mawgan Porth Corn 5 B7
Maw Green Ches E 168 D2
Mawla Corn 4 F4
Mawnan Corn 3 D7
Mawnan Smith Corn 3 D7
Mawsley Northants 120 B6
Mawson Green
S Yorks 198 D6
Mawthorpe Lincs 191 G7
Maxey Pboro 138 B2
Maxstoke Warks 134 F4
Maxted Street Kent 54 E6
Maxton Borders 262 C4
Kent 55 E10
Maxwellheugh
Borders 262 C6
Maxwelltown
Dumfries 237 B11
Maxworthy Corn 11 C11
Mayals Swansea 56 C6
May Bank Staffs 168 F5
Maybole S Ayrs 257 G8
Maybury Sur 50 B4
Maybush Soton 32 E5
Mayer's Green
W Mid 133 E10
Mayes Green Sur 50 F6
Mayeston Pembs 73 E8
Mayfair London 67 C9
Mayfield E Sus 37 B9
Midloth 271 C7
Northumb 243 B7
Staffs 169 F11
W Loth 269 B8
Mayford Sur 50 B3
Mayhill Swansea 56 C6
May Hill Mon 79 C8
May Hill Village Glos 98 G4
Mayland Essex 88 E6
Maylandsea Essex 88 E6
Maynard's Green
E Sus 23 B9
Mayne Ho Moray 302 C2
Mayon Corn 1 D3
Maypole Bromley 68 G3
Dartford 68 E4
Kent 71 G7
Mon 79 B7
Scilly 1 G4
Maypole Green
Essex 107 G9
Norf 143 D8
Suff 125 F8
Suff 126 D5
Mays Green Oxon 65 C8
May's Green N Som 59 G11
Sur 50 B5
Mayshill S Glos 61 C7
Maythorn S Yorks 197 F7
Maythorne Notts 171 D11
Maywick Shetland 313 L5
Mead Devon 13 G11
Devon 24 D2
Mead End Hants 19 B11
Hants 33 E11
Wilts 31 C8
Meadgate Bath 45 B7
Meadle Bucks 84 D4
Meadowbank
Ches W 167 B11
Edin 280 G5
Meadowend Essex 106 C4
Meadowfield
Durham 233 D10
Meadowfoot N Ayrs 266 F4
Meadow Green
Hereford 116 F4
Meadow Hall
S Yorks 186 C5
Meadow Head
S Yorks 186 E4
Meadowley Shrops 132 E3
Meadowmill E Loth 281 G8
Meadows
Nottingham 153 B11
Meadowtown
Shrops 130 C6
Meads E Sus 23 F10
Meadside Oxon 83 G9
Mead Vale Sur 51 D9
Meadwell Devon 12 E4
Meaford Staffs 151 B7
Meagill N Yorks 205 B9
Mealabost W Isles 304 E6
Mealabost Bhuirgh
W Isles 304 C6
Mealasta W Isles 304 F1
Meal Bank Cumb 221 F10
Meal Hill W Yorks 197 F7
Mealrigg Cumb 229 B8
Mealsgate Cumb 229 C10
Meanwood
W Yorks 205 F11
Mearbeck N Yorks 212 G6
Meare Som 44 E3
Meare Green Som 28 B4
Som 28 C3
Mearns Bath 45 B7
E Renf 267 D10
Mears Ashby
Northants 120 D6
Measborough Dike
S Yorks 197 F11
Measham Leics 152 G6
Meath Green Sur 51 E9
Meathop Cumb 211 C8
Meaux E Yorks 209 F7
Meaver Corn 2 F5
Meavy Devon 7 B10
Medbourne Leics 136 E5
M Keynes 102 D6
Medburn Northumb 242 C4
Meddon Devon 24 D3
Meden Vale Notts 171 B9
Medhurst Row Kent 52 D3
Medlam Lincs 174 D4
Medlar Lancs 202 F4
Medlicott Shrops 131 E8
Medlyn Corn 2 C6
Medmenham Bucks 65 C10
Medomsley Durham 242 G4
Medstead Hants 49 F7
Meerbrook Staffs 169 C7
Meer Common
Hereford 115 G7
Meer End W Mid 118 C4
Meerhay Dorset 29 G7
Meers Bridge Lincs 191 D7
Meersbrook
S Yorks 186 E5
Meesden Herts 105 E8
Meeson Telford 150 E3
Meeson Heath
Telford 150 E3
Meeth Devon 25 F8
Meethe Devon 25 C11
Meeting Green Suff 124 F4
Meeting House Hill
Norf 160 D6
Meggernie Castle
Perth 285 C9
Meggethead
Borders 260 E5
Meidrim Carms 92 G5
Meifod Denb 165 D8
Powys 148 G3
Meigle N Ayrs 266 B3
Perth 286 C6
Meikle Earnock S
Lnrk 268 E4
Meikle Ferry Highld 309 L7
Meikle Forter
Angus 292 G3
Meikle Gluich
Highld 309 L6
Meikle Obney Perth 286 D4
Meikleour Perth 286 D5
Meikle Pinkerton
E Loth 282 F4
Meikle Strath
Aberds 293 F8
Meikle Tarty Aberds 303 G9
Meikle Wartle
Aberds 303 F7
Meinciau Carms 75 C7
Meir Stoke 168 G6
Meir Heath Staffs 168 G6
Melbourn Cambs 105 C7
Melbourne Derbys 153 D7
E Yorks 207 E11
S Lnrk 269 G11
Melbury Abbas
Dorset 30 D5
Melbury Bubb Dorset 29 F9
Melbury Osmond
Dorset 29 F9
Melbury Sampford
Dorset 29 F9
Melby Shetland 313 H3
Melchbourne Beds 121 D10
Melcombe Som 43 G9
Melcombe Bingham
Dorset 30 G3
Melcombe Regis
Dorset 17 E9
Meldon Devon 13 C7
Northumb 252 G4
Meldreth Cambs 105 B7
Meldrum Ho Aberds 303 G8
Melfort Argyll 275 B9
Melgarve Highld 290 D6
Meliden / Gallt Melyd
Denb 181 E9
Melinbyrhedyn
Powys 128 D6
Melin Caiach Caerph 77 F10
Melincourt Neath 76 E4
Melincryddan Neath 57 B8
Melinsey Corn 3 B10
Melin-y-coed
Conwy 164 C4
Melin-y-ddôl
Powys 129 B11
Melin-y-grug
Powys 129 B11
Melin-y-Wig Denb 165 F8
Melkington
Northumb 273 G7
Melkinthorpe Cumb 231 F7
Melkridge Northumb 240 E6
Melksham Wilts 62 G2
Melksham Forest
Wilts 62 G2
Mellangaun Highld 307 L3
Mellangoose Corn 2 D5
Melldalloch Argyll 275 F10
Mell Green W Berks 64 D3
Mellguards Cumb 230 B4
Melling Lancs 211 E11
Mers 193 G11
Mellingey Corn 10 G4
Melling Mount
Mers 194 G2
Mellis Suff 126 C2
Mellis Green Suff 125 C11
Mellon Charles
Highld 307 K3
Mellon Udrigle
Highld 307 K3
Mellor Gtr Man 185 D7
Lancs 203 G9
Mellor Brook Lancs 203 G8
Mells Som 45 D8
Suff 127 B8
Mells Green Som 45 D8
Melmerby Cumb 231 D8
N Yorks 213 B11
N Yorks 214 D6
Melon Green Suff 124 F6
Melplash Dorset 16 B5
Melrose Borders 262 C2
Melsetter Orkney 314 H2
Melsonby N Yorks 224 D3
Meltham W Yorks 196 E6
Meltham Mills
W Yorks 196 E6
Melton E Yorks 200 B3
Suff 126 G5
Meltonby E Yorks 207 C11
Melton Constable
Norf 159 C10
Melton Mowbray
Leics 154 F5
Melton Ross
N Lincs 200 E5
Melvaig Highld 307 L2
Melverley Shrops 148 F6
Melverley Green
Shrops 148 F6
Melvich Highld 310 C2
Membland Devon 7 F11
Membury Devon 28 G3
Memsie Aberds 303 C9
Memus Angus 287 B8
Mena Corn 5 C10
Menabilly Corn 5 E11
Menadarva Corn 4 G2
Menagissey Corn 4 F4
Menai Bridge /
Porthaethwy
Anglesey 179 G9
Mendham Suff 142 G5
Mendlesham Suff 126 D2
Mendlesham Green
Suff 125 E11
Menethorpe
N Yorks 216 F5
Mengham Hants 21 B10
Menheniot Corn 6 C5
Menherion Corn 2 B6
Menithwood Worcs 116 D4
Menna Corn 5 E8
Mennock Dumfries 247 B8
Menston W Yorks 205 E9
Menstrie Clack 278 B6
Mentmore Bucks 84 B6
Menzion Borders 260 E3
Meoble Highld 295 G9
Meole Brace Shrops 149 G9
Meols Mers 182 C2
Meon Hants 33 G8
Meonstoke Hants 33 D10
Meopham Kent 68 F6
Meopham Green
Kent 68 F6
Meopham Station
Kent 68 F6
Mepal Cambs 139 G8
Meppershall
C Beds 104 D2
Merbach Hereford 96 B6
Mercaton Derbys 170 G3
Merchant Fields
W Yorks 197 B7
Merchiston Edin 280 G4
Mere Ches E 184 E2
Wilts 45 G10
Mere Brow Lancs 194 D2
Mereclough Lancs 204 G3
Mere Green W Mid 134 D2
Worcs 117 E9
Merehead Wrex 149 B9
Mere Heath
Ches W 183 G11
Meresborough
Medway 69 G10
Mereside Blkpool 202 G2
Meretown Staffs 150 E5
Mereworth Kent 53 C7
Mergie Aberds 293 E9
Meriden Herts 85 F10
W Mid 134 G4
Merkadale Highld 294 B5
Merkland Dumfries 237 B9
N Ayrs 256 B2
S Ayrs 244 E6
Merkland Lodge
Highld 309 G4
Merle Common Sur 52 D2
Merley Poole 18 B6
Merlin's Bridge
Pembs 72 C6
Merlin's Cross Pembs 73 E7
Merridale W Mid 133 D7
Merridge Som 43 G8
Merrie Gardens IoW 21 E7
Merrifield Devon 8 F6
Devon 24 G3
Merrington Shrops 149 E9
Merrion Pembs 72 F6
Merriott Dorset 16 B6
Som 28 E6
Merriottsford Som 28 E6
Merritown Dorset 19 B8
Merrivale Devon 12 F6
Hereford 98 G2
Merrow Sur 50 C4
Merrybent Darl 224 C4
Merry Field Hill
Dorset 31 G8
Merry Hill Herts 85 G10
W Mid 133 D7
Merryhill Green
Wokingham 65 E9
Merrylee E Renf 267 D11
Merry Lees Leics 135 B9
Merrymeet Corn 6 B5
Merry Meeting Corn 11 G7
Merry Oak Soton 32 E6
Mersham Kent 54 F5
Merstham Sur 51 C9
Merston W Sus 22 C5
Merstone IoW 20 E6
Merther Corn 5 G7
Merther Lane Corn 5 G7
Merthyr Carms 93 G7
Merthyr Cynog
Powys 95 D9
Merthyr-Dyfan
V Glam 58 F6
Merthyr Mawr
Bridgend 57 F11
Merthyr Tydfil
M Tydf 77 D8
Merthyr Vale M Tydf 77 F9
Merton Devon 25 E8
London 67 E9
Norf 141 D8
Oxon 83 B9
Merton Park London 67 F9
Mervinslaw Borders 262 G5
Meshaw Devon 26 D3
Messing Essex 88 B5
Messingham
N Lincs 199 G11
Mesty Croft W Mid 133 E9
Mesur-y-dorth
Pembs 87 E11
Metal Bridge
Durham 233 E11
Metfield Suff 142 G5
Metherell Corn 7 B8
Metheringham
Lincs 173 C9
Methersgate Suff 108 B5
Methil Fife 281 B7
Methilhill Fife 281 B7
Methlem Gwyn 144 C3
Methley W Yorks 197 B11
Methley Junction
W Yorks 197 B11
Methley Lanes
W Yorks 197 B11
Methlick Aberds 303 F8
Methven Perth 286 E4
Methwold Norf 140 E4
Methwold Hythe
Norf 140 E4
Mettingham Suff 143 F7
Metton Norf 160 B3
Mevagissey Corn 5 G10
Mewith Head
N Yorks 212 F4
Mexborough
S Yorks 187 B7
Mey Highld 310 B6
Meyrick Park Bmouth 19 C7
Meysey Hampton
Glos 81 F10
Miabhag W Isles 305 H2
W Isles 305 J3
Miabhig W Isles 304 E2
Mial Highld 299 B7
Michaelchurch
Hereford 97 F10
Michaelchurch Escley
Hereford 96 E6
Michaelchurch on Arrow
Powys 114 G4
Michaelston-le-Pit
V Glam 59 E7
Michaelston-y-Fedw
Newport 59 C8
Michaelstow Corn 11 F7
Michealston-super-Ely
Cardiff 58 D6
Michelcombe Devon 8 B3
Micheldever Hants 48 F4
Michelmersh Hants 32 B4
Mickfield Suff 126 E2
Micklebring
S Yorks 187 C8
Mickleby N Yorks 226 C6
Micklefield Bucks 84 G5
W Yorks 206 G4
Micklefield Green
Herts 85 F8
Mickleham Sur 51 C7
Micklehurst
Gtr Man 196 G3
Mickleover Derby 152 C6
Micklethwaite
Cumb 239 G7
W Yorks 205 E8
Mickleton Durham 232 G5
Glos 100 C3
Mickletown
W Yorks 197 B11
Mickle Trafford
Ches W 166 B6
Mickley Derbys 186 F4
N Yorks 214 D5
Shrops 150 C2
Mickley Green Suff 124 F6
Mickley Square
Northumb 242 E3
Midanbury Hants 33 E7
Mid Ardlaw Aberds 303 C9
Mid Auchinleck
Invclyd 276 G6
Midbea Orkney 314 B4
Mid Beltie Aberds 293 C8
Mid Calder W Loth 269 B11
Mid Cloch Forbie
Aberds 303 D7
Mid Clyth Highld 310 F6
Middle Assendon
Oxon 65 B8
Middle Aston Oxon 101 F9
Middle Balnald
Perth 286 B4
Middle Barton Oxon 101 F8
Middle Bickenhill
W Mid 134 G4
Middlebie Dumfries 238 B6
Middle Bockhampton
Dorset 19 B9
Middle Bourne Sur 49 E10
Middle Bridge
N Som 60 D3
Middle Burnham
Som 43 D10
Middle Cairncake
Aberds 303 E8
Middlecave N Yorks 216 E5
Middle Chinnock
Som 29 E7
Middle Claydon
Bucks 102 F4
Middle Cliff Staffs 169 E8
Middlecliffe
S Yorks 198 F2
Middlecott Devon 13 D10
Devon 24 F6
Devon 26 F3
Middle Crackington
Corn 11 B9
Middlecroft Derbys 186 G6
Middle Drums
Angus 287 B9
Middle Duntisbourne
Glos 81 D7
Middlefield Falk 279 E7
Middleforth Green
Lancs 194 B4
Middle Green Bucks 66 C4
Som 27 D10
Suff 124 D4
Middleham N Yorks 214 B2
Middle Handley
Derbys 186 F6
Middle Harling Norf 141 F9
Middle Herrington
T&W 243 G9
Middlehill Corn 6 B5
Wilts 61 F10
Middle Hill Pembs 73 C7
Staffs 133 B9
Middlehope Shrops 131 F9
Middle Kames
Argyll 275 E10
Middle Littleton
Worcs 99 B11
Middle Luxton Devon 28 E2
Middle Madeley
Staffs 168 F3
Middle Maes-coed
Hereford 96 E6
Middlemarsh Dorset 29 F11
Middle Marwood
Devon 40 F4
Middle Mayfield
Staffs 169 G10
Middle Mill Pembs 87 F11
Middlemoor Devon 12 G5
Middlemuir Aberds 303 D9
Aberds 303 E8
Aberds 303 G9
Middleport Stoke 168 F5
Middle Quarter Kent 53 F11
Middle Rainton
T&W 234 B2
Middle Rasen Lincs 189 D9
Middlerig Falk 279 F8
Middle Rigg Perth 286 G4
Middle Rocombe
Devon 9 B8
Middlesbrough
Mbro 234 G5
Middlesceugh
Cumb 230 C4
Middleshaw Cumb 211 B11
Middle Side Durham 232 F4
Middlesmoor
N Yorks 213 E11
Middle Stoford Som 27 C11
Middle Stoke Devon 13 G9
Medway 69 D10
W Mid 119 B7
Middlestone
Durham 233 E11
Middlestone Moor
Durham 233 E10
Middle Stoughton
Som 44 D2
Middlestown
W Yorks 197 D9
Middle Strath
W Loth 279 G8
Middle Street Glos 80 E3
Middle Taphouse Corn 6 C3
Middlethird Borders 272 G3
Middlethorpe York 207 D7
Middleton Aberds 293 B10
Argyll 288 E1
Cumb 212 B2
Derbys 169 C11
Derbys 170 D3
Essex 107 D7
Gtr Man 195 F11
Hants 48 E2
Hereford 115 D10
Hrtlpl 234 E6
IoW 20 D2
Lancs 202 B4
Midloth 271 D7
Norf 158 F3
Northants 136 F6
Northumb 252 F3
Northumb 264 B4
N Yorks 204 E5
N Yorks 205 D8
N Yorks 216 B5
Perth 286 C5
Perth 286 F2
Perth 286 G5
Shrops 115 B10
Shrops 130 D5
Shrops 148 D6
Suff 127 D8

Mosterton Dorset 29 F7
Moston Ches E 168 C2
Ches W 182 G6
Gtr Man 195 G11
Shrops 149 D11
Moston Green
Ches E 168 C2
Mostyn Flint 181 E11
Mostyn Quay Flint 181 E11
Motcombe Dorset 30 B5
Mothecombe Devon 8 F2
Motherby Cumb 230 F4
Motherwell N Lnrk 268 D5
Motspur Park London 67 F8
Mottingham London 68 E2
Mottisfont Hants 32 B4
Mottistone IoW 20 E4
Mottram in Longdendale
Gtr Man 185 B7
Mottram Rise
Gtr Man 185 B7
Mottram St Andrew
Ches E 184 F5
Mott's Green Essex 87 B8
Mott's Mill E Sus 52 F4
Mouldsworth
Ches W 183 G8
Moulin Perth 286 B3
Moulsecoomb
Brighton 36 F4
Moulsford Oxon 64 C5
Moulsham Essex 88 D2
Moulsoe M Keynes 103 C8
Moultavie Highld 300 B6
Moulton Ches W 167 B11
Lincs 156 E6
Northants 120 D5
N Yorks 224 E4
Suff 124 E3
V Glam 58 E5
Moulton Chapel
Lincs 156 F5
Moulton Eaugate
Lincs 156 F6
Moulton Park
Northants 120 E5
Moulton St Mary
Norf 143 B7
Moulton Seas End
Lincs 156 D6
Moulzie Angus 292 F4
Mounie Castle
Aberds 303 G7
Mount Corn 4 D5
Corn 6 B2
Highld 301 E9
W Yorks 196 D5
Mountain Anglesey 178 E2
W Yorks 205 G7
Mountain Air
Bl Gwent 77 D11
Mountain Ash / Aberpennar
Rhondda 77 F8
Mountain Bower
Wilts 61 D10
Mountain Cross
Borders 270 F2
Mountain Street
Kent 54 C5
Mountain Water
Pembs 91 G8
Mount Ambrose Corn 4 G4
Mount Ballan Mon 60 B3
Mount Batten Plym 7 E9
Mountbenger
Borders 261 D8
Mountbengerburn
Borders 261 D8
Mountblow W Dunb 277 G9
Mount Bovers Essex 88 G4
Mount Bures Essex 107 E8
Mount Canisp
Highld 301 B7
Mount Charles Corn 5 B10
Corn 5 E10
Mount Cowdown
Wilts 47 C9
Mount End Essex 87 E7
Mount Ephraim
E Sus 23 B7
Mounters Dorset 30 D3
Mountfield E Sus 38 C2
Mountgerald Highld 300 C5
Mount Gould Plym 7 D9
Mount Hawke Corn 4 F4
Mount Hermon Corn 2 F6
Sur 50 B4
Mount Hill S Glos 61 E7
Mountjoy Corn 5 C7
Mount Lane Devon 12 B3
Mountnessing Essex 87 F10
Mounton Mon 79 G8
Mount Pleasant
Bucks 102 E3
Ches E 168 D4
Corn 5 C10
Derbys 152 D6
Derbys 152 F5
Derbys 170 F4
Devon 27 G11
Durham 233 E11
E Sus 23 E7
E Sus 36 D6
Flint 182 G2
Hants 19 B11
Kent 71 F10
London 85 G8
M Tydf 77 F9
Neath 57 B9
Norf 141 E9
Pembs 73 D8
Shrops 149 G9
Stockton 234 G4
Stoke 168 G5
Suff 106 B4
T&W 243 E7
Warks 135 F7
Worcs 99 D10
Worcs 117 E10
W Yorks 197 C8
Mount Sion Wrex 166 E3
Mount Skippett Oxon 82 B5
Mountsolie Aberds 303 D9
Mountsorrel Leics 153 F11
Mount Sorrel Wilts 31 C8
Mount Tabor
W Yorks 196 B5
Mount Vernon
Glasgow 268 C3
Mount Wise Corn 7 E9
Mousehill Sur 50 E2
Mousehole Corn 1 D5
Mousen Northumb 264 C4
Mousley End Warks 118 D4
Mouswald Dumfries 238 C3
Mouth Mill Devon 24 B3
Mowbreck Lancs 202 G4
Mow Cop Ches E 168 D5
Mowden Darl 224 B5
Essex 88 C3
Mowhaugh Borders 263 E8
Mowmacre Hill
Leicester 135 B11
Mowshurst Kent 52 D3
Mowsley Leics 136 F2
Moxby N Yorks 215 F11
Moxley W Mid 133 D9
Moy Argyll 255 E8
Highld 290 E6
Highld 301 F7
Moy Hall Highld 301 F7
Moy Ho Moray 301 C10
Moyles Court Hants 31 F11
Moylgrove / Trewyddel
Pembs 92 C2
Moy Lodge Highld 290 E6
Muasdale Argyll 255 C7
Muchalls Aberds 293 D11
Much Birch
Hereford 97 E10
Much Cowardne
Hereford 98 B2
Much Cowarne
Hereford 98 B2
Much Dewchurch
Hereford 97 E9
Muchelney Som 28 C6
Muchelney Ham Som 28 C6
Much Hadham Herts 86 B5
Much Hoole Lancs 194 C3
Much Hoole Moss Houses Lancs 194 C3
Much Hoole Town
Lancs 194 C3
Muchlarnick Corn 6 D4
Much Marcle
Hereford 98 E3
Muchrachd Highld 300 F2
Much Wenlock
Shrops 132 C2
Muckairn Argyll 289 F11
Muckernich Highld 300 D5
Mucking Thurrock 69 C7
Muckle Breck
Shetland 312 G7
Muckleford Dorset 17 C8
Mucklestone Staffs 150 B4
Muckleton Norf 158 B6
Shrops 149 E11
Muckletown Aberds 302 G5
Muckley Shrops 132 D2
Muckley Corner
Staffs 133 B11
Muckley Cross
Shrops 132 D2
Muckton Lincs 190 E5
Muckton Bottom
Lincs 190 E5
Mudale Highld 308 F5
Mudd Gtr Man 185 C7
Muddiford Devon 40 F5
Muddlebridge Devon 40 G4
Muddles Green
E Sus 23 C8
Mudeford Dorset 19 C9
Mudford Som 29 D9
Mudford Sock Som 29 D9
Mudgley Som 44 D2
Mugdock Stirl 277 F11
Mugeary Highld 294 B6
Mugginton Derbys 170 G3
Muggintonlane End
Derbys 170 G3
Muggleswick
Durham 232 B6
Mugswell Sur 51 C9
Muie Highld 309 J6
Muir Aberds 292 E2
Muircleugh
Borders 271 F10
Muirden Aberds 303 D7
Muirdrum Angus 287 D9
Muiredge Fife 281 B7
Muirend Glasgow 267 C11
Muirhead Angus 287 D7
Fife 286 G6
Fife 287 F8
N Lnrk 268 B3
S Ayrs 257 C8
Muirhouse Edin 280 F4
N Lnrk 268 D5
Muirhouselaw
Borders 262 D4
Muirhouses Falk 279 E10
Muirkirk E Ayrs 258 D5
Muirmill Stirl 278 E4
Muir of Alford
Aberds 293 B7
Muir of Fairburn
Highld 300 D4
Muir of Fowlis
Aberds 293 B7
Muir of Kinellar
Aberds 293 B10
Muir of Miltonduff
Moray 301 D11
Muir of Ord Highld 300 D5
Muir of Pert Angus 287 D8
Muirshearlich
Highld 290 E3
Muirskie Aberds 293 D10
Muirtack Aberds 303 F9
Muirton Aberds 303 D7
Highld 301 C7
Perth 286 E5
Perth 286 F3
Muirton Mains
Highld 300 D4
Muirton of Ardblair
Perth 286 C5
Muirton of Ballochy
Angus 293 G8
Muiryfold Aberds 303 D7
Muker N Yorks 223 F8
Mulbarton Norf 142 C3
Mulben Moray 302 D3
Mulberry Corn 5 B10
Mulfra Corn 1 C5
Mulindry Argyll 254 B4
Mulla Shetland 313 G6
Mullardoch House
Highld 300 F2
Mullenspond Hants 47 D9
Mullion Corn 2 F5
Mullion Cove Corn 2 F5
Mumbles Hill
Swansea 56 D6
Mumby Lincs 191 G8
Mumps Gtr Man 196 F2
Mundale Moray 301 D10
Munderfield Row
Hereford 116 G2
Munderfield Stocks
Hereford 116 G2
Mundesley Norf 160 B6
Mundford Norf 140 E6
Mundham Norf 142 D6
Mundon Essex 88 E5
Mundurno
Aberdeen 293 B11
Mundy Bois Kent 54 D2
Munerigie Highld 290 C4
Muness Shetland 312 C8
Mungasdale Highld 307 K4
Mungrisdale Cumb 230 E3
Munlochy Highld 300 D6
Munsary Cottage
Highld 310 E6
Munsley Hereford 98 C3
Munslow Shrops 131 F10
Munstone Hereford 97 C10
Murch V Glam 59 E7
Murchington Devon 13 D9
Murcot Worcs 99 C11
Murcott Oxon 83 B9
Wilts 81 G7
Murdieston Stirl 278 B3
Murdishaw Halton 183 E9
Murieston W Loth 269 C11
Murkle Highld 310 C5
Murlaggan Highld 290 D2
Highld 290 E5
Murra Orkney 314 F2
Murrayfield Edin 280 G4
Murrayshall Perth 286 E5
Murraythwaite
Dumfries 238 C4
Murrell Green Hants 49 B8
Murrell's End Glos 98 E4
Glos 98 G5
Murrion Shetland 312 F4
Murrow Cambs 139 B7
Mursley Bucks 102 F6
Murston Kent 70 G2
Murthill Angus 287 B8
Murthly Perth 286 D4
Murton Cumb 231 G10
Durham 234 B3
Northumb 273 F9
Swansea 56 D5
T&W 243 C8
York 207 C8
Murton Grange
N Yorks 215 B10
Murtwell Devon 8 D5
Musbury Devon 15 C11
Muscliff Bmouth 19 B7
Muscoates N Yorks 216 C3
Muscott Northants 120 E2
Musdale Argyll 289 G11
Mushroom Green
W Mid 133 F8
Musselburgh
E Loth 280 G6
Musselwick Pembs 72 D4
Mustard Hyrn Norf 161 F8
Muston Leics 154 B6
N Yorks 217 D11
Mustow Green
Worcs 117 C7
Muswell Hill London 86 G3
Mutehill Dumfries 237 E8
Mutford Suff 143 F9
Muthill Perth 286 F2
Mutley Plym 7 D9
Mutterton Devon 27 G8
Mutton Hall E Sus 37 C9
Muxton Telford 150 G4
Mwdwl-eithin Flint 181 F11
Mwynbwll Flint 165 B11
Mybster Highld 310 D5
Myddfai Carms 94 F5
Myddle Shrops 149 E9
Myddlewood Shrops 149 E9
Myddyn-fych Carms 75 C10
Mydroilyn Ceredig 111 F9
Myerscough Lancs 202 F5
Myerscough Smithy
Lancs 203 G8
Mylor Bridge Corn 3 B8
Mylor Churchtown
Corn 3 B8
Mynachdy Cardiff 59 D7
Rhondda 77 F8
Mynachlog-ddu
Pembs 92 E2
Mynd Shrops 115 C7
Myndd Llandegai
Gwyn 163 B10
Myndtown Shrops 131 F7
Mynydd Bach
Ceredig 112 B4
Mynydd-bach Mon 79 G7
Swansea 57 B7
Mynydd-bach-y-glo
Swansea 56 B6
Mynydd Bodafon
Anglesey 179 D7
Mynydd Fflint / Flint Mountain Flint 182 G2
Mynydd Gilan Gwyn 144 E5
Mynydd-isa Flint 166 C3
Mynyddislwyn
Caerph 77 G11
Mynydd-llan Flint 181 G11
Mynydd Marian
Conwy 180 F5
Mynydd Mechell
Anglesey 178 D5
Mynyddygarreg
Carms 74 D6
Mynytho Gwyn 144 C6
Myrebird Aberds 293 D9
Myrelandhorn
Highld 310 D6
Myreside Perth 286 E6
Myrtle Hill Carms 94 E5
Mytchett Sur 49 B11
Mytchett Place Sur 49 C11
Mytholm W Yorks 196 B3
Mytholmes W Yorks 204 F6
Mytholmroyd
W Yorks 196 B4
Mythop Lancs 202 G3
Mytice Aberds 302 F4
Myton Warks 118 E6
Myton Hall N Yorks 215 F8
Myton-on-Swale
N Yorks 215 F8
Mytton Shrops 149 F8

N

Naast Highld 307 L3
Nab Hill W Yorks 197 D7
Nab's Head Lancs 194 B6
Naburn York 207 D7
Nab Wood W Yorks 205 F8
Naccolt Kent 54 E4
Nackington Kent 55 C7
Nacton Suff 108 C4
Nadderwater Devon 14 C3
Nafferton E Yorks 209 B7
Na Gearrannan
W Isles 304 D3
Nag's Head Glos 80 F5
Naid-y-march
Flint 181 F11
Nailbridge Glos 79 B10
Nailsbourne Som 28 B2
Nailsea N Som 60 D3
Nailstone Leics 135 B8
Nailsworth Glos 80 F5
Nailwell Bath 61 G8
Nairn Highld 301 D8
Nalderswood Sur 51 D8
Nance Corn 4 G3
Nanceddan Corn 2 C2
Nancegollan Corn 2 C4
Nancemellin Corn 4 G2
Nancenoy Corn 2 D6
Nancledra Corn 1 B5
Nangreaves Lancs 195 D10
Nanhoron Gwyn 144 C5
Nanhyfer / Nevern
Pembs 91 D11
Nannau Gwyn 146 E4
Nannerch Flint 165 B11
Nanpantan Leics 153 F10
Nanpean Corn 5 D9
Nanquidno Corn 1 D3
Nanstallon Corn 5 B10
Nant Carms 74 B6
Denb 165 D11
Nant Alyn Flint 165 B11
Nant-ddu Powys 77 B8
Nanternis Ceredig 111 F7
Nantgaredig Carms 93 G9
Nantgarw Rhondda 58 B6
Nant-glas Powys 113 E9
Nantglyn Denb 165 C8
Nantgwyn Powys 113 B9
Nantithet Corn 2 E5
Nantlle Gwyn 163 E8
Nantmawr Shrops 148 E5
Nant Mawr Flint 166 C3
Nantmel Powys 113 D10
Nantmor Gwyn 163 F10
Nant Peris / Old Llanberis Gwyn 163 D10
Nantserth Powys 113 C9
Nant Uchaf Denb 165 D8
Nantwich Ches E 167 E11
Nant-y-Bai Carms 94 C5
Nant-y-Bwch
Bl Gwent 77 C10
Nant-y-cafn Neath 76 D4
Nantycaws Carms 75 B7
Nant y Caws Shrops 148 D5
Nant-y-ceisiad
Caerph 59 B8
Nant-y-derry Mon 78 D4
Nant-y-felin
Conwy 179 G11
Nant-y-ffin Carms 93 E11
Nantyffyllon
Bridgend 57 C11
Nantyglo Bl Gwent 77 C11
Nant-y-gollen
Shrops 148 D4
Nant-y-moel
Bridgend 76 G6
Nant-y-pandy
Conwy 179 G11
Nant-y-Rhiw Conwy 164 D4
Nantyronen Station
Ceredig 112 B3
Napchester Kent 55 D10
Naphill Bucks 84 F4
Napleton Worcs 99 B7
Napley Staffs 150 B4
Napley Heath Staffs 150 B4
Nappa N Yorks 204 C3
Nappa Scar
N Yorks 223 G9
Napton on the Hill
Warks 119 E9
Narberth / Arberth
Pembs 73 C10
Narberth Bridge
Pembs 73 C10
Narborough Leics 135 D10
Norf 158 G4
Narfords Som 28 F3
Narkurs Corn 6 D6
Narracott Devon 24 D5
Narrowgate Corner
Norf 161 F8
Nasareth Gwyn 163 E7
Naseby Northants 120 B3
Nash Bucks 102 E5
Hereford 114 E6
Kent 55 B9
London 68 G2
Newport 59 C10
Shrops 116 C2
Som 29 E8
Nashend Glos 80 D5
Nash End Worcs 132 G5
Nashes Green Hants 49 D7
Nash Lee Bucks 84 D4
Nash Mills Herts 85 E9
Nash Street E Sus 23 C8
Kent 68 F6
Nassington
Northants 137 D11
Nastend Glos 80 D3
Nast Hyde Herts 86 D2
Nasty Herts 105 G7
Natcott Devon 24 C3
Nateby Cumb 222 D5
Lancs 202 E5
Nately Scures Hants 49 C8
Natland Cumb 211 B10
Natton Glos 99 E8
Naughton Suff 107 B10
Naunton Glos 100 G2
Worcs 99 D7
Naunton Beauchamp
Worcs 117 G9
Navant Hill W Sus 34 B6
Navenby Lincs 173 D7
Navestock Heath
Essex 87 F8
Navestock Side Essex 87 F9
Navidale Highld 311 H4
Navity Highld 301 C7
Nawton N Yorks 216 C3
Nayland Suff 107 E9
Nazeing Essex 86 D6
Nazeing Gate Essex 86 D6
Nazeing Long Green
Essex 86 E6
Nazeing Mead Essex 86 D5
Neacroft Hants 19 B9
Nealhouse Cumb 239 G8
Neal's Green Warks 134 G6
Neames Forstal Kent 54 B5
Neap Shetland 313 H7
Near Hardcastle
N Yorks 214 F2
Near Sawrey Cumb 221 F7
Nearton End Bucks 102 F6
Neasden London 67 B8
Neasham Darl 224 C6
Neat Enstone Oxon 101 G7
Neath Abbey Neath 57 B8
Neatham Hants 49 E8
Neath / Castell-nedd
Neath 57 B8
Neath Hill M Keynes 103 C7
Neatishead Norf 160 E6
Neat Marsh E Yorks 209 G9
Neaton Norf 141 C8
Nebo Anglesey 179 C7
Ceredig 111 D10
Conwy 164 D4
Gwyn 163 E7
Nebsworth Warks 100 C3
Nechells W Mid 133 F11
Necton Norf 141 B7
Nedd Highld 306 F6
Nedderton
Northumb 252 G6
Nedge Hill Som 44 C5
Telford 132 B4
Nedging Suff 107 B9
Nedging Tye Suff 107 B10
Needham Norf 142 G4
Needham Green
Essex 87 B9
Needham Market
Suff 125 G11
Needham Street
Suff 124 D4
Needingworth
Cambs 122 C6
Needwood Staffs 152 E3
Neen Savage Shrops 116 B3
Neen Sollars Shrops 116 C3
Neenton Shrops 132 F2
Nefod Shrops 148 B6
Nefyn Gwyn 162 G4
Neighbourne Som 44 D6
Neight Hill Worcs 117 F8
Neilston E Renf 267 D9
Neinthirion Powys 129 B9
Neithrop Oxon 101 C8
Nelly Andrews Green
Powys 130 B5
Nelson Caerph 77 F10
Lancs 204 F3
Nelson Village
Northumb 243 B7
Nemphlar S Lnrk 269 G7
Nempnett Thrubwell
N Som 60 G4
Nene Terrace Lincs 138 B5
Nenthall Cumb 231 B11
Nenthead Cumb 231 C11
Nenthorn Borders 262 B5
Neopardy Devon 13 B11
Nepcote W Sus 35 F10
Nepgill Cumb 229 F7
Nep Town W Sus 36 D2
Nerabus Argyll 254 B3
Nercwys Flint 166 C2
Nerston S Lnrk 268 D2
Nesbit Northumb 263 C11
Ness Ches W 182 F4
Orkney 314 C4
Nesscliffe Shrops 149 F7
Nesstoun Orkney 314 A7
Neston Ches W 182 F3
Wilts 61 F11
Netchells Green
W Mid 133 F11
Netham Bristol 60 E6
Nethanfoot S Lnrk 268 F6
Nether Alderley
Ches E 184 F4
Netheravon Wilts 46 D6
Nether Blainslie
Borders 271 G10
Nether Booth
Derbys 185 D10
Netherbrae Aberds 303 D7
Netherbrough
Orkney 314 E3
Nether Broughton
Leics 154 D3
Netherburn S Lnrk 268 F6
Nether Burrow
Lancs 212 D2
Nether Burrows
Derbys 152 B5
Netherbury Dorset 16 B5
Netherby Cumb 239 C9
N Yorks 206 D2
Nether Cassock
Dumfries 248 C6
Nether Cerne Dorset 17 B9
Nether Chanderhill
Derbys 186 G4
Netherclay Som 28 C3
Nether Compton
Dorset 29 D9
Nethercote Oxon 101 C9
Warks 119 E10
Nethercott Devon 12 B3
Devon 40 F3
Oxon 101 G9
Som 42 G6
Nether Crimond
Aberds 303 G8
Netherdale Shetland 313 H3
Nether Dalgliesh
Borders 249 B7
Nether Dallachy
Moray 302 C3
Nether Edge
S Yorks 186 E4
Netherend Glos 79 E9
Nether End Derbys 186 G3
Leics 154 G4
W Yorks 197 F8
Nether Exe Devon 26 G6
Netherfield E Sus 38 D2
M Keynes 103 D7
Notts 171 G10
Nethergate Norf 159 D11
Nether Glasslaw
Aberds 303 D8
Nether Hall
Leicester 136 B2
Netherhampton
Wilts 31 B10
Nether Handley
Derbys 186 F6
Nether Handwick
Angus 287 C7
Nether Haugh
S Yorks 186 B6
Nether Headon
Notts 188 F2
Nether Heage
Derbys 170 E5
Nether Heyford
Northants 120 F3
Nether Hindhope
Borders 263 G7
Nether Horsburgh
Borders 261 B8
Nether Howecleuch S Lnrk 260 G2
Nether Kellet
Lancs 211 F10
Nether Kidston
Borders 270 G4
Nether Kinmundy
Aberds 303 E10
Nether Kirton
E Renf 267 D9
Netherland Green
Staffs 152 C2
Nether Langwith
Notts 187 G8
Netherlaw Dumfries 237 E9
Netherlay Dorset 28 F6
Nether Leask
Aberds 303 F10
Netherlee E Renf 267 D11
Nether Lenshie
Aberds 302 E6
Netherley Aberds 293 D10
Mers 182 D6
W Yorks 196 E4
Nether Loads
Derbys 170 B4
Nethermill Dumfries 248 F2
Nethermills Moray 302 D5
Nether Monynut
Borders 272 C4
Nether Moor Derbys 170 B5
Nethermuir Aberds 303 E9
Netherne on-the-Hill
Sur 51 B9
Netheroyd Hill
W Yorks 196 D6
Nether Padley
Derbys 186 F3
Nether Park
Aberds 303 D10
Netherplace
E Renf 267 D10
Nether Poppleton
York 207 B7
Netherraw Borders 262 E3
Nether Row Cumb 230 D2
Nether Savock
Aberds 303 E10
Netherseal Derbys 152 G5
Nether Shiels
Borders 271 F8
Nether Silton
N Yorks 225 G9
Nether Skyborry
Shrops 114 C5
Nether St Suff 125 E8
Netherstoke Dorset 29 F8
Nether Stowe Staffs 152 G2
Nether Stowey Som 43 F7
Nether Street Essex 87 C9
Herts 86 B6
Netherthird E Ayrs 258 F3
Netherthong
W Yorks 196 F6
Netherthorpe
Derbys 186 G6
S Yorks 187 E8
Netherton Aberds 303 E8
Angus 287 B9
Ches W 183 F8
Corn 11 G11
Cumb 228 D6
Devon 14 G3
Glos 81 E11
Hants 47 B11
Hereford 97 F10
Mers 193 G11
N Lnrk 268 E5
Northumb 251 B11
Oxon 82 F6
Perth 286 B5
Shrops 132 G4
Stirl 277 F11
W Mid 133 F8
Worcs 99 C9
W Yorks 196 E6
W Yorks 197 D9
Netherton of Lonmay
Aberds 303 C10
Nethertown Cumb 219 D9
Highld 310 B7
Lancs 203 F10
Staffs 152 F2
Nether Urquhart
Fife 286 G5
Nether Wallop
Hants 47 F10
Nether Warden
Northumb 241 D10
Nether Wasdale
Cumb 220 E2
Nether Welton
Cumb 230 B3
Nether Westcote
Glos 100 G4
Nether Whitacre
Warks 134 E4
Nether Winchendon or Lower Winchendon
Bucks 84 C2
Netherwitton
Northumb 252 E4
Netherwood E Ayrs 258 D5
Nether Worton
Oxon 101 E8
Nether Yeadon
W Yorks 205 E10
Nethy Bridge
Highld 301 G10
Netley Hants 33 F7
Netley Hill Soton 33 E7
Netley Marsh Hants 32 E4
Nettacott Devon 14 B4
Netteswell Essex 87 C7
Nettlebed Oxon 65 B8
Nettlebridge Som 44 D6
Nettlecombe Dorset 16 B6
IoW 20 F6
Nettleden Herts 85 C8
Nettleham Lincs 189 F8
Nettlestead Kent 53 C7
Suff 107 B11
Nettlestead Green
Kent 53 C7
Nettlestone IoW 21 C8
Nettlesworth
Durham 233 B11
Nettleton Glos 80 C6
Lincs 200 G6
Wilts 61 D10
Nettleton Green
Wilts 61 D10
Nettleton Hill
W Yorks 196 D5
Nettleton Shrub
Wilts 61 D10
Nettleton Top
Lincs 189 B10
Netton Wilts 46 F6
Neuadd Carms 94 G3
Nevendon Essex 88 G2
Nevern / Nanhyfer
Pembs 91 D11
Nevilles Cross
Durham 233 C11
New Abbey
Dumfries 237 C11
New Aberdour
Aberds 303 C8
New Addington
London 67 G11
Newall W Yorks 205 D10
Newall Green
Gtr Man 184 D4
New Alresford Hants 48 G5
New Alyth Perth 286 C6
Newark Orkney 314 B7
Pboro 138 C4
Newark-on-Trent
Notts 172 E3
New Arley Warks 134 F5
New Arram E Yorks 208 E6
Newarthill N Lnrk 268 D5
New Ash Green Kent 68 F6
New Balderton
Notts 172 E4
Newball Lincs 189 F9
Newbarn Kent 55 F7
New Barn Kent 68 F6
New Barnet London 86 F3
New Barnetby
N Lincs 200 E5
Newbarns Cumb 210 E4
New Barton
Northants 121 E7
New Basford
Nottingham 171 G9
Newbattle Midloth 270 B6
New Beaupre V Glam 58 E4
New Beckenham
London 67 E11
New Bewick
Northumb 264 E3
Newbie Dumfries 238 D5
Newbiggin Cumb 210 F5
Cumb 211 D11
Cumb 219 G11
Cumb 230 F5
Cumb 231 B7
Cumb 231 F8
Durham 232 B5
Durham 232 F4
Durham 233 B8
N Yorks 213 B9
N Yorks 223 G9
Newbiggin-by-the-Sea
Northumb 253 F8
Newbigging Aberds 303 G7
Angus 287 D8
Borders 262 F6
Edin 280 F2
S Lnrk 269 F10
New-bigging Angus 286 C6
Newbiggings
Orkney 314 B6
Newbiggin Hall Estate
T&W 242 D6
Newbiggin-on-Lune
Cumb 222 D4
New Bilton Warks 119 B9
Newbold Derbys 186 G5
Gtr Man 196 E2
Leics 136 B5
Leics 153 F8
Newbold Heath
Leics 135 B8
Newbold on Avon
Warks 119 B9
Newbold on Stour
Warks 100 B4
Newbold Pacey
Warks 118 F5
Newbolds W Mid 133 C8
Newbold Verdon
Leics 135 C8
New Bolingbroke
Lincs 174 D4
New Bolsover
Derbys 187 G7
Newborough Pboro 138 B4
Staffs 152 D2
New Boston Mers 183 B9
New Botley Oxon 83 D7
Newbottle
Northants 101 D10
T&W 243 G8
New Boultham
Lincs 189 G7
Newbourne Suff 108 C5
New Bradwell
M Keynes 102 C6
New Brancepeth
Durham 233 C10
Newbridge Bath 61 F8
Caerph 78 F2
Ceredig 111 F10
Corn 1 C4
Corn 4 G5
Corn 7 B7
Dumfries 237 B11
Edin 280 G2
E Sus 52 G3
Hants 32 D3
IoW 20 D4
Lancs 204 F3
N Yorks 216 B6
Oxon 82 E6
Pembs 91 E8
Shrops 148 D6
W Mid 133 D7
Wrex 166 G3
New Bridge Wrex 166 G3
Newbridge Green
Worcs 98 D6
Newbridge-on-Usk
Mon 78 G5
Newbridge-on-Wye
Powys 113 F10
New Brighton Flint 166 B3
Mers 182 C4
Wrex 166 E3
W Sus 22 B3
W Yorks 197 B9
W Yorks 205 F8
New Brimington
Derbys 186 G6
New Brinsley Notts 171 E7
New Brotton Redcar 235 G9
Newbrough
Northumb 241 D9
New Broughton
Wrex 166 E4
New Buckenham
Norf 141 E11
Newbuildings Devon 26 G3
New Buildings Bath 45 B7
Dorset 18 E5
Newburgh Aberds 303 D9
Aberds 303 G9
Borders 261 F8
Fife 286 F6
Lancs 194 E3
Newburn T&W 242 D5
Newbury Kent 54 B2
W Berks 64 F3
Wilts 45 E10
New Bury Gtr Man 195 F8
Newbury Park
London 68 B2
Newby Cumb 231 G7
Lancs 204 D2
N Yorks 205 D11
N Yorks 212 E4
N Yorks 215 F7
N Yorks 225 C10
N Yorks 227 G10
Newby Bridge Cumb 211 B7
Newby Cote
N Yorks 212 E4
Newby East Cumb 239 F11
Newby Head Cumb 231 G7
New Byth Aberds 303 D8
Newby West Cumb 239 G9
Newby Wiske
N Yorks 215 B7
Newcastle Bridgend 58 D2
Mon 78 B6
Shrops 130 G4
Newcastle Emlyn / Castell Newydd Emlyn
Carms 92 C6
Newcastleton or Copshaw Holm
Borders 249 F11
Newcastle-under-Lyme
Staffs 168 F4
Newcastle upon Tyne
T&W 242 E6
New Catton Norf 160 G4
Newchapel Powys 129 G9
Staffs 168 E5
Sur 51 E11
Newchapel / Capel Newydd Pembs 92 D4
New Charlton London 68 D2

Oridge Street Glos 98 F5
Orlandon Pembs 72 D4
Orlestone Kent 54 G3
Orleton Hereford 115 D9
Worcs 116 D3
Orleton Common
Hereford 115 D9
Orlingbury
Northants 121 C7
Ormacleit W Isles 297 H3
Ormathwaite Cumb 229 F11
Ormesby Redcar 225 B10
Ormesby St Margaret
Norf 161 G9
Ormesby St Michael
Norf 161 G9
Ormiclate Castle
W Isles 297 H3
Ormidale Lodge
Argyll 275 F11
Ormiscaig Highld 307 K3
Ormiston Borders 262 G2
E Loth 271 B8
Ormsaigbeg Highld 288 C6
Ormsaigmore
Highld 288 C6
Ormsary Argyll 275 F8
Ormsgill Cumb 210 E3
Ormskirk Lancs 194 F2
Ornsby Hill Durham 233 B9
Orpington London 68 F3
Orrell Gtr Man 194 F4
Mers 182 B4
Orrell Post Gtr Man 194 G4
Orrisdale IoM 192 C4
Orrock Fife 280 D4
Orroland Dumfries 237 E9
Orsett Thurrock 68 C6
Orsett Heath
Thurrock 68 D6
Orslow Staffs 150 F6
Orston Notts 172 G3
Orthwaite Cumb 229 E11
Ortner Lancs 202 C6
Orton Cumb 222 D2
Northants 120 B6
Staffs 133 D7
Orton Brimbles
Pboro 138 D3
Orton Goldhay
Pboro 138 D3
Orton Longueville
Pboro 138 D3
Orton Malborne
Pboro 138 D3
Orton-on-the-Hill
Leics 134 C6
Orton Rigg Cumb 239 G8
Orton Southgate
Pboro 138 E2
Orton Waterville
Pboro 138 D3
Orton Wistow
Pboro 138 D2
Orwell Cambs 123 G7
Osbaldeston Lancs 203 G8
Osbaldeston Green
Lancs 203 G8
Osbaldwick York 207 C8
Osbaston Leics 135 C8
Shrops 148 E6
Telford 149 F11
Osbaston Hollow
Leics 135 B8
Osbournby Lincs 155 B11
Oscroft Ches W 167 B8
Ose Highld 298 E3
Osea Island Essex 88 D6
Osehill Green
Dorset 29 F11
Osgathorpe Leics 153 F8
Osgodby Lincs 189 C9
N Yorks 207 G8
N Yorks 217 C11
Osgodby Common
N Yorks 207 F8
Osidge London 86 G3
Oskaig Highld 295 B7
Oskamull Argyll 288 E6
Osleston Derbys 152 B4
Osmaston Derby 153 C7
Derbys 170 G2
Osmington Dorset 17 E10
Osmington Mills
Dorset 17 E10
Osmondthorpe
W Yorks 206 G2
Osmotherley
N Yorks 225 F9
Osney Oxon 83 D8
Ospisdale Highld 309 L7
Ospringe Kent 70 G4
Ossaborough Devon 40 E3
Ossemsley Hants 19 B10
Osset Spa W Yorks 197 D9
Ossett W Yorks 197 C9
Ossett Street Side
W Yorks 197 C9
Ossington Notts 172 C3
Ostend Essex 88 F6
Norf 161 C7
Osterley London 66 D6
Oswaldkirk N Yorks 216 D2
Oswaldtwistle Lancs 195 B8
Oswestry Shrops 148 D5
Otby Lincs 189 C10
Oteley Shrops 149 C8
Otford Kent 52 B4
Otham Kent 53 C9
Otham Hole Kent 53 C10
Otherton Staffs 151 G8
Othery Som 43 G11
Otley Suff 126 F4
W Yorks 205 D10
Otterbourne Hants 33 C7
Otterburn Northumb 251 E9
N Yorks 204 B3
Otterburn Camp
Northumb 251 D9
Otterden Place Kent 54 C2
Otter Ferry Argyll 275 E10
Otterford Som 28 E2
Otterham Corn 11 C9
Otterhampton Som 43 E8
Otterham Quay Kent 69 F10
Otterham Station
Corn 11 D9
Otter Ho Argyll 275 F10
Ottershaw Sur 66 G4
Otterspool Mers 182 D5
Otterswick Shetland 312 E7
Otterton Devon 15 D7
Otterwood Hants 32 G6
Ottery St Mary Devon 15 B8
Ottinge Kent 55 E7
Ottringham E Yorks 201 C9
Oughterby Cumb 239 F7
Oughtershaw
N Yorks 213 C7
Oughterside Cumb 229 C8
Oughtibridge
S Yorks 186 C4
Oughtrington
Warr 183 D11
Oulston N Yorks 215 E10
Oulton Cumb 238 G6
Norf 160 D2
Staffs 150 E5
Staffs 151 B8
Suff 143 D10
W Yorks 197 B11
Oulton Broad Suff 143 E10
Oultoncross Staffs 151 C8
Oulton Grange
Staffs 151 B8
Oulton Heath Staffs 151 B8
Oulton Street Norf 160 D3
Oundle Northants 137 F10
Ounsdale Staffs 133 E7
Ousby Cumb 231 E8
Ousdale Highld 311 G4
Ousden Suff 124 F4
Ousefleet E Yorks 199 C10
Ousel Hole W Yorks 205 E8
Ouston Durham 243 G7
Northumb 241 G7
Northumb 242 C3
Outcast Cumb 210 D6
Out Elmstead Kent 55 C8
Outer Hope Devon 8 G3
Outertown Orkney 314 E2
Outgate Cumb 221 F7
Outhgill Cumb 222 E5
Outhill Warks 118 D2
Outhills Aberds 303 D10
Outlands Staffs 150 C5
Outlane W Yorks 196 D5
Outlane Moor
W Yorks 196 D5
Outlet Village
Ches W 182 G6
Outmarsh Wilts 61 G11
Out Newton
E Yorks 201 C11
Out Rawcliffe Lancs 202 E4
Outwell Norf 139 C10
Outwick Hants 31 D10
Outwood Gtr Man 195 F9
Som 28 B4
Sur 51 D10
W Yorks 197 C10
Outwoods Leics 153 F8
Staffs 150 F5
Staffs 152 E4
Warks 134 G4
Ouzlewell Green
W Yorks 197 B10
Ovenden W Yorks 196 B5
Ovenscloss
Borders 261 C11
Over Cambs 123 C7
Ches W 167 B10
Glos 80 B4
S Glos 60 C5
Overa Farm Stud
Norf 141 F9
Overbister Orkney 314 B6
Over Burrow Lancs 212 D2
Over Burrows
Derbys 152 B5
Overbury Worcs 99 D9
Overcombe Dorset 17 E9
Over Compton
Dorset 29 D9
Overend W Mid 133 G9
Over End Cambs 137 E11
Derbys 186 G3
Overgreen Derbys 186 G4
Over Green W Mid 134 E3
Over Haddon
Derbys 170 B2
Over Hulton
Gtr Man 195 F7
Over Kellet Lancs 211 E10
Over Kiddington
Oxon 101 G8
Over Knutsford
Ches E 184 F3
Over Langshaw
Borders 271 G10
Overleigh Som 44 F3
Overley Staffs 152 F3
Overley Green
Warks 117 F11
Over Monnow Mon 79 C8
Overmoor Staffs 169 F7
Over Norton Oxon 100 F6
Over Peover Ches E 184 G3
Overpool Ches W 182 F5
Overs Shrops 131 D7
Overscaig Hotel
Highld 309 G4
Overseal Derbys 152 F5
Over Silton N Yorks 225 G9
Overslade Warks 119 C9
Oversland Kent 54 B5
Oversley Green
Warks 117 F11
Overstone Northants 120 D6
Over Stowey Som 43 F7
Overstrand Norf 160 A4
Over Stratton Som 28 D6
Over Tabley Ches E 184 E2
Overthorpe
Northants 101 C9
W Yorks 197 D8
Overton Aberdeen 293 B10
Aberds 293 B9
Ches W 183 F8
Dumfries 237 C11
Glos 80 C2
Hants 48 D4
Invclyd 276 G5
Lancs 202 B4
N Yorks 207 B7
Shrops 115 C10
Staffs 151 B10
Swansea 56 D3
W Yorks 197 D9
Overton Bridge
Wrex 166 G5
Overton / Owrtyn
Wrex 166 G5
Overtown Lancs 212 D2
N Lnrk 268 E6
Swindon 63 D7
W Yorks 197 D11
Over Town Lancs 195 B11
Over Wallop Hants 47 F9
Over Whitacre
Warks 134 E5
Over Worton Oxon 101 F8
Oving Bucks 102 G5
W Sus 22 C6
Ovingdean Brighton 36 G5
Ovingham Northumb 242 E3
Ovington Durham 224 C2
Essex 106 C5
Hants 48 G5
Norf 141 C8
Northumb 242 E3
Owen's Bank Staffs 152 D4
Ower Hants 32 D4
Owermoigne Dorset 17 D11
Owlbury Shrops 130 E6
Owlcotes Derbys 170 B6
Owl End Cambs 122 B4
Owler Bar Derbys 186 F3
Owlerton S Yorks 186 D4
Owlet W Yorks 205 F9
Owlpen Glos 80 F4
Owl's Green Suff 126 D5
Owlsmoor Brack 65 G11
Owlswick Bucks 84 D3
Owlthorpe S Yorks 186 E6
Owmby Lincs 200 G5
Owmby-by-Spital
Lincs 189 D8
Ownham W Berks 64 E2
Owrtyn / Overton
Wrex 166 G5
Owslebury Hants 33 C8
Owston Leics 136 B5
S Yorks 198 E5
Owston Ferry
N Lincs 199 G10
Owstwick E Yorks 209 G11
Owthorne E Yorks 201 B10
Owthorpe Notts 154 C3
Owton Manor Hrtlpl 234 F5
Oxborough Norf 140 C4
Oxclose S Yorks 186 E6
T&W 243 F7
Oxcombe Lincs 190 F4
Oxcroft Derbys 187 G7
Oxcroft Estate
Derbys 187 G7
Oxen End Essex 106 F3
Oxenhall Glos 98 F4
Oxenholme Cumb 211 B10
Oxenhope W Yorks 204 F6
Oxen Park Cumb 210 B6
Oxenpill Som 44 E2
Oxenton Glos 99 E9
Oxenwood Wilts 47 B10
Oxford Oxon 83 D8
Stoke 168 E5
Oxgang E Dunb 278 G3
Oxgangs Edin 270 B4
Oxhey Herts 85 F10
Oxhill Durham 242 G5
Warks 100 B6
Oxlease Herts 86 D2
Oxley W Mid 133 C8
Oxley Green Essex 88 C6
Oxley's Green E Sus 37 C11
Oxlode Cambs 139 F9
Oxnam Borders 262 F5
Oxnead Norf 160 E4
Oxshott Sur 66 G6
Oxspring S Yorks 197 G9
Oxted Sur 51 C11
Oxton Borders 271 E9
Mers 182 D3
Notts 171 E10
N Yorks 206 E6
Oxton Rakes Derbys 186 G4
Oxwich Swansea 56 D3
Oxwich Green
Swansea 56 D3
Oxwick Norf 159 D8
Oykel Bridge Highld 309 J3
Oyne Aberds 302 G6
Oystermouth
Swansea 56 D6
Ozleworth Glos 80 G3

P

Pabail Iarach
W Isles 304 E7
Pabail Uarach
W Isles 304 E7
Pabo Conwy 180 F4
Pace Gate N Yorks 205 C8
Pachesham Park Sur 51 B7
Packers Hill Dorset 30 E2
Packington Leics 153 G7
Packmoor Staffs 168 E5
Packmores Warks 118 D5
Packwood W Mid 118 C3
Packwood Gullet
W Mid 118 C3
Padanaram Angus 287 B8
Padbury Bucks 102 E4
Paddington London 67 C9
Warr 183 D10
Paddlesworth Kent 55 F7
Kent 69 G7
Paddock Kent 54 C3
W Yorks 196 D6
Paddockhaugh
Moray 302 D2
Paddockhill Ches E 184 F4
Paddockhole
Dumfries 248 G6
Paddock Wood Kent 53 E7
Paddolgreen
Shrops 149 C10
Padfield Derbys 185 B8
Padgate Warr 183 D10
Padham's Green
Essex 87 F10
Padiham Lancs 203 G11
Padney Cambs 123 C10
Padog Conwy 164 E4
Padside N Yorks 205 B9
Padside Green
N Yorks 205 B9
Padson Devon 13 B7
Padstow Corn 10 F4
Padworth W Berks 64 F6
Padworth Common
Hants 64 G6
Paganhill Glos 80 D4
Page Bank Durham 233 D10
Page Moss Mers 182 C6
Page's Green Suff 126 D2
Pagham W Sus 22 D5
Paglesham Churchend
Essex 88 G6
Paglesham Eastend
Essex 88 G6
Paibeil W Isles 296 E3
Paible W Isles 305 J2
Paignton Torbay 9 C7
Pailton Warks 135 G9
Painleyhill Staffs 151 C10
Painscastle Powys 96 B3
Painshawfield
Northumb 242 E3
Pains Hill Sur 52 C2
Painsthorpe
E Yorks 208 B2
Painswick Glos 80 D5
Painter's Forstal
Kent 54 B3
Painters Green
Wrex 167 G8
Painter's Green Herts 86 B3
Painthorpe
W Yorks 197 D10
Paintmoor Som 28 F4
Pairc Shiaboist
W Isles 304 D4
Paisley Renfs 267 C9
Pakefield Suff 143 E10
Pakenham Suff 125 D8
Pale Gwyn 147 B9
Pale Green Essex 106 C3
Palehouse Common
E Sus 23 B7
Palestine Hants 47 E9
Paley Street
Windsor 65 D11
Palfrey W Mid 133 D10
Palgowan Dumfries 245 G9
Palgrave Suff 126 B2
Pallaflat Cumb 219 C9
Pallington Dorset 17 C11
Pallion T&W 243 F9
Pallister Mbro 225 B10
Palmarsh Kent 54 G6
Palmer Moor
Derbys 152 C2
Palmersbridge Corn 11 F9
Palmers Cross
Staffs 133 C7
Sur 50 E4
Palmer's Flat Glos 79 D9
Palmers Green
London 86 G4
Palmer's Green Kent 53 E7
Palmerstown V Glam 58 F6
Palmersville T&W 243 C7
Palmstead Kent 55 D7
Palnackie Dumfries 237 D10
Palnure Dumfries 236 C6
Palterton Derbys 171 B7
Pamber End Hants 48 B6
Pamber Green Hants 48 B6
Pamber Heath Hants 64 G6
Pamington Glos 99 E8
Pamphill Dorset 31 G7
Pampisford Cambs 105 B9
Pan IoW 20 D6
Orkney 314 G3
Panborough Som 44 D3
Panbride Angus 287 D9
Pancakehill Glos 81 C9
Pancrasweek Devon 24 F3
Pancross V Glam 58 F4
Pandy Gwyn 128 C2
Gwyn 146 F4
Gwyn 147 D7
Mon 96 G6
Powys 129 C8
Wrex 148 B3
Wrex 166 G6
Pandy'r Capel Denb 165 E9
Pandy Tudur Conwy 164 C5
Panfield Essex 106 F4
Pangbourne
W Berks 64 D6
Panhall Fife 280 C6
Panks Bridge
Hereford 98 B2
Pannal N Yorks 206 C2
Pannal Ash
N Yorks 205 C11
Pannel's Ash Essex 106 C5
Panpunton Powys 114 C5
Panshanger Herts 86 C3
Pant Denb 166 E2
Flint 181 G10
Gwyn 144 C4
M Tydf 77 D9
Powys 129 C11
Shrops 148 E5
Wrex 166 D5
Wrex 166 F3
Pantasaph Flint 181 F11
Pantdu Neath 57 C9
Panteg Ceredig 111 E9
Torf 78 F4
Pantersbridge Corn 6 B3
Pant-glas Gwyn 163 F7
Pant-glâs Powys 128 D5
Pant-glas Shrops 148 C5
Pantgwyn Carms 93 F11
Ceredig 92 B4
Pant-lasau Swansea 57 B7
Pantmawr Cardiff 58 C6
Pant Mawr Powys 129 G7
Panton Lincs 189 F11
Pant-pastynog
Denb 165 C8
Pantperthog Gwyn 128 C4
Pantside Caerph 78 F2
Pant-teg Carms 93 F9
Pant-y-Caws Carms 92 F3
Pant-y-crûg
Ceredig 112 B3
Pant-y-dwr Powys 113 B9
Powys 113 C9
Pant-y-ffridd
Powys 130 C3
Pantyffynnon Carms 75 C10
Pantygasseg Torf 78 F3
Pantymwyn Flint 165 C11
Pant-y-pyllau
Bridgend 58 C2
Pant-yr-awel
Bridgend 58 B2
Pant-y-Wacco
Flint 181 F10
Panxworth Norf 161 G7
Papcastle Cumb 229 E8
Papermill Bank
Shrops 149 D11
Papigoe Highld 310 D7
Papil Shetland 313 K5
Papley Northants 138 F2
Orkney 314 G4
Papple E Loth 281 G11
Papplewick Notts 171 E8
Papworth Everard
Cambs 122 E5
Papworth St Agnes
Cambs 122 E5
Papworth Village
Settlement Cambs 122 E5
Par Corn 5 E11
Paradise Glos 80 C5
Paradise Green
Hereford 97 B10
Paramoor Corn 5 F9
Paramour Street
Kent 71 G9
Parbold Lancs 194 E3
Parbrook Som 44 F5
W Sus 35 B9
Parc Gwyn 147 C7
Parc Erissey Corn 4 G3
Parc-hendy Swansea 56 B4
Parchey Som 43 F10
Parciau Anglesey 179 E7
Parcllyn Ceredig 110 G4
Parc Mawr Caerph 77 G10
Parc-Seymour
Newport 78 G6
Parc-y-rhôs Carms 93 B11
Pardown Hants 48 D5
Pardshaw Cumb 229 G7
Pardshaw Hall
Cumb 229 F8
Parham Suff 126 E6
Park Corn 10 G6
Devon 14 B2
Dumfries 247 E10
Som 44 G3
Swindon 63 C7
Park Barn Sur 50 C3
Park Bottom Corn 4 G3
Park Bridge
Gtr Man 196 G2
Park Broom Cumb 239 F10
Park Close Lancs 204 E3
Park Corner Bath 45 B9
E Sus 23 C8
E Sus 52 F4
Oxon 65 B7
Windsor 65 C11
Parkend Glos 79 D10
Glos 80 C3
Park End Beds 121 G9
Cambs 123 E11
Mbro 225 B10
Northumb 241 B9
Som 43 G7
Staffs 168 E3
Worcs 116 C5
Parkengear Corn 5 F8
Parker's Corner
W Berks 64 E6
Parker's Green
Herts 104 F6
Kent 52 D6
Parkeston Essex 108 E4
Parkfield Corn 6 B6
S Glos 61 D7
W Mid 133 D8
Parkfoot Falk 278 F6
Parkgate Ches E 184 G3
Ches W 182 F3
Cumb 229 B10
Dumfries 248 F2
Essex 87 B11
Kent 53 G11
Sur 51 E8
S Yorks 186 B6
Park Gate Dorset 30 F2
Hants 33 F8
Kent 55 D7
Suff 124 F4
Worcs 117 C8
W Yorks 197 E8
Park Green Essex 105 F9
Parkhall W Dunb 277 G9
Park Hall Shrops 148 C6
Parkham Devon 24 C5
Parkham Ash Devon 24 C5
Parkhead Cumb 230 C2
Glasgow 268 C2
S Yorks 186 E4
Park Head Cumb 231 C7
Derbys 170 E5
W Yorks 197 F7
Parkhill Aberds 303 E10
Invclyd 277 G7
Park Hill Glos 79 F9
Kent 54 G3
Mers 194 G3
Notts 171 E11
N Yorks 214 F6
S Yorks 186 D5
Parkhill Ho Aberds 293 B10
Parkhouse Mon 79 E7
Parkhouse Green
Derbys 170 C6
Parkhurst IoW 20 C5
Parklands W Yorks 206 F3
Park Lane Staffs 133 B7
Wrex 149 B8
Park Langley London 67 F11
Park Mains Renfs 277 G9
Parkmill Swansea 56 D4
Park Mill W Yorks 197 E9
Parkneuk Aberds 293 F9
Fife 279 D11
Park Royal London 67 C7
Parkside C Beds 103 G10
Cumb 219 B10
Durham 234 B4
N Lnrk 268 D6
Staffs 151 D8
Wrex 166 D5
Parkstone Poole 18 C6
Park Street Herts 85 E10
W Sus 50 G6
Park Town Luton 103 G11
Oxon 83 D8
Park Village
Northumb 240 E5
W Mid 133 C8
Park Villas W Yorks 206 F2
Parkway Hereford 98 D4
Som 29 C9
Park Wood Kent 53 C9
Medway 69 G10
Parkwood Springs
S Yorks 186 D4
Parley Cross Dorset 19 B7
Parley Green Dorset 19 B7
Parliament Heath
Suff 107 C9
Parlington W Yorks 206 F4
Parmoor Bucks 65 B9
Parnacott Devon 24 F4
Parney Heath
Essex 107 E10
Parr Mers 183 C8
Parracombe Devon 41 E7
Parr Brow Gtr Man 195 G8
Parrog Pembs 91 D10
Parsley Hay
Derbys 169 C10
Parslow's Hillock
Bucks 84 E4
Parsonage Green
Essex 88 D2
Parsonby Cumb 229 D8
Parson Cross
S Yorks 186 C5
Parson Drove
Cambs 139 B7
Parsons Green
London 67 D9
Parson's Heath
Essex 107 F10
Partick Glasgow 267 B11
Partington Gtr Man 184 C2
Partney Lincs 174 B6
Parton Cumb 228 G5
Cumb 239 G7
Dumfries 237 B8
Glos 99 G7
Hereford 96 B6
Partridge Green
W Sus 35 D11
Partrishow Powys 96 G5
Parwich Derbys 169 E11
Pasford Staffs 132 D6
Passenham
Northants 102 D5
Passfield Hants 49 G10
Passingford Bridge
Essex 87 F8
Passmores Essex 86 D6
Paston Norf 160 C6
Pboro 138 C3
Paston Green Norf 160 C6
Pasturefields Staffs 151 D9
Patchacott Devon 12 B5
Patcham Brighton 36 F4
Patchetts Green
Herts 85 F10
Patching W Sus 35 F9
Patchole Devon 40 E6
Patchway S Glos 60 C6
Pategill Cumb 230 F6
Pateley Bridge
N Yorks 214 F3
Paternoster Heath
Essex 88 C6
Pathe Som 43 G11
Pather N Lnrk 268 E5
Pathfinder Village
Devon 14 C2
Pathhead Aberds 293 G9
E Ayrs 258 G4
Fife 280 C5
Midloth 271 C7
Path Head T&W 242 E5
Pathlow Warks 118 F3
Path of Condie
Perth 286 F4
Pathstruie Perth 286 F4
Patient End Herts 105 F8
Patmore Heath
Herts 105 F8
Patna E Ayrs 257 G10
Patney Wilts 46 B5
Patrick IoM 192 D3
Patrick Brompton
N Yorks 224 G4
Patricroft Gtr Man 184 B3
Patrington E Yorks 201 C10
Patrington Haven
E Yorks 201 C10
Patrixbourne Kent 55 B7
Patsford Devon 40 F4
Patterdale Cumb 221 B7
Pattiesmuir Fife 279 E11
Pattingham Staffs 132 D6
Pattishall Northants 120 G3
Pattiswick Essex 106 G6
Patton Shrops 131 E11
Patton Bridge
Cumb 221 F11
Paul Corn 1 D5
Paulerspury
Northants 102 B4
Paull E Yorks 201 B7
Paul's Green Corn 2 C4
Paulsgrove Ptsmth 33 F10
Paulton Bath 45 B7
Paulville W Loth 269 B9
Pave Lane Telford 150 F5
Pavenham Beds 121 F9
Pawlett Som 43 E10
Pawlett Hill Som 43 E9
Pawston Northumb 263 C9
Paxford Glos 100 D3
Paxton Borders 273 E8
Payden Street Kent 54 C2
Payhembury Devon 27 G9
Paynes Green Sur 50 F6
Paynter's Cross Corn 7 C7
Paynter's Lane End
Corn 4 G3
Paythorne Lancs 204 C2
Payton Som 27 C10
Peacehaven E Sus 36 G6
Peacehaven Heights
E Sus 36 G6
Peacemarsh Dorset 30 B4
Peak Dale Derbys 185 F9
Peak Forest
Derbys 185 F10
Peak Hill Lincs 156 F5
Peakirk Pboro 138 B3
Pean Hill Kent 70 G6
Pear Ash Som 45 G9
Pearsie Angus 287 B7
Pearson's Green Kent 53 E7
Peartree Herts 86 C2
Pear Tree Derby 153 C7
Peartree Green
Essex 87 F9
Hereford 97 E11
Soton 32 E6
Sur 50 F3
Peas Acre W Yorks 205 E8
Peasedown St John
Bath 45 B8
Peasehill Derbys 170 F6
Peaseland Green
Norf 159 F11
Peasemore W Berks 64 D3
Peasenhall Suff 127 D7
Pease Pottage
W Sus 51 G9
Peas Hill Cambs 139 D8
Peaslake Sur 50 E5
Peasley Cross Mers 183 C8
Peasmarsh E Sus 38 C5
Som 28 E4
Sur 50 D3
Peaston E Loth 271 B8
Peastonbank E Loth 271 B8
Peathill Aberds 303 C9
Peat Inn Fife 287 G8
Peatling Magna
Leics 135 E11
Peatling Parva
Leics 135 F11
Peaton Shrops 131 G10
Peatonstrand
Shrops 131 G10
Peats Corner Suff 126 E3
Pebmarsh Essex 107 E7
Pebsham E Sus 38 F3
Pebworth Worcs 100 B2
Pecket Well
W Yorks 196 B3
Peckforton Ches E 167 D8
Peckham London 67 D10
Peckham Bush Kent 53 D7
Peckingell Wilts 62 E2
Pecking Mill Som 44 F6
Peckleton Leics 135 C9
Pedair-ffordd
Powys 148 E2
Pedham Norf 160 G6
Pedlars End Essex 87 D8
Pedlar's Rest
Shrops 131 G9
Pedlinge Kent 54 F6
Pedmore W Mid 133 G8
Pednor Bottom
Bucks 84 E6
Pednormead End
Bucks 85 E7
Pedwell Som 44 F2
Peebles Borders 270 G5
Peel Borders 261 B10
IoM 192 D3
Lancs 202 G3
Peel Common Hants 33 G9
Peel Green Gtr Man 184 B2
Peel Hall Gtr Man 184 D4
Peel Hill Lancs 202 G3
Peel Park S Lnrk 268 E2
Peene Kent 55 F7
Peening Quarter
Kent 38 B5
Peggs Green Leics 153 F8
Pegsdon C Beds 104 E2
Pegswood Northumb 252 F6
Pegwell Kent 71 G11
Peinaha Highld 298 D4
Peinchorran Highld 295 B7
Peingown Highld 298 B4
Peinlich Highld 298 D4
Peinmore Highld 298 E4
Pelaw T&W 243 E7
Pelcomb Pembs 72 B6
Pelcomb Bridge
Pembs 72 B6
Pelcomb Cross
Pembs 72 B6
Peldon Essex 89 B7
Pelhamfield IoW 21 C7
Pell Green E Sus 52 G6
Pellon W Yorks 196 B5
Pelsall W Mid 133 C10
Pelsall Wood
W Mid 133 C10
Pelton Durham 243 G7
Pelton Fell Durham 243 G7
Pelutho Cumb 229 B8
Pelynt Corn 6 D4
Pemberton Carms 75 E8
Gtr Man 194 G5
Pembles Cross Kent 53 D11
Pembre / Pembrey
Carms 74 E6
Pembrey / Pembre
Carms 74 E6
Pembridge Hereford 115 F7
Pembroke Pembs 73 E7
Pembroke Dock / Doc
Penfro Pembs 73 E7
Pembroke Ferry
Pembs 73 E7
Pembury Kent 52 E6
Pempwell Corn 12 F3
Penallt Mon 79 C8
Pen-allt Hereford 97 F11
Penally / Penalun
Pembs 73 F10
Penalt Hereford 97 F11
Penalun / Penally
Pembs 73 F10
Penare Corn 5 G9
Penarlâg / Hawarden
Flint 166 B4
Penarron Powys 130 F2
Penarth V Glam 59 E7
Penarth Moors
Cardiff 59 E7
Penbeagle Corn 2 B2
Penbedw Flint 165 B11
Pen-bedw Pembs 92 D4
Penberth Corn 1 E4
Penbidwal Mon 96 G6
Penbodlas Gwyn 144 C5
Pen-bont Rhydybeddau
Ceredig 128 G3
Penboyr Carms 93 D7
Penbryn Ceredig 110 G5
Pencader Carms 93 D8
Pencaenewydd
Gwyn 162 G6
Pencaerau Neath 57 B8
Pen-caer-fenny
Swansea 56 B4
Pencaitland E Loth 271 B8
Pencarnisiog
Anglesey 178 G5
Pencarreg Carms 93 B10
Pencarrow Corn 11 E8
Penceiliogi Carms 75 E8
Pencelli Powys 95 F11
Pen-clawdd Swansea 56 B4
Pencoed Bridgend 58 C3
Pencombe
Hereford 115 G11
Pen-common Powys 76 D6
Pencoyd Hereford 97 F10
Pencoys Corn 2 B5
Pencraig Anglesey 179 F7
Hereford 97 G11
Powys 147 D10
Pencroesoped Mon 78 D4
Pencuke Corn 11 C9
Pendas Fields
W Yorks 206 F3
Pendeen Corn 1 C3
Pendeford W Mid 133 C7
Penderyn Rhondda 77 D7
Pendine / Pentwyn
Carms 74 D2
Pendlebury
Gtr Man 195 G9
Pendleton Gtr Man 184 B4
Lancs 203 F11
Pendock Worcs 98 E5
Pendoggett Corn 10 F6
Pendomer Som 29 E8
Pendoylan V Glam 58 D5
Pendre Bridgend 58 C2
Gwyn 110 C2
Powys 95 F10
Pendrift Corn 11 G8
Penegoes Powys 128 C5
Penelewey Corn 4 G6
Penenden Heath
Kent 53 B9
Penffordd Pembs 91 G11
Penffordd Lâs /
Staylittle Powys 129 E7
Pengam Caerph 77 F11
Penge London 67 E11
Pengegon Corn 2 B5
Pengelly Corn 11 E7
Pengenffordd Powys 96 E3
Pengersick Corn 2 D3
Pen-gilfach Gwyn 163 C9
Pengold Corn 11 C8
Pengorffwysfa
Anglesey 179 C7
Pengover Green Corn 6 B5
Pen-groes-oped
Mon 78 D4
Penguithal Hereford 97 G10
Pengwern Denb 181 F8
Penhale Corn 2 F5
Corn 5 D8
Penhale Jakes Corn 2 D4
Penhallick Corn 3 F7
Corn 4 G3
Penhallow Corn 4 E5
Penhalurick Corn 2 B6
Penhalvean Corn 2 B6
Penhelig Gwyn 128 D2
Penhill Devon 40 G4
Swindon 63 B7
Penhow Newport 78 G6
Penhurst E Sus 23 B11
Peniarth Gwyn 128 B2
Penicuik Midloth 270 C4
Peniel Carms 93 G8
Denb 165 C8
Penifiler Highld 298 E4
Peninver Argyll 255 E8
Penisa'r Waun
Gwyn 163 C9
Penistone S Yorks 197 G8
Penjerrick Corn 3 C7
Penketh Warr 183 D9
Penkhull Stoke 168 G5
Penkill S Ayrs 244 D6
Penknap Wilts 45 D11
Penkridge Staffs 151 G8
Pen-Lan Swansea 56 B6
Pen-Lan-mabws
Pembs 91 F7
Penleigh Wilts 45 C11
Penley Wrex 149 B8
Penllech Gwyn 144 C4
Penllergaer Swansea 56 B6
Penllwyn Caerph 77 F11
Ceredig 128 G3
Penllyn V Glam 58 D3
Pen-llyn Anglesey 178 E4
Pen-lon Anglesey 162 B6
Penmachno Conwy 164 E3
Penmaen Caerph 77 F11
Swansea 56 D4

Penmaenan Conwy 180 F2
Penmaenmawr
Conwy 180 F2
Penmaenpool Gwyn 146 F3
Penmaen Rhôs
Conwy 180 F5
Penmark V Glam 58 F5
Penmarth Corn 2 B6
Penmayne Corn 10 F4
Pen Mill Som 29 D9
Penmon Anglesey 179 E10
Penmore Mill Argyll 288 D6
Penmorfa Ceredig 110 G6
Gwyn 163 G8
Penmynydd
Anglesey 179 G8
Penn Bucks 84 G6
W Mid 133 D7
Pennal Gwyn 128 C4
Pennan Aberds 303 C8
Pennance Corn 4 G4
Pennant Ceredig 111 E10
Conwy 164 D5
Denb 147 C10
Denb 165 E8
Powys 129 D7
Pennant Melangell
Powys 147 D10
Pennar Pembs 73 E7
Pennard Swansea 56 D5
Pennar Park Pembs 72 E6
Penn Bottom Bucks 84 G6
Pennerley Shrops 131 D7
Pennington Cumb 210 D5
Gtr Man 183 B11
Hants 20 C2
Pennington Green
Gtr Man 194 F6
Pennorth Powys 96 F2
Penn Street Bucks 84 F6
Pennsylvania Devon 14 C4
S Glos 61 E8
Penny Bridge Cumb 210 C6
Pennycross Argyll 289 G7
Plym 7 D9
Pennygate Norf 160 E6
Pennygown Argyll 289 E7
Penny Green Derbys 187 F8
Penny Hill Lincs 157 D7
W Yorks 196 D5
Pennylands Lancs 194 F3
Pennymoor Devon 26 E5
Pennypot Kent 55 G7
Penny's Green Norf 142 D3
Pennytinney Corn 10 F6
Pennywell T&W 243 F9
Pen-onn V Glam 58 F5
Penparc Ceredig 92 B4
Pembs 91 E7
Penparcau Ceredig 111 B11
Penpedairheol
Caerph 77 F10
Mon 78 E4
Penpergym Mon 78 C4
Penperlleni Mon 78 E4
Penpethy Corn 11 D7
Penpillick Corn 5 D11
Penplas Carms 74 B5
Penpol Corn 3 B8
Penpoll Corn 6 E2
Penponds Corn 2 B4
Penpont Corn 11 G7
Dumfries 247 E8
Powys 95 F9
Penprysg Bridgend 58 C3
Penquit Devon 8 E2
Penrallt Gwyn 145 B7
Powys 129 F9
Penrherber Carms 92 D5
Penrhiw Caerph 78 G2
Penrhiwceiber
Rhondda 77 F8
Pen-Rhiw-fawr
Neath 76 C2
Penrhiwgarreg
Bl Gwent 78 E2
Penrhiw-llan Ceredig 93 C7
Penrhiw-pal Ceredig 92 B6
Penrhiwtyn Neath 57 B8
Penrhos Anglesey 178 E3
Gwyn 144 C6
Hereford 114 F6
Penrhôs Mon 78 C6
Penrhos Mon 78 C6
Powys 76 C3
Pen-rhos Wrex 166 E3
Penrhosfeilw
Anglesey 178 E2
Penrhos-garnedd
Gwyn 179 G9
Penrhyd Lastra
Anglesey 178 C6
Penrhyn Bay / Bae-Penrhyn Conwy 180 E4
Penrhyn Castle
Pembs 92 B2
Penrhyn-coch
Ceredig 128 G2
Penrhyndeudraeth
Gwyn 146 B2
Penrhynside Conwy 180 E4
Penrhyn side Conwy 180 E4
Penrhys Rhondda 77 F8
Penrice Swansea 56 D3
Penrith Cumb 230 E6
Penrose Corn 10 G3
Corn 11 F7
Penrose Hill Corn 2 D4
Penruddock Cumb 230 F4
Penryn Corn 3 C7
Pensarn Carms 74 B6
Conwy 181 F7
Pen-sarn Gwyn 145 D11
Gwyn 162 G6
Pensax Worcs 116 D4
Pensby Mers 182 E3
Penselwood Som 45 G9
Pensford Bath 60 G6
Pensham Worcs 99 C8
Penshaw T&W 243 G8
Penshurst Kent 52 E4
Pensilva Corn 6 B5
Pensnett W Mid 133 F8
Penston E Loth 281 G8
Penstone Devon 26 G3
Penstraze Corn 4 F5
Pentewan Corn 5 F10
Pentiken Shrops 130 G4
Pentir Gwyn 163 B9
Pentire Corn 4 C5
Pentirvin Shrops 130 C6
Pentlepoir Pembs 73 D10
Pentlow Essex 106 B6
Pentlow Street
Essex 106 B6
Pentney Norf 158 G4
Penton Corner
Hants 47 D10
Penton Grafton
Hants 47 D10
Penton Mewsey
Hants 47 D10
Pentonville London 67 C10
Pentowin Carms 74 B3
Pentraeth Anglesey 179 F8
Pentrapeod Caerph 77 E11
Pentre Carms 75 C8
Denb 165 D10
Flint 165 C11
Flint 166 B4
Flint 166 C2
Flint 166 D2
Powys 129 F11
Powys 130 B4
Powys 130 E5
Powys 147 D11
Powys 148 G3
Rhondda 77 F7
Shrops 148 D4
Shrops 149 F7
Wrex 148 B2
Wrex 166 G3
Pentrebach Carms 94 E6
M Tydf 77 E9
Rhondda 58 B5
Swansea 75 D10
Pentre-bâch
Ceredig 93 B11
Pentre-bach Powys 95 E8
Pentrebane Cardiff 58 D6
Pentrebeirdd
Powys 148 G3
Pentre Berw
Anglesey 179 G7
Pentre-bont Conwy 164 E2
Pentre Broughton
Wrex 166 E4
Pentre Bychan
Wrex 166 F4
Pentrecagal Carms 92 C6
Pentre-cefn Shrops 148 D4
Pentre-celyn Denb 165 E11
Powys 129 B7
Pentre-chwyth
Swansea 57 B7
Pentre Cilgwyn
Wrex 148 B4
Pentre-clawdd
Shrops 148 C5
Pentre-coed Shrops 149 B7
Pentre-cwrt Carms 93 D7
Pentre Dolau-Honddu
Powys 95 C9
Pentredwr Denb 165 F11
Pentre-dwr Swansea 57 B7
Pentrefelin
Anglesey 178 C6
Carms 93 G11
Ceredig 94 B2
Conwy 180 G4
Denb 166 G2
Gwyn 145 B10
Pentre-Ffwrndan
Flint 182 G3
Pentrefoelas Conwy 164 E5
Pentref-y-groes
Caerph 77 F11
Pentre-galar Pembs 92 E3
Pentregat Ceredig 111 G7
Pentre-Gwenlais
Carms 75 B10
Pentre Gwynfryn
Gwyn 145 D11
Pentre Halkyn Flint 182 G2
Pentreheyling
Shrops 130 E4
Pentre Hodre
Shrops 114 B6
Pentre Isaf Conwy 164 B5
Pentre Llanrhaeadr
Denb 165 C9
Pentre Llifior
Powys 130 D2
Pentrellwyn Ceredig 93 C8
Pentre-llwyn-llwyd
Powys 113 G9
Pentre-llyn Ceredig 112 C2
Pentre-llyn cymmer
Conwy 165 E7
Pentre Maelor Wrex 166 F5
Pentre Meyrick
V Glam 58 D3
Pentre-newydd
Shrops 148 B5
Pentre-Piod Torf 78 E3
Pentre-Poeth Carms 75 E8
Newport 59 B9
Pentre'r beirdd
Powys 148 G3
Pentre'r Felin
Conwy 164 B4
Pentre'r-felin
Denb 165 B10
Powys 95 E8
Pentre-rhew
Ceredig 112 G3
Pentre-tafarn-y-fedw
Conwy 164 C4
Pentre-ty-gwyn
Carms 94 D6
Pentreuchaf Gwyn 145 B7
Pentre-uchaf
Conwy 180 F5
Pentrich Derbys 170 E5
Pentridge Dorset 31 D8
Pentrisil Pembs 91 E11
Pentwyn Caerph 77 E10
Cardiff 59 C8
Pen-twyn Caerph 78 E2
Carms 75 C9
Mon 79 D8
Torf 78 E3
Pentwyn Berthlwyd
Caerph 77 F10
Pentwyn-mawr
Caerph 77 F11
Pentwyn / Pendine
Carms 74 D2
Pentyrch Cardiff 58 C6
Penuchadre V Glam 57 G11
Pen-Uchar Plwyf
Flint 181 G11
Penuwch Ceredig 111 E11
Penwartha Corn 4 E5
Penwartha Coombe
Corn 4 E5
Penweathers Corn 4 G6
Penwithick Corn 5 D10
Penwood Hants 64 G2
Penwortham Lane
Lancs 194 B4
Penwyllt Powys 76 B5
Pen-y-Ball Top
Flint 181 F11
Penybanc Carms 75 C10
Pen-y-banc Carms 93 G8
Carms 94 G2
Pen-y-bank Caerph 77 E10
Penybedd Carms 74 E6
Penybont Ceredig 128 F2
Powys 114 E2
Pen-y-Bont
Bl Gwent 78 D2
Carms 92 G6
Gwyn 128 C4
Gwyn 146 D2
Powys 148 E4
Pen y Bont ar ogwr / Bridgend Bridgend 58 C2
Penybontfawr
Powys 147 E11
Penybryn Caerph 77 F10
Pen-y-Bryn Gwyn 145 B9
Gwyn 146 F3
Pembs 92 C3
Powys 130 C3
Shrops 148 B6
Wrex 166 G3
Penycae Wrex 166 F3
Pen-y-cae Bridgend 58 C2
Neath 57 D9
Powys 76 C4
Pen-y-cae-mawr
Mon 78 F6
Penycaerau Gwyn 144 D3
Pen-y-cefn Flint 181 F10
Pen-y-clawdd Mon 79 D7
Pen-y-coed Shrops 148 E5
Pen-y-coedcae
Rhondda 58 B5
Penycwm Pembs 90 G6
Pen-y-Darren
M Tydf 77 D9
Penydre Swansea 75 E11
Pen-y-fai Bridgend 57 E11
Pen-y-fan Carms 56 B4
Mon 79 D8
Penyfeidr Pembs 91 F7
Pen-y-felin Flint 165 B11
Penyffordd Flint 166 C4
Pen-y-ffordd Denb 181 F8
Flint 181 E10
Penyffridd Gwyn 163 D8
Pen y Foel Shrops 148 E5
Penygarn Torf 78 E3
Pen-y-garn Carms 93 E11
Ceredig 128 F2
Penygarnedd Powys 148 E2
Pen-y-garnedd
Anglesey 179 F8
Penygelli Powys 130 E2
Pen-y-gop Conwy 164 G6
Penygraig Rhondda 77 G7
Pen-y-graig Gwyn 144 C3
Penygraigwen
Anglesey 178 D6
Penygroes Gwyn 163 E7
Pembs 92 D3
Pen-y-groes Carms 75 C9
Pen-y-groeslon
Gwyn 144 C4
Pen-y-Gwryd Hotel
Gwyn 163 D11
Pen-y-lan Cardiff 59 D7
Newport 59 B9
V Glam 58 D3
Pen-y-maes Flint 181 F11
Pen-y-Myndd Carms 75 E7
Penymynydd Flint 166 C4
Pen-y-Park Hereford 96 C5
Penyraber Pembs 91 D9
Pen-yr-englyn
Rhondda 76 F6
Penyrheol Caerph 58 B6
Swansea 56 B5
Torf 78 F3
Pen-yr-heol
Bridgend 58 C2
Mon 78 C6
Pen-yr-Heolgerrig
M Tydf 77 D8
Pen-y-rhiw Rhondda 58 B5
Penysarn Anglesey 179 C7
Pen-y-stryt Denb 165 E11
Penywaun Rhondda 77 E7
Pen-y-wern Shrops 114 B6
Penzance Corn 1 C5
Peopleton Worcs 117 G8
Peover Heath
Ches E 184 G3
Peper Harow Sur 50 E2
Peppercombe Devon 24 C5
Pepper Hill Som 43 F7
W Yorks 196 B6
Peppermoor
Northumb 264 F6
Pepper's Green
Essex 87 C10
Pepperstock C Beds 85 B9
Perceton N Ayrs 267 G7
Percie Aberds 293 D7
Percuil Corn 3 C9
Percyhorner Aberds 303 C9
Percy Main T&W 243 D8
Per-ffordd-llan
Flint 181 F10
Perham Down Wilts 47 D9
Periton Som 42 D3
Perivale London 67 C7
Perkhill Aberds 293 C7
Perkinsville Durham 243 G7
Perlethorpe Notts 187 G11
Perranarworthal Corn 3 B7
Perrancoombe Corn 4 E5
Perran Downs Corn 2 C3
Perranporth Corn 4 E5
Perranuthnoe Corn 2 D2
Perranwell Corn 3 B7
Corn 4 E5
Perranwell Station
Corn 3 B7
Perran Wharf Corn 3 B7
Perranzabuloe Corn 4 E5
Perrott's Brook Glos 81 D8
Perry Devon 26 F5
Kent 55 B9
W Mid 133 E11
Perry Barr W Mid 133 E11
Perry Beeches
W Mid 133 E11
Perry Common
W Mid 133 E11
Perry Crofts Staffs 134 C4
Perryfields Worcs 117 C8
Perryfoot Derbys 185 E10
Perry Green Essex 106 G6
Herts 86 B6
Som 43 F9
Wilts 62 B3
Perrymead Bath 61 G9
Perrystone Hill
Hereford 98 F2
Perry Street Kent 68 E6
Som 28 F4
Perrywood Kent 54 B4
Pershall Staffs 150 C6
Pershore Worcs 99 B8
Pert Angus 293 G8
Pertenhall Beds 121 D11
Perth Perth 286 E5
Perthcelyn Rhondda 77 F9
Perthy Shrops 149 C7
Perton Hereford 97 C11
Staffs 133 D7
Pertwood Wilts 45 F11
Pested Kent 54 C4
Peterborough
Pboro 138 D3
Peterburn Highld 307 L2
Peterchurch
Hereford 96 D6
Peterculter
Aberdeen 293 C10
Peterhead Aberds 303 E11
Peterlee Durham 234 C4
Petersburn N Lnrk 268 C5
Petersfield Hants 34 C2
Peter's Finger Devon 12 D3
Peter's Green Herts 85 B10
Petersham London 67 E7
Peters Marland
Devon 25 E7
Peterstone Wentlooge
Newport 59 C9
Peterston-super-Ely
V Glam 58 D5
Peterstow Hereford 97 G11
Peter Tavy Devon 12 F6
Petertown Orkney 314 F3
Peterville Corn 4 E4
Petham Kent 54 C6
Petherwin Gate
Corn 11 D11
Petrockstow Devon 25 F8
Petsoe End
M Keynes 103 B7
Pett E Sus 38 E5
Pettaugh Suff 126 F3
Pett Bottom Kent 54 E6
Kent 55 C7
Petteridge Kent 53 E7
Pettinain S Lnrk 269 G9
Pettings Kent 68 G6
Pettistree Suff 126 G5
Pett Level E Sus 38 E5
Petton Devon 27 C8
Shrops 149 D8
Petts Wood London 68 F2
Petty Aberds 303 F7
Pettycur Fife 280 D5
Petty France S Glos 61 B9
Pettymuick Aberds 303 G9
Pettywell Norf 159 E11
Petworth W Sus 35 C7
Pevensey E Sus 23 E10
Pevensey Bay E Sus 23 E11
Peverell Plym 7 D9
Pewsey Wilts 63 G7
Pewsey Wharf Wilts 63 G7
Pewterspear Warr 183 E10
Phantassie E Loth 281 F11
Pharisee Green
Essex 106 G2
Pheasants Bucks 65 B9
Pheasant's Hill Bucks 65 B9
Pheasey W Mid 133 D11
Pheonix Green Hants 49 B9
Phepson Worcs 117 F8
Philadelphia T&W 243 G8
Philham Devon 24 C3
Philiphaugh
Borders 261 D10
Phillack Corn 2 B3
Philleigh Corn 3 B9
Phillip's Town
Caerph 77 E10
Philpot End Essex 87 B10
Philpstoun W Loth 279 F10
Phocle Green
Hereford 98 F2
Phoenix Green Hants 49 B9
Phoenix Row
Durham 233 F9
Phorp Moray 301 D10
Pibsbury Som 28 B6
Pibwrlwyd Carms 74 B6
Pica Cumb 228 G6
Piccadilly S Yorks 187 B7
Warks 134 D4
Piccadilly Corner
Norf 142 F5
Piccotts End Herts 85 D9
Pickburn S Yorks 198 F4
Picken End Worcs 98 C6
Pickering N Yorks 216 C5
Pickering Nook
Durham 242 F5
Picket Hill Hants 31 F11
Picket Piece Hants 47 D11
Picket Post Hants 31 F11
Pickford W Mid 134 G5
Pickford Green
W Mid 134 G5
Pickhill N Yorks 214 C6
Picklenash Glos 98 F4
Picklescott Shrops 131 D8
Pickles Hill W Yorks 204 F6
Pickletillem Fife 287 E8
Pickley Green
Gtr Man 195 G7
Pickmere Ches E 183 F11
Pickney Som 27 B11
Pickstock Telford 150 E4
Pickup Bank
Blkburn 195 C8
Pickwell Devon 40 E3
Leics 154 G5
Pickwick Wilts 61 E11
Pickwood Scar
W Yorks 196 C5
Pickworth Lincs 155 C10
Rutland 155 G9
Picton Ches W 182 G6
Flint 181 E10
N Yorks 225 D8
Pict's Hill Som 28 B6
Piddinghoe E Sus 36 G6
Piddington Bucks 84 G4
Northants 120 G6
Oxon 83 B10
Piddlehinton Dorset 17 B10
Piddletrenthide
Dorset 17 B10
Pidley Cambs 122 B6
Pidney Dorset 30 F2
Piece Corn 2 B5
Piercebridge Darl 224 B4
Piercing Hill Essex 86 F6
Pierowall Orkney 314 B4
Piff's Elm Glos 99 F8
Pigdon Northumb 252 F5
Pightley Som 43 F8
Pig Oak Dorset 31 G8
Pigstye Green
Essex 87 D10
Pike End W Yorks 196 D4
Pikehall Derbys 169 D11
Pike Hill Lancs 204 G3
Pike Law W Yorks 196 D4
Pikeshill Hants 32 F3
Pikestye Hereford 97 B10
Pilford Dorset 31 G8
Pilgrims Hatch Essex 87 F9
Pilham Lincs 188 C5
Pilhough Derbys 170 C3
Pill N Som 60 D4
Pembs 72 D6
Pillaton Corn 7 C7
Staffs 151 G8
Pillerton Hersey
Warks 100 B6
Pillerton Priors
Warks 100 B5
Pilleth Powys 114 D5
Pilley Glos 81 B7
Hants 20 B2
S Yorks 197 G10
Pilley Bailey Hants 20 B2
Pillgwenlly Newport 59 B10
Pilling Lancs 202 D4
Pilling Lane Lancs 202 D3
Pillmouth Devon 25 C7
Pillowell Glos 79 D10
Pillows Green Glos 98 F5
Pillwell Dorset 30 D3
Pilmuir Borders 261 G11
Pilning S Glos 60 B5
Pilrig Edin 280 F5
Pilsbury Derbys 169 C10
Pilsdon Dorset 16 B4
Pilsgate Pboro 137 B11
Pilsley Derbys 170 C6
Derbys 186 G2
Pilsley Green
Derbys 170 C6
Pilson Green Norf 161 G7
Piltdown E Sus 36 C6
Pilton Devon 40 G5
Edin 280 F4
Northants 137 G10
Rutland 137 C8
Som 44 E5
Pilton Green
Swansea 56 D2
Piltown Som 44 F5
Pimhole Gtr Man 195 E10
Pimlico Herts 85 D9
Lancs 203 E10
London 67 D9
Northants 102 C2
Pimperne Dorset 29 F9
Dorset 30 F6
Pinchbeck Lincs 156 D4
Pinchbeck Bars
Lincs 156 D3
Pinchbeck West
Lincs 156 E4
Pincheon Green
S Yorks 199 D7
Pinckney Green
Wilts 61 G10
Pincock Lancs 194 D5
Pineham Kent 55 D10
M Keynes 103 C7
Pinehurst Swindon 63 B7
Pinfarthings Glos 80 E5
Pinfold Lancs 193 E11
Pinfold Hill S Yorks 197 G9
Pinfoldpond C Beds 103 E8
Pinford End Suff 124 F6
Pinged Carms 74 E6
Pingewood W Berks 65 F7
Pin Green Herts 104 F4
Pinhoe Devon 14 C5
Pinkett's Booth
W Mid 134 G5
Pink Green Worcs 117 D11
Pinkie Braes E Loth 281 G7
Pinkney Wilts 61 B11
Pinkneys Green
Windsor 65 C11
Pinksmoor Som 27 D10
Pinley W Mid 119 B7
Pinley Green Warks 118 D4
Pin Mill Suff 108 D4
Pinminnoch
Dumfries 236 D2
S Ayrs 244 E5
Pinmore S Ayrs 244 E6
Pinmore Mains
S Ayrs 244 E6
Pinnacles Essex 86 D6
Pinner London 66 B6
Pinner Green
London 85 G10
Pinnerwood Park
London 85 G10
Pin's Green Worcs 98 B6
Pinsley Green
Ches E 167 F9
Pinstones Shrops 131 F9
Pinvin Worcs 99 B9
Pinwall Leics 134 C6
Pinwherry S Ayrs 244 F5
Pinxton Derbys 171 E7
Pipe and Lyde
Hereford 97 C10
Pipe Aston Hereford 115 C9
Pipe Gate Shrops 168 G2
Pipehill Staffs 133 B11
Pipehouse Bath 45 B9
Piperhall Argyll 266 D2
Piperhill Highld 301 D8
Pipe Ridware
Staffs 151 F11
Piper's Ash Ches W 166 B6
Piper's End Worcs 98 E6
Piper's Hill Worcs 117 D9
Piper's Pool Corn 11 E11
Pipewell Northants 136 F6
Pippacott Devon 40 F4
Pippin Street Lancs 194 C5
Pipps Hill Essex 69 B7
Pipsden Kent 53 G9
Pipton Powys 96 D3
Pirbright Sur 50 B2
Pirbright Camp Sur 50 B2
Pirnmill N Ayrs 255 C9
Pirton Herts 104 E2
Worcs 99 B7
Pisgah Ceredig 112 B3
Stirl 285 G11
Pishill Oxon 65 B8
Pishill Bank Oxon 84 G2
Pismire Hill S Yorks 186 C5
Pistyll Gwyn 162 G4
Pit Mon 78 D5
Pitagowan Perth 291 G10
Pitblae Aberds 303 C9
Pitcairngreen Perth 286 E4
Pitcalnie Highld 301 B8
Pitcaple Aberds 303 G7
Pitchcombe Glos 80 D5
Pitchcott Bucks 102 G5
Pitcher's Green Suff 125 F8
Pitchford Shrops 131 C10
Pitch Green Bucks 84 E3
Pitch Place Sur 49 F11
Sur 50 C3
Pitcombe Som 45 G7
Pitcorthie Fife 280 D2
Fife 287 G9
Pitcot Som 45 D7
V Glam 57 G11
Pitcox E Loth 282 F2
Pitcur Perth 286 D6
Pitfancy Aberds 302 E5
Pitfichie Aberds 293 B8
Pitforthie Aberds 293 F10
Pitgair Aberds 303 D7
Pitgrudy Highld 309 K7
Pithmaduthy Highld 301 B7
Pitkennedy Angus 287 B9
Pitkevy Fife 286 G6
Pitkierie Fife 287 G9
Pitlessie Fife 287 G7
Pitlochry Perth 286 B3
Pitmachie Aberds 302 G6
Pitmain Highld 291 C9
Pitmedden Aberds 303 G8
Pitminster Som 28 D2
Pitmuies Angus 287 C9
Pitmunie Aberds 293 B8
Pitney Som 29 B7
Pitrocknie Perth 286 C6
Pitscottie Fife 287 F8
Pitsea Essex 69 B8
Pitses Gtr Man 196 G2
Pitsford Northants 120 D5
Pitsford Hill Som 42 G6
Pitsmoor S Yorks 186 D5
Pitstone Bucks 84 B6
Pitstone Green Bucks 84 B6
Pitstone Hill Bucks 85 C7
Pitt Hants 33 B7
Pittachar Perth 286 E2
Pitt Court Glos 80 F3
Pittendreich
Moray 301 C11
Pittentrail Highld 309 J7
Pittenweem Fife 287 G9
Pitteuchar Fife 280 B5
Pittington Durham 234 C2
Pittodrie Aberds 302 G6
Pitton Swansea 56 D2
Wilts 47 G8
Pitts Hill Stoke 168 E5
Pittswood Kent 52 D6
Pittulie Aberds 303 C9
Pittville Glos 99 G9
Pityme Corn 10 F5
Pity Me Durham 233 B11
Pityoulish Highld 291 B11
Pixey Green Suff 126 B4
Pixham Sur 51 C7
Worcs 98 B6
Pixley Hereford 98 D3
Shrops 150 D3
Pizien Well Kent 53 C7
Place Newton
N Yorks 217 E7
Plaidy Aberds 303 D7
Corn 6 E5
Plain-an-Gwarry Corn 4 G3
Plain Dealings Pembs 73 B9
Plains N Lnrk 268 B5
Plainsfield Som 43 F7
Plain Spot Notts 171 E7
Plain Street Corn 10 F5
Plaish Shrops 131 D10
Plaistow Bromley 68 E2
Newham 68 C2
W Sus 50 G4
Plaistow Green
Essex 106 F6
Plaitford Wilts 32 D3
Plaitford Green
Hants 32 C3
Plank Lane Gtr Man 194 G6
Plans Dumfries 238 D3
Plantation Bridge
Cumb 221 F9
Plantationfoot
Dumfries 248 E4
Plardiwick Staffs 150 E6
Plasau Shrops 149 E7
Plâs Berwyn Denb 165 G11
Plas-canol Gwyn 145 F11
Plas Coch Wrex 166 E4
Plas Dinam Powys 129 F10
Plas Gogerddan
Ceredig 128 G2
Plashet London 68 C2
Plashett Carms 74 D3
Plasiolyn Powys 129 C11
Plas Llwyngwern
Powys 128 C5
Plas Meredydd
Powys 130 D3
Plas Nantyr Wrex 148 B3
Plasnewydd Powys 129 D9
Plaster's Green Bath 60 G4
Plastow Green Hants 64 G4
Plas-yn-Cefn Denb 181 G8
Platt Kent 52 B6
Platt Bridge
Gtr Man 194 G6
Platt Lane Shrops 149 B10
Platts Common
S Yorks 197 G11
Platt's Heath Kent 53 C11
Plawsworth
Durham 233 B11
Plaxtol Kent 52 C6
Playden E Sus 38 C6
Playford Suff 108 B4
Play Hatch Oxon 65 D8
Playing Place Corn 4 G6
Playley Green Glos 98 E5
Plealey Shrops 131 B8
Pleamore Cross
Som 27 D10
Plean Stirl 278 D6
Pleasant Valley
Pembs 73 D10
Pleasington Blkburn 194 B6
Pleasley Derbys 171 C8
Pleasleyhill Notts 171 C8
Pleck Dorset 30 D3
Dorset 30 E2
W Mid 133 D9
Pleckgate Blkburn 203 G9
Pleck or Little Ansty
Dorset 30 G3
Pledgdon Green
Essex 105 F11
Pledwick W Yorks 197 D10
Plemstall Ches W 183 G7
Plenmeller
Northumb 240 E6
Pleshey Essex 87 C11
Plockton Highld 295 B10
Plocrapol W Isles 305 J3
Plot Gate Som 44 G4
Plot Street Som 44 F5
Ploughfield Hereford 97 C7
Plough Hill Warks 134 E6
Plowden Shrops 131 F7
Ploxgreen Shrops 131 C7
Pluckley Kent 54 D2
Pluckley Thorne Kent 54 E2
Plucks Gutter Kent 71 G9
Plumbland Cumb 229 D9
Plumbley S Yorks 186 E6
Plumford Kent 54 B4
Plumley Ches E 184 F2
Plump Hill Glos 79 B11
Plumpton Cumb 230 D5
E Sus 36 E5
Northants 101 B11
Plumpton End
Northants 102 B4
Plumpton Foot
Cumb 230 D5
Plumpton Green
E Sus 36 D5
Plumpton Head
Cumb 230 E6
Plumstead London 68 D3
Norf 160 C2
Plumstead Common
London 68 D3
Plumstead Green
Norf 160 C2
Plumtree Notts 154 C2
Plumtree Green
Kent 53 D10
Plumtree Park
Notts 154 C2
Plungar Leics 154 C5
Plush Dorset 30 G2
Plusha Corn 11 E11
Plushabridge Corn 12 G2
Plusterwine Glos 79 F9
Plwmp Ceredig 111 G7
Plymouth Plym 7 E9
Plympton Plym 7 D10
Plymstock Plym 7 E10
Plymtree Devon 27 G9
Pobgreen Gtr Man 196 F4
Pochin Houses
Caerph 77 E11
Pocket Nook
Gtr Man 183 B10
Pockley N Yorks 216 B2
Pocklington
E Yorks 208 D2
Pockthorpe Norf 141 D8
Norf 158 D6
Norf 159 E10
Norf 159 F11
Pode Hole Lincs 156 E4
Podimore Som 29 C8
Podington Beds 121 E8
Podmoor Worcs 117 C8
Podmore Norf 159 G9
Staffs 150 B5
Podsmead Glos 80 B4
Poffley End Oxon 82 C5
Pogmoor S Yorks 197 F10
Point Corn 3 B8
Point Clear Essex 89 C9
Pointon Lincs 156 C2
Pokesdown Bmouth 19 C8
Pol a Charra
W Isles 297 K3
Polbae Dumfries 236 B4
Polbain Highld 307 H4
Polbathic Corn 7 D7
Polbeth W Loth 269 C10
Polborder Corn 7 C7
Polbrock Corn 5 B10
Polchar Highld 291 C10
Polebrook
Northants 137 F11
Pole Elm Worcs 98 B6
Polegate E Sus 23 D9
Pole Moor W Yorks 196 D5
Poles Highld 309 K7
Polesden Lacey Sur 50 C6
Poleshill Som 27 C9
Pole's Hole Wilts 45 C10
Polesworth Warks 134 C5
Polgear Corn 2 B5
Polgigga Corn 1 E3
Polglass Highld 307 J5
Polgooth Corn 5 E9
Poling W Sus 35 G8
Poling Corner W Sus 35 F8
Polkerris Corn 5 E11
Polla Highld 308 D3
Polladras Corn 2 C4
Pollard Street Norf 160 C6
Pollhill Kent 53 C11
Poll Hill Mers 182 E3
Pollie Highld 309 H7
Pollington E Yorks 198 D6
Polliwilline Argyll 255 G8
Polloch Highld 289 C9
Pollok Glasgow 267 C10
Pollokshields
Glasgow 267 C11
Polmadie Glasgow 267 C11
Polmarth Corn 2 B6
Polmassick Corn 5 F9
Polmear Corn 5 E11
Polmont Falk 279 F8
Polmorla Corn 10 G5
Polnessan E Ayrs 257 G10
Polnish Highld 295 G9
Polopit Northants 121 B10
Polpenwith Corn 2 D6
Polpeor Corn 2 B2
Polperro Corn 6 E4
Polruan Corn 6 E2
Polsham Som 44 E4
Polsloe Devon 14 C4
Polstead Suff 107 D9
Polstead Heath Suff 107 C9
Poltalloch Argyll 275 D9
Poltesco Corn 2 F6
Poltimore Devon 14 B5
Polton Midloth 270 C5
Polwarth Borders 272 E4
Polwheveral Corn 2 D6
Polyphant Corn 11 E11
Polzeath Corn 10 F4
Pomeroy Derbys 169 B10
Pomphlett Plym 7 E10
Ponciau Wrex 166 F3
Pond Close Som 27 B10
Ponde Powys 96 D2
Pondersbridge
Cambs 138 E5
Ponders End London 86 F5
Pond Park Bucks 85 E7
Pond Street Essex 105 D9
Pondtail Hants 49 C10
Pondwell IoW 21 C8
Poniou Corn 1 B4
Ponjeravah Corn 2 D6
Ponsanooth Corn 3 B7
Ponsford Devon 27 F8
Ponsonby Cumb 219 D11
Ponsongath Corn 3 F7
Ponsworthy Devon 13 G10
Pont Corn 6 E2
Pont Aber Carms 94 G4
Pont Aber-Geirw
Gwyn 146 D5
Pontamman Carms 75 C10
Pontantwn Carms 74 C6
Pontardawe Neath 76 E2
Pontarddulais
Swansea 75 E9
Pontarfynach / Devils Bridge Ceredig 112 B4
Pont-ar-gothi
Carms 93 G10
Pont ar Hydfer Powys 95 F7
Pont-ar-llechau
Carms 94 G4
Pontarsais Carms 93 F8
Pontblyddyn Flint 166 C3
Pontbren Araeth
Carms 94 G3
Pontbren Llwyd
Rhondda 76 D6
Pontcanna Cardiff 59 D7
Pont Cyfyng Conwy 164 D2
Pont Cysyllte Wrex 166 G3
Pontdolgoch
Powys 129 E10
Pont Dolydd Prysor
Gwyn 146 B4
Pontefract W Yorks 198 C3
Ponteland Northumb 242 C5
Ponterwyd Ceredig 128 G4
Pontesbury Shrops 131 B7
Pontesbury Hill
Shrops 131 B7
Pontesford Shrops 131 B7
Pontfadog Wrex 148 B4
Pontfaen Pembs 91 E10
Pont-faen Powys 95 E9
Shrops 148 B5
Pont Fronwydd
Gwyn 146 E6
Pont-gareg Pembs 92 C2
Pontgarreg Ceredig 110 G6
Ponthen Shrops 148 F6
Pont-Henri Carms 75 D7

406 Ros–San

Rose Corn 4 E5
Roseacre Kent 53 B9
Lancs 202 F4
Rose-an-Grouse Corn 2 B2
Rose Ash Devon 26 C3
Rosebank E Dunb 278 G3
S Lnrk 268 F6
Rosebery Midloth 270 D6
Rosebrae Moray 301 C11
Rosebrough
Northumb 264 D4
Rosebush Pembs 91 F11
Rosecare Corn 11 B9
Rosedale Herts 86 E4
Rosedale Abbey
N Yorks 226 F4
Roseden Northumb 264 E2
Rosedinnick Corn 5 B8
Rosedown Devon 24 C3
Rosefield Highld 301 D8
Rose Green Essex 107 F8
Suff 107 C9
Suff 107 D8
W Sus 22 D6
Rose Grove Lancs 204 G2
Rosehall Highld 309 J4
N Lnrk 268 C4
Rosehaugh Mains
Highld 300 D6
Rosehearty Aberds 303 C9
Rosehill Blkburn 195 C8
Corn 4 E5
Corn 5 C10
Gtr Man 184 D3
London 67 F9
Pembs 72 B5
Shrops 150 C3
T&W 243 D8
Rose Hill Bucks 66 C2
Derbys 153 B7
E Sus 23 B7
Gtr Man 195 F8
Lancs 204 G2
Oxon 83 E8
Suff 108 C3
Sur 51 D7
Roseisle Moray 301 C11
Roseland Corn 6 C5
Roselands E Sus 23 E10
Rosemarket Pembs 73 D7
Rosemarkie Highld 301 D7
Rosemary Lane
Devon 27 E11
Rosemelling Corn 5 D10
Rosemergy Corn 1 B4
Rosemount Perth 286 C5
Rosenannon Corn 5 B9
Rosenithon Corn 3 E8
Roser's Cross E Sus 37 C9
Rose Valley Pembs 73 E8
Rosevean Corn 5 D10
Rosevear Corn 2 E5
Roseville W Mid 133 E8
Rosevine Corn 3 B9
Rosewarne Corn 2 B4
Corn 4 G2
Rosewell Midloth 270 C5
Roseworth Stockton 234 G4
Roseworthy Corn 2 B4
Corn 4 F5
Roseworthy Barton
Corn 2 B4
Rosgill Cumb 221 B10
Rosherville Kent 68 E6
Roshven Highld 289 B9
Roskear Croft Corn 4 G3
Roskhill Highld 298 E2
Roskill House
Highld 300 D6
Roskorwell Corn 3 E7
Rosley Cumb 230 B2
Roslin Midloth 270 C5
Rosliston Derbys 152 F4
Rosneath Argyll 276 E5
Ross Borders 273 C9
Dumfries 237 E8
Northumb 264 B4
Perth 285 E11
Rossett Wrex 166 D5
Rossett Green
N Yorks 206 C2
Ross Green Worcs 116 E5
Rossie Ochill Perth 286 F4
Rossie Priory Perth 286 D6
Rossington
S Yorks 187 B10
Rosskeen Highld 300 C6
Rossland Renfs 277 G8
Rossmore Poole 19 C7
Ross-on-Wye
Hereford 98 G2
Roster Highld 310 F6
Rostherne Ches E 184 E2
Rostholme S Yorks 198 F5
Rosthwaite Cumb 220 C5
Cumb 220 G4
Roston Derbys 169 G10
Rosudgeon Corn 2 D3
Rosyth Fife 280 E2
Rotchfords Essex 107 E8
Rotcombe Bath 44 B6
Rothbury Northumb 252 C3
Rotherbridge W Sus 35 C7
Rotherby Leics 154 F3
Rotherfield E Sus 37 B9
Rotherfield Greys
Oxon 65 C8
Rotherfield Peppard
Oxon 65 C8
Rotherham S Yorks 186 C6
Rotherhithe London 67 D11
Rothersthorpe
Northants 120 F4
Rotherwas Hereford 97 D10
Rotherwick Hants 49 B8
Rothes Moray 302 E2
Rothesay Argyll 275 G11
Rothiebrisbane
Aberds 303 F7
Rothiemay Crossroads
Moray 302 E5
Rothiemurchus Lodge
Highld 291 C11
Rothienorman
Aberds 303 F7
Rothiesholm Orkney 314 D6
Rothley Leics 153 G11
Northumb 252 F2
Rothley Plain
Leics 153 G11
Rothley Shield East
Northumb 252 E2
Rothmaise Aberds 302 F6
Rothwell Lincs 189 B11
Northants 136 G6
W Yorks 197 B10
Rothwell Haigh
W Yorks 197 B10
Rotsea E Yorks 209 C7
Rottal Angus 292 G5
Rotten End Essex 106 F4
Suff 127 D7
Rotten Green Hants 49 B9
Rotten Row W Berks 64 E5
W Mid 118 B3
Rottingdean Brighton 36 G5
Rottington Cumb 219 C9
Rotton Park
W Mid 133 F10
Roud IoW 20 E6
Rougham Norf 158 E6
Suff 125 E8
Rougham Green
Suff 125 E8
Rough Bank
Gtr Man 196 E2
Roughbirchworth
S Yorks 197 G9
Roughburn Highld 290 E5
Rough Close Staffs 151 B8
Rough Common Kent 54 B6
Roughcote Staffs 168 G6
Rough Haugh
Highld 308 E7
Rough Hay Staffs 152 E4
Roughlee Lancs 204 E2
Roughley W Mid 134 D2
Roughmoor Som 28 B2
Swindon 62 B6
Roughrigg N Lnrk 278 G6
Roughsike Cumb 240 B2
Roughton Lincs 174 C2
Norf 160 B4
Shrops 132 E5
Roughton Moor
Lincs 174 C2
Roughway Kent 52 C6
Roundbush Essex 88 E5
Round Bush Herts 85 F10
Roundbush Green
Essex 87 C9
Round Green
Luton 103 G11
Roundham Som 28 F6
Roundhay W Yorks 206 F2
Round Maple Suff 107 C9
Round Oak Shrops 131 G7
W Mid 133 F8
Round's Green
W Mid 133 F9
Roundshaw London 67 G10
Round Spinney
Northants 120 D5
Roundstonefoot
Dumfries 248 B4
Round Street Kent 69 F7
Roundstreet Common
W Sus 35 B9
Roundswell Devon 40 G4
Roundthorn
Gtr Man 184 D4
Roundthwaite Cumb 222 E2
Roundway Wilts 62 G4
Roundyhill Angus 287 B7
Rousdon Devon 15 C11
Rousham Oxon 101 G9
Rous Lench Worcs 117 G10
Routenburn N Ayrs 266 C3
Routh E Yorks 209 E7
Rout's Green Bucks 84 F3
Row Corn 11 F7
Cumb 211 B8
Cumb 231 E8
Rowanburn
Dumfries 239 B10
Rowanfield Glos 99 G8
Rowardennan Stirl 277 B7
Rowarth Derbys 185 D8
Row Ash Hants 33 E8
Rowbarton Som 28 B2
Rowberrow Som 44 B3
Row Brow Cumb 229 D7
Rowde Wilts 62 G3
Rowden Devon 13 B8
N Yorks 205 B11
Rowe Head Cumb 210 D5
Rowen Conwy 180 G3
Rowfoot Northumb 240 E5
Rowford Som 28 B2
Row Green Essex 106 G4
Row Heath Essex 89 B10
Rowhedge Essex 107 G10
Rowhill Sur 66 G4
Rowhook W Sus 50 G6
Rowington Warks 118 D4
Rowington Green
Warks 118 D4
Rowland Derbys 186 G2
Rowlands Castle
Hants 34 E2
Rowlands Gill T&W 242 F5
Rowland's Green
Hereford 98 D3
Rowledge Sur 49 E10
Rowlestone Hereford 97 F7
Rowley E Yorks 208 G5
Shrops 130 B6
Rowley Green London 86 F2
Rowley Hill
W Yorks 197 E7
Rowley Park Staffs 151 E8
Rowley Regis
W Mid 133 F9
Rowley's Green
W Mid 134 G6
Rowling Kent 55 C9
Rowly Sur 50 E4
Rownall Staffs 169 F7
Rowner Hants 33 G9
Rowney Green
Worcs 117 C10
Rownhams Hants 32 D5
Row-of-trees
Ches E 184 F4
Rowrah Cumb 219 B11
Rowsham Bucks 84 B4
Rowsley Derbys 170 B3
Rowstock Oxon 64 B3
Rowston Lincs 173 D9
Rowthorne Derbys 171 C7
Rowton Ches W 166 C6
Shrops 149 G7
Telford 150 F2
Rowton Moor
Ches W 166 C6
Row Town Sur 66 G4
Roxburgh Borders 262 C5
Roxburgh Mains
Borders 262 D5
Roxby N Lincs 200 D2
N Yorks 226 B5
Roxeth London 66 B6
Roxton Beds 122 G3
Roxwell Essex 87 D10
Royal British Legion
Village Kent 53 B8
Royal Leamington Spa
Warks 118 D6
Royal Oak Darl 233 G10
Lancs 194 G2
N Yorks 218 D2
Royal's Green
Ches E 167 G10
Royal Tunbridge Wells /
Tunbridge Wells
Kent 52 F5
Royal Wootton Bassett
Wilts 62 C5
Roybridge Highld 290 E4
Royd S Yorks 197 G8
Roydhouse W Yorks 197 E8
Royd Moor S Yorks 197 G8
W Yorks 198 E2
Roydon Essex 86 D6
Norf 141 G11
Norf 158 E4
Roydon Hamlet
Essex 86 D6
Royds Green
W Yorks 197 B11
Royston Glasgow 268 B2
Herts 105 C7
S Yorks 197 E11
Royston Water Som 28 E2
Royton Gtr Man 196 F2
Ruabon / Rhiwabon
Wrex 166 G4
Ruaig Argyll 288 E2
Ruan High Lanes
Corn 3 B10
Ruan Lanihorne Corn 5 G7
Ruan Major Corn 2 F6
Ruan Minor Corn 2 F6
Ruarach Highld 295 C11
Ruardean Glos 79 B10
Ruardean Hill Glos 79 B10
Ruardean Woodside
Glos 79 B10
Rubery Worcs 117 B9
Rubha Ghaisinis
W Isles 297 G4
Rubha Stoer Highld 306 F5
Ruchazie Glasgow 268 B3
Ruchill Glasgow 267 B11
Ruckcroft Cumb 230 C6
Ruckhall Hereford 97 D9
Ruckinge Kent 54 G4
Ruckland Lincs 190 F4
Rucklers Lane Herts 85 E9
Ruckley Shrops 131 C10
Rudbaxton Pembs 91 G9
Rudby N Yorks 225 D9
Ruddington Notts 153 C11
Ruddle Glos 79 C11
Rudford Glos 98 G5
Rudge Shrops 132 D6
Som 45 C10
Rudge Heath
Shrops 132 D5
Rudgeway S Glos 60 B6
Rudgwick W Sus 50 G5
Rudhall Hereford 98 F2
Rudheath Ches W 183 G11
Rudheath Woods
Ches W 184 G2
Rudhja Garbh
Argyll 289 E11
Rudley Green Essex 88 E4
Rudloe Wilts 61 E10
Rudry Caerph 59 B7
Rudston E Yorks 217 F11
Rudyard Staffs 169 D7
Ruewood Shrops 149 D9
Rufford Lancs 194 D3
Rufforth York 206 C6
Ruffs Notts 171 F8
Rugby Warks 119 B10
Rugeley Staffs 151 F10
Ruggin Som 27 D11
Ruglen S Ayrs 245 C7
Rugley Northumb 264 G5
Ruilick Highld 300 E5
Ruishton Som 28 C3
Ruisigearraidh
W Isles 296 C5
Ruislip London 66 B5
Ruislip Common
London 66 B5
Ruislip Gardens
London 66 B5
Ruislip Manor London 66 B6
Ruiton W Mid 133 E8
Ruloe Ches W 183 G9
Rumach Highld 295 G8
Rumbling Bridge
Perth 279 B10
Rumbow Cottages
Worcs 117 B8
Rumburgh Suff 142 G6
Rumbush W Mid 118 B2
Rumer Hill Staffs 133 B9
Rumford Corn 10 G3
Falk 279 F8
Rumney Cardiff 59 D8
Rumsam Devon 40 G5
Rumwell Som 27 C11
Runcorn Halton 183 E8
Runcton W Sus 22 C5
Runcton Holme
Norf 140 B2
Rundlestone Devon 13 G7
Runfold Sur 49 D11
Runhall Norf 141 B11
Runham Norf 143 B10
Norf 161 G9
Runham Vauxhall
Norf 143 B10
Running Hill Head
Gtr Man 196 F4
Runnington Som 27 C10
Running Waters
Durham 234 C2
Runsell Green Essex 88 D3
Runshaw Moor
Lancs 194 D4
Runswick Bay
N Yorks 226 B6
Runwell Essex 88 G2
Ruscombe Glos 80 D4
Wokingham 65 D9
Ruscote Oxon 101 C8
Rushall Hereford 98 E2
Norf 142 G3
Wilts 46 B6
W Mid 133 C10
Rushbrooke Suff 125 E7
Rushbury Shrops 131 E10
Rushcombe Bottom
Poole 18 B5
Rushden Herts 104 E6
Northants 121 D9
Rushenden Kent 70 E2
Rusher's Cross
E Sus 37 B10
Rushey Mead
Leicester 136 B2
Rushford Devon 12 F4
Norf 141 G8
Rushgreen Warr 183 D11
Rush Green Essex 89 B11
Herts 86 C5
Herts 104 G4
London 68 B4
Norf 141 B11
Rush-head Aberds 303 E8
Rush Hill Bath 61 G8
Rushington Hants 32 E5
Rushlake Green
E Sus 23 B10
Rushland Cross
Cumb 210 B6
Rushley Green
Essex 106 D5
Rushmere C Beds 103 F8
Suff 143 F9
Rushmere St Andrew
Suff 108 B4
Rushmere Street
Suff 108 B4
Rushmoor Sur 49 E11
Telford 150 G2
Rushmore Hants 33 E11
Rushmore Hill
London 68 G3
Rushock Hereford 114 F6
Worcs 117 C7
Rusholme Gtr Man 184 B5
Rushton Ches W 167 C9
Dorset 18 D3
Northants 136 G6
N Yorks 217 C9
Shrops 132 B2
Rushton Spencer
Staffs 168 C6
Rushwick Worcs 116 G6
Rushyford Durham 233 F11
Rushy Green E Sus 23 C7
Ruskie Stirl 285 G10
Ruskington Lincs 173 E9
Rusland Cumb 210 B6
Rusling End Herts 104 G4
Rusper W Sus 51 F8
Ruspidge Glos 79 C11
Russel Highld 299 E8
Russell Hill London 67 G10
Russell's Green
E Sus 38 E2
Russell's Hall
W Mid 133 F8
Russell's Water Oxon 65 B8
Russel's Green Suff 126 C5
Russ Hill Sur 51 E8
Rusthall Kent 52 F5
Rustington W Sus 35 G9
Ruston N Yorks 217 C9
Ruston Parva
E Yorks 217 G11
Ruswarp N Yorks 227 D7
Ruthall Shrops 131 F11
Rutherford Borders 262 C4
Rutherglen S Lnrk 268 C2
Ruthernbridge Corn 5 B10
Ruthin Denb 165 D10
V Glam 58 D3
Ruthrieston
Aberdeen 293 C11
Ruthven Aberds 302 E5
Angus 286 C6
Highld 291 D9
Highld 301 F8
Ruthven House
Angus 287 C7
Ruthvoes Corn 5 C8
Ruthwaite Cumb 229 D10
Ruthwell Dumfries 238 D3
Ruxley London 68 E3
Ruxton Hereford 97 F11
Ruxton Green
Hereford 79 B8
Ruyton-XI-Towns
Shrops 149 E7
Ryal Northumb 242 C2
Ryal Fold Blkburn 195 C7
Ryall Dorset 16 C4
Worcs 99 C7
Ryarsh Kent 53 B7
Rychraggan Highld 300 F4
Rydal Cumb 221 D7
Ryde IoW 21 C7
Rydens Sur 66 F6
Rydeshill Sur 50 C3
Rydon Devon 14 G3
Rye E Sus 38 C6
Ryebank Shrops 149 C10
Rye Common Hants 49 C9
Ryecroft S Yorks 186 B6
W Yorks 205 F7
Ryecroft Gate Staffs 168 C6
Ryeford Glos 80 E4
Rye Foreign E Sus 38 C5
Rye Harbour E Sus 38 D6
Ryehill E Yorks 201 B8
Ryeish Green
Wokingham 65 F8
Ryelands Hereford 115 F9
Rye Park Herts 86 C5
Rye Street Worcs 98 D5
Ryeworth Glos 99 G9
Ryhall Rutland 155 G10
Ryhill W Yorks 197 E11
Ryhope T&W 243 G10
Rylah Derbys 171 B7
Rylands Notts 153 B10
Rylstone N Yorks 204 B5
Ryme Intrinseca
Dorset 29 E9
Ryther N Yorks 207 F7
Ryton Glos 98 E4
N Yorks 216 D5
Shrops 132 C5
T&W 242 E5
Warks 135 F7
Ryton-on-Dunsmore
Warks 119 C7
Ryton Woodside
T&W 242 E4

S

Sabden Lancs 203 F11
Sabine's Green Essex 87 F8
Sackers Green Suff 107 D8
Sacombe Herts 86 B4
Sacombe Green
Herts 86 B4
Sacriston Durham 233 B10
Sadberge Darl 224 B6
Saddell Argyll 255 D8
Saddell Ho Argyll 255 D8
Saddington Leics 136 E3
Saddle Bow Norf 158 F2
Saddlescombe
W Sus 36 E3
Saddle Street Dorset 28 G5
Sadgill Cumb 221 D9
Saffron's Cross
Hereford 115 G10
Saffron Walden
Essex 105 D10
Sageston Pembs 73 E9
Saham Hills Norf 141 C8
Saham Toney Norf 141 C8
Saighdinis W Isles 296 E4
Saighton Ches W 166 C6
Sain Dunwyd / St
Donats V Glam 58 F2
St Abbs Borders 273 B8
St Abb's Haven
Borders 273 B8
St Agnes Corn 4 E4
Scilly 1 H3
St Albans Herts 85 D10
St Allen Corn 4 E6
St Andrews Fife 287 F9
St Andrew's Major
V Glam 58 E6
St Andrew's Wood
Devon 27 F9
St Annes Lancs 193 B10
St Anne's Park Bristol 60 E6
St Ann's Dumfries 248 E3
Nottingham 171 G9
St Ann's Chapel Corn 12 G4
Devon 8 F3
St Anthony Corn 3 C9
St Anthony-in-Meneage
Corn 3 D7
St Anthony's T&W 243 E7
St Anthony's Hill
E Sus 23 E10
St Arvans Mon 79 F8
St Asaph / Llanelwy
Denb 181 G8
St Athan / Sain Tathon
V Glam 58 F4
Sain Tathon / St Athan
V Glam 58 F4
St Augustine's Kent 54 C6
St Austell Corn 5 E10
St Austins Hants 20 B2
St Bees Cumb 219 C9
St Blazey Corn 5 E11
St Blazey Gate Corn 5 E11
St Boswells Borders 262 C3
St Breock Corn 10 G5
St Breward Corn 11 F7
St Briavels Glos 79 E9
St Briavels Common
Glos 79 E8
St Bride's Pembs 72 C4
St Brides Major / Saint-
y-Brid V Glam 57 G11
St Bride's Netherwent
Mon 60 B2
St Brides-super-Ely
V Glam 58 D5
St Brides Wentlooge
Newport 59 C9
Saintbridge Glos 80 B5
St Budeaux Plym 7 D8
Saintbury Glos 100 D2
St Buryan Corn 1 D4
St Catherine Bath 61 E9
St Catherine's
Argyll 284 G5
St Catherine's Hill
Dorset 19 B8
St Chloe Glos 80 E4
St Clears / Sanclêr
Carms 74 B3
St Cleer Corn 6 B5
St Clement Corn 4 G6
St Clether Corn 11 E10
St Colmac Argyll 275 G11
St Columb Major Corn 5 C8
St Columb Minor Corn 4 C6
St Columb Road Corn 5 D8
St Combs Aberds 303 C10
St Cross Hants 33 B7
St Cross South Elmham
Suff 142 G5
St Cyrus Aberds 293 G9
St David's Perth 286 E3
St David's / Tyddewi
Pembs 90 F5
St Day Corn 4 G4
St Decumans Som 42 E5
St Dennis Corn 5 D9
St Denys Soton 32 E6
St Devereux Hereford 97 E8
St Dials Torf 78 G3
St Dogmaels /
Llandudoch Pembs 92 B3
St Dominick Corn 7 B8
St Donat's / Sain
Dunwyd V Glam 58 F2
St Edith's Wilts 62 G3
St Endellion Corn 10 F5
St Enoder Corn 5 D7
St Erme Corn 4 E6
St Erney Corn 7 D7
St Erth Corn 2 B3
St Erth Praze Corn 2 B3
St Ervan Corn 10 G3
St Eval Corn 5 B7
St Ewe Corn 5 F9
St Fagans Cardiff 58 D6
St Fergus Aberds 303 D10
St Fillans Perth 285 E10
St Florence Pembs 73 E9
St Gennys Corn 11 B8
St George Bristol 60 E6
Conwy 181 F7
St George in the East
London 67 C10
St Georges N Som 59 G11
St George's
Gtr Man 184 B4
Telford 150 G4
V Glam 58 D5
St George's Hill Sur 66 G5
St George's Well
Devon 27 F8
St Germans Corn 7 D7
St Giles Lincs 189 G7
London 67 C10
St Giles in the Wood
Devon 25 D8
St Giles on the Heath
Devon 12 C3
St Giles's Hill Hants 33 B7
St Gluvias Corn 3 C7
St Godwalds Worcs 117 D9
St Harmon Powys 113 C9
St Helena Warks 134 C5
St Helen Auckland
Durham 233 F9
St Helens Cumb 228 E6
IoW 21 D8
Mers 183 B8
St Helen's E Sus 38 E4
S Yorks 197 F11
St Helen's Wood
E Sus 38 E4
St Helier London 67 F9
St Hilary Corn 2 C3
V Glam 58 E4
Saint Hill Devon 27 F9
W Sus 51 F11
St Ibbs Herts 104 F3
St Illtyd Bl Gwent 78 E2
St Ippollytts Herts 104 F3
St Ishmael's Pembs 72 D4
St Issey Corn 10 G4
St Ive Corn 6 B6
St Ive Cross Corn 6 B6
St Ives Cambs 122 C6
Corn 2 A2
Dorset 31 G10
St James Dorset 30 C5
London 67 C9
Norf 160 E5
St James's End
Northants 120 E4
St James South Elmham
Suff 142 G6
St Jidgey Corn 5 B8
St John Corn 7 E8
St Johns London 67 D11
Warks 118 C5
St John's E Sus 52 G4
IoM 192 D3
Sevenoaks 52 B4
Southborough 52 E5
Sur 50 B3
Worcs 116 G6
W Yorks 206 F4
St John's Chapel
Devon 25 B8
Durham 232 D3
St John's Fen End
Norf 157 G10
St John's Highway
Norf 157 G10
St John's Park IoW 21 C8
St John's Town of Dalry
Dumfries 246 G4
St John's Wells
Aberds 303 F7
St John's Wood
London 67 C9
St Judes IoM 192 C4
St Julians Herts 85 D10
Newport 59 B10
St Just Corn 1 C3
St Justinian Pembs 90 F4
St Just in Roseland
Corn 3 B9
St Katharines Wilts 63 G9
St Katherine's
Aberds 303 F7
St Keverne Corn 3 E7
St Kew Corn 10 F6
St Kew Highway Corn 10 F6
St Keyne Corn 6 C4
St Lawrence Corn 5 B10
Essex 89 E7
IoW 20 F6
Kent 71 F11
St Leonards Dorset 31 G10
E Sus 38 F3
S Lnrk 268 E2
St Leonard's Bucks 84 D6
St Leonard's Street
Kent 53 B7
St Levan Corn 1 E3
St Luke's Derby 152 B6
London 67 C10
St Lythans V Glam 58 E6
St Mabyn Corn 10 G6
St Madoes Perth 286 E5
St Margarets Herts 86 C5
London 67 E7
St Margaret's
Hereford 97 E7
St Margaret's at Cliffe
Kent 55 E11
St Margaret's Hope
Orkney 314 G4
St Margaret South
Elmham Suff 142 G6
St Mark's Glos 99 G8
IoM 192 E3
St Martin Corn 2 E6
Corn 6 E5
St Martins Perth 286 D5
St Martin's Shrops 148 B6
St Martin's Moor
Shrops 148 B6
St Mary Bourne
Hants 48 C2
St Marychurch Torbay 9 B8
St Mary Church
V Glam 58 E4
St Mary Cray London 68 F3
St Mary Hill V Glam 58 D3
St Mary Hoo
Medway 69 D10
St Mary in the Marsh
Kent 39 B9
St Mary's Orkney 314 F4
St Mary's Bay Kent 39 B9
St Maughans Mon 79 B7
St Maughans Green
Mon 79 B7
St Mawes Corn 3 C8
St Mawgan Corn 5 B7
St Mellion Corn 7 B7
St Mellons Cardiff 59 C8
St Merryn Corn 10 G3
St Mewan Corn 5 E9
St Michael Caerhays
Corn 5 G9
St Michael Church
Som 43 G10
St Michael Penkevil
Corn 5 G7
St Michaels Kent 53 F11
Torbay 9 C7
Worcs 115 D11
St Michael's Hamlet
Mers 182 D5
St Michael's on Wyre
Lancs 202 E5
St Michael South
Elmham Suff 142 G6
St Minver Corn 10 F5
St Monans Fife 287 G9
St Neot Corn 6 B3
St Neots Cambs 122 E3
St Newlyn East Corn 4 D6
St Nicholas Herts 104 F5
Pembs 91 D7
V Glam 58 E5
St Nicholas at Wade
Kent 71 F9
St Nicholas South
Elmham Suff 142 G6
St Nicolas Park
Warks 135 E7
St Ninians Stirl 278 C5
St Olaves Norf 143 D9
St Osyth Essex 89 B10
St Osyth Heath
Essex 89 B10
St Owens Cross
Hereford 97 G10
St Pancras London 67 C10
St Paul's Glos 80 B4
St Paul's Cray London 68 F3
St Paul's Walden
Herts 104 G3
St Peters Kent 71 F11
St Peter's Glos 99 G8
T&W 243 E7
St Peter South Elmham
Suff 142 G6
St Peter The Great
Worcs 117 G7
St Petrox Pembs 73 F7
St Pinnock Corn 6 C4
St Quivox S Ayrs 257 E9
St Ruan Corn 2 F6
Saint's Hill Kent 52 E4
St Stephen Corn 5 E8
St Stephens Corn 7 D8
Herts 85 D10
St Stephen's Corn 12 D2
St Teath Corn 11 E7
St Thomas Devon 14 C4
Swansea 57 C7
St Tudy Corn 11 F7
St Twynnells Pembs 73 F7
St Veep Corn 6 E2
St Vigeans Angus 287 C10
St Vincent's Hamlet
Essex 87 G9
St Wenn Corn 5 C9
St Weonards
Hereford 97 G9
St Winnow Corn 6 D2
Saint y Brid / St Brides
Major V Glam 57 G11
St y-Nyll V Glam 58 D5
Saith ffynnon Flint 181 F11
Salcombe Devon 9 G9
Salcombe Regis
Devon 15 D9
Salcott-cum-Virley
Essex 88 C6
Salden Bucks 102 F6
Sale Gtr Man 184 C3
Saleby Lincs 191 F7
Sale Green Worcs 117 F8
Salehurst E Sus 38 C2
Salem Carms 94 F2
Ceredig 128 G3
Corn 4 G4
Salen Argyll 289 E7
Highld 289 C8
Salendine Nook
W Yorks 196 D6
Salenside Borders 261 E11
Salesbury Lancs 203 G9
Saleway Worcs 117 F8
Salford C Beds 103 D8
Gtr Man 184 B4
Oxon 100 F5
Salford Ford
C Beds 103 D8
Salford Priors
Warks 117 G11
Salfords Sur 51 D9
Salhouse Norf 160 G6
Saligo Argyll 274 G3
Salisbury Wilts 31 B10
Salkeld Dykes
Cumb 230 D6
Sallachan Highld 289 C11
Sallachy Highld 295 B11
Highld 309 J5
Salle Norf 160 E2
Salmans Kent 52 E4
Salmonby Lincs 190 G4
Salmond's Muir
Angus 287 D9
Salmonhutch Devon 14 B2
Salperton Glos 99 G11
Salperton Park Glos 81 B9
Salph End Beds 121 G11
Salsburgh N Lnrk 268 C6
Salt Staffs 151 D9
Salta Cumb 229 B7
Saltaire W Yorks 205 F8
Saltash Corn 7 D8
Saltburn Highld 301 C7
Saltburn-by-the-Sea
Redcar 235 G9
Saltby Leics 155 D7
Salt Coates Cumb 238 G5
Saltcoats Cumb 219 F11
E Loth 281 E9
N Ayrs 266 G4
Saltcotes Lancs 193 B11
Saltdean Brighton 36 G5
Salt End E Yorks 201 B7
Salter Lancs 212 G2
Salterbeck Cumb 228 F5
Salterforth Lancs 204 D3
Salters Heath Hants 48 B6
Saltershill Shrops 150 D2
Salters Lode Norf 139 C11
Salter Street W Mid 118 C2
Salterswall
Ches W 167 B10
Salterton Wilts 46 F6
Saltfleet Lincs 191 C7
Saltfleetby All Saints
Lincs 191 C7
Saltfleetby St Clement
Lincs 191 C7
Saltfleetby St Peter
Lincs 190 D6
Saltford Bath 61 F7
Salt Hill Slough 66 C3
Salthouse Cumb 210 F4
Norf 177 E9
Saltley W Mid 133 F11
Saltmarsh Newport 59 C11
Saltmarshe E Yorks 199 C9
Saltness Orkney 314 G2
Shetland 313 J4
Saltney Flint 166 B5
Salton N Yorks 216 D4
Saltrens Devon 25 C7
Saltwell T&W 243 E7
Saltwick Northumb 242 B5
Saltwood Kent 55 F7
Salum Argyll 288 E2
Salvington W Sus 35 F10
Salwarpe Worcs 117 E7
Salwayash Dorset 16 B5
Sambourne Warks 117 E11
Wilts 45 E11
Sambrook Telford 150 E4
Samhla W Isles 296 E3
Samlesbury Lancs 203 G7
Samlesbury Bottoms
Lancs 194 B6
Sampford Arundel
Som 27 D10
Sampford Brett Som 42 E5
Sampford Chapple
Devon 25 G10
Sampford Courtenay
Devon 25 G10
Sampford Moor
Som 27 D10
Sampford Peverell
Devon 27 E8
Sampford Spiney
Devon 12 G6
Sampool Bridge
Cumb 211 B9
Samuel's Corner
Essex 70 B3
Samuelston E Loth 281 G9
Sanachan Highld 299 E8
Sanaigmore Argyll 274 F3
Sanclêr / St Clears
Carms 74 B3
Sancreed Corn 1 D4
Sancton E Yorks 208 F4
Sand Highld 307 K4
Shetland 313 J5
Som 44 D2
Sandaig Highld 295 E9
Sandal W Yorks 197 D10
Sandale Cumb 229 C10
Sandal Magna
W Yorks 197 D10
Sandavore Highld 294 G6
Sandbach Ches E 168 C3
Sandbach Heath
Ches E 168 C3
Sandbank Argyll 276 E3
Sandbanks Kent 70 G4
Poole 18 D6
Sandborough Staffs 152 F2
Sandbraes Lincs 200 G6
Sandend Aberds 302 C5
Sanderstead London 67 G10
Sandfields Glos 99 G8
Neath 57 C8
Staffs 134 B2
Sandford Cumb 222 B4
Devon 26 G4
Dorset 18 D4
Hants 31 G11
IoW 20 E6

N Som 44 B2
Shrops 148 E6
Shrops 149 C11
S Lnrk 268 G4
Worcs 99 B7
W Yorks 205 F11
Sandford Batch N Som 44 B2
Sandfordhill Aberds 303 E11
Sandford Hill Stoke 168 G6
Sandford on Thames Oxon 83 E8
Sandford Orcas Dorset 29 C10
Sandford St Martin Oxon 101 F8
Sandgate Kent 55 G7
Sand Gate Cumb 211 D7
Sandgreen Dumfries 237 D7
Sandhaven Aberds 303 C9
Argyll 276 E3
Sandhead Dumfries 236 E2
Sandhill Bucks 102 F4
Cambs 139 F11
S Yorks 198 F2
Sandhills Dorset 29 E11
Dorset 29 G9
Mers 182 C4
Oxon 83 D9
Sur 50 F2
W Yorks 206 F3
Sandhoe Northumb 241 D11
Sandhole Argyll 275 D11
Sand Hole E Yorks 208 F2
Sandholme E Yorks 208 G2
Lincs 156 B6
Sandhurst Brack 65 G10
Glos 98 G6
Kent 38 B3
Sandhurst Cross Kent 38 B3
Sandhutton N Yorks 215 C7
Sand Hutton N Yorks 207 B9
Sandiacre Derbys 153 B9
Sandilands Lincs 191 E8
S Lnrk 259 B9
Sandiway Ches W 183 G10
Sandleheath Hants 31 E10
Sandling Kent 53 B9
Sandlow Green Ches E 168 B3
Sandness Shetland 313 H3
Sandon Essex 88 E2
Herts 104 E6
Staffs 151 C8
Sandonbank Staffs 151 D8
Sandown IoW 21 E7
Sandown Park Kent 52 E6
Sandpit Dorset 28 G6
Sandpits Glos 98 F6
Sandplace Corn 6 D5
Sandridge Herts 85 C11
Wilts 62 F2
Sandringham Norf 158 D3
Sands Bucks 84 G4
Sandsend N Yorks 227 C7
Sands End London 67 D9
Sandside Cumb 210 D6
Cumb 211 C9
Orkney 314 F2
Sand Side Cumb 210 C4
Lancs 202 C4
Sandside Ho Highld 310 C3
Sandsound Shetland 313 J5
Sandtoft N Lincs 199 F8
Sandvoe Shetland 312 D5
Sandway Kent 53 C11
Sandwell W Mid 133 F10
Sandwich Kent 55 B10
Sandwich Bay Estate Kent 55 B11
Sandwick Cumb 221 B8
Orkney 314 H4
Shetland 313 L6
Sandwith Cumb 219 C9
Sandwith Newtown Cumb 219 C9
Sandy Carms 75 E7
C Beds 104 B3
Sandybank Orkney 314 C5
Sandy Bank Lincs 174 E3
Sandy Carrs Durham 234 C3
Sandycroft Flint 166 B4
Sandy Cross E Sus 37 C9
Sur 49 D11
Sandy Down Hants 20 B2
Sandyford Dumfries 248 E6
Stoke 168 E5
Sandygate Devon 14 G3
IoM 192 C4
S Yorks 186 D4
Sandy Gate Devon 14 C5
Sandy Haven Pembs 72 D5
Sandyhills Dumfries 237 D10
Sandylake Corn 6 C2
Sandylands Lancs 211 G8
Som 27 C10
Sandylane Swansea 56 D5
Sandy Lane Wilts 62 F3
Wrex 166 G5
W Yorks 205 F8
Sandypark Devon 13 D10
Sandysike Cumb 239 D9
Sandy Way IoW 20 E5
Sangobeg Highld 308 C4
Sangomore Highld 308 C4
Sanham Green W Berks 63 F10
Sankey Bridges Warr 183 D9
Sankyns Green Worcs 116 E5
Sanna Highld 288 C6
Sanndabhaig W Isles 297 G4
W Isles 304 E6
Sannox N Ayrs 255 C11
Sanquhar Dumfries 247 B7
Sansaw Heath Shrops 149 E10
Santon Cumb 220 E2
N Lincs 200 E2
Santon Bridge Cumb 220 E2
Santon Downham Suff 140 F6
Sapcote Leics 135 E9
Sapey Bridge Worcs 116 F4
Sapey Common Hereford 116 E4
Sapiston Suff 125 B8
Sapley Cambs 122 C4
Sapperton Derbys 152 C3
Glos 80 E6
Lincs 155 C10
Saracen's Head Lincs 156 D6
Sarclet Highld 310 E7
Sardis Carms 75 D9
Pembs 73 D10
Sarisbury Hants 33 F8
Sarn Bridgend 58 C2
Flint 181 F10
Powys 130 E4
Sarnau Carms 74 B4
Ceredig 110 G6
Gwyn 147 B9
Powys 95 E10
Powys 148 F4
Sarn Bach Gwyn 144 D6
Sarnesfield Hereford 115 G7
Sarn Meyllteyrn Gwyn 144 C4
Saron Carms 75 C10
Carms 93 D7
Denb 165 C8
Gwyn 163 B8
Gwyn 163 D7
Sarratt Herts 85 F8
Sarratt Bottom Herts 85 F8
Sarre Kent 71 G9
Sarsden Oxon 100 G5
Sarsden Halt Oxon 100 G5
Sarsgrum Highld 308 C3
Sasaig Highld 295 E8
Sascott Shrops 149 G8
Satley Durham 233 C8
Satmar Kent 55 F9
Satran Highld 294 B6
Satron N Yorks 223 F8
Satterleigh Devon 25 C11
Satterthwaite Cumb 220 G6
Satwell Oxon 65 C8
Sauchen Aberds 293 B8
Saucher Perth 286 D5
Sauchie Clack 279 C7
Sauchieburn Aberds 293 G8
Saughall Ches W 182 G5
Saughall Massie Mers 182 D3
Saughton Edin 280 G4
Saughtree Borders 250 D3
Saul Glos 80 D2
Saundby Notts 188 D3
Saundersfoot Pembs 73 E10
Saunderton Bucks 84 E3
Saunderton Lee Bucks 84 F4
Saunton Devon 40 F3
Sausthorpe Lincs 174 B5
Saval Highld 309 J5
Savary Highld 289 E8
Saveock Corn 4 F5
Saverley Green Staffs 151 B9
Savile Park W Yorks 196 C5
Savile Town W Yorks 197 C8
Sawbridge Warks 119 D10
Sawbridgeworth Herts 87 B7
Sawdon N Yorks 217 B8
Sawley Derbys 153 C9
Lancs 203 D11
N Yorks 214 F4
Sawood W Yorks 204 G6
Sawston Cambs 105 B9
Sawtry Cambs 138 G3
Sawyers Hill Wilts 81 G8
Sawyer's Hill Som 27 C11
Saxby Leics 154 F6
Lincs 189 D8
W Sus 35 G7
Saxby All Saints N Lincs 200 D3
Saxelbye Leics 154 E4
Saxham Street Suff 125 E11
Saxilby Lincs 188 F5
Saxlingham Norf 159 B10
Saxlingham Green Norf 142 D4
Saxlingham Nethergate Norf 142 D4
Saxlingham Thorpe Norf 142 D4
Saxmundham Suff 127 E7
Saxondale Notts 154 B3
Saxon Street Cambs 124 F3
Saxtead Suff 126 D5
Saxtead Green Suff 126 E5
Saxtead Little Green Suff 126 D5
Saxthorpe Norf 160 C2
Saxton N Yorks 206 F5
Sayers Common W Sus 36 D3
Scackleton N Yorks 216 E2
Scadabhagh W Isles 305 J3
Scaftworth Notts 187 C11
Scagglethorpe N Yorks 216 E6
Scaitcliffe Lancs 195 B9
Scaladal W Isles 305 G3
Scalan Moray 292 B4
Scalasaig Argyll 274 D4
Scalby E Yorks 199 B10
N Yorks 227 G10
Scald End Beds 121 F10
Scaldwell Northants 120 C5
Scaleby Cumb 239 E11
Scalebyhill Cumb 239 E10
Scale Hall Lancs 211 G9
Scale Houses Cumb 231 B7
Scales Cumb 210 E5
Cumb 230 F2
Cumb 231 C7
Lancs 202 G5
Scalford Leics 154 E5
Scaling Redcar 226 C4
Scaliscro W Isles 304 F3
Scallasaig Highld 295 D10
Scallastle Argyll 289 F8
Scalloway Shetland 313 K6
Scalpay W Isles 305 J4
Scalpay Ho Highld 295 C8
Scalpsie Argyll 255 B11
Scamadale Highld 295 F9
Scamblesby Lincs 190 F3
Scamland E Yorks 207 E11
Scammadale Argyll 289 G10
Scamodale Highld 289 B10
Scampston N Yorks 217 D7
Scampton Lincs 189 F7
Scaniport Highld 300 F6
Scapa Orkney 314 F4
Scapegoat Hill W Yorks 196 D5
Scar Orkney 314 B6
Scarborough N Yorks 217 B10
Scarcewater Corn 5 E8
Scarcliffe Derbys 171 B7
Scarcroft W Yorks 206 E3
Scarcroft Hill W Yorks 206 E3
Scardroy Highld 300 D2
Scarff Shetland 312 E4
Scarfskerry Highld 310 B6
Scargill Durham 223 C11
Scar Head Cumb 220 G5
Scarinish Argyll 288 E2
Scarisbrick Lancs 193 E11
Scarness Cumb 229 E10
Scarning Norf 159 G9
Scarrington Notts 172 G2
Scarth Hill Lancs 194 F2
Scarthingwell N Yorks 206 F5
Scartho NE Lincs 201 F9
Scarvister Shetland 313 J5
Scarwell Orkney 314 D2
Scatness Shetland 313 M5
Scatraig Highld 301 F7
Scawby N Lincs 200 F3
Scawsby S Yorks 198 G5
Scawthorpe S Yorks 198 F5
Scawton N Yorks 215 C10
Scayne's Hill W Sus 36 C5
Scethrog Powys 96 F2
Scholar Green Ches E 168 D4
Scholemoor W Yorks 205 G8
Scholes Gtr Man 194 F5
S Yorks 186 B5
W Yorks 197 B7
W Yorks 197 F7
W Yorks 204 F6
W Yorks 206 F3
Scholey Hill W Yorks 197 B11
School Aycliffe Durham 233 G11
Schoolgreen Wokingham 65 F8
School Green Ches W 167 C10
Essex 106 E4
IoW 20 D2
W Yorks 205 G8
Schoolhill Aberds 293 D11
School House Dorset 28 G5
Sciberscross Highld 309 H7
Scilly Bank Cumb 219 B9
Scissett W Yorks 197 E8
Scleddau Pembs 91 E8
Scofton Notts 187 E10
Scole Norf 126 B2
Scole Common Norf 142 G2
Scolpaig W Isles 296 D3
Scone Perth 286 E5
Sconser Highld 295 B7
Scoonie Fife 287 G7
Scoor Argyll 274 B5
Scopwick Lincs 173 D9
Scoraig Highld 307 K5
Scorborough E Yorks 208 D6
Scorrier Corn 4 G4
Scorriton Devon 8 B4
Scorton Lancs 202 D6
N Yorks 224 E5
Sco Ruston Norf 160 E5
Scotbheinn W Isles 296 F4
Scotby Cumb 239 G10
Scotch Corner N Yorks 224 E4
Scotches Derbys 170 F4
Scotforth Lancs 202 B5
Scotgate W Yorks 196 E6
Scot Hay Staffs 168 F4
Scothern Lincs 189 F8
Scotland Leics 136 D3
Leics 153 E7
Lincs 155 C10
W Berks 64 F5
Scotland End Oxon 100 E6
Scotland Gate Northumb 253 G7
Scotlands W Mid 133 C8
Scotland Street Suff 107 D9
Scotlandwell Perth 286 G5
Scot Lane End Gtr Man 194 F6
Scotsburn Highld 301 B7
Scotscalder Station Highld 310 D4
Scotscraig Fife 287 E8
Scots' Gap Northumb 252 F2
Scotston Aberds 293 F9
Perth 286 C3
Scotstoun Glasgow 267 B10
Scotstown Highld 289 C10
Scotswood T&W 242 E5
Windsor 66 F2
Scottas Highld 295 E9
Scotter Lincs 199 G11
Scotterthorpe Lincs 199 G11
Scottlethorpe Lincs 155 E11
Scotton Lincs 188 B5
N Yorks 206 B2
N Yorks 224 F3
Scottow Norf 160 E5
Scott Willoughby Lincs 155 B11
Scoughall E Loth 282 E2
Scoulag Argyll 266 D2
Scoulton Norf 141 C9
Scounslow Green Staffs 151 D11
Scourie Highld 306 E6
Scourie More Highld 306 E6
Scousburgh Shetland 313 M5
Scout Dike S Yorks 197 G8
Scout Green Cumb 221 D11
Scouthead Gtr Man 196 F3
Scowles Glos 79 C9
Scrabster Highld 310 B4
Scraesburgh Borders 262 F5
Scrafield Lincs 174 B4
Scragged Oak Kent 69 G10
Scrainwood Northumb 251 B11
Scrane End Lincs 174 G5
Scrapsgate Kent 70 E2
Scraptoft Leics 136 B2
Scrapton Som 28 E3
Scratby Norf 161 F10
Scrayingham N Yorks 216 G4
Scredda Corn 5 E10
Scredington Lincs 173 G9
Screedy Som 27 B9
Scremby Lincs 174 B6
Scremerston Northumb 273 F10
Screveton Notts 172 G2
Scrivelsby Lincs 174 B3
Scriven N Yorks 206 B2
Scronkey Lancs 202 D4
Scrooby Notts 187 C11
Scropton Derbys 152 C3
Scrub Hill Lincs 174 D2
Scruton N Yorks 224 G5
Scrwgan Powys 148 E3
Scuddaborg Highld 298 C3
Scuggate Cumb 239 C10
Sculcoates Hull 209 G7
Sculthorpe Norf 159 C7
Scunthorpe N Lincs 199 E11
Scurlage Swansea 56 D3
Sea Som 28 E4
Seaborough Dorset 28 F6
Seabridge Staffs 168 G4
Seabrook Kent 55 G7
Seaburn T&W 243 F10
Seacombe Mers 182 C4
Seacox Heath Kent 53 G8
Seacroft Lincs 175 C9
W Yorks 206 F3
Seadyke Lincs 156 B6
Seafar N Lnrk 278 G5
Seafield Highld 311 L3
Midloth 270 C5
S Ayrs 257 E8
W Loth 269 B10
Seaford E Sus 23 F7
Seaforth Mers 182 B4
Seagrave Leics 154 F2
Seagry Heath Wilts 62 C3
Seaham Durham 234 B4
Seahouses Northumb 264 C6
Seal Kent 52 B4
Sealand Flint 166 B5
Seale Sur 49 D11
Seamer N Yorks 217 C10
N Yorks 225 C9
Seamill N Ayrs 266 F4
Sea Mill Cumb 210 F5
Sea Mills Bristol 60 D5
Corn 10 G4
Sea Palling Norf 161 D8
Searby Lincs 200 F5
Seasalter Kent 70 F5
Seascale Cumb 219 E10
Seathorne Lincs 175 B9
Seathwaite Cumb 220 C4
Cumb 220 F4
Seatle Cumb 211 C7
Seatoller Cumb 220 C4
Seaton Corn 6 E6
Cumb 228 E6
Devon 15 C10
Durham 243 G9
E Yorks 209 D9
Kent 55 B8
Northumb 243 B8
Rutland 137 D8
Seaton Burn T&W 242 C6
Seaton Carew Hrtlpl 234 F6
Seaton Delaval Northumb 243 B8
Seaton Ross E Yorks 207 E11
Seaton Sluice Northumb 243 B8
Seatown Aberds 302 C5
Aberds 303 D11
Dorset 16 C4
Seaureaugh Moor Corn 2 B6
Seave Green N Yorks 225 E11
Seaview IoW 21 C8
Seaville Cumb 238 G5
Seavington St Mary Som 28 E6
Seavington St Michael Som 28 D6
Seawick Essex 89 C10
Sebastopol Torf 78 F3
Sebay Orkney 314 F5
Sebergham Cumb 230 C3
Sebiston Velzian Orkney 314 D2
Seckington Warks 134 B5
Second Coast Highld 307 K4
Second Drove Cambs 139 F10
Sedbergh Cumb 222 G3
Sedbury Glos 79 G8
Sedbusk N Yorks 223 G7
Seddington C Beds 104 B3
Sedgeberrow Worcs 99 D10
Sedgebrook Lincs 155 B7
Sedgefield Durham 234 F3
Sedgeford Norf 158 B4
Sedgehill Wilts 30 B5
Sedgemere W Mid 118 B4
Sedgley W Mid 133 E8
Sedgley Park Gtr Man 195 G10
Sedgwick Cumb 211 B10
Sedlescombe E Sus 38 D3
Sedlescombe Street E Sus 38 D3
Sedrup Bucks 84 C3
Seed Kent 54 B2
Seed Lee Lancs 194 C5
Seedley Gtr Man 184 B4
Seend Wilts 62 G2
Seend Cleeve Wilts 62 G2
Seend Head Wilts 62 G2
Seer Green Bucks 85 G7
Seething Norf 142 D6
Seething Wells London 67 F7
Sefton Mers 193 G11
Segensworth Hants 33 F8
Seggat Aberds 303 E7
Seghill Northumb 243 C7
Seifton Shrops 131 G9
Seighford Staffs 151 D7
Seilebost W Isles 305 J2
Seion Gwyn 163 B8
Seisdon Staffs 132 E6
Seisiadar W Isles 304 E7
Selattyn Shrops 148 C5
Selborne Hants 49 G8
Selby N Yorks 207 G8
Selgrove Kent 54 B4
Selham W Sus 34 C6
Selhurst London 67 F10
Selkirk Borders 261 D11
Sellack Hereford 97 F11
Sellack Boat Hereford 97 F11
Sellafirth Shetland 312 D7
Sellan Corn 1 C4
Sellibister Orkney 314 B7
Sellick's Green Som 28 D2
Sellindge Kent 54 F6
Selling Kent 54 B4
Sells Green Wilts 62 G3
Selly Hill N Yorks 227 D7
Selly Oak W Mid 133 G10
Selly Park W Mid 133 G11
Selmeston E Sus 23 D8
Selsdon London 67 G10
Selsey W Sus 22 E5
Selsfield Common W Sus 51 G10
Selside Cumb 221 F10
N Yorks 212 D5
Selsley Glos 80 E4
Selsmore Hants 21 B10
Selson Kent 55 B10
Selsted Kent 55 E8
Selston Notts 171 E7
Selston Common Notts 171 E7
Selston Green Notts 171 E7
Selwick Orkney 314 F2
Selworthy Som 42 D2
Semblister Shetland 313 H5
Semer Suff 107 B9
Sem Hill Wilts 30 B5
Semington Wilts 61 G11
Semley Wilts 30 B5
Sempringham Lincs 156 C2
Send Sur 50 B4
Send Grove Sur 50 C4
Send Marsh Sur 50 B4
Senghenydd Caerph 77 G10
Sennen Corn 1 D3
Sennen Cove Corn 1 D3
Sennybridge / Pont Senni Powys 95 F8
Serlby Notts 187 D10
Serrington Wilts 46 F5
Sessay N Yorks 215 D9
Setchey Norf 158 G2
Setley Hants 32 G4
Seton E Loth 281 G8
Seton Mains E Loth 281 F8
Setter Shetland 312 E6
Shetland 313 H5
Shetland 313 J7
Shetland 313 L6
Settiscarth Orkney 314 E3
Settle N Yorks 212 G6
Settrington N Yorks 216 E6
Seven Ash Som 43 G7
Sevenhampton Glos 99 G10
Swindon 82 G2
Seven Kings London 68 B3
Sevenoaks Kent 52 C4
Sevenoaks Common Kent 52 C4
Sevenoaks Weald Kent 52 C4
Seven Sisters / Blaendulais Neath 76 D4
Seven Springs Glos 81 B7
Seven Star Green Essex 107 F8
Severn Beach S Glos 60 B4
Severnhampton Swindon 82 G2
Severn Stoke Worcs 99 C7
Sevick End Beds 121 G11
Sevington Kent 54 E4
Sewards End Essex 105 D11
Sewardstone Essex 86 F5
Sewardstonebury Essex 86 F5
Sewell C Beds 103 G9
Sewerby E Yorks 218 F3
Seworgan Corn 2 C6
Sewstern Leics 155 E7
Sexhow N Yorks 225 D9
Sezincote Glos 100 E3
Sgarasta Mhor W Isles 305 J2
Sgiogarstaigh W Isles 304 B7
Sgiwen / Skewen Neath 57 B8
Shabbington Bucks 83 D11
Shab Hill Glos 80 B6
Shackerley Shrops 132 B6
Shackerstone Leics 135 B7
Shacklecross Derbys 153 C8
Shackleford Sur 50 D2
Shackleton W Yorks 196 B3
Shacklewell London 67 B10
Shacklford Sur 50 D2
Shade W Yorks 196 C2
Shadforth Durham 234 C2
Shadingfield Suff 143 G8
Shadoxhurst Kent 54 F3
Shadsworth Blkburn 195 B8
Shadwell Glos 80 F3
London 67 C11
Norf 141 G8
W Yorks 206 F2
Shaffalong Staffs 169 E7
Shaftenhoe End Herts 105 D8
Shaftesbury Dorset 30 C5
Shafton S Yorks 197 E11
Shafton Two Gates S Yorks 197 E11
Shaggs Dorset 18 E3
Shakeford Shrops 150 D3
Shakerley Gtr Man 195 G7
Shakesfield Glos 98 E3
Shalbourne Wilts 63 G10
Shalcombe IoW 20 D3
Shalden Hants 49 E7
Shalden Green Hants 49 E7
Shaldon Devon 14 G4
Shalfleet IoW 20 D4
Shalford Essex 106 F4
Som 45 G8
Sur 50 D4
Shalford Green Essex 106 F4
Shalloch Moray 302 D3
Shallowford Devon 25 B11
Devon 41 E8
Staffs 151 D7
Shalmsford Street Kent 54 C5
Shalstone Bucks 102 D2
Shamley Green Sur 50 E4
Shandon Argyll 276 D5
Shandwick Highld 301 B8
Shangton Leics 136 D4
Shankhouse Northumb 243 B7
Shanklin IoW 21 E7
Shannochie N Ayrs 255 E10
Shannochill Stirl 277 B10
Shanquhar Aberds 302 F5
Shanwell Fife 287 E8
Shanzie Perth 286 B6
Shap Cumb 221 B11
Shapridge Glos 79 B11
Shapwick Dorset 30 G6
Som 44 F2
Sharcott Wilts 46 B6
Shard End W Mid 134 F3
Shardlow Derbys 153 C8
Shareshill Staffs 133 B8
Sharlston W Yorks 197 D11
Sharlston Common W Yorks 197 D11
Sharmans Cross W Mid 118 B2
Sharnal Street Medway 69 E9
Sharnbrook Beds 121 F9
Sharneyford Lancs 195 C11
Sharnford Leics 135 E9
Sharnhill Green Dorset 30 F2
Sharoe Green Lancs 202 G6
Sharow N Yorks 214 E6
Sharpenhoe C Beds 103 E11
Sharperton Northumb 251 C11
Sharples Gtr Man 195 E8
Sharpley Heath Staffs 151 B9
Sharpness Glos 79 E11
Sharpsbridge E Sus 36 C6
Sharp's Corner E Sus 23 B9
Sharpstone Bath 45 B9
Sharp Street Norf 161 E7
Sharpthorne W Sus 51 G11
Sharptor Corn 11 G11
Sharpway Gate Worcs 117 D9
Sharrington Norf 159 B10
Sharrow S Yorks 186 D4
Sharston Gtr Man 184 D4
Shatterford Worcs 132 G5
Shatterling Kent 55 B9
Shatton Derbys 185 E11
Shaugh Prior Devon 7 C10
Shavington Ches E 168 E2
Shaw Gtr Man 196 F2
Swindon 62 B6
W Berks 64 F3
Wilts 61 F11
W Yorks 204 F6
Shawbank Shrops 131 G9
Shawbirch Telford 150 G2
Shawbury Shrops 149 E11
Shawclough Gtr Man 195 E11
Shaw Common Glos 98 F3
Shawdon Hall Northumb 264 G3
Shawell Leics 135 G10
Shawfield Gtr Man 195 E11
Staffs 169 C9
Shawfield Head N Yorks 205 C11
Shawford Hants 33 C7
Som 45 C9
Shawforth Lancs 195 C11
Shaw Green Herts 104 E5
Lancs 194 D4
N Yorks 205 C11
Shawhead Dumfries 237 B10
N Lnrk 268 C4
Shaw Heath Ches E 184 F3
Gtr Man 184 D5
Shawhill Dumfries 238 D6
Shawlands Glasgow 267 C11
Shaw Lands S Yorks 197 F10
Shaw Mills N Yorks 214 G5
Shawsburn S Lnrk 268 E5
Shaw Side Gtr Man 196 F2
Shawton S Lnrk 268 F3
Shawtonhill S Lnrk 268 F3
Shay Gate W Yorks 205 F8
Sheandow Moray 302 F2
Shear Cross Wilts 45 E11
Shearington Dumfries 238 D2
Shearsby Leics 136 E2
Shearston Som 43 G9
Shebbear Devon 24 F6
Shebdon Staffs 150 D5
Shebster Highld 310 C4
Sheddens E Renf 267 D11
Shedfield Hants 33 E9
Sheen Staffs 169 C10
Sheepbridge Derbys 186 G5
Sheepdrove W Berks 63 D10
Sheep Hill Durham 242 F5
Sheeplane C Beds 103 E8
Sheepridge Bucks 65 B11
W Yorks 197 D7
Sheepscar W Yorks 206 G2
Sheepscombe Glos 80 C5
Sheepstor Devon 7 B11
Sheepwash Devon 25 F7
Northumb 253 F7
Sheepway N Som 60 D3
Sheepy Magna Leics 134 C6
Sheepy Parva Leics 134 C6
Sheering Essex 87 C8
Sheerness Kent 70 E2
Sheerwater Sur 66 G4
Sheet Hants 34 C3
Shrops 115 C10
Sheets Heath Sur 50 B2
Sheffield Corn 1 D5
S Yorks 186 D5
Sheffield Bottom W Berks 65 F7
Sheffield Green E Sus 36 C6
Sheffield Park S Yorks 186 D5
Shefford C Beds 104 D2
Shefford Woodlands W Berks 63 E11
Sheigra Highld 306 C6
Sheildmuir N Lnrk 268 D5
Sheinton Shrops 132 C2
Shelderton Shrops 115 B8
Sheldon Derbys 169 B11
Devon 27 F10
W Mid 134 G3
Sheldwich Kent 54 B4
Sheldwich Lees Kent 54 B4
Shelf Bridgend 58 C2
W Yorks 196 B6
Shelfanger Norf 142 G2
Shelfield Warks 118 E2
W Mid 133 C10
Shelfield Green Warks 118 E2
Shelfleys Northants 120 F4
Shelford Notts 171 G11
Warks 135 F8
Shell Worcs 117 F9
Shelland Suff 125 E10
Shellbrook Leics 152 F6
Shelley Essex 87 E9
Suff 107 D10
W Yorks 197 E8
Shelley Woodhouse W Yorks 197 E8
Shell Green Halton 183 D8
Shellingford Oxon 82 G4
Shellow Bowells Essex 87 D10
Shellwood Cross Sur 51 D8
Shelsley Beauchamp Worcs 116 E4
Shelsley Walsh Worcs 116 E4
Shelthorpe Leics 153 F10
Shelton Beds 121 D10
Norf 142 E4
Notts 172 G3
Shrops 149 G9
Stoke 168 F5
Shelton Green Norf 142 E4
Shelton Lock Derby 153 C7
Shelton under Harley Staffs 150 B6
Shelve Shrops 130 D6
Shelvin Devon 27 G11
Shelvingford Kent 71 F8
Shelwick Hereford 97 C10
Shelwick Green Hereford 97 C10
Shenfield Essex 87 G10
Shenington Oxon 101 C7
Shenley Herts 85 E11
Shenley Brook End M Keynes 102 D6
Shenleybury Herts 85 E11
Shenley Church End M Keynes 102 D6
Shenley Fields W Mid 133 G10
Shenley Lodge M Keynes 102 D6
Shenley Wood M Keynes 102 D6
Shenmore Hereford 97 D7
Shennanton Dumfries 236 C5
Shennanton Ho Dumfries 236 C5
Shenstone Staffs 134 C2
Worcs 117 C7
Shenstone Woodend Staffs 134 C2
Shenton Leics 135 C7
Shenval Highld 300 G4
Moray 302 G2
Shenvault Moray 301 E10
Shepeau Stow Lincs 156 G6
Shephall Herts 104 G5
Shepherd Hill W Yorks 197 C9
Shepherd's Bush London 67 C8
Shepherd's Gate Norf 157 F11
Shepherd's Green Oxon 65 C8
Shepherd's Hill Sur 50 G2
Shepherd's Patch Glos 80 E2
Shepherd's Port Norf 158 C3
Shepherdswell or Sibertswold Kent 55 D9
Shepley W Yorks 197 F7
Shepperdine S Glos 79 F10
Shepperton Sur 66 F5
Shepperton Green Sur 66 F5
Shepreth Cambs 105 B7
Shepshed Leics 153 F9
Shepton Beauchamp Som 28 D6
Shepton Mallet Som 44 E6
Shepton Montague Som 45 G7
Shepway Kent 53 C9
Sheraton Durham 234 D4
Sherberton Devon 13 G8
Sherborne Bath 44 B5
Dorset 29 D10
Glos 81 C11
Sherborne St John Hants 48 B6
Sherbourne Warks 118 E5
Sherbourne Street Suff 107 C9
Sherburn Durham 234 C2
N Yorks 217 D9
Sherburn Grange Durham 234 C2
Sherburn Hill Durham 234 C2
Sherburn in Elmet N Yorks 206 G5
Shere Sur 50 D5
Shereford Norf 159 D7
Sherfield English Hants 32 C3
Sherfield on Loddon Hants 49 B7
Sherfin Lancs 195 B9
Sherford Devon 8 G5
Dorset 18 C4
Som 28 C2
Sheriffhales Shrops 150 G5
Sheriff Hill T&W 243 E7
Sheriff Hutton N Yorks 216 F3
Sheriff's Lench Worcs 99 B10
Sheringham Norf 177 E11
Sherington M Keynes 103 B7
Sheringwood Norf 177 E11
Shermanbury W Sus 36 D2
Shernal Green Worcs 117 E8
Shernborne Norf 158 C4
Sherrard's Green Worcs 98 B5
Sherrardspark Herts 86 C2
Sherriffhales Shrops 150 G5
Sherrington Wilts 46 F3
Sherston Wilts 61 B11
Sherwood Nottingham 171 G9
Sherwood Green Devon 25 C9
Sherwood Park Kent 52 E6
Shettleston Glasgow 268 C2
Shevington Gtr Man 194 F4
Shevington Moor Gtr Man 194 E4
Shevington Vale Gtr Man 194 F4
Sheviock Corn 7 D7
Shewalton N Ayrs 257 B8
Shibden Head W Yorks 196 B5
Shide IoW 20 D5
Shiel Aberds 292 B4
Shiel Bridge Highld 295 D11
Shieldaig Highld 299 B8
Highld 299 D8
Shieldhall Glasgow 267 B10
Shieldhill Dumfries 248 F2
Falk 279 F7
S Lnrk 269 G10
Shield Row Durham 242 G6
Shielfoot Highld 289 C8
Shielhill Angus 287 B8
Invclyd 276 G4
Shifford Oxon 82 E5
Shifnal Shrops 132 B4
Shilbottle Northumb 252 B5
Shilbottle Grange Northumb 252 B6
Shildon Durham 233 F10
Shillford E Renf 267 D8
Shillingford Devon 27 C7
Oxon 83 G9
Shillingford Abbot Devon 14 D4
Shillingford St George Devon 14 D4
Shillingstone Dorset 30 E4
Shillington C Beds 104 E2
Shillmoor Northumb 251 B9
Shilton Oxon 82 D3
Warks 135 G8
Shilvington Northumb 252 G5
Shimpling Norf 142 G3
Suff 125 G7

Shimpling Street
Suff 125 G7
Shincliffe Durham 233 C11
Shiney Row T&W 243 G8
Shinfield Wokingham 65 F8
Shingay Cambs 104 B6
Shingham Norf 140 C5
Shingle Street Suff 109 C7
Shinner's Bridge
Devon 8 C5
Shinness Highld 309 H5
Shipbourne Kent 52 C5
Shipdham Norf 141 B9
Shipdham Airfield
Norf 141 B9
Shipham Som 44 B2
Shiphay Torbay 9 B7
Shiplake Oxon 65 D9
Shiplake Bottom
Oxon 65 C8
Shiplake Row Oxon 65 D9
Shiplate N Som 43 B11
Shiplaw Borders 270 F4
Shipley Derbys 170 G6
Northumb 264 F4
Shrops 132 D6
W Sus 35 C10
W Yorks 205 F8
Shipley Bridge Sur 51 E10
Shipley Common
Derbys 171 G7
Shipley Shiels
Northumb 251 E7
Shipmeadow Suff 143 F7
Shipping Pembs 73 D10
Shippon Oxon 83 F7
Shipston-on-Stour
Warks 100 C5
Shipton Bucks 102 F5
Glos 81 B8
N Yorks 207 B7
Shrops 131 E11
Shipton Bellinger
Hants 47 D8
Shipton Gorge
Dorset 16 C5
Shipton Green
W Sus 22 C4
Shipton Lee Bucks 102 G4
Shipton Moyne Glos 61 B11
Shipton Oliffe Glos 81 B8
Shipton on Cherwell
Oxon 83 B7
Shipton Solers Glos 81 B8
Shiptonthorpe
E Yorks 208 E3
Shipton-under-
Wychwood Oxon 82 B3
Shirburn Oxon 83 F11
Shirdley Hill Lancs 193 E11
Shirebrook Derbys 171 B8
Shirecliffe S Yorks 186 C4
Shiregreen S Yorks 186 C5
Shirehampton Bristol 60 D4
Shiremoor T&W 243 C8
Shirenewton Mon 79 G7
Shire Oak W Mid 133 C11
Shireoaks Derbys 185 E9
Notts 187 E9
Shires Mill Fife 279 D10
Shirkoak Kent 54 F2
Shirland Derbys 170 D6
Shirlett Shrops 132 D3
Shirley Derbys 170 G2
Hants 19 B9
London 67 F11
Soton 32 E6
W Mid 118 B2
Shirley Heath
W Mid 118 B2
Shirley holms Hants 19 B11
Shirley Warren Soton 32 E5
Shirl Heath Hereford 115 F8
Shirrell Heath Hants 33 E9
Shirwell Devon 40 F5
Shirwell Cross Devon 40 F5
Shiskine N Ayrs 255 E10
Shitterton Dorset 18 C2
Shobdon Hereford 115 E8
Shobley Hants 31 F11
Shobnall Staffs 152 E4
Shobrooke Devon 26 G5
Shoby Leics 154 F3
Shocklach Ches W 166 F6
Shocklach Green
Ches W 166 F6
Shoeburyness Sthend 70 C2
Sholden Kent 55 C11
Sholing Soton 32 E6
Sholing Common
Soton 33 E7
Sholver Gtr Man 196 F3
Shootash Hants 32 C4
Shooters Hill London 68 D2
Shootersway Herts 85 D7
Shoot Hill Shrops 149 G8
Shop Corn 10 G3
Corn 24 E2
Devon 24 E5
Shop Corner Suff 108 E4
Shopford Cumb 240 C3
Shopnoller Som 43 G7
Shopp Hill W Sus 34 B6
Shopwyke W Sus 22 B5
Shore Gtr Man 196 D2
W Yorks 196 B2
Shore Bottom Devon 28 G2
Shoreditch London 67 C10
Som 28 C2
Shoregill Cumb 222 E5
Shoreham Kent 68 G4
Shoreham Beach
W Sus 36 G2
Shoreham-by-Sea
W Sus 36 F2
Shore Mill Highld 301 C7
Shoresdean
Northumb 273 F9
Shores Green Oxon 82 D5
Shoreside Shetland 313 J4
Shoreswood
Northumb 273 F8
Shoreton Highld 300 C6
Shorley Hants 33 B9
Shorncliffe Camp
Kent 55 F7
Shorncote Glos 81 F8
Shorne Kent 69 E7
Shorne Ridgeway
Kent 69 E7
Shorne West Kent 69 E7
Shortacombe Devon 12 D6
Shortacross Corn 6 D5
Shortbridge E Sus 37 C7
Short Cross W Mid 133 G9
Shortfield Common
Sur 49 E10
Shortgate E Sus 23 B7
Short Green Norf 141 F11
Shorthampton Oxon 100 G6
Shortheath Hants 49 F9
Sur 49 E10
Short Heath Derbys 152 G6
W Mid 133 C9
W Mid 133 E11
Shorthill Shrops 131 B8
Shortlands London 67 F11
Shortlanesend Corn 4 F6
Shortlees E Ayrs 257 B10
Shortmoor Devon 28 G2
Dorset 29 G7
Shorton Torbay 9 C7
Shortroods Renfs 267 B9
Shortstanding Glos 79 C9
Shortstown Beds 103 B11
Short Street Wilts 45 D10
Shortwood Glos 80 F4
S Glos 61 D7
Shorwell IoW 20 E5
Shoscombe Bath 45 B8
Shoscombe Vale
Bath 45 B8
Shotatton Shrops 149 E7
Shotesham Norf 142 D5
Shotgate Essex 88 G3
Shotley Northants 137 D8
Suff 108 D4
Shotley Bridge
Durham 242 G3
Shotleyfield
Northumb 242 G3
Shotley Gate Suff 108 E4
Shottenden Kent 54 C4
Shottermill Sur 49 G11
Shottery Warks 118 G3
Shotteswell Warks 101 B8
Shottisham Suff 108 C6
Shottle Derbys 170 F4
Shottlegate Derbys 170 F4
Shotton Durham 234 D4
Durham 234 F3
Flint 166 B4
Northumb 242 B6
Northumb 263 C8
Shotton Colliery
Durham 234 C3
Shotts N Lnrk 269 C7
Shotwick Ches W 182 G4
Shouldham Norf 140 B3
Shouldham Thorpe
Norf 140 B3
Shoulton Worcs 116 F6
Shover's Green
E Sus 53 G7
Shraleybrook Staffs 168 F3
Shrawardine Shrops 149 F8
Shrawley Worcs 116 E6
Shreding Green
Bucks 66 C4
Shrewley Warks 118 D4
Shrewley Common
Warks 118 D4
Shrewsbury Shrops 149 G9
Shrewton Wilts 46 E5
Shripney W Sus 22 C6
Shrivenham Oxon 63 B8
Shropham Norf 141 E9
Shroton or Iwerne
Courtney Dorset 30 E5
Shrub End Essex 107 G9
Shrubs Hill Sur 66 F3
Shrutherhill S Lnrk 268 F5
Shucknall Hereford 97 C11
Shudy Camps
Cambs 106 C2
Shulishadermor
Highld 298 E4
Shulista Highld 298 B4
Shuna Ho Argyll 275 C8
Shurdington Glos 80 B6
Shurlock Row
Windsor 65 E10
Shurnock Worcs 117 E10
Shurrery Highld 310 D4
Shurrery Lodge
Highld 310 D4
Shurton Som 43 E8
Shustoke Warks 134 E4
Shute Devon 15 B11
Devon 26 G5
Shute End Wilts 31 B11
Shutford Oxon 101 C7
Shut Heath Staffs 151 E7
Shuthonger Glos 99 D7
Shutlanger
Northants 120 G4
Shutta Corn 6 E5
Shutt Green Staffs 133 B7
Shuttington Warks 134 B5
Shuttlesfield Kent 55 E7
Shuttlewood Derbys 187 G7
Shuttleworth
Gtr Man 195 D10
Shutton Hereford 98 F3
Shwt Bridgend 57 D11
Siabost bho Dheas
W Isles 304 D4
Siabost bho Thuath
W Isles 304 D4
Siadar W Isles 304 C5
Siadar Iarach
W Isles 304 C5
Siadar Uarach
W Isles 304 C5
Sibbaldbie Dumfries 248 F4
Sibbertoft Northants 136 G3
Sibdon Carwood
Shrops 131 G8
Sibford Ferris Oxon 101 D7
Sibford Gower
Oxon 101 D7
Sible Hedingham
Essex 106 E5
Sibley's Green
Essex 106 F2
Sibsey Lincs 174 E5
Sibsey Fen Side
Lincs 174 E4
Sibson Cambs 137 D11
Leics 135 C7
Sibster Highld 310 D7
Sibthorpe Notts 172 F3
Notts 188 G2
Sibton Suff 127 D7
Sibton Green Suff 127 C7
Sicklesmere Suff 125 E7
Sicklinghall
N Yorks 206 D3
Sid Devon 15 D8
Sidbrook Som 28 B3
Sidbury Devon 15 C8
Shrops 132 F3
Sidcot N Som 44 B2
Sidcup London 68 E3
Siddal W Yorks 196 C6
Siddick Cumb 228 E6
Siddington Ches E 184 G4
Glos 81 F8
Siddington Heath
Ches E 184 G4
Sidemoor Worcs 117 C9
Side of the Moor
Gtr Man 195 E8
Sidestrand Norf 160 B5
Sideway Stoke 168 G5
Sidford Devon 15 C8
Sidlesham W Sus 22 D5
Sidlesham Common
W Sus 22 C5
Sidley E Sus 38 F2
Sidlow Sur 51 D9
Sidmouth Devon 15 D8
Sidway Staffs 150 B5
Sigford Devon 13 G11
Sigglesthorne
E Yorks 209 D9
Sighthill Edin 280 G3
Glasgow 268 B2
Sigingstone / Tresigin
V Glam 58 E3
Signet Oxon 82 C2
Sigwells Som 29 C10
Silchester Hants 64 G6
Sildinis W Isles 305 G4
Sileby Leics 153 F11
Silecroft Cumb 210 C2
Silfield Norf 142 D2
Silford Devon 24 B6
Silian Ceredig 111 G11
Silkstead Hants 32 C6
Silkstone S Yorks 197 F9
Silkstone Common
S Yorks 197 G9
Silk Willoughby
Lincs 173 G9
Silloth Cumb 238 G4
Sills Northumb 251 C8
Sillyearn Moray 302 D5
Siloh Carms 94 D4
Silpho N Yorks 227 G9
Silsden W Yorks 204 D6
Silsoe C Beds 103 D11
Silton Dorset 30 B3
Silverburn Midloth 270 C4
Silverdale Lancs 211 E9
Staffs 168 F4
Silverdale Green
Lancs 211 E9
Silver End Essex 88 B4
W Mid 133 F8
Silvergate Norf 160 D3
Silver Green Norf 142 E5
Silverhill E Sus 38 E3
Silver Hill E Sus 38 B2
Silverhill Park E Sus 38 E4
Silver Knap Som 29 C11
Silverknowes Edin 280 F4
Silverley's Green
Suff 126 B5
Silvermuir S Lnrk 269 F8
Silverstone
Northants 102 C3
Silver Street Glos 80 E3
Kent 69 G11
Som 27 C11
Som 44 G4
Worcs 117 B11
Silverton Devon 27 G7
W Dunb 277 F8
Silvertonhill S Lnrk 268 E4
Silvertown London 68 D2
Silverwell Corn 4 F4
Silvington Shrops 116 B2
Silwick Shetland 313 J4
Sim Hill S Yorks 197 G9
Simister Gtr Man 195 F10
Simmondley Derbys 185 C8
Simm's Cross
Halton 183 D8
Simm's Lane End
Mers 194 G4
Simonburn
Northumb 241 C9
Simonsbath Som 41 F9
Simonsburrow
Devon 27 D10
Simonside T&W 243 E8
Simonstone Lancs 203 G11
N Yorks 223 G7
Simprim Borders 272 F6
Simpson M Keynes 103 D7
Pembs 72 B5
Simpson Cross
Pembs 72 B5
Simpson Green
W Yorks 205 F9
Sinclair's Hill
Borders 272 E6
Sinclairston
E Ayrs 257 F11
Sinclairtown Fife 280 C5
Sinderby N Yorks 214 C6
Sinderhope
Northumb 241 G8
Sinderland Green
Gtr Man 184 C2
Sindlesham
Wokingham 65 F9
Sinfin Derby 152 C6
Sinfin Moor Derby 153 C7
Singdean Borders 250 C3
Singleborough
Bucks 102 E5
Single Hill Bath 45 B8
Singleton Lancs 202 F3
W Sus 34 E5
Singlewell Kent 69 E7
Singret Wrex 166 D4
Sinkhurst Green
Kent 53 E10
Sinnahard Aberds 292 B6
Sinnington N Yorks 216 B4
Sinton Worcs 116 E6
Sinton Green Worcs 116 E6
Sion Hill Bath 61 F8
Sipson London 66 D5
Sirhowy Bl Gwent 77 C11
Sisland Norf 142 D6
Sissinghurst Kent 53 F9
Sisterpath Borders 272 F5
Siston S Glos 61 D7
Sithney Corn 2 D4
Sithney Common Corn 2 D4
Sithney Green Corn 2 D4
Sittingbourne Kent 70 G2
Six Ashes Staffs 132 F5
Six Bells Bl Gwent 78 E2
Sixhills Lincs 189 D11
Six Hills Leics 154 E2
Sixmile Kent 54 E6
Six Mile Bottom
Cambs 123 F11
Sixpenny Handley
Dorset 31 D7
Sizewell Suff 127 E9
Skaigh Devon 13 C8
Skail Highld 308 E7
Skaill Orkney 314 C4
Orkney 314 E2
Orkney 314 F5
Skares E Ayrs 258 F2
Skateraw E Loth 282 F4
Skaw Shetland 312 B8
Shetland 312 G7
Skeabost Highld 298 E4
Skeabrae Orkney 314 D2
Skeeby N Yorks 224 E4
Skeete Kent 54 E6
Skeffington Leics 136 C4
Skeffling E Yorks 201 D11
Skegby Notts 171 C7
Notts 188 G3
Skegness Lincs 175 C9
Skelberry Shetland 313 G6
Shetland 313 M5
Skelbo Highld 309 K7
Skelbo Street
Highld 309 K7
Skelbrooke S Yorks 198 E4
Skeldyke Lincs 156 B6
Skelfhill Borders 249 C11
Skellingthorpe
Lincs 188 G6
Skellister Shetland 313 H6
Skellorn Green
Ches E 184 E6
Skellow S Yorks 198 E4
Skelmanthorpe
W Yorks 197 E8
Skelmersdale Lancs 194 F3
Skelmonae Aberds 303 F8
Skelmorlie N Ayrs 266 B3
Skelmuir Aberds 303 E9
Skelpick Highld 308 D7
Skelton Cumb 230 D4
E Yorks 199 B9
N Yorks 223 E11
Redcar 226 B3
York 207 B7
Skelton-on-Ure
N Yorks 215 F7
Skelwick Orkney 314 B4
Skelwith Bridge
Cumb 220 E6
Skendleby Lincs 174 B6
Skendleby Psalter
Lincs 190 G6
Skene Ho Aberds 293 C9
Skenfrith Mon 97 G9
Skerne E Yorks 208 B6
Skerne Park Darl 224 C5
Skeroblingarry
Argyll 255 E8
Skerray Highld 308 C6
Skerricha Highld 306 D7
Skerryford Pembs 72 C6
Skerton Lancs 211 G9
Sketchley Leics 135 E8
Sketty Swansea 56 C6
Skewen / Sgiwen
Neath 57 B8
Skewes Corn 5 B9
Skewsby N Yorks 216 E2
Skeyton Norf 160 D4
Skeyton Corner
Norf 160 D5
Skiag Bridge Highld 307 G7
Skibo Castle Highld 309 L7
Skidbrooke Lincs 190 C6
Skidbrooke North End
Lincs 190 B6
Skidby E Yorks 208 G6
Skilgate Som 27 B7
Skillington Lincs 155 D7
Skinburness Cumb 238 F4
Skinflats Falk 279 E8
Skinidin Highld 298 E2
Skinner's Bottom Corn 4 F4
Skinners Green
W Berks 64 F2
Skinnet Highld 308 C5
Skinningrove
Redcar 226 B4
Skipness Argyll 255 B9
Skippool Lancs 202 E3
Skiprigg Cumb 230 B3
Skipsea E Yorks 209 B9
Skipsea Brough
E Yorks 209 C9
Skipton N Yorks 204 C5
Skipton-on-Swale
N Yorks 215 D7
Skipwith N Yorks 207 F9
Skirbeck Lincs 174 G4
Skirbeck Quarter
Lincs 174 G4
Skirethorns
N Yorks 213 G9
Skirlaugh E Yorks 209 F8
Skirling Borders 260 B3
Skirmett Bucks 65 B9
Skirpenbeck
E Yorks 207 B10
Skirwith Cumb 231 E8
Skirza Highld 310 C7
Skitby Cumb 239 D10
Skitham Lancs 202 E4
Skittle Green Bucks 84 E3
Skulamus Highld 295 C8
Skullomie Highld 308 C6
Skyborry Green
Shrops 114 C5
Skye Green Essex 107 G7
Skye of Curr Highld 301 G9
Skyfog Pembs 90 F6
Skyreholme
N Yorks 213 G11
Slack Derbys 170 C4
W Yorks 196 B3
W Yorks 196 D5
Slackcote Gtr Man 196 F3
Slackhall Derbys 185 E9
Slackhead Moray 302 C4
Slack Head Cumb 211 D9
Slackholme End
Lincs 191 G8
Slacks of Cairnbanno
Aberds 303 E8
Slad Glos 80 D5
Sladbrook Glos 98 F5
Slade Devon 27 F10
Devon 40 D4
Kent 54 C2
Pembs 72 B6
Slade End Oxon 83 G9
Slade Green London 68 D4
Slade Heath Staffs 133 B8
Slade Hooton
S Yorks 187 D8
Sladen Green Hants 48 C2
Sladesbridge Corn 10 G6
Slades Green Worcs 99 E7
Slaggyford
Northumb 240 G5
Slaidburn Lancs 203 C10
Slaithwaite W Yorks 196 E5
Slaley Derbys 170 D3
Northumb 241 F11
Slamannan Falk 279 G7
Slape Cross Som 43 F10
Slapewath Redcar 226 B2
Slapton Bucks 103 G8
Devon 8 G6
Northants 102 B2
Slateford Edin 280 G4
Slate Haugh Moray 302 C4
Slatepit Dale Derbys 170 B4
Slattocks Gtr Man 195 F11
Slaugham W Sus 36 B3
Slaughterbridge
Corn 11 D8
Slaughterford Wilts 61 E10
Slaughter Hill
Ches E 168 D2
Slawston Leics 136 E5
Slay Pits S Yorks 199 F7
Sleaford Hants 49 F10
Lincs 173 F9
Sleagill Cumb 221 B11
Sleap Shrops 149 D9
Sleapford Telford 150 F2
Sleapshyde Herts 86 D2
Sleastary Highld 309 K6
Slebech Pembs 73 B8
Sledge Green Worcs 98 E6
Sledmere E Yorks 217 G8
Sleeches Cross
E Sus 52 G5
Sleepers Hill Hants 33 B7
Sleetbeck Cumb 240 B2
Sleet Moor Derbys 170 E6
Sleight Dorset 18 B5
Sleights N Yorks 227 D7
Slepe Dorset 18 C4
Sliabhna h-Airde
W Isles 296 F3
Slickly Highld 310 C6
Sliddery N Ayrs 255 E10
Slideslow Worcs 117 C9
Sligachan Hotel
Highld 294 C6
Sligneach Argyll 288 G4
Sligrachan Argyll 276 C3
Slimbridge Glos 80 E2
Slindon Staffs 150 C6
W Sus 35 F7
Slinfold W Sus 50 G6
Sling Glos 79 D9
Gwyn 163 B10
Slingsby N Yorks 216 E3
Slioch Aberds 302 F5
Slip End C Beds 85 B9
Herts 104 D5
Slippery Ford
W Yorks 204 E6
Slipton Northants 121 B9
Slitting Mill Staffs 151 F10
Slochd Highld 301 G8
Slockavullin Argyll 275 D9
Slogan Moray 302 E3
Sloley Norf 160 E5
Sloncombe Devon 13 D10
Sloothby Lincs 191 G7
Slough Slough 66 D3
Slough Green Som 28 C3
W Sus 36 B3
Slough Hill Suff 125 G7
Sluggan Highld 301 G8
Sluggans Highld 298 E4
Slumbay Highld 295 B10
Sly Corner Kent 54 G3
Slyfield Sur 50 C3
Slyne Lancs 211 F9
Smailholm Borders 262 B4
Smallbridge
Gtr Man 196 D2
Smallbrook Devon 14 B3
Glos 79 E9
Smallburgh Norf 160 E6
Smallburn Aberds 303 E10
E Ayrs 258 D5
Smalldale Derbys 185 E11
Derbys 185 F9
Small Dole W Sus 36 E2
Small End Lincs 174 D6
Smalley Derbys 170 G6
Smalley Common
Derbys 170 G6
Smalley Green
Derbys 170 G6
Smallfield Sur 51 E10
Smallford Herts 85 D11
Small Heath W Mid 134 F2
Smallholm Dumfries 238 B4
Small Hythe Kent 53 G11
Smallmarsh Devon 25 C10
Smallrice Staffs 151 C9
Smallridge Devon 28 G4
Smallshaw Gtr Man 196 G2
Smallthorne Stoke 168 E5
Small Way Som 44 G6
Smallwood Ches E 168 C4
Worcs 117 D10
Smallwood Green
Suff 125 F8
Smallwood Hey
Lancs 202 D3
Smallworth Norf 141 G10
Smannell Hants 47 D11
Smardale Cumb 222 D4
Smarden Kent 53 E11
Smarden Bell Kent 53 E11
Smart's Hill Kent 52 E4
Smaull Argyll 274 G3
Smeatharpe Devon 27 E11
Smeaton Fife 280 C5
Smeeth Kent 54 F5
Smeeton Westerby
Leics 136 E3
Smelthouses
N Yorks 214 G3
Smercleit W Isles 297 K3
Smerral Highld 310 F5
Smestow Staffs 133 E7
Smethcott Shrops 131 D9
Smethwick W Mid 133 F10
Smethwick Green
Ches E 168 C4
Smirisary Highld 289 B8
Smisby Derbys 152 F6
Smite Hill Worcs 117 F7
Smithaleigh Devon 7 D11
Smithbrook W Sus 34 C6
Smith End Green
Worcs 116 G5
Smithfield Cumb 239 D10
Smith Green Lancs 202 C5
Smithies S Yorks 197 F11
Smithincott Devon 27 E9
Smithley S Yorks 197 G11
Smith's End Herts 105 D8
Smiths Green
Ches E 184 G4
Smith's Green
Ches E 168 E3
Essex 105 G11
Essex 106 C3
Smithston Aberds 302 G5
Smithstown Highld 299 B7
Smithton Highld 301 E7
Smithwood Green
Suff 125 G8
Smithy Bridge
Gtr Man 196 D2
Smithy Gate Flint 181 F11
Smithy Green
Ches E 184 G2
Gtr Man 184 D5
Smithy Houses
Derbys 170 F5
Smithy Lane Ends
Lancs 194 E2
Smock Alley W Sus 35 D9
Smockington Leics 135 F9
Smoky Row Bucks 84 D4
Smoogro Orkney 314 F3
Smug Oak Herts 85 E10
Smyrton S Ayrs 244 G4
Smythe's Green
Essex 88 B6
Snagshall E Sus 38 C3
Snaigow House
Perth 286 C4
Snailbeach Shrops 131 C7
Snails Hill Som 29 E7
Snailwell Cambs 124 D2
Snainton N Yorks 217 C8
Snaisgill Durham 232 F5
Snaith E Yorks 198 C6
Snape N Yorks 214 C5
Suff 127 F7
Snape Green Lancs 193 E11
Snape Hill Derbys 186 F5
S Yorks 198 G2
Snapper Devon 40 G5
Snaresbrook London 67 B11
Snarestone Leics 134 B6
Snarford Lincs 189 E9
Snargate Kent 39 B7
Snarraness Shetland 313 H4
Snatchwood Torf 78 E3
Snave Kent 39 B8
Sneachill Worcs 117 G8
Snead Powys 130 E6
Snead Common
Worcs 116 D4
Sneads Green
Worcs 117 D7
Sneath Common
Norf 142 F3
Sneaton N Yorks 227 D7
Sneatonthorpe
N Yorks 227 D8
Snedshill Telford 132 B4
Sneinton
Nottingham 153 B11
Snelland Lincs 189 E9
Snelston Derbys 169 G11
Snetterton Norf 141 E9
Snettisham Norf 158 C3
Sneyd Green Stoke 168 F5
Sneyd Park Bristol 60 D5
Snibston Leics 153 G8
Snig's End Glos 98 F5
Snipeshill Kent 70 G2
Sniseabhal W Isles 297 H3
Snitter Northumb 252 C2
Snitterby Lincs 189 C7
Snitterfield Warks 118 F4
Snitterton Derbys 170 C3
Snitton Shrops 115 B11
Snittongate Shrops 115 B11
Snodhill Hereford 96 C6
Snodland Kent 69 G7
Snods Edge
Northumb 242 G3
Snowden Hill
S Yorks 197 G9
Snowdown Kent 55 C8
Snow End Herts 105 E8
Snow Hill Ches E 167 E10
W Yorks 197 C10
Snow Lea W Yorks 196 D5
Snowshill Glos 99 E11
Snow Street Norf 141 G11
Snydale W Yorks 198 D2
Soake Hants 33 E11
Soar Anglesey 178 G5
Carms 94 F2
Devon 9 G9
Gwyn 146 B2
Powys 95 E9
Soar-y-Mynydd
Ceredig 112 G5
Soberton Hants 33 D10
Soberton Heath
Hants 33 E10
Sockbridge Cumb 230 F6
Sockburn Darl 224 D6
Sockety Dorset 29 F7
Sodom Denb 181 G9
Shetland 313 G7
Wilts 62 C4
Sodylt Bank Shrops 148 B6
Soham Cambs 123 C11
Soham Cotes
Cambs 123 B11
Soho London 67 C9
Som 45 D7
W Mid 133 F10
Solas W Isles 296 D4
Soldon Cross Devon 24 E4
Soldridge Hants 49 G7
Sole Street Kent 54 D5
Kent 69 F7
Solfach / Solva
Pembs 90 G5
Solihull W Mid 118 B2
Solihull Lodge
W Mid 117 B11
Sollers Dilwyn
Hereford 115 F8
Sollers Hope
Hereford 98 E2
Sollom Lancs 194 D3
Solva / Solfach
Pembs 90 G5
Somerby Leics 154 G5
Lincs 200 F5
Somercotes Derbys 170 E6
Somerdale Bath 61 F7
Somerford Ches E 168 B4
Dorset 19 C9
Staffs 133 B7
Somerford Keynes
Glos 81 G8
Somerley W Sus 22 D4
Somerleyton Suff 143 D9
Somersal Herbert
Derbys 152 B2
Somersby Lincs 190 G4
Somersham Cambs 123 B7
Suff 107 B11
Somers Town London 67 C9
Ptsmth 21 B8
Somerton Newport 59 B10
Oxon 101 F9
Som 29 B7
Suff 124 G6
Somerton Hill Som 29 B7
Somerwood
Shrops 149 G11
Sompting W Sus 35 G11
Sompting Abbotts
W Sus 35 F11
Sonning Wokingham 65 D9
Sonning Common
Oxon 65 C8
Sonning Eye Oxon 65 D9
Sontley Wrex 166 F4
Sookholme Notts 171 B8
Sopley Hants 19 B9
Sopwell Herts 85 D11
Sopworth Wilts 61 B10
Sorbie Dumfries 236 E6
Sordale Highld 310 C5
Sorisdale Argyll 288 C4
Sorley Devon 8 F4
Sorn E Ayrs 258 D3
Sornhill E Ayrs 258 C2
Sortat Highld 310 C6
Sotby Lincs 190 F2
Sothall S Yorks 186 E6
Sots Hole Lincs 173 C10
Sotterley Suff 143 G9
Soudley Shrops 131 E9
Shrops 150 D4
Soughley S Yorks 197 G7
Soughton / Sychdyn
Flint 166 B2
Soulbury Bucks 103 F7
Soulby Cumb 222 C4
Cumb 230 F5
Souldern Oxon 101 E10
Souldrop Beds 121 E9
Sound Ches E 167 F10
Shetland 313 H5
Shetland 313 J6
Sound Heath
Ches E 167 F10
Soundwell S Glos 60 D6
Sourhope Borders 263 E8
Sourin Orkney 314 C4
Sourlie N Ayrs 266 G6
Sour Nook Cumb 230 C3
Sourton Devon 12 C6
Soutergate Cumb 210 C4
South Acre Norf 158 G6
South Acton London 67 D7
South Alkham Kent 55 E8
Southall London 66 C6
South Allington
Devon 9 G10
South Alloa Falk 279 C7
Southam Cumb 219 C9
Glos 99 F9
Warks 119 E8
South Ambersham
W Sus 34 C6
Southampton Soton 32 E6
South Anston
S Yorks 187 E8
South Ascot Windsor 66 F2
South Ashford Kent 54 E4
South Auchmachar
Aberds 303 E9
Southay Som 28 D6
South Baddesley
Hants 20 B3
South Ballachulish
Highld 284 B4
South Balloch
S Ayrs 245 D8
South Bank Redcar 234 G6
York 207 C7
South Barrow Som 29 B10
South Beach
Northumb 243 B8
South Beach / Marian-y-
de Gwyn 145 C7
South Beddington
London 67 G9
South Benfleet Essex 69 B9
South Bents T&W 243 E10
South Bersted
W Sus 22 C6
South Blainslie
Borders 271 G10
South Bockhampton
Dorset 19 B9
Southborough
Bromley 68 F2
Kent 52 E5
Kingston-upon-Thames 67 F7
Southbourne Bmouth 19 C8
W Sus 22 B3
South Bramwith
S Yorks 198 E6
South Brent Devon 8 D3
South Brewham Som 45 F8
South Bromley
London 67 C11
Southbrook Wilts 45 G10
South Broomage
Falk 279 E7
South Broomhill
Northumb 252 D6
Southburgh Norf 141 C9
South Burlingham
Norf 143 B7
Southburn E Yorks 208 C5
South Cadbury Som 29 B10
South Cairn
Dumfries 236 C1
South Carlton Lincs 189 F7
Notts 187 E9
South Carne Corn 11 E10
South Cave E Yorks 208 G4
South Cerney Glos 81 F8
South Chailey E Sus 36 D5
South Chard Som 28 F4
South Charlton
Northumb 264 E5
South Cheriton Som 29 C11
Southchurch Sthend 70 B2
South Church
Durham 233 F10
South Cliffe E Yorks 208 F3
South Clifton Notts 188 G4
South Clunes Highld 300 E5
South Cockerington
Lincs 190 D5
South Common
Devon 28 G4
Southcoombe Oxon 100 F6
South Cornelly
Bridgend 57 E10
South Corriegills
N Ayrs 256 C2
South Corrielaw
Dumfries 248 G5
Southcote Reading 65 E7
Southcott Corn 11 B9
Devon 24 D6
Wilts 47 B7
Southcourt Bucks 84 C4
South Cove Suff 143 G9
South Creagan
Argyll 289 E11
South Creake Norf 159 B7
Southcrest Worcs 117 D10
South Crosland
W Yorks 196 E6
South Croxton Leics 154 G3
South Croydon
London 67 G10
South Cuil Highld 298 C3
South Dalton
E Yorks 208 D5
South Darenth Kent 68 F5
Southdean Borders 250 B4
Southdene Mers 182 B6
South Denes Norf 143 C10
Southdown Bath 61 G8
Corn 7 E8
South Down Hants 33 C7
Som 28 E2
South Duffield
N Yorks 207 G9
South Dunn Highld 310 D5
South Earlswood Sur 51 D9
Southease E Sus 36 F6
South Elkington
Lincs 190 D3
South Elmsall
W Yorks 198 E3
South Elphinstone
E Loth 281 G7
Southend Argyll 255 G7
Bucks 65 B9
Glos 80 F2
London 67 E11
Oxon 83 E9
W Berks 64 D2
W Berks 64 E5
Wilts 63 E7
South End Beds 103 B10
Bucks 103 F7
Cumb 210 G4
E Yorks 209 E9
Hants 31 D10

South-end Herts 86 B6
South End N Lincs 200 C6
Norf 141 E9
Southend-on-Sea
Sthend 69 B11
Southerhouse
Shetland 313 K5
Southerly Devon 12 D6
Southernby Cumb 230 D3
Southern Cross
Brighton 36 F3
Southernden Kent 53 D11
Southerndown
V Glam 57 G11
Southerness
Dumfries 237 D11
Southern Green
Herts 104 E6
South Erradale
Highld 299 B7
Southery Norf 140 E2
Southey Green
Essex 106 E5
South Fambridge
Essex 88 F5
South Farnborough
Hants 49 C11
South Fawley
W Berks 63 C11
South Ferriby
N Lincs 200 C3
Southfield Northumb 243 B7
South Field E Yorks 200 B4
Windsor 66 D3
Southfields London 67 E9
Thurrock 69 C7
Southfleet Kent 68 E6
South Flobbets
Aberds 303 F7
Southford IoW 20 F6
South Garth
Shetland 312 D7
South Garvan
Highld 289 B11
Southgate Ceredig 111 A11
London 86 G3
Norf 159 C7
Norf 160 E2
Swansea 56 D5
W Sus 51 F9
South Glendale
W Isles 297 K3
South Gluss
Shetland 312 F5
South Godstone
Sur 51 D11
South Gorley Hants 31 E11
South Gosforth
T&W 242 D6
South Green Essex 87 G11
Essex 89 B8
Kent 69 G11
Norf 157 F10
Norf 159 G11
Suff 126 B3
South Gyle Edin 280 G3
South-haa Shetland 312 E5
South Hackney
London 67 C11
South Ham Hants 48 C6
South Hampstead
London 67 C9
South Hanningfield
Essex 88 F2
South Harefield
London 66 B5
South Harrow London 66 B6
South Harting
W Sus 34 D3
South Hatfield Herts 86 D2
South Hayling Hants 21 B10
South Hazelrigg
Northumb 264 C3
South Heath Bucks 84 E6
Essex 89 B10
South Heighton
E Sus 23 E7
South-heog
Shetland 312 E5
South Hetton
Durham 234 B3
South Hiendley
W Yorks 197 E11
South Hill Corn 12 G2
N Som 43 B10
Pembs 72 C4
South Hinksey Oxon 83 E8
South Hole Devon 24 C2
South Holme
N Yorks 216 D3
South Holmwood
Sur 51 D7
South Hornchurch
London 68 C4
South Huish Devon 8 G3
South Hykeham
Lincs 172 C6
South Hylton T&W 243 F9
Southill C Beds 104 C3
Dorset 17 E9
Southington Hants 48 D4
South Kelsey Lincs 189 B8
South Kensington
London 67 D9
South Kessock
Highld 300 E6
South Killingholme
N Lincs 201 D7
South Kilvington
N Yorks 215 C8
South Kilworth
Leics 136 G2
South Kirkby
W Yorks 198 E2
South Kirkton
Aberds 293 C9
South Kiscadale
N Ayrs 256 D2
South Knighton
Devon 14 G2
Leicester 136 C2
South Kyme Lincs 173 F11
South Lambeth
London 67 D10
South Lancing
W Sus 35 G11
Southlands Dorset 17 F9
South Lane S Yorks 197 F9
Southleigh Devon 15 C10
South Leigh Oxon 82 D5
South Leverton
Notts 188 E3
South Littleton
Worcs 99 B11
South Lopham
Norf 141 G10
South Luffenham
Rutland 137 C8
South Malling E Sus 36 E6
Southmarsh Som 45 G8
South Marston
Swindon 63 B7
Southmead Bristol 60 D5
South Merstham Sur 51 C9
South Middleton
Northumb 263 E11
South Milford
N Yorks 206 G5
South Millbrex
Aberds 303 E8
South Milton Devon 8 G4
South Mimms Herts 86 E2
Southminster Essex 89 F7
South Molton Devon 26 B2
Southmoor Oxon 82 F5
South Moor Durham 242 G5
South Moreton Oxon 64 B5
South Mundham
W Sus 22 C5
South Muskham
Notts 172 D3
South Newbald
E Yorks 208 F4
South Newbarns
Cumb 210 F4
South Newington
Oxon 101 E8
South Newsham
Northumb 243 B8
South Newton Wilts 46 G5
South Normanton
Derbys 170 D6
South Norwood
London 67 F10
South Nutfield Sur 51 D10
South Ockendon
Thurrock 68 C5
Southoe Cambs 122 E3
Southolt Suff 126 D3
South Ormsby Lincs 190 F5
Southorpe Pboro 137 C11
South Ossett
W Yorks 197 D9
South Otterington
N Yorks 215 B7
Southover Dorset 17 C8
E Sus 36 F6
E Sus 37 B11
South Owersby
Lincs 189 C9
Southowram
W Yorks 196 C6
South Oxhey Herts 85 G10
South Park Sur 51 D8
South Pelaw
Durham 243 G7
South Perrott Dorset 29 F7
South Petherton
Som 28 D6
South Petherwin
Corn 12 E2
South Pickenham
Norf 141 C7
South Pill Corn 7 D8
South Pool Devon 8 G5
South Poorton
Dorset 16 B6
Southport Mers 193 D10
South Port Argyll 284 E4
Southpunds
Shetland 313 L6
South Quilquox
Aberds 303 F8
South Radworthy
Devon 41 G9
South Rauceby
Lincs 173 F8
South Raynham
Norf 159 E7
South Reddish
Gtr Man 184 C5
Southrepps Norf 160 B5
South Reston Lincs 190 E6
Southrey Lincs 173 B10
Southrop Glos 81 E11
Oxon 101 E7
Southrope Hants 49 E7
South Ruislip London 66 B6
South Runcton Norf 140 B2
South Scarle Notts 172 C4
Southsea Ptsmth 21 B8
Wrex 166 E4
South Shian Argyll 289 E11
South Shields T&W 243 D9
South Shore Blkpool 202 G2
South Side Durham 233 F8
Orkney 314 D5
South Somercotes
Lincs 190 C6
South Stainley
N Yorks 214 G6
South Stainmore
Cumb 222 C6
South Stanley
Durham 242 G5
South Stifford
Thurrock 68 D6
Southstoke Bath 61 G8
South Stoke Oxon 64 C6
W Sus 35 F8
South Stour Kent 54 F4
South Street E Sus 36 D5
Kent 54 B5
Kent 68 G6
Kent 69 G10
Kent 70 F6
London 52 B2
South Tawton Devon 13 C9
South Tehidy Corn 4 G3
South Thoresby
Lincs 190 F6
South Tidworth Wilts 47 D8
South Tottenham
London 67 B10
Southtown Norf 143 B10
Orkney 314 G4
Som 28 D4
Som 44 F5
South Town Devon 14 E5
Hants 49 F7
South Twerton Bath 61 G8
South Ulverston
Cumb 210 D6
South View Hants 48 C6
Southville Devon 8 G4
Torf 78 F3
South Voxter
Shetland 313 G5
Southwaite Cumb 230 C4
South Walsham
Norf 161 G7
Southwark London 67 D10
South Warnborough
Hants 49 D8
Southwater W Sus 35 B11
Southwater Street
W Sus 35 B11
Southway Plym 7 C9
Som 44 E4
South Weald Essex 87 G9
South Weirs Hants 32 G3
Southwell Dorset 17 G9
Notts 172 E2
South Weston Oxon 84 F2
South Wheatley
Corn 11 C10
Notts 188 D3
South Whiteness
Shetland 313 J5
Southwick Hants 33 F10
Northants 137 E10
Som 43 D11
T&W 243 F9
Wilts 45 B10
W Sus 36 F2
South Widcombe
Bath 44 B5
South Wigston
Leics 135 D11
South Willesborough
Kent 54 E4
South Willingham
Lincs 189 E11
South Wimbledon
London 67 E9
South Wingate
Durham 234 E4
South Wingfield
Derbys 170 D5
South Witham Lincs 155 F8
Southwold Suff 127 B10
South Wonford
Devon 24 F5
South Wonston
Hants 48 F3
Southwood Derbys 153 E7
Hants 49 B10
Norf 143 B7
Som 44 G5
Worcs 116 E4
South Woodford
London 86 G6
South Woodham Ferrers
Essex 88 F4
South Wootton Norf 158 E2
South Wraxall Wilts 61 G10
South Yardley
W Mid 134 G2
South Yarrows
Highld 310 E7
South Yeo Devon 25 G8
South Zeal Devon 13 C9
Soval Lodge
W Isles 304 F5
Sowber Gate
N Yorks 215 B7
Sowerby N Yorks 215 C8
W Yorks 196 C4
Sowerby Bridge
W Yorks 196 C5
Sowerby Row Cumb 230 D3
Sower Carr Lancs 202 E3
Sowley Green Suff 124 G4
Sowood W Yorks 196 D5
Sowood Green
W Yorks 196 D5
Sowton Devon 14 C5
Sowton Barton
Devon 14 D2
Soyal Highld 309 K5
Soyland Town
W Yorks 196 C4
Spacey Houses
N Yorks 206 C2
Spa Common Norf 160 C5
Spalding Lincs 156 E4
Spaldington
E Yorks 207 G11
Spaldwick Cambs 122 C2
Spalford Notts 172 B4
Spanby Lincs 155 B11
Spango Invclyd 276 G4
Spanish Green Hants 49 B7
Sparham Norf 159 F11
Sparhamhill Norf 159 F11
Spark Bridge Cumb 210 C6
Sparkbrook
W Mid 133 G11
Sparkford Som 29 B10
Sparkhill W Mid 133 G11
Sparkwell Devon 7 D11
Sparl Shetland 312 G5
Sparnon Corn 1 E3
Sparnon Gate Corn 4 G3
Sparrow Green
Norf 159 G9
Sparrow Hill Som 44 C2
Sparrowpit Derbys 185 E9
Sparrow's Green
E Sus 52 G6
Sparsholt Hants 48 G2
Oxon 63 B10
Spartylea Northumb 232 B3
Spath Staffs 151 B11
Spaunton N Yorks 226 G4
Spaxton Som 43 F8
Spean Bridge Highld 290 E4
Spear Hill W Sus 35 D10
Spearywell Hants 32 B4
Speckington Som 29 C9
Speed Gate Kent 68 F5
Speedwell Bristol 60 E6
Speen Bucks 84 F4
W Berks 64 F3
Speeton N Yorks 218 E2
Speke Mers 182 E6
Speldhurst Kent 52 E5
Spellbrook Herts 87 B7
Spelsbury Oxon 101 G7
Spelter Bridgend 57 C11
Spen W Yorks 197 B7
Spencers Wood
Wokingham 65 F8
Spen Green Ches E 168 C4
Spennells Worcs 116 C6
Spennithorne
N Yorks 214 B2
Spennymoor
Durham 233 E11
Spernall Warks 117 E11
Spetchley Worcs 117 G7
Spetisbury Dorset 30 G6
Spexhall Suff 143 G7
Speybank Highld 291 C10
Spey Bay Moray 302 C3
Speybridge Highld 301 G10
Speyview Moray 302 E2
Spillardsford
Aberds 303 D10
Spilsby Lincs 174 B6
Spindlestone
Northumb 264 C5
Spinkhill Derbys 187 F7
Spinney Hill
Northants 120 E5
Spinney Hills
Leicester 136 C2
Spinningdale Highld 309 L6
Spion Kop Notts 171 B9
Spirthill Wilts 62 D3
Spital Mers 182 E4
Windsor 66 D3
Spitalbrook Herts 86 D5
Spitalfields London 67 C10
Spitalhill Derbys 169 F11
Spital Hill S Yorks 187 C10
Spital in the Street
Lincs 189 D7
Spital Tongues
T&W 242 D6
Spithurst E Sus 36 D6
Spittal Dumfries 236 D5
E Loth 281 F9
E Yorks 207 C11
Highld 310 D5
Northumb 273 E10
Pembs 91 G9
Stirl 277 D10
Spittalfield Perth 286 C5
Spittal Houses
S Yorks 186 B5
Spittal of Glenmuick
Aberds 292 E5
Spittal of Glenshee
Perth 292 F3
Spittlegate Lincs 155 C8
Spixworth Norf 160 F4
Splatt Corn 10 F4
Corn 11 D10
Devon 25 F10
Som 43 F8
Splayne's Green
E Sus 36 C6
Splott Cardiff 59 D7
Spofforth N Yorks 206 C3
Spondon Derby 153 B8
Spon End W Mid 118 B6
Spon Green Flint 166 C3
Spooner Row Norf 141 D11
Spoonleygate
Shrops 132 D6
Sporle Norf 158 G6
Spotland Bridge
Gtr Man 195 E11
Spott E Loth 282 F3
Spratton Northants 120 C4
Spreakley Sur 49 E10
Spreyton Devon 13 B9
Spriddlestone Devon 7 E10
Spridlington Lincs 189 E8
Sprig's Alley Oxon 84 F3
Springbank Glos 99 G8
Spring Bank Cumb 229 G10
Springboig Glasgow 268 C3
Springbourne
Bmouth 19 C8
Springburn Glasgow 268 B2
Spring Cottage
Leics 152 F6
Spring End N Yorks 223 F9
Springfield Argyll 275 F11
Caerph 77 F11
Dumfries 239 D8
Essex 88 D2
Fife 287 F7
Gtr Man 194 F5
Highld 300 C6
M Keynes 103 D7
Moray 301 D10
W Mid 133 D8
W Mid 133 F9
W Mid 133 G11
Springfields Stoke 168 G5
Spring Gardens Som 45 D9
Spring Green Lancs 204 E4
Spring Grove London 67 D7
Springhead
Gtr Man 196 G3
Springhill E Renf 267 D10
IoW 20 B6
N Lnrk 269 D7
Staffs 133 B11
Staffs 133 C9
Spring Hill Gtr Man 196 F2
Lancs 195 B8
W Mid 133 D7
Springholm
Dumfries 237 C10
Springkell Dumfries 239 B7
Spring Park London 67 F11
Springside N Ayrs 257 B9
Springthorpe Lincs 188 D5
Spring Vale S Yorks 197 G9
Spring Valley IoM 192 E4
Springwell Essex 105 C10
T&W 243 F7
T&W 243 F9
Springwells
Dumfries 248 E3
Sproatley E Yorks 209 G9
Sproston Green
Ches W 168 B2
Sprotbrough
S Yorks 198 G4
Sproughton Suff 108 C2
Sprouston Borders 263 B7
Sprowston Norf 160 G4
Sproxton Leics 155 E7
N Yorks 216 C2
Sprunston Cumb 230 B3
Spunhill Shrops 149 C8
Spurlands End Bucks 84 F5
Spurstow Ches E 167 D9
Spurtree Shrops 116 D2
Spynie Moray 302 C2
Spyway Dorset 16 C6
Square and Compass
Pembs 91 E7
Squires Gate
Blkpool 202 G2
Sraid Ruadh Argyll 288 E1
Srannda W Isles 296 C6
Sronphadruig Lodge
Perth 291 F9
Stableford Shrops 132 D5
Staffs 150 B6
Stacey Bank
S Yorks 186 C3
Stackhouse N Yorks 212 F6
Stackpole Pembs 73 F7
Stackpole Quay
Pembs 73 F7
Stacksford Norf 141 E11
Stacksteads Lancs 195 C10
Stackyard Green
Suff 107 B9
Staddiscombe Plym 7 E10
Staddlethorpe
E Yorks 199 B10
Staddon Devon 24 C3
Devon 24 G5
Staden Derbys 185 G9
Stadhampton Oxon 83 F10
Stadhlaigearraidh
W Isles 297 H3
Stadmorslow Staffs 168 D5
Staffield Cumb 230 C6
Staffin Highld 298 C4
Stafford Staffs 151 E8
Stafford Park
Telford 132 B4
Stafford's Corner
Essex 89 B7
Stafford's Green
Dorset 29 C10
Stagbatch Hereford 115 F9
Stagden Cross
Essex 87 C10
Stagehall Borders 271 G9
Stagsden Beds 103 B9
Stagsden West End
Beds 103 B9
Stag's Head Devon 25 B11
Stain Highld 310 C7
Stainburn Cumb 228 F6
N Yorks 205 D10
Stainby Lincs 155 E8
Staincliffe W Yorks 197 C8
Staincross S Yorks 197 E10
Staindrop Durham 233 G8
Staines Green Herts 86 C3
Staines-upon-Thames
Sur 66 E4
Stainfield Lincs 155 D11
Lincs 189 G10
Stainforth N Yorks 212 F6
S Yorks 198 E6
Staining Lancs 202 F3
Stainland W Yorks 196 D5
Stainsacre N Yorks 227 D8
Stainsby Derbys 170 B6
Lincs 190 G4
Stainton Cumb 211 B10
Cumb 230 F5
Cumb 239 F9
Durham 223 B11
Mbro 225 C9
N Yorks 224 F2
S Yorks 187 C9
Stainton by Langworth
Lincs 189 F9
Staintondale
N Yorks 227 F9
Stainton le Vale
Lincs 189 C11
Stainton with Adgarley
Cumb 210 E5
Stair Cumb 229 G10
E Ayrs 257 E10
Stairfoot S Yorks 197 F11
Stairhaven Dumfries 236 D4
Staithes N Yorks 226 B5
Stakeford Northumb 253 F7
Stake Hill Gtr Man 195 F11
Stakenbridge Worcs 117 B7
Stake Pool Lancs 202 D4
Stalbridge Dorset 30 D2
Stalbridge Weston
Dorset 30 D2
Stalham Norf 161 D7
Stalham Green Norf 161 E7
Stalisfield Green
Kent 54 C3
Stallen Dorset 29 D10
Stallingborough
NE Lincs 201 E7
Stalling Busk
N Yorks 213 B8
Stallington Staffs 151 B8
Stalmine Lancs 202 D3
Stalmine Moss Side
Lancs 202 D3
Stalybridge Gtr Man 185 B7
Stambermill W Mid 133 G8
Stamborough Som 42 F4
Stambourne Essex 106 D4
Stambourne Green
Essex 106 D4
Stamford Lincs 137 B10
Stamford Bridge
Ches W 167 B7
E Yorks 207 B10
Stamfordham
Northumb 242 C3
Stamford Hill
London 67 B10
Stamperland
E Renf 267 D11
Stamshaw Ptsmth 33 G10
Stanah Cumb 220 B6
Lancs 202 E3
Stanborough Herts 86 C2
Stanbridge C Beds 103 G9
Dorset 31 G8
Stanbridgeford
C Beds 103 G9
Stanbrook Essex 106 F2
Worcs 98 B6
Stanbury W Yorks 204 F6
Stand Gtr Man 195 F9
N Lnrk 268 B5
Standburn Falk 279 G8
Standeford Staffs 133 B8
Standen Kent 53 E11
Standen Hall Lancs 203 E10
Standen Street
Kent 53 G10
Standerwick Som 45 C10
Standford Hants 49 G10
Standford Bridge
Telford 150 E4
Standingstone
Cumb 229 B11
Cumb 229 E7
Standish Glos 80 D4
Gtr Man 194 E5
Standish Lower Ground
Gtr Man 194 F5
Standlake Oxon 82 E5
Standon Hants 32 B6
Herts 105 G7
Staffs 150 B6
Standon Green End
Herts 86 B5
Stane N Lnrk 269 D7
Stanecastle N Ayrs 257 B8
Stanfield Norf 159 E8
Stoke 168 E5
Stanford C Beds 104 C3
Kent 54 F6
Norf 141 E7
Shrops 148 G6
Stanford Bishop
Hereford 116 G3
Stanford Bridge
Worcs 116 D4
Stanford Dingley
W Berks 64 E5
Stanford End
Wokingham 65 G8
Stanford Hills
Notts 153 E10
Stanford in the Vale
Oxon 82 G4
Stanford-le-Hope
Thurrock 69 C7
Stanford on Avon
Northants 119 B11
Stanford on Soar
Notts 153 E10
Stanford on Teme
Worcs 116 D4
Stanford Rivers
Essex 87 E8
Stanfree Derbys 187 G7
Stanground Pboro 138 D4
Stanhill Lancs 195 B8
Stanhoe Norf 158 B6
Stanhope Borders 260 D4
Durham 232 D5
Kent 54 E3
Stanion Northants 137 F8
Stank Cumb 210 E4
Stanklyn Worcs 117 C7
Stanks W Yorks 206 F3
Stanley Derbys 170 G6
Durham 242 G5
Lancs 194 F3
Notts 171 C7
Perth 286 D5
Shrops 132 G3
Shrops 132 G5
Staffs 168 E6
Wilts 62 E3
W Yorks 197 C10
Stanley Common
Derbys 170 G6
Stanley Crook
Durham 233 D9
Stanley Downton
Glos 80 E4
Stanley Ferry
W Yorks 197 C11
Stanley Gate Lancs 194 G2
Stanley Green
Ches E 184 E5
Poole 18 C6
Shrops 149 B10
Stanley Hill Hereford 98 C3
Stanley Moor Staffs 168 E6
Stanley Pontlarge
Glos 99 E9
Stanleytown Rhondda 77 G8
Stanlow Ches W 182 F6
Staffs 132 D5
Stanmer Brighton 36 F4
Stanmore Hants 33 B7
London 85 G11
Shrops 132 E4
W Berks 64 D3
Stanner Powys 114 F5
Stannergate Dundee 287 D8
Stannersburn
Northumb 250 F6
Stanners Hill Sur 66 G3
Stanningfield Suff 125 F7
Stanningley
W Yorks 205 G10
Stannington
Northumb 242 B6
S Yorks 186 D4
Stanpit Dorset 19 C9
Stansbatch Hereford 114 E6
Stansfield Suff 124 G5
Stanshope Staffs 169 E10
Stanstead Suff 106 B6
Stanstead Abbotts
Herts 86 C5
Stansted Kent 68 G6
Stansted Airport
Essex 105 G11
Stansted Mountfitchet
Essex 105 G10
Stanthorne
Ches W 167 B11
Stanton Glos 99 E11
Mon 96 G6
Northumb 252 F4
Staffs 169 F10
Suff 125 C9
Stantonbury
M Keynes 102 C6
Stanton by Bridge
Derbys 153 D7
Stanton-by-Dale
Derbys 153 B9
Stanton Chare Suff 125 C9
Stanton Drew Bath 60 G5
Stanton Fitzwarren
Swindon 81 G11
Stanton Gate Notts 153 B9
Stanton Harcourt
Oxon 82 D6
Stanton Hill Notts 171 C7
Stanton in Peak
Derbys 170 C2
Stanton Lacy Shrops 115 B9
Stanton Lees
Derbys 170 C3
Stanton Long
Shrops 131 E11
Stanton-on-the-Wolds
Notts 154 C2
Stanton Prior Bath 61 G7
Stanton St Bernard
Wilts 62 G5
Stanton St John
Oxon 83 D9
Stanton St Quintin
Wilts 62 D2
Stanton Street Suff 125 D9
Stanton under Bardon
Leics 153 G9
Stanton upon Hine
Heath Shrops 149 E11
Stanton Wick Bath 60 G6
Stantway Glos 80 C2
Stanwardine in the
Fields Shrops 149 E8
Stanwardine in the
Wood Shrops 149 D8
Stanway Essex 107 G8
Glos 99 E11
Stanway Green
Essex 107 G9
Suff 126 C4
Stanwell Sur 66 E5
Stanwell Moor Sur 66 E4
Stanwick Northants 121 C9
Stanwick-St-John
N Yorks 224 C3
Stanwix Cumb 239 F10
Stanycliffe
Gtr Man 195 F11
Stanydale Shetland 313 H4
Staoinebrig
W Isles 297 H3
Stape N Yorks 226 G5
Stapehill Dorset 31 G9
Stapeley Ches E 167 F11
Stapenhill Staffs 152 E5
Staple Kent 55 B9
Som 42 E6
Staplecross E Sus 38 C3
Staple Cross Devon 27 C8
Essex 88 E6
Staplefield W Sus 36 B3
Staple Fitzpaine Som 28 D3
Stapleford Cambs 123 G9
Herts 86 B4
Leics 154 F6
Lincs 172 D5
Notts 153 B9
Wilts 46 F5
Stapleford Abbotts
Essex 87 G8
Stapleford Tawney
Essex 87 F8
Staplegrove Som 28 B2
Staplehay Som 28 C2
Staple Hill S Glos 61 D7
Worcs 117 C9
Staplehurst Kent 53 E9
Staple Lawns Som 28 D3
Staplers IoW 20 D6
Staples Hill W Sus 35 B8
Staplestreet Kent 70 G5
Stapleton Bristol 60 D6
Cumb 240 C2
Hereford 114 D6
Leics 135 D8
N Yorks 198 D4
N Yorks 224 C5
Shrops 131 C9
Som 29 C7
Stapley Som 27 E11
Staploe Beds 122 E2
Staplow Hereford 98 C3
Stapness Shetland 313 J4
Star Fife 287 G7
Pembs 92 E4
Som 44 B2
Stara Orkney 314 D2
Starbeck N Yorks 206 B2
Starbotton N Yorks 213 E9
Starcross Devon 14 E5
Stareton Warks 118 C6
Stargate T&W 242 E5
Star Hill Mon 79 E7
Starkholmes Derbys 170 D4
Starling Gtr Man 195 E9
Starlings Green
Essex 105 E9
Starr's Green E Sus 38 D3
Starston Norf 142 G4
Start Devon 8 G6
Startforth Durham 223 B10
Start Hill Essex 105 G10
Startley Wilts 62 C2
Startop's End Bucks 84 C6
Starveall S Glos 61 B9
Starvecrow Kent 52 D5
Statenborough Kent 55 B10
Statford St Andrew
Suff 127 E7
Statham Warr 183 D11
Stathe Som 28 B5
Stathern Leics 154 C5
Station Hill Cumb 229 B11
Station Town
Durham 234 D4
Statland Common
Norf 141 D10
Staughton Green
Cambs 122 D2
Staughton Highway
Cambs 122 E2
Staughton Moor
Beds 122 E2
Staunton Glos 79 C8
Glos 98 F5
Staunton in the Vale
Notts 172 G4
Staunton on Arrow
Hereford 115 E7
Staunton on Wye
Hereford 97 B7
Staupes N Yorks 205 B10
Staveley Cumb 211 B7
Cumb 221 F9
Derbys 186 G6
N Yorks 215 G7
Staveley-in-Cartmel
Cumb 211 B7
Staverton Devon 8 C5
Glos 99 G7
Northants 119 E10
Wilts 61 G11
Staverton Bridge
Glos 99 G7
Stawell Som 43 F11
Stawley Som 27 C9
Staxigoe Highld 310 D7
Staxton N Yorks 217 D10
Staylittle Ceredig 128 F2
Staylittle / Penffordd-
Lâs Powys 129 E7
Staynall Lancs 202 E3
Staythorpe Notts 172 E3
Stead W Yorks 205 D8
Steam Mills Glos 79 B10
Stean N Yorks 213 E11
Steanbow Som 44 F5
Stearsby N Yorks 216 E2
Steart Som 29 B9
Som 43 D9
Stebbing Essex 106 G3
Stebbing Green
Essex 106 G3
Stechford W Mid 134 F2
Stede Quarter Kent 53 F11
Stedham W Sus 34 C5
Steel Northumb 241 F10
Northumb 251 G9
Steel Bank S Yorks 186 D4
Steel Cross E Sus 52 G4
Steelend Fife 279 C10
Steele Road Borders 250 E2
Steeleroad-end
Borders 250 E2
Steel Green Cumb 210 D3
Steel Heath Shrops 149 B10
Steen's Bridge
Hereford 115 F10
Steep Hants 34 B2
Steephill IoW 21 F7
Steep Lane
W Yorks 196 C4
Steeple Dorset 18 E4
Essex 88 E6
Steeple Ashton Wilts 46 B2
Steeple Aston Oxon 101 F9
Steeple Barton
Oxon 101 G8
Steeple Bumpstead
Essex 106 C3
Steeple Claydon
Bucks 102 F3
Steeple Gidding
Cambs 138 G2
Steeple Langford
Wilts 46 F4
Steeple Morden
Cambs 104 C5
Steep Marsh Hants 34 B3
Steeraway Telford 132 B3
Steeton W Yorks 204 E6
Stein Highld 298 D2
Steinmanhill Aberds 303 E7
Stella T&W 242 E5
Stelling Minnis Kent 54 D6
Stelvio Newport 59 B9
Stembridge Som 28 C6
Swansea 56 C3
Stemster Highld 310 C5
Stemster Ho Highld 310 C5
Stenalees Corn 5 D10
Stenaquoy Orkney 314 C5
Stencoose Corn 4 F4
Stenhill Devon 27 E9
Stenhouse Dumfries 247 E8
Edin 280 G4
Stenhousemuir Falk 279 E7
Stenigot Lincs 190 E3
Stennack Corn 2 B5
Stenness Shetland 312 F4
Stenscholl Highld 298 C4
Stenso Orkney 314 D3
Stenson Derbys 152 D6
Stenton E Loth 282 G2
Fife 280 B5
Stentwood Devon 27 F10
Stenwith Lincs 154 B6
Stepaside Corn 5 F9
Pembs 73 D10
Powys 129 F11
Stepping Hill
Gtr Man 184 D6
Steppingley
C Beds 103 D10
Stepps N Lnrk 268 B3
Sterndale Moor
Derbys 169 B10
Sternfield Suff 127 E7
Sterridge Devon 40 D5
Stert Wilts 46 B4
Sterte Poole 18 C6
Stetchworth Cambs 124 F2
Stevenage Herts 104 G4
Steven's Crouch
E Sus 38 D2
Stevenston N Ayrs 266 G5
Stevenstone Devon 25 D8

Sutton Scarsdale
Derbys 170 B6
Sutton Scotney Hants 48 F3
Sutton Street Suff 108 C6
Sutton under Brailes
Warks 100 D6
Sutton-under-Whitestonecliffe
N Yorks 215 C9
Sutton upon Derwent
E Yorks 207 D10
Sutton Valence
Kent 53 D10
Sutton Veny Wilts 45 E11
Sutton Waldron
Dorset 30 D5
Sutton Weaver
Ches W 183 F8
Sutton Wick Bath 44 B5
Oxon 83 G7
Swaby Lincs 190 F5
Swadlincote Derbys 152 F6
Swaffham Norf 140 B6
Swaffham Bulbeck
Cambs 123 E11
Swaffham Prior
Cambs 123 E11
Swafield Norf 160 C5
Swaile's Green E Sus 38 C3
Swainby N Yorks 225 E9
Swain House
W Yorks 205 F9
Swainshill Hereford 97 C9
Swainsthorpe Norf 142 C4
Swainswick Bath 61 F9
Swaithe S Yorks 197 G11
Swalcliffe Oxon 101 D7
Swalecliffe Kent 70 F6
Swallow Lincs 201 G7
Swallow Beck Lincs 173 B7
Swallowcliffe Wilts 31 B7
Swallowfield
Wokingham 65 G8
Swallowfields Devon 8 C5
Swallowhurst Cumb 220 G2
Swallownest
S Yorks 187 E7
Swallows Cross
Essex 87 F10
Swalwell T&W 242 E6
Swampton Hants 48 C2
Swanage Dorset 18 F6
Swanbach Ches E 167 G11
Swanbister Orkney 314 F3
Swanborough
Swindon 81 G11
Swan Bottom Bucks 84 D6
Swanbourne Bucks 102 F6
Swanbridge V Glam 59 F7
Swan Green
Ches W 184 G2
Suff 126 C6
Swanland E Yorks 200 B3
Swanley Glos 80 F2
Kent 68 F4
Swanley Bar Herts 86 E3
Swanley Village Kent 68 F4
Swanmore Hants 33 D9
IoW 21 C7
Swannay Orkney 314 D2
Swannington Leics 153 F8
Norf 160 F2
Swanpool Lincs 189 G7
Swanscombe Kent 68 E6
Swansea / Abertawe
Swansea 56 C6
Swanside Mers 182 C6
Swanston Edin 270 B4
Swan Street Essex 107 F7
Swanton Abbott
Norf 160 D5
Swanton Hill Norf 160 D5
Swanton Morley
Norf 159 F10
Swanton Novers
Norf 159 C10
Swanton Street
Kent 53 B11
Swan Village
W Mid 133 E9
Swanwick Derbys 170 E6
Hants 33 F8
Swanwick Green
Ches E 167 F9
Swarby Lincs 173 G8
Swarcliffe W Yorks 206 F3
Swardeston Norf 142 C4
Swarister Shetland 312 E7
Swarkestone
Derbys 153 D7
Swarland Northumb 252 C5
Swarraton Hants 48 F5
Swartha W Yorks 205 D7
Swarthmoor Cumb 210 D5
Swartland Orkney 314 D2
Swathwick Derbys 170 B5
Swaton Lincs 156 B2
Swavesey Cambs 123 D7
Sway Hants 19 B11
Swayfield Lincs 155 E9
Swaythling Soton 32 D6
Sweet Green Worcs 116 E2
Sweetham Devon 14 B3
Sweethaws E Sus 37 B8
Sweethay Som 28 C2
Sweetholme Cumb 221 B11
Sweethouse Corn 5 C11
Sweets Corn 11 B9
Sweetshouse Corn 5 C11
Sweffling Suff 126 E6
Swell Som 28 C5
Swelling Hill Hants 49 G7
Swepstone Leics 153 G7
Swerford Oxon 101 E7
Swettenham Ches E 168 B4
Swetton N Yorks 214 E3
Swffryd Caerph 78 F2
Swiftsden E Sus 38 B2
Swift's Green Kent 53 E11
Swilland Suff 126 G3
Swillbrook Lancs 202 G5
Swillington
W Yorks 206 G3
Swillington Common
W Yorks 206 G3
Swimbridge Devon 25 B10
Swimbridge Newland
Devon 40 G6
Swinbrook Oxon 82 C3
Swincliffe N Yorks 205 B10
W Yorks 197 B8
Swincombe Devon 41 E7
Swinden N Yorks 204 C3
Swinderby Lincs 172 C5
Swindon Glos 99 G8
Staffs 133 E7
Swindon 63 C7
Swine E Yorks 209 F8
Swinefleet E Yorks 199 C9
Swineford S Glos 61 F7
Swineshead Beds 121 D11
Lincs 174 G2
Swineshead Bridge
Lincs 174 G2
Swinethorpe Lincs 172 B5
Swiney Highld 310 F6
Swinford Leics 119 B11
Oxon 82 D6
Swingate Notts 171 G8
Swingbrow Cambs 139 F7
Swingfield Minnis
Kent 55 E8
Swingfield Street
Kent 55 E8
Swingleton Green
Suff 107 B9
Swinhoe Northumb 264 D6
Swinhope Lincs 190 B2
Swining Shetland 312 G6
Swinister Shetland 312 E5
Shetland 313 L6
Swinithwaite
N Yorks 213 B10
Swinmore Common
Hereford 98 C3
Swinnie Borders 262 F4
Swinnow Moor
W Yorks 205 G10
Swinscoe Staffs 169 F10
Swinside Cumb 229 G10
Swinside Townfoot
Borders 262 F6
Swinstead Lincs 155 E10
Swinton Borders 272 F6
Glasgow 268 C3
Gtr Man 195 G9
N Yorks 214 D4
N Yorks 216 E5
S Yorks 186 B6
Swinton Bridge
S Yorks 187 B7
Swinton Hill Borders 272 F6
Swintonmill Borders 272 F6
Swinton Park
Gtr Man 195 G9
Swiss Valley Carms 75 E8
Swithland Leics 153 G10
Swordale Highld 300 C5
Highld 309 K6
Swordland Highld 295 F9
Swordly Highld 308 C7
Sworton Heath
Ches E 183 E11
Swyddffynnon
Ceredig 112 D3
Swynnerton Staffs 151 B7
Swyre Dorset 16 D6
Sycamore Devon 28 F3
Sychdyn / Soughton
Flint 166 B2
Sychtyn Powys 129 B9
Sydallt Wrex 166 D4
Syde Glos 81 C7
Sydenham London 67 E11
Oxon 84 E2
Som 43 F10
Sydenham Damerel
Devon 12 F4
Syderstone Norf 158 C6
Sydling St Nicholas
Dorset 17 B8
Sydmonton Hants 48 B3
Sydney Ches E 168 D2
Syerston Notts 172 F2
Syke Gtr Man 195 D11
Sykehouse S Yorks 198 D6
Sykes Lancs 203 C8
Syleham Suff 126 B4
Sylen Carms 75 D8
Symbister Shetland 313 G7
Symington Borders 271 F8
S Ayrs 257 C9
S Lnrk 259 B11
Symondsbury Dorset 16 C4
Symonds Green
Herts 104 F4
Symonds Yat
Hereford 79 B9
Synderford Dorset 28 G5
Synod Inn / Post Mawr
Ceredig 111 G8
Synton Borders 261 E11
Synton Mains
Borders 261 E11
Synwell Glos 80 G3
Syre Highld 308 E6
Syreford Glos 99 G10
Syresham Northants 102 C2
Syster Highld 310 C6
Syston Leics 154 G2
Lincs 172 G6
Sytchampton Worcs 116 D6
Sytch Ho Green
Shrops 132 E5
Sytch Lane Telford 150 E2
Sywell Northants 120 D6

T

Taagan Highld 299 C10
Tabley Hill Ches E 184 F2
Tabor Gwyn 146 F5
Tàbost W Isles 304 B7
Tabost W Isles 305 G5
Tachbrook Mallory
Warks 118 E6
Tacker Street Som 42 F4
Tackley Oxon 101 G9
Tacleit W Isles 304 E3
Tacolneston Norf 142 D2
Tadcaster N Yorks 206 E5
Tadden Dorset 31 G7
Taddington Derbys 185 G10
Glos 99 E11
Taddiport Devon 25 D7
Tadhill Som 45 D7
Tadley Hants 64 G6
Oxon 64 B4
Tadlow Beds 104 B5
C Beds 104 B5
Tadmarton Oxon 101 D7
Tadnoll Dorset 17 D11
Tadwick Bath 61 E8
Tadworth Sur 51 B8
Tafarnau-bach
Bl Gwent 77 C10
Tafarn-y-bwlch
Pembs 91 E11
Tafarn-y-gelyn
Denb 165 C11
Taff Merthyr Garden
Village M Tydf 77 F10
Taff's Well Rhondda 58 C6
Tafolwern Powys 129 C7
Tai Conwy 164 C3
Taibach Neath 57 D9
Tai-bach Powys 148 D3
Taigh a Ghearraidh
W Isles 296 D3
Taigh Bhalaigh
W Isles 296 D3
Tai-mawr Conwy 165 G7
Tai-morfa Gwyn 144 D5
Tain Highld 309 L7
Highld 310 C6
Tai-nant Wrex 166 F3
Tainlon Gwyn 162 E6
Tairbeart W Isles 305 H3
Tai'r-Bull Powys 95 F9
Tairgwaith Neath 76 C2
Tai'r-heol Caerph 77 G10
Tai'r-ysgol Swansea 57 B7
Tai-Ucha Denb 165 D8
Takeley Essex 105 G11
Takeley Street
Essex 105 G10
Talacharn / Laugharne
Carms 74 C4
Talachddu Powys 95 E11
Talacre Flint 181 E10
Talardd Gwyn 147 D7
Talaton Devon 15 B7
Talbenny Pembs 72 C4
Talbot Green
Rhondda 58 C4
Talbot Heath Poole 19 C7
Talbot's End S Glos 80 G2
Talbot Village Poole 19 C7
Talbot Woods
Bmouth 19 C7
Tale Devon 27 G9
Talerddig Powys 129 C8
Talgarreg Ceredig 111 G8
Talgarth Powys 96 E3
Talgarth's Well
Swansea 56 D2
Talisker Highld 294 B5
Talke Staffs 168 E4
Talke Pits Staffs 168 E4
Talkin Cumb 240 F3
Talladale Highld 299 B9
Talla Linnfoots
Borders 260 E4
Tallaminnoch
S Ayrs 245 D10
Talland Corn 6 E4
Tallarn Green Wrex 166 G6
Tallentire Cumb 229 D8
Talley Carms 94 E2
Tallington Lincs 137 B11
Talmine Highld 308 C5
Talog Carms 92 F6
Talsarn Carms 94 F5
Tal-sarn Ceredig 111 F10
Talsarnau Gwyn 146 B2
Talskiddy Corn 5 B8
Talwrn Anglesey 179 F7
Wrex 166 F3
Tal-y-bont Ceredig 128 F3
Conwy 164 B3
Gwyn 145 E11
Gwyn 179 G10
Talybont-on-Usk
Powys 96 G2
Tal-y-cafn Conwy 180 G3
Tal-y-coed Mon 78 B6
Talygarn Rhondda 58 C4
Talyllyn Powys 96 F2
Tal-y-llyn Gwyn 128 B4
Talysarn Gwyn 163 E7
Tal-y-waenydd
Gwyn 163 F11
Talywain Torf 78 E3
Tal-y-wern Powys 128 C6
Tamanabhagh
W Isles 304 F2
Tame Bridge
N Yorks 225 D10
Tamer Lane End
Gtr Man 194 G6
Tamerton Foliot Plym 7 C9
Tame Water
Gtr Man 196 F3
Tamfourhill Falk 279 E7
Tamworth Staffs 134 C4
Tamworth Green
Lincs 174 G5
Tancred N Yorks 206 B5
Tandem W Yorks 197 D7
Tanden Kent 54 F2
Tandlehill Renfs 267 C8
Tandridge Sur 51 C11
Tanerdy Carms 93 G8
Tanfield Durham 242 F5
Tanfield Lea
Durham 242 G5
Tang N Yorks 205 B10
Tangasdal W Isles 297 M2
Tang Hall York 207 C8
Tangiers Pembs 73 B7
Tangley Hants 47 C10
Tanglwst Carms 92 E6
Tangmere W Sus 22 B6
Tangwick Shetland 312 F4
Tangy Argyll 255 E7
Tan Hills Durham 233 B11
Tan Hinon Powys 129 F7
Tanhouse Lancs 194 F3
Tanis Wilts 62 G3
Tankersley
S Yorks 197 G10
Tankerton Kent 70 F6
Tanlan Flint 181 E10
Tan-lan Conwy 164 C3
Gwyn 163 G10
Tanlan Banks Flint 181 E10
Tannach Highld 310 E7
Tannachie Aberds 293 E9
Tannadice Angus 287 B8
Tanner's Green
Worcs 117 C11
Tannington Suff 126 D4
Tannington Place
Suff 126 D4
Tannochside N Lnrk 268 C4
Tan Office Suff 126 E2
Tan Office Green
Suff 124 F5
Tansley Derbys 170 D4
Tansley Hill W Mid 133 F9
Tansley Knoll
Derbys 170 C4
Tansor Northants 137 E11
Tanterton Lancs 202 G6
Tantobie Durham 242 G5
Tanton N Yorks 225 C10
Tanwood Worcs 117 C8
Tanworth-in-Arden
Warks 118 C2
Tan-y-bwlch
Gwyn 163 G11
Tanyfron Wrex 166 E3
Tan-y-fron Conwy 165 C7
Tan-y-graig
Anglesey 179 F8
Gwyn 144 B6
Tanygrisiau Gwyn 163 F11
Tan-y-groes Ceredig 92 B5
Tan-y-mynydd
Gwyn 144 C6
Tan-y-pistyll
Powys 147 D11
Tan-yr-allt Denb 181 E9
Gwyn 163 E7
Tanyrhydiau
Ceredig 112 D4
Tanysgafell Gwyn 163 B10
Taobh a Chaolais
W Isles 297 K3
Taobh a' Ghlinne
W Isles 305 G5
Taobh a Thuath Loch
Aineort W Isles 297 J3
Taobh a Tuath Loch
Baghasdail
W Isles 297 J3
Taobh Siar W Isles 305 H3
Taobh Tuath
W Isles 296 C5
Taplow Bucks 66 C2
Tapnage Hants 33 E9
Tapton Derbys 186 G5
Tapton Hill S Yorks 186 D4
Tarbat Ho Highld 301 B7
Tarbert Argyll 255 B7
Argyll 275 E7
Argyll 275 G9
Tarbet Argyll 285 G7
Highld 295 F9
Highld 306 E6
Tarbock Green
Mers 183 D7
Tarbolton S Ayrs 257 D10
Tarbrax S Lnrk 269 D10
Tardebigge Worcs 117 D10
Tardy Gate Lancs 194 B4
Tarfside Angus 292 F6
Tarland Aberds 292 C6
Tarleton Lancs 194 C3
Tarleton Moss
Lancs 194 C2
Tarlogie Highld 309 L7
Tarlscough Lancs 194 E2
Tarlton Glos 81 F7
Tarn W Yorks 205 F9
Tarnbrook Lancs 203 B7
Tarnock Som 43 C11
Tarns Cumb 229 B8
Tarnside Cumb 221 G8
Tarporley Ches W 167 C9
Tarpots Essex 69 B9
Tarr Som 42 G6
Tarraby Cumb 239 F10
Tarrant Crawford
Dorset 30 G6
Tarrant Gunville
Dorset 30 E6
Tarrant Hinton
Dorset 30 E6
Tarrant Keyneston
Dorset 30 G6
Tarrant Launceston
Dorset 30 F6
Tarrant Monkton
Dorset 30 F6
Tarrant Rawston
Dorset 30 F6
Tarrant Rushton
Dorset 30 F6
Tarrel Highld 311 L2
Tarring Neville
E Sus 36 G6
Tarrington Hereford 98 C2
Tarrington Common
Hereford 98 D2
Tarryblake Ho
Moray 302 E5
Tarsappie Perth 286 E5
Tarskavaig Highld 295 E7
Tarts Hill Shrops 149 B8
Tarves Aberds 303 F8
Tarvie Highld 300 D4
Perth 292 G2
Tarvin Ches W 167 B7
Tarvin Sands
Ches W 167 B7
Tasburgh Norf 142 D4
Tasley Shrops 132 E3
Taston Oxon 101 G7
Tat Bank W Mid 133 F9
Tatenhill Staffs 152 E4
Tatenhill Common
Staffs 152 E3
Tathall End
M Keynes 102 B6
Tatham Lancs 212 F2
Tathwell Lincs 190 E4
Tatling End Bucks 66 B4
Tatsfield Sur 52 B2
Tattenhall Ches W 167 D7
Tattenhoe
M Keynes 102 E6
Tatterford Norf 159 D7
Tattersett Norf 158 C6
Tattershall Lincs 174 D2
Tattershall Bridge
Lincs 173 D11
Tattershall Thorpe
Lincs 174 D2
Tattingstone Suff 108 D2
Tattingstone White
Horse Suff 108 D2
Tattle Bank Warks 118 E3
Tatton Dale Ches E 184 E2
Tatworth Som 28 F4
Taunton Gtr Man 196 G2
Som 28 C2
Taverham Norf 160 G3
Taverners Green
Essex 87 B9
Tavernspite Pembs 73 C11
Tavistock Devon 12 G5
Taw Green Devon 13 B9
Tawstock Devon 25 B9
Taxal Derbys 185 F8
Tay Bridge Dundee 287 E8
Tayinloan Argyll 255 C7
Taymouth Castle
Perth 285 C11
Taynish Argyll 275 E8
Taynton Glos 98 G4
Oxon 82 C2
Taynuilt Argyll 284 D4
Tayport Fife 287 E8
Tayvallich Argyll 275 E8
Tea Green Herts 104 G2
Tealby Lincs 189 C11
Tealing Angus 287 D8
Teams T&W 242 E6
Team Valley T&W 242 E6
Teanford Staffs 169 G8
Teangue Highld 295 E8
Teanna Mhachair
W Isles 296 E3
Teasley Mead E Sus 52 F4
Tebay Cumb 222 E2
Tebworth C Beds 103 F9
Tedburn St Mary
Devon 14 C2
Teddington Glos 99 E9
London 67 E7
Teddington Hands
Worcs 99 E9
Tedsmore Shrops 149 D7
Tedstone Delamere
Hereford 116 F3
Tedstone Wafer
Hereford 116 F3
Teesville Redcar 225 B10
Teeton Northants 120 C3
Teffont Evias Wilts 46 G3
Teffont Magna Wilts 46 G3
Tegryn Pembs 92 E4
Teigh Rutland 155 F7
Teigncombe Devon 13 D9
Teigngrace Devon 14 G2
Teignmouth Devon 14 G4
Teign Village Devon 14 E2
Telford Telford 132 B3
Telham E Sus 38 E3
Tellisford Som 45 B10
Telscombe E Sus 36 G6
Telscombe Cliffs
E Sus 36 G5
Templand Dumfries 248 F3
Temple Corn 11 G8
Glasgow 267 B10
Midloth 270 D6
Wilts 45 E10
Windsor 65 C10
Temple Balsall
W Mid 118 B4
Temple Bar Carms 75 B9
Ceredig 111 G10
W Sus 22 B5
Templeborough
S Yorks 186 C6
Temple Cloud Bath 44 B6
Templecombe Som 30 C2
Temple Cowley Oxon 83 E8
Temple End Essex 106 C6
Suff 124 G3
Temple Ewell Kent 55 E9
Temple Fields Essex 87 C7
Temple Grafton
Warks 118 G2
Temple Guiting
Glos 99 F11
Templehall Fife 280 C5
Temple Herdewyke
Warks 119 G7
Temple Hill Kent 68 D5
Temple Hirst
N Yorks 198 C6
Templeman's Ash
Dorset 28 G6
Temple Normanton
Derbys 170 B6
Temple Sowerby
Cumb 231 F8
Templeton Devon 26 E5
Pembs 73 C10
W Berks 63 F11
Templeton Bridge
Devon 26 E5
Templetown
Durham 242 G4
Tempsford C Beds 122 G3
Ten Acres W Mid 133 G11
Tenandry Perth 291 G11
Tenbury Wells
Worcs 115 D11
Tenby / Dinbych-y-
Pysgod Pembs 73 E10
Tencreek Corn 6 E4
Tendring Essex 108 G2
Tendring Green
Essex 108 F2
Tendring Heath
Essex 108 F2
Ten Mile Bank Norf 140 D2
Tenston Orkney 314 E2
Tenterden Kent 53 G11
Terfyn Conwy 180 F6
Gwyn 163 C9
Terhill Som 43 G7
Terling Essex 88 B3
Ternhill Shrops 150 C2
Terpersie Castle
Aberds 302 G5
Terras Corn 5 E8
Terregles Banks
Dumfries 237 B11
Terrible Down E Sus 23 B7
Terrick Bucks 84 D4
Terriers Bucks 84 G5
Terrington N Yorks 216 E3
Terrington St Clement
Norf 157 E10
Terrington St John
Norf 157 G10
Terryhorn Aberds 302 F4
Terry's Green
Warks 118 C2
Terwick Common
W Sus 34 C4
Teston Kent 53 C8
Testwood Hants 32 E5
Tetbury Glos 80 G5
Tetbury Upton Glos 80 F5
Tetchill Shrops 149 C7
Tetchwick Bucks 83 B11
Tetcott Devon 12 B2
Tetford Lincs 190 G4
Tetley N Lincs 199 E9
Tetney Lincs 201 G10
Tetney Lock Lincs 201 G10
Tetsworth Oxon 83 E11
Tettenhall W Mid 133 D7
Tettenhall Wood
W Mid 133 D7
Tetworth Cambs 122 G4
Teuchan Aberds 303 F10
Teversal Notts 171 C7
Teversham Cambs 123 F9
Teviothead
Borders 249 B10
Tewel Aberds 293 E10
Tewin Herts 86 C3
Tewin Wood Herts 86 B3
Tewitfield Lancs 211 E10
Tewkesbury Glos 99 E7
Teynham Kent 70 G3
Teynham Street Kent 70 G3
Thackley W Yorks 205 F9
Thackley End
W Yorks 205 F9
Thackthwaite Cumb 229 G8
Thainston Aberds 293 F8
Thakeham W Sus 35 D10
Thame Oxon 84 D2
Thames Ditton Sur 67 F7
Thames Haven
Thurrock 69 C8
Thames Head Glos 81 F7
Thamesmead London 68 C3
Thanington Kent 54 B6
Thankerton S Lnrk 259 B11
Tharston Norf 142 E3
Thatcham W Berks 64 F4
Thatto Heath Mers 183 C8
Thaxted Essex 106 E2
The Aird Highld 298 D4
Theakston N Yorks 214 B6
Thealby N Lincs 199 D11
The Alders Staffs 134 C3
Theale Som 44 D3
W Berks 64 E6
The Arms Norf 141 D7
Thearne E Yorks 209 F7
The Bage Hereford 96 C5
The Balloch Perth 286 F2
The Bank Ches E 168 D4
The Banks Gtr Man 185 D7
Wilts 62 D4
The Barony
Ches E 167 E11
Orkney 314 D2
The Barton Wilts 62 D5
The Batch S Glos 61 E7
The Beeches Glos 81 E8
The Bell Gtr Man 194 F4
The Bents Staffs 151 C10
Theberton Suff 127 D8
The Blythe Staffs 151 D10
The Bog Shrops 131 D7
The Borough Dorset 30 E2
London 67 D10
The Bourne Sur 49 E10
Worcs 117 F9
The Bows Stirl 285 G11
The Braes Highld 295 B7
The Brampton
Staffs 168 F4
The Brand Leics 153 G10
The Bratch Staffs 133 E7
The Breck Orkney 314 F3
The Brents Kent 70 G4
The Bridge Dorset 30 E3
The Broad Hereford 115 E9
The Brook Suff 125 B11
The Brushes Derbys 186 F5
The Bryn Mon 78 D4
The Burf Worcs 116 D6
The Butts Hants 49 F8
Som 45 D9
The Camp Glos 80 D6
Herts 85 D11
The Cape Warks 118 D5
The Chart Kent 52 C3
The Chequer Wrex 167 G7
The Chuckery
W Mid 133 D10
The City Bucks 84 F3
The Cleaver
Hereford 97 F10
The Close W Sus 22 C5
The Colony Oxon 100 D6
The Common Bath 60 G6
Bucks 102 E5
Dorset 30 E3
Shrops 150 D3
Suff 108 B2
Swansea 56 C4
Wilts 47 G8
Wilts 61 G11
Wilts 62 C4
W Sus 51 G7
The Corner Kent 53 E8
Shrops 131 F8
The Cot Mon 79 F8
The Craigs Highld 309 K4
The Crofts E Yorks 218 E4
The Cronk IoM 192 C4
The Cross Hands
Leics 134 C6
The Cwm Mon 79 G7
Theddingworth
Leics 136 F3
Theddlethorpe All Saints
Lincs 191 D7
Theddlethorpe St Helen
Lincs 191 D7
The Dell Suff 143 D9
The Delves W Mid 133 D10
The Den N Ayrs 266 E6
The Dene Durham 242 G4
Hants 47 C11
The Down Kent 53 F7
Shrops 132 E3
The Downs Sur 50 F3
The Dunks Wrex 166 E4
The Eals Northumb 251 F7
The Eaves Glos 79 D10
The Fall W Yorks 197 B10
The Fence Glos 79 D8
The Flat Glos 80 B3
The Flatt Cumb 240 B3
The Flourish Derbys 153 B8
The Folly Herts 85 C11
S Glos 61 E8
The Fording Hereford 98 F3
The Forge Hereford 114 F6
The Forstal Kent 54 F4
The Forties Derbys 152 F6
The Four Alls
Shrops 150 C3
The Fox Wilts 62 B6
The Foxholes
Shrops 132 G2
The Frenches Hants 32 C4
The Frythe Herts 86 C2
The Garths Shetland 312 B8
The Gibb Wilts 61 D10
The Glack Borders 260 B6
The Gore Shrops 131 G11
The Grange Norf 160 E2
N Yorks 225 F11
The Green Cambs 122 D5
C Beds 85 B8
Cumb 210 C3
Cumb 211 D7
Essex 88 B3
Hants 32 B3
M Keynes 103 C7
Norf 141 C11
Norf 159 B11
Northants 102 C5
Oxon 101 F9
Shrops 130 G6
S Yorks 197 G8
Warks 118 F4
Wilts 45 G11
The Grove
Dumfries 237 B11
Durham 242 G3
Herts 85 F9
Shrops 131 B7
Shrops 131 G8
Worcs 99 C7
The Gutter Derbys 170 F5
Worcs 117 B9
The Hacket S Glos 61 B7
The Hague Derbys 185 C8
The Hall Shetland 312 D8
The Hallands
N Lincs 200 C5
The Ham Wilts 45 C11
The Handfords
Staffs 151 E7
The Harbour Kent 53 D10
The Haven W Sus 50 G5
The Headland Hrtlpl 234 E6
The Heath Norf 159 D8
Norf 160 E3
Norf 160 E4
Staffs 151 C11
Suff 108 D2
The Hem Shrops 132 B4
The Hendre Mon 79 C7
The Herberts V Glam 58 E3
The Hermitage
Cambs 123 C7
The High Essex 86 C6
The Highlands E Sus 38 F2
The Hill Cumb 210 C3
The Hobbins Shrops 132 E4
The Hollands Staffs 168 D6
The Hollies Notts 172 E4
The Holmes Derbys 153 B7
The Holt Wokingham 65 D10
The Hook Worcs 98 C6
The Hope Shrops 115 B10
The Howe Cumb 211 B9
IoM 192 F2
The Humbers
Telford 150 G3
The Hundred
Hereford 115 E10
The Hyde London 67 B8
Worcs 98 C6
The Hythe Essex 107 G10
The Inch Edin 280 G5
The Knab Swansea 56 D6
The Knap V Glam 58 F5
The Knapp Hereford 116 G3
S Glos 79 G11
The Knowle W Mid 133 F9
The Laches Staffs 133 B8
The Lake Dumfries 237 E8
The Lakes Worcs 116 B5
The Lawe T&W 243 D9
The Lawns E Yorks 208 G6
Thelbridge Barton
Devon 26 E3
The Leacon Kent 54 G3
The Leath Shrops 131 F11
The Lee Bucks 84 E6
The Lees Kent 54 C4
The Leigh Glos 99 F7
The Leys Staffs 134 C4
The Lhen IoM 192 B4
The Ling Norf 142 D6
The Lings Norf 141 B10
S Yorks 199 F7
The Linleys Wilts 61 F11
Thelnetham Suff 125 B10
The Lunt W Mid 133 D9
Thelveton Norf 142 G3
Thelwall Warr 183 D10
The Manor W Sus 22 C4
The Marsh Ches E 168 C4
Hereford 115 F9
Powys 130 D6
Shrops 150 D3
Staffs 150 D6
Suff 125 B11
Suff 126 B2
Wilts 62 C5
Themelthorpe
Norf 159 E11
The Middles
Durham 242 G6
The Mint Hants 34 B3
The Moor Flint 166 B4
Kent 38 B3
The Moors Hereford 97 E10
The Mount Hants 64 G2
Reading 65 E8
The Mumbles / Y
Mwmbwls Swansea 56 D6
The Murray S Lnrk 268 E2
The Mythe Glos 99 E7
The Nant Wrex 166 E3
The Narth Mon 79 D8
The Neuk Aberds 293 D9
Thenford Northants 101 C10
The Node Herts 104 G4
The Nook Shrops 149 C11
Shrops 150 E3
The North Mon 79 D8
Theobald's Green
Wilts 62 F4
The Oval Bath 61 G8
The Park Glos 99 G8
The Parks S Yorks 198 F6
The Pitts Wilts 31 B9
The Platt Oxon 83 E9
The Pludds Glos 79 B10
The Point Devon 14 E5
The Pole of Itlaw
Aberds 302 D6
The Port of Felixstowe
Suff 108 E5
The Potteries Stoke 168 F5
The Pound Glos 98 E4
The Quarry Glos 80 F2
Shrops 149 G9
The Quarter Kent 53 E11
Kent 53 G11
The Rampings Worcs 99 E7
The Rectory Lincs 156 G2
The Reddings Glos 99 G8
Therfield Herts 104 D6
The Rhos Pembs 73 C8
The Rhydd Hereford 97 E9
The Riddle Hereford 115 E9
The Ridge Wilts 61 F11
The Ridges
Wokingham 65 G10
The Ridgeway Herts 86 E3
The Riding
Northumb 241 D10
The Riggs Borders 261 C8
The Rink Borders 261 C11
The Rise Windsor 66 F2
The Rock Telford 132 B3
The Rocks Kent 53 B8
S Glos 61 C8
The Roe Denb 181 G8
The Rookery Herts 85 G10
Staffs 168 D5
The Row Lancs 211 D9
The Rowe Staffs 150 B6
The Ryde Herts 86 D2
The Sands Sur 49 D11
The Scarr Glos 98 F4
The Shoe Wilts 61 E10
The Shruggs Staffs 151 C8
The Slack Durham 233 F8
The Slade W Berks 64 F4
The Smeeth Norf 157 G10
The Smithies
Shrops 132 D3
The Spa Wilts 62 G2
The Spring Warks 118 C5
The Square Torf 78 F3
The Stocks Kent 38 B6
Wilts 62 G2
The Straits Hants 49 F9
W Mid 133 E8
The Strand Wilts 46 B2
The Swillett Herts 85 F8
The Sydnall Shrops 150 C3
Thetford Lincs 156 F2
Norf 141 G7
The Thrift Cambs 104 D6
The Throat
Wokingham 65 F10
The Toft Staffs 151 F8
The Towans Corn 2 B3
The Town Scilly 1 F3
The Twittocks Glos 99 D7
The Tynings Glos 80 B6
The Vale W Mid 133 G11
The Valley Ches E 167 D11
Kent 54 C3
Leics 154 F4
Pembs 73 D10
The Vauld Hereford 97 B10
The Village Newport 78 G4
Windsor 66 E3
W Mid 133 F7
The Walshes Worcs 116 C6
The Warren Kent 54 E3
Wilts 63 F8
The Waterwheel
Shrops 131 C7
The Weaven
Hereford 97 E10
The Wells Sur 67 G7
The Wern Wrex 166 E3
The Willows
NE Lincs 201 F8
The Wood Shrops 148 E6
Shrops 149 D9
The Woodlands
Leics 136 D3
Suff 107 C11
Suff 108 D3
The Woods W Mid 133 D10

The Wrangle Bath 44 B4
The Wrythe London 67 F9
The Wyke Shrops 132 B4
The Wymm Hereford 97 B10
Theydon Bois Essex 86 F6
Theydon Garnon Essex 87 F7
Theydon Mount Essex 87 F7
The Yeld Shrops 131 G11
Thicket Mead Bath 45 B7
Thick Hollins W Yorks 196 E6
Thickthorn Hall Norf 142 B3
Thickwood Wilts 61 E10
Thimbleby Lincs 190 G2
N Yorks 225 F9
Thimble End W Mid 134 E2
Thinford Durham 233 E11
Thingley Wilts 61 E11
Thingwall Mers 182 E3
Thirdpart N Ayrs 266 F3
Thirlby N Yorks 215 C9
Thirlestane Borders 271 F11
Thirn N Yorks 214 B4
Thirsk N Yorks 215 C8
Thirtleby E Yorks 209 G9
Thistleton Lancs 202 F4
Rutland 155 F8
Thistley Green Essex 88 B2
Suff 124 B3
Thixendale N Yorks 216 G6
Thockrington Northumb 241 B11
Tholomas Drove Cambs 139 B7
Tholthorpe N Yorks 215 F9
Thomas Chapel Pembs 73 D10
Thomas Close Cumb 230 C4
Thomastown Aberds 302 F5
Rhondda 58 B4
Thompson Norf 141 D8
Thomshill Moray 302 D2
Thong Kent 69 E7
Thongsbridge W Yorks 196 F6
Thoralby N Yorks 213 B10
Thoresby Notts 187 G10
Thoresthorpe Lincs 191 F7
Thoresway Lincs 189 B11
Thorganby Lincs 190 B2
N Yorks 207 E9
Thorgill N Yorks 226 F4
Thorington Suff 127 C8
Thorington Street Suff 107 D10
Thorlby N Yorks 204 C5
Thorley Herts 87 B7
IoW 20 D3
Thorley Houses Herts 105 G9
Thorley Street Herts 87 B7
IoW 20 D3
Thormanby N Yorks 215 E9
Thorn Devon 13 D9
Powys 114 E5
Thornaby on Tees Stockton 225 B9
Thornage Norf 159 B11
Thornborough Bucks 102 E4
N Yorks 214 D5
Thornbury Devon 24 F6
Hereford 116 F2
S Glos 79 G10
W Yorks 205 G9
Thornby Cumb 239 G7
Northants 120 B3
Thorncliff W Yorks 197 E8
Thorncliffe Staffs 169 D8
Thorncombe Dorset 28 G5
Dorset 30 G5
Thorncombe Street Sur 50 E4
Thorncote Green C Beds 104 B3
Thorncross IoW 20 E4
Thorndon Suff 126 D2
Thorndon Cross Devon 12 C6
Thorne Corn 24 G2
S Yorks 199 E7
Thorne Coffin Som 29 D8
Thornehillhead Devon 24 D6
Thorne Moor Devon 12 D3
Thornend Wilts 62 D3
Thorner W Yorks 206 E3
Thornes Staffs 133 C11
W Yorks 197 D10
Thorne St Margaret Som 27 C9
Thorney Bucks 66 D4
Notts 188 G5
Pboro 138 C5
Som 28 C6
Thorney Close T&W 243 G9
Thorney Crofts E Yorks 201 C8
Thorney Green Suff 125 E11
Thorney Hill Hants 19 B9
Thorney Island W Sus 22 C3
Thorney Toll Pboro 138 C6
Thorneywood Notts 171 G9
Thornfalcon Som 28 C3
Thornford Dorset 29 E10
Thorngrafton Northumb 241 D7
Thorngrove Som 43 G11
Thorngumbald E Yorks 201 B8
Thornham Norf 176 E2
Thornham Fold Gtr Man 195 F11
Thornham Magna Suff 126 C2
Thornham Parva Suff 126 C2
Thornhaugh Pboro 137 C11
Thornhill Cardiff 59 C7
Cumb 219 D10
Derbys 185 E11
Dumfries 247 D9
Soton 33 E7
Stirl 278 B3
Torf 78 F3
Wilts 62 D5
W Yorks 197 D9
Thorn Hill S Yorks 186 C6
Thornhill Edge W Yorks 197 D8
Thornhill Lees W Yorks 197 D8
Thornhill Park Hants 33 E7
Thornhills W Yorks 197 C7
Thornholme E Yorks 218 G2
Thornicombe Dorset 30 G5
Thornielee Borders 261 B10
Thornley Durham 233 D8
Durham 234 D3
Thornliebank E Renf 267 D10
Thornly Park Renfs 267 C9
Thornroan Aberds 303 F8
Thorns N Yorks 223 E7
Suff 124 F4
Thornseat S Yorks 186 C2
Thornsett Derbys 185 D8
Thorns Green Ches E 184 E3
Thornthwaite Cumb 229 F10
N Yorks 205 B9
Thornton Angus 287 C7
Bucks 102 D5
E Yorks 207 D11
Fife 280 B5
Lancs 202 E2
Leics 135 B9
Lincs 174 B2
Mbro 225 C9
Mers 193 G10
Northumb 273 F9
Pembs 72 D6
W Yorks 205 G8
Thornton Curtis N Lincs 200 D5
Thorntonhall S Lnrk 267 D11
Thornton Heath London 67 F10
Thornton Hough Mers 182 E4
Thornton in Craven N Yorks 204 D4
Thornton in Lonsdale N Yorks 212 E3
Thornton-le-Beans N Yorks 225 G7
Thornton-le-Clay N Yorks 216 F3
Thornton-le-Dale N Yorks 216 C6
Thornton le Moor Lincs 189 B9
Thornton-le-Moor N Yorks 215 B7
Thornton-le-Moors Ches W 182 G6
Thornton-le-Street N Yorks 215 B8
Thorntonloch E Loth 282 G4
Thornton Park Northumb 273 F8
Thornton Rust N Yorks 213 B9
Thornton Steward N Yorks 214 B3
Thornton Watlass N Yorks 214 B4
Thornwood Common Essex 87 D7
Thornydykes Borders 272 F2
Thoroton Notts 172 G3
Thorp Gtr Man 196 F2
Thorp Arch W Yorks 206 D4
Thorpe Cumb 230 F5
Derbys 169 E11
E Yorks 208 D5
Lincs 191 E7
Norf 143 D8
Notts 172 F3
N Yorks 213 G10
Sur 66 F4
Thorpe Abbotts Norf 126 B3
Thorpe Acre Leics 153 E10
Thorpe Arnold Leics 154 E5
Thorpe Audlin W Yorks 198 D3
Thorpe Bassett N Yorks 217 E7
Thorpe Bay Sthend 70 B2
Thorpe by Water Rutland 137 D7
Thorpe Common Suff 108 D5
Thorpe Constantine Staffs 134 B5
Thorpe Culvert Lincs 175 C7
Thorpe Edge W Yorks 205 F9
Thorpe End Norf 160 G5
Thorpe Fendykes Lincs 175 C7
Thorpe Green Essex 108 G3
Lancs 194 C5
Suff 125 G8
Sur 66 F4
Thorpe Hamlet Norf 142 B4
Thorpe Hesley S Yorks 186 B5
Thorpe in Balne S Yorks 198 E5
Thorpe in the Fallows Lincs 188 E6
Thorpe Langton Leics 136 E4
Thorpe Larches Durham 234 F3
Thorpe Latimer Lincs 156 B2
Thorpe Lea Sur 66 E4
Thorpe-le-Soken Essex 108 G3
Thorpe le Street E Yorks 208 E2
Thorpe le Vale Lincs 190 C2
Thorpe Malsor Northants 120 B6
Thorpe Mandeville Northants 101 B10
Thorpe Market Norf 160 B4
Thorpe Marriot Norf 160 F3
Thorpe Morieux Suff 125 G8
Thorpeness Suff 127 F9
Thorpe on the Hill Lincs 172 B6
W Yorks 197 B10
Thorpe Row Norf 141 B9
Thorpe St Andrew Norf 142 B5
Thorpe St Peter Lincs 175 C7
Thorpe Salvin S Yorks 187 E8
Thorpe Satchville Leics 154 G4
Thorpe Street Suff 125 B10
Thorpe Thewles Stockton 234 G4
Thorpe Tilney Lincs 173 D10
Thorpe Underwood Northants 136 G5
N Yorks 206 B5
Thorpe Waterville Northants 137 G10
Thorpe Willoughby N Yorks 207 G7
Thorpe Wood N Yorks 207 G7
Thorpland Norf 140 B2
Thorrington Essex 89 B9
Thorverton Devon 26 G6
Thoulstone Wilts 45 D10
Thrandeston Suff 126 B2
Thrapston Northants 121 B9
Thrashbush N Lnrk 268 B5
Threapland Cumb 229 D9
N Yorks 213 G9
Threapwood Ches W 166 F6
Staffs 169 G8
Three Ashes Hants 64 G6
Hereford 97 G10
Shrops 115 B7
Som 45 D7
Three Bridges Argyll 284 F4
Lincs 190 D6
W Sus 51 F9
Three Burrows Corn 4 F4
Three Chimneys Kent 53 F10
Three Cocked Hat Norf 143 D8
Three Cocks / Aberllynfi Powys 96 D3
Three Crosses Swansea 56 C5
Three Cups Corner E Sus 37 C10
Three Fingers Wrex 167 G7
Three Gates Dorset 29 F10
Threehammer Common Norf 160 E6
Three Hammers Corn 11 D10
Three Holes Norf 139 C10
Three Holes Cross Corn 10 G6
Threekingham Lincs 155 B11
Three Leg Cross E Sus 53 G7
Three Legged Cross Dorset 31 F9
Threelows Staffs 169 F9
Three Maypoles W Mid 118 B2
Threemile Cross Wokingham 65 F8
Three Mile Cross Wokingham 65 F8
Threemilestone Corn 4 G5
Threemiletown W Loth 279 F11
Three Oaks E Sus 38 E4
Threepwood Borders 271 G10
Three Sisters Denb 165 C9
Threewaters Corn 5 B10
Threlkeld Cumb 230 F2
Threshers Bush Essex 87 D7
Threshfield N Yorks 213 G9
Thrigby Norf 161 G9
Thringarth Durham 232 G4
Thringstone Leics 153 F8
Thrintoft N Yorks 224 G6
Thriplow Cambs 105 B8
Throapham S Yorks 187 D8
Throckenholt Lincs 139 B7
Throcking Herts 104 E6
Throckley T&W 242 D5
Throckmorton Worcs 99 B9
Throop Dorset 18 C2
Throphill Northumb 252 F4
Thropton Northumb 252 C2
Throsk Stirl 279 C7
Througham Glos 80 D6
Throughgate Dumfries 247 G9
Throwleigh Devon 13 C9
Throwley Kent 54 B3
Throwley Forstal Kent 54 C3
Throxenby N Yorks 217 B10
Thrumpton Notts 153 C10
Notts 188 E2
Thrumster Highld 310 E7
Thrunton Northumb 264 G3
Thrupe Som 44 D6
Thrupp Glos 80 E5
Oxon 82 F3
Oxon 83 B7
Thruscross N Yorks 205 B9
Thrushelton Devon 12 D4
Thrussington Leics 154 F2
Thruxton Hants 47 D9
Hereford 97 E8
Thrybergh S Yorks 187 B7
Thulston Derbys 153 C8
Thunder Bridge W Yorks 197 E7
Thundergay N Ayrs 255 C9
Thunder Hill Norf 161 F8
Thunder's Hill E Sus 23 C9
Thundersley Essex 69 B9
Thundridge Herts 86 B5
Thurcaston Leics 153 G11
Thurcroft S Yorks 187 D7
Thurdon Corn 24 E3
Thurgarton Norf 160 C3
Notts 171 F11
Thurgoland S Yorks 197 G9
Thurlaston Leics 135 D10
Warks 119 C9
Thurlbear Som 28 C3
Thurlby Lincs 156 F2
Lincs 172 C6
Lincs 191 F7
Thurleigh Beds 121 F11
Thurlestone Devon 8 G3
Thurloxton Som 43 G9
Thurlstone S Yorks 197 G8
Thurlton Norf 143 D8
Thurlton Links Norf 143 D8
Thurlwood Ches E 168 D4
Thurmaston Leics 136 B2
Thurnby Leics 136 C2
Thurne Norf 161 F8
Thurnham Kent 53 B10
Lancs 202 C5
Thurning Norf 159 D11
Northants 137 G11
Thurnscoe S Yorks 198 F3
Thurnscoe East S Yorks 198 F3
Thursby Cumb 239 G8
Thursford Norf 159 C9
Thursford Green Norf 159 C9
Thursley Sur 50 F2
Thurso Highld 310 C5
Thurso East Highld 310 C5
Thurstaston Mers 182 E2
Thurston Suff 125 D8
Thurston Clough Gtr Man 196 F3
Thurston End Suff 124 G5
Thurstonfield Cumb 239 F8
Thurstonland W Yorks 197 E7
Thurton Norf 142 C6
Thurvaston Derbys 152 B2
Derbys 152 B4
Thuxton Norf 141 B10
Thwaite N Yorks 223 F7
Suff 126 D2
Thwaite Flat Cumb 210 E4
Thwaite Head Cumb 220 G6
Thwaites W Yorks 205 E7
Thwaite St Mary Norf 142 E6
Thwaites Brow W Yorks 205 E7
Thwing E Yorks 217 E11
Tibbermore Perth 286 E4
Tibberton Glos 98 G5
Telford 150 E3
Worcs 117 F8
Tibenham Norf 142 F2
Tibshelf Derbys 170 C6
Tibshelf Wharf Notts 171 C7
Tibthorpe E Yorks 208 B5
Ticehurst E Sus 53 G7
Tichborne Hants 48 G5
Tickencote Rutland 137 B9
Tickenham N Som 60 E3
Ticket Wood Devon 8 G4
Tickford End M Keynes 103 C7
Tickhill S Yorks 187 C9
Tickleback Row Brack 65 E11
Ticklerton Shrops 131 E9
Tickmorend Glos 80 F4
Ticknall Derbys 153 E7
Tickton E Yorks 209 E7
Tidbury Green W Mid 117 B11
Tidcombe Wilts 47 B9
Tiddington Oxon 83 E11
Warks 118 F4
Tidebrook E Sus 37 B10
Tideford Corn 6 D6
Tideford Cross Corn 6 C6
Tidenham Glos 79 F9
Tidenham Chase Glos 79 F9
Tideswell Derbys 185 F11
Tidmarsh W Berks 64 E6
Tidmington Warks 100 D5
Tidnor Hereford 97 D11
Tidpit Hants 31 D9
Tidworth Wilts 47 D8
Tiers Cross Pembs 72 C6
Tiffield Northants 120 G3
Tifty Aberds 303 E7
Tigerton Angus 293 G7
Tigh-na-Blair Perth 285 F11
Tighnabruaich Argyll 275 F10
Tighnacachla Argyll 274 G3
Tighnafiline Highld 307 L3
Tighness Argyll 284 G6
Tigley Devon 8 C5
Tilbrook Cambs 121 D11
Tilbury Thurrock 68 D6
Tilbury Green Essex 106 C4
Tilbury Juxta Clare Essex 106 C5
Tile Cross W Mid 134 F3
Tilegate Green Essex 87 D8
Tile Hill W Mid 118 B5
Tilehouse Green W Mid 118 B3
Tilehurst Reading 65 E7
Tilekiln Green Essex 105 G10
Tiley Dorset 29 F11
Tilford Sur 49 E11
Tilford Common Sur 49 E11
Tilford Reeds Sur 49 E11
Tilgate W Sus 51 G9
Tilgate Forest Row W Sus 51 G9
Tilkey Essex 106 G6
Tilland Corn 6 C6
Tillathrowie Aberds 302 F4
Tillers' Green Glos 98 E3
Tilley Shrops 149 D10
Tilley Green Shrops 149 D10
Tillicoultry Clack 279 B8
Tillietudlem S Lnrk 268 F6
Tillingham Essex 89 E7
Tillington Hereford 97 B9
Staffs 151 E8
W Sus 35 C7
Tillington Common Hereford 97 B9
Tillislow Devon 12 C3
Tillworth Devon 28 G4
Tillyarblet Angus 293 G7
Tillybirloch Aberds 293 C8
Tillycorthie Aberds 303 G9
Tilly Down Hants 47 D10
Tillydrine Aberds 293 D8
Tillyfour Aberds 293 B7
Tillyfourie Aberds 293 B8
Tillygarmond Aberds 293 D8
Tillygreig Aberds 303 G8
Tillykerrie Aberds 303 G8
Tilly Lo Aberds 293 C7
Tillynaught Aberds 302 C5
Tilmanstone Kent 55 C10
Tilney All Saints Norf 157 F11
Tilney cum Islington Norf 157 G11
Tilney Fen End Norf 157 G10
Tilney High End Norf 157 F11
Tilney St Lawrence Norf 157 G10
Tilsdown Glos 80 F2
Tilshead Wilts 46 D4
Tilsmore E Sus 37 C9
Tilsop Shrops 116 C2
Tilstock Shrops 149 B10
Tilston Ches W 167 E7
Tilstone Bank Ches W 167 D9
Tilstone Fearnall Ches W 167 C9
Tilsworth C Beds 103 G9
Tilton on the Hill Leics 136 B4
Tilts S Yorks 198 F5
Tiltups End Glos 80 F4
Tilty Essex 105 F11
Timberden Bottom Kent 68 G4
Timberhonger Worcs 117 C8
Timberland Lincs 173 D10
Timbersbrook Ches E 168 C5
Timberscombe Som 42 E3
Timble N Yorks 205 C9
Timbold Hill Kent 54 B2
Timbrelham Corn 12 E3
Timperley Gtr Man 184 D3
Timsbury Bath 45 B7
Hants 32 C4
Timsgearraidh W Isles 304 E2
Timworth Suff 125 D7
Timworth Green Suff 125 D7
Tincleton Dorset 17 C11
Tindale Cumb 240 F4
Tindale Crescent Durham 233 F9
Tindon End Essex 106 E2
Tingewick Bucks 102 E3
Tingley W Yorks 197 B9
Tingon Shetland 312 E4
Tingrith C Beds 103 E10
Tingwall Orkney 314 D3
Tinhay Devon 12 E3
Tinkers End Bucks 102 F5
Tinshill W Yorks 205 F11
Tinsley S Yorks 186 C6
Tinsley Green W Sus 51 F9
Tintagel Corn 11 D7
Tintern Parva Mon 79 E8
Tintinhull Som 29 D8
Tintwistle Derbys 185 B8
Tinwald Dumfries 248 G2
Tinwell Rutland 137 B10
Tipner Ptsmth 33 G10
Tippacott Devon 41 D9
Tipper's Hill Warks 134 F5
Tipperty Aberds 302 C6
Aberds 303 G9
Tipple Cross Devon 12 D3
Tipps End Norf 139 D10
Tip's Cross Essex 87 E9
Tiptoe Hants 19 B11
Tipton W Mid 133 E8
Tipton Green W Mid 133 E9
Tipton St John Devon 15 C7
Tiptree Essex 88 B5
Tiptree Heath Essex 88 B5
Tirabad Powys 95 C7
Tiraghoil Argyll 288 G5
Tircanol Swansea 57 B7
Tirdeunaw Swansea 57 B7
Tirinie Perth 291 G10
Tirley Glos 98 F6
Tirley Knowle Glos 98 F6
Tiroran Argyll 288 G6
Tirphil Caerph 77 E10
Tirril Cumb 230 F6
Tirryside Highld 309 H5
Tir-y-berth Caerph 77 F11
Tir-y-dail Carms 75 C10
Tisbury Wilts 30 B6
Tisman's Common W Sus 50 G5
Tissington Derbys 169 E11
Titchberry Devon 24 B2
Titchfield Hants 33 F8
Titchfield Common Hants 33 F8
Titchfield Park Hants 33 F8
Titchmarsh Northants 121 B10
Titchwell Norf 176 E3
Titcomb W Berks 63 F11
Tithby Notts 154 B3
Tithebarn Staffs 169 G9
Tithe Barn Hillock Mers 183 B9
Titley Hereford 114 E6
Titlington Northumb 264 F4
Titmore Green Herts 104 F4
Titsey Sur 52 C2
Titson Corn 24 G2
Tittenhurst Windsor 66 F3
Tittensor Staffs 151 B7
Tittleshall Norf 159 E7
Titton Worcs 116 D6
Titty Hill W Sus 34 B5
Tiverton Ches W 167 C9
Devon 27 E7
Tivetshall St Margaret Norf 142 F3
Tivetshall St Mary Norf 142 F3
Tividale W Mid 133 E9
Tivington Som 42 D2
Tivington Knowle Som 42 E2
Tivoli Cumb 228 G5
Tivy Dale S Yorks 197 F9
Tixall Staffs 151 E9
Tixover Rutland 137 C9
Toab Orkney 314 F5
Shetland 313 M5
Toadmoor Derbys 170 E4
Toad Row Suff 143 F10
Tobermory Argyll 289 D7
Toberonochy Argyll 275 C8
Tobha Beag W Isles 296 D5
Tobha Mor W Isles 297 H3
Tobhtarol W Isles 304 E3
Tobson W Isles 304 E3
Toby's Hill Lincs 191 C7
Tocher Aberds 302 F6
Tockenham Wilts 62 D4
Tockenham Wick Wilts 62 C4
Tockholes Blkburn 195 C7
Tockington S Glos 60 B6
Tockwith N Yorks 206 C5
Todber Dorset 30 C4
Todding Hereford 115 B8
Toddington C Beds 103 F10
Glos 99 E10
W Sus 35 G8
Toddlehills Aberds 303 E10
Todd's Green Herts 104 F4
Todenham Glos 100 D4
Todhill Angus 287 D8
Todhills Cumb 239 E9
Durham 233 E10
Todlachie Aberds 293 B8
Todmorden W Yorks 196 C2
Todpool Corn 4 G4
Todrig Borders 261 F10
Todwick S Yorks 187 E7
Toft Cambs 123 F7
Lincs 155 F11
Shetland 312 F6
Warks 119 C9
Toft Hill Durham 233 F9
Lincs 174 C2
Toft Monks Norf 143 E8
Toft next Newton Lincs 189 D8
Toftrees Norf 159 D7
Tofts Highld 310 C7
Toftshaw W Yorks 197 B7
Toftwood Norf 159 G9
Togston Northumb 252 C6
Tokavaig Highld 295 D8
Tokers Green Oxon 65 D8
Tokyngton London 67 C7
Tolastadh a Chaolais W Isles 304 E3
Tolastadh bho Thuath W Isles 304 D7
Tolborough Corn 11 F9
Tolcarne Corn 2 B5
Corn 2 C5
Tolcarne Wartha Corn 2 B5
Toldish Corn 5 D8
Tolgus Mount Corn 4 G3
Tolhurst E Sus 53 G7
Tolladine Worcs 117 F7
Tolland Som 42 G6
Tollard Farnham Dorset 30 D6
Tollard Royal Wilts 30 D6
Toll Bar Mers 183 C7
Rutland 137 B10
S Yorks 198 F5
Tollbar End W Mid 119 B7
Toll End W Mid 133 E9
Tollerford Dorset 17 B7
Toller Fratrum Dorset 17 B7
Toller Porcorum Dorset 17 B7
Tollerton Notts 154 C2
N Yorks 215 G10
Toller Whelme Dorset 29 G8
Tollesbury Essex 89 C7
Tollesby Mbro 225 B10
Tolleshunt D'Arcy Essex 88 C6
Tolleshunt Knights Essex 88 C6
Tolleshunt Major Essex 88 C5
Tollie Highld 300 D5
Toll of Birness Aberds 303 F10
Tolm W Isles 304 E6
Tolmers Herts 86 E4
Tolpuddle Dorset 17 C11
Tolskithy Corn 4 G3
Tolvaddon Downs Corn 4 G3
Tolvah Highld 291 D10
Tolworth London 67 F7
Tomaknock Perth 286 E2
Tom an Fhuadain W Isles 305 G5
Tomatin Highld 301 G8
Tombreck Highld 300 F6
Tombui Perth 286 B2
Tomchrasky Highld 290 B4
Tomdoun Highld 290 C3
Tomich Highld 300 B6
Highld 300 G3
Tomich House Highld 300 E5
Tomintoul Aberds 292 D3
Moray 292 B3
Tomlow Warks 119 E9
Tomnaven Moray 302 F4
Tomnavoulin Moray 302 G2
Tomperrow Corn 4 G5
Tompkin Staffs 168 E6
Tompset's Bank E Sus 52 G2
Tomsleibhe Argyll 289 F8
Tomthorn Derbys 185 F9
Ton Mon 78 F5
Ton Breigam V Glam 58 D3
Tonbridge Kent 52 D5
Tonderghie Dumfries 236 F6
Tondu Bridgend 57 E11
Tone Som 27 C10
Tonedale Som 27 C10
Tone Green Som 27 C11
Tong Kent 53 D10
Shrops 132 B5
W Yorks 205 G10
Tonge Leics 153 E8
Tonge Corner Kent 70 F2
Tonge Fold Gtr Man 195 F8
Tonge Moor Gtr Man 195 E8
Tong Forge Shrops 132 B5
Tong Green Kent 54 C3
Tongham Sur 49 D11
Tongland Dumfries 237 D8
Tong Norton Shrops 132 B5
Tong Park W Yorks 205 F9
Tong Street W Yorks 205 G9
Tongue Highld 308 D5
Tongue End Lincs 156 F3
Tongwell M Keynes 103 C7
Tongwynlais Cardiff 58 C6
Tonmawr Neath 57 B10
Tonna / Tonnau Neath 57 B9
Tonnau / Tonna Neath 57 B9
Ton-Pentre Rhondda 77 F7
Ton-teg Rhondda 58 B5
Tontine Lancs 194 G4
Tonwell Herts 86 B4
Tonypandy Rhondda 77 G7
Ton-y-pistyll Caerph 77 F11
Tonyrefail Rhondda 58 B4
Toot Baldon Oxon 83 E9
Toothill Hants 32 D5
Swindon 62 C6
W Yorks 196 C6
Toot Hill Essex 87 E8
Staffs 169 G9
Tooting Graveney London 67 E9
Topcliffe N Yorks 215 D8
W Yorks 197 B9
Topcroft Norf 142 E5
Topcroft Street Norf 142 E5
Top End Beds 121 E10
Top Green Notts 172 F3
Topham S Yorks 198 D6
Topleigh W Sus 34 D6
Top Lock Gtr Man 194 F6
Top of Hebers Gtr Man 195 F11
Top o' th' Lane Lancs 194 C5
Top o' th' Meadows Gtr Man 196 F3
Toppesfield Essex 106 D4
Toppings Gtr Man 195 E8
Toprow Norf 142 D3
Topsham Devon 14 D5
Top Valley Nottingham 171 F9
Torbeg N Ayrs 255 E10
Torboll Farm Highld 309 K7
Torbothie N Lnrk 269 D7
Torbreck Highld 309 J7
Torbrex Stirl 278 C5
Torbryan Devon 8 B6
Torbush N Lnrk 268 D6
Torcross Devon 8 G6
Torcroy Highld 291 D9
Tore Highld 300 D6
Torfrey Corn 6 E2
Torgyle Highld 290 B5
Torinturk Argyll 275 G9
Torkington Gtr Man 184 D6
Torksey Lincs 188 F4
Torlum W Isles 296 F3
Torlundy Highld 290 F3
Tormarton S Glos 61 D9
Tormisdale Argyll 254 B2
Tormitchell S Ayrs 244 E6
Tormore Highld 295 E8
N Ayrs 255 D9
Tornagrain Highld 301 E7
Tornahaish Aberds 292 C4
Tornapress Highld 299 E8
Tornaveen Aberds 293 C8
Torness Highld 300 G5
Toronto Durham 233 E9
Torpenhow Cumb 229 D10
Torphichen W Loth 279 G9
Torphin Edin 270 B4
Torphins Aberds 293 C8
Torpoint Corn 7 E8
Torquay Torbay 9 C8
Torquhan Borders 271 F8
Torr Devon 7 E11
Devon 8 C2
Torra Argyll 254 B4
Torran Argyll 275 C9
Highld 298 E5
Highld 301 B7
Torrance E Dunb 278 G2
Torrans Argyll 288 G6
Torranyard N Ayrs 267 G7
Torre Som 42 E4
Torbay 9 C8
Torridon Highld 299 D9
Torridon Ho Highld 299 D8
Torries Aberds 293 B8
Torrin Highld 295 C7
Torrisdale Highld 308 C6
Torrisdale Castle Argyll 255 D8
Torrisdale-Square Argyll 255 D8
Torrish Highld 311 H3
Torrisholme Lancs 211 G9
Torroble Highld 309 J5
Torroy Highld 309 K5
Torrpark Corn 11 D10
Torry Aberdeen 293 C11
Aberds 302 F4
Torryburn Fife 279 D10
Torsonce Borders 271 G9
Torsonce Mains Borders 271 G9
Torterston Aberds 303 E10
Torthorwald Dumfries 238 B2
Tortington W Sus 35 F8
Torton Worcs 116 C6
Tortworth S Glos 80 G2
Torvaig Highld 298 E4
Torver Cumb 220 G5
Torwood Falk 278 E6
Torwoodlee Mains Borders 261 B11
Torworth Notts 187 D11
Tosberry Devon 24 C3
Toscaig Highld 295 B9
Toseland Cambs 122 E4
Tosside N Yorks 203 B11
Tostock Suff 125 E9
Totaig Highld 295 C10
Highld 298 D2
Totardor Highld 294 B5
Tote Highld 298 E4
Totegan Highld 310 C2
Tote Hill Hants 32 C4
W Sus 34 C5
Totford Hants 48 F5
Totham Hill Essex 88 C5
Totham Plains Essex 88 C5
Tothill Lincs 190 E6
Tot Hill Hants 64 G3
Totland IoW 20 D2
Totley S Yorks 186 F4
Totley Brook S Yorks 186 E4
Totley Rise S Yorks 186 E4
Totmonslow Staffs 151 B9
Totnell Dorset 29 F10
Totnes Devon 8 C6
Totnor Hereford 97 E11
Toton Notts 153 C10
Totronald Argyll 288 D3
Totscore Highld 298 C3
Tottenham London 86 G4
Tottenham Hale London 67 B10
Tottenhill Norf 158 G2
Tottenhill Row Norf 158 G2
Totteridge Bucks 84 G5
London 86 G2
Totternhoe C Beds 103 G9
Totteroak S Glos 61 C8
Totterton Shrops 131 F7
Totties W Yorks 197 F7
Tottington Gtr Man 195 E9
Norf 141 D7
Tottlebank Cumb 210 C6
Tottleworth Lancs 203 G10
Totton Hants 32 E5
Touchen End Windsor 65 D11
Toulston N Yorks 206 E5
Toulton Som 43 G7
Toulvaddie Highld 311 L2
Tournaig Highld 307 L3
Toux Aberds 303 D9
Tovil Kent 53 C9
Towan Corn 10 G3
Towan Cross Corn 4 F4
Toward Argyll 266 B2
Towcester Northants 102 B3
Towednack Corn 1 B5
Towerage Bucks 84 G4
Tower End Norf 158 F3
Tower Hamlets Kent 55 E10
Towerhead N Som 44 B2
Tower Hill Ches E 184 F6
Devon 12 C3
Essex 108 E5
Herts 85 E8
Mers 194 G2
Sur 51 D7
W Mid 133 E11
W Sus 35 B11
Towersey Oxon 84 D2
Tow House Northumb 241 E7
Towie Aberds 292 B6
Aberds 302 G5
Aberds 303 C8
Towiemore Moray 302 E3
Tow Law Durham 233 D8
Town Barton Devon 14 C2
Townend Derbys 185 E9
Staffs 151 B9
W Dunb 277 F8
Town End Bucks 84 F3
Cambs 139 D8
Cumb 211 B7
Cumb 211 C8
Cumb 212 C2
Cumb 220 D6
Cumb 221 E8
Cumb 221 F7
Cumb 231 F8

Derbys 185 F11
E Yorks 207 C10
Mers 183 D7
W Yorks 196 D5
Townfield Durham 232 B5
Town Fields
Ches W 167 B10
Towngate Cumb 230 B6
Lincs 156 G2
Town Green
Gtr Man 183 B9
Lancs 194 F2
Norf 161 G7
Townhead Argyll 275 G11
Cumb 229 D7
Cumb 230 D6
Cumb 231 E8
Dumfries 237 E8
N Lnrk 268 B4
Northumb 251 E9
S Ayrs 244 C6
S Yorks 186 E4
S Yorks 197 G7
Town Head Cumb 220 D6
Cumb 221 E8
Cumb 222 C2
Cumb 222 C3
Cumb 231 F7
Cumb 231 F8
Cumb 231 G8
Cumb 231 G9
Derbys 185 F11
N Yorks 204 B2
N Yorks 212 F5
Staffs 169 F8
W Yorks 204 D6
Townhead of Greenlaw
Dumfries 237 C9
Townhill Fife 280 D2
Swansea 56 C6
Townhill Park Hants 33 E7
Town Kelloe
Durham 234 D3
Townlake Devon 12 G4
Townland Green
Kent 54 G2
Town Lane
Gtr Man 183 B11
Town Littleworth
E Sus 36 D6
Town of Lowton
Mers 183 B10
Town Park Telford 132 B3
Town Row E Sus 52 G5
Townsend Bath 44 B5
Bucks 84 D2
Devon 25 B10
Herts 85 D10
Oxon 63 B11
Pembs 72 D4
Som 44 C4
Stoke 168 F6
Wilts 46 B3
Wilts 46 B4
Towns End Hants 48 B5
Som 30 D2
Town's End Bucks 102 G2
Dorset 18 B3
Dorset 18 E5
Dorset 29 F9
Som 45 D7
Townsend Fold
Lancs 195 C10
Townshend Corn 2 C3
Town Street Glos 98 F6
Townwell S Glos 79 G11
Town Yetholm
Borders 263 D8
Towthorpe E Yorks 217 G8
York 207 B8
Towton N Yorks 206 F5
Towyn Conwy 181 F7
Toxteth Mers 182 D5
Toynton All Saints
Lincs 174 C5
Toynton Fen Side
Lincs 174 C5
Toynton St Peter
Lincs 174 C6
Toy's Hill Kent 52 C3
Trabboch E Ayrs 257 E10
Traboe Corn 2 E6
Trabrown Borders 271 F10
Tracebridge Som 27 C9
Tradespark Highld 301 D8
Orkney 314 F4
Trafford Park
Gtr Man 184 B3
Traigh Ho Highld 295 F8
Trallong Powys 95 F9
Trallwn Rhondda 77 G9
Swansea 57 B7
Tramagenna Corn 11 E7
Tram Inn Hereford 97 E9
Tranch Torf 78 E3
Tranent E Loth 281 G8
Tranmere Mers 182 D4
Trantlebeg Highld 310 D2
Trantlemore Highld 310 D2
Tranwell Northumb 252 G5
Trapp Carms 75 B11
Traprain E Loth 281 F11
Trap's Green Warks 118 D2
Trapshill W Berks 63 G11
Traquair Borders 261 C8
Trash Green W Berks 65 F7
Travellers' Rest
Carms 74 B5
Trawden Lancs 204 F4
Trawscoed Powys 95 E11
Trawsfynydd Gwyn 146 B4
Trawsnant Ceredig 111 D11
Treadam Mon 78 B5
Treaddow Hereford 97 G10
Treal Corn 2 F6
Trealaw Rhondda 77 G8
Treales Lancs 202 G4
Trearddur Anglesey 178 F3
Treaslane Highld 298 D3
Treath Corn 3 D7
Treator Corn 10 F4
Tre-Aubrey V Glam 58 E4
Trebanog Rhondda 77 G8
Trebanos Neath 76 E2
Trebarber Corn 5 C7
Trebartha Corn 11 F11
Trebarwith Corn 11 D7
Trebarwith Strand
Corn 10 D6
Trebeath Corn 11 D11
Tre-Beferad V Glam 58 F3
Trebell Green Corn 5 C11
Treberfydd Powys 96 F2
Trebetherick Corn 10 F4
Trebilcock Corn 5 C9
Treble's Holford Som 43 G7
Tre-boeth Swansea 57 B7
Treborough Som 42 F4
Trebudannon Corn 5 C7
Trebullett Corn 12 F2
Treburgett Corn 11 F7
Treburgie Corn 6 C4
Treburley Corn 12 F3
Treburrick Corn 10 G3
Trebyan Corn 5 C11
Trecastle Powys 95 F7
Trecenydd Caerph 58 B6
Trecott Devon 25 G10
Trecwn Pembs 91 E9
Trecynon Rhondda 77 E7
Tredannick Corn 10 G6
Tredaule Corn 11 E10
Tredavoe Corn 1 D5
Treddiog Pembs 91 F7
Tredegar Bl Gwent 77 D10
Trederwen Powys 148 F5
Tre-derwen Powys 148 F4
Tredethy Corn 11 G7
Tredington Glos 99 F8
Warks 100 C5
Tredinnick Corn 1 C4
Corn 5 D10
Corn 6 B3
Corn 6 D4
Corn 10 G4
Tredogan V Glam 58 F5
Tredomen Caerph 77 G10
Powys 96 E2
Tredown Devon 24 D2
Tredrizzick Corn 10 F5
Tredunnock Mon 78 G5
Tredustan Powys 96 E2
Tredworth Glos 80 B4
Treen Corn 1 B4
Corn 1 E3
Treesmill Corn 5 D11
Treeton S Yorks 186 D6
Trefaes Gwyn 144 C5
Trefanny Hill Corn 6 D4
Trefasser Pembs 91 D7
Trefdraeth Anglesey 178 G6
Trefdraeth / Newport
Pembs 91 D11
Trefecca Powys 96 E2
Trefechan Ceredig 111 A11
M Tydf 77 D8
Wrex 166 F3
Trefeglwys Powys 129 E9
Trefeitha Powys 96 E2
Trefenter Ceredig 112 D2
Treffgarne Pembs 91 G9
Treffynnon Pembs 90 F6
Treffynnon / Holywell
Flint 181 F11
Trefgarn Owen
Pembs 91 F7
Trefil Bl Gwent 77 C10
Trefilan Ceredig 111 F11
Trefin / Trevine
Pembs 90 E6
Treflach Shrops 148 D5
Trefnanney Powys 148 F4
Trefnant Denb 181 G9
Trefonen Shrops 148 D5
Trefor Anglesey 178 E5
Gwyn 162 F5
Treforda Corn 11 E7
Treforest Rhondda 58 B5
Treforgan Ceredig 92 B4
Tre-Forgan Neath 76 D3
Treforys / Morriston
Swansea 57 B7
Trefriw Conwy 164 C3
Trefrize Corn 12 F2
Tref y Clawdd /
Knighton Powys 114 C5
Trefynwy / Monmouth
Mon 79 C8
Tregada Corn 12 E2
Tregadgwith Corn 1 D4
Tregadillett Corn 12 E2
Tre-gagle Mon 79 D8
Tregaian Anglesey 178 F6
Tregajorran Corn 4 G3
Tregamere Corn 5 C8
Tregardock Corn 10 E6
Tregare Mon 78 C6
Tregarland Corn 6 D5
Tregarlandbridge
Corn 6 D4
Tregarne Corn 3 E7
Tregaron Ceredig 112 F3
Tregarrick Mill Corn 6 D4
Tregarth Gwyn 163 B10
Tregath Gwyn 163 B10
Tregatillian Corn 5 C8
Tregatta Corn 11 D7
Tregavarah Corn 1 D4
Tregear Corn 2 E5
Tregeare Corn 11 D10
Tregeiriog Wrex 148 C3
Tregele Anglesey 178 C5
Tregellist Corn 10 F6
Tregeseal Corn 1 C3
Tregew Corn 3 C8
Tre-Gibbon Rhondda 77 E7
Tregidden Corn 3 E7
Treginnis Pembs 90 G4
Treglemais Pembs 90 F6
Tregole Corn 11 B9
Tregolls Corn 2 B6
Tregolwyn / Colwinston
V Glam 58 D2
Tregona Corn 5 B7
Tregonce Corn 10 G4
Tregonetha Corn 5 C9
Tregonna Corn 10 G4
Tregonning Corn 5 D7
Tregony Corn 5 G8
Tregoodwell Corn 11 E8
Tregorden Corn 10 G6
Tregorrick Corn 5 E10
Tregoss Corn 5 C9
Tregoyd Powys 96 D4
Tregoyd Mill Powys 96 D3
Tregreenwell Corn 11 E7
Tregrehan Mills Corn 5 E10
Tregroes Ceredig 93 C8
Tregullon Corn 5 C11
Tregunna Corn 10 G5
Tregurrian Corn 5 B7
Tregurtha Downs
Corn 2 C2
Tre Gwyr / Gowerton
Swansea 56 B5
Tregyddulan Pembs 91 D7
Tregynon Powys 129 D11
Tre-gynwr Carms 74 B6
Trehafod Rhondda 77 G8
Trehafren Powys 129 E11
Trehan Corn 7 D8
Treharris M Tydf 77 F9
Trehemborne Corn 10 G3
Treherbert Rhondda 76 F6
Tre-hill V Glam 58 E5
Trehunist Corn 6 C6
Trekeivesteps Corn 11 G10
Trekenner Corn 12 F2
Trekenning Corn 5 C8
Treknow Corn 11 D7
Trelales / Laleston
Bridgend 57 F11
Trelan Corn 2 F6
Tre-lan Flint 165 B11
Trelash Corn 11 C9
Trelassick Corn 5 E7
Trelawnyd Flint 181 F9
Trelech Carms 92 E5
Treleddyd-fawr
Pembs 90 F5
Treleigh Corn 4 G4
Treletert / Letterston
Pembs 91 F8
Trelew Corn 3 B8
Trelewis M Tydf 77 F10
Treligga Corn 11 E7
Trelights Corn 10 F5
Trelill Corn 10 F6
Trelion Corn 5 E8
Treliske Corn 4 F6
Trelissick Corn 3 B8
Treliver Corn 5 B9
Trellech Mon 79 D8
Trelleck Grange Mon 79 E7
Trelogan Flint 181 E10
Treloquithack Corn 2 D5
Trelowia Corn 6 D5
Trelowth Corn 5 E9
Trelystan Powys 130 C5
Tremadog Gwyn 163 G9
Tremail Corn 11 D9
Tremain Ceredig 92 B4
Tremaine Corn 11 D10
Tremains Bridgend 58 D2
Tremar Corn 6 B5
Trematon Corn 7 D7
Trematon Castle Corn 7 D8
Tremayne Corn 2 B4
Trembraze Corn 6 B5
Tremedda Corn 1 B5
Tremeirchion Denb 181 G9
Tremethick Cross
Corn 1 C4
Tremore Corn 5 C10
Tremorebridge Corn 5 C10
Tremorfa Cardiff 59 D8
Tre-Mostyn Flint 181 F10
Trenance Corn 4 C6
Corn 5 B7
Corn 5 C9
Corn 10 G4
Trenant Corn 6 B4
Corn 10 G5
Trenarren Corn 5 F10
Trenay Corn 6 B3
Trench Telford 150 G3
Trench Green Oxon 65 D7
Trench Wood Kent 52 D5
Trencreek Corn 4 C6
Trencrom Corn 2 B2
Trendeal Corn 5 E7
Trenear Corn 2 C5
Treneglos Corn 11 D10
Trenerth Corn 2 B4
Trenewan Corn 6 E3
Trengune Corn 11 C9
Trenhorne Corn 11 F11
Treningle Corn 5 B10
Treninnick Corn 4 C6
Trenoon Corn 2 F6
Trenoweth Corn 3 C7
Trent Dorset 29 D9
Trentham Stoke 168 G5
Trentishoe Devon 40 D6
Trentlock Derbys 153 C9
Trent Vale Stoke 168 G5
Trenwheal Corn 2 C4
Treoes V Glam 58 D2
Treopert / Granston
Pembs 91 E7
Treorchy / Treorci
Rhondda 77 F7
Treorci / Treorchy
Rhondda 77 F7
Treowen Caerph 78 F2
Powys 130 E2
Tre-pit V Glam 58 E2
Trequite Corn 10 F6
Tre'r-ddôl Ceredig 128 E3
Trerhyngyll V Glam 58 D4
Trerise Corn 2 F6
Trer llai / Leighton
Powys 130 B4
Trerose Corn 3 D7
Trerulefoot Corn 6 D6
Tresaith Ceredig 110 G5
Tresamble Corn 3 B7
Tresarrett Corn 11 G7
Tresavean Corn 2 B6
Tresawle Corn 5 F7
Tresawsen Corn 4 F5
Trescoll Corn 5 C10
Trescott Staffs 132 D6
Trescowe Corn 2 C3
Tresean Corn 4 D5
Tresevern Croft Corn 2 B6
Tresham Glos 80 G3
Tresigin / Sigingstone
V Glam 58 E3
Tresillian Corn 5 F7
Tresimwn / Bonvilston
V Glam 58 E5
Tresinney Corn 11 E8
Tresinwen Pembs 91 C7
Treskerby Corn 4 G4
Treskillard Corn 2 B5
Treskilling Corn 5 D10
Treskinnick Cross
Corn 11 B10
Treslothan Corn 2 B5
Tresmeer Corn 11 D10
Tresowes Green Corn 2 D3
Tresoweshill Corn 2 D4
Tresparrett Corn 11 C8
Tresparrett Posts
Corn 11 C8
Tressady Highld 309 J7
Tressait Perth 291 G10
Tresta Shetland 312 D8
Shetland 313 H5
Treswell Notts 188 F3
Treswithian Corn 4 G2
Treswithian Downs
Corn 4 G2
Tre-Taliesin Ceredig 128 E3
Trethellan Water Corn 2 B6
Trethevy Corn 11 D7
Trethewell Corn 3 B9
Trethewey Corn 1 E3
Trethillick Corn 10 F4
Trethomas Caerph 59 B7
Trethosa Corn 5 E8
Trethowel Corn 5 E10
Trethurgy Corn 5 D10
Tretio Pembs 90 F5
Tretire Hereford 97 G10
Tretower Powys 96 G3
Treuddyn Flint 166 D3
Trevadlock Corn 11 F11
Trevail Corn 4 D5
Trevalga Corn 11 D7
Trevalgan Corn 1 A5
Trevalyn Wrex 166 D5
Trevance Corn 10 G4
Trevanger Corn 10 F5
Trevanson Corn 10 G5
Trevarrack Corn 1 C5
Trevarren Corn 5 C8
Trevarrian Corn 4 B6
Trevarrick Corn 5 G9
Trevarth Corn 4 G4
Trevaughan Carms 73 B11
Carms 93 G7
Tre-vaughan Carms 93 G8
Treveal Corn 1 A5
Trevegean Corn 1 D3
Treveighan Corn 11 F7
Trevellas Corn 4 E4
Trevelmond Corn 6 C4
Trevelver Corn 10 G5
Trevemper Corn 4 D6
Treven Corn 11 D7
Trevena Corn 2 D4
Trevenen Corn 2 D5
Trevenen Bal Corn 2 D5
Trevenning Corn 11 F7
Treveor Corn 5 G9
Treverbyn Corn 5 D10
Corn 6 B4
Treverva Corn 3 C7
Trevescan Corn 1 E3
Trevethin Torf 78 E3
Trevia Corn 11 E7
Trevigro Corn 6 B6
Trevilder Corn 10 G6
Trevilla Corn 3 B8
Trevilson Corn 4 D6
Trevine Corn 10 F5
Trevine / Trefin
Pembs 90 E6
Treviscoe Corn 5 D8
Treviskey Corn 2 B6
Trevithal Corn 1 D5
Trevoll Corn 4 D6
Trevone Corn 10 F3
Trevor Wrex 166 G3
Trevorrick Corn 10 G4
Trevor Uchaf Denb 166 G2
Trevowah Corn 4 D5
Trevowhan Corn 1 B4
Trew Corn 2 D4
Trewalder Corn 11 E7
Trewarmett Corn 11 D7
Trewartha Corn 2 B2
Corn 3 B10
Trewassa Corn 11 D8
Treween Corn 11 E10
Trewellard Corn 1 C3
Trewen Corn 11 E7
Corn 11 E11
Mon 79 G7
Trewennack Corn 2 D5
Trewennan Corn 11 E7
Trewern Powys 148 G5
Trewetha Corn 10 E6
Trewethen Corn 10 F6
Trewethern Corn 10 F6
Trewey Corn 1 B5
Trewidland Corn 6 D5
Trewindle Corn 6 C2
Trewint Corn 6 C5
Corn 11 B9
Corn 11 E10
Trewithian Corn 3 B9
Trewithick Corn 11 D11
Trewollock Corn 5 G10
Trewoodloe Corn 12 G2
Trewoofe Corn 1 D4
Trewoon Corn 2 F5
Corn 5 E9
Treworga Corn 5 G7
Treworgan Common
Mon 78 D6
Treworlas Corn 3 B9
Treworld Corn 11 C8
Trewornan Corn 10 G5
Treworrick Corn 6 B4
Treworthal Corn 3 B9
Trewyddel / Moylgrove
Pembs 92 C2
Tre-wyn Mon 96 G6
Treyarnon Corn 10 G3
Treyford W Sus 34 D4
Trezaise Corn 5 D9
Trezelah Corn 1 C5
Triangle Glos 79 E8
Staffs 133 B11
W Yorks 196 C4
Trickett's Cross
Dorset 31 G9
Triffleton Pembs 91 G9
Trillacott Corn 11 D11
Trimdon Durham 234 E3
Trimdon Colliery
Durham 234 D3
Trimdon Grange
Durham 234 D3
Trimingham Norf 160 B5
Trimley Lower Street
Suff 108 D5
Trimley St Martin
Suff 108 D5
Trimley St Mary
Suff 108 D5
Trimpley Worcs 116 B5
Trims Green Herts 87 B7
Trimsaran Carms 75 E7
Trimstone Devon 40 E3
Trinafour Perth 291 G9
Trinant Caerph 78 E2
Tring Herts 84 C6
Tringford Herts 84 C6
Tring Wharf Herts 84 C6
Trinity Angus 293 G8
Devon 27 F7
Edin 280 F4
Trinity Fields Staffs 151 D8
Trisant Ceredig 112 B4
Triscombe Som 43 F7
Trislaig Highld 290 F2
Trispen Corn 4 E6
Tritlington
Northumb 252 E6
Troan Corn 5 D7
Trochry Perth 286 C3
Trodigal Argyll 255 E7
Troearhiwgwair
Bl Gwent 77 D11
Troedrhiwdalar
Powys 113 G9
Troedrhiwffenyd
Ceredig 93 C8
Troedrhiwfuwch
Caerph 77 E10
Troedyraur Ceredig 92 B6
Troedyrhiw M Tydf 77 E9
Trofarth Conwy 180 G5
Trolliloes E Sus 23 C10
Tromode IoM 192 E4
Trondavoe Shetland 312 F5
Troon Corn 2 B5
S Ayrs 257 C8
Trooper's Inn Pembs 73 C7
Trosaraidh W Isles 297 K3
Trossachs Hotel
Stirl 285 G9
Troston Suff 125 C7
Trostre Carms 56 B4
Trostrey Common
Mon 78 E5
Troswell Corn 11 C11
Trotshill Worcs 117 F7
Trotten Marsh
W Sus 34 B4
Trottiscliffe Kent 68 G6
Trotton W Sus 34 C4
Trough Gate Lancs 195 C11
Troutbeck Cumb 221 E8
Cumb 230 F3
Troutbeck Bridge
Cumb 221 F8
Troway Derbys 186 F5
Trowbridge Cardiff 59 C8
Wilts 45 B11
Trowell Notts 153 B9
Trow Green Glos 79 D9
Trowle Common
Wilts 45 B10
Trowley Bottom
Herts 85 C9
Trows Borders 262 C5
Trowse Newton
Norf 142 B4
Troydale W Yorks 205 G10
Troy Town Kent 52 D2
Kent 54 E5
Medway 69 F8
Truas Corn 11 D7
Trub Gtr Man 195 F11
Trudoxhill Som 45 E8
Trueman's Heath
Worcs 117 B11
True Street Devon 8 C6
Trull Som 28 C2
Trumaisgearraidh
W Isles 296 D4
Trumfleet S Yorks 198 E6
Trumpan Highld 298 C2
Trumpet Hereford 98 D3
Trumpington Cambs 123 F8
Trumpsgreen Sur 66 F3
Trunch Norf 160 C5
Trunnah Lancs 202 E2
Truro Corn 4 G6
Truscott Corn 12 D2
Trusham Devon 14 E3
Trusley Derbys 152 B5
Trussall Corn 2 D5
Trussell Corn 11 D10
Trusthorpe Lincs 191 E8
Truthan Corn 4 E6
Truthwall Corn 2 C2
Trwstllewelyn
Powys 130 D3
Tryfil Anglesey 178 E6
Trysull Staffs 133 E7
Trythogga Corn 1 C5
Tubbs Mill Corn 5 G9
Tubney Oxon 82 F6
Tubslake Kent 53 G9
Tuckenhay Devon 8 D6
Tuckermarsh Devon 7 B8
Tuckerton Som 28 B3
Tuckhill Shrops 132 F5
Tuckingmill Corn 4 G3
Corn 11 F7
Wilts 30 B6
Tucking Mill Bath 61 G9
Tuckton Bmouth 19 C8
Tuddenham Suff 108 B3
Suff 124 C4
Tuddenham St Martin
Suff 108 B3
Tudeley Kent 52 D6
Tudeley Hale Kent 52 D6
Tudhay Devon 28 G4
Tudhoe Durham 233 D11
Tudhoe Grange
Durham 233 E11
Tudor Hill W Mid 134 D2
Tudorville Hereford 97 G11
Tudweiliog Gwyn 144 B4
Tuebrook Mers 182 C5
Tuesley Sur 50 E3
Tuesnoad Kent 54 E2
Tuffley Glos 80 C4
Tufnell Park London 67 B9
Tufton Hants 48 D3
Pembs 91 F10
Tugby Leics 136 C5
Tugford Shrops 131 F11
Tughall Northumb 264 D6
Tulchan Lodge
Angus 292 F3
Tullecombe W Sus 34 B4
Tullibardine Perth 286 F3
Tullibody Clack 279 B7
Tullich Argyll 284 F4
Highld 299 E9
Highld 300 G6
Tullich Muir Highld 301 B7
Tulliemet Perth 286 B3
Tulloch Aberds 293 F9
Aberds 303 F8
Highld 290 E5
Perth 286 E4
Tulloch Castle
Highld 300 C5
Tullochgorm
Argyll 275 D10
Tulloch-gribban
Highld 301 G9
Tullochroisk Perth 285 B11
Tullochvenus
Aberds 293 C7
Tulloes Angus 287 C9
Tullybannocher
Perth 285 E11
Tullybelton Perth 286 D4
Tullycross Stirl 277 D9
Tullyfergus Perth 286 C6
Tullymurdoch Perth 286 B5
Tullynessle Aberds 293 B7
Tulse Hill London 67 E10
Tumbler's Green
Essex 106 F6
Tumble / Y Tymbl
Carms 75 C8
Tumby Lincs 174 D2
Tumby Woodside
Lincs 174 D3
Tummel Bridge
Perth 285 B11
Tumpy Green Glos 80 E2
Tumpy Lakes
Hereford 97 B10
Tunbridge Hill
Medway 69 E10
Tunbridge Wells / Royal
Tunbridge Wells
Kent 52 F5
Tunga W Isles 304 E6
Tungate Norf 160 D5
Tunley Bath 45 B7
Glos 80 E6
Tunnel Hill Worcs 98 C6
Tunnel Pits N Lincs 199 G8
Tunshill Gtr Man 196 E2
Tunstall E Yorks 209 G12
Kent 69 G11
Lancs 212 E2
Norf 143 B8
N Yorks 224 F4
Staffs 150 D5
Stoke 168 E5
Suff 127 G7
T&W 243 G9
Tunstead Derbys 185 G10
Gtr Man 196 G4
Norf 160 E5
Tunworth Hants 49 D7
Tupsley Hereford 97 C10
Tupton Derbys 170 B5
Turbary Common
Poole 19 C7
Turfdown Corn 5 B11
Turf Hill Gtr Man 196 E2
Turfholm S Lnrk 259 B8
Turfmoor Devon 28 G3
Shrops 149 F7
Turgis Green Hants 49 B7
Turin Angus 287 B9
Turkdean Glos 81 B10
Turkey Island Hants 33 E9
W Sus 34 D3
Turkey Tump
Hereford 97 F10
Tur Langton Leics 136 E4
Turleigh Wilts 61 G10
Turleygreen Shrops 132 F5
Turlin Moor Poole 18 C5
Turmer Hants 31 F10
Turn Lancs 195 D10
Turnalt Argyll 275 C9
Turnastone Hereford 97 D7
Turnberry S Ayrs 244 B6
Turnchapel Plym 7 E9
Turnditch Derbys 170 F3
Turner Green Lancs 203 G8
Turner's Green
E Sus 23 B10
E Sus 52 G6
Warks 118 D3
W Berks 64 F4
Turners Hill W Sus 51 F10
Turners Puddle
Dorset 18 C2
Turnerwood
S Yorks 187 E8
Turnford Herts 86 E5
Turnhouse Edin 280 G3
Turnhurst Stoke 168 E5
Turnstead Milton
Derbys 185 E8
Turnworth Dorset 30 F4
Turrerich Perth 286 D2
Turriff Aberds 303 D7
Tursdale Durham 234 D2
Turton Bottoms
Blkburn 195 D8
Turves Cambs 138 D6
Turves Green
W Mid 117 B10
Turvey Beds 121 G8
Turville Bucks 84 G3
Turville Heath Bucks 84 G2
Turweston Bucks 102 D2
Tushielaw Borders 261 F8
Tutbury Staffs 152 D4
Tutnall Worcs 117 C9
Tutnalls Glos 79 E10
Tutshill Glos 79 G8
Tutt Hill Kent 54 D3
Tuttington Norf 160 D4
Tutts Clump W Berks 64 E5
Tutwell Corn 12 F3
Tuxford Notts 188 G2
Twatt Orkney 314 D2
Shetland 313 H5
Twechar E Dunb 278 F4
Tweedale Telford 132 C4
Tweeddaleburn
Borders 270 E5
Tweedmouth
Northumb 273 E9
Tweedsmuir
Borders 260 E3
Twelve Heads Corn 4 G5
Twelve Oaks E Sus 37 C11
Twelvewoods Corn 6 B4
Twemlow Green
Ches E 168 B3
Twenties Kent 71 F10
Twenty Lincs 156 E3
Twerton Bath 61 G8
Twickenham London 67 E7
Twigworth Glos 98 G6
Twineham W Sus 36 D3
Twineham Green
W Sus 36 C3
Twinhoe Bath 45 B8
Twinstead Essex 107 D7
Twinstead Green
Essex 106 D6
Twiss Green Warr 183 B11
Twist Devon 28 G3
Twiston Lancs 204 E2
Twitchen Devon 41 G9
Shrops 115 B7
Twitchen Mill Devon 41 G9
Twitham Kent 55 B9
Twitton Kent 52 B4
Two Bridges Devon 13 G8
Glos 79 D11
Two Burrows Corn 4 F4
Two Dales Derbys 170 C3
Two Gates Staffs 134 C4
Two Mile Ash
M Keynes 102 D6
W Sus 35 B10
Two Mile Hill Bristol 60 E6
Two Mile Oak Cross
Devon 8 B6
Two Mills Ches W 182 G5
Two Pots Devon 40 E4
Two Waters Herts 85 D9
Twr Anglesey 178 E2
Twycross Leics 134 C6
Twydall Medway 69 F9
Twyford Bucks 102 F3
Derbys 152 D6
Dorset 30 D5
Hants 33 C7
Leics 154 G4
Lincs 155 E8
Norf 159 E10
Oxon 101 D9
Shrops 148 D6
Wokingham 65 D9
Worcs 99 B10
Twyford Common
Hereford 97 D10
Twyn-Allws Mon 78 C3
Twynholm Dumfries 237 D8
Twyning Glos 99 D7
Twyning Green Glos 99 D8
Twynllanan Carms 94 G5
Twynmynydd Carms 75 C11
Twyn Shôn-Ifan
Caerph 77 G11
Twynyrodyn M Tydf 77 D9
Twyn-yr-odyn
V Glam 58 E6
Twyn-y-Sheriff Mon 78 D6
Twywell Northants 121 B9
Tyberton Hereford 97 D7
Tyburn W Mid 134 E2
Tyby Norf 159 D11
Ty-coch Swansea 56 C6
Tycroes Carms 75 C10
Tycrwyn Powys 148 F2
Tyddewi / St Davids
Pembs 90 F5
Tydd Gote Lincs 157 F9
Tydd St Giles Cambs 157 F8
Tydd St Mary Lincs 157 F8
Tyddyn Powys 129 F9
Tyddyn Angharad
Denb 165 F9
Tyddyn Dai Anglesey 178 C6
Tyddyn-mawr Gwyn 163 G9
Ty-draw Conwy 164 D5
Swansea 57 C7
Tye Hants 22 C2
Tye Common Essex 87 G11
Tyegate Green Norf 161 G7
Tye Green Essex 87 C10
Essex 87 D7
Essex 87 F11
Essex 105 D11
Essex 105 G10
Essex 106 G5
Tyersal W Yorks 205 G9
Ty-fry Mon 78 F6
Tyganol V Glam 58 E4
Ty-hen Carms 92 G6
Gwyn 144 C3
Ty-isaf Carms 56 B4
Tyla Mon 78 C2
Tylagwyn Bridgend 58 B2
Tyldesley Gtr Man 195 G7
Tyle Carms 94 F3
Tyle-garw Rhondda 58 C4
Tyler Hill Kent 70 G6
Tylers Causeway
Herts 86 D3
Tylers Green Bucks 84 G6
Tyler's Green Essex 87 D8
Sur 51 C11
Tyler's Hill Bucks 85 E7
Ty Llwyn Bl Gwent 77 D11
Tylorstown Rhondda 77 F8
Tylwch Powys 129 G9
Ty-mawr Anglesey 179 D7
Ty Mawr Carms 93 C10
Ty-mawr Conwy 181 F7
Ty Mawr Cwm
Conwy 164 F6
Tynant Rhondda 58 B5
Ty-nant Conwy 165 G7
Gwyn 147 D8
Tyncelyn Ceredig 112 E2
Tyndrum Stirl 285 D7
Tyne Dock T&W 243 D9
Tyneham Dorset 18 E3
Tynehead Midloth 271 D7
Tynemouth T&W 243 D9
Tyne Tunnel T&W 243 D8
Tynewydd Ceredig 92 B4
Neath 76 D4
Rhondda 76 F6
Ty-Newydd
Ceredig 111 D10
Tyning Bath 45 B7
Tyninghame E Loth 282 F2
Tyn-lon Gwyn 163 D7
Tynron Dumfries 247 E8
Tyntesfield N Som 60 E4
Tyntetown Rhondda 77 F9
Ty'n-y-bryn Rhondda 58 B4
Tyn-y-celyn Wrex 148 B3
Tyn-y-coed Shrops 148 D4
Ty'n-y-coedcae
Caerph 59 B7
Tyn-y-cwm
Swansea 75 E10
Tynyfedw Conwy 165 B7
Tyn-y-fedwen
Powys 148 C2
Ty'n-y-ffordd Denb 181 G8
Tyn-y-ffridd Powys 148 C2
Ty'n-y-garn
Bridgend 57 E11
Tynygongl Anglesey 179 E8
Tynygraig Ceredig 112 D3
Tyn-y-graig
Powys 113 G10
Ty'n-y-groes Conwy 180 G3
Ty'n-y-maes Gwyn 163 C10
Tyn-y-pwll
Anglesey 178 D6
Ty'n-yr-eithin
Ceredig 112 E3
Tynyrwtra Powys 129 F7
Tyrells End C Beds 103 E9
Tyrell's Wood Sur 51 B7
Ty'r-felin-isaf
Conwy 164 C5
Ty Rhiw Rhondda 58 C6
Tyrie Aberds 303 C9
Tyringham
M Keynes 103 B7
Tyseley W Mid 134 G2
Ty-Sign Caerph 78 G2
Tythecott Devon 24 D6
Tythegston Bridgend 57 F11
Tytherington
Ches E 184 F6
S Glos 61 B7
Som 45 D9
Wilts 46 E2
Tytherleigh Devon 28 G4
Tytherton Lucas
Wilts 62 E2
Tyttenhanger Herts 85 D11
Ty-uchaf Powys 147 E10
Tywardreath Corn 5 E11
Tywardreath Highway
Corn 5 D11
Tywyn Conwy 180 F3
Gwyn 110 C2

U

Uachdar W Isles 296 F3
Uags Highld 295 B9
Ubberley Stoke 168 F6
Ubbeston Green
Suff 126 C6
Ubley Bath 44 B4
Uckerby N Yorks 224 E4
Uckfield E Sus 37 C7
Uckinghall Worcs 99 D7
Uckington Glos 99 G8
Shrops 131 B11
Uddingston S Lnrk 268 C3
Uddington S Lnrk 259 C9
Udimore E Sus 38 D5
Udley N Som 60 G3
Udny Green Aberds 303 G8
Udny Station
Aberds 303 G9
Udston S Lnrk 268 D3
Udstonhead S Lnrk 268 F4
Uffcott Wilts 62 D6
Uffculme Devon 27 E9
Uffington Lincs 137 B11
Oxon 63 B10
Shrops 149 G10
Ufford Pboro 137 C11
Suff 126 G5
Ufton Warks 119 E7
Ufton Green W Berks 64 F6
Ufton Nervet
W Berks 64 F6
Ugadale Argyll 255 E8
Ugborough Devon 8 D3
Ugford Wilts 46 G5
Uggeshall Suff 143 G8
Ugglebarnby
N Yorks 227 D7
Ughill S Yorks 186 C3
Ugley Essex 105 F10
Ugley Green Essex 105 F10
Ugthorpe N Yorks 226 C5
Uidh W Isles 297 M2
Uig Argyll 276 E2
Argyll 288 D3
Highld 296 F7
Highld 298 C3

Corn 2 E5
Corn 5 D7
Hereford 97 C9
Som 43 D10
Wilts 45 G9
White Cross Hill
Cambs 123 B9
White End Worcs 98 E5
Whiteface Highld 309 L7
Whitefarland
N Ayrs 255 C9
Whitefaulds S Ayrs 245 B7
Whitefield Aberds 303 G7
Dorset 18 C4
Gtr Man 195 F10
Perth 286 D5
Som 27 B9
Whitefield Lane End
Mers 183 D7
Whiteflat E Ayrs 258 D2
Whiteford Aberds 303 G7
Whitegate Ches W 167 B10
White Gate
Gtr Man 195 G11
Som 28 F4
White Grit Shrops 130 D6
Whitehall Blkburn 195 C7
Bristol 60 E6
Devon 27 E10
Devon 40 F4
Hants 49 C8
Herts 104 E6
W Sus 35 C10
White Hall Herts 104 G5
Whitehall Village
Orkney 314 D6
Whitehaven Cumb 219 B9
Shrops 148 E5
Whitehawk Brighton 36 G4
Whiteheath Gate
W Mid 133 F9
Whitehill E Sus 37 B8
Hants 49 G9
Kent 54 B4
Midloth 271 B7
Moray 302 D5
S Lnrk 268 D4
Staffs 168 E3
White Hill Bath 45 B8
Wilts 45 G10
W Yorks 204 E6
Whitehills Aberds 302 C6
S Lnrk 268 E2
T&W 243 E7
White Hills
Northants 120 E4
Whiteholme Blkpool 202 E2
Whitehough Derbys 185 E8
Whitehouse Aberds 293 B8
Argyll 275 G9
White House Suff 108 B2
Whitehouse Common
W Mid 134 D2
Whitehouse Green
W Berks 65 F7
White Houses Notts 188 F2
Whiteinch Glasgow 267 B10
Whitekirk E Loth 281 E10
Whiteknights Reading 65 E8
Whiteknowes
Aberds 293 C7
Whitelackington
Som 28 D5
White Lackington
Dorset 17 B10
White Ladies Aston
Worcs 117 G8
Whitelaw S Lnrk 268 G2
Whiteleaf Bucks 84 E4
Whiteleas T&W 243 E9
Whiteleaved Oak
Glos 98 D5
Whitelee Borders 262 C3
Northumb 250 B6
White Lee W Yorks 197 B8
Whitelees S Ayrs 257 C9
White-le-Head
Durham 242 G5
Whiteley Bank IoW 21 E7
Whiteley Green
Ches E 184 F6
Whiteley Village Sur 66 G5
White Lund Lancs 211 G8
Whitelye Mon 79 E8
Whitemans Green
W Sus 36 B4
White Mill Carms 93 G9
Whitemire Moray 301 D9
Whitemoor Corn 5 D9
Nottingham 171 G8
Warks 118 C5
White Moor Derbys 170 F5
Whitemore Staffs 168 C5
Whitenap Hants 32 C5
White Ness Shetland 313 J5
White Notley Essex 88 B3
White Oak Kent 68 F4
Whiteoak Green
Oxon 82 C4
White Ox Mead Bath 45 B8
Whiteparish Wilts 32 C2
White Pit Lincs 190 F5
Whitepits Wilts 45 F10
White Post Kent 52 E4
Notts 171 D10
Whiterashes Aberds 303 G8
Whiterigg Borders 262 C3
Whiterock Bridgend 58 D2
White Rocks
Hereford 97 G8
White Roding or White
Roothing Essex 87 C9
Whiterow Highld 310 E7
White's Green W Sus 34 B6
Whiteshill Glos 80 D4
S Glos 60 D6
Whiteside Northumb 240 D6
W Loth 269 B9
Whitesmith E Sus 23 C8
Whitespots
Dumfries 247 F10
White Stake Lancs 194 B4
Whitestaunton Som 28 E3
Whitestone Aberds 293 D8
Devon 14 C3
Devon 27 B8
Warks 135 F7
White Stone
Hereford 97 C11
Whitestones Aberds 303 D8
Whitestreet Green
Suff 107 D9
Whitewall Common
Mon 60 B2
Whitewall Corner
N Yorks 216 E5
White Waltham
Windsor 65 D10
Whiteway Bath 61 G8
Dorset 18 E3
Glos 80 C6
Glos 80 F4
Whitewell Aberds 303 C9
Corn 11 E7
Highld 291 C11
Lancs 203 D9
Wrex 167 G7
Whitewell Bottom
Lancs 195 C10
Whiteworks Devon 13 G8
Whitfield Kent 55 D10
Northants 102 E2
Northumb 241 F7
S Glos 79 G11
Whitfield Court Sur 50 B3
Whitfield Hall
Northumb 241 F7
Whitford Devon 15 B11
Whitford / Chwitffordd
Flint 181 F10
Whitgift E Yorks 199 C10
Whitgreave Staffs 151 D7
Whithaugh Borders 249 F11
Whithebeir Orkney 314 C5
Whithorn Dumfries 236 E6
Whiting Bay N Ayrs 256 D2
Whitington Norf 140 D4
Whitkirk W Yorks 206 G3
Whitland / Hendy-Gwyn
Carms 73 B11
Whitlaw Borders 271 F9
Whitleigh Plym 7 C9
Whitletts S Ayrs 257 E9
Whitley Gtr Man 194 F5
N Yorks 198 C5
Reading 65 E8
S Yorks 186 C4
Wilts 61 F11
W Mid 119 B7
Whitley Bay T&W 243 C9
Whitley Bridge
N Yorks 198 C5
Whitley Chapel
Northumb 241 F10
Whitley Head
W Yorks 204 E6
Whitley Heath
Staffs 150 D6
Whitley Lower
W Yorks 197 D8
Whitley Reed
Ches W 183 E10
Whitley Row Kent 52 C3
Whitley Sands T&W 243 C9
Whitley Thorpe
N Yorks 198 C5
Whitley Wood
Reading 65 F8
Whitlock's End
W Mid 118 B2
Whitminster Glos 80 D3
Whitmoor Devon 27 E9
Whitmore Dorset 31 F9
Staffs 168 G4
Whitmore Park
W Mid 134 G6
Whitnage Devon 27 D8
Whitnash Warks 118 E6
Whitnell Som 43 F8
Whitney Bottom Som 28 E4
Whitney-on-Wye
Hereford 96 B5
Whitrigg Cumb 229 D10
Cumb 238 F6
Whitriggs Borders 262 F3
Whitsbury Hants 31 D10
Whitslaid Borders 271 G11
Whitsome Borders 273 E7
Whitsomehill
Borders 273 F7
Whitson Newport 59 C11
Whitstable Kent 70 F6
Whitstone Corn 11 B11
Whittingham
Northumb 264 G3
Whittingslow
Shrops 131 F8
Whittington Glos 99 G10
Lancs 212 D2
Norf 140 D4
Shrops 148 C6
Staffs 133 G7
Staffs 134 B3
Staffs 150 C5
Warks 134 D5
Worcs 117 G7
Whittington Moor
Derbys 186 G5
Whittlebury
Northants 102 C3
Whittleford Warks 134 E6
Whittle-le-Woods
Lancs 194 C5
Whittlesey Cambs 138 D5
Whittlesford Cambs 105 B9
Whittlestone Head
Blkburn 195 D8
Whitton Borders 263 E7
Hereford 115 C8
London 66 E6
N Lincs 200 C2
Northumb 252 C3
Powys 114 D5
Shrops 115 C11
Stockton 234 G3
Suff 108 B2
Whittonditch Wilts 63 E9
Whittonstall
Northumb 242 F3
Whittytree Shrops 115 B8
Whitway Hants 48 B3
Whitwell Derbys 187 F8
Herts 104 G3
IoW 20 F6
N Yorks 224 F5
Rutland 137 B8
Whitwell-on-the-Hill
N Yorks 216 F4
Whitwell Street
Norf 160 E2
Whitwick Leics 153 F8
Whitwood W Yorks 198 C2
Whitworth Lancs 195 D11
Whixall Shrops 149 C10
Whixley N Yorks 206 B4
Whoberley W Mid 118 B6
Wholeflats Falk 279 E8
Whome Orkney 314 G3
Whorlton Durham 224 C2
N Yorks 225 E9
Whydown E Sus 38 F2
Whygate Northumb 241 B7
Whyke W Sus 22 C5
Whyle Hereford 115 E11
Whyteleafe Sur 51 B10
Wibdon Glos 79 F9
Wibsey W Yorks 205 G8
Wibtoft Leics 135 F9
Wichenford Worcs 116 E5
Wichling Kent 54 B2
Wick Bmouth 19 C8
Devon 27 G11
Highld 310 D7
S Glos 61 E8
Shetland 313 K6
Som 28 B6
Som 43 C10
Som 43 E8
V Glam 58 E2
Wilts 31 C11
Worcs 99 B9
W Sus 35 G8
Wicken Cambs 123 C11
Northants 102 D4
Wicken Bonhunt
Essex 105 E9
Wickenby Lincs 189 E9
Wicken Green Village
Norf 158 C6
Wick Episcopi
Worcs 116 G6
Wickersley S Yorks 187 C7
Wicker Street Green
Suff 107 C9
Wickford Essex 88 G3
Wickham Hants 33 E9
W Berks 63 E11
Wickham Bishops
Essex 88 C4
Wickhambreaux Kent 55 B8
Wickhambrook Suff 124 G4
Wickhamford
Worcs 99 C11
Wickham Green
Suff 125 D11
W Berks 63 E11
Wickham Heath
W Berks 64 F2
Wickham Market
Suff 126 F6
Wickhampton Norf 143 B8
Wickham St Paul
Essex 106 D6
Wickham's Cross
Som 44 G4
Wickham Skeith
Suff 125 D11
Wickham Street
Suff 124 G5
Suff 125 D11
Wick Hill Brack 65 E11
Kent 53 E10
Wokingham 65 G9
Wickhurst Kent 52 D4
Wicklane Bath 45 B7
Wicklewood Norf 141 C11
Wickmere Norf 160 C3
Wickridge Street
Glos 98 F6
Wick Rocks S Glos 61 E8
Wick St Lawrence
N Som 59 F11
Wickstreet E Sus 23 D8
Wick Street Glos 80 D5
Wickwar S Glos 61 B8
Widbrook Wilts 45 B10
Widcombe Bath 61 G9
Widdington Essex 105 E10
Widdrington
Northumb 253 D7
Widdrington Station
Northumb 252 E6
Widecombe in the Moor
Devon 13 F10
Widegates Corn 6 D5
Widemarsh
Hereford 97 C10
Widemouth Bay Corn 24 G2
Wideopen T&W 242 C6
Widewall Orkney 314 G4
Widewell Plym 7 C9
Widford Essex 87 D11
Herts 86 B6
Widgham Green
Cambs 124 F3
Widham Wilts 62 B5
Widley Hants 33 F11
Widmer End Bucks 84 F5
Widmerpool Notts 154 D2
Widmoor Bucks 66 B2
Widmore London 68 F2
Widnes Halton 183 D8
Wierton Kent 53 D9
Wig Powys 130 F2
Wigan Gtr Man 194 F5
Wiganthorpe
N Yorks 216 E3
Wigbeth Dorset 31 F8
Wigborough Som 28 D6
Wig Fach Bridgend 57 F10
Wiggaton Devon 15 C8
Wiggenhall St Germans
Norf 157 G11
Wiggenhall St Mary
Magdalen Norf 157 G11
Wiggenhall St Mary the
Virgin Norf 157 G11
Wiggenhall St Peter
Norf 158 G2
Wiggens Green
Essex 106 C3
Wiggington Staffs 134 B4
Wigginstall Staffs 169 C9
Wigginton Herts 84 C6
Oxon 101 E7
Shrops 148 B6
Staffs 134 B4
York 207 B7
Wigginton Bottom
Herts 84 D6
Wigginton Heath
Oxon 101 D7
Wigglesworth
N Yorks 204 B2
Wiggonby Cumb 239 G7
Wiggonholt W Sus 35 D9
Wighill N Yorks 206 D5
Wighton Norf 159 B8
Wightwick Manor
Staffs 133 D7
Wigley Derbys 186 G4
Hants 32 D4
Wigmarsh Shrops 149 D7
Wigmore Hereford 115 D8
Medway 69 G10
Wigsley Notts 188 G5
Wigsthorpe
Northants 137 G10
Wigston Leics 136 D2
Wigston Magna
Leics 136 D2
Wigston Parva Leics 135 F9
Wigthorpe Notts 187 E9
Wigtoft Lincs 156 B5
Wigton Cumb 229 B11
Wigtown Dumfries 236 D6
Wigtwizzle S Yorks 186 B2
Wike W Yorks 206 E2
Wike Well End
S Yorks 199 E7
Wilbarston
Northants 136 F6
Wilberfoss E Yorks 207 C10
Wilberlee W Yorks 196 E5
Wilburton Cambs 123 C9
Wilby Norf 141 F10
Northants 121 D7
Suff 126 C4
Wilcot Wilts 62 G6
Wilcott Shrops 149 F7
Wilcott Marsh
Shrops 149 F7
Wilcove Corn 7 D8
Wilcrick Newport 60 B2
Wilday Green
Derbys 186 G4
Wildboarclough
Ches E 169 B7
Wilden Beds 121 F11
Worcs 116 C6
Wildern Hants 33 E7
Wildernesse Kent 52 B4
Wilderspool Warr 183 D10
Wilderswood
Gtr Man 194 E6
Wilde Street Suff 124 B4
Wildhern Hants 47 C11
Wildhill Herts 86 D3
Wildmanbridge S
Lnrk 268 E6
Wild Mill Bridgend 58 C2
Wildmoor Hants 49 B7
Oxon 83 F7
Worcs 117 B9
Wildridings Brack 65 F11
Wildsworth Lincs 188 B4
Wildwood Staffs 151 E8
Wilford Nottingham 153 B11
Wilgate Green Kent 54 B3
Wilkesley Ches E 167 G10
Wilkhaven Highld 311 L3
Wilkieston W Loth 270 B2
Wilkinthroop Som 29 C11
Wilkin Throop Som 29 C11
Wilksby Lincs 174 C3
Willacy Lane End
Lancs 202 F5
Willand Devon 27 E8
Som 27 E11
Willand Moor Devon 27 E8
Willard's Hill E Sus 38 C2
Willaston Ches E 167 E11
Ches W 182 F4
Shrops 149 B11
Willen M Keynes 103 C7
Willenhall W Mid 119 B7
W Mid 133 D9
Willerby E Yorks 208 G6
N Yorks 217 D10
Willersey Glos 100 D2
Willersley Hereford 96 B6
Willesborough Kent 54 E4
Willesborough Lees
Kent 54 E4
Willesden London 67 C8
Willesden Green
London 67 C8
Willesley Leics 152 G6
Wilts 61 B11
Willett Som 42 G6
Willey Shrops 132 D3
Warks 135 G9
Willey Green Sur 50 C2
Willhayne Som 28 E4
Williamhope
Borders 261 C10
Williamscott Oxon 101 B9
William's Green
Suff 107 C9
Williamslee Borders 270 G6
Williamstown
Rhondda 77 G8
Williamthorpe
Derbys 170 B6
Willian Herts 104 E4
Willicote Pastures
Worcs 100 B3
Willingale Essex 87 D9
Willingcott Devon 40 E3
Willingdon E Sus 23 E9
Willingham Cambs 123 C8
Suff 143 G8
Willingham by Stow
Lincs 188 E5
Willingham Green
Cambs 124 G2
Willington Beds 104 B2
Derbys 152 D5
Durham 233 D9
Kent 53 C9
T&W 243 D8
Warks 100 D5
Willington Corner
Ches W 167 B8
Willington Quay
T&W 243 D8
Willisham Suff 125 G11
Willisham Tye Suff 125 G11
Willitoft E Yorks 207 F10
Williton Som 42 E5
Willoughbridge
Staffs 168 G3
Willoughby Lincs 191 G7
Warks 119 D10
Willoughby Hills
Lincs 174 F4
Willoughby-on-the-
Wolds Notts 154 D2
Willoughby Waterleys
Leics 135 E11
Willoughton Lincs 188 C6
Willowbank Bucks 66 B5
Willow Green
Ches W 183 F10
Worcs 116 F5
Willow Holme Cumb 239 F9
Willows Gtr Man 195 F8
Willows Green Essex 88 B2
Willowtown
Bl Gwent 77 C11
Will Row Lincs 191 D7
Willsbridge S Glos 61 E7
Willslock Staffs 151 C11
Willstone Shrops 131 D9
Willsworthy Devon 12 E6
Wilmcote Warks 118 F3
Wilmington Bath 61 G7
Devon 15 B10
E Sus 23 E8
Kent 68 E4
Wilmington Green
E Sus 23 D8
Wilminstone Devon 12 F5
Wilmslow Ches E 184 E4
Wilmslow Park
Ches E 184 E5
Wilnecote Staffs 134 C4
Wilney Green Norf 141 G11
Wilpshire Lancs 203 G9
Wilsden W Yorks 205 F7
Wilsden Hill
W Yorks 205 F7
Wilsford Lincs 173 G8
Wilts 46 B6
Wilts 46 F6
Wilsham Devon 41 D9
Wilshaw W Yorks 196 F6
Wilsic S Yorks 187 B9
Wilsill N Yorks 214 G3
Wilsley Green Kent 53 F9
Wilsley Pound Kent 53 F9
Wilsom Hants 49 F8
Wilson Hereford 97 G11
Leics 153 E8
Wilsontown S Lnrk 269 D9
Wilstead Beds 103 C11
Wilsthorpe Derbys 153 C9
Lincs 155 G11
Wilstone Herts 84 C6
Wilstone Green
Herts 84 C6
Wilthorpe S Yorks 197 F10
Wilton Borders 261 G11
Cumb 219 C10
Hereford 97 G11
N Yorks 217 C7
Redcar 225 B11
Som 28 C2
Wilts 46 G5
Wilts 63 G9
Wilton Park Bucks 85 G7
Wiltown Devon 27 D11
Som 28 C5
Wimbish Essex 105 D11
Wimbish Green
Essex 106 D2
Wimblebury Staffs 151 G10
Wimbledon London 67 E8
Wimble Hill Hants 49 D10
Wimblington Cambs 139 E8
Wimboldsley
Ches W 167 C11
Wimbolds Trafford
Ches W 182 G6
Wimborne Minster
Dorset 18 B6
Wimborne St Giles
Dorset 31 E8
Wimbotsham Norf 140 B2
Wimpole Cambs 104 B6
Wimpson Soton 32 E5
Wimpstone Warks 100 B4
Wincanton Som 30 B2
Winceby Lincs 174 B4
Wincham Ches W 183 F11
Winchburgh
W Loth 279 G11
Winchcombe Glos 99 F10
Winchelsea E Sus 38 D6
Winchelsea Beach
E Sus 38 D6
Winchester Hants 33 B7
Winchestown
Bl Gwent 77 C11
Winchet Hill Kent 53 E8
Winchfield Hants 49 C9
Winchfield Hurst
Hants 49 C9
Winchmore Hill
Bucks 84 G6
London 86 G4
Wincle Ches E 169 B7
Wincobank S Yorks 186 C5
Winder Cumb 219 B10
Windermere Cumb 221 F8
Winderton Warks 100 C6
Windhill Highld 300 E5
S Yorks 198 G3
W Yorks 205 F9
Wind Hill Cumb 210 E5
Pembs 73 F9
Windhouse Shetland 312 D6
Winding Wood
W Berks 63 E11
Windle Hill Ches W 182 F4
Windlehurst
Gtr Man 185 D7
Windlesham Sur 66 G2
Windley Derbys 170 F4
Windmill Corn 10 G3
Flint 181 G11
Flint 182 G2
Windmill Hill Bristol 60 E5
E Sus 23 C10
Halton 183 E9
Kent 69 F10
Som 28 D4
Worcs 99 B8
W Yorks 197 D11
Windrush Glos 81 C11
Windsor N Lincs 199 E9
Windsor 66 D3
Windsoredge Glos 80 E4
Windsor Green Suff 125 G7
Windwhistle Som 28 F5
Windy Arbor Mers 183 D7
Windy Arbour
Warks 118 C5
Windydoors
Borders 261 B10
Windygates Fife 287 G7
Windyharbour
Ches E 184 G4
Windy Hill Wrex 166 E4
Windyknowe
W Loth 269 B9
Windy Nook T&W 243 E7
Windywalls Borders 263 C7
Windy-Yett E Ayrs 267 E9
Wineham W Sus 36 C2
Winestead E Yorks 201 C9
Winewall Lancs 204 E4
Winfarthing Norf 142 F2
Winford IoW 21 E7
N Som 60 F4
Winforton Hereford 96 B5
Winfrith Newburgh
Dorset 18 E2
Wing Bucks 103 G7
Rutland 137 C7
Wingate Durham 234 D4
Wingates Gtr Man 195 F7
Northumb 252 D4
Wingerworth
Derbys 170 B5
Wingfield C Beds 103 F10
Suff 126 B4
S Yorks 186 B6
Wilts 45 B10
Wingfield Green
Suff 126 B4
Wingfield Park
Derbys 170 E5
Wingham Kent 55 B8
Wingham Green Kent 55 B8
Wingham Well Kent 55 B8
Wingmore Kent 55 D7
Wingrave Bucks 84 B5
Winkburn Notts 172 D2
Winkfield Brack 66 E2
Winkfield Place
Brack 66 E2
Winkfield Row
Brack 65 E11
Winkhill Staffs 169 E9
Winkhurst Green
Kent 52 D3
Winklebury Hants 48 C6
Winkleigh Devon 25 F10
Winksley N Yorks 214 E5
Winkton Dorset 19 B9
Winlaton T&W 242 E5
Winlaton Mill T&W 242 E5
Winless Highld 310 D7
Winllan Powys 148 E4
Winmarleigh Lancs 202 D5
Winmarleigh Moss
Lancs 202 D4
Winnal Hereford 97 E9
Winnal Common
Hereford 97 E9
Winnall Hants 33 B7
Worcs 116 D6
Winnard's Perch Corn 5 B8
Winnersh Wokingham 65 E9
Winnington
Ches W 183 G10
Staffs 150 B4
Winnington Green
Shrops 148 G6
Winnothdale Staffs 169 G8
Winscales Cumb 228 F6
Winscombe N Som 44 B2
Winsdon Hill Luton 103 G11
Winsford Ches W 167 B10
Som 42 G2
Winsham Devon 40 F3
Som 28 F5
Winshill Staffs 152 E5
Winsh-wen Swansea 57 B7
Winsick Derbys 170 B6
Winskill Cumb 231 D7
Winslade Devon 24 D5
Hants 49 D7
Winsley N Yorks 214 G4
Wilts 61 G10
Winslow Bucks 102 F5
Winslow Mill
Hereford 98 D2
Winson Glos 81 D9
Winson Green
W Mid 133 F10
Winsor Hants 32 E4
Winstanley Gtr Man 194 G5
Winstanleys
Gtr Man 194 F5
Winster Cumb 221 G8
Derbys 170 C2
Winston Durham 224 B2
Suff 126 E3
Winstone Glos 81 D7
Winston Green Suff 126 E3
Winswell Devon 25 E7
Winterborne Bassett
Wilts 62 E6
Winterborne Came
Dorset 17 D10
Winterborne Clenston
Dorset 30 G4
Winterborne
Herringston Dorset 17 D9
Winterborne Houghton
Dorset 30 G4
Winterborne Kingston
Dorset 18 B3
Winterborne Monkton
Wilts 62 E6
Winterborne Muston
Dorset 18 B3
Winterborne Stickland
Dorset 30 G4
Winterborne Tomson
Dorset 18 B3
Winterborne
Whitechurch
Dorset 30 G4
Winterborne Zelston
Dorset 18 B3
Winterbourne Kent 54 B5
S Glos 60 C6
W Berks 64 E3
Winterbourne Abbas
Dorset 17 C8
Winterbourne Bassett
Wilts 62 E6
Winterbourne Dauntsey
Wilts 47 G7
Winterbourne Down
S Glos 61 D7
Winterbourne Earls
Wilts 47 G7
Winterbourne Gunner
Wilts 47 F7
Winterbourne Monkton
Dorset 17 D9
Winterbourne
Steepleton Dorset 17 D8
Winterbourne Stoke
Wilts 46 E5
Winterbrook Oxon 64 B6
Winterburn N Yorks 204 B4
Winterfield Bath 45 B7
Winter Gardens
Essex 69 C9
Winterhay Green
Som 28 D5
Winterhead N Som 44 B2
Winteringham
N Lincs 200 C2
Winterley Ches E 168 D2
Wintersett
W Yorks 197 D11
Wintershill Hants 33 D8
Winterton N Lincs 200 D2
Winterton-on-Sea
Norf 161 F9
Winter Well Som 28 C3
Winthorpe Lincs 175 B9
Notts 172 D4
Winton Bmouth 19 C7
Cumb 222 C5
E Sus 23 E8
Gtr Man 184 B3
N Yorks 225 F8
Wintringham
N Yorks 217 E7
Winwick Cambs 138 G2
Northants 120 C2
Warr 183 C10
Winwick Quay
Warr 183 C10
Winyard's Gap Dorset 29 F7
Winyates Worcs 117 D11
Winyates Green
Worcs 117 D11
Wirksworth Derbys 170 E3
Wirksworth Moor
Derbys 170 E4
Wirswall Ches E 167 G8
Wisbech Cambs 139 B9
Wisbech St Mary
Cambs 139 B8
Wisborough Green
W Sus 35 B8
Wiseton Notts 188 D2
Wishanger Glos 80 D6
Wishaw N Lnrk 268 D5
Warks 134 E3
Wisley Sur 50 B5
Wispington Lincs 190 G2
Wissenden Kent 54 E2
Wissett Suff 127 B7
Wistanstow Shrops 131 F8
Wistanswick Shrops 150 D3
Wistaston Ches E 167 E11
Wistaston Green
Ches E 167 E11
Wiston Pembs 73 B8
S Lnrk 259 C11
W Sus 35 E10
Wiston Mains S
Lnrk 259 C11
Wistow Cambs 138 G5
Leics 136 D2
N Yorks 207 F7
Wiswell Lancs 203 F10
Witcham Cambs 139 G9
Witchampton Dorset 31 F7
Witchford Cambs 123 B10
Witcombe Som 29 C7
Withacott Devon 24 D6
Witham Essex 88 C4
Witham Friary Som 45 E8
Witham on the Hill
Lincs 155 F11
Witham St Hughs
Lincs 172 C5
Withcall Lincs 190 E3
Withdean Brighton 36 F4
Witherenden Hill
E Sus 37 B10
Withergate Norf 160 D5
Witheridge Devon 26 E4
Witheridge Hill Oxon 65 C7
Witherley Leics 134 D6
Withermarsh Green
Suff 107 D10
Withern Lincs 190 E6
Withernsea
E Yorks 201 B10
Withernwick
E Yorks 209 E9
Withersdale Street
Suff 142 G5
Withersdane Kent 54 D5
Withersfield Suff 106 B3
Witherslack Cumb 211 C8
Witherwack T&W 243 F9
Withial Som 44 F5
Withiel Corn 5 B9
Withiel Florey Som 42 G3
Withielgoose Corn 5 B10
Withielgoose Mills
Corn 5 B10
Withington Glos 81 B8
Gtr Man 184 C5
Hereford 97 C11
Shrops 149 G11
Staffs 151 B10
Withington Green
Ches E 184 G4
Withington Marsh
Hereford 97 C11
Withleigh Devon 26 E6
Withnell Lancs 194 C6
Withnell Fold Lancs 194 C6
Withybed Green
Worcs 117 C10
Withybrook Som 45 D7
Warks 135 G8
Withybush Pembs 73 B7
Withycombe Som 41 F11
Som 42 E4
Withycombe Raleigh
Devon 14 E6
Withyditch Bath 45 B8
Withyham E Sus 52 F3
Withy Mills Bath 45 B7
Withymoor Village
W Mid 133 F8
Withypool Som 41 F10
Withystakes Staffs 169 F7
Withywood Bristol 60 F5
Witley Sur 50 F2
Witnells End Worcs 132 G5
Witnesham Suff 126 G3
Witney Oxon 82 C5
Wittensford Hants 32 E3
Wittering Pboro 137 C11
Wittersham Kent 38 B5
Witton Angus 293 F7
Norf 142 B6
W Mid 133 E11
Worcs 117 E7
Witton Bridge Norf 160 C6
Witton Gilbert
Durham 233 B10
Witton Hill Worcs 116 E5
Witton-le-Wear
Durham 233 E8
Witton Park Durham 233 E9
Wiveliscombe Som 27 B9
Wivelrod Hants 49 F7
Wivelsfield E Sus 36 C4
Wivelsfield Green
E Sus 36 C5
Wivenhoe Essex 107 G10
Wivenhoe Cross
Essex 107 G10
Wiveton Norf 177 E8
Wix Essex 108 F3
Wixams Beds 103 C10
Wixford Warks 117 G11
Wixhill Shrops 149 D11
Wixoe Suff 106 C4
Woburn C Beds 103 E8
Woburn Sands
M Keynes 103 D8
Wofferwood Common
Hereford 116 G3
Wokefield Park
W Berks 65 F7
Woking Sur 50 B4
Wokingham
Wokingham 65 F10
Wolborough Devon 14 G3
Woldhurst W Sus 22 C5
Woldingham Sur 51 B11
Woldingham Garden
Village Sur 51 B11
Wold Newton
E Yorks 217 E10
NE Lincs 190 B2
Wolfclyde S Lnrk 260 B2
Wolferd Green Norf 142 D5
Wolferlow Hereford 116 E3
Wolferton Norf 158 D3
Wolfhampcote
Warks 119 D10
Wolfhill Perth 286 D5
Wolf's Castle Pembs 91 F9
Wolfsdale Pembs 91 G8
Wolfsdale Hill Pembs 91 G8
Woll Borders 261 E11
Wollaston Northants 121 E8
Shrops 148 G6
W Mid 133 G7
Wollaton
Nottingham 153 B10
Wollerton Shrops 150 C2
Wollerton Wood
Shrops 150 C2
Wollescote W Mid 133 G8
Wollrig Borders 261 E11
Wolsingham
Durham 233 D7
Wolstanton Staffs 168 F5
Wolstenholme
Gtr Man 195 D11
Wolston Warks 119 B8
Wolsty Cumb 238 G4
Wolterton Norf 160 C3
Wolvercote Oxon 83 D7
Wolverham Ches W 182 F6
Wolverhampton
W Mid 133 D8
Wolverley Shrops 149 C9
Worcs 116 B6
Wolverstone Devon 27 G10
Wolverton Hants 48 B5
Kent 55 E9
M Keynes 102 C6
Shrops 131 F9
Warks 118 E4
Wilts 45 G9
Wolverton Common
Hants 48 B5
Wolvesnewton Mon 79 F7
Wolvey Warks 135 F8
Wolvey Heath
Warks 135 F8
Wolviston Stockton 234 F5